THIRD EDITION

The Harvard Guide to Psychiatry

Edited by Armand M. Nicholi, Jr., M.D.

The Belknap Press of Harvard University Press

Cambridge, Massachusetts, and London, England · 1999

Copyright © 1988, 1999 by the President and Fellows of Harvard College
All rights reserved
Printed in the United States of America

Library of Congress Cataloging-in-Publication Data

The Harvard guide to psychiatry / edited by Armand M. Nicholl, Jr.—3rd ed.
    p. cm.
  Rev. ed. of: The new Harvard guide to psychiatry. 1988.
  Includes bibliographical references and index.
  ISBN 0-674-37570-X (alk. paper)
  1. Psychiatry.   I. Nicholi, Armand M., 1928–   .
  II. New Harvard guide to psychiatry.
  [DNLM: 1. Mental Disorders—diagnosis.
  2. Mental Disorders—therapy.   WM 141H339   1999]
RC454.N47   1999
616.89—dc21
DNLM/DLC
for Library of Congress   98-41672

To my wife, Ingrid
and my teacher, the late Elvin Semrad

Marilyn S. Albert, Ph.D.
Professor of Psychiatry and Neurology, Harvard Medical School; Director, Gerontology Research Unit, Massachusetts General Hospital

James Bakalar, J.D.
Lecturer in Law, Department of Psychiatry, Harvard Medical School; Associate Editor, *Harvard Medical School Mental Health Letter*

Ross J. Baldessarini, M.D.
Professor of Psychiatry (Neuroscience), Harvard Medical School; Director, Laboratories for Psychiatric Research, McLean Hospital

Anne E. Becker, M.D., Ph.D.
Clinical Assistant in Psychiatry, Massachusetts General Hospital; Director of Training and Research, Harvard Eating Disorders Center

Lee Birk, M.D.
Director, Learning Therapies, Inc., Concord, Massachusetts; Associate Clinical Professor of Psychiatry, Harvard Medical School

Deborah Blacker, M.D., Sc.D.
Assistant Professor of Psychiatry, Harvard Medical School; Assistant Professor of Epidemiology, Harvard School of Public Health

Jonathan F. Borus, M.D.
Professor of Psychiatry, Harvard Medical School; Psychiatrist in Chief, Brigham and Women's Hospital

Edwin H. Cassem, M.D.
Chairman, Department of Psychiatry, Massachusetts General Hospital; Professor of Psychiatry, Harvard Medical School

Nicholas A. Covino, Psy.D.
Assistant Professor of Psychology, Department of Psychiatry, Harvard Medical School; Director, Psychology Division, Beth Israel Deaconess Medical Center

Ken Duckworth, M.D.
Assistant Professor of Psychiatry, Harvard Medical School; Clinical Director, Massachusetts Mental Health Center

Felton Earls, M.D.
Professor of Child Psychiatry, Harvard Medical School; Professor of Human Behavior and Development, Harvard School of Public Health

Stephen V. Faraone, Ph.D.
Associate Professor, Harvard Medical School Department of Psychiatry at the Massachusetts Mental Health Center and Harvard Institute of Psychiatric Epidemiology and Genetics

Fred H. Frankel, M.B.CH.B., D.P.M.
Psychiatrist-in-Chief, Emeritus, Beth Israel Deaconess Medical Center; Professor of Psychiatry, Emeritus, Harvard Medical School

Jean A. Frazier, M.D.
Instructor in Psychiatry, Harvard Medical School; Clinical Assistant and Director of the Psychotic Disorders Program for Children and Adolescents, Joint Pediatric Psychopharmacology Program at Massachusetts General and McLean Hospitals

Gregory Fricchione, M.D.
Associate Professor of Psychiatry, Harvard Medical School; Director, Medical Psychiatry Service, Brigham and Women's Hospital

Randy S. Glassman, M.D.
Director, Women's Psychiatric Services, Brigham and Women's Hospital; Instructor in Psychiatry, Harvard Medical School

Donald C. Goff, M.D.
Associate Professor of Psychiatry, Harvard Medical School; Director, Psychotic Disorders Program, Massachusetts General Hospital

Alan I. Green, M.D.
Associate Professor of Psychiatry, Harvard Medical School; Director of the Commonwealth Research Center, Massachusetts Mental Health Center

Lester Grinspoon, M.D.
Associate Professor of Psychiatry, Harvard Medical School

Jon E. Gudeman, M.D.
Professor of Psychiatry and Behavioral Medicine, Medical College of Wisconsin, Milwaukee; Medical Director, Milwaukee County Mental Health Complex

John G. Gunderson, M.D.
Director, Psychosocial Research Programs, McLean Hospital; Professor of Psychiatry, Harvard Medical School

David B. Herzog, M.D.
Director, Eating Disorders Unit, Massachusetts General Hospital; Professor of Psychiatry (Pediatrics), Harvard Medical School

J. Allan Hobson, M.D.
Professor of Psychiatry, Harvard Medical School

Edward M. Hundert, M.D.
Professor of Psychiatry and Medical Humanities, and Senior Associate Dean for Medical Education, University of Rochester School of Medicine and Dentistry

Steven E. Hyman, M.D.
Professor of Psychiatry, Harvard Medical School (on leave); Director, National Institute of Mental Health

Michael S. Jellinek, M.D.
Chief, Child Psychiatry Service, Massachusetts General Hospital; Professor of Psychiatry and of Pediatrics, Harvard Medical School

Michael A. Jenike, M.D.
Professor of Psychiatry, Harvard Medical School

Arthur Kleinman, M.D.
Presley Professor of Anthropology and Psychiatry, and Chair, Department of Social Medicine, Harvard Medical School; Professor of Psychiatry, The Cambridge Hospital

Benjamin Liptzin, M.D.
Chairman, Department of Psychiatry, Baystate Health System; Professor and Deputy Chair, Department of Psychiatry, Tufts University School of Medicine

W. W. Meissner, S.J., M.D.
University Professor of Psychoanalysis, Boston College; Training and Supervising Analyst, Boston Psychoanalytic Society and Institute, Inc.

M.-Marsel Mesulam, M.D.
Ruth and Evelyn Dunbar Professor of Neurology and Psychiatry, and Director, Cognitive Neurology and Alzheimer's Disease Center, Northwestern University Medical School

Eran D. Metzger, M.D.
Instructor in Psychiatry, Harvard Medical School; Associate Director of Geropsychiatry, Hebrew Rehabilitation Center for Aged

Jane M. Murphy, Ph.D.
Professor of Psychiatry, Harvard Medical School; Professor in Epidemiology, Harvard School of Public Health

John C. Nemiah, M.D.
Professor of Psychiatry, Dartmouth Medical School; Professor of Psychiatry, Emeritus, Harvard Medical School

Armand M. Nicholi, Jr., M.D.
Associate Clinical Professor of Psychiatry, Harvard Medical School; Clinical Associate, Department of Psychiatry, Massachusetts General Hospital

Ralph A. Nixon, M.D., Ph.D.
Professor of Psychiatry, New York University Medical School; Director, Neuroscience Research, Nathan S. Kline Institute for Psychiatric Research

Michael W. Otto, Ph.D.
Associate Professor of Psychology, Harvard Medical
School; Director, Cognitive-Behavior Therapy Program,
Massachusetts General Hospital

Chester M. Pierce, M.D.
Professor of Education and Psychiatry, Emeritus,
Harvard University; Senior Psychiatrist, Massachusetts
General Hospital

Stephen L. Pinals, M.D.
Assistant Professor of Psychiatry, Case Western Reserve
University School of Medicine; University Hospitals of
Cleveland

Mark H. Pollack, M.D.
Associate Professor of Psychiatry, Harvard Medical
School; Director, Anxiety Disorders Program,
Massachusetts General Hospital

Scott L. Rauch, M.D.
Director of Psychiatric Neuroimaging Research,
Massachusetts General Hospital; Associate Professor of
Psychiatry, Harvard Medical School

Peter Reich, M.D.
Chief of Psychiatry, MIT Medical Department; Professor
of Psychiatry, Harvard Medical School

Perry F. Renshaw, M.D., Ph.D.
Director, Brain Imaging Center, McLean Hospital;
Associate Professor of Psychiatry, Harvard Medical
School

Malcolm P. Rogers, M.D.
Associate Professor of Psychiatry, Harvard Medical
School; Attending Psychiatrist, Psychiatry Division,
Brigham and Women's Hospital

Jerrold F. Rosenbaum, M.D.
Director, Outpatient Psychiatry Division, Massachusetts
General Hospital

Anthony J. Rothschild, M.D.
Irving S. and Betty Brudnick Professor of Psychiatry and
Director of Clinical Research, Department of Psychiatry,
University of Massachusetts Medical Center;
Lecturer in Psychiatry, Harvard Medical School

Carl Salzman, M.D.
Director of Education and Director of
Psychopharmacology, Massachusetts Mental Health
Center; Professor of Psychiatry, Harvard Medical School

Kathy M. Sanders, M.D.
Assistant Professor of Psychiatry, Harvard Medical
School; Director, Acute Psychiatry Service,
Massachusetts General Hospital

Andrew Satlin, M.D.
Assistant Professor of Psychiatry, Harvard Medical
School; Associate Director, CNS Research, Novartis
Pharmaceuticals Corp.

Larry J. Seidman, Ph.D.
Director of Neuropsychology, Massachusetts Mental
Health Center; Associate Professor in Psychology,
Department of Psychiatry, Harvard Medical School

Rosalia Silvestri, M.D.
Assistant Professor of Neurology, Harvard Medical
School

Alan Abraham Stone, M.D.
Touroff-Glueck Consultant in Psychiatry, McLean
Hospital; Professor of Law and Psychiatry, Faculty of
Law and Faculty of Medicine, Harvard University

Paul Summergrad, M.D.
Director, Psychiatry Network, Partners Health Care
System, Inc.; Assistant Professor of Psychiatry, Harvard
Medical School

Mauricio Tohen, M.D., Dr. P.H.
Associate Clinical Professor of Psychiatry, Harvard
Medical School; Medical Adviser, Lilly Research
Laboratories

Rosemary Toomey, Ph.D.
Instructor in Psychology, Harvard Medical School;
Department of Psychiatry, Massachusetts Mental Health
Center and Brockton/West Roxbury Veterans Affairs
Medical Center

Ming T. Tsuang, M.D., Ph.D., D.Sc.
Stanley Cobb Professor of Psychiatry and Director,
Harvard Institute of Psychiatric Epidemiology and
Genetics, Harvard Schools of Medicine and Public
Health; Superintendent and Head, Harvard Department
of Psychiatry at Massachusetts Mental Health Center

George E. Vaillant, M.D.
Professor of Psychiatry, Harvard Medical School;
Director of Research, Division of Psychiatry, Brigham
and Women's Hospital

Jeffrey B. Weilburg, M.D.
Assistant Professor of Psychiatry, Harvard Medical
School; Department of Psychiatry, Massachusetts
General Hospital

Roger D. Weiss, M.D.
Associate Professor of Psychiatry, Harvard Medical
School; Clinical Director, Alcohol and Drug Abuse
Program, McLean Hospital

Contents

A wealth of new scientific knowledge, the publication of the *Diagnostic and Statistical Manual of Mental Disorders,* fourth edition (DSM-IV), and the emergence of managed care with its widespread, intrusive impact on the practice of psychiatry set the stage for this third edition of *The Harvard Guide to Psychiatry.* As with the first two editions, the editor invited an advisory group of senior faculty members to begin formal planning of the project. This advisory group included Drs. Ross Baldessarini, Jonathan Borus, Edward Cassem, Joseph Coyle, Fred Frankel, Chester Pierce, Ming Tsuang, and Carl Salzman.

The first task of the group involved discussing new research and selecting the members of the Harvard Medical School faculty they thought best qualified to present this new information. We wanted to choose people not only with the knowledge and research experience to write authoritatively but also with the ability to write clearly and concisely. This selection process involved reading and assessing the published works of many faculty members and proved a demanding editorial task—but one that we believe produced a distinguished group of contributors.

The second task was to include the considerable amount of new knowledge while keeping the size of the volume manageable. By limiting both the number of contributors and the space allotted to their topic, we imposed on each author the responsibility of deciding what to omit as well as what to include, and of maintaining brevity without sacrificing thoroughness. As with the previous editions, we attempted to avoid the stylistic criticism directed against most medical writing by focusing on style as well as on content. (Most authors continue to follow the practice of using "he" or "his" whenever the gender of an individual is not specified. Likewise, many authors have used the more concise wording to refer to individuals with specific conditions: for example, "the mentally retarded person" rather than "the person with mental retardation.") Many of the chapters underwent several revisions before being sent to outside authorities for further critical review.

Our objective was to produce an up-to-date, well-integrated, and technically sound text that will enhance the knowledge and technical skills of all clinicians. We also realize, however, that success as a clinician requires considerably more than clinical knowledge and technical skill. In every field of medicine, but especially in the practice of psychiatry, the art is as important as the science, and the clinician's character as important as his intellect. Throughout the text we assume the existence of an attitude, a quality of character, a set of values—above all, a capacity to step outside one's own needs sufficiently to become acutely aware of the patient's needs. This crucial aspect of the art of clinical practice can never be taught in courses on medical ethics or on the doctor-patient relationship. Perhaps it can be taught only by example and learned through the process of identification. The Greek term *agape* refers to this quality—a disinterested, objective willing of the best for a person and acting accordingly, regardless of how one feels toward him. This basic principle, already as old as the Bible, remains the key to all human relationships, especially the one between therapist and patient.

The two individuals to whom I dedicate this volume have provided me with examples of this ideal code of conduct—one in a personal relationship in the context of the family, the other in a professional relationship in the context of the classroom and clinic. The late Dr. Elvin Semrad unfailingly combined care and compassion for his patients with vast clinical knowledge and extraordinary skill. We hope this third edition reflects this ideal.

The planning and writing of this book during the past four years required an immense amount of time and work on the part of many people. I am especially indebted to Dr. Fred Lee, who helped ease the heavy editorial chores, and to all the contributors for their splendid cooperation—especially to the many suggestions given freely and frequently by Drs. Baldessarini, Borus, Cassem, Frankel, Pierce, and Salzman.

A.M.N.   Concord, Massachusetts

Introduction

Scientific research continues to increase our understanding of the human mind. Recent findings have shed new light on the development of the mind, on its complex relationship with the body, and on the diagnosis and treatment of its disorders. In presenting these new findings, the contributors to this volume worked to produce a text sufficiently up-to-date to be valuable to the experienced clinician and researcher, and sufficiently clear to be understood by the beginning student.

This edition, like the preceding two editions, strives not only to maintain a rigorous scientific approach with an emphasis on current research but also to focus on the patient as a person, giving no less attention to the individual suffering from a specific disorder than to the disorder itself. From the first chapter, demonstrating the positive correlation between the strength of the therapist-patient relationship and a successful therapeutic outcome, to the last chapter, discussing the influence of new laws and of managed care on this relationship, the focus remains on the patient, the doctor, and the highly complex interaction between them.

The new knowledge incorporated in this volume comes from a variety of sources, including: (1) recent clinical and laboratory research and new technology that facilitates this research, such as the vastly improved brain-scanning methods of computed tomography (CT), positron emission tomography (PET), and magnetic resource imaging (MRI); the advances in molecular biology prompting the search for a specific gene in the transmission of schizophrenia and other psychiatric disorders; computed brain electrical activity mapping (BEAM); and new biomedical techniques for assessing enzymes, metabolites, and neurotransmitters in human tissues; (2) the emergence of diseases such as acquired immune deficiency syndrome (AIDS) whose first—and sometimes only—manifestation may be severe psychiatric symptoms; (3) the increased incidence of disorders such as bulimia and the recent intensive investigation of others

such as Alzheimer's disease and obsessive-compulsive disorder; (4) environmental and cultural changes that result from or contribute to psychiatric disorder, such as the rapid rise in nontherapeutic psychoactive drug use and in adolescent suicide; (5) new interests in psychiatry, such as the current emphasis on psychiatric diagnosis and classification, on ethics, and on recovered memory under hypnosis; and (6) the obtrusive and pervasive impact of managed care on the practice of psychiatry.

The following paragraphs offer an introduction to some of the material and a brief overview of the general format.

Part One focuses on the examination and assessment of patients with psychiatric disorders and on the diagnosis and classification of those disorders. For the reader unfamiliar with DSM-IV, Chapter 4 reviews the evolution of the current emphasis on classification and on precise definition of psychopathology. Its detailed explanation of the structure of these documents will prove helpful both to the student and to the experienced clinician. In addition, the reader will find the DSM-IV categories discussed throughout the text. In response to the section in DSM-IV on defense mechanisms, a later chapter—Chapter 10—discusses these mechanisms in detail, traces their history in psychoanalytic theory, explains how the individual uses them, categorizes them according to the degree of psychopathology associated with them, and illustrates how they can be identified and altered clinically. A new chapter—Chapter 5—focuses on modern neuroimaging techniques used in assessment.

Part Two reflects the concentrated effort of psychiatrists to establish the neurological and biological substrates of the major psychiatric disorders. In these chapters the contributors discuss questions such as: Does a specific biological abnormality distinguish these disorders? And how do genetic, biochemical, environmental, and psychological factors influence the pathogenesis of these diseases? They review current knowledge concerning the neural basis of affect and cognition and discuss the most recent theories of how these disorders develop—for example, the current hypothesis that schizophrenia results from abnormal brain development. Another new chapter—Chapter 7—presents a clear and concise overview of the most recent research findings concerning the biology of schizophrenia, depression, anxiety, and the addictive disorders.

Part Three introduces new research on the psychological aspects of mental illness, with chapters on theories of personality (including the contributions of major theorists, such as Heinz Kohut and his colleagues, to the area of "self psychology"); the dynamic understanding of psychopathology; anxiety disorders (including posttraumatic stress, panic, and obsessive-compulsive disorders); the mood disorders; schizophrenia and other psychotic disorders; personality disorders; and delirium, dementia, and other cognitive disorders. Chapter 17 on psychosomatic medicine reviews recent findings concerning the effects of acute stress, bereavement, and other emotional disturbances on the immune system; and the relationship of type A behavior, hostility, and depression to cardiovascular disease and of certain premorbid psychological profiles to cancer. Other contributors review the adverse effects of drugs currently used for nontherapeutic purposes among a large segment of our population and the epidemiology, pathogenesis, diagnosis, and treatment of eating disorders.

Part Four addresses the treatment and management of patients with psychiatric illness. The contributors discuss principles of individual psychotherapy, group therapy, behavior therapy, new treatment approaches to sexual dysfunction, crisis intervention, and psychiatric emergencies. Because a significant proportion of current biological research on the major psychiatric disorders arises from knowledge of the effects of psychotropic drugs, the chapter on psychopharmacology—Chapter 21—reviews not only the new drugs used in treatment of the disorders but also a theoretical understanding of their actions. This section includes a new chapter on indications for the use of hypnosis.

Part Five focuses on special groups of patients and on environmental and psychosocial factors that play a role in the pathogenesis of the major psychiatric illnesses. Chapters on the child and adolescent review recent studies that support the vast body of research during past decades underscoring the importance to the developing child of the physical presence and emotional accessibility of both parents. In the chapter on the child (Chapter 27), the authors discuss not only DSM-IV criteria for the major psychiatric disorders of childhood but also the current emphasis

on early intervention to prevent them, the treatment of these disorders, and the impact of divorce, and of child abuse and neglect. Chapter 28 on the adolescent reviews research on adolescent drug use and on the psychological effects of currently popular drugs—especially the form of cocaine called "crack"—and delineates the psychological differences between users and nonusers. It also reviews research indicating that changes in child-rearing practices and in the structure of the family play a significant role in the recent epidemic of adolescent drug use, pregnancy, and suicide. Other contributors present detailed discussions of the treatment of the elderly person, the mentally retarded person, the alcohol-dependent and the drug-dependent person, the problems of deinstitutionalization and homelessness among patients with chronic mental illness, and the management of the person confronting death.

Part Six explores the relationship between psychiatry and culture. These chapters explore racial, cultural, and ethical issues in psychiatry, survey the extensive research in psychiatric epidemiology during the past two decades, describe recent developments in the organization of resources devoted to psychiatric care, and outline the plethora of new laws that profoundly influence the practice of psychiatry in the United States. The last two chapters present a vivid description of the profound influence of managed care on the practice of psychiatry and a clear prognosis of the future. The last sentence of the last chapter sounds a warning: "Managed care and the courts will have more to say about the doctor-patient relationship than does the medical profession."

These six parts complement one another. The clinician interested in AIDS, for example, will find helpful the discussion of the neuropsychological tests used in assessing brain damage and brain dysfunction in AIDS patients (Chapter 3); the chapter on neural substrates of behavior (Chapter 6); and the description of the neurological and psychiatric symptoms caused by direct infection of the brain by the human immune deficiency virus, the neural pathology involved, and the appropriate psychiatric management of the disease (Chapter 17); and the discussion of the psychotherapies will prove helpful in the treatment not only of the AIDS patient but also of his family (Chapter 20). Because no cure for AIDS appears imminent, the clinician caring for AIDS patients will also find practical information on the care of the person confronting death (Chapter 33). Finally, in view of ongoing legal developments, the sections on Tarasoff and on confidentiality may prove crucially relevant to psychiatrists in determining how they understand their legal responsibilities to AIDS patients. The last two chapters will help the clinician understand the resources available to his patient under managed care (Chapters 37 and 38).

Progress in psychiatry continues in many directions. More rigorously controlled studies have replaced the relatively unsophisticated research of the past. Investigators have focused on establishing the neurological substrates of psychiatric disorders—that is, on ascertaining the specific parts of the brain associated with the disturbed thinking, feeling, and behavior of these disorders. They continue to search for structural, metabolic, and physiological abnormalities that may be clues to the cure of particular illnesses. And they do so with the full realization that even the identification of such abnormalities will leave unanswered the question of whether they are the cause or the result of the disorder. New discoveries have come from explorations both within cells, to find the gene or genes involved in genetic transmission of a disorder, and between the cells, especially at "synaptic clefts," the spaces that exist between each of the billions of brain cells.

We have made great strides in increasing our knowledge of the biochemistry and neurophysiology of the brain and in understanding the mind. The excitement of discovery prevails as we approach new breakthroughs. Paradoxically, however, the more we learn about the mind, the more we realize that we can never reduce human thought, feeling, or behavior to a biochemical reaction. Our knowledge of biology by no means rules out the significance of psychological factors, nor our knowledge of genetics the significance of environmental factors. The more we develop and use psychopharmacologic drugs, the more we realize that these drugs usually must be combined with psychotherapy to be most effective. Perhaps once we discover the elusive abnormal metabolite, we may find it influenced by a combination of genetic, environmental, biological, and psychological factors. The integration of these factors may constitute psychiatry's greatest challenge.

New knowledge of the mind reveals not only its paradoxical nature but also its enormous complexity. Above all, it leaves us with an acute awareness of how little we really know. In 1977 Dr. Lewis Thomas wrote in the *New England Journal of Medicine:* "The only solid piece of scientific truth about which I feel totally competent is that we are profoundly ignorant about nature. Indeed I regard this as the major discovery of the past one hundred years of biology . . . It is this sudden confrontation with the depth and scope of ignorance that represents the most noteworthy contribution of twentieth-century science to the human intellect." This awareness of our ignorance may be the first sign of real progress, indicating perhaps that as our island of knowledge increases, so does our shoreline of ignorance. Awareness of how much we do not know fosters not only humility but also the desire to continue the search.

Progress in our understanding of the development and functioning of the mind and of the diagnosis, treatment, and prevention of its disorders will determine in no small measure the quality of life on this planet as we enter the twenty-first century.

PART ONE

Examination and Evaluation

ARMAND M. NICHOLI, JR.

The Therapist-Patient Relationship

As the practice of medicine leans more heavily on modern technology and struggles with the obtrusive constraints of managed care, the complex interactions between doctor and patient have come under intense scrutiny and severe criticism. Critics charge that excessive emphasis on the science and technology of medicine has forced neglect of the art of medicine, and excessive emphasis on the cost of medical care has sacrificed the quality of that care. Consequently the relationship between physician and patient has suffered serious erosion. Concern over the deterioration of this relationship has resulted in a plethora of books and articles during the past few years. These publications explore every conceivable aspect of the doctor-patient interaction, including authoritarian control of patients (Katz, 1984; Merrill, 1995; Friedman, 1996), misuse of power by the doctor (Raven, 1986; Greenblatt, 1986; Briggs, 1990; Owen, 1995), attachment and termination of the relationship (Berlin, 1986; Kantrowitz, Katz, and Paolitto, 1990; Tapper, 1994; Bostic, 1996), dehumanization of the relationship (Fink, 1982; Zelm, 1986; Kass, 1996), sexual contact between doctor and patient (Pope, 1990; Appelbaum, 1994; Bayer, Coverdale, and Chiang, 1996; Adler, 1997), communication with patients (Quill, 1989; Trad, 1993; Cesario, 1996), informed consent (Jensen, 1989; Weil, 1993), patient compliance (Evans and Spellman, 1983; Holm, 1993), the impact of managed care on the relationship (Hunt, 1990; Book, 1991; Gabbard, 1992; Tuttman, 1997), confidentiality (Kleinman et al., 1997; Razis, 1990; Goldstein and Calderone, 1992), illness or death of the doctor (Gurtman, 1990; Lasky, 1990; Kleinman, 1990), what the doctor calls the patient (Rosenman and Goldney, 1991), and what the patient calls the doctor (Walter, 1991), and the ethical considerations of the relationship (APA, 1985, 1995; Kleinman et al., 1997). The American Psychiatric Association (1985) reviewed 85 studies of psychotherapy in an attempt to explore the influence of the therapist-patient relationship on the effectiveness of treatment.

Though significant in all medical specialties, the quality of the doctor-patient relationship becomes crucial in the practice of psychiatry.* In no other branch of medicine do the course and outcome of treatment rest so heavily on the highly complex and extremely sensitive interaction between doctor and patient. A review of hundreds of research studies confirms the hypothesis that the strength of the doctor-patient relationship is more positively correlated with successful therapeutic outcome than increased understanding or any of several other factors investigated (Hartley, 1985; Luborsky and Auerbach, 1985; Frank and Gunderson, 1990; Mohl et al., 1991; Hansson, 1992; Weiss, 1997).

From the first moment of contact, the doctor or therapist initiates a process that involves a multiplicity of factors within himself as well as within the patient and determines in large measure whether or not the patient recovers. In this process the patient's personality becomes the primary therapeutic focus; the therapist's personality (the vehicle for his skills, sensitivity, and experience), the primary therapeutic instrument; and the interaction between the two, the matrix in which all psychotherapy either succeeds or fails. Even before therapy actually begins, the quality of the initial encounter facilitates or impedes the therapist's attempt to complete a successful evaluation. Lack of initial rapport hinders his efforts to establish an accurate diagnosis, to determine the indications for treatment, and to choose the appropriate treatment modality.

Although systematic study and controlled research on the therapist-patient relationship remain surprisingly limited, some recent studies shed light on the reasons why many of these relationships fail (Luborsky et al., 1983; Hartley, 1985; Mohl et al., 1991; Weiss, 1997). These stud-

---

*The principles discussed here apply to all therapist-patient relationships, regardless of their duration or the form and intensity of the therapy. Physicians in other specialties aver that these principles indeed apply, by and large, to all doctor-patient relationships.

ies investigate patients who left therapy against medical advice either after an initial interview or after a few sessions. They point out that one component of the therapist-patient relationship supersedes all others in determining whether the patient continues with therapy: the therapist's ability to convey an intrinsic interest in the patient has been found to be more important than his position, appearance, reputation, clinical experience, training, and technical or theoretical knowledge. Although this finding, like many significant research findings on human behavior, appears obvious once we become aware of it,* the practical application of this knowledge is by no means obvious. Close, detailed attention must therefore be given to how, within the confines of a professional relationship, and without patronizing or condescending, the therapist conveys genuine interest in the patient.

This question can best be considered by focusing particularly on what happens between therapist and patient during the initial evaluation. This chapter describes not only the basic principles and dynamics of an effective therapist-patient relationship but also the tone, or emotional ambience; it emphasizes specific details of the initial encounter that are often taken for granted, seldom discussed, and frequently unheeded but nevertheless crucial.†

The major elements of this initial encounter are (1) the therapist's attitude toward the patient; (2) the therapist's emotional resources and standard of conduct; (3) the professional versus the social relationship; (4) the concepts of resistance and therapeutic alliance; (5) obstacles in the patient: manifestation of resistance; (6) feelings toward the therapist: reality and transference; (7) obstacles in the therapist: impediments to listening; (8) feelings toward the patient: reality and countertransference; (9) jargon and humor as obstacles; and (10) ethical considerations: sexual relations within therapy.

The Therapist's Attitude toward the Patient

The therapist's approach to the patient sets the tone for the initial interview. Whether the patient is young or old, neatly groomed or disheveled, outgoing or with-

drawn, articulate or inarticulate, highly integrated or totally disintegrated, of high or low socioeconomic status, the skilled clinician realizes that the patient, as a fellow human being, is considerably more like himself than he is different and that even if he understands only a fraction of a patient's mental functioning, that patient will contribute significantly to the therapist's understanding of himself and of every other patient. The therapist also realizes that each patient, regardless of how prosaic in appearance and background, is considerably more complex than can be grasped or described, no matter how brilliantly detailed the therapist's dynamic and genetic formulation; that each patient offers the therapist the potential for increasing his own professional skills and understanding, as well as for contributing to the body of knowledge in this relatively new specialty he practices. These realizations motivate the skilled and sensitive therapist to approach each patient with no little degree of humility, care, and respect.

The Therapist's Emotional Resources and Standard of Conduct

When a therapist first introduces himself to a patient— whether in a hospital ward, an outpatient clinic, or a private office—he brings to that first contact a reservoir of feelings, attitudes, and past experiences. His confidence in his clinical skills, his tolerance of the perplexity inherent in the diagnostic process, his ability to step out of his own needs and conflicts sufficiently to become aware of those of the patient, his attitude toward sickness, his sensitivity to suffering, his ability to recognize and to confront directly intense feelings of anxiety, depression, anger, dependency, and sexuality both in his patients and in himself, his intrinsic desire to help, his awareness of nuances of what people feel and subtleties in the expression of feelings, his ability to relate warmly, his respect for himself and for others, his value for human life, indeed, his very philosophy of life—all influence his approach to the patient and his capacity for establishing an effective therapist-patient relationship. In essence, the therapist must draw upon those resources within himself and observe the same courtesies he uses in his social and family relationships. The therapist must guard against the widespread tendency to neglect these common courtesies or to allow traditional scientific and medical formalities or externally imposed time constraints to supersede them in his relationship with his patients.

A patient consulting any doctor suffers stress, not only because of conflicts prompting the consultation but also because of conditions inherent in the doctor-patient rela-

---

*"It seems to be my fate," said Freud, "to discover only the obvious: that children have sexual feelings, which every nursemaid knows; and that night dreams are just as much a wish-fulfillment as day dreams" (Jones, 1953, p. 350).

†We shall view the therapist-patient relationship from a psychodynamic perspective, not because this perspective surpasses others, but because most training centers teach psychotherapy from this perspective and because psychoanalytic theory currently is more richly developed.

tionship. The patient, for example, is usually confused about the significance of his symptoms, unaware of their cause, apprehensive about what the doctor will recommend, and often embarrassed or humiliated at exposing what he considers exceedingly personal details of his life. Under such circumstances he is particularly vulnerable, and for this reason he deserves even more consideration than in ordinary social interactions. Too often, however, he receives less. Even the simple introductory handshake is often neglected—perhaps because of the doctor's hectic schedule, because the doctor shares a common human tendency to withdraw from emotional illness, because he adheres to a distorted concept of the psychoanalytic model in which the doctor never touches the patient (see Chapter 20), or, more likely, because he has never been formally taught to heed such issues.

The mundane yet often neglected practice of shaking hands helps set the tone for the initial relationship between therapist and patient. Shaking hands firmly with a patient brings to the first moments of contact an element of personal warmth and respect. This simple gesture eases the tension preceding the initial interview and reassures the patient, who almost always approaches the doctor with a degree of apprehension. To the patient, the doctor represents not only an awesome stranger who will probe the most intimate aspects of his life but also a highly knowledgeable authority with the power to make life and death decisions—or, in the case of a psychiatrist, what may be even more anxiety provoking, decisions concerning sanity and soundness of mind. Because so many people harbor this threatening image, a simple handshake at the beginning and at the end of the first session helps the doctor appear more human. The following example illustrates this point.

> After presenting the history of a patient to the staff of a large teaching hospital, a resident doctor attempted to bring the patient from the ward to the conference to be interviewed. The patient, somewhat suspicious and fearful of confronting a large group, refused to enter the conference room. Another resident then went to persuade the patient. Again he refused. A third and fourth resident also tried unsuccessfully. Then a fifth resident spoke briefly to the patient, who immediately followed him into the conference room. When the staff reviewed the incident later, the only difference in approach appeared to be that the successful resident had taken the time to introduce himself and to shake the patient's hand.

The therapist's general attitude sets the stage for the development of initial rapport and for the establishment of a constructive working relationship, even as he meets the patient and asks him to be seated in his office. How does the therapist, for example, address the patient? Does he use the first or last name only, dispensing with the title Mr., Miss, or Mrs. before the patient has granted that liberty? Does the doctor dismiss these common courtesies as stuffy formality? Or does he use them to express respect for the patient as a fellow human being? (Some studies indicate that some patients may prefer to be called by their first name [Rosenman and Goldney, 1991] but they reserve the right to decide.) Is the therapist relaxed and at ease? Does he sit comfortably in his chair—close enough to hear a soft-spoken person but far enough to avoid causing discomfort to those sensitive to physical closeness? Or is he tense and on edge, giving the impression of being more interested in obtaining the necessary facts and moving on quickly to the next patient than in the patient as a person? The skillful clinician carefully observes the impact of his words and behavior, realizing that all he says and does conveys his attitude toward his patient.

In essence, every aspect of the initial stages of the therapist-patient relationship can be measured against a single, simple standard: Is the therapist, in his exchange of initial courtesies, as warm and respectful to the patient as he would be to a dignitary visiting his home? Meeting such a visitor for the first time, the therapist would introduce himself, offer his hand, and take pains to make the visitor welcome and comfortable. The therapist would honor the visitor's title until given permission to dispense with it. He would strive to be relaxed and composed without being aloof or stilted and to be warm and responsive without being familiar or effusive. He should do the same in his first meeting with the patient.

The Professional versus the Social Relationship

If the therapist follows this standard of conduct, is there a risk of blurring the lines between a professional and a social relationship? How does the doctor-patient relationship differ from others? Although a doctor is expected to have a clear understanding of the differences, his medical school experience seldom helps him achieve it. Although he may express the same amenities in both his professional and social relationships, the skilled clinician seldom confuses one with the other. He realizes that as long as his patient remains his patient, their interaction must, for the benefit of the patient, remain within the context of a professional relationship. This relationship differs from the social one in that it exists to perform a unique task— namely, to evaluate and treat the conflicts prompting the patient to seek psychiatric help.

The professional relationship is therefore a somewhat constrained, though nevertheless spontaneous, relationship in which the therapist directs his clinical skills and experience toward this evaluation and treatment. Whereas a social relationship focuses on the needs of both parties, a professional relationship focuses solely on the needs of the patient—never on the needs of the therapist. This principle helps him maintain objectivity and develop an acute sensitivity to the ways the patient's emotional conflicts manifest themselves in the interaction with the therapist. The therapist keeps his input into the relationship as stable and consistent as possible to help gauge subtle changes in the patient's reaction to him. He carefully directs his words and behavior to what he judges to be, in both the short and the long term, the best interests of the patient.

This constraint imposes limitations on the relationship, providing a degree of frustration for both parties. The patient becomes frustrated because his emotional conflicts and his tendency to regress often create expectations and demands that cannot be met. The therapist experiences frustration, and a degree of loneliness as well, because some of his patient's needs, and all of his own, must by and large be filled elsewhere. It cannot be emphasized too strongly, however, that although a professional relationship sets clearly defined limits and demands some restraint and reserve, it by no means precludes warmth and kindness. Furthermore, to the extent that most patients need to see the therapist as a friend, as someone strongly *for* them, and to the extent that they consider a friend to be "a person with whom one is allied in a common struggle" or "a person whom one knows and trusts," as the *American Heritage Dictionary* defines the term, then to that extent a professional relationship also does not preclude friendship.*

The Concepts of Resistance and Therapeutic Alliance

Once the patient is seated, the therapist focuses his attention on facilitating in every way possible the patient's efforts to tell his story. His story comprises the events and conflicts in his life that prompted him to consult a psychiatrist or other professional. More than in any other branch of medicine, the diagnostic formulation leans heavily on the patient's description of his symptoms and his explanation of the reasons for his visit. Although

*Both ancient Romans and ancient Greeks described the doctor-patient relationship in terms of friendship (see Seneca *De beneficiis* 6.16 and Hippocratic *Praecepta* 50.9.258).

the patient may be eager to tell his story, partly to find relief from inner stress, and although the therapist may be eager to hear this story, realizing its indispensable contribution to his evaluation, the process of communication often runs into obstacles in both patient and therapist.

Dynamic psychiatry focuses considerable attention on understanding the manifestations and sources of obstacles in the patient. These observations have led to the clinical concept of *resistance*—those forces within the patient, conscious and unconscious, that oppose the purpose of the evaluation and the goals of the therapeutic process and that may be expressed in behavior, feelings, attitudes, ideas, impulses, and fantasies. This concept is fundamental to understanding the puzzling complexities of the interaction between therapist and patient. Close scrutiny of the therapist-patient relationship has revealed, paradoxically, that although patients come seeking relief from pain, they overtly or covertly oppose the therapist's efforts to effect that relief. A part of the patient strongly opposes not only the therapist but also the part of himself that seeks help.

The concepts of resistance, transference, and countertransference represent the most basic elements of dynamic psychiatry and illuminate many confusing and paradoxical aspects of the therapist-patient relationship. Though observed primarily in the context of intensive therapy, they often occur early in the therapist-patient interaction (see Chapter 20).

The clinical manifestations of resistance are myriad. The patient may be several minutes late for his sessions; he may stare at the floor and avoid looking at the therapist, slouch in his chair or hide behind his hands, sit stiffly and not move at all or move incessantly, announce that he has nothing to say, that his symptoms have disappeared (the so-called flight into health), that he sees no reason for his being there, or that he refuses to discuss what prompted him to make an appointment. He may use jargon to avoid expressing what he feels, assume ignorance or stupidity, automatically reject every comment made by the therapist, joke incessantly, express his utter hopelessness of ever being helped, attempt to talk about the psychiatrist, or express overt hostility and uncooperativeness, excessive compliance, or an overeagerness to please. He may be seductive; he may stutter, stammer, or become mute; or he may respond in one- or two-word sentences, as in the following:

"What brings you to see me?"

"My wife."

"You called for an appointment because your wife suggested it?"

"Yes."

"How do you understand her suggesting you see a psychiatrist?"

"I don't."

"Did you ask her?"

"No."

The skilled clinician learns to recognize the many forms of resistance in the patient, for he realizes that their detection and resolution determine whether his relationship with the patient will progress or founder.

The *therapeutic alliance* refers to those aspects of the therapist-patient relationship based on the patient's conscious and unconscious desires to cooperate with the therapist's efforts to help him. Whereas resistance represents all those forces in the patient opposing help from the therapist, the treatment alliance represents all the rational, nonneurotic parts of the patient desiring help.

Conceptually, the notion of the therapeutic alliance developed from theories of ego psychology and involves those ego functions relatively independent of the instinctual drives—the autonomous ego functions (Hartmann, 1964; A. Freud, 1966). The concept has received considerable attention in the literature of psychodynamics under such terms as *treatment alliance, working alliance,* and *therapeutic contract* (Sandler, Dare, and Holder, 1973; Hartley and Strupp, 1986; Meissner, 1992; Hanley, 1994; Hentschel, 1997).

Obstacles in the Patient: Manifestations of Resistance

Tension and anxiety may interfere with the patient's ability to think and speak clearly and thus provide resistance to free expression. This tension arises not only from the stresses inherent in the therapist-patient relationship but also, to a greater extent, from the repression of unconscious material underlying the psychological symptoms. The most superficial probing of this repressed, emotionally charged material may arouse intense anxiety and cause the most articulate person to stammer, grope for the right word, misuse or mispronounce words, or make grammatical errors he would seldom otherwise make.

Furthermore, subjective experience often defies easy verbalization. Physicians who become patients attest to the difficulty of translating their own symptoms into words, their extensive medical vocabulary notwithstanding, even when their symptoms are physical, localized to one part of the body, and acute in onset. Patients find psychological symptoms, with their frequently irrational, unconscious determinants, and with their onset usually extending over months or years, extremely difficult to verbalize or describe clearly.

When a patient struggles with such difficulties, the therapist must take steps not only to reduce this initial tension in every way possible but also to avoid intensifying it, deliberately or unthinkingly. If the patient at first refuses to talk about a topic, it is best merely to make note of it and go on to some other area. The therapist may explore briefly what makes the patient reticent, but the all-important issues of trust and confidentiality can be discussed with the patient at a later moment (see Chapter 2). Some therapists deliberately increase anxiety for the avowed purpose of observing how the patient reacts under stress. Because most patients already suffer enormous stress, however, such measures are uncalled for and are usually counterproductive. Other therapists, influenced by a distorted notion of the analytic model, may be aloof, distant, and distressingly unresponsive during the initial interview. To refuse to answer a patient's question, for example, without first explaining the reason why this and other customary modes of communication must be modified during the interview, unnecessarily increases the discomfort of the patient and reflects insensitivity on the part of the therapist. To express impatience by looking at the clock or moving restlessly as the patient struggles to express himself, to attempt to hurry the interview by offering alternative words or phrases as a patient gropes for the right one, to correct a patient's mispronunciation, misuse of a word, or grammatical error (a temptation, for example, when the therapist is insecure and the patient a learned professor) are all ways therapists may unthinkingly increase the tension and discomfort of the patient, impede the history-taking process, and thereby make the evaluation more difficult.

Whatever steps the therapist takes to mitigate this initial anxiety will facilitate both the patient's efforts to communicate and ultimately his own evaluation. A brief comment as the patient is being seated, for example, may help ease initial tension: "Did you have trouble finding the office?" "Has it stopped raining?" To the inexperienced therapist this banter may seem unprofessional, a waste of time. But the skilled clinician begins his evaluation from the first moment of contact with the patient. During this initial exchange of amenities, the therapist can observe a great deal about the patient's demeanor and his interaction with people. He can avoid any risk of the patient's using these friendly comments to carry on a lengthy social conversation (and thus delay confronting the emotionally charged issues) by focusing immediately on the basic information needed for his evaluation: birth date, marital status, previous psychiatric help, and other information the patient knows well and can relate with ease. This approach makes possible a gradual transition from the initial exchange of amenities to the more difficult but central question, "What brings you to see me?" Whatever steps the therapist takes to help the patient confront this question with a minimum of inner fear and anxiety will set the stage for the establishment of further rapport and for a successful first interview.

The therapist's *mannerisms* can cause negative reactions in certain patients, and he must be sensitive to these reactions when they occur. For example, the 60-year-old president of a large corporation requested consultation with a university psychiatrist to help resolve some long-standing difficulties with his son, who was attending that institution. During the second interview the executive stormed out of the office and failed to return. "What bothered me more than anything else," he said later, "was that every other word the psychiatrist used was a four-letter word. Perhaps he does this to show he is 'with it,' but I found it insulting and disrespectful. I left with the impression that he had more maturing to do and needed more help than I."

This incident points to the tendency of some clinicians who work with adolescents and young adults to tailor their dress and speech to those of their patients to help establish rapport. Such efforts usually fall short of success, the adolescent's dress and speech being an effort to establish distance from the adult world and to find his own identity. The therapist must be alert to the effects of his dress, speech, and other mannerisms on particular patients so he can deal with barriers that emerge. Most of the errors the therapist makes, however, are far less obvious than offensive mannerisms. More often they result in his inability to listen sympathetically, an insensitive comment, premature reassurance, a judgmental tone ("Why did you do that?"), or a patronizing air ("Come into the office, dear"). All may evoke negative feelings in the patient that interfere with the establishment of rapport.

Other obstacles the therapist may encounter early on may arise from the patient's *misconceptions* about psychotherapy, secondary gains from illness, displaced motivation, or the use of psychological defenses to avoid meaningful material. A common misconception arises from the fear that the doctor will pass on information about the patient to others or compile a record of the patient to which future employers or other agencies will have access. The therapist must assure the patient that standards of the utmost confidentiality will be followed, even when discussing clinical material with supervisors or other clinicians; the name of the patient must be revealed only with the patient's consent. Erosion of confidentiality inevitably erodes the relationship with the patient. Another misconception is that the therapist will "brainwash" an

individual or influence the patient against his will to give up a certain philosophy or lifestyle—for example, a woman may fear that the therapist will influence her to settle for a traditional role she views as that of a second-class citizen; a devout person may fear that the therapist will ridicule or destroy his faith; or a homosexual seeking help for nonsexual problems may fear that the therapist will attempt to change his sexual orientation. Direct reassurance and clarification of the goals of evaluation and therapy will help remove such barriers.

Secondary gain (as opposed to "primary gain") refers to certain benefits the patient enjoys in being ill that cause him to take advantage of his illness and to prolong it. Such benefits include increased personal attention, disability compensation, and decreased responsibility, as well as more subtle gratifications such as satisfaction of the need for self-punishment or the vengeful punishment of others who are forced to take responsibility for the patient or to share his suffering. Such secondary satisfactions from illness may cause the patient to refuse to cooperate with therapy and must be detected and dealt with at the outset of treatment.

Displaced motivation may also be a barrier. Not infrequently a patient comes to the therapist only because a parent, a spouse, or a family physician sends him. If the patient sees no need for help, the first task of the therapist is to shift motivation from the referring person to the patient himself. By carefully exploring the patient's conflicts, the therapist can help the patient understand how these conflicts impair functioning in important areas of the patient's life. This understanding will often help the patient realize his need for therapy. (Sometimes, of course, the patient may not in fact need help, and the therapist can be immeasurably reassuring by conveying this to the family or other referring person.)

Among the psychological defenses, in addition to repression, that become obstacles is the use of intellectual reasoning to avoid painful feelings.* This kind of *intellectualization* involves expressing complaints with the use of jargon: "I seem to be suffering from severe ego diffusion," or "I think I have a number of unresolved pregenital conflicts." This obstacle occurs frequently in patients who work or study in hospital or university communities. The therapist must halt this tendency immediately by explain-

*Recent attempts to categorize obstacles or resistance according to source have led to terms such as (1) *defense resistance,* including repression and intellectualization; (2) *transference resistance,* in which feelings displaced onto the doctor act as resistance; (3) *secondary gain resistance,* wherein gratifications of being ill outweigh the distress of the illness; and (4) *superego resistance,* stemming from the patient's sense of guilt and need for punishment.

ing that the patient's task is to express what he feels and experiences in his own words.

Feelings toward the Therapist: Reality and Transference

The sources of resistance providing the most powerful obstacles to diagnostic and therapeutic efforts are the patient's feelings toward the therapist. All feelings in relationships as we now understand them run on a double track. We react and relate to another person not only on the basis of how we consciously experience that person in reality, but also on the basis of our unconscious experience of him in reference to our experiences with significant people in infancy and childhood—particularly parents and other family members. We tend to displace our feelings and attitudes from these past figures onto people in the present, especially if someone has features similar to a person in the past. An individual may, therefore, evoke intense feelings in us—strong attraction or strong aversion—totally inappropriate to our knowledge of or experience with that person. This process may, to varying degrees, influence our choice of a friend, roommate, spouse, or employer.

Feelings toward the therapist also have this twofold basis. They arise first from reactions to what the therapist is in reality—how he treats the patient, his manner, his dress, the length of his hair, the tone of his voice, the warmth or coldness of his personality, the firmness of his handshake—to all that he says and does in his interaction with the patient. Second, they arise from what he represents to the patient's unconscious. Feelings toward the therapist, therefore, stem not only from the real, factual aspects of the therapist-patient interaction but also from feelings displaced onto the therapist from unconscious representation of people important to the patient early in his childhood experiences. These displaced or transferred feelings tend to distort his perception of the therapist, making him appear to be an important figure in the patient's past; they create, in one sense, an illusion (Sandler, Dare, and Holder, 1973; Chused, 1992). This phenomenon of *transference,* of displacing feelings from a person in the past to a person in the present, gives rise to some of the most intense, colorful, complex, perplexing, potentially destructive, and eventually most therapeutically useful aspects of the entire therapist-patient relationship.

Although transference reactions occur in all relationships, they occur most frequently and most intensely in relationships with authority. This happens especially in doctor-patient relationships, partly because patients often view the doctor as an authority figure and tend to displace onto him feelings once directed toward their parents, the first authorities in their lives. In addition, illness fosters regression to childlike patterns of response that may in turn lead to a strong passive dependence on the doctor. While doctors have been aware of transference phenomena for centuries, they failed to appreciate their complexity and therapeutic value until Freud studied and described them in detail (S. Freud, 1895, 1905, 1912).

Not all feelings toward the therapist, of course, interfere with the patient's telling his story. Positive feelings, because they evoke a desire to please the therapist, usually facilitate the patient's efforts to communicate. Such feelings may cause a sudden, marked improvement in the patient when the disappearance of symptoms results primarily from a desire to please the therapist. These so-called transference cures (not to be confused with "flight into health," a form of resistance) may be temporary, disappearing as soon as the intensity of the positive feelings toward the therapist diminishes. When positive feelings become too intense, however, when the need to please and to win approval becomes excessive, positive feelings may have the reverse effect, causing the patient to withhold information he feels may provoke the therapist's disapproval. In addition to the excessive need to please, positive feelings may also give rise to strong erotic feelings toward the therapist, that may in turn increase the patient's anxiety and interfere with easy communication. Negative feelings toward the therapist, not surprisingly, almost always pose a barrier to easy communication. Anger and hostility evoke a reluctance to confide in the therapist and a tendency consciously or unconsciously to withhold significant details.

Transference feelings that become barriers to communication (whether the feelings are positive or negative) usually become manifest during the course of intensive therapy and will be discussed in greater detail in Chapter 20. Sometimes, however, such barriers manifest themselves early in the therapist-patient relationship and seriously interfere with its progress. Because the therapist and patient have not yet established a therapeutic alliance, this obstacle may not only impede the therapist's evaluation but also, unless resolved, abruptly and prematurely terminate the relationship.

During the first few sessions of an evaluation, a 33-year-old woman experienced great difficulty speaking to the doctor. She entered the office and immediately began to cry. When she apologized for her loss of control, the doctor waited patiently for her to regain her composure and encouraged her to express all her feelings. The intensity of the crying, however, continued throughout several sessions and made it impossible for the patient to speak. The doctor's efforts to explore the cause of her crying only increased her sobbing. She would feel fine until she entered the waiting room, then be overcome with fear and remorse. She expressed confusion over her fear of the doctor and her inability to talk to him. Entering the office, she would burst into tears, clench her fists, and press her arms against her body as though protecting herself. Her face would twitch, her hands tremble, and her whole body shake uncontrollably. Out of desperation, she consulted another doctor. The consultant suggested she return to her doctor and make one more effort to resolve the impasse; if that proved unsuccessful, he would find another therapist for her.

When she returned to her doctor and discussed in detail her session with the consultant, it became clear that her description of her doctor to the consultant paralleled word for word her description of her father given during the initial interview. When the doctor pointed this out to her, she said she had often noticed that the doctor's eyes were "exactly the same" as her father's. The doctor then explored with the patient her early and current relationship with her father, described by her as "a very special relationship." As a child, she had been his favorite and held him in awe. She spoke in glowing terms of his intelligence, his handsome appearance, and his strength. She mentioned also that he was cold, highly critical, somewhat cruel, and much hated by the rest of the family. Although she loved him, she feared him, and as a child she had found it impossible to talk with him. She recalled that her older, 11-year-old sister had failed to respond quickly when her father called and had been "beaten by him with a belt until she bled." Even as an adult, she trembled when speaking with him on the phone. As she explored her relationship with her father, she realized how much her feelings toward the doctor paralleled those feelings experienced repeatedly as a small child toward her father. Once recognized and explored with the patient, the obstacle was overcome, the evaluation completed, and the relationship continued into a prolonged, constructive therapeutic experience.

Transference resistance, because it poses such a powerful obstacle, must be recognized early and dealt with immediately by the therapist, especially when it occurs during the initial evaluation or during the early stages of therapy. The therapist may recognize that a barrier exists and that it obviously relates to how the patient feels toward him, but how does he diagnose such feelings as transference reactions? His ability to distinguish between transferred and "reality" aspects of the patient's reactions may prove vital to a continuation of the therapist-patient relationship.

Transference reactions have characteristics that the skilled clinician readily recognizes. First, transference is essentially an unconscious process. Although the patient may be aware of what he feels and perceive that his feelings are somewhat strange or bizarre, at the beginning of therapy he has little or no awareness of the source of these feelings or of their displacement from that source to the therapist. In the case described above, the patient was acutely aware of her own anxiety and realized she feared the doctor, but she had no idea what caused these fears or of their relation to an early figure in her life whom she loved and at the same time feared intensely. Second, transference feelings are inappropriate in time and in intensity to the circumstances in which they occur. The patient may underreact or overreact—and may be fully aware that the reaction is inappropriate; the patient in the illustration expressed confusion because her fear of the therapist was out of keeping with what she described as his warmth and compassion. Third, transference reactions are characterized by ambivalence, that is, by the coexistence of opposing feelings or emotions toward the same person. In this case, the patient felt fear and a degree of hostility toward the doctor but also had feelings of respect, admiration, and sexual attraction.

Because transference reactions are so prevalent, so colorful in their intensity, and so helpful in understanding the patient's dynamics, the therapist may become entranced by them and neglect the reality aspects of his relationship with the patient. Although his patient may be hypersensitive, may struggle with impaired self-esteem, may be insatiably dependent, and may manifest other conflicts causing frequent interpersonal difficulty, the therapist must not be lulled into neglecting the part he may be playing in provoking barriers within the patient.

If the therapist mistakenly treats feelings based on the reality of the relationship as transference feelings, he may permanently destroy the possibility of a good working relationship with the patient. If, for example, he makes a mistake in scheduling the initial interview and the patient arrives only to be told to come at some other time, or if he is late for the patient's first appointment, the patient may be furious with the therapist, even before making contact with him. If the therapist then treats the patient's anger as transference, ignoring the reality on which the anger is based, he may never see that patient again. Once the anger is recognized, the therapist must explore the anger with the patient to help to determine its source. Anger and other negative feelings may stem from transference or reality aspects of the relationship, or both, and neither can be ignored.

Obstacles in the Therapist: Impediments to Listening

Just as serious obstacles to the diagnostic and therapeutic process may arise within the patient, they may also arise within the therapist. The latter become especially destructive to the therapist-patient relationship when they interfere with the therapist's capacity to listen. The therapist's ability to convey a genuine interest in his patient, to facilitate the patient's communication, and to establish a solid therapeutic alliance depends in large measure on his capacity to listen effectively. Before discussing obstacles that interfere with listening, this section will attempt to define it.

How can one describe the all-important, seemingly simple, yet enormously complex process of effective listening? Listening effectively involves first and foremost keeping out of the patient's way as he attempts to tell his history. To keep from obtruding, to keep quiet, to keep the spotlight focused completely on the patient—these are among the therapist's most difficult tasks. Effective listening involves several elements: having sufficient awareness and resolution of one's own conflicts to avoid reacting in a way that interferes with the patient's free expression of thoughts and feelings; avoiding subtle verbal or nonverbal expressions of disdain or judgment toward the content of the patient's story, even when that content offends the therapist's sensibilities; waiting patiently through periods of silence or tears as the patient summons up courage to delve into painful material or pauses to collect his thoughts or his composure; hearing not only what the patient says but what he is trying to say and what he leaves unsaid; using both ears and eyes to detect confirming or conflicting messages in verbal content and affect (from tone of voice, posture, and other nonverbal clues); scanning one's own reactions to the patient; avoiding looking away from the patient as he speaks; sitting still; limiting the number of mental excursions into one's own fantasies; controlling those feelings toward the patient that interfere with an accepting, sympathetic, nonjudgmental attitude; and realizing that full acceptance of the patient is possible without condoning or sanctioning attitudes and behavior destructive to him or to others.

Although it takes place in a setting of physical inactivity, listening involves an intensely active emotional and intellectual process. The therapist absorbs a vast array of complex, often confusing and conflicting data. He then sifts what he considers relevant from irrelevant detail and uses this detail continuously to refine his diagnostic impression. Effective listening provides the key to moving beyond the crude and often dehumanizing method of diagnosing by attaching labels; it enables the therapist to formulate his diagnosis on conflicts specific to the patient and eventually to use this information for appropriate therapeutic intervention. In essence, effective listening is the focus of all one's mental and physical processes onto the patient, so that for that span of time between the patient's entrance into the office and his departure, he has the therapist's unwavering attention.

Just as anxiety within the patient may interfere with his efforts to communicate, *anxiety within the therapist* may also erect barriers to communication. Though usually less intense and more subtle, anxiety within the therapist may impede not only the patient's telling his history but also the therapist's ability to hear that history. Tension and anxiety within the therapist may have many sources, the most common being the nature of the material explored in the psychiatric interview. Unconscious thoughts and feelings are highly charged emotionally, and whether overtly manifest, as in a psychotic patient, or carefully defended against, as in a less disturbed patient, they may create considerable tension in both patient and therapist. Extreme anxiety in the patient may arouse anxiety in the therapist, and the contagious quality of depression may cause the therapist to feel despondent and emotionally drained. The absence of the usual verbal responses in a schizophrenic patient may cause the therapist to feel uneasy or apprehensive.

If the patient's conflicts parallel unresolved conflicts in the therapist, the anxiety aroused in the therapist may cause "blind spots," making it difficult for him to hear or to understand aspects of the patient's story. For example, a first-year resident experienced unusual discomfort working with patients whose problems were primarily sexual. The resident's own background and conflicts severely inhibited him sexually, so that he dated little and found it necessary to avoid even plays and movies with sexual scenes. During his own analysis, he discovered that when his patients focused on sexual problems, his intense anxiety not only made it difficult for him to hear what they were saying but also caused him to interrupt them frequently and change the subject.

In another instance, a resident became pregnant unexpectedly. Her ambivalence toward this unplanned pregnancy caused her to deny it and to avoid thinking or talking about it. As her pregnancy became increasingly evident, she reported to her supervisor that her patients "all seemed suddenly to be falling apart." On further exploration with her supervisor, she realized she had failed to mention her pregnancy to her patients and to tell them that she would soon be leaving them. She had not previously seen that the recurrence of symptoms in many of these patients accompanied expressions of dissatisfaction with her and of anger toward earlier figures who had left them. Once she recognized this blind spot, she discussed these issues with her patients and observed an immediate lessening of their agitation and discontent. (For more on pregnant therapists, see Nadelson et al., 1974; Cullen-Drill, 1994.)

The therapist's professional insecurity may also add to his tension, making it difficult for him to tolerate a patient's hostility or criticism, especially if it stems from the intuitive ability many disturbed patients display for detecting specific weaknesses and insecurities in others. Confidence in his own clinical skills, gained through training and experience, helps the therapist tolerate these attacks quietly, with a minimum of anxiety, anger, or other defensive reactions. Another source of anxiety in the therapist is the confusion inherent in the early phases of every evaluation. The interviewer must, for varying periods of time, tolerate working in the dark. As is not the case with medical and surgical patients, causes of the psychiatric patient's symptoms are rarely discoverable through physical examination, x-rays, and laboratory procedures. Each patient presents a complex puzzle that may take considerable time and effort to solve.

How a therapist handles his anxiety determines whether or not the anxiety becomes an obstacle. People handle anxiety in different ways—some by talking excessively, others by becoming excessively quiet. If a therapist characteristically handles anxiety by becoming quiet, he may run some risk of appearing distant and withdrawn from the patient. This is by far the lesser of two evils, however, for if he handles anxiety by talking excessively, he will inevitably obstruct progress. When a therapist is talking, he cannot be listening. He may, for example, give premature reassurance, conveying the impression that he does not really understand the seriousness of the patient's symptoms. A patient may reveal thoughts of killing himself or of killing others. The therapist, made anxious by this, may respond that many people have such thoughts, or that thinking is not the same as acting, then quickly change the subject and thus fail to explore conflicts underlying such thoughts and the possibility of their being expressed in action.

One young woman with metastatic carcinoma searched in vain for a doctor or a member of her family who would discuss her illness with her or acknowledge it seriously. Even a therapist she consulted found confronting a young, dying person so anxiety provoking that he would not at first allow her to discuss her illness. When he realized this, he struggled for words that would recognize her grave condition and yet not contribute to her despair. When he told her that he understood the seriousness of her illness but also realized that she, like everyone else, did not know whether tomorrow she would live or die, she found relief, some degree of hope, and freedom to express her feelings.

Fatigue may act as another obstacle to effective listening. Being battered by anxiety-provoking, emotionally charged material hour after hour while physically immobile can be emotionally exhausting and physically debilitating for even the most experienced clinician. Perhaps for this reason Freud expressed horror that a doctor was seeing 10 patients a day and called it a concealed attempt at suicide. It betrays no professional secret to acknowledge that many patients have observed their therapists falling asleep—not only those sitting behind a couch but also those in a face-to-face interview. Such experiences, though humorous on one level, do little to convince the patient of the therapist's intrinsic interest. Regular physical exercise, a well-ventilated office, proper spacing of patients, and light lunches to minimize postprandial drowsiness can help to reduce fatigue and its influence on the difficult task of listening effectively. A therapist who sleeps is not listening.

Impatience is still another obstacle to listening, involving excessive eagerness to make the diagnosis. This may be particularly prevalent when the therapist plans to present his material to a supervisor or at a case conference. The diagnostic process ought to be continuous throughout the evaluation and refined during the various stages of therapy. If the therapist arrives at a diagnosis prematurely, he risks hearing only material confirming his diagnosis. This kind of overeagerness may also lead to impatience. Rather than waiting calmly for the patient to express in words the circumstances and the complexity of the feelings prompting him to seek help, the therapist may attempt to hurry the process by asking several questions at once: "How did your father die, where were you when it happened, and how did you feel when you heard about it?" Or, if the patient pauses to answer one question, the therapist may ask a second question before the first is answered. Such attempts to accelerate the process—even if the therapist has only one session to complete his evaluation—usually confuse the patient, make him more tense, and impede his efforts to tell his story. The imposed time constraints of managed care make clinicians vulnerable to the dangers of impatience.

Another obstacle—*inattentiveness*—results from the failure of the therapist to use both ears and eyes for the acute perception that is part of effective listening. The clinician must listen attentively to what the patient says, to what he avoids saying, and to subtle changes in tone that may point to important areas to explore. In one instance, a 39-year-old woman, relating some of her family history during an initial interview, mentioned the name of a young man she knew as a teenager. The therapist noticed a slight change in the tone of her voice when she spoke his name and asked her if this young man had any special significance. She burst into tears as she explained he was the first and only man she really loved, that he had rejected her, and that she had never completely resolved her grief. That particular loss and its many ramifications proved to be a central issue in a consequent successful course of psychotherapy.

Although some therapists find it difficult to confront patients face to face, to look at them openly and directly, the listening process does nevertheless involve looking at and observing the patient. (Freud used a couch because he had difficulties looking at patients and having patients look at him.) A patient feels he does not have the therapist's full attention if the therapist keeps looking away. A patient may become openly hostile if, when speaking, he notices the therapist shift his gaze to his fingernails, to papers on the desk, or to the window. Although an unblinking stare obviously distracts, an attentive, level gaze reassures the patient and helps focus the therapist's attention on signs easily overlooked; the twitch of an eyelid, the slight watering of an eye, a transient flush, the almost imperceptible tremble of the chin, and subtle, fleeting facial expressions may all provide clues to emotionally charged areas. The therapist may, of course, look away when he comments or when the patient pauses, but his eye contact with the patient helps both him and the patient to communicate.

Restlessness, the inability to sit still, may also impede communication. A fidgety, restless therapist may appear impatient, inattentive, and uninterested. The clinician should realize that his time with the patient belongs totally to the patient and attempt to settle down comfortably to give the patient his full attention. The stresses peculiar to the psychiatric interview make it difficult for the therapist to sit still and sustain a composed demeanor. This difficulty can be minimized if the clinician, in developing his potential as a therapist, comes to terms with what he considers the passive, receptive aspects of his character.

Daydreaming erects yet another barrier, since listening effectively requires focusing one's full mental faculties.

Keeping the mind focused on the patient for a prolonged period of time is the most important and often the most difficult aspect of effective listening. The emotionally charged content of the patient's history, the unmet physical and emotional needs of the therapist, and the combination of all other obstacles interfere with concentrated listening. The therapist must limit his natural tendency to take brief mental excursions into his own thoughts and daydreams. The more frustrated the therapist is in his extraprofessional life, the more frequent will be these excursions and the greater the tendency to use, in fantasy, details of the patient's life to satisfy vicariously the therapist's own unmet needs. When the therapist's attention wanes, when he leaves on one of these mental excursions, the patient senses his absence; a vacant stare or a brief glance away from the patient may telegraph this departure. Not infrequently, the patient's suspicion that the therapist has left is confirmed by the therapist's asking a question the patient has just answered. Although it may be unrealistic to expect these excursions to cease entirely, the skilled clinician limits them by continually refocusing his mind on the patient. The ideal is to work toward "session-tight compartments," wherein the therapist shuts out his own concerns, needs, and preoccupations and focuses entirely on those of the patient.

Feelings toward the Patient: Reality and Countertransference

The therapist's feelings toward the patient may also impose a barrier. As is the case with the feelings of the patient toward the therapist, those of the therapist toward the patient have a twofold basis. First, they are based on the reality of the patient's appearance, personality, character, and conflicts; second, they are based on what the patient represents to the therapist's unconscious in terms of early significant figures. The tendency of the therapist to displace feelings from these earlier figures onto the patient is referred to as *countertransference.* (The "counter" in this term means "parallel to" or "complementary to," as in *counterpart,* and not "opposite" or "contrary to," as in *counterphobic.*)

If a therapist feels strongly negative toward a patient, he must determine whether these negative feelings arise from the reality or from the transferred aspects of the relationship. Some therapists feel it is unfair to the patient and to themselves to begin therapy with a patient they do not like. One must keep in mind, however, that most patients have some unlikable quality—defects of character; pockets of immaturity; regressive, dependent, and manipulative features of their illness. These features have created difficulties in their relationships with people generally and will eventually manifest themselves in their relationship with the therapist. The therapist, therefore, will probably encounter in most patients some qualities he does not like. The sensitive clinician makes careful distinctions between the symptoms of the patient, on the one hand, and the patient as a person, on the other, and will not permit the negative feelings provoked by the symptoms to interfere with his desire to understand and to help the person.

If the negative feelings of the therapist stem from countertransference feelings, he may have considerably more difficulty understanding and controlling them. Early in the therapist-patient relationship, for example, a therapist may find himself experiencing intense feelings toward a patient that appear to have no basis in reality.

A resident found himself curiously depressed and upset after evaluating a young woman for therapy. The interview had gone well. The patient was intelligent, personable, and articulate; she had classic symptoms, appeared to be psychologically minded, was well motivated, and readily accepted the doctor's suggestion for therapy. Although the doctor had time to see the patient in therapy, he decided to refer her to another doctor. After the interview the doctor found himself struggling with a sadness that persisted throughout the day. Only when reviewing his notes that evening did he realize that during the course of the interview the patient had mentioned that she was pregnant and discussed the necessity of her leaving her proposed therapy briefly for her confinement. This led the doctor to recall a recent experience of his own, when his wife had left him to enter the hospital to give birth to their first child; this recollection in turn flooded him with early memories of the desertion he had felt when his mother had left him as a small boy to deliver his younger brother.

As with transference, countertransference involves inappropriately intense feelings and the unconscious displacement of such feelings from a person in the past to one in the present.

Jargon and Humor as Obstacles

The counterproductivity of the patient's use of psychological jargon in describing his symptoms or giving his history has already been mentioned. The therapist must also avoid this tendency in his communication with the patient. Technical terms purportedly facilitate communication within a specialized field. In psychiatry, where the terms often lack precise and standardized definitions, they confuse more often than they clarify. An inexperienced therapist with an uncertain grasp of psychiatry may become entranced with this language and use it freely with both his peers and his patients. Because one tends to fear what one does not understand, such terms may unnecessarily frighten the patient.

Technical terms not only confuse; they also dehumanize, oversimplify, and, when used pejoratively, express veiled hostility. H. Bruch (1974) writes that "young psychiatrists are apt to acquire an extensive psychoanalytic vocabulary, and this excess verbiage may act like shining but distorting glasses . . . Instead of sympathetically observing and responding to his patient . . . he will label him with accusing, punitive, and essentially invalidating [epithets] . . . 'passive-aggressive,' 'masochistic,' 'compulsive.'" Such terms often convey "badness" as well as sickness, and no therapist would tolerate others' using them to refer to his own family. Bruch continues, "The less secure a therapist is, the more likely he will cling to stereotyped concepts and a cliché-ridden vocabulary" (p. 25). Insecurity, however, does not always fade with experience, and the tendency to use obsolete and confusing terms is not limited to young therapists.

The ability to describe human behavior with psychodynamic understanding but without psychoanalytic jargon requires a good grasp of basic concepts. As a therapist grows in understanding, he ought to be able to express himself to both colleagues and patients without jargon. Observers sitting in on the workshops of Anna Freud, for example, were impressed at the almost complete absence of psychoanalytic terms.

Humor can exert a wonderful humanizing influence in interpersonal relationships, easing tension and facilitating communication. Often during the arduous process of psychotherapy, a hearty laugh between therapist and patient underscores Addison's comment that "mirth is like a flash of lightning, that breaks through a gloom of clouds." Yet humor also has destructive potential in the therapist-patient relationship and can become an obstacle to progress.

To avoid the destructive aspects of humor, the therapist must be alert to what the patient actually feels from moment to moment. A patient may smile, laugh, or giggle not because he feels amused but because he feels anxious. A 28-year-old woman, for no apparent reason, would suddenly flush crimson during her therapy sessions and begin to giggle uncontrollably. As she explored these reactions she realized that erotic thoughts and feelings toward the therapist precipitated this anxious giggling and paralleled childhood and adolescent feelings experienced when her nude father entered her room each night to lock her windows. A 26-year-old man would giggle suddenly and uncontrollably while experiencing toward his therapist the same apprehension he experienced as a child toward a harsh, punitive father. Both patients expressed embarrassment and annoyance at these episodes.

Joking and other forms of humor may be a form of resistance. A witty, intelligent graduate student, for example, announced suddenly to the interviewer that he had been out with a beautiful girl the night before. He said, "She had long black hair flowing down her back; none on her head, just down her back," and laughed uproariously. The sudden, unexpected joke and the contagiousness of his laugh caused the therapist to join in. Several such episodes later, when the therapist focused on the process as well as the content of the interview, he realized the patient told a joke whenever he approached emotionally charged topics. The joke served to release anxiety and to change the subject quickly. Patients may use humor to deal with painful topics or to screen feelings that would overwhelm them if confronted directly. A young woman, recently notified that her father was dying, introduced this subject by laughingly describing a number of his amusing idiosyncrasies.

Anxiety in the therapist may cause him to smile inappropriately or otherwise to use humor destructively. The anxiety aroused by an enraged patient threatening violence may cause the therapist to smile and to provoke the patient's rage further. Explicitly sexual material may also make an inexperienced therapist smile anxiously, giving the patient the impression of being laughed at. Even the simple rule of smiling with and not at the patient (Kubie, 1971) needs to be followed judiciously. If the therapist had joined in the uncontrollable giggling of the 2 patients mentioned above, he would have increased their discomfort, and if he had continued to laugh with the graduate student, he would have encouraged the student's resistance. Realizing the dangers of humor must not, however, preclude a warm smile or appropriate spontaneous laughter. A dour therapist who makes no response to a patient's humorous overtures can be a tedious bore and may increase the patient's discomfort.

The key to using humor appropriately is being tuned in to the patient's feelings, to his mood as it changes from session to session and from topic to topic. The therapist must remember that most psychiatric patients are extremely sensitive to being laughed at, that although others may have found the patients' symptoms and irrational behavior amusing, the patients find them painful. Sometimes a patient will suddenly see a ludicrous aspect to his

behavior and burst into laughter. The therapist can, of course, join in the laughter; but laughing at the patient or making fun of his symptoms through mockery, sarcasm, or irony will inevitably set a discordant tone and become an obstacle to the relationship.

Ethical Considerations: Sexual Relations within Therapy

No discussion of the therapist-patient relationship would be adequate without mention of the ethical and moral issues involved—an area of increasing interest in the psychiatric literature. All the aspects discussed so far imply that this relationship must be focused completely on the welfare of the patient and conducted within the framework of high ethical standards. The lowering of these standards, many believe, has impaired the quality of the relationship, provoked widespread concern over patients' rights, and contributed to passage of recent laws that attempt not only to protect these rights but also to define and regulate the therapist's conduct (see Chapters 35 and 38). These laws reflect society's insistence that high standards be maintained (Veatch, 1981; APA, 1985, 1995; Haddox, 1986).

The striking recent increase in interest in medical and psychiatric ethics has centered on a number of ethical issues. In this chapter only the issue of sexual activity between patient and therapist will be considered—an issue that concerns the ethics of the professional relationship itself. (For discussion of other ethical issues, the reader is referred to the references at the end of this chapter and to Chapters 35 and 38.)

Sexual relations between therapist and patient have become a topic of open discussion not only in the lay press but also in the most recent medical literature (Herman et al., 1987; Pope, 1990; Appelbaum, 1994; Bayer, Coverdale, and Chiang, 1996). Although changes in sexual mores and other aspects of our culture have contributed to this discussion, the Hippocratic oath—the traditional ethical guideline for physicians—proscribes sexual relationships with patients, as does the American Psychiatric Association (1985) code of ethics.

Until the 1970s doctors discussed this topic sotto voce. The evidence consisted primarily of anecdotes, and the general impression was that only a tiny percent of highly disturbed individuals practiced such behavior. Since 1970, a few documented studies have been published. S. H. Kardener (1974) surveyed 460 physicians and reported that "between 5 and 13 percent . . . engaged in erotic behaviors, including and excluding sexual intercourse, with a limited number of patients" and that the psychiatrists in this sample were "least likely to engage in erotic acts, particularly compared with obstetrician-gynecologists and general practitioners" (p. 1134).

A national random-sample survey of 1423 practicing psychiatrists revealed that 98% of respondents considered therapist-patient sexual contact "always inappropriate and usually harmful to the patient" (Herman et al., 1987).

Yet psychiatrists, and other therapists, for reasons discussed throughout this chapter, may be most vulnerable. As already discussed, the therapist-patient relationship, especially when carried out over an extensive period of time, fosters complex, intense, and often confusing feelings in both patient and therapist. These may include romantic and sexual feelings that the patient insists on expressing physically and demands that the therapist reciprocate. Although this situation occurs less frequently than novels and movies imply, its occurrence presents a delicate problem for the therapist. While he must encourage the free expression of all thoughts, feelings, and wishes, he must limit the patient to expressing them verbally. He must reject the patient's physical expression of such feelings but must be exceedingly careful never to reject the patient. Because these intensely positive feelings create unfulfilled yearnings and are therefore often stressful for the patient, the therapist must not dismiss them lightly or insensitively.

Sexual activity between therapist and patient may reflect an acting out of the patient's pathology—or the therapist's pathology.

Sometimes the patient's demands are overt. But as Freud wisely observed: "It is not a patient's crudely sensuous desires which constitute the temptation. These are more likely to repel . . . It is rather, perhaps, a woman's subtler and aim-inhibited wishes which bring with them the danger of making a man forget his technique and medical task for the sake of a fine experience" (1915, p. 170). The patient may convey these "subtler wishes" by expressing an inability to confide fully in a person without being close physically, or by expressing sexual dreams or fantasies about the therapist in a manner calculated more to arouse than to explore or enlighten. As a first step, the patient may attempt to change the restrained, formal relationship into a more familiar one by asking the therapist personal questions concerning his age, his marital status, and his residence. The therapist will do well to remember that although patients may press to make the relationship more intimate, they often become extremely uncomfortable when they succeed. Motives for changing the relationship are at best mixed, and a part of the patient is usually greatly relieved to keep the relationship a professional

one. Because romantic and sexual feelings may be a form of resistance and impede therapeutic progress, they must be confronted, explored, and resolved so that therapy can proceed. Such exploration soon makes clear that these feelings have little to do with the personal charm of the therapist but would be directed toward anyone sitting in his chair. Thus, analyzing these feelings not only reduces their intensity in the patient but also reduces the tendency of the therapist to be flattered by them.

The issue of a physical relationship becomes more complicated if the therapist experiences romantic and sexual feelings toward the patient. Until the late 1950s erotic feelings toward the patient were seldom discussed in the literature except to state they must never be tolerated (Tower, 1956). But in 1959 Harold Searles described such feelings in the therapist as a frequent and normal occurrence during the course of intensive therapy. Current authors agree with Searles, and it no longer seems necessary for therapists to view these feelings as an intolerable aberration in themselves. By and large, however, the psychiatric profession considers *acting* on these feelings to be an expression of pathology in the therapist (Davidson, 1976). And some authors have stressed the ethical obligation of psychiatrists to expose colleagues who "sexually abuse patients" (Strasburger, Jorgenson, and Randles, 1990). Though recognizing sexual love as one of the most fulfilling of pleasures, medical and psychiatric organizations have traditionally taken an unequivocal stand against sexual activity within the therapeutic relationship (APA, 1985; 1995).

As part of the recent widespread discussion of medical ethics, some therapists have questioned this traditional moral stance. A recent study of psychiatric residents reports that 4.9% acknowledged sexual interaction with supervisors (Pope, 1990). And if N. Wagner's findings (1972) are representative—that 25% of freshman medical students he studied thought that physical expressions of feelings were acceptable if both parties' feelings were genuine—we may expect students and young clinicians to question this traditional stance with increasing frequency. Do sufficient reasons exist to justify this standard, or have present-day mores made it passé? The following, based on a review of recent literature, on clinical observations of a few who transgressed this standard, and on interviews with colleagues serving on national and local ethics committees, are some reasons why wisdom dictates that the therapist adhere to the traditional standard.

Perhaps most important, a breach of this standard may be destructive to the patient. First, erotic feelings in the patient are usually a source of resistance, and physical expression of them with the therapist impedes their resolution and obstructs therapeutic progress. Acting out feelings interferes with their verbal expression and thus with the work of therapy. Second, a large percentage of patients come to psychiatrists today seeking help in controlling impulses (in contrast to overcoming inhibition of impulses, as occurred more frequently in the past). The physical expression of sexual impulses in therapy not only indicates that the therapist also lacks this control but may also exacerbate the very problem—the patient's lack of control—for which the patient seeks help.

A physical relationship may also be destructive to the therapist-patient relationship. Sexual activity changes the professional relationship to an intimate social one and thereby reduces or destroys its therapeutic effectiveness. The therapist can no longer function as an objective, caring source of healing. To find a therapist to whom one can relate effectively, whose qualities of character one can respect, in whose integrity and competence one can have confidence, and to whom one can entrust one's life is indeed a rare experience. A patient may travel great distances and make considerable sacrifices to consult such a therapist. To deprive a patient of this source of professional help and healing is, as S. H. Kardener states, "psychologically a frighteningly high price the patient must pay" (1974, p. 1135).

Such a relationship may be destructive to the therapist. When a therapist has sexual relations with a patient, the experience often exerts a negative influence on the way he sees himself and the ways others see him. The concern that he may have harmed a patient or lowered his professional standards may lead to a loss of confidence. In addition, the sexual activity almost inevitably becomes known to colleagues and to others in the community. Although the therapist may choose to ignore traditional moral standards in the conduct of his personal life, society and his professional colleagues expect, and indeed demand, that he heed them in his professional life (Redlich and Mollica, 1976). When a therapist fails to do so, he compromises his integrity and his reputation. Even when the therapist follows the questionable recommendation (Marmor, 1972) that those who cannot control their countertransference feelings should terminate treatment and marry the patient, difficulties persist. V. Davidson (1976) raises several cogent questions: "What is to be done when the therapist enters into the same situation with another patient in the future? . . . Is it possible for the psychiatrist ever to terminate his moral and ethical obligations to the patient? . . . There is some legal precedent for believing that duties of a physician toward a patient

continue after termination of the contractual agreement." One might also ask what effect this marriage will have on other patients in the therapist's practice and in his community.

The sexual relationship may be a source of potential legal liabilities. Alan Stone (1976) writes that sexual activity between therapist and patient creates the possibility of "malpractice liability" if the patient claims some psychological harm as a result. Courts have construed the doctor-patient relationship as comparable to a fiduciary relationship, or the relationship between guardian and ward (Runion, 1984). Thus the legal validity of consent from the patient becomes dubious as a legal defense.

The therapist's own breach of the traditional moral code represents a departure from the ethics of his profession. If a therapist belongs to the American Medical Association or the American Psychological Association, he swears to uphold its canon of ethics, which proscribes sexual activity between therapist and patient. Some authors (Jonsen and Hellegers, 1974; Redlich and Mollica, 1976) criticize this canon for lack of moral substance and for failing to define professional character, virtue, right action, or duty. Others, however, argue that laws and codes can only define the lowest acceptable standards and that virtue, character, and right action can never be legislated; instead, they must ultimately reflect an individual's personal ethics, philosophy of life, professional integrity, and commitment to the welfare of his patients.

Although Freud worried that "those who are still youngish and not yet bound by strong ties" may find it particularly difficult "to keep within the limits prescribed by ethics and technique" (1915, p. 169), ethics committees have found that complaints of sexual activity with patients have been primarily against older therapists—perhaps those who have had close ties and lost them. Whether young or old, the therapist must be careful to avoid using the patient to fulfill needs that otherwise would be met in his extraprofessional life.

The silence previously accorded the subject of sexual activity between doctor and patient may be that any discussion of it inevitably risks sounding moralistic and judgmental. Nevertheless, as the literature continues to focus on this issue in the future, we may find it helpful to keep in mind the following: although sexual feelings may arise naturally within the therapeutic relationship because of the nature of that relationship, sexual activity, regardless of the circumstances, is considered by law and by the profession an exploitation of the patient; although mores change, basic moral principles endure, and the wise therapist adheres closely to these principles—in the best interest of his patient, of himself, and of his profession.

Perhaps because of the dehumanizing effects of modern medical technology, the physician-patient relationship has been receiving increasing attention in the medical literature. The more we understand this interaction, the more we realize its complexities and the ways in which it differs from what we expect.

The importance of the attitude of the psychiatrist in setting the tone for his relationship with the patient has already been stressed. The therapist may approach the patient merely as a "case," whose character structure, symptoms, and defenses must be assessed in order to attach the appropriate diagnostic label. Or he may look beyond the patient's pathology to see a fellow human being with unique characteristics, and with the same hopes, fears, aspirations, feelings, and perhaps, except for differences in degree, the same conflicts as his own—a suffering human being who may have skills and areas of knowledge superior to those of the therapist but whose illness has made him dependent on the therapist and particularly vulnerable. The latter approach will ensure a degree of humility in the therapist and prevent the patronizing arrogance afflicting some who hold a measure of power over others. It will also facilitate giving the patient the same warmth and courtesy accorded a respected guest, a cherished relative, or, one would hope, the therapist himself should he become a patient. More important, the therapist will more likely have a desire to help the patient—to give him hope, to allay his fears, and to alleviate his pain.

Wanting to help the patient, wanting the best for the patient and acting accordingly—whether a particular patient evokes positive or negative feelings—necessitates no little degree of maturity on the part of the therapist. It requires him, regardless of feelings he may have to the contrary and regardless of the particular status of the patient, always to act in the best interest of that patient. Perhaps this indiscriminate, unbiased concern—the Greeks called it *agape*—encompasses all that we mean when we speak of sympathy, empathy, and compassion.

Although the therapist has a moral obligation to attain and to maintain his maximum clinical competence, no theoretical knowledge or technical skill can ever compensate for the absence of this quality of sensitive concern. Its presence not only will convey that intangible but clearly perceived "intrinsic interest" in the patient but also will help the relationship weather the multitude of errors and ignorance that is the lot of every psychotherapist.

In psychiatry, unlike other branches of medicine, therapeutic progress rests entirely on the therapist's ability to relate effectively to his patient. Once a therapist makes contact with his patient, he begins a journey strewn with obstacles arising both within himself and within his patient. An understanding of these obstacles helps the therapist avoid the usual pitfalls and snags that bog down his diagnostic and therapeutic efforts and, more important, helps him know what to do once these barriers arise. This understanding necessitates an acute sensitivity to the needs and reactions of his patients, as well as an acute self-awareness that provides him ready access to his own emotional resources and limitations. If the therapist fails to gain this understanding, he may find the arduous task of psychotherapy frustrating and ultimately intolerable. If, however, he strives consciously and continuously throughout his professional life to increase this understanding, if he uses his teaching, research, administrative, and other experiences, not to escape from his patients but to enhance his understanding of them, he will in time—despite the loneliness and isolation of his work—be recognized as a competent clinician. This recognition will come not only from increasing numbers who need and seek his help but also from the other skilled craftsmen in his field—those who do the work for which psychiatry exists and who are responsible for whatever respect the profession enjoys. More important, as the therapist increases his understanding of his relationship with his patients and uses this understanding to relieve their suffering, he will find few endeavors in life more deeply gratifying.

References

Adler, R. 1997. Post-termination patient-therapist sexual contact. *Aust. N.Z. J. Psychiatry* 31:149.

American Psychiatric Association. 1985. *The principles of medical ethics with annotations especially applicable to psychiatry.* Washington, D.C.: American Psychiatric Press.

———— 1995. *Opinions of the Ethics Committee on the principles of medical ethics.* Washington, D.C.: American Psychiatric Press.

Appelbaum, P. S. 1994. Sexual relationships between physicians and patients. *Arch. Intern. Med.* 154:2561–2565.

Bayer, T., J. Coverdale, and E. Chiang. 1996. A national survey of physicians' behaviors regarding sexual contact with patients. *South. Med. J.* 89:977–982.

Berlin, M. 1986. Attachment behavior in hospitalized patients. *JAMA* 255:3391–93.

Book, H. E. 1991. Is empathy cost efficient? *Am. J. Psychother.* 45:21–30.

Bostic, J. Q. 1996. Our time is up: forced terminations during psychotherapy training. *Am. J. Psychther.* 50:347–359.

Briggs G. W. 1990. Some pitfalls of the authoritarian doctor-patient relationships in primary care medicine. *J. Miss. State Med. Assoc.* 31:77–84.

Bruch, H. 1974. *Learning psychotherapy: rationale and ground rules.* Cambridge, Mass.: Harvard University Press.

Cesario, F. J. 1996. Supreme Court protects communication in psychotherapy. *J. Law Med. Ethics* 24:388–389.

Chused, J. F. 1992. The patient's perception of the analyst: the hidden transference. *Psychoanal. Q.* 61:161–184.

Cullen-Drill, M. 1994. The pregnant therapist. *Perspect. Psychiatric Care* 4:7–13.

Davidson, V. 1976. Psychiatry's problem with no name: therapist-patient sex. Paper presented at the 129th annual meeting of the American Psychiatric Association, Miami.

Docherty, J., and S. Fiester. 1985. The therapeutic alliance and compliance with psychopharmacology. In *American Psychiatric Association annual review.* Vol. 4, ed. A. J. Frances and R. E. Hales. Washington, D.C.: American Psychiatric Press.

Evans, L., and M. Spellman. 1983. The problem of non-compliance with drug therapy. *Drugs* 25:63–76.

Fink, E. 1982. Psychiatry's role in the dehumanization of health care. *J. Clin. Psychiatry* 43:137–138.

Frank, A. F., and J. G. Gunderson. 1990. The role of the therapeutic alliance in the treatment of schizophrenia: relationship to course and outcome. *Arch. of Gen. Psychiatry* 47:228–236.

Freud, A. 1966. *Normality and pathology in childhood.* London: Hogarth Press.

Freud, S. 1895. Studies on hysteria. In *Standard edition,* ed. J. Strachey. Vol. 2. London: Hogarth Press, 1968.

——— 1905. Fragment of an analysis of a case of hysteria. In *Standard edition,* ed. J. Strachey. Vol. 7. London: Hogarth Press, 1968.

——— 1912. The dynamics of transference. In *Standard edition,* ed. J. Strachey. Vol. 12. London: Hogarth Press, 1958.

——— 1915. Observations on transference-love. In *Standard edition,* ed. J. Strachey. Vol. 12. London: Hogarth Press, 1958.

Friedman, L. 1996. Overview: knowledge and authority in the psychoanalytic relationship. *Psychoanal. Q.* 65:254–265.

Gabbard, G. O. 1992. The therapeutic relationship in psychiatric hospital treatment. *Bull. Menninger Clin.* 56:4–19.

Garrity, T. 1981. Medical compliance and the doctor-patient relationship: a review. *Soc. Sci. Med.* 15:215–222.

Goldstein, R. I., and J. M. Calderone. 1992. The Tarasoff raid: a new extension of the duty to protect. *Bull. Am. Acad. Psychiatry* 20:335–342.

Greenblatt, M. 1986. The use and abuse of power in the administration of systems. *Psychiatric Annals* 16:650–652.

Greenson, R. R. 1965. The problem of working through. In *Drives, affects, behavior,* ed. M. Schur. New York: International Universities Press.

——— 1967. *The technique and practice of psychoanalysis.* Vol. 1. New York: International Universities Press.

Gurtman, J. H. 1990. The impact of the psychoanalyst's serious illness on psychoanalytic work. *J. Am. Acad. Psychoanal.* 18:613–625.

Gutheil, T., J. N. Burszta, and H. Brodsky. 1984. Malpractice prevention through the sharing of uncertainty: informed consent and the therapeutic alliance. *N. Engl. J. Med.* 311:49–51.

Haddox, V. 1986. What power does the patient possess? *Psychiatric Annals* 16:640–644

Hanley, C. 1994. Reflections on the place of the therapeutic alliance in psychoanalysis. *Int. J. Psychoanal.* 75:457–467.

Hansson, L. 1992. Stability of therapeutic alliance and its relationship to outcome in short-term inpatient psychiatric care. *Scand. J. Soc. Med.* 20:45–50.

Hartley, D. 1985. Research on the therapeutic alliance in psychotherapy. In *American Psychiatric Association annual review.* Vol. 4, ed. A. J. Frances and R. E. Hales. Washington, D.C.: American Psychiatric Press.

Hartley, D., and H. Strupp. 1986. The therapeutic alliance: its relationship to outcome in brief psychotherapy. In *Empirical studies of psychoanalytic theories,* ed. J. Masling. Vol. 2. Hillsdale, N.J.: Lawrence Erlbaum Associates.

Hartmann, H. 1964. *Essays on ego psychology.* London: Hogarth Press.

Heimann, P. 1960. Counter-transference. *Br. J. Med. Psychol.* 33:9–15.

Hentschel, U. 1997. Therapeutic alliance and transference: an exploratory study of their empirical relationship. *J. Nerv. Ment. Dis.* 185:254–262.

Herman, J., N. Gartrell, S. Olarte, M. Feldstein, and R. Localio. 1987. Psychiatrist-patient sexual contact: results of a national survey. II. Psychiatrists' attitudes. *Am. J. Psychiatry* 144:164–169.

Holm, S. 1993. What is wrong with compliance? *J. Med. Ethics* 19:108–110.

Hunt, W. R. 1990. A psychoanalyst does psychopharmacology. *J. Psychiatric Clin. North Am.* 13:323–331.

Jensen, P. S. 1989. Informed consent as a framework for treatment: ethical and therapeutic considerations. *Am. J. Psychother.* 43:378–386.

Jones, E. 1953. *The life and work of Sigmund Freud.* Vol. 1. New York: Basic Books.

Jonsen, A. R., and A. E. Hellegers. 1974. Conceptual foundations for an ethics of medical care. In *Ethics of health care,* ed. L. Tancredi. Washington, D.C.: National Academy of Sciences.

Kantrowitz, J. L., A. L. Katz, and F. Paolitto. 1990. Followup of psychoanalysis five to ten years after termination. III. The relation between the resolution of the transference and the patient-analyst match. *J. Am Psychoanal. Assoc.* 38:655–678.

Kardener, S. H. 1974. Sex and the physician-patient relationship. *Am. J. Psychiatry* 131:1134–36.

Kardener, S. H., M. Fuller, and I. N. Marsh. 1973. A survey of physicians' attitudes and practices regarding erotic and non-erotic contact with patients. *Am. J. Psychiatry* 130:1077–81.

Kass, L. R. 1996. Dehumanization triumphant. *Conn. Med.* 60:619–620.

Katz, J. 1984. *The silent world of doctor and patient.* New York: Free Press.

Kernberg, O. 1965. Notes on countertransference. *J. Am. Psychoanal. Assoc.* 13:38–56.

Kleinman, I. 1990. Death of the analyst. *Can. J. Psychiatry.* 35:426–429.

Kleinman, I., F. Bayless, S. Rodgers, and P. Singer. 1997. Bioethics for Clinicians. 8. Confidentiality. *Can. Med. Assoc. J.* 156(4):521–524.

Kubie, L. 1971. The destructive potential of humor in psychotherapy. *Am. J. Psychiatry* 127:861–866.

Lasky, R. 1990. Catastrophic illness in the analyst and the analyst's emotional reaction to it. *Int. J. Psychoanal.* 71:455–473.

Luborsky, L., and A. Auerbach. 1985. The therapeutic relationship and psychodynamic psychotherapy: the research evidence and its meaning for practice. In *American Psychiatric Association annual review.* Vol. 4, ed. A. J. Frances and R. E. Hales. Washington, D.C.: American Psychiatric Press.

Luborsky, L., P. Crits-Christoph, L. Alexander, et al. 1983. Two helping alliance methods for predicting outcomes of psychotherapy. *J. Nerv. Ment. Dis.* 171:480–491.

Marmor, J. 1972. Sexual acting out in psychotherapy. *Am. J. Psychoanal.* 22:3–8.

Marziali, E. 1984. Prediction of outcome in brief psychotherapy and therapist interpretive interventions. *Arch. Gen. Psychiatry* 41:301–304.

Meissner, W. W. 1992. The concept of the therapeutic alliance. *J. Am. Psychoanal. Assoc.* 40:1059–87.

Menninger, K. A. 1958. *Theory of psychoanalytic technique.* New York: Basic Books.

Merrill, J. M. 1995. Authoritarian's role in medicine. *Am. J. Med. Sci.* 310:87–90.

Mohl, P. C., D. Martinez, C. Ticknor, M. Huang, and L. Cordell. 1991. Early dropouts from psychotherapy. *J. Nerv. Ment. Dis.* 179:478–481.

Nadelson, C., M. Notman, E. Arons, and J. Feldman. 1974. The pregnant therapist. *Am. J. Psychiatry* 131:1107–11.

Osler, Sir William. 1963. *Aequanimitas and other papers that have stood the test of time.* New York: Norton.

Owen, I. R. 1995. Power, boundaries, intersubjectivity. *Br. J. Med. Psychol.* 68:97–107.

Pope, G. G. 1990. Abuse if psychotherapy: psychotherapist-patient intimacy. *Psychother. Psychosom.* 53:191–198.

Quill, T. E. 1989. Recognizing and adjusting to barriers in the doctor-patient communication. *Ann. Intern. Med.* 111:51–57.

Raven, B. 1986. A taxonomy of power in human relations. *Psychiatric Annals* 16:633–636.

Razis, D. V. 1990. Medical confidentiality. *Quality Assur. Health Care* 2:353–357.

Redlich, F., and R. F. Mollica. 1976. Ethical issues in contemporary psychiatry. *Am. J. Psychiatry* 133:125–141.

Rosenman, S. J., and R. D. Goldney. 1991. Naming of patients by therapists. *Aust. N.Z. J. Psychiatry* 25:129–131.

Runion, J. 1984. Whatsoever things are true: means and values in modern psychiatry. *Can. J. Psychiatry* 29:223–227.

Sandler, J., C. Dare, and A. Holder. 1970. Basic psychoanalytic concepts. VIII. Special forms of transference. *Br. J. Psychiatry* 117:561–568.

———— 1973. *The patient and the analyst.* New York: International Universities Press.

Searles, H. F. 1959. Oedipal love in the countertransference. *Int. J. Psychoanal.* 40:180–190.

Stone, A. 1976. Legal implications of sexual activity between psychiatrist and patient. *Am. J. Psychiatry* 133:1138–41.

Stone, L. 1967. The psychoanalytic situation and transference: postscript to an earlier communication. *J. Am. Psychoanal. Assoc.* 15:3–58.

Strasburger, L. H., L. Jorgenson, and R. Randles. 1990. Mandatory reporting of sexually exploitative psychotherapy. *Bull. Am. Acad. Psychiatry Law* 18:379–384.

Tapper, C. M. 1994. Unilateral termination of treatment by a psychiatrist: guidelines of the Canadian Psychiatric Association. *Can. J. Psychiatry* 39:2–7.

Tower, L. E. 1956. Countertransference. *J. Am. Psychoanal. Assoc.* 4:224–255.

Trad, P. V. 1993. The paradox of confidential communications. *Am. J. Psychother.* 47:1–4.

Tuttman, S. 1997. Protecting the therapeutic alliance in this time of changing health-care delivery systems. *Int. J. Group Psychother.* 47:3–16.

Veatch, R. 1981. *A theory of medical ethics.* New York: Basic Books.

Wagner, N. 1972. Ethical concerns of medical students. Paper read at the Western Workshop of the Center for the Study of Sex Education in Medicine, Santa Barbara, Calif.

Walter, G. 1991. The naming of our species: appellations for the psychiatrist. *Aust. N.Z. J. Psychiatry* 25:123–128.

Weil, F. 1993. The right of the mental patient to be medically informed. *Med. Law* 12:681–686.

Weiss, M. 1997. The role of the alliance in the pharmacologic treatment of depression. *J. Clin. Psychiatry* 58:196–204.

Zelm, G. 1986. Don't let technology diminish humanity. *Can. Med. Assoc. J.* 135:1186–89.

Zetzel, E. R. 1956. Current concepts of transference. *Int. J. Psychoanal.* 37:369–376.

Recommended Reading

Bloch, S., and P. Chodoff. 1991. *Psychiatric ethics.* New York: Oxford University Press.

Entralgo, P. L. 1969. *Doctor and patient.* New York: McGraw-Hill.

Fromm-Reichman, F. 1950. *Principles of intensive psychotherapy.* Chicago: University of Chicago Press.

Meissner, W. W. 1992. The concept of the therapeutic alliance. *J. Am. Psychoanalytic Assoc.* 40:1059–87.

Osler, Sir William. 1963. *Aequanimitas and other papers that have stood the test of time.* New York. Norton.

Veatch, R. M. 1981. *A theory of medical ethics.* New York: Basic Books.

ARMAND M. NICHOLI, JR.

History and
Mental Status

The previous chapter described the influence of the therapist-patient relationship on the success or failure of the psychiatric interview, especially those interviews directed toward the initial evaluation. During the evaluation, the therapist not only interacts with the patient but also simultaneously observes this interaction carefully and critically. The information obtained through this observation, together with biographical and other data from the psychiatric interview and psychological and laboratory tests, provides the basis for assessing the patient's emotional status.

As the assessment of physical illness is based on a history, a physical examination, and indicated laboratory tests, psychiatric assessment also includes a history (the anamnesis), a psychiatric (mental status) examination, and, when indicated, psychological and laboratory tests. This chapter deals with the psychiatric history and examination; psychological testing is covered in the following chapter; and laboratory tests are discussed in the various chapters on neuroimaging and on the organic and biological aspects of mental illness.

Because the psychiatric evaluation involves answering questions critical to the patient's welfare (Is he suicidal? Does he need hospitalization? Are his symptoms psychogenic or organic in origin?), the evaluation ought to be conducted or at least supervised by an experienced psychiatrist. Some psychiatric hospitals have their most experienced staff members perform or supervise the initial evaluation of patients. An individual may come to the clinic or hospital or to a psychiatrist's private office on his own, or he may be referred by his family, a friend, or his family physician. On the basis of the evaluation, the examiner must decide whether or not the patient is ill, the nature of his illness, and the treatment most appropriate for that illness, and must relate his findings to the referring source.

A psychiatric evaluation requires the examiner to perform the challenging task of grasping in a limited amount of time the past and present difficulties that prompt the patient to consult a psychiatrist. His goal is to discover the nature and intensity of the patient's inner conflicts, the extent they interfere with important areas of functioning, and whether or not they warrant therapeutic intervention. In addition to considering differential diagnosis among the mental disorders, the interviewer must be especially alert to the possibility of organic illness, particularly organic mental disorder, and must determine whether and to what extent such disease contributes to the patient's psychological symptoms. Some psychiatric symptoms may be direct expressions of certain organic disorders—brain tumors, acquired immune deficiency syndrome, uremia, or drug reactions, for example—and not just emotional reactions to their physically incapacitating effects. Such conditions demand immediate medical or surgical intervention and must be diagnosed promptly.

Evaluation of the psychiatric patient may take one or several interviews to complete. However many sessions are needed, the interviewer will make optimal use of his time if he has a clear idea of the general areas to explore and the specific kinds of information needed for an accurate assessment. The traditional approach to the evaluation derives from the older, descriptive psychiatry and follows the structured, systematic method of history taking and physical examination used in general medicine. With the arrival of the newer, dynamic psychiatry, many psychiatrists found the traditional approach rigid, confining, and incompatible with their efforts to explore the human personality. Consequently several modifications of the traditional approach have been introduced, notably by Finesinger (1948), Sullivan (1954), Deutsch and Murphy (1955), Menninger (1963), and Scheflen (1963). Although a structured question-and-answer approach to the psychiatric patient may yield a wealth of objective facts, analytically oriented psychiatrists have stressed that this approach interferes with obtaining the kinds of information they find essential to an accurate psychiatric assessment—an empathic understanding of the patient's inner conflicts, some indication of the unconscious determinants of these conflicts, and an awareness of how these conflicts manifest themselves in the therapist-patient relationship.

This emphasis on the limitations of the structured question-and-answer approach has led some psychiatrists to the extreme stance of using no structure at all, approaching the patient in a haphazard, disorganized way, and collecting incomplete psychiatric records. As in other medical disciplines, the key to accurate assessment is thoroughness. The skilled clinician often makes a diagnosis others have missed simply on the basis of looking carefully where others have neglected to look. Thoroughness demands that the diagnostician have in mind a clear outline of the important areas to cover and the specific details to elicit within these areas. Familiarity with 2 readily available documents will help the examiner establish this mental outline. First, *A Psychiatric Glossary,* published by the American Psychiatric Association (1988), will help the examiner think about and formulate his evaluation in the most recently defined psychiatric terms and concepts. These terms and concepts undergo continuous revision, and the clinician will find keeping conversant with the latest edition of the *Glossary* helpful in communicating his findings to his colleagues. Second, the new revised fourth edition of the *Diagnostic and Statistical Manual of Mental Disorders* (DSM-IV [1994]) will help the interviewer classify the disorders he observes and establish a specific diagnosis (see Chapter 4). Although this most recent publication emphasizes classifying psychiatric disorders in terms of descriptive pathology and the specific behavior impaired, the dynamic mechanisms of emotional illness have also been considered with the inclusion of a section on defense mechanisms (cf. Chapters 4 and 10). With a general outline in mind based on both clinical experience and knowledge of recent nosology and classification, the interviewer will be less likely to make serious omissions. His approach to the patient, however, must never be rigid or routine but tailored to the specific needs, conflicts, and personality of the individual patient.

The Psychiatric History

Although the psychiatrist must be flexible and spontaneous in his approach to the patient, he must nevertheless record the historical data obtained during the evaluation in a meaningful and organized form. Good record keeping makes it possible for not only the interviewer but also others to read and understand the record at a later date. If

the interviewer has clearly in mind an outline of the specific categories of information to ascertain, he can readily check his notes at the end of an interview to see what types of information have been omitted and cover those areas during the next interview.

Format for the Psychiatric History

Attention to the topics suggested below may contribute to the interviewer's thoroughness and help him to organize and record data without imposing a rigid question-and-answer approach. The psychiatric history ought to include the following categories:

1. *Identifying data.* The psychiatrist needs to know the patient's name, address, phone number, date and place of birth, sex, marital status, and education, the referring source, and the name and address of the patient's closest relative.

2. *Chief complaint.* A brief statement of the patient's current difficulty—the "presenting problem"—is usually given in reply to the question "What brings you to see me?" or "What brings you to the hospital?" More than any other, this part of the patient's history ought to be quoted verbatim, even when the information comes from a relative or other informant.

3. *Present illness.* Once a patient describes his main complaint, he will usually, with the encouragement of the doctor, describe other complaints, both recent and long-standing. Although this information may be presented in a disorganized and haphazard way, the doctor must formulate and record an orderly chronological summary of the development of the patient's signs and symptoms, the nature and intensity of his conflicts, previous episodes of illness and their outcome, and past psychiatric treatment and hospitalization. The patient's awareness of and attitude toward his illness—the tendency to deny, minimize, or exaggerate, as well as evidence of primary and secondary gains—should be noted.

4. *Personal history.* The record should include a summary of the patient's life with emphasis on events in his past not covered in the preceding category but pertinent to understanding his present illness. If the patient's symptoms point to certain diagnostic possibilities, the clinician's knowledge of etiological factors will indicate areas to be explored in depth. If, for instance, the examination reveals that the patient has lost the ability to pronounce words or to name common objects (amnestic aphasia), the interviewer will focus his attention on questions confirming or ruling out organic mental disorder (see Chapter 16). The interviewer's knowledge of predictable crises in an individual's development—the beginning of school,

the birth of a sibling, the loss of a parent through death or divorce, the onset of puberty, departure from home for boarding school or college—also provides clues to areas that may prove helpful to explore. Recording this information in chronological order will help give an overview of the emotionally significant aspects of the patient's life. Some potentially fruitful categories of information are suggested below.

Infancy. Among the facts that should be noted carefully are the place and condition of birth; whether the patient was breast- or bottle-fed; whether the pregnancy was planned and the child wanted; the emotional climate of the home; illness and hospitalizations; age at toilet training, of sitting, walking, and talking; any unusual circumstances of birth; and any discontinuities in the infant-mother relationship. Much of this information must be obtained, of course, by the patient from his parents or older siblings.

Childhood. Important information about this period includes childhood diseases and hospitalizations; the patient's relationship with each parent and that between parents; the emotional climate of the home; any discontinuities in relationships with either parent through divorce, death, or other causes; the patient's relationships with other members of the family; temper tantrums, stuttering, nightmares, phobias, bed-wetting, or other psychological difficulties; earliest memories, daydreams, and repetitive dreams; childhood personality traits; his reaction to discipline; and any tendency to excessive dependence or independence.

Adolescence. The psychiatrist must explore the patient's preparation for and reaction to onset of puberty; his degree of impulse control (how did the patient express aggression and the intensification of sexual interests and desires?); his adaptation to parental demands; his relationship with members of the family; peer relationships—the number of friends and the quality of friendships with both sexes; the physical and emotional accessibility of each parent; his reaction to sexual experience; his adoption or rejection of parental moral standards; and any special gifts or talents.

Adulthood. The important facts about the adult's establishment of emotional and financial independence and his career planning and career identity themselves fall into several categories. All the types of information discussed below are important in the patient's adult life and

ought to be explored in this part of the history-taking process; some aspects of the patient's adult life, however, grow naturally out of its earlier phases and thus may overlap with other sections of the history.

Educational and occupational history. Difficulties in starting school; school phobias; academic and emotional adjustment throughout the school and college years; relationship with classmates and especially with teachers; unusual experiences in school or in college; successes and failures. Job experiences, reasons for changing jobs, conflicts with peers, repetitive conflicts with superiors, and job performance and satisfaction.

Social history. Relationships with peers of both sexes; community activities; hobbies, religious interests, philosophy of life; cultural interests; ethical standards and concerns; attitudes toward aging and death.

Sexual and marital history. How and from whom first sexual information was obtained; sexual experiences in childhood and adolescence; control of sexual impulses as an adult; onset and history of menses; reactions to wet dreams; premarital sexual experiences and emotional reactions to them; courtship and marriage; sexual relationship with spouse—frequency, satisfaction, climax, conflicts; birth control, pregnancies, abortions; sexual deviations; extramarital relationships; conflicts in marriage; feelings and attitudes toward menopause.

Medical history. All illnesses, accidents, hospitalizations, and operations, in chronological order; attitudes toward illness, hospitalization, and treatment; past medications, drugs now being ingested—especially abuses of alcohol, nicotine, tranquilizers, amphetamines, and other drugs.

Family history. A detailed record of the parents, siblings, grandparents, and other relatives important to the patient, especially during his early years; the dominant parent and the parent with whom the patient has identified most; which parent enforced discipline and how; family values; ethnic, economic, and social background; age of parents at death, divorce, or separation; any family history of physical and emotional illnesses, suicides, or alcoholism; description of patient's own family (spouse and children).

Spiritual history. All patients have a worldview or philosophy of life that includes religious or spiritual convictions. Whether naturalistic or theistic, the worldviews of patients influence their concept of self, their relationships, and their attitude toward their illness. How and when was this worldview formed? How does it influence understanding of their symptoms?

Technique

While the evaluating psychiatrist's general approach to the patient will be similar to any other initial therapist-patient relationship (see Chapter 1), a few additional techniques may prove particularly useful in ascertaining the chief complaint and in taking the psychiatric history. When asked why he has come to the hospital or the doctor's office, the patient may not only describe his chief complaint but also provide considerable information concerning his history. The doctor ought to explore specifically and in detail the events that immediately precipitated the patient's seeking help. Such exploration will often reveal details not at first mentioned by the patient. The patient may, for example, give complaints he has had for months or years as reasons for his seeking help. If, however, the interviewer asks, "But what led you to seek help at this particular time?" and follows up with, "Can you think of any other reasons why you sought help now?" the patient may recall a whole series of precipitating events that influenced his decision to consult a psychiatrist.

The doctor can help make the interview more spontaneous and free-flowing by using clues from the patient to broach the various subjects he wishes to explore. If, for example, the patient mentions his parents while describing his chief complaint, the doctor may say, "You mentioned your parents a few minutes ago; can you tell me more about them?" To ask a general question like this one and then to focus on specific details—"Do your parents live together?" "How old are they?"—is usually the most fruitful way of obtaining in a spontaneous manner the details of the family history.

Obtaining historical information by this method rather than by following a rigid outline may present some difficulty in organization, but the interviewer can arrange the material later when he enters it into the patient's permanent record or prepares it for presentation to a supervisor or staff conference. The interviewer ought to feel free to take notes during the initial evaluation to help him recall specific dates and other details accurately. If he uses his own shorthand to make his notes brief, he can usually take them unobtrusively. Patients sometimes wait until the interviewer stops writing in order to have his full attention. If this situation occurs, the doctor can encourage the patient not to wait, reassuring him that the doctor will continue to listen even while jotting down notes. Some patients may find the doctor's writing too great a distraction. In such cases the doctor must limit himself to taking down a date or a key word and write more extensive notes at the end of the hour. Still other patients may object to note taking out of fear that the notes will become accessible to those who will use them against the patient. Such an objection may offer the doctor his first opportunity to discuss the important issue of confidentiality (see Chapters 1 and 38).

Because most psychiatric patients suffer from emotional conflicts, the interviewer will find it helpful—not just while taking the history but throughout his contact with the patient—to focus on the patient's feelings. Questions to the patient ought therefore to begin with the phrase "How do you feel . . . ?" rather than "What do you think . . . ?"

Although the interviewer ought to refrain from making interpretations during the evaluation, he may indicate areas that will be fruitful for the patient to explore further if therapy is indicated. He might say, for example, "You may find it helpful to explore the possibility of a relationship between the angry feelings you described toward your father and your reactions to your many different employers over the years." Though not an interpretation, such statements help clarify issues and point to areas of conflict for the patient to work on later.

The first person mentioned by the patient during the initial interview may give the interviewer a clue to his most significant current relationship. Exploring this relationship may open the door to a great deal of information concerning the present difficulty.

When a patient answers "I don't know" to a question, the interviewer can sometimes help him by not going on to another question immediately. If the interviewer responds, instead, with "What comes to mind?" the patient may reveal a great deal about the topic not at first readily accessible to him. In this way the patient will begin a process of exploring his own thoughts and feelings through free association. This method will prove especially helpful to him if at the end of the evaluation he is referred for psychoanalytically oriented psychotherapy.

When the patient relates information that appears illogical, confusing, or contradictory or that seems to have no basis in reality, the doctor may find it helpful to give him the benefit of the doubt and say, "I don't understand," rather than "You aren't being clear" or "You don't make sense." The doctor may also help establish rapport by reminding the patient that although the interview will focus on the part the patient plays in the difficulty he encounters, the doctor realizes that other people may have contributed to these difficulties. Sometimes patients feel that the doctor thinks they are to blame for all of the difficulty described in their history, when they know that spouses or parents or employers play a predominant role. Focusing solely on the patient's conflicts may also give him the impression that he has no strengths and is more severely ill than he really is. The doctor can reassure a highly sensitive patient by acknowledging, when possible, the part others play in the patient's problem as well as the patient's own strengths and assets; he must nevertheless remind the patient that their primary task is to understand the patient's conflicts and the part, however major or minor, these conflicts play in his impaired functioning.

Throughout the evaluation the interviewer should encourage the patient to express all of his thoughts and feelings freely. The doctor should not hesitate to point out that an accurate evaluation necessitates knowing as much as possible about the patient. He can encourage this free flow of expression by being responsive. He may nod or say, "I understand," or acknowledge the patient's feelings by saying, "That must have been difficult for you." If the patient suddenly stops talking, the interviewer may encourage him to continue by repeating the patient's last phrase. This particular method of eliciting information encourages the patient to use free association as a means of eliciting information from his unconscious. Felix Deutsch called this method of history taking the "associative anamnesis" and found it especially effective in patients with psychosomatic complaints. Deutsch writes:

If the examiner allows [the patient] to talk without asking leading questions the patient will usually give a detailed account of his complaints and ideas about his illness. When he has exhausted his ideas and recollections about his disturbances he will stop and wait to be asked a question. The examiner waits until it is clear that the patient will not continue spontaneously, then he repeats one of the points of the patient's last sentences in an interrogative form. Usually the examiner repeats one of the . . . complaints last mentioned, being careful to use the same words as the patient. The patient then usually gives new information centering around his symptoms and is stimulated to further associations. (1939, p. 357)

Although the doctor ought to encourage the patient to speak freely, he must guard against obviously irrelevant chatter and ought not to hesitate to ask a question directing the patient to more relevant material. Free association is used primarily by psychoanalytically oriented psychiatrists as a means of obtaining historical data during the evaluation. For a comparison of this method with others, the reader is referred to L. H. Havens's paper "Clinical Methods in Psychiatry" (1972) and to Ekkehard Othmer's (1994) discussion of interviewing techniques developed by different schools.

The skillful clinician may use the patient's associations and references to elicit a rather complete history, the patient elaborating on what he himself has introduced. Toward the end of the evaluation, however, the doctor may see gaps in the information he has obtained; he must pursue this material by direct questioning. He will usually find it more productive even when eliciting specific details to avoid questions that can be answered simply yes or no and to make his questions open-ended. "Tell me about your relationship with your brother" will usually yield more information than "Do you have a good relationship with your brother?" Furthermore, questions ought always to be couched in terms and asked in a context that the patient finds least humiliating and embarrassing. If a patient says she experiences great anxiety when physically close to men, the doctor may suspect from this and similar comments that the patient may be struggling with homosexual feelings. He would err, however, if he approached this subject directly. Instead he might ask the patient to tell him more about her discomfort with men. She might state that her close relationships have always been with women. If the doctor then asks, "Has this closeness included a physical relationship?" she might reply, "No, but I have thought about it often." In this gradual and non-threatening way, the doctor can open the door for the patient to discuss her homosexual feelings and fantasies—a topic she might never discuss with a stranger if his approach were less tactful and less appropriately timed. Patients seldom speak of their difficulties in terms of "homosexuality," "frigidity," or "impotence," and the doctor's sensitivity to the comfort of the patient will usually preclude his use of such terms.

The technique of history taking can be refined by observing skilled clinicians and by recording interviews and listening to or observing them with supervisors. A tape recorder or video recorder ought never to be used, however, without the permission of the patient and without informing him explicitly how and by whom the tape will be used. The presence of a recorder may make it difficult for some patients to speak freely. The doctor's efforts to be factual and to make the patient comfortable must be natural and unobtrusive. Like that of a good musical accompanist, the better the doctor's technique in taking a history, the less noticeable it will be to both interviewer and patient. But tact must never be used as an excuse for avoiding sensitive areas and thus failing to explore pertinent subjects. For example, failure to rule out suicidal thoughts whenever they might possibly be present may have disastrous consequences. "Have you had thoughts of injuring yourself?" ought to be asked whenever the examiner has the slightest suspicion that the patient may be suicidal.

The Psychiatric Examination

The purpose of the psychiatric, or mental status, examination is to observe and record in a systematic way the current emotional state and the specific mental functions of the patient.

Prior to the nineteenth century, physicians recorded their observations on psychological disorders in a highly personalized narrative style. Then, beginning with Pinel, Esquirol, and Falret in the early 1800s and culminating in Emil Kraepelin's classification, published in 1899, psychiatrists began to stress a more scientific and objective clinical approach. Not until 1918, however, was there a systematic form for reporting the psychiatric examination; in that year Adolf Meyer (who first referred to such an exam as the *mental status*) published his "Outlines of Examinations" (see Meyer, 1951). His structured format, with slight modifications, has been taught to psychiatrists in the United States for over 50 years (Donnelly, Rosenbert, and Fleeson, 1970).

Dynamic psychiatrists have long resisted and criticized the use of any standard form for recording the mental status examination, considering it timeworn, rigid, stereotyped, dehumanizing, offensive to sensitive patients, and an impediment to observing unique characteristics of the patient. They have also pointed to widespread inconsistencies in the categories and definitions of terms on which standardized forms rest (Weitzel et al., 1973). Rather than the standardized descriptive format, they have advocated a free-form, narrative approach. Other psychiatrists, however, have argued that the free-form method has produced a generation of psychiatrists with no idea how to conduct a mental status examination (Weitzel et al., 1973) and has resulted in hospital records that are disorganized, incomplete, and useless for statistical analysis and carefully controlled research (Donnelly, Rosenbert, and Fleeson, 1970). Because recent studies have found the free-form style of recording to be less efficient and less thorough, especially in providing information for data-processing equipment used in many hospitals, a great deal of interest exists in developing a form with widespread acceptance (Donnelly, Rosenbert, and Fleeson, 1970; Weitzel et al., 1973; Greist, Klein, and Erdman, 1983; Klerman et al., 1984). These considerations, plus the time constraints imposed by managed care, increased interest in standardized interviews and

prompted clinicians and researchers to develop many forms of these interviews over the past several years. These include completely structured interviews such as the Diagnostic Interview Schedule (DIS), and semistructured ones such as the Structured Clinical Interview for DSM-III-R (SCID) and more recently for DSM-IV. The semistructured interview provides the interviewer some flexibility in the order and content of the interview (Spitzer et al., 1992; Steinberg, 1993; Bremmer et al., 1993). Recent studies focus on the reliability of the SCID and how it compares with the unstructured interview of experienced clinicians (Segal, 1994; Steiner et al., 1995).

Format for the Psychiatric Examination

The format proposed here is based on a consensus among professors of psychiatry from medical schools across the country on what they think essential in a mental status examination (Weitzel et al., 1973). Such a form ought never to be used like a physical examination form; rather, it is intended primarily to help organize and record data. The examiner can explore most of the categories while taking the psychiatric history; indeed, the history will give him clues to which items he needs to focus on and which he can ignore. A graduate student currently doing honors work in mathematics, for example, need not be given IQ tests. The mental status examination, therefore, varies with each patient. (Terms are based primarily on the 1988 edition of the American Psychiatric Association's *Psychiatric Glossary*.)

1. *General appearance.* Specific idiosyncratic characteristics of dress and grooming ought to be noted, as well as posture, gait, facial expression, and gestures. The interviewer should note any distinctive feature that would identify the individual immediately.
2. *Attitude.* What is the patient's attitude toward his illness, toward the interview, and toward the doctor? If ill, is he aware that he is ill? Is he cooperative or evasive, arrogant or ingratiating, aggressive or submissive, outgoing or withdrawn? Does he express feelings freely or does he avoid them obviously? These observations give clues to the patient's main defense mechanisms as well as to patterns of relating to people generally.
3. *Motor behavior.* The posture and gait of the patient should be noted in detail, as well as tics, tremors, posturing, pacing, grimaces, and other abnormal bodily movements. Nail biting, wringing of the hands, tapping of the foot, chewing movements, and other manifestations of anxiety may appear or inten-

sify during the interview and give clues to emotionally charged content. Some types of abnormal motor behavior point to specific disorders—the psychomotor excitement of a manic patient, for instance, or the psychomotor retardation of the depressed patient.

4. *Speech.* Tone of voice, pitch, rate of speech (very fast and pressured as in a manic state or very slow as in a depressed state), affectations, and mutism or other abnormalities should be noted. These disturbances characterize the patient's form of speech, that is, the way he speaks, rather than what he says. What the patient says, that is, the content of his speech, will be mentioned under thought processes.

5. *Affective states.* The term *affect* refers to what the patient is feeling at the moment, to the feeling tone or emotional state and its outward manifestations. The feeling tone (affect) may be flat or blunted with little emotion expressed. Anger, fear, euphoria, elation, ecstasy, depression, irritability, and other emotional states should be noted. Affect that appears to be inappropriate to the patient's circumstances or thought content has important diagnostic implications. The patient's subjective description of his feeling tone over time, that is, his *mood,* ought to be noted and recorded.

6. *Thought processes.* From attending to the content of the patient's speech, the interviewer can observe disturbances in thought processes, in the structure and rate of associations, and in the flow of ideas. Does one thought logically follow another, or are the patient's thoughts loosely connected?

7. *Thought content.* The content of a patient's thinking can be assessed by listening to his history. The patient's preoccupations, ambitions, repetitive dreams, and daydreams will give some idea of this content. Pathological content must be noted carefully (for example, unusual suspiciousness, depressive ideas, expressions of worthlessness, hypochondriacal ideas, ideas of unreality, obsessions, phobias, and delusions).

8. *Perception.* Perception is the capacity to be aware of objects and to discriminate among them. The interviewer must observe and record any distortions in the patient's perceptions of reality; illusions and hallucinations constitute the more serious forms of perceptual distortion.

9. *Intellectual functioning.* A general impression of the patient's intellectual capacity will be gained from listening to his history. His general level of knowledge must be measured against the years of formal education he has completed and his particular family and cultural background. If the interviewer suspects certain forms of schizophrenia or certain kinds of organic mental disorder, he ought to look for disturbances in abstract thinking. This disturbance can be measured by asking the patient the meaning of some of the more common proverbs.

10. *Orientation.* Disorientation in terms of person, place, or time must be noted. Disturbances in orientation occur primarily, though not exclusively, in organic mental disorders.

11. *Memory.* Disorders of memory can usually be detected while taking the patient's history. His ability to recall past and recent events can be tested as the doctor elicits dates and other details of his life. If there appear to be gaps in his memory or if the dates he gives conflict, the doctor can explore this possibility in more detail (cf. Chapters 6 and 16).

12. *Judgment.* The examiner must evaluate the patient's ability to compare and assess alternatives in deciding on a course of action. (The patient's ability to make and carry out plans, to take the initiative, to discriminate accurately, and to behave appropriately in social and other situations reflects his judgment.) His ability to compare facts or ideas and to draw correct conclusions from facts is also a reflection of his judgment, as are his capacity to carry out his responsibilities appropriately and his ability to meet academic, business, and family obligations adequately. All may be assessed in the course of the psychiatric history.

The Significance of Abnormalities

Observation of abnormalities in any of these 12 general categories will guide the clinician toward ruling in or out a particular diagnosis or conclusion about the patient's mental status. Some signs and symptoms will indicate the necessity for psychological or neurological tests. The clinician must always keep in mind the possibility of organic illness as he reviews the various areas of the psychiatric evaluation, since such disorders must be diagnosed and treated promptly.

Abnormal appearance. If a patient appears disheveled and unkempt, the examiner ought to determine from family or friends whether he was neat in appearance before the onset of his present difficulties. A deterioration in dress and grooming sometimes marks the onset of schizophrenia or depression. The examiner should also be aware of the seductive dress and manner of some patients with hysterical character disorders, the exhibitionistic dress of some male homosexuals, the drab, excessively loose clothing worn by some sexually inhibited women, and the dark glasses worn continuously by some paranoid patients. Overly fastidious dress and grooming may indicate obsessive-compulsive traits. Although most individuals fall between the extremes of dress, appearance must never serve as a basis for diagnosis but only as an indicator of conflicts worthy of further exploration.

Abnormal attitude. Certain disturbances in attitude will alert the examiner to specific diagnostic possibilities. The doctor ought to be aware of the suspiciousness, evasiveness, and arrogance that characterize some paranoid patients; the uncooperativeness or impatience of severely manic patients; the reserved, remote, and unfeeling attitude of the schizophrenic; the resistant, uncooperative attitude of the passive-aggressive patient; the apprehensive attitude of the patient suffering from acute anxiety neurosis; the apathetic, helpless attitude of the depressed patient; and the easily distracted, seemingly indifferent attitude of the patient suffering from an acute brain disorder.

Abnormal motor behavior. A number of disorders may show themselves in motor abnormalities. A few are discussed here. *Echopraxia* is the pathological repetition, by imitation, of the movements of another person; this motor disturbance is often seen in catatonic schizophrenics. In *cerea flexibilitas* ("waxy flexibility") a patient maintains his body position for long periods of time; the patient's arm or leg will remain passively in the position in which it is placed. This motor disturbance is characteristic of catatonic schizophrenia but may also occur in organic mental disorders. *Catalepsy,* a generalized condition of diminished responsiveness usually characterized by trancelike states and immobility, occurs in various organic and psychological disorders. *Cataplexy,* a temporary loss of muscle tone and weakness, may be precipitated by laughter, anger, or surprise. The term *automatism* refers to automatic and apparently undirected motor behavior that is not consciously controlled and is seen often in psychomotor epilepsy. *Stereotypy,* the persistent, mechanical repetition of speech or motor activity, is observed in some schizophrenics.

Hyperactivity in an adult suggests the possibility of a manic condition. *Hyperkinesia,* a state of restless, destructive, and assaultive activity, may occur in a child during periods of great emotional stress or following encephalitis and other forms of organic mental disorder. Chronic restless activity in an adult may be a manifestation of anxiety or of an agitated depression. *Akathisia* refers to the

particular type of restlessness and uncontrolled motor activity associated with certain psychotropic drugs such as the phenothiazines. A *compulsion* is an insistent, repetitive, intrusive, and unwanted urge to perform an act that is contrary to the person's ordinary wishes or standards; failure to perform the compulsive act leads to overt anxiety. A person with an obsessive-compulsive neurosis manifests obsessive ideas, pervasive doubts, and compulsive rituals, such as repeated hand washing or checking to see that the gas or lights have been turned off. The suffix *-mania* is used with a number of Greek roots to indicate a morbid preoccupation with certain kinds of activity or a compulsive need to behave abnormally. Some examples follow:

Dipsomania: compulsion to drink alcoholic beverages
Egomania: pathological preoccupation with self
Erotomania: pathological preoccupation with erotic fantasies or activities
Kleptomania: compulsion to steal
Megalomania: pathological preoccupation with delusions of power or wealth
Monomania: pathological preoccupation with one subject or idea
Necromania: pathological preoccupation with death or dead bodies
Nymphomania: abnormal and excessive need for sexual intercourse, used to describe women
Pyromania: morbid compulsion to set fires
Satyromania: pathological or exaggerated sexual drive or excitement in the man, more often referred to as *satyriasis*
Trichotillomania: compulsion to pull out one's hair

Manic patients may be in constant motion with an apparent inexhaustible supply of energy. *Catatonic excitement* also involves extreme overactivity. Decreased activity is seen in some depressed patients *(psychomotor retardation)* and some catatonic patients *(catatonic stupor)*. *Paralysis* or muscular weakness *(asthenia)* may be present as a hysterical symptom. *Hysterical aphonia* is the loss of speech and *astasia-abasia,* the inability to walk or stand; both are associated with hysterical conversion.

Abnormal speech. Like abnormalities in motor activity, abnormalities in speech are associated with particular disorders. *Mutism* is the refusal to speak for conscious or unconscious reasons and is often present in severely psychotic patients. *Punning* and *rhyming* occur in manic states and in schizophrenic disorders. *Verbigeration,* the stereotyped and seemingly meaningless repetition of words or sentences, is seen in certain types of schizophrenia. *Aphasia* refers to a loss of previously possessed facility of language comprehension or production caused by lesions located in specific regions of the brain. *Amnestic* (or *anomic) aphasia* is the loss of the ability to name objects; *Broca's aphasia,* the loss of the ability to produce spoken and (usually) written language, with comprehension retained; and *Wernicke's aphasia,* the loss of ability to comprehend language, with the ability to produce it retained (see Chapter 6).

Abnormal affect. A broad range of mental disorders manifest disturbances of affect. Rage, anger, or hostility may characterize the paranoid schizophrenic; tension and apprehension, patients with acute anxiety reaction or with a phobia; and extreme anxiety associated with personality disorganization, patients with homosexual or other states of panic. The examiner should also be aware of the feeling of unreality concerning the environment or the self *(depersonalization)* and the ambivalence seen in certain schizophrenic patients, and of the inappropriate giggling and silliness seen in hebephrenic schizophrenia. Other disturbances in affect are *euphoria,* an exaggerated feeling of physical and emotional well-being not consonant with outward events, which occurs in organic mental disorders and toxic or drug-induced states; excessive *elation,* a feeling of confidence and enjoyment associated with increased motor activity; *exultation,* an intense elation with feelings of grandeur; and *ecstasy,* a feeling of intense rapture and joy. All of them may occur under inappropriate circumstances in acute manic states in patients suffering from manic-depressive psychosis or schizophrenia. *Anxiety,* the apprehension or uneasiness that results from the anticipation of danger, usually of intrapsychic origin and therefore unconscious, is often distinguished from *fear,* the apprehension resulting from a consciously recognized, usually external threat or danger. Anxiety is ordinarily present in all neurotic illness.

Abnormal thought processes. Abnormalities observed in patients' thought processes may indicate the presence of particular disorders. *Circumstantiality* is a disturbance in the associative thought processes in which a patient digresses into unnecessary detail and inappropriate thoughts before communicating the central idea; it is observed in schizophrenia, in obsessional disorders, and in some cases of epileptic dementia. *Neologisms,* seen in some schizophrenic patients, are new words or condensations of several words formed in an effort to express a highly complex idea. Neologisms may also occur in patients with organic mental disorders. *Word salad* is an in-

coherent mixture of words and phrases that is commonly seen in advanced states of schizophrenia.

Perseveration is the pathological repetition of the same response to different questions. This repetition results from the patient's clinging to a specific thought or idea and is observed in some patients with organic mental disorders, in catatonic schizophrenics, in patients suffering from senile dementia, and in those who have suffered an injury to the speech centers of the brain. *Incoherence,* a type of disjointed, confusing speech, results when one idea runs into another so that both thought and speech disregard the laws of logic. Incoherence is seen in severely disturbed psychotic patients, usually those suffering from schizophrenia. *Echolalia* is the pathological repetition of one person's words by another and sometimes represents a regression to childlike forms of mocking behavior in a patient expressing hostility and resentment. Some clinicians, however, believe that this behavior represents a neurological deficit and is an attempt to maintain a continuity of thought processes. Echolalia occurs in certain cases of schizophrenia, particularly in catatonic schizophrenics.

Condensation refers to a thinking process in which one symbol stands for a number of others and results in the fusion of various ideas or concepts into one; it is observed primarily in schizophrenics. *Flight of ideas* describes a succession of thoughts without logical connections and with a rapid shifting from one idea to another. Ideas follow in quick succession but do not progress, so that the point of the conversation is never reached. Flight of ideas may occur in the early stages of schizophrenia and in patients in the manic phase of a manic-depressive psychosis. *Retardation* of thought involves a slowing of the thought processes reflected in slow speech; the patient often comments that his thoughts come slowly and with great difficulty. It may be observed in depressed patients and in certain schizophrenic patients. *Blocking* is another obstruction to the flow of thought or speech where the thought processes suddenly appear to cease entirely. The blockage appears to be related to strong feelings such as anger or terror that accompany certain thoughts and interrupt their progression. Whatever the interruption in the train of thinking, it appears to be totally unconscious. Blocking occurs primarily in schizophrenia, though it may occur to a lesser degree in acute anxiety.

Abnormal thought content. Abnormalities in thought content may appear as delusions, hypochondriacal ideas, obsessions, or phobias. A *delusion* is a firm, false, fixed idea or belief that is inconsistent with the patient's educational and cultural background. The important aspect of a delusion is its fixed nature; the patient adheres to the false belief against all reason, logic, and evidence to the contrary. Delusions of grandeur arise from feelings of inadequacy or inferiority and involve an exaggerated idea of one's own importance. Delusions of persecution involve a false belief that one is being harassed or oppressed; delusions or ideas of reference, a false belief that the remarks or actions of others have special meaning for oneself; and delusions of self-accusation, false ideas of self-blame and remorse. Delusions of control involve false feelings that one is being controlled by others. Delusions of infidelity derive from pathological jealousy that one's spouse is unfaithful. Paranoid delusions involve an intense over-suspiciousness leading to persecutory delusions. The presence of a delusion in a patient is of great diagnostic significance, because it indicates that a patient is psychotic. Therefore delusions are pathognomonic of the psychoses, although they do not, of course, occur in all psychotics. Delusions occur primarily in schizophrenia but may appear in any of the psychoses, including those associated with organic mental disorders.

Hypochondriasis or hypochondria, is an exaggerated concern for one's own health that is not based on any physical illness, although the patient feels ill. A patient may be preoccupied with a particular organ of his body or with an idea that he is incurably ill with a specific physical disease. Hypochondriasis may occur during the involutional period of life (that is, after age 45), during depressions, and in certain schizophrenics.

An *obsession* is a pathological persistence of a thought, feeling, or impulse that can neither be dispelled by conscious processes nor be influenced by logical reasoning. The obsessive thought is usually unwanted by the patient and consciously distasteful to him, but it is often unconsciously desired. Obsessive thoughts frequently occur in combination with compulsive acts. Both occur in obsessive-compulsive neurosis.

Phobia is the persistent, obsessive, unrealistic fear or pathological dread of an object or situation; it is believed to arise through a process of displacing an unconscious conflict onto a symbolically related external object. Some of the more common phobias are acrophobia (fear of heights), agoraphobia (fear of open places), ailurophobia (fear of cats), algophobia (fear of pain), claustrophobia (fear of closed spaces), erythrophobia (fear of blushing), hematophobia (fear of the sight of blood), mysophobia (fear of dirt and germs), panophobia (fear of everything), pathophobia (fear of disease or suffering), and xenophobia (fear of strangers).

Abnormal perception. A number of disorders characterized by abnormalities in perception are described here. An *illusion* is a disorder of perception defined as the misinterpretation of a real experience—hearing one's name in the distant sound of a train, for instance, or seeing shadows of trees as animals. Illusions occur frequently in toxic states and in schizophrenia. In contrast, a *hallucination* is a false sensory perception in the absence of external stimuli. Hallucinations may be induced by factors such as drugs, alcohol, and stress and may involve taste, touch, sound, sight, or smell.

Hypnagogic hallucinations are false sensory perceptions occurring in healthy people midway between falling asleep and being awake. (Both hallucinations and illusions may be induced in healthy people by prolonged isolation or by the influence of certain drugs such as mescaline.) *Auditory hallucinations* (those involving hearing) are the most frequent forms of perceptual disturbance; they are common in schizophrenic patients, who often will speak to or quarrel with the "voices" they hear. *Visual hallucinations* (involving sight) occur much less frequently than auditory hallucinations but are seen occasionally in the deliria of acute infectious diseases and toxic psychoses. *Olfactory hallucinations* (involving smell) sometimes occur in schizophrenic reactions and with organic lesions of the temporal lobe. *Gustatory hallucinations* (involving taste) are rare false perceptions of taste; when they occur, they are usually associated with hallucinations of smell. Both occur in uncinate fits. *Tactile hallucinations* (involving touch) occur principally in toxic states and in certain drug addictions. The sensation that insects are crawling under the skin *(formication)* occurs commonly in delirium tremens and cocainism. *Kinesthetic hallucinations* are false perceptions of movement or sensation and commonly occur after the loss of a limb ("phantom limb"), in toxic states, and in certain schizophrenic reactions. Atropine and its derivatives may cause a patient to see people in miniature *(Lilliputian hallucinations)*, and other drugs such as alcohol, marihuana, and phenothiazines may evoke hallucinations in some people. Withdrawal of drugs such as alcohol, barbiturates, and tranquilizers may precipitate visual hallucinations in people addicted to them.

Agnosia is the inability to recognize objects. This disturbance in perception is caused by organic mental disorders and not by a defect in elementary sensation or a reduced level of consciousness.

Abnormal intellectual functioning. Intelligence, an extremely difficult quality to define, usually refers to the ability to understand, recall, and mobilize previous experience in adapting to new situations; it encompasses a number of mental processes such as accuracy of thinking, the capacity for complex thought, and the ability to manipulate ideas in a constructive way. The examiner can obtain a fairly good estimate of the patient's intelligence in taking the history. The patient's vocabulary and general fund of information, interpreted in light of his educational and cultural background, will give the examiner some idea of the patient's intelligence. If a question of serious impairment exists, intelligence may be more accurately assessed by means of one of several standardized intelligence tests (see Chapter 3). *Mental retardation* is usually defined as an organically caused lack of intelligence to a degree that interferes with social and vocational performance, although not all authorities agree with this definition (see Chapter 30). *Dementia* may be considered an irreversible loss of mental functioning owing to organic causes (see Chapter 16).

Abnormal orientation. In certain severe psychiatric disorders, orientation is impaired. Disorientation to time consists of a loss of awareness of the hour, the day, the date, the month, the season, or the year; disorientation to person, a lack of awareness of one's identity; disorientation to place, a lack of awareness of one's location and spatial orientation; and disorientation to situation, a lack of awareness of why one is in a particular place. Disorientation may occur in any psychiatric disorder where impairment of memory or disturbance of perception or attention exists. Disorientation may therefore be present in organic mental disorders, as well as in acute episodes of the affective disorders and of schizophrenia.

Abnormal memory. Memory may be defined as the ability to recall to consciousness previously registered experiences and information. The examiner can obtain from the history a fairly good assessment of the patient's ability to recall both recent and remote events. *Amnesia,* absence of memory, may be complete or partial and may have either an emotional or an organic basis. Some patients may recall very little before an emotionally traumatic event, such as the death of a significant figure in their lives, even when that event has occurred relatively late in childhood or early adolescence. *Hysterical amnesia* is a highly selective loss of memory involving emotionally charged events. *Anterograde amnesia* is loss of memory for recent events and is usually progressive; it occurs frequently in arteriosclerotic cerebral degeneration. *Retrograde amnesia* involves past events and is not usually progressive. Brain trauma may sometimes give rise to amnesia for events im-

mediately before or immediately after the accident. Delirium, epilepsy, and certain dissociative reactions such as fugues often give rise to memory disorders. A *fugue* is a personality dissociation characterized by amnesia and involving actual physical flight from the area of conflict.

Hypermnesia, the excessive retention of memories, occurs in certain disorders such as paranoia and hypomania. *Paramnesia* is the falsification of memory by distortion of recall. Types of paramnesia include *retrospective falsification,* a recollection of the true memory to which the patient adds false details; *confabulation,* an unconscious filling in of gaps in memory with experiences that the patient believes to be true but that have no basis in fact; and *déjà vu,* an illusion of visual recognition in which a new situation is incorrectly regarded as a repetition of a previous memory. The patient may feel that a new scene is familiar or that he has previously lived through a current experience. Déjà vu usually occurs when the present situation has a link in the patient's mind with some past experience that he can no longer remember. In *jamais vu,* the patient experiences a false unfamiliarity with situations that he has actually experienced. Déjà vu and jamais vu may occur in schizophrenics, in patients suffering from certain psychoneuroses, in those with lesions of the temporal lobe including epilepsy, with patients in states of fatigue or intoxication, and sometimes in normal individuals. The examiner must therefore be especially alert for defects in memory when examining patients suffering from fugues or other dissociative reactions, from head trauma and delirium, or from epilepsy.

Abnormal judgment. A patient's judgment is impaired if his thoughts and actions are inconsistent with reality. Judgment is impaired in various organic mental disorders as well as in certain psychogenic disorders—for example, in the manic phase of a manic-depressive psychosis.

Technique

It has already been stressed that the examiner can conduct most of the mental status examination while taking the history and that neither the history nor the examination should follow a rigid, stereotyped format. If the interviewer is skillful and a keen observer, he will be able to tailor his approach to the specific needs of the patient and, in a relaxed, natural manner and without embarrassment to the patient, obtain all the information needed for the examination. Through keen observation and careful listening, the examiner can note the patient's general appearance, his speech, his attitude during the interview, his behavior, and his affective state, as well as his thought processes and thought content. While taking the history, the interviewer can also note whether or not the patient is oriented and can assess the state of his memory by noting his ability to recall recent and remote experiences. How the patient relates to people and whether or not he handles social and other affairs appropriately and with discernment can also be observed while taking a history and used to assess the patient's judgment.

The techniques to be followed in the examination depend in large part on what the interviewer has observed while taking the history. If the content of the interview raises the possibility of defects in the patient's judgment, for instance, the doctor may say, "You mentioned that your family complained of your suddenly spending too much money. Can you tell me more about this complaint?" Later the doctor may ask, "Has your family had other complaints?" Similarly, the doctor may use a clue from the patient to test the patient's memory: "You said earlier that you had difficulty remembering things lately. Can you remember my name?" "Can you remember the name of this hospital?" "Can you tell me today's date? What year it is?" (Forgetting the day may have little significance, but forgetting the year will always be significant.)

If the examiner has doubts about the patient's thought processes or content, he can focus on these areas with specific questions: "Do you have difficulty concentrating?" "Do you have difficulty controlling your thoughts?" "Can you tell me what you daydream about most?" These and similar questions may help focus on specific difficulties that the doctor may feel it necessary to explore. If the patient gives evidence of disturbances in perception, the doctor ought to guide the patient toward this area in a conversational and indirect manner. If the patient alludes to people controlling his thoughts or telling him what to do, the doctor may ask, "Can you tell me more about these people?" or "Who are these voices that you hear?" and then explore them in detail.

With experience, the examiner will learn to use specific kinds of questions to explore various areas of the mental status examination. If the interviewer thinks it necessary to test the patient's span of attention or the speed of his thought processes, he may ask him to subtract 7 from 100 and to keep subtracting by 7s. If the interviewer suspects that the patient has difficulty with abstract thinking, he may ask the patient to interpret a number of proverbs: "What is the meaning of 'a stitch in time saves nine'?"

Whatever questions the examiner uses to test specific functions, his judgment of whether or not they are appropriate for a given patient and his manner in asking them determine, in large measure, their effectiveness. If the questions are inappropriate or asked in a stilted, unnatural manner, the patient may consider them insulting, crude, or humiliating. Although a complete psychiatric examination is vitally important for the evaluation of the patient, the doctor must be careful to conduct the examination with respect for the patient and his comfort. A friendly and tactful manner will make the patient's cooperation more likely and thus ensure a thorough and accurate assessment.

A patient who is unwilling or unable to speak poses a difficult problem in evaluation. The doctor's observational and descriptive powers must come into full play here. He should note whether the patient will shake hands, say hello, speak spontaneously, answer questions, or be willing to write even if he is unwilling to speak. Does he talk to himself, appear to be listening to voices, or appear suspicious, preoccupied, or inattentive? Does he exhibit abnormal facial expressions, posture, or bodily movements? Every unusual detail of the patient's general appearance and emotional reaction ought to be noted and recorded. This information may be extremely helpful in understanding the patient, especially when his inaccessibility is the first stage of a gradually developing emotional disorder.

The Physical Examination

Every evaluation of a psychiatric patient ought to include a complete physical examination. The neurological aspects of such an examination are often of great significance, especially in patients with intellectual deficit or disturbances of memory and attention and those with aphasias, agnosias, and apraxias. If any of these symptoms is present, the psychiatrist may choose to refer the patient to a neurologist for a thorough neurological workup. In hospital practice, a psychiatrist will usually give a physical examination as part of the patient's general workup. In private practice, some psychiatrists refer their patients to internists and general practitioners for the physical examination. Regardless of who performs the physical examination, the doctor evaluating the psychiatric patient must assume responsibility for seeing that it gets done.

Diagnostic Formulation and Assessment for Treatment

The diagnostic formulation includes a summary of the patient's history and of the examination and a provisional diagnosis based on these findings. It also includes a clear description of the present symptoms and emotional conflicts, of the genetic factors involved (that is, of the constitutional and early life experiences contributing to the disorder), and of the dynamic or psychological processes resulting in the conflicts. A diagnostic classification from the revised *Diagnostic and Statistical Manual of Mental Disorders* (DSM-IV) may also be included.

After formulating the diagnosis, the examiner confronts the most important part of the evaluation—determining whether treatment is indicated and what type of treatment will be most effective. A competent examiner will strive to avoid bias toward any one form of therapy and will be sufficiently informed to determine the most effective therapeutic modality for each patient. To refer a patient for behavior therapy, for short-term psychotherapy, for electroconvulsive therapy, for psychoanalysis, or for other forms of therapy without specific and clear indications for such a referral is irresponsible. Like unnecessary surgery, unnecessary therapy ought to be discouraged. Often therapy is prescribed even when the indications for it are unclear because the doctor feels it can do no harm. It can. In addition to wasting time, effort, and financial resources, it may result in a number of untoward complications.

To determine whether treatment is indicated, the doctor must assess the degree to which the patient's conflicts seriously interfere with his functioning in important areas of his life. If they do not interfere, or if they interfere in an area of functioning not currently important to the patient, they do not warrant therapeutic intervention. A doctor may be enormously reassuring to such a patient simply by helping him to understand that he does not need treatment. (For a more detailed discussion of various therapies, see Chapter 20.)

Concluding the Interview

In bringing the initial session to a close, the examiner must avoid cutting the patient off in the middle of an important part of his history or making him feel that he is being summarily dismissed. Terminating a session smoothly is not always easy—particularly if either the patient or the doctor has conflicts over leaving people or being left—and a degree of firmness and technical skill is often necessary in the examiner. If he will see the patient again, of course, the examiner can close by saying, "Let's continue here the next time." In this way he notifies the patient that the hour is up, expresses interest in the patient's history by saying he would like to hear more about it, and encourages the patient to maintain continuity with the next session.

At the end of an evaluation, the examiner should ask whether the patient has any questions about the examiner's impressions or recommendations. Information about the nature of the evaluation, about a particular type of therapy recommended, or about the qualifications of the clinic or therapist to whom the patient is being referred will reduce the patient's anxiety and help him to follow through with the examiner's recommendations.

The evaluation of a psychiatric patient comprises a thorough history, a detailed psychiatric examination, and, when indicated, psychological tests. The examiner's primary purpose is to assess within a limited number of sessions the nature and intensity of the patient's emotional conflicts and to determine the most effective treatment for their alleviation or resolution. Because a misdiagnosis may have untoward consequences for the patient, the evaluation ought to be conducted by therapists still in training only under the supervision of senior and experienced staff members. In addition to his experience and knowledge, an examiner's thoroughness determines, in large measure, the accuracy and effectiveness of his evaluation; the clinician's ability to be thorough will be enhanced if he has clearly in mind the important areas to cover in both the history and the examination. Finally, although tact and sensitivity must always characterize his questioning, they must never interfere with the completeness and accuracy of his evaluation.

References

American Psychiatric Association. 1980. *Diagnostic and statistical manual of mental disorders.* 3rd ed. Washington, D.C.

———— 1987. *Diagnostic and statistical manual of mental disorders.* 3rd ed., rev. Washington, D.C.

———— 1988. *A psychiatric glossary.* Washington, D.C.: American Psychiatric Press.

———— 1994. *Diagnostic and statistical manual of mental disorders.* 4th ed., rev. Washington, D.C.

Bremner, J. D., M. Steinberg, S. M. Southwick, D. R. Johnson, and D. S. Charney. 1993. Use of the structured interview for DSM IV dissociative disorders for systematic assessment of dissociative symptoms in posttraumatic stress disorder. *Am. J. Psychiatry* 150:1011–14.

Deutsch, F. 1939. The associative anamnesis. *Psychoanal. Q.* 8:354–381.

Deutsch, F., and N. F. Murphy. 1955. *The clinical interview.* New York: International Universities Press.

Donnelly, J., M. Rosenbert, and W. Fleeson. 1970. The evolution of the mental status—past and future. *Am. J. Psychiatry* 125:997–1002.

Finesinger, J. E. 1948. Psychiatric interviewing. I. Some principles and procedures in insight therapy. *Am. J. Psychiatry* 105:187–195.

Greist, J., M. Klein, and H. Erdman. 1983. Computers and psychiatric diagnosis. *Psychiatric Annals* 13:785–792.

Havens, L. H. 1972. Clinical methods in psychiatry. *Int. J. Psychiatry* 10:7–28.

Klerman, G. L., G. E. Vaillant, R. L. Spitzer, and R. Michels. 1984. A debate on DSM-III. *Am. J. Psychiatry* 141:539–553.

Menninger, K. A. 1963. *The vital balance.* New York: Viking Press.

Meyer, A. 1951. *The collected papers of Adolf Meyer,* ed. E. E. Winters. Vol. 3. Baltimore: Johns Hopkins University Press.

Othmer, Ekkehard. 1994. *The clinical interview using DSM IV.* Vol. 2. *The difficult patient.* Washington, D.C.: American Psychiatric Press.

Scheflen, A. E. 1963. Communication and regulation in psychotherapy. *Psychiatry* 26:126–1.

Segal, Daniel L. 1994. Reliability of the structured clinical interview for DSM-III-R: an evaluative review. *Compr. Psychiatry* 35:316–327.

Smelson, D. A. 1997. Evaluating the diagnostic interview: obstacles and future directions. *J. Clin. Psychol.* 53:497–505.

Spitzer, R. L., J. B. Williams, M. Gibbon, and M. B. First. 1992. The Structured Clinical Interview for DSM III-R (SCID). I. History, rationale, and description. *Arch. Gen. Psychiatry* 49:624–629.

Steinberg, M. 1993. *The structured clinical interview for DSM-IV dissociative disorders.* Washington, D.C.: American Psychiatric Press.

Steiner, J. L., J. K. Tebes, W. H. Sledge, and M. L. Walker. 1995. A comparison of the structured clinical interview for DSM-III and clinical diagnoses. *J. Nerv. Ment. Dis.* 183:365–369.

Sullivan, H. S. 1954. *The psychiatric interview.* New York: Norton.

Weitzel, W., D. Morgan, T. Guyden, and J. Robinson. 1973. Toward a more efficient mental status examination. *Arch. Gen. Psychiatry* 128:215–218.

Climent, E. C., R. Plutchik, H. Estrada, L. Gaviria, and W. Arevalo. 1975. A comparison of traditional and symptom-checklist based histories. *Am. J. Psychiatry* 132:450–453.

Fauman, A. 1983. The emergency evaluation of organic mental disorders. *Psychiatr. Clin. North Am.* 6:233–257.

Halleck, S. L. 1991. *Evaluation of the psychiatric patient: a primer.* New York: Plenum Press.

Kovess, V. 1992. Why discrepancies exist between structured diagnostic interviews and clinicians' diagnoses. *Social Psychiatry and Psychiatric Epidemiology* 27:185–191.

Pohl, R., R. Lewis, and R. Niccolini. 1982. Teaching the mental status examination: comparison of three methods. *J. Med. Educ.* 57:626–629.

Strub, R. I., and F. W. Black. 1993. *The mental status examination in neurology.* 3d ed. Philadelphia: Davis.

Recommended Reading

Akiskal, H. S. 1994. Mental status examination: the art and science of the clinical interview. In *Diagnostic Interviewing,* ed. M. Hersen and S. Turner. 2nd ed. New York: Plenum Press.

LARRY J. SEIDMAN
ROSEMARY TOOMEY

The Clinical Use of Psychological and Neuropsychological Tests

Psychological and neuropsychological tests are used in psychiatry to provide a descriptive, dynamic, and diagnostic understanding of the patient, including an assessment of adaptive strengths and weaknesses. Factors important in this understanding include cognitive processes, such as thinking, perception, and memory; the experiencing and expression of emotions; significant inner conflicts and the mechanisms for defense and coping with stress; characteristic personality styles; perceptions of the self and others and their expression in interpersonal behavior; diagnostic clarification, including the nature and implications of central nervous system (CNS) dysfunction; and the possible means through which the individual can be helped to achieve relief from distress and to move toward improved functioning, adaptation, learning, and growth.

This chapter focuses on the use of psychological and neuropsychological tests in clinical assessment, after briefly reviewing the history of testing and addressing the fundamentals of test construction and measurement. We shall focus on adult assessment, reflecting our experience with this population and recognizing that coverage of child assessment is beyond the scope of this chapter. A full description of child assessment can be found in J. M. Sattler's (1988) excellent text. Our coverage includes the rationale, composition, and use of various batteries of psychological tests; illustrative referral questions; a focus on the characteristics and utility of individual intelligence and personality tests; and the assessment of brain dysfunction through neuropsychological testing.

History of Testing

Psychological testing rests on the central assumption that individuals differ with respect to identifiable and measurable dimensions that have implications for some aspects of mental functioning. This idea, with roots in Western thought since the time of the Greek city-state, took its modern quantitative direction from Francis Galton's 1869 study of individual differences via brief psychophysical tests and his demonstration that psychological characteristics were normally distributed.

The era of mental tests as we know them today began when Alfred Binet was asked to devise a method to determine which children might benefit most from public school in France. With Theodore Simon (Binet and Simon, 1905) he assembled 30 different tasks, which formed the basis of the original Binet intelligence test. Lewis Terman of Stanford University standardized his revision of the Binet scale by testing 1000 native-born California children and 400 adults. Intelligence testing was established in this country through the first edition of the Stanford-Binet test in 1916. The Stanford-Binet was revised in 1937, 1960, and again in 1986 (Thorndike, Hagen, and Sattler, 1986).

The Binet approach used the age-scale format, with items grouped according to the percentage of children able to complete them. This led in turn to the introduction of the concept of mental age, which is the sum of credits obtained for the tests passed at different age levels. The original intelligence quotient (IQ = mental age divided by chronological age) was introduced in the 1916 test. These methods were also applied to group intelligence tests (Army Alpha and Beta) that were developed in order to assign World War I military personnel and were forerunners of the many group intelligence tests designed to evaluate intellectual ability.

David Wechsler, while at New York City's Bellevue Hospital, developed and standardized a new kind of individually administered intelligence test, with the assessment of adolescent and adult psychiatric patients in mind. Published in 1939 and known as the Wechsler-Bellevue Scale, it consisted of 11 different subtests, 6 verbal and 5 performance, selected to measure various aspects of intellectual ability. Wechsler tested enough subjects to establish standardization tables for each age group from 16 to 64 and to convert the scores on the subtests into Verbal, Performance, and Full-Scale IQs that placed an individual accurately in relation to his age peers and were comparable across age groups. Wechsler also introduced the current concept of IQ, the deviation quotient, which was superior to Binet's mental age approach because it did not fluctuate with age. The 1955 *Wechsler Adult Intelligence Scale* (WAIS) and its more recent revision, the WAIS-R (1981) are the successors to the Wechsler-Bellevue Scale.

The early part of the twentieth century was also a time of burgeoning developments in the measurement of individual differences in personality. We can trace the origins of the clinical application of individual personality testing to Carl Jung and Hermann Rorschach. Starting with the free association of psychoanalysis, Jung developed the familiar word association test as a key to unconscious "complexes" (1918). Rorschach, a Swiss psychiatrist, discovered what he claimed to be a method for assessing the "whole" of an individual's personality (1942). The inkblot technique he first described in 1921 was brought to this country at the start of the 1930s, and a small number of psychologists began to teach and use it before and during World War II. S. J. Beck (1944) and B. Klopfer (Klopfer and Kelley, 1942) published the most influential pioneering guides to Rorschach procedures and interpretation, and Rapaport, Gill, and Schafer (1945) at the Menninger Clinic made the test the cornerstone of their classic diagnostic studies. Exner's (1990) adaptation of the Rorschach scoring system over the previous 25 years has increased the reliability of this test and led to research efforts that have strengthened its validity.

In the 1930s Henry Murray led a group of students at Harvard's Psychological Clinic in extensive and intensive studies of personality, and included explorations of psychoanalytic concepts with special interest in the "unconscious" (1938). From this work came the Thematic Apperception Test (TAT), first marketed as a test in 1943.

During this same decade Hathaway and McKinley at the University of Minnesota were exploring an objective and empirical method to improve the accuracy of psychiatric diagnosis. Their search resulted in the 1943 publication of the *Minnesota Multiphasic Personality Inventory* (MMPI), which utilizes the true-false responses of patients to 566 psychiatrically relevant statements and has come to be the most widely used psychological test in the world. The MMPI format was for use in many other self-report personality tests over the past 50 years. The MMPI was revised (MMPI-2) in 1989, and a specialized version for adolescents (MMPI-A) has also been developed (Butcher et al., 1992).

Neuropsychology is the most recent subdivision of psychological assessment, stimulated to a great degree by traumatic brain injuries to combat soldiers in World War II. Investigators such as K. Goldstein (1942), H. L. Teuber (1948), B. Milner (1963), and A. R. Luria (1980) provided the foundation of the neuropsychological approach based on clinical and experimental observations, whereas W. C. Halstead (1947) developed his battery of tests to measure "biological intelligence." R. M. Reitan (1986; Reitan and Davison, 1974) expanded and developed Halstead's battery and demonstrated the validity of neuropsychological investigation with neurological and neurosurgical patients, contributing to widespread utilization of neuropsychological assessment in psychiatry. Different approaches to clinical neuropsychological investigation have developed (Golden, Hammeke, and Purisch, 1980; Luria, 1980; Milberg, Hebben, and Kaplan, 1996), and we shall discuss them in detail later.

Sophisticated computer technology has made possible the on-line scoring and interpretation of many tests, most prominently the MMPI and other self-administered instruments, including the *Millon Clinical Multiaxial Inventory* (MCMI) (Millon, 1983, 1987) and neuropsychological measures.

Fundamentals of Test Construction and Administration

The term *test* implies a systematic approach to the development and use of some set of tasks, questions, or other stimuli in order to obtain samples of behaviors of specific interest. Although tests vary considerably in the degree to which they have been systematically derived, they generally arise from a context of controlled experimentation, in contrast to the usual clinical investigative stance for observation or interview in psychiatry. The intelligence, personality, and neuropsychological tests of today represent a blend of items taken from earlier tests, modified items, and new concepts and operations. Sophisticated techniques are used to determine the combination of items and procedures that will best sample the behaviors of interest and meet a variety of other needs. A standardized test, such as one of the widely used intelligence tests, is likely to have the following characteristics: items or questions selected on the basis of empirical studies; directions for administration and scoring; norms based on the performance of identified samples of subjects; and quantitative estimates of the reliability, validity, and utility of the test.

Administration and scoring are done in accordance with specific directions to ensure that test results are comparable from one individual or situation to another. The most important such comparison makes use of normative data. Some tests—again the standardized intelligence test is the model—are used with normative tables based on the scores of groups of subjects who have been carefully selected in accordance with sampling procedures. These procedures must take into account the intended applications of the test. For example, standardization of an intelligence test requires that a large number of subjects in each age group be covered by the test, because intellectual performance is known to vary with age. Similarly, if the norms are to be applicable to a given population—to American adolescents and adults, for instance—the sampling procedures should provide appropriate representation of such variables as education, occupation, race, urban versus rural residence, and, so far as possible, any other factors that could bias the data if not taken into account.

The *reliability* of a test refers to its consistency and stability. Split-half, test-retest, and interjudge agreement are the most common methods of determining reliability. The reliability of a long spelling test, for example, may be estimated by splitting the test in half; the scorer correlates the number of correct responses to odd-numbered and even-numbered items. Correlations between scores obtained from the same individuals on 2 occasions, 1 week apart, would be an appropriate means of assessing reliability using the test-retest method. This procedure, however, would be less reliable when applied to the scores of psychiatric patients on a scale measuring depressive mood, which is likely to fluctuate over time. Interjudge agreement would be the method of choice if one wished to develop a scoring system for the content of thematic stories; here we need to know that 2 or more scorers can apply the concepts and rules of the system in the same ways.

The *validity* of a test refers to the degree to which it measures what it is supposed to measure. Three types of validity are usually delineated: content, predictive, and construct. *Content* validity is concerned with how well the test samples the behaviors of interest. *Predictive* validity refers to the accuracy of the test in measuring relevant characteristics or events. Predictive validity need not be limited to future events; *concurrent* and *postdictive* validity are self-explanatory terms for other kinds of "predictions." Certain concepts that one may wish to measure,

however, lack simple or agreed-upon criteria. Tests of anxiety or ego strength, for example, cannot be easily validated by reference to external events. Their *construct* validity is established by the gradual accumulation of evidence that they correlate with a variety of other measures or behaviors commonly accepted as manifestations of the construct in question.

The *utility* of a test refers to how useful it is for a particular purpose. In clinical practice one should be concerned with what a test will add to information that could be derived easily, quickly, or inexpensively from other available sources. Tests are unlikely to have great utility in predicting outcomes with either very high or very low base rates of occurrence in the population of interest.

The Assessment Process

A full psychological evaluation of a patient in a psychiatric setting can be time-consuming and expensive. The traditional administration, scoring, analysis, and report of a battery of tests may take as much as 5 to 15 hours, depending on the patient's capacity and the questions being evaluated. For example, a very lengthy evaluation may occur in the case of a patient who has suffered a serious stroke and who wishes to return to her professional occupation. Such an evaluation may require extensive testing to determine cognitive and emotional capacities, and the patient may work rather slowly on the high-level tasks required to test her competence. Not all evaluations may require comprehensive testing. Moreover, in this era of managed health care (see Chapter 37), clear, focused questions for the evaluation are particularly important. When resources are limited, an assessment may aim at elucidating one or two areas, rather than providing a comprehensive picture. It is therefore of great importance to consider what the testing will contribute to the clinical needs of the patient—in other words, its incremental utility. The answers to this question will depend on a clear understanding of what the clinical issues are in the particular case and on knowledge of what may reasonably be expected from testing. Discussion of referral issues with the psychologist is also helpful in providing a focus for organizing and presenting the test results and interpretations.

An extensive psychological study will typically provide a basis for a comprehensive report that assesses and evaluates the patient's overall and specific cognitive functions; offers hypotheses about the dynamic and developmental aspects of his personality and psychopathology; provides information on the likely course of cognitive abilities;

comments on his or her strengths and vulnerabilities; contributes to the diagnosis of DSM-IV Axis I clinical syndromes and Axis II personality patterns and disorders; and offers recommendations regarding treatment. (DSM-IV refers to the American Psychiatric Association's *Diagnostic and Statistical Manual of Mental Disorders,* fourth edition, 1994.)

Referrals for Testing

Referral questions for psychological testing can vary widely. Differential diagnosis is perhaps the most common referral issue. For example, testing may contribute to diagnosis by assessing the relative prominence of thought disorder and reality testing on structured (WAIS-R) and unstructured (Rorschach) tests to help distinguish schizophrenic-type psychoses from borderline personality disorder. A combination of personality and neuropsychological measures may help in clarifying whether an individual's decline in functional capacity is secondary to depression or to a dementing illness.

Characterizing the patient's attitudes, capacities, and limitations may have important implications for treatment. For example, a deeply cynical and suspicious attitude toward authority reflected in themes on the TAT and in responses to items on the WAIS-R comprehension subtest will undoubtedly be reflected in the patient's relationship to the therapist in psychotherapy. Alternatively, the patient's capacity to withstand stress without regressing in the testing situation may help the therapist judge whether supportive treatment with a disturbed individual might move safely toward an emphasis on uncovering problems. The data that the psychologist uses to make these statements will be clearer as we discuss the nature of the different tests.

Preparation of the Patient

The psychiatrist should always discuss the testing with the patient before the psychologist is seen. If this is done in a perfunctory or evasive manner, the patient's feelings of anxiety or resentment will reduce the value of the examination and hinder the establishment of a working alliance. The patient's previous experience with testing, either in clinical settings or in school or business, should be explored in order to discover and assist with negative feelings and unrealistic expectations. The psychiatrist should know what the testing is like and should make clear, but not exaggerate, its importance in his or her planning for the patient.

The Battery Approach

In most clinical assessment situations the psychologist uses a combination of tests designed to answer the referral questions. In general, composite batteries are selected to sample varied aspects of behavior and do so by presenting different types of stimuli under varying test conditions. Although each test may have specific purposes, and complementary data are expected from different tasks, hypotheses based on one test may be supported or disconfirmed by data from another. A clinical interview (as described in Chapter 1) often accompanies formal testing and provides an important behavioral and historical context in which to interpret formal testing. Hypotheses generated from one or more tests may also be supported or disconfirmed by information revealed in the interview.

Rapaport, Gill, and Schafer (1945) were the first to integrate individually administered intelligence, personality, and cognitive tests into a battery to sample widely a person's adaptive capacities and limitations. The core elements of their battery—a Wechsler intelligence test and two projective tests, the Rorschach and TAT—continue to be central in the clinical assessment of personality in the United States. The projectives are supplemented or, in some settings, supplanted by objective personality measures such as the MMPI or the MCMI. Human figure drawings and sentence completion tests are frequently added to assess psychodynamic issues, while other tasks are used to screen for possible brain dysfunction. Additional special-purpose tests that examine abstraction, memory, attention, or other mental functions in greater detail may be added to the basic battery. Different batteries of tests are constructed for the assessment of children or for examining more specific areas, as in neuropsychological, vocational, educational, or behavioral assessment.

The Psychological Report and Patient Feedback

The psychological report is the formal, detailed statement of the psychologist's understanding of the patient as interpreted from the test data, with particular focus on the issues raised in the referral question. A give-and-take discussion between the psychiatrist and the psychologist may arise from the report, permit the raising of additional questions, and add to the psychiatrist's understanding of how testing can help in her work.

The most enlightening reports tend to be person oriented rather than test oriented. Although some of the raw data may be included for illustrative purposes, it is neither necessary nor helpful for the psychologist to justify every interpretation by citing the evidence or to submit a laboratory report full of figures. (However, a separate data sheet may be appended to the text of the report, so that test data can be compared in the event that repeat testing is required.) It is the psychologist's reponsibility to express the conclusions based on the strength and convergence of the evidence collected. The psychiatrist will naturally find most useful the reports of psychologists who share the same theoretical and diagnostic frames of reference. Psychiatrists and psychologists collaborate with mutual respect and understanding, and it is under these conditions that the psychiatrist is able to make optimal use of the psychologist's skill and experience for the benefit of the patient.

Feedback to the patient is a crucial component of the assessment process. The patient expects that his time and effort will have been put to productive use, but may be worried about negative evaluations or implications based on his performance. Feedback can take a variety of forms, including the psychologist meeting with the patient, the psychiatrist discussing the findings with the patient after receiving the psychologist's feedback, or, finally, all parties meeting together to discuss the findings. The last is a good option for the patient who is apt to distort the feedback, or the patient with limited verbal comprehension or memory. In some cases it may be useful to have other parties present to hear the feedback, such as the parents of a child who has been evaluated, or the vocational rehabilitation counselor working with the patient to identify viable work options. Regardless of who provides the feedback, the patient can best use feedback that is communicated in a language he understands, that summarizes a limited number of main conclusions, and that emphasizes strengths or adaptive coping skills as well as noting problem areas. Recommendations for treatment, schooling, or special training should take into account the capacity of the patient to mobilize his or her resources in these directions.

Factors Influencing Test Results

Optimal use of testing requires that the psychologist take into account the motivational state of the patient. Test performance may be lowered by ongoing depressive, anxious, confused, or hostile states or by particular wishes, fears, or concerns about the testing or its consequences. Medications are likely to have some influence on performance; this issue is discussed later in the chapter (see

"Limitations of Reliability and Validity" under "Assessment of Brain Dysfunction"). The psychologist should also be alert to any situational factors influencing the performance of the patient, such as sleep deprivation, family strife, or concurrent medical problems.

The psychologist needs to understand the many concerns regarding the applicability of testing procedures to various racial and ethnic groups both within and outside the American culture. Some of these concerns have been outlined by Suzuki and Kugler (1995) in relation to various aspects of the assessment process. Differences in culture, race, or ethnicity between the examiner and examinee may affect the development of rapport and overall communication during the assessment process. Specific test content and test-taking procedures will probably be most familiar to those in the dominant Caucasian middle-class culture. Test norms are most applicable to people similar to those in standardization samples, but often minority groups have been underrepresented in standardization samples. Thus, interpretations of test scores may need to be qualified for certain individuals with varying backgrounds. In addition, the clinician may need to consider more seriously the impact of social explanations for individual deficits for minority clients. Factors that may moderate all these influences include proficiency with the English language, education level, socioeconomic status, degree of racial identity and acculturation status, and living situation. Discrepancies in performance between different groups tend to diminish as similarities increase on these other demographic variables (see Chapter 34).

The good clinician should be sensitive to all the issues discussed in the above paragraph. However, there will always remain unique situations for the clinician to evaluate. For example, a college student who recently emigrated from Russia is referred to evaluate his performance in college. Cultural and language differences will likely limit validity of the data. Testing by a Russian language examiner or in Russian versions of the tests would likely increase the validity of the test results. However, such adaptations may not be available. Thus, the clinician must be quite cautious in the strength of his conclusions and indicate the relative limits to confidence in his interpretation. Good general rules to guide all assessments include the gathering of information through history taking from the subject as well as from independent sources (e.g., schools, previous test results, family members, previous and current therapists), evaluating consistency of results between various tests and the history before making firm conclusions, and reporting on moderating variables or alternative explanations to the findings. When feasible, follow-up testing can support or disconfirm the initial findings.

Computers and Testing

Today the administration, scoring, and interpretation of an ever increasing list of tests, questionnaires, and interviews can be done entirely by computer. The patient can sit at a console and enter responses that are immediately processed, either by telephone transmission or by on-site software, and transformed into a complex report. Adaptive programs that can vary administration in accordance with the subject's responses are widely available. Speed, volume, reliability, storage capacity, and minimal involvement of professional time are among the advantages of computerized testing. The current ethical assumption is that a professional-to-professional consultation is involved, but new guidelines are evolving. Although the validity of computerized reports is most difficult to evaluate, it is clear that this approach can simulate successfully the expert test interpreter and produce reports that are acceptable for many purposes. Nevertheless, the professional psychologist must be responsible for reporting such findings in the test report.

Standardized Intelligence Tests

The concept of intelligence as a unitary trait or a set of modular capacities has been widely researched, discussed, and disputed (Gardner, 1983; Kaufman, 1990). As experience in the use of standardized intelligence tests grew, it became apparent that the patterning of different abilities and the ways in which problems were solved were valuable supplements to the measurement of the IQ; this recognition marked the beginning of the intelligence test as a clinical instrument (Lezak, 1995). In the clinical context, Wechsler's definition of intelligence as "the aggregate or global capacity of the individual to act purposefully, to think rationally and to deal effectively with his environment" (1958, p. 7) expresses the concept well. However, as knowledge of the brain-intelligence relationship increases, the concept of intelligence, especially biological intelligence, will no doubt be revised. Moreover certain talents, especially in creative or technical pursuits, are not adequately evaluated by current intelligence tests (Gardner, 1983). Other aspects of cognition (social and emotional "intelligence") are measured only in indirect ways on current intelligence tests, and these characteristics may someday be incorporated into such tests. Al-

though the meaning and value of the IQ score itself have been the center of controversy (Lezak, 1988), clinicians have found the individually administered intelligence tests (Stanford-Binet, Wechsler series) to produce very rich data reflecting the adaptive capacities of the individual.

Despite the limitations noted above, the Wechsler intelligence tests have been the cornerstone of the clinical assessment of adult intellectual functioning. The standardization of the Wechsler series was an improvement on that of the Stanford-Binet; the Wechsler series norms have become increasingly representative of American English-speaking adults with respect to education, occupation, race, socioeconomic level, and geographic region, reflecting the census data of each era as accurately as possible. The WAIS-R retains about 80% of the WAIS items, the others having been replaced or modified to make them more current, culturally fair, or otherwise improved. The subtests are the same, though administered in a new order, and the age range now extends from 16 through 74. Periodic revisions of the test are also necessary because items get easier over time. For example, studies of individuals given both tests in randomized order indicate that WAIS-R IQs average about 8 points lower than those of the WAIS (Flynn, 1987). A new revision of the WAIS-R is under way and will be published in the near future with norms likely to reflect the increased life expectancy of the United States population.

The WAIS-R comprises 11 subtests: information, comprehension, arithmetic, similarities, digit span, and vocabulary in the verbal scale; and digit symbol, picture completion, block design, picture arrangement, and object assembly in the performance scale. Although the scales differ in terms of length, content, and process (verbalization versus psychomotor function), they can be compared with one another because each subtest is converted into a standard score with a mean of 10. The standard scores are summed separately for the verbal and performance subtests to provide a Verbal and a Performance IQ in addition to the Full-Scale IQ. These IQs have the same meaning at all ages because for each age group a mean IQ of 100 and a standard deviation of 15 have been established.

Factor analytic studies have demonstrated that the 11 subtests do not reflect 11 different components of intelligence. Most factor analytic studies have suggested three factors which can be compared (Kaufman, 1990). The Verbal Comprehension factor is composed of the information, vocabulary, comprehension, and similarities subtests; the Perceptual Organization factor is composed of the picture completion, block design, and object assembly subtests; and the Attention/Freedom from Distractibility factor is composed of the digit span, arithmetic, and digit symbol subtests. The 11 subtests do, however, represent a range of tasks that allows the clinician to describe and interpret not only the patient's general level of attainment but also the specific patterning of intellectual functioning as suggested by subtest comparisons along with observations of the manner in which the problems are approached and solved. Profile patterns that appear distinctive are a fruitful source of clinical hypotheses, and some observations can be made with confidence.

Verbal–Performance IQ discrepancies are often interpreted with respect to psychopathology, neurological impairment, professional and technical aptitudes, and other characteristics of human behavior. Discrepancies of at least 15–20 points between Verbal and Performance IQ are ordinarily sufficient to warrant interpretation. The meaning of the discrepancy will vary according to the individual context. In clinical psychiatric practice it is usually the Performance IQ that is lower, and this difference may be associated with a variety of conditions. Depression will have this effect, especially as a function of slowing down on the timed tests. The discrepancy may reflect cerebral damage, especially to the right hemisphere. Alternatively, professionals and others at the highest educational levels may have relatively higher Verbal than Performance IQs primarily on the basis of their differential experience and learning. The opposite pattern, a Verbal IQ that is 15 or more points below the Performance IQ, is more likely to be associated with certain cognitive dysfunctions, such as those caused by developmentally based language disabilities. In general, unusual variability or "scatter," either between subtests or within a subtest, is often of significance and may reflect a deficit from a higher level of functioning.

Since this review is concerned with the assessment of adults, we shall merely note that scales incorporating the same structure were developed for use with children. The *Wechsler Intelligence Scale for Children* (WISC) appeared in 1949 and was revised in 1974 (WISC-R). The latest revision (WISC-III, 1991) covers the age range from 6 to 16 and is one of the predominant tests of cognitive functions in children. The *Wechsler Preschool and Primary Scale of Intelligence* (WPPSI), published in 1967 and revised in 1989 (WPPSI-R), is intended for ages 4–6. The structure is the same as that of the WISC, but 3 new subtests suitable for the younger age group were introduced. Adaptations to these tests are available for certain purposes. In the 1970s, legal cases challenged the use of these tests for school placement purposes, arguing that they were dis-

criminatory against minorities. The System of Multicultural Pluralistic Assessment (SOMPA) was presented as one alternative model (Mercer and Lewis, 1978); it incorporated medical and social information into the formal assessment of adaptive capabilities for grade school children. The SOMPA employed the WISC-R, but used multiple norms and adjustments based on social variables to yield an Estimated Learning Potential (ELP) to complement the standard IQ.

It is important at least to mention briefly another kind of intelligence test, the self-administered type such as the *Raven Progressive Matrices* (Raven, Court, and Raven, 1985). This test, primarily a measure of nonverbal, inductive reasoning, may be used to supplement or supplant the individually administered test. It tends to correlate well with the WAIS-R (approximate $r = 0.70$) and yet at times provides a dramatic contrast with it. For example, some patients with severe developmentally based learning disabilities may have major compromise on many WAIS-R tasks owing to interference in the acquisition of knowledge because of verbal, perceptual, or motor deficits, yet they may demonstrate very high reasoning ability on the Raven Matrices. This kind of comparison can lead to a more accurate picture of the person's capacities and to the development of a more appropriate educational or vocational treatment plan. Nonverbal tests may also provide a more accurate estimate of intellectual capacity for the educationally underprivileged whose verbal skills are limited by their environmental circumstances. Although nonverbal tests have been touted as more "culture fair" (Rogers, 1993), available evidence does not totally support this claim (Sattler, 1988), and thus, use of these tests for this purpose should be approached with caution (Suzuki and Kugler, 1995).

Under certain circumstances clinicians or researchers may want to obtain an estimate of IQ, often because administration of the entire WAIS-R is too time-consuming. There are many such short-form methods available (Silverstein, 1990). Most methods utilize a combination of the vocabulary and block design subtests to estimate IQ (Brooker and Cyr, 1986). Tests such as the Raven Matrices and others are also used for this purpose. These estimates usually vary slightly from an IQ obtained from the entire test.

Another issue that frequently arises is how to obtain an accurate "premorbid IQ" in the case of someone who has had significant neuropsychiatric illness. The interpretation of IQ test data such as those obtained from the WAIS-R is invariably affected by the potentially deleterious influence of functional and/or neurocognitive dysfunctions associated with the patient's condition. Such conditions, including schizophrenia or Alzheimer's disease, may lead to deterioration of IQ. This effect has been known for many years, leading to recommendations that selected WAIS-R subtests (usually vocabulary or information) be used to obtain "premorbid" IQ estimates (Wechsler, 1958). While these methods have some degree of effectiveness for this purpose, recent evidence suggests that such subtests are often affected by some illnesses as well. Thus, alternative measures, usually oral word recognition reading tests such as the National Adult Reading Test (NART; Nelson and O'Connell, 1978) or Reading subtest from the Wide Range Achievement Test-3 (WRAT-3; Wilkinson, 1993) may be substituted. These tests have the advantage that they are normed on the same numerical scale (mean score = 100) as the WAIS-R and are thus easily compared. In typical situations, oral reading (but not comprehension) tests are relatively unaffected by mental and neurological illnesses. This is so probably because they measure rote knowledge that is automatically retrieved in the recognition testing format (Kremen et al., 1996). A limitation on their use is that certain developmental cognitive disorders, particularly those affecting language such as dyslexia, will underestimate IQ because the syndrome directly impairs reading ability.

Personality Assessment: Projective Tests

When a stimulus with some degree of ambiguity is presented to an individual and an appropriate response set is established, we assume that to some degree the responses will reflect the individual's particular ways of organizing and describing experience. Depending on the specific characteristics of the stimuli and the task, basic psychological processes such as associative thinking, imagination, cognitive style, conflicts, defense mechanisms, adaptive techniques, and modes of interpersonal relationships may be brought into play. Projective tests are therefore a potentially rich source for the understanding of the individual in depth, in breadth, and as a unique person.

A common attribute of projective tests is that there is no "right" answer. When asking the subject to describe what an inkblot suggests or to make up a story in response to a picture, the examiner gives minimal guidelines concerning expected or typical performance. This situation in itself often arouses anxiety; for this reason, analysis and interpretation of projective tests are especially useful in understanding how an individual is likely to react under stress and uncertainty and in conflicted situations.

The value and utility in interpreting projective tests are dependent on both the examiner's experience and knowledge of personality and psychopathology within a theoretical framework and the appropriate application of empirical and normative data where available. The psychologist's inferences from projective tests emerge from the same set of concepts used to observe and describe the development and functioning of people in general and people with psychiatric difficulties in particular. We have selected the Rorschach test for lengthy presentation because of its unique place among the many projective tests; we shall also take up the TAT and then, very briefly, sentence completion methods and human figure drawings as representative of this type of assessment.

The Rorschach Technique

The Rorschach stimuli consist of 10 symmetrical "inkblots," each on a piece of white cardboard; 5 are entirely in shades of black and gray, 2 include areas of red, and 3 are entirely multicolored. They are presented to all subjects in a standard sequence with instructions to say "what might this be." No further guidance is provided. The examiner records accurately not only the patient's words but also relevant aspects of his behavior. After these "free associations," the examiner repeats back the patient's responses and conducts a nonleading inquiry in order to understand how the patient sees the reported percepts. In particular, the examiner aims to understand the *location* of the percept, the *content* of the percept, and what aspects of the blot suggested the percept (the *determinants,* such as form, color, shading, and movement).

Rorschach originally published the "Form Interpretation Test" in 1921 in a monograph entitled *Psychodiagnostik.* One of Rorschach's supervisors was Bleuler, who had recently coined the term "schizophrenia." Rorschach had noticed the unusual responses of schizophrenics on the popular "Blotto game" involving inkblots. He then became primarily interested in the perceptual processing of the inkblots, rather than the content of responses. He devised the original codes for location and determinants and noticed some relationships between certain codes and psychological aspects of respondents.

The concept of projection in psychological testing did not really emerge until later, as discussed by Murray (1938) and Frank (1939). However, once discussed, the Rorschach test became an obvious application. The 1940s and 1950s saw a vast blossoming in the use of projective tests and in their interpretation from a psychoanalytic perspective. During this era, the content of a person's responses was deemed worthy of interpretation. The content was interpreted in accordance with the psychologist's understanding of the implications of images and symbols and the sequential manner in which they are given by the patient. R. Schafer (1954) formulated a useful guide for the interpretation of Rorschach content, deriving his meanings from psychoanalytic theory. Dependent, sado-masochistic, or authoritarian orientations, for example, may be suggested by images of food, a person being torn apart, or Napoleon, respectively. Sexual identity, guilt, different emotional states, and other themes may be inferred from the content of responses.

Content interpretation is not a simplistic "dreambook" process; major trends of the personality cannot be identified merely by equating them with symbols. Valid and meaningful interpretations of content depend on the convergence of evidence and the integration of content hypotheses with inferences from the formal and behavioral data. Behavior during the test also reveals information about the person; thus, careful observation of the predominant modes of interaction with the tester may be included in the analysis. One may note collaborative, enthusiastic, active, submissive, challenging, evasive, seductive, euphoric, passive-aggressive, or suspicious tendencies—the possibilities are endless. The degree to which the patient is aware of his seriously deviant responses and behavior is of particular importance.

By the late 1950s, five interpretive approaches were in practice, authored by Beck, Klopfer, Hertz, Piotrowski, and Rapaport and Schafer. A comparison of these approaches was published by J. E. Exner in *The Rorschach Systems* in 1969. Although the different systems addressed similar features and codes, definition and interpretations varied. In addition, through various surveys Exner and his colleagues discovered wide variability in the application of the systems. Exner began the process of integrating the divergent procedural, scoring, and interpretive strategies into an atheoretical, empirically based comprehensive system built on the formal and structural qualities of the Rorschach.

Exner's *The Comprehensive System* was initially published in 1974 with subsequent editions in 1978, 1982, 1986, and 1990. Exner and his colleagues (Exner, 1990) have amassed thousands of protocols and have established expectancy tables for many test variables in clinical and nonclinical populations and in different age groups. With this foundation he has been able to test successfully many old and new hypotheses about the meanings and correlates of Rorschach data. This approach has transformed the clinical use of the Rorschach around the United States. Exner's accomplishments, buttressed by his active teaching of the "comprehensive system" through workshops across the country, have had a significant ef-

fect on practice. Exner's approach is amenable to computerized scoring, and interpretation systems are widely used. Where there used to be a variety of systems, the Exner system has now become the standard and is routinely taught in graduate courses in psychological assessment. However, the rich history of the previous systems continues to influence current Rorschach interpretation.

The psychologist scores the protocol and examines trends in the scoring summary against the backdrop of his own experience, which includes knowledge of normative data from published studies. The most important formal qualities are those of location, determinants, form level, content categories, and deviations of thought and language. For example, in terms of the location codes, one patient may show a strong tendency to use tiny and unusual areas of the blots, while another may tend to organize major elements into coherent wholes. It is a short inferential leap to suggesting that the first individual usually organizes experience in a piecemeal or analytic fashion, attending to details at the expense of the larger view, and that the second is more able to integrate and to generalize.

Each of the determinants is associated with interpretive characteristics. To oversimplify considerably, the degree to which color in the blots is represented in the individual's responses is related to reactivity to emotional stimulation; the frequency of responses involving humans in motion may be indicative of the relationship of fantasy or anticipation to action; and responses to the shading or textural aspects may suggest the quality and intensity of anxiety. The patient's reality testing—the capacity to perceive the experiential world as it is and as others perceive it—is inferred primarily from the *form level* of the Rorschach responses. Using both published norms and clinical judgment, the examiner scores each percept as a plus or a minus on the basis of the general correspondence of the inkblot area used to the actual shape of what the patient has seen. The percentage of plus responses is the form level.

The Rorschach can be scored for special indices to serve as warning signs for major problem areas. The suicide constellation index measures the potential for suicide and was based on protocols of cases where the Rorschach was given within 60 days of a successful suicide (Exner, 1990). Both the depression index and the schizophrenia index attempt to discriminate these disorders from others. The unstructured nature of the Rorschach lends itself well to the clinical assessment of thought disorder. The Rorschach is quite useful in demonstrating the organization of thought, reasoning and logical operations, the perceptual processes of differentiation and integration, the quality of language and communication, and the degree of insight and self-awareness. Rapaport, Gill, and Schafer (1945) delineated 24 types of pathological thought and verbalizations that were found in the Rorschachs of schizophrenic patients, and these "signs" continue to have widespread acceptance in clinical work.

More recently, Johnston and Holzman (1979) have provided a system for coding and quantifying the Rapaport, Gill, and Schafer manifestations of thought and language disorder. Their "thought disorder index" (TDI) is a reliable measure for both research and clinical purposes, and they have extended the overall framework to analysis of the verbal subtests of the WAIS as well. Within their 4 general categories—associative, combinatory, disorganized, and unconventional verbalizations—they have described and differentially weighted 4 levels of response in each category. Consider the following illustration of the levels of combinatory response, each involving the same 2 inkblot elements: a man sitting on a tree stump (normal); a man with a dog's face sitting on a tree stump (incongruous); a man sitting on the head of a butterfly (fabulized combination); a huge man crushing a butterfly that was trying to poison him through his bottom (confabulation); a man looking like a man-butterfly (contamination). The detailed descriptions and definitions of the TDI not only enhance research and theory but may also introduce greater reliability among clinicians in describing thought disorder. Similarly, the Exner system captures thought disorder through the use of special scores delineating unusual verbalizations, including deviant verbalizations or responses and inappropriate combinations or condensations of percepts, not unlike those in the TDI.

The development of self psychology (Kohut, 1971) and object relations (Kernberg, 1966) in contemporary psychoanalytic theory and the related interest in concepts associated with borderline personality organization have led to a resurgence of Rorschach studies with promising clinical implications. For example, among the many important contributions of S. Blatt and his colleagues is their "concept of the object scale," which integrates stages of perceptual development with psychoanalytic "object representations" (Blatt, 1983). Human responses on the Rorschach are scored with regard to level of differentiation, articulation, degree of internality in motivation, degree of integration of object and action, and nature of interaction. In each of these categories human responses are scored along a developmental continuum and weighted differentially, as well as rated separately for good or poor form level. Krohn and Mayman (1974) have also described a system for assessing object relations from Rorschach human responses.

The Rorschach has played an important role in validating the construct of borderline personality organization and in turn has been useful in making the diagnosis. R. Knight's (1953) observation that borderline patients appear to be neurotic but regress dramatically in psychoanalysis is paralleled by the observation that such patients show no signs of serious disturbance on structured intelligence tasks and yet may appear to be psychotic on the unstructured Rorschach (Singer and Larson, 1981). The Rorschachs of borderline patients, as compared with those of neurotics, tend to show strong oral-aggressive and sexual content; polarization of self-other representations (for example, good-bad); primitive or merged content (for example, engulfment); variable reality testing; primitive defenses, such as splitting, devaluation, and projection, and primitive idealization (Cooper, Perry, and Arnow, 1988); and inappropriate combinatory perceptions (Smith, 1980). Compared with psychotics, borderline personalities are more anxious about their atypical responses and are more able to respond accurately to testing of the limits. Borderlines tend not to produce contaminations and show more definite character dispositions (Smith, 1980). Illustrative of contemporary psychoanalytic research is the preliminary study based conceptually on the work of D. Winnicott (1953), in which borderlines showed substantially more "transitional object phenomena" responses in the Rorschach than did schizophrenics (Greenberg et al., 1987). The volume of papers on borderline phenomena and the Rorschach test is an especially valuable resource (Kwawer et al., 1980).

The Thematic Apperception Test

The TAT (Morgan and Murray, 1935) had its origins in the explorations of normal personalities conducted by Henry A. Murray and his colleagues at Harvard (Murray, 1938). It has since been a part of the typical clinical psychological examination and a major instrument in personality research, particularly in studies of motivation. The TAT consists of a series of black and white pictures, chiefly drawings or woodcuts, most of which portray one or more persons in situations designed to elicit themes of psychological significance. The subject is asked to make up a story for each picture and to specify what led to the situation, what is happening, what the characters are thinking and feeling, and how the story ends. The stimuli are sufficiently ambiguous to allow the subject to project individual fantasies, feelings, patterns of relationship, needs, and conflicts. There are 30 pictures in the complete set, including some alternative versions for males and females and for adults and adolescents. Twenty pictures were intended to be shown to each subject, but because of the length of time involved, most clinicians tend to use a shorter subset of 10–12 cards.

Formal scoring systems are not typically employed in analysis of the TAT. There are limited data on the reliability and validity of this test, often because studies investigate only a limited number of cards that vary between studies (Keiser and Prather, 1990). In one systematic and promising approach to measuring object relations with the TAT, Westen and colleagues (1990) utilized a Q-sort technique. However, most clinicians currently use a less systematic approach than they do on the Rorschach. Clinical analysis is a matter of carefully developing hypotheses from each story, taking into account the nature of the subject's identification with the characters, the feelings expressed, the conflicts and resolutions presented, the overall richness and tone of the stories, and the defensive and adaptive activities. The clinician uses his experience, aided by published accounts of the prominent themes brought out by each picture, to determine whether a particular story deserves special emphasis because of its idiosyncratic quality.

One TAT card, for example, depicts a young man reclining with eyes closed while an older man stands over him with one arm raised. The patient may see the young man as asleep, ill, or dead; the older man as praying, hypnotizing, caring, curing, or attacking. The figures may be strangers or in an intense relationship; the antecedent and consequent elements may be logically and emotionally congruent with the scene described, or they may be magical or arbitrary; the narrative may be coherent, or it may reflect blocking or disorganization of thought. Sophisticated TAT interpretation requires thoroughness and skill in assigning appropriate weight and meaning to the various aspects of the data and in drawing a psychological portrait that is both valid and useful.

Variations of the TAT have been devised for different minority groups including the Thompson TAT (1949), where the original TAT cards have been redrawn with African American characters, and the Tell Me a Story Test (TEMAS; Costantino, Malgady, and Vasquez, 1981) with new cards portraying themes culturally relevant to urban Hispanic characters. There also exists a child version of the TAT, the Children's Apperception Test (CAT; Bellack and Bellack, 1949), in which the pictures involve animals instead of humans.

The TAT and Rorschach are typically used together, allowing the clinician to cross-check and supplement hypotheses arising from these and other sources. The TAT is more structured than the Rorschach and tends to elicit material that may be closer to a conscious level of thinking. Psychosocial developmental issues in particular are illuminated by TAT stories; for example, a picture of a boy playing a violin may bring forth themes of mastery, ambition, competence, or inferiority.

Other Projective Tests

More than a few test instruments have projective properties, but we shall limit our attention to the two that are best known and most often used, ordinarily as supplements to the usual battery. The *Incomplete Sentences Blank* (Rotter and Rafferty, 1950) consists of a list of sentence beginnings for the subject to complete, such as "My mother . . ." and "My greatest mistake was . . ." There are typically 4 or 5 such items relevant to each of several content areas, and subjects are instructed to respond quickly. Interpretation involves a judgment of adjustment or disturbance as well as the personal dynamic meaning of the content. The sentence completion method is less disguised than the Rorschach and TAT, making it useful as a source of feelings and perceptions that are closer to conscious awareness.

Human figure drawings are considered to be another projective device. Typically the subject is asked to draw a person (almost always a whole person), after which another sheet is provided for drawing a person of the opposite sex. There are variations, one of the earliest of which was the house-tree-person technique of J. N. Buck (1948). A later change involved the addition of action instructions in Burns and Kaufman's (1970) Kinetic Family Drawing (KFD), in which the patient is asked to draw a picture of his or her family doing something. Handler and Habenicht (1994) discuss the notion that action drawings tend to reveal more about conflicts than static pictures. A number of scoring approaches to the KFD exist, but evidence on reliability and validity is scant since studies focus on different variables. Burns's (1982) scoring system focuses on the action of characters, their physical characteristics, the organization of the figures on the page, and their distance and position in reference to one another. For example, if everyone in the family is closely drawn together except the patient, who is in the far opposite corner of the page, one might consider themes of isolation or alienation from the family. Figure drawings may be stylized or highly expressive of one's individuality. Most interpreters of human figure drawings place emphasis on the portrayal of "body image" and its disturbance. Size, stance, facial expression, dress, and emphasis on particular body parts are among the characteristics to be noted. Some examiners supplement the drawings with a few open-ended questions, such as "What kind of person is this?" Perceptions of the self and others may be brought to light in this way.

Personality Assessment: Objective Tests

In contrast to projective tests, which elicit the individual's responses in an open-ended and relatively unstructured fashion, objective personality tests, inventories, and questionnaires typically consist of standardized items in response to which the subject answers true or false or expresses preference or agreement-disagreement. These objective tests are usually constructed for the purpose of measuring specific psychological characteristics, such as personality traits, factors, patterns, or disorders. These test items ordinarily have *face validity*. That is, they are manifestly samples of, or otherwise relevant to, the characteristics or variables of interest. Items may also be included on purely empirical grounds, however, because they have a demonstrated relationship to those characteristics, even though their content is not recognizable as such.

A *response set* is a predisposition to answer test items in a specifically biased manner. Answering mostly true to a true-false questionnaire, giving "socially desirable" answers, or portraying oneself as significantly more or significantly less emotionally disturbed than is warranted are examples of response sets. Some objective tests include scales (e.g., the "validity" scales on the MMPI) or other devices to measure such tendencies and take them into account in the scoring or interpretation of the data.

Objective tests are reliably scored and readily quantified and are therefore quite comparable from one context to another. These attributes are especially amenable to administration, scoring, and interpretation by computer.

The Minnesota Multiphasic Personality Inventory

By far the most widely used objective test in clinical practice and research is the MMPI, published originally by Hathaway and McKinley (1943). Designed as an aid to psychiatric diagnosis, the MMPI began as a pool of more than a thousand true-false items taken from case reports, texts, and similar sources. The responses of groups of patients with confirmed psychiatric diagnoses of various kinds were compared with those of a sizable group of pre-

sumably normal people (visitors to a hospital). Validity and "clinical" scales were developed on an entirely empirical basis. For example, the schizophrenia scale consisted of items on which schizophrenics and normals differed significantly in the proportion of true and false answers. Items were eliminated for various statistical reasons but never because their content seemed unrelated to schizophrenia; the criterion was whether the item discriminated schizophrenics from normals. The revised MMPI (MMPI-2; Hathaway and McKinley, 1989) consists of 567 true-false items; however, shorter forms, such as an MMPI version with 168 items (Vincent et al., 1984), have been used with success for screening purposes.

The authors intended the MMPI to render accurate diagnostic judgments very simply—schizophrenics were expected to have their highest score on the schizophrenia scale; depressives would peak on the depression scale. Two observations were soon made: quite a few individuals with no psychiatric history scored high on one or more scales; and interpretation of a more complex analysis of configurations would permit not only more accurate diagnosis but personality description as well. This method of interpretation is termed actuarial (Meehl, 1954), and the MMPI pioneered in the use of actuarial methods (Marks, Seeman, and Haller, 1974).

The revised MMPI (MMPI-2) was published in 1989. The primary reason for revision was a need to restandardize the test according to current norms. The norm group for the original MMPI was collected in the 1930s and consisted of primarily Caucasian rural Minnesotans with an average eighth grade education. An additional purpose in revising the MMPI was to update the language in the item descriptions and to delete items whose content was no longer relevant based on current social norms. The new normative sample included 2600 subjects (1462 women and 1138 men). Demographic data are comparable to the 1980 U.S. census, with the exception that the normative sample has a higher mean education level and socioeconomic status.

The basic MMPI consists of 3 validity scales and 10 clinical scales. The validity scales were designed to aid in estimating response predispositions that might alter scores on the clinical scales. The items in the validity scales of the two versions are basically comparable. The clinical scales of the MMPI-2 are also very comparable to the old clinical scales, yielding very similar raw scores. T-scores tend to be lower for the MMPI-2, so the threshold for a clinical elevation was changed from 70 (2 standard deviations above the mean) to 65. An advancement of the MMPI-2 over the previous MMPI is the use of uniform T-scores; thus, the same T-score corresponds to the same percentile so that clinicians can more directly compare elevations on different scales. Additional supplementary scales were generated from the addition of new items in the MMPI-2, including two new substance abuse scales.

The original validity scales included a *Lie* (L) scale assessing basic naïveté, lack of frankness about self, rigidity, and moralistic and conventional attitudes; a *Deviant response* (F) scale, which may be elevated owing to random responding, intention to look "sick," pronounced subjective distress, severe psychopathology, confusion, or inadequate English reading skills; and a *Defensiveness* (K) scale, which can reflect inhibition, an intention to look "good," or low insight. The MMPI-2 adds three new validity scales. These include the Fb, which is similar to F, but allows the examiner to see if the subject's response pattern changes between the first and second halves of the test. The variable response inconsistency scale (VRIN) measures contradictory responding between pairs of items. Although the F scale was originally constructed to measure careless responding, it can also be elevated in cases of severe psychopathology or "faking bad." Thus, the VRIN can help the examiner determine whether random responding contributes to a high F. The true response inconsistency scale (TRIN) contains pairs of items opposite in meaning, and can detect yes or no response sets.

Translation of MMPI scales into meaningful statements about personality and psychopathology begins with an examination of the validity scales. If the F or K scale is unduly elevated, the psychologist will either qualify his interpretations or, in extreme cases, judge the entire test to be invalid on the basis of deviant response (F) or massive defensiveness (K).

The basic clinical scales are listed below, together with the most common correlates or interpretations of high elevations.

Clinical scales

1. *Hypochondriasis* (Hs): exaggerated concern with physical symptoms, with or without organic basis; demanding behavior; narcissism.
2. *Depression* (D): sadness, low morale, apathy, lethargy, lack of hope, overcontrol.
3. *Hysteria* (Hy): blandness, emotional displays, naïveté, bodily symptoms, seeking of affection and attention.
4. *Psychopathic deviate* (Pd): characterological social adjustment problems, with delinquent or antisocial behavior; impulsivity; immaturity; hostility.
5. *Masculinity-femininity* (Mf): rejection of traditional sex-role attributes; creativity, sensitivity (males); assertiveness, competitiveness, unemotional behavior (females).
6. *Paranoia* (Pa): suspiciousness, sensitivity, delusions of persecution, ideas of reference, rigidity, externalizing defenses.
7. *Psychasthenia* (Pt): anxiety, phobias, obsessive rumination, compulsive behavior, guilt, insecurity.
8. *Schizophrenia* (Sc): social withdrawal, inappropriate behavior, bizarre ideas, hallucinations, delusions, thought disorder.
9. *Hypomania* (Ma): overactivity, elevated mood, excitement, distractibility, denial of distress, impulsivity.
10. *Social introversion* (Si): sensitivity, shyness, introversion, overcontrol.

Assuming that the validity scales are within acceptable limits, one then considers the 2 or 3 clinical scales with the highest elevations. Most systems for classifying MMPI profiles utilize this method; the different categories of profiles are called *code types*. Let us take the 2–7 type (i.e., elevations on "depression" and "psychasthenia" scales) as an example and mention here only a few of the common attributes (Graham, 1977). This knowledge is derived from the accumulation over the years of both empirical and clinical experience (Butcher et al., 1989; Ben-Porath, 1994). Patients of the 2–7 type are anxious, tense, worried, and overreactive to stress. Somatic complaints and clinical signs of depression, such as retardation of thought and speech and loss of weight, are common, along with pessimism, low self-esteem, and brooding. These individuals have high goals and feel guilty when they fall short. They may be intropunitive, indecisive, rigid, and perfectionistic. Relations with others tend to be passive-dependent; docility and lack of assertiveness are often found. Because they show intense discomfort and distress, the subjects elicit nurturant behavior from others and are usually motivated for therapy or change. Confidence in the validity of this clinical picture is greatest when the elevations of scales 2 and 7 are high and stand out considerably from the others.

The psychologist does not mechanically copy these descriptions from the "cookbook." He will take into account elevations on other scales, as well as information from content scales (Wiggins, 1966) and "critical items" that have been derived from the MMPI item pool. He may integrate scores and profiles from a psychodynamic point of view (Trimboli and Kilgore, 1983). Above all, he will analyze and integrate all the information at his disposal, including non-MMPI information specific to the patient, in order to prepare a useful, valid, and meaningful descriptive and diagnostic summary. Computer-based interpretive reports, though having the appearance of a finished product, require on both clinical and ethical grounds a review by a trained MMPI analyst.

Computers were first used in the 1960s to generate psychological reports at the Mayo Clinic in Minnesota (Fowler, 1985). The MMPI was employed to screen out from thousands of medical patients those who had psychological problems. Subsequently, many MMPI computer programs for interpretation have developed and are utilized routinely throughout the world. The MMPI, like many self-report tests, can be administered to the subject directly on the computer.

The Millon Clinical Multiaxial Inventory

The MCMI (Millon, 1983) is an objective, computer scored and interpreted test for the assessment of personality patterns and disorders described in DSM-III (1980). Revised in 1987, the MCMI-2 is more closely aligned with DSM-III-R (1987). These instruments are designed to be used with clinical populations. Theodore Millon was a prominent participant in the development of Axis II (personality disorders), and the taxonomy and criteria of these standards bear the stamp of his thinking and research (Millon and Green, 1996).

The MCMI and MCMI-2 are self-report inventories containing 175 true-false items. The original MCMI measures 8 personality pattern scales: schizoid, avoidant, dependent, histrionic, narcissistic, antisocial, compulsive, and passive-aggressive. In addition, the MCMI measures the 3 Axis II personality disorders considered to represent more serious pathology: schizotypal, borderline, and paranoid. Axis I clinical syndromes are also included and demarcated into basic syndromes—anxiety, somatoform, hypomania, dysthymia, alcohol abuse, and drug abuse—and more severe syndromes: thought disorder, psychotic depression, and delusional disorder. The MCMI-2 adds 2 new personality scales—aggressive-sadistic and self-defeating—and 3 validity scales that assess various kinds of response bias. The disclosure scale (Scale X) measures the degree to which a patient freely discusses himself or herself versus being more secretive. The desirability scale (Scale Y) measures the degree to which the patient attempts to present himself or herself in a positive light. The debasement scale (Scale Z) is the opposite of Scale Y, measuring the degree to which the patient discloses negative aspects of the self.

MCMI norms were initially developed from a sample of 1591 patients (inpatients and outpatients in a wide variety of clinical settings) and cross-validated on 256 patients. The norms for the MCMI-2 were based on two samples. In the first sample, 519 clinicians from around the country provided MCMI data, MCMI-2 data, and DSM-III-R diagnoses for 825 of their patients. In the second sample, 93 clinicians from various settings provided MCMI-2 profiles and DSM-III-R diagnoses on 467 of their patients. The MCMI-2 normative group underrepresents minorities; nevertheless, the manual offers separate norms for Caucasian, African American, and Hispanic patients. In both versions, raw scores are transformed to base-rate scores, such that the proportion of patients scoring above critical thresholds corresponds to the prevalence of these symptoms in the clinical norm groups. One threshold of these transformed scores (75 or above) demarcates the presence of some personality features associated with the disorder the scale measures, and a second threshold (85 or above) demarcates the predominance of features associated with that disorder.

External validation ensuring that clinical groups with certain disorders scored high on scales measuring those disorders was performed. An advancement of the MCMI-2 involves a system of weighting items more central to a diagnosis more heavily, in order to optimize diagnostic accuracy.

Assessment of Brain Dysfunction: Neuropsychological Testing

In psychiatric settings until the 1970s, psychological evaluation of patients with suspected brain dysfunction usually consisted of the same basic test battery we described earlier (Rapaport, Gill, and Schafer, 1945). A clinical psychologist would attempt to determine the presence or absence of "organicity" (brain damage) on the basis of pathognomonic "organic" signs (Reitan and Davison, 1974) derived primarily from the WAIS, Bender-Gestalt (Bender, 1949), Draw-a-Person, MMPI, and Rorschach tests, supplemented by data from specialized tests such as the Wechsler Memory Scale, which was revised in 1987 (Wechsler, 1987). Although this clinical process had some success in identifying brain dysfunction (Spreen and Benton, 1965), it was limited on both empirical and conceptual grounds (Reitan and Davison, 1974; Lezak, 1995): many of the organic test impairments were associated with irrelevant factors (poor motivation, psychosis, low IQ) and thus produced "false positive" diagnoses, and many manifestations of brain damage (language deficits, memory problems) were not reflected on the single visuomotor test most often used to assess organicity, the

Bender-Gestalt (Bender, 1949), leading to "false negative" diagnoses.

The basic assumption underlying the concept of organicity—that brain damage is unitary—was faulty. Rather, the manifestations of brain dysfunction vary dramatically depending on the size, location, and type of lesion, to name just a few influential factors (Lezak, 1995). The organicity construct has been gradually replaced by the neuropsychological approach, the clinical discipline concerned with brain-behavior relationships. In this model the neuropsychologist attempts to determine whether the clinical picture and test data represent some neurobehavioral syndrome (Luria, 1980).

The traditional psychological battery remains useful in adding neuropsychological information when no brain pathology is suspected by the referring clinician (Weinstein et al., 1991, 1994). That is, when a psychologist is asked to do a psychological evaluation of intellectual capacity and personality dynamics, she may identify previously unsuspected brain impairment on the basis of the organic signs or test patterns. These may then be validated by the more differentiated and in-depth assessments of neuropsychology or neurology (Weinstein et al., 1994). When brain dysfunction is clearly part of the original differential diagnosis, or if there is known brain damage and the referring clinician wants an assessment of functional strengths and weaknesses, a neuropsychological assessment should be requested. The 2 approaches may appropriately be used conjointly when both personality and neuropsychological factors are to be assessed, as in articulating various aspects of complex neuropsychiatric disorders such as temporal lobe epilepsy (Greenberg and Seidman, 1992). For such cases a careful evaluation of personality and neuropsychological function may enhance goal setting and choice of type of psychotherapy or other treatment interventions (Allen and Lewis, 1986; Leftoff, 1983; Weinstein et al., 1991).

Since the 1950s the practice of clinical neuropsychological assessment has progressed dramatically. Whereas neuropsychological testing was initially a series of specialized procedures known to only a few (Luria, 1980) and utilized primarily in neurological and neurosurgical settings (Costa, 1983), it has been used increasingly of late in medical, rehabilitation, and psychiatric settings (Allen and Lewis, 1986). In psychiatric settings the growth of clinical neuropsychology corresponds to increased knowledge of biological factors associated with the etiology and expression of psychopathology and with the rapid development of increasingly sophisticated neurodiagnostic technology and its subsequent application to the study of psychiatric disorders such as schizophrenia (Seidman, 1983).

Neuropsychological testing in psychiatry provides information regarding diagnosis; cognitive, perceptual, and motor capacities or deficits; and treatment recommendations. It is now possible for an experienced clinician to use test data reliably to determine the presence or absence of brain dysfunction, to localize the damage, and to establish the etiology of the lesion (Milberg, Hebben, and Kaplan, 1996). Moreover, a comprehensive functional assessment can lead to neurologically meaningful subgroups (for example, in different types of developmental disorders, verbal and nonverbal) that may have relevance to treatment, as in the application of differential strategies of cognitive rehabilitation (Gianutsos, 1980; Yozawitz, 1986).

Relationship of the Neuropsychological Exam to Other Exams

Most neuropsychologists regardless of theoretical orientation agree on several basic characteristics that define clinical neuropsychological evaluations. The aim of the neuropsychological exam is to assess reliably, validly, and as completely as possible the behavioral correlates of brain functions (Reitan, 1986). The major emphasis in the neuropsychological examination is placed on central processing functions that involve "higher" (cognitive) functions (Weintraub and Mesulam, 1985; Reitan, 1986). The greatest relevance of testing lies in treatment planning and implications for daily life (Milberg, Hebben, and Kaplan, 1996; Keefe, 1995).

All neuropsychological approaches ought to assess some aspects of intelligence, reasoning and abstraction, attention (sustained and selective), "executive" and self-control functions (shift of set, planning, and organizational capacity), learning and memory, language, perceptual (auditory and visual) and constructional tasks, and sensory and motor functions. Comprehensive test batteries are long because the human brain-behavior relationship is quite complex (Luria, 1980). Test data are interpreted in the context of many factors, including the age, sex, education, and handedness of the patient (Lezak, 1995).

Although the data gathering approach of the neuropsychologist can be well integrated with a psychodynamic orientation (Allen and Lewis, 1986), a few distinctions are noteworthy. In the psychodynamic approach the examiner minimizes test structure in order to assess projective components and to discern underlying motives, wishes, and thought processes (Rapaport, Gill, and Schafer,

1945). By contrast, the neuropsychologist usually is structuring and encouraging, attempting to find out what the patient can best achieve and by what process (Milberg, Hebben, and Kaplan, 1996). Moreover, neuropsychologists doing a clinical assessment typically make greater use of history and medical records.

The neuropsychological evaluation covers the same functions as the mental status exam (see Chapter 2) but in a more elaborated, deep, and quantified manner (Weintraub and Mesulam, 1985). When contrasted with the mental status exam, neuropsychological testing is broader in that more differentiated functions are assessed; deeper in that far more items constitute a task or function, usually arranged from simple to difficult; and more quantified in that there is more standardized scoring of data, as well as the provision of normative data on different samples. In addition, its administration is more standardized. The neurologist's assessment of cranial nerves, sensory and motor functions, and coordination (more "elementary" functions) and the neuropsychologist's assessment of "higher" cognitive functions complement each other well (Weintraub and Mesulam, 1985).

Types of Referral Questions in Psychiatry

The neuropsychological exam has 3 general aims: (1) identification of neuropsychological dysfunction leading to inferences regarding presence, type, and etiology of brain dysfunction; (2) comprehensive assessment of cognitive, perceptual, and motor strengths and weaknesses as a guide for treatment; and (3) assessment of the level of performance of many mental functions, for both initial evaluation and measurement of change over time.

Differential diagnosis. While experienced neuropsychologists may achieve a greater than 90% "hit rate" in diagnosing brain dysfunction (Milberg, Hebben, and Kaplan, 1996; Reitan, 1986), the referring clinician needs to discuss with the neuropsychologist the relative merits of using neuropsychological examination (comprehensive or brief) compared with those of other methods such as the neurological evaluation or specialized neurodiagnostic techniques. On the one hand, for example, neuropsychological evaluation is labor-intensive (a full battery typically takes 2–8 hours to administer, not to mention scoring, interpretation, and report writing) and is thus expensive. On the other hand, it has very low invasiveness compared with such diagnostic procedures as x-ray computerized tomographic (CT) scanning or lumbar puncture. Moreover, the neuropsychological exam is unique in

providing a comprehensive, empirically grounded picture of mental function. Neuropsychological evaluation may be especially helpful when the clinician wants both differential diagnostic information and a profile of adaptive strengths and weaknesses, or when a patient who is resistant to other testing perceives it as a less threatening diagnostic procedure.

Some disorders, such as major depression or Alzheimer's disease, do not have reliable and valid laboratory tests and can best be diagnosed with the aid of neuropsychological profiles (Moss and Albert, 1992). In other diseases, such as AIDS, neuropsychological assessment may be helpful in identifying early manifestations of dementia, which may precede the overt syndrome (Beason-Hazen, Nasrallah, and Bornstein, 1994). These symptoms may include subtle cognitive deficits (such as memory loss, impaired concentration, or mental slowing) and motor problems that are sometimes attributed to depression or misconstrued as concomitants of systemic illness or general malaise (Navia and Price, 1986).

Disorders such as schizophrenia or schizophreniform psychoses associated with temporal lobe epilepsy may have broadly overlapping and confusing pictures on the clinical psychiatric and electroencephalographic evaluation that may be clarified by neuropsychological testing (Seidman et al., 1992). For example, a distinctly focal and lateralized neuropsychological deficit (such as short-term verbal memory deficit and mild word-finding difficulty in the absence of other neuropsychological deficits) is far more characteristic of idiopathic temporal lobe epilepsy than of schizophrenia (Seidman, 1990; Greenberg and Seidman, 1992). The neuropsychologist may identify a clinical symptom picture and a cluster of deficits that characterize a subtype of neurobehavioral syndrome, as in schizophrenia with frontal-executive dysfunction (Goldberg and Seidman, 1991). Alternatively, the neuropsychologist may conclude that cognitive dysfunction is indeed present but may be static or not essential to the syndrome being evaluated (for example, a developmentally based spelling problem in a case of schizophrenia).

Characterization of adaptive strengths and weaknesses as a guide for treatment. Probably the greatest contribution of the neuropsychological exam relative to that of neurological or other neurodiagnostic evaluations is in providing a broad description of the patient's capacities and deficits and their impact on his adaptation to the world (Weiss and Seidman, 1988; Keefe, 1995). This profile is essential for treatment planning, which may include rehabilitation efforts generally and psychotherapy specifically.

For example, although the clinician may clearly know that a patient is schizophrenic, the disorder is heterogeneous with respect to manifestations of brain dysfunction (Seidman, 1983, 1990), and the neuropsychological exam may help in determining the types of vocational or educational training the patient can utilize. Subtle learning disabilities may be identified in a student who is anxious and depressed about failures in school but is unable to pinpoint the cause. Such referrals are wide-ranging: they include high school students who have a specific spelling disability, college students who are intelligent but unable to learn required foreign languages, and graduate students in math, science, or medicine who are failing subjects requiring visual-spatial analysis. All may benefit from the neuropsychological exam in terms of counseling as to career choice, recommendations for compensatory learning strategies, and psychotherapy to deal with the impact on self-esteem, mastery, and identity (Seidman, 1994).

The identification of a person's cognitive deficits has definite ramifications for psychotherapy. For example, even mild verbal memory and abstraction problems secondary to left hemisphere temporal lobe damage may interfere with the utilization of dynamic psychotherapy, which relies heavily on verbal abstract interpretation and learning. The therapist might explore what other modalities are more efficient (for example, art therapy) or whether special techniques are necessary to facilitate learning, such as writing down insights, memories, and recommendations.

Identification of a neurologically based cognitive deficit may also help a patient come to terms more realistically with narcissistic injuries associated with experiences of failure. Some patients are greatly relieved when they learn that the origin of their problem is in their brain, not in their mind or "self." Others, of course, become depressed because the brain damage may be irremediable or progressive (Seidman, 1994). Neuropsychological data can aid the family of a handicapped or vulnerable child (schizophrenic, learning disabled, and so on) by helping them develop realistic expectations for their child so that secondary emotional problems can be minimized and a supportive environment developed.

Neuropsychological data can be used to support the validity of a disorder that is difficult and sometimes controversial to diagnose such as attention deficit hyperactivity disorder (ADHD) in adults (Spencer, Biederman, Wilens, and Faraone, 1994). For example, the presence of attention and executive dysfunctions are useful validating criteria for ADHD because they do not share method variance with other measures (Seidman et al., 1997). In contrast to neuropsychological measures, assessments of psychiatric symptoms rely on the self-report of subjects, or on the reports of teachers or parents which may be influenced by recall biases, halo effects, and other potentially confounding factors. In adults this problem is magnified because an informant is often unavailable to verify behaviors that may have occurred many years earlier. Thus, the presence of a cluster of attention-executive deficits in a person with symptoms characteristic of ADHD may result in a more confident clinical diagnosis. Moreover, the presence of such difficulties can validate the self-report of a patient, whose complaints had been previously misinterpreted or ignored (Seidman, 1994, 1997).

Assessment of change of state. Many patients have fluctuating mental states, as in schizophrenia and affective disorder, medical illness (renal disease, diabetes, and the like), drug or alcohol abuse, or as a result of somatic therapies (medication or electroconvulsive therapy [ECT]). Repeated testing is often desirable to assess the patient's cognitive capacities. The effects of a treatment such as ECT on cognitive function (for example, impairment of short-term memory) can be long lasting (Squire, 1986). Monitoring cognitive status by repeated testing allows an objective measure of subjective complaints and of recovery of function. Baseline testing early in the course of an illness such as schizophrenia or brain tumor can be compared with later evaluations to clarify the course of the disorder or to assess the impact of various interventions, such as medication trials. As new medications are developed, their effect on cognition and information processing ought to be assessed so as to contribute to a determination of the cognitive costs and benefits for the patient.

Types of Batteries

Assessment of the multiple functions described above can be performed with varying degrees of depth and flexibility. For example, we have noted that a comprehensive exam may typically last from 2 to 8 hours, whereas a shortened screening exam may take only an hour or two, covering the same functions more superficially. Moreover, "bedside" evaluation may be most appropriate for patients who cannot be tested by conventional methods (Weintraub and Mesulam, 1985).

It is important to note that constraints on the use of services, imposed in part by managed care (see Chapter 37), has led to the increasing use of briefer batteries. Thus, brief "micro-batteries" have been developed for specific purposes, such as the assessment of Alzheimer's disease or other late-life dementias (Milberg, 1996) in elderly people who can tolerate only brief evaluations. A clinician might then supplement the brief battery with additional appropriate tests as hypotheses are developed in the course of the examination.

An example of this approach is offered for the assessment of ADHD (Seidman, 1997; Seidman et al., 1997). In our approach, the core neuropsychological assessment takes approximately two hours and consists of the following clinical tests: (1) the WAIS-R Vocabulary and Block Design subtests to estimate IQ; (2) the WAIS-R/WISC-3 Digit Span, Digit Symbol/Coding and Arithmetic subsets to estimate "freedom from distractibility"; (3) the Stroop Test (Golden, 1978) to measure selective attention and response inhibition; (4) the Wisconsin Card Sorting Test (WCST [Grant and Berg, 1948; Heaton, 1981]) to measure concept formation, perseveration, and shift of set; (5) the Rey-Osterrieth Complex Figure to measure organization, planning, and visual memory (Rey, 1941; Osterrieth, 1944); (6) the auditory continuous performance test (CPT) to measure vigilance or sustained attention (Rosvold et al., 1956; Weintraub and Mesulam, 1985); (7) the scattered letters version of the visual cancellation test (Weintraub and Mesulam, 1985) to measure selective attention and planning; and (8) the California Verbal Learning Test (CVLT [Delis et al., 1987, 1994]), adult or child version, to examine verbal learning and memory. If, as is common, the ADHD patient has a comorbid learning disability (LD), additional specialized tests are added to the battery of screening achievement tests, such as Arithmetic, Reading, and Spelling tests. For a verbal LD, tests of phonological awareness (e.g., phoneme deletion tasks) and rapid naming supplement the core battery (Fletcher et al., 1994). Techniques used to measure the strategy of performing specific tasks, such as the Rey-Osterrieth figure, are often influenced by knowledge of developmental processes (Waber and Holmes, 1985; Seidman et al., 1995, 1997).

In the next section we briefly address the relative merits of 3 major comprehensive neuropsychological approaches and explore the rationale behind our use of the "process" approach in the psychiatric context.

The *Halstead-Reitan Battery* (HRB) pioneered clinical neuropsychological testing, which developed from Halstead's attempt to measure biological intelligence (Halstead, 1947). It consists of a combination of tests measuring motor speed and agility, spatial relations, complex psychomotor function, conceptual ability, speech-sound perception, and nonverbal auditory perception and is usually administered with a WAIS-R and the Trail-Making Test (Reitan, 1958), a test of mental tracking.

Other tests are added as needed, such as an aphasia-screening exam when language disorder is suspected (Halstead and Wepman, 1949). Administration of the battery usually takes 6–8 hours and is typically performed by a trained technician or, in academic settings, by a neuropsychologist in training; the test data are interpreted by a clinical neuropsychologist.

Reitan (1986) has delineated 4 types of analyses that clinicians use to evaluate HRB data: *level of performance,* the absolute deviation and dispersion of individual test scores compared with normative expectancies and the patient's own variable performance across different tests; *left-right comparisons,* the relative sensory, perceptual, and motor performances of the 2 sides of the body; *pathognomonic signs,* the features of poor performance or the clusters of test scores that point clearly to the existence of discrete disorders, and *differential patterns,* the large arrays of test profiles that are predictive of disease or damage.

As an analytical tool the HRB has evident strengths. Not only is it the most extensively studied of all neuropsychological batteries, but it also has excellent predictive validity in neurosurgical or neurological settings, where it is widely utilized (Reitan and Davison, 1974; Reitan, 1986). Because different tests in the HRB were normed on the same subjects, and in some approaches converted to standard scores, accurate between-test comparisons can be obtained. When used in psychiatric settings, however, the HRB may have certain limitations. The core battery is quite long, and the time and cost of administration may become prohibitive if additional tests must be added (as is often the case in functional assessment). Because the core battery does not thoroughly measure certain key functions that are often impaired in neuropsychiatric populations, tests of memory and attention are often added (Halperin, 1991; Weintraub and Mesulam, 1985). Moreover, the ability to establish rapport, to get cooperation, to obtain reliable and valid data, to evaluate the validity of test results, and to observe problem solving carefully is crucial in testing psychiatric patients, because level of performance may be grossly affected by agitation or poor motivation. Therefore it is often necessary to adapt the HRB in psychiatric settings by making the battery more flexible.

The *Luria Nebraska Neuropsychological Battery* (LNNB) is a standardization of items drawn from *Luria's Neuropsychological Investigation* (Christensen, 1975), a compendium and systematization of some of A. R. Luria's assessment procedures and techniques (Luria, 1980). The developers of the LNNB (Golden, Hammeke, and Purisch, 1980) have attempted to transform the flexible, patient-centered, qualitative clinical investigation advocated by Luria into a more psychometrically based battery format. This effort reflects the critique by some neuropsychologists that Luria's techniques are unscientific and not subject to cross-validation because the individual procedures recommended by Christensen cannot be repeated in any precise way.

The LNNB is a test battery that takes 2–3 hours to administer (usually by a technician). It rates the patient's performance on a scaled scoring system and is composed of 14 scales designed to offer a comprehensive neuropsychological evaluation (Golden, Hammeke, and Purisch, 1980). These include scales of motor, acousticomotor (rhythm), kinesthetic (tactile), and visual functions; writing, reading, and arithmetic skills; receptive and expressive speech; memory and intelligence; and 3 summary scales.

Despite the apparent utility of the battery, some neuropsychologists have criticized the LNNB on the fundamental methodological issues of reliability and validity. Problems in the standardization samples (Adams, 1980), item selection, scoring, and validation (Spiers, 1981), and interpretation, particularly of language disorder (Delis and Kaplan, 1982), indicate that results from this approach need to be viewed cautiously.

Moreover, the LNNB has been criticized as a distortion of Luria's method, which should not be confused with his approach (Spiers, 1981). Many of the scales have an inadequate number of items to assess the functions named (Spiers, 1981). Although the LNNB seems to have had some success in differentiating schizophrenics with and without brain dysfunction, it is limited in testing several functions known to be impaired in that illness, including executive functions (for example, planning and set shifting), complex language functions, short-term memory, abstraction, and attention (Seidman, 1983, 1990; Goldberg and Seidman, 1991; Seidman et al., 1992; Gur, 1986). Perhaps the greatest limitation of the LNNB is that it is a fixed battery. As noted above, because clinical presentations vary so greatly, clinicians may need to supplement the LNNB with other tests.

The *Boston process neuropsychological approach* (Milberg, Hebben, and Kaplan, 1996) is not a battery of identical items or tests routinely administered, as in the HRB and LNNB, but rather reflects a flexible, hypothesis-testing, qualitative approach to neurobehavioral syndrome analysis (Lezak, 1995; Goldberg and Costa, 1986). The Boston process approach is a combination of qualitative and psychometric features that reflects the integration of the behavioral neurological orientation exemplified by Geschwind (1979) and Luria (1980), with the rigorous quantification of the American research tradition in psychology. Many neuropsychologists worldwide use variations of the qualitative process approach in that their orientation to battery construction is flexible and they include the problem-solving strategies of patients in their analysis (Lezak, 1995).

The process approach starts with a smaller set of core measures than that of the HRB; then it focuses in on certain cognitive processes more specifically and intensively as hypotheses are developed. On the assumption that neurological dysfunction will be reflected in psychological tests, the examiner looks for nonspecific indicators of impairment while scanning for highly selective deficits, or a configuration of deficits, which allows him or her to infer that a lateralized or localized brain dysfunction is present (Goodglass and Kaplan, 1979).

Some of the nonspecific (nonlocalizing) deficits commonly found include impairment in conceptual thinking, slowing and "stickiness" of ideational processes, perseveration, reduced scope of attention, stimulus boundedness, and impairment of memory (Goodglass and Kaplan, 1979). The set of lateralizing and localizing signs and deficits is too extensive to list completely here—it reflects the whole field of neuropsychology—but, broadly speaking, it includes the disorders of functions previously addressed, such as many aspects of language, visual-spatial performance, and memory (Geschwind, 1979; Goodglass and Kaplan, 1979).

The Boston test battery often includes the WAIS-R; the Wechsler Memory Scale–Revised (Wechsler, 1987) or the California Verbal Learning Test (Delis et al., 1987); the Rey-Osterreith Complex Figure, a test of visuoconstructional and planning ability; the Wisconsin Card Sorting Test, which assesses the capacity to shift set; the Boston Naming Test, a measure of visual-confrontation naming ability (Kaplan, Goodglass, and Weintraub, 1983); the Visual-Verbal Test, a measure of abstraction ability (Feldman and Drasgow, 1981); and some form of the CPT. Certain tasks or brief batteries, such as the Boston Diagnostic Aphasia Exam (Goodglass and Kaplan, 1983), may be utilized for specific patient populations. Descriptions of many of these tasks can be found in more comprehensive texts (Lezak, 1995).

The process approach utilizes the 4 basic principles of interpretive analysis described by Reitan (1986), but more strongly emphasizes the way the patient attains a score and the preserved functions that the scores reflect rather than the achievement per se (Kaplan, 1988, 1990). Because most tests are multifactorial, people may arrive at correct (or incorrect) solutions via diverse routes. Thus, the subject's approach to the task is carefully observed and placed in the context of the task demands. The different processes or styles of solving a task may be indicative of the integrity of different brain structures. For example, a dynamic serial picture of the problem-solving process is recorded while a patient is putting the WAIS-R block designs together. In this way, behaviors such as featural priority (emphasis on details), contextual priority (emphasis on the gestalt), and hemispatial priority (the tendency to work on one side of visual space) can be assessed (Kaplan, 1990). Right hemisphere–damaged patients tend to work on the right side of visual space and to use a detail-oriented strategy, whereas left hemisphere–damaged patients tend to work in the reverse field and with the reverse strategy (Milberg, Hebben, and Kaplan, 1996).

The Boston group suggests that qualitative data may, in fact, better reflect an underlying brain lesion because impairment may be demonstrated even if the final score is correct (Kaplan, 1990). This perspective is partially supported by a study done by Heaton and associates (1981). They demonstrated that clinicians who rated HRB results had better success in classifying brain damage cases than did a psychometric-formula approach rooted heavily in level of performance. The authors believed that the superiority of the clinicians was related to their ability to supplement test scores with consideration of the qualitative and configural features of their data. In most current neuropsychological practice, including clinicians and technicians who utilize the HRB and the LNNB, both psychometric and process data are used. The flexible, hypothesis-testing approach seems well suited to psychiatry because process features may be less likely to be affected by motivational deficits than are level of performance and pathognomonic signs. Process variables are probably less susceptible to conscious faking, as a patient would be unlikely to know the neurological rules governing the process, and they may also be less susceptible to the effects of practice and repetition, which can confound the interpretation of scores.

Limitations of Reliability and Validity

Despite the obvious role of quantification in neuropsychological testing, interpretation of test data ultimately depends on the knowledge base, training, and skill of the clinician. Neuropsychological tests are only indirect measures of brain function, and test scores thus represent an inference regarding the status of the brain. This is in contrast to direct measures of structure by CT scan or of function by positron emission tomography scan (see Chapter 5). In a psychiatric setting, where problems of motivation, effort, cooperation, and state of the illness are common, analysis of neuropsychological data must go beyond the level of performance deficits, since many studies have shown this dimension to be especially affected by "functional" factors (Yozawitz, 1986). Process analyses oriented to focal syndromes and focused on the relative efficiency of the 2 sides of the body and hemispace may enhance predictive validity (Milberg, Hebben, and Kaplan, 1996; Yozawitz, 1986).

Because the patient's clinical state may change, repeat testing when the patient is at optimal clinical status often clarifies the nature of the diagnosis. Selective deficits found in the context of otherwise good performance obtained when patients are tested at their best state can be considered most valid. A repeat evaluation need not include the entire initial examination. It is often sufficient to select a number of measures that may change and compare them to some tests that are likely to remain stable. Because validity increases with more test items or multiple measurements, a second evaluation often helps to clarify the diagnosis.

Neuropsychologists must also carefully take into account the role of medications in neuropsychological function and distinguish their effects from the patient's adaptive ability. Different medications are likely to produce different effects. On the one hand, for example, Trimble and Thompson (1986) have demonstrated that in both epileptic patients and normal subjects, some adverse effects are caused by anticonvulsants on some measures of neuropsychological testing. On the other hand, Cassens and associates (1990) have reported that antipsychotic medications have negligible or mildly positive effects on most measures of neuropsychological testing in chronic schizophrenia. However, the neuropsychological effects of even a single medication may be complex. For example, in treating schizophrenic patients, some antipsychotic medications may improve sustained attention but impair motor function because of mild sedation (Cassens et al., 1990). Adding to the complexity is that patients may be receiving multiple drugs at the same time (for one or more conditions), whose neuropsychological effects may be unclear.

In the best of all possible worlds, testing would be performed on a person when in an unmedicated state, and then perhaps repeated (to assess drug effects) after systematic administration of a single drug. Because this ideal is difficult to achieve in real world practice, certain practical guidelines may be helpful. First, in non-emergency circumstances, testing ought to be done when the patient has been stable on his or her particular medication regimen. Because clinically significant neuropsychological indications of overmedication may be present (Weinstein et al., 1994), despite an absence of observable signs of medication toxicity (excessive sedation, confusion, gait disturbance), the clinician must be very alert to the possibility of subtle impairments as a result of medications. We find that a common outcome of the results of neuropsychological testing in such cases (on patients who are otherwise well treated) is a reduction in dose of medication in patients who can tolerate it clinically. Such interventions can have surprisingly dramatic positive results (Weinstein et al., 1994).

The Role of Computers in Neuropsychological Testing

Many clinical and research neuropsychological tests are computerized for administration and scoring, and this trend will undoubtedly grow. The utility of computers for clinical interpretation of test data, however, cannot be currently advocated. Studies by Adams and Brown (1986) indicated that 3 computer programs were far less adequate in interpreting data than were neuropsychological "experts." On the one hand, although fairly accurate predictions were made regarding the presence of cerebral dysfunction, Adams and Brown (1986), like others (Heaton et al., 1981), found that more subtle distinctions concerning lateralization or localization were not made consistently by any of the current computer algorithms. On the other hand, fears that assessment would be "dehumanized" have not been confirmed. Sitting at a console is preferred by some patients to a paper-and-pencil session. A battery of tests administered by a psychologist, however, is a personal clinical encounter that is much to be preferred when circumstances call for it.

This chapter contains a relatively broad overview of the role of psychological and neuropsychological tests used in clinical practice. The use of such tests is based on the concept that understanding individual differences is crucial for treatment. The art of clinical psychological assessment has evolved over the past 75 years in keeping with changes in the mental sciences. We expect that this evolution will continue. The current view that many psychiatric syndromes are heterogeneous (such as ADHD or schizophrenia), and that many patients with these disorders have neuropsychological problems, requires greater attention to the functional capacities and deficits of individuals with these disorders. Moreover, the fact that neuropsychological deficits have real world consequences (Green, 1996) suggests that neuropsychological understanding is important in the planning of treatment

(Seidman, 1994). The growing prevalence of patients presenting with disorders of cognitive function, especially in the elderly, is increasing the need for neuropsychological assessment. At the same time, changes in the organization of health care services will likely place a greater premium on briefer evaluations than in the past (Milberg, 1996; Seidman, 1997). We fully expect that psychological and neuropsychological tests will continue to be helpful in diagnosis, treatment planning, and assessing change over time, such as in response to treatment interventions. We believe that assessment which appropriately integrates neuropsychological, personality, and behavioral tests can effectively measure the person's experience, adaptive capacity, and conflict and the meaning of his or her difficulties. The flexible use of assessment, at the bedside or in extended evaluation, may be of great benefit to both patient and clinician.

References

Adams, K. 1980. In search of Luria's battery: a false start. *J. Consult. Clin. Psychol.* 48:511–516.

Adams, K. M., and G. G. Brown. 1986. The role of the computer in neuropsychological assessment. In *Neuropsychological assessment of neuropsychiatric disorders,* ed. I. Grant and K. M. Adams. New York: Oxford University Press.

Allen, J., and L. Lewis, eds. 1986. Neuropsychology in a psychodynamic setting. *Bull. Menninger Clin.* 50:1–132.

American Psychiatric Association. 1994. *Diagnostic and Statistical Manual of Mental Disorders–IV.* Washington, D.C.: American Psychiatric Association.

Beason-Hazen, S., H. A. Nasrallah, and R. A. Bornstein. 1994. Self-report of symptoms and neuropsychological performance in asymptomatic HIV-positive individuals. *J. Neuropsychiat. Clin. Neurosci.* 6:43–49.

Beck, S. J. 1944. *Rorschach's test.* Vol. 1. New York: Grune & Stratton.

Bellack, L., and S. S. Bellack. 1949. *Children's Apperception Test.* New York: C.P.C.

Bender, L. 1949. *A visual motor gestalt test and its clinical use.* American Orthopsychiatric Association research monographs, no. 8.

Ben-Porath, Y. S. 1994. The MMPI and MMPI-2: Fifty years of differentiating normal and abnormal personality. In *Differentiating normal and abnormal personality,* ed. S. Strack and M. Lorr. New York: Springer Publishing Company.

Binet, A., and T. Simon. 1905. Méthodes nouvelles pour le diagnostic du niveau intellectuel des anormaux. *Année psychologique* 11:191–244.

Blatt, S., and H. Lerner. 1983. The psychological assessment of object representation. *J. Pers. Assess.* 47:7–28.

Brooker, B. H., and J. J. Cyr. 1986. Tables for clinicians to use to convert WAIS-R short forms. *Journal of Clinical Psychology* 42:982–986.

Buck, J. N. 1948. The H-T-P test. *J. Clin. Psychol.* 4:151–159.

Burns, R. 1982. *Self-growth in families: Kinetic Family Drawings (K-F-D) research and application.* New York: Brunner/Mazel.

Burns, R., and S. Kaufman. 1970. *Kinetic Family Drawings (K-F-D): an introduction in understanding children through kinetic drawings.* New York: Brunner/Mazel.

Butcher, J. N., W. G. Dahlstrom, J. R. Graham, A. Tellegen, and B. Kaemmer. 1989. Manual for administration and scoring MMPI-2. Minneapolis: University of Minnesota Press.

Butcher, J. N., C. L. Williams, J. R. Graham, R. P. Archer, A. Tellegen, Y. S. Ben-Porath, and B. Kaemmer. 1992. *MMPI-A (Minnesota Multiphasic Personality Inventory–Adolescent): manual for administration, scoring, and interpretation.* Minneapolis: University of Minnesota Press.

Cassens, G., A. K. Inglis, P. S. Appelbaum, and T. G. Gutheil. 1990. Neuroleptics: effects on neuropsychological function in chronic schizophrenic patients. *Schizophr. Bull.* 16:477–499.

Christensen, A. L. 1975. *Luria's neuropsychological investigation.* New York: Spectrum Press.

Cooper, S., J. C. Perry, and D. Arnow. 1988. An empirical approach to the study of defense mechanisms: reliability and preliminary validity of the Rorschach defense scales. *J. Pers. Assess.* 52:187–203.

Costa, L. 1983. Clinical neuropsychology: a discipline in evolution. *J. Clin. Neuropsychol.* 5:1–11.

Costantino, G., R. Malgady, and C. Vasquez. 1981. A comparison of the Murray-TAT and a new thematic apperception test for urban Hispanic children. *Hispanic Journal of Behavioral Science* 3:291–300.

Craig, R. J., ed. 1993. *The Millon Clinical Multiaxial Inventory: a clinical research information synthesis.* Hillsdale, N.J.: Lawrence Erlbaum Associates.

Delis, D. C., and E. Kaplan. 1982. The assessment of aphasia with the Luria-Nebraska neuropsychological battery: a case critique. *J. Consult. Clin. Psychol.* 50:32–39.

Delis, D. C., J. H. Kramer, E. Kaplan, and B. A. Ober. 1987. *California verbal learning test: adult edition.* San Antonio: The Psychological Corporation, Harcourt, Brace and Jovanovich.

——— 1994. *California verbal learning test: children's version.* San Antonio: Harcourt Brace.

Exner, J. E. 1969. *The Rorschach systems.* New York: Grune and Stratton.

——— 1990. *The Rorschach: a comprehensive system.* Vol. 1. *Basic foundations.* 3rd ed. New York: Wiley.

Feldman, M. J., and J. Drasgow. 1981. *The visual-verbal test.* Los Angeles: Western Psychological Services.

Fletcher, J. M., S. E. Shaywitz, D. P. Shankweiler, L. Katz, I. Y. Lieberman, K. K. Stuebing, D. J. Francis, A. E. Fowler, and B. A. Shaywitz. 1994. Cognitive profiles of reading disability: comparisons of discrepancy and low achievement definitions. *J. Ed. Psychol.* 86:6–23.

Flynn, J. R. 1987. Massive IQ gains in 14 nations: what IQ tests really measure. *Psychological Bulletin* 101:171–191.

Fowler, R. 1985. Landmarks in computer-assisted psychological assessment. *J. Consult. Clin. Psychol.* 53:748–759.

Frank, L. K. 1939. Projective methods for the study of personality. *Journal of Psychology* 8:389–413.

Gardner, H. 1983. *Frames of mind: theory of multiple intelligences.* New York: Basic Books.

Geschwind, N. 1979. Specializations of the human brain. *Sci. Am.* 241:108–117.

Gianutsos, R. 1980. What is cognitive rehabilitation? *J. Rehabilitation* 23:36–40.

Goldberg, E., and L. D. Costa. 1986. Qualitative indices in neuropsychological assessment: extension of Luria's approach to executive deficit following prefrontal lesions. In *Neuropsychological assessment of neuropsychiatric disorders,* ed. I. Grant and K. M. Adams. New York: Oxford University Press.

Goldberg, E., and L. J. Seidman. 1991. Higher cortical functions in normals and in schizophrenia: a selective review. In *The handbook of schizophrenia.* Vol. 5. *Neuropsychology, psychophysiology, and information processing,* ed. S. Steinhauer, J. H. Gruzelier, and J. Zubin. New York: Elsevier Science Publishing Co.

Golden, C. J. 1978. *Stroop color and word test: a manual for clinical and experimental use.* Chicago: Stoelting.

Golden, C. J., T. Hammeke, and A. Purisch. 1980. The Luria-Nebraska neuropsychological battery: manual. Rev. ed. Los Angeles: Western Psychological Services.

Goldstein, K. 1942. *After effects of brain injuries in war.* New York: Grune & Stratton.

Goodglass, H., and E. Kaplan. 1979. Assessment of cognitive deficit in the brain-injured patient. In *Handbook of behavioral neurobiology.* Vol. 2, ed. M. Gazzaniga. New York: Plenum Publishing.

——— 1983. *The assessment of aphasia and related disorders.* 2nd ed. Philadelphia: Lea & Febiger.

Graham, J. R. 1977. *The MMPI: a practical guide.* New York: Oxford University Press.

Grant, D. A., and E. A. Berg. 1948. A behavioral analysis of degree of reinforcement and ease of shifting to new responses in a Weigl-type card sorting program. *J. Exp. Psychol.* 38:404–411.

Green, M. F. 1996. What are the functional consequences of neurocognitive deficits in schizophrenia? *Am. J. Psychiat.* 153:321–330.

Greenberg, M., and L. J. Seidman. 1992. The neuropsychology of temporal lobe epilepsy. In *Clinical syndromes in adult neuropsychology: the practitioner's handbook,* ed. R. White. Amsterdam: Elsevier.

Greenberg, R., S. Craig, L. J. Seidman, S. Cooper, and A. Teele. 1987. Transitional phenomena and the Rorschach: a test of a clinical theory of borderline personality organization. In *The borderline patient: emerging concepts in diagnosis, psychodynamics, and treatment,* ed. J. S. Grotstein, M. Solomon, and J. A. Lang. New York: Analytic Press.

Gur, R. 1986. Cognitive aspects of schizophrenia. In *American Psychiatric Association annual review.* Vol. 5, ed. A. J. Frances and R. E. Hales. Washington, D.C.: American Psychiatric Press.

Halperin, J. M. 1991. The clinical assessment of attention. *International Journal of Neuroscience* 58:171–182.

Halstead, W. C. 1947. *Brain and intelligence: a quantitative study of the frontal lobes.* Chicago: University of Chicago Press.

Halstead, W. C., and J. M. Wepman. 1949. The Halstead-Wepman aphasia screening test. *J. Speech Hear. Disord.* 14:9–13.

Handler, L., and D. Habenicht. 1994. The Kinetic Family Drawing Technique: a review of the literature. *J. Per. Assess.* 62:440–464.

Hathaway, S. R., and J. C. McKinley. 1943. *The Minnesota Multiphasic Personality Inventory.* New York: Psychological Corp.

———— 1989. *The Minnesota Multiphasic Personality Inventory–2.* New York: Psychological Corp.

Heaton, R. K. 1981. *Wisconsin Card Sorting Test manual.* Odessa, Fla.: Psychological Assessment Resources, Inc.

Heaton, R. K., I. Grant, W. Z. Anthony, and R. A. W. Lehman. 1981. A comparison of clinical and automated interpretation of the Halstead-Reitan battery. *J. Clin. Neuropsychol.* 3:121–141.

Johnston, M. H., and P. S. Holzman. 1979. *Assessing schizophrenic thinking: a clinical and research instrument for measuring thought disorder.* San Francisco: Jossey-Bass.

Jung, C. 1918. *Studies in word association.* London: Heinemann.

Kaplan, E. 1988. A process approach to neuropsychological assessment. In *Clinical neuropsychology and brain function: research, measurement, and practice,* ed. T. Boll and B. K. Bryant. Washington, D.C.: American Psychological Association.

———— 1990. The process approach to neuropsychological assessment of psychiatric patients. *J. Neuropsychiat Clin. Neurosci.* 2:51–66.

Kaplan, E., H. Goodglass, and S. Weintraub. 1983. *The Boston Naming Test.* Philadelphia: Lea & Febiger.

Kaufman, A. S. 1990. Verbal-performance IQ discrepancies: Base rates, lateralized brain damage, and diverse correlates. In *Assessing adolescent and adult intelligence.* Boston: Allyn and Bacon.

Keefe, R. S. E. 1995. The contribution of neuropsychology to psychiatry. *Am. J. Psychiatry* 152:6–15.

Keiser, R. E., and E. N. Prather. 1990. What is the TAT? A review of ten years of research. *J. Per. Assess.* 55:800–803.

Kernberg, O. 1966. Structural derivatives of object relations. *Int. J. Psychoanal.* 47:236–253.

Klopfer, B., and D. M. Kelley. 1942. *The Rorschach technique.* Yonkers-on-Hudson, N.Y.: World Book.

Knight, R. 1953. Borderline states. In *Psychoanalytic psychiatry and psychology,* ed. R. Knight and C. Friedman. New York: International Universities Press.

Kohut, H. 1971. *The analysis of the self.* New York: International Universities Press.

Kremen, W. S., L. J. Seidman, S. V. Faraone, J. R. Pepple, M. J. Lyons, and M. T. Tsuang. 1996. The "3R's" and neuropsychological function in schizophrenia: an empirical test of the matching fallacy. *Neuropsychol.* 10:22–31.

Krohn, A., and M. Mayman. 1974. Object representations in dreams and projective tests. *Bull. Menninger Clin.* 43:515–524.

Kwawer, J. S., H. D. Lerner, P. M. Lerner, and A. Sugarman, eds. 1980. *Borderline phenomena and the Rorschach test.* New York: International Universities Press.

Leftoff, S. 1983. Psychopathology in the light of brain injury: a case study. *J. Clin. Neuropsychol.* 5:51–64.

Lezak, M. D. 1988. IQ: R.I.P. *J. Clin. Exp. Neuropsychol.* 10:351–361.

———— 1995. *Neuropsychological assessment.* 3rd ed. New York: Oxford University Press.

Luria, A. R. 1980. *Higher cortical functions in man.* 2nd ed. New York: Basic Books.

Marks, P. A., W. Seeman, and D. L. Haller. 1974. *The actuarial use of MMPI with adolescents and adults.* New York: Oxford University Press.

Meehl, P. 1954. *Clinical versus statistical prediction: a theoretical analysis and a review of the evidence.* Minneapolis: University of Minnesota Press.

Mercer, J. R., and J. F. Lewis. 1978. *System of multicultural pluralistic assessment.* New York: Psychological Corporation.

Milberg, W. P. 1996. Issues in the assessment of cognitive function in dementia. *Brain and Cognition* 31:114–132.

Milberg, W. P., N. Hebben, and E. Kaplan. 1996. The Boston process neuropsychological approach to neuropsychological assessment. In *Neuropsychological assessment of neuropsychiatric disorders,* ed. I. Grant and K. M. Adams. 2nd ed. New York: Oxford University Press.

Millon, T. 1983. *Millon Clinical Multiaxial Inventory manual.* 3rd ed. Minneapolis: Interpretive Scoring Systems, National Computer Systems.

——— 1987. *Millon Clinical Multiaxial Inventory II Manual.* Minneapolis: National Computer Systems.

Millon, T., and C. Green. 1996. Interpretive guide to the Millon Clinical Multiaxial Inventory (MCMI-II). In *Major Psychological Assessment instruments,* Vol. 2, ed. C. S. Newmark. Boston: Allyn and Bacon.

Milner, B. 1963. Some effects of different brain lesions on card sorting: the role of the frontal lobes. *Arch. Gen. Neurol.* 9:90–100.

Morgan, C. D., and H. A. Murray. 1935. A method for investigating fantasies: the thematic apperception test. *Arch. Neurol. Psychiatry* 34:289–306.

Moss, M. B., and Albert, M. S. 1992. Neuropsychology of Alzheimer's disease. In *Clinical syndromes in adult neuropsychology: the practitioner's handbook,* ed. R. White. Amsterdam: Elsevier.

Murray, H. A. 1938. *Explorations in personality.* New York: Oxford University Press.

Navia, B. A., and R. W. Price. 1986. Dementia complicating AIDS. *Psychiatric Annals* 16:158–166.

Nelson, H. E., and A. O'Connell. 1978. Dementia: the estimation of premorbid intelligence levels using the New Adult Reading Test. *Cortex* 14:234–244.

Osterrieth, P. A. 1944. Le test de copie d'une figure complexe. *Arch. de Psychologie* 30:206–356.

Rapaport, D., M. M. Gill, and R. Schafer. 1945. *Diagnostic psychological testing.* Vols. 1 and 2, rev., ed. R. R. Holt. New York: International Universities Press, 1968.

Raven, J. G., J. H. Court, and J. Raven. 1985. *Manual for Raven progressive matrices and vocabulary scales.* London: Lewis.

Reitan, R. M. 1958. Validity of the trail making test as an indicator of organic brain damage. *Percept. Mot. Skills* 8:271–276.

——— 1986. Theoretical and methodological bases of the Halstead-Reitan neuropsychological test battery. In *Neuropsychological assessment of neuropsychiatric disorders,* ed. I. Grant and K. M. Adams. New York: Oxford University Press.

Reitan, R. M., and L. A. Davison. 1974. *Clinical neuropsychology: current status and applications.* Washington, D.C.: Winston.

Rey, A. 1941. L'examen psychologique dans les cas d'encephalopathie traumatique. *Arch. de Psychologie* 28:286–340.

Rogers, M. R. 1993. Psychoeducational assessment of racial/ethnic minority children and youth. In *Best practices in assessment for school and clinical settings,* ed. H. B. Vance. Brandon, Vt.: Clinical Psychology Publishing.

Rorschach, H. 1921. *Psychodiagnostik.* Berne: Hans Huber.

——— 1942. *Psychodiagnostics: a diagnostic test based on perception.* Berne: Hans Huber.

Rosvold, H. E., A. F. Mirsky, I. Sarason, E. D. Bransome, and L. H. Beck. 1956. A continuous performance test of brain damage. *J. Consult. Psychol.* 20:343–350.

Rotter, J. B., and J. E. Rafferty. 1950. *Manual: the Rotter incomplete sentences blank.* New York: Psychological Corp.

Sattler, J. M. 1988. *Assessment of children's intelligence.* 3rd ed. San Diego: Author.

Schafer, R. 1954. *Psychoanalytic interpretation in Rorschach testing.* New York: International Universities Press.

Seidman, L. J. 1983. Schizophrenia and brain dysfunction: an integration of recent neurodiagnostic findings. *Psychol. Bull.* 94:195–238.

——— 1990. The neuropsychology of schizophrenia: a neurodevelopmental and case study approach. *J. Neuropsychiat. Clin. Neurosci.* 2:301–312.

——— 1994. Listening, meaning, and empathy in neuropsychological disorders: case examples of assessment and treatment. In *Psychotherapist's guide to neuropsychiatric patients: diagnostic and treatment issues,* ed. J. Ellison, C. S. Weinstein, and T. Hodel-Malinofsky. Washington, D.C.: American Psychiatric Press.

——— 1997. The role of neuropsychology in psychiatry. In *Psychiatry,* ed. A. Tasman, J. Kay, and J. A. Lieberman. Philadelphia: W. B. Saunders.

Seidman, L. J., G. Cassens, W. S. Kremen, and J. R. Pepple. 1992. The neuropsychology of schizophrenia. In *Clinical syndromes in adult neuropsychology: the practitioner's handbook,* ed. R. White. Amsterdam: Elsevier.

Seidman, L. J., K. B. Benedict, J. Biederman, J. H. Bernstein, K. Seiverd, S. Milberger, D. Norman, E. Mick, and S. V. Faraone. 1995. Performance of ADHD children on the Rey-Osterrieth complex figure: a pilot neuropsychological study. *J. Child Psychol. Psychiat.* 36:1459–73.

Seidman, L. J., J. Biederman, S. V. Faraone, W. Weber, and C. Oulette. 1997. Towards defining a neuropsychology of ADHD: performance of children and adolescents from a large clinically referred sample. *J. Consult. Clin. Psychol.* 65:150–160.

Silverstein, A. B. 1990. Short forms of individual intelligence tests. *Psychol. Assess.* 2:3–11.

Singer, M., and D. Larson. 1981. Borderline personality and the Rorschach test. *Arch. Gen. Psychiatry* 38:693–698.

Smith, K. 1980. Object relations concepts as applied to the

borderline level of ego functioning. In *Borderline phenomena and the Rorschach test,* ed. J. S. Kwawer et al. New York: International Universities Press.

Spencer, T., J. Biederman, T. Wilens, and S. V. Faraone. 1994. Is attention-deficit hyperactivity disorder in adults a valid disorder? *Harv. Rev. Psychiat.* 1:326–335.

Spiers, P. A. 1981. Have they come to praise Luria or to bury him? The Luria-Nebraska battery controversy. *J. Consult. Clin. Psychol.* 49:331–341.

Spreen, O., and A. L. Benton. 1965. Comparative studies of some psychological tests for cerebral damage. *J. Nerv. Ment. Dis.* 140:323–333.

Squire, L. R. 1986. The neuropsychology of memory dysfunction and its assessment. In *Neuropsychological assessment of neuropsychiatric disorders,* ed. I. Grant and K. M. Adams. New York: Oxford University Press.

Suzuki, L. A., and J. F. Kugler. 1995. Intelligence and personality assessments: multicultural perspectives. In *Handbook of multicultural counseling,* ed. J. G. Ponterotto, J. M. Casas, L. A. Suzuki, and C. M. Alexander. Thousand Oaks, Calif.: Sage Publications.

Teuber, H. L. 1948. Neuropsychology. In *Recent advances in diagnostic psychological testing,* ed. M. R. Harrower. Springfield, Ill.: Thomas.

Thompson, C. 1949. The Thompson modification of the Thematic Apperception Test. *J. Proj. Tech.* 13:469–478.

Thorndike, R. L., E. P. Hagen, and J. A. Sattler. 1986. *Stanford-Binet intelligence scale.* 4th ed. Chicago: Riverside.

Trimble, M. R., and P. J. Thompson. 1986. Neuropsychological aspects of epilepsy. In *Neuropsychological assessment of neuropsychiatric disorders,* ed. I. Grant and K. M. Adams. New York: Oxford University Press.

Trimboli, F., and R. Kilgore. 1983. A psychodynamic approach to MMPI interpretation. *J. Pers. Assess.* 47:614–626.

Vincent, K. R., I. M. Castillo, R. I. Hauser, J. A. Zapata, H. J. Stuart, C. K. Cohn, and G. J. O'Shanick. 1984. *MMPI-168 Codebook.* Norwood, N.J.: Ablex.

Waber, D., and Holmes, J. M. 1985. Assessing children's copy productions of the Rey-Osterrieth Complex Figure. *J. Clin. Exp. Neuropsychol.* 7:264–280.

Wechsler, D. 1958. *The measurement and appraisal of adult intelligence.* 4th ed. Baltimore: Williams & Wilkins.

——— 1981. *Wechsler Adult Intelligence Scale—revised.* New York: Psychological Corp.

——— 1987. *Wechsler Memory Scale—revised.* New York: Psychological Corp.

——— 1989. *Manual for the Wechsler preschool and primary scale of intelligence—revised.* New York: Psychological Corp.

——— 1991. *Manual for the Wechsler intelligence scale for children—III.* New York: Psychological Corp.

Weinstein, C. S., L. J. Seidman, J. J. Feldman, and J. J. Ratey. 1991. Neurocognitive disorders in psychiatry: a case example of diagnostic and treatment dilemmas. *Psychiatry* 54:65–75.

Weinstein, C. S., L. J. Seidman, G. Ahern, and K. McClure, 1994. Integration of neuropsychological and behavioral neurologic assessment in psychiatry: a case example involving brain injury and polypharmacy. *Psychiatry* 57:62–76.

Weintraub, S., and M.-M. Mesulam. 1985. Mental state assessment of young and elderly adults in behavioral neurology. In *Principles of behavioral neurology,* ed. M.-M. Mesulam. Philadelphia: Davis.

Weiss, J., and L. J. Seidman. 1988. The clinical use of psychological and neuropsychological tests. In *The new Harvard guide to modern psychiatry,* ed. A. Nicholi. Cambridge, Mass.: Harvard University Press.

Westen, D., N. E. Lohr, K. Silk, L. Gold, and K. Kerber. 1990. Object relations and social cognition in borderlines, major depressives, and normals: a thematic apperception test analysis. *Psychol. Assess.* 2:355–364.

Wiggins, J. S. 1966. Substantive dimensions of self-report in the MMPI item pool. *Psychological Monographs* 80:22 (whole no. 630).

Wilkinson, G. S. 1993. *The Wide Range Achievement Test manual.* 3rd ed. Wilmington, Del. Wide Range.

Winnicott, D. 1953. Transitional objects and transitional phenomena. *Int. J. Psychoanal.* 34:89–97.

Yozawitz, A. 1986. Applied neuropsychology in a psychiatric center. In *Neuropsychological assessment of neuropsychiatric disorders,* ed. I. Grant and K. M. Adams. New York: Oxford University Press.

Recommended Reading

Damasio, A. R. 1994. *Descartes' error: emotion, reason, and the human brain.* New York: Avon Books.

Gould, S. J. 1996. *The mismeasure of man.* 2nd ed. New York: W. W. Norton.

Luria, A. R. 1973. *The working brain.* London: Harmondsworth.

Newmark, C. S., ed. 1985. *Major psychological assessment instruments.* Newton, Mass.: Allyn and Bacon.

Acknowledgments

We gratefully acknowledge the substantial contributions made to this chapter by Dr. Justin Weiss, who authored or coauthored this chapter in previous editions. We also thank Dr. William S. Stone for his helpful suggestions.

DEBORAH BLACKER

MING T. TSUANG

Classification and DSM-IV

The official classification system in American psychiatry is embodied in the *Diagnostic and Statistical Manual,* fourth edition (DSM-IV), which provides detailed diagnostic criteria and diagnostic codes covering a full range of psychiatric problems. This volume represents the most recent efforts on the part of the American Psychiatric Association (APA) to provide on a solid research base a uniform and usable set of diagnostic criteria for mental disorders. It is an effort to develop a scientific *nosology,* or classification system (Kendler, 1990), following principles of classification used elsewhere in medicine, and drawing on the *psychometric* or "mind-measuring" skills of psychology.

This chapter begins with a description of DSM-IV, including its goals, format, and organization. We then discuss the roots of DSM-IV in the prior editions of the APA's *Diagnostic and Statistical Manual* dating back to 1952, and, more critically, in the Feighner and Research Diagnostic Criteria that played a critical role in the development of the landmark third edition (DSM-III). We then review the process of development for DSM-IV and successive revisions. We close with a discussion of the limitations and future directions of psychiatric classification. The actual diagnostic categories and their numerical codes are available in an appendix following the chapter.

The Goals of DSM-IV

DSM-IV, like its predecessors, has three main goals: broad coverage of mental disorders, improved reliability of diagnosis (and thus better communication), and improved validity of diagnosis (and thus greater utility).

Coverage of Mental Disorders

DSM-IV is meant to allow psychiatrists to communicate clearly among themselves, and with other physi-

cians, other mental health professionals, and with non-clinicians, particularly in the legal and human services systems. For this reason, it must provide diagnostic codes covering all mental disorders, and even other conditions or situations that might be encountered in clinical, forensic, or other settings (e.g., "V codes" for issues such as relational problems or malingering). It also must accommodate "no diagnosis" (V71.09) and various levels of provisional diagnosis (options include: "diagnosis deferred" [799.9], "unspecified mental disorder [non-psychotic]" [300.9], "psychotic [or other] disorder not otherwise specified [NOS]," and statements that the diagnosis is to be regarded as provisional.

A *mental disorder* is defined broadly in DSM-IV as a clinically significant behavioral or psychological syndrome or pattern that occurs in an individual and that is associated with present distress (e.g., a painful symptom) or disability (e.g., impairment in one or more important areas of functioning) or with a significantly increased risk of suffering death, pain, disability, or an important loss of freedom. In addition, this syndrome or pattern must not be merely an expectable and culturally sanctioned response to a particular event, for example, the death of a loved one. Whatever its original cause, it must currently be considered a manifestation of a behavioral, psychological, or biological dysfunction in the individual. Neither deviant behavior (e.g., political, religious, or sexual) nor conflicts that are primarily between the individual and society are mental disorders unless the deviance or conflict is a symptom of dysfunction in the individual, as described above.

The authors of DSM-IV readily acknowledge that this term and its definition reflect an outmoded dichotomy between the physical and the mental, but maintain that it describes nonetheless the kinds of patients seen by psychiatrists and other mental health professionals. How one defines *disorder* becomes important because of the critical role it plays in insurance reimbursement, disability, and forensic settings. Although the authors of DSM-IV justify use of the term *disorder* by focusing on distress and disability, this definition remains problematic.

Improved Reliability of Diagnosis

Another goal of DSM-IV and its predecessors is improved reliability of classification (Shrout, 1995; Carmines and Zeller, 1979). Reliability is the consistency or repeatability of classification over time or across different observers. It is generally assessed by a measure of the agreement between or among different raters or at different times, corrected for agreement expected by chance alone. The most common reliability measure for studies of diagnosis is the kappa coefficient. The use of a uniform and at least partially operationalized set of diagnostic criteria focused on observable characteristics has vastly improved the reliability of psychiatric diagnosis, as described below.

The principal benefit of improved reliability in clinical and other settings is improved communication. Good reliability facilitates communication among clinicians (e.g., caring for the same patient across time or across settings), between researchers and clinicians (e.g., in the research literature), and between clinicians and other groups (e.g., in forensic or social service settings). In addition, for the same reason, good reliability is a prerequisite to scientific progress in nosology, etiology, pathophysiology, and treatment.

Improved Validity of Diagnosis

Validity is defined as the correspondence of classification with an underlying truth, that is, that the diagnostic entities we describe are "real" (Goldstein and Simpson, 1995; Carmines and Zeller, 1979). In the context of diagnostic boundaries (e.g., between schizophrenia and bipolar disorder), this is sometimes described as "carving nature at its joints," although most nosologists readily concede that this image suggests cleaner boundaries than are discernible in nature (Kendell, 1989; Grove and Andreasen, 1989). Validity is generally measured by the percent of true cases that are correctly identified (sensitivity) and the percent of non-cases that are correctly identified (specificity), judged against a gold standard classification. With the rare exception of disorders such as Alzheimer's disease for which autopsy confirmation stands as the gold standard, there is no higher standard in diagnosis than the DSM criteria themselves. Especially at the early stages of drafting diagnostic criteria, clinical judgment about whether patients are or are not suffer-

ing from a given disorder is sometimes used in place of a gold standard. However, in order to improve on validity, one generally assesses whether the syndromes defined by diagnostic criteria show meaningful correlations with "external validators" such as treatment response, family history, and prognosis, as described below.

Although the assessment of validity is as much a theoretical as an empirical issue, validity has major practical significance. In clinical terms, validity means that the criteria describe syndromes with clinical relevance, e.g., to the selection of therapies, to guidance regarding risky behaviors, to prediction of prognosis. Similarly, the most valid category definitions are those that best help us to identify specific etiologies or better treatments. Thus, the final arbiter of the validity of diagnostic constructs is their utility in clinical and research practice (Kendell, 1989).

The Structure of DSM-IV

Several key features of DSM-IV help it reach the goals outlined above. They include (1) descriptive rather than theoretical formulation; (2) specific, operationalized diagnostic criteria; (3) syndromic definitions; (4) diagnostic hierarchies; and (5) a multiaxial system.

Descriptive Formulations

Because of the controversy both within psychiatry and between psychiatry and other disciplines regarding theoretical frameworks and the etiology of mental disorders, it was decided early in the development of DSM-III to attempt to be descriptive rather than theoretical. Although it is clear that no observation is truly theory-neutral, the criteria in DSM-IV are defined on the whole in terms of descriptive psychopathology and manifest behavior, with minimal inferences as to possible motivation (conscious or unconscious) or causation (developmental, psychological, or environmental). The focus on description also led to the use of observable features rather than those requiring extensive clinical judgment. It thus greatly enhanced the reliability of the diagnostic criteria.

Operationalized Diagnostic Criteria

The specification of operational criteria for each disorder is a key feature of DSM-IV. The criteria generally begin with a description of the essential features of a diagnostic entity, followed by additional symptoms which are expected to be present, with the number of such symptoms required to make a diagnosis and, where applicable, their duration, consistency, or intensity. Like the focus on observable attributes, operationalized descriptions have greatly improved diagnostic reliability.

Syndromic Definitions

DSM-IV focuses on ordering psychiatric symptomatology into *syndromes,* or clusters of symptoms that tend to occur together. These syndromes are then organized into sections of the document according to the primary mental faculty that is disturbed, the classic triad being thinking, feeling, and acting. The disorders of thinking are the psychoses, of which schizophrenia is paramount. The disorders of feeling, or affect, encompass mania and depression, as well as the anxiety states. The disorders of behavior involve disturbances in eating, sexual functioning, and the like. This principle has been extended in DSM-IV beyond the earlier versions in that even disorders of known cause (e.g., a brain disease or the effects of a drug) are classified according to shared phenomenology. For example, substance-induced depression now appears with the mood disorders, while in DSM-III and DSM-III-R it appeared with the substance-related disorders.

Diagnostic Hierarchies

For many decades textbooks and diagnostic systems organized the classification of mental disorders hierarchically. An early diagnosis made in the sequence preempts other diagnoses. For example, patients first diagnosed as having schizophrenic disorders and who are labeled schizophrenic often display anxiety and depressive symptoms as well, but these disorders would not be diagnosed. To an extent this practice is continued in DSM-IV: disorders that are due to a known cause (e.g., depression due to alcohol abuse) preempt those whose cause is unknown (major depression), and more pervasive disorders (e.g., autistic disorder) preempt less pervasive ones (expressive language disorder). However, the hierarchies have been curtailed to a significant extent. Most notably, personality disorders are considered on a separate axis precisely so that they may be diagnosed along with psychotic, mood, anxiety, or other disorders. In addition, while in DSM-III a diagnosis of major depressive disorder precluded a diagnosis of panic disorder, in DSM-III-R and DSM-IV both diagnoses may be coded. Similarly, depressive symptoms are not simply viewed as part of schizophrenia: although major depressive disorder cannot be diagnosed in the presence of schizophrenia, a diagnosis of major depressive disorder not otherwise specified is given (and, it should be noted, DSM-IV provides a set of research criteria for a proposed diagnosis of "postpsychotic depressive disorder of schizophrenia" in Appendix B).

Multiaxial System

In order to capture more of the complexity of real patients, DSM-IV allows them to be described on multiple "axes," which basically correspond to domains of function (or dysfunction). Axis I and Axis II are specific to psychiatry, with Axis II reserved for long-standing "trait" disorders including personality disorders and mental retardation, and Axis I including everything else. Axis III is for general medical conditions. Axis IV allows for the coding of specific stressors that may be contributing to or responsible for the Axis I or Axis II conditions. Axis V provides a quantitative assessment of functional status.

Axis I: clinical syndromes and V codes. Axis I is the largest section of DSM-IV and corresponds to the traditional categorization of disorders as reflected in most diagnostic classifications. It includes all major and minor mental disorders, except those coded on Axis II. It also includes the V codes, which are used to describe conditions that may be encountered in clinical or forensic practice but are not considered mental disorders (e.g., interpersonal problems, antisocial behavior).

Axis II: mental retardation and personality disorders. Axis II, which includes disorders that persist through the life span, is meant to allow (and encourage) clinicians to seek out long-standing conditions that might underlie a major Axis I disorder and might otherwise be overlooked (e.g., borderline personality with episodes of major depression).

It is critical to be aware of the presence of personality disorders because they may predispose to certain Axis I disorders (e.g., borderline personality disorder and major depressive disorder), and may affect their course and treatment. *Personality* refers to relatively enduring patterns of relating to, perceiving, and thinking about oneself, significant others, and the environment. All individuals have such patterns. Personality *disorder* occurs only when the patterns become inflexible and maladaptive and/or significantly impair the individual's social or occupational functioning. Axis II may also be used to indicate a maladaptive personality style or persistent defense mechanisms that fall short of criteria for a personality disorder.

Axis II is also used to code mental retardation, and can be used to indicate borderline intellectual functioning as well. In DSM-III and III-R, Axis II also included developmental disorders (problems in reading, mathematics, language, articulation, and the like). However, these were moved to Axis I in DSM-IV because it was felt that they were generally not overlooked, and were more appropriately classed with other Axis I disorders.

Axis III: general medical conditions. Axis III provides an opportunity for the clinician to indicate the presence or absence of a current or past general medical disorder or condition that is considered potentially relevant to understanding, treating, or managing the individual with an Axis I or Axis II disorder.

The World Health Organization codes for general medical conditions commonly encountered in psychiatric practice are listed in Appendix G of DSM-IV. However, no detailed operational criteria exist for Axis III, and the clinician must exercise considerable judgment in designating the conditions to be coded under this axis and in determining the extent of medical evaluation, including the use of laboratory tests.

Axis IV: psychosocial and environmental problems. Axis IV provides a coding system for the type of problem(s) judged clinically to contribute to the development or exacerbation of the mental disorders coded on Axis I or Axis II. In former versions of DSM, this axis focused on the severity of stressors, but in DSM-IV the format was switched to allow for more focus on the type of problems in a patient's life such as "occupational problem," "problem with the primary support group," or "educational problem." Clinicians are asked to identify the broad type of problem involved, and then briefly characterize the issue for the individual patient.

Axis V: global assessment of functioning. Axis V permits the communication of an individual's level of adaptive function. This is generally coded using the 100-point GAF (Global Assessment Functioning) scale presented in the text, which is a minor revision of an earlier version (found in DSM-III) called the Global Assessment Scale (GAS). The assessment of function can be made with reference to current functioning, functioning at 2 points in time (e.g., admission and discharge from the hospital), or the highest level attained in the past year. The highest level of function in the past year gives an overall impression of baseline functional status, and is particularly helpful in anticipating the expected degree of improvement in patients in the midst of an acute decompensation.

The GAF scale has been criticized by some because it represents an amalgam of pure functional descriptors (e.g., "unable to work") and symptom-based ones (e.g.,

"occasional panic attacks"). Although one can expect to find a moderate correlation between severity of symptoms and global assessment of functioning, there are many patients with very intense symptoms who maintain apparently high levels of social and occupational functioning, and individuals with mild symptoms who suffer almost complete social disability and impaired functioning. Thus, some favor the alternate functional scale known as the Social and Occupational Functioning Assessment Scale (SOFAS), which appears in DSM-IV Appendix B, and is more clearly focused on functional descriptors.

Proposed new axes: defense mechanisms and relational functioning. During the development of DSM-III, psychoanalysts and other dynamically oriented psychiatrists complained that insufficient attention was being given to dynamic mechanisms, such as conflicts, ego functions, and defense mechanisms. A work group attempted to develop criteria for such evaluations, and provided several definitions for defense mechanisms (e.g., acting out, denial, displacement, projection) derived mainly from psychodynamic principles. During the DSM-IV development process, these were elaborated into a more comprehensive Defensive Functioning Scale on which the overall level of defensive functioning and most prominent defense mechanisms can be indicated. This proposed axis appears in Appendix B of DSM-IV for purposes of research and testing.

There has also been considerable pressure to include a specific measure of functioning in personal relationships, one of the major foci of mental health treatment. Thus, the Global Assessment of Relational Functioning (GARF), a 100-point scale rating the domains of problem solving, organization, and emotional climate, is presented for research purposes in Appendix B of DSM-IV.

Historical Background

During the nineteenth century, advances in scientific thinking contributed to the concept of specific diseases, each with its own signs, symptoms, natural course, outcome, and prognosis. This concept was most clearly enunciated by Thomas Sydenham in England, who has been called the father of modern medical nosology. These views of disease were afforded scientific support and intellectual acceptance by discoveries from the biological sciences, including advances in clinico-pathological correlations, the discovery of the role of bacteria and other microorganisms in disease, the dawn of diagnostic radiology, and the development of rudimentary laboratory studies such as testing of blood glucose and hematologic indices.

As psychiatry emerged as a medical specialty in the early- to mid-nineteenth century, advances in biology were rapidly brought to bear on disturbances of thinking, mood, and behavior. There was a strong interest in the careful characterization of the clinical phenomenology, and notable successes were achieved in correlating specific mental syndromes with autopsy and bacteriological findings. By 1895, clinical and epidemiologic studies had shown that central nervous system syphilis was associated with the syndrome of general paresis, and this association was confirmed by the development of the Wassermann test in 1905 and the isolation of the syphilitic spirochete in the brain by H. Noguchi in 1911. After World War I, J. Goldberger and his associates in the U.S. Public Health Service discovered the relationship of the psychiatric complications of pellagra to vitamin B deficiency. In addition to elucidating the biological basis of the disorder, Goldberger's discovery paved the way for effective treatment and, ultimately, prevention. In the following decades, the discovery of chromosomal anomalies led to an understanding of Down syndrome and other forms of retardation, and the discovery of multiple aminoacidurias further elucidated the pathogenesis of some other forms.

Revival of Interest in Diagnosis, Nosology, and Classification

In the years following World War II, psychoanalysis rapidly came into prominence in American psychiatry. The remaining "functional" disorders, i.e., those not explained by the first wave of biological discoveries, were largely understood—and treated—within psychoanalysis. Because psychoanalysis is focused on unconscious processes thought to be related to early childhood experience, it is relatively unconcerned with classification. Thus, there was relatively little attention paid to nosology during this period.

Beginning in the early 1960s a number of factors contributed to a revival of interest in diagnosis and nosology in psychiatry. These include: (1) therapeutic advances; (2) an interest in scientific investigation, coupled with methodological developments facilitating research, and (3) concerns regarding the effect of inconsistent terminology on the credibility of the profession.

Changes in available therapies may have been the most important stimulus to the development of clear-cut diagnostic descriptors. With the arrival of at least somewhat specific treatments for anxiety, depression, psychosis, and mania, careful diagnosis became critical to treatment decision making. Concomitant with therapeutic developments, there was increased interest in treatment and etiologic research, which required the careful delineation of diagnostic categories and the measurement of change over time. To meet this need, diagnostic instruments identifying patients for research protocols and scales quantifying changes in symptoms and behaviors after therapeutic interventions were developed. In this effort there was active interchange of information among clinical psychiatrists, clinical psychologists, psychopathologists, and psychopharmacologists. The psychologists in particular contributed their extensive knowledge of psychometrics, initially developed in the assessment of intelligence and other forms of cognitive and social performance and gradually applied to psychopathology and abnormal behavior. These new tools, along with developments in statistics and computers rendering large-scale studies more feasible, greatly advanced research during this period.

One of the first major areas to be addressed was psychiatric diagnosis itself. Mounting evidence of the unreliability of psychiatric diagnosis left both clinicians and researchers dissatisfied with existing clinical assessment procedures. Moreover, the absence of agreement on diagnoses among clinicians, especially in dramatic court cases, undermined the credibility of the mental health profession. On the international level, the large gap observed between the reported rates of schizophrenia in the United States and those in England and Wales, despite similar rates of hospitalization (Kramer, 1961), suggested major differences in diagnostic practices. The U.S.-U.K. study, using a newly developed European diagnostic rating instrument known as the Present State Exam (PSE), showed that careful attention to disease definition resolved the discrepancy: the rates were actually similar when similar diagnostic criteria and procedures were employed (Cooper et al., 1972). At about the same time, the International Pilot Study of Schizophrenia demonstrated, using the PSE and a set of structured diagnostic criteria, that schizophrenia could be identified—and had similar core features—across a wide range of cultures and languages (World Health Organization, 1973). This progress in classification led to an appreciation of the role of formal diagnostic criteria and associated rating scales, and paved the way for the development of DSM-III, as described below.

The Pedigree of DSM-IV

As the official nomenclature of the American Psychiatric Association, DSM-IV can trace its lineage through DSM-I in 1952, DSM-II in 1968, DSM-III in 1980, and DSM-III-R in 1987. However, it bears only a superficial resemblance to DSM-I and DSM-II, which provided only descriptive guidelines for diagnosing psychopathology and a glossary, and contained no diagnostic criteria. The primary focus of DSM-I was the need to provide accurate statistics on the prevalence of mental disorders in hospitals and other settings. Under the influence of the great psychiatrist Adolf Meyer, who had a strong belief in the role of psychobiological and social factors in the development of mental illness, most disorders were termed "reactions" to a presumed social stressor (e.g., "manic-depressive reaction," "schizophrenic reaction"). DSM-II was similar, but dropped the term *reaction*. Neither DSM-I nor DSM-II told psychiatrists how to diagnose any of these conditions, providing neither clear definitions nor explicit criteria for diagnosis.

The more relevant lineage for DSM-IV consists of the explicit sets of operational diagnostic criteria developed for psychiatric research in the late 1960s and early 1970s, leading to DSM-III in 1980. The first of these was the criteria formulated by the Washington University group in St. Louis, led by Eli Robins, Samuel Guze, and George Winokur, and codified in an article by John Feighner (Feighner et al., 1972). These criteria covered a limited set of diagnostic entities (14 in total), and were aimed at identifying a relatively homogeneous group of patients with fairly typical forms of each disorder. They were utilized, and validated, in a wide range of clinical and epidemiological studies, including, for example, the Iowa 500 study, which focused on the long-term outcome and familial aggregation of schizophrenia and mood disorders (Tsuang and colleagues, 1979, 1980).

A few years later, in the context of planning the National Institute of Mental Health's Psychobiology of Depression collaborative study (Katz and Klerman, 1979), which needed a more extensive set of criteria to make accurate diagnosis in both inpatients and outpatients and their often less severely affected relatives, the Research Diagnostic Criteria (RDC) were developed (Spitzer, Endicott, and Robins, 1978). The RDC drew heavily on the Feighner criteria, but were much broader, covering 24 categories, many of which had several subtypes.

The innovations embodied in the RDC, along with many of the specific criteria, were then incorporated directly into DSM-III, which appeared in 1980. Many individuals involved in the development of the Feighner criteria and RDC contributed to the formation of DSM-III, and DSM-III drew extensively on the RDC. However, because of the broader mandate of the APA's diagnostic and statistical manuals, which needed to account for every individual encounter in a broad range of settings, this time the criteria were dramatically expanded to cover a much broader range of psychopathology.

The Contribution of DSM-III

DSM-III was a landmark in the development of psychiatric classification, drawing on the best available research from the preceding decades, and placing psychiatry firmly back in the medical model of basing treatment decisions on diagnosis. It is noteworthy for the following innovations:

1. It was the first official nomenclature to provide operational criteria, both inclusionary and exclusionary.

2. For the most part, these criteria were based on manifest descriptive psychopathology rather than on inferences from presumed causation or etiology, whether psychodynamic, social, or biological. The exception was the "organic" disorders, whose presumed biological causes were known. Notably, the choice of descriptive rather than etiological criteria did not, in itself, represent an abandonment of the ideal of classification and diagnosis based on causation; rather it represented a heuristic decision to deal with the dilemma that the pathophysiology of most of the disorders we currently encounter in psychiatry is unknown.

3. DSM-III introduced a multiaxial system to accommodate the multiple aspects of patients' lives and experience. The system was a response to the criticism, mainly from clinicians, that individual patients are more complex than their assignment to a single diagnostic class can indicate. Previous efforts to develop multiaxial systems had been initiated in child psychiatry, but had previously not been included in an official classification system.

4. DSM-III was the first official nomenclature to be tested for reliability in a field study. Never before had statistical evidence been produced concerning the acceptance, reliability, feasibility, and utility of a diagnostic scheme.

5. With DSM-III, the American Psychiatric Association embarked on an implicit principle of periodic revision of the diagnostic system, leading to DSM-III-R in 1987, and DSM-IV in 1994.

The Development of DSM-IV

The editions of the *Diagnostic and Statistical Manual* since DSM-III constitute an effort to use the scientific method to develop better—i.e., more reliable and valid—

diagnostic definitions. While the measurement of reliability is relatively straightforward, and there is little doubt that DSM-III and its successors have vastly improved the reliability of psychiatric diagnosis, validity is more problematic. We describe below the nature of evidence used in establishing the validity of diagnostic constructs, along with the specific process used to gather and interpret this evidence in the development of the diagnostic criteria for DSM-IV.

Principles of Establishing Diagnostic Validity

Because diagnostic criteria developers have limited ability to appeal to a higher gold standard, most efforts to validate diagnostic constructs depend on some kind of triangulation between observations about a diagnostic entity and theories about its expected attributes, in a process sometimes referred to as construct validation (Cronbach and Meehl, 1955). Well-delineated diagnostic entities are expected to be internally coherent and to display correlations with "external validators," or features not included in the definition but expected to be related. This means that by knowing that certain individuals meet criteria for a certain diagnosis, one can predict to a greater or lesser degree other attributes such as what medications they might respond to, how they can be expected to be functioning in 10 years' time, and so on.

In 1970, Eli Robins and Samuel Guze outlined a series of steps that they hoped would lead to the development of an improved diagnostic system in psychiatry. The process they described has been elaborated to an extent over the years, but has not fundamentally changed through the development of the Feighner, RDC, DSM-III, and successive DSM criteria. The first step in defining a diagnosis is to describe a clinical syndrome with a focus on observable (and reliable) characteristics that delineate its key features and differentiate it from other syndromes. Then one seeks evidence from correlations with external validators that the syndrome has meaning over and above pure description. The external validators highlighted by Robins and Guze and subsequently (Kendell, 1989; Akiskal, 1980) include response to treatment, long-term course or prognosis, family history (which can represent either genetic or cultural transmission, but in either case is common in psychiatric disorders), associated symptoms (beyond those required to make the diagnosis), and biological and psychometric tests. Other validators might have been selected, but these made sense in the context of the remedicalization of psychiatry in the late 1960s, and they have remained the cornerstone of evaluating validity

through successive rounds of revision of the diagnostic system.

The Development Process

Kendler (1990) describes the process of developing psychiatric diagnostic systems prior to DSM-III as involving either the expertise of a single expert professor (e.g., Pinel, Bleuler, or Kraepelin) or a consensus of experts (e.g., the panels involved in drafting DSM-I and DSM-II). DSM-III transformed this process by insisting that the panel of experts rely not only on their own experience but on the available data, following the validation process described above. The process for editions from DSM-III on has involved a work group with clinical expertise and a knowledge of the available literature; field trials, initially focused on achieving diagnostic reliability and then addressing issues of validity; and review and comments from practitioners and academicians.

For DSM-IV, this process has been extended and made somewhat more formal, with a greater insistence on making—and documenting—data-driven changes (Davis, 1997). In the development of DSM-IV, there were 13 work groups, each focused on a group of disorders (e.g., mood disorders, cognitive disorders). At every stage the work groups' decisions were reviewed by a large and broad group of advisers representing clinical and research experience, methodologic expertise, other professional disciplines, and international and cross-cultural perspectives. The process began with a formal literature review: 175 reviews were performed, covering virtually all of the conditions mentioned in the manual, plus others that have not been included. These can be reviewed in the *DSM-IV Sourcebook* (Widiger et al., 1994, 1996, 1997). In addition, for critical questions on which there were insufficient data, data reanalyses—also following a specified protocol—were sometimes performed; these can also be reviewed in the *Sourcebook*. In areas where data necessary to make critical decisions were still lacking, 12 field trials were performed, each involving at least 5 sites with a diverse patient population. Beyond these focused trials, a larger effort was undertaken (and is ongoing) to evaluate the reliability of DSM-IV as a whole based on a set of videotapes covering a range of typical and atypical patients.

Decisions on changes in diagnostic criteria and new diagnostic entities were reviewed by each work group with the input of the group's advisers based on the accumulation of data. The decision-making process for each proposed change was documented in the *Sourcebook*. All changes were designed to enhance the reliability, validity, or clinical utility of the criteria. The changes made between DSM-III-R and DSM-IV are listed in Appendix D of DSM-IV. Specific reasons advanced for these changes include: streamlining of criteria to make them easier to remember and use; conformity with other organizations (either in nomenclature or in specific criteria); clarification of criteria found to be ambiguous in practice (thus increasing reliability); data suggesting a shift that would increase the validity (e.g., omitting false negatives missed because of a too stringent requirement; adding an impairment requirement or an exclusion criterion to reduce false positives); data suggesting that a boundary should be shifted based on external validators (e.g., bipolar II disorder as a distinct entity); and addition of subtypes found to have clinical significance (e.g., bipolar disorder with rapid cycling).

Proposed new diagnoses, almost 100 in number, received still greater scrutiny. The handful accepted were designed to increase the homogeneity of existing categories where data suggested this was warranted, or to increase the coverage of the diagnostic system. After extensive literature review and discussion, there remained 20 proposed new categories that could be neither adopted nor definitively rejected, and so were relegated to an appendix as deserving of further study.

During the development of DSM-IV there was ongoing collaboration with the groups involved in the development of the World Health Organization's International Classification of Diseases, tenth edition (ICD-10) (World Health Organization, 1992). This helps ensure international input into the DSM system and American psychiatrists' input into the international system. In addition, it is critical because ICD codes are required for reimbursement in the United States, based on ICD-9, with ICD-10 expected to be implemented in about 2000. The ICD-10 codes for each DSM-IV disorder appear in Appendix H of DSM-IV. The collaboration between DSM and ICD developers dates all the way back to ICD-6, which was the first version of the ICD to have a specific section on mental disorders, and DSM-I. However, the collaboration has been particularly close and fruitful in recent years, and the diagnostic systems have become progressively more similar.

Limitations of Classification in Psychiatry

Psychiatry has made enormous strides in reliability and some progress in validity since the publication of DSM-III in 1980, and these changes have in turn fostered impressive progress in our understanding of psycho-

pathology and our ability to treat mental disorders. Nonetheless, the diagnostic system and the method we use to define it have some serious limitations. These limitations have been discussed by numerous commentators (Kendler, 1990; Coryell and Zimmerman, 1987; Faust and Miner, 1986; Follette and Houts, 1996), and can be reviewed only briefly here. One way to view the various concerns is to ask whether they pertain to the process, the science, or the phenomena themselves.

The current process based on expert opinion guided by data generates several problems. First are the complex and sometimes awkward sets of criteria that often emerge in the process of committee negotiations (bringing to mind the old joke that a camel is a horse designed by a committee). Another is the expectation that we can design a single set of criteria for clinical practice, research, and forensic purposes: each task has a different level of reliance on clinical judgment, calls for a different level of detail in the diagnostic criteria, and requires a different level of homogeneity in the resulting categories. ICD-10 has two versions: one for clinicians, which uses descriptive categories to guide clinical judgment, and one for researchers with formal operationalized criteria (which had not been part of any prior version of the ICD). Another arises from the decision to make the criteria cover all possible reasons for a clinical encounter. This is a necessity in a system designed for reimbursement and certain other statistical purposes, but greatly limits validity in several areas: those diagnoses specifically introduced to increase the homogeneity of adjacent categories (e.g., schizoaffective disorder), those designed to be provisional (e.g., schizophreniform disorder), and those not particularly amenable to the medical model (e.g., V codes). The last facet of the process that often generates problems is the need for periodic revision: if this comes too often, practice, training, and research are compromised, and there is danger that clinicians in particular will simply ignore the criteria. If it does not come often enough, there is a risk that the categories will become reified, and clinicians and investigators alike will forget that the current system offers a provisional attempt at making useful distinctions, rather than objective descriptions of "real" entities.

Another set of limitations relates to the state of our nosologic science. First among these is the decision, in the interest of maximizing reliability, to focus on observable characteristics. This tends to sacrifice certain kinds of information that may be hard to measure for potentially more valid ones, especially those involving the expert judgment of experienced clinicians. Another perhaps more critical issue concerns the choice of external validators. First, as Kendler (1990) has pointed out, there is nothing to validate the choice of validators, and there is no a priori reason why the different validators should validate the same choices of diagnostic criteria. A second issue is the lack of an absolute standard regarding how much difference should be required to define a subtype, and how much more to define a separate disorder. Although scientific considerations can inform this decision, it is ultimately a judgment call. In order to keep the number of categories manageable, it is best to avoid too many divisions; but in order to keep them homogeneous, it is helpful to divide them into smaller subtypes, or use specifiers to break them down further.

Most critically, the problems may be in the phenomena we are studying. For instance, some phenomena may be better characterized using a dimensional model. Many critics have pointed out that no sharp boundaries divide the normal from the abnormal and that many of the phenomena involved in diagnosis, such as anxiety and depression, are extensions of normal phenomena. Personality in particular has been "resistant" to the categorical approach, and many observers feel that it is more usefully defined dimensionally. Different but equally thorny issues surround those disorders that may represent milder forms of major axis I disorders, e.g., schizotypal disorder, which appears to be related to schizophrenia, and cyclothymic disorder, which is probably related to bipolar disorder. Another major issue is the extensive comorbidity among psychiatric disorders (Kessler et al., 1994), which calls into question whether we are really seeing the coexistence of multiple disorders, or whether the joints at which we seek to carve psychopathology simply do not exist.

Future Directions

The two major organizations involved in the preparation of psychiatric nomenclatures and diagnostic systems—the American Psychiatric Association and the World Health Organization—are both committed to making periodic revisions and to incorporating new scientific knowledge. Changes that may appear in the subsequent versions of DSM include the incorporation of more information from laboratory, imaging, and genetic studies; dimensional systems for some attributes, especially personality disorders and some aspects of psychotic illness; the use of multiple formats from the most fully specified for research to the less so for clinical practice; and the development of additional axes to provide a more comprehensive description of the patient.

The development of DSM-III and its successors has been a major impetus to improvement in communication among investigators and clinicians, and has paved the way for burgeoning high-quality systematic research into the nature of psychopathology and a host of other areas from neurochemistry and physiology to brain imaging to genetics and beyond (Andreasen, 1997). This research has been made possible to a significant extent by improvements in diagnosis over the last 25 years, and, reciprocally, has contributed and will continue to contribute to improvements in our diagnostic nomenclature.

Appendix: DSM-IV Classification: Axes I and II Categories and Codes

DSM-IV-30
Appendix H: DSM-IV Classification with ICD-10 Codes*

As of the publication of this manual (in early 1994), the official coding system in use in the United States is the *International Classification of Diseases,* Ninth Revision, Clinical Modification (ICD-9-CM). At some point within the next several years, the U.S. Department of Health and Human Services will require for reporting purposes in the United States the use of codes from the *International Statistical Classification of Diseases and Related Health Problems,* Tenth Revision (ICD-10). To facilitate this transition process, the preparation of DSM-IV has been closely coordinated with the preparation of Chapter V, "Mental and Behavioural Disorders," of ICD-10 (developed by the World Health Organization). Consultations between the American Psychiatric Association and the World Health Organization have resulted in DSM-IV codes and terms that are fully compatible with the codes and terms in the tabular index of ICD-10. Presented below is the DSM-IV Classification with the ICD-10 codes. Each entry of Appendix H links first to the corresponding text section of DSM-IV, then to the corresponding criteria set.

NOS = Not Otherwise Specified.

An *x* appearing in a diagnostic code indicates that a specific code number is required.

An ellipsis (. . .) is used in the names of certain disorders to indicate that the name of a specific mental disorder or general medical condition should be inserted when re-

*Reprinted with permission from the *Diagnostic and Statistical Manual of Mental Disorders, Fourth Edition* (Washington, D.C.: American Psychiatric Association, 1994). Copyright 1994 by the American Psychiatric Association.

cording the name (e.g., F05.0 Delirium Due to Hypothyroidism).

If criteria are currently met, one of the following severity specifiers may be noted after the diagnosis:

Mild

Moderate

Severe

If criteria are no longer met, one of the following specifiers may be noted:

In Partial Remission

In Full Remission

Prior History

Disorders Usually First Diagnosed in Infancy, Childhood, or Adolescence

MENTAL RETARDATION

Note: These are coded on Axis II.

F70.9 Mild Mental Retardation

F71.9 Moderate Mental Retardation

F72.9 Severe Mental Retardation

F73.9 Profound Mental Retardation

F79.9 Mental Retardation, Severity Unspecified

LEARNING DISORDERS

F81.0 Reading Disorder

F81.2 Mathematics Disorder

F81.8 Disorder of Written Expression

F81.9 Learning Disorder NOS

MOTOR SKILLS DISORDER

F82 Developmental Coordination Disorder

COMMUNICATION DISORDERS

F80.1 Expressive Language Disorder

F80.2 Mixed Receptive-Expressive Language Disorder

F80.0 Phonological Disorder

F98.5 Stuttering

F80.9 Communication Disorder NOS

PERVASIVE DEVELOPMENTAL DISORDERS

F84.0 Autistic Disorder

F84.2 Rett's Disorder

F84.3 Childhood Disintegrative Disorder

F84.5 Asperger's Disorder

F84.9 Pervasive Developmental Disorder NOS

ATTENTION-DEFICIT AND DISRUPTIVE BEHAVIOR DISORDERS

—.– Attention-Deficit/Hyperactivity Disorder

F90.0 Combined Type

F98.8 Predominantly Inattentive Type

F90.0 Predominantly Hyperactive-Impulsive Type

F90.9 Attention-Deficit/Hyperactivity Disorder NOS

F91.8 Conduct Disorder

Specify type: Childhood-Onset Type/Adolescent-Onset Type

F91.3 Oppositional Defiant Disorder

F91.9 Disruptive Behavior Disorder NOS

FEEDING AND EATING DISORDERS OF INFANCY OR EARLY CHILDHOOD

F98.3 Pica

F98.2 Rumination Disorder

F98.2 Feeding Disorder of Infancy or Early Childhood

TIC DISORDERS

F95.2 Tourette's Disorder

F95.1 Chronic Motor or Vocal Tic Disorder

F95.0 Transient Tic Disorder

Specify if: Single Episode/Recurrent

F95.9 Tic Disorder NOS

ELIMINATION DISORDERS

—.– Encopresis

R15 With Constipation and Overflow Incontinence *(also code K59.0 constipation on Axis III)*

F98.1 Without Constipation and Overflow Incontinence

F98.0 Enuresis (Not Due to a General Medical Condition)

Specify type: Nocturnal Only/Diurnal Only/Nocturnal and Diurnal

OTHER DISORDERS OF INFANCY, CHILDHOOD, OR ADOLESCENCE

F93.0 Separation Anxiety Disorder

Specify if: Early Onset

F94.0 Selective Mutism

F94.x Reactive Attachment Disorder of Infancy or Early Childhood

.1 Inhibited Type

.2 Disinhibited Type

F98.4 Stereotypic Movement Disorder

Specify if: With Self-Injurious Behavior

F98.9 Disorder of Infancy, Childhood, or Adolescence NOS

Delirium, Dementia, and Amnestic and Other Cognitive Disorders

DELIRIUM

F05.0 Delirium Due to...*[Indicate the General Medical Condition] (code F05.1 if superimposed on Dementia)*

—.– Substance Intoxication Delirium *(refer to Substance-Related Disorders for substance-specific codes)*

—.– Substance Withdrawal Delirium *(refer to Substance-Related Disorders for substance-specific codes)*
—.– Delirium Due to Multiple Etiologies *(code each of the specific etiologies)*
F05.9 Delirium NOS

DEMENTIA
F00.xx Dementia of the Alzheimer's Type, With Early Onset *(also code G30.0 Alzheimer's Disease, With Early Onset, on Axis III)*
   .00 Uncomplicated
   .01 With Delusions
   .03 With Depressed Mood
   Specify if: With Behavioral Disturbance
F00.xx Dementia of the Alzheimer's Type, With Late Onset *(also code G30.1 Alzheimer's Disease, With Late Onset, on Axis III)*
   .10 Uncomplicated
   .11 With Delusions
   .13 With Depressed Mood
   Specify if: With Behavioral Disturbance
F01.xx Vascular Dementia
   .80 Uncomplicated
   .81 With Delusions
   .83 With Depressed Mood
   Specify if: With Behavioral Disturbance

DEMENTIA DUE TO OTHER GENERAL MEDICAL CONDITIONS
F02.4 Dementia Due to HIV Disease *(also code B22.0 HIV disease resulting in encephalopathy on Axis III)*
F02.8 Dementia Due to Head Trauma *(also code S06.9 Intracranial injury on Axis III)*
F02.3 Dementia Due to Parkinson's Disease *(also code G20 Parkinson's disease on Axis III)*
F02.2 Dementia Due to Huntington's Disease *(also code G10 Huntington's disease on Axis III)*
F02.0 Dementia Due to Pick's Disease *(also code G31.0 Pick's disease on Axis III)*
F02.1 Dementia Due to Creutzfeldt-Jakob Disease *(also code A81.0 Creutzfeldt-Jakob disease on Axis III)*
F02.8 Dementia Due to. . .[Indicate the General Medical Condition not listed above](also code the general medical condition on Axis III)*
—.– Substance-Induced Persisting Dementia *(refer to Substance-Related Disorders for substance-specific codes)*
F02.8 Dementia Due to Multiple Etiologies *(instead code F00.2 for mixed Alzheimer's and Vascular Dementia)*
F03 Dementia NOS

AMNESTIC DISORDERS
F04 Amnestic Disorder Due to. . .[Indicate the General Medical Condition]*

Specify if: Transient/Chronic
—.– Substance-Induced Persisting Amnestic Disorder *(refer to Substance-Related Disorders for substance-specific codes)*
R41.3 Amnestic Disorder NOS

OTHER COGNITIVE DISORDERS
F06.9 Cognitive Disorder NOS

Mental Disorders Due to a General Medical Condition Not Elsewhere Classified

F06.1 Catatonic Disorder Due to. . .*[Indicate the General Medical Condition]*
F07.0 Personality Change Due to. . .*[Indicate the General Medical Condition]*
Specify type: Labile Type/Disinhibited Type/Aggressive Type/Apathetic Type/Paranoid Type/Other Type/Combined Type/Unspecified Type
F09 Mental Disorder NOS Due to. . .*[Indicate the General Medical Condition]*

Substance-Related Disorders

[a]*The following specifiers may be applied to Substance Dependence:*
   Specify if: With Physiological Dependence/Without Physiological Dependence
Code course of Dependence in fifth character:
   0 = Early Full Remission/Early Partial Remission
   0 = Sustained Full Remission/Sustained Partial Remission
   1 = In a Controlled Environment
   2 = On Agonist Therapy
   4 = Mild/Moderate/Severe
The following specifiers apply to Substance-Induced Disorders as noted:
[I]With Onset During Intoxication/[W]With Onset During Withdrawal

ALCOHOL-RELATED DISORDERS
Alcohol Use Disorders
F10.2x Alcohol Dependence[a]
F10.1 Alcohol Abuse

Alcohol-Induced Disorders
F10.00 Alcohol Intoxication
F10.3 Alcohol Withdrawal
   Specify if: With Perceptual Disturbances
F10.03 Alcohol Intoxication Delirium
F10.4 Alcohol Withdrawal Delirium
F10.73 Alcohol-Induced Persisting Dementia
F10.6 Alcohol-Induced Persisting Amnestic Disorder

F10.xx Alcohol-Induced Psychotic Disorder
 .51 With Delusions[I,W]
 .52 With Hallucinations[I,W]
F10.8 Alcohol-Induced Mood Disorder[I,W]
F10.8 Alcohol-Induced Anxiety Disorder[I,W]
F10.8 Alcohol-Induced Sexual Dysfunction[I]
F10.8 Alcohol-Induced Sleep Disorder[I,W]

F10.9 Alcohol-Related Disorder NOS

AMPHETAMINE (OR AMPHETAMINE-LIKE)–RELATED DISORDERS
Amphetamine Use Disorders
F15.2x Amphetamine Dependence[a]
F15.1 Amphetamine Abuse

Amphetamine-Induced Disorders
F15.00 Amphetamine Intoxication
F15.04 Amphetamine Intoxication, With Perceptual Disturbances
F15.3 Amphetamine Withdrawal
F15.03 Amphetamine Intoxication Delirium
F15.xx Amphetamine-Induced Psychotic Disorder
 .51 With Delusions[I]
 .52 With Hallucinations[I]
F15.8 Amphetamine-Induced Mood Disorder[I,W]
F15.8 Amphetamine-Induced Anxiety Disorder[I]
F15.8 Amphetamine-Induced Sexual Dysfunction[I]
F15.8 Amphetamine-Induced Sleep Disorder[I,W]
F15.9 Amphetamine-Related Disorder NOS

CAFFEINE-RELATED DISORDERS
Caffeine-Induced Disorders
F15.00 Caffeine Intoxication
F15.8 Caffeine-Induced Anxiety Disorder[I]
F15.8 Caffeine-Induced Sleep Disorder[I]

F15.9 Caffeine-Related Disorder NOS

CANNABIS-RELATED DISORDERS
Cannabis Use Disorders
F12.2x Cannabis Dependence[a]
F12.1 Cannabis Abuse

Cannabis-Induced Disorders
F12.00 Cannabis Intoxication
F12.04 Cannabis Intoxication, With Perceptual Disturbances
F12.03 Cannabis Intoxication Delirium
F12.xx Cannabis-Induced Psychotic Disorder
 .51 With Delusions[I]
 .52 With Hallucinations[I]
F12.8 Cannabis-Induced Anxiety Disorder[I]

F12.9 Cannabis-Related Disorder NOS

COCAINE-RELATED DISORDERS
Cocaine Use Disorders
F14.2x Cocaine Dependence[a]
F14.1 Cocaine Abuse

Cocaine-Induced Disorders
F14.00 Cocaine Intoxication
F14.04 Cocaine Intoxication, With Perceptual Disturbances
F14.3 Cocaine Withdrawal
F14.03 Cocaine Intoxication Delirium
F14.xx Cocaine-Induced Psychotic Disorder
 .51 With Delusions[I]
 .52 With Hallucinations[I]
F14.8 Cocaine-Induced Mood Disorder[I,W]
F14.8 Cocaine-Induced Anxiety Disorder[I,W]
F14.8 Cocaine-Induced Sexual Dysfunction[I]
F14.8 Cocaine-Induced Sleep Disorder[I,W]

F14.9 Cocaine-Related Disorder NOS

HALLUCINOGEN-RELATED DISORDERS
Hallucinogen Use Disorders
F16.2x Hallucinogen Dependence[a]
F16.1 Hallucinogen Abuse

Hallucinogen-Induced Disorders
F16.00 Hallucinogen Intoxication
F16.70 Hallucinogen Persisting Perception Disorder (Flashbacks)
F16.03 Hallucinogen Intoxication Delirium
F16.xx Hallucinogen-Induced Psychotic Disorder
 .51 With Delusions[I]
 .52 With Hallucinations[I]
F16.8 Hallucinogen-Induced Mood Disorder[I]
F16.8 Hallucinogen-Induced Anxiety Disorder[I]

F16.9 Hallucinogen-Related Disorder NOS

INHALANT-RELATED DISORDERS
Inhalant Use Disorders
F18.2x Inhalant Dependence[a]
F18.1 Inhalant Abuse

Inhalant-Induced Disorders
F18.00 Inhalant Intoxication
F18.03 Inhalant Intoxication Delirium
F18.73 Inhalant-Induced Persisting Dementia
F18.xx Inhalant-Induced Psychotic Disorder
 .51 With Delusions[I]
 .52 With Hallucinations[I]
F18.8 Inhalant-Induced Mood Disorder[I]
F18.8 Inhalant-Induced Anxiety Disorder[I]

F18.9 Inhalant-Related Disorder NOS

NICOTINE-RELATED DISORDERS
Nicotine Use Disorder
F17.2x Nicotine Dependence[a]

Nicotine-Induced Disorder
F17.3 Nicotine Withdrawal

F17.9 Nicotine-Related Disorder NOS

OPIOID-RELATED DISORDERS
Opioid Use Disorders
F11.2x Opioid Dependence[a]
F11.1 Opioid Abuse

Opioid-Induced Disorders
F11.00 Opioid Intoxication
F11.04 Opioid Intoxication, With Perceptual Disturbances
F11.3 Opioid Withdrawal
F11.03 Opioid Intoxication Delirium
F11.xx Opioid-Induced Psychotic Disorder
    .51 With Delusions[I]
    .52 With Hallucinations[I]
F11.8 Opioid-Induced Mood Disorder[I]
F11.8 Opioid-Induced Sexual Dysfunction[I]
F11.8 Opioid-Induced Sleep Disorder[I,W]

F11.9 Opioid-Related Disorder NOS

PHENCYCLIDINE (OR PHENCYCLIDINE-LIKE)–RELATED DISORDERS
Phencyclidine Use Disorders
F19.2x Phencyclidine Dependence[a]
F19.1 Phencyclidine Abuse

Phencyclidine-Induced Disorders
F19.00 Phencyclidine Intoxication
F19.04 Phencyclidine Intoxication, With Perceptual Disturbances
F19.03 Phencyclidine Intoxication Delirium
F19.xx Phencyclidine-Induced Psychotic Disorder
    .51 With Delusions[I]
    .52 With Hallucinations[I]
F19.8 Phencyclidine-Induced Mood Disorder[I]
F19.8 Phencyclidine-Induced Anxiety Disorder[I]

F19.9 Phencyclidine-Related Disorder NOS

SEDATIVE-, HYPNOTIC-, OR ANXIOLYTIC-RELATED DISORDERS
Sedative, Hypnotic, or Anxiolytic Use Disorders
F13.2x Sedative, Hypnotic, or Anxiolytic Dependence[a]
F13.1 Sedative, Hypnotic, or Anxiolytic Abuse

Sedative-, Hypnotic-, or Anxiolytic-Induced Disorders
F13.00 Sedative, Hypnotic, or Anxiolytic Intoxication

F13.3 Sedative, Hypnotic, or Anxiolytic Withdrawal
    Specify if: With Perceptual Disturbances
F13.03 Sedative, Hypnotic, or Anxiolytic Intoxication Delirium
F13.4 Sedative, Hypnotic, or Anxiolytic Withdrawal Delirium
F13.73 Sedative-, Hypnotic-, or Anxiolytic-Induced Persisting Dementia
F13.6 Sedative-, Hypnotic-, or Anxiolytic-Induced Persisting Amnestic Disorder
F13.xx Sedative-, Hypnotic-, or Anxiolytic-Induced Psychotic Disorder
    .51 With Delusions[I,W]
    .52 With Hallucinations[I,W]
F13.8 Sedative-, Hypnotic-, or Anxiolytic-Induced Mood Disorder[I,W]
F13.8 Sedative-, Hypnotic-, or Anxiolytic-Induced Anxiety Disorder[W]
F13.8 Sedative-, Hypnotic-, or Anxiolytic-Induced Sexual Dysfunction[I]
F13.8 Sedative-, Hypnotic-, or Anxiolytic-Induced Sleep Disorder[I,W]
F13.9 Sedative-, Hypnotic-, or Anxiolytic-Related Disorder NOS

POLYSUBSTANCE-RELATED DISORDER
F19.2x Polysubstance Dependence[a]

OTHER (OR UNKNOWN) SUBSTANCE-RELATED DISORDERS
Other (or Unknown) Substance Use Disorders
F19.2x Other (or Unknown) Substance Dependence[a]
F19.1 Other (or Unknown) Substance Abuse

Other (or Unknown) Substance-Induced Disorders
F19.00 Other (or Unknown) Substance Intoxication
F19.04 Other (or Unknown) Substance Intoxication, With Perceptual Disturbances
F19.3 Other (or Unknown) Substance Withdrawal
    Specify if: With Perceptual Disturbances
F19.03 Other (or Unknown) Substance-Induced Delirium (*code F19.4 if onset during withdrawal*)
F19.73 Other (or Unknown) Substance-Induced Persisting Dementia
F19.6 Other (or Unknown) Substance-Induced Persisting Amnestic Disorder
F19.xx Other (or Unknown) Substance-Induced Psychotic Disorder
    .51 With Delusions[I,W]
    .52 With Hallucinations[I,W]
F19.8 Other (or Unknown) Substance-Induced Mood Disorder[I,W]
F19.8 Other (or Unknown) Substance-Induced Anxiety Disorder[I,W]

F19.8 Other (or Unknown) Substance-Induced Sexual Dysfunction[I]

F19.8 Other (or Unknown) Substance-Induced Sleep Disorder[I,W]

F19.9 Other (or Unknown) Substance-Related Disorder NOS

Schizophrenia and Other Psychotic Disorders

F20.xx Schizophrenia
   .0x Paranoid Type
   .1x Disorganized Type
   .2x Catatonic Type
   .3x Undifferentiated Type
   .5x Residual Type
Code course of Schizophrenia in fifth character:
   2 = Episodic With Interepisode Residual Symptoms (*specify if:* With Prominent Negative Symptoms)
   3 = Episodic With No Interepisode Residual Symptoms
   0 = Continuous (*specify if:* With Prominent Negative Symptoms)
   4 = Single Episode In Partial Remission (*specify if:* With Prominent Negative Symptoms)
   5 = Single Episode In Full Remission
   8 = Other or Unspecified Pattern
   9 = Less than 1 year since onset of initial active-phase symptoms
F20.8 Schizophreniform Disorder
   Specify if: Without Good Prognostic Features/With Good Prognostic Features
F25.x Schizoaffective Disorder
   .0 Bipolar Type
   .1 Depressive Type
F22.0 Delusional Disorder
   Specify type: Erotomanic Type/Grandiose Type/Jealous Type/Persecutory Type/Somatic Type/Mixed Type/Unspecified Type
F23.xx Brief Psychotic Disorder
   .81 With Marked Stressor(s)
   .80 Without Marked Stressor(s)
   Specify if: With Postpartum Onset
F24 Shared Psychotic Disorder
F06.x Psychotic Disorder Due to. . .*[Indicate the General Medical Condition]*
   .2 With Delusions
   .0 With Hallucinations
—.– Substance-Induced Psychotic Disorder (*refer to Substance-Related Disorders for substance-specific codes*)
   Specify if: With Onset During Intoxication/With Onset During Withdrawal
F29 Psychotic Disorder NOS

Mood Disorders

The following specifiers apply (for current or most recent episode) to Mood Disorders as noted:
   [a]Severity/Psychotic/Remission Specifiers/[b]Chronic/[c]With Catatonic Features/[d]With Melancholic Features/[e]With Atypical Features/[f]With Postpartum Onset
The following specifiers apply to Mood Disorders as noted:
   [g]With or Without Full Interepisode Recovery/[h]With Seasonal Pattern/[i]With Rapid Cycling

DEPRESSIVE DISORDERS

F32.x Major Depressive Disorder, Single Episode[a,b,c,d,e,f]
F33.x Major Depressive Disorder, Recurrent[a,b,c,d,e,f,g,h]
Code current state of Major Depressive Episode in fourth character:
   0 = Mild
   1 = Moderate
   2 = Severe Without Psychotic Features
   3 = Severe With Psychotic Features
   Specify: Mood-Congruent Psychotic Features/Mood-Incongruent Psychotic Features
   4 = In Partial Remission
   4 = In Full Remission
   9 = Unspecified
F34.1 Dysthymic Disorder
   Specify if: Early Onset/Late Onset
   Specify: With Atypical Features
F32.9 Depressive Disorder NOS

BIPOLAR DISORDERS

F30.x Bipolar I Disorder, Single Manic Episode[a,c,f]
   Specify if: Mixed
Code current state of Manic Episode in fourth character:
   1 = Mild, Moderate, or Severe Without Psychotic Features
   2 = Severe With Psychotic Features
   8 = In Partial or Full Remission
F31.0 Bipolar I Disorder, Most Recent Episode Hypomanic[g,h,i]
F31.x Bipolar I Disorder, Most Recent Episode Manic[a,c,f,g,h,i]
Code current state of Manic Episode in fourth character:
   1 = Mild, Moderate, or Severe Without Psychotic Features
   2 = Severe With Psychotic Features
   7 = In Partial or Full Remission
F31.6 Bipolar I Disorder, Most Recent Episode Mixed[a,c,f,g,h,i]
F31.x Bipolar I Disorder, Most Recent Episode Depressed[a,b,c,d,e,f,g,h,i]
Code current state of Major Depressive Episode in fourth character:
   3 = Mild or Moderate
   4 = Severe Without Psychotic Features
   5 = Severe With Psychotic Features
   7 = In Partial or Full Remission

F31.9 Bipolar I Disorder, Most Recent Episode Unspecified[g,h,i]

F31.8 Bipolar II Disorder[a,b,c,d,e,f,g,h,i]
Specify (current or most recent episode): Hypomanic/Depressed

F34.0 Cyclothymic Disorder

F31.9 Bipolar Disorder NOS

F06.xx Mood Disorder Due to. . .*[Indicate the General Medical Condition]*
.32 With Depressive Features
.32 With Major Depressive-Like Episode
.30 With Manic Features
.33 With Mixed Features

—.– Substance-Induced Mood Disorder *(refer to Substance-Related Disorders for substance-specific codes)*
Specify type: With Depressive Features/With Manic Features/With Mixed Features
Specify if: With Onset During Intoxication/With Onset During Withdrawal

F39 Mood Disorder NOS

Anxiety Disorders

F41.0 Panic Disorder Without Agoraphobia

F40.01 Panic Disorder With Agoraphobia

F40.00 Agoraphobia Without History of Panic Disorder

F40.2 Specific Phobia
Specify type: Animal Type/Natural Environment Type/Blood-Injection-Injury Type/Situational Type/Other Type

F40.1 Social Phobia
Specify if: Generalized

F42.8 Obsessive-Compulsive Disorder
Specify if: With Poor Insight

F43.1 Posttraumatic Stress Disorder
Specify if: Acute/Chronic
Specify if: With Delayed Onset

F43.0 Acute Stress Disorder

F41.1 Generalized Anxiety Disorder

F06.4 Anxiety Disorder Due to. . .*[Indicate the General Medical Condition]*
Specify if: With Generalized Anxiety/With Panic Attacks/With Obsessive-Compulsive Symptoms

—.– Substance-Induced Anxiety Disorder *(refer to Substance-Related Disorders for substance-specific codes)*
Specify if: With Generalized Anxiety/With Panic Attacks/With Obsessive-Compulsive Symptoms/With Phobic Symptoms
Specify if: With Onset During Intoxication/With Onset During Withdrawal

F41.9 Anxiety Disorder NOS

Somatoform Disorders

F45.0 Somatization Disorder

F45.1 Undifferentiated Somatoform Disorder

F44.x Conversion Disorder
.4 With Motor Symptom or Deficit
.5 With Seizures or Convulsions
.6 With Sensory Symptom or Deficit
.7 With Mixed Presentation

F45.4 Pain Disorder
Specify type: Associated With Psychological Factors/Associated With Both Psychological Factors and a General Medical Condition
Specify if: Acute/Chronic

F45.2 Hypochondriasis
Specify if: With Poor Insight

F45.2 Body Dysmorphic Disorder

F45.9 Somatoform Disorder NOS

Factitious Disorders

F68.1 Factitious Disorder
Specify type: With Predominantly Psychological Signs and Symptoms/With Predominantly Physical Signs and Symptoms/With Combined Psychological and Physical Signs and Symptoms

F68.1 Factitious Disorder NOS

Dissociative Disorders

F44.0 Dissociative Amnesia

F44.1 Dissociative Fugue

F44.81 Dissociative Identity Disorder

F48.1 Depersonalization Disorder

F44.9 Dissociative Disorder NOS

Sexual and Gender Identity Disorders

SEXUAL DYSFUNCTIONS
The following specifiers apply to all primary Sexual Dysfunctions:
Lifelong Type/Acquired Type/Generalized Type/Situational Type Due to Psychological Factors/Due to Combined Factors

Sexual Desire Disorders
F52.0 Hypoactive Sexual Desire Disorder
F52.10 Sexual Aversion Disorder

Sexual Arousal Disorders
F52.2 Female Sexual Arousal Disorder
F52.2 Male Erectile Disorder

Orgasmic Disorders
F52.3 Female Orgasmic Disorder
F52.3 Male Orgasmic Disorder
F52.4 Premature Ejaculation

Sexual Pain Disorders
F52.6 Dyspareunia (Not Due to a General Medical Condition)
F52.5 Vaginismus (Not Due to a General Medical Condition)

Sexual Dysfunction Due to a General Medical Condition
N94.8 Female Hypoactive Sexual Desire Disorder Due to. . .*[Indicate the General Medical Condition]*
N50.8 Male Hypoactive Sexual Desire Disorder Due to. . .*[Indicate the General Medical Condition]*
N48.4 Male Erectile Disorder Due to. . .*[Indicate the General Medical Condition]*
N94.1 Female Dyspareunia Due to. . .*[Indicate the General Medical Condition]*
N50.8 Male Dyspareunia Due to. . .*[Indicate the General Medical Condition]*
N94.8 Other Female Sexual Dysfunction Due to. . .*[Indicate the General Medical Condition]*
N50.8 Other Male Sexual Dysfunction Due to. . .*[Indicate the General Medical Condition]*
—.– Substance-Induced Sexual Dysfunction (*refer to Substance-Related Disorders for substance-specific codes*)
  Specify if: With Impaired Desire/With Impaired Arousal/With Impaired Orgasm/With Sexual Pain
  Specify if: With Onset During Intoxication

F52.9 Sexual Dysfunction NOS

PARAPHILIAS
F65.2 Exhibitionism
F65.0 Fetishism
F65.8 Frotteurism
F65.4 Pedophilia
  Specify if: Sexually Attracted to Males/Sexually Attracted to Females/Sexually Attracted to Both
  Specify if: Limited to Incest
  Specify type: Exclusive Type/Nonexclusive Type
F65.5 Sexual Masochism
F65.5 Sexual Sadism
F65.1 Transvestic Fetishism
  Specify if: With Gender Dysphoria
F65.3 Voyeurism
F65.9 Paraphilia NOS

GENDER IDENTITY DISORDERS
F64.x Gender Identity Disorder
  .2 in Children
  .0 in Adolescents or Adults
  Specify if: Sexually Attracted to Males/Sexually Attracted to Females/Sexually Attracted to Both/Sexually Attracted to Neither
F64.9 Gender Identity Disorder NOS

F52.9 Sexual Disorder NOS

Eating Disorders

F50.0 Anorexia Nervosa
  Specify type: Restricting Type; Binge-Eating/Purging Type
F50.2 Bulimia Nervosa
  Specify type: Purging Type/Nonpurging Type
F50.9 Eating Disorder NOS

Sleep Disorders

PRIMARY SLEEP DISORDERS
Dyssomnias
F51.0 Primary Insomnia
F51.1 Primary Hypersomnia
  Specify if: Recurrent
G47.4 Narcolepsy
G47.3 Breathing-Related Sleep Disorder
F51.2 Circadian Rhythm Sleep Disorder
Specify type: Delayed Sleep Phase Type/Jet Lag Type/Shift Work Type/Unspecified Type
F51.9 Dyssomnia NOS

Parasomnias
F51.5 Nightmare Disorder
F51.4 Sleep Terror Disorder
F51.3 Sleepwalking Disorder
F51.8 Parasomnia NOS

SLEEP DISORDERS RELATED TO ANOTHER MENTAL DISORDER
F51.0 Insomnia Related to. . .*[Indicate the Axis I or Axis II Disorder]*
F51.1 Hypersomnia Related to. . .*[Indicate the Axis I or Axis II Disorder]*

OTHER SLEEP DISORDERS
G47.x Sleep Disorder Due to. . .*[Indicate the General Medical Condition]*
  .0 Insomnia Type

.1 Hypersomnia Type
.8 Parasomnia Type
.8 Mixed Type
—.– Substance-Induced Sleep Disorder (refer to Substance-Related Disorders for substance-specific codes)
Specify type: Insomnia Type/Hypersomnia Type/Parasomnia Type/Mixed Type
Specify if: With Onset During Intoxication/With Onset During Withdrawal

Impulse-Control Disorders Not Elsewhere Classified

F63.8 Intermittent Explosive Disorder
F63.2 Kleptomania
F63.1 Pyromania
F63.0 Pathological Gambling
F63.3 Trichotillomania
F63.9 Impulse-Control Disorder NOS

Adjustment Disorders

F43.xx Adjustment Disorder
.20 With Depressed Mood
.28 With Anxiety
.22 With Mixed Anxiety and Depressed Mood
.24 With Disturbance of Conduct
.25 With Mixed Disturbance of Emotions and Conduct
.9 Unspecified
Specify if: Acute/Chronic

Personality Disorders

Note: These are coded on Axis II.
F60.0 Paranoid Personality Disorder
F60.1 Schizoid Personality Disorder
F21 Schizotypal Personality Disorder
F60.2 Antisocial Personality Disorder
F60.31 Borderline Personality Disorder
F60.4 Histrionic Personality Disorder
F60.8 Narcissistic Personality Disorder
F60.6 Avoidant Personality Disorder
F60.7 Dependent Personality Disorder
F60.5 Obsessive-Compulsive Personality Disorder
F60.9 Personality Disorder NOS

Other Conditions That May Be a Focus of Clinical Attention

PSYCHOLOGICAL FACTORS AFFECTING MEDICAL CONDITION
F54 . . .[Specified Psychological Factor] Affecting. . .[Indicate the General Medical Condition]
Choose name based on nature of factors:
Mental Disorder Affecting Medical Condition
Psychological Symptoms Affecting Medical Condition
Personality Traits or Coping Style Affecting Medical Condition
Maladaptive Health Behaviors Affecting Medical Condition
Stress-Related Physiological Response Affecting Medical Condition
Other or Unspecified Psychological Factors Affecting Medical Condition

MEDICATION-INDUCED MOVEMENT DISORDERS
G21.0 Neuroleptic-Induced Parkinsonism
G21.0 Neuroleptic Malignant Syndrome
G24.0 Neuroleptic-Induced Acute Dystonia
G21.1 Neuroleptic-Induced Acute Akathisia
G24.0 Neuroleptic-Induced Tardive Dyskinesia
G25.1 Medication-Induced Postural Tremor
G25.9 Medication-Induced Movement Disorder NOS

OTHER MEDICATION-INDUCED DISORDER
T88.7 Adverse Effects of Medication NOS

RELATIONAL PROBLEMS
Z63.7 Relational Problem Related to a Mental Disorder or General Medical Condition
Z63.8 Parent-Child Relational Problem (code Z63.1 if focus of attention is on child)
Z63.0 Partner Relational Problem
F93.3 Sibling Relational Problem
Z63.9 Relational Problem NOS

PROBLEMS RELATED TO ABUSE OR NEGLECT
T74.1 Physical Abuse of Child
T74.2 Sexual Abuse of Child
T74.0 Neglect of Child
T74.1 Physical Abuse of Adult
T74.2 Sexual Abuse of Adult

ADDITIONAL CONDITIONS THAT MAY BE A FOCUS OF CLINICAL ATTENTION
Z91.1 Noncompliance With Treatment
Z76.5 Malingering
Z72.8 Adult Antisocial Behavior

Z72.8 Child or Adolescent Antisocial Behavior
R41.8 Borderline Intellectual Functioning
R41.8 Age-Related Cognitive Decline
Z63.4 Bereavement
Z55.8 Academic Problem
Z56.7 Occupational Problem
F93.8 Identity Problem
Z71.8 Religious or Spiritual Problem
Z60.3 Acculturation Problem
Z60.0 Phase of Life Problem

Additional Codes

F99 Unspecified Mental Disorder (nonpsychotic)
Z03.2 No Diagnosis or Condition on Axis I
R69 Diagnosis or Condition Deferred on Axis I
Z03.2 No Diagnosis on Axis II
R46.8 Diagnosis Deferred on Axis II

References

Akiskal, H. S. 1980. External validating criteria for psychiatric diagnosis: their application in affective disorders. *J. Clin. Psychiatry* 41:6–15.

American Psychiatric Association. 1952. *Diagnostic and statistical manual of mental disorders* (DSM-I). Washington, D.C.: American Psychiatric Association Press.

——— 1968. *Diagnostic and statistical manual of mental disorders,* 2d ed. (DSM-II). Washington, D.C.: American Psychiatric Association Press.

——— 1980. *Diagnostic and statistical manual of mental disorders,* 3d ed. (DSM-III). Washington, D.C.: American Psychiatric Association Press.

——— 1987. *Diagnostic and statistical manual of mental disorders,* 3d ed., rev. (DSM-III-R). Washington, D.C.: American Psychiatric Association Press.

——— 1994. *Diagnostic and statistical manual of mental disorders,* 4th ed. (DSM-IV). Washington, D.C.: American Psychiatric Association Press.

Andreasen, N. C. 1997. Linking mind and brain in the study of mental illness: a project for a scientific psychopathology. *Science* 275:1586–93.

Carmines, E., Zeller, R. 1979. *Reliability and validity assessment.* Beverly Hills, Calif.: Sage Publications.

Cooper, J. E., Kendell, R. E., Gurland, B. J., Sharpe, L., Copeland, J. R. M., Simon, R. 1972. *Psychiatric diagnosis in New York and London: a comparative study of mental hospital admissions.* Institute of Psychiatry Maudsley Monographs no. 20. London: Oxford University Press.

Coryell, W., and Zimmerman, M. 1987. Progress in the classification of functional psychoses. *Am. J. Psychiatry* 144:1471–74.

Cronbach, L., and Meehl, P. 1955. Construct validity in psychological tests. *Psychological Bulletin* 42:281–301.

Davis, W. 1997. Introduction. In *DSM-IV sourcebook,* vol. 4, ed. Widiger, T. A., Frances, A. J., Pincus, H. A., Ross, R., First, M. B., Davis, W. W. Washington, D.C.: American Psychiatric Association Press.

Faust, D., and Miner, R. A. 1986. The empiricist and his new clothes: DSM-III in perspective. *Am. J. Psychiatry* 143:962–967.

Feighner, J. P., Robins, E., Guze, S. B., Woodruff, R. A., Winokur, G., Munoz, R. 1972. Diagnostic criteria for use in psychiatric research. *Arch. Gen. Psychiatry* 26:57–63.

Follette, W. C., and Houts, A. C. 1996. Models of scientific progress and the role of theory and taxonomy development: a case study of the DSM. *J. Consulting Clin. Psychology* 64:1120–32.

Goldstein, J. M., and Simpson, J. G. 1995. Validity: definitions and applications to psychiatric research. In *Textbook in psychiatric epidemiology,* ed. Tsuang, M., Tohen, M., and Zahner, G. E. P. New York: John Wiley and Sons. 229–242.

Grove, W. M., and Andreasen, N. C. 1989. Quantitative and qualitative distinctions between psychiatric disorders. In *The validity of diagnosis,* ed. Robins, L. N. and Barrett, J. E. New York: Raven Press.

Katz, M. M., and Klerman, G. L. 1979. Introduction: overview of the clinical studies program. *Am. J. Psychiatry* 136:49–51.

Kendell, R. E. 1989. Clinical validity. *Psychological Medicine* 19:45–55.

Kendler, K. S. 1990. Toward a scientific psychiatric nosology: strengths and limitations. *Arch. Gen. Psychiatry* 47:969–973.

Kessler, R. C., McGonagle, K. A., Zhao, S., Nelson, C. B., Hughes, M., Eshleman, S., Wittchen, H. U., Kendler, K. S. 1994. Lifetime and 12-month prevalence of DSM-III-R psychiatric disorders in the United States: results from the National Comorbidity Survey. *Arch. Gen. Psychiatry* 51:8–19.

Kramer, M. 1961. Some problems for international research suggested by observations on differences in first admission rates to mental hospitals of England and Wales and of the United States. In *Proceedings of the Third World Congress of Psychiatry.* Montreal: University of Toronto and McGill University Press.

Robins, E., and Guze, S. B. 1970. Establishment of diagnostic validity in psychiatric illness: its application to schizophrenia. *Am. J. Psychiatry* 126:983–987.

Shrout, P. E. 1995. Reliability. In *Textbook in psychiatric epi-*

demiology, ed. Tsuang, M., Tohen, M., and Zahner, G. E. P. New York: John Wiley and Sons. 213–227.

Spitzer, R. L., Endicott, J., and Robins, E. 1978. Research diagnostic criteria: rationale and reliability. *Arch. Gen. Psychiatry* 35:773–782.

Tsuang, M. T., Winokur, G., and Crowe, R. R. 1980. Morbidity risks of schizophrenia and affective disorders among first-degree relatives of patients with schizophrenia, mania, depression and surgical conditions. *Br. J. Psychiatry* 137:497–504.

Tsuang, M. T., Woolson, R. F., and Fleming, J. A. 1979. Long-term outcome of major psychoses. I. Schizophrenia and affective disorders compared with psychiatrically symptom-free surgical conditions. *Arch. Gen. Psychiatry* 66:1295–1301.

Widiger, T. A., Frances, A. J., Pincus, H. A., Ross, R., First, M. B., and Davis, W. W. 1994. *DSM-IV sourcebook,* vol. 1. Washington, D.C.: American Psychiatric Association Press.

——— 1996. *DSM-IV sourcebook,* vol. 2. Washington, D.C.: American Psychiatric Association Press.

——— 1997. *DSM-IV sourcebook,* vol. 3. Washington, D.C.: American Psychiatric Association Press.

World Health Organization. 1973. *The international pilot study of schizophrenia.* Geneva: World Health Organization.

——— 1992. *The ICD-10 classification of mental and behavioural disorders.* Geneva: World Health Organization.

Recommended Reading

Kendler, K. S. 1990. Toward a scientific psychiatric nosology: Strengths and limitations. *Arch. Gen. Psychiatry* 47:969–973.

Robins, E., and Guze, S. B. 1970. Establishment of diagnostic validity in psychiatric illness: Its application to schizophrenia. *Am. J. Psychiatry* 126:983–987.

Widiger, T. A., Frances, A. J., Pincus, H. A., Ross, R., First, M. B., and Davis, W. W. *DSM-IV sourcebook,* vols. 1–3. Washington, D.C.: American Psychiatric Association Press, 1994 (vol. 1), 1996 (vol. 2), 1997 (vol. 3).

Acknowledgments

This chapter is based on an earlier version, "Classification and DSM-III-R," by the late Gerald L. Klerman.

5

PERRY F. RENSHAW
SCOTT L. RAUCH

Neuroimaging in Clinical Psychiatry

Over the last three decades a series of rapid technical developments has provided a range of noninvasive methods for the assessment of brain anatomy, chemistry, and metabolism in man. At a fundamental level, these techniques are demonstrating that the traditional dichotomy between structural and functional brain disorders, as might be evaluated by a neurologist and a psychiatrist, respectively, does not hold up well. Thus, research studies are consistently documenting brain dysfunction in a range of psychiatric illnesses (Andreasen, 1989; Krishnan and Doraiswamy, in press).

However, for a variety of reasons, the clinical applications of this technical progress remain much less clearly defined. Psychiatry residents are expected to learn about "the use, reliability, and validity of the generally accepted diagnostic techniques, including . . . imaging" during the course of their training (American Council for Graduate Medical Education, 1996). Similarly, the American Board of Psychiatry and Neurology requires that candidates for board certification in psychiatry answer questions regarding clinical diagnostic procedures, including neuroimaging (American Board of Psychiatry and Neurology, 1996). However, the rapid rate of advancement in neuroimaging makes it difficult to assess the current state of the art at any given time. Additionally, relatively few reports exist on the utility of neuroimaging in the assessment of specific psychiatric populations. In turn, this makes it more difficult to obtain permission from third party payers to cover the costs of a brain imaging evaluation. Therefore, with increasing emphasis on cost containment, psychiatrists must be familiar with the range of available neuroimaging modalities, and appreciate their optimal utilization in clinical practice.

In clinical practice, neuroimaging is primarily used to aid in differential diagnosis. In most cases, the clinical utility of neuroimaging stems from its ability to demonstrate organic pathology as a possible substrate of disturbed mental status. Thus, neuroimaging studies are routinely used to "rule in" or "rule out" general medical conditions, as opposed to primary mental disorders. Current understanding of the pathobiology underlying primary psychiatric disorders is quite limited, and pathognomonic imaging profiles indicative of specific psychiatric disorders have not been identified. Consequently, for the time being, neuroimaging studies are of limited utility in the identification of specific primary psychiatric conditions. In the future, however, neuroimaging techniques may be used to make or confirm psychiatric diagnoses, and neuroimaging profiles may even be incorporated into the diagnostic criteria for certain psychiatric disorders. The potential for future clinical applications extends beyond diagnosis. Ultimately, neuroimaging data may be valuable for predicting the natural course of psychiatric illness as well as treatment response.

In this chapter the principles of currently available neuroimaging methods will be reviewed. These methods include computed axial tomography (CT), magnetic resonance imaging (MRI), and single photon emission computed tomography (SPECT). Based on data from the research literature, guidelines for the use of neuroimaging studies in clinical psychiatry will be presented. Finally, imaging techniques with emerging clinical applications, such as magnetic resonance spectroscopy (MRS), functional magnetic resonance imaging (fMRI), and positron emission tomography (PET), will be discussed.

Currently Available Diagnostic Imaging Techniques

Computed Axial Tomography (CT)

CT, developed in the early 1970s, is the result of innovative modifications to the technology of plain x-ray imaging (Gibby and Zimmerman, 1992). Plain x-ray imaging relies on the principle that an x-ray beam is differentially attenuated, owing to both scatter and absorption, as it passes through material, according to the density of that material. For instance, an x-ray beam is highly attenuated when passing through bone, minimally attenuated when passing through air, and attenuated across a spectrum of degrees when passing through materials of intermediate densities. Thus, if the initial intensity of the x-ray beam is known, a detection device can be used to determine the residual beam intensity after it has passed through an object of interest.

In the case of plain x-ray imaging, the detection device is x-ray sensitive film, and the image is formed as a simple two-dimensional projection. In the case of CT, multiple x-ray beam generators and detectors are arranged in a ringlike fashion, with the object to be imaged placed in the middle of the ring. Each volume element (i.e., "voxel") within the object is penetrated by beams (i.e., sampled) from multiple directions, and images are generated using image processing techniques. The development of CT scanners was facilitated by a large number of scientists in different fields who worked on fundamental problems in image reconstruction during the 1950s and 1960s (Bracewell, 1956; Kuhl and Edwards, 1963; DeRosier and Klug, 1968).

In this way, a ring of beam generators and detectors is used to image one slice through the brain. The patient is advanced through the gantry of the CT scanner after each slice is acquired so that multiple contiguous slices can be imaged sequentially. "Computed" refers to the computational process that allows for the calculation of attenuation values for each voxel; "axial" refers to the transaxial orientation in which the data are acquired and presented; and "tomography" refers to this slab-wise or slice-wise imaging. CT images are typically displayed in a gray scale, with the highest attenuation values (e.g., corresponding to bone) appearing white, the lowest attenuation values (e.g., corresponding to gas) appearing black, and intermediate attenuation values (e.g., corresponding to soft tissues) appearing in shades of gray.

Contrast agents and their use. High density (radio-opaque) contrast media are introduced intravenously, and produce characteristic enhancement of CT images (Osborn, 1994). The contrast material normally travels intravascularly, and yields a high attenuation signal. When there is blood brain barrier (BBB) compromise, the contrast leaks out and serves as a marker. In many forms of pathology, including frank bleeding, as well as neoplasm, infection, and inflammation, characteristic contrast enhancement occurs. Thus, a CT study with contrast may allow for identification of a lesion that would otherwise have been missed without contrast, or provide additional information about a given lesion, which aids in dif-

ferential diagnosis of pathology (e.g., tumor versus abscess).

CT contrast media are typically iodine based, and there are two types: ionic and non-ionic. Ionic contrast is far less expensive, but presents greater risks (Gibby and Zimmerman, 1992). Adverse contrast reactions can be divided into idiosyncratic and chemotoxic reactions (Zweiman, Mishkin, and Hildreth, 1975). Idiosyncratic reactions include vasomotor symptoms, hypotension, nausea, flushing, or urticarial skin reactions, up to and including frank anaphylaxis. Idiosyncratic reactions occur in approximately 5% of cases, with known risk factors including age < 1 or > 60 years old, history of asthma or allergies, cerebrovascular disease, or prior contrast reactions (Shehadi, 1982). Patients who develop reactions are treated according to the nature of their reaction: urticaria is treated with intravenous diphenhydramine, respiratory distress is treated with intravenous epinephrine, and hypotension is treated with intravenous fluids. For patients at higher risk, pretreatment with steroids may be recommended (Gibby and Zimmerman, 1992). Chemotoxic reactions to CT contrast may involve the brain or kidneys. Brain contrast chemotoxicity is characterized by seizure, occurring in 1/10,000 cases overall, but in up to 1–10% of cases where gross BBB compromise is present (Witten, Hirsch, and Hartman, 1973). Renal toxicity takes the form of impaired renal function, and has as its primary risk factor preexisting impaired renal function (Hayman et al., 1980). Non-ionic contrast media are less likely to cause idiosyncratic reactions, anaphylaxis, or chemotoxicity, but at up to 25 times the cost of ionic forms (White and Halden, 1986).

Advantages and limitations. Since CT uses ionizing radiation, it is contraindicated during pregnancy, and, when possible, women of childbearing potential should have pregnancy ruled out prior to having a CT scan. Anxiety reactions are minimized with CT because patients are not tightly confined within the scanner, there is little extraneous noise during the scan, and the scanning times are relatively brief. Each slice of the scan can be acquired in about 1 minute, and an entire brain scan can be completed in less than 10 minutes. Thus, this modality is excellent for patients who might have difficulty lying still for an extended time period (e.g., agitated or arthritic patients). CT is relatively effective at distinguishing tissues with markedly different x-ray attenuation properties, such as bone vs. soft tissue vs. fluid vs. gas, with excellent spatial resolution (<1 mm).

Unfortunately, CT does not distinguish well between different soft tissue densities. In particular, CT is limited in its capacity to identify white matter lesions. Whereas fresh bleeding (<48–72 hrs old) is well identified by CT, sub-acute bleeding (>72 hrs) or acute bleeding in the context of severe anemia (i.e., Hgb ≤10g/dl) may appear "isodense" with respect to normal brain tissue (Osborn, 1994). Soft tissue surrounded by bone can be obscured by artifacts, making certain brain regions, such as the contents of the posterior fossa, difficult to visualize effectively with CT. Nonetheless, CT is very reliable for imaging bone itself (e.g., to evaluate fracture), calcifications, and acute bleeding and is the imaging modality of choice in the context of acute trauma.

Utility in psychiatric populations. The first clinical CT scanner was installed at Atkinson Morley's Hospital in 1971 (Coffman, 1989), and the advantages of CT, as opposed to plain skull x-rays, for the evaluation of psychiatric populations were demonstrable as early as 1978 (Tsai and Tsuang, 1978). In a comparison of results from 125 patients admitted to the Iowa Psychiatric Hospital over a 3-year period, these investigators noted that CT scanning detected more than 5 times as many intracranial abnormalities as did skull x-rays in this population. Subsequently, a plethora of investigators reported on the utility of CT scanning in psychiatric populations (Table 5.1).

Table 5.1 Use of CT scanning in psychiatric populations

	Total Studied	Atrophy (Diffuse)	Focal Finding	Population and Risk Factors for Abnormalities
Woods (1976)	190	62 (33%)	26 (14%)	Psychiatric inpatients referred by neurological consultant; increased age.
Owens et al. (1980)	136	—	12 (9%)	Randomly selected chronic schizophrenics; increased age.
Larson et al. (1981)	123	43 (35%)	11 (9%)	Consecutive referrals for CT because of psychiatric illness, average age 49; focal neurological examination.
Tsai and Tsuang (1981)	135	27 (20%)	5 (4%)	Psychiatric inpatients with suspected organic brain disease, 3% of total patients, average age 41.
Evans (1982)	100	66 (66%)	7 (7%)	Consecutive referrals for CT by psychiatrists, average age 56; dementia.
Beresford et al. (1986)	165	—	38 (23%)	Psychiatric inpatients with clinical indication for scan, 4% of total patients, median age 52; focal neurological exam, abnormal mental status.
Emsley et al. (1986)	100	50 (50%)	23 (23%)	Consecutive referrals of psychiatric inpatients; alcohol abuse, head trauma, focal neurological signs.
McClellan, Eisenberg, and Giyananni (1988)	261	27 (10%)	4 (1.5%)	All psychiatric inpatients without known medical or neurological disorders, median age 41.
Battaglia and Spector (1988)	45	—	3 (7%)	Consecutive inpatients with first episode psychosis, average age 26.
Chandler and Patten (1989)	37	10 (27%)	22 (60%)	Consecutive geriatric psychiatric inpatients with clinical indications; mean age 77.
Colohan et al. (1989)	54	10 (19%)	15 (28%)	Psychiatric inpatients with clinical indications, 1% of total patients, median age 51; abnormal mental status.
Total	1,346	295/1000 (29.5%)	166 (12%)	

Across all of these studies, 12% of patients demonstrated focal abnormalities. The likelihood of detecting an abnormal finding increased with age, with an abnormal neurological examination, with an altered mental status, and with a history of head trauma or alcohol abuse.

Attempts to propose guidelines for the use of CT scanning to evaluate psychiatric patients on a cost effectiveness basis (Larson et al., 1981) have been complicated by the difficulty of evaluating the benefit of a negative (normal) result (Holt et al., 1982). Weinberger (1984) emphasized that the total radiation exposure, 2–3 rads, is relatively low and should not be viewed as an important disincentive in most instances. Despite a lack of objective empirical data, several investigators have proposed guidelines for the use of CT scanning (Weinberger, 1984; Emsley et al., 1986). Possible indications for scanning include: confusion and dementia of unknown cause; a first episode of psychosis; new psychiatric syndromes after the age of 50; the presence of focal neurological signs; and a history of craniocerebral trauma or seizures.

Magnetic Resonance Imaging (MRI)

Basic principles. MRI exploits the intrinsic magnetic properties of the human body, which is mainly composed of water. The hydrogen atoms in water molecules contain nuclei which act as dipoles. Within a static magnetic field, each of the nuclei, or dipoles, will align either with or against the field. Those nuclei aligned with the magnetic field will have a slightly lower energy level than those nuclei which are aligned against the field. Radiofrequency (RF) irradiation at the proper frequency (e.g., a resonance frequency of ~64 MHz for a 1.5 Tesla magnetic field) will allow some of the lower energy nuclei to absorb RF energy and align against the field. When the RF pulse is turned off, some of the nuclei at the higher energy level will emit RF energy and return to the lower energy state, aligning with the magnetic field. The emission of RF energy can be detected by an appropriate coil (or antenna), and this is the signal that is measured by MR scanners. Images, or spatial maps of RF signals, are constructed by applying magnetic field gradients during the period of RF irradiation. The rate at which excited nuclei return to their equilibrium (low energy) state is described in terms of two tissue relaxation times, T1 and T2.

Brain MR images are representations of brain structure, as opposed to actual pictures. Images may be obtained using different acquisition parameters and are often referred to as being T1-weighted, T2-weighted, or proton density images. T1-weighted images appear to represent neuroanatomy with great clarity; gray matter is dark, white matter is light, and CSF is very dark (Figure 5.1). T2-weighted images look very different and are designed to highlight areas of pathology; regions which contain extravasated blood appear dark because of the paramagnetic effects of iron, and regions containing tumor or edema appear light because of a relatively increased water content.

Contrast agents. Contrast agents are also used to enhance MRI images (Bradley, Yuh, and Bydder, 1993). While CT contrast media are high density and typically iodine based, MR contrast agents in clinical practice are strongly paramagnetic and typically contain chelated gadolinium. These agents work by altering the local magnetic environment and, by extension, tissue relaxation times. As with CT, MR contrast agents will diffuse from the intravascular to the extracellular space when there is some compromise of the blood brain barrier (e.g., in the case of cerebral neoplasm or inflammation). MR contrast is well tolerated, and the most common severe reaction is the induction of an asthma attack in patients with preexisting reactive airway disease.

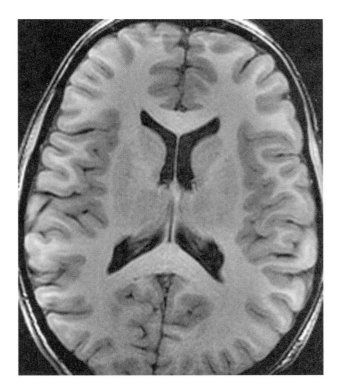

Figure 5.1 High-resolution, T1-weighted brain MR image through an axial slice at the level of the basal ganglia. The unusually high degree of resolution in this image is obtained by using a specially designed, phased array coil set (Wald et al., 1995).

Advantages and limitations. MRI does not require exposure to ionizing radiation. Thus, patients can safely have multiple serial scans without concerns about aggregate radiation dose. MRI, although probably quite safe, is still deemed relatively contraindicated during early pregnancy (Magin, Liburdy, and Persson, 1992), but is preferable to ionizing radiation exposure. Because of the strong magnetic field associated with MRI, the presence of metallic implants of any kind are relative contraindications to MRI (Kanal and Shellock, 1994). Specifically, metal aneurysm clips can be twisted off, shrapnel remnants can be drawn through tissue and heated to scalding temperatures, and cardiac pacemakers can be deprogrammed or stimulated to misfire, all owing to the force of the magnetic field. Metallic orthopedic pins may be permissible as long as they are far from the site to be imaged, since although they will not pose substantial risk, they will produce local image artifacts. Other equipment with metallic components is also prohibited from the scanner suite. Therefore, MRI may also be contraindicated for medical inpatients connected to ancillary devices (e.g., intravenous pumps, cardiac monitors, or respirators).

MRI scanner bores are usually 2–3 feet wide and several feet deep, thereby producing a considerable sense of confinement for many patients. This factor, coupled with the loud clanking noise of the scanner and scanning times from 20–40 minutes or more, cause ~10% of patients to report significant discomfort or anxiety, with up to 1% experiencing frank claustrophobic or panic reactions (Melendez and McCrank, 1993). Oral administration of a benzodiazepine or other sedative agent (i.e., alprazolam 0.5–1.0 mg or chloral hydrate 500–1000 mg) 30 minutes prior to beginning the scanning procedure is effective as prophylaxis against such anxiety reactions (Klein, 1991; Greenberg et al., 1993).

MRI produces images with excellent soft tissue contrast, as well as excellent spatial resolution. MRI is especially sensitive to white matter lesions and provides excellent visualization of posterior fossa contents. Moreover, MRI data can be resliced in any plane without substantial loss of spatial resolution. Bone and other mineral deposits produce an MRI signal void, because the dipoles trapped in a solid matrix cannot be perturbed by the RF pulse. Fresh blood from an acute bleed (<48–72 hours) is not easily distinguished from gray matter, although sub-acute bleeding (>48–72 hours) or chronic hematomas can be reliably identified.

Utility in psychiatric populations. As compared with CT scanning, substantially fewer studies on the utility of MRI for the evaluation of patients with psychiatric disorders

have been published. In 1992, Wahlund and colleagues reported that 121 of 731 consecutively referred subjects with a primary psychiatric disorder had evidence for a focal abnormality on brain MRI. Subsequently, Woods et al. (1995) noted that 58 of 536 (11%) consecutively referred psychiatric inpatients had evidence of focal brain pathology. More recently, we reported on the prevalence of unanticipated findings that might lead to a change in treatment in a cohort of 6200 consecutively referred psychiatric inpatients at a single institution (Rauch and Renshaw, 1995). Of this sample, 99 subjects (1.6%) were noted to have findings which might lead to a change in clinical management. The most common new diagnosis was that of multiple sclerosis (MS), which was present in approximately 0.8% of all subjects, a rate which is roughly 13 times higher than the prevalence of MS in the general population (Lyoo et al., 1996). The majority of subjects with unsuspected MS had been diagnosed as having refractory affective illness. Finally, in a comprehensive literature review, Becker and colleagues (1995) have presented data which strongly suggest that subcortical and white matter pathology are observed at increased rates in patients with late life onset depressive and psychotic disorders.

On the basis of existing data, we have recently suggested that structural brain imaging may be most appropriate for subjects with a new onset psychosis, a new onset dementia or delirium, or for subjects with other acute mental status changes in the presence of specific risk factors (i.e., advanced age, history of head trauma, or neurological signs; Rauch and Renshaw, 1995). Additionally, imaging may be valuable in the evaluation of treatment of refractory patients as well as those who are about to undergo an initial course of electroconvulsive therapy. The strongest data which suggest that brain MRI may be useful for the detection of intracranial pathology in patients with psychotic disorders come from large scale autopsy studies of patients who were chronically hospitalized (Patton and Sheppard, 1956; Raskin, 1956). These studies indicate that intracranial neoplasms are approximately 60% more common at death in patients with psychotic disorders (3.7%) than in age matched individuals who die of general medical illness (2.3%). Data from neuroimaging research studies continue to demonstrate that subtle brain pathology is present in a much larger percentage of schizophrenic patients (Chua and McKenna, 1995; Yurgelun-Todd et al., 1996a).

Weytingh and colleagues (1995) have recently reviewed the literature regarding "reversible dementia" and concluded that treatable conditions were likely to be found in only approximately 1% of patients. Although normal pressure hydrocephalus, neoplasm, and subdural hematoma may be detected on brain MRI in patients with dementia, the most common reversible causes of new onset memory loss are depression, medication effects, and metabolic derangements. As with schizophrenia, structural brain imaging studies have consistently demonstrated morphological changes, especially in the temporal lobes, in patients with Alzheimer's disease (Jagust, 1996), although these differences do not appear to be useful for the clinical evaluation of patients.

In clinical practice, preapproval for the use of diagnostic imaging procedures is now commonly required, and decisions on whether to order a scan must often take into account the policies of the third party payer. In the Commonwealth of Massachusetts, the only neuropsychiatric diagnoses for which MRI is a reimbursable procedure under Medicare are psychosis and dementia (Table 5.2).

CT vs. MRI. In general, it is most prudent to proceed directly to an MRI scan. Moreover, in most cases a contrast study should be suggested, although we recommend that this decision be deferred to the radiologist. In the vast majority of settings CT is less expensive than MRI (Table 5.3), although the rates that are charged are typically much higher than the negotiated fees which are actually paid by insurers. At McLean Hospital, for example, overall revenues for performing brain MRI are approximately 60% of billed charges. Moreover, as capitation becomes increasingly common, there may be no additional reimbursement for diagnostic brain imaging. In some areas, CT may also be more widely or readily available than MRI.

However, as noted above, MRI is the higher yield modality. Therefore, CT is often followed by MRI regardless of the CT result, and thus proceeding directly to MRI may

Table 5.2   Reimbursable indications for a brain MRI scan: Commonwealth of Massachusetts, Medicare, January 1996

Neoplasm

Epilepsy

Cerebrovascular disease

Cerebral degeneration

Unspecified psychosis

Skull fracture

Myasthenia gravis

Dementia of unknown etiology

Table 5.3   Total charges for noncontrast brain imaging of an uninsured patient: Greater Boston Area, November 1996

	CT	MRI
Teaching Hospital A	$343	$867
Teaching Hospital B	$539	$1,521
Community Hospital A	$703	$1,700
Freestanding Center A	$600	NA
Freestanding Center B	$402	$975

be more cost efficient. Exceptions occur in the context of acute trauma, when there is a high suspicion of acute bleeding, or when MRI is relatively contraindicated. For each individual case it is most helpful if, in the requisition to radiology, the referring psychiatrist specifies the clinical question(s) to be addressed by the scan. The better the information provided to the radiologist, the better the chances that an optimal study will be performed.

Single Photon Emission Computed Tomography (SPECT)

Basic principles. In clinical practice, SPECT brain imaging is most commonly used to construct images of regional cerebral blood flow. Since metabolic activity and cerebral perfusion are typically tightly coupled, SPECT imaging is regarded as a type of "functional," as opposed to structural, brain imaging. SPECT may also be used for receptor imaging, although this is not routinely available as a clinical technique (Schlosser and Schlegel, 1995; Innis, 1992). As the name suggests, SPECT exploits single photon emitting nuclides, and narrow filters called "collimators" are arranged as entry portals for each photon detector. Thus, only those photons traveling along a specific trajectory reach a given detector. In this way, the site of the photon source is determined geometrically. As a consequence of these mechanics, SPECT provides limited sensitivity and spatial resolution (~6–12 mm), with a gradient whereby spatial resolution is best at the surface of the brain and worse for deep structures.

The tracer xenon-133 is a freely diffusable gas that is introduced via inhalation and used to produce images reflective of cerebral blood flow (Ingvar and Lassen, 1961). Because of the very low energy of photons from ^{133}Xe, deep structures cannot be well characterized in this manner, and images are often displayed as simple two-dimensional projections rather than tomographically.

The tracer 99m-Technetium-HMPAO is introduced via intravenous injection, and is also used to produce images reflective of blood flow (Leonard, Nowotnik, and Neirinck, 1986). With ^{99m}Tc-HMPAO, the tracer redistributes over a matter of a few minutes following injection, and then remains "frozen" in its initial distribution pattern. Because of the long half-life of ^{99m}Tc, the patient can be imaged several hours later, and the brain image will still be reflective of the state at the time of initial tracer redistribution. Other tracers used to image blood flow in conjunction with SPECT include ^{123}I-iodoamphetamine and the new agent Tc-Ethyl cysteinate dimer.

Advantages and limitations. As with other nuclear medicine procedures, SPECT requires the use and safe handling of radioactive substances. Thus, SPECT imaging may not be available at some institutions, and, as image quality is heavily dependent upon the type of scanner used, it may not be possible to obtain high resolution brain images. The radiochemistry of single photon emitters is such that they have long half-lives, and they can be synthesized from commercially available precursors with the tools available in a general radiochemistry lab. Positron emission tomography (PET) is discussed later in this chapter. Although PET remains the gold standard nuclear medical technique for functional imaging, its greater cost and limited availability often make SPECT a more practical option. SPECT is more reasonably priced and more widely accessible than PET. SPECT provides good spatial resolution for superficial brain structures (i.e., cortical convexities), but provides limited resolution for deep structures. Charges for a brain SPECT scan are similar to those for a brain MRI scan (Table 5.4).

Utility in psychiatric populations. Several reviews which highlight the promise of SPECT for the evaluation of individuals with neuropsychiatric impairment have recently been published (Krausz et al., 1996; Weinberger, 1993). Almost certainly, the most progress has been made in the use of SPECT for the evaluation of patients with dementia, where characteristic decreases in temporo-

parietal blood flow are present in the majority of patients with probable Alzheimer's disease (PRAD). Masterman and colleagues (1997) have recently published a critical appraisal of the SPECT perfusion literature, which consists of at least 36 independent studies including approximately 1000 subjects with PRAD, 500 subjects with dementias due to other etiologies, and 250 healthy controls. Overall, the sensitivity and specificity of temporoparietal perfusion deficits for distinguishing patients with PRAD from healthy controls were 83% and 93%, respectively. The sensitivity and specificity of these deficits in distinguishing subjects with PRAD from those with dementia of other etiologies were 77% and 84%, respectively.

Historically, the clinical psychiatrist rarely needs such an expensive test to make this distinction. The early and accurate identification of individuals with PRAD has recently become increasingly important for at least two separate reasons. First, two independent research groups (Small et al., 1995; Reiman et al., 1996) have used positron emission tomography (PET) to demonstrate that cognitively normal older subjects who are homozygous for the apolipoprotein E epsilon 4 allele, and thus at increased risk for the development of PRAD, have reduced temporoparietal glucose metabolism. At the present time, a number of different agents either are in clinical use or are being evaluated for the treatment of PRAD (Aisen and Davis, 1994; Secades and Frontera, 1995; Muller, Mutschler, and Riederer, 1995; Boller, Orgogozo, and Tacrine, 1995). Thus, functional brain imaging may provide a means to identify those individuals with PRAD before they are symptomatic, thereby creating opportunities for early therapeutic intervention.

SPECT also has a clinical role in the evaluation of partial complex seizure disorders, which may be accompanied by a range of affective, cognitive, and behavioral symptoms (Smith et al., 1986). Interictal SPECT studies, in which one expects to see decreased temporal lobe perfusion, have a sensitivity and specificity of 66% and 68%, respectively, when compared with EEG localization (Krausz et al., 1996). More encouraging is the use of ictal SPECT, in which the temporal lobe focus is hyperperfused, and the literature predicts a sensitivity and specificity of 90% and 77%, respectively, compared to EEG localization.

Research Neuroimaging Modalities

Clinical neuroimaging is a rapidly evolving discipline owing to the extraordinary pace of basic and clinical research on new methods and technologies. Two newer magnetic resonance techniques include magnetic resonance spec-

Table 5.4   Total charges for brain SPECT imaging of an uninsured patient: Greater Boston Area, November 1996

	SPECT
Teaching Hospital A	$1,182
Teaching Hospital B	$1,414

troscopy (MRS), which permits the assessment of brain chemistry, and functional magnetic resonance imaging (fMRI), which exploits intrinsic magnetic properties of brain and blood to measure changes in regional cerebral hemodynamics. Positron emission tomography (PET) is an older nuclear imaging method which is not widely available. Some of the benefits and limitations of MRS, fMRI and PET are discussed below.

Magnetic Resonance Spectroscopy (MRS)

Magnetic resonance spectroscopy (MRS) employs standard magnetic resonance imaging devices to make measurements of chemical levels within the brain. MRS-visible compounds which can be measured noninvasively in the human brain include psychotropic medications such as lithium (Renshaw and Wicklund, 1988) and some fluorinated polycyclic drugs (Komoroski et al., 1990; Renshaw et al., 1992) and endogenous cerebral metabolites. Two different MRS-visible nuclei are evaluated in most studies of brain biochemistry: phosphorus (31P) and hydrogen (1H). Phosphorus MR spectra provide information on the concentration of high energy phosphate compounds (e.g., phosphocreatine, adenosine triphosphate, etc.) and phospholipid metabolites (phosphomonoesters and phosphodiesters). Changes in the brain 31P MR spectra of patients with schizophrenia (Pettegrew et al., 1991), bipolar disorder (Kato et al., 1991), and major depression (Moore et al., 1997) have been reported. Proton MR spectra detect signals from N-acetyl aspartate (NAA, a putative neuronal marker), cytosolic, choline containing compounds (Cho), and myo-inositol (Myo-Inos). Decreased levels of NAA have been measured in the temporal lobes of patients with schizophrenia (Yurgelun-Todd et al., 1996b), a state dependent increase in the basal ganglia Cho resonance has been reported in patients with major depression (Renshaw et al., in press), and an increase in the concentration of Myo-Inos has been detected in patients with Alzheimer's disease (Miller et al., 1993).

The potential that MRS studies have for advancing our understanding of mental illness has been the subject of several recent reviews (Dager and Steen, 1992; Maier, 1995; Soares, Krishnan, and Keshavan, 1996). The clinical utility of MRS has not yet been established, but the technical capability to perform studies is now available on most commercial MR scanners. In practice, the major limitation in the use of MRS is the low sensitivity of the technique, which in turn leads to poor spatial resolution (1–10 cm^3 for proton MRS and 25–150 cm^3 for phosphorus MRS) (Dager and Steen, 1992).

Functional Magnetic-Resonance Imaging (fMRI)

Functional brain imaging studies have historically been limited both by the need to use radioactive tracers as well as by poor temporal resolution. Recent developments in the area of magnetic resonance imaging (MRI) may largely surmount these limitations. First, the development of high speed, echo planar imaging (EPI) devices (Stehling, Turner, and Mansfield, 1991) has greatly enhanced the temporal resolution of MRI. With EPI, single image planes can be acquired in 50–100 msec or multiple image planes can be acquired each second. However, fMRI, which may be performed with or without a high speed MR scanner, selectively detects image parameters which are proportional to cerebral blood flow or blood volume. This strategy capitalizes on the fact that, in general, focal changes in neuronal activity are closely coupled to changes in cerebral blood flow (Fox et al., 1986) and blood volume (Fox and Raichle, 1986).

The fMRI studies may be divided into two separate classes: (1) those which make use of endogenous physiological factors to detect changes in cerebral activation, the "noncontrast" techniques (Ogawa et al., 1990; Kwong et al., 1992), and (2) those which require the intravenous administration of a paramagnetic agent, the "contrast" techniques (Belliveau et al., 1990). Noncontrast techniques make use of either T1-weighted pulse sequences to detect changes in blood flow or, more commonly, T2-weighted pulse sequences to detect changes in the local concentration of paramagnetic deoxyhemoglobin. The latter method has been referred to as "blood oxygen–level dependent" imaging (or BOLD). In a BOLD experiment, regional brain activation is associated with changes in both blood flow and blood volume, the magnitude of the former exceeding that of the latter, leading to a washout of paramagnetic deoxyhemoglobin, decreased phase dispersion of surrounding tissue proton molecules, and increased local signal intensity (Ogawa et al., 1993). One major drawback to BOLD studies is low sensitivity; at 1.5 T, the magnitude of the observed signal intensity changes is relatively small. For instance, photic stimulation, which induces a 70% increase in occipital cortical blood flow, produces a 2–4% MR signal intensity increase (Kwong et al., 1992; Hathout et al., 1994). Additionally, recent work suggests that the magnitude of BOLD signal intensity changes may vary with subject age (Ross et al., 1997) and gender (Levin et al., 1996).

The contrast method is a tracer kinetic technique. It utilizes the bolus injection of a paramagnetic contrast agent to produce changes in tissue magnetic susceptibility and MR image intensity (Belliveau et al., 1990). During the first pass of the contrast agent, MR signal intensity may decrease by as much as 20–40%. This method may be used to map the distribution of cerebral volume at rest or to measure changes in response to cerebral activation (Belliveau et al., 1991). Resting CBV maps (Figure 5.2) have been shown to correlate well with PET images of fluorodeoxyglucose uptake (Gonzalez et al., 1995) and with HMPAO SPECT images of cerebral blood flow (Johnson et al., 1995). Levin and colleagues (1995) have developed a multiple bolus method for performing dynamic susceptibility contrast studies which are designed to measure the effects of drugs on cerebral hemodynamics.

The promise that fMRI studies hold for the evaluation of patients with mental illness has recently been reviewed (David, Blamire, and Breiter, 1994; Levin, Ross, and Renshaw, 1995), but the applications of fMRI to clinical populations has been limited to date. BOLD fMRI studies of motor (Schroder et al., 1995; Wenz et al., 1994) and visual stimulation (Renshaw, Yurgelun-Todd, and Cohen, 1994) in schizophrenic subjects have been reported. More recently, Yurgelun-Todd and colleagues (1996c) have used BOLD fMRI to evaluate changes in

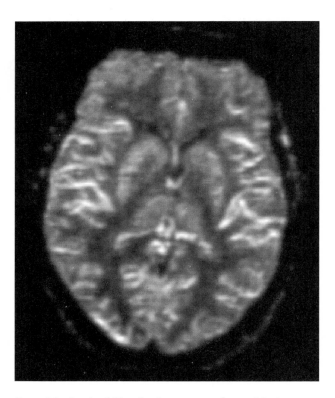

Figure 5.2 Cerebral blood volume map of an axial plane. Note that subcortical structures, such as the basal ganglia and the thalamus, are clearly seen. This degree of spatial resolution, 1.5 mm × 1.5 mm in plane, is not possible using either SPECT or PET imaging. Images were produced as described by Maas and colleagues (1997).

frontal and temporal lobe perfusion during word production in schizophrenic subjects and matched comparison subjects. Patients with obsessive-compulsive disorder have been studied during symptom provocation using BOLD fMRI (Breiter et al., 1996). Dynamic susceptibility contrast MRI has been used by several groups to evaluate changes in regional cerebral perfusion in patients with Alzheimer's disease (Gonzalez et al., 1995; Harris et al., 1996). Based on the data in these early studies, CBV maps appear to provide data equivalent to those obtained by SPECT for establishing a diagnosis of probable Alzheimer's disease. However, data to generate CBV maps are acquired over the course of 1 to 2 minutes and without the use of radiotracers. Thus, susceptibility contrast MRI may be particularly well suited, relative to SPECT, for the evaluation of demented subjects. Susceptibility contrast MRI is also being actively investigated as a tool for the evaluation of patients with a range of neurological disorders, including cerebral ischemia and infarction, cancer, and epilepsy (Levin, Ross, and Renshaw, 1995).

Positron Emission Tomography (PET)

As the name suggests, PET tracers are positron emitters and are radioactive by virtue of having proton rich (or neutron deficient) nuclei. Consequently, they decay by conversion of a proton into a neutron, with release of a "positron" (essentially a positively charged particle of approximately electron-like size and mass). This released positron has positive charge, high energy, and low mass. It travels a short distance (~1–2 mm) until it encounters an electron. Upon collision with an electron, annihilation occurs, resulting in the release of two photons of light/energy which are emitted in opposite directions (180° apart). It is this factor of dual photon emission that is critical to the high resolution of PET (4–8 mm).

The nuclide oxygen-15 (injected as ^{15}O-water, ^{15}O-butanol, or inhaled as ^{15}O-carbon dioxide) is used to produce images of regional cerebral blood flow. Since these oxygen-containing compounds diffuse freely within the blood, regional concentrations of ^{15}O reflect the magnitude of blood flow to each area over the initial uptake and equilibration period (≤90 seconds). Since blood flow is tightly coupled to neuronal activity, these images serve as an index of gross neuronal activation. Each scan takes only 1–2 minutes. Moreover, because of its short half-life (~2 minutes), only a 10-minute washout (5 x half-life) is necessary to return to background counts post-scan. Therefore, up to 12 serial scans can be performed in a ~1–2 hour scanning session. This technique is well suited to studying state-dependent brain characteristics, since patients can be scanned several times in each of several different conditions. Currently this technique is widely used in research, since patients can be scanned multiple times while performing different cognitive tasks (e.g., Roland, 1993). In such paradigms, by subtracting one data set from another (i.e., test condition minus control condition), statistical or difference images can be produced that provide information about the spatial distribution of brain systems that mediate specific brain functions (Kosslyn et al., 1993) or states (Rauch et al., 1994).

The tracer ^{18}F-fluoro-deoxy-glucose (FDG) (injected intravenously) is used to produce images of cerebral glucose metabolism (Reivich et al., 1977). FDG is taken up by neurons via the same active transport system as glucose. Glucose or FDG uptake is proportional to the metabolic demands of the cell. Once in the neuron, FDG initially proceeds along the same metabolic pathway as glucose. Unlike glucose, however, FDG cannot proceed beyond a certain point in this pathway, and becomes stranded within the cell (primarily within the neuropil), wherein it serves as a marker of metabolic activity. Since glucose metabolism is likewise tightly coupled with neuronal activity, this is an alternative marker of gross neuronal activation. In the case of FDG, the agent is injected prior to the patient entering the scanner. Uptake proceeds for 20–40 minutes and then scanning is performed. Although scanning protocols vary, a single FDG scan typically requires approximately 1 hour in the scanner. The result is a high signal to noise image that reflects the integrated neuronal activation over the ~40 minute FDG uptake period. Therefore, this technique is well suited for producing high quality images characterizing states that last ≥20 minutes (i.e., enduring states or traits). When available, PET-FDG represents the gold standard functional imaging technique for the evaluation of seizures or brain tumors.

PET receptor characterization studies represent a more complex analog to receptor binding studies that are routinely performed in vitro (Tamminga et al., 1993). High affinity receptor ligands labeled with a variety of nuclides (usually carbon-11 or fluoride-18) are used as tracers. They redistribute within the brain based upon the regional density of and affinity to the relevant receptor population. A wide variety of ligands have been effectively radiolabeled for use in PET and are available for the study of monoaminergic as well as other receptor systems. In particular, there is an emerging capability for the multifaceted characterization of dopaminergic systems, including D1 and D2 receptors as well as dopamine reuptake sites (Tamminga et al., 1993). Already, investigators have used this approach to study dopamine receptor density in schizophrenia (Farde et al., 1992; Wong et al.,

1986) and movement disorders (Wong et al., 1989). Although these techniques currently serve only as research tools, clinical applications may be established in the near future. Receptor neuroimaging studies may be used to demonstrate receptor characteristics associated with neuropsychiatric disease vs. non-disease states and therefore aid in diagnosis, predict treatment response, quantify receptor occupation by psychotropic medications, and aid in the development of new medications with sought-after receptor binding profiles.

Only PET can be used to produce images reflective of glucose metabolism. There is tremendous flexibility in the range of tracers which can be used in conjunction with PET because of the chemical characteristics of positron emitters. This is a critical issue in developing tracers for receptor characterization studies. Positron emitters must be generated, however, via a cyclotron. Cyclotrons are highly expensive to purchase and to maintain. Moreover, since positron emitters used in PET are short-lived, the cyclotron must be onsite or very nearby the PET scanner. These factors explain the relative scarcity of PET centers (<100 in the U.S.), and contribute to the high cost of PET scanning.

In sum, neuroimaging technology provides a powerful, relatively noninvasive means for assessing brain structure and function. The vast majority of patients tolerate these studies well. CT and MRI are useful for assessing brain structure, thereby allowing the clinician to rule in or rule out a variety of general medical conditions known to cause abnormal mental status. MRI represents the gold standard modality with few exceptions; CT is the modality of choice for assessing trauma or suspected hemorrhage when acute (<48 hrs). SPECT images that reflect cerebral blood flow may be produced on a routine basis, whereas PET, a more expensive modality, can provide images of glucose metabolism as well. In contemporary psychiatry, the clinical utility of functional brain imaging with SPECT or PET is limited to an adjunctive role in the assessment of dementia and seizure disorders. MRS and fMRI, as well as PET and SPECT, are imaging modalities that offer great promise as tools for research and clinical application in the future.

References

Aisen, P. S., and Davis, K. L. 1994. "Inflammatory mechanisms in Alzheimer's disease: Implications for therapy." *American Journal of Psychiatry* 151:1105–1113.

American Board of Psychiatry and Neurology. 1996. *Information for Applicants.*

American Council for Graduate Medical Education. 1996.

Program Requirements for Residency Education in Psychiatry.

Andreasen, N. C., ed. 1989. *Brain imaging: applications in psychiatry.* Washington, D.C.: American Psychiatric Press.

Battaglia, J., and Spector, I. C. 1988. Utility of the CAT scan in a first psychotic episode. *Gen. Hosp. Psych.* 10:398–401.

Becker, T., Retz, W., Hofmann, E., Becker, G., Teichmann, E., Gsell, W. 1995. Some methodological issues in neuroradiological research in psychiatry. *J. Neural Trans.* 99:7–54.

Belliveau, J. W., Rosen, B. R., Kantor, H. L., Rzedzian, R. R., Kennedy, D. N., McKinstry, R. C., Vevea, J. M., Cohen, M. S., Pykett, I. L., Brady, T. J. 1990. Functional cerebral imaging by susceptibility contrast imaging. *Magn. Reson. Med.* 14:538–546.

Belliveau, J. W., Kennedy, D., McKinstry, R. C., Buchbinder, B. R., Weisskoff, R. M., Veve, M. S., Brady, T. J., Rosen, B. R. 1991. Functional mapping of the human visual cortex by magnetic resonance imaging. *Science* 254:716–719.

Beresford, T. P., Blow, F. C., Hall, R. C. W., Nichols, L. O., Langston, J. W. 1986. CT scanning in psychiatric inpatients: clinical yield. *Psychosomatics* 27:105–112.

Boller, F., Orgogozo, J. M. 1995. Tacrine. Alzheimer's disease and the cholinergic theory: a critical review. *Neurologia* 10:194–199.

Bracewell, R. N. 1956. Strip integration in radio astronomy. *Australian J. Physics* 9:188–217.

Bradley, W. G., Yuh, W. T. C., Bydder, G. M. 1993. Use of M. R. imaging contrast agents in the brain. *JMRI* 3:199–218.

Breiter, H. C., Rauch, S. L., Kwong, K. K., Baker, J. R., Weisskoff, R. M., Kennedy, D. N., Kendrick, A. D., Davis, T. L., Jiang, A., Cohen, M. S., Stern, C. E., Belliveau, J. W., Baer, L., O'Sullivan, R. L., Savage, C. R., Jenike, M. A., Rosen, B. R. 1996. Functional magnetic resonance imaging of symptom provocation in obsessive-compulsive disorder. *Archives of General Psychiatry* 53:595–606.

Chandler, J., and Patten, J. 1989. Head C. T. in new geriatric psychiatry patients: a prospective study. *J. Geriatric Psych. and Neurol.* 2:101–105.

Chua, S. E., and McKenna, P. J. 1995. Schizophrenia—a brain disease? A critical review of the structural and functional cerebral abnormality in the disorder. *Br. J. Psychiatry* 166:563–582.

Coffman, J. A. 1989. *Computed tomography in psychiatry, in brain imaging: applications in psychiatry,* ed. N. Andreason. Washington, D.C.: APA Press.

Colohan, H., O'Callaghan, E. O., Larkin, C., Waddington, J. L. 1989. An evaluation of cranial C. T. scanning in clinical psychiatry. *Irish J. Med. Sci.* 7:178–181.

Dager, S. R., and Steen, R. G. 1992. Applications of magnetic resonance spectroscopy to the investigation of neuropsychiatric disorders. *Neuropsychopharmacology* 6:249–266.

David, A., Blamire, A., and Breiter, H. 1994. Functional magnetic resonance imaging: a new technique with implications for psychology and psychiatry. *Br. J. Psychiatry* 164:2–7.

DeRosier, D. J., and Klug, A. 1968. Reconstruction of three-dimensional structures from electron micrographs. *Nature* 217:130–134.

Emsley, R. A., Stander, D., Bell, P. S. H., Gledhill, R. F. 1986. Computed tomography in psychiatric patients. *S. Afr. Med. J.* 70:212–214.

Evans, N. J. R. 1982. Cranial computerized tomography in clinical psychiatry: 100 consecutive cases. *Comprehensive Psych.* 23:445–450.

Farde, L., Wiesel, F. A., Halldin, C., et al. 1988. Central D2-dopamine receptor occupancy in schizophrenic patients treated with antipsychotic drugs. *Arch. Gen. Psychiatry* 45:71–76.

Farde, L., Norstrom, A. L., Weisel, F. A., et al. 1992. Positron emission tomographic analysis of central D1 and D2 dopamine receptor occupancy in patients treated with classic neuroleptics and clozapine: relation to extrapyramidal side effects. *Arch. Gen. Psychiatry* 49:538–544.

Fox, P. T., and Raichle, M. E. 1986. Focal physiological uncoupling of cerebral blood flow and oxidative metabolism during somatosensory stimulation in human subjects. *Proc. Natl. Acad. Sci. USA* 83:1140–44.

Fox, P. T., Mintun, M. A., Raichle, M. E., Miezin, F. M., Allman, J. M., Van Essen, D. C. 1986. Mapping human visual cortex with positron emission tomography. *Nature* 323:806–809.

Gibby, W. A., and Zimmerman, R. A. 1992. X-ray computed tomography. In *Clinical brain imaging: principles and applications,* ed. J. C. Mazziotta and S. Gilman. Philadelphia: F.A. Davis. 2–38.

Gonzalez, R. G., Fischman, A. J., Guimaraes, A. R., Carr, C. A., Stern, C. E., Halpern, E. F., Growdon, J. H., Rosen, B. R. 1995. Functional M. R. in the evaluation of dementia: correlation of abnormal dynamic cerebral blood volume measurements with changes in cerebral metabolism on positron emission tomography with fludeoxyglucose F18. *AJNR* 16:1763–70.

Greenberg, S. B., Faerber, E. N., Aspinall, C. L., Adams, R. C. 1993. High dose chloral hydrate sedation for children undergoing M. R. imaging: safety and efficacy in relation to age. *AJR* 161:639–641.

Harris, G. J., Lewis, R. F., Satlin, A., English, C. D., Scott, T. M., Yurgelun-Todd, D. A., Renshaw, P. F. 1996. Dynamic susceptibility contrast MRI of regional cerebral blood volume in Alzheimer's disease. *Am. J. Psychiatry* 153:721–724.

Hathout, G. M., Kirlew, K. A. T., So, G. J. K., Hamilton, D. R., Zhang, J. X., Sinha, U., Sinha, S., Sayre, J., Gozal, D., Harper, R. M., Lufkin, R. B. 1994. MR imaging signal response to sustained stimulation in human visual cortex. *JMRI* 4:537–543.

Hayman, L. A., Evans, R. A., Fahr, L. M., Hinck, V. C. 1980. Renal consequences of rapid high dose contrast CT. *AJR* 134:553–555.

Hollister, L. E., and Shah, N. N. 1996. Structural brain scanning in psychiatric patients: a further look. *J. Clinical Psychiatry* 57:241–244.

Holt, R. E., Rawat, S., Beresford, T. P., Hall, R. C. W. 1982. Computed tomography of the brain and the psychiatric consultation. *Psychosomatics* 23:1007–19.

Ingvar, D. H., and Lassen, N. A. 1961. Quantitative determination of regional cerebral blood flow in man. *Lancet* 2:806–807.

Innis, R. B. 1992. Neuroreceptor imaging with SPECT. *J. Clin. Psychiatry* 53(11, suppl.):29–34.

Jagust, W. J. 1996. Functional imaging patterns in Alzheimer's disease: relationships to neurobiology. *Annals N.Y. Acad. Sci.* 777:30–36.

Johnson, K. A., Renshaw, P. F., Becker, J. A., Satlin, A., Holman, B. L. 1995. Comparison of functional MRI and SPECT in Alzheimer's Disease. *Neurology* (suppl.) 45:874S.

Kanal, E., and Shellock, F. G. 1994. The value of published data on M. R. compatibility of metallic implants and devices. *AJNR* 15:1394–1396.

Kato, T., Shiori, T., Takahashi, S., et al. 1991. Measurement of brain phosphoinositide metabolism in bipolar patients using in vivo 31P MRS. *J. Aff. Disorders* 22:185–190.

Klein, D. S. 1991. Prevention of claustrophobia induced by M. R. imaging: use of alprazolam. *AJR* 156:633.

Komoroski, R. A., Newton, J. E. O., Karson, C., Cardwell, D., Sprigg, J. 1990. Detection of psychoactive drugs in vivo in humans using 19F NMR spectroscopy. *Biol. Psychiatry* 29:711–714.

Kosslyn, S. M., Alpert, N. M., Thompson, W. L., Maljkovic, V., Weise, S. B., Chabris, C. F., Hamilton, S. E., Rauch, S. L., Buonanno, F. S. 1993. Visual mental imagery activates topographically organized visual cortex: PET investigations. *J. Cogn. Neurosci.* 5:263–287.

Krausz, Y., Bonne, O., Marciano, R., Yaffe, S., Lerer, B., Chisin, R. 1996. Brain SPECT imaging of neuropsychiatric disorders. *European Journal of Radiology* 21:183–187.

Krishnan, K. R. R., and Doraiswamy, P. M., eds. In press. *Brain imaging in clinical psychiatry*. New York: Marcel Dekker.

Kuhl, D. E., and Edwards, R. Q. 1963. Image separation isotope scanning. *Radiology* 80:653–661.

Kwong, K. K., Belliveau, J. W., Chesler, D. A., Goldberg, I. E., Weisskoff, R. M., Poncelet, B. P., Kennedy, D. N., Hoppel, B. E., Cohen, M. S., Turner, R., Cheng, H. M., Brady, T. J., Rosen, B. R. 1992. Dynamic magnetic resonance imaging of human brain activity during primary sensory stimulation. *Proc. Natl. Acad. Sci. USA* 89:5675–79.

Larson, E. B., Mack, L. A., Watts, B., Cromwell, L. D. 1981. Computed tomography in patients with psychiatric illnesses advantage of a "rule-in" approach. *Ann. Int. Med.* 95:360–364.

Leonard, J.-P., Nowotnik, D. P., and Neirinck, R. D. 1986. Technetium-99m-d,1-HM-PAO: a new radiopharmaceutical for imaging regional brain perfusion using SPECT: a comparison with iodine-123 HIPDM. *J. Nuc. Med.* 27:1819–23.

Levin, J. M., Ross, M. H., and Renshaw, P. F. 1995. Clinical applications of functional MRI in neuropsychiatry. *J. Neuropsychiatry and Clinical Neurosci.* 7:511–522.

Levin, J. M., Kaufman, M. J., Ross, M. H., Mendelson, J. H., Maas, L. C., Cohen, B. M., Renshaw, P. F. 1995. Sequential dynamic susceptibility contrast M. R. experiments in human brain: residual contrast agent effect, steady state, and hemodynamic perturbation. *Magnetic Resonance in Medicine* 34:655–663.

Levin, J. M., Ross, M. H., Mendelson, J. H., Mello, N. K., Cohen, B.M., Renshaw, P. F. 1996. Gender differences in BOLD response to photic stimulation. In *Proceedings of the 4th Annual Meeting of the International Society for Magnetic Resonance in Medicine*, New York. 278.

Lyoo, I. K., Seol, H. Y., Byun, H. S., Renshaw, P. F. 1996. Unsuspected multiple sclerosis in patients with psychiatric disorders: a magnetic resonance imaging study. *J. Neuropsychiatry and Clinical Neurosci.* 8:54–59.

Maas, L. C., Harris, G. J., Satlin, A., English, C. D., Lewis, R. F., Renshaw, P. F. 1997. Regional cerebral blood volume measured by dynamic susceptibility contrast MRI in Alzheimer's disease: a principal components analysis. *JMRI* 7:215–219.

Magin, R. L., Liburdy, R. P., and Persson, B. 1992. Biological effects and safety aspects of nuclear magnetic resonance imaging and spectroscopy. *Annals of the New York Academy of Sciences* 649.

Maier, M. In vivo magnetic resonance spectroscopy: Applications in psychiatry. *Br. J. Psychiatry* 167:299–306.

Masterman, D. L., Mendez, M. F., and Cummings, J. L. 1997. Sensitivity, specificity, and positive predictive value of Tc99m-HMPAO SPECT in discriminating Alzheimer's disease from other dementias. *J. Geriatric Psychiatry and Neurology* 10:15–21.

McClellan, R. L., Eisenberg, R. L., and Giyananni, V. L. 1988. Routine C. T. screening of psychiatry inpatients. *Radiology* 169:99–100.

Melendez, C., and McCrank, E. 1993. Anxiety-related reactions associated with magnetic resonance imaging examinations. *JAMA* 270:745–747.

Miller, B. L., Moats, R. A., Shonk, T., Ernst, T., Woolley, S., Ross, B. D. 1993. Alzheimer disease: depiction of increased cerebral myo-inositol with proton M. R. spectroscopy. *Radiology* 187:433–437.

Moore, C. M., Christensen, J. D., Lafer, B., Fava, M., Renshaw, P. F. 1997. Decreased adenosine triphosphate in the basal ganglia of depressed subjects: a phosphorous-31 magnetic resonance spectroscopy study. *American Journal of Psychiatry* 154:116–118.

Muller, W. E., Mutschler, E., and Riederer, P. 1995. Noncompetitive NMDA receptor antagonists with fast open-channel blocking kinetics and strong voltage-dependency as potential therapeutic agents for Alzheimer's dementia. *Pharmacopsychiatry* 28:113–124.

Ogawa, S., Lee, T. M., Kay, A. R., Tank, D. W. 1990. Brain magnetic resonance imaging with contrast dependent on blood oxygenation. *Proc. Natl. Acad. Sci. USA* 87:9868–72.

Ogawa, S., Menon, R. S., Tank, D. W., Kim, S. G., Merkle, H., Ellerman, J. M., Ugurbil, K. 1993. Functional brain mapping by blood oxygenation level-dependent contrast magnetic resonance imaging. *Biophys. J.* 6:803–812.

Osborn, A. G. 1994. *Diagnostic neuroradiology.* St. Louis: Mosby Year Book.

Owens, D., Johnstone, E. C., Bydder, G. M., Kreel, L. 1980. Unsuspected organic disease in chronic schizophrenia as demonstrated by computed tomography. *J. Neurol. Neurosurg. Psychiatr.* 43:1065–69.

Patton, R. B., and Sheppard, J. A. 1956. Intracranial tumors at autopsy in mental patients. *Am. J. Psych.* 113:319–324.

Pettegrew, J. W., Keshavan, M. S., Panchalingham, K., Strychor, S., Kaplan, D. B., Tretta, M. G., Allen, M. 1991. Alterations in brain high energy phosphate metabolism in first episode, drug naive schizophrenics. *Arch. Gen. Psychiatry* 48:563–568.

Raskin, N. 1956. Intracranial neoplasms in psychotic patients: survey of 2430 consecutive complete autopsies performed at Boston State Hospital during the period 1930–1950. *Am. J. Psych.* 113:461–484.

Rauch, S. L., and Renshaw, P. F. 1995. Clinical neuroimaging in psychiatry. *Harvard Review of Psychiatry* 2:297–312.

Rauch, S. L., Jenike, M. A., Alpert, N. M., Baer, L., Breiter, H. C. R., Savage, C. R., Fischman, A. J. 1994. Regional cerebral blood flow measured during symptom provocation in obsessive-compulsive disorder using oxygen-15 labeled carbon dioxide and positron emission tomography. *Arch. Gen. Psych.* 51:62–70.

Reiman, E. M., Caselli, R. J., Yun, L. S., Chen, K., Bandy, D., Minoshima, S., Thibodeau, S. M., Osborne, D. 1996. Preclinical evidence of Alzheimer's disease in persons homozygous for the epsilon 4 allele for apolipoprotein E. *New England Journal of Medicine* 334:752–758.

Reivich, M., Kuhl, D., Wolf, A., et al. 1997. Measurement of local cerebral glucose metabolism in man with 18-F-2 fluoro-2-deoxy-D-glucose. *Acta Neurol. Scand.* 56(64, suppl):190–191.

Renshaw, P. F., and Wicklund, S. 1988. In vivo measurement of lithium in humans by nuclear magnetic resonance spectroscopy. *Biol. Psychiatry* 23:465–475.

Renshaw, P. F., Yurgelun-Todd, D. A., and Cohen, B. M. 1994. Increased hemodynamic response to photic stimulation in schizophrenic patients: an echo planar MRI study. *Am. J. Psychiatry* 151:1493–95.

Renshaw, P. F., Guimaraes, A. R., Fava, M., Rosenbaum, J. F., Pearlman, J. D., Flood, J. G., Puopolo, P. R., Clancy, K., Gonzalez, R. G. 1992. Accumulation of fluoxetine and norfluoxetine in human brain during therapeutic administration. *Am. J. Psychiatry* 149:1592–94.

Renshaw, P. F., Lafer, B., Babb, S. M., Fava, M., Stoll, A. L., Christensen, J. D., Moore, C. M., Yurgelun-Todd, D. A., Bonello, C. M., Pillay, S. S., Rothschild, A. J., Nierenberg, A. A., Rosenbaum, J. F., Cohen, B. M. In press. Basal ganglia choline levels in depression and response to fluoxetine treatment: an in vivo proton magnetic resonance spectroscopy study. *Biological Psychiatry.*

Roland, P. E. 1993. *Brain Activation.* New York: Wiley-Liss.

Ross, M. H., Yurgelun-Todd, D. A., Renshaw, P. F., Maas, L. C., Mendelson, J. H., Mello, N. K., Cohen, B. M., Levin, J. M. 1997. Age-related reduction in functional MRI response to photic stimulation. *Neurology* 48:173–176.

Schlosser, R., and Schlegel, S. 1995. D2-receptor imaging with [123I] IBZM and single photon emission tomography in psychiatry: a survey of current status. *J. Neural Transmission* 99:173–185.

Schroder, J., Wenz, F., Schad, L. R., Baudendistel, K., Knopp, M. V. 1995. Sensorimotor cortex and supplementary motor area changes in schizophrenia: a study with functional magnetic resonance imaging. *British Journal of Psychiatry* 167(2):197–201.

Secades, J. J., and Frontera, G. 1995. CDP-choline: pharmacological and clinical review. *Methods and findings in experimental and clinical pharmacology* 17 (suppl. B):2–54.

Shehadi, W. H. 1982. Contrast media adverse reactions: occurrence, recurrence, and distribution patterns. *Radiology* 143:11–17.

Small, G. W., Mazziotta, J. C., Collins, M. T., Baxter, L. R., Phelps, M. E., Mandelkern, M. A., Kaplan, A., La Rue, A., Adamson, C. F., Chang, L. 1995. Apolipoprotein E type 4 allele and cerebral glucose metabolism in relatives at risk for familial Alzheimer disease. *JAMA* 273:942–947.

Smith, D. B., Craft, B. R., Collins, J., Mattson, R. H., Cramer, J. A. 1986. Behavioral characteristics of epilepsy patients compared with normal controls. Results from V. A. cooperative study #118. *Epilepsia* 27:760–768.

Soares, J. C., Krishnan, K. R. R., and Keshavan, M. 1996. Nuclear magnetic resonance spectroscopy: new insights into the pathophysiology of mood disorders. *Depression* 4:14–30.

Stehling, M. K., Turner, R., and Mansfield, P. 1991. Echoplanar imaging: magnetic resonance imaging in a fraction of a second. *Science* 254:43–49.

Tamminga, C. A., Dannals, R. F., Frost, J. J., Wong, D. F., Wagner, H. N. 1993. Neuroreceptor and neurochemistry studies with positron emission tomography in psychiatric illness: promise and progress. In *Review of Psychiatry*, ed. J. M. Oldham, M. B. Riba, and A. Tasman. Washington, D.C.: American Psychiatric Press. 487–510.

Tsai, L., and Tsuang, M. T. 1978. Computerized tomography and skull x-rays: relative efficacy in detecting intracranial disease. *Am. J. Psych.* 135:1556–57.

——— 1981. How can we avoid unnecessary C. T. scanning for psychiatric patients? *J. Clin. Psychiatry* 42:453–454.

Wahlund, L. O., Agartz, I., Saaf, J., Wetterberg, L., Marions, O. 1992. MRI in psychiatry: 731 cases. *Psychiatry Research: Neuroimaging* 45:139–140.

Wald, L. L., Carvahal, L., Moyher, S. E., et al. 1995. Phased array detectors and an automated intensity correction algorithm for high resolution imaging of the human brain. *Magn. Reson. Med.* 34:433–439.

Weinberger, D. R. 1984. Brain disease and psychiatric illness: When should a psychiatrist order a CAT scan? *Am. J. Psych.* 141:1521–1527.

——— 1993. SPECT imaging in psychiatry: introduction and overview. *J. Clin Psychiatry* 54 (suppl.):3–5.

Wenz, F., Schad, L. R., Knopp, M. V., Baudendistel, K. T., Flomer, F., Schroder, J., van Kaick, G. 1994. Functional magnetic resonance imaging at 1.5 T: activation pattern in schizophrenic patients receiving neuroleptic medication. *Magnetic Resonance Imaging* 12(7):975–82.

Weytingh, M. D., Bossuyt, P. M., van Crevel, H. 1995. Reversible dementia: more than 10% or less than 1%? A quantitative review. *J. Neurol.* 242:466–471.

White, R. I., and Halden, W. J. 1986. Liquid gold: low-osmolality contrast media. *Radiology* 159:559–560.

Witten, D. M., Hirsch, R. D., and Hartman, G. W. 1973. Acute reactions to urographic contrast medium: incidence, clinical characteristics, and relationship to history of hypersensitivity states. *AJR* 119:832–840.

Wong, D. F., Wagner, H. N., Tobe, L. E., et al. 1986. Positron emission tomography reveals elevated D2 dopamine receptors in drug-naive schizophrenics. *Science* 234:1558–63.

Wong, D., Pearlson, G., Young, L., Singer, H., Villemagne, V., Tune, L. 1989. D2 dopamine receptors are elevated in neuropsychiatric disorders other than schizophrenia. *J. Cereb. Blood Flow Metab.* 9(suppl. 1):S593.

Woods, B. T., Brennan, S., Yurgelun-Todd, D. A., Young, T., Panzarino, P. 1995. MRI abnormalities in major psychiatric disorders: an exploratory comparative study. *J. Neuropsychiatry and Clinical Neurosciences* 7:49–53.

Yurgelun-Todd, D. A., Kinney, D. K., Sherwood, A. R., Renshaw, P. F. 1996a. Magnetic resonance in schizophrenia. *Seminars in Clinical Neuropsychiatry* 1:4–19.

Yurgelun-Todd, D. A., Renshaw, P. F., Gruber, S. A., Waternaux, C., Cohen, B. M. 1996b. Proton magnetic resonance spectroscopy of the temporal lobes in schizophrenics and normal controls. *Schizophrenia Research* 19:55–59.

Yurgelun-Todd, D. A., Waternaux, C. M., Cohen, B. M., Gruber, S. A., English, C. D., Renshaw, P. F. 1996c. Functional magnetic resonance imaging of schizophrenic patients and comparison subjects during word production. *American Journal of Psychiatry* 153:200–205.

Zweiman, R., Mishkin, M. M., and Hildreth, E. A. 1975. An approach to the performance of contrast studies in contrast material-reactive persons. *Ann. Intern. Med.* 83:159–162.

Recommended Reading

Andreasen, N. C., ed., *Brain imaging: Applications in psychiatry.* Washington, D.C.: American Psychiatric Press, 1989.

Krishnan, K. R. R., and Doraiswamy, P. M., eds. 1997. *Brain imaging in clinical psychiatry.* New York: Marcel Dekker.

Seminars in Clinical Neuropsychiatry, vol. 1, no. 1, 1996.

Acknowledgments

Portions of this manuscript are based on a review published by the authors in the *Harvard Review of Psychiatry* 2 (1995):297–312. The authors wish to thank Dr. Lawrence Wald for providing the high-resolution brain MRI in Figure 5.1 and Luis Maas S.M. for providing the map of cerebral blood volume in Figure 5.2.

Dr. Rauch is supported in part by grant MH01215 from the National Institute of Mental Health, Bethesda, and a Young Investigator Award from the National Alliance for Research on Schizophrenia and Depression, Chicago. Dr. Renshaw was supported in part by grants from the National Institute on Drug Abuse (DA09448), the Stanley Foundation, and a Young Investigator Award from the National Alliance for Research on Schizophrenia and Depression.

PART TWO

Brain and Behavior

M.-MARSEL MESULAM

Neural Substrates of Behavior: The Effects of Focal Brain Lesions upon Mental State

The clinical syndromes associated with focal brain lesions provide important insights into the biological substrates of mental function. The behavioral features and pathophysiological mechanisms of these syndromes have already become the focus of extensive monographs. The purpose of this chapter is to provide a highly selective introduction to this subject and to explore its relevance to differential diagnosis in psychiatry.

Brain Organization and Large-Scale Networks

The central nervous system is engaged in 3 major operations: (1) reception of sensory stimuli from outside and from within *(input)*; (2) execution of motor acts *(output)*; and (3) *intermediary processing* interposed between input and output. Thought, language, memory, self-awareness, and even many aspects of mood and affect constitute different manifestations of intermediary processing. The neural substrates for these intermediary processes are located principally within the limbic system and cortical association areas. From a behavioral point of view, therefore, the cerebral hemispheres can be divided into 4 major components: primary sensory cortex, primary motor cortex, association cortex, and the limbic system (Figure 6.1; Table 6.1). It is the latter 2 components, those associated with intermediary processing, that are most relevant to the substance of this chapter. Of these, the limbic component is involved predominantly in the modulation of mood, motivation, and memory, whereas the association component is involved predominantly in perceptual elaboration and motor planning.

The hypothalamus is the head ganglion of the internal milieu and the chief repository of neural programs for instincts and drives. Among the structures listed in Table 6.1, only limbic regions have substantial monosynaptic interconnections with the hypothalamus. The limbic system is therefore polarized toward the internal environment and its requirements. In contrast, the primary sensory and motor areas are polarized toward the outside world: the sensory areas provide portals for the entry of information about extrapersonal events, and the motor areas coordinate the movements through which the environment is manipulated. Hypothalamic nuclei have very few direct connections with primary sensory and motor cortical areas. This arrangement ensures that motor proficiency and perceptual accuracy are not unduly influenced by sudden shifts in the emotional state of the individual. Communications between the sensorimotor apparatus and the hypothalamus occur through obligatory relays within limbic and association cortex. The limbic and association regions therefore provide neural bridges that mediate between the inner urges of the individual and the contingencies of the extrapersonal environment (Mesulam, 1985).

Intermediary processing increases the flexibility of behavior so that drives can be satisfied according to the limitations and opportunities that exist within the extrapersonal world. Animals comparatively lower in the phylogenetic scale have relatively underdeveloped association cortex and display remarkable behavioral rigidity. In these animals specific stimuli can automatically trigger predetermined responses that are described as instinctive. For example, a turkey hen with a newly hatched brood will attack every moving object that does not utter the specific "peep" of its chicks. If a turkey hen is made deaf, it will proceed to kill its own progeny (Schleidt and Schleidt, 1960). The behavioral repertoire of higher species, especially humans, is characterized by greater flexibility. The neural substrate for much of this flexibility is provided by the interposition of limbic and association areas between stimuli and responses, between hypothalamic urges and external reality. These intermediary areas of the brain act like *and* gates and *or* gates in a programming board. Hence identical stimuli can trigger vastly different responses depending on situational context, past experience, and present needs. It is the phylo-

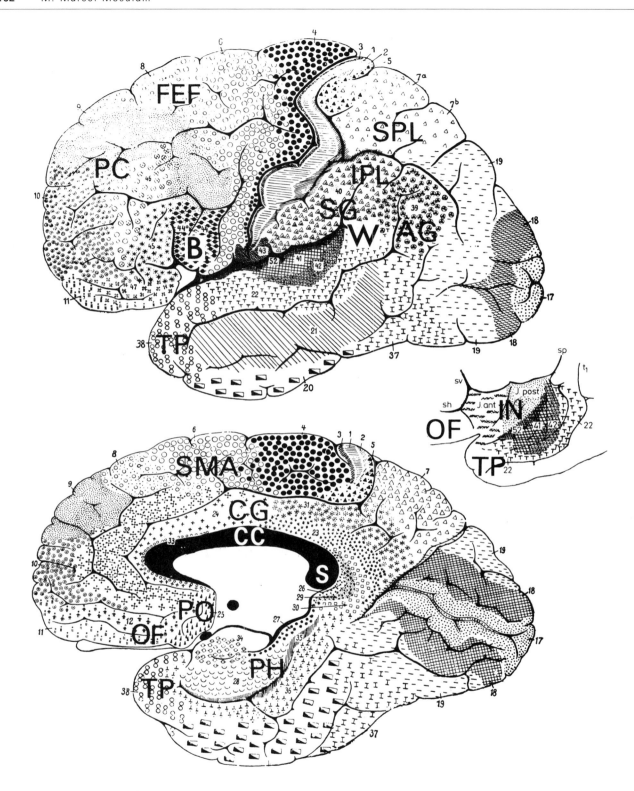

Figure 6.1 Brodmann's (1914) map of the human brain. Abbreviations: *AG*, angular gyrus; *B*, Broca's area; *CC*, corpus callosum; *CG*, cingulate gyrus; *FEF*, frontal eye fields; *IN*, insula; *IPL*, inferior parietal lobule; *OF*, orbitofrontal region; *PC*, prefrontal cortex; *PO*, parolfactory region; *S*, splenium; *SG*, supramarginal gyrus; *SMA*, supplementary motor area; *SPL*, superior parietal lobule; *TP*, temporopolar region; *W*, Wernicke's area.

genetic development of this intermediary processing that is responsible for choice among options, flexible shifts away from unsuccessful responses, adaptation to new situations, delay of premature gratification, and even for self-awareness, thought, and play behavior. As in so many other areas of biology, however, advantages rarely come without special vulnerabilities. In this case intermediary processing could be said to bring with it the susceptibility for apprehension, doubt, rumination, and excessive inhibition. Some of these more speculative aspects of brain-behavior interactions are not yet accessible to direct analysis by the neurological approach. But the examination of patients with lesions in limbic and association areas has provided substantial insights into the neural substrates of many other behavioral and cognitive realms.

The relationships between mental function and brain structure are complex. There are no dedicated centers for memory, emotion or language. According to current thinking, cognitive and behavioral functions (domains) are coordinated by intersecting large-scale networks which contain interconnected cortical and subcortical components. The network approach to higher cortical function has at least four implications of clinical relevance: (1) a single domain such as language or memory can be disrupted by damage to any one of several areas, as long as these areas belong to the same network; (2) dam-age confined to a single area can give rise to multiple deficits, involving the functions of all networks that intersect in that region; (3) damage to a network component may give rise to minimal or transient deficits in the relevant domain if other parts of the network undergo compensatory reorganization; and (4) individual anatomical sites within a network display a relative (but not absolute) specialization for different behavioral aspects of the relevant function. Five anatomically defined large-scale networks are most relevant to clinical practice: a perisylvian network for language; a parieto-frontal network for spatial orientation; an occipito-temporal network for object recognition; a limbic network for memory, emotion, and motivation; and a prefrontal network for attention and comportment.

The Limbic Network

The term *limbic system* is used to designate a heterogeneous set of structures in the brain stem, diencephalon, striatum, basal forebrain, and cortex (Table 6.1; Figures 6.1 and 6.2). Four major reasons can be identified for lumping these structures into a single network: (1) The components that make up the limbic system are tightly interconnected through monosynaptic pathways (Figure 6.2). In the 1930s Papez pointed out that the relatively few

Table 6.1 Some behavioral subdivisions of the cerebral cortex

Primary sensory cortex
    Visual (area 17 in Figure 6.1)
    Auditory (areas 41, 42)
    Somatosensory (areas 3, 1, 2, but mostly area 3b)

Primary motor cortex
Area 4 and caudal part of area 6

Association cortex
    Unimodal motor (rostral area 6, caudal area 8, area 44)
    Unimodal visual (areas 18, 19, 20, 21, 37)
    Unimodal auditory (area 22)
    Unimodal somatosensory (area 5, rostral area 7)
    Heteromodal prefrontal (areas 9, 10, 11, 45, 46, 47, rostral area 8, rostral area 12, rostral area 32)
    Heteromodal parietotemporal (areas 39, 40, caudal area 7, banks of superior temporal sulcus, area 36)

Limbic system (cortical and subcortical components)
    Paralimbic cortex (insula; temporopolar cortex—area 38; caudal orbitofrontal cortex—caudal areas 12, 13; cingulate complex—areas 23, 24, 33, 31, 26, 29; parolfactory region—area 25, caudal area 32; parahippocampal cortex—areas 28, 34, 35, 30)
    Core limbic formations (hippocampus, amygdala, substantia innominata, septal nuclei, pyriform olfactory cortex)
    Limbic basal ganglia and related structures (nucleus accumbens, medial globus pallidus, ventral tegmental area of Tsai, habenula)
    Limbic thalamus (midline nuclei, anterior tubercle nuclei, laterodorsal nucleus, dorsomedial nucleus, medial pulvinar nucleus)
    Hypothalamic nuclei

connections then known formed a mammillo-thalamo-cingulo-hippocampo-mammillary loop. This circuit now bears his name. Many additional neural connections have been described since then, and it is important to realize that the Papez circuit is only one of many possible limbic loops. (2) Components of the limbic system may contain common immunological properties. For example, the herpes simplex virus has a preferential affinity for the cortical components of the limbic system. Conceivably this virus recognizes a common antigenic site shared by limbic cortical areas. (3) Limbic regions display common pharmacological properties. For example, cholinergic, dopaminergic, and opioid innervations are particularly intense within limbic structures. Furthermore, procaine, lidocaine, and cocaine have an activating effect that is selectively targeted to the limbic and paralimbic parts of the cerebral cortex (Mesulam, 1987b; Ketter et al., 1996). (4) Components of the limbic system have common behavioral affiliations. Thus even substantial limbic lesions can leave most sensory and motor functions intact while profoundly impairing behaviors related to memory and emotion. The limbic network can be divided into amygdaloid and hippocampal spheres of influence (see Figure 6.2). The hippocampus and its connections are more closely affiliated with memory function, whereas the amygdala and its pathways are more closely affiliated with emotion and motivation.

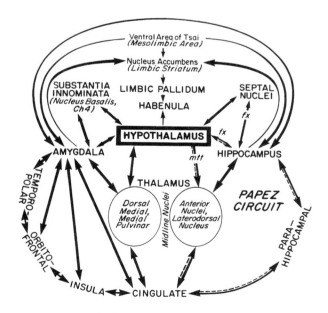

Figure 6.2 Some limbic connections. Only selected pathways are demonstrated. The dashed lines outline the Papez circuit. The term *hippocampus* is used to designate not only Ammon's horn but also the subicular complex. Abbreviations: *fx,* fornix; *mtt,* mammillothalamic tract.

Emotion and Limbic Epilepsy

The limbic system provides a crucial anatomical substrate for the coordination of *emotion and motivation.* Depth electrodes in patients who are being investigated for the surgical treatment of intractable epilepsy, for example, show that strong emotional experiences are associated much more commonly with discharges from limbic structures (especially the amygdala) than with discharges from the nonlimbic components of the temporal lobe (Gloor et al., 1982). Moreover, sensory stimuli that do not initially activate the amygdala or hypothalamus do so when they are associated with an emotionally relevant stimulus (LeDoux et al., 1983).

Each component of the limbic system participates in neural events related to mood and emotion. The hypothalamus seems to act as a neural repository for triggering skeletomotor and autonomic patterns associated with specific emotions. The amygdala and the paralimbic regions with which it is interconnected (see Figure 5.2) appear to play a crucial role in the channeling of emotion to the proper object and mental content. Downer (1962) showed that complex visual stimuli triggered appropriate emotional responses in rhesus monkeys only if the visual information had access to an intact amygdala. This finding helps in understanding the neural basis of the *Klüver-Bucy syndrome,* wherein bilateral damage to the amygdala and surrounding temporopolar cortex in monkeys results in 3 dramatic behavioral changes: incessant and inappropriate mouthing of inedible objects, attempts to copulate with unlikely sexual objects, and an uncharacteristic friendliness to human beings. Although the drives that are being expressed in this syndrome are part of the physiological behavioral repertoire, they are no longer directed to the proper extrapersonal target, reflecting the presence of a sensory-limbic disconnection (Geschwind, 1965). Some components of the Klüver-Bucy syndrome can be seen in patients who develop bilateral degeneration of the temporal pole in the course of Pick's disease or herpes simplex encephalitis.

Temporolimbic epilepsy. The limbic components of the temporal lobe (amygdala, hippocampus, parahippocampal gyrus, temporal pole) and the paralimbic cortices of the insula, frontal lobe, and cingulate gyrus have a low seizure threshold and frequently become the source of epileptic activity. Such seizures may be associated with characteristic automatisms such as staring, lip smacking, head turning, forced walking, running *(epilepsia cursiva),* and epigastric sensations. These symptoms readily raise the suspicion of temporolimbic epilepsy, especially when accompanied by olfactory or gustatory hallucinations. In other patients these characteristic features may be absent, and the manifestations of temporolimbic epilepsy may be confined to behavioral and psychiatric symptoms. Some of these symptoms are brief and related mostly to *ictal* epileptic discharges; others are more prolonged and tend to occur during the *interictal* state.

Ictal manifestations include déjà vu, jamais vu, feelings of unreality, depersonalization, fear, panic attacks (with or without associated autonomic discharges), elation, erotic sensations, depression, and forced thoughts that may take obsessive-compulsive proportions. These are designated as the *experiential phenomena* of temporolimbic epilepsy. The sudden, transient, unprovoked, repetitive, and stereotyped nature of the symptomatology provides a clue to the underlying epileptic etiology.

It is relatively easy to understand how transient epileptic discharges in the brain can be associated with transient (ictal) experiential phenomena. It is more difficult to understand the relationship of temporolimbic epilepsy to long-term behavioral changes. Some of these changes take the form of altered *personality traits,* whereas others may resemble conventional *psychiatric syndromes.* Anecdotal observations, as well as quantitative studies, have hypothesized the existence of a relatively characteristic cluster of behavioral traits in these patients. Some patients with temporolimbic epilepsy are said to act as if the entire world were saturated with intense emotional significance. These patients may lack a sense of humor, become overly serious and brooding, develop excessive philosophical interests, an obsessive hyperreligiosity, a curious tendency to write excessively, and a low threshold for moral outrage and aggressive outbursts. Many show difficulty in getting to the point during conversation, become lost in interminable detail, and display a characteristic circumstantiality of thought patterns. Patients may manifest wide mood swings, unpredictable explosive behaviors in response to minor provocations, and diverse alterations of sexual practice. The circumstantiality, obsessive rumination, humorlessness, and intense emotionality lead to a rather striking style of interpersonal interaction that has been described as "interpersonal viscosity."

There is a good deal of debate whether these traits are peculiar to temporolimbic epilepsy and whether they constitute a specific interictal behavioral syndrome. Hypergraphia is the one component of this hypothetical interictal syndrome that appears to have the most specific association to temporolimbic epilepsy (Spiers et al., 1985). Not all patients with temporolimbic epilepsy have this cluster of behavioral traits. Conversely, not all patients with these traits turn out to have temporolimbic

epilepsy. But when these behaviors are marked (especially the tetrad of viscosity, hyperreligiosity, hyposexuality, and hypergraphia), the clinician should have a higher index of suspicion for the presence of temporolimbic epilepsy. It is important to understand that this description refers to truly extraordinary deviations from normal behavior. Some of these patients will have multiple religious conversions from one faith to another. Others may maintain detailed diaries and compose exceedingly long letters (that they may never mail) for the sheer pleasure of writing. A patient who developed temporolimbic epilepsy in middle age and had no prior literary tendencies explained that the urge to express her thoughts and feelings in writing was so intense that she would sit with a pencil in her hand in front of a pad to make sure that nothing worth writing down would be missed. Another patient decided to copy Webster's dictionary page by page in longhand.

A great deal has been written about violence and limbic epilepsy (Pincus, 1981; Hood, Siegfried, and Wieser, 1983). In animals, amygdaloid damage seems to have an overall taming effect, whereas amygdaloid stimulation may trigger unprovoked aggressive attacks. These observations have led to the suggestion that some abnormally violent individuals (e.g., those with the episodic dyscontrol syndrome) may have amygdaloid overactivity, perhaps in the form of covert seizures, and that they may benefit from the surgical ablation of the amygdala when other therapeutic modalities prove ineffective (Mark and Ervin, 1970). This association between violence and temporolimbic epilepsy has to be interpreted in light of clinical experience which shows that excessive aggression occurs only in a very small minority of patients with temporolimbic epilepsy. In some of the epileptic patients who do become violent, dramatic and murderous acts of violence can be committed during fugues and related dissociative episodes. Others display sudden and unprovoked episodes of violence, occasionally associated with surprising feats of strength. The associated acts of violence usually occur without premeditation, but this is not a general rule. Amnesia for the episode may not be a consistent feature. In contrast to psychopathic conditions where the patient may experience little guilt, patients who are aggressive in conjunction with temporolimbic epilepsy tend to be very remorseful. In addition to ictal aggressive outbursts, which are probably quite rare, temporolimbic epilepsy is also associated with personality traits that increase the likelihood of explosive behaviors. In between the infrequent explosive outbursts, the patient with temporolimbic epilepsy has no difficulty controlling aggressive outbursts. The only limbic lesions which trigger uncontrolled and consistent attack and biting behaviors in humans are those associated with a direct involvement of the hypothalamus (Reeves and Plum, 1969).

Temporolimbic epilepsy has also been described in conjunction with more conventional psychiatric syndromes such as schizophreniform psychosis, affective disorders, multiple personality, conversion reactions, and obsessive-compulsive disorders. The strongest association is with schizophreniform conditions and depression. The frequency of such disturbances is much higher among temporolimbic epileptics than in the general population (Slater and Beard, 1963; Mendez, Cummings, and Benson, 1986). In contrast to idiopathic schizophrenia, patients with the schizophreniform reaction of temporolimbic epilepsy generally lack a family history of psychosis, rarely show temporal deterioration, tend to maintain adequate interpersonal contact, and do not show flattening of affect. But these patients do have hallucinations, delusions, and distinctly idiosyncratic paranoid ideation. There is some evidence indicating that left-handed women who develop temporolimbic epilepsy on the basis of cystic or hamartomatous lesions in the left hemisphere are the most prone to develop schizophreniform reactions (Taylor, 1975). In clinical practice, it is prudent to consider the possibility of temporolimbic epilepsy in patients with schizophreniform states, affective disorders, multiple personality, and especially panic attacks.

Women with the psychiatric manifestations of temporolimbic epilepsy usually show a characteristic exacerbation of epileptic discharges and behavioral symptoms in synchrony with the menstrual cycle. Sometimes this *catamenial* effect is very much exaggerated and can assist in raising the suspicion of underlying temporolimbic epilepsy. The amygdala, which is very frequently the site of abnormal epileptic discharges, is monosynaptically interconnected with the hypothalamus. Patients with temporolimbic epilepsy may therefore develop abnormalities in the hypothalamopituitary regulation of endocrine function, leading to infertility, testicular atrophy, decreased sperm motility, endometriosis, cystic mastitis, and other manifestations of polycystic ovarian disease (Herzog et al., 1986). Sometimes these endocrinological abnormalities improve on antiepileptic medication. The characteristic hyposexuality and some of the other behavioral manifestations in patients with temporolimbic epilepsy may be influenced by these endocrinological consequences of temporolimbic epilepsy.

The cerebral abnormality caused by temporolimbic epilepsy is not confined either to the site of the primary focus or to the period of ictal discharges. Ictal activity originating at one limbic structure very frequently spreads to other components of the limbic system. Evidence obtained with positron emission tomography shows that the epileptic focus is in an abnormal hypometabolic state even during interictal states (Kuhl et al., 1980). Patients with temporolimbic epilepsy therefore have a baseline limbic dysfunction accentuated by ictal discharges that invade the entire limbic system. In view of the pivotal role that the limbic system plays in channeling emotion, these disturbances could lead to a distorted and inappropriate mapping of feelings onto thought and experience (Mesulam, 1981). The resultant chaos and the patient's attempts at reintroducing internal coherence into the fabric of mental life may collectively lead to the associated psychiatric symptomatology. In some of the patients, temporolimbic epilepsy leads to an intensification of affective coloring (e.g., "limbic hyperconnectivity") that can promote behavioral traits such as hyperreligiosity and hypergraphia (Bear, 1979). In others, the incongruity of affective mapping may lead to schizophreniform and dissociative states.

Epileptic discharges can result from many different causes that alter the electrical stability of the neuron. In most cases the triggers for specific seizure events remain unknown. In a small number of patients, however, epileptic discharges are triggered by identifiable experiences. This condition is known as *reflex epilepsy*. In some patients the trigger may be a certain color or a certain visual pattern. In others it is extremely specific, such as a certain piece of music or the chiming of a particular church bell. When such complex triggers exist, the focus of the epilepsy is commonly located within the temporal lobe. Sometimes the reflex epilepsy leads to intense experiential phenomena. For example, in a now famous case, the sight of a safety pin induced epileptic discharges that were associated with intensely pleasurable erotic feelings (Mitchell, Falconer, and Hill, 1954). In time, looking at or thinking about the safety pin became a major source of sexual gratification for the patient, suggesting that reflex epilepsy could conceivably become an etiological factor in fetishism. Another example is provided by a patient who complained of abrupt and unprovoked mood fluctuations. She reported feeling intensely depressed and tearful when listening to a certain piece of dance music. The music did not sound particularly moody to other observers, and was not associated with any particularly sad event in her life. When the music was played in the electrophysiological laboratory, it triggered spike discharges in the electroencephalogram (EEG), depression, and crying. There were no other sensory, motor, or autonomic manifestations of epilepsy. In a minority of patients, the reflex epilepsy leads to a feeling of elation. Such patients may seek the triggering event and work to induce seizures

(Ames and Saffer, 1983; Faught et al., 1986). In other patients the reflex epilepsy can be triggered by cognitive activities, such as reading, doodling, or mental arithmetic (Anderson and Wallis, 1986).

Diagnosis and management of temporolimbic epilepsy. The seizure focus in temporolimbic epilepsy is located in the basal and medial parts of the brain and may therefore elude detection by routine surface EEGs. A thorough workup should include activation procedures such as the induction of sleep. Obtaining the tracing during periods of particularly intense symptomatology is also useful. Negative EEGs do not rule out temporolimbic epilepsy: it is possible that the patient was studied at a time when spiking activity was absent or that the placement of the electrodes was not optimal. It is also important to keep in mind that behavioral manifestations that appear to be interictal by surface recording may turn out to be ictal if invasive procedures for depth recording are used.

When psychiatric disorders occur in a patient with temporolimbic epilepsy, the clinician should consider two possible types of relationships. One possibility is that the two conditions are causally related, in which case the treatment of the epilepsy should have a beneficial effect on the psychiatric state. Alternatively, the epilepsy and the psychiatric symptoms may each constitute independent manifestations of an underlying limbic disease, in which case the treatment of the epilepsy should have little impact on the psychiatric state. In some patients who manifest some of the symptomatology described above, neurodiagnostic tests occasionally reveal the presence of non-epileptic temporolimbic abnormalities such as a cyst in the medial temporal lobe or a focal temporal slowing of the EEG. The term *temporolimbic dysfunction* (TLD) can be used to designate this condition and to set it apart from temporolimbic epilepsy (TLE).

I have seen patients with temporolimbic epilepsy in whom antiepileptic medication has helped to alleviate depression, panic attacks, hallucinations, memory disturbances, and circumstantiality. Such medication is usually less helpful for the schizophreniform and dissociative conditions. In general, patients with the conjunction of temporolimbic epilepsy and psychiatric symptomatology need an integrated program of treatment that includes antiepileptic management, psychotherapy, and psychoactive medication. Group therapy for patients with temporolimbic epilepsy may be particularly effective for sharing highly unusual experiences and dispelling the sense of uniqueness. The physician who manages such patients usually finds himself in the midst of a most challenging mind-body dilemma. When dealing with disturbing symptomatology the patient may frequently ask,

"Is this me or is this a seizure?" The answer to this very difficult question needs to be individualized for each patient.

Limbic Control of Autonomic and Endocrine Function

Emotional states are associated with specific patterns of autonomic responses. It is therefore not surprising that limbic regions should also participate in the regulation of autonomic tone. The amygdala and hypothalamus have a powerful influence on autonomic function, reflecting the direct connections they have with autonomic nuclei in the brain stem. Electrical stimulation in the cortical components of the limbic system (for example, anterior insula, caudal orbitofrontal cortex, temporal pole, cingulate gyrus) also results in marked and consistent autonomic responses. Insular stimulation tends to produce gastrointestinal responses, whereas stimulation of the other cortical components leads to cardiovascular and respiratory changes. Some of these responses are quite dramatic and may include inhibition of gastric peristalsis, respiratory arrest, and blood pressure changes of as much as 100 mm of mercury. Even multifocal cardiac necrosis can be obtained when monkeys with no intrinsic cardiovascular disease receive electrical stimulation into the caudal orbitofrontal cortex (Hall and Cornish, 1977).

The importance of interactions between mental state and autonomic activation patterns is well known in medical practice. Mental stress can increase blood pressure, promote the formation of ulcers, lead to abnormal esophageal motility, and even induce cardiac arrhythmias in the absence of cardiovascular predisposing factors. Individual emotions, and even different cognitive states, may be associated with relatively specific patterns of autonomic activation. Conceivably the influence of mental state upon autonomic activation in both normal and abnormal conditions is coordinated principally by cortical components of the limbic network. Future research may well determine that these parts of the brain provide a potential anatomical substrate for psychosomatic disease, essential hypertension, and certain types of heart disease. These are some of the considerations that have led to the alternative designation of the limbic system as "the visceral brain" (MacLean, 1949).

Memory and Amnesia

Memory permeates all aspects of mental life. Common sense may therefore lead to the expectation that this faculty should have a large safety margin and that it should be impaired only by the largest of brain lesions. The facts, however, lead to a different conclusion: neurological diseases frequently lead to severe memory deficits, and the responsible lesions can be quite small, as long as they are located within the confines of the limbic system.

The amnestic syndrome. This is the most severe form of memory disturbance and displays the following characteristics: (1) There is a *retrograde amnesia* for information acquired before the onset of the illness. The retrograde amnesia obeys a temporal gradient, also known as Ribot's law, so that memories acquired just before the onset of the amnesia are less accessible than more remote ones. This probably reflects the fact that more remote information is highly overlearned and more extensively incorporated into the contents of consciousness. Thus patients with the amnestic form of senile dementia have relatively little difficulty remembering intimate details of distant events at a time when they cannot recall more recent events. The fact that amnestic patients almost never forget their own names or birthplaces is also consistent with Ribot's law. (2) The patient has severe *anterograde amnesia,* which interferes with the conscious (e.g., declarative or explicit) recall of new experience. Patients may not recall what they had to eat a few minutes ago or who visited them the day before. Disorientation to time and also to persons and places new to the patient arises as a consequence of this anterograde amnesia. Patients with the amnestic syndrome are extremely vulnerable to interference. They can retain information for many minutes if undisturbed, but even the briefest distraction leads to the loss of the pertinent memory traces. (3) One of the most colorful consequences of the amnesia is *confabulation.* If the examiner asks, "Do you know who I am?" the patient may provide a confabulatory response such as: "Of course I know you. Weren't you the salesman who sold me a car?" This confabulation (a false-positive retrieval response) may occur because the patient is not fully aware of his memory problem and also because he lacks the mechanisms for critically evaluating whether a retrieved item fits the present context and his past experience. Confabulation is not a necessary feature and is present mostly during the acute states of the amnestic syndrome. (4) The patient is alert, attentive, and motivated. In contrast to devastated explicit memory function, other cognitive faculties such as language and visuospatial skills are quite intact. In fact, severely amnestic patients may obtain superior scores in IQ tests.

The patient with an amnestic syndrome is usually unaware of current news, cannot learn the route to a new destination, loses personal items within the house, may leave the stove on, and may pay the same bill several times or not at all. The acute amnestic syndrome is not compatible with independent existence and frequently leads to institutionalization. Although the ability to give an *explicit* verbal account of newly acquired experience is always severely impaired in the amnestic syndrome, *implicit* memory, as assessed by the acquisition of new motor skills, autonomic conditioning, and perceptual priming, can be preserved. In this context, implicit learning refers to diverse settings where prior exposure to a task or stimulus influences future responses even when the subject is unable to recall explicitly the prior exposure. On a motor coordination task such as mirror drawing, for example, an amnestic patient may show a learning curve indistinguishable from that of normal subjects. At the beginning of each daily training session, however, the same patient may deny knowledge of any prior exposure to the task (Milner, Corkin, and Teuber, 1968).

Components of emotionally relevant experiences may also be retained, though not necessarily at the level of explicit knowledge. For example, patients who have a condition known as *prosopagnosia* (inability to recognize faces by sight) emit an autonomic response indicative of physiological arousal when shown the face of a familiar person, even though they give no verbal indication of having recognized that individual (Bauer, 1984; Tranel and Damasio, 1985). A similar conclusion emerges from a clinical anecdote reported by Claparède (Claparède, 1911). He was taking care of an amnesic patient who showed no signs of recognizing him despite his daily visits. Apparently annoyed at this ingratitude, Claparède concealed a thumbtack in his hand and gave the patient a powerful pinprick during his customary daily handshake. The next morning the patient still denied recognizing the doctor, but was most reluctant to shake his hand. Clearly the painful consequence of the handshake had been stored in some implicit form and influenced subsequent behavior, although no verbalizable conscious knowledge was associated with the event. The phenomenon of implicit memory may provide useful models for exploring the biological foundations of unconscious mental processes.

When the amnestic syndrome occurs in isolation, it is always associated with a focal destructive lesion in the limbic system. Many neurological diseases can give rise to an amnestic state. These include tumors (of the sphenoid wing, posterior corpus callosum, thalamus, or medial temporal lobe), infarctions (in the territories of the anterior or posterior cerebral arteries), head trauma, herpes simplex encephalitis, Wernicke-Korsakoff encephalopathy, paraneoplastic limbic encephalitis, and degenerative dementias such as Alzheimer's or Pick's disease. The one common denominator of all these diseases is that they lead to bilateral lesions in one or more components in the limbic network. Occasionally left-sided unilateral damage to the limbic network may give rise to an amnestic state, but this is usually transient. Not all the limbic structures shown in Figure 5.2 have to be involved to produce an amnesia. For example, bilateral infarctions confined to the limbic thalamus, bilateral anterior temporal lobectomy, bilateral damage to the septum or basal forebrain, and bilateral medial diencephalic lesions (as in the Wernicke-Korsakoff syndrome) have each been associated with amnestic states (Signoret, 1985). Although the site of damage does influence the clinical details of the amnesia, the major aspects of the amnestic state listed above are present in most of these patients. In general, bilateral damage to structures in the Papez circuit tend to yield the most severe amnestic states. Damage confined to the amygdala may selectively interfere with the facilitatory effect of emotional arousal upon recall without giving rise to a full-fledged amnestic state (Cahill et al., 1995).

Although the limbic network is the site of damage for amnestic states, it is almost certainly not the storage site for memories or motor skills. The sensory data related to experienced events constitute the essential building blocks of memory and are stored in widely distributed form throughout association cortex. The role attributed to the limbic network is to bind these distributed fragments into events and experiences that have the level of coherence necessary for conscious recall. Damage to the limbic network does not necessarily destroy memories but interferes with their conscious (declarative) recall in coherent form. The individual fragments of information remain preserved in sensory association cortex and sustain implicit memory (Mesulam, 1994).

Partial amnesias. The full-fledged amnestic syndrome is global and influences the declarative recall of all aspects of experience, in all sensory modalities. Occasionally, when the limbic damage is unilateral, material- or modality-specific amnesias arise. Right-sided lesions may selectively impair memory for complex perceptual patterns, whereas lesions confined to left-sided structures may preferentially impair memory for words. Left hemisphere lesions result in amnesias for verbal material that are usually more severe than the amnesias for nonverbal material that result from lesions in the right hemisphere (Signoret, 1985). This may indicate a left hemisphere dominance for memory or the fact that even nonverbal items may be memorized through some verbal mediation. The binding function attributed to the limbic system necessitates the integrity of sensory-limbic interconnections. Lesions in the temporal lobe can disrupt visuo-limbic, auditory-limbic or somatosensory-limbic interactions and can lead to partial amnesias confined to the relevant sensory modality (Ross, 1980). A visuo-limbic disconnection, for example, may disrupt the ability to learn new visual associations without interfering with the learning of information acquired through other modalities of input.

Transient global amnesia. This dramatic syndrome is usually seen in middle-aged individuals, especially after a period of physical stress (sexual activity, a dip in cold water, exercise, and so on). The onset of the memory loss is quite sudden. A component of retrograde amnesia occurs and can encompass a period ranging from a few hours to several years preceding the onset of the illness. During the ictus the patient manifests severe anterograde amnesia similar to the one described for the amnestic state. Total disorientation is the rule, and the patient may even forget biographical information. In contrast to the amnestic syndrome, there is usually considerable anxiety and even agitation. The patient continually asks what is happening to him, what he is doing here, and who the other person is. The episode may last from 12 to 72 hours and sometimes even longer. Following recovery, the patient usually cannot recall events that occurred during the ictus. Vascular insufficiency in the territory of the posterior cerebral artery, migraine, temporolimbic epilepsy, and even brain tumor have been associated as etiological factors for this syndrome, but it is also fairly common to find no obvious cause in some patients. In most instances there is a single episode without recurrence. However, transient global amnesia could also be the harbinger of a stroke in the posterior cerebral circulation. Transient global amnesia can be misinterpreted as having psychogenic causes.

Epileptic and narcoleptic memory disturbances. Temporolimbic epilepsy may result in powerful feelings of déjà vu (illusion of familiarity) or jamais vu (illusion of unfamiliarity). Prolonged episodes of jamais vu could give rise to states during which the patient denies being acquainted with familiar persons, places, and facts. This condition may give the impression of an amnestic state. When these patients are questioned, however, they will readily distinguish the feeling of unfamiliarity from a true loss of the relevant factual memory.

Temporolimbic epilepsy can also lead to dissociative fugue states. The patient may lose memory for past information, including biographical data and identity. During the fugue state—which can last from minutes to hours and in unusual circumstances even days—the patient may engage in complex acts ranging from routine to criminal.

External appearance may be quite unremarkable. Occasionally behavior seems automatic, driven, and inflexible. Despite the marked retrograde amnesia, the patient may show little if any anterograde amnesia, so that new information can be acquired during the ictus. Following the episode, the patient may not retain any knowledge of events that occurred during the fugue state. Some patients with frequent fugues complain that they "lose time." Similar, but usually briefer, fugue states can also be seen in narcolepsy.

Many patients with temporolimbic epilepsy complain of memory difficulties. Neuropsychological testing frequently reveals abnormal memory function, but the deficits are usually material-specific and rarely severe. In a few patients, temporolimbic epilepsy can lead to severe amnestic conditions, occasionally with unusual clinical features. Some of these patients may show an abnormal acceleration of forgetting. Anterograde memory may appear unremarkable when retention is tested within relatively short intervals of minutes to hours, but the patient may not be able to retain information related to experiences that happened a few days ago (Ahern et al., 1994). Some other patients show multiple "islands" of amnesia for isolated significant events in the past. These unusual amnesias may reflect an impairment of memory *consolidation*.

Depression, aging, and memory function. Depressed patients frequently complain of memory failure. In some individuals this is part of the self-deprecation characteristic of depression, and objective testing fails to reveal memory difficulties. In others, the syndrome of endogenous depression may contain a bona fide component of memory loss. The deficit is neither as severe nor as generalized as the one in the amnestic syndrome. In contrast to the patient with the fully developed amnestic syndrome, those who suffer memory loss in conjunction with depression are very much concerned about this deficit. Testing may reveal that the memory loss is due mainly to ineffective registration and retrieval (Weingartner et al., 1981). If additional drilling is allowed at the stage of registration or if cues are provided during recall, the deficit is usually overcome. In sharp contrast to the amnestic state, where confabulation may be a central feature, patients who have the memory loss of depression tend to give false negative responses in the form of "I don't know." When the patient is coaxed to provide an answer, the memory loss turns out to be less severe than reported. The memory loss of endogenous depression appears to be particularly marked in the aged individual. Young patients with depression usually do not have significant cognitive deficits.

Many modalities of treatment for depression (electroconvulsive therapy, lithium salts, antidepressants with anticholinergic effects) can also lead to memory impairment. In managing a depressed patient who complains of faulty memory, one must decide whether the symptom is associated with the underlying disease or with its treatment. Treatment of the depression or withdrawal of the offending medication is often associated with an improvement of memory function in some of these patients.

Aging itself may lead to a decrease in memory capacity, but this deficit is usually mild and rarely interferes with age-appropriate daily living activities. This type of memory disturbance has been called *benign senescent forgetfulness* to set it apart from the more rapidly progressive and malignant amnesia of dementia (Kral, 1962). The benign forgetfulness of aging impedes mostly the ability to remember names and dates rather than events. As most of the difficulty appears to be at the stage of retrieval, peripheral cues in the forms of written reminders and date books can be very helpful. Although no fixed structural brain lesion has been associated with the memory disturbances of depression and aging, impairments of cholinergic transmission (in aging) and norepinephrine innervation (in depression) could play a role in these conditions.

Psychogenic amnesias. Many disparate states have been included under the rubric of psychogenic amnesia. Some individuals tend to retain little if any conscious recollection of unpleasant or traumatic events. The process of repression is invoked to explain this phenomenon. The resultant memory discontinuity can sometimes be eliminated by hypnosis, sodium amytal injections, or during psychotherapy. These patients have isolated lacunae in memory but no other manifestations of amnesia. In contrast to patients with fugue states, the memory gaps are for specific events rather than for time periods. In patients with the condition of multiple personality, some of the personalities may be amnesic for the experience of the others.

The malingerer has a vested interest in failing to recall a certain event. Some malingering may take the form of "theatrical (or Hollywood) amnesia," whereby a person is suddenly found to have lost all prior memory, including who he is (Signoret, 1985). The person gives no evidence of ongoing anterograde amnesia, however, and can acquire new information quite normally. This condition needs to be distinguished from fugue states, which usually last for short periods and rarely if ever for days on end. The loss of information about personal identity is an important differentiating feature because patients with organic amnesias (with the possible exception of fugue states and the late stages of dementia) ordinarily do not forget their own names, birthplaces, or birthdates.

Distorted memory. Reduplicative paramnesia and the Capgras syndrome are closely allied conditions of distorted memory (Alexander, Stuss, and Benson, 1979). *Reduplicative paramnesia* (a term coined by Arnold Pick) refers to the delusional belief that a place (usually new to the patient) is actually situated in a different and usually more familiar geographic site. For example, a resident of Providence hospitalized at the Beth Israel Hospital in Boston may insist that he is at the Providence Beth Israel Hospital. When confronted with the information that the sign at the entrance indicates that this is the Boston Beth Israel Hospital and that Providence does not have a Beth Israel Hospital, or when shown evidence that his present surroundings exactly match those of Boston, the patient may express wonderment but remain unshaken in his conviction. He may suggest that there could be an exact duplicate or branch of the Boston Beth Israel Hospital situated in Providence, perhaps built just recently. Sometimes the patient may wonder why anybody would go to such lengths as to reproduce the Boston skyline in Providence. Although the patient is capable of comprehending the implausibility of such circumstances, logical arguments usually have little if any effect in altering this belief. Sometimes the patient confesses that he "knows" this to be impossible but that it nonetheless "feels" true. Patients with reduplicative paramnesia usually have no additional thought disturbances, delusions, or hallucinations. Temporal disorientation may be present, but patients with this syndrome do not usually have other features of an anterograde amnesia. They can retain new information, which makes their persistence in this delusional mislocation of their environment even more puzzling.

The *Capgras syndrome* refers to the strongly held delusional belief that others (usually family members) and sometimes even the self have been replaced by doubles or impostors. Often the patient believes that an underlying plot is motivating the impostors. At other times no paranoid features are present. In one clinical case that was reported, a patient insisted that his wife and 5 children had been replaced by doubles. He assumed that his original wife had deserted him, and he was very thankful that she had been thoughtful enough to find a replacement (Alexander, Stuss, and Benson, 1979). It has been pointed out that the Capgras syndrome is not based on a perceptual problem, since the patient will clearly state that the putative impostor looks "exactly like" the original person. Therefore, as in reduplicative paramnesia, the problem is mostly one of distorted belief associated with the process of recognition (Berson, 1983).

In neurological practice the most common setting for reduplicative paramnesia and the Capgras syndrome occurs in patients with relatively severe head trauma who initially develop an amnestic syndrome (indicative of limbic involvement) but who subsequently recover most memory functions. These patients will usually also have bifrontal damage that is almost always more severe in the right side. In normal waking life, the sensory impressions related to familiar persons and places do change from time to time. The intact brain tends to assume continuity and to use this new information to update and expand the relevant associations. In patients who recover from an amnestic state and who also have bifrontal lesions, the mechanisms for updating knowledge and for critically assessing contextual plausibility seem to be disrupted, leading to the dramatic occurrences of the Capgras syndrome and reduplicative paramnesia. In clinical practice these conditions must be distinguished from experiences of jamais vu, which can lead to transient feelings of unfamiliarity associated with places and persons.

The biological vulnerability to memory distortion. The dramatic manifestations of reduplicative paramnesia, the Capgras syndrome, epileptic fugues, déjà vu, and jamais vu help to show that memory is not an all-or-none phenomenon and that it is vulnerable to various forms of distortion. This vulnerability has recently attracted a great deal of attention in relation to hypnotic suggestibility, the effect of emotional trauma on the accuracy of recall, and the reliability of eyewitness accounts (Schacter et al., 1995). A review of pertinent physiological studies suggests that each neuron is likely to participate in the storage of hundreds of thousands of memories. In turn, the storage of a new experience is likely to represent a distributed process involving hundreds of thousand of neurons, each of which already contains information related to components of past experience. Consequently, past memories are likely to influence the way in which new experience is stored at the same time that they are being modified by the new experience.

The distributed mode of memory storage enables the same experience to be recalled in many different combinatorial forms and through many different associative approaches. Although this organization enriches the process of recall, it also makes it vulnerable to distortion. Memory is both fragile and resilient. Traces of consciously experienced events may never completely disappear from memory, but they are rarely, if ever, reproduced with complete fidelity. All acts of recall are also acts of imagination and reinterpretation. The tendency for distortion is a byproduct of this complex organization. The ultimate goal of memory is not to maximize the accuracy of recall but to optimize its value for adaptive survival. It can even be argued that a superior talent for accurate factual recall could constitute a sign of brain disease. In some types of autism, for example, otherwise mentally retarded individuals, also known as idiots savants, are capable of remarkable feats of accurate recall. These individuals cannot reorganize facts creatively, and their phenomenal memory ability is of little benefit (and often an impediment) in the pursuit of life achievements.

Although memories are naturally prone to distortion and reinterpretation, adaptive conduct requires that the resultant re-creations remain within the boundaries of the reality principle. The limbic system helps to bind fragments of information into coherent experiences, whereas the frontal lobes play an important role in determining boundaries of contextual plausibility. Under severe emotional stress or after damage to fronto-limbic structures, this boundary is crossed and the re-creation of reality takes the form of implausible confabulations. The frontal lobes tend to mature relatively late, and this may explain why children are particularly prone to confabulation.

The foregoing discussion suggests that the neural substrate of memory can be conceptualized as containing three interacting components. The *limbic system* provides the basic machinery for encoding, retrieval, and binding; *sensory association cortex* contains the factual building blocks of experience; high order association cortex, including *prefrontal cortex,* introduces contextual boundaries for constraining the creativity with which the past is reconstructed. Considering all this complexity, what is surprising is not that we occasionally forget a fact or a face, but that we can remember at all (Mesulam, 1995b).

Language and Aphasia

The ultimate product of mental activity is thought. Language is one of the most important vehicles through which thought is encoded, modeled, and transmitted. I once read an evocative description comparing thought to an April cloud that sheds a shower of words. Although the biological study of thought is in its mere infancy, great strides have been made in the study of words and language, especially through the examination of brain lesions that give rise to aphasias (Benson, 1985; Mesulam, 1990; Damasio, 1992). The neural substrate of language takes the form of a distributed network centered in the perisylvian region of the left hemisphere. The posterior pole of this network is known as *Wernicke's area* and includes the posterior third of the superior temporal gyrus and a surrounding rim of the inferior parietal lobule. An

essential function of Wernicke's area is to transform sensory inputs into their neural word representations so that these can enter the distributed associations that lead to meaning. The anterior pole of the language network, known as *Broca's area,* includes the posterior part of the inferior frontal gyrus and a surrounding rim of prefrontal heteromodal cortex. An essential function of this area is to transform neural word representations into their articulatory sequences so that the words can be uttered in the form of spoken language. The sequencing function of Broca's area also appears to involve the ordering of words into sentences so that the resulting statement has a meaning-appropriate syntax (grammar). Wernicke's and Broca's areas are interconnected with each other and with additional perisylvian, temporal, prefrontal, and posterior parietal regions, making up a large-scale distributed network subserving the various aspects of language function. Damage to any one of these components or to their interconnections can give rise to language disturbances *(aphasia).* Aphasia should be diagnosed only when there are deficits in the formal aspects of language such as naming, word choice, comprehension, spelling, or syntax. Dysarthria and mutism do not, by themselves, lead to a diagnosis of aphasia.

In almost all dextrals and in about 60% of sinistrals, the left hemisphere is dominant for language. In these individuals damage to the left hemisphere yields severe and occasionally permanent aphasias, whereas even large right hemisphere lesions have no such effect. Some individuals display a pattern of mixed dominance, so that damage to either hemisphere may give rise to aphasias. Very few individuals have a clear-cut right hemispheric dominance for language functions. Because 80–90% of all individuals are right-handed, the cerebral hemisphere that is dominant for complex movements is often (but not always) also dominant for language. This hemispheric asymmetry for handedness and language functions is one of the most fundamental biological facts about the human brain. There is at least one anatomical basis for this behavioral asymmetry: the posterior language area in the left hemisphere is anatomically larger than the equivalent region in the right hemisphere in about 60% of right-handers (Geschwind and Levitsky, 1968).

Wernicke's aphasia. Wernicke's aphasia is characterized by two cardinal deficits: the patient cannot understand language in any modality of input and cannot express thoughts in meaning-appropriate words. Language output is fluent and maintains appropriate melody but is highly paraphasic and circumlocutious. Occasionally, the tendency for paraphasic errors is so pronounced that it leads to strings of neologisms which form the basis of what is known as *jargon aphasia*. Speech contains large numbers of function words (e.g., prepositions, conjunctions) but few substantive nouns or verbs denoting specific actions. The output is therefore voluminous but uninformative. For example, a 76-year-old man was brought to the emergency room because he started to talk "funny" while playing cards. In the following passage he is trying to describe how his wife accidentally threw away something important, perhaps his dentures:

We don't need it anymore, she says. And with it when that was downstairs was my teethtick . . . a . . . den . . . dentith . . . my dentist. And they happened to be in that bag . . . see? How could this have happened? How could a thing like this happen . . . So she says we won't need it anymore . . . I didn't think we'd use it. And now if I have any problems anybody coming a month from now, four months from now, or six months from now, I have a new dentist. Where my two . . . two little pieces of dentist that I use . . . that I . . . all gone. If she throws the whole thing away . . . visit some friends of hers and she can't throw them away.

Gestures and pantomime do not improve communication. The patient does not seem to realize that his language is incomprehensible and may appear angry and impatient when the examiner fails to decipher the meaning of a severely paraphasic statement. In some patients this type of aphasia can be associated with severe agitation and paranoid behaviors. Testing comprehension in these patients can be challenging. If asked to raise a hand, touch an ear, or perform other actions with the limbs, the patient gives no indication of comprehension. If asked simple questions that require a yes or no answer, such as "Can a dog fly?" the patient answers at random if at all. Yet the same patient will usually follow commands for whole body movements or movements that use axial musculature (such as "Close your eyes; stand up; turn around") with extreme care and rapidity. If the examiner confined the testing to opening and closing the eyes, the existence of severe comprehension deficits could be overlooked. It is said that this dramatic dissociation occurs because the ability to follow whole body and axial commands is subserved by pathways that remain outside the basic language network (Geschwind, 1965). An alternative possibility is that these movements are coordinated by the right hemisphere. In either case this dissociation emphasizes that "comprehension" is not a unitary mental phenomenon, that it can be fractionated with brain damage, and that the examiner has to look into several independent modes of comprehension. The dramatic dissociation between the failure to understand simple questions (e.g., "What is your name?") in a patient who rapidly closes his/her eyes, sits up, or rolls over when asked to do so is characteristic of Wernicke's aphasia and helps to differentiate it from deafness, psychiatric disease, or malingering. In addition to the paraphasic speech and poor comprehension of spoken language, patients with Wernicke's aphasia also have impaired repetition, naming, reading, and writing.

The lesion site most commonly associated with Wernicke's aphasia is located in the posterior parts of the language network, and tends to involve at least parts of Wernicke's area. A cerebrovascular lesion (commonly embolic and in the distribution of the angular branch of the middle cerebral artery) or neoplasm is the most common etiology. With the occasional exception of a right hemi- or quadrantanopia and mild nasolabial flattening, the conventional neurological examination may be quite normal. The paraphasic, neologistic speech in an agitated patient with an otherwise uneventful neurological examination may lead to the suspicion of a primary psychiatric disorder such as schizophrenia or mania but the other components characteristic of acquired aphasia and the absence of prior psychiatric disease usually settle the issue.

Broca's aphasia. Speech is non-fluent, labored, dysarthric, and interrupted by many word-finding pauses. It is impoverished in function words but enriched in meaning-appropriate nouns and verbs. Abnormal word order and the inappropriate deployment of bound morphemes (e.g., word endings used to denote tenses, possessives, or plurals) lead to a characteristic agrammatism. The resultant output is telegraphic and pithy but quite informative. In the following passage, a 45-year-old man with Broca's aphasia is describing his medical history: "I see . . . the dotor, dotor sent me . . . Bosson. Go to hospital. Dotor . . . kept me beside. Two, tee days, doctor send me home."

Occasionally output is reduced to a grunt or single word ("yes" or "no") which is emitted with different intonations in an attempt to express approval or disapproval. In addition to fluency, naming and repetition are also impaired. Comprehension of spoken language is intact, except for syntactically difficult sentences with passive voice structure or embedded clauses. Reading comprehension is also preserved, with the occasional exception of a specific inability to read small grammatical words such as conjunctions and pronouns. The last two features indicate that Broca's aphasia is not just an "expressive" or "motor" disorder and that it may also involve a comprehension deficit for function words and syntax. Patients with Broca's aphasia can be tearful, easily frustrated, and profoundly depressed. Even when spontaneous speech is severely dysarthric, the patient may be able to display a relatively preserved articulation of words when singing. This dissociation has been used to develop specific therapeutic approaches (e.g., melodic intonation therapy) for treating patients with Broca's aphasia. Additional neurological deficits that are usually encountered in these patients include right hemiparesis (or hemiplegia) and right facial weakness. The most characteristic lesion site tends to include parts of Broca's area. Cerebrovascular lesions (usually based on occlusive disease in the internal carotid or middle cerebral arteries) are the most frequent etiological processes.

Global aphasia. Some patients suffer damage to both Broca's and Wernicke's areas. They develop a very severe aphasia characterized by an almost total failure of speech output and comprehension. Even some of these patients, however, can attentively follow commands aimed at axial musculature. This syndrome is designated as *global aphasia.*

Disconnection aphasias. Some aphasias occur not because of direct damage to Wernicke's or Broca's area but because of a disconnection of these areas with each other and with other parts of the language network. In *conduction aphasia* the lesion is located either in fiber bundles (such as the arcuate fasciculus) that interconnect Wernicke's area to Broca's area or in intervening cortical areas that are likely to act as relays between the two (such as the insula, parietal operculum, and inferior parietal lobule). Since the 2 major cortical "centers" of the language network are intact, these patients have relatively few difficulties with language comprehension or with speech fluency. But they do have paraphasic speech that is relatively empty of content and that does not express the intended meaning. During the examination, patients with conduction aphasia have the most difficulty when asked to *repeat* speech, especially small function words (for example, "No ifs, ands, or buts").

Damage to the dorsolateral parietotemporal aspect of the left hemisphere may leave Wernicke's area intact while disconnecting it from other posterior association regions of the brain. These patients, who are said to have a *transcortical sensory (fluent) aphasia,* experience severe difficulties in comprehending language and expressing their thoughts. Because the 2 cortical centers and their interconnections are intact, however, they have no problem repeating speech. An analogous lesion in the dorsolateral frontal lobe interferes with the interactions between Broca's area and the rest of the frontal lobe, including the medially situated supplementary motor area. This condition gives rise to a *transcortical motor (non-fluent) apha-*

sia. Patients show a dramatic paucity of spontaneous speech output. When they are forced to speak, the output is generally telegraphic and pithy. Several features of this type of aphasia are reminiscent of Broca's aphasia. But because Broca's area and its interactions with Wernicke's area are intact, the ability to repeat is preserved (see Table 6.2).

Anomic aphasia. A disturbance of naming is not a very specific finding because it is a feature of virtually all the aphasias described above and can even occur in conjunction with metabolic encephalopathies. When naming is the only language disorder that exists, the patient is said to have an *anomic aphasia.* Such patients have no problem with comprehension or repetition and they are able to express themselves reasonably well except for occasional paraphasias. They fail in tests of naming, especially when asked to name small parts of common objects, such as the crystal of a watch, the hem of a coat, or the tip of a pencil. Writing may or may not be impaired. Left hemisphere lesions that do not give rise to one of the aphasic syndromes described above are usually associated with an anomic aphasia. Anomic aphasia is also the most common type of aphasia seen after head injury and in the dementias of the Alzheimer and Pick types. The presence of anomia is a very sensitive indicator of left hemisphere dysfunction.

The angular gyrus and the Gerstmann syndrome. The inferior parietal lobule is one of the most important high-order association areas of the brain. Some lesions (not as extensive as those giving rise to a transcortical sensory aphasia) destroy parts of the inferior parietal lobule while leaving Wernicke's area mostly intact. The consequence of such damage may include difficulties with naming, reading, writing, and calculations, a cluster that is referred to as the *angular gyrus syndrome.* Comprehension of spoken language is generally intact, whereas reading comprehension is often impaired. Other patients develop a combination of 4 symptoms: difficulty with calculations (dyscalculia), impaired writing (dysgraphia), an inability to name fingers (finger agnosia), and an inability to distinguish left from right (left-right confusion). This tetrad is known as the *Gerstmann syndrome.* When it occurs in isolation, it is frequently associated with a left inferior parietal lobule (usually angular gyrus) lesion. The correlation of finger-naming difficulties with calculation difficulties is said to reflect the importance of fingers in the acquisition of arithmetic skills.

Pure word deafness. In some patients, brain lesions disconnect the language network from a single sensory modality. These relatively rare lesions give rise to the dramatic manifestations of pure word deafness and pure alexia without agraphia. In *pure word deafness,* either bilateral lesions or a strategically placed unilateral lesion in the left superior temporal gyrus prevents auditory information from reaching the language network. These patients are neither deaf nor aphasic. They have no difficulty registering and comprehending environmental sounds—they will open the door upon hearing a knock and will pick up the phone when it rings. Although these patients have no problem understanding written language, they react to spoken language as if this were in an alien tongue they cannot decipher. Thus a patient who picks up the telephone as it rings will assume a puzzled and occasionally frustrated expression when realizing his inability to comprehend what is being said on the other end of the line. The language output is almost entirely normal. Occasionally, belligerent and paranoid reactions are associated with this syndrome. Because these patients may have no deficits in the routine neurological examination, they can easily be mistaken as having primarily a psychiatric disturbance. The dramatic dissociation between the comprehension of written versus spoken language is diagnostic and distinguishes these patients from those with psychiatric disease.

Pure alexia without agraphia. The alexia associated with the angular gyrus syndrome is called a *central alexia* because it results from the destruction of a brain region necessary for the relevant multimodal interactions. This type of alexia is almost always associated with dysgraphia. *Pure alexia,* in contrast, is a disconnection syndrome. It is the visual analogue of pure word deafness. Most characteristically, this syndrome is seen when 2 regions, each supplied by the posterior cerebral artery, are simultaneously damaged. One component of the lesion is usually located in the left occipital cortex. By itself this only creates a right homonymous hemianopia. Patients with a right homonymous hemianopia are not necessarily alexic because visual information from the left visual field can

Table 6.2 Clinical features of aphasias and related conditions

| Syndrome | Spoken Language | | Repetition | Naming | Writing | Reading |
	Output	Comprehension				
Wernicke's aphasia	Fluent, paraphasic, circumlocutional, empty of content	Impaired except for axial commands	Impaired	Impaired	Impaired	Impaired
Broca's aphasia	Nonfluent, reduced, pithy, agrammatic	Intact except for complex grammatical structure	Impaired	Impaired	Impaired	Impaired for grammatical words
Global aphasia	Nonfluent, sometimes mute	Impaired	Impaired	Impaired	Impaired	Impaired
Conduction aphasia	Fluent, paraphasic, circumlocutional	Intact	Impaired	Impaired	Usually impaired	Intact comprehension
Transcortical sensory aphasia	Fluent, paraphasic, circumlocutional	Impaired except for axial commands	Intact	Impaired	Impaired	Impaired
Transcortical motor aphasia	Nonfluent, pithy	Intact	Intact	Sometimes impaired	Sometimes impaired	Intact comprehension
Anomic aphasia	Fluent, paraphasic, circumlocutional	Intact	Intact	Impaired	Usually impaired	Usually intact
Pure word deafness	Intact	Impaired	Impaired	Intact	Intact	Intact
Pure alexia	Intact	Intact	Intact	Intact except for colors	Intact	Impaired

reach the right hemisphere and then cross the splenium of the corpus callosum to access the language network in the left hemisphere. If a patient with left occipital damage also sustains an infarction of the splenium (this is not uncommon because this part of the corpus callosum is supplied by the same artery that supplies the occipital cortex), the left hemisphere language network becomes completely disconnected from visual input. These patients have no aphasia, because the language network is intact. They understand and produce spoken language quite normally. They can also write very well, but they cannot read, even what they have written seconds ago, because the pertinent visual information cannot reach the left hemisphere language network. These patients may also have a generalized color-naming deficit or a true color blindness in the spared parts of the right visual field. The latter condition is known as a *central achromatopsia*.

Transcallosal anomia. Information from the right hemisphere needs to be transferred across the corpus callosum into the left hemisphere in order to elicit appropriate language behavior. If a patient with a corpus callosum lesion is blindfolded and given an object to palpate with the right hand, he will have no problem naming the object or describing its use because somatosensory pathways are crossed and the information from the right hand is conveyed to the left hemisphere. But when a similar object is placed in the left hand, it cannot be named, because the somatosensory information that reaches the right hemisphere cannot be conveyed to the left side of the brain. Such a patient could demonstrate with his left hand how to use the object, thus indicating that he "knows" what the object is. His inability to name the object, however, could also lead to the inference that he "does not know" its identity. This syndrome shows that brain lesions can fragment mental processes and that knowledge is not necessarily a unitary phenomenon (Geschwind, 1965). The most dramatic instances of this syndrome are seen with vascular lesions in the territory of the anterior cerebral arteries.

Mutism. Absence of speech is described as *mutism*. Mute patients need not be aphasic. In addition to bilateral lesions that directly damage oropharyngeal motor pathways, mutism is also seen with medial frontal damage in either hemisphere (in the region of the supplementary motor area) or with basal ganglia, white matter, and frontal cortex lesions of the left hemisphere. The absence of aphasia can be demonstrated by the fact that some of these patients have no difficulty with language comprehension or with writing. The stages of recovery from mutism may include whispered, breathy, and eventually dysarthric speech. On occasion, the term *aphemia* is used to describe this syndrome and its variants.

Apraxia. Apraxia can be defined as an impairment of learned movement that cannot be explained by deficits of motor function, sensation, or language comprehension. *Ideomotor apraxia* is said to occur if a patient is unable to convert spoken commands that are clearly understood into the corresponding movements. The patient can be asked to show how he would use a hammer, stamp out a cigarette, and suck through a straw. In the absence of the appropriate objects (hammer, cigarette, and straw), his response to these commands enables the examiner to assess ideomotor praxis in the upper limb, lower limb, and buccofacial musculature, respectively.

When a patient cannot follow a command used to test ideomotor apraxia, the examiner can test comprehension by performing several movements including the correct one. If the patient identifies the correct movement, one may assume he has understood the command. The examiner can test the fact that the patient has no relevant motor impediment either by spontaneous observation, by handing the patient the actual tool or object, or by performing the correct movement and asking the patient to imitate it. Ideomotor apraxia does not interfere with the ability to use real objects or tools and therefore has little impact on daily living activities. Ideomotor apraxia is generally associated with lesions that disconnect components of the language network from the motor areas of the frontal lobe. Patients with Wernicke's aphasia cannot be tested because they do not comprehend the command. Patients with conduction aphasia and Broca's aphasia will frequently show limb and buccofacial apraxia.

Visual Recognition and Agnosias

Perceptual information about faces and objects is initially encoded in primary (striate) visual cortex and adjacent upstream peristriate visual association areas. This information is subsequently relayed first to the downstream visual association areas of occipito-temporal cortex and then to other heteromodal and paralimbic areas of the cerebral cortex. Bilateral lesions in the fusiform and lingual gyri of occipito-temporal cortex disrupt this process and interfere with the ability of otherwise intact perceptual information to activate the distributed multimodal associations that lead to the recognition of faces and objects. The resultant face and object recognition deficits are known as *prosopagnosia* and *visual object agnosia*.

The patient with prosopagnosia cannot recognize familiar faces, including, sometimes, the reflection of his/

her own face in the mirror. This is not a perceptual deficit since prosopagnosic patients can easily tell if two faces are identical or not. Furthermore, a prosopagnosic patient who cannot recognize a familiar face by visual inspection alone can use auditory cues to reach appropriate recognition if allowed to listen to the person's voice. The deficit in prosopagnosia is therefore modality specific and reflects the existence of a lesion that prevents the activation of otherwise intact multimodal templates by relevant visual input. The deficit in prosopagnosia is not limited to the recognition of faces but can also extend to the recognition of individual members of larger generic object groups (Damasio, Damasio, and Van Hoesen, 1982; Damasio, 1985; Mesulam, 1994). For example, prosopagnosic patients characteristically have no difficulty with the generic identification of a face as a face, or of a car as a car, but cannot recognize the identity of an individual face or the make of an individual car. This reflects a visual recognition deficit for proprietary features that characterize individual members of an object class. When recognition problems become more generalized and extend to the generic identification of common objects, the condition is known as a visual object agnosia. In contrast to prosopagnosic patients, those with object agnosia cannot recognize a face as a face or a car as a car. The characteristic lesions in prosopagnosia and visual object agnosia consist of bilateral infarctions in the territory of the posterior cerebral arteries and involve the lingual and fusiform gyri. Associated deficits can include visual field defects (especially superior quadrantanopias) or achromatopsia. Rarely, the responsible lesion is unilateral. In such cases, prosopagnosia is associated with lesions in the right hemisphere and object agnosia with lesions in the left.

Right Hemisphere Syndromes

Patients with right hemisphere injury do not ordinarily display obvious language difficulties. Upon rapid bedside examination these patients may therefore seem to have behavioral impairments that are substantially milder than the frankly aphasic and superficially incoherent patients with left hemisphere injury. This distinction has led to the designation of the right hemisphere as the minor or nondominant side of the brain. Subsequent research, however, has shown that the right hemisphere does have important, possibly dominant, roles in several realms of behavior. These areas include spatial orientation, visuospatial skills, affect, and paralinguistic communication. In contrast to left hemisphere damage, which leads to aphasia, acalculia, and apraxia, damage to the right hemi-

sphere is characterized by hemispatial neglect, dressing apraxia, constructional apraxia, anosognosia (denial of illness), and impaired paralinguistic skills.

The differences in the behavioral specializations of the 2 hemispheres has generated a number of dichotomies. In contrast to the logical and verbal left hemisphere, the right hemisphere has been characterized as mediating processes that are creative, intuitive, and holistic. Furthermore, some investigators have suggested that the right hemisphere may be the site of unconscious processing. There is little support for these sweeping generalizations, which have permeated much of the popular literature on hemispheric specialization. The association of the right hemisphere with unconscious processes arises from the mistaken impression that nonverbal mental operations can be equated with those that are unconscious. The one clearly established fact is that the 2 hemispheres have widely divergent behavioral specializations but the biological mechanisms responsible for these differences are not yet fully understood.

Hemispatial neglect. The dorsal parieto-frontal cortices of the human brain play an important role in coordinating spatial orientation. Damage to these parts of the brain yield syndromes of spatial disorientation such as hemispatial neglect, Balint's syndrome, anosognosia, dressing apraxia and construction apraxia. Contralesional hemispatial neglect is a relatively common and devastating consequence of brain injury. It is said to be present when the impact of sensory events upon explicit (conscious) behaviors displays a spatial bias that cannot be attributed to elementary sensory-motor deficits such as weakness, clumsiness, or poor acuity. Patients with severe neglect may fail to shave, groom, or dress the side of the body contralateral to the brain lesion; they may fail to eat the food placed on that side of the tray; and they may fail to read the contralesional half of each sentence. If the patient is asked to draw the face of a clock or to copy a simple figure, he may omit detail on the left side; if given pencil and paper and asked to write, he may squeeze all the words onto the right side of the page. Neglect for the extrapersonal space is not a disorder of seeing, hearing, or moving, but one of looking, listening, and exploring (Mesulam, 1994).

Contralesional neglect is far more common, lasting, and severe after right than after left hemisphere lesions. This asymmetry leads to a model of right hemispheric specialization for spatial orientation whereby the left hemisphere contains the neural mechanisms for attending only to the contralateral right hemispace, whereas the right hemisphere contains the mechanisms for attending to the entire extrapersonal space. According to this model, left hemisphere damage leads to relatively minor contralateral neglect because the ipsilateral attention mechanisms of the right hemisphere take over attentional processes within the right hemispace. Right hemisphere damage, however, leads to severe left unilateral neglect because the left hemisphere does not have ipsilateral attention mechanisms.

At least 3 behavioral components can be identified in neglect. The first is a sensory-representational component: events occurring within the left hemispace have a diminished impact on awareness, especially if competing events are simultaneously taking place in the right side. This is best demonstrated with the phenomenon of extinction. In this maneuver the patient successfully detects sensory stimulation from either side of space as long as it is presented unilaterally. When the same stimulation is presented simultaneously from both sides of space, the patient fails to report the stimulus on the left side. Lesser degrees of extinction can also occur in the context of other clinical syndromes (for example, callosal disconnection or sensory dysfunction). But when extinction is multimodal or severe or when it emerges in conjunction with other manifestations of spatial inattention, it reflects

the sensory-representational component of the neglect syndrome. The second component of neglect is a motor-exploratory deficit: the patient shows a reluctance to direct orienting and exploratory movements toward the left hemispace. This can be demonstrated by visual target cancellation tasks or by blindfolding the patient and asking him to retrieve a small target from the top of a table with the unaffected right hand. Visual search and manual exploration under these conditions are much more efficient on the right side of space (Figure 6.3). There is also a limbic-motivational component to neglect: the patient behaves as if nothing of importance could be expected to occur in the left side of space. It seems as if the left side of space becomes subjected to an emotional devaluation. As part of this devaluation, some patients develop the curious phenomenon of *anosognosia:* they deny the existence of left hemiplegia and sometimes even express the delusional belief that the arm belongs to another person. The phenomenon of anosognosia may provide a model for studying the biological bases of denial states.

In keeping with the behavioral complexity of neglect behavior, investigators have shown that the brain regions involved in neglect make up a complex cerebral network (Mesulam, 1981a; Mesulam, 1990). The 3 major cortical

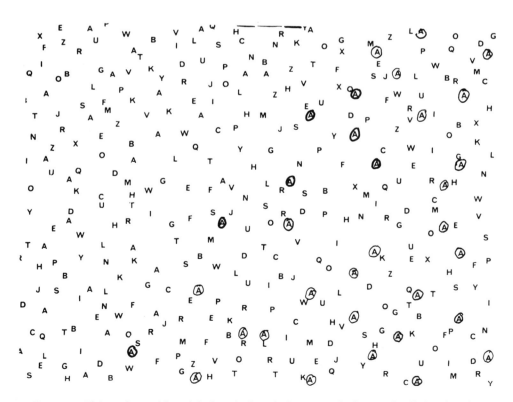

Figure 6.3 This patient with a right hemisphere lesion was asked to circle all the A's. Although the patient had no visual-field defect, he had a marked left neglect.

components of this network are in the *frontal cortex* (including premotor cortex, area 6, and the frontal eye fields, area 8; see Figure 6.1), the *posterior parietal cortex* (areas 39, 40, 7), and the *cingulate gyrus*. Subcortical components of this network are found in the basal ganglia, the thalamus, and the brain stem reticular formation. A different but complementary mapping of the environment may exist within each of the major cortical components of this network: a sensory representational map of the extrapersonal world in posterior parietal cortex, a map for the distribution of motor exploration in frontal cortex, and a motivational map for the distribution of relevance in the cingulate gyrus. These 3 cortical regions are interconnected by monosynaptic pathways. The interactions among the cortical and subcortical components of this network are necessary for the effective distribution of spatial orientation. Damage to any one of these components or to their interconnections may give rise to neglect. This large-scale network organization explains why neglect behavior can occur after lesions not only in the parietal cortex but also in the cingulate region, the frontal lobe, the basal ganglia, and the thalamus. This large-scale neural network organization of spatial orientation and its dominant control by the right hemisphere have now been confirmed with the help of functional imaging experiments in neurologically intact subjects (Corbetta et al., 1993; Gitelman et al., 1996).

Balint's syndrome and simultanagnosia. Bilateral damage to dorsal parieto-frontal cortices gives rise to a dramatic and global impairment of spatial orientation. The associated clinical picture, known as *Balint's syndrome,* has three components. First, the patient cannot scan the visual environment in a systematic way, a condition designated as an *oculomotor apraxia.* A second component, an inability to extend the hand appropriately to a visual target, is known as *optic ataxia.* When viewing a complex visual scene or a large object, the patient tends to base identification exclusively on the feature that falls within the central part of the visual field without being able to integrate this information with additional information contained in the more peripheral aspects of the stimulus field. Thus, when facing a door the patient may initially detect the doorknob alone and verbally try to reason out what a doorknob would be doing by itself, only then reaching the conclusion that he must be looking at a door. This third component of Balint's syndrome is also known as *simultanagnosia.* Patients with Balint's syndrome experience severe visual recognition difficulties based on their inability to integrate visual percepts. The resulting face and object recognition deficits are known as *apperceptive*

visual agnosias, whereas the prosopagnosia and visual object agnosias described above are known as *associative* agnosias because they result from the failure of an intact percept to evoke the relevant multimodal associations.

The clinical manifestations of neglect and Balint's syndrome help to highlight the anatomical and behavioral subdivision of visual association pathways into dorsal and ventral components (Ungerleider and Mishkin, 1982; Mesulam, 1994). The dorsal visuofugal pathway is directed toward the dorsal parietal and frontal lobes and is important for visuospatial and visuomotor function. Its unilateral interruption in the right hemisphere leads to the neglect syndrome; its bilateral interruption leads to Balint's syndrome. The ventral visuofugal pathway relays visual information into the limbic system, temporoparietal language areas, and downstream visual association areas of occipitotemporal cortex. Destruction of this ventral component is associated with visual amnesias, the Klüver-Bucy syndrome, pure alexia, prosopagnosia, and visual object agnosia.

Complex perceptual tasks. Patients with right brain lesions, especially in the posterior aspects of the hemisphere, experience a much greater impairment in complex perceptual tasks than those with equivalent lesions in the left hemisphere. In keeping with this relationship, it can be shown that the right hemisphere of the intact brain is more effective in the processing of complex nonlinguistic perceptual information. Experiments based on dichotic listening show a consistent right ear (and therefore left hemisphere) advantage for word and number recognition but a left ear advantage for melody identification (Kimura, 1973). Tachistoscopic experiments have shown a left visual field (and therefore right hemisphere) superiority for depth perception, spatial localization, and the identification of complex geometric shapes (Springer and Deutsch, 1981).

A left visual field (and therefore right hemisphere) superiority has been demonstrated for the processing of perceptual information related to unfamiliar faces. This asymmetry acquires potential behavioral relevance because most faces are distinctly asymmetrical. Thus, when an experimental subject is briefly exposed to a new face, the information in the left visual field (coming from the right side of the other person's face) can be shown to play the most important role in the storage of pertinent information. If the subject in such an experiment is subsequently presented with 2 photographic composites, one consisting of the 2 left sides and the other of the 2 right sides of the same face, he will tend to conclude that the composite made of the right side (which had been viewed through the left visual field) more closely resembles the original face. Despite this crucial role of the right hemisphere in the *perceptual analysis* of information related to faces, severe prosopagnosia is usually seen in the context of bilateral lesions, suggesting that both hemispheres take part in the *recognition* of faces.

Left hemispatial neglect and complex perceptual deficits contribute to the emergence of 3 additional clinical features associated with the right hemisphere syndrome: (1) *constructional apraxia,* that is, major difficulties in copying simple figures, especially if they also include three-dimensional perspective; (2) *dressing apraxia,* reflecting a major difficulty in aligning the body axis with the axis of the garment (dressing apraxia can be demonstrated by presenting the patient with a coat that has been inverted or with a sleeve turned inside out: unable to rearrange the garment into the proper orientation, the patient may keep looking at it with a puzzled expression while unsuccessfully fumbling with it); and (3) difficulties in spatial orientation and route finding, even in familiar surroundings. Some difficulties with constructional tasks may also emerge after left hemisphere damage, but in much milder form.

Affect

The limbic system plays a crucial role in the generation and channeling of emotions. But other cortical areas, especially those of the right hemisphere, also play important roles in the modulation of feeling and its expression. In the neurologically intact individual one generally assumes that affect conveyed through tone of voice, gestures, and facial expression is consistent with the underlying feeling state. In patients with brain damage, however, experience and expression can be dissociated from each other. In pseudobulbar palsy, for example, the patient may display crying or laughing behavior that bears little if any relationship to underlying sadness or happiness. The potential for such dissociation indicates that the expression and the experience of emotion may need to be considered independently in patients with brain injury.

Emotional experience and its expression are differentially influenced by each cerebral hemisphere. The literature on this subject can be divided into 2 camps. Some authors suggest that each hemisphere introduces a different emotional valence to experience and behavior. Others, however, suggest that the right hemisphere is dominant for the experience and expression of all emotions. A closer examination of these 2 positions shows that the divergence of opinion is more apparent than real.

Lack of concern and even inappropriate jocularity

(anosognosia) in response to hemiplegia is a striking feature of some patients with right hemisphere lesions but is almost never seen after damage to the left hemisphere. In contrast, right hemiplegia and left hemisphere damage are often associated with severe frustration and depression. These observations have led to the hypothesis that normal emotional state represents the outcome of a reciprocal balance between a negatively biased right hemisphere and a positively biased left hemisphere. Experiments in neurologically intact volunteers have provided partial support for this hypothesis (Dimond, Farrington, and Johnson, 1976). Two potential problems are associated with this line of reasoning. First, the expression of jocularity in left hemiplegics may have little relationship to the underlying state of feeling as major discrepancies may arise between emotional state and its expression in patients with brain damage. Despite apparent jocularity, for example, some left hemiplegics may be severely depressed (Ross, 1985). Second, the assumption is usually made that the despondency of the right hemiplegic is analogous to the jocularity of the left hemiplegic, except that it is of the opposite valence. One could argue, however, that despondency is an entirely appropriate reaction to a devastating event such as hemiplegia, whereas jocularity is always inappropriate. This reasoning leads to the somewhat different inference that right hemisphere lesions are more likely to result in abnormal emotional responses to life experiences, an interpretation that is more consistent with the existence of a relative right hemisphere specialization for the modulation of affect and emotion.

Several additional observations support this conclusion. For example, patients with right hemisphere damage may show profound deficits in their ability to express emotional state (positive or negative) through variations in the tone of voice (emotional prosody), facial expression, body posture, and hand gestures. On occasion, the most salient feature in the entire clinical picture of a patient with right hemisphere injury will be a loss of emotional prosody and an inability to impart the proper affective tone onto behavior (Ross and Mesulam, 1979; Ross, 1985). A teacher with this kind of lesion complained that she could no longer maintain discipline in her classroom, which she had previously regulated largely through changes in her tone of voice. Another patient was thought to be inconsiderate and depressed because his demeanor and tone of voice lacked the proper variations (Ross and Mesulam, 1979).

Patients with right hemisphere lesions may also have difficulty understanding (decoding) the emotional expressions of others (Heilman, Scholes, and Watson, 1975;

Ahern et al., 1991). Equivalent difficulties are not seen after analogous damage to the left side of the brain. Deficits in the display (encoding) of emotional expression are associated with lesions in the more anterior frontal parts of the right hemisphere, whereas deficits in the decoding of emotional expressions tend to arise after lesions in the more posterior temporoparietal parts (Ross, 1985). These encoding and decoding deficits are confined to the expression of relatively subtle affective modulations. Outbursts of extreme fear or anger, however, may remain preserved because their primary neural substrate is probably located bilaterally within limbic structures (Ross, 1985).

Evidence obtained in neurologically intact volunteers support the contention that the *intact* right hemisphere is more effective in both the encoding and decoding of emotional expression. Thus emotional expressions are more accentuated on the left side of the face, and a left visual field advantage exists for the identification of emotional expressions (Sackeim, Gur, and Savey, 1978; Heller and Levy, 1981). This asymmetry leads to a potential paradox. In face-to-face encounters, information from the more expressive left half of the face is likely to fall within the right visual field of the observer, an arrangement that would engender an intrinsic inefficiency in the communication of affective states. Possibly, this arrangement might reflect the adaptive value of making one's emotions less than perfectly obvious.

In addition to these observations related to the *expression* of emotion, indirect evidence suggests the possible existence of a right hemisphere specialization also for the *experience* of emotions. For example, autonomic responses to emotional stimuli are attenuated in patients with right hemisphere lesions but not in those with left hemisphere injury (Zoccolatti, Scabini, and Violani, 1982). In a different and rather remarkable experiment, neurologically intact subjects were asked to stimulate themselves into sexual climax while their EEGs were being monitored. The results showed that EEG amplitude during orgasm was greater over the right hemisphere (Cohen, Rosen, and Goldstein, 1976).

Even the relationship between altered affective states and the motor system is tighter in the right hemisphere. For example, the left side of the body appears more suggestible to hypnosis (Sackeim, 1982), and unilateral hysterical paralysis is more frequently encountered in the left side of the body, even in left-handers (Stern, 1977). In further support of a putative right hemisphere specialization for emotion, the observation has been made that affective disorders may be more closely associated with dysfunction of the right than of the left hemisphere. For example,

neurological signs indicative of right hemisphere dysfunction may be seen in depressed patients and may disappear upon treatment (Weintraub and Mesulam, 1983; Brumback, Stanton, and Wilson, 1984). In patients with temporolimbic epilepsy, left-sided foci are more likely to be associated with thought disorders, whereas right-sided foci are more likely to be associated with affective disease (Bear and Fedio, 1977). Affective disorders are also more common in conjunction with right-sided brain damage (Lishman, 1968). In patients with otherwise typical manic-depressive disturbances, the EEG power spectra tend to show greater disturbances over the right hemisphere in the manic as well as the depressed state (Flor-Henry, 1979); and the performance of such patients in dichotic listening tasks is similar to that of individuals with right temporal lobectomy (Yozawitz et al., 1979). A potentially discrepant but controversial observation comes from Robinson and colleagues, who report that depression is more common after left than after right hemisphere lesions (Robinson et al., 1984; House et al., 1990).

The limbic system plays a critical role in the generation and channeling of emotion. The observations reviewed in this section show that other parts of the cerebral cortex also participate in this process by modulating the expression and perhaps also the experience of emotion. Each cerebral hemisphere may impart a differential valence to this process, and it appears that there is an overall right hemisphere specialization in this realm of behavior.

Paralinguistic Aspects of Communication

The formal aspects of language (e.g., phonetics, morphology, semantics, and syntax) are under the dominant control of the left hemisphere. Effective communication involves additional *paralinguistic* components. The encoding and decoding of emotional expression through variations of prosody and facial expression constitute paralinguistic aspects of communication. As already mentioned, these paralinguistic functions are under right hemisphere control. In addition to imparting emotional tone, speech prosody is also used to denote emphasis and attitude ("She *is* pretty" versus "She is *pre*tty?"). These aspects of prosody also appear to be influenced by right hemisphere activity (Weintraub, Mesulam, and Kramer, 1981). Another aspect of paralinguistic communication is the ability to comprehend situational context through nonverbal channels of information processing. Patients with right hemisphere injury are more severely impaired than those with left hemisphere injury in this type of paralinguistic task (Benowitz et al., 1983).

The modulation of verbal output according to contextual demands, the choice of appropriate forms of address (*tu* versus *vous*), and the choice of proper diction or pitch (using a higher frequency when addressing a child) each constitutes additional paralinguistic functions about which we have relatively little neurological information. Some patients have developed major and salient deficits in these areas of behavior following right hemisphere damage. For example, one patient, known to be shy and considerate before suffering a right temporal lobe infarction, became uncharacteristically brazen and abrasive following the stroke. From his hospital room he would keep calling the physician's office and use forms of address and conversational styles that reflected inappropriate familiarity. The same patient also talked excessively and would not take cues to yield the floor during conversation (Mesulam, 1985).

The commonly observed socially inappropriate behaviors of patients with right hemisphere injury may reflect, at least in part, difficulties at the level of paralinguistic behaviors. The patient may not be able to decode nonverbal messages and may not be able to modulate his behavior to fit contextual cues. These difficulties, the denial of disability (anosognosia), and the potential discrepancy between affect and underlying emotional state pose considerable challenges in the rehabilitation and management of patients with damage to the right hemisphere.

The Frontal Lobes, Comportment, and Executive Functions

The frontal lobes account for almost one-third of the total cortical volume in the human cerebral hemispheres. The frontal lobes can be divided into motor-premotor, heteromodal, and paralimbic components. The terms *prefrontal cortex* and *frontal lobe syndrome* generally refer only to the paralimbic (i.e., caudal orbitofrontal, anterior cingulate, and parolfactory areas) and heteromodal (i.e., areas 9, 10, 11, 12, 45, 46, and 47) components of the frontal lobes (see Figure 6.1). These cortical areas and the subcortical regions (e.g., the head of the caudate nucleus and the mediodorsal nucleus of the thalamus) with which they are interconnected make up a large-scale *prefrontal network*. The clinical case of Phineas Gage (also known as the Boston crowbar case), described more than a century ago by Harlow (Harlow, 1868), has been used as a model for the frontal lobe syndrome. Phineas Gage was a reliable and conscientious foreman who became profane, irascible, and irresponsible following an accident during which a tamping rod was blown through his frontal lobes. The many reports published since Harlow's paper have pro-

vided additional support for the conclusions that frontal lobe damage can lead to dramatic alterations of personality and conduct while leaving basic cognitive and sensorimotor functions relatively intact.

The orbitofrontal and anterior cingulate areas provide a convergence site for neural inputs from association, paralimbic, and limbic cortices and constitute a zone of intersection for the prefrontal and limbic networks. In keeping with this organization, the prefrontal network plays an important role in behaviors that require an integration of cognition with emotion and motivation. There is no simple formula for summarizing the diverse functional affiliations of the prefrontal network. Its integrity appears important for the simultaneous (on-line) awareness of context, options, consequences, relevance, and perspectives so as to allow the formulation of adaptive inferences, decisions, and actions. Damage to this part of the brain impairs mental flexibility, foresight, judgment, and the ability to inhibit inappropriate responses. Behaviors impaired by prefrontal cortex lesions are often referred to as *executive functions*.

A wide range of behavioral changes can be observed in patients with prefrontal lesions (Mesulam, 1986). Some become puerile, profane, slovenly, facetious, irresponsible, grandiose, and irascible; others lose spontaneity, curiosity, and initiative and develop an apathetic blunting of feeling, drive, mentation, and behavior (abulia); others show an erosion of foresight, judgment, and insight and lose the ability to delay gratification and often the capacity for remorse. Still others show an impairment of abstract reasoning, creativity, problem solving, and mental flexibility; jump to premature conclusions; and become excessively concrete or stimulus bound. The orderly planning and sequencing of complex behaviors, the ability to attend to several components simultaneously and then flexibly alter the focus of concentration, the capacity for grasping the context and gist of a complex situation, the resistance to distraction and interference, the ability to follow multistep instructions, the inhibition of immediate but inappropriate response tendencies, and the ability to sustain behavioral output without perseveration may each become markedly disrupted.

On neuropsychological investigation (see Weintraub and Mesulam, 1985, for a description of the procedures), patients with prefrontal damage may show deficits in tasks of concentration (e.g., digit span), inhibition (e.g., the go–no go task, the Stroop test), motor sequencing (e.g., the Luria alternating hand postures), mental flexibility (e.g., the visual/verbal test), and hypothesis formation (e.g., the Wisconsin card sort task). The disruption of attentional functions contributes to the emergence of "working memory" impairments. Working memory refers to the amount of information that can be kept *on-line* at any given time. Working memory impairments interfere with the ability to maintain a coherent trend of thought and lead to confusion, especially in complex situations that require the simultaneous consideration of several variables. The attentional deficits also disrupt the registration and retrieval of new information and lead to secondary memory deficits. These memory difficulties can be differentiated from those of the amnestic state by showing that they improve when the attentional load of the task is decreased. Working memory (also known as immediate memory) is an attentional function based on the temporary on-line holding of information. It is closely associated with the integrity of the prefrontal network and the ascending reticular activating system. Retentive memory, by contrast, depends on the stable (off-line) storage of information and is associated with the integrity of the limbic network. The distinction of the underlying neural mechanisms is illustrated by the observation that severely amnestic patients who cannot remember events that occurred a few minutes ago may have intact if not superior working memory capacity, as shown in tests of digit span.

Some patients with sizable frontal lobe lesions and severe behavioral disturbances may have routine neurological and even neuropsychological examinations that are quite unremarkable. This paucity of "objective" findings is sometimes responsible for the clinician's overlooking the possibility of large and treatable frontal lesions. Even patients with a history of major behavioral difficulties associated with frontal lobe damage may behave impeccably in the office. This is in keeping with the clinical observation that such patients are most impaired under circumstances with minimal external control of behavior: the office setting may introduce just enough external structure to suppress some of these behavioral tendencies. Furthermore, a patient who gives perfect answers to questions about hypothetical social or moral dilemmas may act with a total lack of judgment when faced with the real situation. The clinical adage that judgment and complex comportment cannot be tested in the office is particularly pertinent to the evaluation of patients with frontal lobe damage. Numerous case reports describe patients with massive frontal lobe pathology (for example, meningioma, lipoma, or carniopharyngioma) who have carried psychiatric diagnoses for many years. In general, the abulia and apathy can be misinterpreted as depression, whereas the labile, inappropriate, and impulsive behaviors may raise the possibilities of mania, hysteria, psychosis, or character disorder. Such misdiagnoses can have

grave consequences, because some of the underlying frontal lobe lesions are treatable if detected early.

Although the term *frontal syndrome* is used to designate the entire spectrum of these behavioral changes, each patient may have a different cluster of salient deficits. The specific pattern of behavioral deficits is probably determined by the site, size, laterality, nature, and temporal course of the lesion and perhaps also by the past personality of the patient and the age of onset. The most common clinical manifestations of damage to the prefrontal network take the form of two relatively distinct syndromes. In the *frontal abulic syndrome,* the patient shows a loss of initiative, creativity, and curiosity and displays a pervasive emotional blandness and apathy. In the *frontal disinhibition syndrome,* the patient becomes socially disinhibited and shows severe impairments of judgment, insight, and foresight. In this second group of patients, the dissociation between intact intellectual function and a total lack of even rudimentary common sense is striking. Despite the preservation of all essential memory functions, the patient cannot learn from experience and continues to display inappropriate behaviors without appearing to experience emotional pain, guilt, or regret when such behaviors repeatedly lead to disastrous consequences.

The abulic syndrome tends to be associated with damage to dorsolateral prefrontal cortex, whereas the disinhibition syndrome is more likely to be associated with damage to medial prefrontal or orbitofrontal cortex. These behavioral syndromes tend to arise almost exclusively after bilateral lesions, most frequently in the setting of head trauma, ruptured aneurysms, glioblastomas, and falx or olfactory groove meningiomas. Unilateral lesions confined to prefrontal cortex are very difficult to diagnose clinically and may remain silent until the pathology spreads to the other side. The emergence of developmentally primitive reflexes such as grasping, rooting, and sucking is often considered a sign of frontal lobe disease. However, these reflexes are seen only in patients with very large lesions that extend into the premotor components of the frontal lobes. Occasionally, these reflexes also emerge in the context of metabolic encephalopathies where there are no structural lesions in the frontal lobes. The vast majority of patients with prefrontal lesions and frontal lobe behavioral syndromes do not display these reflexes. The suck, root, and grasp reflexes are therefore not helpful for either detecting or excluding a frontal lobe lesion.

Physiological observations in laboratory primates provide some clues about frontal lobe function. Visual cortex (area 17) neurons sensitive to a certain stimulus orientation will almost always fire when an object in that orientation enters their receptive field. In contrast, many of the visually responsive neurons in the prefrontal cortex have little specificity for color, size, orientation, or movement. Instead, these neurons are very sensitive to the behavioral relevance of the environmental event. Thus a neuron that responds briskly to a stimulus associated with reward may drastically alter its response to the same visual stimulus when it becomes associated with an aversive or neutral outcome (Kojima, 1980; Thorpe, Rolls, and Maddison, 1983). It could be suggested that this sensitivity to the behavioral relevance rather than to the physical dimensions of stimuli provides the neural substrate for realizing that "all is not gold that glitters." Without this type of neuron, a given stimulus would automatically call up a predetermined response regardless of context, so that neither autonomy from the environment nor abstract thinking would be possible.

Despite all we have learned in the past few decades, a certain sense of uniqueness is still associated with frontal lobe function. It is quite remarkable, for example, that sizable frontal lobe lesions can remain clinically silent for many years. Even after massive bifrontal lesions, change can often be detected only in comparison with the previous personality of the individual rather than in reference to any set of absolute behavioral standards. Many of the alterations associated with prefrontal lesions appear to overlap with the range of normal human behavior. A vast number of improvident, irresponsible, inappropriate, and facetious individuals, for example, give no evidence of demonstrable brain damage. In contrast, the lack of visible damage to the pertinent cerebral area is a rare occurrence in individuals with aphasia, amnesia, apraxia, or unilateral neglect. A major computational function of prefrontal cortex may be to integrate the activity of multiple cortical areas so as to reach an optimal match between context and response. Damage to this part of the brain would thus result in behavioral deficits that are context dependent rather than static.

The network approach postulates that the same cognitive domain can be impaired after damage to different parts of the brain as long as these parts belong to the same large-scale neural network. Accordingly, lesions in the caudate nucleus or in the mediodorsal nucleus of the thalamus (structures which can be considered subcortical components of the prefrontal network) can also give rise to the clinical picture of a frontal lobe syndrome. This is one reason why the mental state changes associated with degenerative basal ganglia diseases such as Parkinson's or Huntington's disease so often take the form of a frontal lobe syndrome. Bilateral multifocal lesions, none of

which are individually large enough to cause specific cognitive deficits such as aphasia or neglect, can collectively interfere with the connectivity and therefore with the integrating function of prefrontal cortex. This is one reason why a frontal lobe syndrome is the single most common behavioral profile associated with a variety of bilateral multifocal brain diseases including metabolic encephalopathy, multiple sclerosis, B-12 deficiency, and others. In fact, the vast majority of patients with the clinical diagnosis of a frontal lobe syndrome tend to have lesions that do not involve prefrontal cortex but that involve either the subcortical components of the prefrontal network or its connections with other parts of the brain. In order to avoid the paradox of making a diagnosis of frontal lobe syndrome in a patient with no evidence of frontal cortex disease, it is advisable to use the diagnostic term "prefrontal network syndrome," with the understanding that the responsible lesions can lie anywhere within this distributed network.

Modulatory Pathways and the Ascending Reticular Activating System

The neural connections of the cerebral cortex can be divided into two main functional groups. One group contains discrete point-to-point interconnections (e.g., corticocortical, corticostriatal, and thalamocortical) that subserve specific *channel* functions. The connections between Wernicke's area and Broca's area or those between the frontal eye fields and posterior parietal cortex belong to this group of connections. These connections tend to employ excitatory amino acids as transmitter substances and convey *content-specific* information. The destruction of this type of pathway leads to impairments in the relevant functional domains, and the resultant interruption of information processing cannot be reversed by pharmacological agents.

The second group of cortical connections can be designated as *modulatory*. They arise from relatively small nuclei in the basal forebrain and brain stem, reach all parts of the cerebral cortex, and regulate overall behavioral states related to all cognitive and comportmental domains. These modulatory connections employ acetylcholine, dopamine, serotonin, and norepinephrine as the transmitter substances. They convey *state-specific* information. Their dysfunction is implicated in abnormalities of behavioral states related to arousal, attention, mood, and motivation. The activity of these modulatory pathways, and the behavioral states they modulate, can be altered by existing pharmacological agents. There are four major corticopetal modulatory pathways in the human brain: cholinergic projections originating in the basal forebrain Ch1-Ch4 cell groups, dopaminergic projections originating in the substantia nigra–ventral tegmental area, serotonergic projections originating in the raphe nuclei, and noradrenergic projections originating in the nucleus locus coeruleus (Mesulam, 1990, 1995).

The ascending cholinergic pathway from the basal forebrain to the cerebral cortex acts as an excitatory neuromodulator for cortical neurons. Its activity enhances the response of cortical neurons to novel and behaviorally relevant stimuli. This pathway contributes to the modulation of arousal and attention and may also play an important role in gating sensory-limbic interactions related to memory processes. In keeping with these relationships, cholinergic antagonists suppress the arousal-related low-voltage fast activity of the cortical EEG and the novelty-related P300 response. The degeneration of these ascending cholinergic projections in Alzheimer's disease may contribute to the emergence of memory and attentional disturbance in these patients.

The behavioral affiliations of ascending monoaminergic pathways have been investigated extensively. The dopaminergic cells of the substantia nigra–ventral tegmental area are sensitive to motivationally relevant stimuli and to cues that signal their existence (Schultz, 1994). The dopaminergic pathways from the ventral tegmental area and substantia nigra to the cerebral cortex and striatum have therefore been implicated in the modulation of motivational arousal and may contribute to the establishment and maintenance of behaviors related to substance addiction (Fontana, Post, and Pert, 1993; Wilson et al., 1995). Noradrenergic projections from the nucleus locus coeruleus to the cerebral cortex are thought to increase the signal-to-noise ratio and the sharpness of tuning in the response of cortical neurons to sensory stimuli (Foote, Bloom, and Aston-Jones, 1983; Levin, Craik, and Hand, 1988). The activity of neurons in the nucleus locus coeruleus appears to be correlated with the level of arousal and overall efficiency in tasks requiring attentive behavior (Ray, Mirsky, and Pragay, 1982; Aston-Jones et al., 1994). In addition to this role in attention and arousal, the ascending noradrenergic pathway is thought to play an important role in regulating mood and in the influence of emotional arousal on memory and learning (Cahill et al., 1995). The efficacy of noradrenergic reuptake inhibitors in the treatment of depression and the finding of a decreased number of neurons in the nucleus locus coeruleus in suicide victims provide indirect support for this behavioral affiliation (Arango, Underwood, and Mann, 1996). The ascending serotonergic projections from the raphe nuclei to the cerebral cortex are thought to

exert additional regulatory influences on emotion and motivation. Serotonergic denervation may promote aggressive behaviors, whereas drugs that increase the availability of serotonin decrease appetite and can relieve depression and obsessive-compulsive symptomatology (Olivier et al., 1995).

Moruzzi and Magoun (1949) had introduced the concept of a brain stem reticular activating system (ARAS) that acted to desynchronize the cortical electroencephalogram via a relay in the thalamus. The foregoing discussion indicates that the original concept of the ARAS needs to be expanded to include the additional ascending corticopetal cholinergic and monoaminergic projections listed above. According to this expanded concept, the ARAS is a network of direct and transthalamic corticopetal connections that modulate overall behavioral states related to arousal, attention, mood, and motivation.

The cerebral cortex is not only the target of ascending modulatory projections from the brain stem, basal forebrain, and thalamus, but also the source of descending feedback projections to several components of the ARAS. Almost all parts of the cerebral cortex project to the reticular nucleus of the thalamus and therefore influence its inhibitory effect upon other thalamic relay nuclei (Jones, 1975). The projection from the cerebral cortex to the reticular nucleus of the thalamus is mostly excitatory, whereas the projections to this thalamic nucleus from the brain stem cholinergic nuclei are inhibitory. The reticular nucleus of the thalamus is thus in a position to act as a site for integrating the reciprocal influence of the cerebral cortex and of the brain stem reticular formation upon the transthalamic processing of information. Although the basal forebrain projects to the entire cerebral cortex, it receives feedback projections from a very limited set of cortical areas, namely, those that belong to the limbic and paralimbic zones of the cerebral cortex (Mesulam and Mufson, 1984). This asymmetry is a feature of all the other ascending modulatory pathways of the ARAS: they project widely to the cerebral cortex but receive very few reciprocal connections from the cerebral cortex (Mesulam, 1987a).

The modulatory pathways reviewed in this section highlight the multiple factors involved in the coordination of cognition and comportment. Language, spatial orientation, attention, memory, emotion, and motivation are each coordinated by the individual large-scale networks reviewed in previous sections. The ARAS introduces a complementary level of control which modulates the overall behavioral states within which the specific behaviors related to these domains can unfold. In the process of remembering, for example, the content of what is recalled is likely to be determined primarily by the information that flows along the point-to-point sensory-limbic interconnections. However, the speed of recall, and even the emotional coloring of the recollection, may be regulated by the activity of the modulatory pathways that innervate the relevant regions of limbic and association cortex. Among all the complex factors involved in the neural control of comportment and cognition, those that represent the contributions of the ARAS and its modulatory pathways are the most accessible to therapeutic manipulation by existing pharmacological agents.

Attention and Confusional States (Delirium)

The waking individual is bombarded by vast quantities of sensory inputs emanating from the environment and a nearly unlimited supply of thoughts generated by the brain itself. Only a fraction of this information can be processed at any given time. Furthermore, the part of the stimulus field that is most relevant for achieving goals of immediate importance (and these could range from food scavenging to resolving deep ethical dilemmas) keeps shifting from one moment to another in a manner that reflects the inner needs of the individual, the dictates of the environment, and the experience gained in the past. Hence there is a need for postulating a neural mechanism that helps to focus awareness on the behaviorally relevant aspects of the stimulus space. The word *attention* is used as a generic term to designate a family of neural mechanisms for selecting the part of the stimulus array that is to capture the center of awareness and for holding the other, potentially distracting, stimuli at bay.

Attentional processes can be divided into 2 major classes. First, there is a *matrix* or *state* function that regulates the power of concentration, the span of vigilance, the efficiency of detection, and the signal-to-noise ratio. This type of attentional process has been associated with the ARAS, including its cortical components in the frontal lobes. The second class of attentional processes could be conceptualized in terms of *vector* or *channel* functions that regulate the target of attention in one of the many behaviorally relevant spaces (extrapersonal, mnemonic, semantic, visceral, and so forth). This component is more akin to selective attention and is generally associated with a complex network of cortical structures and their subcortical connections. Spatial orientation represents one aspect of selective attention. The organization of this function and its disruption in the form of hemispatial neglect has been described above.

Disturbances in the matrix aspects of attention are frequently encountered in clinical practice. The term *confusional state* is used to designate a condition where an impairment of the attentional matrix is the most salient aspect of the clinical picture. Additional impairments in other areas of cognition and comportment may also exist, but they are either secondary to the attentional deficit or of lesser severity. The clinical picture of a patient in an acute confusional state is familiar to most physicians. Attention either wanders aimlessly or is suddenly focused on an irrelevant stimulus that becomes the source of distraction. Thought and skilled movement also become vulnerable to interference. The patient may volunteer that "concentration" and "thinking straight" require great effort. The stream of thought loses its coherence because of frequent intrusions by competing thoughts and sensations. Skilled-movement sequences, even those as automatic as dialing the telephone or using eating utensils, lose their coherence and show signs of disintegration, perseveration, and impersistence. When asked to recite the months of the year in reverse order, the patient may say, "December, November, October, September . . . October, November, December, January," showing the inability to inhibit intrusion from familiar but inappropriate response tendencies. This clinical description highlights the 3 major features of confusional states: (1) disturbance of vigilance, heightened distractibility, impersistence, and perseveration; (2) inability to maintain a coherent stream of thought; and (3) inability to carry out a sequence of goal-directed movements.

Additional mental state deficits are also common in confusional states. Perceptual distortions may lead to illusions and even hallucinations. The patient is often, but not always, disoriented and shows evidence of faulty memory. Mild anomia, dysgraphia, dyscalculia, and constructional deficits are common. Judgment may be faulty, insight appears blunted, and affect is quite labile, with a curious tendency for facetious witticism. Some of these deficits are probably secondary to attentional difficulties. For example, if the patient is allowed sufficient drilling during the acquisition stage of a learning task, memory improves. Calculations that appear devastated when tested mentally may prove quite accurate when the patient is allowed to use pencil and paper. Other deficits of mental state (for example, poor judgment and hallucinations) may be affected independently by the underlying pathogen that gives rise to the confusional state.

The most common cause of a confusional state is a toxic or metabolic encephalopathy caused by polypharmacy, renal failure, and the like. Some toxic metabolic encephalopathies, especially those associated with withdrawal states, may lead to agitated and psychotic deliria. When aspects such as hallucinations, delusions, and agitation become more prominent than the attentional deficit in a metabolic encephalopathy, then the designation of "delirium" or "toxic psychosis" may be more appropriate than that of a "confusional state." Confusional states may also arise as the sole manifestation of subdural hematoma, seizures, multifocal brain disease (such as systemic lupus erythematosis, fat emboli, vasculitis, or degenerative dementia), and even focal cerebral lesions.

Strokes in the medial temporo-occipital cortex of either hemisphere can trigger agitated confusional states. These patients usually also have visual field deficits. In another group of patients, acute confusional states may arise as the major manifestation of stroke in the inferior parietal lobule and the inferior frontal gyrus of the right hemisphere. These patients may have very few, if any, additional neurological signs, and the presence of a cerebrovascular accident can be overlooked. The occurrence of confusional states with unilateral strokes in the right side of the brain has led to the suggestion that the right hemisphere may have a specialized function in regulating not only spatial orientation but also the matrix aspect of attention. In further support of this hypothesis, some investigators have reported that patients with right hemisphere damage tend to show greater deficits in vigilance (arousal) functions than those with equivalent left hemisphere damage (Boller et al., 1986). As noted above, the prefrontal network plays an important role in regulating the "executive" aspects of the attentional matrix and can give rise to confusional states when damaged bilaterally. The one common denominator of all cortical areas associated with confusional states is that they belong to the group of heteromodal cortex.

Other Neurobehavioral Syndromes

Primary Degenerative Dementia

Dementia is said to exist when a disease of the brain causes a gradual decline of mental function that interferes with daily living activities appropriate for age and background. Dementia can arise at any age but is particularly prevalent in old age. Dementias can be associated with several distinct clinical profiles. The single most common clinical pattern involves an initial deterioration of memory and attention that is soon accompanied by additional impairments of language, visuospatial perception, and comportment. Social graces and concern for external appearance may initially appear relatively preserved, and the patient may look healthy and alert until the terminal stages. The vast majority of patients with this clinical pattern suffer from Alzheimer's disease. Alzheimer's disease is characterized by histological lesions known as senile plaques and neurofibrillary tangles. The disease causes a gradual loss of neurons, synapses, and several transmitter systems, especially the cholinergic innervation of the cerebral cortex. The pathology starts in the limbic system and eventually spreads to other components of association cortex in the temporal, parietal, and frontal lobes. This anatomical predilection pattern of the neuropathology is in keeping with the early and severe impairment of memory function and the subsequent involvement of other cognitive and comportmental domains. Psychiatric manifestations such as depression, hallucinations, delusions, and a variety of obstreperous behaviors are part of the syndrome, especially in its more advanced stages.

Less common clinical patterns in dementia are characterized by a relative preservation of memory in patients who display the gradual dissolution of language functions or the progressive emergence of a frontal network syndrome. These syndromes have been designated as Primary Progressive Aphasia and Frontal Dementia, respectively. In patients with the latter syndrome, uninhibited and bizarre behaviors or apathy may dominate the clinical picture. This is the one group of patients with dementia where erroneous diagnoses of primary psychiatric diseases are common. In contrast to patients with Alzheimer's disease, who usually display anorexia and decreased libido, those with frontal dementias may manifest overeating and hypersexuality. The neuropathological examination in patients with Primary Progressive Aphasia and Frontal Dementia characteristically shows the lesions of Pick's disease or a focal cortical neuronal loss without specific histopathological features. Some patients with these unusual clinical patterns show the neuropathological lesions of Alzheimer's disease, but with an atypical anatomical distribution.

Basal Ganglia Disorders

Traditional neurology tends to associate the basal ganglia almost exclusively with motor function. However, extensive clinical evidence indicates that almost every disease of the basal ganglia is also associated with major changes in mental state. One possibility is that the basal ganglia are directly involved in the coordination of complex behavior. In keeping with this suggestion, it is well known that the basal ganglia have extensive connections with association and limbic cortex. The striatum (i.e., the caudate, putamen, nucleus accumbens) is a component of almost all large-scale neurocognitive networks. In monkeys, lesions confined to the head of the caudate nucleus may give rise to deficits in cognitive tasks without necessarily interfering with motor function. The behavioral affiliations of individual striatal sectors tend to be identical to those of the cortical areas with which they are most closely interconnected. Degenerative basal ganglia diseases associated with major mental state alterations include Huntington's chorea, Parkinson's disease, Wilson's disease, supranuclear ophthalmoplegia (Steele-Olszewski-Richardson syndrome), olivopontocerebellar degeneration, corticobasalganglionic degeneration, and Hallervorden-Spatz disease. Many degenerative basal ganglia diseases are associated with a certain degree of cortical pathology that could also contribute to the mental state alterations.

The mental state alterations of Huntington's and Parkinson's diseases have been studied extensively. Huntington's disease is genetically transmitted in an autosomal dominant fashion. The genetic defect is based on the mutation of a gene on chromosome 4 that encodes a protein of unknown function known as huntingtin. The disease leads to severe atrophy of the caudate nuclei and sometimes to an additional loss of cortical neurons. Its 2 major clinical components are chorea and mental state alterations. The changes in mental state may precede the chorea by many years. The mental changes are usually very similar to components of the frontal lobe syndrome but can also include psychotic features. Patients show deficits in insight and judgment and may develop a pervasive state of apathy and abulia. Depression is also common and may represent another biological manifestation of the underlying neurological disease. As the degenerative changes of Huntington's disease become established, the depression tends to blend into a state of apathetic dementia.

Parkinson's disease is associated with a severe loss of the pigmented cells in the substantia nigra–ventral tegmental area and in the nucleus locus coeruleus. At least one-fourth of elderly patients with Parkinson's disease develop severe progressive mental state changes compatible with a diagnosis of dementia. The most customary change is an overall slowing of mentation known as bradyphrenia. The resultant attentional deficits tend to cause secondary problems in almost all other cognitive functions. Drugs that alleviate the motor components of Parkinson's disease are rarely useful for reversing the mental changes. Occasionally an amnestic condition similar to Alzheimer's dementia may develop, but this is probably associated with the concomitant occurrence of pathological changes characteristic of Alzheimer's disease. In the late stages of the disease, visual hallucinations of a frightening nature can occur. Patients may not volunteer this information unless they are specifically questioned. Depression is very common. Some have argued that this is a reactive depression to a disabling disease. Others have pointed out that this may reflect the loss of cortical norepinephrine resulting from the loss of neurons in the nucleus locus coeruleus. Antidepressants are useful in the management of these patients.

The Gilles de la Tourette Syndrome

The Tourette syndrome includes three features: (1) *motor tics* in the neck, face, and sometimes lower limbs; (2) *vocal tics,* which can range from throat clearing to snorting, barking, swearing, and profanity (coprolalia); and (3) *obsessive-compulsive symptomatology,* which includes recurring thoughts (for example, that family members will get into an accident), repetitive touching, collecting, obsessive orderliness, and sometimes compulsive self-mutilation. The entire triad is present in less than a third of the population with this syndrome. Generally the diagnosis requires one of the first 2 components to be present. It is conceivable, however, that a subset of patients with Tourette's syndrome will have salient obsessive-compulsive component while the tics may be subtle or perhaps even absent. This possibility introduces additional considerations to the differential diagnosis of obsessive-compulsive disorders. There is a familial pattern of occurrence, even though the exact mode of inheritance has not been determined. This disorder is more common in males and has a typical age of onset between 6 and 20 years.

The colorful symptomatology in these patients may have grave consequences. The tendency for coprolalia or for emitting bizarre noises can make it extremely difficult to continue with schooling or to keep a job. Occasionally the coprolalia will lead to altercations with passers-by or with the police. Sometimes the tics can be so violent that they lead to cervical disc disease and major dental problems. The obsessive-compulsive tendencies are sometimes marked. One patient almost faced divorce because of his compulsive tendency to keep pinching his wife's cheeks. With the exception of these specific behavioral problems, patients with Tourette's syndrome tend to be bright, intelligent, and insightful. Treatment of the Tourette syndrome is usually very successful, providing relief to approximately 80 percent of patients (Mesulam and Petersen, 1987). The mainstay of therapy is dopamine-blocking neuroleptics. Success in isolated cases has also been reported with a variety of other agents, especially clonidine.

Corpus Callosum Syndromes

The corpus callosum provides a large white-matter tract for interconnecting the 2 hemispheres of the brain. When this commissure is intact, the brain functions as an integrated whole. Damage to the corpus callosum leads to disconnection syndromes (such as anomia for objects placed in the left hand or ideomotor apraxia in the left limbs). Another and most dramatic syndrome of callosal disconnection has been designated as the "alien hand." This syndrome occurs when a callosal lesion is combined with damage to the frontal lobes. In this condition the patient may report that one hand (usually the left) is out of his control and behaves independently, sometimes in ways that cause physical harm to the patient himself. This clinical condition illustrates how the fabric of volition can be fragmented in patients with brain damage.

Hallucinations

Hallucinations may occur in a large variety of neurological syndromes. They are particularly frequent in toxic metabolic encephalopathies, especially those associated with fever, infection, drug overdose, and withdrawal syndromes. Hallucinations are common in conditions such as Parkinson's disease and narcolepsy. Hallucinations are also seen in several other conditions and can be divided into 2 classes: ictal hallucinations and release hallucinations. *Ictal hallucinations* are associated with partial epilepsy, especially in the occipital and temporal lobes. These can occur in any modality, but the visual and olfactory hallucinations are probably the most common. If the site of the epileptic discharge is in the occipital lobe, then the visual hallucinations may take the form of flashes, simple geometric shapes, and colors. If the site is in the temporal lobe, especially in the right hemisphere, complex images and scenes are hallucinated. Ictal hallucinations are brief, stereotyped, and sometimes localized to a certain part of the visual field. Similar hallucinations may also occur in patients with migraine, especially as part of the aura.

Release hallucinations occur either when there is a major problem with the peripheral sensory apparatus or when there is central pathology in the brain (McNamara, Heros, and Boller, 1982). Loss of peripheral acuity, as in progressive deafness, macular degeneration, and cataracts, may lead to vivid visual and auditory hallucinations in elderly individuals, even when no other evidence of psychiatric disturbance exists. The visual hallucinations may include small animals and complex colorful scenes, and the auditory hallucinations may take the form of continuously repeating jingles, fragments of tunes, or entire songs. In contrast to the ictal hallucinations, these are continuous and repetitive. Initially these release hallucinations are associated with fear, but eventually they result in annoyance and then resignation. The combination of

pathological alterations in the peripheral sensory apparatus and also in visually responsive cortical areas appears to be associated with the most florid hallucinations. On rare occasions brain lesions alone, especially in the distribution of the basilar artery, may result in release hallucinations (for example, *peduncular hallucinosis*). In those instances investigators have suggested that such lesions permanently release hypothetical mechanisms that inhibit the daytime occurrence of dreaming. A physiological disturbance of the same mechanisms may underlie the hypnagogic hallucinations seen in narcolepsy.

Relevance of Neurological Disease to Psychiatric Practice

The relevance of neurological disease to psychiatric practice can be reviewed from the vantage point of at least 4 patient groups. The great majority of patients who seek psychotherapy have no demonstrable structural or physiological abnormality in the brain. Patients in this group seek help either because they face intolerable circumstances or because they have acquired maladaptive response patterns to life experiences. Except for the symptomatic prescription of medication, the biological approach to brain function is of relatively little assistance in the management of these patients.

Recent observations suggest the existence of another group of individuals in whom genetic (constitutional) or developmental peculiarities in brain organization could impede normal emotional and behavioral maturation without necessarily leaving other traces of a static brain lesion (Weintraub and Mesulam, 1983; Price et al., 1990). From the clinical vantage point, individuals in this hypothetical second group might not be easily differentiated from those in the first. They are, however, likely to develop relatively atypical syndromes that are generally less responsive to traditional treatment.

A third group contains patients with the major psychoses, severe characterological problems, intractable phobias, and pervasive obsessive-compulsive disorders. Increasing evidence suggests that these patients may have underlying abnormalities of brain physiology such as abnormal response to lactate in panic attacks, dopaminergic dysfunction or fronto-limbic pathology in schizophrenia, fronto-striatal dysfunction in obsessive-compulsive disorders, and monoaminergic dysfunction in depression. Despite the putative cerebral pathology within the latter 2 categories, none of the patients in these first 3 groups can be said to have a neurological disease in the traditional sense of the term.

This chapter has focused on yet a fourth group of patients who suffer disorders of mental state and behavior in conjunction with acquired neurological disease. Sometimes the presence of the underlying brain disease is obvious, whereas in other instances the findings on the traditional neurological examination may be quite subtle or even elusive. The term *organic* is most commonly associated with syndromes in this fourth group of patients. This chapter has endeavored to show that the spectrum of these syndromes is exceedingly wide, that the nature of the lesion determines the clinical features of the behavioral deficit, and that an understanding of the relevant brain-behavior interactions is essential for accurate differential diagnosis and effective management.

Detecting the neurological disease responsible for behavioral problems is an important exercise. But the task of the psychiatrist does not end there. Even patients with an organic brain syndrome are often in need of psychiatric help. In addition to providing emotional support, the aims of such treatment include teaching new strategies for coping with the disability and for circumventing it. Educating the patient and the family about those behavioral problems that are the immediate consequences of brain damage also helps to lessen frustration and to alleviate misplaced feelings of guilt and anger. The psychiatrist needs to realize, however, that traditional psychodynamic models of mental function and psychotherapy may be only partially applicable to the population of individuals with neurological disease. In the course of treating these patients, for example, the therapist's nonverbal messages (in the form of the approving, disapproving, or questioning "hmm-hmm's") may be misconstrued, the patient's tone of voice may have little relation to his state of feeling, the mechanisms for insight may be shattered, strong affect may reflect seizure activity rather than psychological antecedents, the ability for abstraction may be deficient, memory may be faulty, and bizarre language may not reflect an underlying thought disturbance. In addition to these clinical considerations, new sets of indications may need to be entertained in prescribing psychoactive medication. The use of neuroleptics and antidepressants in temporal lobe epilepsy, for example, must take into account the putative effect of these agents on seizure thresholds (Clifford et al., 1985).

Despite these potential obstacles, the psychiatric treatment of individuals with neurological disease can become a rewarding experience for the patient as well as for the therapist. The expertise needed for managing these patients may eventually lead to the establishment of a multidisciplinary specialty based on closer interactions between neurology and psychiatry. The insights likely to emerge from this interaction could then pave the way for important advances in exploring the neurobiological foundations of mental function.

References

Ahern, G. L., D. L. Schomer, J. Kleefield, H. Blume, G. R. Cosgrove, S. Weintraub, and M. M. Mesulam. 1991. Right hemisphere advantage for evaluating emotional facial expressions. *Cortex* 27(2):193–202.

Ahern, G. L., M. O'Connor, J. Dalmau, A. Coleman, J. B. Posner, D. L. Schomer, A. G. Herzog, D. A. Kolb, and M.-M. Mesulam. 1994. Paraneoplastic temporal lobe epilepsy with testicular neoplasm and atypical amnesia. *Neurol.* 44:1270–1274.

Alexander, M. P., D. T. Stuss, and D. F. Benson. 1979. Capgras syndrome: a reduplicative phenomenon. *Neurol.* 29:334–339.

Ames, F. R., and D. Saffer. 1983. The sunflower syndrome. *J. Neurol. Sci.* 59:1–11.

Anderson, N. E., and W. E. Wallis. 1986. Activation of epileptiform activity by mental arithmetic. *Arch. Neurol.* 43:624–626.

Arango, V., M. D. Underwood, and J. J. Mann. 1996. Fewer pigmented locus coeruleus neurons in suicide victims: preliminary results. *Biol. Psych.* 39:112–120.

Aston-Jones, G., J. Rajkowski, P. Kubiak, and T. Alexinsky. 1994. Locus coeruleus neurons in monkey are selectively activated by attended cues in a vigilance task. *J. Neurosci.* 14:4467–4480.

Bauer, R. M. 1984. Autonomic recognition of names and faces in prosopagnosia. *Neuropsychol.* 22(4):457–469.

Bear, D., and P. Fedio. 1977. Quantitative analysis of interictal behavior in temporal lobe epilepsy. *Arch. Neurol.* 34:454–467.

Bear, D. M. 1979. Temporal lobe epilepsy: a syndrome of sensory-limbic hyperconnection. *Cortex* 15:357.

Benowitz, L. I., D. M. Bear, R. Rosenthal, M. M. Mesulam, E. Zaidel, and R. W. Sperry. 1983. Hemispheric specialization in nonverbal communication. *Cortex* 19(1):5–11.

Benson, F. 1985. Aphasia and related disorders: a clinical approach. In *Principles of behavioral neurology,* ed. M.-M. Mesulam. Philadelphia: F. A. Davis. 193–238.

Berson, R. J. 1983. Capgras' syndrome. *Am. J. Psychiat.* 140:969–978.

Boller, F., K. Yokoyama, P. Ackles, P. Hood, and R. Jennings. 1986. Lack of heart rate changes during an attention task in patients with right hemisphere lesions. *Neurol.* 36(S):131.

Brumback, R. A., R. D. Stanton, and H. Wilson. 1984. Right cerebral hemispheric dysfunction. *Arch. Neurol.* 41:248–249.

Cahill, L., R. Babinsky, H. J. Markowitsch, and J. L. McGaugh. 1995. The amygdala and emotional memory. *Nature* 377:295–296.

Claparède, M. 1911. Recognition et moiite. *Archives de neurologie* 11:79–90.

Clifford, D. B., J. L. Rutherford, F. G. Hicks, and C. F. Zorumski. 1985. Acute effects of antidepressants on hippocampal seizures. *Ann. Neurol.* 18:692–697.

Cohen, H. D., R. C. Rosen, and L. Goldstein. 1976. Electroencephalographic laterality changes during human sexual orgasm. *Archives of Sexual Behavior* 5:189–199.

Corbetta, M., F. M. Miezin, G. L. Shulman, and S. E. Petersen. 1993. A PET study of visuospatial attention. *J. Neurosci.* 13:1202–26.

Damasio, A. R. 1985. Disorders of complex visual processing: agnosias, achromatopsia, Balint's syndrome, and related difficulties of orientation and construction. In *Principles of behavioral neurology,* ed. M.-M. Mesulam. Philadelphia: F. A. Davis. 259–288.

——— 1992. Aphasia. *New Eng. J. Med.* 326:531–539.

Damasio, A. R., H. Damasio, and G. W. Van Hoesen. 1982. Prosopagnosia: anatomic basis and behavioral mechanisms. *Neurol.* 32:331–341.

Dimond, S. J., L. Farrington, and P. Johnson. 1976. Differing emotional response from right and left hemisphere. *Nature* 261:690–692.

Downer, De C. J. L. 1962. Interhemispheric integration in the visual system. In *Interhemispheric relations and cerebral dominance,* ed. V. B. Mountcastle. Baltimore: Johns Hopkins University Press.

Faught, E., J. Falgout, D. Nidiffer, and F. Dreifuss. 1986. Self-induced photosensitive absence seizures with ictal pleasure. *Arch. Neurol.* 43:408–410.

Flor-Henry, P. 1979. On certain aspects of the localization of the cerebral systems regulating and determining emotion. *Biol. Psych.* 14:677–698.

Fontana, D. J., R. M. Post, and A. Pert. 1993. Conditioned increases in mesolimbic dopamine overflow by stimuli associated with cocaine. *Brain Res.* 629:31–39.

Foote, S. L., F. E. Bloom, and G. Aston-Jones. 1983. Nucleus locus coeruleus: new evidence of anatomical and physiological specificity. *Physiol. Rev.* 63:844–914.

Geschwind, N. 1965. Disconnection syndromes in animals and man. *Brain* 88:237–294.

Geschwind, N., and W. Levitsky. 1968. Human brain: left-right asymmetries in temporal speech region. *Science* 161:186–187.

Gitelman, D. R., N. M. Alpert, S. M. Kosslyn, K. Daffner, L. Scinto, W. Thompson, and M.-M. Mesulam. 1996. Functional imaging of human right hemispheric activation for exploratory movements. *Ann. Neurol.* 39:174–179.

Gloor, P., A. Olivier, A. F. Quesney, F. Andermann, and S. Horowitz. 1982. The role of the limbic system in experiential phenomena of temporal lobe epilepsy. *Ann. Neurol.* 12:129–144.

Hall, R. E., and K. Cornish. 1977. Role of the orbital cortex in cardiac dysfunction in unanesthetized rhesus monkey. *Exper. Neurol.* 56:289–297.

Harlow, J. M. 1868. Recovery from the passage of an iron bar through the head. *Massachusetts Medical Society Publications* 2:327–346.

Heilman, K. M., R. Scholes, and R. T. Watson. 1975. Auditory affective agnosia: disturbed comprehension of affective speech. *J. Neurol. Neurosurg. Psych.* 38:69–72.

Heller, W., and J. Levy. 1981. Perception and expression of emotion in right-handers and left-handers. *Neuropsychol.* 19:263–272.

Herzog, A. G., M. M. Seibel, D. L. Schomer, J. L. Vaitukaitis, and N. Geschwind. 1986. Reproductive endocrine disorders in women with partial seizure of temporal lobe origin. *Arch. Neurol.* 43:341–346.

Hood, T. W., J. Siegfried, and H. G. Wieser. 1983. The role of stereotactic amygdalectomy in the treatment of temporal lobe epilepsy associated with behavioral disorders. *Appl. Neurophysiol.* 46:19–25.

House, A., M. Dennis, C. Warlow, K. Hawton, and A. Molyneux. 1990. Mood disorders after stroke and their relation to lesion location: a CT scan study. *Brain* 113:1113–29.

Jones, E. G. 1975. Some aspects of the organization of the thalamic reticular complex. *J. Comp. Neurol.* 162:285–308.

Ketter, T. A., P. J. Andreason, M. S. George, C. Lee, D. S. Gill, P. I. Parekh, M. W. Willis, P. Herscovitch, and R. M. Post. 1996. Anterior paralimbic mediation of procaine-induced emotional and psychosensory experiences. *Arch. Gen. Psychiatr.* 53:59–69.

Kimura, D. 1973. The asymmetry of the human brain. *Sci. Amer.* 228:70–78.

Kojima, S. 1980. Prefrontal unit activity in the monkey: relation to visual stimuli and movements. *Exper. Neurol.* 69:110–123.

Kral, V. A. 1962. Senescent forgetfullness: benign and malignant. *Canad. Med. Assoc. J.* 86:257–260.

Kuhl, D. E., J. Engel, M. E. Phelps, and C. Selin. 1980. Epileptic pattern of local cerebral metabolism and perfusion in man determined by emission computed tomography of 18 FDG and 13 NH3. *Ann. Neurol.* 8:348–360.

LeDoux, J. E., M. E. Thompson, C. Iadecola, L. W. Tucker, and D. J. Reis. 1983. Local cerebral blood flow increases during emotional processing in the conscious rat. *Science* 221:576–578.

Levin, B. E., R. L. Craik, and P. J. Hand. 1988. The role of epinephrine in adult rat somatosensory (SmI) cortical metabolism and plasticity. *Brain. Res.* 443:261–271.

Lishman, W. A. 1968. Brain damage in relation to psychiatric disability after head injury. *Br. J. Psychiat.* 114:373–410.

MacLean, P. D. 1949. Psychosomatic disease and the visceral brain: recent developments bearing on the Papez theory of emotion. *Psychosom. Med.* 11:338–353.

Mark, V. H., and F. R. Ervin. 1970. *Violence and the brain.* New York, Harper & Row.

McNamara, M. E., R. C. Heros, and F. Boller. 1982. Visual hallucinations in blindness: the Charles Bonnet syndrome. *Int. J. Neurosci.* 17:13–15.

Mendez, M. F., J. L. Cummings, and D. F. Benson. 1986. Depression in epilepsy. *Arch. Neurol.* 43:766–771.

Mesulam, M.-M. 1981a. A cortical network for directed attention and unilateral neglect. *Ann. Neurol.* 10(4):309–325.

——— 1981b. Dissociative states with abnormal temporal lobe EEG: multiple personality and the illusion of possession. *Arch. Neurol.* 38:176–181.

——— 1985. Patterns in behavioral neuroanatomy: association areas, the limbic system, and hemispheric specialization. In *Principles of behavioral neurology,* ed. M.-M. Mesulam. Philadelphia: F. A. Davis. 1–70.

——— 1986. Frontal cortex and behavior. *Ann. Neurol.* 19(4):320–325.

——— 1987a. Asymmetry of neural feedback in the organization of behavioral states. *Science* 237(4814):537–538.

——— 1987b. Lidocaine toxicity and the limbic system. *Am. J. Psychiat.* 144(12):1623–24.

——— 1990. Large-scale neurocognitive networks and distributed processing for attention, language, and memory. *Ann. Neurol.* 28(5):597–613.

——— 1994a. Higher visual functions of the cerebral cortex and their disruption in clinical practice. In *Principles and practice of ophthalmology,* ed. D. M. Albert and F. A. Jakobiec. Philadelphia: Saunders. 2640–53.

——— 1994b. The multiplicity of neglect phenomena. *Neuropsych. Rehab.* 4:173–176.

——— 1994c. Neurocognitive networks and selectively distributed processing. *Rev. Neurol. (Paris)* 150:564–569.

——— 1995a. Cholinergic pathways and the ascending reticular activating system of the human brain. *Ann. N.Y. Acad. Sci.* 757:169–179.

——— 1995b. Notes on the cerebral topography of memory and memory distortion: a neurologist's perspective. In *Memory distortion,* ed. D. L. Schacter, J. T. Coyle, G. D. Fischbach, M.-M. Mesulam, and L. E. Sullivan. Cambridge, Mass.: Harvard University Press. 379–385.

Mesulam, M.-M., and E. J. Mufson. 1984. Neural inputs into the nucleus basalis of the substantia innominata (Ch4) in the rhesus monkey. *Brain* 107:253–274.

Mesulam, M.-M., and R. C. Petersen. 1987. Treatment of Gilles de la Tourette's syndrome: eight-year practice-based experience in a predominantly adult population. *Neurol.* 37:1828–33.

Milner, B., S. Corkin, and H. L. Teuber. 1968. Further analysis of the hippocampal amnesic syndrome: 14-year follow-up study of HM. *Neuropsychol.* 6:215–234.

Mitchell, W., M. A. Falconer, and D. Hill. 1954. Epilepsy with fetishism relieved by temporal lobectomy. *Lancet* 2:626–630.

Moruzzi, G., and H. W. Magoun. 1949. Brain stem reticular formation and activation of the EEG. *Electroenceph. Clin. Neurophysiol.* 1:459–473.

Olivier, B., J. Mos, R. van Oorschot, and R. Hen. 1995. Serotonin receptors and animal models of aggressive behaviors. *Pharmacopsychiatry* 28:80–90.

Pincus, J. H. 1981. Violence and epilepsy. *New Eng. J. Med.* 305:696–698.

Price, B. H., K. R. Daffner, R. M. Stowe, and M. M. Mesulam. 1990. The comportmental learning disabilities of early frontal lobe damage. *Brain* 113(pt. 5):1383–93.

Ray, C. L., A. F. Mirsky, and E. B. Pragay. 1982. Functional analysis of attention-related unit activity in the reticular formation of the monkey. *Exper. Neurol.* 77:544–562.

Reeves, A. G., and F. Plum. 1969. Hyperphagia, rage, and dementia accompanying a ventromedial hypothalamic neoplasm. *Arch. Neurol.* 20:616–624.

Robinson, R. G., K. L. Kubos, L. B. Starr, K. Rao, and T. R. Price. 1984. Mood disorders in stroke patients. Importance of location of lesion. *Brain* 107:81–93.

Ross, E. D. 1980. Sensory-specific and fractional disorders of recent memory in man. *Arch. Neurol.* 37:193–200.

——— 1985. Modulation of affect and nonverbal communication by the right hemisphere. In *Principles of behavioral neurology,* ed. M.-M. Mesulam. Philadelphia: F. A. Davis. 239–258.

Ross, E. D., and M. M. Mesulam. 1979. Dominant language functions of the right hemisphere? Prosody and emotional gesturing. *Arch. Neurol.* 36:144–148.

Sackeim, H. A. 1982. Lateral asymmetry in bodily response to hypnotic suggestion. *Biol. Psych.* 17:437–447.

Sackeim, H. A., R. C. Gur, and M. C. Savey. 1978. Emotions are expressed more intensely on the left side of the face. *Science* 202:434–436.

Schacter, D., J. T. Coyle, G. D. Fischbach, M.-M. Mesulam, and L. E. Sullivan, eds. 1995. *Memory distortion.* Cambridge, Mass.: Harvard University Press.

Schleidt, W., and M. Schleidt. 1960. Störung der Mutter-Kind-Beziehung bei Truthühnern durch Gehorverlust. *Behaviour* 16:3–4.

Schultz, W. 1994. Behavior-related activity of primate do-pamine neurons. *Rev. Neurol. (Paris)* 150:634–639.

Signoret, J.-L. 1985. Memory and amnesias. In *Principles of behavioral neurology,* ed. M.-M. Mesulam. Philadelphia: F. A. Davis. 169–192.

Slater, E., and A. W. Beard. 1963. The schizophrenic-like psychoses of epilepsy. *Br. J. Psychiat.* 109:95–150.

Spiers, P. A., D. L. Schomer, H. W. Blume, and M.-M. Mesulam. 1985. Temporolimbic epilepsy and behavior. In *Principles of behavioral neurology,* ed. M.-M. Mesulam. Philadelphia: F. A. Davis. 289–326.

Springer, S. P., and G. Deutsch. 1981. *Left brain, right brain.* San Francisco: Freeman.

Stern, D. B. 1977. Handedness and the lateral distribution of conversion reactions. *J. Nerv. Ment. Dis.* 164:122–128.

Taylor, D. C. 1975. Factors influencing the outcome of schizophrenia-like psychosis in patients with temporal lobe epilepsy. *Psychol. Med.* 5:249–254.

Thorpe, S. J., E. T. Rolls, and S. Maddison. 1983. The orbitofrontal cortex: neuronal activity in the behaving monkey. *Exp. Brain. Res.* 49:93–115.

Tranel, D., and A. R. Damasio. 1985. Autonomic recognition of familiar faces by prosopagnosics: evidence for knowledge without awareness. *Neurol.* 35:119–120.

Ungerleider, L. G., and M. Mishkin. 1982. Two cortical visual systems. In *The analysis of visual behavior,* ed. D. J. Ingle, R. J. W. Mansfield, and M. D. Goodale. Cambridge, Mass.: MIT Press. 549–586.

Weingartner, H., R. M. Cowan, D. L. Murphy, J. Martello, and C. Gerdt. 1981. Cognitive processes in depression. *Arch. Gen. Psychiatr.* 38:42–47.

Weintraub, S., and M. M. Mesulam. 1983. Developmental learning disabilities of the right hemisphere: emotional, interpersonal, and cognitive components. *Arch. Neurol.* 40:463–8.

————— 1985. The examination of mental state. In *Principles of behavioral neurology,* ed. M.-M. Mesulam. Philadelphia: F. A. Davis. 71–123.

Weintraub, S., M. M. Mesulam, and L. Kramer. 1981. Disturbances in prosody: a right-hemisphere contribution to language. *Arch. Neurol.* 38:742–4.

Wilson, C., G. G. Nomikos, M. Collu, and H. C. Fibiger. 1995. Motivational correlates of motivated behavior: importance of drive. *J. Neurosci.* 15:5169–78.

Yozawitz, A., G. Bruder, S. Sutton, L. Sharpe, B. Gurland, J. Fleiss, and L. Costa. 1979. Dichotic perception: evidence for right hemisphere dysfunction in affective psychosis. *Br. J. Psychiat.* 135:224–237.

Zoccolatti, P., D. Scabini, and C. Violani. 1982. Electrodermal responses in patients with unilateral brain damage. *J. Clin. Neuropsychol.* 4:143–150.

Recommended Reading

Critchley, M. 1953. *The parietal lobes.* London: Arnold.

Ferrier, D. 1876. *The functions of the brain.* London: Smith, Elder.

Geschwind, N. 1974. *Selected papers on language and the brain.* Boston: Reidel.

Nielsen, J. M. 1936. *Agnosia, apraxia, aphasia.* New York: Hoeber.

Penfield, W., and T. C. Erickson. 1971. *Epilepsy and cerebral localization.* Springfield, Ill.: Thomas.

7

STEVEN E. HYMAN

The Neurobiology of Mental Disorders

We traditionally describe a subset of human brain diseases as mental disorders because their primary pathophysiology affects the most complex, integrative functions of the brain. Because we are only beginning to understand the neurobiology of these disorders, this chapter represents an early progress report. Throughout history many attempts to understand these terrible illnesses have been made; but only recently have adequate scientific tools existed to make possible cumulative progress. In no small part this lag reflects the extremely difficult scientific problems posed by mental disorders. The brain is not only the most complex organ in the body, it is also the most complex object of human inquiry. Unraveling the pathophysiology of mental disorders requires an understanding of: the function and dysfunction of neural circuits that subserve cognition, emotion, and behavior; the cells that make up those circuits; and the molecular constituents of those cells. We also must understand how genes and environment collaborate to build our brains, including brains vulnerable to mental disorders, and how our brains change throughout life. Despite the difficulty of these tasks, progress is not merely possible, it is visibly occurring. The goal of this chapter is not to be encyclopedic, but, after a brief description of relevant genetics and neurobiology, to illustrate recent progress made in the biology of several common, serious mental disorders: a subset of the anxiety disorders, addictive disorders, mood disorders, and schizophrenia.

Overview of Genetics

Genetics promises to be a powerful approach for understanding what goes wrong in the brain of individuals with mental disorders. The goal of genetics research is to identify and clone the particular versions of genes (alleles) that create vulnerability to mental disorders. This is accomplished by using molecular genetics to find linkage of a trait (in this case the trait is a disease) to known DNA markers, followed by the application of other molecular techniques to identify the actual disease gene. In an alternative approach, one uses knowledge about the pathophysiology of a disorder to make an educated guess about which genes might be dysfunctional, and then employs molecular genetics to prove that the gene is actually responsible. This latter "candidate gene" approach is increasingly applied, but our understanding of pathophysiology, and the number of identified genes expressed in the brain, are still so limited that success with this approach remains several years away. The isolation and cloning of vulnerability alleles will provide critical tools for investigating the brain, potentially novel molecular targets for drug development, and tools for epidemiologists to investigate not only genetic but also nongenetic factors that contribute to the risk of illness.

Genes give rise to proteins, which are the critical building blocks of cells. When genetic variation has functional consequences, it is generally because an important protein is expressed in a different amount, at a different time or place, or with a different structure (and hence function) from the norm. Even before identifying vulnerability alleles, investigators have made substantial progress by studying spatial and temporal patterns of gene expression in normal brain development and function. The resulting "molecular maps" have been particularly enlightening when combined with systems level analyses of neural circuits involved in cognition, emotion, and behavior. Building on these approaches are technologies that are increasingly permitting us to mutate, overexpress, or inactivate any gene of our choosing in the mouse brain. These methods have produced significant progress in understanding, for example, mechanisms underlying certain types of memory in the mouse that serve as models of explicit human memory formation (Tsien et al., 1996).

The identification of alleles that produce vulnerability to mental disorders will permit us to focus rapidly developing molecular neurobiologic approaches on the pathophysiology of mental illness. We will be able to ask where such genes function in the brain, at what stages of development, and under what circumstances. We can also ask how disease vulnerability alleles alter the normal function of cells, and what might occur if these genes were not expressed at all. Beyond neurobiology, disease vulnerability genes will become critical epidemiologic tools, defining risk groups and perhaps helping narrow the search for modifiable environmental risk factors which act together with vulnerability genes to produce mental illness. While the importance of finding vulnerability genes is clear, the search has proved to be far more difficult than originally hoped.

There is no question that vulnerability to mental disorders, and indeed to almost all human disease, has a significant genetic component. For various mental disorders the contribution of genes has been demonstrated by family, twin, and adoption studies. At the same time, however, genetic epidemiology and molecular genetics have shown that in all cases analyzed to date, vulnerability to mental disorders is genetically complex; specifically, no single gene causes manic depressive illness, schizophrenia, or for that matter any mental disorder or normal cognitive or emotional trait. Rather, multiple alleles found at multiple loci within the genome interact to produce vulnerability to mental disorders. In all cases it also appears that nongenetic factors must interact with the relevant genes to convert vulnerability into illness. It is also possible that no single allele is required for any mental disorder, i.e., in different families, different combinations of alleles may influence vulnerability. This complex genetic scenario is not unique to mental disorders. Serious diseases that are due to a single genetic locus (often called Mendelian disorders after Gregor Mendel, who initially described the inheritance of traits due to the operation of a single locus), such as cystic fibrosis or Huntington's disease, are relatively rare. The genetics of most common human disorders such as coronary artery disease, diabetes mellitus, mood disorders, hypertension, and schizophrenia are characterized by complexity—many alleles, each contributing small effects and interacting with the environment.

Not surprisingly, it is easier to identify alleles that contribute major effects than to identify multiple alleles each of which contributes small effects or which contribute effects only when other critical alleles are also present (Lander and Schork, 1994). Thus many genes that cause Mendelian disorders such as cystic fibrosis and Huntington's disease have already been identified and cloned. This has permitted the development of tools to study the pathogenesis of these disorders. In the case of Huntington's disease, for example, antibodies have been raised which specifically recognize the abnormal protein product of the Huntington's disease gene, and have been used to investigate the processes that actually kill cells. In addi-

tion, for Huntington's disease and for certain forms of familial Alzheimer's disease (a small percentage of Alzheimer's disease is "Mendelian"; the vast bulk of the disease is, however, genetically complex), transgenic mice have been produced which reproduce some of the pathology of the human disorder. Such mice will be useful not only for investigating the pathophysiology of these diseases but also for developing treatments. In contrast, no genetically complex human disorder has yet been satisfactorily solved. The molecular and statistical technologies to do so, however, are under active development, and indeed all of medicine is entering the era of grappling with genetically complex disorders.

Compounding technical difficulties are also difficulties in defining phenotypes; indeed, for mental disorders this may be the most difficult problem. While the *Diagnostic and Statistical Manual of Mental Disorders* of the American Psychiatric Association, DSM-IV (American Psychiatric Association, 1994), is a useful tool for communication, it would be foolhardy to think that its criteria represent "natural kinds" that map onto the genome. The hardest task for psychiatric geneticists is the identification of groups of individuals with mental symptoms genetically homogeneous enough to permit the tools of complex genetic analysis to work. Such analyzable phenotypes may be very similar to clinical schizophrenia, bipolar disorder, or early onset depression, but what maps onto the genome may be only simpler symptom complexes or clusters of symptoms that are not readily predictable a priori. During the coming decade, the field will have a great deal of work to do to solve the problem of phenotype in mental disorders.

Overview of Neurobiology

Complexity

It has been estimated crudely that there are 100 billion neurons in the human brain; however, this number reveals little of the brain's complexity. Unlike other organs, the cells of the brain are composed of thousands of distinct types, with specific structural and functional phenotypes. Even this enormous number of cell types underestimates the complexity of the brain, in part because the primary elements of communication are not neurons but synapses, the specialized gaps across which neurons communicate with one another. In the simplest synaptic arrangement, one neuron releases a neurotransmitter that diffuses across a synaptic cleft and binds to specific receptors on the postsynaptic neuron. Neurons in the brain generally form thousands of synapses; some form more than 100,000 synapses with other neurons. Overall more than 100 trillion synapses may exist in a single human brain, perhaps tenfold more. The number of connections that each individual cell within the brain makes is unlike any computer ever devised in its complexity. Moreover, this connectivity is highly specific. Neurons form nodes in both local circuits and circuits involving long-distance interactions; in addition, any given neuron may form a node on not just one but many different circuits that process the inputs and outputs of the brain.

Overlying the complexity of connections in the brain is the complexity of communication modes. Neurons use more than 100 identified chemicals to signal one another, and additional trophic substances released by both neurons and glia also affect communication. Single neurons may synthesize and release multiple neurotransmitters, and probably every neuron in the brain responds to many different neurotransmitters. In addition, each neurotransmitter may interact with many different types of receptors. For example, the neurotransmitter serotonin has at least 14 different receptors in the human brain, with each receptor linked to complex post-receptor signaling mechanisms. Much of the specificity and nuance of communication in the brain results from the combinatorial interactions of multiple neurotransmitters, receptors, and post-receptor signaling pathways acting on each individual neuron.

The crowning aspect of the brain's complexity, however, is its plasticity. The brain undergoes significant changes in the structure and function of neurons and synapses based on experience. Not only during brain development but even in the mature brain, every memory that lasts beyond a few minutes, whether a conscious, explicit memory, a new motor program, or an emotional memory of the type described below, involves the activation of a cascade of genes within critical neurons resulting in the synthesis of a set of new proteins that alter the structure of synapses. Ultimately, alterations in the strength of existing synapses, the production of new synapses, and the pruning of others change the function of circuits in the brain and thus behavior.

Circuitry

The brain receives, processes, and interprets sensory information and controls motor, autonomic, and neuroendocrine outputs. It carries out both emotional and cognitive processing. This includes the decoding of information carried by complex symbols such as language, and the appraisal of the survival value of experiences. The brain selects among sensory inputs for those worthy of attention, and records significant experiences

and procedures in different types of memory. All of these functions are carried out in the brain by neurons arrayed in remarkably complex but precise networks. Thus, for example, visual processing involves the transmission of information from the retina to a way station in the thalamus (the lateral geniculate nucleus) to the primary visual cortex in the occipital lobe. Visual information is then analyzed by many parallel circuits into components such as form, motion, and color, and then synthesized into our picture of the visual world along with information from other sensory modalities and that stored as explicit and implicit memories, including, for example, the emotional valence of a visual experience. This type of precise point-to-point communication in the brain is carried out by large numbers of axons operating in parallel. Synaptic communication within such circuits is fast (occurring in the millisecond range) and is largely accomplished by excitatory amino acid neurotransmitters, most notably glutamate. Fast inhibitory transmission in the brain also largely utilizes amino acids. The most significant inhibitory neurotransmitter is gamma aminobutyric acid (GABA). In the brain stem and spinal cord, many of the functions of GABA are shared by yet another amino acid, glycine. As might be expected for neurotransmitters serving such roles, glutamate and GABA are synthesized by a very large number of different neurons throughout the brain.

Monoamine Systems in the Brain

Superimposed on these precise, parallel circuits which use fast excitatory transmission are systems of neurotransmitters that serve complex modulatory roles (reviewed in Hyman and Nestler, 1993). Neurotransmitters that serve primarily modulatory roles include the neuropeptides and the purines, such as adenosine, which have diverse roles, e.g., dampening or facilitating communication within local circuits and in long projection neurons in the brain. Perhaps the most remarkable modulatory systems, however, are those which utilize the monoamine neurotransmitters (norepinephrine, serotonin, dopamine, and histamine), and the related neurotransmitter acetylcholine. These are particularly important in psychiatry because many psychotherapeutic drugs, and also drugs of abuse, interact initially with monoamine systems.

In contrast to glutamate and GABA, the monoamine neurotransmitters and acetylcholine are synthesized in a highly restricted number of nuclei in the reticular core of the brain stem (and in the case of acetylcholine, also in the basal forebrain) which project widely to cortical and subcortical targets as well as to the spinal cord. For example, norepinephrine is produced by the locus coeruleus (LC), a small nucleus in the dorsal pons, and by several smaller nuclei nearby. Essentially all of the norepinephrine in the cerebral cortex is derived from the LC. Serotonin is produced by a small number of nuclei lying near the brain stem raphe. The projections of the serotonin neurons are the most widely divergent of all the monoamines, innervating essentially every structure in the central nervous system, albeit with varying densities. Dopamine is synthesized by neurons in the midbrain, in the substantia nigra pars compacta, which projects to the caudate and putamen (these are the neurons that die in Parkinson's disease), and in the ventral tegmental area (VTA), which projects to the nucleus accumbens, hippocampus, amygdala, and cerebral cortex. In addition, there are restricted dopaminergic systems within the hypothalamus which are involved in neuroendocrine control.

The anatomic organization of monoamine systems, in which a small number of neurons innervate wide areas of the central nervous system, combined with their known physiology (e.g., all LC norepinephrine and dopamine neurons appear to fire in unison), is consistent with the hypothesis that they perform a unique set of intrinsic regulatory functions in the brain. These neurotransmitters are thought to set the responsiveness of large areas of brain circuitry, acting via G protein–linked receptors and second messenger systems (reviewed in Hyman and Nestler, 1993; 1996) rather than transmitting precise data about the external world. These intrinsic regulatory functions are thought to play critical roles in determining whether an organism is awake or asleep, in regulating its level of attention and its degree of motivation toward a particular goal, in determining whether the organism is inattentive, paying focused attention, or engaged in scanning vigilance, and in determining which stimuli are worth recording in memory. These systems are also involved in relaying the emotional significance of an object or event throughout the brain, after emotional processing nuclei have determined, for example, whether objects or experiences are to be approached and repeated, avoided, escaped, or treated neutrally. Given the functional architecture of the monoamine systems in the brain, it is not surprising that they are critically involved in the actions of antidepressant and antipsychotic drugs, and many other drugs that affect emotion and cognition.

Applications to Mental Disorders

Because mental disorders affect the higher integrative functions of the human brain, animal models that fully

replicate these diseases may not be possible. However, animal models used to investigate particular aspects of cognitive and emotional processing and to predict responses to some psychotropic drugs have been useful. The utility of animal models to study emotion becomes obvious if one uses the conceptual tools of cognitive and integrative neuroscience, focusing on the mechanisms and circuits underlying cognitive and emotional processing rather than on the delineation of subjective states, which are difficult to study with rigor in humans and essentially impossible in animals (Rogan and LeDoux, 1996). Significant progress has been made, for example, in understanding the neural substrates of negative emotion related to fear and avoidance (LeDoux, 1996; Davis, 1997) and positive emotion related to reward (Schultz, Dayan, and Montague, 1997). With the additional tools of functional neuroimaging, it has been possible to move from animal-based studies of emotional processing to the investigation of pathways involved in cognition and emotion in humans. Increasingly armed with neural circuit–based hypotheses and cognitive and emotional tasks aimed at isolating particular neural circuits in the brain, investigators have begun to examine specific functional abnormalities in a variety of mental disorders such as anxiety disorders (Rauch et al., 1995), obsessive-compulsive disorder (Baxter et al., 1992; Rauch et al., 1994), depression (Drevets et al., 1997; Mayberg, 1997), and addictive disorders (Breiter et al., 1997).

Functional neuroanatomic studies in psychiatry have been complemented by morphometric imaging and postmortem studies which have reported anatomic abnormalities in schizophrenia (Suddath et al., 1990; Pakkenberg, 1990; Andreasen et al., 1994) and autism (Courchesne, Townsend, and Saitoh, 1994), diseases in which abnormal brain development might be expected to leave clear anatomic traces. In addition, postmortem human studies have begun to identify putative cellular and molecular abnormalities in a variety of mental disorders such as depression (Klimek et al., 1997) and schizophrenia (Benes et al., 1991; Heckers et al., 1991; Akbarian et al., 1993a, b).

Specific Disorders

Anxiety Disorders

The DSM-IV (American Psychiatric Association, 1994) classifies panic disorder, post-traumatic stress disorder, simple phobias, social phobia, generalized anxiety disorder, and obsessive-compulsive disorder as anxiety disorders. The neural substrates and genetic, developmental, and other environmental factors that contribute to these disorders will no doubt turn out to be varied. Nevertheless, for those disorders such as post-traumatic stress disorder, panic disorder, or phobias in which an inability to regulate fear appears to be the core symptom, there is increasing evidence that circuits involving the amygdala play a central role. In contrast, obsessive-compulsive disorder (OCD) appears preliminarily to reflect abnormal function of the striatum. However, our understanding of the neurobiology of OCD is not well developed. This section on the neurobiology of anxiety disorders will therefore focus on the "core" anxiety disorders where substantial progress has been made.

Genetics. Of the core anxiety disorders, the genetics of panic disorder have been best investigated. Other disorders, such as social phobia and vulnerability to post-traumatic stress disorder, are in earlier stages of investigation, and generalized anxiety disorder as currently diagnosed may be too heterogeneous for genetic investigation. Recent reports of genes that might be linked to normal anxiety or "worry" are too tenuous in terms of statistical power or underlying neurobiologic hypotheses to warrant extensive comment at this point.

In one family study of anxiety disorders, 17.3% of the first-degree relatives of probands with panic disorder also had panic disorder; an additional 7.4% were characterized as having probable panic disorder (Crowe et al., 1983). In contrast, among the first-degree relatives of normal controls, only 1.8% had panic disorder and 0.4% had probable panic disorder. The risk of generalized anxiety disorder was found to be no different in the families of the probands versus controls. Overall, first-degree relatives of probands with panic disorder exhibit a risk ranging between 3.4 and 14.7% greater than among the first-degree relatives of normal controls (Crowe et al., 1983; Mendlewicz, Papadimitrious, and Wilmotte, 1993; reviewed in National Institute of Mental Health, 1997). Data from twin studies of anxiety disorders also support a genetic basis. Monozygotic twins had a significantly higher concordance rate for panic disorder than did dizygotic twins (Torgerson, 1983; Kendler, Neale, et al., 1993). There have been no published adoption studies. The existing studies have not provided a convincing model of the mode of inheritance, and no reproducible linkage to DNA markers has been demonstrated.

Studies of OCD in adults are consistent with a genetic contribution but are few in number. In one twin study monozygotic twins showed 33% concordance for OCD and dizygotic twins 7% concordance (Carey and Gottesman, 1981). There are no adoption studies to date.

Neural substrates of anxiety disorders. Neural systems involved in the processing of cognitive and emotional information are highly interdependent, as is well illustrated by many functions of the prefrontal cortex. Thus, making too great a distinction between cognitive and emotional pathways is somewhat arbitrary. Nonetheless, certain neural circuits in the brain have as their central function what might be called emotional processing, i.e., appraising the significance of objects, events, and other organisms, (e.g., dangerous, edible, desirable) and then regulating the functioning of sensory, motor, and neuroendocrine systems to respond adaptively. Additionally, in humans, subjective emotional responses occur in parallel with these physiologic responses (LeDoux, 1996).

The older psychiatric literature often ascribed emotional processing to a group of subcortical structures lumped together as the "limbic system." While "limbic" remains a useful anatomic term, this older formulation is neither fully accurate nor useful (LeDoux, 1996). For example, the hippocampus is anatomically part of the limbic system but is critical to explicit (cognitive) memories, not emotional memories. In investigations of emotional disorders, it is more useful to analyze the particular pathways associated with a given emotion, e.g., to analyze separately the circuits involved in fear or the circuits involved in reward, both of which affect "limbic" and "non-limbic" structures. This pathway- or circuit-based view of the brain is more accurate than one thought of in terms of separate autonomous regions.

The survival of an organism is dependent on its ability to predict dangerous circumstances or, alternatively, circumstances under which food, water, or other requirements of life can be obtained. Thus, beyond producing the immediate response to a stimulus, a critical role for emotional systems is to put novel stimuli into adaptive behavioral and physiologic repertoires, which, depending on the nature of the stimulus, may be defensive or appetitive, for example. This requires that emotional circuits be able to control the encoding of memories; in general, the greater the survival relevance of an event, the stronger the resulting memory will be and the more powerfully it will modify subsequent behavior.

Investigators take advantage of this learning function to analyze pathways involved in emotion. For example, they use simple classical conditioning experiments, similar to those first described by Pavlov, to analyze the mechanisms by which animals predict danger or reward. In such experiments, a neutral stimulus (conditioned stimulus) such as a tone or a light consistently precedes an emotionally laden stimulus (the unconditioned stimulus), which can be aversive, such as foot shock, or rewarding, such as food. After a period of learning (conditioning), the animal behaves as if the conditioned stimulus predicted the time of arrival and magnitude of the aversive or rewarding event. (Pavlov used a bell to signal food.) The ability to activate emotional systems with a simple tone or light has permitted analysis of the relevant pathways using careful brain lesions or pharmacologic blockers to interrupt the behavioral outputs of the circuit at different points. In the analysis of conditioned fear, investigators have paired a neutral tone with foot shock, and mapped the pathways from sensory input to behavioral response. Different investigators have used the freezing response, startle response, or autonomic responses as the end point to identify fear in laboratory rats. These mapping studies have identified the amygdala, a complex structure within the temporal lobes, as critical to fear responses (LeDoux, 1996; Rogan and LeDoux, 1996; Davis, 1997).

When a tone comes to signal danger, the information reaches the amygdala via two pathways. Rapidly processed but only approximate information comes from the thalamus (the medial geniculate nucleus of the thalamus is a way station in auditory processing), and more highly processed but more slowly arriving information comes from the auditory areas of the cerebral cortex. The rapid pathway from the thalamus permits an organism to get ready to respond to danger before the sensory and cognitive processing that can distinguish a real danger from a false alarm is complete. Survival favors erring on the side

of preparedness (LeDoux, 1996). From these sensory systems, information is transmitted to the major input nucleus of the amygdala, the lateral nucleus. Recent electrophysiology experiments have found that with fear conditioning that pairs a tone with foot shock, there is strengthening of the synaptic connections made by neurons projecting from the auditory thalamus to the lateral amygdala. The mechanism by which these synapses are strengthened is an alteration in cellular physiology called long-term potentiation, in which subsequent stimuli produce greater responses in the lateral amygdala. Long-term potentiation is thought to be one of the major mechanisms underlying many forms of memory. As at some synapses in the hippocampus, where explicit memories are encoded, long-term potentiation in the amygdala requires activation of one type of glutamate receptor, the N-methyl-D-aspartic acid (NMDA) receptor (Davis, 1997).

From the lateral amygdala, information is passed to the central nucleus, the major output nucleus of the amygdala, which projects, in turn, to effector sites for fear responses. (See Figure 7.1.) Projections to different regions of the hypothalamus activate the sympathetic nervous system and induce the release of stress hormones such as corticotropin-releasing hormone (CRH). The production of CRH in the paraventricular nucleus of the hypothalamus activates a cascade leading to release of glucocorticoids from the adrenal cortex. These put the

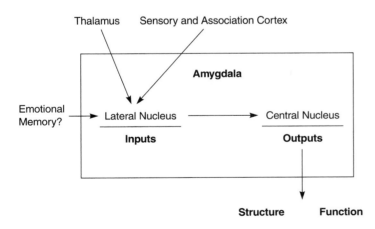

Figure 7.1 Summary of the flow of information into and out of the amygdala. Fear-related information enters the amygdala via its lateral nucleus. It is thought that the synaptic connections made in the lateral nucleus may be an important site of emotional memory. Information is passed from the lateral nucleus to the central nucleus, from which projection fibers to the central gray matter, hypothalamus, and other brain regions produce the physiological responses characteristic of fear.

body in a catabolic state and also suppress inflammatory responses. (This hypothalamic-pituitary-adrenal axis is often chronically hyperactive in depression, as will be discussed below.) The central nucleus also projects to different parts of the periaqueductal gray matter (PAG), which initiates descending analgesic responses via endogenous opioids that can suppress pain in an emergency, and which also activates species-typical defensive responses (e.g., many animals freeze when fearful). Under normal circumstances these are adaptive responses that enhance survival; but when dysregulated, such pathways can produce disabling anxiety disorders.

Information that requires invasive experiments can be obtained only in animals. With functional neuroimaging such as positron emission tomography (PET), single photon emission tomography (SPECT), and functional magnetic resonance imaging (fMRI), however, investigators can now extend what has been learned in animals to humans. For example, fearful facial expressions have been shown to activate the amygdala in fMRI studies of normal human subjects (Breiter et al., 1996). There have also been functional imaging studies in anxiety disorders, such as PET studies of brain activation in phobias (Rauch et al., 1995). Functional imaging using circuit-based hypotheses and well-chosen emotional and cognitive tasks should help elucidate the role of these pathways in both health and mental disorders.

Relevance to anxiety disorders. Anxiety differs from fear in that the fear-producing stimulus is either not present or not immediately threatening. In anticipation of danger, however, the same arousal, vigilance, physiologic preparedness, and negative affects and cognitions occur. Different types of internal or external factors or triggers act to produce the anxiety symptoms of panic disorder, agoraphobia, post-traumatic stress disorder, simple phobias, generalized anxiety disorder, and the prominent anxiety that commonly occurs in major depression. However, the core anxiety symptoms in all of these disorders may result from a "final common pathway"—an inability of the brain to regulate its fear circuitry, specifically that involving the amygdala.

The emotional memories produced by fear have both cognitive and affective components. The cognitive component (which requires the hippocampus) records the precise setting in which danger was experienced and the details of the experience; the emotional component (which requires the amygdala) can reinitiate the entire physiologic cascade of the fear response. Under normal circumstances, such emotional memories are adaptive.

We avoid putting ourselves in harm's way a second time after being burned, bitten, or chased once. Faced with cues that predict danger, we are physiologically ready to escape or to fight. However, the strength and long-lived nature of emotional memories are the central problem for individuals with post-traumatic stress disorder (PTSD), and possibly for individuals with agoraphobia who have come to associate the terribly aversive experience of a panic attack with a variety of previously neutral contexts. PTSD follows one or more experiences of overwhelming trauma. Individuals have nightmares, increased startle responses, "numbing" of normal feelings, and cue-dependent reliving of the traumatic experience. The pathophysiology of PTSD is hypothesized to involve overstimulation of amygdala-based fear pathways and the development of powerful, maladaptive emotional memories. Any cue reminiscent of the original trauma can bring the entire experience flooding back, including the aversive aspects. The price we pay for having such powerful survival systems in the brain is the possibility of their usurpation by overpowering stimuli. A similar picture is emerging with respect to the biology of reward as the basis for addiction, as discussed below.

The type of stimulus that might activate and perhaps overwhelm amygdala-based fear pathways is fairly clear for PTSD. In agoraphobia, a panic attack might be the unconditioned stimulus, and the context in which the attack occurs now becomes a conditioned cue generating anticipatory anxiety and even a triggered panic attack. But what initiates the "false alarms" in panic disorder? Are the fear pathways in these individuals hypersensitive to begin with? Do panic attacks arise elsewhere in the brain and then alter the physiology of the fear pathways, sensitizing them so that panic becomes spontaneous or easily triggered by conditioned cues? These are important questions for further research. One leading hypothesis is that interoceptive information may be the initial trigger for panic attacks (Papp, Klein, and Gorman, 1993). An infusion of sodium lactate can provoke panic attacks in individuals with panic disorder but generally not in unaffected control subjects or successfully treated patients. One hypothesis is that lactate acts similarly to CO_2 inhalation (another inducer of panic). Lactate is rapidly metabolized to bicarbonate (HCO_3), which does not cross the blood-brain barrier, but which leads to an increase in central P_{CO2} (i.e., an increase in carbon dioxide concentrations in the fluid perfusing the brain). Increased central P_{CO2} would secondarily cause hyperventilation, but more important, CO_2 could represent a "suffocation alarm" acting via medullary chemoreceptors. It is known, for example, that increased central P_{CO2} increases locus coeruleus firing rates and likely activates other stress systems.

Treatment for panic attacks and other anxiety disorders now focuses on selective serotonin reuptake inhibitor (SSRI) antidepressants, benzodiazepines, and cognitive-behavioral therapies. The actual targets in the brain for these drugs is not known, although there are high levels of serotonin, GABA$_A$/benzodiazepine, and neuropeptide receptors in the amygdala. One advantage of understanding brain circuitry is the ability to target novel medications to specific receptors in specific structures. Thus, if there is confirmation that the lateral amygdala is critically involved in fearful emotional memories, it might prove worthwhile to identify the serotonin, benzodiazepine, and other receptor types found in this area in order to develop potentially new drug treatments.

It has long been known that fear conditioning can be extinguished. If a rat that has been conditioned with a tone and foot shock is exposed repeatedly to the tone without any foot shock, the fear responses to the tone will abate. Cognitive behavioral therapies are aimed at extinguishing fear responses in anxiety disorder. There is interesting (LeDoux, 1996), albeit controversial (Davis, 1997), evidence that emotional memories are not erased with extinction but suppressed by the frontal lobes. This is consistent with the clinical observation that under stress or with an intercurrent depression, anxiety disorder patients may relapse even after successful prior treatment.

Obsessive-compulsive disorder. There is growing evidence that obsessive-compulsive disorder differs from the other traditional anxiety disorders in its neurobiologic substrates. Current hypotheses have focused on the loop from the frontal cortex to the striatum, to the thalamus, and then back to the striatum. Much of the direct evidence has focused on the striatum, which is composed of the caudate nucleus and the putamen. Structural neuroimaging studies have given varied results; however, a well-conducted morphometric MRI study found a reduced caudate volume in OCD patients compared with control subjects (Robinson et al., 1995). PET studies have also implicated the caudate nucleus in OCD (Baxter et al., 1992). In addition, neurologic diseases that affect the striatum may include obsessive-compulsive symptoms. These include Tourette's syndrome (Palumbo, Maughan, and Kurlan, 1997), in which motor and phonic tics, thought to be of striatal origin, often coexist with obsessions (which have been speculatively conceptualized as cognitive tics) and compulsions. There are, in addition, preliminary ob-

servations that have correlated a fraction of cases of acute onset pediatric obsessive-compulsive disorder with Sydenham's chorea, the latter being a classic symptom of acute rheumatic fever. In these children the symptoms of OCD begin before the movement disorder. The hypothesized pathogenesis is that antibodies against streptococci mimic a striatal antigen which is then attacked as an "innocent bystander." Some children develop obsessive-compulsive disorder following streptococcal infections even in the absence of movement disorder (Swedo et al., 1997). The major pharmacologic treatment for OCD is serotonin reuptake inhibitors, and indeed the striatum contains many types of serotonin receptors in high concentration.

Addictive Disorders

Genetics. Among the addictive disorders, genetic analyses are most advanced in the study of alcoholism. Indeed, little is known about the genetics of vulnerability to opiate, cocaine, or nicotine addiction. Alcoholism has long been known to run in families; twin and adoption studies have established that the familial nature of alcoholism is genetically based (Cloninger, Bohman, and Sigvardsson, 1981). As in other mental disorders, it is now abundantly clear that vulnerability to alcoholism is genetically complex, involving multiple genes and nongenetic factors. For both males and females, genetic factors operate most powerfully in pedigrees with early onset alcoholism (Heath et al., 1991; Kendler et al., 1992). Although there is controversy as to whether a particular allele of the dopamine D2 receptor is associated with vulnerability to alcoholism or other addictive disorders, the preponderance of evidence is strongly against such an association (Gelernter, Goldman, and Risch, 1993).

The kinds of genes that might contribute to the risk of alcoholism or other addictions are not yet known. It has been hypothesized that alleles predisposing to alcoholism are so common that they may have conferred some selective advantage prior to the time when humans learned how to ferment grain or grapes. Indeed, the genetic factors which are best understood in relation to alcohol abuse and dependence actually appear to be protective. These are variations in genes encoding 2 principal enzymes involved in alcohol metabolism, alcohol dehydrogenase and aldehyde dehydrogenase, which give rise to the alcohol flush reaction (Thomasson et al., 1991). This reaction is characterized by facial flushing, tachycardia, and headache following the consumption of alcohol, thus creating an aversive response similar to that of disulfiram

(Antabuse). Some degree of flushing occurs in approximately half of individuals of Chinese or Japanese ancestry and approximately one-third with Korean ancestry. The most alcohol-sensitive individuals are homozygous at the aldehyde dehydrogenase locus for a variant that causes a serious deficiency in acetaldehyde metabolism. Among these individuals alcoholism is almost unknown.

Pending more specific knowledge, risk factors for alcoholism and other addictions may be divided into factors that increase the likelihood of drug use and factors that increase the likelihood that with use, the individual will be "captured" by the drug. It has been hypothesized that the interaction of a person's genes and environment during brain development might influence both the willingness of an individual to experiment with drugs and alcohol and the risk of becoming dependent upon experimentation. The study of environmental factors that produce risk versus resilience with respect to drug use and addiction is also in its early stages. Environmental factors that influence drug-taking behavior include drug availability and acceptability in an individual's subculture, behavioral alternatives to drug use, coexisting psychiatric illness, and chronic pain. Factors that influence the "capture rate" include the intrinsic addictiveness of the drug used, including the form in which it is administered (e.g., smoked crack cocaine is more addictive than chewed coca leaves). Intrinsic addictiveness depends on the ability of a substance to be reinforcing and to produce neural adaptations that lead to addiction, as will be described below.

Neural substrates of addiction. The core feature of addictive disorders is compulsive drug use and inability to control use, despite negative consequences. Tolerance may also occur, but is neither necessary nor sufficient to make the diagnosis. In the case of opiates and alcohol, physical dependence as manifested by a somatic withdrawal syndrome may also occur. As in studies of fear and anxiety, investigations of the neural substrates of drug abuse and addiction have profited from the development of animal models. Rodents and nonhuman primates, for example, can be trained to self-administer drugs abused by humans. Though not equivalent to human addiction, these models have permitted important investigations into the behaviorally relevant substrates of drug abuse in the brain. They have made possible studies in which lesions or pharmacologic agents have been used to block drug-induced reinforcement and have also permitted focused application of the tools of molecular biology and neurophysiology to brain areas required for reinforcement. The result is an increasingly precise understanding of how drugs such as cocaine, amphetamines, and opiates pro-

duce long-term alterations in the function of neurons that control behavior (Self and Nestler, 1995; Hyman, 1996). Recently, investigators began using noninvasive neuroimaging approaches to test in human subjects hypotheses developed using animal models. They observed, for example, that the brain regions implicated in animal models of cocaine action also appear to be involved in humans (Volkow et al., 1997, Breiter et al., 1997).

Despite some important drug-specific properties, all highly addictive drugs (e.g., cocaine, amphetamines, opiates, nicotine, and ethyl alcohol) act on a common "reward" circuit in the brain. The first information about this system derived from experiments initially performed in the 1950s (Olds and Milner, 1954). In these experiments, investigators probed the brains of rats with a stimulating electrode, asking a simple question: Are there locations of the electrode in the brain for which a rat will work for electrical stimulation? It was found that there were indeed a small number of such brain regions giving rather dramatic results: a rat would press a lever repeatedly for stimulation, even ignoring normal needs for food, water, and rest. A great deal of research since the 1950s has established that the critical system mediating this type of reinforcement is a dopaminergic pathway extending from the ventral tegmental area (VTA) of the midbrain to the nucleus accumbens (NAc), which is the major component of the ventral striatum. This meso-accumbens circuit is often described as a "brain reward" circuit (see Figure 7.2), where reward is an operational concept that describes the positive value that an animal ascribes to an object, physiological state, or behavioral act as evidenced by its behavior. In the nucleus accumbens, precise sensorimotor information, carried by glutamatergic projection neurons from the cerebral cortex, is integrated with information about the motivational state of the organism carried by dopamine projections from

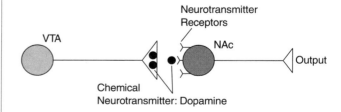

Figure 7.2 Schematic diagram of the brain reward circuitry. VTA neuron releases dopamine in the NAc in response to a rewarding stimulus; or if the reward is expected, in response to cues that predict the reward (Shultz, Dayan, and Montague, 1997). The downstream projections of the NAc neuron (arrow) that give rise to "brain reward" are not yet fully understood.

the VTA, and information about the arousal state of the organism carried by serotonin fibers from the raphe nuclei.

The mesoaccumbens dopamine pathway is part of an emotional circuit that appears to motivate behaviors required for survival and reproductive success, including the act of reproduction itself (Mirenowicz and Schultz, 1996; Shultz, Dayan, and Montague, 1997). As new rewarding stimuli (such as a highly palatable new food) are discovered by an organism, the dopaminergic reward pathway plays a key role in adding such stimuli to adaptive behavioral repertoires. The function of dopamine in the mesoaccumbens pathway is thus more complex than simply signaling "euphoria" or consumption of "something good." As described above in the discussion of fear, survival demands that an organism be able to predict future reward (or danger) based on learned environmental cues and then to produce the appropriate physiologic and behavioral responses to approach or escape. When a monkey is trained to recognize cues associated with a reward, an interesting transition occurs. During the training period, dopamine neurons are activated when the monkey touches or tastes a rewarding food or juice (Mirenowicz and Schultz, 1996). But once conditioning has occurred, the firing of dopamine neurons moves earlier in time from just after delivery of the reward to the appearance of the cue that predicts the reward. If a reward is not delivered at the appropriate time after the cue, the firing of dopamine neurons is depressed below their basal rate of firing; if it exceeds expectation, greater dopamine firing apparently occurs (Mirenowicz and Schultz, 1996; Shultz, Dayan, and Montague, 1997). The conclusion of this and other research is that dopamine plays a major role in learning the circumstances under which rewarding events occur. As will be seen, the role played by dopamine in this type of learning (positive emotional memory formation) is likely highly relevant to the cue-induced desire for drugs that occurs in addicted individuals (O'Brien et al., 1992).

By unfortunate serendipity, this mesoaccumbens dopamine system, meant to signal rewarding, life-enhancing events, makes our brains vulnerable to drug addiction, because certain alkaloids found in nature (e.g., coca, nicotine, and opium), as well as the short-chain alcohol products of fermentation, directly or indirectly enhance the actions of dopamine within this circuit. Each of these highly addictive drugs mimics or enhances the actions of 1 or more neurotransmitters in the brain that are involved in the regulation of VTA dopamine neurons or which have receptors in the NAc itself. Thus, for example, cocaine and amphetamine act directly on VTA neurons to increase the synaptic concentration of dopamine, acting via the dopamine reuptake transporter (see Figure 7.3).

Opiates have 2 effects on the mesoaccumbens pathway. There are opiate receptors on NAc neurons so that opiates can act directly; in addition, morphine-like opiates cause VTA neurons to release dopamine. This is because VTA dopamine neurons are tonically inhibited by interneurons, which in turn possess opiate receptors. Since opiates are inhibitory, endogenous opiates (e.g., enkephalins) or opiate drugs (e.g., morphine or heroin) inhibit the inhibitory interneurons and thereby disinhibit the VTA dopamine neurons. Although the precise mechanism is less well understood, both ethyl alcohol and nicotine disinhibit VTA neurons and cause dopamine release.

An understanding of these pathways can help in designing treatments for addiction. Naltrexone, a long-acting opiate receptor antagonist, appears to decrease craving for alcohol (Volpicelli et al., 1995) and may have a useful place in the treatment of alcoholism. This action of naltrexone may reflect an action on the interneurons that regulate the firing of the VTA, theoretically decreasing alcohol-induced dopamine release by blocking endogenous opioids. Similarly, the apparent efficacy of bupropion in treating nicotine addiction may reflect an as yet poorly understood action in the mesoaccumbens dopamine circuit.

Because drugs such as cocaine or opiates stimulate the brain reward system with a longevity and power exceeding that of normally occurring, positively reinforcing stimuli, their motivational effects are profound. The drug

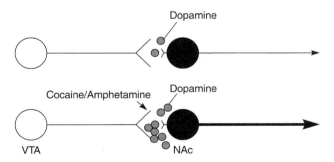

Figure 7.3 The effects of cocaine and amphetamine. Normally, following its release, dopamine action is terminated by a reuptake transporter that takes the dopamine back into the presynaptic neuron. Cocaine mimics dopamine enough to bind to the reuptake transporter, but not enough to enter the cell. Instead, cocaine blocks the transporter, causing a buildup of dopamine in the synapse. Amphetamine enters the cell via the transporter but causes the presynaptic neuron to release dopamine, essentially putting the transporter into "reverse."

abuser literally learns to short-circuit the normal processes by which naturally rewarding stimuli produce their effect. Abusers find that at least initially, they can produce a reliable sense of euphoria and well-being. Of course, the efficacy and reliability of addictive drugs turn out to be a two-edged sword. It is precisely because of their potent ability to stimulate cells in the mesolimbic dopamine system that these drugs activate powerful homeostatic mechanisms, producing adaptations in the biochemistry and physiology of these cells that lead to tolerance and dependence (Self and Nestler, 1995; Hyman and Nestler, 1996). In addition, since dopamine signals the presence of something rewarding to be approached, drugs of abuse also produce powerful conditioning that marks the circumstances (both environmental and interoceptive) under which drug use occurs as highly significant and predictive of something of positive value. The result is deeply etched emotional memories that are the basis of cue-conditioned craving which may occur even years after detoxification (O'Brien et al., 1992). Over time, in fact, the addicted person often has decreased enjoyment of his or her chosen substance because of the development of tolerance or of drug-related medical conditions, such as alcoholic gastritis. Despite diminished enjoyment, distress, and failures in life roles, the addicted person continues to want drugs or alcohol intensely (Robinson and Berridge, 1993).

Overall, it appears that in vulnerable individuals, addiction is the result of taking drugs that stimulate the mesoaccumbens reward pathway. If these drugs are taken with adequate dose and frequency for a long enough period of time, they can cause long-lived alterations in the biochemical and functional properties of neurons. These long-lived changes result behaviorally in uncontrolled drug use. The specific syndrome of dependence and withdrawal for each drug depends on where, in addition to the mesoaccumbens pathway, receptors for that drug are found, and by implication which particular brain pathways undergo long-term alterations in response to repeated drug exposure.

The types of long-term changes that addictive drugs produce in the brain can be divided conceptually into 3 categories. First, opiates and ethyl alcohol, but not cocaine, produce compensatory adaptations in brain regions that control somatic functions, thus producing physical dependence (Self and Nestler, 1995). As a result, discontinuation of opiates or alcohol can produce a physical withdrawal syndrome, such as the well-known alcohol withdrawal syndrome that includes hypertension, tachycardia, tremor, nystagmus, insomnia, and often grand mal seizures.

Second, all addictive drugs appear to produce adaptations within the brain reward circuitry itself (Maldonado et al., 1992; Self and Nestler, 1995; Hyman, 1996). These are quite complex and far from fully understood. A subset of these adaptations results in tolerance, decreasing some of the reinforcing effects of the drug and therefore contributing to increases in dosage. The same types of adaptations that contribute to tolerance also contribute to dependence, i.e., putting the brain in a state that will lead to emotional and motivational symptoms of withdrawal (such as dysphoric mood, inability to experience pleasure, and drug craving) following drug cessation (Hyman, 1996). Human fMRI experiments have found that following cocaine infusion in cocaine-dependent subjects, prolonged NAc activation occurs, and that this activation continues well beyond the period of euphoria and into the period of dysphoria and drug craving (Breiter et al., 1997). The combination of noninvasive human investigation with investigation in animal models should help us understand the timing and types of alterations in neural function that occur, and how they contribute to the addicted state. In addition to adaptations that lead to dependence and withdrawal, there is evidence for adaptations that produce sensitization, i.e., a subset of the effects of drugs may actually increase. Some aspects of sensitization increase the desire for the drug (Robinson and Berridge, 1993); others, such as the syndrome of cocaine-induced paranoia which may develop with chronic use, create additional serious problems for drug users.

In addition to the 2 types of drug-induced adaptations described, the third type of long-term alteration in brain function produced by drugs of abuse is the production of emotional memories related to drug use. Well-known examples of cue-induced desire for drugs include the craving for a cigarette produced by a large meal or the re-experiencing of some withdrawal symptoms by detoxified heroin addicts who return to the site at which they had previously used drugs. The precise relationship of these cue-dependent emotional memories to relapse in previously detoxified individuals remains a matter of study (O'Brien et al., 1992), but it creates a rationale for behavioral therapies to help detoxified individuals cope with circumstances that elicit craving.

These different types of long-term changes in the brain have varied time courses of onset and decay. Somatic withdrawal may last from days to 1 or 2 weeks; the motivational aspects of withdrawal may last from several weeks to months; emotional memories related to drug use may last a lifetime.

In summary, a great deal is known about addictive disorders at both the neural systems level and the biochemical and molecular levels. The key to this understanding is the availability of adequate animal models and knowledge of the key pathogenic factors, the drugs themselves. The situation in mood disorders and schizophrenia is more difficult, as animal models are far less adequate, and the pathogenic factors are unknown. As for other mental disorders, however, the genetics of vulnerability to addictive disorders remains unsolved.

Mood Disorders

Genetics. The lifetime prevalence of serious major depression in the United States is 5% (Regier et al., 1988), making depression arguably the most common serious brain disease. Less severe forms of depression may affect perhaps an additional 10% of the population. Females have approximately a twofold greater risk of unipolar depression than men in almost all cultures studied. The lifetime prevalence of bipolar disorder is approximately 1% of the population worldwide. Bipolar disorder affects men and women approximately equally.

The prevalence of mood disorders in first-degree relatives of depressed individuals is at least twice that in relatives of randomly selected individuals (Weissman, Kidd, and Prusoff, 1982). The familial nature of bipolar disorder is especially clear, with an 8–25% incidence of bipolar disorder in the first-degree relatives of bipolar probands, compared with 1% in the general population. Family studies have supported the clinical distinction between unipolar (depressions only) and bipolar disorder (as defined by the occurrence of mania). Most studies indicate that relatives of bipolar probands have an excess of both unipolar and bipolar disorders, whereas relatives of unipolar probands have an excess of unipolar disorder only (Andreasen et al., 1987; McGuffin and Katz, 1989). The status of individuals with unipolar depression in bipolar pedigrees is complex. Any given case may be due to the co-occurrence of 2 relatively common disorders in one pedigree, milder expression of bipolarity in some members of the pedigree, or delayed onset of manias with respect to depressions in that individual.

Based on twin and adoption studies, strong evidence exists that the tendency for mood disorders to run in families is due in part to shared genes. Indeed, the weight of evidence for a genetic contribution to bipolar disorder is the strongest for any mental disorder. For unipolar depression the evidence for a genetic contribution is greater in early onset than in late onset cases. In one adoption study the biological and adoptive relatives of adult adoptees with mood disorders were compared with the biological and adoptive relatives of matched unaffected adoptees. There was an eightfold increase in unipolar depression and a fifteenfold increase in suicide among the biological relatives of the probands (Wender et al., 1986). These data provided evidence for a genetic contribution to both unipolar depression and suicide. Twin studies also support a role for genes, with a stronger role in bipolar than unipolar disorder (Gershon et al., 1975). In one study, among unipolar twin pairs the concordance rate for illness was 54% for monozygotic pairs and 24% for dizygotic pairs (approximately 2:1), but for bipolar pairs the concordance was 69% for monozygotic pairs and 19% for dizygotic pairs (Bertelson, Harvald, and Hauge, 1977). Despite the strong evidence for genetic transmission of vulnerability, especially in bipolar disorder, molecular genetic analyses have not yet yielded reproducible linkage data. This is similar to the current situation for all common complex genetic disorders, and reflects the issues described at the beginning of this chapter.

Most current models of the heritability of depression and manic-depressive illness suggest that multiple genetic loci and nongenetic factors are involved. Moreover, the critical nongenetic factors that influence disease penetrance and course may be unshared within a family, and therefore difficult to analyze. For example, stress has often been implicated as a factor in onset of depression (Kendler et al., 1995), but events that function as stressors are, in many cases, specific to individuals.

Neural substrates of mood disorders. Mood disorders are among the most prevalent causes of morbidity worldwide. Based on course and genetics, as described above, the best-validated subtyping of mood disorders is into unipolar and bipolar. Both unipolar and bipolar disorders have additional subtypes (e.g., atypical depression and bipolar II disorder) which are clinically useful, but which have not been shown to be genetically distinct. Mood disorders generally exhibit an episodic course, although they may also become chronic. Depression is characterized by many abnormalities, including disordered mood, sleep, appetite, energy, sex drive, and motivation. There may be psychomotor retardation or agitation, and abnormal thoughts, such as guilt, and suicidal ideas. The features of the depressive syndrome are the same whether the patient is unipolar or bipolar. Mania is characterized by euphoria which may be brittle, increased energy, and decreased need for sleep. Patients are often intrusive, hypersexual, and impulsive; they have inflated self-esteem, which may be delusional. Cognitively they are distractible; their speech is often rapid and pressured. Psychotic symptoms are common.

The neurobiologic substrates of mood disorders are

not well understood, but one striking feature is the abnormal functioning of many different brain regions. Thus sleep disturbances might be referable to the brain stem monoamine or cholinergic nuclei or, given the stereotyped diurnal pattern of sleep disturbance, to the circadian pacemaker in the suprachiasmatic nucleus of the hypothalamus. Altered appetite and energy might reflect abnormalities of different hypothalamic nuclei. Low mood and lack of interest occurring in depression and euphoria and increased involvement in goal-directed activities occurring in mania may reflect opposite abnormalities in the nucleus accumbens/ventral striatum (which is also the substrate of cocaine and amphetamine action as described above), as well as abnormalities in the prefrontal cortex and the amygdala. Anxiety, a common symptom of depression, may also reflect abnormalities of amygdala function. The excessive release of stress hormones results from hyperfunctioning of the paraventricular nucleus of the hypothalamus with downstream effects on the pituitary and adrenal glands. Alterations in the content of thought reflect abnormal functioning of the cerebral cortex.

A neurobiologic understanding of mood disorders must explain how such diverse brain regions are affected, how the abnormalities are episodic, and what the impact of both genes and environment is in pathogenesis. Emotional circuits which can impact the functioning of all of these structures directly or indirectly are currently a matter of study. Because of their widespread projections and role in antidepressant action, monoamine systems have historically been considered important in the pathophysiology of mood disorders. Even if not the primary cause of mood disorders, monoamine systems could generalize an abnormality initiated elsewhere to affect much of the rest of the brain.

Animal models of depression (e.g., forced swim or learned helplessness models) have been useful in predicting drug responses, but the problem of mood regulation has been more difficult to model in animals than fear or reward. Thus, much research has utilized human subjects. Investigators have focused on documenting abnormalities in monoamine systems because of the known efficacy of antidepressant drugs which target norepinephrine, serotonin, and, less commonly, dopamine systems. While it is widely recognized that pharmacologic agents in the brain could be acting many synapses away from the pathophysiology, many experiments have nonetheless been performed to study monoamine turnover, monoamine receptors on accessible peripheral cells, and the effects of various pharmacologic challenges on monoamine systems. Unfortunately, these approaches have yielded relatively little.

More recently, investigators have used functional neuroimaging to study both depression and mania. Compared with studies of anxiety or addiction, there are less satisfactory animal models to guide hypotheses, making the research more difficult. Indeed, there are still too few studies using neural circuit–based hypotheses or of specific cognitive or emotional tasks aimed at identifying the precise pathways involved in mood disorders. However, such work is commencing (Lane et al., 1997; Mayberg, 1997). In one set of studies using PET, patterns of regional glucose metabolism in depressed subjects were compared to those of induced sadness in healthy volunteers. Decreases in metabolism in the dorsal neocortex and increases in the ventral paralimbic cortex characterized both states. The changes seen in the depressed subjects normalized when they were treated (Mayberg, 1997). In another study that used PET imaging to study resting cerebral blood flow and glucose utilization, there was an area of abnormally decreased activity in the prefrontal cortex in a region ventral to the genu of the corpus callosum in both familial unipolar and bipolar depressives. This decrement in activity was ascribed to a surprising reduction in cortical volume in this region as measured by MRI in both the unipolar and bipolar samples (Drevets et al., 1997). These results, which need independent replication, are interesting because the putative abnormality occurs within a brain region that is highly interconnected with the striatum and amygdala, structures that have been associated (as described above) with both positive and negative emotion, and also associated with the hypothalamus, which is involved in many of the neuroendocrine and visceral outputs of emotional processing (Damasio, 1997). The medial prefrontal cortex sits at the crossroads between thoughts and emotions. Lesions of the ventromedial prefrontal cortex result in impairment of emotional reactions to complex situations without impairing simple emotional responses (Damasio, 1994, 1997). A question about these results is raised by the fact that metabolism in the subgenual prefrontal cortex was found to be increased compared with controls during mania, a result which is inconsistent with the apparent loss of tissue volume in the bipolar group overall. It must be stressed that an understanding of pathways involved in emotion and their relationship to mood disorders is in its early stages. Circuits involving the medial prefrontal cortex, amygdala, ventral striatum, and hypothalamus are proving to be important.

Neuroendocrine abnormalities in depression. The most reproducible neuroendocrine finding in psychiatry is the abnormal activation of the hypothalamic-pituitary-adrenal (HPA) axis in perhaps half of all cases of major depression. Subsets of subjects with depression may exhibit increased cortisol production, as measured by increases in urinary free cortisol and decreased ability of the potent synthetic glucocorticoid dexamethasone to suppress plasma cortisol, adrenocorticotropic hormone (ACTH), and beta-endorphin. (See Figure 7.4.) There is both direct and indirect evidence for hypersecretion of corticotropin-releasing hormone (CRH); ACTH responses to intravenously administered CRH are blunted, and increased concentrations of CRH have been reported in cerebrospinal fluid (reviewed in Heit et al., 1997). In a postmortem study of depressed individuals, CRH was found to be increased in the paraventricular nucleus of the hypothalamus (Raadsheer et al., 1995).

Increases in cortisol result in a catabolic state, suppress the immune system, and may have direct effects on mood, energy, and cognition. While exogenously administered glucocorticoids often produce euphoria and increased energy, the potential impact of endogenous glucocorticoids in depression must take into account the complex adaptations that would occur in response to chronic hypercortisolemia and other neuroendocrine abnormalities. There have been speculative concerns that depression may increase cortisol to levels toxic to hippocampal neurons in humans (Sapolsky, 1992). The hippocampus is required for feedback inhibition of CRH neurons. It has therefore been hypothesized that episodes of depression marked by severe hypercortisolemia might produce further impairment in feedback regulation of the HPA axis and predispose to chronicity of depression or at least to future recurrences.

In addition to potential effects of cortisol, there are striking parallels between some aspects of the stress response, symptoms of melancholic depression, and the effects of CRH injected into the cerebral ventricles in animal models. These include increased arousal and vigilance, decreased appetite, decreased sexual behavior, and increased heart rate and blood pressure (Gold, Goodwin, and Chrousos, 1988). Whether hypothalamic abnormalities are primary or more likely secondary to the initiating cause of depression, a strong case can be made for their role in the generation of serious symptoms, and for an impact on the course of the disease and its somatic sequelae.

Monoamine systems and antidepressant action. Historically, hypotheses linking mood disorders to norepinephrine and serotonin systems in the brain were based not on their anatomy and physiology but on pharmacological observations. It was observed clinically that approximately 15% of patients treated chronically with the antihypertensive drug reserpine developed a syndrome indistinguishable from naturally occurring depression. Reserpine was found to deplete neurons of norepinephrine, serotonin, and dopamine. The first antidepressants discovered also affected monoamines. Thus, the monoamine oxidase (MAO) inhibitors were found to inhibit the enzyme that metabolizes monoamine neurotransmitters. Because this enzyme is found in presynaptic terminals, its inhibition would prolong the life of monoamine neurotransmitters found in the presynaptic cytoplasm and thereby increase the amounts available for re-

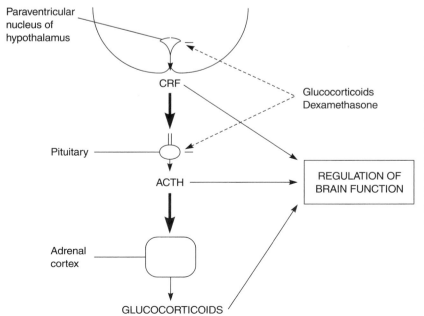

Figure 7.4 Under normal circumstances, a wide variety of stressors induce the paraventricular nucleus of the hypothalamus to synthesize and release corticotropin-releasing hormone (CRF). This travels via the portal hypophyseal circulation to the anterior pituitary, where it causes release of adrenocorticotropic hormone (ACTH) into the systemic circulation. ACTH acts in the adrenal cortex to cause release of cortisol. Normally cortisol feeds back (minus signs) at the level of the PVN and pituitary to decrease CRF and ACTH release respectively.

lease. Imipramine and the other tricyclic antidepressants were found to inhibit the reuptake of norepinephrine and serotonin in varying ratios. Because reuptake is the primary mechanism by which the synaptic actions of monoamines are terminated, the tricyclic antidepressants acutely increase the amount of these neurotransmitters within synapses (reviewed in Hyman and Nestler, 1993).

Taken together, pharmacological observations such as these led to a simple hypothesis that depression was the result of inadequate monoamine neurotransmission and that clinically effective antidepressants work by increasing the synaptic availability of monoamines.

A major problem with all versions of these early "monoamine deficiency" hypotheses was the observation that the inhibitory actions of different antidepressants on monoamine reuptake or monoamine oxidase activity are immediate, whereas clinical efficacy requires weeks of treatment. This therapeutic delay has led more recently to the view that it is chronic adaptations in brain function, rather than increases in synaptic norepinephrine and serotonin per se, that underlie the therapeutic effects of antidepressant drugs. The focus of research on antidepressant mechanisms has, as a result, shifted increasingly from the immediate effects of antidepressants to effects which develop more slowly. The anatomic focus of research on antidepressants also has shifted: while monoamine synapses are the immediate target of antidepressant drugs, attention is increasingly focused not on monoamine neurons themselves, but on the brain structures innervated by monoamines wherein chronic alterations in monoaminergic inputs caused by antidepressant drugs could lead to long-lasting adaptations that effectively treat depression. The actual molecular and cellular adaptations that are produced by antidepressants, and the cells and circuits in which they must occur, are, thus, currently the critical targets of research on antidepressant mechanisms. (The molecular aspects of this view are reviewed in detail in Hyman and Nestler, 1993, 1996.)

Schizophrenia

Genetics. As twin and adoption studies indicate, a genetic component to the risk of schizophrenia is well established. Adoption studies show that excess risk of schizophrenia is conferred by biological rather than adoptive parents, while twin studies reveal a higher concordance rate among monozygotic than dizygotic twins. More than 40 family studies of schizophrenia in aggregate suggest a six- to tenfold increased risk to first-degree relatives of probands with schizophrenia over relatives of normal controls, who have a 1% risk worldwide (National Institute of Mental Health, 1997). Based on 6 twin studies that used relatively modern definitions of schizophrenia, the concordance rate for monozygotic twins is approximately 46% compared to 14% for dizygotic twins (Farmer, McGuffin, and Gottesman, 1987; Prescott and Gottesman, 1993). Adoption studies have found a significantly greater rate of schizophrenia in the biological relatives of adoptees with chronic schizophrenia than in the biologic relatives of control adoptees (Kety et al., 1994; Kendler et al., 1994).

Despite strong evidence for genetic transmission of risk, molecular genetic analyses of schizophrenia over the past decade have failed to identify reproducible linkage to known genetic markers. Thus the state of genetic research in schizophrenia is similar to that for mood disorders, as discussed above. Most models of the heritability of schizophrenia suggest that multiple genetic loci are involved and that nongenetic factors (e.g., pre- or perinatal viral infection, prenatal malnutrition, perinatal anoxia, or other birth complications) are likely to be unshared among siblings. As illustrated by the maximal concordance rate of 46% for monozygotic twins, nongenetic factors play an important role in converting genetic vulnerability into illness. Nongenetic factors which predispose to schizophrenia may include stochastic developmental factors as well as specific environmental insults. Possible environmental risk factors that have been identified by epidemiological means include problems in utero such as starvation, influenza, and Rh incompatibilities, and perinatal complications (Hultman et al., 1997).

As in the case of other mental disorders, genetic analyses of schizophrenia are hampered by the lack of pathognomonic diagnostic features. A unique problem in this disorder is the decreased fertility of individuals with schizophrenia. For example, one study found that individuals with schizophrenia reproduced at a rate about one-quarter that of control subjects (Kendler, McGuire, et al., 1993).

Neural substrates of schizophrenia. Schizophrenia is an extremely serious disorder that typically exhibits a chronic course, punctuated by acute exacerbations. Core features include psychotic symptoms and disabling abnormalities in cognition, emotion, and social functioning. The likely heterogeneity of schizophrenia in humans and its lack of pathognomonic features have hampered not only genetic studies but also studies of its neurobiology. Because there are no satisfactory animal models, gross and microscopic anatomic studies are limited to humans. Remarkably, despite the numerous difficulties posed by this situation, a combination of neuroradiologic and neuropathologic approaches has produced a consensus that schizophrenia is indeed characterized by gross anatomic abnormalities. The most compelling evidence exists for ventricular enlargement (Suddath et al., 1990), but there are also findings consistent with loss of tissue volume and a possible decrease in cell number in the prefrontal cerebral cortex, hippocampus, and thalamus (Suddath et al., 1990; Shenton et al., 1992; Pakkenberg, 1990; Andreasen et al., 1994). Data from magnetic resonance spectroscopy is consistent with that from other techniques, suggesting a reduction in concentration of multiple neuronal markers in the dorsolateral prefrontal cortex and the hippocampal region (Bertolino et al., 1996). There is less consensus about microscopic neuropathology; a variety of abnormalities with potential biological significance have been reported (Benes et al., 1991, Heckers et al., 1991, Arnold et al., 1991, Akbarian et al., 1993a, b), but convincing reproducibility across laboratories is lacking.

One useful approach to the problem of studying schizophrenia against the backdrop of normal variation in brain size and ventricular volume was employed by Suddath et al. (1990). They used a cohort of 15 sets of monozygotic twins in which twin pairs were discordant for schizophrenia. In 14 out of the 15 pairs the co-twin with schizophrenia had a smaller anterior hippocampus on the left and for 13 out of 15 pairs a smaller anterior hippocampus on the right. Among the twins with schizophrenia as compared with their unaffected co-twins, the lateral ventricles were larger on the left in 14 and on the right in 13. The third ventricle was also larger in 13 of the affected co-twins. No such differences in the hippocampus or ventricular volume were found in 7 sets of monozygotic twins without schizophrenia who were studied as controls. Since monozygotic twins have 100% of their DNA in common, this study also highlighted the role of nongenetic factors in the pathogenesis of schizophrenia.

Some differences between monozygotic twins are likely the result of stochastic factors operating during development; examples include differences in fingerprints, immunoglobulins, and T-cell receptors. Thus, some variation in brain morphology between monozygotic twins is expected, for example, differences in gyral patterns. However, the striking differences in gross brain morphology between the affected and unaffected co-twins in the study of Suddath et al. (1990) are consistent with a specific unshared environmental factor or factors that have derailed normal brain development.

The current leading hypothesis of the pathogenesis of schizophrenia proposes that it results from abnormal brain development, with early pathologic events becoming clinically apparent in the late teens or early 20s owing to ongoing brain maturation which unmasks a preexisting problem. This view has been based partly on the observation that except in the relatively rare case of childhood onset schizophrenia, ventricular enlargement can be detected even at the first onset of active schizophrenic symptoms (Lim et al., 1996). Whether ventricular enlargement is stable or progressive in at least some subtypes of schizophrenia remains to be definitively established. Ventricular enlargement progressing more rapidly than expected for age might suggest an active neurodegenerative process rather than a purely developmental one. Arguing against a neurodegenerative process is the absence of gliosis or inflammatory cells in neuropathologic specimens; however, more detailed examination of the brain with histologic stains to identify reactive astrocytes or microglia is warranted. Other evidence for a neurodevelopmental origin of schizophrenia includes evidence from one series of postmortem studies consistent with abnormal cell migration during formation of the cerebral cortex (Akbarian et al., 1993a, b). One difficulty that a neurodevelopmental hypothesis of schizophrenia must address is the delay in onset of symptoms to the late teens or early 20s. During the burst of brain development that coincides with puberty, marked changes in behavior and judgment occur in normal individuals. In an individual with schizophrenic pathology, the process of brain development might reveal neurodevelopmental abnormalities that produced only mild symptoms in childhood. Animal models have been produced which show this in principle, e.g., that hippocampal lesions made during the neonatal period can produce new neurochemical and behavioral abnormalities that appear only in maturity (Lipska et al., 1995).

Complementary to morphometric and neuropathologic studies are neuropsychologic studies using functional neuroimaging. Functional neuroimaging has been used to investigate pathways that might be used in the production of hallucinations and has found involvement not only of sensory pathways but also of brain regions usually involved in emotional processing (Silbersweig et al., 1995). Many studies have investigated cognitive deficits in patients with schizophrenia, with the most significant group of findings demonstrating abnormalities of frontal lobe functioning. The pattern of functional deficits observed is generally consistent with the putative locations of tissue loss that have been reported in the frontal lobes and in the mediodorsal nucleus of the thalamus (Pakkenberg, 1992), which is interconnected with the prefrontal cortex. Studies with both PET and

SPECT in patients with schizophrenia reveal a pattern of decreased metabolism in the dorsolateral prefrontal cortex, independent of medication status (Berman et al., 1992). When patients with schizophrenia are given tasks dependent on frontal lobe function, such as the Wisconsin Card Sort, they perform the task poorly; this impaired performance correlates with failure of normal frontal lobe activation as determined by SPECT, PET, and fMRI (Weinberger et al., 1992). The Wisconsin Card Sort is a complex, effortful task. Simpler frontal lobe tasks, however, at least preliminarily give similar results. Physiological experiments in nonhuman primates, for example, have revealed that the prefrontal cerebral cortex is required for what has been called "working memory," the ability to hold information "on line" and to update it based on ongoing experience. Studies in nonhuman primates, humans with frontal lobe injuries, and subjects with schizophrenia suggest that deficits in working memory, and therefore in the ability to guide behavior by representations, may be a fundamental cognitive impairment in schizophrenia (Goldman-Rakic, 1994).

The efficacy of dopamine D2 receptor family antagonists in treating the psychotic symptoms of schizophrenia have led to the hypothesis that dopaminergic function is abnormally increased in at least part of the brain in schizophrenia. More recently, the psychotomimetic effects of the noncompetitive NMDA (N-methyl D-aspartate) receptor antagonists phencyclidine (PCP) and ketamine have suggested that a deficiency in glutamatergic neurotransmission might also be responsible for symptoms of schizophrenia (Tamminga, 1998). Finally, the ability of the atypical antipsychotic drugs clozapine, risperidone, olanzapine, and quetiapine to block serotonin 5-HT2A receptors has led some investigators to argue that serotonin plays a role in the pathogenesis of schizophrenia.

It is widely recognized that the action of a drug in treating or producing symptoms does not imply that the target of the drug is involved in the natural pathogenesis of those symptoms. Therefore additional evidence beyond a role in therapeutics or symptom provocation is needed to implicate these neurotransmitters in symptoms formation. Direct evidence for any of these neurotransmitters has been difficult to obtain. For example, postmortem studies have not identified convincing up-regulation of dopamine receptors in the brains of unmedicated individuals with schizophrenia (Davis et al., 1991). Similarly, resting studies using SPECT and PET to quantitate D2-like receptors in drug-naive patients with schizophrenia have also been inconclusive. While still indirect, newer approaches using SPECT and PET have attempted to study dopamine transmission. These studies employ stimuli such as amphetamine to induce dopamine release, and then observe the degree of displacement of a radioactive tracer bound to D2 dopamine receptors in the striatum of living patients. One such study has reported increased dopamine release in schizophrenic patients (i.e., increased sensitivity to amphetamine) compared with controls (Laruelle et al., 1996). Such dynamic approaches to neurotransmission may increasingly contribute to understanding abnormalities in the brains of patients with mental disorders; but it is difficult to interpret the significance of something as complex as amphetamine-induced neurotransmitter release. Interestingly, it has been reported that dopamine D1 receptors are decreased in the prefrontal cortex of drug-naive and drug-free individuals with schizophrenia (Okubo et al., 1997). If replicated, this finding is of interest because D1 dopamine receptors have been shown to play a role in working memory, which, as described above, is impaired in schizophrenia (Goldman-Rakic, 1994). Of course, a decrease in expression of a receptor type cannot be interpreted in isolation since it could be primary or, alternatively, could represent an adaptation to increased stimulation.

D3 and D4 dopamine receptor types related to the D2 receptor but encoded by different genes have been identified. Most antipsychotic drugs bind the entire D2 family (D2, D3, and D4) with high affinity. The D4 dopamine receptor has aroused substantial interest because the uniquely efficacious atypical antipsychotic drug clozapine has a relatively high affinity for the D4 receptor compared to its affinity for the D2 receptor (Van Tol et al., 1991). Clozapine also has actions at 5-HT2A, alpha adrenergic, and other neurotransmitter receptors. Nonetheless, the D4 receptor, along with the 5-HT2A receptor, has become an important target of antipsychotic drug development. There is no convincing evidence to date of alterations in D3 or D4 receptor number in the brain in unmedicated patients with schizophrenia.

Overall it remains unclear whether there is an abnormality in the release of dopamine, glutamate, or serotonin or in the postsynaptic actions of these neurotransmitters in schizophrenia. The possibility has also been raised that putative dopaminergic abnormalities in schizophrenia might reflect an abnormal "balance" between dopamine pathways and glutamate, serotonin, or other neurotransmitter pathways.

References

Akbarian, S., Bunney, W. E., Potkin, S. G., Wigal, S. B., Hagman, J. O., Sandman, C. A., and Jones, E. G. 1993a. Altered distribution of nicotinamide-adenine dinucleotide phosphate-diaphorase cells in frontal lobe of schizophrenics implies disturbances of cortical development. *Arch. Gen. Psychiatry* 50:169.

Akbarian, S., Vinuela, A., Kim, J. J., Potkin, S. G., Bunney, W. E., and Jones, E. G. 1993b. Distorted distribution of nicotinamide-adenine dinucleotide phosphate-diaphorase neurons in temporal lobe of schizophrenics implies anomalous cortical development. *Arch. Gen. Psychiatry* 50:178.

American Psychiatric Association. 1994. *Diagnostic and statistical manual of mental disorders,* 4th ed. Washington, D.C.: American Psychiatric Press.

Andreasen, N. C., Rice, J., Endicott, J., Coryell, W., Grove, W. N., and Reich, T. 1987. Familial rates of affective disorder. *Arch. Gen. Psychiatry* 44:461–469.

Andreasen, N. C., Arndt, S., Swayze, V., Cizadlo, T., Flaum, M., O'Leary, D., Ehrhardt, J. C., and Yuh, W. T. 1994. Thalamic abnormalities in schizophrenia visualized through magnetic resonance image averaging. *Science* 266:294–298.

Andreasen, N. C., O'Leary, D. S., Cizadlo, T., Arndt, S., Rezai, K., Ponto, L. L., Watkins, G. L., and Hichwa, R. D. 1996. Schizophrenia and cognitive dysmetria: a positron-emission tomography study of dysfunctional prefrontal-thalamic-cerebellar circuitry. *Proc. Natl. Acad. Sci. USA* 93:9985–90.

Arnold, S. E., Hyman, B. T., Van Hoesen, G. W., and Damasio, A. R. 1991. Some cytoarchitectural abnormalities of the entorhinal cortex in schizophrenia. *Arch. Gen. Psychiatry* 48:625.

Baxter, L. R. Jr., Schwartz, J. M., Bergman, K. S., Szuba, M. P., Guze, B. H., Mazziotta, J. C., Alazraki, A., Selin, C. E., Ferng, H. K., Munford, P., and Phelps, M. E. 1992. Caudate glucose metabolic rate changes with both drug and behavior therapy for obsessive-compulsive disorder. *Arch. Gen. Psychiatry* 49:681.

Benes, F. M., McSparren, J., Bird, E. D., SanGiovanni, J. P., and Vincent, S. L. 1991. Deficits in small interneurons in prefrontal and cingulate cortices of schizophrenic and schizoaffective patients. *Arch. Gen. Psychiatry* 48:996.

Berman, K. F., Torrey, F., Daniel, D. G., and Weinberger, D. R. 1992. Regional cerebral blood flow in monozygotic twins discordant and concordant for schizophrenia. *Arch. Gen. Psychiatry* 49:927.

Bertelson, A., Harvald, B., and Hauge, M. A. 1977. Danish twin study of manic-depressive disorder. *Br. J. Psychiatry* 130:330–351.

Bertolino, A., Nawroz, S., Mattay, V. S., et al. 1996. Regionally specific pattern of neurochemical pathology in schizophrenia as assessed by multislice proton magnetic resonance spectroscopic imaging. *Am. J. Psychiatry* 153:1554.

Breiter, H. C., Etcoff, N. L., Whalen, P. J., Kennedy, W. A., Rauch, S. L., Buckner, R. L., Strauss, M. M., Hyman,

S. E., and Rosen, B. R. 1996. Response and habituation of the human amygdala during visual processing of facial expression. *Neuron* 17:875–887.

Breiter, H. C., Gollub, R. L., Weisskoff, R. M., Kennedy, D. N., Makris, N., Berke, J. D., Goodman, J. M., Kantor, H. L., Gastfriend, D. R., Riorden, J. P., Mathew, R. T., Rosen, B. R., and Hyman, S. E. 1997. Acute effects of cocaine on human brain activity and emotion. *Neuron* 19:591–611.

Carey, G., and Gottesman, I. I. 1981. Twin and family studies of anxiety, phobic, and obsessive disorders. In *Anxiety: new research and changing concepts,* ed. Klein, D. F., and Rabkin, J. New York: Raven Press. 117–136.

Cloninger, C. R., Bohman, M., and Sigvardsson, S. 1981. Inheritance of alcohol abuse: cross-fostering analysis of adopted men. *Arch. Gen. Psychiatry* 38:861.

Courchesne, E., Townsend, J., and Saitoh, O. 1994. The brain in infantile autism: posterior fossa structures are abnormal. *Neurology* 44:214–223.

Crowe, R. R., Noyes, R., Pauls, D. L., and Slymen, D. 1983. A family study of panic disorder. *Arch. Gen. Psychiatry* 40:1065–69.

Damasio, A. R. 1994. *Descartes' error: emotion, reason, and the human brain.* New York: G. P. Putnam.

——— 1997. Towards a neuropathology of emotion and mood. *Nature* 386:769–770.

Davis, K. L., Kahn, R. S., Ko, G., and Davidson, M. 1991. Dopamine in schizophrenia: a review and reconceptualization. *Am. J. Psychiatry* 148:1474–1486.

Davis, M. 1997. Neurobiology of fear responses: the role of the amygdala. *J. Neuropsychiatry Clin. Neurosci.* 9:382–402.

Drevets, W. C., Price, J. L., Simpson, J. R., Todd, R. D., Reich, T., Vannier, M., and Raichle, M. E. 1997. Subgenual prefrontal cortex abnormalities in mood disorders. *Nature* 386:824–827.

Farmer, A. E., McGuffin, P., and Gottesman, I. I. 1987. Twin concordance for DSM-III schizophrenia. *Arch. Gen. Psychiatry* 44:634.

Gelernter, J., Goldman, D., and Risch, N. 1993. The A1 allele at the D2 dopamine receptor gene and alcoholism: a reappraisal. *JAMA* 269:1673–77.

Gershon, E. S., Mark, A., Cohen, et al. 1975. Transmitted factors in morbid risk of affective disorders. *J. Psychiatr. Res.* 12:283–299.

Gold, P. W., Goodwin, F. K., and Chrousos, G. P. 1988. Clinical and chiochemical manifestations of depression: relation to the neurobiology of stress. *N. Engl. J. Med.* 319:413–420.

Goldman-Rakic, P. S. 1994. Working memory dysfunction in schizophrenia. *J. Neuropsychiatry Clin. Neurosci.* 6:348–357.

Heath, A. C., Meyer, J., Eaves, L. J., and Martin, N. G. 1991. The inheritance of alcohol consumption patterns in a general population twin sample. Parts I and II. *J. Studies on Alcohol* 52:345–352, 425–433.

Heckers, S., Heinsen, H., Geiger, B., and Beckmann, H. 1991. Hippocampal neuron number in schizophrenia. *Arch. Gen. Psychiatry* 48:1002.

Heit, S., Owens, M. J., Plotsky, P., and Nemeroff, C. B. 1997. Corticotropin-releasing factor, stress, and depression. *Neuroscientist* 3:186–194.

Hultman, C. M., Ohman, A., Cnattingius, S., et al. 1997. Prenatal and neonatal risk factors for schizophrenia. *Brit. J. Psychiatry* 170:128.

Hyman, S. E. 1996. Addiction to cocaine and amphetamine. *Neuron* 16:901–904.

Hyman, S. E., and Nestler, E. J. 1993. *The molecular foundations of psychiatry.* Washington, D.C.: American Psychiatric Association.

———— 1996. Initiation and adaptation: a paradigm for understanding psychotropic drug action. *Am. J. Psychiatry* 153:151–162.

Kendler, K. S., Heath, A. C., Neale, M. C., Kessler, R. C., and Eaves, L. J. 1992. A population-based twin study of alcoholism in women. *JAMA* 268:1877–82.

Kendler, K. S., McGuire, M., Gruenberg, A. M., O'Hare, A., Spellman, M., and Walsh, D. 1993. The Roscommon family study. *Arch. Gen. Psychiatry* 50:527.

Kendler, K. S., Neale, M. C., Kessler, R. C., Heath, A. C., and Eaves, L. J. 1993. Panic disorder in women: a population-based twin study. *Psychological Medicine* 23:397–406.

Kendler, K. S., Gruenberg, A. M., Kinney, D. K., et al. 1994. Independent diagnoses of adoptees and relatives as defined by DSM-III in the provincial and national samples of the Danish Adoption Study of Schizophrenia. *Arch. Gen. Psychiatry* 51:456–468.

Kendler, K. S., Kessler, R. C., Walters, E. E., et al. 1995. Stressful life events, genetic liability, and onset of an episode of major depression in women. *Am. J. Psychiatry* 152:833–842.

Kety, S. S., Wender, P. H., Jacobsen, B., et al. 1994. Mental illness in the biological and adoptive relatives of schizophrenic adoptees: replication of the Copenhagen Study in the rest of Denmark. *Arch. Gen. Psychiatry* 51:442–455.

Klimek, V., Stockmeier, C., Overholser, J., Meltzer, H. Y., Kalka, S., Dilley, G., and Ordway, G. A. 1997. Reduced levels of norepinephrine transporters in the locus coeruleus in major depression. *J. Neurosci.* 17:8451–58.

Kovacs, M., Devlin, B., Pollock, M., et al. 1997. A controlled family history study of childhood-onset depressive disorder. *Arch. Gen. Psychiatry* 54:613.

Lander, E. S., and Schork, N. J. 1994. Genetic dissection of complex traits. *Science* 265:2037–48.

Lane, R. D., Reiman, E. M., Ahern, G. L., et al. 1997. Neuroanatomical correlates of happiness, sadness, and disgust. *Am. J. Psychiatry* 154:926.

Laruelle, M., Abi-Dargham, A., van Dyck, C. H., Gil, R., D'Souza, C. D., Erdos, J., McCance, E., Rosenblatt, W., Fingado, C., Zoghbi, S. S., Baldwin, R. M., Seibyl, J. P., Krystal, J. H., Charney, D. S., and Innis, R. B. 1996. Single photon emission computerized tomography imaging of amphetamine-induced dopamine release in drug-free schizophrenic subjects. *Proc. Natl. Acad. Sci. USA* 93:9235–40.

LeDoux, J. 1996. *The emotional brain.* New York: Simon and Schuster.

Lim, K. O., Tew, W., Kushner, M., et al. 1996. Cortical gray matter volume deficit in patients with first-episode schizophrenia. *Am. J. Psychiatry* 153:1548.

Lipska, B. K., Chrapusta, S. J., Egan, M. F., and Weinberger, D. R. 1995. Neonatal excitotoxic ventral hippocampal damage alters dopamine response to mild repeated stress and to chronic haloperidol. *Synapse* 20:125–130.

Maldonado, R., Stinus, L., Gold, L. H., and Koob, G. F. 1992. Role of different brain structures in the expression of the physical morphine withdrawal syndrome. *J. Pharm. Exp. Ther.* 261:669–677.

Mayberg, H. S. 1997. Limbic-cortical dysregulation: a proposed model of depression. *J. Neuropsychiatry Clin. Neurosci.* 9:471–481.

McGuffin, P., and Katz, R. 1989. The genetics of depression and manic-depressive disorder. *Br. J. Psychiatry* 155:294–304.

Mendlewicz, J., Papadimitrious, G., and Wilmotte, J. 1993. Family study of panic disorder: comparison with generalized anxiety disorder, major depression, and normal subjects. *Psychiatric Genetics* 3:73–78.

Mirenowicz, J., and Schultz, W. 1996. Preferential activation of midbrain dopamine neurons by appetitive rather than aversive stimuli. *Nature* 379:449–451.

National Institute of Mental Health. 1997. Genetics and mental disorders. Report of the National Institute of Mental Health Genetics Working Group.

O'Brien, C. P., Childress, A. R., McLellan, A. T., and Ehrman, R. 1992. Classical conditioning in drug-dependent humans. *Ann. New York Acad. Sci.* 654:400–415.

Okubo, Y., Suhara, T., Suzuki, K., et al. 1997. Decreased prefrontal dopamine D1 receptors in schizophrenia revealed by PET. *Nature* 385:634.

Olds, M. E., and Milner, P. 1954. Positive reinforcement produced by electrical stimulation of septal area and other regions of the rat brain. *J. Comp. Physiol. Psych.* 47:419–427.

Pakkenberg, B. 1990. Pronounced reduction of total neuron number in mediodorsal thalamic nucleus and nucleus accumbens in schizophrenics. *Arch. Gen. Psychiatry* 47:1023–28.

———— 1992. The volume of the mediodorsal thalamic nucleus in treated and untreated schizophrenics. *Schizophr. Res.* 7:95–100.

Palumbo, D., Maughan, A., and Kurlan, R. 1997. Hypothesis III: Tourette's syndrome is only one of several causes of a developmental basal ganglia syndrome. *Arch. Neurol.* 54:475–483.

Papp, L. A., Klein, D. F., and Gorman, J. M. 1993. Carbon dioxide hypersensitivity, hyperventilation, and panic disorder. *Am. J. Psychiatry* 150:1149.

Prescott, C. A., and Gottesman, I. 1993. Genetically mediated vulnerability to schizophrenia. *Psychiatric Clinics of North America* 16:245–267.

Price, R. A., Kidd, K. K., and Weissman, M. M. 1987. Early onset (under age 30 years) and panic disorder as markers for etiologic homogeneity in major depression. *Arch. Gen. Psychiatry* 44:434.

Raadsheer, F. C., van Heerikhuize, J. J., Lucassen, P. J., et al. 1995. Corticotropin-releasing hormone mRNA levels in the paraventricular nucleus of patients with Alzheimer's disease and depression. *Am. J. Psychiatry* 152:1372–76.

Rauch, S. L., Jenike, M. A., Alpert, N. M., Baer, L., Breiter, H. C. R., Savage, C. R., and Fischman, A. J. 1994. Regional cerebral blood flow measured during symptom provocation in obsessive-compulsive disorder using oxygen 15–labeled carbon dioxide and positron emission tomography. *Arch. Gen. Psychiatry* 51:62.

Rauch, S. L., Savage, C. R., Alpert, N. M., Miguel, E. C., Baer, L., Breiter, H. C., Fischman, A. J., Manzo, P. A., Moretti, C., and Jenike, M. A. 1995. A positron emission tomographic study of simple phobic symptom provocation. *Arch. Gen. Psychiatry* 52:20–28.

Regier, D. A., Boyd, J. H., Burke, J. D. Jr., Rae, D. S., Myers, J. K., Kramer, M., Robins, L. N., George, L. K., Karno, M., and Locke, B. Z. 1988. One-month prevalence of mental disorders in the United States: based on five Epidemiological Catchment Areas sites. *Arch. Gen. Psychiatry* 45:977.

Rice, J., Reich, T., Andreasen, N. C., et al. 1987. The familial transmission of bipolar illness. *Arch. Gen. Psychiatry* 44:441.

Robinson, D., Wu, H., Munne, R. A., Ashtari, M., Alvir, J. M. J., Lerner, G., Koreen, A., Cole, K., and Bogerts, B. 1995. Reduced caudate nucleus volume in obsessive-compulsive disorder. *Arch. Gen. Psychiatry* 52:393–398.

Robinson, T. E., and Berridge, K. C. 1993. The neural basis of drug craving: an incentive-sensitization theory of addiction. *Brain Res. Rev.* 18:247–291.

Rogan, M. T., and LeDoux, J. E. 1996. Emotion: systems, cells, synaptic plasticity. *Cell* 85:469–475.

Sapolsky, R. M. 1992. *Stress, the aging brain, and the mechanisms of neuron death.* Cambridge, Mass.: MIT Press.

Self, D., and Nestler, E. J. 1995. Molecular mechanisms of drug reinforcement and addiction. *Ann. Rev. Neurosci.* 18:463–496.

Shenton, M. E., Kikinis, R., Jolesz, F. A., Pollak, S. D.,

LeMay, M., Wible, C. G., Hokama, H., Martin, J., Metcalf, D., Coleman, M., and McCarley, R. W. 1992. Abnormalities of the left temporal lobe and thought disorder in schizophrenia. *N. Engl. J. Med.* 327:604.

Shultz, W., Dayan, P., and Montague, P. R. 1997. A neural substrate of prediction and reward. *Science* 275:1593–99.

Silbersweig, D. A., Stern, E., Frith, C., Cahill, C., Holmes, A., Grootoonk, S., Seaward, J., McKenna, P., Chua, S. E., Schnorr, L., et al. 1995. A functional neuroanatomy of hallucinations in schizophrenia. *Nature* 378:176–179.

Suddath, R. L., Christison, G. W., Torrey, E. F., Casanova, M. F., and Weinberger, D. R. 1990. Anatomical abnormalities in the brains of monozygotic twins discordant for schizophrenia. *N. Engl. J. Med.* 322:790.

Swedo, S. E., Leonard, H. L., Mittleman, B. B., Allen, A. J., Rapoport, J. L., Dow, S. P., Kanter, M. E., Chapman, F., and Zabriskie, J. 1997. Identification of children with pediatric autoimmune neuropsychiatric disorders associated with streptococcal infections by a marker associated with rheumatic fever. *Am. J. Psychiatry* 154:110–112.

Tamminga, C. A. 1998. Schizophrenia and glutamatergic transmission. *Crit. Rev. Neurobiol.* 12:21–36.

Thomasson, H. R., Edenberg, H. J., Crabb, D. W., Mai, X.-L., Jerome, P. E., Li, T.-K., Wang, S. P., Liu, Y. T., Lu, R. B., and Yin, S. J. 1991. Alcohol and aldehyde genotypes and alcoholism in Chinese men. *Am. J. Hum. Genet.* 48:677–681.

Torgersen, S. 1983. Genetic factors in anxiety disorders. *Arch. Gen. Psychiatry* 40:1085–89.

Tsien, J. Z., Chen, D. F., Gerber, D., Tom, C., Mercer, E. H., Anderson, D. J., Mayford, M., Kandel, E. R., and Tonegawa, S. 1996. Subregion- and cell type–restricted knockout in mouse brain. *Cell* 87:1317–26.

Van Tol, H. M. V., Bunzow, J. R., Guan, H. C., et al. 1991. Cloning of the gene for a human dopamine D4 receptor with high affinity for the antipsychotic clozapine. *Nature* 350:610.

Volkow, N. D., Wang, G. J., Fischman, M. W., Fltin, R. W., Fowler, J. S., Abumrad, N. N., Vitkun, S., Logan, J., Gatley, S. J., Pappas, N., Hitzemann, R., and Shea, C. E. 1997. Relationship between subjective effects of cocaine and dopamine transporter occupancy. *Nature* 386:827–833.

Volpicelli, J. R., Watson, N. T., King, A. C., Sherman, C. E., and O'Brien, C. P. 1995. Effect of naltrexone on alcohol "high" in alcoholics. *Am. J. Psychiatry* 152:613.

Weinberger, D. R. 1995. Schizophrenia as a neurodevelopmental disorder. In *Schizophrenia*, ed. Hirsch, S. R., and Weinberger, D. R. London: Blackwell Science.

Weinberger, D. R., Berman, K. F., Suddath, R., and Torrey, E. F. 1992. Evidence of dysfunction of a prefrontal-limbic network in schizophrenia: a magnetic resonance imaging and regional cerebral blood flow study of discordant monozygotic twins. *Am. J. Psychiatry* 149:890.

Weissman, M. M., Kidd, K. K., and Prusoff, B. A. 1982. Variability in rates of affective disorders in relatives of depressed and normal probands. *Arch. Gen. Psychiatry* 39:1397.

Wender, P. H., Kety, S. S., Rosenthal, D., Schulsinger, F., Ortmann, J., and Lunde, I. 1986. Psychiatric disorders in the biological and adoptive families of adopted individuals with affective disorders. *Arch. Gen. Psychiatry* 43:923–929.

Recommended Reading

Hyman, S. E., and Nestler, E. J. 1996. Initiation and adaptation: a paradigm for understanding psychotropic drug action. *Am. J. Psychiatry* 153:151–162.

Lander, E. S., and Schork, N. J. 1994. Genetic dissection of complex traits. *Science* 265:2037–48.

LeDoux, J. 1996. *The emotional brain.* New York: Simon and Schuster.

Shultz, W., Dayan, P., and Montague, P. R. 1997. A neural substrate of prediction and reward. *Science* 275:1593–99.

Weinberger, D. R. 1995. Schizophrenia as a neurodevelopmental disorder. In *Schizophrenia,* ed. Hirsch, S. R., and Weinberger, D. R. London: Blackwell Science.

Disclaimer

The views expressed in this chapter do not necessarily represent the views of the agency or the United States.

J. ALLAN HOBSON

ROSALIA SILVESTRI

Sleep and Its Disorders

The Neurobiology of Sleep

The Natural History of Sleep

Modern research supports three important changes in our understanding of sleep (see Table 8.1). First, sleep is a complex biological function whose length and depth is extremely variable: individuals may vary in their baseline sleep need between 4 and 10 hours. Normally, short sleepers tend to be hyperactive but productive and well adjusted, while long sleepers tend to be low-key underachievers and mildly depressed. It is difficult, in humans, to know the degree to which traits are inherited or acquired, but genetically controlled experiments in animals show marked strain differences in sleep length. There thus appears to be a bell-shaped distribution of sleep length, so the duration variable cannot, per se, be taken as an index of pathology; the physician should be aware of pushing patients against powerful biological gradients.

The variable quality of sleep experienced is a function of the extreme sensitivity of sleep to environmental perturbations. As these include diet, exercise, interpersonal conflict, and intrapersonal stress, a careful history is key to understanding sleep pathology and to its management.

Perhaps the most reassuring point to remember and communicate is that normal sleep is not only variable and responsive but also carefully regulated. Experiments show that sleep resembles New England's weather: if you don't like it, wait a minute. Thus good sleep follows poor. Put another way, the longer the sleep deprivation, the greater the drive to sleep. And, despite highly publicized initial results, sleep deprivation studies have not revealed specific or long-lasting ill effects, so conservative management is not likely to be dangerous even to the insomniac who may ultimately need pharmacological treatment. Fortunately the nature of the regulatory processes are beginning to be understood, as will be pointed out in the next section.

Setting the Hypothalamic Clock: Circadian Rhythms

All organisms, from unicellular yeast to multicellular humans, show predictable rises and falls in physiological functions throughout each 24-hour day. These rhythms are called circadian (*cira,* "about," and *dies,* "a day"), because in the absence of time cues (zeitgebers) they become free-running at a period of about one day. In most organisms, synchrony with cosmic forces is achieved by the light-dark cycle which resets the rhythms each day. In humans the synchronizing function of light cues is usually replaced by social schedules, but some individuals appear to escape from, or be intrinsically out of phase with, the diurnal rhythmicity that characterizes most human society.

Endogenous circadian rhythms are regulated by hypophyseal and epiphyseal structures comprising one or more biological clocks with circadian periodicity (see Figure 8.1). For example, the temperature and rest-activity rhythms, which have been uncoupled during free-run experiments, appear to be regulated by different brain oscillators. The neural basis of these rhythms is still incompletely known, but evidence indicates that the suprachiasmatic nucleus of the hypothalamus plays a central role in the rest-activity cycle of several mammalian species. This nucleus receives direct input from optic tract fibers which carry information about light-dark conditions from the retina. The inferior accessory optic pathway to the pineal gland may also provide information

Table 8.1 Natural history of sleep

Sleep is variable
Sleep is sensitive
Sleep is regulated
Sleep is reciprocal to waking

about light conditions which are translated by changing enzyme levels (e.g., 5 hydroxyl-indole methyltransferase, acetylcholine acetylase, and tryptophan hydroxylase) into periodic changes in output of hormones (e.g., melatonin) and neurotransmitters (e.g., acetylcholine [ACh], serotonin [5-HT], and norepinephrine [NE]).

A Pontine Brain Stem Clock Controlling the NREM-REM Cycle

In adult humans, the EEG sleep cycle is a shorter (ultradian) rhythm with a periodicity of 100 minutes; it is most prominent at the nadir of the circadian rhythm. This setting of the ultradian sleep dream cycle within one circadian rhythm phase suggests that the controlling oscillators are normally coupled, but REM (rapid eye move-

ment) sleep can also become dissociated from other circadian rhythms under free-running conditions.

Sleep can be objectified in the laboratory by recording brain waves (EEG), muscle tone (EMG), and eye movements (EOG). By using the EEG, it is possible to classify segments of the record as wake stage and sleep stages I, II, III, and IV. The EOG and EMG help to distinguish the Stage I EEG of sleep onset (NREM; non-rapid eye movement) from that which emerges later (Stage I REM) and is associated with rapid eye movements and the abolition of postural muscle tone.

NREM Sleep Stage II is defined by the presence of a distinctive EEG waveform called the sleep spindle because of the stereotyped augmenting-decrementing voltage pattern at 15–18 c/s. When these spindles give way to higher voltage, slow waves begin to be mixed with the spindles

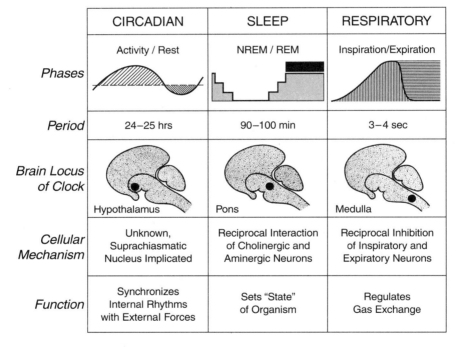

	CIRCADIAN	SLEEP	RESPIRATORY
Phases	Activity / Rest	NREM / REM	Inspiration/Expiration
Period	24–25 hrs	90–100 min	3–4 sec
Brain Locus of Clock	Hypothalamus	Pons	Medulla
Cellular Mechanism	Unknown, Suprachiasmatic Nucleus Implicated	Reciprocal Interaction of Cholinergic and Aminergic Neurons	Reciprocal Inhibition of Inspiratory and Expiratory Neurons
Function	Synchronizes Internal Rhythms with External Forces	Sets "State" of Organism	Regulates Gas Exchange

Figure 8.1 Some biological rhythms and their brain stem clocks. Three rhythms interact to determine the order and disorder of sleep. Circadian rhythms are endogenous fluctuations of many bodily functions, including rest and activity, with a period of about 24 hours. As seen in the schematic sagittal brain sections, the suprachiasmatic nucleus of the hypothalamus is a key part of this control system which synchronizes internal processes with external forces. The ultradian sleep cycle, with its 90–100 minute period of non-rapid eye movement (NREM) alternating with rapid eye movement (REM) states, is controlled by reciprocal interaction of cholinergic and aminergic pontine reticular neurons which oscillate out of phase (see also Figure 8.2). This clock determines the behavioral state (wake, NREM, and REM sleep) of the organism. The mechanism by which the circadian clock sets the threshold of the sleep cycle clock is unknown. Many homeostatic regulatory functions, including respiration, are influenced by the circadian rhythm and the sleep-wake cycle. The respiratory oscillator is similar in neuronal design to the sleep cycle clock but has a shorter period (3 seconds) determined by reciprocal inhibition of expiratory and inspiratory neurons in the medulla.

such that they occupy up to half the record, NREM Stage III is scored. In Stage IV the entire record is dominated by high voltage (>150 mV) slow waves (<4 c/s).

Each 90–100 minute epoch of sleep consists of a stereotyped sequence of brain and body events with two distinctly different phases constituting the trough and peak of the rhythm. The initial phase, occurring at sleep onset, is called slow wave or non-REM sleep. It is characterized by progressive EEG slowing and a corresponding decrease in muscle tone, heart rate, respiratory rate, and blood pressure. Movements are rare on the descending limb of this curve, and dramatic spurts of growth hormone release can be recorded. When this deactivation process is maximal—at about mid-cycle—subjects may require 5 minutes of active mobilization to achieve full arousal when awakened (physicians should not give medical advice when aroused from NREM sleep, especially early in the first two cycles, when the NREM troughs are particularly deep).

The later, peak phase of the cycle, called fast wave or REM sleep, marks the culmination of progressive reactivation of the EEG and autonomic functions. Paradoxically, muscle tone is even further depressed in REM sleep; this is caused by active inhibitory mechanisms which obliterate tonus and paralyze all but the ocular musculature. Silently signaling the intense internal activation of brain stem sensorimotor systems, the eyes execute spectacular runs of nystagmiform movement. Upon awakening from REM sleep, subjects are easily aroused and often give detailed dream reports.

The NREM-REM cycle repeats itself, usually without interruption, four to five times each night. The later cycles have shallower NREM troughs with relatively more time devoted to REM toward morning. Major shifts in posture—of which the subject is generally unaware—occur at NREM-REM phase transitions, hence at least 8 or 10 times per night. Thus even one who claims to have "slept like a log" actually "tossed and turned all night." The physiological systems underlying mentation, movement, and cardiorespiratory control undergo dynamic and dramatic changes through the night. The sleep disorders can be readily appreciated and understood in these terms. Given the complexity of organismic orchestrations, it is remarkable that any of us ever sleeps without dysfunctional consequence or complaint.

The Reciprocal Interaction Model

Lesion and ablation studies indicate that the oscillator controlling the sleep-dream cycle is located in the pons. Single cell recordings suggest that this pontine clock is composed of two interconnected neuronal populations whose activity levels fluctuate symmetrically (see Figure 8.2). This out-of-phase oscillation appears to be due to reciprocal interaction of oppositely signed excitatory and inhibitory neurotransmitters.

During waking, the resting activity level of neurons in the brain stem aminergic nuclei is high. The nuclei containing these waking-on cells include the noradrenergic locus coeruleus and the serotonergic dorsal raphe, which have been implicated in control of sleep state, mood, and learning. In waking, aminergic inhibition suppresses resting activity of cholinergic neurons in nuclei such as the reticular giant cells. During NREM, aminergic inhibition gradually declines; simultaneously cholinergic excitation increases so that at mid-cycle the balance between aminergic inhibition and cholinergic excitation shifts. This is followed by the REM period, when aminergic inhibition nadirs and cholinergic excitation becomes maximal. The time constant of this system, which oscillates in the range of minutes, cannot depend solely on millisecond synaptic duration delays. The fact that period length is a function of brain size within and across species suggests that a distance factor may be involved. Protein transport of neurotransmitter enzymes is one plausible mechanism for phase conversion.

As predicted by the reciprocal interaction model, microinjection of either cholinergic agonists or aminergic antagonists into the pons can convert an animal's state from waking to REM sleep. This account of change in consciousness in terms of shifting ratios of sympathetic to parasympathetic drive carries the classical conceptions of Cannon and Hess to the level of the single neuron. It allows us to interpret sleep physiology, pathophysiology, and pharmacology specifically, consistently, and rationally.

A Pathophysiological Model of Sleep Disorders

Human organismic state may be a function of reciprocally shifting activity levels of inhibitory and excitatory neuronal populations. Two kinds of problems, one static, the other dynamic, may perturb such a control system (see Table 8.2). A *static shift* in net drive of one or both opposing neuronal populations results in an increasing propensity for one state or the other. Thus insomnia (or too much waking) occurs if there is either aminergic overactivity or cholinergic underactivity—or both. Reciprocally, hypersomnia (or too little waking) occurs if there is either aminergic underactivity or cholinergic overactivity—or both. This formulation views the probability of waking or sleep to be a function of the set point of the controlling oscillator. Set point level is not independent of environmental influences: exogenous (e.g., noise) and endogenous (e.g., cortical or muscular) inputs both play their part.

The *dynamics* of the system are such that timing errors may occur, resulting in a temporal dissociation of state components. For example, if the subsystems controlling mentation and motor activity are not precisely coordinated, there may be hallucinosis (hypnagogic hallucinations) when falling asleep or persistent immobility (sleep paralysis) when aroused from REM, as in narcolepsy; conversely, motor activity may emerge during deep NREM sleep, as in somnambulism (sleepwalking) or enuresis.

Dynamic shifts in activity level of multiple subsys-

tems integrated reciprocally also have predictable consequences for autonomic control systems. Thus the decreasing aminergic drive on brain stem reticular neurons that is integral to sleep onset may result in cessation of breathing (as in central sleep apnea) if the set point of the respiratory oscillator—itself a reticular system—is suddenly changed. Similarly, the deactivation (probably a disfacilitation) of motor systems that is integral to sleep onset may compromise a marginal airway via decreasing tonus of glossal and hypoglossal muscles (as in peripheral or obstructive sleep apnea). Reestablishment of adrenergic tone on arousal from sleep may be delayed,

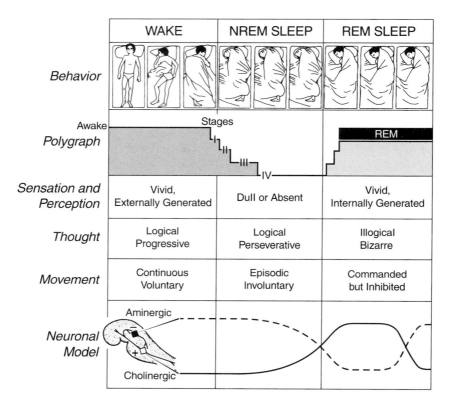

Figure 8.2 Reciprocal interaction model of state control. The states of waking, NREM, and REM sleep have behavioral, polygraphic, and psychological manifestations, all of which appear to be orchestrated by a pontine brain stem control system. Posture shifts, detectable by time lapse photography or video, occur during waking and with phase changes in the sleep cycle. Two different mechanisms account for sleep immobility: disfacilitation (during the stages I–IV of NREM sleep) and inhibition (during REM sleep). The motor inhibition of REM prevents motor commands from being acted upon. In dreams, we imagine that we move but we do not. The neuronal model of the clock which programs these states is depicted as reciprocal interconnections between aminergic inhibitory (filled cell) and cholinergic excitatory (open cell) neurons whose activity levels, recorded by microelectrodes in cats, are also reciprocal. Aminergic cells *(broken lines)* are most active in waking, decline in NREM, and reach their nadir in REM. Cholinergic cells *(solid lines)* have low resting levels in waking, increase progressively in NREM, and reach their peak activity in REM. Note that state changes and movements occur at the crossover point of the two activity curves.

Table 8.2 A pathophysiological model of sleep

Causes	Effects
Level changes in sleep cycle oscillator	Level change in attention, motoric, and homeostatic regulatory systems
Aminergic underactivity or cholinergic overactivity (or both)	Hypersomnia (e.g., narcolepsy)
Aminergic overactivity or cholinergic underactivity (or both)	Insomnia (e.g., anxiety states)
Timing errors between sleep cycle oscillator and other systems	Parasomnia (e.g., sleepwalking)

as in sleep drunkenness associated with deficient blood pressure regulation.

The foregoing underscores our main point: the pathophysiology of sleep disorders can be understood as functional disturbance of multiple interacting neuronal control systems. As such, sleep disorders fall into no existing medical specialty but are situated at the intersection of medicine, neurology, and psychiatry. These three levels of analysis—the medical, the neurological, and the psychiatric—are as important to the individual physician as they are to the sleep disorders specialist, since every patient is likely to demonstrate derangement in all three domains. Therein lies one great challenge of this new field of clinical investigation.

The Evaluation of Sleep Complaints

Until recently sleep was neither observed nor objectively measured, so the physician was literally groping in the dark in his diagnostic efforts. Sleep laboratory studies reveal two kinds of errors in subjective reporting: overestimation of time spent awake in insomnia and underestimation of the physiologically significant respiratory disturbances that occur in sleep. Thus the insomniac perceives his 1 or 2 hours of sleep loss as 3 or 4, while the apneic patient is completely unaware of the hundreds of arousals that occur when he is cyanotic with an oxygen saturation of 50%! The insomniac, who is often anxious, may compound this irony by exerting great pressure on the physician for a prompt, uncritical, and even potentially dangerous therapeutic response, while the apneic patient, urgently needing a tracheotomy, sits lethargically uncomplaining.

Documentation can be accomplished in several direct

and simple ways prior to referral for sleep lab evaluation (see Table 8.3). One is the sleep log, kept for at least 2 and preferably for 4 weeks following an initial visit. On a single sheet (each line represents 24 hours) the patient records the times of retiring, falling asleep, arousals, awakening, and arising. Dated entries corresponding to the lines indicate subjective state and behavioral data for the intervening waking periods. The sleep log has several uses beyond establishing baseline symptoms: (1) it involves the patient in an observational effort that looks at his entire lifestyle; (2) it provides data about the relation of waking activity to sleep; (3) it provides data on night-to-night variability that can be enlightening and didactic; and (4) it buys time, which often brings change.

So sensitive is sleep to situational variables that vigorous efforts should be made to document normal and abnormal sleep in its natural habitat. Since movement distinguishes waking from sleep and punctuates sleep in a predictable pattern, simple actigraphic monitoring provides useful data about circadian and ultradian rhythms. Long-term temperature monitoring is also possible. A related technique is time-lapse photography and/or video monitoring, which yields complex behavioral data including interaction between bed partners. From an analysis of major posture shifts that normally accompany NREM-REM transition, home-based recording provides objective data to correlate with subjective estimates. If eyelid movement is recorded together with accelerometer-generated signals from head movement, the states of waking, NREM sleep, and REM sleep can be reliably discriminated by a simple, portable, self-applicable system called the Nightcap. The Nightcap is sensitive to most of the parameters relevant to the diagnosis and treatment of insomnia.

Sleep lab studies still provide the only definitive means of documenting the diagnostic signs of the major sleep disorders. If narcolepsy, nocturnal myoclonus, or sleep apnea cannot be ruled out by the simple means described above, referral to a sleep lab is indicated (see Table 8.4). Since so much has been made of the value of sleep lab evaluations, it may be worthwhile to point out some of their limitations. Adaptation effects have already been

Table 8.3 Diagnostic adjuncts

1. Sleep log
2. Bed partner interview
3. Audio tape recording
4. Home-based sleep monitoring
5. Sleep lab polysomnography

Table 8.4 Sleep lab signs of specific disorders

Narcolepsy	REM periods at nocturnal sleep onset REM sleep in daytime attacks
Sleep apnea syndrome	Respiratory arrests Airway obstruction Oxygen desaturation Frequent arousals
Nocturnal myoclonus	Periodic contraction of limb musculature

mentioned: it is common especially for anxious subjects to sleep poorly for 1, 2, or even 3 nights in an unfamiliar place; little confidence can be placed in studies of insomnia lasting less than 4 successive nights. While the occurrence of sleep onset REM periods may support the diagnosis of narcolepsy, their absence does not rule out that diagnosis, and they also occur in sleep apnea. Thus sleep lab evaluation, an expensive and disruptive procedure, may not provide definitive diagnosis, especially for the most common problems; the referring physician may not be enlightened, and the patient may remain unimproved, so reliance may well be placed on more direct means of investigation and management.

Diagnosis and Treatment of Sleep Disorders

A classification scheme proposed by the American Sleep Disorders Association in 1990 divides sleep disorders into 4 major categories (see Table 8.5). This groups most of the known sleep symptoms and signs in syndromes corresponding to the International Classification of Diseases (ICD-9) nomenclature.

It is beyond the scope of this chapter to give an account of all the presently coded sleep disorders. However, there are general concepts and guidelines which must be considered to diagnose correctly and treat the most serious and common sleep disorders.

Dyssomnias

Dyssomnias are primary disorders of sleep. They can be due to intrinsic causes (idiopathic or psychological) or extrinsic environmental factors such as high altitude, behavioral problems as in the insufficient sleep syndrome, nocturnal eating syndrome, and inadequate sleep hygiene. They include disorders characterized by insufficient or qualitatively poor sleep as well as others in which excessive daytime sleep (EDS) is the primary symptom. The two conditions are often causally related, EDS being the natural consequence of a poor night's sleep. Among the intrinsic dyssomnias are psychophysiological insomnia, idiopathic insomnia, sleep state misperception, and the main hypersomnias such as narcolepsy, idiopathic, and recurrent hypersomnias and some mixed forms of sleep disturbance in which insomnia and hypersomnia may alternate, such as sleep apnea, periodic limb movement disorder (PLM), and the restless legs syndrome (RLS). This chapter focuses on the most

Table 8.5 Classification of sleep disorders

1. Dyssomnias
   intrinsic—e.g., psychophysiological insomnia, narcolepsy, idiopathic hypersomnia, recurrent hypersomnia, obstructive sleep apnea syndrome, central sleep apnea syndrome, periodic limb movement disorder, restless legs syndrome disorder
   extrinsic—e.g., inadequate sleep hygiene, insufficient sleep syndrome, environmental sleep disorder
   circadian rhythms sleep disorders—e.g., jet lag syndrome, shift work sleep disorder, advanced sleep phase syndrome, delayed sleep phase syndrome

2. Parasomnias
   arousal disorders—e.g., confusional arousals, sleep terrors, sleepwalking
   sleep-wake transition disorders—e.g., rhythmic movement disorder, sleep starts
   parasomnias usually associated with REM sleep—e.g., nightmares, sleep paralysis, REM sleep behavior disorder
   other parasomnias—e.g., enuresis, bruxism

3. Sleep Disorders associated with:
   mental disorders—e.g., psychoses, mood disorders, anxiety disorders, alcoholism
   neurological disorders—e.g., parkinsonism, sleep-related epilepsy, sleep-related headaches
   medical disorders—e.g., nocturnal cardiac ischemia, sleep-related asthma, sleep-related gastroesophageal reflux

4. Proposed Sleep Disorders—e.g., short sleeper, long sleeper, fragmentary myoclonus, sleep hyperhidrosis, pregnancy-associated sleep disorder

important dyssomnias and then discusses sleep problems most commonly encountered by psychiatrists.

Insomnias. The insomnias can be subdivided into initial, midterm, and terminal, respectively characterized by difficulties falling asleep, maintaining sleep throughout the night, and awakening early in the morning. These variants can present simultaneously, as for instance in insomnia due to anxiety disorder (initial + midterm insomnia) or depression (midterm and terminal insomnia). The insomnias can also be classified according to duration of symptoms as transient, short-term, medium-term, and persistent or chronic.

This temporal distinction is important for correct treatment. While a short-term (less than 2 weeks) pharmacological trial of sleeping pills is indicated for transient and short-term insomnias, a thorough etiological search is encouraged for medium-term cases and for the chronic insomnias for which sleeping pills can be only a short-term adjunct to the etiologically based therapeutic plan (e.g., benzodiazepines added to antidepressive or neuroleptic agents).

Most experts maintain that although short-acting hypnotic benzodiazepines are safer than older barbiturates, they should not be used for longer than 2–3 weeks. Benzodiazepines provide only symptomatic relief, and subjects habituate rapidly to them and may experience rebound insomnia when they are stopped. Insomnias related to chronic anxiety disorders are thus problematic because effective treatment usually requires longer-term trials. Some of the new, non-benzodiazepine agents such as zolpidem or zopiclone minimize withdrawal effects and allow longer, safer periods of treatment, especially in persistent insomnias of the elderly.

Case I Insomnia
M.P., a 26-year-old woman, was, like many ambitious graduate students, reluctant to stop her always seemingly inadequate studying. When she finally did get into bed, she was then unable to fall asleep because of persistent rumination and anxiety about her school performance. Because she was always shy of sleep, she had trouble paying attention in class, which increased her concerns about her scholastic performance.

Immediate relief of the sleep onset insomnia was obtained with a short-acting sedative. Helpful behavioral changes included relaxation training (to reduce performance anxiety), regular afternoon exercise (to increase physiological readiness for sleep), and a changed schedule (to permit adequate opportunity for sleep). Psychotherapy focused on the traumatic origins of her self-doubt

and fostered a realistic increase in self-confidence. She completed graduate school, married happily, and gave up sedative medications when she conceived a child.

Hypersomnias. Narcolepsy is a syndrome characterized by a tetrad of symptoms: EDS and sleep attacks, cataplexy (a sudden loss of postural muscle tone), hypnagogic/hypnopompic hallucinations, and sleep paralysis. The first two symptoms are mandatory for diagnosis and distinguish this syndrome from other hypersomnias. As pointed out previously, some of these symptoms can be considered timing errors resulting in a temporal dissociation of state components, with REM inhibition of muscle tone and vivid dreamlike imagery gaining access to the waking state. This, and other aspects of the pathophysiology of narcolepsy, are illustrated in Figure 8.3. The neurophysiological hallmark of narcolepsy is a markedly reduced REM latency in both nocturnal sleep and daytime naps (≥ than 2 Sleep onset REM [SoREMS] occurring in 4 of 5 naps recorded in the Multiple Sleep Latency Test). This HLA DR2 and DW2 haplotypes are biological markers of this disorder.

Narcoleptic patients usually have disrupted nocturnal sleep with multiple arousals sometimes related to breathing disorders but more often to periodic limb movements. Treatment is symptomatic, aiming first to reduce EDS with aminergic agonists (amphetamines, methylphenidate, pemoline, and new noradrenaline agonists such as Modaffinil) and second to reduce cataplectic attacks with aminergic potentiating drugs such as the tricyclic antidepressants protriptyline, clomipramine, and veloxazine or with selective serotonin reuptake inhibitors (SSRIs).

Case II Narcolepsy
B.C. was a 36-year-old married apple grower who had suffered from irresistible sleep attacks since adolescence. He had been unsuccessfully treated by a psychiatrist who assumed that his sleep attacks were psychogenic. While describing his fear of having an attack and falling from a ladder at work, he laughed and immediately entered a brief REM sleep period complete with eye movements, loss of responsiveness, and collapse of muscle tone. Upon arousal a few minutes later he recounted having dreamed of skiing and falling in the snow when he was surprised to see a long-lost college classmate skiing down the slope.

To reduce the risk of more serious bodily harm, the patient was educated about his cyclical propensity to sleep attacks and encouraged to take brief, protective naps every 70–80 minutes while working or driving. At the same time he was placed on a low dose of an amine reuptake blocker with anticholinergic properties to potentiate waking and oppose REM. He was also referred to a narcolepsy support group and became an advocate for public education and political action in research on the brain.

Less common forms of hypersomnia include the idiopathic and recurrent hypersomnias. Idiopathic hypersomnia is marked by excessive nocturnal sleep of good quality and by EDS which is not as severe as in the narcoleptic patient and which is not REM related. Recurrent hypersomnia is thought to be a pervasive functional disorder of the hypothalamus with hypersexuality, binge eating, and irritability associated with periods of EDS and sleep periods as long as 18–20 hours.

Movement disorders. Periodic limb movement disorder (PLM) and restless legs syndrome (RLS) are very common sleep disorders. They may present as insomnia or EDS. In PLM, periodic movements occur during NREM

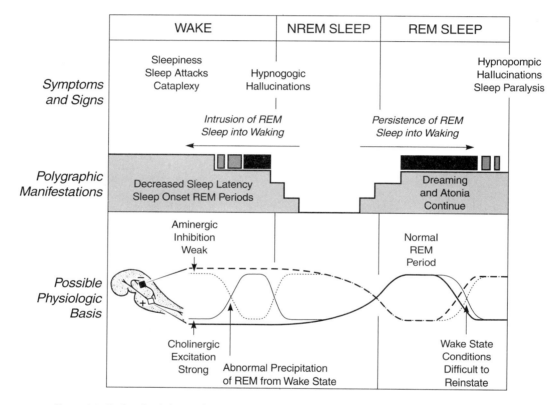

Figure 8.3 Pathophysiology of narcolepsy. Narcoleptic patients have several abnormalities of sleep-waking state control that appear to result from changes in set point of the REM state oscillator. During waking, REM sleep signs intrude as sleepiness, sleep attacks, and cataplexy. This increased propensity to REM is measured in multiple-sleep latency tests and may manifest itself as hypnogogic hallucinations or sustained sleep-onset REM period. On arousal from REM sleep, there may be persistence of mental phenomena of REM (hypnopompic hallucinations) and/or REM sleep motor inhibition (sleep paralysis). Reciprocal interaction models account for these phenomena by hypothesizing decreased aminergic inhibition *(light broken line)* and/or increased cholinergic excitation *(light solid line)* in the pontine oscillator. During waking there is increased propensity for the REM generator to reach threshold. At sleep onset there is brief escape from aminergic restraint and sleep-onset REM period is triggered. The system then resets and cycles normally until end of REM, when there is a lag in reinstitution of waking-state conditions and REM phenomena again escape their normal temporal bounds. Clinical efficacy of aminergic agonists (e.g., amphetamine) or amine reuptake blockers (e.g., imipramine) may be due to their capacity to reset aminergic inhibition to normal levels *(heavy broken line)*. By reciprocal interaction, this would also reset the cholinergic generator *(heavy solid line)*.

sleep, and the continuous arousals impede the patient from entering deeper stages of sleep. In RLS, uncomfortable sensations in the limbs occur during the first part of the night and prevent normal transition from wakefulness to sleep. Treatment options include the benzodiazepine clonazepam and other muscle relaxants for PLM and codeine, opioids, and several vitamin cocktails for RLS. Dopaminergic agonists have recently been found effective in both disorders, suggesting that a change in the aminergic-cholinergic set point of the basal ganglia may be a pathophysiological factor.

The sleep apnea syndromes. Sleep apnea or sleep disordered breathing is the second most common sleep disorder. In contrast to more frequent but less disabling insomnias, sleep apnea is a severe, potentially life threatening disorder characterized by impaired patency of the upper airway during sleep. There are two types of sleep apnea, obstructive and central. In the latter, by far less common, the absence of ventilatory effort parallels collapse of the upper airway with consequent lack of airflow. The pathophysiology of these two apneic processes is illustrated in Figure 8.4.

Most obstructive sleep apnea patients begin their lives as snorers who evolve into the full-blown syndrome in their forties. Risk factors are male gender, middle age, obesity, and facial bone abnormalities. As a consequence of chronic nocturnal hypoxemia and its attendant baro-

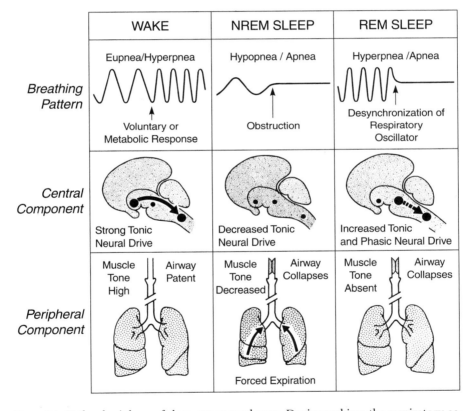

Figure 8.4 Pathophysiology of sleep apnea syndrome. During waking, the respiratory oscillator of the medulla receives tonic drive from other neural structures and can respond to voluntary and metabolic signals to change breathing pattern. Ventilation is assured by active maintenance of the upper airway via tonus of oropharyngeal musculature. In NREM sleep, central drive on both respiratory oscillator and peripheral muscles declines owing to disfacilitation. Respiratory rate and amplitude thus diminish and the airway is subject to collapse. If obstruction occurs, forced expiratory effort may actually aggravate airway obstruction, and prolonged apneas with marked hypoventilation and hypoxia may occur. During REM sleep, activation of pontine generator neurons produces tonic and phasic driving of the respiratory oscillator, which may desynchronize leading to hyperpnea and/or to apnea. In addition, medullary oscillator becomes unresponsive to metabolic signals. In patients with tendency to airway collapse, these processes may multiply deleterious effects.

receptor stimulation, sleep apnea patients go on to develop hypertension and cardiac arrhythmias and become more prone to myocardial infarction, left and right heart failure, and cerebrovascular accidents.

Nocturnal symptoms include chronic loud snoring and gasping or choking episodes during the night with fragmented shallow sleep owing to recurrent arousals. Daytime symptoms include EDS, fatigue-related work or car accidents, and personality changes with cognitive impairment resulting from vigilance-related problems.

The diagnosis can easily be made by several simple ambulatory devices (Mesam 4, Edentrace, and voice-operated tape recorders) which provide indirect measures of respiratory effort via sleep posture, heart rate, snoring sounds, and oxygen saturation data. Traditional sleep laboratory recordings are nonetheless recommended to inform treatment decisions documenting the severity of symptoms and their sleep stage relationship during the night.

Treatment options include behavioral approaches such as weight loss, abstinence from alcohol, and withdrawal of sedative medication. Because some sleep apnea patients complain of insomnia, the obvious danger of sedative treatment must be emphasized. Specific recommendations for sleep posture control may also help. Mechanical (oral-dental) devices are applicable only in mild to moderate cases. Nasal CPAP (continual positive air pressure) during sleep is often dramatically helpful if it can be tolerated. Surgical procedures such as UPPP (uvulo-palato-pharyngoplasty), LAUP (laser assisted uvuloplasty), nasal surgery, adeno-tonsillectomy, tracheostomy, and maxillofacial surgery are indicated when structural abnormalities exist.

Parasomnias

Among the parasomnias, three disorders are of particular interest to psychiatrists: sleepwalking, sleep terrors, and nightmares. Sleepwalking and sleep terrors are considered to be disorders of arousal, as subjects struggle to awaken from deep slow wave sleep. They are usually age-dependent conditions, being fairly common in children with a positive family history. Unless they persist after adolescence, they do not require specific treatment (benzodiazepines or psychotherapy). Nightmares are frightening dreams occurring in REM, but they do not evince the autonomic driving seen in sleep terrors. They are seen in acute stress disorder, in depressed patients, and in some patients with schizoid and borderline personality disorders. Tricyclic and other REM-suppressant agents may be added to the treatment of the underlying primary disorder.

REM sleep behavior disorder (RBD) is a dramatic and recently identified condition which reflects the acting out of dream content owing to loss of physiological muscle tone inhibition of normal REM. The disorder can be idiopathic in rare instances but is more often associated with brain stem degenerative diseases such as the Shy Drager syndrome, olivo-ponto-cerebellar degeneration (OPCD), or bilateral thalamic lesions. Functionally related conditions may temporarily emerge following alcohol or antidepressant medication withdrawal, or during chronic treatment of depressed or narcoleptic patients with REM suppressant agents.

Sleep Disturbances in Psychiatric Patients

Sleep complaints are commonly reported in patients with psychiatric disorders. Because they are rarely associated with specific polygraphic findings, discretion should be exercised before referring these patients to a sleep lab. Clinical relevance of the sleep symptoms is not to be denied, however, and the patient's report of sleep quality may be used to support a psychiatric diagnosis or to evaluate its prognosis after a therapeutic trial has been started. For example, the recent onset of difficulty falling asleep and/or of nightmares can point to the rapidly mounting anxiety of impending psychosis, while the sudden occurrence of frequent nightmares in a previously unaffected patient can herald a post-traumatic stress disorder, a depressive disorder, or simply a normal reaction to acute stress. A sudden reduction in sleep length without complaint of insomnia is often an early symptom of a manic episode.

Sleep in the Anxiety Disorders

Patients with anxiety disorders usually report difficulty falling asleep and maintaining sleep throughout the night. This is particularly true in generalized anxiety disorders. Because of the chronicity of their disturbance and their low threshold to stressful or painful situations, these patients are surely among the biggest consumers of sleeping pills. Hypnotics should be considered only as one part of the general therapeutic plan, since the insomnia is only one manifestation of a 24-hour problem. Besides the commonly used benzodiazepines and amytriptiline, buspirone (a new anxiolytic interfering with serotonin neurotransmission) may be helpful.

Patients with obsessive-compulsive disorder (OCD) have objective sleep findings resembling those of depressed patients, i.e., shortened REM sleep, decreased Stages III and IV, and decreased total sleep time. They also usually have a difficult transition to sleep owing to time-consuming presleep rituals. The most effective approach to the sleep symptoms is etiologic and involves both serotoninergic agents and behavioral techniques.

Chronic anxiety with generalized hyperarousal is the hallmark of post-traumatic stress disorder. Symptoms are usually worsened by secondary substance abuse and by frequent occurrence of major depressive episodes. REM latency is usually reduced, and episodes of REM behavior disorder may also occur. Effective treatment includes buspirone (for the insomnia) and a combination of clonidine and imipramine (for nightmares).

Patients with panic attacks, especially those which occur at night, must be differentiated from those suffering from nightmares, night terrors, hypnagogic hallucinations, and sleep paralysis. Nocturnal panic attacks are more likely to occur during NREM sleep, especially in the transition from light to deep sleep. They are usually accompanied by significant tachycardia and gross body movements, but the respiratory rate is absolutely regular. Sleep deprivation and relaxation both seem to trigger nocturnal panic attacks which create a vicious circle by aggravating anticipatory anxiety at bedtime. Pharmacological treatment options include the tricyclic clomipramine, SSRIs (excluding fluoxetine because of its disrupting action on sleep continuity), and the benzodiazepines bromazepam and alprazolam. Cognitivebehavioral techniques are strongly indicated to counteract the phobic avoidance behavior that may cripple these patients.

Sleep in the Mood Disorders

Depression-associated insomnia constitutes 80% of all cases of insomnia seen by psychiatrists. Midterm and terminal insomnia associated with increased wakefulness after sleep onset and early morning awakening are the main clinical features. The severity of insomnia is directly related to the severity of depression and is more strongly expressed in male patients.

The polygraphic findings include reduced Stages III–IV in the first cycle of sleep and a reduced REM latency. The duration and REM density of the first REM period are often increased. According to some authors, this is a specific state marker of depressive disorder, while for others it is a trait marker indicating genetic predisposition even in clinically unaffected subjects. It is clear that a reduced REM latency is nonspecific since it occurs in psychotic depression, OCD, and some schizophrenic patients as well as in a variety of patients afflicted by such non-psychiatric sleep disorders as sleep apnea and narcolepsy.

The REM sleep alterations are promptly reversed by tricyclic agents probably because of their anticholinergic

and proaminergic properties. It has been suggested that a rapid normalization of REM latency predicts good clinical outcome. The SSRIs are less effective in correcting REM sleep parameters and generally show alerting properties that limit their effectiveness in the treatment of depressed patients with severe insomnia. Monoamineoxidase inhibitors (MAOIs) and electroconvulsive therapy (ECT) both share REM-suppressing effects as well as antidepressant efficacy. Other commonly employed drugs do not have the same effect on REM (e.g., trazodone, amineptine, nefazodone). Both total and partial sleep deprivation induce mood improvement on the following day, whereas REM sleep naps cause a worsening of symptoms. These findings are compatible with the theory of cholinergic hypersensitivity in depression.

Possibly reflecting a shift from cholinergic to aminergic dominance, manic episodes are characterized by reduced total sleep time and by increased early morning awakening. Deep sleep and normal REM are better preserved than in major depression.

Sleep in Schizophrenia

Sleep is severely disturbed in schizophrenic patients. The reduction of total sleep time and REM with inversion of the sleep-wake rhythm is often the first symptom of an acute psychotic episode.

REM latency is generally reduced, especially in chronic illness. This finding could be related to cholinergic hypersensitivity and/or to increased serotonin turnover, which are found in schizophrenic patients. REM percentage, however, is reduced during the acute phase and consequently increased in chronic patients during remission. REM density is also reduced in acute patients, especially in the hallucinatory phase, probably as a function of intense aminergic activation. A distinctive feature of schizophrenia is the lack of REM rebound following REM deprivation during the acute phase. This finding has been ascribed to defective serotonin metabolism and to dopaminergic hyperactivity. NREM sleep is also conspicuously altered in schizophrenia with more than a 50% reduction of Stages III and IV in both acute and chronic patients. There is also a Stage II percentage reduction with an increased number of spindles, while Stage I is increased with atypical high frequency EEG activity. These changes all relate to the initial insomnia, the highly fragmented sleep, and the early morning awakenings.

An interesting observation in schizophrenic patients is the instability of the sleep-wake cycle and of oral temperature, suggesting a desynchronization of hypothalamic pacemakers. Both sleep phase and body temperature low points are advanced in schizophrenic patients. It is unclear whether this finding is related to the disease itself or to chronic use of neuroleptics.

Sleep in Eating Disorders

Insomnia is not an issue for patients with eating disorders. Anorexic patients usually feel less need to sleep, while bulimic patients may sleep more following a binge episode. Several parasomnias are common in bulimic patients. Sleepwalking episodes may occur with food intake that cannot be remembered by the patient. Sleep-talking and bruxism are also seen. Nocturnal bulimic episodes always occur in NREM sleep and respond to fluoxetine and amineptine therapy.

Both bulimia and anorexia share some polygraphic features with major depressive disorders. These include a reduced REM latency, reduced total sleep time, and reduced sleep efficiency. Cholinergic hypersensitivity may mediate the rapid REM induction following arecoline administration in patients affected by eating disorders.

In severe anorexia, both REM and NREM are severely reduced during periods of weight loss characterized by increased protein catabolism. This process is reversed when weight is regained during rehabilitation. In addition to medication, family therapy and cognitive-behavioral treatment may help to correct abnormal personality traits and ritual behaviors.

Sleep in Alcoholism

Chronic alcohol excess and acute or chronic alcohol abstinence are both related to major sleep disruption. Moderate alcohol intake has a biphasic effect: it first potentiates NREM and suppresses REM; this is followed by REM rebound and fragmented sleep. With chronic alcohol intake the initial sedative effect is likely to decline, requiring increased dosages to facilitate sleep induction. Chronic alcoholism potentiates such parasomnias as sleepwalking, enuresis, nightmares, sleep terrors, and snoring. Sleep apnea symptoms may also be exacerbated by alcohol-induced muscle relaxation of the upper airway, with a resultant worsening of cognitive impairment and increased EDS.

Acute abstinence is accompanied by NREM sleep suppression and by REM rebound. In delirium tremens, sleep is characterized by low-voltage fast EEG activity, by REM bursts, and by persistent tonic mental EMG, indicating a dissociation of REM sleep signs leading to multiple arousals.

NREM may never return to baseline in some patients, and when it does, it normalizes only after up to 2 years of abstinence. The "low NREM" syndrome seen in some post-alcoholic patients is thought to reflect residual alcoholic dependence and functional tolerance. These subjects have a heightened sensitivity to alcohol with marked REM and NREM suppression.

Sleep disorders of alcoholics are difficult to treat since any commonly used pharmacologic approach is potentially harmful. Sedative hypnotics can worsen respiratory problems and aggravate cognitive deficits, while antidepressants can only be used with caution given their side effects and potential risk for overdosage. Sleep hygiene, cognitive psychotherapy, relaxation techniques, and sleep restriction are preferred as both more beneficial and safe.

Sleep in Dementia

Sleep is severely altered in demented patients. Alzheimer's disease causes more consistent sleep changes than cerebrovascular dementia. During the first stages of the disease, total sleep time is reduced by major difficulties in falling asleep and sleep fragmentation caused by numerous arousals, with worsening of cognitive impairment. EDS is an early consequence. As the disease progresses, episodes of nocturnal confusion, delirium, and confabulation may ensue with even more severe alteration of the sleep-waking cycle. The so-called sundown syndrome is marked by psychomotor agitation and restlessness at night together with behavioral disturbances and EDS in the daytime.

Polygraphic findings include initial marked deterioration of NREM sleep with decreased spindles followed by such severe REM reduction that all sleep stage distinctions are blurred or lost.

The 24-hour rest-activity cycle is also deconstructed as sleep-wake rhythm disruption progresses and a true vegetative state is reached. The marked cholinergic degeneration, especially in the nucleus basalis of Meynert, contributes to sleep and cognitive alterations.

Sedative hypnotics do not help these patients and may actually have a paradoxically arousing effect. Low doses of neuroleptics such as thioridazine may be more helpful, especially in the management of the sundown symptoms.

Sleep is a complex function of the brain whose state is regulated by a coupled set of neural oscillators. The circadian alteration of rest and activity (and of body temperature) is programmed by the suprachiasmatic nucleus of the hypothalamus. This structure normally confines the cyclic alternation of NREM and REM sleep to the rest phase. But the pontine oscillator controlling NREM and REM via the reciprocal interaction of aminergic and cholinergic neurons can escape from circadian control (as in narcolepsy) and is itself subject to shifts in its set point, causing insomnias and hypersomnias. Because these two central oscillators modulate the entire brain, precise synchronization and balance in recruitment of their multiple outputs is critical to normal sleep and dreaming. The parasomnias can thus be understood as disorders of synchronicity and balance. In discussing the specific sleep disorders and those which affect psychiatric patients, we have illustrated these pathophysiological principles. We have also shown how their treatment with psychopharmacological agents acts to reset or shift the balance of the neuromodulatory control systems of the brain.

References

Allen, R. B., Wagman, A. M. I., and Funderburk, F. R. 1977. Slow wave sleep changes: alcohol tolerance and treatment implication. *Adv. Exp. Med. Biol.* 85A:629–640.

Evans, F. J. 1983. Sleep, eating, and weight disorders. In *Eating and weight disorders,* ed. R. K. Goodstein. New York: Springer Publishing Company. 147–178.

Evans, L. K. 1987. Sundown syndrome in institutionalized elderly. *J. Am. Geriatr. Soc.* 35:101–108.

Feinberg, M., Gillin, J. C., Carrol, B. J., Greden, J. F., Zis, A. P. 1982. EEG studies of sleep in the diagnosis of depression. *Biol. Psychiatry* 305–316.

Gillin, J. C., Smith, T. L., Irwin, M., Kripke, D. F., Schuckit, M. 1990. EEG sleep studies in "pure" primary alcoholism during subacute withdrawal: relationship to normal controls, age, and other clinical variables. *Biol. Psychiatry* 27:477–488.

Insel, T. R., Gillin, J. C., Moore, A., Mendelson, W. B., Loewenstein, R. J., Murphy, D. L. 1982. The sleep of patients with obsessive-compulsive disorder. *Arch. Gen. Psychiatry* 39:1372–77.

Katz, J. L., Kuperberg, A., Pollack, C. P., et al. 1984. Is there a relationship between eating disorder and affective disorder: new evidence from sleep recordings. *Am. J. Psychiatry* 141:753–759.

Kupfer, D. J., and Foster, F. G. 1978. EEG sleep and depression. In *Sleep disorders: diagnosis and treatment,* ed. R. L. Williams and I. Karacan. New York: John Wiley and Sons. 163–205.

Lesser, I. M., Poland, R. E., Holcomb, C., Rose, D. E. 1985. Electroencephalographic study of nighttime panic attacks. *J. Nerv. Ment. Dis.* 173:744–746.

Maggini, C., Guazzelli, M., Piere, M., et al. 1986. REM latency in psychiatric disorders: polygraphic study on major depression, bipolar disorder, manic and schizo-phrenic disorder. *New Trends in Experimental and Clinical Psychiatry* 1 (no. 2):93–101.

Mills, J. N., Morgan, R., Minors, D. S., et al. 1977. The free running circadian rhythms of two schizophrenics. *Chronobiologia* 4:353–360.

Montplaisir, J., Petit, D., Lorrain, P., Gauthier, S., Neilsen, T. 1995. Sleep in Alzheimer's disease: further consideration on the role of brainstem and forebrain cholinergic populations in sleep-wake mechanisms. *Sleep* 18:145–148.

Zarcone, V. P., Benson, K. L., and Berger, P. A. 1987. Abnormal rapid eye movement latencies in schizophrenia. *Arch. Gen. Psychiatry* 44:45–48.

Recommended Reading

Diagnostic Classification Steering Committee. 1990. *ICSD international classification of sleep disorders: diagnostic and coding manual.* Rochester, Minn.: American Sleep Disorders Association.

Kryger, M. H., Roth, T., and Dement, W. C. 1994. *The principles and practice of sleep medicine.* Philadelphia: W. B. Saunders.

Steriade, M., and McCarley, R. W. 1990. *Brainstem control of wake-sleep states.* New York: Plenum.

Thorpy, M. J. 1990. *Handbook of sleep disorders.* New York: Marcel Dekker.

Acknowledgments

The research on which this chapter is based was supported by the National Institute of Health (Grants M. H. 13.923 and M. H. 48.832) and the Mind-Body Network of the John D. and Catherine T. MacArthur Foundation.

PART THREE

Psychopathology

W. W. MEISSNER

Theories of Personality

This discussion of the more influential personality theories in psychiatry begins with the contributions of Sigmund Freud, followed by consideration of some of his disciples and followers. We then consider their modification and enrichment by later successors. These developments in analytic theory are followed by more succinct discussions of the contributions of other nonanalytic theorists, whose views derive primarily from psychological personality research and tend to play a less central role in psychiatric thinking about personality and character.

Classic Psychoanalysis

Sigmund Freud (1856–1939) revolutionized psychiatric thinking and laid the groundwork for the psychodynamic understanding of mental disorders. Although many of his ideas have been superseded, basic Freudian concepts are still the foundation of psychoanalytic understanding.

Origins of Freud's Views

The Concept of Hysteria

Freud's earliest observations centered on the relation between hysteria and hypnosis. His study of hypnotic and posthypnotic suggestion led him to conclude that unconscious ideas persisted in the mind and continued to influence the subject's actions and behavior, even though the patient remained totally unaware of such influence. For Freud's colleague Josef Breuer, hysterical phenomena were caused by "hypnotic states"—spontaneous dissociative states like those produced by hypnotic suggestion. Freud, however, noted that hysterical symptoms disappeared when the patient's memory of specific traumatic events connected with the onset of the symptom was made conscious.

Repression and Resistance

He observed, further, that powerful mental forces excluded these traumatic ideas from consciousness, and that they could become conscious only by dint of psychical effort. These observations led Freud to formulate his concepts of *repression* and *resistance*. Although conscious expression of a pathogenic idea and its associated affect helped alleviate hysterical symptoms, he also concluded that powerful repressive forces had expelled the idea from consciousness, and that these same forces were the cause of resistance to any therapeutic attempts to bring the idea back into awareness.

Since pathogenic ideas usually proved to involve conflicts over sexuality, Freud postulated that such ideas related to specific traumatizing (sexual) events occurring earlier in childhood. At first, basing this "seduction hypothesis" on his patients' recollections and the intense associated affects, he attributed the trauma more or less exclusively to actual physical seduction, practiced on or by the child, that had so overwhelmed and threatened the child that powerful repressive defenses were required to prevent reemergence of memory of the trauma into awareness.

This early theory of hysteria was a theory of defense, based on repression, resistance, and the seduction hypothesis. Repression and the related notion of defense are fundamental in psychoanalytic theory, based on the assumption that dynamic forces or drives exist in the mind as powerful sources of motivation, which are opposed by defense mechanisms. The opposition of drives and defenses gives rise to psychic conflict.

As his clinical experience grew and as his own self-analysis deepened, Freud began to wonder whether confirmation of his seduction hypothesis by his patients was more a result of suggestion than of actual historical events; rather, some appeared to be expressions of unconscious sexual wishes and fantasies from the infantile period. This insight led him to abandon the seduction hypothesis as *the* explanation of neurosis, and to focus more on the child's inner motivations, wishes, and fantasies. While Freud did not completely discount seduction, as has frequently been charged, his interest and theorizing did change course. On the ruins of the seduction hypothesis Freud constructed a theory of the psychology of dynamic mental forces, expressed in repression, resistance, and conflict. He developed the theory of psychoneurosis based on the vicissitudes of infantile sexuality, in terms of which persistent infantile wishes, primarily libidinal, escape control of repressing forces and erupt into consciousness in the distorted form of neurotic symptoms.

Dream Theory

Freud then turned his attention to the manifestation of these dynamic forces in dreams (Freud, 1900). During this period, when his patients frequently reported dreams and their related material, he evolved the technique of free association, whereby the patient was encouraged to express whatever thoughts, feelings, fantasies, or images came to awareness. He gradually came to realize that dreams had meanings, which could be deciphered through these associations. Patients often reported material related to repressed memories and ideas of which they were otherwise unaware.

The study of dreams became for Freud the "royal road of the unconscious," and his development of dream theory paralleled his analysis of psychoneurotic symptoms. Freud saw the dream as a conscious expression of an unconscious fantasy or wish. The *dream work* (the process by which the dream is created) produced the conscious material of the dream (manifest content), which expressed underlying unconscious ideas (latent content) in a distorted or disguised form. Associations revealed the hidden links between dream symbols and the repressed ideas. Freud postulated that a dream censor opposed conscious access of unconscious ideas during the waking state, but during the regressive relaxation of sleep, the censor allowed some of the unconscious content to be incorporated into dream material. The dream work consisted of 4 transforming processes—displacement, condensation, symbolism, and projection—which transformed latent dream ideas. The disguise of latent ideas made them sufficiently tolerable to the patient's ego to bypass the restrictive control of the censor. This relaxation of repression, allowing unconscious content to surface, was analogous to the loosening of repression in the pro-

duction of hysterical symptoms—the "return of the repressed."

These contending forces, repressed and repressing, and the nature of the conflicts between them, became central in Freud's thinking. They led him to envision 2 contrasting psychic systems, one producing a rational organization of dream thoughts similar to normal thinking and another creating bewildering and irrational dream thoughts. The *primary process* acted to discharge psychic tension, whereas *secondary process* involved inhibition and delay and served to correct and regulate the primary system. All psychic functions involve participation in both primary and secondary processes in varying degrees.

The Topographic Model

During the quarter-century after Freud abandoned the seduction hypothesis, the *topographic model* dominated his thinking. The model described a mental topography in terms of the relationships of various psychic elements to consciousness. The model was based on the following assumptions: (1) symptoms and dreams have specific, demonstrable meaning within a causal psychological network (psychological determinism); (2) unconscious repressed elements influence present experience as regulated by the pleasure principle and primary process (theory of unconscious psychological processes); (3) unconscious psychological conflicts exist in the mind (the basis for a theory of psychoneurosis, expressed in resistance and repression); and (4) unconscious processes, forces, and conflicts derive from psychological energies originating in instinctual drives, and repression of such energies and their subsequent distortions and transformations give rise to neurotic symptoms and anxiety.

The divisions of the mental topography are the conscious, preconscious, and unconscious. The *conscious system* is the region of the mind in which perceptions derived from internal or extrinsic stimuli are integrated and brought into awareness. The objects of such perceptions include bodily processes, mental processes, thoughts, and affects. The *preconscious system* consists of mental processes and contents that can enter conscious awareness relatively easily when the individual focuses attention on them. Preconscious thought organization ranges from relatively reality-based or problem-solving thought sequences (secondary process) to more primitive fantasies, daydreams, or dreamlike images, reflecting primary process organization. The preconscious can be influenced by both conscious and unconscious sources, but also has the function of maintaining a repressive barrier or censorship against unconscious wishes and desires. The transformation of unconscious processes to preconscious or conscious levels takes place only by the expenditure of energy to overcome the repressive barrier.

The unconscious can be defined descriptively as nonconscious mental events, applying to both unconscious and preconscious events. In more systematic and dynamic terms, the unconscious refers to mental contents and processes excluded from consciousness by repression, thus distinguishing unconscious from preconscious events. In this dynamic sense, unconscious content consists of drive representations or wishes that are in some sense unacceptable, threatening, or incongruous with the conscious intellectual or ethical standards of the individual. Nonetheless, as Freud thought, the drives constantly strive for discharge and thus give rise to intrapsychic conflict between repressed and repressing forces of the mind. The *unconscious system* is that region of the mind in which unconscious dynamic processes operate and repressed mental content or memory traces are organized according to primary process. As in the dream process, these elements tend to be divorced from verbal symbols, express unconscious wishes, and derive from instinctual, particularly sexual, forces.

Freud struggled to achieve an adequate formulation of instinctual drives. His best-known definition describes the instinctual as a "concept on the frontier between the mental and the somatic, as the psychical representative of the stimuli originating from within the organism and reaching the mind, as a measure of the demands made upon the mind for work in consequence of its connections with the body" (1915, pp. 121–122). The nature of the connection between biological and psychological factors continues to trouble analytic thinking. Analysts tend to emphasize one or another aspect of this definition, variously stressing the biological or the psychological.

Sexuality played a primary role in Freud's thinking, but his ideas were not clearly articulated until his *Three Essays on the Theory of Sexuality* (1905), in which he presented a schema of stages in the development of sexual drives that has become the classic paradigm of analytic theory. Although he had freed himself from the seduction hypothesis and the conviction that early sexual trauma was the sole cause of neurosis, he remained convinced that neurotic disturbances had their roots in disturbances of the sexual drive. This conviction, and his attempts to build a theory to support it, would eventually yield to a deeper appreciation of the roles of narcissism and aggression, but at this early point he saw the energy of the psychic apparatus almost exclusively in libidinal terms. The relation of energies involved in narcissism and aggression, as well as in ego functions, to the sexual energy of libido remained problematic.

Freud described 4 major characteristics of instincts: source, impetus, aim, and object. The *source* was the part of the body from which instinctual drives arose, for libidinal drives the specific erotogenic zones: mucous membranes of the mouth, anus, and genitalia. *Impetus* was the degree or intensity of the demand made by the instinctual drive, and *aim* was the action by which the drive achieved satisfaction and reduced the intensity of stimulation. Finally, the *object* was the person or thing that satisfied the instinctual drive and became the target for instinctual discharge. Although Freud regarded the object as the most variable and interchangeable aspect of the instinct, increased understanding of the importance of specific objects (such as parents) in the infant's experience has considerably modified this point of view.

In infancy and early childhood, stimulation of the mucous membranes of the mouth, anus, or external genitalia causes erotic sensations. These pregenital instincts are gradually integrated under domination of the genital zone during normal development. Nonetheless, pregenital erotic components from oral and anal zones persist in adult sexual activity, particularly in foreplay or perversions. Infantile sexuality is polymorphous perverse, lacking integration under the primacy of adult genital drives, and gradually undergoes selective repression. The resultant transformations, distortions, and fixations of these component instincts may become the basis for adult personality characteristics and forms of psychopathology.

The emergence and predominance of specific erotogenic zones and their respective erotic drives follow a sequence of progressive biologically determined developmental phases: the oral phase of early infancy is followed by the anal phase, which then gives way to a phallic or oedipal phase. In the *oral phase,* the infant cannot survive without relief from painful inner physiological states; for this he depends on external caretaking objects. Oral hunger needs gain satisfaction by feeding. The experience of unsatisfied need and frustration in the absence of the breast, followed by need-satisfying release of tension in the presence of the breast, provides the infant's first awareness of external objects. The mother's capacity to respond empathically to the infant's needs permits homeostatic balancing of physiological needs within the child.

According to this theory, the oral zone maintains its dominant role in the organization of behavior through approximately the first 18 months of life. Oral drives are both libidinal and aggressive: oral erotic needs to take in, suck, swallow, and thus achieve quiescence dominate early in the oral phase, but later become mixed with more aggressive components (oral sadism) expressed in biting, chewing, spitting, or crying. Positive oral character traits include capacities for giving and receiving without excessive dependence or envy and for trust and reliance on others. Pathological traits include excessive optimism, pessimism, demandingness, dependence, and envy.

The *anal phase* of psychosexual development extends roughly from 1½ to 3 years of age. Maturation of neuromuscular control over sphincters permits greater voluntary control, particularly over retention and expulsion of feces. At the same time, parents require the child to relinquish some of his control and accede to toilet training. Voluntary sphincter control is part of the increasing shift from the relative passivity of the oral phase to greater activity and autonomy. Conflicts arise over issues of control, to a degree in the child's struggle with the parents over retaining or expelling feces, but also in other negotiations with parents.

Anal eroticism refers to sexual pleasure in anal functioning, both in retaining the precious feces and in presenting them as a gift to the parent. *Anal sadism* expresses aggressive wishes connected with discharging feces as powerful and destructive weapons. The child can exert power over the parent by control of evacuative functions, yielding and giving up the fecal mass or refusing to yield and withholding. The child's sense of control is fragile and easily threatened: if his stubborn withholding is excessively punished or his loss of control excessively shamed, the child may regress to oral patterns of behavior, such as thumb sucking, mouthing, and so forth. Positive anal traits include a sense of personal autonomy and a capacity for independence without shame or self-doubt. Pathological traits include excessive orderliness, obstinacy, stubbornness, willfulness, frugality, ambivalence, defiance, and sadomasochistic tendencies.

In the transition to the *phallic* or *genital phase,* pregenital components (oral and anal) are integrated into a new configuration in which the primary focus of sexual interest and stimulation is genital. This phase begins in the third year and continues to the end of the fifth year. The child becomes aware of sexual differences, and the penis becomes the organ of principal interest to children of both sexes. This period is critical in the early formation of gender identity. The genital character of the libidinal organization at this phase justifies calling it a "genital" or "phallic" phase, but the quality of genital drive organization remains infantile and differs radically from the genital reorganization that takes a more mature and decisive form in adolescence (puberty).

In the pregenital period, the child's relationships primarily involve interactions with each parent separately. In the phallic period, the child develops a new level of complexity in object relationships involving both parents at once; this triadic relationship is referred to as the *oedipal situation.* The Oedipus complex involves two complementary configurations: the *positive oedipal configuration,* a loving (sexual) attachment to the parent of the opposite sex and ambivalent rivalry with the parent of the same sex, and the *negative oedipal configuration,* in which the attachment is toward the same-sex parent with negative attitudes toward the opposite-sex parent; together they form the final and crucial stage in the development of infantile sexuality.

As Freud viewed the process, oedipal involvement is less complicated for boys than for girls, because the boy remains attached to his first love object, the mother. But his interest in the mother takes a strong erotic turn, as he desires to possess her exclusively and sexually. This can take the form of wanting to touch her, trying to get into bed with her, and expressing wishes to replace his father. He cannot tolerate competition from siblings for his mother's affection, but primarily the little lover wants to eliminate his archrival, the mother's husband, his father. Such destructive wishes evoke fears of retaliation and severe anxiety. Freud postulated that the punishment fit the crime so that the basic anxiety for the male child in this period was fear of castration. Castration anxiety arouses a fear of bodily or narcissistic injury stronger than the erotic attachment to the mother. Under pressure of castration anxiety, the boy must renounce his oedipal love for his mother and identify with his father. The picture is not this simple, however, because he also loves his father and at times feels anger toward his mother. He also seeks approval and affection from his father, and this homosexual component may have a powerful influence in shaping the child's personality.

Freud felt that the oedipal situation was considerably more involved for girls, who must shift their primary attachment from mother to father under oedipal pressures and thus prepare for a future sexual role. Freud thought that the anatomical difference between the sexes, specifically the girl's lack of a penis, precipitated the oedipal situation; he posited that the lack of a penis provoked an intense sense of loss and narcissistic injury, as well as envy of the larger male organ. Freud believed that once the girl realized that she did not have a penis, her attitude toward her mother changed, and she began to hold the mother responsible for bringing her into the world with inferior genital equipment. This hostility could be intense and color the child's future relationship to the mother. The further discovery that the mother also lacked a penis increased the child's antipathy toward and devaluation of her mother, resulting in her turning to her father in the vain hope that he would give her a baby as a substitute for the missing penis. These early theories of female sexuality have been radically revised in current thinking.

According to Freud, the girl's sexual love toward her father meets continuing disappointment and frustration. The wish to be loved by the father fosters identification with the mother, whom the father loves and with whom he sleeps. The threat to the girl is not castration but rather loss of —love—at one level, loss of the father's love in competition with the mother, but at a deeper and more infantile level, loss of the mother's love as well. Resolution of the oedipal attachment involves renunciation of the father in order to gain a more suitable, nonincestuous love object.

Freud regarded the Oedipus complex as the nucleus for the development of the child's personality and for the genesis of neuroses and symptom formations. He also held that internalizations derived from the oedipal situation profoundly influenced the development of character. These internalizations, by which parental standards and prohibitions, as well as other aspects of the parental models, were internalized were one of the means by which oedipal conflicts and tensions in the child's relationship to the parents were resolved. They formed the core of the child's emerging psychic structure, especially the superego.

Narcissism

The notion of narcissism led to important modifications in Freud's instinct theory (Freud, 1914). In certain clinical states—schizophrenic withdrawal, physical illness and hypochondriasis, deep sleep, and certain forms of object choice, particularly homosexual—Freud argued that libido was withdrawn from outside objects and redirected toward the patient's own ego. This could be seen dramatically in certain megalomaniacal delusions characterized by grandiosity (an enormously inflated sense of one's own importance). Freud ascribed these conditions to *primary narcissism,* a hypothetical state existing at birth in which the infant's libidinal energies seek only satisfaction of physiological needs and preservation of inner equilibrium and well-being. Involvement with significant objects in the environment is necessary for survival and draws the infant's libido outward from this initial objectless state. The infant's libido attaches to these external objects, becoming *object libido.* But in traumatic situations, whether physical or psychological (physical injury or threat of in-

jury, object loss, excessive deprivation or frustration), object libido may detach from objects and reinvest in the self as *narcissistic libido.* Freud referred to this regressive reinvestment in the self as *secondary narcissism.*

The concept of narcissism created a dilemma for Freud's instinct theory, in which instincts were either sexual-libidinal or ego (self-preservative) instincts. Narcissism seemed to be a form of libidinal investment in the self, but it also appeared to overlap both sexual-libidinal and ego instincts. The sexual instinct would be in conflict with itself—narcissistic vs. object libido rather than sexual vs. ego instincts. This assumed dualism was also questionable because it seemed that although the component instincts (oral, anal, and phallic) were derived from a single sexual instinct, they could oppose one another. How could conflicting forces arise from a single instinct? The question of narcissism and its relation to other instinctual and libidinal processes remains an important and controversial area of psychoanalytic investigation.

Aggression

Aggression is the second primary motivating force in human behavior. Freud originally thought aggression was related to libido expressed in the perversion of sadism. This relationship was questionable, however, because the aims of these instincts differ: the sexual aim is to obtain pleasure or gratification; the aim of aggression to inflict or to avoid pain. One seeks to preserve the object as a source of pleasure, the other to destroy it as a source of pain. Freud tried to solve the problem by making the aggressive component independent of libido and including it with the ego instincts. But the dualism of libidinal vs. ego instincts was further challenged when evidence of self-destructive tendencies in depressed and masochistic patients made it clear that sadistic or aggressive impulses are not always self-preserving. This led Freud finally to remove aggression from the ego instincts and to consider it a separate instinct, on an equal footing with libido.

Life and Death Instincts

When Freud formulated the notions of life and death instincts in *Beyond the Pleasure Principle* (1920), he returned to the basic dualism in his instinct theory which had been challenged by his intermediate theories on narcissism and aggression. The life and death instincts represent his attempt to link the theory of instincts to a biological framework. The essential frame of reference came from his earliest attempts to provide a physiological model as the basis for explaining mental phenomena, especially in his *Project* (1895). The model proposed that the tendency of the nervous system to rid itself of stimuli and reduce levels of tension by energic discharge (constancy principle) was the basis for gaining pleasure and minimizing pain. Freud based his understanding of the instincts on the economic principles regulating drive discharge with which he had started his theoretical career—entropy and constancy.

The death instinct *(thanatos)* stipulated a tendency of all living organisms to return to a state of total quiescence as an extension of the constancy principle, according to which all organisms tend to return to a state of minimal stimulation. In opposition to this force, Freud posited the life instinct *(eros)*, the tendency for organisms to reunite and to reorganize into more complex and differentiated forms. Arguments over the validity of the basic instincts, which tend to center on the death instinct, often lose sight of the importance of the life instinct, which stands in opposition to the closed-system "economics" of the death instinct and provides a basis for an open-system concept of instinctual motivation.

Freud's final formulations of the dual-instinct theory took the form of a general biological speculation. The relevance of this speculation to clinical observation or practice has been a matter of considerable controversy. Freud tried to connect his theory to the clinical phenomena of the repetition compulsion (the general tendency in human behavior to repeat painful experiences) and masochism (the tendency to find gratification in suffering and pain) as supportive evidence for the death instinct, but even these phenomena can be understood adequately on other grounds and do not require appeal to such ultimate instinctual tendencies. Freud's speculations on the primal instincts have persisted among Kleinian theorists, but otherwise have fallen into disuse.

The Structural Theory

Transition. The topographic model provided a framework for development of Freud's instinct theory, but it had deficiencies in accounting for certain clinical findings. First, the defense mechanisms appeared as unconscious resistances during treatment and were themselves not easily made conscious. Freud concluded that the agency of repression (defense) could not be preconscious, but had to be unconscious. Second, Freud's patients frequently exhibited an unconscious need for punishment or sense of guilt. But in terms of the topographic model, the guilt-inducing moral agency making this demand was allied with the anti-instinctual repressive forces that should have been readily available to awareness in the precon-

scious level of the mind. These difficulties with the topographic model led Freud to replace it with the structural model proposed in *The Ego and the Id* (1923). The structural or tripartite theory initiated a new era in the theory of psychoanalysis, dominated by the 3 psychic structures—id, ego, and superego—that were thought to account for all mental phenomena, conscious and unconscious.

Development of the ego concept. The ego concept evolved through the phases of Freud's thinking as well as post-Freudian developments. In the first phase, ending in 1897, Freud saw the ego as a dominant mass of conscious ideas and values distinct from the impulses and wishes of the repressed unconscious. This ego was primarily concerned with defense, more or less synonymous in this phase with repression. The second phase, from 1897 to 1923, reflected Freud's abandonment of the seduction hypothesis and his focusing on instinctual drives, their representations and transformations. The concept of the ego was connected with the ego instincts, which he was struggling to clarify. He limited defense primarily to repression and viewed it as consisting of an instinctual force directed against unconscious derivatives. The ego's functions followed the reality principle and secondary process and included the capacity for delay of gratification. The third phase, from 1923 to 1937, saw development of the structural theory, in which the ego was defined as a structural entity definitively separated from the instinctual drives, now housed in the id. The ego was a coherent organization of mental processes and functions oriented toward the perceptual-conscious system, but including mechanisms responsible for resistance and unconscious defense.

This ego was still relatively passive and weak, reactive to pressures from id, superego, and reality. The position of the ego was soon strengthened in Freud's reanalysis of anxiety in *Inhibitions, Symptoms, and Anxiety* (1926). The ego was no longer merely passively responsive to the turbulent demands of the id by way of defensive repression, but assumed an active role in regulating drive derivatives to produce signal anxiety, an anticipation of danger, which set defensive processes in motion. Signal anxiety became, for Freud, an autonomous ego function for initiation of defense, allowing the ego to turn passively experienced anxiety into active mastery; that is, the anxiety signal triggered a defensive response in the ego to overcome or avoid the threatening danger. The danger here was presumed to be coming from instinctual impulses, such as incestuous wishes, castration fears, and fears of separation and loss. Toward the end of this period, Freud introduced the notion that the ego developed from sources independent of instinctual drives. He no longer viewed the ego as deriving from the instincts by way of confrontations with reality, but as having its own autonomous genetic roots.

The fourth phase of the ego concept began with Anna Freud's *The Ego and the Mechanisms of Defense* (1936) and culminated in the systematizing elaborations of Heinz Hartmann and David Rapaport. Hartmann's key contributions were his development of a theory of ego autonomy and his emphasis on the principle of adaptation. *Ego autonomy* referred to the innate or acquired capacity of the ego to function independently of instinctual impulses and the influence of drive derivatives. *Adaptation* referred to the capacity of the organism to fit in and adjust harmoniously to the environment. The adaptational approach not only linked psychoanalytic theory with biological thinking but also pointed in the direction of elaborating analytic principles into a general psychology of behavior.

The id. In the tripartite structural theory, Freud placed sexual and aggressive instincts in a special part of the mind called the *id,* which he believed to be a completely unorganized, primordial reservoir of instinctual energies under domination of primary process. The id, therefore, belonged to the unconscious, though was not coextensive with it. The instinctual drives were biologically given, hereditary, and concerned only with seeking immediate discharge. These drives, however, were not simply random sources of energy, but were specifically ordered by primary process organization. The degree of structure in the id and the manner of its integration with other structural components remain matters of theoretical debate.

The ego. The *ego* in the tripartite theory is closely related to consciousness and external reality, yet has unconscious operations in relation to the drives and their regulation, for example, unconscious defense mechanisms. Freud provided a comprehensive definition of the ego:

Here are the principal characteristics of the ego. In consequence of the pre-established connection between sense perception and muscular action, the ego has voluntary movement at its command. It has the task of self-preservation. As regards external events, it performs that task by becoming aware of stimuli, by storing up experiences about them (in the memory), by avoiding excessively strong stimuli (through flight), by dealing with moderate stimuli (through adaptation), and finally by learning to bring about expedient changes in the external world to its own advantage (through activity). As regards internal events in relation to the id, it

performs that task by gaining control over the demands of the instinct, by deciding whether they are to be allowed satisfaction, by postponing that satisfaction to times and circumstances favorable in the external world, or by suppressing their excitations entirely. It is guided in its activity by consideration of the tension produced by stimuli, whether these tensions are present in it or introduced into it. (1940, pp. 145–146)

The ego serves as an intrapsychic agency with a variety of functions. First, it controls and regulates instinctual drives. To ensure the integrity of the individual and to mediate between the id and the outside world, the ego must be able to delay immediate discharge of urgent wishes and impulses. This involves progressing from regulation by the pleasure principle to the more adaptive reality principle, along with a shift from primary process to secondary process cognitive organization. The ego also concerns itself with the individual's relationship to reality, particularly in maintaining the sense of reality and the capacity for adaptive reality testing (the capacity to evaluate the external world and its meaning correctly). In addition, the ego carries out a variety of defensive functions. At first the concept of defense was synonymous with repression, but later, in relation to the signal theory of anxiety, it became more differentiated. Signal anxiety enabled the ego to call into operation a variety of defense mechanisms in response to specific signals of instinctual danger (for example, denial, reaction formation, rationalization).

Another primary function of the ego is synthesis—uniting, organizing, and binding together various drives, tendencies, and functions, thus enabling the individual to think, feel, and act in an organized and integrated manner. The synthetic function is concerned with the organization of the self and its operations into a consistent and coherent adaptive pattern.

The superego. The *superego* is the structural modification of the ego responsible for unconscious guilt, masochism, and negative therapeutic reactions. The superego superseded the old censor of Freud's early dream theories. He believed that it arose from internalization of parental prohibitions and prescriptions (ideals) in the resolution of the oedipal involvement. Thus, the oedipal boy internalized the potentially castrating father to avoid the oedipal guilt associated with incestuous sexual wishes toward his mother and murderous wishes against his father. The superego resulted from this internalization with (introjection of) the punishing father, based on the parental superego, which prohibits ("Thou shalt not") and prescribes ("Thou shalt").

Freud derived the mechanisms for internalization of the superego from his earlier analysis of mourning and melancholia (1917), both of which result from object loss. In mourning, the ego gradually withdraws its libidinal attachment to the lost object; the detached libido then redirects itself to other substitute objects. But in melancholia (depression), the libido cannot free itself from the object and instead takes the object into the ego, where it becomes a split-off part of the ego. As Freud put it, "The shadow of the object fell upon the ego," so that the original ambivalence toward the object—love and hate—is redirected toward the self (p. 249). He called this mechanism "introjection" or "narcissistic identification." In the case of superego formation, to which Freud applied this analysis, love and hate of the parental objects are thus internalized or introjected.

The internalized superego and ego structures are the basis of the personality development of the child. While the superego originates in parental internalization, it also involves the internalization of social ethical standards, moral ideals, values, and prohibitions of conscience. The superego includes both protective, rewarding functions associated with ideals and values (ego ideal) and punitive, critical functions related to the unconscious sense of guilt and moral conscience (superego aggression). While Freud's analysis of the superego derived from his experience with depressed, obsessional, and paranoid patients, significant areas of superego-ego integration remain that require further exploration. The formation and integration of value systems is one such area. The further understanding of adaptive superego functions has implications for the evolution of human culture.

Early Variations: Rebellious Disciples

The group that Freud gathered around him consisted of both devoted followers and men and women of independent mind and considerable creative capacity who disagreed with some of his formulations. The history of the psychoanalytic movement is a fascinating study in the interplay of personality conflicts and the genesis of revolutionary ideas. The deviating views of some of Freud's followers served as nodal points, not only in the development of his own thinking, but in the history of analysis as well.

Alfred Adler

Some of these disciples found it difficult to accept without question or rebellion the powerful hegemony of Freud's thinking. In his emphases on the role of libido in the etiology of neurosis and on the vicissitudes of sexual drives, Freud remained somewhat impervious to other viewpoints. But as the scope and complexity of psychoanalytic theory grew over the years, some of the differing perspectives contributed to the larger body of analytic thinking. This is particularly true of the work of Alfred Adler (1870–1937), the first of the rebellious disciples.

Turning against the biological emphasis of Freud's ideas, particularly the role of instincts and sexuality in the neuroses, Adler split from the ranks of Freud's disciples in 1911. His own work then focused on issues of inferiority vs. superiority, at first emphasizing organ inferiority, but later expanding his view to include general issues of human inferiority. Adler thought that inferiority as a universal human feeling originated in the child's feelings of inferiority because of his smallness and helplessness, and that inferiority was countered by a compensatory need to seek a dominating or superior position. He regarded this striving for power as essentially masculine in character—the "masculine protest"—whereas passivity and inferiority were more feminine. The struggle for superiority expressed the "will to power"; thus Adler reinterpreted the role of the oedipal complex in terms of its inherent power relationships, that is, the need to subjugate the mother and compete successfully with the father. For Adler, the will to power was the guiding force in human behavior—a formulation that forced Freud to deal more explicitly with aggression and the nature of defense.

Adler later emphasized social aspects of human involvement, particularly "social interest," which could channel and restrain the will to power more constructively. He appealed to an innate potential for relating with others beyond merely instinctual needs. He recognized the importance of the child's experience with significant caretakers in the development of mutual dependency, but he diverged from Freud's intrapsychic and biological orientation. He also regarded education as an important means to achieve and amplify social interest. Recent developments in psychoanalysis have broadened the mainstream of psychoanalytic thought to include some of Adler's viewpoints. Although he has been criticized for oversimplifying the complexity of human experience, his psychology can be regarded as the equivalent of an ego psychology before its time.

Carl Jung

Carl Jung (1875–1961) was an independent thinker who was at first quite taken with Freud's ideas, but increasingly followed his own path. Freud early thought of him as his successor, but the tension between them intensified through the years of their collaboration. Jung split with Freud in 1916 by publishing his *Psychology of the Unconscious,* in which he attacked Freud's notion of libido and reformulated the libido theory. He suggested that sexual libido was only a variant of a more primal libido, synonymous with a more general and undifferentiated form of energy. For Jung, such energy emerged in the prepuberty period and only then began to play its predominant role.

Jung emphasized the role of opposites in psychic life—conscious vs. unconscious, love vs. hate, thought vs. feeling, and so on. If one aspect became dominant consciously, the unconscious tended to emphasize its correlative opposite. Jung developed a character typology on the basis of opposition between parameters of conscious-unconscious, sensation-intuition, thinking-feeling, and extraversion (turning outward of libido)–introversion (turning inward of libido). The balance of these opposites determined the character style. The ways of responding to the inner and outer world differed depending on the basic orientation of libido, whether extraversive or introversive. Extraversive thinking, for example, stressed facts about the external world and the rules of law and nature. Introversive thinking, in contrast, emphasized subjective experience and ideas. The unconscious of both would favor the opposite disposition—the extraversive having an introspective unconscious bent and vice versa.

Jung had more clinical experience with psychotic patients and their thinking than did Freud. Furthermore, his writings reflected his deep immersion in the rich mythic and symbolic lore of many cultures, particularly those of the Orient. He gave symbols a broader and deeper interpretation than the restrictively sexual interpretation advanced by Freud. Jung was more sensitive to the transmission of neurotic difficulties from parents to children and emphasized the role of the mother. Only late in his career did Freud begin to appreciate the influence of the child's early interaction with the mother—an important area of interest for contemporary psychoanalysts.

Jung's notion of the collective unconscious (the deepest level of the unconscious mind, containing universal psychic elements derived from phylogenetic experience) influenced Freud's thinking, particularly his idea of the "primal horde" as the origin of social structures (1913). Although Freud thought that the taboo against incest was the result of racial memory of primal experiences, the notion of the collective unconscious never became a functional part of his theory. For Jung, the collective unconscious was a vital component in the patient's individual psyche, manifested through dreams and symbols, which provided a source of great therapeutic potential. He interpreted the dream as an expression of archetypes or primordial images from the collective unconscious.

Jung differed from Freud in his theory of libido and in his conception of the nature and function of the unconscious. Jung's libido theory postulated a more general form of psychic energy that tended to play down the sexual derivation of the neuroses. Moreover, Jung saw the unconscious as the repository of phylogenetic or racial experience, in contrast to Freud's more ontogenetic view of the unconscious as related to infantile experience and repression. In Jung's later work his ideas took a pseudo-mystical and religious direction, becoming increasingly remote from clinical experience and having limited clinical applicability.

Otto Rank

Rank (1884–1939) was for many years Freud's devoted follower and secretary, only gradually defining his own divergent ideas. Rank did not accept Freud's formulations of the Oedipus complex; instead he related all neurotic anxiety to the birth trauma, which in his view produced a primal anxiety, expressed in neurotic manifestations, that slowly diminished throughout life. Separation anxiety was thus essential to his theory, since he felt that all later forms of separation reactivated the primal anxiety of the birth trauma.

Rank saw his theory as the basis for a method of therapy that he felt could abbreviate the long, laborious course of analysis by actively emphasizing the birth trauma from the beginning of therapy. Freud objected to this increased activity by the analyst and to focusing the analytic process in such a narrow way. Rank interpreted the response of his patients to his active interventions as related to conflicts over dependence and independence. He concluded that the basic problem was really the patient's difficulty in asserting his own will—another reflection of birth trauma, the birth of individuality. He began to view Freud's technique as fostering the tendency of the patient to submit, thus undermining his will. Rank stressed the present interaction with the analyst, rather than emphasizing past relationships, and focused on issues of separation from the mother. He set a definite time limit for the treatment in order to intensify and precipitate separation issues. Rank's will therapy did not differ greatly from Adler's and Jung's ideas and influenced later experimentation by Ferenczi, Alexander, and others attempting to modify and shorten analytic treatment.

Sándor Ferenczi

Sándor Ferenczi (1873–1933) was a member of Freud's early circle. A brilliant innovator, he experimented with the psychoanalytic method seeking to shorten the course of analytic treatment by intensifying the patient's emotional experiences—a procedure he called "active therapy." He was partially analyzed by Freud and maintained close, if ambivalent, personal ties with Freud despite their disagreements over theory and technique. Ferenczi emphasized the role of trauma as the source of neurotic disturbances and sought to modify his clinical technique accordingly. He advocated a more active form of therapy, even to the point of mutual analysis, in which analyst and patient took turns analyzing each other, though he found it necessary to curtail this approach because it began to infringe on the confidentiality of other patients. Ferenczi employed several forms of suggestion and behavioral modification, using a technique of forced fantasies that antedated certain contemporary therapeutic developments. His work emphasized emotional rather than intellectual and interpretive aspects of analysis—a precursor of more flexible, active approaches to treatment that adapt the therapeutic process to the patient's special needs and personality organization. He disagreed with Freud's more conservative approach and argued that more intimate and affectionate involvement with patients was at times indicated, even embracing and kissing—a practice that Freud strongly disapproved. In general, however, Ferenczi was more attuned to the role of the analyst, and particularly countertransference issues, as they impacted the therapy—an aspect of his thinking that has found sympathetic reverberations in current analytic approaches. The points of difference between himself and Freud remain active and controversial to this day.

The Next Generation

In contrast to the rebellious disciples, the post-Freudians were more faithful followers who did not break with the master but extended and deepened his ideas. This group provided the core of more orthodox psychoanalytic thinking after Freud.

Karl Abraham

Karl Abraham (1877–1925) was one of Freud's first and most faithful disciples. He founded the Berlin Institute and enjoyed a prolific, if abbreviated, career as a psychoanalyst and psychiatrist. His work in applying psychoana-lytic insights to the psychoses, particularly differentiating between hysteria and dementia praecox, is classic. His observation that psychotic patients lack the capacity for meaningful libidinal involvement with others contributed significantly to Freud's views on narcissism. Abraham elaborated Freud's instinct theory, crystallizing stages of infantile libidinal development and relating them to forms of adult character pathology; he presented detailed descriptions of oral, anal, and genital character types. Moreover, starting from Freud's views on mourning and melancholia, Abraham developed the psychoanalytic understanding of depression, particularly the role of introjection in such pathological states.

Melanie Klein

Melanie Klein (1882–1960) trained under Abraham in Berlin and then moved to London. Her research and teachings became a source of germinal inspiration and sharp controversy and still profoundly influence psychoanalytic thinking. Klein took her point of departure from Freud's later instinct theory, particularly the death instinct. Working primarily with very young children, she described instinctual dynamics in the first years of life. She held that the child, driven by the death instinct, is compelled to rid himself of intolerable, destructive impulses (predominantly oral) and to project them externally. The earliest recipient of these projected impulses is the mother's breast, which provides need-satisfying nourishment and satiation (good breast), but also often deprives and fails to satisfy (bad breast). At this stage the images of the breast are part-objects that the infant has yet to combine into a single whole object, the mother. Early frustration of oral needs, even in the first year of life, reinforces these trends so that the bad breast becomes a persecutory object that is hated, feared, and envied.

The experience of the bad breast and its associated persecutory anxiety form the earliest developmental stage in Klein's theory—the paranoid/schizoid position. The bad breast withholds gratification and thus stimulates the child's primitive oral envy, provoking sadistic wishes to penetrate and destroy the mother's breasts and body. In boys, these primitive destructive impulses give rise to the fear of retaliation (based in part on projection) in the form of castration anxiety; in girls, the primitive envy is expressed in envy of the mother's breast during the oral developmental phase, later transforming into penis envy during the genital phase. Klein held that by the time of weaning, the child is capable of recognizing the mother as a whole object possessing good and bad qualities. But the combination of good and bad qualities in a single object—previously separated in part-objects—creates a dilemma: destructive attacks on the bad object will also destroy the good and needed object. This prevents the child from unleashing aggressive impulses against the object and lays the basis for the depressive position, in which aggression is directed against the self rather than against the object. The guilt associated with destructive wishes against the object is the precursor of conscience.

Even at this early level of development, Klein postulated a primitive superego. In the anal-sadistic phase, this primitive superego directs aggression against the self, so that the child seeks to eject it. Projection of destructive superego elements permits acceptance of good introjects (internalization of good objects), alleviating the underlying paranoid anxiety. The projected superego elements are later reintrojected to become the agency of guilt and early forms of obsessional behavior. The Kleinian emphasis on good and bad introjects, following Abraham's lead, concentrates on vital relationships to objects at the earliest level of child development. This aspect of Klein's thinking became the point of departure for later object-relations theories.

Wilfred Bion

Klein's influence has given rise to a prominent school of psychoanalysis embodying and extending her ideas. Among a number of distinguished figures, the most significant may be Wilfred Bion (1897–1979). Bion extended and applied Klein's orientation, especially developing the ramifications of the notion of projective identification—a process, originally described by Klein, by which a subject displaces a part of the self into an object and then identifies with that object or elicits a response in the object corresponding to qualities of the projection. Bion applied this notion to a wide range of psychotic and cognitive operations. He developed the metaphor of the "container" and the "contained" to express the manner in which projective identification occurs, especially in the contexts of mother-child and analyst-patient interaction. The child-patient projects toxic or destructive contents onto the mother-analyst, who in turn absorbs, modifies, or "contains" it so that it becomes available in more benign form for subsequent reinternalization by the child-patient, resulting in a healthier modification of the child-patient's pathogenic introjects. Bion also contributed significantly to the understanding of group processes by demonstrating the "basic assumptions" that operate on an unconscious emotional level in therapeutic groups and are expressed in patterns of fight-flight, pairing, and dependence (see Chapter 17).

Wilhelm Reich

Wilhelm Reich (1897–1957) rose to prominence in the 1920s as a creative contributor to psychoanalysis. Later in his career, his quest for the biological roots of the libido theory led him to formulate the orgone theory, an unfortunate pseudoscientific aberration. Reich's contributions to psychoanalytic thinking were his ideas of character structure and character analysis. He viewed character as a defensive structure, an armor for the ego against both internal instinctual pressures and external environmental stimuli. Character armor became an automatic pattern of reaction, retaining a certain flexibility in healthier characters but becoming rigid and unyielding in the neurotic personality. Reich's character analysis derived from his hypothesis that resistances are inherent in the character structure of neurotic patients. Resistances reveal themselves in the patient's characteristic ways of acting and reacting, exemplified by traits such as passivity, arrogance, and argumentativeness. He felt that character traits and character resistance have to be repeatedly confronted until the patient begins to experience them as foreign bodies requiring removal. This then opens the way for the revival of repressed infantile material and its analysis along more strictly Freudian lines.

Franz Alexander

Franz Alexander (1891–1964), one of the younger generation of German analysts, spent most of his career in the United States. His contributions to psychosomatic medicine, particularly his theory of psychosomatic specificity and specific organ vulnerability, strongly influenced psychosomatic research in the 1940s and 1950s. The specificity hypothesis suggested that some organic diseases have not only a specific pathophysiology but also a specific psychopathology.

Alexander also contributed to the application of analytic principles to dynamic psychotherapy. He adopted a flexible position, questioning traditional psychoanalytic ideas about therapy, such as whether length and intensity of therapy necessarily implied depth of therapeutic effect, or whether a small number of interviews necessarily precluded more stable and profound therapeutic effects. He focused on what he considered the essence of the psychoanalytic process—bringing unconscious motivations and feelings into awareness, thus extending conscious control over behavior. He experimented with several parameters of therapy, including deliberate interruptions of treatment as a way of increasing the emotional intensity and efficacy of the therapeutic process. Such artificial separations confronted the patient with his dependency and were intended to enable the patient to recognize and accept his independence.

Alexander emphasized emotional aspects of therapy in his concept of the "corrective emotional experience." Under the favorable conditions of therapy, he attempted to expose the patient to emotional conflicts handled unsuccessfully in the past. Rather than stressing repetitive aspects of infantile conflicts in the transference relationship, Alexander emphasized the differences between the infantile conflict situation and the current therapy situation. He thought that these emotional aspects of the treatment process were necessary for therapeutic results, thus underplaying therapeutic effects of insight gained through interpretation—the more traditional analytic view. Alexander's formulations have profoundly influenced the technique of analytically oriented psychotherapy.

Ego Psychology

The ego psychology movement emerged in the late 1930s as a development of Freud's views regarding the ego and its place in psychic functioning. This development, largely stimulated by the work of Anna Freud and Heinz Hartmann and his collaborators, made the ego the centerpiece of personality theory as the integrating and regulating component of the structural theory.

Anna Freud

Anna Freud (1895–1982) became the leading interpreter of orthodox analytic views after her father. Her work *The Ego and the Mechanisms of Defense* (1936) brought the ego and its defenses into the center of clinical interest. In her view, attention to and analysis of the patient's defenses are mandatory, along with the analysis of instinctual components. She was also a major contributor and guide in the development of child analysis, one of the first to adapt analytic techniques, particularly play techniques, to the treatment of children. Later she became the central figure in the more orthodox reaction to Melanie Klein's views about child analysis and development. She insisted on the need to modify analytic techniques in work with children, especially in view of the immaturity of the child's psychic structures and defenses and relative inability to distinguish reality from fantasy. She disagreed with Klein's views of early superego formation and Kleinian attempts to use direct interpretation in therapy with young children.

Heinz Hartmann

Anna Freud's work extended the ego psychology of her father, in which the ego was primarily occupied with the work of defense and reaction to instinctual pressures. Heinz Hartmann's (1894–1970) monograph *Ego Psychology and the Problem of Adaptation* (1939) opened the way to a new set of problems and concepts that turned the ego's face more explicitly to the outside world. His insistence on ego autonomy and adaptive capacities initiated the systematic elaboration of a more powerful ego psychology and the development of a broader psychosocial understanding of the ego's activity and involvement in the external environment.

Freud had suggested that the ego was formed by gradual modification of the id owing to the impact of external reality on instinctual drives, resulting in gradual replacement of the pleasure principle by the reality principle. Freud thus emphasized the effect of instincts on ego development. Hartmann introduced some important modifications to this theory by postulating primary autonomous ego functions developing independently of drives and conflicts. Together with Ernst Kris (1900–1957) and Rudolph Loewenstein (1898–1976), he suggested that the ego did not differentiate from the id, as Freud had thought, but that both id and ego developed from a common undifferentiated matrix. Furthermore, he believed that the rudimentary apparatuses underlying primary autonomous ego functions (perception, motility, memory, and intellect) were present from birth and may undergo congenital or genetically determined variations. These rudimentary ego apparatuses enable the infant to fit in with objects and the environment in order to gain satisfaction of instinctual needs and drives. The balance of controlling forces—ego autonomy from the demands of the id, as well as ego autonomy from the demands of the environment—required for optimal functioning of the organism formed the basis for Hartmann's theory of the adaptive functions of the ego in mediating between external reality and the demands of internal psychic systems. He introduced the adaptational point of view as one of the basic assumptions of psychoanalytic theory and linked it to the concept of the autonomy of the ego.

Hartmann designated an area in which the ego functions without intrapsychic conflict, which he called "conflict free." This area of ego functioning includes capacities for perception, intuition, comprehension, thinking, language, certain aspects of motor development, learning, and intelligence. When any of these functions becomes secondarily involved in conflict, the conflict-free operation may be impeded. The guarantee of conflict-free functioning depends on the primary autonomous structure of the ego as an independent realm of psychic organization that is not totally dependent on or derived from instincts. Emergence of primary autonomous factors requires stimulation by an "average expectable environment" that guarantees and supports their autonomous development and functioning.

The ego may also retrieve certain functions from the domination of drive influences, contributing to the development of secondary ego autonomy. Thus a mechanism arising in the service of defense may become an independent structure, such that the drive impulse merely triggers the "automatized" function. For example, reaction formations (such as emphasizing cleanliness to defend against anal impulses related to filth and dirt) may lose their defensive quality and become nonconflictual and adaptive aspects of character. This change of function requires a different form of energy. Hartmann related the conflict-free area of functioning to neutralized energies derived from libidinal or aggressive energies by the desexualization of libidinal drives or the deaggressivization of aggressive drives. Neutralization provides autonomous ego functions with energies whose drive interference or dependence is minimal.

Hartmann's ego psychology dealt primarily with ego mechanisms and structures and the formal aspects of their organization, and only incidentally with instinctual drives and derivatives. Hartmann tried to shift the focus of psychoanalysis from a clinically oriented, conflict-based theory to a more general theory of the psychic apparatus and human behavior.

David Rapaport

The major architect of this domain was David Rapaport (1911–1960), the great systematizer of ego psychology, who developed Hartmann's ideas about the functioning of the ego, with particular attention to the ego's cognitive functioning. Rapaport's work gave rise to a number of hypotheses that have stimulated major efforts to test psychoanalytic theories by extra-analytic experimental designs. Rapaport, more than any other analytic thinker, spurred the effort by which psychoanalysis could evolve into a general theory of psychological behavior.

Contemporary Theorists

The work of these major contributors to ego psychology opened the way to further refinements that have engendered a much greater and more effective integration of the insights of earlier ego theorists with other dimensions of analytic thinking. Among these contributors, Roy Schafer's (1922–) efforts to refocus the adaptive aspects of defensive functioning, his reconstruction of many aspects of psychic functioning in terms of personal action and responsibility in an effort to circumvent the metapsychology, and more current interests in translating structural terms into narrative and experiential forms have been both stimulating and controversial. Another important contribution to deepening understanding of psychic functioning in developmental terms came from Margaret Mahler (1897–1985). Her intensive study of infantile psychoses and the developmental process led to her ideas concerning the patterns of growth of both ego and self in terms of the separation-individuation process—studies that have exercised a major impact on views of the emergence of psychic structures.

Other significant contributors include Otto Kernberg (1928–), who sought to integrate aspects of ego psychology with object relations perspectives in an effort to understand borderline psychopathology. Influences on his views of psychic structure and object relations stem from a variety of sources, including Klein, Fairbairn, Jacobson, and Hartmann, in addition to Freud. He regards the basic units of intrapsychic structure as constellations of self-images, object-images, and affective dispositions. Self-object-affect units are forms of internalized object relations that coalesce into more complex psychic structures. These dynamic structures constitute the basis for personality organization and integration and provide the focus for therapeutic intervention. Structural change in patients who have consolidated the intrapsychic agencies (id, ego, and superego) is quite different from that in patients who have not achieved this level of integration. In the former group of patients, activation of an object relationship in treatment reflects conflicts between and within these psychic structures. In more primitive patients, in whom there is a lack of such integration, ego functions, infiltrated by drive derivatives and primitive defense mechanisms (splitting, denial, projection), protect the psyche against conflict by resorting to dissociation into primitive ego states based on the organization of subject-object-affect constellations.

Among other contemporary theorists, Joseph Sandler has clarified many aspects of ego psychology and the structural theory, especially in their application to clinical practice; and George Klein's (1918–1973) theoretical and research efforts, especially regarding cognitive controls, added new dimensions to the understanding of ego functioning and effective psychic integration. Klein's separation of clinical theory from metapsychology has been an influential point of view—one developed more extensively by Robert Holt (1917–). Theoretical and research efforts in this area remain active and productive.

The Neo-Freudians

The neo-Freudians came into prominence in the 1930s, rebelling against basic analytic orientations, particularly the instinct theory, and emphasizing social and cultural factors. These developments emerged as reactions against previous analytic concepts, largely because analytic theory had not matured sufficiently to assimilate these new directions. But the divergence has become less striking over time, since contemporary psychoanalytic theories tend increasingly to integrate orthodox with later neo-Freudian perspectives.

Karen Horney

Although Karen Horney (1885–1952) was trained in the orthodox psychoanalytic tradition, her early contributions not only stamped her as a distinguished contributor to psychoanalytic thinking but also presaged the direction of her later thinking. Early in her career she challenged Freud's ideas on feminine psychology, on the nature of the neurotic process, on the death instinct, and particularly on the role of cultural factors in neurosis.

Many of her ideas had an Adlerian quality, though her thinking was strikingly original. She formulated a holistic notion of the personality as an individual unit functioning within a social framework and continually interacting with its environment. Although she recognized the role of biological needs and drives, she shifted the emphasis in her theory of personality and neurosis to the dynamic influences of cultural and social factors. She rejected Freud's structural theory and psychic energy and stressed current interactions and motivations rather than infantile libidinal derivatives operating through repetition compulsion.

At the center of her theory was the concept of the self, including an actual self, a real self, and an idealized self as the main facets of the personality. The *actual self* was the sum total of the individual's experience. The *real self* was a more central force or principle, unique within each individual and equivalent to a sense of healthy integration or harmonious wholeness. The *idealized self*, however, was potentially a source of neurosis that overcame and avoided psychic conflict by adopting an attitude of superiority or self-sufficiency or by demands for special consideration. The idealized self was a form of glorified self-image that could progressively encompass more aspects of the personality and, when relatively or totally unconscious, provide the source of neurotic claims and demands. Fears, inhibitions, and feelings of deprivation could thereby be transformed into unbalanced demands for and expectations of attention or support that could control the individual's inner life and external behavior. Horney referred to this imbalance as the "pride system," which manifested itself in unrealistically high standards and expectations on the one hand and excessive self-hatred and self-contempt on the other. This pathological system produced alienation from the self and characteristically neurotic resolutions of inner tension. Horney's ideas on the idealized self and the pride system anticipated current psychoanalytic ideas on narcissism and the psychology of the self.

In regard to therapy, Horney rejected symptom relief or social adjustment as adequate therapeutic goals. Rather, she emphasized self-realization and self-actualization, dealing with here-and-now manifestations of the pride system and other neurotic adjustments in contrast to derivatives of past experience. Further, she emphasized the activity of the analyst in the therapeutic process and rejected the stereotype of the analyst as a detached, unfeeling, unresponding mirror. She felt, much like Ferenczi, that emotional involvement between therapist and patient was an important aspect of the therapeutic process.

Harry Stack Sullivan

Harry Stack Sullivan (1892–1949) was the first of the neo-Freudians to receive his psychoanalytic training and experience entirely in the United States. Following theorists such as Adolf Meyer and William Alanson White, Sullivan turned away from the biological and instinctual bias of classic psychoanalytic theories and concentrated on interpersonal relations as the central concept of his thinking.

His theory of personality development did not altogether abandon basic biological drives or needs. But rather than seeing bodily zones as the determining source of developmental changes, he regarded them as the critical areas through which the child establishes interpersonal contact with the significant figures in his environment. Rejecting any concept of psychic energy, Sullivan highlighted the need for security, which he felt could be satisfied only through meaningful, gratifying interpersonal relationships. The basic need for others became a central facet of his theory. According to Sullivan, the confidence derived from these relationships created a sense of self-esteem that overcame feelings of powerlessness and helplessness that are part of the human condition. The lack of a sense of security or self-esteem, exacerbated by an abiding sense of disapproval by the significant figures (parents), became a source of anxiety.

Sullivan saw anxiety as the propelling force for personality development and the central element in the etiology of neuroses, psychoses, and other forms of psychopathology. The "self-system" discharges tension in acceptable ways, preventing the individual from being overwhelmed by anxiety, and maintaining the personality as an effectively functioning entity. When the anxiety-containing resources of the self-system are exceeded, clinical symptoms result, particularly in the form of prototaxic or parataxic distortions that violate canons of logic and causality. Both neuroses and psychoses stem from disturbances in interpersonal relationships. Freud regarded psychosis as the result of conflict between the ego and reality, and neurosis as an intrapsychic conflict among the id, ego, and superego. For Sullivan, however, the basic conflict was between the individual and the human environment of significant others. He believed that intrapsychic conflicts were derived from interpersonal conflicts by internalization of external objects and conflicted relationships.

Sullivan's approach to therapy was to view it as essentially a learning process, centered on the interpersonal relationship between therapist and patient. He focused specifically on anxiety and the interpersonal context in which it occurred. He saw the therapist as an active participant-observer in an exploratory process and experimented with corresponding modifications of the therapy situation. Sullivan emphasized current patterns of interpersonal interaction rather than historical or genetic aspects of the individual's behavior.

Erich Fromm

Erich Fromm (1900–1980) originally took his psychoanalytic training at the Berlin Institute, later emigrating to the United States. His theory contained strong social inclinations, reflecting the influence of the Frankfurt school of social thought. He saw human nature as fundamentally motivated by self-preservation, requiring regulation of organic drives to suit this purpose. Added to this was the need for others to accomplish the social and cultural objectives that distinguish man from animals. Fromm envisioned personality organization as the product of the interaction of biological with sociocultural influences that shape the personality orientation. He developed a typology of character types reflecting these forces which could take either a productive or nonproductive form. Productive characters represented the ideal or optimal form of personality, corresponding to the Freudian genital character. Nonproductive forms included the *authoritarian character,* marked by desires for submission (masochistic) to authority or authoritarian domination (sadistic) related to having or not having power; the *receptive character,* based on oral-dependency needs, viewing the sources of all good as external, and constantly seeking love and support from others; the *exploitative character,* seeking to gain external goods through force, manipulation, or deception; the *hoarding character,* denoted by miserly, compulsive, and obstinate qualities (similar to Freud's anal character), fearful of losing and compelled to husband his resources; and the *marketing orientation,* in which the individual views himself as a commodity requiring adaptation to the demands and expectations of others, repressing needs for self-realization and expression to gain acceptance and value in others' eyes.

In therapy, Fromm accepted much of the Freudian approach, including free association, transference, resistance, countertransference, and dream interpretation, but emphasized the analyst's role as a rational authority and resolution of the patient's character pathology to gain more productive status. Fromm also made important contributions to religion, distinguishing immature from more mature forms of religious experience, and to social criticism.

Object Relations Theorists

Historically the impetus for the theory of object relations came from Melanie Klein's notion of intrapsychic introjects representing the internalization of significant relations with infantile objects. This trend has been reinforced by the increasing proportion of patients with severe character problems or personality disorders in which major patterns of relatedness to others are disturbed. Analytic attempts to treat such patients have led to explorations of personality organization as well as problems in early object relations and their effect on personality development.

Ronald Fairbairn

If Melanie Klein's theory was an instinctual theory without an ego, the theory of object relations developed by

Ronald Fairbairn (1889–1964) was an ego theory without instincts. Fairbairn tried to separate psychological science from its biological roots and thereby dissociate his theory of the ego from instincts as biological drives. He stressed that instincts were inherently object-seeking rather than concerned with energy discharge. Rather he postulated that the mental apparatus consisted of inherently dynamic structures from the beginning of life and that the ego likewise is integrated, whole, and object related from the beginning. These aspects of dynamic functioning and structure were for Freud the outcome of a developmental process, but for Fairbairn they were simply postulated. Consequently his theory bypasses any real concept of ego development or the development of object relations; it also bypasses problems of self-object differentiation simply by postulating that the ego is related to its objects from the beginning.

Fairbairn's theory predicates an initially undivided ego. All subsequent psychic structures evolve as ego substructures by a process of splitting (a defensive mechanism by which good and bad impulses and objects are separated) and introjection (a defense in which representations of loved or hated objects are internalized and serve as quasi-autonomous sources of psychic activity); both processes involve parallel splitting of objects and the ego. These formulations reflect Fairbairn's preoccupation with schizoid patients in whom inner splitting of the ego and withdrawal from object relatedness is central.

Fairbairn, along with his interpreter Guntrip and other object relations theorists, address ambiguities regarding the personal ego in classic analytic structural theory. As long as the ego is viewed as an organization of functions, it provides no place for the personal, subjectively apprehended and sensed ego as a source of inner activity (the subjective sense of "I"). Fairbairn's object relations theory challenges the structural viewpoint by postulating a personal (subjectively perceived) ego, but does not resolve the inherent ambiguity between the personal and the structural ego, that is, between a subjective source of personal activity and an intrapsychic organization of functions.

Michael Balint

Michael Balint (1896–1970) focused on the earliest stages of mother-child involvement. He rejected Freud's primary narcissism, in which the infant's attachment to objects derives from a primary state of self-contained, objectless libidinal investment. Instead, Balint substituted a stage of "primary love," in which the infant begins life in a condition of relatedness and libidinal investment in the maternal object. He accepted the lack of differentiation between self and object so characteristic of this early stage and emphasized the need for a harmonious fitting together of mother and child, especially at the beginning of the child's life.

From this early symbiotic matrix, 2 basic life attitudes develop as the infant's perceptions of himself and of the mother differentiate and the infant's sense of self becomes more individuated. One is the tendency to feel safe and secure by maintaining close, clinging attachments to objects (ocnophilic), with the result that separation becomes the central anxiety. The opposite tendency seeks safety and security through the exercise of ego capacities in exploring the world away from objects of dependence (philobatic). A corollary of the latter tendency is the fear of danger by engulfment, motivating development of skills in dealing with people without getting deeply involved or attached. These extreme tendencies are usually mixed to varying degrees in individual personalities.

Balint concerned himself with manifestations of developmental failure reflected in the therapeutic process. He distinguished between phases of benign and malignant regression. During benign regression in analysis, the analyst provides a form of empathic recognition enabling the patient to bear the unstructured experience with at least manageable anxiety. Lost infantile objects can then be mourned and the patient's orientation to the object world can be recast. In malignant regression, the ego is overwhelmed by unmanageable anxiety, preventing the patient from doing the work of therapy. Balint referred to this level of personality structure as the "basic fault," a fundamental disturbance in the capacity for object relations prior to the acquisition of language. He felt that the basic fault could not be repaired by merely verbal techniques and interpretation, but required nonverbal interventions specifically derived from the object relationship between patient and analyst.

Donald Winnicott

Donald Winnicott (1897–1971), a gifted pediatrician turned psychoanalyst, contributed ingeniously to the study of early object relations and character pathology by focusing on the earliest stages of mother-child interaction. He described the emergence of what he called "transitional objects," the infant's first object possession perceived as separate from the infant's self. Winnicott argued from close study of infant behavior in using transitional objects that the object stands for the maternal breast or the mother, the first external object to which the infant relates. Emergence of the transitional object antedates capacities for reality testing. Winnicott held that the transitional object could become a fetish object and persist as part of adult sexual adjustment.

The transitional object exists in an intermediate realm of illusion, which involves both an objective external reality (the mother's breast) and a subjectively experienced internal object (the introjected breast), yet is distinct from both and cannot be reduced to either one or the other. This intermediate area of experience, shared by both inner and outer reality, absorbs the greater part of the infant's experience and is retained in adult experiences of creativity and imagination. The transitional object itself is usually decathected—that is, it becomes less and less an object of emotional investment—rather than repressed, and its importance thus diminishes as it is replaced by emerging cultural interests, including art and religion.

The mother's participation in this intermediate realm of illusion, which the transitional object inhabits, depends on her responsiveness to the infant's need to create her as a good mother. From the point of view of an observer, the mother's breast exists independently of the baby; but from the point of view of the baby, he creates it as a means of satisfying his need. In this attuned responsiveness to the baby's need, the mother functions as a "good-enough mother." Failure to provide good-enough mothering can result in emergence of a false self in the child, representing a failure in developmental experience and resulting in a variety of character pathologies. Winnicott's notions of the formation of the false self are similar to Balint's formulations regarding the basic fault and to Fairbairn's notion of the schizoid personality. Such patients are neither neurotic nor psychotic, but relate to the world through a compliant shell that is not quite real to them or to us. These disturbed personality types reflect deficits in very early object relations, specifically in the mutuality and reciprocal responsiveness of the early mother-child object relationship.

Winnicott, along with other object relations theorists, was intensely concerned with the modifications of the analytic process that may be required to meet the needs of such defective personalities. The model for such modifications in Winnicott's approach was good-enough mothering, which found expression in his notion of "holding" as a central therapeutic technique, primarily in most primitive personalities, but the idea has gradually been expanded to include most analyses.

Self Psychology

Self as Structural

The self psychology movement came into prominence largely as the result of Heinz Kohut's efforts in the late 1960s, but there was a history of development of a self-concept in psychoanalysis well before that. The concept of the self within the structural theory was inaugurated by Hartmann's distinction between ego and self, terms that had been left ambiguous by Freud: the ego was an intrapsychic organization of functions, while the self was cast in terms of a self-representation that then became the object of narcissistic libido, but also was specifically connected with object relations. This clarified the distinction between object libido and narcissistic libido, since the self was the repository for secondary narcissism and as such distinct from the ego.

Hartmann's distinction between the ego and the self cast the self in representational terms. The self was conceptualized either as a complex representation, organized and synthesized as a function of the ego, or, by later theorists, in structural terms as a more complex and supraordinate integration of the tripartite structures (that is, embracing the tripartite entities as subordinate substructures). The former view regarded the self as part of the representational world, whereas the latter assigned it to the realm of internal psychic structure. The differences of emphasis and formulation regarding these 2 perspectives remain unresolved.

Edith Jacobson. Following in Hartmann's footsteps, Edith Jacobson (1897–1978) elaborated the development of the self as distinct from ego. She further developed the notion of the self as connected explicitly to the context of object relationships (1964). In her view, development of the self took place in relation with objects by means of specific forms of internalization by which characteristics of objects and object relations were transformed into internal psychic structures. Jacobson tried to link the issues of identity formation and the emergence of the self to the exigencies of a psychic model based on drives, conflicts, defenses, and structures.

Erik Erikson. Erik Erikson (1902–1994) made 2 important contributions to psychoanalytic thinking with his elaboration of instinctual theory and his epigenetic theory. Erikson's (1963) modification of instinctual theory suggested a relationship between instinctual zones as formulated by Freud and development of specific modalities of ego functioning. He linked aspects of ego development to the genetic timetable of instinctual development, whereby particular erotogenic zones become the loci of stimulation for the development of particular forms of ego functioning.

The first mode of psychosexual development was the oral-incorporative or "taking-in" mode, followed by the oral-retentive mode, consisting of taking and holding on to things. These elements of getting, getting what is given, or getting to be a giver lay the groundwork for a basic sense of trust, a primary psychosocial attainment. Similarly, in the later anal-urethral muscular stage, retentive and eliminative modes operate through the capacity for self-control over impulses of letting go and holding on. These modalities of retention and elimination underlie the second nuclear psychosocial crisis, establishment of basic autonomy or, conversely, basic shame or doubt.

Erikson proposed an epigenetic schema spanning the entire life cycle. At each stage, basic psychosocial crises, or phases of developmental conflict, must be resolved. The resolution of each crisis provides the basis and starting point for the resolution of succeeding crises. Erikson designated 8 such psychosocial crises: (1) basic trust vs. basic mistrust, (2) autonomy vs. shame and doubt, (3) initiative vs. guilt, (4) industry vs. inferiority, (5) identity vs. role confusion, (6) intimacy vs. isolation, (7) generativity vs. stagnation, and (8) ego integrity vs. despair. The qualities resulting from these critical resolutions were ambiguously attributed to the ego or the self, but advanced a set of terms readily open to and applicable to a self cast in structural terms.

Erikson's notion of identity has had a great impact on contemporary thinking, but difficulties arose in integrating this elusive notion within the traditional psychoanalytic framework. Erikson described identity in the following terms: "At one time, then, it will appear to refer to a conscious sense of individual identity; at another to an unconscious striving for a continuity of personal character; at a third, as a criterion for the silent doings of ego synthesis; and finally as a maintenance for an inner solidarity with a group's ideals and identity" (1959, p. 102). Thus identity seemed to have at the same time an internal and an external frame of reference: internally related to the integration of the self; externally related to those aspects of social and cultural organization by which the individual is accepted into and becomes a functioning part of his society and culture.

The notion of identity served as an integrating concept at a point in the history of psychoanalysis when attempts were being made to join psychoanalytic theory with broader aspects of social and cultural influence. Such theoretical integration remains a serious problem, however. One could view identity as an aspect of the integration of the self-concept, but the status of the self-concept itself in psychoanalytic theory is by no means secure—that is, whether the self can be viewed as structural in nature or as merely experiential. Nevertheless, with his concept of identity and the epigenetic schema of psychosocial crises, Erikson opened up a rich and provocative area for future exploration which awaits further theoretical elaboration.

Additional contributions to this line of structural thinking about the self came from Douglas Levin (1921–19??), who attempted to explore the implications of Hartmann's distinction of self vs. ego for integrating the structural viewpoint with Erikson's epigenetic categories; from Heinz Lichtenstein (1904–1990), who further articulated the integration of narcissistic dynamics with a structuralized version of the self; and also, in my view, from John Gedo (1927–), who has progressively articulated a version of the self that is fundamentally structural in conception and more closely connected with biological foundations.

Self as Experiential

Self psychology, specifically designated as such, is a more recent addition to psychoanalytic thinking that takes its origin from contributions by Heinz Kohut (1913–1981) and his followers. Kohut linked the origin of the self to narcissism, viewing the self as the result of a separate line of narcissistic development that progresses through a series of archaic narcissistic structures toward establishing a mature and cohesive self-organization.

Kohut's view departs from earlier ones in that, rather than the self serving as the object of narcissistic cathexis, it now becomes a narcissistic structure independent of the development of id, ego, and superego. Kohut (1966, 1971) argued that narcissism undergoes a separate line of development independent from object libido and object relations. In his view, the original primary narcissism differentiates in the course of development and in response to lapses in parental empathy into 2 archaic configurations, the grandiose self and the idealized parental imago. The *grandiose self* involves an exaggerated and exhibitionistic image of the self that becomes the repository for infantile perfection; the *idealized parental imago,* in contrast, transfers the previous perfection to an admired omnipotent object. Further development of the grandiose self leads to more mature ambition, self-esteem, self-confidence, and pleasure in accomplishment. The idealized parental imago becomes integrated into the ego ideal with the mature values, ideals, and standards it represents. Pathological persistence of the grandiose self results in intensification of grandiosity, exhibitionism, shame, envy, depression, hypochondriacal concerns, and undermining of self-esteem. Loss of the idealized object or the idealized object's love can result in narcissistic imbalance, leaving the individual vulnerable to depression, depletion, poor self-esteem, failure of ideals and values, and even fragmentation.

Kohut bases his self psychology on the need, both during the course of development and during the course of life, for empathic interaction with "selfobjects" (1971, 1977). The original selfobject is the mother or caretaking person who provides empathic response to selfobject needs in the infant in the form of love, admiration, acceptance, joyful participation, warmth, and responsiveness, communicating a sense of valued and cherished existence to the child. Human beings continue to seek objects to fulfill these basic selfobject needs throughout life. Failures to fulfill such needs can result in the formation of pathological psychic structures and patterns of behavior during development and pathological character structures during adult life. (This analysis comes close to Winnicott's views on good-enough mothering.)

Selfobject needs are the basis of transferences that can be described in both narcissistic and selfobject terms (Kohut, 1984). To the extent that archaic narcissistic structures remain relatively stable, they serve as the basis for narcissistic transferences: the idealized imago expresses itself in idealizing transferences, and the grandiose self in mirror transferences. In *idealizing transferences,* the lost narcissistic perfection of infancy is recaptured by assigning it to an idealized analytic object to whom all power and strength are attributed. Union with the idealized object (analyst) thus becomes essential for maintaining the coherence and stability of the subject's self. In *mirror transferences,* the object is experienced as an extension of the subject's own grandiose self, so that the object (analyst) becomes the repository for the grandiosity and exhibitionism of the grandiose self. The object thus becomes merged with the grandiose self (merger transference), or is seen as a reflection of the grandiose self (twinship transference), or is accepted as important to the individual only to the extent that he responds to the narcissistic needs for approval and admiration of the reactivated grandiose self (mirror transference in the narrow sense).

Kohut extended this view of narcissistic transferences in terms of selfobject needs to formulate so-called selfobject transferences. Selfobject transferences tend to follow patterns of self-disordered pathology and include transferences based on selfobject needs for idealizing, mirroring, merging, seeking an alter ego, or shunning contact. The therapist's efforts are directed to meeting and satisfying these selfobject needs in a way that can be therapeutically useful. The basic technical approach to these needs is through empathy and acceptance, allowing the patient to gain the satisfaction denied through failures of parental empathy, and opens the way to transformation of these pathological needs to more adaptive forms of realization. Only when these needs have been adequately met and the self has been sufficiently consoli-

dated through the sustaining empathy in the selfobject transference, and by the interpretation of earlier selfobject failures, is therapeutic change possible. Controversy has developed among self psychologists between those who regard empathy as curative in its own right and those who see it as a necessary propaedeutic to interpretation by which therapeutic effects are achieved, and between those who maintain close adherence to Kohut's tenets and those who seek to integrate self psychology perspectives with other theoretical persuasions. Other developments of self psychology, starting from Kohut's emphasis on the experience of the self, have moved in the direction of viewing the relation of self and selfobjects in intersubjective terms such that nothing takes place in the domains of psychic experience or relationships that is not the result of intersubjective interactions involving two or more persons. Particularly applications of this view focus on developmental experience and the mutual intersubjective interchange between analyst and patient.

Kohut's views have been controversial but have added another dimension to the understanding of narcissism and its treatment. The extent to which his theory of the self and its origins can be integrated with previous metapsychological perspectives is still unsettled, and questions concerning the clinical and therapeutic validity of his approach remain debatable. Whether his views regarding the bipolar self and the persistent role of selfobject needs can be integrated with previous psychoanalytic notions of the self and the closely related notions of character and identity is a matter of theoretical exploration and debate. Nonetheless, his work has opened new inroads into the study of narcissistic pathology and has lent new vitality to the psychoanalytic study of the self and its vicissitudes.

Psychological Theories of Personality

The theories discussed in this section represent a variety of models of personality based on psychological investigation rather than on clinical experience. Although these theories have not arisen within a clinical context and thus lack the relevance and immediate application to clinical concerns of psychoanalytic theories, their importance for psychiatric thinking cannot be underestimated. They have stimulated a considerable body of research, and some have provided a basis for understanding more specific areas of psychiatric work. Finally, they provide perspectives on human experience and behavior that often reach beyond the limited psychopathological view of more specifically clinical theories. An important work of the future is integration of these psychological approaches with more explicitly clinical theories.

Humanistic Theories

Humanistic theories approach behavior in relatively holistic and dynamic terms. They are primarily concerned with what is unique and distinctive about human behavior and experience.

Gordon Allport. Gordon Allport (1897–1967) was for years the dean of American personality theorists. He taught at Harvard throughout his career. Impressed by the complexity and uniqueness of the individual human personality, he envisioned personality as an open system in constant interaction with its environment, not subject to the laws of entropy, as are closed physical systems. Allport distinguished between the historical roots of motives and their current functioning. He held that motivation may be, and in healthy individuals usually is, independent of its origins. He termed this the *functional autonomy* of motives, a formulation very close to, if not identical with, Hartmann's notion of secondary autonomy.

Central to Allport's theory of personality was the *trait,* by which he meant a determining tendency or predisposition to action resulting from integration of several habits. These combinations are never exactly the same in different individuals, but show certain biological and cultural similarities that form comparable modes of adjustment. Traits, then, are generalized predispositions to behavior providing the basis for personality description.

Allport took a staunch position against scientific reductionism in psychology, particularly with respect to personality. He described 2 contrasting orientations toward the study of personality: the first from a Lockean tradition, the second from a Leibnizian or Kantian tradition. In the Lockean position, the mind begins as a tabula rasa, and its development is determined by environmental influences. By contrast, the Leibnizian or Kantian position postulates a perpetually self-activating mind whose development comes from its own inner potentiality and spontaneous dynamisms. Allport referred to this unifying core of the personality as the *proprium,* his equivalent for the self as the source of agency and self-esteem. He believed that a dynamic synthesis was required to integrate these respective orientations and thus provide an adequate understanding of personality.

Henry Murray. Henry Murray (1893–1988) was Allport's colleague at Harvard for many years. He elaborated a theory based on concepts of *need* and *press.* Needs represented forces in the brain that energize and organize perceptions, thoughts, and actions and direct them toward specific goals. He developed an elaborate taxonomy of such needs. Press referred to aspects of the environment that help or hinder efforts to achieve goals. Murray articulated his theory in relation to the *Thematic Apperception Test* (TAT), which has become a staple instrument in clinical personality assessment.

Abraham Maslow. Abraham Maslow (1908–1970) developed a holistic theory of psychic health rather than of sickness. It postulated a hierarchy of needs underlying human motivation; when needs with the greatest potency are satisfied, the next higher level of needs presses for fulfillment. The hierarchy extends from the most basic physiological needs to the highest aesthetic and spiritual needs. For Maslow, man is essentially good: development and behavior of the individual can be subverted only by the interference of society, which places impediments to the fulfillment of human inner needs. Needs for esteem, knowledge, and beauty are particularly important, but social institutions and processes can also help in facilitating self-actualization—the highest value of Maslow's system. The self-actualized person, who makes full use of his capacities and potentialities, is the central and idealized prototype of Maslow's theory. Such individuals are characterized by high levels of objectivity, humility, and creativity, lack of inner conflict, and a capacity for joy. The notion of "peak experiences," in which an individual feels especially fulfilled, intensely satisfied, and functions to the full limits of his potentiality, are important in Maslow's theory. Such moments may be found at times in the lives of ordinary people, but they are particularly characteristic of self-actualized individuals.

In therapy, Maslow aimed at increasing self-knowledge and understanding and at mobilizing the potentialities and resources of the individual toward greater self-actualization. His approach was eclectic, emphasizing kindness and concern, but allowing room for a more structured and interpretive approach with some patients. He stressed man's inherent goodness and capacity for love, and made therapeutic efforts to mobilize these capacities by generating intense, highly emotional peak experiences. He felt positive about sensitivity and encounter groups and the development of growth centers connected with the human potential movement, because he thought they might prove to be vehicles for unleashing such experiences.

Factor Analytic Theories

The mathematical approach to personality relies on objective methods of personality measurement and the application of mathematical techniques, particularly forms of analysis of variance and covariance and factor analysis, to assess the role of personality factors in an individual personality. These factors are similar to the traits defined by humanistic theories. Quantitative methods of personality study, particularly the method of multivariate design, derive from the work of Francis Galton, Carl Spearman, and L. L. Thurstone. This approach involves the simultaneous measurement and correlation of multiple variables, which can be reduced to a limited set of underlying functional unities and then used to identify specific patterns of personality.

The underlying factors or source traits give rise to surface traits, that is, to behaviors that regularly appear and disappear in combination with one another. Functional psychological testing tries to discover the inherent dynamic, temperamental, or functional capacities of the human personality. A specific act expresses the total personality, which is evaluated by a profile of source trait scores. The act, therefore, represents an intersection of a multidimensional personality functioning within a multidimensional context.

The multivariate factor analyst attempts to make a diagnosis similar to that of the clinician. The difference is that the factor analyst actually measures the changing strength of symptoms and calculates their covariation to elucidate the interconnection of symptoms, rather than assessing them on a relatively intuitive basis, as does the clinician. For example, R. B. Cattell (b. 1905) developed a personality factor test involving 16 quantitatively determined factors providing a profile of the functioning personality. Cattell's factors include warmth of affect, intelligence, ego strength, excitability, dominance, superego strength, shrewdness, guilt proneness, self-sufficiency, and so on. Further efforts are needed to apply sophisticated quantitative techniques to clinical work. The advent of computer scoring has facilitated this development.

Systems-Information Theory

Stimulated by the mathematical concepts of servomechanisms and cybernetics in the work of Norbert Wiener (1894–1964) and by information theory, the general systems approach arose in areas foreign to psychiatry, such as engineering, and only gradually has it found application within psychiatry in Juergen Ruesch's (b. 1909) communications theory and others.

The crucial mechanism in the cybernetic process is the feedback circuit, along which the output of the system sends a modifying feedback signal modulating the ongoing activity of the system. Positive feedback increases the level of output, whereas negative feedback reduces it. The biological organism consists of aggregates of interacting feedback circuits that maintain internal homeostasis. Homeostasis is the basic steady state of the organism that depends on interlocking regulations to maintain critical variables within a constant range and direct the organism toward specific goals. The system is constantly monitored by feedback mechanisms to maintain its internal stability and/or its target direction.

Living organisms are open systems with continual exchange of input from and output to the environment. Feedback mechanisms maintain this open system in a steady state of homeostasis requiring continuous exchange of energy or information or both. Such systems may maintain themselves in a state of negative entropy, that is, in a condition of greater improbability, order, and complexity. They increase their level of order, complexity, and differentiation through development and adaptation. Within this framework, the human personality has the properties of an open system with dynamic ordering of parts and processes in mutual interaction and regulation. Psychopathology stems from disruption of the system rather than a loss of single functions. Personality itself is an integration of biological or physiological subsystems, at the lowest level, with broader social and cultural subsystems integrated as a hierarchical structure into the functioning personality system. At each level of system integration, feedback mechanisms and homeostatic regulations are qualitatively different. The systems perspective, however, provides an overall integrating schema by which the various parts can be studied and understood in relation to one another.

One variant of the systems approach is Ruesch's (1957) application of communications theory to psychiatry. Communication is a process of social interchange, determined by the organs of communication, the social environment with which the individual interacts and communicates, and the manner in which the individual's knowledge, skills, and capacities for adaptation are influenced by his basic experience. Various parts of social systems regulate each other by the exchange of messages. Communication of messages can be disturbed or disrupted when messages are given or received in a distorted way: when they are not perceived at all; when they are poorly timed, arriving too early or too late; or when they are inappropriate to the situation. Disruption in the communication system may occur in any of the components of the process: in the communicator, in the message, or in the environment in which the communication is given.

Therapeutic interventions within this framework try to determine the causes of disordered communication and to correct them. These functions consist not of energy transformations but rather of the transformation of information in the form of messages, a process that involves encoding and decoding, coordination, and combination of messages. In the therapeutic setting, the focus on processes of communication helps to increase the individual's awareness of his own disordered communications and the ways in which they affect other people. This may lead to abandonment of unnecessary assumptions and distorted beliefs and to modification of certain attitudes that may distort communications to and from others.

An additional development in this area is the application of information and systems theory to psychoanalysis. A number of attempts have been made to translate and reformulate psychoanalytic notions into the language of servomechanisms and information feedback (Peterfreund, 1971, 1983; Rosenblatt and Thickstun, 1977). These efforts have had partial success, particularly in increasing awareness of the extent to which systems concepts seem to be implicit in much of psychoanalytic thinking. The further question whether information theory has the resources to substitute entirely for more traditional psychoanalytic concepts, particularly in regard to complex affective understandings, remains a matter of controversy.

Phenomenological-Existential Theories

Phenomenological and existential theories focus on the uniqueness of the individual and his self-actualizing potential. They explicitly oppose the reductionism of behaviorist approaches; on this point they concur with humanistic approaches. They differ, however, in their emphasis on the individual's present experience in defining the psychological field.

Carl Rogers. The theory of Carl Rogers (1902–1987) is unique among psychological theories in that it derives from a primary concern with therapy, specifically his client-centered psychotherapy. Within Rogers's phenomenological and organismic theory, the phenomenological field is equivalent to the totality of the individual's experience. The self is a differentiated portion of the phenomenological field consisting of the individual's image and evaluation of himself.

Rogers postulated and based his therapy on an inherent self-actualizing tendency and an innate valuing process, not unlike Maslow's. Conflict arises when the need for approval comes into conflict with the self-actualizing tendency. His nondirective, client-centered approach stressed the attitudes of the therapist as they are communicated to the client, much like the stress on empathy in

self psychology. Critical attitudes include the therapist's genuineness and openness in dealing with the client, his attitude of unconditional positive regard for the client, and, finally, the therapist's accurate, empathic understanding of the client's feelings, sentiments, and attitudes. The therapist's empathic and understanding acceptance allows the client to express his thoughts and feelings and increasingly to be able to listen to his own communications. Slowly, he comes to accept and integrate the therapist's attitudes toward himself, and thus is increasingly able to express himself more openly and to become free to grow in more natural and self-actualizing directions. To this extent, the client-centered approach shares certain common notes with Kohut's self psychology.

Rollo May. A major exponent of the existential approach was Rollo May (1909–1994). Philosophical and phenomenological in orientation, the existential approach to human behavior stands in diametrical opposition to reductionistic or behavioristic orientations toward the human personality. In the existential perspective, man's self-awareness is his most basic experience. Existential psychiatrists emphasize the uniqueness and individuality of each human being, of each human existence *(Dasein)*. They look to the phenomenological aspects of the individual's experience of himself and the world in which he exists. These include various modes of *being-in-the-world:* the world of objects, external and internal, forming our environment *(Umwelt);* the social world of other persons *(Mitwelt);* and the world of oneself, one's inner values and potentials *(Eigenwelt)*. May focuses on the ontological anxiety arising from threats to one's existence as a personality as a core element of pathological adjustment. Pathology is equivalently constriction of *Dasein* that can be released only through love and care experienced in an empathic relationship with the therapist. In this vein, existential psychotherapy examines the actual encounter between 2 human beings and tries to describe and understand it in terms of current, actual experience. In this respect, the psychiatric existential approach attempts to describe the unique communication of the human dyad in terms formulated by existential philosophers— what Heidegger called *Mitsein,* or being-with-others, and what Buber referred to as the *I-Thou relationship.* Existential approaches emphasize actual, immediate, usually emotional experience as opposed to historical (developmental) determinants, accentuating self-actualizing tendencies characteristic of other humanistic, phenomenological, and existential theories.

Jacques Lacan. Despite his avowedly psychoanalytic involvement and theoretical orientation, I include Lacan here more for his phenomenological or existential emphasis than for his uniquely analytic and linguistic perspectives. Jacques Lacan (1901–1990) became the enfant terrible of French psychoanalysis and exercised a significant influence not just in European circles but more widely. He professed a return to the basic Freudian texts, but brought to them his own unique blend of linguistic and structural interpretation. With particular reference to Freud's dream theory, Lacan stressed the symbolic role of metonymy and metaphor in expressing unconscious derivatives. He argued that the unconscious is structured like a language and that meaning involves chains of signifiers—the revealing of these chains of signification being the work of analysis. He described metaphor (as substitution of signifier for signified or the condensation of signifiers, based on similarity) and metonymy (part for whole, analogous to analytic displacement, based on contiguity) as processes by which unconscious roots of desire find expression in language. Experience is divided into the imaginary (the order of perception, hallucination, and their derivatives), the symbolic (the order of language, discursive and symbolic action, and subjective interaction), and the real, which Lacan defines in his own sense as beyond the imaginary and symbolic—not external reality but what is real for the subject yet beyond the reach of symbolic comprehension. Lacan's theories are complex, often obscure and confusing, but have stimulated great interest, especially insofar as they draw a variety of contemporary philosophical currents—especially Husserlian phenomenology, Heideggerian existentialism, Hegelian perspectives on consciousness, the structural linguistics of Saussure and Jakobson, and the structural anthropology of Lévi-Strauss—into closer proximity with analytic perspectives and concerns.

Learning Theories

Theories of learning deal more or less exclusively with cognitive aspects of the personality. But their influence on psychiatric thinking has been profound, particularly in the wake of Jean Piaget's work on child development; and behavioral learning theories have been applied in behavioral therapy and behavior modification (see Chapter 22 for detailed discussion). Learning theories have proliferated and developed, particularly through experimental studies of behavior and development.

Social learning. Perhaps the most significant development is the application of learning theories to social learning. This application, begun by Neal Miller (b. 1909) and John Dollard (1900–1980), was advanced by Robert Sears (1908–1989), and more recently has been enlarged by the contributions of Albert Bandura (1925–) on questions of modeling. Dollard and Miller developed a theory of primary (hunger, thirst, sex, avoidance of pain) and secondary or learned drives (anger, guilt, anxiety, sexual preferences, needs for money, power, conformity, and so on). The primary cannot be extinguished but only satisfied; the secondary can be modified by new learning.

The basic theory is that children learn to become human beings only through contacts with other people in society. Individuals must learn to regulate behavior according to social norms and standards. The principal agents of this teaching are the parents. Learning is accomplished by rewarding social behaviors, thus reinforcing them, and by punishing behaviors that violate social rules. Generally, actions requiring protracted socialization involve sex, aggression, dependency, status seeking, power, and striving for affection (secondary drives). Punishment, which may be physical or symbolic—the threat of loss of parental love and approval—associates these basic impulses with anxiety. This association may establish a link between the anticipation of punishment and the punished impulses, so that the child comes to fear his own desires and has to find ways of dealing with this fear.

Within the family context, because parents both punish and reward, they are both loved and hated. The loving and protecting, on the one hand, and the fear and dislike, on the other hand, lay the basis for the ambivalence children feel toward their parents in our culture. The necessity for regulating and dealing with these emotions generates certain mechanisms calculated to reduce anxiety and fear. The child uses repression and the other mechanisms of defense to minimize these feelings. Diminution of anxiety reinforces such defenses, as well as other defense mechanisms or neurotic symptoms that may develop.

The influence of imitation, especially imitation of parental models, is particularly important in social learning, and holds a central place in the work of Miller and Dollard. Imitative behavior can be reinforced either extrinsically, as when the mother praises a child for copying desirable behavior or scolds or punishes him for copying undesirable behavior, or intrinsically, as when imitation gains rewards similar to those granted the copied behavior. Imitative behavior may also be self-reinforcing, and social behavior can also be acquired vicariously by observation of a model's behavior. In modeling, the behavior of the copier approximates that of a model. The potentialities of vicarious learning through the experience of modeled behavior have been explored by Bandura, and the importance of this avenue for acquisition and development of social behaviors cannot be underestimated.

Warm interaction with and affectionate attachment to a model increase the likelihood of imitation and copying.

Imitative behavior, thus reinforced, tends to generalize into a tendency to behave like the caretaking model. Such generalized imitation, copying multiple aspects of the model's behavior, is the behavioral equivalent of identification. Thus the child's socialization involves internalization not only of specific behavioral patterns, but also of the beliefs, attitudes, and values of the caretaking object.

Cognitive controls and cognitive styles. One aspect of the application of learning models to personality organization has been the study of cognitive controls. The examination of cognitive structure came about from the work of Herman Witkin (1916–1979), Jerome Kagan (1929–), and George Klein (1918–1971), among others. Witkin and Kagan focused on the notion of cognitive style (the consistency of individual differences in the organization of cognitive functions and the experience of the perceptual field). Witkin developed the rod-and-frame test and the embedded-figures test, from which he defined the characteristics of field dependence and field independence, that is, the extent to which the subject's perception is influenced by background factors, or the extent to which the subject has difficulty in keeping an object or item separate from its surroundings. Field-independent subjects are better able to prescind from the specific context in which information is embedded. Kagan later formulated global vs. articulate extremes of style as a further development of these ideas. These extremes define a continuum of varying degrees of differentiation of experience: at one extreme, there is a consistent tendency for experience to be global and diffuse, with the organization of the field as a whole dictating the way in which parts are perceived; at the opposite extreme, experience tends to be more articulated and structured, so that parts are experienced as discrete and organized within the total field.

Klein's studies of cognitive controls took their point of departure from Rapaport's earlier psychoanalytic formulations. Klein postulated stable individual differences in cognitive functioning that represent specific ego controls operating within the conflict-free sphere. Ego controls organize and manage information input and thus coordinate ego functions with environmental demands and internal impulses and drives. The main cognitive control principles are focal attention (scanning behavior, diffuse vs. focal); field articulation (adaptive processing of information from a stimulus field, field dependence vs. independence, and inclusion vs. exclusion of irrelevant information); leveling-sharpening (integration of sequentially experienced stimuli—levelers tend to assimilate new experiences with old; sharpeners tend to maintain discrete impressions of sequential stimuli); and equivalence range (the breadth and number of categories used to relate objects and their properties, that is, few categories and exact standards for inclusion vs. broad categories and less concern with differences between informational units). Although these approaches have stimulated active research on the development and functioning of cognitive capacities, they seem to have fallen into disregard, with only a handful of applications to developmental or therapeutic considerations.

This survey is highly selective and can hardly represent the rich complexity and diversity of the clinical and psychological theoretical approaches impinging on our attempts to understand human behavior and experience in psychiatry. Too often in the history of psychiatry, such theories have been approached with a closed mind, as though one theory had an exclusive claim on a valid view of the human mind, to the exclusion of others. It is to be hoped that even a limited survey such as this might sustain the view that these theories do not stand in opposition to one another but, rather, that each has grasped its own fragmentary perspective of a far-reaching and endlessly complex reality. I hope that this review has at least stimulated interest in further theoretical integration and in deepening clinical understanding. It is only in this direction that we can hope ultimately to help our patients understand themselves and thus direct their lives more adaptively and creatively.

References

Erikson, E. H. 1959. *Identity and the life cycle: selected papers.* Psychol. Issues 1, monograph no. 1. New York: International Universities Press.

———— 1963. *Childhood and society.* New York: Norton.

Freud, A. 1936. *The ego and the mechanisms of defense.* New York: International Universities Press, 1946.

Freud, S. 1895. Project for a scientific psychology. In *Standard edition,* ed. J. Strachey. Vol. 1. London: Hogarth Press, 1966.

———— 1900. The interpretation of dreams. In *Standard edition,* ed. J. Strachey. Vols. 4 and 5. London: Hogarth Press, 1953.

———— 1905. Three essays on the theory of sexuality. In *Standard edition,* ed. J. Strachey. Vol. 7. London: Hogarth Press, 1953.

———— 1913. Totem and taboo. In *Standard edition,* ed. J. Strachey. Vol. 13. London: Hogarth Press, 1955.

———— 1914. On narcissism. In *Standard edition,* ed. J. Strachey. Vol. 14. London: Hogarth Press, 1957.

———— 1915. Instincts and their vicissitudes. In *Standard*

edition, ed. J. Strachey. Vol. 14. London: Hogarth Press, 1957.

——— 1917. Mourning and melancholia. In *Standard edition,* ed. J. Strachey. Vol. 14. London: Hogarth Press, 1958.

——— 1920. Beyond the pleasure principle. In *Standard edition,* ed. J. Strachey. Vol. 18. London: Hogarth Press, 1955.

——— 1923. The ego and the id. In *Standard edition,* ed. J. Strachey. Vol. 19. London: Hogarth Press, 1961.

——— 1926. Inhibitions, symptoms, and anxiety. In *Standard edition,* ed. J. Strachey. Vol. 20. London: Hogarth Press, 1959.

——— 1940. An outline of psychoanalysis. In *Standard edition,* ed. J. Strachey. Vol. 23. London: Hogarth Press, 1964.

Hartmann, H. 1939. *Ego psychology and the problem of adaptation,* trans. D. Rapaport. New York: International Universities Press, 1958.

Jacobson, E. 1964. *The self and the object world.* New York: International Universities Press.

Jung, C. G. 1916. *Psychology of the unconscious: a study of the transformations and symbolisms of the libido, a contribution to the history of the evolution of thought,* trans. B. M. Hinkle. New York: Moffat, Yard.

Kohut, H. 1966. Forms and transformations of narcissism. In *Search for the self,* ed. P. H. Ornstein. New York: International Universities Press.

——— 1971. *The analysis of the self.* New York: International Universities Press.

——— 1977. *The restoration of the self.* New York: International Universities Press.

——— 1984. *How does analysis cure?* Chicago: University of Chicago Press.

Peterfreund, E. 1971. *Information, systems, and psychoanalysis: an evolutionary biological approach to psychoanalytic theory.* New York: International Universities Press.

——— 1983. *The process of psychoanalytic therapy: models and strategies.* Hillsdale, N.J.: Analytic Press.

Rosenblatt, A. D., and J. T. Thickstun. 1977. *Modern psychoanalytic concepts in a general psychology.* New York: International Universities Press.

Ruesch, J. 1957. *Disturbed communication.* New York: Norton.

Hartmann, H. 1964. *Essays on ego psychology.* New York: International Universities Press.

Kurzweil, E. 1989. *The Freudians: a comparative perspective.* New Haven: Yale University Press.

Laplanche, J., and J.-B. Pontalis. 1973. *The language of psychoanalysis.* New York: Norton.

Moore, B. E., and B. D. Fine, eds. 1990. *Psychoanalytic terms and concepts.* New Haven: American Psychoanalytic Association and Yale University Press.

Munroe, R. L. 1955. *Schools of psychoanalytic thought.* New York: Dryden.

Yankelovich, D., and W. Barrett. 1970. *Ego and instinct: the psychoanalytic view of human nature—revised.* New York: Random House.

Recommended Reading

Ellenberger, H. F. 1970. *The discovery of the unconscious.* New York: Basic Books.

Greenberg, J. R., and S. A. Mitchell. 1983. *Object relations in psychoanalytic theory.* Cambridge, Mass.: Harvard University Press.

GEORGE E. VAILLANT

Defense Mechanisms

Phenomenology and pathophysiology both play an important role in our understanding of disease. Whereas nineteenth-century medical phenomenologists viewed pus, fever, pain, and coughing as evidence of disease, twentieth-century pathophysiologists have regarded these symptoms as evidence of the body's healthy efforts to cope with physical or infectious insult. In parallel fashion much of what modern psychiatric phenomenologists classify as disorders according to the *Diagnostic and Statistical Manual of Mental Disorders,* fourth edition (DSM-IV), can be reclassified by those with a more psychodynamic viewpoint as manifestations of the ego's adaptive efforts to cope with psychological stress. Such adaptive efforts are subsumed under the general term *defense mechanisms.* In recognition of the association between psychological homeostasis and psychopathology, DSM-IV has included a Defensive Functioning Scale as a proposed diagnostic axis for further study.

Definition

It is important to place defense mechanisms within the broader framework of stress and coping. Response to stress may be considered from 2 perspectives. The first emphasizes relatively nonspecific psychophysiological responses to stress, such as elevated Hamilton depression scales or elevations in blood epinephrine levels. This is the perspective of Hans Selye and other phenomenologists. The second perspective focuses on how an individual's integrated central nervous system perceives and copes with the stressor. In this case the result of stress is seen not as nonspecific depression and anxiety but as highly differentiated synthetic behaviors that may range from arcane delusional systems to the writing of a great novel. This second perspective, that of ego psychology, is the orientation of this discussion.

If stress can be viewed from 2 vantage points, coping responses can be viewed as divided into 3 broad categories. The first coping category involves eliciting help from appropriate others, for example, by mobilizing social supports. The second coping category involves voluntary cognitive efforts such as information gathering, anticipating danger, and rehearsing responses to danger. The third coping category entails deploying involuntary adaptive mechanisms or automatic psychological processes that protect the individual from the awareness of internal or external dangers or stressors. These processes are often subsumed under the psychoanalytic term *ego mechanisms of defense.* This mode of coping is the focus of this chapter.

The use of ego mechanisms of defense usually alters perception of both internal and external reality, and often, as with hypnosis, the use of such mechanisms compromises other facets of cognition. Awareness of instinctual "wishes" is usually diminished; alternatively, antithetical wishes may be passionately adhered to. Ego mechanisms of defense keep affects within bearable limits during sudden changes in emotional life, such as following the death of a loved one. They can deflect or deny sudden increases in biological drives, such as heightened sexual awareness and aggression during adolescence. Defenses also allow individuals a period of respite to master changes in self-image that cannot be immediately integrated, as might result from puberty, an amputation, or a promotion. Finally, defenses enable individuals to mitigate unresolved conflicts with important people, living or dead. In each case the individual appears to deal with a sudden stress by *denial* or *repression.* But used indiscriminately, these two terms lose the explanatory power of the conceptual scheme—ego mechanisms of defense.

Defense mechanisms involve far more than simple neglect or repression of reality. They reflect integrated dynamic psychological processes. Like their physical analogues—rubor, calor, dolor, and turgor—defenses reflect healthy, often highly coordinated responses to stress rather than a deficit state or a learned voluntary strategy.

Thus a defense mechanism has more in common with an opossum involuntarily but skillfully playing dead than with either the involuntary but nonspecific anesthesia of a neurologically denervated limb or the consciously controlled evasive maneuvers of a halfback.

Classification

Historically, defense mechanisms were first described by Sigmund Freud in 1894. Both Freud and his students, however, tended to ignore the importance of differentiating defense mechanisms. It took James Strachey, Freud's final editor, and Anna Freud, his daughter, to appreciate and to emphasize what Freud did not—the variety and the power of the concept, ego mechanisms of defense (A. Freud, 1937).

In 1894 Freud observed not only that affect could be "dislocated or transposed" from ideas (by the unconscious mechanisms that he would later call dissociation, repression, and isolation), but also that affect could be "reattached" to other ideas (by the mechanism of displacement). Over a period of 40 years, Freud outlined most of the defense mechanisms of which we speak today. He identified 5 of their important properties:

1. Defenses are a major means of managing both cognitive dissonance and affect.
2. Defenses are unconscious.
3. Defenses are discrete from one another.
4. Although often the hallmarks of major psychiatric syndromes, defenses are reversible.
5. Defenses can be adaptive as well as pathological.

During the first decade after he identified them, Freud clearly conceptualized defense mechanisms as distinct from one another. Thus by 1905, in *Jokes and Their Relation to the Unconscious*, Freud described the separate mechanisms of humor, distortion, displacement, repression, suppression, fantasy, and isolation. After 1905, however, the term *defense (Abwehr)* no longer figured prominently in his work and was replaced by "'repression' (as I now began to say instead of 'defense')" (1906, p. 276).

For 20 years the distinction between individual ego mechanisms was blurred in Freud's writings, and despite his efforts (1926), it remains so for many writers today. Modern students of psychiatry must learn to separate an individual's defensive operations into component parts, much as an analytic chemist might use a prism to break the nonspecific glow of an unknown gas into the discrete spectral colors that identify it. Studying the individual defenses that constitute a patient's pattern of psychopathology and "denial" of stress can be most revealing.

For only as we learn to differentiate defensive processes from one another can we decipher the dynamics of a patient's choice of symptoms.

In 1936 Freud advised the interested student that there is "an extraordinarily large number of methods (or mechanisms, as we say) used by our ego in the discharge of its defensive function . . . my daughter, the child analyst, is writing a book upon them" (1936, p. 245). He was referring, of course, to Anna Freud's *The Ego and Mechanisms of Defense* (1937), which to this day remains one of the definitive texts on the subject. Thirty years later Anna Freud wrote: "Defenses have their own chronology . . . they are more apt to have pathological results if they come into use before the appropriate age or are kept up too long after it. Examples are denial and projection which are 'normal' in early childhood and lead to pathology in later years; or repression and reaction formation, which cripple the child's personality if used too early" (1965, p. 177). Indeed, in terms of a continuum of defenses from pathological to adaptive, many early contributors to ego psychology recognized the likelihood of such a hierarchy, but none provided specific outlines or empirical underpinnings.

Freud and his early followers had chosen to study children and psychologically impaired individuals; they paid relatively little attention to the fate of a given defense as the child matured and as the patient recovered. Recognition of hierarchically differentiated defenses, however, requires a highly developed appreciation of the healthy ego, and it was not until World War II that psychoanalytically trained researchers began to study the vicissitudes of unconscious adaptation in normal populations. Ernst Kris, Heinz Hartmann, George Engel, Robert White, David Hamburg, Lois Murphy, Elvin Semrad, and Karl Menninger belong on anyone's list of individuals who deserve special credit for underscoring our need to define a hierarchy of defense mechanisms. Every one of these investigators, however, presented a different nomenclature and schema for assessing defenses. None supplied mutually exclusive definitions, sought the reliability of raters, or provided empirical evidence beyond clinical anecdote.

In the last 30 years several empirical studies have suggested that it is possible to arrange defense mechanisms into a hierarchy of relative psychopathology (Vaillant, 1986, 1992), and DSM-IV has offered a tentative glossary of consensually validated definitions. Table 10.1 arranges these defense mechanisms into 7 general classes of relative psychopathology.

All classes of defenses are effective in "repressing" conflict and in "denying" stress; but the individual defenses differ greatly in the diagnoses associated with their use and perhaps in their consequences for long-term biopsychosocial adaptation. In the first, most pathological category are found denial and distortion of external reality. These mechanisms are common in our dreams, in young children, and in psychosis. Schizophrenics can experience perforated duodenal ulcers without complaint of physical pain. Labeling psychotic denial, as in Table 10.1, Level I, as "denial of external reality" is a far more narrow but specific use of the term than simply making denial synonymous with all defenses. The same is true of distortion: in their delusions manics distort reality and believe that their wishes have come true. These psychotic defenses

Table 10.1   Defense levels and individual defense mechanisms (adapted from DSM-IV)

I.   *Level of Defensive Deregulation.* This level is characterized by failure of defensive regulation to contain the individual's reaction to stressors, leading to a pronounced break with objective reality. Examples are:
• delusional projection
• psychotic denial
• psychotic distortion

II.   *Action Level.* This level is characterized by defensive functioning that deals with internal or external stressors by action or withdrawal. Examples are:
• acting out
• apathetic withdrawal
• passive aggression

III.   *Major Image-distorting Level.* This level is characterized by gross distortion or misattribution of the image of self or others. Examples are:
• autistic fantasy
• projective identification
• splitting of self-image or image of others

IV.   *Disavowal Level.* This level is characterized by keeping unpleasant or unacceptable stressors, impulses, ideas, affects, or responsibility out of awareness with or without a misattribution of these to external causes. Examples are:
• denial
• projection
• rationalization

V.   *Minor Image-distorting Level.* This level is characterized by distortions in the image of the self, body, or others that may be employed to regulate self-esteem. Examples are:
• devaluation
• idealization
• omnipotence

VI.   *Mental Inhibitions (compromise formation) Level.* Defensive functioning at this level keeps potentially threatening ideas, feelings, memories, wishes, or fears out of awareness. Examples are:
• displacement
• dissociation
• intellectualization
• isolation of affect
• reaction formation
• repression
• undoing

VII.   *High Adaptive Level.* This level of defensive functioning results in optimal adaptation in the handling of stressors. These defenses usually maximize gratification and allow the conscious awareness of feelings, ideas, and their consequences. They also promote an optimum balance among conflicting motives. Examples of defenses at this level are:
• anticipation
• affiliation
• altruism
• humor
• self-assertion
• self-observation
• sublimation
• suppression

rarely respond to simple psychological intervention. To breach them requires altering the brain by neuroleptics or waking the dreamer. Over the long term these defenses are invariably maladaptive. Psychotics are unhappy, and they often die young.

More common in everyday life are the "immature" defenses, Levels II–IV. These categories are associated with adolescents, with immature adults, and with personality disorders. They include the paranoid's projection, the schizoid's autistic fantasy, the mutual passive-aggression (sadomasochism) of the wife-beater and his wife, the sociopath's impulsive, "mindless" translation of inner conflict into "acting out," and the hypochondriac's magnification of pain and help-rejecting complaining. Like cigarette smoking in a crowded elevator, such behavior seems innocent to the user and deliberately irritating and provocative to the observer. Immature defenses externalize responsibility and allow individuals with personality disorders to refuse help. Defenses in this category rarely respond to verbal interpretation alone. They can be breached in two ways: first, by confrontation—often by a group of supportive peers—or by videotaped empathic but focused psychotherapy; and second, by improving intrapsychic competence by rendering the individual less anxious and lonely through empathy, less tired and hungry through rest, or less intoxicated through abstinence. Such techniques are outlined in depth in Leigh McCullough Vaillant's focused textbook on psychotherapy, *Changing Character* (1996).

The third class of defenses is associated with the old-fashioned neuroses (recently relabeled *anxiety disorders* by DSM-IV) and is common to the psychopathology of everyday life. For the purpose of the hierarchy in Table 10.1, this class is labeled Level VI. It includes mechanisms such as repression, intellectualization, isolation of affect, reaction formation, and displacement. In contrast to the "immature" defenses, the defenses of neurosis are manifested clinically by phobias, compulsions, obsessions, somatizations, and amnesias. Such defenses, like a stone in a shoe, create problems for no one but their owners. Thus users often seek help, and neurotic defenses do respond easily to interpretation.

The fourth and theoretically more mature class of defenses includes Level VII defenses of humor, altruism, sublimation, and suppression. These mechanisms still distort and alter feelings, conscience, relationships, and reality, but they perform these tasks gracefully and flexibly. Writing great tragedy (i.e., sublimation), for example, is financially rewarding, instinctually gratifying, and sometimes life-saving for the author. The "distortion" involved in stoicism (suppression), humor, and altruism seems as ethical and as mentally healthy to an observer

as the immature defenses seem immoral and antisocial. Living one's life by laughter, the Golden Mean, and the Golden Rule leads to living a life of happiness, and often to old age.

Less mature defenses may evolve into more mature defenses. The adolescent's autistic fantasies may become the scholar's intellectualized obsession. The bigot's projected prejudice may develop into the displacement of the phobic. Mary Baker Eddy's hypochondriasis evolved first into reaction formation against any complaint of physical illness and then into the highly rewarding altruistic founding of the Christian Science Church.

Over time we may not always adapt to the same stress in the same way. Just as some children outgrow allergies, so the second-grader's irritating sadomasochistic pleasure of putting thumbtacks on chairs may evolve into the adolescent's enjoyment of the displaced hostility of *Mad* magazine and finally into mature, enjoyable humor where the hostile intent is invisible.

In summary, the so-called immature defenses listed in Table 10.1 correspond to those inferred intrapsychic mechanisms commonly observed in the Axis II disorders of DSM-IV. Such defenses are consistently and negatively correlated with global assessment of mental health and, like smoking in crowded elevators, profoundly distort the affective component of interpersonal relationships. In contrast, the so-called mature defenses identify inferred intrapsychic mechanisms that have been consistently correlated with successful psychological adaptation. These mechanisms allow the individual consciously to experience the affective component of interpersonal relationships, but in a tempered fashion. Across studies the intermediate defenses show mixed positive and negative correlations that are of minimal statistical significance. Such defenses cause more suffering to the individual than to those in the environment.

One must appreciate, however, that, like hypnosis or an artist's sublimation, the "mechanisms" in Table 10.1 do not reflect actual neuronal assemblies but rather serve as metaphors to describe higher integrated processes of the central nervous system. If defenses are the building blocks of psychopathology, their division into "levels" of categories is as arbitrary as our division of colors. There will always be as many different colors—and as many defenses—as there are angels that dance on the head of a pin.

Case Example

Let me offer an example to illustrate how deploying different defenses to solve the same conflict would lead to very different diagnoses.

A 30-year-old Chinese-American businessman finds himself dishonored and threatened by his 65-year-old business partner–father, whom he has never before consciously mistrusted. Ethically he believes that he should continue to honor his father; but in his limbic system and amygdala he feels, "I hate my father; my father is my enemy." The fact is that the father has defrauded his son's customers. The young businessman is presented a reality, a fact of life, for which he has had no time to prepare. He finds that he can neither live with his father nor abandon his filial relationship.

In short, the young man's conflict extends beyond a psychoanalytic model in which his conscience (superego) and his impulses (id) are at war. Defenses are as important in our adjustment to other people, to reality, and to our culture as they are to inner tranquillity. Changes in the son's reality and in his personal relationships have produced *external* social conflict as dynamically important as his *internal* conflict over his patricidal impulses. And conflicts over anger, grief, and dependency are just as distressing as conflicts over forbidden "Freudian" sexual wishes. Either the son must consciously experience both the *idea* and the *feeling* of hating his father, which will lead to profound anxiety, depression, and physiological stress, or in some way he must alter his inner and/or outer reality. This process of psychological alteration may lead to his being classified by DSM-IV as mentally ill. Table 10.2 gives a series of possible homeostatic transformations that his mind might effect to protect him from conscious stress. These transformations illustrate in a more differentiated fashion the mechanisms listed in Table 10.1.

Diagnosis

How does one identify a defense mechanism that one cannot see? A major challenge in using psychodynamic formulation as an explanatory concept in mental illness is to avoid unwarranted inference and superstition. After all, psychodynamics is no more than a system of metaphors, a metapsychology devised to explain the unknown, and it is not readily susceptible to experimental proof. To put ego psychology on a firmer footing than alchemy, phrenology, or astrology, let me suggest that defenses can be identified in much the same way that we measure the height of mountains and trees we cannot climb—by triangulation. We must contrast a patient's *symptoms* (or a healthy person's *creative product*) with his self-report or *mental content* and with someone else's *objective report,* biography, or old charts. In this way an unconsciously motivated slip of the tongue can be distinguished from a simple mistake, a true paralysis from paresis owing to psychogenic conversion, and a delusion from true political persecution. To

quote Freud, the patient's symptom is thereby rendered "no longer nonsensical, nor incomprehensible. It is full of meaning, well motivated and an integral part of the patient's emotional experience" (1926, p. 218).

The following true case history illustrates how understanding defenses can render a bizarre, perhaps pathological obsession into a healthy form of coping with stress. A physician developed a hobby of cultivating living cells in test tubes. In a recent interview (autobiography/mental content), he described to me with special enthusiasm an interesting tissue culture (symptom or creative product) that he had grown from a biopsy from his mother's leg. Only toward the end of the interview did he casually reveal that his mother had died from a stroke only 3 weeks previously (objective biography). His mention of her death was as emotionless as his description of his mother's still-living tissue culture had been affectively colored. Ingeniously and unconsciously, he had used his hobby and his special skills as a physician to mitigate temporarily his grief. Although his mother was no longer alive, by shifting his attention and affection he was still able, in a sense, to care for her in his home laboratory. The vignette could be labeled "displacement and intellectualization."

Treatment

The best way to alter a person's choice of defensive style under stress is to make his social milieu more predictable and supportive. We are all a little schizoid and paranoid when among strangers who we fear may treat us harshly. We are all more adept at altruism, suppression, and playful sublimation when among friends and others empathic toward our pain. As physicians, we can learn to accept the distortions of inner and outer events that accompany the defensive maneuvers of our patients as often as we challenge or grow angry at them. Schizoid and paranoid personalities in the consulting room are rarely attractive, but they respond better to empathy and forbearance than to confrontation or rejection. Remember, ego mechanisms of defense—like cough, pain, and leukocytosis—are as likely to be evidence of adaptation as they are evidence of sickness. In psychiatry as in general medicine, we need to treat the underlying cause, not the symptom. Pain at McBurney's point is not a diagnosis but may be a lifesaving symptom drawing the surgeon's attention to an inflamed appendix.

We also can help patients to deploy more mature defenses by altering the internal milieu. Toxic brain syndrome makes almost anyone project; intoxication leads to fantasy; unlanced abscesses of grief and anger lead to rage turned upon the self. We are all more mature when not hungry, tired, and lonely.

Finally, if we breach a patient's defense, we must be sure we have his permission. If in the course of examination we ask a patient to remove his protective covering, we must protect him with something else. Either we must offer ourselves—a luxury rarely available to busy doctors—or we must offer and facilitate a substitute defense. Psychopharmacology is rarely specific enough to do the job. More than one hypochondriac has evolved from berating others with his own pain to becoming altruistically concerned about the pain of others. Such an evolution must not be dismissed as a flight into health, but accepted as the wisdom of the ego.

References

Bond, M., S. T. Gardiner, J. Christian, and J. J. Sigel. 1983. An empirical examination of defense mechanisms. *Arch. Gen. Psychiatry* 40:333–338.

Conte, H. R., and R. Plutchik. 1995. *Ego defenses: theory and measurement.* New York: John Wiley & Sons.

Freud, A. 1937. *The ego and mechanisms of defense.* London: Hogarth Press.

——— 1965. *Normality and pathology of childhood: assessments of development.* New York: International Universities Press.

Freud, S. 1894. The neuro-psychosis of defense. In *Standard edition,* ed. J. Strachey. Vol. 1. London: Hogarth Press, 1964.

——— 1905. Jokes and their relation to the unconscious. In *Standard edition,* ed. J. Strachey. Vol. 8. London: Hogarth Press, 1964.

——— 1906. My views on the part played by sexuality in the etiology of the neuroses. In *Standard edition,* ed. J. Strachey. Vol. 7. London: Hogarth Press, 1964.

——— 1926. Inhibitions, symptoms, and anxiety. In *Standard edition,* ed. J. Strachey. Vol. 20. London: Hogarth Press, 1964.

——— 1936. A disturbance of memory on the acropolis.

Table 10.2 Contrasting ways of altering the conscious representation of a conflict

Defense	Conscious Representation of Idea, Feeling, or Behavior	DSM-IV Phenomenological Diagnosis[a]	
No defense	I HATE (!) MY FATHER.	309.9	Adjustment disorder unspecified
Psychotic defense			
Denial	I WAS BORN WITHOUT A FATHER.	298.8	Brief psychotic disorder
Immature defenses			
Projection	MY FATHER HATES (!) ME.	301.0	Paranoid personality disorder
Passive aggression	I HATE (!) MYSELF (suicide attempt).	300.4	Dysthymic disorder
Acting out	WITHOUT REFLECTION, I HIT 12 POLICEMEN.	301.7	Antisocial personality disorder
Fantasy	I DAYDREAM OF KILLING GIANTS.	301.2	Schizoid personality disorder
Neurotic (intermediate) defenses			
Dissociation	I TELL MY FATHER JOKES.	300.15	Dissociative disorder
Displacement	I HATE (!) MY FATHER'S DOG.	300.29	Simple phobia
Isolation (or intellectualization)	I DISAPPROVE OF FATHER'S BEHAVIOR.	300.3	Obsessive-compulsive disorder
Repression	I DO NOT KNOW WHY I FEEL SO HOT AND BOTHERED.	300.02	Generalized anxiety disorder
Reaction formation	I LOVE (!) MY FATHER OR I HATE (!) FATHER'S ENEMIES.		—
Mature defenses			
Suppression	I AM CROSS AT FATHER BUT WILL NOT TELL HIM.		—
Sublimation	I BEAT FATHER AT TENNIS.		—
Altruism	I COMFORT FATHER HATERS.		—

a. Diagnosis assumes that conscious representation of the conflict was carried to pathological extremes and that the other criteria for the diagnosis were met.

In *Standard edition*, ed. J. Strachey. Vol. 22. London: Hogarth Press, 1964.

Haan, N. 1977. *Coping and defending.* San Francisco: Jossey-Bass.

Vaillant, G. E. l977. *Adaptation to life.* Boston: Little, Brown (rpt. Harvard University Press).

———— 1992. *Ego mechanisms of defense: a guide for clinicians and researchers.* Washington, D.C.: American Psychiatric Press.

Vaillant, G. E., ed. 1986. *Empirical studies of ego mechanisms of defense.* Washington, D.C.: American Psychiatric Press.

Vaillant, G. E., and R. Drake. 1985. A theoretical hierarchy of adaptive ego mechanisms and Axis II. *Arch. Gen. Psychiatry* 42:597–601.

Vaillant, L. M. 1996. *Changing character.* New York: Basic Books.

Recommended Reading

American Psychiatric Association. 1994. *Diagnostic and statistical manual of mental disorders,* 4th ed. Washington, D.C.

Freud, A. 1937. *The ego and mechanisms of defense.* London: Hogarth Press.

Loevinger, J. 1976. *Ego development.* San Francisco: Jossey-Bass.

Vaillant, G. E. 1992. *Ego mechanisms of defense: a guide for clinicians and researchers.* Washington, D.C.: American Psychiatric Press.

Vaillant, L. M. 1996. *Changing character.* New York: Basic Books.

JOHN C. NEMIAH

The Psychodynamic Basis of Psychopathology

Psychopathology may be viewed from two different aspects, the phenomenological and the explanatory. From a phenomenological aspect, psychopathology is concerned with pathological distortions of psychic functions as these may be seen and described either by the individual experiencing them or by an external observer. Self-observation is private and subjective and deals with consciously experienced events such as feelings, sensations, and perceptions; observations made by others are public and objective and are primarily concerned with the behavior of the individual being observed. Phenomenological psychopathology is a descriptive discipline and is not concerned with explanations. It attemps to delineate, define, and categorize symptoms and behavior and to ascertain how they are related to one another in the various pathological syndromes that constitute psychiatric illness.

Psychopathologists, however, commonly move beyond pure description and endeavor to explain the genesis of the phenomena they observe. Their explanations may be in terms of neuropathological states that are correlated with psychological and behavioral abnormalities, or they may remain conceptually within the sphere of psychology, viewing psychopathological phenomena as the result of underlying psychological processes. The nature of these explanations depends on the theoretical models used to frame them, and it is the variety of such models that has led to the confusion and frequent lack of communication among those concerned with understanding mental disorders.

The phenomenological approach to psychopathology will receive fuller treatment elsewhere in this volume in those sections dealing with the description of clinical syndromes. The central concern in what follows here is with the psychological explanation of the observed phenomena. Our attention will be focused on the psychodynamic model of mental functioning, which is derived from psychoanalysis and has proved to be a clinically useful theoretical approach. The main emphasis in this chapter is on the elucidation of psychological conflict and the mental mechanisms underlying major psychoneurotic disorders. The more primitive defense mechanisms and defects in ego function that play a role in the production of the psychoses and severe personality disorders are discussed in other chapters.

Mental Mechanisms

Basic to the understanding of mental mechanisms are two key concepts, unconsious mental processes and psychological conflict, which can best be understood by viewing them through the history of their development.

The Unconscious: Development of the Concept

Although the origins of psychodynamic concepts may perhaps be traced back to Anton Mesmer and animal magnetism in the latter part of the eighteenth century, it was not until the end of the nineteenth that they emerged as specific psychodynamic formulations in the clinical investigations and writings of Charcot, Janet, and Freud.

Charcot, hysteria, and hypnosis. Jean-Martin Charcot (Goetz, Bonduelle, and Gelfand, 1995) is commonly remembered for his seminal pathophysiological studies of amyotrophic lateral sclerosis and tabes dorsalis. Those, however, were only a fraction of the many important clinical investigations that flourished during his creative leadership of the medical service of the Salpêtrière hospital in Paris. Of equal importance was Charcot's rehabilitation of hypnosis as an investigative and therapeutic tool and his application of it to the study of a large number of patients with a wide spectrum of somatoform and dissociative disorders then referred to as "hysteria." In this setting, the essential identity of hypnotic and hysterical phenomena became evident and the important role of psychological processes in their production was demonstrated.

Janet and dissociation. Pierre Janet, one of Charcot's most illustrious pupils and head of the Salpêtrière's psychological laboratory, played a central part in the development of those studies. His investigations led to a basic formulation of psychopathological processes and symptom formation that remains central to psychodynamic conceptualization to this day (Janet, 1889).

Hypnosis was a major investigative procedure in Janet's evaluation of patients with hysterical symptoms. Its use enabled him to determine the existence of unconscious mental phenomena and to demonstrate their fundamental importance in the production of clinical symptoms. The unconscious mental contents were commonly memories of traumatic life experiences that had been "dissociated" from conscious awareness and were unavailable to voluntary recall. However, although thus rendered unconscious (or "subconscious" in Janet's terminology), the traumatic memories retained the capacity to affect the individual's surface behavior and function in the form of ego-alien symptoms beyond the individual's voluntary control.

One of Janet's earliest patients graphically demonstrates the nature of those psychopathological mechanisms. Marie, a young woman of 18, suffered from a number of hysterical somatic symptoms, among them blindness in her left eye and numbness in the surrounding area of her face. Marie reported that she had had those symptoms for as long as she could remember, and she insisted that she had no idea whatsoever where, when, or how her dysfunction had begun. Under hypnosis, however, Marie readily remembered a traumatic episode at the age of 6 that had immediately preceded the onset of her symptoms. She had been forced one day, despite her screams of horror and protest, to take a nap in the same bed with a little playmate, the left side of whose face was covered with festering impetiginous lesions. Her own symptoms developed shortly thereafter in the same distribution, never to disappear.

Based on those findings, Janet treated Marie with a therapeutic maneuver that was an early forerunner of the procedures of modern cognitive therapy. Reviving Marie's traumatic memories once again under hypnosis, Janet altered her visual memories of the episode through vigorous hypnotic sugestion. "I caused her to believe," he wrote, "that the child was very attractive and had no scabs, but she was only half convinced. After making her repeat the scene a second time, I was successful, and she fearlessly caressed the imaginary child. The sensation in the left side of her face returned without difficulty, and when I woke her up, Marie saw clearly with her left eye." Janet's psychological maneuver had succeeded in produc-

ing a dramatic cure for a condition that, at the time he wrote his account, had lasted for some 5 months.

As Marie and many other of his patients demonstrated, Janet's discovery of dissociated unconscious mental contents provided a useful explanation of the immediate mechanisms underlying the production of hysterical and other neurotic symptoms. That explanation did not, however, account for the occurrence of the process of dissociation that had rendered pathogenic mental events unconscious in the first place. To provide such an explanation, Janet turned to a more complex, more speculative, and less tangible formulation of the nature of human psychological functioning.

Each human being, Janet postulated, is born with a genetically determined quantum of nervous energy. In a normal person, that energy serves to bind together all the neural processes and their associated mental functions (especially memories) into a unified, integrated whole under the dominance of the self, or ego. In certain people, however, there is a deficiency of nervous energy *(la misère psychologique)* either on a genetic basis or as the result of some severe intercurrent illness. In such individuals, the expenditure of nervous energy during the expression of emotions aroused by traumatic events compromises its binding power and leads to a loosening of the normal synthesis of the personality and a falling away of mental elements from conscious awareness and the control of the self—a process that Janet termed "dissociation." Thus dissociated, the lost memories and mental processes now formed the unconscious pathogenic nucleus for the production of the observable, consciously experienced, ego-alien symptoms of neurotic illness.

Freud and psychological conflict. In 1886 Sigmund Freud went to the Salpêtrière to study neuropathology under Charcot. By that time Charcot's investigations of hypnotic and hysterical phenomena were well established, and Freud soon found himself swept up by the enthusiasm of those around him for the study of hysterical patients. Indeed, he was soon diverted from working in the pathological laboratory as he learned to recognize the clinical characteristics that distinguished hysteria from neurological illness, became acquainted with the techniques and phenomena of hypnosis, and absorbed Charcot's concepts of the role of suggestion and autosuggestion in the production of hysterical symptoms. After several intellectually stimulating months he returned to Vienna inspired to turn his clinical attention in a new direction.

The way was opened for Freud to exploit his recently gained knowledge through his association with Josef

Breuer, an older, established, and respected Viennese neurologist. In 1880 Breuer had undertaken the case of Anna O., a well-to-do young woman suffering from a host of incapacitating hysterical symptoms (Breuer and Freud, 1895). Breuer began to treat her with hypnosis, using it initially to remove symptoms by direct suggestion. He discovered, however, that his patient responded in an unorthodox manner. Under the influence of hypnosis, and at times spontaneously, she lapsed into somnambulistic states of altered consciousness in which she appeared to experience vivid hallucinations, which she described at length. As Breuer listened to her recitals, he realized that she was reliving past traumatic events, each of which was represented symbolically by her various symptoms. Furthermore, he discovered that when she had recounted in detail the memory of a traumatic episode, giving vent to all the emotions associated with it, the hysterical symptoms disappeared. On one occasion, for example, when she was suffering from a hysterical inability to drink, she recounted seeing a colleague's dog drinking from a water glass. At the time she had been disgusted and angered but had said nothing, only to develop her hysterical hydrophobia shortly thereafter. In the hypnotic treatment session she recalled this episode, expressed aloud the anger she had felt but suppressed at the time of the event, asked for a glass of water, and awoke from the hypnotic trance in the act of drinking. From that point on she was free of the symptom.

Breuer capitalized on his chance finding and, over a series of hypnotic sessions, actively directed the patient's recall to the events and emotions behind a variety of her symptoms, which disappeared as a result. In their subsequent collaboration Breuer and Freud applied what they called their "cathartic treatment" to several other hysterical patients, ultimately publishing their results in *Studies on Hysteria,* a monograph presenting their clinical findings and theoretical formulations (Breuer and Freud, 1895).

In discovering and recognizing the importance of emotional catharsis, Breuer carried the use of hypnosis a step beyond the practice of the Salpêtrière school. As we have seen in Janet's treatment of Marie, hypnosis had until then been employed therapeutically to remove symptoms by suggestion alone designed to alter the character of the traumatic memories underlying the symptoms or to suppress the symptoms directly. To this therapeutic maneuver Breuer and Freud added the important technical innovation of raising to consciousness not only the patient's traumatic memories but the associated feelings as well, thus permitting a discharge of the previously withheld emotional response. Those observations were the first

step toward the formulation of a truly psychodynamic psychology, which Freud was shortly to elucidate in his theoretical considerations of dissociation.

Psychological Conflict: Emergence of a Basic Model

Freud and Breuer, it should be noted, adopted Janet's formulation that hysterical symptoms were the result of dissociated, unconscious memories of traumatic events. "Hysterics," they agreed, "suffer from reminiscences." However, in their explanation of the occurrence of the basic process of dissociation itself, Janet and Freud revealed a fundamental schism in their conceptual models. Janet, as we have already seen, had explained dissociation as the result of a pathological lowering of nervous energy that weakened the binding power of the self and its synthesis of mental functions so that certain elements escaped from voluntary control and consciousness. In his theoretical formulation in *Studies on Hysteria,* Breuer followed Janet's conceptual approach in ascribing the production of symptoms to a hypnoid mental state. According to Breuer, an individual who underwent an emotionally traumatic experience while in a spontaneously occurring hypnoid state of altered consciousness would fail to carry the memories of the event into consciousness upon returning to normal consciousness. The memories and associated emotions would consequently remain behind in a condition of dissociation, acting as a pathogenic focus for the formation of symptoms. In both Janet's and Breuer's etiological formulations, dissociation was viewed as the passive falling away of mental elements from the totality of the ego.

Repression and defense hysteria. Freud initially concurred wth Breuer's formulation, only briefly alluding in *Studies on Hysteria* to the mechanism of repression and to the syndrome of "defence hysteria" resulting from it. The conception behind these two terms was, however, the leading edge of a theoretical explanation of dissociation that resulted in a radically new formulation of the functioning of the human mind. As he subsequently developed his ideas (Freud, 1894, 1895, 1896), it became clear that Freud had laid the foundation for a psychodynamic psychology.

Freud proposed that certain mental elements (ideas, emotions, impulses) were unacceptable to the individual's ego because they were frightening, unethical, disgusting, or otherwise undesirable. Accordingly, the ego *actively forced* these unpalatable elements from consciousness and held them beyond voluntary recall in an unconscious dissociated state. Dissociation, in this theoretical model, was the result of the occurrence of psychodynamic mental processes as one part of the mind came into active conflict with another. The passive, static explanatory models of Janet and Breuer were replaced in Freud's formulation by a psychodynamic view of the mind that ultimately developed into the sophisticated psychoanalytic concepts of normal and pathological psychic functioning.

Freud's subsequent clinical work led to alterations in his therapeutic techniques and additions to his theoretical formulations. He gave up formal hypnosis and adopted instead the method of free association, which required patients to report every and all thoughts entering their mind during therapeutic sessions, however trivial or unpleasant they seemed. It soon became evident that this was an impossible task and that, however motivated to comply, patients either exhibited involuntary gaps and hesitations in their associations or consciously withheld information—a "resistance" that Freud recognized as the outward manifestation of the inner forces of repression he had postulated as causing dissociation. At the same time, as he worked with his patients over an extended period, he found them developing unrealistic feelings and attitudes about himself that appeared to be more appropriate to, and to result from, relationships formed in the early years of their lives—a phenomenon that he termed and that we now know as *transference*.

Early etiological formulations. Such was the state of Freud's thinking when he advanced his first etiological formulations of the neuroses. The traumatic theory of neurosis was basic to these early explanations, and in particular he learned from his patients that sexual traumas were involved in almost every instance (Freud, 1896). After such an event, Freud suggested, individuals initially protected themselves from the painful emotions associated with the subsequent traumatic memories by repressing both memories and affect. As a result, the undischarged emotional energy associated with memories of the trauma had to be processed further to prevent it from forcing its way back into consciousness. This was accomplished by specific mechanisms of defense: in hysterical neurosis, by *converting* the excess psychic energy into a somatic symptom; in obsessions and phobias, by *displacing* it to other seemingly harmless ideas. The choice of defensive process—and hence of symptoms—was determined by the patient's constitutional disposition, although Freud strongly disagreed with the French insistence that neuroses resulted from hereditary degeneracy. In Freud's view, neurotic symptoms could occur in people with sound heredity when they were confronted by a sufficiently painful trauma. Furthermore, as the number of his hysterical patients, most of them women, increased, he

discovered that although the outbreak of neurotic symptoms might follow an adult sexual trauma, his patients almost invariably reported an earlier painful sexual experience in childhood involving seduction by an adult—in most instances the father (Freud, 1896). These clinical observations led him to propose that the cause of hysteria lay in a sexual assault suffered passively in childhood.

As his clinical observations increased, Freud was forced reluctantly to modify this initial traumatic model of the pathogenesis of hysteria (Masson, 1985). In the course of his analysis of his own dreams and related associations, he became aware of memories of sexual feelings and fantasies extending back into his childhood—an awareness that was instrumental in his ultimate recognition that human sexuality, contrary to general belief, antedated the occurrence of puberty, and that early in life children normally experienced vivid sexual feelings and fantasies referable to a variety of bodily zones and directed at the significant people in their lives. From this realization the concept of the universal and orderly development of the child's libidinal drives from their earliest oral manifestations to their final stage of genital primacy gradually emerged. Concurrently, the child's personal relationships ran their course from the initial dyadic tie to the mother, through the triangular oedipal situation involving both parents, and then beyond to adult genital relationships with members of the opposite sex. In individuals who suffered distortions and arrests during these developmental stages, either from overtly traumatic experiences or from more subtly distorting patterns of relationships, internal psychological conflicts arose over unresolved infantile sexual drives and relationships—conflicts leading in adult life to psychoneurotic symptoms (Freud, 1905). In Freud's revised formulation, it should be noted, psychological trauma was viewed as being only one of a number of possible pathogenic factors. Janet's concept of the purely traumatic etiology of neurotic disorders was thus broadened to include a wide variety of chronic, internalized psychological conflicts as causal elements.

The topographic model. In the light of his observations, Freud fashioned a psychodynamic scheme of the human psyche and of symptom formation that guided his thinking and practice during the early years of the twentieth century (Freud, 1910). In this theoretical framework, which came to be known as the topographic model of the mind, two important forces, the libidinal and the life-preserving instincts, were in conflict. The life-preserving instincts were viewed as residing in the ego and as motivating the ego to control the libidinal instincts and to regulate their discharge in such a way as to preserve the individual's psychological and social integrity. An important element in the ego's control of the libido was the mechanism of repression, which rendered unconscious the dangerous and unacceptable elements of the sexual drive, along with the emotions and fantasies deriving from it. Furthermore, the psyche was seen as being made up of a conscious portion, the ego, and an unconscious portion containing the repressed libidinal elements. Though thus relegated to the unconscious by the ego's repression, the banished drives were not necessarily rendered inactive. Indeed, they tended to maintain a steady pressure for reemergence into consciousness and overt expression—often achieving this in the disguised form of ego-alien psychoneurotic symptoms.

The structural model. The topographic model functioned well as a guide for early psychoanalytic investigators and clinicians when their interest was focused on psychoneurotic disorders. However, with the application of psychoanalytic techniques and formulations to a wider range of emotional illnesses, it was found to be inadequate to encompass all the facts. When Freud turned his attention to clinical depression, he was forced to recognize a need to revise his theoretical conceptions. First of all, it became apparent from the observations of the vagaries of self-esteem in depression (and equally in megalomania) that narcissism, or "self-love," of which self-esteem and self-preservation were important elements, was a function of the libido's investiture of the self. If self-preservation was in fact merely a manifestation of self-directed libidinal instincts, then the topographic model's view of libidinal and self-preserving instincts as separate and conflicting forces could not be maintained (Freud, 1914, 1920).

Furthermore, it became evident that aggression had not been dealt with adequately in the earlier theoretical model, where it had been considered to be merely an intergral part of the masochistic and sadistic forms of the libidinal drive. From his exploration of the nature of aggression in the form of suicidal, self-mutilating, and self-castigating behavior in depressed patients, Freud was led to the conclusion that aggression was more than a shading of libido; it was a full-fledged drive in itself (Freud, 1917, 1920). His further discovery of unconscious ego functions (especially the defenses) and of the role of the superego (a mental agency neither clearly part of the ego nor an instinct) in producing clinical depression led Freud to recognize the inadequacy of the topographic model to encompass these facts. The consequent need to refashion his theoretical structure resulted in his proposing a new map of the mind, the so-called *structural model.*

With the transition from the topographic to the structural model, we come into the familiar territory of the id, ego, and superego, that troika of mental agencies into which the mind is divided in modern psychoanalytic theory. The focus of attention is no longer on topographically locating a mental event in the conscious or unconscious parts of the psyche but on the functional aspects of the 3 structural elements constituting the mental apparatus. The nature of these agencies is described in greater detail elsewhere (see Chapter 9). Their function will only be summarized here (see Freud, 1923).

The id is viewed as being the source of the instincts, or drives, which are experienced in consciousness by the ego as urges to action along with their accompanying emotions and fantasies, whose nature is determined by the motivating drive. The libidinal and aggressive drives provide the basic motivation for human behavior, normal and abnormal, and are the source of psychological conflict.

The ego is conceived of as a set of functions that enables the organism to adapt to its internal and external environment. Sensation, perception, logical thought, control of the motor apparatus, use of language, and testing of reality are all ego functions that underlie the purposeful behavior and survival of the individual in the universe. In particular, the ego controls the instinctual drives and channels their discharge in ways that bring gratification through behavior that is socially acceptable and physically harmless to the individual. Central to this controlling funtion are the ego defenses, which will shortly be more fully described.

The superego, a developmental offshoot of the ego, is the locus of the ego ideals, the individual's set of images of the kind of person one ought or would like to be. Vested in the superego is the capacity to observe oneself and one's behavior, and to judge whether that behavior accords with one's ideals. Finally, in its role as judge, or conscience, the superego causes the ego to experience a raising or a lowering of self-esteem as the individual does or does not live up to those ideals.

In the structural model the unconscious is no longer conceived of as being one of the component parts of the psyche. Rather, the term *unconscious* is now used to describe a quality of each of the 3 major divisions of the mental apparatus. The whole of the id and its drives is viewed as being unconscious, whereas the various component functions of the ego and superego may be either conscious or unconscious. Anxiety is also conceived of differently in the structural model. In the topographic model, anxiety was thought to be a direct somatic translation of undischarged repressed libido into physiological processes. In the structural model, anxiety becomes a property of the ego. As an ego affect, it acts as a signal of a forbidden id drive that is threatening to escape from control. Depression, the ego's response to the loss of either an important object or ideal self-image, is also an ego affect important for the maintenance of psychic equilibrium. Both anxiety and depression are painful ego affects that motivate the ego to undertake defensive operations designed to prevent or remove the conscious experience of psychic pain. Thus a more or less stable psychodynamic equilibrium is established among the various psychic agencies that are in psychological conflict with one another.

Before discussing the role of psychological conflict in the production of psychiatric disorders, it will be helpful to review in more detail the nature and variety of the ego defenses. The focus in what follows is on those defense mechanisms that play a role in the production of the psychoneurotic disorders discussed in Chapters 12, 14, 15. (For a more general discussion of the nature and variety of defense mechanisms, see Chapter 10.)

Ego Defense Mechanisms

Repression. The fundamental mechanism of ego defense, repression forces drives, affects, memories, and fantasies into the unconscious, and then maintains their active and continued exclusion from conscious awareness. Repression occurs automatically, outside the boundaries of consciousness. It thus differs from suppression, which is the volitional exclusion of thoughts and feelings from conscious attention. Repression is a universal and normal human mechanism. It is characteristically activated during the course of human growth and development at the end of the oedipal period, thus ushering in the latency phase around the age of 7 and rendering unconscious much of what had gone on before in the individual's life. This results in the phenomenon of infantile amnesia which underlies the universal inability of adults to remember their early childhood in any but the most fragmentary fashion. Repression, however, continues to be employed in later life as a mechanism of defense against specific anxiety-provoking thoughts and feelings that are aroused by the pressure of inner drives or by the stimuli of external events.

The effect of repression may be observed in the almost universal occurrence of forgetting a well-known name or of being unable to remember a dream on awakening. We know that we know the name or that we have dreamed vividly in the night just passed, but no amount of mental effort enables us to recall the forgotten contents. Indeed, in the attempt to recall them we catch repression in the act of excluding it from our consciousness. It becomes evident that the memory or image is not permanently erased from our minds when, at some later point in time, the "forgotten" name or dream suddenly flashes quite unbidden into our conscious awareness.

In a more clinical setting repression is responsible for the gaps in patients' memories of significant events in their lives. It is most strikingly manifested in the clinical condition of dissociative amnesia, in which the memory of whole segments of past life is lost to voluntary recall.

Susan H., a young woman of 18, was brought to the hospital in a state of confusion. Her mental clouding rapidly cleared after admission, but it was then evident that her mind was completely blank for the events of the 7 hours prior to coming to the hospital. She had no idea where she had been or what she had been doing and was surprised to find herself on a psychiatric ward. No amount of struggling to remember enabled her to recall what had happened, and it was only when she was put into a state of light hypnosis that her memory was restored. It was then discovered that the period covered by the amnesia had been one in which she had suffered an intolerable disappointment—abandonment by her boyfriend at a time when she desperately needed his help. By employing the defense of repression, she was able to protect herself against the emotional pain aroused by this event.

Denial. In the strict sense of the word, denial refers to denying the reality of an external fact. Its universality is evident in the immediate response of most people to being informed of an unexpected personal catastrophe: "It's not true!" Ordinarily reality rapidly asserts itself, and the individual confronts the painful fact with appropriate emotions and actions, but in some cases denial continues as a prolonged reaction of varying degrees of severity.

A young widow complained of headaches and an inability to grieve for her husband, who had hanged himself in the cellar some weeks before. In the initial clinical interviews the patient described how she could not bring herself to believe that her husband was dead. She kept everything in the house as it had been when he was alive, preserving his personal effects in the living room and keeping his clothes in the bedroom closet. Every evening she found herself setting his place at the dinner table and listening for the noise of his car in the driveway as she anticipated his return from work. Her sense of reality was not entirely shattered, however, for even while she was quite involuntarily behaving as if he were alive, intellectually she knew he was dead, although she could not experience it emotionally.

Denial is commonly seen in patients suffering from a physical illness who refuse to recognize the signficance of symptoms despite having information that should lead them to know better. Thus individuals frequently delay consulting their physician about the signs and symptoms of cancer even though they have repeatedly been exposed to information on cancer detection in the media. Or they will ignore chest pains suggesting a myocardial infarction despite the fact that a close relative has recently died of a heart attack after suffering similar symptoms.

If the defensive operations of repression and denial were entirely effective in banishing memories and affects from the mind, that would be the end of the matter. But as we have seen, the process of rendering something unconscious does not necessarily make it inoperative. On the contrary, an equilibrium of forces is created, with the excluded material, especially the drives and affects, constantly pressing for conscious expression and discharge. Thus repression and denial are not simply isolated, single acts of defense; rather, they continuously exert a countering energy against the material they have intially pushed from consciousness. In addition to repression and denial, a number of other ego defenses allow a partial representation in consciousness of the unacceptable mental contents in ways that render them tolerable to the ego. Each of these may constitute the primary defensive operation in itself, or they may individually or in combination be employed as defenses auxiliary to repression when the repressed material exerts an unusual degree of pressure and threatens to break through into consciousness.

Isolation. Isolation involves the separation of an idea from its associated affect, usually with the disappearance of the latter from conscious awareness. It is seen particularly in the ego's attempt to defend itself against the aggressive drive and is a common mental mechanism in those whose approach to the world is more thoughtful and intellectual than emotional. If not overdone, it is a useful psychological maneuver for professional people such as physicians who must deal with human misery and pain with sufficient detachment to be able to provide effective and rational clinical management. But when carried to an extreme, isolation compromises the full development of the human personality and leads to characterological abnormalities or overt psychiatric symptoms.

A patient with a pathologically exaggerated obsessional personality was almost totally devoid of feelings, especially those of anger and aggression. During one therapeutic session he reported having a fantasy that he had seen the therapist struck down by a truck on the street, and he described in almost too vivid detail his imagery of the therapist lying crumpled, bleeding, and broken on the pavement. He would infer from his fantasy, commented the patient, that he was angry at the therapist. "Do you feel that way?" asked the latter, to which the patient replied, "No," in a flat, emotionless, dry, matter-of-fact tone of voice. His response demonstrated the effect of the defense of isolation, which had excluded all feeling from conciousness but had permitted him to remain comfortably aware of a gory tapestry of destructive thoughts.

Isolation also less commonly refers to a process whereby the individual is prevented from seeing the connection between emotionally or causally related events. A patient may, for example, feel annoyed about something the therapist has said or done and shortly thereafter report a hostile fantasy about the therapist with no recognition of the relation of the one event to the other, despite the fact that their close temporal association would suggest a significant connection.

Displacement. In displacement, a drive or emotion is severed from its original connection with a person or event and is attached to a substitute person or object. With its origin thus disguised, the drive or emotion may more safely be expressed. Anger that cannot be shown to a superior at work is commonly unleashed on someone lower in the workplace hierarchy or on a member of the individual's family. The sexual fantasies of an adolescent for a teacher or for the parent of a friend often reveal the displacement of forbidden if thinly disguised libidinal desires for a parent. Displacement also forms an element in the transference that routinely develops in the doctor-patient relationship. The effect of displacement is often clearly observed in the transformations of anxiety that occur in the formation of phobic symptoms.

In a young woman with a severe phobia of boats, it was discovered in the course of analytic psychotherapy that her first serious sexual encounter had taken place in the cockpit of a sailboat—an event that had aroused in her simultaneously great sexual excitement and tremendous anxiety and guilt over feelings and behavior that she felt were utterly taboo. From that point on, as a result of the displacement of her sexual feelings and anxiety to the incidental and neutral setting in which her sexual arousal had occurred, boats came symbolically to represent the forbidden affects and to remain a lasting source of neurotic phobic anxiety. In the language of learning theory, boats had become a conditioned stimulus. Indeed, in the mechanism of displacement are to be found ego processes that provide a link between the concepts of psychoanalysis and learning theory.

Turning against the self. Similar to displacement, in that the drive or emotion is deflected from its initial object, turning against the self is a defense mechanism commonly employed in the psychological processing of anger and aggression, particularly as these feelings are related to depression.

A young woman came to the psychiatric clinic complaining of depression. It was discovered in the course of her evaluation that her depression was related to a recent move to a new house which had caused her to lose contact with several close friends and, in particular, with her mother, with whom she had an unusually close relationship. Furthermore, as it turned out, she had made the move not because she herself had wanted to but because she thought it would be better for her children in the new home. In an attempt to discover what she felt about the move, including possible elements of resentment toward her children for being in part responsible for her deprivations, it became apparent that not only did she experience no conscious resentment toward them, but, as we shall see in more detail in the discussion of the defense of reaction formation, she had *never* experienced any anger whatsoever toward them, no matter what they did or how provoking they might have been. She had never punished them in any way for fear of harming them. Indeed, she said that "rather than hurt them, I'd rather hurt myself," thus demonstrating a turning inward on herself of feelings of anger and aggression that would in fact have been quite appropriately directed toward her children.

Negation. In negation the underlying anxiety-provoking drive or emotion is readily evident, but it is expressed negatively. This occurs through the simple expedient of prefixing a negative to the expression of the feeling, impulse, or fantasy. A middle-aged man, for instance, had spent six months in a hospital for chronic, incapacitating back pain. He seemed on the surface quite blandly unperturbed by the absence of any significant relief of symptoms or improvement in his condition despite all of his physician's therapeutic efforts during this time. When asked how he felt about having literally been bedridden

throughout this entire period, he replied, "Do you mean, did I want to take that doctor and punch his nose all bloody and out of shape? Oh, no Doc, I never had any thoughts like that!"

Undoing. Undoing is generally associated with obsessive-compulsive disorder. With this defense the patient attempts to reduce the anxiety accompanying frightening impulses or fantasies, usually aggressive in nature, by retracting them in thoughts or actions. A young man, for example, would think each time he turned off a light switch, "My father is going to die." Then, overcome by anxious concern about this idea, he would say to himself, "I take back that idea," and his anxiety would be quieted. A patient described by Freud (1909) threw a branch of a tree lying on the sidewalk into the bushes beside the walk. Shortly thereafter he became obsessed with the thought that in its new position the branch might stick out so as to harm a passer-by. At some inconvenience to himself, he felt obliged to return to the spot and to replace the limb where he had originally found it. It should be noted in these episodes that both the original thought or action and the countering move of undoing have no relation to reality. They are a form of magical thinking stemming entirely from inner psychological processes.

Reaction formation. The defenses that have been discussed thus far are mental mechanisms that play a central part in the formation of discrete psychiatric symptoms. Reaction formation, however, is a defense mechanism that results in the creation of enduring behavior patterns that help to determine the nature and quality of the individual's character structure and personality.

Reaction formation is characteristically a defense against aggression, against dependency, and against passivity. In protecting themselves against the anxiety those mental elements arouse, individuals adopt and exhibit attitudes and patterns of behavior that are the exact opposite in character, thereby excluding the frightening elements from conscious awareness and expression.

Reaction formation against dependency needs (counterdependence) is perhaps best seen in those patients who deny a serious illness or who, when incapacitated by an illness or injury, fight against assuming the sick role. Closely related to counterdependency, reaction formation against passivity is commonly found in men who have underlying doubts about their masculinity and their physical strength and capabilities. Such individuals are bluff, tough, and rugged in their manner and their pursuits; they enjoy work demanding physical prowess and strength, will seek out tasks that present danger and challenge, and like to take on tasks and problems that have defeated other men. A patient, for example, who was hospitalized for a back injury sustained at work described his lifelong enjoyment of construction work that required him to operate huge cranes and powerful earth movers. He had always volunteered for dangerous assignments and boasted about his bravery in the face of physical hazards or personal injury. On one occasion, he reported proudly, he had continued working all day long after the terminal portion of his little finger had been torn off by a conveyor belt. He merely wrapped the injured hand in a makeshift bandage and reported to his doctor only after the workday was over.

Counterphobia. Related to, if not a special form of, reaction formation, the counterphobic defense is aimed specifically at the anxiety associated with phobic symptoms. As such it represents an attempt by the individual to turn the passive experience of a phobic situation into active mastery in such a way that the activity or situation that formerly caused painful anxiety is now a source of pleasure. Thus a person with a phobia of flying will learn to pilot an airplane, or one suffering from a fear of heights will take up rock climbing as a hobby.

Identification. The mechanism of identification is employed to protect oneself against the pain of the loss of a person with whom one has had an important relationship. Unlike imitation, in which there is a conscious attempt to mimic the behavior of others, identification involves unconscious processes that lead to the unwitting adoption of attitudes, attributes, and behavior patterns of the lost person—a mechanism that eases or obviates the experience of grief. A common form of such identification is seen in the display by a bereaved survivor of the symptoms of the illness from which a close friend or relative has died. A woman, for example, whose mother had succumbed to a myocardial infarction consulted her physician shortly thereafter because of chest pain and breathlessness that mimicked her mother's primary symptoms, but for which no pathophysiological basis could be detected. Similarly, through identification with the aggressor, one can often master the anxiety aroused by a person one fears. One commonly sees such a defense in children who, after a visit to the doctor or a trip to the hospital for surgery, subject a doll or sibling or companion to a playful reproduction of the shots received or the operation undergone.

Projection. A mechanism of defense that leads to both neurotic and psychotic phenomena, projection is most commonly found in that universal if unpleasant human propensity for creating scapegoats. One can relieve one's sense of guilt by blaming other people or external circumstances for events that are primarily of one's own doing. The projection of anxiety-provoking impulses is more serious for it often leads to paranoid delusions.

A young man began to feel that strangers talking to each other across the car from him in the subway were calling him homosexual. Not long after, when a man pressed against him in a subway rush hour crowd, he was convinced that this was a homosexual advance. A few days later an acquaintance held a lighted match to his mouth, requesting him to blow it out in order, he thought, to demonstrate his homosexuality to other people. Thereafter he was tortured by the conviction that everyone where he worked knew and talked constantly about his sexual preference. These conclusions were, of course, false; they arose from his own unrecognized unconscious homosexual drives, projected and played out in the external world.

Unlike most of the other defenses discussed thus far, projection causes a distortion in the perception and interpretation of the environment. However, the distortion alone does not constitute a full-blown delusion, for the individual may be fully aware that the perceptions, no matter how vivid and compelling, are not actually true. It is only when the capacity to distinguish inner fantasy from outer reality is lost—that is, when reality testing is absent—that the individual develops a delusional conviction that his perceptions are in fact "real"—a conviction that no amount of argument, fact, or evidence to the contrary can dispel.

Regression. The term *regression* is used in a general sense to refer to the retreat from a more mature developmental level of personality organization to behavior and thinking characteristic of an earlier phase of growth and development. Regression is often employed in a defensive way that enables patients to avoid the anxiety associated with psychological conflicts derived from the oedipal-genital phase of development by turning their attention to more primitive, pregenital stages of organization.

A young woman undertook psychotherapy because of an incapacity to form a lasting emotional tie with men. She would repeatedly enter into a new heterosexual relationship with hope and enthusiasm, only to find her ardor inexplicably cooling within a few weeks, leading eventually to a breaking off of the liaison. Early in the course of therapy she approached the subject of her strong sexual attraction to men, a topic that made her visibly anxious. She reported in her next therapeutic session that she had been anxious for a day or two following her previous session and then, in what seemed to be an abrupt change of subject, began talking quite freely, and in considerable detail, about her close attachment to and dependency on her mother. Her sudden, spontaneous shift to a preoccupation with her relationship with her mother, which she described easily and readily, without any sense of anxious discomfort, was a defensive response to her earlier anxiety when confronting her heterosexual feelings and fantasies. The regressive flow of her associations away from her anxiety-producing sexual feelings and fantasies to memories having to do with her preoedipal, little-girl ties to her mother allowed her to avoid the painful anxiety aroused by confronting her central pathogenic psychological conflict over heterosexuality.

Conversion and sublimation. Before leaving the subject of defense mechanisms, we should briefly consider two mental processes, conversion and sublimation, that are important for processing mental energies and helping the ego in its attempts to remain free of anxiety.

The term *conversion* appeared early in Freud's theoretical conceptions (Breuer and Freud, 1895) and represented for him the means by which repressed psychic excitation could be transformed into a somatic expression of the energies involved—a transformation manifested clinically as a sensory or motor hysterical symptom. The term *conversion hysteria* soon became, and remains today, as *conversion disorder,* indissolubly linked with somatic pseudo-neurological sensorimotor dysfunctions. *Sublimation* is another psychodynamic concept introduced early into psychoanalytic theory. It involves the neutralization of instinctual energy in such a manner as to render it conflict-free and available for derivative socially acceptable and useful activities—notably those involved in scientific and artistic pursuits. The concept is more relevant to psychoanalytic theory as a general system of psychology applicable to all of human behavior than to psychodynamic explanations of clinical psychopathology.

Dynamic Processes in the Development of Psychiatric Disorders

In our consideration of psychological structure and function, we have thus far been concerned mainly with what Hartmann and Kris (1945) have termed the "dynamic" aspect—that is, with "the interaction and the conflict of forces within the individual and with their reaction to the external world at any given time." However, as Hartmann and Kris have pointed out, the cross-sectional, dynamic view of the psyche is complemented by the equally important "genetic" aspect, which reveals "how any condition under observation has grown out of an individual's past, and extended throughout his entire life span." (The term "genetic," it should be noted parenthetically, is used here to refer to early developmental psychological phenomena, not to biological hereditary factors.) Accordingly, as we turn now to a consideration of the psychodynamic processes that underlie the development of clinical psychiatric disorders, we must examine both their dynamic and psychogenetic characteristics.

The Role of Psychological Conflict in the Development of Psychiatric Disorders

Normal Psychological Equilibrium

In the psychologically normal human being (a mythical figure, perhaps, but one that many persons approximate), the conflicting forces of the various psychic elements result in a stable equilibrium that permits the individual to function in a mature, adaptive, self-fulfilling way. Realistic about and responsive to the surrounding world, the individual is capable of experiencing a wide range of feelings, of entering into lasting and satisfying human relationships, and of working creatively and effectively. The person's drives, although controlled by the ego, find ready avenues to expression in constructive activities without being warped, stunted, or constricted. In such individuals the balance among the psychological elements and a flexibility in their interaction maintain their mental equilibrium or facilitate its prompt restitution if it is temporarily disrupted by emotional stress.

Distortions of the Psychological Equilibrium

In many people, permanent distortions of their psychic structure lead to constrictions in their lives (often visible in their behavior and human relationships), even though, within limitations, they may function for long periods of time with a measure of success. Individuals, for example, in whom isolation of affect is a central defense mechanism often appear to their acquaintances to be emotionally distant and reserved; yet they may at the same time be very effective at jobs requiring intelligence, reason, and logical thought. Such distortions, however, though compatible with living a conventional and successful life, render them vulnerable to the outbreak of psychiatric symptoms in the face of environmental stresses to which their emotional conflicts make them specifically sensitive.

The young woman with a phobia of boats, mentioned in the earlier discussion of displacement, had functioned reasonably well in her daily life at school and at home during the greater part of her adolescence. She was, however, unusually naive and ignorant about sexual matters that were commonplace knowledge among her friends. Her virginal innocence was matched by the absence of curiosity about sexuality and a lack of interest in the exploratory sexual behavior usual in adolescents. Her behavior and the quality of her relationships, in other words, appeared to be the result of a repression of libido that brought about an exaggerated inhibition and constriction of normal adolescent sexuality.

The patient's defense functioned effectively for several years, and her psychological equilibrium remained stable and unshifting until her later teens. It was then that she met a young man of more than passing interest to her, who put mounting pressure on her to engage in physical sexual activity. Though growing increasingly anxious, she controlled herself until one day, when they were out sailing, her own desires were roused to a point where she finally yielded to his demands and indulged in extensive foreplay short of intercourse. For a few days thereafter she was overcome by profound guilt and a mounting anxiety that persisted until ultimately their defensive displacement onto boats resulted in the emergence of her crippling phobic disorder.

In psychological terms these developments can be understood as follows: For several years the patient's psychological equilibrium had allowed her to function reasonably smoothly and comfortably, although it had caused a marked constriction of her sexual life and activities. However, as the relationship with her boyfriend developed, increasing stress was imposed on her psychic equilibrium as the repressed libido was stimulated to more open expression. The initial effect of the stress was evident in her growing anxiety, but no major shift in her inner equilibrium occurred until the episode on the boat. At that point the defense of repression was momentarily overpowered, resulting in her sudden surge of acute guilt and anxiety. The ego was motivated by those emotions to bring forth auxiliary defenses, first by displacing the libido and associated anxiety to the image of boats. As the result of that displacement, boats now became the primary source of the patient's anxiety, which she could keep under control by using the further defense of avoiding the anxiety-provoking object. A new equilibrium was thus established that enabled the ego to regain its control over the instinctual impulse and the anxiety associated with it. It was, however, an equilibrium quite different in structure from the one that had existed before. It was now characterized by the emergence of a clinical psychiatric symptom, the phobia, which imposed greater restrictions on the patient's life and freedom of motion than she had experienced before the shift in equilibrium had occurred. Now, in addition to her restrictions in engaging in sexual activity, she could not venture near the oceanfront of the town in which she lived for fear of seeing a boat, nor could she look at television, attend the movies, or read the daily paper without an acute fear that she might run across the picture of one—a state of affairs that was as incapacitating and limiting as a severe physical illness.

Anger and the impulse toward aggressive behavior are equally powerful sources of psychological conflict and anxiety. Harvey M., a man in his mid-30s, was admitted to a psychiatric unit in a general hospital for the evaluation of chronic pain and weakness in his legs. During the early part of his hospitalization the patient was observed to be consistently cheerful, mild-mannered, compliant with ward routines, uncomplaining, and totally undemanding. In clinical interviews he expressed concern that the pain and weakness in his legs had forced him to give up work, but denied any emotional problems or conflicts in his personal relationships. Indeed, he reported, he had always got along well with everyone at home and at work. He could not remember a time in his life when he had been angry or been in an argument; he had always been amiable, easygoing, and adaptable to the wishes of others. He was particularly close to his wife, with whom he exhibited the same equitable, smooth, unruffled kind of relationship that characterized his general social behavior. He found himself now increasingly dependent on her because of the incapacitation resulting from his symptoms, but he denied any tensions or difficulties between them because of that dependency.

The patient's stay in the hospital coincided with the Thanksgiving holiday, which occurred about ten days after his admission. It marked a sudden and radical change in his behavior, which was immediately evident in his clinical interview the following day. He came into the doctor's office trembling, hyperventilating, sweating, agitated, and complaining of intense anxiety that had begun the night before, had steadily increased in intensity, and had kept him awake all night long. Despite his agitation, however, he was able to talk readily in the interview and indeed seemed to gain relief from being able to express and describe his feelings of anxiety. He had never experienced anything like them before, and he was totally mystified and bewildered by them. Nothing had happened, he insisted; why should he feel that way?

Initially the patient talked only about his feelings of anxiety. Then, well into the session, he mentioned spontaneously that he had been surprised to find that in addition to being anxious, he had begun to feel irritable as well. Furthermore, as the evening before had worn on, he had been deeply distressed to find himself preoccupied with increasingly destructive thoughts and urges—such as smashing the dishes in the ward kitchen, or tearing up all his bedclothes, or destroying the furniture in the day room. As the patient revealed more and more of these feelings and images, he became increasingly anxious. Finally, the doctor said to him quietly, "Perhaps this is what you are so anxious about." At that, the patient burst into tears and sobs, exclaiming, "Yes! I was afraid I'd just go totally berserk—do a real job on everything and everybody over there on the ward!"

With that outburst the patient became noticeably calmer, and his anxiety gradually subsided. From then on he talked quietly and easily about his inner experiences during the day on Thanksgiving. He had, he said, been "half hoping, half expecting" that his wife would call him. As the day wore on and there was no word from her, he began to feel increasingly sad and lonely. Then, late in the afternoon, he suddenly had a momentary flash of annoyance at his wife. "Dammit! Why couldn't she call!" he thought to himself, and then immediately felt guilty and made excuses for her, reminding himself that she was busy making Thanksgiving dinner for all the rest of the family at home. With that, he put the whole subject out of his mind. It was shortly thereafter that he went to bed and began to experience the early phases of the anxiety that led to the sequence of events that has been described.

It takes little in the way of reflection to recognize the origins of Harvey M.'s anxiety, which, by the time he arrived at his doctor's office the day after Thanksgiving, had reached the level of outright panic. From what had been learned about his personality structure and the nature of his personal relationships, it had become evident that anger and aggression had been a lifelong source of psychological conflict for him and that he had controlled his aggressive drive by the ego defense mechanisms of isolation of affect and reaction formation. These had functioned effectively for him throughout his adult life, until the equilibrium between the drive and the defenses against it had been severely stressed by the arousal of the patient's underlying rage when his wife failed to call him on Thanksgiving day. As a consequence, the anger began to overcome the constraining defense mechanisms and to emerge into conscious expression, thus arousing anxiety that represented a reaction to and a signal of its escape from control.

Finally, as demonstrated by these two clinical vignettes, it should be noted that anxiety occupies a central position in the realm of psychiatric disorders. On the one hand, from a diagnostic point of view, anxiety is a ubiquitous phenomenon, either constituting a syndrome in its own right or appearing as a prominent symptom in other psychiatric disorders. On the other hand, from a psychodynamic point of view, anxiety serves as a marker of psychological conflict and is thus an important guide to the exploration and understanding of the psychological processes that underlie psychiatric illness. Whenever anxiety is a feature of the patient's disorder, it should alert the clinician to the necessity for including a psychodynamic assessment in the patient's overall clinical evaluation.

The Developmental (Psychogenetic) Component of Psychiatric Disorders

As we have noted earlier, the interplay of psychological forces that make up the psychic structure of the adult is the result of a long period of growth and development. It has a history that includes an infinitude of shaping experiences in childhood that have helped to determine the adult personality. The roots of psychiatric disorders lie in psychological disturbances during those early formative years, and it is as important (if often more difficult) for the psychiatrist to uncover and understand those psychogenetic factors in illness as it is to dissect the psychodynamic forces involved.

Developmental Arrests and Adult Symptoms

George M., a married man of 34, consulted a doctor because of increasing anxiety over an obsessional thought that he had bumped into people he passed, especially "older persons," causing them to fall and injure themselves. He was particularly concerned that he had knocked bystanders on subway platforms onto the tracks, where they had been run over by a train and killed. He had grown so alarmed over this fantasied possibility that he had given up traveling by subway, and had called the transit authority's main office on several occasions to make sure that no one had been killed in that fashion. In direct association to that symptom, he reported that when he was 3½ his father had shot himself in a state of depression following injuries from a fall at work that had left him incapacitated. As, over 30 years later, the patient recounted the circumstances of his father's death, he burst into deep sobs, lamenting his loss and the fact that he had never had the chance to know and enjoy a paternal relationship. The patient was particularly surprised by this uprush of feelings, for he could not remember ever having experienced them before.

From a dynamic point of view it was evident that the patient's anxiety was a marker of a serious conflict over aggression, the destructiveness and intensity of which were indicated by the violent nature of his fantasies. Further evidence of the importance of this conflict lay in the fact that he had always been concerned about being aggressive. He could remember only one occasion in his life when he had been angry, and he described himself as a person who had consistently tried to be friendly, agreeable, and "easygoing" no matter what provocation he might have had to become angry. Reaction formation had clearly been a central ego defense throughout his life.

In the search for the psychogenetic roots of the patient's psychoneurosis, two observations are helpful: (1) the marked similarity between the patient's obsessional concern that he would harm others by knocking them down and the circumstances of his father's suicide in a state of depression that had had its inception in an incapacitating fall; and (2) the fact that 30 years after that event, the patient for the first time in his memory had experienced and expressed sadness over his father's loss with a keenness as if it had occurred only yesterday. The normal process of mourning that would ordinarily have attenuated his grief appeared to have been blocked, leaving the emotion alive and poignantly fresh over the many years that had elapsed since the tragic event.

Let us reflect for a moment on the psychological state of a little boy of 3½ years in the normal course of his growth and development. At that age he is emerging from the anal-aggressive phase, with all of the attendant ambivalence, aggression, and concern over control of emotions and body functions. He is entering the early phase of the oedipal period, characterized not only by erotic fantasies and longings for the mother but also by a highly ambivalent relationship with the father—a mixture of admiration and love and of intense rivalry and aggressive competition accompanied by hostile and destructive fantasies. At the same time, the ego's perception of reality is not yet

firmly established; the child believes that his thoughts are omnipotent and that he can effect changes in the physical world merely by thinking that they will happen.

It is not surprising that, occurring at the time of a developmental phase when such a mental set was predominant, the death of his father should have had a profound and lasting effect on the patient. The magical conviction of the omnipotence of his infantile thought was confirmed as reality matched his fantasy. As a result, he experienced a strong sense of guilty responsibility for his father's demise and developed a fearful respect for the power of his aggressive drive. From then on it was necessary to keep aggression under strict control. Reinforced by the fateful events in his environment, the mental constellation characteristic of that age remained fixed, impervious to the forces of normal development that would ordinarily have tempered his aggressive drive and modified his ego functions in the direction of more mature and rational thinking. The distortion in his psyche that was thus created persisted as a fixation point into his adult years, to reemerge in a psychoneurotic illness that had many of the qualities characteristic of the childhood stage of development in effect at the time of the original trauma.

Much of the foregoing reconstruction of the psychogenesis of George M.'s illness is inferential, based on general knowledge of the sequential phases of human psychological development, not on his own memories of that period of his life and the sad occurrence that disrupted it. In Sally K., however, a married woman of 26, we can see directly and convincingly the connection between adult symptoms and traumatic childhood events.

Sally K. was admitted to the psychiatric ward of a general hospital because of severe anxiety mixed with depression. Her symptoms had started some six months before in response to the abrupt appearance of a phenomenon that puzzled and shocked her. One morning, for no apparent reason and without forewarning, she suddenly thought of herself and her father clinging naked together in a sexual embrace. From that time on the thought occurred regularly, totally against her will and despite her attempts to banish it from her mind, and she found herself repeatedly preoccupied with the erotic vision. It was the mounting anxiety and despair in the face of this unshakable phantom that caused her to seek medical help.

As her history unfolded over a series of interviews, several additional important facts emerged. The imagined scene had initially appeared at a time when the patient's father, after a long period during which they had had no communication, had generously offered to help her over some financial difficulties. She was surprised and troubled by his overtures, since, as she vehemently insisted, she and her father had absolutely nothing in common. Indeed, in a lengthy protest, she elaborated on the fact that, far from being close to him, she had always hated him, had always felt tense and uncomfortable in his presence, and had consistently avoided all contact with him whatsoever.

Questioned by the interviewer about the passionate (and suspicious) urgency of her denial of her closeness to her father, she at length reported that they had not always been so distant. As a little girl she had, in fact, been his favorite, and he had regularly showered affection and attention on her, at times going so far as to take her into bed with him in innocent but affectionate play. One day, when she was 11, and was hanging on the arm of his chair while he read the paper, she suddenly had the image of the two of them locked in a naked embrace. Shocked and terrified, she ran to her mother. Although the image had not recurred, she had kept emotional and physical distance from her father thereafter.

As the patient revealed this information in a therapeutic session, her anxiety became intense and she was for a time unable to talk. At length, however, as the interview came to an end, she brought forth a new fact: she had regularly slept in a crib in her parents' bedroom until she was nearly 6. The following day she reported yet a further fact: the night before her distressing symptoms had suddenly appeared, she had had a nightmare in which she saw and heard animals noisily mating in a zoo. In direct association to her dream she recaptured a long-lost memory of having waked in the middle of the night at the age of 5 to observe her parents having sexual intercourse. When they noticed her watching them, they sprang apart, and her father angrily ordered her back to sleep. As she described this event, the patient was once again consumed by almost paralyzing anxiety that took several minutes to abate. The recitation was, however, followed by an immediate and complete disappearance of all her symptoms—a clinical remission still present on a follow-up visit several months after her discharge from the hospital.

Even in this condensed history, the psychogenetic roots of the patient's adult neurosis are clear. As a part of her normal growth and development she was, at the age of 5, in the midst of an oedipal attachment to her father, with all its attendant erotic fantasies and wishes. Occurring at this phase of her psychosexual evolution, the witnessing of her parents' sexual activity (not only on the occasion recounted but quite possibly on others as well, in view of the fact that she slept regularly in their bedroom) intensified her libidinal attachment to her father to an abnormal degree. As a result, the process of normal development, which would ordinarily bring about an attenuation of this attachment, was distorted, and the patient remained fixated in her incestuous ties. Subjected to the repression that accompanied the onset of latency, the whole complex went underground. It emerged from its unconscious state in the transient initial outbreak of her symptom when the patient was 11, following which she redoubled her defensive efforts against the dangerous incestuous impulse through her angry avoidance of any relationship with her father. Thus protected, she was able to move through adolescence to adulthood, marriage, and motherhood, but the unresolved oedipal tie rendered her liable to further neurotic difficulty, which erupted under the stressful stimulation of her father's attempt to help her—an approach that activated the underlying incestuous impulse and intensified it to the point where it once again emerged in the form of a psychoneurotic illness.

Developmental Arrests and Patterns of Adult Relationships

In the two patients whom we have just examined, our focus has been on the role of early life events in the production of adult neurotic symptom disorders. It is important to recognize that early life events may also lead in adulthood to pathological patterns of behavior and human relationships. Although the latter are perhaps more subtle and harder to describe than overt psychiatric symptoms, they are often equally incapacitating and distressing to the individuals who suffer from them. That fact is readily apparent in a final patient to be considered now, who not only suffered from serious neurotic symptoms but also found her relationships with men seriously compromised by pathological patterns of behavior whose origins could be traced back to her childhood.

In 1910 Cécile V., an unmarried schoolteacher in her mid-40s, consulted Dr. Theodore Flournoy, professor of psychology at the University of Geneva, because of a deeply troubling and recurrent pattern of behavior. Although most of the time she lived the sedate, chaste, and proper life of an Edwardian schoolmistress, she would on occasion find herself invaded by lewd sexual fantasies and dreams, accompanied by an overpowering libidinal drive that led her to masturbate and, she hinted, more rarely to sexual encounters with men. After a week or two the storm would pass, and she would return to being her usual prim self, troubled, guilty, and filled with remorse at her loss of control.

Flournoy saw the patient over a long period of time during which he obtained a detailed history of her life, in part directly from her verbal account and in part from the frequent letters she sent him and from a journal in which she described the course of her difficulties (Flournoy, 1915). From these sources the unusually virginal and sexually innocent quality of her adolescence becomes apparent. As she reported to Flournoy, she had always been aware that her sisters and her school classmates had had their sexual "secrets," but she herself had remained totally ignorant of their substance and had had no curiosity or desire to learn about them.

During her nineteenth year she was seduced by a man considerably her senior, who, as she put it, precipitated her "completely unprepared into the furnace of sexual emotions and of brutal, filthy revelations." Panic-stricken and sick at heart, she consulted a textbook in her father's library to seek enlightenment about what had happened but succeeded only in becoming terrified that she was pregnant. From then on, however, she led an active social life, with numerous male friends and suitors until the death of her father some 12 years later. His demise coincided with her experiencing a religious conversion, which gave her a measure of control over her passionate feelings, broken only by the periodic eruptions of uncontrolled erotic emotions and behavior for which she eventually consulted Flournoy.

Of particular interest was the nature of the pattern of her relationships with men. She would repeatedly be attracted to individuals much older than herself, who usually were married and who, as she quite openly recognized, strongly resembled her father. Initially the friendship would be based on mutual intellectual and artistic interests, but invariably sexual passion would emerge, producing in the patient a crisis of conscience of such turbulence that she would be forced to break off the liaison, only to start the process all over again with another man. As a result the patient had reached middle age without having married and without having allowed herself the human satisfaction of a lasting, loving relationship.

The dynamic aspects of the patient's disorder are clear. Central to her difficulty was a profound conflict over her sexual drive. During the greater part of her adolescence it had been controlled by the defense of repression—so tightly controlled that the patient not only had had none of the libidinal strivings and fantasies normal for girls of

her age but had lived in total ignorance of all things sexual. After her rude awakening at the age of 18, the full force of her sexual drive was unleashed, and the conflict over sexuality became overt, not only causing her deep mental anguish but also determining the course of her frustrating, repeatedly abortive relationships with men.

It is in her journals and her letters to Flournoy that we discover the psychogenetic roots of her adult conflict, for there she reveals to us two important facts. First, she describes her emotional isolation in childhood from all the members of her family save her father. He, she reported, "was alone able to win my heart," and from her earliest years there existed between them a "delicious intimacy." She developed for him an "affection that was exclusive, passionate, and jealous"—an affection that continued through the first decade of her life into the early part of her adolescence. The second psychogenetic element arose from events in her sixth year. At that time she was taught to masturbate by one of the maids in the family ménage, a practice that she initially adopted with wild abandon, mixed from the start with intense shame, guilt, and emotional conflict. Although she is not explicit in her written account, she apparently soon gained control over her sexual activity and during her latency period and adolescence had no memory of this earlier behavior, which, like everything associated for her with sexuality, was subjected to the massive repression noted earlier. Only with the reappearance of her libidinal drive after her seduction at 18 did she recall these experiences, feelings, and practices of her childhood, a recollection colored by the same guilty horror that attended and blighted her ensuing adult sexual life.

Despite the differences in their adult behavior and neurotic disorders, a central feature is common to Cécile V. and Sally K.—namely, the failure of both to resolve their oedipal ties to their fathers. During the period of Cécile V.'s early childhood before the latency phase, an intense attachment to her father and a marked conflict over genital sexuality were present. The disappearance of much of this conflict during her adolescence was more apparent than real. It was merely rendered unconscious by a pathological degree of repression that prevented any awareness whatsoever of her libidinal strivings. With this degree of inhibition, she was unable to engage in the usual adolescent exploratory heterosexual behavior and relationships that normally attenuate childhood ties to the father and open up new channels for an eventual mature, adult experience of love and marriage with a suitable man. In Cécile V. the normal processes of growth and development had been blocked, and her sexual drive remained fixated at the oedipal phase. When it reemerged into consciousness with her seduction at 18, it was unchanged. With its incestuous coloring unmodified, not only did it determine her repeated choice of paternal men in relationships that bore the stamp of her unresolved tie to her father, but also in each instance, as sexual feelings for her partner grew in intensity, their unmodified oedipal character made them a source of intense anxiety and conflict. As a consequence, the patient was forced to reject such forbidden desires and to break off the relationship. Imprisoned in her past, she could only repeat it endlessly in her future.

Preoedipal Fixations and Borderline Characteristics

In the patients whom we have examined thus far, the emphasis has been on the psychogenetic origins of their adult disorders in fixations at the oedipal phase of their development. In each of them existed a potential capacity for forming a positive, adult relationship with other human beings—a capacity inhibited and distorted by conflicts arising from those fixations that set the stage for the emergence of psychoneurotic illness in adulthood.

In many individuals, however, the potential for such adult relationships is severely limited or does not appear to exist at all. Instead of reaching out to others with a love (however circumscribed by psychological conflicts) that altruistically recognizes the other's emotional needs and attempts to satisfy them, such individuals form relationships that are based on a narcissistic dependency that seeks selfishly to gratify their own wants without regard for the needs of others. Hand in hand with such a degree of dependency goes a potential for violent and destructive aggression if the dependent needs are not gratified. (Though strongly controlled by his ego defenses, such a reactive aggression could be observed in Harvey M., whose attack of acute anxiety was described earlier.) The relationships established by such individuals are characterized by a profound ambivalence, by repeated attempts to manipulate others to gain their own ends, by a tendency to see others as either completely good or totally bad, by a propensity for experiencing slights and rejections where none has occurred, and by distortions in ego functions characterized by the use of projective defense mechanisms and by a difficulty in distinguishing fantasy from reality.

In this large group of individuals with narcissistic and borderline personality traits (whose clinical and psychodynamic features are described in greater detail in Chapter 15, "Personality Disorders"), the psychogenesis of their disorder lies in the preoedipal phase of their development. Inadequacies in parental care during their earliest stages of psychological growth, when the child's needs for nurturing are paramount, lead to fixations at

the level of oral dependency, primitive aggression, and immature ego functions that are carried on into adult life. f particular importance is the fact that such individuals do not develop the capacity for a basic trust in the goodwill, concern, and caring qualities of other people. They approach every relationship with the conviction that it will bring them pain and harm, and until they are certain of their ground, they maintain a guarded distance from emotional ties.

This fundamental suspiciousness of others has an important bearing on the psychotherapy of such patients, as contrasted with those whose psychoneurotic disorders stem primarily from oedipal conflicts. The latter enter into therapy with the expectation that the physician is there to help them. They at once form a therapeutic alliance with the therapist, within the framework of which they are enabled from the start to examine their inner conflicts with an objective self-observation and an emotional distance from their feelings and fantasies that allows them to achieve therapeutic insights. With borderline patients, however, the initial phases of treatment must be devoted to establishing their sense of trust and to creating the therapeutic alliance without which insight psychotherapy cannot be carried out. Indeed, in many borderline patients the capacity to develop insight may be severely limited if not completely absent, and the improvement they achieve in therapy is based mainly on the positive relationship they are gradually able to form with their physician. In such patients, furthermore, the attempt of the therapist to focus on their dependency needs and primitive aggression may result in their being overwhelmed with unmanageable emotions and fantasies—a situation that will preclude the formation of a stable therapeutic relationship. All too often, thoughtless and uncritical attempts to probe the emotional depths of borderline patients will make them worse rather than better.

In the light of these clinical facts, it is evident that as one assesses each new patient, it is important to distinguish between those whose problems arise primarily from oedipal conflicts and those whose disorders are mainly preoedipal in origin. The planning of appropriate treatment measures must rest on a careful evaluation of the dynamic and psychogenetic aspects not only of patients' symptoms but of their personality characteristics and patterns of relationships as well.

The fact that the vocabulary used throughout this discussion of the psychodynamic aspects of psychiatric disorders has been psychological in nature should not be construed to mean that the function of the brain is irrelevant. On the contrary, modern clinical research has not only elucidated the biological underpinnings of affective and cognitive processes but also resulted in the development of pharmaceutical agents that have revolutionized the treatment of many affective and cognitive disorders. Indeed, the success of the psychopharmacological management of psychiatric illness has in recent years tended to push psychodynamic observation and treatment into the wings—to the detriment of patients' often vital needs for emotional understanding and support. The biological and psychodynamic elements of psychiatric disorders, far from being mutually exclusive, provide complementary information about their etiology and offer important indications for the proper combination of medical and psychological treatment measures. Only by evaluating both aspects of the illness of each patient they examine will psychiatric clinicians escape the dangerous error of restricting their outlook to what William Blake has called "Single vision and Newton's sleep" (Keynes, 1932).

References

Breuer, J., and S. Freud. 1895. Studies on hysteria. In *Standard edition,* ed. J. Strachey. Vol. 2. London: Hogarth Press, 1955.

Flournoy, T. 1915. Une mystique moderne. *Arch. Psychol.* 15:1–224.

Freud, S. 1894. The neuro-psychoses of defence. In *Standard edition,* ed. J. Strachey. Vol. 3. London: Hogarth Press, 1962.

——— 1895. On the grounds for detaching a particular syndrome from neurasthenia under the description "anxiety neurosis." In *Standard edition,* ed. J. Strachey. Vol. 3. London: Hogarth Press, 1962.

——— 1896. The aetiology of hysteria. In *Standard edition,* ed. J. Strachey. Vol. 3. London: Hogarth Press, 1962.

——— 1905. Three essays on sexuality. In *Standard edition,* ed. J. Strachey. Vol. 7. London: Hogarth Press, 1953.

——— 1909. A case of obsessional neurosis. In *Standard edition,* ed. J. Strachey. Vol. 10. London: Hogarth Press, 1955.

——— 1910. Five lectures on psycho-analysis. In *Standard edition,* ed. J. Strachey. Vol. 11. London: Hogarth Press, 1957.

——— 1914. On narcissism: an introduction. In *Standard edition,* ed. J. Strachey. Vol. 14. London: Hogarth Press, 1958.

——— 1917. Mourning and melancholia. In *Standard edition,* ed. J. Strachey. Vol. 14. London: Hogarth Press, 1958.

——— 1920. Beyond the pleasure principle. In *Standard edition,* ed. J. Strachey. Vol. 18. London: Hogarth Press, 1955.

——— 1923. The ego and the id. In *Standard edition,* ed. J. Strachey. Vol. 19. London: Hogarth Press, 1955.

Goetz, C., M. Bonduelle, and T. Gelfand. 1995. *Charcot: constructing neurology.* New York: Oxford University Press.

Hartmann, H., and E. Kris. 1945. The genetic approach in psychoanalysis. *Psychoanal. Study Child* 1:11–30.

Janet, P. 1889. *L'automatisme psychologique.* New ed. Paris: La Société Pierre Janet, 1989.

Keynes, G., ed. 1932. *Poetry and prose of William Blake.* London: Nonesuch Press.

Masson, J., trans. and ed. 1985. *The complete letters of Sigmund Freud to Wilhelm Fliess, 1887–1904.* Cambridge, Mass.: Harvard University Press.

Recommended Reading

Ellenberger, H. 1970. *The discovery of the unconscious.* New York: Basic Books.

Freud, S. 1915–1917. Introductory lectures on psycho-analysis. In *Standard edition,* ed. J. Strachey. Vols. 15 and 16. London: Hogarth Press.

Gabbard, G. 1994. *Psychodynamic psychiatry in clinical practice: the DSM-IV edition.* Washington, D.C.: American Psychiatric Press.

Janet, P. 1907. *The major symptoms of hysteria.* New York: Macmillan.

Nemiah, J. 1961. *Foundations of psychopathology.* New York: Oxford University Press.

Nersessian, E., and R. Kopff, Jr. 1995. *Textbook of psychoanalysis.* Washington, D.C.: American Psychiatric Press.

Anxiety Disorders and Their Treatment

MICHAEL W. OTTO

MARK H. POLLACK

MICHAEL A. JENIKE

JERROLD F. ROSENBAUM

The ability to identify and avoid harm is a crucial feature of adaptive functioning. Anxiety, the body's warning signal of potential harm, is a powerful inhibitor of ongoing behavior, helping the organism attend to potential threat and prepare for defensive behavior. Arousal is heightened, attention narrows toward available threat cues, and the body may mobilize the fight-or-flight response. A general correspondence between the intensity and duration of the anxiety and the actual aversive event defines normal anxiety. When the intensity or duration of the anxiety experience is excessive or when attempts to terminate the anxiety lead to regular disruptions in functioning, a diagnosis of pathologic anxiety may be warranted.

Anxiety disorders as a group are the second most common psychiatric disorder behind drug and alcohol abuse, occurring at a lifetime prevalence of about 25% in the general population (Kessler et al., 1994). The prevalence appears even higher in medical populations, in whom excessive utilization of medical resources and increased levels of dependence and disability are common (Simon and von Korff, 1991; Klerman et al., 1991). Anxiety manifests with physical, affective, cognitive, and behavioral symptoms. Physical symptoms associated with anxiety reflect autonomic arousal, including tachycardia, hyperventilation, tremor, light-headedness, and gastrointestinal distress. The affective state may range from uneasiness and edginess to extreme terror and panic. The cognitive symptoms include worry, apprehension, and a focus on potential harm. Behaviorally, anxiety results in a wide range of avoidance or compulsive behavior designed to minimize discomfort associated with feared situations or events. Although anxiety may be a universal experience and an expected transient response to stress, pathological levels of anxiety cause marked levels of distress and interfere with functioning.

Etiology of Anxiety Disorders

Genetic and family studies provide evidence of the heritability of emotional reactivity (Barlow, 1988; McNally, 1994). One temperamental construct that has received converging empirical support is Kagan's "behavioral inhibition to the unfamiliar" (Kagan, 1994; Kagan, Reznick, and Snidman, 1987). This term is used to describe children characterized by a predisposition to be irritable as infants, shy and fearful as toddlers, and quiet, cautious, and introverted at school age. These children, characterized by physiological arousal and behavioral restraint in response to unfamiliar situations, are also at risk for the development of anxiety disorders (Biederman et al., 1990; Rosenbaum et al., 1991). Presumably, both the elevated physiological response to external cues as well as strong tendencies toward inhibition and avoidance place behaviorally inhibited children at risk for anxiety disorders. The actual emergence of an anxiety disorder, however, appears to be a function of the shaping experiences to which the developing child is exposed and the cognitive and behavioral coping skills or deficits developed over time. On the negative side, dysfunctional thinking patterns (cognitions), particularly inflated expectations about the likelihood or seriousness of aversive events, can influence the ease by which pathological anxiety may be elicited. These faulty expectations may be a product of a variety of logical errors resulting from misinformation (e.g., "All dogs are dangerous," or "It is dangerous for my heart to beat fast"), overestimation of the probability of negative outcomes (e.g., "I will be fired for my errors," or "My plane will crash"), or direct exposure to traumatic experiences (e.g., "I was attacked on a night like this"), as well as the failure to discriminate between currently safe and past unsafe or aversive conditions (e.g., "I will be criticized just like I was at home"). Regardless of the source of these thoughts, they share in common the ability to elicit anxiety in response to relatively innocuous events, setting the stage for the development of anxiety disorders.

Once anxiety is elicited, avoidance and neutralization responses represent attempts to turn off the anxiety signal. These strategies bring with them additional problems that may perpetuate anxiety disorders. Avoidance prevents individuals from learning more adaptive responses to feared situations and deprives them of the opportunity to learn that expected dire consequences do not emerge following exposure to the phobic stimulus. Moreover, the illusion of escape from "dire circumstances" can help maintain phobic concerns and anticipatory anxiety and motivate future avoidance behavior (e.g., "I would have lost control if I hadn't left the seminar"). With chronic avoidance, individuals lack the opportunity to reestablish a sense of safety in feared situations.

These learning perspectives on the etiology of anxiety are complemented by attention to central nervous system activity in anxiety disorders. A number of lines of evidence suggest that there are at least two central systems involved in pathologic anxiety. Central noradrenergic mechanisms, particularly related to the locus ceruleus (LC), the primary source of brain norepinephrine, have been implicated in panic attacks (Redmond and Huang, 1979). When the LC is stimulated, an acute fear response can be elicited. Agents that alter LC firing rates (e.g., antidepressants or high potency benzodiazepines) are used in clinical practice as anti-panic agents. Benzodiazepine receptors in central nervous areas, including the septohippocampal area, appear to play an important role in generalized anxiety, worry, vigilance, and anticipation (Gray, 1985). Benzodiazepine receptors in relevant limbic structures may modulate alert, arousal, and behavioral inhibition by increasing binding of the inhibitory neurotransmitter gammaaminobutyric acid (GABA) (Tallman and Gallagher, 1985). There are extensive neuronal connections between the LC and limbic system structures. In addition, abnormalities in central serotonin function appear important in the genesis of pathologic anxiety, although the exact nature of this relationship remains to be fully elucidated (Westenberg and Den Boer, 1994). Peptides such as corticotropin-releasing factor and cholecystokinin also appear important in the activation of pathologic levels of anxiety (Bradwejn et al., 1992; Yehuda and Nemeroff, 1994). The redundancy and control of the central anxiety system is reflected in the variable mechanism of action of pharmacologic agents and other interventions used to treat anxiety disorders.

Psychodynamic perspectives on anxiety disorders emphasize developmental experiences. Freud's early work implied a physiological basis for anxiety attacks in terms of undischarged libido; later emphasis suggested that anxiety was a signal of threat to the ego, with these signals elicited because certain events and situations (symbolic or actual) were similar to early developmental experiences threatening to the vulnerable child, such as separation or loss. More recent psychodynamic postulations suggest a focus on the importance of separation experiences, object relations, and the use of internalized resources to maintain affective stability under stress (Shear, 1996).

The major explanatory models of anxiety disorders are not mutually exclusive. Constitutional vulnerabilities to pathologic anxiety may become manifest in the face of specific developmental experiences, sustained adversity, or trauma, and be maintained by faulty cognitive and behavioral patterns. A constitutional vulnerability is presumably shaped by developmental experience, either harmful or protective, and activated by environmental factors. Likewise, individual differences in one's ability to tolerate anxiety as well as the likelihood of responding to anxiety with avoidance appear to help determine whether a full anxiety pattern is developed.

Treatment Considerations

Well-controlled studies provide clinicians with the ability to see beyond the biases of their own clinical experience and to observe the outcome of large numbers of patients described in controlled treatment protocols. Large clinical trials, however, provide a perspective based on the average responses that can be expected with a well-characterized group of patients at a defined level of severity; it is up to the clinician to expand upon these initial findings with individual treatment efforts. Empirical studies, then, provide one source of information to inform, guide, and improve clinical practice.

To date, the most studied and the most efficacious treatments for anxiety disorders include pharmacologic and cognitive behavioral treatments. This does not mean that treatments based on other approaches and using other methods are not effective; instead, it suggests that at this point in time, pharmacotherapy and cognitive behavior therapy (CBT) have been most exposed to the bright lights of empirical scrutiny and have demonstrated efficacy under these conditions (for meta-analytic reviews of the anxiety treatment outcome literature, see Feske and Chambless, 1995; Christensen et al., 1987; Clum, Clum, and Surls, 1993; Durham and Allen, 1993; Gould, Otto, and Pollack, 1995; Gould et al., 1997; Gould et al., in press;

Greist et al., 1995; Hunt and Singh, 1991; Otto et al., 1996).

Both cognitive behavioral and pharmacologic treatments intervene in the self-perpetuating patterns characterizing anxiety disorders but tend to intervene at different points. Cognitive behavioral treatments for anxiety disorders are designed to bring a variety of exposure, cognitive restructuring, and symptom management techniques to target the core fears and behavioral patterns of each disorder. Pharmacologic treatments are aimed most directly at the attenuation or suppression of the affective and somatic symptoms of anxiety. With the anxiety symptoms more under control, patients are in a better position to eliminate maladaptive cognitive and avoidance responses. Pharmacologic agents for anxiety disorders are summarized in Table 12.1.

The degree to which cognitive behavioral and pharmacologic treatments are successful in bringing about long-term changes depends on the degree to which they can chronically alter anxiety-producing (anxiogenic) patterns. Cognitive behavioral treatments target changes in cognitive and overt behavior; and if new patterns of behavior are established, treatment changes should be maintained over time (Juster and Heimberg, 1995; Otto and Whittal, 1995). In contrast, pharmacologic treatment can be expected to be most effective when: (1) ongoing pharmacologic suppression of anxiety symptoms is maintained, (2) patients make enduring changes in cognitive and behavioral responses to anxiety sensations and phobic situations during the course of medication treatment, or (3) patients experience changes in their environment such that the anxiety response is no longer elicited. Research findings support these basic observations. When anxiolytic medications are continued, treatment responses tend to be maintained over follow-up periods (Mavissakalian and Perel, 1992). In contrast, when medi-

Table 12.1 Standard pharmacopoeia for anxiety disorders

Agent	Initial Dose (mg/d)	Typical Dosage Range (mg/d)	Limitations/Primary Side Effects
Serotonin Selective Reuptake Inhibitors (SSRI)			
clomipramine (Anafranil)	25	25–250	Sedation, weight gain, TCA side effects
fluoxetine (Prozac)	10	20–80	Jitteriness
fluvoxamine (Luvox)	50	150–300	Sedation, GI distress
paroxetine (Paxil)	10	20–50	Sedation, GI distress
sertraline (Zoloft)	25	50–200	GI distress
Other Novel Antidepressants			
nefazodone (Serzone)	50	300–500	Sedation, GI distress
venlafaxine (Effexor)	18.75	75–300	Jitteriness, GI distress
Tricyclic Antidepressants (TCA)			
imipramine (e.g., Tofranil)	10–25	100–300	Jitteriness, TCA side effects
Monoamine Oxidase Inhibitors (MAOI)			
phenelzine (e.g., Nardil)	15–30	45–90	Diet restrictions, MAOI side effects
tranylcypromine	10	30–60	
Benzodiazepines			
alprazolam (Xanax)	0.25 qid	2–8/day	Sedation, discontinuation difficulties, potential for abuse, psychomotor and memory impairment
clonazepam (Klonopin)	0.25 hs	1–5/day	As above
lorazepam (Ativan)	0.5 tid	3–12	As above
oxazepam (Serax)	15	30–60	As above
Buspirone (Buspar)	5 tid	15–60/day	Dysphoria
Beta-Blockers			
propranolol (e.g., Inderal)	10–20	10–160	Depression (maintenance use)

cation is discontinued, relapse is common unless additional treatment is instituted (Noyes et al., 1989; Noyes et al., 1991; Schweizer, 1995; Pato et al., 1988).

Because both pharmacologic and cognitive behavioral treatments are effective options, the choice of treatment depends in part on patient preference, treatment availability, and contraindications to one or another treatment modality. Also, in the context of these empirically validated treatments, it is difficult to evaluate the role of more traditional psychotherapy in selecting an initial intervention. Supportive and psychodynamic treatments seldom have been examined in controlled treatment trials, and the available evidence provides a mixed picture. For example, supportive therapy, enhanced with a strong informational component, performed well for the treatment of panic disorder in one short-term trial (Shear et al., 1994). In other trials, supportive treatments for panic disorder (Beck et al., 1992) or social phobia (Heimberg et al., 1990) were found to offer treatment benefits that were clearly inferior to those of cognitive behavioral interventions. As noted, the absence of empirical evidence does not imply that a treatment is not effective, only that the magnitude and time course of benefit is not known. Consequently, the assumed benefit of supportive or psychodynamic treatments for anxiety disorders must be evaluated against the relatively better-known benefits of cognitive behavioral or pharmacologic alternatives. In addition, for select patients, couples or family therapy may need to be considered as supplemental strategies.

For any intervention, patients should be given clear expectations about the nature of treatment, alternative strategies, and the benefits expected to emerge with each. With this information, clinicians and patients can collaboratively select an initial treatment strategy, evaluate the progress of treatment, and decide if and when an alternative strategy should be implemented. As reflected by the results of empirical trials, clear benefit can be expected for a number of empirically supported interventions well within the first 2 to 3 months of treatment; the absence of such benefit should motivate consideration of the need for alternative or adjunctive strategies.

In summary, the choice of treatment for each patient is a decision that incorporates clinical availability, patient preference, potential for adverse effects, and efficacy over both the short and long term. Ongoing monitoring of treatment response will help ensure that the outcome of treatment is evaluated relative to other logical options. With these considerations in place, we will focus in the remainder of this chapter on the modalities of treatment that have consistent empirical support: cognitive behavioral and pharmacologic interventions.

Panic Disorder

Patients with panic disorder experience recurrent and unexpected panic attacks followed by at least a month of persistent concerns about additional attacks, worry about the implications of the attack, anticipatory anxiety, or significant changes in behavior (e.g., avoidance) related to the attacks (American Psychiatric Association, 1994). As with other psychiatric disorders, the anxiety attacks cannot be viewed as the physiological effects of a substance and cannot be better accounted for by anxiety episodes occurring during other anxiety disorders, such as social phobia, specific phobia, or post-traumatic stress disorder. Panic attacks themselves are defined as a period of intense fear or discomfort developing abruptly and reaching a peak within 10 minutes. Panic attack symptoms include: (1) rapid heart rate, (2) palpitations, (3) sweating, (4) hot flashes or chills, (5) shaking or trembling, (6) shortness of breath, (7) choking sensations, (8) chest pain or discomfort, (9) abdominal distress or nausea, (10) dizziness and light-headedness, (11) derealization or depersonalization, (12) fears of losing control or of going crazy, and (13) fears of dying.

The severity and frequency of panic attacks vary widely. While some patients may have panic attacks once or twice a week, other patients may have attacks on a daily basis. Some patients may reduce the frequency of attacks by avoiding situations which trigger them. An additional diagnosis of agoraphobia is given if there is the presence of fears or avoidance of situations from which escape may be difficult or embarrassing or where help may not be readily available in the event of a panic attack. Agoraphobic situations commonly include being alone; traveling in a bus, car, or train; being in or on bridges, elevators, grocery stores, long lines; or reexperiencing any situation in which the patient previously experienced a panic attack. Some patients push themselves through this fear and enter these feared situations despite considerable anxiety, while others avoid these situations or require a companion to accompany them.

In comparison to the criteria in the third edition of the *Diagnostic and Statistical Manual of Mental Disorders* (DSM-III-R; American Psychiatric Association, 1987), the fourth edition (DSM-IV) deemphasizes the number of panic attacks required for the diagnosis and places much more emphasis on the fear of attacks. It is this fear that leads to avoidance and to the development of chronic arousal and anxious apprehension about further attacks. The focus on the fear of anxiety symptoms in panic disorder is also consistent with the recognition of additional avoidance behaviors that frequently occur with the disorder, including the development of fears of exercise, caffeine, sexual activity, or other activities or events that produce sensations of arousal reminiscent of anxiety or panic situations.

Associated Disorders

Complications with panic disorder include other anxiety disorders, depression, alcohol abuse, excessive use of medical facilities, somatization, decreased physical and social functioning, increased financial dependence, and vocational dysfunction (Markowitz et al., 1989). In addition, men with panic disorder and phobic anxiety appear to be at increased risk for premature death from cardiovascular causes (Coryell, Noyes, and Clancy, 1982; Kawachi et al., 1994).

Social phobia frequently co-occurs with panic disorder, and when panic attacks occur in a social situation, the differential diagnosis between panic and social phobia is sometimes difficult; nonetheless, examination of the patient's core fears aids diagnosis. In panic disorder the core fear is of having a panic attack, and this fear should be evident outside of social situations. In contrast, patients with social phobia may panic upon exposure to social scrutiny, although their concern centers on the possibility of humiliation or embarrassment in social situations.

Generalized anxiety disorder (GAD) also frequently co-occurs with panic disorder, and may occur in up to 30% of cases (Brown and Barlow, 1992; Pollack et al., 1990). In GAD, patients are excessively worried about a number of life events or stressors in addition to the typical anticipatory anxiety focusing on the possible recurrence of a panic attack. A lifetime history of *major depression* occurs in approximately two-thirds of patients with panic disorder (Ball et al., 1994; Uhde et al., 1985). This depression may either predate or emerge after the onset of panic disorder. For some patients the depression may reflect a reactive demoralization to the negative effects of panic on their lives, while for others the comorbidity may reflect the emergence of an independent condition.

Epidemiology and Course

Panic disorder with and without agoraphobia has been found to occur in approximately 3–6% of the population (Kessler et al., 1994). It is more commonly diagnosed in

women than in men; there is approximately a 3:1 ratio of patients with agoraphobia and a 2:1 ratio of patients without agoraphobia. The average age of onset for panic disorder is typically in the third decade; however, consistent with the diathesis model for panic disorder discussed above, more than half of adult patients with panic disorder begin experiencing significant difficulties with anxiety in the form of overanxiousness, social phobia, or separation anxiety during childhood (Pollack et al., 1996). Initial panic attacks appear to occur spontaneously, but most individuals with panic disorder are able to identify a life stressor that appeared to herald the disorder (Manfro et al., in press).

Treatment of patients with panic disorder involves pharmacologic and/or cognitive behavioral interventions. For many patients, combined treatment with both types of therapy may provide optimal short-term outcome.

Pharmacologic Treatment

Tricyclic antidepressants, serotonin selective reuptake inhibitors, monoamine oxidase inhibitors, and high potency benzodiazepines are all effective treatments for panic disorder. The tricyclic antidepressant imipramine has the longest history of use for panic disorder, and along with clomipramine, has been intensively studied. The typical dose of tricyclic is approximately 2.25 mg/kg/d (100–300 mg/d) aimed at achieving a blood level of 75–150 ng/ml of imipramine plus desipramine or its metabolites (Mavissakalian & Perel, 1995). Initial antidepressant treatment may be associated with increased anxiety; consequently, treatment should be initiated with low doses on the order of 10 mg/d, with gradual titration upward as tolerated. In addition, treatment with tricyclic antidepressants is associated with a variety of side effects which make both acute and long-term treatment difficult, including anticholinergic effects such as dry mouth, blurred vision, constipation, orthostatic hypotension, cardiac conduction defects, weight gain, and fatality in overdose. Studies suggest that a significant proportion of panic patients treated over the long term discontinue treatment with antidepressants because of side effects, particularly weight gain (Noyes et al., 1989). More recently, the serotonin selective reuptake inhibitors (SSRIs, including fluoxetine 20–80 mg/d, sertraline 50–200 mg/d, paroxetine 20–50 mg/d, fluvoxamine 150–300 mg/d) have become first line agents for the treatment of panic disorder as well as the other anxiety conditions because of their broad spectrum of efficacy and favorable side effect profile. Positive clinical experience in open trials has been bolstered by data from large-scale controlled trials demonstrating the effectiveness of SSRIs for panic disorder. Like the tricyclic antidepressants, these agents may worsen anxiety on initiation of treatment, and accordingly treatment of panic patients or the anxious depressed should be initiated at half the usual starting dose for depression (i.e., 5–10 mg fluoxetine, 25 mg sertraline, 10 mg paroxetine, 25 mg fluvoxamine) and titrated upward after the first week.

Onset of benefit for the SSRIs and other antidepressants usually begins after 2 to 3 weeks of treatment. The SSRIs are generally better tolerated for acute and long-term treatment than the older antidepressants, yet may be associated with transient or persistent side effects including anxiety or sleep disturbance, gastrointestinal symptoms, and sexual disturbance. Other newer agents such as venlafaxine, nefazodone, and mirtazapine are also probably effective for the treatment of panic disorder, though they have not been widely tested for this indication. Limited data suggest bupropion and trazodone may be relatively less effective for panic disorder than the other standard agents.

The monoamine oxidase inhibitors (MAOIs) (phenelzine 45–90 mg/d, tranylcypromine 30–60 mg/d) have demonstrated efficacy for panic disorder in clinical use and controlled trials and are considered by many clinicians to be the most comprehensively effective agents for treating panic disorder and its complications, including atypical depressive features. MAOIs do not generally cause the early anxiogenic response associated with other antidepressants, but over time may be associated with side effects including insomnia, weight gain, edema, sexual dysfunction, and myoclonus that make treatment difficult. In addition, the need for careful dietary monitoring and concerns about hypertensive reactions associated with MAOI treatment may be particularly daunting to anxious patients. Generally, the SSRIs offer a similar spectrum of efficacy as the MAOIs with a superior safety and side effect profile and are generally used first in most patients, with MAOIs reserved for patients failing to respond to other first line interventions.

All benzodiazepines are effective for the treatment of generalized anxiety symptoms and sleep disturbance. The high potency benzodiazepines (HPBs; e.g., alprazolam, clonazepam) appear to have particular efficacy for the treatment of panic disorder at typically used therapeutic dosages. The HPBs have the advantage of being well tolerated with a relatively rapid onset of effect and high safety profile. The disadvantages of benzodiazepines include early sedation associated with initiation of treatment (managed by keeping the initial dose low), memory impairment, and the potential for abuse in individuals with a history or tendency toward drug or alcohol abuse. Although dose escalation does not typically emerge as an issue in patients with panic disorder, patients do become physiologically dependent on the benzodiazepines and may have trouble discontinuing them because of emergent withdrawal symptomatology. Consequently, benzodiazepines need to be tapered very gradually in order to decrease the propensity for emergent symptomatology, although many patients continue to have difficulties despite slow taper strategies. In addition to these issues, benzodiazepines are not generally effective as a monotherapy for comorbid moderate to severe depression in individuals with panic disorder. Some clinicians may initiate combined treatment with antidepressants and the high potency benzodiazepines in order to combine the rapid antianxiety effects associated with the benzodiazepines and decrease activation associated with the initiation of the antidepressants, as well as provide coverage of comorbid or benzodiazepine-induced depression. For some of these individuals, benzodiazepines may be tapered a few weeks after the antidepressant begins to take effect, although patients may often remain on combined treatment.

Alprazolam is commonly administered in doses of 2–8 mg/d, with most patients achieving benefit at around 4–6 mg/d. Treatment is generally initiated at 0.5 mg tid to minimize early sedation, with a gradual stepwise increase thereafter (over weeks to months) to a maintenance dose. Because of its relatively short half-life, alprazolam is administered on a qid basis, and patients may experience rebound anxiety because of its pharmacokinetic properties. In addition, patients who miss doses or are discontinuing treatment may also experience increased anxiety, particularly with shorter-acting agents. Clonazepam is a longer-acting benzodiazepine that can be given twice a day and, because of its longer half-life, is associated with less interdose rebound anxiety. Clonazepam is twice as potent as alprazolam and is administered on a bid basis at 1–5 mg/d, with most patients achieving benefit at 2–3 mg/d.

Cognitive Behavioral Treatments

Historically, cognitive behavioral treatments for panic disorder focused primarily on the agoraphobia that accompanies panic disorder. Stepwise exposure techniques encouraged patients to reenter and remain in feared situations despite initial anxiety, and helped patients learn that their catastrophic fears did not materialize. Such treatment, applied alone or in combination with medications, was found to be markedly successful for the treatment of agoraphobia. Moreover, the last decade has brought a refinement in cognitive behavioral techniques, with the development of new strategies to target the fears of panic symptoms that are a core feature of panic disorder itself. These newer treatments emphasize cognitive restructuring and exposure interventions to help patients modify and eliminate anxious apprehension and fears of panic.

Cognitive techniques tend to focus on patients' distortions of the probability and degree of catastrophe associated with the feared consequences of panic attacks. Informational interventions, Socratic questioning, logical analysis, and behavioral experiments (direct examination of the sequelae of feared activities) are the mainstay of cognitive interventions. In addition, fears of the somatic sensations of anxiety (anxiety sensitivity) are directly modified with "interoceptive" exposure procedures that expose patients to feared bodily sensations. For example, purposeful hyperventilation may be used to induce numbness, tingling, and dizziness to help patients eliminate the fear of these symptoms. As fears of symptoms decrease, patients no longer respond to sensations of arousal with panic, and regular evocation of panic attacks can be eliminated.

Cognitive behavioral programs emphasizing cognitive restructuring and interoceptive exposure typically begin with a strong informational component that provide patients with a cognitive behavioral model of the disorder and the rationale for the interventions to follow. Breathing retraining (emphasizing slow, diaphragmatic breaths) and muscle relaxation training may also be applied to help patients eliminate anxiogenic responses. For patients with agoraphobia, additional situational exposure sessions are assigned (for manualized treatment programs, see Barlow and Craske, 1993; Otto et al., 1996).

Treatment programs emphasizing such interventions are frequently delivered in 12 to 15 sessions and are associated with panic-free rates of above 74% (Barlow et al., 1989; Beck et al., 1992; Clark et al., 1994). Maintenance of gains also tends to be high with these treatments, although waxing and waning of panic-free status among treated patients (Brown and Barlow, 1995; Otto and Whittal, 1995), suggests that some patients may require "booster" sessions over time to maintain treatment gains.

Combined Treatments

A variety of studies suggest that adding exposure therapy alone to pharmacologic treatment improves acute treatment outcome and leads to greater retention of treatment gains over time (Gould, Otto, and Pollack, 1995; Telch and Lucas, 1994). These findings argue for the regular application of exposure instruction in all pharmacologic care of patients with panic disorder. In addition, CBT has been found to be effective for improving outcome for patients who are non-responders or partial responders to pharmacologic treatment (Pollack et al., 1994). Cognitive behavioral treatment packages have also been applied successfully to problems of medication (particularly benzodiazepine) discontinuation in patients with panic disorder (Otto et al., 1993; Spiegel et al., 1994).

The addition of medications to cognitive behavioral treatment also appears to aid treatment response in the short term; however, the limited evidence available to date suggests that over the long term the efficacy of CBT alone approximates that for combined pharmacologic and cognitive behavioral treatment (Telch and Lucas, 1994).

Social Phobia

Social phobia is characterized by a persistent fear of one or more social or performance situations that invoke intense anxiety, distress, or avoidance and result in significant impairment in a person's social or role functioning (American Psychiatric Association, 1987). At the core of the phobic concern are fears that the individual may act in a way that is embarrassing or humiliating; these fears may include fears of saying something foolish, appearing foolish, showing anxiety symptoms, or making mistakes. Although public speaking fears are not uncommon in the general population, it is the intensity of the distress and the interference with the patient's functioning that result in the diagnosis of social phobia.

Social phobia may be defined in terms of a generalized or specific subtype. The specific subtype refers to difficulties with circumscribed situations or performance anxiety, the most common being public speaking, but also including actions such as using a public bathroom, or eating or writing in front of others. The generalized subtype of social phobia is diagnosed if fears extend to most social situations including participating in small groups, dating, initiating and maintaining conversations, or speaking to authority figures. The generalized subtype, if severe and chronic, is very difficult to discern from avoidant personality disorder. Indeed, it has been suggested that there is no qualitative difference between these two disorders, although there is a quantitative difference, with the most severe social phobics tending to earn the additional diagnosis of avoidant personality disorder (Turner, Beidel, and Townsley, 1992).

Epidemiology and Course

The lifetime prevalence of social phobia is approximately 13%, making it the third most common psychiatric disorder in the community after alcohol dependence and major depression. In the community, social phobia is more prevalent in women than men (Schneier et al, 1992). The average age of onset of social phobia is approximately 16 years, although the distribution of age at onset is both bimodal and positively skewed. The first peak age of onset occurs at approximately 5 years of age followed by a second peak at 13 years (Schneier et al., 1992).

As with the other anxiety disorders, social phobia is associated with a chronic and unremitting course without treatment, and tends to run in families (Fyer et al., 1995; Juster and Heimberg, 1995). Social phobia is often comorbid with other anxiety disorders, including panic disorder and generalized anxiety disorder, and individuals with these co-occurring anxiety disorders also tend to have high rates of depression. Rates of alcohol abuse and dependence are particularly high in social phobics (Kushner, Sher, and Beitman, 1990), perhaps because anxiety and distress for social phobics occurs in situations where alcohol is available as a maladaptive coping response.

Pharmacologic Treatment

The MAOIs (phenelzine and tranylcypromine) have been the most widely studied agents for the treatment of social phobia, and have repeatedly demonstrated efficacy. More recently, an expanding body of clinical research and some data from controlled trials suggest the efficacy of the SSRIs (e.g., fluoxetine, sertraline, paroxetine, and fluvoxamine) for social phobia as well (Pollack and Gould, 1996). Tricyclic antidepressants appear less effective for social phobia than the other agents. In addition, the HPB clonazepam has demonstrated efficacy for the treatment of social phobia in doses similar to those used in panic disorder (Davidson et al., 1991). The beta-blockers (i.e., propranolol 20–80 mg/d, and atenolol 50–150 mg/d) have also been found to be effective for the treatment of the performance subtype of social phobia. The beta-blockers are generally administered an hour before the patient undergoes the performance situation (e.g., recital, public speaking). They presumably work by eliminating some of the peripheral autonomic symptoms such as tremor and tachycardia and decrease the patient's perception that he or she is visibly anxious. Beta-blockers are generally less effective for the cognitive symptoms of fear and are not as effective as the other agents mentioned for the treatment of generalized social phobia.

Cognitive Behavioral Treatment

Cognitive behavioral formulations of social phobia emphasize the role of expectations of embarrassment or humiliation in intensifying anxiety and disrupting performance in social situations (Heimberg and Barlow, 1991). Because of predictions of negative outcomes (e.g., "Others will notice my anxiety and think I am odd"; "I will say something stupid and be rejected"), patients with social phobia are predisposed to experience excessive autonomic arousal in social situations. This arousal helps increase attention to the expected adverse consequences of poor performance, thereby escalating anxiety and motivating avoidance.

Cognitive behavioral treatments for social phobia have traditionally included cognitive interventions, exposure interventions, their combination, and social skill training interventions (Heimberg, 1989; Juster and Heimberg, 1995). Studies of exposure-based treatments have provided consistent evidence for their efficacy. Exposure interventions help patients enter situations and allow them to dissipate their fear by staying and performing adequately in these situations. The elimination of safety signals (e.g., tensing to minimize trembling hands or having a drink at a party) is associated with greater benefit following exposure (Wells et al., 1995), presumably because it allows patients to learn fully that social situations are "safe" rather than "lucky escapes" owing to safety behaviors. Exposure also provides patients with an opportunity to enhance their competence in social situations while building confidence in their ability to meet their goals despite initial anxiety. Cognitive restructuring interventions seek to enhance any exposure effects by helping patients better direct their attention and cognitive abilities toward relevant cues (e.g., their speech or the conversation) rather than anxiogenic thoughts. Social skills training—including instruction, modeling by the therapist, and practice by the patient with corrective feedback—is aimed most prominently at enhancing social competence. In addition, relaxation procedures for social anxiety may also be a useful adjunct to other interventions.

In initial cognitive behavioral sessions, patients are provided with a wealth of information on the nature of anxiety conditions and self-perpetuating cycles between anxiogenic cognitions, anxiety responses, and avoidance behaviors. Patients are taught to identify both their cognitive distortions in social situations and the logical flaws in their thinking. They are then introduced to stepwise exposure with practice in the group setting. That is, the social phobia group provides an audience for exposure and rehearsals (to a variety of social situations and interactions) in role-playing situations.

After its long being considered a "neglected anxiety disorder," the recognition of social phobia as a highly prevalent, distressing, and disabling disorder has increased research efforts toward understanding its nature and treatment (Liebowitz et al., 1985). Both pharmacologic and cognitive behavioral treatments have demonstrated efficacy for the treatment of social phobia (Gould and Otto, 1996), with future research aimed at the relative benefits of these interventions used individually or in combination for particular patients.

Post-traumatic Stress Disorder

Patients with post-traumatic stress disorder (PTSD) have experienced a catastrophic event that would be clearly distressing to anybody (i.e., facing a serious threat to one's life, having one's home destroyed, being assaulted or raped, or being in a combat situation with a threat to physical integrity of self or others) and an emotional response characterized by intense fear, helplessness, or horror. PTSD is characterized by symptoms in three domains, including reexperiencing phenomena, avoidance reactions, and high levels of autonomic arousal (American Psychiatric Association, 1994).

Reexperiencing symptoms include recurrent, intrusive recollections and dreams of the trauma, perceiving and acting as if the trauma were recurring ("flashbacks"), and the experience of significant distress upon exposure to events that represent aspects of the traumatic event. Avoidance of thoughts, feelings, and activities associated with the trauma, as well as difficulties recalling important aspects of the trauma, a sense of a foreshortened future, emotional blunting (including decreased interest in usual activities), feelings of detachment or estrangement from others, and a decreased ability to feel emotions (especially those associated with intimacy, tenderness, and sexuality) are all defined as avoidance symptoms. Finally, symptoms of increased arousal may include difficulties falling or staying asleep, difficulties concentrating, hypervigilance, an exaggerated startle response, and irritability or angry outbursts. Duration of these symptoms must be at least 1 month, and must result in clinically significant distress or impairment in social or role functioning.

Acute Stress Disorder, a new diagnostic category in the DSM-IV, describes reactions to extreme stress lasting up to 1 month. An acute stress disorder is characterized by reexperiencing, avoidance, and increased arousal symptoms that last for a minimum of 2 days and a maximum of 4 weeks and that occur within 4 weeks of the traumatic event.

PTSD is hypothesized to be most likely to develop when the traumatic event is perceived as both uncontrollable and life-threatening (Foa, Steketee, and Rothbaum, 1989), and symptom profiles are remarkably similar among PTSD sufferers regardless of the source of their trauma (e.g., combat, rape, physical assault, etc.; Keane and Wolfe, 1990). Higher levels of social support and economic status as well as low levels of avoidance of trauma cues are associated with a lower likelihood of emergence of PTSD (Burnam et al., 1988; Jones and Barlow, 1990; Steketee and Foa, 1987).

Epidemiology

According to the Epidemiologic Catchment Area survey, the prevalence of PTSD is 1% in the general population, with PTSD occurring in civilians who suffer life-threatening accidents or assaults, or who have survived natural disasters (Helzer, Robins, and McEvoy, 1987). Estimates of the lifetime prevalence rates for PTSD range from 1–9% (Breslau et al., 1991; Davidson et al., 1991), with significantly higher rates among high-risk groups such as combat veterans (Keane, Litz, and Blake, 1990).

Pharmacologic Treatment

Traditionally the pharmacotherapy of PTSD has been targeted at the most prominent associated symptoms (i.e., antidepressants for depression and panic symptoms, benzodiazepines for anxiety, anticonvulsants for mood and stability and rage, clonidine for autonomic arousal, and neuroleptics for psychotic symptoms). Recently the SSRIs have been applied to the treatment of PTSD, with data from open and controlled trials supporting the clinical impression of efficacy of these agents. Although there are no clear guidelines for dosing of the SSRIs for PTSD, general clinical practice is to use doses typical for the treatment of other anxiety and depressive disorders. At least one study with fluoxetine suggested potentially greater benefit for some patients at higher dose levels (i.e., 60 mg/d) than lower doses (van der Kolk et al., 1994)

Given the high levels of co-occurring mood and anxiety disorders in patients with post-traumatic stress disorder, initiating pharmacotherapy with an SSRI is a reasonable clinical strategy, either alone or in combination with cognitive behavioral interventions.

Cognitive Behavioral Treatment

A variety of theoretical approaches emphasize the importance of exposure to memories of the trauma to aid in the emotional reprocessing of the experience. The goal of this exposure is to help individuals reestablish a sense of safety and control in their lives following exposure to a traumatic stressor, and to eliminate the many conditioned emotional responses to trauma cues that may impair adaptive functioning (Foa and Kozak, 1986; Otto et al., 1996). Exposure therapy can be conducted in a range of formats including discussions of the trauma, structured review of memories (in verbal or written form), guided imagery, hypnosis, or exposure to trauma cues in vivo (e.g., returning to the site of a trauma).

One goal of exposure is to help patients discriminate between the terrifying conditions of the original trauma, trauma-related emotional memories and fears, and the current degree of safety and control available to them. Patients are provided with adaptive coping skills to deal with the symptoms and emotions emerging in the wake of this exposure. In addition, review of the meaning of the trauma provides patients with a format for evaluating changes in belief systems caused by the trauma and its aftermath. The efficacy of exposure-based treatments is supported by numerous case reports and open trials as well as a select number of controlled studies. Although the treatment outcome literature is limited by the small number of controlled studies conducted to date, it appears that CBT currently offers some of the most optimal treatment outcome for PTSD (for review, see Otto et al., 1996). Empirically validated treatment packages for specific types of PTSD are currently available (e.g., treatment of rape-related PTSD; Resnick and Schnicke, 1993).

Combined Treatments

As conceptualized by van der Kolk (1994), the goal of treatment for PTSD is to aid current functioning by helping patients differentiate past traumatic experiences from current reality. He suggests that medications "are often essential for patients to begin to achieve a sense of safety and perspective from which to approach their tasks" (p. 261). From a cognitive behavioral perspective, medications and cognitive behavioral affect-regulation skills provide a means to manage the intense symptoms of hyperarousal, intrusive reliving, dissociation, and numbing so that exposure and cognitive restructuring proce-

dures can be applied constructively. There is little systematic data on whether combined pharmacologic and cognitive behavioral strategies provide additive treatment effects. Recent encouraging evidence for the utility of SSRIs for PTSD suggests that these agents should receive attention in studies of combined treatment. As noted, a program of exposure and cognitive restructuring should be considered a standard element of treatment for patients with PTSD.

Obsessive-Compulsive Disorder

A typical individual with obsessive-compulsive disorder (OCD) may spend hours a day washing his hands (although he recognizes no real reason to do so), or checking and rechecking to be sure that a stove is turned off, a door is locked, or some catastrophe has not befallen his children. An internist may repeatedly call the laboratory to be absolutely certain that she heard the result correctly. Other individuals with OCD may have no rituals but may endure endless hours of intrusive obsessive thoughts.

DSM-IV criteria (American Psychiatric Association, 1994) require either obsessions or compulsions which are a significant source of distress, are time-consuming, or significantly interfere with the person's normal routine, occupational functioning, or usual social activities or relationships with others. Obsessions are defined as recurrent and persistent thoughts, impulses, or images (not simply excessive worries) that are recognized as a product of one's own mind, but are experienced, in at least some phase of the disorder, as intrusive and inappropriate. To meet DSM-IV critiera, the individual must attempt to suppress or ignore (or otherwise neutralize) these thoughts. Clinically, the most common obsessions are repetitive thoughts of violence (e.g., killing one's child), contamination (e.g., becoming infected by shaking hands), and doubt (e.g., repeatedly wondering whether one has performed some act, such as having hurt someone in a traffic accident).

Compulsions are repetitive behaviors (or mental acts) aimed at neutralizing distress or a dreaded event, and are performed according to rigid rules or in response to an obsession, but are not realistically connected to the obsession or feared outcome or are clearly excessive (American Psychiatric Association, 1994). Typical compulsions include handwashing, ordering, and checking. A change from DSM-III-R to DSM-IV is reflected in the addition of mental compulsions such as praying, counting, or repeating words silently. In DSM-III-R these would have been called obsessions; but because such repetitive mental actions generally serve to decrease anxiety, it was felt that they would be better characterized as mental compulsions. Usually obsessions are anxiety-provoking while compulsions are anxiety-relieving.

DSM-IV also notes that if another Axis I disorder is present, the content of the obsessions or compulsions is not restricted to it (e.g., preoccupation with food in the presence of an eating disorder, hair pulling in the presence of trichotillomania, concern with appearance in the presence of body dysmorphic disorder, preoccupation with drugs in the presence of a substance use disorder, preoccupation with having a serious illness in the presence of hypochondriasis, or guilty ruminations in the presence of a major depressive disorder).

Prevalence and Etiology

OCD is common as demonstrated by the Epidemiologic Catchment Area study, which found a 6-month point prevalence of about 1.6% and lifetime prevalence of 2–3% (Karno et al., 1988). Thus in the United States alone, between 5 and 7 million people suffer from OCD. Recent pharmaceutical industry data indicate that far fewer than 50% of these patients are being treated.

In rare cases one can identify a brain insult such as encephalitis or head injury as an antecedent to OCD, but typically there is no identifiable neurologic precipitant. With the advent of precise neuroimaging techniques such as morphometric magnetic resonance imaging (mMRI) and positron emission tomography (PET), new ways to look at the brain are now available. PET scans have indicated hyperactivity in the frontal lobes, cingulum, and basal ganglia of OCD patients when compared to depressed individuals and normal controls. In addition, MRI studies have demonstrated occasional patients who have lesions in the striatum. Also, mMRI reveals that OCD patients have significantly more gray matter and less white matter, suggesting a developmental abnormality. This combination of findings from several high technology imaging studies supports a neurologic hypothesis for OCD (Rauch and Jenike, 1993; Rauch et al., 1994).

Clinically there is much overlap between patients with OCD, chronic motor tic disorder, and Tourette's syndrome (TS), and a genetic relationship among these disorders seems likely. Further strengthening a possible link, clinically researchers find that about 20% of OCD patients exhibit tics (Jenike, Baer, and Minichiello, 1990).

Although the treatment effectiveness of serotonergic drugs suggests that alteration of brain serotonergic systems may be one mechanism through which these agents have their therapeutic effects, there remains no evidence of baseline serotonergic dysfunction in OCD pa-

tients. There are, however, some data suggesting that serotonergic perturbations can modify symptoms of OCD (Rauch and Jenike, 1993). It is important to keep in mind that the serotonergic system does not function in a vacuum; other transmitter systems may play an equally important role in OCD. A comprehensive model of OCD must likely consider multiple transmitter systems.

Obsessive-Compulsive Personality Disorder

Obsessive-compulsive disorder is frequently confused with obsessive-compulsive *personality* disorder. These are quite distinct from each other in terms of symptomatology and, more important, in terms of treatment. Traditional psychotherapy produces little change in OCD obsessions and compulsions; it may, however, be of some value in the treatment of patients with obsessive-compulsive personality disorder. Conversely, although CBT and psychopharmacologic treatments have been found in controlled trials to be very effective for OCD symptoms, there has been little research in using these approaches for obsessive-compulsive personality disorder.

Course and Prognosis

The mean age of onset of OCD is between ages 20 and 24; over 80% develop symptoms prior to age 35. Some patients describe the onset of symptoms after a stressful event, such as a pregnancy, a sexual problem, or the death of a relative, and in many cases the onset is acute. Because many patients manage to keep their symptoms secret, there is often a delay of 5 to 10 years before patients come to psychiatric attention.

Precise predictions of the general course and prognosis of OCD are precluded by the lack of detailed knowledge about the natural history of the illness. There are no carefully conducted studies that evaluate longitudinal course. In general, OCD is a chronic illness that exhibits a waxing and waning course, even with treatment. Although complete cures do occasionally occur, such an outcome is unusual. However, approximately 90% of patients can expect moderate to marked improvement with optimum treatment. There is some evidence that good premorbid functioning is an optimistic prognostic sign, but hard evidence of this is lacking. The actual obsessional content does not seem to be related to prognosis.

Pharmacologic Treatment

The treatment of patients suffering from OCD often requires the clinician to integrate various approaches to maximize patient outcome. Patients with OCD rarely respond fully to either psychotherapeutic or pharmacologic approaches alone; and for optimal response, patients must generally receive medication in combination with other approaches, particularly CBT. This combined approach improves the condition of most patients substantially, and occasionally completely, within a few months.

Case reports of successful treatment of OCD have involved almost every antidepressant on the market including imipramine, clomipramine, amitriptyline, doxepin, desipramine, sertraline, zimelidine, fluoxetine, trazodone, and fluvoxamine (Jenike, Baer, and Minichiello, 1990). Recent placebo–double-blind controlled trials have found that clomipramine (up to 250 mg/d), fluvoxamine (up to 300 mg/d), sertraline (up to 200 mg/d), paroxetine (up to 60 mg/d), and fluoxetine (up to 80 mg/d) are effective treatments for OCD (Clomipramine Collaborative Study Group, 1991; Tollefson et al, 1994; Rasmussen et al., in press; Chouinard et al., 1991; Paroxetine OCD Study Group, submitted for publication)

Anecdotal evidence suggest that MAOIs may be helpful for patients who suffer concomitantly from OCD and panic attacks or severe anxiety. Also, one double-blind crossover trial of 6 OCD patients carried out in Denmark reported that lithium was not effective as a treatment for OCD (Geisler and Schou, 1970). There are, however, a few case reports of patients with classic OCD who improved with lithium carbonate (Stern and Jenike, 1983; van Putten and Sander, 1975; Forssman and Walinder, 1969).

Only a few case reports outline success with antipsychotic agents; most of these patients were atypical, and some resembled the clinical picture of schizophrenia rather than classic OCD. It may be that the schizophrenic features were partly, or even substantially, responsible for the good results. One group of researchers reported that neuroleptics enhanced the effects of fluvoxamine alone or in combination with lithium carbonate in OCD patients who had concomitant tics, while it did not help those OCD patients who did not have tics (McDougle et al., 1991). However, in view of the scarcity of data on the efficacy of these agents and the frequency of toxic side effects, neuroleptic use can be recommended only for the more acutely disturbed obsessional patient, for the shortest possible period.

Anxiolytic agents are of little use in the treatment of obsessions or compulsions, but they do help with the anxiety that many OCD patients report. If antiobsessional agents improve OCD, anxiety usually decreases without the use of anxiolytics.

Neurosurgery

With the advent of restricted and relatively safe neurosurgical operations, such as cingulotomy and capsulotomy, and the recognition that some patients are severely disabled and remain refractory even to modern treatments, interest has reawakened in neurosurgery. Since most OCD patients who undergo neurosurgery have had very severe illness that has not responded to multiple therapeutic approaches (including pharmacotherapy and CBT), the results of surgical intervention are impressive.

A recent study confirmed the relative safety and partial efficacy (at least 25–30% of patients improved) of stereotactic cingulotomy as a treatment for refractory, severely disabled OCD patients (Jenike et al., 1991). The main complication—seizures, which occurred in 3 (9%) patients—was easily controlled by phenytoin. Four patients committed suicide, but each had been very ill with complicating disorders, especially severe depression, among which population suicide is a common complication. All 4 patients were noted to be severely depressed with strong suicidal ideation at the time of operation. It remains possible that disappointment secondary to failure of this "last resort" treatment could have contributed to suicide in these patients. There is some evidence that other treatments, including pharmacotherapy and behavior therapy, are more likely to be successful after neurosurgery than before. The bulk of the literature supports the need for continued research in this area. Based on the above findings, we continue to offer neurosurgery for patients with severe and refractory OCD. Commonly, patients do not benefit immediately; a few weeks to months are required for optimal improvement.

A number of operations are in use around the world for treating disabling OCD. Reviewing the worldwide literature on 4 neurosurgical procedures (anterior cingulotomy, limbic leucotomy, tractotomy, and anterior capsulotomy), one finds that anterior cingulotomy has a very low complication rate and a moderate success rate. Limbic leucotomy combines bilateral cingulate lesions with lesions in the orbitomedial frontal areas containing fibers of a fronto-caudate-thalamic tract that may be critical in the formation of obsessive-compulsive symptoms. Anterior capsulotomy and tractotomy have also been reported to provide significant improvement rates. The identification of patient subgroups with a high likelihood of improvement after neurosurgical procedures merits further study. Currently it is impossible to determine in advance which patients might improve and which procedure is the best for an individual patient.

Overall, modern site-specific operations are quite safe.

It is still unclear which OCD patients should be referred for surgical procedures, and definite recommendations must await further data from ongoing prospective studies. However, there does appear to be a role for neurosurgery in the severely disabled and treatment-refractory OCD patient.

Cognitive Behavioral Treatment

The cognitive behavioral techniques most consistently effective in reducing compulsive rituals and obsessive thoughts are *exposure* to the feared situation or object, and *response prevention*, in which the patient resists the urge to perform the compulsion after exposure. Simple relaxation therapy is an ineffective treatment for OCD symptoms. CBT typically produces the largest changes in rituals, such as compulsive cleaning or checking, whereas changes in obsessive thoughts are less predictable. Consequently CBT is regarded as one of the treatments of choice when behavioral rituals predominate, and is frequently combined with pharmacotherapy to enhance outcome.

Behavioral techniques have been understood for over a century; in fact, Janet (Marks, 1981) gave a remarkably accurate description of what is now termed exposure therapy, including the name itself:

The guide, the therapist, will specify to the patient the action as precisely as possible. He will analyze it into its elements if it should be necessary to give the patient's mind an immediate and proximate aim. By continually repeating the order to perform the action, that is, exposure, he will help the patient greatly by words of encouragement at every sign of success, however insignificant, for encouragement will make the patient realize these little successes and will stimulate him with the hopes aroused by glimpses of greater successes in the future. Other patients need strictures and even threats and one patient told [Janet], "Unless I am continually being forced to do things that need a great deal of effort I shall never get better. You must keep a strict hand over me."

Exposure therapy as described by Janet remains a major behavioral treatment of OCD a century later. Unfortunately, it was not until the late 1960s that these techniques were widely and effectively employed in the treatment of OCD. Soon after Janet gave his description of exposure therapy, Freud published his analysis of semantic conditioning in the formation of obsessions and compulsions in the patient known as the Rat Man, and interest turned toward the meaning of obsessions and compulsions and away from considering the compulsive behaviors as treatment targets in and of themselves. Although psychodynamic formulations have descriptive value, they have not yielded reliable techniques for modifying obsessions and compulsions.

Inexperienced clinicians are sometimes fearful of the effects or unaware of the potential of behavioral treatment. A number of common misconceptions have developed. It is important for the clinician to know that: (1) CBT will not lead to the formation of substitute symptoms, (2) interrupting compulsive rituals is not dangerous in any way to the patient, (3) the patient's thoughts and feelings are not ignored in behavior therapy, (4) modern behavior therapists do not assume that all maladaptive behavior is learned through simple conditioning processes, (5) the use of medication is not incompatible with behavior therapy, and (6) behavior therapists recognize that their therapeutic techniques are not equally effective for all patients. Controlled outcome studies of exposure and response prevention for OCD over a period of 15 years with more than 200 patients in various countries have found that 60–70% of OCD patients were much improved after behavioral treatment (Jenike, Baer, and Minichiello, 1990). At follow-up of 2 years or more, improvements in rituals had been maintained in almost all patients (Jenike, Baer, and Minichiello, 1990). Thus there are, in fact, many reports that demonstrate the efficacy of exposure and response prevention, and preliminary results of a recent study indicate that behavior therapy may well be more effective than pharmacotherapy when compared head to head (Foa and Liebowitz, unpublished data). Patients with only obsessive thoughts and no rituals have been studied separately, but treatment remains focused on exposure, sometimes employing a tape loop to provide exposure to anxiety-provoking thoughts (Salkovskis, 1983).

Occasional studies have attempted to tease apart the differential effects of exposure and response prevention components of behavior therapy. For example, with washers, exposure therapy was found to help mainly in reducing the anxiety component, while response prevention had its greatest effect in reducing the ritualistic washing. The combined treatment was more effective than either component in isolation.

Cognitive interventions have also been applied successfully to the treatment of OCD (van Oppen et al., 1995). These interventions focus on correction of dysfunctional thought patterns that fuel obsessions and compulsions. For example, Salkovskis's (1985, p. 579) account of the etiology of OCD emphasizes dysfunctional beliefs that may predispose individuals to overreact to intrusive thoughts (e.g., "Having a thought about an action is like performing the action," or "Failing to prevent—or failing to try to prevent—harm to self or to others is the same as having caused the harm in the first place"). Ongoing research will need to determine which patients at what level of severity best respond to cognitive, behavioral, or combination interventions.

Generalized Anxiety Disorder

In DSM-IV generalized anxiety disorder (GAD) is defined as a disorder of excessive anxiety and worry about a number of events or activities (American Psychiatric Association, 1994). Worry is a common feature of mood disturbances, and to help discriminate GAD from other disorders, the diagnostic criteria also require that the worry not occur exclusively in the context of a depressive disorder. Likewise, the topic of the worry cannot be exclusively the focus of another anxiety disorder. For a diagnosis of GAD, the anxiety and worry must be present more days than not for at least 6 months, and must be accompanied by at least 3 of the following 6 symptoms: (1) difficulties concentrating or loss of train of thought, (2) restlessness or feeling on edge, (3) irritability, (4) muscle tension, (5) easy onset of fatigue, and (6) sleep disturbances. This symptom list is markedly shorter than the 18-item list that was used to define the disorder in DSM-III-R. An additional change is criterion B in DSM-IV, which requires difficulties *controlling* the worry. These changes place greater emphasis on the worry process as central to the disorder and less emphasis on the range of somatic symptoms that may accompany this worry.

Comorbidity

Generalized anxiety disorder frequently co-occurs with other conditions, including major depression, panic disorder, and social phobia (Kessler et al., 1994). Large-scale epidemiological studies suggest that only a very small percentage of patients experience generalized anxiety disorder in the absence of other comorbid mood and anxiety conditions, which underscores the critical observation in clinical practice that patients presenting with GAD symptoms should be carefully assessed for the presence of depression and receive appropriate interventions (e.g., antidepressant medication or CBT for depression).

Prevalence and Course

The lifetime prevalence of generalized anxiety disorder is 5%, with the disorder being diagnosed more frequently in men (Kessler et al., 1994). Many individuals with generalized anxiety disorder have a significant history of anxiety dating back to childhood, although some patients experience onset of the disorder after the age of 20. The course appears chronic, though fluctuating with worsening of symptoms during periods of stress and quiescence at other times.

Pharmacological Treatment

Benzodiazepines have long been a mainstay of the pharmacotherapy of GAD. The benzodiazepines, when compared to barbituates and the nonbarbituate sedative and hypnotic agents used in the past (e.g., meprobamate), are more selectively anxiolytic with less sedation, less withdrawal symptomatology, and lower morbidity and mortality in overdose. Concerns about physical dependence and difficulties in discontinuing treatment for some patients do need to be seriously considered in weighing the risks and benefits of benzodiazepine therapy for the anxious patient. All benzodiazepines are effective for generalized anxiety symptoms, with drug selection often made on the basis of the pharmacokinetic properties of the agent; the clinician may use a benzodiazepine with a fast onset of action (e.g., diazepam or alprazolam) for greater clinical impact, an agent with a slower onset of action (e.g., oxazepam) to minimize sedation or confusion, a short-acting agent (e.g., alprazolam) to allow rapid clearing, or a longer-acting agent (e.g., clonazepam) to eliminate interdose or post-treatment rebound in withdrawal symptomatology. Treatment is usually initiated at low doses (e.g. diazepam 5–10 mg/d or its equivalent) and gradually titrated up relative to remaining symptoms and emerging side effects, with a dose range of 30–40 mg of diazepam or its equivalent being common for most patients.

High rates of comorbid depression in patients with generalized anxiety disorder, as well as comorbid anxiety disorders such as panic disorder and social phobia, encourage the use of antidepressants for generalized anxiety disorder, although studies demonstrate an effect for the tricyclic antidepressants for GAD regardless of the presence of the comorbid conditions (Kahn, McNair, and Frankenthaer, 1987). There is little data regarding the SSRIs for use in the generalized anxiety patient, but clinical experience suggests that these agents are also effective. As with patients with panic disorder, use of antidepressants for patients with GAD requires the initial use of low doses, with gradual upward titration. For some patients, benzodiazepines are employed for acute management of anxiety, with antidepressant addition or substitution considered for patients requiring ongoing maintenance therapy. Benzodiazepine therapy is to be avoided in patients with a significant comorbid substance abuse problem. This is not uncommon in patients with generalized anxiety disorder.

Buspirone is a non-benzodiazepine anxiolytic with effects on postsynaptic serotonin receptors and partial agonist effects on dopamine receptors which lacks significant sedative or anticonvulsant properties or abuse potential. Buspirone is indicated for generalized anxiety disorder and is typically initiated at doses of 5–10 mg bid and titrated up to about 60 mg/d, as tolerated in bid or tid doses. Similar to the antidepressants, there is a therapeutic lag of at least 2 to 3 weeks for treatment of GAD with buspirone. Although many patients do not respond despite an adequate dose and duration of treatment, buspirone may be useful for some persistently anxious patients, and, over course of treatment, discontinuation may be less complicated than with benzodiazepines.

Beta-blockers have also been used for the treatment of GAD. Though effective in reducing the somatic symptoms associated with anxiety, including tachycardia and tremor, they are generally less effective against the cognitive and affective symptoms associated with significant anxiety and thus are generally used as an adjunctive treatment for patients with GAD.

Cognitive Behavioral Treatment

Three core strategies have been applied to the treatment of GAD: relaxation training, cognitive restructuring, and worry exposure (e.g., Borkovec and Costello, 1993; Barlow, Rapee, and Brown, 1992; Durham and Allen, 1993). Relaxation training is targeted at decreasing autonomic arousal and may include a number of strategies including progressive muscle relaxation, biofeedback-assisted relaxation training, and self-hypnosis. Progressive muscle relaxation has received particular attention in GAD, and patients are asked to apply relaxation skills when confronted by worry or somatic sensations of anxiety. The relaxation may specifically reduce symptoms of arousal but may also interrupt ongoing worry cycles by providing an alternative response to initial worry cues.

Cognitive restructuring interventions are aimed directly at the uncontrolled worry process characterizing GAD, and generally include education on the role of cognitions in generating and maintaining anxiety, monitoring and labeling of negative and catastrophic thoughts, and instruction in methods to challenge and replace dysfunctional thoughts and anxiety-related beliefs. Attention is given to the tendency to overestimate the likelihood and severity of negative outcomes and to underestimate the ability to cope should a negative outcome occur. During sessions the therapist and patient work collaboratively to challenge dysfunctional thoughts and provide more rational evaluations of the likelihood and manageability of

negative events; between sessions the patient is asked to monitor and challenge dysfunctional thoughts.

Exposure-based interventions for GAD are targeted directly at changing emotional and cognitive responses to distressing images or catastrophic thoughts (Gould and Otto, 1996). Exposure procedures may be combined with "worry time interventions," which attempt to gain control over worry behavior by assigning it to a specific time and place each day. During the designated worry time, patients are instructed to worry, but the worry process is constrained to more adaptive problem solving that includes problem definition, identification of feared outcomes, evaluation of the likelihood of these outcomes, and identification and evaluation of available coping responses should the negative outcome occur.

Current treatment packages tend to combine cognitive restructuring, relaxation, and exposure treatment, and treatment manuals for therapists and patients are available (e.g., Craske, Barlow, and O'Leary, 1992). There is evidence that combination treatments are superior to relaxation treatments alone, and have been found to be equivalent or superior to medication treatments (Gould and Otto, 1996). In addition to offering a treatment outcome that tends to be maintained over time, CBT avoids the problems of oversedation, memory disturbances, discontinuation difficulties, and abuse that have been identified as potential issues for benzodiazepine treatment of GAD (Schweizer, 1995). Nonetheless, despite encouraging results in controlled trials, it is clear that treatments for GAD are in an early stage of development, and that the field must improve upon the modest successes of current treatment alternatives (for review, see Barlow, 1988; Durham and Allen, 1993; Gould and Otto, 1996).

Combined Treatment

There has been little investigation of combined cognitive behavioral and pharmacologic treatment strategies. At present we are aware of only one well-controlled treatment trial. This trial examined the efficacy of CBT delivered alone or in combination with diazepam treatment (Power et al., 1990). These treatments were not significantly different, and both were superior to treatment with diazepam alone. Hence, to date there is no strong evidence for additive efficacy of combined strategies for GAD relative to CBT alone.

Specific Phobias

A diagnosis of specific phobia is given when there is evidence of persistent, marked fear of a specific object or event. The feared stimulus must reliably evoke avoidance or distress and interfere with routine functioning, and the anxiety response must be excessive and unreasonable given the stimulus (American Psychiatric Association, 1994). As with most of the anxiety disorders, anticipatory anxiety and avoidance is common, and the anxiety response upon exposure to the feared stimulus may reach panic proportions.

Specific phobias are differentiated from panic disorder by the focus on the feared stimulus and the absence of panic attacks in other situations. Specific types of phobias include fears of animals (e.g., dogs or snakes, as well as fears of insects), the natural environment (e.g., storms, heights, or water), blood-injection-injury (e.g., fears of seeing blood or of receiving an injection or other invasive medical procedure; this subtype may include a strong vasovagal reaction), and situational events (e.g., fears of trains, buses, tunnels, bridges, elevators, flying, driving, or closed places) (American Psychiatric Association, 1994).

Prevalence and Course

Specific phobias affect approximately 5–10% of the population according to 6-month prevalence estimates (Myers et al., 1984). Onset is typically in childhood (Öst, 1987), and because of sustained avoidance, phobias tend to remain chronic conditions without treatment.

Treatment

Benzodiazepines (e.g., alprazolam 0.5–2.0 mg prn) or beta-blockers can be used on a "prn" basis to help patients cope acutely with feared situations (e.g., fear of flying). However, cognitive behavioral techniques are generally considered more comprehensively effective for the treatment of specific phobias. Exposure is the mainstay of cognitive behavioral treatments for specific phobias, and research has not indicated a significant advantage for one type of exposure over another (for review, see Barlow, 1988). Patients who are especially reluctant to follow through on self-paced exposure may be aided by modeling by the therapist as a prelude to direct exposure. Informational and cognitive interventions may also aid in modulating the anticipatory anxiety that can induce patients to avoid exposure assignments. Both multiple and single-session treatments have been tested and appear to offer patients long-lasting benefit; as with other anxiety disorders, eliminating fears of anxiety sensations independent of the situations that elicit anxiety may provide benefit to patients with specific phobias (Zarate et al., 1988). Finally, there appears to be little sustained benefit

in adding medications to exposure procedures for specific phobias (for review, see Barlow, 1988).

An increasing recognition that the anxiety disorders are highly prevalent and associated with marked distress and disability has spurred an interest in research to elucidate their underlying pathophysiology, to improve their recognition and diagnosis, and to develop effective treatment strategies for these disorders. The development of safer, more effective pharmacologic treatments and the refinement of cognitive behavioral strategies will offer patients more advanced and effective forms of treatment for the anxiety disorders over the next decade.

References

American Psychiatric Association. 1987. *Diagnostic and statistical manual of mental disorders.* 3rd ed., rev. Washington, D.C.: American Psychiatric Association.

———— 1994. *Diagnostic and statistical manual for mental disorders.* 4th ed. Washington, D.C.: American Psychiatric Association.

Ball, S. G., Otto, M. W., Pollack, M. H., and Rosenbaum, J. F. 1994. Predicting prospective episodes of depression in patients with panic disorder: a longitudinal study. *Journal of Consulting and Clinical Psychology* 62:359–365.

Barlow, D. H. 1988. *Anxiety and its disorders: the nature and treatment of anxiety and panic.* New York: Guilford Press.

Barlow, D. H., and Craske, M. G. 1993. *Mastery of your anxiety and panic II.* Albany, N.Y.: Graywind Publications.

Barlow, D. H., Rapee, R. M., and Brown, T. A. 1992. Behavioral treatment of generalized anxiety disorder. *Behavior Therapy* 23:551–570.

Barlow, D. H., Craske, M. G., Cerny, J. A., and Klosko, J. S. 1989. Behavioral treatment of panic disorder. *Behavior Therapy* 20:261–282.

Beck, A. T., Sokol, L., Clark, D. A., Berchick, R., and Wright, F. 1992. A crossover study of focused cognitive therapy for panic disorder. *American Journal of Psychiatry* 149:778–783.

Biederman, J., Rosenbaum, J. F., Hirshfeld, D. R., Faraone, S. V., Bolduc, E. A., Gersten, M., Meminger, S. R., Kagan, J., Snidman, N., and Reznick, J. S. 1990. Psychiatric correlates of behavioral inhibition in young children of parents with and without psychiatric disorders. *Archives of General Psychiatry* 47:21–26.

Borkovec, T. D., and Costello, E. 1993. Efficacy of applied relaxation and cognitive-behavioral therapy in the treatment of generalized anxiety disorder. *Journal of Consulting and Clinical Psychology* 61:611–619.

Bradwejn, J., Koszycki, D., Payeur, R., Bourin, M., and Borthwick, H. 1992. Study of the replication of action of cholecystokinen in panic disorder. *American Journal of Psychiatry* 149:962–964.

Breslau, N., Davis, G. C., Andreski, P., and Peterson, E. 1991. Traumatic events and post-traumatic stress disorder in an urban population of young adults. *Archives of General Psychiatry* 48: 216–222.

Brown, T. A., and Barlow, D. H. 1992. Comorbidity among anxiety disorders: implications for treatment in DSM-IV. *Journal of Consulting and Clinical Psychology* 6: 835–844.

——— 1995. Long-term outcome in cognitive-behavioral treatment of panic disorder: clinical predictors and alternative strategies for assessment. *Journal of Consulting and Clinical Psychology* 63, 754–765.

Burnam, M. A., Stein, J. A., Golding, J. M., Siegel, J. M., Sorenson, S. B., Forsythe, A. B., and Telles, C. A. 1988. Sexual assault and mental disorders in a community population. *Journal of Consulting and Clinical Psychology* 56:843–850.

Chouinard, G., Goodman, W., Greist, J., Jenike, M., Rasmussen, S., White, K., Hackett, E., Gaffney, M., and Bick, P. A. 1991. Results of a double-blind placebo controlled trial using a new serotonin uptake inhibitor, sertraline, in obsessive-compulsive disorder. *Psychopharmacology Bulletin* 26:279–284.

Christensen, H., Hadzi-Pavlovic, D., Andrews, G., and Mattick, R. 1987. Behavior therapy and tricyclic medication in the treatment of obsessive-compulsive disorder: a quantitative review. *Journal of Consulting and Clinical Psychology* 55:701–711.

Clark, D. M., Salkovskis, P. M., Hackmann, A., Middleton, H., Pavlos, A., and Gelder, M. 1994. A comparison of cognitive therapy, applied relaxation and imipramine in the treatment of panic disorder. *British Journal of Psychiatry* 164:759–769.

Clomipramine Collaborative Study Group. 1991. Efficacy of clomipramine in OCD: results of a multicenter double-blind trial. *Archives of General Psychiatry* 48:730–738.

Clum, G. A., Clum G. A., and Surls, R. 1993. A meta-analysis of treatments for panic disorder. *Journal of Consulting and Clinical Psychology* 61:317–326.

Coryelle, W., Noyes, R., and Clancy, J. 1982. Excess mortality in panic disorder. *Archives of General Psychiatry* 39:701–703.

Craske, M. G., Barlow, D. H., and O'Leary, T. A. 1992. *Mastery of your anxiety and worry.* Albany, N.Y.: Graywind Publications.

Davidson, J. R. T., Ford, S. M., Smith, R. D., and Potts, N. L. S. 1991. Long-term treatment of social phobia with clonazepam. *Journal of Clinical Psychiatry* 52(suppl):16–20.

Davidson, J. R., Hughes, D., Blazer, D. G., and George, L. K. 1991. Post-traumatic stress disorder in the community: an epidemiological study. *Psychological Medicine* 21:713–721.

Durham, R. C., and Allen, T. 1993. Psychological treatment of generalized anxiety disorder: a review of the clinical significance of results in outcome studies since 1980. *British Journal of Psychiatry* 163:19–26.

Feske, U., and Chambless, D. L. 1995. Cognitive behavioral versus exposure only treatment for social phobia: a meta-analysis. *Behavior Therapy* 26:695–720.

Foa, E. B., and Kozak, M. J. 1986. Emotional processing of fear: exposure to corrective information. *Psychological Bulletin* 99:20–35.

Foa, E. B., and Liebowitz, M. Unpublished data.

Foa, E. B., Steketee, G., and Rothbaum, B. O. 1989. Behavioral/cognitive conceptualizations of post-traumatic stress disorder. *Behavior Therapy* 20:155–176.

Forssman, H., and Walinder, J. 1969. Lithium in treatment failures. *Journal of Nervous and Mental Disease* 161:255–264.

Fyer, A. J., Mannuzza, S., Chapman, T. F., Liebowitz, M. R., and Klein, D. F. 1995. A direct interview family study of social phobia. *Archives of General Psychiatry* 50:286–293.

Geisler, A., and Schou, M. 1970. Lithium ved tvangsneuroser. *Nordisk Psykiatrisk Tidsskrift* 23:493–495.

Gould, R. A., and Otto, M. W. 1996. Cognitive-behavioral treatment of social phobia and generalized anxiety disorder. In *Challenges in clinical practice: pharmacologic and psychosocial strategies,* ed. M. H. Pollack, M. W. Otto, and J. F. Rosenbaum. New York: Guilford Press. 171–200.

Gould, R. A., Otto, M. W., and Pollack, M. H. 1995. A meta-analysis of treatment outcome for panic disorder. *Clinical Psychology Review* 15:819–844.

Gould, R. A., Otto, M. W., Pollack, M. P., and Yap, L. 1997. Cognitive-behavioral and pharmacological treatment of generalized anxiety disorder: a preliminary meta-analysis. *Behavior Therapy* 28:285–305.

Gould, R. A., Buckminster, S., Pollack, M. H., Otto, M. W., and Yap, L. In press. Cognitive-behavioral and pharmacological treatment for social phobia: a meta-analysis. *Clinical Psychology: Science and Practice.*

Gray, J. A. 1985. Issues in the neuropsychology of anxiety. In *Anxiety and the anxiety disorders,* ed. A. H. Tuma and J. D. Maser. Hillsdale, N.J.: L. Earlbaum. 5–26.

Greist, J. H., Jefferson, J. W., Kobak, K. A., Katzelnick, D. J., and Serlin, R. C. 1995. Efficacy and tolerability of serotonin transport inhibitors in obsessive-compulsive disorder. *Archives of General Psychiatry* 52:53–60.

Heimberg, R. G. 1989. Cognitive and behavioral treatments for social phobia: a critical analysis. *Clinical Psychology Review* 9:107–128.

Heimberg, R. G., and Barlow, D. H. 1991. New developments in cognitive-behavioral therapy for social phobia. *Journal of Clinical Psychiatry* 52(suppl.):21–30.

Heimberg, R. G., Dodge, C. S., Hope, D. A., Kennedy, C. R., Zolloo, L. J., and Becker, R. E. 1990. Cognitive behavioral group treatment for social phobia: comparison with a credible placebo control. *Cognitive Therapy and Research* 14:1–23.

Helzer, J. E., Robins, L. N., and McEvoy, L. 1987. Post-traumatic stress disorder in the general population: findings of the epidemiologic catchment area survey. *New England Journal of Medicine* 317:1630–34.

Hunt, C., and Singh, M. 1991. Generalized anxiety disorder. *International Review of Psychiatry* 3:215–229.

Jenike, M. A., Baer, L., and Minichiello, W. E., eds. 1990. *Obsessive-compulsive disorders: theory and management.* 2nd ed., Chicago: Year Book Medical Publishers.

Jenike, M. A., Baer, L., Ballantine, H. T., Martuza, R. L., Tynes, S., Giriunas, I., Buttolph, L., and Cassem, N. 1991. Cingulotomy for refractory obsessive-compulsive disorder: a long-term follow-up of 33 patients. *Archives of General Psychiatry* 48:548–555.

Jenike, M. A., Breiter, H. C. R., Baer, L., Kennedy, K. N., Savage, C. R., Olivares, M. J., O'Sullivan, R. L., Shera, D. M., Rauch, S. L., Keuthen, N., Rosen, B. R., Caviness, V. S., and Filipek, P. A. 1996. Cerebral structural abnormalities in patients with obsessive-compulsive disorder: A quantitative morphometric magnetic resonance imaging study. *Archives of General Psychiatry* 53:625–632.

Jones, J. C., and Barlow, D. H. 1990. The etiology of posttraumatic stress disorder. *Clinical Psychology Review* 10:299–328.

Juster, H. R., and Heimberg, R. G. 1995. Social phobia: longitudinal course and long-term outcome of cognitive-behavioral treatment. *Psychiatric Clinics of North America* 18:821–842.

Kagan, J. 1994. *Galen's prophecy.* New York: Harper Collins.

Kagan, J., Reznick, J. S., and Snidman, N. 1987. Biological bases of childhood shyness. *Science* 240:167–171.

Kahn, R. J., McNair, D. M., and Frankenthaer, L. M. 1987. Tricyclic treatment of generalized anxiety disorder. *Journal of Affective Disorders* 13:145–151.

Karno, M., Golding, J. M., Sorenson, S. B., and Burnam, A. 1988. The epidemiology of obsessive-compulsive disorder in five U.S. communities. *Archives of General Psychiatry* 45:1094–99.

Kawachi, I., Colditz, G. A., Ascherio, A., Rimm, E. B., Giovannucci, E., Stampfor, M. J., and Willet, W. C. 1994. Prospective study of phobic anxiety and risk of coronary heart disease in men. *Circulation* 89:1992–97.

Keane, T. M., and Wolfe, J. 1990. Comorbidity in post-traumatic stress disorder: an analysis of community and clinical studies. *Journal of Applied Social Psychology* 20:1776–88.

Keane, T. M., Litz, B. T., and Blake, D. D. 1990. Post-traumatic stress disorder in adulthood. In *Handbook of child and adult psychopathology: a longitudinal perspective,* ed. M. Hersen and C. G. Last. New York: Pergamon Press. 275–291.

Kessler, R. C., McGonagle, K. A., Zhao, S., Nelson, C. B., Hughes, M., Eshleman, S., Wittchen, H. U., and Kendler, K. S. 1994. Lifetime and twelve month DSM-III-R psychiatric disorders in the United States. *Archives of General Psychiatry* 51:8–19.

Klerman, G. L., Weissman, M. M., Ouellette, R., Johnson, J., and Greenwald, S. 1991. Panic attacks in the community: social morbidity and health care utilization. *Journal of the American Medical Association* 265:742–746.

Kushner, M. G., Sher, K. J., and Beitman, B. D. 1990. The relation between alcohol problems and the anxiety disorders. *American Journal of Psychiatry* 147:685–695.

Liebowitz, M. R., Gorman, J. M., Fyer, A. J., and Klein, D. F. 1985. Social phobia: review of a neglected anxiety disorder. *Archives of General Psychiatry* 42:729–736.

Manfro, G. G., Otto, M. W., McArdle, E. T., Worthington, J. J. III, Rosenbaum, J. F., and Pollack, M. H. In press. Relationship of antecedent stressful life events to childhood and family history of anxiety and the course of panic disorder. *Journal of Affective Disorders.*

Markowitz, J. S., Weissman, M. M., Ouellette, R., Lish, J. D., and Klerman, G. L. 1989. Quality of life in panic disorder. *Archives of General Psychiatry* 46:984–992.

Marks, I. M. 1981. Review of behavioral psychotherapy I: obsessive-compulsive disorder. *American Journal of Psychiatry* 584–592.

Mavissakalian, M., and Perel, J. M. 1992. Clinical experiments in maintenance and discontinuation of imipramine therapy in panic disorder with agoraphobia. *Archives of General Psychiatry* 49:318–323.

———— 1995. Imipramine treatment of panic disorder with agoraphobia: dose ranging and plasma level-response relationships. *American Journal of Psychiatry* 152:673–682.

McDougle, C. J., Price, L. H., Goodman, W. K., Charney, D. S., and Hennger, G. R. 1991. A controlled trial of lithium augmentation in fluvoxamine-refractory obsessive-compulsive disorder: lack of efficacy. *Journal of Clinical Psychopharmacology* 11:175–184.

McNally, R. J. 1994. *Panic disorder: a critical analysis.* New York: Guilford Press.

Myers, J. K., Weissman, M. M., Tischler, G. L., Holzer, C. E. III, Leaf, P. J., Orvaschel, H., Anthony, J. C., Boyd, J. H., Burke, J. D. Jr., Kramer, M., and Stoltzman, R. 1984. Six-month prevalence of psychiatric disorders in three communities: 1980 to 1982. *Archives of General Psychiatry* 41:959–967.

Noyes, R., Garvey, M. J., Cook, B. L., and Samuelson, L. 1989. Problems with tricyclic antidepressant use in patients with panic disorder or agoraphobia: results of a naturalistic follow-up study. *Journal of Clinical Psychiatry* 50:163–169.

Noyes, R., Garvey, M. J., Cook, B., and Suelzer, M. 1991. Controlled discontinuation of benzodiazepine treatment for patients with panic disorder. *American Journal of Psychiatry* 148:517–523.

Öst, L. G. 1987. Age of onset in different phobias. *Journal of Abnormal Psychology* 96:223–229.

Otto, M. W., and Whittal, M. L. 1995. Cognitive-behavior therapy and the longitudinal course of panic disorder. *Psychiatric Clinics of North America* 18:803–820.

Otto, M. W., Pollack, M. H., Sachs, G. S., Reiter, S., Meltzer-Brody, S., and Rosenbaum, J. F. 1993. Discontinuation of benzodiazepine treatment: efficacy of cognitive-behavior therapy for patients with panic disorder. *American Journal of Psychiatry* 150:1485–90.

Otto, M. W., Jones, J. C., Craske, M. G., and Barlow, D. H. 1996. *Stopping anxiety medication: panic control therapy for benzodiazepine discontinuation.* San Antonio, Tex.: Psychological Corporation.

Otto, M. W., Penava, S. J., Pollock, R. A., and Smoller, J. W. 1996. Cognitive-behavioral and pharmacologic perspectives on the treatment of post-traumatic stress disorder. In *Challenges in clinical practice: pharmacologic and psychosocial strategies*, ed. M. H. Pollack, M. W. Otto, and J. F. Rosenbaum. New York: Guilford Press. 219–260.

Paroxetine Obsessive-Compulsive Disorders Study Group. Submitted for publication. Efficacy of fixed doses of paroxetine in the treatment of obsessive-compulsive disorder: a randomized, double-blind, placebo-controlled trial.

Pato, M. T., Zohar-Hadouch, R., Zohar, J., and Murphy, D. L. 1988. Return of symptoms after discontinuation of clomipramine in patients with obsessive-compulsive disorder. *American Journal of Psychiatry* 145:1521–25.

Pollack, M. H., and Gould, R. A. 1996. The pharmacotherapy of social phobia. *International Clinical Psychopharmacology* 11(suppl. 3):71–75.

Pollack, M. H., Otto, M. W., Rosenbaum, J. F., Sachs, G. S., O'Neil, C., Asher, R., and Meltzer-Brody, S. 1990. Longitudinal course of panic disorder: findings from the Massachusetts General Hospital Naturalistic Study. *Journal of Clinical Psychiatry* 51:12–16.

Pollack, M. H., Otto, M. W., Kaspi, S. P., Hammerness, P. G., and Rosenbaum, J. F. 1994. Cognitive-behavior therapy for treatment-refractory panic disorder. *Journal of Clinical Psychiatry* 55:200–205.

Pollack, M. H., Otto, M. W., Sabatino, S., Majcher, D., Worthington, J. H., McArdle, E. T., and Rosenbaum, J. F. 1996. Relationship of childhood anxiety to adult panic disorder: correlates and influence on course. *American Journal of Psychiatry* 153:376–381.

Power, K. G., Simpson, R. J., Swanson, V., and Wallace, L. A. 1990. A controlled study of cognitive behavior therapy, diazepam, and placebo, alone and in combination for the treatment of generalized anxiety. *Journal of Anxiety Disorders* 4:267–292.

Rasmussen, S. A., Goodman, W. K., Greist, J. H., Jenike, M. A., Kozak, M. J., Liebowitz, M., Robinson, D. G., and White, K. L. In press. Fluvoxamine in the treatment of obsessive-compulsive disorder: a multicenter double-blind placebo-controlled study in outpatients. *American Journal of Psychiatry.*

Rauch, S. L., and Jenike, M. A. 1993. Neurobiological models of obsessive-compulsive disorder. *Psychosomatics* 34:20–32.

Rauch, S. L., Jenike, M. A., Alpert, N. M., Baer, L., Breiter, H. C. R., and Fischman, A. J. 1994. Regional cerebral blood flow measured during symptom provocation in obsessive-compulsive disorder using 15-o labeled CO_2 and positron emission tomography. *Archives of General Psychiatry* 1:62–70.

Redmond, D. E., and Huang, Y. H. 1979. New evidence for a locus ceruleus–norepinephrine connection with anxiety. *Life Sciences* 25:2149–62.

Resnick, P. A., and Schnicke, M. K. 1993. *Cognitive processing therapy for rape victims: a treatment manual.* Newbury Park, Calif.: Sage.

Rosenbaum, J. F., Biederman, J., Hirshfeld, D. R., Bolduc, E. A., and Chaloff, J. 1991. Behavioral inhibition in children: a possible precursor to panic disorder or social phobia. *Journal of Clinical Psychiatry* 52(suppl. 11):5–9.

Salkovskis, P. M. 1983. Treatment of an obsessional patient using habituation to audiotaped ruminations. *British Journal of Clinical Psychology* 22:311–313.

——— 1985. Obsessional-compulsive problems: a cognitive-behavioural analysis. *Behavior Research and Therapy,* 23(5):571–583.

Schneier, F. R., Hohnson, H., Hornig, C. D., Liebowitz, M. R., and Weissman, M. M. 1992. Social phobia: comorbidity and morbidity in an epidemiologic sample. *Archives of General Psychiatry* 49:282–288.

Schweizer, E. 1995. Generalized anxiety disorder: longitudinal course and pharmacologic treatment. *Psychiatric Clinics of North America* 18:843–858.

Shear, M. K. 1996. Factors in the etiology and pathogenesis of panic disorder: revisiting the attachment/separation paradigm. *American Journal of Psychiatry* (Festschrift suppl.) 153:125–136.

Shear, K. S., Pilkonis, P. A., Cloitre, M., and Leon, A. C. 1994. Cognitive behavioral treatment compared with nonprescriptive treatment of panic disorder. *Archives of General Psychiatry* 51:395–401.

Simon, G., and von Korff, M. 1991. Somatisation and psychiatric disorders in the Epidemiologic Catchment Area Study. *American Journal of Psychiatry* 148:1494–1500.

Spiegel, D. A., Bruce, T. J., Gregg, S. F., and Nuzzarello, A. 1994. Does cognitive behavior therapy assist slow-taper alprazolam discontinuation in panic disorder? *American Journal of Psychiatry* 151:876–881.

Steketee, G., and Foa, E. B. 1987. Rape victims: post-traumatic stress responses and their treatment. A review of the literature. *Journal of Anxiety Disorders* 1:69–86.

Stern, T. A., and Jenike, M. A. 1983. Treatment of obsessive-compulsive disorder with lithium carbonate. *Psychosomatics* 24:671–673.

Tallman, J. F., and Gallager, D. W. 1985. The GABA-ergic system: a locus of benzodiazepine action. *Annual Review of Neuroscience* 8:21–44.

Telch, M. J., and Lucas, R. A. 1994. Combined pharmacological and psychological treatment of panic disorder: current status and future directions. In *Treatment of panic disorder,* ed. B. E. Wolfe and J. D. Maser. Washington, D.C.: American Psychiatric Press.

Thyer, B. A. 1985. Audio-taped exposure therapy in a case of obsessional neurosis. *Journal of Behaviour Therapy and Experimental Psychiatry* 16:271–273.

Tollefson, G. D., Rampey, A. H., Potvin, J. H., Jenike, M. A., Rush, J. A., Dominguez, R. A., Koran, L. M., Shear, K., Goodman, W., and Genduso, L. A. 1994. A multicenter investigation of fixed-dose fluoxetine in the treatment of obsessive-compulsive disorder. *Archives of General Psychiatry* 51:559–567.

Turner, S. M., Beidel, D. C., and Townsley, R. M. 1992. Social phobia: a comparison of specific and generalized subtypes and avoidant personality disorder. *Journal of Abnormal Psychology* 101:326–331.

Uhde, T. W., Boulenger, J. P., Roy Byrne, P. P., Geraci, M., Vittone, J., and Post, R. M. 1985. Longitudinal course of panic disorder: clinical and biological considerations. *Progress in Neuropsychopharmacology and Biological Psychiatry* 9:39–51.

van der Kolk, B. A. 1994. The body keeps the score: memory and the evolving psychobiology of posttraumatic stress. *Harvard Review of Psychiatry* 1:253–265.

van der Kolk, B. A., Dreyfuss, D., Michaels, M., Shera, D., Berkowitz, R., Fisler, R., and Saxe, G. 1994. Fluoxetine in post-traumatic stress disorder. *Journal of Clinical Psychiatry* 55:517–522.

van Oppen, P., de Haan E., van Balkom A. J. L. M., Spinhoven, P., Hoogduin, K., and van Dyck, R. 1995. Cognitive therapy and exposure in vivo in the treatment of obsessive-compulsive disorder. *Behavior Research and Therapy* 33:379–390.

van Putten, T., and Sander, D. G. 1975. Lithium in treatment failures. *Journal of Nervous and Mental Disease* 161:255–264.

Wells, A., Clark, D. M., Salkovskis, P., Ludgate, J., Hackmann, A., and Gelder, M. 1995. Social phobia: the role of in-situation safety behaviors in maintaining anxiety and negative beliefs. *Behavior Therapy* 26:153–161.

Westenberg, H. G., and Den Boer, J. A. 1994. The neuropharmacology of anxiety: a review of the role of serotonin. In *Handbook of Depression and Anxiety,* ed. J. A. Den Boer and J. M. A. Sitsen. New York: Marcelle Decker. 405–446.

Yehuda, R., and Nemeroff, C. B. 1994. Neuropeptide alterations in affective and anxiety disorders. In *Handbook of Depression and Anxiety,* ed. J. A. Den Boer and M. A. Sitsen. New York: Marcelle Decker. 543–572.

Zarate, R., Rapee, R. M., Craske, M. G., and Barlow, D. H. 1988. The effectiveness of interoceptive exposure in the treatment of simple phobia. Paper presented at the 22nd Annual Association for Advancement of Behavior Therapy Convention, New York.

Recommended Reading

Barlow, D. H. 1988. *Anxiety and its disorders: the nature and treatment of anxiety and panic.* New York: Guilford Press.

Foa, E. B., and Kozak, M. J. 1986. Emotional processing of fear: exposure to corrective information. *Psychological Bulletin* 99:20–35.

Jenike, M. A., Baer, L., and Minichiello, W. E., eds. 1990. *Obsessive-compulsive disorders: theory and management.* 2nd ed. Chicago: Year Book Medical Publishers.

Lydiard, R. B., Brawman-Mintzer, O., and Ballenger, J. C. 1996. Recent developments in the psychopharmacology of anxiety disorders. *Journal of Consulting and Clinical Psychology* 64:660–668.

Mavissakalian, M. R., and Prien, R. F., eds. 1996. *Long-term treatments of anxiety disorders.* New York: American Psychiatric Press.

Pollack, M. H., and Otto, M. W., eds. 1995. Anxiety disorders: longitudinal course and treatment. *Psychiatric Clinics of North America* 18(4).

Pollack, M. H., Otto, M. W., and Rosenbaum, J. F., eds. 1996. *Challenges in clinical practice: pharmacologic and psychosocial strategies.* New York: Guilford Press.

Rosenbaum, J. F., Pollack, M. H., Otto, M. W., and Bernstein, J. G. 1997. Anxiety patients. In *Massachusetts General Hospital handbook of general hospital psychiatry,* ed. N. H. Cassem, T. A. Stern, J. F. Rosenbaum, and M. S. Jellinek. 4th ed. St. Louis: Mosby Year Book. 173–210.

13

MING T. TSUANG
STEPHEN V. FARAONE
ALAN I. GREEN

Schizophrenia and Other Psychotic Disorders

Schizophrenia and other psychotic disorders that manifest massive disruptions of perception, cognition, emotion, and behavior are difficult to treat and even more difficult to explain from an etiological or pathophysiological perspective. Their consequences, for both the individual and society, are nothing short of tragic. For many patients the disorders result in lifetime psychiatric disability, periodic hospitalizations, poor social adjustment, and disrupted family relationships. Because approximately 1 of every 100 people will be afflicted with schizophrenia at some time in their life, the costs to society are tremendous, more than $20 billion per year in the United States.

Historical Review

Psychosis has been described for at least 3400 years. Sanskrit writings mentioned such disorders as early as 1400 B.C. The Greek physicians of the Hippocratic school in the fifth century B.C. called them "dementia" and distinguished them from mania and melancholia. During the second century and for more than a thousand years thereafter, psychosis was considered a form of possession by the devil and was dealt with accordingly in religious courts, jails, and asylums.

During the nineteenth century modern psychiatry progressed from observing symptoms, to defining symptom clusters as part of specific illnesses with common manifestations, to focusing on related groups of illnesses, and eventually to studying their underlying somatic and psychological factors. Classificatory efforts in the late eighteenth and early nineteenth centuries led to descriptions of symptoms, illness groups, and patterns of recovery. Toward the end of the nineteenth century, the science of descriptive psychopathology approached a watershed with Emil Kraepelin's differentiation of dementia praecox and manic-depressive psychoses in 1896. Before Eugen Bleuler coined the term *schizophrenia,* the term *dementia praecox* was used because of the disorder's pervasive disruption of perceptual and cognitive processes *(dementia)* and its early onset *(praecox).* These features contrast with the relatively intact mentation and later onset of the manic-depressive psychoses, where disturbances of mood dominate the clinical picture. Kraepelin is also credited with differentiating the psychoses on the basis of course and outcome. Patients with dementia praecox were observed to have a progressively deteriorating course with no return to their premorbid level of functioning. Manic-depressive patients had an episodic course of illness with periods of normal functioning punctuated by severe but time-limited episodes of psychopathology. In delineating the characteristic presentation and course of dementia praecox, Kraepelin clearly recognized that there was no pathognomonic sign or symptom for the disorder.

Eugen Bleuler used Kraepelin's systematic classification of psychoses and a theoretical model of etiological processes to redefine the disorder as *schizophrenia,* from the Greek words for "splitting of the mind." He described 4 fundamental symptoms (Bleuler's 4 *A*'s): ambivalence, disturbance of association, disturbance of affect, and a preference for fantasy over reality (autism). Hallucinations, delusions, negativism, and stupor were not considered crucial for diagnosis. For Bleuler the 4 *A*'s were most important because they reflected the presumed fundamental defect, that is, a splitting of the normally integrated functions that coordinate thought and affect. This emphasis on theory as a means for determining the diagnostic relevance of signs and symptoms contrasts sharply with Kraepelin's reliance on empirical observations to determine clusters of signs and symptoms corresponding to putative disease entities. Bleuler's approach is also notable for his redefinition of dementia praecox as "the group of schizophrenias." This foreshadowed the commonly held contemporary view that schizophrenia is an etiologically heterogeneous group of disorders with similar clinical presentations.

Ivan Pavlov saw schizophrenia as a generalized inhibition or chronic hypnotic state arising from excessive stimulation of a nervous system weakened by hereditary or acquired damage. He demonstrated that dogs, when faced with an increasingly difficult learning task that became impossible to perform, would display bizarre and aggressive behavior. These studies of "experimental neuroses" in animals provided the impetus for extensive theoretical formulation and experimental research in various forms of conditioning and their relationship to psychopathology. Although Pavlov's work led to tremendous advances in learning theory with applications to anxiety disorders, a successful explanation of schizophrenia was not achieved.

Sigmund Freud believed that the content of schizophrenic speech confirmed his theories of the unconscious motivation of human behavior and the stages of psychosexual development. He ultimately concluded, however, that schizophrenia represented such a degree of narcissistic regression that treatment was impossible owing to the schizophrenic's inability to develop a true transference relationship. Despite his pessimism concerning the psychotherapeutic treatment of schizophrenics, Freud's formulations have been used by subsequent theorists and therapists in attempts to develop a more comprehensive understanding of the etiology and treatment of the illness.

Carl Jung was influenced by Freud's concepts of unconscious motivation in human behavior and used word associations to explore networks of related memories, events, interactions, and feelings. Jung saw these unconscious complexes as powerful forces in individuals' lives. His formulations of introverted and extroverted personalities, developed subsequent to his break with Freud, have been used to describe the emotional life of the schizophrenic.

Adolf Meyer, working during the first quarter of the twentieth century, considered schizophrenia a reaction to a traumatic life situation, a view basic to his psychobiological approach to all mental illness. Referring to schizophrenia as a group of "reaction" disorders, Meyer viewed them as the outcome of habitual patterns of maladaptive responses based on organic, psychological, and sociocultural factors. He considered clinical symptoms less basic to conceptualizing mental disturbance than the nature of the stress and the individual's reaction to it. This approach contributed to a unitary view of all mental and emotional illness as points along a continuum extending from neurosis to psychosis.

The work of Harry Stack Sullivan spanned the 1920s to 1940s. He stressed deeply disturbed interpersonal relationships as the basis for schizophrenia, rather than the intrapsychic mechanisms emphasized by the followers of Freud. In his view the psychological and behavioral mechanisms needed to attain security, self-esteem, and the fulfillment of physiological drives are damaged in schizophrenia.

Heinz Hartmann related schizophrenic psychopathology to severe conflicts over uncontrolled aggression, which can interfere with the development of autonomous ego functions and thus disturb perception and disrupt logical thought and human relationships. Frustration, the danger of threatened or actual separation, and interference with achievement of aims were hypothesized precipitants of aggression. Dependent people who dread separation and loss were seen as particularly vulnerable to such events. Hartmann viewed aggression and its consequences as crucial issues in psychiatric disorders and held that both the amount of aggression and the nature of the defenses used to deal with it determine diagnosis.

William and Karl Menninger, who worked in many areas of psychiatric research, treatment, and education from World War I to the 1970s, and who derived their theoretical bases from Meyer and Freud, were instrumental in changing the view of the American psychiatric community toward schizophrenia. They regarded schizophrenia less as an illness than as a reaction to stress. In 1958 Karl Menninger formulated a unitary theory of the progression of mental illnesses from "simple nervousness" through neurotic illness, undisguised aggression, psychotic disorganization, and repudiation of reality to malignant anxiety and depression ending in death. Thus he moved in the direction of stressing the importance of unmastered aggression in the schizophrenic as a factor in the psychosis.

In the 1940s psychoanalytic theorists turned their attention to object relations in general, focusing particularly on the earliest version—the mother-child relationship. Margaret Mahler noted that schizophrenic children's inordinate attachment to their mothers stunted their psychosocial abilities; from this observation she developed the concept of "separation-individuation." This process occurs within the first 3 years of life, beginning with normal symbiosis with the mother and culminating in the child's recognition of himself as a separate individual. The schizophrenic child and the psychotic adult fail to negotiate this process of separation-individuation and are therefore both severely and decidedly emotionally dependent on a valued person ("a compliant object") for emotional sustenance and support.

Analytic theory has also focused on the function of the ability to bear anxiety and depression in leading to normal development. In this view schizophrenics lack both capacities, and part of the therapeutic strategy is to help patients face psychic situations they have avoided because of their incapacity to handle anxiety in situations of interpersonal closeness and sadness in situations of loss. The ability to experience anxiety and sadness appropriately was seen as a sign of increasing strength in patients.

The influence of object relations theory and of Sullivan's focus on interpersonal relations has led other theorists to apply psychoanalytic theory to disturbed family communication. Ruth and Theodore Lidz studied the mothers of schizophrenic patients and found that they had nurtured a parasitic attitude in their children. The patients, feeling that they were important to their mothers, complied with parental expectations in order to receive support. Observations suggesting that the irrationality of the family is transmitted directly to the child led the investigators to conceptualize 2 forms of family interaction or bonding patterns. In "marital skew" one partner dominates the emotional life of the family. Such families usually consist of either a domineering, hostile wife and a passive, dependent husband or a tyrannical, narcissistic husband and a fearful, acquiescent wife. In either case, the weaker partner diverts hatred of the spouse toward the spouse's favored child. In "marital schism" each partner is disappointed and disillusioned with the other and relies on the child for support and comfort. The partners live together in mutual isolation, the family splits into warring camps, and the child bears the guilt of allying himself with one parent against the other. By 1965 the Lidzes' investigations had led them to conclude that parents of schizophrenics, fundamentally unable to nurture offspring, create a family that fails to transmit modes of behavioral reciprocity and accommodation and thus fails as a social institution.

By 1973 Theodore Lidz placed more emphasis than he had previously on schizophrenic thinking as a basis for the illness. He suggested that the patient develops his own egocentric overinclusiveness in order to adapt to that of his parents. Lidz and his school have consistently ascribed the illness more specifically to the direct impact of these patterns on the child than to the role of the patient's intrapsychic and ego reactions and adaptations.

Gregory Bateson and his associates studied another form of family bonding and developed the concept of the "double bind," a special form of ambivalence in which mother, father, or siblings make overt requests or imply demands for a strong reaction that conflicts with the one required by the situation (such as telling a child with a father who has just been particularly brutal and hateful, "You know your father loves you"). According to Bateson,

failure to acknowledge or accede to the irrational demand incurs either a threat to inner equilibrium or the possibility of punishment; thus no reasonable, acceptable response is possible. The child cannot flee the conflict, and feelings of paralysis, anger, anxiety, and helplessness result. In Bateson's view psychosis develops to deal with such situations. The child eventually learns to use the double bind (a means of identifying with the aggressor) against other people. Bateson holds that these situations occur repeatedly in the childhood of the schizophrenic.

Lyman Wynne and his associates described the bond of "pseudomutuality," wherein constricted roles are assigned to family members at the expense of their individuality. Even when these roles are interchanged, their shared rigidity and narrowness maintain a superficial togetherness. Like Lidz, Wynne held that the child learns irrationality, which becomes a pattern of living for him; his internalization of the pathological aspects of the family leads to disturbances such as fragmentation of experience, identity diffusion, and disturbed perception and communication. Once internalized, however, this system of mutuality cannot break down without leading to overt schizophrenia. According to Wynne and associates, the style of interpersonal relations in the family is also tied to cognitive development; inappropriate cognitive and affective distance or closeness among family members leads to a sense of purposelessness.

Don Jackson was struck by the underlying order in the apparent disorder, coldness, and cruelty of the schizophrenic's family and held that such families are in fact not at all disorganized. On the contrary, they are structured to allow family members little access to the wide repertoire of behavior available to most people; the bizarre behavior observed in such families is a sign of the restrictions they impose. Within this framework the patient learns irrational behavior directly from his family.

The many currents of psychoanalytic theory led to a wealth of psychotherapeutic procedures for the treatment of schizophrenic patients. Most notable in this regard is the work of Elvin Semrad, who felt that the basic therapeutic attitude should be an acceptance of the patient as he is, of his aims in life, his values, and his nonpsychotic modes of operating. Semrad emphasized the importance of providing the patient with a series of interpersonal experiences to help him differentiate between psychotic and socially appropriate behavior. Thus the development of interpersonal skills was seen as a necessary adjunct to the basic techniques of dynamic psychotherapy.

In Semrad's view the psychotherapist has 3 major functions. The first is to make a personal diagnostic summary of the patient, describing his needs, defense mechanisms, aims, and love objects. Next the therapist has to supply what the patient needs, either directly, through candid, respectful therapeutic interaction, or indirectly, through other people provided for this purpose. In the process of providing effective interpersonal and coping skills, the therapist helps the patient give up infantile behavior. The goal is to help the patient confront the details of the traumatic experience that led to chronic frustration and, ultimately, to psychosis.

Semrad encouraged a thorough, though painful, investigation of the psychotic episode to help the patient understand what the therapist did to be helpful and to focus therapy on the causes of the decompensation. By understanding the series of interpersonal relationships and impasses that led to the psychotic episode, the patient could learn to cope with the emotional turmoil that precipitated psychosis and thereby avoid future decompensations. Providing the patient with behavioral and cognitive coping skills was considered to be the end point of psychotherapy, because clinical experience indicated that the analysis of the psychosis-vulnerable ego was impossible in most cases.

Diagnostic Issues

Contemporary Diagnosis of Schizophrenia

Although the development of cognitive and psychoanalytic theories of schizophrenia has provided a rich source of clinical description and hypotheses, none of these theories has convincingly explained the phenomenon of schizophrenia in all its manifestations. As a result, contemporary diagnostic systems rely solely on descriptive psychopathology as a source of diagnostic information; inferences about presumed underlying psychological processes are *not* considered relevant for making a diagnosis.

The move toward diagnostic systems based solely on observable or reportable psychopathology was motivated primarily by the unreliability of diagnostic categories that allowed room for diagnostic inference based on putative underlying mechanisms. It is intuitively obvious that if well-trained mental health clinicians cannot agree that a person is or is not schizophrenic, then the diagnostic category cannot be very meaningful. In addition to creating problems in the diagnosis of individual patients, unreliable diagnostic criteria made it difficult, if not impossible, to pursue research with homogeneous groups of patients that would be comparable to those studied by other investigators.

The problem with the vague, inference-based diagnosis of schizophrenia that had evolved by the 1960s was

dramatically demonstrated by epidemiological comparisons between the United States and the United Kingdom. Morton Kramer (1961) reported that the hospital rate of schizophrenia in the United States (28.0 per 100,000) was nearly 1.5 times the rate in the United Kingdom (17.9 per 100,000). The hospital rate of mood disorders in the United Kingdom (36.0 per 100,000) was approximately 5 times the rate in the United States (7.0 per 100,000). Were these differences artifacts of poor diagnostic systems, or did they constitute a true differential distribution of psychotic disorders in the 2 countries?

A collaborative study between American and British researchers was undertaken to answer this question (Cooper et al., 1972). Patients in the 2 countries were interviewed with a common structured psychiatric interview, and diagnoses were made with a common diagnostic standard. The study groups consisted of 250 patients in a New York hospital, 65% of whom were given a hospital diagnosis of schizophrenia, and 250 patients in a London hospital, 34% of whom were given a hospital diagnosis of schizophrenia. Although hospital-diagnosed schizophrenia was nearly twice as common in the New York group, the project diagnoses of schizophrenia resulted in similar rates: 32% of the New York sample and 26% of the London sample were schizophrenic according to standardized criteria. Most of the hospital-diagnosed schizophrenics in New York who did not meet research criteria for schizophrenia met research criteria for mood disorders. Thus, as Kramer (1961) had suggested, the rates for schizophrenia in Great Britain and the United States were due to diagnostic artifacts and were not true population differences.

By the mid-1970s structured diagnostic criteria based on observable or reportable aspects of psychopathology and course had become the standard for use in psychiatric research. The World Health Organization's (WHO) international pilot study of schizophrenia (World Health Organization, 1973) had demonstrated that it was possible to develop valid and reliable diagnostic instruments that could identify a common syndrome of schizophrenia in 9 countries. Researchers at Washington University in St. Louis (Feighner et al., 1972), Columbia University in New York (Spitzer, Endicott, and Robins, 1978), and elsewhere continued developing and validating operational definitions of psychiatric disorders. These definitions entered the clinical arena with the publication in 1980 of the third edition of the *Diagnostic and Statistical Manual* of the American Psychiatric Association (DSM-III). During the subsequent decade, with publication of the fourth edition, these criteria evolved into the current DSM-IV criteria for schizophrenia.

The DSM-IV criteria for schizophrenia (Table 13.1) require diagnosticians to make judgments about 6 major criteria. Criterion A requires the presence, in some form, of the massive disruptions in cognition and/or perception that have been seen as characteristic of schizophrenia since Kraepelin's time. As Table 13.1 indicates, criterion A is met when the patient expresses certain types of delusions, auditory hallucinations, thought disorder, catatonia, or negative symptoms.

Criteria B and C in the DSM-IV nomenclature reflect the Kraepelinian belief that schizophrenia is characterized by a chronic deteriorating course. Thus the patient must manifest some clear indication of deterioration in social or occupational functioning and must show continuous signs of the illness for at least 6 months.

Criterion D excludes a full depressive or manic syndrome; if it is present, it must have developed after the active phase of the disorder or been brief relative to the duration of active-phase symptoms. This exclusionary criterion is necessary to create a more homogeneous diagnostic category that is not contaminated by manic or depressive disorders with psychotic features. Criterion E requires that the illness is not better accounted for by a general medical condition, substance use, or a pervasive developmental disorder. This exclusion is necessary because other conditions are known to mimic the signs and symptoms of schizophrenia (Slater and Beard, 1963; Davison and Bagley, 1969).

Clinical Features

As Table 13.1 indicates, the structured, criterion-based approach of DSM-IV does not allow clinicians to diagnose schizophrenia based on unobservable psychological processes. Although the structured approach minimizes inference and improves reliability, it must be emphasized that sound clinical judgment is still required to formulate a diagnosis. With structured criteria, clinical judgment enters into the evaluation of whether a specific, well-defined criterion is present or absent. Although clearly defined in DSM-IV, the clinical features that constitute the diagnosis of schizophrenia can be difficult to determine in clinical situations. Thus structured diagnostic criteria have not eliminated the need for clinical judgment; they have merely focused this judgment on the data-collection process of the diagnostic enterprise.

Clinical features of schizophrenia are usually divided into 2 categories. Positive features refer to manifestations in which the patient produces behaviors that are outside the usual behavioral repertoire of human beings. Positive symptoms predominate during the *active* phase of the illness, when the patient is most disturbed. The active phase usually precipitates the patient's hospitalization or referral for care. Negative features correspond to manifestations in which the patient has eliminated important behaviors from his behavioral repertoire. Negative symptoms predominate during the *prodromal* and *residual* phases of the illness. The prodromal phase precedes the first active phase; the residual phase follows the active phase.

Positive symptoms. In DSM-IV positive symptoms correspond primarily to criterion A. Historically they have been prominent in diagnostic approaches to schizophrenia. Most notable in this regard is the approach of Kurt

Table 13.1 DSM-IV criteria for schizophrenia

A. Presence of two or more during a 1-month period (unless successfully treated)
  1. delusions
  2. hallucinations
  3. disorganized speech
  4. grossly disorganized or catatonic behavior
  5. affective flattening, alogia, or avolition
  Only one of the above is required if delusions are bizarre or patient hears a running commentary on his or her behavior or hears voices conversing

B. Deterioration in functioning in such areas as work, social relations, and self-care

C. Continuous signs of the disturbance for at least 6 months

D. Schizoaffective and Mood Disorders have been ruled out

E. The disturbance is not due to substance use or a general medical condition

F. If there is a history of Pervasive Developmental Disorder, prominent hallucinations or delusions must be present for at least 1 month (unless successfully treated)

Schneider. He believed that the most important, or "first-rank," diagnostic indicators of schizophrenia were delusions, somatic hallucinations, auditory hallucinations commenting on the patient's behavior, hearing one's thoughts spoken aloud, and the belief that one's thoughts are controlled by or broadcast to others. Positive symptoms can be classified as perceptual, cognitive, emotional, or motoric, depending on which area of behavior is involved. These symptoms are not diagnostic for schizophrenia if the sensorium is clouded or confused.

The most common perceptual aberration is *auditory hallucinations.* In some cases the hallucination maintains a running commentary on the patient's behavior or thoughts. In others 2 or more voices converse with each other. Less elaborate auditory hallucinations can also occur but must be unrelated to depressive or manic themes to be diagnostic for schizophrenia. Although less common, visual, olfactory, and gustatory hallucinations are also observed in schizophrenia. Patients may also experience somatic hallucinations; these are perceptions in body organs that cannot be accounted for by physiological mechanisms (for example, "People are touching me" when that is not happening, or "My liver is rotting").

Hallucinations must not be confused with illusions. A *hallucination* is a perception that occurs in the absence of a stimulus. An *illusion* is a perception that occurs when an ambiguous stimulus is misinterpreted. For example, in response to probes about visual hallucinations, a patient indicated that he had seen his dead mother one evening. Further questioning revealed that the patient had seen someone who resembled his mother, and this resemblance was accentuated in the dim light. Although this episode may be informative about the patient's reactions to his mother's death, it was an illusion, not a hallucination indicative of schizophrenia. Recurrent illusions occur during the prodromal and residual phases of the illness. Visual hallucinations should also not be confused with the hypnagogic imagery that many individuals experience before falling asleep.

Cognitive disruption in schizophrenia is observed commonly in the form of *delusions,* false beliefs not amenable to change by reason or experience even though the person is in a clear state of consciousness. Although the source of a delusion is often personal, content is usually related to the patient's cultural context. In Franz Mesmer's day, patients spoke of being influenced by magnetism; 80 years ago, by electricity; and 40 years ago, by television. Now they may speak of being influenced by atomic radiation or computers. Patients with *paranoid delusions* believe that one or more individuals or organizations are trying to harm them. Like other delusions, these are often easy to recognize because their components are

clearly absurd (for example, a patient may complain that her mother is plotting with extraterrestrial creatures to prevent her from graduating from high school). In some cases, however, a persecutory belief may appear false because it is improbable, but may actually be grounded in fact. One of the authors, for example, had a patient whose fear of being assaulted by Mafia thugs was shown to be nondelusional after careful assessment of his previous criminal activities.

Paranoid delusions should not be confused with *delusions of sin or guilt,* in which the patient believes he is being punished for some misdeed. The misdeed may be real (the patient wrecked his friend's car) or it may be fictional (the patient made a deal with the devil). Even when the misdeed is real, the punishment is usually out of proportion (the patient feels condemned to remain in a closet for the rest of his life because he forgot to mow the lawn for his father). Paranoid and guilty delusions differ in that the paranoid patient believes the claimed persecution is undeserved, whereas the delusionally guilty patient believes the punishment is deserved. Since delusions of sin or guilt are often seen in psychotic depressives, patients should be carefully evaluated for affective features.

Delusions of jealousy involve the belief that a spouse or lover has been unfaithful and are often difficult to evaluate. If bizarre components are lacking, presence of the delusion can be confirmed by observing how the patient integrates the relevant evidence. The delusional patient will ignore or rationalize any evidence contesting the delusion, no matter how convincing the evidence. In contrast, the most minute piece of evidence supporting the delusion will be presented and discussed with great emotion and elaboration.

Somatic delusions are often related to somatic hallucinations. They are usually bizarre and involve the belief that something abnormal and dangerous is happening to the patient's body. For example, one patient believed his intestines were being devoured by a giant worm. Another was certain he would soon die because his body was rotting from the inside outward. Somatic delusions also occur in psychotic depression and delusional disorder. Somatic delusional disorders are rare and resemble other hypochondriacal disturbances in that concerns with and fear about physical health are prominent. The difference lies in the degree of conviction: for the delusional patient, the disease or change in appearance is real, usually bizarre, and not grounded in reality.

The patient with *grandiose delusions* expresses unrealistic and sometimes bizarre beliefs about his own talents or accomplishments. An extreme example would be a patient who claimed to be "king of the universe" because of his special relationship with God. In milder cases the patient may claim to have extraordinary talents that are not substantiated (for example, the patient claims to be a great mathematician although his alleged mathematical proofs are meaningless scrawls). Because grandiosity is commonly seen in hypomania and mania, patients should be carefully evaluated for affective features.

Religious delusions are false beliefs that involve religious or spiritual themes. The delusional status of a religious belief may be obvious, as in the case of a patient who collected a roomful of grapefruits because she believed they contained the essence of God. More than with other delusions, however, the delusional status of religious beliefs may be difficult to establish. A religious belief is not delusional if consistent with the patient's cultural context. For example, many Jehovah's Witnesses believe in the imminent end of the world. Such a belief would not be delusional if expressed by a member of that sect, but it might be delusional if expressed by a nonreligious person. Some schizophrenics may be attracted by unusual religious sects. If this is suspected, then the putative religious delusion should be explored for either a history that precedes the patient's joining the sect or components that are absurd even in the context of the sect. A delusional religious belief is likely to lead to functional impairment.

Bizarre delusions are beliefs whose content is obviously absurd and has no possible basis in fact. Several fairly frequent bizarre delusions have been reported in the clinical and research literature. *Delusions of being controlled* involve beliefs that one's body or mind is controlled by an outside agency. The patient's subjective experience of being controlled must exceed the simple feeling of being persuaded or coerced and include some sense of being mechanically or pseudomechanically manipulated. For example, an individual who feels pressured by a peer group to dress or think in a certain way is not delusional. But one who believes his friends are using personal computers to send electronic messages to his brain to control the way he dresses and thinks is delusional. *Thought broadcasting* is observed when a patient believes his thoughts can be heard by others. The patient may indicate that his thoughts are loud enough to be heard or that someone has implanted a radio transmitter inside his brain. *Thought insertion* is the subjective experience that thoughts are being inserted into one's stream of consciousness by some outside agency. These thoughts are usually unpleasant or disturbing and may direct the patient to engage in bizarre or aggressive behaviors. *Thought withdrawal* is the reverse of thought insertion. The patient reports episodes of thoughts simply vanishing from his mind and attributes their loss to some outside agency.

This is often manifested as blocking, a sudden stop in the stream of speech.

As Andreasen (1986) suggested, the diagnostician should attend to several dimensions of delusional thought when making a judgment of the delusion's severity. These dimensions are persistence, complexity, bizarreness, behavioral impact, and degree of doubt. The *persistence* of a delusion is measured in terms of the frequency with which it engages the patient's thoughts or actions. Some patients will report delusions that have affected them on a daily basis for months or even years. Others will report episodic delusions that come and go and last only several hours at a time.

The *complexity* of a delusion refers to the degree to which the patient's false beliefs form a cohesive, interconnected set of themes. Some patients may have relatively fragmentary delusions. For example, a patient may believe he is the president of the United States but does not develop any elaborate themes or stories associated with his high office. A similar but very complex delusion is illustrated by the case of a patient who believed he was the president of the United States in disguise because of assassination threats by the KGB. He had chosen a job as a bank teller because it would allow him to control the money supply of the country, which was his ultimate source of power. Such a delusion might elaborate into greater levels of complexity and include friends, relatives, or even strangers who played some role in this unusual story.

The *bizarreness* of a delusion refers to its level of credibility. Some delusions are clearly absurd: they involve Martians, special powers, or impossible or contradictory experiences. Other delusions may seem objectively unusual but appear reasonable for the patient's subculture. This situation often occurs when the patient comes from a deviant cultural context (for example, the criminal community or an unusual religious sect) and expresses beliefs consistent with that context. If a belief is possibly delusional, it is useful to allow the patient to discuss the implications of the belief and associated ideas. With further discussion, a culturally reasonable but unusual belief may blossom into a complex and bizarre delusional system.

The *behavioral impact* of a delusion refers to the degree to which the patient acts on his false beliefs. At one extreme the patient may only discuss a delusion when asked about it and may never perform any related actions. At the other extreme the patient may constantly preach his delusional belief to strangers and take extreme, self-damaging actions based on it (for example, the patient may burn his house down because he believes it is contaminated with evil spirits that are trying to kill him). Patients also vary on the *degree of doubt* attached to delusions. Some patients believe their delusion with full conviction; others may have bizarre ideas that they think might be true with varying degrees of certainty.

Delusions of all kinds are often accompanied by another cognitive disruption, *markedly illogical thinking.* For example, a schizophrenic might reason, "The president of the United States is Protestant; I am Protestant; therefore I am the president of the United States." A patient's reasoning may also be impaired by *loosening of associations,* that is, the connection of ideas or images that have no apparent relationship to one another. Thought and language usually have a high degree of sequential cohesiveness that emerges from the stringing together of ideas and/or images that are consensually related to one another. Obliquely related responses to questions are examples of *tangentiality.* For example, in a normal conversation it is reasonable for a person to respond to another's description of a fishing vacation by describing his own vacation or asking questions about the other's vacation. A schizophrenic might respond by talking about a tuna fish sandwich he had the other day. For the schizophrenic, the loose association between a fishing vacation and tuna fish is enough to justify the transition. Associations can become so idiosyncratic and remote that no connection at all is observed between different components of a schizophrenic's speech. In the extreme case the patient emits *word salad;* that is, most of the words in any given sentence appear to have no syntactic or semantic connection to one another.

The disruption of emotional functioning is usually observed in one of two forms: inappropriate affect and excessive emotional excitement. *Inappropriate affect* refers to giggling, self-absorbed smiling, or a mood incongruent with expressed ideas. For example, one patient may grin or chuckle while discussing the death of his brother whom he loved dearly. Another may continually grin or scowl in a bizarre fashion regardless of context. *Excessive emotional excitement* is often seen in agitated schizophrenic patients. They may experience appropriate emotions, but because of delusional thinking or other factors the intensity of these emotions may be too extreme.

Disruptions of motor behavior are termed *catatonic excitement.* This consists of episodes of uncontrolled, agitated, and disorganized behavior. The patient may be hyperactive, gesticulate excessively, and be destructive or violent. Motor dysfunction is also seen in repetitive, apparently meaningless movements known as *stereotypies.* Schizophrenic patients also exhibit *mannerisms,* habitual movements that usually involve a single body part (gri-

maces, tics, moving lips soundlessly, fidgeting with fingers, hand wringing, thigh rubbing).

Negative symptoms. Negative symptoms affect the cognitive, emotional, and behavioral spheres of functioning in the direction of decreased expressiveness and responsiveness. Negative symptoms may be more chronic and in some ways more devastating than positive symptoms. But they usually do not precipitate hospitalization because, unlike positive symptoms, they usually do not impinge upon others and therefore do not bring the patient to the attention of legal or medical authorities. Negative symptoms are more difficult to define and, until a psychometrically validated scale was developed by Andreasen (1982), have been difficult to rate reliably.

Negative cognitive symptoms reflect diminished productivity of thought. *Poverty of speech* simply means that the patient says very little on his own initiative or in response to questions or situations that would normally evoke verbal behavior. The extreme case is *mutism,* in which a patient does not speak at all even though he is physically capable of doing so. *Poverty of content of speech* is evident when the patient's verbal productivity is normal but the verbalization conveys very little information. *Increased latency of response* refers to the situation in which the patient responds meaningfully to questions, but the time between question and response is abnormally long. *Blocking* occurs when the patient's stream of speech suddenly stops and he is incapable of continuing. This behavior is often seen in conjunction with thought withdrawal.

The negative symptoms associated with emotional responding are often called *flat, blunt,* or *restricted affect.* This term refers to a variety of phenomena that indicate a reduced degree or lack of emotional expressivity. As Andreasen (1982) notes, restricted affect may be observed in the patient's lack of vocal inflections, paucity of expressive gestures, poor eye contact, decreased spontaneous movements, unchanging facial expression, or affective nonresponsivity. In the interview situation these affective features are often experienced as difficulty in establishing rapport with the patient. Negative affective disruption is also seen in *anhedonia,* the inability to experience pleasure. Anhedonia may be reflected in lack of interest in recreation, friendships, and sexuality. Diminished emotional responsiveness is also seen in the schizophrenic's muted ability to feel intimacy or closeness with others.

Negative motor symptoms are seen, in an extreme form, in *catatonic stupor.* Catatonic stupor is not commonly observed. It consists in a total lack of movement and verbal behavior. Patients exhibit *waxy flexibility;* they passively allow others to manipulate their limbs into sometimes uncomfortable positions. *Posturing* (also known as *catalepsy*) refers to holding unusual or uncomfortable positions for long periods during a catatonic stupor.

Negativism refers to a resistance, without apparent motive, to all instructions or attempts to be moved. More common behavioral impairments are poor grooming and hygiene, inability to persist at a task, and withdrawal from social activities. The systematic study of social behavior in schizophrenic patients has indicated that the disorder results in a marked loss of the basic behavioral components necessary for effective social interaction (Curran and Monti, 1982).

Subtypes of Schizophrenia

In DSM-IV the use of the term *schizophrenic disorders* instead of *schizophrenia* emphasizes the contemporary belief that the constellation of signs and symptoms that Kraepelin identified as dementia praecox can be the result of different underlying disorders. Although Kraepelin believed that dementia praecox was a unitary disease category, he and his contemporaries had observed that the disorder had several different clinical manifestations. He distinguished hebephrenic, catatonic, and paranoid subtypes of schizophrenia, to which Bleuler added a subtype called simple schizophrenia. It is a tribute to the observational acumen of these early psychopathologists that these subtypes are still recognized in DSM-IV.

Five major subtypes of schizophrenia are recognized by DSM-IV: paranoid, disorganized, catatonic, undifferentiated, and residual.

Paranoid schizophrenia is predominantly characterized by a preoccupation with one or more delusions or frequent auditory hallucinations. Although the delusions are typically persecutory or grandiose, other types of delusion may occur. Hallucinations are usually related to the content of the patient's delusions. The patient may be tense, suspicious, guarded, and reserved to the point of vagueness or even mutism. Some individuals may be hostile or aggressive yet conduct themselves well socially; others may be angry, argumentative, and even violent. Paranoid patients show only mild, if any, impairments on neuropsychological tests. Their long-term outcome is usually better than that for other schizophrenia subtypes.

Disorganized schizophrenia, called *hebephrenia* in other classifications, shows disorganized speech, disorganized behavior, and flat or inappropriate affect. Although the patient may have fragmentary delusions or hallucinations, they are never systematized and are without a coherent theme. Behavior may be characterized by hypo-

chondriacal complaints, extreme social withdrawal, and bizarre actions or thoughts. Disorganized schizophrenics manifest a poor premorbid personality structure, show an early and insidious onset for the illness, suffer from extreme social impairment, and endure a chronic course without significant remission.

Catatonic schizophrenia typically appears in the form of marked psychomotor disturbances, ranging from negativism, rigidity, excitement, and posturing to the extreme of stupor. At times one sees stereotypical movements, mannerisms, and waxy flexibility. At the extreme of negativism, mutism may occur. Some patients may rapidly alternate between extremes of stupor and excitement. The danger during stupor or excitement is that the individual may harm himself or others. Without medical supervision the patient may develop malnutrition, exhaustion, and hyperpyrexia or may injure himself. Common several decades ago, this subtype is now rare in Europe and North America.

Undifferentiated schizophrenia is diagnosed if all DSM-IV criterion A symptoms are present but the clinical picture does not fit any of the 3 subtypes already described.

Residual schizophrenia is diagnosed when the patient gives a history of at least 1 episode of schizophrenia and residual signs of the illness still exist, but there is no prominent psychotic symptom. The patient often shows emotional blunting, social withdrawal, eccentric behavior, illogical thinking, and loosening of association. Delusions and hallucinations are not prominent and do not have much affect connected with them.

Differential Diagnosis of Other Psychotic Disorders

Psychotic disorder due to a general medical condition. Before a diagnosis of schizophrenia is made, it is crucial to rule out nonpsychiatric medical disorders by history, clinical examination, or laboratory findings. For example, although many patients who experience cerebral trauma will not develop schizophrenia-like symptoms, the prevalence of apparently schizophrenic psychosis among brain-damaged patients is significantly greater than expected. Davison and Bagley (1969) suggest a possible association with temporal lobe lesions, although early development of post-traumatic psychosis appears related to severe closed-head injuries having diffuse cerebral consequences. Other examples of medical conditions that may cause psychosis are given in Table 13.2.

Substance-induced psychotic disorder. The increasing prevalence of drug and alcohol abuse among admissions to psychiatric facilities makes the differential diagnosis of schizophrenia and substance-induced mental disorders a common diagnostic problem. Drug abuse in psychiatric patients has become an increasingly important clinical problem over the past few decades. Fischer and associates (1975), for example, studied consecutive admissions to a psychiatric hospital during 3 months in 1971. Almost one-third of 335 patients had abused drugs at some time. Half the patients younger than 31 had abused drugs. Hall and associates (1979) studied a group of 57 consecutive admissions. Of these patients, 58% were found to have a history of drug abuse. A major difficulty in the differential diagnosis of schizophrenia and substance-induced disorders stems from the practical problem of distinguishing between the effects of certain substances and the psychotic features of schizophrenia (Davison, 1976).

Although there is evidence that abuse of particular drug types can be characterized by specific symptom patterns, the relationships are complex and further complicated by the possibility of polydrug abuse. For example, Bell (1965) reported that amphetamine psychosis can be distinguished from paranoid schizophrenia by both the prominence of visual hallucinations and the relative absence of thought disorder in the former. Ellinwood and Petrie (1981) reported that, compared with schizophrenia, amphetamine psychosis was more likely to manifest visual hallucinations and distortion of body image. Other reports, however, suggest that the most common features of amphetamine psychosis are indistinguishable from schizophrenia (Jonsson and Gunne, 1970).

Abraham (1980) distinguished LSD psychosis from schizophrenia on the basis of visual disturbances, mystical preoccupation, and subtle gaps in the logic of conversation in the drug abusers. Bowers (1972) attributed more conceptual disorganization, less motor retardation, less blunt affect, more excitement, and less lack of energy to drug (primarily LSD) abusers with psychosis compared with acute psychotic reactions unrelated to drug abuse. Nevertheless, others have found LSD psychosis to be virtually indistinguishable from schizophrenia (Rinkel et al., 1952). After a comprehensive literature review, Davison (1976) concluded that "*typical* model psychoses (acute reaction to LSD, mescaline or related drugs) are not identical with *typical* examples of schizophrenia, but individual features of the drug reaction are remarkably similar to some of the experiences of the acute schizophrenic psychoses" (p. 111).

Luisada and Reddick (1980) suggested that phencyclidine (PCP) psychosis can be distinguished from schizophrenia by the violence, aggression, extreme anxiety, and tension of PCP abusers. A study by Erard, Luisada, and Peele (1980), however, did not substantiate these results. They found that the only significant difference in symptoms was the greater rate of extreme anxiety or panic state in schizophrenia. These investigators concluded that their clinical data could not differentiate PCP psychosis from an acute schizophrenic episode.

As this brief review makes clear, symptomatology alone is not an adequate guide for distinguishing drug psychoses from schizophrenia. This is especially true if drug histories are unreliable, if there is polydrug abuse, or if the duration of psychosis exceeds the duration of drug action. If the patient's premorbid history is relatively normal and the duration of psychosis does not exceed the duration of drug action, then it is reasonable to assume the psychosis to be substance induced. Data collected by Tsuang, Simpson, and Kronfol (1982) suggest that psychotic drug abusers having psychotic symptoms that exceed the duration of drug action but persist less than 6 months have better premorbid personalities, shorter hospitalization, less need for pharmacotherapy, better discharge dispositions, and lower familial risks for psychiatric disorders than do psychotic drug abusers whose

Table 13.2 Examples of general medical conditions that can cause psychosis

Neurologic Conditions
neoplasms, cerebrovascular disease, Huntington's disease, epilepsy, auditory nerve injury, deafness, migraine, central nervous system infections

Endocrine Conditions
hyperthyroidism, hypothyroidism, hyperparathyroidism, hypoparathyroidism, hypoadrenocorticism

Metabolic Conditions
hypoxia, hypercarbia, hypoglycemia

Other Conditions
fluid or electrolyte imbalances, hepatic or renal diseases, autoimmune disorders with central nervous system involvement

Source: Adapted from American Psychiatric Association (1994), *Diagnostic and Statistical Manual of Mental Disorders* (4th ed., rev.). Washington, D.C.: American Psychiatric Association. Reprinted with permission. Copyright 1994 by the American Psychiatric Association.

psychoses exceed 6 months' duration. Thus it appears that the effective differential diagnosis of schizophrenia and substance-induced psychoses cannot be made without adequate observations of the course of the disorder.

Delusional disorder. Delusional (paranoid) disorders are a group of disorders whose cardinal feature is the delusion—a fixed false belief maintained in the face of contradictory evidence and not shared by members of cultural or religious groups to which the individual belongs. Generally, the patient's delusions are well systematized and logically developed. In prior versions of the DSM nomenclature, delusional disorder had been called paranoid disorder. In DSM-IV, the term *delusional* emphasizes that the category includes conditions in which delusions other than the persecutory or jealous type are present. The patient, however, does not meet criterion A for schizophrenia.

This disorder is relatively infrequent (Winokur, 1977) and easily confused with paranoid schizophrenia. A critical distinction between the 2 disorders is that paranoid disorder is not accompanied by hallucinations of any type and that, except for the paranoid or jealous delusion, none of the positive symptoms of schizophrenia predominates the clinical picture. The paranoid delusion is usually somewhat plausible and in no way bizarre.

Occasionally, mania with delusions must be differentiated from delusional disorder. In mania, the affective state is more intense and labile in the manic, readily turning to elation or tearful sadness during the interview. In contrast, the patient with delusional disorder will maintain a steady mood, which may be appropriate for the delusional concerns. Moreover, the manic will be expansive, while the delusional disorder patient will be cautious, reserved, and constricted in his approach.

Drug intoxication and other organic mental disorders usually present symptoms that contrast dramatically with those manifest in delusional disorder. In drug-induced hallucinatory disorders, stemming from the use of phencyclidine, THC, LSD, or mescaline, frightening hallucinations with bizarre, poorly systematized delusions may occur. In delirium, a common organic mental disorder, marked distractibility, confusion, disorientation, and defects in judgment and affect are often apparent. In dementia, by contrast, delusions may be prominent, but a careful mental status examination tends to reveal the presence of cognitive disturbance. Amphetamine or cocaine disorder can cause an organic delusional syndrome that may be difficult to diagnose unless a drug history and screen are collected. A host of medical and psychiatric disorders are associated with delusions, especially in older patients.

Psychotic disorder, not otherwise specified. In practice it is not uncommon to find patients who are psychotic but do not meet the criteria for schizophrenia or the other differential diagnostic categories mentioned above. Many of them will be diagnosed as psychotic disorder, not otherwise specified, a residual category reserved for such patients. Examples of psychosis NOS are transient psychotic episodes associated with the menstrual cycle, psychoses with unusual features, persistent auditory hallucinations as the only disturbance, some "postpartum psychoses," and psychoses with confusing clinical features.

Schizophreniform disorder. Patients with schizophreniform disorder meet the A, D, and E diagnostic criteria for schizophrenia, but the duration of the condition is between 1 and 6 months. Evidence of social or occupational dysfunction is not required, but if it occurs, the diagnosis of schizophreniform disorder can still be made. In many cases the diagnosis of schizophreniform disorder is coded as "provisional." This means that the patient meets the schizophreniform duration criteria, but because he has not yet recovered, the possibility of a condition having a longer duration must also be considered.

Brief psychotic disorder. If the duration of the disorder is less than 1 month, then the diagnosis of brief psychotic disorder may be appropriate. In this disorder the patient has delusions, hallucinations, disorganized speech, or grossly disorganized behavior with a duration between 1 day and 1 month. Brief psychotic disorders are usually precipitated by a profoundly upsetting event. These patients are often overwhelmed with emotional turmoil or confusion. Although this is a brief disorder, patients can show severe impairment and are at risk for adverse outcomes owing to poor judgment, cognitive impairment, or acting on the basis of delusional thoughts. In some cases of brief psychotic disorder, the existence of a personality disorder similar to the schizophrenic prodrome may suggest schizophrenia. Careful examination of the personality structure and observation of the clinical course will clarify this distinction.

Shared psychotic disorder. In DSM-IV, shared psychotic disorder (also known as folie à deux) is diagnosed when the patient has a delusion that is similar in content to an already-established delusion in another person with whom he or she has a close relationship. In cases of shared psychotic disorder, the 2 patients are usually related to each other and, in their relationship, the first one to become psychotic is often the dominant member of the dyad. Shared psychoses usually occur between 2 individuals (hence folie à deux), but may also occur among members of a large group.

Schizoaffective disorder. Although Kraepelin's separation of schizophrenia from mood disorders is generally accepted, there are some severely disturbed patients who appear to have a hybrid disorder. The term *schizoaffective psychosis* was first used by Kasanin (1933) to describe patients having a sudden onset in a state of marked emotional turmoil, distortion of the outside world (including false sensory impressions in some), and recovery following a short-lived psychosis of a few weeks to a few months. DSM-IV criterion A requires schizoaffective patients to have had an uninterrupted period of illness that includes both an episode of mood disorder (manic, depressive, or mixed) and symptoms that meet citerion A for schizophrenia.

Criterion B facilitates the differential diagnosis of schizoaffective and mood disorders by requiring that the patient exhibit delusions or hallucinations for at least 2 weeks in the absence of prominent mood symptoms. If the psychotic symptoms occur only when mood symptoms are prominent, a diagnosis of mood disorder with psychotic features would be more appropriate.

Criterion C facilitates the differential diagnosis of schizoaffective disorder and schizophrenia. It requires that the mood disorder symptoms be present for a *substantial* portion of the active and residual periods of the illness. Here it is crucial to remember that the "period of illness" is not simply the acute or active phase of symptoms that brings the patient to the attention of the clinician; it includes the entire period during which the patient shows clinically significant signs of the disturbance. This is a key point because many schizophrenic patients will remain ill for years if not decades. If their illness is punctuated by episodes of mood disturbance, the diagnosis of schizoaffective disorder would not be appropriate—unless the episodes lasted for a substantial period of time.

Differential Diagnosis with Mood Disorders

Another important and sometimes difficult differential diagnosis is between schizophrenia and major mood disorders with psychotic features. The dividing line between schizophrenia and major mood disorders remains a source of controversy. Many manic and depressed patients experience hallucinations and/or delusions that are similar in form to those observed in schizophrenia. DSM-IV differentiates the two disorders by excluding the diagnosis of schizophrenia if the duration of depressive or manic syndrome has not been brief in duration relative to the duration of criterion A symptoms during the active and residual phases of the illness.

Unfortunately, judgments of relative duration can be difficult. As an aid to differential diagnosis, the clinician should examine the content of hallucinations and delusions. When psychotic symptoms are mood congruent, a mood disorder may be indicated. For example, manic patients often have grandiose delusions, and depressed patients often have delusions of sin or guilt. Similarly, the content of an auditory hallucination may reveal themes of elation or dysphoria. Patients who cannot be clearly diagnosed as either schizophrenic or affective, because of the presence of equally pronounced features of both, qualify for the diagnosis of "schizoaffective disorder."

On rare occasions schizophrenic symptoms will appear to be under the voluntary control of the patient, suggesting malingering or a factitious disorder.

The misdiagnosis of other disorders as schizophrenia will be avoided if the clinician collects all available data and remembers that no clinical feature is pathognomonic to the disorder. If, after a thorough clinical interview, the diagnosis of a psychotic patient remains unclear, it is sometimes useful to collect information about psychiatric illness in biological relatives. Although family psychiatric history is not considered a diagnostic criterion in DSM-IV, family, twin, and adoption research suggests that a psychotic patient with schizophrenic relatives is likely to be schizophrenic; one with manic or depressed relatives is likely to have a mood disorder.

The Schizophrenia Spectrum

Our understanding of schizophrenia is complicated by the fact that, in addition to the observed heterogeneity within strictly defined DSM-IV schizophrenia, a variety of disorders resemble schizophrenia without meeting DSM-IV criteria. Kety and associates (1968) suggested that strictly defined schizophrenia represented one end of a spectrum of disorders of varying severity. Instead of viewing schizophrenia as a dichotomous trait that was either present or absent, the spectrum concept views individuals as having varying degrees of vulnerability to schizophrenia, ranging from normal individuals through personality-disordered individuals to the extreme of classical schizophrenia.

The spectrum concept was motivated by 2 developments in the genetics of schizophrenia. Several decades ago, Gottesman and Shields (1967) presented a multi-factorial polygenic (MFP) model of schizophrenia. Originally formulated by D. S. Falconer (1965), the MFP model assumes that all individuals have some degree of unobservable liability or predisposition to develop schizophrenia. This liability is composed of genetic and environmental components, each of which has small additive effects. If a person's liability is more than a certain threshold value, she will develop schizophrenia; otherwise she will not.

The spectrum concept suggests that there are several thresholds on the liability continuum. Persons below the lowest threshold remain unaffected; those above the lowest threshold but below the next one develop the mildest form of schizophrenia; those above the second threshold but below the third develop a more severe form of schizophrenia, and so on. As Faraone and Tsuang's (1985) review indicates, the MFP model has received substantial support in the research literature.

The MFP model was consistent with observations of schizophrenia families showing that non-schizophrenic relatives were at high risk for other psychiatric disorders (Tsuang and Faraone, 1994). These include schizophrenia-like psychoses (schizophreniform disorder, schizoaffective disorder, psychosis NOS) and several personality disorders whose clinical presentations are similar to non-psychotic schizophrenic phenomenology (schizotypal personality disorder, paranoid personality disorder, and schizoid personality disorder).

For example, Kety and associates (1978) found an excess of "borderline" schizophrenia among the biological but not the adoptive relatives of schizophrenic probands. Their criteria for borderline schizophrenia included relatively mild distortions of cognition and language, anhedonia, impairments in interpersonal behavior, multiple neurotic manifestations, and feelings of depersonalization or strangeness. Their concept of borderline schizophrenia eventually evolved into the DSM-III category of schizotypal personality disorder. The criteria for this disorder require that an individual manifest 4 of the following: magical thinking, ideas of reference, social isolation, recurrent illusions, odd speech, inadequate rapport in face-to-face interaction, suspiciousness, and undue social anxiety or hypersensitivity to real or imagined criticism.

In addition to schizophrenia-like psychiatric disorders, the schizophrenia spectrum includes several neurobiological abnormalities that do not qualify for a specific psychiatric diagnosis (Faraone et al., 1995a). These anomalies include eye tracking dysfunction (Levy et al., 1994), attentional impairment (Cornblatt and Keilp, 1994), allusive thinking (Catts et al., 1993), neurologic signs (Erlenmeyer-Kimling et al., 1982), thought disorder (Shenton et al., 1989), characteristic auditory evoked potentials (Friedman and Squires-Wheeler, 1994), neuropsychological impairment (Kremen et al., 1994), and structural brain abnormalities (Weinberger et al., 1981; Cannon et al., 1993; Liddle, Spence, and Sharma, 1995; Seidman et al., 1996).

Treatment of Schizophrenia

Currently no known cure exists for schizophrenia. There are, however, several modes of treatment that can, when skillfully applied, reduce the impact of schizophrenic disorders on both the patient and the community. Moreover, the new generation of medications (introduced in the 1990s) have the potential for improving the long-term outcome of schizophrenia beyond what had been possible before. Although for clarity we shall discuss the treatment modalities independently, effective management usually requires a combination of interventions tailored to the patient's needs. The approaches discussed here include pharmacotherapy and the psychosocial therapies.

Pharmacotherapy

The treatment of schizophrenic patients was revolutionized in the mid-1950s with the recognition of the antipsychotic effects of chlorpromazine. Since then, the use of this and other "major tranquilizers" or "typical neuroleptic (or antipsychotic) drugs" improved the outcome of patients enough that many long-term hospitalization wards were emptied, and many schizophrenic patients were able to live in the community. In recent years the atypical antipsychotic drug clozapine has produced as much advance in treating psychotic disorders as did the typical agents in the 1950s. Moreover, a new generation of post-clozapine "novel antipsychotic" drugs have just been introduced into clinical practice at the time of this writing. Characteristics of the antipsychotic drugs and indications for their use are discussed more fully in Chapter 21. In this section we focus on their application to the psychotic disorders.

Effectiveness. Neuroleptic drugs are effective in the treatment of acute schizophrenia (Davis, 1975). Their ability to control psychosis was dramatically demonstrated in the National Institute of Mental Health's (NIMH) double-blind, placebo-controlled studies (Cole, Goldberg, and Klerman, 1964; Goldberg, Klerman, and Cole, 1965). Over a 6-week period clinically significant reductions in psychotic symptoms were observed in approximately 70% of neuroleptic-treated schizophrenics and 25% of placebo-treated schizophrenics. Psychosis worsened in about 45% of the placebo-treated group and in less than 5% of the neuroleptic-treated group. Approximately 25% of the neuroleptic-treated patients in the NIMH trials showed no change. Subsequent studies of neuroleptic nonresponders showed that such patients did not routinely respond to "megadoses" of medication (McCreadie et al., 1979; Bjorndal et al., 1980; Hollister and Kim, 1982). In addition, studies of serum neuroleptic levels in treatment-resistant schizophrenics indicated that most of these patients achieved high serum neuroleptic levels (Van Putten, May, and Jenden, 1981; Van Putten, 1984).

Although the relationship between serum neuroleptic levels and neuroleptic bioavailability at the site of antipsychotic activity is poorly understood, these results suggest that nonresponse is not due to simple pharmacokinetic phenomena. Moreover, data regarding D_2 occupancy imply that even modest doses of most "typical" or "atypical" agents achieve as much effect at the D_2 receptor as do megadoses (Wolkin et al., 1989). Fortunately, many of the nonresponders to typical neuroleptics have some response to clozapine (see below).

In addition to their beneficial effects acutely, neuroleptic medication appears more effective than placebo in preventing future psychotic relapses in remitted schizophrenic patients. In 29 double-blind, placebo-controlled studies involving a total of 3519 patients, the 1-year relapse rate in the drug-treated group was found to be substantially less than that for the placebo-treated group: 19% versus 55% (Davis et al., 1980). However, although neuroleptics unquestionably reduce the risk of psychotic relapse for many schizophrenic patients, it is clear that over time many patients relapse despite continued treatment, and some patients may function well even without the medication.

For example, Johnson (1979) reported that 25% of neuroleptic-free schizophrenics did not relapse over a 4-year period, and Rosen and associates (1968) found that maintenance neuroleptic treatment reduced the rate of relapse for patients categorized as "hospitalization prone" but had no effect on the clinical stability of other patients. Moreover, there is a subgroup of patients who remain clinically stable despite having low serum neuroleptic levels, which suggest low neuroleptic bioavailability (Kolakowska et al., 1985; Faraone et al., 1986). The existence of a subgroup of schizophrenic patients who may not need chronic neuroleptic medication is also consis-

tent with studies of schizophrenic prognosis before the advent of antipsychotic drugs. These reported clinical improvement in 17–40% of untreated schizophrenic disorders (Hastings, 1958; Beck, 1968; Langfeldt, 1969; Bleuler, 1978). In summary, although many schizophrenic patients benefit greatly from maintenance with typical neuroleptics, many patients either do not respond or relapse despite treatment. And there may be other patients who can function as well without medication as with it.

Novel antipsychotic agents. In recent years a number of new or "novel" agents have been introduced. Clozapine, the first of these agents, is clearly more effective than the older "typical" antipsychotic drugs for patients who do not respond to these older agents. In an international multicenter study (Kane et al., 1988), 30% of treatment-resistant patients had a meaningful response to clozapine over a 6-week period. More recent studies suggest that the rate of response in such patients can be up to 50% (Lieberman et al., 1994). Clozapine decreases positive psychotic symptoms, and may also alleviate negative symptoms according to some (Miller et al., 1994) but not all (Carpenter et al., 1995) reports. Moreover, it improves overall quality of life and decreases the suicide rate in treatment-resistant patients with schizophrenia (Meltzer et al., 1990; Meltzer and Okayli, 1995). Finally, some health economics studies demonstrate that clozapine use may be associated with cost savings, largely owing to a decrease in the rate of hospitalization (Revicki et al., 1990; Meltzer et al., 1993). Despite its efficacy, clinicians restrict clozapine use mainly to schizophrenic patients resistant to or intolerant of the older antipsychotic drugs, because of a rare but sometimes fatal side effect—agranulocytosis (discussed below).

The introduction of clozapine has "changed the landscape" for the pharmacology of psychotic disorders. Clearly, "treatment-resistant" patients may respond to clozapine, but "suboptimal responders" may do so as well (Breier et al., 1993). Green (1996) suggested that the success of clozapine may indicate that our expectations for pharmacologic agents may be too low, and that optimal use of clozapine (and the post-clozapine generation of agents) may improve the short- and long-term outcome of many patients. The severe side effects of clozapine (principally agranulocytosis and seizures) have thus far generally limited its use to treatment-resistant patients. Fortunately, a number of new "post-clozapine" agents are in the process of being introduced into clinical practice.

The first of these agents, risperidone, has a similar ratio of $5HT_2/D_2$ affinity in in vitro systems as clozapine, and appears to be more effective (particularly for negative symptoms) and to lead to fewer extrapyramidal side effects than typical agents (Marder and Meibach, 1994). The second novel drug, olanzapine, has a broad spectrum pharmacologic profile that resembles clozapine and also appears better than the standard agents, particularly in negative symptoms (Beasley et al., 1996). To determine ways to improve the long-term outcome of patients, investigators have been examining the efficacy of clozapine, risperidone, and olanzapine for first-episode patients. The next edition of this chapter may very well contain exciting new information about the benefits of these new agents.

Side effects. The side effects produced by the older agents have limited their use. For purposes of description, they can be divided into non-neurological and neurological side effects. Non-neurological effects include, among others: sedation, hypotension, dry mouth, blurred vision, tachycardia, galactorrhea, amenorrhea, decreased libido, weight gain, hyperpyrexia, retinopathy, and seizures (Hollister, 1977). The neurological side effects include: acute dystonia, parkinsonism, akathisia, and tardive dyskinesia (Marder and VanPatten, 1995). Dystonia (muscle spasms appearing in the head and neck) occurs most often shortly after the medications are begun; it occurs in a minority of cases and is easily treated with anticholinergic agents. Akathisia (a subjective sense of restlessness often associated with pacing or moving the feet) may occur in up to 75% of patients and be a source of extreme discomfort. Lowering the medication dose or adding a beta-blocker may be helpful. The rigidity, akinesia, and tremors of parkinsonism, which may occur in about 30% of patients, is improved by the addition of an anticholinergic medication.

Prolonged use of neuroleptic medication can produce a sometimes irreversible syndrome known as tardive dyskinesia (TD), which consists of uncontrollable movements usually involving the mouth, lips, and tongue. A review of the epidemiology of TD found the rate among neuroleptic-treated patients to range from 5.6% to 46%, with a mean of 17.6% across 37 different studies examining a total of 12,930 patients (Jeste and Wyatt, 1982). Older women, those treated at high doses for long periods of time, and psychotic patients with affective disorders may be at greater risk than others (Marder and VanPatten, 1995). In the 1980s, an increase in malpractice litigation regarding tardive dyskinesia complicated the clinical use of the standard neuroleptic drugs (Applebaum, Schaffner, and Meisel, 1985). Fortunately, discontinuing treatment with standard neuroleptic agents is often accompanied by a decrease in dyskinetic symptoms. The atypical anti-

psychotic drug clozapine may not cause TD, and its use may allow symptoms of tardive dyskinesia to improve. At this writing it is not clear whether risperidone or olanzapine will be associated with tardive dyskinesia.

An uncommon but sometimes fatal reaction to neuroleptic medication is neuroleptic malignant syndrome (NMS). The clinical signs of the syndrome are fever, tachycardia, rigidity, altered consciousness, abnormal blood pressure (high, low, or labile), tachypnea, and diaphoresis (Levenson, 1985). Laboratory data usually indicate elevated serum creatinine phosphokinase levels and increased white blood cell counts. Treatment usually involves stopping the neuroleptic and monitoring vital functions. It appears that clozapine is rather unlikely to cause NMS, but it is too early to be sure whether the novel agents are as likely to produce NMS as the standard agents.

The newer agents (clozapine, risperidone, and olanzapine) have different side effect profiles than the older agents. Clozapine causes agranulocytosis, which can be fatal. With the weekly white blood count monitor's system currently in place, the rate of agranulocytosis over the first 6 years of its use in the United States has been 0.37%, with 13 deaths from agranulocytosis out of over 150,000 people given the drug (M. Kramer, Sandoz Pharmaceuticals, personal communication). Seizures are dose related and can occur in more than 5% of cases at high doses. Valproic acid is sometimes used with clozapine for seizure control. Other side effects include tachycardia, drooling, sedation, enuresis, orthostatic hypotension, hyperthermia, myoclonic jerks, drop attacks, and liver function changes. However, unlike the typical (older) agents, clozapine does not produce neurologic side effects or elevate the hormone prolactin.

Risperidone produces fewer neurological side effects than standard agents (Marder and Meibach, 1994) but more than clozapine. It also elevates prolactin and may be associated with galactorrhea. Olanzapine also appears to produce a low level of neurologic effects (but they can occur at high doses) and no significant elevation of prolactin.

Increasing awareness of the prevalence and severity of side effects caused by the older antipsychotic drugs led to strategies to minimize the cumulative neuroleptic dose a patient could be exposed to during his life, and thus prevent or lessen the risk of side effects, especially TD. Most clinicians have believed that an intensive acute period of neuroleptic therapy is appropriate, but there have been questions raised about the protracted use of neuroleptics without evidence of improvement. For patients responsive to the older agents, low dose (or at times, intermittent) medication strategies have often been tried (Carpenter and Heinrichs, 1984). Although these medication strategies may put the patient at increased risk for relapse, their use has at times been recommended because they reduce the risk of side effects.

Fortunately, the introduction of the new antipsychotic agents (which seem less likely to cause severe neurologic side effects) changes the calculation of benefits and risks of these agents. It may be that prolonged use of some of these newer agents may improve overall outcome without significant risk of severe side effects. More research, however, will be needed to determine the optimal treatment strategies using these new agents.

Behavior Therapy

In this section we consider some specific applications of behavioral techniques to the management of schizophrenic disorders.

Operant techniques. The principles of operant conditioning developed by B. F. Skinner and his colleagues define how the systematic manipulation of rewards and punishment can increase or decrease the frequency of specific human behaviors in specified contexts. Research suggests that these principles can be successfully applied to schizophrenic patients in a systematic and comprehensive program known as the *token economy* (Kazdin, 1977). Such programs are most effectively implemented on an inpatient, day hospital, or halfway house basis, where the therapeutic staff can control the rewards and punishments. A token is a small, easily identified object, such as a poker chip, that the patient can earn and then use to buy rewards. If possible, tokens should be individualized for each patient to avoid theft, gambling, and other interpatient exchanges. When patients first enter the token economy, they are given free tokens that they may use to buy rewards controlled by the staff. Rewards may include both concrete items, such as special foods, and access to valued activities, such as television and game rooms. To promote the generalization of behavioral change to real-life settings, rewards should be similar to those that occur naturally in the patient's life situation. Patients may have to be exposed to the rewards and experience their enjoyment value before they begin to buy them with tokens.

Once the patient has learned that tokens can be used to acquire rewards, the tokens are no longer given free. At this point the staff designs an individual behavioral program for the patient, which specifies the types and degree of behavioral change required to earn tokens. The initial requirements should be relatively easy. As the patient

learns the rules and begins to change, the rules can be modified to require more difficult levels of behavioral change. Enough staff should be available to observe patients' behavior.

When staffing is adequate, rewards are well chosen, and rules well defined, then the token economy can be an effective means of modifying behavior in schizophrenic patients (Kazdin and Bootzin, 1972). Reductions in bizarre and aggressive behaviors and increases in self-maintenance are relatively easy to achieve. Development of interactive social behaviors, however, has been less clearly demonstrated. This problem is due primarily to the fact that many schizophrenic patients emit very little, if any, appropriate social behavior. Social behavior cannot be improved by operant procedures if it does not already exist in some rudimentary form. Special techniques to modify social behavior are discussed in the next section.

Although modifying target behaviors in a token economy is fairly easy, generalizing these changes to the community is more difficult (Kazdin and Bootzin, 1972). As a rule, generalization of behavioral change to situations where tokens are unavailable is unlikely to occur unless systematic procedures are applied. To be successful, the target behaviors should, to some extent, be rewarded in the community (for example, behaviors related to job success). It is also useful to pair the earning of tokens with social reinforcement, such as praise and affection; gradually the tokens can be replaced with social rewards. If possible, behavioral training should take place in community as well as hospital settings. Because many patients are discharged to an environment that includes some authority figure, such as the owner of a halfway house or a relative, that person should be familiarized with behavioral principles, if possible, so the patient's behavioral training can continue. In addition, some patients can learn techniques of self-reinforcement to maintain behavioral change.

Response acquisition procedures. The basic idea of a response acquisition procedure is to teach the patient to emit a behavior that he rarely or never performs. Because many chronic psychiatric patients have few social behaviors, response acquisition techniques are often termed *social skills training* (Curran and Monti, 1982). This training is usually performed with groups of patients to provide the necessary social context.

Social behaviors that can be taught with such an approach include starting a conversation, self-disclosure, listening skills, giving and receiving criticism, and assertiveness. In addition to learning the elements of social behavior, patients are taught appropriate placement, timing, and sequencing of behavior. Response acquisition techniques can also be applied to daily living skills, such as self-care, cooking, and job hunting. Although more research is needed, social skills training appears to be an effective means of improving the social functioning of severely impaired psychiatric patients.

Family therapy. Many family therapy approaches assume that a patient's illness is directly or indirectly caused by deviant family structures or functions. The "behavioral" family therapy used to treat schizophrenia, however, does not. It does assume that family members have an impact on the course of illness, inasmuch as stress in the family environment has been associated with propensity to relapse (Vaughn and Leff, 1976; Vaughn et al., 1982). Behavioral family therapy not only reduces stress in the patient's life but also trains family members to participate actively in the community management of schizophrenia (Falloon et al., 1986). As described by Curran, Faraone, and Graves (1986), family therapy for schizophrenia has 3 major components: education, communication, and problem solving.

A primary goal of the educational component is to reduce the family's guilt and self-blame for the patient's illness. Educating family members about the genetic and biological bases of schizophrenia usually alleviates guilty feelings, allowing the family to use their emotional energy to cope more productively with their schizophrenic relative. The family must also understand that schizophrenic symptoms are outside the patient's control. This insight relieves tensions resulting from the belief that the patient is using psychotic symptoms to avoid adult responsibility; it also directly reduces unrealistic expectations that family members may hold for their schizophrenic relative. Such expectations (for example, that the patient will go to law school or be successful in business) are often a source of great stress for the patient. Understanding the biological aspects of schizophrenia helps family members to recognize and accept the importance of neuroleptic medication. A full discussion of the purpose, effectiveness, and potential side effects of the medicine also reinforces the patient's adherence to a neuroleptic regimen.

Family members must be informed about potential stresses within the home that could increase the likelihood of schizophrenic relapse. Discussion might include topics from the research literature, such as "expressed emotion" (Vaughn and Leff, 1976) and stressful life events (Rabkin, 1980). One should look for idiosyncratic stresses within each family. Asking the patient to describe to family members what he finds distressing is often useful. Curran, Faraone, and Graves (1986) have emphasized

that families should not confuse maintenance of a low-stress environment with permissiveness; the family needs to set limits on undesirable and disruptive behaviors as much as possible. Teaching the family principles of behavioral management, such as those used in token economy programs, might help them in managing their schizophrenic relative.

Although many families understand the information imparted in behavioral family therapy, they often do not have the communication skills to implement needed changes effectively. Communication training for families is similar to the response acquisition procedures described for schizophrenic patients; the only difference is that family members usually function at a higher level than the patient does. Common communication skills lacking in families include effective listening, giving and receiving positive feedback, giving and receiving criticism, making requests, talking about feelings, and being assertive (Falloon and Liberman, 1983; Curran, Faraone, and Graves, 1986).

A major source of family stress is often the inability to solve problems that arise from the schizophrenic illness or from other factors. A family management program emphasizing the development of problem-solving skills can significantly reduce schizophrenic relapse (Falloon et al., 1986). Curran, Faraone, and Graves (1986) recommend the following steps: (1) clearly define the problem; (2) have family members jointly generate as many possible solutions as they can think of; (3) systematically evaluate each potential solution; (4) choose the best solution based on the systematic evaluation; (5) implement the chosen solution; and (6) review the results of implementation and repeat the problem-solving process if necessary.

Psychotherapy

Individual psychotherapy is effective in the treatment of schizophrenia only when combined with pharmacotherapy. For example, May and associates (1976) compared neuroleptic therapy with (1) psychotherapy, (2) psychotherapy plus neuroleptic therapy, and (3) neither treatment. Neuroleptic therapy was markedly more effective than psychotherapy alone or the no-treatment control. Patients receiving psychotherapy alone did no better than the no-treatment group. There was, however, a nonsignificant trend for neuroleptics plus psychotherapy to be more effective than neuroleptics alone. In 1982, following a comprehensive review of the research literature, the American Psychiatric Association's Commission on Psychotherapies concluded:

Psychotherapy as the sole therapeutic modality seems to be useful in such conditions as some psychoneuroses, personality disorders, and maladjustments. Psychotherapy alone has been shown to be less effective for the major mood disorders and much less so for schizophrenia. The prototypic relationship between psychotherapy and pharmacotherapy seems reciprocal, favoring psychotherapy for personality disorders and favoring pharmacotherapy for psychotic disorders. For many conditions the interrelationship seems to be additive. (American Psychiatric Association, 1982, p. 227)

Although psychotherapy alone is not an effective treatment for schizophrenia, our experience indicates that a strong therapeutic alliance is necessary for the success of other treatments. The therapeutic skills required for the development of a productive therapist-patient relationship are also useful tools for maintaining compliance with drug regimens and motivation for behavior therapy. Although on the surface drug and behavior therapies appear to be easily and mechanically implemented, their success is facilitated by engaging the patient with the interpersonal therapeutic skills characteristic of psychotherapy.

Course and Outcome

For Kraepelin (1971), writing in 1919, one of the cardinal characteristics of schizophrenia was a progressively deteriorating course with little, if any, recovery from the illness. In contrast, manic-depressive illness was thought to have an episodic course with good intermorbid functioning and a relatively benign outcome. In this century, as psychiatry has moved from clinical observation to rigorous investigation, a more complex view of schizophrenic outcome has emerged.

Manfred Bleuler (1978), son of Eugen Bleuler, reported a 20-year follow-up of over 200 schizophrenic patients. He excluded from his study patients who either had died or had not been in a relatively stable psychiatric condition for a 5-year period. Surprisingly, 20% of his study sample had fully recovered from their psychoses. They were free of psychotic symptoms and demonstrated normal levels of social functioning. A mild outcome was observed in 33% of the patients. They continued to have hallucinations and delusions, but their observable behavior was normal, with only mild impairments in social functioning. A moderate or severe outcome was observed in 47% of the follow-up sample. These patients had severe impairments in all areas of social functioning, along with marked schizophrenic symptoms.

Tsuang, Woolson, and Fleming (1979) reported a 35–40-year follow-up study of 186 schizophrenics, 86 manics, and 212 depressives. The proportion of each group that married was 21% of the schizophrenics, 70% of the manics, 81% of the depressives, and 89% of a surgical control group. Ability to function outside an institutional setting was seen in 34% of the schizophrenics, 69% of the manics, 70% of the depressives, and 90% of the controls. Productive occupational functioning characterized 35% of the schizophrenics, 67% of the manics, 67% of the depressives, and 88% of the controls. The percentage of each group with no psychiatric symptoms at follow-up was 20% for schizophrenics, 50% for manics, 61% for depressives, and 85% for controls.

The World Health Organization (1973, 1979) performed an international 2-year follow-up study of over 1000 psychotic patients. An examination of the length of the psychotic episode that brought the patients to the project's attention indicates no marked differences between diagnostic groups. There was a trend in the data, however, suggesting that the average length of episode was greater for schizophrenia. The schizophrenic patients were psychotic for a greater percentage of the 2-year follow-up period than the affective patients. The percentage of patients psychotic at follow-up was greater for schizophrenia (37%) compared with mania (26%) and psychotic depression (14%). Overall, the pattern of course was most severe for the schizophrenic patients.

L. Ciompi (1980) was able to follow nearly 300 patients for as long as 50 years after hospitalization. Using Bleuler's categories of outcome, Ciompi found 27% of the patients to be fully recovered, 22% to have mild symptoms, 24% to have moderately severe symptoms, and 18% to have severe symptoms; 9% of the sample had an uncertain outcome. A progressively deteriorating, insidious onset was observed in 49% of the patients, the rest having a sudden or acute onset of illness with little or no difficulties in premorbid functioning. In addition, 48% of the patients had a continuous course of illness; the rest had an episodic course. Episodic course was more likely among patients with acute onset. Acute onset and episodic course were both associated with better long-term outcome.

Overall, studies of course and outcome support Kraepelin's original conclusions: the course and outcome of schizophrenia are, on the average, worse than those of mood disorders. But a substantial proportion of schizophrenics have been observed to have a fairly benign course and outcome. This is most marked in the studies of Bleuler and Ciompi, which suggest full recovery in approximately 25% of the patients. Notably, a retrospective follow-up study from Vermont suggested that favorable outcome may be more common among schizophrenic patients than was previously believed (Harding et al., 1987). This study examined 82 DSM-III defined schizophrenic patients 32 years after their index hospital admissions. At follow-up, most of these patients were free of schizophrenic symptomatology (68%), required little or no help to meet basic needs (81%), and led a moderately to very full life (73%).

Unfortunately, the ability to predict outcome among schizophrenic patients is limited. From their analyses of the WHO outcome data, Strauss and associates (1978) concluded that previous levels of work functioning and social relationships are significant predictors of outcome; thus different outcome variables may represent semi-independent processes.

Many clinicians believe that the presence of affective symptoms during a schizophrenic decompensation is a favorable prognostic sign. This connection was strongly emphasized by the work of George Vaillant (1964), who observed that 11 of 13 earlier studies had reported an association between symptoms suggestive of psychotic depression and recovery in schizophrenia. He found that 80% of 30 recovered schizophrenics and 33% of 30 nonrecovered schizophrenics had manifested depressive symptomatology. His 1964 data on patients followed for up to 15 years found the correlation between remission and depressive symptoms to be .40. Although a majority of studies report similar findings (Levenstein, Klein, and Pollack, 1966; McCabe et al., 1972; Taylor and Abrams, 1975), some have been less supportive. For example, Bland, Parlner, and Orn (1978) report that whereas factors relating to consumption of care and morbidity are highly correlated with outcome ratings, the correlation between depressive symptoms and outcome in schizophrenia is only .10. Similar results were reported by Carpenter and associates (1978) in their discussion of predictors of outcome derived from schizophrenics participating in the WHO study. The study of Welner and associates (1977) also failed to find any relation between affective symptoms and prognosis. More research is needed to understand more fully whether affective symptoms are a sign of good-prognosis schizophrenia or a misdiagnosed affective or schizoaffective disorder.

Depression is common in the course of schizophrenia. Over a 6- to 12-year span, Guze et al. (1983) reported that 25 of 44 schizophrenics (57%) had one or more depressive episodes. Relatives of these schizophrenics were not at increased risk for mood disorder compared with relatives of schizophrenics without depressive episodes. It is important to note that these schizophrenics had an otherwise typical course of schizophrenic symptoms. Their illness did not appear to begin with affective symptoms and was not episodic.

Obsessive or compulsive features also occur in patients with schizophrenia. Although early studies suggested that the presence of such features was associated with a benign course (Rosen, 1956), more recent studies (Fenton and McGlashan, 1986; Berman et al., 1995a) suggest that their presence is associated with a poor outcome. Berman et al. (1995a) suggested that 14–47% of inpatients with schizophrenia may have such features. Preliminary data suggest that addition of a serotonin reuptake blocking medication to typical neuroleptic drugs may be helpful for psychotic patients with obsessive-compulsive features (Berman et al., 1995b). Further studies are needed to determine whether the presence of such obsessive and compulsive features identifies a true subtype of schizophrenia, and to explore optimal treatment options.

One aspect of the course of an illness is the stability of the symptoms over time as reflected in diagnostic stability. Personal interviews of 93 of 117 living patients who had been diagnosed schizophrenic 35 to 40 years earlier and who met Washington University criteria on chart review confirmed the diagnosis in 93%. Only 4% were found to have mood disorders at follow-up (Tsuang et al., 1981). Guze et al. (1983) reported similar results in a prospective follow-up of 19 narrowly defined schizophrenics. None were re-diagnosed with a mood disorder.

Mortality in schizophrenics is elevated compared with the general population (Tsuang and Woolson, 1977; Ciompi, 1980; Simpson, 1988). A good portion of this increased mortality is due to suicide (Simpson, 1988). Tsuang (1978) found that 10% of the deceased schizophrenics died by suicide; this represents 4% of the total sample of 195 who could be traced to either death or present residence. Schizophrenics have an increased risk of death owing to physical illness as well. However, a reported decreased risk for cancer death appears to be an artifact of inappropriate statistical analysis (Tsuang et al., 1980b). As noted earlier, recent data suggest that the atypical neuroleptic clozapine may lessen the suicide risk in such patients (Meltzer and Okayli, 1995).

Although psychosocial factors have not been convincingly shown to influence the etiology of schizophrenia, a growing body of data indicates the importance of these factors in determining the course of the disorder. Much research is focused on the role of stressful life events. Although some controversy exists over the best definition of a stressful event, most researchers agree that stressful events are those life circumstances that require physical or psychological adaptation on the part of the patient. Life events may be negative, as in the death of a spouse, or positive, as in the birth of a child. J. G. Rabkin's (1980) comprehensive review of the relevant research literature found no support for the hypothesis that life events are associated with onset of illness. Schizophrenics who relapse, however, *tend* to have more stressful life events than those who do not relapse, although relapse can occur in the absence of such events and remission can be maintained in their presence. More stressful life events are found for relapsing schizophrenics taking neuroleptic medication than for relapsing schizophrenics who are drug free (Birley and Brown, 1970; Leff et al., 1973). This suggests that the prophylactic effects of neuroleptics and the absence of stressful life events may be additive. That is, the availability of one protective factor may compensate for the lack of the other.

An important focus of psychosocial research has been the emotional environment in the family of the schizophrenic patient. This research has examined a construct known as *expressed emotion* (EE) (Kavanagh, 1992). EE is defined in terms of the degree to which family members are critical of the patient, the amount of hostility they express toward him, and their degree of emotional overinvolvement with him. Vaughn and Leff (1976) examined 9-month relapse rates in 128 schizophrenic patients living with their families. The relapse rate among patients living with high-EE families was 51%. This contrasted sharply with the 13% relapse among patients living with low-EE families. Among patients living with high-EE families the relapse rate was strongly related to the amount of contact the patient had with the family. Patients having more than 35 hours of family contact per week had a relapse rate of 69%, compared with a 28% relapse rate for patients having fewer than 35 hours of contact. The prophylactic effect of neuroleptic medication differed for patients returning to low-EE and high-EE families. Among the low-EE group, the relapse rate was not different between patients on drugs and those not on drugs. In contrast, patients from high-EE families were significantly more likely to relapse if they were not taking neuroleptic medication. This outcome was most marked for patients having more than 35 hours of contact per week with their relatives. Among this latter group of patients, 92% of those not on drugs relapsed, compared with a 53% relapse rate for those who continued to take neuroleptic medication.

Vaughn and Leff's (1976) study of a British sample was replicated in a 9-month study of schizophrenic patients from California. The relapse rate for patients from high-EE families (56%) was substantially higher than that for patients returning to low-EE families (17%). The effect of family contact for high-EE families was similar to that observed in the British study. Patients having more than 35

hours of contact per week with high-EE families had a 77% relapse rate, compared with the 46% relapse rate for patients having less contact with high-EE family members. The California study agreed with the British study in finding that a combination of low family contact and regular medication mitigated the effects of having a high-EE family. The California study, however, found no medication effect for patients having more than 35 hours of contact per week with high-EE families. Studies designed to reduce expressed emotion in families have demonstrated reduced relapse rates in the treated families (Falloon et al., 1982; Leff et al., 1982; Falloon and Liberman, 1983; Falloon et al., 1986).

Epidemiology

Prevalence and Incidence

A large number of studies have provided reasonably consistent answers to 2 fundamental questions of psychiatric epidemiology: how many individuals in the general population suffer from schizophrenic disorders at a given point or period in time *(prevalence)*, and how many new cases of schizophrenia are observed in the general population during a specified period of time *(incidence)?* Table 13.3 presents the results of 51 published studies of the prevalence of schizophrenia in population samples from 24 countries. The results range from a low of 0.6 cases per 1000 in Ghana to a high of 17.0 cases per 1000 in one of the Swedish samples. Altogether, these studies suggest that at any given point in time 0.5% of the population is suffering from a schizophrenic disorder. The prevalence results in Table 13.3 are remarkably consistent, given the high degree of cultural and methodological variability among these studies. The results clearly indicate that schizophrenia is not specific to one type of culture. The disorder does not discriminate between East and West or between developed and less developed countries. The unusually high prevalence of 17 per 1000 reported by Böök and associates (1978) may be caused by special environmental factors. The population studied was a north Swedish isolate separated from the rest of the country and located in an austere environment. It has been suggested that such environments may be more conducive to the withdrawn, isolated lifestyle preferred by many schizophrenic patients.

The prevalence figures in Table 13.3 underestimate the lifetime risk for schizophrenia, because recovered cases are counted as unaffected, and the estimate of risk is not corrected for the variable age of onset of the disorder. Estimates of the lifetime prevalence for schizophrenia range from 0.3% to 2.7%, with a mean of 1% (Table 13.4). Thus, about 1 in every 100 people will develop a schizophrenic disorder during his or her lifetime.

Table 13.5 presents the results of 17 studies of the incidence of schizophrenia in population samples from 10 countries. The expected annual appearance of new cases in these populations ranges from a low of 0.10 per 1000 to a high of 0.69 per 1000. On average this suggests an incidence of 0.35 new cases of schizophrenia per 1000 members of the general population. W. W. Eaton (1985) noted that lifetime prevalence figures for schizophrenia are lower than expected, given the reported incidence rates for schizophrenia and the fact that the disorder is usually chronic. He accounts for this in part by the finding that the rate of mortality among schizophrenics is approximately twice that of the general population (Tsuang, Woolson, and Fleming, 1980a).

Risk Factors

A major goal of psychiatric epidemiology is to examine the differential distribution of schizophrenic disorders among well-defined subsamples of the general population. This research strategy has led to an empirical compilation of factors associated with an elevated risk for schizophrenia. In this section we briefly discuss risk factors that have been found to be relevant to schizophrenia. The discovery of factors that increase an individual's likelihood of developing schizophrenia clearly has implications for an etiological and pathophysiological understanding of the disorder.

As discussed in detail in Chapter 36, family, twin, and adoption studies provide strong evidence that individuals with a schizophrenic biological relative are much more likely to develop the disorder than individuals with no

Table 13.3 Prevalence of schizophrenia

Study	Location	Prevalence per 1000
Brugger (1931)	Germany	2.4
Brugger (1933)	Germany	2.2
Klemperer (1933)	Germany	10.0
Strömgren (1935)	Denmark	3.3
Lemkao (1936)	U.S.A.	2.9
Roth and Luton (1938)	U.S.A.	1.7
Brugger (1938)	Germany	2.3
Lin (1946–1948)	China	2.1
Mayer-Gross (1948)	Scotland	4.2
Bremer (1951)	Norway	4.4
Böök (1953)	Sweden	9.5
Larson and Sjogren (1954)	Sweden	4.6
National Survey (1954)	Japan	2.3
Essen-Möller (1956)	Sweden	6.7
Yoo (1961)	Korea	3.8
Juel-Nielsen et al. (1962)	Denmark	1.5
Ivanys et al. (1963)	Czechoslovakia	1.7
Krasik (1965)	U.S.S.R.	3.1
Hagnell (1966)	Sweden	4.5
Wing et al. (1967)	England	4.4
	Scotland	2.5
	U.S.A.	7.0
Lin et al. (1969)	Taiwan	1.4
Jayasundera (1969)	Ceylon	3.2
Kato (1969)	Japan	2.3
Dube (1970)	India	3.7
Roy et al. (1970)	Canada	
	Indians	5.7
	Non-Indians	1.6
Crocetti et al. (1971)	Yugoslavia	
	Rijeka	7.3
	Zagreb	4.2

Study	Location	Prevalence per 1000
Kulcar et al. (1971)	Yugoslavia	
	Lubin	7.4
	Sinj-Trogir	2.9
Bash et al. (1972)	Iran	2.1
Zharikov (1972)	U.S.S.R.	5.1
Babigian (1975)	U.S.A.	4.7
Temkov et al. (1975)	Bulgaria	2.8
Rotstein (1977)	U.S.S.R.	3.8
Nielsen and Nielsen (1977)	Denmark	2.7
Ouspenskaya (1978)	U.S.S.R.	5.3
Böök et al. (1978)	Sweden	17.0
Lehtinen et al. (1978)	Finland	15.0
Wijesinghe et al. (1978)	Ceylon	5.6
Weissman (1980)	New Haven	4.0
Hafner and Klug (1980)	Germany	1.2
Walsh et al. (1980)	Ireland	8.3
Rin and Lin (1982)	Taiwan	0.9
Sikanartey et al. (1984)	Ghana	0.6
Meyers et al. (1984)	New Haven	11.0
	Baltimore	10.0
	St. Louis	6.0
Von Korff et al. (1985)	Baltimore	6.0
Hwu (1989)	Taiwan	2.4
Astrup (1989)	Norway	7.3
Hwu (1989)	Taiwan	2.4
Bøjholm (1989)	Denmark	3.3
Lee (1990)	Korea	3.1
Stefánsson (1991)	Iceland	3.0
Youssef (1991)	Ireland	3.3

ill relatives. The accumulated evidence suggests that the transmission of the disorder between relatives is primarily genetic, not environmental. The exact genetic mechanism, however, is unknown (Faraone and Tsuang, 1985; Tsuang and Faraone, 1994).

In industrialized societies, schizophrenia is more prevalent among lower socioeconomic groups (Cooper, 1978). Dunham's (1965) work suggests that the excess of schizophrenics in the lowest socioeconomic group results either from downward drift or from the schizophrenic's failure to move into a higher class. Goldberg and Morrison (1963) found that the social class distribution of the fathers of schizophrenics did not differ from that of the general population. Male schizophrenics tended to have lower job achievement than did fathers, brothers, and other male relatives. Whereas fathers tended to rise in job status, schizophrenic sons tended to fall into jobs of lower and lower status or become disabled. Thus it appears that,

although low socioeconomic status is known to have deleterious effects, it is primarily an effect of schizophrenia rather than its cause.

Many studies have found increased rates of obstetric complications (OCs) in the births of children who eventually became schizophrenic. For example, schizophrenic patients are more likely to have been born prematurely and to have had relatively low birth weights (Lane and Albee, 1966; Woerner, Pollack, and Klein, 1971). The finding that OCs are predictive of subsequent schizophrenia has been confirmed in other studies (McNeil and Kaij, 1978; Jacobsen and Kinney, 1980), and a review by McNeil (1988) suggested that complications leading to oxygen deprivation or trauma appear to be most relevant to the subsequent development of schizophrenia.

Several studies have found that obstetric complications tend to be more common in sporadic compared with familial cases of schizophrenia (Kinney and Jacobsen, 1978; Reveley, Reveley, and Murray, 1984; Schwarzkopf et al., 1989; O'Callaghan et al., 1990). Notably, McNeil et al. (1994) found that obstetric complications among monozygotic (MZ) twin pairs were more common among those discordant for schizophrenia than those concordant for schizophrenia. A similar trend had been reported by Onstad et al. (1992). Also, among MZ twins discordant for schizophrenia, obstetric complications are more frequent in the history of the schizophrenic twin compared with the co-twin (Pollin and Stabenau, 1968). However, birth weight differences were not found between schizophrenic and well MZ co-twins in a review of 6 systematically ascertained twin samples (Shields and Gottesman, 1977).

In contrast to twin studies, data from several non-twin family studies are not consistent with the assertion that a history of obstetric complications is more frequent among sporadic schizophrenic patients (Pearlson et al., 1985; Nimgaonkar et al., 1988; O'Callaghan et al., 1992; Roy et al., 1994). However, studies comparing schizophrenic patients with their well siblings find more OCs among the patients (Woerner, Pollack, and Klein, 1971; DeLisi et al., 1988), although some studies disagree (McCreadie et al., 1992). Discrepancies among studies may reflect either the greater statistical power of the twin study (Eaves, Kendler, and Schulz, 1986), or differences among studies in the methods of OC assessment or the specific OCs studied. Nevertheless, taken together, these results suggest that OCs are probably an etiological risk factor for schizophrenia, but that they are neither necessary nor sufficient causes of the disorder. This is consistent with prospective studies showing that most individuals who experience OCs do not develop psychoses or

Table 13.4 Lifetime prevalence of schizophrenia

Study	Location	Lifetime Prevalence per 1000
Hagnell (1966)	Sweden	14.0
Brugger (1931)	Germany	3.8
Brugger (1933)	Germany	4.1
Klemperer (1933)	Germany	14.0
Brugger (1938)	Germany	3.6
Strömgren (1938)	Denmark	5.8
Ødegard (1946)	Norway	18.7
Fremming (1947)	Denmark	9.0
Böök (1953)	Sweden	26.6
Sjögren (1954)	Sweden	16.0
Helgason (1964)	Iceland	8.0
Helgason (1977)	Iceland	4.9
Böök (1978)	Sweden	24.8
Robins (1984)	New Haven, U.S.A.	19.0
	Baltimore, U.S.A.	16.0
	St. Louis, U.S.A.	10.0
Widerlov (1989)	Denmark	37.0
Lehtinen (1990)	Finland	13.0
Hwu (1989)	Taiwan	2.6
Youssef (1991)	Ireland	6.4

other psychiatric disorders (Buka, Tsuang, and Lipsitt, 1993).

It may be that the effect of OCs is to activate the genetic predisposition to schizophrenia. For example, in the study of DeLisi et al. (1988) that found more OCs among schizophrenic compared with non-schizophrenic siblings, each family had at least 2 siblings with schizophrenia, suggesting that OCs work in combination with familial factors. A similar effect was shown more dramatically in a series of studies of children born to schizophrenic mothers. These "high-risk" children are not more likely than other children to have OCs (Mednick and Schulsinger, 1968). However, among the high-risk children, OCs are predictive of subsequent psychiatric abnormality (Mednick, 1970). Among the same high-risk sample, Parnas et al. (1982) reported a tendency for the children who became schizophrenic to have had more OCs. They also found that those with the least complicated births had "borderline schizophrenia" (i.e., schizotypal personality disorder). The investigators suggested that children with the schizophrenic genotype would not develop schizophrenia if they had unusually uncomplicated births.

J. G. Knight (1985) speculated that schizophrenia may be an autoimmune disease triggered by infection. This hypothesis is supported by the fact that schizophrenia and autoimmune diseases share common features, such as variable age of onset, incomplete penetrance, and a course characterized by periods of remission and relapse. The autoimmune hypothesis is also consistent with findings regarding another risk factor, lack of rheumatoid arthritis. This fairly common disorder, which probably involves other autoimmune mechanisms, is rarely found among schizophrenic patients. A common autoimmune genetic mechanism facilitating one disorder and preventing the other could explain this finding (Knight, 1985). The socioeconomic class findings are probably due to a combination of the direct effects of inadequate medical care and the indirect effects of downward drift. In any case, it is clear that the epidemiologic study of well-defined populations provides a useful data base for the generation of hypotheses about the etiology of schizophrenic disorders.

The theory that schizophrenia is caused by a virus has been put forward to explain several epidemiological and clinical observations (Torrey and Kaufmann, 1986). Fore-

Table 13.5 Incidence of schizophrenia

Study	Location	Annual Number of New Cases per 1000
Ødegaard (1946)	Norway	.24
Hollingshead and Redlich (1958)	U.S.A.	.30
Norris (1959)	U.K.	.17
Jaco (1960)	U.S.A.	.35
Dunham (1965)	U.S.A.	.52
Warthen (1967)	U.S.A.	.70
Adelstein et al. (1968)	U.K.	.26–.35
Walsh (1969)	Ireland	.46–.57
Hafner and Reimann (1970)	Germany	.54
Lieberman (1974)	U.S.S.R.	.19–.20
Hailey et al. (1974)	U.K.	.10–.14
Babigian (1975)	U.S.A.	.69
Nielsen (1976)	Denmark	.20
Helgason (1977)	Iceland	.27
Krupinski (1983)	Australia	.18
Folnegovic (1990)	Croatia	.22
Youssef (1991)	Ireland	.16

most among these is the finding that the births of schizophrenic patients are more likely to occur during the late winter and spring months, when the fetus is at increased risk for exposure to viruses (Hare, Price, and Slater, 1974; Dalen, 1975; Hare, 1976). Moreover, studies of immunological parameters have found in the serum and cerebral spinal fluid of schizophrenic patients excess levels of herpes antibody titre, immunoglobulins, cytomegalovirus antibody titre, interleukin-2 receptors, alpha interferon, and autoantibodies (Libikova et al., 1979; Torrey, Yolken, and Winfrey, 1982; Kaufmann et al., 1983; van Kammen et al., 1984; Kirch et al., 1985; Ganguli et al., 1987; Rapaport et al., 1989). Also, some studies report an association between schizophrenia and the Human Leukocyte Antigen (HLA) A9 locus (Goldin, DeLisi, and Gershon, 1987). Since the HLA loci are known to be associated with autoimmune diseases, these data led Wright, Gill, and Murray (1993) to suggest that some cases of schizophrenia may have an autoimmune basis.

Evidence supportive of the viral hypothesis also comes from studies of persons born during influenza epidemics. Mednick et al. (1988) studied a Finnish cohort who had been fetuses during a 1957 epidemic of influenza. They reported that those exposed to the epidemic during their second trimester of development were at increased risk for subsequently being diagnosed with schizophrenia. However, this finding was not replicated in a Scottish study that failed to consistently find an increased risk for schizophrenia associated with influenza epidemics in 1918, 1919, or 1957; analyses limited to the city of Edinburgh in 1957 supported the viral hypothesis, but the nationwide data did not (Kendell and Kemp, 1989). Also, only limited evidence of an association between viral epidemics and schizophrenia was found in an American study (Torrey, Rawlings, and Waldman, 1988). Barr and associates (1990) criticized these studies on methodological grounds and replicated the Finnish results in a Danish sample. Data presented by Sham et al. (1992) supported a link between schizophrenia and maternal influenza but suggested that it would account for fewer than 2% of schizophrenia cases. In contrast, Crow and Done (1992) did not support the hypothesis that maternal influenza was a risk factor for schizophrenia. Takei et al. (in press) found that females—but not males—exposed to influenza epidemics 5 months prior to birth had an increased rate of schizophrenia in adulthood. Although more research is needed, it seems reasonable to conclude that viral infection during fetal development may play a role in the etiology of schizophrenia.

Several studies examining season of birth show that non-familial schizophrenic probands are more likely to be born during winter months than familial schizophrenic probands (Shur, 1982; Goldstein et al., 1990; O'Callaghan et al., 1991; Roy et al., 1994). For example, Roy et al. (1994) reported that 32% of sporadic schizophrenic patients were born between December 21 and March 21, compared with 18% of familial patients. Goldstein et al. (1990) delineated a cluster of schizophrenic patients characterized by poor premorbid history, flat affect, winter birth, and no family history of schizophrenia. This cluster was more common in male sporadic cases. This may be similar to the "neurodevelopmental subtype" characterized by Castle and Murray (1991) as having early onset, poor premorbid social adjustment, restricted affect, and a male to female ratio of 7 to 3.

In contrast to the 5 studies showing increased winter birth among sporadic schizophrenic patients, several studies have implicated winter-spring births as a risk factor for familial schizophrenia. For example, Pulver et al. (1992) found the highest rates of schizophrenia among relatives when the proband had been born between February and May. The lowest rates occurred when the proband's birth was between October and January. This effect was observed for all female probands and for male probands for relatives younger than 30 years of age. The older relatives of male probands were less likely to have schizophrenia if the proband had been born between February and May.

The season of birth results are, admittedly, difficult to reconcile. In part, this is due to the different time windows used to define winter birth. Notably, all studies find some evidence for seasonality, but until the causes of seasonality are better understood and data are reported on similar time scales, the connection between putative viral infections and familial schizophrenia will be difficult to evaluate.

Brain Dysfunction in Schizophrenia

In a review of schizophrenia and brain dysfunction, L. J. Seidman (1983) concluded that neurodiagnostic studies provide evidence for 3 distinct categories of schizophrenic patients. The most severely and clearly brain-damaged group manifests a variety of abnormalities, including cerebral atrophy, enlarged ventricles, diffuse neuropsychological deficits, electroencephalographic abnormalities, and predominantly negative symptoms. A second group of patients exhibits moderate brain dysfunction with some evidence for atypical structural asymmetries and hemispheric asymmetries of function. It is likely that brain dysfunction in this group is relatively mild and localized to left hemisphere functions. Seidman concluded that the third group, paranoid schizophrenics, was less well understood from a neurological perspective.

Structural Brain Abnormalities

We use the phrase "structural brain abnormalities" to refer to any unusual changes in the form or configuration of the brain observed in schizophrenic patients but not in healthy people. The most direct way to observe such changes is literally to look at the brain, after death, using methods from neuropathology. Many such studies have been done thanks to the generosity of individuals who agreed to donate their brain to research following their death. We can draw 2 major conclusions from the results of these neuropathologic studies of schizophrenia (Weinberger, Wagner, and Wyatt, 1983; Bogerts, 1993). First, abnormalities of the brain are common among schizophrenic patients. For example, some studies have reported atypical cell architecture and neuronal loss in prefrontal cortex (Benes, Davidson, and Bird, 1986; Akbarian et al., 1993a), cingulate cortex (Benes et al., 1987), entorhinal cortex (Falkai, Bogerts, and Rozumek, 1988), and the temporal lobe (Jakob and Beckmann, 1986; Akbarian et al., 1993b). Second, no single abnormality is found in all or even most brains from schizophrenic patients. This is a curious result, which we will see mirrored by other methods of studying the schizophrenic brain. Whereas most well-defined brain diseases leave a distinct pathophysiological signature on the brain, this is not the case for schizophrenia.

The study of brain dysfunction in schizophrenia has been greatly facilitated by the increasingly sophisticated neurodiagnostic techniques that have become available in the last few decades. Computed tomography (CT) and magnetic resonance imaging (MRI) have been used to study gross structural brain pathology by many investigators. A review by Weinberger and Kleinman (1986) found that 24 of 29 CT scan studies of lateral ventricular size report ventricular enlargement in schizophrenic patients. Nine of 11 CT scan studies of the third ventricle report it to be enlarged in schizophrenia. Cortical sulcal enlargement has been observed in 14 of 17 studies. Shenton et al. (1992) have demonstrated a relationship between thought disorder and volume of the left superior temporal gyrus. The observation of CT scan abnormalities among untreated schizophrenics suggests that the findings are not due to neuroleptic treatment (Weinberger, 1984). Subsequent MRI studies have confirmed these early findings of structural brain anomalies in schizophrenic patients (Weinberger et al., 1992; Andreasen et al., 1994).

Patients with enlarged ventricles tend to have negative symptoms, cognitive impairment, more neurological signs, less independent residential living, longer inpatient hospital stays, and a poor response to neuroleptic treatment (Johnstone et al., 1976; Golden et al., 1980; Weinberger et al., 1980; Andreasen et al., 1982; Weinberger, 1984; Zec and Weinberger, 1986; Raz and Raz, 1990). After reviewing 10 studies, Lewis (1987) concluded that ventricular enlargement was more common among schizophrenic patients without a family history of schizophrenia. A subsequent review of additional studies also supported this conclusion (Lyons et al., 1989b). These results initially suggested that ventricular enlargement might be a useful means for identifying subtypes of schizophrenia. However, researchers have not yet been able to isolate a homogeneous subtype with this feature (Daniel et al., 1991).

The ventricular enlargement associated with schizophrenia is present at the onset of the illness; it is probably not due to progressive deterioration through the course of the illness (Weinberger, 1984). This abnormality, however, is not confined to schizophrenia. It has also been reported in mania, schizoaffective disorder, and adolescent obsessive-compulsive disorder (Nasrallah, McCalley-Whitters, and Jacoby, 1982; Rieder et al., 1983; Behar et al., 1984).

Most investigators favor a neurodevelopmental model to explain the focal abnormalities detected in patients with schizophrenia (Weinberger, 1995). The apparent lack of progressive ventricular enlargement, apparent prenatal pathology, and absence of gliosis seem to favor this model. Some authors, however, have proposed that certain aspects of schizophrenia may be consistent with a neurodegenerative process (Olney and Farber, 1995; Coyle, 1996). Further research will be required to clarify this issue.

Functional Brain Abnormalities

Sophisticated studies of brain function have become possible with the development of positron emission tomography (PET), magnetic resonance spectroscopy (MRS), brain potential imaging (BPI), and regional cerebral blood flow (RCBF) procedures such as photon computerized tomography (SPECT) and functional MRI (fMRI). The PET scanning procedure measures the metabolism of radioactively tagged glucose. This allows a computer to reconstruct an image that reflects relative degrees of glucose use throughout the brain. Several studies suggest that schizophrenics have relatively decreased levels of metabolism in the frontal cortex (Farkas et al., 1984; Weinberger and Berman, 1988; Buchsbaum et al., 1990). Hypofrontality in schizophrenics, however, was not consistently observed in these studies, and it has not been observed by some others (Sheppard et al., 1983). Wolkin and associates (1985) did PET studies of 10 chronic schizophrenic subjects before and after neuroleptic treatment. Compared with normal controls, the schizophrenics had lower metabolic activity levels in frontal and temporal regions. The schizophrenics tended to have greater metabolic activity in the basal ganglia area. After neuroleptic treatment, the schizophrenics manifested normal metabolic activity except for the persistence of hypofrontality. Unfortunately, the finding of hypofrontality may not be specific to schizophrenia, as it has been reported among patients with mood disorders (Buchsbaum et al., 1984).

Some studies of regional cerebral blood flow (RCBF) use a radioactive isotope, either inhaled or injected, to measure cerebral blood flow; others use rapid MRI procedures. Studies of RCBF in schizophrenics and controls have yielded equivocal results. Some studies find that total brain blood flow is reduced in schizophrenia (Mathew et al., 1982; Ariel et al., 1983), and regional blood flow measurements suggest a particular reduction in frontal blood flow (Buchsbaum and Ingvar, 1982; Ariel et al., 1983). Work by Weinberger, Berman, and Zec (1986) suggests that RCBF results are sensitive to the cognitive state of the subject. They have demonstrated that differences between patients and controls were most marked when they were required to perform the Wisconsin card-sorting task (WCST). Normal subjects manifested increased cerebral blood flow to the dorsolateral prefrontal cortex during this task; unmedicated schizophrenic patients did not. These findings were replicated in a sample of medicated patients but could not be repeated when the task was changed to the visual continuous performance task (CPT). This outcome is consistent with the nature of the 2 tasks. The WCST is a clinical test for functional impairments related to frontal lobe functions, whereas the CPT is considered a measure of *attention* or distractibility.

A number of investigators have postulated left hemisphere dysfunction in schizophrenia. Gur (1979) concluded from her own work and a review of the literature that schizophrenics had a dysfunctional left hemisphere, overactivation of the dysfunctional hemisphere, and failure to shift processing to the right hemisphere. Left hemisphere dysfunction may include an attentional deficit (Niwa et al., 1983).

In schizophrenics, Gur et al. (1983) found that the relative amount of blood flow to the left and right hemispheres differentiated schizophrenic patients from controls. For a verbal task the patients showed no flow asymmetries, and controls showed an increase in left hemisphere flow. For a spatial task the patients showed greater left hemisphere increases than right hemisphere increases; the controls showed a larger right hemisphere increase on the same task. Left temporal lobe epilepsy has been associated with an increased risk of a psychosis with schizophrenic symptomatology, and right temporal epilepsy with an increased risk of affective symptoms (Flor-Henry, 1983).

Brain potential imaging (BPI) creates a topographic distribution of EEG spectral energy from all regions of the scalp simultaneously. Morstyn and associates (1983a; 1983b) found increases in theta and delta activity that were localized to frontal regions and increases in beta activity in postcentral areas bilaterally and in the left anterior temporal region. These investigators used the BPI method to examine the P300 component of the average evoked potential. Compared with controls, schizophrenics were most deficient in activity localized to the left upper middle and posterior temporal regions. In more recent reports of this group, the P300 deficit in patients with schizophrenia has been shown to correlate with reduction in the volume of the left posterior superior temporal gyrus (McCarley et al., 1993). Guenther and Breitling (1985) also found increased delta and theta activity bifrontally. The results also suggested widespread left hemisphere dysfunction during sensory motor activation.

Magnetic resonance spectroscopy (MRS) is a new technique that can allow for the assessment of neurochemistry in vivo. With MRS (particularly at high field strength), a number of chemicals of interest in schizophrenia may be detected, including N-acetyl asparate (a marker of neurons) and glutamate (which has been implicated in neurotoxicity). In recent years this technique has begun to be applied to the study of patients with schizophrenia (Bertolino et al., 1996; Kegeles et al., 1996).

Overall, the rapid growth in the sophistication of neurodiagnostic technology has produced a series of fascinating, though sometimes inconsistent, descriptions of the structure and function of the schizophrenic brain. Further studies are needed to understand better the specific role of brain abnormalities in schizophrenia, their specificity for the disorder, and their utility in delineating homogeneous subtypes of schizophrenia.

Neuropsychological Abnormalities

The physiological measures of brain functioning discussed above provide clear evidence that the schizophrenic brain does not function correctly. However, because they measure physical aspects of the brain, they tell us little about how brain abnormalities in schizophrenia affect the patients' behavior. The study of how brain abnormalities affect behavior is a subspecialty of psychology known as *neuropsychology*. In a neuropsychological study of schizophrenia, the neuropsychologist asks the patient to perform a variety of tasks. These tasks measure specific aspects of brain functioning. For example, to test verbal memory the neuropsychologist may read a story and then ask the patient questions to see if key points are remembered. To test visual memory we show the patient designs and see if they can be recalled.

Neuropsychological studies have consistently found schizophrenic patients to have serious neuropsychological deficits (Seidman, 1983, 1990; Seidman et al., 1992; Saykin et al., 1994). Schizophrenic patients perform poorly on standardized intelligence tests. On the average, the intelligence quotients (IQs) of schizophrenic patients are 5 to 10 points lower than normal. The lower average IQ scores of schizophrenic patients suggest that the abnormalities of brain structure and function discussed above lead to decreased abilities to perform mental tasks. The goal of neuropsychological studies has been to separate the abilities that are impaired in schizophrenic patients from those that are not.

Several types of attention are impaired in schizophrenia: *immediate attention,* the ability to focus on the aspects of a task for a short period of time; *sustained attention,* the ability to focus on a task for a long period of time; and *selective attention,* the ability to focus on one thing (e.g., a conversation) while ignoring another (e.g., background music). Schizophrenic patients show problems in each of these areas of attention. In general, their ability to attend becomes worse as the task becomes more difficult.

In most studies, schizophrenic patients show consistently slower *motor speed* than healthy subjects. It is difficult for the neuropsychologist to know if this slowness is due to problems with attention or other abilities. Whatever the cause of this slow response speed, it makes it difficult for a schizophrenic patient to work as efficiently as a healthy person.

Deficits in *abstraction* and *concept formation* have long been observed among schizophrenic patients. Both of these are necessary components of effective higher level thinking. These functions are closely related to the planning and organizational skills we need in everyday life. It is not surprising that many schizophrenics do poorly on these tasks since clinical observations of schizophrenic patients show them to be deficient in many of these skills. Notably, the poor performance of schizophrenic patients on these tasks is related to reduced activity of the frontal cortex measured in blood flow studies. Thus, the neuropsychological studies are consistent with the imaging studies discussed above.

Because thought disorder is a common feature of schizophrenic patients, it is not surprising that these patients also have difficulties on neuropsychological measures of *verbal ability and language.* It is important to note, however, that these problems are different from the speech and language problems that neurologists describe in many neurology patients. For example, schizophrenic patients usually have mild language disturbances in which simple language functions such as naming objects and understanding speech are not affected. These simple functions are often disturbed in people with neurological conditions. In contrast, schizophrenic patients usually have problems with complex language tasks.

Research consistently finds schizophrenic patients to have difficulties with *learning* and *memory.* They have learning and memory problems for both verbal information (words, sentences, and stories) and visual information (pictures). In both these areas the memory deficits are seen if patients are asked to remember items over short or long periods of time.

Schizophrenic patients tend to do reasonably well on simple *visual-spatial tasks.* These tasks require the patient to observe a problem and determine its solution based on the spatial relationships of items that are seen. For example, organizing a group of blocks to match a design is a visual-spatial task. Relative to other neuropsychological skills, visual-spatial functioning appears to be less impaired in schizophrenia. This may be related to the issue of brain asymmetry.

Abnormalities in brain laterality are found in some schizophrenic patients. Studies usually find these patients to have greater left brain than right hemisphere dysfunction. As we discussed above, they tend to have problems with verbal and language abilities (a function of the left hemisphere), but not with visual-spatial abilities (a function of the right hemisphere). Schizophrenic patients are also more likely to be left-handed, which may be a sign of abnormal brain laterality. However, most are right-handed. Thus, the unusual patterns of brain asymmetry seen in schizophrenia probably indicate relatively small differences in left and right hemisphere functioning. That is, in schizophrenia the left hemisphere is not completely useless, but it functions less efficiently than the right side.

Neurotransmitter Dysfunction

Neurotransmitter-based theories of the etiology of schizophrenia include the dopamine hypothesis (Snyder, 1976; Wyatt, 1985), and other hypotheses based on noradrenergic (Lake et al., 1987), serotonergic (Stahl and Wets, 1987), glutamatergic (Olney and Farber, 1995; Coyle, 1996), neuropeptide (Nemeroff and Bissette, 1987), and phospholipid and prostaglandin (Brody,

Wolkin, and Rotrosen, 1987) pathways. These 3 monoamines are interrelated in their metabolism and share some of the enzymes for their synthesis and degradation. For example, norepinephrine (NE) is derived from dopamine (DA) by the action of dopamine-b-hydroxylase (DBH) and therefore shares the 2 preceding steps with the dopamine pathway. These 2 steps are catalyzed by the enzymes tyrosine hydroxylase (TH), which converts tyrosine to L-dopa, and L-dopa decarboxylase (DDC), which converts L-dopa to dopamine. DDC is also shared between the catecholamines (DA, NE, and epinephrine) and the 5-HT pathways. Moreover, monoamine oxidase (MAO), particularly the type A isoenzyme, is a major enzyme in degradation pathways of all 3 monoamines.

A common theme of the neurotransmitter hypotheses of schizophrenia is that imbalances in the concentration of neurotransmitters or abnormal activities in the transmitter pathways cause symptoms of the syndrome. For example, in the DA hypothesis the positive symptoms of schizophrenia are due to hyperactivity of the mesolimbic dopamine system. However, decreased activity in the frontal cortex may be related to negative symptoms. Based on animal experiments reported by Pycock and colleagues (1980), Weinberger suggests that the decreased activity of prefrontal cortex may, in fact, be related to the mesolimbic system by hyperactivity. While the focus here may be on the DA system, it is important to remember that connectivity between prefrontal and mesolimbic systems involves other transmitters—particularly glutamate, (discussed below).

The dopamine hypothesis of schizophrenia initially emerged from several lines of evidence. First, drugs that increase brain DA activity, such as amphetamine (Snyder, 1972) and L-dopa (Davis, 1978), can exacerbate schizophrenic symptoms, and even cause psychotic symptoms in normals. Second, the antipsychotic drugs can suppress psychotic symptoms caused by such agents. Third, the antipsychotic drugs appear to work, in part, through their antagonistic effects in DA activity (Carlsson and Lindqvist, 1963), specifically through blocking D2 receptors. The potency of the standard antipsychotic drugs seems to correlate with the D2 receptor affinity (Creese, Burt, and Snyder, 1976).

Some, but not all, work has continued to support certain aspects of the theory. DA receptor density is elevated in the postmortem brains of both medicated and unmedicated schizophrenic patients (Wong et al., 1986; Jaskiw and Kleinman, 1988; Wong, 1990). Using PET scanning, Wong et al. (1986) demonstrated that the D2 receptor density in the caudate nucleus was significantly higher in both 5 treated and 10 drug-naive schizophrenia patients, compared to 11 normal volunteers. However, Farde et al.

(1987) could not confirm this finding. This discrepancy in these 2 reports may be due to differences in techniques used. Seeman and associates (1993) suggests that there is an increase in the density of D_4 receptors in patients with schizophrenia. The affinity of the atypical antipsychotic drug for D_4 receptors may be of some importance in this regard (Van Tol et al., 1991). This is an area of continuing research.

A number of groups have used neurochemical techniques to assess the activity of the DA system in patients with schizophrenia. Some, but not all, groups have reported lower levels of the enzyme DBH (which converts NE to DA) in patients with schizophrenia (Wise and Stein, 1973; Wyatt et al., 1978; Sternberg et al., 1982). Other investigators have shown that the dopamine metabolite homovanillic acid (HVA) is elevated in the plasma of those schizophrenic patients with increased levels of psychosis (Green et al., 1993), but lower in schizophrenics compared to normals (Davidson and Davis, 1988). Once again, these data point to relative imbalances in the DA system rather than an overall hyperactivity.

Despite the obvious appeal of the DA theory of schizophrenia, a number of investigators have also evaluated the potential role of norepinephrine (NE). Some have reported an increase in noradrenergic activity in some patients with schizophrenia—particularly paranoid patients (Lake et al., 1980; Kemali, Del Vecchio, and Maj, 1982; van Kammen et al., 1990). Antelman and Caggiula (1977) and van Kammen et al. (1989) have suggested that NE may function as a modulator of schizophrenic symptoms through its action on the DA system. Some groups have suggested that clozapine's potent action on the noradrenergic system may be related to its clinical effects (Green et al., 1993; Breier et al., 1994).

The serotonin hypothesis of schizophrenia, which initially emerged in the 1950s following observations of the striking similarities between serotonin and the hallucinogen lysergic acid (LSD), was replaced by the DA hypothesis. In recent years, however, many investigators have begun to focus once again on the importance of the serotonin system in psychosis, largely because of the known interactions between the serotonin and DA systems in the brain (Waldmeier, 1980; Jenner, Sheehy, and Marsden, 1983; Agren et al., 1986), and the potent serotonin receptor blocking actions of clozapine and many of the novel antipsychotic drugs (Waltzer, 1991).

In recent years the glutamate hypothesis of schizophrenia has been proposed by a number of investigators (Olney and Farber, 1995; Coyle, 1996). The basis for this hypothesis rests on early data regarding reduced cerebrospinal fluid glutamate levels in chronic patients (Kim et al., 1980) and the production of psychosis by the dissociative anesthetic phencyclidine (PCP), an N-methyl-D-aspartate (NMDA) noncompetitive antagonist. This theory suggests that hypoactivity of glutamate transmission through the NMDA receptor could lead to increased activity at non-NMDA glutamate receptors, producing signs of neurodegeneration (Coyle, 1996).

It is probably obvious from this brief review that any simple assertions of the role of any one neurotransmitter system in the symptoms of schizophrenia or psychosis itself is overly simplistic. The evidence suggesting a role for DA in the production of positive symptoms seems compelling, yet contributions from the norepinephrine, serotonin, glutamate, and other transmitter systems are quite important. Further understanding of the interactions of these transmitter systems is likely to lead to development of new pharmacologic treatment approaches.

Genetic Heterogeneity and Brain Dysfunction in Schizophrenia

In a review of the etiology of schizophrenia, Tsuang and Faraone (1995) concluded that the inconsistency of results across different studies was consistent with genetic heterogeneity. The presence of genetic heterogeneity suggests that several genetic forms of schizophrenia as well as nongenetic forms may exist. There is a growing literature that compares schizophrenics having a family history of the disorder with schizophrenics having no family history. Lyons et al. (1989b) presented a detailed review of the familial-sporadic distinction in schizophrenia. Their review indicated that the neuropsychological function of attention, particularly sustained attention or vigilance as measured by the Continuous Performance Test, is impaired more often in familial schizophrenics (Orzack and Kornetsky, 1971; Walker and Shayer, 1982), although that finding was not replicated by Roy et al. (1994). However, on another measure of attention, Alm et al. (1984) found that familial schizophrenics did better on a digit span task than their sporadic counterparts. Notably, there is consistent evidence for poor attentional performance among the relatives of schizophrenic patients (Erlenmeyer-Kimling, 1975; Erlenmeyer-Kimling et al., 1982, 1983, 1991; Neuchterlein and Dawson, 1984; Kremen et al., 1994; Faraone et al., 1995b).

Evidence from electrophysiologic studies showed that electroencephalogram (EEG) abnormalities were more common among sporadic cases of schizophrenia (Hays, 1977; Kendler and Hays, 1982). In contrast, abnormalities elicited by visual- and auditory-evoked potential paradigms are more strongly associated with familial cases (Asarnow, Cromwell, and Rennick, 1978; Romani et al.,

1986, 1987; Schwarzkopf et al., 1988). As with attention deviance, there is solid evidence that the relatives of schizophrenic patients are at risk for evoked potential abnormalities (Blackwood, St. Clair, and Muir, 1991; Blackwood et al., 1991; Kremen et al., 1994).

Based on a review of 10 computed tomography (CT) studies, Lewis et al. (1987) concluded that structural brain abnormalities were more strongly associated with sporadic as compared to familial schizophrenia. Although not all studies could confirm that conclusion, the later review of Lyons et al. (1989b) concluded that the weight of evidence supported the hypothesis of more CT abnormalities among sporadic schizophrenic patients. Reveley, Reveley, and Murray (1984) reported data on 21 MZ pairs from the Maudsley Hospital Twin Register; 9 were concordant for schizophrenia and 12 were discordant. There was no significant difference in cerebral ventricular size between the schizophrenic members of discordant and concordant pairs. However, when the pairs were divided on the basis of family history, those with a negative family history had significantly larger cerebral ventricles.

Vita et al. (1994) performed a statistical meta-analysis of 8 studies of cerebral structural abnormalities in familial and sporadic schizophrenia that provided numerical values for the ventricular brain ratio (VBR). The VBR was 21% greater in 325 family history negative subjects compared with 122 family history positive subjects. Notably, studies that did not find this effect had relatively small samples (mean N = 35) compared with those that did find the effect (mean N = 77). Thus, failures to find familial-sporadic differences could be due to small sample sizes. This may explain why Roy and Crowe (1994) concluded that only 2 of 10 studies supported the hypothesis of ventricular enlargement in non-familial schizophrenia. The statistical power of the method has been discussed in detail elsewhere (Eaves, Kendler, and Schulz, 1986; Kendler, 1987; Lyons et al., 1989a).

Vita et al.'s (1994) meta-analysis suggests there is a subgroup of non-familial schizophrenic patients who, compared with other schizophrenic patients, have increased VBRs. However, if increased VBR were limited to a subgroup of patients, one would expect to find a bimodal distribution of VBR among schizophrenic patients. This was not the case in one analysis of 691 schizophrenic patients (Daniel et al., 1991). However, the authors noted important limitations to their analyses, and bimodality is difficult to demonstrate (Everitt, 1981; Ghosh and Sen, 1985). Thus, these results cannot definitively rule out the existence of a distinct group of schizophrenic patients.

The hypothesis that increased brain abnormalities are associated with environmental etiological factors is also supported by several twin studies that found greater neurodiagnostic abnormalities among the affected co-twins of monozygotic twin pairs discordant for schizophrenia compared with their unaffected co-twins. Since MZ twins are genetically identical, any differences between co-twins can be attributed to environmental factors. In these twin studies, the affected co-twin has had more neuropsychological dysfunction (Goldberg et al., 1990, 1993), larger cerebral ventricles (Reveley, Reveley, and Clifford, 1982), more abnormalities on magnetic resonance imaging (Casanova et al., 1990), and greater "hypofrontality" in the regional cerebral blood flow paradigm (Berman et al., 1992). Studies of non-twin siblings also find larger cerebral ventricles in the schizophrenic compared to the well sibling (DeLisi et al., 1986). Thus, like the familial-sporadic studies, these twin studies suggest that environmental factors account for some of the brain abnormalities observed in schizophrenic patients.

Cannon et al. (1993) proposed that structural brain abnormalities among schizophrenic patients could be attributed to the effects of the genetic risk for schizophrenia in combination with obstetric complications (OCs). In the high-risk sample of Mednick and colleagues (Mednick and Schulsinger, 1968; Mednick et al., 1971; Parnas et al., 1982; Schulsinger et al., 1984; Silverton et al., 1988), Cannon et al. (1993) showed linear increases in cortical and ventricular cerebrospinal fluid–brain ratios with increasing level of genetic risk for schizophrenia. Moreover, the genetic risk for schizophrenia interacted with OCs: the effect of OCs on ventricular enlargement increased with the subject's genetic risk. Notably, OCs did not predict ventricular enlargement for subjects who were not at genetic risk for schizophrenia.

Clearly, more research is needed to further our understanding of the heterogeneity of schizophrenia. It is unlikely that the etiology and pathophysiology of schizophrenia will be well understood unless patients can be separated into homogeneous subgroups based on clinical features and biological parameters. This should lead to a better understanding of course, outcome, response to neuroleptic medication, and the role of psychosocial factors. The diagnostic nomenclature of the future should allow clinicians to choose more effectively among currently available treatment regimens. Until then, extensive knowledge of the individual patient, clinical skill, and compassion must be combined for the effective treatment of schizophrenic disorders.

Schizophrenia: A Neurodevelopmental Brain Disorder

The research we have discussed suggests that schizophrenia occurs when abnormal genes lead to brain dysfunction. In some cases an environmental agent may be needed to trigger this process. In the past decade, several researchers have concluded that schizophrenia may well be a neurodevelopmental brain disorder (Seidman, 1990; Weinberger, 1994; Goldman-Rakic, 1995).

To understand this concept, it is useful to consider brain disorders that do not have a neurodevelopmental origin. Simple examples are acquired brain syndromes which occur after an injury to the head and disorders that are due to the ingestion of toxic substances (e.g., drugs, lead). In each of these cases, some external agent has acted on a normal brain to make it abnormal.

In contrast, in neurodevelopmental disorders the brain does not develop (i.e., grow) properly. In other words, it is never really normal to begin with. We know that genes contain the "blueprint" for building the brain. In schizophrenia this blueprint contains errors so that the brain is not "built" correctly. Goldman-Rakic (1995) suggested that certain brain cells in schizophrenic patients do not "migrate" correctly during development. That is, normal brain development requires that cells locate themselves in the right spot and connect to one another in specific patterns. In schizophrenia it may be that some cells are in the wrong place to begin with, and because of that, they do not make the appropriate connections with other brain areas as the normal aging process of the central nervous system unfolds through adolescence.

Evidence for the neurodevelopmental hypothesis is seen in studies which find that children of schizophrenic mothers have deviant scores on neuropsychological measures of brain functioning (Erlenmeyer-Kimling, Cornblatt, and Golden, 1983; Erlenmeyer-Kimling et al., 1995), and that those who eventually become psychotic have measurable neurologic abnormalities (Fish, 1984). Such studies suggest that the brains of people who become schizophrenic may not be completely normal even in childhood, well before the onset of the illness. An animal model of perinatal excitotoxic damage to the ventral hippocampus to the rat created by Weinberger's group is also consistent with the neurodevelopmental theory. In this model the rats appear normal until puberty (despite the hippocampal damage), but then develop hyperdopamingeric behaviors after puberty (Lipska and Weinberger, 1993a, 1993b).

The brain abnormalities of pre-schizophrenic children probably impair their functioning at school and make it difficult to form friendships. Walker and Lewine (1990) collected the home movies made of schizophrenic patients when they were children, prior to their first schizophrenic episode. The movies also pictured some children who did not become schizophrenic. Clinical raters viewed these movies with the goal of deciding which children in the movies eventually became schizophrenic. Although they made some errors, these raters were able to classify many of the children correctly.

The late onset (following puberty) of psychotic symptomatology could relate to the continued development of the brain (especially the frontal cortex) through adolescence. Consistent with Weinberger's animal model described above, patients with schizophrenia may express psychosis as the frontal cortex "comes on-line" in a deficient fashion as a result of the long-standing neurologic abnormalities. Thus, the onset of schizophrenia may need to wait for certain areas of the brain to develop incorrectly. When these brain areas cannot perform functions necessary for people to cope with the transition from adolescence to adulthood, schizophrenia may ensue. Of course, in many patients the onset of illness occurs in the late twenties and early thirties, long after the brain has completed its development. In such people, environmental factors may "stress" the abnormal pre-schizophrenic brain and result in the development of symptoms of the disorder.

References

Abraham, H. 1980. Psychiatric illness in drug abusers. *N. Engl. J. Med.* 302:868–869.

Agren, H., Mefford, I., Rudorfer, M., Linnoila, M., and Potter, W. 1986. Interacting neurotransmitter systems: a non-experimental approach to the 5HIAA-HVA correlation in human CSF. *J. Psychiat. Res.* 20:175–193.

Akbarian, S., Bunney, W. E. Jr., Potkin, S. G., Wigal, S. B., Hagman, J. O., Sandman, C. A., and Jones, E. G. 1993a. Altered distribution of nicotinamide-adenine dinucleotide phosphate-diaphorase cells in frontal lobe of schizophrenics implies disturbances of cortical development. *Arch. Gen. Psychiat.* 50:169–177.

Akbarian, S., Vinuela, A., Kim, J. J., Potkin, S. G., Bunney, W. E. Jr., and Jones, E. G. 1993b. Distorted distribution of nicotinamide-adenine dinucleotide phosphate-diaphorase neurons in temporal lobe of schizophrenics implies anomalous cortical development. *Arch. Gen. Psychiat.* 50:178–187.

Alm, T., Lindstrom, L. H., Ost, L. G., and Ohman, A. 1984. Electrodermal non-responding in schizophrenia: relationships to attentional, clinical, biochemical, computed tomographical, and genetic factors. *Int. J. Psychophysio.* 1:195–208.

American Psychiatric Association. 1982. *Commission on Psychotherapies: psychotherapy research: methodological and efficacy issues.* Washington, D.C.: American Psychiatric Association.

Andreasen, N. C. 1982. Negative symptoms in schizophre-

nia: definition and reliability. *Arch. Gen. Psychiat.* 39:784–788.

——— 1986. Comprehensive assessment of symptoms and history. Unpublished manuscript.

Andreasen, N. C., Olsen, S. A., Dennert, J. W., et al. 1982. Ventricular enlargement in schizophrenia: relationship to positive and negative symptoms. *Am. J. Psychiatry* 139:297–302.

Andreasen, N. C., Flashman, L., Flaum, M., Arndt, S., Swayze, V. II, O'Leary, D. S., Ehrhardt, J. C., and Yuh, W. T. C. 1994. Regional brain abnormalities in schizophrenia measured with magnetic resonance imaging. *JAMA* 272:1763–69.

Andrews, G., Hall, W., Goldstein, G., Lapsley, H., Bartels, R., and Silove, D. 1985. The economic costs of schizophrenia: implications for public policy. *Arch. Gen. Psychiat.* 42:537–543.

Antelman, S., and Caggiula, A. 1977. Norepinephrine-dopamine interactions and behavior. *Science* 195:646–653.

Applebaum, P. S., Schaffner, K., and Meisel, A. 1985. Responsibility and compensation for tardive dyskinesia. *Am. J. Psychiatry* 142:806–810.

Ariel, R. N., Golden, C. J., and Berg, R. A., et al. 1983. Regional cerebral blood flow in schizophrenics: tests using the Xenon Xe 133 inhalation method. *Arch. Gen. Psychiat.* 40:258–263.

Asarnow, R. F., Cromwell, R. L., and Rennick, P. M. 1978. Cognitive and evoked response measures of information processing in schizophrenics with and without a family history of schizophrenia. *J. Nerv. Ment. Dis.* 166:719–730.

Barr, C. E., Mednick, S. A., and Munk-Jorgensen, P. 1990. Exposure to influenza epidemics during gestation and adult schizophrenia: a 40-year study. *Arch. Gen. Psychiat.* 47:869–874.

Beasley, C. J., Sanger, T., Satterlee, W., et al. 1996. Olanzapine versus placebo: results of a double-blind, fixed-dose olanzapine trial. *Psychopharmacol.* 124:159–167.

Beck, M. 1968. Twenty-five and thirty-five year follow-up of first admissions to mental hospital. *Can. Psychiatr. Assoc. J.* 13:219–229.

Behar, D., Rapoport, J. L., Berg, C. J., et al. 1984. Computerized tomography and neuropsychological test measures in adolescents with obsessive-compulsive disorder. *Am. J. Psychiatry* 141:363–369.

Bell, D. 1965. Comparison of amphetamine psychosis and schizophrenia. *Br. J. Psychiat.* 111:701–707.

Benes, F. M., Davidson, J., and Bird, E. D. 1986. Quantitative cytoarchitectural studies of the cerebral cortex of schizophrenics. *Arch. Gen. Psychiat.* 43:31–35.

Benes, F. M., Majocha, R., Bird, E. D., and Marotta, C. A.

1987. Increased vertical axon numbers in cingulate cortex of schizophrenia. *Arch. Gen. Psychiat.* 44:1017–21.

Berman, I., Kalinowski, A., Berman, S., Lengua, J., and Green, A. 1995a. Obsessive and compulsive symptoms in chronic schizophrenia. *Compr. Psychiat.* 36:6–10.

Berman, I., Sapers, B., Chang, H., Losonczy, M., Schmilder, J., and Green, A. 1995b. Treatment of obsessive-compulsive symptoms in schizophrenic patients with clomipramine. *J. Clin. Psychopharmacol.* 15:206–210.

Berman, K. F., Torrey, E. F., Daniel, D. G., and Weinberger, D. R. 1992. Regional cerebral blood flow in monozygotic twins discordant and concordant for schizophrenia. *Arch. Gen. Psychiat.* 49:927–934.

Bertolino, A., Callicott, J., Nawroz, S., Knable, M., Mattay, V., Duyn, J., Tedeschi, G., Frank, J., and Weinberger, D. 1996. Reproducibility of proton magnetic resonance spectroscopic imaging in patients with schizophrenia and normal controls. *Biol. Psychiat.* 39:634.

Birley, J., and Brown, G. 1970. Crises and life changes preceding the onset or relapse of acute schizophrenia. *Br. J. Psychiat.* 110:327–333.

Bjorndal, N., Bjerve, M., Gerlach, J., et al. 1980. High dosage haloperidol therapy in chronic schizophrenic patients: a double blind study of clinical response, side effects, serum haloperidol, and serum prolactin. *Psychopharmacol.* 67:17–23.

Blackwood, D., St. Clair, D., and Muir, W. 1991. DNA markers and biological vulnerability markers in families multiply affected with schizophrenia. *Eur. Arch. Psychiatr. Neurol. Sci.* 240:191–196.

Blackwood, D. H. R., St. Clair, D., Muir, W. J., and Duffy, J. C. 1991. Auditory P300 and eye tracking dysfunction in schizophrenic pedigrees. *Arch. Gen. Psychiat.* 49:899–909.

Bland, R., Parlner, J., and Orn, H. 1978. Prognosis in schizophrenia. *Arch. Gen. Psychiat.* 35:72–77.

Bleuler, M. 1978. *The schizophrenic disorders: long-term patient and family studies.* New Haven: Yale University Press.

Bogerts, B. 1993. Recent advances in the neuropathology of schizophrenia. *Schiz. Bull.* 19:431–445.

Böök, J. A., Wetterberg, L., and Modrzewska, K. 1978. Schizophrenia in a North Swedish geographical isolate, 1900–1977: epidemiology, genetics, and biochemistry. *Clin. Gen.* 14:373–394.

Bowers, M. 1972. Acute psychosis induced by psychotomimetic drug abuse. I. Clinical findings. *Arch. Gen. Psychiat.* 27:437–440.

Breier, A., Buchanan, R., Irish, D., et al. 1993. Clozapine treatment of outpatients with schizophrenia: outcome and long-term response patterns. *Hosp. Commun. Psychiat.* 44:1145–49.

Breier, A., Buchanan, R., Waltrip, R. I., et al. 1994. The effect of clozapine on plasma norepinephrine: relationship to clinical efficacy. *Neuropsychopharmacology* 10:1–17.

Brody, D., Wolkin, A., and Rotrosen, J. 1987. Phospholipids and prostaglandins in schizophrenia. In *Neurochemistry and neuropharmacology of schizophrenia,* ed. F. A. Henn and L. E. DeLisi. Amsterdam: Elsevier. 319–336.

Buchsbaum, M., DeLisi, L., Holcomb, H., et al. 1984. Anteroposterior gradients in cerebral glucose use in schizophrenia and affective disorders. *Arch. Gen. Psychiat.* 41:491–498.

Buchsbaum, M. S., and Ingvar, D. H. 1982. New visions of the schizophrenic brain: regional differences in electrophysiology, blood flow, and cerebral glucose use. In *Schizophrenia as a brain disease,* ed. F. A. Henn and H. A. Nasrallah. New York: Oxford University Press.

Buchsbaum, M. S., Nuechterlein, K. H., Haier, R. J., Wu, J., Sicotte, N., Hazlett, E., Asarnow, R., Potkin, S., and Guich, S. 1990. Glucose metabolic rate in normals and schizophrenics during the continuous performance test assessed by positron emission tomography. *Br. J. Psychiat.* 156:216–227.

Buka, S. L., Tsuang, M. T., and Lipsitt, L. P. 1993. Pregnancy/delivery complications and psychiatric diagnosis: a prospective study. *Arch. Gen. Psychiat.* 50:151–156.

Cannon, T. D., Mednick, S. A., Parnas, J., Schulsinger, F., Praestholm, J., and Vestergaard, A. 1993. Developmental brain abnormalities in the offspring of schizophrenic mothers. I. Contributions of genetic and perinatal factors. *Arch. Gen. Psychiat.* 50:551–564.

Carlsson, A., and Lindqvist, M. 1963. Effect of chlorpromazine and haloperidol on formation of 3-methoxytyramine and normetanephrine in mouse brain. *Acta Pharmacological Toxicology* 20:140–144.

Carpenter, W., and Heinrichs, D. 1984. *Intermittent pharmacotherapy of schizophrenia.* Washington, D.C.: American Psychiatric Press.

Carpenter, W., Bartko, J., Strauss, J., and Hawk, A. 1978. Signs and symptoms as predictors of outcome: a report from the international pilot study of schizophrenia. *Am. J. Psychiatry* 35:340–345.

Carpenter, W., Conley, R., Buchanan, R., et al. 1995. Patient response and resource management: another view of clozapine treatment of schizophrenia. *Am. J. Psychiatry* 152:827–832.

Casanova, M. F., Sanders, R. D., Goldberg, T. E., Bigelow, L. B., Christison, G., Torrey, E. F., and Weinberger, D. R. 1990. Morphometry of the corpus callosum in monozygotic twins discordant for schizophrenia: a magnetic resonance imaging study. *J. Neurol. Neurosurg. Psychiat.* 53:416–421.

Castle, D. J., and Murray, R. M. 1991. The neurodevelopmental basis of sex differences in schizophrenia. *Psychol. Med.* 21:565–575.

Catts, S. V., McConaghy, N., Ward, P. B., Fox, A. M., and Hadzi-Pavlovic, D. 1993. Allusive thinking in parents of schizophrenics: meta-analysis. *J. Nerv. Ment. Dis.* 181:298–302.

Ciompi, L. 1980. Catamnestic long-term study on the course of life and aging in schizophrenics. *Schiz. Bull.* 6:606–618.

Cole, J., Goldberg, S., and Klerman, G. 1964. Phenothiazine treatment in acute schizophrenia. *Arch. Gen. Psychiat.* 10:246–261.

Cooper, B. 1978. Epidemiology. In *Schizophrenia towards a new synthesis,* ed. J. K. Wing. New York: Grune and Stratton.

Cooper, J. E., Kendell, R. E., and Gurland, B. J., et al. 1972. *Psychiatric diagnosis in New York and London: a comparative study of mental hospital admissions.* Institute of Psychiatry, Maudsley Monographs, no. 20. London: Oxford University Press.

Cornblatt, B. A., and Keilp, J. G. 1994. Impaired attention, genetics, and the pathophysiology of schizophrenia. *Schiz. Bull.* 20:31–46.

Coyle, J. 1996. The glutamatergic dysfunction hypothesis for schizophrenia. *Harv. Rev. Psychiat.* 3:241–253.

Creese, I., Burt, D. R., and Snyder, S. H. 1976. Dopamine receptor binding predicts clinical and pharmacological potencies of antischizophrenic drugs. *Science* 192:481–482.

Crow, T. J., and Done, D. J. 1992. Prenatal exposure to influenza does not cause schizophrenia. *Br. J. Psychiat.* 161:390–393.

Curran, J. P., and Monti, P. M. 1982. *Social skills training: a practical handbook for assessment and treatment.* New York: Guilford.

Curran, J. P., Faraone, S. V., and Graves, D. 1986. Behavioral family therapy in an acute inpatient setting. In *Handbook of behavioral family therapy,* ed. I. A. Fallon. New York: Guilford,

Dalen, P. 1975. *Season of birth: a study of schizophrenia and other mental disorders.* Amsterdam: Elsevier.

Daniel, D. G., Goldberg, T. E., Givvons, R. D., and Weinberger, D. R. 1991. Lack of a bimodal distribution of ventricular size in schizophrenia: a Gaussian mixture analysis of 1056 cases and controls. *Biol. Psychiat.* 30:887–903.

Davidson, M., and Davis, K. L. 1988. A comparison of plasma homovanillic acid concentrations in schizophrenic patients and normal controls. *Arch. Gen. Psychiat.* 45:561–563.

Davis, J., Schaffer, C., Killian, G., Kinard, C., and Chan, C. 1980. Important issues in the drug treatment of schizophrenia. *Schiz. Bull.* 6:70–87.

Davis, J. M. 1975. Maintenance therapy in psychiatry. I. Schizophrenia. *Am. J. Psychiatry* 132:1237–45.

———— 1978. Dopamine theory of schizophrenia: a two-factor theory. In *The nature of schizophrenia: new approaches to research and treatment,* eds. Wynne, L. C., Cromwell, R. L., Matthyse, S. New York: John Wiley.

Davison, K. 1976. Drug-induced psychoses and their relationship to schizophrenia. In *Schizophrenia today,* ed. D. Kemali, G. Bartholini, and D. Richter. Oxford: Pergamon Press.

Davison, K., and Bagley, C. 1969. Schizophrenia-like psychoses associated with organic disorders of the central nervous system: a review of the literature. *Br. J. Psychiat.* spec. publ. no. 4:113–184.

DeLisi, L. E., Dauphinais, I. D., and Gershon, E. S. 1988. Perinatal complications and reduced size of brain limbic structures in familial schizophrenia. *Schiz. Bull.* 14:185–191.

DeLisi, L. E., Goldin, L. R., Hamovit, V. R., Maxwell, M. E., Kurtz, D., and Gershon, E. S. 1986. A family study of the association of increased ventricular size in schizophrenia. *Arch. Gen. Psychiat.* 43:48.

Dunham, H. W. 1965. *Community and schizophrenia: an epidemiological analysis.* Detroit: Wayne State University Press.

Eaton, W. W. 1985. Epidemiology of schizophrenia. *Epidemiologic Reviews* 7:105–126.

Eaves, L. J., Kendler, K. S., and Schulz, S. C. 1986. The familial sporadic classification: its power for the resolution of genetic and environmental etiological factors. *J. Psychiat. Res.* 20:115–130.

Ellinwood, E. J., and Petrie, W. 1981. Drug-induced psychoses. In *Psychiatric factors in drug abuse,* ed. R. W. Pickens and L. L. Heston. New York: Grune and Stratton.

Erard, R., Luisada, P., and Peele, R. 1980. The PCP psychosis: prolonged intoxication or drug-precipitated functional illness? *Journal of Psychedelic Drugs* 12:235–251.

Erlenmeyer-Kimling, L. 1975. A prospective study of children at risk for schizophrenia: methodological considerations and some preliminary findings. In *Life history research in psychopathology,* ed. R. Wirt, G. Winokur, and M. Ross. Minneapolis: University of Minnesota Press. 22–46.

Erlenmeyer-Kimling, L., Cornblatt, B., and Golden, R. R. 1983. Early indicators of vulnerability to schizophrenia in children at high genetic risk. In *Childhood psychopathology and development,* ed. S. B. Guze, F. J. Earls, and J. E. Barrett. New York: Raven Press. 247–264.

Erlenmeyer-Kimling, L., Cornblatt, B., Friedman, D., Marcuse, Y., Rutschmann, J., Simmens, S., and Devi, F. 1982. Neurological, electrophysiological, and attentional deviations in children at risk for schizophrenia. In *Schizophrenia as a brain disease,* ed. F. A. Henn and H. A. Nasrallah. New York: Oxford University Press. 61–98.

Erlenmeyer-Kimling, L., Rock, D., Squires-Wheeler, E.,

Roberts, S., and Yang, J. 1991. Early life precursors of psychiatric outcomes in adulthood in subjects at risk for schizophrenia or affective disorders. *Psychiat. Res.* 39:239–256.

Erlenmeyer-Kimling, L., Squires-Wheeler, E., Adamo, U. H., Bassett, A. S., Cornblatt, B. A., Kestenbaum, C. J., Rock, D., Roberts, S. A., and Gottesman, I. I. 1995. The New York high-risk project: psychoses and cluster A personality disorders in offspring of schizophrenic parents at 23 years of follow-up. *Arch. Gen. Psychiat.* 52:857–865.

Everitt, B. S. 1981. A Monte Carlo investigation of the likelihood ratio test for the number of components in a mixture of normal distributions. *Multivariate Behavioral Research* 16:171–180.

Falconer, D. S. 1965. The inheritance of liability to certain disease, estimated from the incidence among relatives. *Ann. Hum. Genet.* 29:51–71.

Falkai, P., Bogerts, B., and Rozumek, M. 1988. Limbic pathology in schizophrenia: the entorhinal region—a morphometric study. *Biol. Psychiat.* 24:515–521.

Falloon, I. R. H., and Liberman, R. P. 1983. Behavioral family intervention in the management of chronic schizophrenia. In *Family therapy in schizophrenia,* ed. W. R. McFarlane. New York: Guilford.

Falloon, I. R. H., Boyd, J. L., and McGill, C. W., et al. 1982. Family management in the prevention of exacerbations of schizophrenia: a controlled study. *N. Engl. J. Med.* 306:1437–40.

Falloon, I. R. H., Boyd, J. L., McGill, C. W., Williamson, M., Razani, J., Moss, H. B., Gilderman, A. M., and Simpson, G. M. 1986. Family management in the prevention of morbidity of schizophrenia: clinical outcome of a two-year controlled study. *Arch. Gen. Psychiat.* 42:887–896.

Faraone, S. V., and Tsuang, M. T. 1985. Quantitative models of the genetic transmission of schizophrenia. *Psychol. Bull.* 98:41–66.

Faraone, S. V., Curran, J. P., Laughren, T., Faltus, F., Johnston, R., and Brown, W. A. 1986. Neuroleptic bioavailability, psychosocial factors, and clinical status: a 1-year study of schizophrenic outpatients after dose reduction. *Psychiat. Res.* 19:311–322.

Faraone, S. V., Kremen, W. S., Lyons, M. J., Pepple, J. R., Seidman, L. J., and Tsuang, M. T. 1995a. Diagnostic accuracy and linkage analysis: how useful are schizophrenia spectrum phenotypes? *Am. J. Psychiatry* 152:1286–90.

Faraone, S. V., Seidman, L. J., Kremen, W. S., Pepple, J. R., Lyons, M. J., and Tsuang, M. T. 1995b. Neuropsychological functioning among the nonpsychotic relatives of schizophrenic patients: a diagnostic efficiency analysis. *J. Abnorm. Psychol.* 104:286–304.

Farde, L., Wiesel, F.-A., Hall, H., Halldin, C., Stone-Elander, S., and Sedvall, G. 1987. No D2 receptor increase in PET study of schizophrenia. *Arch. Gen. Psychiat.* 44:671–672.

Farkas, T., Wolf, A. P., and Jaeger, J., et al. 1984. Regional brain glucose metabolism in chronic schizophrenia: a positron emission transaxial tomographic study. *Arch. Gen. Psychiat.* 41:293–300.

Feighner, J. P., Robins, E., and Guze, S. B., et al. 1972. Diagnostic criteria for use in psychiatric research. *Arch. Gen. Psychiat.* 26:57–63.

Fenton, W., and McGlashan, T. 1986. The prognostic significance of obsessive-compulsive symptoms in schizophrenia. *Am. J. Psychiatry* 143:437–441.

Fischer, D. E., Halikar, J. A., Baker, J., and Smith, J. 1975. Frequency and patterns of drug abuse in psychiatric patients. *Disorders of the Nervous System* 36:550–553.

Fish, B. 1984. Characteristics and sequelae of the neurointegrative disorder in infants at risk for schizophrenia: 1952–1982. In *Children at risk for schizophrenia: a longitudinal perspective,* ed. N. F. Watt, E. J. Anthony, L. C. Wynne, and J. E. Rolf. Cambridge: Cambridge University Press. 423–439.

Flor-Henry, P. 1983. Determinants of psychosis in epilepsy: laterality and forced normalization. *Biol. Psychiat.* 18:1045–57.

Friedman, D., and Squires-Wheeler, E. 1994. Event-related potentials (ERPs) as indicators of risk for schizophrenia. *Schiz. Bull.* 20:63–74.

Ganguli, R., Rabin, B. S., Kelly, R. H., Lyte, M., and Ragu, U. 1987. Clinical and laboratory evidence of autoimmunity in acute schizophrenia. *Ann. N.Y. Acad. Sci.* 496:676–685.

Ghosh, J. K., and Sen, P. K. 1985. On the asymptotic performance of the log likelihood ratio statistic for the mixture model and related results. Proceedings of the Berkeley Conference in Honor of Jerzy Neyman and Jack Kiefer. II:789–806.

Goldberg, E. M., and Morrison, S. L. 1963. Schizophrenia and social class. *Br. J. Psychiat.* 109:785–802.

Goldberg, S., Klerman, G., and Cole, J. 1965. Changes in schizophrenic psychopathology and ward behavior as a function of phenothiazine treatment. *Br. J. Psychiat.* 111:120–123.

Goldberg, T. E., Ragland, D., Torrey, E. F., Gold, J. M., Bigelow, L. B., and Weinberger, D. R. 1990. Neuropsychological assessment of monozygotic twins discordant for schizophrenia. *Arch. Gen. Psychiat.* 47:1066–72.

Goldberg, T. E., Torrey, E. F., Gold, J. M., Ragland, J. E., Bigelow, L. B., and Weinberger, D. R. 1993. Learning and memory in monozygotic twins discordant for schizophrenia. *Psychol. Med.* 23:71–85.

Golden, C. J., Moses, J. A., and Zelazowski, R., et al. 1980. Cerebral ventricular size and neuropsychological impairment in young chronic schizophrenics: measurement by the standardized Luria-Nebraska neuropsychological battery. *Arch. Gen. Psychiat.* 37:619–623.

Goldin, L. R., DeLisi, L. E., and Gershon, E. S. 1987. Genetic aspects to the biology of schizophrenia. In *Neurochemistry and neuropharmacology of schizophrenia,* ed. F. A. Henn and L. E. DeLisi. Amsterdam: Elsevier. 467–487.

Goldman-Rakic, P. S. 1995. More clues to "latent" schizophrenia point to developmental origins. *Am. J. Psychiatry* 152:1701–3.

Goldstein, J. M., Santangelo, S. L., Simpson, J. C., and Tsuang, M. T. 1990. The role of gender in identifying subtypes of schizophrenia: a latent class analytic approach. *Schiz. Bull.* 16:263–275.

Gottesman, I., and Shields, J. 1967. A polygenic theory of schizophrenia. *Proc. Natl. Acad. Sci.* 58:199–205.

Green, A. 1996. Treatment-resistant and treatment-intolerant schizophrenia. *Journal of Clinical Psychiatry Monograph* 14:8–9.

Green, A., Alam, M., Sobieraj, J., Pappalardo, K., Waternaux, C., Salzman, C., Schatzberg, A., and Schildkraut, J. 1993. Clozapine response and plasma catecholamines and their metabolites. *Psychiat. Res.* 46:139–149.

Guenther, W., and Breitling, D. 1985. Predominant sensorimotor area left hemisphere dysfunction in schizophrenia measured by brain electrical activity mapping. *Biol. Psychiat.* 20:515–532.

Gur, R. E. 1979. Cognitive concomitants of hemispheric dysfunction in schizophrenia. *Arch. Gen. Psychiat.* 36:269–274.

Gur, R. E., Skolnick, B. E., and Gur, R. C., et al. 1983. Brain function in schizophrenic disorders. I. Regional blood flow in medicated schizophrenics. *Arch. Gen. Psychiat.* 40:1250–54.

Guze, S. B., Cloninger, R., Martin, R. L., and Clayton, P. 1983. A follow-up and family study of schizophrenia. *Arch. Gen. Psychiat.* 40:1273–76.

Hall, R., Strickney, S., Gardner, E., Perl, M., and LeCann, A. 1979. Relationship of psychiatric illness to drug abuse. *Journal of Psychedelic Drugs* 11:337–342.

Harding, C. M., Brooks, G. W., Ashikaga, T., Strauss, J. S., and Breier, A. A. 1987. The Vermont longitudinal study of persons with severe mental illness. I. Methodology, study sample, and overall status 32 years later. *Am. J. Psychiatry* 144:718–726.

Hare, E. 1976. The season of birth of siblings of psychiatric patients. *Br. J. Psychiat.* 129:49.

Hare, E., Price, J., and Slater, E. 1974. Mental disorder and season of birth. *Br. J. Psychiat.* 124:81.

Hastings, D. 1958. Follow-up results in psychiatric illness. *Am. J. Psychiatry* 40:1057–66.

Hays, P. 1977. Electroencephalographic variants and genetic predisposition to schizophrenia. *Journal of Neurology, Neurosurgery, and Psychiatry* 40:753–755.

Hollister, L., and Kim, D. 1982. Intensive treatment with haloperidol of treatment-resistant chronic schizophrenic patients. *Am. J. Psychiatry* 139:1466–68.

Hollister, L. E. 1977. Antipsychotic medications and the treatment of schizophrenia. In *Psychopharmacology: from theory to practice,* ed. J. D. Barchas, P. A. Berger, R. D. Ciaranello, and G. R. Elliot. New York: Oxford University Press.

Jacobsen, B., and Kinney, D. K. 1980. Perinatal complications in adopted and non-adopted schizophrenics and their controls: preliminary results. *Acta Psychiatr. Scand.* suppl. 285:337.

Jakob, H., and Beckmann, H. 1986. Prenatal developmental disturbances in the limbic allocortex in schizophrenics. *J. Neural. Trans.* 65:303–326.

Jaskiw, G., and Kleinman, J. 1988. *Postmortem neurochemistry studies in schizophrenia.* New York: Oxford University Press.

Jenner, P., Sheehy, M., and Marsden, C. 1983. NE and 5HT modulation of brain DA function. *British Journal of Clinical Pharm.* 15:277s–289s.

Jeste, D. V., and Wyatt, R. J. 1982. Therapeutic strategies against tardive dyskinesia. *Arch. Gen. Psychiat.* 39:803–816.

Johnson, D. 1979. Further observations on the duration of depot neuroleptic maintenance therapy in schizophrenia. *Br. J. Psychiat.* 135:524–530.

Johnstone, E. C., Crow, T. J., and Frith, C. D., et al. 1976. Cerebral ventricular size and cognitive impairment in chronic schizophrenia. *Lancet* 2:924–926.

Jonsson, L., and Gunne, L. 1970. Clinical studies of amphetamine psychosis. In *Amphetamines and related compounds,* ed. E. Costa and S. Garattini. New York: Raven Press.

Kane, J., Honigfeld, G., Singer, J., Meltzer, H., and Group, C. C. S. 1988. Clozapine for the treatment-resistant schizophrenic. *Arch. Gen. Psychiat.* 45:789–796.

Kasanin, J. 1933. The acute schizoaffective psychoses. *Am. J. Psychiatry* 90:97–126.

Kaufmann, C. A., Weinberger, D. R., Yolken, R. H., Torrey, E. F., and Potkin, S. F. 1983. Viruses and schizophrenia. *Lancet* 2:1136–37.

Kavanagh, D. J. 1992. Recent developments in expressed emotion and schizophrenia. *Br. J. Psychiat.* 160:601–620.

Kazdin, A. E. 1977. *The token economy: a review and evaluation.* New York: Plenum Publishing.

Kazdin, A. E., and Bootzin, R. R. 1972. The token economy: an evaluative review. *Journal of Applied Behavior Analysis* 5:343–372.

Kegeles, L., Kaufmann, C., Chan, S., Gorman, J., Mann, J.,

and Malaspina, D. 1996. Proton magnetic resonance study of the hippocampus in schizophrenia. Society of Biological Psychiatry Annual Meeting, Research Abstract 462.

Kemali, D., Del Vecchio, M., and Maj, M. 1982. Increased noradrenaline levels in CSF and plasma of schizophrenic patients. *Biol. Psychiat.* 17:711–7.

Kendell, R. E., and Kemp, J. W. 1989. Maternal influenza in the etiology of schizophrenia. *Arch. Gen. Psychiat.* 46:878–882.

Kendler, K. S. 1987. Sporadic vs. familial classification given etiologic heterogeneity: sensitivity, specificity, and positive and negative predictive power. *Genet. Epidemiol.* 4:313–330.

Kendler, K. S., and Hays, P. 1982. Familial and sporadic schizophrenia: a symptomatic, prognostic, and EEG comparison. *Am. J. Psychiatry* 139:1557–62.

Kety, S. S., Rosenthal, D., Wender, P. H., and Schulsinger, F. 1968. The types and prevalence of mental illness in the biological and adoptive families of adopted schizophrenics. *J. Psychiat. Res.* 1:345–362.

Kety, S. S., Rosenthal, D., Wender, P. H., Schulsinger, F., and Jacobson, B. 1978. The biologic and adoptive families of adopted individuals who became schizophrenic: prevalence of mental illness and other characteristics. In *The nature of schizophrenia: new approaches to research and treatment,* ed. L. C. Wynne, R. L. Cromwell, and S. Matthysse. New York: John Wiley and Sons.

Kim, J., Kornhuber, H., Schmid-Burgk, W., and Hollander, B. 1980. Low cerebrospinal fluid glutamate in schizophrenic patients and a new hypothesis on schizophrenia. *Neuroscience Letters* 20:379–383.

Kinney, D. K., and Jacobsen, S. 1978. Environmental factors in schizophrenia: new adoption evidence. In *The nature of schizophrenia: new approaches to research and treatment,* ed. L. C. Wynne, R. L. Cromwell, and S. Matthysse. New York: John Wiley & Sons.

Kirch, D. G., Kaurmann, C. A., Papadopoulous, N. M., Martin, B., and Weinberger, D. R. 1985. Abnormal cerebrospinal fluid indices in schizophrenia. *Biol. Psychiat.* 20:1039–46.

Knight, J. G. 1985. Possible autoimmune mechanisms in schizophrenia. *Integr. Psychiatry* 3:134–143.

Kolakowska, T., Williams, A., Ardern, M., Reveley, K., Jambor, K., Gelder, M., and Mandelbrote, B. 1985. Schizophrenia with good and poor outcome. I. Early clinical features, response to neuroleptics, and signs of organic dysfunction. *Br. J. Psychiat.* 146:229–239.

Kraepelin, E. 1971. *Dementia praecox and paraphrenia.* Huntington, N.Y.: Robert Krieger (facs. of 1919 ed.).

Kramer, M. 1961. Some problems for international research suggested by observations on differences in first admission rates to the mental hospitals of England and Wales and of the United States. Proceedings of the Third World Congress of Psychiatry 3:153–160.

Kremen, W. S., Seidman, L. J., Pepple, J. R., Lyons, M. J., Tsuang, M. T., and Faraone, S. V. 1994. Neuropsychological risk indicators for schizophrenia: a review of family studies. *Schiz. Bull.* 20:103–119.

Lake, C., Sternberg, D., van Kammen, D., Ballenger, J., Ziegler, M., Post, R., Kopin, J., and Bunney, W. 1980. Schizophrenia: elevated CSF norepinephrine. *Science* 207:331–333.

Lake, C. R., Kleinman, J. E., Kafka, M. S., Ko, G. N., Smith Moore, S., and Ziegler, M. 1987. Norepinephrine metabolism in schizophrenia. In *Neurochemistry and neuropharmacology of schizophrenia,* ed. F. A. Henn and L. E. DeLisi. Amsterdam: Elsevier. 227–256.

Lane, E. A., and Albee, G. W. 1966. Comparative birthweights of schizophrenics and their siblings. *Journal of Psychology* 64:227.

Langfeldt, G. 1969. Schizophrenia: diagnosis and prognosis. *Behavioral Science* 14:173–182.

Leff, J., Hirsch, S., Gaind, R., Rhode, P., and Stevens, B. 1973. Life events and maintenance therapy in schizophrenic relapse. *British Journal of Psychiatry* 123:659–660.

Leff, J., Kuipers, L., and Berkowitz, R., et al. 1982. A controlled trial of social intervention in the families of schizophrenic patients. *Br. J. Psychiat.* 141:121–134.

Levenson, J. L. 1985. Neuroleptic malignant syndrome. *Am. J. Psychiatry* 142:1137–45.

Levenstein, S., Klein, D., and Pollack, M. 1966. Follow-up study of formerly hospitalized voluntary psychiatric patients: the first two years. *Am. J. Psychiatry* 122:1102–9.

Levy, D. L., Holzman, P. S., Matthysse, S., and Mendell, N. R. 1994. Eye tracking and schizophrenia: a selective review. *Schiz. Bull.* 20:47–62.

Lewis, S. W., Reveley, A. M., Reveley, M. A., Chitkara, B., and Murray, R. M. 1987. The familial/sporadic distinction as a strategy in schizophrenia research. *Br. J. Psychiat.* 151:306–313.

Libikova, H., Breir, S., Kosikova, M., Pagady, J., Stunzer, D., and Ujhazyova, D. 1979. Assay of interferon and viral antibodies in the cerebrospinal fluid in clinical neurology and psychiatry. *Acta Biologica Medica Germanica* 38:879–893.

Liddle, P. F., Spence, S. A., and Sharma, T. 1995. A PET study of obligate carriers of the predisposition to schizophrenia. *Schiz. Res.* 15:90.

Lieberman, J., Scafferman, A., Pollack, S., et al. 1994. Clinical effects of clozapine in chronic schizophrenia: response to treatment and predictors of outcome. *Am. J. Psychiatry* 151:1744–52.

Lipska, B. K., and Weinberger, D. R. 1993a. Cortical regulation of the mesolimbic dopamine system: implications for schizophrenia. In *Limbic motor circuits and neuropsychiatry,* ed. P. W. Kalivas and C. D. Barnes. Boca Raton: CRC Press. 329–349.

——— 1993b. Delayed effects of neonatal hippocampal damage on haloperidol-induced catalepsy and apomorphine-induced stereotypic behaviors in the rat. *Developmental Brain Research* 75:213–222.

Luisada, P., and Reddick, C. 1980. An epidemic of drug-induced schizophrenia. *Journal of Psychedelic Drugs* 12:235–251.

Lyons, M. J., Faraone, S. V., Kremen, W. S., and Tsuang, M. T. 1989a. Familial and sporadic schizophrenia: a simulation study of statistical power. *Schiz. Res.* 2:345–353.

Lyons, M. J., Kremen, W. S., Tsuang, M. T., and Faraone, S. V. 1989b. Investigating putative genetic and environmental forms of schizophrenia: methods and findings. *Int. Rev. Psychiat.* 1:259–276.

Marder, S., and Meibach, R. 1994. Risperidone in the treatment of schizophrenia. *Am. J. Psychiatry* 151:825–835.

Marder, S., and VanPatten, T. 1995. Antipsychotic medications. In The American Psychiatric Press *Textbook of psychopharmacology,* ed. A. F. Schatzberg, C. B. Nemeroff. Washington, D.C.: APA Press. 1–26.

Mathew, R. J., Duncan, G. C., and Weinman, M. L., et al. 1982. Regional cerebral blood flow in schizophrenia. *Arch. Gen. Psychiat.* 39:1121–24.

May, P., Tuma, A., Yale, C., Potepan, P., and Dixon, W. 1976. Schizophrenia—a follow-up study of results of treatment. II. Hospital stay over two or five years. *Arch. Gen. Psychiat.* 33:481–506.

McCabe, M., Fowler, R., Cadoret, R., and Winokur, G. 1972. Symptom differences in schizophrenia with good and poor prognosis. *Am. J. Psychiatry* 128:1239–43.

McCarley, R. W., Shenton, M. E., O'Donnell, B. F., Faux, S. F., et al. 1993. Auditory P300 abnormalities and left posterior superior temporal gyrus volume reduction in schizophrenia. *Arch. Gen. Psychiat.* 50:190–197.

McCreadie, R., Flanagan, W., McKnight, J., et al. 1979. High dose flupenthixol decanoate in chronic schizophrenia. *Br. J. Psychiatry* 135:175–179.

McCreadie, R. G., Hall, D. J., Berry, I. J., Robertson, L. J., Ewing, J. I., and Geals, M. F. 1992. The Nithsdale Schizophrenia Surveys. X. Obstetrical complications, family history, and abnormal movements. *Br. J. Psychiat.* 161:799–805.

McNeil, T. F. 1988. Obstetric factors and perinatal injuries. In *Nosology, epidemiology, and genetics of schizophrenia,* ed. M. T. Tsuang and J. C. Simpson. New York: Elsevier. 319–344.

McNeil, T. F., and Kaij, L. 1978. Obstetric factors in the development of schizophrenia: complications in the births of preschizophrenics and in reproduction by schizophrenic parents. In *The nature of schizophrenia: new ap-*

proaches to research and treatment, ed. L. C. Wynne, R. L. Cromwell, and S. Matthysse. New York: John Wiley and Sons. 401–429.

McNeil, T. F., Cantor-Graae, E., Torrey, E. F., Sjostrom, K., Bowler, A., Taylor, E., Rawlings, R., and Higgins, E. S. 1994. Obstetric complications in histories of monozygotic twins discordant and concordant for schizophrenia. *Acta Psychiatr. Scand.* 89:196–204.

Mednick, S. A. 1970. Breakdown in individuals at high risk for schizophrenia: Possible predispositional perinatal factors. *Ment. Hyg.* 54:50.

Mednick, S. A., and Schulsinger, F. 1968. Some premorbid characteristics related to breakdown in children with schizophrenic mothers. In *The transmission of schizophrenia,* ed. D. Rosenthal and S. S. Kety. Oxford: Pergamon Press. 267–291.

Mednick, S. A., Mura, E., Schulsinger, F., and Mednick, B. 1971. Perinatal conditions and infant development in children with schizophrenic parents. *Soc. Bio.* suppl. 18:103.

Mednick, S. A., Machon, R. A., Huttunen, M. O., and Bonett, D. 1988. Adult schizophrenia following prenatal exposure to an influenza epidemic. *Arch. Gen. Psychiat.* 45:189–192.

Meltzer, H., and Okayli, G. 1995. Reduction of suicidality during clozapine treatment of neuroleptic-resistant schizophrenia: impact on risk-benefit assessment. *Am. J. Psychiatry* 152:183–190.

Meltzer, H., Burnett, S., Bastani, B., et al. 1990. Effects of six months of clozapine treatment on the quality of life of chronic schizophrenic patients. *Hosp. Commun. Psychiat.* 41:892–897.

Meltzer, H., Cola, P., Way, L., et al. 1993. Cost effectiveness of clozapine in neuroleptic-resistant schizophrenia. *Am. J. Psychiatry* 150:1630–38.

Miller, D., Perry, P., Cadoret, R., et al. 1994. Clozapine's effect on negative symptoms in treatment-refractory schizophrenics. *Compr. Psychiat.* 35:8–15.

Morstyn, R., Duffy, F., and McCarley, R. 1983a. Altered P300 topography in schizophrenia. *Arch. Gen. Psychiat.* 40:729–734.

——— 1983b. Altered topography of EEG spectral content in schizophrenia. *Electroencephalogr. Clin. Neurophysiol.* 56:263–271.

Nasrallah, H. A., McCalley-Whitters, M., and Jacoby, C. G. 1982. Cerebral ventricular enlargement in young manic males: a controlled CT study. *J. Affect. Disor.* 4:15–19.

Nemeroff, C. B., and Bissette, G. 1987. The role of neuropeptides in schizophrenia. In *Neurochemistry and neuropharmacology of schizophrenia,* ed. F. A. Henn and L. E. DeLisi. Amsterdam: Elsevier. 297–317.

Neuchterlein, K. H., and Dawson, M. E. 1984. Information processing and attentional functioning in the developmental course of schizophrenic disorders. *Schiz. Bull.* 10:160–203.

Nimgaonkar, V. L., Wessely, S., Tune, L. E., and Murray, R. M. 1988. Response to drugs in schizophrenia: the influence of family history, obstetric complications, and ventricular enlargement. *Psychol. Med.* 18:583–592.

Niwa, S. I., Hiramatsu, K. I., and Kameyama, T., et al. 1983. Left hemisphere's inability to sustain attention over extended time periods in schizophrenics. *Br. J. Psychiat.* 142:477–481.

O'Callaghan, E., Larkin, C., Kinsella, A., and Waddington, J. L. 1990. Obstetric complications, the putative familial-sporadic distinction, and tardive dyskinesia in schizophrenia. *Br. J. Psychiat.* 157:578–584.

O'Callaghan, E., Gibson, T., Colohan, H. A., Walshe, D., Buckley, P., Larkin, C., and Waddington, J. L. 1991. Season of birth in schizophrenia: evidence for confinement of an excess of winter births to patients without a family history of mental disorder. *Br. J. Psychiat.* 158:764–769.

O'Callaghan, E., Gibson, T., Colohan, H. A., Buckley, P., Walshe, D. G., Larkin, C., and Waddington, J. L. 1992. Risk of schizophrenia in adults born after obstetric complications and their associations with early onset of illness: a controlled study. *Br. Med. J.* 305:1256–59.

Olney, J., and Farber, N. 1995. Glutamate receptor dysfunction and schizophrenia. *Arch. Gen. Psychiat.* 52:998–1007.

Onstad, S., Skre, I., Torgersen, S., and Kringlen, E. 1992. Birthweight and obstetric complications in schizophrenic twins. *Acta Psychiatr. Scand.* 85:70–73.

Orzack, M. H., and Kornetsky, C. 1971. Environmental and familial predictors of attention behavior in chronic schizohrenics. *J. Psychiat. Res.* 9:21–29.

Parnas, J., Schulsinger, F., Teasdale, T. W., Feldman, P. M., and Mednick, S. A. 1982. Perinatal complications and clinical outcome within the schizophrenia spectrum. *Br. J. Psychiat.* 140:416.

Pearlson, G. D., Garbacz, D. J., Moberg, P. J., Ahn, H. S., and DePaulo, J. R. 1985. Symptomatic, familial, perinatal, and social correlates of CAT changes in schizophrenics and bipolars. *J. Nerv. Ment. Dis.* 173:42.

Pollin, W., and Stabenau, J. R. 1968. Biological, psychological, and historical differences in a series of monozygotic twins discordant for schizophrenia. In *The transmission of schizophrenia*, ed. D. Rosenthal and S. Kety. New York: Pergamon Press,

Pulver, A. E., Liang, K.-Y., Brown, C. H., Wolyniec, P., McGrath, J., Adler, L., Tam, D., Carpenter, W. T., and Childs, B. 1992. Risk factors in schizophrenia: season of birth, gender, and familial risk. *Br. J. Psychiat.* 160:65–71.

Pycock, C., Kerwin, R., and Carter, C. 1980. Effect of lesions of cortical dopamine terminals on subcortical dopamine in rat. *Journal of Neurochem.* 34:91–99.

Rabkin, J. G. 1980. Stressful life events and schizophrenia: a review of the research literature. *Psychol. Bull.* 87:408–425.

Rapaport, M. H., McAllister, C. G., Pickar, D., Nelson, D. L., and Paul, S. M. 1989. Elevated levels of soluble interleukin 2 receptors in schizophrenia. *Arch. Gen. Psychiat.* 46:291–292.

Raz, S., and Raz, N. 1990. Structural brain abnormalities in the major psychoses: a quantitative review of the evidence from computerized imaging. *Psychol. Bull.* 108:93–108.

Reveley, A. M., Reveley, M. A., and Clifford, R. M. 1982. Cerebral ventricular size in twins discordant for schizophrenia. *Lancet* 1:540–541.

Reveley, A. M., Reveley, M. A., and Murray, R. M. 1984. Cerebral ventricular enlargement in non-genetic schizophrenia: a controlled twin study. *Br. J. Psychiat.* 144:89–93.

Revicki, D., Luce, B., Weschler, J., et al. 1990. Cost-effectiveness of clozapine for treatment-resistant schizophrenic patients. *Hosp. Commun. Psychiat.* 41:850–854.

Rieder, R. O., Mann, L. S., and Weinberger, D. R., et al. 1983. Computed tomographic scans in patients with schizophrenia, schizoaffective, and bipolar affective disorder. *Arch. Gen. Psychiat.* 40:735–739.

Rinkel, M., DeShon, H., Hyde, R., and Solomon, H. 1952. Experimental schizophrenia-like symptoms. *Am. J. Psychiatry* 108:572.

Romani, A., Zerbi, F., Mariotti, G., Callieco, R., and Cosi, V. 1986. Computed tomography and pattern reversal visual evoked potentials in chronic schizophrenic patients. *Acta Psychiatr. Scand.* 73:566–573.

Romani, A., Merello, S., Gozzoli, L., Zerbi, F., Grassi, M., and Cosi, V. 1987. P300 and CT scan in patients with chronic schizophrenia. *Br. J. Psychiat.* 151:506–513.

Rosen, B., Engelhardt, D., Freedman, N., and Margolis, R. 1968. The hospitalization proneness scale as a predictor of response to phenothiazine treatment. *J. Nerv. Ment. Dis.* 146:476–480.

Rosen, I. 1956. The clinical significance of obsessions in schizophrenia. *Journal of Mental Science,* 103:773–785.

Roy, M.-A., and Crowe, R. R. 1994. Validity of the familial and sporadic subtypes of schizophrenia. *Am. J. Psychiatry* 151:805–814.

Roy, M.-A., Flaum, M. A., Gupta, S., Jaramillo, L., and Andreasen, N. C. 1994. Epidemiological and clinical correlates of familial and sporadic schizophrenia. *Acta Psychiatr. Scand.* 89:324–328.

Saykin, A. J., Shtasel, D. L., Gur, R. E., Kester, D. B., Mozley, L. H., Stafiniak, P., and Gur, R. C. 1994. Neuropsychological deficits in neuroleptic naive patients with first-episode schizophrenia. *Arch. Gen. Psychiat.* 51:124–131.

Schulsinger, F., Parnas, J., Petersen, E. T., Schulsinger, H., Teasdale, T. W., Mednick, S. A., Moller, L., and Silverton, L. 1984. Cerebral ventricular size in offspring of schizophrenic mothers. *Arch. Gen. Psychiat.* 41:602.

Schwarzkopf, S. B., Chapman, R. M., Jimenez, M., Treglia, L., Kane, C. F., Lamberti, J. S., and Nasrallah, H. A. 1988. Familial and sporadic schizophrenia: visual evoked potential differences. *Biol. Psychiat.* 24:828–833.

Schwarzkopf, S. B., Nasrallah, H. A., Olson, S. C., Coffman, J. A., and McLaughlin, J. A. 1989. Perinatal complications and genetic loading in schizophrenia: preliminary findings. *Psychiat. Res.* 27:233–239.

Seeman, P., Guan, H., and Van Tol, H. H. 1993. Dopamine D4 receptors elevated in schizophrenia. *Nature* 365:441–445.

Seidman, L. J. 1983. Schizophrenia and brain dysfunction: an integration of recent neurodiagnostic findings. *Psychol. Bull.* 94:195–238.

——— 1990. The neuropsychology of schizophrenia: a neurodevelopmental and case study approach. *J. Neuropsychiat.* 2:301–312.

Seidman, L. J., Cassens, G. P., Kremen, W. S., and Pepple, J. R. 1992. Neuropsychology of schizophrenia. In *Clinical syndromes in adult neuropsychology: the practitioner's handbook*, ed. R. F. White. Amsterdam: Elsevier. 381–449.

Seidman, L. J., Faraone, S. V., Goldstein, J. M., Goodman, J. M., Matsuda, G., Kremen, W. S., Kennedy, D. N., Makris, N., Caviness, V. S., and Tsuang, M. T. 1996. Reduced subcortical brain volumes in nonpsychotic siblings of schizophrenic patients. *Biol. Psychiat.* 39:602.

Sham, P. C., O'Callaghan, E., Takei, N., Murray, G. K., Hare, E. H., and Murray, R. M. 1992. Schizophrenia following prenatal exposure to influenza epidemics between 1939 and 1960. *Br. J. Psychiat.* 160:461–466.

Shenton, M. E., Solovay, M. R., Holzman, P. S., Coleman, M., and Gale, H. J. 1989. Thought disorder in the relatives of psychotic patients. *Arch. Gen. Psychiat.* 46:897–901.

Shenton, M., Kikinis, R., Jolesz, F., Pollack, S., LeMay, M., Wible, C., Hokama, H., Martin, J., Metcalf, D., Coleman, M., and McCarley, R. 1992. Abnormalities of the left temporal lobe and thought disturbances in schizophrenia: a qualitative magnetic resonance imaging study. *N. Engl. J. Med.* 327:604–612.

Sheppard, G., Gruzelier, J., Manchanda, R., et al. 1983. Positron emission tomography scanning in predominantly never-treated acute schizophrenic patients. *Lancet* 2:1448–52.

Shields, J., and Gottesman, I. I. 1977. Obstetric complications and twin studies of schizophrenia: clarification and affirmation. *Schiz. Bull.* 3:351–354.

Shur, E. 1982. Season of birth in high and low genetic risk schizophrenics. *Br. J. Psychiat.* 140:410–415.

Silverton, L., Mednick, S. A., Schulsinger, F., Parnas, J., and Harrington, M. E. 1988. Genetic risk for schizophrenia, birthweight, and cerebral ventricular enlargement. *J. Abnorm. Psychol.* 97:496–498.

Simpson, J. 1988. Mortality studies in schizophrenia. In *Nosology, epidemiology and genetics of schizophrenia*, ed. M. T. Tsuang and J. C. Simpson. Amsterdam: Elsevier. 245–273.

Slater, E., and Beard, A. W. 1963. The schizophrenia-like psychoses of epilepsy. I. Psychiatric aspects. *Br. J. Psychiat.* 109:95–150.

Snyder, S. 1976. The dopamine hypothesis of schizophrenia: focus on the dopamine receptor. *Am. J. Psychiatry* 133:197–202.

Snyder, S. H. 1972. Catecholamines in the brain as mediators of amphetamine psychosis. *Arch. Gen. Psychiat.* 27:169–179.

Spitzer, R. L., Endicott, J., and Robins, E. 1978. Research diagnostic criteria: rationale and reliability. *Arch. Gen. Psychiat.* 35:773–782.

Stahl, S. M., and Wets, K. 1987. Indoleamines and schizophrenia. In *Neurochemistry and neuropharmacology of schizophrenia*, ed. F. A. Henn and L. E. DeLisi. Amsterdam: Elsevier. 257–296.

Sternberg, D. E., VanKammen, D. P., Lerner, P., and Bunney, W. E. 1982. Schizophrenia: dopamine beta-hydroxylase activity and treatment response. *Science* 216:1423–25.

Strauss, J., Kokes, R., Carpenter, W., and Ritzler, B. 1978. The course of schizophrenia as a developmental process. In *The nature of schizophrenia*, ed. L. C. Wynne, R. L. Cromwell, and S. Matthysse. New York: Wiley.

Takei, N., Sham, P., O'Callaghan, E., Murray, G. K., Glover, G., and Murray, R. M. In press. Prenatal influenza and schizophrenia: is the effect confined to females? *Am. J. Psychiatry.*

Taylor, M., and Abrams, R. 1975. Manic depressive illness and good prognosis schizophrenia. *Am. J. Psychiatry* 132:741–742.

Torrey, E. F., and Kaufmann, C. A. 1986. Schizophrenia and neuroviruses. In *The neurology of schizophrenia*, ed. H. A. Nasrallah and D. R. Weinberger. Amsterdam: Elsevier. 361–376.

Torrey, E. F., Rawlings, R., and Waldman, I. N. 1988. Schizophrenic births and viral diseases in two states. *Schiz. Res.* 1:73–77.

Torrey, E. F., Yolken, R. H., and Winfrey, C. J. 1982. Cytomegalovirus antibody in cerebrospinal fluid of schizophrenic patients detected by enzyme immunoassay. *Science* 216:892–893.

Tsuang, M. T. 1978. Suicide in schizophrenics, manics, depressives, and surgical controls: a comparison with general population suicide mortality. *Arch. Gen. Psychiat.* 35:153–155.

Tsuang, M. T., and Faraone, S. V. 1994. Epidemiology and

behavioral genetics of schizophrenia. In *Biology of schizophrenia and affective disease,* ed. S. J. Watson. New York: Raven Press.

———— 1995. The case for heterogeneity in the etiology of schizophrenia. *Schiz. Res.* 17:161–175.

Tsuang, M. T., and Woolson, R. F. 1977. Mortality in patients with schizophrenia, mania, depression, and surgical conditions. *Br. J. Psychiat.* 130:162–166.

Tsuang, M. T., Simpson, J. C., and Kronfol, Z. 1982. Subtypes of drug abuse with psychosis: demographic characteristics, clinical features, and family history. *Arch. Gen. Psychiat.* 39:141–147.

Tsuang, M. T., Woolson, R. F., and Fleming, J. A. 1979. Long-term outcome of major psychoses. I. Schizophrenia and affective disorders compared with psychiatrically symptom-free surgical conditions. *Arch. Gen. Psychiat.* 36:1295–1301.

———— 1980a. Causes of death in schizophrenia and manic-depression. *Br. J. Psychiat.* 136:239–242.

———— 1980b. Premature deaths in schizophrenia and affective disorders: an analysis of survival curves and variables affecting the shortened survival. *Arch. Gen. Psychiat.* 37:979–983.

Tsuang, M. T., Woolson, R. F., Winokur, G., and Crowe, R. R. 1981. Stability of psychiatric diagnosis: schizophrenia and affective disorders followed up over a 30- to 40-year period. *Arch. Gen. Psychiat.* 38:535–539.

Vaillant, G. 1964. Prospective prediction of schizophrenic remission. *Arch. Gen. Psychiat.* 11:509–518.

van Kammen, D., Peters, J., van Kammen, W., Nugent, A., Goetz, K., Yao, J., and Linnoila, M. 1989. CSF norepinephrine in schizophrenia is elevated prior to relapse after haloperidol withdrawal. *Biol. Psychiat.* 26:176–188.

van Kammen, D., Peters, J., van Kammen, W., Neylan, T., Yao, J., Shaw, D., and Docherty, G. 1990. Noradrenaline, state dependency, and relapse prediction in schizophrenia. In *International perspectives in schizophrenia,* ed. M. Weller. London: John Libbey. 253–268.

van Kammen, D. P., Mann, L., Scheinin, M., van Kammen, W. B., and Linnoila, M. 1984. Spinal fluid monoamine metabolites and anti-cytomegalovirus antibodies and brain scan evaluation in schizophrenia. *Psychopharmacol. Bull.* 20:519–522.

Van Putten, T. 1984. Guidelines to the use of plasma levels: a clinical perspective. *J. Clin. Psychiatry* (monograph) 2:27–32.

Van Putten, T., May, P., and Jenden, D. 1981. Does a plasma level of chlorpromazine help? *Psychol. Med.* 11:729–734.

Van Tol, H., Bungow, J., Guan, H., et al. 1991. Cloning of the gene for a human dopamine D4 receptor with high affinity for the antipsychotic clozapine. *Nature* 350:610–614.

Vaughn, C., and Leff, J. 1976. The influence of family and social factors on the course of psychiatric illness: a comparison of schizophrenic and depressed neurotic patients. *Br. J. Psychiatry.* 129:125–137.

Vaughn, C., Snyder, K., Freeman, W., Jones, S., Falloon, I., and Liberman, R. 1982. Family factors in schizophrenic relapse: a replication. *Schiz. Bull.* 8:425–426.

Vita, A., Dieci, M., Giobbio, G. M., Garbarini, M., Morganti, C., Braga, M., and Invernizzi, G. 1994. A reconsideration of the relationship between cerebral structural abnormalities and family history of schizophrenia. *Psychiat. Res.* 53:41–55.

Waldmeier, P. 1980. Serotonergic modulation of mesolimbic and frontal cortical dopamine neurons. *Experientia* 36:1092–94.

Walker, E., and Lewine, R. J. 1990. Prediction of adult-onset schizophrenia from childhood home movies of the parents. *Am. J. Psychiatry* 147:1052–56.

Walker, E., and Shayer, J. 1982. Familial schizophrenia: a predictor of neuromotor and attentional abnormalities in schizophrenia. *Arch. Gen. Psychiat.* 39:1153–56.

Weinberger, D. 1995. Neurodevelopmental perspectives on schizophrenia. In *Psychopharmacology: the fourth generation of progress,* ed. F. E. Bloom and D. Kupfer. New York: Raven Press. 1171–83.

Weinberger, D., and Kleinman, J. 1986. Observations on the brain in schizophrenia. In *American psychiatric association annual review,* ed. A. J. Frances and R. E. Hales. Washington, D.C.: American Psychiatric Press.

Weinberger, D., Berman, K., and Zec, R. 1986. Physiologic dysfunction of dorsolateral prefrontal cortex in schizophrenia. I. Regional cerebral blood flow evidence. *Arch. Gen. Psychiat.* 43:114–124.

Weinberger, D. R. 1984. CAT scan findings in schizophrenia: speculation on the meaning of it all. *J. Psychiat. Res.* 18:477–490.

———— 1994. Schizophrenia as a neurodevelopmental disorder: a review of the concept. In *Schizophrenia,* ed. S. R. Hirsch and D. R. Weinberger. London: Blackwood Press,

Weinberger, D. R., and Berman, K. F. 1988. Speculation on the meaning of cerebral metabolic hypofrontality in schizophrenia. *Schiz. Bull.* 14:157–168.

Weinberger, D. R., Wagner, R. I., and Wyatt, R. J. 1983. Neuropathological studies of schizophrenia: a selective review. *Schiz. Bull.* 9:193–212.

Weinberger, D. R., Llewellyn, B. B., and Kleinman, J. E., et al. 1980. Cerebral ventricular enlargement in chronic schizophrenia: an association with poor response to treatment. *Arch. Gen. Psychiat.* 37:11–13.

Weinberger, D. R., DeLisi, L. E., Neophytides, A. N., and Wyatt, R. J. 1981. Familial aspects of CT scan abnormalities in chronic schizophrenic patients. *Psychiat. Res.* 4:65–71.

Weinberger, D. R., Berman, K. F., Suddath, R., and Torrey, E. F. 1992. Evidence of dysfunction of a prefrontal-limbic network in schizophrenia: a magnetic resonance imaging and regional cerebral blood flow study of discordant monozygotic twins. *Am. J. Psychiatry* 149:890–897.

Welner, A., Croughan, J., Fishman, R., and Robins, E. 1977. The group of schizoaffective and related psychoses: a follow-up study. *Compr. Psychiatry* 18:413–422.

Winokur, G. 1977. Delusional disorder (paranoia). *Compr. Psychiat.* 18:511–521.

Wise, C. D., and Stein, L. 1973. Dopamine-beta-hydroxylase deficits in the brains of schizophrenic patients. *Science* 181:344–347.

Woerner, M. G., Pollack, M., and Klein, D. F. 1971. Birthweight and length in schizophrenics personality disorders and their siblings. *Br. J. Psychiat.* 118:461.

Wolkin, A., Jaeger, J., Brodie, J., Wolf, A., Fowler, J., Rotrosen, J., Gomez-Mont, F., and Cancro, R. 1985. Persistence of cerebral metabolic abnormalities in chronic schizophrenia as determined by positron emission tomography. *Am. J. Psychiatry* 142:564–571.

Wolkin, A., Brodie, J. D., Barouche, F., Rotrosen, J., Wolf, A. P., Smith, M., Fowler, J., and Cooper, T. B. 1989. Dopamine receptor occupancy and plasma haloperidol levels. *Arch. Gen. Psychiat.* 46:482–483.

Wong, D. F. 1990. Elevated dopamine receptors in psychosis. Annual Meeting of the American Psychiatric Association. 209.

Wong, H. N., Tune, L. E., and Dannals, R. F., et al. 1986. Positron Emission Tomography reveals elevated D2 dopamine receptors in drug-naive schizophrenics. *Science* 234:1558–63.

World Health Organization. 1973. *The international pilot study of schizophrenia.* Geneva: World Health Organization.

———— 1979. *Schizophrenia: an international followup study.* New York: Wiley.

Wright, J., Gill, M., and Murray, R. M. 1993. Schizophrenia: genetics and the maternal immune response to viral infection. *Am. J. Med. Genet. Neuropsychiat. Genet.* 48:40–46.

Wyatt, R. J. 1985. The dopamine hypothesis: variations on a theme. In *Research in the schizophrenic disorders: the Stanley R. Dean Award lectures,* ed. R. Cancro and S. R. Dean. Jamaica, N.Y.: Spectrum. 225–247.

Wyatt, R. J., Erdelyi, E., Schwartz, M., Herman, M., and Barchas, J. D. 1978. Difficulties in comparing catecholamine-related enzymes from the brains of schizophrenics and controls. *Biol. Psychiat.* 13:317–334.

Zec, R. F., and Weinberger, D. R. 1986. Relationship between CT scan findings and neuropsychological performance in chronic schizophrenia. *Psychiatric Clinics of North America* 9:49–61.

Recommended Reading

Gottesman, I. I. 1991. *Schizophrenia genesis: the origin of madness.* New York: Freeman.

Green, A. I., and Schildkraut, J. J. 1995. Should clozapine be a first-line treatment for schizophrenia? The rationale for a double-blind clinical trial in first-episode patients. *Harvard Review of Psychiatry* 3:1–9.

Seidman, L. J., Cassens, G. P., Kremen, W. S., and Pepple, J. R. 1992. Neuropsychology of schizophrenia. In *Clinical syndromes in adult neuropsychology: the practitioner's handbook,* ed. R. F. White. Amsterdam: Elsevier. 381–449.

Tsuang, M. T., and Faraone, S. V. 1994. Epidemiology and behavioral genetics of schizophrenia. In *Biology of schizophrenia and affective disease,* ed. S. J. Watson. New York: Raven Press.

Tsuang, M. T., Faraone, S. V., and Johnson, P. 1997. *Schizophrenia: the facts.* Oxford: Oxford University Press.

Weinberger, D. R. 1995. Neurodevelopmental perspectives on schizophrenia. In *Psychopharmacology: the fourth generation of progress,* ed. F. E. Bloom and D. Kupfter. New York: Raven Press.

Acknowledgments

Preparation of this chapter was supported in part by the National Institute of Mental Health Grants 1-R01MH41879-01, 5-UO1 MH46318-02, and 1-R37MH43518-01 to Dr. Ming T. Tsuang, by NIMH grants R01MH49891-02A and R01MH52376-03 to Dr. Alan I. Green, and by funds from the Commonwealth Research Center of Massachusetts. The authors gratefully acknowledge the contributions made by Max Day, M.D., to a previous version of this chapter.

ANTHONY J. ROTHSCHILD

Mood Disorders

Mood disorders are well described in ancient history. The dominant features common to these disorders are disturbances of the patient's mood and affect—most often depression, but also elation and mania. Efforts at classification of mood disorders date from Egypt (around 3000 B.C.), including Hippocrates' enlightened approach in conceptualizing mental disorders as due to natural vs. supernatural causes (around 400 B.C.). In the early twentieth century, Kraepelin (1921) was one of the first to distinguish "manic-depressive insanity" from schizophrenia by the presence of a deteriorating vs. nondeteriorating course. In the past several decades, impressive progress has been made in the effectiveness of drug therapies (detailed in Chapter 21), especially those using tricyclic antidepressants (TCAs), monoamine oxidase (MAO) inhibitors, selective serotonin reuptake inhibitors (SSRIs), and mood stabilizers such as lithium, divalproex, and carbamazepine. New forms of psychotherapy have increased the diversity of available treatments, and their efficacy has improved the prognosis for mood disorders.

This chapter describes the clinical, diagnostic, epidemiologic, etiological, and treatment aspects of mood disorders. Clinicians now diagnose the mood disorders by the symptomatic and behavioral criteria codified in the American Psychiatric Association's *Diagnostic and Statistical Manual of Mental Disorders,* fourth edition (DSM-IV). However, the pathophysiology of mood disorders may involve many causes, even though the syndrome varies little across a broad range of patients. Multiple etiological factors—genetic, biochemical, psychodynamic, and socioenvironmental—may interact in complex ways. In any given patient, the specific etiology of the mood disorder is usually uncertain, and clinicians thus need to weigh varying combinations of stress, personality, central nervous system changes, and other factors.

The Depressions

The term *depression* has many different meanings. Current evidence suggests that depression is a heterogeneous group of disorders characterized by a broad spectrum of symptom type, severity, and course of illness. Depression is a rather vague descriptive term used to describe conditions ranging from normal sadness and disappointment to severe and incapacitating psychiatric illness. William Styron in his book *Darkness Visible* aptly describes the unsatisfactory descriptive nature of the term *depression:* "a noun with bland tonality and lacking any magisterial presence, used indifferently to describe an economic decline or rut in the ground. A true wimp of a word for such a major illness" (Styron, 1990, p. 37).

Distinguishing Normal Mood from Depressive Illness

Feelings of sadness, disappointment, and frustration are part of the normal human experience. Distinguishing between normal mood and abnormal depression can at times be difficult. As with other disease states in medicine, mood disorders involve an accentuation in the intensity or duration of otherwise normal emotional states. Furthermore, as discussed below, the diagnosis of depressive illness requires the presence of specific signs and symptoms in addition to a depressed mood. Because all human beings experience sad, depressed, and discouraged states, depressed patients readily gain the empathic understanding of clinicians and family members. The familiarity of depressed mood may at times hinder the clinical assessment and differential diagnosis, since it may obscure the boundary between normality and abnormality. Family and friends may tend to minimize the clinical significance of the patient's difficulties, because the manifestations of the illness may appear to be a normal emotional state.

Clinicians diagnose a depressive illness by the intensity,

pervasiveness, and persistence of the mood symptoms as well as by the degree of interference of the depressed mood with the person's social and physiological functioning. Several features distinguish clinically ill patients from those with normal mood. These patients exhibit a combination of the following features: (1) impairment of body functioning, including disturbances in sleep, appetite, sexual interest, and autonomic nervous system and gastrointestinal processes; (2) reduced desire and ability to perform the expected social roles in family, work, marriage, or school; (3) suicidal thoughts or acts; and (4) disturbances in reality testing, manifested by delusions, hallucinations, or confusion. Suicidal thoughts and acts and impairment of reality testing indicate a need for psychiatric attention and often for hospitalization.

Symptoms of Depression

The central feature of depression is a subjective experience of marked sadness (depressed mood) or a pervasive loss of interest and pleasure in the individual's activities (anhedonia). Irritability or anxiety may be the predominant mood disturbance in some patients and agitation in others. Many experience feelings of lowered self-esteem and of helplessness. Depressed patients frequently become preoccupied or obsessed with work, family, finances, and health, and view these matters with marked pessimism and hopelessness. They often feel guilty about past or current actions. The combination of hopelessness, pessimism, low self-esteem, and guilt may prompt morbid and/or suicidal thoughts. Patients with depression almost always experience several of the symptoms listed in Table 14.1.

Depressed mood, the most characteristic symptom, occurs in over 90% of patients. Patients with a major depressive episode often describe their mood as depressed, sad, hopeless, discouraged, or "down in the dumps." Along with this state of inner distress, the physician often observes changes in posture, speech, facial expression, dress, and grooming consistent with the patient's self-report. A small percentage of patients with "masked depression" do not report sadness, but the physician may subsequently elicit this information by interview and observe the depressed mood in the person's facial expression and demeanor. Some patients may complain of somatic symptoms such as body aches and pains rather than reporting feelings of sadness.

Loss of interest or pleasure in usual activities is nearly always present to some degree in depressed patients. The patient may report that activities which previously provided gratification such as hobbies, sports, eating, sex, social events, time spent with family, children, or friends—are no longer enjoyable. Family members may notice the neglect of formerly pleasurable avocations (e.g., a once avid tennis player no longer plays). In severe forms the patient is described as anhedonic.

Table 14.1 Criteria for major depressive episode

1. Depressed mood most of the day, nearly every day, as indicated by either subjective report (e.g., feels sad or empty) or observation made by others (e.g., appears tearful).

2. Markedly diminished interest or pleasure in all, or almost all, activities most of the day, nearly every day (as indicated by either subjective account or observation made by others).

3. Significant weight loss when not dieting or weight gain (e.g., a change of more than 5% of body weight in a month), or decrease or increase in appetite nearly every day.

4. Insomnia or hypersomnia nearly every day.

5. Psychomotor agitation or retardation nearly every day (observable by others, not merely subjective feelings of restlessness or being slowed down).

6. Fatigue or loss of energy nearly every day.

7. Feelings of worthlessness or excessive or inappropriate guilt (which may be delusional) nearly every day (not merely self-reproach or guilt about being sick).

8. Diminished ability to think or concentrate, or indecisiveness, nearly every day (either by subjective account or as observed by others).

9. Recurrent thoughts of death (not just fear of dying), recurrent suicidal ideation without a specific plan, or a suicide attempt or a specific plan for committing suicide.

Source: Reprinted with permission from the *Diagnostic and Statistical Manual of Mental Disorders, Fourth Edition.* Copyright 1994 by the American Psychiatric Association.

Many patients will experience a *decrease in appetite* (anorexia) and marked *weight reduction;* however, a subset of patients experience increased appetite (hyperphagia) and weight gain.

Sleep disturbances in patients suffering from major depression include difficulty falling asleep, difficulty remaining asleep, and/or early morning awakening (initial, middle, and terminal insomnia). Less frequently, patients present with an increase in sleeping (hypersomnia) in the form of prolonged sleep episodes at night or increased daytime sleep.

Some depressed patients exhibit an *increase in psychomotor activity* (agitation). Patients with an agitated depression may demonstrate pacing, hand-wringing, nail-biting, and incessant smoking or talking. They complain of being jittery or fidgety. Other patients may exhibit decreased psychomotor activity (psychomotor retardation). These patients typically complain of lethargy and fatigue, and their body movements may appear slowed and limited. Their speech is often impoverished, monotonic, and increasingly slowed.

Fatigue, loss of energy, and tiredness are common symptoms in depression. The patient often feels run down, as if energy were being drained from the body, and may complain of heaviness in the arms and legs. Patients may interpret these feeling states as "nervous exhaustion," being "overworked," a "nervous breakdown," or "vitamin or nutritional deficiency." The patient often reports fatigue with even the simplest tasks.

Feelings of worthlessness or excessive or inappropriate guilt associated with a major depressive episode may include unrealistic negative evaluations of one's worth or guilty preoccupations with or ruminations over minor past failings. Depressed patients often will misinterpret trivial day-to-day occurrences as evidence of personal defects and have an exaggerated sense of responsibility for negative events. In his classic paper "Mourning and Melancholia" (1917), Freud postulated that guilt and self-reproach characterized depression (melancholia) but not normal grief. Subsequent clinical research has revealed inaccuracies in both parts of this formulation: many grieving persons feel shameful and guilt ridden, and many depressed people do not consciously experience or report guilt. Guilt appears to be associated in Western societies with conflicts generated by the moral lessons of child-rearing practices and religious beliefs, which become internalized as superego and conscience. Cross-cultural studies indicate that guilt and feelings of worthlessness are less common in depressed patients in African and Asian societies, while shame and complaints of bodily dysfunction and loss of energy are more prevalent. In severe forms of depression, the sense of worthlessness or guilt may be of delusional proportions.

Depressed patients often complain of *difficulty in concentration,* slowed thinking, poor memory, and similar symptoms. They often have trouble making decisions even over minor matters. They may appear easily distracted or complain of memory difficulties. Those in intellectually demanding occupations are often unable to function adequately, even with mild concentration problems (e.g., an attorney who can no longer perform complicated but previously manageable tasks). On formal psychological testing, accurate answers are usually obtained but speed and performance are slowed. In elderly patients the differential diagnosis between a major depression and the early stages of a dementia may be difficult. In some individuals the major depressive episode may be the initial presentation of an irreversible dementia.

Suicidal thoughts are common in patients suffering from major depression, but only a few have suicidal intent. These thoughts range from the feeling that they would not care if they died in their sleep or that others would be better off if they were dead, to transient but recurrent thoughts of committing suicide, to actual specific plans for committing suicide. The frequency, intensity, and lethality of these thoughts may vary considerably. The risk of suicide is present until the psychological mood state of dysphoria has improved, which is often the last symptom to do so, following improvement in energy level, somatic complaints, and other symptoms. The dysphoric mood is what the patient experiences most intensely, but it is the least observable by others. The period of highest risk extends from the acute episode into the months after symptomatic remission, with the highest suicide mortality occurring during the period of 6–9 months after symptomatic improvement. Although the causes of this phenomenon are not clear, possible explanations are that (1) the patient's *apparent* symptomatic improvement reflects a decision to commit suicide, and the outward calm reflects a resolution of the patient's internal struggle whether to live or die; or that (2) after a period of remission, the patient experiences a return of symptoms (relapse), resulting in feelings of hopelessness and helplessness and a belief that he will never get better.

Elations and Mania

Although manic episodes occur far less frequently than depressions, their dramatic onset and character continue to fascinate psychiatrists and laymen. More than 2000 years ago, Aretaeus of Cappadocia first described the condition of mania (Adams, 1856). Hippocrates also described early symptomatology (Goodwin and Jamison, 1990). Kraepelin (1921) helped distinguish important differences between manic-depressive illness and dementia praecox (schizophrenia). Kraepelin noted that patients with manic depression have an episodic course interspersed with occasional euthymic periods and, in general, a better prognosis than patients with schizophrenia. The widely used term *mania* stems from earlier experience with psychotic states; recent clinical experience indicates a spectrum of euphoric and elated states. In the United States, the first edition of the *Diagnostic and Statistical Manual of Mental Disorders* (DSM-I) described 2 types of manic-depressive illness: manic-depressive reaction, manic type, and manic-depressive reaction, other, which included mixed mania. Psychotic features were not mentioned; and as a result, patients with psychotic mania were classified within the schizophrenia spectrum (American Psychiatric Association, 1952). When DSM-II was published in 1968, the term *manic-depressive reaction* was changed to *manic-depressive illness.* It was then classified as a major affective disorder and was grouped under the affective psychoses, thus emphasizing the presence of the psychotic symptoms as part of manic-depressive illness (American Psychiatric Association, 1968). With the publication of DSM-III (American Psychiatric Association, 1980), the term *manic-depressive illness* was changed to *bipolar disorder,* which, together with unipolar disorder, became part of the mood disorders.

DSM-IV (American Psychiatric Association, 1994), described an acute manic episode as a distinct period of abnormal and persistently elevated expansive or irritable mood lasting at least 1 week or requiring hospitalization. In addition, 3 or more of a number of symptoms must be persistent to a significant degree, and 4 or more if the mood is irritable. Symptoms of a manic episode include:

1. inflated self-esteem or grandiosity
2. decreased need to sleep
3. pressured speech or increased talkativeness
4. racing thoughts or flight of ideas
5. distractibility
6. increased goal-directed activity or psychomotor agitation at school or work
7. excessive involvement in pleasurable activities with a high degree of harmful consequences

The mood disturbance cannot be due to a substance (e.g., a medication or drug of abuse) or a general medical condition. In a departure from previous diagnostic conceptualizations, mania precipitated solely by antidepressant medications is not classified as mania associated with bipolar disorder. The episode must be severe enough to cause marked occupational impairment or interference with social activities or a relationship, or it must be severe enough to necessitate hospitalization to prevent harm to the patient or others.

A number of descriptive studies have closely examined the mood, behavioral, and cognitive features of the manic state. Most manic patients experience depression (72%), irritability (80%), expansiveness (60%), and mood liability, the classic "mood swings" of manic-depressive illness (69%) as often as euphoria (71%) (Keck et al., 1996). The combination of mood symptoms in mania is determined, in part, by the degree of severity or stage of mania (Carlson and Goodwin, 1973). The course of a manic episode can be divided into 3 stages, based primarily on the predominant mood: Stage I is characterized by euphoria; Stage II by irritability, dysphoria, and depression; and Stage III by severe anxiety (often escalating to panic), dysphoria, and delirium (Carlson and Goodwin, 1973). The changes in mood symptoms from Stages I through III, as mania escalates, are often recapitulated in reverse as mania subsides by switching into the depressive phase or with treatment.

Psychotic and nonpsychotic cognitive symptoms are now recognized to be common in mania (Goodwin and Jamison, 1990). The most common nonpsychotic cognitive symptoms seen in mania include grandiosity, racing thoughts, and distractibility/poor concentration (Keck et al., 1996). Over 25 studies (summarized in Goodwin and Jamison, 1990) have demonstrated that all forms of psychosis (e.g., delusions, hallucinations, formal thought disorder) can be present during mania. These include the classic symptoms of grandiose and religious delusions, mood-incongruent delusions, and first-rank Schneiderian symptoms (e.g., hearing voices, thought broadcasting, thought insertion) (Pope and Lipinski, 1978).

The most common behavioral disturbances in mania include pressured speech, hyperverbosity, physical hyperactivity, decreased sleep, hypersexuality, and extravagance. Less commonly occurring behavioral symptoms include violent or assaultive acts, religiosity, head decoration, public sexual exposure, pronounced regression, catatonia, and fecal smearing or incontinence (Keck et al., 1996).

Clinical experience suggests that manic patients often lack insight and fail to recognize their symptoms. Their poor recognition of the behavioral manifestations of their illness and their need for treatment are commonly associated with noncompliance and poor outcome (Jamison et al., 1979; O'Connell et al., 1991). This lack of insight may be one of the most insidious symptoms of mania.

Manic episodes have a high tendency to recur. Follow-up studies reveal that before the introduction of lithium, about 75% of manic patients had more than 1 episode in their lifetime. Almost all patients with manic episodes also experience depressive episodes. Several studies (Keller et al., 1986; Tohen, 1988; Tohen and associates, 1990a, b) suggest that bipolar illness has a variable prognosis ranging from complete recovery to functional incapacitation. Other studies (Tohen et al., 1990a, 1995) have reported that outcome in single-episode cases differs from multiple-episode cases.

Diagnosis and Classification

Major Depressions

For clinicians, diagnosing depression can be challenging, given the variability of its presentation. One patient may present with prominent self-reproach and tearfulness while another patient will present with multiple physical complaints. One patient may present with classic neurovegetative signs and symptoms of depression while another patient presents with "reverse" neurovegetative symptoms (e.g., hyperphagia, hypersomnia). Moreover, diagnosing depression in patients with medical illness can also be challenging, since many of the symptoms and signs of depression, such as weight loss, apathy, insomnia, and low energy, may be due to the medical condition itself or to a complication of the medical treatment. Despite its clinical variability, depression carries a significant morbidity and mortality for the sufferer. In DSM-IV, major depression is now referred to as "major depressive disorder" to emphasize that it is a syndrome that includes both psychological and somatic symptoms (Hales, Yudofsky, and Talbott, 1994). To meet the diagnosis of major depressive disorder according to DSM-IV, 5 of the 9 symptoms listed in Table 14.1 must be present for at least 2 weeks; at least 1 of the symptoms must be either depressed mood or loss of interest or pleasure. The diagnostic criteria can be grouped into 4 general categories: (1) *disturbances in mood:* feelings of being sad, blue, depressed, hopeless, "blah," irritable, "down in the dumps," worried; (2) *disturbances in cognition:* loss of interest, difficulty concentrating, low self-esteem, negative thoughts, indecisiveness, guilt, suicidal ideation, delusions, hallucinations; (3) *behavioral disturbances:* social withdrawal, psychomotor retardation; (4) *somatic disturbances:* fatigue, sleep disturbance, changes in appetite, weight loss, or weight gain (Hales, Yudofsky, and Talbott, 1994).

To avoid a functional vs. organic dichotomy, the authors of DSM-IV transferred 2 diagnostic categories—mood disorder owing to a general medical condition and substance-induced mood disorder—from the organic mental disorder section in DSM-III-R (American Psychiatric Association, 1987) to the general category of mood disorders. The essential feature of this diagnostic category is that the mood disturbance is etiologically related to the general medical condition or to substance abuse. The clinician will often observe temporal association between the onset, exacerbation, or remission of the general medical condition (or substance abuse) and that of the mood disturbance.

There has been significant debate in the literature regarding the potential shortcomings of an overreliance on categorizing disorders primarily by their presenting symptoms. Some have argued that treatment response should also be included as a key variable in categorizing psychiatric disorders (Fink, 1993; Schatzberg and Rothschild, 1992). Although recent editions of the *Diagnostic and Statistical Manual* avoid using specific treatment response as a criteria for categorization, data exist that provide evidence of differential treatment response in specific disorders such as catatonia (Rosebush et al., 1990; Fink and Taylor, 1991) and delusional depression (Schatzberg and Rothschild, 1992). DSM-IV uses "specifiers" which describe the most recent categorizations of mood disorder. These include: (1) with psychotic features, (2) with catatonic features, (3) with melancholic features, (4) with atypical features, (5) with postpartum onset, and (6) with seasonal pattern.

Psychotic (delusional) depression. Schatzberg and Rothschild (1992) argue that sufficient data and clinical reasons exist to designate major depression with psychotic features—a disorder with considerable morbidity and mortality—as a distinct depressive syndrome. However, in DSM-IV, the term *psychotic features* indicates the presence of either delusions or hallucinations. Generally, the content of the delusions or hallucinations is consistent with the depressive themes. Such mood-congruent psychotic features include delusions of guilt, delusions of deserved punishment, nihilistic delusions, somatic delusions, and delusions of poverty. Less commonly, the content of the hallucinations or delusions has no apparent relationship to depressive themes. Such mood-incongruent psychotic features include persecutory delusions, delusions of thought insertion, delusions of thought broadcasting, and delusions of control.

Unfortunately for the clinician, unlike patients with other psychotic disorders (e.g., schizophrenia or mania), patients with psychotic depression are often able to keep their unusual thoughts and feelings to themselves. Because the detection of delusions and hallucinations is often difficult in patients with psychotic depression, a number of investigators have attempted to study whether other characteristics may help distinguish between psychotic and nonpsychotic depressed patients. Several investigators report that patients with psychotic depression demonstrate a more frequent and severe psychomotor disturbance (either retardation or agitation) than do patients with nonpsychotic depression (Charney and Nelson, 1981; Coryell, Pfohl, and Zimmerman, 1984; Frances et al., 1981; Glassman and Roose, 1981; Lykouras et al., 1986; Nelson and Bowers, 1978). Psychotically depressed patients have also been reported to exhibit more pronounced paranoid symptoms (Frances et al., 1981; Lykouras et al., 1986), cognitive impairment (Rothschild et al., 1989), hopelessness (Frances et al., 1981), hypochondriasis (Coryell, Pfohl, and Zimmerman, 1984; Glassman and Roose, 1981), anxiety (Charney and Nelson, 1981; Glassman and Roose, 1981), early insomnia (Frances et al., 1981; Lykouras et al., 1986), middle insomnia (Lykouras et al., 1986), and constipation (Parker et al., 1991) than nonpsychotic depressed patients. Patients with psychotic depression also fail to show a diurnal variation in mood compared with endogenous depressed nonpsychotic patients (Parker et al., 1991).

Patients with psychotic depression experience greater short-term morbidity and mortality in the acute episode than do nonpsychotic depressed patients. Some investigators report the incidence of suicidal thoughts as well as the act of suicide to be greater among hospitalized patients with psychotic depression than among nonpsychotic depressed patients (Roose, Glassman, and Walsh, 1983; Nelson, Khan, and Orr, 1984). However, other studies that compare the 2 groups on suicidal ideation or suicide attempts fail to find statistically significant differences between them (Charney and Nelson, 1981; Feighner et al., 1972; Frances et al., 1981; Glassman and Roose, 1981; Lykouras et al., 1986; Nelson and Bowers, 1978). In general, patients with psychotic depression have longer recovery times then patients with nonpsychotic depression (Coryell et al., 1984; Robinson and Spiker, 1985). Some studies suggest that psychotically depressed patients have residual social impairment but not depression or psychosis at 1 year (Rothschild et al., 1993b) and 5 years (Coryell et al., 1990) after an episode.

Antidepressant medications have made it more important to distinguish between psychotic and nonpsychotic depression. Previously, most severely depressed patients,

both psychotic and nonpsychotic, received electroconvulsive therapy. Today it is more important to make the distinction, because patients with psychotic depression respond better to a combination of a tricyclic antidepressant and a neuroleptic (Spiker et al., 1985; Schatzberg and Rothschild, 1992). Selective serotonin reuptake inhibitors in combination with neuroleptics are less well studied but may be effective as well (Rothschild et al., 1993a; Wolfersdorf et al., 1995). For some patients, especially those with a history of mania, the addition of lithium to the antidepressant-neuroleptic combination may prove helpful (Price, Conwell, and Nelson, 1983).

Catatonic features. In DSM-IV the specifier "with catatonic features" can be applied to the patient's current or most recent major depressive episode (or manic episode) when the clinical picture is characterized by marked psychomotor disturbance that may involve motoric immobility, excessive motor activity, extreme negativism, mutism, peculiarities of voluntary movement, and echolalia or echopraxia. Fink and others have argued that catatonia should be designated as a distinct syndrome in part because of its unique responsivity to electroconvulsive therapy (ECT) and benzodiazepines (e.g., lorazepam) rather than to neuroleptics (Fink, 1993; Schatzberg and Rothschild, 1993; Gelenberg, 1976; Rosebush et al., 1990; Fink and Taylor, 1991; Fricchione et al., 1983; Vingradov and Reiss, 1986; Greenfield et al., 1987).

Melancholic features. The specifier "with melancholic features" refers to loss of interest or pleasure in all, or almost all, activities or lack of reactivity to usually pleasurable stimuli. In addition, the patient's depressed mood does not improve when something good happens. These criteria are reminiscent of the older term *endogenous.* At least 3 of the following symptoms also must be present to meet the criteria for melancholia: (1) a distinct quality of the depressed mood, (2) depression that is regularly worse in the morning, (3) early morning awakening, and (4) psychomotor retardation or agitation, significant anorexia or weight loss, or excessive or inappropriate guilt. The subtyping of major depression with melancholic features allows for assembling a more homogeneous group of patients in whom biological studies can be undertaken than with the major depressive category as a whole. Thus, melancholic features are more frequently associated with abnormal laboratory findings such as dexamethasone nonsuppression, hyperadrenocorticism, reduced rapid eye movement (REM) latency, abnormal tyramine challenge test, and an abnormal asymmetry on dichotic listening tasks (American Psychiatric Association, 1994).

Atypical features. The term *atypical depression* has been used for many years by clinicians to refer to a patient with *nonendogeneous* depression who responded well to monoamine oxidase inhibitor (MAOI) antidepressants. Over the past few decades, the operational criteria for diagnosing atypical depression have been refined and are enumerated in DSM-IV. These criteria apply only when the patient has a diagnosis of a DSM-IV major depressive disorder and include mood reactivity (the mood improves in response to positive events) and 2 or more of the following features: (1) hypersomnia, (2) significant weight gain or increase in appetite, (3) leaden paralysis, i.e., heavy feeling in arms or legs, and (4) a long-standing pattern of interpersonal rejection sensitivity that results in significant social or occupational impairment (American Psychiatric Association, 1994; Quitkin et al., 1989, 1990, 1991; Liebowitz et al., 1984).

Postpartum onset. The "postpartum onset" specifier is a new addition to DSM-IV and has important implications for both prognosis and treatment. Postpartum onset may be applied to either major depressive or manic episodes in bipolar disorder, major depressive disorder, or brief psychotic disorder. In general, the symptoms that characterize a postpartum depression do not differ from symptoms in a non-postpartum episode. Typically, symptom onset occurs within 4 weeks postpartum (Dean and Kendell, 1981; Meltzer and Kumar, 1985). Psychotic features appear from 1 in 500 to 1 in 1000 deliveries and are typically more common in primiparous women (Kendell, Chalmers, and Platz, 1987). In both the psychotic and nonpsychotic presentations, there may be associated suicidal ideation, obsessional thoughts regarding violence to the child, early morning awakening, spontaneous crying after the usual duration of "baby blues" (i.e., 3–7 days postpartum), panic attacks, and lack of interest in the infant (American Psychiatric Association, 1994; Davidson and Robertson, 1985; Meltzer and Kumar, 1985; Platz and Kendell, 1988; Dean and Kendell, 1981).

Seasonal pattern. In DSM-IV, "seasonal pattern" refers to the onset and remission of any affective disorder (unipolar or bipolar depression) at characteristic times of the year. In unipolar disorders, this represents a subtype of depression in which episodes generally begin in fall or winter and remit in spring (Rosenthal et al, 1984, 1985). This pattern must be consistent over the 2 years prior to diagnosis. Major depressive episodes that occur in a seasonal pattern are often characterized by anergia, hyperphagia, and hypersomnia. In the spring, some patients may experience a remission in their symptoms and others a hypomanic or manic episode. Patients with a seasonal pattern to their depression may respond well to phototherapy (Rosenthal et al., 1984, 1985). Though limited data exist on long-term treatment with phototherapy, clinicians generally reserve it for patients with less severe and well-defined winter depressions.

Bipolar Disorders

The value of distinguishing depressed patients with a history of manic episodes (the bipolar group) from those with recurrent episodes of depression only (the unipolar group) was initially suggested by Leonhard, Korff, and Schulz (1962) as an elaboration of Kraepelin's concept of manic-depressive illness. Their proposal was adopted by Angst, Perris, Winokur, Robins, and others involved in family and psychopathological studies of affective disorders in the 1950s and 1960s.

Since then, considerable evidence of genetic, familial, personality, biochemical, physiological, and pharmacologic differences between bipolar and unipolar patients has accumulated. For example, genetic studies have shown that the families of patients with bipolar illness have a far higher frequency of previous psychiatric disorders than families of patients with depression alone. Psychopharmacologic studies indicate differences in the response of bipolar and unipolar patients to many psychoactive drugs, especially lithium.

A number of important modifications in the diagnostic criteria for bipolar disorder were introduced in DSM-IV. First, DSM-IV reinstated the stipulation of a minimum duration of 1 week of a sufficient number of manic symptoms to meet criteria for a manic episode, although manic symptoms may be of less than 1 week's duration if hospitalization is necessary. Second, DSM-IV defined separate criteria for a *mixed episode* which specify that the symptom criteria for both a manic episode and a major depressive episode must be met concurrently nearly every day for at least 1 week. Third, DSM-IV provides separate criteria for *hypomania;* these specify a duration of at least 4 days of mood change (distinct from the usual nondepressed mood) and an unequivocal change in functioning observable by others. By definition, hypomania is not severe enough to cause marked impairment or to require hospitalization. In conjunction with the specific criteria for hypomania, DSM-IV has also introduced *bipolar II disorder* as a separate diagnostic category distinct from bipolar I disorder. Patients with bipolar II disorder have a clinical course characterized by the occurrence of 1 or more episodes of major depression and at least 1 hypomanic episode. In general, patients with bipolar II disorder often do not view the hypomanic episodes as a problem, but rather are brought to the clinician's attention when they seek treatment during a depressive episode. Finally, DSM-IV introduced a number of diagnostic specifiers (see above).

Rapid cycling

DSM-IV has adopted the original description of Dunner and Fieve (1974) in defining rapid cycling as "the occurrence of four or more mood episodes during the previous 12 months" (American Psychiatric Association, 1994). These episodes can occur in any combination and order. The mood episodes that occur during a period of rapid cycling are not different from those that occur during a non–rapid cycling interval and must meet both the symptom and duration criteria for a manic, hypomanic, mixed, or major depressive episode.

Rapid cycling is an important clinical distinction because it is associated with increased morbidity (Fawcett, Scheftner, and Clark, 1987) and is often difficult to treat pharmacologically. Patients with rapid cycling respond poorly to lithium, and standard treatments for bipolar disorder such as antidepressants and antipsychotics may induce or exacerbate cycling (Roy-Byrne, Joffe, and Uhde, 1987; Alarcon, 1985; Kukopulos, Reginaldi, and Laddomada, 1980; McElroy and Keck, 1993). Patients with rapid cycling may have a more favorable response to valproate or carbamazepine (McElroy et al, 1988; Calabrese and Delucci, 1990; Post, Uhde, and Roy-Byrne, 1987). Surveys of clinical populations suggest that rapid cycling is not uncommon, occurring in 5–20% of adult patients with bipolar disorder (Wehr et al., 1988; Calabrese and Delucci, 1990; McElroy and Keck, 1993).

Course and Outcome

Until recently clinicians tended to view depression as a discrete illness with a self-limiting course. However, in the last 2 decades, long-term studies have revealed that depression can be a lifelong disease with periods of relapse and recurrence. Although many individuals return to a state of "normalcy" and euthymia, others achieve only a partial recovery or experience a number of relapses and recurrences. Most studies have found that severity of depression at baseline and clinical features such as history of

chronicity are the best predictors of favorable recovery. Approximately 50–60% of individuals who suffer from a major depressive disorder can be expected to have a second episode at some point in the future. Individuals who have had 2 episodes have a 70% chance of having a third, and individuals who have had 3 episodes have a 90% chance of having a fourth. Approximately 5–10% of individuals who have had a single episode of major depression subsequently develop a manic episode.

Follow-up naturalistic studies indicate that 1 year after the diagnosis of a major depressive episode, 40% of individuals still have symptoms that are sufficiently severe to meet criteria for a full major depressive episode, while another 20% continue to have some symptoms that while no longer meeting full criteria for a major depressive episode do meet criteria for major depressive disorder in partial remission. Patients with major depression with psychotic features (psychotic depression) recover at a slower rate than nonpsychotic patients. Some studies suggest that patients with psychotic depression have residual social impairment but no depression or psychosis at 1 year (Rothschild et al., 1993b) and 5 years (Coryell et al., 1990) after the initial index episode. Recent studies indicate that poor outcome in major depression is associated with chronic endogenous hypercortisolemia (Rothschild et al., 1993b; Ribeiro et al., 1993).

Bipolar I disorder is a recurrent disorder, with more than 90% of individuals who have had a single manic episode going on to have future episodes. Approximately 60–70% of manic episodes occur immediately before or after a major depressive episode. Prior to the introduction of lithium maintenance treatment, patients with bipolar I disorder had an average of 4 episodes over a 10-year period. In general, the interval between episodes tends to decrease as the individual ages.

While the majority of individuals with bipolar I disorder return to a fully functional level between episodes, approximately 20–30% continue to display mood lability and interpersonal or occupational difficulties. Data from the National Institutes of Mental Health (NIMH) Collaborative Studies (Keller et al., 1986) suggest that patients who present with mania recover at a faster rate than patients who present depressed or in a mixed state. Early age of onset is associated with a multiepisodic course (Winokur and Kadrmas, 1989), and female sex has been reported to be a predictor of rapid cycling (Coryell, Endicott, and Keller, 1992). Patients whose first episode is purely manic recover at a much faster rate than those whose first episode is mixed or cycling. Co-morbid substance abuse is also a predictor of poor outcome in bipolar disorder (Tohen et al., 1995).

The majority of patients with bipolar II disorder return to a fully functional level between episodes, but 15% continue to display mood lability and interpersonal or occupational difficulties. Approximately 60–70% of hypomanic episodes in bipolar II disorder occur immediately before or after a major depressive episode. Over a period of five years, approximately 5–15% of patients with bipolar II disorder will develop a full manic episode.

Other Forms of Mood Disorders

DSM-III introduced the concept of *dysthymia* to include the large group of patients who have chronic depressions lasting more than 2 years but whose symptoms are less intense and less numerous than those that fit the criteria for major depression. This diagnostic concept brought together cases previously labeled "depressive character," "depressive personality," "neurotic depression," and "characterlogic depression." Multicenter collaborative research studies indicate that 25% of patients seen in clinics and university hospitals with the diagnosis of major depression also demonstrate a history of dysthymia. Those with both major depression and dysthymia are said to suffer from "double depression" (Keller and Shapiro, 1982; Keller et al., 1983). The longer the duration of the chronic low-grade depression, the greater the probability of relapse into major depression and of consequent chronicity (Akiskal, 1983). Dysthymic disorder appears to respond to a variety of antidepressant agents, including tricyclic antidepressants, monoamine oxidase inhibitors, and selective serotonin reuptake inhibitors (Howland, 1991; Rosenthal et al., 1992).

Cyclothymic disorder is a chronic, fluctuating mood disturbance involving numerous periods of hypomanic symptoms and numerous periods of depressive symptoms. The hypomanic symptoms are of insufficient number, severity, pervasiveness, or duration to meet full criteria for a manic episode, and the depressive symptoms are of insufficient number, severity, pervasiveness, or duration to meet full criteria for a major depressive episode.

Patients with *personality disorders* often demonstrate mood symptoms. For example, patients with obsessive-compulsive and dependent personality disorder may show signs of depression when their self-esteem is low or when a loss has occurred. Moreover, patients with borderline personality disorder may have marked mood swings in the context of many other symptoms. In all cases of personality disorders, the basis for making a diagnosis of a mood disorder is the presence of a DSM-IV constellation of mood and physical symptoms.

Physicians should rule out a *medical problem* that may be presenting as a major depression. The presence of a potential precipitating psychosocial event or a past history of depression should not bias physicians against considering an underlying medical condition as a potential cause of a depressive episode. Table 14.2 lists medical conditions that may commonly present as major depressive disorder. Many endocrinological disorders, including hypo- or hyperthyroidism and Cushing's syndrome, may present with depressive symptoms. Patients with diabetes mellitus are also at increased risk for major depression, which, if untreated, can increase the morbidity from the diabetes (Goodnick, Henry, and Buki, 1995). Fibro-

Table 14.2 Some organic causes of depression

I. Neurological Disorders
   Parkinson's disease
   Huntington's disease
   Multiple sclerosis
   Primary degenerative dementia
   Post-concussion syndromes
   Chronic subdural hematomas

II. Metabolic Abnormalities and Endocrinopathies

Hyper- or hypothyroidism	Diabetes
Hyponatremia	Uremia
Hypokalemia	Cushing's disease
Pernicious anemia	Addison's disease
Pellagra	Hepatic disease
Hyperparathyroidism	Wernicke-Korsakoff syndrome

III. Neoplastic Disease
   Pancreatic carcinoma
   Primary cerebral tumor
   Cerebral metastasis

IV. Drugs and Poisons

Alcohol	Sedatives
Amphetamine	Digitalis
Cocaine	Steroids
Barbiturates	Oral contraceptives
Opiates	Lead poisoning
Anti-hypertensives	Other heavy metals

V. Infectious Diseases

TB	Hepatitis
CNS syphilis	Encephalitis
Mononucleosis	Post-encephalitis states

VI. Other Medical Conditions
   Acquired immune deficiency syndrome (AIDS)
   Cardiovascular disease (e.g., CAD, hypertension)
   Systemic lupus erythematosus
   Fibromyalgia
   Postpartum syndromes

myalgia and systemic lupus erythematosus are 2 common rheumatologic disorders that can present with symptoms of major depression. Cardiovascular diseases such as hypertension and coronary artery disease are associated with major depression. Cardiovascular disorders should be ruled out because, as with diabetes mellitus, a concurrent major depression may increase morbidity and mortality from these illnesses (Frasure-Smith, Lesperance, and Talajic, 1993, 1995). A careful history, a full review of systems, a physical and neurological examination, and appropriate laboratory tests will assist the physician in ruling out the presence of a medical condition.

Adjustment disorder with depressed mood is a residual category used to describe presentations that are a response to an identifiable stressor and that do not meet the criteria for another specific Axis I disorder such as major depression. By definition, the disturbance of mood in an adjustment disorder begins within 3 months of onset of a stressor and lasts no longer than 6 months after the stressor or its consequences have ceased. No systematic treatment studies of adjustment disorder have been conducted, although clinical experience indicates the value of brief forms of psychotherapy, at times combined with medication. If the depression persists or the symptoms are intense, the disorder is then classified as major depression, and the category of major depression overrides the diagnosis of adjustment disorder.

Epidemiology

Incidence and Prevalence

It has been estimated that more than 15% of adults are at risk to develop a clinical depression during their lifetime (Regier et al., 1993; Kessler et al., 1994). If dysthymia is included, the risk of developing depression in the course of a lifetime appears to increase to 20–30% of the adult population. Since only a small percentage of patients with clinical depression actually seek out medical or psychiatric care, these numbers may actually be low (Regier et al., 1993). The 1-year prevalence for a manic episode in the National Comorbidity Study (NCS) was 1.3% (Kessler et al., 1994), although in the Epidemiologic Catchment Area (ECA) Study, the 1-year prevalence rate for manic episodes ranged in the 5 sites from as low as 0.1% to 0.6% (Regier et al., 1988). The cumulative prevalence rate of major depression across the 5 sites in the ECA study averaged 1.5% in the 2 weeks prior to subject interview. A 4.4% lifetime prevalence rate for major depressive disorder was demonstrated in the ECA study (Regier et al.,

1993). The NCS reported a 10.3% prevalence rate of major depressive disorder and a 17.1% lifetime prevalence rate (Kessler et al., 1994).

Age, Gender, and Race

Depression may occur at any age. The ECA data found a mean age for major depression of 27 years (Regier et al., 1993). Depressive disorders are approximately twice as prevalent in women as they are in men (Regier et al., 1993; Kessler et al., 1994). This finding appears to be true for the range of depressive disorders and is especially the case for the less severe forms of depression. Weissman and Klerman (1977) demonstrated that the prevalence differences between men and women appear to be multifactorial, with biological influences (either genetic or endocrinological) as well as psychosocial elements (women's need to balance multiple roles in today's society). In bipolar disorder, female sex has been reported to be a strong predictor of rapid cycling (Coryell, Endicott, and Keller, 1992).

Data from the ECA study, NCS, and smaller community and clinical samples have not demonstrated significant differences in the prevalence of major depression or bipolar disorder across racial or ethnic lines. However, major depressive disorder may have differences in clinical presentation across cultures. For example, several ethnic groups may tend to have a more somatic presentation of major depression (Jones-Webb and Snowden, 1993).

Socioeconomic and Marital Status

Researchers once thought that bipolar disorder was a condition of the upper and middle classes (Weissman and Klerman, 1977). Subsequent studies have found no consistent relationship of social class to depressive disorders when educational achievement and occupational level are used as indexes of social status.

Rates of depression are highest in the unmarried and widowed. Evidence also suggests that the stress of marital separation and/or divorce may be related to increased rates of depressive illness (Kiecolt-Glaser and Glaser, 1987). Overall rates are lowest among those who are married; however, if the marriage is described as unsatisfactory, particularly by females, the rates of major depression are high during the period of marital discord. In contrast, among males the risk period for depression is highest after the period of marital discord, during the 6 months following separation.

Etiology

Genetic Factors

The possibility of a genetic factor in the etiology of mood disorders has been investigated in Scandinavia, Germany, the United Kingdom, and the United States. Evidence that supports the genetic transmission of mood disorders includes: (1) an increased frequency of depression in relatives of the patient compared with the general population; (2) a greater concordance rate for the disease in monozygotic twins than dizygotic twins; (3) an increased frequency of psychiatric abnormalities in relatives of the affective illness patient than in the general population; and (4) an onset of the illness at a characteristic age without any evidence of a precipitating event. Concordance rates for mood disorder (unipolar and bipolar I) in monozygotic twins are estimated to be 75%, whereas concordance rates for dizygotic twins are 20%, which approximates the morbidity risk among siblings (Rosanoff, Handy, and Plesset, 1935; Allen et al., 1974; Kendler et al., 1996). No studies report one twin developing a mood disorder and another schizophrenia.

Family studies of major depressive disorder indicate that first-degree relatives have a morbidity risk of approximately 15%. Male first-degree relatives have a risk rate of 11%, compared to 18% for female first-degree relatives. Morbidity risk for mood disorders among parents of patients is 13%, among siblings 15%, and among children 20% (Perris, 1966; Gershon et al., 1975; James and Chapman, 1975; Tsuang, Winokur, and Crowe, 1980).

While the specific mode of transmission of mood disorders remains to be established, some investigators have proposed an autosomal dominant gene with incomplete penetrance—autosomal dominant because of the similar morbidity risk (15%) among parents, children, and siblings, but incomplete penetrance to explain the less than 100% concordance in monozygotic twins. The heterogeneity of major depressive illness makes progress with this illness limited in contrast to bipolar disorder, which is believed to be more genetically homogeneous. The data clearly support the utility of the bipolar classification and also indicate that mood disorders are genetically distinct from schizophrenia.

Life Events and Environmental Stress

Most clinicians and investigators have long believed that a relationship exists between stressful life events and clinical depression, and in general, research has confirmed the existence of this relationship (Ilfeld, 1988; Lloyd, 1980; Paykel, 1976; Fava et al., 1981). Major losses, including death, divorce, and health and money crises, frequently are associated with depression. These stressful life events may, in some people, be a necessary but not sufficient cause for depression. However, in a specific patient it can often be impossible to ascertain the time line of events. For example, did the depression occur first and lead to trouble in the marriage and to divorce, or did difficulties in the relationship lead to divorce, which in turn led the patient to become depressed?

Social models of depression stress that adaptiveness and helplessness are learned. To the extent that depression is a learned form of helplessness, it is important to look for role models of helplessness within the family. Disruptions in the family early in the patient's life—and, more specifically, disturbances in early parent-child relationships—can leave a person vulnerable to depression.

Since less than 20% of the population who experience losses develop clinical depression, other significant factors must play a role in the etiology of depression. Clearly, there must be some predisposition for the development of depression whether genetic, psychosocial, or characterological.

Personality Factors

Clinicians since the time of Hippocrates have noted that certain "temperaments" are related to depressions and elations, but not until the twentieth century, following the observations of Sigmund Freud (1917), Karl Abraham (1927), Edward Bibring (1953), and other psychoanalysts, were these relationships explored in depth. It is widely believed that persons prone to depression are characterized by low self-esteem, strong superego, clinging and dependent interpersonal relations, and limited capacity for mature and enduring object relations.

Abraham (1927) was the first to psychodynamically link grief and melancholy. He stated that normal mourning, or grief, becomes melancholy, or depression, when anger and hostility accompany love for the lost object. Freud, in his famous paper on mourning and melancholia (1917), advanced Abraham's ideas. In addition to ambivalent feelings toward the lost object, Freud considered melancholia a "disturbance of self-regard." The melancholic, unlike the mourner, suffers a loss of self-respect. Furthermore, he described mourning as occurring only in response to a realistically lost object, whereas melancholia could occur in reaction to the unconsciously perceived or imagined loss of an object.

In melancholia, the anger experienced toward the real or imagined loss of the loved object is hypothetically turned upon the self (Fenichel, 1945). This formulation helps to explain the self-reproach and loss of self-esteem seen in depression as well as the melancholic patient's need for punishment. However, this hypothesis is not consistent with the group of patients known as "hostile depressives," who exhibit concomitant anger and depression (Paykel, 1971; Weissman et al., 1973). In addition, the expression of hostility by depressed patients toward the lost object does not correlate with clinical improvement and can even result in a worsening of the depression (Klerman and Gershon, 1970).

Bibring viewed depression as a disorder of esteem. Mourning was not just for the lost object but for the mourner's loss of self-esteem. The lost person or object was viewed as the symbol of the individual's lost self-esteem.

The cognitive behavioral model of depression is based on the hypothesis that depression is built on negative expectations and beliefs (Beck, 1974; Rush et al., 1977; Kovacs and Beck, 1978). Hopelessness and helplessness are central to the experience of depression. The cognitive behavioral model's hypothesis is that depressive mood succeeds (not precedes) a set of cognitive processes involving a negative self-conception, negative interpretations of one's life events, and a pessimistic view of the future. In this model, helplessness and hopelessness are the result of this cognitive set. Cognitive psychotherapy, which has demonstrated efficacy for depression, is aimed at altering these negative cognitive processes. Although cognitive behavioral treatment is effective for depression, it cannot be established that negative adaptive attitudes actually cause depression rather than exist as a symptom of the disorder (Silverman et al., 1984; Simons et al., 1984).

Childhood Loss and Separation

Research on the role of infancy and early childhood in depression and mania is focused on possible impairments of ego function and sensitivities to separation and loss that arise from experiences of the early mother-child relationship. Melanie Klein (1945) hypothesized that the capacity for depression exists in all of us and postulated a "normal depressive position" as the stage of life from 6–12 months. During this stage the infant experiences a fall from the impotence of early infancy to the stage of being separate, dependent, and vulnerable. Attempts to test this hypothesis have relied on direct observation of infants and young children, particularly those in institutions. Spitz (1946)

studied normal infants over 6 months of age who had been separated from their mothers and placed in institutions. He described a triphasic reaction of protest, despair, and detachment which he called "anaclitic depression." Bowlby (1961) postulated that an interruption in the normal course of development, by separation or loss, produces "anxious attachment." Investigations into the frequency of parental loss or other kinds of psychic trauma in the childhood of patients with depression indicate that as a group, patients with depression seem to experience more parental loss from death, separation, or other causes than normal or other diagnostic groups. However, this factor alone does not seem sufficiently universal to account for all forms of depression. Since no single psychodynamic process, personality type, stressful life event, or developmental experience is unique to depressive states, at the present time the psychodynamic hypotheses are primarily of heuristic value, contributing to case formulation, guidance of psychotherapeutic practice, and research design.

Pathophysiology

Research over the past 3 decades has led to a better understanding of the biologic basis of mood disorders. Animal models of depression further our understanding of the pathophysiology of depressive symptomotology in humans. These models demonstrate that medications used in humans as antidepressants or mood-stabilizing drugs can correct changes in neurotransmitters in regulatory systems. In humans, depression consists essentially of 2 types of symptoms: disturbances of mood and feelings, which cannot be tested in animals; and vegetative symptoms and alterations in observable behaviors, including sleep, activity, sexual interest and activity, appetite, weight, and ability to concentrate. Animals subjected to specific stressors exhibit weight loss, sleep difficulties, loss of sexual activity, inability to learn, and decreased motor activity—which closely resemble the clinical signs of endogenous depressions (Weiss et al., 1976)—and alterations in immune and hormonal functioning (Bartrop et al., 1977; Schleifer et al., 1984). Animal models of depression have increased our understanding of the physiologic basis of depressive symptomatology in humans, the mechanisms of antidepressant and mood-stabilizing drugs, and the development of new medications for the treatment of mood disorders. Animal models also demonstrate that specific stressors such as separation and loss can alter brain biogenic amines as well as immune and endocrine systems. For example, infant monkeys separated from their mothers or from groups of peers develop symptoms characterized by agitation, sleeplessness, distress calls, and screaming, followed after 1–2 days by "depression," characterized by a decrease in activity, appetite, play, and social interaction, and the development of a "sad" facial expression (McKinney and Bunney, 1969; Kraemer and McKinney, 1979; Suomi, Harlow, and Domek, 1970; Suomi, Collins, and Harlow, 1976). Treatment with antidepressants modifies the development of these symptoms caused by the separation (Hrdina, Von Kulmiz, and Stretch, 1979).

In the late 1950s several investigators proposed that catecholamines might be involved in the pathophysiology of depression. They observed that reserpine and tetrabenzamine could cause depression as a side effect (both medications cause a profound depletion of norepinephrine, or NE, in the brain), that inhibitors of MAO (the first effective antidepressants) elevated NE levels, and tricyclic antidepressants, such as imipramine, worked by blocking the reuptake mechanism and prolonging the synaptic effects of NE in the brain. The original catecholamine hypothesis of major depression hypothesized that depression occurred from a functional deficit of NE at critical effector sites in the central nervous system (Bunney and Davis, 1965; Schildkraut, 1965). Initial studies by fluorometric assays of the NE metabolite 3-methoxy-4-hydroxyphenylglycol (MHPG) showed generally decreased levels in the cerebrospinal fluid (CSF), plasma, and urine of patients with major depression (Schildkraut, 1965; Bunney and Davis, 1965; Schildkraut, 1978). More recent studies that have reported normal or increased activity of the NE system in depression have led to new hypotheses which view depression as a failure of the regulation of NE systems (Siever and Davis, 1985).

Further studies suggest that other transmitter systems also may play a role in depression. Coppen and colleagues (1972) hypothesize that indoleamines play a role in the pathogenesis of depression. Several studies have demonstrated that there is a reduction in CSF concentration of 5-hydroxyindolacetic acid (5-HIAA), the principal metabolite of serotonin, in some depressed patients (Asberg et al., 1976; Asberg, Traskman, and Thoren, 1976; Gibbons and Davis, 1986; Roy, De Jong, and Linnoila, 1989). In addition, Asberg et al. (1976) reported that low concentrations of 5-HIAA may be a marker for suicidal behavior and for suicide risk in depressed patients. Other major lines of evidence that serotonin is important in depressive disorders include: (1) increased efficacy of CNS serotonergic transmission with virtually all known antidepressant agents, regardless of their receptor-specific properties; (2) decreased CSF concentrations of the major serotonin metabolite 5-HIAA in postmortem brains of suicide victims (Stanley and Mann, 1983); (3) decreased 5-HT reuptake in the platelets of depressed patients (Tuomisto and Tukiainen, 1976); (4) possible reversal of antidepressant-induced remissions with depletion of plasma tryptophan precursors (Delgado et al., 1990); and (5) reversal of the clinical efficacy of antidepressants by p-chlorophenylalamine, which decreases 5-HT synthesis (Shopsin, Freedman, and Gershon, 1976). The introduction of the selective serotonin reuptake inhibitors (SSRIs) into clinical practice in 1988 has led to a considerable increase in research into the role of serotonin in the pathophysiology of major depression. Acetylcholine has been suggested as an etiologic agent based on data that centrally active cholinomimetic drugs rapidly induce depressed moods (Janowsky and Overstreet, 1995). Decreased CSF and plasma gamma-aminobutyric acid (GABA) levels have been observed in depressed patients (Berrettini et al., 1982; Gold et al., 1980), which has led to speculation about its potential role in depression (Morselli et al., 1980). The GABA agonist progabide has an antidepressant effect (Thaker, Moran, and Tomminga, 1990; Petty et al., 1995), and various benzodiazepines, such as alprazolam, facilitate GABA neurotransmission (Morselli et al., 1980).

Another focus of research has been on receptor sensitivity. Almost all antidepressants decrease the number of postsynaptic B-adrenergic receptors. In addition, medications that increase postsynaptic receptors (e.g., reserpine, propranolol) can induce depression (Sulser, 1983; Richelson, 1984). This decrease in receptors has been termed "down regulation." This "down regulation" hypothesis is not inconsistent with the monoamine hypotheses of depression which postulate that disturbances in norepinephrine and serotonin could be etiologic in origin and corrected by antidepressants. This correction could be achieved by a process that involves "down regulation" of synaptic receptors both presynaptically and postsynaptically (Hyman and Nestler, 1986; Baron et al., 1988).

Investigations of neurotransmitters as well as studies of second-messenger systems, neuroimaging, and neuroendocrine functioning support the view that mood disorders involve a profound alteration in multiple body systems, including many hypothalamic functions such as the regulation of sleep and wakefulness and of appetite and eating, and neuroendocrine control of peripheral endocrine organs, particularly the adrenal glands, thyroid, and gonads. The patient experiences these bodily changes as feelings of fatigue, change in appetite, decrease in sexual interest, and slowing of movements and thinking. Physicians do a disservice to their patients when they tell them,

"There's nothing wrong with you, it's all in your head." Unfortunately, conventional diagnostic techniques, including x-rays, MRI scanning, and blood laboratory tests, are not useful at this time in the clinical setting; however, significant abnormalities on biological testing seen in depressed patients are being pursued in the research setting. The focus of research into the pathophysiology of mood disorders indicates that these biological changes are profound and that most of the systems, although not all (Rothschild et al., 1993b; Ribeiro et al., 1993), return to normal when the patient experiences symptomatic remission.

Treating Depression

The treatment of depression can be a challenging and gratifying experience for patients, their families, and psychiatrists. It is challenging because the diagnosis is sometimes unclear, co-morbid psychiatric morbidity is common, and, unfortunately, depression may end in suicide. It is gratifying because most patients respond quite well to therapeutic intervention. The options for treatment of major depression include somatic therapies such as antidepressant medications or electroconvulsive therapy (ECT), and psychotherapeutic approaches (including cognitive, interpersonal, behavioral, family, and psychoanalytic). The skillful psychiatrist maintains a flexible approach, applying the treatment most appropriate for the individual patient without commitment to theoretical schools or treatment ideologies.

Medication Treatment of Acute Depressions

Over the past half-century, remarkable advances have been made in the development of medications to treat depressive illness. In general, approximately 65–80% of depressed outpatients receiving an antidepressant will show marked improvement (Chan et al., 1987; Baldessarini, 1989). To date, no evidence exists that any one antidepressant or class of antidepressants is more efficacious or works at a faster rate of speed than any other antidepressant. However, antidepressants differ in their mechanisms of action, side effect profile, and toxicity in overdose. Recent years have seen a dramatic increase in the number of antidepressants available to treat depression with the advent of the SSRIs and other new antidepressant agents. These newer medications, which have an improved side effect profile over older classes of medications such as the tricyclic antidepressants (TCAs) and monoamine oxidase inhibitors (MAOIs), were developed specifically to treat depression. The development of these antidepressants differs from the serendipitous "discovery" of the TCAs and MAOIs.

The medications commonly used to treat depressions are summarized in Table 14.3. In general, a clinical trial of an antidepressant medication lasts 4–6 weeks. The response rate of patients to antidepressants is slow and subtle, and it is important for patients and their families to be educated about this. In addition, when side effects of antidepressant use occur, they are likely to occur early in the treatment before the positive beneficial effects of the medication begin.

Tricyclic antidepressants. The tricyclic antidepressants (TCAs), one of the older classes of antidepressants, are rather broadly acting drugs, blocking the reuptake of both norepinephrine and serotonin, but with primary effects on the norepinephrine system. Unfortunately, the side effect profile of the TCAs remains suboptimal because of considerable anticholinergic and cardiovascular side effects, weight gain, and sedation. These side effects often lead to poor compliance. In general, the older tertiary amine tricyclics, (e.g., amitriptyline, imipramine) have more side effects than the secondary amine tricyclics (e.g., desipramine, nortriptyline).

The prescription of TCAs requires gradual titration of the patient's dose until a therapeutic dose is achieved. For most TCAs the usual starting dose is 25 mg or 50 mg at bedtime with gradual increases by 25 mg or 50 mg increments to a dose range of approximately 150–300 mg per day (with the exception of nortriptyline, for which the dose is usually half these amounts). One should not start a patient on the therapeutic dose because most patients would be unable to tolerate that amount of tricyclic without gradual titration. By contrast, with some of the newer agents such as the SSRIs (see below), the starting dose for many patients is the same as the therapeutic dose.

A disadvantage of the TCAs is their toxicity when taken in overdose. With most of the TCAs 1500 mg is lethal if taken in overdose (Baldessarini, 1989), and thus a 7–10 day supply or more of a TCA could be fatal. When first prescribing TCAs (or any antidepressant), the clinician should write small prescription amounts until the patient feels better, because the risk of suicide in depression remains until the psychological mood state is improved. While somatic complaints, energy level, and sleep disturbance improve early during recovery from depression, the psychological mood state—which is what the patient feels and is correlated with risk for suicide (Fawcett, Scheftner, and Clark, 1987)—is often the last symptom to improve. Once the patient is better, the risk of suicide decreases, and larger prescription amounts can be given.

Heterocyclic antidepressants. Heterocyclic antidepressants (e.g., amoxapine, maprotiline, trazodone) were introduced in the United States in the early 1980s in an attempt by the pharmaceutical industry to develop antidepressants with better side effect profiles than the TCAs. Their mechanism of action (and efficacy) is similar to the TCAs, and in general they exhibit fewer TCA-like side effects.

Maprotiline has not been widely used because of concerns regarding a higher rate of seizures (Dessain et al., 1986). Amoxapine, although an antidepressant, is converted by the liver to the neuroleptic loxapine (Cohen, Harris, and Altesman, 1982), and patients on amoxapine exhibit anti-dopaminergic side effects such as galactorrhea, pseudoparkinsonian side effects, and tardive dyskinesia. Trazodone is a very sedating antidepressant which can produce acute dizziness and fainting when taken on an empty stomach (particularly in high dosages). Its sedative properties are sometimes useful as a sleeping pill when combined with non-sedating antidepressants such as the SSRIs (see below).

Monoamine oxidase inhibitors. The monoamine oxidase inhibitors (MAOIs), like the TCAs, are an older class of antidepressant medication. A little over a decade ago, MAOIs were generally the second-line medications after the TCAs for the treatment of depression. Their use has declined in recent years because of the advantages of the newer antidepressant agents, and they generally are reserved for those patients who have not responded to TCAs and SSRIs.

MAOIs can have activating side effects and can also cause insomnia at night with considerable sedation during the day (Teicher et al., 1988). Patients prescribed MAOIs may develop hypertensive crises from drug-drug or food-drug interactions (*Physician's Desk Reference,* 1994). Patients on MAOIs need to be on special tyramine-free diets, avoiding foods with high levels of tyramine. However, on a day-to-day basis, the most problematic side effect with MAOIs is orthostatic hypotension.

Bupropion. Bupropion is a newer agent whose specific mechanism of action has not been elucidated, although it is nonserotonergic, and appears to exert its effects primarily on the noradrenergic system. In double-blind studies it is comparable in efficacy to TCAs (Feighner et al., 1986; Mendels et al., 1983). Bupropion has a low rate

Table 14.3 Dose ranges of antidepressants

Generic Name	Brand Name	Usual Therapeutic Dose Range (mg/day)[a]
Tricyclics		
amitriptyline	Elavil, Endep	150–300
desipramine	Norpramin, Pertofrane	150–300
imipramine	Tofranil, Janimine Sk-Pramine	150–300
nortriptyline	Pamelor, Aventyl	50–150
Heterocyclics		
amoxapine	Asendin	150–450
maprotiline	Ludiomil	150–200
trazodone	Desyrel	150–300
MAOIs		
phenelzine	Nardil	45–90
tranylcypramine	Parnate	30–50
SSRIs		
fluoxetine	Prozac	20–80
paroxetine	Paxil	20–50
sertraline	Zoloft	50–200
Other		
bupropion	Wellbutrin	200–450
venlafaxine	Effexor	75–375
nefazodone	Serzone	300–500
mirtazapine	Remeron	15–45

a. Dosage ranges are approximate. Many patients will respond at relatively low dosages (even below ranges given above); others may require higher dosages.

of anticholinergic side effects (Lineberry et al., 1990), orthostatic hypotension (Farid et al., 1983), and effects on cardiac conduction (Wenger, Cohn, and Bustrack, 1983). It can occasionally be activating and is reported to have a fourfold higher incidence of grand mal seizures as compared with TCAs (*Physician's Desk Reference*, 1994). The rate of grand mal seizures in patients taking bupropion increases if the total daily dose of bupropion is greater than 450 mg per day or if any single dose is greater than 150 mg (*Physician's Desk Reference*, 1994). For this reason, it is recommended that bupropion be prescribed in divided dosages (tid) with no single dose greater than 150 mg (*Physician's Desk Reference*, 1994).

Selective serotonin reuptake inhibitors (SSRIs). The SSRIs are a new class of antidepressants which are now quite widely prescribed for the treatment of depression in the United States. The SSRIs inhibit free synaptic serotonin reuptake and, in contrast to the TCAs, have negligible effects on norepinephrine and dopamine uptake (Richelson, 1988; Tulloch and Johnson, 1992; Heym and Koe, 1988). When compared with the TCAs in double-blind studies, the SSRIs have been found to be equally effective but better tolerated than the TCAs (Baldessarini, 1989; Grimsley and Jann, 1992). Distinct advantages of the SSRIs (as compared to TCAs) are their low potential for causing seizures and their safety when taken in overdose (Baldessarini, 1988; Grimsley and Jann, 1992).

The dose ranges of the SSRIs currently available in the United States are shown in Table 14.3. For patients being treated for major depression, the vast majority who respond will do so at either the starting dose or approximately in the mid-range. High doses of SSRIs, although well tolerated by patients (Stoll, Pope, and McElroy, 1991), are usually not required, although an extended treatment time may be advisable (Schweitzer, Rickels, and Amsterdam, 1990).

Fluoxetine became available in 1988 and was the first SSRI on the market in the United States. As an SSRI, it has few of the tricyclic-like side effects and tends not to cause weight gain. It can be given in once-a-day dosing and has a wide margin of safety in overdose (Baldessarini, 1989). The common side effects of fluoxetine include nausea, anxiety, nervousness, and insomnia (*Physician's Desk Reference*, 1994). There have also been reports of akathisia (Lipinski et al., 1989; Rothschild and Locke, 1991; Wirshing et al., 1992), a side effect more commonly seen with antipsychotic medications (Rothschild and Locke, 1991; Wirshing et al., 1992). The akathisia responds well to low doses of propranolol (Lipinski et al., 1989; Rothschild and Locke, 1991). These side effects tend to be

dose related, so if they occur and are problematic for the patient, reducing the dose is advised.

Sertraline was the second SSRI on the market in the United States, becoming available in early 1992. It has some similarities to fluoxetine and also some differences, particularly in the areas of pharmacokinetics and drug-drug interactions. Similar to fluoxetine, sertraline is a highly selective SSRI equal in efficacy to the TCAs, but with few tricyclic-like side effects (Grimsley and Jann, 1992). Unlike fluoxetine, sertraline's metabolite, N-desmethylsertraline, is substantially less active than the parent compound, sertraline (Koe et al., 1983; Leonard, 1988), and the half-life of sertraline and its metabolite is considerably shorter than the half-life of fluoxetine and its equipotent metabolite norfluoxetine (Doogan and Caillard, 1988). Thus, sertraline reaches a steady state plasma level of active drug faster and has a shorter washout period than fluoxetine.

Sertraline can be given in once-a-day dosing since its mean half-life is 26 hours (Doogan and Caillard, 1988). A steady state plasma level of the active drug is achieved in approximately 1 week (Doogan and Caillard, 1988; Ronfeld, Shaw, and Termaine, 1988). The most common side effects of sertraline include nausea, diarrhea, loose stools, tremor, and insomnia (*Physician's Desk Reference*, 1994). These side effects tend to be dose related, so if they occur and are problematic for the patient, decreasing the dose would be indicated. Like fluoxetine, sertraline is associated with significantly less anticholinergic, antihistaminic, and cardiovascular side effects than the TCAs, and patients taking large overdoses have survived without sequelae (Grimsley and Jann, 1992).

Paroxetine became available in the United States in 1993. Paroxetine has no active metabolites and a mean half-life of approximately 24 hours (DeVane, 1992), so that steady state plasma levels are reached in approximately 1 week (similar to sertraline). The recommended dose range is 20–50 mg per day, although the recommended maximum dose in the geriatric population is 40 mg per day (*Physician's Desk Reference*, 1994). The most commonly reported adverse side effects of paroxetine include nausea, somnolence, insomnia, dizziness, headache, dry mouth, constipation, and tremor (*Physician's Desk Reference*, 1994). Paroxetine exhibits some affinity for the muscarinic cholinergic receptor (Thomas, Nelson, and Johnson, 1987) and in multicenter studies of paroxetine it was observed to cause mild anticholinergic side effects such as dry mouth and constipation (Boyer and Blumhardt, 1992).

The SSRIs should not be given concomitantly with MAOIs because the combination can result in the potentially fatal serotonin syndrome (Sternbach, 1991). The symptoms of the serotonin syndrome include hyperthermia, muscle rigidity, and autonomic hyperactivity, which can progress to coma and death. It is also important to remember not to prescribe SSRIs and MAOIs close in time to each other. When switching from an MAOI to any of the SSRIs, a washout period of 2 weeks is recommended. When switching from an SSRI to an MAOI, a washout period of 2 weeks is recommended for sertraline and paroxetine, while a 5-week washout period is recommended when switching from fluoxetine to an MAOI. This is because of the long half-life of fluoxetine and its equipotent metabolite norfluoxetine.

Venlafaxine. Venlafaxine, which became available in the United States in 1994, has been shown in the animal model to block the reuptake of norepinephrine, serotonin, and dopamine (Muth, Haskins, and Moyer, 1986). In in vitro studies it appears to lack anticholinergic, antihistaminergic, and antiadrenergic activity. In multicentered trials (Montgomery, 1993), side effects of venlafaxine versus placebo included nausea (35% versus 10%), somnolence (24% versus 10%), dizziness (18% versus 6%), dry mouth (22% versus 11%), and sweating (12% versus 2%). Venlafaxine treatment is associated with sustained increases in blood pressure, and it is therefore recommended to check the patient's blood pressure both before and after the prescription of venlafaxine (Manufacturer's Prescribing Information, 1994). An increased pulse rate has also been reported with venlafaxine (Manufacturer's Prescribing Information, 1994).

The half-life of venlafaxine is 3–5 hours (Schweizer et al., 1991), and the active metabolite o-Desmethylvenlafaxine has a half-life of 9–11 hours (Schweizer et al., 1991), so it should be prescribed in divided dosages. Venlafaxine may be particularly useful in treatment-resistant depressed patients (Nierenberg et al., 1994).

Nefazodone. Nefazodone, released in 1995, is a weak inhibitor of neuronal serotonin uptake and a potent 5-HT$_2$-receptor antagonist (Fontaine, 1992). Nefazodone has been shown to be as effective as imipramine for the treatment of major depression (Fontaine, 1992; Rickels et al., 1994; Fontaine et al., 1994). Side effects include somnolence, dizziness, orthostatic hypotension, asthenia, dry mouth, nausea, constipation, headache, and blurred and impaired vision (Fontaine, 1992). As with trazodone, to which it is chemically related, sedation may limit patient acceptance. Because of the short half-lives of the parent compound and active metabolites, twice-daily dosing is recommended. The recommended initiating dose is 200

mg/d, administered in 2 divided doses, although in many patients a smaller starting dose may be necessary. The optimal therapeutic range is 300–500 mg/d with a maximum recommended total daily dose of 600 mg/d.

Mirtazapine. Mirtazapine was approved for the treatment of major depression in 1996. It increases both noradrenaline and serotonin reuptake and specifically blocks 5-HT$_2$ and 5-HT$_3$ receptors. Its efficacy in depression has been established in placebo- and amitriptyline-controlled trials in moderate to severe depressive disorders (Smith et al., 1990; Bremner, 1995). The most common reported side effects are somnolence, increased appetite, and dizziness. The effective dose range of mirtazapine is between 15–45 mg a day, usually given at bedtime. The starting dose is 15 mg/day at bedtime.

Augmentation strategies. The addition of lithium carbonate or thyroid hormone (T$_3$) to an antidepressant is a popular strategy for treatment of nonresponders or partial responders to antidepressants (deMontigny et al., 1981; Prange et al., 1976). Although clinical experience has suggested that T$_3$ is less efficacious than the addition of lithium carbonate, double-blind placebo-controlled studies have observed that lithium carbonate and T$_3$ are equally effective, and both are more effective than placebo, when added to a tricyclic antidepressant (Joffe et al., 1993).

Sexual Dysfunction

Decreased libido and sexual satisfaction have been associated with the occurrence of depression in unmedicated individuals (Mathew and Weinman, 1982; Howell et al., 1987) and have been associated with almost all of the antidepressant medications currently prescribed (Segraves, 1992). Thus, it is important to ask about sexual dysfunction in depressed patients before prescribing an antidepressant.

If sexual dysfunction occurs as a side effect of antidepressants, several steps can be taken. First, lowering the dose of the antidepressant may occasionally alleviate the sexual dysfunction side effects. Other strategies include the addition of cyproheptadine (Steele and Howell, 1986; Sovner, 1984; McCormick Olin, and Brotman, 1990), bethanacol (Yager, 1986; Gross, 1982; Segraves, 1987), amantadine (Balogh et al., 1992), yohimbine (Price and Grunhaus, 1990), buspirone (Norden, 1994), or bupropion (Labbate and Pollack, 1994), a switch to another antidepressant (Walker et al., 1993; Feiger et al., 1996), or delaying the intake of the antidepressant until after coitus (Olivera, 1994). With the short half-life SSRIs such as sertraline and paroxetine, a weekend "drug holiday" can provide relief from sexual dysfunction side effects in some patients without resulting in recurrence of depressive symptoms (Rothschild, 1995).

General Comments Regarding Antidepressants

Rate of response. When evaluating the response of patients being treated with antidepressants, the clinician must remember that the symptoms of depression resolve gradually (usually over several weeks). As noted, the dysphoric mood state is often the last symptom of depression to improve. The patient may, therefore, report improvement in energy level, sleep disturbance, or somatic complaints, and the physician may observe that the patient smiles for the first time in weeks or shows improvement in cognitive processes. Simultaneously, the patient may report feeling "lousy" and that the "medication is not working." If the physician observes signs of improvement in depression (or the patient's family reports improvement), it is important to continue the antidepressant currently being prescribed. These early signs of improvement may be a harbinger of a full antidepressant response.

Although patients may experience significant improvement in the symptoms of major depression within the first week, this is not common. In fact, if the patient contacts the physician shortly after the antidepressant is prescribed and profusely thanks the physician for starting the antidepressant, 2 possibilities need to be considered: that the patient is bipolar and has switched into a manic episode; or that treatment has had a placebo effect. Although the occurrence of mania with antidepressant therapy is not always predictable, the physician must take a good personal and family history for bipolar disorder before starting medications. If a placebo effect is a possibility, the physician should encourage the patient to continue to take the medication. He should not be surprised, however, if 7–10 days later the patient reports that the medication "has stopped working."

Presence of anxiety. Anxiety is a symptom commonly seen in patients with major depression (Coryell, 1990). While the patient may be more distressed by the anxiety symptoms, this should not distract the physician from looking for the key symptoms of depression. However, the clinician often finds it difficult to know whether the patient is suffering primarily from a mood disorder (e.g., major depression) or primarily from an anxiety disorder (e.g., generalized anxiety disorder). Distinguishing differences between these 2 diagnostic possibilities include the following: patients with major depression exhibit anhedonia (loss of interest or pleasure in usual activities), fatigue,

weight or appearance changes, sad affect, and excessive guilt more commonly than patients with pure anxiety disorders; while patients with anxiety and mood disorders often have difficulty falling asleep, the patients with major depression will exhibit early morning awakening (waking up at 3:00 or 4:00 A.M. and not being able to fall back asleep), and anxiety disorder patients, while often having trouble falling asleep, usually do not exhibit early morning awakening once they are asleep.

To the degree to which anxiety is one of the symptoms of the major depressive episode, antidepressants will help alleviate the anxiety symptoms. In contrast, an anxiolytic medication (e.g., buspirone, benzodiazepines) will alleviate only anxiety symptoms; there is little evidence that they are effective for the many other symptoms of major depression (e.g., anhedonia, suicidal ideation). Thus, if a patient with major depression and symptoms of anxiety is given only an anxiolytic medication, the full syndrome of major depression will not be adequately treated.

Sedating vs. nonsedating antidepressants. Some physicians have been reluctant to prescribe SSRIs in patients with a significant degree of insomnia because the SSRIs are not sedating. However, like all antidepressants, the SSRIs alleviate not only the depression but also the insomnia associated with depression. While the prescription of a very sedating antidepressant such as amitriptyline or trazodone will result in a depressed patient with insomnia initially sleeping better, it is important to remember that insomnia is only 1 of the many symptoms of depression. A starting dose of 50 mg of amitriptyline or trazodone will do little for the total syndrome of major depression and its accompanying symptoms of hopelessness, poor energy, anhedonia, and suicidal ideation. One would need to raise the dose of the amitriptyline or trazodone more toward the therapeutic antidepressant dose level of 150–300 mg per day. When one does this with sedating antidepressants, however, one is often faced with the problem of next-day oversedation.

While the SSRIs are often effective in alleviating the sleep disturbance seen in major depression, they occasionally fail to do so, and sometimes they cause insomnia as a side effect. If a sleep disturbance develops during SSRI treatment, adding a small amount of a sedating antidepressant (e.g., trazodone) to the SSRI as a sleeping medication is often effective (Nierenberg et al., 1994).

Antidepressant overdose. TCAs are the highest cause of drug-related death after alcohol-drug combinations and heroin (Beaumont, 1989). They are also the fourth highest cause of overdose seen in emergency rooms in the United States (Callahan, 1985), and 70–80% of patients who take overdoses of TCAs do not reach the hospital alive (Kulig, 1986). In this regard, the newer agents offer the advantage of a wider margin of safety in overdose.

Electroconvulsive Therapy

Electroconvulsive therapy (ECT) is the oldest and one of the most effective somatic therapies for patients suffering from major depression. The literature reports an overall response rate of 75–85% for ECT in the treatment of depression (Chan et al., 1987). It is particularly indicated for patients with major depression and psychotic features, or for patients who are in acute danger to themselves or others (acutely suicidal or catatonic patients who are unable to care for themselves). This treatment should be considered for those who relapse during antidepressant drug treatment, and who have responded favorably to ECT in the past.

The initial workup of a patient for ECT includes a complete history and physical examination, laboratory studies, an EKG, and an anesthesiology consultation. Many clinicians also prefer a structural brain imaging study—computerized tomography (CT) or magnetic resonance imaging (MRI)—as well. While there are no absolute contraindications to ECT, the laboratory studies and an EKG can help identify medical conditions that need to be addressed prior to the patient's receiving general anesthesia and ECT.

ECT is usually administered 2 or 3 days per week for an average course of 6–12 treatments. ECT treatments are administered either unilaterally or bilaterally on an inpatient or an outpatient basis. The bilateral positioning of the electrodes has been reported to cause more severe cognitive side effects, including disorientation or a sustained confusional state.

Considerable misinformation and misunderstanding surround ECT. Patients and their families should be reassured by an open and honest discussion of the procedure with the treating clinician. Several books and videos are available and should be recommended or provided to receptive patients and families. ECT is a safe and highly effective treatment for major depression. All clinicians should be familiar with this treatment; for some patients it may be the only remedy to which they respond.

Psychotherapeutic Management of Acute Depressions

Individual psychotherapy plays an important role in the treatment of depressed patients. Somatic treatments and psychotherapy complement each other in specific ways. Medications or ECT can be efficacious in treating the neurovegetative symptoms of depression (e.g., appetite, sleeping, energy level, and cognitive disturbances), while psychotherapy acts as a specific and effective treatment for the interpersonal and social disturbances that accompany depression (e.g., isolation, dependence, and diminished work performance). Evidence suggests that the combination of psychotherapy and pharmacotherapy is more effective than either treatment alone (Conte et al., 1986).

The types of therapy used in the treatment of patients with major depressive disorder include psychodynamic, cognitive-behavioral, and interpersonal. The selection of a specific psychotherapeutic technique should be based on an individual patient's presentation and preferences.

Psychotherapy for the acutely ill depressed patient should be supportive and restitutive. The psychotherapy involves empathic listening because the depressed patient wants to share his or her grief. The therapist should convey a sense of hope to the depressed patient, but not in the form of simple reassurance or universal optimism. Therapists must seek out and understand the patient's fears and anxiety such as the belief that he or she will never get better and that the depression may last forever.

Since patients suffering from depression often view the world in a negative way and may suffer from cognitive dysfunction, they should be advised to avoid making major life decisions while depressed. In particular, decisions regarding marriage, divorce, changing jobs, or selling a home should be postponed if possible. Many patients suffering from depression may make decisions which they will later regret once they have recovered. Clinicians should avoid taking responsibility for the decisions the patient must make.

Conventional dynamic or exploratory psychotherapy is often not appropriate for the acutely depressed patient. Non-directive, exploratory psychotherapy may unduly stress the severely depressed person and can reinforce an unconscious view of the caregiver as unavailable and uncaring.

Cognitive therapy is a process whereby dysfunctional thought patterns in major depression are modified through verbal and action-oriented procedures. Cognitive therapy utilizes a cooperative partnership between the therapist and the patient and uses an active, directive, time-limited structured treatment course. Common goals are clearly identified, and the rationale behind each attempted intervention is clearly explained. Cognitive therapy is believed to exert its greatest effect on dysfunctional attitudes, automatic negative thinking, and irrational beliefs.

Interpersonal psychotherapy (IPT) is a brief, dynamically oriented therapy developed to alleviate depressive symptoms and improve interpersonal functioning. The patient is assisted in developing more effective strategies to deal with current interpersonal problems. Controlled clinical trials have demonstrated the efficacy of IPT alone or in combination with antidepressant medication (Elkin et al., 1989).

Family members of depressed patients often feel left out and uncared for, often because the identified patient generally has been the focus of previous professional contact. An effective alliance with the patient's spouse, significant other, or family is critical for several reasons. First, additional history can be obtained which may be important for differential diagnosis. Second, contact with the family also promotes a clearer exploration and identification of stressors. Third, since the patient is often the last one to recognize that he or she is improving, an outside observer reporting on progress or lack of progress can be quite helpful. A supportive family can influence treatment compliance in a positive way, which correlates with a good outcome.

Treatment of Acute Manic Episodes

Lithium. The efficacy of lithium monotherapy in the treatment of acute mania has been clearly documented with 7 double-blind, placebo-controlled trials conducted between 1954 and 1972 with a total of 162 patients (Baldessarini et al., 1996). Some 80–85% of manic episodes will respond to lithium treatment. Lithium is typically begun at 600 mg per day and modified according to blood levels. The recommended blood levels are 0.8–1.0 mEq/L (Gelenberg et al., 1989). Blood levels should be drawn 12 hours after the last dose has been administered. Blood monitoring after the patient is stable includes lithium blood levels every 3–6 months; thyroid-stimulating hormone (TSH) and creatinine blood levels should be obtained at least twice a year. In individuals over age 45, an annual EKG is recommended.

Although serious adverse effects of lithium are rare, mild adverse effects appear to be common. Kidney damage, long regarded as the most serious adverse effect, is relatively rare. The most frequent adverse effects of lithium include polyuria and polydipsia, which can be present in up to 50% of patients. In 10% of cases, reversible enlargement of the thyroid gland has been reported. Another adverse effect, neurocognitive impairment, is especially common in the elderly and in neurocognitively impaired individuals. Dermatologic side effects are also common.

Divalproex. Divalproex was the second drug approved by the Food and Drug Administration (FDA) for the treatment of acute mania. Double-blind studies have shown equal efficacy between lithium and divalproex, and both drugs are statistically significantly superior to placebo. Lithium and divalproex appear equally effective in the treatment of pure mania, but divalproex is superior in patients with mixed symptoms and in those who cannot tolerate or have failed to respond to lithium. The literature suggests a broader-spectrum efficacy and superior patient satisfaction for divalproex.

The recommended blood level for divalproex is 50–120 ng/ml. The most common adverse effects are drowsiness, anorexia, hair loss, and nausea. Liver toxicity is a rare but recognized adverse effect associated with divalproex. There are 2 types of hepatotoxic reactions. The most common is an asymptomatic, transient, dose-related elevation of liver enzymes; the incidence of liver enzyme elevation ranges between 2.4% and 44%, with higher rates in patients taking multiple drugs. The second reaction type is an idiosyncratic irreversible hepatic failure; it is rare, non–dose related, and usually appears in the first 6 months of treatment. The *Physician's Desk Reference* recommends monitoring liver enzymes in patients receiving divalproex. Baseline liver function tests should be obtained before treatment initiation and at intervals thereafter, especially in the first 6 months. The frequency of monitoring liver enzymes remains controversial. Some investigators have suggested quarterly monitoring while others have suggested that none is needed. Most experts agree that liver enzymes should be monitored at baseline, 2 weeks, at months 2 and 3, and quarterly thereafter.

Other treatments. Other treatments which have been efficacious in the treatment of mania include carbamazepine. The adverse side effect profile of carbamazepine, which includes sedation, confusion, nausea, rash, and blood dyscrasias, have resulted in a low acceptability by patients.

Neuroleptic medications are often useful in the management of the acute manic episode until a mood stabilizer such as lithium, divalproex, or carbamazepine begins to work. A few recent studies have suggested that newer atypical neuroleptics (clozapine, risperidone, olanzapine) may also have efficacy for the treatment of mania both in the acute episode and perhaps for maintenance. More studies are needed to ascertain the role of newer antipsychotics in the treatment of mania.

Although the primary indication for ECT is major depression (see above), it has also been used as a treatment for acute mania. Some 80% of manic patients treated with ECT will have significant clinical improvement, including those patients who fail to respond to lithium or neuroleptics. Most clinicians do not use ECT as a first-line treatment for mania, and further studies are needed regarding its efficacy as a maintenance treatment.

In summary, research over the past 4 decades has led to more precise diagnostic criteria and a better understanding of the biologic basis of mood disorders. As with most diseases, there is no single type of mood disorder nor a single cause. Mood disorders are as treatable as any disorder confronting physicians. With proper evaluation, treatment, and follow-up, restoration to euthymia is an attainable goal in most patients. The hope for the future is that with further refinements in our ability to subtype mood disorders, combined with advances in the fields of neurochemistry, neuroendocrinology, molecular genetics, and brain imaging, the clinician will be better equipped to characterize and rapidly treat patients with these disorders.

References

Abraham, K. 1927. *Notes on the psychoanalytical investigation and treatment of manic-depressive insanity and allied conditions.* Selected Papers of Karl Abraham. London: Hogarth Press.

Adams, F. 1856. *The extant works of Aretaeus, the Cappadocian.* London: Sydenham Society.

Akiskal, H. S. 1983. Dysthymic disorder: psychopathology of proposed chronic depressive subtypes. *Am. J. Psychiatry* 140: 11–20.

Alarcon, R. D. 1985. Rapid cycling affective disorders: a clinical review. *Compr. Psychiatry* 26:522–540.

Allen, M. G., Cohen, S., Pollin, W., et al. 1974. Affective illness in veteran twins: a diagnostic review. *Am. J. Psychiatry* 131:1234–39.

American Psychiatric Association. 1952. *Diagnostic and Statistical Manual of Mental Disorders.* Washington, D.C.: American Psychiatric Association.

——— 1968. *Diagnostic and Statistical Manual of Mental Disorders,* 2d ed. Washington, D.C.: American Psychiatric Association.

——— 1980. *Diagnostic and Statistical Manual of Mental Disorders,* 3d ed. Washington, D.C.: American Psychiatric Association.

——— 1987. *Diagnostic and Statistical Manual of Mental Disorders,* 3d. ed., rev. Washington, D.C.: American Psychiatric Association.

——— 1994. *Diagnostic and Statistical Manual of Mental Disorders,* 4th ed. Washington, D.C.: American Psychiatric Association.

Asberg, M., Traskman, L., and Thoren, P. 1976. 5-HIAA in the cerebrospinal fluid: a biochemical suicide predictor? *Arch. Gen. Psychiatry* 33:1193–97.

Asberg, M., Thoren, P., Traskman, L., et al. 1976. Serotonin depression: a biochemical subgroup within the affective disorders? *Science* 191:478–483.

Baldessarini, R. J. 1989. Current status of antidepressants: clinical pharmacology and therapy. *J. Clin. Psychiatry* 50:117–126.

Baldessarini, R. J., Tondo, L., Suppes, P., et al. 1996. Pharmacological treatment of bipolar disorder throughout the life cycle. In *Mood disorders across the life span,* ed. Tohen, M., Shulman, K. I., and Kutcher, M. T. New York: John Wiley & Sons.

Balogh, S., Hendricks, S. E., and Kang, J. 1992. Treatment of fluoxetine-induced anorgasmia with amantadine [letter]. *J. Clin. Psychiatry* 53:212–213.

Baron, F. M., Ogden, A. M., Siegel, B. W., et al. 1988. Rapid down-regulation of beta-adrenoreceptors by co-administration of desipramine and fluoxetine. *Eur. J. Pharmacol.* 154:125–134.

Bartrop, R. W., Luckhurst, E., Lazarus, L., et al. 1977. Depressed lymphocyte function after bereavement. *Lancet* 83:834–836.

Beaumont, G. 1989. The toxicity of antidepressants. *Br. J. Psychiatry* 154:454–458.

Beck, A. T. 1974. Depressive neurosis. *American handbook of psychiatry,* 2d ed. Vol. 3, ed. Brody, E. B., and Areti, S. New York: Basic Books. 61–90.

Berrettini, W. H., Nurnberger, J. I., Hare, T. A., et al. 1982. Plasma and CSF GABA in affective illness. *Br. J. Psychiatry* 141:483–487.

Bibring, E. 1953. The mechanism of depression. In *Affective disorders,* ed. Greenacre, P. New York: International Universities Press.

Bowlby, J. 1961. The process of mourning. *Int. J. Psychoanal.* 42:317–340.

Boyer, W. F., and Blumhardt, C. L. 1992. The safety profile of paroxetine. *J. Clin. Psychiatry* 53(suppl. 2):61–66.

Bremner, J. 1995. A double-blind comparison of Org 3770, amitriptyline, and placebo in major depression. *J. Clin. Psychiatry* 56:519–525.

Bunney, W. E., and Davis, J. M. 1965. Norepinephrine in depressive reactions. *Arch. Gen. Psychiatry* 13:483–494.

Calabrese, J. R., and Delucci, G. A. 1990. Spectrum of efficacy of valproate in 55 patients with rapid-cycling bipolar disorder. *Am. J. Psychiatry* 147:431–434.

Callahan, M. 1985. Epidemiology of fatal tricyclic antidepressant ingestion: implications for management. *Annals of Emergency Medicine* 14:109.

Carlson, G. A., and Goodwin, F. K. 1973. The states of mania: a longitudinal analysis of the manic episode. *Arch. Gen. Psychiatry* 28:221–228.

Chan, C. H., Janicak, P. G., Davis, J. M., et al. 1987. Response of psychotic and nonpsychotic depressed patients to tricyclic antidepressants. *J. Clin. Psychiatry* 48:197–200.

Charney, D. S., and Nelson, J. C. 1981. Delusional and nondelusional unipolar depression: further evidence for distinct subtypes. *Am. J. Psychiatry* 138:328–333.

Cohen, B., Harris, P., and Altesman, R. 1982. Neuroleptic as well as antidepressant? *Am. J. Psychiatry* 139:1165–67.

Conte, H. R., Plutchik, R., Wild, K. V., et al. 1986. Combined psychotherapy and pharmacotherapy for depression: a systematic analysis of the evidence. *Arch. Gen. Psychiatry* 43:471–479.

Coppen, A., Prange, A. J. Jr., Whybrow, P. C., et al. 1972. Abnormalities of indoleamines in affective disorders. *Arch. Gen. Psychiatry* 26:474–478.

Coryell, W. 1990. Anxiety secondary to depression. *Psychiatric Clin. North Am.* 13:685–698.

Coryell, W., Endicott, J., and Keller, M. 1992. Rapid cycling affective disorder. *Arch. Gen. Psychiatry* 49:126–131.

Coryell, W., Pfohl, B., and Zimmerman, M. 1984. The clinical and neuroendocrine features of psychotic depression. *J. Nerv. Ment. Dis.* 172:521–528.

Coryell, W., Lavori, P., Endicott, J., et al. 1984. Outcome in schizoaffective, psychotic, and nonpsychotic depression. *Arch. Gen. Psychiatry* 41:787–791.

Coryell, W., Keller, M., Lavori, P., et al. 1990. Affective syndromes, psychotic features, and prognosis. I. Depression. *Arch. Gen. Psychiatry* 47:651–657.

Davidson, J., and Robertson, E. 1985. A follow-up study of postpartum illness. *Acta Psychiatr. Scand.* 71:451.

Dean, C., Kendell, R. E. 1981. The symptomatology of postpartum illness. *Br. J. Psychiatry* 139:128.

Delgado, P. L., Charney, D. S., Price, L. H., et al. 1990. Neuroendocrine and behavioral effects of dietary tryptophan restriction in healthy subjects. *Life Sci.* 45:2323–32.

deMontigny, C., Grunberg, F., Mayer, A., et al. 1981. Lithium induces rapid relief of depression in tricyclic antidepressant drug non-responders. *Br. J. Psychiatry* 138:252–256.

Dessain, E. C., Schatzberg, A. F., Woods, B. T., et al. 1986. Maprotiline treatment in depression: a perspective on seizures. *Arch. Gen. Psychiatry* 43:86–90.

DeVane, C. L. 1992. Pharmacokinetics of the selective serotonin reuptake inhibitors. *J. Clin. Psychiatry* 53(suppl. 2):13–20.

Doogan, D. P., and Caillard, V. 1988. Sertraline: a new antidepressant. *J. Clin. Psychiatry* 49 (8, suppl.):46–51.

Dunner, D. L., and Fieve, R. R. 1974. Clinical factors in lithium carbonate prophylaxis failure. *Arch. Gen. Psychiatry* 30:229–233.

Elkin, I., Shea, T., Watkins, J., et al. 1989. National Institute of Mental Health treatment of depression collaborative

program: general effectiveness of treatments. *Arch. Gen. Psychiatry* 46:971–982.

Farid, F. F., Wenger, T. L., Tsai, S. Y., et al. 1983. Use of bupropion in patients who exhibit orthostatic hypotension on tricyclic antidepressants. *J. Clin. Psychiatry* 44:170–173.

Fava, G. A., Munari, F., Pavan, L., et al. 1981. Life events and depression: a replication. *J. Affect. Dis.* 3:159–165.

Fawcett, J., Scheftner, W., and Clark, D. 1987. Clinical predictors of suicide in patients with major affective disorders: a controlled prospective study. *Am. J. Psychiatry* 144:35–40.

Feiger, A., Kiev, A., Shrivastava, R. K., et al. 1996. Nefazodone versus sertraline in outpatients with major depression: focus on efficacy, tolerability, and effects on sexual function and satisfaction. *J. Clin. Psychiatry* 57:53–62.

Feighner, J. P., Hendrickson, G., Miller, L., et al. 1986. Double-blind comparison of doxepin versus bupropion in outpatients with a major depressive disorder. *J. Clin. Psychopharmacol.* 6:27–32.

Feighner, J. P., Robins, E., Guze, S. B., et al. 1972. Diagnostic criteria for use in psychiatric research. *Arch. Gen. Psychiatry* 26:57–73.

Fenichel, O. 1945. *Depression and mania: the psychoanalytic theory of neurosis.* New York: Norton.

Fink, M. 1993. Catatonia and psychotic (delusional) depression: distinct syndromes in DSM-IV [letter]. *Am. J. Psychiatry* 150:1130.

Fink, M., and Taylor, M. A. 1991. Catatonia: a separate category for DSM-IV? *Integrative Psychiatry* 7:2–10.

Fontaine, R. 1992. Novel serotonergic mechanisms and clinical experience with nefazodone. *Clin. Neuropharmacol.* 15:99A.

Fontaine, R., Ontiveros, A., Elie, R., et al. 1994. A double-blind comparison of nefazodone, imipramine, and placebo in major depression. *J. Clin. Psychiatry* 55:234–241.

Frances, A., Brown, R. P., Kocsis, J. H., et al. 1981. Psychotic depression: a separate entity? *Am. J. Psychiatry* 138:831–833.

Frasure-Smith, N., Lesperance, F., and Talajic, M. 1993. Depression following myocardial infarction: impact on 6-month survival. *JAMA* 270:1819–25.

——— 1995. Depression and 18-month prognosis after myocardial infarction. *Circulation* 91:999–1005.

Freud, S. 1917. Mourning and melancholia. In *Standard edition,* ed. Strachey, J. Vol. 14. London: Hogarth Press, 1958.

Fricchione, G. L., Cassem, N. H., Hooberman, D., et al. 1983. Intravenous lorazepam in neuroleptic induced catatonia. *J. Clin. Psychopharmacol.* 3:338–342.

Gelenberg, A. J. 1976. The catatonic syndrome. *Lancet* 1:1339–41.

Gelenberg, A. J., Kane, J. M., Keller, M. B., et al. 1989. Comparison of standard and low serum levels of lithium for maintenance treatment of bipolar disorder. *N. Engl. J. Med.* 321:1489–93.

Gershon, E., Mark, A., Cohen, N., et al. 1975. Transmitted factors in the morbid risk of affective disorders: a controlled study. *J. Psychiatric Res.* 12:283–299.

Gibbons, R. D., and Davis, J. M. 1986. Consistent evidence for a biological subtype of depression characterized by low CSF monoamine levels. *Acta Psychiatr. Scand.* 74:8–12.

Glassman, A. H., and Roose, S. P. 1981. Delusional depression: a distinct clinical entity? *Arch. Gen. Psychiatry* 38:424–427.

Gold, B. I., Bowers, M. J. Jr., Roth, R. H., et al. 1980. GABA levels in CSF of patients with psychiatric disorders. *Am. J. Psychiatry* 137:362–364.

Goodnick, P. J., Henry, J. H., and Buki, V. M. V. 1995. Treatment of depression in patients with diabetes mellitus. *J. Clin. Psychiatry* 56:4.

Goodwin, F. K., and Jamison, K. R. 1990. *Manic-depressive illness.* New York: Oxford University Press.

Greenfield, D., Conrad, C., Kincare, P., et al. 1987. Treatment of catatonia with low-dose lorazepam. *Am. J. Psychiatry* 144:1224–25.

Grimsley, S. R., and Jann, M. W. 1992. Paroxetine, sertraline, and fluvoxamine: new selective serotonin reuptake inhibitors. *Clin. Pharm.* 11:930–957.

Gross, M. D. 1982. Reversal by bethanechol of sexual dysfunction caused by anticholinergic antidepressants. *Am. J. Psychiatry* 139:1193–94.

Hales, R. E., Yudofsky, S. C., and Talbott, J. A. 1994. *Textbook of psychiatry, 2d ed.* Washington, D.C.: American Psychiatric Press. 465–494.

Heym, J., and Koe, K. 1988. Pharmacology of sertraline: a review. *J. Clin. Psychiatry* 48(suppl. 8):40–45.

Howell, S. R., Reynolds, C. F., Thase, M. E., et al. 1987. Assessment of sexual function, interest, and activity in depressed men. *J. Affective Disord.* 13:61–66.

Howland, R. H. 1991. Pharmacotherapy of dysthymia: a review. *J. Clin. Psychopharmacol.* 11:83–92.

Hrdina, P. D., Von Kulmiz, P., and Stretch, R. 1979. Pharmacological modifications of experimental depression in infant macaques. *Psychopharmacology* 64:89–93.

Hyman, S. E., and Nestler, E. J. 1996. Initiation and adaptation: a paradigm for understanding psychotropic drug action. *Am. J. Psychiatry* 153:151–162.

Ilfeld, F. W. 1988. Current social stressors and symptoms of depression. *Am. J. Psychiatry* 134:161–166.

James, N. M., and Chapman, C. J. 1975. A genetic study of bipolar affective disorder. *Br. J. Psychiatry* 126:449–456.

Jamison, K. R. 1989. Mood disorders and seasonal patterns in British writers and artists. *Psychiatry* 52:125–134.

Jamison, K. R., Gerner, R. H., and Goodwin, F. K. 1979. Patient and physician attitudes toward lithium: relationship to compliance. *Arch. Gen. Psychiatry* 36:866–869.

Janowsky, D. S., and Overstreet, D. H. 1995. The role of acetylcholine mechanisms in mood disorders. In *Psychopharmacology: the fourth generation of progress*, ed. Bloom, F. E., and Kupfer, D. J. New York: Raven Press. 945–956.

Joffe, R. T., Singer, W., Levitt, A., et al. 1993. A placebo-controlled comparison of lithium and triodlothyronine augmentation of tricyclic antidepressants in unipolar refractory depression. *Arch. Gen. Psychiatry* 50:387–393.

Jones-Webb, R. J., and Snowden, L. R. 1993. Symptoms of depression among blacks and whites. *Am. J. Public Health* 83:240–244.

Keck, P. E., McElroy, S. L., Kmetz, G. F., Sax, K. W. 1996. Clinical features of mania in adulthood. In *Mood disorders across the life span,* ed. Shulman, K. I., and Tohen, M. New York: Wiley-Liss. 265–279.

Keller, M. B., and Shapiro, R. W. 1982. "Double depression": superimposition of acute depressive episodes on chronic depressive disorders. *Am. J. Psychiatry* 139:438–442.

Keller, M. B., Lavori, P. W., Endicott, J., et al. 1983. "Double depression": two-year follow-up. *Am. J. Psychiatry* 140:689–694.

Keller, M. B., Lavori, P. W., Coryell, W., et al. 1986. Differential outcome of pure manic, mixed/cycling, and pure depressive episodes in patients with bipolar illness. *JAMA* 255:3138–42.

Kendell, R. E., Charlmers, J. C., and Platz, C. 1987. Epidemiology of puerperal psychoses. *Br. J. Psychiatry* 150:662–673.

Kendler, K. S., Eaves, L. J., Walters, E. E., et al. 1996. The identification and validation of distinct depressive syndromes in a population-based sample of female twins. *Arch. Gen. Psychiatry* 153:391–399.

Kessler, R. C., McGonagle, K. A., Zhao, S., et al. 1994. Lifetime and 12-month prevalence of DSM-III-R psychiatric disorders in the United States. *Arch. Gen. Psychiatry* 51:8–19.

Kiecolt-Glaser, J. K., and Glaser, R. 1987. Psychosocial moderators of immune function. *Ann. Behav. Med.* 9:16–20.

Klein, M. 1945. A contribution to the psychogenesis of manic-depressive states. In *Contributions to psychoanalysis.* London: Hogarth Press. 228–310.

Klerman, G., and Gershon, E. 1970. Imipramine effects upon hostility in depression. *J. Nerv. Ment. Dis.* 150:127–132.

Koe, B. E., Weissman, A., Welsh, W. M., et al. 1983. Sertraline 15, 45-N-methyl-4(3,4 dichlorophenyl)-

1,2,3,4-tetrahydro-1-naphthylamine, a new uptake inhibitor with selectivity for serotonin. *J. Pharm. Exp. Ther.* 226:686–700.

Kovacs, M., and Beck, A. T. 1978. Maladaptive cognitive structures in depression. *Am. J. Psychiatry* 135:525–533.

Kraemer, G. W., and McKinney, W. T. 1979. Interactions of pharmacological agents which alter biogenic amine metabolism and depression. *J. Affect. Dis.* 1:33–54.

Kraepelin, E. 1921. *Manic-depressive insanity and paranoia,* trans. Barclay, R. M., ed. Robertson, G. M. Edinburgh: Livingstone.

Kukopulos, A., Reginaldi, D., and Laddomadda, P. 1980. Course of the manic-depressive cycle and changes caused by treatments. *Pharmacopsychiatr.* 13:156–167.

Kulig, K. 1986. Management of poisoning associated with "newer" antidepressant agents. *Annals of Emergency Medicine* 15:1039–45.

Labbate, L. A., and Pollack, M. H. 1994. Treatment of fluoxetine-induced sexual dysfunction with bupropion: a case study. *Ann. Clin. Psychiatry* 6:13–15.

Leonard, B. E. 1988. Pharmacological effects of serotonin reuptake inhibitors. *J. Clin. Psychiatry* 49(suppl 8):12–17.

Leonhard, K., Korff, I., and Schulz, H. 1962. Temperament in families with monopolar and bipolar phasic psychoses. *Psychiatr. Neurol.* 143:416–434.

Liebowitz, M. R., Quitkin, F. M., Stewart, J. W., et al. 1984. Phenelzine and imipramine in atypical depression: a preliminary report. *Arch. Gen. Psychiatry* 41:669–677.

Lineberry, C. G., Johnston, A., Raymond, R. N., et al. 1990. A fixed-dose efficacy study of bupropion and placebo in depressed outpatients. *J. Clin. Psychiatry* 51:194–199.

Lipinski, J. F. Jr., Mallya, G., Zimmerman, P., et al. 1989. Fluoxetine-induced akathisia: clinical and theoretical implications. *J. Clin. Psychiatry* 50:339–342.

Lloyd, C. 1980. Life events and depressive disorder reviewed. I. Events as precipitating factors. *Arch. Gen. Psychiatry* 37:541–548.

Lykouras, E., Malliaras, D., Christodoulou, G. N., et al. 1986. Delusional depression: phenomenology and response to treatment, a prospective study. *Acta Psychiatr. Scand.* 73:324–329.

Mathew, R. J., and Weinman, M. L. 1982. Sexual dysfunction in depression. *Arch. Sex. Behav.* 11:323–328.

McCormick, S., Olin, J., and Brotman, A. W. 1990. Reversal of fluoxetine-induced anorgasmia by cyproheptadine in two patients. *J. Clin. Psychiatry* 51:383–384.

McElroy, S. L., and Keck, P. E. Jr. 1993. Rapid cycling. In *Current Psychiatry Therapy,* ed. Dunner, D. L. Philadelphia: W. B. Saunders.

McElroy, S. L., Keck, P. E. Jr., Pope, H. G. Jr., et al. 1988. Treatment of rapid cycling bipolar disorder with sodium valproate. *J. Clin. Psychopharmacol.* 8:275–279.

McKinney, W. T., and Bunney, W. E. 1969. Animal model of depression: review of evidence and implications for research. *Arch. Gen. Psychiatry* 21:240–248.

Meltzer, E. S., and Kumar, R. 1985. Puerperal mental illness, clinical features and classification: a study of 142 mother-and-baby admissions. *Br. J. Psychiatry* 147:647.

Mendels, J., Amin, M. M., Chouinard, G., et al. 1983. A comparative study of bupropion and amitriptyline in depressed outpatients. *J. Clin. Psychiatry* 44:118–120.

Montgomery, S. A. 1993. Venlafaxine: a new dimension in antidepressant pharmacotherapy. *J. Clin. Psychiatry* 54:119–126.

Morselli, P. L., Bossi, L., Henry, J. F., et al. 1980. On the therapeutic action of S. L. 76–002, a new GABA-mimetic agent: preliminary observations in neuropsychiatric disorders. *Brain Research Bulletin* 5(suppl. 2):411–414.

Muth, E. A., Haskins, J. T., and Moyer, J. A. 1986. Antidepressant biochemical profile of the novel bicyclic compound Wy-45, 030, an ethyl cyclohexanol derivative. *Biochem. Pharmacol.* 35:4493–97.

Nelson, J. C., and Bowers, M. B. 1978. Delusional unipolar depression. *Arch. Gen. Psychiatry* 35:1321–28.

Nelson, W. H., Khan, A., and Orr, W. W. 1984. Delusional depression, phenomenology, neuroendocrine function, and tricyclic antidepressant response. *J. Affect. Disord.* 6:297–306.

Nierenberg, A., Feighner, J. P., Rudolph, R., et al. 1994. Venlafaxine for treatment-resistant unipolar depression. *J. Clin. Psychopharmacol.* 14:419–423.

Nierenberg, A. A., Adler, L. A., Peselow, E., et al. 1994. Trazodone for antidepressant-associated insomnia. *Am. J. Psychiatry* 151:1069–72.

Norden, M. J. 1994. Buspirone treatment of sexual dysfunction associated with selective serotonin re-uptake inhibitors. *Depression* 2:109–112.

O'Connell, R. A., Mayo, J. A., Flatow, L., et al. 1991. Outcome of bipolar disorder on long-term treatment with lithium. *Br. J. Psychiatry* 159:123–129.

Olivera, A. A. 1994. Sexual dysfunction due to clomipramine and sertraline: nonpharmacological resolution. *J. Sex Education and Therapy* 20:112–119.

Oswald, I., and Adam, K. 1986. Effects of paroxetine on human sleep. *Br. J. Clin. Pharmacol.* 22:97–99.

Parker, G., Hadzi-Pavlovic, D., Hickie, I., et al. 1991. Distinguishing psychotic and nonpsychotic melancholia. *J. Affect. Disord.* 22:135–148.

Paykel, E. 1971. Classification of depressed patients: a cluster analysis of derived grouping. *Br. J. Psychiatry* 118:275–288.

Paykel, E. S. 1976. Life stress, depression, and attempted suicide. *J. Hum. Stress* 2:3–12.

Perris, C. 1966. A study of bipolar (manic-depressive) and unipolar recurrent depressive psychoses. *Acta Psychiatr. Scand.* 194(suppl.):1–18.

Petty, F., Trivedi, M. H., Fulton, M., et al. 1995. Benzodiaz-epines as antidepressants: does GABA play a role in de-pression? *Biol. Psychiatry* 38:578–591.

Physician's desk reference. 1994. 49th ed. Oradell, N.J.: Med-ical Economics Co.

Platz, C., and Kendell, R. E. 1988. A matched control fol-low-up and family study of "puerperal psychosis." *Br. J. Psychiatry* 153:90.

Pope, H. G. Jr., and Lipinski, J. F. Jr. 1978. Diagnosis in schizophrenia and manic-depressive illness: a reassess-ment of the specificity of "schizophrenic" symptoms in light of current research. *Arch. Gen. Psychiatry* 35:811–828.

Post, R. M., Uhde, T. W., and Roy-Byrne, P. P. 1987. Corre-lates of antimanic response to carbamazepine. *Psychiatry Res.* 21:71–83.

Prange, A. J. Jr., Wilson, I. L., Breese, G. R., et al. 1976. Hor-monal alteration of imipramine response: a review. In *Hormones, Behavior, and Psychopathology,* ed. E. J. Sachar. New York: Raven Press. 41–67.

Price, J., and Grunhaus, L. J. 1990. Treatment of clomipramine-induced anorgasmia with yohimbine: a case report. *J. Clin. Psychiatry* 51:32–33.

Price, L. H., Conwell, Y., and Nelson, J. C. 1983. Lithium augmentation of combined neuroleptic-tricyclic treat-ment in delusional depression. *Am. J. Psychiatry* 140:318–322.

Quitkin, F. M., McGrath, P. J., Stewart, J. W., et al. 1989. Phenelzine and imipramine in mood reactive depres-sives: further delineation of the syndrome of atypical de-pression. *Arch. Gen. Psychiatry* 46:787–793.

———— 1990. Atypical depression, panic attacks, and re-sponse to imipramine and phenelzine. *Arch. Gen. Psychi-atry* 47:935–941.

Quitkin, F. M., Harrison, W., Stewart, J. W. et al. 1991. Re-sponse to phenelzine and imipramine in placebo nonresponders with atypical depression: a new applica-tion of the crossover design. *Arch. Gen. Psychiatry* 48:318–323.

Regier, D. A., Boyd, J. H., Rae, D. S., et al. 1988. One-month prevalence of mental disorders in the United States: based on five epidemiologic catchment area sites. *Arch. Gen. Psychiatry* 45:977–986.

Regier, D. A., Narrow, W. E., Rae, D. S., et al. 1993. The de facto U. S. mental and addictive disorders service sys-tem: epidemiological catchment area prospective 1-year prevalence rates of disorders and services. *Arch. Gen. Psychiatry* 50:85–94.

Ribeiro, S. C. M., Tandon, R., Grunhaus, L., et al. 1993. The DST as a predictor of outcome in depression: a meta-analysis. *Am. J. Psychiatry* 150:1618–29.

Richelson, E. 1988. Synaptic pharmacology of antidepres-sants: an update. *McLean Hosp. J.* 13:67–88.

Richelson, E. L. 1984. The new antidepressants: structures, pharmacokinetics, pharmacodynamics, and proposed mechanisms of action. *Psychopharmacol. Bull.* 20:213–223.

Rickels, K., Schweizer, E., Clary, C., et al. 1994. Nefazodone and imipramine in major depression: a placebo-controlled trial. *Br. J. Psychiatry* 164:802–805.

Robinson, D. G., and Spiker, D. G. 1985. Delusional depres-sion: a one-year follow-up. *J. Affect. Disord.* 9:79–83.

Ronfeld, R. A., Shaw, G. L., and Termaine, L. M. 1988. Dis-tribution and pharmacokinetics of the selective 5-HT blocker sertraline in man, rat, and dog [abstract]. *Psychopharmacol.* 96:269.

Roose, S. P., Glassman, A. H., and Walsh, B. J. 1983. De-pression, delusions, and suicide. *Am. J. Psychiatry* 140:1159–62.

Rosanoff, A. J., Handy, L. M., and Plesset, I. R. 1935. The etiology of manic-depressive syndromes with special ref-erence to their occurrence to twins. *Am. J. Psychiatry* 91:725–762.

Rosebush, P. I., Hildebrand, A. M., Furlong, B. G., et al. 1990. Catatonic syndrome in a general psychiatric inpa-tient population: frequency, clinical presentation, and re-sponse to lorazepam. *J. Clin. Psychiatry* 51:357–362.

Rosenthal, J., Hemlock, C., Hellerstein, D. J., et al. 1992. A preliminary study of serotonergic antidepressants in treatment of dysthymia. *Prog. Neuropsychopharmacol. Biol. Psychiatry* 16:933–941.

Rosenthal, N. E., Sack, D. A., Gillin, J. C., et al. 1984. Sea-sonal affective disorder: a description of the syndrome and preliminary findings with light treatment. *Arch. Gen. Psychiatry* 41:72–80.

Rosenthal, N. E., Sack, D. A., Carpenter, C. J., et al. 1985. Antidepressant effects of light in seasonal affective disor-der. *Am. J. Psychiatry* 142:163–170.

Rothschild, A. J. 1995. Selective serotonin reuptake inhibi-tor–induced sexual dysfunction: efficacy of a drug holi-day. *Am. J. Psychiatry* 152:1514–16.

Rothschild, A. J., and Locke, C. A. 1991. Reexposure to fluoxetine after serious suicide attempts by three pa-tients: the role of akathisia. *J. Clin. Psychiatry* 52:491–493.

Rothschild, A. J., Benes, F., Hebben, N., et al. 1989. Rela-tionships between brain C. T. scan findings and cortisol in psychotic and nonpsychotic depressed patients. *Biol. Psychiatry* 26:565–575.

Rothschild, A. J., Samson, J. A., Bessette, M. P., et al. 1993a. Efficacy of the combination of fluoxetine and perphenazine in the treatment of psychotic depression. *J. Clin. Psychiatry* 54:338–342.

Rothschild, A. J., Samson, J. A., Bond, T. C., et al. 1993b. Hypothalamic-pituitary-adrenal axis activity and one-year outcome in depression. *Biol. Psychiatry* 34:392–400.

Roy, A., De Jong, J., and Linnoila, M. 1989. Cerebrospinal fluid monoamine metabolites and suicidal behavior in depressed patients. *Arch. Gen. Psychiatry* 46:609–612.

Roy-Byrne, P. P., Joffe, R. T., and Uhde, T. W. 1987. Approaches to the evaluation and treatment of rapid-cycling affective illness. *Br. J. Psychiatry* 145:543–550.

Rush, A. J., Beck, A. T., et al. 1977. Comparative efficacy of cognitive therapy and pharmacotherapy in the treatment of depressed outpatients. *Cognit. Ther. Res.* 1:17–37.

Schatzberg, A. F., and Rothschild, A. J. 1992. Psychotic (delusional) major depression: should it be included as a distinct syndrome in DSM-IV? *Am. J. Psychiatry* 149:733–745.

——— 1993. Letter to the editor [reply to Fink, M.]. *Am. J. Psychiatry* 150:1131.

Schildkraut, J. J. 1965. Current status of the catecholamine hypothesis of affective disorders. In *Psychopharmacology: a generation of progress*, ed. Lipton, M. A., DiMascio, A., and Killam, K. F. New York: Raven Press. 1223–34.

——— 1978. The catecholamine hypothesis of affective disorders: a review of supporting evidence. *Am. J. Psychiatry* 122:509–522.

Schleifer, S. J., Keller, S. E., Meyerson, A. T., et al. 1984. Lymphocyte function in major depressive disorder. *Arch. Gen. Psychiatry* 41:484–486.

Schweizer, E., Rickels, K., Amsterdam, J. D., Fox, I., et al. 1990. What constitutes an adequate antidepressant trial for fluoxetine? *J. Clin. Psychiatry* 51:8–11.

Schweizer, E., Weise, C., Clary, C., et al. 1991. Placebo-controlled trial of venlafaxine for the treatment of major depression. *J. Clin. Psychopharmacol.* 11:233–236.

Segraves, R. T. 1987. Reversal by bethanechol of imipramine-induced ejaculatory dysfunction [letter]. *Am. J. Psychiatry* 144:1243–44.

——— 1992. Overview of sexual dysfunction complicating the treatment of depression. *J. Clin. Psychiatry Monograph* 10:4–10.

Shopsin, B., Freedman, E., and Gershon, S. 1976. PCPA reversal of tranylcypromine effects in depressed patients. *Arch. Gen. Psychiatry* 33:811–819.

Siever, L. J., and Davis, K. L. 1985. Overview: toward a dysregulation hypothesis of depression. *Am. J. Psychiatry* 142:1017–31.

Silverman, J. S., Silverman, J. A., et al. 1984. Do maladaptive attitudes cause depression? *Arch. Gen. Psychiatry* 41:28–30.

Simons, A. D., Garfield, S. L., et al. 1984. The process of change in cognitive therapy and pharmacotherapy for depression. *Arch. Gen. Psychiatry* 41:45–51.

Smith, W., Glaudin, V., Papagides, J., et al. 1990. Mirtazapine vs. amitriptyline vs. placebo in the treatment of major depressive disorder. *Psychopharm. Bull.* 26(2):191–196.

Sovner, R. 1984. Treatment of tricyclic antidepressant–in-duced orgasmic inhibition with cyproheptadine [letter]. *J. Clin. Psychopharmacol.* 4:169.

Spiker, D. G., Weiss, J. C., Dealy, R. S., et al. 1985. The pharmacological treatment of delusional depression. *Am. J. Psychiatry* 142:430–436.

Spitz, R. A. 1946. *Anaclitic depression: the psychoanalytic study of the child.* Vol. 2. New York: International Universities Press.

Stanley, M., and Mann, J. J. 1983. Increased serotonin-2 binding sites in frontal cortex of suicide victims. *Lancet* 1:214–216.

Steele, T. E., and Howell, E. F. 1986. Cyproheptadine for imipramine-induced anorgasmia [letter]. *J. Clin. Psychopharmacol.* 6:326–327.

Sternbach, H. 1991. The serotonin syndrome. *Am. J. Psychiatry* 148:705–713.

Stoll, A. L., Pope, H. G., and McElroy, S. L. 1991. High dose fluoxetine: safety and efficacy in 27 cases. *J. Clin. Psychopharmacol.* 11:225–226.

Styron, W. 1990. *Darkness visible.* New York: Random House.

Sulser, F. 1983. Mode of action of antidepressant drugs. *J. Clin. Psychiatry* 44:14–20.

Suomi, S. J., Collins, M. L., and Harlow, H. F. 1976. Effects of maternal and peer separations of young monkeys. *J. Child Psychol. Psychiatry* 17:101–112.

Suomi, S. J., Harlow, H. F., and Domek, C. J. 1970. Effects of repetitive infant-infant separation of young monkeys. *J. Abnorm. Psychology* 76:161–172.

Teicher, M. H., Cohen, B. M., Baldessarini, R. J., et al. 1988. Severe daytime somnolence in patients treated with an MAOI. *Am. J. Psychiatry* 145:1552–56.

Thaker, G. K., Moran, M., and Tamminga, C. A. 1990. GABA-mimetics: a new class of antidepressant agents. *Arch. Gen. Psychiatry* 47:287–288.

Thomas, D. R., Nelson, D. R., and Johnson, A. M. 1987. Biochemical effects of the antidepressant paroxetine, a specific 5-hydroxytryptamine uptake inhibitor. *Psychopharmacology* 93:193–200.

Tohen, M. 1988. Outcome in bipolar disorder. Ph.D. diss., Harvard University.

Tohen, M., Waternaux, C. M., and Tsuang, M. T. 1990. Outcome in mania: a 4-year prospective follow-up of 75 patients utilizing survival analysis. *Arch. Gen. Psychiatry* 47:1106–11.

Tohen, M., Waternaux, C. M., and Tsuang, M. T., et al. 1990. Four-year follow-up of twenty-four first episode manic patients. *J. Affect. Disord.* 19:79–86.

Tohen, M., Zarate, C. A. Jr., Turvey, C., et al. 1995. The McLean first-episode mania project. Am. Psychiatric Association, 148th Annual Meeting, Miami.

Tsuang, M. T., Winokur, G., and Crowe, R. 1980. Morbidity risks of schizophrenia and affective disorders among first degree relatives of patients with schizophrenia, mania, depression, and surgical conditions. *Br. J. Psychiatry* 137:497–504.

Tulloch, I. F., and Johnson, A. M. 1992. The pharmacologic profile of paroxetine, a new selective serotonin reuptake inhibitor. *J. Clin. Psychiatry* 53(suppl. 2):7–12.

Tuomisto, J., and Tukiainen, E. 1976. Decreased uptake of 5-hydroxytryptamine in blood platelets from depressed patients. *Nature* 262:596–598.

Vinogradov, S., and Reiss, A. L. 1986. Use of lorazepam in treatment-resistant catatonia. *J. Clin. Psychopharmacol.* 6:323–324.

Walker, P. W., Cole, J. O., Gardner, E. A., et al. 1993. Improvement in fluoxetine-associated sexual dysfunction in patients switched to bupropion. *J. Clin. Psychiatry* 54:459–465.

Wehr, T. A., Sack, D. A., Rosenthal, N. E., et al. 1988. Rapid cycling affective disorder: contributing factors and treatment responses in 51 cases. *Am. J. Psychiatry* 145:179–184.

Weiss, J. M., Glazer, H. I., and Pohoreeky, L. A. 1976. Coping behavior and neurochemical changes: an alternative explanation for the original "learned helplessness" experiments. In *Animal Models in Human Psychobiology*, ed. G. Serban and A. Kling, pp. 141–173. New York: Plenum.

Weissman, M., Fox, K., et al. 1973. Hostility and depression associated with suicide attempts. *Am. J. Psychiatry* 130:450–455.

Weissman, M. M., and Klerman, G. L. 1977. Sex differences and the epidemiology of depression. *Arch. Gen. Psychiatry* 34:98–111.

Wenger, T. L., Cohn, J. B., and Bustrack, J. 1983. Comparison of the effects of bupropion and amitriptyline on cardiac conduction in depressed patients. *J. Clin. Psychiatry* 44:174–175.

Winokur, A., Lexon, N., Allen, K., et al. 1994. Sertraline administered for eight weeks to depressed patients did not alter sleep architecture: a preliminary study. Paper presented at the New Research Program and Abstracts, American Psychiatric Association Annual Meeting.

Winokur, G., and Kadrmas, A. 1989. A polyepisodic course in bipolar illness: possible clinical relationships. *Compr. Psychiatry* 30:121–127.

Wirshing, W. C., VanPutten, T., Rosenberg, J., et al. 1992. *Arch. Gen. Psychiatry* 49:580–581.

Wolfersdorf, M., Barg, T. H., Konig, F., et al. 1995. Paroxetine as antidepressant in combined antidepressant-neuroleptic therapy in delusional depression: observation of clinical use. *Pharmacopsychiat.* 28:56–60.

Yager, J. 1986. Bethanechol chloride can reverse erectile and ejaculatory dysfunction induced by tricyclic antidepressants and mazindol: case report. *J. Clin. Psychiatry* 47:210–211.

Recommended Reading

Schatzberg, A. F., and Nemeroff, C. B. (eds.). 1995. *The American Psychiatric Press textbook of psychopharmacology.* Washington, D.C.: American Psychiatric Press.

Sederer, L. I., and Rothschild, A. J. (eds.). 1998. *Acute care psychiatry: diagnosis and treatment.* Baltimore: Williams and Wilkins.

Shulman, K. I., Tohen, M., and Kutcher, S. P. (eds.). 1996. *Mood disorders across the lifespan.* New York: John Wiley and Sons.

JOHN G. GUNDERSON

Personality Disorders

Psychiatrists have viewed the personality disorders with considerable ambivalence because of the problems posed by their diagnosis and because their treatment is widely perceived as futile. Moreover, many patients with personality disorders create problems for the people with whom they come in contact—including those who attempt to help them. Whether it is the man whose arrogance offends, the boy who tortures cats, the compulsively promiscuous housewife, or the daughter in headphones who will not leave her room—all have personality styles that are disturbing to others. It is disruptions such as these that have led society to turn to psychiatry in the hope that it can offer the therapeutic answers to the social problems such disorders represent.

Indeed, psychiatry has given increased attention to the personality disorders in recent decades. This interest is partly due to the more central role they attained in 1980, when, with publication of the third edition of the *Diagnostic and Statistical Manual of Mental Disorders* (DSM-III), the personality disorders were placed on a separate diagnostic axis (Axis II). Earlier diagnostic manuals gave priority to diagnoses of symptoms and mental states. Diagnoses of personality disorder were frequently reserved for those patients to whom neither a psychotic nor a neurotic diagnosis could be assigned. This approach relegated personality diagnoses to a rearguard role, in which they were frequently overlooked. This role contrasted sharply with the model introduced by Wilhelm Reich (1933), and subsequently accepted by many psychoanalysts, suggesting that many symptomatic disturbances are essentially epiphenomena or secondary extensions of underlying and more enduring personality disorders.

Since the introduction of a separate axis for personality diagnoses in DSM-III, research has shown that about half of any population of psychiatric inpatients or outpatients will have 1 or more categories of personality dis-

order. Moreover, diagnosing the presence of a personality disorder is an important way to anticipate treatment resistance—whether psychosocial, such as noncompliance or demandingness, and biological, such as diminished responsiveness to medications for Axis I disorders. Finally, it has become increasingly clear that the heritable disposition to Axis I mental s\tate disturbances is also present in preexisting and enduring personality traits or disorders.

Interest in the personality disorders has been stimulated, too, by the availability of improved methodologies for their study. The advent of specific criteria sets in DSM-III and the development of structured interviews for diagnostic assessment were the cornerstones for research. In addition, the advances achieved by epidemiologic, biological, and genetic studies of other major psychiatric conditions have set valuable precedents that have increasingly been extended to studies of the personality disorders.

A final stimulus for this growing interest derives from the change in attitudes about the treatability of people with even severe forms of personality disorder. This shift originated in the enthusiastic reports of the successful application of both psychoanalytic psychotherapy and long-term residential treatments which appeared in the 1960s and 1970s (for example, Rinsley, 1965; Kohut, 1971; Masterson, 1972; Kernberg, 1975). More recently, endorsements have emerged regarding the possible benefits of group, behavioral, and pharmacologic therapies. The quantity and quality of empirical evidence for these claims remain uneven, but the prospects for changing personality disorders have been further improved by the growing evidence that these disorders are not uniformly stable—that is, patients with different forms of personality disorder have different prognoses—and that considerable variability occurs among patients having the same type of disorder.

Demographics

Studies on the prevalence and demographics of personality disorders are still limited in number and sophistication. Available data indicate that about 13% of a general population can be expected to have personality disorders (Weissman, 1993), with higher rates in lower socioeconomic classes and in unstable or disadvantaged communities. Research has documented the presence of personality disorders in widely differing cultures (Loranger et al., 1994), but has not yet shown whether, as might be expected, the prevalence of specific types varies from culture to culture. Borderline, histrionic, and dependent personality disorders are more common in women, whereas paranoid, narcissistic, antisocial, and obsessive-compulsive types are more common in men.

Comorbidity

While 30–50% of clinical populations will have personality disorders, the prevalence of specific disorders varies greatly in different clinical settings. For example, 70–90% of substance abusers and criminals have personality disorders. Table 15.1 shows the very high rates at which the types of personality disorders have been found to co-occur with major Axis I conditions. The most likely explanation for high rates of co-occurrence is that the person-

ality psychopathology precedes and predisposes to the development of the Axis I disorder; this is not always the case, however, and further study is needed (Tyrer et al., 1996).

Development

Longitudinal studies of children have documented the importance of "fit" between psychopathological vulnerability and environmental demands in the development and evolution of behavioral disturbances (Thomas and Chess, 1984). This model may help to explain the later evolution of personality disorders. Children are born with inborn dispositions, called *temperaments,* that make them more or less alert, active, and sociable. These temperaments undergo modifications based on their interactions with their environments, not only being shaped by the environment but also helping to create the environment by the influence they have on it (Reiss et al., 1995). There is only a modest level of continuity between the personality traits, believed to constitute temperaments, seen in children and those observed when they grow up. Such findings have increasingly suggested that the heritable temperamental aspects of personality may, rather than being most evident in childhood, become increasingly expressed in adulthood. But the stable attitudes, expectations, defenses, and interactive styles that evolve and consolidate as the result of such interaction during that

Table 15.1 Rates of personality disorder in Axis I clinical samples

Axis I Disorder	Most Common Axis II Disorders	Rates
Bipolar	Cluster B	25–50%
Depressive	Cluster B (esp. Borderline and Histrionic)	25–50%
	Cluster C (esp. Avoidant and Dependent)	>50%
Eating	Cluster B	25–50%
	Cluster C	25–50%
Post-traumatic Stress	Cluster B (esp. Borderline)	25–50%
	Cluster C (esp. Avoidant)	25–50%
Schizophrenia	Cluster A	13–50%
(**Schizoaffective**)	Cluster A & B	25–50%
Social Phobia	Cluster A	10–20%
	Cluster B	5–15%
	Cluster C (esp. Avoidant)	25–75%
Somatoform	Cluster C	>50%
Substance Abuse	Cluster B (esp. Antisocial and Borderline)	>50%

Source: This table is derived from Gunderson et al. (1996) and Tyrer et al. (1996).

period constitute the components of personality called *character*.

Developmental vicissitudes make it hazardous to identify a personality as disordered during adolescence, but it has generally been thought that personality disorders are consolidated by the early adult years and thereafter remain stable. Long-term follow-up studies that could demonstrate whether disordered personality traits are stable and enduring have not been done. Certainly we now know that some of the more socially disturbing behaviors of personality-disordered people (theft, promiscuity, exploitiveness, self-destructiveness, unemployment) often diminish with time. This fact in itself suggests that less interpersonally and socially disruptive adaptations are possible. Vaillant (1977) has provided evidence that, rather than being simply context-dependent adaptations, basic changes in defensive style (character "armor") can occur in the aging personality-disordered person. The existing longitudinal studies suggest that personality traits have greater flexibility and adaptability than would be expected according to traditional definitions that stress their stability or clinicians who have stressed their immutability.

Treatment

Since the development of standardized criteria for personality disorders, much attention has been given to identifying specific treatments. Before the 1970s, largely because of the claims made for curative changes in patients with borderline personality organization, many ambitious programs for their psychodynamic treatment were initiated. Since then the role of such therapies has receded, and they are now deployed with more discriminating indications. Moreover, as shown in Table 15.2 multiple other modalities have earned a place in therapeutic planning. While much of the evidence about their effectiveness remains within the realm of informed clinical wisdom, there has been a growing reliance on controlled outcome studies to bolster the claims for their efficacy.

The DSM-IV Categorical System

DSM-III (1980) represented a major advance over earlier efforts to classify personality disorders insofar as it provided a clear set of criteria for their identification, and, by placing these disorders on a separate axis, it drew attention to their potential interaction with other psychiatric conditions. Nonetheless, clinicians often disagree about their Axis II diagnoses. In part, this lack of reliability has been due to the overlapping criteria sets. The subsequent revisions in DSM III-R and DSM-IV have deliberately attempted to make more use of clinical wisdom and the growing research literature to improve differentiation. The relative unreliability undoubtedly also reflects the uncertain validity of some categories. The number of categories is larger than most clinicians and most factor analytic studies suggest is optimal (Lazare, Klerman, and Armor, 1966; Presley and Walton, 1973; Tyrer and Alexander, 1979).

The existing system utilizes a modification of the classical categorical model that is employed for medical conditions; that is, clinicians are encouraged to identify a patient as either having or not having the diagnosis. However, this model is modified in that clinicians are invited to identify subthreshold cases as having traits of the disorder.

Categorical models originate in clinical observations. Such models posit prototypic features that make the personality disorder recognizable, and implicitly these features become "core," such that diagnoses are rarely made in their absence. Categorical systems have developed naturalistically, without any overriding, comprehensive conceptual scheme. Examples range from Hippocrates' 4 humors to contributions in this century as diverse as Kretschmer's (1925) and Sheldon's (1940) somatotypes

Table 15.2 Modalities of treatment

Treatment Type	PPD	STPD	SPD	BPD	ASPD	NPD	HPD	OCPD	AVPD	DPD
Psychodynamic	−	−	+	+		+	+	+	+	+
Cognitive-Behavioral			+	+					+	+
Pharmacologic	+	+		+	−	−	−			−
Sociotherapies			+	+	+	−			+	+

ASPD = Antisocial; AVPD = Avoidant; BPD = Borderline; DPD = Dependent; HPD = Histrionic; NPD = Narcissistic; OCPD = Obsessive-compulsive; PPD = Paranoid; SPD = Schizoid; STPD = Schizotypal.
+ = Often beneficial.
− = Not beneficial.

and Freud's (1908) and Abraham's (1949) descriptions of oral (dependent), anal (obsessive), and phallic (hysterical) types. The most important contributor to the modern classification system was the German nosologist Kurt Schneider (1958). He identified 10 categories, most of which involve the same constructs, with name changes, that are present in the modern DSM-IV and ICD-10 (*International Classification of Diseases*, tenth edition) systems.

The polythetic descriptive model found in the DSM-IV attempts to be "atheoretical." As shown in Table 15.3, it is actually an amalgam of types derived from clinical traditions and dimensional and categorical research. Many of the categories found in the current system (i.e., histrionic, obsessive-compulsive, dependent, borderline, narcissistic) derive from psychoanalytic observations, and while offering the hope of psychological coherence and developmental pathogenesis, these categories are not comprehensive and provide only modest guides to specific therapies.

Significant questions persist about the definition or utility of many of the existing personality disorder types. In the current system, the 10 personality types are clustered into 3 clusters based on descriptive similarities: (1) odd and eccentric (schizoid, paranoid, and schizotypal); (2) dramatic, emotional, or erratic (histrionic, narcissistic, antisocial, and borderline); and (3) anxious, fearful (avoidant, dependent, and obsessive-compulsive). The division into these 3 clusters has generally been validated by several factor-analytic studies, but these studies also sug-

gest that the obsessive-compulsive type may constitute a fourth cluster. Two other personality disorders, passive-aggressive and depressive, are in Appendix II of DSM-IV, indicating that they are viable categories whose inclusion awaits further study.

Alternative Systems for Classifying Personality Disorders

An important controversy exists about whether personality disorders are best classified on the basis of psychological traits (e.g., intrapsychic, interpersonal, or behavioral) or on the basis of biogenetic features (neurophysiological or heritable). These differing conceptual bases have different clinical advantages, the psychological (i.e., characterological) basis providing better guides to psychotherapists, and the biogenetic (i.e., temperamental) basis offering better guides for psychopharmacological treatments. A variety of systems for classifying the personality disorders have been developed, and while each can claim advantages over the others, none has established sufficient familiarity or clinical applicability to surpass the variable assets of the existing system.

Dimensional Models

Academic psychologists have a proud tradition of attempts to develop a comprehensive and theoretically unified way to organize personality traits. By examining a broad range of normally occurring personality traits in

Table 15.3 DSM-IV personality disorders

	Defining Domain	DSM Exemplars	Advocates	Strengths	Weakness
Dynamic	Psychology	Histrionic Obsessive-compulsive Dependent Narcissistic Borderline Self-defeating*	Psycho-therapists	Vivid, explanatory	Inferential
Trait	Traits	Avoidant Negativistic*	Academics	Comprehensive, empirical	Non-clinical
Biological	Biology	Schizotypal, Cyclothymic* Depressive*	Physicians	Basic, explanatory	Not comprehensive
Sociological	Social deviance	Antisocial Passive-aggressive* Sadistic*	Sociologists	Recognizable, socially relevant	Context-dependent

*Options considered for inclusion in DSM-IV.

Table 15.4 The Five Factor Model: dimensions of
personality

Dimension	Qualities
Neuroticism	anxious, negative emotionality
Extraversion	outgoing, positive emotionality
Openness	inquiring, intellectual, creative
Agreeableness	cooperative, trusting
Conscientiousness	responsible, persevering

Source: Adapted from Costa and McCrae, 1990; reprinted with permission.

order to see how they cluster in the general population, these studies have distinguished a discrete number of personality dimensions. Those individuals with the most extreme forms of these dimensions are expected to have personality disorders.

Dimensional (trait) models have the advantages of both empirical testability and broad generalizability. Table 15.4 shows the Five Factor Model—a model that involves 5 dimensions, each of which has demonstrated some heritability, and each of which has established good long-term stability and universality. The evolution of these factors within academic psychology has involved many investigators, and while controversy about them persists, these 5 dimensions have achieved a considerable consensus.

Figure 15.1 illustrates how Millon's (1981) well-known system organized around the dimensions of affiliation and emotionality has been adapted to link with DSM-IV categories. Even with adaptations such as Millon's, however, dimensional models pose certain problems. The fit with traditional categories is uneven, and they require familiarity with logic and constructs not customary to clinicians. In addition, because these models rely on cross-sectional descriptors, they are not founded on the clinically useful ties to the developmental and prognostic issues that traditionally make diagnoses useful to clinicians.

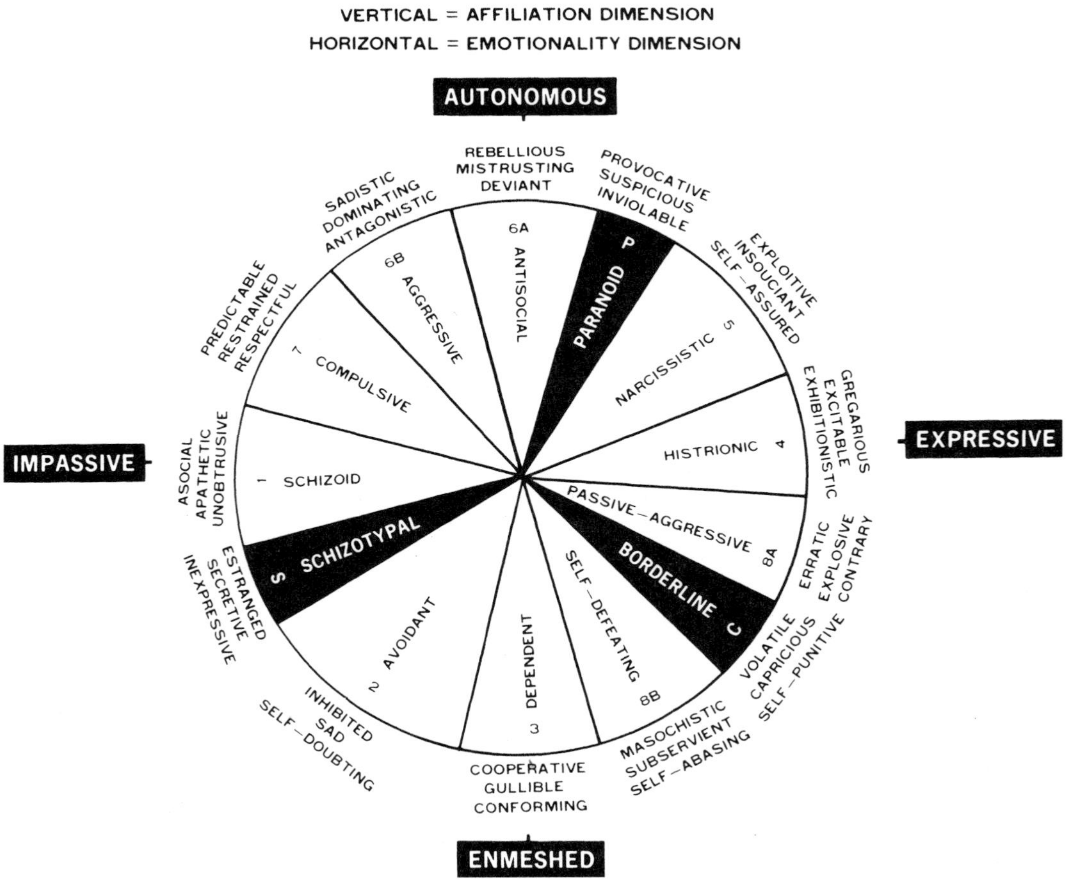

Figure 15.1 A circumplex model for classifying personality types. *Source:* T. Millon, On the nature of taxonomy in psychopathology, in *Issues in diagnostic research*, ed. C. Last and M. Hersen (New York: Plenum, 1987), p. 42. Reprinted with permission.

Finally, while such systems show promise of offering better perspectives about the relationships of personality with Axis I diagnoses, this promise has not yet been confirmed. In sum, they are appealing for their heuristic value and comprehensiveness, but limited because they still seem removed from clinical realities.

A Psychobiological Model

In recent years Cloninger and associates (1993) have developed a new system for classifying personality disorders that is based on personality dimensions (behavioral tendencies) believed to be under genetic control. Whereas 3 dimensions were originally conceptualized—novelty-seeking, harm-avoidance, and reward-dependence—factor analytic studies have now yielded a fourth dimension, persistence. These 4 dimensions have been identified as independently heritable temperaments. The model is now usefully complicated by the addition of 3 environmentally conditioned character types—cooperativeness, self-directness, and self-transcendence. The latter 2 correspond to what an earlier psychiatric literature called autonomous and sublimated. Notably, the lack of self-directness or cooperativeness is what characterizes individuals who have personality disorders.

The Cloninger system derives from a complex interweaving of basic biological and social scientific findings

with original reconceptualizations. Its empirical validity and its potential advantages over other systems are actively being examined.

An Integrative Model

Figure 15.2 illustrates a classification system in which the existing personality types are grouped according to level of severity (Gunderson, 1984). This system is built on the clinical and research literature that has already established dynamic or biogenetic affinity between existing categories and other diagnostic conditions. It thus utilizes the same data sets that have informed the seminal conceptualization by Siever and Davis (1991), who identified 4 underlying psychobiological dispositions to Axis I and Axis II psychopathology—cognitive, impulsive, affective, and anxiety.

The most severe disorders present either prepsychotic disorders or atypical phenotypic expressions of psychotic disorders and should therefore be considered *spectrum disorders.* This group includes paranoid, schizotypal, and cyclothymic disorders, and possibly another, still being investigated personality disordered variant of psychotic depression. A second level of disorders, which could be considered *self disorders,* is characterized by severely restricted interpersonal or functional capacities, or both. This intermediate level includes the narcissistic, border-

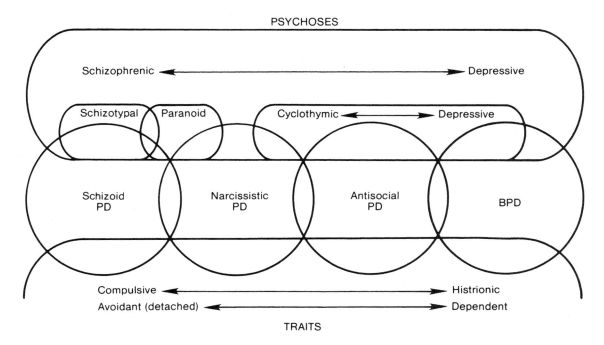

Figure 15.2 Classification of personality. *Source:* J. Gunderson, *Borderline personality disorder* (Washington, D.C.: American Psychiatric Press, 1984), p. 20. Reprinted with permission.

---

line, antisocial, and schizoid categories. These disorders involve major developmental failures related to dysfunctional environments. This level is linked to the spectrum disorders and to their related Axis I disorders by virtue of genetic, prognostic, dynamic, and therapeutic considerations. The third level, *trait disorders,* grades imperceptibly into neurotic problems and into normally occurring trait dimensions. This least dysfunctional group encompasses what the psychoanalytic literature calls neurotic characters. These disorders can also be conceptualized as extreme forms of normally occurring dimensions. As such they can be linked to those dimensions described in Table 15.4 and Figure 15.1 that were empirically derived from normal populations. Trait disorders include the compulsive, passive-aggressive, dependent, histrionic, and avoidant (phobic) personality types.

This system grows naturally out of existing knowledge and clinical traditions, but it has several advantages over the DSM clusters. It takes into account the variable level of severity among these disorders and formalizes the hierarchy among them in ways that diminish the confusing need for identifying multiple personality disorders. Moreover, this system reflects what is known about the relationship of these disorders to other diagnostic conditions and their complicated interface with normal personality. Finally, the divisions contained in this model also have prognostic and therapeutic significance (see Table 15.5).

DSM-IV Categories

What follows is an overview of DSM-IV personality disorder categories. It summarizes current thinking about each disorder's essential features, psychodynamics, epidemiology and course, etiology, and treatment. They are grouped into the 3 clusters of spectrum disorders, self disorders, and trait disorders, with recognition that there are, as noted above, other viable ways to subdivide them.

Spectrum Disorders

The first and most severe group of personality disorders, with the strongest connection to Axis I psychoses, includes the paranoid and schizotypal personality disorders. Cyclothymic and depressive personality also belong in this group, but the cyclothymic type has been placed with the affective disorders, and the depressive type is not yet an official category (it is described among the DSM-IV Appendix B categories).

Paranoid Personality Disorder

Definition. The essential feature of paranoid personality disorder is a pervasive suspiciousness and mistrust based on the unwarranted belief in others' malevolence. These attitudes are intense and strongly defended. Patients search for evidence of deception, threat, or malevolence in others and are extremely sensitive and resistant to any suggestion of their own guilt or responsibility.

Psychodynamics. Paranoid people disavow their own hostile motives by the defensive use of projection. As a result, they attribute hostility to the world they live in and are left feeling weakly vulnerable but morally righteous. They often feel unfairly treated and are quick to argue, threaten, bear grudges, and pursue revenge.

Table 15.5 Personality disorder type

Subclass	Defined by	Defensive Style	Prognosis
•Spectrum Disorders (Paranoid, Schizotypal, Cyclothymic)	Relation to psychoses and social deficits	*maladaptive* projection withdrawal externalization	Stable, poor response to treatment
•Self Disorders (Borderline, Antisocial, Narcissistic, Schizoid)	Social and interpersonal dysfunction	*image distortion* acting out fantasy splitting idealization/devaluation	Unstable, can get better or worse from treatment
•Trait Disorders (Histrionic, Obsessive-compulsive, Avoidant, Dependent)	Interpersonal and intrapsychic conflict	*self-sacrificing* inhibition, intellectualization, passive-aggression, repression	Stable, good response to treatment

Epidemiology and course. The prevalence of paranoid personality disorder is less than 1%. Within clinical populations the disorder is rare because the paranoid person is guarded about seeking help or being in a position of vulnerability or subordination. This condition is more common in men than in women.

Paranoid features are identifiable by adolescence and become increasingly consolidated by the early adult years. This disorder is a particularly stable and syntonic form of adaptation. Except for interpersonal difficulties with those in authority or with those who attempt to become too close, paranoid individuals are likely to function stably.

Etiology. Little is known about the etiology of this disorder. It is thought to have a weak genetic link to more psychotic forms of paranoia, that is, to paranoid disorder and possibly to the paranoid subtype of schizophrenia. Families tend to show rigidly organized roles and communications.

Treatment. A cool, nonintrusive, respectful, noninterpretative psychotherapist may establish sufficient trust that the paranoid person will use the therapist to deal with ongoing very stressful life circumstances. There is no evidence, however, that deeper examination of projective dynamics or a basic modification of character style is possible.

The group and behavioral therapies involve too much disclosure and compliance, respectively, for paranoid patients. Low doses of neuroleptics may, in some cases, manage anxiety and other specific target symptoms. If basic trust has not been established, the paranoid patient can be expected to resist such treatment because of fear that medication will render him weak and controllable.

Schizotypal Personality Disorder

Definition. The essential feature of schizotypal personality disorder combines oddities and eccentricities in thinking or perceptions with a need for interpersonal distance. Social isolation, somatic concerns, constricted effort, and interpersonal suspiciousness are useful in identifying this group.

The diagnosis was born out of adoptive studies that showed that a personality variant of schizophrenia was genetically related to schizophrenia. This is the first explicit effort to identify a personality disorder diagnosis because of its "spectrum" relationship to a parent Axis I condition.

Psychodynamics. Little is known about the dynamics of schizotypal patients other than those which have been attributed to people with schizoid personality. The lack of a psychodynamic conceptual framework for the core features around which the schizotypal syndrome is organized reflects the degree to which its origins are tied to studies of genetic transmission, while the relevant psychodynamic observations are tied to schizoid personality.

Epidemiology and course. A prevalence of 3–5% of the general population is magnified in clinical settings by virtue of the disorder's common comorbid conditions— somatization, obsessive-compulsive disorder, and social phobias. Its use by clinicians as a primary diagnosis is unusual. It appears to be a stable form of maladaptation associated with considerable ongoing disability in terms of persistent symptoms, employment history, and social isolation (McGlashan, 1986). The vocational dysfunction is worse than for borderline personality disorder and is comparable to that observed in schizophrenic persons.

Etiology. Schizotypal personality is found with increased prevalence among the relatives of schizophrenics, and a higher risk of schizophrenia-related disorders is found among the relatives of schizotypal persons. Aside from the familial linkage to schizophrenia, a twin study indicates a 33% concordance in monozygotic twin pairs, as opposed to only 4% in dizygotic co-twins (Torgersen, 1984). Because some schizotypal patients share with schizophrenics impaired smooth eye movement, backward masking, continuous performance tasks, and increased cerebrospinal fluid homovanillic acid (CSF HVA), it is generally believed that they have the same basic central nervous system (CNS) dysfunction.

Unlike with most of the other personality disorders, little has been written about the possibility of developmentally based deficits in this disorder or other pathogenic environmental influences.

Treatment. Schizotypal patients are highly resistant to exploratory psychotherapy and are better suited to a nonintensive, more supportive form of therapy. They rarely need institutional care, but they may profit from rehabilitative approaches that include behavioral techniques. Sheltered work programs and other task-oriented groups may provide useful socializing experiences.

Neuroleptics in low doses may help to diminish severe and enduring symptoms such as ideas of reference, depersonalization, anxiety, obsessive-compulsive ruminations, and somatization (Goldberg et al., 1986). Medications do not, however, seem to effect core impairments in social and interpersonal adaptation.

Self Disorders

The disorders of self, including schizoid, narcissistic, antisocial, and borderline personality disorders, include the most socially and behaviorally maladaptive types. People with these disorders can be considered less severely handicapped than those with spectrum disorders because they do not have high vulnerability to psychoses and because their prognosis can be influenced greatly for better or for worse by their psychosocial environment. These categories have all been major topics in the psychiatric literature and thus have relatively high recognizability by clinicians. Therapeutic efforts predictably encounter major problems requiring special expertise and long-term strategies.

Schizoid Personality Disorder

Definition. The essential feature of schizoid personality disorder is social detachment from relationships and emotional contact. The patient manifests a lifelong pattern of social isolation characterized by a lack of friendships and by indifference to the attitudes and feelings of others. Such individuals are inclined to engage in solitary activities, which often involve mechanical, scientific, futuristic, or other nonhuman subjects.

This category is one of the oldest and most widely used personality diagnoses. It was originally thought to be a genetic variant of schizophrenia, but DSM-III explicitly created the schizotypal personality category to target that subgroup. As a result, the schizoid category is no longer meant to imply such a genetic relationship. Although schizoid personality is common premorbidly in people who develop schizophrenia (perhaps with a frequency as high as 50%), it is unusual for someone with this disorder to develop schizophrenia.

Psychodynamics. The basic dynamic for a schizoid person is defensive withdrawal from attachments because of the expectation that they will be painful. This behavior is accompanied by an extensive use of denial or dissociation of bodily feelings. Sometimes the social detachment is compensated for by a reliance on fantasy life, typically involving science fiction theses, but in any event an imaginary world in which people and situations are more gratifying than in reality.

Epidemiology and course. Available data suggest that this disorder is found in 2% or more of the population. Schiz-

oid individuals are rare in clinical populations because they are averse to seeking treatment.

Schizoid personality disorder is believed to be a stable, lifelong adaptation that begins very early. Schizoid people may find a comfortable niche in a variety of employments where social interaction is minimal (e.g., night security) or where their mental activities can be channeled to constructive purposes (e.g., writing). Because such people can find a good "fit" with the right environment, schizoid individuals appear increasingly adaptive over time by forming a stable but distant network of relationships with people around work tasks and even recreational activities.

Etiology. Most theories suggest that the schizoid person's social detachment begins in early life. A shy, introverted, harm-avoidant temperament is thought to be a predisposing factor. These people fail to develop a basic attachment to primary caretakers, and some theories suggest that this is due to grossly inadequate, cold, or neglectful early parenting. Such histories suggest that this experience begins early (the oral phase) and that the patient's withdrawal from relationships is secondary.

Treatment. Because of their interpersonal detachment, schizoid people rarely seek treatment. Vocational counselors and clergymen are more commonly in a position to introduce them to relationships that may eventually yield possibilities for greater intimacy. Individual therapists should be active, patient, nonintrusive, and openly respectful of the patient's wishes for privacy. A more formal, structured, intellectual style may be more comfortable for the patient than one that is warm or interpretative. Any relationship in which an attachment occurs will be of value.

Group therapies may also be useful for such patients, especially if they are directed toward building social skills and provide a structured framework for the development of new relationships that extend beyond the therapy itself.

Narcissistic Personality Disorder

Definition. The essential feature of narcissistic personality disorder is grandiosity—a persistent and unrealistic overvaluation of one's own importance and achievements. This trait may be evident in arrogance, entitlement, and the need for attention and admiration, but this is often covert. The narcissistic person tends to see others hierarchically: those above are either envied or idealized, whereas those below are seen as inferior and treated with contempt. Such persons are intolerant of criticism, rejection, or indifference; they are likely to respond to these perceived insults with feelings of humiliation and rage.

Their relationships are emotionally shallow and endure only if they provide some reflection that supports their grandiosity. Narcissistic persons view themselves as self-sufficient and consider dependency a sign of weakness.

This category was introduced into DSM-III because of its clinical value in guiding psychotherapeutic interventions. It has not evolved from dimensional research, but it overlaps considerably with the interpersonal style of antisocial personality—so much so that narcissistic individuals are sometimes considered "white-collar" psychopaths.

Psychodynamics. Because grandiosity is—by definition—not reality based, the narcissistic person lives in a constant state of tension with an environment from which disconfirming evidence is potentially forthcoming. Input that is inconsistent with maintaining grandiosity is often ignored by denial or by devaluation of the source. Otherwise it can rapidly lead to a sense of extreme failure and shame, reflecting an exaggerated sense of the importance of the defeat, the criticism, or the rejection. Grandiosity is also threatened by perceptions that others have more power, talent, achievements, and the like. Under these circumstances a narcissistic person is likely to experience intense envy, from which ruthless behaviors may ensue. Conversely, he may identify himself with an enviable person and thereby use the other's accomplishments as reflections on himself. Sometimes narcissistic persons sustain their grandiosity by narrowing their social exposure and experience. Such people are most likely to seek psychiatric care as a result of depression in circumstances of failure or diminished admiration.

Epidemiology and course. The prevalence of this disorder in the general population is unknown, but it is common in office practices and other outpatient settings. It is more common in men than in women (60–75%). This diagnosis is difficult to make in adolescence but is found in a broad range of adult ages. Available evidence suggests that it is a relatively unstable personality type, perhaps because the overt features may become evident—i.e., diagnosable—when situational stress makes them observable (Ronningstam, Gunderson, and Lyons, 1995).

Etiology. Heinz Kohut (1971) theorized that a grandiose sense of self is a part of normal early development and that narcissistic personality disorder occurs when the grandiosity gets sustained because of the failure of parents to provide an adequate empathic experience or adequate exposure to disillusioning realities. In contrast, Kernberg (1975) suggests that pathological narcissism is an active defensive adaptation against conflicts centered on early rage and helplessness. Narcissistic individuals will often report a general absence of parental warmth and support that is supplemented by parental overvaluation of some characteristic, such as beauty, intelligence, or talent.

Treatment. Individual psychotherapy, including psychoanalysis, is the basic form of treatment for patients with narcissistic personality disorder. Less intensive dynamic psychotherapies are preferable for those who also have ego deficits in impulse control or affect regulation. However, the techniques and processes by which psychotherapy can be useful are controversial. Kernberg (1975) views the basic narcissistic issues as anger and envy and the need to be self-sufficient. He emphasizes active interpretation and confrontation of the patient's defenses against acknowledging these affects and needs and of the patient's defensive efforts to idealize the therapist.

In contrast, Kohut (1971) defines the core of the disorder as the stunted development of the patient's grandiose self based on parental failures to mirror and allow idealization in phase-appropriate ways. He therefore suggests that the therapist allow an idealizing transference to develop and to persist uninterpreted until disillusion gradually develops through the therapist's unintended but inevitable empathic failures. Interpretations are focused on the patient's positive transference wishes for a more satisfying and perfect relationship.

A third view is offered by A. H. Modell (1975), who agrees with the importance of allowing an idealizing transference to develop but then, like Kernberg, encourages therapists to become quite active in interpreting and confronting the patient with his lack of genuine relatedness and self-sufficiency.

Narcissistic patients are hospitalized because of associated Axis I disorders such as severe depression related to career or marital impasses, anorexia nervosa, or bipolar disorder. In residential settings they will try to reestablish a sense of superiority by seeking evidence of their specialness from caretakers and by comparing themselves favorably with others. As their grandiosity returns, they are likely to offend their caregivers and other patients by their sudden devaluation of them and by their condescending and entitled attitudes.

It is difficult to engage or sustain such individuals in group therapy. There is no evidence that medications or behavioral therapies play a significant role in the treatment of such patients.

Antisocial Personality Disorder

Definition. The essential feature of antisocial personality disorder is a chronic disregard for the rights of others, and an absence of remorse for the harmful effects of these behaviors on others. Most of the cardinal signals of this disorder involve aggressive or illegal activities, deceit, repeated thefts, assaults, evasion of financial obligations, and lying. Other features include impulsivity and recklessness. The antisocial person's lack of fidelity, loyalty, and honesty prevents him from forming enduring or close relationships.

The diagnosis of antisocial personality disorder requires a history of conduct disorder before the age of 15.

Psychodynamics. Because antisocial persons view their external world as affectively cold and self-serving, they expect that nothing can be freely given. They feel that behaviors are largely determined externally by coercion or opportunities. To survive, they believe they must extort whatever they can by virtue of their mental or physical resources. They value other people egocentrically for what they can provide, and their relationships are unburdened by guilt or loyalty. Hence antisocial people may appear enviably free from care, but the essential flatness and barrenness of their inner experience surfaces when their externally directed activities are curtailed. Then the absence of meaningful attachments may become apparent, and depression commonly develops.

Epidemiology and course. Antisocial personality disorder has a lifetime prevalence of 2–3%, is about 4 times more frequent among males than among females, and its prevalence is increased in lower socioeconomic urban areas.

Evidence of this disorder usually appears in early adolescence in the form of typically antisocial behaviors such as lying, truancy, vandalism, or promiscuity (Robins, 1966). Other early predictors include evidence of poor impulse control, poor attention in school, and remorseless acts of cruelty. Antisocial actions become more prevalent in adolescence, when they characteristically expand to aggressive sexual behaviors and substance abuse. The young adult antisocial person's failure to function responsibly at work or in a role as a parent or a spouse completes the clinical picture. Peak prevalence occurs in the 24–44 age group and then drops off abruptly in the over-45 age group. The more flagrant aspects of the disorder gradually but significantly diminish as antisocial persons enter their 30s and 40s. For a significant number antisocial behaviors may cease altogether, but the related issues of callousness and exploitiveness may persist. The distinction from narcissistic personality disorder is then unclear.

Etiology. Both genetic and environmental influences are known to operate in the pathogenesis of antisocial personality disorder. Twin and adoptive studies have pointed to a heritable predisposition, i.e., a temperament, involving impulsivity and social detachment. These studies have also indicated that its development can be modified by good parental care. Most developmental theories suggest that the pathogenic environmental process begins early in life and is due to the absence of sustained, stable parenting. The pathogenesis then depends on ongoing social reinforcements. Antisocial children usually come from home environments characterized by large families, frequent divorce, and grossly inconsistent or neglectful parenting. The parental role models often include antisocial behaviors, notably substance abuse and violence. Occasionally one may observe parental conflicts in which antisocial behaviors are covertly encouraged.

Treatment. Treatment usually fails because of the patient's lack of motivation, the tendency to explain and discharge affects externally, and the habitual distrust of authority.

Therapies that depend on peer pressure and socially corrective experiences are preferable to individual therapies. The best results have generally been reported from therapeutic communities—closed, structured environments involving confrontational experiences with peers and intensive group therapies (Jones, 1956; Sturup, 1978). Such institutional group programs focus on the antisocial person's need to assume responsibility for actions and to behave responsibly toward others. Effective institutional programs invoke clear and consistent environmental consequences for behaviors, which help the impulsive antisocial person to anticipate such consequences (for example, being late for a group therapy meeting would result in less access to television). Such programs remain unusual, because society is ambivalent about investing resources to aid a group that already taxes existing social institutions, especially under circumstances where only limited and occasional success can be expected.

When residential settings (including prisons) limit antisocial behaviors, underlying feelings of emptiness, depression, and anxiety can become evident. Talking therapies may help antisocial persons learn to tolerate these feelings and to develop more socially acceptable behavioral responses. Adolescents whose delinquency occurs while they are still part of an involved family that has implicitly encouraged antisocial actions may be helped by family therapy. No pharmacotherapies are thought to be helpful.

Borderline Personality Disorder

Definition. The essential feature of borderline personality disorder is fear of and intolerance for being alone.

Typically this fear leads to behavioral "markers" such as the repetitive engagement in self-destructiveness, substance abuse, promiscuity, and other desperate impulsive actions. Borderline individuals report sustained feelings of loneliness, emptiness, and rage. Their intense, unstable relationships are characterized by devaluation, manipulation, dependency, and self-denial. They may at times have psychotic-like perceptual, dissociative, or paranoid experiences.

Of all the personality disorders, the repertoire of behaviors and symptoms associated with this category is the most varied and unstable. Borderline personality was originally thought to be an atypical form of schizophrenia, but the focus has since shifted to questions of its being an atypical form of affective disorder or posttraumatic stress disorder. Considerable evidence has accumulated in the efforts to connect the borderline syndrome to these Axis I disorders. The results have failed to confirm strong or specific associations, but they have helped provide, by default, considerable evidence that this diagnosis may be a discernible and well-validated form of personality disorder (Gunderson and Sabo, 1993).

Psychodynamics. Various theories have emphasized either the patient's severe aggression or his problems with object relations. Kernberg (1984) has postulated that an excessive aggressive instinct interacts with usual or exaggerated frustrations in the early mother-child relationship. This conflict causes the child either to integrate his aggression, which causes an inner sense of destructiveness, or to project it, which leads to both paranoid fears and a search for an ideal mother elsewhere. Adler and Buie (1979) have emphasized failures to acquire soothing introjects that can provide comfort in periods of separation. This deficit is evident in the patient's sensitivity to abandonment, the use of self-destructiveness to prevent separation, and the psychotic-like experiences that arise when separation or abandonment does occur. The borderline person's reality testing is uniquely sensitive to the degree of contextual structure and support in his environment. It can lapse in diverse settings such as unstructured work, treatment, or psychological testing.

Epidemiology and course. The prevalence of borderline personality is about 2–3%. It occurs about 3 times as frequently in females as in males. Its presence has been documented in numerous industrialized and underdeveloped cultures. It is the most common personality disorder found in outpatient and inpatient psychiatric populations, where it generally occurs in 15–25% of all patients. The use of this psychiatric diagnosis dramatically increased after its inclusion in the DSM. It is now included in the official international classification system as "Unstable" personality disorder.

Substance abuse, promiscuity, reliance on transitional objects, and the search for clinging, exclusive relationships during adolescence are early indicators of borderline personality. Because many borderline characteristics may constitute part of normal adolescence, the diagnosis often cannot be made with confidence until after the age of 16, when the individual has developed more stable patterns. The disorder is most often apparent in late adolescence and young adulthood but tapers during the 30s and later. Studies on the longitudinal course suggest severe morbidity in terms of recidivism, social disruption, role dysfunction, and severe symptoms 3–7 years after the diagnosis is made. Longer follow-up studies indicate that for many the most disruptive behaviors diminish over time. Many cease their efforts to find "better parenting" from mental health caregivers and resign themselves to seeking comfort from substance abuse, self-help groups, doctrinaire religious sects, or sadomasochistic relationships. The risk of suicide (about 10%) is 3 times higher than in the general population, but is not high compared to the number of "attempts" that fail.

Etiology. Borderline patients have uniformly failed to establish a secure attachment to their primary caretakers. The environmental contributions to this failure are usually notable. Borderline patients often describe enduring patterns of inconsistency, unpredictability, and unavailability in their parenting. Broken families, traumatic separations, frequent relocations, and adoption are also common. The pathogenic consequences of such patterns are frequently observed in the siblings of borderline patients as well. The literature describes 2 family constellations associated with the development of borderline personality. One is characterized by neglect—parental failure to provide adequate support, discipline, and attention. Such families often project precocious independence onto the child. A second, less common family constellation is characterized by overinvolvement. In such families the patient's efforts to develop autonomy are covertly resisted by parental withdrawal or punitive actions. An influential early theory by Masterson (1972) focused on the preborderline child's problems in the rapprochement subphase (16–30 months) of development. Rather than permitting successful experimentation with separation and autonomy, parental resistance to independence prompts the child to be submissive and to dissociate from his aggression. This remains a valuable theory for some borderline patients, but it is neither a necessary nor a sufficient precondition.

Other factors, both heritable and traumatic, are also

believed to have a role in the failed attachment of borderline patients. Many borderline persons have childhood histories that include sexual abuse (about 60%), including incest (about 25%) and violence (about 60%). When emotional abuse and parental separations are added, about 90% of borderlines will have had some form of childhood trauma. These traumas are thought to have a significant etiological role in about half of the patients with BPD. They probably act by priming the neurophysiological system to render the children vulnerable to later stress (such as exposure to anger or separations) as well as the distorted interpersonal expectations that are typical of borderline patients.

Studies of the familial relationship of borderline personality disorder to other diagnoses have failed to show a familial relationship to schizophrenia, bipolar disorder, or major depression (the last of particular importance because borderline patients frequently have comorbid depression). These studies have, however, documented a marked increase in borderline personality, antisocial personality disorder, and substance abuse in the relatives. A small twin study failed to show evidence for heritability, but most theorists believe that borderline patients have a genetically based predisposition that takes the form of extreme separation sensitivity, heightened aggressiveness, and, as with antisocials, impulse dysregulation.

Treatment. Long-term individual psychotherapy can be very helpful to patients with borderline personality disorder, but it is difficult to engage them in this process. Even with experienced therapists, nearly 50% drop out in the first 6 months. Many borderline patients see a series of therapists, each of whom they reject angrily and impulsively. The intense affects, demands for care, and repetitious crises that permeate the early stage of treatment often evoke intense feelings of helplessness and anger among the caregivers. The difficulties associated with treatment here give a pejorative connotation to this diagnosis, which can be evident in its being applied carelessly for patients who are unresponsive or demanding.

Nonintensive therapy (1–2 visits per week) that begins with a series of short-term contractors based on discrete goals and a "Let's see if this helps" agreement can diminish and help establish a collaborative alliance. Psychoanalysis is usually contraindicated because borderline patients easily regress in response to the lack of structure. The "borderline" patients reportedly treated through psychoanalysis do not meet usual criteria.

Successful therapies are characterized by a period of overt dependency and progressively diminished acting out. Consistency, reliability, and adherence to boundaries are important nonspecific elements of individual therapy that reassure and stabilize many patients. Management of the borderline patient's efforts to test the boundaries of the therapy and to evoke parental responses from therapists by provocative or self-destructive behaviors is a major problem during the first year of treatment. Therapists need to respond to these behaviors in ways that convey concern but do not reinforce their recurrence. If a diminution of suicidality and a creation of a positive dependency have not occurred within the first year, consultation should be sought. Clinicians agree on the necessity and value of confrontation and limits during this period. Interpretations require judicious use. Some borderline patients systematically misunderstand them in ways that are counterproductive (e.g., invasions, invalidations, criticism), and this can lead to negative therapeutic reactions. For other patients, interpretations of hostile controlling motivations or fears of dependency can diminish the testing and manipulative behaviors and facilitate the formation of a therapeutic alliance.

A broad range of adjunctive treatments is often needed to sustain and add to the benefits of individual therapy. Intermittent short-term hospitalizations are common. In the hospital, constrained action, clear structure, and the presence of focused groups and confrontation can make stays beneficial and limit the development of a regressive tie to the institutional care. Longer-term care is often required such that borderline patients can profit from the social learning vocational rehabilitation opportunities of partial hospital programs. It should be noted, however, that staff frequently respond to these patients with either overly nurturant or harshly punitive attitudes that can lead to disruptive staff disagreements. Such "splitting" occurs so often that institutional care can easily have introgenic effects of aggravating the borderline patient's desperation, impulsivity, and unrealistic expectations. Experienced, well-supervised staff and good communication are necessary for milieu programs to be beneficial.

Intermittent educative contacts with the parents of borderline patients who live at home are useful to consolidate support for treatment. Ongoing family therapy, however, is not indicated except when the patient comes from an enmeshed, overinvolved, separation-resistant family. Under these circumstances family therapy may be critical for a successful outcome.

Mounting evidence suggests that, while virtually all classes of medications may be helpful in the pharmacologic treatment of patients with borderline personality disorder, none are uniformly or dramatically so. Moreover, because the effects of medications are usually modest, and misuse and side effects are likely to be common, caution should be exercised in prescribing them. Pharmacotherapies should be initiated with statements that enlist the borderline patient's alliance, such as "You will need to help me evaluate whether this is of use," rather than giving assurances or high expectations. Hostile, impulsive, and depressive symptom behaviors are most likely to be helped by the serotonin-reuptake inhibitors, and, conversely, are most likely to be aggravated by benzodiazepines. Neuroleptics and anticonvulsants may have a role in the treatment of particularly agitated, volatile, and impulsive borderline patients.

Trait Disorders

The third and least severe group of personality disorders are those that may be considered trait disorders. This group includes the histrionic, avoidant, dependent, and obsessive-compulsive types. Most may have related Axis I anxiety disorders and are of the type that were called neurotic characters in the earlier literature. People with this group of disorders are thought to have little problem with reality testing and to be the most amenable to psychological interventions, including short-term strategies.

Histrionic Personality Disorder

Definition. The essential feature of histrionic personality disorder is the excessive expressiveness (in actions, appearance, and affects) that evokes and maintains the attention of others. Histrionic persons are colorful, dramatic, and extroverted. Their awareness of their "audience" and desire to evoke appreciative and positive responses give their emotions and relationships a superficial and insincere quality. Their cognitive style too seems imprecise, fanciful, and transitory. Such individuals appear flirtatious and seductive, and tend also to eroticize other people's behaviors and motives. Somatic complaints and submissiveness are characteristic secondary features of such patients.

Psychodynamics. The preoccupation of histrionic persons with appearances and with being erotically pleasing to others is used to compensate for a lack of knowledge or competence, i.e., inner insecurities about their functional abilities. The excessive attention to the impressions made upon others reflects an inability to understand or to take responsibility for internal motives and feelings. It also serves a defensive role, permitting the individual to avoid and ignore his own opinions, wishes, and feelings—especially hostile or fearful ones. Histrionic people will often evoke protective or directive responses, for example, by

displays of emotion. The protection or direction thus attained will, in turn, support their dependency, help them to avoid responsibility, and reinforce their insecurities.

Epidemiology and course. The prevalence of histrionic personality disorder is unknown. It is more commonly diagnosed in females, though research suggests that it may be equally prevalent in males. Possibly this is because characterizations such as "seductive," "superficial charm," and "appealing" have feminine connotations in Western societies. Histrionic traits become increasingly socially conspicuous and maladaptive with advancing age. Inner insecurities and inconsistencies are often revealed when the histrionic person is confronted with the pragmatic routines involved in being a parent or spouse. Because the histrionic person has often depended on being found seductive or charming by others, such individuals often turn to fantasized or actual infidelity, or to hypochondriacal preoccupations.

Etiology. Unlike the symptoms of the hysterical neurotic, which Freud attributed to oedipal conflicts, i.e., unconscious guilt about incestuous impulses, the more dysfunctional symptoms of histrionic personality disorder (called "primitive" or "oral" hysteria in earlier literature) are thought to stem from insufficiency and disapproval in the early mother-child relationship. Adult patients often identify a familial pattern in which the mother's failures caused them to turn to their father for nurturance, which is offered in response to the child's excessively dramatic behavior and emotional displays (Hollander, 1971). Development of the disorder is likely effected by a heritable temperament that favors extraversion, expressiveness, and attention seeking. Family history studies suggest a prevalence of antisocial and alcoholic problems in relatives.

Treatment. Dynamic therapies of variable duration and intensity are the major therapeutic vehicle. Horowitz (1995) advocates integrating cognitive behavioral methods to clarify irrational cognitions, and systematically disrupting maladaptive expressions of emotion while reinforcing adaptive actions is important. Histrionic patients often have problems terminating short-term therapy on schedule, whereas psychoanalysis often requires the use of extensive parameters (for example, talks with medical doctors or meeting with spouses). Therapists can anticipate that the patient will use seductive overtures reflexively, including rapid insights and acclaim for the therapist's skill, in the hope of winning the therapist's affection, though these can easily distract from the stated goals of the therapy. These goals include diminishing the histrionic patient's excessive emotional reactivity to others and deployment of vague externalized rationalizations. Therapists need to insist that histrionic patients attend to, value, and express their own feelings, opinions, and motives, all the while requiring clarification of "what exactly do you mean?" The therapist will need to clarify and interpret the patient-therapist interaction from the beginning of therapy. Rather than interpreting the patient's overly dramatic or shallow behavior, therapists should empathically ask for more facts and more detail, helping patients structure their experience.

Both couples therapy and group therapy are often useful. The tendencies of histrionic patients to adapt themselves in a complementary way to what they perceive as the wishes of others and to cling dependently to them can be readily identified and confronted in these treatment settings. Such treatments also provide an opportunity to attain ongoing extratherapeutic supports for change.

Institutional and pharmacologic therapies do not have significant roles in the treatment of histrionic patients.

Avoidant Personality Disorder

Definition. The essential feature of avoidant personality disorder is the fearful avoidance of persons or situations when a risk of failure, rejection, or strong emotions can be foreseen. Coexisting with a fearful, shy, and self-effacing demeanor, however, are strong desires for relationships and accomplishments.

This category is linked to Fenichel's (1945) category of phobic personality. In DSM-III a single trait, interpersonal avoidance because of fear of rejection, was highlighted. The definition has now been expanded to include avoidance of situations and strong feelings and, in contrast to schizoid personality, a conscious wish to be more social. Since this category's inclusion in DSM-III, it has gradually assumed wider recognition and is now acknowledged to be quite common in clinical populations.

Psychodynamics. People with this disorder avoid risky situations to diminish anxiety associated with potential disappointment, rejection, or failure. This behavior may be caused by an exaggerated desire for acceptance, an intolerance of criticism or inaccuracies (i.e., perfectionism), or a willingness to constrict one's life to maintain a sense of control.

Epidemiology and course. Although its prevalence in the population is believed to be only about 1%, avoidant personality disorder is common in both inpatient and outpatient settings (5–15%). This syndrome is found among a broad spectrum of psychiatric patients but especially in patients with depression, post-traumatic stress disorder (PTSD), and the anxiety disorders. Clinicians rarely employ this as a primary diagnosis, and no information is available on its course or stability.

Etiology. A temperamental predisposition involving being highly anxious and self-conscious (neuroticism), shy, harm-avoidant, or unreceptive to new experiences may precede the defensive elaboration of this trait into a personality type.

Treatment. A wide variety of psychotherapeutic treatments can benefit such individuals. Generally the goals are to help patients confront what they avoid at a pace they can learn from. Short-term psychotherapy using supportive and directive methods may be effective. Behavior modification aimed at desensitizing patients in specific situations that elicit phobic avoidance can be useful. Group therapy and other therapies emphasizing socialization skills with peers can also help. Pharmacotherapies are rarely needed and are usually feared by avoidant patients.

Dependent Personality Disorder

Definition. The essential feature of dependent personality disorder is an excessive need to be taken care of. This will usually manifest as submissiveness, seeking and accepting direction from others, and a persistent need for reassurance. A sense of inferiority, self-doubt, suggestibility, and lack of perseverance are additional characteristics.

This category is linked to early psychoanalytic theories and in previous editions of the DSM was called passive-dependent personality. Dependency has emerged as a major dimension of interpersonal relationships in studies of both normal and pathological personalities.

Psychodynamics. Dependent behaviors allow individuals to dissociate their own aggressive or assertive impulses. Such behaviors reflect not only fear of the consequence of self-assertion (rejection or criticism) but also the wish to ingratiate oneself with and bind others through guilt and indebtedness for services.

Epidemiology and course. No data are available on its prevalence as a specific type of personality disorder, but it often co-occurs with many other psychiatric and medical conditions. In these instances it may have developed as a consequence of prolonged disability. It is about 3 times more common in women than in men. As a primary diagnosis it is more apt to occur in outpatients. Patients with this disorder will present for psychiatric treatment with major symptomatic disturbances such as substance abuse, depression, and anxiety. Because of the severity of somatic symptoms, medical hospitalizations are also common. Little is known about the course of this disorder.

Etiology. Dependent personality disorder is thought to stem from overintrusive, oversolicitous early parenting combined with criticism or rejection of the child's signs of assertiveness and independence. Early theorists such as Freud (1908) and Abraham (1949) focused on the "oral" stage of development, but it is now recognized that ongoing reinforcement patterns that are not phase specific are important in the development of this personality type. Kagan and Moss (1960) have shown that dependent behaviors observed at ages 6–10 are likely to continue into young adulthood, and that such continuity is more common in females than in males.

Submissiveness in attachment behaviors may be a genetically determined or temperamental factor that could predispose an individual to the development of dependent personality disorder.

Treatment. Dependent patients are responsive to a broad range of psychological treatments. Both dynamic and behavioral therapies support the patient's need to bear the anxiety of making decisions and asserting his own wishes. Dynamic therapies vary in the amount of attention they give to examination and interpretation of the dependency manifested in the transference. Although the duration of psychotherapies may be quite variable, short-term treatments are frequently successful. In any event, therapists use the dependent patient's readiness to please as leverage to get him involved in anxiety-provoking situations involving assertiveness and independence elsewhere in his life.

Pharmacotherapies have no known effectiveness in the treatment of such patients, and institutional treatments are contraindicated, unless required by a comorbid major illness, because they inevitably reinforce passivity and dependency.

Obsessive-Compulsive Personality Disorder

Definition. The essential feature of obsessive-compulsive personality disorder is preoccupation with mental and interpersonal control and orderliness at the expense of flexibility and openness. This trait is manifested by a restricted ability to express strong emotions and by orderliness, parsimony, and obstinacy. Obsessive-compulsive persons constantly struggle between compliance and defiance—a struggle that is evident cognitively in indecision and interpersonally in control struggles. They are fearful of situations or feelings that are unfamiliar or intense or that threaten their sense of control. This diagnosis is widely used clinically, has become a stable component of the diagnostic system, and its diagnostic integrity has been well-established. It emerges as a wide range of conceptual and empirical schemes as a distinct dimension involving conscientiousness, persistence, and intellectual and/or cognitive reliance.

Psychodynamics. Early psychoanalysts (Freud, 1908; Abraham, 1949) proposed that prolonged and exaggerated toilet training struggles give way to the "anal triad" of character traits: obstinacy, parsimony, and orderliness. These theories proposed that the obsessive-compulsive character develops from defensive efforts to control unacceptable aggressive (defiant, controlling, sadistic) impulses. Later formulations added that obsessive-compulsive traits such as indecision and perfectionism originate in struggles between mother and child in which the child alternates between defiance and guilty fear. Major defenses, in addition to the obsessive thinking and compulsive actions, are reaction formation, isolation, and undoing.

Epidemiology and course. The limited data on the epidemiology of obsessive-compulsive personality disorder indicate a prevalence of less than 1% in the general population and that it occurs about twice as often in men as in women. It is no more prevalent among people with higher educations or IQs than among others. In clinical populations it is unusual among inpatients but more common among outpatients.

Etiology. Early psychoanalytic theories proposed that this personality type arose in the struggles of the child and the parents around issues of control, authority, and autonomy during the so-called anal phase, ages 2–4 of development. More recent studies have raised the possibility that hypersensitivity to change (high arousal secondary to novel situations) or even the excessive need for organization and control may be phenotypic variants expressions of a genetically determined dimension of personality.

Treatment. The preferred treatment of obsessive-compulsive personality disorder is usually dynamic psychotherapy, including psychoanalysis. Struggles over control, affectless recitations, and the wish for tidy, perfectionistic formulas are issues that the therapist commonly encounters. Psychoanalysis may be effective in bringing about a profound change in the defensive structure of some individuals. Cognitive therapies for obsessive-compulsive patients are increasingly being used to identify and modify rigid cognitive schemata and to learn techniques for interrupting obsessional preoccupations. Short-term dynamically oriented group therapy with a focus on the current situation and the use of confrontation can allow the patients to identify and decipher the source of feelings and to overcome inhibitions toward decisions or change.

Recent interest in pharmacotherapy has led to promising but variable claims. Results remain too inconclusive to justify endorsing a role for medications at present.

Other Personality Disorders

Categories of personality disorder that are surrounded by controversy and lack sufficient empirical support to justify inclusion in DSM-IV have been listed in Appendix B. In DSM-III-R this appendix included self-defeating (masochistic) and sadistic personality disorder. Both are now gone. New categories include depressive personality disorder and passive-aggressive (negativistic) personality disorder. While the latter was a diagnosis in prior editions, it required an expanded definition to cover multiple areas of functioning, and when this was done, it then lacked sufficient empirical or clinical support. Depressive personality is a diagnosis with great historical significance, and its appearance in the appendix is a testimonial to its conceptual significance and to promising, albeit still insufficient, research support. Future classification systems will include these 2 disorders if further study confirms their validity and clinical value.

Passive-Aggressive (Negativistic) Personality Disorder

Definition. The essential feature of passive-aggressive personality disorder is passive resistance (covert noncompliance) to demands for social and occupational performance. More so than in other personality disorders, this pattern may be context dependent, appearing only in certain situations.

Although this category has been included in every diagnostic system since DSM-I, and it is widely recognized, its dependence on situational stressors, its failure to be verified in clinical factor analytic studies, and the fact that the prior criteria set defined a specific trait rather than a constellation of concurrent traits led to this disorder's "demotion" to the appendix in DSM-IV. Its definition now has been expanded to include a broader range of "negativistic" traits that include interpersonal and self-concept criteria.

Psychodynamics. As suggested by the name, the principal dynamic consists of aggressive impulses and motives expressed by passivity, that is, inaction, obstructionism, procrastination, and inefficiency. It is essentially an interpersonal dynamic: its recognition depends on the seemingly unjustified frustration and hostility others feel toward such individuals. The passive-aggressive person's verbal expressions of compliance or agreement conceal his actual noncompliance and the secret sadistic satisfaction he derives from the frustration he thereby causes. This dynamic involving inhibitions and conflict about hostility links this disorder with masochistic and depressive personality disorders. The ambivalence and indecision found in passive-aggressive disorder is similar to that observed in obsessive-compulsive persons, who may appear similarly obstructionistic, but these disorders can be distinguished because the latter group is not motivated by a wish to evoke frustration in others.

Epidemiology and course. The prevalence of this disorder is low. As a primary clinical diagnosis it is rare. Passive-aggressive behaviors, however, are highly common, especially where there is a hierarchy of authority and power.

Small et al. (1970) followed 100 inpatients diagnosed as passive-aggressive for 10–15 years. They found that these patients remained irritable, anxious, and depressed; had many somatic complaints; and experienced significant dysfunction at work and in their relationships. It is difficult to generalize from their findings, however, because it seems likely that many of their patients would now be given other Axis II diagnoses.

Etiology. The little that has been written about the etiology of passive-aggressive personality disorder focuses on disturbed parent-child interactions in which struggles over self-assertion and control are prominent.

Treatment. Individual psychotherapy is generally considered the treatment of choice. Therapists must be ready to confront and interpret the patient's inevitable (conscious and unconscious) efforts to frustrate the agreed-upon goals and to resist the contractual framework under which therapy was established.

Short-term psychotherapy and group therapy are often sufficient for identifying, interpreting, and clarifying the reasons for the maladaptive aspects of passive-aggressive behaviors. If the trait is broadly displayed and causes severe dysfunction, more extensive dynamically oriented therapies, including psychoanalysis, may be indicated.

Behavioral therapy techniques directed at assertiveness training can be useful. There is no pharmacotherapy of known usefulness for this condition; and because compliance problems should be expected, medications may be contraindicated.

Depressive Personality Disorder

Definition. The essential feature of depressive personality disorder is the predominantly negative thoughts and feelings that these individuals experience, associated with a relative inability to experience enthusiasm or pleasure across a wide variety of situations.

The origins of this disorder can be traced to Hippocrates' melancholic temperament. It was revived by German phenomenologists, most notably Kurt Schneider (1958), and it has been present in the ICD-9 and ICD-10 as a variant of depressive disorder.

Psychodynamics. Being aware of negative (often hostile or critical) thoughts and feelings, but then believing that such thoughts and feelings are wrong, leads to reaction formations that take the form of persistent self-criticisms, anxiety, self-consciousness, and defensiveness.

Epidemiology and course. Prevalence of this disorder has not been studied. Existing research makes it clear that it exists in many nonclinical subjects, who, though impaired, have often had no treatment (Klein and Miller, 1993). It is believed to originate early in life and to become consolidated into a stable constellation of traits only in adult years. Its stability over time has been shown for 1 year and is not modified by comorbid major depressive episodes.

Etiology. Little is known but much has been theorized about the origins of this disorder. Akiskal (1992), following Hippocrates, identifies it as a heritable subaffective temperament that, like cyclothymic personality, may be adaptive or normal in some situations, but at its extreme is dysfunctional. Whether dysfunctional or not, it reflects a type of vulnerability to major affective disorders. A related construct derived from academic psychology is the dimension of neuroticism. In contrast, psychoanalysts have identified this as a type of neurotic character, a type that Kernberg (1984) argues is a close cousin to masochistic (self-defeating) personality disorder. As such it is thought to have its origins in early developmental experiences that inhibit expression of anger and encourage affects such as guilt and shame as being evidence of virtue and requirements for lovability.

Treatment. Nothing is known about treatment, but the competing themes of etiology suggest a wide range of possibilities. There may be instances where psychodynamic therapies, including psychoanalysis, could be appropriate. Alternately, this disorder may be so genetically determined as to be relatively unchangeable by any means. The third possibility is that it will be discovered to have associated neurophysiological abnormalities that prove responsive to pharmacotherapies.

This chapter has reviewed the current diagnostic categories for personality disorders found in DSM-IV. Notable progress is being made in developing better definitions for these categories and in providing scientific bases for their validity. The types of personality disorder are clustered in DSM-IV by descriptive similarities. It is expected that the future system of classifying personality disorders will reflect ongoing research in ways that will integrate descriptive features with level of severity, knowledge about spectrum relationships with Axis I disorders, and the dimensions of personality found in normal personality.

References

Abraham, K. 1949. *Selected papers on psychoanalysis (1921–1925)*. London: Hogarth Press.

Adler, G., and Buie, D. 1979. Aloneness and borderline psychopathology: the possible relevance of child development issues. *Int. J. Psychoanal.* 60:83–96.

Akiskal, H. S. 1992. The distinctive mixed states of bipolar I, II, and III. *Clin. Neuropharmacol.* 15(suppl.):632A–633A.

Beck, A. T., and Freeman, A. 1990. *Cognitive theory of personality disorders.* New York: Guilford Press.

Cattell, R. 1965. *The scientific analysis of personality.* Chicago: Aldine.

Cleckley, H. 1964. *The mask of sanity,* 4th ed. St. Louis: C. V. Mosby.

Cloninger, C. R., Svrakic, D. M., and Pyzybeck, T. R. 1993. A psychological model of temperament and character. *Arch. Gen. Psychiatry* 50:975.

Costa, P. T., and McCrae, R. R. 1990. Personality disorders and the five factor model of personality. *J. Personality Disorders* 4:362–371.

Eysenck, H. J. 1952. *The scientific study of personality.* London: Routledge and Kegan Paul.

Fenichel, O. 1945. *The psychoanalytic theory of the neurosis.* New York: Norton.

Freud, S. 1908. *Character and anal erotism.* In *Standard edition,* ed. J. Strachey. Vol. 9. London: Hogarth Press, 1959.

Goldberg, S., Schulz, S., Schulz, P., Resnick, R., Hamer, R., Friedel, R. 1986. Borderline and schizotypal personality disorders treated with low dose thiothixene versus placebo. *Arch. Gen. Psychiatry* 43:680–686.

Gunderson, J. G. 1984. *Borderline personality disorder.* Washington, D.C.: American Psychiatric Press.

——— 1992. Severe personality disorders: diagnostic controversies. In *Annual review of psychiatry,* ed. A. Tasman and M. B. Riba. Vol. 1. Washington, D.C.: American Psychiatric Press. 9–24.

Gunderson, J. G., and Sabo, A. 1993. The phenemonological and conceptual interface of borderline posttraumatic stress disorder. *Am. J. Psychiatry* 150:19–27.

Gunderson, J. G., Triebwasser, J. T., Phillips, K. A., Sullivan, C. N. 1996. Personality and vulnerability to affective disorders. In *Personality and psychopathology,* ed. R. Cloninger. Washington, D.C.: American Psychiatric Press.

Hollander, M. 1971. The hysterical personality. *Contemp. Psychiatry* 1:17–24.

Horowitz, M. J. 1995. Histrionic personality disorder. In *Treatments of psychiatric disorders,* ed. G. Gabbard. Washington, D.C.: American Psychiatric Press. 2312–26.

Jones, M. 1956. The concept of a therapeutic community. *Am. J. Psychiatry* 112:647–650.

Kagan, J., and Moss, H. 1960. The stability of passive and dependent behavior from childhood through adulthood. *Child Dev.* 31:577–591.

Kernberg, O. 1975. *Borderline conditions and pathological narcissism.* New York: Aronson.

——— 1984. *Severe personality disorder.* New Haven: Yale University Press.

Klein, D. N., and Miller, G. A. 1993. Depressive personality in a nonclinical sample. *Am. J. Psychiatry* 150:1718–24.

Kohut, H. 1971. *The analysis of self.* New York: International Universities Press.

Kretschmer, E. 1925. *Physique and character.* London: Kegan Paul.

Lazare, A., Klerman, G., and Armor, D. 1966. Oral, obsessive, and hysterical patterns: an investigation of psychoanalytic concepts by means of factor analysis. *Arch. Gen. Psychiatry* 14:624.

Leary, T. 1957. *Interpersonal diagnosis of personality: a functional theory and methodology for personality evaluation.* New York: Ronald Press.

Livesley, J. W., Jang, K. L., Jackson D. N., Vernon, P. A. 1993. Genetic and environmental contributions to dimensions of personality disorder. *Am. J. Psychiatry* 150:1826.

Loranger, A. W., Sartorius, N., Andreoli, A., Berger, P., Dickstra, R. F. W., Ferguson, B., Jacobsberg, L. B., Mombour, W., Pull, C., Ono, Y., Regier, D. A. 1994. International personality disorder examination. WHO/ADAMHA. *International Pilot Study of Personality Disorders* 51:215–224.

Masterson, J. 1972. *Treatment of the borderline adolescent: a developmental approach.* New York: Wiley.

McGlashan, T. H. 1986. The Chestnut Lodge follow-up study. *Arch. Gen. Psychiatry* 43:20–30.

Millon, T. 1981. *Disorders of personality: DSM-III Axis II.* New York: Wiley.

——— 1995. *Disorders of personality: DSM-IV and beyond.* New York: Wiley.

Modell, A. H. 1975. A narcissistic defense against affects and the illusion of self-sufficiency. *Int. J. Psychoanal.* 56:275–282.

Presley, A., and Walton, H. 1973. Dimensions of abnormal personality. *Br. J. Psychiatry* 122:269–276.

Reich, W. 1949. *Character analysis.* New York: Orgone Institute Press.

Reiss, D., Hetherington, E. M., Plomin, R., Howe, G. W., Simmens, S. J., Henderson, S. H., O'Connor, T. J., Bussell, D. A., Anderson, E. R., Law, T. 1995. Genetic questions for environmental studies: differential parenting and psychopathology in adolescence. *Arch. G. Psychiatry* 52:925–936.

Rinsley, D. 1965. Intensive psychiatric hospital treatment of adolescents. *Psychiatr. Q.* 39:405–429.

Robins, L. N. 1966. *Deviant children grown up: a sociological and psychiatric study of sociopathic personality.* Baltimore: Williams & Wilkins.

Ronningstam, E. R., Gunderson, J. G., and Lyons, M. 1995. Changes in pathological narcissism. *Am. J. Psychiatry* 152:253–257.

Rutter, M. 1987. Temperament, personality and personality disorder. *Br. J. Psychiatry* 150:443–458.

Schneider, K. 1958. *Psychopathic personalities.* Springfield, Ill.: Thomas.

Shapiro, D. 1965. *Neurotic styles.* New York: Basic Books.

Sheldon, W. H. 1940. *The varieties of human physique: an introduction to constitutional psychology.* New York: Harper.

Siever, L. J., and Davis, K. L. 1991. A psychobiological perspective on the personality disorders. *Am. J. Psychiatry.* 148:1647–58.

Small, I. F., Small, J. G., Alig, V. B., Moore, D. F. 1970. Passive-aggressive personality disorder: a search for a syndrome. *Am. J. Psychiatry* 126:973–983.

Soloff, P. 1993. Pharmacological therapies of borderline personality disorder. In *Borderline personality disorder: etiology and treatment,* ed. J. Paris. Washington, D.C.: American Psychiatric Press. 319–348.

Stone, M. 1993. *Abnormalities of personality: within and beyond the realm of treatment.* New York: W. W. Norton and Co.

Sturup, G. K. 1978. Changing patterns of treatment. *Bull. Am. Acad. Psychiatry Law* 6:176–194.

Thomas, A., and Chess, S. 1984. Genesis and evolution of behavioral disorders: from infancy to early adult life. *Am. J. Psychiatry* 141:1–9.

Torgersen, S. 1984. Genetic and nosologic aspects of schizotypal and borderline disorders: a twin study. *Arch. Gen. Psychiatry* 41:546–554.

Tyrer, P., and Alexander, J. 1979. Classification of personality disorder. *Br. J. Psychiatry* 135:163–167.

Tyrer, P., Gunderson, J. G., Lyons, M., and Tohen, M. 1996. The extent of comorbidity between mental state and personality disorders. In *New perspectives in personality disorders,* ed. P. Pilkonis. New York: Guilford Press.

Vaillant, G. E. 1977. *Adaptation to life.* Boston: Little, Brown.

Waldinger, R., and Gunderson, J. G. 1987. *Effective psychotherapy with borderline patients.* Washington, D. C.: American Psychiatric Press.

Weissman, M. 1993. The epidemiology of personality disorder: a 1990 update. *J. Pers. Dis.* 7(suppl.):44–62.

Recommended Reading

Gunderson, J. G. 1984. *Borderline personality disorder.* Washington, D.C.: American Psychiatric Press.

Gunderson, J. G., and Gabbard, G. O., eds. 1995. Personality disorders. In *Treatments of psychiatric disorders,* ed. G. Gabbard. Vol. 2. Washington, D.C.: American Psychiatric Press. 2243–93.

Kernberg, O. 1985. *Severe personality disorders.* New Haven: Yale University Press.

Livesley, J. W., ed. 1995. *The DSM-IV personality disorders.* New York: Guilford Press.

Millon, T. 1995. *Disorders of personality: DSM-IV and beyond.* New York: Wiley.

Siever, L. J., and Davis, K. L. 1991. A psychobiological perspective on the personality disorders. *Am. J. Psychiatry* 148:1647.

Stone, M. 1993. *Abnormalities of personality: within and beyond the realm of treatment.* New York: W. W. Norton and Co.

Thomas, A., and Chess, S. 1984. Genesis and evolution of behavioral disorders: from infancy to early adult life. *Am. J. Psychiatry* 141:1–9.

Vaillant, G. E. 1994. *The wisdom of the ego.* Boston: Little, Brown.

RALPH A. NIXON
MARILYN S. ALBERT

Disorders of Cognition

Cognition encompasses the realms of memory, attention, language, visuospatial ability, conceptualization, and general intelligence. In cognitive disorders, disturbances of memory are common, but alterations in the other spheres of cognition are often present and may even dominate the clinical picture. A systematic approach to evaluating the various cognitive faculties is therefore key to distinguishing among the three major classes of cognitive disorder described in the *Diagnostic and Statistical Manual of Mental Disorders,* fourth edition (DSM-IV): dementia, delirium, and amnestic disorder. Dementia is characterized by a chronic decline in multiple cognitive functions occurring in clear consciousness. Delirium is a global decline in cognitive function, accompanied by alterations in consciousness and attention. Amnestic disorder is a disability in learning new information or recalling previously leaarned information in the absence of other intellectual deficits. Collectively, the cognitive disorders are among the most commonly encountered psychiatric conditions in the elderly. As many as one-fourth of hospitalized patients over the age of 65 develop delirium. More than half of all the beds in nursing homes are occupied by individuals suffering from dementia. Their number may grow to nearly 9 million by the year 2000 and will nearly double by the year 2030 as the percentage of the total population reaching the age of 65 increases. Countering these sober projections, however, are the strides that have been made toward refining the differential diagnosis of cognitive disorders and understanding the genetics and pathophysiology of these cognitive conditions. Because the prospects for effectively treating individual conditions are now bright and increasingly immediate, recognizing cognitive disturbances in clinical practice and distinguishing among the possible causes is more critical than ever. In this chapter we first describe a general approach to the medical and psychiatric evaluation of individuals who present with cognitive disturbances and show how a detailed cognitive assessment can aid in the differential diagnosis. Next, we describe features of the major cognitive disorders, following the classification system described in the DSM-IV and a general approach to their management. Specific etiologies of dementia are considered in some detail, the more common of which have received the greatest attention.

A patient with dementia experiences a chronic and substantial decline in 2 or more areas of cognitive function. Dementia, therefore, differs from syndromes, such as amnesia and aphasia, in which significant cognitive decline is primarily limited to 1 major area of ability (e.g., memory or language).

Approximately 50 disorders are known to cause dementia (Table 16.1). Some forms of dementia are extremely common, particularly within specific age ranges. For example, there is general agreement that the prevalence of Alzheimer's disease among individuals over 85 years of age is at least 25% (REF); some studies indicate that the prevalence may be as high as 48% (REF). Moreover, dementing disorders produce a considerable personal and financial toll, since the affected individual is commonly sick for many years and must be cared for by others. Although, at the present time, few dementing disorders can be prevented from progressing, the welfare of most dementing patients can be improved with good management. Thus, this chapter will focus on how to identify and manage dementing conditions.

Diagnostic Features of Dementia

The definition of dementia in DSM-IV is somewhat different from that in previous editions. It has been simplified, and now emphasizes that memory impairment is a necessary but not sufficient sign of the syndrome. At least 1 of the following additional findings must also be present: aphasia (language disturbance), apraxia (impaired ability to perform motor activities despite intact motor function), agnosia (failure to recognize or identify objects despite intact sensory function), or disturbances of executive function (including the ability to think abstractly as well as to plan, initiate, sequence, monitor, and stop complex behavior). The cognitive deficits must be sufficiently severe to cause impairment in occupational or social functioning. The diagnosis of dementia should not be made unless it is clear that the cognitive status of the individual has declined from a previously higher level of function and that the symptoms are not solely apparent during an episode of delirium.

Impaired judgment, poor insight, and personality change (which previously were primary diagnostic features) are now considered "associated features." Other associated characteristics include psychiatric symptoms,

Table 16.1 Dementia: Diagnosis by categories with representative examples

Degenerative
Dementia of Alzheimer's Type
Frontal Lobe Dementia with/without Motor
    Neuron Disease
Pick's Disease
Diffuse Cortical Lewy Body Disease
Corticobasal Degeneration
Huntington's Disease
Wilson's Disease
Parkinson's Disease
Multiple System Atrophy
Progressive Supranuclear Palsy

Psychiatric
Pseudo-dementia of Depression

Vascular
Vascular Dementia
Binswanger's Encephalopathy
Amyloid Dementia
Diffuse Hypoxic/Ischemic Injury

Obstructive
Normal Pressure Hydrocephalus
Obstructive Hydrocephalus

Traumatic
Chronic Subdural Hematoma
Dementia Pugilistica
Post-concussion Syndrome

Neoplastic
Tumor—Malignant—1o/2o
Tumor—Benign—e.g., Frontal Meningioma
Paraneoplastic Limbic Encephalitis

Infectious
Chronic Meningitis (e.g., TB)
Post Herpes Encephalitis
Focal Cerebritis/Abscesses
HIV Dementia
HIV-associated Infection
Syphilis
Lyme Encephalopathy
Subacute Sclerosing Panencephalitis
Creutzfeldt-Jakob Disease
Progressive Multifocal Leukoencephalopathy
Parenchymal Sarcoidosis
Chronic Systemic Infection

Demyelinating
Multiple Sclerosis
Adrenoleukodystrophy
Metachromatic Leukodystrophy

Autoimmune
Systemic Lupus Erythematosis
Polyarteritis Nodosa

Drugs/Toxins
  Medications:
    Anticholinergics
    Antihistamines
    Anticonvulsants
    Beta-blockers
    Sedative-hypnotics

Substance Abuse:
Alcohol
Inhalants
PCP

Toxins:
Arsenic
Bromide
Carbon monoxide
Lead
Mercury
Organophosphates

e.g., persecutory delusions and hallucinations (particularly visual). Motor disturbances (e.g., falls, ataxia, and extrapyramidal signs), as well as dysarthria or slurred speech, may be associated with certain dementing disorders.

Dementia of the Alzheimer Type

Because of the prevalence of Alzheimer's disease (AD), DSM-IV provides a separate diagnostic subsection for this disorder. The subsection is labeled Dementia of the Alzheimer Type (DAT), to emphasize that a definite diagnosis of AD cannot currently be made without obtaining brain tissue for examinination. Therefore the diagnosis is generally considered presumptive. To make this diagnosis during life, the clinician must conduct a comprehensive evaluation (Table 16.2) to rule out other causes of cognitive decline and to determine whether the symptoms and course are characteristic of AD (Figure 16.1).

Vascular Dementia

The term *vascular dementia* now replaces the term *multi-infarct dementia*. Vascular causes account for the second most common form of dementia, but it is still far less common than AD. Moreover, patients with AD commonly have coexisting vascular disease, which often exacerbate their symptoms.

Dementia Due to Other Medical Conditions

This subsection of DSM-IV includes a broad range of disorders that are etiologically associated with a dementia: structural lesions; trauma; infections; endocrine, nutritional, and metabolic disorders; and autoimmune diseases. In addition, certain disorders principally affecting brain tissue are included in this section. Dementias due to Pick's disease, Parkinson's disease, Huntington's disease, and Creutzfeldt-Jakob disease are represented here.

Substance-Induced Persisting Dementia

To establish a diagnosis of substance-induced persisting dementia, there must be evidence through history, physical, or laboratory data that cognitive deficits consistent with dementia are probably caused by the substance. The term *persisting* is important since the diagnosis cannot be made during a period of acute intoxication or during withdrawal. The most common cause of this type of disorder is chronic alcohol abuse, but toxins, poisons, inhal-

ants, sedatives-hypnotics, and other medications are included in this section. If one suspects AD in an individual with substance abuse problems, it is essential to eliminate the abuse before a diagnosis of AD can be made.

Dementia Due to Multiple Etiologies

The final diagnostic subsection of the DSM-IV emphasizes that a patient can have more than 1 cause of cognitive decline. While many combinations occur, the most common is the coexistence of DAT and vascular disease. Some authorities refute this assertion, suggesting that diffuse Lewy body disease is the second most common dementing disorder and that its combination with DAT is not sufficiently recognized. However, a recent interna-

Table 16.2 Recommended laboratory studies in dementia workup

Blood studies
Complete blood count
B_{12}
Folate
Sedimentation rate
Glucose
Calcium
Phosphorus
Magnesium
Electrolytes
Liver function tests
Thyroid-stimulating hormone
Creatinine, Blood urea nitrogen
Cholesterol (high density lipoprotein/low density
   lipoprotein)
Triglycerides
Syphilis serology

Urinalysis

Other studies
Electrocardiogram
Computed axial tomography or Magnetic resonance
   imaging

**Representative additional studies based on history and
   physical findings**
Chest x-ray
Electroencephalogram
Noninvasive carotid studies
Human immunodeficiency virus testing
Rheumatoid factor, Anti-nuclear antibody, and other
   autoimmune disorder screens
Lumbar puncture
Drug levels
Heavy metal screening

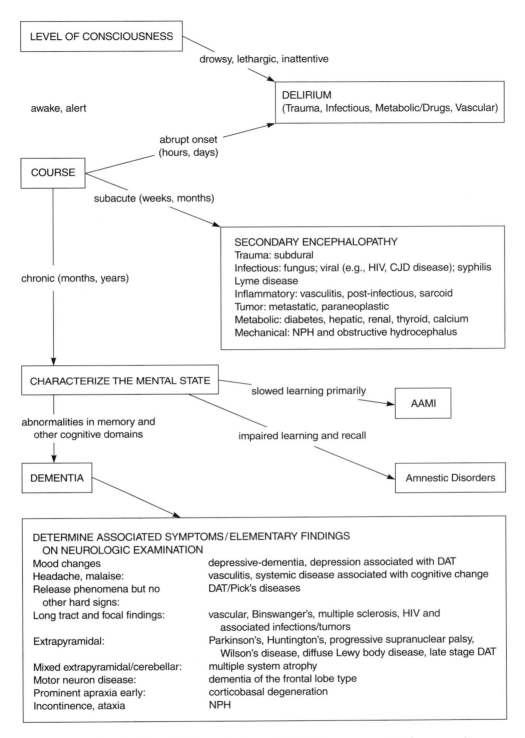

Figure 16.1 An algorithm for dementia diagnosis. AAMI = age-associated memory impairment; HIV = human immunodeficiency virus; CJD = Creutzfeldt-Jakob disease; DAT = dementia of the Alzheimer's type; NPH = normal pressure hydrocephalus. *Source:* Adapted with permission from J. D. Schmahmann, "Neurobehavioral manifestations of focal cerebral lesions," presented at the Massachusetts General Hospital course in Geriatric Psychiatry, Boston, September 1995.

tional conference estimated the prevalence of pure Lewy body disease (in the absence of AD) at 3% of dementia patients.

Scores of specific disorders can cause dementia (see Table 16.1). The clinician cannot have in-depth knowledge of all, but can identify common/typical and rare/unusual presentations. In addition, certain associated findings on examination can direct the consultant to particular diagnoses (see Figure 16.1).

Evaluation of Dementia

Dementia, or brain failure, deserves at least as careful an assessment as the failure of any other organ. Only through thoughtful evaluation will remediation of the cognitive decline be possible.

The evaluation requires a reliable history (cognitive, medical, psychiatric, and family), complete medical and neurological examinations, appropriate laboratory testing, and assessments of mental status and cognitive function.

History

Cognitive history, taken by a skilled clinician, is an extremely sensitive diagnostic tool. Onset, course, and associated symptoms must be elicited carefully because these details of history are often the most important diagnostic clues. A good cognitive history must establish the time at which cognitive changes first became apparent. Because some diseases are well known for their particularly rapid rate of decline, any suggestion that the symptoms began within the year should be very carefully explored. The clinician must also determine the nature of the cognitive and/or behavioral changes evident when the disease began. Since the primary progressive dementias (which display no characteristic neurologic abnormality early in their course), such as Alzheimer's disease and Pick's disease, are most easily differentiated by the nature of the symptoms at onset, this information is critical to elicit with care. Finally, it is important to determine whether the symptoms came on gradually or suddenly. The onset of delirium, which can be a life-threatening disorder, is generally days or weeks. Thus, the manner in which the symptoms have progressed over time will affect the speed with which the clinician must proceed. Because the cognitive history is so essential to an accurate diagnosis, the patient (who is, by definition, experiencing cognitive problems) should never be the sole informant.

Medical history and medications are important to re-

view. The clinician must consider whether or not identified surgical procedures (e.g., gastrectomy predisposing to B_{12} deficiency) or medical illness (e.g., hypertension or lupus) contribute to the symptoms of cognitive dysfunction. Query regarding blood transfusions (particularly during the early to mid-1980s, when human immunodeficiency virus testing was not readily available), exposure to toxins (such as lead, other heavy metals, carbon monoxide), as well as any history of head trauma is crucial. Careful questioning should cover an alcohol usage history (not just current patterns), including past history of abuse or overuse. Drug history—prescribed, over-the-counter, and illicit—should also be reported. Although making up only 12% of the population, those over the age of 65 are prescribed 30% of all prescription medications. Many non-psychotropic agents, including those sold over-the-counter, can have negative effects on cognition. For example, antihistamines and antispasmodic drugs can cause cognitive difficulties.

Psychiatric history, looking particularly for reports of past mood or psychotic disorder, may assist in the differentiation of cognitive changes observed in depression from those of primary dementing disorder. Although cognitive changes can be seen in depression, the history and mental status examination usually allow one to separate depression and dementia or to suggest that both are present. Neurovegetative symptoms of depression may be difficult to link specifically to mood or cognitive disorder, since anergia, sleep disturbance, and appetite change can be seen in both depression and dementia. Thus, it is important to modify the questions asked to encompass the possibility of cognitive impairment. For example, if the tasks are simplified and within the capabilities of a non-depressed demented patient, the patient will typically be able to carry them out. Similarly, if food is presented in a manner that the patient can manage (e.g., meat cut into bite-size pieces), then the patient may manifest gusto in his eating where none had been seen before (see Table 16.1).

Family history is also helpful for diagnosis. Certain dementing disorders (e.g., Huntington's disease) have definite genetic modes of transmission (e.g., autosomal dominant), while for others (e.g., certain vascular dementias), though the specific mode of transmission may be unclear, their prevalence is much higher in affected families than in the population at large. Recently, several familial subtypes of DAT with genetic loci have been identified. To date, familial subtypes with a dominant mode of transmission affect only those under the age of

60. The majority of patients with DAT appear to have a complex interaction between genetics and other factors.

Medical and Neurological Examination

The consultant should review carefully recent examinations in the medical record to assess their adequacy and accuracy. Typically, the cardiac examination may be fastidious and extensive. In contrast, the neurological examination may be cursory, detailing only elemental findings. The cognitive portion of the examination may note only that the patient is alert and oriented. Additionally, if notes report "disorientation," it is often unclear from the chart whether the patient could not remember the day of the week or whether he was confused or psychotic. Consequently, the psychiatric consultant should look for medical and neurological findings that are associated with dementing disorders. For example, focal areas of muscle weakness and pyramidal signs may suggest vascular dementia. The presence of extrapyramidal movements may point to one of the dementias principally affecting subcortical motor areas. However, mild to moderate DAT may be associated with extrapyramidal symptoms and other neurologic signs. A comprehensive neurologic examination should include careful assessment of ocular function as well as the presence of any frontal release signs.

Laboratory Examination

Table 16.2 lists hematologic and other tests that are typically a part of dementia evaluation. Whenever possible and appropriate, results of prior testing in other settings should be obtained. For example, a chest x-ray or computed axial tomography scan should not be reordered if one was recently done unless an acute change has occurred. Additional tests (e.g., serum copper and ceruloplasmin or serum and urine porphyrins) should be requested if history and examination suggest particular disorders.

Psychiatric Mental Status Examination

The bedside psychiatric examination covers considerable territory but focuses on assessments of affective and psychotic symptoms and signs. One should probe for mood symptoms, irritability, or tearfulness, and nihilistic or suicidal thinking. Depressed elderly patients may, among their somatic complaints, describe decrements in memory. However, depressed patients, as opposed to DAT patients, may perform better on more difficult memory tasks than on simple ones.

Psychotic symptoms can be present in primary psychiatric disorders, such as psychotic depression or schizophrenia, but they can also be associated signs of delirium or dementia. The prevalence of psychosis in moderate to severe DAT is estimated to be in the range of 40–80%. Usually, delusions in patients with DAT are of a paranoid nature, often with the mistaken belief that misplaced items have been stolen. With progression of the disease, the patient may come to believe that spouses are parents or that they are actually impostors (i.e., Capgras syndrome). Illusions and hallucinations, usually of a visual nature, also occur with advanced DAT. For example, some patients describe seeing "little people" entering their homes. Despite such unusual occurrences, not all hallucinations or delusions are troublesome to the patient. Mood and psychotic symptoms can occur as part of the clinical picture of many dementing disorders. Generally, they are nonspecific. However, taken together with other elements of the assessment, such symptoms can provide clues as to whether a psychiatric disorder or a dementing disorder is present.

Cognitive Assessment

Domains of cognitive function that require an accurate bedside assessment include the following: *A*ttention, *C*onceptualization, *A*ppearance/Behavior, *L*anguage, *M*emory, *VIS*uospatial, *A*gnosia and *A*praxia, and *GE*neral intelligence. A useful mnemonic for these critical areas of assessment is: A CALM VISAGE.

Delirium

Delirium, also called an acute confusional state, is by definition a cognitive disorder of acute onset, usually of hours or days. The DSM-IV criteria specify that there must be: (1) a disturbance of consciousness (i.e., reduced clarity of awareness of the environment) with reduced ability to focus, sustain, or shift attention; (2) a change in cognition *or* the development of a perceptual disturbance that is not better accounted for by a preexisting condition (e.g., a dementia, a sensory deficit); (3) a disturbance that develops over a short period of time (usually hours or days) and tends to fluctuate during the course of the day; and (4) evidence from the history, physical examination, or laboratory findings that the disturbance is caused by the direct physiological consequences of the general medical condition (e.g., medication, substance withdrawal, etc.). This definition differs from earlier ones in that associated conditions such as incoherent speech, disturbance of the sleep-wake cycle, or change in psychomotor activity are no longer considered core symptoms.

Since delirium can be confused with a dementia, and rapid treatment of a delirium is essential, it is necessary to differentiate a delirium from a dementia. Some of the hallmark differences are summarized in Table 16.3. However, as emphasized in the DSM-IV criteria, delirium can be superimposed on a preexisting dementia, and therefore the possibility of coexisting conditions must be entertained.

Evaluation and Management of Organic Brain Disorders

Assessment of Cognitive Function by the Clinician

It is neither cost-effective nor optimal for the patient's well-being for a detailed workup to be conducted every time concerns arise about the cognitive status of an elderly individual. Therefore the clinician must develop the means for determining the necessity for further evaluation. The ideal way to accomplish this is for the clinician to incorporate brief cognitive testing into the regular clinical evaluation, as an initial means of assessing mental abilities in the patient. If this is done prior to complaints of cognitive change, the baseline evaluation can serve as a standard against which all other testing can be compared. Non-standard testing, developed by the clinician, can be used for this purpose. Alternatively, there are a va-

riety of standardized, but brief, mental status tests that can be employed. The most commonly used screening tests are the Mini-Mental State Exam (Folstein, Folstein, and McHugh, 1975), the Blessed Dementia Scale (Blessed, Tomlinson, and Roth, 1968) and the Short Portable Mental Status Questionnaire (Pfeiffer, 1975). All have high test-retest reliability and are relatively brief to administer (5–15 minutes).

Of these, the Mini-Mental State Exam (MMSE) is most commonly used in clinical settings. It is excellent for this purpose because it assesses a broad range of cognitive abilities (including memory, language, spatial ability, and set-shifting) in a simple and straightforward manner. The other screening tests mentioned above primarily evaluate memory and orientation. The wide use of the MMSE in epidemiologic studies has yielded cutoff scores that facilitate the identification of patients with cognitive dysfunction. The other screening tests have been applied in a variety of experimental settings, but epidemiologic data are limited. Finally, the extensive use of the MMSE has produced widespread familiarity with its scoring system, facilitating communication among clinicians. For all of these reasons, the MMSE seems most appropriate for inclusion in the standard clinical evaluation of a patient.

Scores on the MMSE range from 0–30. Scores above 26 are generally considered to be excellent and reflective of normal cognitive function. Mildly impaired patients typically obtain scores of 20–26, moderate impairment is reflected by scores of 11–20, and severe impairment by scores of 10 or below. A cutoff score of 23 is generally recommended as indicative of cognitive dysfunction. How-

Table 16.3 Clinical features of delirium, depression, and dementia of the Alzheimer's type

	Delirium	Depression	Dementia of the Alzheimer's Type
Onset	Abrupt	Relatively discrete	Insidious
Initial symptoms	Difficulty with attention and disturbed consciousness	Dysphoric mood or lack of pleasure	Memory deficits— verbal and/or spatial
Course	Fluctuating—over days to weeks	Persistent—usually lasting months if untreated	Gradually progressive, over years
Family history	Not contributory	May be positive for depression	May be positive or DAT
Memory	Poor registration	Patchy/inconsistent	Recent > remote
Memory complaints	Absent	Present	Variable—usually absent
Language deficits	Dysgraphia	Increased speech latency	Confrontation naming difficulties
Affect	Labile	Depressed/irritable	Variable—may be neutral

Key: DAT = Dementia of the Alzheimer's Type.

ever, the application of this cutoff must be modified by knowledge of the educational level of the patient. For example, subjects with a substantial amount of education can experience a considerable degree of cognitive decline before a score of 23 is achieved. On the other hand, persons with little education may obtain a score of 23 at baseline. This is because some items on the MMSE (or comparable screening tests) require a minimal educational background. For example, serial 7s, which contribute heavily to the score on both the MMSE and the Mental Status Questionnaire, is difficult for most very elderly individuals with limited education to perform. This may lower their total score sufficiently so that, with a few other minor errors, they fall below the cutoff point on the test. Several recent studies indicate that for a person with less than 8 years of education, it is better to use a cutoff score of 17. For persons of very high levels of education (i.e., ≥16), a cutoff score of 27 may be appropriate (Heeren et al., 1990; Bleeker et al., 1988; Murden et al., 1991). Recent studies also indicate that there are no consistently significant differences between blacks and whites of equal education, indicating that education, but not race, is the important factor that influences test performance.

One can also improve the utility of brief mental status tests by examining the nature of the patient's errors. For example, numerous studies indicate that tests of delayed recall are best at differentiating mildly impaired AD patients from controls and from patients with other causes of cognitive decline (Moss et al., 1986; Beardsall and Huppert, 1991; Welsh et al., 1991). Thus a patient who obtains a score of 27 on the MMSE but fails to recall all 3 of the items on the recall aspect of the test should definitely be examined in greater detail for evidence of a dementing disorder. Strokes, particularly those that affect the language system, also produce selective deficits. Thus a patient with a left anterior infarct in the distribution of the anterior communicating artery may have difficulty in naming 2 common objects on the MMSE but be able to recall all 3 items after having repeated their names.

Obtaining a Cognitive History

If evidence of cognitive decline is suggested by brief cognitive testing, it is important to determine if the patient or family members are aware of cognitive problems and, if so, to obtain a history of the evolution of the cognitive decline. Such a "cognitive history" is best obtained from a family member or close friend of the patient, since a patient with suspected cognitive dysfunction is obviously not the ideal informant. It is also best to question the informant separately from the patient, since family members and friends are generally uncomfortable discussing evidence of cognitive decline in the presence of the patient.

A good cognitive history must establish the time at which cognitive changes first became apparent. This will provide important clues regarding the nature of the disorder, since some diseases are well known for their particularly rapid rate of decline (e.g., Creutzfeldt-Jakob disease). It will also enable the clinician to give the family some tentative feedback regarding the future course of the illness. If the point at which the disorder began is known, the rate of decline can be determined by seeing how long it has taken the patient to reach the present level of function. While estimates of the rate of progression can be only roughly approximated, it is extremely helpful for the family to have an estimate in making plans for the future. Repeated testing can provide further help in establishing the course of disease.

Next, the clinician must determine the nature of the behavioral changes that were evident when the disease began. This will also provide essential information regarding the diagnosis. For example, an early symptom of Pick's disease is generally thought to be a change in personality (e.g., inappropriate behavior), while the most common early symptom of Alzheimer's disease is a gradual progressive decline in the ability to learn new information. Several years after these diseases begin, when most patients are actually diagnosed, the cognitive symptoms of the 2 disorders may be very similar, so that information regarding the initial symptoms may be critical.

It is important to determine whether the initial symptoms came on suddenly or gradually. If the onset of illness is gradual and insidious, as in Alzheimer's disease, it is often only in retrospect that the family realizes that a decline has occurred. In contrast, a series of small strokes, even if not evident on CT scan or MRI, produce a history of sudden onset and stepwise progression. There is generally an incident (a fall, a period of confusion) that marks the beginning of the disorder. Acute confusional states generally have an acute onset as well, though if they are the result of a condition such as drug toxicity, this may not be the case.

The manner in which the symptoms have progressed over time also provides important diagnostic information. A stepwise deterioration characterized by sudden exacerbations of symptoms is most typical of multi-infarct dementia. However, a physical illness in an Alzheimer patient (e.g., pneumonia, a hip fracture, etc.) can cause a rapid decline in cognitive function. The sudden worsening of symptoms in a psychiatric patient (e.g., depression) can also produce an abrupt decrease in mental status.

Careful questioning is therefore necessary to determine the underlying cause of a stepwise decline in function.

Getting a good cognitive history is one of the most difficult yet most important aspects of an evaluation for cognitive dysfunction. Cognitive histories are difficult to obtain because most patients and family members are not attuned to subtle behavioral symptoms. They do not know how to isolate important aspects of the medical history or how to focus on individual cognitive functions in isolation from one another. For example, the family may state that the first symptom of disease was the patient's anxiety and depression about work, and only when asked may remember several episodes that preceded the onset of work-related anxiety in which the patient could not remember how to deal with a complex situation or how to use new equipment.

Family members may also have difficulty understanding why certain subtle distinctions are important for diagnosis. For example, a family member may say that the patient's first symptom was forgetfulness but, when asked to provide instances of this forgetfulness, may explain that the patient had trouble installing a new drawer pull in the kitchen or had trouble knowing how to find a familiar location, both of which would suggest spatial difficulty more than memory difficulty. In addition, an unwillingness to admit that certain impairments exist can also prevent family members from providing accurate information.

Finally, family members can sometimes misinterpret even fairly direct questions. For example, a history of a gradually progressive disorder is essential to the diagnosis of Alzheimer's disease. Yet family members frequently say that a disorder came on suddenly because their awareness that something was wrong came on suddenly. This realization on the part of the family often coincides with external events such as a trip to an unfamiliar place that prevented the patient from employing overlearned habits and routines, and thus exposed the cognitive decline. However, the family may interpret this as a sudden onset. If this misconception appears to be the case, it is then necessary to determine whether any symptoms of cognitive change preceded the external event. Most commonly, family members then recall episodes which they had previously ignored but are, in fact, evidence of an earlier change in cognitive function.

It is also important to determine the patient's current functional status. This may be done in an informal manner by asking how the patient spends a typical day or by using a standardized instrument developed to assess activities of daily living (e.g., Lawton et al., 1982). A sub-

stantial discrepancy between the functional and cognitive status of the patient generally suggests the presence of a psychiatric illness.

Referral for Neuropsychological Assessment

If both brief mental status testing and the cognitive history suggest that the patient has experienced a cognitive decline, then the clinician must determine whether detailed neuropsychological testing would be helpful. Neuropsychological testing is generally most helpful in the differential diagnosis of mildly and moderately impaired patients. This is because each of the disorders that can cause cognitive decline in the elderly has a characteristic pattern of spared and impaired abilities, and these are easiest to demonstrate early in the course of disease. Appropriate neuropsychological testing can also be helpful in moderately to severely impaired patients, particularly if the goal of the testing is to identify areas of spared ability that can be used to improve patient management. For example, patients with little expressive language ability can still comprehend a considerable amount of information, and a test that can determine a patient's level of comprehension (e.g., Albert and Cohen, 1992) can enable the caregiver to communicate with him or her most effectively.

In referring a patient for detailed neuropsychological evaluation, it is therefore important that the clinician communicate the goal of the testing (i.e., diagnosis and/or management). It is also helpful if the neuropsychologist can receive as much background as possible pertaining to the history of the disorder (i.e., the medical and cognitive history, current medical illnesses and medications, recent neurologic assessment, etc.). The neuropsychologist can then interpret the test results with all of the background in mind.

By the same token, it is reasonable for the nonpsychologist who refers a patient for testing to expect that information be provided in a framework that is easy to interpret. One approach that neuropsychologists often use to clarify their results is to summarize them in terms of 6 major areas of ability: attention, language, memory, spatial ability, conceptualization, and general fund of knowledge. This type of summary should be possible, regardless of the neuropsychologist's approach to test selection.

Neuropsychological Assessment

There are at least 2 basic approaches that neuropsychologists take to the selection of a neuropsychological test protocol. Some individuals use a predetermined test battery, such as the Halstead-Reitan Battery (Boll, 1981) or the Luria-Nebraska Battery (Golden, 1981). Others select from a group of tests ones which seem particularly relevant to the diagnostic question. However, even in the latter case, there tends to be a core group of tests that are relied upon more heavily than others. The types of tests that are frequently utilized and the rationale for their selection are described briefly below (see Lezak, 1983, for further details of neuropsychological tests in use).

Attention. Attention is important to consider because simple attentional abilities must be preserved for any other task to be performed adequately. If the subject has difficulty keeping his or her mind on the task for 1–3 minutes at a time, it will not be possible to assess other areas of function. For this reason, attention is often assessed before other cognitive domains have been evaluated. Auditory and visual attention can be assessed easily by means of digit span and letter cancellation. A variety of continuous performance tasks are also available for this purpose. Many of these have been adapted for computer so that both accuracy and latency can be recorded.

Language. Language testing for aphasia would generally include an evaluation of comprehension, repetition, reading, writing, and naming. Several standardized batteries are available for this purpose (Goodglass and Kaplan, 1972; Kertesz, 1980). Some include brief aphasia screening tests that are useful for identifying the existence of a problem without giving a detailed analysis (Halstead and Wepman, 1949). If aphasia has been ruled out, or is not suspected, confrontation naming (Kaplan, Goodglass, and Weintraub, 1983) is almost always part of the assessment of an older individual, since decreases in naming ability occur with age and are also a prominent symptom of a number of disorders common among the elderly (e.g., Alzheimer's disease). Alterations in verbal fluency (Benton and Hamsher, 1976) are also seen in many dementing diseases (Welsh et al., 1992; Milberg and Albert, 1989).

Memory. Memory dysfunction occurs in almost all of the cognitive disorders common in the elderly, and the nature and severity of the memory impairment can serve as one of the major guidelines to the diagnosis. The assessment of memory is complicated by the fact that changes in memory capacity occur as people age. Therefore, careful testing is often necessary to differentiate normal from pathological memory performance. Fortunately, there is a

Table 16.4 Memory tests

Wechsler Memory Scale (Wechsler, 1945)
Wechsler Memory Scale-Revised (Wechsler, 1988)
CERAD Word List Learning Test (Morris et al., 1989)
Rey Auditory Verbal Learning Test (Rey, 1964)
Selective Reminding Test (Buschke and Fuld, 1974)
Delayed Recognition Span Test (Moss et al., 1986)
California Verbal Learning Test (Delis et al., 1987)
Randt Memory Test (Randt, Brown, and Osborne, 1980)
Fuld Object Memory Test (Fuld, 1980)

wide variety of memory tests from which one can choose. Table 16.4 lists the ones in most common use today. While some were specifically developed for use with the elderly, most were originally designed for younger populations and are now being applied to older individuals.

Visuospatial ability. The assessment of visuospatial ability is more difficult in the elderly than in the young because of the prevalence of visual sensory deficits in this age range. In all of the cognitive domains previously discussed, function can be evaluated either orally or visually. However, this is not the case for visuospatial ability, and alternate means of administration are more difficult to develop. It is, for example, difficult to enlarge test stimuli such as blocks or sticks. Therefore, figure copying is the method of assessment that is most likely to be successful. Figures can be chosen to span a great range of difficulty and, as mentioned earlier, can be adapted (by using photographic enlargement or a felt-tipped pen) for individuals with moderate sensory impairments. Even then it may be necessary to allow for a greater margin of error. In addition to constructional ability, one should assess perceptual capacity. Figure matching tasks are a good analogue for figure copying. They have the added advantage that they can be administered to patients with severe cognitive deficits, patients in whom it is otherwise difficult to assess spatial function meaningfully.

Executive function. Tasks that examine executive function include tests of concept formation, abstraction, set shifting, and set maintenance. Table 16.5 lists some of the tests that are available. Many of them are lengthy (e.g., the Wisconsin Card Sorting Test), and shortened versions are often selected for clinical assessment (e.g. Nelson, 1976). The Trail Making Test (Reitan, 1958) is extremely brief

Table 16.5 Executive function tests

Similarities Subtest of WAIS (Wechsler, 1944; 1981)
Proverbs Test (Gorham, 1956)
Trail Making Test (Reitan, 1958)
Modified Card Sorting Test (Nelson, 1976)
Visual-Verbal Test (Feldman and Drasgow, 1951)
Odd Man Out Test (Flowers and Robertson, 1985)

(approximately 5 minutes in length) and is one of the most sensitive to subtle impairments in set-shifting ability (Lafleche and Albert, 1995). The advantage of tasks such as proverb interpretation or Similarities from the WAIS-R is that they are generally arranged in order of difficulty. Thus the harder items can be omitted if the individual fails on easier items. There are, in addition, tasks that have been designed to assess abstraction in patients with moderate to severe cognitive impairments who fail the standard tests (Mattis, 1976).

General knowledge. It is also helpful to assess a patient's general intelligence. This will allow one to determine whether the individual has access to previously acquired knowledge. The Vocabulary Subtest of the Wechsler Adult Intelligence Scale—Revised (WAIS-R) is well-known as the best quick estimate of IQ (Wechsler, 1981). Shortened versions of the WAIS-R are also available (Satz and Mogel, 1962). However, in order to interpret the results, one must have a general sense of the individual's premorbid level of ability. Since tests that are purported to assess premorbid ability, such as the Vocabulary Subtest of the WAIS-R and the Nelson Adult Reading Test (NART) (Nelson and O'Connell, 1978), for which extensive norms are now available (Grober and Sliwinski, 1991), often show declines in even mildly impaired patients, information regarding education and occupation is probably the best guide to determining premorbid cognitive status.

The Dementias

There are dozens of disorders that lead to dementia, but only a handful account for more than 90% of all dementing cases. Alzheimer's disease and related disorders are active in more than half of all cases, vascular dementia and stroke account for 15–20%, and Parkinson's disease and brain injury lead to about 8% and 5%, respectively. In the following sections, features of these conditions are described that show how the pathophysiology and neuroanatomy help to explain the presenting clinical features and aid in the diagnosis and treatment of individual dementing disorders.

Alzheimer's Disease

Although forms of dementia arising late in life had been identified by Kraepelin and his colleagues by the 1800s, it was not until 1907 that Alois Alzheimer identified the presenile form of dementia with unique neuropathologic features which now bears his name. His description of the disease captures the clinical and pathological essence of the condition as it is diagnosed today (Alzheimer, 1907). Alzheimer's patient, a 51-year-old woman, presented with jealousy toward her husband. Soon she showed a progressively worsening memory loss and disorientation to time and place, delusions of persecution, and language disturbances in the face of a relatively normal neurologic exam. Mental deterioration progressed, and she died 4½ years later. By the time of her death, she showed little response and remained bedridden with her legs drawn up to her body (Alzheimer, 1907). On autopsy, her brain showed clear evidence of cerebral atrophy. Using new histologic staining methods, Alzheimer examined cortical neurons under the microscope and discovered that many contained fibrous structures—neurofibrillary tangles—which existed in the same affected brain regions as extracellular plaque-like lesions. In 1910 Kraepelin suggested that this neuropathologic picture was pathognomic of a new presenile dementing disease, and introduced the eponymn "Alzheimer's disease" (Kraepelin, 1910).

Epidemiology. Initially considered relatively uncommon, Alzheimer's disease remained a footnote in neuropsychiatry literature until the late 1960s, when investigators noticed that many cases of senile dementia, a much more common condition, displayed the same neuropathologic features. Now about 50% of all late-life dementias are attributable to Alzheimer's disease, and an additional 15–20% have combined Alzheimer and vascular pathology. Alzheimer's disease afflicts individuals of all socioeconomic backgrounds and spares no major cultural subgroup. Clinical symptoms may appear as early as the fourth decade, and the age-specific prevalence increases logarithmically, doubling approximately every 5 years (Katzman and Kawas, 1994). Individuals who reach the age of 65 have a lifetime risk of 5–10%, depending on the diagnostic criteria used. Owing to the post–World War II population boom, the proportion of senior citizens in the total population will double by 2020, dramatically increasing the incidence of Alzheimer's disease.

Recent genetic advances have shown Alzheimer's disease to be the common pathologic outcome of a family of diseases with different primary etiologies (Schellenberg, 1995). Gene mutations on at least 3 different chromosomes account for the familial forms of Alzheimer's disease (FAD)—the 15–20% of cases that follow a typical autosomal dominant inheritance pattern and include most cases of early-onset Alzheimer's disease. In FAD, a single gene defect, interacting with the brain aging process, causes the disease. In the other 80–85% of cases, designated "sporadic" Alzheimer's disease, emergence of disease is influenced by various environmental factors as well as by genes with either neuroprotective or disease-facilitating effects. Topping the list of known risk factors for late-onset Alzheimer's disease, other than advancing age, is inheritance of the ε-4 allele of the single gene encoding apolipoprotein E (ApoE), a molecule that transports cholesterol and certain phospholipids into cells (Poirier et al., 1995). The three ApoE isoforms, ε2, ε3, and ε4, vary by only a single amino acid substitution but are markedly different in their binding affinities for low density lipoprotein (LDL) receptors and other proteins (Roses, 1995a). Inheritance of a single ε4 allele increases risk of Alzheimer's disease threefold, while homozygosity for ε4 is associated with an eightfold increase in risk (Corder et al., 1993). Fortunately, the incidence of the ε4/ε4 genotype in the general human population is relatively low (1–2%). The ApoE ε4 allele appears to influence the age of onset rather than the duration and severity of the disease. Because Alzheimer's disease does not develop in all individuals with the ε4 allele and not all Alzheimer patients have the ε4 allele, the presence of the Apoε4 allele is not a diagnostic test, nor is its determination a useful screening measure (Roses, 1995b).

Down syndrome is another strong genetic risk factor for Alzheimer's disease. Nearly all individuals who reach their fifth decade have the neuropathologic stigmata of Alzheimer's disease (Wisniewski, Wisniewski, and Wen, 1985), and most decline cognitively in later years (Lai and Williams, 1989). This increased risk is suspected of being related to the gene for amyloid precursor protein (APP) located on the region of chromosome 21 that is trisomic in Down syndrome (Delebar et al., 1987).

Even in "sporadic" Alzheimer's disease, a family history of dementia is important. First-degree relatives of patients with Alzheimer's disease have a fourfold increased risk over that of the general population (Corey-Blum, Galasko, and Thal, 1995). Inheritance of the ε4 allele of ApoE is the major contributor to this risk. In a study of 285 twin individuals in Finland, monozygotic twins were nearly 4 times more likely than dizygotic twins to be concordant for Alzheimer's disease (Raiha et al., 1996). Fur-

ther observations that the age of onset differed by as much as 15 years in some twin pairs underscore the additional role of environmental influences on the penetrance of Alzheimer's disease (Raiha et al., 1996).

Other factors considered to increase Alzheimer's risk include head injury, education below the secondary school level, major depression, exposure to environmental toxins (e.g., aluminum), alcohol abuse, birth to a mother older than 40, and female gender (Katzman and Kawas, 1994). In each of these examples, however, the relative increased risk is less than twofold, the findings are not fully established, and in some cases the apparent effect may have alternative explanations. Nevertheless, these and other risk factors may prove to have significantly more clinical relevance when they are present together. In one study, for example, individuals with an ε4 allele and a history of head injury associated with loss of consciousness were 5 times more likely to be diagnosed with Alzheimer's disease than individuals with ε4 alone (Mayeux et al., 1995).

Pathology. The brain in Alzheimer's disease displays varying degrees of cortical atrophy and ventricular enlargement. At the microscopic level, neurofibrillary tangles and senile plaques are the characteristic lesions. Neurofibrillary tangles are skeins of twisted abnormal filaments whose presence in neurons reflects a global disorganization of the neuronal cytoskeleton (Goedert, 1993). The microtubule-associated protein tau, present in a hyperphosphorylated state, forms abnormal paired helical filaments that, along with fragments of various cytoskeletal proteins, compose the tangle. Senile plaques are complex spherical lesions of varying size, usually many times larger than a single neuron, which typically contain an extracellular core of amyloid surrounded by degenerating dendrites and axons, as well as various phagocytic cells (Selkoe, 1991). Amyloid in plaques is principally composed of the ß-amyloid peptide, a 40–43 amino acid peptide derived by the normal processing of a larger ubiquitous membrane glycoprotein, the amyloid precursor protein (Checler, 1995).

Neuronal loss in Alzheimer's disease is extensive and may be preceded by synapse loss (Terry, Masliah, and Hansen, 1994). Cellular dysfunction is first detected in the transentorhinal cortex of the temporal lobe and spreads to the subiculum, hippocampus, and eventually to the frontal and parietal lobes and amygdala, suggesting an anatomical basis for the principal cognitive features of the disease (Hyman et al., 1986). Loss of subcortical neurons, such as the cholinergic basal forebrain nucleus of Meynert and septal nuclei and, to a lesser extent, noradrenergic neurons of the locus coeruleus and serotonergic neurons of the dorsal raphe nuclei, is associated with reduced concentrations of neurotransmitter system components in these neurons (Hof and Morrison, 1994). Losses of other neuropeptides, such as vasopressin, somatostatin, substance P, neuropeptide Y, and certain receptors, parallel the dropout of neurons of various functional types (Francis, Cross, and Bowen, 1994; Young and Penney, 1994). Neuronal loss, however, is selective: some neuronal populations, even in the neocortex, are remarkably well preserved at late stages of the disease (Hof and Morrison, 1994).

Alzheimer's disease is a histopathological diagnosis. According to one current set of criteria, a definite diagnosis of Alzheimer's disease can be made only when senile plaques reach a requisite number, adjusted for age, in the most affected region of the neocortex (Mirra et al., 1991). More stringent research criteria require a count of numbers of both plaques and neurofibrillary tangles (Khachaturian, 1985). The number of either lesion correlates more or less with the severity of clinical dementia (Terry, Masliah, and Hansen, 1994), but it is not clear whether these lesions are directly related to cognitive decline or are simply indirect markers of the neuronal dysfunction underlying dementia.

Pathophysiology. The cellular and molecular basis for Alzheimer's disease is the subject of intense investigation, and while definitive answers are not available, important clues have emerged from the integration of pathologic, biochemical, and genetic information. Various lines of evidence point to an important role for the amyloid precursor protein (ß-APP) in Alzheimer's disease pathogenesis. After ß-APP was discovered to be the precursor of the ß-amyloid that accumulates in senile plaques, suspicions of its involvement in AD were heightened by the discovery that at least 4 mutations of the ß-APP gene cause Alzheimer's disease in the 10% of FAD cases attributable to chromosome 21.

How ß-APP figures as an etiologic factor is not yet fully resolved. Current hypotheses suggest involvement of either an alteration in one of the still unknown functions of ß-APP itself or neurotrophic or neurotoxic effects of processed derivatives of ß-APP. One hypothesis places the ß-amyloid peptide at the center of disease pathogenesis, based on its ability, under experimental conditions in vitro, to form fibrillar aggregates that are toxic to neurons. According to this hypothesis, known etiologic factors are suspected of causing overproduction of the ß-amyloid peptide or promoting its aggregation into fibrils that ac-

cumulate and are neurotoxic (Cotman and Pike, 1994; Selkoe, 1996). An alternative but not mutually exclusive hypothesis is that Alzheimer's disease involves the brain's failure to repair cumulative neuronal damage arising from normal aging processes, ischemic and environmental insults, and genetic factors that increase cellular vulnerability (Regland and Gottfries, 1992; Nixon and Cataldo, 1994). Therefore, a putative impairment in the known neurotrophic actions of ß-APP or APP's mobilization during neuronal injury are most relevant to this hypothesis. Indeed, cells normally secrete a large fragment of ß-APP—protease nexin II or APPS—which promotes neuron growth and increases neuron survival after certain types of injury (Mattson, 1994).

ApoE's importance as a risk factor is compatible with either hypothesis. On the one hand, ApoE exhibits relatively strong interactions with the ß-amyloid peptide, which may be relevant to its aggregation or clearance (Roses, 1995a). On the other hand, transport of cholesterol and phospholipids by ApoE is critical to the process of membrane turnover in injured cells, and ApoE production is dramatically elevated after nervous system injury (Poirier, Minnich, and Davignon, 1995). Interestingly, ApoE ε3, but not the more sinister ApoE ε4, promotes the outgrowth and branching of neuronal processes, suggesting how the ApoE genotype may influence risk for Alzheimer's disease (Weisgraber, Pitas, and Mahley, 1994).

Genes on chromosome 14 and chromosome 1, which account for about 70% and 20% of early-onset familial Alzheimer cases, have recently been identified and shown to harbor mutations in individuals with FAD (Sherrington et al., 1995; Levy-Lahad et al., 1995). A high degree of sequence homology between these 2 genes suggests that they may have similar biological functions. These functions are not yet known.

Clinical features. The essential features of general dementia described in previous sections also apply to dementia of the Alzheimer type. The onset of clinical symptoms is insidious. Memory loss is most often the earliest symptom, but impaired performance in intellectually demanding tasks at work or a change in personality may also herald AD's onset. The patient may respond in varying ways to these early symptoms. Recognition of impaired performance may trigger depressive symptoms, exacerbating the cognitive changes and perhaps dominating the presenting clinical picture. Some individuals may successfully hide disabilities from friends and relatives for months or years until symptoms become obvious. Still others, because of the heightened public awareness of

Alzheimer's disease, may seek evaluation at such an early stage that it is difficult to make the distinction between early Alzheimer's disease and age-associated memory impairment, a benign form of senescent forgetfulness. At these early stages, the memory lapses are similar to, but more frequent than, those experienced by most elderly such as forgetting appointments, the location of a parked car, the thread of a conversation, or previously familiar traffic routes. An acute worsening, often accompanied by disorientation, may occur when a person is hospitalized for an unrelated condition or visits relatives or friends in an unfamiliar environment. Alcohol, medications, or intercurrent illnesses may provoke exacerbations of this occurrence or delirium. Although patients may acknowledge symptoms at the early stages, denial of memory impairment in the face of obvious cognitive deficits is remarkably common. As time goes on, orientation becomes impaired, and other features, including language and praxis difficulties, decreased spontaneity, and increasingly inflexible patterns of behavior become obvious to family members and colleagues. Tasks that allow the person to live independently, including driving, cooking, financial management, and, later, dressing and personal hygiene, eventually require supervision.

Other psychiatric symptoms are common throughout these stages. Depressive symptoms occur frequently at early disease stages in 30–50% of cases, but the degree of depression is usually mild (Cummings et al., 1995). These symptoms often benefit from pharmacologic treatment but usually remit spontaneously as the disease progresses. Delusions or hallucinations are seen in 30–40% of Alzheimer's cases (Folstein and Bylsma, 1994). Individuals' distress over losing objects may be accompanied by paranoid ideas that others are trying to steal from them or harm them, fears that a spouse is unfaithful, or fears that others are plotting to commit them to an institution. Also common is a delusional misidentification in which the patient's spouse is believed to be a double or an impersonator (Capgras syndrome) or that strangers are living in the house (phantom boarder syndrome). Visual hallucinations may occur in 15–20% of patients and auditory hallucinations in another 10% (Forstl, Sattel, and Bahro, 1993).

Treatment. Although success in treating the progressive cognitive deterioration of Alzheimer's disease and other dementias has been modest thus far, research in this area is very active and centers on 3 general strategies. Until recently, most efforts have been directed toward the first strategy—palliative approaches aimed at augmenting neurotransmission impaired by the degeneration of specific neuronal populations. This approach is necessarily limited because many transmitter systems are affected in AD, and enhancing neurotransmission is not likely to alter the progression of the disease. A second and potentially more promising strategy targets specific events in the cellular pathogenesis of the disease in order to block its progression. Potential interventions include slowing the production and aggregation of ß-amyloid in the brain, inhibiting steps in the cell death process, blocking secondary cell damage due to immune and inflammatory responses to neurodegeneration, enhancing deficient or defective repair mechanisms in neurons, providing growth factors for regeneration, and protecting neurons against the effects of excitotoxins, free radicals, and ischemic injury. The third approach, although less well advanced, is a strategy to restore brain function by regenerating lost brain tissue or replacing it by neurotransplantation. This approach will likely have the greatest potential benefit in disorders which primarily affect a single neuronal population, such as in Parkinson's disease.

Drug treatments shown to have some therapeutic benefits for certain populations of Alzheimer's patients have been developed based on enhancing the functioning of surviving cholinergic neurons using cholinomimetic agents. The design rationale for these therapies derives from the well-established role of the cholinergic system in memory function and the early, prominent loss of cholinergic neurons in Alzheimer's disease. However, even after several decades of investigation into the ability of various agents to enhance cholinergic function, only acetylcholinesterase (AChE) inhibitors have proven clinically useful, and these only in a limited way. Tetrahydroaminoacridine (Tacrine), the first FDA-approved agent for the treatment of Alzheimer's disease, is a prototype of a class of AChE-inhibitors now becoming available for Alzheimer therapy. Though cognitive improvement has been reported, there is no evidence that Tacrine influences the rate of progression of the disease itself. Taking daily doses of 80 mg or more of Tacrine, approximately one-third of individuals with early Alzheimer's disease will experience mild to moderate improvement in global clinical functioning and cognitive performance (Davis and Powchick, 1995). The best responses are equivalent to a 6–12 month slowing of cognitive deterioration; the longest studies thus far reported extend over only a 30-week period, so whether these early benefits of the drug are preserved is still unknown. Positive responses are most likely at the highest recommended doses of 160 mg, but this dose is often poorly tolerated. Tacrine's use is limited by various factors, including the modest improvement rate, the relatively low frequency of responders, the lack of effect on the overall progression of the disease, the risk of hepatotoxicity (usually asymptomatic) in as much as half the patient population, the incidence of nausea, vomiting, and diarrhea in up to one-third of patients, the need for weekly ALT (alanine amino transferase) tests to monitor hepatotoxicity, the small potential for hypotensive cholinergic crises, and this medication's very high cost.

Although patients who respond to Tacrine are a minority within the general Alzheimer population, specific subpopulations may respond at a higher frequency. For example, Alzheimer patients carrying either ApoE 2 or ApoE 3 alleles may respond better than those with 1 or 2 ApoE 4 alleles (Poirer et al., 1995). Hormone status may also be important: estrogen influences cholinergic function by increasing choline acetyltransferase activity and has both trophic and protective effects on cholinergic neurons and possibly other neuron types (Paganini-Hill, 1996). Also, estrogen has been shown to enhance cognitive function in animal studies, as well as trials with postmenopausal women (Paganini-Hill, 1996). In small clinical trials, some postmenopausal women with Alzheimer's disease treated with estrogen showed improved memory, orientation, and calculation ability, as well as better global functioning, especially those with mild to moderate dementia. The effects were lost when treatment was discontinued. Tacrine may also be more effective in women who are receiving estrogen replacement therapy (Schneider et al., 1996).

New treatments targeting known pathogenetic events in Alzheimer's disease have not yet reached the clinic. However, one existing class of approved drugs, certain anti-inflammatory agents (NSAIDs and steroids), might qualify to do so. The presence of immune or inflammatory cells in senile plaques has suggested that secondary brain damage might arise as a result of this inflammatory response and that anti-inflammatory treatments may therefore be beneficial. In support of this view, Alzheimer's disease is less prevalent in patients with histories of rheumatoid arthritis who had been treated with anti-inflammatory agents (McGeer et al., 1990). Furthermore, steroids or nonsteroidal anti-inflammatory agents, such as indomethacin, appear to have protective effects against Alzheimer's disease (Breitner et al., 1994; Rogers et al., 1993). Given the gastrointestinal toxicity of NSAIDs and the systemic toxicity of steroids, it would be premature at this stage of the study to recommend chronic use of anti-inflammatory agents in the general Alzheimer's disease

patient, but the development of gastrointestinal-sparing anti-inflammatory agents seems to be a promising direction for therapy in the near future.

Frontotemporal Dementia

Over a century ago Arnold Pick (1892) described patients with a progressive disturbance in personality and cognition in association with atrophy of the frontal and temporal lobes. Later, Alois Alzheimer (1911) reported that swollen neurons and intraneuronal inclusion bodies were associated with this clinical picture. This disorder was subsequently called Pick's disease (Gans, 1922). However, it remained poorly understood until an interest in Alzheimer's disease produced a parallel interest in disorders that were frequently confused with it. The work of Neary and his colleagues (Neary et al., 1988; Snowden, Neary, and Mann, 1996) has begun to clarify the clinical characteristics and neuropathology of this disorder, recently termed frontotemporal dementia (FTD).

Epidemiology. FTD is primarily a disorder of presenile onset, with the most common age of onset between 45 and 60 (Gustafson, 1987; Neary et al., 1988). Within this age range it may represent at least 20% of patients with primary progressive dementia, although careful epidemiological studies regarding FTD remain to be done. A family history of dementia in first-degree relatives has been reported in almost half of the cases seen in clinics that specialize in this disorder (Gustafson, 1987; Snowden, Neary, and Mann, 1996), but it is unclear whether or not this is related to a referral bias of such families. An autosomal dominant mode of transmission is nevertheless clear in some families. In one study (Petersen et al., 1995) a gene on chromosome 17 was said to be related to the development of progressive subcortical gliosis (PSG) (Neumann and Cohn, 1967), a disorder with some clinical similarities to FTD but a differing neuropathological profile; thus its relevance to FTD remains unclear.

Pathology. The pathological picture of FTD consists of atrophy involving primarily the frontal and temporal lobes, with the parietal lobe relatively spared. Accompanying this atrophy are 2 general types of pathology. One pathological profile consists of extensive neuronal loss and astrocytosis. The astrocytosis predominates in the upper layers of the cortex, layers II and III. In about 25% of these cases, inclusion bodies and swollen neurons called Pick bodies are also present. There is a loss of myelin and axons in the white matter. In the second pathological profile associated with FTD, there is widespread neuronal loss and microvacuolar degeneration (spongiosis) in the upper layers of the cortex, layers II and III, but little astrocytosis. There is a loss of myelin and axons in the white matter. A subset of these patients also show evidence of motor neuron disease and at autopsy have loss of anterior horn cells.

When the pathology includes the presence of Pick bodies, the patients meet the criteria of Pick's disease, as mentioned above. In the absence of Pick bodies and dramatic atrophy (also called "knife edge" atrophy), the pathological picture appears nonspecific (Knopman et al., 1990) and can confuse the neuropathologist unfamiliar with this disorder. The link between the neuropathology and the clinical presentation is often what clarifies the diagnosis.

Investigators in England and Sweden have recently published a consensus statement regarding the neuropathology of FTD in which the pathological hallmarks presented above are described and classical Pick's disease is proposed as belonging at one end of the spectrum of FTD. There remains, however, uncertainty about whether Pick's disease should be considered a separate disorder or, instead, as one end of a continuum with other types of FTD. This definitional issue increases the difficulty for pathologists in consistently identifying FTD on the basis of autopsy alone.

Clinical features. Frontotemporal dementia is a progressive dementing disorder which, like Alzheimer's disease, has an insidious onset, although the earliest symptom is not memory loss. Instead 2 types of presentation are seen.

The most common presentation is a major alteration in personality and social behavior. Lack of conformity to social conventions (of recent onset) is often a very early sign. Patients tend to show poor judgment, lack foresight, and neglect their personal responsibilities. There are changes in reactivity as well, such that patients become either hyperactive (i.e., restless, distractible, disinhibited) or hypoactive (i.e., apathetic, lacking initiative). Early in the course of disease, patients often neglect their personal hygiene. Changes in eating and drinking patterns are common; patients often overeat or develop a preoccupation with eating specific foods (e.g., bananas). Stereotyped behavior, which is reminiscent of obsessive-compulsive disorder, is also common.

The alternate presentation of FTD is insidious and progressive difficulty with language. These patients typically begin with word finding problems that make communication increasingly problematic. In some patients this problem spreads to other aspects of language; thus repetition, reading, writing, and comprehension eventually become affected. As these difficulties emerge, the disorder resembles a nonfluent aphasia. An alternative pattern of difficulty is seen in the patients who develop a loss of word meaning. Thus, early in the course of disease patients often are unable to understand the meaning of very common words (e.g., window, comb, etc.). As problems with word meaning progress, they interfere with other aspects of language function (e.g., reading and writing). Patients with this "semantic" version of FTD are likely to also develop some of the obsessive characteristics seen in the more common presentation of FTD; for example, they prefer fixed routines and become preoccupied with exactness and neatness.

Vascular Dementia

Cardiovascular disease, whether thrombotic, embolic, or hemorrhagic, may cause regional brain tissue injury that leads to a syndrome of multiple cognitive deficits and focal neurologic signs known as vascular dementia. Most commonly, vascular dementia is caused by vessel occlusion, which may give rise to different clinical and pathologic pictures depending on whether large or small vessels are involved. Alzheimer's disease coexists in as many as one-third of vascular dementias, and misdiagnosis of vascular dementia as Alzheimer's disease is not uncommon. Distinguishing these 2 clinical entities is critically important because many stroke risk factors that predispose an individual to vascular dementia are preventable, and therapeutic approaches to the 2 dementias are different.

About 15% of late-life dementias in the United States are attributable to cerebrovascular causes alone, and an additional 10% are "mixed" dementia, reflecting the coexistence of Alzheimer's disease and vascular dementia (Tatemichi, Sacktor, and Mayeux, 1994). In other countries, however, the prevalence of vascular dementia may range from 10% to 59%, and is diagnosed 2–3 times more frequently in Asia than in the United States (Tatemichi, Sacktor, and Mayeux, 1994). At least part of this variability may reflect the absence of widely accepted criteria for the diagnosis (Erkinjuntti, 1994). The increasing incidence beginning in the sixth decade parallels prevalence patterns for cardiovascular disease. Not unexpectedly, factors that increase the likelihood of cerebrovascular accident are risk factors for vascular dementia, including hypertension, heart disease, diabetes mellitus, severe hyperlipidemia, disorders affecting clotting mechanisms or blood viscosity, cigarette smoking, and excessive alcohol consumption. Additional factors, some still unknown, increase the risk of dementia early after stroke such as the individual's age and education and the collaterality and size of the brain lesion. Thus, a 90-year-old is twice as likely to develop dementia after a stroke as a 60-year-old (Tatemichi, Sacktor, and Mayeux, 1994).

Pathophysiology. Interrupted brain tissue perfusion, regardless of the vascular insult, has the same end point, namely, neuron cell death in the central infarcted area and dysfunction of additional neurons extending concentrically from the infarct. Much is known about cellular mechanisms underlying hypoxic and ischemic neuronal injury (Whetsell, 1996). Most senile dementia used to be attributed to "hardening of the arteries" until the late 1960s, when Alzheimer's disease was recognized as the basis for most of these cases. Later, the concept emerged that infarction at multiple sites in the brain, termed "multi-infarct dementia," was the neuropathologic basis of vascular dementia; however, because there is no strong correlation between dementia and infarct location, research has now come full circle to the theory that many cases of vascular dementia are indeed causally related to arteriosclerosis, leading to progressive white matter degeneration. This still-evolving concept has given rise to the designation of at least 4 types of vascular dementia.

Multi-infarct dementia (MID) involves the moderate to severe loss of tissue by infarction within cortical areas, and to a lesser extent subcortical areas, supplied by branches of the major cerebral arteries. The clinical course is usually punctuated by multiple transient ischemic attacks or strokes. Except when the infarcts are large, their size does not necessarily correlate with dementia severity. This observation and the fact that most infarcts are caused by arteriosclerosis has suggested that dementia severity in MID may have additional determinants as in other types of vascular dementia. *Lacunar state* is a type of MID wherein the infarcts are smaller than those in MID. Arising in the basal ganglia, pons, and white matter, these smaller infarcts result from arteriosclerosis and the occlusion of deep-penetrating arterioles. White matter lesions may be the common neuropathologic basis for dementia in this condition, as well as in *Binswanger's disease.* Binswanger's disease is a chronic ischemic disorder leading to irregular focal periventricular lesions which extend into subjacent white matter, and ventricular enlargement, both of which abnormalities are evident by MRI. Although it often develops in the context of hypertension and arteriosclerosis, this condition may also be caused by other conditions that reduce blood flow in the microcirculation, such as changes in cardiac output or blood pressure, poor blood volume, functional abnor-

malities in the arteries, and alterations in blood serum viscosity and coagulability. The possible involvement of these different hemodynamic factors suggests various strategies for altering the course of the disease in those at high risk for Binswanger's disease (Caplan, 1995). A subcortical dementia is typical in each of these three subtypes of vascular dementia.

Dementia following stroke is particularly likely when specific regions of brain tissue are damaged (Erkinjuntti et al., 1988; Delay and Brion, 1962). For example, infarct in cortical association areas, such as the angular gyrus, produces a cortical dementia similar to that in Alzheimer's disease, as well as a syndrome that includes fluent aphasia, alexia with agraphia, constructional disturbances, and Gerstmann syndrome. Another important pattern is bilateral involvement of the thalamus or basal ganglia (putamen and caudate) and white matter projections from these areas to the frontal cortex, which provides a possible basis for the prominent frontal lobe symptoms in vascular dementia.

Diagnosis and treatment. The DSM-IV diagnosis of vascular dementia is made by satisfying the criteria for dementia and demonstrating, in addition, focal neurologic signs and symptoms or neuroimaging evidence of cerebrovascular disease that is considered etiologically related to the disturbance. The neurologic signs are often multifocal. Gait abnormalities, including unprovoked falls, occur frequently; walking is usually slow, unsteady, and composed of smaller than normal steps. Pyramidal tract dysfunctions may include weakness, hyperreflexia, spasticity, and extensor plantar reflexes. In multi-infarct dementia, clinical examination may reveal asymmetric neurological signs such as visual field deficits, hemiparesis, and reflex abnormalities. In Binswanger's disease and lacunar state, pseudobulbar signs with dysarthria, dysphagia, and labile laughing and crying are particularly common. Urinary urgency and incontinence, like gait disturbances, may be early markers of the condition. Parkinson-like deficits such as slowness, decreased associative movement, and rigidity are frequently seen. The neurologic signs tend to parallel the cognitive and behavioral symptoms. Typically, there is an acute onset of dysfunction in 1 or more cognitive or neurologic domains, which may be followed by periods of stabilization or even a partial improvement in functional level, but generally not completely back to baseline. The typical stepwise course of deterioration emphasized in the older literature may not be seen, and indeed the course usually fluctuates, with periods of distinct improvement (Meyer et al., 1988).

The cognitive and behavioral abnormalities seen in

vascular dementia correspond to a frontal-subcortical pattern of impairment. Apathy and inertia predominate. The majority of patients exhibit blunted affect and are withdrawn; they have decreased spontaneity, prolonged latency in responding to queries and commands, and difficulty persevering with tasks that they understand. Patients are laconic and seldom initiate conversation (Caplan, 1995). Patients with vascular dementia report depressed mood, early insomnia, anxiety, and general somatic complaints more frequently than do patients with Alzheimer's disease (Sultzer et al., 1993). Their own insight into their deficits is usually reduced, judgment is poor, and computation and mathematical functions are usually deficient. Abnormalities of memory, language, and visuospatial functions are more variable but not as prominent as in patients with Alzheimer's disease, who tend to have a more cortical involvement. Although intellectual deterioration is evident in every case, the range is wide.

The major reason for distinguishing vascular dementia from Alzheimer's disease is the potential for slowing the progression of vascular dementia by reducing risk factors and applying specific therapies for preventing stroke recurrence. For example, controlling hypertension reduces risk of recurrent cerebral infarction (Dunbabin and Sandercock, 1990). Reducing blood viscosity and platelet aggregation and, depending on the vascular cause, endarterectomy should prevent clot formation and help maintain the patency of arteries. Aspirin, at 325 mg daily, is effective in preventing transient ischemic attack (TIA) and reducing strokes and, in one controlled study of patients with vascular dementia, actually improved cognitive function over the first 2 years of a 3-year study, while the untreated group deteriorated slightly. The platelet antiaggregant Ticlopidine, at 250 mg b.i.d., may actually be more effective than aspirin in preventing stroke in some patients (Hass et al., 1989; Grotta et al., 1992). This agent may cause diarrhea, skin rash, and, rarely, neutropenia.

Diffuse Lewy Body Disease

Lewy bodies, described nearly 100 years ago as intracytoplasmic eosinophilic inclusions in neurons, were first observed in the substantia nigra and brain stem nuclei of patients with Parkinson's disease. More sensitive methods for detecting these structures have recently revealed a form of dementia, called diffuse Lewy body disease (DLBD), associated with a wide distribution of Lewy bodies within cortical and subcortical areas, and often a loss of pigmented neurons (Beck, 1995; Hansen et al.,

1989). The presence of dementia may be related to additional loss of cholinergic projections from the substantia innominata to the cortex (Gibb, Ersi, and Lees, 1985) which correlates with the presence of Lewy bodies. DLBD is now recognized as the cause of 5–10% of all dementias, ranking it among the most common types (Hansen et al., 1990). It remains unclear whether DLBD is a distinct disease or a variant of Alzheimer's disease or Parkinson's disease, the neuropathology of which (i.e., senile plaques and nigral degeneration, respectively) often but not invariably coexists with diffuse Lewy bodies. In any event, the diffuse Lewy body pattern has both diagnostic and therapeutic importance. The clinical presentation, for example, may be distinctive. DLBD patients have been described as having delirium-like fluctuations and cognitive impairment, prominent visual and auditory hallucinations, paranoid ideation, repeated unexplained falls, and transient clouding and/or loss of consciousness (McKeith, Fairbairn, et al., 1992; Beck, 1995). The memory loss may resemble Alzheimer's, but unlike an Alzheimer's patient, the DLBD patient displays a greater degree of impairment in attention, verbal fluency, and visuospatial function (Hansen et al., 1989) and is more likely to progress to severe dementia over a period of months. Mild parkinsonism, particularly rigidity and gait disturbance, typically follows dementia onset and responds relatively poorly to anti-parkinson medication. Notably, extrapyramidal responses to standard neuroleptic doses may be exaggerated (McKeith, Perry, et al., 1992). Although the clinical features of this disease are still being established, recognizing DLBD identifies dementia patients for whom neuroleptics are contraindicated and may identify a group that shows a particularly good response to cholinergic agonists (Perry et al., 1994).

Parkinson's Disease

Parkinson's disease, which afflicts 0.1–0.2% of the population, begins to increase in incidence in the sixth decade and may afflict as many as 1% of persons reaching 80 years of age. Its diagnosis is entirely clinical and requires, as the core system, upper body akinesia, a symptom complex that may include slowed movements (bradykinesia), poverty of movements, difficulty initiating movement, and progressive fatiguing of repetitive movement (Quinn, 1995). Rigidity, either of the cogwheel or lead pipe type, is usually present. The classic 3–5 hz resting tremor is frequent but may be absent in 30% of patients. These symptoms arise when 60% or more of the dopamine neurons are lost from the pars compacta of the substantia nigra and other pigmented brain stem nuclei, which project to the limbic system, forebrain, and basal ganglia. A hallmark of Parkinson's neuropathology is the presence of Lewy bodies in the cytoplasm of surviving nigral neurons. Parkinson's disease is most commonly idiopathic, but toxic factors in the environment are suspected to be important. At least one type is caused by injecting a synthetic form of heroin, N-methyl-4-phenyl-1,2,3,6-pyridine.

Dementia is 2–3 times more common in Parkinson's disease than in an age-matched control population, but it still affects only a minority (10–20%) of afflicted individuals (Mayeux et al., 1988; Marder et al., 1993). Younger patients are rarely affected even though motor disease may be severe. This suggests that Parkinson's disease itself may be insufficient to cause dementia. Age-related factors are evidently important because the cumulative incidence of dementia may rise to 65% in those Parkinson patients who survive to age 85 (Mayeux et al., 1990). Besides advanced age, however, there are few predictors of dementia risk. Notably, Alzheimer's disease occurs with higher than expected frequency in Parkinson's disease (Hofman et al., 1989).

Subtle forms of cognitive impairment are common in Parkinson patients in the absence of overt dementia. For example, slowness of thought processes, termed bradyphrenia, associated with decreased concentration, attention span, and reaction time, may sometimes give the impression of dementia (Mayeux et al., 1987). Parkinson dementia displays the recent and retrograde memory deficits seen in Alzheimer's disease but involves greater deficits of verbal memory and greater visuospatial impairments, reflecting disturbed frontal lobe basal ganglion interconnections (Pillon et al., 1991; Richards et al., 1991). However, the frequent coexistence of Alzheimer's disease and depression in up to 40% of patients (Sano et al., 1989) may overshadow clinical distinctions between Alzheimer and Parkinson dementias.

Considerably less common than Parkinson's disease is a distinct group of akinetic-rigid disorders with unique non-cognitive features and varying levels of cognitive impairment, usually of the milder variety. In most of these conditions, cognitive deficits correspond to the fronto-cortical or frontal system type. These are characterized by bradyphrenia, personality change (apathy or depression), and impaired calculation and abstracting (Cohen and Freedman, 1995). The best known of these is progressive supranuclear palsy (PSP), a rare disorder (1–4 per 100,000) that typically manifests in the sixth decade of life as a symptom triad consisting of supranuclear ophthalmalplegia (mainly affecting vertical gaze), pseudobulbar palsy, and dystonic rigidity (particularly of the neck). Mild to moderate dementia, dysarthria, and disturbances of gait and posture are common.

Huntington's Disease

Despite its low incidence (4–8 per 100,000) (Harper, 1992), Huntington's disease has been extensively studied as the classic example of an autosomal dominant disorder with complete penetrance (Huntington's Disease Collaborative Research Group, 1993). The causative mutation on the short arm of chromosome 4 has been traced to a gene, designated Huntington, that encodes a novel protein important in cellular oxidative metabolism. The mutation in the disease consists of a DNA sequence containing multiple repeats of the trinucleotide sequence CAG which is abnormally extended to as many as 37–86 repeats (Huntington's Disease Collaborative Research Group, 1993). The mutation leads to the loss of various types of transmitter neurons in the caudate nucleus and putamen, which can be detected by clinical imaging at early disease stages as glucose hypometabolism in the striatum using positron emission tomography (PET) and, later, as atrophy of the same regions using MRI (Young et al., 1986). Dementia severity, however, correlates most strongly with the development of fronto-parietal and temporo-occipital hypometabolism, which leads to predominantly frontal type dementia (Kuwert et al., 1990). Onset typically occurs between 35 and 50 years of age and progresses inexorably over a 10- to 20-year period (Harper, 1992). Commonly, cognitive or affective personality changes such as apathy, irritability, and poor impulse control are the presenting symptoms. As in other frontal dementias, impaired memory is largely a consequence of attentional deficits and manipulation of previously acquired information (Pillon et al., 1991). Poor judgment, reduced verbal fluency, and impaired visuospatial function are relatively prominent, while aphasia and other cortical features are less common. The diagnosis is suggested by the presence of dementia with choreiform movements, a family history of Huntington's disease, and characteristic PET or MRI findings.

Dementias Associated with Infective Agents

HIV. The human immunodeficiency virus (HIV-1) infects 1–2 million Americans and 25–35 million individuals worldwide. About one-third of adults and one-half of children with acquired immunodeficiency syndrome (AIDS) eventually develop neurologic complications characterized by impaired concentration, slowness of hand movement, and difficulty walking. The syndrome, termed HIV-1–associated cognitive/motor complex, may be classified as either "severe" or "mild" form, evident only in the context of a demanding life style. Unlike other viral encephalitides, AIDS dementia manifests itself clinically without direct infection of neurons with the virus. Cellular damage correlating with clinical severity is mediated by various toxic molecules produced by infective macrophages in both the blood and brain (Lipton & Gendelman, 1995). Neuronal loss and myelin pallor are prominent in subcortical areas and usually seen in CT or MRI as atrophy (ventricular enlargement) and diffuse signal change, respectively, in the subcortical white matter (Broderick et al., 1993). Functional imaging shows early hypermetabolism in the thalamus and subsequent hypometabolism spreading to the temporal cortex (Van Gorp et al., 1992).

Creutzfeldt-Jakob Disease. Subacute spongiform encephalopathy (SSE), or Creutzfeldt-Jakob disease (CJD) (Cohen and Freedman, 1995), is one of several rare dementing disorders caused by prions, which are transmissible proteinaceous particles containing little or no nucleic acid. Most cases arise sporadically; about 10% of cases are inherited in an autosomal dominant fashion; and, rarely, the disease occurs by accidental inoculation from transplanted tissue, contaminated neurosurgical instruments, or injected human growth hormone. The patients deteriorate rapidly and die within 6–12 months. Progressive mental decline is accompanied by extrapyramidal, pyramidal, cerebellar, and visual changes, lead pipe rigidity, and myoclonus. Typical 1 Hz biphasic and triphasic periodic complexes are commonly seen by electroencephalogram (EEG). The cognitive deficits are those of a cortical dementia, with prominent aphasia, agnosia, apraxia, and psychosis. Neuropathologic findings include diffuse cerebral atrophy, neuronal loss, astrocytosis, and spongiform vacuolation of neurons and glia. Neuroimaging studies reveal nonspecific atrophy. The diagnosis is confirmed by detecting the prion protein in the brain (Serban et al., 1990).

General Paresis

Once an important cause of dementia, general paresis (dementia paralytica), a form of tertiary neurosyphilis, is a rare disorder since the advent of antibiotics. The disorder is characterized by florid frontal lobe syndromes, memory impairment accompanied by small irregular pupils (sometimes the classic Argyll Robertson pupil), dysarthria, spasticity, and polyradiculopathy, and the diagnosis is confirmed by the presence of a cellular reaction in cerebrospinal fluid (CSF) and a positive serologic test in blood and CSF.

Dementias Associated with Brain Injury

Traumatic brain injuries usually exert their maximal effects immediately and improve gradually; one of the varied clinical syndromes that often persists is cognitive impairment. Although amnesia is the most common sequela, dementia with aphasia and frontal lobe features may also be seen (Levin, 1989; Mattson and Levin, 1990). One exception to this pattern is subdural hematoma, in which symptoms persist long after the actual injury as the extra cerebral collection of blood slowly expands. This is an important cause of cognitive impairment in alcoholic individuals and in elderly persons with subacute worsening of cognition; it should be suspected even when a history of head trauma is equivocal. Localizing neurologic signs support the diagnosis but may be absent. The diagnosis may be confirmed by CT or MRI evidence of local hypodensity and by EEG evidence of reduced voltage in the affected area, as well as by CSF xanthochromia. Repetitive head trauma of the kind experienced by boxers ruptures microvessels and causes microinfarction in cortical and subcortical areas. This leads to a condition known as dementia pugilistica, a syndrome characterized by dementia with cortical and subcortical features, ataxia, dysarthria, and parkinsonian features (Jordan, 1987).

Normal pressure hydrocephalus is an uncommon but potentially reversible dementia that may arise after brain trauma, subarachnoid hemorrhage, brain infection, or, in some cases, idiopathic causes. An abnormal resistance to CSF outflow and intermittent pressure waves is believed to lead to a ventricular enlargement (Bradley et al., 1991), the cardinal finding revealed by CT or MRI and, ultimately, to neuronal loss and cortical atrophy (Kaye et al., 1990; Vanneste et al., 1992). The clinical syndrome is classically characterized by the triad of dementia, gait disturbance (magnetic or apraxic gait), and urinary incontinence, although the last symptom is an inconsistent and often late feature (Benzel, Pelletier, and Levy, 1990). The cognitive deficits are commonly those of abulia, a syndrome of slowness, apathy, and lack of spontaneity—symptoms which, in their extreme, constitute akinetic mutism.

Reversible Dementias

Some dementias are fully reversible with appropriate treatment. More commonly, however, dementias considered in this category represent the reversible component of 2 or more coexisting conditions: a potentially treatable condition that exacerbates a second condition causing incipient but previously unrecognized dementia. An example of the latter is the dementia syndrome of depression (DSD). Depression frequently occurs either as a response to or symptom of a dementing disorder (e.g., vascular dementia, Parkinson dementia), or as an Axis I disorder in a person with emergent Alzheimer's disease. In many cases, treatment with antidepressants may result in substantial, if not full, recovery of intellectual function. In fact, a therapeutic response to antidepressants in this setting is highly suggestive of DSD (Folstein and McHugh, 1978). Follow-up of these patients over the next decade, however, will show that the majority develop Alzheimer's type dementia (Kral and Emery, 1989). Because depression can promote earlier onset of dementia, its recognition and appropriate treatment in the context of dementia are crucial. Clues that should heighten the suspicion of DSD include personal or family histories of affective disorders, sleep disturbances (especially early morning awakening), and reports or awareness of depressed mood. Compared to individuals with Alzheimer's disease alone, patients with DSD are more likely to be concerned about their cognitive symptoms and will tend to seek medical attention at an earlier stage of cognitive impairment. Rather than understating or denying their cognitive deficits, they are acutely aware of these deficits and may even express greater distress over the level of impairment than might be expected from objective cognitive testing. Behavioral deterioration may also exceed the severity of cognitive dysfunction (Emery and Oxman, 1992). Asymmetric frontal hypometabolism evident by PET, distinct from the biparietal and temporal hypometabolism seen in Alzheimer patients, may provide additional support for the diagnosis. Given the possible benefits of antidepressant treatment and the promise of new antidepressants having relatively favorable side effect profiles and lower anticholinergic activity, there should be a low threshold for initiating an antidepressant trial with a demented patient when a possible component of depression cannot clearly be excluded.

Among potentially reversible dementias, those caused by drugs, chemical toxins, and metabolic disturbances are the most common. Most of these present acutely with delirium, but a few are more insidious and resemble a progressive dementia instead. For many of the examples in Table 16.1, it has not been established whether the factors are etiologic or if they merely provoke dementia in individuals with a preexisting vulnerability. Long-acting benzodiazepines, hypnotics, and anticholinergic medications may precipitate a dementia syndrome, particularly

in older individuals. Chronic alcohol abuse may also lead to dementia, typically with frontal lobe features, in about 3% of alcoholic inpatients (Cutting, 1982) but more frequently causes amnestic syndromes, as described later. Abstinence from drinking may result in significant improvement for the alcoholic patient, especially in the first few weeks (Victor, 1994). An alarming trend in children and young adults is the increasing practice of inhaling organic solvent vapors, such as toluene, in paints, glues, and other commercial products to achieve an altered state of consciousness. Persistent cognitive impairment tends to be a late consequence of this practice but can be quite profound (Fornazzari et al., 1983). Metal poisoning gives rise to various encephalopathic states that may satisfy the criteria for dementia but more commonly cause delirium. Furthermore, deficiencies of certain vitamins can cause dementia. For example, vitamin B_{12} deficiency may present as an insidious intellectual deterioration with associated affective disturbances and delusions. These symptoms may precede the onset of the hallmark neurologic complication, subacute combined degeneration of the spinal cord, and may even occur in the absence of hematologic findings of pernicious anemia. Vitamin B_{12} replacement therapy may benefit some patients, but many show little improvement from it (Hector and Burton, 1988). Folic acid deficiency causes a similar syndrome (Strachan and Henderson, 1967). Cognitive impairment is associated with vitamin deficiencies that are rarely seen in this country except in the alcoholic population; these include thiamine (vitamin B_1) deficiency causing Wernicke's syndrome and Korsakoff's syndrome (discussed later), and nicotinic acid deficiency (pellagra) causing dermatitis, diarrhea, and dementia. Various metabolic disturbances are customarily included in lists of reversible dementias but are more likely to cause apathy, attentional and concentration deficits, or clouding of consciousness than dementia.

Management of Dementia

Although dementia is irreversible and progressive in many cases, the symptoms that are often most disturbing to patients or their families are amenable to treatment. In one study, 87% of caregivers reported depression, anger, and fatigue as a consequence of caring for a demented family member. The greatest contribution to the caregiver's burden was not memory dysfunction per se but behaviors such as physical agitation, accusatory behavior, and suspiciousness—symptoms that are largely manageable. Relieving these symptoms not only improves the quality of life for these patients but, by reducing burdens on families or other caregivers, also enables patients to function independently and remain with their families for longer periods of time.

Dementia management involves a judicious balance of nonpharmacologic and pharmacologic approaches tailored to the individual's specific needs, which may change markedly over the course of the illness. The degree of disruption caused by behavioral symptoms is not necessarily proportional to dementia severity. It is important for caregivers and families to recognize that some of the most disturbing behaviors, such as agitation and violent outbursts, may arise relatively early in the course but then become considerably less intense later. Caregivers who are not aware of the natural course may believe that the burdens will only increase over time and may make premature judgments about their ability to manage a demented family member at home.

Intervention should begin with identifying troublesome behaviors that may be modified without medications. Even when pharmacotherapy is necessary, nonpharmacologic approaches greatly reduce the number and dosages of required medication. A history and physical examination will determine whether or not medications or medical conditions are contributing to confusion, agitation, sedation, psychosis, or sleep disturbance. Specific questions should be asked about alcohol intake or the use of over-the-counter medications and "natural" remedies.

Providing an understanding of the dementing process to family members and caregivers and conveying the intention of developing a real partnership to work through problems that may arise is essential to long-term management. Education about the natural course of the dementing illness, the factors that may influence day-to-day functioning, and the repertoire of available therapeutic interventions provides reassurance to the family and readjusts their expectations to match the patient's limitations, thereby modifying their responses to the patient— all of which is likely to have beneficial consequences. For example, variations in cognitive performance that are typical during the early course of dementia often lead family members to believe that the patient has voluntary control over his or her level of performance. As a result, they may fail to recognize the patient's limitations and interpret repetitive questioning and other signs of memory loss as attention-seeking or passive-aggressive behavior. The patient's inability to meet these expectations, coupled with frustration or anger on the part of the caregiver, reinforces the patient's sense of failure and fears of abandonment and may promote depression, anxiety, isolation, and worsening cognitive performance. An understanding

of the patient's functional limitations encourages the caregiver to be supportive when the patient performs up to his or her potential and discourages challenging the patient beyond his or her limits.

Anxiety and other psychiatric symptoms also arise in situations that require the patient to learn new information or retrieve recently acquired memories—the areas of greatest dysfunction in the demented individual. For example, unfamiliar environments encountered on vacations or trips to the city, or social interactions involving groups of new people or recent acquaintances, often provoke considerable anxiety and may be vigorously resisted against the wishes of family members who may incorrectly see these activities as "therapeutic." Daily activities need to be continually simplified to avoid a sense of failure while encouraging as much autonomy as possible. Activities requiring a considerable degree of new learning should be replaced with activities that rely on skills previously mastered by the patient in his or her occupation or hobbies. Daily and weekly routines should be structured to provide a feeling of constancy and predictability. Living environments should preserve orienting stimuli such as the individual's furniture and memorabilia, as well as calendars, clocks, and message boards. Hearing and vision impairments should be corrected to maximize communication.

Behavioral disturbances also develop when cognitive deficits create the sense of losing control over one's environment. Patients may compensate for this loss of control by hiding or denying deficits and by resisting offers of support. Extreme conflicts often arise when families take necessary steps to safeguard the patient by restricting driving, cooking, and other activities of independent living, or by introducing additional caregivers into the house. The patient may resist doctor visits, fearing that the detection of deficits will catalyze a further loss of autonomy and prompt nursing home placement. Sensitivity to the issue of maximizing the patient's autonomy is crucial to allaying anxiety. Decision making and assumption of responsibility should be allowed to the maximal extent possible within the limits of safety. Preservation of and respect for the patient's personal space and possessions creates needed constancy in the environment and promotes a sense of autonomy. Anxieties arising from the fear of abandonment may be minimized by avoiding unnecessary confrontations, anger, and conflict, by providing repeated reassurances of support, and by preserving caregiver continuity.

Even with the most assiduous application of nonpharmacologic approaches, dementia management usually requires additional pharmacologic intervention. Certain behaviors that are generally responsive to medication include depression, sleep disturbances, delusions, hallucinations, verbal and physical agitation, and regressed behaviors (Maletta, 1994).

Depression is common at early stages of dementia and may frequently herald dementia onset. Indeed, a mild to moderate cognitive deficit occurring in the elderly in the context of major depression has been well recognized and was previously termed "pseudo dementia" because cognitive symptoms often improve as the depression is treated. It is now known that, even after successful antidepressant treatment, dementia emerges in most of these cases within a few years, implying that depression provoked a preclinical stage of dementia to become clinically manifest. Moreover, the emergence of depression at any stage during dementia is usually associated with worsening cognitive performance and deteriorating function. Even when depressed mood is not evident, anxiety, sleep disturbance, or psychosis may be responsive to antidepressants. Newer antidepressants are generally well tolerated by the elderly, and because the consequences of untreated depressive symptoms are considerable, clinicians should maintain a relatively low threshold for initiating an antidepressant trial if 1 or more target symptoms is identified. The selective serotonin reuptake inhibitors (SSRI) fluoxetine, sertraline, and paroxetine are the antidepressants of choice in the demented individual because of their minimal cholinergic, antihistaminic, and antiadrenergic side effects. Although well tolerated, these medications should be initiated in low doses in the elderly. Individuals unresponsive to SSRIs, particularly those with psychomotor retardation and apathy, may respond to norepinephrine reuptake inhibitors. Among the best tolerated and least cardiotoxic are desipramine and bupropion; however, either may cause agitation, and the latter may lower seizure threshold to a greater extent than other antidepressants. Electroconvulsive therapy (ECT) should be considered for melancholic or psychotic depression where the severity of symptoms or debilitated physical state of the patient precludes a pharmacologic approach.

Sleep-wake disturbances arise commonly in depressed or psychotic individuals with dementia, and in SDAT may become more prominent later, when brain centers controlling circadian rhythms begin to degenerate. Initial management should begin by (1) maintaining a constant bedtime schedule; (2) maximizing daytime activities to avoid napping and reducing factors that increase daytime sedation; and (3) eliminating stimulants and activating stimuli at night. Bright-light therapy during the day has also been used effectively to reduce sundowning behavior,

a worsening CF cognition that occurs in the early evening, and may promote more normal sleep patterns (Satlin et al., 1992). Pharmacologic treatment should first be aimed toward correcting primary psychiatric symptoms such as psychosis and depression that may underlie the sleep disturbance. The sedative antiserotonergic antidepressant trazodone in low doses (50–100 mg) often induces sleep and reduces daytime anxiety while causing few adverse side effects. Short-acting benzodiazepines, such as oxazepam (Serax, 15 mg) or the more sedative medication lorazepam (Ativan, 0.5 mg), may be considered for acute situations, but are rarely indicated for continual use because of their potential for exacerbating cognitive impairment.

The presence of hallucinations should prompt evaluation and appropriate treatment if indicated for delirium or an epileptic focus. Both hallucinations and delusions are relatively common in SDAT and respond well to very low doses of high potency neuroleptics such as haloperidol (e.g., 0.5 mg daily) or trifluoperazine (e.g., 4 mg), although extrapyramidal side effects are common and are sometimes confused with target symptoms. Newer neuroleptics such as risperidone, which have a lower potential for extrapyramidal effects, may have some advantages as an alternative.

Agitation and disinhibited behavior are among the most frequently encountered associated symptoms of dementia. Some of the major causes of anxiety and agitation have been discussed above, and management begins with the nonpharmacologic approaches previously described and by treating primary psychiatric conditions. For agitation not attributable to these conditions, neuroleptics remain the most widely used pharmacologic intervention. Their use in this situation, despite the fact that they are frequently ineffective and commonly cause side effects, simply reflects the lack of systematic investigation of alternative therapies. However, anecdotal experience and small uncontrolled studies are beginning to provide some support for alternative treatments. For example, trazodone in low doses during the day or at bedtime diminishes agitation effectively in some anxious patients. SSRIs, such as sertraline, may also be effective for anxiety and agitation, even in patients who appear minimally depressed. The anticonvulsants carbamazepine or valproic acid may be effective in some patients with severe agitation unresponsive to other treatments. While relatively well tolerated, these medications may cause ataxia, gastrointestinal side effects, and, rarely, hepatoxicity. In the case of carbamazepine, the slight risk of leukopenia or, rarely, aplastic anemia requires regular monitoring of the white blood cell count. The short-acting benzodiazepine oxazepam may be useful for occasional acute episodes of agitation. More severe agitation may be effectively treated acutely with the more sedative benzodiazepine lorazepam, which can also be administered intramuscularly. As previously mentioned, the benzodiazepines are poor choices for chronic treatment of anxiety or agitation.

The foregoing overview is only a general approach to management and suggests only initial pharmacologic strategies. The reader is referred to several reviews (Lake and Grossberg, 1996) for more detailed discussion of approved and experimental pharmacologic treatments for the behavioral and psychiatric symptoms associated with dementia and for the cognitive deficits themselves. Research to develop cognitive enhancers is particularly active, although no agent has yet been found to improve cognitive function unequivocally in demented patients as a general group. Hydergine, a mixture of 3 ergoloid mesylates, has been widely prescribed for patients with dementia for over 50 years. Numerous studies at conventional doses (e.g., 1 mg t.i.d.) have shown little efficacy in SDAT and only modest clinical effects in vascular dementia, which may relate to mild stimulant effect or antidepressant effects. Higher doses (6–9 mg daily), however, are well tolerated with few side effects and, in anecdotal experiences, may modestly improve overall levels of function in certain demented individuals.

Delirium

Delirium is the most commonly encountered psychiatric syndrome in a general hospital setting. While it is not restricted to any age group, its prevalence is considerably higher among the elderly, especially those with preexisting brain dysfunction. Its emergence in an elderly person is an ominous prognostic sign and requires prompt medical attention to identify and treat the underlying causes. Despite its clinical significance, delirium remains, as Lipowski has called it, "the Cinderella of American Psychiatry—taken for granted, ignored, and seldom studied" (Lipowski, 1983).

The lack of agreement about the fundamental nature of this disorder and the criteria for its diagnosis have spawned a confusing array of clinical terms to denote this state and its apparent subvariants. While some investigators stress the importance of distinguishing a syndrome of hyperactivity, autonomic arousal, and hallucinations from the state of quiet confusion and disorientation (Adams and Victor, 1989), DSM-IV considers delirium as one general syndrome. The cardinal clinical feature is a deficit

in maintaining, shifting, and focusing attention, thereby reducing an individual's ability to perceive the environment correctly and respond to it appropriately. Global disturbance of perception, thinking, and memory, the 3 major aspects of cognition, is a second core feature. These symptoms arise acutely or subacutely and fluctuate during the course of the day. The syndrome is usually transient and reversible, although these are not among the DSM-IV criteria. Prevalence rates for delirium vary widely as a result of epidemiological analyses being influenced by the composition of the patient population under study, the diagnostic and exclusion criteria applied, and the rigor of the assessment methods. In hospitalized patients over the age of 65, estimates range between 10% and 35% for those diagnosed (Lipowski, 1983). About 25% of those judged to be cognitively intact on admission may be expected to develop delirium during the first month of hospitalization (Hodkinson, 1973). A sobering statistic is the further observation that 1 in 4 elderly patients exhibiting delirium on admission to the hospital dies within a month (Hodkinson, 1973; Bedford, 1959; Simon and Cahan, 1963). It is important to bear in mind, however, that mortality in this setting seems to depend more on the nature of the medical condition or conditions than on the presence or absence of delirium (van Hemert et al., 1994; Kishi et al., 1995). In one study, for example, mortality rates varied twelvefold among groups of delirious patients with different medical illnesses.

The risk for developing delirium increases markedly in individuals over the age of 60. The presence of preexisting brain damage or other central nervous system (CNS) neurologic abnormalities also greatly increases this risk (Lipowski, 1990). Many medical conditions predispose individuals to delirium, but certain populations are considered to be especially vulnerable. These include individuals with advanced AIDS, alcoholics or chronic abusers of barbiturates and benzodiazepines in acute withdrawal, burn patients, and post-surgical patients. In any hospitalized patient, the use of multiple medications, particularly those with anticholinergic activity (Dyer, Ashton, and Teasdale, 1995), malnutrition (Inouye and Charpentier, 1996), and the use of physical restraints are additional factors that increase the risk of delirium.

Clinical Features

In delirium, impairments in attention, cognition, sleep-wake cycle, and psychomotor behavior wax and wane unpredictably during the course of a day (Lipowski, 1983). Cognition frequently worsens in the early evening, a phenomenon known as sundowning. Transient lucid intervals may occur, and their presence distinguishes delirium from dementia.

Although delirium presents in many different ways, attention is invariably disrupted (Beresin, 1988; Levkoff et al., 1986, 1991; Lipowski, 1983, 1990; Seltzer, 1986). The level of arousal, one aspect of attention, may be increased or decreased, giving rise to a state of hyperactivity associated with agitation, and autonomic symptoms or a state of quiet confusion and apathy which is sometimes mistaken for depression. Hypoactive and hyperactive periods often oscillate in the course of the day. In both states concentration is diminished and less selective. On the one hand, the patient loses the ability to focus on incoming stimuli well enough to organize and fix them clearly mentally. On the other hand, attention may at times transiently become fixated on a distracting stimulus, such as an indistinct conversation or noise outside the room, which is often misinterpreted and may inspire a loosely organized delusional system. With a shortened attention span, the patient's stream of thought loses its goal directedness and conversation becomes rambling, fragmentary, and disjointed. These attentional deficits exacerbate, or may actually cause, other deficits in cognition. For example, failing to attend to appropriate environmental cues may lead the patient to become disoriented to time and place. Personal identity is almost always preserved. Attentional deficits also impede the registration of new information and impair recent memory.

Not all cognitive deficits, however, are attention related. Memory in all of its aspects is impaired, although remote memory is less affected. Executive functions, including the ability to reason, think abstractly, plan, and organize, are usually disrupted. Performance in constructional tasks, writing, and naming is poor. The perception of objects, people, and surroundings is commonly distorted, which may lead to illusions, delusions, or hallucinations, more commonly visual than auditory. Unfamiliar surroundings or people are often misidentified as familiar. These perceptual deficits, coupled with heightened arousal and rapid shifts in focus, give rise to a kaleidoscope of erratic behaviors and shifting emotional states, the intensity of which may actually overshadow the cognitive features. Wakefulness and general activity may be reduced during the day and increased at night. Sleep becomes fragmented, and agitation, hallucinations, and disorientation increase as dream states intrude into waking, especially in settings of reduced sensory input. The heightened states of arousal that typify drug and alcohol withdrawal are accompanied by autonomic hyperactivity including tachycardia, diaphoresis, and anxiety. Intention

tremor, myoclonus, and asterixis ("liver flap") also appear in delirious states associated with drug withdrawal or metabolic encephalopathy.

Differential Diagnosis

Differentiating delirium from other cognitive disorders is usually not difficult. "Acute onset of global cognitive and attentional deficits and abnormalities, the severity of which fluctuates during the day and tends to be highest at night, is practically diagnostic of delirium" (Lipowski, 1983). By contrast, "pre-existing cognitive impairment present for months or years; varying little over the course of the day; relatively normal alertness, attention, and level of consciousness; and lack of concurrent physical illness or drug intoxication all suggest the diagnosis of dementia" (Lipowski, 1990). These distinctions are not always clear-cut, however, because of the high frequency with which delirium is superimposed on a preexisting dementia. Under these conditions, the contributions of each state to the clinical picture may be difficult to assess and may become evident only after the delirium is appropriately treated. Given the markedly different prognostic and treatment implications for these 2 conditions, the misidentification of delirium as dementia could have serious consequences. Accordingly, upon any acute or subacute change in cognitive status, delirium should be immediately suspected and evaluation initiated, regardless of whether or not a previous cognitive dysfunction exists. Acute confusional states can also arise in the absence of a demonstrable neurologic or systemic cause. While these states may be attributable to functional psychosis, it is unwise to presume a functional basis for any acute confusional state, even when a past history of psychiatric disorder exists.

Although delirium is diagnosed on the basis of behavioral signs and symptoms, the electroencephalogram may be a useful diagnostic tool. Bilateral diffuse slowing of EEG background activity correlates with the severity of cognitive impairment in delirious patients. Abnormal low voltage fast activity characterizes the state of heightened arousal associated with delirium tremens and other withdrawal states, as well as hyperthyroidism (Pro and Wells, 1977). These EEG abnormalities may be most helpful in distinguishing delirium from the acute confusional states associated with functional psychosis, in which the EEG is usually normal. Although rarely indicative of a specific etiology, certain EEG patterns may suggest the presence of certain metabolic disorders (e.g., hepatic encephalopathy), encephalitis, some drug interactions, epilepsy, or focal neurologic processes (e.g., stroke, abscess, or tumor). EEG slowing may also be seen in elderly patients with dementia and is therefore less useful in distinguishing dementia and delirium.

Once the presence of delirium is established, identifying its cause or causes relies on routine medical diagnosis. Precipitating organic factors can be identified in 80–95% of elderly individuals with delirium (Hodkinson, 1973; Simon and Cahan, 1963; Purdie, Honigman, and Rosen, 1981). A list of possible organic causes would include nearly every known illness, intoxication, or metabolic disturbance (Table 16.6), but these can be conveniently sub-

Table 16.6 Etiologies of delirium

Drug Intoxication
  Anticholinergics, sympathomimetics, opiates, antiparkinson drugs
  Lithium
  Antiarrythmics (e.g., lidocaine)
  H$_2$-receptor blockers
  Sedative-hypnotics
  Alcohol
  Toxins: pesticides, solvents
  Heavy metals: mercury, lead, manganese

Drug Withdrawal
  Alcohol
  Sedative-hypnotics

Trauma
  Heat stroke, postoperative states, severe burns
  Cerebral contusion
  Subdural hematoma

CNS Pathology
  Seizures
  Tumor
  Normal pressure hydrocephalus

Infection
  Cerebral (e.g., meningitis, encephalitis, HIV, syphilis, abscesses)
  Systemic (e.g., sepsis, urinary tract infection, pneumonia)

Vascular
  Cerebrovascular (e.g., infarcts, hemorrhage, vasculitis, hypertensive encephalopathy)
  Cardiovascular (e.g., low output states, congestive heart failure, shock)

Physiological or Metabolic
  Hypoxemia, anemia, electrolyte disturbances, hyposmolality, renal or hepatic failure, acidosis, carbon monoxide poisoning
  Endocrine disorders
    thyroid disturbance, hyper- or hypoglycemia
  Nutritional
    Thiamine, niacin, or vitamin B$_{12}$ deficiency

divided into 4 general categories: (1) primary cerebral diseases; (2) systemic diseases affecting the brain secondarily, notably metabolic encephalopathies, neoplasms, infections, and cardiovascular and collagen diseases; (3) intoxication with exogenous substances, including medical and recreational drugs and poisons of plant, animal, and industrial origin; and (4) withdrawal from substances of abuse in a person addicted to them, mostly alcohol and sedative hypnotic drugs (Lipowski, 1990). Working in concert with these organic factors are sleep deprivation, psychological stress, exposure to unfamiliar surroundings, and excessive or deficient sensory input (Lipowski, 1983). Adverse effects of prescribed medications, especially those with anticholinergic activities, are perhaps the most common cause of delirium in the elderly. Other common causes include congestive heart failure, pneumonia, urinary tract infection, cancer, uremia, hypokalemia, dehydration and/or sodium depletion, and cerebral infarction involving the right hemisphere (Lipowski, 1990). Although a complete assessment should consider all possible causes in Table 16.6, the clinician should be particularly vigilant in identifying emergent conditions that require urgent medical treatment to avoid irreversible damage.

Pathophysiology

The pathophysiologic basis for delirium is poorly understood (Trzepacz, 1994). Current concepts still draw heavily on the hypothesis of Engel and Romano from the 1940s that delirium involves a reduction in cerebral metabolism, reflected in a slowing of EEG background activity (Romano and Engel, 1944; Engel and Romano, 1944). The observation that decreased oxidative metabolism, among its many other effects, depresses the synthesis of acetylcholine spawned a further hypothesis that impaired cholinergic transmission underlies the global deficits in cognition and, possibly, alterations in the sleep cycle observed in delirium (Blass and Plum, 1983). This notion is consistent with known functions of the basal forebrain and pontine cholinergic projections to cortical, subcortical, and brain stem areas. Supporting the key role of cholinergic mechanisms in delirium is the ability of anticholinergic medications to induce delirium, the reversibility of this state by physostigmine, and the correlation between cognitive impairment and serum anticholinergic levels in delirium (Mach et al., 1995). Central noradrenergic activity increases in delirium tremens (Hawley et al., 1981) and may, along with altered dopaminergic transmission, contribute to an elevated state of arousal. Other neurotransmitter systems have also been implicated, but the evidence for their involvement is fragmentary and circumstantial (Trzepacz, 1994).

Management

Delirium management centers on treating the underlying illness, keeping in mind that the underlying cause may, in fact, be many causes. Management should begin by identifying and correcting emergent states that require particularly urgent attention (Table 16.6). For example, parental thiamine should be given to all patients suspected of having Wernicke's encephalopathy, a syndrome of confusion, ataxia, and ophthalmoplegia that may evolve to the irreversible amnestic state, Korsakoff's psychosis. Rapid assessment of other emergent conditions including hypoglycemia, hypoxia, hyperthermia, and severe hypertension should likewise have highest priority in the evaluation process. The course of subsequent medical treatment depends on the underlying causes, but most commonly involve discontinuing a medication or toxic agent, correcting an electrolyte imbalance, treating an infection, or improving a nutritional factor. Alcohol and barbiturate/benzodiazepine withdrawal require specific approaches involving readministration of the intoxicating agent or its pharmacologic equivalent and allowing a slower, more controlled withdrawal process.

Pharmacologic therapy is often necessary to reduce inappropriate behavior that interferes with medical care or is harmful to the patient or others. Although criteria for choosing a particular agent are based on anecdotal evidence, there is general agreement that low doses of a high potency neuroleptic, such as haloperidol, given orally or parentally up to several times per day can produce considerable benefits without depressing respiration, causing hypotension, or contributing to anticholinergic activity. Haloperidol is quite well tolerated when given intravenously in doses similar to those used orally. Low potency neuroleptics (e.g., chlorpromazine, thioridazine) and antihistamines have unfavorable side effects that may exacerbate the delirium. Except in drug withdrawal states, the role of benzodiazepines in treating delirium is not established. Although they should generally be avoided in routine treatment of delirium, benzodiazepines may be helpful in low doses when short-term sedation is necessary to complete a critical imaging study, or as an adjunct to high potency neuroleptics when agitation is potentially life threatening and does not respond to a neuroleptic alone.

Given the normal fluctuating course of delirium, continuous follow-up is essential to evaluate the response and modify the treatment plan when needed. Close and consistent observation is facilitated by situating the patient near the nursing station. The company of a family member during and after the delirium may provide calming reassurance to an agitated patient and increase the level of vigilance against inappropriate behavior. It is usually helpful to eliminate extremes of sensory input to the patient, for example, by providing adequate room lighting at night and avoiding contact with other delirious patients. Measures that reorient the patient to his or her surroundings are also helpful, such as placing a clock, a calendar, and familiar objects or photographs in the room.

Amnestic Disorders

Amnesia

The amnesic syndrome, thought rare, represents the most striking pattern of memory disorder. The most famous amnesic patient, HM, was first described in 1957 (Scoville and Milner, 1957). His profound difficulty with the ability to learn new information resulted from the surgical removal of the medial temporal lobes as a treatment for epilepsy. Since then, it has become evident that a wide variety of disorders can produce an amnesic disorder (e.g., alcoholic Korsakoff's syndrome, herpes encephalitis, ischemia, and surgical excision).

Pathology. When HM was first described, it was thought that his anterograde amnesia was primarily the result of damage to the hippocampus. However, systematic work since that time, in both humans and non-human primates, has revealed that the areas of cortex adjacent to the hippocampus (including the entorhinal, the perirhinal and the parahippocampal cortices) are as necessary as the hippocampus itself in producing normal anterograde explicit memory (see Zola-Morgan and Squire, 1990, for a review). The amygdala, once thought to be part of this explicit memory system, appears to be involved in the recall of emotionally charged information but, if damaged in isolation, does not produce a significant deficit in the ability to learn new material that has no affective impact (e.g., LeDoux et al., 1990). Damage to structures in the medial diencephalon, such as the intralaminar nuclei of the thalamus, also produces an anterograde amnesia (Winocur et al., 1984; Langlais et al., 1992). The most common form of diencephalic amnesia can be seen in patients with alcoholic Korsakoff's syndrome, in which the dorsomedial nucleus of the thalamus and the mammillary bodies are lesioned as a result of thiamine deficiency and chronic alcohol abuse (Butters and Cermak, 1980).

Clinical features. All amnesic patients share with HM a common pattern of anterograde memory deficit in that they have a severe disability in learning new information in the absence of other intellectual deficits. For example, if one reads a word list repeatedly to an amnesic patient, he or she learns and retains little of it. The difficulty with new learning experienced by amnesic patients is, however, primarily limited to information that they are explicitly trying to remember, and is therefore often called "explicit" memory. Learning a route to a new location or remembering the plot of a new movie is an example of explicit memory.

Amnesic patients also have difficulty with remote memory. For example, they have difficulty remembering information from the past, such as important historical events that occurred during their lifetime. This remote memory deficit generally, though not always, has a temporal gradient, with the most remote events being better preserved than the most recent ones. The pattern and extent of this remote memory deficit varies according to the etiology of the disorder (Albert, Butters, and Brandt, 1981).

However, amnesic patients are typically unimpaired on tests of "implicit" memory, where memory is inferred from a change in performance on a task, without the subject's having made a conscious effort to learn something new (Graf and Schacter, 1985). Motor skill learning (e.g., learning to ride a bicycle), where the individual generally does not consciously learn each movement needed to become skilled, is one example of the type of implicit learning that is not impaired in amnesic patients.

Despite the devastating effect that an amnesia has on an individual's ability to function independently, it is uncommon for amnesic patients to develop behavioral abnormalities. They rarely become upset when they have difficulty recalling new information. Some amnesic patients, such as those with alcoholic Korsakoff's syndrome, have clear affective changes that explain this behavior (e.g., Oscar-Berman et al., 1990), but others do not.

References

Adams, R. D., and Victor, M. 1989. *Principles of neurology.* 4th ed. New York: McGraw-Hill.

Albert, M., Butters, N., and Brandt, J. 1981. Patterns of remote memory in amnesic and dementing patients. *Arch. Neurol.* 38:401–408.

Albert, M., and Cohen, C. 1992. The test for severe impairment: an instrument for the assessment of patients with severe cognitive dysfunction. *J. Am. Geriatr. Soc.* 40:449–453.

Albert, M. S., and Moss, M. 1988. *Geriatric neuropsychology.* New York: Guilford Press.

Alzheimer, A. 1907. A new disease of the cortex. *Allg. Z. Psychol.* 64:146–148.

Beardsall, L., and Huppert, F. 1991. A comparison of clinical, psychometric, and behavioural memory tests: findings from a community study of the early detection of dementia. *Int. J. Ger. Psychiat.* 6:295–306.

Beck, B. J. 1995. Neuropsychiatric manifestations of diffuse Lewy body disease. *J. Geri. Psych. Neurol.* 8(3):189–196.

Bedford, P. D. 1959. General medical aspects of confusional states in elderly people. *Br. Med. J.* 2:185–188.

Benton, A. L., and Hamsher, K. 1976. Multilingual aphasia examination. Iowa City: University of Iowa Press.

Benzel, C. C., Pelletier, A. L., and Levy, P. G. 1990. Communicating hydrocephalus in adults: prediction of outcome after ventricular shunting procedures. *Neurosurgery* 26:660–665.

Beresin, E. V. 1988. Delirium in the elderly. *J. Geri. Psych. Neurol.* 1:127.

Blass, J. P., and Plum, F. 1983. Metabolic encephalopathies. In *The neurology of aging,* ed. Katzman, R., and Terry, R. D. Philadelphia: F. A. Davis.

Bleeker, M. L., Colla-Wilson, K., Kawas, C., Agnew, J. 1988. Age-specific norms for the Mini-Mental State Exam. *Neurology* 38:1565–68.

Blessed, G., Tomlinson, B. E., and Roth, M. 1968. The association between quantitative measures of dementia and of senile changes in the cerebral gray matter of elderly subjects. *British Journal of Psychiatry* 114:797–811.

Boll, T. 1981. The Halstead-Reitan neuropsychology battery. In *Handbook of clinical neuropsychology,* ed. Fliskov, S., and Boll, T. New York: Wiley-Intersciences.

Braak, H., and Braak, E. 1995. Staging of Alzheimer's disease–related neurofibrillary changes. *Neurol. Aging* 16(3):271–284.

Bradley, W. G. Jr., Whittemore, A. R., Kortman, K. E., et al. 1991. Marked cerebrospinal fluid void: indicator of successful shunt in patients with suspected normal-pressure hydrocephalus. *Radiology* 178:459–466.

Breitner, J. C. S., Gau, B. A., Welsh, K. A., et al. 1994. Inverse relationship of anti-inflammatory treatments and Alzheimer's disease: initial results of a co-twin control study. *Neurol.* 44:227–232.

Broderick, D. F., Wippold, F. J., Clifford, D. B., et al. 1993. White matter lesions and cerebral atrophy on M. R. images in patients with and without AIDS dementia complex. *Am. J. Roentgenology* 161:177–181.

Buschke, H., and Fuld, P. A. 1974. Evaluating storage, retention, and retrieval in disordered memory and learning. *Neurology* 11:1019–25.

Butters, N., and Cermak, L. 1980. *Alcoholic Korsakoff's syndrome.* New York: Academic Press.

Caplan, L. R. 1995. Binswanger's disease, revisited. *Neurol.* 45:626–633.

Checler, F. 1995. Processing of the ß-amyloid precursor protein and its regulation in Alzheimer's disease. *J. Neurochem.* 65(4):1431–44.

Chiu, H. F. K. 1995. Psychiatric aspects of progressive supranuclear palsy. *Genl. Hosp. Psychiatry* 17:135–143.

Cohen, S,. and Freedman, M. 1995. Cognitive and behavioral changes in the Parkinson-plus syndromes. *Behav. Neurol. Movement Disorders* 65:139–157.

Corder, E. H., Saunders, A. M., Strittmatter, W. J., et al. 1993. Gene dose of apolipoprotein E type 4 allele and the risk of Alzheimer's disease in late onset families. *Science* 261:921–923.

Corey-Blum, J., Galasko, D., and Thal, L. J. 1995. Is it Alzheimer's? A strategy for diagnosis. *Im. Intern. Med. Spec.* 16:28–37.

Cotman, C. W., and Pike, C. J. 1994. ß-amyloid and its contributions to neurodegeneration in Alzheimer's disease. In *Alzheimer's disease,* ed. Terry, R. D., Katzman, R., and Bick, K. L. New York: Raven. 305.

Cummings, J. L., Ross, W., Absher, J., Gornbein, J., Hadjiaghai, L. 1995. Depressive symptoms in Alzheimer disease: assessments and determinants. *Alz. Dis. Rel. Disorders* 9:87–93.

Cutting, J. 1982. Alcoholic dementia. In *Psychiatric aspects of neurologic disease.* Vol. 2, ed. Benson, D. F., and Blumer, D. New York: Grune & Stratton. 149–165.

Davis, K. L., and Powchik, P. 1995. Tacrine. *Lancet* 345:625–630.

Delay, J., and Brion, S. 1962. *Les Démences Tardives.* Paris: Masson & Cie.

Delebar, J.-M., Goldgaber, D., Lamour, Y., et al. 1987. ß-amyloid gene duplication in Alzheimer's disease and karyotypically normal Down syndrome. *Science* 235:1390–92.

Delis, D. C., Kramer, J. H., Kaplan, E., Ober, B. A. 1987. California verbal learning test. New York: Psychological Corporation.

Dunbabin, D. W., and Sandercock, P. A. G. 1990. Preventing stroke by the modification of risk factors. *Stroke* 21(suppl. 4):IV36–IV39.

Dyer, C. B., Ashton, C. M., and Teasdale, T. A. 1995. Postoperative delirium: a review of 80 primary data–collection studies. *Arch. Intern. Med.* 155(5):461–465.

Emery, V. O., and Oxman, T. E. 1992. Update on the dementia spectrum of depression. *Am. J. Psych.* 149:305–317.

Engel, G. L., and Romano, J. 1944. Delirium: reversibility of the electroencephalogram with experimental procedures. *Arch. Neurol. Psychiatry* 51:378–392.

———— 1959. Delirium, a syndrome of cerebral insufficiency. *J. Chron. Dis.* 9:260–277.

Erkinjuntti, T. 1994. Clinical criteria for vascular dementia: the NINDS-AIREN criteria. *Dementia* 5:189–192.

Erkinjuntti, T., Haltia, M., Palo, J., Sulkava, R., Paetau, A. 1988. Accuracy of the clinical diagnosis of vascular dementia: a prospective clinical and post-mortem neuropathological study. *J. Neurol. Neurosurg. Psych.* 51:1037–44.

Farlow, M. R., Yee, R. D., Dlouhy, S. R., Conneally, P. M., Azzarelli, B., Ghetti, B. 1989. Gerstmann-Straussler-Scheinker disease: extending the clinical spectrum. *Neurology* 39:1446–52.

Feldman, M. J., and Drasgow, J. A. 1951. A visual-verbal test for schizophrenia. *Psychiatric Quarterly Supplement* 25:55–64.

Flowers, K., and Robertson, C. 1985. The effect of Parkinson's disease on the ability to maintain a mental set. *J. Neurol. Neurosurg. Psychiat.* 48:517–529.

Folstein, M. F., and Bylsma, W. 1994. Noncognitive symptoms of Alzheimer's disease. In *Alzheimer's disease,* ed. Terry, R. D., Katzman, R., and Bick, K. L. New York: Raven. 27–40.

Folstein, M. F., and McHugh, P. R. 1978. Dementia syndrome of depression. In *Alzheimer's disease, senile dementia, and related disorders,* ed. Katzman, R., Terry, R. D., and Bick, K. L. New York: Raven. 87–93.

Folstein, M. F., Folstein, S. E., and McHugh, P. R. 1975. "Mini-Mental State": a practical method for grading cognitive state of patients for the clinician. *J. Psychiatr. Res.* 12:189–198.

Fornazzari, L., Wilkinsin, D. A., Kapur, B. M., et al. 1983. Cerebellar, cortical, and functional impairment in tuolene abusers. *Acta Neurol. Scand.* 67:319–329.

Forstl, H., Sattel, H., and Bahro, M. 1993. Alzheimer's disease: clinical features. *Int. Rev. Psych.* 5:327–349.

Francis, P. T., Cross, A. J., and Bowen, D. M. 1994. Neurotransmitters and neuropeptides. In *Alzheimer's disease,* ed. Terry, R. D., Katzman, R., and Bick, K. L. New York: Raven. 247.

Fuld, P. A. 1980. Guaranteed stimulus-processing in the evaluation of memory and learning. *Cortex* 16:255–272.

Gans, A. 1922. Betrachtungern uber Art und Ausbreitung des krankhaften Prozesses in einem Fall von Pickscher Atrophie des Stirnhirns. *Zeitschrift fur die Gesante Neurologie und Psychiatrie* 80:10–28.

Gibb, W. R. G. 1989. Dementia and Parkinson's disease. *Br. J. Psychiatry* 154:596–614.

Gibb, W. R. G., Ersi, M. M., and Lees, A. J. 1985. Clinical and pathological features of diffuse cortical Lewy body disease (Lewy body dementia). *Brain* 110:1131–53.

Gibb, W. R. G., Scott, T., and Lees, A. J. 1991. Neuronal inclusions of Parkinson's disease. *Mov. Disord.* 6:2–11.

Goedert, M. 1993. Tau protein and the neurofibrillary pathology of Alzheimer's disease. *Trends Neurosci.* 16:460–465.

Golden, C. J. 1981. A standardized version of Luria's neuropsychological tests. In *Handbook of clinical neuropsychology,* ed. Fliskov, S., and Boll, T. New York: Wiley-Intersciences.

Goldgaber, D., Goldfarb, L., Brown, P., et al. 1989. Mutations in familial Creutzfeldt-Jakob disease and Gerstmann-Straussler-Schenkman syndrome. *Exp. Neurol.* 106:204–206.

Goodglass, H., and Kaplan, E. 1972. *The assessment of aphasia and related disorders.* Philadelphia: Lea & Febiger.

Gorham, D. R. 1956. A proverbs test for clinical and experimental use. *Psychological Reports* 1:1–12.

Graf, P., and Schacter, D. 1985. Implicit and explicit memory for new associations in normal and amnesic subjects. *J. Exper. Psychol. Learning, Memory, and Cognition* 11:501–518.

Gray, K. F. 1996. Dementia: Lewy body disease. *Geri. Psych. News* 2(2):6.

Grober, E., and Sliwinski, M. 1991. Development and validation of a model of estimating premorbid verbal intelligence in the elderly. *J. Clin. Exper. Neuropsychol.* 13:933–949.

Grotta, J. G., Norris, J. W., and Kamm, B. 1992. Prevention of stroke with ticlopidine: who benefits most? *Neurol.* 42:111–114.

Gustafson, L. 1987. Frontal lobe degeneration of non-Alzheimer type. I. Clinical picture and differential diagnosis. *Arch. Gen. Geriatr.* 6:209–223.

Halstead, W. C., and Wepman, J. M. 1949. The Halstead-Wepman aphasia screening test. *Journal of Speech and Hearing Disorders* 14:9–15.

Hansen, L., Salmon, D., Galasko, D., et al. 1990. The Lewy body variant of Alzheimer's disease: a clinical and pathological entity. *Neurol.* 40:1–8.

Hansen, L. A., Masliah, E., Terry, R. D., et al. 1989. A neuropathological subset of Alzheimer's disease with concomitant Lewy body disease and spongiform change. *Acta Neuropathol.* (Berlin) 78:194–201.

Harper, P. S. 1992. The epidemiology of Huntington's disease. *Hum. Genet.* 89:365–376.

Hass, W. K., Easton, J. D., Adams, H. P., et al. 1989. A randomized trial comparing ticlopidine hydrochloride with aspirin for the prevention of stroke in high-risk patients. *N. Engl. J. Med.* 321:501–507.

Hawley, R. J., Major, L. F., Schulman, E. A., et al. 1981. CSF levels of norepinephrine during alcohol withdrawal. *Arch. Neurol.* 38:289–292.

Hector, M., and Burton, J. R. 1988. What are the psychiatric manifestations of vitamin B12 deficiency? *J. Am. Geriatr. Soc.* 36:1105–12.

Heeren, T., Lagaay, A., Beek, W., Rooymans, H., Hijmans,

W. 1990. Reference values for the Mini-Mental State Examination (MMSE) in octo- and nonagenerians. *JAGS* 38:1093–96.

Hodkinson, H. M. 1973. Mental impairment in the elderly. *J. R. Coll. Physicians Lond.* 7:305–317.

Hof, P. R., and Morrison, J. H. 1994. The cellular basis of cortical disconnection in Alzheimer's disease and related dementing conditions. In *Alzheimer's disease,* ed. Terry, R. D., Katzman, R., and Bick, K. L. New York: Raven. 197.

Hofman, A., Schulte, W., Tanja, T. A., et al. 1989. History of dementia and Parkinson's disease in 1st-degree relative of patients with Alzheimer's disease. *Neurol.* 39:1589–92.

Huntington's Disease Collaborative Research Group. 1993. A novel gene containing a trinucleotide repeat that is expanded and unstable on Huntington's disease chromosomes. *Cell* 72:971–983.

Hyman, B. T., Van Hoesen, G. W., and Damasio, A. R. 1990. Memory-related neural systems in Alzheimer's disease: an anatomic study. *Neurol.* 40:1721–30.

Hyman, B. T., Van Hoesen, G. W., Kromer, L. J., Damasio, A. R. 1986. Perforant pathway changes and the memory impairment of Alzheimer's disease. *Ann. Neurol.* 20:472–481.

Inouye, S. K., and Charpentier, P. A. 1996. Precipitating factors for delirium in hospitalized elderly persons: predictive model and interrelationship with baseline vulnerability. *JAMA* 275(11):852–857.

Jordan, B. D. 1987. Neurologic aspects of boxing. *Arch. Neurol.* 44:453–454.

Kaplan, E., Goodglass, H., and Weintraub, S. 1983. *Boston Naming Test.* Philadelphia: Lea & Febiger.

Katzman, R.,, and Kawas, C. H. 1994. The epidemiology of dementia and Alzheimer's disease. In *Alzheimer's disease,* ed. Terry, R. D., Katzman, R., and Bick, K. L. New York: Raven. 105–122.

Kaye, J. A., Grady, C. L., Haxby, J. V., et al. 1990. Plasticity in the aging brain: reversibility of anatomic, metabolic, and cognitive deficits in normal-pressure hydrocephalus following shunt surgery. *Arch. Neurol.* 47:1336–41.

Kertesz, A. 1980. *Western Aphasia Battery.* London, Ontario: University of Western Ontario Press.

Khachaturian, Z. S. 1985. Diagnosis of Alzheimer's disease. *Arch. Neurol.* 42:1097–1105.

Kishi, Y., Iwasaki, Y., Takezawa, K., Kurosawa, H., Endo, S. 1995. Delirium in critical care unit patients admitted through an emergency room. *Gen. Hosp. Psychiatry* 17(5):371–379.

Knopman, D., Mastri, A., Frey, W., Sung, J., Rustan, T. 1990. Dementia lacking distinctive histologic features: a common non-Alzheimer degenerative dementia. *Neurology* 40:251–256.

Kraepelin, E. 1910. *Psychiatrie: Ein Lehrbuch für Studierende und Arzte,* vol. 2, *Klinische Psychiatrie,* part 1, pp. 616–632. Leipzig.

Kral, V. A., and Emery, O. B. 1989. Long-term follow-up of depressive pseudodementia of the aged. *Can. J. Psych.* 34:445–446.

Kuwert, L., Lange, H. W., Langen, K. J., et al. 1990. Cortical and sub-cortical glucose consumption measured by PET in patients with Huntington's disease. *Brain* 113:1405–23.

Lafleche, G., and Albert, M. 1995. Executive function deficits in mild Alzheimer's disease. *Neuropsychology* 9:313–320.

Lai, F., and Williams, R. S. 1989. A prospective study of Alzheimer disease in Down syndrome. *Arch. Neurol.* 46(8):849–853.

Lake, J. T., and Grossberg, G. T. 1996. Management of psychosis, agitation, and other behavioral problems in Alzheimer's disease. *Psych. Annl.* 25(5):274–279.

Langlais, P., Mandel, R., and Mair, R. 1992. Diencephalic lesions, learning impairments, and intact retrograde memory following acute thiamine deficiency in the rat. *Behav. Brain Res.* 48:177–185.

Lawton, P., Moss, M., Fulcomer, M., Kleban, M. 1982. A research and service-oriented multilevel assessment instrument. *J. Gerontol.* 37:91–99.

LeDoux, J., Cicchetti, P., Xagoraris, A., Romanski, L. 1990. The lateral amygdaloid nucleus: sensory interface of the amygdala in fear conditioning. *J. Neurosci.* 10:1062–1069.

Levin, H. S. 1989. Memory deficit after closed-head injury. *J. Clin. Exp. Neuropsych.* 12:129–153.

Levkoff, S. E., Besdine, R. W., and Wetle, T. 1986. Acute confusional states (delirium) in the hospitalized elderly. *Ann. Rev. Geron. Geri.* 6:1–26.

Levkoff, S. E., Liptzin, B., Cleary, P., et al. 1991. Review of research instruments and techniques used to detect delirium. *Int. Psychogeri.* 3:253–271.

Levy-Lahad, E., Wasco, W., et al. 1995. A familial Alzheimer's disease locus on chromosome 1. *Science* 269:970–972.

Lezak, M. 1983. *Neuropsychological assessment.* New York: Oxford University Press.

Lipowski, Z. J. 1983. Transient cognitive disorders (delirium, acute confusional states) in the elderly. *Am. J. Psychiatry* 11(140):1426–36.

——— 1990. *Delirium: acute confusional states.* New York: Oxford University Press.

Lipton, S. A., and Gendelman, H. E. 1995. Dementia associated with the acquired immunodeficiency syndrome. *N. Engl. J. Med.* 332(14):933–940.

Mach, J. R. Jr., Dysken, M. W., Kuskowski, M., Richelson, E., Holden, L., Jilk, K. M. 1995. Serum anticholinergic activity in hospitalized older patients with delirium: a preliminary study. *J. Am Geri. Soc.* 43(5):491–5.

Maletta, G. 1994. Pharmacologic treatment and management of the aggressive demented patient. *Psych. Anns.* 20:446–455.

Marder, K., Tang, M. X., Cote, L. J., Stern, Y., Mayeux R. 1993. Predictors of dementia in community-dwelling elderly patients with Parkinson's disease. *Neurol.* 43:S115.

Mattis, S. 1976. Dementia rating scale. In *Geriatric Psychiatry,* ed. Bellack, R., and Karasu, B. New York: Grune & Stratton. 71–121.

Mattson, M. P. 1994. Calcium and neuronal injury in Alzheimer's disease. Contributions of beta-amyloid precursor protein mismetabolism, free radicals, and metabolic compromise. *Ann. N.Y. Acad. Sci.* 747:50–76.

Mattson, A. J., and Levin, H. S. 1990. Frontal lobe dysfunction following closed head injury: a review of the literature. *J. Nerv. Ment. Dis.* 178:282–291.

Mattson, M. P., Furukawa, K., Bruce, A. J., Mark, R. J., Blanc, E. 1997. Calcium homeostasis and free radical metabolism as convergence points in the pathophysiology of dementia. In *Molecular mechanisms of dementia,* ed. Wasco, W., and Tanzi, R. E. Totowa, N.J.: Humana Press.

Mayeux, R., Chen, J., Mirabello, E., Marder, K., Bell, K., Dooneief, G., Stern, Y. 1990. An estimate of the incidence of dementia in patients with idiopathic Parkinson's disease. *Neurol.* 40:1513–17.

Mayeux, R., Ottman, R., Maestre, G., et al. 1995. Synergistic effects of traumatic head injury and apolipoprotein-E4 in patients with Alzheimer's disease. *Neurol.* 45:555–557.

Mayeux, R., Stern, Y., Rosenstein, R., Marder, K., Hauser, A., Cote, L., Fahn, S. 1988. An estimate of the prevalence of dementia in idiopathic Parkinson's disease. *Arch. Neurol.* 45:260–262.

Mayeux, R., Stern, Y., Sano, M., Cote, L. 1987. Bradyphrenia in Parkinson's disease: clinical features and biochemistry. *Neurol.* 37:1130–34.

Meyer, J. S., Rogers, R. L., Judd, B. W., Mortel, K. F., Sims, P. 1988. Cognition and cerebral blood flow fluctuate together in multi-infarct dementia. *Stroke* 19:163–169.

McGeer, P. L., McGeer, E., Rogers, J., et al. 1990. Antiinflammatory drugs and Alzheimer's disease. *Can. J. Neurol. Sci.* 16:516–527.

McKeith, I., Fairbairn, A., Perry, R., et al. 1992. Neuroleptic sensitivity in patients with senile dementia of Lewy body type. *BMJ* 305:673–678.

McKeith, I. G., Perry, R. H., Fairbairn, A. F., et al. 1992. Operational criteria for senile dementia of Lewy body type (SDLT). *Psychol. Med.* 22:911–922.

McKeith, I. G., Fairbairn, A. F., Bothwell, R. A., et al. 1994. An evaluation of the predictive validity and inter-rater reliability of clinical diagnostic criteria for senile dementia of Lewy body type. *Neurol.* 44:872–877.

Milberg, W., and Albert, M. 1989. Cognitive differences between patients with PSP and Alzheimer's disease. *J. Clin. Exper. Neuropsychol.* 11:605–614.

Mirra, S. S., Heyman, A., McKeel, D., Sumi, S. M., Crain, B. J., Brownlee, L. M., Vogel, F. S., Hughes, J. P., van Belle, G., Berg, L. 1991. The Consortium to Establish a Registry for Alzheimer's Disease (CERAD). *Neurol.* 41:479–486.

Morris, J. C., Heyman, A., Mohs, R. C., Hughes, J. P., van Belle, G., Fillenbaum, G., Mellits, E. D., Clark, C. 1989. The Consortium to Establish a Registry for Alzheimer's Disease (CERAD). 1. Clinical and neuropsychological assessment of Alzheimer's disease. *Neurol.* 39:1159–65.

Moss, M., Albert, M., Butters, N., Payne, M. 1986. Differential patterns of memory loss among patients with Alzheimer's disease, Huntington's disease and alcoholic Korsakoff's syndrome. *Archives of Neurology* 43:239–246.

Murden, R., McRae, T., Kaner, S., Bucknam, M. 1991. Mini-Mental State Exam scores vary with education in blacks and whites. *JAGS* 39:149–155.

Myer, J. S., Rogers, R. L., Judd, B. W., Mortel, K. F., Sims, P. 1988. Cognition and cerebral blood flow fluctuate together in multi-infarct dementia. *Stroke* 19:63–169.

Neary, D., Snowden, J., Northen, B., Goulding, P. 1988. Dementia of frontal lobe type. *J. Neurol Neurosurg. Psychiatr.* 51:353–361.

Nelson, H. E. 1976. A modified card sorting test sensitive to frontal lobe defects. *Cortex* 12:313–324.

Nelson, H. E., and O'Connell, A. 1978. Dementia: the estimation of premorbid intelligence levels using the new adult reading test. *Cortex* 14:234–244.

Neumann, M., and Cohn, R. 1967. Progressive subcortical gliosis, a rare form of presenile dementia. *Brain* 90:405–418.

Nixon, R. A., and Cataldo, A. M. 1994. Free radicals, proteolysis, and the degeneration of neurons in Alzheimer disease: how essential is the ß-amyloid link? *Neuro. Aging* 15(4):1–7.

Organic mental impairment in the elderly. 1981. *J. R. Coll. Physicians Lond.* 15:141–167.

Oscar-Berman, M., Hancock, M., Mildworf, B., Hutner, N., Weber, D. 1990. Emotional perception and memory in alcoholism and aging. *Alcoholism: Clinical and Experimental Research* 14:383–393.

Paganini-Hill, A. 1996. Estrogen replacement therapy and Alzheimer's disease. *Br. J. ObGyn.* 103(13):80–86.

Perry, E. K., Haroutunian, V., Davis, K. L., Levy, R., Lantos, P., Eagger, S., Honavar, M., Dean, A., Griffiths, M., McKeith, I. G., et al. 1994. Neocortical cholinergic activities differentiate Lewy body dementia from classical Alzheimer's disease. *Neuroreport* 5:747–749.

Petersen, R., Tabaton, M., Chen, S., Monari, L., Richardson, S., Lynches, T., Manetto, V., Lanska, D., Markesbury, W., Currier, R., Autilio-Gambetti, L., Wilhelmsen, K., Gambetti, P. 1995. Familial progressive subcortical

gliosis: presence of prions and linkage to chromosome 17. *Neurol.* 45:1062–67.

Pfeiffer, E. 1975. SPMSQ: Short Portable Mental Status Questionnaire. *Journal of the American Geriatric Society* 23:433–441.

Pick, A. 1892. Uber die Beziehungen der senilen Hirnatrophie zur Aphasie. *Prager Medizinische Wochsenschrift* 17:165–167.

Pillon, B., Dubois, B., Ploska, A., Agid, Y. 1991. Severity and specificity of cognitive impairment in Alzheimer's and Huntington's diseases: a controlled prospective study. *J. Neurol. Neurosurg. Psych.* 53:1089–95.

Poirier, J., Minnich, A., and Davignon, J. 1995. Apolipoprotein E, synaptic plasticity and Alzheimer's disease: trends in molecular medicine. *Ann. Med.* 27:663–670.

Poirier, J., Delisle, M. C., Quirion, R., Aubert, I., Farlow, M., Lahiri, D., Hui, S., Bertrand, P., Nalbantoglu, J., Gilfix, B. M., et al. 1995. Apolipoprotein E4 allele as a predictor of cholinergic deficits and treatment outcome in Alzheimer disease. *PNAS/USA* 92(26):12260–64.

Pro, J. D., and Wells, C. E. 1977. The use of the electroencephalogram in the diagnosis of delirium. *Diseases Nerv. Sys.* 38:804–808.

Purdie, F. R., Honigman, T. B., and Rosen, P. 1981. Acute organic brain syndrome: a review of 100 cases. *Ann. Emerg. Med.* 10:455–461.

Quinn, N. 1995. Parkinsonism: recognition and differential diagnosis. *Fortnightly Rev. Inst. Neurol. Lond.* 310:447–452.

Raiha, I., Kaprio, J., Koskenvuo, M., Rajala, T., Sourander, L. 1996. Alzheimer's disease in Finnish twins. *Lancet* 347:573–578.

Randt, C. T., Brown, E. R., Osborne, D. J. 1980. A memory test for longitudinal measurement of mild to moderate deficits. *Clinical Neuropsychology* 2:184–194.

Regland, B., and Gottfries, C.-G. 1992. The role of amyloid beta-protein in Alzheimer's disease. *Lancet* 340:467–470.

Reitan, R. M. 1958. Validity of the Trail Making Test as an indication of organic brain damage. *Perceptual and Motor Skills* 8:271–276.

Rey, A. 1964. L'examen clinique en psychologie. Paris: Presses Universitaires de France.

Richards, M., Stern, Y., Sano, M., et al. 1991. Patterns of neuropsychological impairments are distinct in Parkinson's disease: Alzheimer's disease and Parkinson's dementia. *Neurol.* 41:177.

Rogers, J., Kirby, L. C., Hempelman, S. R., et al. 1993. Clinical trial of indomethacin in Alzheimer's disease. *Neurol.* 43:1609–11.

Romano, J., and Engel, G. L. 1944. Delirium: electroencephalogram data. *Arch. Neurol. Psychiatry* 51:356–377.

Roses, A. D. 1995a. Perspective on the metabolism of

apolipoprotein E and Alzheimer disease. *Exper. Neuro.* 132:149–156.

———— 1995b. Apolipoprotein E genotyping in the differential diagnosis, not prediction, of Alzheimer's disease. *Ann. Neurol.* 38:6–14.

Sano, M., Stern, Y., Williams, J., Cote, L., Rosenstein, R., Mayeux, R. 1989. Co-existing dementia and depression in Parkinson's disease. *Arch. Neurol.* 46:1284–87.

Satlin, A., Volicer, L., Ross, V., et al. 1992. Bright light treatment of behavioral and sleep disturbances in patients with Alzheimer's disease. *Am. J. Psych.* 149:1028–32.

Satz, P., and Mogel, S. 1962. An abbreviation of the WAIS for clinical use. *Journal of Clinical Psychology* 18:77–79.

Schellenberg, G. D. 1995. Genetic dissection of Alzheimer disease, a heterogeneous disorder. *Proc. Natl. Acad. Sci. USA* 92:8552–58.

Schneider, L. S., Farlow, M. R., Henderson, V. W., Pogoda, J. M. 1996. Effects of estrogen replacement therapy on response to Tacrine in patients with Alzheimer's disease. *Neurol.* 46(6):1580–84.

Schorer, C. E. 1985. Historical essay: Kraepelin's description of Alzheimer's disease. *Intl. J. Aging Hum. Dev.* 21(3):235–239.

Scoville, W., and Milner, B. 1957. Loss of recent memory after bilateral hippocampal lesions. *J. Neurol. Neurosurg. Psychiatr.* 20:11–21.

Selkoe, D. J. 1991. The molecular pathology of Alzheimer's disease. *Neuron* 6:487–498.

———— 1996. Amyloid beta-protein and the genetics of Alzheimer's disease. *J. Biol. Chem.* 271:18295–98.

Seltzer, B. 1986. Organic mental disorders. In *Harvard Guide to Modern Psychiatry.* Cambridge, Mass.: Belknap Press of Harvard University Press. 358–386.

Serban, D., Taraboulos, A., DeArmond, S. J., et al. 1990. Rapid detection of Creutzfeldt-Jakob disease and scrapie prion proteins. *Neurol.* 40:110–117.

Sherrington, R., Rogaev, E. I., Liang, Y., Rogaeva, E. A., Levesque, G., Ikeda, M., Chi, H., Lin, C., Li, G., Holman, K., Tsuda, T., Mar, L., Foncin, J. F., Bruni, A. C., Montesi, M. P., Sorbi, S., Rainero, I., Pinessi, L., Nee, L., Chumakov, I., Pollen, D., Brookes, A., Sanseau, P., Polinsky, R. J., Wasco, W., DaSilva, H. A. R., Haines, J. L., Pericak-Vance, M. A., Tanzi, R. E., Roses, A. D., Fraser, P. E., Rommens, J. M., St. George-Hyslop, P. H. 1995. Cloning of a gene bearing missense mutations in early-onset familial Alzheimer's disease. *Nature* 375:754–760.

Siest, G., Pillot, T., Regis-Baily, A., Leninger-Muller, B., Steimetz, J., Galteau, M. M., Visvikis, S. 1995. Apolipoprotein E: an important gene and protein to follow in laboratory medicine. *Clin. Chem.* 41(8):1068–86.

Simon, A., and Cahan, R. B. 1963. The acute brain syndrome in geriatric patients. *Psych. Res. Repts.* 16:8–21.

Snowden, J., Neary, D., and Mann, D. 1996. *Fronto-temporal lobar degeneration: frontotemporal dementia, progressive aphasia, semantic dementia.* London: Churchill Livingstone.

Strachan, R. W., and Henderson, J. G. 1967. Dementia and folate deficiency. *Q. J. Med.* 36:189–204.

Sultzer, D. L., Levin, H. S., Mahler, M. E., High, W. M., Cummings, J. L. 1993. A comparison of psychiatric symptoms in vascular dementia and Alzheimer's disease. *Am. J. Psych.* 150(12):1806–12.

Tatemichi, T. K., Sacktor, N., and Mayeux, R. 1994. Dementia associated with cerebrovascular disease, other degenerative diseases, and metabolic disorders. In *Alzheimer's Disease,* ed. Terry, R. D., Katzman, R., and Bick, K. L. New York: Raven. 123.

Terry, R. D., Masliah, E., Hansen, L. A. 1994. Structural basis of the cognitive alterations in Alzheimer's disease. In *Alzheimer's Disease,* ed. Terry, R. D., Katzman, R., and Bick, K. L. New York: Raven. 179.

Tomlinson, B. E., Blessed, G., and Roth, M. 1970. Observations on the brains of demented old people. *J. Neurol. Sci.* 11:205–242.

Trzepacz, P. T. 1994. The neuropathogenesis of delirium: a need to focus our research. *Psychosom.* 35(4):374–391.

Van Gorp, W. G., Mandelfern, M. A., Gee, M., et al. 1992. Cerebral metabolic dysfunction in AIDS: findings in a sample with and without dementia. *J. Neuropsych. Clin. Neurosci.* 4:280–287.

Van Gorp, W. G., Hinkin, C., Satz, P., et al. 1993. Neuropsychological findings in HIV infection, encephalopathy, and dementia. In *Neuropsychology of Alzheimer's disease and other dementias,* ed. Parks, R. W., Zec, R. F., and Wilson, R. S. New York: Oxford University Press. 153–185.

van Hemert, A. M., van der Mast, R. C., Hengeveld, M. W., et al. 1994. Excess mortality in general hospital patients with delirium: a 5-year follow-up of 519 patients seen in psychiatric consultation. *J. Psychosom. Res.* 38(4):339–346.

Vanneste, J., Aughustijn, P., Davies, G. A. G., et al. 1992. Normal pressure hydrocephalus: is cisternography still useful in selecting patients for a shunt? *Arch. Neurol.* 49:366–370.

Victor, M. 1994. Alcoholic dementia. *Can. J. Neurol. Sci.* 21:88–99.

Wechsler, D. 1944. *The measurement of adult intelligence.* Baltimore: M. D. Williams & Wilkins.

———— 1945. A standardized memory scale for clinical use. *Journal of Psychology* 19:87–95.

———— 1981. *The Wechsler Adult Intelligence Scale–Revised.* New York: Psychological Corporation.

Weiner, M. F., ed. 1996. *The dementias: diagnosis, management, and research.* Washington, D.C.: American Psychiatric Press.

Weisgraber, K. H., Pitas, R. E., and Mahley, R. W. 1994. Lipoproteins, neurobiology, and Alzheimer's disease: structure and function of apolipoprotein E. *Curr. Op. Struc. Bio.* 4:507–515.

Welsh, K., Butters, N., Hughes, J., Mohs, R., Heyman, A. 1991. Detection of abnormal memory decline in mild cases of Alzheimer's disease using CERAD neuropsychological measures. *Arch. Neurol.* 48:278–281.

———— 1992. Detection and staging of dementia in Alzheimer's disease. *Arch. Neurol.* 49:448–452.

Whetsell, W. O. Jr. 1996. Current concepts of excitotoxity. *J. Neuro. Exper. Neuro.* 55(1):1–13.

Winocur, G., Oxbury, S., Roberts, R., Agnetti, V., Davis, D. 1984. Amnesia in a patient with bilateral lesions to the thalamus. *Neuropsychologia* 2:123–143.

Wisniewski, K. E., Wisniewski, H. M., and Wen, G. Y. 1985. Occurrence of neuropathological changes and dementia of Alzheimer's disease in Down's syndrome. *Ann. Neurol.* 17:278.

Young, A. B., Penney, A. B. Jr. 1994. Neurotransmitter receptors in Alzheimer's disease. In *Alzheimer's disease,* ed. Terry, R. D., Katzman, R., and Bick, K. L. New York: Raven. 293.

Young, A. B., Penney, J. B., Starosta-Rubenstein, S., et al. 1986. PET scan investigations of Huntington's disease: cerebral metabolic correlates of neurological features and functional decline. *Ann. Neurol.* 20:296–303.

Zola-Morgan, S., and Squire, L. 1990. The neuropsychology of memory: parallel findings from humans and nonhuman primates. *Ann. New York Acad. Sci.* 608:434–456.

Recommended Reading

Folstein, M. F. (ed.). 1998. *Neurobiology of primary dementia.* Washington, D.C.: American Psychiatric Press.

Terry, R. D., Katzman, R., and Bick, K. L. (eds.). 1994. *Alzheimer's disease.* New York: Raven.

Weiner, M. F. (ed.). 1996. *The dementia diagnosis, management, and research.* Washington, D.C.: American Psychiatric Press.

Psychosomatic Medicine and Consultation-Liaison Psychiatry

MALCOLM P. ROGERS

GREGORY FRICCHIONE

PETER REICH

The relationship between the mind and the body has intrigued physicians throughout the history of medicine. Although terminology and theories of causality have changed over the years to reflect the status of medical knowledge, the clinical phenomena subsumed under the modern concept of psychosomatic medicine can be found in the writings of every era. Precipitation of sudden death by strong emotions, the kindness of the physician as an adjunct to healing, the importance of social supports in health maintenance, and the pathogenic effects of depression are examples of current issues in psychosomatic medicine that can be traced to the writings of early Greek physicians. During the twentieth century, discoveries in physiology and psychology have shed new light on the interactions between the mind and the body. Psychoanalysis, learning theory, neurophysiology, neuroradiology, endocrinology, genetics, and immunology are among the many disciplines that have made contributions. Further, a new subspecialty within psychiatry has emerged as the practical branch of psychosomatic medicine: consultation-liaison psychiatry, which deals with the psychological problems of medical and surgical patients. In spite of these advances, at a basic level "the mysterious leap from the mind to the body" remains as puzzling today as it was in ancient times.

The terminologies used in psychiatric nomenclature to describe psychosomatic phenomena reflect the concepts of the times. *Organ neurosis* was a term used by early psychoanalysts to indicate that body parts could become the targets of psychological conflicts; *psychophysiologic autonomic and visceral disorders,* used in the *Diagnostic and Statistical Manual of Mental Disorders* (DSM, 1952), implicated an overactive autonomic nervous system; and the later term *psychophysiological disorders* (DSM-II, 1967) implied the selection of specific organ systems as objects of the stress response.

Defining the territory covered by psychosomatic med-

icine today presents a formidable challenge, because the concept is used so widely and in so many different ways. Beginning with DSM-III (third edition) in 1980 and continuing though DSM-III-R (third edition, revised) in 1987 and DSM-IV (fourth edition) in 1994, psychosomatic disorders appear under two headings. The first category, *somatoform disorders,* includes somatization disorder, conversion disorder, hypochondriasis, and chronic pain disorder—conditions characterized by physical complaints and symptoms without organic findings or explanation. These symptoms are responses to psychological factors but are often intertwined with the manifestations of real physical disorders. Patients with these presentations are usually seen by nonpsychiatric physicians in general hospitals or in practice, and the patients do not readily accept the notion that they have a mental disorder or that they need psychiatric treatment. The second category, *psychological factors affecting physical conditions,* encompasses all situations in medicine in which physical conditions appear to be precipitated or exacerbated by "psychologically meaningful environmental stimuli." Examples are rheumatoid arthritis and migraine headache. Almost all medical conditions are now known to be responsive to psychological factors, and psychosomatic processes can be identified in the clinical courses of most patients in medical practice.

Beyond these discrete concepts in DSM-IV, many psychosomatic concepts are an integral part of modern medicine. Examples are stress and stress management, social supports, behavioral risk factors, educational and economic factors, loss, and relaxation. The concept of specific psychosomatic medical disorders is no longer widely accepted; instead clinicians and investigators are coming to recognize the role of psychosocial factors in all physical disorders and in patient care throughout clinical practice. This chapter describes the development of psychosomatic concepts in medicine and presents an overview of areas of current interest.

Historical Development of Psychosomatic Medicine

Throughout most of history, technologically primitive societies have not drawn sharp distinctions between mental and physical disease. Native American tribes, for example, attributed illness to disharmony or imbalance in the relationship of the individual to nature and his social milieu. To this day indigenous healing involves religious ceremonies designed to restore a sense of harmony.

The early Greeks emphasized the interrelationship between mind and body. In the fifth century B.C. Socrates is said to have stated, "It is not proper to cure the eyes without the head nor the head without the body, so neither is it proper to cure the body without the soul." Hippocrates espoused a similar philosophy and emphasized the relationship between the physician and the patient in the healing process. Physicians, he said, should look upon patients with kindly expressions and never impatience, which could inhibit healing. Galen, a Greek physician living in Rome in the second century A.D., compiled a summary of Greek medicine that served as a foundation of European medicine for the next thousand years. He posited a rational soul, centered in the brain, and two irrational subsouls, one the energetic, irascible male soul located in the heart, the other the sensuous female soul situated in the liver. These souls were material slaves rather than masters of the body.

After the early classical attempts to join the mind and the body in a more integrated approach to the causes and treatment of disease, there was a shift toward religious and mystical views of illness in the Middle Ages. Outside forces, such as witches and demons, were believed to bring on disease. The Renaissance sharply reversed that trend, and interest prevailed in the natural and physical sciences. With the development of a more laboratory-based practice of medicine in the tradition of Louis Pasteur and Rudolf Virchow, physicians largely discarded earlier views of the psychological influences on disease and related the origin of disease to structural changes within the cell. In 1818 Johann Heinroth, a German psychiatrist, first used the term *psychosomatic* in his efforts to explain insomnia. He wrote with intuitive grasp of inner conflict, though in religious terms, and viewed body and psyche as but two aspects, internal and external, of the same entity. Not until more than 100 years later, however, did the modern era of systematic investigation of psychosomatic relationships truly begin.

Early Psychophysiological Observations

William Beaumont, an American physician, made in 1833 what may be the earliest empirical observations of a psychophysiological relationship. Beaumont's opportunity resulted from a gunshot wound to the abdomen of a young French-Canadian trapper, Alexis St. Martin. Beaumont, a military surgeon, managed to save the life of the young man. His patient, however, was left with a large gastric fistula. Over a number of years Beaumont studied the process of peptic digestion and observed the gastric mucosa of a sometimes reluctant St. Martin under various circumstances. He reported: "In febrile dyathesis, or predisposition, from whatever cause, obstructed perspiration, undue excitement by stimulating liquors, overloading the stomach with food—fear, anger or whatever distresses or disturbs the nervous system—the villous coat becomes sometimes red and dry, at other times, pale and moist, and loses its smooth and healthy appearance" (Beaumont, 1838, p. 98).

At the turn of the twentieth century, the great Russian physiologist Ivan P. Pavlov attempted to explain abnormal behavior by developing experimental models of conflict and neurosis in laboratory animals. He made remarkable observations about the impact of learning and experience on psychophysiological reactions. In his work on gastric secretions in dogs, for example, he demonstrated that stimuli present when the dogs were offered food eventually evoked salivation in the animals in the absence of food. Even the footsteps of the experimenter as he entered the room came to evoke salivation. From these detailed observations grew concepts of the conditioned response and the role of conditioned and unconditioned stimuli. Pavlov (1927) provided the basis for the study of conditioning and learning within the autonomic nervous system, continuing a line of investigation with enormous implications for the development of psychosomatic disorders.

In the 1920s the experimental work of Walter B. Cannon, an American physiologist, also helped to build the foundation of modern psychosomatic medicine. His most important contribution demonstrated the involvement of chemical factors in mediating the effects of emotional and neurological changes on distant organs. He observed that psychological threat or the stimulation of sympathetic nerves produced effects on distant, sensitized smooth muscles and the heart. The chemical mediator was epinephrine, released by the adrenal medulla. Cannon (1932) theorized that the bodily changes caused by emotional responses to stress prepared the organism for the struggle for existence, the "fight-or-flight" response. He elaborated the concept of homeostasis, drawing on earlier work by Claude Bernard in 1859, namely, that the organism attempts to maintain a stable internal equilibrium in response to external challenges, whether physiological or psychological.

According to Cannon's theory, in the fight-or-flight response the blood supply to the muscles, the heart, and the brain increased as it decreased to the visceral organs. The organism, when not engaged in fending off stress by fight or flight, reconstituted itself by activities such as eating or reproduction. In the reconstitution phase the parasympathetic nervous system predominated, whereas in the fight-or-flight response the sympathetic nervous system predominated. Thus a reciprocal relationship existed between the sympathetic and the parasympathetic nervous systems. Cannon outlined a number of additional physiological changes that occurred during the fight-or-flight response: an alteration in carbohydrate metabolism that mobilized sugar; a polycythemia that prolonged muscular relaxation; an increase in blood pressure, heart rate, and respiration that facilitated a higher rate of oxygen pickup and delivery; and a rise in blood coagulability to prevent excessive blood loss. The nuances of these reactions continue to be important targets of psychosomatic investigation.

Psychodynamic Approaches to the Mind-Body Relationship

Franz Anton Mesmer's experience at the turn of the nineteenth century revealed the powerful influence of suggestion on bodily symptoms. The French neurologist Jean-Martin Charcot extended these observations by demonstrating that hypnosis could reverse paralysis and other conversion symptoms (see Chapter 11). Their work began to reveal the startling power of unconscious mental processes in these somatic symptoms. Freud based his work on further use of hypnosis and free association to uncover hidden psychological factors in physical symptoms lacking an organic basis. Indeed, the existence of the somatoform disorders, characterized by the psychological need for expression of somatic symptoms, strengthens the concept of a psychosomatic process. If somatic symptoms express so powerfully the hidden emotional conflicts of the individual, then surely these emotions could also influence somatic processes to pro-

duce structural changes or physiological disorders in the body.

Historically the growing popularity of psychoanalysis in the United States in the 1930s strongly influenced the modern era of psychosomatic research. The first journal devoted to psychosomatic research, *Psychosomatic Medicine*, began publication in 1939. Its first editorial defined psychosomatic medicine as the study of "the interrelationship of the psychological and physiologic aspects of all normal and abnormal bodily functions." It also set as its initial mission the attempt to integrate somatic therapy and psychotherapy.

The psychoanalytic movement and the early influences of psychophysiological observations led to the formation of the American Psychosomatic Society in 1942. One of the original founders of the society, Flanders Dunbar, produced a comprehensive work on the "psychosomatic disorders" (1947) that helped to crystallize the field and emphasized the association between particular personality types and medical disorders. Subsequently Franz Alexander, a psychoanalyst in Chicago, focused his attention on certain diseases that came to be known as the "holy 7" psychosomatic disorders: ulcerative colitis, peptic ulcer, rheumatoid arthritis, hyperthyroidism, neurodermatitis, bronchial asthma, and migraine headache. Alexander's (1950) focus on these disorders inadvertently narrowed the concept of psychosomatic disorder to this list. Unfortunately it both drew attention away from other disorders (which by implication were not viewed as psychosomatic) and overstated the role of psychological factors in causing the identified disorders. Alexander's view of the psychogenesis of certain diseases became a predominant principle of psychosomatic medicine in the 1940s and 1950s and eventually led to a backlash from other parts of the medical community. He postulated that specific unresolved conflicts could lead to chronic emotional tensions; the physiological consequences of these tensions might result in dysfunction and ultimately in structural changes in certain "target organs." His concept that specific psychodynamic conflicts could lead to specific diseases came to be known as the *specificity hypothesis*.

Although some clinicians currently find it fashionable to point out the limitations of Alexander's interpretations, in fact he and his colleagues conducted careful clinical studies in a scientific manner. He supported his notion of specificity on data drawn from the ratings of blinded observers who analyzed the content of recorded interviews with patients. The observers used the patterns of conflict they discerned to identify, with some success, the particular disease from which the patient suffered.

Alexander's work reflected the tendency of American psychiatry during this era to deemphasize biological factors in psychiatric disease and perhaps to overemphasize psychological factors as the sole cause. In its effort to join the psyche to the soma, the psychoanalytic approach sometimes tended to combine language from different levels of reality; thus urticaria, for example, represented suppressed "weeping from the skin."

The current interest in personality type as a risk factor for the development of coronary artery disease (discussed below in detail) is reminiscent of Dunbar's observations, although the role of genetic and other physiological predisposing factors that contribute to the pathogenesis of this disease is now better understood.

The role of personality in the development of psychosomatic illness is also central to the concept of *alexithymia* ("no words for mood"). As first articulated by Peter Sifneos (1967), this hypothesis suggests that many patients with psychosomatic disorders have a particular inability to express their feelings. Although the concept may lead to useful scientific study in the future, it remains largely theoretical and tends to perpetuate the myth that certain presumed "psychosomatic disorders" exist (Lesser, 1981). Uncertainty about the relationship of psychological factors to the onset of physical illness prompted the change from the category "psychophysiologic disorders" in DSM-II (1968) to "psychological factors affecting physical disease" beginning in DSM-III (1980).

The Concept of Stress

The work of Hans Selye (1950) put the concept of stress on the map. In conducting experiments to produce a new sex hormone in the mid-1940s, Selye gave rats multiple doses of crude ovarian extracts. The rats developed adrenal enlargement, involution of the thymus and lymph nodes, and gastric ulcers. He discovered that extracts of other organs produced identical changes in the rats, as did several other stimuli, such as extremes of temperature, pain, epinephrine, and infectious agents. Psychologists called this common response to a variety of stimuli the general adaptation syndrome. Although Selye at first referred to the external stimuli as *stresses,* he later used the term to describe the nonspecific response of the general adaptation syndrome.

In current research the issue of whether the stress response is primarily physiological or psychological has generated some controversy, particularly in the transition from animal to human research. We can define an animal's response to an external threat in physiological or behavioral terms, such as freezing or defecation, but can only infer its subjective response. In contrast, we define the human stress response chiefly in terms of subjective, mental experience, although the physiological dimension has also been investigated extensively. The problem of definition arises, for example, when a research subject denies any emotional distress in response to a threat but vastly increases his output of serum cortisol or epinephrine. In such a case can we conclude that this person is experiencing stress?

Despite problems of definition, the concept of stress has become a central, unifying theme in psychosomatic research (Elliot and Eisdorfer, 1982). It is inherent in Cannon's (1932) notion of homeostasis and the organism's adaptation to external threats through the fight-or-flight response. In his later investigations he specifically looked at stimuli that could disrupt the equilibrium of the internal environment and strain the adaptive capacity of the organism. Psychoanalysts viewed this disturbance, or stress, in terms of an internal, intrapsychic conflict. Conceptually, however, it is important to differentiate between the external stimulus and the internal response. Unfortunately the term *stress* has been used to describe both. This confusion is not surprising, because the process of converting an external stimulus into an internal response lies at the heart of our understanding of the psychosomatic mystery. H. Weiner (1972) describes this process as the "transduction of experience," emphasizing that mental experience is only one of several routes by which external stimuli are converted into measurable physiological processes.

Psychological theorists investigating the conversion of external stimuli to internal responses began to challenge the concept of psychological specificity. Some suggested that a given psychosomatic disease was produced by the impact of a nonspecific psychological stress on a specific but unknown physical vulnerability. G. F. Mahl (1953), who articulated this "nonspecificity hypothesis," made a strong case for the role of a generalized stress response in triggering various psychosomatic diseases. He induced states of stress experimentally in humans as well as in animals, measuring such physiological concomitants as gastric secretions and adrenal activity.

Harold Wolff and his associates also conducted a series of careful psychophysiological studies in human beings (Wolff, Wolf, and Hare, 1950). Like Mahl, they stressed the adaptive and nonspecific nature of stress as a precipitant of illness. Wolff emphasized the role of culture in defining how an individual perceives a given life stress. He developed meticulous methods for observing psychophysiological responses such as the galvanic skin response and redness, swelling, hypersecretion, and hypomotility within the gastrointestinal system. He studied both the manifest behaviors of subjects and these physiological variables as indicators of experimentally induced emotional states.

The clinical observations of Arthur Schmale and George Engel (1967) enriched the concept of the generalized stress response and its effect on human health. These investigators identified many patients whose illness had begun in a state they characterized as the "giving-up, given-up complex." In this version of stress, the individual's hopeless and helpless state, like clinical depression, overwhelms his adaptive capacity.

The Measurement of Stress

The problem of quantifying the level of stress, often described retrospectively, was addressed in the work of Thomas Holmes and Richard Rahe (1967). From an initial study of the role of psychosocial factors on the course of tuberculosis, they developed a list of 43 life changes, the Schedule of Recent Events, ranging from the death of a spouse to minor violations of the law. Their subjects indicated which changes had occurred during the previous 6 or 12 months and then weighted each according to the amount of effort required (or stress experienced) in adapting to it. Based on the ratings of 1000 normal subjects, each life change was given a score: the death of a spouse, 100 life change units (LCU); getting married, 50 LCUs; a minor violation of the law, 11 LCUs. Some changes were usually considered positive, such as getting married or receiving a promotion, but these events also require adaptation and so were included in the overall score. This methodological approach to the measurement of stress has been widely adapted and has generated a host of studies.

Holmes and Rahe's hypothesis, seemingly confirmed by initial data, was that the greater the number of LCUs, the more likely the subject was to experience physical illness (Rahe, 1975). When they applied this theory prospectively, as they did in a study of U.S. and Norwegian naval enlisted men who were to embark on a period of active shipboard duty, higher LCUs were associated with a statistical increase in the frequency of illness. Subjects in the highest as compared to the lowest tenth percentile of LCUs showed a 25% increase in risk of illness. For the most part they had minor viral illnesses, which probably reflected health care–seeking behavior rather than an actual increased incidence of viral disease.

By necessity most studies of the more serious diseases, such as multiple sclerosis and juvenile rheumatoid arthritis, were done retrospectively (using a modified Schedule of Recent Events for children) and were probably subject to significant distortion of memory. One of the major methodological problems stems from the need for many patients to give meaning to their otherwise unexplained illnesses by attributing them to recent life events, which affects recall on the Schedule of Recent Events. Another limitation of this measurement is its focus on a broad range of events, or external stimuli, and the lack of precision on their subjective meaning and hence on the subject's likely internal physiological response. Moreover, some of the life events might have occurred in association with the early manifestations of a disease (Rabkin and Streuning, 1976).

Further refinements of this methodological approach added other dimensions of the individual's social environment and psychological state. Sidney Cobb (1976) was one of the first to emphasize the importance of social support in modifying the effects of external stressors. He defined social support as information leading a person to believe that (1) he is cared for and loved, (2) he is esteemed and valued, and (3) he belongs to a network of communication and mutual obligation. Although difficult to develop, some scales do measure this kind of support, and a large number of studies have revealed impressive correlations with medical illness (Dimsdale, 1995). As discussed later in the section on heart disease, social support is a powerful buffer against the adverse health effects of stress.

Other design modifications have added measures of either subjective levels of distress (such as the Brief Symptom Inventory) or personality characteristics reflecting the individual's capacity to cope. For example, S. C. Kobasa (1979) has developed a measure of hardiness traits to differentiate between individuals likely to become ill and those not likely to do so in spite of high stress. The hardiness test measures commitment (belief in the importance and value of who one is and what one is doing), control (the tendency to believe or act as if one can influence the course of events), and challenge (the ability to embrace change rather than stability as the normative state and to expect to respond positively to change).

The concept of helplessness (lack of control) has gradually gained recognition. Martin Seligman, a research psychologist, has developed experimental models of helplessness—originally for the insights they could provide on the development of depression. His early experiments with dogs provided a model for the learning of helplessness in response to a challenge. Dogs presented early in their development with situations in which they were helpless learned to respond as if they were helpless (although they were not) when confronted with challenges later in life. Animal models using helplessness as a psychological component of experimental stress have provided a great deal of insight on physiological responses to stress and have proved relevant to the human experience.

Both the quantitative approach to the measurement of stress, as in the Schedule of Recent Events, and detailed individual studies have identified loss of a significant person as a major stressor. Interesting similarities have been noted between an overwhelmed stress response and clinical depression, especially with respect to feelings of exhaustion, helplessness, and hopelessness. For these reasons investigators have focused on bereavement in an effort to understand better the relationship between stress and disease. Bereavement has the additional advantage of being a clearly demarcated and recorded event and is therefore well suited to an epidemiologic approach. Although several early studies showed a dramatic increase in mortality and morbidity in spouses after bereavement, subsequent studies have drawn more modest conclusions (Van Eijk, Smits, and Huygen, 1988). Although this kind of approach does not address the mechanisms underlying the increased incidence of mortality following bereavement, it does demonstrate its clinical importance.

Biological Responses to Stress

While Selye (1976) continued to study the stress response in light of newer physiological advancement, John Mason (1975) explored the range of the hormonal response elicited by stress. Not only was the adrenal gland involved, but changes occurred in other hormones as well, including growth hormone, thyroid hormone, prolactin, insulin, and sex hormones.

Indeed, many studies have examined not only hormonal changes in the periphery but also changes of hormonal-releasing factors and neurotransmitters directly within the central nervous system (CNS) in response to stress. Roy-Byrne and his colleagues (1986), for example, have related lower responses to corticotropin-releasing hormone (CRH) stimulation in patients with panic disorder, the onset of which was significantly correlated with an increase in adverse life events. Others have identified changes in rodents in the more traditional neurotransmitters, such as norepinephrine, as a result both of stress and, in some cases, of deprivation in early development. Since 1975 the neurosciences have discovered

many new neurotransmitters and neuropeptides active in the CNS. We know that the endorphins, for example, are released in response to experimental stressors in animals. Although the effect of endorphins in the modulation of pain has been documented, we are only beginning to discover their effects on a range of other physiological parameters relevant to stress research.

The discipline of physiology itself has gained a new level of sophistication in the understanding of circadian rhythms and the interrelationship between internal clocks that regulate temperature and the sleep-wakefulness cycle. Indeed, many of the animal models of stress effects on the vulnerability to infection, autoimmune disorders, and malignancy have demonstrated sensitivity to the timing and duration of stress. As with most biological research, the more we study, the greater our appreciation for the complexity of the biological response to stress.

Stress Management Approaches

The concept of stress continues to hold the public's interest as a result of unprecedented media attention to health issues and to the individual's responsibility for regulating his own health. The belief that one should assume responsibility for the onset or the course of one's illnesses may place an unwarranted burden on individuals. Popular approaches epitomized by the use of guided imagery to influence immune responses in the treatment of cancer may in some cases lead to premature intervention strategies based on limited scientific understanding.

Stress management programs have sprung up across the country as a way of dealing with the popularized version of the stress response known as "burnout" (teacher burnout, nurse burnout, and so forth). Many stress management programs employ useful strategies, such as the relaxation response, improving interpersonal skills to enhance social support, improving stamina, redefining priorities, recognizing and avoiding maladaptive behaviors, and reframing situations in a more positive way (McCue and Sachs, 1991). But group stress management programs carried out over several sessions often naively assume that individuals can, in what amounts to a behavioral hygiene approach, simply eliminate many of the sources of stress by restructuring their lives. Indeed, some of the programs seem to ignore what psychoanalysis has taught us about conflict and the deeper roots of behavior. While the mushrooming of stress reduction programs across the nation may offer some useful approaches to public health, an enormous gulf separates psychophysiological investigations of stress and its complex role in disease from these popular implementations.

Current Frontiers of Psychosomatic Research

Historically psychosomatic research has been linked to advances in biology and medicine. New insights into pathophysiology inevitably create new opportunities for psychophysiological understanding.

Psychoimmunology

The burgeoning of psychoimmunologic investigation has mirrored the explosion of knowledge in the field of immunology. In many ways the focus on the immune system is appropriate, because that system regulates the body's defenses against infection and appears to influence the pathophysiology of autoimmune disorders and malignancies. George Solomon was among the first to suggest that emotional states might influence the immune system. His hypothesis evolved from his clinical interests in the relationship of emotions to rheumatoid arthritis. In experimentally probing the effects of different kinds of stress on the immunologic responses of mice to immunization, he discovered that the stress of overcrowding could dampen and handling in early life could enhance the antibody response to immunization (Solomon, Levine, and Kraft, 1968).

Solomon's work was the beginning of a long series of animal studies that have examined the effects of various stressors on both the humoral immune system (involving B-lymphocytes and their production of antibodies) and the cellular immune system (involving T-lymphocytes and their role in delayed hypersensitivity reactions, such as organ transplantation rejection and the tuberculin skin response). Many investigations have focused on the effects of experimental stress on T-lymphocyte activity. Monjan and Collector (1977), using the chronic stress of a loud noise, showed a biphasic response of the immune system in mice. An initial decrease in T-lymphocyte activity for the first 2 weeks was followed by an increase over the next 2 weeks.

Keller and his associates (1981) have shown a direct correlation between the degree of stress in rats and the lymphocyte proliferative response to mitogens, a general measure of immune strength. Rats subjected to an electrical stress showed significant diminution in the strength of their lymphocyte response, the mechanism of which, as subsequent work showed, could not be explained by an elevation in adrenal corticosteroids. Even in adrenalectomized rats, the investigators were able to

show a similar diminution in lymphocyte response after electric shock.

Laudenslager and Ryan (1983) carried this experimental situation one step further. They were able to show that it was not the electric shock itself that created the immunologic change but the helplessness of the rat to stop it. Two groups of animals receiving the same amount of electric shock, one able to turn it off and the other helpless but passively yoked to the first, had entirely different immune responses. In fact, when electric shock alone was used, animals that had some capacity to turn it off showed a slight (though not significant) augmentation in their cellular immune response.

In addition to the experimental induction of stress, researchers have investigated naturally imposed stresses on laboratory animals. For example, Vernon Riley (1981) demonstrated that in rodents the stress of shipping and handling led to thymic involution and an elevation in corticosteroid levels at the time of their arrival in the laboratory. He also showed that the endocrine and immunologic changes that resulted from these inadvertent stresses could have a dramatic bearing on the course of a disease. Using the mouse model of mammary tumor produced by the Bittner oncogenic virus, Riley demonstrated that the reduction of the usual stresses could change the time course of tumor growth. Mice protected from handling and noise stress showed only a 7% incidence of tumor at 400 days, as opposed to 92% in the unprotected group. Several experiments have shown that helplessness affects the growth rate of animal tumor systems, and this change is presumably related to changes in immunologic response. In fact, the same experimental situations that affect immunologic responses have in other experiments influenced the outcome of a variety of animal models of disease, including malignancy, autoimmune arthritis, and infection (Moynihan and Ader, 1996). The results have usually been complicated and at times paradoxical, depending on the particular stressor chosen and its timing and duration.

Other animal experiments have also pointed to important connections between emotional states and the brain and immunologic response. For example, Marvin Stein and his colleagues (1991), as well as some early Russian investigators, have shown that experimental lesions in specific parts of the hypothalamus are associated with decreased humoral and cellular immunity.

In another intriguing line of research, Ader and Cohen (1975) demonstrated a conditioning effect on the immune response. Using a taste aversion paradigm in rats, Ader showed that a conditioned stimulus, such as a novel saccharin-flavored solution, when paired with an unconditioned stimulus such as cyclophosphamide (an immunosuppressive and emetic agent), could produce a subsequent conditioned immunosuppressive response in a rat. Others have replicated this basic finding; subsequent research using a similar conditioning paradigm has shown specific effects of this conditioning on T- and B-cells separately, as well as both augmentation and diminution of immune response in laboratory animals. Although the magnitude of the effect is small, it has been shown to modify the degree of kidney involvement in a mouse model of systemic lupus erythematosis. The mechanism accounting for the conditioned immunosuppressive or immunoenhancing effect remains one of the more intriguing mysteries in psychosomatic research. Recent work has demonstrated that cyclophosphamide-induced leukopenia in humans can be conditioned (Giang et al., 1996).

Investigators have increasingly observed in human beings similar immunologic changes related to life stress. It is important to recognize, however, that in no case have these immunologic changes been clearly shown to be responsible for the onset or exacerbation of illness. In one of the first such studies, Roger Bartrop (Bartrop et al., 1977), an Australian investigator, showed a decrease in human lymphocyte response to mitogens following bereavement. A further and even more convincing demonstration of this effect was shown by Schleifer and his colleagues (1983) at Mt. Sinai Hospital in New York. Fifteen men whose wives were dying from breast cancer underwent, prospectively, serial measures of lymphocyte function as well as psychological evaluations. The investigators were able to demonstrate in these subjects a significant decrease in lymphocyte response to mitogens in the few weeks immediately following bereavement, a response that subsequently returned to normal levels. In a continuing series of clinical studies, they have shown immunologic changes in patients with major affective disorder when compared to patients with dysthymic disorders or schizophrenia and to inpatients undergoing hernia repair.

Kiecolt-Glaser and colleagues (1984) have shown similar changes in immunologic activity—specifically changes in natural killer cell responses as a function of the stress of final exams in a group of medical students. Other investigators have shown comparable effects of acute stress on the magnitude of natural killer cell activity (which is thought to provide a natural defense against malignancy and viral infections). These studies confirm earlier observations on the importance of social support in modifying the effect of stress. For example, the same investigators have shown diminished cellular immune re-

sponse in women separated within the previous year as opposed to a demographically controlled group of married women. Within the married group those reporting poor marriages showed significant reductions in 3 immune measures, all indicating a relative decrease in the strength of the immune response. Another group of investigators (Thomas, Goodwin, and Goodwin, 1985) has shown an inverse relationship between social support and total lymphocyte count in a group of healthy but elderly nursing home subjects, a relationship seen in female but not in male subjects. Arnetz and his colleagues (1987) have shown a decrease in lymphocyte response to mitogens in unemployed women. They also found a decrease in reactivity to tuberculin skin testing but no changes in the number or ratio of T-cell subpopulations or serum cortisol. In a more recent review of studies of stress and altered immunity in human beings, Herbert and Cohen (1993) demonstrated that there is substantial evidence between stress and alteration in some measures of immune function—principally natural killer cell activity and response to mitogens. Their review also notes that the degree of immune alteration is often greater than subjective self-reports of stress, that it varies with length of stressors, and that social and interpersonal event stressors have different effects from non-social ones.

While we must remain cautious about the significance and even the reproducibility of these stress-related immunologic changes, they at least begin to provide a plausible mechanism for some of the observed and long-suspected relationships of a variety of stressors to subsequent illness. For the moment these findings are helping investigators explore and answer some intriguing questions at the forefront of biological research. One wonders why a connection exists between the nervous system and immunologic responses. Yet it is clear that the nervous system does have some regulatory influence, not only from the studies cited but also from evidence that lymphocytes have receptors for substances such as acetylcholine and norepinephrine, long known to be important neurotransmitters. Although we are a long way from understanding the significance of these connections, we know that the mechanisms involve neuroendocrine pathways including but not confined to the adrenal corticosteroids and the autonomic nervous system, which has direct anatomical connections (some would suggest synapses with lymphocytes) in the body of the thymus and spleen. These mechanisms involve not only efferent pathways but also afferent pathways capable of bringing information to the hypothalamus from the periphery (Besedovsky et al., 1979). Indeed, Fricchione and Stefano (1994) have proposed a macrophage-focused, bidirectional immune hypothesis. The macrophage, as the antigen presenting cell, is at the forefront of any acute phase response cascade ending in both cellular and humoral immune activity. While macrophage behavior is subject to stress hormone regulation, its monokine products are stimulating regulators of the stress response at the hypothalamic level (Reichlin, 1993). Those wishing to pursue this topic in more detail can find excellent summaries by Ader, Felten, and Cohen (1991), Stein, Miller, and Trustman (1991), and Kiecolt-Glaser and Glaser (1995).

Psychosomatic Aspects of Coronary Heart Disease

If a public opinion poll were taken on which disorders are influenced by the emotions, an overwhelming majority of Americans would very likely list heart disease among the top contenders. The assumption that chronic stress plays an etiological role in coronary disease is so widely held that it may surprise people to learn that scientific support for this relationship is still quite shaky. The cardiovascular system remains one of the most challenging frontiers in psychosomatic medicine. The fact that known risk factors such as smoking, hypertension, and serum lipids account for only about half the cases of coronary disease leaves plenty of room for psychosocial variables. The cardiovascular system is quite accessible to physiological observations, and its basic mechanisms have been understood for decades. Although the enormous public health problem caused by coronary disease has been a great stimulus to research on the etiology and prevention of heart disease, the uncertainties that still surround psychosomatic aspects show how difficult it is to elucidate the role of emotional factors in the pathogenesis of disease.

The likelihood that stress plays an important role in the pathogenesis of coronary heart disease has made psychosomatic research part of the mainstream of scientific investigation in cardiology and related fields. Sophisticated, large-scale epidemiologic studies of the natural history of heart disease routinely include the assessment of behavioral and psychosocial factors. Scientists engaged in basic research on heart disease are giving increasing attention to psychophysiological relationships. Because of the widespread interdisciplinary interest in stress and heart disease, a review of the research in this area gives some understanding of where the field of psychosomatic medicine stands today and of the problems it faces in the future.

The literature on the relationship of stress to coronary heart disease is voluminous. A few examples will illustrate the main trends, approaches, and areas of controversy. To begin with, the disease is actually a process that extends over many years and involves a series of events of different durations. Coronary disease may progress silently for decades. Once a critical degree of arterial blockage is reached, ischemic changes begin and symptoms develop, including angina and arrhythmias. Symptomatic disease may continue for months or years before the occurrence of a heart attack, which represents an acute event lasting minutes or hours. Each stage of the disease process involves specific pathophysiological changes, and stress and other behavioral factors may well have specific relationships to each stage. The psychosomatic aspects of atherogenesis may be quite different from the relationship of stress to the occurrence of a heart attack. The specificity of the relationship of stress to elements of a complex disease process is often overlooked. Long-term behavioral factors that may relate to atherogenesis may have no bearing on the evolution of ischemic symptoms or on the acute occurrence of a heart attack. Likewise, those factors that precipitate angina or destabilize the myocardium may not relate to the development of coronary disease itself.

Research on stress and coronary disease has taken 3 general forms. In the first, the natural history of the disease is related to psychological factors and events. In the second, the cardiovascular responses of human subjects are studied under experimental stress conditions. And in the third, animal models are used to simulate human heart disease and to elucidate potentially pathogenic relationships between stress and the heart. As in other areas of psychosomatic medicine, the definition of stress in regard to the role of psychosomatic factors in heart disease remains ambiguous. Studies vary greatly in what is observed and defined as stressful. Many define stress in terms of life events; others use psychophysiological changes; and still others consider the subjective experiences of the patient. Some presume the presence of stress from the personality style of the patient. Deriving general conclusions from a picture that includes such a diversity of approach, method, definition, and research strategy is one of the challenges that face the student of psychosomatic medicine.

Natural history studies. Although most people believe that life stress and intense emotions have an effect on the heart, it is surprisingly difficult to demonstrate a relationship between naturally occurring stresses and the onset of coronary heart disease. In the Grant Study, George Vaillant (1978) found that poor mental health between the ages of 21 and 47 was associated with deteriorating physical health between the ages of 42 and 53 in a cohort of 204 healthy men drawn from the Harvard College classes of 1942, 1943, and 1944. The men with coronary artery disease, however, were distributed evenly across the mental health categories. Two were in the best mental health category, and of the 18 sick people in the worst mental health category, only 3 had coronary disease. In another well-known prospective longitudinal study of a cohort of healthy individuals, the Precursor Study of Johns Hopkins medical students, coronary disease was associated with earlier traits of anger, hypochondriasis, and depression, although the association was relatively weak. The 50 who developed cancer, from the total of 1337 male medical students, showed a different premorbid profile—that of a lack of closeness to parents and a relative inability to express emotions (Thomas et al., 1983).

Several studies have called into question the relationship of type A behavior to coronary heart disease. Type A behavior was originally defined by a structured interview that now includes videotaped observations of speech and behavior (Friedman and Rosenman, 1974). Its characteristics include competitiveness, time urgency, aggression, impatience, lack of pleasure, and visible mannerisms such as abrupt gestures and explosive speech. A self-administered questionnaire was developed by David Jenkins in collaboration with Rosenman and Zyzanski (1974). Subsequently other investigators created different measures of type A behavior. The Framingham Study developed its own type A scale, and many of the epidemiologic projects in Europe have employed the Bortner rating scale, a list of 14 paired adjectives that the patient is asked to use for self-evaluation. It is not clear whether these instruments measure the same traits. The original enthusiasm for type A as a predictor of heart disease was based on the discovery that it seemed to predict the development of heart disease in populations that were initially disease-free. In 4 of 5 major prospective studies of multiple risk factors, type A behavior predicted coronary heart disease end points at a ratio of about 2 to 1. In the fifth study, on Japanese-Americans in Honolulu, no such relationship was found. Westernization may favor coronary heart disease, which raises the question of whether type A behavior is culture-dependent. Most of the studies were done on white males, although the Framingham Study included women.

Several studies have tried to relate type A behavior to prognosis in high-risk patients and to the extent of coronary disease found on angiography. Weak and ambiguous results have emerged, suggesting that type A behavior is not a powerful predictor of mortality or morbidity in populations with existing coronary disease and is at best a weak projector of objective coronary artery disease. When

Redford Williams and his colleagues (1986) measured type A behavior by the structured interview technique in 2289 men at the time of angiography, the behavior was predictive of the extent of coronary disease only in patients under age 45. In the older group (over age 55), type B behavior (meaning essentially the opposite of type A) appeared to be slightly more prevalent among patients with significant coronary narrowing.

Efforts have been made to purify the active principle in type A behavior by studying the components of type A traits. The most promising relationship appears to be that of hostility to coronary disease. In one study Barefoot and colleagues (1983) found that in 255 physicians studied over a 25-year period, the hostility score on the *Minnesota Multiphasic Personality Inventory* (MMPI) predicted a fivefold difference in the occurrence of coronary disease. Physicians with a hostility score above the median had 5 times the number of coronary events as those below the median. In another study, hostility, cynicism, and aggression appeared to be significant risk factors for mortality in patients with coronary artery disease (Goldstein and Niaura, 1992). When hostility is looked at as a general risk factor for all diseases and mortality, it also proves to be a strong predictor. In the Western Electric Study, begun in 1960, the hostility scale of the MMPI predicted total mortality over a 20-year period from ages 40–45 to ages 60–65.

The present status of type A behavior as a predictor of coronary disease can be summarized as follows: (1) in a white, Westernized population without coronary disease, type A behavior favors the development of coronary disease; (2) in a population at high risk for coronary disease, type A behavior will not predict subsequent morbidity and mortality; (3) in patients who have had a myocardial infarction, type A behavior will not predict a recurrence; (4) type A behavior will not predict an arrhythmia or sudden cardiac death; (5) type A behavior will not predict the extent of coronary narrowing seen on angiography; and (6) if hostility is parceled out as a component of type A behavior, it may have predictive value (the role of hostility needs further study). Type A behavior is a psychosomatic concept that was oversold before completion of critical studies. It was a simple concept that had a basis in folklore and intuition. Many patients and physicians still believe it is important as a risk factor in coronary disease. Psychosomatic medicine must lift this burden of misconception.

Studies exploring the possibility that stress may lead to the emergence of symptomatic heart disease were foreshadowed in the 1930s by Adolph Meyer, who proposed that life events were related to health. A number of early studies using the Holmes and Rahe Schedule of Recent Events to measure the pressure of life events before disease onset seemed to demonstrate that most adverse health changes, particularly heart attacks, were preceded by increased pressure. Prospective studies, however, have failed to confirm the relationship of stressful events to the onset of heart disease. For example, in a study of over 5000 middle-aged construction workers who were followed for 15 months after a life events inventory, no association was found between the 32 heart attacks that occurred during the study period and the life events scores. More recent work has emphasized the personal meaning of life events and the factors that modify their impact, notably the role of social supports and the context in which these events occur.

A more compelling strategy than using a simple life events inventory is to isolate a specific event as a marker for the onset of stress. The study of health changes after retirement utilizes this approach. Although common intuition may suggest that people fall apart after retirement, in fact studies have failed to demonstrate a consistent pattern of health change following this important life event. Investigators have used the same strategy to study health changes after bereavement, with similar results. On the Holmes and Rahe scale, loss of a spouse was listed as the most traumatic life event. Several studies seemed to indicate that the mortality rates of bereaved individuals rose during the period immediately after the loss of a spouse. In 1969 a well-known article reported a study of 4000 Welshmen who had lost their wives. During the first 6 months after bereavement, their mortality from heart disease appeared to be 67% higher than the rate expected by actuarial statistics. Subsequently, however, a sophisticated epidemiologic study from Johns Hopkins University failed to replicate these results (Helsing, Szklo, and Comstock, 1981). The study paired 4032 widowed men and women with nonwidowed controls and followed them for 12 years. A slight increase in mortality in the bereaved males in the 55–75 age group began to appear in the second year after death of the spouse. No increase in death after bereavement could be demonstrated in the older men, and no statistically significant difference occurred in any of the groups of women after loss of the spouse. The causes of death were spread over various conditions that seemed to be associated with changes in lifestyle and in moving to nursing homes rather than with the grief process itself. Cardiovascular deaths did not increase as much as other deaths. The fact that no increase in death occurred during the first year after bereavement was further evidence that the trauma of loss was not a factor. Social isolation and lack of support appeared to be more relevant. Once men remarried, they returned to the mortality curve of the control group. Other studies have also failed to demonstrate a health consequence from bereavement alone. The myth of the effects of bereavement on the heart, however, still persists.

The role of social support in protecting individuals from the effects of stress has been demonstrated more convincingly in a 9-year prospective study of almost 7000 adults in Alameda County, California (Berkman and Syme, 1979). Those who lacked social and community ties were more likely to die of all causes by a factor of almost 3. Similar results were obtained in a longitudinal study of 331 people in North Carolina, where the crucial factor seemed to be the individual's perception of the availability of social support. And in a large-scale study of the usefulness of beta-blockers in the prevention of mortality after myocardial infarction, the combined effect of life stress and social isolation was associated with a fourfold increase in mortality. In the same study, the type A behavior pattern had no predictive value for mortality. The protective effect of social support is confirmed in the work of Oxman and associates (1995), which shows lower mortality in the 6-month period after cardiac surgery in patients with greater religious faith and group affiliation. The absence of socioeconomic resources enhances the risk of death in patients with coronary artery disease (Williams et al., 1992).

The affective state most often noted as an indicator of poor prognosis in patients with heart disease is depression—which corroborates the importance of social isolation as a risk factor. Studies of depression are not as well designed or as extensive as the epidemiologic studies of type A behavior or life events, but they present a rather convincing picture. After myocardial infarction (MI), depression, noted clinically or on rating scales, is a marker for the risk of recurrence and increased mortality. In one study at Albert Einstein Montefiore Medical Center in New York, 88 patients at risk for sudden death were followed for 18 months (Kennedy et al., 1985). The only predictors of poor outcome were depression and mild brain damage. Of the two, depression was the more powerful. Fatal secondary arrhythmias were associated with depression at a significance level of $p < 0.006$. Lesperance and her colleagues (1996) noted that one-third of patients developed depression following MI. Those who did were 3–4 times more likely to die in the year or so following MI than non-depressed patients. These studies bear out the widely held clinical impression that depression, especially when combined with agitation and obsessive preoccupations, is a danger sign in patients with heart disease. The psychophysiological connection between depression and the cardiovascular system is still unclear (Cameron, 1996). Depression is known to be associated with increased levels of circulating catecholamines, adrenal cortical hormones, and increased sympathetic tone. Depression also can disturb the sleep cycle and other diurnal patterns. Perhaps these perturbations have adverse effects on the cardiovascular system.

Everson and her colleagues (1996) have documented that in a community-based population of middle-aged men, hopelessness is associated with a higher incidence of myocardial infarction as well as cancer.

More systematic information is available on the relationship of acute stress to heart attacks. Folklore and anecdotal evidence support the belief that emotional disturbances can precipitate sudden death. (In 1971 George Engel, for example, published a collection of 170 newspaper stories of sudden deaths that occurred after acute emotional disturbance.) Among the few studies that have approached the problem more systematically is Greene, Goldstein, and Moss's (1972) report on the events preceding sudden death in 26 employees of the Kodak company. He found that half the patients were significantly depressed in the weeks before death and had a sudden attack during a state of acute arousal. Meyers and Dewar (1975) reconstructed the events of the day preceding death in 100 men who died suddenly; in 23 cases they found evidence of acute emotional stress in the hour prior to death. No other behavioral factor appeared as frequently in their study. Rissanen and colleagues (1978) reported similar results in 117 sudden-death victims in Helsinki. A study of 117 survivors of life-threatening arrhythmias, which used data drawn from the memories of the patients and their relatives, found that 25 had suffered their arrhythmias during acute emotional disturbances (Reich et al., 1981). The most common disturbance was anger, often associated with anxiety. A comparison of the cardiac pathology of patients who had arrhythmias during emotional stress with that of the other patients in the series revealed that the patients with emotional triggers had a more benign structural pathology, were younger, and had a more severe arrhythmia profile—that is, they had ventricular fibrillation rather than ventricular tachycardia. This study suggested that susceptibility to emotional stress contributed to fatal arrhythmias in younger patients with more benign pathology.

The fact that only 20% of the patients in the 3 larger studies experienced sudden death during emotional stress suggests that a susceptible subgroup exists that needs to be identified and studied more thoroughly. The possibility that those patients who develop arrhythmias during emotional stress constitute a group of "hot reactors" with special cardiac susceptibility to stress is currently under consideration in several centers. This possibility is in line with the psychosomatic concept of a vulnerable organ system. Psychosomatic research would make an important contribution to the prevention of cardiac fatalities if this vulnerable subgroup of patients could be identified and protected. A promising new approach may involve brain positron emission tomographic (PET) studies during cardiac symptoms. Some of these approaches are already furthering our knowledge of the central nervous system pathways mediating cardiac events in disorders such as silent myocardial ischemia (Rosen et al., 1994).

It seems less likely from epidemiologic studies that emotional stress precipitates myocardial infarction. The sudden-death victims who died during emotional upsets were probably suffering from acute episodes of ventricular fibrillation rather than myocardial infarction. Ventricular fibrillation, however, is the most common form of sudden death, and any contribution to the protection of vulnerable patients from the occurrence of arrhythmias would constitute a major advance. Psychoactive medications could, in effect, take their place among antiarrhythmic drugs.

Experimental studies of human subjects. Psychophysiological studies of the effects of stress on the cardiovascular system of human subjects, both normal and with coronary heart disease, have provided some insight into the role of psychosomatic factors in coronary heart disease, although the evidence is largely circumstantial. Investigators who have monitored subjects during stressful experiences have demonstrated that public speaking, driving through rush-hour traffic, and watching exciting athletic events, as well as other stimulating experiences, can provoke ventricular arrhythmias in susceptible individuals. Patients with a prolonged Q-T syndrome—a rare, sometimes inherited disorder in which fatal ventricular arrhythmias can be provoked by sudden surges of sympathetic nervous activity (Schwartz, 1975)—have been monitored while experiencing emotional stress, and the actual onset of ventricular fibrillation has been observed. One young woman developed serious arrhythmias when her alarm clock rang or when she heard loud, frightening noises, including thunder. Angina pectoris episodes can be provoked by emotional stress and can be conditioned to occur in response to signal stimuli. A. P. Selwyn and colleagues (1986) have shown that episodes of silent ischemia, presumably from coronary artery spasm, occur frequently during all life stresses and can be provoked in the laboratory by asking susceptible patients with coronary disease to perform mental arithmetic.

Artificial stress tests have occasionally been disappointing because patients can isolate themselves emotionally quite successfully. In a susceptible patient, however, the effects of laboratory stress can be dramatic. Recalling disturbing life events is one approach that has recreated cardiac symptoms in some patients. Standard tests, such as mental arithmetic, have been less effective. However, Rozanski and his colleagues (1988) have shown that personally relevant mental stress stimulated by an emotionally arousing personalized speaking task produced wall-motion abnormalities on thallium scintigraphy in 23 of 39 (59%) coronary artery disease patients, indicating that mental stress may indeed be an important myocardial ischemia precipitant rivaling exercise. Many investigators have tried to demonstrate differences in the cardiovascular activity of type A and type B individuals. The results of these tests have not been impressive. When type A and type B individuals are challenged to a competitive game and are made angry by their opponents, the type A subjects show a greater cardiovascular response. This experiment is often cited as evidence to support the notion that type A individuals are more susceptible to heart disease because of their competitiveness and hostility. Psychosomatic research could make a major contribution to the evaluation of patients with heart disease if investigators could devise a psychological stress test that reliably distinguishes individuals who respond to life stress by disturbances of cardiovascular physiology. It has become routine to measure arrhythmia threshold in patients with malignant arrhythmias by running a wire into the heart and provoking extrasystoles by electrical stimulation. This technique enables clinicians to test the efficacy of antiarrhythmic agents. Although it also offers a unique opportunity to evaluate the effects of psychological stress on arrhythmia threshold by direct observation, the lack of an adequate psychological stress test limits this approach.

Some studies (Malkoff et al., 1993) of acute experimental stress in healthy subjects have noted the increased secretion of adenosine triphosphate (ATP) by platelets, an indicator of platelet activation, which may have important links to acute coronary events.

Animal studies. The accessibility of the cardiovascular system makes it relatively easy to create animal models of clinical situations relating stress to heart disease. The heart must be sufficiently large to develop arrhythmias, however, and it is difficult to reproduce coronary artery disease in animals.

For many years researchers have known that brain stimulation can alter cardiovascular physiology and even produce fatal arrhythmias (Verrier and Lown, 1984). The areas of the brain that produce the most dramatic effects are related functionally to the sympathetic outflow. When a dog's heart is subjected to experimental ischemia, increased sympathetic traffic produced by stimulation along the sympathetic outflow can trigger a fatal episode of ventricular fibrillation. It is extremely difficult to provoke ventricular fibrillation in a normal dog heart. When a dog is conditioned to show signs of fear in a sling where it has received electric shocks, it will develop spontaneous arrhythmias when moved from its own cage to the sling, provided that the dog's heart has been damaged by an experimental myocardial infarction. The move from the home cage to the sling lowers the ventricular fibrillation threshold by a factor of 2 or more.

Animals without experimental infarcts also show a decrease in ventricular fibrillation threshold when subjected to experimental stress. The same effects can be demonstrated in pigs that are moved from familiar surroundings to a new and threatening environment. Recently the same changes in ventricular fibrillation threshold have been induced by making dogs angry. When a restrained dog that has been fasted is made to watch another dog eat its dinner out of its own dish, the restrained dog displays angry reactions and has a marked fall in ventricular fibrillation threshold. All these effects are traceable to the sympathetic nervous system and can be abrogated by sympathetic blockade.

A more difficult model to create is one that demonstrates the effects of subacute or chronic stress on the cardiovascular system. In one study socially stressed adult male monkeys fed on a low-fat, low-cholesterol diet developed more extensive coronary artery atherosclerosis than did unstressed controls (Kaplan, Clarkson, and Manuck, 1984). Social stress was produced by periodically altering group membership by redistributing animals every 12 weeks and forcing the stressed monkeys to develop new group memberships and relationships. The introduction of strangers to a group of monkeys creates a high degree of social instability. Antagonistic encounters and extreme forms of submission occurred with significantly greater frequency in these periodically reorganized groups than among control animals.

Another animal model that simulates the effects of long-term stress on the cardiovascular system involves primates that have prematurely been separated from their mothers. These experimental animals have a relatively unstable cardiovascular system and tend to develop tachycardia and arrhythmias under stress in greater frequency than the controls. The maternally deprived animals appear to be models for various forms of psychosomatic susceptibility, including cardiovascular reactivity.

Research on possible psychosomatic factors of coronary heart disease has progressed relatively rapidly because heart disease is such an important health problem and because so many investigators in the mainstream of cardiovascular research have considered stress to be an important variable. Nevertheless, the role of psychosomatic factors in the pathogenesis of coronary disease needs to be established more rigorously, and many questions remain unanswered on the importance of stress in the clinical management of patients and in primary and secondary prevention of coronary disease. In spite of this uncertainty, stress management programs are widely used on a routine basis for patients with heart disease, and a surprising number of patients seem to believe that some form of life stress has brought on their heart disease.

The medical profession owes the public a more balanced and realistic view of the role of stress and of the definition of stress in this condition. All too often patients become afraid of their own emotions and retreat from the hurly-burly of the workplace. Psychosomatic research on coronary disease is impeded by issues that have plagued it from the beginning. The concept of stress is often used imprecisely, without reference to time, duration, or the patient's own experiences. Animal models serving as analogies or metaphors for human disorders sometimes provide the basis for uncritical generalizations. Relationships are oversimplified and popularized. Psychosomatic concepts tend to be reduced to a level of folklore and intuition, and once disseminated, they develop the power of myth and are exceedingly difficult to modify or eradicate. By contrast, intervention strategies designed to reduce sympathetic tone are not likely to be dangerous and may well have protective effects on the heart. In any event, there is a need for continuing scientific rigor in the approach to these issues. Whether stress does in fact play a significant role in the pathogenesis of coronary disease remains an open question.

Types of Psychosomatic Research

An in-depth description of all areas of psychosomatic research is beyond the scope of this chapter. The interested reader can find reviews of psychiatric aspects of specific medical illnesses in the *Comprehensive Textbook of Psychiatry* (Kaplan and Sadock, 1985) and McDaniel et al. in *Synopsis of Psychiatry* (1994). Our intent here is to highlight some of the best examples of the range of approaches taken to investigate the intriguing questions in psychosomatic medicine.

Psychosomatic research has had a long tradition of studying individual patients in great depth from both a biological and a psychological perspective. Probably no investigator has epitomized this approach more than George Engel during his long and productive career. One particular case, which first captured his attention in 1955, was that of Monica, a 15-month-old infant with esophageal atresia and a surgically created gastric fistula (Engel, 1987). Like William Beaumont 150 years earlier, Engel and his colleagues observed the activity of Monica's gastric mucosa in relationship to her mood and behavior over a period of many years. When she was depressed and withdrawn in response to strangers or losses, the secretion of acid decreased markedly. Conversely, more assertive, aggressive behaviors correlated with a substantial increase in acid secretion. Engel studied Monica's psychological and physical health over the ensuing 32 years. One of numerous fascinating observations was that Monica's style of infant feeding resembled the manner in which she herself was fed as an infant. With hundreds of psychological tests, interviews, and recorded observations since age 2, her life has been documented like no other.

Long-term prospective group studies have provided some of the more interesting insights into the psychosomatic process. As previously discussed, Vaillant's Grant Study identified some of the factors that may predispose individuals toward the subsequent development of physical illness and psychosomatic disorders (Vaillant, 1978). In one part of his analysis, he compared the characteristics of those who developed both physical and psychosomatic illness with the characteristics of those who did not. As his measure of psychosomatic illness, he took 5 common types of illness frequently called psychosomatic: peptic ulcer, colitis, allergy, hypertension, and musculoskeletal complaints. He identified these problems in 50 of his 95 subjects, whom he compared with the 45 who did not develop psychosomatic disease. He found only a slightly greater incidence of psychopathology in the former group. Of interest, the "psychosomatic" patients more commonly sought out doctors, both in childhood and as adults; they were less likely to take vacations and engage in athletic activities and were more likely to resort to alcohol and drugs to relieve stress. They also had more somatic symptoms in general when under stress, but the symptoms varied from situation to situation and did not consistently refer to a particular target organ. In the same study Vaillant observed a much greater difference between the 20 subjects who developed chronic and irreversible physical illnesses and the 75 who did not (we have already noted, however, the absence of such a correlation in those with coronary heart disease). The chronically ill group had a significantly greater level of premorbid psychopathology. Thus if one uses the more expanded definition of psychosomatic illness in regard to chronic physical disease, his data strongly suggest that early psychological ill health predisposes one toward the development of serious physical disease. Interestingly, over time, genetic and biological factors seem to outweigh psychosomatic ones in the development of some disorders, such as hypertension (Vaillant and Gerber, 1996).

Prospective studies are particularly useful in psychosomatic research because, in contrast to retrospective studies, they avoid confusing the patient's psychological response to his illness with his premorbid psychological characteristics. Methodologically, however, it has been difficult to study prospectively a large enough population to accumulate sufficient numbers of patients who develop relatively uncommon diseases. One way around this dilemma is to pick a population at risk for a particular disease, evaluate the subjects thoroughly at baseline, and then follow them through a relatively short-term environmental exposure that would tend to precipitate the disease. One of the classics of psychosomatic research is such a study of peptic ulcer disease (Mirsky, 1958). Because patients with duodenal ulcer have higher levels of pepsinogen in the urine and blood than those without the disease, serum pepsinogen was used as a biological marker for increased gastric acid secretion. Mirsky and his colleagues studied a large number of healthy men immediately prior to their undergoing the stress of entering basic training in the army. In addition to measuring pepsinogen levels, they performed a variety of psychological tests, including the Rorschach test, the Saslow questionnaire, and the Blacky test, and gave the men psychoanalytically oriented interviews focusing on styles of interpersonal interaction. Neither high pepsinogen levels nor a specific psychological pattern of dependency conflict alone was sufficient, but in combination they could predict the development of duodenal ulcer. The discovery that *H. pylori* may have a causative role in the development of peptic ulcer suggests that these psychological factors can influence immunologic defenses as well.

Another outstanding example of this approach can be found in Kasl, Evans, and Neiderman's (1979) investigation of psychosocial risk factors in the development of infectious mononucleosis—a study that also carefully differentiated between illness and illness behavior in the setting of an acute onset of disease. This 4-year prospective study of a class of 1400 cadets at the West Point Military Academy included immunologic measurements, evaluations of actual clinical disease, and extensive psychological assessments of the subjects. On entry about one-third of the freshman cadets lacked Epstein-Barr virus (EBV) antibody, and about 20% of this group became infected, as evidenced by their subsequent development of EBV antibody titers. Among those seroconverters about one-quarter developed definite clinical infectious mononucleosis. Several psychosocial factors, when taken in combination, were found to correlate significantly with the increased risk of developing clinical disease. The best predictor was a combination of high motivation and poor academic performance. Having an "overachiever" father was also related significantly to the onset of clinical disease. The investigators further showed that the same psychosocial factors were correlated significantly with the likelihood of seroconversion, as well as with the length of hospitalization among cadets who developed clinical infectious mononucleosis.

Using an epidemiologic approach to investigate psychosomatic relationships, Kasl and Cobb (1982) studied the impact of job loss on blue-collar workers. They identified two plants, one in an urban and one in a rural setting, that were going to close permanently. They studied both the anticipation of job loss among employees and the aftereffects of termination. A control group of 74 men whose jobs were stable was compared with the 100 men whose jobs were abolished. All were married blue-collar workers with about 19 years of seniority. The results revealed the buffering effects of social support. During the weeks before and after job termination, cholesterol and uric acid levels in the serum were found to be higher in those with diminished social support. No significant increases were found in hypertension and peptic ulcer disease, although an increase in arthritis did occur, in inverse proportion to the level of social support.

Erich Lindemann's (1944) description of the reactions of the Coconut Grove fire survivors highlighted the frequency of somatic symptoms occurring in the aftermath of disasters. Numerous studies have shown that post-traumatic stress disorder is a common aftereffect of the experience of sudden disaster or assault. The impact of disaster on the development of physical disease, however, is less clear. Part of the problem, of course, is that many of the disasters have some direct or delayed impact on health through nonpsychological mechanisms, such as increases in infection after floods or earthquakes. One report did find an association between chronic pain syndromes and post-traumatic stress disorder: Benedikt and Kolb (1986) found that 10% of 225 patients referred to a pain clinic met the DSM-III criteria for chronic post-traumatic stress disorder. In all 22 cases (all male), the chronic pain was localized at the sites of former injuries, the majority of which had occurred directly in combat.

Other studies have examined the relationship of psychological experience to physiological events, or vice versa. Though not directly pertaining to disease development, many of them offer interesting insights into the connection between life experience and physiological fluctuation. One of the most interesting is the Three Investigators' Study, in which 3 psychosomatic researchers (Rahe, Rubin, and Arthur, 1974) kept careful diaries over a 6-month period documenting the stresses of their own everyday lives. Concomitantly they measured their serum cholesterol, cortisol, and uric acid levels at frequent intervals. In one of the subjects the prospect of an unpleasant residential move was associated with a marked increase in cholesterol. Another had repeated peak elevations in cortisol levels during the time of an extreme disappointment related to his work. In association with other stressful life events, 2 of the subjects had elevations in uric acid similar to levels seen in clinical gout.

Another approach has been to induce experimentally a stress experience in humans and look at some of the physiological responses. Although this approach has a long tradition in psychosomatic research and may provide some clues about a subject's biological vulnerability to the development of illness, one is often left wondering exactly what the physiological responses mean and whether they are adaptive or maladaptive. Kosten and his colleagues (1984) observed the effects of a stressful interview on 52 subjects, whose average age was 61, to determine whether or not the stress provoked a change in growth hormone (GH), and if so, whether that hormonal change was correlated with anxiety and "defensiveness." In response to a review of the subjects' experience of the death or serious illness of a spouse, 54% of the sample demonstrated an elevated serum level of GH (2.0 nanograms per milligram). About half the positive responders were "anticipatory" responders (that is, for them the anticipation of the interview was more potent than the actual interview). Furthermore, subjects who had a high GH response to the interview tended to have higher anxiety scores. When combined with a defensiveness profile characterized primarily by denial, this high anxiety score was even more strongly correlated with an elevated GH level response to stress. Such a study represents an effort to refine our understanding of the relationship of subjective experience and personality to psychoendocrine responses to stress.

Another study looked at the long-term endocrinologic effects of practicing transcendental meditation (TM), a stress-relieving intervention. Werner and his colleagues (1986) at the Maharishi International University in Fairfield, Iowa, evaluated prospectively 11 male subjects before and after a 3-year program of TM-Sidhi meditation. Over this period they observed a progressive decrease in the serum thyroid-stimulating hormone (TSH) and prolactin, but no change in cortisol T_3 or T_4 levels. The health implications for these and other similar hormonal changes related to psychological experience, however, are unknown.

Finally, psychosomatic researchers have often used animal models of disease or stress to gain further insights into psychophysiological responses. One excellent example of the use of an animal model to understand the multiplicity of factors in the onset of disease was Robert Ader's (1971) series of investigations on peptic ulcer formation in the rat. He demonstrated that increased vulnerability to developing an ulcer depended on a variety of factors, including: (1) the duration of enforced immobility; (2) the timing of the imposed immobilization during the 24-hour activity cycle; (3) the biological predisposition of the rat as indicated by its sex and by high inherited plasma pepsinogen levels; (4) prenatal influences, such as handling of the pregnant females; (5) various other early life and environmental factors, such as the way the animals were housed and the degree to which they were handled; and (6) analogous to current emphasis on social support, whether the rats were facing the stress alone or with other rats. Although it is difficult, of course, to move from an animal model to the human system, animal models frequently allow a clearer and cleaner demonstration of the role of a range of variables in the onset of disease.

Another example has been the work of Myron Hofer (1984), whose creative use of an animal model of early infant-mother interaction has provided considerable insight into the regulation of psychophysiological responses to separation. Hofer has identified at least a dozen independent and specific "hidden regulators" within the mother-infant interaction. For example, maternal body warmth acts as a regulator of the activity level of the infant rat, while maternal touch regulates the pup's growth hormone. From the experience of this animal model, Hofer has suggested that specific physiological regulation might also exist within the context of human relationships and be vulnerable to disruption as a consequence of separation and bereavement. The emphasis here is on the importance of interpersonal and social relationships in the regulation of multiple physiological responses in an individual. Creative animal research such as Hofer's has generated the development of new concepts and hypotheses worthy of exploration in humans.

Consultation-Liaison Psychiatry

No discussion of psychosomatic medicine would be complete without considering the development and role of consultation-liaison psychiatry. Z. J. Lipowski (1983, 1992) has been a particularly strong voice in identifying consultation-liaison psychiatry as a distinct subspecialty within psychiatry and viewing it as part of the psychosomatic movement. As a subspecialty, it deals with the psychiatric problems of medical and surgical patients. It is the clinical, practical arm of psychosomatic medicine. While researchers have explored the role of psychological factors in the onset of physical disorders, clinicians have increasingly applied such knowledge to psychiatric problems encountered in medical and surgical patients. For the patient, the stress of having a medical disorder often gives rise to an immediate and urgently felt problem that challenges the skill of the consultation-liaison psychiatrist. The problem may be acute or chronic, depending on the nature of the medical disorder. Adjusting to a medical illness requires a complex adaptation and in some cases is associated with specific psychiatric conditions.

In the 1920s and 1930s general hospitals began to include psychiatric units to provide a link between psychiatry and medicine in matters of patient care. The term *consultation-liaison* reflects the dual activity of psychiatrists in providing direct consultation to the patient and in assisting the medical staff in patient management. *Liaison* conveys the broader role of fostering the integration of psychiatry into medicine by teaching psychiatric concepts to medical students and non-psychiatric physicians and by developing collaborative relationships with them. Since 1970 consultation-liaison psychiatry has developed rapidly, stimulated in part by the National Institute of Mental Health's effort to bring psychiatry closer to medicine.

The development of new professional societies and journals also reflects the widening attention to psychiatric aspects of medical and surgical illness. For example, in 1960 the new Academy of Psychosomatic Medicine first published its journal, *Psychosomatics,* subtitled *Exploring the Interaction of Mind and Body and Disease.* This journal continues to present clinical observations and controlled studies that have helped to disseminate the experience of consultation-liaison psychiatrists using pharmacotherapy and psychotherapeutic approaches. There are, of course, other societies with their own journals that offer slightly different orientations. For example, *Health Psychology,* the official journal of the Division of Health Psychology of the American Psychological Association, focuses on the need for more practical intervention in the behavioral aspects of illness and is oriented toward behaviorism as a theoretical framework. Other journals such as *General Hospital Psychiatry* explore the relationship of psychiatry to medicine and primary care.

A psychiatrist working in a general hospital with medically and surgically ill patients receives several different kinds of requests for assistance. Probably the most frequent request is for help with patients who exhibit severe anxiety and depression. Another common request is for help in understanding somatic complaints that appear to lack an organic basis, which is the typical presentation of somatoform disorders. These complex, sensitive situations require tact and a particularly good working relationship between medical and psychiatric staff. The next most frequent request is for assistance in brief episodes of psychosis, usually manifesting as delirium or dementia in elderly patients, an increasingly large segment of the population in general hospitals. Finally, the consultation-liaison psychiatrist often receives calls for help from the medical staff in "managing" a difficult medical or surgical patient. The root of the problem is usually a personality disorder, often combined with a substance abuse disorder.

Lipowski and Wolston (1981) have documented the referral patterns for psychiatric consultation based on 2 samples of 1000 medical and surgical patients. They concluded that depressive disorders were consistently at the top of the list, averaging about 40% of referrals, followed by organic brain syndromes, about 15%. The average rate of psychiatric consultation among hospital admissions in their study samples was 4%. Using an estimated incidence of psychiatric morbidity among patients with medical and surgical problems of 30–50%, they concluded that only about 10% of patients needing consultation were actually referred. The frequency of psychiatric consultation in a general hospital tends to be a function of the visibility and perceived usefulness of the consultation-liaison psychiatrist.

Gonzales (1994) and others have focused attention on the role of psychiatry in primary care practice—which is often viewed as the "de facto" mental care system. Research has clearly indicated that despite the large number of visits which are being made for mental health reasons, and despite the high prevalence of psychiatric disorders, the recognition and treatment of these disorders by primary care physicians is suboptimal (Borus et al., 1988; Ormel and Tiemens, 1995).

Adaptation to Medical and Surgical Illness

Clinical experience has increased our understanding of how people react and adapt to medical and surgical illness. Primarily it has taught us to focus on the specific meaning of the illness for an individual in a given situation. To appreciate what the illness means to the individual, the clinician must consider various dimensions of the patient and the disease (Leigh and Reiser, 1985).

The clinician's first task is to assess the patient's personality. Kahana and Bibring (1964) have described several personality types often encountered in a general hospital, each of which has a characteristic response to illness.

Their list includes: (1) dependent demanding patients; (2) orderly, controlling (obsessive-compulsive) patients; (3) dramatizing, emotional, histrionic patients; (4) long-suffering, self-sacrificing masochistic patients; (5) guarded, suspicious (paranoid) patients; (6) superior, special, narcissistic patients; and (7) seclusive, aloof, schizoid patients. Others have added impulsive patients and patients with mood swings to the list. The consultation-liaison psychiatrist understands that under the challenge of hospitalization, the defensive styles of most patients become temporarily magnified. The dependent patient, for example, may experience the supportiveness of the hospital environment as extremely comforting, whereas the seclusive, schizoid patient may experience the intrusiveness and loss of privacy as extremely threatening.

Second, the clinician should consider the patient's age and developmental stage. Clearly the meaning of illness is different for a 19-year-old college student who is developing an independent identity and learning intimacy than for a 50-year-old married woman who is anticipating freedom from the responsibilities of child rearing. In each case the patient's perception of her illness will be greatly influenced by the circumstances immediately preceding hospitalization.

Third, the clinician must assess the nature of the disease itself, including rate of onset, degree of impact on interpersonal and occupational functioning, and likely course (fixed, reversible, progressive, and so on).

Finally, the clinician needs to consider the illness both in terms of the patient's family and in terms of the broader cultural and social context. The level of social support available to the patient from family, employer, and community has critical practical importance in planning for discharge and sometimes even in recommending certain kinds of treatment.

Serious illness is usually a pivotal event in a person's life—a time for enforced reflection and stocktaking and often a period of intense emotional experience and change. Affective ties to family and friends may be strengthened or perhaps disrupted. Memories of prior losses and challenges are revived. With the threat of death or drastic change in lifestyle, one often sees the meaning of life and of personal priorities with unusual clarity. Patients may feel isolated and need to talk to an understanding person. Not surprisingly, many are very amenable to brief psychotherapy, providing the consultation-liaison psychiatrist with the opportunity to help and to know intimately people not ordinarily seen in psychiatric practice.

How patients cope with the stress of illness depends to a great extent on the meaning of the illness to them, that is, on their cognitive appraisal of the situation. For most people coping implies more than an unconscious psychological defense. Rather, it involves an active, conscious problem-solving strategy. Coping is a process critically linked to the dimension of time, with different manifestations at different phases of the illness.

In sudden major illness, common reactions include denial and even distortion and projection. The more acute and life-threatening the illness, the more the reaction resembles post-traumatic stress disorder, with the individual experiencing a tendency toward numbing yet intrusive thoughts about the illness while awake and in nightmares. This pattern generally occurs in the early stages of integration after a traumatic event. Indeed some have speculated that the persistence and clarity of memories formed during an acute, traumatic incident reflects the recording of memory by an altered biological process.

The experience of an acute heart attack is one such event that has been studied extensively from a psychological point of view. Hackett and Cassem (1974) constructed an interview based on a denial scale to explore an individual's immediate response to having a heart attack. They evaluated denial both in cognitive terms and in terms of related behaviors, such as minimization of symptoms, delay in seeking medical care, denial of fear, and the use of humorous clichés about death. Their observations suggested that denial was the most common ego defense used by patients suffering from acute myocardial infarction while in the coronary care unit, and, interestingly, they found that denial was positively related to the likelihood of survival in the immediate post-MI period.

Different illnesses pose different challenges to patients. Consultation-liaison psychiatrists have helped to define some of the novel and extraordinary situations encountered by patients in modern medicine. For example, 10 years after the introduction of the cardiac pacemaker, Greene and Moss (1969) looked at the psychological factors that influenced the adjustment of patients with permanently implanted pacemakers. They found that ancillary good health and a meaningful interpersonal relationship tended to be associated with satisfactory adjustment to the pacemaker. Patients who had had symptoms for a longer period before implantation also adjusted better than those who had been sick only a short time. Patients who had a history of poor adjustment to other prostheses, such as eyeglasses, dentures, hearing aids, or artificial limbs, exhibited a higher incidence of concern over the pacemaker than did those who had adjusted well. For most, however, adjustment did improve over time. More recently, observations about how patients cope with implantable ventricular defibrillators have been made (Morris et al., 1991). On occasion, psychiatric morbidity in these patients will include secondary panic disorder and post-traumatic stress disorder related to the experience of cardioversion and/or difibrillator discharge (Fricchione and Vlay, 1994).

Consultation-liaison psychiatrists have helped other practitioners to understand the psychological issues raised by new medical treatments. For example, as burn units improve the likelihood of survival for patients with extensive burns, the psychiatric consultant has helped to define the psychological ramifications of both the accident and the treatment (Andreason, 1974). To begin with, a high incidence of alcohol and other substance abuse is found in extensively burned patients. Some "burn-prone" patients appear to have a specific version of accident proneness. Beyond the acute life-threatening phase, in which problems of electrolyte disturbance and sepsis frequently lead to brief episodes of delirium, there follows a lengthy hospitalization with time-consuming and painful dressing changes, rehabilitation therapy, and multiple plastic surgeries to improve functional mobility and to minimize the disfiguring effects of the burn. During the first year after discharge, many patients continue to have symptoms of depression, anxiety, and phobic behavior, although those with good premorbid psychological health generally recover fully. Andreason observes that the psychiatric prognosis for children who have been burned is worse.

The field of organ transplantation, which began with kidneys and now includes bone marrow, heart, lung, and liver transplantations, poses new psychological issues and challenges for the adaptive capacity of patients. Each kind of transplantation has its own special psychological and biological features. The consultation-liaison psychiatrist plays a role in the selection of patients for kidney transplantation and in the evaluation of psychological pressures on potential donors (Levy, 1986). The psychiatric side effects associated with prednisone and other immunosuppressive drugs, the intense emotional experience of being given a "new life," the dependency problems, the fatigue, and other symptoms of what may be chronic secondary illnesses resulting from the treatment, as well as the sexual dysfunction and cognitive changes of those on chronic dialysis, have all been well documented.

There has been increasing interest in the psychological health of long-term survivors of extraordinary treatments such as bone marrow transplantation. Preliminary work suggests that bone marrow transplantation is not associated long-term with any greater psychosocial risk than conventional chemotherapy (Lesko et al., 1992).

Other psychological issues are involved in coping with other chronic medical disorders, such as multiple sclerosis, rheumatoid arthritis, spinal cord injuries, or cancer, to name a few. A. Weisman (1979) described 4 psychosocial phases related to the stages of treatment and progression of cancer: existential plight, accommodation and mitigation, recurrence and relapse, and deterioration and decline. To obtain information about coping strategies used by cancer patients throughout these stages, he developed an interview rating procedure in which he divided coping responses into 3 categories: *appraisal-focused* responses, which involved logical analysis such as cognitive redefinition and cognitive avoidance; *problem-focused* responses, which involved a more active seeking of information, problem solving, or development of alternative rewards; and *emotion-focused* responses, which involved affective regulation, emotional discharge, and resigned acceptance. In his view the more disturbed patients tended to use withdrawal and disengagement from others, externalization with projection of blame, tension reduction through excessive use of alcohol or drugs, and passive acceptance or submission. Healthier patients were more likely to confront the problem, accept but redefine the situation, and seek medical direction and comply with treatment. Occasionally the same behaviors could have equivocal relationships with problem resolution and emotional functioning. For example, Weisman and Worden (1976–77) pointed out that some of the more constructive strategies, such as seeking information, could also be used as a defense to postpone an acceptable course of action. The particular psychological problems and coping demands of almost all medical and surgical problems have been and continue to be explored in depth.

Most patients cope very well and adapt to extraordinary situations. One rarely sees a breakdown of ego functioning of psychotic proportions or suicide as a psychological response to medical illness. Suicidal behavior in hospitalized medical and surgical patients is uncommon and generally reflects an underlying psychotic illness or delirium or an unresolved problem in the doctor-patient relationship (Reich and Kelly, 1976). Some epidemiologic studies, however, have shown a positive correlation between physical and psychiatric disorders (Lipowski, 1979). Published estimates of psychiatric morbidity among general hospital inpatients have ranged from 20% (a figure not particularly different from what might be expected from the community at large) to 70%. The wide discrepancy in the reported prevalence reflects unresolved methodological difficulties in the definition of psychiatric morbidity, particularly of depression in medical patients.

Some surveys of patients with chronic medical illness have suggested that psychiatric maladjustment is considerably less prevalent than in the population of psychiatrically ill patients and no more so than in the general population (Cassileth et al., 1984). Cassileth and her colleagues measured mental health scores of patients with arthritis, diabetes, cancer, renal disease, and dermatological disorders and found them all significantly higher than those of patients under treatment for depression but no different from those of the general public. Within the patient groups, those whose illnesses had been diagnosed for 3 months or less had greater anxiety, depression, and loss of control and poorer overall mental health than those whose illnesses had been diagnosed for longer periods. The authors concluded that psychological adaptation among patients with chronic illnesses was indeed remarkably effective and fundamentally independent of the specific diagnoses.

More sensitive psychological measures, however, are likely to show strain in patients from adaptation to chronic physical disease. A chronic disabling disease may impose complex and subtle burdens both on the patient and on his family. Many patients have written eloquently of their experiences with chronic illness, particularly of the isolation and the subtle way in which they are treated differently by others (Rabin, Rabin, and Rabin, 1982).

On some psychological tests, such as the MMPI, patients with chronic disorders have shown abnormalities. One study provided evidence of a possible clustering of personality characteristics resulting from chronic disease (Spergel, Ehrlich, and Glass, 1978). The MMPI profiles of patients with rheumatoid arthritis, chronic pulmonary disease, multiple sclerosis, low back pain, and chronic peptic ulcer disease were virtually indistinguishable from one another, all showing elevated scores in depression, hypochondriasis, and hysteria. It is unclear whether these changes represent an adaptive adjustment to disease—by grieving and by self-monitoring of symptoms—or whether they reflect maladaptive functioning.

As noted earlier, estimates indicate that depression occurs in 20–40% of medically ill patients. The difficulty of differentiating primary affective disorder from adjustment disorder with depressed mood and organic affective disorders in medically ill patients has led some to propose new frameworks for the classification and study of medical depression (Popkin, Callies, and Colon, 1987). As a first step in their classification, Popkin and co-workers suggest that the clinician characterize the nature of the patient's medical illness as either discrete or ongoing. Second, he should describe the status of the patient's brain structure and physiological function as either intact or compromised. Brain function would be identified as compromised on the basis of objective evidence from laboratory or diagnostic studies, diagnosis of a medical illness presumed or understood to involve the brain, or clinical diagnosis of an organic mental disorder. And third, the clinician should define the status of the patient's cognition and memory as either unimpaired, transiently impaired, or permanently impaired. By defining the nature of the population more precisely, such a system would shed light on the development of depression in the medically ill.

Psychiatric Morbidity Associated with Specific Medical Disorders

Specific medical problems have an unexpectedly high degree of morbidity. Many involve subtle or unexpected organic brain syndromes. Some cases have elucidated the underlying pathophysiology of these psychiatric disorders. Robinson and Szetela (1981) have described an increased incidence of mood change following left hemispheric brain injury. Using several mood scales, they compared 18 patients with left hemispheric strokes with 11 patients suffering traumatic brain injury for frequency and severity of depression. More than 60% of the stroke patients had clinically significant depressions, versus about 20% of the trauma patients, even though all showed comparable impairments in daily living activities and global cognitive functions. Although both groups had similar-sized lesions, CAT scans revealed that the areas of ischemic injury were more anterior in the stroke patients than in the trauma patients. In fact, the severity of depression was directly correlated with the closeness of the lesion to the frontal pole. These clinical findings led the authors to postulate that depression following left hemispheric brain injury, rather than being a nonspecific psychological response, was a symptom of injury to specific pathways in the brain. In related animal research Robinson (1980) was able to demonstrate a differential effect of right versus left hemispheric cerebral infarction on catecholamine levels at distant sites in the rat brain.

Robinson and his group have also demonstrated the increased mortality risk associated with post-stroke depression (Robinson, 1993) as well as the benefits of post-stroke antidepressant therapy (Lipsey et al., 1984). They and others have also identified the development of post-stroke generalized anxiety disorder, a phenomenon which occurs in over 20% of patients and often becomes chronic (Astrom, 1996).

Panic disorder has also been noted to be more prevalent after not only postpartum states (Metz, Sichel, and Goff, 1988) but pulmonary disease as well (Pollack et al., 1996).

In the field of organ transplantation, Levenson and others (1993) have systematically described some of the specific psychiatric issues associated with donors and recipients, especially as they pertain to compliance and course following transplantation.

Clinicians have long noted that patients with temporal lobe epilepsy have an unexpectedly high incidence of psychosis. Schizophreniform psychosis is more likely to be associated with left temporal lobe dysfunction, major affective disorders with right temporal lobe dysfunction. Further, D. Bear (1977) has documented interictal personality changes in patients with temporal lobe epilepsy, such as hypergraphia and hyperreligiosity. Such observations have fostered the development of new hypotheses for the development of psychosis, such as limbic kindling (lowering of seizure threshold by repetitive, subclinical electrical discharges), leading to the use of Tegretol and other anticonvulsant medications in lithium-resistant cases of manic-depressive psychosis.

Psychiatric problems associated with systemic lupus erythematosis represent another interesting and complex area of investigation. Lupus cerebritis may produce such problems as psychosis, seizures, or cognitive impairment, but the psychologically and socially disruptive aspects of the disease may also produce depression, anxiety, and insomnia. Although these effects are well known, in actual practice it may be extremely difficult to diagnose accurately the etiology of psychiatric difficulties in patients with lupus and many other types of medical disorder.

Finally, Reich and colleagues (1983) have found that survivors of cardiac arrest and resuscitation show a high incidence of subtle personality and behavioral changes, presumably related to areas of hypoxic brain injury incurred during the arrest. Specific psychiatric morbidity associated with newly developed medical treatments will continue to be the subject of investigation. The findings will not only help doctors to inform the patient about the potential hazards of new treatment but may also shed light on whether new medical approaches, taken in their entirety, do improve the patient's quality of life.

Psychosocial Factors Influencing the Course of Disease

That the psychological reactions of patients to disease could have an effect on the course of a disease seems intuitively obvious but remains relatively unexplored from a scientific perspective. Many of the available studies have focused on the behaviors relating directly to compliance with medical therapy (Zisook and Gammon, 1981; Garrity, 1981; Prince, Frasure-Smith, and Rolicz-Woloszyk, 1982). Compliance applies not only to the cessation of behaviors such as smoking and substance abuse but also to the willingness of patients to follow prescribed regimens, whether medications, exercise, or other mo-

dalities. For example, the progress of internal medicine in demonstrating that antihypertensive treatment limits the morbidity and mortality of patients has stimulated interest in the patient's compliance with antihypertensive medications. The result has been a more balanced understanding of what is involved in compliance, namely, that there are competing demands on the patient, and a trade-off between short-term disadvantages of compliance (for example, the risk of depression or sexual dysfunction) but future health, on the one hand, and short-term benefits of noncompliance but a poorer prognosis, on the other hand.

Some investigators have defined the psychological issues involved in noncompliance in particular groups of patients with specific disorders. For example, Voehnert and Popkin (1986) found that consistent, long-term noncompliance in diabetics was characteristic of patients who met the criteria for borderline personality disorder. In many cases impaired family dynamics, magical hope for cure, and resentment of physicians for not providing such cure lay beneath the noncompliant behavior. Another study found noncompliance with hemodialysis to be far more prevalent in younger than in older patients, presumably because of the additional developmental demands of the early adult years (Gonsalves-Ebrahim et al., 1987).

Not only have such clearly defined behavioral factors influenced the outcome of medical disorders, but the more mysterious psychophysiological interactions also presumably play a role, although relationships have been difficult to establish and tend to be highly specific in nature. Stress has been associated with a worse outcome of rheumatoid arthritis, asthma (Gorman, 1990), and more unstable glucose levels in diabetes mellitus (Halford, Cuddily, and Mortimer, 1990). Depression, as noted above, is an ominous risk factor in coronary artery disease. Overall, however, there is a relative dearth of studies that have carefully looked at the role of psychological factors on long-term outcomes in medical disease.

Psychiatric Interventions

Significant changes have occurred in the medical care system partly as a result of consultation-liaison services (Kornfeld, 1996) and partly through the evolution of medical care itself. The nature of the doctor-patient relationship has changed, with greater recognition of the need for an alliance. The right of the patient, when competent, to refuse medical treatment is now widely accepted. Both doctors and patients expect medical treatments to be more effective than they once did, which generally improves the patient's level of compliance and strengthens the physician's conviction about the need for compliance. An increased awareness and sensitivity to the psychological experiences of hospitalized patients and their families has become standard procedure in many hospitals. For example, to accommodate patients in pediatrics and obstetrics, many hospitals allow families to remain in the hospital overnight and to be present in the delivery room.

Many more patients receive psychiatric assistance in hospitals for problems in coping with their medical or surgical illnesses than was the case a decade ago. Documenting the efficacy of psychiatric intervention among such patients is in some ways more difficult than in the primary psychiatric disorders, where target symptoms and problems are often better defined. The focus has therefore been on the more quantifiable medical and cost outcomes of psychiatric intervention in the general hospital. For example, Levitan and Kornfeld (1981) have demonstrated that psychiatric consultation early in the course of hospitalization for elderly patients with hip fractures has reduced the psychiatric morbidity, decreased the length of hospital stay, and increased the likelihood that patients will return home rather than be placed in nursing homes. A large body of research also indicates that preoperative psychiatric intervention shortens the length of hospital stay, decreases the need for pain medication, and reduces the incidence of postoperative delirium (Rogers and Reich, 1986). A series of classic studies reported 20 years ago showed that a 5-minute preoperative visit with the anesthesiologist, in which he outlined the plan of care for the day of surgery and anticipated and normalized the postoperative pain experience, greatly reduced the patient's preoperative anxiety and postoperative use of pain medication (Egbert et al., 1964). Such studies are more difficult to conduct today because of pressures that have shortened the length of hospital stay, in some cases to the point of causing psychological distress in patients and in the medical and nursing staff. But preoperative intervention and teaching have become commonplace in the care of patients in general hospitals.

In an era when the cost of medical care has become a predominant issue, it is not surprising that the benefits of psychiatric intervention in a general hospital are most often quantified in terms of money. Smith and colleagues (1986) have reported that psychiatric consultation for patients with somatization disorder, a common problem in general hospitals, greatly reduced the frequency of costly medical visits and diagnostic studies in primary care settings. Conventional wisdom has long held that many patients with somatoform disorders are best treated by frequent and continuing interpersonal support, which can obviate some of the diagnostic testing and referrals to specialists, as well as excessive doctor-shopping.

Many other changes have occurred within the general hospital. Appreciation has grown for the psychosocial factors involved in many illnesses, particularly chronic pain. Chronic pain is a disease with recognized psychological factors but is best treated by a team of specialists—internists, surgeons, anesthesiologists, and psychiatrists—using a multimodal approach (tricyclic antidepressants, physical therapy, nerve blocks, relaxation response, and the like). Behavioral medicine divisions have emerged in many departments of medicine. Specialists in behavioral medicine focus on specific behavioral interventions and analysis. One of the best-known examples of behavioral intervention is the use of the relaxation response to reduce blood pressure in patients with borderline essential hypertension. Another example is the use of specific biofeedback techniques to retrain dysfunctional physiological reflexes, such as irritable colon, tension headaches, incompetent sphincters, or Raynaud's phenomenon.

Two of the most frequently cited studies documenting the effect of psychiatric intervention in disease course are those of David Spiegel and associates (1989) on breast cancer and Fawzy and associates (1993) on melanoma. Spiegel's study demonstrated that weekly support groups (including relaxation and self-hypnosis techniques) prolonged the life of women with metastatic breast cancer, and Fawzy's study showed a similar effect for patients with melanoma.

Patients themselves expect, and indeed have created, reservoirs of social support in the form of self-help groups to deal with specific illnesses. These groups clearly reduce the isolation felt by patients and their families and provide ongoing social support. In many cases they offer patients hope through substantial fundraising for the support of research efforts to find cures. Although these groups are largely patient-initiated, they involve physicians actively in advisory and educational capacities.

The Future: AIDS, Managed Care, and Other New Challenges

The psychosomatic movement and consultation-liaison psychiatry will continue to promote a broad understanding and appreciation of the interaction between the mind and the body in health and disease. Indeed, much of the current excitement and challenge of psychiatry lies in the integration of psychological and biological factors in primary psychiatric disorders, as well as in medical and surgical illnesses. Much remains to be done. We have only begun to understand the impact of medical and surgical disorders on psychological health and, conversely, the impact of psychological factors on the course of medical diseases.

We shall continue to confront new diseases that require a biopsychosocial approach. One of the clearest examples of such diseases is acquired immunodeficiency syndrome, AIDS. It has been clear for some time that AIDS can produce an organic brain syndrome by direct brain infection with the human immunodeficiency virus (HIV). As many as 40% of AIDS patients have neurological complications at some point in their illness, typically an organic brain syndrome with demented, delusional, and affective features (Detmer and Lu, 1986). Although opportunistic central nervous system (CNS) infections, such as toxoplasmosis or cryptococcal infections, may cause similar symptoms in these immunosuppressed patients, it is now clear that presence of HIV virus in the brain and associated indirect effects of microglia and macrophages (Glass et al., 1995) account for most of the neuropsychiatric symptoms. Neuroimaging (Aylward et al., 1995), neuropathological (Van Gorp et al., 1989), and clinical (Navia, 1990) studies all support the notion of AIDS dementia as a subcortical dementia, beginning with atrophy in white matter and progressing to gray matter areas, particularly caudate nucleus and posterior cortex. In the CNS the virus has been found most frequently in macrophages, pleomorphic microglia, multinucleated giant cells, and (rarely) neurons (Stoler et al., 1986). Lesions in deep gray and white matter predominate and are associated with cortical atrophy and ventricular enlargement, although exactly how the viral infection produces such extensive damage to the brain remains a mystery. Although AIDS dementia is usually associated with later stages of the disease, there is some evidence that neurological infiltration may precede lymphocytic involvement. In one series 13% of patients at risk for AIDS first presented with neuropsychiatric symptoms prior to any other manifestations (Levy, Bredeson, and Rosenblum, 1985).

The neurological involvement has profound implications for treatment, in that even with more adequate treatment for the systemic, lymphocytic involvement, the dementing process might continue as a separate process. Moreover, the neuropsychiatric problems interfere with compliance and with the overall management of such patients—already a difficult enough problem.

The psychological impact of a life-threatening disease without a cure in a young population is extraordinary, and, not surprisingly, consultation experience has revealed a high incidence of depression, categorized pri-

marily as adjustment disorder. Recurrent themes include the problems of dealing with a life-threatening illness, uncertainty about the implications of an AIDS diagnosis, social isolation, and guilt over previous lifestyle (Dilley et al., 1985). The widespread irrational fear of contagion seen in schools, the workplace, and even among health care professionals adds to the isolation and burdens of this disease. Such patients do now and will continue to consume an increasing proportion of the total bill for hospital care. As many accounts in the popular press have conveyed, approximately 2 million Americans are currently thought to be infected with the virus, and the majority are expected eventually to come down with the clinical disease.

Another extraordinary aspect of this disease is that the extent of the epidemic potential within the heterosexual community will depend on future sexual behavior. The use of safe sex practices and society's willingness to accept the realities of the AIDS threat will determine the future. The possible role of psychological factors in the development of clinical illness in patients who have developed antibodies to the virus raises some of the intriguing psychophysiological questions addressed by Kasl, Evans, and Neiderman (1979) in their study of infectious mononucleosis. In fact, in the tradition of earlier psychosomatic research, Theorell et al. (1995) have noted that lack of social support is associated with a more rapid deterioration in CD4 counts. Advances in psychoneuroimmunology may well contribute even further to our understanding of AIDS.

Medicine will develop more new and startling technologies both for diagnosis and for treatment. Consultation-liaison psychiatrists will be at the forefront of the ethical and psychological ramifications of these events. University teaching hospitals are also likely to develop new brain-imaging techniques that will help to define psychiatric problems, especially organic brain syndromes.

We are confronted with new illnesses such as chronic fatigue syndrome, multiple chemical sensitivities, chronic candidiasis, and repetitive stress injuries, which challenge our ability to differentiate real organic disorders from somatoform disorders in new disguises (Johnson, DeLuca, and Natelson, 1996).

Finally, pressure for containing the cost of medical care and reducing the cost of illness is likely to continue in the coming years, which will focus even more attention on how the behaviors and habits of patients can either promote or damage health. Smoking, obesity, alcoholism, other substance abuse, lack of exercise, noncompliance with prescribed medical therapy, and other dimensions of living not yet identified will increasingly be the target of intervention studies. To acquire enough scientific information to avoid premature conclusions and to handle intervention sensitively so that the doctor-patient relationship is enhanced rather than weakened is likely to be high on the list of challenges for the future.

References

Ader, R. 1971. Experimentally induced gastric lesions: results and implications of studies in animals. In *Advances in psychosomatic medicine.* Vol. 6. *Duodenal ulcer,* ed. H. Weiner. Basel: Karger.

Ader, R., and N. Cohen. 1975. Behaviorally conditioned immunosuppression. *Psychosom. Med.* 37:333–340.

Ader, R., D. L. Felten, and N. Cohen, eds. 1991. *Psychoneuroimmunology.* San Diego, CA: Academic Press.

Alexander, F. 1950. *Psychosomatic medicine: its principles and applications.* New York: Norton.

Andreason, N. J. 1974. Neuropsychiatric complications in burn patients. *Int. J. Psychiatry Med.* 5:161–171.

Arnetz, B. B., J. Wasserman, B. Petrini, S.-O. Brenner, L. Levi, P. Eneroth, H. Salovaara, T. Theorell, and I.-L. Petterson. 1987. Immune function in unemployed women. *Psychosom. Med.* 49:3–12.

Astrom, M. 1996. Generalized anxiety disorder in stroke patients. A 3-year longitudinal study. *Stroke* 27:270–5.

Aylward, E. H., P. D. Brettschneider, J. C. McArthur, G. J. Harris, T. E. Schlaepfer, J. D. Henederer, P. E. Barta, A. Y. Tien, and G. D. Pearlson. 1995. Magnetic resonance imaging measurement of gray matter volume reductions in HIV dementia. *Am. J Psychiatry* 152:987–994.

Barefoot, J. C., W. G. Dahlstrom, and R. B. Williams. 1983. Hostility, CHD incidence and total mortality: a 25-year follow-up study of 255 physicians. *Psychosom. Med.* 45:59–63.

Bartrop, R. W., E. Lockhurst, L. Lazarus, L. G. Kiloh, and R. Penny. 1977. Depressed lymphocyte function after bereavement. *Lancet* 1:834–836.

Bear, D. 1977. The significance of behavior change in temporal lobe epilepsy. *McLean Hosp. J.* spec. issue, 9–21.

Beaumont, W. 1838. *Experiments and observations on the gastric juice and the physiology of digestion.* Edinburgh: Maclachlan and Stewart.

Benedikt, R. A., and L. C. Kolb. 1986. Preliminary findings on chronic pain and post traumatic stress disorder. *Am. J. Psychiatry* 143:908–910.

Berkman, L. F., and S. L. Syme. 1979. Social networks, host resistance, and mortality: a nine-year follow-up study of Alameda County residents. *Am. J. Epidemiol.* 109:186–203.

Besedovsky, H. O., A. DelRey, E. Sorkin, et al. 1979. Immunoregulation mediated by the sympathetic nervous system. *Cell Immunol.* 48:346–355.

Borus, J. F., M. J. Howes, N. P. Devins, R. Rosenberg, and W. W. Livingston. 1988. Primary health care providers' recognition and diagnosis of mental disorders in their patients. *Gen. Hosp. Psychiatry* 10:317–321.

Cameron, O. 1996. Depression increases post-MI mortality: how? *Psychosom. Med.* 58:111.

Cannon, W. B. 1932. *The wisdom of the body.* New York: Norton.

Cassileth, E. R., E. J. Lusk, T. B. Strouse, et al. 1984. Psychological status in chronic illness: a comparative analysis of six diagnostic groups. *N. Engl. J. Med.* 311:506–511.

Cobb, S. 1976. Social support as a moderator of life stress. *Psychosom. Med.* 38:300–314.

Detmer, W. M., and F. G. Lu. 1986. *Neuropsychiatric complications of AIDS: a literature review.* San Francisco: Baywood.

Dilley, J. W., H. N. Ochitill, M. Perl, and P. A. Volberding. 1985. Findings in psychiatric consultations with patients with acquired immune deficiency syndrome. *Am. J. Psychiatry* 142:82–85.

Dimsdale, J. E. 1995. Social support—a lifeline in stormy times. *Psychosom. Med.* 57:1–2.

Dunbar, F. 1947. *Emotions and bodily changes.* 3d ed. New York: Columbia University Press.

Egbert, L. D., G. E. Battit, C. E. Welch, and M. K. Barlett. 1964. Reduction of post-operative pain by encouragement and instruction of patients. *N. Engl. J. Med.* 270:825.

Elliot, G. R., and C. Eisdorfer, eds. 1982. *Stress and human health: analysis and implications of research.* New York: Springer.

Engel, G. L. 1971. Sudden and rapid death during psychological stress. *Ann. Intern. Med.* 74:771–782.

——— 1981. The clinical applications of the biopsychosocial model. *Am. J. Psychiatry* 137:535–544.

——— 1987. Monica, an infant with a gastric fistula: some lessons from 32 years of continuous observations. Paper presented at the annual meeting of the American Psychosomatic Society, Philadelphia.

Everson, S. A., D. E. Goldberg, G. A. Kaplan, R. D. Cohen, E. Pukkala, J. Tuomilehto, and J. T. Salonen. 1996. Hopelessness and the risk of mortality and incidence of myocardial infarction and cancer. *Psychosom. Med.* 58:113–121.

Fawzy, F., N. W. Fawzy, C. S. Hyun, et al. 1993. Malignant melanoma: effects on an early structured psychiatric intervention, coping, and affective state of recurrence and survival 6 years later. *Arch. Gen. Psychiatry* 50:681–689.

Fricchione, G., and G. B. Stefano. 1994. The stress response and autoimmunoregulation. *Adv. Neuroimmunol.* 4:388–395.

Fricchione, G., and S. C. Vlay. 1994. Psychiatric aspects of the implantable cardioverter-difibrillator. In *Implantable cardioverter defibrillators: a comprehensive textbook,* ed. N. A. M. Estes, A. S. Manolis, and P. J. Wang. New York: Marcel Dekker. 405–423.

Friedman, M., and R. H. Rosenman. 1974. *Type A behavior and your heart.* New York: McGraw-Hill.

Garrity, T. F. 1981. Medical compliance in the clinician patient relationship: a review. *Soc. Sci. Med.* 15:215–222.

Giang, D. W., A. D. Goodman, R. B. Schiffer, et al. 1996. Conditioning of cyclophosphamide-induced leukopernia in humans. *J. Neuropsychiatry Clin. Neurosci.* 8:194–201.

Glass, J. D., H. Fedor, S. L. Wesselingh, and J. C. McArthur. 1995. Immunocytochemical quantitation of human immunodeficiency virus in the brain: correlations with dementia. *Ann. Neurol.* 38:755–762.

Goldstein, M. G., and R. Niaura. 1992. Psychological factors affecting physical condition: cardiovascular disease literature review. Part I. Coronary artery disease and sudden death. *Psychosomatics* 33:134–145.

Gonsalves-Ebrahim, L., G. Sterin, A. D. Gulledge, et al. 1987. Noncompliance in younger adults on hemodialysis. *Psychosom.* 28:34–41.

Gonzales, J. J. 1994. Psychiatric problems in primary care: what are the problems, how will we recognize them, and how can we treat them. *Psychosom. Med.* 56:94–96.

Gorman, J. M. 1990. Psychobiological aspects of asthma and the consequent research implications (editorial). *Chest* 97:514–5.

Greene, W. A., and A. J. Moss. 1969. Psychosocial factors in the social adjustment of patients with permanently implanted cardiac pacemakers. *Ann. Intern. Med.* 70:897–902.

Greene, W. A., S. Goldstein, and A. J. Moss. 1972. Psychosocial aspects of sudden death. *Arch. Intern. Med.* 129:725–731.

Hackett, T., and N. Cassem. 1974. Development of a quantitative rating scale to assess denial. *J. Psychosom. Res.* 18:93–100.

Halford, W. K., Cuddily, S., and Mortimer, R. H. 1990. Psychological stress and blood glucose regulation in type 1 diabetic patients. *Health Psychol.* 9:516–528.

Heaton, R. K., R. A. Velin, J. A. Mccutchan, et al. 1994. Neuropsychological impairment in human immunodeficiency virus infection: implications for employment. *Psychosom. Med.* 56:8–17.

Helsing, K. J., M. Szklo, and G. M. Comstock. 1981. *J. Public Health* 71:802–809.

Herbert, T. B., and S. Cohen. 1993. Stress and immunity in humans: a meta-analytic review. *Psychosom. Med.* 55:364–379.

Hofer, M. A. 1984. Psychobiologic perspective on bereavement. *Psychosom. Med.* 46:183–197.

Holmes, T. H., and R. H. Rahe. 1967. The social readjustment rating scale. *J. Psychosom. Res.* 11:213–218.

Jenkins, C. D., R. H. Rosenman, and S. J. Zyzanski. 1974. Prediction of clinical coronary heart disease by a test for the coronary prone behavior pattern. *N. Engl. J. Med.* 290:1271–75.

Johnson, S. K., J. DeLuca, and B. H. Natelson. 1996. Assessing somatization disorder in the chronic fatigue syndrome. *Psychosom. Med.* 58:50–57.

Kahana, R. J., and G. L. Bibring. 1964. Personality types and medical management. In *Psychiatry and medical practice in a general hospital,* ed. N. Zinberg. New York: International Universities Press.

Kaplan, H. I., and B. J. Sadock, eds. 1985. *Comprehensive textbook of psychiatry.* Vol. 4. Baltimore: Williams and Wilkins.

Kaplan J. R., T. B. Clarkson, and S. B. Manuck. 1984. Pathogenesis of carotid bifurcation atherosclerosis in cynomolgus monkeys. *Stroke* 15:994–1000.

Kasl, S. V., and S. Cobb. 1982. Variability of stress effects among men experiencing job loss. In *Handbook of stress: theoretical and clinical aspects,* ed. L. Goldberger and S. Breznitz. New York: Free Press.

Kasl, S. V., A. S. Evans, and J. C. Neiderman. 1979. Psychosocial risk factors in the development of infectious mononucleosis. *Psychosom. Med.* 41:445–466.

Keller, S., J. Weiss, S. Schleifer, N. E. Miller, and M. Stein. 1981. Suppression of immunity by stress: effect of graded series of stressors on lymphocyte stimulation in the rat. *Science* 213:1397–1400.

Kennedy, G. J., M. Hofer, D. Cohen, and J. Fisher. 1985. Significance of depression and dementia in patients at risk for sudden death. *Psychosom. Med.* 47:90–91.

Kiecolt-Glaser, J. K., W. Garner, C. E. Speicher, et al. 1984. Psychosocial modifiers of immunocompetence in medical students. *Psychosom. Med.* 46:7–14.

Kiecolt-Glaser, J. K., and R. Glaser. 1986. Psychological influences on immunity. *Psychosom. Med.* 27:621–624.

———— 1995. Psychoneuroimmunology and health consequences: data and shared mechanisms. *Psychosom. Med.* 57:269–274.

Kobasa, S. C. 1979. Stressful life events, personality, and health: an inquiry into hardiness. *J. Pers. Soc. Psychol.* 37:1–11.

Kornfeld, D. S. 1996. Consultation-liaison psychiatry and the practice of medicine. The Thomas P. Hackett Award lecture given at the 42nd annual meeting of the Academy of Psychosomatic Medicine, 1995. *Psychosomatics* 37:236–248.

Kosten, T. R., S. Jacobs, J. Mason, et al. 1984. Psychological correlates of growth hormone response to stress. *Psychosom. Med.* 46:49–58.

Laudenslager, M. L., and S. M. Ryan. 1983. Coping and immunosuppression: inescapable but not escapable shock suppresses lymphocyte proliferation. *Science* 221:568–570.

Leigh, H., and M. F. Reiser. 1985. *The patient: biological, psychological, and social dimensions of medical practice.* 2d ed. New York: Plenum Publishing.

Lesko, L. M., J. S. Ostroff, G. H. Mumma, D. E. Mashberg, and J. C. Holland. J. C. 1992. Long-term psychological adjustment of acute leukemia survivors: impact of bone marrow transplantation versus conventional chemotherapy. *Psychosom. Med.* 54:30–47.

Lesperance, F., N. Frasure-Smith, and M. Talajiic. 1996. Major depression before and after myocardial infarction: its nature and consequences. *Psychosom. Med.* 58:99–110.

Lesser, I. M. 1981. A review of the alexithymia concept. *Psychosom. Med.* 43:531–543.

Levenson, J. L., and M. E. Olbrisch. 1993. Psychosocial evaluation of organ transplant candidates: a comparative study of process, criteria, and outcomes in heart, liver, and kidney transplantation. *Psychosomatics* 34:314–323.

Levitan, S. J., and D. S. Kornfeld. 1981. Clinical and cost benefits of liaison psychiatry. *Am. J. Psychiatry* 138:790–793.

Levy, N. B. 1986. Renal transplantation and the new medical era. *Adv. Psychosom. Med.* 15:167–179.

Levy, R. M., D. E. Bredeson, and M. L. Rosenblum. 1985. Neurological manifestations of the acquired immune deficiency syndrome (AIDS): experience at UCSF and review of the literature. *J. Neurosurg.* 62:475–495.

Lindemann, E. 1944. Symptomatology and management of acute grief. *Am. J. Psychiatry* 101:141–148.

Lipowski, Z. J. 1979. Physical illness and psychiatric disorder: a neglected relationship. *Psychiatrica Fennica* (suppl.) 32–57.

——— 1983. Current trends in consultation-liaison psychiatry. *Can. J. Psychiatry* 28:329–338.

——— 1992. Consultation-liaison psychiatry at century's end. *Psychosomatics* 33:128–133.

Lipowski, Z. J., and E. J. Wolston. 1981. Liaison psychiatry: referral patterns and their stability over time. *Am. J. Psychiatry* 138:1608–11.

Lipsey, J. R., R. G. Robinson, G. D. Pearlson, et al. 1984. Nortriptyline treatment of post-stroke depression: a double-blind study. *Lancet* 8372:297–299.

Mahl, G. F. 1953. Psychological changes during chronic fear. *Ann. N.Y. Acad. Sci.* 56:240.

Malkoff, S. B., M. F. Muldoon, Z. R. Zeigler, and S. B. Manuck. 1993. Blood platelet responsivity to acute mental stress. *Psychosom. Med.* 55:477–482.

Mason, J. W. 1975. Emotion as reflected in patterns of endocrine integration. In *Emotions—their parameters and measurement,* ed. L. Levi. New York: Raven Press.

McCue, J. D., and C. L. Sachs. 1991. A stress management workshop improves residents' coping skills. *Arch. Intern. Med.* 151:2273–77.

McDaniel, J. S., M. G. Moran, J. L. Levenson, and A. Stoudemire. 1994. Psychological factors affecting medical conditions. In *Synopsis of psychiatry,* ed. R. E. Hales and S. C. Yudofsky. Washington, D.C.: American Psychiatric Press. 525–545.

Metz, A., D. A. Sichel, and D. C. Goff. 1988. Post-partum panic disorder. *J. Clin. Psychiatry* 49:278–279.

Meyers, A., and H. A. Dewar. 1975. Circumstances attending 100 sudden deaths from coronary artery disease with coroner's necropsies. *Br. Heart I.* 37:1133–43.

Mirsky, I. A. 1958. Physiologic, psychologic, and social detriments in the etiology of peptic ulcer. *Am. J. Dig. Dis.* 3:285–313.

Monjan, A. A., and M. I. Collector. 1977. Stress-induced modulation of the immune response. *Science* 196:307–308.

Morris, P. L., J. Badger, C. Camielewski, et al. 1991. Psychiatric morbidity following the implantation of cardioventer defibrillator. *Psychosomatics* 32:58–64.

Moynihan, J. A., and R. Ader. 1996. Psychoneuroimmunology: animal models of disease. *Psychosomatic Med.* 58:546–558.

Navia, B. 1990. The AIDS dementia complex. In *Subcortical dementia,* ed. J. L. Cummings. New York: Oxford University Press.

Ormel, J., and B. Tiemens. 1995. Recognition and treatment of mental illness in primary care: towards a better understanding of a multifaceted problem. *Gen. Hosp. Psychiatry* 17:160–164.

Ostrom, M. 1996. Generalized anxiety disorder in stroke patients: a 3-year longitudinal study. *Stroke* 27:270–275.

Oxman, T. E., D. H. Freeman, and E. D. Manheimer. 1995. Lack of social participation or religious strength and comfort as risk factors for death after cardiac surgery in the elderly. *Psychosom. Med.* 57:5–15.

Pavlov, I. P. 1927. *Conditioned reflexes.* London: Oxford University Press.

Pollack, M. H., R. Kradin, M. W. Otto, J. Worthington, R. Gould, S. A. Sabitino, and J. F. Rosenbaum. 1996. Prevalence of panic in patients referred for pulmonary function testing at a major medical center. *Am. J. Psychiatry* 153:110–113.

Popkin, M. K., A. L. Callies, and E. A. Colon. 1987. A framework for the study of medical depression. *Psychosomatics* 28:27–33.

Prince, R., M. Frasure-Smith, and E. Rolicz-Woloszyk. 1982. Life stress, denial, and outcome in ischemic heart disease patients. *J. Psychosom. Res.* 26:23–31.

Rabin, D., P. L. Rabin, and R. Rabin. 1982. Compounding the ordeal of ALS. *N. Engl. J. Med.* 307:506–509.

Rabkin, J., and E. Streuning. 1976. Life events, stress, and illness. *Science* 194:1013–20.

Rahe, R. 1975. Epidemiological studies of life change and illness. *Int. J. Psychiatry Med.* 6:133–146.

Rahe, R. H., R. T. Rubin, and R. J. Arthur. 1974. The three investigators' study: serum uric acid, cholesterol, and cortisol variability during stresses of everyday life. *Psychosom. Med.* 36:258–268.

Reich, P., R. A. DeSilva, B. Lown, and B. J. Murawski. 1981. Acute psychological disturbances preceding life-threatening ventricular arrhythmias. *JAMA* 246:233–235.

Reich, P., and M. J. Kelly. 1976. Suicide attempts by hospitalized medical and surgical patients. *N. Engl. J. Med.* 294:298–301.

Reich, P., Q. R. Regestein, B. J. Murawski, R. A. DeSilva, and B. Lown. 1983. Unrecognized organic mental disorders in survivors of cardiac arrest. *Am. J. Psychiatry* 140:1194–97.

Reichlin, S. L. 1993. Neuroendocrine-immune interactions. *N. Eng. J. Med.* 329:1246–53.

Riley, V. 1981. Psychoneuroendocrine influences on immunocompetence and neoplasia. *Science* 212:1100–9.

Rissanen, V., M. Rome, and P. Siltanen. 1978. Premonitory symptoms and stress factors preceding sudden death from ischemic heart disease. *Acta Med. Scand.* 204:389–396.

Robinson, R. G. 1980. The differential effect of right vs. left hemisphere cerebral infarction on catecholamines in behavior in the rat. *Brain Research* 188:63–78.

——— 1993. Association of depression with 10-year post-stroke mortalities. *Am. J. Psychiatry* 150:124–129.

Robinson, R. G., and B. Szetela. 1981. Mood change following left hemispheric brain injury. *Ann. Neurol.* 9:447–453.

Rogers, M., and P. Reich. 1986. Psychological intervention with surgical patients: evaluation outcome advances. *Psychosom. Med.* 15:23–50.

Rosen, S. D., E. Paulesu, C. D. Frith, R. S. J. Frackowiak, G. J. Davies, T. Jones, and P. G. Comici. 1994. Central nervous system pathways in angina pectoris. *Lancet* 344:147–150.

Roy-Byrne, P. P., T. W. Uhde, R. M. Post, W. Gallucci, G. P. Chrousos, and P. W. Gold. 1986. The corticotropin-releasing hormone stimulation test in patients with panic disorder. *Am. J. Psychiatry* 143:896–899.

Rozanski, A., C. N. Bairey, D. S. Krantz, et al. 1988. Mental stress and the induction of silent myocardial ischemia in patients with coronary artery disease. *N. Eng. J. Med.* 318:1005–12.

Schleifer, S. J., S. E. Keller, and M. Stein. 1985. Stress effects on immunity. *Psychiatric J. of Univ. of Ottawa* 10:125–131.

Schleifer, S. J., S. E. Keller, M. Camerino, et al. 1983. Suppression of lymphocyte stimulation following bereavement. *JAMA* 250:374–377.

Schmale, A. H., and G. L. Engel. 1967. Psychoanalytic theory of somatic disorder: conversion, specificity, and the disease onset situation. *J. Amer. Psychoanal. Assoc.* 15:344–365.

Schwartz, P. J. 1975. The long Q-T syndrome. *Am. J. Cardiol.* 89:378–390.

Seigel, D., J. R. Bloom, H. C. Kramer, et al. 1989. Effect of psychosocial treatment on survival of patients with metastatic breast cancer. *Lancet* 2:888–891.

Selwyn, A. P., M. Shea, J. E. Deanfield, R. Wilson, P. Horlock, and H. A. O'Brien. 1986. Character of transient ischemia in angina pectoris. *Am. J. Cardiol.* 58:21B-25B.

Selye, H. 1950. *Physiology and pathology of exposure to stress.* Montreal: Acta Press.

——— 1976. Forty years of stress research: principal remaining problems and misconceptions. *Can. Med. Assoc. J.* 115:53–56.

Sifneos, P. E. 1967. Clinical observations on some patients suffering from a variety of psychosomatic diseases. Proceedings of the Seventh European Conference on Psychosomatic Research, Rome. *Acta Med. Psychosom.* 1.

Smith, G. R. Jr., et al. 1986. Psychiatric consultation and somatization disorder: a randomized controlled study. *N. Engl. J. Med.* 314:1407.

Solomon, G. F., S. Levine, and J. K. Kraft. 1968. Early experience and immunity. *Nature* (London) 220:821–822.

Spergel, P., G. E. Ehrlich, and D. Glass. 1978. The rheumatoid arthritic personality: a psychodiagnostic myth. *Psychosomatics* 19:79–86.

Spiegel, D., J. R. Bloom, H. C. Kraemer, and E. Gottheil. 1989. Effect of psychosocial treatment on survival of patients with metastatic breast cancer. *Lancet* 2:888–891.

Stein, M., A. H. Miller, and R. L. Trustman. 1991. Depression, the immune system, and health and illness. *Arch. Gen. Psychiatry* 8:171–177.

Stoler, M. H., T. A. Eskin, S. Benn, R. C. Angerer, and L. M. Angerer. 1986. Human T-cell lymphotropic virus type III infection of the central nervous system: a preliminary in situ analysis. *JAMA* 256:2360–64.

Theorell, T., V. Blomkvist, H. Jonsson, S. Schulman, E. Berntorp, and L. Stigendal. 1995. Social support and the development of immune function in human immunodeficiency virus infection. *Psychosom. Med.* 57:32–36.

Thomas, C. B., et al. 1983. *The precursors study: a prospective study of a cohort of medical students.* Vol. 5. Baltimore: Johns Hopkins University Press.

Thomas, P. D., J. M. Goodwin, and J. S. Goodwin. 1985. Effect of social support on stress-related changes in cholesterol level, uric acid level, and immune function in an elderly sample. *Am. J. Psychiatry* 142:735–737.

Vaillant, G. E. 1978. Natural history of male psychological health. IV. What kinds of men do not get psychosomatic illness? *Psychosom. Med.* 40:420.

Vaillant, G. E., and P. D. Gerber. 1996. Natural history of male psychological health. XIII. Who develops high blood pressure and who responds to treatment. *Am. J. Psychiatry* 153(7, Festschrift suppl.):24–29.

Van Eijk, J., A. Smits, F. Huygen, and H. Van den Hoogen. 1988. Effect of bereavement on the health of remaining family members. *Fam. Pract.* 5:278–282.

Van Gorp, W. D., M. A. Mandelkern, J. R. Ropchan, G. Evans, W. H. Blahd, and F. Flynn. 1989. Cerebral metabolic (PET), neuropsychologic, and neurologic abnormalities in patients with AIDS. *Int. Conf. AIDS* 5:459 (abstract no. Th.B. P.259).

Verrier, R. L., and B. Lown. 1984. Behavior, stress, and cardiac arrhythmias. *Ann. Rev. Physiol.* 46:155–176.

Voehnert, C. E., and M. K. Popkin. 1986. Psychological issues in treatment of the severely noncompliant diabetics. *Psychosom.* 27:11–20.

Weiner, H. 1972. Presidential address: some comments on the transduction of experience by the brain: implications for our understanding of the relationship of mind to body. *Psychosom. Med.* 34:355–380.

Weisman, A. 1979. *Coping with cancer.* New York: McGraw-Hill.

Weisman, A., and J. Worden. 1976–77. The existential plight in cancer: significance of the first 100 days. *Int. J. Psychiatry Med.* 7:1–15.

Werner, O. R., R. K. Wallace, B. Charles, et al. 1986. Long-term endocrinological changes in subjects practicing transcendental meditation in TM-sidhi program. *Psychosom. Med.* 48:59–66.

Williams, R. B., J. C. Barefoot, R. M. Califf, T. L. Haney, W. B. Saunders, D. B. Pryor, M. A. Hlatky, I. C. Siegler, and D. B. Mark. 1992. Prognostic importance of social and economic resources among medically treated patients with angiographically documented coronary artery disease. *JAMA* 267:520–524.

Williams, R. B., J. C. Barefoot, T. L. Haney, F. E. Harrell, J. A. Blumenthal, D. E. Pryor, and B. Peterson. 1986. Type A behavior and angiographically documented coronary atherosclerosis in a sample of 2,298 patients. *Psychosom. Med.* 48:302.

Wolff, H. G., S. Wolf Jr., and C. E. Hare, eds. 1950. *Life stress and bodily disease.* Baltimore: Williams & Wilkins.

Zisook, S., and E. Gammon. 1981. Medical noncompliance. *Int. J. Psychiatry Med.* 10:291–303.

Recommended Reading

Cassem, N. H., et al., eds. 1997. *Massachusetts General Hospital: Handbook of general hospital psychiatry,* 4th ed. St. Louis: Mosby.

Kornfeld, D. S. 1996. Consultation-liaison psychiatry and the practice of medicine. *Psychosomatics* 37:236–248.

Rundell, J. R., and M. G. Wise, eds. 1996. *Textbook of consultation-liaison psychiatry.* Washington, D.C.: American Psychiatric Press.

Stein, M., A. H. Miller, and R. L. Trestman. 1991. Depression, the immune system, and health and illness: findings in search of meaning. *Arch. Gen. Psychiatry* 48:171–177.

Stoudemire, A., and B. S. Fogel, eds. 1993. *Psychiatric care of the medical patient.* New York: Oxford University Press.

Strain, J. J., J. S. Hammer, and G. Fulop. 1994. APM task force on psychosocial interventions in the general hospital inpatient setting: a review of cost-offset studies. *Psychosomatics* 35:253–262.

18

LESTER GRINSPOON

JAMES BAKALAR

ROGER WEISS

Substance Use Disorders

The *Diagnostic and Statistical Manual of Mental Disorders,* fourth edition (DSM-IV), defines *substance abuse* as a maladaptive pattern of substance use as indicated by 1 or more of the following, occurring within a 12-month period: (1) continued use despite a persistent or recurrent social or interpersonal problem caused or exacerbated by use of the substance, (2) recurrent use when use is physically hazardous, (3) recurrent substance-related legal problems, (4) a failure to fulfill role obligations as a result of recurrent substance use. Although interpretations of drug abuse are vulnerable to cultural biases, for the purposes of this chapter it means taking drugs repeatedly at dose levels or in circumstances and settings that either cause or significantly augment the potential for harm.

The DSM-IV definition of *substance dependence* calls for the presence of at least 3 of the following symptoms in the same 12-month period, as part of a maladaptive pattern of use leading to clinically significant impairment or distress: (1) much time spent obtaining the drug or recovering from its effects, (2) often taking more of the drug than intended, (3) tolerance, (4) withdrawal symptoms, (5) use of the drug to avoid or relieve withdrawal symptoms, (6) a persistent or repeated desire or effort to cut down use, and (7) continued drug use despite the fact that use is causing or exacerbating a physical or psychological problem. The overarching term *substance use disorder* is used to refer to either substance abuse or substance dependence. *Physical dependence* on a drug implies a biochemical or physiological change in the body that makes the continued presence of the drug necessary to avoid a withdrawal syndrome. *Tolerance* refers to a declining effect of the drug upon repeated administration of the same dose and the consequent necessity to increase the dose to obtain the original euphoric effect. Physical dependence and tolerance are neither necessary nor sufficient for the diagnosis of substance dependence or substance abuse.

The causes of substance use are complex, involving genetic, family, psychological, social, environmental, and behavioral influences that interact in variable ways. For example, of two people who become euphoric upon first taking a particular drug, one may be inclined by temperament or personality to seek out the drug again, while the other, more cautious, avoids it for fear of abuse or dependence. Vulnerability to drug abuse can be conceived on the same public health model that is used for studying vulnerability to infectious disease: host (the drug user), agent (the drug), and environment. Thus, the likelihood that a given person will abuse a drug depends on which drug it is and under what circumstances the drug is used. For example, someone who is given an opioid for relief of pain after surgery is less likely to become an abuser than someone who takes it for the first time after buying it from a street dealer. Nevertheless, not everyone who is exposed to illicit opioids becomes dependent on them; dependency arises from the interactions among many physiological, psychological, and social factors.

Opioids

Opioid drugs can be divided into several categories: natural opium alkaloids, such as morphine and codeine; semisynthetic derivatives of morphine, such as heroin; synthetic opioids, such as meperidine and methadone; and mixed agonist-antagonists, such as buprenorphine and pentazocine. The commonly abused opioids are semisynthetic and synthetic drugs, especially heroin.

Intravenous administration of heroin produces a "rush" of euphoria that typically lasts from 30 seconds to 1 minute. This is followed by a period of calm and apparent drowsiness ("nodding") that may last for several hours. Users sometimes describe this experience as "being wrapped in warm cotton." Potential physical side effects include nausea and vomiting (although tolerance generally develops), miosis, and constipation.

Adverse Effects

One of the great dangers of opioid use is respiratory depression. Although tolerance to this effect develops, death from overdose remains possible for 2 reasons. First, many illicit drug users do not know how much they are taking. Second, opioid addicts who are detoxified lose their tolerance and are therefore in danger if they resume use at the level at which they quit.

An acute overdose of opioids can lead to stupor or coma, with miosis and diminished pulse and respiration. Acute overdose is treated by providing life support (e.g., establishing an adequate airway) and by intravenous administration of 0.4 mg of the narcotic antagonist naloxone, which ordinarily reverses the symptoms within 2 minutes. If there is no response, the dose of naloxone should be repeated twice at 5-minute intervals. If there is still no response, the coma probably has some other cause. The effect of naloxone lasts only 1–4 hours, and some opioids, methadone in particular, are longer-acting. To avoid the danger of relapse into a coma after the naloxone wears off, patients who have taken an opioid overdose should be observed for at least 24–48 hours. Furthermore, most people who overdose on opioids are physically dependent, and naloxone may induce severe withdrawal symptoms in them.

In physically dependent patients, abstinence symptoms typically begin 6–12 hours after the last dose. These symptoms include dilation of the pupils, sweating, yawning, gooseflesh, tearing, runny nose, nausea or vomiting, insomnia, muscle aches, diarrhea, and general dysphoria. Heart rate, blood pressure, and respiration are generally elevated. In the case of long-acting opioids such as methadone, withdrawal symptoms may begin up to 2–4 days after the last dose. Although the acute symptoms usually peak within a few days and diminish in a week, irritability, anxiety, dysphoria, insomnia, and drug craving may persist for months.

Methadone taken orally at 10–40 mg per day will usually prevent abstinence symptoms in a patient who is physically dependent on other opioid drugs. Since methadone is longer-acting than heroin and synthetic opioids, the dose can be tapered over several days to several weeks. The antihypertensive drug clonidine is also an effective treatment for opioid withdrawal in doses ranging from 0.3 mg to 1.2 mg per day. A more rapid detoxification technique, developed recently, uses a combination of clonidine and the oral narcotic antagonist naltrexone, sometimes along with the mixed opioid agonist/antagonist drug buprenorphine. Ultrafast detoxification under general anesthesia is being studied but is still considered experimental.

Treatment

The first major decision is whether to recommend opioid maintenance or opioid-free treatment. Opioid maintenance (usually with methadone) substitutes a long-acting, pharmacologically pure, legal, inexpensive oral drug for a short-acting, illicit, expensive drug that is often taken intravenously and may contain impurities. The goal is rehabilitation, not abstinence. This treatment has a high rate of compliance, protects the patient from HIV infection through contaminated needles, and often reduces illegal drug use and criminal activity. But some patients continue to use other drugs, including alcohol, cocaine, and benzodiazepines; some divert methadone into the illicit market; and there are occasional accidental overdose deaths. A long-acting form of methadone, LAAM, has recently received Food and Drug Administration (FDA) approval for opioid maintenance.

The other major pharmacologic treatment of opioid dependence involves the narcotic antagonist naltrexone, which blocks the effects of opioids without producing serious side effects. Unfortunately, most heroin addicts either will not take naltrexone or stop taking it almost immediately. Family support and leverage from a probation officer or (in the case of a physician) a licensing board can be helpful in persuading patients to take naltrexone.

Psychosocial treatments of opioid dependence include the residential self-help programs known as therapeutic communities, which use a confrontational approach focusing on honesty and hard work. Other modes of treatment are drug counseling based on 12-step principles and multimodal programs combining individual, group, and family therapy with vocational rehabilitation.

Cocaine

Cocaine is an alkaloid derived from the shrub *Erythroxylon coca*, a plant indigenous to the Andes, where some natives chew its leaves for their stimulating effect. Cocaine was isolated from the coca leaf in 1859 and became important after 1884 as the first effective local anesthetic; this is also its only current medical use. In 1914 cocaine was subjected to the same laws as morphine and heroin, and since then it has been legally classified with the narcotics. The use of cocaine in the United States increased dramatically between the mid-1970s and the mid-1980s. It has diminished since then, but the number of heavy users has remained constant. About 3 million Americans used cocaine in one recent year.

The most common ways of taking cocaine are intranasal use of cocaine hydrochloride (snorting); intramuscular or intravenous injection of cocaine hydrochloride; and smoking cocaine freebase or "crack," an alkaloidal form that is prepared by adding a base (usually baking soda) to a solution of cocaine hydrochloride and water. Intranasal use produces euphoria in 30 seconds to 2 minutes; the effect peaks at about 10 minutes and ends after 15 minutes to an hour. Intravenous injection results in euphoria after 15 seconds, with a peak effect at 5 minutes and a duration of 15–20 minutes. Smoking crack produces an effect that begins in 6–10 seconds, peaks at 3–5 minutes, and lasts 10–15 minutes. Because cocaine works so quickly and wears off so quickly, it has a high liability for dependence, especially in the smokeable form. There are no dramatic physical withdrawal symptoms, but heavy users who stop taking the drug often suffer depression, craving, fatigue, and drowsiness.

Adverse Effects

Cocaine produces medical complications mainly by constricting blood vessels and increasing the activity of the sympathetic nervous system (e.g., raising blood pressure and heart rate), thus increasing the danger of irregular heart rhythms and myocardial infarction. Grand mal seizures and intracranial hemorrhage may also occur. Crack smokers may develop bronchitis and lose the capacity to diffuse carbon monoxide. Intranasal users are subject to ulceration of the nasal mucosa and occasionally perforation of the septum. Needle sharing and the exchange of cocaine for sex create a high risk of human immunodeficiency virus (HIV) infection. Use of cocaine during pregnancy has been associated with premature birth, low birth weight, genitourinary malformations, and other fetal defects.

Intensive and compulsive users become jittery, irritable, and self-absorbed. Other behavioral complications include decreased appetite (and potential weight loss), insomnia, perceptual disturbances, paranoid thinking, and at times full-blown psychosis. Cocaine may be sexually stimulating, but chronic abusers tend to lose sexual interest. They may also become hypersensitive to sound, light, and touch. Users often take alcohol, sedatives, marihuana, or opioids to calm cocaine-induced agitation, and this practice may create a dual dependence that is particularly hard to treat. The combination of paranoia, agitation, and concurrent alcohol use increases the likelihood of aggression.

Treatment

There is no single treatment that is best for all persons dependent on cocaine. Most clinicians and researchers recommend total abstinence not only from cocaine but from all other nonmedical drug use as well, since it increases the likelihood of relapse to cocaine use. Drug treatment for cocaine abusers has generally been disappointing. Some studies have found that the tricyclic antidepressant desipramine reduces cocaine use and craving, but results are conflicting. Another drug with some promise is amantadine, but it too has not been consistently effective. Disulfiram may be helpful because it discourages alcohol consumption, and some patients relapse to cocaine use only under the influence of alcohol.

Several psychosocial treatments show some promise. Researchers are studying behavioral therapies in which patients are reinforced by a significant other or by payments of money or vouchers for negative urine screens. Relapse prevention treatments based on the principles of cognitive behavioral therapy and drug counseling based on 12-step principles have also had some success.

Amphetamines

Amphetamines and amphetamine congeners are a large group of central stimulant drugs; among the best known are dextroamphetamine (Dexedrine), methamphetamine (Methedrine), and methylphenidate (Ritalin). Racemic amphetamine sulfate (Benzedrine) was first introduced as a medicine in 1932. In 1937 it became available in tablet form. Soon amphetamine was receiving sensational publicity, and many physicians came to regard it as a versatile remedy second only to a few other extraordinary drugs such as aspirin. In 1971 the annual legal U.S. production of amphetamines of all kinds reached more than 10 billion tablets. From the mid-1960s on, there was also considerable growth in illicit laboratory synthesis and black market diversion of legitimately produced drugs.

Since 1970, amphetamine abuse has declined, partly because of legal restrictions. Amphetamines now have accepted therapeutic applications only in treating narcolepsy and attention deficit disorder and as an occasional adjunct to antidepressants in the treatment of depression. Few physicians now prescribe amphetamines for weight loss because of well-founded doubts concerning efficacy and safety.

The most commonly abused amphetamine is methamphetamine, which is taken either intravenously ("crystal") or by smoking ("ice"). The effects resemble those of cocaine but last longer. Like cocaine abusers, amphetamine abusers also commonly abuse sedative-hypnotics or alcohol as well.

Adverse Effects

Both acute amphetamine intoxication and chronic use have numerous adverse physical effects. Symptoms of acute poisoning include flushing, pallor, cyanosis, fever, tachycardia, nausea, vomiting, difficulty breathing, tremor, elevated blood pressure, hemorrhages, strokes, seizures, loss of consciousness, and coma. Death from overdose is usually associated with high fever, seizures, and shock. Injection abuse can produce HIV infection, hepatitis, lung abscesses, endocarditis, and necrotizing angiitis.

Adverse psychological effects include restlessness, logorrhea, insomnia, dysphoria, irritability, hostility, tension, confusion, anxiety, panic, and sometimes psychosis.

The initial symptoms of amphetamine-induced psychotic disorder include restlessness, increased irritability, and heightened perceptual sensitivity. These may be followed by delusions of persecution, ideas of reference, and auditory and visual hallucinations. The symptoms disappear within a period of days to several weeks, but suspiciousness and ideas of reference may persist longer. Psychosis usually occurs when an abuser who is already taking large doses takes even larger amounts than usual for a period of time.

Patterns of Abuse

Chronic amphetamine abusers often find that the drug begins to dominate their lives through a craving severe enough to be called a compulsion. Their irritability and paranoia may cause unprovoked violence and drive their friends away; their preoccupation with the drug has a disastrous effect on family relationships and work. A high degree of tolerance develops; an abuser may eventually need up to 20 times the original dose to recover the euphoric effect.

A letdown or "crash" often occurs when an amphetamine abuser is forced to stop using the drug for a time because it is producing agitation, paranoia, and malnutrition. A debilitating cycle of "runs" (heavy use for several days to a week) and crashes is a common pattern of abuse. The physical symptoms of withdrawal include headache, sweating, muscle and stomach cramps, and hunger. The characteristic psychological symptom is a lethargic depression, suicidal at times, which peaks several days after the last dose of amphetamine but may persist at lesser intensity for weeks. Often a vicious cycle develops. Patients

who suffer from chronic depression or feelings of inadequacy experience initial relief from amphetamine and become dependent on the drug. When they try to stop using it, they become depressed even further and feel a strong desire to start again.

Treatment

Because amphetamine-induced psychosis is generally self-limiting, treatment usually requires only supportive measures. The clinician may facilitate elimination of the drug by acidifying the urine with ammonium chloride. Antipsychotics may be prescribed for the first few days; after that there is usually little need for drug treatment. Proposed treatments for chronic amphetamine abuse resemble those for cocaine abuse, but few studies are available.

Sedative, Hypnotic, and Anxiolytic Drugs

There are several categories of these drugs, which are prescribed for anxiety and insomnia. Barbiturates, such as secobarbital, phenobarbital, and pentobarbital, can cause serious respiratory depression leading to a lethal overdose, as well as physical dependence and a potentially fatal acute withdrawal reaction. They have been largely supplanted by safer drugs. Other sedative-hypnotics such as glutethimide, meprobamate, and chloral hydrate are not commonly used. The most commonly prescribed anxiolytic drugs are the benzodiazepines, which include diazepam, flurazepam, oxazepam, chlordiazepoxide, alprazolam, and clonazepam. These drugs are also used as muscle relaxants, anticonvulsants, and anesthetics. Mild to moderate levels of intoxication resemble alcohol intoxication; the symptoms include drowsiness, unsteady gait, and weakness. Some benzodiazepines have a disinhibiting effect that may cause hostile or aggressive behavior in susceptible people.

Adverse Effects

Benzodiazepines by themselves cause relatively little respiratory depression, and they have a higher ratio of lethal to effective dose than other sedative-hypnotic drugs. However, the risk increases when they are mixed with other agents, especially alcohol. In some cases "drug automatism" may occur; people whose judgment and memory are already impaired by the drug may forget or disregard previous use and unintentionally take a dose that proves to be fatal.

Tolerance and Withdrawal

Benzodiazepines produce less euphoria than other sedative-hypnotic drugs, so the risk of abuse and dependence is relatively low in the general population. But these drugs are sometimes used to buffer the effects of stimulant withdrawal or enhance the effects of opioids and alcohol. Patients with a history of alcohol or other substance abuse are likely to abuse benzodiazepines and should be given them only as a last resort. Furthermore, benzodiazepines can induce both tolerance and physical dependence. A withdrawal syndrome may occur even at therapeutic doses if the drug is used for a month or more. The symptoms include anxiety, tremulousness, numbness in the extremities, insomnia, irritability, dysphoria, intolerance for bright lights and loud noises, nausea, sweating, and muscle twitching. The most severe, although uncommon, withdrawal symptoms are seizures, which typically occur 1–3 days after the last dose of a short-acting benzodiazepine, and a state of delirium characterized by anxiety, disorientation, nightmares, and visual hallucinations. Withdrawal is not usually accompanied by craving for the drug. Because some benzodiazepines are eliminated from the body slowly, symptoms may persist for several weeks or more.

Treatment of Withdrawal

In general, withdrawal is treated by gradual dose reduction. Some patients who have been taking short-acting benzodiazepines such as alprazolam may benefit if a longer-acting agent such as phenobarbital or clonazepam is substituted and later gradually withdrawn. The rate of dose reduction depends on the patient's age, size, and physical and psychiatric condition and length of time the drug has been used.

Psychedelics (Hallucinogens)

There are many psychedelic or hallucinogenic drugs, some natural and some synthetic. The best known are mescaline, derived from the peyote cactus; psilocybin, found in about 100 mushroom species; and the synthetic drug lysergic acid diethylamide (LSD), which is related to psychoactive alkaloids found in morning glory seeds, the lysergic acid amides. Other psychedelic drugs include dimethyltryptamine (DMT), and 2,5,-dimethoxy-4methyl-amphetamine (DOM, also known as STP). The average active dose varies considerably. For example, it is 50 micrograms for LSD, about 1 mg for lysergic acid

amides, 5 mg for DOM, 10 mg for psilocybin, 50 mg for DMT, and 200 mg for mescaline. Only LSD and mushrooms containing psilocybin are now available in any quantity on the illicit market.

The subjective effects of these drugs differ somewhat in quality and duration, but LSD produces the widest range of effects and can be taken as a prototype. The reaction varies greatly with personality, expectations, and setting, but usually involves profound alterations in perception, mood, and thinking. Perceptions become unusually intense: colors and textures seem richer, contours sharpened, music more emotionally profound, smell and taste heightened. Normally unnoticed details capture the attention, and ordinary things are seen with wonder, as if for the first time. Synesthesia is common: colors are "heard" or sounds "seen." Changes in body image and alterations of time and space perception also occur. Intensely vivid dreamlike kaleidoscopic imagery appears before closed eyes. True hallucinations are infrequent, but visual distortions and illusions are common. Emotions become unusually intense and may change abruptly and often; two seemingly incompatible feelings may be experienced at once. Suggestibility is greatly heightened, and sensitivity to nonverbal cues is increased. Exaggerated empathy with or detachment from other people may arise. A heightened sense of reality and significance suffuses the experience; introspective reflection and feelings of religious and philosophical insight are common. The sense of self is greatly changed, sometimes to the point of depersonalization, merging with the external world, separation of self from body, or total dissolution of the ego in mystical ecstasy.

Adverse Effects

The most common adverse effect of LSD and related drugs is the "bad trip," which resembles the acute panic reaction to cannabis (see below) but is generally more severe and occasionally produces true psychotic symptoms, such as hallucinations and paranoid delusions. The bad trip typically ends when the immediate effect of the drug wears off—in the case of LSD, in about 8–12 hours. Under most circumstances the best treatment is protection, companionship, and reassurance; sedative drugs (e.g., a short-acting benzodiazepine) are useful in some cases. The bad trip is classified in DSM-IV as a hallucinogen-induced anxiety, mood, or psychotic disorder, with onset during intoxication.

Another adverse effect of hallucinogenic drugs is persistent flashbacks, or *hallucinogen persisting perception disorder.* Flashbacks are episodes of visual distortion, time expansion, or relived intense emotion lasting usually a few seconds to a few minutes but sometimes longer. Probably about a quarter of all hallucinogen users have experienced some form of flashback. As a rule they are mild and transient, sometimes even pleasant, but sometimes they involve repeated frightening images and in that case may require psychiatric attention. Flashbacks ordinarily decrease in number and intensity with time, but some individuals report persistent perceptual difficulties lasting for years after the last use of psychedelics. The perceptual disturbances include visions of geometric shapes, trails of light moving through the air, and difficulty in reading because words seem to swirl around the page. Flashbacks are most likely to occur under stress and can be induced by fatigue or alcohol or marihuana intoxication.

Other prolonged adverse reactions to LSD present the same variety of symptoms as bad trips. They have been classified as anxiety disorders, depressive disorders, and psychoses. Most of these adverse reactions end after 24–48 hours, but sometimes they last weeks or even months.

Craving does not occur, and substance dependence, according to the DSM-IV definition, is almost unknown. There is no physical dependence; tolerance develops quickly but also disappears, usually within 2–3 days.

MDMA

An illicit drug that first became popular in the 1980s is 3,4-methylenedioxymethamphetamine (MDMA), known on the street as "ecstasy." Although it is structurally related to both amphetamine, a stimulant, and mescaline, a psychedelic or hallucinogenic drug, MDMA is neither. It produces neither a stimulant effect nor perceptual distortions, body image alterations, or changes in the sense of self. Instead it is primarily a euphoriant that generates a sense of emotional openness and intimacy. The effects last 2–4 hours. Common physical side effects include a rise in heart rate and blood pressure, dry mouth, loss of appetite, jaw clenching or teeth grinding, and sometimes a mild hangover with fatigue for a day afterward. There have been a few reports of deaths, mainly from overstimulation and dehydration leading to a stroke or heart attack in people who had been dancing for hours in a hot, crowded room while not consuming any liquids.

MDMA involves no craving or withdrawal reaction. At high doses and with repeated use, tolerance to the desired effects usually develops, and the physical side effects tend to become more uncomfortable. As a result, long-term

heavy or habitual use is rare. Nevertheless, there are serious questions about chronic effects. In animal experiments, repeated high doses of MDMA have been found to damage neurons producing the neurotransmitter serotonin. Depletion of serotonin metabolites has been found in the spinal fluid of some people who have taken MDMA 20 times or more. The physical or psychological consequences of these changes are unclear.

Phencyclidine

Phencyclidine (PCP) was first investigated as a surgical general anesthetic and analgesic. Because of disorientation, agitation, and delirium on emergence from anesthesia, it is now medically available only for veterinary use. Illicit PCP may be taken intranasally, orally, or intravenously, but it is usually smoked in a cigarette because this is the best means of titrating the dose. The most popular street names are "angel dust," "T," "rocket fuel," and "hog." Phencyclidine is occasionally misrepresented as mescaline, psilocybin, or THC, although this is less common now than in the past.

Phencyclidine is relatively cheap and easy to synthesize in illicit laboratories. There are about 30 chemical analogs, some of which have appeared on the illicit market. Another related drug is ketamine ("K"), a short-acting anesthetic with psychoactive properties similar to those of phencyclidine.

One gram of PCP may be used to make as few as 4 or as many as several dozen cigarettes. This variability, together with the extreme uncertainty of PCP content in street samples, makes it difficult to predict the effect, which also depends on the setting and the user's previous experience. Less than 5 mg of PCP is considered a low dose, and doses above 10 mg are considered high. The effects of 2–3 mg of smoked PCP begin within 5 minutes and plateau in half an hour.

In the early phases, users are often uncommunicative and lost in fantasy. They experience "speedy" feelings, euphoria, bodily warmth, tingling, peaceful floating sensations, and occasional feelings of depersonalization or isolation. Some users describe PCP intoxication as similar to "feeling dead." Striking alterations of body image, distortions of space and time perception, and delusions or hallucinations may occur, although PCP is not primarily classified as a hallucinogen. Thought may become confused and disorganized. The user may be sympathetic, sociable, and talkative at one moment, hostile and negative at another. Anxiety is often the most prominent presenting symptom in an adverse reaction. Head-rolling movements, stroking, grimacing, and repetitive chanting speech may occur. The intoxication lasts about 4–6 hours, sometimes giving way to a mild irritable depression. Users may find that it takes from 24 to 48 hours to recover completely from the high.

Adverse Effects

Mild cases of adverse PCP reaction or overdose usually do not come to medical attention; when they do, they may often be treated as an emergency in the outpatient department. Symptoms at low doses may range from mild euphoria and restlessness to increasing levels of anxiety, fearfulness, confusion, and agitation. Patients may exhibit difficulty in communication, a blank staring appearance, disordered thinking, depression, and occasionally self-destructive or belligerent and irrationally assaultive behavior. Accidents, homicide, and suicide are the main causes of death from PCP use.

Like the other effects of PCP intoxication, neurological and physical symptoms are typically dose-related. Among the common symptoms in cases brought to emergency rooms are systolic hypertension and nystagmus. At low doses, patients may have dysarthria, gross ataxia, and muscle rigidity, particularly in the face and neck. Increased deep tendon reflexes and diminished response to pain are commonly observed. Higher doses may lead to high fever, agitated and repetitive movement, and athetosis or clonic jerking of the extremities. Involuntary isometric muscle contraction can lead to acute rhabdomyolysis, myoglobinuria, and even kidney failure. Patients may become drowsy, stuporous, or even comatose. Vomiting, hypersalivation, and sweating are common. Clonic movements and muscle rigidity sometimes precede generalized seizure activity, and status epilepticus has been reported. Death from respiratory arrest may also occur.

A period of 2–3 days may elapse before psychiatric help is sought, because friends are trying to deal with the psychosis by providing resources and support; patients who lose consciousness present earlier. While most will recover within 1–2 days, some will remain psychotic for as long as 2 weeks. Patients who are first seen in a coma often show disorientation, hallucinations, confusion, and difficulty in communication upon regaining consciousness—symptoms also seen in noncomatose patients. Other symptoms of PCP psychosis are staring, echolalia, posturing, sleep disturbances, paranoid ideation, and depression. The behavioral disturbance may include inappropriate laughing and crying, public masturbation, urinary incontinence,

and violence. Often the patient has amnesia for the entire period of the psychosis.

These symptoms must be distinguished from sedative-hypnotic or opioid overdose, psychosis resulting from the use of psychedelic drugs, and acute psychotic episodes. Laboratory analysis and the characteristic physical findings are helpful in establishing the diagnosis, especially when the drug history is unreliable.

Treatment

Unconscious patients must of course be carefully monitored, especially because excessive salivation may interfere with already compromised breathing. In an alert patient who has recently taken PCP, forced vomiting is risky because of possible laryngeal spasm. Muscle spasms and seizures are best treated with diazepam. The environment should afford minimal sensory stimulation; reassurance or talking down is generally useless and may lead to more agitation or violence. Ideally one person should stay with the patient in a quiet, dark room. Four-point restraint is dangerous, because it may lead to rhabdomyolysis; total body immobilization may occasionally be necessary. Diazepam is often effective in reducing agitation, but a patient with severe behavioral disturbance may require short-term antipsychotic medication. A hypotensive drug may occasionally be needed. Ammonium chloride at the acute stage and ascorbic acid and cranberry juice (which contains benzoic acid) later on are used to acidify the urine and thus promote elimination of the drug.

Inhalants

Some abused inhalants are gasoline, varnish remover, lighter fluid, airplane glue, rubber cement, cleaning fluid, and aerosols (especially spray paints). The active ingredients include toluene, acetone, benzene, and halogenated hydrocarbons. Because these substances are legal, cheap, and accessible, they are used mostly by the young (ages 6–16) and poor, who inhale them from a tube, a can, a plastic bag, or a rag held over the nose. The intoxication usually lasts 15–30 minutes.

Acute Effects

Inhalant intoxication has a central depressant effect, characterized by euphoria, excitement, a floating sensation, dizziness, slurred speech, ataxia, and a sense of heightened power. Like alcohol, inhalants may cause impaired judgment leading to impulsive and aggressive behavior, and amnesia may occur for the period of intoxication. Other acute effects are nausea, anorexia, and in high doses stupor and even unconsciousness. Death may be caused by central respiratory depression, asphyxiation, or accident.

Chronic Effects

Substantial tolerance develops after repeated sniffing. A serious risk is irreversible damage to the liver, kidneys, and other organs from benzene or halogenated hydrocarbons. Peripheral neuritis has also been reported. Permanent neuromuscular and brain damage must be considered a possibility because inhalants often contain high concentrations of copper, zinc, and heavy metals. Some clinicians report brain atrophy and chronic motor impairment in toluene users.

Marihuana

Marihuana has been known for thousands of years as a medicine and intoxicant, and it was widely used in the nineteenth century as an analgesic, anticonvulsant, and hypnotic. Recently there has been interest in using it to treat the nausea and vomiting produced by cancer chemotherapy, the AIDS weight loss syndrome, and a number of other symptoms and syndromes. But throughout history marihuana has served chiefly as a euphoriant. A resin that covers the flowers and leaves of the hemp plant (*Cannabis sativa*) contains the active substances in marihuana, chief of which is delta-9-tetrahydrocannabinol. The drug can be taken in the form of a drink or in foods, but in this country it is usually smoked, either in a pipe or in a cigarette called a "joint." There is considerable public concern about its widespread use, and especially about the effects of acute intoxication on driving, school performance, and other activities. National surveys have shown a recent increase in marihuana use among adolescents in the United States.

Marihuana Intoxication

Marihuana intoxication varies a great deal, but common symptoms are euphoria, rapid flow of ideas, decreased short-term memory, and sometimes impairment of concentration and judgment. The intoxication heightens sensitivity to external stimuli, alters sensory and perceptual functions, and sometimes causes a discontinuity in thought sequence that may result in irrelevant associations. Time seems to slow down, and appetite increases.

Physiological changes include increased heart rate and reddening of the conjunctiva. Although many users report that marihuana enhances the enjoyment of sexual intercourse, there is little evidence that it stimulates or weakens sexual desire or potency. The effects of smoking last 2–4 hours, the effects of ingestion 5–12 hours.

Curiously, a splitting of consciousness may occur: while experiencing the high, smokers may at the same time objectively observe their own intoxication. They may, for example, have paranoid thoughts yet at the same time laugh at them. This ability to retain objectivity, in conjunction with the *behavioral tolerance* (learning how to act normal even when under the influence of the drug), may explain why many experienced users behave soberly in public even when highly intoxicated.

Adverse Effects

Although generally not classified as a hallucinogen, marihuana can produce some of the same effects as hallucinogens: distorted perception of body parts, spatial and temporal distortion, depersonalization, increased sensitivity to sound, synesthesia, heightened suggestibility, and a sense of deeper awareness.

Although the nightmarish reactions that even the experienced LSD user may endure are unlikely to afflict experienced marihuana smokers, some cannabis users may also suffer from short-lived acute anxiety states, sometimes accompanied by paranoid thoughts. The anxiety may become intense enough to be called panic. Although uncommon, this is probably the most frequent adverse reaction to the moderate use of smoked marihuana. Sufferers may believe that body image distortions mean that they are ill or dying; they may interpret the psychological changes as an indication that they are losing their sanity. Rarely, the panic becomes incapacitating, usually for a relatively short time. Simple reassurance is the best treatment; it is dangerous to mistake this for toxic psychosis and subject the user to physical intervention that heightens the panic. The anxiety reaction is not psychotic because the ability to test reality remains intact.

Anxiety reactions and paranoid thoughts are more likely to occur in those taking the drug for the first time or in unpleasant or unfamiliar settings; they are rare in experienced users. The likelihood varies directly with the dose and inversely with the user's experience; thus the most vulnerable person is an inexperienced user who inadvertently (often precisely because of unfamiliarity with the drug) takes a large dose that produces unexpected perceptual and somatic changes.

Among new users of marihuana, an acute depressive syndrome occasionally occurs. It is generally rather mild and transient but sometimes requires psychiatric intervention. This reaction is most likely in a user with underlying depression. Paradoxically, some people who suffer from chronic depression find cannabis useful as an antidepressant.

One rather rare reaction to cannabis is the flashback. Although some reports suggest that this may occur even without prior use of any other drug, in general it seems to arise only when people who have used the more powerful psychedelic drugs smoke marihuana at a later time.

Chronic heavy use is sometimes said to cause an "amotivational syndrome." Reports by many investigators, particularly in Egypt and in parts of Asia, indicate that long-term users of the potent versions of cannabis are passive, unproductive, and lacking in ambition. However, the existence and the nature of this syndrome has generated substantial controversy, since it is difficult to disentangle the effects of marihuana from preexisting psychological factors that may have led to chronic heavy use of the drug.

The most clearly documented adverse physical effects of marihuana use are produced in the lungs. Mild airway constriction is reported in studies of both animals and human beings. Marihuana smoke also contains many of the same carcinogenic hydrocarbons as tobacco smoke. Although not yet confirmed clinically, chronic respiratory disease and lung cancer must be considered dangers for long-term heavy users.

Tolerance and Withdrawal

The significance of tolerance and withdrawal after regular heavy use of cannabis remains uncertain. Some indications of tolerance and a mild discontinuation syndrome after frequent use at high doses exist, and there may be some difficulty in stopping use as part of a pattern of long-term regular heavy use. There is little clinical evidence that either tolerance or withdrawal symptoms present serious problems to users or cause them to continue using cannabis.

References

American Psychiatric Association. 1994. *Diagnostic and statistical manual of mental disorders.* 4th ed. Washington, D. C.: American Psychiatric Press.

Carroll, K. M., Rounsaville, B. J., and Keller, D. S. 1991. Relapse prevention strategies for the treatment of cocaine abuse. *Am. J. Drug Alcohol Abuse* 17(3):249–265.

Galanter, M., and Kleber, H. D. 1994. *Textbook of substance abuse treatment.* Washington, D.C.: American Psychiatric Press.

Greenfield, S. F. 1996. Women and substance use disorders. In *Psychopharmacology and women,* ed. Jensvold, M. F., Halbreich, U., and Hamilton, J. A. Washington, D. C.: American Psychiatric Press. 299–321.

Greenfield, S. F., Weiss, R. D., and Mirin, S. M. In press. Psychoactive substance use disorders. In *The practitioner's guide to psychoactive drugs.* 4th ed., ed. Gelenberg, A. J., and Bassuk, E. L. New York: Plenum Press.

Grinspoon, L. 1977. *Marihuana reconsidered.* 2d ed. Cambridge, Mass.: Harvard University Press.

Grinspoon, L., and Bakalar, J. B. 1979. *Psychedelic drugs reconsidered.* New York: Basic Books.

——— 1985. *Cocaine: a drug and its social evolution.* 2d ed. New York: Basic Books.

Grinspoon, L., and Hedblom, P. 1975. *The speed culture: amphetamine use and abuse in America.* Cambridge, Mass.: Harvard University Press.

Institute of Medicine. 1982. *Marijuana and health.* Washington, D.C.: National Academy Press.

Kosten, T. R., and McCance, E. 1996. A review of pharmacotherapies for substance abuse. *Am. J. Addict.* 5(4 suppl.):S30–S37.

Mendelson, J. H., and Mello, N. K. 1996. Management of cocaine abuse and dependence. *N. Engl. J. Med.* 334:965–972.

Najavits, L. M., and Weiss, R. D. 1994. The role of psychotherapy in the treatment of substance use disorders. *Harvard Rev. Psychiatry* 2:84–96.

Peroutka, S. J., ed. 1990. *Ecstasy: the clinical, pharmacological, and neurotoxicological effects of the drug MDMA.* Boston: Kluwer.

Petersen, L. C., and Stillman, R. C., eds. 1978. *Phencyclidine (PCP) abuse: an appraisal.* National Institute on Drug Abuse research monographs no. 21. Washington, D.C.: Government Printing Office.

Rubin, V., and Comitas, L. 1975. *Ganja in Jamaica.* The Hague: Mouton.

Szara, S. I., and Ludford, J. P., eds. 1980. *Benzodiazepines: a review of research results.* National Institute on Drug Abuse research monographs no. 33. Washington, D.C.: Government Printing Office.

Weiss, R. D., Mirin, S. M., and Bartel, R. 1994. *Cocaine.* 2d ed. New York: Plenum Press.

Recommended Reading

Grinspoon, L. 1977. *Marihuana reconsidered.* 2d ed. Cambridge, Mass.: Harvard University Press.

Grinspoon, L., and Bakalar, J. B. 1979. *Psychedelic drugs reconsidered.* New York: Basic Books.

——— 1985. *Cocaine: a drug and its social evolution,* 2d ed. New York: Basic Books.

Grinspoon, L., and Hedblom, P. 1975. *The speed culture: amphetamine use and abuse in America.* Cambridge, Mass.: Harvard University Press.

Waldorf, D., Reinarman, C., and Murphy, S. 1991. *Cocaine changes: the experience of using and quitting.* Philadelphia: Temple University Press.

DAVID B. HERZOG

ANNE E. BECKER

Eating Disorders

Eating disorders comprise a set of syndromes relating to weight preoccupation and disordered eating, including anorexia nervosa, bulimia nervosa, binge-eating disorder, and atypical patterns of disordered eating. This chapter describes the epidemiology, clinical features, diagnosis, etiology, and treatment of eating disorders.

Epidemiology

Incidence and Prevalence

A number of methodologic difficulties complicate estimates of the prevalence of the eating disorders, including changing diagnostic criteria and difficulty of case detection (Drewnowski, Hopkins, and Kessler, 1988). Among young females, the point prevalence of anorexia is 0.28% (Hoek, 1995) and of bulimia nervosa 1% (Hoek, 1995; Fairburn and Beglin, 1990). Prevalence of partial syndrome eating disorders may be twice that of full syndrome disorders in community populations. The recently defined binge-eating disorder is the most prevalent eating disorder, with a prevalence in college student samples of 2.6% and among those seeking treatment in weight control programs 29% (Spitzer et al., 1993). Estimates of lifetime prevalence of bulimia nervosa are as high as 4.2% (Kendler et al., 1991).

Age, Sex, Ethnicity, and Social Class

The onset of anorexia tends to occur at a younger age than that of bulimia. The general range for anorexia nervosa is between 12 years and the mid-30s, with a bimodal age of onset at 13–14 and 17–18 years; bulimia usually begins in females between 17–18 years of age (Halmi et al., 1979) and in males between 18–26 (Carlat and Camargo, 1991). While uncommon, late onset bulimia and anorexia can occur as well (Beck, Casper, and Anderson, 1996). All of the eating disorders are more prevalent in females than

males, with 90% of anorectics being female and 85–90% of bulimics being female. Binge-eating disorder, while still more prevalent in females, is the most common eating disorder among men, with a female to male ratio of 1.5:1 (American Psychiatric Association, 1994). While eating disorders are less common among Asian and African American women than among Caucasian women, they are more common among Native American women (Crago, Shisslak, and Estes, 1996); moreover, binge eating and bulimia may be increasing among ethnic minorities in the United States (Pike and Walsh, 1996). Eating disorders have long been perceived to be associated with high socioeconomic status; however, the data do not support this relationship in anorexia and actually suggest that bulimia may be more common among low socioeconomic status groups (Gard and Freeman, 1996).

The Clinical States

Although this discussion analyzes anorexia and bulimia nervosa separately, the 2 syndromes may coexist. Many bulimics have a history of anorexia nervosa; others may subsequently lose weight and become anorexic. Approximately half the anorexic population engages in bingeing and purging behaviors. Alternatively, persons can present with symptoms of either or both of these disorders without meeting full diagnostic criteria for either one. Indeed, there has been controversy over the degree to which eating disorders represent discrete disorders or simply an extreme on the continuum of dieting behaviors and weight and body image preoccupations. Many of those diagnosed with partial syndrome disorders, or even categorized as "pathological dieters," progress to full syndrome eating disorders in longitudinal studies (Shisslak, Crago, and Estes, 1995). Conversely, persons originally meeting full criteria for the disorders can go on to develop partial syndrome disorders (Norring and Sohlberg, 1993; Herpertz-Dahlmann et al., 1996). The clinical significance of treatment and outcome for these subsyndromal patterns of disordered eating is not yet known. Among a number of atypical forms of disordered eating, consisting of bingeing on and spitting out food, purging without bingeing, and bingeing without purging, the last pattern, now labeled binge-eating disorder (BED), has emerged as an important and prevalent subtype.

Anorexia nervosa most commonly begins in a teenager who is overweight or perceives herself to be overweight. The young woman then starts a diet that escalates into an obsessive preoccupation with being thin. She may achieve extreme and often rapid weight loss through severe restriction of her caloric intake or through the use of purging or other compensatory techniques (fasting, vomiting, laxatives, or diuretics) to eliminate the calories she has consumed. Excessive physical activity is another method of weight loss and control which anorectics commonly use, and it may be an early sign of incipient anorexia nervosa, predating any weight loss.

Anorexia nervosa may begin abruptly as a single circumscribed episode or as an insidious process lasting from months to many years. It may manifest a fluctuating course with several exacerbations and remissions, or it may in some tragic instances progress unremittingly to death. Follow-up studies indicate that 20% of cases continue on a chronic course, whereas 30% improve over time and about half recover (Steinhausen, 1995). The mortality rate due to anorexia nervosa is 5.6% per decade; the annual mortality rate among anorectics is more than twice that of female psychiatric inpatients age 10–39 and more than 12 times higher than that of females 15–24 in the general population (Sullivan, 1995). Causes of death are generally suicide or complications of the disorder (Crisp et al., 1992). Favorable prognostic indicators for anorexia include early age of onset, high social status or education, and a short interval between onset of symptoms and intervention (Steinhausen, 1995).

The bulimic is typically a late adolescent or young adult woman who has attempted various diets. She may learn about purging techniques as a form of weight management via a friend, a family member, or even the media and embark upon a course of self-induced vomiting, laxative abuse, or other compensatory measures to pursue often unrealistic weight goals. Bulimics typically binge on "junk food" high in carbohydrates during a time they have set aside for solitary bingeing, often purchasing such foods in anticipation of a binge. Binges by definition consist of consuming an unusually large amount of food and are associated with a sense of lack of control over the episode. Afterward there is frequently self-loathing relating to the episode and accompanying low self-esteem and shame relating to weight or body shape; alternatively, a bulimic may experience emotional numbing or relief in association with her bingeing and purging. The bulimic's preoccupation with food and preparation for bingeing frequently isolate her socially and may interfere with work or study. The bulimic woman is often ashamed of her eating symptoms, going to great lengths to conceal this information from family, friends, spouse, or physician. Unlike the anorectic, the bulimic is usually distressed by her symptoms and willing to accept help. Bulimia is frequently associated with other impulsive behaviors such as alcohol or drug use, stealing or shoplifting, and suicidal behavior (Herzog, 1982). Bulimia is commonly a chronic, episodic disorder. The majority of patients treated for bulimia have some relapse into bulimic behavior (Mitchell et al., 1989). In one 10-year follow-up study, for example, 9% of patients continued to have bulimia, 39% continued with some symptoms, and 52% recovered fully (Collings and King, 1994).

Physical Manifestations and Sequelae

Anorexia and bulimia can cause harmful and potentially life-threatening medical complications. The chief complication of binge-eating disorder is obesity. Binge eating after a gastroplasty can result in pouch dilatation or staple line disruption (Shikora, Benotti, and Forse, 1994) and potentially even gastric rupture in unoperated individuals (Evans, 1968).

The complications of anorexia nervosa are largely those of starvation, whereas those of bulimia result from the effects of bingeing and purging. Anorexia nervosa has been associated with cardiovascular, hematological, gastrointestinal, renal, endocrine, neurologic, and skeletal changes. Physical manifestations include bradycardia, hypotension, arrhythmias, mild anemia, leukopenia, delayed gastric motility, increased blood urea nitrogen, renal calculi, amenorrhea, hypothyroidlike state, osteoporosis, and profound hypoglycemia. The gastrointestinal abnormalities may produce an exaggerated sense of stomach fullness, abdominal pain, and constipation. Brain abnormalities in anorexia include ventricular and cortical sulcal enlargement; there may also be impairment in attention, concentration, planning, and insight. Potential complications in adolescents also include pubertal delay, peak bone mass reduction, and growth retardation (Fisher et al., 1995). It is noteworthy that with refeeding, peripheral edema is common with anorexia nervosa.

The bulimic frequently presents for a health problem that developed as a result of her bingeing and purging behaviors. The diagnosis of bulimia nervosa may be suspected on the basis of dental enamel erosion, electrolyte abnormalities, abrasion of the knuckles from induced vomiting (Russell's sign), or otherwise unexplained enlarged parotid glands. Other physical manifestations include amenorrhea (in 40% of cases), hypokalemia, and esophagitis. Repeated induction of vomiting with ipecac can lead to chronic absorption of the drug and cause a neuromyopathy or a potentially fatal myocardial dysfunction. Vomiting, diuretic abuse, and laxative abuse can all lead to electrolyte disturbances. In addition, diuretic abuse can cause idiopathic edema; laxative abuse can lead to laxative dependency and a dilated, atonic colon; and diet pill use can result in elevated blood pressure, palpitations, seizures, renal failure, and intracerebral hemorrhage (Mehler, 1996b).

Diagnosis

Diagnostic criteria for the eating disorders have undergone substantial revision and remain somewhat controversial. For both anorexia and bulimia nervosa, the diagnosis rests partly on an inappropriate or undue concern with weight or body shape. The 2 disorders are further defined by behavioral symptoms aimed (at least originally) at weight management and often resulting in patterns of disordered eating such as restricting or bingeing. Binge-eating disorder, by contrast, does not require a concern with weight or body shape, but rather involves a consistent pattern of disordered eating.

Anorexia nervosa is further defined by its 2 physiologic characteristics, amenorrhea and low weight, the latter defined as less than 85% of expected weight within DSM-IV (*Diagnostic and Statistical Manual of Mental Disorders,* fourth edition) criteria or less than or equal to a body mass index of 17.5 by ICD-10 (*International Classification of Diseases,* tenth revision) Diagnostic Criteria for Research (American Psychiatric Association, 1994). Pro-

visional diagnostic criteria for binge-eating disorder were introduced in the DSM-IV and include regular, episodic binge-pattern eating with associated distress. DSM-IV diagnostic criteria for anorexia nervosa and bulimia nervosa, as well as provisional diagnostic criteria for binge-eating disorder, are summarized in Tables 19.1–3.

Making the diagnosis of an eating disorder is not simple. The usual practice of applying diagnostic criteria to symptoms endorsed by a patient is often not possible for these patients. Eliciting symptoms is a great clinical challenge. Anorectics are typically invested in maintaining their behaviors and are reluctant to seek help. They may not disclose or may even actively conceal their symptoms. Indeed, there is a frequent inability to recognize the severity of one's emaciation in anorexia. Anorectics commonly share a repertoire of methods to evade clinical intervention, including wearing loose clothing to conceal their frame, "water-loading," or carrying weights to falsely elevate a low weight. Although many bulimics find their symptoms genuinely distressing, they can be equally ambivalent about giving up symptoms that they see as essential to weight management or that they have come to experience as an intrapsychic solution to emotional distress. Even when they present to a clinical setting, disclosure of symptoms is frequently inhibited by shame in describing or acknowledging them. It is typical for either bulimics and anorectics to conceal their symptoms from family, friends, and physicians alike.

Diagnostic evaluation for the eating disorders requires a full psychiatric interview, with additional information from a family evaluation, primary care clinician, and dietitian. When a patient is unable or unwilling to disclose information about symptoms, relevant clinical information from family and friends proves essential. These syndromes may also be inferred from a number of laboratory and physical findings that often suggest the sequelae of weight loss or purging behaviors. While an empathic,

Table 19.1 Diagnostic criteria for anorexia nervosa

A. Refusal to maintain a body weight at or above a minimally normal weight for age and height

B. Intense fear of gaining weight or becoming fat, even though underweight

C. Disturbance in the way in which one's body weight or shape is experienced, undue influence of body weight or shape on self-evaluation, or denial of the seriousness of current low body weight

D. In postmenarcheal females, amenorrhea, i.e., the absence of at least 3 consecutive menstrual cycles

Types:
Restricting Type: no regular binge-eating or purging behavior during the current episode

Binge-Eating/Purging Type: Regular binge-eating or purging behavior during the current episode

Source: Adapted from American Psychiatric Association (1994), *Diagnostic and Statistical Manual of Mental Disorders, Fourth Edition.* Reprinted with permission. Copyright 1994 by the American Psychiatric Association.

nonjudgmental approach is helpful in overcoming hesitation to disclose owing to shame, a patient whose physical findings suggest medical compromise often needs to be confronted with the potential severity and associated risks of her condition so that appropriate limits can be set around symptoms and essential clinical data can be obtained for treatment planning.

Often a straightforward approach in history taking is quite successful. Since adolescent and young adult women can be quite sophisticated about disordered eating symptoms, they can be asked directly about weight concerns, dietary patterns, purging and other compensatory behaviors, as well as impairment in social, school, or occupational functioning. Questions should include specifics

about the range of possible symptoms and frequency, including questions regarding self-induced vomiting, the means and frequency, whether there is associated use of ipecac, and other modalities of purging.

Etiology

Sociocultural Factors

There is little doubt that the cultural value placed on thinness in Western society plays an important role in the development of eating disorders, and the prevalence of these disorders does appear to be greater in Westernized societies. Dieting is understood to be a risk factor for the devel-

Table 19.2 Diagnostic criteria for bulimia nervosa

A. Recurrent episodes of binge eating characterized by both (1) eating a larger than usual amount of food in a discrete period of time and (2) a sense of lack of control over eating during the episode

B. Recurrent inappropriate compensatory behaviors in order to prevent weight gain, including self-induced vomiting, misuse of laxatives, enemas, diuretics, or other medications, fasting, or excessive exercise

C. The binge-eating and inappropriate compensatory behaviors both occur, on average, at least twice a week for 3 months

D. Self-evaluation is unduly influenced by body shape and weight

E. The disturbance does not occur exclusively during episodes of anorexia nervosa

Types:
Purging Type: Regular use of purging behaviors (such as self-induced vomiting or misuse of laxatives, diuretics, or enemas) during the episode

Nonpurging Type: Use of inappropriate compensatory behaviors but not purging during the episode

Source: Adapted from American Psychiatric Association (1994), *Diagnostic and Statistical Manual of Mental Disorders, Fourth Edition.* Reprinted with permission. Copyright 1994 by the American Psychiatric Association.

Table 19.3 Research criteria for binge-eating disorder

A. Recurrent episodes of binge eating, characterized by both
   (1) eating, in a discrete period of time (e.g., within any 2-hour period), an amount of food that is definitely larger than most people would eat in a similar period of time under similar circumstances
   (2) a sense of lack of control over eating during the episode

B. The binge-eating episodes are associated with 3 (or more) of the following:
   • eating much more rapidly than normal
   • eating until feeling uncomfortably full
   • eating large amounts of food when not feeling physically hungry
   • eating alone because of being embarrassed by how much one is eating
   • feeling disgusted with oneself, depressed, or very guilty after overeating

C. Marked distress regarding binge eating is present

D. The binge eating occurs, on average, at least 2 days a week for 6 months

E. The binge eating is not associated with the regular use of inappropriate compensatory behaviors and does not occur exclusively during the course of anorexia nervosa or bulimia nervosa

Source: Adapted from American Psychiatric Association (1994), *Diagnostic and Statistical Manual of Mental Disorders, Fourth Edition.* Reprinted with permission. Copyright 1994 by the American Psychiatric Association.

opment of eating disorders, and it has been proposed that cultural pressures to be slim induce dieting that may increase the risk of disordered eating. Studies have demonstrated that cultural "ideals" have shifted toward a thinner, more tubular shape over the past few decades as the population as a whole has gained weight (Garner et al., 1980; Wiseman et al., 1992). Conflicts generated by cultural transition, such as changing expectations for women (Gordon, 1990), may contribute to the pathogenesis of these disorders. It is likely that other factors, such as culturally conditioned body experience (Becker and Hamburg, 1996) or body satisfaction (Pike and Walsh, 1996) play an important role in the cultural mediation of these disorders as well. The media also play an instrumental part in disseminating and routinizing culturally idealized images and practices that support the development of disordered eating (Becker and Hamburg, 1996).

Psychological Factors

Psychological dysfunction in eating disorders manifests itself in distorted attitudes, depression, early developmental failure, and family dysfunction. Anorectics and bulimics commonly show an excessive concern for achieving perfection and avoiding self-indulgence. To them, weight gain means that one is bad or out of control.

Hilde Bruch, a primary contributor to our understanding of eating disorders, relates the anorectic's sense of ineffectiveness, interoceptive disturbance, and body image disturbance to early childhood experiences. She proposes that when appropriate responses from the mother are chronically lacking, as in the case of mothers who feed their children primarily to quiet them or to make them sleep, the child does not learn to differentiate her own needs from those imposed by others. As a result, the child feels helpless. In order to sustain a connection with her mother, she feels a desperate need to comply with what she perceives to be her mother's needs. When the child grows older, she achieves feelings of competence, effectiveness, and control by rejecting her own appetitive needs and becoming thin (Bruch, 1973).

Substantial evidence indicates that the eating-disordered patient is often the family member identified as troubled in a generally disturbed family. Anorectic families are typified by enmeshment, overprotection, rigidity, lack of conflict resolution, and use of the child to diffuse parental conflict (Minuchin, Rosman, and Baker, 1978). Salvador Minuchin and others have observed that the child does in fact occupy a triangulated position between her parents. The families appear to be in deep conflict, with separation of the parents a recurrently

veiled or real threat. These conflicts are rarely acknowledged directly or resolved but instead are frequently detoured through the symptomatic child. The child's maturation threatens the balance of the family system. The anorectic's position in the family reinforces her sense of insecurity, distrust, and hyperresponsibility, as well as her fears regarding mating and sexuality.

Comorbidity between eating disorders and depression and anxiety raises the issue of whether patterns of disordered eating are a coping response to affective instability or anxiety. Data on the onset of eating and affective disorders are variable. Sometimes the affective disorder precedes the eating disorder or vice versa, and sometimes they present simultaneously. Clinically, eating-disordered symptoms often appear to serve in the management of affect; moreover, it is not uncommon to have them present in the context of other self-destructive coping mechanisms such as self-mutilation or substance abuse.

Biological Factors

Anorectic and bulimic patients have various neurochemical abnormalities. The search for a specific abnormality in anorexia is hindered by the patient's starvation state, which itself produces extensive changes in hypothalamic and metabolic functioning. Abnormalities in cerebrospinal fluid levels of 3-methoxy-4-hydroxy-phenylglycol, homovanillic acid, 5-hydroxyindoleacetic acid, and tyrosine (central nervous system metabolites) have been noted in anorexia nervosa. Nearly all these conditions become normal with weight restoration. Some hormonal alterations, however, cannot be attributed to starvation. For example, about one-fifth of anorectics lose menses prior to weight loss (Herzog and Copeland, 1985). Furthermore, the rate of cortisol production increases in anorexia and decreases in starvation.

Since serotonin is known to modulate appetitive behaviors and satiety, a number of studies have examined its role in anorexia and bulimia nervosa. Although abnormalities in central serotonin function have been investigated in the pathogenesis of anorexia, there are conflicting data concerning whether a significant serotonin abnormality may persist in weight-recovered anorectics (O'Dwyer, Lucey, and Russell, 1996; Kaye, Gwirtsman, et al., 1991), making it difficult to implicate serotonergic abnormalities in the pathogenesis of anorexia. Similarly, there is evidence of serotonergic dysregulation (reduced activity) in bulimia nervosa; whether this represents a cause or an effect of the disorder remains unclear, however (Brewerton, 1995). Nonetheless, serotonergic abnormalities, once present, may play a role in sustaining pathologic feeding behavior (Weltzin, Fernstrom, and Kaye, 1994). In fact, the efficacy of antidepressant medications in the reduction of bingeing behavior, irrespective of effects on mood, may hinge on their role in regulating one of the monoamine neurotransmitters that impact on appetitive behavior (Kaye and Weltzin, 1991).

Whether or not bulimia or anorexia nervosa may have a genetic basis remains unclear. Some studies have shown a discrepancy in concordance for anorexia between monozygotic and dizygotic twins with higher rates in the monozygotic group, which suggests a genetic component to the illness (Strober, 1991). Nevertheless, a subsequent study found that while the co-twin of a twin with anorexia was at significantly higher risk for the illness than the general population, the concordance was higher in dizygotic than monozygotic pairs, arguing for a familial component rather than a genetic one (Walters and Kendler, 1995). Other studies support a genetic basis of bulimia nervosa by twin concordance data (Strober, 1991; Kendler et al., 1991).

Treatment

Treatment of the eating disorders generally demands a multimodal, multidisciplinary team approach which includes input from 1 or more mental health professionals (e.g., a psychotherapist, a psychopharmacologist, or a family therapist), a primary care internist or pediatrician, as well as a nutritionist. Although some eating-disordered patients can benefit from treatment by a single clinician, most patients, particularly those with severe personality disorder, will require a team approach. A treatment team and plan can be identified in an initial evaluation process which may include individual and family evaluation as well as assessment of nutritional status and physical health. This plan should be presented clearly to the patient and, when appropriate, to the patient's family.

Clinicians involved on the team should communicate frequently and clearly for several reasons. First, since nondisclosure or minimalization of symptoms is common among this population, communication among team members supplements information essential to the patient's safety and treatment which might not otherwise emerge in an individual encounter. Second, certain clinical information (such as frequency or modality of purging or weight) is less accessible to particular members of the treatment team yet essential to management. Finally, splitting is common among team members. Especially when the family communication system is pathological, families tend to recreate their family environment among clinicians involved in treatment. Rather than focus on divisive issues within the family unit, the family focuses on differences of opinion among the treating clinicians and uses this information to split them. Clinicians must communicate frequently to avoid this situation and to help the families refocus their energies on restoring the patient and family to health.

The onset of these disorders generally precedes their presentation by several years, and their management is frequently complicated by a patient's resistance to engaging in treatment. Anorectic patients and their families often deny the illness, evade treatment, and engender negative reactions among medical personnel. In her extreme thinness, the anorectic feels she has found the perfect solution to her deep-seated sadness and feelings of inadequacy. Her chief complaint is that everyone is always on her back, and she wants the clinician to get those people off. Bulimic patients are distressed by their symptoms and are generally receptive to treatment, yet they often have a low tolerance for frustration and experience difficulty accepting therapeutic interventions that do not produce immediate symptomatic relief. At the same time, these patients often dread relinquishing symptoms that have perhaps served an organizing or self-soothing function for them.

Outpatient Treatment

The outpatient treatment program should be designed to meet the needs of the individual. The evaluation will guide construction of a treatment plan comprising psychotherapy, nutritional guidance, and medical monitoring, with adjuvant pharmacotherapy, family therapy, and group therapy when appropriate. It is important that both the patient and the treatment team agree on the initial plan, which minimally must include provision for safety from medical risks and self-harm. Some patients may accept some of the treatment recommendations later in the treatment despite rejecting them initially.

Psychotherapy. Individual psychotherapy is the modality clinicians most commonly prescribe for outpatient treatment. The therapist's initial task is to establish trust by acknowledging the patient's ongoing pain and recognizing the multiple determinants of the disorder (social, psychopathological, genetic, biological, behavioral, and familial). The goal of therapy is to help the patient achieve the ability to regulate herself in a more adaptive manner than through her eating behavior. The patient must uncover her own inner resources—her potential for thinking, judging, and feeling—in order to permit self-directed action.

It is often helpful for patient and therapist to view the eating disorder as a compromise solution to a set of unresolvable psychological dilemmas. These conflicts may include the simultaneous desire for autonomy and for childlike dependence, the experience of inner life as an unpredictable roller coaster, the need to feel completely in control of a body that nevertheless refuses to stop having appetites, and the confusion over sexual desire and its absolute rejection. Within a family, the anorectic may feel that her own will to be free clashes with her fear that the family will fall apart without her. During psychotherapy, the patient and the therapist recognize, define, question, and challenge erroneous assumptions and attitudes so that they can eventually modify them. They liberate conflicts from the frozen realm of the eating symptom to discuss them in the growing safety of the therapeutic relationship. The therapist needs to have the patience to proceed slowly, using small, concrete events to cast doubt on deeply held maladaptive convictions. The treatment of eating-disordered patients often requires an unusual level of flexibility on the part of the therapist, who may at times need to be quite active, speak frequently, support, encourage, educate, question, challenge, reassure, weigh, set behavioral limits, and prescribe medication all within the framework of careful, ongoing attention to the therapeutic relationship and its difficulties of transference and countertransference. The medically ill patient will require vigilant attention to safety and nutritional balance, whereas a medically stable patient may not even need to address eating behavior directly for months during an intense period of therapy. The therapist should be able to tailor his or her therapeutic style to the individual needs of the patient at a given time and resist becoming immobilized within his or her theoretical certainties.

Many patients benefit from a thorough description of anorexia nervosa or bulimic disorder. Not infrequently, they are surprised to learn that other people have had the same ideas and feelings. They may be relieved to find that, painful though their symptoms may be, the therapist can value them as partial solutions to psychological dilemmas and will not launch a single-minded crusade against them. The therapist should also be able to listen to his or her patients' concepts about the etiology and function of the eating disorder. Many patients have remarkable insight concerning the nature of their dilemma, despite its tenacity.

In the treatment of anorectics, establishing a weight contract within the first few sessions of therapy is often helpful. The continuation of therapy can be contingent on the patient's staying above a specified weight. (The therapist, for example, might say, "We can continue our attempt to understand your situation through words as long as your nutritional state is reasonably healthy; if you are at risk of death, we simply cannot talk about it.") Although anorectics are often manipulative and deceitful in their efforts to defeat a weight-gaining program, they should be reminded that the goal of therapy is not to impose weight gain but to explore ways to improve one's quality of life. Only if low weight reaches the point of peril does weight itself become the focus of therapy, and then only because it is impossible to improve one's quality of life when the risk of death by starvation is imminent. Maintaining a therapeutic position that protects life while respecting the patient's psychological need to be very thin requires considerable finesse.

Psychotherapy with the eating-disordered patient is slow and difficult. Ultimately the therapist faces the challenge of helping the patient build a new personality structure after many years of superficial existence. During the course of treatment, patients may become critically ill and require hospitalization; develop angry, devaluing transference reactions toward the therapist; suspend therapy before they are entirely well; struggle about payment and the scheduling of sessions; and force the therapist to set limits and then accuse him or her of always trying to run the patient's life. Patients may appear to improve in an attempt to placate the therapist, only to relapse in defiant rebellion. Many patients get better only after experiencing the constancy of the therapist's care through these permutations of setbacks and progress.

Specific treatment approaches. Eating-disordered symptoms respond to a variety of individual psychotherapeutic treatment approaches. Cognitive-behavioral therapy (CBT) is the best-established treatment for bulimia nervosa and shows promise for the treatment of binge-eating disorder, although it has been used less widely in anorexia nervosa, and its efficacy relative to other psychological therapies requires further study (Wilson and Fairburn, 1993). The goals of CBT are to help the patient eradicate or control the unwanted behaviors and to change the distorted cognitions the patient may have developed. CBT for bulimia comprises 3 stages over a 20-week period: (1) introduction of behavioral techniques such as self-monitoring and stimulus control; (2) identification and modification of "dysfunctional thoughts and attitudes" concerning body and eating; and (3) relapse prevention strategies (Wilson and Fairburn, 1993). Symptom reduction in bulimia nervosa with this treatment modality is impressive and includes a mean reduction of binge eating and purging of 73–93% and 77–94%, respectively, and mean remission rates of 51–71% and 36–56% for binge eating and purging, respectively (Wilson and Fairburn, 1993). The limited information available about the usefulness of combining psychotherapy with medication suggests that a combination of CBT and a tricyclic or selective serotonin-reuptake inhibitor (SSRI) may be superior to either therapy alone.

Although less studied, interpersonal therapy (IPT) has been found equally effective as CBT in the treatment of bulimia nervosa (Agras, 1991; Fairburn et al., 1993) despite their presumably working by different mechanisms. Unlike CBT, IPT does not focus on eating behavior, but rather assists the patient in exploring how interpersonal stress triggers maladaptive patterns of eating (Agras, 1991).

Psychodynamic psychotherapy is also a useful treatment modality for disordered eating. Although this modality of psychotherapy focuses on distal rather than proximal antecedents to the disordered eating, there is evidence that symptom-oriented work early in the process is often essential (Tobin, 1993). Notwithstanding the efficacy of CBT in the treatment of bulimia nervosa, many patients who present with disordered eating bring a variety of interpersonal difficulties, characterologic problems, and comorbid disorders to the therapeutic setting that may be more amenable to a psychodynamic approach. While it is appropriate to address symptom control in the therapy—especially when symptoms either are distressing or pose a medical risk—many patients are quite capable of exploring affective states, conflicts, and stressors that precipitate their symptoms and can do this best in a psychodynamic therapy.

Group therapy. Group therapy is emerging as a favored treatment modality for patients with bulimia. It may be prescribed in conjunction with other treatment or as the sole therapy for the mildly to moderately ill bulimic who feels isolated by her symptoms. Group cognitive behavioral therapy and group interpersonal therapy have been adapted for individuals with binge-eating disorder and have shown some efficacy in reducing symptoms (Bruce and Wilfley, 1996). There is also a rationale for including group treatment as an adjunctive approach in the treatment of anorexia nervosa as well since it may counteract the sense of alienation and isolation these patients experience (Piazza et al., 1983). Major models of outpatient group therapy for bulimics include psychodynamically oriented psychotherapy, cognitive-behavioral therapy, psychoeducational therapy, and self-help therapy.

Family therapy. In treating the adolescent with an eating disorder, it is frequently helpful to prescribe both individual and family therapy. Family therapy can also be a successful intervention for young adults. Usually family therapy is used as an adjunct to an individual therapy, but in one controlled trial, family therapy was actually found more effective than individual therapy alone for anorectics whose illness had begun before age 19 and was not chronic (Russell et al., 1987). There is also evidence that individual therapy can impact favorably upon family processes even when the family is not seen in therapy (Robin, Siegel, and Moye, 1995). Four treatment approaches have been applied to the family treatment of eating disorders: structural family therapy, structural-strategic therapy, systemic family therapy, and symbolic experiential family therapy.

Pharmacotherapy. Because most eating-disordered patients have substantial character pathology and psychosocial impairment, medication is rarely indicated except in the context of psychotherapy. While a number of classes of agents have been studied, there is no generally accepted pharmacologic treatment for anorexia nervosa. There is preliminary evidence that fluoxetine may be useful in preventing relapse in weight-recovered anorectics, but this requires further investigation (Walsh and Devlin, 1992).

In contrast, there is good evidence to support the role of pharmacotherapy in the management of bulimia nervosa. The most convincing data support the use of antidepressant medication to treat the symptoms of bulimia. Among the trials of antidepressants conducted, treatment with medication overall decreased binge frequency by an average of 56%, while there was an average decrease of only 11% with placebo; decrease in the frequency of self-induced vomiting appears similar to that in binge eating (Jimerson, Herzog, and Brotman, 1993). Generally, improvement occurs after 1–3 weeks of treatment in this population (Mitchell and de Zwaan, 1993). It is of note that the response of bulimic symptoms to antidepressant medication is not predicted by whether or not there is comorbid depression.

It remains unclear whether any particular agent is superior in treating this population since few data exist comparing antidepressants (Jimerson, Herzog, and Brotman, 1993), and indeed, there is evidence that a number of trials of agents may be necessary in an individual to achieve an optimal regimen (Pope et al., 1985; Walsh, 1991). Although many agents are effective in reducing symptoms, some are clearly less desirable because of their side effect profile or association with adverse events in this population. Monoamine oxidase inhibitors (MAOIs) are generally avoided as a first-line agent because of the risks associated with dietary indiscretion; there is some evidence, nonetheless, that phenelzine may be the most appropriate agent for bulimic patients with comorbid atypical depression (Rothschild et al., 1994). Bupropion is relatively contraindicated in this population because of an associated risk of seizure (Horne et al., 1988), and trazodone has been associated with delirium in bulimic patients (Damlouji and Ferguson, 1984).

The most promising family of medications for the treatment of bulimia is the SSRIs, since they are generally well tolerated by patients. Fluoxetine is the only agent to date that has been approved by the Food and Drug Administration (FDA) for the treatment of bulimia nervosa. It has been shown effective in diminishing bulimic symptoms, with a dosage of 60 mg daily superior to 20 mg daily (Fluoxetine Bulimia Nervosa Collaborative Study Group, 1992). Among the tricyclic antidepressants, imipramine and desipramine are the most effective. There is evidence that desipramine is most effective if continued for at least 24 weeks; efficacy is also enhanced by combining it with CBT (Agras et al., 1994). Despite short-term efficacy of desipramine in the treatment of bulimia nervosa, limitations to long-term efficacy are suggested by considerable relapse rates (Walsh et al., 1991).

The pharmacologic treatment of binge-eating disorder is emerging. Preliminary data would suggest that SSRIs, tricyclic antidepressants, and appetite suppressants may be effective in the reduction of binge eating.

Guidelines for prescribing psychotropic medication to bulimic patients include the following steps:

1. Medication should be prescribed in the context of a supportive psychotherapeutic relationship for 2 reasons: first, patients will find it easier to adhere to a medication trial if ambivalence toward both the medication and control of the symptoms can be explored; and second, there is evidence that a combination of medication and therapy is superior to medication alone.
2. Medication should be dosed on a schedule when it is most likely to be absorbed, in other words, at times when a patient is unlikely to purge.
3. Several drug trials may be necessary before an optimal regimen is identified.
4. Comorbid disorders (i.e., depression or anxiety) should be treated when appropriate.

Medical monitoring. As a general rule, the eating-disordered patient should be followed by an internist or pediatrician for any potential complications of malnutrition or purging. Given the chronicity of these illnesses, medical monitoring for potential complications and deterioration is essential to a comprehensive care plan. The role of education is critical in this patient population. For example, patients are often not aware of the sometimes irreversible or life-threatening complications of their symptoms. They can often be steered away from behaviors that are especially dangerous, such as ipecac use to induce vomiting, and encouraged to report frequency and intensity of purging behaviors. In addition, anticipating transient unpleasant side effects associated with cessation of disordered behavior (e.g., constipation, fluid retention, and bloating associated with laxative withdrawal or the early satiety and exaggerated postprandial fullness with refeeding; see Mehler, 1996a) helps the patient adhere to the treatment plan.

In the outpatient setting, the eating-disordered patient should have a full physical examination and should be seen regularly for weight, blood pressure, and pulse readings—all parameters that can help the clinician assess whether inpatient care may be indicated. Serum electrolytes and an electrocardiogram should also be obtained at the outset of treatment as well as when indicated by any initial abnormalities, chronic malnutrition, or purging symptoms in follow-up. Serum potassium should be followed regularly for the patient who purges, since most modalities of purging risk depletion of potassium. On the initial evaluation, a complete blood count, renal function tests, and a urinalysis should also be obtained, with the addition of calcium, magnesium, phosphorus, amylase, and liver function for patients with either severe symptoms or malnutrition; these studies should be repeated as indicated by the clinical situation (American Psychiatric Association, 1992). Serum glucose should be followed in anorectic patients, since hypoglycemia is common in this population and severe hypoglycemia is associated with sudden death (Mehler, 1996a). Other studies, such as hormonal assays or bone densitometry, may be indicated if amenorrhea is present. Patients who induce vomiting should have close follow-up dental care as well because of dental caries associated with repeated vomiting.

Hospitalization

While outpatient treatment for eating disorders is generally adequate and even preferable, inpatient or partial hospitalization will be an essential step in the treatment for some anorectic and bulimic patients. Partial hospitalization is an attractive option when patients require intensive support to achieve control over symptoms that are not responding adequately. In some cases partial hospitalization may provide support through the transition from inpatient to outpatient care.

A decision to hospitalize a patient is based on consideration of medical or psychiatric risk or failure to respond to outpatient management. Since medical risk is likely to be more gradual than acute in this population of patients, the team will find it helpful to set the parameters for hospitalization well before it is actually necessary. For example, the team might decide on a "hospitalizable weight" for a patient—that is, a weight at which the patient knows she must enter the hospital. Such parameters should be agreed upon by the entire team and made quite explicit with a patient; in some cases it is helpful for the patient and team members to have a written or verbal treatment contract for the patient to refer to in such a situation. These parameters need to be adhered to firmly by the team, both for safety and because the patient may be looking for containment and may be unable to articulate the need other than by transgressing her contract.

The risk of mortality from anorexia is substantially higher when body weight is at or below 60% of standard weight (Okabe, 1993), but most clinicians agree that hospitalization should occur in the setting of rapid weight loss, or at least when an individual's weight is at or below 75% of ideal body weight. When weight restoration is the goal of hospitalization, the inpatient treatment program requires a nutritional rehabilitation protocol to which all treating clinicians can agree. The physician must explain the treatment regimen in detail to the patient prior to hospitalization. Further, when appropriate, he or she should tell the patient that anorexia nervosa is a potentially life-threatening illness and that the purpose of the treatment program is to prevent her death. It is essential that staff members remind themselves, as well as the patient and her family, that the administration of a feeding regimen is a lifesaving act and not a punishment.

At the time of admission, the physician should establish with the patient a target weight for discharge. Preliminary evidence suggests that anorectics who are discharged while still severely underweight are more symptomatic and at greater risk for rehospitalization for their eating disorder than those who achieve normal weight prior to discharge (Baran, Weltzin, and Kaye, 1995). Minimally, the goal weight should allow resumption of normal reproductive function and reversal of bone demineralization (American Psychiatric Association, 1992). The suc-

cess of the protocol depends on the ability of the staff to be open, honest, and firm about implementing the treatment program.

References

Agras, W. S. 1991. Nonpharmacologic treatments of bulimia nervosa. *J. Clin. Psychiatry* 52(suppl.):29–33.

Agras, W. S., E. M. Rossiter, B. Arnow, C. F. Telch, S. D. Raeburn, B. Bruce, and L. M. Koran. 1994. One-year follow-up of psychological and pharmacologic treatments for bulimia nervosa. *J. Clin. Psychiatry* 55:179–183.

American Psychiatric Association. 1992. Practice guideline for eating disorders. *Am. J. Psychiatry* 150:207–228.

——— 1994. *Diagnostic and Statistical Manual of Mental Disorders.* 4th ed. Washington, D.C.: American Psychiatric Association.

Baran, S. A., T. E. Weltzin, and W. H. Kaye. 1995. Low discharge weight and outcome in anorexia nervosa. *Am. J. Psychiatry* 152:1070–72.

Beck, D., R. Casper, and A. Andersen. 1996. Truly late onset of eating disorders: a study of 11 cases averaging 60 years of age at presentation. *International Journal of Eating Disorders* 20:389–395.

Becker, A. E., and P. Hamburg. 1996. Culture, the media, and eating disorders. *Harvard Rev. Psychiatry* 4:163–167.

Brewerton, T. D. 1995. Toward a unified theory of serotonin dysregulation in eating and related disorders. *Psychoneuroendocrinology* 20:561–590.

Bruce, B., and D. Wilfley. 1996. Binge eating among the overweight population: a serious and prevalent problem. *Journal of the American Dietetic Association* 96:58–61.

Bruch, H. 1973. *Eating disorders: obesity, anorexia nervosa, and the person within.* New York: Basic Books.

Carlat, D. J., and C. A. Camargo. 1991. Review of bulimia nervosa in males. *Am. J. Psychiatry* 148:831–843.

Collings, S., and M. King. 1994. Ten-year follow-up of 50 patients with bulimia nervosa. *British Journal of Psychiatry* 164:80–87.

Crago, M., C. M. Shisslak, and L. S. Estes. 1996. Eating disturbances among American minority groups: a review. *International Journal of Eating Disorders* 19:239–248.

Crisp, A. H., J. S. Callender, C. Halek, and L. K. G. Hsu. 1992. Long-term mortality in anorexia nervosa: a 20-year follow-up of the St. George's and Aberdeen cohorts. *British Journal of Psychiatry* 161:104–107.

Damlouji, N. F., and J. M. Ferguson. 1984. Trazodone-induced delirium in bulimic patients. *Am. J. Psychiatry* 141:434.

Drewnowski, A., S. A. Hopkins, and R. C. Kessler. 1988. The prevalence of bulimia nervosa in the U. S. college student population. *American Journal of Public Health* 78:1322–25.

Evans, D. S. 1968. Acute dilatation and spontaneous rupture of the stomach. *Br. J. Surg.* 55:940–942.

Fairburn, C. G., and S. J. Beglin. 1990. Studies of the epidemiology of bulimia nervosa. *Am. J. Psychiatry* 147:401–408.

Fairburn, C. G., R. Jones, R. C. Peveler, R. A. Hope, and M. O'Connor. 1993. Psychotherapy and bulimia nervosa. *Arch. Gen. Psychiatry* 50:419–428.

Fisher, M., N. H. Golden, D. K. Katzman, R. E. Kreipe, J. Rees, J. Schebendach, G. Sigman, S. Ammerman, and H. M. Hoberman. 1995. Eating disorders in adolescents: a background paper. *Journal of Adolescent Health* 16:420–437.

Fluoxetine Bulimia Nervosa Collaborative Study Group. 1992. Fluoxetine in the treatment of bulimia nervosa: a multicenter, placebo-controlled, double-blind trial. *Arch. Gen. Psychiatry* 49:139–147.

Gard, M. C. E., and C. P. Freeman. 1996. The dismantling of a myth: a review of eating disorders and socioeconomic status. *International Journal of Eating Disorders* 20:1–12.

Garner, D. M., P. E. Garfinkel, D. Schwartz, and M. Thompson. 1980. Cultural expectations of thinness in women. *Psychological Reports* 47:483–491.

Gordon, R. A. 1990. *Anorexia and bulimia: anatomy of a social epidemic.* Cambridge: Blackwell Publishers.

Halmi, K. A., R. C. Casper, E. D. Eckert, S. C. Goldberg, and J. M. Davis. 1979. Unique features associated with the age of onset of anorexia nervosa. *Psychiatr. Res.* 1:209–215.

Herpertz-Dahlmann, B. M., C. Wewetzer, E. Schulz, and H. Remschmidt. 1996. Course and outcome in adolescent anorexia nervosa. *International Journal of Eating Disorders* 19:335–345.

Herzog, D. B. 1982. Bulimia: the secretive syndrome. *Psychosomatics* 23:481–487.

Herzog, D. B., and P. M. Copeland. 1985. Eating disorders. *N. Engl. J. Med.* 313:295–303.

Hoek, H. 1995. The distribution of eating disorders. In *Eating disorders and obesity,* ed. K. D. Brownell and C. G. Fairburn. London: Guilford Press. 207–211.

Horne, R. L., J. M. Ferguson, H. G. Pope Jr., J. I. Hudson, C. B. Lineberry, J. Ascher, and A. Cato. 1988. Treatment of bulimia with bupropion: a multicenter controlled trial. *J. Clin. Psychiatry* 49:262–266.

Jimerson, D. C., D. B. Herzog, and A. W. Brotman. 1993. Pharmacologic approaches in the treatment of eating disorders. *Harvard Review of Psychiatry* 1:82–93.

Kaye, W. H., and T. E. Weltzin. 1991. Serotonin activity in anorexia and bulimia nervosa: relationship to the modu-

lation of feeding and mood. *J. Clin. Psychiatry* 52(suppl.):41–48.

Kaye, W. H., H. E. Gwirtsman, D. T. George, and M. H. Ebert. 1991. Altered serotonin activity in anorexia nervosa after long-term weight restoration. *Arch. Gen. Psychiatry* 48:556–562.

Kaye, W. H., T. E. Weltzin, L. K. G. Hsu, and C. M. Bulik. 1991. An open trial of fluoxetine in patients with anorexia nervosa. *J. Clin. Psychiatry* 52:464–471.

Kendler, K. S., C. MacLean, M. Neale, R. Kessler, A. Heath, and L. Eaves. 1991. The genetic epidemiology of bulimia nervosa. *Am. J. Psychiatry* 148:1627–37.

Mehler, P. S. 1996a. Eating disorders: anorexia nervosa. *Hospital Practice* 31(1):109–118.

———— 1996b. Eating disorders: bulimia nervosa. *Hospital Practice* 31(2):107–126.

Minuchin, S., B. L. Rosman, and L. Baker. 1978. *Psychosomatic families: anorexia nervosa in context.* Cambridge, Mass.: Harvard University Press.

Mitchell, J. E., and M. de Zwaan. 1993. Pharmacological treatments of binge eating. In *Binge eating: nature, assessment, and treatment,* ed C. G. Fairburn and G. T. Wilson. New York: Guilford Press. 250–269.

Mitchell, J. E., R. L. Pyle, D. Hatsukami, G. Goff, D. Glotter, and J. Harper. 1989. A 2–5 year follow-up study of patients treated for bulimia. *International Journal of Eating Disorders* 8:157–165.

O'Dwyer, A.-M., J. V. Lucey, and G. F. M. Russell. 1996. Serotonin activity in anorexia nervosa after long-term weight restoration: response to D-fenfluramine challenge. *Psychological Medicine* 26:353–359.

Okabe, K. 1993. Assessment of emaciation in relation to threat to life in anorexia nervosa. *Internal Medicine* 32:837–842.

Norring, C. E. A., and S. S. Sohlberg. 1993. Outcome, recovery, relapse, and mortality across six years in patients with clinical eating disorders. *Acta Psychiatrica Scandinavica* 87:437–444.

Piazza, E., J. D. Carni, J. Kelly, and S. K. Plante. 1983. Group psychotherapy for anorexia nervosa. *Journal of the American Academy of Child Psychiatry* 22:276–278.

Pike, K. M., and B. T. Walsh. 1996. Ethnicity and eating disorders: implications for incidence and treatment. *Psychopharmacology Bulletin* 32:265–274.

Pope, H. G., J. I. Hudson, J. M. Jonas, and D. Yurgelun-Todd. 1985. Antidepressant treatment of bulimia: a two-year follow-up study. *Journal of Clinical Psychopharmacology* 5:320–327.

Robin, A. L., P. T. Siegel, and A. Moye. 1995. Family versus individual therapy for anorexia: impact on family conflict. *International Journal of Eating Disorders* 17:313–322.

Rothschild, R., M. H. Quitkin, F. M. Quitkin, J. W. Stewart, K. Ocepak-Welikson, P. J. McGrath, and E. Tricamo. 1994. A double-blind placebo-controlled comparison of phenelzine and imipramine in the treatment of bulimia in atypical depressives. *International Journal of Eating Disorders* 15:1–9.

Russell, G. F., G. I. Szmukler, C. Dare, and M. A. Eisler. 1987. An evaluation of family therapy in anorexia nervosa. *Arch. Gen. Psychiatry* 44:1047–56.

Shikora, S. A., P. N. Benotti, and R. A. Forse. 1994. Surgical treatment of obesity. In *Obesity: pathophysiology, psychology, and treatment,* ed. G. L. Blackburn and B. S. Kanders. New York: Chapman & Hall.

Shisslak, C. M., M. Crago, and L. S. Estes. 1995. The spectrum of eating disturbances. *International Journal of Eating Disorders* 18:209–219.

Spitzer, R. L., S. Yanovski, T. Wadden, R. Wing, M. D. Marcus, A. Stunkard, M. Devlin, J. Mitchell, D. Hasin, and R. L. Horne. 1993. Binge eating disorder: its further validation in a multisite study. *International Journal of Eating Disorders* 13:137–153.

Steinhausen, H.-C. 1995. Treatment and outcome of adolescent anorexia nervosa. *Horm. Res.* 43:168–170.

Strober, M. 1991. Family-genetic studies of eating disorders. *J. Clin. Psychiatry* 52(suppl):9–12.

Sullivan, P. F. 1995. Mortality in anorexia nervosa. *Am. J. Psychiatry* 152:1073–74.

Tobin, D. L. 1993. Psychodynamic psychotherapy and binge eating. In *Binge eating,* ed. C. G. Fairburn and G. T. Wilson. 287–313.

Walsh, B. T. 1991. Psychopharmacologic treatment of bulimia nervosa. *J. Clin. Psychiatry* 52(suppl.):35–38.

Walsh, B. T., and M. J. Devlin. 1992. The pharmacologic treatment of eating disorders. *Psychiatric Clinics of North America* 15:149–160.

Walsh, B. T., B. A. Hadigan, M. J. Devlin, M. Gladis, and S. P. Roose. 1991. Long-term outcome of antidepressant treatment for bulimia nervosa. *Am. J. Psychiatry* 148:1206–12.

Walters, E. E., and K. S. Kendler. 1995. Anorexia nervosa and anorexic-like syndromes in a population-based female twin sample. *Am. J. Psychiatry* 152:64–71.

Weltzin, T. E., M. H. Fernstrom, and W. H. Kaye. 1994. Serotonin and bulimia nervosa. *Nutrition Reviews* 52:399–408.

Wilson, G. T., and C. G. Fairburn. 1993. Cognitive treatments for eating disorders. *Journal of Consulting and Clinical Psychology* 61:261–269.

Wiseman, C. V., J. G. Gray, J. E. Mosimann, and A. H. Aherns. 1992. Cultural expectations of thinness in women: an update. *International Journal of Eating Disorders* 11:85–89.

Recommended Reading

American Psychiatric Association. 1993. Practice guideline for eating disorders. *Am. J. Psychiatry* 150:207–228.

Brownell, K. D., and C. G. Fairburn, eds. 1995. *Eating disorders and obesity.* New York: Guilford Press.

Fairburn, C. G., and G. T. Wilson, eds. 1993. *Binge eating: nature, assessment, and treatment.* New York: Guilford Press.

PART FOUR

Principles of Treatment and Management

W. W. MEISSNER

The Psychotherapies: Individual, Family, and Group

From its earliest beginnings, when the Viennese physician Josef Breuer and his younger colleague Sigmund Freud (1895) began their investigations of the therapy of hysterical illnesses, the idea that physical pains and dysfunctions could be alleviated by talking—the "talking cure"—seemed revolutionary. In our own day, when the phenomenon of psychotherapy seems so solidly embedded in our cultural matrix, we do not often pause to consider the mystery of it. But the idea of remedying the discomforts, anxieties, depressions, and failures of development and adjustment by merely talking seems wondrous and challenges our understanding.

From his first observations of the removal of a hysterical symptom solely through verbal communication between patient and physician in his treatment of the now famous case of Anna O., Breuer made the momentous discovery that both physical and psychological symptoms could effectively be removed when the patient, under hypnosis, verbalized thoughts and feelings related to them. His observations set the stage for Freud's investigations that led to the development of psychoanalysis and formulation of some of the technical and theoretical concepts underlying major forms of psychotherapy practiced today.

Psychotherapy as a technical term has come to acquire a broad and nonspecific meaning referring to any form of communication between a psychotherapist and a patient which involves a relationship between them and some form of communication for the purpose of remedying whatever disturbance, physical or psychic, the patient brings for treatment. The number of persons involved, either as treaters or as patients, is left open, as is the determination of the modality and techniques deemed to be therapeutic. This broad definition encompasses a wide variety of therapies that differ in intensity and duration—ranging from hypnosis, Gestalt therapy, reality therapy, logotherapy, psychodrama, and transactional analysis to supportive therapy, brief psychotherapy, group therapy, marital therapy, and psychoanalysis.

Although many forms of psychotherapy are practiced today, this chapter discusses only the most representative forms. Classical psychoanalysis and psychoanalytic psychotherapy, for example, are two closely related types of therapy employing psychoanalytic concepts and techniques to modify human behavior; I will discuss them together, differentiating between them when suitable. This form of therapy is applicable to a broad continuum of emotional disorders, including neuroses, personality disorders, and the reconstituted psychoses (in patients no longer overtly psychotic). Behavior therapy is discussed in Chapter 22.

To evaluate and treat patients with emotional disorders, the clinician must have a solid grounding not only in various forms of psychopathology but also in major forms of psychotherapy. Only then can he direct the patient to the form of therapy most effective in treating his disorder. Psychotherapy is a serious undertaking with enormous potential for harm as well as for healing. It must therefore be practiced only by professionals with solid understanding of the limits of their training and experience and the limited potential of their discipline and skill to serve therapeutic objectives. An inexperienced therapist ought always to conduct therapy under the supervision of a more experienced clinician. Even more experienced therapists are well advised to seek consultation from more experienced colleagues when they are brought to the limits of their resources in treating difficult cases.

General Principles

Before discussing specific techniques of psychotherapy—techniques best mastered through closely supervised work with individual patients—we shall consider some dimensions of the therapeutic process common to all forms of psychotherapy: (1) the relationship between diagnosis and the most suitable form of therapy, (2) the therapeutic relationship, (3) defenses and resistance, (4) therapeutic objectives and goals, and (5) the ethical issues embedded in the therapeutic experience.

Diagnostic Concerns

Diagnosis plays an important role in all aspects of the therapeutic process. The therapist must determine what the nature of the patient's difficulties is and what capacity the patient has for successfully undertaking any projected course of therapy. In many patients for whom individual psychotherapy is indicated, a major discrimination lies between more intensive forms of expressive psychotherapy and more supportive or short-term forms. The expressive forms rely on a degree of regression to mobilize sources of unconscious conflict and draw them into conscious awareness. Supportive psychotherapy tends to work more directly with conscious material and makes less of an attempt to challenge the patient's defenses, but offers forms of support to the ego and facilitates the efforts of the patient to deal with issues and problems in the here-and-now. The therapist's diagnostic impression guides him not only in his determination of the most suitable form of treatment during the initial evaluation, but also in his immediate moment-to-moment interactions with the patient throughout the course of therapy. Last but not least, diagnosis helps both therapist and patient decide when therapy must end. That decision requires a diagnostic evaluation of the extent to which therapeutic goals have been achieved and the degree to which changes in the patient represent an enduring achievement that will not undergo dissolution after treatment stops.

Because no single form of therapy is appropriate for all patients, the therapist must make important diagnostic distinctions in deciding on the most effective form of treatment. Although his decision may leave room for discussion and difference of opinion, this basic principle holds: any scientific approach to the treatment of emotional disorders must be based on detailed knowledge of the efficacy of specific forms of therapy for specific forms of psychopathology. The therapist must decide which patients are capable of sustaining and profiting from particular forms of therapy. In addition, psychotherapy, even given the broad range of its forms and modalities, is inappropriate for some patients. Such patients may be treated by a variety of somatic therapies and/or management techniques. Ideally, the majority of these patients can be brought to a point at which psychotherapy becomes useful and appropriate.

Although the therapist begins to develop his diagnostic impression during the initial evaluation of the patient (see Chapters 1, 2, and 3), he continues to refine and modify this impression as long as the therapy continues. The accuracy and sensitivity of the therapist's diagnosis contribute in some measure to his therapeutic effectiveness. In establishing his diagnosis, the clinician avoids simply attaching a diagnostic label to the patient, fitting him into the appropriate category from the American Psychiatric Association's *Diagnostic and Statistical Manual of Mental Disorders,* fourth edition (DSM-IV). Not only do numbers of patients fit poorly into these categories, but also this relatively descriptive and multiple axis–oriented method of categorizing illness contributes more to the need for classification and record keeping than to psychotherapeutic utility. Diagnosis, in a more clinically relevant and refined sense, and in the hands of a skilled clinician, empathically captures aspects of the patient's inner world and leads to increased understanding of the patient's conflicts, anxieties, affects, strengths, and aspirations. Throughout the therapeutic process, therefore, the therapist refines his diagnosis by observing and assessing the patient's accessibility, his level of anxiety or depression or other affective states, his levels of regression and resistance, his defenses, and his readiness for therapeutic intervention.

The skilled clinician recognizes that during the course of therapy the patient's inner world undergoes constant modification. Recognizing and evaluating these changes helps the therapist to determine the dosage and timing of his therapeutic interventions. Because these factors are always critical, the therapist's capacity to evaluate accurately the patient's state of mind is a major contributing factor to his effectiveness. Hence he must be able to evaluate the quality, nature, and intensity of the therapist-patient relationship. This capacity, though important in all phases of therapy, is particularly significant during the final stages, when therapeutic goals must be evaluated and the all-important mutual decision to terminate is made. Thus the diagnostic process contributes to all stages of therapy, from the initial evaluation, through the sometimes long and tedious phases of alleviating symptoms and resolving conflicts, to the decision to bring therapy to a close.

The Therapeutic Relationship

To a degree, psychotherapy follows the medical model, both in its emphasis on diagnosis and in the significance it attributes to the relationship between therapist and patient. It differs from the general medical approach, however, in that the therapist-patient relationship becomes the primary factor in the treatment (see the discussion of the therapist-patient relationship in Chapter 1). The quality and nature of the relationship can enhance or severely impair the potential for effective therapeutic intervention. Thus the skilled therapist makes specific interventions only in terms of his evaluation of the overall dynamics of his relationship with his patient. The therapeutic relationship can be analyzed in terms of 3 significant components: therapeutic alliance, transference and its correlative countertransference, and the real relation. This triad forms the 3 legs of the therapeutic stool: they are all concurrently and consistently operative within the therapeutic situation and the therapeutic relation. They come into play in different forms and to different degrees in all forms of psychotherapy, and provide the essential constituents of the therapeutic process and of therapeutic effectiveness. Although these processes are at work in all psychotherapy, they are particularly important in individual forms of therapy. I will undertake a more detailed treatment of each component in discussing individual psychotherapy below.

Defenses and Resistance

Resistance comprises all those elements and forces within the patient, both conscious and unconscious, that oppose the treatment process. The therapist may encounter resistance in all forms of therapy expressed as lack of cooperation with therapeutic efforts or other indirect forms of inhibiting or countering therapeutic effectiveness. But in the individual psychotherapies, such resistances are addressed directly and worked on as part of the therapeutic regimen. Despite the patient's wish for treatment, he may find himself reacting to internal forces opposing therapeutic progress. The therapeutic process tends to shift the patient's inner psychic equilibrium and to create anxiety in him. Through resistance he mobilizes his defensive resources to diminish anxiety and maintain internal equilibrium. Because the therapist, by his interventions, provokes this disequilibrium, the patient unconsciously blames the therapist and the therapy for the anxiety he suffers. Consequently his ego mobilizes defenses that act to resist or oppose the therapeutic process.

In all forms of individual psychotherapy, the therapist must make a critical decision: should he leave the patient's resistances intact, or should he try to reduce them? If he attempts to reduce these resistances by bringing them into awareness, his efforts may arouse extreme anxiety and induce excessive regression in certain patients. When this happens, he must change direction, at least temporar-

ily, and leave the patient's defensive organization intact. In better-integrated and better-functioning patients, in whom his efforts do not produce these untoward effects to an excessive degree, the therapist directs his efforts to undermining the resistance in order to promote therapeutic regression, unmask deeper material, and help the patient to attain additional insight.

Each patient has, in the course of his development and life experience, evolved a repertoire of defenses organized to fend off anxiety or other dysphoric affects and to maintain the stability and integration of the self. In considering the patient's resistances, therefore, the therapist must be sensitive to the patient's capacity for dealing with and resolving the resistance without being overwhelmed. The therapist's respect for the patient's defenses and resistances is especially important in the initial phase of therapy, particularly in establishing a secure therapeutic alliance. If the patient observes this sensitive respect in the therapist, he may be more willing to form an alliance. If the patient's resistance precludes the formation of an alliance, however, the therapist may have no choice but to deal with the resistance at the outset by confrontation or interpretation (discussed later). When to support the patient's defenses and when to confront and attempt to resolve them are questions that challenge the diagnostic skills and empathic sensitivity of every therapist.

Therapeutic Objectives and Goals

Progress in therapy is difficult to assess if either therapist or patient does not have clearly in mind the goals to be achieved. Therapeutic objectives are therefore an important factor in the therapeutic interaction. Therapist and patient should have a clear idea of what they are looking for in the therapy and how they are to attain it. The therapeutic goals should be correlated with the diagnosis and motivation of the patient, the motivation of the therapist, and other practical considerations. When setting therapeutic objectives with the patient, the therapist must consider a number of determinants. The patient's diagnosis limits the kind and extent of therapy prescribed. Since diagnosis is an ongoing process, the therapeutic objectives are similarly open and modifiable. In addition, the patient's motivation must be considered. For many patients the achievement of symptomatic relief or the resolution of an immediate crisis is the sole objective. The therapist's zeal must therefore be tempered by an awareness of the patient's motivation and therapeutic needs. Therapist and patient arrive at therapeutic objectives by mutual agreement, never by unilateral decision. Both must keep in mind that therapeutic goals are not the same as life goals.

Often enough, attaining therapeutic goals is only a step toward the further attainment of life goals. Such a distinction often becomes crucial in reaching a decision to terminate.

Therapeutic objectives may range from narrowly focused and short-term goals, such as symptom relief or crisis resolution, to long-term objectives, such as profound characterological change and resolution of the patient's basic conflicts—or, more realistically, reduction in the intensity of these conflicts. In some cases the goal may be merely to provide a supportive relationship, to sustain the patient during a particular crisis or period of stress or in making a crucial life decision. Supportive efforts may be limited in time or may extend over a long period, particularly with patients whose capacity for therapeutic work and for adequate functioning without a sustaining therapeutic relationship is limited. Certain fragile personalities function relatively well when provided with a supportive substitute ego in the therapist.

Goals set at the beginning of therapy may of course be modified or replaced by new ones as therapy progresses. Patients, for example, often come into treatment because of an acute crisis or an exacerbation of symptoms that resolve after a short period of therapy. During the therapeutic work, however, they uncover deeper personality dysfunctions or conflicts, which they decide must also be resolved. This decision leads therapist and patient to reassess and refocus the therapeutic objectives to longer-term perspectives and more extensive personality change. In regard to therapeutic goals, D. W. Winnicott (1965) distinguished management from treatment. In the management of patients, he suggested that the goal was to do as little as possible in dealing with the patient's difficulties; in treatment, however, the goal was to accomplish as much as possible for and with the patient. Management involves a limited, short-term objective, whereas treatment involves a more extensive, long-term goal.

In setting goals, the therapist must also consider his own motivation. Lack of interest in treating a particular patient can undermine the effectiveness of treatment. Other considerations include financial resources (the patient may not be able to afford extensive or intensive treatment with a private therapist but may qualify for such treatment at a community psychiatric clinic with scaled fees), as well as available therapy time and the limits of the therapist's skills or training. The effect of the patient's financial circumstances on therapeutic objectives is becoming a more significant problem with the increase in prepaid treatment plans and forms of third-party payment.

In summary, the therapeutic objectives are established early in therapy by mutual agreement and must be reviewed and modified throughout the course of therapy. In this way the therapist and patient can decide which old goals are no longer feasible, choose new goals on the basis of what has been uncovered during the therapeutic process, assess overall therapeutic progress, and establish the best time to terminate.

Ethical Issues

The psychotherapeutic enterprise is an ethical undertaking in every respect and has embedded in it a therapeutic morality as an essential constituent. The discussion of these ethical issues belongs more properly to the therapeutic alliance, but I focus on them here since they are general issues that pervade all forms of therapy. Ethical principles require that therapy be conducted with openness, candor, honesty, and integrity without compromise. Nothing should take place in the therapeutic interactions that the patient is not informed about or to which he does not give his consent. There is no room for deception, trickery, or withholding or concealing of information.

In addition, specific ethical issues can be discussed under the headings of values, confidentiality, and responsibility. Values are an integral aspect of the therapeutic interaction. There are values inherent in the therapeutic structure itself, and there are values that are brought to that framework by both therapist and patient. The inherent values have to do with the focus on open and honest inquiry for the purpose of gaining self-understanding and insight, the insistence on the validity of the patient's authentic personality—the assumption that in every human being there is a core selfhood that if allowed free and unconflicted expression would provide the basis for creative, adaptive, and productive living—and finally the value of values, that is, a basic commitment to the proposition that values are an integral aspect of the patient's personality and capacity to function meaningfully and adaptively in the world. These inherent values guide and inspire the therapeutic effort, in the first instance in the therapist, but increasingly as therapy progresses and exercises its effects, in the patient as well. The ultimate internalization of these and other operative therapeutic values is an aspect of therapeutic outcome and change.

In addition to the values inherent in the process, both therapist and patient bring their respective value systems into the therapeutic interaction. The therapist operates under the ethical constraint that he will not impose or otherwise induce his personal values on the patient; but at the same time his personal values are operative within the therapeutic situation by reason of the fact that his participation is a function of his total personality, including his value system. The same is true of the patient, but with a different emphasis and perspective. To the extent that his personal values are involved in his pathology, they may come under scrutiny and be open to therapeutic exploration and modification. This requires not only that the process be engaged in with willing and free commitment, but also that the exploration and acquisition of more constructive and less neurotically determined values be conducted without ethical or moral pressures or suasions of any kind. It is in this fundamental sense that the therapeutic encounter can be said to be value-free, but not in the sense that it is not concerned with or engaged in the understanding, processing, and modification of values.

Basic issues of confidentiality and responsibility pervade the whole realm of psychotherapy and are particularly important in individual psychotherapy. Confidentiality is an essential part of the therapeutic contract and of an effective therapeutic alliance. Consequently the therapist must resist intrusions into the privacy of the therapeutic relationship from a variety of sources, including family members, institutions, civil authorities, and—quite pressingly and increasingly—third-party insurance carriers. Limited space makes it impossible to resolve here all the complex issues of confidentiality; one must note, however, that it is an area of profound conflicting interests and that infringement of confidentiality unavoidably undermines the therapeutic alliance. Otherwise legitimate interests in peer review and the demands of fiscal constraint have increasingly created pressures for impinging on and diluting the confidentiality of the psychotherapy relation, to the detriment and undermining of therapeutic essentials. How these conflicting demands and requirements are to be reconciled in our society remains to be seen.

The second important ethical issue is responsibility, embracing both the therapist's responsibility to the patient, spelled out in the *therapeutic contract*—an informal verbal agreement to work together within the confines of the therapist-patient relationship toward the therapeutic goals, and enacted in the therapeutic alliance—and the patient's responsibility for the process and its outcome. In all psychotherapy, the therapist's ultimate commitment to the welfare of his patient governs and directs his therapeutic interventions toward what he understands to be ultimately in the patient's best interest. This principle implies that the therapist always uses his therapeutic skills to promote and accomplish for his patient the most effective course of treatment.

The patient's participation in the therapeutic process also involves a specific responsibility. In committing himself to a therapeutic process, he assumes a responsibility to participate productively, work cooperatively with the therapist, come to appointments on time, pay the agreed fee regularly and responsibly, and involve himself as effectively as he can in the therapeutic work. Failure to accept these responsibilities breaches the therapeutic contract and impedes therapeutic progress. In summary, these ethical dimensions of the therapeutic relationship cannot be compromised without undermining the therapeutic structure and thereby the effectiveness of therapy.

Individual Psychotherapies

Psychoanalytic Psychotherapy

Psychoanalytic psychotherapy derives its theory from the psychoanalytic model, but it should be adequately distinguished from classical psychoanalysis, a more intensive form of expressive-exploratory individual psychotherapy, on the one hand, and more limited and supportive psychotherapy, on the other hand.

In general, *psychoanalysis* strives for the most intense and all-encompassing resolution of the patient's conflicts and revision of his personality structure. *Psychoanalytic psychotherapy* aims at symptom reduction and the adaptive functioning of the patient; it undertakes less profound structural and personality modifications. Psychoanalytic psychotherapy is usually conducted face-to-face rather than with the use of the psychoanalytic couch as in psychoanalysis proper. The therapist is more active, allowing a briefer time lapse prior to his interventions, in contrast to the analyst, who employs indefinite delay to foster the maximum tolerable regression and the emergence of unconscious conflict. While analysis focuses on the relationship between analyst and patient and its emotional tensions, psychoanalytic psychotherapy tends to emphasize the patient's life situation. Consequently the relationship between therapist and patient in psychoanalytic psychotherapy has more definitive boundaries and is usually less intense than in the analytic situation.

Psychoanalytic psychotherapy, as an insight-oriented form of expressive therapy, can be distinguished from more supportive psychotherapies—therapies more concerned with bolstering ego defenses and minimizing regression and anxiety. Supportive psychotherapy will be discussed later in this chapter.

Indications. Criteria for patients optimally suited for psychoanalytic psychotherapy roughly parallel those for psychoanalysis itself. When conflicts are deeply embedded or have a long-standing characterological quality, psychoanalysis is probably the treatment of choice. The question of whether psychoanalytic psychotherapy or psychoanalysis is more suitable for a given patient is not only a difficult matter of clinical judgment but also often open to discussion. The criteria for analyzability include: (1) the capacity for a therapeutic alliance, that is, a reasonably well integrated ego and some ability to relate effectively; (2) sufficient resourcefulness for effective therapeutic work; (3) the capacity to sustain therapeutic regression and to master the resulting anxiety; (4) the capacity to form a transference neurosis; and (5) the capacity to maintain the distinction between fantasy and reality. Patients can be effectively treated in psychoanalytic psychotherapy if they demonstrate some degree of these characteristics; consequently this form of therapy can play an effective role in treating a broader range of psychopathology than is possible with psychoanalysis. Psychoanalytic psychotherapy has evolved in the context of the widening scope of psychoanalytic treatment in which analytically oriented treatment has been extended to include patients experiencing narcissistic, borderline, and other forms of relatively more primitive or severe personality disorder.

Certain distinctions must be made in the application of psychoanalytic psychotherapy. The patients best suited to this method are those suffering from neurotic conflicts and symptom complexes, from reactive conditions (particularly depression), and from the whole realm of nonpsychotic character disorders. It is also the treatment of choice for patients with borderline personalities, though the management of these patients' regressive episodes may require a blending of supportive therapeutic techniques with those of insight-oriented psychotherapy. Although these cases require occasional modification of therapeutic technique, the basic objectives of the analytically oriented approach remain in force.

This form of psychotherapy has a more limited role in the management of acute psychotic regression, but it certainly has a place in the treatment of more compensated psychotic patients, who have some capacity for long-term intensive treatment. Once again, the analytic approach may need to be significantly modified to include more supportive elements, especially during severe and repeated regressive episodes. These modifications will be discussed in the section on supportive psychotherapy.

Therapeutic relationship. The therapeutic relation is a central dimension of all psychotherapies, but it assumes an especially crucial status in psychoanalytic therapy. This centrality has been increasingly emphasized as the under-

standing of psychoanalytic processes has shifted from a 1-person to a 2-person perspective. To a much greater extent than previously, aspects of analytic therapy are considered as taking place in and through the interaction of the 2 participants—therapist and patient. The shift in perspective affects all aspects of the therapy, but has particular relevance for the understanding of the 3 components of the therapeutic relation: alliance, transference/countertransference, and the real relationship.

Therapeutic alliance. The therapeutic alliance (see Chapter 1) involves primarily the conscious (or preconscious), rational, and nonneurotic aspects of the relationship between patient and therapist. It includes those components that make effective therapeutic and collaborative effort between therapist and patient possible and potentially beneficial. It is based on their explicit or implicit agreement to work together toward a mutually desired objective, the improvement and maturation of the patient.

As the therapist attempts to form an alliance with more responsible and mature aspects of the patient, a therapeutic split occurs on both sides of the relationship. In the patient a split occurs between the observing part of his ego and those parts of himself caught up in neurotic conflict. In the therapist a split occurs between functions involved in the therapeutic process and those caught up in his own neurotic conflicts, which may cause the therapist to respond with anxiety to unconscious impulses within the patient or within himself. Thus an effective alliance occurs ideally between the more responsible aspects of both therapist and patient.

The concept of the therapeutic alliance is by no means simple or uncomplicated. It involves multiple aspects of the therapeutic relationship and should be carefully distinguished from both transference in the patient and countertransference in the therapist, and from the real aspects of the relationship between them. While it involves elements of the therapeutic framework and contract (scheduling, arrangements for payment of fee, explicit or implicit boundaries, and so on), it also includes components of empathy, trust, autonomy, initiative, responsibility, and fundamental ethical considerations, among others. All these elements are called into play in varying proportions and with varying emphases as the therapeutic process moves forward. Issues of trust may predominate in the early phases but may become less central and give way to problems related to autonomy later in the therapy. This in turn may fade in the face of the intensification of issues of responsibility or other value orientations as the therapeutic work advances. The ground of the alliance constantly shifts and evolves during the course of therapy. One perspective that attempts to articulate some of this process comes from the *developmental analogue.* This view compares phases of the therapeutic process to phases of development: the issues pertinent in phases of development follow an epigenetic progression, and the therapeutic effort may follow a similar pattern. If trust and issues of dependence dominate the earliest interactions, more adolescent issues may dominate the closing stages of therapy, with an emphasis on issues of separation, independence, responsibility, and the like (Meissner, 1992, 1996).

The therapeutic alliance enables the therapist to make specific interventions even when they arouse considerable anxiety in the patient. It also sustains the patient's capacity to accept and to integrate these interventions. (An *intervention* is an action by the therapist—such as interpretation, confrontation, or clarification, discussed later—that tends to increase a patient's self-awareness or influence his behavior.) In addition, the therapeutic alliance provides a stable basis allowing both parties to experience, observe, and overcome barriers to the therapeutic process that may arise in either patient or therapist. For example, the therapeutic alliance helps the process of therapy weather the patient's negative, hostile, or distrustful feelings, especially when such feelings stem from the negative transference. While alliance and transference are antithetical—in the general sense that where transference prevails, alliance does not, and vice versa—it is also valid that alliance can provide the context of safety and security that will allow deeper and more meaningful dimensions of transference to emerge into awareness. The same holds true for distortions and disturbances arising within the therapist, especially those stemming from unresolved unconscious conflicts (countertransference). The therapeutic alliance therefore helps to keep the therapeutic relationship intact and to resolve stresses, distortions, and forces that would otherwise destroy it or compromise its therapeutic effectiveness.

The therapist must pay attention to alliance building and alliance maintenance throughout the therapy. A good therapeutic alliance depends on the establishment and continual reinforcement of a therapeutic contract with the patient, the appropriate degree of activity on the part of the therapist, and the therapist's ability to convey to the patient an empathic understanding of what the patient is feeling and experiencing. If the therapeutic contract is broken, if the therapist fails to convey empathy or is excessively passive or withholding at certain critical stages of the therapy, the therapeutic alliance may become unraveled and therapy disrupted. In working with unstable personalities, the therapist may have to adopt at times a supportive or holding stance in order to stabilize the patient's ego resources and minimize regression and the intensity of anxiety. Regressive episodes inevitably tend to destabilize the alliance, particularly with borderline patients, with the result that efforts to bolster the alliance run the risk of increasing the patient's fear of dependence. But the therapist must frequently allow this dependence to develop in such patients as a side effect of facilitating the alliance. The dependence may never be totally resolved but may become a focus of later therapeutic attention.

Therapeutic *misalliances,* distinct from transferences, can also play an important role in psychotherapy. Failures in the alliance may relate to or even result from transference distortions, but the misalliance itself is not the same as the transference. Distortions of the alliance may also come from factors having little to do with transference—from the side of reality, for example. To the extent that misalliances enter into the therapeutic interaction, they take therapeutic priority because they tend to distort or disrupt the alliance and therefore undermine any effective therapeutic effort. Misalliances do not reflect the patient's more mature wishes for symptom relief or for resolution of intrapsychic conflict; rather, they derive from the neurotic need to suffer, to maintain symptoms, to avoid change, to manipulate others, to gain narcissistic gratification, and so on. They often arise from more or less characterological dispositions and expectations that the patient brings with him to therapy, such as the wish to gain relief without effort, magical expectations, and intolerance of ambiguity or frustration. When such misalliances derive from transference distortions (often narcissistic or negative transference), exploration of the transference can help to resolve the alliance difficulty; but the alliance issues should be dealt with as having their own implications and meaning.

To decide on the method of therapy most appropriate for a given patient, the therapist must closely observe and carefully assess the patient's capacity to establish a therapeutic alliance. If the patient has generally been able to form healthy, trusting, mutually satisfying relationships, he probably has the capacity to establish an effective alliance. Conversely, a patient with a limited ability to establish trusting relationships, or who deals with important relationships, especially authority relations, in terms of power struggles over dominance and submission, may have a limited capacity to form an effective therapeutic alliance. This limited capacity may reflect an impairment in early one-to-one relationships, particularly at the level of trust-generating and autonomy-building interaction with the mother. The firmness or solidity of the therapeutic alliance determines in large measure the patient's tolerance for therapeutic regression and for the relative passivity of the therapist. In severely disturbed patients with minimal capacity for alliance, the therapist must pay particular attention to the vicissitudes of the alliance and constantly support and reinforce it. In some more primitive character disorders, the capacity for alliance may be sufficiently compromised to allow little more than an effort by the therapist to provide a "holding environment"—as much of a semblance of alliance as can be tolerated at that juncture. The skilled therapist will therefore tend to use more supportive therapeutic techniques with these patients because they usually tolerate poorly the induced regression of more insight-oriented approaches.

The therapeutic alliance may be undermined by positive or negative transferences. As discussed in Chapter 1, *positive transference* may create in the patient such a desire to please the therapist or gain his approval that he refuses to expose his conflicts or less praiseworthy impulses; *negative transference* may make the therapist seem hostile and persecuting, so that the patient no longer sees his interventions as helpful. Negative transference can thus override any empathic connection of the patient with the therapist's benign and therapeutic intentions. Transference resistance is the most powerful form of unconscious resistance. The working through and resolution of such resistance is essential for permanent therapeutic benefit to the patient and often forms the central issue to be worked on in intensive psychoanalytically oriented psychotherapy.

Transference. The second aspect of the therapeutic relationship is transference, the process of experiencing toward a person in the present the patterns of feeling and behavior that originated in the past (see Chapter 1). This unconscious process results in a repetition of attitudes, fantasies, and affects originally experienced in early relationships—primarily with parents but also with other family members, such as siblings or grandparents, or with extrafamilial figures, such as teachers or doctors. Transference occurs in all human relationships, more or less intensely in proportion to their duration and emotional significance. Because therapy often extends over a long period of time and because it deals with strong emotions, the therapeutic relationship provides a natural matrix for the development of transference feelings.

Transference may take various forms and may reflect a diversity of developmental levels. Transference may occur by *displacement* when attributes or characteristics originally experienced in relationships with significant figures earlier in life are experienced in a current relationship with a new object. It may also occur by *projection* when certain attributes or characteristics derived from an earlier object relationship have been internalized (become part of the patient's self-organization) and are subsequently reexternalized in relation to the new object. Thus the patient's own attributes are experienced as in the object by way of projection. The manner in which the transference is formed may have different dynamic and affective implications. Although a mixture of transference forms can occur in any patient, the balance tends to shift toward projective transference in the more primitive character disorders.

Transference feelings may appear at any time during the therapeutic process; they tend to become more intense and create more resistance as therapy progresses. The patient experiences transference feelings in proportion to the degree of regression he undergoes. Because transference occurs unconsciously, and because transference feelings have such a peculiar vitality and forcefulness, the patient often mistakes them for real love or anger. As regression continues, the transference feelings may increase in intensity to the point where they interfere with therapeutic progress. The patient may experience strong erotic feelings toward the therapist, which may interfere with effective therapy. Or he may experience intensely hostile feelings toward the therapist and even break off therapy. In this respect, it is worth noting that in every therapeutic process there is a powerful tendency for the patient to draw the basis or certain aspects of the relation with the therapist into the transference interaction and away from the alliance sector, thus undermining the alliance or forming a misalliance.

Transference feelings may be so intensely focused on the therapist that they give rise to a *transference neurosis,* a condition in which early neurotic feelings and reactions make up the bulk of the patient's feelings toward the therapist, and the original childhood conflicts between instinctual drives and the defenses against them are reactivated in the new relation. Transference neurosis provides a powerful therapeutic tool, to the extent that the therapist can help the patient to observe his transference feelings and neurotic conflicts as they manifest themselves in the therapist-patient relationship. The intensity and unique vividness of these feelings make them useful for demonstration and interpretation. The transference neurosis, however, also provides the most powerful resistance to the therapeutic process because it involves longstanding, unresolved conflicts and feelings that are more intense and more highly charged emotionally than those usually involved in less developed transference reactions. Effective therapeutic processing of such transference manifestations remains a function of the intactness and effectiveness of the alliance.

Transference feelings, particularly the transference

neurosis, provide powerful resistance insofar as the patient seeks to keep the therapeutic interaction solely on a transference basis rather than on the basis of effective analysis leading to change. The resistance arises primarily from the patient's wish to use the transference as a source of gratification, as when a female patient prefers to regard transferred sexual and loving feelings toward a male therapist as real and clings to them rather than face the painful work of understanding and working through required by the therapeutic process.

Although transference feelings occur in all forms of psychotherapy, the skilled therapist handles transference phenomena according to the patient's diagnosis and the particular form of therapy used. With some patients the therapist will foster development and expression of transference feelings, whereas with others he will minimize or avoid them. In general, the therapist will foster the development and expression of transference feelings when he feels that this will not disturb the patient's capacity to distinguish reality from fantasy (the reality of the therapeutic relationship from the fantasy relationship implied in the transference); when he feels sure of a strong enough therapeutic alliance against which to test out the transference elements; and when he has sufficient time to help the patient work through and resolve the transference involvement. These conditions are optimally present in the psychoanalytic situation. They may also be found to lesser degrees in other briefer or more superficial forms of therapy. Many patients either tend to form more dilute or less obvious transference derivatives rather than a full-blown transference neurosis or have difficulty maintaining a therapeutic alliance. Forms of therapy that do not rely on the mobilization and working through of transference may therefore be more appropriate for these patients.

If the therapist chooses to focus on transference feelings, he realizes that only a firm therapeutic alliance enables the patient to gain enough distance from his transference feelings to identify them, recognize their source, and integrate the therapist's interpretation of them. Through these interpretations, the patient gradually recognizes the distinction between transference feelings and real feelings toward the therapist. He recognizes that transference feelings come from an earlier time in his life and are inappropriate to his present life situation, and he comes to see the therapist in a less distorted way.

In determining the most appropriate form of therapy for a given patient, the therapist must assess the patient's capacity to tolerate transference feelings while maintaining an effective therapeutic alliance. By working through these transference feelings, the patient will also work through and resolve his underlying neurotic conflicts. In terms of diagnosis, patients with neuroses, neurotic characters, and some narcissistic personality disorders may be capable of this form of intense therapeutic work. It is less likely that patients with more primitive forms of personality organization—the forms of more primitive borderline and psychotic pathology in which ego defects are prominent and ego strengths are impaired—would benefit from this sort of transference-based treatment. For such patients, therapy aims more at maintaining a consistent alliance and dealing with the ongoing, present-day context of the patient's experience.

Countertransference. The therapist must be aware of another important aspect of the therapeutic relationship, namely, his own countertransference. Countertransference (see Chapter 1) is the displacement onto the patient of attitudes and feelings derived from the therapist's own inner world, including earlier life experiences. The term also refers to unconscious reactions taking place in the therapist in response to the patient's transference. It has been used at times to refer to all of the therapist's emotional reactions to the patient, and at other times only to those emotional reactions that derive from or are influenced by the therapist's unconscious—analogous to the patient's transference. These reactions are usually evoked by interaction with the patient, but may result from influences extrinsic to the therapy. They express derivatives of the therapist's unresolved intrapsychic conflicts, unconscious fantasies, and introjects.

Some useful distinctions can be made in thinking about countertransference. In the therapist's reaction to the patient, we can differentiate the following elements: intellectual understanding, based on information received from the patient and on the therapist's knowledge; a general response to the patient's personality; the therapist's transference to the patient; the therapist's counterreaction to the patient, that is, his unconscious reaction based on the role he is assigned by the patient's transference; and finally empathic identification with the patient. In these terms countertransference would generally include both the therapist's transference and his unconscious counterreaction to the patient. Rather than lumping together all affective reactions of the therapist to the patient as countertransference, it is more useful to keep clearly in focus what may be countertransference and what may not. The therapist's anger at repeated and insulting attacks from the patient is more likely to be a real reaction than a countertransferential response or some combination of the two.

Countertransference was originally thought only to distort or interfere with the therapeutic interaction, but more recent views have emphasized the role of countertransference in providing clues to the patient's unconscious or to distortions in the therapeutic relationship. On the one hand, these at times intense and often inappropriate feelings may arise from unresolved, unconscious conflicts in the therapist and may cloud his understanding and responsiveness. On the other hand, he may, if aware of these countertransference feelings, use them as valuable clues to the latent meaning of the patient's behavior, thoughts, or feelings. In this way the therapist may use his own unconscious as an instrument in establishing contact with the patient's unconscious. In addition, especially in the context of greater emphasis on interactional aspects of the therapy situation, attention has been focused on *countertransference enactments,* in which a combination of transferential and countertransferential derivatives get acted out in the therapeutic interaction. At times such enactments can serve as indicators of previously unrecognized or unacknowledged aspects of countertransference or a transference-countertransference interaction between therapist and patient (Jacobs, 1991).

Real relation. The real relation is the third component of the therapeutic relation along with the alliance and transference-countertransference. Reality pervades the therapeutic relation—the location of the therapist's office, the decor of the office, the comportment and manner of dress of therapist and patient, and so on. The primary reality, outweighing all others, is the person of the therapist on the one hand and the person of the patient on the other. In addition to the realities inherent in the structure of the therapy situation, external realities can impinge on the therapy and shape its course. Financial considerations, third-party payers, legal prescriptions (peer review), requirements and requests for information from insurance carriers, and other factors constituting the social and cultural context within which therapy is practiced can play a role. And no one can escape the inevitable or adventitious factors of life—death, illness, pregnancy, race, divergent cultural backgrounds, and so on—all of which can play a role in influencing the course of any therapeutic process (Meissner, 1996). Each of these real factors can stir up transferential reactions and can create distortions and problems for the alliance.

In terms of the real relation between therapist and patient, a careful distinction should be made between what is real in the relation and what pertains to the alliance. The distinction between the real and transference is more easily made, but too often alliance is then amalgamated to the real aspects of the relation. Alliance pertains to specific elements of the relation between patient and therapist that are pertinent to the therapeutic context and set the conditions for therapeutic work. Payment of the fee may serve as an example: exchange of legal tender for services rendered—checks, money, dealings with insurance companies, and so on—is real enough, as is the medium of exchange. But the negotiation over these matters, the specific arrangements for conducting them in the course of therapy, and the acceptance and observance of responsibilities undertaken with respect to them are all matters pertaining to the alliance, since they are part of the structure generated by patient and therapist within which they will conduct the work of the therapy.

We can also note here that, similar to the previously noted tendency for the patient to draw the therapist away from his footing in the alliance into a transference-based interaction, there is an analogous tendency for patients to seek to draw the therapist away from alliance into reality. The need to make the therapeutic relationship into something real is in this sense universal. But to the extent that either tactic succeeds—whether in the direction of transference or in the direction of reality—the alliance suffers to the detriment of the therapeutic effort. The pull to reality can be seen in efforts to make the relationship into something more like a friendship, or to use it in a real context unrelated to the therapy, as in efforts to engage the therapist socially, or in business, or even in attempts to arrange friendly meetings in contexts other than the place and time for therapy. More extreme instances are the efforts of some patients in the throes of intense erotic transferences to make the erotic relation to the therapist something real rather than fantasy. The therapist's task in these instances is to maintain or restore the integrity of the alliance and do what he can to bring the therapy back on line.

Regression. A prominent feature of the therapeutic process is *regression,* the tendency of a patient to return to earlier, more childish or infantile patterns of thinking, feeling, and functioning. This phenomenon may be observed outside the treatment situation in the series of progressions and regressions of normal childhood development. A child may revert to bed-wetting or lose bowel control when hospitalized or under stress. Regression may also be observed in adults during play, during certain kinds of creative activity, or during physical illness, when a person becomes clinging and excessively demanding.

Regression may be constructive and therapeutic or obstructive and pathological. *Therapeutic regression* emerges as part of the therapeutic process and provides the therapist with a vehicle for demonstrating important data from the patient's past in an unusually clear and convincing way. In analytic therapy, such regression is essential for gaining access to unconscious elements that are normally repressed and defended against. *Pathological regression,* in contrast, has a destructive influence on therapy and results when the regression occurs too rapidly or is too intense or too prolonged. This kind of regression overwhelms the patient with uncontrollable anxiety and interferes with his ability to understand and meaningfully integrate insights gained from observing regressive patterns. Because it interferes with his capacity for self-observation, pathological regression makes it difficult for the patient to work effectively with the therapist. Pathological regression may be seen in neurotic patients who are overwhelmed with anxiety and express the fear that they are becoming too dependent and are losing all control over their thoughts and feelings. Extreme forms of pathological regression may be seen in psychotic patients who retreat into primary process thinking and/or infantile patterns of behavior.

The therapist may encourage or facilitate regression in patients undergoing psychoanalytically oriented psychotherapy or psychoanalysis by using an office setting that offers minimum sensory stimulation; by use of the analytic couch; by assuming a relatively passive role; by encouraging the patient to focus entirely on himself and his inner mental processes; by instructing the patient to express all thoughts, fantasies, and feelings regardless of how foolish or childish they sound; and by various other techniques common to the more intensive forms of individual psychotherapy. As regressive phenomena emerge, the patient may develop a childlike dependence on the therapist, demand to be held or taken care of, speak in a whiny, childlike tone, or experience temporary changes in body image. He may say that he feels like a small child, and as he leaves the office express surprise that he is as tall as the therapist. How the patient reacts and relates to the therapist during this phase of therapy provides important data from early life experiences for understanding and reworking conflicts.

As a critical part of his diagnostic task, the therapist must assess the patient's capacity to tolerate therapeutic regression and determine to what degree this regression can be productively induced. The quality of the therapeutic alliance and the patient's inner resources determine in large measure his capacity to tolerate regression and to integrate meaningfully the data such regression provides. When regression is already a significant part of the patient's pathological picture, further regression is undesirable, and the therapist must try to minimize it. If regression threatens a patient's ability to discriminate between fantasy and reality, or if it generates overwhelming anxieties, the regression will be unproductive and possibly harmful. Therapeutic regression is more likely to be fruitful if it remains within the limits of the patient's capacity to maintain ego functioning and a working therapeutic alliance. A carefully induced therapeutic regression fosters the emergence of transference feelings and the development of the transference neurosis. (This in turn can confront the therapist with perhaps the most powerful source of resistance—indicating that even therapeutic regression has both positive and negative features.)

The degree to which regression can be safely induced is always a difficult question for the therapist. Even in neurotic patients with substantial ego strengths, the therapist may find it necessary to induce regression to the level of early primary relationships. Some clinicians also believe that deep regressions are useful in borderline or psychotic patients if carried out in fairly intensive therapy extending over many months or years. Even in these patients, however, such regressions rarely prove effective without the prior attainment of some degree of significant therapeutic alliance. The question of whether the regressive aspects of therapy should be maximized or minimized and to what degree depends on diagnostic criteria and continues to generate discussion and controversy among therapists.

The working through of the patient's resistances not only increases the availability of unconscious content but also fosters therapeutic regression. As the potential for regression increases, resistance tends to increase correspondingly. Therapeutic regression stirs up considerable anxiety against which the patient must defend himself. In relatively intense and long-term psychotherapy, the increasing regression facilitates both transference and its correlative transference resistances.

Many patients cannot be treated with long-term, anxiety-producing therapy, the model for which is psychoanalysis. They lack the required ego strength to allow them to continue the work of the therapy in a state of therapeutic regression. Patients whose tolerance of regression is poor, and whose capacity to maintain adaptive ego functions in spite of such regression is compromised, obviously run the risk of a structural or ego regression and should not be subjected to such therapy. The range of individual psychotherapy, however, is quite broad, and therapists can perform meaningful therapeutic work (with proper adaptation of the therapeutic approach to the patient's needs) on most forms of psychopathology. In acutely decompensated or psychotic patients, the therapist may need to interrupt the therapy or combine it with other supportive and management techniques to help the patient through the period of acute regression and enable him to return to the therapeutic work. With patients who cannot tolerate the therapy or who lack motivation to work in therapy, it is better not to undertake it and to utilize whatever other management approaches can be employed to help the patient deal with his difficulties.

Techniques. The techniques of psychoanalytic psychotherapy are derived from the model of psychoanalysis. The primary technique, *free association,* requires the patient to express his thoughts freely, to say all that comes to mind without selectiveness or modification and without concern about whether the thoughts are relevant or appropriate. Free association requires passivity and patience on the part of the therapist and encourages significant regression in the patient. The more active the therapist, the more he risks deterring the patient's efforts to associate.

Free association requires a peculiar split in the patient's ego functioning which is related to the alliance. Part of the patient's mind passively allows unconscious thoughts to rise to consciousness, while another part actively collaborates with the therapist in the evaluation and assessment of these thoughts. The capacity to drift into regression and to work within the therapeutic alliance, required by free association, varies considerably among patients. With patients who cannot sustain regression without undue anxiety—often the case in borderline patients—the therapist may have to assume a more active therapeutic stance.

Among the major therapeutic techniques, the therapist's capacity to listen empathically, meaningfully, and constructively is indispensable (see Chapter 1). Observation of the patient's behavior and attention to what he means, as well as to what he says, provide the foundation for therapeutic understanding. In insight-oriented therapy, the therapist listens not only to the patient's manifest content but also to the latent unconscious meanings that underlie it. Furthermore, the empathic listening attitude of the therapist fosters therapeutic regression and thus aids in the emergence of transference.

Questions are a significant part of the therapist's technique; they may be used to acquire information or to focus the patient's attention on a specific issue. Appropriate, sensitive, tactful questions facilitate the patient's understanding and insight, underline the mutual concern with the patient's problem, and support and reinforce the therapeutic alliance. Inappropriate, insensitive, and excessively challenging questions increase the patient's anxiety, arouse a sense of frustration and inadequacy in him, and consequently undermine the therapeutic alliance. The skilled therapist develops techniques of questioning that reflect sensitivity to what the patient feels and facilitate the patient's efforts at free association. For example, a patient may describe a pattern of behavior; comment, "I

don't know why I do that"; and then become silent. Or, because the patient's conflicts are in large measure unconscious, he may reply to questions he or the therapist raises by saying, "I don't know." The skilled therapist will avoid meeting silence with silence here and will not usually attempt to provide a possible answer for the patient. More often he will encourage the patient to explore the issue by free association and thus help the patient discover answers for himself.

The therapist's sensitivity to the patient's specific needs determines how a question is asked. "How long have you had difficulty responding sexually?" may be considerably easier for some patients to deal with than "How long have you been frigid?" "What led to your changing jobs this time?" may sound less judgmental to a highly sensitive patient than "Why did you get fired again?" Asking questions in terms of "what" and "how" will usually yield more information than questions about "why." By and large the patient does not know why, so the question can become unduly challenging and anxiety provoking. These subtle variations in the way a therapist couches his questions help make the difference between a refined approach and an unskilled one.

The therapist may also seek *clarification* of ambiguities by asking questions. Or he may repeat something the patient has said or done as a way of prompting further consideration or associations. Clarification may thus serve as a mild form of confrontation or even interpretation and may bring the particular issues with which the patient struggles into sharper focus.

In *confrontation* the therapist directs the patient's attention to a behavior or issue of which both are aware and which the patient has been avoiding. Confrontations usually occur more frequently in psychotherapy than in classical psychoanalysis. They generally relate to the patient's conscious thought or real situations. When carried out from the perspective of a solid therapeutic alliance, confrontations help the patient stand aside and observe his own thoughts and actions.

Confrontations may help the therapist set limits to the patient's tendency to act out or deal with the patient's resistances, with crises arising within or outside of therapy, or with disruptions of the therapeutic alliance. (In these instances the therapist must be particularly attentive to his own countertransference distortions or difficulties.) Confrontation may therefore help the therapist deal with therapeutic stalemates, misuse of treatment, attempts to manipulate, attempts to seduce or attack the therapist, serious misconceptions about treatment, and persistent defenses and resistances that threaten to subvert the therapeutic process.

The primary and most important therapeutic tool is *interpretation*. Interpretations are verbal interventions directed toward conveying additional meaning or understanding that might help the patient become aware of previously repressed material in a meaningful and affectively significant way. The interpretation brings into conscious awareness and intellectually illuminates an area of conflict that the patient has previously repressed. Interpretations may be either dynamic or genetic. Dynamic interpretations focus on the current operation of psychic forces and motivations, whereas genetic interpretations focus on connections between past and present emotional reactions and experiences.

The therapist often uses interpretation to combat the patient's resistance, to make the patient aware of his efforts to block the work of treatment. Through interpretation the therapist brings into focus the unconscious meanings and genetic roots of resistance. Resistances are overdetermined, in that they rest on multiple unconscious fantasies; only by bringing these fantasies into consciousness and specifically dealing with them can the therapist help the patient overcome the resistance. Frequently the fantasies underlying specific resistances merge with those underlying the neurotic symptoms, so that the therapist's attempt to resolve defenses also provides him with insight into the unconscious roots of the patient's illness.

Thus the therapist's interpretation of resistance, the uncovering of unconscious motivations and their genetic origins, is an essential part of the therapeutic process. Interpretations that fail to touch on specific life experiences and concrete fantasies of the patient tend to be ineffective and diffuse. A common error in psychoanalytic psychotherapy is moving too quickly to the interpretation of unconscious content. The therapist must first prepare the way by helping the patient deal with and overcome his defenses. Otherwise the therapist's interpretations may precipitate excessive anxiety or regression and thus undermine the treatment process, or they may make little impression because the patient's resistance has not been adequately resolved. Often interpretations can be accepted intellectually by the patient but make little impression and lead to little or no change.

The therapist also uses interpretation to help resolve transferences. The patient's real feelings toward the therapist must be distinguished from transference feelings, those displaced from earlier relationships or projected. While the patient's real feelings may constitute an important area for discussion, clarification, and resolution in therapy, transference feelings serve as the primary focus for interpretation. When the transference elements emerge with sufficient clarity and force, they provide significant insight into basic conflicts and their origins. But insights derived from transference must always be integrated with the patient's current real-life difficulties and their resolution.

One of the most difficult tasks confronting the therapist is determining the right time to make an interpretation. His ability to sense the right moment and to make the interpretation with appropriate intensity and depth requires a combination of training, intuition, and experience. This ability in large measure determines his effectiveness in conducting insight-oriented therapy, and the skilled therapist seeks to refine this ability throughout his professional life. The most appropriate time to make an interpretation is when the patient has brought sufficient unconscious material into awareness and accomplished enough work to be on the verge of arriving at the interpretation himself. At this point, a simple question or observation from the therapist will often suffice to help the patient make his own interpretation. A properly timed interpretation will often strike the patient with significant emotional impact and clarity. He will suddenly see and understand an aspect of his life or a specific pattern of behavior that has puzzled him for years. Such therapeutic experiences are among the most gratifying for both patient and therapist. When an interpretation has the proper timing and depth, the patient will not only be able to accept it but will also be able to confirm and integrate it with past and current experiences both within and outside of therapy.

Premature interpretations can heighten the patient's resistance and impede the unfolding of further unconscious material. Erroneous interpretations, which no therapist can entirely avoid, may not necessarily impair therapy. If, however, they reflect the therapist's countertransference feelings, they may intensify the patient's resistance and undermine the therapeutic alliance. Incomplete or inexact interpretations may be less damaging if stated in a conjectural tone or as tentative hypotheses offered for the patient's consideration. In this way they may serve as a first step toward a more complete interpretation. The therapist may suggest, for example, "I wonder if there is any relationship between your inability to tolerate your roommate and the long-standing conflicts you described with your brother?"

However, in a context of therapeutic interaction, and within the parameters set by the alliance, interpretation is less a function of the therapist than of the collaboration between therapist and patient. In this sense, interpretations are arrived at through the combined efforts of both participants. In this tentative, exploratory venture involving both partners, the issues of exactness and timing of interpretations recede in importance. More important are the aspects of the collaborative interaction. Here, interpretations arise within the alliance and are developed and articulated in terms conditioned by the alliance, with respect for the respective roles and contributions of both members of the dyad.

The therapist must guard against superficial and general interpretations that fail to reach an adequate and therapeutically appropriate depth. He must also avoid interpretations that explore unconscious material before the patient is prepared to deal with it. Such inappropriate probing often reflects the therapist's own unresolved voyeurism or seductiveness and may stem from countertransference difficulties. Deep interpretation of unconscious material must take place gradually and only after the patient has been adequately prepared. This preparation increases the patient's capacity to accept and to integrate such interpretations.

The therapist may also use *reconstruction,* a technique closely related to interpretation. Reconstruction attempts to correlate, understand, and tie together forgotten, repressed, but psychologically significant early life experiences. The patient's free associations, behavior, dreams, and transference reactions may suggest traces of these experiences. The therapist bases his reconstruction not only on the patient's overt material but also on the significant aspects that appear to be missing from it; he attempts through further exploration to attain fuller understanding of the patient's symptoms and conflicts by filling in the gaps. Like interpretation, reconstruction may be a gradual process; it may also involve collaborative contributions from both patient and therapist. The therapist may develop the reconstruction over an extended period, gradually making it more complete as he gains access to more material. This evolution supplies the basis for still more complete reconstruction and deeper understanding.

Once a patient gains insight through his free associations and through interpretation or other therapeutic intervention, his therapeutic work has only begun. Insight alone seldom produces significant changes. Rather, it must undergo a laborious process called *working through,* which often constitutes the bulk of psychotherapeutic work. In working through, the insight—that is, the understanding of the particular unconscious conflict brought to consciousness—and all its ramifications must be explored, extended, and tested again and again. By tracing the conflict back to its origins and exploring its past and current manifestations in all aspects of the patient's life, the patient and therapist can overcome re-

sistances to the insight, and the patient learns to accept, integrate, and understand it both intellectually and emotionally. The process of working through helps reduce the intensity of the conflict, giving the patient increased control over it and thus effecting significant change. Thus change depends not only on insight but also on the working through of that insight and, perhaps most important, on the continual exertion of the patient's will to change.

In psychoanalytic psychotherapy the therapist explores the patient's transference feelings, especially when these feelings impede therapy by acting as resistances and when they reflect regression and the emergence of transference neurosis. When this neurosis emerges with sufficient clarity and force, the patient's basic conflicts are often focused in dramatic ways in relation to the therapist and thus provide an opportunity for the patient to gain insight into his conflicts and progressively work them through. Resolution of basic conflicts in the context of the transference is one of the major objectives of the therapy. Success in gaining this particular objective depends on the nature of the patient's psychopathology and his inherent capacity for the therapeutic work.

Outcome. The outcome of psychoanalytic psychotherapy can be measured against therapeutic objectives. Psychoanalytic psychotherapy implies that the therapist undertakes to accomplish as much with the patient as is possible within obvious limitations. As a long-term, intensive, expressive-exploratory, insight-oriented therapy, it aims at fundamental changes in the patient's adaptive functioning and personality organization. Realistic considerations may of course require therapist and patient to settle for more modest objectives. Frequently patients find themselves significantly less motivated to continue therapy after achieving relief of symptoms. The time the therapist has available to work with the patient may be limited, or the patient may be forced to move to another city within a particular time span. The decision that sufficient work has been done, within the given limitations, for therapy to be brought to a close must be arrived at by patient and therapist together.

In general, the ideal course of therapy would achieve the following aims: (1) removal or improvement of symptoms; (2) resolution or reduction in the intensity of basic conflicts; (3) resolution of the patient's therapeutic dependence, allowing him greater autonomy and increased self-esteem; and (4) an adequate degree of adaptive and mature functioning. These criteria must often be modified and less than optimal goals accepted. When compromise occurs, both therapist and patient must be aware that their settling for modified objectives may result in difficulties for the patient later on and necessitate additional therapeutic work.

Assessment. Attempts to assess psychoanalytic psychotherapy have had an unfortunate history. H. J. Eysenck's critique (1965) suggested that the effects of therapeutic intervention on patients differed little from normal life experience without treatment. He reported that roughly a third of patients improved, another third got worse, and another third showed little or no change. Subsequent investigators, however, have questioned Eysenck's data and conclusions (Kiesler, 1966; Luborsky et al., 1971; Luborsky, Singer, and Luborsky, 1975; Strupp, Hadley, and Gomes-Schwartz, 1977; Luborsky, 1984; Luborsky and Crits-Christoph, 1990).

Assessment based on more careful studies, with particular attention to patient selection and outcome criteria (the guidelines used to measure therapeutic change) that do justice to the complexity of the human personality and the psychotherapeutic process, leads to a much more optimistic conclusion. Such studies suggest that psychoanalytic psychotherapy, properly utilized, is the most effective form of therapeutic intervention for specific groups of patients. The Menninger Clinic study (Kernberg et al., 1972) indicated that for borderline patients, purely supportive treatment is relatively ineffective, and that an insight-oriented approach based on working through the transference relationship (with supplemental hospitalization) was most effective. Thus support is increasing for the position that psychoanalytic psychotherapy is the optimal treatment for patients with neurotic disorders and conflicts and for some patients with borderline personality organization (Meissner, 1988). There is controversy in this area with respect to the extent to which exploratory or supportive techniques are more appropriate and effective in the treatment of relatively severe character disorders (Wallerstein, 1986).

Other extensive studies indicate a more limited applicability of psychotherapy in the treatment of psychosis (Grinspoon, Ewalt, and Shader, 1972; May, 1968). The use of drugs, particularly the various classes of neuroleptics, seems to be more effective than psychotherapy in many psychotic patients. But even in this area, a select group of patients appears to respond more positively to drugs in combination with group or individual psychotherapy (Robbins, 1993).

Additional research is required to provide specific criteria for selecting patients who will respond positively to psychotherapeutic intervention. Current trends suggest that particular types of patients respond best to particular psychotherapeutic techniques. Attempts to extend psy-

chotherapeutic skills beyond the realm of their appropriate application are counterproductive.

Supportive Psychotherapy

Supportive psychotherapy is a form of therapy that seeks to leave the patient's defenses intact and helps him to suppress and control disturbing thoughts and feelings by measures such as reassurance, suggestion, inspiration, and persuasion. Unlike psychoanalytic psychotherapy, supportive therapy focuses primarily on present difficulties and avoids probing into the past or the unconscious. It is limited in therapeutic objectives rather than duration. The specific indications for this therapy can be considered in terms of the patient's current situation or in terms of his specific diagnosis.

Indications. Situationally, a therapist can use supportive psychotherapy most effectively when a patient experiences acute stress and turmoil or when a patient with psychotic potential goes into acute decompensation (that is, deteriorates and becomes overtly psychotic). Thus the therapist uses supportive psychotherapy primarily in dealing with life crises or regressive episodes. The death of a loved one, divorce, illness, the loss of a job, or a developmental crisis may precipitate such episodes. Supportive psychotherapy is the therapist's response to the patient's acute disorganization and inability to cope with such crises, to master anxiety, and to maintain effective functioning under great emotional turmoil. Such crises may occur frequently in extremely fragile patients.

In diagnostic terms, the therapist can provide supportive therapy to psychotic patients and, intermittently, to borderline patients; he will rarely use this approach with patients who have neurotic difficulties or character disorders except when therapeutic goals are limited accordingly. With fragile and disorganized patients, a supportive involvement may be the most that can be accomplished, and such patients may be seen at irregular intervals over extended periods of time.

Techniques. While a therapist using insight-oriented approaches fosters regression by undermining patients' resistances and probes the unconscious by exploratory interventions, the therapist using supportive treatment moves in the opposite direction. He minimizes the intensity of therapeutic involvement by limiting the frequency and duration of patient visits. He also attempts to minimize the patient's regressive tendency, to stabilize and maintain the patient's functioning defensive structure and other ego functions, and to contain the patient's sometimes overwhelming anxiety within manageable limits.

In supportive therapy, therefore, the therapist uses reassurance and supportive reinforcement to reduce anxiety and assumes an active therapeutic stance to promote a sense of alliance and helpfulness and to minimize regression. In this way the therapist offers himself as a constant and readily available support with whom the patient may achieve a stable and therapeutically consistent relationship. He avoids, however, premature reassurance, which the patient may interpret as a lack of understanding of the severity of his illness and the intensity of his suffering.

In supportive therapy the therapist may also use extrapsychotherapeutic means to achieve these ends. He is more likely than in insight therapy to use medication as a means of calming the patient or hospitalization to help the patient control his behavior and to remove him from excessive stimulation contributing to the crisis or regressive stress. The therapist regards medication and hospitalization as protective devices that act as buffers between the patient and overwhelming anxiety and turmoil. He may offer the patient advice, supply him with information, or educate him explicitly in regard to aspects of his life and experience. In general, the therapeutic stance of the therapist is relatively active, offering himself to the patient as a supportive, friendly, protective, and constant object and adopting a firmly but gently authoritative attitude. He accepts and tolerates the patient's needs for dependency and attachment instead of attempting to explore and change them. Hence the quality of the alliance differs considerably from that in psychoanalytic psychotherapy.

In the supportive context the therapist offers the patient a surrogate ego he can depend on. Although conflicts over dependency may develop even in patients who need such a relationship, the advisability of attempting to modify the patient's dependency toward increasing self-reliance remains controversial. Usually the prolonged course of supportive psychotherapy leads to a gradual decrease in the frequency of therapeutic sessions with a gradual weakening in the intensity of the therapeutic relationship, but the ties of dependency to the supportive therapist are generally left relatively intact. These ties may remain strong even when therapeutic contacts are spaced over months or years.

In a supportive relationship the therapist focuses on the patient's current life experience—his contacts, relationships, stresses, emotions, disappointments, hopes, and gratifications. The therapist seeks to mobilize the patient's available resources to deal with these aspects of his ongoing experience and to manage the difficulties he encounters in a more effective and adaptive manner.

Outcome. The therapeutic objectives of supportive psychotherapy must necessarily be modest, but modesty by no means implies simplicity or ease of achievement. Supportive therapy aims at the reconstitution and stabilization of the patient's functioning. This process may require short-term involvement or a relationship extending over considerable time.

Frequently, however, particularly in cases of episodic regression, the supportive approach achieves in a relatively short time its primary objective of returning the patient to a more effective, pre-decompensation level of functioning. Once the goal is achieved, the usefulness of merely supportive therapy is limited, and the therapist may shift to a more insight-oriented approach. He will gradually change his techniques to those of psychoanalytic psychotherapy, while constantly testing the patient's capacity to sustain this type of treatment. Even so, the therapist must be ready to respond to transient regressive episodes or decompensations, which the shift to insight-oriented therapy may precipitate. In working with more regressed psychotic patients, the therapist may encounter great resistance to the acceptance of responsibility and relinquishment of dependence on the therapist that such a change in approach necessitates.

Assessment. Although supportive psychotherapy may serve as an effective short-term holding action, it may also be the optimal treatment modality over a more extended period. The therapist may also find it useful in the management of disruptive turmoil or regressive episodes and in the regressive phases of more insight-oriented treatment. In the original Menninger study, Kernberg et al. (1972) indicated that in the treatment of borderline patients and some others, supportive interventions at critical junctures can increase the effectiveness of insight-oriented approaches. Supportive measures were most effective in the reconstitution of acutely decompensated patients, particularly in the hospital setting. Within this context, when the supportive measures have achieved their objectives, hospitalization is no longer necessary. The therapist must then decide whether such patients will benefit from further therapeutic intervention. Subsequent reevaluation of the Menninger data (Wallerstein, 1986) suggests that the role and effectiveness of relatively supportive techniques are greater than previously appreciated. Not only were supportive approaches more broadly utilized in that study, but also the effects in terms of long-term change and extent of meaningful personality modification were underestimated. The relative effectiveness of supportive and exploratory techniques remains open to further clarification, but it seems safe to say that most psychotherapy processes involve some mixture of both supportive and exploratory approaches utilizing one or the other in complementary fashion as required by the therapeutic context.

Many such patients profit immeasurably from an insight-oriented approach that examines the origins and causes of their acute decompensation. Other patients, however, languish in a continuing state of dependence and disorganization, which prevents them from benefiting from further insight-oriented therapy. For these patients a continuing supportive relationship, together with the resources of psychopharmacology and hospital facilities, may help maintain adequate stabilization and level of functioning in the outside world.

Brief Psychotherapy

Brief psychotherapy is a limited, insight-oriented therapy—limited both in its objectives and in number of patient visits. It can be distinguished from psychoanalytic psychotherapy, where greater emphasis is placed on the role of insight into unconscious dynamics, and also from supportive psychotherapy, in which the role of insight is reduced.

Indications. In brief psychotherapy, the therapist uses fundamental psychodynamic principles to help the patient achieve limited insight into a specifically defined area of emotional conflict. Consequently this form of therapy works best with patients whose ego functioning is relatively intact and whose presenting complaint centers on a specific area of conflict. Brief psychotherapy requires the capacity to relate to the therapist in a cooperative and productive manner (alliance), the ability to openly share pertinent feelings, the capacity for insight, and, above all, a basic motivation to achieve insight. Despite these cautions, recent opinion, driven by social demands for fiscal restraint and cost containment, has advocated extending the reach of short-term therapy to a broader range of patient types and conditions (Davanloo, 1992; Mann, 1990). Studies of brief psychotherapy (Sifneos, 1972, 1992) also indicate that motivation is a primary predictor of successful outcome. The therapist uses brief psychotherapy, therefore, as a form of crisis intervention (see Chapter 26), but also for situations in which therapeutic goals can be rapidly focused and achieved. Helping the patient gain insight into the reasons for his acute emotional turmoil enables him to mobilize ego capacities in the service of reducing this area of conflict.

Techniques. Brief psychotherapy is time limited, and the therapist and patient set the limits either in reference to the attainment of specific therapeutic goals or in terms of a specific number of visits. Ideally, the therapist seeks an optimal time span to achieve limited objectives. The patient's initial positive transference reactions motivate him to work toward these therapeutic objectives, but optimally an at least workable alliance around these goals must take hold before the emergence of any transference resistance. The therapist deals with transference reactions, positive or negative, promptly and directly in the interest of maintaining the alliance and minimizing transference effects that would impede therapeutic efforts. The therapist should be wary of patients who expect magical cures in the specified, limited number of clinic visits, since these attitudes will frustrate effective therapeutic work.

Brief psychotherapy is explicitly focused, concentrating on immediate areas of emotional conflict. Separating a manageable area of conflict from deeper and more extensive areas of personality dysfunction is often technically difficult. Frequently a number of interrelated conflicts from different psychic levels coexist, but brief psychotherapy strives to avoid deeper characterological issues, particularly those involving dependency needs. It therefore specifically avoids early dependent needs and problems with passivity, which can create entanglements and lead to complications during treatment. These are issues more appropriate for long-term psychotherapy.

Thus in brief psychotherapy the therapist attempts to stay reality oriented and to keep the focus on the patient's current life conflicts without emphasizing past experience. This limited focus does not exclude all aspects of the patient's past, however, because acquired patterns of reaction may play a significant role in current conflicts. Patients may attach characteristic meanings to a variety of everyday experiences. Such a bias may, for example, take the form of imagining themselves to be totally controlled by, or to have total control over, the environment. These attitudes reflect diverse underlying, unconscious determinants and often lead to a single predominant and repetitive pattern of ordering and responding to external situations and stimuli. Insight into such patterns contributes significantly to the patient's ability to deal with current difficulties. Throughout the process, the emphasis falls on recognizing, defining, and reinforcing the patient's strengths and bringing them to bear in dealing with his problems.

Brief psychotherapy may also be defined as a problem-solving process, but one in which the therapist helps the patient mobilize his own resources to deal with the problem rather than solving it for the patient. The task orientation keeps the objective clearly in focus and emphasizes reaching a solution within a short time. The problem-solving process has several phases: the first is *perceptual organization,* during which the therapist helps define the conflict and the limits of therapeutic effort. During this phase the therapist can also evaluate the patient's capacity for the requisite reorganization and reordering. The second phase, *perceptual reorganization,* calls for reordering conscious material by clarification and occasional confrontation. The therapist connects newly uncovered thoughts and feelings to the structure of the defined conflict. The patient's resistances may limit this reordering and uncovering. A phase of *transference interpretation* may follow, in which the therapist uses the patient's previously achieved insights and feelings toward him to provide a more emotionally vivid and experiential context for the patient's new insights into his conflicts. In the final phase, *termination and integration,* if the therapist has been correct in his interpretation, the patient will begin to work through his problem with an accompanying decrease of symptoms.

Outcome. Brief psychotherapy seeks to reduce the presenting distress and bring about symptomatic relief. The therapist's goal of helping the patient gain insight into an explicitly defined area of conflict removes brief psychotherapy from the realm of transference cure, which by definition is achieved without insight (see Chapter 1). The insight gained helps mobilize the patient's resources to master the disturbing anxiety and to resolve the conflict. Resolution of the immediate difficulties may leave long-term difficulties requiring further work untouched.

Assessment. Brief psychotherapy was developed and has been used most effectively on outpatient clinics, particularly when offered to selected groups of patients best able to profit from it. Partly because of the proliferation of third-party insurance plans with benefits covering only a limited number of outpatient visits, brief psychotherapy has come to play an increasingly significant role in patient management. Pressures to use it as a replacement for longer-term therapy ignore the nature and purpose of short-term therapy. Such pragmatic and extrinsic considerations aside, however, the limited objectives of brief psychotherapy may or may not satisfy the patient's needs. The option of more extensive psychotherapeutic work should be left open to the patient when he demonstrates the need and the capacity for it. But in a significant number of properly selected and well-motivated patients, brief psychotherapy may be all that is required.

Group Psychotherapies

The group approach to psychotherapy has established itself as a major form of psychiatric treatment. With in-

creasing pressures on the psychiatric profession to treat greater numbers of patients, group therapy takes on particular significance and utility. Material in this section is intended primarily for potential group therapists, as well as for those evaluating or referring patients for group therapy.

While individual psychotherapy involves the interaction between 2 parties, the therapist and the patient, group psychotherapy involves combinations of individuals occupying the patient or therapist roles. The typical configuration is that of a single therapist or leader and a number of patients (usually 6–8) participating in a single group process. Variants on this basic configuration include multiple therapists and smaller or larger groups. Thus in group therapy there may be 1 or more cotherapists, and in family therapy there may be 1 or more therapists and 1 or more families.

I shall discuss basic principles underlying group therapy in general and then focus on intensive group therapy, family therapy, and psychodrama.

General Principles

Patient selection. Opinions regarding patient selection for group therapy have changed as experience with the group process has deepened and broadened. Like all other forms of therapy, group therapy is better suited to some patients than to others; like their counterparts in individual psychotherapy, group therapists consider relatively healthy, neurotic, non-narcissistic patients who function well to be ideal for the group process. At one time group therapists considered certain patients poor risks for the group approach: severe psychoneurotics, psychotics, patients with organic difficulties, patients with psychosomatic problems, and depressed, narcissistic, and paranoid patients. Increasing experience, however, suggests that most of these patients can use group settings effectively, but that patients with more severe pathology require modifications in approach and technique.

The therapist must carefully select his patients for group therapy. Before recommending a patient for this therapy, the therapist should make an adequate diagnostic appraisal, including assessment of the patient's presenting problem, history, pathology, and suitability for joining the particular group under consideration. Because patients often interact with the group in patterns predetermined by previous family involvements, the therapist may also find it helpful to explore the patient's important interpersonal involvements, specifically those within his family of origin. Some recent research suggests that good sibling and peer relationships are predictive of successful group participation.

The decision to treat patients in a group rather than in individual therapy is not always clear-cut. In general, patients capable of forming a workable transference and sustaining the difficult work of therapy deserve that opportunity in a one-to-one context; but such patients often also do well in groups. Those who have difficulty with inappropriate interpersonal relationships, who tend to act out feelings, or who may develop a transference that would excessively complicate individual therapy can sometimes be treated effectively in groups. By the same token, certain narcissistic or paranoid patients may be excessively disruptive to the group effort or may find it too difficult to become a functioning member of the group. Such patients may do better in individual therapy. In addition, patients may have a preference for or against group treatment, and this preference must also enter into the therapist's decision. Even so, referral to group treatment may be made simply on the ground that no other form of treatment is available.

Group organization. How large a group should be, how long and how frequently it should meet, and how homogeneous the members should be are important issues to consider in establishing a therapy group. Although no ironclad rules prevail, the therapist determines these specific parameters only after deciding on the nature, purpose, and function of the group. The size of a group will be roughly inversely proportional to the intensity of the therapeutic interaction. In intensive, analytically oriented groups, for example, the optimal number of group members is 7 or 8. Increasing the number above 8 dilutes the intensity of group interaction, and decreasing the number below 7 heightens the intensity of interaction with the leader and undercuts the effectiveness of the group process. But if groups are less exploratory and more supportive or problem oriented, larger numbers can be involved effectively.

The organization and function of a group determine the frequency and duration of meetings. More frequent meetings increase the intensity of the interaction among members and correspondingly deepen the level of responsiveness among members and between members and the leader. Although most groups meet once a week, the number of meetings may be altered according to group purposes.

The duration of individual meetings also affects the intensity of the members' interaction. The group process requires adequate time to develop, yet excessively long meetings may discourage the group from concentrating on serious issues. In general, 1 hour is considered the minimum time required for the group to accomplish some work; 2 hours has been found excessive. The ideal length for most group meetings falls somewhere in the middle, from an hour and a quarter to an hour and a half. The group itself may decide how often and how long to meet. Groups have their own style and pacing, and, within limits, the members may feel that they need more time or can work more effectively with less time.

Groups may be homogeneous or heterogeneous in terms of patients' age, educational level, race, sex, and diagnosis. Therapy groups appear to do better when they are heterogeneous and balanced. The group ought not to be too heavily weighted with members of one sex, with schizophrenic or borderline patients, or with patients significantly removed in age from the rest of the group. There are exceptions to this rule of thumb, however. Disturbed adolescents, geriatric patients, acute psychotics, alcoholics, homosexuals, and patients with serious physical handicaps often work more effectively in homogeneous groups.

The group may operate in an open or a closed fashion. A closed group comprises patients selected to work together within a limited time frame. The termination date may be preset or determined as the group proceeds, but the group works together toward its termination. Although members may be replaced if they drop out in the early phases of therapy, the group is gradually closed to new members during the later phases. Open groups accept and terminate patients continually in the course of the group process, so that termination becomes an issue for individual patients rather than for the group as a whole. An open group will have a continual turnover of members, while the group itself may persist for many years. Problems of engagement and separation are active in both group settings but in different ways. The open group has to deal with the recurrent problem of integrating and losing individual members; the closed group has to deal with the problems of commitment to and loss of the group itself.

Each type of structure has advantages. The closed group allows for greater intensity of group interaction, deeper involvement in the group process, and the opportunity to work through the process of termination more thoroughly. Closed groups also are advantageous when the therapist is available for only a specified period—as in training programs. The open group, in contrast, can develop an ongoing group process and can share the benefits of group experience and insight with incoming patients over an extended time frame.

Group process. Three basic phases characterize the life of a group, bringing specific issues into focus and dominating group interaction. In the initial stage, the patient is concerned with the question of inclusion, whether he will be accepted and become a part of the group. He no longer functions as an isolated individual but is gradually incorporated into the body of the group. Dominant issues are membership and sharing, or, in more analytic terms, concerns about narcissism and symbiotic longing. In the second phase, questions of power and autonomy preoccupy the patient. Can the patient function as an independent person within the group, and can he maintain autonomy in the face of the leader's presumed power? Is power focused in the leader or distributed and shared among the group members? In the third phase of group interaction, issues of equality and the give-and-take between members influence their acceptance of one another as individuals, the expression of real affection and support, and the capacity for mature and healthy mutuality. This equality promotes and sustains the autonomy of each group member.

Group formation is the process by which a number of individuals become an effectively functioning group. Group life gradually generates a therapeutic context in which patients can resolve their underlying conflicts and work toward maturity and self-sustaining autonomy. The nature of this evolution may vary among groups or may fluctuate in intensity as the group develops. The group leader must constantly keep this evolution in focus as he attempts to understand and respond to the flow of events in the group interaction.

Role of the leader. The group therapist or leader plays a central role in group development, even though his role can vary considerably within different groups. When the leader adopts a more active and manipulative stance, the group consolidates around the leader so that effective therapeutic action tends to occur between him and the members. An active leader diminishes the level of anxiety within the group but also generates expectations and transference difficulties. A less active leader raises the level of group anxiety and forces the group to consolidate itself, often against the leader. The more passive stance of the leader thus fosters evolution of the group itself as a therapeutic instrument and brings more sharply into focus patterns of interaction and individual distortions that contribute to the group process and reflect individual and collective pathologies. Thus the locus of therapeutic action lies more among members than between members and the leader.

The role of the leader is particularly significant in the initial phases of group formation. His position vis-à-vis the group determines whether the initial issues of inclusion and acceptance will be focused on the leader or diffused around the group itself. In either case, the leader

sets the course for the group's further development and evolution.

Throughout the life of the group, its particular characteristics, the specific phase of its development, and the personality and theoretical orientation of the leader will help to define his role. Within the group, however, the therapist must maintain a flexible stance, varying his interaction and responsiveness in terms of the ongoing activity of the group and the apparent needs of the members. He must avoid a preselected, fixed, theoretically determined role. Groups that have developed a considerable degree of solidarity have less need for therapeutic activity from the leader. Unstable and more fragmented groups may require greater activity from the leader to maintain cohesiveness and to facilitate group efforts.

Nonetheless, the leader's character traits—exhibitionism, narcissism, tendencies toward omnipotence, or need for control—may exert a powerful influence on his style. The therapist must therefore be as alert to problems of countertransference and their enactments as he would be in individual psychotherapy. Out of another set of neurotic conflicts and needs—such as excessive passivity or fear of appearing less than perfect—therapists may also err in the direction of withdrawal from the group process, isolation, or failure to intervene directly and actively when required.

Within a group, each member's psychodynamics and personality are unique. The ultimate effectiveness of the group leader depends on his capacity to detect and respond to the members' varying needs and, through appropriate intervention, to facilitate the group process. The therapist must deal actively with patients' tendencies to regress, particularly in the case of psychotic or borderline patients, and their tendencies to act out, either within or outside the group. One member may, for example, threaten another verbally within the group meeting, or 2 members may carry out a destructive relationship outside the group. The skillful therapist acts to mobilize group resources to deal with such problems rather than dealing with members on an individual basis himself, a tactic that can undermine group efforts and frustrate the group process. The underlying intent of disruptive events in the group is often precisely such an undermining of group work, and the therapist must avoid aiding this unconsciously determined activity.

Several styles characterize group interaction patterns. At one end of a continuum of such patterns is the *analytic* approach, in which the leader adopts a relatively inactive role and encourages the evolution of the group process. In this process the group gradually consolidates and gains a degree of cohesiveness, and the material brought to the group interaction gradually deepens from a superficial level to more basic conflicts. These conflicts then can become available for corrective action, either by the ongoing group interaction or by the leader's interpretation. The other extreme of interaction patterns is the *existential* approach, in which the therapist no longer stands aside as a separate leader but engages as much as possible in the group interaction as a member among members. In this participatory approach, the therapist shares his own feelings, attitudes, and countertransference difficulties with the group, along with observations stemming from his own greater experience of group phenomena. Midway between these extremes stands the *transactional* approach, in which the leader focuses on current patterns of interaction among group members and between himself and group members. Although the leader acts more as a participating member of the group, the focus remains on the transactional aspects of the group process, and he makes no attempt to delve into the patients' past experiences or the elements of underlying conflict or transference distortion.

One cannot predetermine whether one style will be more advisable or more therapeutically effective than another. Different leaders feel comfortable with different styles and, as a general principle, work most effectively with the style best suited to their own personalities. The group leader, however, must recognize the role that countertransference may play in his choice of style and must be open to using other forms of interaction to achieve therapeutic results when indicated. In addition, the most suitable style or modality may vary from group to group, depending on the group's purposes and organization.

Although therapy groups most often have several patients and a single group leader, groups may also have multiple therapists. Male and female cotherapists may provide advantages for some groups. This arrangement diversifies the skills and personality dispositions contributed by the leaders to the group process and facilitates emergence of transference patterns derived from earlier family interactions. Patients' transference reactions may be split between male and female therapists in such a way that the pattern becomes more easily discernible and more readily available for interpretation. The interaction between therapists can also be useful in providing a model for male-female interactions and perhaps a healthier source of identification than the patients' original models. In heterosexual groups, with inevitable male-female conflicts and significant transference distortions, this combination of therapists may be particularly helpful.

Also important are the so-called leaderless groups—not only those in which the leader abstains from exercising leadership but also those specifically organized to function without any designated leader. Such *self-help groups* have proven of some usefulness to individuals manifesting high levels of resistance to any form of authoritative or expert leadership. Self-help groups for drug addicts have been particularly effective. Leaderless groups may also provide a mutually supportive context for interaction among alcoholics or the elderly.

In addition, groups with a leader may occasionally meet without the leader, when the leader cannot be present. Such occasional leaderless meetings may foster expression of feelings and attitudes about the leader and stimulate aspects of group interaction that might not otherwise have surfaced. It is important that the group review and analyze such leaderless sessions subsequently with the leader present.

Group versus individual psychotherapy. Group psychotherapy has advantages that differ from those of individual psychotherapy. Both forms of treatment encompass a wide variety of approaches, levels of intensity, and applicability. They differ in that generally the group experience does not expose basic conflicts and subtle forms of defense in as great a depth as individual insight-oriented psychotherapy nor work them through as thoroughly. The group process, however, adds a different dimension to the patient's therapeutic experience, one unavailable through individual psychotherapy alone.

Although the group process does not induce a transference neurosis, as more analytically oriented forms of individual psychotherapy might, it nonetheless mobilizes a variety of transference phenomena. Consequently the emphasis in group work shifts from the resolution of individual patients' nuclear neurotic conflicts to the study of group dynamics and the understanding of disturbances in interpersonal relationships. The development of more effective ways of relating interpersonally and the influence of corrective emotional experiences within the group compensate for the loss of depth in patient material.

Ethical issues. Along with issues of openness, honesty, and candor, the primary ethical issues in group therapy are confidentiality and responsibility, already discussed in regard to psychotherapy as a whole. As in individual therapy, the therapist must maintain the confidentiality of the group work; he must ensure that communications within the group remain privileged and are not discussed with persons outside the group. Obviously the members must share this responsibility; their capacity for maintaining confidentiality is directly related to how well they function as a group. Group members may tend to discuss issues raised in the group with spouses, friends, or other individuals, thus infringing on the expectations of confidentiality of other members; the therapist must make clear that such discussion undermines the sense of trust and cohesiveness essential to the group's functioning.

In a more general sense, responsibility for the group and the functioning of the group process is shared by the leader and the members. The leader's primary responsibility is to facilitate the group process and to maximize its benefits for individual patients. As the group evolves, members gradually accept responsibility for its functioning and the welfare of its members. Patients' social interaction with one another outside group sessions touches on the important issue of responsibility. Such activity is often a form of acting out and undermines group cohesiveness. As a general rule, the leader should minimize his own contacts with individual patients outside the group. Where appropriate, extragroup contacts, such as individual sessions with individual members, should be worked back into the fabric of the group process by discussing them during group sessions.

In the rapidly expanding field of group therapy, the ethical aspects of the treatment situation, particularly the responsibility of the group leader, cannot be overemphasized. Failure to discuss them sufficiently has often resulted in group techniques deleterious to patients. Situations in which patients' defenses have been overwhelmed, leading to unfortunate consequences, in which inappropriate techniques have been applied with countertherapeutic effects, or in which patients are forced into compromised positions of emotional or physical exposure or manipulation can be counted among such ethically questionable results.

Intensive Group Therapy

Intensive group therapy adheres to a more analytic model and usually involves fairly small, heterogeneous groups of 7 or 8 members. In intensive group work the leader assumes a relatively passive stance. He tends to allow material and patterns of interaction to develop more fully within the group before intervening. The leader oversees the group process, allows it to emerge, and intervenes only to focus the group's attention on specific issues and on patterns of group interaction that might otherwise escape notice. The leader's unwillingness to give answers, solve problems, or adopt an active position vis-à-vis the group turns the initiative back to the members and forces them

to deal with specific questions and anxieties. Thus the group is encouraged to use its own resources and to mold itself into a functioning, cohesive unit. In the beginning, the group members may work together, joining their efforts against and in spite of the leader, rather than in submission to or collaboration with him.

Indications. Intensive group therapy may be useful for a broad spectrum of patients with neurotic and characterological problems, as well as for patients with a more borderline personality organization. Reasonably well compensated psychotic patients also may benefit from such groups, but it is advisable to limit their number to 1 or 2 in any given group. Psychotic patients' sensitivity to unconscious issues may facilitate the group work, but the presence of too many such patients can be disorganizing and disruptive. The tendency for psychotic patients to regress can be tolerated and responded to by the healthier resources of other group members, but only within limits.

Group process. Cohesion is the sense of mutual belonging and participation that members of a group experience when sharing common goals. This feeling does not occur automatically but must be worked on and achieved. By gaining cohesiveness, the group becomes a functioning unit capable of therapeutic work. As cohesiveness evolves, members recognize that they share personality traits, defenses, conflicts, and problems, and a sense of common effort emerges. A degree of regression may be induced that encourages sharing of more personal, painful, and often more primitive material. When the group reaches an optimal degree of cohesion, it can accomplish the most effective therapeutic work; at this time the group also becomes more responsive to the interventions and interpretations of the leader. Group cohesiveness creates an accepting and empathic emotional atmosphere that makes possible significant identifications with the leader and with healthier aspects of other members. Individual patients must work to separate themselves as individuals out of the group matrix, thus gaining greater maturity and autonomy.

Conflicts in the group setting differ from those in other forms of psychotherapy only in that they are expressed in a more externalized form in relation to other group members. Patients may split ambivalent feelings and assign them to different members of the group at different times. The leader must identify and be sensitive to underlying conflicts and to the way a patient displays them in the group interaction. Intensive groups tend to experience regression which deepens as the group work progresses. Often the most significant changes occur only after the group as a whole reaches an adequate level of regression. The depth of material manifested by group members (from earlier developmental levels), the degree of mutual projection, and the tendency for primary process forms of expression and organization to dominate the group interaction all reflect the depth of regression.

The group's *basic assumptions* (Bion, 1961) reflect the unconscious dynamics in the emotional (non–task-oriented) level of its interaction. Basic assumptions of fight-flight, pairing, and dependency reflect the group's underlying trends toward regression. *Fight* may appear as hostility, antagonism, or disruptive behavior; *flight* may take the form of running away from stress by joking, disrupting the meeting, daydreaming, intellectualizing, rambling incoherently, missing sessions, or even attempting to escape from the group. *Pairing* behavior may involve 2 members making private remarks to each other, or one member reaching out continually to another with expressions of warmth, approval, and agreement. *Dependency* may be manifest in behavior eliciting aid from the leader or other members or appealing to tradition, experts, or events from prior periods of group interaction.

The group always engages in some degree of work (task-directed effort) that inevitably produces strain in some part of the group system. This strain may give rise to conflict, tension, anxiety, ambiguity, and confusion. Problems of orientation, evaluation, and control relate primarily to the work area; problems of decision, tension management, and integration relate to the emotional area. Emotionality is an inner-directed, unlearned pattern of response to the group's unconscious need to maintain itself as a unit under the strain caused by forces external or internal to it. The basic assumptions are the patterns of emotional interaction that come to dominate the group process.

Group transferences have the same origins and significance as transference in any other setting. In a heterogeneous group, however, transferences are manifested in different ways. Group members displace transference feelings onto the leader(s), especially when male and female cotherapists serve as the bearers of parental images. Feelings and attitudes may also be displaced onto other group members. Indeed, the variety of members provides many transference opportunities: patients may transfer elements from significant figures in their lives, such as siblings or spouses, onto other group members. Aspects of the family configuration can often be identified in the patient's reaction to the group. A frequent manifestation of transference is "sibling rivalry" with other group members for the attention or interest of the leader/parent.

By acting out, the patient expresses his conflicts and fantasies in behavioral terms outside the group session instead of in words within the session. For example, a patient may express hostile feelings toward another member by calling him on the phone and objecting to his taking sides during a group session. Acting out impedes group inquiry and understanding. Psychopathic or borderline patients with poor tolerance for tension have the greatest tendency to act out. The group's capacity to control this tendency is proportional to its degree of cohesion. Patients may act out as a way of drawing the leader into a controlling or limit-setting posture. More often than not, the leader can call upon group resources for limit setting, but on occasion the leader must take the responsibility himself in order to prevent excessive destructiveness. The leader must also distinguish acting out from the patient's attempts to seek a greater degree of autonomy and mastery.

In contrast, *acting in* is the expression of a patient's conflicts within the group in actions instead of words. One patient, for example, may physically assault another. This nonverbal behavioral reenactment of the patient's conflicts may disorganize the group and destroy its interaction. Resistance in any form is as critical in group therapy as in any other form of therapy, but may be focused in terms of the group's basic assumptions. Group resistance may be expressed by all or by some of the group members; it may take the form of prolonged silences, periods of dependency on and overvaluation of the leader, or hostility toward and attacks on the leader. Reactive defensive patterns may arise in connection with events in the group history, such as interruptions for vacations, introduction of new members, termination or departure of longer-term members, and enactments of countertransference difficulties by the leader. These resistances must be clarified, interpreted, and to some extent worked through before underlying emotions, conflicts, and fantasies can be examined. Emergence of group resistances indicates the need for more active confrontation and interpretation by the leader. In group work, as in other forms of therapy, the rigidity of resistances impedes the therapeutic process. The leader may inadvertently reinforce group resistance by playing into the unconscious needs and defensive structure of the members. Thus group resistance often represents the sum total of the mutually reinforcing resistances of group members.

The group process of *working through* mobilizes resources in the group to deal with such resistances and defenses and gradually modify them over time. The success of working through depends on the ability of various group members to recognize transference distortions and help other members to abandon such neurotic involvements. Working through and deepening of the material, in order to make basic conflicts available for modification, distinguishes intensive group therapy from other more superficial reality-based or supportive group approaches.

Termination systematically brings to a close the patient's involvement in the group when he has achieved certain predetermined goals. It must be carefully distinguished from premature flight, which occurs when the individual feels compelled to flee the group because of anxiety he cannot master. In an open group, where individual members terminate at different times, the usual criteria for termination of therapy apply. The decision to leave the group depends largely on the patient's continuing motivation and his felt need for treatment, but the final decision to terminate is an appropriate subject for group discussion. Successful termination can raise group morale and contribute substantially to other members' sense of accomplishment and self-esteem. Premature departures from the group, however, may represent failure of the group process and, by implication, failure of the other members to deal effectively with the difficulties of the patient who has left.

In the closed group, the criteria for termination depend on the level of development of the group process. The therapist must assess whether the group has become an effectively functioning therapeutic matrix allowing free and easy communication, whether the members of the group have achieved some sense of individuation and autonomy, whether the patients function on the basis of reality rather than fantasy, whether narcissistic and dependency needs have been resolved or reduced, and whether the patients' life difficulties outside the group have improved. Although the therapist should regard these criteria as optimal and never fully achieved, he can expect significant progress to be made toward them.

Termination, a significant process both for individual patients and for the group as a whole, brings the critical issues of attachment, autonomy, and dependence into focus, enabling them to be worked through and resolved to a degree. In this final stage of the group, the basis for the stabilization and integration of the patient's emerging autonomy can be consolidated. Termination must always be discussed at length within the group and a consensus regarding its timing reached whenever possible.

Assessment. Intensive group therapy, properly conducted and given sufficient time to deal with the members' basic conflicts, has proven its clinical worth. The therapeutic results compare favorably with those of individual psychotherapy. Although group therapy may not work through

basic issues with as much thoroughness and depth as individual approaches, its value has been amply substantiated within the compass of its intents and limits.

One must remember that even symptomatic improvement in patients suffering from symptom neuroses (in contrast to character neuroses) often takes an intense group experience and considerable time, sometimes several years. Deeply embedded characterological problems require even more extensive therapeutic efforts. When patients can be kept involved in the group process, and when this process develops properly with competent leadership, significant therapeutic gains can be expected—specifically a decrease in the intensity of inner conflicts and an increase in control over them.

Family Therapy

Indications. Family therapy, which has evolved as a form of group therapy over the last quarter-century or so, is usually possible only in treatment of children, adolescents, or young adult patients. Its advisability depends on the degree of family involvement with the patient as well as on the availability of family members to participate. This approach is indicated when a patient's difficulties reflect ongoing disturbed relationships with the family, particularly families with identifiable psychopathology in other members or in the family as a whole. The family itself is regarded as the unit of treatment rather than as a group of individuals. Generally all members of the nuclear family, including younger children, should be involved in the evaluation. Members of the extended family may also play an important role in the family dynamics, and to that extent should be included as well. The approach and aims of family therapy are similar to those of group therapy, except that the family is a natural, preformed group with a significant psychological history prior to treatment. Family members, of course, often live together and have ties of mutual dependency and intrafamilial transference developed over years of interaction.

The therapist usually encounters significant resistances to involving the family in treatment of any kind. The process of evaluation and therapy poses a threat to the matrix of psychological forces, compromises, and adjustments that allow a measure of homeostasis in the family system. Family members are invested in maintaining the system because of the equilibrium, both intrapsychic and interactional, that the system provides. Attempts to alter it are opposed because of the threat not only to the system but also to individual members. Not uncommonly certain members try to undermine or thwart the therapy. Efforts of one member to individuate and become more independent are usually met with undermining counterattacks to bring him back into line. This is particularly the case for the "designated patient," who often serves as a repository for some of the family pathology, thus stabilizing the family system.

Generally the therapist encounters difficulties keeping the father and the patient's siblings in the therapeutic situation. Frequently one parent will, behind the scenes, pressure the rest of the family into treatment, intensifying their resistance. In a typical pattern, the father and other family members will attend a few sessions and then find excuses not to come, ultimately leaving the therapist with the patient and the patient's mother. The therapy is more effective if all family members participate, because they are all involved in the emotional interaction of the family and thus contribute in their separate ways to its pathology. But even if, in addition to the patient, only one other member is available for treatment, the effect on the family can be indirectly continued through that member.

Family process. The family differs from other therapeutic groups in that it is a natural rather than an artificial grouping, bound together by marriage, blood, and a mutual history spanning a number of years. Moreover, the family naturally includes members of both sexes and at least 2 generations. Consequently, certain aspects of the group process—such as regression and conflict—are relatively well developed and articulated at the beginning of therapy and play a role in the therapy process.

The family may be looked at from several perspectives. Perhaps the most important is that of the family as an emotional system. In this view, each member contributes a portion of unconscious, unresolved affective material to the family's emotional interaction. Thus a system emerges involving specific family members in varying degrees and exercising powerful emotional influences between and among them. A set of interlocking projections and introjections (see Chapter 10) characterizes this system, lending a specific quality to family interactions, and defining each member's sense of self. In a pathological family, the parents may project undesirable or conflictual aspects of their own personalities onto the child, who internalizes (introjects) these elements and makes them a part of his own growing personality. A mother, for example, may project her feelings of inferiority and lack of value onto her daughter; the daughter is then seen and treated as inferior and devalued and comes to experience herself as such.

Within the family emotional system, some members may manifest a relative lack of self-differentiation, leaving them more susceptible to conflicting emotional influences derived from other family members. Thus the child's emerging sense of self may be shaped by unexpressed but nonetheless active projections from other family members. The family therapist must define this unconsciously functioning family system and examine the pattern of projections and introjections, related distortions, and patterns of behavioral interaction resulting from them.

The family system may also be viewed in terms of homeostatic principles. From this perspective the family works to preserve an equilibrium; any disturbance in the balance of forces activates counterforces tending to reduce the disequilibrium and bring the system back into balance. As a result of therapeutic intervention, one of the family members may attempt to define a more coherent sense of self and free himself from entanglement in the family emotional system. Such an attempt elicits powerful counterpressures from other family members to defeat this bid for autonomy and to return the deviant member to his proper place within the system. These powerful forces underlie family rigidity, impede the patient's bid for greater emotional maturity, and serve as the basic rationale for family therapy as opposed to other forms of therapy.

Other family therapists have focused on patterns of transactional interaction among family members. Transactions are communications at many levels transmitted by verbal, nonverbal, affective, behavioral, or gestural means. These transactional patterns are extremely important channels of communication and also serve as indicators of underlying affective involvements. Important pathogenic transactional mechanisms include double binding, pseudomutuality, and pseudohostility. *Double binding* involves conflicting communications, usually between parent and child: one message is explicit and verbal, the other implicit and nonverbal. A parent may thus tell the child to grow up and be more independent, while withdrawing affection and approval when the child behaves in a more independent, adult manner. In *pseudomutuality* the appearance of a sense of relationship is maintained to cover underlying conflicts, tensions, and lack of affectively valid, real relationships. Conversely, in *pseudohostility* the appearance of hostility masks underlying anxiety related to intimacy and the sharing of affection. Such mechanisms serve to blur significant differences among family members, prevent achievement of effective individuality by any of them, and hinder development of real relationships between family members.

The family system in this view may be characterized by alliances and splits among members: such as parents versus children, or a mother and one child versus father and another child; difficulties or ambiguities in the power hierarchy (who decides; who has the last word); firmness or permeability of boundaries between generations; and tolerance for ambivalence without scapegoating. Therapeutic focus falls on the immediate pattern of interaction and the delineation of each participant's role. Interventions aim at elucidating these patterns, uncovering their underlying motivations, reestablishing parental authority, clarifying boundaries, and readjusting splits and alignments.

The most prominent emotional constellation is the emotional triad—the smallest stable emotional relationship system. A 2-person or dyadic system is relatively unstable, insofar as communication between the partners becomes open and meaningful or tends to break down, leading to disruption of the dyad. The 3 members involved in the triad work to preserve its integrity. If 2 of the members move toward each other and establish a more open communication, the third member will interrupt this communication and attempt to establish a closer involvement with 1 of the other 2. Within the triad, the sense of emotional integrity and cohesiveness of the self depends on the involvement of and emotional communication from the others. Conversely, when the level of tension and anxiety rises between any pair, they work to escape the tension in the dyad by involving the third member.

A family system may exhibit stable or shifting patterns of triadic involvement with different family members at different times. The triadic patterns repeat themselves over and over throughout the family history. One of the most characteristic involves the "emotional divorce" between mother and father, in which the father is forced into a passive, weak position, leaving the mother to hold the more aggressive, dominating, and forceful (sometimes castrating) position. The child caught up in this interaction as the third member may become chronically infantilized and dependent on the mother. If the father and mother become more emotionally involved, the child is shunted to the side and must recreate the emotional divorce to reestablish his dependent relationship with the mother. Therapeutic intervention must identify these triadic involvements and allow the members to disengage and to achieve a higher level of self-differentiation.

Techniques. Family therapy is conducted with as many family members as possible and may involve treatment of more than one member of the family at a time. This should include both parents, their children, and any other significant figures involved in the family interaction who are able to participate effectively in the therapy. There may be 1 or more therapists: male and female cotherapists

may provide sex-differentiated role models. One of the major difficulties in family work is that the therapist must constantly keep in focus the family process and relate to the family as a functioning unit rather than to individual members.

Family dynamics create constant pressures on the therapist to become involved in the preestablished family emotional patterns and to take sides, that is, to become part of the family system. Frequently the therapist tries to stand apart from the interaction and facilitate communication between family members. Gradually helping the family to become aware of underlying emotional patterns allows for a loosening of triadic configurations and opens up the potential for further growth. The therapist contributes to this process by supporting attempts by individuals to gain a more autonomous stance. The success of this effort often requires uncovering the techniques by which other family members counteract the individual's attempt to differentiate and clarifying the underlying motivations in both individual and family terms. In these transactions one must keep in mind that the actions of individuals are determined not merely by personal motives, but also by the dynamic patterns at work in the family system.

One variation of family therapy is *multiple family therapy,* with more than 1 family meeting together with 1 or more therapists. This approach broadens the base of interaction and communication. Members of the other families uninvolved in the emotional system of any given family are better able to make astute observations and freer to communicate those observations. Another variation of family treatment is *couples therapy,* in which a single couple or a group of couples may meet with 1 or more therapists. These groups focus on present patterns of interaction, with only occasional reference to their origins in transferences or other patterns of interaction derived from the respective families of origin. Elucidating patterns of projection and opening channels of communication contribute to resolution of problems. The way in which marriage partners interact to elicit undesirable responses from each other is central. Through the group process, for example, a wife may discover how her own behavior and projective distortions elicit or contribute to her husband's ill treatment of her. These patterns are often mutual and reciprocally reinforcing. Progressive pathological interaction between spouses can be clarified, understood, and interrupted in this type of therapy.

Assessment. Family therapy is firmly established as an effective modality of treatment when used appropriately for acceptable objectives. Theoretical foundations supporting the therapeutic rationale have achieved wider consensus and evaluative studies support the impression that therapeutic outcomes are comparable to other approaches, and in certain contexts and with selected cases may be preferable to other forms of intervention. It is often useful in a short-term setting to deal with specific problems and to open channels of communication within a family. It may be useful combined with other forms of therapy— most often with individual therapy for one or more family members. Such combined approaches may promote therapeutic work but may also create complications and difficulties (see the discussion, in the next section, of combined therapies).

Psychodrama

Psychodrama is a form of group therapy, originated by J. L. Moreno (1889–1974) in which patients act out roles and characterizations in dramatic form on a stage. It encourages patients to enact inner tensions, conflicts, and feelings, with an emphasis on spontaneity and uninhibited expression. The roles include director, actor, auxiliary ego, and protagonist. The specific techniques are role playing, role reversal, soliloquy, and the use of doubles and mirrors to express, through auxiliary egos, aspects of the patient that he cannot express directly himself. The auxiliary ego is usually a staff member trained to enact different roles so as to intensify the patient's emotional reactions. He may represent some important figure in the patient's life (reflecting implicit transference derivatives), or he may express the patient's hidden impulses, wishes, and attitudes or unacceptable parts of the patient's self.

Psychodrama stands at one end of the spectrum of group therapy approaches, among those that rely on spontaneity and expressiveness. Such expressive, supportive, inspirational group approaches seem to have beneficial short-term effects. They enable patients to feel better and often to modify specific pathological behaviors. But the long-term effects and the persistence of change wrought through such approaches remain open to question.

Acting in psychodrama is not the same as "acting out" in psychoanalysis. The latter is an expression of unconscious conflicts through activity rather than recall and verbalization. This nonverbal expression works against the therapeutic need to experience and analyze conflicts in order to gain greater insight. Acting out in the analytic context, then, is a form of resistance expressing in behavior the rigid and repetitive qualities of the unconscious. In contrast, acting in psychodrama through dramatic performance is a vehicle for making more conscious, and thus more available for therapeutic processing, the unconscious, repressed aspects of the patient's personality— his conflicts, wishes, feelings, and attitudes.

For those patients whose capacities for verbalization are minimal or for whom verbal expression is difficult, dramatizing and enacting a role may be effective, often achieving therapeutic breakthroughs. Psychodramatic techniques can have specific applicability when other therapeutic forms have proved unsuccessful in reaching the patient. They may also be used to open up untouched areas of the patient's experience for further exploration. The development of firm guidelines for the use of psychodrama will depend on future experience and continued systematic evaluation.

Combined Therapies

Combined therapies integrate group or family therapy with individual psychotherapy. Clinical opinion ranges from the belief that combined approaches should never be used to the belief that they should always be used. There are no clear indications for combined approaches, and at this point the decision to use them with a given patient is a matter of clinical judgment. Patients in individual therapy may benefit from the multiplicity of transference opportunities and social interactions provided by a group. Similarly, certain patients in group therapy may deepen their level of insight and working through in supplemental individual sessions. The decision regarding combined therapies should be made cautiously and with good reasons for this move, and not because the therapist does not know what else to do.

The technical aspects of combined approaches will depend on whether the therapist and the group leader are the same or different individuals. When the therapist is also the group leader, transference intensification may increase the patient's dependence and/or resistance; they may also have a clarifying effect. Another problem is that the increased individual attention may intensify the patient's narcissism and wish for intimacy with the therapist. When therapist and group leader are different, other kinds of transference difficulties may arise. Splitting of the transference may sometimes occur, so that the patient's negative feelings focus on one therapist and his positive feelings on the other. The patient may externalize conflicts by provoking disagreement between therapists, who then make conflicting recommendations to the patient. Therapeutic success depends in large measure on effective collaboration between therapists and on their capacity to resolve personality differences. When a therapist's narcissism or interpersonal difficulties contaminate the therapeutic collaboration, combined therapy will flounder. Disparities between therapists invite acting-out behavior. The therapists must establish clear guidelines and agreement on their respective areas of therapeutic responsibility.

Combined therapies have not been sufficiently practiced to permit a sound appraisal. Evaluations have tended to be unsystematic and anecdotal. In this as in all other areas of therapy, the selection of patients for whom a particular therapeutic approach will be appropriate poses a challenge to clinical judgment and an important research problem for future evaluation.

This discussion of the main forms of psychotherapeutic intervention has emphasized the importance of careful and accurate diagnosis, both in initially deciding what form of therapy will help the patient and, as the therapeutic process develops, in guiding the course of the therapy. The therapist-in-training should first master one therapeutic modality; as experience, necessity, or interest dictates, he can then enlarge the range of his therapeutic skills by learning to work in other forms. Two important results of this training should be an awareness of his own therapeutic limitations and the realization that one therapist cannot and should not be expected to treat all kinds of patients with all kinds of therapy. Not only therapists but also therapeutic forms have inherent limitations. A therapist who masters a given technique will also learn and gain considerable respect for its limitations.

Despite our growing knowledge of and experience in treating various types of psychopathology, much of our information remains impressionistic, intuitive, or anecdotal. Only in recent years have we begun to collect hard data to reinforce and often correct our clinical impressions. However difficult and problematic such research may be, it offers us solid hope that psychotherapeutic efforts will gain an increasingly firm and scientifically validated place in the armamentarium of psychiatric interventions.

References

American Psychiatric Association. 1994. *Diagnostic and statistical manual of mental disorders.* 4th ed. Washington, D.C.: American Psychiatric Press.

Bion, W. R. 1961. *Experiences in groups.* London: Tavistock.

Breuer, J., and Freud, S. 1895. Studies on hysteria. In *Standard edition,* ed. J. Strachey. Vol. 2. London: Hogarth Press, 1955.

Davanloo, H. 1992. *Short-term dynamic psychotherapy.* Northvale, N.J.: Jason Aronson.

Eysenck, H. J. 1965. The effects of psychotherapy. *Int. J. Psychiatry* 1:99–144.

Grinspoon, L., Ewalt, J. R., and Shader, R. I. 1972. *Schizophrenia: pharmacotherapy and psychotherapy.* Baltimore: Williams & Wilkins.

Jacobs, T. J. 1991. *The use of the self: countertransference and communication in the analytic situation.* Madison, Conn.: International Universities Press.

Kernberg, O. F., Burstein, E. D., Coyne, L., Applebaum, A., Horwitz, L., and Voth, H. 1972. Psychotherapy and psychoanalysis. *Bull. Menninger Clin.* 36:1–275.

Kiesler, D. J. 1966. Some myths of psychotherapy research and the search for a paradigm. *Psychol. Bull.* 65:110–136.

Luborsky, L. 1984. *Principles of psychoanalytic psychotherapy: a manual for supportive-expressive treatment.* New York: Basic Books.

Luborsky, L., and Crits-Christoph, P. 1990. *Understanding transference: the core conflictual relationship theme method.* New York: Basic Books.

Luborsky, L., Singer, B., and Luborsky, L. 1975. Comparative studies of psychotherapies: is it true that "everyone has won and all must have prizes"? *Arch. Gen. Psychiatry* 35:995–1008.

Luborsky, L., Chandler, M., Auerbach, A. H., Cohen, J., and Bachrach, H. M. 1971. Factors influencing the outcome of psychotherapy: a review of quantitative research. *Psychol. Bull.* 75:145–185.

Mann, J. 1990. *Time-limited psychotherapy.* Cambridge, Mass.: Harvard University Press.

May, P. R. A. 1968. *Treatment of schizophrenia.* New York: Science House.

Meissner, W. W., S. J. 1988. *Treatment of patients in the borderline spectrum.* Northvale, N.J.: Jason Aronson.

——— 1992. The concept of the therapeutic alliance. *J. Amer. Psychoanal. Assoc.* 40:1059–87.

——— 1996. *The therapeutic alliance.* New Haven: Yale University Press.

Robbins, M. 1993. *Experiences of schizophrenia: an integration of the personal, scientific, and therapeutic.* New York: Guilford Press.

Sifneos, P. E. 1972. *Short-term psychotherapy and emotional crisis.* Cambridge, Mass.: Harvard University Press.

——— 1992. *Short-term anxiety-provoking psychotherapy: a treatment manual.* New York: Basic Books.

Strupp, H. H., Hadley, S. W., and Gomes-Schwartz, B. 1977. *Psychotherapy for better or worse: the problem of negative effects.* New York: Aronson.

Wallerstein, R. S. 1986. *Forty-two lives in treatment: a study of psychoanalysis and psychotherapy.* New York: Guilford Press.

Winnicott, D. W. 1965. *The maturational processes and the facilitating environment.* New York: International Universities Press.

Recommended Reading

Bowen, M. 1978. *Family therapy in clinical practice.* New York: Aronson.

Gabbard, G. O. 1994. *Psychodynamic psychiatry in clinical practice: the DSM-IV edition.* Washington, D.C.: American Psychiatric Press.

Luborsky, L., Mintz, J., Auberbach, A., et al. 1987. *Psychotherapy: who will benefit and how.* New York: McGraw-Hill.

Meissner, W. W., S. J. 1986. *Psychotherapy and the paranoid process.* Northvale, N. J.: Aronson.

Oremland, J. D. 1991. *Interpretation and interaction: psychoanalysis or psychotherapy?* Hillsdale, N.J.: Analytic Press.

Walsh, F., ed. 1982. *Normal family processes.* New York: Guilford.

Werman, D. S. 1984. *The practice of supportive psychotherapy.* New York: Brunner/Mazel.

ROSS J. BALDESSARINI

Psychopharmacology

Throughout the history of medicine, attempts have been made to utilize chemical or medicinal means to modify emotional pain and abnormal behavior. Alcohol and opiates have been used for centuries, not only therapeutically by physicians and healers but also spontaneously by people for their soothing or mind-altering effects. Stimulant and hallucinogenic plant products have also been a part of folk practices for centuries. More recently, modern technology has been applied, first in "rediscovering" and purifying many folk medicines or other natural products, and later in synthesizing and manufacturing their active principles or chemical variants with desired effects. Throughout the discussion that follows, the classes of chemicals used for their "psychotropic" effects (altering feelings, thinking, and behavior) will be referred to by the somewhat awkward terms *antipsychotic, antidepressant,* and *antianxiety* agents. This system of terminology grows out of the "allopathic" tradition of modern scientific medicine based on treatment by drugs producing effects opposite or antagonistic to those of a given illness. Estimates are that perhaps 10% of the American population uses psychotropic agents by prescription and that a similar percentage of all prescriptions are for psychotropic medicines, representing perhaps 150 million prescriptions and a market in billions of dollars annually in the United States alone.

The modern era of psychopharmacology can be dated from 1949, when the antimanic effects of the lithium ion were rediscovered, or from 1952, when reserpine was isolated and the special properties of chlorpromazine discovered. Also in the early 1950s, the antidepressant monoamine oxidase (MAO) inhibitors and, soon thereafter, the tricyclic antidepressant agents were discovered. Meprobamate was introduced in 1954, and chlordiazepoxide was being developed before 1960. Thus, by the end of the 1950s, psychiatry had available therapeutic agents for the major idiopathic psychoses, including schizophrenia, mania, and severe depression, as well as for anxiety disorders. Until recently, remarkably few fundamentally new kinds of psychotropic agents appeared. The period from the 1950s to the late 1980s was characterized largely by accumulation of structural analogues of the earlier agents and other chemically different but pharmacologically similar drugs, and important advances in understanding the biological and clinical actions of these drugs and their appropriate use, as well as advances in psychiatric diagnosis.

The impact of the modern psychopharmaceuticals on the practice of psychiatry since the 1950s compares well with the impact of antibiotics on medicine. In the first decade of its availability, the antipsychotic drug chlorpromazine, for example, was given to approximately 50 million patients, and about 10,000 scientific papers were written about it. The vast and growing use of psychotropic medicines underscores the revolutionary impact of these drugs on clinical as well as theoretical psychiatry.

Prior to the 1950s most severely disturbed psychiatric patients were managed in relatively isolated, secluded public or private institutions, usually with locked doors, barred windows, and other physical restraints. The few medical means of managing them included the use of barbiturates, bromides, narcotics, and anticholinergic drugs such as scopolamine for sedation, as well as soothing baths and wet packs, shock therapies with insulin or convulsant drugs or electrically induced convulsions and neurosurgical techniques, including prefrontal leukotomy. Most of those forms of treatment, except for electroconvulsive therapy (ECT), have since virtually disappeared. Most locked doors have opened; patients and psychiatric treatment facilities themselves have been returned to the community, to general hospitals, and to open day hospitals, or to outpatient units. Most psychiatric hospitalizations currently are brief, usually to deal with crises or acute dangerousness, with a rapid return within days to less restrictive and less costly alternatives.

To conclude that the availability of modern drugs alone has been responsible for these changes would be an exaggeration. During the past several decades, changes in the management of psychiatric patients also evolved; these included early application of group and milieu therapies, an appreciation of the regressive effects of institutions upon behavior, a strongly increased social consciousness, as well as cost consciousness throughout medicine, and the growth of community psychiatry. A fair conclusion is that these social and administrative changes and the new drugs had mutually facilitating and enabling effects. These earlier trends are now strongly reinforced by a pre-occupation with cost containment in American medicine.

Statistics that confirm the important impact of modern psychotropic drugs on hospital practice include the observation that in the United States the number of hospitalized psychiatric patients reached a peak of close to 0.6 million in 1955 to a fraction of that number currently, despite an increase in the total population. This change has resulted not only from the beneficial effects of modern drugs but also from policy decisions to alter the pattern of health care delivery, including contemporary trends in managed care. Rates of new admissions and of re-admissions have not kept pace with the potentially misleading decline in the prevalence of hospitalization; in certain categories, especially among the very young and the very old, new admission rates have increased since the 1950s, and readmission rates have climbed steadily over the same decades, with a suspected acceleration accompanying sharp declines in length of hospitalization since the 1980s. Although some patients who might formerly have been hospitalized are now kept "in the community," often under conditions of marginal or inadequate adjustment, causing considerable distress to their families, certainly a large proportion of patients formerly held in hospitals for many months are now capable of returning to useful and productive lives in weeks or even days, thanks to the current philosophy of care, improvements in non–hospital-based treatment alternatives (including partial hospital, day treatment, and sheltered living programs), as well as the effects of modern psychopharmacology.

Despite the striking improvements in treatment and care of patients with psychotic and other severe and disabling mental illnesses, serious problems remain. While many acute episodes of psychotic, major affective, and anxiety disorders can be interrupted or shortened with modern therapies, and highly disturbed and disorganized behavior is now relatively infrequent even in public mental institutions, available pharmacotherapies have significant shortcomings. These include limitations of efficacy and potentially serious toxicity. Many chronically ill patients do not respond satisfactorily to any treatment. In such cases the temptation to "do something" by using psychotropic agents indefinitely, aggressively, and in various combinations has become hard to resist, despite a risk

of potentially serious adverse effects and increased cost offset by sometimes quite limited benefits.

The development of novel psychotropic agents is extraordinarily costly and time-consuming, with little assurance that an effective and safe new drug will result after nearly a decade of development at a cost of perhaps a quarter-billion dollars. The costs and risks involved, coupled with many failures during clinical development owing to lack of effectiveness in targeted clinical indications or to unanticipated adverse effects, contribute to unprecedentedly high prices for innovative psychotropic medicines. The current era in new drug development for the central nervous system (CNS) is characterized by dramatic gains in the ability to define a burgeoning number of potential molecular and cellular targets for novel agents whose interactions with those sites can be predicted with increasing precision. However, the ability to predict behavioral and clinical consequences of innovative agents is disproportionately limited as knowledge of the physiology of novel receptor proteins and other potential macromolecular drug targets lags far behind the discovery of such molecules and their genetic messages.

At the outset of this overview of contemporary psychopharmacology, it is important to emphasize that the appropriate use of psychotropic medication is but one component of the increasingly precise, specific, research-supported, and challenging practice of psychiatric therapeutics. Other components of sound current practice are covered in other chapters of this book. Important clinical challenges for American psychiatry at the present time are implicit in what follows. They include: (1) skillfully integrating biomedical and psychosocial components of comprehensive and cost-effective psychiatric therapeutics; (2) defining individual and shared professional responsibilities for psychiatric patients in socially, administratively, and economically complex clinical environments; and (3) resisting growing pressures toward an increasingly technologically oriented, grossly simplistic, and essentially "mindless cookbook" form of psychiatry, often based on the shortsighted and almost certainly erroneous basic assumption that treating complex human illnesses with pills is more cost-effective than other supposedly more time-consuming, costly, or ineffectual approaches (Baldessarini, 1985, 1997b).

Antipsychotic Agents

Many chemical compounds have proved effective in the management of a broad range of psychotic symptoms, and particularly useful in the treatment of schizophrenia and mania. Nearly all currently available antipsychotic agents are antagonists of the function of dopamine as a central neurotransmitter and produce a variety of neurological effects in animals and in patients. Efforts at present are focused on attempting to limit the formerly typical neurological effects of antipsychotic drugs on the control of posture and movement. Traditionally, psychopharmacologists were sufficiently struck by the regular association between antipsychotic and extrapyramidal effects of drugs (such as parkinsonism, restlessness, dystonias, and dyskinesias) to suggest the term *neuroleptic* ("nervous system affecting," or producing signs of neurological disorder) for this class of drugs. The carefully controlled clinical acceptance in the 1980s of clozapine, which is highly atypical in virtually lacking acute extrapyramidal side effects, and the more recent development of a growing series of other novel agents with limited risk of such adverse effects encourages use of the more optimistic general term *antipsychotic* for this class of psychotropic agents.

The earliest antipsychotic drugs introduced in the 1950s were the Rauwolfia alkaloids (no longer used in psychiatry) and the phenothiazines. The first antipsychotic phenothiazine, chlorpromazine (Thorazine and other trade names), was developed in Paris as a preanesthetic sedative that was soon found to have beneficial

Table 21.1 Antipsychotic agents in current use in the United States, typical daily doses, and representative side effects

Chemical Type and Name[a]	Doses (mg)			Side Effects		
	Usual	Extreme	Single IM	Extrapyramidal	Sedation	Hypotension
Alphatic Phenothiazines						
Chlorpromazine HCl (Thorazine)	300–800	25–1,500	25–50	+ +	+ + +	+ +
Triflupromazine HCl (Vesprin)	100–150	25–300	20–50	+ +	+ +	+ +
Piperidine Phenothiazines						
Mesoridazine besylate (Serentil)	75–300	10–400	25	+	+ + +	+ +
Piperacetazine (Quide)	20–160	5–200	NA	+ +	+ +	+
Thoridiazine HCl (Mellaril)	200–600	10–800	NA	+	+ + +	+ +
Piperazine Phenothiazines						
Acetophenazine maleate (Tindal)	60–120	20–600	NA	+ +	+ +	
Fluphenazine HCl (Prolixin)[b]	10–25	1–30	1–5	+ + +	+	+
Perphenazine (Trilafon)	8–24	4–64	5–10	+ +	+ +	+
Trifluoperazine HCl (Stelazine)	5–25	2–60	1–2	+ + +	+	+
Thioxanthenes						
Chlorprothixene (Taractan)	50–400	30–600	25–50	+ +	+ + +	+ +
Thiothixene HCl (Navane)	5–30	2–60	2–6	+ + +	+	+
Phenylpiperidines[c]						
Haloperidol (Haldol)[b]	5–20	1–100	2.5–5	+ + +	+	+
Pimozide (Orap)	2–10	0.5–20	NA	+ + +	+	+
Dibenzazepines						
Clozapine (Clozaril)	100–500	50–800	NA	±	+ + +	+ +
Loxapine succinate (Loxitane)	50–100	10–250	10–25	+ +	+ +	+
Miscellaneous Heterocyclics						
Olanzapine (Zyprexa)	10–15	5–20	NA	±	+ +	+ +
Risperidone (Risperdal)	1–6	0.5–10	NA	+ +	+	+ +
Molindone (Moban)	50–225	15–400	NA	+	+ +	±

Note: Side effects are rated as follows: ±, minor or uncommon; +, mild; + +, moderate; + + +, severe or common. NA = not available in parenterally injected forms.

a. Some older agents (e.g., chlorpromazine) are also available as generic compounds; loxapine is also marketed as Daxolin, and molindone as Lidone.

b. Fluphenazine and haloperidol are also available as long-acting decanoate esters for IM administration in 2–4-week intervals (fluphenazine typically in doses of 12.5–25 mg every 2–3 weeks; haloperidol at 50–100 mg every 3–4 weeks); a shorter-acting enanthate ester of fluphenazine is no longer commonly used; other decanoate or palmitate esters are used in other countries, including prodrugs of thioxanthenes.

c. Haloperidol is a butyrophenone (phenylbutylpiperidine); pimozide is a benzimidazole-diphenylbutylpiperidine recommended for the treatment of Tourette's syndrome in the US; droperidol (Inapsine) is a benzimidazole-phenylbutylpiperidine used in anesthesia and occasionally for psychiatric emergencies (2.55.0 mg IM or IV).

effects in psychotic and manic patients (Delay, Deniker and Harl, 1952; Swazey, 1974). More than 20 *phenothiazines* have reached clinical application since the introduction of chlorpromazine; they include several types that differ in the chemical structure of the side-chain moiety (see Table 21.1 and Figure 21.1). The terminal amino group may have aliphatic carbon-chain substituents (amino-alkyl phenothiazines, such as chlorpromazine [Thorazine] and triflupromazine [Vesprin]), or the terminal amino nitrogen atom may be incorporated into a cyclic structure, as in the piperidine derivatives, such as thioridazine (Mellaril) and mesoridazine (Serentil), and the potent piperazine derivatives, such as trifluoperazine (Stelazine) and fluphenazine (Prolixin). The tricyclic core of the molecules was also altered, without loss of antipsychotic effects, and the *thioxanthenes* became the first nonphenothiazine antipsychotic agents; they also include aliphatic types, such as chlorprothixene (Taractan), and several potent piperazines, such as thiothixene (Navane).

More extensive modifications of the central ring of the phenothiazines led to piperazine derivatives of *dibenzepine* tricyclic molecules, including the typical neuroleptic loxapine (Loxitane) and clozapine (Clozaril). Clozapine has particular importance as an atypical agent, lacking the extrapyramidal neurological actions of most other antipsychotic agents, and has convincing evidence for clinical superiority as an antipsychotic, although it also carries a high risk of potentially fatal agranulocytosis (Baldessarini and Frankenburg, 1991; Wagstaff and Bryson, 1995). Experience with clozapine has strongly encouraged development of a growing series of novel antipsychotic agents which share either structural (olanzapine [Zyprexa], quetiapine [Seroquel]) or functional (risperidone [Risperdal], sertindole [Serlect], ziprasidone) similarities to clozapine, but seem to lack some of its adverse effect risks. These developments support hope that additional drugs can be developed that retain desired antipsychotic effects without producing extrapyramidal reactions.

Another discovery occurred independently in 1959 in Belgium, where experimentation with a series of derivatives of meperidine (Demerol) in search of novel analgesics led to discovery of the *butyrophenones* (phenylbutylpiperidines) (Janssen 1970; see Table 21.1). The only butyrophenone in regular clinical psychiatric use in the United States as an antipsychotic agent at present is haloperidol (Haldol). Droperidol (Inapsine), highly sedating and short acting, is available as an injectable anesthetic agent, but is also sometimes used in psychiatric emergencies. Other analogues of the butyrophenones are the *diphenylbutylpiperidines,* including pimozide (Orap), an effective antipsychotic drug recommended in the United States primarily for the treatment of Tourette's syndrome. Butyrophenones share with the piperazine phenothiazines high potency and a strong tendency to affect the extrapyramidal motor system, and both have limited tendencies to produce sedation, hypotension, and anticholinergic or other adverse autonomic effects.

Long-acting antipsychotic agents include long-chain aliphatic fatty-acid esters (commonly, the 10-carbon decanoate) of fluphenazine or haloperidol, and other esters and agents are available abroad. These preparations are injected in an oily vehicle intramuscularly, usually every 2–4 weeks, and are useful in the management of chronically psychotic outpatients who may be unreliable in taking oral medications, or who are responding unsatisfactorily to oral medication.

Pharmacology

The antipsychotic agents are generally well absorbed after oral or parenteral administration, are sparingly water soluble, and bind avidly to membranes and lipids. Their nominal plasma elimination half-life is typically 20–40 hours, but their effects and tissue levels in the CNS may persist for weeks, particularly following repeated dosing. Most have a complex metabolism, mainly by hepatic enzymatic oxidation, dealkylation, and conjugation, and yield both active and inactive by-products. Correlations between plasma levels of most of these drugs and their effects in patients are weak and are rarely employed clinically. An exception is haloperidol; its relatively simple metabolism produces inactive fragments by oxidative separation of the phenylpiperidine ring system from the side chain and its keto moiety is reversibly reduced to an alcohol. Clinical benefits are found in a majority of patients at serum haloperidol concentrations of 5–20 ng/ml (Baldessarini, Cohen, and Teicher, 1988).

Actions of antipsychotic drugs include selective antagonism of dopamine receptors, most consistently type D_2 in the limbic forebrain and cerebral cortex, basal ganglia, hypothalamus, and anterior pituitary (Meltzer and Stahl, 1979; Baldessarini, 1985, 1996a, 1997a). These interactions probably contribute to the various antipsychotic, extrapyramidal, and neuroendocrine (hyperprolactinemia) actions of typical antipsychotic agents. The effects of stimulating these receptors by dopamine are mediated by ubiquitous second-messenger mechanisms that include inhibiting production of cyclic-adenosine monophosphate (cyclic-AMP) and modulation of the phosphoinositol pathway (Baldessarini and Tarazi, 1996; Baldessarini, 1997a). D_2 type receptors occur not only postsynaptically, but also presynaptically to function as autoreceptors that inhibit the production and release of dopamine. It follows that treatment with their antagonists blocks both the postsynaptic D_2 receptors as well as those mediating presynaptic negative feedback, leading to short-lasting stimulation of dopamine release. This compensatory dopaminergic response may underlie acute dystonia, typically observed between days 1 and 10 of initial antipsychotic treatment. Eventually, the presynaptic dopamine neurons become silenced owing to depolarization inactivation, as postsynaptic D_2 blockade continues, with the result that parkinsonism evolves and antipsychotic actions become clinically evident within 1–3 weeks of treatment.

A series of dopamine receptors has been genetically cloned and sequenced in recent years. These include the traditional and most abundant types, D_1 and D_2, as well as D_1-like (D_1 and D_5) and D_2-like (D_2 with long and less common short peptide chain variants, as well as D_3 and D_4). All are members of a large family of membrane proteins with 7 highly conserved hydrophobic transmembrane a-helical regions that include the receptors for most monoamine neurotransmitters. These receptor proteins operate through interactions of their intracellular peptide segments with intracellular cyclic-guanosine triphosphate (GTP), associated proteins (G-proteins), and effector molecules (such as adenylyl cyclase and phospholipase C) involved in the metabolism of cyclic-AMP and in the phosphoinositol pathway (Baldessarini and Tarazi, 1996). D_1 receptors are the most abundant, and their major cellular action of simulating production of cyclic-AMP has long been known, though their behavioral and emotional effects remain elusive. Experimental D_1-selective antagonists have shown little extrapyramidal effect, but lacked antipsychotic efficacy. The D_3 and D_4 receptor types are particularly attractive targets for novel antipsychotics since the atypical agent clozapine is at least weakly selective for D_4 over other D_2-like receptors, and D_3 receptors are localized to the limbic basal forebrain. Both D_3 and D_4 receptors are, however, expressed in very low relative abundance, making it difficult to develop

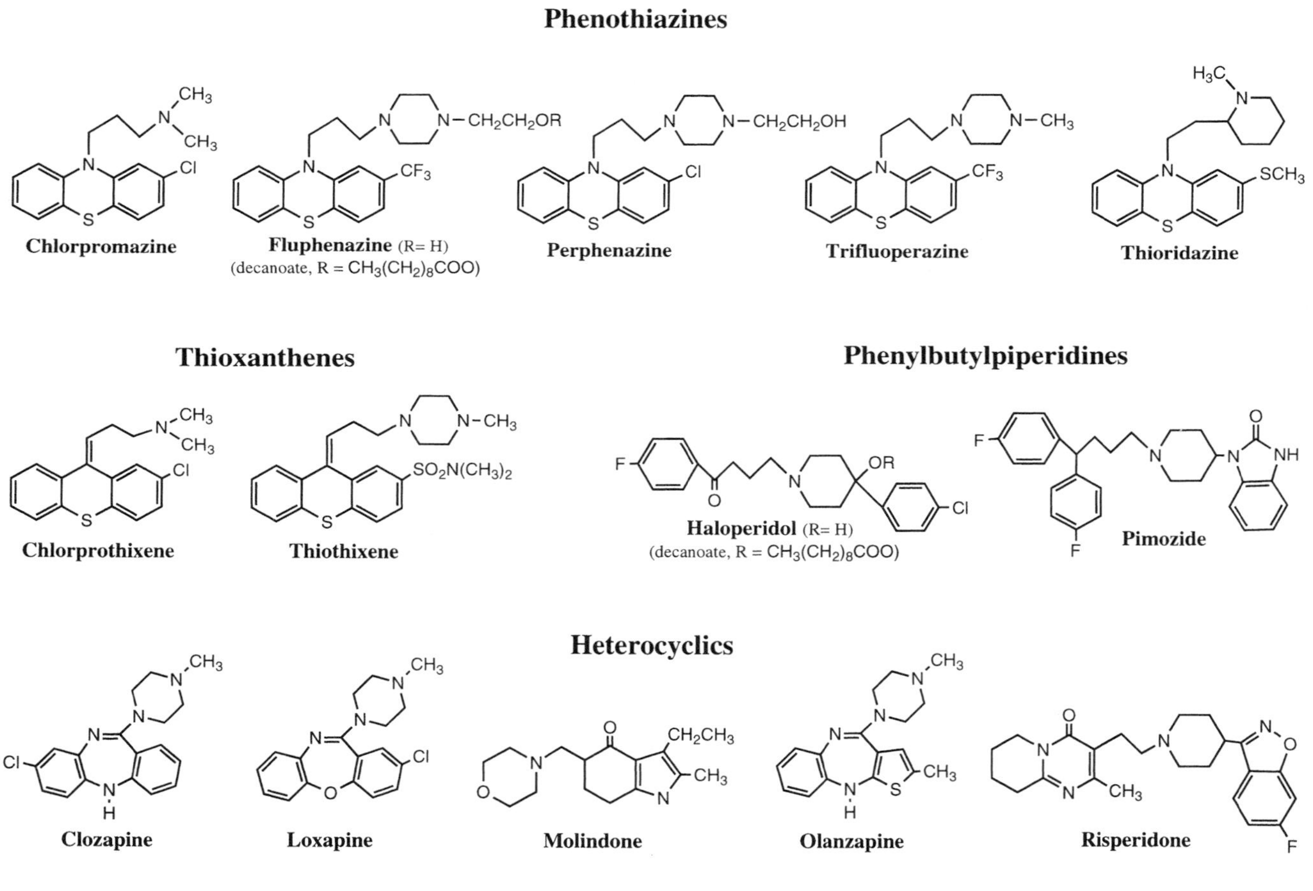

Figure 21.1 Antipsychotics.

agents that are highly selective for these sites in vivo. At least one potent and selective D$_4$ antagonist has lacked antipsychotic efficacy or neurological side effects in preliminary clinical testing.

Most antipsychotic agents also have some anti–a-adrenergic activity, and low-potency neuroleptics have other effects (including antimuscarinic and antihistaminic), sometimes yielding sedative and unwanted autonomic or CNS-intoxicating effects. In contrast to low-potency antipsychotic drugs, most potent antipsychotics, including piperazine phenothiazines and thioxanthenes, butyrophenones, and risperidone, have a relatively high risk of dystonia, parkinsonism, and other adverse extrapyramidal effects (see Table 21.1). Clozapine has a particularly complex neuropharmacology that includes strong anticholinergic actions combined with weak D$_1$ and D$_2$ antidopaminergic effects that both probably contribute to low risk of extrapyramidal side effects. Additional effects include prominent antihistaminic and antiadrenergic actions, and its relatively strong antagonism of serotonin, 5-HT$_2$ receptors has encouraged development of novel agents with mixed antidopaminergic and antiserotonergic activity as potential atypical antipsychotic agents, including risperidone, olanzapine, the currently experimental agents sertindole, quetiapine, and ziprasidone, and others (Baldessarini and Centorrino, 1997).

Clinical Use

Antipsychotic agents are clinically useful for short- and long-term treatment in a broad range of severe mental illnesses, particularly those marked by agitation, delusions and hallucinations ("positive" psychotic symptoms), often with gradual disappearance of thought disorder and improved functioning. Antipsychotic agents have a particularly prominent role in the treatment of schizophrenia but are also useful in other severe psychiatric illnesses including mania, major depression with psychotic features, paranoid or delusional disorders, involutional and senile psychoses, the agitation of dementia and acute delirium, as well as reactions to hallucinogens such as amphetamine (for which benzodiazepines are also effective and perhaps safer), and in certain neuropsychiatric disorders, including Tourette's syndrome and early Huntington's disease (see Table 21.2).

Not only are the benefits of antipsychotic treatment diagnostically unspecific and palliative, but also their immediate effects in acute psychotic agitation may well be indistinguishable from those of sedatives (Baldessarini, Cohen, and Teicher, 1988). High doses of benzodiaze-pines as well as of antipsychotic agents can both provide useful quieting effects in acutely psychotic persons, and both are commonly used in emergencies. Although excessive doses of antipsychotics were commonly used in the past, similar short-term benefits can be obtained more safely with moderate doses of an antipsychotic agent and liberal temporary use of a sedative. Within several days to weeks, however, the unique beneficial effects of antipsychotic agents become clinically apparent, as the more characteristic symptoms of psychotic illness, including delusional thinking and hallucinatory perceptions, diminish. Sedative and antianxiety agents have proved ineffectual in later phases of treatment of psychotic disorders, and particularly in schizophrenia. Improvement in moti-

Table 21.2 Indications for short- and long-term use of antipsychotic agents

Short-term Use
Acute psychotic episodes of any type
Exacerbations in chronic schizophrenia
Acute mania while awaiting effects of lithium or an anticonvulsant
Adjunctively in major depression with psychotic features
For severe agitation in delirium or dementia while seeking specific remediable causes
For agitation and abnormal movements in Tourette's and Huntington's syndromes
Childhood psychotic disorders of uncertain type
Miscellaneous medical uses, including nausea and vomiting or intractable hiccups

Long-term Use
Primary Indications
  Schizophrenia
  Delusional disorders (paranoia)
  Childhood psychoses
  Tourette's and Huntington's syndromes
Secondary Indications
  Unstable bipolar or schizoaffective disorders not adequately managed otherwise
  Otherwise unmanageable agitation in mental retardation or pervasive developmental disorders
  Otherwise unmanageable agitation in dementia
  Schizotypal personality not adequately managed otherwise
Questionable Indications
  Recurrent major mood disorders in which more specific treatments have not failed
  Personality disorders without prominent psychotic features (including schizoid and borderline)

Note: In addition to the short-term uses listed above, continued antipsychotic treatment for more than 3 months can be considered when clinical indications, responses, and lack of credible alternatives are encountered. Long-term treatment is usually considered 6 months or more.

vation, insight, judgment, and cognition, however, typically requires more time and varies with the nature of the illness—schizophrenic and demented patients being least likely to show marked improvement of these features of chronic illness. The sometimes modest benefits gained in chronic conditions need to be evaluated clinically in individuals against the risks involved, particularly the possibility of potentially irreversible dyskinesias or sustained akathisia and akinesia, with impairment of psychomotor skills.

Controlled studies using 300 mg or more of chlorpromazine a day, or equivalent doses of other antipsychotic drugs, have consistently and convincingly demonstrated the efficacy of agents listed in Table 21.1, usually in patients considered to have schizophrenia (Baldessarini, 1985, 1996a). Accordingly, acute psychosis or exacerbations of chronic psychosis, especially of schizophrenia, are routinely treated with antipsychotic medications in adequate doses. While the *potency* (effect per milligram) of antipsychotic agents can vary by more than a hundredfold (e.g., 1 mg of pimozide or risperidone may be equivalent to nearly 100 mg of chlorpromazine; see Table 21.1), the overall clinical *efficacy* of most agents, as determined in controlled comparisons of large numbers of psychotic patients, is remarkably similar, provided that adequate doses were used (at least the equivalent of 250–300 mg of chlorpromazine a day). In about 100 studies that have made direct comparisons of antipsychotic agents in schizophrenia, no agent except clozapine has been consistently more effective than chlorpromazine. Clozapine proved to be superior or possibly superior in efficacy to standard comparison agents in over 80% of some 16 controlled comparisons (Baldessarini and Frankenburg, 1991). The relative efficacy of newly emerging agents remains to be tested directly against clozapine or other agents. Several older agents (e.g., mepazine [Pacatal], prochlorperazine [Compazine], promazine [Sparine]) have yielded inferior results in controlled trials and are not recommended as antipsychotics. Molindone also is not consistently as effective as other antipsychotic drugs, and it and loxapine are not extensively investigated. However, they both offer the advantage of chemical dissimilarity to other agents for cases of dangerous sensitivity reactions. Nearly every other antipsychotic agent in common use currently in American medicine (Table 21.1) produced better results than placebo in at least 80–90% of controlled, usually short-term, trials.

Typical short-term clinical outcomes in comparing most antipsychotic agents with an inactive placebo have shown that about 66–75% of schizophrenic patients improved within 6 weeks and only 5–10% became clinically worse, while of those given a placebo, perhaps 10–25% improved and about 50% were unchanged or became worse. Ordinary sedatives such as phenobarbital or benzodiazepines have consistently failed to produce better results with chronically psychotic patients than an inactive placebo. Yet sedatives can be useful clinically in managing acutely psychotic or manic patients temporarily, while neuroleptic doses are held at moderate levels. Currently, high-potency benzodiazepines such as lorazepam (Ativan) are commonly employed liberally for this purpose, usually with doses scaled back as the patient improves over several days or weeks.

The degree of early improvement in an acutely psychotic or exacerbated chronically psychotic patient with antipsychotic therapy is usually limited, commonly to levels of 33–50% of baseline psychopathology symptom ratings within 4–6 weeks. Nevertheless, such levels of response are sufficient to permit further treatment of a majority of psychotic patients outside of a hospital. To help in the implied selection and triage process, the rate of early improvement is often predictable by the nature of the past, premorbid, and prodromal history and current symptom pattern. More acute and affect-laden illnesses tend to improve more rapidly and fully. Psychotic patients with a poor premorbid level of achievement and adjustment, those with multiple acute episodes or chronic disability, and those with coarse brain disease or dementia are least likely to respond rapidly and well. Nevertheless, full gains for both acutely and chronically psychotic patients typically require weeks or even months to be realized—nowadays, usually in ambulatory treatment settings, in the absence of dangerous behavior, following initial partial stabilization.

There is an erroneous impression that the high-potency agents (particularly the piperazine phenothiazines or thioxanthenes and the butyrophenones) are somehow more "incisive" in their ability to interrupt florid delusions and hallucinations, or that the same agents are uniquely beneficial for withdrawn and apathetic schizophrenics owing to putative "activating" effects. Few firm data derived from controlled clinical trials support these concepts, and several randomized comparisons of agents of high and low potency have shown no consistent differences in efficacy between highly aroused and emotionally withdrawn psychotic patients (Baldessarini, 1985). Although scientific support for these practices is lacking, it is not unreasonable to select the more potent agents for floridly psychotic or withdrawn patients, provided that the higher incidence of acute extrapyramidal side effects of such agents is tolerated. Antipsychotic agents of low potency (such as aliphatic side-chain phenothiazines or thioxanthenes, and clozapine) have prominent sedative effects and thus are a reasonable choice for agitated, manic, and sleepless patients. Their autonomic and central anticholinergic actions also present relatively greater risks of hypotension, falls, confusion, or delirium. All drugs may not be equally effective for a given patient, and so it is reasonable to try a number of dissimilar drugs serially, in adequate and increasing or injected doses for several weeks or months, to give a patient who responds poorly to an initial medication trial the benefit of any doubt.

Administering most or all of a daily dose of a neuroleptic agent at bedtime for patients with insomnia or for those troubled by sedation during the day is reasonable. Once-daily dosing is safest after an initial period of adaptation to gradually increasing divided daily doses. The favorable margin of general safety (therapeutic index) or tolerability and the relatively slow clearance of the antipsychotic agents permit this practice. In general, attempts to tailor therapy to the individual patient's requirements can include trying a different type of agent, experimenting with high doses for limited periods if little progress is observed within several weeks, as well as anticipating and making clinical use of differences in side effects among various drugs. Selection of appropriate dosages can be guided by Table 21.1. With the possible exception of elderly and infirm senile patients, it is usual to employ doses of the equivalent of 250–500 mg of chlorpromazine a day, particularly early in treatment, sometimes supplemented temporarily with a potent benzodiazepine or other sedative agent. There is some research support for the impression that the dose-effect relationship of neuroleptic agents may be biphasic, and clear evidence that unusually high doses are associated with an increased risk of potentially serious adverse effects (Baldessarini, Cohen, and Teicher, 1988). In acute psychosis the median or half-maximally effective dose (ED_{50}) of many antipsychotics is equivalent to about 5 mg of haloperidol (or 200–300 mg of chlorpromazine) per 24 hours. Daily doses above 20–30 mg of a potent agent such as haloperidol or fluphenazine is unlikely to yield greater efficacy and carries a high risk of dystonia, akathisia, akinesia, and other neurological side effects that are unwanted in themselves and may also lead to apparent psychiatric worsening (Baldessarini, Cohen, and Teicher, 1988). In long-term maintenance treatment, effective doses of neuroleptic drugs usually can be even lower than are used in treating acute psychotic or manic illness, and again, doses only 2–3 times higher than the ED_{50} are associated with little or no further gain of benefit and carry an increased risk of adverse CNS effects (Hogarty and Ulrich, 1977; Kane et al., 1983; Baldessarini, Cohen, and Teicher, 1988). For virtually all antipsychotic agents, increasing doses to seek superior beneficial effects involves balancing these hoped-for gains against a rising risk of adverse effects and reduced tolerability and acceptance of the treatment. Sensitive clinical balancing of the effectiveness and tolerability of antipsychotic medication is a critical component of the art of treating chronically psychotic patients.

Standard practice is to continue antipsychotic medication for several months or even a year or longer after initial improvement, guided by the past history and progress of individual patients. Individualized clinical determination is also required to decide how much medication is required, and for how long. Most research concerning long-term treatment is based on limited periods of maintenance (6–12 months) and relatively few types of drugs (mostly phenothiazines), as well as treatment of diagnostically and clinically heterogeneous groups of patients (Baldessarini, 1985; Baldessarini, Cohen, and Teicher, 1988; Gilbert et al. 1995; Viguera et al., 1997a). Such studies indicate appreciable relapse rates following recovery from an acute psychotic illness or exacerbation of schizophrenia, particularly when active medication is discontinued soon after discharge from hospital. In patients diagnosed as schizophrenic, relapse on a placebo occurs at rates of 5–7% per month, and 1-year relapse rates average 60–70%, although many patients who maintain stability for 6 months have done surprisingly well thereafter, particularly in earlier studies that involved relatively broad diagnostic criteria. There is some evidence that abrupt discontinuation of antipsychotic medication is associated with more frequent and earlier relapses, and that gradual discontinuation or stopping long-acting depot injections are followed by slower and later recurrences of illness (Viguera et al. 1997a). Rapid shifts from clozapine to a standard neuroleptic or risperidone appear to carry especially high risks of early relapse. Many attempts have been made to obtain superior benefits in chronically psychotic patients by increasing doses of potent antipsychotic agents to the daily equivalent of as much as 100 mg of haloperidol or fluphenazine. Such efforts have yielded rare or minimal added benefits, with dose-dependent risks of sometimes severe adverse effects (Baldessarini, Cohen, and Teicher, 1988; Bollini et al. 1994).

In the management of patients with chronic psychotic illnesses over many years, the conduct of a medication regimen requires considerable clinical judgment, knowledge of individual patients and their life circumstances, and flexibility with respect to the changing clinical needs of each patient, and routine formulas are best avoided. In some systems, the prescribing physician may not know the patient best, and, with special care and effort, sharing of information and of clinical responsibility in a team effort can often be done safely and effectively. The safest guideline is to use the least medication for the shortest time necessary to obtain the desired results, with later occasional attempts to reduce dosage or, sometimes, to consider gradual removal of antipsychotic medication altogether, particularly for patients with intermittent or affective, nonschizophrenic psychotic disorder. Conservative dosing with antipsychotic agents, with careful individual adjustment in response to favorable and undesirable reactions in individual patients, can enhance tolerability and adherence to treatment recommendations (Van Putten, 1974). In addition, skillful clinicians watch closely for prodromal or early warning signs of psychotic relapse that signal the need for more medication and closer follow-up or protection. Rarely do psychotic patients require a rigidly fixed dose of medication indefinitely. A very common reason for apparent failure of antipsychotic treatment is not taking the medication prescribed. Moreover, there is some suspicion that repeated stopping and restarting antipsychotic medication may increase risks of late neurological side effects including tardive dyskinesia, as well as having deleterious effects on the overall course of psychotic illnesses. Sound practice includes gradual determination of individual minimum effective doses, sustained and not interrupted in chronically psychotic patients, and modified flexibly as changing circumstances and clinical status may require.

With the introduction of innovative antipsychotic agents, new challenges are emerging with respect to initial drug selection. It may seem plausible to consider use of clozapine early, or even as an antipsychotic agent of first choice (Kane et al., 1983; Baldessarini and Frankenburg, 1991; Wagstaff and Bryson, 1995). However, the medical risks involved, including potentially lethal agranulocytosis, and the high costs and inconvenience of avoiding these by the current requirement for weekly monitoring of white blood cell counts, strongly limit acceptance of this option. An even more challenging, and unresolved, question is when to employ the emerging novel and safer antipsychotic agents, such as risperidone, olanzapine, and others, particularly in emergencies, when they are usually combined with a potent benzodiazepine for rapid sedation, and in long-term maintenance therapy. Their efficacy in comparison to standard agents or clozapine, as well as clinical and economic cost-benefit considerations, remain to be tested, although their safety appears to be superior to that of clozapine (Baldessarini and Centorrino, 1997). An additional challenge is to develop protocols for optimally safe and tolerated transitions between pharmacologically dissimilar antipsychotic agents.

Other psychotropic medicines, including antidepressants, antianxiety agents, anticonvulsants, and antihypertensive agents, have been tried in the treatment of abulic emotional withdrawal and apathy ("negative" symptoms) of chronic psychosis. Evidence for their efficacy remains weak (Christison, Firch, and Wyatt, 1991; Plasky, 1991; Meltzer, 1992; Baldessarini, 1996a; Baldessarini and Centorrino, 1997). However, the treatment of depressive or anxiety symptoms with adjunctive antidepressant or antianxiety medication is a common and appropriate clinical practice, and such symptoms or syndromes, with the demoralizing effects of chronic disability, are common in schizophrenic and psychotic affective illnesses.

A final question is whether nonpharmacological forms of treatment contribute importantly to the management of schizophrenic and other chronically psychotic patients. This topic is addressed in other chapters of this book. Briefly, however, the evaluation of psychotherapies in schizophrenia has been much less extensive than that of the pharmacotherapies. Several provocative controlled comparisons of chemotherapy and psychosocial forms of treatment have been made, however. They indicate that the presence or absence of an antipsychotic agent made a marked difference in the clinical course in schizophrenia, whereas supportive milieu treatment and rehabilitation efforts, group or family therapies, or intensive psychotherapy, even when conducted by experienced therapists, contributed relatively less and were largely ineffective or simply not feasible when used without medication. Nevertheless, there is growing research support for the practice of most psychiatrists to include supportive and rehabilitative efforts with medications in their work with chronically psychotic patients, as has been done traditionally on clinical and humanitarian grounds. Indeed, combinations of rational antipsychotic drug treatment with cost-effective psychosocial interventions (particularly supportive milieu treatment, rehabilitation efforts, and group or family therapies) can yield rates of psychotic exacerbation or relapse two- to threefold lower than are obtained with medication alone, and these added benefits have been sustained for up to 2 years (Christison, Firch, and Wyatt, 1991; Meltzer, 1992; Baldessarini and Centorrino, 1997).

Adverse Effects

The most important point to clarify concerning the systemic adverse effects of the antipsychotic agents is that they are relatively safe drugs; acute overdoses are rarely fatal. This safety in no small measure accounts for their enormous acceptance and widespread use. The overall incidence of important systemic side effects during the short-term use of these drugs is a few percent, although effects that are more annoying than dangerous occur regularly. These side effects include feelings of sluggishness, weakness, or faintness, and a variety of mild anticholinergic autonomic effects, including dry mouth and blurred vision.

In contrast to such general effects, the neuroleptic drugs regularly induce troublesome and sometimes dangerous neurological effects involving motility and posture, presumably mediated by drug effects on the extrapyramidal motor system (Keepers, Clappison, and Casey, 1983; Shah and Donald, 1986). For example, the common drug-induced Parkinson syndrome probably reflects the ability of the antipsychotic agents to block the actions of dopamine as a synaptic neurotransmitter in the caudate nucleus and putamen of the brain, much as spontaneously occurring Parkinson's disease reflects the selective degeneration of the nigrostriatal dopamine pathway to the same basal ganglia. Several discrete extrapyramidal syndromes are associated with the use of neuroleptic antipsychotic agents. They include acute dystonias, parkinsonism, motor restlessness (akathisia), late or tardive dyskinesia, and less common reactions such as withdrawal dyskinesias and the malignant syndrome (Table 21.3). Except for parkinsonism, the pathophysiological basis of these reactions is not well understood.

Acute dystonias occur within the first few days of treatment and are most common with the potent neuroleptic agents, including the butyrophenones, piperazine derivatives, and even risperidone. Seen more frequently in younger male patients, they involve moderate or dramatic and distressing tonic contractions of the muscles of the neck, mouth, tongue, eyes, and back, and may include opisthotonos or oculogyric crisis. Occasionally, dystonic signs are prominent in the late-emerging tardive dyskinesias, particularly in young men. Tolerance develops rapidly, and acute dystonia is uncommon after a week or two of antipsychotic treatment, except occasionally on infrequent reinjection of depot ester preparations. This timing, and the gradual replacement of risk of dystonia with that of parkinsonian bradykinesia, theoretically supports suggestions that dystonia may reflect early compensatory responses of dopaminergic neural systems to increase the production and release of dopamine. A main problem with this frightening and occasionally life-threatening syndrome (due to laryngeal spasm or otherwise compromised function of respiratory muscles) is to recognize it and not to ascribe it to a seizure disorder,

tetany, tetanus, a conversion reaction, or a manifestation of psychosis. When the diagnosis is considered, treatment by parenteral injection of an antiparkinsonism agent can be dramatically effective (Table 21.4; e.g., diphenhydramine [Benadryl, 25–50 mg intramuscularly or 25 mg intravenously] and benztropine mesylate [Cogentin, 2 mg parenterally]). It is best to continue similar medication orally for at least a few days thereafter. While some clinicians provide an antiparkinsonism agent routinely, and especially in the treatment of young male outpatients with high doses of a potent neuroleptic, the protective effects expected may not be adequate, and patients should be forewarned.

Drug-induced parkinsonism is strikingly similar to idiopathic Parkinson's disease (paralysis agitans), except that resting tremor is less prominent in the drug-induced disorder. Bradykinesia and some muscle rigidity, stooped posture, festinating gait, masklike inexpressive facies, and sometimes drooling are usual signs of this reaction. The syndrome usually begins after the first days of treatment, and gradually becomes more evident. Tolerance to extrapyramidal effects is highly variable. While it is usual with dystonia, it may or may not develop in parkinsonism over several months to decreasing requirements for antiparkinsonism medication. Many patients show requirements for anticholinergic co-medication for many months after their removal in patients receiving typical neuroleptic agents, even under double-blind and placebo-controlled observation. An unusual reaction, called the *"rabbit" syndrome* or perioral tremor, may occur after months of neuroleptic treatment. Its timing and involvement of the mouth sometimes lead to confusion with tardive dyskinesia, but unlike the latter, the "rabbit" syndrome tends to improve when the neuroleptic is discontinued and an antiparkinsonism agent is added. Generally, antipsychotic agents with higher potency induce dystonic reactions and parkinsonism with greater frequency than less potent agents (see Table 21.1), whereas the less potent agents tend to induce sedation and autonomic effects more frequently. Moreover, agents with low potency and relatively strong central anticholinergic actions, notably clozapine (Clozaril), mesoridazine (Serentil), and thioridazine (Mellaril), are particularly unlikely to induce extrapyramidal effects. Among recently introduced novel antipsychotic agents, risperidone (Risperdal) is only quantitatively atypical in that daily doses above 2–4 mg produce acute extrapyramidal effects at rates that are not much less than for some older agents, whereas olanzapine (Zyprexa) has a very low risk, and other new atypical antipsychotic agents may also share that property.

The agents used most widely to counteract neuroleptic-induced dystonias and parkinsonism are the anticholinergic and antihistaminic agents (see Table 21.4). Amantadine has almost no anticholinergic activity but may facilitate central catecholamine function. Dopamine agonists such as L-dopa and bromocriptine are used to treat spontaneous Parkinson's disease, but their tendency to induce agitation and psychotic exacerbation usually contraindicates their use by psychotic patients. Use of antiparkinsonism agents can often be minimized or avoided by lowering the dose of antipsychotic drug or by use of an agent with less potential for inducing extrapyramidal reactions. Use of antiparkinsonism medications "prophylactically" before manifestation of extrapyramidal side effects is usually not necessary; their continued use for longer than 2 or 3 months at constant dosage and without objective evidence of their continued necessity is less reasonable. The lowest effective doses of antiparkinsonism drugs should be sought. They are often difficult to discontinue following prolonged use. The potent anticholinergic properties of most antiparkinsonism agents, as well as unknown central effects of high doses of amantadine (Symmetrel), can induce toxic confusional syndromes that are not always recognized in psychotic patients.

An infrequent early reaction to antipsychotic agents is the *neuroleptic malignant syndrome (NMS)*. These severe akinetic and catatonic, stuporous reactions, classically involving fever and unstable pulse, blood pressure, and respirations, are typically associated with release of muscle proteins into the serum with severe muscle rigidity. Milder bradykinesia and rigidity may precede this potentially catastrophic reaction. Risk factors include use of high doses of potent antipsychotic agents such as fluphenazine, haloperidol, or risperidone, or intramuscular injections of a neuroleptic, although they occasionally

Table 21.3 Extrapyramidal syndromes associated with typical neuroleptic-antipsychotic agents

Reaction	Features	Maximum Risk	Proposed Mechanisms	Treatments
Acute dystonias	Muscle spasms: tongue, face, neck, back; terrifying; rarely fatal from asphyxia	1–5 days or with each injection of decanoates	Dopamine excess?	Injected antiparkinsonism agents, then oral
Parkinsonism	Bradykinesia, rigidity, variable tremor, mask facies, shuffling gait	Evolves slowly in 1–4 weeks, often persists	Dopaminergic deficiency	Oral anticholinergics, amantadine; dopaminergics are too risky
Malignant syndrome	Catatonia, stupor, fever, unstable pulse, blood pressure and respirations, elevated serum creatine kinase and myoglobin; can be fatal	Days to weeks	Hypothalamic and extrapyramidal dysfunction likely; not muscle calcium influx problem as in hyperthermia of anesthesia	Stop neuroleptic; expert intensive care; dantrolene or bromocriptine may help
"Rabbit" syndrome	Rare perioral tremor; usually reversible	Months to years	Parkinsonism variant?	Oral anticholinergics
Akathisia	Motor restlessness with anxiety and agitation	Can start immediately and usually persists	Unknown; adrenergic component?	Reduce dose or change drug propranolol; antiparkinson agents and benzodiazepines
Tardive dyskinesias	Oral-facial dyskinesia, choreoathetosis, variable dystonia; often slowly reversible; rarely progressive	6–120 months; worse when drug stopped	Dopaminergic excess likely	Prevention best; treatment unsatisfactory; vitamin E (400–1200 units/day) may help; slow spontaneous remission

Note: Akathisia and early tardive dyskinesias are often overlooked unless specifically considered at examination. The risks of most reactions is greater with high-potency, typical neuroleptics, and all but acute dystonia (young males at greatest risk for both acute and tardive dystonias) and akathisia (any age) are more likely in the elderly. Children may also be at elevated risk for parkinsonism as well as reversible neuroleptic withdrawal–associated dyskinesias.

also occur after moderate oral doses of chlorpromazine or thioridazine. Their rarity offers limited insights into other risk factors based on pharmacoepidemiological methods, but the elderly are probably at increased risk of danger from this reaction. They seem to be much less common now than formerly in psychiatric and nursing home settings, probably owing to more conservative use of neuroleptic agents, but are not rare in emergency room practice. The pathophysiology of the profound muscle rigidity in most cases is probably not based on the disorder of calcium transport associated with the malignant hyperthermia of general anesthesia, but it can include rhabdomyolysis with release of creatine kinase and myoglobin into the blood, with associated renal damage. Without expert medical care the risk of fatality in the neuroleptic malignant syndrome can be over 10%. Lesser forms of profound extrapyramidal toxicity, with catatonic rigidity, stupor, and labile pulse and blood pressure, without high fever, may represent milder forms or precursors of the malignant syndrome and are sometimes overlooked or misdiagnosed in psychotic patients, who may be given even more neuroleptic if the catatonia is not recognized as a toxic reaction. This dangerous condition requires early recognition, immediate discontinuation of neuroleptic treatment, intensive medical and nursing care, and a search for infection or other treatable conditions. Antiparkinsonism agents are usually unhelpful and may contribute to cerebral intoxication. Cautious use of the dopamine agonist bromocriptine mesylate (Parlodel, in oral or intramuscular doses of 5–60 mg a day) or the muscle relaxant dantrolene (Dantrium) may help, but these empirical practices lack secure research support.

Another important early and sustained neurological syndrome is the sometimes highly distressing motor restlessness, fidgeting, pacing, "restless legs," and drive to move about known as *akathisia*. This reaction is frequently overlooked or dismissed as a manifestation of psychotic anxiety or agitation, and sometimes inappropriately treated by increasing the dose of the antipsychotic drug. It may be associated with or induce clinical worsening or aggressive behavior in some psychotic patients, and it typically persists indefinitely, producing severe distress and doubtless contributing heavily to noncompliance with prescribed medication. The reaction can sometimes be managed by reducing the dose of antipsychotic medication or by changing to a less potent or atypical agent. Antiparkinsonism drugs or antianxiety agents with muscle-relaxing properties, such as diazepam (Valium), may have some beneficial effects, and moderate doses of propranolol (Inderal, 20–80 mg daily) with little cardiovascular effect appear to be more consistently effective (Lipinski et al., 1984). Many cases respond poorly to treatment, and a clinical decision must be made, weighing the distress of the akathisia against the need for antipsychotic medication.

Table 21.4 Agents used to counteract extrapyramidal reactions to neuroleptic agents

Drug Type Agents	Trade Names	Indications	Usual Doses (mg/24 hr)
Anticholinergics		Dystonia, parkinsonism	
Benztropine mesylate	Cogentin and others		1–6
Biperidin HCl	Akineton		2–10
Trihexyphenidyl HCl	Artane		5–15
Antihistaminic-anticholinergics		Dystonia, parkinsonism	
Diphenhydramine HCl	Benadryl and others		25–100
Orphenadrine citrate	Norflex and others		50–300
Adrenergic-dopaminergic		Parkinsonism	
Amantadine HCl	Symmetrel		100–300
Dopaminergics		Malignant syndrome	
Bromocriptine mesylate	Parlodel		2.5–60
Pergolide mesylate	Permax		0.1–5
Muscle relaxant		Malignant syndrome	
Dantrolene sodium	Dantrium		60–600
Beta-blocker		Akathisia	
Propranolol HCl	Inderal and others		20–120

A late-appearing ("tardive") extrapyramidal syndrome that has led to a reappraisal of the value of uninterrupted and indefinitely prolonged antipsychotic chemotherapy of chronic psychosis is called *tardive dyskinesia* (Baldessarini and Tarsy, 1979; Jeste and Wyatt, 1983). This syndrome has an incidence of about 3–5% a year for at least 10 years of neuroleptic treatment. Spontaneous remissions also occur at about 2–4% a year, even with continued antipsychotic treatment, though with higher remission rates with less medicine and younger patients. Prevalence (corrected for spontaneous dyskinesias) averages about 15–25% overall, with much higher rates in elderly populations. Tardive dyskinesia consists of involuntary or semivoluntary choreiform (ticlike) movements, often with an athetotic or dystonic component; it classically involves tongue, face, and neck muscles but often affects the extremities and muscles controlling posture and sometimes those involved in breathing. Early signs include subtle movements of the surface or body of the tongue, increased eye blinking, and chorea of fingers or toes. Although "lingual-buccal-masticatory" movements are a classic form of the syndrome, and are especially common in older patients, abnormalities of posture and at least mild choreiform movements of the extremities are also common. Younger patients may have impressive involvement of the extremities and trunk, including mainly dystonic forms of this or a related disorder *(tardive dystonia)*, particularly in young men. Tardive dyskinesia may be associated with any of the older typical neuroleptic agents, and has been observed with other antidopaminergic agents including the antidepressant amoxapine and the gastroenterological benzamide compound metoclopramide (Reglan), though not with clozapine. Risks with more recently introduced agents remain to be clarified. Tardive dyskinesia, though painless, can be embarrassing, stigmatizing, and distressing, especially in outpatients who otherwise function relatively well. In some cases vocational and self-care skills can be impaired. This syndrome has been the basis of a number of malpractice suits. This medicolegal aspect of the disorder as well as its clinical significance strongly encourage more cautious and thoughtful use of antipsychotic agents. A thorough neurological evaluation of cases of tardive dyskinesia includes a vigorous attempt to exclude other forms of choreiform disease such as Huntington's disease, rheumatic chorea, Meige's oral-mandibular dystonia, Wilson's disease, and other rare toxic or degenerative dyskinetic syndromes. Rapid withdrawal of relatively high doses of potent neuroleptic drugs is sometimes complicated by the development of acute choreoathetotic reactions, similar in appearance to tardive dyskinesia but usually lasting for only a few days. Tardive dyskinesia may reflect a functional overactivity of dopamine as a neurotransmitter in the CNS, possibly arising to compensate for the chronic blockade of dopaminergic receptors by the antipsychotic drugs. Tardive dyskinesia is sometimes irreversible or may last for many months after withdrawal of the antipsychotic agents, and other irreversible neurotoxic effects on central neurons may also be involved. Other risk factors that may represent clues to the pathophysiology of tardive dyskinesia include age, major depression, and diabetes mellitus (Jeste and Wyatt, 1983).

Treatment of tardive dyskinesia remains unsatisfactory. Antiparkinsonism agents usually have negligible effects. The most effective short-term treatment is to suppress the manifestations of the disorder with any potent antipsychotic or amine-depleting agent (reserpine or tetrabenazine), but this approach usually requires increasing doses of the suppressing agent, fails eventually, and may contribute further to the underlying problem. Yet there is no evidence that continued suppression of the symptoms results in their eventual worsening, even though continued neuroleptic treatment may prevent or delay spontaneous remission of tardive dyskinesia. The fat-soluble antioxidant vitamin E (in daily doses ranging from 400 to 1200 international units) may have some therapeutic effects in tardive dyskinesia, but its potential preventive effects are unproved (Lohr and Galigiuri, 1996). The tendency toward eventual spontaneous remission in tardive dyskinesia offers hope, particularly in young patients and when antipsychotic agents can be reduced to a minimum dose or discontinued altogether. Perhaps the best means of dealing with the problem as the development of less neurotoxic antipsychotic agents continues is to seek to avoid it by thoughtful and conservative use of antipsychotic medications in low but effective doses, and only as indicated by objectively discernible and clinically responsive signs of improvement in psychotic disorders.

Additional CNS adverse effects of antipsychotic agents are also known. Some may increase the incidence of *seizures* in epileptic patients. This risk is particularly high with clozapine, with which it is dose-dependent (Baldessarini and Frankenburg, 1991). Usually a clinical decision must be made to balance the need for antipsychotic medication and the control of seizures with anticonvulsants, the dosage of which may need to be increased. An anticonvulsant, such as sodium valproate, can be combined safely with clozapine when it is required at daily doses above 500 mg. High doses of thioridazine (over 800 mg daily) have been associated with irreversible pigmentary retinopathy. The lethal dose of most antipsychotic agents in humans is unknown, and it is virtually impossible to commit suicide by an acute overdosage involving only an antipsychotic agent. Since ingestions are often mixed, however, it is essential to consider the presence of other central depressants or agents with prominent central anticholinergic activity.

Systemic adverse effects of antipsychotics include peripheral *anticholinergic actions* of antipsychotic agents, which are modest and are usually limited to annoying symptoms such as dry mouth and blurred vision, although ileus and urinary retention can occur, particularly in older patients. The most anticholinergic antipsychotic agents are clozapine and thioridazine, and other agents of low potency. Glaucoma is rare with antipsychotic or antidepressant drugs and is usually associated with "narrow angle" or acute, obstructive glaucoma, itself unusual. Acute glaucoma is an ophthalmologic emergency; chronic glaucoma can almost always be managed with pilocarpine or other cholinomimetic eye drops. Oral daily doses of 5–15 mg of neostigmine, 5–10 mg of pilocarpine, or 150–225 mg of bethanechol (Urecholine) to increase salivation or to reverse other anticholinergic effects have not been particularly helpful in countering side effects of the antipsychotic or antidepressant agents, although bethanechol may help to reverse urinary retention. Clozapine may produce enuresis that can sometimes be controlled with the antispasmodic acid oxybutynin (Ditropan; 5–10 mg) or nasal insufflation of the synthetic antidiuretic peptide desmopressin (DDAVP; 20–40 μg). Clozapine may also suppress clearance of oral liquids to produce nocturnal sialorrhea and perhaps increase the risk of pneumonia.

Orthostatic hypotension is the most common cardiovascular problem with antipsychotic therapy, and is especially common with low-potency phenothiazines, clozapine, and rapid dosing with risperidone or olanzapine, particularly in elderly patients and in combination with a drug-metabolism inhibiting serotonin-reuptake inhibitor (Meyer et al., 1996). Pimozide and sertindole may have mild depressant effects on cardiac conduction parameters in the electrocardiogram (ECG). Other annoying side effects of antipsychotic agents include presumably *autonomic* or *hypothalamic effects* such as changes in appetite, weight gain, and fluid retention; breast enlargement, engorgement, and galactorrhea; and changes in libido and ejaculatory incompetence. Many of these autonomic effects are commonly associated with the less potent agents. Weight gain is particularly striking with clozapine, and may be less with molindone, but occurs with most antipsychotic agents, including newer drugs. Most neuroleptic agents (probably not clozapine) have a prolactin-elevating effect that may contribute to breast enlargement or sexual changes. Although drug-induced hyperprolactinemia has not been associated with increased risk or spread of carcinoma of the breast, some breast tumors are prolactin-dependent and may grow faster in a hyperprolactinemic state. Jaundice is infrequently associated with antipsychotic treatment and is almost always of an allergic, cholestatic type, appearing within the first month of treatment and reversing spontaneously. Skin reactions include photosensitivity early in treatment and occasional rashes.

Severe bone marrow depression, aplastic anemia, or *agranulocytosis* are rare (overall incidence is less than 0.01% for antipsychotic drugs other than clozapine), with the maximum risk within the first 2 months of treatment. Low-potency agents appear to carry the highest risk, and the reaction is strongly associated with clozapine (in about 1% of unmonitored cases), limiting its widespread use, and leading to the current requirement of weekly white blood cell monitoring for access to the drug; even with close monitoring of leukocyte counts, there have been several deaths due to clozapine-associated agranulocytosis, particularly within the first 3–6 months of treatment, when the risk is highest. Agranulocytosis associated with phenothiazines usually reflects direct cytotoxicity, whereas indirect, and possibly genetically determined, immunologically based effects are suspected with clozapine (Mendelowitz et al., 1995). Agranulocytosis is a potentially catastrophic, rapidly developing medical emergency with high mortality. It must be suspected and promptly evaluated in cases of malaise, fever, or sore throat that occur early in the course of treatment.

The question of the safety of antipsychotic agents in *pregnancy and lactation* is unresolved. These agents do pass the blood-placenta barrier as well as the blood-brain barrier and are to some extent secreted in human milk; they can induce a mild degree of sedation followed by motoric excitement in the newborn. There is no evidence, however, that they are responsible for an increased incidence of fetal malformations. Still, the current consensus is that the use of antipsychotic agents should be avoided in pregnancy and lactation, certainly in the first trimester of pregnancy, although clinical judgment must be exercised when the indications for medication or psychiatric hospitalization are compelling. Small, divided doses of the well-known older, high-potency agents may be preferable.

Summary

The availability of modern, effective, and safe antipsychotic drugs has contributed to almost revolutionary changes in the delivery of psychiatric care. These agents have supported and reinforced the melioristic expectations of modern psychiatry. Most psychotic patients can be managed in open psychiatric hospitals or in general hospitals, and the duration of hospitalization has been markedly reduced. Many psychotic patients can be maintained at home, and many incipient attacks of acute psychosis can be managed by psychiatrists or primary care physicians without hospitalization.

Although there are many chemical types of antipsychotic drugs, they are pharmacologically similar, partly as a result of the methods for predicting the antipsychotic activity of new agents by their essentially neurological or antidopaminergic actions in animals or tissues. The main shortcoming of the available antipsychotic agents is their regular tendency to produce disorders of the extrapyramidal motor system. A second shortcoming is that their efficacy is easiest to demonstrate in patients with acute illnesses with the best prognosis; lesser effects are obtained in chronic psychosis, particularly in schizophrenia or dementia. Better agents are being sought that can produce antipsychotic effects with minimal neurological toxicity.

Antimanic and Mood-Stabilizing Agents

Antipsychotic drugs are commonly used in the treatment of mania, but the lithium ion and several anticonvulsants (notably, carbamazepine and sodium valproate) have unique utility and some selectivity in the treatment of bipolar manic-depressive disorders. All of these agents are, however, inferior to the antipsychotic agents in the treatment of other forms of psychosis, and particularly chronic schizophrenia, although they may have beneficial adjunctive effects in idiopathic psychotic illnesses in which an affective component, agitation, or aggression is prominent. Lithium salts also have a unique place in the long-term maintenance of patients with severe recurrent mood disorders, including bipolar disorders and major depression (Jefferson, Greist and Ackerman, 1983). The differential effectiveness of antipsychotic and antimanic or mood-stabilizing agents strongly stimulated modern interest in the differentiation of the various idiopathic psychotic disorders and reconsideration of a former tendency in American psychiatry to use the term *schizophrenia* inappropriately, almost as a synonym for psychosis.

In 1949 John Cade of Melbourne reported several striking anecdotes of beneficial responses to lithium carbonate among severely disturbed manic patients (Cade, 1949). This report led to an intense investigation of the biology and clinical actions of lithium salts in Europe in the 1950s and 1960s (Schou, 1969). Several studies led to early acceptance of lithium into European and English psychiatric practice as an effective and safe treatment for bipolar disorders, both for the treatment of acute mania and for reducing the frequency and severity of recurrent mania and depression, and in recurring major (unipolar) depression—both of which are included among "manic-depressive" syndromes abroad. Lithium salts were not accepted into American psychiatric practice until 1970 for several reasons. One was strong skepticism among American physicians about the safety of lithium salts, following reports in 1949–50 of several cases of severe intoxication and even of death among medically ill patients using large uncontrolled amounts of lithium-containing salt substitutes while on a sodium-restricted regimen for cardiac or renal failure. Sodium restriction and diuretic treatment are now known to increase the retention and toxicity of the lithium ion, and lithium salts cannot be used safely in gram quantities without careful monitoring of blood levels of lithium ion, a substance with a very narrow margin of safety, or low therapeutic index. Another factor contributing to the slow development of lithium therapy was lack of commercial interest in this inexpensive, unpatentable mineral and, consequently, lack of industrial support to demonstrate the efficacy and safety of its use. Before lithium was accepted into contemporary American psychiatric practice, compelling evidence was accumulated for its support, largely by academic researchers.

Pharmacology

Lithium is usually administered as 300 mg (8.1 mEq) tablets or capsules of the dibasic carbonate salt Li_2CO_3, or as a liquid preparation of the dilithium citrate salt ($Li_2C_6H_6O_7$; 8.1 mEq/teaspoon or 5.0 ml), as the generic substances or as various commercially available preparations. Lithium ion is readily absorbed after oral administration (injectable forms are not used); it is easily measured by chemical techniques used to assay sodium and potassium (atomic absorption spectrometry or flame photometry), and can also be measured in brain tissue with magnetic resonance spectroscopy (Baldessarini et al., 1996b). Unlike sodium and potassium ions, lithium lacks a strongly preferential distribution across cell membranes, though it penetrates the blood-brain barrier and cell membranes with some difficulty, leading to brain and intracellular concentrations that are typically about half those in plasma. Lithium ion is eliminated almost entirely by renal excretion. As with sodium, 70–80% of the lithium ion, which readily passes into the glomerular filtrate, is reabsorbed in the proximal renal tubules, and there is almost no absorption of lithium in the distal tubules. Sodium diuresis and deficiency of sodium tend to increase retention of lithium and hence to increase its toxicity. The average half-life of lithium in the body falls somewhat with age from about 18 to 36 hours (Table 21.5). It is not possible to increase the rate of removal of lithium by the administration of most diuretic drugs; most of these, by removal of sodium, can even increase lithium retention and the risk of toxicity, and thiazides or other potassium-losing diuretics can further complicate the electrolyte imbalance. Use of lithium in patients on salt restriction or in sodium-wasting states requires extra caution in monitoring blood levels of lithium and avoiding intoxication. Fluid loading, solute-induced diuresis (as with mannitol) and theophylline may contribute to some increased renal excretion of lithium in cases of intoxication, but dialysis techniques are highly effective in cases of serious acute overdosage.

The mechanism of action of lithium ion in affective disorders is still not clearly defined, although several interesting pharmacologic effects have been described (Table 21.6; Johnson, 1984). Some attention has been directed to the effects of lithium on electrolyte balance across membranes, including neurons, but mechanisms by which lithium might thus exert a beneficial or mood-stabilizing effect are not known, nor are maldistributions of cations in affective illness well established. Lithium, in clinically attainable concentrations, may exert certain antagonistic or sensitivity-modifying actions at synapses mediated by catecholamines in the brain (see Table 21.6). These actions include inhibition of the release of nor-

epinephrine and dopamine, as well as weak actions on the uptake (increases) and retention (decreases) of catecholamine neurotransmitters in presynaptic nerve terminals, but possible facilitation of release of serotonin in some forebrain regions. Lithium ion interferes with the ability of some hormones to produce cyclic-AMP by stimulating adenylyl cyclase, which is believed to be an important component of the receptor mechanism of several hormones, including the catecholamines and antidiuretic hormone (ADH). These findings accord well with the old hypothesis that catecholamines may be functionally overactive in the brain in mania, but they do not help to explain the reported mood-normalizing actions of the lithium ion in recurrent bipolar or depressive illnesses. These effects may be mediated by growing evidence that lithium in clinically relevant concentrations may modify the sensitivity of neurotransmitter receptors. In addition, there is growing evidence that lithium can alter responses of post-receptor, molecular *effector* and *second-messenger* mechanisms that mediate the actions of many neurotransmitters. Lithium has a selective inhibitory effect on inositol-1-phosphatase, an enzyme involved in the metabolism of the ubiquitous second-messenger phosphatidyl inositol, and may also modify the activity of protein kinases associated with this pathway (Manji, Potter, and Lenox, 1995; Baldessarini, 1996b; Baldessarini et al., 1996b).

Neuropharmacological actions of the other established antimanic agents, carbamazepine (5-carbamyl-imino-stilbene; Tegretol) and valproic acid (2-propylpentanoic acid; Depakene) or its sodium salt in enteric-coated cap-

Table 21.5 Antimanic agents used in the United States: typical doses, serum concentrations, and half-life

Agents	Trade Names	Typical Dose (mg/24 hr)	Therapeutic Serum Levels	Half-Life (hr)
Lithium salts		600–2400	0.6–1.2 mEq/L	18–30
Lithium carbonate	Eskalith and others			
Slow release lithium carbonate	Eskalith, Lithobid			
Lithium citrate	Cibalith and others			
Anticonvulsants				
Carbamazepine	Tegretol	400–1000	0.6–1.2 μg/ml	10–20
Valproate sodium	Depakote	500–2000	50–120 μg/ml	12–20

Note: Half-life is for the elimination phase from plasma. It tends to rise in the elderly, and carbamazepine tends to induce its own metabolism, with a lower half-life after weeks of treatment (8–12 hours), as well as that of many other agents; valproic acid has a weak metabolic effect of the opposite kind.

Lithium citrate (dibasic) is available as a liquid, of which 5 ml (1 teaspoonful) contains the equivalent of 300 mg of a tablet of the dibasic carbonate (8.1 mEq of lithium ion). Valproic acid (Depakene) is less commonly used owing to a greater risk of gastrointestinal side effects than with the enteric-coated sodium valproate preparation (Depakote), which can be given in initial loading doses of up to 20 mg/kg body weight in the first 24 hours for a more rapid onset of effect.

Other newer anticonvulsants including gabapentin (Neurontin) and lamotrigine (Lamictal) remain investigational with respect to the treatment of manic-depressive disorders.

sules (Depakote) that may be specific to mania are not known, but it is suspected that their anticonvulsant effects may contribute (see Figure 21.2 and Table 21.6). Carbamazepine and valproic acid both act like many other anticonvulsants to alter the function of cation channels in neuronal membranes, particularly by inhibiting the neuron-polarizing function of voltage-sensitive sodium channels. In addition, carbamazepine has an antagonistic effect at adenosine receptors, may alter the release or function of ADH, interacts with a subtype of benzodiazepine receptors linked to calcium transport, and can increase neuronal firing of noradrenergic neurons in the locus coeruleus (opposite to the effect of structurally similar tricyclic antidepressants). In addition to an anticonvulsant action through inhibiting sodium transport, at relatively high doses, valproate and its prominent double-bonded metabolite (2-propyl-2-pentenoic, or D²-valproic acid) may also increase cerebral concentrations of the ubiquitous central inhibitory neurotrans-

mitter γ-aminobutyric acid (GABA) by enhancing its synthesis by glutamate decarboxylase or diminishing its metabolism by GABA transaminase, but probably not through interactions with cerebral GABA receptors.

By imitation of the treatment of epilepsy, doses of carbamazepine used empirically in the treatment of bipolar disorders provide plasma levels of 6–12 µg/ml, and valproate is given to provide plasma concentrations of 50–100 µg/ml, or as high as 150 µg/ml in acute mania. The powerful hepatic drug oxidation–inducing effect of carbamazepine can enhance its own elimination, as reflected in a decrease of its plasma half-life, from about 20 to 10 hours with continued exposure, and usually requires divided daily dosing. It is metabolized extensively to the neuropharmacologically active but more rapidly cleared 10,11-epoxide (oxidized at the central ring), as well as side-ring oxidized products and glucuronide conjugates. Valproate has a relatively short elimination half-life of about 15 hours (shorter if combined with carbamaze-

Table 21.6 Proposed pharmacodynamic actions of antimanic agents

Lithium salts

Blocks neuronal release of norepinephrine and dopamine, but may increase release of serotonin (5-HT) in some brain regions.
May increase acetylcholine (ACh) production and potentiate some actions of muscarinic agonists.
May increase activity of γ-aminobutyric acid (GABA) through increased synthesis or decreased transport.
Increases cerebral production of many neuropeptides (e.g., enkephalins, dynorphin, substance P, neurokinins, tachykinins).
Blocks receptor-mediated actions of some hormones on adenylyl cyclase (AC) and the 3′,5′-(cyclic)-adenosine monophosphate (cyclic-AMP) second-messenger system (e.g., antidiuretic hormone, thyroid-stimulating hormone, ß-adrenergic agonists, and prostaglandins E).
May stabilize catecholamine and muscarinic (ACh$_m$) receptor sensitivity during altered neurotransmitter availability (limiting supersensitivity of ß, D$_2$ and ACh$_m$ receptors), but evidence is inconsistent.
Interacts with the inositol trisphosphate (IP$_3$)–diacylglycerol (DAG) phosphatidyl inositol (PI) second-messenger pathway regulated by phospholipase C (PLC) and used by α$_1$, ACh$_m$, D$_1$, D$_2$, 5-HT$_1$, and 5-HT$_2$ receptors, including inhibiting inositol-1-phosphatase to reduce hydrolysis of phosphatidylinositol bisphosphate and increase accumulation of inositol monophosphate.
Complexly alters activity or abundance or phosphokinase C (PKC) as regulated by the PI second-messenger pathway, with early activation and possibly later inactivation (possibly through accumulation of DAG); alters interaction of PKC with phorbol esters after repeated treatment but may mimic them acutely.
May alter coupling of guanosine triphosphate (GTP)–associated proteins (G-proteins) to AC or PLC and can decrease mRNA for several G-proteins or their α subunits.
Can stimulate expression of proto-oncogenes that regulates genetic expression in cell nuclei.
May alter distribution or actions of other cations (Mg^{2+}, Ca^{2+}, K$^+$, and Na$^+$).
Has subtle interactions with circadian and ultradian biorhythms of activity, sleep phases, and temperature, possibly slowing cycling or reducing phase-advances implicated in mood disorders.

Anticonvulsants

Carbamazepine and valproate both slow recovery of voltage activated Na$^+$ channels after physiological inactivation, and suppress repetitive neuronal firing.
Carbamazepine may interfere with the actions of antidiuretic hormone.
Valproate can alter metabolism of GABA by activating glutamate decarboxylase required for GABA synthesis and decreasing activity of GABA transaminase, which inactivates GABA, but with questionable physiological effects on the activity of GABA as an inhibitory neurotransmitter.
Valproate may affect Ca^{2+} T-currents across neuronal membranes in a minor way.

pine), and usually is given in divided doses; it may be taken up and secreted by the brain by a carrier-mediated process and not merely by diffusion. Its metabolism is mainly to glucuronide conjugates, but oxidation of the side chains at positions 2 and 4 to form double-bonds can occur (2-propyl-2-pentenoic acid predominates but it can convert to the 4-pentenoic congener sparingly). Estimates of elimination half-life and commonly accepted therapeutic serum concentrations of these antimanic anticonvulsants are provided in Table 21.5.

Clinical Use

Lithium carbonate was only gradually accepted into general psychiatric practice in the United States, is still recommended by manufacturers mainly for mania and acute recurrences of mania, and remains underutilized, its acceptance probably limited by social stigma associated with stereotyped conceptions of maniacal behavior. Acceptance of the anticonvulsants (perhaps as "neurological" drugs) by bipolar disorder patients is sometimes easier. Only a small fraction (<10%) of more than 2 million Americans with bipolar or other recurrent major mood disorders are treated with any form of mood-stabilizing treatment for more than a few months at a time.

Several controlled studies demonstrate the efficacy of lithium carbonate, carbamazepine, and valproate in acute mania, with improvement rates typically of 70–80% in 10–14 days. Even though the usefulness of these agents in the treatment of acute mania is securely based on experimental evidence, clinical response to each drug by itself is, in fact, usually impractically slow. The addition of an

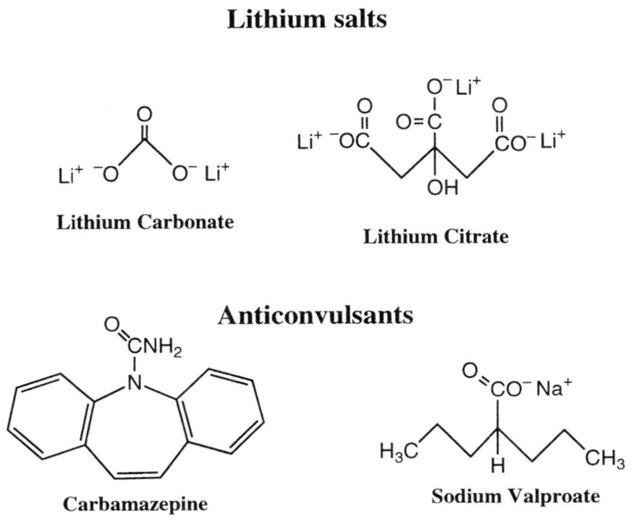

Lithium salts

Lithium Carbonate

Lithium Citrate

Anticonvulsants

Carbamazepine

Sodium Valproate

Figure 21.2 Antimanics.

antipsychotic or a sedating agent (commonly a high-potency benzodiazepine such as lorazepam or clonazepam) within the first few days of treatment is usually necessary to bring about prompt behavioral control of mania, particularly in an open psychiatric unit. In addition, aggressive loading doses of valproate (of perhaps 20 mg/kg on the first day) in those who can tolerate the nausea commonly found early in valproate treatment may also bring about a rapid antimanic response.

There is also excellent evidence that lithium has significant prophylactic utility in preventing recurrent attacks of mania and of manic and depressive episodes in recurring major affective disorders, and particularly bipolar disorders (type I with mania, type II with hypomania, and both with severe depression). Among 15 controlled studies of the prophylactic effects of lithium in over 900 manic-depressive patients (most, but not all, bipolar), the overall relapse rate was 85% among patients given a placebo and only 33% among patients maintained on a lithium salt for over 2 years (Baldessarini, 1985; 1996b; Baldessarini et al., 1996b). The initial indication for which lithium carbonate was licensed was the treatment of mania per se, although at present the prolonged use of lithium for prevention of recurrent mania or acute episodes of mania or depression in bipolar disorder is also a widely accepted practice. Evidence for beneficial effects of lithium on preventing both mania and depression in bipolar disorders is increasingly convincing. Although the difference between lithium and a placebo is greater for mania than depression, the risk of morbidity due to both polarities is almost identical during lithium maintenance treatment (Baldessarini, 1996b; Baldessarini et al., 1996b). Evidence for the utility of lithium salts in the long-term treatment of nonbipolar recurrent major depression suggests a more moderate effect. Support for the usefulness of lithium as a primary treatment for depression is inconclusive, but its place as a supplemental treatment in otherwise treatment-resistant unipolar major depression is convincing.

Studies of both short-term and prophylactic maintenance treatment with the antimanic anticonvulsants are much more limited than the extensive, well-controlled studies of lithium. Carbamazepine and valproate both have substantial short-term antimanic effects, but studies of the long-term use of carbamazepine are limited in number and confounded by including subjects with treatment-resistant bipolar disorders as well as other psychotic conditions. Long-term studies of valproate have yet to be reported and critically evaluated. Nevertheless, both anticonvulsants (and other drugs recently accepted for neurological indications) are used empirically, with remaining uncertainty about their potential usefulness in comparison to lithium. Anecdotal evidence supports the suggestion that the anticonvulsants may have particular utility in rapidly cycling, mixed manic-depressive, and psychotic bipolar disorders and perhaps some cases of poorly characterized schizoaffective illnesses that remain difficult to differentiate from bipolar disorders and schizophrenia. The usefulness of carbamazepine and valproate in depression is not established, although some rapidly cycling bipolar II patients have done well with valproate. These agents are increasingly employed empirically as a supplemental treatment in patients who have unsatisfactory responses to lithium alone. They also have a growing application in juvenile and geriatric mania, and among these age groups may be better accepted or tolerated than lithium, even though controlled studies of such uses also are lacking (Baldessarini et al., 1996b). Use of these agents in various psychiatric conditions is summarized in Table 21.7.

In most cases mood-stabilizing treatment is started in an episode of acute mania or hypomania. If lithium, carbamazepine, or valproate is started mainly for its prophylactic actions in a period of normal or depressed mood, or if its use is to be continued indefinitely after an acute attack of mania, 2 important guidelines should be followed. First, the indications should be convincing, and second, the patient should be reliable enough to follow the required medical regimen. Infrequent episodes of even severe mania or depression separated by several years, or more frequent episodes of milder abnormalities of mood, require clinical judgment to balance the inconvenience and risk of the treatment against the indications for it. Highly unreliable, impulsive, or suicidal patients are not good candidates for the sustained use of lithium treatment on an outpatient basis, because the ingestion of even a few days' supply of a lithium salt can be highly toxic or even lethal. This warning is paradoxical, since lithium is one of the few psychotropic treatments with strong evidence of an antisuicide effect, and this may or may not be tied to benefits in recurring depression (Baldessarini et al., 1996b).

When antimanic treatment is initiated in mania, it is usual to hospitalize manic patients, at least briefly, although treatment can sometimes be started on an outpatient basis in milder cases and with cooperative patients. Initial medical evaluation should include a physical examination and laboratory tests of renal, electrolyte, liver, and thyroid function (including radioimmunoassays of T_4 and thyroid-stimulating hormone, TSH), fasting blood sugar, complete blood count, and electrocardiogram. Although lithium has been used safely and successfully in cases of severe cardiovascular and renal disease, these conditions require close monitoring of electrolyte balance and expert medical consultation. Sound practice also calls for reevaluation of renal, electrolyte, cardiac, and thyroid functions and general medical status quarterly or at least twice a year with lithium. In addition, valproate requires close monitoring of liver function, particularly in early weeks, owing to a low but finite risk of hepatotoxic effects of valproate or one of its oxidized metabolites, particularly in children, as well as in adults exposed simultaneously to multiple anticonvulsants capable of inducing hepatic microsomal oxidative enzyme activity. Blood counts are followed closely in early use of carbamazepine and valproate because of the risk of at least mild bone marrow suppression.

When lithium carbonate is started in manic patients, the initial dose is usually 600 or 900 mg/day, in divided oral doses. The goal is to increase the dose gradually over several days to attain blood levels of about 1.0 and as high as 1.25 mEq/L. Rapid increases in the dose and blood level of lithium often produce gastrointestinal distress, which

Table 21.7 Clinical indications for antimanic treatments

Acute mania
Lithium is effective but slow and usually supplemented with a neuroleptic or sedative.
Valproate is effective and can act rapidly in loading doses.
Carbamazepine is probably effective but slow.

Recurrences of mania and bipolar depression
Lithium is highly effective in preventing recurrence of mania and depression in bipolar I and II disorders and reduces suicide risk markedly in these conditions.
There is some evidence for long-term efficacy of carbamazepine in bipolar I disorder and schizoaffective disorders.
Valproate is commonly used for long-term prevention of recurrences of mania and depression in bipolar I and II disorders, but the research evidence supporting the practice remains preliminary.

Recurrences of nonbipolar depression
Only lithium has substantial research support for efficacy in recurrent unipolar depression and as a supplement to antidepressants in acute unipolar depression.

can usually be avoided by increasing the dose gradually and by using the medication initially 3 or 4 times a day with or just after a meal. The required final oral dose to attain the desired blood level varies considerably; younger and larger patients require larger doses. Typical daily doses of lithium carbonate range between 1200 and 3600 mg for manic patients. The benefits of later maintenance treatment follow a dose-dependent risk-benefit relationship, such that optimal reduction of time ill over 2 years was found at serum levels of about 0.7–0.8 mEq/L, with moderate risk of side effects, whereas the risk of adverse effects increases with further increases in dose or drug concentration (Baldessarini, 1996b). Extensive international practice has found that average serum concentrations of lithium of about 0.6 mEq/L are quite effective and well accepted and tolerated by patients compared to higher levels commonly sought, but often not actually sustained, in American practice.

Doses of carbamazepine used in the treatment of mania typically range from 400 to 1000 mg daily by mouth, and valproate is given at daily oral doses gradually increased to 1000–1500 mg, seeking serum drug concentrations noted in Table 21.5. Valproate is sometimes given aggressively for rapid short-term control of acute mania, in oral doses starting at 20 mg/kg daily (ca. 1200–1500 mg over 24 hours), so as to attain blood concentrations of 50–100 µg/ml within 1–2 days, and daily doses of 3600 mg or even more have occasionally been used safely.

The most important principle in the use of lithium is that, unlike most other medicines used in psychiatry, its oral dose is not an adequate guide, and assured maintenance of safe blood concentrations of the agent is crucial. Blood levels of lithium vary markedly over the 24-hour cycle; accordingly, for most patients, doses are best divided to minimize risk of acute intoxication, and blood levels are assayed according to a strict protocol. The accepted convention defines appropriate blood levels as those measured 8–12 hours after the final dose of the day and prior to the first morning dose. In the first few weeks of lithium therapy in manic patients, blood assays are usually obtained 2 or 3 times a week. An antipsychotic or sedative drug will probably be required in the first week of treatment. While ECT was formerly common in the treatment of mania, its use now is rarely necessary. Once the appropriate dose of lithium carbonate is known, it can be continued until the mania begins to abate; at that time changes in the fluid and electrolyte balance often occur, with an increased risk of lithium intoxication, calling for gradual reductions in the dose and blood concentration, guided by the individual patient's clinical responses and tolerability.

For prophylaxis after discharge from hospital, blood levels of lithium of 0.7–0.9 mEq/L are adequate and safe, and many patients may eventually remain stable at levels as low as 0.6–0.7 mEq/L. Usually each patient has a rather stable requirement of the total daily dose to obtain the desired blood level of lithium (typically between 600 and 1500 and, most commonly, 900 mg/day), although considerable variation occurs among patients. After a few weekly blood assays to establish the appropriate maintenance dose for the individual patient, blood assays can be performed infrequently, at first monthly and eventually quarterly, with random and unannounced blood samples taken as a check on the reliability of the patient's use of the drug. Normally salt supplements are not necessary, but the maintenance of a normal sodium intake and output is important. Patients have been maintained on stable doses of lithium carbonate between episodes of mania or depression for many years without problems. Optimal serum concentrations of anticonvulsants have not been specifically established in manic-depressive disorders, and so tentatively follow guidelines developed in the treatment of epilepsy, in which levels of 6–12 µg/ml of carbamazepine and 50–100 µg/ml of valproic acid are considered safe and effective in mania as well as for long-term prophylaxis against mania and bipolar depression. The possible usefulness of these agents in unipolar depression is not established.

Recent research has documented a high risk of early recurrences of mania or depression in bipolar type I or II patients following the abrupt or rapid discontinuation of lithium, with a 50% risk of a new episode within 6 months (Suppes et al., 1993). This response probably includes an increased rate of suicide attempts, and so is of grave concern. Circumstances that may lead to rapid removal of lithium include the emergence of severe adverse effect, pregnancy, or simple and common defaulting by the patent. The risk of an early recurrence of major affective illness can be reduced by slow discontinuation of lithium over several weeks or longer (Baldessarini et al., 1996a). It is not known whether changing to a pharmacologically dissimilar mood-stabilizing agent such as an anticonvulsant can protect against such risks. Similar responses have been documented with antipsychotic agents in schizophrenia, and are also strongly suspected with antidepressants in major depression (Baldessarini, Suppes, and Tondo, 1996; Viguera et al., 1997a, b). In general, it is good practice to discontinue any long-term psychotropic therapy slowly over at least several weeks, and with close clinical monitoring for untoward reactions or emergence of clinical worsening, particularly over the first several months.

Other than carbamazepine and valproate, alternatives to lithium for the long-term maintenance of bipolar manic-depressive patients are not established. Antipsychotic agents are given to a majority of American bipolar disorder patients at some time, often on an intermittent basis when standard mood-stabilizing regimens prove unsuccessful in preventing recurrences of mania or depression, or when psychotic features persist. This common practice is not supported with extensive research, and there is some epidemiological evidence of an increased risk of tardive dyskinesia in association with mood disorders, particularly unipolar major depression. Clozapine is sometimes used alone or with a standard mood-stabilizing agent when other treatments of severe bipolar disorder, particularly with sustained psychotic features, prove insufficiently effective. Although this practice is not supported with extensive research, it has been found effective empirically in many patients who are very difficult to treat otherwise. Newer atypical antipsychotic agents with lower risk of adverse effects surely will also be investigated for similar indications. A growing list of novel anticonvulsant agents has been introduced in recent years. Some, including gabapentin (Neurontin) and lamotrigine (Lamictal), appear to have mood-altering effects, and are under investigation as well as empirical extension of their current neurological indications for potential psychiatric applications. Potent benzodiazepines with anticonvulsant as well as sedative actions are very useful in the short-term control of mania, and may help to abort emerging recurrences of mania, but remain untested for long-term prevention of recurrences of major mood disturbances. Several antihypertensive agents, including the a_2-autoadrenoceptor agonist clonidine and the calcium channel blocker verapamil, may have weak antimanic effects, but these are rarely useful clinically, and the long-term protective effects of such drugs against recurrences of mania or depression are not established.

Adverse Effects

The most common problems associated with the use of lithium salts are mild or occasionally distressing nausea, vomiting, and diarrhea, usually when doses are increased rapidly (Table 21.8). Subtle but surprisingly subjectively important effects on the nervous system may also be felt, and they contribute to inconsistent acceptance of lithium or its outright refusal. These may be difficult to verify objectively without sensitive neuropsychological assessments, but include loss of mental acuity, spontaneity, and verve, minor memory impairments, and defects in fine motor control. Motor effects can be seen as resting tremor and unsteady handwriting, which typically worsen with

incipient intoxication (for severe, sustained tremor small doses of propranolol [Inderal] may help). Signs of cerebral intoxication, with confusion, slurred speech, and ataxia, are especially common in elderly patients, who clear and tolerate lithium less well than young adults. Moreover, it is important to realize that even nominally "therapeutic" serum concentrations of lithium assayed at their daily nadir are typically associated with much higher peak levels, and these can be at least two- to threefold higher than the morning level, even when divided doses of lithium salts are employed. Ratios of peak-to-trough serum concentrations of lithium are much more limited with slow-release pharmaceutical preparations of lithium carbonate.

The most important means of detecting serious intoxication early are clinical signs, and blood assays should be considered only as secondary and confirmatory. When signs of intoxication are noted, the intake of lithium should be decreased or stopped without waiting for the results of a blood lithium assay. Early signs of *intoxication* with lithium include increasing tremor, weakness, ataxia, giddiness, drowsiness, slurred speech, blurred vision, and tinnitus. More severe intoxication includes increased neuromuscular irritability, increased deep tendon reflexes, nystagmus, and increasing lethargy and stupor leading to coma, sometimes with generalized seizures. Extrapyramidal reactions are rare with ordinary doses of lithium, but choreoathetosis can occur in severe intoxication. The electroencephalogram (EEG) of patients receiving lithium ordinarily reveals generalized slowing, with a prominent activity at 4–6 Hz (cycles/second), even without toxic levels. Toxicity can be expected at blood levels of 2–4 mEq/L, and levels much above 5 mEq/L may be fatal. In acute lithium overdoses the usual causes of death are the secondary complications of coma, including pneumonia and shock. Lithium probably also has some effect of lowering seizure threshold, particularly in patients with established epilepsy; such patients are probably more safely treated with carbamazepine or valproate. A few cases of uncertain significance have been reported that raise the question whether the combination of lithium in high doses with haloperidol (Haldol) may produce severe forms of potentially irreversible and even fatal CNS intoxication, although this combination has been used safely throughout the world for many years and continues to be used. The crucial lesson from experiences with lithium intoxication, alone or in combination with other drugs, is to appreciate the potential of lithium, alone, in excessive and neurotoxic doses, to produce severe cerebral intoxication, often with residual cognitive, motor, or other neurological sequelae. In addition, it is particularly important to watch for subtle forms of organic mental disorder (delirium or reversible "dementia") in elderly patients receiving prolonged lithium treatment. Finally, since bipolar disorders have among the highest known rates of comorbid substance abuse (alcohol and stimulants are especially common choices), many cases of apparent lithium intoxication are complicated by the intake of multiple cerebrotoxins.

Cardiovascular problems are unusual in patients given controlled quantities of lithium salts. Hypotension and cardiac arrhythmias are rare, although electrocardiographic changes can occur. With doses likely to be encountered clinically, the most typical ECG changes are similar to those associated with hypokalemia, even though blood levels of potassium are usually normal. These changes include flattening and even inversion of the T-waves; effects are dose-dependent and reversible and probably have little pathophysiological significance. In experimental animals extraordinarily high, toxic concentrations of lithium (above 10 mEq/liter) have been reported to produce more profound changes in the ECG.

Renal tubular damage due to lithium had been a concern, partly because pathological changes were reported in early cases of gross overdosage with lithium in patients with preexisting circulatory and renal disease. Renal tubular damage in the rat has also been reported, but these findings are difficult to relate to the clinical situation because the studies involved toxic doses of lithium salts. Sev-

---

Table 21.8 Adverse effects of antimanic agents

Lithium salts
Light-headedness, lethargy, weakness, mild confusion, tremor
Severe intoxication and coma on overdose, occasionally with irreversible brain damage (dialysis helps)
Myasthenia gravis may worsen
Early polyuria and thirst; later tolerance usual
Later diabetes insipidus with elevated levels and poor response to ADH
Weight gain is prominent
Creatinine rarely rises gradually with granulomatous changes in renal biopsy (associated with polyuria)
Occasional diffuse, nontoxic, nonmalignant goiter
Borderline or mild hypothyroidism, occasionally severe; TSH elevated early
Minor changes in serum calcium; uncertain effects on bone maturation or osteoporosis
Mild nonleukemic leukocytosis (extra caution when stopping lithium with clozapine or carbamazepine)
Marked worsening of acne vulgaris
Variable, usually mild, alopecia
Rare skin eruptions, folliculitis (resembling keratosis pilaris), or ulcerations
Mild fluid retention or local edema
Most diuretics retain lithium; loss of K^+ can increase toxicity
Teratogenic effects (especially Ebstein's tricuspid valve and cardiac septal defects, ca. 1/7500 risk)

Anticonvulsants
Sedation, dizziness, ataxia (carbamazepine and valproate)
Nausea, vomiting, cramps, diarrhea (valproate > carbamazepine)
Weight gain (carbamazepine and valproate)
Headache (carbamazepine more than valproate)
Occasional hepatic dysfunction, rare damage
Carbamazepine: rash, systemic inflammatory syndromes; valproate: rash and alopecia
Early marrow suppression, occasionally severe (carbamazepine: leukocytes, erythrocytes; valproate: platelets)
Carbamazepine rarely associated with inappropriate ADH with hyponatremia
Reduced cardiac conduction (usually minor unless overdose)
Hypotension (carbamazepine >> valproate)
Valproate may decrease bone density (including children)
Valproate may induce masculinization in women
Valproate: rare toxic hepatic damage (especially in children or when mixed with other hepatic inducing agents including carbamazepine; fatal in ca. 1/50,000 exposures)
Teratogenic effects (spina bifida with valproate > carbamazepine, ca. 1/100; carbamazepine: dysmorphic face)
Altered drug metabolism (carbamazepine induces metabolism of many other agents, including itself; valproate interferes moderately with metabolism of many other agents)

Note: > = greater than; >> = much greater than.

eral studies of renal biopsies in bipolar patients treated with lithium for several years have also found evidence of nonspecific degenerative and granulomatous reactions. These are uncommon and most likely to be found when persistent diabetes insipidus is present clinically. The most common adverse renal effects of lithium treatment are early, usually temporary, appearance of thirst and polyuria. Use of once-daily dosing with lithium may limit polyuria, but this effect is minor (<10% reduction in 24-hour urine volume) in most patients, and should be balanced against the increased risk of cerebral intoxication at peak serum concentrations, which can be several times above the trough concentrations on which the preceding dosing recommendations are based (Baldessarini et al., 1996b). Later a minority of patients develop a form of nephrogenic diabetes insipidus, resulting in the intake of many liters of water per day and the output of large quantities of dilute urine (over 5 liters a day), with elevations of circulating concentrations of ADH and loss of a renal concentrating response to exogenous ADH peptides. This syndrome is probably due to the ability of lithium ion to interfere with the activity of ADH on the renal tubules, including blockade of the response of adenylyl cyclase mediated by ADH receptors. This syndrome is reversible and is usually managed conservatively by reducing the intake of lithium or discontinuing its use. In contrast, carbamazepine has been associated with excesses of ADH, with water retention and sometimes intoxication. When there are compelling indications to continue the use of lithium, the syndrome often responds paradoxically to thiazides and other diuretics, as do other forms of nephrogenic diabetes insipidus, and their use may require supplemental daily doses of potassium. This treatment might be considered after appropriate medical consultation and usually requires reducing the dose of lithium and close monitoring of potassium and other electrolytes. It is probably done more safely with diuretics which do not induce hypokalemia, such as amiloride (Milodor), whose toxic effects are probably increased with lithium.

Another uncommon metabolic abnormality is the development of *goiter* in patients receiving ordinary doses of lithium salts for prolonged periods. Patients almost always remain euthyroid or only slightly hypothyroid, although the circulating levels of TSH may increase, and benign, diffuse nontoxic goiter is sometimes found in association with long-term lithium treatment. Some patients who formerly maintained high normal circulating levels of thyroid hormone may become medically symptomatic or depressed when levels fall into the low end of the nominally normal range, and for them use of supplemental thyroid hormone may be beneficial. Lithium can interfere with thyroid metabolism at several points, including the iodination and release of iodinated thyronines, and some evidence of interference with their actions on target tissues. There is no known serious danger from the goiter (it is reversible and not precancerous), but judgment must be exercised, with the help of endocrinological consultation, as to whether to continue the treatment with lithium rather than considering an alternative such as an anticonvulsant. Rarely does significant functional hypothyroidism or myxedema occur, although middle-aged women with occult thyroiditis or struma and marginal thyroid function are at risk of becoming clinically hypothyroid when treated with lithium for prolonged periods. Adding supplemental exogenous thyroxine or triiodothyronine often leads to regression of the goiter and maintenance of the euthyroid status while lithium therapy is pursued.

Other adverse effects of lithium include the occasional development of localized edema and eruptions or even ulcerations of the *skin.* Use of antihistaminic agents or shifting to a different lithium preparation may help eliminate the rashes. Worsening of acne vulgaris is a common dermatologic problem during lithium treatment, and psoriasis may also worsen. For rare skin ulcers associated with use of lithium, topical steroids are beneficial. Hepatic and bone marrow toxicity are rarely associated with lithium therapy, although mild elevations of the leukocyte count in the peripheral blood of uncertain significance (not preleukemic) are not unusual. Occasionally, when lithium has been combined with an agent having bone marrow–suppressing (carbamazepine) or toxic effects (clozapine), leukocyte counts will fall precipitously when lithium is removed, calling for particularly close clinical monitoring and blood cell counting.

Appropriate concern surrounds the use of lithium in *pregnancy* and *lactation,* partly based on evidence in experimental animals that very high doses of lithium are associated with fetal wastage and anomalies of the CNS. Together with other alterations in fluid and electrolyte metabolism in pregnancy, lithium clearance increases; with physiological diuresis after delivery, there may be increased retention of lithium and increased risk of intoxication. Fetal distress may occur when lithium is used near term, and hypotonia and listlessness may follow hyperkinesis in the newborn infants of mothers taking lithium. Reports of human fetal anomalies associated with the use of lithium in pregnancy (especially cardiovascular malformations) are sufficiently alarming to urge avoidance of its use in the early months of pregnancy, to advise caution and discontinuation of lithium before term, and to advise the use of lithium in pregnancy only for the most urgent indications.

The most consistently suspected teratogenic effect is

Ebstein's anomaly of the right heart, with a malformed tricuspid valve and variable septal defects. This condition is often detectable in utero by ultrasonography, is associated with a range of physiological impairments, and can usually be repaired surgically early in life. Most of the evidence for an association of this cardiac anomaly with fetal exposure to lithium in the first trimester of pregnancy has arisen from registries of children born after exposure to lithium in utero. Such data are unreliable owing to selective reporting of adverse events more often than normal outcomes. Better-controlled epidemiological investigations continue to support this association, but suggest that risk may rise from a base rate of spontaneous Ebstein's anomalies of about 1/20,000 live births to levels that are only 2 or 3 times higher (about 1/7500). Given this relatively low level of risk and availability of options for managing the problem if it does arise, the decision whether to discontinue lithium during pregnancy should be balanced against the past frequency and severity of psychiatric illness and the high risk of early recurrence associated with abrupt discontinuation of lithium (Cohen et al., 1994). Options may include avoiding exposure to lithium in the several months involved in attaining pregnancy and through the first trimester, with gradual removal of lithium in the time preceding a planned pregnancy. Relatively safe treatment options for severe exacerbations of mania or depression during pregnancy include use of ECT, neuroleptics, antidepressants, and hospitalization, but the anticonvulsants carbamazepine and particularly valproate are not considered safe in pregnancy.

Adverse effects of the antimanic anticonvulsants carbamazepine and valproate include suppression of bone marrow function, usually to a moderate degree, but sometimes with clinically significant anemia, leukopenia, or thrombocytopenia. In addition, valproic acid has rarely (ca. 1/10,000 treated cases) produced potentially fatal (1/50,000) hepatic damage, most often in infants. This effect may be mediated, at least in part, by the uncommon oxidized metabolite (2-propyl-4-pentenoic acid or D^4-valproic acid) with a reactive double-bond in the side chain of the drug; its formation may be made more likely with simultaneous use of anticonvulsants which induce the activity of hepatic microsomal oxidases. For this reason, the combination of valproate with carbamazepine is not recommended as a routine practice. More common side effects of these anticonvulsants include excessive sedation, mild cerebral intoxication, and common nausea, particularly with valproate. Carbamazepine is also associated frequently with rashes that may limit its use, and it may induce inapppropriate secretion of ADH. Lithium and the antimanic anticonvulsants have all been associated with weight gain, which is a common reason for non-

acceptance of their long-term use. Another prominent complicating property of valproic acid is its striking ability to induce the hepatic oxidative metabolism and clearance of itself and many other agents, including antidepressants and antipsychotic agents. Valproate is one of the few older anticonvulsants without such microsomal inducing effects; in fact, valproate can compete with the clearance of some other drugs to produce moderate increases in their circulating concentrations (Meyer et al., 1996). Valproate is not considered safe in pregnancy owing to its strong association with potentially crippling and irreparable spina bifida at risk of more than 1/100 cases (mainly epileptic women, whose comparability to bipolar women is not established); carbamazepine may also carry some increased risk of spina bifida and has also been associated with other suspected fetal anomalies, including dysmorphic facial development (Cohen et al., 1994).

Summary

Lithium ion provides a useful and relatively specific form of chemotherapy for manic and hypomanic episodes, although its clinical actions may be delayed for a week or more, requiring the use of an antipsychotic or sedative agent in the initial period to control the behavior of very disturbed patients. Lithium also has beneficial effects in preventing recurrences of bipolar depression, and probably also exerts beneficial actions in unipolar major depression. The main limitations of lithium are its narrow therapeutic index and requirement of close medical supervision. The most promising aspect of the use of lithium is its prophylactic effectiveness in reducing the frequency and severity of manic and depressive attacks in bipolar illness and conditions that may be related to it. Some anticonvulsants, notably carbamazepine and valproic acid, have antimanic actions, though their long-term benefits for preventing recurrences of mania or depression are not securely established by compelling research evidence. Nevertheless, these anticonvulsants have found increasing empirical clinical acceptance as alternatives or supplements to lithium in recent years.

Antidepressant Agents

Before the 1950s, medical treatments of depression included the amphetamines for psychomotor retardation and the barbiturates for agitation. Stimulants are still occasionally used for some cases of mild or secondary depression as well as in geriatric practice for mild dementia and anergic depression and in pediatrics for attention deficit–hyperactivity disorder (ADHD). However, there is little reason to use these agents in most cases of major depression; their efficacy in severe depression is unproved, and they can worsen agitation and psychosis. In the late 1940s structural analogues of nicotinic acid developed for the treatment of tuberculosis included the hydrazine compound *iproniazid* (Marsilid). This drug was found to have euphoriant or mood-elevating and behaviorally activating properties in some patients, and in the mid-1950s it was reported to have useful antidepressant properties in psychiatric patients and found to be a potent and irreversible inhibitor of the amine-catabolizing enzyme monoamine oxidase. Other hydrazine compounds and nonhydrazines with MAO-inhibiting properties were also introduced into psychiatry. In the late 1950s the second important and long-dominant class of mood-elevating agents, the *tricyclic antidepressants* (TCAs), was introduced with the discovery of mood-elevating properties of imipramine (Tofranil and others; Hollister, 1978). These include clomipramine (Anafranil), the chlorinated derivative of imipramine, which can be considered a forerunner of the now clinically dominant selective serotonin potentiating agents.

The TCAs have two benzene rings joined through a 7-member central ring (Figure 21.3). The original compound of this class, imipramine (Tofranil), was developed and initially tested clinically in psychotic patients because its preclinical properties and structure were superficially similar to those of the phenothiazines. In one of its initial clinical trials in Switzerland, Roland Kuhn found in 1957–58 that imipramine had little antipsychotic efficacy but had mood-elevating and behavior-activating properties (Kuhn, 1958). Soon thereafter, imipramine and several other structurally related tricyclic agents were demonstrated to be effective in major depression in controlled comparisons with either a placebo or a stimulant. These beneficial clinical effects have not always been as demonstrable as those of the antipsychotic agents in placebo-controlled trials. Moreover, the TCAs have a high risk of adverse effects and can be lethal on acute overdose. Nevertheless, they rapidly emerged in the 1960s as the standard agents for major depression, and have been particularly successful in severe and classically melancholic forms of depression.

Since the late 1980s, after nearly two decades of little progress, several new antidepressants have been introduced in the United States. The most important new class of agents are the selective serotonin-reuptake inhibitors (SRIs or SSRIs), which potentiate the actions of serotonin (5-hydroxytryptamine) as a neurotransmitter. Clomipramine has many properties of an SRI, but it is also a TCA and potentiates norepinephrine as a neurotransmitter as well as serotonin. Zimelidine can be considered the first

truly selective SRI, but it was withdrawn from clinical use owing to association with a serum sicknesslike febrile syndrome and ascending paralysis of the Guillain-Barré type. The first clinically successful selective serotonin-reuptake inhibitor was fluoxetine (Prozac). In recent years several additional SRI agents have entered general clinical use, and others remain in experimental status. In order of their licensing in the United States, they include sertraline (Zoloft), paroxetine (Paxil), venlafaxine (Effexor), and fluvoxamine (Luvox).

Finally, several agents with novel structures and incompletely defined actions have been added, including the older sedative-antidepressant agent trazodone (Desyrel) and its newer congener nefazodone (Serzone), which also interact with serotonin neurotransmission, the stimulantlike drug bupropion (Wellbutrin), and a new drug mirtazapine (Remeron), which is a close structural analogue of an older European antidepressant mianserin.

Pharmacology

Historically, the monoamine-potentiating effects of the MAO inhibitors, which prevent the metabolic destruction of serotonin and norepinephrine, and later the TCAs, which prevent inactivation of these monoamines by blocking their neuronal transport, gave important encouragement to the "amine hypotheses" of the pathophysiology of affective disorders, which suggest that depression is associated with a deficient activity of norepinephrine and serotonin as neurotransmitters in the brain, while mania may be an expression of the overactivity of norepinephrine or dopamine (Baldessarini, 1985). While this theory is oversimplified, it has guided development of antidepressant drugs of all types up to the present time. Indeed, the discovery of the MAO inhibitors and of imipramine in the 1950s led to a minor revolution in conceptualizations of depressive disorders as having an important neurobiological and not purely psychosocial basis.

MAO inhibitors were the first clinically successful antidepressants (Murphy et al., 1987). Their use since their introduction in the 1950s has, however, been limited as a result of their complex and often unpredictable interactions with many other drugs, early association of some of them with liver-damaging toxic effects, and lack of knowledge about their optimal clinical indications and dosing. Many physicians and patients are reluctant to use MAO inhibitors for these reasons. Until recently, the 2 most commonly used antidepressant MAO inhibitors in American medicine were phenelzine (Nardil) and tranylcypromine (Parnate); a third agent, isocarboxazid (Marplan), is no longer marketed. These agents persist in

Tricyclics: Tertiary Amines

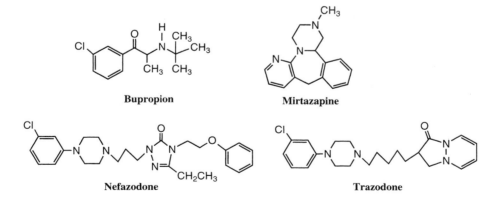

Amitriptyline **Clomipramine** **Doxepin** **Imipramine** **Trimipramine**

Tricyclics: Secondary Amines

Desipramine **Nortriptyline** **Protriptyline** **Amoxapine** **Maprotiline**

Selective Serotonin Reuptake Inhibitors

Fluoxetine **Fluvoxamine** **Paroxetine** **Sertraline** **Venlafaxine**

Figure 21.3 Antidepressants: A

Atypical Antidepressants

Bupropion **Mirtazapine**

Nefazodone **Trazodone**

Monoamineoxidase Inhibitors

Phenelzine **Tranylcypromine** **Selegiline**

Figure 21.3 Antidepressants: B

activity long after they have been cleared, and their disposition and metabolism are not considered clinically important. Because of their virtually irreversible interactions with MAO or its flavin cofactor in the outer membrane of mitochondria, synthesis of new MAO molecules is required to overcome the inhibition by protein synthesis which requires 1–2 weeks and so accounts for the duration of action of the older MAO inhibitors. It is generally assumed that MAO inhibitors are effective antidepressants owing to their preventing the metabolic breakdown of monoamines in nerve endings, with an increased amount of transmitter release per nerve impulse. This very plausible theory is not proved, however, and other ill-defined effects may be involved.

Subsequent developments include discovery of 2 different genetically specified molecular forms of MAO enzyme proteins and development of drugs which inhibit them selectively. Both phenelzine and tranylcypromine are long-acting inhibitors of both of the major molecular forms of the enzyme MAO, types A and B (Finberg and Youdim, 1983). Type A is characteristic of monoamine nerve terminals, where it is localized to mitochondrial membranes, and can also be found in liver and in human intestinal mucosa; its inhibition typically produces mood elevation. Type B is found in human liver and blood platelets, and to some extent in brain tissues (possibly including dopamine neurons). Relatively selective inhibition of each MAO type has been achieved in a series of propargyl (triple bond–containing) compounds that alkylate MAO irreversibly and are thus destroyed. An experimental agent of this type, clorgyline, is selective for MAO-A and an effective antidepressant. Another, selegiline (formerly [-]-deprenyl; Eldepril), is selective for MAO-B, at least at low daily doses (10–20 mg). It was recently introduced into American medicine to enhance the diminishing availability of dopamine in early Parkinson's disease, but it also may have mild mood-elevating and perhaps antianxiety effects, and is sometimes employed empirically in psychiatry (Wiseman and McTavish, 1995). High doses of selegiline can inhibit both forms of MAO, and may also produce amphetaminelike by-products that can block the neuronal transport of monoamines, including norepinephrine and tyramine. An attractive feature of selective inhibition of MAO-B is a low risk of producing potentially catastrophic hypertensive effects. These are associated with intake of indirect sympathomimetic amines such as tyramine, found in many foods and beverages (Walker et al., 1996), or others found in commonly used medicines, including nonprescription decongestants. This safety may in part reflect a lack of increased levels of norepinephrine at nerve terminals following inhibition of

MAO-B, and perhaps limited access of tyramine to such nerve terminals. Additional innovative MAO inhibitors with relatively low risk of potentiating pressor amines are short-acting, reversible inhibitors selective for MAO-A (sometimes referred to as RIMAs), including brofaromine and moclobemide (Manerix in Canada). These are effectively antidepressant but are not currently available in the United States (Danish University Group, 1993).

More is known about the pharmacology of the TCAs than other antidepressants, based on their study for nearly 4 decades. There are currently 10 antidepressants of the tricyclic, imipraminelike type in clinical use in the United States (see Figure 21.3). Five of these—amitriptyline (Elavil, Endep, and others), clomipramine (Anafranil), doxepin (Adapin, Sinequan), imipramine (Tofranil and others), and trimipramine (Surmontil)—have tertiary-amine side chains. Another 5—amoxapine (Asendin), desipramine (Norpramin, Pertofrane), maprotiline (Ludiomil), nortriptyline (Aventyl, Pamelor), and protriptyline (Vivactil)—have secondary-amine side chains. Several of these are N-dealkylated metabolic derivatives of tertiary-amine precursors (desipramine and nortriptyline from imipramine and amitriptyline, respectively, and amoxapine (norloxapine) from the neuroleptic loxapine; see Table 21.9). Although amoxapine has its terminal nitrogen atom located within an accessory piperazine ring, and maprotiline has an ethylene bridge across its central 6-carbon ring, considering these molecules "tetracyclic" obscures their striking pharmacological similarities to other TCA-type agents.

The TCAs are well absorbed after oral administration and are not usually administered by injection, though this is sometimes done with amitriptyline and imipramine. Their plasma elimination half-lives average about 20–48 hours, with generally slower elimination of the secondary amines (30–48 hours) than their tertiary-amine precursors (12–20 hours); protriptyline has an unusually slow rate of elimination (half-life more than 90 hours). Most TCAs have a sufficient margin of safety and sufficiently slow elimination to encourage once-daily dosing, at least in moderate amounts (below 200 mg of imipramine, or its equivalent).

Clinically appropriate serum or plasma concentrations of TCAs typically average 100–250 ng/ml of the parent drug plus its N-dealkylated metabolite (for example, imipramine plus desipramine), although one of the best-evaluated agents, nortriptyline, has optimal plasma levels of about 50–150 ng/ml (see Table 21.9). Assays of the pharmacologically active and possibly cardiotoxic ring-hydroxy metabolites of the TCAs would be of additional clinical value, but are not usually available from clinical chemistry laboratories. Levels above 300 ng/ml are associated with increased risk of adverse effects, including cerebral intoxication and suppression of cardiac conduction, and concentrations over 1000 ng/ml are likely to be quite toxic and potentially lethal when associated with acute overdoses, particularly in elderly or cardiac patients and probably also in children (Glassman, Roose, and Bigger, 1993).

Serum TCA levels vary by more than ten-fold between individuals given the same dose, but genetically determined activity of hepatic cytochrome P450 microsomal oxidases that are largely responsible for eliminating TCAs and most other psychotropic agents tends to be stable within individuals over long periods. These drug-metabolizing systems also diminish in activity with maturation and aging, so that children are most efficient at clearing TCAs and the elderly least so. The relationships of dose, plasma level, and clearance of TCAs are sufficiently robust that it is possible to predict clinical dosing requirements in individuals based on determining a serum drug concentration at 24 hours after a small, safe test dose of a TCA such as nortriptyline. This form of quantitative, pharmacokinetically predicted dosing emphasizes the predictability of genetically based drug clearance processes, and it seems to be cost-effective, but it is not used in contemporary clinical practice (Simmons et al., 1985).

Assays of TCA concentrations in blood can provide clinically useful information (APA, 1985; Perry, Zeilman,

Table 21.9 Antidepressants used in the United States: typical doses, serum concentrations, and half-life

Generic Names	Trade Names	Elimination Half-life (hr)[a]	Doses (mg/24 hr)		Typical Serum Levels (ng/ml)[b]
			Typical	Extreme	
Tricyclic-type norepinephrine reuptake inhibitors					
Tertiary amines (affect norepinephrine and serotonin)					
Amitriptyline HCl	Elavil and others	16+30	100–200	25–300	100–200
Doxepin HCl	Sinequan and others	16+30	100–200	25–300	150–250
Imipramine HCl	Tofranil and others	12+30	100–200	25–300	150–300
(+)Trimipramine	Surmontil	16+30	75–200	25–300	100–300
Secondary amines (affect mainly norepinephrine)					
Amoxapine HCl	Asendin	24	200–300	50–600	150–500
Desipramine HCl	Norpramin and others	30	100–200	25–300	125–300
Maprotiline HCl	Ludiomil	48	100–150	25–250	200–400
Nortritplyine HCl	Pamelor and others	30	75–150	25–250	75–150
Protriptyline HCl	Vivactil	80	15–40	10–60	75–250
Selective serotonin-reuptake inhibitors					
Clomipramine HCl	Anafranil	30+70	100–200	25–250	200–600
(±)Fluoxetine HCl	Prozac	50+200	20–40	5–80	175–500
Fluvoxamine HCl	Luvox	18	100–200	50–300	100–200
Paroxetine HCl	Paxil	22	20–40	10–50	30–100
Sertraline HCl	Zoloft	25+66	100–150	50–200	20–40
(±)Venlafaxine HCl	Effexor	5+11	75–225	25–375	
Atypical antidepressants					
Bupropion HCl	Wellbutrin	12	200–300	100–450	50–100
Mirtazapine	Remeron	26	20–30	10–60	—
Nefazodone	Serzone	3	200–400	100–600	—
Trazodone HCl	Desyrel and others	5	150–200	50–600	800–1600
Monoamine-oxidase inhibitors					
Phenelzine sulfate	Nardil	ca. 100	30–60	15–90	<10
Tranylcypromine sulfate	Parnate	ca. 48	20–30	10–60	<10
(−)Selegiline HCl	Eldepryl	2–20	10–15	5–20	<10

Note: Amitriptyline and imipramine are available in injectable (IM) forms.

a. Second value is for the prominent secondary amine derivative (nor-metabolite) of the parent compound.

b. Use of serum concentration to guide clinical dosing (therapeutic drug monitoring) is not secure except for nortriptyline and perhaps amitriptyline, desipramine, and imipramine; levels cited include the secondary-amine metabolites.

and Arndt, 1994). For example, high levels may be found in patients showing pronounced side effects after low doses, or very low concentrations may be found in patients showing neither improvement nor side effects after a high nominal dose of an antidepressant. Standards for antidepressant drug level monitoring are most secure for nortriptyline, with good research also available for amitriptyline, desipramine, and imipramine, but only limited support to guide interpretation of serum concentrations of most SRIs or other atypical antidepressants (DeVane, 1992; Van Harten, 1993; Perry, Zeilman, and Arndt, 1994). Potentially clinically important variations in blood levels or effects of antidepressants (or other psychotropic agents) of different commercial brands ("bioequivalence") have been considered but not proved.

The TCAs have as an evidently primary pharmacodynamic action the ability to block the neuronal uptake or transport process that serves as the crucial means of physiologically inactivating released norepinephrine in the brain and in the peripheral sympathetic nervous system. For that reason, their functional designation as selective norepinephrine-reuptake inhibitors (NRIs), to contrast them with the SRIs, might be considered. Division of the TCAs and related compounds into those with tertiary versus secondary amine side chains emphasizes their pharmacological dissimilarities. The tertiary-amine TCAs are generally more complex pharmacologically. They interact with both norepinephrine and serotonin transporters. This effect is particularly prominent in clomipramine, which shares many clinical properties with the SRIs, including powerful antianxiety effects and gastrointestinal side effects. They are also strongly antimuscarinic and antihistaminic (mainly acting at H_1 receptors), accounting for their propensity to induce sedation and parasympathetic dysfunction. The secondary-amine TCAs are much more selective NRIs, with little effect on serotonin, and they have somewhat less anticholinergic activity than the tertiary-amine TCAs, with the notable exception of protriptyline, which is also the most potent and long-acting TCA (see Table 21.9). Other exceptional TCAs include trimipramine, which is a relatively weak blocker of norepinephrine transport, and amoxapine, which shares some antidopamine activity with its N-methylated congener the neuroleptic agent loxapine, and has been associated with extrapyramidal symptoms (EPS) including tardive dyskinesia, making it a risky candidate for long-term applications.

The later actions of TCAs are complex and involve several slowly evolving responses of the CNS that may represent secondary or compensatory effects (Heninger and Charney, 1987; Baldessarini, 1989, 1996b). These ac-

tions are summarized in Table 21.10. Their immediate and sustained blocking of the transport-inactivation of norepinephrine probably persists indefinitely. However, the resulting increased extracellular availability of the catecholamine in the synapse leads to rapid compensatory responses, including reduced firing rates of noradrenergic neurons in the brainstem's locus coeruleus and reduced synthesis and release of the neurotransmitter—most likely through the agency of presynaptic α_2 adrenergic autoreceptors. Since most TCAs have low affinity for the α_2 and postsynaptic β-adrenoceptors, both are exposed to an excess of their endogenous ligand, norepinephrine, by sustained blockade of the uptake process, and eventually their availability diminishes (downregulation) and their functionality is reduced (desensitization) (Cusack, Nelson, and Richelson, 1994). Loss of β-adrenoceptors probably does not contribute to mood-elevating effects, and, indeed, some centrally acting β-blockers such as propranolol can probably induce depression in some susceptible persons. As the efficacy of the α_2 autoreceptors is lost, the presynaptic activity of adrenergic neurons gradually returns, and may even rise to supranormal levels.

A direct attack on the α_2 autoreceptor has been considered as a potential means of developing additional novel mood-elevating agents. Whereas α_2 agonists like the antihypertensive drug clonidine (Catapres) suppress production and release of norepinephrine to lower blood pressure and perhaps exert minor antimanic effects, the α_2 antagonist yohimbine (Yocan) is transiently mood-elevating and stimulantlike. The recently introduced atypical antidepressant mirtazapine (Remeron), like its predecessor and close structural congener mianserin (which lacks a ring-methyl group; see Figure 21.3), is a potent antagonist of serotonin type 2 receptors (5-HT$_2$), and this effect may or may not contribute to the psychotropic properties of both agents. In addition, mirtazapine probably acts in part by inhibiting α_2 receptors, but it also facilitates serotonin transmission, perhaps in part through α_2 receptors located as regulatory heteroceptors on serotonin nerve terminals.

One route of postsynaptic transmission that is retained in the process of adaptation to TCA treatment is through the postsynaptic α_1 adrenoceptors. They may even become somewhat supersensitive, probably because they are a site of partial early blockade by TCAs, leaving them relatively protected against desensitization by excess intrasynaptic norepinephrine. These adaptive processes during early treatment with a TCA typically require 1–3 weeks in laboratory animals—timing that closely parallels the typical lag in clinical response to the TCAs and most other antidepressants. The receptor interactions of TCAs and other agents with sustained mood-elevating effects may represent an important distinction between true antidepressants and stimulants, which lack affinity for adrenergic, dopaminergic, or serotonergic receptors and tend to develop rapid loss of behavioral activation on repeated administration.

In contemporary medical practice, the selective serotonin-reuptake inhibitors have emerged since the late 1980s as the dominant and most frequently prescribed antidepressants. They have rapidly displaced the older TCAs and MAO inhibitors, mainly because of their relative safety, tolerability, and ease of use by nonpsychiatric physicians (Baldessarini, 1996b). These agents are generally believed to exert their useful psychotropic effects by increasing the availability of serotonin as a synaptic neurotransmitter by preventing its physiological inactivation by reuptake into presynaptic nerve terminals (Fuller and Wong, 1987; Koe, 1990; Dechant and Clissold, 1991; Beasley, Masica, and Potvin, 1992; Grimsley and Jann, 1992). Neuronal reuptake of serotonin occurs through the mediation of a selective transporter protein that is structurally similar to those selective for dopamine and stimulant drugs (including cocaine, amphetamines, methylphenidate, and

probably also the atypical antidepressant bupropion), or for norepinephrine and the TCAs, particularly the secondary-amine TCAs as well as some stimulants. All are members of a family of large neuroproteins which are believed to cross cell membranes 12 times, and to interact functionally with the sodium transport system. This complex mechanism requires energy derived from adenosine triphosphate (ATP), probably produced locally from oxidative metabolism within the abundant mitochondria of monoaminergic nerve terminals.

As with TCAs and noradrenergic neurotransmission, complex changes occur in serotonin receptors in animal brain tissue following repeated treatment with SRIs that are not found after treatment with TCAs, MAO inhibitors, or electroconvulsive shock. These include inconsistent loss of postsynaptic forebrain serotonin (5-HT) receptors of types 1 or 2, with unclear functional consequences, as well as desensitization of presynaptic autoreceptors (type 1A, mainly on midbrain raphe cell bodies and dendrites, or type 1B or 1D, found mainly on serotonergic nerve terminals) that may further enhance the synaptic availability of serotonin (Heninger and Charney, 1987; Wamsley et al., 1987; Romero et al., 1996; Stahl, 1996).

Table 21.10 Actions of antidepressants

Tricyclic-type norepinephrine (NE) reuptake inhibitors
Produce immediate and sustained inhibition of physiological inactivation of NE
Variable antihistaminic (H_1) and anticholinergic (muscarinic) blockade, with minor anti-α_1 effects
Induce rapid reduction of firing rates of locus coeruleus NE neurons and reduce NE synthesis and release
Increased synaptic abundance of NE leads to down-regulation of presynaptic α_2 adrenergic autoreceptors
Desensitization of α_2 autoreceptors leads to increased synthesis and release of NE
Induce secondary down-regulation of postsynaptic β_1-adrenoceptors with no known benefit
Postsynaptic α_1 adrenoceptors remain or may become supersensitive to provide a functional outlet
Dopamine (DA) autoreceptors may undergo secondary desensitization

Selective serotonin (5-HT) reuptake inhibitors
Produce immediate and sustained inhibition of physiological inactivation of 5-HT
Induce rapid reduction of firing rates of raphe 5-HT neurons and reduce 5-HT synthesis and release
Increased synaptic abundance of 5-HT leads to down-regulation of 5-HT_{1A} autoreceptors
Loss of 5-HT_{1A} feedback leads to increased synthesis and release of 5-HT
Induce secondary down-regulation of postsynaptic 5-HT_2 receptors
Some agents have mixed effects on 5-HT and NE transporters (e.g., clomipramine, venlafaxine)

Monoamine oxidase (MAO) inhibitors
Inhibit oxidative inactivation of NE, 5-HT and DA by MAO in nerve terminal mitochondria (mainly type A)
Can produce secondary alterations in β-adrenergic, 5-HT_2, and other monoamine receptors

Atypical agents
Nefazodone and trazodone weakly inhibit neuronal reuptake of 5-HT and may block 5-HT_2 receptors; nefazodone also has weak effects against NE reuptake
Bupropion weakly inhibits neuronal reuptake of NE and DA, partly by active metabolites
All may produce secondary alterations in monoamine receptors

Additional late adaptations to repeated antidepressant treatment have been suggested. These include effects on GABA receptors of unknown significance, desensitization of D_2 autoreceptors to indirectly enhance forebrain dopaminergic mechanisms, and emerging changes in neurotransmitter effector and second-messenger systems, as well as in the activity of cyclic AMP–dependent kinases affecting cytoskeletal proteins involved in neuronal growth and sprouting (Heninger and Charney, 1987; Wong, Bruck, and Farabman, 1991; Baldessarini, 1996b). There may even be changes at the level of gene expression, for example, through increased abundance of glucocorticoid receptors in monoaminergic neurons (Kitayana, Janson, and Cintra, 1988).

Several other types of antidepressants have important effects on serotonin neurotransmission, including possible indirect effects of the TCAs (Baldessarini, 1996b). Venlafaxine (Effexor) inhibits serotonin transport about 5 times more potently than norepinephrine uptake, compared to selectivity ratios of tenfold or more for other more typical SRIs (Muth et al., 1986; Bolden-Watson and Richelson, 1993). Also, in addition to its norepinephrine-potentiating effects, the new atypical antidepressant mirtazapine may increase the metabolic turnover and release of serotonin, while blocking some postsynaptic serotonin receptors, and perhaps some presynaptic serotonin autoreceptors. Such agents herald the development of mixed SRI-NRI agents, which in some ways resemble the tertiary-amine TCAs, but lack anticholinergic, cardiac-depressant, and other adverse autonomic effects characteristic of the TCAs. Other mixed SRI-NRI agents (such as duloxetine) remain investigational. They may provide some of the benefits of combining an agent of each type. For example, combining a typical SRI with low doses of desipramine may produce beneficial effects not obtained with either agent alone (Nelson et al., 1991). In general, mixing of dissimilar antidepressants has become increasingly common, particularly since many cases of depression respond unsatisfactorily to single agents (Thase, 1992).

The primary actions of the triazolopyridine, atypical sedative-antidepressant trazodone (Desyrel) and its triazolopiperazine congener nefazodone (Serzone) are less well established (Eison et al., 1990; Rickels et al., 1995; Taylor et al., 1995; see Figure 21.3). These relatively short-acting agents (see Table 21.10) have weak actions against serotonin reuptake, and nefazodone also has weak activity against norepinephrine transport. This effect of trazodone, for example, is several hundred times weaker than that of paroxetine (Bolden-Watson and Richelson, 1993). These agents (and some TCAs) also act as direct antago-

nists at postsynaptic serotonin 5-HT_2 receptors, with uncertain behavioral effects. Loss of the same 5-HT_2 receptors is also a later, indirect consequence of sustained blockade of serotonin transport by the classic SRIs. Trazodone and nefazodone are not anticholinergic, but trazodone does have antagonistic effects at α_1 adrenergic and H_1 histamine receptors that may contribute to its sedative effects and popularity as a relatively safe and nondependency-producing hypnotic agent; the anti-adrenergic effect probably also contributes to rare but potentially troublesome priapism associated with trazodone. Trazodone and its active metabolite m-chlorophenylpiperazine (mCPP) also may have agonist actions at some 5-HT_1 receptors and may indirectly facilitate noradrenergic transmission.

Stimulant drugs are still sometimes used clinically, including for the treatment of depression and early dementia in the elderly, and they have a well-established place in the treatment of ADHD (particularly d-amphetamine [Dexedrine and others], methylphenidate [Ritalin], and sodium pemoline [Cylert]). Their interactions with dopamine transporters to increase the activity of dopamine and induce behavioral arousal has been surprisingly little explored as a principle of novel antidepressants. One such agent with sustained mood-elevating agents was nomifensine, which was withdrawn from clinical use owing to association with blood dyscrasias. Another stimulantlike atypical antidepressant is the short-acting propiophenone bupropion (Blackwell, 1987; Settle, 1989). Its mechanism of action remains incompletely defined. Bupropion itself is a weak inhibitor of the neuronal uptake of monoamines, with a slight preference for dopamine transporters; however, it may be converted in vivo to active metabolites, including a hydroxylated derivative with amphetaminelike activity against both dopamine and norepinephrine uptake. Methylphenidate and low doses of bupropion have been combined safely with SRIs, and may help to control or reverse anergic or sedative effects sometimes associated with SRIs.

Clinical Use

Major depression is one of the most common of the severe mental illnesses and, as such, results in high levels of morbidity, early mortality, and enormous costs to society that sustain a high level of interest in improving recognition and treatment of these disorders (Kind and Sorensen, 1993). The diversity of conditions subsumed under the generic term *depression* and the inconsistency with which clinicians and investigators categorize depressions make evaluation of the treatment of depression difficult. Regardless of the categorization scheme followed, it is generally agreed that depressions vary in severity. The more severe forms include those that have been referred to as "major," "melancholic," "endogenous," "psychotic," "manic-depressive," "involutional," "agitated," or "vital," depending on the clinical form of the illness and the patient's personal and family history, and would include the depressive phases of bipolar I and II syndromes (Zornberg and Pope, 1993). In contrast, the less severe forms have been referred to as "minor," "reactive," "neurotic," "situational," or "anxious" depressions, or "dysthymia" in the case of chronic depression of moderate severity. The short-term prognosis for less severe depressions is usually better than for the more severe forms, although depression of mild to moderate severity can be a chronic condition, and can be difficult to distinguish from a personality disorder. Demonstrations of the efficacy of medical treatments over a placebo are much clearer for the more serious or more classic depressions, with pronounced "biological" symptoms. These include anorexia and insomnia (or hyperphagia and hypersomnic anergy in bipolar or atypical depressions), and increased rapid-eye-movement (REM or dream) sleep, loss of drive and sexual interest, and circadian changes in activity or mood, as well as increased secretion of adrenocorticosteroids or other stress hormones.

Responsiveness of major depression to an antidepressant versus a placebo is predicted by both the *form* and *severity* of the syndrome: classic melancholic unipolar depression and bipolar depressions, particularly when they arise acutely on a relatively healthy premorbid status, are most likely to respond well, particularly if psychotic, highly agitated, or mixed manic-depressive features are absent; in addition, responsiveness may relate to severity biphasically, in that depression of moderate severity is more likely to respond well than very severe depression. (Fairchild et al,, 1986; Kocsis et al., 1990; Brown and Kahn, 1994; Baldessarini, 1985, 1996b). Furthermore, many cases of lesser depressive illnesses tend to recover more rapidly, to remit spontaneously, and to respond to environmental influences, as well as to treatment with psychotherapy or to sedatives, antianxiety medications, or stimulants, or to nonspecific treatments including placebos, about as well as to standard antidepressants.

A difficulty in evaluating medical treatments of depression is that spontaneous remission rates for unselected depressions are as high as 20–30% within the first 4–6 weeks and exceed 50% within a few months, even for many relatively severe depressions. Moreover, a placebo

can increase the remission rates of acute depression to about 25–40% in the first month or two. Although the preceding considerations can guide predictions of treatment response, the potential for sustained morbidity or increased mortality is sufficiently high in major depression and bipolar depression, and the ability to predict treatment response sufficiently low, that empirical trials of standard antidepressants in adequate doses and times should be considered routinely when the diagnosis of a clinically significant depressive syndrome has been made (Greenberg et al., 1993; Kind and Sorensen, 1993). Contemporary medical practice continues to underdiagnose and undertreat medical depression to an alarming extent, despite better training of physicians and the introduction of safer and simpler treatments in recent years: only a minority of depressed patients are correctly diagnosed, and a minority of them adequately treated (Keller et al., 1986; McCombs et al., 1990; Greenberg et al., 1993).

Currently, virtually all of the commonly employed antidepressants (MAO inhibitors, TCAs, SRIs, and atypical agents) have their clearest effects in the more serious and classically medical or melancholic depressions, for which their performance in controlled clinical trials has been fairly consistent, though not dramatic (Morris and Beck, 1974; Rogers and Clay, 1975; Montgomery, 1980). The best performance of the drugs has been documented in trials that attempted to exclude the less severe depressions, that used adequate doses of medication (at least 150 mg of imipramine, 20 mg of fluoxetine, or their equivalent; see Table 21.9), and that persisted for at least a month. Information on dose-response relationships for older and newer antidepressants is surprisingly limited, and is not well supported by therapeutic drug monitoring by assays of serum concentrations except for a few TCAs, and particularly nortriptyline. Moreover, the very long half-life of fluoxetine, in particular, has led to the paradoxical finding of no apparent dose-effect relationship in short-term trials (Gram, 1994). Several studies of the treatment of depression or panic disorder with imipramine also indicate a clear trade-off of dose versus benefit and tolerability, with high dropout rates found at daily doses of 200 mg or more (Mavissakalian and Perel, 1989).

In controlled trials involving a mixture of depressive syndromes of varying subtypes and severity, overall improvement rates with TCAs have been about 66–75%, in contrast to about 25–40% with a placebo; that is, only an additional 35% of patients with significant depressive illnesses responded to the active medication. Perhaps half who respond poorly to a TCA or other standard antidepressant respond satisfactorily to an MAO inhibitor or to

ECT (Thase, 1992). While ECT has consistently outperformed antidepressant drugs, particularly in severe or psychotic forms of major depression, the overall gain is only on the order of 10–20% (Sackheim et al., 1990; Riddle and Scott, 1995).

Among the specific antidepressants, more similarities than differences in overall effectiveness are found, particularly in the syndrome of major depression. However, as the pharmacological diversity of the antidepressants and their range of clinical uses in conditions other than major depression broadens, their selection can be guided by the presence of indications other than, or in addition to, depression itself. Indeed, it is questionable that all of the agents considered in this section can rationally be lumped together as "antidepressants," and clarification of the advantages and disadvantages of specific agents in specific syndromes is still evolving (Nelson et al., 1995). Tentative guidelines for their clinical use are provided in Table 21.11.

As might be expected, as newer treatments are integrated into contemporary clinical practice, questions remain about the relative efficacy of older and newer agents. This is a particularly pressing matter in comparing SRIs and TCAs, the most commonly employed antidepressants. Research on which to base a rational choice between these types of antidepressants in regard to efficacy

is limited and inconclusive (Roose et al., 1994). Typically, however, an SRI will be tried first because of its relative safety and tolerability, but a TCA trial should be considered when an SRI has been unsuccessful. Some antidepressants may be less effective in severe depression than others, including trazodone and low doses of bupropion; trazodone is helpful with insomnia, and bupropion may worsen insomnia when given at bedtime. Bupropion and the SRIs may be somewhat safer in bipolar depression owing to a possibly lower risk of inducing mania (Peet, 1994; Sachs et al., 1995). Certain agents may be particularly helpful when anxiety symptoms are prominent and for the primary indication of an anxiety syndrome, such as panic or severe phobia (TCAs, MAO inhibitors, SRIs, and possibly nefazodone), whereas others may be ineffective (trazodone), or even worsen anxiety (bupropion and stimulants) (Davis, Janicak, and Bruninga, 1987; Den Boer and Westenberg, 1995; Mavissakalian and Ryan, 1996). In contrast, when depression is associated with lethargy or an attentional disorder, bupropion or another stimulant, or a TCA, may be useful (Zametkin and Rappoport, 1987; Biederman et al., 1989; Spencer et al., 1993). In obsessive-compulsive disorder (OCD) or related habitual behavioral disorders (e.g., kleptomania, trichotillomania), the SRIs, including the TCA clomipramine, are clearly superior to TCAs (particularly the NRI

Table 21.11 Indications for treatment with antidepressants

Acute major depression (unipolar or bipolar), including secondary depression with classic symptoms (all antidepressant types)

Prevention of early relapse or recurrent unipolar depression for at least 6–12 months (all antidepressant types)

Some forms of chronic depression or dysthymia (any agent may help, but MAOIs may have special benefits)

"Atypical" depression (with hypersomnia, lassitude, and hyperphagia that may represent bipolar II disorder) and "hysteroid dysphoria" may particularly benefit from MAOIs

Depressive symptoms in borderline and other personality disorders[a]

Panic component of panic-agoraphobia syndrome (TCAs and MAOIs, perhaps SRIs, possibly nefazodone)

Some cases of generalized anxiety and social phobias (SRIs may be best)[a]

Post-traumatic stress disorder (PTSD; SRIs tend to be preferred)[a]

Attention disorder with hyperactivity (ADHD; especially TCAs and perhaps bupropion and SRIs)

Bulimia nervosa (TCAs and SRIs best studied), but probably not other eating disorders

Obsessive-compulsive disorder (OCD) and related habit syndromes (e.g., kleptomania, trichotillomania, and others; SRIs only)

Mild geriatric "pseudodementia" with depressive symptoms[a]

Some forms of chronic pain, including peripheral neuropathies (tertiary-amine TCAs probably outperform SRIs)[a]

Tics with ADHD and perhaps Tourette's syndrome (TCAs best, SRIs uncertain; bupropion worsens)

Chronic fatigue syndrome[a]

Enuresis (geriatric and pediatric, especially low doses of imipramine at bedtime)[a]

Neurological disorders (migraine and narcolepsy [especially clomipramine], sleep apnea [especially protriptyline])[a]

Aggression, dyscontrol, and agitation in mental retardation and brain injury[a]

Inflammatory disorders (ulcer, colitis, myositis, dermatitis [especially tertiary-amine TCAs])[a]

Abbreviations: TCAs = tricyclic-type antidepressants; MAOIs = monoamine oxidase inhibitors;
SRIs = selective serotonin-reuptake inhibitors.
a. Clinical indications not backed with extensive, rigorous research.

secondary-amine TCAs) or bupropion, but often require doses several times greater than are effective in major depression (Greist et al., 1995; Jefferson et al., 1995). In some chronic pain syndromes, the older tertiary-amine TCAs appear to be superior to secondary amines, and much more so than the SRIs (Max et al., 1992).

Additional bases on which to select a specific agent include consideration of risks or potential utility of side effects. Thus, the sedative effects of tertiary-amine TCAs can be particularly useful when anxiety or insomnia is present, whereas bupropion and some SRIs (notably fluoxetine, which may have a relatively high risk of inducing akathisialike restlessness or insomnia) may have opposite effects. For elderly and cardiac patients, and others at high risk of anticholinergic delirium, glaucoma, ileus, or urinary retention, the TCAs (particularly the tertiary-amines and protriptyline) are best avoided, and persons on complex medical regimens or receiving a phenyl-piperidine analgesic (such as meperidine) or an SRI should avoid MAO inhibitors owing to the risk of potentially catastrophic drug interactions, considered further below.

The possibility of predicting responses to a specific antidepressant by biological tests has been suggested. Such predictive techniques include unusually low or high excretion of the urinary metabolite of norepinephrine 3-methoxy-4-hydroxyphenethylene glycol (MHPG), failure to suppress secretion of cortisol by dexamethasone, an acute behavioral or mood-activating response to amphetamine, or early delay in the onset of REM sleep have all been suggested for such use and have some research support (Baldessarini, 1985, 1996b). These techniques, however, are not sufficiently well supported or practical, nor are they sufficiently powerful predictors of response, to support their routine clinical use. Clinical methods of diagnosis of major or endogenous depression with melancholic features, and the aggressive use of tolerated high doses of standard antidepressants, sometimes guided by assays indicating adequate serum concentrations, are much more powerful and practical methods of predicting responses to antidepressant therapy (APA, 1985; Baldessarini, 1996b).

An elaborate medical evaluation before starting antidepressant treatment is usually not necessary in younger and healthy individuals, but a good appreciation of the cardiovascular, cerebrovascular, gastrointestinal, urinary, and ophthalmological status is well advised, especially in elderly depressed patients, who are at greater risk of the toxic effects of antidepressants. Usually treatment is started with moderate doses of an SRI in outpatients or elderly patients. The amount is usually increased by 5 or 10 mg every few days to doses of 20–30 mg/day of fluoxetine or the equivalent of another agent; if a TCA is used, starting daily doses of 50–100 mg are typical, with rapid increases to at least 150 mg, and sometimes up to 200 mg, based on tolerability and individual responses (see Table 21.9). With inpatients it is common to start with similar doses of an SRI, or to use a TCA somewhat more aggressively, starting at 100–150 mg of imipramine or its equivalent daily, and seeking daily doses of 200–250 mg as soon as possible. Doses above 300 mg/day of imipramine or its equivalent are associated with increased risks of adverse effects, including cardiovascular toxicity and psychotic agitation and confusion, and are best reserved for carefully supervised hospitalized patients, preferably after a trial of several weeks up to 200–300 mg/day in divided doses. Current indications for psychiatric hospitalization for depression are typically narrower than formerly, and based heavily on ongoing assessment of dangerousness or inability to care for oneself. Special situations that may modify dose selection include patients with prominent anxiety symptoms, who tend to be intolerant of rapid dose increases of antidepressants, and persons with OCD (obsessive-compulsive disorder) symptoms, which are unlikely to respond to a TCA and may require daily doses of an SRI as high as 40–80 mg of fluoxetine or its equivalent. Severe agitation and the presence of psychotic features may require temporary addition of an antipsychotic agent or early consideration of ECT, as would severe suicidality.

In severe depression and in cases of refusal of food and oral medications, an injectable form of imipramine or amitriptyline can be used (initially 100 mg/day in divided doses, intramuscularly), although the efficacy or speed is not necessarily increased in this way, and intravenous clomipramine (Anafranil) is sometimes used abroad, and experimentally in the United States. It is usually not necessary to add a hypnotic medication for sleep, although trazodone is commonly used for sleep in combination with an SRI, and a benzodiazepine can be added to a TCA or SRI when anxiety symptoms are prominent, especially early in the introduction to antidepressant treatment. If ECT is used, it can be administered safely while antidepressants are being used, although it is wise to omit the first dose of antidepressant on the morning of ECT, to avoid use of lithium on days of ECT, and to use pre-ECT anticholinergic agents (to minimize secretions and vagal effects on the heart) sparingly if a TCA is being employed so as to minimize risks of adverse effects, particularly toxic delirium. Although it might seem a good idea, it is not usual to give a stimulant in the first few days of treatment while awaiting the antidepressant effects of a standard antidepressant, because of the meager benefits likely to be realized and the added complexity of medical management.

An important feature of virtually all antidepressants is their delay in clinical onset of antidepressant effect, typically at least a week and sometimes up to 3 weeks. The failure of objective improvement in activity, sleep, appetite, mood, or social interest within 1–2 weeks is an unfavorable prognostic sign, suggesting that the final result will be unsatisfactory. If the objective response is poor (the patient is usually the last to acknowledge improvement) after 4–6 weeks of seemingly adequate doses of an antidepressant, and if there is not even slight improvement in 2–3 weeks, there is little likelihood that changing to another similar agent or increasing doses above 40 mg of fluoxetine or its equivalent will help. At that point the main choices are to try a TCA if one has not been used, to add a trial of lithium as an adjuvant even in unipolar depression, or to switch to an MAO inhibitor or ECT, and there is little reason not to go directly to ECT, as it is the most likely to have additional benefit when the illness is severe or the patient requires hospitalization. With outpatients, a period in hospital at that point may also provide additional nonspecific benefits, although current medical economics limit this option. If an MAO inhibitor is used—for example, in a patient who refuses ECT—it is safest to allow at least a week for TCAs to be metabolized and excreted before adding the MAO inhibitor in order to avoid rare but potentially catastrophic drug interactions that may occur, including hyperpyrexia and convulsions. Even longer intervals are warranted if an SRI had been used, as long as 1 month in the case of long-acting fluoxetine, owing to the potentially fatal risk of similar but even more common cerebral and generalized toxic reactions, usually designated the "serotonin syndrome," discussed below.

Owing to the potentially severe toxicity and limited margin of safety of TCAs, MAO inhibitors, and bupropion, dispensing more than a week's supply to a depressed and possibly suicidal outpatient is unwise, and consideration of risks should be given in programs which prefer to dispense larger amounts of medications for economic reasons. The risk of suicide probably rises with *inadequate* antidepressant treatment and may increase with initial improvement, since activity usually increases before mood elevation. Recent concerns that some antidepressants (particularly fluoxetine) may specifically increase suicidal risk are unproved, but prudence suggests that increases of agitation, restlessness, and insomnia due to any type of antidepressant should be minimized, in part to avoid increased risk of aggressive behavior including self-injury or suicide (Teicher, Glod, and Cole, 1993). Safe and well-tolerated use of antidepressants also requires changing gradually from one agent to another, even at an equivalent dose, and preferably by using gradually increasing, divided doses over at least several days, and discontinuing long-term treatment even more gradually over some weeks or even months, while monitoring closely for an emerging recurrence. The expense of antidepressant agents can be minimized by prescribing their generic preparations, which are commonly available for older agents, and the largest unit dose available, with small prescriptions provided initially both for safety and to ensure tolerability and continued use.

After appreciable clinical improvement of a severe depressive illness has been achieved with an antidepressant, it is usual to continue the treatment with a well-tolerated dose similar to that found effective in the acute phase of treatment (commonly, 20 mg of fluoxetine or 100–150 mg of imipramine or their equivalent) for several months, and perhaps up to a year or more. Longer continuation (months) or maintenance treatment (years) is indicated for severe illness or in patients with a history of frequently recurrent depression or sustained minor symptoms or dysfunction between major episodes (so-called "double depression"); low doses (half or less than those used in acute depression) in this phase of treatment may be less effective in preventing relapses (Keller et al., 1984; Kupfer et al., 1992; Frank et al., 1993). Continuation and maintenance antidepressant treatment is often helpful for patients treated initially with ECT, probably even when ECT was used because of unsatisfactory responses to antidepressant trials (Sackheim et al., 1990; Riddle and Scott, 1995).

Later benefits and the prevention of recurrent episodes of major depression after 12 months of follow-up have some research support, but interpretation and applicability to clinical policy remain uncertain. More than 2 dozen trials of long-term maintenance treatment in unipolar major depression with various types of agents have yielded a nearly fourfold longer median interval between major episodes (just over 1 year without medication versus over 4 years with it; Viguera et al., 1997b). However, it is not clear to what extent the removal of medication itself may contribute to the risk of relapse within the first months after discontinuation, as appears to be the case with antipsychotic agents and lithium (Suppes et al., 1993; Baldessarini, Suppes, and Tondo, 1996; Viguera et al., 1997a). Moreover, many studies indicate a tendency to failure of antidepressant maintenance treatment with more than 1–2 years of follow-up, possibly owing largely to noncompliance (Baldessarini, 1985; Baldessarini and Tohen, 1988). The long intervals typically encountered between episodes of major depression suggest a less favorable risk or cost-benefit relationship for indefinite maintenance treatment in unipolar depression than in conditions with more rapid recurrences or sustained morbidity. Current conceptualizations of major depression in contemporary American and international nosologies are extraordinarily broad and include a wide range of risks of recurrence, severity, and chronicity in an indubitably heterogeneous syndrome. It follows that international practices and opinions with respect to routine recommendation of indefinitely prolonged maintenance treatment with high doses of antidepressants vary widely. A proposed tentative resolution of the matter is to consider prolonged treatment on an individual basis, taking into account the patient's frequency and severity of past illness, current progress, and estimated vulnerability.

Attempts have been made to increase the efficacy or to diminish the typical 1–3 week delay in onset of clinical benefit of antidepressant agents. Thyroid status may alter the efficacy of antidepressants, and should be evaluated in patients who fail to respond to adequate doses of an antidepressant within about a month. The addition of thyroid hormone, even to euthyroid patients, might improve or hasten the response to TCAs, though other types of antidepressants have not been evaluated. For instance, 25–50 μg of (-)-tri-iodothyronine (T3, Cytomel) daily, but not thyroxin (T4), and perhaps thyrotropin-stimulating hormone (TSH), but not TSH-releasing hormone (TRH), may have such beneficial effects (Lasser and Baldessarini, 1997). Addition of lithium, in doses and serum concentrations used in the treatment of bipolar disorders, is consistently effective in perhaps one-third or one-half of depressed patients found resistant to antidepressant monotherapy, as well as in long-term maintenance treatment of recurring major depression (Baldessarini and Tohen, 1988; Souza and Goodwin, 1991; Baldessarini et al., 1996b). Starting patients on the combination of lithium and an antidepressant is also an option, particularly in severe depression or cases suggestive of bipolar depression, although it lacks systematic study. Antipsychotic agents also have a place as adjunctive agents in cases of major depression with psychotic features, or involutional depression with a great deal of agitation and guilty or morbid rumination of delusional proportions; in such cases, and when trials of antidepressant medications fail, ECT still has an important, and sometimes life-saving, place. Adding pindolol (Visken and others; an indole b-adrenergic blocker with prominent inhibitory effects on

serotonin 5-HT$_{1A}$ autoreceptors) may increase the speed of antidepressant action of SRIs (Romero et al., 1996). As the numbers of safe drug combinations that can be used increase, a growing number of combinations of antidepressants with one another or with anxiolytic, mood-stabilizing, or other agents are being used empirically, even without systematic research support (Nelson et al., 1991; Sokolov and Joffe, 1995; Zajecka, Jeffriess, and Fawcett, 1995). Although there is a wise tendency in medical practice to avoid "polypharmacy," it is sometimes a rational option in cases found resistant to more standard and conservative treatments, as is common in major depressive disorders and with even the best of contemporary antidepressants, which are far from being universally effective.

Although the record of achievement of even the best available older and newer antidepressants is uneven in major depression, with response rates typically averaging two-thirds to three-quarters of patients responding within 4–6 weeks, the range of clinical utility of these drugs is growing. This phenomenon challenges traditional categorizations of psychotropic drugs, or emphasizes the overlap between mood disorders and anxiety-related conditions (Hudson and Pope, 1990). Disorders in which there is substantial research and abundant clinical experience to support the effectiveness of antidepressant treatment include typical forms of major depression found in association with other medical or psychiatric conditions (such as in the months following stroke; Morris et al., 1993), the panic component of panic-agoraphobia syndrome, obsessive-compulsive and related habit disorders (the OCD group of syndromes), attention disorder with hyperactivity in children and adults (ADHD), tic disorders including some cases of Gilles de la Tourette's disorder, bulimia nervosa, and some cases of post-traumatic stress disorder (PTSD), premenstrual dysphoria, or chronic fatigue, as well as some chronic pain syndromes (Max et al., 1992). Many of these conditions are underdiagnosed and undertreated. These indications are summarized in Table 21.11.

Not all antidepressants provide all of these benefits, and specific rankings by effectiveness within class of agents are also unclear (Kasper and Heiden, 1995). SRIs are particularly and differentially effective in the OCD group, and perhaps in bulimia, though not usually in OCD-like anorexia nervosa (Pope and Hudson, 1986; Den Boer and Westenberg, 1995). They are also emerging, more broadly, as plausible alternatives to benzodiazepines and other sedative-anxiolytics in generalized forms of anxiety. SRIs are probably also effective in panic disorder, although TCAs (particularly amitriptyline, clomipramine, imipramine) and MAO inhibitors may be superior, trazodone is probably ineffective, and stimulants including bupropion are contraindicated (Den Boer and Westenberg, 1995; Greist et al., 1995). While stimulants remain agents of first choice for ADHD, TCAs represent an alternative when stimulants fail or provide uneven results at different times of the day, induce abnormal movements, insomnia, or anorexia, or when their abuse is likely (Zametkin and Rappoport, 1987; Biederman et al., 1989). In chronic pain, tertiary-amine TCAs may be more effective than secondary amine TCAs or SRIs (Max et al., 1992). In addition to differential effectiveness of specific types of antidepressants in specific disorders, it is also important to emphasize that many of the conditions just listed are complex and require judicious application of more comprehensive clinical management, including cognitive, behavioral, other psychological, and rehabilitative components for optimally effective care.

The recent renaissance of interest in developing new antidepressant agents and expanding their spectrum of clinical applications has helped to clarify several problems for the assessment of antidepressant treatment. While many of the newer antidepressants have less likelihood of inducing autonomic and other side effects that are characteristic of older TCAs and MAO inhibitors, and they are much less likely to prove fatal on acute overdoses, their efficacy is not greater, in general. Most of the placebo-controlled clinical trials of new antidepressants now rely on moderately ill outpatients, in part because of practical considerations of patient availability and both clinical and ethical concerns about the use of placebos in hospitalized or severely melancholic, psychotic, bipolar, or suicidal patients. In addition, the less frequent contemporary studies of relatively severe depression have tended to rely on comparison of a new agent with a standard drug such as imipramine. Given the uneven performance of imipraminelike agents versus placebo, the evident heterogeneity among depressive disorders, and the substantial rate of placebo responses even in patients meeting current criteria for major depression, the available body of research provides less than compelling support for the efficacy of some newer agents in the most severe depressions. Drugs usually considered antianxiety agents may have useful effects on some symptoms in some forms of depression, especially in outpatients with anxious, phobic, or obsessive-ruminative features, even though they probably are not truly mood-elevating or effective for the anhedonic core features of melancholia, and the distinction between the range of utility of these classes of drugs in mildly ill populations is not clear. Moreover, the obverse distinction is also becoming increasingly blurred, in

that many drugs developed as antidepressants are proving superior in efficacy and safety to some traditional antianxiety agents in the most severe forms of anxiety-related disorders, including panic-agoraphobia and OCD. Finally, while newer antidepressants are often less toxic and less likely to be lethal on acute overdosage than the older agents, they too have limitations and side effects, as discussed in the following section. While the search continues for more effective and safer antidepressant therapies, the cornerstones of the medical therapy of severe depressive illness are the SRIs, TCAs, and ECT.

Adverse Effects

The SRIs carry a high risk of inducing nausea and vomiting or sexual dysfunction; high doses of bupropion, clomipramine, and maprotiline can induce epileptic seizures; amoxapine can produce extrapyramidal side effects; trazodone can induce excessive sedation or even confusion (especially in elderly patients), its efficacy in melancholia is not secure, and it has been associated with priapism in men; bupropion can induce agitation and insomnia and is best not given at night; and all effective antidepressants carry some risk of inducing manic switching in bipolar depression (Zornberg and Pope, 1993).

Many older drugs used for the treatment of mood disorders (TCAs, MAO inhibitors, and lithium salts) are toxic in acute overdosage and are given to patients at increased risk of attempting suicide. Nevertheless, the risk of suicide (and possibly of medical deaths) is probably higher in untreated and inadequately treated depression. The most common toxic side effects of the TCAs are extensions of their pharmacologic activities (Table 21.12). These include anticholinergic actions leading to dry mouth, sweating, and ophthalmological effects, including variable but usually mild mydriatic effects and often some degree of cycloplegia, leading to blurred near vision due to the impairment of accommodation. These problems are more annoying than dangerous and can usually be managed by simple means, including sugar-free candy (to avoid dental caries and oral infections) or mouthwashes and reading lenses. There is also a risk of inducing acute glaucoma, as discussed previously in regard to the antipsychotic agents. Cholinergic eyedrops, mouthwashes, or systemic medications have been tried for these symptoms but are usually not very helpful. Moreover, some degree of tolerance to these side effects normally develops.

More serious antivagal effects of the highly anticholinergic TCAs include paralytic *ileus* and *urinary retention;* thus extra caution is necessary in elderly patients and men with prostatism, and urgent medical intervention is required when these conditions develop. Treatment includes eliminating or reducing the dose of antidepressant, giving cholinergic smooth-muscle stimulants such as bethanechol (Urecholine, 2.5 or 5.0 mg subcutaneously or 25–50 mg by mouth, as needed). When severe inhibition of gastrointestinal or urinary function occurs with even small doses of antidepressants, it may be necessary to change the treatment to an atypical agent with low anticholinergic activity, to tranylcypromine (Parnate), or to ECT. Among the tricyclic agents, amitriptyline is the most potently anticholinergic (about 5% as potent as atropine, but given in doses more than 100 times greater than atropine); others, such as desipramine, are relatively less antimuscarinic but are not free of antiparasympathetic side effects.

A serious consequence of the anticholinergic and direct quinidinelike cardiac depressant effects of the TCAs is their *cardiac toxicity*. Tachycardia and impaired conduction are not unusual and are to be expected in cases of acute overdosage of the older imipraminelike antidepressants. ECG changes include tachycardia, prolongation of the Q-T interval, and flattening of the T-waves. Decreased strength of contraction (negative inotropic effect) may occur, and there is some risk of syncope. *Postural hypotension* is perhaps the most common and troublesome

cardiovascular effect of tricyclic and MAO inhibitor antidepressants, although the mechanisms underlying this effect are not clear. Important cardiovascular risk factors are cardiac conduction defects (especially bundle branch block syndromes) and advanced age. Because there is a potential risk of malignant ventricular arrhythmias, cardiac arrest, syncope, and congestive heart failure with the TCAs, they must be used in lower doses and with great caution in elderly patients with known cardiac disease, especially with impaired intracardiac conduction, and those at risk of stroke. An important consideration in choosing the treatment for serious depression in elderly or infirm patients is that with its modern modifications, ECT is an acceptably safe alternative.

The untoward effects of TCAs on the *central nervous system* include mild dizziness and lightheadedness, insomnia and restlessness, or fatigue and somnolence. Fine and occasionally gross resting tremors are common and may respond to diazepam (Valium) or propranolol (Inderal). TCAs must be used with caution for patients receiving anticholinergic antiparkinsonism medications. Large doses of TCAs can induce toxic delirium resembling that which is due to atropine poisoning. This condition is not always easy to diagnose in severely depressed patients who are already agitated and psychotic. Seizures and the worsening of epilepsy have also been associated

Table 21.12 Common adverse effects of antidepressants

Agents	Characteristic Adverse Effects
Tricyclic-type antidepressants	
Amoxapine	Extrapyramidal reactions including tardive dyskinesia
Tertiary amines	Anticholinergic, cognitive, sedating, hypotensive, cardiac depressant; fatal on overdose; weight gain, mild leukopenia
Secondary amines	Less anticholinergic and sedating, cardiac depressant; fatal on overdose
Maprotiline	Seizures (>200 mg/day), rashes
Protriptyline	Anticholinergic, occasional photosensitivity
Serotonin-reuptake inhibitors	
Clomipramine	Sedation, anticholinergic, nausea, seizures, rare hemolysis
Fluoxetine, fluvoxamine, paroxetine, etc.	Agitation (especially fluoxetine) or anergy, insomnia, sexual, nausea, headache, little weight gain; raise drug levels (sertraline may have somewhat lower risk); may induce mania less than other agents in bipolar depression
Paroxetine	Mild anticholinergic effects
Monoamine oxidase inhibitors	
Phenelzine, tranylcypromine	Hypotension, mild hypertension, severe drug interactions, sexual, liver toxicity
Selegiline	Low risk of hypertensive crisis with low doses
Atypical antidepressants	
Bupropion	Seizures (>450 mg/day), overstimulation, insomnia, anorexia, weight loss; may induce mania less than other antidepressants in bipolar depression
Mirtazapine	Sedation, infrequent leukopenia
Trazodone, nefazodone	Sedation, hypotension, priapism (trazodone only)

with antidepressants, especially maprotiline and bupropion.

Various skin reactions have been described, and an allergic-obstructive type of jaundice may occur, rarely, early in the course of treatment. Blood dyscrasias are uncommon, and agranulocytosis is very rare. There is a tendency to gain weight during treatment with TCAs that is less with SRIs and low with bupropion or other stimulants.

TCAs are highly toxic when taken in large *overdoses,* and they had been a common choice in suicide attempts. Acute doses above the equivalent of 1000 mg of imipramine are almost always toxic, but doses as low as a few hundred milligrams, especially of amitriptyline, have been severely toxic in adults and can be fatal to elderly patients and children; acute doses in excess of 2000 mg can be fatal to healthy young adults. Most newer antidepressants, including the SRIs, are much less likely to be lethal on acute overdoses. Bupropion, clomipramine, and maprotiline often induce epileptic seizures on overdoses. Overdoses of the TCAs commonly induce signs of *anticholinergic poisoning* early: restless agitation, confusion, disorientation, perhaps seizures and hyperthermia, dry, sometimes flushed skin, tachycardia, sluggish and at least moderately dilated pupils, decreased bowel sounds, and often acute urinary retention; later, severe CNS depression and coma (rarely lasting more than 24 hours) sometimes result. The early toxic effects probably include peripheral and central anticholinergic and antivagal actions of these potent muscarinic blocking agents. Because of the relatively low therapeutic index (margin of safety) of these agents and the TCAs, it is unwise to dispense more than a week's supply of medication, and certainly never more than 1000 mg of imipramine or the equivalent of another agent (see Table 21.9). The cardiac toxicity of overdoses of imipraminelike agents is particularly dangerous and may include severe depression of myocardial conduction, with various forms of heart block, atrial fibrillation, malignant ventricular arrhythmias, the syndrome of Torsade de Pointes (undulating ventricular tachycardia), or cardiac arrest. Removal of these antidepressant agents from the blood by dialysis techniques is not feasible, and forced diuresis adds little and may contribute to cardiac failure. Physostigmine (eserine, Antilirium), a reversible anticholinesterase with central as well as peripheral cholinergic activity, may be useful in the treatment of mild intoxication with agents possessing significant anticholinergic activity, but it can complicate management of severe overdoses and cannot replace vigorous use of appropriate life-support measures by medical experts. Many of the agents commonly employed to manage ventricular arrhythmias can lead to further conduction blockade and cardiac depression; electrical defib-

rillation, conversion, and cardiac pacing may be necessary and are often safer; magnesium salts are used to treat Torsade de Pointes. Cases of severe antidepressant poisoning should ideally be managed in a medical intensive care unit, with constant cardiac monitoring, excellent medical and cardiological supervision, and immediately available defibrillating and resuscitation equipment. Although the risk of cardiac arrhythmia can continue for a week or more after the initial overdose, it is unlikely given at least 24 hours of alert mental status and of a normal, monitored ECG.

Antidepressants have many *interactions with other drugs.* TCAs increase CNS depression due to alcohol, barbiturates, and other sedatives as well as antipsychotic agents and anticonvulsants by pharmacodynamic interactions. Moreover, the effects of any anticholinergic agent, including antiparkinsonism drugs, are increased by the antimuscarinic activity of the TCAs, and such combinations have a high risk of inducing delirium. Most SRIs are powerful inhibitors of the metabolic clearance of other agents, including the TCAs and bupropion, through the important hepatic microsomal cytochrome P450 oxidative enzymes (Crewe et al., 1992; Meyer et al., 1996). Sertraline may be somewhat less likely to do this. Carbamazepine, barbiturates, and phenytoin induce increased activity of the same enzymes and so can lower circulating concentrations of the TCAs to decrease their efficacy. Lithium lacks such effects, and valproate, in contrast to most other anticonvulsants, can produce mild interference with the hepatic clearance of many other agents.

A particularly dangerous effect of combining certain antidepressants with one another or with other drugs is a reaction commonly designated the *serotonin syndrome.* It is marked by initial muscle twitches or myoclonus, evolving into agitated delirium, seizures, fever, coma, and death (Sternbach, 1991). The high risk of such potentially fatal interactions contraindicates combinations of any SRI with any agent with MAO-inhibiting properties. Such reactions have been reported even with modern MAO inhibitors including selegiline. Another rare interaction with similar features has been observed with combinations of TCAs and MAO inhibitors. Similar reactions have been reported when an MAO inhibitor was combined with the phenylpiperidine analgesic meperidine, though not with morphine. The long-acting SRI fluoxetine requires particular care to allow it sufficient time (at least 2 weeks) to wash out before an MAO inhibitor is added to the regimen.

Another potentially dangerous effect of the MAO inhibitors is their ability to provoke *acute hypertensive crises,* sometimes associated with intracranial bleeding and cardiovascular collapse. The risk of these severe vascular reactions can be minimized by the scrupulous avoidance of medications, foods, and beverages containing appreciable quantities of sympathomimetic amines such as tyramine, which can be produced by fermentation. Since more than 10 mg of tyramine is usually required to produce hypertension, the most risky foods are the ripe cheeses and certain yeast products used as food supplements (Walker et al., 1996). In addition, some prescription drugs and proprietary medications including cold and sinus medications and decongestant inhalers contain sympathomimetic agents (ephedrines, amphetamines, and phenylephrine) or other compounds that can induce hypertension or other untoward reactions in the presence of an MAO inhibitor. Since tyramine and other indirect sympathomimetic amines require uptake into noradrenergic nerve terminals to act by releasing norepinephrine present there in increased abundance during treatment with an MAO inhibitor, the presence of a TCA agent can limit the hypertensive actions of tyramine, although the clinically appropriate strategy is to avoid hypertensive crises by avoiding intake of pressor amines. If such a hypertensive reaction is encountered, specific treatment is the immediate, but slow, intravenous injection of a potent alpha-adrenergic blocking agent, such as phentolamine (Regitine), in doses of 5 mg as needed. Associated vascular head pain should never be treated with meperidine (Demerol). The selective inhibitor of MAO-B (at low doses only) selegiline has a lower risk of potentiating pressor amines, probably by having a limited norepinephrine-increasing effect, and the newer, short-acting, reversible MAO-A inhibitors (RIMAs) are relatively less likely to potentiate tyramine, though neither type of agent can be assumed to be free of such risk. Some drugs other than antidepressants have MAO-inhibiting effects. These include the antihypertensive agent pargyline (Eutonyl), the nitrofuran antibiotics such as furazolidone (Furoxone), and a cancer chemotherapy agent, procarbazine (Matulane).

A difficult combination to manage satisfactorily is *depression and hypertension*. Many antihypertensive agents (including reserpine, methyldopa, and propranolol, but not diuretics, noncentrally acting beta-blockers, calcium channel blockers or angiotensin-converting enzyme [ACE] inhibitors), possibly owing to their central antiadrenergic properties, are sometimes associated with depression or, at least, intolerable sedation, anergy, and loss of libido.

The safety of all antidepressant drugs in *pregnancy and lactation* is not adequately established, although there is no convincing epidemiological evidence of teratogenic effects. Many antidepressants pass the placental barrier and can be secreted in low levels in human milk. In severe prepartum and postpartum depression, ECT can be used safely.

Summary

The modern medical treatment of depression is based on agents which act by potentiating neurotransmission due to norepinephrine, serotonin, or other monoamines in the central nervous system. Currently the most widely used antidepressant medicines are the selective inhibitors of the physiological inactivation of serotonin reuptake into neurons (SRIs). The current popularity of the SRIs is based on their relative safety, tolerability, and simplicity of use, although the effectiveness of all currently available antidepressants appears to be similar on average. In addition, the older tricyclic-type or imipraminelike antidepressants (TCAs) and related drugs act mainly by inhibiting the transport of norepinephrine, usually with lesser effects on serotonin transport. The inhibitors of monoamine oxidase (MAO) act by preventing the enzymatic oxidative inactivation of the various monoamine neurotransmitters. Other atypical antidepressants (bupropion, mirtazapine, nefazodone, trazodone) also exert complex effects on central monoaminergic neurotransmission.

Beneficial effects of all clinically employed antidepressants have been demonstrated in controlled clinical trials among outpatients as well as smaller numbers of hospitalized and other severely depressed patients. However, their performance is imperfect, with about two-thirds to three-quarters of patients responding to an active agent, compared to 20%–40% response rates with an inactive placebo and only slightly higher rates (for some symptoms) with sedative-anxiolytic agents. Standard antidepressants are most likely to be effective in depressive disorders marked by the presence of classic melancholic features, bipolarity, lack of psychotic features, and moderate but not extreme severity. Prediction of their efficacy is not powerfully enhanced by application of various biological measures of research importance. Selection of patients for a trial of antidepressant treatment is based empirically on the presence of a classic syndrome of major depression or depressive symptoms with clinically significant severity and dysfunction. Nearly all antidepressants require several weeks to provide clinically appreciable benefits, perhaps paralleling gradual adaptive adjustments in the presynaptic production of cerebral monoamines and the functional sensitivity of their receptors.

In very severe cases of depression, more consistent and more rapid effects are obtained with ECT, which is still used in the treatment of some cases of acute, severe psychotic depression, especially with dangerously suicidal patients and when antidepressants fail to work within a month or so, as happens in as many as 30% of cases of severe depression. Antipsychotic agents also have a useful adjunctive role in the treatment of agitated and psychotic forms of depression, and lithium salts can potentiate tricyclic antidepressants, at least. Bipolar depression is insufficiently recognized, and use of most antidepressants without a mood-stabilizing agent for such conditions risks inducing potentially dangerous agitation or mania. The MAO inhibitors are effective antidepressants in high doses, and they can benefit perhaps half of patients who respond inadequately to standard antidepressants; however, their use is complicated by the many restrictions required by their toxic interactions with other agents, including the SRIs and pressor amines. Stimulants now have a limited role in the treatment of depressive illnesses but are useful in attention deficit hyperactivity disorder (ADHD) and are sometimes employed in geriatric depressive syndromes or early dementia.

A most encouraging aspect of the clinical application of antidepressant therapy is the broadening range of indications of these drugs. SRI, TCA, and MAO inhibitor antidepressants have powerful anxiolytic actions that are particularly effective in the panic component of panic-agoraphobia, and the SRIs are selectively effective in obsessive-compulsive disorder (OCD) and related habitual behavior disorders. The TCAs are also effective in ADHD and some chronic pain syndromes.

Antianxiety Agents

There is no ideal generic term for antianxiety agents. The use of the synonyms *antianxiety, anxiolytic,* or *tranquilizer* to some degree represents wishful thinking, based on a long search for drugs that are specific for anxiety and distinctly different from sedative or hypnotic agents. Antianxiety agents have been of interest throughout the history of medicine. At the start of this century the main antianxiety agents were the bromides, along with ethanol and its analogues, paraldehyde and chloral hydrate. Next, the barbiturates became the standard sedatives and hypnotics. Introduction of the alcohol-like propanediols led to the development of meprobamate (Miltown, Equanil) in the 1950s. Soon thereafter, the search for safer antianxiety agents lacking the potentially lethal central and respiratory depressant and addicting properties of all the previously mentioned sedative-hypnotic tranquilizing agents led to the development of the benzodiazepines (Figure 21.4).

The first antianxiety benzodiazepine, chlordiazepoxide

(Librium), was introduced in 1960. It was found to have potent taming effects in animals and anticonvulsant, skeletal-muscle relaxant, and sedative-antianxiety effects in humans (Malizia and Nutt, 1995). Chlordiazepoxide (Librium) and later diazepam (Valium), and more recently alprazolam (Xanax) and lorazepam (Ativan), have been among the most commonly prescribed drugs of all kinds, recently at rates approaching 100 million prescriptions a year in the United States and a cost of hundreds of millions of dollars annually. The benzodiazepines have useful antianxiety effects, are relatively safe, and virtually completely displaced older sedatives, although some antidepressant drugs, particularly the SRIs, are increasingly accepted for the treatment of severe anxiety disorders, including panic and OCD, as is discussed above.

A recently introduced class of agents with beneficial effects for anxiety or dysphoria of moderate severity are the *azaspirones* (azaspirodecanediones), currently represented clinically by buspirone (Figure 21.4; Table 21.13). Originally developed as a potential antipsychotic agent with weak antidopaminergic activity, buspirone has pharmacological properties as a serotonin 5-HT$_{1A}$ receptor partial agonist distinct from those of both neuroleptics and sedatives including the benzodiazepines (Eison and Temple, 1986; Rickels and Schweizer, 1987; Sussman, 1994; Yocca, 1990). Their antidopaminergic actions are limited in vivo, and they do not produce clinical extrapyramidal side effects. Also, they do not interact with binding sites for benzodiazepines or facilitate GABA, are not anticonvulsant, lack tolerance or withdrawal reactions, and do not show cross-tolerance with benzodiazepines or other sedatives.

Pharmacology

Most agents used to treat anxiety depress the central nervous system, approximately in proportion to the dose. Mild central depression can provide clinically useful antianxiety effects more or less separable from sedation. Large amounts of older sedatives can produce cerebral intoxication (delirium) that may result in coma, respiratory depression, and death. All sedative-tranquilizers, including the benzodiazepines, have some tendency to be required in increasing doses because of tolerance and to produce psychological habituation and, potentially, physiological dependence (addiction). A trend in the development of these agents has been a gradual improvement of their therapeutic index, with consequent separation of antianxiety and sedative effects and a lessening of addictive potential, notably with the benzodiazepines. The sedative-tranquilizers also have very limited, if any, antipsychotic or mood-stabilizing activity but are very useful temporarily to sedate acutely agitated psychotic or manic patients, and currently lorazepam (Ativan) is commonly used for such purposes, in part owing to its excellent bioavailability in various forms of administration.

The barbiturates and propanediols such as meprobamate are now rarely used for the management of anxiety, but phenobarbital is still used as an anticonvulsant. It can induce the synthesis and activity of hepatic cytochrome P450 microsomal enzymes to increase its own rate of metabolism and that of many other drugs. Addiction to meprobamate occurs after prolonged use of doses not much greater than the upper limits of

recommended doses. None of these older sedatives can be recommended for clinical use in modern psychiatric practice. Certain sedative antihistamines, including diphenhydramine (Benadryl) and hydroxyzine (Atarax, Vistaril) are occasionally employed to treat mild anxiety or insomnia. Other approaches to the pharmacotherapy of anxiety disorders have included trials of antiadrenergic compounds usually employed for hypertension or other cardiovascular disorders, including the β-adrenergic antagonists propranolol and atenolol, and the α₂ agonist clonidine. Such compounds are not effective in severe anxiety disorders, but may modify autonomic expression of situational phobias such as performance anxiety (Rickels and Schweizer, 1987; Dubovsky, 1990).

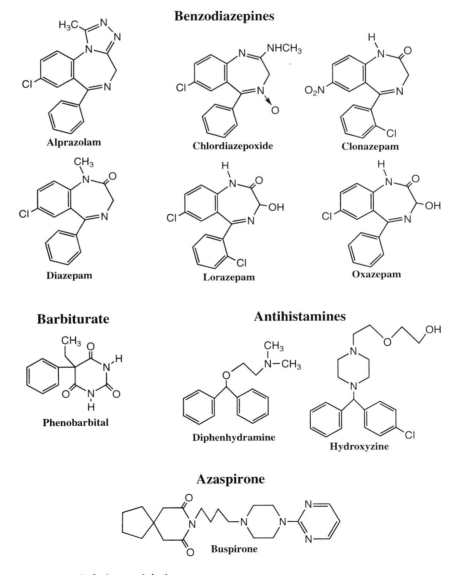

Figure 21.4 Sedative anxiolytics.

The benzodiazepines have rather widespread and diffuse inhibitory effects in the central nervous system and important anticonvulsant as well as muscle-relaxant activity. The benzodiazepines and nearly all the sedatives produce slow-wave and low-voltage fast (beta) activity in the EEG. The benzodiazepines have depressant actions in the limbic system at lower doses than are associated with more generalized depressant effects on the cerebral cortex and the reticular activating system. This partial selectivity correlates with relatively selective suppression of conditioned (especially "avoidance") behaviors more than unconditioned responses—and with their clinical antianxiety effect and relative lack of sedation in comparison with older sedatives.

Current theory accounts for the actions of benzodiazepines as facilitators of inhibitory neurotransmission mediated by the ubiquitous neuroactive compound γ-aminobutyric acid (GABA) (Paul et al. 1983; Malizia and Nutt, 1995; Stahl, 1996). An important class of GABA receptors (type A) are membrane proteins associated with chloride channels as well as receptive sites for benzo-diazepines (and probably also barbiturates, alcohol, the imidazopyridine hypnotic zolpidem, and other central depressants). This ring-shaped collection of transmembrane proteins includes representatives of at least 16 subunit peptides of 5 groups (α, β, γ, δ, ρ); benzodiazepines are believed to bind to type α subunits (also designated the BZ site, or omega receptor which occurs in at least 3 subtypes [ω_1, ω_2, ω_3] that vary in expression in brain regions), and GABA to β subunits. GABA acts by increasing the flow of the anion chloride across neural membranes to produce hyperpolarization and diminish neurophysiological activity, and the benzodiazepines act to facilitate this main effect of GABA. Other agents, including some benzodiazepines and β-carbolines, exert a range of agonist, partial-agonist, inverse agonist (reduce GABA effects on chloride influx), and antagonist actions (block full, partial, and inverse agonists) (Baldessarini, 1996a). The imidazobenzodiazepine flumazenil (Romazicon) is the first clinically developed benzodiazepine antagonist, and can be used to reverse the central depressant actions of benzodiazepines rapidly (Brogden and Goa, 1988).

Table 21.13   Selected sedative and antianxiety agents used in the United States: half-life and typical doses

Generic Names	Trade Names	Elimination Half-life (hr)	Doses (mg/24 hr)	
			Typical	Extreme
Anxiolytic benzodiazepines				
Alprazolam	Xanax and others	12	1–3	0.5–10
Chlordiazepoxide HCl	Librium and others	18	15–60	10–100
Clonazepam	Klonopin	34	2–10	0.5–2
Clorazepate dipotassium	Tranxene and others	100	20–30	10–90
Diazepam	Valium and others	60	5–30	2–60
Lorazepam	Ativan and others	15	2–6	1–10
Oxazepam	Serax and others	8	30–60	10–120
Azaspirone				
Buspirone HCl	BuSpar	2.5	15–30	5–60
Barbiturate				
Phenobarabital	Phenobarbital	80	30–120	15–400
Antihistamines				
Diphenhydramine HCl	Benadryl and others	4	50–100	10–300
Hydroxyzine HCl	Atarax and others	4	100–200	50–400
Hypnotics				
Flurazepam HCl	Dalmane and others	24	15–30	15–30
Temazepam	Restoril and others	11	15–30	15–30
Triazolam	Halcion and others	2	0.125–0.25	0.125–0.5
Zolpidem	Ambien	2.5	10	5–10

Note: Most anxiolytic benzodiazepines are rapidly absorbed orally, particularly diazepam; oxazepam is not.
All are converted to prominent, long-acting metabolites except lorazepam, oxazepam, and alprazolam.
Lorazepam is recommended for parenteral (IM) administration.
Hydroxyzine is also available as the pamoate (Vistaril).

Most sedative-tranquilizers and alcohol, but not the azapirones such as buspirone or the sedative antihistamines such as hydroxyzine, exhibit "cross-tolerance," or the ability of one to produce tolerance to the effects of the others, probably caused in large part by shared pharmacodynamic effects on chloride channels and GABA$_A$ receptor function. It follows that withdrawal of addicting doses of agents showing cross-tolerance can be accomplished with gradually diminishing doses of any one of them, as is commonly done with benzodiazepines in alcohol dependence or a long-acting barbiturate with dependence on many sedatives. The benzodiazepines (and antihistamines) are less likely than other sedatives to produce dangerous withdrawal syndromes, but some patients may gradually increase doses to maintain efficacy and may experience worsening of anxiety or even physiological symptoms including seizures on rapid withdrawal, particularly from high doses of potent, short-acting agents given for prolonged periods. Withdrawal reactions to the azapirones are unknown. The danger of severe coma, respiratory depression, and death following an acute overdose of a benzodiazepine or buspirone is much less than after a comparable multiple of the average daily dose of a barbiturate, propanediol, or other sedative.

Benzodiazepines differ among themselves in several ways (see Table 21.13). Diazepam (Valium) is particularly rapidly absorbed after oral (but not intramuscular) administration and induces euphoria and acute intoxication, which have contributed to its popularity as a drug of abuse. Lorazepam (Ativan) is remarkably efficiently and consistently absorbed by intramuscular as well as oral or sublingual administration, and, as with oxazepam (Serax), its elimination is dependent not on oxidation through active metabolites but on direct inactivation by conjugation with glucuronic acid (Greenblatt, Shader, and Abernethy, 1983). Oxazepam, alprazolam (Xanax), lorazepam, and the hypnotic agents triazolam (Halcion) and temazepam (Restoril) are the most rapidly metabolized and cleared benzodiazepines; they do not have active metabolites or a tendency to accumulate in tissue. In the elderly or in patients with impaired hepatic function, oxazepam in small, divided doses is currently favored owing to its brief action and direct conjugation and elimination. The last property is shared by lorazepam, but not by alprazolam, which requires ring-oxidation before conjugation, though its elimination half-life is somewhat shorter than that of lorazepam. Clonazepam, diazepam, and oxazepam are also especially effective as anticonvulsants. Long-acting benzodiazepines typically produce pharmacologically active metabolites; *desmethyldiazepam* is a common product.

Buspirone and several other experimental azapirones (e.g., gepirone, ipsapirone, tandospirone, tiaspirone) have selective affinity for serotonin receptors of the 5-HT$_{1A}$ type, for which they appear to be partial agonists, with complex agonist and antagonist actions, but a potential for net diminution of serotonergic neurotransmission. Their selective affinity at serotonin 5-HT$_{1A}$ receptors is demonstrated by potent competition with the selective 5-HT$_{1A}$ ligand radiolabeled 8-hydroxy-2-(dipropylamino)tetralin (8-OH-DPAT), and they have weaker interactions with other serotonin receptor types. Their agonist and antagonist effects on serotonin neurotransmission vary with abundance of serotonin. They are relatively active agonists of somatodendritic 5-HT$_{1A}$ autoreceptors and so can reduce the synthesis and release of serotonin, as well as exerting some postsynaptic 5-HT$_{1A}$ antagonism that increases when there is less serotonin to compete. These effects are blocked selectively by 5-HT$_{1A}$ antagonists such as (-)-pindolol. Long-term antiserotonergic actions of azapirones may lead to receptor adaptations, including decreases of 5-HT$_2$ (but probably not 5-HT$_{1A}$) receptors in cerebral cortex. Azapirones also have minor effects on cerebral dopaminergic and noradrenergic systems, and they fail to produce extrapyramidal side effects or hyperprolactinemia at ordinary doses. Unlike the barbiturates and benzodiazepines, the azapirones fail to compete with benzodiazepine binding sites or facilitate GABA, and may even have weak antagonist effects on GABA transmission.

Clinical Use

None of the sedative-tranquilizer antianxiety drugs alone is useful as a primary therapeutic agent in psychotic or major affective psychiatric illnesses, although these drugs have important specialized applications in patients with these and other major disturbances, particularly for short-term or emergency sedation. Benzodiazepines are now drugs of choice in severe anxiety disorders, and high-potency benzodiazepines are effective in the treatment of the panic-agoraphobia syndrome, in which antidepressants can be used if benzodiazepines fail (Sheehan, Ballenger, and Jacobsen, 1980; Rosenbaum, 1982; Balestrieri, Ruggeri, and Bellantuono, 1989; Coplan, Gorman, and Klein, 1992). Benzodiazepines of low potency probably also have beneficial effects against panic, but their usefulness is limited by their lack of potency and by excessive sedation in high doses. In general medicine, benzodiazepines are useful in the *short-term treatment* of relatively transient forms of anxiety, fear, and tension. They are also used as preoperative sedatives and in the management of short-lived, painful syndromes and psychosomatic and other illness with unexplained physical manifestations.

The benzodiazepines (Table 21.13) continue to be the most commonly employed antianxiety agents for generalized anxiety disorder. Benzodiazepines of very high potency (alprazolam, clonazepam, and lorazepam) also are effective in blocking panic attacks, as are several antidepressant agents (Rosenbaum, 1982; Rickels and Schweizer, 1987; Dubovsky, 1990; Hollister et al., 1993; Lader, 1994; Romach et al., 1995). For generalized or nonspecific anxiety, the specific agent selected seems to make little difference. Benzodiazepines are sometimes given to outpatients with anxiety mixed with symptoms of depression, though their specific efficacy in the core features of severe major depression is unlikely. Treatment of severe anxiety disorders usually requires a combination of the use of antianxiety agents with psychological and rehabilitative interventions, particularly cognitive and behavioral treatments in panic-agoraphobia.

Although benzodiazepines are ideally used for limited periods in low but effective doses, many anxiety disorders treated by psychiatrists are recurrent or chronic, requiring prolonged treatment. In long-term use, most patients continue to derive benefits and do not show tolerance (loss of efficacy at constant dose) or dose escalation over time, despite a great deal of concern about these possibilities (Lader, 1994; Romach et al., 1995). Despite some controversy surrounding their use in recent years (Salzman, 1990), benzodiazepines continue to be popular and useful drugs because their effects in anxiety are consistently superior to a placebo and because they are relatively safe agents, with relatively low risk of addiction or suicide. Diazepam (Valium) was the most popular drug of any kind in the United States in the 1970s, and currently popular agents are the more expensive high-potency benzodiazepines including lorazepam and alprazolam.

Buspirone has beneficial actions in anxious patients, particularly those with generalized anxiety of limited severity. Unlike potent benzodiazepines and many antidepressant drugs, it lacks beneficial actions in severe anxiety or panic (Sussman, 1994). It also does not share with antidepressants their efficacy as a monotherapy in OCD and ADHD, but it may have some adjunctive utility in OCD when added to an SRI antidepressant. Buspirone may require 2 weeks or more to become clinically effective, or much longer than benzodiazepines. Its lack of cross-tolerance with benzodiazepines correlates with a lack of protection against withdrawal-emergent anxiety when changing abruptly from a benzodiazepine to buspirone, requiring a gradual transition to buspirone. The mild central adrenergic facilitating actions of buspirone may worsen withdrawal responses to benzodiazepines, but might contribute to moderate mood-elevating or anti-dysphoric effects sometimes found with buspirone. Better understanding of the actions and optimal clinical application of the azapirones awaits further research.

Adverse Effects

Adverse effects of antidepressants used as antianxiety agents are discussed above. For all sedatives the most commonly encountered problem is daytime sedation, with drowsiness, decreased mental acuity, some decrease in coordination and occupational productivity, and increased risk of accidents, particularly when sedatives are combined with alcohol. Autonomic and extrapyramidal side effects are not usually encountered with the sedatives. Liver damage and blood dyscrasias are rare. Interactions with other medications occur with the barbiturates and propanediols, but rarely with the benzodiazepines and azapirones.

It would be a mistake to conclude that the benzodiazepines are totally innocuous. Occasionally overdoses equivalent to about 2 weeks' supply, especially when mixed with alcohol, have led to death. The common use of high doses of chlordiazepoxide or oxazepam in the treatment of alcoholic withdrawal and the use of benzodiazepines intravenously to control seizures or cardiac arrhythmias are rarely complicated by apnea or cardiac arrest. Some patients become dysphoric, agitated, angry, or otherwise apparently "disinhibited" while taking benzodiazepines. This effect resembles that of alcohol. Rarely, rage reactions have been observed. Triazolam (Halcion) has been associated with daytime anxiety and dissociative or amnestic reactions, particularly at doses above 0.25 mg.

The most serious problems of the older sedatives are related to their tendency to produce tolerance and physiological dependence or addiction, in addition to psychological habituation. The phenomenon of tolerance to both the antianxiety and the sedative effects of sedatives can contribute to innocent self-medication in increasing doses. Rapid intoxication and euphoria with the short-acting barbiturates, most of the nonbarbiturate sedative-hypnotics, and most impressively with diazepam among the benzodiazepines contribute to their abuse. Physicians can deal with the problems associated with sedative-tranquilizing agents by selecting those with the least potential for abuse, dependence, and lethality and by using the drugs for clear indications and for short periods when possible. Patients with a previous history of substance abuse, particularly of alcohol or other central depressants, or other dyssocial or impulsive traits should be treated with this class of agents very cautiously, if at all. In general, the use of sedative-tranquilizers in patients with personality disorders and more characterological forms of psychiatric disorder is unlikely to be helpful except in acute exacerbations of turmoil or anticipatory anxiety and can lead to abuse.

Risk of physical dependence on sedatives rises with daily dose and duration of use. Meprobamate is highly addicting. With short-acting barbiturates, signs and symptoms of withdrawal can be expected after the intake of about 4–5 times the usual daily dose for more than a month, and severe withdrawal reactions, with hypotension, seizures, delirium tremens, and hallucinosis, can be expected to occur 2 or 3 days after discontinuation of prolonged dosage more than 5 times the ordinary daily dose, and certainly above 10 times this dose. The withdrawal syndrome is strikingly similar to that associated with alcohol. Withdrawal from addiction to barbiturates and other sedatives is a serious and life-threatening medical problem. Physical dependence on the benzodiazepines has been studied most extensively with the oldest agents of that group, chlordiazepoxide and diazepam, although it seems more likely to develop with the newer, high-potency agents including alprazolam and lorazepam. Physical dependence is not likely unless abuses reach at least 10, or more likely 20, times the usual daily dose of a barbiturate or a low-potency benzodiazepine or perhaps 3–5 times that of a high-potency congener, and continue for several months. The onset of a withdrawal syndrome with the low-potency benzodiazepines, glutethimide (Doriden), and phenobarbital is considerably later than with either the short-acting barbiturates (2–3 days) or alcohol (3–5 days); it is usually seen at 4–8 days but sometimes as long as 2 weeks after withdrawal from the long-acting benzodiazepines including diazepam and clonazepam. Even when a withdrawal syndrome is encountered after abuse of the long-acting benzodiazepines, it is likely to be of only moderate intensity and is rarely associated with seizures. Benzodiazepines of high potency and relatively short action (such as alprazolam, lorazepam, and triazolam) probably carry an appreciable risk of habituation and induce physiological as well as psychiatric withdrawal reactions, especially when relatively high doses are discontinued rapidly (Woods, Katz, and Winger 1987; Salzman, 1990; Robertson and Treasure, 1996). These may include EEG changes and rapid exacerbation of anxiety symptoms; the latter can be hard to differentiate from relapse of a primary anxiety disorder and may lead to increased or more frequent dosing. In addition, triazolam has been associated with amnestic or dissociative reactions during the waking state, particularly when used as a hypnotic in single doses above 0.25 mg.

Benzodiazepines have a comfortable margin of safety in comparison with other sedatives. Although suicide with a benzodiazepine is very unlikely, many deliberate overdoses involve more than 1 agent, typically whatever the victim has at hand, and can present complicated toxicological problems. Recommendation of a specific number of days' supply of a benzodiazepine that can be dispensed safely is difficult; rare deaths have been reported following the acute ingestion of 600–1000 mg of chlordiazepoxide or diazepam, and there are reports of survival at doses of more than 2000 mg. With other sedatives and hypnotics, as a general rule, the acute ingestion of 10 days' supply at one time will regularly produce severe intoxication and may be lethal, and the ingestion of 20 times the daily or hypnotic dose is very likely to be fatal. Thus, even though fatality is less likely and more unpredictable with acute overdoses of the benzodiazepines, dispensing more than perhaps a 2-week supply of a low-potency benzodiazepine or a week's supply of a high-potency benzodiazepine or other sedative is unwise, particularly early in the treatment of a patient who is not well known to the clinician.

The safety of the sedative-tranquilizers and anxiolytic antidepressants in pregnancy has not been established. Little compelling evidence indicates that the benzodiazepines are teratogenic, although a possible association between cleft lip or palate and the use of diazepam in the first trimester is suspected. The barbiturates can alter fetal hepatic metabolism and should be avoided. The safety of the increasingly commonly and widely employed SRIs in pregnancy also remains to be clarified.

Summary

Anxiety and dysphoria are ubiquitous human experiences, and the history of psychopharmacology has been marked by the partially successful search for more effective and less toxic or dependency-producing antianxiety agents, and has included the replacement of alcohol and the bromides by the barbiturates in the early twentieth century and the later addition of nonbarbiturate sedatives, including the propanediols. All these agents are severely toxic and potentially lethal when taken acutely in doses above 20 times the normal daily dose, and they can be addicting when used for several months at doses only a few times above the usual daily doses. Their withdrawal can be managed by the substitution of a short-acting barbiturate and the *slow* withdrawal of the same barbiturate or of phenobarbital over several weeks. After the 1960s the benzodiazepines became the most widely employed antianxiety agents with a substantial margin of safety and a limited potential for producing dependence.

Anxiety symptoms are most effectively and appropriately treated pharmacologically when they represent symptomatically significant, function-limiting manifestations of psychiatric disorders, including generalized anxiety disorder (GAD), the panic-agoraphobia syndrome as well as severe social or situational phobias, and other syndromes presumably related to the anxiety disorder, including obsessive-compulsive disorder and related habit disorders such as kleptomania and trichotillomania. Antianxiety agents also have a useful place in managing reactive or anticipatory features of medical or surgical illness. Benzodiazepines, in particular, should be used ideally for brief periods even though their tendency to induce tolerance to their antianxiety and sedative effects and their risk of psychological habituation and even physical dependence is much more limited than with older sedative drugs. Routine and sustained use of sedative-antianxiety drugs for psychiatric patients with a personality disorder or a history of abuse of alcohol or other central depressants is of questionable value and may lead to abuse. However, since anxiety disorders treated by psychiatrists are frequently recurrent or chronic, long-term treatment is sometimes required and can yield sustained long-term benefits. Agents developed as antidepressants, including the TCAs and MAO inhibitors, but particularly the SRIs, provide an attractive alternative for long-term use in many severe anxiety disorders. Optimal treatment of anxiety disorders requires thoughtful and closely monitored use of medications within a comprehensive and coordinated program of psychopharmacological, psychosocial (particularly behavioral and cognitive), and rehabilitative interventions.

Concerning psychopharmacology in general, effective and relatively safe medical treatments are now available for most major psychiatric disorders. Their usefulness is most apparent in the more acute and severe forms of psychiatric illness. Unfortunately, many persistent forms of psychosis, mood disorder, anxiety syndromes, and personality disorders respond unsatisfactorily to pharmacological interventions—particularly to their use in isolation from more comprehensive treatment programs. When psychotropic drugs are required for extended use, adherence to the prescribed regimen is often a problem. Suggestions concerning factors that can reduce compliance are summarized in Table 21.14 (Baldessarini, 1994). Even in syndromes that are responsive to medications, the most efficient and humane use of psychopharmacological therapies in psychiatry, as in any medical specialty, requires a careful balance of applied medical technology and attention to the patient as both an individual and a member of a social network—aspects of psychiatric care that are emphasized in other chapters of this book.

Psychopharmacology has had important influences on the development of contemporary psychiatry; many of these were discussed in the introduction to this chapter (Baldessarini, 1997b). To reiterate, the availability of agents with impressive beneficial or deleterious effects on mental activity, mood, and behavior has led to an in-

Table 21.14 Conditions that may limit adherence to recommended treatment

Excessively complex regimen (multiple small doses of several agents given on different schedules)
Early onset and persistence of side effects with subjective discomfort
Slow onset of subtle beneficial effects that are not obvious to the patient
Misleading apparently low risk of immediate relapse when treatment discontinued
Contributions of patient's condition (psychosis, depression, mania, confusion, mental retardation, dementia, impaired hearing or vision, illiteracy, lack of language fluency, and cultural differences)
Simple ignorance and need for ongoing education and encouragement
Contributions of specific psychopathology (denial, grandiosity, obsessionality, demoralization, dependency, passive aggression, fear, ambivalence, splitting, sociopathy, substance abuse)
Avoidance of stigma, resentment of illness by patient or family
Clinician-patient disparity in aims and expectations of treatment
Involvement of multiple clinicians without clearly defined responsibilities and regular communication
Insufficient contact with or confidence in primary prescribing clinician
Clinician aloof, authoritarian, rigid, passive, angry, inclined to "psychologize" medical problems, overworked, insufficiently compensated, or insufficiently trained and experienced
Financial hardship and conflicts about use of available financial support by patient or clinicians; intrusions or denial of services by insurers, managers, or other third parties
Inevitable human error

creased interest in the biological and medical aspects of psychiatry since the 1950s—aspects that had lost some influence owing to the prominence in mid–twentieth-century American psychiatry of psychosocial and particularly psychoanalytic theories and techniques. In addition, the development of psychopharmacology has interacted with other positive biomedical and psychosocial research and clinical approaches to psychiatric illness that evolved in the post–World War II era, reinforcing an atmosphere of optimism about the treatability and rehabilitation of severely ill psychiatric patients, and reinforcing the professional identity of psychiatric physicians.

References

American Psychiatric Association (APA) Task Force on the Use of Laboratory Tests in Psychiatry. 1985. Tricyclic antidepressants: blood level measurements and clinical outcome. *Am. J. Psychiatry* 142:155–162.

Baldessarini, R. J. 1985. *Chemotherapy in psychiatry: principles and practice,* 2nd ed. Cambridge, Mass.: Harvard University Press.

——— 1989. Update on pharmacology and treatment with antidepressants. *J. Clin. Psychiatry* 50:117–126.

——— 1994. Enhancing treatment with psychotropic medicines. *Bull. Menninger Clinic* 58:224–241.

——— 1996a. Drugs and the treatment of psychiatric disorders: antipsychotic and antianxiety agents. Chap. 18 in *Goodman and Gilman's the pharmacological basis of therapeutics,* 9th ed., ed. J. G. Hardman, L. E. Limbird, P. B. Molinoff, R. W. Ruddon, and A. G. Gilman. New York: McGraw-Hill. 399–430.

——— 1996b. Drugs and the treatment of psychiatric disorders: antimanic and antidepressant agents. Chap. 19 in *Goodman and Gilman's the pharmacological basis of therapeutics,* 9th ed., ed. J. G. Hardman, L. E. Limbird, P. B. Molinoff, R. W. Ruddon, and A. G. Gilman. New York: McGraw-Hill. 431–459.

——— 1997a. Dopamine receptors and clinical medicine. In *The dopamine receptors,* ed. K. A. Neve and R. L. Neve. Totowa, N.J.: Humana Press. 457–498.

——— In press. Fifty years of biomedical psychiatry and psychopharmacology in America. In *Fifty years of American psychiatry,* a volume celebrating the 150th anniversary of the founding of the American Psychiatric Association, ed R. Menninger and J. Nemiah. Washington, D.C.: APA Press.

Baldessarini, R. J., and F. Centorrino. 1996. Results and limits of antipsychotic pharmacotherapy. *Nóos. Aggiornamenti in Psichiatria* (Rome) 4:249–273.

——— and F. R. Frankenburg. 1991. Clozapine—a novel antipsychotic agent. *New Engl. J. Med.* 324:746–754.

——— and F. I. Tarazi. 1996. Brain dopamine receptors: a primer on their current status, basic and clinical. *Harvard Rev. Psychiatry* 3:301–325.

——— and D. Tarsy. 1979. Relationship of the actions of neuroleptic drugs to the pathophysiology of tardive dyskinesia. *Intl. Rev. Neurobiol.* 21:1–45.

——— and M. Tohen. 1988. Is there a long-term protective effect of mood-altering agents in unipolar depressive disorder? In *Psychopharmacology: current trends,* ed. D. E. Casey and A. V. Christensen. Heidelberg: Springer-Verlag. 130–139.

Baldessarini, R. J., B. M. Cohen, and M. H. Teicher. 1988. Significance of neuroleptic dose and plasma level in the pharmacological treatment of psychoses. *Arch. Gen. Psychiatry* 45:79–91.

——— T. Suppes, and L. Tondo. 1996. Lithium withdrawal in bipolar disorder: implications for clinical practice and experimental therapeutics research. *Am. J. Therapeutics* 3:492–496.

Baldessarini, R. J., L. Tondo, G. L. Faedda, G. Floris, T. Suppes, and N. Rudas. 1996a. Effects of the rate of discontinuing lithium maintenance treatment in bipolar disorders. *J. Clin. Psychiatry* 57:441–448.

——— L. Tondo, T. Suppes, G. L. Faedda, and M. Tohen. 1996b. Pharmacological treatment of bipolar disorder throughout the life-cycle. In *Bipolar disorder through the life-cycle,* ed. K. I. Shulman, M. Tohen, and S. Kutcher. New York: John Wiley & Sons. 299–338.

Balestrieri, M., M. Ruggeri, and C. Bellantuono. 1989. Drug treatment of panic disorder—a critical review of controlled clinical trials. *Psychiatr. Devel.* 7:337–350.

Beasley, C. M., D. N. Masica, and J. H. Potvin. 1992. Fluoxetine: review of receptor and functional effects and their clinical implications. *Psychopharmacology* 107:1–10.

Biederman J., R. J. Baldessarini, V. Wright, D. Knee, and J. S. Harmatz. 1989. A double-blind placebo controlled study of desipramine in the treatment of ADD: efficacy. *J. Acad. Child Adolesc. Psychiatry* 28: 777–784.

Blackwell, B. 1987. Newer antidepressant drugs. Chap. 105 in *Psychopharmacology: the third generation of progress,* ed. H. Y. Meltzer. New York: Raven Press. 1041–49.

Bolden-Watson, C., and E. Richelson. 1993. Blockade by newly developed antidepressants of biogenic amine uptake into rat brain synaptosomes. *Life Sciences* 52:1023–29.

Bolini, P., S. Pampallona, M. J. Orza, M. E. Adams, and T. C. Chalmers. 1994. Antipsychotic drugs: is more worse? A meta-analysis of the published randomized control trials. *Psychol. Med.* 24:317–326.

Brogden, R. N., and K. L. Goa. 1988. Flumazenil: review of its benzodiazepine antagonist properties, intrinsic activity, and therapeutic use. *Drugs* 35:448–467.

Brown, W. A., and A. Kahn. 1994. Which depressed patients should receive antidepressants? *CNS Drugs* 1:341–347.

Cade, J. F. J. 1949. Lithium salts in the treatment of psychotic excitement. *Med. J. Austral.* 2:349–352.

Christison, G. W., D. G. Firch, and R. J. Wyatt. 1991. When symptoms persist: Choosing among alternative somatic treatments for schizophrenia. *Schizophrenia Bull.* 17:217–245.

Cohen, L. S., J. M. Friedman, J. W. Jefferson, E. M. Johnson, and M. L. Weiner. 1994. A reevaluation of risk of in utero exposure to lithium. *JAMA* 271:146–150.

Coplan, J. D., J. M. Gorman, and D. F. Klein. 1992. Serotonin related functions in panic-anxiety: a critical overview. *Neuropsychopharmacology* 6:189–200.

Crewe, H. K., M. S. Lennard, G. T. Tucker, F. R. Woods, and R. E. Haddock. 1992. The effect of selective serotonin reuptake inhibitors on cytochrome P450–2D6 (CYP2D6) activity in human liver microsomes. *Br. J. Clin. Pharmacol.* 34:262–265.

Cusack, B., A. Nelson, and E. Richelson. 1994. Binding of antidepressants to human brain receptors: focus on newer generation compounds. *Psychopharmacology* 114:559–565.

Danish University Antidepressant Group. 1993. Moclobemide: a reversible MAO-A inhibitor showing weaker antidepressant effect than clomipramine in a controlled multicenter study. *J. Affect. Disord.* 28:105–116.

Davis, J. M., P. G. Janicak, and K. Bruninga. 1987. The efficacy of MAO inhibitors in depression: a meta-analysis. *Psychiatric Ann.* 17:825–831.

Dechant, K. L., and S. P. Clissold. 1991. Paroxetine: a review of its pharmacodynamic and pharmacokinetic properties, and therapeutic potential in depressive illness. *Drugs* 41:225–253.

Delay, J., P. Deniker, and J. Harl. 1952. Utilisation thérapeutique psychiatrique d'une phenothiazine d'action centrale élective (4560 RP). *Ann. Med. Psychol.* 110:112–117.

Den Boer, J. A., and H. G. Westenberg. 1995. Serotonergic compounds in panic disorder, obsessive-compulsive disorder and anxious depression: a concise review. *Hum. Psychopharmacol.* 10(suppl.):S173–S183.

DeVane, C. L. 1992. Pharmacokinetics of the selective serotonin reuptake inhibitors. *J. Clin. Psychiatry* 53(suppl. 2):13–20.

Dubovsky, S. L. 1990. Generalized anxiety disorder: new concepts and psychopharmacologic therapies. *J. Clin. Psychiatry* 51(suppl.):3–10.

Eison, A. S., and D. L. Temple, Jr. 1986. Buspirone: review of its pharmacology and current perspectives on its mechanism of action. *Am. J. Medicine* 80(suppl. 3B):1–9.

Eison, A. S., M. S. Eison, J. R. Torrente, R. N. Wright, and F. D. Yocca. 1990. Nefazodone: preclinical pharmacology of a new antidepressant. *Psychopharmacol. Bull.* 26:311–315.

Enna, S., J. B. Malick, and E. Richelson, eds. 1981. *Antidepressants: neurochemical, behavioral, and clinical perspectives.* New York: Raven Press.

Fairchild, C. J., J. A. Rush, N. Vasavada, D. E. Giles, and M. Khatami. 1986. Which depressions respond to placebo? *Psychiatry Res.* 18:217–226.

Finberg, J. P. M., and M. B. H. Youdim. 1983. Selective MAO A and B inhibitors: their mechanism of action and pharmacology. *Neuropharmacology* 22(3B):441–446.

Frank, E., D. J. Kupfer, J. M. Perel, C. Cornes, A. G. Mallinger, M. E. Thase, A. B. McEachran, and V. J. Grochocinski. 1993. Comparison of full-dose vs. half-dose pharmacotherapy in the maintenance treatment of recurrent depression. *J. Affect. Disord.* 27:139–145.

Fuller, R. W., and T. Wong. 1987. Serotonin reuptake blockers in vitro and in vivo. *J. Clin. Psychopharmacol.* 7:14–20.

Gilbert, P. L., M. J. Harris, and D. V. Jeste. 1995. Neuroleptic withdrawal in schizophrenic patients: a review of the literature. *Arch. Gen. Psychiatry* 52:173–188.

Glassman, A. H., S. P. Roose, and J. T. Bigger, Jr. 1993. The safety of tricyclic antidepressants in cardiac patients: Risk-benefit reconsidered. *JAMA* 269:2673–75.

Gram, L. F. 1994. Fluoxetine. *N. Engl. J. Med.* 331:1354–61.

Greenberg, P. E., L. E. Stiglin, S. N. Finkelstein, and E. R. Berndt. 1993. Depression: a neglected major illness. *J. Clin. Psychiatry* 54:419–424.

Greenblatt, D. J., R. I. Shader, and D. R. Abernethy. 1983. Current status of benzodiazepines. *N. Engl. J. Med.* 309:354–358.

Greist, J. H., J. W. Jefferson, K. A. Kobak, D. J. Katzelnick, and R. C. Serlin. 1995. Efficacy and tolerability of serotonin transport inhibitors in obsessive-compulsive disorder: a meta-analysis. *Arch. Gen. Psychiatry* 52:53–60.

Grimsley, S. R., and M. J. Jann. 1992. Paroxetine, sertraline, and fluvoxamine: new selective serotonin reuptake inhibitors. *Clin. Pharmacy* 11:930–957.

Heninger, G. R., and D. S. Charney. 1987. Mechanisms of action of antidepressant treatments: implications for the etiology and treatment of depressive disorders. Chap. 54 in *Psychopharmacology: the third generation of progress,* ed. H. Y. Meltzer. New York: Raven Press. 535–544.

Hogarty, G. E., and R. F. Ulrich. 1977. Temporal effects of drug and placebo in delaying relapse in schizophrenic outpatients. *Arch. Gen. Psychiatry* 34:297–301.

Hollister, L. E. 1978. Tricyclic antidepressants. *N. Engl. J. Med.* 299:1106–9, 1168–72.

Hollister, L. E., B. Müller-Oerlinghausen, K. Rickels, and R. I. Shader, eds. 1993. Clinical uses of benzodiazepines. *J. Clin. Psychopharmacology* 13(suppl. 1):1–169.

Hudson, J. I., and H. G. Pope, Jr. 1990. Affective spectrum disorder: does antidepressant response identify a family of disorders with a common pathophysiology? *Am. J. Psychiatry* 147:552–564.

Janssen, P. A. J. 1970. Chemical and pharmacological classification of neuroleptics. In *Modern problems in pharmacopsychiatry: the neuroleptics,* ed. O. P. Bokon, P. A. J. Janssen, and J. Bokon. Basel: S. Karger.

Jefferson, J. W., J. H. Greist, and D. L. Ackerman. 1983. *Lithium encyclopedia for clinical practice.* Lithium Information Center, Department of Psychiatry, University of Wisconsin, Madison.

Jefferson, J. W., M. Altemus, M. A. Jenicke, T. A. Pigott, and D. J. Stein. 1995. Algorithm for the treatment of obsessive-compulsive disorder (OCD). *Psychopharmacol. Bull.* 31:487–480.

Jeste, D. V., and R. J. Wyatt. 1983. *Understanding and treating tardive dyskinesia.* New York: Guilford.

Johnson, F. N. 1984. *The psychopharmacology of lithium.* New York: Macmillan.

Kane, J. M., A. Rifkin, M. Woerner, G. Reardon, S. Sarantoakos, D. Schiebel, and J. Ramos-Lorenzi. 1983. Low-dose neuroleptic treatment of outpatient schizophrenics. *Arch. Gen. Psychiatry* 40:893–896.

Kasper, S., and A. Heiden. 1995. Do SSRIs differ in their antidepressant efficacy? *Hum. Psychopharmacol.* 10(suppl.):S163–S172.

Keepers, G. A., V. J. Clappison, and D. E. Casey. 1983. Initial anticholinergic prophylaxis for neuroleptic-induced extrapyramidal syndromes. *Arch. Gen. Psychiatry* 40:1113–17.

Keller, M. B., G. L. Klerman, P. W. Lavori, W. Coryell, J. Endicott, and J. Taylor. 1984. Long-term outcome of episodes of major depression: clinical and public health significance. *JAMA* 252:788–792.

——— P. W. Lavori, G. L. Klerman, N. C. Andreasen, J. Endicott, W. Coryell, J. Fawcett, J. P. Rice, and R. M. Hirschfeld. 1986. Low levels and lack of predictors of somatotherapy and psychotherapy received by depressed patients. *Arch. Gen. Psychiatry* 43:458–466.

Kind, P., and J. Sorensen. 1993. The costs of depression. *Intl. Clin. Psychopharmacol.* 7:191–195.

Kitayana, I., A. M. Janson, and A. Cintra. 1988. Effects of chronic imipramine treatment on glucocorticoid receptor immunoreactivity in various regions of the rat brain. *J. Neural Transm.* 73:119–203.

Kocsis, J. H., J. L. Croughan, M. M. Katz, M. T. P. Butler, S. Secunda, C. L. Bowden, and J. M. Davis. 1990. Response to treatment with antidepressants of patients with severe or moderate nonpsychotic depression and of patients with psychotic depression. *Am. J. Psychiatry* 147:621–624.

Koe, K. B. 1990. Preclinical pharmacology of sertraline: a potent and specific inhibitor of serotonin reuptake. *J. Clin. Psychiatry* 51(suppl. 12B):14–17.

Kuhn, R. 1958. The treatment of depressive states with G22355 (imipramine hydrochloride). *Am. J. Psychiatry* 115:459–464.

Kupfer, D. J., E. Frank, J. M. Perel, C. Cornes, A. G. Mallinger, M. E. Thase, A. B. McEachran, and V. J. Grochocinski. 1992. Five-year outcome for maintenance therapies in recurrent depression. *Arch. Gen. Psychiatry* 49:769–773.

Lader, M. 1994. Benzodiazepines: a risk-benefit profile. *CNS Drugs* 1:377–387.

Lasser, R., and R. J. Baldessarini. 1997. Thyroid hormones in depressive disorders: reappraisal of clinical utility. *Harvard Rev. Psychiatry* 4:291–305.

Lipinski, J. F., G. Zubenko, B. M. Cohen, and P. Barreira. 1984. Propranolol in the treatment of neuroleptic-induced akathisia. *Am. J. Psychiatry* 141:412–415.

Lohr, J. B., and M. P. Galigiuri. 1996. A double-blind placebo-controlled study of vitamin-E treatment of tardive dyskinesia. *J. Clin. Psychiatry* 57:167–173.

Malizia, A. L., and D. J. Nutt. 1995. Psychopharmacology of benzodiazepines—an update. *Hum. Psychopharmacol.* 10:S1–S14.

Manji, H. K., W. Z. Potter, and R. H. Lenox. 1995. Signal transduction pathways: molecular targets for lithium's actions. *Arch. Gen. Psychiatry* 42:431–543.

Mavissakalian, M. R., and J. M. Perel. 1989. Imipramine dose-response relationship in panic disorder with agoraphobia. *Arch. Gen. Psychiatry* 46:127–131.

Mavissakalian, M. R., and M. T. Ryan, 1996. Recent advances in pharmacologic and psychosocial treatments of panic disorder. *Essential Psychopharmacol.* 1:108–126.

Max, M. B., S. A. Lynch, J. Muir, S. E. Shoaf, B. Smoller, and R. Dubner. 1992. Effects of desipramine, amitriptyline, and fluoxetine on pain in diabetic neuropathy. *N. Engl. J. Med.* 326:1250–56.

McCombs, J. S., M. B. Nichol, G. L. Stimmel, D. A. Sclar, C. M. Beasley, Jr., and L. S. Gross. 1990. The cost of antidepressant drug therapy failure: a study of antidepressant use patterns in a Medicaid population. *J. Clin. Psychiatry* 51(Suppl. 6):60–69.

Meltzer, H. Y. 1992. Treatment of the neuroleptic-nonresponsive schizophrenic patient. *Schizophrenia Bull.* 18:515–542.

Meltzer, H. Y., and S. M. Stahl. 1976. The dopamine hypothesis of schizophrenia: a review. *Schizophrenia Bull.* 2:19–76.

Mendelowitz, A. J., S. L. Gerson, J. M. J. Alvir, and J. A. Lieberman. 1995. Clozapine-induced agranulocytosis: risk factors, monitoring and management. *CNS Drugs* 4:412–421.

Meyer, M., R. J. Baldessarini, D. Goff, and F. Centorrino.

1996. Clinically significant interactions of psychotropic drugs with antipsychotic agents. *Drug Safety* 15:333–346.

Montgomery, S. A. 1980. Review of antidepressant efficacy in inpatients. *Neuropharmacology* 19:1185–90.

Morris, J. B., and A. Beck. 1974. The efficacy of antidepressant drugs. *Arch. Gen. Psychiatry* 30:667–674.

Morris, P. L. P., R. G. Robinson, P. Andrejewski, J. Samuels, and T. R. Price. 1993. Association of depression with 1-year poststroke mortality. *Am. J. Psychiatry* 150:124–129.

Murphy, D. L., C. S. Aulakh, N. A. Garrick, and T. Sunderland. 1987. Monoamine oxidase inhibitors as antidepressants. Chap. 55 in *Psychopharmacology: the third generation of progress*, ed. H. Y. Meltzer. New York: Raven Press. 545–552.

Muth, E. A., J. T. Haskins, J. A. Moyer, G. E. Husbands, S. T. Nielsen, and E. B. Sigg. 1986. Antidepressant biochemical profile of the novel bicyclic compound Wy-45,030, an ethyl cyclohexanol derivative [venlafaxine]. *Biochem. Pharmacol.* 24:4493–97.

Nelson, J. C., C. M. Mazure, M. B. Bowers, Jr., and P. I. Jatlow. 1991. A preliminary, open study of the combination of fluoxetine and desipramine for rapid treatment of major depression. *Arch. Gen. Psychiatry* 48:303–307.

——— J. P. Docherty, G. M. Henschen, S. Kasper, A. A. Nierenberg, and N. G. Ward. 1995. Algorithms for the treatment of subtypes of unipolar major depression. *Psychopharmacol. Bull.* 31:475–485.

Paul, S., J. Skolnick, J. Tallman, and E. Usdin. 1983. *Pharmacology of benzodiazepines*. New York: Macmillan.

Peet, M. 1994. Induction of mania with selective serotonin re-uptake inhibitors and tricyclic antidepressants. *Br. J. Psychiatry* 164:549–550.

Perry, P. J., C. Zeilman, and S. Arndt. 1994. Tricyclic antidepressant concentrations in plasma: an estimate of their sensitivity and specificity as a predictor of response. *J. Clin. Psychopharmacol.* 14:230–240.

Plasky, P. 1991. Antidepressant usage in schizophrenia. *Schizophrenia Bull.* 17:649–657.

Pope, H. G., Jr., and J. I. Hudson. 1986. Antidepressant drug therapy for bulimia: current studies. *J. Clin. Psychiatry* 47:339–345.

Rickels, K., and E. E. Schweizer. 1987. Current pharmacotherapy of anxiety and panic. Chap. 122 in *Psychopharmacology: the third generation of progress*, ed. H. Y. Meltzer. New York: Raven Press. 1193–1203.

Rickels, K., D. S. Robinson, E. Schwiezer, R. N. Marcus, and D. J. Roberts. 1995. Nefazodone: aspects of efficacy. *J. Clin. Psychiatry* 56(suppl. 6):43–46.

Riddle, W. J. R., and A. I. F. Scott. 1995. Relapse after successful electroconvulsive therapy: the use and impact of continuation antidepressant drug treatment. *Hum. Psychopharmacol.* 10:201–205.

Robertson, J. R., and W. Treasure. 1996. Benzodiazepine abuse: nature and extent of the problem. *CNS Drugs* 5:137–146.

Rogers, S. C., and P. M. Clay. 1975. A statistical review of controlled studies of imipramine and placebo in the treatment of depressive illnesses. *Br. J. Psychiatry* 127:599–603.

Romach, M., U. Busto, G. Somer, H. L. Kaplan, and E. Sellers. 1995. Clinical aspects of chronic use of alprazolam and lorazepam. *Am. J. Psychiatry* 152:1161–67.

Romero, L., N. Bel, F. Artigas, D. de Montigny, and P. Blier. 1996. Effect of pindolol on the function of pre- and postsynaptic 5-HT$_{1A}$ receptors: in vitro microdialysis and electrophysiological studies in the rat brain. *Neuropsychopharmacology* 15:349–360.

Roose, S. P., A. H. Glassman, E. Attia, and S. Woodring. 1994. Comparative efficacy of selective serotonin reuptake inhibitors and tricyclics in the treatment of melancholia. *Am. J. Psychiatry* 151:1735–39.

Rosenbaum, J. F. 1982. The drug treatment of anxiety. *N. Engl. J. Med.* 306:401–404.

Sachs, G. S., B. Lafer, A. L. Stoll, M. Banov, A. B. Thibault, M. Tohen, and J. F. Rosenbaum. 1994. A double-blind trial of bupropion vs. desipramine for bipolar depression. *J. Clin. Psychiatry* 55:391–393.

Sackeim, H. A., J. Prudic, D. P. Devanand, P. Decina, B. Kerr, and S. Malitz. 1990. The impact of medication resistance and continuation pharmacotherapy on relapse following response to electroconvulsive therapy in major depression. *J. Clin. Psychopharmacol.* 10:96–104.

Salzman, C., ed. 1990. *Benzodiazepine dependence, toxicity, and abuse* (APA Task Force Report). Washington, D.C.: American Psychiatric Association.

Schou, M. 1969. The biology and pharmacology of lithium: a bibliography. *NIMH Psychopharmacol. Bull.* 5:33–62.

Settle, E. C. 1989. Bupropion: a novel antidepressant, update. *Intl. Drug Ther. Newsletter* 24:29–36.

Shah, N., and A. Donald, eds. 1986. *Movement disorders*. New York: Plenum Press. 365–389.

Sheehan, D. V., J. Ballenger, and G. Jacobsen. 1980. Treatment of endogenous anxiety with phobic, hysterical, and hypochondriacal symptoms. *Arch. Gen. Psychiatry* 36:51–59.

Simmons, S. A., P. J. Perry, E. D. Rickert, and J. L. Bourne. 1985. Cost-benefit analysis of prospective pharmacokinetic dosing of nortriptyline in depressed inpatients. *J. Affect. Dis.* 8:47–53.

Sokolov, S. T., and R. T. Joffe. 1995. Practical guidelines for combination drug therapy of treatment-resistant depression. *CNS Drugs* 4:341–350.

Souza, F. G. M., and G. M. Goodwin. 1991. Lithium treatment and prophylaxis in unipolar depression: a meta-analysis. *Br. J. Psychiatry* 158:666–675.

Spencer, T., J. Biederman, T. Wilens, R. Steingard, and D. Geist. 1993. Nortriptyline treatment of children with attention-deficit hyperactivity disorder and tic disorder or Tourette's syndrome. *J. Am. Acad. Child, Adolesc. Psychiatry* 32:205–210.

Stahl, S. 1996. *Essential psychopharmacology: neuroscientific basis and practical applications.* New York: Cambridge University Press.

Sternbach, H. 1991. The serotonin syndrome. *Am. J. Psychiatry* 148:705–713.

Suppes, T., R. J. Baldessarini, G. L. Faedda, L. Tondo, and M. Tohen. 1993. Discontinuing maintenance treatment in bipolar manic-depression: risks and implications. *Harvard Rev. Psychiatry* 1:131–144.

Sussman, N. 1994. The uses of buspirone in psychiatry. *J. Clin. Psychiatry Monogr.* 12:3–19.

Swazey, J. P. 1974. *Chlorpromazine in psychiatry: a study in therapeutic innovation.* Cambridge, Mass.: MIT Press.

Taylor, S. P., R. B. Carter, A. S. Eison, U. L. Muillins, H. L. Smith, J. P. Torrente, R. N. Wright, and F. D. Yocca. 1995. Pharmacology and neurochemistry of nefazodone, a novel antidepressant drug. *J. Clin. Psychiatry* 56(suppl. 6):3–11.

Teicher, M. H., C. A. Glod, and J. O. Cole. 1993. Antidepressant drugs and the emergence of suicidal tendencies. *Drug Safety* 3:186–212.

Thase, M. E. 1992. Long-term treatments of recurrent depression. *J. Clin. Psychiatry* 53(suppl. 9):32–44.

Van Harten, J. 1993. Clinical pharmacokinetics of selective serotonin reuptake inhibitors. *Clin. Pharmacokinetics* 24:203–220.

Van Putten, T. 1974. Why do schizophrenic patients refuse to take their drugs? *Arch. Gen. Psychiatry* 31:67–72.

Viguera, A. C., R. J. Baldessarini, J. Hegarty, D. P. van Kammen, and M. Tohen. 1997a. Risk of discontinuing maintenance medication in schizophrenia. *Arch. Gen. Psychiatry.* 54:49–55.

Viguera, A. C., R. J. Baldessarini, and J. Friedberg. 1998. Risks of interrupting continuation or maintenance treatment with antidepressants in major depressive disorders. *Harvard Review of Psychiatry* 5:293–306.

Wagstaff, A. J., and H. M. Bryson. 1995. Clozapine: a review of its pharmacological properties and therapeutic use in patients with schizophrenia who are unresponsive to or intolerant of classical antipsychotic agents. *CNS Drugs* 4:370–400.

Walker, S. E., K. I. Shuman, S. A. Tailor, and D. Gardner. 1996. Tyramine content of previously restricted foods in monoamine oxidase inhibitor diets. *J. Clin. Psychopharmacol.* 16:383–388.

Wamsley, J. K., W. F. Byerley, R. T. McCabe, E. J. McConnell, T. M. Dawson, and B. I. Grosser. 1987. Receptor alterations associated with serotonergic agents: an autoradiographic analysis. *J. Clin. Psychiatry* 48(suppl. 3):19–25.

Wiseman, L. R., and D. McTavish. 1995. Selegiline: a review of its clinical efficacy in Parkinson's disease and its clinical potential in Alzheimer's disease. *CNS Drugs* 4:230–246.

Wong, K. L., R. C. Bruck, and I. A. Farabman. 1991. Amitriptyline-mediated inhibition of neurite outgrowth from chick embryonic cerebral explants involves a reduction in adenylate cyclase activity. *J. Neurochem.* 57:1223–30.

Woods, J. H., J. L. Katz, and G. Winger. 1987. Abuse liability of benzodiazepines. *Pharmacol. Rev.* 39:251–413.

Yocca, F. D. 1990. Neurochemistry and neurophysiology of buspirone and gepirone: interactions at presynaptic and postsynaptic 5-HT$_{1A}$ receptors. *J. Clin. Psychopharmacology* 10:6S–12S.

Zajecka, J. M., H. Jeffries, and J. Fawcett. 1995. The efficacy of fluoxetine combined with a heterocyclic antidepressant in treatment-resistant depression: a retrospective analysis. *J. Clin. Psychiatry* 56:338–343.

Zametkin, A. J., and J. L. Rappoport. 1987. Noradrenergic hypothesis of attention deficit disorder with hyperactivity: a critical review. Chap. 83 in *Psychopharmacology: the third generation of progress,* ed. H. Y. Meltzer. New York: Raven Press. 837–842.

Zornberg, G. L., and H. G. Pope, Jr. 1993. Treatment of depression in bipolar disorder: new directions for research. *J. Clin. Psychopharmacol.* 13:397–408.

Recommended Reading

Baldessarini, R. J. 1985. *Chemotherapy in psychiatry: principles and practice.* Cambridge, Mass.: Harvard University Press.

——— 1996. Drugs and the treatment of psychiatric disorders: antipsychotic and antianxiety agents. Chaps. 18 and 19 in *Goodman and Gilman's the pharmacological basis of therapeutics,* 9th ed., ed. J. G. Hardman, L. E. Limbird, P. B. Molinoff, R. W. Ruddon, and A. G. Gilman. New York: McGraw-Hill. 399–459.

Bassuk, E. L., S. C. Schoonover, and A. J. Gelenberg. 1991. *The practitioner's guide to psychoactive drugs,* 3rd ed. New York: Plenum Publishing.

Bloom, F. E., and D. J. Kupfer, eds. 1994. *Psychopharmacology: the fourth generation of progress.* New York: Raven Press.

Ciraulo, D. A., R. I. Shader, D. J. Greenblatt, and W. Creelman, eds. 1995. *Drug interactions in psychiatry,* 2nd ed. Baltimore: Williams & Wilkins.

Cooper, J. R., F. E. Bloom, and R. H. Roth. 1991. *The biochemical basis of neuropharmacology,* 6th ed. New York: Oxford University Press.

Gallicchio, V. S., and N. J. Birch, eds. 1996. *Lithium: biochemical and clinical advances.* Cheshire, Conn.: Weidner Publishing.

Janicek, P. G., J. M. Davis, S. H. Preskorn, and F. J. Ayd, Jr., eds. 1993. *Principles and practice of psychopharmacotherapy.* Baltimore: Williams & Wilkens.

Johnson, F. N. 1984. *The psychopharmacology of lithium.* New York: Macmillan.

Kane, J. M., and D. V. Jeste, eds. 1992. *Tardive dyskinesia: a task force report.* Washington, D.C.: American Psychiatric Association.

Kane, J. M., and J. A. Lieberman, eds. 1992. *Adverse effects of psychotropic drugs.* New York: Guilford Press.

Klein, D. F., R. Gittelman, F. Quitkin, and A. Rifkin. 1980. *Diagnosis and drug treatment of psychiatric disorders: adults and children,* 2nd ed. Baltimore: Williams & Wilkins.

Mountgomery, S., and F. Rouillon, eds. 1992. *Long-term treatment of depression.* New York: John Wiley & Sons.

Neve, K. A., and R. L. Neve, eds. 1997. *The dopamine receptors.* Totowa, N.J.: Humana Press.

Prien, R. F., and D. S. Robinson, eds. 1994. *Clinical evaluation of psychotropic drugs: principles and guidelines.* New York: Raven Press.

Schatzberg, A. F., and C. B. Nemeroff, eds. 1995. *The American Psychiatric Press textbook of psychopharmacology.* Washington, D.C.: American Psychiatric Press.

Shulman, K. I., M. Tohen, and S. P. Kutcher, eds. 1996. *Mood disorders across the life span.* New York: John Wiley & Sons.

Stahl, S. 1996. *Essential psychopharmacology: neuroscientific basis and practical applications.* New York: Cambridge University Press.

LEE BIRK

Cognitive Behavior Therapy and Systemic Behavioral Psychotherapy

Behavior therapy may be defined as the array of clinical concepts and therapeutic procedures that have been systematically developed from the experimental observation and modification of animal and human behavior. In its most sophisticated clinical form, behavior therapy is not limited to simple motor reflex learning, or even to the whole range of learned external behaviors mediated by skeletal muscles—from crude and simple actions (such as bar pressing) to subtle and complex behavioral sequences, or "chained responses" (such as parallel skiing, violin playing, or sculpting). Rather, despite its historical origins in pure behaviorism, as with other psychotherapeutic approaches, modern behavior therapy now includes and even emphasizes techniques for modifying those problematic and difficult-to-measure internal responses that we call feelings and thoughts. It is this new ability to deal with thinking and feeling that has made it a versatile and broadly applicable approach and resulted in its being widely known for over a decade now as cognitive behavior therapy.

Historical Background

Although behavior therapy as a significant clinical enterprise dates back only to the early 1960s, its scientific origins date back to Pavlov (1928, 1941), Thorndike (1898), and even earlier. In 1920, Watson and Rayner reported their classic experiment with the 11-month-old infant Albert, demonstrating that a "phobia" could be created by classical conditioning and that it obeyed familiar principles of stimulus generalization; this term refers to the experimentally observed fact that stimuli very similar to a conditioned stimulus will elicit the same conditioned response, though in a progressively weaker form as the stimulus used becomes less and less similar to the one used in the original conditioning.

Watson later sparked widespread enthusiasm and criticism by advocating a radical, sweeping, and simplistic "behaviorism" which he claimed could explain not only all phobias but all of human personality, by simple stimulus-response (S-R) bonds.

More realistically, as early as 1924, Mary Cover Jones successfully treated phobias in children by a behavioral method that we would now call in vivo systematic desensitization, using eating as a competitive response. W. Horsley Gantt (1944, 1953), working in the Pavlovian Laboratory in Adolf Meyer's psychiatry department at Johns Hopkins Medical School in the 1930s, 1940s, and 1950s, almost single-handedly sustained in the United States the ideal of a behavioral approach to psychiatry.

It was not until the late 1950s, however, that—almost simultaneously and on 3 continents—3 major research traditions began to coalesce into a set of clinically useful ideas and methods. The work of Wolpe, Lazarus, and Rachman (Wolpe, 1958), first in South Africa and later in the United States, emphasized competitive response or "counter-conditioning" treatment strategies. In the United States, the research of B. F. Skinner and his students, especially Ogden Lindsley, in operant conditioning emphasized precise analysis and contingency control of the clinical situation (Lindsley and Skinner, 1954). And at the Maudsley Hospital in London, M. B. Shapiro (1961) and his colleagues, especially Isaac Marks (1972, 1976), following in the footsteps of Claude Bernard in medicine, emphasized the value of treating the single psychiatric case as an experiment in itself.

Throughout the 1960s behavior therapy grew prodigiously into a fully recognized and at times almost oversold approach to treatment problems in clinical psychiatry. Early in 1970 the American Psychiatric Association chartered a task force to evaluate the achievements and potential of the behavioral approach. In mid-1973 its report, *Behavior Therapy in Psychiatry,* concluded that "behavior therapy and behavioral principles employed in the analysis of clinical phenomena have reached a stage of development where they now unquestionably have much to offer informed clinicians in the service of modern clinical and social psychiatry" (Birk et al., 1973, p. 64).

The following year Birk and Brinkley-Birk (1974) proposed a conceptual synthesis of behavioral and psychoanalytic elements to permit the development of therapeutic strategies more efficacious than either approach alone.

Since then, the "integration," or at least the at times useful combination, of behavioral and psychodynamic methods (Wachtel, 1977; Woods and Marmor, 1980; Goldfried, 1982; Arkowitz and Messer, 1984) has become widely accepted, in marked contrast to the narrow focus on specific maladaptive behaviors and the factional belligerence characteristic of the 1950s and 1960s. The aggressive competitiveness of that period gradually, but now rather completely, has been replaced by a tendency to combine and "integrate" widely disparate theories and therapies in a way that too often has been much less than optimally thoughtful and critical (Lazarus, 1996; Grunebaum, 1997). Perhaps (as suggested in the second edition of this volume) this huge shift, between about 1956 and 1996, represents something like the extreme points on a historical pendulum. In any case, the important practical point is that between these two extremes, for over 20 years now, considerable practical clinical wisdom has been accumulating.

Consider, for example, this summary written by Cyril Franks, in 1984, after having been the senior editor of the *Annual Review of Behavior Therapy* for the 11 years since its inception in 1973:

[Early] behavior therapy was simplistic in its understandable focus upon specific responses and the treatment of circumscribed maladaptive behaviors. It was all we were able to deal with at that stage of our evolution. Early behavior therapists [then] deliberately ignored cognitive processes and were ill-equipped to deal with complex *social systems.* [Yet the evolution eventually produced both] *cognitive behavior therapy* and the extension of behavior therapy into the external environment by way of *systems theory.* (quoted in Arkowitz and Messer, 1984, p. 353)

This concession, though laudable, did follow by 5 to 10 years both the robust development of cognitive behavior therapy (Mahoney, 1974; Beck, 1976; Meichenbaum, 1977; Beck et al., 1979) as well as the beginning pragmatic synthesis of behavioral psychotherapy with social systems theory (Birk, 1974, 1982a, b, 1984, 1988).

In the slow evolution toward psychodynamic/behavioral "integration"/combination there have been 4 identifiable quantum leaps. First, beginning in the late 1960s and early 1970s, a number of researchers and clinicians (Goldiamond and Dyrud, 1968; Birk, 1968, 1970, 1972, 1973a, b; Sloane, 1969; Marmor, 1971; Feather and Rhoads, 1972) advocated the use of behavior therapy together with a psychodynamic approach. Second, the publication of *Behavior Therapy in Psychiatry* by the American Psychiatric Association (Birk et al., 1973) called for explicit recognition of the behavioral elements not only in "dynamic psychotherapy," but also in group, family, couple, and sex therapy. Third, in 1974, three influential papers were published. The first, by Rhoads and Feather, reported a successful hybrid therapy which employed the behavioral method of systematic desensitization but used stimulus hierarchies based on psychodynamically relevant themes. The second, by Birk, also described a successful hybrid therapy, an integrated behavioral psychoanalytic method of group therapy found to be quite effective with patients who had previously remained quite treatment resistant, even with very extensive psychoanalyis and/or individual psychodynamic therapy. The third, by Birk and Brinkley-Birk, outlined a working conceptual synthesis between psychoanalytic and behavioral frameworks which they had successfully employed across a variety of differing patients. (This paper's title, then considered jarring if not brash, was, quite simply, "Psychoanalysis and Behavior Therapy.") Fourth, P. L. Wachtel's book (1977) used the same title, but added an enticing subtitle: *Psychoanalysis and Behavior Therapy: Toward an Integration.* Wachtel's book was unprecedented in its thorough treatment of psychoanalytic theory, and in its attempt, epistemologically, to sift the wheat from the chaff in terms of clinically indispensable psychoanalytic concepts.

The founding in 1985 of the Society for the Exploration of Psychotherapy Integration (SEPI) brought together leading behavioral, psychoanalytic, and cognitive therapists into a cross-fertilizing dialogue, one which has led not to total merger, but rather, much more promisingly, to "hybrid vigor" and to the useful combination, when appropriate, of 3 previous largely separate traditions, literatures, and phenomenological legacies.

The combination of psychoanalysis and behavior therapy has strengthened both and has led to a new hybrid strength in psychotherapy as a whole. It is now more commonly recognized that "diagnosis" is almost always better (that is, more complete and useful) if a thorough behavioral analysis is done in addition to the therapist's making a real effort to understand the "psychodynamics" of the case. Furthermore, there is an increasingly widespread recognition that all cases occur within systems—i.e., within a family and social matrix—and this is leading toward a pragmatic integration of systems thinking and methods within psychiatric practice.

The other major development has been the discovery and refinement of nonbehavioral treatment methods that in many cases have proved to be more efficient than behavior therapy. This has led to a number of inroads on what had been primarily the territory of behavior therapy. For example, the drug pimozide works better and is quicker than behavior therapy in treating Gilles de la Tourette syndrome (Shapiro, Shapiro, and Eisenkraft, 1983; Shapiro and Shapiro, 1983), as is intramuscular haloperidol for potentially life-threatening intractable hiccups (Ives, 1985). Antidepressant and other drugs (principally imipramine, paroxetine and sometimes phenelzine or valproate) are now recognized as important to the treatment and management of panic attacks and the unconditional panic portion of agoraphobia (Sheehan, Ballenger, and Jacobsen, 1980; Sheehan, 1982; Ballenger, 1986; Woodman and Noyes, 1994). In addition, of course, the late 1980s and 1990s witnessed the birth of important behavioral techniques for treating panic (Wolpe, 1995). For panic attacks leading to agoraphobia, behavioral exposure therapies are combined with drugs which reduce spontaneous panic attacks but do not in themselves help conditioned phobic avoidance, while behavioral exposure therapies reduce learned phobic avoidance but do not significantly alter spontaneous panic attacks (Sheehan, 1982; Ballenger, 1986). In addition, for treating bulimia, whether or not via antidepressant mechanisms, antidepressant drugs such as imipramine (Pope et al., 1983; Hudson and Pope, 1985; Pope and Hudson, 1986), phenelzine (Walsh et al., 1984), and possibly lithium (Hsu, 1985) now have surpassed behavior therapy in clinical importance. And although response prevention is still a mainstay for treating severe obsessive-compulsive states, it is now often used with drugs—clomipramine, sertraline, or fluoxamine. Since obsessions are cognitive, not motor, they cannot be treated with response prevention. Compulsions, which are repetitive rituals, can be directly observed and thus can be prevented; obsessions, which are recurrent thoughts, cannot (Abel, 1993).

Even more surprisingly, for severe chronic obesity (defined as body weight 100% or more above ideal weight), surgery is now the primary treatment of choice, rather than any form of behavior therapy or psychotherapy (Stunkard, Stinnett, and Smoller, 1986); and family therapy is now deservedly more popular than behavior therapy in the treatment of anorexia nervosa (Minuchin et al., 1975; Minuchin, Rosman, and Baker, 1978).

Since the first edition of this volume in 1976, in a historic "first," a form of psychotherapy (a subtype of behavior therapy, Aaron Beck's "cognitive therapy for depression") was proved superior in controlled trials to pure

pharmacotherapy (Beck et al., 1979; Simons et al., 1986). Also, biofeedback has become the recognized treatment of choice for tension headache, migraine, Raynaud's disease, and chronic pain syndromes (Surwit, 1982). Not surprisingly, cognitive therapy and drug therapy, used together, have now been reported to be better than either alone (Conte et al., 1986).

Since the second edition, in 1988, we have witnessed another landmark event—the demonstration of common brain mechanisms for improvement in obsessive-compulsive symptoms, whether produced by behavior therapy (response prevention) or by pharmacotherapy (fluoxetine). Patients who improve, no matter with which treatment, have been found to have PET scan studies (positron emission tomography scans) which are very similar. Patients who improve with either treatment show the same kind of microanatomical neurochemical changes in the caudate nucleus of the thalamus (Abel, 1993). This is exciting, because we are now at the edge of a dawning new ability to look directly inside the behaviorists' "black box"—the brain.

Distinguishing Characteristics of Behavior Therapy

Insistence on the Observable

What distinguishes behavior therapy and behavioral psychotherapy from other therapies is an insistence on observable phenomena, as opposed to inferred processes, in guiding diagnosis and treatment. Historically, this very significant difference between behavioral and dynamic psychotherapies arises from the rootedness of the behavioral therapies in experimental scientific method. When behavior therapists work toward modifying feelings or behaviors, they adopt a rigorous standard of evidence for evaluating the phenomena in question; that is, they insist on having some way to observe, validate, and at least crudely quantify those feelings (internal behaviors) that are being treated as the target symptom. The purest of behaviorists would insist on some method of direct observation and actual measurement, such as the use of an electromyogram (EMG) to monitor precise levels of tension in the frontalis muscle. Such precise electromyographic measurement of a feeling and its electronic translation into a moment-to-moment, quantitative, and highly accurate auditory display to the patient—in the form of a series of small clicks varying in frequency per minute—constitute the basis for a highly effective and efficient behavioral method for the treatment of tension headache. Less pure behaviorists—the majority of clinical behavior therapists—are willing to address much more difficult-to-measure behaviors, such as unwelcome sexual or aggressive impulses, acute feelings of depression, or repetitive obsessional thoughts. In the latter cases, no analogue for the electromyogram has yet become available. The behavioral clinician must therefore either define these phenomena as out of his purview and job description because of the impossibility of direct observation and measurement, or lower his epistemological standards and be willing to accept and work with self-report data. There are and can be no other alternatives, because impulses and thoughts are, by their very nature, purely subjective and private events, never directly observable in themselves nor subject to external validation.

Indirect Methods of Observation

By collaborating with patients toward a precise specification of what constitutes a systematic response, and by asking patients actually to tally their own subjective perception of the occurrence of these responses, one can obtain highly useful data. For instance, a patient who habitually pulls out his eyebrows, bites his fingernails, or smokes and is motivated to break the habit can be asked to keep a careful day-by-day record on index cards of particular impulses to pull, bite, or smoke.

Having patients keep records of this kind, tallying the occurrence and the precise timing of impulses, overt behaviors, and their thoughts and feelings at the time, generates a fairly accurate frequency record of target internal behaviors. (Of course, this record keeping in itself influences the behavior being monitored, producing an inevitable built-in distortion, secondary to the measurement process. Despite this inherent distortion, the clinical value of carefully collected self-report data can be enormous.) It also provides both the patient and the therapist with a large amount of useful clinical information about the precise external and internal conditions under which the target behavior occurs. The target behavior is the particular, carefully specified element of the patient's total behavioral repertoire being treated as the chief complaint, the modification of which helps the patient's life situation. In many cases the target behavior is obvious (such as head banging). In other instances subtle behavioral analysis is necessary to refine a vague complaint, such as "shyness," into its separate and complex behavioral components, which usually include avoidance of eye contact, a soft speaking voice, and submissive body postures. In addition, however, many other very subtle and idiosyncratic observable responses must be recognized and addressed if a particular shy individual is to be helped optimally.

The clinical utility of such records is generally astonishing to both patients and fledgling behavior therapists. In most cases the patient simply is not aware of the situational and thematic details revealed by such tally records and could never provide such a rich history, even with very extended retrospective history taking. After being collected in this way, these contextual data surrounding symptom occurrence are used in a continuing, ever-broadening behavioral analysis: a precise specification of the variables that influence the frequency of the target behavior. For example, from the tally the patient and the therapist may conclude inductively that the patient feels like biting his nails when he is frustrated and angry and that he has in his current behavioral repertoire no apparent alternative to nail biting that would be an effective outlet for these feelings. If a history of underassertiveness (or inappropriate assertiveness) corroborates the lack of a more adaptive response functionally equivalent to nail biting, such a tally might indicate that assertiveness training should be a part of a comprehensive behavioral approach to help the patient learn an alternative response to nail biting.

In addition to the typically voluminous index card tally, the raw data thus accumulated should be periodically summarized quite concisely in a day-to-day trends graph. Usually the therapist does this with the patient, at least in the beginning. If the therapist treats graph making with genuine enthusiasm, regarding it as a cooperative, mutual, and social task in which patient and therapist share, he reinforces the patient's labors in collecting accurate and complete data. Since the data should include notations about subjective, internal responses (private events), only the patient himself *can* collect a complete record, and it is therefore very important that the therapist attend carefully to his own behavior so as to influence optimally the patient's data collection behavior. The therapist must elicit this behavior, shape it toward completeness and relevance, and maintain it through continued reinforcement.

Figure 22.1 shows a small segment of an actual graph constructed with a severely obsessional patient. Here the target behavioral symptom was any irrational avoidance behavior associated with the patient's profound fear of cancer, which he viewed delusionally as an illness to which he was uniquely susceptible. Thus the patient felt he could not safely touch doorknobs, money, a bar of soap, his own clothes, and many, many other items without elaborate precautionary rituals. He used waxed paper to grasp a doorknob, kicked doors shut with his shoe, and routinely discarded soap he had used only once and refused to touch it, even to throw it away. The graph summarizes a period in the treatment during which the patient was asked to make earnest efforts not to reinforce all these impulses to avoid imagined contamination by allowing himself to engage in actual avoidance behaviors. The patient was most reluctant to do this because, a priori, he felt that if he were to inhibit actual avoidance behaviors, he would feel in greater danger of cancer, leading to more fear, and therefore would actually increase the frequency of avoidance impulses. In this false expectation he had failed to recognize that his high level of fearful thoughts was in part being reinforced and maintained by his high level of overt avoidance responses, inasmuch as avoidance behaviors served temporarily to reduce the patient's high level of anxiety. The graph illustrates 2 typical patterns: the number of subjective impulses exceeds the number of overt behavioral responses, and the number of

impulses does not diminish to zero (by extinction) until well after the number of overt behavioral responses has reached zero and remained there for some time.

A common example of the latter phenomenon is that of the reformed heavy smoker who may have to wait months or even years before he not only never smokes but also rarely experiences a compelling urge to smoke. A more experimental example, and one with ubiquitous and pivotally important clinical analogues, is the experimentally observed much greater resistance to extinction of cardiac-conditioned reflexes than to motor-conditioned reflexes. One example of a simple cardiac-conditioned reflex is the occurrence of marked tachycardia in response to an auditory signal that was originally a neutral stimulus but that, after repeated pairing with a

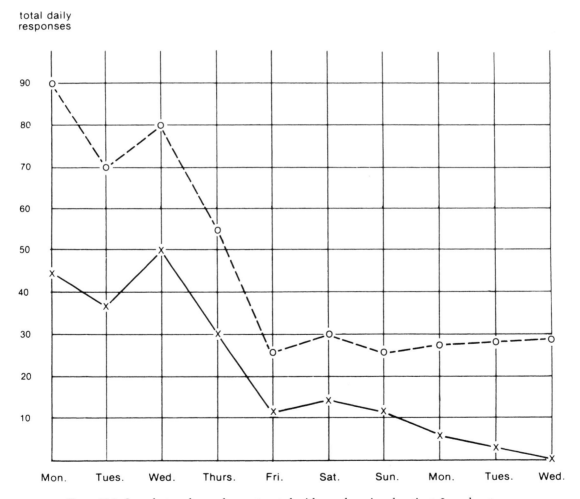

total daily responses

Figure 22.1 Sample trends graph constructed with an obsessional patient. Impulses toward avoidance behavior are indicated by the Os and actual avoidance behaviors by Xs. This patient expected that inhibiting actual avoidance behaviors would increase the frequency of impulses, that is, that line O-O-O would rise as line X-X-X fell. In fact, he was wrong and the behavioral analysis of his problem was correct: his impulses toward avoidance *decreased* as he voluntarily inhibited actual avoidance behaviors.

painful electric shock, comes through learning to produce a sharp increase in heart rate in response to the tone alone. Gantt (1953), who first observed this phenomenon experimentally in dogs, called it "schizokinesis" and reported a ratio of 100:1 or more, in terms of the number of learning trials required to produce extinction of the "cardiac CR" (the cardiac component of a conditioned reflex) in comparison with "motor CR" (the muscular component). Since the cardiac CR is a response to a conditioned tone that signals an impending electric shock, it may be thought of as part of the dog's "feeling" about the coming shock as well as part of his "impulse" to flex—that is, withdraw—the forepaw that is about to receive the shock.

Epistemological Levels in Behavior Therapy

Internal medicine has reached its present relatively advanced level through precise and careful observation of normal physiological processes, the effects of various disease processes on them, and, finally, the modifications of physiological and disease processes by drugs or other treatments. In medicine, the day-to-day management of cases that are diagnostically or therapeutically especially difficult remains very much rooted in the careful collection of relevant data on the individual case. Yet in medicine, experience indicates that always relying on a full battery of expensive, time-consuming diagnostic tests can be monumentally inefficient and certainly not in the patient's interest. Often the clinician's knowledge of the high probability of a fully successful outcome permits him to recommend definite treatment without such elaborate assessment beforehand. In a parallel manner, experienced behavior therapists may offer apparently simple cases presumptive treatment directly, without collecting detailed baseline data. In such cases, often only an hour or two of consultation is necessary before presumptive treatment begins. Prime examples would be the use of assertiveness training with individuals who are habitually meek or sporadically explosive or both and the use of systematic desensitization for people with unrealistic and maladaptive fears. Behavior therapists should be, and are, quite pragmatic and empirical. In many puzzling or difficult cases, however, or when specific research goals make this necessary, such an investment of time and energy is clearly warranted and worthwhile.

Epistemologically, then, in behavior therapy as in internal medicine, there is often no substitute for detailed study of the individual case. In psychiatry this is very often best done within the social system in which the problem arose (such as couple therapy or family therapy) or within a replica of the peer environment in which the patient is malfunctioning (group therapy). Such study may be vital for the development of enough understanding to permit a favorable clinical outcome, or it may be important for the scientific advancement of the field as a whole. This is an area where accumulated clinical wisdom, mature scientific and human balance, and a proper ethical concern for the patient and the immediacy of his problem ideally should lead to well-balanced, cost-effective judgments. Many times placing the patient's welfare first will dictate prompt initiation of presumptive treatment. When this is the case, lofty ideas of behavioral science should not be used to rationalize an obsessively meticulous approach to helping people with life problems.

Cognitive Processes as Indirectly Observable "Behaviors"

Behavior therapists have increasingly acknowledged the importance of thoughts and feelings within psychotherapy. (After all, most patients come for psychotherapy because they *feel bad* or are disturbed by certain *thoughts.* Few come because of neatly circumscribed maladaptive and purely motor habits that are directly observable in a scientifically pure and handy way.) Fortunately, this trend includes many former "radical" behaviorists, who previously dismissed out of hand all "mental phenomena," including all thoughts and feelings, because of the impossibility of observing them directly. Such matters were in some quarters summarily dismissed as being unscientific, "mere self-report data."

A good example of the new broader neobehavioral epistemology, which is much more useful clinically, can be found in a state-of-the-art summary by Franks: "Private events—the cognitive mediators of behavior—are no longer beyond the psychological pale . . . a major role is now attributed to vicarious and indirect learning processes . . . [involving cognition]" (quoted in Arkowitz and Messer, 1984, p. 354).

Behavioral Analysis

The seminal work of Beck, first with depression (Beck, 1976; Beck et al., 1979), and then with anxiety, stands as an impressive monument to the usefulness and at times the centrality, indeed necessity, of working with thoughts and feelings in understanding and treating many psychiatric disorders. More recently Mahoney (1995), speaking masterfully from the point of view of philosophy of science, has addressed the same issue.

An adequate behavioral analysis is the sine qua non of effective behavior therapy. And this, as Beck's work has convincingly demonstrated, needs to include thoughts, especially thoughts about self and the feelings linked to them.

Although the behavior therapist will not in every case spend several weeks collecting a detailed behavioral baseline before beginning his efforts at modification, he should *in every case* arrive at a functionally sound behavioral analysis before beginning treatment. That is, he should know precisely what the presenting problematic behaviors are: how frequently and under what circumstances (stimulus conditions) they occur; what factors and persons may be operating to reinforce and maintain them; what factors and persons may be operating to punish nascent, more adaptive behaviors that might otherwise emerge as satisfactory alternatives to the problematic behaviors; and what effective behaviors the patient has in his current repertoire that might be used as a competing response system or as reinforcing stimuli for more adaptive behavioral patterns. Gaining an overall, contextual view not just of the problematic behaviors but of the patient's life as a whole is also necessary. Information regarding the learned origins of the problematic behaviors is also helpful in designing a program of treatment. Therapeutic outcome will be much improved if the therapist is incessantly curious about how, when, why, and from whom the patient learned his present behaviors, including both the presenting problematic behaviors and any persistent idiosyncratic attitudes (habitual cognitive sets) the patient seems to live by. If possible, a thorough behavioral evaluation should include at least brief interviews of the important people in the patient's life, usually with the patient and in various other combinations, in order to observe directly how each person elicits, reinforces, or punishes his behavior.

As an applied clinical discipline, behavior therapy always involves 2 related steps: conducting a behavioral analysis, and carrying out a program of treatment based on this analysis. The first step is by far the more difficult, requiring much clinical experience, skill, and sophistication, a good grasp of learning theory, and enough patience and persistence to track down all the relevant environmental determinants of the presenting symptom. *If the behavioral analysis is wrong or incomplete, a positive outcome from treatment cannot be expected.*

A preliminary behavioral analysis is always made before formal treatment begins and is then progressively refined and modified as more and more is learned about the patient, his environment, and his responses to ongoing events, including the treatment itself.

Indications for Behavior Therapy

In general, any patient who complains of a discrete symptom—such as a specific fear, compulsion, obsession, psychosomatic symptom, or behavioral deficit—deserves at least an evaluation for behavior therapy. An evaluation is even more emphatically indicated if a careful history suggests that external stimuli trigger the symptom or significantly influence its frequency or intensity. Patients with multiple symptoms can also be treated behaviorally, sometimes by more than one technique. By contrast, patients with "migratory complaints" and problems where no clear correlations can be discovered between particular antecedent stimulus situations and particular maladaptive responses are usually better treated in psychotherapy and very often best treated in systemic behavioral psychotherapy. Some of these patients apparently have a psychotic core and thus are responding to shifting and chaotic internal stimuli, while others may be constantly creating new symptoms because of the presence of strong guilt or anger as an acquired idiosyncratic drive state. For either of these nonpsychotic types of patients, behavioral psychotherapy affords a much fuller opportunity for a subtle and sophisticated behavioral analysis. A broad, thorough, psychodynamically sophisticated behavioral analysis is the crucial factor for maximizing favorable outcome because it clarifies why, for example, a patient who would ordinarily be expected to be punished by a certain event is in fact reinforced (masochistically) by it.

The following specific disorders are eminently treatable behaviorally: PTSD, or (post-traumatic stress disorder; the full range of phobias, simple and complex; panic attacks with and without agoraphobia; obsessive-compulsive disorders, even severe ones; facial and other tics; stuttering, tension headache, migraine headache, and Raynaud's disease; so-called impotence and frigidity; vaginismus, premature ejaculation, ejaculatory incompetence, and genital psychoanesthesia.

In addition, behavior therapy may be the treatment of choice or at least the principal treatment for eliminating a wide range of maladaptive habits: hair and eyebrow pulling; pathological scratching; nail biting; exhibitionism; ego-dystonic transvestism or fetishism; head banging and other self-destructive behaviors in children; intractable hiccuping, sneezing, or vomiting; and difficult voiding, to cite a few. Behavioral techniques may also be used with other approaches, such as group therapy or individual psychotherapy, to help people control or eliminate smoking, drinking, or overeating behaviors. For such habit problems in patients with high hypnotizability and unambivalent motivation, treatment by hypnosis may be more efficient than behavior therapy. For alcoholism and obesity, behavior therapy should be combined with behavioral psychotherapy, which in turn typically involves both group and family work. Finally, behavioral techniques can and should be used to ameliorate symptoms of mental retardation, autism, hospitalism, and repetitive self-destructive behaviors in both childhood and adult psychoses.

This chapter cannot attempt to describe the myriad of specific techniques used for all these extremely wide-ranging problems. However, it does discuss the bases of all behavior therapy, and does offer more details on truly "core" treatment techniques. The aim is to cover those fundamentals that every psychiatrist must know in order to use behavioral analysis and behavioral treatment methods competently, and to recognize when to refer to a behavioral specialist for 4 core treatment methods.

For the 4 major techniques discussed—systematic desensitization, assertiveness training, sex therapy, and operant conditioning—most psychiatrists now in training should seek out enough supervised clinical experience with these techniques to be able to use these approaches with competence and confidence in their own future practices.

Core Behavioral Techniques

If therapists learning systematic desensitization, assertiveness training, sex therapy, and operant conditioning view them as a collection of prespecified procedures, these core techniques will seem to have very little in common with one another, and therapeutic outcome will necessarily suffer. In using all the core techniques, the therapist must pay specific attention to the behavior to be changed, to its *antecedents* (the stimuli preceding it), and to the consequences of that behavior. Thus for each of the core techniques the therapist must devote his attention to 3 key questions. First, what is the behavior to be changed? (That is, what is the target behavior?) Second, what are the stimuli leading to the behavior? Third, what are the events that follow the behavior, serving either to reinforce or to punish it?

Systematic Desensitization and Other "Exposure" Techniques

Developed in the 1950s by Joseph Wolpe and popularized courageously (if at times provocatively) by him against strong opposition from psychoanalytically oriented therapists, systematic desensitization is one of the most important and commonly employed behavioral treatment techniques. For years much of the psychiatric community reacted against behavioral treatment with a fervor now recognizable as an artifact of tradition and a priori theorizing rather than as a corollary of empirically established fact. Literally dozens of studies have now demonstrated that systematic desensitization is both more efficient and

more effective than traditional psychotherapy in the treatment of maladaptive fears (Wolpe et al., 1973). In contrast to the situation of several decades ago, current psychoanalytic literature emphasizes theoretical "integration" of the accepted effectiveness of systematic desensitization—and of behavior therapy as a whole—rather than attempting to demonstrate how it cannot and does not work or how it inevitably leads to "symptom substitution." In fact, no solid evidence exists that symptom substitution, as earlier conceived, occurs at all.

Wolpe developed his now famous method for human patients after making a crucial observation during his earlier work on the experimental induction of neurotic behavior in cats. He discovered that when cats with experimentally induced "phobias" could be induced to engage in a competitive response (eating) in a series of rooms progressively more similar to the one in which they had developed a conditioned fear response, their experimentally induced (learned) fear responses could be reduced and eventually eliminated. Before such "therapy," the cats were demonstrably "neurotic" all the time, in a constant fear state with no apparent stimulus, and showing crouching, piloerection, and even defecation with only slight provocation. Quite predictably, in accordance with the principle of stimulus generalization, they showed the most fear in the room where the original traumatic conditioning had occurred. After "therapy" they were free of all these anxiety symptoms, even in the original chamber. Wolpe constructed an elaborate theory permeated with rather abstruse concepts from Hullian learning theory to explain why this worked. The theory also involved borrowing a legitimate neurophysiological term from Sherrington—*reciprocal inhibition*—to refer to the fact that a competitive response (in this case, eating) served to block the neural connection between the sensory perception of the conditioned fear stimuli and the conditioned anxiety responses, thus paving the way for a restoration of normal behavior. Wolpe was struck by the stimulus generalization aspects of experimental neuroses: the closer the stimulus properties of a given room were to those of the room in which the original traumatic learning took place, the more intense was the phobic response to that room. From this he developed the idea of pairing a competitive response (such as eating, relaxation, sexual arousal, or animated conversation) with a hierarchy of progressively more intense and difficult conditioned stimulus situations to inhibit a *previously learned anxiety response* (such as fear of heights or closed spaces or *phobias* about snakes, spiders, or boats). *Learned fears* may be very intense and even severe, sometimes (rarely) even crippling, but they do not involve a learned association between an external stimulus and an unsolved and unconscious or partially conscious personal conflict, as do *phobias.*

Although Wolpe pioneered the development of desensitization techniques, he was not the solitary inventor of systematic desensitization any more than Freud was the solitary discoverer of the unconscious. Watson and Rayner (1920) described an experimentally induced fear, and Jones (1924) employed processes essentially similar to desensitization 30 years before Wolpe developed and popularized this type of treatment strategy.

In classic systematic desensitization, the patient is taught a method of muscular relaxation that will function later as the competitive response. Hypnosis may be used as an aid in learning relaxation, but it is not a necessary part of the process. Furthermore, desensitization can be accomplished in cases in which the patient cannot be hypnotized. In fact hypnosis may add an element of apparent magic and thus increase the patient's tendency to relate to the behavior therapist in a dependent, childlike way rather than working with him collaboratively as an adult. Such regressive side effects of hypnosis are especially troublesome if the systematic desensitization is part of a more wide-ranging psychotherapy, since the latter depends in part on new learning mediated by the patient's recognition and understanding of transference feelings. The use of biofeedback in relaxation training, by contrast, has been shown to be a valuable aid, both in learning relaxation and in monitoring the actual level of muscular relaxation as treatment proceeds.

Although individual preferences in teaching relaxation vary, many behavior therapists use what is known as a modified Jacobson technique (Jacobson, 1938), based on the principle of contrasting effects. During the initial sessions, in addition to learning relaxation, the patient is asked to construct and bring in a hierarchy of hypothetical stimulus situations that he has reason to believe would cause him to experience increasingly intense fear. The lowest level of such a hierarchy would be a peaceful, effectively neutral scene, and just above that a mild scene with some attenuated and distant elements of what the patient fears most, and so on through progressively graded steps. At the top of the hierarchy, the pinnacle scene should elicit a maximally intense fear response. For example, 2 separate general themes are common in flight phobias: the fear of being closed in and the fear of crashing or falling out of the sky to one's death. Still other themes may be relevant and crucial for success, such as fear of making a spectacle of oneself, fear of being thought a coward, and so forth. Hierarchies must reflect *all* the themes underlying a particular phobia in a particular patient.

A patient who sought treatment for severe sleep-onset insomnia was found to have an underlying fear of dying, which made him avoid sleep. He had undergone surgery in which he was convinced he was going to die, and he had visited battlefields littered with dismembered dead and dying men, so his hierarchy included these scenes. Near the bottom of his hierarchy were activities such as "driving past a hospital" and "getting ready to go to bed at night." At the very top was "being locked in a morgue overnight, surrounded by dozens of dead bodies and having to stay there alone until morning." This patient, who had a 14-year history of severe insomnia, with substantial weight loss, frequent viral infections, and—since they increased his fear—a paradoxical wakeful response to sedatives, made a full and lasting recovery in only 7 hours of treatment by systematic desensitization. The treatment would have failed, however, if each of the themes of death, dying, hospitals, dead bodies, and confinement had not been included in the hierarchies.

Usually the patient is asked to rate each scene on the hierarchy in terms of its anticipated potential to evoke anxiety, in units called subjective units of distress (SUDs). The peaceful scene at the bottom of the hierarchy can be set at zero, representing the maximum freedom from anxiety the patient ever feels, and the most terrifying one at the very top at 100, representing the maximum anxiety the patient ever feels. For those scenes in between, the patient assigns a numerical level that he believes approximates the fear-producing potential of the scene relative to the others. Although SUD scale "measurements" are only crudely quantitative and depend on self-report, this method has obvious clinical advantages. It should, for example, protect the therapist from unwittingly working with a hierarchy containing huge gaps. SUD scale ratings should also be combined with more direct and physiological measures of fear, such as heart rate, and for research purposes with measures such as the palmar sweat test. (Although the latter is too cumbersome for routine use, it supplies sound quantitative data.)

Once the hierarchy has been constructed and the patient has learned relaxation (to serve as a competitive response), the therapist helps the patient to remain relaxed while the latter vividly imagines each of the scenes. The patient uses a digital signaling system, usually the brief raising of the index finger, to indicate an uncomfortably high level of anxiety. The therapist should supplement this information by direct observation of the patient's breathing, facial expression, and vascular state. It can be supplemented also by EMG feedback. If the patient signals a high degree of anxiety, he may be asked to imagine an already practiced scene and work up again to the difficult scenes. When a scene evokes very little anxiety, the therapist goes on to the next step in the hierarchy.

As treatment proceeds, it is imperative for the therapist to encourage (and if necessary insist upon) real-life exposure to the phobic stimulus situation that the patient has already mastered in the imagined situation. The therapist should not, however, encourage the patient to tackle tasks he is not yet prepared for, as the resulting failure will reinforce the link between fear-conditioned stimuli and fear responses. If an overload of intense fear stimuli elicits anxiety responses so strong that they overwhelm and undermine the intended competitive response (relaxation), the phobic response will obviously be strengthened.

Although Wolpe's contribution to behavior therapy (Wolpe, 1958) was a great one, and although his was an unprecedentedly parsimonious view of neurotic processes and of psychotherapy, subsequent experience and research, especially that of Marks (1972, 1976), has indicated clearly the need for a further refinement of theory and practice in the direction of still greater parsimony: controlled studies show that the prior teaching of relaxation as a competitive response is not necessary for success in systematic desensitization. Other research has indicated that neither prior relaxation training nor the use of carefully graded hierarchies is crucial for success in systematic desensitization. This fact, however, is not tantamount to proof that they are without clinical value in all cases. Perhaps imaginal desensitization will eventually prove to be required only in patients whose resistance to in vivo desensitization procedures is sufficient to warrant initial treatment of a less threatening sort. The same kind of point might be made for the construction of carefully graded hierarchies, and even for the use of imaginal scenes at all. All this leaves undisputed only the effectiveness of systematic exposure in vivo to feared but realistically harmless stimuli.

It may be that the classic form of desensitization introduced by Wolpe for use with human patients served, at times quite usefully, merely as a complex persuasive maneuver to get phobic patients to undergo real-life extinction experiences that previously they had strenuously avoided. The original desensitization procedure used by Wolpe to treat his experimentally neurotic cats was, of course, an in vivo desensitization technique, employing actual exposure to rooms increasingly similar to the one where the experimental neurosis was learned. The future of desensitization, as well as its most sophisticated and efficient use in the present, seems to lie in emphasizing in vivo exposure to feared but realistically harmless stimuli and in de-emphasizing, whenever possible, all the other components—relaxation, hierarchical subtleties, and imaginal rehearsal.

Not only is in vivo desensitization usually faster, but it also provides more directly observable data. Moreover, the classic imaginal form of desensitization, with its emphasis on the therapist's teaching the patient to be thoroughly relaxed, followed by the therapist's taking the responsibility for actively and vividly describing a series of scenes that the patient is to imagine while remaining totally passive and relaxed, may tend to foster undue dependency. (A further potential disadvantage is the possibility that the whole procedure may counterproductively activate sexual feelings toward the therapist.) In contrast, in vivo desensitization not only does not encourage the patient to adopt a dependent and childlike stance with respect to the therapist but actually requires him to exercise courage and adult responsibility. Thus, in working with an agoraphobic patient, for example, the therapist may begin immediately, even in the first hour, by going outside with the patient and requesting that he—or more usually she—walk as far as possible away from the therapist. Such an active, real-life approach, early in the treatment, communicates that the goal of therapy is behavioral change and that the patient and the therapist together are responsible for working actively to maximize such change. In an in vivo approach, each feared response performed by a phobic patient constitutes a real-life "extinction trial," because, realistically, no feared consequences follow the responses. (*Extinction* is the process in which a learned or conditioned response—in this case a fear response—is repeated over and over without reinforcement or punishment and so eventually returns to its preconditioning baseline of intensity.) Thus an unrealistic fear response treated by exposure in vivo eventually becomes zero or nearly zero.

By accompanying patients on some of their assigned extinction trials, the therapist gains access to an important source of self-report data: in this situation of induced stress, the patient often produces a flood of thematically relevant, associatively rich material that can be used to discover and to help the patient understand how and why he learned the particular fear now undergoing extinction by in vivo desensitization. Thus in vivo desensitization usually generates useful cognitions, which can be used to facilitate the change process. Dynamically trained therapists will recognize this phenomenon as a form of structuring the "working through" of insights *before* those insights actually develop.

The behavior therapist thus gives strategic primacy to what dynamic therapists call "working through" and uses it to facilitate useful insight, rather than working toward insight with the vague hope that, once acquired, such insight will one day be actualized and worked through as real change.

There are several dangers inherent in the fact that systematic desensitization has been naively and destructively oversold. First, there is a tendency, which occurs even among some otherwise sophisticated psychiatrists, to equate systematic desensitization with behavior therapy as a whole—a fallacy analogous to equating internal medicine not just with antibiotics but with a particular brand of one of the tetracyclines. Second, the field of behavior therapy is rife with novices whose behavioral enthusiasm exceeds their clinical wisdom, and these inexperienced practitioners may indiscriminately use a rote desensitization paradigm with almost any kind of patient or any type of clinical situation, sometimes with very bad results. Thus patients with ungrieved losses or violently unstable marriages, among other problems, may be run through mindless hierarchies that contribute more to the problem than to its solution.

Systematic desensitization is only one of a number of particular techniques for the reduction or elimination of maladaptive fears. *If there is no fear*—if the main problem is unresolved grief, guilt, or anger—*then desensitization is not appropriate.* Furthermore, not every patient who comes labeled—even self-labeled—as having a phobia really has one. Many patients experience obsessional symptoms as phobias or have institutionalized avoidances that are maintained by a web of social reinforcement ("secondary gain") rather than by real fear. Before embarking on a course of desensitization, it is therefore important to ask specifically about autonomic signs of fear, about the thematic elements of the phobic situation, and about the social consequences of the phobic behavior. When the patient attempts to approach the phobic stimulus, does his heart beat fast? Does it pound? Does he sweat, or do his palms become moist? Does someone else routinely offer comfort and reassurance or assume responsibility during the period of phobic avoidance? Finally, before embarking on a course of imaginal desensitization, the therapist must ascertain that the patient is capable both of visualizing scenes at will and of experiencing palpable fear in response to an imagined representation of the phobic stimulus.

Two other procedures should be mentioned along with desensitization because they are also extinction-based fear reduction procedures. One is *flooding*—an abbreviation of "stimulus flooding" (Marks, 1972). Its aim is to saturate, or flood, the phobic patient with maximally fear-producing stimuli without permitting him to terminate the stimuli or to escape. Obviously, then, flooding is a "cold turkey," forced extinction situation—one that can be very rapidly effective but is for most purposes unnecessarily unpleasant and has the potential to do real harm. If the patient should manage to escape the flooding situa-tion before his fear responses have begun to subside, the procedure will actually operate to make the original fear worse.

Flooding is related to the "implosive therapy" approach of Stampfl (Stampfl and Levis, 1967) as Wolpe's desensitization is related to Feather and Rhoads's psychodynamic-theme-desensitization (1972). Implosive therapy is flooding not with actual physical stimuli but with mental images of intensely disturbing psychoanalytic themes. Because it involves assumed mental images and presumptively relevant psychoanalytic themes, and probably also partly because some of the themes used (such as castration and violent aggression) are so upsetting to so many of us, implosive therapy remains less well researched and more controversial than flooding.

The second procedure, *response prevention* (Mills et al., 1973), is much like flooding but depends on the fact that anxiety regularly issues in a behavioral response. It is used with patients who have severe obsessive-compulsive rituals such as hand washing. These rituals typically occur after the patient encounters some external stimulus, such as a doorknob. Often, however, only a thought that he regards as bad or dirty or dangerous is sufficient to produce the ritual response. Subjectively, the particular ritual is apparently intended magically to undo or neutralize the contact that has just occurred. Even if the patient "knows" intellectually that the ritual is superstitious, it still has the capacity to reduce temporarily a very high level of anxiety and thus is maintained by negative reinforcement—the temporary reduction of an ongoing aversive drive (in this case, high anxiety). Response prevention forces the patient to undergo extinction of his rituals and his obsessional fears through eliminating the possibility of his making the ritualized response. For example, if his problem is hand washing, the handles are taken off the water faucets, and the water is turned off except during brief and narrowly defined periods each day. The patient is therefore compelled to learn viscerally, not just intellectually, that the ritual is superfluous to his real safety. In behavioral terms, his avoidance responses, previously maintained by negative reinforcement, are forced to undergo extinction.

Assertiveness Training and "Training in Emotional Freedom"

In assertiveness training, strong self-assertion is used as a competitive response to inhibit conditioned anxiety and fear in conceptually much the same way as the use of relaxation in systematic desensitization. The technique utilizes the principle that the most rapid way to dissipate strong premonitory anxiety is actually to begin an activity. Thus one may be very nervous before giving a lecture or a dramatic performance or before taking an examination, but this anxiety usually diminishes sharply when the actual performance begins. Assertion as an active performance begins to serve successfully as a competitive response capable of inhibiting the anxiety that previously existed unopposed, provided one learns to experiment with *strong* self-assertion.

Clinically, assertiveness training is a technique for individuals who chronically fail to stand up for their own rights in a firm, effective, and appropriate way. Patients who can profit from it are not limited to meek Caspar Milquetoast types. It is equally indicated for patients who "hold it all in" as long as they can and then explode in a self-defeating rage. It is also extremely useful, especially when combined with group therapy, for many patients with chronic, unremitting depression, the manifest affect of which is helplessness. It is in fact helpful in some form to a very wide spectrum of people who are situationally underassertive—people who can be effectively assertive with strangers, or even with their bosses, but not with their spouses, for example. (In this case, assertiveness training should be combined with some form of therapy, such as couple group therapy.) Other people can secure their rights and can express anger appropriately and without great difficulty, but they may be almost paralyzed by inhibition and embarrassment when they attempt to express warmth, liking, and affection toward another person. In this case, modified assertiveness training techniques may be used, sometimes called "training in emotional freedom" (Lazarus, 1971).

Both assertiveness training and "training in emotional freedom" are usually best carried out within a more broadly ranging therapy group, because the social interactions there are "real," not just staged and playacted. In patients whose primary problem is learning to express (and usually also receive) emotional warmth, the advantages are especially marked. In this natural (unstaged) social setting genuinely warm feelings occur that facilitate such learning and its subsequent generalization to "the outside world," as patients so often put it. In addition, there are other helpful mechanisms: modeling and identification with the therapist and other more expressive group members. This learning from those who have learned already is a particularly potent source for people of a transforming conviction that they too can change.

In other cases, patients may have striking deficits in particular social skills, such as introducing themselves, saying hello, making or responding to social invitations. These patients may be helped with a variant of assertiveness training that is often called "social skills training."

All types of assertiveness training techniques rely cen-

trally on *behavioral shaping,* the process in which successive approximation is used to condition a complex desired response. First, the organism is reinforced for any response that is in the direction of the desired response (or even any response that vaguely resembles the first phase of a complex desired response); next, the criterion for reinforcement is slowly, steadily, and progressively raised. An animal analogue would be teaching the response "three turns to the right." First, any rightward-turning or rightward-looking response is reinforced; then, by successive approximation, rightward movement of the shoulder girdle, then of the pelvic girdle, then of the legs, becomes a criterion for reinforcement. After one full turn is learned, the criterion for reinforcement is raised still further, until finally the organism performs the exact response desired. In this way organisms can be taught very complex responses that they could never learn by simple respondent conditioning.

As Wolpe pointed out (1958), certain types of questions are invaluable in determining the need for assertiveness training. For example:

"Suppose you are waiting in a line for theater tickets and someone cuts in front of you. What would you do?" A patient starkly in need of assertiveness training might well say something like this:

"Well, inside I'd be knotted up, burning. It would probably spoil my whole evening, and the knot in my stomach would still be there when I went to bed that night, but I wouldn't say anything—because I wouldn't want to make a scene."

Other valuable screening questions are:

Suppose you go to a department store and buy a sweater, then later after leaving the store you discover it has a hole in it? What would you do?

Suppose you go to a restaurant and want a quiet table in a darkish corner where you can talk, but the hostess seats you at a table right in the center of the room, bustling with people, light, and noise. What would you do?

Suppose a friend [some patients are assertive enough with strangers, but not with friends] borrows ten dollars from you and promises to pay you back the next day at lunch. The next day lunch comes and goes but nothing happens. What would you do?

Suppose your husband or wife does or says something at your expense, something you regard as clearly unfair. What would you do?

In addition to talking with the patient, observe him! Waiting room behavior often provides a much richer source of more reliable data by affording an opportunity for directly observing the patient's assertive and other social behaviors in a segment of his actual life. What is he like in the waiting room, with the other people there? How does he deal with the secretary or receptionist? How does he behave in a joint interview situation with his wife? What is he like with the whole family? How does he react in a group? These questions of course all relate to discussion of behavioral psychotherapy as a process of in vivo observation and behavioral shaping. However, in many cases classic, single goal–oriented behavior therapy techniques are used most effectively when they arise from or are embedded in the context of a more broadly ranging behavioral psychotherapy. The latter permits enough direct observation of social behaviors to effect a more accurate behavioral diagnosis, reflecting subtleties of the life situation that the patient cannot report fully because he does not yet recognize and understand them.

If the therapist can make a clear diagnosis of a broad or a narrow deficit in assertive behavior by using any or all of these kinds of probes, then assertiveness training would be useful and is indicated. Not only do early treatment sessions typically remove all doubt as to the relevance of enhancing assertive responses, but also they usually lead to a spontaneous outpouring of diverse social situations in the patient's actual life in which he feels stymied and frustrated because of his difficulty with assertive responses. Treatment begins with a further probe for recent actual situations in which the patient did not assert himself optimally. These situations are then discussed in detail, together with the patient's and the therapist's ideas as to what specific responses might have been more effective.

Before the end of the hour, the patient is asked to be alert during the coming week to similar situations requiring assertive behavior and to note how he responds to them. In the next session the therapist asks the patient about these situations—what he actually said and did, and what the outcome was. The patient is then asked, "If you had it all to do over again, how would you handle it, what actually would you say?" Usually the therapist can make at least a few suggestions that improve further on the patient's initial attempt at redesigning a response that the patient would regard as ideal. He can also help by giving his reasons for preferring a particular version, and, either then or later, he can also help by role-playing or modeling a desirable response, like an actor.

In systematic behavioral psychotherapy (in an ongoing therapy group, for example), the therapist can accomplish much the same thing, almost in passing, by first asking the patient what he *did* say and what he *now* thinks he might better have said, and then by volunteering what he himself might have done ("If that had happened to me, I think I might have said . . .").

In the more structured, classic version of assertiveness training, the patient is asked repeatedly to role-play such troublesome situations, each time trying to respond in a more nearly ideal way. After each attempt, the patient is offered a gentle critique of his assertive "act." The therapist points out soft and apologetic tones or overly belligerent tones, diffident postures, lack of direct or sustained eye contact, and telltale hesitations. The therapist can use mimicry effectively if he is skillful at ensuring that the patient realizes that this use of mimicry is never derisive but is, rather, intended for his benefit and his own therapeutic goals. Then the therapist asks the patient to try again, "*Much* louder and stronger this time, and without the apologetic gestures." This role-playing is repeated as many times as necessary, with constantly responsive gestural feedback (reinforcement and punishment). The gestural feedback offered during the performance is in the form of frowns, fortissimo gestures, "OK" signs, and affirmative nods. In his criticism the therapist should be constructive and good-natured, and humor may at times be used to advantage if it is clearly shared with the patient. In any event, the central idea is to use behavioral shaping (successive approximation) to produce an assertive performance that has been enhanced in content, directness, volume, and tone. In this final, enhanced performance, residual signs of apologetic diversions and hesitations or of sagging emphasis, either verbal or nonverbal, should not appear.

To achieve this result, role reversal is at times employed; in role reversal the patient is asked to play the role of his oppressor, while the therapist plays the patient's role. This reversal affords further opportunities for the use of modeling; in this way the therapist can demonstrate the possibility of formulating a strong, confident, assertive response, regardless of what his adversary says. Thus learning proceeds through a mixture of instruction, coaching, modeling, role rehearsal, role reversal, and behavioral shaping, all with the aim of bringing easy assertive responses into the patient's repertoire.

Since the strongest component of this technique is the behavioral shaping, it is very important never to praise or otherwise reinforce diminished assertive performances. It can be tempting to offer encouragement to a disheartened patient on his fifth or seventh attempt to master a role-played assertive situation, but if, as often happens, he does less well on his fifth try than he did on the previous one, he must be bluntly told so. Praise—as distinct from reassurance or encouragement—is useful only after a performance that successively approximates the agreed-upon goal. Praise should never directly follow (that is, be contingent upon) a diminished assertive performance. (Between trials the patient may need encouragement or reassurance, but if this is needed and offered, it should by all means be done noncontingently.) Anticipatory role-playing of situations and confrontations that are expected or needed may also help the patient prepare for the week to come.

As in systematic desensitization, the patient should be urged to try out his newly practiced skills in real life, especially when his skill seems great enough to master the particular hierarchical level of difficulty represented by the actual situation. He should not be forced prematurely into precipitating assertive situations that are still clearly too difficult in terms of his skill or confidence level. Such precipitation will only be counterproductive, because it will very likely result in a confrontation in which the patient's nascent assertive repertoire will be punished, not reinforced. Such an outcome would operate to confirm the patient's pretreatment conviction that no assertion is the only safe stance for him.

In the very first few sessions it is usually necessary to deal with the patient's objections that "this is all so artificial." Usually the best way to overcome this objection is to reassure patients that their new assertiveness will seem artificial to them at first but that, as they continue to use and profit from the use of assertive behaviors, assertiveness will in time not only seem quite natural but actually become part of them. Thus, eventually, they will find themselves quite naturally using assertive behaviors that at first seemed to require great effort and forethought. After 3 to 5 sessions of learning progressively more assertive behavior, patients become (appropriately) very excited about increasing assertiveness in their expressive styles because they begin to grasp the potential for enhancing the quality of their lives. Thus the need to convince patients of the value of assertiveness training, despite its "artificiality," is usually short-lived; the patient soon begins to bring to the sessions a tried and definite enthusiasm.

Sex Therapy

Because of its immense clinical importance, and also because of the appreciable differences in treatment strategy and therapeutic stance, sex therapy is a specialty unto itself, and one that can be mastered fully only by those with a thorough grasp of couple therapy. The clinical practice of sex therapy is covered in Chapter 23. For the purposes of this chapter, it is enough to highlight the fact that the prescriptive techniques of sex therapy are behaviorally based interventions that require guidance via both "learning theory" on the one hand and experience with couple and individual dynamics on the other.

The prescriptive learning techniques of sex therapy are behaviorally based therapies. Sex therapy is behavioral not just because it involves the brief treatment of specific problems but, more important, because specific sex therapy techniques can best be understood in terms of a learning theory model.

It is essential, however, in locating these techniques among the behaviorally based therapies, to acknowledge the great debt that sex therapy, and all of psychiatry, owes first to Kinsey, more recently to Masters and Johnson, and most recently to Helen Kaplan, for opening the field of sexual functioning first to scientific inquiry and now to direct therapeutic influence. None of these pioneers has been a behavior therapist. In addition to providing the first accurate scientific description of the basic physiology of sexual arousal, intercourse, and orgasm, Masters and Johnson made a great therapeutic advance by emphasizing direct work with both members of a couple when one or both partners were sexually dysfunctional. As early as 1958, however, Wolpe, a behavior therapist, wrote about the treatment of impotence and frigidity and advocated the use of sexual arousal itself as a competitive response.

Shorn of all complexity, sex therapy "works" through a series of successful, confidence-restoring, hierarchically graded sexual experiences. In effect, it is a form of in vivo systematic desensitization, which employs sexual pleasure rather than relaxation as a response competitive with anxiety.

Operant Conditioning

The concepts and facts derived from studies of operant conditioning are central to *all* clinical work in behavior therapy and behavioral psychotherapy. Indeed, no therapist or analyst can ever be in the same room with any patient or exchange words, looks, nods, or gestures without operant conditioning being involved. Both patient and therapist, aware of it or not, will be reinforcing some responses and punishing other responses in the behavior of the other person.

Nevertheless, operant conditioning as a pure treatment technique is not one of the most commonly used behavior therapies. Because of its pervasive great importance in all psychotherapies (and in everyday life), it is classified as a "core" behavior therapy treatment modality.

The principles of operant conditioning seem alarmingly (and deceptively) simple. *Punishment* is anything that decreases the frequency of the response immediately preceding it, such as spanking a dog immediately after he jumps up on a person. A more clinical example, and one to avoid, especially in dealing with underassertive patients, is that of a therapist exploding with angry criticism immediately after the patient criticizes him. If the criticism is unwarranted or distorted, the therapist can make this point, *after a brief delay,* without punishing a patient's valuable nascent assertiveness. In contrast, a therapeutically useful example of punishment drawn from couple therapy, where the point *is* to punish a particular category of response, would be a therapist's strong negative interpretation *immediately after* a spouse inappropriately asserts some infantile entitled "right" with respect to his marital partner. It is often strategically important, in clinical practice, to use punishment not just *after* a maladaptive response but actually *during* such a response; such punishment can effectively interrupt the full response, which is part of a complex chain of maladaptive behavior, and make way for new, more adaptive behavior.

Positive reinforcement is anything that increases the frequency of the response immediately preceding it, such as delivering a bit of food or water to an experimental animal immediately after the response of bar pressing. A more clinical example is that of expressing interest or making an effectively positive interpretation immediately after a habitually meek person expresses some annoyance.

Negative reinforcement is the temporary interruption of a continuous negative stimulus, which serves to reinforce (*increase* the frequency of) the immediately preceding response. A simple example would be putting on sunglasses in bright light; this response removes the mildly aversive stimulus of glaring brightness and therefore negatively reinforces the response of putting on the sunglasses. In a laboratory example, an experimental animal in a room with a shock-grid floor might turn the shock off for 5 seconds each time it pressed a bar. In this way the response of bar pressing would be negatively reinforced. A clinical example, drawn from work with severely disturbed phobic-obsessional patients, is the therapist's continuously and purposefully violating the patient's magical safety rituals (an aversive stimulus for the patient) and then ceasing to do this immediately after the patient himself makes some response in which he atypically confronts one of his fears directly. Such a strategy is rarely needed, but, when it is, there may be no real substitute for it; it can literally be life-saving.

Neither past general experience nor a priori judgments establish whether a given stimulus is in fact reinforcing or punishing; this varies from person to person and must always be established empirically. Fully confident specification of reinforcers and punishers thus requires a number of observed trials. Nevertheless, an increase or decrease in frequency can be effected by a single application of a reward or punishment. This is called "one-trial learning" or, if the consequence is punishing, "traumatic learning."

Operant methods capitalize on all these principles to change behavior in desirable ways. Largely because of the negative views of Skinner (1953) on the use of aversive stimuli, particularly for punishment, and because of Skinner's association with the word *operant,* it is in fact true that most people referring to operant methods in behavior therapy are talking about systematically using positive reinforcement to increase desirable behaviors. Aversive stimuli may, however, be used beneficially after a response to decrease the frequency of that response (punishment); or they may be used as continuing negative stimuli, the temporary cessation of which, contingent on a particular response, can be used to increase the frequency of that response (negative reinforcement). Aversive techniques are therefore customarily categorized separately from operant methods, even though punishment is as much a part of operant conditioning theory as is reinforcement.

It is part of the fundamental pragmatism and empiricism of behaviorism that no stimulus is assumed to be "positive" or "negative"; rather, stimuli can be judged to be reinforcing or punishing only through observed trials. This is important clinically because for some schizophrenic patients, for example, the stimulus of a smile or a friendly hello is in fact punishing and because some stimuli that are punishing for most people are reinforcing for some guilty or masochistic patients.

Habitual or high-frequency behaviors can serve as reinforcers if they are made to follow and be contingent on low-frequency behaviors; this is known as the *Premack principle.* For example, a person who habitually watches television as a high-frequency behavior but rarely exercises can effectively increase the frequency of his exercising behavior if he permits himself to watch television only after a period of exercising. The Premack principle is extremely useful clinically in designing made-to-order behavioral programs for self-control and for correcting maladaptive deficits of particular behaviors.

The most important use of an operant strategy is in behavioral psychotherapy, where the use of punishment, positive reinforcement, and behavioral shaping of problematic behaviors can be used to modify target behaviors directly, in vivo, in a natural social setting. The next most important use is as a component in assertiveness training, described in the section on core techniques. A third important application of operant treatment methods is in developing more successful inpatient ward management programs. Operant methods of behavior therapy are also being used effectively in classrooms and institutions dealing with disadvantaged, hyperactive, retarded, and emotionally disturbed children.

Operant conditioning within psychotherapies: punishment a necessary component. In psychotherapy, especially in behavioral psychotherapy within social systems, such as in couple or family therapy and group therapy, patients do often present certain behaviors that urgently require not just reduction but reduction to zero if any progress is to be made, if there is to be no lasting damage to human relationships, and if the very therapy itself is to be able to continue. How can the clinician deal with this problem? Even the experimental psychologist working under easily controllable laboratory conditions has at his disposal only a few ways to reduce ongoing conditioned behaviors: satiation, stimulus change, physical restraint, extinction, and punishment. In clinical work with human beings, only extinction and punishment are both possible and ethically acceptable. Extinction, however, especially after a response has been learned via intermittent reinforcement—as is usually the case in everyday life—typically requires literally hundreds or even thousands of stimulus trials. This leaves the clinician only punishment as a practical, ethically acceptable way quickly to reduce to zero certain pivotal and destructive behaviors that otherwise could block progress.

And yet punishment is widely ignored or misused by psychodynamic therapists because they falsely equate punishment with vindictiveness, and so try to avoid it altogether, and by behavior therapists, who are much more likely to use punishment, but to use it badly and ineffectively, primarily through failing always to be sure to use it together with the strategy of reinforcing an alternative, more adaptive response.

However, if a therapist will only make the effort to "switch gears," and for a scant few minutes think as a laboratory scientist does, he will be amply rewarded. He will not master the whole extensive and detailed body of experimentally derived knowledge about punishment, but he *will* genuinely understand "the basics" about it, which are of fundamental importance in all clinical work. These necessary basic points are conveyed in Figures 22.2, 22.3, and 22.4.

The most effective way to eliminate inappropriate or maladaptive behavior appears to be to punish it while simultaneously reinforcing some desired alternative behavior (Azrin and Holz, 1966; Birk, 1973b). Thus punishment has an important place in behavior therapy and even more so in behavioral psychotherapy (especially couple, group, and family therapy). Such use of punishment should never become an excuse for the therapist to be vindictive or sadistic, but a therapist must be able to use it consciously and well when it is needed: to be a couple, group, or family therapist and not know how and when to use punishment would be as irresponsible as to be a surgeon who knows how to make incisions but not how to tie off bleeders!

Nevertheless, any therapist using punishment alone in any form—from disinterested facial expressions and effectively negative interpretations to aversive conditioning—should remember that the most he can expect from pure punishment is a period of response suppression.

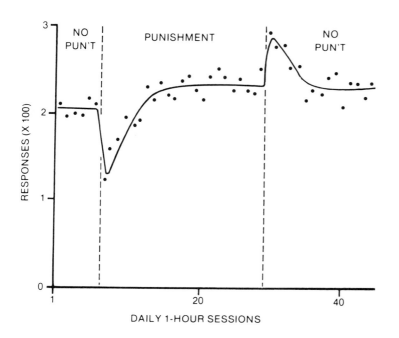

Figure 22.2 Effect of the addition and removal of punishment upon the food-reinforced response of one subject. The punishment was a brief electric shock that followed every response on the days between those represented by the vertical dashed lines. *Source:* N. H. Azrin, Sequential effects of punishment, *Science* 181 (1960): 605–606. © 1960 American Association for the Advancement of Science.

Punishment does not produce extinction, and therefore ordinarily does not in itself permanently eliminate responses.

Figure 22.2 shows that with these ordinary intensity levels of punishment—the only ones acceptable in clinical work—even the temporary suppresser effect is a weak one. Moreover, when punishment ceases, there is a "double rebound" effect: after temporarily decreasing slightly, the response frequency increases even while punishment continues. The second, and more prominent, effect occurs when punishment ceases, and there is a sharp and larger increase in response frequency. In some cases, *very strong* punishments may produce marked, long-lasting response suppression but not true extinction (Holland and Skinner, 1961).

Figure 22.3 shows that mild levels of punishment do not have any response-suppressive effect. Abruptly, when a middle level of intensity is reached (at about 40 volts), response suppression occurs. With pure punishment, very high levels must be used together with reinforcement of an alternative response, even when only a moderate level (about 50 volts) is used. *Punishment should therefore always be employed together with reinforcement of some new, desired behavior.*

Pure punishment at acceptable levels produces only partial response suppression (Figure 22.4). As is also shown in Figure 22.3, however, punishment used together with a strategy of reinforcing an alternative response produces a complete change in behavior. If the alternative response is well chosen, it brings more reinforcement than did the old, punished response, thus supplanting it so that the change produced is permanent—very much in contrast to the highly temporary change produced by pure punishment. Punishment alone must be continued indefinitely even to maintain change through response suppression; if punishment is discontinued, the previously suppressed behavior rebounds to a higher level than before. Advocating punishment in this shortsighted way is as seriously counterproductive as advocating drinking seawater in order to treat thirst and dehydration!

Operant conditioning within aversive therapies. Self-damaging behaviors in autistic children may be interrupted by aversive conditioning, using brief noninjurious but painful electric shock as a punishing stimulus. In these and similar circumstances in which self-injury or even death is a likely result without such intervention,

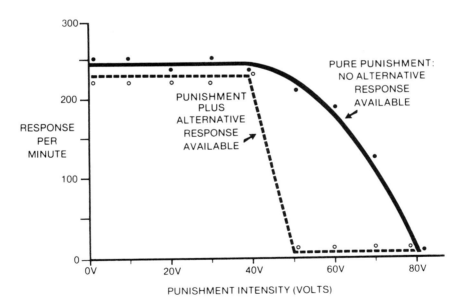

Figure 22.3 The rate of punished responses as a function of the punishment intensity. The data are from a pigeon reinforced under a fixed ratio (FR) schedule with reinforcement occurring every 25 trials. Two response keys were available; responses on both keys were effective in fulfilling the FR requirement. Punishment was delivered for all responses on the preferred key concurrently with the FR food schedule. The intensity of the punishing shock was increased in steps of 10 volts, allowing at least 5 days at each intensity. This procedure was carried out both with the nonpreferred key covered (no alternative response available) and with both response keys uncovered (alternative response available). *Source:* N. H. Azrin and W. C. Holz, 1966.

classical aversive conditioning may make sense. With all consenting nonpsychotic adults, it is important to emphasize the collaborative quality of the treatment. The patient should regard the shock sessions as something facilitating his own choice for his own behavior, something the therapist is doing *with* him, not *to* him.

Most of the modern work on aversive conditioning has been done with electric shock because, quite unlike nausea-producing drugs, electric shock has sharp and precisely controllable onset-offset properties. (Much early disenchantment with the use of aversive conditioning in alcoholism and addiction came from very poorly executed behavior therapy, in which insufficient attention was paid to the need for precise time and contingency control of the punishing stimulus; virtually all of the early work done with apomorphine and other drugs suffers from this disqualifying defect.)

Other Behavioral Therapies

Biofeedback

Biofeedback is the use of monitoring instruments (usually electrical) to detect and amplify internal physiological processes in order to make this ordinarily inaccessible information available to the individual—literally, to feed it back to him in some form. Thus through biofeedback a patient with a tension headache (one caused by abnormal levels of tension or contraction in the frontalis or occipitalis muscles of the head) ordinarily knows only that the front or the back of his head hurts or does not hurt. With biofeedback he can know precisely from moment to moment what is the level of tension (contraction) in his frontalis and occipitalis muscles by two different means:

(1) through the use of an electromyogram to detect activity in those muscles, and (2) through an amplification and display system by means of which he can "hear" the level of muscular activity as a series of small clicks spaced in time as a function of the level of tension or "see" the level of tension by reading a dial.

The clinical importance of utilizing such organ-specific artificial feedback is that, with continued exposure and practice (biofeedback training), individuals can learn to bring under partial conscious control particular body functions that are not ordinarily subject to conscious control (such as heart rate and blood pressure) or that are ordinarily under only minimal conscious control (such as tension in the frontalis and occipitalis muscles). Currently, the most important and common clinical application is in the treatment of headache symptoms.

Like other psychosomatic disorders, tension headache begins with life stress and usually also involves unresolved inner conflicts. The familiar psychophysiological paradigm is this:

Life stress and unsolved inner conflicts → physical symptoms.

For psychophysiological headache syndromes—including both tension headache and migraine headache—suppressed or poorly recognized anger is very often the most important "inner conflict." Psychotherapy emphasizing insight and the cognitive uncovering of such anger and the reasons for it can deal with one part of the problem. Assertiveness training can also help because it helps individuals learn to be more able to speak up effectively for themselves and their rights, and so operates to reduce the amount of frustration and anger inherent in daily living. Psychotherapy and assertiveness training are both

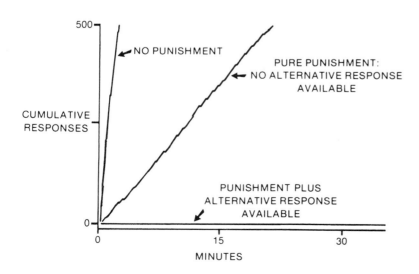

Figure 22.4 Cumulative response records of the punished responses of human subjects under a variable interval schedule of reinforcement. The reinforcement deliveries are not indicated. The punishment was an annoying buzzing sound that was delivered for each response. *Source:* Based on data from R. L. Herman and N. H. Azrin, Punishment by noise in an alternative response situation, *J. Exp. Anal. Behav.* 7 (1964): 185–188.

ways of dealing with the left or "input" side of the psycho-physiological paradigm.

Biofeedback is a way of dealing directly with the right or "output" side of that paradigm. This is the side that, for tension headache patients, means that, for whatever reasons, they have increased levels of tension in the occipitalis and frontalis muscles and resultant pain. Whatever the sources, in external life stress or in internal conflict or both, for tension headache patients, increased muscle tension in the occipitalis and frontalis muscles is the final common pathway, and biofeedback can enable the patient to learn to reduce that level of tension in order to relieve the pain of headache or to abort a headache in the making.

Biofeedback training can also facilitate useful cognitive learning about what an individual's triggering stimuli are for such psychosomatic reactions, thus enriching the work concomitantly being done in psychotherapy and assertiveness training.

In the treatment of the complex neurovascular migraine syndrome by biofeedback, the headache itself is treated as the target symptom. The headache is apparently secondary to a situation of excessive sympathetic outflow resulting finally in painfully pulsating and distended extracranial arteries. Thus hand warming (possible only with decreased sympathetic outflow) is used as a target physiological response, and temperature feedback is used to achieve this. Temperature feedback also may be used to alleviate the painfully cold hands and feet which derive from the vascular insufficiency caused by Raynaud's disease.

EMG feedback is also useful in the treatment of tics, in relaxation training, in monitoring the course of imaginal desensitization, in the treatment of sleep-onset insomnia, and in stroke rehabilitation.

Behavioral Medicine

In 1973 I first used the term *behavioral medicine* in a book describing the usefulness of biofeedback in the treatment of medical disorders such as tension and migraine headaches, Raynaud's disease, and certain cardiac arrhythmias (Birk, 1973a; also see Surwit, 1982; Gentry, 1984). At that time I made the cautious prediction that "it is perhaps not an exaggeration to point out that a new 'behavioral medicine' [in which, literally, the patient learns not to be sick] may in fact represent a major new developing frontier of clinical medicine and psychiatry" (Birk, 1973a, p. 2). In 1978 the *Journal of Behavioral Medicine* was founded. Since then, behavioral medicine has evolved and grown rapidly to include many diverse learning-based methods

of ameliorating symptoms and promoting health. Behavioral medicine differs very markedly from traditional *psychosomatic medicine,* which began with a search for psychodynamic root causes in 7 disorders then considered to be "the" psychosomatic diseases: duodenal ulcer, asthma, Graves's disease, essential hypertension, ulcerative colitis, neurodermatitis, and rheumatoid arthritis (Alexander, 1939, 1946, 1950; Dunbar, 1943, 1947; Surwit, 1982).

Psychosomatic medicine certainly still holds an important place in the history of psychiatry, and also in our knowledge base for understanding individual patients in depth, as Nemiah has wisely pointed out (Nemiah, 1996). But because psychosomatic medicine has so heavily focused on "intrapsychic conflict" as a presumed cause, and on the patient's spontaneous verbal productions in psychotherapy as the chosen way to understand conflicts presumptively assumed to be causative, the hope of developing "insight" into root conflicts, which in turn might lead to the significant amelioration of symptoms, has proved elusive to say the least. The practical results of all this over more than half a century have been largely disappointing, and no one has ever been able to document clear intrapsychic cause-effect links, or to produce replicable demonstrations that verbal psychotherapy can produce substantial symptom amelioration in medical diseases.

In marked contrast, *behavioral medicine* does not posit that it is necessary to discover root intrapsychic causes, modify personality structures, or produce insight in order to effect significant symptom amelioration. In contrast to those of psychosomatic medicine, the methods of behavioral medicine are empirical: if disease-linked deviant physiological processes can be reliably observed, *and also measured continuously,* then it is possible at least to try out ways of systematically using the laws of learning to manipulate the relevant physiological behavior, employing a kind of autonomic nervous system behavior therapy, or "biofeedback."

For instance, as already noted, since it is possible to measure continuously the level of tension in the frontalis muscle of the forehead, it was possible to try out biofeedback as a behavioral medicine learning technique aimed at teaching patients how to eliminate the pain of tension headache. Empirical studies then established, first, that patients could indeed utilize biofeedback to establish new and artificial but effective cybernetic loops, which in turn enabled them to learn how to lower frontalis muscle tension voluntarily; and, second, that this new learning did indeed enable them to avoid or abort headaches.

Other kinds of physiological interventions that are less "elegant"—less target-organ specific—than biofeedback may also be used, such as relaxation training, meditation, or both, to lower diastolic blood pressure in early hypertension.

Beyond this, for a large variety of medical disorders, *any* workable method capable of altering behaviors so as to lead to a reduction in known "risk factors" may be successfully employed as a "preventive" behavioral medicine technique. An important example is the use of behavioral, educational, persuasive, incentive-based, and group-support methods to reduce or eliminate smoking (which of course is an important risk factor in coronary artery disease) in order to reduce the incidence and severity of heart attacks. Exercise habits may also be modified in much the same ways, thus effecting a reduction in sedentary lifestyle and poor aerobic condition as risk factors.

For all these examples, and for all established legitimate behavioral medicine interventions, *empirical validation of the effectiveness of presumed "treatments" is a sine qua non.*

The most compellingly important difference between traditional psychosomatic medicine and behavioral medicine is the latter's well-established greater effectiveness in actually helping patients with "such physical disorders as headache, chronic pain, and Raynaud's disease—disorders that heretofore had proven unusually resistant to the application of the traditional approaches of biomedicine" (Surwit, 1982, p. 4).

Systemic Behavioral Psychotherapy

In systemic behavioral psychotherapy the therapist works in vivo inside social systems (Birk, 1982a, 1984, 1988). Optimally, this is done within multiple and purposely juxtaposed natural systems (couple and family systems) and artificial systems (therapy groups). In the first phase, behavioral analysis, again optimally, the patient is observed both inside her or his own natural systems, usually briefly, and then much more extensively inside a therapy group. When the behavioral analysis is complete, the therapist should be able to specify what "target behaviors" are appropriate for therapeutic modification. The target behaviors should be chosen openly and with the agreement of the group and the patient. Modification within the group can then proceed by the deliberate use of the operant conditioning method of "behavioral shaping," used here for the direct learning of new, more adaptive behaviors. This shaping—indeed, direct new learning—is powerfully catalyzed by concomitant cognitively mediated learning, which in turn advances not just through the interpretations of a single therapist, but also from the parallel processing of a wealth of cognitive feedback from other group members, as well as from cognitive insights arising from the multiple identifications and counteridentifica-

tions found within a therapy group (Guttmacher and Birk, 1971). It is impossible to function as a skilled behavioral psychotherapist without first being an accomplished and experienced behavior therapist who has deliberately acquired an almost unthinking mastery of learning theory as it applies to clinical situations, a ready understanding of defense mechanisms in action, and a cultivated gift for accurate empathy. One cannot become a ski racer without first becoming a skier.

In classic behavior therapy, the therapist has the luxury of dealing with a single problem, or at most with a few well-defined problems, using well-defined techniques such as assertiveness training, systematic desensitization, biofeedback, or aversive conditioning, once he has articulated a satisfactory behavioral analysis. Of course in his most difficult cases the classical behavior therapist must actually invent and continually modify as necessary a composite treatment technique, based on a detailed and continuing behavioral baseline study, in order to solve complex individual problems of behavioral engineering.

In his work with patients chosen for systemic behavioral psychotherapy, by contrast, the patient's complaints, at least initially, are much more vague, ill defined, multiple, and amorphous. Or the patient may complain about others: he cannot get along with his wife or make good relationships with people, and he has no idea, or only the vaguest idea, what *in his own habitual behavior* contributes to his problems. Thus the initial behavioral analysis, which in simple, classical behavior therapy may require an hour or two of interviewing, or in complex behavior therapy a week or two of index card data gathering, may require 20, 40, or more hours of direct observation of the patient's actual functioning within one or more natural social systems, preferably including the very social system—the family—in which he learned and/or experienced his amorphous dissatisfaction, or a replica of it. Typically, with varying emphases depending on the nature of the case, the patient is observed in several different social settings—for example, in couple therapy, in family therapy with his parents or in-laws, and also with his children, as well as in therapy with a group of his peers. The natural social systems, on display in couple therapy and family therapy, are invaluable for early accurate diagnosis of the central issues, problems, and "target symptoms." The artificial social systems (mixed therapy groups, couple groups), because they are much less encumbered by the "ruts" of long-practiced emotionally defensive habits, are much more effective for behavior change treatment. Thus, in the first phase of systemic behavioral psychotherapy, the preeminently important work is that which is done diagnostically, within the natural social systems of the presenting patient: in other words, her or his marital or couple system, family of origin system, family of procreation system, and sometimes also her or his in-law system. The central questions to be pursued in all these systems are these: Who is doing what to whom? What interactional patterns and processes need to change? What behavior of the patient, *or other members of the system,* needs to change?

In the second phase, most of the work takes place within an artificial social system, a therapy group of one kind or another such as a mixed therapy group or couple therapy group, or a combination of both of these. Habitual defenses, maladaptive communication styles, and other behavioral patterns are much less rigidly established in the artificial social systems, less reflexive and "encrusted," making these ideal settings in which people can learn new, more adaptive behaviors and communicative styles, without the interference of well-established and predictable marital or family "short circuits." Once new, useful behavior patterns have been learned *(and also practiced adequately!),* the stage is set for the third phase of systemic behavioral psychotherapy. This last phase involves the evocation and practice of the newly learned, more adaptive behavior and styles back in the old natural systems, the couple and family systems, despite the predictable short circuits characteristic of those systems, while the strength of the newly learned behaviors is being supported and maintained by reinforcement occurring concurrently within the same ongoing therapy groups in which the new behaviors were originally learned.

Because of the accumulated strength of family systems, prior work on new learning within the artificial systems, the therapy groups, needs to be overrepresented by a factor of 50, 100, or even 150:1, in the experience of this systemic behavioral psychotherapist (Birk, 1982b).

The full details of how a learning model is optimally employed within overlapping group, family, and couple systems constitute a subject clearly beyond the scope of this or any other single chapter. The important features to be stressed here are (1) the deliberate combination of elements of a psychoanalytic or psychodynamic approach with a behavioral approach in order to enhance the therapeutic power of the former, the breadth of the latter, and the therapist's overall effectiveness (Birk and Brinkley-Birk, 1975); and (2) the use of direct observation within the relevant natural social systems to ensure precise, comprehensive, and relevant behavioral analysis and to improve both the results of treatment and the range of human life problems that can be usefully approached through a natural science methodology (Birk, 1973a, 1974, 1982a, b, 1984, 1988).

Use of a natural science methodology—second nature for laboratory-trained behaviorists—leads to direct

therapeutic power, power to produce *direct* behavioral changes that can revolutionize the way a couple communicates, the way a family deals with grief or anger, or the way one person in a group relates to another (Birk, 1968; Shapiro and Birk, 1967). Insight is not a necessary prerequisite for far-reaching change; insight also helps but may at times lag behind direct behavioral change. In couple and family therapy formats, the therapist observes the actual social systems in which the patient experiences his difficulty, however amorphously. In a group therapy format, however, the group is not at first a natural social group. Like a jury, a therapy group is an assemblage of somewhat randomly chosen peers, which eventually becomes a natural social group as a result of their working together. And, as in couple or family therapy, in group therapy an individual can learn, and a therapist can directly observe, not only that a patient's behavior is socially isolating, hostile, provocative, seductive, or maladaptive, but also *precisely* what about it is so and how it can be usefully modified.

The systemic behavioral psychotherapist uses this unique vantage point to forge an increasingly refined, subtle, and comprehensive behavioral analysis. As the therapist becomes sure of elements of the problem, such as a subtle pattern of sulky underassertiveness limited to relations with the spouse or an inability to make eye contact with opposite-sex peers, he shares this information with the patient and the group. The therapist's observations and formulations are refined and validated—or revised—by the group as a whole. Once this refinement is accomplished, the therapist must establish a specific treatment contract to which the patient subscribes. The therapist can then begin direct use of operant methods to modify the contributory problematic behaviors. These operant methods do include punishment in the form of interrupting the old behavior with negative interpretations, but they always employ simultaneous positive reinforcement of a more acceptable and effective alternative behavior.

In systemic behavioral psychotherapy the therapist consciously uses behavioral shaping, or successively raising the criterion level for reinforcing a response. Put another way, behavioral shaping is a technique of successive approximation in which the desired new behavior occurs fully only near the end of the shaping process. In pursuing therapeutic goals through behavioral shaping, the therapist functions as a punisher, as a reinforcer, and also as a catalytic source of "discriminative stimuli" signaling the availability of reinforcement if a response is emitted. In using discriminative stimuli to catalyze new behaviors, the therapist also consciously uses the principle of *stimulus fading*—gradually doing less and less to discourage (punish) the old behaviors and to encourage the new behaviors (by direct reinforcement or by supplying discriminative stimuli).

When therapeutic goals are reached, the behavioral psychotherapist strives for phased and very gradual termination, still following the principle of stimulus fading. Thus the patient or couple frequently progresses from weekly meetings, to biweekly meetings, to monthly meetings, to quarterly meetings, to follow-up visits about a year apart, then as needed.

All this emphasis on the principle of stimulus fading increases the durability of the new behavioral patterns learned and thus increases the probability that the new behavior will maintain itself *with natural consequences only following it*. The new behavior will of course maintain itself naturally only if it truly "works better" than the old behavior and brings more reinforcement from the world at large.

In work of this kind the behavioral psychotherapist is often assisted by group process: other group (or family) members, by identification and by modeling, typically adopt some version of the therapist's reinforcement-and-punishment stance with respect to individuals within the group. Thus, after some considerable shared experience, the therapist himself may supply only a minimal discriminative stimulus, and another group member may provide the reinforcement.

In addition to consciously using reinforcement, punishment, discriminative stimuli, modeling, and stimulus fading, the behavioral psychotherapist systematically employs stimulus generalization in the service of therapeutic goals. In a behaviorally oriented therapy group, patients typically see one another socially, in various combinations outside the group and in places and situations outside those of the usual therapy meeting. All of this of course promotes the transfer of newly learned behaviors to the larger life situation and accelerates the useful breakdown of patients' destructively rigid but all too common compartmentalizations of "therapy behavior" and "life behavior."

The Impact of Behavioral Science and Behavior Therapy on Psychiatry

Psychiatry is, or should be, an art. But it should be an art based on the application of scientific methodology to human life problems as well as on the relevant, always expanding findings of its multiple root sciences: psychology, especially cognitive psychology and the psychology of object relations, experimental psychology and learning theory; the brain sciences, including neuroanatomy, neurophysiology, neurochemistry, and neuro-

pharmacology; the social sciences, including anthropology, sociology, and non-human primate studies, to name only a few of the most important. Yet the average psychiatrist, including those still in training, has had very little education in basic behavioral science.

It is now belatedly obvious that those planning to be psychotherapists of any type need to prepare themselves with basic science courses in conditioning and learning. Those courses should include supervised laboratory experience with animal learning processes, including extinction, punishment, stimulus generalization, behavioral shaping, and stimulus fading. Those who intend to specialize in behavior therapy, and especially in systemic behavioral psychotherapy, should have particularly thorough backgrounds in the basic sciences underlying this field. Like other clinicians, of course, they should also have long, broad, and adequately supervised experience across a large range of diagnoses, cultural settings, types of patients and problems, and therapeutic modalities. Specifically, they should know how and when to use phenothiazines and other neuroleptics, lithium, valproate, carbamazapine, the tricyclic antidepressants and SSRIs (selective serotonin-reuptake inhibitors) plus buproprion, nefazadone, venlafazine, and the MAOIs (monoamine oxidase inhibitors); when to consider organic treatments such as electroconvulsive therapy; and when to arrange for special neurological study or tests, such as electroencephalography to look for psychomotor seizures. In addition, they should know enough about themselves psychoanalytically to understand their own countertransference reactions.

Behavioral science has already added to the practice of psychiatry a multiplicity of treatment techniques of established clinical value. Beyond this, the field, especially with its current growing interest in cross-fertilization with social systems therapies such as family therapy, group therapy, and couple therapies, seems to be on the threshold of a new and perhaps even greater contribution through the further development of systemic behavioral psychotherapy. This field, true to its natural science origins, relies on direct in vivo observation of the social systems relevant to the problems of individuals for precise behavioral analysis and subsequent therapy using operant social learning techniques. The natural science origins of these behavioral contributions represent one stream among many confluent ones, all of which clamor for a renewed appreciation of the basic scientific foundations of modern psychiatry.

In this larger venture, a major specific contribution of behavior therapy has been the proper recapture of *responsibility for outcome* in psychiatry, which for a while had partially and improperly split off from the rest of medicine in accepting this responsibility. Unconscious "resistance" is a real phenomenon; it should not, however, be used as a large, all-purpose shield to ward off blame when the patient undergoes years of therapy yet makes very little progress or actually becomes worse.

Behavior therapists generally accept an appropriately large share of responsibility for clinical outcome. When they do something that does not "work" clinically, they tend to look for the reason not in patient "resistance" but in one or more of the following: (1) an inadequate (incomplete or wrong) behavioral analysis; (2) poor execution of well-designed therapy based on an adequate behavioral analysis; (3) an inappropriate choice of treatment method, as in clinical situations where behavior therapy in itself is quite ineffective, such as psychosis or temporal lobe epilepsy masquerading as a simple learned eating disorder; or (4) insufficient therapeutic leverage—instances in which the therapist could not or simply did not get adequate control of the significant reinforcers and punishers in the patient's life.

The fact that this field requires full acceptance of professional responsibility is a large part of what makes working within it both exhilarating and a learning experience in itself.

New Developments and Trends for the Future

Since the publication of the second edition of the *Harvard Guide to Psychiatry* in 1988, a number of refinements in clinical practice, in addition to new useful drugs, and new knowledge about old drugs, have led to changes in how behavioral therapies can most effectively be combined with psychopharmacotherapy. Here I attempt to highlight some of the major changes which have occurred and to predict which of the new trends will prove to be of lasting significance. What are these trends?

First, we have learned much more about posttraumatic stress disorder (PTSD), its previously underestimated importance, and its effective treatment. A recent article by Foa, Riggs, and Gershuny suggested that "there are two patterns of post trauma symptoms, one characterizing PTSD, and one characterizing . . . phobic [reactions]" (1995). Since some phobias and many posttraumatic stress reactions can arise as enduring psychopathological reactions to a single traumatic event (stimulus), both PTSD and phobias can be seen to be instances of one-trial learning, at least in some cases. (And for those cases stemming from multiple traumatic stimuli, it is equally true that they can be seen to be instances of multiple-trial learning.) *It should therefore come as no surprise that the backbone of effective treatment for PTSD, like that for phobias, is necessarily behaviorally based, and relies on*

exposure. In both phobias and PTSD, for successful therapy, exposure needs to occur which is both repeated and without the punishment which occurred as a part of the genesis of the traumatically learned problem. This clinical recipe, repeated exposure without punishment, precisely defines "extinction" as it is well known to operate in both respondent and operant conditioning. For both disorders, we are dealing with the "extinction" of an aversive conditional reflex, a core concept in learning theory thoroughly investigated for over half a century and demonstrated both in laboratory studies of Pavlovian (or "respondent") conditioning (Gantt, 1944), and by research in "operant conditioning" (Skinner, 1948; Azrin and Holz, 1966). So it is certainly no accident that behavior therapy cut its "baby teeth" clinically in the treatment of phobias (Wolpe, 1958) and now, a half century later, is proving itself also to be at the center of all the effective treatments for PTSD (Dyck, 1993). This includes the much-vaunted method of EMDR, or eye movement desensitization and reprocessing.

Second, we now have much more effective behavioral therapies for the treatment of panic disorder (Wolpe, 1995), and we now know more about the utility of combining behavioral treatment with appropriate pharmacotherapy—with, for example, imipramine, paroxetine, phenelzine, or valproate, but *not* with alprazolam (because of the marked tolerance and addiction problems which occur with most benzodiazapines. Clonazepam is a qualified exception to this generalization).

Third, there has been an increase in the use of prescriptive strategies (Hersen and Ammerman, 1994) for the treatment of a wide variety of clinical problems. In using prescriptive strategies, the therapist employs patients' willingness to do what they are told will make them well. For example, patients with panic disorder can be given prescriptions to produce at will sensations of panic which they gradually learn (through extinction) are not in fact evidence that they are "dying" or "going crazy." The work of Masters and Johnson, and later that of Helen Kaplan, who specifically employed prescriptive strategies in sex therapy, were important forerunners of the "new" trend toward prescriptive treatments. Though neither Masters (a gynecologist) nor Kaplan (a psychoanalyst) was behaviorally trained, both deserve credit as pioneers in the use of prescriptive strategies in behavior therapy.

Fourth, the health care crisis and the effort by managed care organizations to limit payments to techniques proven to be effective have placed new emphasis on "empirically validated treatment techniques" (Chambless, 1995; Hersen and Ammerman, 1994; Mueser and Glynn, 1995; Barlow, 1988; Barlow and Craske, 1989). Without ignoring its devastating effect on psychiatry in general and psychotherapy in particular, one can acknowledge that managed care has led to an increased emphasis on documenting which kinds of treatments work best for specific problems.

Nevertheless, it is to be hoped that the resulting "guidelines" will not prove to be a straitjacket, or to inhibit and discourage useful innovation and the reasonable trial of plausible new approaches to a problem. In some cases effective treatment must first be "invented," then proved to be effective. This principle is important in cases where "documented" treatments fail to work, and in recalcitrant disorders (such as alcoholism) where no treatments have yet been documented to work consistently.

Fifth, many who have worked in the field of behavioral therapy for decades acknowledge that behavioral therapy has become so mainstream that there is now a loss of enthusiasm, ferment, and excitement. Although this loss dates back roughly 20 years (Lazarus, personal communication, 1996), behavior therapy, in almost all its forms, continues to be healthily rooted in observation, critical thinking, and empirical study.

Take the technique of EMDR, or eye movement desensitization and reprocessing, as a salient example: although this technique has been reported in many case studies to be dramatically effective, particularly for traumatically driven nightmares and other intrusive imagery (Young, 1995, to cite one example), and although it has been used enthusiastically, it is heartening to see the amount of critical research and thinking which the many sweeping claims about it have already generated (Herbert and Mueser, 1992; Dyck, 1993; Bauman and Melnyk, 1994; Montgomery and Ayllon, 1994; Tallis and Smith, 1994; Vaughan et al., 1994; Carrigan and Cahill, 1995; Foley and Spates, 1995; Lohr et al., 1995; Rosen, 1995; Spates and Burnette, 1995).

The specific prescription of rapid eye movements as part of exposure therapy may mimic a possible motor component of the imagery necessarily reproduced as exposure-based therapy proceeds. (This line of reasoning is particularly compelling for nightmares.) Specific studies, however, have so far failed to show significant differences between exposure with "rapid eye movements," versus exposure with "slow eye movements," and using imagery alone, with no eye movements. Although EMDR needs further rigorous research, it is controversial, because comparative studies fail to support assertions that it is a significantly more effective and specific treatment than other exposure-based therapies. One wonders whether EMDR may not eventually parallel the exposure treatment method of systematic desensitization introduced by Wolpe. Although it represented a significant advance for

both the field of behavioral therapy and for psychiatry as a whole, Wolpe's early belief that the specifics of his original procedure (such as relaxation training or some other assumed "competitive response" and the use of stimulus hierarchies) were crucial for clinical success eventually proved to be quite unfounded (Marks, 1976).

Exposure therapies "work," in whatever form, because they are based on extinction: for this reason they are likely to survive. By contrast, eye movement desensitization and reprocessing is a specific *technique* of therapy, and "emotional reprocessing," like "reciprocal inhibition" before it, may well remain an unproved theory.

Sixth, the further integration of the social system therapies—group, couple, and family therapies—with psychotherapy and with cognitive behavior therapy will prove to be more and more important clinically. Also, systemic behavioral psychotherapy, involving as it does strategically purposeful combinations of artificial and natural social groups, will come into much wider and more effective use.

References

Abel, J. L. 1993. Exposure with response prevention and serotonergic antidepressants in the treatment of obsessive compulsive disorder. *Behav. Res. Ther.* 315:463–478.

Alexander, F. 1939. Emotional factors in essential hypertension. *Psychosom. Med.* 1:173–179.

———1946. Training principles in psychosomatic medicine. *Am. J. Orthopsychiatry* 16:410–412.

———1947. Treatment of a case of peptic ulcer and personality disorder. *Psychosom. Med.* 9:320–330.

———1950. *Psychosomatic medicine: its principles and applications.* New York: Norton.

Arkowitz, H., and S. B. Messer, eds. 1984. *Psychoanalytic therapy and behavior therapy: is integration possible?* New York: Plenum Publishing.

Azrin, N. H., and W. C. Holz. 1966. Punishment. In *Operant behavior: areas of research and application,* ed. W. K. Honig and J. E. R. Staddon. New York: Appleton-Century-Crofts.

Ballenger, J. C. 1986. Pharmacotherapy of the panic disorders. *J. Clin. Psychiatry* (suppl.)47:27–32.

Barlow, D. H. 1988. *Anxiety and its disorders.* New York: Guilford Press.

Barlow, D. H., and M. G. Craske. 1989. *Mastery of your anxiety and panic.* Albany, N.Y.: Graywind Publications.

Bauman, N., and N. T. Melnyk. 1994. A controlled comparison of eye movements and finger tapping in the treatment of test anxiety. *J. Behav. Ther. & Exp. Psychiat.* 251:29–33.

Baxter, L. R. Jr., J. M. Schwartz, K. S. Bergman, M. P. Szuba, B. H. Guze, J. C. Mazziotta, A. Alazraki, C. E. Selin, H. K. Ferng, P. Munford, et al. 1992. Caudate glucose metabolic rate changes with both drug behavior therapy for obsessive compulsive disorder. *Arch. Gen. Psychiatry* 49(9):681–689.

Beck, A. I. 1976. *Cognitive therapy and the emotional disorders.* New York: International Universities Press.

Beck, A. I., A. J. Rush, B. E. Shaw, and G. Emery. 1979. *Cognitive therapy of depression.* New York: Guilford.

Birk, L. 1968. Social reinforcement in psychotherapy. *Cond. Reflex* 3:116–123.

———1970. Behavior therapy—integration with dynamic psychiatry. *Behav. Ther.* 1:522–526.

———1972. Psychoanalytic omniscience and behavioral omnipotence: current trends in psychotherapy. *Semin. Psychiatry* 4:113–120.

———1973a. *Biofeedback: behavioral medicine.* New York: Grune & Stratton.

——— ed. 1973b. Psychoanalysis and behavioral analysis: natural resonance and complementarity. *Int. J. Psychiatry* 11:160–166.

———1974. Intensive group therapy: an effective behavioral-psychoanalytic method. *Am. J. Psychiatry* 131:499–510.

———1982a. Brief family therapy used to catalyze extended psychotherapy. In *Questions and answers in family therapy,* ed. A. Gurman. Vol. 2. New York: Brunner/Mazel.

———1982b. Psychotherapy within social systems. In *Psychoanalysis: critical explorations in contemporary theory and practice,* ed. A. Jacobson and D. Parmelee. New York: Brunner/Mazel.

———1984. Combined concurrent/conjoint psychotherapy for couples: rationale and efficient new strategies. In *Marriage and divorce,* ed. C. C. Nadelson and D. L. Polonsky. New York: Guilford.

———1988. Behavioral/psychoanalytic psychotherapy within overlapping social systems: a natural matrix for diagnosis and therapeutic change. *Psychiatric Annals* 118(5):296–308.

Birk, L., and A. Brinkley-Birk. 1974. Psychoanalysis and behavior therapy. *Am. J. Psychiatry* 131:11–16.

———1975. The learning therapies. In *Overview of the psychotherapies,* ed. G. Usdin. New York: Brunner/Mazel.

Birk, L., S. Stolz, J. V. Brady, A. Lazarus, J. Lynch, A. Rosenthal, W. D. Skelton, J. Stevens, and E. Thomas. 1973. *Behavior therapy in psychiatry.* Washington, D.C.: American Psychiatric Association.

Carrigan, M. H., and S. P. Cahill. 1995. The relevance of the anxiety literature to research on eye movement desensitization. *J. Behav. Ther. & Exp. Psychiat.* 26(4):365–366.

Chambless, D. 1995. Training in and dissemination of empirically validated psychological treatments: report and recommendations. *The Clinical Psychologist* 48:3–23.

Conte, H. R., R. Plutchik, K. W. Wild, and I. B. Karasu. 1986. Combined psychotherapy and pharmacotherapy for depression. *Arch. Gen. Psychiatry* 43:471–479.

Dunbar, F. 1943. *Psychosomatic diagnosis.* New York: Harper, Hoeber.

———1947. *Emotions and bodily changes.* 3rd ed. New York: Columbia University Press.

Dyck, M. J. 1993. A proposal for a conditioning model of eye movement desensitization treatment for post traumatic stress disorder. *J. Behav. Ther. & Exp. Psychiat.* 24(3):201–210.

Foa, E. B., D. S. Riggs, and B. S. Gershuny. 1995. Arousal, numbing, and intrusion: symptom structure of PTSD following assault. *AMJ Psychiatry.* 152:116–120.

Feather, V. W., and J. M. Rhoads. 1972. Psychodynamic behavior therapy. *Arch. Gen. Psychiatry* 26:503–511.

Foley, T., and C. R. Spates. 1995. Eye movement desensitization of public speaking anxiety: a partial dismantling. *J. Behav. Ther. & Exp. Psychiatry* 26(4):321–329.

Gantt, W. A. H. 1944. *Experimental basis for neurotic behavior.* New York: Harper and Brothers.

———1953. Principles of nervous breakdown in schizokinesis and autokinesis. *Ann. N. Y. Acad. Sci.* 56:143–163.

Gentry, W. D., ed. 1984. *Handbook of behavioral medicine.* New York: Guilford.

Goldfried, M. R., ed. 1982. *Converging themes in psychotherapy: trends in psychodynamic, humanistic, and behavioral practice.* New York: Springer.

Goldiamond, I., and J. E. Dyrud. 1968. Some applications and implications of behavioral analysis for psychotherapy. In *Proceedings of the annual conference on research in psychotherapy.* Vol. 3. Washington, D.C.: American Psychological Association.

Grunebaum, H. 1997. Commentary: Why integration may be a misguided goal for family therapy. *Fam. Process* 36:19–21.

Guttmacher, J., and L. Birk. 1971. Group therapy: what specific therapeutic advantages? *Compr. Psychiatry* 12:546–556.

Herbert, J. D., and K. T. Mueser. 1992. Eye movement desensitization: a critique of the evidence. *J. Behav. Ther. Exp. Psychiatry* 23:169–174.

Hersen, M., and R. T. Ammerman, eds. 1994. *Handbook of prescriptive treatments for adults.* New York: Plenum Press.

Holland, J., and B. F. Skinner. 1961. *The experimental analysis of behavior.* New York: McGraw-Hill.

Hsu, L. K. 1985. The treatment of bulimia with lithium. *Am. J. Psychiatry* 142:271.

Hudson, J. I., and H. G. Pope, Jr. 1985. Treatment of anorexia nervosa with antidepressants. *J. Clin. Psychopharmacol.* 5:17–23.

Ives, I. J. 1985. Treatment of intractable hiccups with intramuscular haloperidol. *Am. J. Psychiatry* 142:1368–69.

Jacobson, E. 1938. *Progressive relaxation.* Chicago: University of Chicago Press.

Jones, M. C. 1924. The elimination of children's fears. *J. Exp. Psychol.* 7:382–390.

Lazarus, A. A. 1971. *Behavior therapy and beyond.* New York: McGraw-Hill.

Lazarus, A. 1996. The utility and futility of combining treatment in psychotherapy. *Clin. Psychology: Science and Practice* 3:59–68.

Lindsley, O. R., and B. F. Skinner. 1954. A method for the experimental analysis of behavior of psychotic patients. *Am. Psychol.* 9:419–420.

Logan, C. G., and S. I. Grafton. 1995. Functional anatomy of human eyeblink conditioning determined with regional cerebral glucose metabolism and positron-emission tomography. *Proceedings of the National Academy of Sciences of the United States of America:* 92(16):7500–7504.

Lohr, J. M., R. A. Kleinknecht, D. F. Tolin, and R. H. Barret. 1995. The empirical status of the clinical application of eye movement desensitization and reprocessing. *J. Behav. Ther. & Exp. Psychiatry* 26(4):285–302.

Lovibond, S. H. 1970. Aversive control of behavior. *Behav. Ther.* 1:80–91.

Mahoney, M. J. 1974. *Cognition and behavior modification.* Cambridge, Mass.: Ballinger.

——— 1995. Cognition and causation in human experience. *J. Behav. Ther. & Exp. Psychiatry* 26(3):275–278.

Marks, I. M. 1972. Perspective on flooding. *Semin. Psychiatry* 4:129–138.

———1976. The current status of behavioral psychotherapy. *Am. J. Psychiatry* 133:253–261.

———1983. Are there anticompulsive or antiobsessional drugs? A review of the evidence. *Br. J. Psychiatry* 143:338–347.

Marmor, J. 1971. Dynamic psychotherapy and behavior therapy. *Arch. Gen. Psychiatry* 24:22–28.

Mavissakalian, M., L. M. Turner, L. Michelson, and K. Jacob. 1985. Tricyclic antidepressants in obsessive-compulsive disorders: antiobsessional or antidepressant agents. *Am. J. Psychiatry* 142:572–576.

Meichenbaum, D. 1977. *Cognitive behavior modification: an integrative approach.* New York: Plenum Publishing.

Mills, H. L., W. S. Agras, D. H. Barlow, and J. R. Mills. 1973. Compulsive rituals treated by response prevention. *Arch. Gen. Psychiatry* 28:524–529.

Minuchin, S., B. Rosman, and L. Baker. 1978. *Psychosomatic families: anorexia nervosa in context.* Cambridge, Mass.: Harvard University Press.

Minuchin, S., B. Rosman, B. Liebman, L. Milman, and I. A. Todd. 1975. A conceptual model of psychosomatic illness in children. *Arch. Gen. Psychiatry* 32:1031–37.

Montgomery, R. W., and T. Ayllon. 1994. Eye movement desensitization across images: a single case design. *J. Behav. Ther. & Exp. Psychiatry* 25(1):23–28.

Mueser, K. T., and S. M. Glynn. 1995. *Behavioral family therapy for psychiatric disorders.* Needham Heights, Mass.: Allyn & Bacon.

Nemiah, J. C. 1996. Alexithymia: present, past—and future? *Psychosomatic Medicine* 58:217–218.

Pavlov, I. P. 1928. *Lectures on conditioned reflexes,* ed. W. A. H. Gantt. Vol. 1. New York: International Publishers.

———1941. *Lectures on conditioned reflexes,* ed. W. A. H. Gantt. Vol. 2. New York: International Publishers.

Pope, H. G. Jr., and J. I. Hudson. 1986. Antidepressant drug therapy of bulimia: current status. *J. Clin. Psychiatry* 47:339–345.

Pope, H. G. Jr., J. I. Hudson, J. M. Jonas, and D. Yurgelun-Todd. 1983. Bulimia treated with imipramine: a placebo-controlled double blind study. *Am. J. Psychiatry* 140:554–558.

Rhoads, J. M., and V. W. Feather. 1974. Application of psychodynamics to behavior therapy. *Am. J. Psychiatry* 131:17–20.

Rosen, G. M. 1995. On the origin of eye movement desensitization. *J. Behav. Ther. & Exp. Psychiatry* 26(2):121–122.

Seligman, M. E. P. 1994. *What you change and what you can't.* New York: Knopf.

Shapiro, A. K., and E. Shapiro. 1983. Controlled study of pimozide vs. placebo in Tourette's syndrome. *J. Am. Acad. Child Psychiatry* 23:161–173.

Shapiro, A. K., E. Shapiro, and G. J. Eisenkraft. 1983. Treatment of Gilles de la Tourette syndrome symptoms with pimozide. *Am. J. Psychiatry* 140:1183–86.

Shapiro, D., and L. Birk. 1967. Group therapy in experimental perspective. *Int. J. Group Psychotherapy* 17:211–224.

Shapiro, F. 1995. *Eye movement desensitization and reprocessing.* New York: Guilford Press.

Shapiro, M. B. 1961. The single case in fundamental clinical psychological research. *Br. J. Med. Psychol.* 34:255–262.

Sheehan, D. V. 1982. Panic attack and phobias. *N. Engl. J. Med.* 307:156–159.

Sheehan, D. V., J. Ballenger, and G. Jacobsen. 1980. Treatment of endogenous anxiety with phobic, hysterical, and hypochondriacal symptoms. *Arch. Gen. Psychiatry* 37:51–59.

Simons, A. D., G. E. Murphy, J. L. Levine, and R. D. Wetzel. 1986. Cognitive therapy and pharmacotherapy for depression. *Arch. Gen. Psychiatry* 43:43–48.

Skinner, B. F. 1953. *Science and human behavior.* New York: Macmillan.

———— 1966. *The behavior of organisms: An experimental analysis.* Englewood Cliffs, N.J.: Prentice-Hall.

Sloane, R. B. 1969. The converging paths of behavior therapy and psychotherapy. *Int. J. Psychiatry* 7:493–503.

Spates, C. R., and M. M. Burnette. 1995. Eye movement desensitization: three unusual cases. *J. Behav. Ther. & Exp. Psychiatry* 26(1):51–55.

Stampfl, T. G., and D. J. Levis. 1967. Essentials of implosive therapy: a learning-theory-based psychodynamic behavioral therapy. *J. Abnorm. Psychol.* 6:496–503.

Stunkard, A. J., J. L. Stinnett, and J. W. Smoller. 1986. Psychological and social aspects of the surgical treatment of obesity. *Am. J. Psychiatry* 143:417–429.

Surwit, R. S. 1982. Behavioral treatment of disease: introduction. In *Behavioral treatment of disease,* ed. R. S. Surwit, R. B. Williams, A. Stepton, and R. Biersner. New York: Plenum Publishing.

Szabo, Z., et al. 1995. Position emission tomography imaging of serotonin transporters in the human brain using (11c) (+) Mc N 5652. *Synapse* 20(1):37–43.

Tallis, F., and E. Smith. 1994. Does rapid eye movement desensitization facilitate emotional processing? *Behav. Res. Ther.* 32(4):459–461.

Thorndike, E. L. 1898. *Animal intelligence: an experimental study of the associated processes in animals.* New York: Macmillan.

Vaughan, K., et al. 1994. A trial of eye movement desensitization compared to image habituation training and applied muscle relaxation in post-traumatic stress disorder. *J. Behav. Ther. & Exp. Psychiatry* 25(4):283–291.

Wachtel, P. L. 1977. *Psychoanalysis and behavior therapy: toward an integration.* New York: Basic Books.

Walsh, B. I., J. W. Stewart, S. P. Roose, M. L. Gladis, and A. Glassman. 1984. Treatment of bulimia with phenelzine: a double-blind placebo-controlled study. *Arch. Gen. Psychiatry* 41:1105–9.

Watson, J. B., and R. Rayner. 1920. Conditioned emotional reactions. *J. Exp. Psychol.* 3:1–14.

Wolfe, B. E., and J. D. Maser, eds. 1994. *Treatment of panic disorder: a consensus development conference.* Washington, D.C.: American Psychiatric Press.

Wolpe, J. 1958. *Psychotherapy by reciprocal inhibition.* Stanford: Stanford University Press.

Wolpe, J., J. P. Brady, M. Serber, W. S. Agras, and R. P. Lieberman. 1973. The current status of systematic desensitization. *Am. J. Psychiatry* 130:961–965.

Wolpe, J., and V. C. Rowan. 1988. Panic disorder: a product of classical conditioning. *Behav. Res. Ther.* 26:441–450.

Woodman, C. L. and R. Noyes, Jr. 1994. Panic disorder: treatment with valprocite. *J. Clin. Psychiatry* 55(4):134–136.

Woods, S. M., and J. Marmor, eds. 1980. *The interface between the psychodynamic and behavioral therapies.* New York: Plenum Publishing.

Young, W. C. 1995. Eye movement desensitization/reprocessing: its use in resolving the trauma caused by the loss of a war buddy. *Am. J. Psychother.* 49(2) Spring:282–291.

Recommended Reading

Barlow, D. H. 1988. *Anxiety and its disorders.* New York: Guilford Press.

Barlow, D. H., and M. G. Craske. 1989. *Mastery of your anxiety and panic.* Albany, N. Y.: Graywind Publications.

Beck, A. I. 1976. *Cognitive therapy and the emotional disorders.* New York: International Universities Press.

Beck, A. I., A. J. Rush, B. E. Shaw, and G. Emery. 1979. *Cognitive therapy of depression.* New York: Guilford Press.

Birk, L. 1972. Psychoanalytic omniscience and behavioral omnipotence. In *Psychotherapy and behavior change,* ed. I. Marks, A. Bergin, et al. Chicago: Aldine Publishing Company. 36–43.

———— 1982. Psychotherapy within social systems. In *Exploration in psychoanalysis,* ed. A. Jacobson and D. Parmalee. New York: Brunner/Mazel.

———— 1986. The demise of dogma in psychotherapy. *Contemp. Psychiatry* 5:107–110.

———— 1988. Behavioral/psychoanalytic psychotherapy within overlapping social systems: a natural matrix for change. *Psychiatric Annals* 118(5):296–308.

Birk, L., and A. Brinkley-Birk. 1974. Psychoanalysis and behavior therapy. *Am. J. Psychiatry* 131(5):499–510.

Birk, L., et al. 1973. *Behavior therapy in psychiatry.* Washington, D.C.: American Psychiatric Association.

Chambless, D. 1995. Training in and dissemination of empirically validated psychological treatments: report and recommendations. *Clinical Psychologist* 48:3–23.

Crisp, A. H. 1966. "Transference," "symptom emergence," and "social repercussion" in behavior therapy: a study of fifty-four treated patients. *Br. J. Med. Psychol.* 39:179–196.

Dyck, M. J. 1993. A proposal for a conditioning model of eye movement desensitization: treatment for post-traumatic stress disorder. *J. Behav. Ther. & Exp. Psychiatry* 24(3):201–210.

Ferster, C. B. 1972. Clinical reinforcement. *Semin. Psychiatry* 4:101–111.

Foa, E. B., and P. M. Emmelkamp. 1983. *Failures in behavior therapy.* New York: Wiley.

Guttmacher, J., and L. Birk. 1971. Group therapy: what specific therapeutic advantages? *Compr. Psychiatry* 12:546–556.

Hersen, M., and R. J. Ammerman, eds. 1994. *Handbook of prescriptive treatments for adults.* New York: Plenum Press.

Lohr, J. M., R. A. Kleinknecht, D. F. Tolin, and R. H. Barret. 1995. The empirical status of the clinical application of eye movement desensitization and reprocessing. *J. Behav. Ther. & Exp. Psychiatry* 26(4):285–302.

Mahoney, M. J. 1995. Cognition and causation in human experience. *J. Behav. Ther. & Exp. Psychiatry* 26(3):275–278.

Marks, I. M. 1976. The current status of behavioral psychotherapy: theory and practice. *Am. J. Psychiatry* 133:253–261.

Mueser, K. T., and S. M. Glynn. 1995. *Behavioral family therapy for psychiatric disorders.* Needham Heights, Mass.: Allyn & Bacon.

Rachman, S., R. Hodgson, and I. M. Marks. 1971. Treatment of chronic obsessive-compulsive neurosis. *Behav. Res. Ther.* 9:237–247.

Seligman, M. E. P. 1974. Depression and learned helplessness. In *The psychology of depression,* ed. R. J. Friedman and M. M. Katz. Washington, D. C.: Wiley, Halsted Press.

——— 1994. *What you can change and what you can't.* New York: Knopf.

Seligman, M. E. P., S. F. Maier, and R. L. Solomon. 1971. Unpredictable and uncontrollable aversive events. In *Aversive conditioning and learning,* ed. F. R. Brush. New York: Academic Press.

Shapiro, I. 1995. *Eye movement desensitization and reprocessing.* New York: Guilford Press.

Walton, D., and M. D. Mather. 1964. The application of learning principles to the treatment of obsessive-compulsive states in the acute and chronic phases of illness. In *Experiments in behavior therapy,* ed. H. J. Eysenck. New York: Macmillan.

Wolpe, J. 1985. Differentiation between classically conditioned and cognitively based neurotic fears. *J. Beh. Res. and Exp. Psychiatry* 16:287–293.

Acknowledgments

The author thanks Ken R. LaCerte, M.Ed., L.C.S.W., L.M.F.T., L.M.H.C., for his close collaboration, help, and support in updating this chapter for the third edition. The author is also grateful to Henry Grunebaum, M. D., and Arnold A. Lazarus, Ph.D., for their invaluable perspectives, as well as for their specific suggestions.

23

LEE BIRK

Sex Therapy

Since the publication of the second edition of this volume in 1988, the core of sex therapy, which is behavioral, has not changed. In every clinical case there is a progressively unfolding process which occurs as an outcome of the therapist's behavioral prescriptions (Hersen and Ammerman, 1994). In this process one needs to be continually guided in choosing (and not infrequently inventing!) what the next prescription(s) need to be in order to help the couple take one more step, first toward, then eventually into, a new pattern of sexual experience with each other. Each case begins with at least one of the partners, and not rarely both, experiencing nonpleasurable responses to situational stimuli which would be quite pleasurable and also erotic for other people (not patients) who are neither psychologically impaired nor suffering from learned sexual dysfunction. Learned dysfunctions can impair, either totally or partially, desire, arousal, or orgasm, and/or the full pleasure and enjoyment which normally attend each of these phases of the human sexual response. Sex therapy is the behaviorally based art of systematically helping patients to move their sexual response through a designed series of graded experiences, from an avoided, partial, or pleasureless response to a fully unimpaired, fully pleasurable response. So the fundamental principles of this art have not changed.

Similarly, there has been no change in the background of general clinical experience which is desirable if not necessary for a therapist to be optimally effective in doing sex therapy. Because the therapist must be very skilled in simultaneously sparking *and also in tenaciously maintaining* a strong collaborative and therapeutic alliance with each of 2 partners; this alliance must be capable of surviving the inevitable anxieties and temporary setbacks which always occur in sex therapy. Since some of the behavioral prescriptions will prove at least temporarily egodystonic, "pulling off" all this requires a high level of intuitive clinical "savvy" about each of the partners, and about the couple as a functional unit. Ordinarily, this level of experienced intuitiveness occurs only in therapists who are both somewhat gifted to begin with and also long experienced in the vicissitudes of individual and couple psychotherapy.

In short, neither the fundamental *principles* of learning which underlie the prescriptive strategies nor the kinds of *clinical experience* necessary to implement these strategies and do the work of sex therapy have changed. Still, however, it seems useful to ask and briefly answer the following two-part question: What then *has* changed? What *is* new and important in sex therapy? An attempt to address these questions has been added at the end of the chapter.

Sex therapy, the science and art of diagnosing and treating psychogenic sexual dysfunction, is a highly focused subspecialty both of the broad field of psychotherapy and of the narrower field of couple therapy. With its sharp focus on sexual behavior and its prescriptive strategies, sex therapy can be relatively brief and dramatically effective. Yet these same characteristics inevitably limit its scope. Because human problems are ordinarily complex, sex therapy is vastly more useful clinically when combined with individual psychotherapy and couple therapy according to the particular needs of the couple.

Nearly all readers of this book will bring to it considerable experience in individual therapy; they will in addition find a great deal to guide them in this area in Chapter 22; fewer readers, however, will have much experience in couple therapy. Yet couple therapy is a special art, the mastery of which is vital to practicing sex therapy successfully. Moreover, to be effective, couple therapy usually needs to be combined (with judicious restraint) with individually based therapies and also with relevant family therapy work. The individual work can be done solo (with a single therapist) or in a therapy group; group work is often superior (Guttmacher and Birk, 1971; Birk, 1974, 1982). The conjoint couple therapy work can be done solo or in a couple group; for more difficult and longer cases, couple group therapy typically is usually vastly superior (Grunebaum and Crist, 1968; Grunebaum, Crist, and Neiberg, 1969; Birk, 1984; Grunebaum, 1985).

This chapter discusses in detail only sex therapy itself, a subspecialty of a subspecialty. The reader should, however, be aware that sex therapy requires more than thorough knowledge of medical and psychogenic causes of sexual dysfunction and competence in the behavioral elements of sex therapy. Sex therapy also requires broad clinical confidence based on training and experience in psychotherapy, couple therapy, and family therapy. For all these reasons, the "Recommended Reading" section at the end of this chapter includes a select list of works on couple therapy, couple group therapy, and family therapy.

Ironically, although Freud forced society to confront sexuality as an important and pervasive reality, psychoanalysis and psychoanalytic psychotherapy have been conspicuously unsuccessful in the treatment of the 6 major psychogenic sexual dysfunctions: "impotence" (erectile dysfunction), "frigidity" (female arousal dysfunction), female orgasmic dysfunction, "ejaculatory incompetence" (male orgasmic dysfunction), premature ejaculation, and vaginismus.

Perhaps because people feel fear, shame, embarrassment, and personal inadequacy when suffering from symptoms of sexual dysfunction, the number who present themselves for treatment is vastly lower than the actual incidence of the problems. Frank, Anderson, and Rubenstein (1978), for example, in a pilot survey of 100 well-educated, stably married couples, found that 63% of the women and 40% of the men reported one or more dysfunctions. More than half the dysfunctional women reported multiple dysfunctions, affecting both arousal and orgasm. Authors from Kinsey to Kaplan have estimated that for women the frequency of "absolute" orgastic dysfunction, with no orgasm ever, under any circumstances, is in the range of 10%. This problem therefore may affect 10 million women in the United States. These facts make it clear that all psychiatrists working with nonpsychotic outpatients should learn at least the rudimentary principles of treating psychogenic sexual dysfunction, and, by appropriate referral or by direct work, be able to incorporate sex therapy into their practices.

Overview

Throughout the early twentieth century Freud and his followers demonstrated the relevance and ubiquity of conscious and unconscious sexual thoughts and impulses. Then in the late 1940s and early 1950s Kinsey immersed the culture in a mass of interview-documented facts about overt sexual behavior (Kinsey, Pomeroy, and Martin, 1948; Kinsey et al., 1953). In 1954 William Masters, a gynecologist, and his collaborator, Virginia Johnson, established a scientifically sophisticated laboratory of sexuality at the Washington University Medical School in St. Louis; together they published 2 landmark volumes on their work, *Human Sexual Response* (1966) and *Human Sexual Inadequacy* (1970). Their pioneering scientific and clinical work was powerfully cross-fertilized with dynamic psychiatry by psychoanalyst Helen Singer Kaplan in her influential *The New Sex Therapy* (1974) and *Disorders of Sexual Desire* (1979). Subsequent books by LoPiccolo and LoPiccolo (1978), Leiblum and Pervin (1980), Arentewicz and Schmidt (1983), Kaplan again (1983), Rosen and Beck (1988), Leiblum and Rosen (1991), and Rosen and Leiblum (1995a), have progressively added to the base of our scientific and clinical knowledge.

In the ebullient early years of sex therapy, Kinsey, Masters and Johnson, and their followers thought that psychogenic sexual dysfunction resulted from specific learned blocks involving either *arousal* or *orgasm* or both; during that time therapists used strategies of corrective relearning. They based their methods on the experimental study of animal learning by Pavlov, Skinner, Wolpe (1958), and others. Their work had shown beyond a doubt that sexual responses are as susceptible to conditioning as other animal or human behaviors and that in fact sexual function in animals and humans is particularly easy to disrupt with punishing external stimuli, and so is especially vulnerable to learned inhibition (as in male or female arousal dysfunctions) or learned distortion (as in premature ejaculation or vaginismus). Because sexual dysfunctions are in fact learned aberrations of the "normal" sexual response, learning theory, the discipline that studies how organisms learn and unlearn behavior patterns, is crucial in guiding the technical aspects of sex therapy.

Beginning in the late 1970s, however, therapists recognized the need to enlarge their biphasic view of sexual response to a triphasic one in which "desire" is considered to be the first phase. Although this change has been both heuristically and practically useful, behavioral treatment of the "desire disorders" has been markedly less successful than the treatment of arousal/orgasm disorders. Brief focused behavioral sex therapy often can be done with the arousal/orgasm disorders but not ordinarily with "desire disorders." All sex therapists, including the most ardently behavioral ones, have had to look at their results and at the necessary length of treatment and have had to concede that desire problems are at the very least extremely difficult to treat successfully. This may be because the underlying phenomenology of sexual desire and of fluctuations in sexual desire is extremely complex. If sexual desire is to be, and especially to remain, healthy and strong for both partners within a couple system, then both partners need to have achieved certain developmental levels of maturity: authentic love requires successful individuation within the family of origin, a degree of separation from parents and siblings, and the capacity for (relatively) transference-free mutuality. Thus for some couples sexual desire (or the lack of it in one partner) comes to function almost as a crude barometer for the success of the *other* partner in having achieved authentic love versus entitlement/narcissism, true mutuality versus mutual transference distortions, and successful individuation versus "fusion" with a spouse. Sexual desire waxes and wanes with all of these as a component of the characteristic ambivalence toward the spouse that inevitably attends marital fusion instead of successful individuation, transference distortion instead of accurate knowing of the real person, and entitlement/narcissism instead of genuine caring love.

Whereas arousal and orgasm occur by reflex, conditioned or unconditioned, "desire" is a complex cerebral phenomenon more complicated than personality itself, because it involves 2 personalities, with all the complexities of their mature and immature (narcissistic) parts impinging on one another. It should therefore not have surprised us to discover, in the 1980s, the failure of brief behavioral sex therapy when used alone to deal with desire disorders. Currently there is general agreement that therapy for "inhibited sexual desire" problems must include and emphasize psychotherapy and couple therapy. Used in this broader context, behavioral sex therapy assignments can uncover and bring into focus previously shadowy feeling-problems.

The Need to Shift Gears in Treating Sexual Dysfunction

The following case history illustrates the need for combining sex therapy with psychotherapy.

The couple were in their thirties, married to each other for about 7 years. He was an engineer/junior executive and she an aspiring artist. There were 2 children, one theirs and an older one hers by a prior marriage. He complained of "impotence" or inability to achieve and maintain erections during lovemaking and she of inability to reach orgasm during lovemaking. After many months of largely unsuccessful self-prescription, they specifically requested help via professional sex therapy by a male-female cotherapy team.

Treatment went well, and within a few sessions both were enjoying the sensate focus exercises prescribed. He was experiencing full and sustained erections during these "pleasure sessions," and she, though considerably more aroused than before, still was not experiencing orgasm during the sessions. As treatment proceeded, more and more genital touching and caressing was "faded into" the prescriptions; the effects of these suggestions began to summate with those of the already intensely pleasurable sensate focus assignments.

After only a few sessions of the new genital prescriptions, the wife arrived presenting a dream: "Bernie and I were in our own bed . . . having a real good time . . . and I was getting really turned on. Both of you were there, too, standing at the foot of our bed, watching us. Both of you were smiling and urging us on, saying 'Go ahead, it feels really good, it's fun, you'll enjoy it,' and so on. I was getting more and more turned on and thinking maybe I was about to climax. But just then my bedroom door opened, and my mother came in. She stood at the foot of the bed beside you both, shaking her head sternly and saying, 'Don't have an orgasm—you'll get cancer!'"

In this behavioral treatment approach based on that of Masters and Johnson and more directly on that of Helen Kaplan, the therapists suddenly encountered a resistance to further therapeutic progress. This resistance involved an irrational but significant preconscious (previously unconscious) fear of punishment for the pleasure of orgasm and a fear-ridden attachment to and identification with a mother whose worldview stood in marked contrast, if not to the therapist's worldviews, then at least to their unified and thoroughly hedonistic therapeutic stance with this patient. This dream signaled that it was time to shift gears and work through previously unconscious resistance unexpectedly uncovered through the early change produced by behavioral sex therapy.

Taking time to deal in a nonbehavioral way with important phenomena of this kind does not necessitate abandoning the focused goals and methods of sex therapy. It does require that the therapist feel comfortable in temporarily suspending work as a *sex therapist* to work as a *psychotherapist* in helping one member of the couple resolve inner difficulties that impede sexual functioning. Though sometimes indicated, the diversion from sex therapy to scheduled individual psychotherapy sessions with one or both spouses is usually unproductive; a psychotherapeutic intervention should be brief enough to occupy only part of an hour, and, if conducted with both partners present, the "auditing" spouse learns more about the partner and his or her emotions than could ever be communicated through retrospective narration. Couple therapy interventions undertaken before the resolution of all sexual dysfunctions in both partners should ordinarily be limited to removing obstructions to further progress in the sex therapy. Otherwise the unresolved sexual problem may destroy the couple's relationship even while couple therapy continues.

Knowing when and how to shift during the therapeutic enterprise, which approach to change to, and when to shift back are crucial skills in sex therapy. Problems of sexual dysfunction are rarely if ever monochromatically sexual; most people have mixed problems that require judicious blending of couple therapy, psychotherapy with both partners present, and sex therapy. (Many also have undiagnosed medical problems contributing to their sexual symptoms.) Another crucial skill is knowing when *not* to yield to a resistance to the focused behavioral work of sex therapy—when a shift either to evaluating medical factors or to a psychotherapeutic mode would be an unnecessary and counterproductive diversion.

General Clinical Method

Sex therapy is a brief, focused therapy designed specifically for the treatment of sexual dysfunctions. It focuses on the immediate causes of sexual dysfunction (such as "monitoring," and inadequate or inappropriate stimulation) rather than on remote causes (such as oedipal conflict, repressive upbringing, rape, incest, unwanted pregnancies, or other traumatic sexual episodes from the past). It may require only 4–6 hours of treatment or as many as 50 hours if the resistances are exceptionally complex and tenacious; usually 15–30 hours are needed. Most modern sex therapists see couples for a series of weekly appointments rather than for a 2-week period of intensive treatment as originally practiced by Masters and Johnson. The meetings involve discussion and prescription of a series of graded experiences to be carried out by the couple in their own home with full privacy. To reduce complexity and expense, most sex therapists no longer routinely recommend male-female cotherapist teams except in exceptionally difficult and psychotherapeutically fragile situations.

Initial Evaluation

Typically the initial evaluation begins on the telephone when one member of the couple calls. Which one calls? Does the call come from the one with the more salient problem or from the one who has been agitating for treat-

ment? Is the person not calling really interested in treatment or only agreeing to "see somebody" under duress? How hard is it to schedule the first hour? (Many professional couples have such exacting schedules that when both finally arrive, they soon discover that an extremely high-pressure lifestyle has become a significant part of the problem. Because of intense ambition, learned avoidance of conflictual behaviors, or both, many of these couples have forged adaptations giving themselves little time or energy for easygoing pleasure, sexual or otherwise.) Are there any obvious potential medical causes or contributants to sexual dysfunction? Two examples are diabetes and drugs; many antihypertensive and all but a few antidepressant drugs are sexually problematic.

Does he sometimes have full erections (including morning erections), and can he through self-stimulation attain orgasm? Can she attain orgasm in this manner with full arousal and pleasure? If the answer to these questions is yes, the therapists can conclude that at least the primary causes for dysfunction are psychogenic.

During the first meeting the therapist needs to get an idea of each individual's personality, work, attitudes about fun and pleasure, family and religious background, education, sexual development, previous sexual history with other partners, and history of masturbation, both during adolescence and at present. A detailed history of each person's feeling about and practice of masturbation, from the earliest time to the present, is often crucial for later treatment. With many couples it may be wise to use the term *self-stimulation to orgasm* rather than *masturbation*. Medically prescribed self-stimulation is quite acceptable to some people to whom even the word *masturbation* is repugnant. Other individuals would object to this as an evasive euphemism; the therapist needs to use his best clinical judgment, subordinating semantics to the core need to reduce "resistance" to a minimum.

The therapist will find it helpful to spend at least 1 appointment with each member of the couple alone so as to learn of important issues each may be unwilling or embarrassed to discuss in the presence of the other. (Common topics for inhibition are fantasies about other sexual partners, details of experience with past sexual partners, fantasies that are uncomfortable, current masturbatory behavior, and reservations about the sexual appeal of a spouse. Less common, but obviously crucial when present, are homosexual urges or fantasies—or heterosexual attractions in treating homosexual couples—and actual current, usually secret, extramarital affairs.)

The therapist must also obtain an impression of the couple as an interacting dyadic system. The most crucial question is, *Do they like each other?* They may "love" each other, but this is not so crucial as simple, uncomplicated liking. Do they possess a sense of humor and perspective? (If so, the prognosis vastly improves.) How, when, and where did they meet, and what attracted them to each other? Does each person perceive these positive traits as still existing in the other? How did the relationship change when they moved in together and/or married and/or had children together?

How precisely are they interacting sexually now? What is their current baseline of sexual behavior with each other, and also alone, with masturbation? Who usually initiates lovemaking? How? What actually happens when they do make love? Who does what to add to or detract from the ambiance? Do they usually enjoy touching and caressing each other, or do they go at sex in a goal-oriented genital way? How do they each respond, at best and at worst, and also typically? Does either have a tendency to "spoil" romantic moods or to postpone lovemaking until a romantic, close, affectionate mood has passed or been transformed into impatience or a quarrel? Do they feel unfree about oral or even manual genital stimulation? Can both parties communicate honestly and fluently about what happens during lovemaking and what was felt?

What actually happens after lovemaking? Does one person have a need to punish the other after intercourse? (Examples of punishment are interrupting postcoital drowsiness or sleep or bringing up controversial subjects.

Frequently one partner apologizes for its not having been "good"—which punishes both parties—or reveals, in a guilt-inducing fashion, immediately after the fact, that he or she had a pain, a headache, or an upset stomach while they were having intercourse.) How frequently—or infrequently—does the couple make love? Is there a significant difference in desired frequency? How does their pattern of lovemaking now, in terms of frequency, tenderness, and pleasure, compare with their best experience earlier? Does one spouse use withholding sex as a form of leverage? As a punishment? As a substitute for effective self-assertion?

The Behavioral Core of Sex Therapy: Defining the Dysfunctions and Their Controlling Stimuli

What are the "target symptoms," the current dysfunctional responses that bring the couple for treatment? Do these occur consistently or only part of the time? If there are variations in degree, what factors influence this? Therapists find it helpful to think schematically in terms of a flowchart (Figure 23.1) and to employ precise behavioral terminology.

Discriminative stimuli, or S_D's, signal the availability of reinforcement for a particular emitted response and so set the stage for the occurrence of that response: thus a friendly look sets the stage for a "hello," just as a tone signal or a green light may set the stage for a bar-pressing

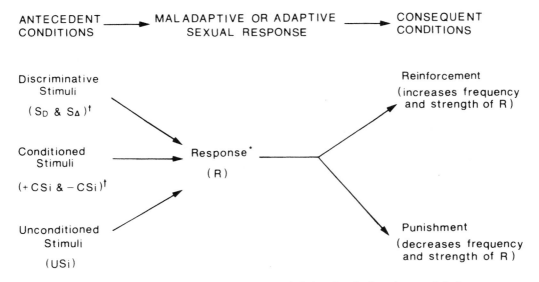

Figure 23.1 The behavioral core of sex therapy: defining the dysfunctions and their controlling stimuli. The response, for example, may be a "normal" sexual response, or sexual behavior but no erection (loss of erection with penetration), or sexual behavior but no lubrication and no vasocongestive orgasmic platform. With repetition, $S_D \rightarrow +CS_i$ and $S_\Delta \rightarrow -CS_i$.

response in a laboratory learning situation. In the sexual situation, warm conversation with eye contact and the sharing of feeling and affection serve as an effective S_D for the response of sexual arousal and pleasurable lovemaking. A host of other cues, such as candlelight, soft music, a clean shave, or a hint of perfume, can also contribute to a romantic ambiance as effective S_D's. With repetition, these S_D's actually become +CSi, or positive conditioned stimuli, so that even fragmentary exposure to these stimuli may elicit powerful sexual feeling and interest.

S_Δ's signal the *unavailability* of reinforcement and so set the stage not for a sexual response but for no response. Examples include television in the background, cigar smoke, hair curlers and face cream, unbrushed teeth, or other deficiencies in personal hygiene.

The basic technical stratagems in sex therapy utilize weekly behavioral prescriptions to implement a systematic and graded manipulation of the antecedent and consequent conditions, which, as shown in Figure 23.1, temporally bracket the dysfunctional sexual response. Because sensual and sexual stimulation are inherently strongly reinforcing, in manipulating consequent conditions the therapist's major role is simply to ensure that both partners do not find ways, usually unconscious, to self-sabotage and so undo the natural reinforcement inherent in sexual pleasure. The sex therapist must swiftly detect such sabotage and respond quickly with psychotherapeutic or couple-system interventions as ways to undo the undoing of natural pleasure and reinforcement.

Another legacy of both the behavioral and the Masters and Johnson traditions is the careful use of gradualism, especially via the use of stimulus hierarchies or stimulus fading. (See Figure 23.2 and the discussion of systematic desensitization in Chapter 22.) In sex therapy, stimulus fading is more effective than use of a stimulus "hierarchy," because most patients come to treatment already quite

sensitized to failure. Such patients tend to regard discrete "steps" as threatening but scarcely notice their own gradual, smooth progress via stimulus fading. By analogy, a person seated in a comfortable restaurant would be more disturbed if someone abruptly turned on one or more bright lights than if a rheostat mechanism gradually and continuously increased the light level. Optimally, at least, patients in treatment for sexual dysfunction have a parallel need to remain comfortable and to keep their attention on pleasure, not on "step 5."

Medical Assessment

Although psychologists and others can learn to treat psychogenic sexual dysfunction, only physicians—especially psychiatrists, internists, family practitioners, urologists, gynecologists, endocrinologists, and neurologists—possess the necessary medical training and experience to distinguish organic (or organic plus psychogenic) from purely psychogenic sexual dysfunction and to refer those cases with an organic component. Table 23.1 summarizes the medical conditions that may cause or contribute to sexual dysfunction.

The differential diagnosis involves first ruling out (or establishing) organic causes for the dysfunctional symptoms and then doing the same for organic contributants. In most cases a detailed and careful history is sufficient to rule out organic causes. If a careful history reveals a clear situation linkage—that is, if the dysfunctional symptoms are clearly stimulus bound, occurring only after certain antecedent conditions and not after others—one may safely conclude that the major cause of the dysfunction is psychogenic, not organic. Examples of situation linkages are a man's impotence with one partner and not with another, a woman's ability to achieve orgasm manually or orally but not during intercourse, or during intercourse

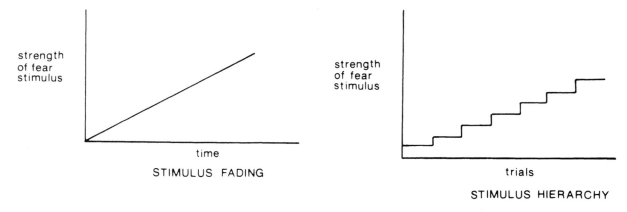

Figure 23.2 Stimulus fading and stimulus hierarchy.

with one partner and not with another, and either's ability to achieve fully successful masturbation under some circumstances but not under others. A history of normal morning erections, however, does not in itself rule out important or even crucial organic causes such as a heavy afternoon or evening intake of alcohol or other drugs, or a hormonal imbalance (Spark, White, and Connolly, 1980). Measurement of free and total serum testosterone and serum prolactin should therefore be done in every case of male arousal dysfunction and of both female and male desire dysfunction as well as in a number of other clinical situations.

The question of organic contributants must be approached even more cautiously. Again, only a careful history can help determine the need for laboratory testing and/or referral to an experienced specialist for consultation. Possible organic contributants are alcohol and drugs (including steroids) or antihypertensive therapy; diabetes, multiple sclerosis, and other neurologically or neuropathy-mediated causes; endocrine disorders, renal disease, and liver disease (see Table 23.1).

If there are both apparent psychogenic factors and important potential biogenic contributants, the diagnostic problem requires careful collaboration between the therapist and the consulting neurologist, endocrinologist, vascular studies specialist, gynecologist, or internist. One common diagnostic problem—"impotence" coexisting with diabetes—can be solved with unique efficiency through the use of the REM test, which can document that physiological processes subserving erection are intact. In this test, more accurately called evaluation of "nocturnal penile tumescence," or NPT, a strain gauge is used to detect, measure, and record the cycles of full erection, which in physically unimpaired males occur every 90 minutes during periods of REM sleep (see Karacan, 1978).

The experienced sex therapist should assume responsibility for the total case management of patients with mixed medical and psychogenic sexual problems or with mixed medical and psychiatric ones. Psychiatrists serving in this role and dealing with the impressive technical sophistication and expertise of specialized consultants must not lose sight of their responsibility for total case management. For example, when a patient is referred by an endocrinologist, urologist, or gynecologist as presumptively psychiatric, he often bears the message: "Dr. X did every possible medical study and said I was perfectly normal medically and so needed to see you." Usually the referring physician meant to convey only that he found no evidence of abnormality relating to his particular specialty. (For example, internists, endocrinologists, and even urologists

seldom perform appropriate vascular studies on patients they refer. The therapist must assume responsibility for ensuring that *all* plausible causes of a presenting sexual dysfunction are investigated by appropriate diagnostic testing and specialized consultation.)

"Simple" (Arousal/Orgasm) Dysfunctions and Specific Relearning Strategies

The 6 major dysfunctions can be classified (with reference to *The Diagnostic and Statistical Manual of Mental Disorders,* fourth edition, or DSM-IV) as either inhibitory (the male and female arousal and orgastic dysfunctions) or hyperexcitatory (premature ejaculation and vaginismus). Although each case must be approached on its own merits and with its own particular timetable and strategy, the following general principles of strategy are usually useful.

Arousal Dysfunctions: Male and Female (DSM-IV, 302.72)

Arousal dysfunctions in men take the form of "impotence," or inability to achieve an erection, and in women of "frigidity," or lack of lubrication or genital vasocongestion. A typical treatment strategy would include the following steps:

1. Proscribe intercourse and, if fear is great, also breast and genital caressing. This needs to be done to reduce performance anxiety and permit the full undistracted appreciation of sensual and sexual pleasure without monitoring, so that pleasure can function as a strong competitive response able to supplant anxiety, guilt, shame, or embarrassment.
2. Proscribe orgasm, both during early "sensate focus" exercises and during manual stimulation, to increase sexual drive.
3. Prescribe nondemand, nongenital caressing "sensate focus" exercises, using a pleasant greaseless lotion such as Keri Lotion or Curel. A good way to help many people break the ice and set a tone of fun, lightheartedness, and sensual pleasure is to ask them to begin by showering together. In bed, the partners then take turns "pleasuring" the other person, with one partner being the giver or receiver of pleasure throughout one full session. The "giver" is asked to begin with a "total body back rub," literally from head to toe, using creative variation in alternating light touch with deeper massage and very faint, fine touch, and so forth. Next follows a total "front

rub," but there should be no touching of breasts or genitals.

4. Use stimulus fading to include at first very brief, fleeting periods of breast touching, then genital touching, then gradually less fleeting but still nondemand caressing of breasts and genitals.

5. Instruct the couple to use "cycling" in their pleasuring sessions; that is, ask them to go through several cycles of switching from genital to nongenital touching and caressing, making the switch in order to let the erection (or, for women, the high arousal state) subside. This gives people direct experiential knowledge of their own and their partner's various phases of arousal. Also it clearly demonstrates that these arousal levels are stimulus-linked and are therefore not subject to mysterious and permanent disappearance.

6. Use stimulus fading to move to fleeting mutual geni-

tal contact, then partial containment, then fleeting full containment, then gradually longer periods of containment. Continue, however, to proscribe full, vigorous thrusting and to use cycling, but with brief containment at the high point. By ordinary semantic standards, intercourse of course occurs early in step 6. However, it is often useful in reducing performance fears to restructure ordinary semantics so that the word *intercourse* is reserved to mean full and prolonged penetration with vigorous, pleasurable thrusting by both partners, with orgasm for both. Using this kind of semantic restructuring, the therapist would begin desensitization to the word *intercourse* only after a couple had been enjoying it together for some time.

7. Fade in quiet, gentle motion during containment, but continue to proscribe full thrusting and to emphasize cycling.

Table 23.1 Outline of organic factors in sexual dysfunction

Major medical causes of sexual dysfunction, male and female	
Liver disease and renal disease	Decreased desire
Temporal lobe lesions (including temporal lobe epilepsy)	Decreased desire (or increased)
Diabetes	Arousal dysfunction
Endocrine disorders (e.g., hypothyroidism, hypopituitarism, Addison's disease, Cushing's disease)	Decreased desire and arousal dysfunction
Low back pain	Decreased desire and arousal dysfunction
Most chronic systemic diseases	Decreased desire and arousal dysfunction
Other organic factors, male dysfunctions	
Infectious mononucleosis	Decreased desire
Urethritis or prostatitis	Impotence, premature ejaculation
Local/psychological problems (e.g., phimosis, hypospadias, herpes simplex of penis)	Decreased desire, impotence
Mechanical/psychological problems (e.g., large inguinal hernia, or large hydrocele)	Impotence
Radical perineal prostatectomy	Impotence but desire normal
Abdominoperineal bowel resections	Impotence but desire normal
Abdominal aortic surgery	Ejaculatory disturbance
Lumbar sympathectomy	Ejaculatory disturbance
Some rhizotomies for pain relief	Impotence and ejaculatory disturbance
Castration	Loss of desire, impotence, and retarded ejaculation
Other organic factors, female dysfunctions	
Infectious mononucleosis	Decreased desire
Vulvitis and vaginitis; pelvic inflammatory disease, endometriosis; fibroids; ovarian cysts; uterine tumors; pelvic masses; Bartholin's cyst infection	Dyspareunia, with secondary decreased interest, arousal dysfunction, vaginismus
Painfully adherent clitoral hood; weak pubococcygeus muscles	Orgastic dysfunction
Poor episiotomy; obstetrical trauma; poor hysterectomy	Dyspareunia and impaired sexual response but normal desire
Oophorectomy plus adrenalectomy	Decreased desire

8. Fade in brief periods of mutual movement, still proscribing intercourse and emphasizing cycling.

9. Fade in spontaneous mutual movement during intercourse but stress that orgasm is not the goal. Continue to emphasize fading.

10. In the first session after nature has taken over, resulting in highly pleasurable lovemaking, share the couple's enthusiasm.

11. Continue to emphasize cycling to make sure that the couple has enough favorable experiences with lovemaking to dispel fears of "losing it."

12. Fade out the therapy.

Female Orgasmic Disorder (DSM-IV, 302.73)

If the woman has never experienced an orgasm under any circumstances, work with her first; if orgasm is inhibited only during intercourse, begin at step 6.

1. Teach self-stimulation (masturbation) with pleasure and without guilt in a "total body pleasure" fashion, with orgasm eventually as a by-product.

2. Prescribe Kegel exercises to strengthen the pubococcygeal muscles subserving the orgasm response.

3. Interrupt monitoring for orgasm with competitive responses: vivid fantasies, attention to sensual feelings, concentration on rhythmic breathing, breath-holding if necessary.

4. Instruct patient to contract her abdominal and perineal muscles voluntarily when sexual excitement levels are very high.

5. *If necessary only,* have the patient use a vibrator to achieve the first orgasm. It should be the type of vibrator that delivers the vibrating sensation by the fingertips, not by itself. (This facilitates later stimu-

Table 23.1 (continued)

Pharmacological factors	
Progesterone and estrogens (e.g., pregnancy, birth control pills)	Decreased desire
Alcohol and sedatives	Decreased sexual response, and decreased desire (high doses)
Narcotics (including methadone)	Orgasmic dysfunction
Antiandrogens (e.g., estrogens, ACTH, cortisone)	Decreased desire
Androgens (or high androgen/estrogen ratio)	Increased desire
Levodopa	Increased desire
Cocaine and amphetamines (acutely only)	Increased desire
Alcohol, sedatives, and minor tranquilizers (low doses only, and weakly only)	Increased desire
Antipsychotics	
Phenothiazines	Retrograde ejaculation
Thioridazine	Retarded ejaculation; also impotence and arousal dysfunctions
Fluphenazine (Prolixin)	Impotence
Haloperidol	Decreased desire, arousal and/or orgasmic dysfunctions
Antidepressants (MAOI and tricyclics)	Arousal and/or orgasmic dysfunctions
Lithium	Arousal and/or orgasmic dysfunctions
Anticholinergic drugs (e.g., Banthine, Probanthine, Atropine, Cogentin, Artaine, etc.)	Arousal dysfunctions
Antiadrenergic drugs (e.g., many antihypertensives, especially guanethidine; ergot alkaloids)	Orgastic dysfunctions
Mellaril (Thioridazine)	Frequently causes retarded ejaculation
Index of suspicion for organic factors, ranked highest to lowest	
Retrograde ejaculation	
Loss of desire	
Impotence	
Premature ejaculation	(If recent and acute, rule out infection)
Ejaculatory incompetence	Rule out psychotropic medications
Female arousal dysfunctions	Rule out psychotropic medications

Source: L. Birk, Shifting gears in treating psychogenic sexual dysfunction: medical assessment, sex therapy, psychotherapy, and couple therapy, *Psychiatr. Clin. North Am.,* 3 (1980), table 1, pp. 162–163.

lus generalization away from vibrator with fingertips to fingertips alone.)

6. After the patient has become able to achieve orgasm reliably via masturbation, fade in her partner (or, if necessary, partner plus vibrator) as the primary source of genital stimulation in masturbation to orgasm. In order to reduce the patient's perfectionistic "performance" worries and pressures, instruct the couple to have intercourse, with orgasm for him, before he stimulates her.

7. Fade in penetration by the partner while continuing stimulation to orgasm by the partner.

8. Eventually, the patient should have one experience of being brought very near orgasm by her partner's manual stimulation of her, then of experiencing orgasm just after penetration.

9. Repeat this experience periodically, gradually fading in more and more penetration/containment time during lovemaking. If necessary use "bridging" manual stimulation during the penetration experience.

10. Educate that it is pleasurable and good to reach orgasm in a *variety* of ways, only one of which is during vaginal containment.

Male Orgasmic Disorder (DSM-IV, 302.74)

1. Instruct (or if necessary teach) the patient to masturbate to orgasm.

2. Prescribe masturbation by the patient at home, with his partner in the house but not in his immediate presence.

3. Fade in the physical presence of the partner, first in the bedroom not looking, then looking, then closer, then next to, then touching bodies but not looking, then touching bodies and looking.

4. Fade in the partner as a participant in manual penile stimulation; at first the patient does nearly all the stimulation himself; then his partner stimulates him at the point of ejaculatory inevitability.

5. Fade in a more and more important role for the partner in the manual stimulation; finally she will be able to provide all the stimulation.

6. Fade in intercourse, using ejaculatory inevitability to achieve first intravaginal orgasm.

Premature Ejaculation (DSM-IV, 302.75)

This extremely common dysfunction, experienced by 20–30% of all men at some time, can usually be treated briefly and easily. The therapist must *not* prescribe anesthetic creams or other well-known folk strategies aimed at blocking or distracting the man's attention from erotic feelings. Inattention is in fact an important root cause of this dysfunction; typically the patient is situationally or chronically unable to attend to or observe sufficiently his own erotic feelings to permit the appropriate pacing of incoming sensory input, with the result that he quickly reaches the stage of ejaculatory inevitability. At this point he abruptly becomes aware of a flood of erotic feelings, but his awareness comes too late for him to avoid ejaculation. Treatment usually follows this general scheme:

1. The patient is instructed to give his partner an orgasm after the sessions, ordinarily manually or orally, and the partner is instructed to take charge of his therapy.

2. The partner is asked to stimulate the patient manually through 4 full cycles, during which the patient is to *concentrate his attention on his erotic feelings,* then signal her to stop stimulation when he is near ejaculatory inevitability. In very severe cases it may be necessary to use the "squeeze technique," originally described by Semans, grasping the penis between the thumb and forefinger and administering a firm and fairly prolonged squeeze, until excitement and the sense of being near ejaculatory inevitability fade.

3. The partner repeats step 2 on 2 or 3 occasions, each time with 4 full cycles, now using a lubricant such as Keri Lotion.

4. Repeat step 2 with the partner still in charge but using containment instead of manual stimulation to stimulate the patient. (Use the female-superior position only if that "works" historically and empirically; that position can sometimes be counterproductive.)

5. Fade in gentle movement by the patient, then gentle thrusting by him, before orgasm is allowed to occur.

6. If relevant, prescribe gentle, slow intercourse in male-superior position.

7. Fade in more spontaneous movement by the patient during intercourse.

Vaginismus (DSM-IV, 306.51)

1. Prescribe Kegel exercises to help the patient learn how to contract and relax perivaginal muscles voluntarily.

2. Prescribe extensive Kegel exercises to point of muscle fatigue *immediately before* containment experiences.

3. If patient has an intact arousal/orgasm response, prescribe self-stimulation to arousal followed by minimally threatening containment experience, such as only the tip of one of her own fingers. If the arousal/orgasm response is not intact, teach and prescribe

progressive relaxation as a competitive response to inhibit the anxiety of the penetration/containment experiences, rather than using sexual arousal as a competitive response.

4. Fade in more substantial containment experiences with gradually larger objects.
5. Prescribe sensate focus exercises with the partner, gradually fading in genital stimulation by him.
6. Prescribe vaginal containment experiences with one or more fingers, in which the partner is first merely present in the house, then in the room, then participates more and more, finally using his fingers rather than hers.
7. Prescribe partial, then complete penile penetration with *quiet* containment.
8. Fade in very gentle motion during containment; gradually increase level of movement.
9. Fade in spontaneous movement during containment.

Treatment protocols such as these are useful as general guides, particularly for learners; but they should never be used as a substitute for a methodical case analysis or for careful thinking about each individual case. At times a thoughtful behavioral/psychodynamic/systems review of an individual case will dictate the use of a wholly different treatment approach.

Other "Simple" (Arousal/Orgasm) Dysfunctions

In addition to the 6 major psychogenic dysfunctions, there are 2 other fairly common dysfunctions:

1. Functional dyspareunia (DSM-IV, 306.76). This is "recurrent or persistent genital pain in either a male or a female, occurring before, during, or after sexual intercourse," with the pain presumed to be psychogenic in origin. A particularly heavy burden of reasonable proof, excluding possible "biogenic" sources for the pain, rests with any clinician who would make this diagnosis.
2. Premature and less than fully satisfying orgasm in women. This is analogous to premature ejaculation in men; it is much more common than generally realized. (In fact, it is probably more common than vaginismus.)

Other, less common learned or "psychogenic" dysfunctions, also treatable, with enough ingenuity and skill, include:

1. Intercourse-dependent orgastic dysfunction (that is, orgasm possible *only* with intercourse, not with manual or oral stimulation).

2. Partial ejaculatory incompetence, with "seepage" secondary to intact emission (the first phase of male orgasm) but blocked ejaculation.
3. Genital psychoanesthesia.
4. Ejaculation without orgasm.
5. Functional dyspareunia.

Of these other dysfunctions, only functional dyspareunia has its own number code in DSM-IV. The others are grouped together as "sexual dysfunction NOS" (DSM-IV, 302.70). All are treatable via appropriately designed sex therapy. By contrast, retrograde ejaculation does not call for sex therapy. If it is postsurgical, it is generally untreatable; if it occurs as a result of the use of phenothiazine or certain antihypertensive drugs, it can be addressed by discontinuing these drugs and using alternative nonproblematic medications.

Desire Dysfunctions

Desire dysfunctions, originally described and later discussed by Lief (1977, 1985), are not only psychologically complex; they may also have a large neurobiological component. Schreiner-Engel and Schiavi (1986), for example, have published data showing that people with desire disorders show a much-increased lifetime prevalence rate of depressive disorder. In early research, Lief (1986) reported that bupropion may be effective in ameliorating low desire.

What Is Behavioral about Therapy for Hypoactive Desire?

The behavioral prescriptions for producing direct and rapid behavior change in the arousal/orgasm dysfunctions are used almost adjunctively in patients with hypoactive sexual desire as a way to facilitate psychotherapy, which must be the major avenue for change. In desire dysfunctions, the prescriptions are generally *not* important because they produce direct and therapeutic change in the target behavior, sexual desire.

Instead, the "behavioral" prescriptions—behavioral because they are therapist requests to engage in certain sexual behaviors—have their effect nonbehaviorally, by way of new insight: the attempt to carry out these prescriptions and the subsequent analysis of "what went wrong" are often useful in bringing to light and into sharp focus feeling-problems that previously had been shadowy and amorphous at best. The life experience of trying to carry out the sexual prescriptions assists people in recognizing that they have been routinely "turning themselves off" in order to avoid sexual arousal because they wish to avoid it with that person, whether out of transference, unworked-through hostility, or a loss of respect for the partner. Psychotherapy or couple therapy, used as the major avenue of treatment, helps to ferret out—and sometimes to correct—the underlying reason(s) for the patient's unconscious blocking of desire. When successful, this hybrid approach can sometimes restore a person's capacity to enjoy sexual desire and fulfillment with his or her valued mate. Thus desire disorders require both psychotherapy (couple and individual) and sex therapy; when success is achieved, it is rarely in fewer than 100 treatment hours, versus 15–30 hours for most other sex therapy cases. Treatment tends to last a year or more, in contrast to 3 or 4 months for arousal/orgasmic dysfunctions.

Hypoactive Sexual Desire Disorder (DSM-IV, 302.71)

All clinicians dealing with hypoactive sexual desire must look very carefully for symptoms of depression, for biogenic factors such as undiagnosed major medical illness, and for use of medications that block desire: not just steroids, estrogen, and progesterone but also sedatives, benzodiazepines, and (especially) alcohol.

Sexual Aversion Disorder (DSM-IV, 302.79)

A much less common dysfunction involves not just simple lack of desire but "persistent or recurrent extreme *aversion* to and avoidance of all or almost all genital contact with a sexual partner" (emphasis added). The clinician must avoid confusing this disorder with the more common, and at least somewhat less prognostically bleak, problem of hypoactive sexual drive disorder.

Nonbehavioral Ingredients in Sex Therapy

Even without shifting to couple therapy or psychotherapy, sex therapists achieve results in a number of important ways. Among them are:

Education. Many men and some women are unaware of the crucial role of clitoral stimulation in the female sexual response. Many women do not know that men experience a refractory period after an orgasm. Many men and women, and an uncomfortable number of doctors, believe that one overcomes premature ejaculation by directing attention away from the erotic aspects of intercourse.

Modeling. The therapist provides an example for patients, not only for free unembarrassed discussion of sex

but also in establishing an attitude toward sex of unconflicted pleasure, lightheartedness, and fun.

Being the doctor in charge. Patients often enter sex therapy discouraged and self-traumatized by dashed efforts at self-prescription. This often occurs in physicians and psychotherapists who need sex therapy, paralleling what may happen in almost every other sphere of medicine. Patients who come blaming each other are difficult, but those who come blaming themselves, not only for bad sex and/or a bad relationship but also for self-treatment that has not worked, are particularly unfortunate. With rare exceptions, couples need a doctor, a therapist who will assess, rule out organic causes or contributants, formulate a treatment strategy, prescribe, troubleshoot and modify prescriptions, and take the blame when something goes wrong.

Proscribing feared responses, such as intercourse and breast or genital stimulation during the initial phases of treatment.

Mobilizing hope. Some couples come for treatment after 2 or more decades of frustration with partial dysfunction. The therapist, armed with specific technical knowledge and favorable experience treating other couples, needs to be confident, active, and direct in helping the couple realize they can change if they will use the therapy being offered.

Promoting prompt, accurate, nonpunitive feedback. People often need help in learning the vast superiority of positive feedback (reinforcing "what goes right" by breathing, sighs, and body movements indicating pleasure) versus negative feedback (instant critique and analysis of what is not quite right).

Providing a neutral perspective of both partners as individuals and as a couple.

Effectiveness

More complete outcome data are available for most forms of sex therapy than for most other areas of psychotherapy. The following list briefly summarizes outcome data (Heiman, LoPiccolo, and LoPiccolo, 1981, pp. 620–621; see also Arentewicz and Schmidt, 1983) for each major type of dysfunction in order of success:

Premature ejaculation and vaginismus: 90–95% success.

Absolute female orgasmic dysfunction (no orgasm ever): 85–95% success if orgasm with partner is criterion, but only 30–50% if orgasm during intercourse is criterion.

Partial female orgasmic dysfunction (patient seldom orgastic or orgasmic only with solo masturbation): 70–80% success, but only 30–50% if criterion is orgasm during intercourse.

Secondary erectile dysfunction (patient has had erections in past): 60–80% success.

Primary erectile dysfunction (no erections ever in sexual situations): 40–60% success.

Retarded or blocked ejaculation: 50–82% success.

Low or inhibited sexual desire: no reliable outcome studies of sex therapy; sporadic successes at best after much longer therapies.

Indications for Sex Therapy

Sex therapy is generally both effective and highly efficient for psychogenic dysfunctions unless complicating factors exist, such as the coexistence of an important relationship problem, a previously unsuspected problematic sexual preference in terms of homosexual/heterosexual arousal patterns, or a blocking internal problem, such as severe depression, in one or both partners. Sex therapy may or may not be indicated, depending on the outcome of a behavioral/psychodynamic/systems analysis of the particular case. In such cases the treatment tends to be as good or as poor as the treatment for the other problems, whether with psychotherapy, couple therapy, or both. If a couple like each other, love each other, and generally get along and communicate reasonably well, and one or both suffer from a "simple" sexual dysfunction or a compound sexual dysfunction (such as inhibited arousal or inhibited orgasm), sex therapy is indicated and ordinarily should succeed in resolving the presenting problems. In view of the checkered results of psychoanalysis and psychoanalytic psychotherapy, sex therapy should be initiated first, without subjecting the patient to the frustrations of a "trial" of individual psychotherapy, group therapy, or psychoanalysis. What is often at risk from initially ineffective treatment is nothing less than the painful, unnecessary demise of a highly valued relationship. Even when the relationship itself survives the inappropriate postponement of direct treatment, the very postponement typically makes later specific treatment with sex therapy longer and more difficult. Many patients, for different reasons, may profit from *both* psychoanalysis *and* sex therapy, *but one form of therapy cannot substitute for the other.*

Desire dysfunctions are more difficult and take longer to treat; they also carry a more precarious prognosis and generally require psychotherapy and couple therapy in addition. This leads to large differences in the length of treatment. For most uncomplicated arousal or orgasm dysfunctions, 5–25 hours of treatment should suffice, whereas desire dysfunctions are rarely treatable in less than 50–100 hours. (Time is usually needed for the 2 partners separately as well as for regular conjoint meetings.) Also, treatment tends to last a year or more versus an average duration of 3–4 months for "simple" dysfunctions.

Patients with relationship problems *and* sexual dysfunction problems are difficult to generalize about. In some cases, adding sex therapy to couple therapy or individual psychotherapy may be undesirable or contraindicated. In other cases, combining these therapies may not only help patients directly to sexual gains but may also facilitate the patient's work in psychotherapy or psychoanalysis.

Contraindications for Sex Therapy

"Sex therapy" is sometimes requested as a means of bullying a marriage partner into sexual compliance. At other times, as is often true for hypnotherapy and for other kinds of behavior therapy, people may urgently request or demand sex therapy as a way of avoiding other underlying or intertwined problems. No substitute exists for the alert clinician who can use his eyes and ears and his common sense to think his way through the multiple issues. A few general truisms may, however, be offered to help in this process. First, the clinician must keep in mind that *a request for sex therapy is not an indication for sex therapy;* unusual pressure about such a request should raise one's suspicion that sex therapy may in fact be contraindicated. Second, the therapist must guard against being used unwittingly as an accomplice in the manipulation or domination of one partner by the other. Sex therapy, no matter how urgently demanded, must never be used to ride roughshod over ethics, relationships, common sense, or the full free choice of either of the 2 individuals involved.

Avenues for Improvement

Psychiatrists, and all psychotherapists, must learn more about sexual dysfunction and be more attuned when referring people with sexual problems; some patients may be treated intensively for years with other forms of therapy for problems that could be resolved quickly with sex therapy (Simpson, 1985). Sex therapists need to learn more about when and how to broaden their efforts to other modalities, and when not to do so.

Most important, sex therapy should be used with more flexibility. It should be used together with medical assessment and treatment when needed, for mixed "biogenic"/"psychogenic" cases, and when practical it should be used together with couple therapy and psychotherapy in the treatment of couples who present with significant couple problems and sexual dysfunction. For this to happen, psychiatrists need to become good medical diagnosticians and good case managers as well as broadly trained and experienced therapists who know how, when, and when not to "shift gears" in approaching couples with problems of sexual dysfunction.

Couple and Sex Therapy: Need for Integration

Couple therapy and sex therapy are both important branches of psychotherapy; indeed, one cannot do well at either without well-honed general psychotherapy skills. But beyond this, the 2 fields are also intimately related and intertwined branches of psychotherapy. Both may involve seeing and working with unhappy couples together, couples with sexual symptoms and relationship symptoms.

Many times the couples seen by couple therapists and the couples seen by sex therapists are—or could be—the very same couples! Marital turbulence can spawn sexual dysfunction, and sexual dysfunction can exacerbate marital conflict, and both may occur in the same couple. Although historically couple therapy has roots in the family therapy movement, and sex therapy is a form of behavior therapy, clinicians must recognize that troubled couples need skilled psychotherapists trained and experienced in thoughtfully integrated "couple and sex therapy," not in "couple therapy" or "sex therapy."

What's New and Important in Sex Therapy?

Naturally, this is a question that can be answered only by adopting a broad editorial overview in an attempt to select a few of the salient and most important new developments.

First, sex therapy has become "medicalized" (Lief, personal communication, 1996). This is particularly true for the treatment of erectile dysfunction. The pendulum has swung very far indeed from the important 1980 paper by endocrinologist Richard Spark and colleagues, "Impotence Is Not Always Psychogenic." The time is now ripe for a mirror-image companion paper, "Impotence Is Not Always Medical," making the point that impotence is not always or even usually best treated by purely medical interventions.

Obviously, with or without psychogenic factors, testosterone deficiency needs to be considered, looked for, diagnosed, and treated, if fully pleasurable sexual function is to be restored. Similarly, if there is a vascular deficit or a neurological deficit or both, or an abnormality impairing the competence of the valvular system of the corpora cavernosa, these problems must be effectively identified and either treated medically or "bypassed" via such treatment stratagems such as those involving the use of penile vacuum pumps (Bosshardt et al., 1995), intracavernosal injections (Levitt and Mulcahy, 1995), or penile implants (Subrini, 1994). Implants may be of the "pump" variety or may employ flexible semi-rigid implants.

Our colleagues in urology have been pragmatic, ingenious, and skilled in devising, developing, and refining surgical and other physical interventions which have rendered treatable many people who would otherwise have been untreatable. All of us in the field, and especially the many previously untreatable people they have helped, owe them a debt of gratitude for their significant contributions, but with them we need to be vigilant in ensuring that these medical-mechanical solutions are not employed unnecessarily.

Thus we in psychiatry who are actively practicing sex therapy need to become *even more competent diagnostically, both medically and psychiatrically,* to ensure that patients who could have been fully and effectively treated by the relearning techniques of sex therapy not be unnecessarily treated with medical or surgical procedures which are intrinsically invasive, and which in the sexual lives of people are much less than fully optimal, especially in comparison to the outcomes that can be achieved with patients whose real problems are both psychogenic and amenable to the relearning procedures inherent in "traditional" sex therapy. It would be a miscarriage of the good practice of medicine and psychiatry if, through inattention or ignorance, we as psychiatrists were to contribute to any false, unnecessary "medicalization" of the problems of people whose dysfunctions are learned problems maintained through a vicious cycle of performance anxiety and pleasure and erection monitoring. Such patients should be *positively diagnosed psychiatrically,* not just run blindly through a series of medically negative tests, *and should be treated behaviorally, not medically,* by the sex therapy relearning techniques outlined in this chapter.

Second, *there needs to be an increased emphasis on using sex therapy adjunctively to help patients who do have sexual problems that are in part due to a very real medical problem.* There are a host of medical disorders such as diabetes, multiple sclerosis, vascular insufficiency, or noncompetence of the valvular system of the corpora cavernosa (the intactness of which is necessary for full arousal to occur), and it is crucially important for us to bear in mind that in many (if not most) such cases people are also highly likely to have performance anxiety superimposed on their particular medically and physiologically based dysfunctions. These people are worried, anxious, and attempting to muddle through because they *know* they have a real problem, and they are anxious to see just how good/bad their sexual function actually is. Without treatment aimed specifically at this performance anxiety dynamic, they tend to do much worse than they would strictly because of the limitations imposed by their organic problems. Their sexual function without adjunctive sex therapy is much worse, and the level of sexual pleasure available to them in their lives is often catastrophically worse.

In fact, many of the sensual, pleasure-enhancing, and anxiety-reducing techniques of sex therapy may be employed with benefit and increased physical pleasure even when there are extremely glaring physical abnormalities and organic limitations, such as in spinal cord injuries.

Third, *changes are coming because of the advent of the SSRIs* (selective serotonin-reuptake inhibitors). The great popularity of fluoxetine, sertraline, paroxetine, and fluoxamine as antidepressants has led to the fact that we are now encountering a new and very common cause for multiple kinds of sexual dysfunctions in both males and females. The incidence of desire, arousal, and orgasm problems, especially if one appropriately includes relatively mild cases not leading to *absolute* dysfunction, is very high indeed.

Looked at searchingly, the incidence of sexual dysfunction is *much* higher than is reported in the *Physician's Desk Reference:* the manufacturers of fluoxetine, whose introduction marked the dawn of the age of the SSRIs listed the frequency of ejaculatory problems in patients, taking it to be "less than 2%." Shockingly, however, Patterson (1991), after carefully interviewing 60 male patients on fluoxetine, found that fully 75% experienced a significant delay in attaining orgasm.

The *actual* reported evidence of sexual side effects needs to be borne in mind when we are choosing antidepressants for our patients.

Agent	Percentage of Patients with Sexual Side Effects
imipramine	30%
phenelzine	40%
fluoxetine	75%
sertraline	16%
paroxetine	13%

This principle is further highlighted by the fact that there are now effective antidepressants with an incidence of sexual side effects which approaches zero. Buproprion is a long-established and effective drug; it is not an SSRI, but it is an appropriate first-line drug. Other drugs without sexual side effects also now exist: nefazadone, for one, and perhaps also mirtazepine.

So we need to be alert to and actively on the lookout for the new importance of antidepressant drugs as a significant factor in causing sexual dysfunction. With the tricyclics, people did not usually stay on high doses once the acute, severe symptoms of depression had abated, mostly because their anticholinergic side effects could not be overlooked. Unlike sexual side effects, these are punishing side effects which are continuous, not sporadic. The SSRIs, by contrast, with their vaunted very low anticholinergic profile, their once-daily dosage, and their current cultural popularization, have for many become almost a long-term way of life.

When possible, I believe it is optimal to prescribe bupropion or some other drug which is also predictably very much less sexually problematic. When use of an SSRI does seem to be clinically vital, one can usually still choose one of the SSRIs which has a much lower incidence of sexual side effects than the 75% reported by Patterson (1991) for fluoxetine. (At the other end of the spectrum, one finds clomipramine, used primarily in depression with obsessive-compulsive disorder; for it, the reported incidence of sexual side effects, even in the *Physician's Desk Reference,* is 96%!)

When in those rather unusual instances in which a problematic SSRI must be used, there are a couple of treatment possibilities to counteract and minimize sexual side effect problems:

1. Using an adrenergic antidepressant, such as bupropion 100mg b.i.d., late in the day, together with the SSRI (Labbate and Pollack, 1994).
2. Co-administration of a stimulant, such as pemoline, 18–75 mg once daily.
3. The use of carefully timed specific antagonists to sexual side effects, such as cyproheptadine. These agents, however, act to "undo" temporarily the basic therapeutic (antidepressant) action for which the drug was prescribed. Furthermore, such antagonist strategies at best create only a highly temporary (and necessarily *very* carefully timed) window of physiological opportunity for lovemaking. Such strategies appear to be the worst of all the options. In dealing with a phenomenon normally so spontaneously and serendipitously expressive, and so important for mated bonding with true emotional intimacy, the disadvantage of having to be chained to such meticulous planning ahead is an overwhelmingly important one. (And, more prosaically, in many cases an effective

dysfunction-relieving dose of cyproheptadine is likely to cause extreme drowsiness, and even involuntary sleep, before lovemaking can occur!)

The review paper by Seagraves (1995) is an excellent resource for more detailed information on the subject of antidepressants and sexual dysfunctions.

Fourth, *the female androgen deficiency syndrome, described by Kaplan and Owett (1993), is one of the most important advances in sex therapy during the last 20 years.* Their work, representing 5 years of clinical study of the sexual complaints and behaviors of 11 women with documented androgen deficiency states, served to confirm observations and conclusions originally made much earlier, by Waxenberg (1959, 1960). Waxenberg posited that loss of androgens (testosterone) in women was associated with a marked decrease in desire; further, he predicted that exogenous testosterone should restore libido in androgen-deficient women.

The work of Shervin (1985), who first reported empirically that exogenous testosterone does indeed enhance sexual desire in such women, also supported Waxenberg's hypotheses. The idea finally became clinically popular in 1993 with the publication of Kaplan and Owett's paper.

These are landmark advances. They make it clear that one of the final common pathways for desire dysfunction in some women is androgen deficiency. They fail to tell us whether chronic hostility toward a husband or other emotional factors can cause abnormally low testosterone levels.

These important findings are stimulating new inquiry and research. Now that we have a toehold in understanding (female) sexual desire problems, we may by the time of the fourth edition of this volume find desire dysfunctions in general to be less puzzling, and less notoriously difficult to treat.

References

Arentewicz, G., and G. Schmidt. 1983. *The treatment of sexual disorders.* New York: Basic Books.

Balon, R. 1995. Fluoxetine and sexual dysfunction. *JAMA* 273(19):216.

Bartlik, B., P. Kaplan, and H. Kaplan. 1995. Psychostimulants apparently reverse sexual dysfunction secondary to selective serotonin re-uptake inhibitors. *J. Sex Marital Ther.* 21(4):264–271.

Birk, L. 1974. Intensive group therapy: an effective behavioral-psychoanalytic method. *Am. J. Psychiatry* 131:1, 11–16.

———— 1982. Psychotherapy within social systems. In *Psychoanalysis: critical explorations in contemporary theory and practice,* ed. A. Jacobson and D. Parmalee. New York: Brunner/Mazel.

———— 1984. Combined concurrent/conjoint psychotherapy for couples: rationale and efficient new strategies. In *Marriage and divorce,* ed. C. C. Nadelson and D. L. Polansky. New York: Guilford.

———— 1992. Behavioral/psychoanalytic psychotherapy with overlapping social systems: a natural matrix for diagnosis and therapeutic change. *Integrative psychotherapy.*

Birk, L., S. Stolz, J. P. Brady, J. V. Brady, A. Lazarus, J. Lynch, A. Rosenthal, W. D. Skelton, J. Stevens, and E. Thomas. 1973. *Behavior therapy in psychiatry.* Washington, D.C.: American Psychiatric Association.

Bosshardt, R. J., R. Farwerk, R. Sikora, M. Sohn, and G. Jakse. 1995. Objective measurement of the effectiveness, therapeutic success and dynamic mechanisms of the vacuum device. *Br. J. Urol.* 75(6):786–791.

Crowe, M., and M. Jones. 1992. Sex therapy: the successes, the failures, the future. *Br. J. Hosp. Med.* 48(8):474–479, 482.

Donahey, K., and R. Carroll. Gender differences in factors associated with hypoactive sexual desire. *J. Sex Marital Ther.* 19(1):25–40.

Frank, E., C. Anderson, and D. Rubenstein. 1978. Frequency of sexual dysfunction in "normal" couples. *N. Engl. J. Med.* 299:111–115.

Grunebaum, H. 1985. Inside the group. In *Casebook of marital therapy,* ed. A. S. Gurman. New York: Guilford.

Grunebaum, H., and J. Crist. 1968. Interpretation and the task of the therapist with couples and families. *Int. J. Group Psychother.* 18:495–503.

Grunebaum, H., J. Crist, and N. Neiberg. 1969. Diagnosis and treatment planning for couples. *Int. J. Group Psychother.* 19:185–202.

Guttmacher, J., and L. Birk. 1971. Group therapy: what specific therapeutic advantages? *Compr. Psychiatry* 12:546–556.

Heiman, J. R., L. LoPiccolo, and J. LoPiccolo. 1981. The treatment of sexual dysfunction. In *Handbook of family therapy,* ed. A. L. Gurman and D. P. Kniskern. New York: Brunner/Mazel.

Hersen, M., and T. R. Ammerman, eds. 1994. *Prescriptive therapies, handbooks of prescriptive treatment for adults.* New York: Plenum.

Holzapfel, S. 1993. Sexual medicine in family practice, pt. 2, Treating sexual dysfunction. *Canadian Family Physician* 39:618–624.

Kaplan, H. S. 1974. *The new sex therapy: active treatment of sexual dysfunctions.* New York: Brunner/Mazel.

————1979. *Disorders of sexual desire*. New York: Simon & Schuster.

————1983. *The evaluation of sexual disorders: psychological and medical aspects*. New York: Brunner/Mazel.

Kaplan, H. S., and T. Owett. 1993. The female androgen deficiency syndrome. *J. Sex Marital Ther.* 19(1, spring):3–24.

Karacan, I. 1978. Advances in the psychophysiological evaluation of male erectile impotence. In *Handbook of sex therapy*, ed. J. LoPiccolo and L. LoPiccolo. New York: Plenum.

Kayigil, O., O. Ataham, and A. Metin. 1996. Electrical activity of the corpus cavernosum in patients with corporal veno-occlusive dysfunction. *Br. J. Urol.* 77:261–265.

Kinsey, A. C., W. B. Pomeroy, and C. E. Martin. 1948. *Sexual behavior in the human male*. Philadelphia: Saunders.

Kinsey, A. C., W. B. Pomeroy, C. E. Martin, and P. H. Gebhard. 1953. *Sexual behavior in the human female*. Philadelphia: Saunders.

La Pera, G., and A. Nicastro. 1996. A new treatment for premature ejaculation: the rehabilitation of the pelvic floor. *J. Sex Marital Ther.* 22(1, spring):22–26.

Leiblum, S. R., and L. A. Pervin, eds. 1980. *Principles and practice of sex therapy*. New York: Guilford Press.

Leiblum, S., and R. Rosen. 1991. *Sexual Desire Disorders*. New York: Guilford.

Levitt, E. E., and J. Mulcahy. 1995. The effect of intracavernosal injection of paperverine hydrochloride on orgasm latency. *J. Sex Marital Ther.* 21(1, spring):39–41.

Lief, H. I. 1977. What's new in sex research? Inhibited sexual desire. *Med. Asp. Hum. Sexuality* 2:94–95.

———— 1985. Evaluation of inhibited sexual desire: relationship aspects. In *A comprehensive evaluation of disorders of sexual desire*, ed. H. S. Kaplan. Washington, D.C.: American Psychiatric Press.

———— 1986. Sex and depression. *Med. Asp. Hum. Sexuality* 20:38–53.

LoPiccolo, J., and L. LoPiccolo, eds. 1978. *Handbook of sex therapy*. New York: Plenum.

Masters, W. H., and V. E. Johnson. 1966. *Human sexual response*. Boston: Little, Brown.

———— 1970. *Human sexual inadequacy*. Boston: Little, Brown.

———— 1979. *Homosexuality in perspective*. Boston: Little, Brown.

Murray, F. T., M. Geisser, and T. C. Murphy. 1995. Evaluation and treatment of erectile dysfunction. *Am. J. Med. Sci.* 309(2):99–109.

O'Keefe, M., and D. K. Hunt. 1995. Assessment and treatment of impotence. *Med. Clin. North Am.* 79(2, March):415–434.

Patterson, W. M. 1991. Fluoxetine-associated orgasm dysfunction. *J. Clin. Psychiatry* 52:66–68.

Rosen, R. C., and A. K. Ashton. 1993. Prosexual drugs: empirical status of the "new aphrodisiacs." *Arch. Sex. Behav.* 22(6):521–543.

Rosen, R. C., and G. Beck. 1988. *Patterns of Sexual Arousal*. New York: Guilford.

Rosen, R. C., and S. R. Leiblum. 1995a. Treatment of sexual disorders in the 1990s: an integrated approach. *J. Consult. Clin. Psychol.* 63(6):877–890.

———— 1995b. *Case studies in Sex Therapy*. 3rd ed. New York: Guilford.

Rosen, R. C., S. R. Leiblum, and I. P. Spector. 1994. Psychologically based treatment for male erectile disorder: a cognitive-interpersonal model. *J. Sex Marital Ther.* 20(2, Summer):67–85.

Rowland, D. L., and A. K. Shob. 1995. Understanding and diagnosing sexual dysfunction: recent progress through psychophysiological and psychophysical methods. *Neurosci. Biobehav. Rev.* 19(2):201–209.

Schreiner-Engel, P., and R. C. Schiavi. 1986. Lifetime psychopathology in individuals with low sexual desire. *J. Nerv. Ment. Dis.* 174:646–651.

Segraves, R. T. 1995. Antidepressant-induced orgasm disorder. *J. Sex Marital Ther.* 21(3, Fall):192–201.

Shapiro, D., and L. Birk. 1967. Group therapy in experimental perspective. *Int. J. Group Psychother.* 17:211–224.

Simpson, W. 1985. Psychoanalysis and sex therapy: a case report. *Bull. Menninger Clin.* 49:565–582.

Spark, R. E., A. R. White, and P. B. Connolly. 1980. Impotence is not always psychogenic: newer insights into hypothalamic-pituitary-gonadal dysfunction. *JAMA* 243:750–755.

Subrini, L. 1994. Flexible penile implants: an experience over 60 cures. *Annales de Chirurgie Plastique et Esthetique* 39(1):15–26.

Wolpe, J. 1958. *Psychotherapy by reciprocal inhibition*. Stanford: Stanford University Press.

Recommended Reading

Berman, E. M., and H. I. Lief. 1975. Marital therapy from a psychiatric perspective: an overview. *Am. J. Psychiatry* 132:583–592.

Birk, L. 1980. Shifting gears in treating psychogenic sexual dysfunction: medical assessment, sex therapy, psychotherapy, and couple therapy. *Psychiatr. Clin. North Am.* 3:153–172.

———— 1984. Combined concurrent/conjoint psychotherapy for couples: rationale and efficient new strategies. In

Marriage and divorce, ed. C. C. Nadelson and D. C. Polansky. New York: Guilford.

Birk, L. 1992. *Behavioral/psychoanalytic psychotherapy within overlapping social systems: a natural matrix for diagnosis and therapeutic change. Integrative psychotherapy.*

Gurman, A. S., D. P. Kniskern, and W. M. Pinsof. 1986. Research on the process and outcome of marital and family therapy. In *Handbook of psychotherapy and behavior change,* ed. S. Garfield and A. Bergin. 3rd ed. New York: Wiley.

Haley, J. 1963. Marriage therapy. In *Strategies of psychotherapy.* New York: Grune & Stratton.

Jacobson, N. S., and A. S. Gurman, eds. 1986. *Clinical handbook of marital therapy.* New York: Guilford.

Jacobson, N. S., and G. Margolin. 1979. *Marital therapy: strategies based on social learning and behavior exchange principles.* New York: Brunner/Mazel.

Labbate, L. A., and M. H. Pollack. 1994. Treatment of fluoxetine-induced sexual dysfunction with bupropion: a case report. *Ann. Clin. Psychiatry* 6:13–15.

Leiblum, S., and R. Rosen. 1991. *Sexual Desire Disorders.* New York: Guilford Press.

Rosen, R., and G. Beck. 1988. *Patterns of Sexual Arousal.* New York: Guilford Press.

Rosen, R. C., and S. R. Leiblum. 1995. *Case Studies in Sex Therapy,* 3rd ed. New York: Guilford.

Seagraves, R. L. 1980. *Marital therapy: a combined psychodynamic-behavioral approach.* New York: Plenum.

Waxenberg, S. F., N. G. Drellick, and A. N. Sutherland. 1959. The role of hormones in human behavior I: Changes in female sexuality after adrenalectomy. *J. Clin. Endocrin.* 19:193.

Waxenberg, S. F., J. A. Finkbiner, N. D. Drellick, and A. N. Sutherland. 1960. The role of hormones in human behavior II: Changes in sexual behavior in relation to vaginal smears of breast-cancer patients after oophorectomy and adrenalectomy. *Psychosom. Med.* 22:435–439.

Wolman, B. B., and G. Stricker, eds. 1983. *Handbook of family and marital therapy.* New York: Plenum.

Acknowledgments

The author wishes to thank two people in particular for their help and collaboration in the preparation of this chapter. The first is Ken LaCerte, M.Ed., LMFT, LCSW, LMHC. Mr. LaCerte's steadfast help and support took many forms, was enormously helpful, and elevated notably the overall quality of this updated chapter. The second is Harold I. Lief, M.D. Dr. Lief's extensive experience in sex therapy and couple therapy—and also in psychoanalysis—his specific suggestions, and most especially his invaluable senior perspective have made this chapter immeasurably better than it would otherwise have been.

ERAN D. METZGER

Electroconvulsive Therapy

No current treatment in psychiatry draws more public skepticism than electroconvulsive therapy (ECT). That ECT—a series of electrically induced generalized seizures—should continue to be an important component of psychiatric somatic therapy is testimony to its safety and efficacy as well as to the accomplishments of its contemporary proponents. Indeed, it is due to the refinements in technique resulting from their efforts that ECT, whose origins date back to before the discovery of the first psychotropic medications, remains a modern treatment.

Recent historians have provided detailed accounts of the origins of ECT (Endler, 1988; Abrams, 1992). The Hungarian neuropsychiatrist Ladislas von Meduna is credited with the first systematic study of convulsions to treat mental illness in the early 1930s (Meduna, 1956). He based his clinical trials on postmortem brain studies of schizophrenics and epileptics, from which he incorrectly deduced a "biological antagonism" between schizophrenia and epilepsy. Initial work with camphor was succeeded by trials with the less toxic pentylenetetrazol, which still had the disadvantage of precipitating a feeling of impending death prior to the onset of the seizure. Based on their observations from the slaughterhouses in Rome, where pigs were killed after first being made to seize by an electric shock, Cerletti and Bini introduced electricity as a convulsant (1938). Their initial work with dogs led to the discovery that confining both electrodes to the scalp was sufficient to evoke a seizure without serious side effects.

Advances in anesthesia have been among the most important modifications to affect the safety and comfort of ECT. The muscle relaxant succinylcholine was first introduced as an adjunct for ECT procedures in 1951. Real-time monitoring of blood oxygen saturation levels by photocell oximetry has significantly reduced the likelihood of prolonged hypoxia, previously a major source of ECT morbidity and mortality.

Modern ECT machines deliver alternating current in a brief-pulse square waveform. Compared to the sine wave form delivered by earlier machines, this waveform minimizes patient exposure to sub-threshold energy, thereby decreasing accompanying cognitive impairment. In the presence of high impedance caused by a faulty circuit or insufficient electrode contact, modern machines will abort stimulus delivery and prevent patient exposure to excessively high energy. These instruments may be equipped to monitor one or more EEG channels, which, among other purposes, helps determine the duration of seizure activity.

Sociopolitical Issues

Public acceptance of ECT has not kept pace with the technologic advancements described above, nor has it kept pace with increased public acceptance of psychotropic medication. Modern entertainment media reinforce images, first evoked by literature and Hollywood decades ago, of ECT as an instrument of punishment, where treatment sessions are pandemonium and the aftereffects inhumane (Kesey, 1962). News media have hardly been more sympathetic; witness the opening paragraph of a front-page article in the newspaper USA Today:

The electrodes were placed on her head. With the push of a button, enough electricity to light a 50-watt bulb passed through her skull. Her teeth bit hard into a mouth guard. Her heart raced. Her blood pressure soared. Her brain had an epileptic style grand mal seizure. Then, O—— S——had a heart attack. (Cauchon, 1995)

Psychiatrists continue to face efforts by special interest groups to ban and criminalize the procedure (Kellner, 1995a).

Clinicians who recognized the variability in both the readiness to refer a patient for ECT and technique prompted departments of mental health, professional societies, and colleges to sponsor surveys to develop a more informed opinion. The first survey, published in Massachusetts (Frankel, 1973), was followed by reports in several other states and then by the ECT Task Force of the American Psychiatric Association (APA, 1978). The Royal College of Psychiatrists issued a statement regarding the value of ECT (1977), followed some years later by a detailed survey of a wide range of facilities in Great Britain (Pippard and Ellam, 1981). The 1990 APA Task Force Report was another milestone in the effort to educate clinicians and standardize practice; it provides guidelines and supportive rationale for every aspect of ECT, from informed consent to post-procedure care. Founded in 1976 as the International Psychiatric Association for the Advancement of Electrotherapy, the Association for Convulsive Therapy now boasts a membership of over 300 physicians. The association and its journal, *Convulsive Therapy*, are well-established resources for research, communication, and education. Significant regional differences in the use of ECT in the United States nevertheless persist (Hermann et al., 1995). Clearly there remains a need for professional organizations to continue to foster communication and increased understanding of this treatment among clinicians, legislators, and the general public.

Pretreatment

Screening

While no absolute contraindications to ECT exist (APA, 1990), medical screening is key to ECT without complications. The procedure must be adapted to compensate for various medical conditions. Tests of blood chemistry will rule out abnormalities which may affect seizure threshold or cardiac rhythm, and a complete blood count will indicate the patient's oxygen transport capacity. Similar rationale dictates the procurement of electrocardiogram and chest radiograph. While not a contraindication to ECT, pregnancy must be confirmed. Brain imaging and electroencephalography (EEG) are indicated only if the clinical picture presents a differential diagnosis which these studies would shorten (e.g., rule out brain neoplasm, rule out seizure disorder). In the absence of symptoms or signs, spine films are not indicated. Dental evaluation is indicated if the history and physical exam uncover painful or unstable dentition.

Few medications pose a problem for ECT if the clinician takes adequate precautions. Anithypertensive medications are generally continued but may be cause for anticholinergic pretreatment (see Physiological Events,

below). Oral hypoglycemics and insulin are usually dosed in a manner similar to that for other procedures requiring fasting. Theophylline, prescribed with decreasing frequency, poses a serious risk of status epilepticus (Rasmussen and Zorumski, 1993). Psychotropic medications also require consideration. Benzodiazepines, which are anticonvulsants, clearly shorten seizure duration in ECT, prompting some to argue for their discontinuation before treatment (Greenberg and Pettinati, 1993). The subject of lithium use concurrent with ECT has spawned much debate but little in the way of convincing evidence that lithium either significantly prolongs the effects of succinylcholine used for the procedure or results in neurotoxicity (Mukherjee, 1993). Reports have failed to demonstrate adverse effects from the combination of ECT and monoamine oxidase inhibitor (MAOI) antidepressants (Kellner et al., 1992), and their use is no longer considered grounds for postponement of ECT.

Education and Consent

Given the prevalence of misconceptions about ECT, one cannot overemphasize the importance of the role of the ECT clinician as educator. Although it should not replace an unhurried informational meeting, an introductory pamphlet including, for example, the rationale, the sequence of events, and the anticipated side effects of the treatments, can be very helpful. Similarly, brief educational videotapes are available for viewing by patients and their families. A consent form unique to ECT should be used, as described by the APA (1990). At a minimum, this form should document the patient's understanding of the indications for ECT, the availability of alternative treatments, the risks and possible benefits, and the expected duration of treatment and convalescence.

Treatment

Clinicians use various clinical locations for ECT, ranging from the operating room to the specially designed ECT suite. Whatever the physical locale, the ideal location for the practice of ECT provides privacy, not only for the procedure itself but also for pre- and post-procedure evaluations; adequate space for equipment and personnel; and convenience for both outpatients and inpatients. The fasting patient empties her bladder and is connected to oximetry, cardiac, and blood pressure monitoring. The points of contact on the scalp for EEG and treatment electrodes are cleaned so as to reduce impedance. Through an intravenous line, the patient receives a short-acting anesthetic (usually methohexital) and, once asleep, the short-acting muscle relaxant succinylcholine. A blood pressure cuff located below the knee and inflated above the systolic blood pressure just before administration of the succinylcholine permits visualization of the unmodified seizure in this isolated extremity. A mouthguard is inserted, as succinycholine does not prevent brisk contraction of the temporalis and masseter muscles with the stimulus. The stimulus, ranging from 0.5 to 2.0 seconds in duration and from 5 to 100 joules in energy, is administered via electrodes usually placed in either a nondominant unilateral or bilateral configuration. A generalized seizure ensues and typically lasts 30 to 90 seconds. The patient is ventilated and monitored while awakening and ideally is allowed to complete the waking process in a quiet, low-lit environment. Frequency of treatments varies from center to center but is typically 3 days per week in the United States. A twice per week schedule is equally efficacious and is used in the majority of British and European centers. Recent evidence suggests the less frequent schedule results in a longer response latency but fewer cognitive side effects (Lerer et al., 1995). Multiple stimulus sessions are also used in some centers, even though no improved response has been demonstrated using this technique.

Treatment Variables

Electrode Placement and Stimulus Dosing

The principal factors affecting electrode placement are efficacy and side effects. Most clinicians agree that the most commonly employed nondominant temporo-frontal, or D'Elia, unilateral placement results in a decreased incidence of post-treatment cognitive impairment (D'Elia and Raotma, 1975) when compared to bilateral ECT. They differ, however, over whether this improvement in side effects is achieved at the expense of efficacy. Work by H. A. Sackeim and colleagues suggests that this is the case (1993). The study is strong testimony that, in a discussion of efficacy and side effects, electrode placement and stimulus energy should be considered jointly. In this study, unilateral ECT was more successful when performed using a "high dose" protocol (administration of an electrical intensity 2.5 times the seizure threshold) than when using a "low dose" protocol (minimum electrical intensity required to produce a seizure of adequate duration). However, even high dose unilateral ECT failed to achieve the success rates of bilateral ECT. High energy bilateral ECT resulted in faster response but in a success rate which was not markedly improved over

low dose bilateral ECT. Short-term cognitive side effects were worse for both bilateral groups than for the unilateral groups. It remains to be seen whether these findings reverse the trend of the 1980s away from bilateral ECT. Regardless, at least for the near future the ultimate decision about electrode placement will continue to be based on characteristics of the individual patient. Factors such as the patient's wishes, severity of illness, baseline memory function, and past response must all be part of this decision.

Number of Treatments

Although formulaic approaches have been advocated and have their appeal, there exists no proven algorithm for determining "how much is enough" when it comes to number of ECTs. There is no minimum number of treatments required. Some patients simply respond with fewer treatments (Kellner, 1995b). As is the case with psychotropic medications, objective signs of response typically precede a patient's subjective sense of improvement and may become evident as early as the first treatment. Treatments are continued as long as there is further improvement with each session, and one of several available research rating scales for depression may be useful in documenting this (Hamilton, 1960). Resolution of symptoms and "plateauing" of the rate of improvement are indications of adequate treatment. This typically occurs after 6–12 treatments.

Seizure Length

The production of bilaterally generalized seizures lasting a minimum of 25 seconds is the goal of the treatment session. The origins of this now universal duration criterion are unclear, and studies document successful outcome, particularly with bilateral ECT, even when seizure length dropped below this minimum (Sackeim et al., 1987a). Conversely, adequate seizure length does not guarantee a good response (Sackeim, Devanand, and Prudic, 1991). Longer seizures produce neither faster response nor better outcomes, and they may cause more postictal confusion. ECT itself has anticonvulsant properties; consequently, seizure length commonly decreases over a series of treatments (Sackeim et al., 1987b). Interventions to minimize seizure threshold and maximize seizure length include hyperventilating the patient (carbon dioxide is an anticonvulsant), decreasing the dose of methohexital or changing anesthetic, and administering caffeine intravenously 5 minutes before the stimulus (McCall et al., 1993).

Physiological Events Associated with ECT

Neurologic

The supra-threshold electrical stimulus is defined as that dose which causes depolarization of a sufficient number of neurons to produce a generalized seizure (Abrams, 1992). Seizure threshold varies significantly between individuals and is generally higher with increased age. Dispersion and duration of the seizure is dependent on the stimulus waveform and electrode placement. Nevertheless, the EEG generally follows a predictable pattern, with a high frequency, low amplitude polyspike (tonic) phase soon replaced by a polyspike and slow wave (clonic) phase. The seizure may end abruptly or gradually, and electroencephalogram (EEG) seizure activity not uncommonly persists 10–60 seconds beyond the cessation of motor activity. A period of postictal suppression of variable duration often follows, with a return of the baseline pattern after 90 seconds to a few minutes. After repeated treatments, slowing of the EEG may persist for anywhere from 30 days to a year, depending on treatment variables (Abrams, 1992). Numerous studies of EEG morphology have been undertaken to better characterize the ECT-induced seizure but also with the hope of identifying an EEG marker for therapeutic treatments. Studies correlating degree of EEG slowing with outcome have yielded inconsistent results. Interest has focused on the regularity of the ictal EEG (Krystal et al., 1993) and the duration of postictal suppression (Nobler et al., 1993) as possible markers. As reviewed by Devanand and colleagues, a plethora of animal and human studies employing imaging and histological techniques have failed to produce evidence of neurologic damage that might be attributed to the electrical stimulus or repeated seizures (1994).

Neuroendocrine

Studies of the neuroendocrine changes associated with ECT in patients have been plagued by inconsistent techniques, statistically non-significant findings (often because of small sample size), and contradictory results. The literature on electroconvulsive shock in animals, while extensive, must be interpreted with caution because of the limits of generalizability of these data to human brains. At best, the neuroendocrine literature to date is descriptive and offers little to explain the mode of action of ECT.

The increase in serum prolactin observed after epilep-

tic seizures is also observed after ECT (Öhman et al., 1976). The hypothesis that adequate stimulation of hypothalamic centers is required for the therapeutic effect of ECT (Abrams et al., 1976) has led to efforts to correlate prolactin response with clinical outcome. Although bilateral ECT has been reported to yield higher postictal prolactin levels than unilateral ECT (Swartz and Abrams, 1984), numerous studies have failed to find an association between the magnitude or course of this increase and the antidepressant effect of ECT (Deakin et al., 1983; Abrams and Swartz, 1985; Clark, Alexopoulos, and Kaplan, 1995). Preliminary data support earlier studies suggesting this increase in prolactin may be connected to an ECT-related antidopaminergic effect (Zis et al., 1992).

Serum cortisol is also increased after ECT in the postictal period. As with prolactin, correlation with clinical outcome has been lacking (Hodges et al., 1964). The observed decrease in baseline and postictal cortisol levels during a course of ECT is nonspecific and may be caused by a reduction of depression-related stress (Abrams, 1992).

Cardiovascular

Though infrequent, cardiac complications are the most common source of morbidity and mortality associated with ECT. A brief overview of the cardiac response to ECT indicates why this is so. The electrical stimulus evokes a sizable vagal discharge. This may produce bradycardia or a sinus pause ranging from 2 to 5 seconds. The generalized seizure which follows produces a sympathetic discharge resulting frequently in significant tachycardia and hypertension. The principal risk, then, of a subthreshold stimulus (one insufficient to produce a seizure) is sinus arrest which does not reverse. For this reason, many centers pretreat patients with an anticholinergic medication, usually atropine or glycopyrrolate. Their use has been advocated when the individual patient's seizure threshold is being determined by a titration method, where subthreshold stimuli are more likely. Nevertheless, the use of anticholinergic medication, even in the aforementioned scenario, remains controversial, as these medications carry risks of their own (Kramer, 1993).

Associated with the sympathetic phase tachycardia and hypertension is the risk of arrhythmia and cardiac ischemia. Treatment with intravenous beta-blocker medication (e.g., labetalol or esmolol), either before or after the stimulus and when not contraindicated by a preexisting medical condition, may effectively reduce the risk of hypertension and ectopy. The effectiveness of these medications has permitted the use of ECT in such high-risk situations as cerebral and abdominal aortic aneurysm (Farah, McCall, and Amundson, 1996; Dowling and Francis, 1993). In a prospective study of ECT-related cardiac complications in 40 patients with cardiac disease, Zielinski and colleagues found that complications, most of which were minor, were strongly associated with the nature of the underlying disease and that all but 2 of the patients were able to complete their courses (1993).

Indications

Mood Disorders

Treatment of major depressive episode is the most frequent role for ECT. While 80–90% of patients in early studies showed significant response, success rates have dropped as ECT has come to be reserved largely for patients who have failed to respond to antidepressant medication (APA, 1990; Prudic et al., 1996). Predictors of outcome such as duration of the depressive episode, severity of symptoms, and measures of "endogenous" features have not held up over numerous studies. Clinicians' empirical observations that presence of psychotic features predicts good response have been supported by some studies (Buchan et al., 1992; Nobler and Sackeim, 1996). When catatonia is present, resolution can be rapid and dramatic (Fink, 1992).

Although the literature on ECT in mania is limited, retrospective studies (Alexander et al., 1988) as well as one prospective study (Small et al., 1988) have consistently documented efficacy. Obtaining consent for ECT in mania may pose particular challenges (Miller, 1995).

ECT offers a safe alternative to psychotropic use for the treatment of severe mood disorder in all trimesters of pregnancy (APA, 1990). While its practice should be limited to centers with experience in this area and an obstetrical staff, complications, mostly in the form of premature labor, are extremely rare (Ferrill, Kehoe, and Jacisin, 1992; Walker and Swartz, 1994).

Only a sparse case report literature exists on the use of ECT in child and adolescent mood disorders. These data support ECT as safe and effective in younger patients with unipolar and bipolar mood disorders and indicate these patients tolerate ECT particularly well (Schneekloth, Rummans, and Logan, 1993).

Schizophrenia

As recounted at the beginning of this chapter, convulsive therapy's earliest patients were diagnosed with schizophrenia, and had they not suffered from catatonia and

thus responded dramatically, the advancement of ECT might at least have been delayed. With the development of effective neuroleptic medications, the use of ECT in schizophrenia has become increasingly rare. Studies of ECT in schizophrenia are difficult to interpret because of problems in diagnosis and variable methods. A review of the literature shows generally varied results, with evidence that initial response may be faster with ECT than with medication and that the combination of ECT and neuroleptic may have some advantages in treatment-resistant patients (Weiner and Coffey, 1988; Klapheke, 1993).

Other Disorders

A small case report literature describes improvement of symptoms in some patients with intractable anorexia nervosa (Ferguson, 1993). A larger body of literature describes the use of ECT in patients with obsessive-compulsive disorder, with unimpressive results. One retrospective study of 32 patients, however, found significant improvement independent of mood state (Maletzky, McFarland, and Burt, 1994). ECT has been used to treat neuroleptic malignant syndrome since this syndrome was first identified, and a review of the 31 cases in the literature found an 84% success rate (Scheftner and Shulman, 1992).

Fromm first reported improvements of parkinsonism in psychiatric patients with Parkinson's disease (1959). Numerous subsequent studies have been consistently favorable, to the point that experts in the field have recommended ECT for refractory, incapacitating Parkinson's even in the absence of mood disorder (Fink, 1988; Abrams, 1992). Duration of improvement is quite variable, ranging from days to several months. Patients with Parkinson's disease seem especially vulnerable to the development of postictal delirium (Figiel et al., 1991).

Post-treatment

Cognitive Effects

ECT's effects on memory often produce the most anxiety in patients. The cognitive effects of ECT have been studied exhaustively. As described earlier, degree of impairment is in part related to ECT technique. Nevertheless, the typical reaction is one of delirium in the immediate postictal period, anterograde and retrograde amnesia both during the treatment course and immediately following, and some persistent retrograde amnesia lasting up to several weeks after the last treatment (Steif et al.,

1986; Squire, Slater, and Miller, 1981; Squire, 1986). For this reason, patients are often recommended a "convalescence period" of up to a few weeks after ECT, and are advised against such activities as driving and transacting business during this time (APA, 1990). The severity of cognitive impairment may determine whether a patient completes a course of ECT as an inpatient or from home. The occasional testimonials by patients who claim to have had their memory "wiped out" by ECT gain media attention; however, such cases have not been substantiated by neuropsychological testing. While some patients may never retrieve memory for some events occurring during the course of treatments, patients generally demonstrate both objective and subjective memory *improvement* in comparison to their pre-ECT baseline (Sackeim, 1992).

Maintenance Treatment

One of the major challenges facing the practice of ECT is how best to maintain the benefits achieved. Robust response does not guarantee long-term remission, and unfortunately, relapse is common (Aronson, Shuka, and Hoff, 1987). Treatment with antidepressant medication (Kay et al., 1970; Sackeim et al., 1990) and lithium (Shapira et al., 1995) after ECT appears to reduce the rate of relapse. Relapse rates nevertheless range from 20% to 50%. The majority of patients who relapse on maintenance medication tend to do so within the first few months after ECT and have a history of medication resistance. Continuation ECT (treatment for up to 6 months after the index course) and maintenance ECT (treatment beyond 6 months) (APA, 1990) are areas of renewed interest, and preliminary findings include decreased relapse rates and decreased rates of hospitalization (Vanelle et al., 1994; Schwarz, Lowenstein, and Isenberg, 1995).

Future Investigation

The dawning of the era of intensive research into the biology of thought and emotion brings with it the potential for discovering the mode of action of the somatic therapies. New brain imaging techniques hold the potential vastly to increase the sensitivity of our measurements of the physiological events associated with ECT and other treatments (Nobler et al., 1994). Research into transcranial magnetic stimulation may help elucidate the mechanism of ECT and raises the possibility of a nonconvulsive, nonpharmacologic treatment for depression (Pascual-Leone et al., 1996). In the meantime, more research is needed into each of the areas described in this chapter: to improve how we screen, educate, and prepare

patients for treatment; to standardize technique in the areas of electrode placement and stimulus dose; to reduce side effects further; and to discover how best to maintain the benefits that are achieved with this treatment. To foster such research will require continued efforts by psychiatric training programs to interest residents in this important but still underutilized modality.

References

Abrams, R. 1992. *Electroconvulsive therapy.* 2nd ed. New York: Oxford University Press.

Abrams, R., Essman, W. B., Taylor, M. A., Fink, M. 1976. Concentration of 5-hydroxyindoleacetic acid, homovanillic acid, and tryptophan in the cerebrospinal fluid of depressed patients before and after ECT. *Biol. Psychiatry* 11:85–90.

Abrams, R., and Swartz, C. M. 1985. ECT and prolactin release: relation to treatment response in melancholia. *Convulsive Ther.* 1:38–42.

Abrams, R., and Taylor, M. A. 1976. Diencephalic stimulation and the effects of ECT in endogenous depression. *Br. J. Psychiatry* 129:482–485.

Alexander, R. C., Salomon, M., Ionescu-Pioggia, M., Cole, J. 1988. Convulsive therapy in the treatment of mania: McLean Hospital, 1973–1986. *Convulsive Ther.* 4:115–125.

American Psychiatric Association (APA). 1978. Task Force on Electroconvulsive Therapy report no. 14. Washington, D.C.

——— 1990. Task Force Report on electroconvulsive therapy. The practice of electroconvulsive therapy: recommendations for treatment, training, and privileging. Washington, D.C.

Aronson, T. A., Shuka, S., and Hoff, A. 1987. Continuation therapy after ECT for delusional depression: a naturalistic study of prophylactic treatments and relapse. *Convulsive Ther.* 3:251–259.

Buchan, H., Johnstone, E., McPherson, K., Palmer, R. L., Crow, T. J., Brandon, S. 1992. Who benefits from electroconvulsive therapy? Combined results of the Leicester and Northwick Park trials. *Br. J. Psychiatry* 160:355–359.

Cauchon, D. 1995. "Patients often aren't informed of full danger." *USA Today.* December 6.

Cerletti, U., and Bini, L. 1938. Un nuovo metodo di shock-terapie "l'eletro-shock." *Boll. Acad. Med. Roma* 64:136–138.

Clark, C. P., Alexopoulos, G. S., and Kaplan, J. 1995. Prolactin release and clinical response to electroconvulsive therapy in depressed geriatric patients: a preliminary report. *Convulsive Ther.* 11:24–31.

Deakin, J. F., Ferrier, I. N., Crow, T. J., Johnstone, E. C., Lawler, P. 1983. Effects of ECT on pituitary hormone release: relationship to seizure, clinical variables, and outcome. *Br. J. Psychiatry* 143:618–624.

D'Elia, Y., and Raotma, H. 1975. Is unilateral ECT less effective than bilateral ECT? *Br. J. Psychiatry* 126:83–89.

Devanand, D. P., Dwork, A. J., Hutchinson, E. R., Bolwig, T. G., Sackeim, H. A. 1994. Does ECT alter brain structure? *Am. J. Psychiatry* 151:957–970.

Dowling, F. G., and Francis, A. 1993. Aortic aneurysm and electroconvulsive therapy. *Convulsive Ther.* 9:121–127.

Endler, N. S. 1988. The origins of electroconvulsive therapy (ECT). *Convulsive Ther.* 4:5–23.

Farah, A., McCall, W. V., and Amundson, R. H. 1996. ECT after cerebral aneurysm repair. *Convulsive Ther.* 12:165–170.

Ferguson, J. M. 1993. The use of electroconvulsive therapy in patients with intractable anorexia nervosa. *Int. J. Eating Dis.* 13:195–201.

Ferrill, M. J., Kehoe, W. A., and Jacisin, J. J. 1992. ECT during pregnancy: physiologic and pharmacologic considerations. *Convulsive Ther.* 8:186–200.

Figiel, G. S., Hansen, M. A., Zorumski, C., Krishnan, K. R., Doraiswamy, P. M., Jarvis, M. R., Smith, D. S. 1991. ECT-induced delirium in depressed patients with Parkinson's disease. *J. Neuropsychiatry Clin. Neurosci.* 3:405–411.

Fink, M. 1979. *Convulsive therapy: theory and practice.* New York: Raven Press.

——— 1988. ECT for Parkinson's disease? [editorial]. *Convulsive Ther.* 4:189–191.

——— 1992. Catatonia and DSM-IV. *Convulsive Ther.* 8:159–162.

Frankel, F. H. 1973. ECT in Massachusetts: a task force report. *Massachusetts Journal of Mental Health* 3:3–29.

Fromm, G. H. 1959. Observation on the effects of electroshock treatment in patients with parkinsonism. *Bulletin of Tulane University* 18:71–73.

Greenberg, R. M., and Pettinati, H. M. 1993. Benzodiazepines and electroconvulsive therapy. *Convulsive Ther.* 9:262–273.

Hamilton, M. 1960. A rating scale for depression. *J. Neurology, Neurosurgery, and Psychiatry* 23:56–62.

Hermann, R. C., Dorwart, R. A., Hoover, C. W., Brody, J. 1995. Variation in ECT use in the United States. *Am. J. Psychiatry* 152:869–875.

Hodges, J. R., Jones, M., Elithorn, A., Bridges, P. 1964. Effect of electroconvulsive therapy on plasma cortisol levels. *Nature* 204:754–756.

Kay, D. W., Fahy, T., Garside, R. F. 1970. A seven-month double-blind trial of amitriptyline and diazepam in ECT-treated depressed patients. *Br. J. Psychiatry* 117:667–671.

Kellner, C. H. 1995a. Anti-ECT legislation in Texas. *Convulsive Ther.* 11:148.

——— 1995b. Defining a course of ECT. *Convulsive Ther.* 11:229–231.

Kellner, C. H., Rubey, R. N., Burns, C., Bernstein, H. J., Monroe, R. R. Jr. 1992. Safe administration of ECT in a patient taking selegiline. *Convulsive Ther.* 8:144–147.

Kesey, K. 1962. *One flew over the cuckoo's nest.* New York: Signet.

Klapheke, M. M. 1993. Combining ECT and antipsychotic agents: benefits and risks. *Convulsive Ther.* 9:241–255.

Kramer, B. A. 1993. Anticholinergics and ECT. *Convulsive Ther.* 9:293–300.

Krystal, A. D., Weiner, R. D., McCall, W. V., Shelp, F. E., Arias, R., Smith, P. 1993. The effects of ECT stimulus dose and electrode placement on the ictal electroencephalogram: an interindividual crossover study. *Biol. Psychiatry* 34:759–767.

Lerer, B., Shapira, B., Calev, A., Tubi, N., Drexler, H., Kindler, S., Lidsky, D., Schwartz, J. E. 1995. Antidepressant and cognitive effects of twice- versus three-times weekly ECT. *Am. J. Psychiatry* 152:564–570.

Maletzky, B., McFarland, B., and Burt, A. 1993. Refractory obsessive compulsive disorder and ECT. *Convulsive Ther.* 10:34–42.

McCall, W. V., Reid, S., Rosenquist, P., Foreman, A., Kiesow-Webb, N. 1993. A reappraisal of the role of caffeine in ECT. *Am. J. Psychiatry* 150:1543–45.

Meduna, L. J. 1956. The convulsive treatment: a reappraisal. In *The great physiodynamic therapies in psychiatry,* ed. F. Marbi-Ibanez, A. M. Sackler, M. D. Sackler, and R. R. Sackler. New York: Hoeber-Harper.

Miller, M. C. 1995. ECT and mania [letter]. *Am. J. Psychiatry* 152:654.

Mukherjee, S. 1993. Combined ECT and lithium therapy. *Convulsive Ther.* 9:274–284.

Nobler, M. S., and Sackeim, H. A. 1996. Prediction of response to electroconvulsive therapy: clinical and biological aspects. In *Predictors of response in mood disorders,* ed. P. J. Goodnick. Washington, D.C.: American Psychiatric Press. 177–198.

Nobler, M. S., Sackeim, H. A., Solomou, M., Luber, B., Devanand, D. P., Prudic, J. 1993. EEG manifestations during ECT: effects of electrode placement and stimulus intensity. *Biol. Psychiatry* 34:321–340.

Nobler, M. S., Sackeim, H. A., Prohovnik, I., Moeller, J. R., Mukherjee, S., Schnur, D. B., Prudic, J., Devanand, D. P. 1994. Regional cerebral blood flow in mood disorders, III. *Arch. Gen. Psychiatry* 51:884–897.

Öhman, R., Balldin, J., Walinder, J., Wallin, L., Abrahamsson, L. 1976. Prolactin response to electroconvulsive therapy. *Lancet* 2:936–937.

Pascual-Leone, A., Rubio, B., Pallardo, F., Catala, M. D.

1996. Rapid-rate transcranial magnetic stimulation of left dorsolateral prefrontal cortex in drug-resistant depression. *Lancet* 348:233–237.

Pippard, J., and Ellam, L. 1981. *Electroconvulsive treatment in Great Britain, 1980.* London: Gaskell.

Prudic, J., Haskett, R. F., Mulsant, B., Malone, K. M., Pettinati, H. M., Stephens, S., Greenberg, R., Rifas, S. L., Sackeim, H. A. 1996. Resistance to antidepressant medications and short-term clinical response to ECT. *Am. J. Psychiatry* 153:985–992.

Rasmussen, K. G., and Zorumski, C. F. 1993. Electroconvulsive therapy in patients taking theophylline. *J. Clin. Psychiatry* 54:427–431.

Royal College of Psychiatrists. 1977. Memorandum on the use of electroconvulsive therapy. *Br. J. Psychiatry* 131:261–272.

Sackeim, H. A. 1992. The cognitive effects of electroconvulsive therapy. In *Cognitive disorders: pathophysiology and treatment,* ed. W. H. Moos, E. R.Gamzu, and L. J. Thal. New York: Marcel Dekker.

Sackeim, H. A., Devanand, D. P., and Prudic, J. 1991. Stimulus intensity, seizure threshold, and seizure duration: impact on efficacy and safety of electroconvulsive therapy. *Psychiatr. Clin. North Am.* 14:803–843.

Sackeim, H. A., Decina, P., Portnoy, S., Neeley, P., Malitz, S. 1987a. Studies of dosage, seizure threshold, and seizure duration in ECT. *Biol. Psychiatry* 22:249–268.

Sackeim, H. A., Decina P., Prohovnik, I., Malitz, S. 1987b. Seizure threshold in electroconvulsive therapy: effects of sex, age, electrode placement, and number of treatments. *Arch. Gen. Psychiatry* 44:355–60.

Sackeim, H. A., Prudic, J., Devanand, D. P., Decina, P., Kerr, B., Malitz, S. 1990. The impact of medication resistance and continuation pharmacotherapy on relapse following response to electroconvulsive therapy in major depression. *J. Clin. Psychopharmacol.* 10:96–104.

Sackeim, H. A., Prudic, J., Devanand, D. P., Kiersky, J. E., Fitzsimmons, L., Moody, B. J., McElhiney, M. C., Coleman, E. A., Settembrino, J. M. 1993. Effects of stimulus intensity and electrode placement on the efficacy and cognitive effects of electroconvulsive therapy. *N. Engl. J. Med.* 328:839–846.

Scheftner, W. A., and Shulman, R. B. 1992. Treatment choice in neuroleptic malignant syndrome. *Convulsive Ther.* 8:267–279.

Schneekloth, T. D., Rummans, T. A., and Logan, K. M. 1993. Electroconvulsive therapy in adolescents. *Convulsive Ther.* 9:158–166.

Schwarz, T., Lowenstein, J., and Isenberg, K. E. 1995. Maintenance ECT: indications and outcome. *Convulsive Ther.* 11:14–23.

Shapira, B., Gorfine, M., and Lerer, B. 1995. A prospective study of lithium continuation therapy in depressed pa-

tients who have responded to electroconvulsive therapy. *Convulsive Ther.* 11:80–85.

Small, J. G., Klapper, M. H., Kellams, J. J., Miller, M. J., Millstein, V., Sharpley, P. H., Small, I. F. 1988. ECT compared with lithium in the management of manic states. *Arch. Gen. Psychiatry* 45:727–732.

Squire, L. R. 1986. Memory functions as affected by electroconvulsive therapy. *Ann. N.Y. Acad. Sci.* 462:307–314.

Squire, L. R., Slater, P. C., and Miller, P. L. 1981. Retrograde amnesia and bilateral electroconvulsive therapy: long-term follow-up. *Arch. Gen. Psychiatry* 38:89–95.

Steif, B. L., Sackeim, H. A., Portnoy, S., Decina, P., Malitz, S. 1986. Effects of depression and ECT on anterograde memory. *Biol. Psychiatry* 21:921–930.

Swartz, C., and Abrams, R. 1984. Prolactin levels after bilateral and unilateral ECT. *Br. J. Psychiatry* 144:643–645.

Vanelle, J.-M., Loo, H., Galinowski, A., de Carvalho, W., Bourdel, M.-C., Brochier, P., Bouvet, O., Brochier, T., Olie, J.-P. 1994. Maintenance ECT in intractable manic-depressive disorders. *Convulsive Ther.* 10:195–205.

Walker, R., and Swartz, C. M. 1994. Electroconvulsive therapy during high-risk pregnancy. *Gen. Hosp. Psychiatry* 16:348–353.

Weiner, R. D., and Coffey, C. E. 1988. Indications for use of electroconvulsive therapy. In *Review of Psychiatry.* Vol. 7, ed. A. J. Frances and R. E. Hales. Washington, D.C.: American Psychiatric Press. 458–481.

Zielinski, R. J., Roose, S. P., Devanand, D. P., Woodring, S., Sackeim, H. A. 1993. Cardiovascular complications of ECT in depressed patients with cardiac disease. *Am. J. Psychiatry* 150:904–909.

Zis, A. P., McGarvey, K. A., Clark, C. M., Lam, R. W., Adams, S. A. 1992. The role of dopamine in seizure-induced prolactin release in humans. *Convulsive Ther.* 8:126–130.

Recommended Reading

Abrams, R. 1992. *Electroconvulsive therapy.* 2nd ed. New York: Oxford University Press.

American Psychiatric Association. 1990. Task Force Report on electroconvulsive therapy. The practice of electroconvulsive therapy: recommendations for treatment, training, and privileging. Washington, D.C.

Endler, N. S. 1988. The origins of electroconvulsive therapy (ECT). *Convulsive Ther.* 4:5–23.

Nobler, M. S., and Sackeim, H. A. 1996. Prediction of response to electroconvulsive therapy: clinical and biological aspects. In *Predictors of response in mood disorders,* ed. P. J. Goodnick. Washington, D.C.: American Psychiatric Press. 177–198.

Sackeim, H. A., Prudic, J., Devanand, D. P., Kiersky, J. E., Fitzsimmons, L., Moody, B. J., McElhiney, M. C., Coleman, E. A., Settembrino, J. M. 1993. Effects of stimulus intensity and electrode placement on the efficacy and cognitive effects of electroconvulsive therapy. *N. Engl. J. Med.* 328:839–846.

Acknowledgments

The author thanks Fred Frankel, M. B.Ch.B., D. P. M., for his kind mentorship and encouragement.

NICHOLAS A. COVINO
FRED H. FRANKEL

Clinical Hypnosis

In a manner that would inspire Charles Darwin, clinical hypnosis has survived centuries of change in psychological theory and medical practice. Hypnosis was as useful to the medical practitioners of the 1700s as to the clinical researcher J. M. Charcot (1825–1893) in his work on hysteria, the early psychoanalytic efforts of Sigmund Freud (1856–1939), and to those who currently work in the managed care settings of mental health and medical departments. It is a technique that fits with equal comfort into the work of cognitive, behavioral, and psychodynamic clinicians and one that has been present under various appellations since antiquity.

The Elements of Hypnosis

The following definition of hypnosis elucidates the essential elements of this technique along with an emphasis on the relational aspects that are central to clinical practice.

Hypnosis is an event. . .involving a subject and an operator and dependent for its occurrence on the trance capabilities of the subject, his or her motivation, the situation and the relationship between subject and operator. When these are appropriate, the subject can be guided to experience reality differently. This includes distorted perceptions of various kinds; and unusual achievements of memory such as hypermnesia or amnesia can be part of it. The experience has a beginning and an end and includes a tolerance for logical inconsistencies. (Frankel, 1976)

The subject brings a certain motivation to engage in hypnosis along with a degree of hypnotizability. A relationship of trust must exist between the subject and operator, otherwise very little will happen. Finally, certain conditions favor the accomplishment of hypnotic tasks while others will defeat it. In general, subjects who experience the appropriate conditions with adequate hypnotizability can produce alterations in perception, cognition, emotion, behavior, and memory.

One of the essential elements of hypnosis is the *conveyance of an idea to a subject for uncritical acceptance.* This suggestive aspect of hypnosis is similar to the mechanism of action in a placebo response, where a subsequent change following the administration of an elixir is often unanalyzed by the patient or erroneously attributed to the power of the medication. In a trance, ideas are embraced by the subject, and often acted upon, without regard to logic or objective reality (Shor, 1959). These powerful ideas are thought to be instrumental in producing changes in thinking, behavior, memory, and even physiological functioning.

Human behavior is known to be influenced by direct and indirect suggestions, with certain factors more facilitative of a suggestive effect. When a stimulus is vague, ambiguous, faint, novel, or linked to another with strong emotional properties, it is easier to influence a subject to interpret its meaning along predetermined lines. When the maker of the suggestion is believed to be attractive, trustworthy, intelligent, prestigious, or an expert, it is likely that suggestions will be followed. Group pressure or an opportunity for the subject to become imaginatively or emotionally involved with a task or idea will also increase the probability of an unreflective response (Gheorghiu, 1989; Lundy, 1989). This concept of a forceful idea influencing another has been the cornerstone of clinical hypnosis throughout the ages.

The marquis de Puysegur (1755–1848) described the treatment of his servant, Victor Race.

When I thought his ideas might affect him in a disagreeable way, I stopped them and tried to inspire more cheerful ones . . . At length, I saw him content, imagining that he was shooting at a target, dancing at a festival and so on. I fostered these ideas in him and forced him to move around on his chair as though to dance to a tune which I was able to make him repeat by singing in my mind. By this means I produced in him abundant sweat. After an hour of crisis I calmed him down and left the room. He was given a drink and I made him some soup. The following day, being unable to remember my visit of the previous evening, he told me of his improved state of health. (Gauld, 1992, p. 41)

In the nineteenth century the surgeon James Braid (1795–1860) opposed the popular magnetic theory of Franz Anton Mesmer (1734–1815) and asserted that suggestion alone was the mechanism contributing to the effects of hypnosis. He wrote:

By engendering a state of mental concentration . . . upon some unexciting and empty thing . . . the faculties of the minds of some patients are . . . thrown out of gear . . . so that the higher faculties . . . become dethroned from their supremacy and give place and power to imagination, easily docility or passive obedience; so that even whilst apparently awake . . . they become susceptible of being influenced and controlled entirely by the suggestions of others. (Gauld, 1992, p. 285)

The special nature of this type of attention and the use of the patient's imagination could be called upon to assist the surgeon and patient with a surgical procedure. If the patient were taught to focus more on a benign idea or healthy body part, Braid believed that the subject could ignore painful sensations during surgery. Indeed, James Esdaile (1957) reported that he undertook more than 1000 successful operations in India with hypnosis serving as the anesthetic.

For the first 9 years of his practice, Sigmund Freud states that he had only hypnosis and "a few haphazard and unsystematic psychotherapeutic methods" at his disposal (Freud, 1925). Later, he began to explore the use of this technique as a vehicle for uncovering unconscious conflicts, but his initial use was in the application of direct suggestions for attitude and behavior change.

The real therapeutic value of hypnosis lies in the suggestions made during it. These suggestions consist in an energetic denial of the ailments of which the patient has complained or an assurance that he can do something or a command to perform it. (Freud, 1891)

Freud's early report of "A case of successful treatment by hypnotism" (Freud, 1892–93) revealed a technique that consisted principally of offering new ideas for uncritical acceptance to a woman who seems to have been experiencing a postpartum depression. He writes that he hypnotized her and said: "Have no fear. You will make an excellent nurse. Your baby will thrive and your stomach will be quiet."

Subjects in hypnosis report that the experience is relaxing and that their hypnotized responses (e.g., anesthesia for pain; posthypnotic amnesia) are subjectively experienced as *involuntary*. This reflexive, compliant response differs from the deliberate in the same way that a response to an invitation is distinct from a command (Hilgard, 1991).

In Charcot's model of hysteria, it is the subject who generates symptoms via autosuggestion or self-hypnosis (Gauld, 1992). When a person with a hereditary predisposition to hysteria is exposed to a psychologically traumatic situation, an idea might come to mind (e.g., "I can't move my legs!") that will resist evidence to the contrary and persist after the trauma recedes. Current hypnotic practice remains firmly attached to the importance of the patient's ability to embrace an idea for uncritical acceptance, whether it is presented by hypnotist or subject.

Freud's subsequent immersion into the world of psychoanalysis was largely responsible for emphasizing a second common element of hypnosis: *the relationship between hypnotist and patient is intensified and is central to the cure*. Freud, of course, used the term *transference* to describe the exaggerated notions that a patient might hold regarding the psychological and personal qualities of the therapist as well as the influential nature of their interaction. Hypnotists call this aspect of hypnosis "archaic involvement," where an authoritative, parental-type relationship in hypnosis increases patient motivation, openness to suggestion, and willingness to relax the usual logic, reason, and reality testing that meet a newly presented idea (Shor, 1959).

In many of his writings, but most notably in the paper on group psychology (Freud, 1922), Freud wrestled with this idea of psychological influence. His best examples for explaining the type of influential relationship that occurs between analysand and analyst were what happens to people in hypnosis treatment, when falling in love, and as members of groups.

In a group, the particular acquirements of an individual are obliterated and their distinctiveness vanishes. The mental superstructure which is unique to the individual is removed. The conscious personality has entirely vanished. Will and discernment are lost. All feelings about thoughts are bent in the direction determined by the hypnotizer. He is no longer himself but an automaton who has ceased to be guided by his will. (Freud, 1922)

Freud felt that in a group, individuals think, feel, and act in a manner different from their experience in isolation. In groups people are subjected to profound alterations of mental activity. They become increasingly vulnerable to emotions which intensify at the same time that intellectual abilities are reduced, and individuals yield to instructions that they would ordinarily resist. In hypnosis, Freud believed, the same things happen: individual personality is lost; certain faculties are destroyed or exalted; and an individual experiences a state of fascination with the hypnotizer similar to that which occurs in a group or when one is in love.

Hypnosis, then, is more than just following orders; it is an "emotional tie" between subject and operator (Borch-Jacobsen, 1991). Research indicates that hypnotized subjects, like those in love, will retain some measure of control and cannot be directed to do something that they find truly objectionable. However, good hypnotic subjects, in the context of trusting relationships, can be easily influenced to alter their perception, mood, and behavior. The quality and intensity of this relationship, like the transference developed in psychoanalysis, draws heavily upon earlier relationships with parents and significant others as well as the fantasies and desires of the subject.

Finally, *hypnotized persons can reliably experience alterations in sensation, perception, cognition, emotion, and behavior.* Hypnotic ability seems to be a stable characteristic that is not evenly distributed in the population. The best estimates are that some 15% of the population possesses very high levels of hypnotizability and about 25% are relatively unresponsive to it (Bowers, 1976). Those who have hypnotic ability are able to become absorbed in their imaginative world and might enjoy such activities as reading, watching films, distance running, art, drama, and design, which rely less on cognitive activities such as scanning, attention, concentration, judgment, and reality testing.

In hypnosis, a good subject can experience increased motivation to pursue some aim, mentally rehearse an upcoming performance, or, in the tradition of cognitive psychology (Lazarus and Folkman, 1984; Meichenbaum, 1974), replace a previous understanding in a manner that opens the way for new behaviors and feelings. Alterations in sensory input (e.g., visual, olfactory, gustatory, auditory, kinesthetic) can produce helpful effects such as analgesia (numbness), catalepsy (inability to flex a body part), negative hallucination (not seeing something present), dissociation, alterations in memory, and time distortion. Oftentimes the simple use of imagery to distract the patient from an alarming thought or feared stimulus can be especially effective by producing a relaxation response.

Since antiquity, the priest, the healer, and the hypnotist have issued commands in an authoritarian fashion to subjects who were expected to obey. In Charcot's laboratory, demonstration subjects were thought to be in such an altered state that discussions about their treatment and

behavior could be held in their presence with the mistaken idea that they could not hear. As we shall see, the practice of clinical hypnosis changed dramatically when Freud began to apply "the method of Breuer" to his patients. Although medicine and psychotherapy acknowledge the importance of the relationship between provider and patient in clinical practice, more has been made of the imaginative ability and aims of the patient in hypnotic treatment along with a partnership that resembles collaboration more than command.

Putative Mechanisms

Less is known about what facilitates the changes observed in hypnosis than we would expect of a technique that has reached such an advanced age. It is possible that this theoretical ambiguity contributes to the ability of hypnosis to blend with prevailing practices. However, a number of efforts have been made to discern the possible mechanisms of effect in hypnosis.

The *magnetic theories* of the physician Franz Anton Mesmer guided most understandings of the efficacy of hypnosis with medical patients through the mid-1700s until almost the beginning of the twentieth century. Mesmer believed that a variety of diseases were caused by an imbalance of magnetic fluid in the body. This fluid was thought to unite the heavenly bodies and to create homeostasis, unity, and health in humans. For him and his thousands of followers, the redistribution of magnetic fluid by those with a gift for magnetism was thought to be central to healing a variety of diseases. Indeed, even the renowned neurologist-scientist Charcot was reported to have applied magnets along with suggestions in his treatment of patients, despite the disputation of this technique by several French commissions (Ellenberger, 1970).

Freud, in keeping with early theory, first believed that a new idea presented to the mind of a patient in hypnosis could replace the erroneous, symptom-generating one. Again, he believed that patients were motivated to follow the *suggestions* of the hypnotizer out of love in the same way that a tribe obeys a chief or the group follows the leader (Freud, 1922). A variation of this thinking persists today in the importance given by psychotherapists to hypnotic *rapport* between operator and subject and with one understanding of the psychoanalytic concept of transference.

In the manner taught to him by Josef Breuer, Freud later used hypnosis as a vehicle to access repressed memories, connect the relevant emotions to them, and discharge attendant tensions by means of *abreaction.* Psychological theory at this point held that patients, who were unmotivated or unable to remember traumata from their earlier life, developed psychiatric symptoms because they could not think productively about these experiences, reconcile them, or rid themselves of the troublesome emotions associated with the events. Hypnosis was thought to be a method of returning the patient to the scene of the crime, where the undischarged emotions could be experienced again "in statu nascendi," released, and brought under cognitive control.

Modern researchers find that *perception* plays a crucial role as mediator for the body's fight/flight and stress reaction. The judgments that subjects make about the danger, impact, consequence, and controllability of stimuli seem to determine the level of *autonomic arousal* and the subsequent stress response, rather than any inherent quality of danger common to the stimulus (Lazarus and Folkman, 1984). At the psychophysiological level, there have been reports of changes in heart rate, arterial blood pressure, and oxygen consumption in hypnosis that are similar to those which occur in yoga, biofeedback, Zen, and other meditative practices (Benson, 1975). Some argue that high degrees of hypnotizability influence patients to react to stressful stimuli in their environment with greater intensity and to experience increased psychophysiologic symptoms (Wickramasekera, 1995). The imaginative ability of these patients is thought to serve as an *amplifier* for the experience of a noxious event which triggers an elevated psychophysiological response. In illness and in health, the power of perception or an idea appears to be the basis for the mind-body connection.

Neurological research finds patients who are measured by electroencephalograph (EEG) to demonstrate increased production of alpha and theta rhythms with some uncertainty as to whether this activity is the result of state variables (relaxation alone) or a neurological trait of hypnotizable individuals (Barabasz and Gregson, 1979; Crawford and Gruzelier, 1992; Morgan, Macdonald, and Hilgard, 1974). Highly hypnotizable subjects show neurological differences at the p300 and N1 and P1 components in cortical event-related brain potential (ERP) experiments (Schnyer and Allen, 1995; Spiegel, Cutcomb, Ren, and Pribram, 1985). Shifts in amplitude that coincide with their efforts to restrict peripheral awareness and attention while increasing self-absorption have also been reported. Again, researchers are unable to be certain whether these observations are a neurological cause or the consequence of the relaxed state (Spiegel and Barabasz, 1988).

For many years, investigators have debated whether the observed changes in hypnotized subjects result from a special state of *dissociation* or from *social-psychological*

factors (e.g., role-play, compliance) (Kirsh and Lynn, 1995). Following the work of the early dynamic psychiatrists, many researchers posited that a special quality of consciousness occurs in hypnosis that might be responsible for the phenomena observed. For these theorists, the "trance" that people experience when watching a film, reading a book, driving along a highway, daydreaming, meditating, or responding to a hypnotist's suggestions is thought to be a unique state with special properties.

Janet (1907) believed that attention, thoughts, feelings, memories, and behaviors could exist in *separate streams of consciousness.* From the automatic behaviors of shifting a car while driving, to the seemingly unmotivated compliance of raising an arm at the hypnotist's invitation, to the more serious absences found in the dissociative disorders, the psychological material in these states is thought to be unavailable to the person's immediate conscious awareness. Neodissociation theory (Hilgard, 1991) is a modern expression of these ideas of divided consciousness. Its proponents describe a hierarchy of cognitive abilities with some separation among them that allows, for example, a bilingual person to respond to a question in one language while suppressing another or a pain patient to tolerate increased noxious stimulation while reporting a sense of comfort.

Social and cognitive psychologists dispute the existence of a special state of hypnosis. Instead, they attribute hypnotic responsiveness to a more intentional aspect of consciousness (Sarbin and Coe, 1972; Spanos, 1982). They believe that hypnotized subjects adopt particular social roles and play the parts assigned to them by the hypnotist. Hypnotized persons are thought to carry out the suggestions of hypnotists in the manner reminiscent of nonhypnotized persons assuming the cooperative roles of worker, partner, and friend rather than out of blind obedience. Recent work suggests that these distinctions, especially the special state versus social role debate, are not as sharp as previously thought (Kirsh and Lynn, 1995).

Clinical Applications

A rich body of experimental and clinical evidence supports the application of hypnosis in psychotherapeutic and medical settings. The scholarly literature in this area is uneven in terms of methodology, scope, and focus. While most authorities agree that hypnosis is to be used as an adjunctive technique rather than a comprehensive therapy, some authors focus on the relationship between the degree of hypnotizability and symptom acquisition or maintenance, while other studies explore the relationship between hypnotic interventions and treatment outcome.

A number of methodological problems limit the generalizability of many research findings: failure to describe their hypnotic technique or approach in any detail; absent measures of hypnotizability; unclear targets for hypnotic intervention; and undeveloped rationale for the effectiveness of this technique. Nonetheless, the combination of hypnosis and other psychological treatments has been an effective intervention in a number of areas of medicine and psychotherapy.

Pain

The anesthesiologist Beecher (1969) wrote that an initial physiological event always causes an injury, but the subsequent psychological reaction is intimately involved in creating the experience of pain. As a result of his observations of hospitalized surgical patients and wartime casualties who coped successfully with minimal pain medication, Beecher posited that the patient's level of anxiety and psychological perspective played a central role in determining the degree of suffering experienced with tissue damage (Beecher, 1968; 1969).

Several studies have discovered a linear relationship between the degree of noxious stimulation and pain report, heart rate, and blood pressure readings (Hilgard, 1969; Hilgard and Hilgard, 1975; Hilgard, Macdonald, Marshall, and Morgan, 1974). Hypnotic suggestions for analgesia and distraction have been found to alter this relationship, with hypnotizable subjects reporting the alleviation of pain and highly hypnotizable subjects demonstrating the best reduction (Barber, 1996; Hilgard and Hilgard, 1975). According to the previously mentioned neodissociation hypothesis, researchers propose that a barrier to the conscious awareness of pain exists similar to an amnestic barrier which permits an overt experience of pain freedom, relaxation, and the absence of grimace despite the presence of painful stimulation (Hilgard, 1977). As in the case of posthypnotic amnesia or when a subject is asked to ignore a visually presented object (negative hallucination), adherents of the neodissociation hypothesis believe that the brain of the hypnotized subject makes information regarding painful stimuli temporarily unavailable to conscious perception and capable of being ignored.

In addition to dissociation, most researchers posit some combination of relaxation, distraction, motivation, and cognitive restructuring as operative factors that permit hypnotized subjects to tolerate laboratory-induced or clinical pain. Experimental subjects tolerated electric shock better with hypnosis than at baseline or with placebo (McGlashan, Evans, and Orne, 1969). Miller and Bowers (1986) tested hypnotic suggestions for analgesia

against distraction fantasies and stress inoculation training for cold pressor pain. They found that highly hypnotizable subjects performed well in all conditions, but they did the best when they were offered hypnosis. In another study, ischemic pain was controlled by hypnotically induced suggestions for analgesia, despite having little impact on the subjects' level of anxiety (DeBenedittis, Panerai, and Villamira, 1989).

A number of authors propose a dual mechanism of pain perception which contains a sensory-discriminative function to locate and evaluate the intensity of pain and a motivational-affective function employed to assess the aversive impact and negative emotional resonance. Suggestions for analgesia are thought to control the sensory system, with those for relaxation influencing affects (Barber, 1996; Price and Barber, 1987; Malone, Kurtz, and Strube, 1989; Miller, Barabasz, and Barabasz, 1991).

In a study of children with cancer who were expected to undergo lumbar puncture and bone marrow transplantation, hypnosis helped to manage the associated pain and anxiety better than relaxation and distraction techniques alone (Zeltzer and LeBaron, 1982). Adult patients have been found to tolerate the anxiety and pain associated with cancer (Spiegel and Bloom, 1983; Ali, 1990), bone marrow transplant (Syrjala, Cummings, and Donaldson, 1992), colonoscopy (Cadranel, Benhamou, Zylberberg et al., 1994), angioplasty (Weinstein and Au, 1991), wound debridement (Patterson, Everett, Burns, and Marvin, 1992), arthritis (Domangue, Margolis, Lieberman, and Kaji, 1985), reflex sympathetic dystrophy (Gainer, 1993), and interventional radiography (Lang and Hamilton, 1994) with the aid of hypnosis.

In addition to the cognitive explanations for the role of hypnosis in pain relief, several physiological mechanisms have recently been proposed. Crawford and her colleagues (Crawford, Gur, Skolnick, Gur, and Benson, 1993) discovered increased brain activity in the somatosensory region in response to hypnotic suggestions for analgesia. Researchers found a reduction in spinal nociception as measured by the R-III response in a group of 17 subjects who were instructed to reduce their pain and distress in response to an electric shock (Kiernan, Dane, Phillips, and Price, 1995). The R-III is a spinal nociceptive reflex which, when reduced, can prevent the awareness of the pain signal by the brain. In this study, decreased pain sensation following suggestions for analgesia is thought to have diminished the subjects' awareness of the pain sensation processed by the spinal cord antinociceptive mechanism (R-III). Thus, the higher centers of the brain did not register the full degree of painful stimulation presented. An added benefit to the study is the presence of a physiological parameter to replace the always suspect verbal report as a measure of change (Gracely, 1995).

Asthma

The mind-body connection in bronchial asthma has numerous points of contact. In common parlance, expressions such as "breathtaking beauty," "breathless with anticipation," "inspiring rhetoric," and "panting with excitement" convey our colloquial understanding of the connection between human emotions and respiratory functioning. Anxious-dependent asthmatics have been found to overutilize their medications and medical services as well as to influence their doctors to prescribe more intensive medication regimens than their non-anxious counterparts (Jones, Kinsman, Dirks, and Dahlem, 1979).

A series of studies demonstrate that respiratory symptoms can be produced in human asthmatics by means of *suggestion.* Bronchoconstriction has been induced in asthma sufferers by inviting them to believe that they were inhaling a bronchoconstricting drug or coming into contact with a known allergen, when they were not (Horton, Suda, Kinsman et al., 1978; Spector, Luparello, Kopetzky et al., 1976). Several highly hypnotizable subjects were asked in one study to inhale a saline mist, with their pulmonary functions taken beforehand and afterwards. Pulmonary function tests declined when they were told that they were breathing a bronchoconstricting agent. Subjects reversed their performance when told that they were inhaling a bronchodilator. In each condition, however, the subjects were breathing the same saline mist (Neild and Cameron, 1985).

Clinical research findings show hypnosis to be effective in reducing subjective symptoms of asthma distress as well as medication use. In several early studies, hypnosis was found to be superior to the use of relaxation training alone (British Tuberculosis Association, 1968) and medication control (Maher-Loughnan, 1970) in reducing wheezing and medication usage. More recent studies have found similar reports of symptomatic relief and medication reduction in patients whose chronic asthma had been inadequately controlled by medication (Morrison, 1988) and whose hypnotic capacity predicted symptomatic relief versus a bronchodilator (Ewer and Stewart, 1986).

Unlike in the work with pain, there are few proposed mechanisms of action for hypnosis in asthma. Most of the experimental work seems geared to the suggestion hypothesis developed earlier. Since imaginative ability appears to be involved in creating asthma-like symptoms in

the laboratory, it is reasonable to propose that a new idea can serve to relax the patient enough to permit subjective relief. This assistance might well translate into diminished use of p.r.n. medications. However, those with heightened imaginative ability and hyperreactive personalities may trigger an exacerbation of their illness by imagining themselves to be in danger. As the personality style is addressed and more adaptive imagery suggested, perhaps the calmer patient may experience only baseline disease. The power of the idea might directly reduce the patient's asthma or divert the imaginative trigger to a more benign or adaptive image.

Eating Disorders

In controlled samples from a variety of clinical settings, patients with bulimia have been found to possess unusual amounts of hypnotic ability. In one of the earliest observations, Pettinati and her colleagues (Pettinati, Horne, and Staats, 1985) discovered that hospitalized bulimics scored higher on 3 measures of hypnotizability than a comparison group of anorectic patients. The same elevations of hypnotizability were found in a report of bulimic inpatients (Kranhold, Baumann, and Fichter, 1992). University students with bulimia have also demonstrated higher levels of hypnotizability in several studies (Barabasz, 1990; Groth-Marnat and Schumaker, 1990). These findings were also present in an outpatient clinic sample where women with bulimia also demonstrated higher ratings of hypnotizability compared to normal controls (Covino, Jimerson, Wolfe et al., 1994). Common to all of these studies is the added observation that bulimic patients scored in the high range of hypnotizability. Whereas it is common to find only about 15% of the population in the high range of hypnotizability scores, the majority of the patients in the above-cited studies fell into this rare group. This suggests that there is likely to be a role involving some aspect of hypnosis in symptom acquisition or maintenance in bulimia.

Several investigators propose a beneficial effect for hypnosis in the treatment of bulimia. Clinicians will combine hypnosis with cognitive-behavioral treatments (Holgate, 1984). Suggestions for relaxation, distraction, rehearsal of new behaviors, and control of dissociative and dysphoric feelings are integrated with reframing and other cognitive techniques (Griffiths, Touyz, Mitchell, Bacon, 1987; Vanderlinden and Vandereycken, 1990).

Again, theoretical interpretations of these findings are not abundant, but several possibilities present themselves. As proposed for asthma, perhaps a vivid imagination in the company of an uncritical cognitive style permits self-generated distortions of food or societal emphasis on thinness to persist in the mind of the bulimic, despite corrective information. Since a negative emotional experience often precedes a binge-purge cycle with relaxation following, negative reinforcement theory can also be called upon to understand the maintenance of this behavior. This theory holds that any behavior which reliably reduces a preceding noxious experience will increase in frequency and be reinforced. In keeping with this perspective, perhaps bulimic patients are suggestible people who discover that their symptoms can successfully reduce negative emotions that are difficult for them to put into words (Covino, Jimerson, Wolfe et al., 1994).

Smoking and Weight Control

A persistent and popular myth regarding hypnosis is that the suggestions offered in treatment can motivate reluctant patients to accomplish something that they do not wish to do. Studies involving suggestions for antisocial actions find that subjects truly cannot be driven by hypnosis to perform in ways that oppose their value system (Orne and Evans, 1965). Ambivalent subjects can be invited by the hypnotist to focus with intensity on one side of their conflict in an effort to increase motivation for behavior change. Anxious patients who utilize maladaptive behaviors to regulate their emotions can be trained to employ hypnotic relaxation strategies or to rehearse better coping skills. But forcing a reluctant patient to change is no more possible for the hypnotist than the psychotherapist, physician, or spouse.

Recent research provides some important insights into what motivates people to change and what permits successful transformation (Marlatt and Gordon, 1985; Prochaska, DiClemente, and Norcross, 1992). Prochaska and colleagues propose a series of change stages: precontemplation, contemplation, preparation, action, and termination. Each is thought to have its own character and most appropriate intervention strategy. For example, when a patient is at the contemplation stage, consciousness raising and educational interventions are the most successful. As the person moves toward making and maintaining change, behavioral techniques and environmental controls are helpful (DiClemente and Prochaska, 1982). An understanding of the process of relapse is added to this model by Marlatt and Gordon (1985), who suggest that reframing a relapse as a "lapse" will change the patient's model of treatment to an educational one and invite continued efforts to change.

These theories of change have been employed to address the problems of alcoholism, cigarette smoking, and weight control. Clinicians target specific processes for change and judge success in terms of patient retention and progression to the next stage (Prochaska, Norcross, Fowler et al., 1992). However, little has been done to utilize the imagery, suggestion, behavioral rehearsal, and relaxation potential of hypnosis in combination with this model.

There have been reports of successful uses of hypnosis for weight control (Barabasz and Spiegel, 1989; Cochrane and Friesen, 1986). Some emphasize the advantage of heightened hypnotizability (Anderson, 1985) and length of treatment (Kirsch, Montgomery, and Sapirstein, 1995), yet all of these studies show only a modest number of pounds lost with treatment. Likewise, research on the efficacy of hypnosis for smoking cessation (Lambe, Osier, and Franks, 1986; Perry, Gelfand, and Marcovitch, 1979; Perry and Mullen, 1975) demonstrates only marginal success. Furthermore, this literature has generally failed to employ any physiological outcome measures (e.g., serum thiocyanate) that would enhance the credibility of results beyond the use of patient self-report. Studies that combine the use of hypnosis with nicotine replacement would be useful contributions to clinicians who work in this area.

Persistent Nausea and Vomiting

This common symptom may result from a number of medical causes, but it is most commonly one of the side effects of chemotherapy or a consequence of pregnancy. Classical conditioning paradigms permit us to understand how a previously neutral or even benign stimulus (e.g., a friendly nurse or helpful hospital) can elicit the same problematic response (e.g., nausea and vomiting) when it becomes paired with a noxious stimulus (e.g., cyclophosphamide). The resulting association can trigger anticipatory nausea and vomiting when the patient prepares to return for another chemotherapy treatment or hears the food cart coming up the hall in the hospital.

A group of clinical researchers observed that many inpatients with hyperemesis gravidarum (i.e., persistent nausea and vomiting in pregnancy) left the hospital symptom-free and remained so for the duration of their pregnancy (Apfel, Kelly, and Frankel, 1986). Since no direct treatment had been offered for the hyperemesis (i.e., patients were merely rehydrated), they thought that some suggestive component was more likely the agent of cure and could possibly be involved in the maintenance of the symptom. Indeed, when they assessed a group of patients with hyperemesis, they discovered them to be highly hypnotizable. Moreover, those with more serious symptoms were determined to have the highest levels of hypnotizability.

Although limited, treatment studies have found that hypnosis reduced the symptoms of nausea and vomiting for both groups of sufferers. After only a brief treatment, 122 hyperemesis patients of 138 previous treatment failures reported symptomatic relief regardless of whether they experienced hypnosis in a group or individually (Fuchs, Paldi, Abramovici, and Peretz, 1980). The same success was reported for a hypnotic intervention with oncology patients with anticipatory emesis in a study comparing counseling and no treatment controls (Morrow and Morrell, 1982). In a study where patients served as their own controls, 6 oncology patients were asked to report their symptoms of emesis during and after chemotherapy (Redd, Andresen, and Minagawa, 1982). The application of hypnosis was able to suppress nausea and vomiting each time the hypnotist was present. On the several occasions when the hypnotist was absent for an unscheduled reason, the emesis recurred.

Psychological theory suggests that hypnosis permits the patient to experience a more relaxed or peaceful response in the presence of a noxious stimulus (real or conditioned) allowing the power of the stimulus to be extinguished when frequently repeated. These patients are often referred for hypnotic treatment when their medical providers have become exasperated with the intransigent nature of their symptoms. Clearly, additional clinical research in this area is needed to better establish the utility of hypnotic interventions for this population. However, earlier referral and prophylactic training for at-risk groups might be very helpful to patients distressed by these symptoms and their sequelae.

Immune Disorders

Always a most exciting area of research in the mind-body area is the relationship between suggestion and immune response. A number of stressful events including separation, bereavement, depression, academic stress, and incarceration have been examined for their effects on immune response by researchers in the new field of psychoneuroimmunology. Most writers conclude that those who have been exposed to a high degree of life stress have more compromised physical health (Jemmott and Locke, 1984). The thinking about hypnosis in this area is that suggestions for relaxation, self-absorption, cognitive reframing, and distraction might be powerful factors in offsetting the effects of stress on immune function. Some believe that directing the activity of cells is a useful strategy to employ with hypnosis.

Some of the earliest work in this area was undertaken by A. A. Mason and his colleagues, who utilized hypnosis for the treatment of asthma (Mason and Black, 1958; Maher-Loughnan, MacDonald, Mason, and Fry, 1962) and several dermatologic problems (Mason, 1952, 1963). The results of these studies indicated that suggestion alone could influence the immune response in humans. A group of researchers at the Massachusetts General Hospital found hypnosis to be effective in eliminating a variety of warts that had been unresponsive to traditional treatment (Surman, Gottlieb, Hackett, and Silverberg, 1973). It is not clear whether the mechanism for their success was due to autonomic activity and vasodilatation or a change in immune function.

More recently, Mason (1994) reviewed his earlier work and revised his findings. Instead of finding that immune function was altered with hypnosis, he believes that his study subjects offered the results they believed the investigators were expecting. Thus, psychology rather than physiology was responsible for the successful outcome. In a fashion that resembles a folie à deux, the investigators were also fooled by their wish to believe in the hypnosis hypothesis as much as the subjects were motivated to shape their response in support of the suggestion hypothesis.

Several studies in our laboratory also question the relationship between suggestion and immune response. In one (Locke, Ransil, Covino et al., 1987), highly hypnotizable subjects were unable to alter their immune response to delayed-type hypersensitivity (DTH) antigens. In a second, subjects were first trained to alter hand temperature with suggestion then asked to alter the DTH response to the varicella-zoster antigen (Locke, Ransil, Zachariae et al., 1994). Both studies failed to demonstrate any ability of subjects, trained or otherwise, to alter their immune response with suggestion.

Psychotherapy

In addition to assisting those with medical illnesses, hypnosis has been useful in the treatment of mental health complaints. A recent meta-analysis of 18 studies in which hypnosis was compared to traditional cognitive-behavioral treatments found that the addition of this technique improved the treatment outcome for more than 70% of the hypnotized patients (Kirsch, Montgomery, and Sapirstein, 1995). When means and standard deviations of the outcome variables were compared, hypnosis added about 0.5 standard deviation to treatment success. The authors credit the vivid imagery, suggestibility, and qualities of thinking associated with a dissociative state, as well as altered patient expectations and beliefs. Their conclusion was that most patients who are treated with cognitive-behavioral techniques could benefit from the addition of hypnosis.

Anxiety

Patients with phobias often experience dissociation and panic out of proportion to the stimulus (Frankel, 1976). Although psychodynamic treatments usually fall short of success for these patients, an approach that utilizes graded, imaginative exposure appears to work quite rapidly (Wolpe, 1981).

Frankel and Orne (1976) suggest that the same imaginative ability that assists in managing the panic of the phobic could be involved in the acquisition of the disorder. Their study found not only that phobic patients demonstrated inordinately high degrees of hypnotizability, but also that this trait related to the number of fears. In many ways these findings mirror the psychophysiologic hypothesis of Wickremasekera (1995) and others that heightened imaginative ability acts like an amplifier to the perception of noxious events, prompting an overreaction of the autonomic nervous system.

A number of studies with surgical patients found that psychological techniques can be of benefit at a number of points (Kessler and Dane, 1996). In comparison studies, hypnosis appears to be of greater benefit in the management of presurgical anxiety than a group discussion or patient information (Goldmann, Ogg, and Levey, 1988; Syrjala, Cummings, and Donaldson, 1992). Patients who were taught to use hypnosis before surgery have been found to require less anesthesia during their procedure and to tolerate pain better and be discharged earlier than their counterparts (Goldmann, Ogg, and Levey, 1988; Flaherty and Fitzpatrick, 1978; Matheson and Drever, 1990).

Recovery of Memory

In keeping with the early thinking of Charcot and Freud, a number of psychotherapists have promoted the use of hypnosis in treatment, especially for victims of trauma. Again, they think that this dissociative technique can mirror earlier traumatic experiences and rekindle the attendant emotions and memories. Proponents of the use of hypnosis for memory enhancement believe that the special concentration that comes with this relaxed state can be used to access a repressed memory and permit it to enter consciousness. Sensational cases such as the bus driver who recalled the license number of the kidnapper's van or

the young girls who recalled details about a rapist with the help of hypnosis (Kroger and Douce, 1979) are used to support its efficacy.

Hypnotists in this tradition might employ a videotape metaphor to explain how memory functions, and they invite the subject to slow down, freeze, or magnify what comes to mind (Reiser and Nielson, 1980). Hypnosis is utilized to explore past experiences and articulate the details of an abuse experience with the patient (Phillips, 1993). Other therapists use hypnosis to stabilize patients and teach them ways to cope with intrusive thoughts and dissociative experiences before inviting them to speak about the memories, thoughts, and feelings about traumatic events in an effort to integrate these into consciousness (Brown, 1995).

Although the majority of psychotherapists may believe that hypnosis can help to recover memory (Yapko, 1994), experimental research makes clear that the use of hypnosis in this area is fraught with difficulty.

In experimental situations, the application of hypnosis does not improve recall of word lists by subjects more than encouragement in the nonhypnosis state (Orne, Whitehouse, Dinges, and Orne, 1988). An increase in the production of memories in hypnosis may derive as easily from repetition, review, context, or other psychological factors as from its ability to lift a veil of repression (Erdelyi, 1994). Many researchers believe that subjects who are hypnotized and encouraged to offer additional information relax their caution about what they are willing to report as memory, which invites increased production of material. However, the results are that more errors ("false memories") are produced as additional pieces of truth (Dywan and Bowers, 1983).

The vivid imagery and strong emotions that can be experienced in hypnosis invite the subject to have faith in the validity of the memory even though the event did not occur (Sanders and Simmons, 1983). False memories have been implanted by hypnosis researchers whose subjects remain committed to the truth of these memories, even after the experiment is terminated and the hoax is revealed (Laurence and Perry, 1983; Lynn, Weeks, and Milano, 1989; Sheehan, Statham, and Jamieson, 1991).

Clinicians who favor the use of hypnosis to uncover traumatic memories assert that experimental work in the emotionally sterile environment of a laboratory is not "ecologically valid" and should not be the basis of our understanding of clinical work which draws on deep emotions. Those who argue the case against the use of hypnosis for uncovering memories point to the heightened emotion in the clinical context as the very factor that casts doubt on the truth of what is recovered.

There is much in the literature to suggest that clinical accounts are heavily influenced by explicit suggestion and the expectation of both therapist and patient (Frankel, 1993; Ofshe, 1992). Patients in hypnosis have reported incestuous events in the earliest months of infancy, though the scientific evidence indicates that the nervous system is not yet sufficiently developed at that early state to record memories (Schacter, 1995). People have recalled satanic ritual abuse in early infancy, but the FBI, despite considerable investigation, has never been able to uncover any physical evidence of the burials alleged to have taken place (Lanning, 1989).

It is difficult to believe that a highly hypnotizable individual who is encouraged to let his or her imagination roam to the past will not "recover" events of trauma, even when no formal hypnotic induction has taken place. Likewise, "journaling" (Bass and Davis, 1988), in which patients are encouraged to write down everything that comes to mind, is a process that many critics consider to be vulnerable to hypnotic-like suggestions and questionable conclusions.

Those who appeal to Freud for theoretical support for the use of hypnosis in psychotherapy miss his later writings. As mentioned earlier, Freud did use hypnosis as a suggestive and uncovering technique almost exclusively for the first 8 or 9 years of his practice. He remained theoretically fascinated by hypnosis and often used it as an analogy to explain the workings of the unconscious and his notion of psychoanalytic transference.

There are several legends in psychoanalytic and hypnosis circles regarding Freud's rejection of hypnosis as a therapeutic technique. One story presents Freud's disappointment with his ability as a hypnotist and the failure of the technique to effect permanent enough cures. A second relates a clinical incident in which a patient threw her arms around Freud following a hypnotic treatment. Indeed, there is evidence from a number of Freud's writings for the first (Freud, 1910) and the second (Freud, 1925). While intriguing, these stories miss the point of Freud's struggle with hypnotic technique and psychoanalysis.

In an early paper on psychotherapeutic technique, Freud likens the difference between psychoanalysis and hypnosis to Leonardo da Vinci's famous distinction between painting and sculpture. Hypnosis is like the former, a technique that applies something to a waiting object (suggestion is to an open mind as pigment is to canvas). Psychoanalysis is an effort to uncover the underlying character of the person by gradually eliminating defenses, much as the sculptor peels away layers of rock to free the form within. Far from being an inexperienced hypnotist, Freud had more clinical experience than most masters of

hypnosis and was intimately connected with the writings and works of the field's most prominent leaders in Charcot and Hippolyte Bernheim (1840–1919). However, he ultimately found that hypnosis imposed ideas on a patient whose ego was compromised by an overly intense relationship wherein analysis, logic, and critical thinking were constrained from occurring. His subsequent move to the technique of free association in psychoanalysis was an effort to deal with the limitations that this technique posed in uncovering psychological material along with his evolving theory of the mind.

In a number of ways, hypnosis is a poor technique for use in an uncovering (or psychodynamic) psychotherapy. If Freud could have made it work, it certainly would have saved him a good deal of time and effort! When this technique is applied to already suggestible people in an effort to sharpen memory, research suggests that it yields questionable results. There is little reason to believe that what is uncovered in the clinical context is any different from that of the laboratory or that the patient or therapist can determine what "recovered facts" are indeed true. Given the clinical, theoretical, and research evidence on the questionable nature of memories facilitated by hypnosis, its use in forensic cases is particularly risky business and should be discouraged.

Certain clinical problems in medicine and mental health invite the use of hypnosis as an adjunct to a variety of psychological, medical, and pharmacological treatments. This is especially true for conditions in which an alteration in perception (cognitive or sensory) can influence the activity of the autonomic nervous system. Hypnosis can be helpful in a number of direct and indirect ways by reducing the influence of a hyperreactive personality on a symptom; facilitating the beneficial physiological effects of relaxation; distracting the mind to permit the body to tolerate uncomfortable conditions or procedures; rehearsing new behaviors; or acquiring motivation or a new perspective. These benefits can be the direct result of the application of hypnosis or the consequence of interaction with other factors (e.g., reducing the need for certain medications and saving their side effects).

The multidimensional nature of this technique, with elements of suggestion, motivation, dissociation, role-play, behavior rehearsal, autonomic nervous system influences, perceptual (cognitive, sensory, and memory) alteration, intensified relationship, and so on, most likely accounts for its affinity with a number of medical and psychological theories and clinicians and its survival. Scientists, medical practitioners, psychological clinicians, and a variety of patients have found a myriad of applications for this method across time. The plurality and changing nature of the theories that support clinical hypnosis beg for close collaboration between the scientists and clinicians who are involved in it and a careful reading of their work by consumers.

References

Ali, F. F. 1990. The effect of individual hypnosis on stress, anxiety, and intractable pain experienced by Lebanese cancer patients. *Dissertation Abstract International* [B] 51(6):3111.

Andersen, M. S. 1985. Hypnotizability as a factor in the hypnotic treatment of obesity. *International Journal of Clinical and Experimental Hypnosis* 33:150–159.

Apfel, R. J., Kelly, S. F., and Frankel, F. H. 1986. The role of hypnotizability in the pathogenesis and treatment of nausea and vomiting of pregnancy. *Journal of Psychosomatic Obstetrics and Gynaecology* 5:179–186.

Barabasz, M. 1989. Treatment of bulimia with hypnosis involving awareness and control in clients with high dissociative capacity. *International Journal of Psychosomatics* 36:58.

———— 1990. Treatment of bulimia with hypnosis involving awareness and control in clients with high dissociative capacity. *International Journal of Psychosomatics* 37:53–56.

Barabasz, A. F., and Gregson, R. A. 1979. Antarctic wintering-over, suggestion, and transient olfactory stimulation: EEG-evoked potential and electrodermal responses. *Biological Psychology* 9:285–295.

Barabasz, A., and Spiegel, D. 1989. Hypnotizability and weight loss in obese subjects. *International Journal of Eating Disorders* 8:335–341.

Barber, J. 1996. *Hypnosis and suggestion in the treatment of pain.* New York: W. W. Norton & Co.

Bass, E., and Davis, L. 1988. *The courage to heal: A guide for women survivors of child sexual abuse.* New York: Perennial Library/Harper & Row.

Beecher, H. K. 1968. X. I. Some complexities of the pain experience as seen in comparative studies of pathological and experimental pain. *Research Publications Association for Research in Nervous and Mental Diseases* 46:157–165.

———— 1969. Anxiety and pain. *Journal of the American Medical Association* 209:1080.

Benson, H. 1975. *The relaxation response.* New York: Avon Books.

Borch-Jacobsen, M. 1991. *The emotional tie.* Stanford: Stanford University Press.

Bowers, K. S. 1976. *Hypnosis for the seriously curious.* New York: W. W. Norton & Co.

British Tuberculosis Association. 1968. Hypnosis for asthma: a controlled trial. *British Medical Journal* 4:71–76.

Brown, D. 1995. Pseudomemories: the standard of science and the standard of care in trauma treatment. *American Journal of Clinical Hypnosis* 37:1–24.

Cadranel, J. F., Benhamou, Y., Zylberberg, P., Novello, P., Luciani, F., Valla, D., and Opolon, P. 1994. Hypnotic relaxation: a new sedative tool for colonoscopy? *Journal of Clinical Gastroenterology* 18:27–129.

Cochrane, G., and Friesen, J. 1986. Hypnotherapy in weight loss treatment. *Journal of Consulting and Clinical Psychology* 54:489–492.

Covino, N. A., Jimerson, D. C., Wolfe, B. E., Franko, D. L., and Frankel, F. H. 1994. Hypnotizability, dissociation, and bulimia nervosa. *Journal of Abnormal Psychology* 103:455–459.

Crawford, H. J., and Gruzelier, J. H. 1992. A midstream view of the neuropsychology of hypnosis: recent research and future directions. In *Contemporary hypnosis research,* ed. E. Fromm and M. R. Nash. New York: Guilford Press.

Crawford, H. J., Gur, R. C., Skolnick, B., Gur, R. E., and Benson, D. M. 1993. Effects of hypnosis on regional cerebral blood flow during ischemic pain with and without suggested hypnotic analgesia. *International Journal of Psychophysiology* 15:181–195.

DeBenedittis, G., Panerai, A. A., and Villamira, M. A. 1989. Effects of hypnotic analgesia and hypnotizability on experimental ischemic pain. *International Journal of Clinical and Experimental Hypnosis* 37:55–69.

DiClemente, C. C., and Prochaska, J. O. 1982. Self-change and therapy change of smoking behavior: a comparison of processes of change in cessation and maintenance. *Addictive Behaviors* 7:133–142.

Domangue, B. B., Margolis, C. G., Lieberman, D., and Kaji, H. 1985. Biochemical correlates of hypnoanalgesia in arthritic pain patients. *Journal of Clinical Psychiatry* 46:235–238.

Dywan, J., and Bowers, K. 1983. The use of hypnosis to enhance recall. *Science* 222:184–185.

Ellenberger, H. F. 1970. *The discovery of the unconscious: the history and evolution of dynamic psychiatry.* New York: Basic Books.

Erdelyi, M. H. 1994. Hypnotic hypermnesia: the empty set of hypermnesia. *International Journal of Clinical and Experimental Hypnosis* 42:379–390.

Esdaile, J. 1957. *Hypnosis in medicine and surgery.* New York: Julian.

Ewer, T. C., and Stewart, D. E. 1986. Improvement in bronchial hyper-responsiveness in patients with moderate asthma after treatment with a hypnotic technique: a randomized controlled trial. *British Medical Journal* (clinical research ed.) 293:1129–32.

Flaherty, G. G., and Fitzpatrick, J. J. 1978. Relaxation technique to increase comfort level of postoperative patients: a preliminary study. *Nursing Research* 27:352–355.

Frankel, F. H. 1976. *Hypnosis: trance as a coping mechanism.* New York: Plenum Medical Books.

———— 1993. Adult reconstruction of childhood events in the multiple personality literature. *American Journal of Psychiatry* 150:954–958.

Frankel, F. H., and Orne, M. T. 1976. Hypnotizability and phobic behavior. *Archive of General Psychiatry* 33:1259–69.

Freud, S. 1891. Hypnosis. In *Standard edition*, ed. J. Strachey. Vol. 1. London: Hogarth Press, 1950. 105.

———— 1892–93. A case of successful treatment by hypnotism. In *Standard edition*, ed. J. Strachey. Vol. 1. London: Hogarth Press, 1950. 11–25.

———— 1922. *Group psychology and the analysis of the ego.* London: International Psychoanalytical Press.

———— 1910. The original development of Psychoanalysis. In *Standard edition*, ed. J. Strachey. Vol. 11. London: Hogarth Press, 1950. 1–57.

———— 1925. An autobiographical study. In *Standard edition*, ed. J. Strachey. Vol. 20. London: Hogarth Press, 1950. 3–74.

Fuchs, K., Paldi, E., Abramovici, H., and Peretz, B. A. 1980. Treatment of hyperemesis gravidarum by hypnosis. *International Journal of Clinical and Experimental Hypnosis* 28:313–323.

Gainer, M. J. 1993. Somatization of dissociated traumatic memories in a case of reflex sympathetic dystrophy. *American Journal of Clinical Hypnosis* 36:124–131.

Gauld, A. 1992. *A history of hypnotism.* New York: Cambridge University Press.

Gheorghiu, V. A. 1989. The development of research in suggestibility: critical considerations. In *Suggestion and suggestibility: advances in theory, research, and application*, ed. V. A. Gheorghiu, P. Netter, H. J. Eysenck, and R. Rosenthal. New York: Routledge.

Goldmann, L., Ogg, T. W., and Levey, A. B. 1988. Hypnosis and daycase anesthesia: a study to reduce pre-operative anxiety and intra-operative anesthetic requirements. *Anaesthesia* 43:466–469.

Gracely, R. H. 1995. Hypnosis and hierarchical pain control systems. *Pain* 60:1–2.

Griffiths, R. A., Touyz, S. W., Mitchell, P. B., and Bacon, W. 1987. The treatment of bulimia nervosa. *Australian and New Zealand Journal of Psychiatry* 21:5–15.

Groth-Marnat, G., and Schumaker, J. F. 1990. Hypnotizability, attitudes toward eating, and concern with body size in a female college population. *American Journal of Clinical Hypnosis* 32:194–200.

Hilgard, E. R. 1969. Pain as a puzzle for psychology and physiology. *American Psychologist* 24:103–113.

———— 1977. Divided consciousness: multiple controls in

human thought and action. New York: John Wiley & Sons.

Hilgard, E. R. 1991. A neodissociation interpretation of hypnosis. In *Theories of hypnosis: Current models and perspectives*, ed. S. J. Lynn, Steven Jay, J. W. Rhue, et al. The Guilford clinical and experimental hypnosis series. New York: Guilford Press. 83–104.

Hilgard, E. R., and Hilgard, J. R. 1975. *Hypnosis in the relief of pain.* Los Altos: William Kaufmann.

Hilgard, E. R., and Morgan, A. H. 1975. Heart rate and blood pressure in the study of laboratory pain in man under normal conditions and as influenced by hypnosis. *Acta Neurobiologiae Experimentalis* 35:741–759.

Hilgard, E. R., Macdonald, H., Marshall, G., and Morgan, A. H. 1974. Anticipation of pain and of pain control under hypnosis: heart rate and blood pressure responses in the cold pressor test. *Journal of Abnormal Psychology* 83:561–568.

Holgate, R. A. 1984. Hypnosis in the treatment of bulimia nervosa: A case study. *Australian Journal of Clinical Experimental Hypnosis* 12:105–112.

Horton, D. J., Suda, W. L., Kinsman, R. A., Souhrada, J., and Spector, S. L. 1978. Bronchoconstrictive suggestion in asthma: a role for airways hyperreactivity and emotions. *American Review of Respiratory Disease* 117:1029–38.

Janet, P. 1907. *The major symptoms of hysteria.* New York: Macmillan.

Jemmott, J. B., and Locke, S. E. 1984. Psychosocial factors, immunologic mediation, and human susceptibility to infectious diseases: how much do we know? *Psychological Bulletin* 95:78–108.

Jones, N. F., Kinsman, R. A., Dirks, J. F., and Dahlem, N. W. 1979. Psychological contributions to chronicity in asthma: patient response styles influencing medical treatment and its outcome. *Medical Care* 17:1103–18.

Kessler, R., and Dane, J. R. 1996. Psychological and hypnotic preparation for anesthesia and surgery: an individual differences perspective. *International Journal of Clinical and Experimental Hypnosis* 44:189–207.

Kiernan, B. D., Dane, J. R., Phillips, L. H., and Price, D. D. 1995. Hypnotic analgesia reduces R-III nociceptive reflex: further evidence concerning the multifactorial nature of hypnotic analgesia. *Pain* 60:39–47.

Kirsch, I., and Lynn, S. J. 1995. Altered state of hypnosis: Changes in the theoretical landscape. *American Psychologist* 50:846–858.

Kirsch, I., Montgomery, G., and Sapirstein, G. 1995. Hypnosis as an adjunct to cognitive-behavioral psychotherapy: a meta-analysis. *Journal of Consulting and Clinical Psychology* 163:214–220.

Kranhold, C., Baumann, U., and Fichter, M. 1992. Hypnotizability in bulimic patients and controls: a pilot study. *European Archives of Psychiatry and Clinical Neuroscience* 242:72–76.

Kroger, W. S., and Douce, R. G. 1979. Hypnosis in criminal investigation. *International Journal of Clinical and Experimental Hypnosis* 27:358–374.

Lambe, R., Osier, C., and Franks, P. 1986. A randomized controlled trial of hypnotherapy for smoking cessation. *Journal of Family Practice* 22:61–65.

Lang, E. V., and Hamilton, D. 1994. Anodyne imagery: an alternative to i.v. sedation in interventional radiology. *American Journal of Roentgenology* 162:1221–26.

Lanning, K. V. 1991. Ritual abuse: a law enforcement view or perspective. *Child Abuse and Neglect* 15:171–173.

Lanning, K. V., and Burgess, A. W. 1989. Child pornography and sex rings. In *Pornography: Research advances and policy considerations,* ed. D. Zillmann, J. Bryant, et al. Hillsdale, N.J.: Lawrence Erlbaum. 235–255.

Laurence, J. R., and Perry, C. 1983. Hypnotically created memory among highly hypnotizable subjects. *Science* 222:523–524.

Lazarus, R. S., and Folkman, S. 1984. Stress appraisal and coping. New York: Springer Publishing.

Locke, S. E., Ransil, B. J., Covino, N. A., Toczydlowski, J., Lohse, C. M., Dvorak, H. F., Arndt, K. A., and Frankel, F. H. 1987. Failure of hypnotic suggestion to alter immune response to delayed-type hypersensitivity antigens. *Annals of the New York Academy of Sciences* 496:745–749.

Locke, S. E., Ransil, B. J., Zachariae, R., Molay, F., Tollins, K., Covino, N. A., and Danforth, D. 1994. Effect of hypnotic suggestion on the delayed-type hypersensitivity response. *Journal of the American Medical Association* 272:47–52.

Lundy, R. M. 1989. Measurement and individual differences of suggestibility: some comments. In *Suggestion and suggestibility: new advances in theory, research, and application,* ed. V. A. Gheorghiu, P. Netter, H. J. Eysenck, and R. Rosenthal. New York: Routledge.

Lynn, S.., Weeks, J. R., and Milano, M. J. 1989. Reality versus suggestion: pseudomemory in hypnotizable and simulating subjects. *Journal of Abnormal Psychology* 98:137–144.

Maher-Loughnan, G. P. 1970. Hypnosis and autohypnosis for the treatment of asthma. *International Journal of Clinical and Experimental Hypnosis* 18:1–14.

Maher-Loughnan, M. A., MacDonald, N., Mason, A. A., and Fry, L. 1962. Controlled trials of hypnosis in the symptomatic treatment of asthma. *British Medical Journal* 2:371–376.

Malone, M. D., Kurtz, R. M., and Strube, M. J. 1989. The effects of hypnotic suggestion on pain report. *American Journal of Clinical Hypnosis* 31:221–230.

Marlatt, G. A., and Gordon, J. R., eds. 1985. *Relapse prevention: Maintenance strategies in the treatment of addictive behaviors.* New York: Guilford Press.

Mason,. A. A. 1952. The treatment of congenital ichthyosiform erythrodermia of Braq by hypnotism. *British Medical Journal* 2:422.

——— 1958. Allergic skin responses in a case of asthma and hay fever abolished by hypnotic suggestion. *Lancet* 2:877.

——— 1963. Hypnosis and allergy. *British Medical Journal* 1:1675–76.

——— 1994. A psychoanalyst looks at a hypnotist: a study of folie à deux. *Psychoanalytic Quarterly* 63:641–679.

Mason, A. A., and Black, S. 1958. Allergic skin responses in a case of asthma and hay fever abolished by hypnotic suggestion. *Lancet* 2:877.

Matheson, G., and Drever, J. M. 1990. Psychological preparation of the patient for breast reconstruction. *Annals of Plastic Surgery* 24:238–247.

McGlashan, T. H., Evans, F. J., and Orne, M. T. 1969. The nature of hypnotic analgesia and placebo response to experimental pain. *Psychosomatic Medicine* 31:227–246.

Meichenbaum, D. 1974. *Cognitive-behavior modification.* New York: Plenum Publishing.

Miller, M. E., and Bowers, K. S. 1986. Hypnotic analgesia and stress inoculation in the reduction of pain. *Journal of Abnormal Psychology* 95:6–14.

Miller, M. F., Barabasz, A. F., and Barabasz, M. 1991. Effects of active alert and relaxation hypnotic inductions on cold pressor pain. *Journal of Abnormal Psychology* 100:223–226.

Morgan, A. H., Macdonald, H., and Hilgard, E. R. 1974. EEG alpha: lateral asymmetry related to task, and hypnotizability. *Psychophysiology* 11:275–282.

Morrison, J. B. 1988. Chronic asthma and improvement with relaxation induced by hypnotherapy. *Journal of the Royal Society of Medicine* 81:701–704.

Morrow, G. R., and Morrell, C. 1982. Behavioral treatment for the anticipatory nausea and vomiting induced by cancer chemotherapy. *New England Journal of Medicine* 307:1476–80.

Neild, J. E., and Cameron, I. R. 1985. Bronchoconstriction in response to suggestion: its prevention by an inhaled anticholinergic agent. *British Medical Journal* (clinical research ed.) 290:674.

Ofshe, R. 1992. Inadvertent hypnosis during interrogation: false confession due to dissociative state; misidentified multiple personality and satanic cult hypothesis. *International Journal of Clinical and Experimental Hypnosis* 50:125–156.

Orne, M. T., and Evans, F. 1965. Social control in the psychological experiment: antisocial behavior and hypnosis. *Journal of Personality and Social Psychology* 1:189–200.

Orne, M. T., Whitehouse, W. G., Dinges, D. F., and Orne,

E. C. 1988. Reconstructing memory through hypnosis: forensic and clinical implications. In *Hypnosis and memory,* ed. H. M. Pettinati. New York: Guilford Press.

Patterson, D. R., Everett, J. J., Burns, G. L., and Marvin, J. A. 1992. Hypnosis for the treatment of burn pain. *Journal of Consulting and Clinical Psychology* 60:713–717.

Perry, C., and Mullen, G. 1975. The effects of hypnotic susceptibility on reducing smoking behavior treated by an hypnotic technique. *Journal of Clinical Psychology* 31:498–505.

Perry, C., Gelfand, R., and Marcovitch, P. 1979. The relevance of hypnotic susceptibility in the clinical context. *Journal of Abnormal Psychology* 188:592–603.

Pettinati, H. M., Horne, R. L., and Staats, J. M. 1985. Hypnotizability in patients with anorexia nervosa and bulimia. *Archives of General Psychiatry* 42:1014–16.

Phillips, M. 1993. Turning symptoms into allies: utilization approaches with posttraumatic symptoms. *American Journal of Clinical Hypnosis* 35:179–189.

Price, D. D., and Barber, J. 1987. An analysis of factors that contribute to the efficacy of hypnotic analgesia. *Journal of Abnormal Psychology* 96:46–51.

Prochaska, J. O., DiClemente, C. C., and Norcross, J. C. 1992. In search of how people change: applications to addictive behaviors. *American Psychologist* 47:1102–14.

Prochaska, J. O., Norcross, J. C., Fowler, J. L., Follick, M. J., and Abrams, D. B. 1992. Attendance and outcome in a work site weight control program: processes and stages of change as process and predictor variables. *Addictive Behaviors* 17:35–45.

Redd, W. H., Andresen, G. V., and Minagawa, R. Y. 1982. Hypnotic control of anticipatory emesis in patients receiving cancer chemotherapy. *Journal of Consulting and Clinical Psychology* 50:14–19.

Reiser, M., and Nielson, M. 1980. Investigative hypnosis: a developing specialty. *American Journal of Clinical Hypnosis* 23:75–84.

Sanders, G. S., and Simmons, W. L. 1983. Use of hypnosis to enhance eyewitness accuracy: does it work? *Journal of Applied Psychology* 68:70–77.

Sarbin, T. R., and Coe, W. C. 1972. *Hypnosis: a social psychological analysis of influence communication.* New York: Holt, Rinehart and Winston.

Schacter, D., ed. 1995. *Memory distortion.* Cambridge, Mass.: Harvard University Press.

Schnyer, D. M., and Allen, J. J. 1995. Attention-related electroencephalographic and event-related potential predictors of responsiveness to suggested posthypnotic amnesia. *International Journal of Clinical and Experimental Hypnosis* 43:295–315.

Sheehan, P. W., Statham, D., and Jamieson, G. A. 1991. Pseudomemory effects over time in the hypnotic setting. *Journal of Abnormal Psychology* 100:39–44.

Shor, R. E. 1959. Hypnosis and the concept of generalized reality orientation. *American Journal of Psychotherapy* 12:582–602.

Spanos, N. P. 1982. Hypnotic behavior: a cognitive social psychological perspective. *Research Communications in Psychology, Psychiatry, and Behavior* 7:199–213.

Spector, S., Luparello, T. J., Kopetzky, M. T., Souhrada, J., and Kinsman, R. A. 1976. Response of asthmatics to methacholine and suggestion. *American Review of Respiratory Disease* 113:43–50.

Spiegel, D., and Barabasz, A. F. 1988. Effects of hypnotic instructions on p300 event-related potential amplitudes: research and clinical applications. *American Journal of Clinical Hypnosis* 31:11–17.

Spiegel, D., and Bloom, J. R. 1983. Group therapy and hypnosis reduce metastatic breast carcinoma pain. *Psychosomatic Medicine* 45:333–339.

Spiegel, D., Cutcomb, S., Ren, C., and Pribram, K. 1985. Hypnotic hallucination alters evoked potentials. *Journal of Abnormal Psychology* 94:249–255.

Surman, O. S., Gottlieb, S. K., Hackett, T. P., and Silverberg, E. L. 1973. Hypnosis in the treatment of warts. *Archives of General Psychiatry* 28:439–441.

Syrjala, K. L., Cummings, C., and Donaldson, G. W. 1992. Hypnosis or cognitive behavioral training for the reduction of pain and nausea during cancer treatment: a controlled clinical trial. *Pain* 48:137–146.

Vanderlinden, J., and Vandereycken, W. 1990. The use of hypnosis in the treatment of bulimia nervosa. *International Journal of Clinical and Experimental Hypnosis* 38:101–111.

Weinstein, E. J., and Au, P. K. 1991. Use of hypnosis before and during angioplasty. *American Journal of Clinical Hypnosis* 34:29–37.

Whitehouse, W. G., Dinges, D. F., Orne, E. C., and Orne, M. T. 1988. Hypnotic hypermnesia: enhanced memory accessibility or report bias? *Journal of Abnormal Psychology* 97:289–295.

Wickramasekera, I. 1994. Psychophysiological and clinical implications of the coincidence of high hypnotic ability and high neuroticism during threat perception in somatization disorders. *American Journal of Clinical Hypnosis* 37:22–33.

———— 1995. Somatization: concepts, data, and predictions from the high risk model of threat perception. *Journal of Nervous and Mental Disease* 183:15–23.

Wolpe, J. 1981. Behavior therapy versus psychoanalysis: therapeutic and social implications. *American Psychologist* 36:159–164.

Yapko, M. D. 1994. Suggestibility and repressed memories of abuse: a survey of psychotherapists' beliefs. *American Journal of Clinical Hypnosis* 36:163–187.

Zeltzer, L., and LeBaron, S. 1982. Hypnotic and non-hypnotic techniques for reduction of pain and anxiety during painful procedures in children and adolescents with cancer. *Journal of Pediatrics* 101:1032–35.

Recommended Reading

Barber, J. 1996. Hypnosis and suggestion in the treatment of pain. New York: W. W. Norton.

Frankel, F. H. 1976. *Hypnosis: Trance as a coping mechanism.* New York: Plenum.

Gheorghiu, V. A., Netter, P., Eysenck, H. J., and Rosenthal, R., eds. 1989. *Suggestion and suggestibility: Advances in theory, research, and application.* New York: Routledge.

26

Patient Management

PAUL SUMMERGRAD

KATHY SANDERS

JEFFREY B. WEILBURG

RANDY S. GLASSMAN

The care and management of psychiatric illness has changed significantly in recent years, prompted primarily by scientific and economic forces. During this time a wealth of information has become available concerning accurate and comprehensive psychiatric diagnosis (Regier, Goldberg, and Taube, 1978; Kessler et al., 1994), the nature and course of psychiatric illness (APA, 1997), experience with psychopharmacologic treatments (Joffe, Sokolov, and Streiner, 1996), neuroimaging (Reiman et al., 1989a, b), and molecular biology (Kandel, 1983; Hyman, 1988). The ever-expanding list of psychopharmacologic agents now available for the care of specific psychiatric disorders used singly or in combination has dramatically altered our approach to patients, and enhanced our understanding of the symptoms most likely to be changed by acute psychiatric management (Rosenbaum, 1982; Jenike et al., 1989). Studies combining psychopharmacologic with psychotherapeutic regimens including cognitive-behavioral, interpersonal, and psychodynamic psychotherapy have led to a clearer understanding of how these modes of treatment apply to the care of patients with different diagnostic and presenting problems (Rush, 1996; Waldinger and Frauch, 1989). At no other time in the history of psychiatry have patients with serious and intractable emotional disorders—including depression, manic-depressive illness, schizophrenia, obsessive-compulsive disorder (OCD), panic, and other illnesses—been treated as effectively.

Coinciding with this change has been the emergence of "managed mental health care." The proliferation of managed care companies occurred after a period of relatively unlimited growth—especially in the for-profit sector—of inpatient psychiatric and substance abuse treatment (Jellinek and Nurcombe, 1993). These managed care organizations, often operating from a model of psychiatric care based on short-term psychotherapeutic intervention, have often separated psychiatric care from the rest of general medical-surgical services or imposed severe limits on the ability of patients to seek psychiatric treatment (Summergrad et al., 1995). The demand for quality and outcome measures and defined standards of care, including clinical protocols, have further accelerated a shift away from open-ended psychotherapeutic modalities and from care based on psychodynamic models. These trends focus on diagnostic definition, symptom profiles, rating scales, and outcome measures in an attempt to objectify the care of psychiatric patients (Zarin et al., 1997) for research, clinical, or reimbursement purposes. However, these changes in no way diminish the importance of understanding the patient and the particular, unique circumstances of his or her life.

The patient who presents for emergent or inpatient care is usually seriously ill. The acute turmoil of a depressive episode requires not only accurate diagnosis but an in-depth understanding of the patient as a person as well. This includes not just historical and developmental data but an awareness of the significance of the patient's current circumstances. In the case of acutely suicidal patients or patients with severe character disorders, the need to evaluate a patient's level of despair and safety requires a grounding in psychodynamic psychiatry (Summergrad, 1991).

Psychodynamic evaluation is an essential component of evaluation and management of patients. Despite the improvement of diagnostic precision and the addition of treatment options for the care of patients with significant mental disorders, the value of the broad psychiatric evaluation—the observation of a patient's interrelatedness and the description of past personal and social relationships—remains critical to understanding how a particular disorder affects this individual at this moment in the course of his or her illness (Perry, Cooper, and Michels, 1987).

All medical evaluation and psychiatric evaluation depends upon the construction of a differential diagnosis. This can include—in psychiatry—conditions which may cause disturbances in mood, thought, interpersonal relationships, or other specific elements of behavior. Likewise, gathering information regarding a patient's past and current styles of functioning and relationships and enduring patterns of behavior may generate hypotheses or differential estimates of the degree to which a particular situation or setting may place a patient at substantial risk. Not all patients are equally vulnerable, for example, to loss. The patient who has been traumatized in early life by the loss of a parent or sibling—whatever else his psychiatric symptoms—may be more vulnerable to disruptions in treatment relationships than patients who have known stable family relationships. Individuals whose need for intensely close relationships is marked by ambivalence may respond differently to the structure and support of an inpatient psychiatric setting—a different pattern of reaction from that of patients who have stable interpersonal relationships (Gordon and Beresin, 1983; Gabbard, 1989). The interweaving of diagnostic assessment, knowledge of the scientific and treatment literature, medical evaluation, information about cultural background, and hypotheses derived from psychodynamic formulation are essential elements in the comprehensive evaluation of patients with psychiatric disorders (Eisenberg, 1986).

Likewise, it is important to note that for some patients with specific psychiatric disorders, psychodynamic understanding, while important, may nevertheless not necessarily lead to specific treatments which will reduce the patient's symptoms. The following example illustrates such a situation:

A 31-year-old business executive requested a psychiatric evaluation for help with anxiety symptoms. The son of a well-to-do family, he had previously left home while attending college and then began his own business career. While in his teens, he began to be troubled by increasing symptoms of self-doubt, self-criticism, and recurrent anxiety experiences. These were characterized by the need to wash his hands for extended periods after using the bathroom, touching doorknobs, or using public telephones.

He described his parents as perfectionists. His father in particular was a hard-driving, successful businessman who traveled frequently. In adolescence, he had noted the presence of concerns about knives or other sharp instruments in the house, particularly when his father was home. While living elsewhere he had entered into twice-weekly psychodynamic psychotherapy. While this course of psychotherapy had helped him understand his difficulties in dealing with his family, his obsessional and compulsive symptoms had only worsened. When seen for psychiatric evalua-

tion, he was hand-washing approximately 3 to 4 hours daily, with intrusive obsessional thoughts about contamination and other concerns which interfered with his ability to function at work and in his intimate relationships. Despite a good understanding of the anger he had experienced toward his father and the demands which were placed upon him, psychotherapeutic treatment had been of minimal symptomatic benefit. An interview using a structured obsessive-compulsive disorder rating scale showed the presence of moderate to severe obsessions and compulsions. Treatment with a selective serotonin-reuptake inhibitor (SSRI) led to an 80% reduction in obsessive-compulsive symptoms over an 8-week period. Continued treatment with an SSRI, as well as continued psychotherapeutic contact, led to a persistent reduction in his obsessive-compulsive symptoms.

The above case indicates that the presence of psychodynamic information and fomulation, while valuable in leading to self-understanding, may not be beneficial in managing the difficulties of a particular disorder when specific pharmacologic interventions are required. The next case represents the opposite situation: how the specific psychopharmacologic treatment may be undermined by failure to take into account important dynamic features of a patient's presentation.

A 42-year-old female patient sought psychiatric consultation for symptoms consistent with an atypical major depression, characterized by increased sleep and increased appetite. A review of her past psychiatric history indicated several significant depressive episodes, along with experiences of chronic dysthymia. These were thought by the evaluating psychiatrist to be representative of a rejection-sensitive mood disorder. The patient had had one prior hospitalization for suicidality associated with a worsening depressive illness. The treatment at that time with a tricyclic antidepressant had been reported to be effective. She also had periods of increased use of alcohol, and a sister with a significant substance abuse history.

Despite multiple trials of psychopharmacologic agents, the patient reported ongoing depressive symptoms and began to call the psychiatrist's office frequently. Over the course of the next several months, escalating phone calls, emergency visits, and frequent episodes of alcohol intoxication prompted a reconsideration of the diagnostic evaluation. During hospitalization for worsening suicidal symptoms and substance abuse, the patient's long history of early neglect and abandonment by her mother, absence of a significant relationship with her father, and past history of prior intense and unstable transference relationships with therapists prompted an additional diagnosis of borderline personality disorder. Failure of the original psychiatric evaluation to consider this diagnosis, and the absence of a psychodynamic evaluation which might have revealed it, led to an ineffective treatment plan. To diminish aggressive behavior, the patient was transitioned from individual psychotherapy and psychopharmacologic treatment to group psychotherapy with continued psychopharmacologic management and greater emphasis on substance abuse treatment, including attendance at Alcoholics Anonymous and other structured ambulatory activities.

In this example the lack of a full psychodynamic evaluation, including early history and response to caregivers in previous treatments, led to failure to diagnose a significant personality disorder and to the use of a psychotherapeutic regime which was more likely to lead to regression and an unstable and highly negative transference. Despite other accurate psychiatric diagnoses, the absence of attention to these issues ultimately required a major change in treatment in order to stabilize the patient.

How do the changing paradigms of psychiatric evaluation and treatment and current financial constraints influence patient evaluation, management, and care? In this chapter we will review principles of patient management in several settings: emergency and crisis services, inpatient and diversionary care, as well as the dilemmas of managing care under budgetary constraints.

Excellent psychiatric treatment begins with a comprehensive evaluation and differential diagnosis. In addition to the more open-ended evaluation procedures used in psychoanalysis and in psychodynamic psychotherapy, current psychiatric practice emphasizes a method of gathering data similar to that used in other branches of medicine. This includes review of presenting complaints, history of the present illness, and a clear description of the nature, pattern, duration, and course of symptoms. Many psychiatrists utilize the equivalent of a psychiatric "review of systems" to determine the range of psychiatric disorders or syndromes present in the patient (Hyman and Jenike, 1991).

The evaluating clinician must also obtain information about the patient's background, early development, family relationships, and personality styles. Personality style may be difficult to interpret, given the shifting patterns of defenses and personality presentation in the setting of acute psychiatric syndromes. A complete psychiatric evaluation must include a review of family and personal psychiatric history, history of substance abuse, perinatal and birth information, childhood development of psychiatric difficulties, medical problems, and use of prescribed medications. Given the high comorbidity of medical and substance abuse disorders with psychiatric illness, the clinician must also inquire about past medical illness to order necessary laboratory and medical studies or refer the patient to another physician for such studies.

Many clinicians today use structured rating scales and interviews for diagnostic purposes. The interviews may be automated or used in some other screening format in busy primary care practices. Rating scales frequently used include the Beck Depression Inventory, the Hamilton D for depression, and the Yale-Brown Obsessive-Compulsive Survey, which rates the intensity of obsessive-compulsive symptoms and their interference with daily functioning (Jenike et al., 1989). Screening measures help detect unsuspected psychiatric illness or lifetime comorbidities, while rating scales track a specific patient's response to treatment.

The utilization of rating scales, structured interviews, and a more syndromic model of psychiatric care stems from empirical and other studies demonstrating the response of patients with particular disorders to specific interventions. The increased use of randomized clinical trials in psychopharmacologic studies and the development of short-term psychotherapy studies have led to increasingly specific recommendations for psychopharmacologic and psychotherapeutic interventions (Persons, Thase, and Crits-Christoph, 1996; Dulcan and Benson, 1997). This specificity becomes especially important for patients who may have a number of comorbid psychiatric diagnoses and may be at high risk for multiple hospitalizations. For proper patient care under these circumstances, clinicians must pay close attention not only to mental status examination and formal review of psychiatric and medical symptoms, but to psychodynamically derived data as well. They need to observe the character and quality of interactions with patients, and the types and style of defenses—especially primitive defenses such as splitting and projection—are important.

The next sections review emergency, crisis, and diversionary care, inpatient care, and management of care under limited budgets, including capitation.

Emergency and Crisis Care

The ability of emergency psychiatric staff to contain safely a patient with acute mental status changes and evaluate his or her medical and psychiatric symptoms allows for clear decisions about treatment and the best use of mental health services. The emergency psychiatric service is the center of services that acutely ill patients need for the diagnosis and management of psychiatric, substance abuse, and medical problems (Hillard, 1994; Hyman and Tesar, 1994). This growing trend in the delivery of health care is molded by the changing climate of health care, with its emphasis on cost containment, least restrictive care, quality assurance, and outcome measures. The emergency response system often includes a community-based crisis team with telephone access to an emergency room service. A well-integrated continuum of care makes an array of resources available in a crisis. The decision to admit a patient to a psychiatric hospital or service involves a complex process that takes into consideration other alternatives.

The emergency psychiatric service plays several key roles in crisis management. First, it provides a safe environment for evaluating patients—often over a period of several hours or longer. Second, it offers immediate medical evaluation when substance abuse and/or medical illness are part of the patient's presentation. Third, the emergency psychiatric service provides both insured and uninsured patients and their families help in accessing specialized services. This can be of particular importance during periods of crisis, especially when patients and families have not previously navigated the mental health system or specific insurance plans.

Observation in the Emergency Room

When a patient already in established treatment comes to emergency services, the clinician may be unclear about the cause of the acute crisis. Often, the ability to observe the patient safely over a period of time results in the resolution of a crisis. For example, a patient with chronic mental illness, living in a group home or supervised setting, may experience behavioral difficulties, create concerns about harm to self or others, and be sent to an emergency room for containment. A 24-hour period of observation in the emergency room with additional medication may be what the patient needs to regain self-control and resume his or her usual living arrangements.

A 27-year-old male schizophrenic patient lived in a group home where staff managed medication and privileges under assertive case management principles. The patient was sent to the emergency room when unexpectedly he came home late for dinner and had an angry outburst with staff when confronted about his tardiness. This uncharacteristic behavior frightened the staff and other residents in the group

home. His outburst also included threats of physical violence. Upon arrival in the emergency room, the patient was calm and cooperative. He discussed his feelings of anger and frustration and his struggle with self-control that seemed to be eroded by his illness.

He presented a history of a long, difficult course of treatment following his initial psychotic break, which had caused him to drop out of college. His last psychiatric hospitalization was a year prior to this incident. The emergency room psychiatrist talked with the group home staff to determine the patient's baseline functioning and his symptoms when ill. Realizing this behavior was not usual for the patient, the psychiatrist decided to hold the patient overnight in the emergency room until he would be able to see his usual case manager. The patient was thus removed from a volatile situation until further review of the problem by his regular care providers could occur.

The emergency room setting provided a safe place for the patient while an assessment occurred. Understanding the history of this patient's illness—knowing that he had rarely required hospitalization and that he generally became calmer when temporarily removed from the group home—allowed the emergency room psychiatrist to formulate a plan for care.

Medical Psychiatric Evaluation in the Emergency Room

An important function for a psychiatric emergency service is to evaluate medical issues that may contribute to an acute psychiatric presentation (Marshall, 1949). Intoxication (intentional or unintentional) can be a life-threatening medical emergency. No clinician can adequately evaluate suicidal or homicidal ideation in a patient under the influence of alcohol or other substances. The emergency psychiatric service contains and manages patients while waiting for drugs or alcohol to metabolize sufficiently to permit a valid psychiatric assessment. Additionally, medical illness may sometimes present as a change in mental status and must be diagnosed and treated (Hall et al., 1978).

A 67-year-old homeless woman with long-standing bipolar illness and alcoholism was brought to the emergency room by ambulance. Concerned neighbors called the ambulance when the patient collapsed while exploring garbage cans in their neighborhood. Her vital signs were normal, but her level of consciousness was diminished. She talked in an incoherent yet agitated manner and refused to cooperate with medical examination. The emergency clinician observed that the patient was drunk and that she had not been taking her usual medication. Although her blood alcohol level was twice the legal limit, the examining psychiatrist did not think that explained the severity of her mental status changes. He pursued a medical evaluation while treating her agitation with neuroleptics. An electrocardiogram showed acute changes suggesting myocardial ischemia. No other signs on physical examination pointed to a cardiac event. When enzymes returned positive for an acute myocardial infarction, she was further stabilized and admitted to the cardiac intensive care unit. The patient had no previous history of cardiac problems before this change in mental status.

A 40-year-old businessman came to the emergency room with complaints of chest pain and anxiety. The emergency medicine physician found no evidence of acute cardiopulmonary problems. The patient seemed desperate to discuss his business concerns with the doctor. He spoke of deals falling through because he had failed to connect the proper street names with numbers that appeared in the daily lotto, and then clutched the doctor, desperately looking for understanding. This behavior prompted a consultation from the emergency psychiatric service. The psychiatrist ordered a serum toxicology screen that revealed the presence of cocaine. When the patient was confronted about his use of cocaine, he became guarded and refused to discuss the issue. He was then placed in observation status in the emergency room to give sufficient time for the cocaine to metabolize and allow an adequate psychiatric evaluation. After 6 to 8 hours in the emergency room under observation, the patient was able to engage in a realistic and nonparanoid discussion about his life and his use of cocaine. He agreed to enter detoxification and a structured rehabilitation program.

In both of these cases the evaluation of the patient included a broad differential diagnosis and—in the second case—a willingness to consider the patient's atypical presentation in reaching a more accurate diagnosis.

Managing Emergencies under Managed Care

The mental health benefits of different insurance policies vary widely. Access to care depends on whether the policy is fee for service, preferred provider network, health maintenance organization, or capitated managed care. These types of insurance benefits can be confusing even to knowledgeable clinicians, let alone patients and families. Thorough knowledge of the different policies in a particular geographic region which the emergency psychiatric service covers is crucial in providing the patient with the necessary services without financial liability (Sederer and Summergrad, 1993).

A 35-year-old lab technician was brought to the emergency room by her husband when she was unable to stop crying after an argument they had had after dinner. He was concerned because she kept expressing a desire to die and remarking how meaningless her life had become. Unfamiliar and frightened with this change in his wife as well as being unsure about what to do, he came to the emergency room with her. Neither of the two had a previous psychiatric history, and they did not know where to turn in this family crisis. Their medical health insurer had "carved out" the mental health benefit to another company which handled only mental health and substance abuse treatment. During the psychiatric evaluation in the emergency room, the patient's insurance benefits had to be accessed by calling the separate capitated managed care organization which managed her mental health benefit.

The patient calmed down considerably during the first hour of the evaluation process. The clinician observed that she was suffering from a major depression that had worsened over the last 2 to 3 weeks. Her ability to function at work had diminished, resulting in conflicts with supervisors and co-workers over her performance. This added to her sense of personal failure and futility. During the interview, although not actively suicidal, she was not coping adequately. Her husband was stressed and failed to understand what was going on with his wife. When the clinician explained the diagnosis of major depression to the couple, both were relieved and cooperated with treatment planning.

To plan for appropriate treatment, an awareness of the patient's mental health benefits was crucial in order for treatment to begin without unnecessary delays and frustration. This patient's mental health benefit was based on the integration of an emergency response team with an outpatient network of providers and a psychiatric hospital. The first step in accessing what was available to this patient was to call the clinical crisis team contracted by her insurance company. A crisis team clinician came to the emergency room and met with the patient and her husband to facilitate a covered treatment plan.

With the help of the emergency room psychiatrist who had started the evaluation, the crisis team recommended initiation of medication for depression and a week of partial hospitalization. They determined that the patient needed to take a medical leave from work until her functioning improved with treatment for her depression. Although she lacked suicidal ideation and had a supportive husband, she could not function at work or at home without serious symptoms erupting. The use of partial hospitalization allowed for close observation and rapid use of medication, helped her understand the nature of her illness, and increased her coping skills with specific cognitive behavioral techniques. This choice allowed her to remain with her husband in the evenings without her condition deteriorating. Finally, an appointment with an appropriate outpatient provider was made.

In this situation, the patient's evaluation required not only appropriate diagnosis and an assessment of the patient's social support and coping skills, but also a comprehensive knowledge of how to obtain services for the patient. Absent the expertise which the emergency service provided, even an accurate evaluation would have been of limited benefit if the patient could not have received ongoing care.

Although these cases have focused on the individual patient in crisis, the team approach to the delivery of care is crucial in managing an emergency. Nurses, support staff, case managers, social workers, and doctors each play important roles in the effective understanding and management of disruptive behavior, the identification of resources, and case-specific disposition planning. Good working relationships among co-workers are required to assist patients through the many phases of an evaluation. With the initial triage evaluation, staff must assess safety to decide if a patient can remain in the waiting room or if he or she requires a holding room or mechanical restraint while undergoing evaluation. Other simultaneous activities include insurance identification and verification; medical evaluation including vital signs, observation, and physical examination with or without laboratory studies; use of medication to manage agitated behavior or facilitate the patient's regaining self-control; communication with known outpatient care providers, including case managers; and gathering of information from family and significant others. The emergency service provides ongoing observation; determines the need for restraint or seclusion; and establishes with patient, providers, and at times third-party payers an ongoing plan of care. These steps require extensive communication with clinicians from different medical and mental health disciplines. The psychiatrist is in the middle of numerous relationships that require attention, goodwill, respect, and frequent additional communication before final disposition occurs.

Safety and Restraint

All of these complex activities are done in the service of maintaining the safety of patients in distress. The use of physical restraint to guarantee the safety of a patient undergoing medical and psychiatric evaluation in a busy emergency room is the last resort when less restrictive measures cannot maintain a patient safely. It is usually the severe and involuntary nature of a patient's illness that makes mechanical restraint the best option to keep the patient contained until the evaluation is complete and transfer to a psychiatric, medical, or medical-psychiatric facility can be arranged. Other less restrictive means include sitting with family members in a waiting room, using a professional sitter on a one-to-one basis, and observing a patient in a locked holding room. These issues of patient safety are attended to in the initial triage phase when the patient presents to the emergency room. When a patient is safely secured, staff then can feel safe in caring for the patient in crisis. If the staff do not feel safe, they will avoid contact with, and compromise the care of, that patient. If safety has been afforded, adequate evaluation, diagnosis, and treatment planning can proceed without danger to the patient or staff.

Principles of Inpatient Management

Current Challenges for Inpatient Psychiatry

Inpatient psychiatric care has changed significantly over the past few decades (Mattes, 1982). We now hospitalize only those patients with the most severe psychiatric illnesses, and then only for the most limited period of time. Even prior to managed care, psychiatric units were caring for increasingly varied patient populations (Jayaram et al., 1996). This has been especially true in general hospitals, with the development of medical psychiatry units that care for patients with both active medical and psychiatric disorders (Summergrad, 1994; Stoudemire and Fogel, 1986). Underlying this has been a shift from a model of inpatient treatment which aimed at the definitive treatment of psychiatric conditions to a more symptom- and syndrome-based psychiatric care model, understanding that many serious psychiatric disorders are recurrent and persistent. The latter model often emphasizes symptom recognition, syndrome profiling, and use of rating scales. Psychopharmacologic regimens have become the norm for inpatient psychiatric care. While important psychotherapeutic goals need to be integrated into the hospital care of patients, the clinician uses inpatient hospitalizations to help reduce symptoms, provide focused psychotherapy, and arrange multimodal ambulatory care.

Additionally, the development of integrated delivery systems or integrated behavioral health care networks has led to the reconceptualization of inpatient psychiatric services as being part of a broad continuum of services. These include observation and respite beds, partial hospital services, ambulatory detoxification, and day treatment for patients with substance abuse illnesses (Summergrad et al., 1995). Along with the development of increased residential services for patients with more severe psychiatric illness, the utilization of inpatient services has changed significantly. The average length of stay at leading psychiatric institutions, which once averaged 60 days or more, has fallen to the low double- or high single-digit range. All of these forces have led to a reconsideration of the functions which the inpatient psychiatric unit serve in the continuum of care (Sederer, 1984). In general, we now admit patients for inpatient psychiatric care when they have one or several types of difficulty:

• When they are clearly a danger to themselves or others, or are unable to care for themselves in major activities of daily living.
• When lower levels of treatment fail and they continue to be significantly symptomatic, or when significant social, marital, or family difficulties make it impossible to provide interventions which will treat a significant psychiatric disorder.
• When patients have active medical and/or psychiatric disorders which require multiple psychopharmacologic drug adjustments, electroconvulsive therapy (ECT), or special medical services in a hospital setting.

How do these changes influence the decision to hospitalize a patient? In many circumstances, the use of inpatient services requires an initial evaluation in an emergency or office setting, followed by approval either by an external review agency or a medical director. In lieu of inpatient services, a larger variety of residential, partial, holding, respite, and home health care services are now available. These services, including observation beds or partial hospital services, are often employed by emergency psychiatric services in an attempt to forestall a hospitalization or by inpatient services to shorten length of stay and allow briefer hospitalizations to be incorporated into longer courses of total treatment. The psychiatrist

evaluating a patient is thus no longer faced with a choice between hospitalizing a patient or sending him home, but can choose from a broader range of options.

What Are the Current Goals of Inpatient Psychiatric Care?

With these changes in inpatient populations, lengths of stay, and range of services, the clinician must decide when to hospitalize a patient and must set reasonable goals for that hospitalization.

The clinician may hospitalize a patient to make a detailed diagnostic assessment and to provide a safe environment for psychopharmacologic, medical, or behavioral intervention. Psychotherapy often focuses on specific conflicts, symptom reduction, or psychoeducation within the framework of a broad treatment plan. This includes a psychodynamic formulation and a reasonable assessment of when the patient may be ready to leave the hospital.

The shift of inpatient psychiatric services from a psychotherapeutically open-ended to a symptom-focused model has other implications. Previously, patients with more severe, violent, or difficult psychiatric illnesses were not admitted to open psychiatric units with therapeutic milieu models. Today, most psychiatric units are locked and admit a broader range of psychiatric patients for briefer periods of time. Previously, it was unusual for patients not to attend all group or community meetings on inpatient units. Today, some patients are so seriously ill with either psychotic illness, obsessive-compulsive symptoms, or comorbid medical illness that they cannot leave their rooms, let alone attend meetings (Billig and Leibenluft, 1987). As the following examples indicate, inpatient psychiatric services and care require a broad range of psychiatric expertise.

Protection and Containment

Hospitalization provides increased protection for patients who may harm themselves through self-destructive behaviors, who may harm others, or who are at risk of harm from others or from the environment because their impaired judgment leaves them unable to take appropriate care of themselves. This lack of judgment may result from a variety of psychiatric problems, including delirium or dementia, psychotic illnesses, profound regression in patients with severe character disorders, and acute mania in which grandiose or psychotic thinking may place the patient in personal, financial, or professional jeopardy.

Hospitalization can protect a patient from committing

violent acts that would have serious consequences for both themselves and the community. Violent patients require hospitalization in units that are appropriately staffed and equipped for their safe management.

Suicidal patients frequently require hospitalization for their own protection during diagnostic assessment and treatment. Effective management of a patient who considers, threatens, or attempts suicide depends on accurate assessment of suicidal intent (Sifneos, 1966). A patient who is found to have significant suicidal intent requires hospitalization. To make this assessment, the clinician must first attempt to establish rapport with the patient and understand the various factors involved in the development of the crisis, then must establish the seriousness of a suicidal act, considering both its intent and its lethality. Reliance on either factor alone will be inadequate. For example, a patient with no intention of dying may ingest a drug to manipulate another person, but may choose a drug that is more dangerous than she realizes. Similarly, a patient who seriously contemplates suicide may ingest a medication that is more benign than he thinks and fail in his attempt. In each of these situations, the evaluating clinician must know the patient's intentions to be able to understand the behavior. The clinician must never assume that a patient is knowledgeable about pharmacology and anatomy or that he or she knows precisely which drugs or dosages are lethal.

The clinician must take the patient's communications or subtle messages of despair seriously. If, for example, a patient mentions the possibility of suicide casually during an interview and then dismisses the statement as not serious, the clinician should pursue the subject and inquire more closely about the patient's suicidal thoughts until convinced that the patient has no intention of destroying himself. The clinician must ask whether the patient has thought of the method he would use to kill himself. If the patient answers in the affirmative, further information should be obtained. For example, the clinician should ask whether the patient has managed to procure the means to carry out his plan. Does he have barbiturates or tricyclic antidepressants on hand? How many pills? Does he have a gun? Is it loaded? Has he thought about jumping, hanging, drowning? Are there fantasies that suicide will lead to reunion with lost loved ones, or revenge on those who remain? Such explicit questions can help the psychiatrist evaluate seriousness of intent.

Sudden changes in mood, sudden decisions, or quick solutions to problems also merit careful attention, as the following examples illustrate:

A seriously depressed 19-year-old college student was admitted to the hospital after attempting suicide. She was an orphan who had spent her childhood with her maternal grandmother, whom she detested. She had recently ended a relationship with a boyfriend who had forced her to have sexual intercourse, and she described the experience as painful. To avoid her feelings, she dissociated herself from the sexual act by fantasizing that she was sitting on the sofa watching her boyfriend have intercourse with her.

The resident in charge of her care left for a different service, and the patient was assigned to a new doctor. During the first interview with her new therapist, the patient's depression appeared to have lifted. She claimed she was feeling better and asked whether she could be discharged. The new resident agreed and gave her an appointment for an outpatient visit for the following week. She kept this appointment but appeared to be seriously depressed and asked to be readmitted to the hospital. The resident hesitated because of the shortage of beds. She insisted that she be readmitted, however, and he reluctantly gave in. At this point she suddenly seemed to become preoccupied and said that she wanted to visit her mother's grave before returning for admission the following day. Smiling vaguely, she added that she needed to obtain a toothbrush and a pair of pajamas before returning to the hospital. The doctor agreed, indicating that a bed would be ready for her the following day. The patient failed to return. She was found hanged in her grandmother's basement.

A 72-year-old businessman with a history of several episodes of severe depression became depressed following financial reverses in the stock market. He was treated by a psychiatrist on an outpatient basis twice a week, but his mood remained unchanged. He talked about suicide as a solution for his financial difficulties but reassured the therapist that he would never take such action. The psychiatrist accepted this statement and failed to inquire further about his concrete plans. In the next-to-last interview, the patient looked very depressed, withdrawn, and preoccupied. Alarmed by his appearance, the psychiatrist suggested hospitalization. The patient refused, and the psychiatrist did not press him further but made an appointment with him for the following day. The patient came back, and a marked change seemed to have taken place overnight. He was smiling and said he had worked all night putting his financial affairs in order. He claimed to feel much better and added, "Doctor, it seems as if a big weight has been removed. Now I feel relieved." The psychiatrist, pleased by this apparent change, commented accordingly. The patient smiled as he was leaving and said, "So you think that I am really improving, doctor?" The patient shot himself in his apartment, leaving a note saying that no one had understood the complexity of his problems and that he considered suicide the best way out. The doctor had misunderstood the implication of the "smiling depression" and misinterpreted the patient's statement about straightening out his financial affairs. He had indeed done so, but only in preparation for his death.

Assessment and management of the suicidal patient and appropriate decision making regarding hospitalization depend on an understanding of both the conscious and the unconscious meanings of the patient's suicidal ideas or actions. This understanding must be based on knowledge of the patient's long-standing conflicts, characteristic adaptational modes, and reactions to extreme psychological stress. With some patients, exploration of the method employed in a suicide attempt can yield valuable information about these conscious and unconscious wishes. For example, taking one's mother's heart medication may reveal some of the patient's unconscious feelings.

The most common situations creating a suicidal crisis concern loss—not only of a loved one but also of property, a job, or health. These experiences, in turn, may arouse morbid feelings of hostility and hopelessness. A particular event can then result in a crushing loss of self-esteem. Unable to cope with such feelings, the patient sees the desperate act of suicide as the only solution.

Perhaps more than all other psychiatric emergencies, manipulative suicide attempts tax the physician's capabilities and patience (Maltsberger and Buie, 1974). Manipulative patients strive to rearrange the environment in order to continue living as they desire and to achieve their ends by controlling others. Because suicide manipulators often wish for life rather than death, they may give the impression that their attempts are less than serious. Moreover, when the mode used does not appear particularly lethal, the doctor may dismiss the attempt as a gesture and make no serious effort to investigate it. This failure may prove disastrous.

The patient who attempts suicide in order to manipulate others or his environment may be "successful" in obtaining everything he wants. But the suicidal behavior may be effective for only a limited time. It may satisfy the patient but be unrealistic, with success occurring only in the patient's imagination. Or it may fail in terms of both reality and fantasy (Sifneos, 1966). In any case, the patient's attempt to effect change at the risk of such enormous personal cost reflects desperation. The patient is often in a state of great emotional turmoil, with poor judgment and poor impulse control. Hospitalization provides the patient with some security against further suicide attempts as well as an opportunity to gain perspective on his manipulative behavior.

In evaluating and treating both actively and potentially suicidal patients, the psychiatrist must beware allowing extraneous concerns to hamper his or her ability to assess a patient's clinical needs. Mismanagement is sure to result from a clinician's belief that the patient cannot survive without him or from a preoccupation with possible criticism from colleagues if a patient attempts suicide. In the latter case the clinician's insecurity will be communicated to the patient, who may respond with manipulative behavior, and the clinician may fail to take the calculated risks necessary to reverse the patient's self-destructive patterns. Similarly, to accord special privileges to physicians, colleagues, or well-known people admitted as suicidal patients—such as altering the usual admission criteria or, after admission, relaxing routine suicide precautions in order to make psychiatric treatment more tolerable—courts unnecessary risk. The social status of a patient must never interfere with sound clinical judgment. Once the recommendation for hospitalization or suicide precautions has been made, it must be scrupulously carried out, regardless of the patient's social or professional standing. Likewise, the psychiatrist cannot allow insurance status or the decision of managed care reviewers to have the last word about whether or not to admit or treat a suicidal patient.

The psychiatrist may also be unaware of the negative countertransference feelings that suicidal patients can evoke. If this is the case, treatment recommendations can be adversely affected by the clinician's feelings. This problem often arises in the long-term psychotherapeutic treatment of borderline patients who are chronically suicidal. John T. Maltsberger and Dan H. Buie (1974) have described the variety of ways in which "countertransference hate" can affect the clinician's interventions. For example, such feelings may lead the clinician to attempt to remove him from the patient by recommending hospitalization unnecessarily or too quickly, thereby needlessly risking the regression that often develops secondary to hospitalization. Or the clinician may become overinvolved and tend to take too much responsibility for the patient. This, too, may lead to further regression. The clinician's discomfort with the hostility evoked by such patients may lead to a psychological abandonment of the patient and, as a result, inadequate attention to suicidal behaviors or ideas. Because of the wide variety of conscious and unconscious responses evoked by these patients, clinicians must take special notice of their motives for recommending hospitalization or discharge from the hospital.

Although the types of protection described above can be thought of as containment, we use the term here in a more limited sense to apply to patients who feel overwhelmed by affects, thoughts, or impulses to a degree that is enormously painful but does not leave them in danger of destructive or suicidal behavior. These patients are unable to mobilize the normal adaptive capacities that others have or that they themselves may have when not ill. They include patients with acute affective or psychotic illness, patients with severe character pathology who are very regressed, and acutely agitated, anxious, demented, or delirious patients. For such patients, hospitalization often provides a sense of protection and safety that is as important to them as the concrete protection provided to the self-destructive or violent patients described above (Leeman, 1983).

In making a decision to hospitalize a patient, the clinician must consider the patient's social context in addition to his or her symptoms and diagnosis.

Patient A is a 30-year-old married woman who has carried a diagnosis of bipolar disorder for 7 years. Throughout this period she has been followed by the same psychiatrist and has been taking lithium carbonate. Since her first manic episode she had 2 subsequent manic episodes and 1 episode of major depressive disorder. She is now acutely manic, with grandiose delusions, hypersexuality, auditory hallucinations, and decreased sleep. Her husband calls the treating psychiatrist to say that his wife is ill again. The patient willingly comes to see the psychiatrist that afternoon with her husband. Although she is delusional, she says she knows she is sick and agrees to stay at home with her husband, increase her dosage of lithium, and begin to use neuroleptics. Her husband agrees with the plan. Furthermore, the couple agrees to see the psychiatrist the following day, and the psychiatrist is available to see the patient as frequently as necessary during the next several days.

Patient B is a 26-year-old single male graduate student who has recently moved to this area from another part of the country. He has no family in the area. He has no previous history of psychiatric illness. He has been quite successful in the past both academically and socially. He has been somewhat anxious about his academic workload, but his biggest problem has been his sense of loneliness. He has become acutely manic with grandiose delusions, auditory hallucinations, increased energy, and decreased sleep. He is brought to the emergency unit of a general hospital by his roommate, who has known him for only a few weeks. The patient is not happy about being in the emergency unit because he has "big plans" and "important things to attend to." He refuses to stay in the hospital and leaves in a huff. Two days later, after considerable pressure from his roommate and his academic adviser, he reluctantly agrees to be admitted to the psychiatric unit of the hospital.

These two acutely manic patients require different approaches. Patient A has a history of compliance with a treatment program, is aware that she is ill, and is readily willing to comply with current treatment recommendations. Moreover, her husband is a reasonable observer who is committed to her and eager to see her appropriately treated for her illness. He will probably call the psychiatrist if the patient accelerates or fails to comply with the treatment recommendations. In addition, the patient is in a treatment relationship with a psychiatrist who is willing to see the patient frequently during the psychosis. Patient B has no experience with manic psychosis and therefore has little appreciation of the fact that he is ill. He has few social ties in his current situation. His roommate is concerned and responsible, but his commitment to the patient is limited. Moreover, there is no clinician in the area with whom the patient has an ongoing relationship. There is little likelihood that he will respond to an outpatient treatment approach even under pressure from his roommate and adviser. He needs to be in the hospital.

The clinician must always assess the interplay between clinical presentation and social situation in determining the need for hospitalization. In fact, sometimes a relatively benign clinical presentation is best treated in the hospital because of a particularly chaotic or disturbed situation at home. In addition, patients with chronic psychiatric disorders may at times be admitted to a hospital or a residential treatment center not because their illness has worsened but because their social situation has changed.

A 38-year-old chronic schizophrenic woman lives with her mother, who is her only caretaker and who routinely compensates for her daughter's poor judgment and paranoid thinking. The patient's mother is forced to leave town because another family member is ill. During the previous extended absences of her mother, the patient has not taken her medications and has quickly decompensated and required lengthy admissions to the hospital. The patient again stops taking her medication after her mother's departure, and her psychotic symptoms increase. Keeping her psychiatric history in mind, the patient's psychiatrist recommends hospitalization or a residential treatment unit to prevent a further decompensation. The patient is discharged several days later, when her mother returns.

Intensive or Rapid Diagnostic Evaluation

Hospitalization, or periods of intensive observation, may be appropriate for patients whose symptoms and functioning the clinician finds difficult to understand and diagnose on a routine outpatient basis. Extended observation provides an opportunity for around-the-clock data gathering that may be essential for psychiatric diagnosis. It may also provide an opportunity to observe the patient with his or her family or facilitate the use of sophisticated diagnostic tools.

A 67-year-old retired man had been treated weekly for more than a year for what appeared to be a major depressive disorder, though with some atypical components. Treatment involved the use of appropriate doses of antidepressant medications; exploration of recent losses, both real and symbolic; and meetings with the patient and his wife to explore the possibility of marital adjustment difficulties as a contributing factor in the patient's depression. Despite the clinician's sophisticated efforts, the patient seemed to be increasingly sad and depressed and was less and less able to perform routine household chores or to participate in social activities. Moreover, the clinician felt that he still lacked a good understanding of the patient's concerns and conflicts. The patient was hospitalized and within days looked much brighter. He interacted with other patients and staff members and apparently derived much satisfaction from these interactions. By contrast, when his wife visited, he reverted to a rather sullen and depressed presentation. This observation permitted first the inpatient staff and, subsequently, the outpatient clinician to focus with greater success on the patient's conflicted relationship with his wife, which was exacerbated by his retirement and their increased time together.

A 36-year-old laborer was evaluated on an outpatient basis for a particularly confusing clinical presentation that included rapid and marked fluctuations of mood, episodes of irritability, and infrequent periods of hostility with paranoia. A number of diagnoses had been considered, including rapid-cycling bipolar disorder, temporal lobe epilepsy, and mixed character disorder. He was followed by both a neurologist and a psychiatrist, who worked closely together. A series of electroencephalograms (EEGs) revealed no seizure focus, and trials of lithium carbonate, carbamazapine, and antidepressant medications produced limited clinical improvement. In this context, the clinicians requested hospitalization in order to obtain more data about the patient's complaints of rapid

fluctuation in mood, to observe how the patient interacted with other patients and staff, and to obtain 24 hours of telemetric EEG monitoring. During this monitoring, the patient and staff would note any unusual behaviors or striking fluctuations in mood to ascertain whether there was any correlation between subjective experiences, objective behaviors, and EEG changes.

A 23-year-old graduate student was hospitalized because of increasing withdrawal and inability to leave his room while attending graduate school. The patient had a past history of learning disabilities, but had nevertheless been able to complete college. He had been thought to have suffered from depressive episodes characterized by withdrawal and impaired work and school performance. When the patient's family, who had been unable to reach him, finally found him, they discovered his apartment strewn with garbage. The patient was hospitalized because of his inability to care for himself. A careful diagnostic evaluation revealed the presence of a preexisting attention deficit disorder (ADD) in childhood and the onset of significant obsessive-compulsive disorder, characterized by procrastination and hoarding beginning in his teenage years. Treatment for his obsessive-compulsive disorder, including structured cognitive behavioral therapies, in addition to pharmacologic intervention aimed at ameliorating his residual ADD symptoms as well as OCD, along with a more structured and supportive approach to his graduate studies, led to his successful discharge and return to graduate work.

In this situation, a complex and difficult diagnostic picture was only elaborated in the context of a hospitalization. Hospitalization was needed owing to the deterioration of the patient's living circumstances. Meticulous diagnostic evaluation required the collation of multiple sources of information, including past treatment records, childhood medical evaluations, and the reformulation of his diagnosis to highlight the presence of chronic obsessive-compulsive disorders since early adolescence. The use of specific structured interviews as well as psychological testing and consultation was essential for the accurate diagnosis to be made.

Initiation of Treatment in a Supervised or Medically Safe Setting

Some patients who do not require hospitalization for protection, containment, or diagnosis are admitted because the initiation of their treatment is deemed to be most appropriate in a hospital setting.

An elderly woman with a history of a myocardial infarction, congestive heart failure, and periods of orthostatic hypotension was diagnosed as having a major depressive disorder. Her psychiatrist decided that the appropriate treatment was an antidepressant medication, but both the psychiatrist and the patient's internist agreed that the medication should be started slowly and in an inpatient setting so that vital signs could be monitored frequently. If problems such as orthostatic hypotension or electrocardiogram (EKG) changes did develop, they would be noted quickly and acted on.

Diagnostic and Treatment Dilemmas

Patients misdiagnosed with psychiatric illness when their disorders are actually medical in nature pose a special problem on the inpatient psychiatric service.

A 64-year-old woman was admitted to the inpatient psychiatric service of a general hospital after several months of weight loss and chronic pain. Extensive medical evaluation by her internist including multiple radiologic and ultrasound studies revealed no medical cause for her preoccupation with pain. She was admitted with a presumptive diagnosis of major depression and treated with psychopharmacologic agents.

After a week of continued non-response to these medications, her case was reevaluated by her psychiatrist. As the psychiatrist reviewed both her symptoms and history, the patient expressed concern about her ongoing back pain. She denied any ruminative or cognitive depressive symptoms such as hopelessness, nor did she have significant neurovegetative symptoms such as awakening at night not otherwise attributable to her chronic pain. Because of the penetrating and intense nature of her persistent back pain, a CT scan of the abdomen was undertaken; this revealed the presence of a large pancreatic carcinoma. The patient was transferred to the medical service for pain management, palliation, and preparation for hospice care. She lived for several weeks subsequent to the accurate diagnosis, which allowed important closure for her and her family.

This case demonstrates that psychiatrists and other inpatient clinicians must be alert to the possibility that an intercurrent medical illness may be present during hospitalization. Such patients may be recognized by their failure to respond to psychopharmacological agents and by

the absence of cognitive and other mental components of depression. Neurovegetative signs prove less accurate in this population.

A 74-year-old woman was admitted from home on referral from her primary care physician because of failure to thrive and a question of major depressive disorder. The patient, who had had prior depressive episodes, was initially responsive and alert upon admission to the unit. Within 2 hours of admission, however, she developed a fever of 103.3 degrees, became obtunded, and developed a stiff neck. A lumbar puncture revealed a large number of white cells including polymorphonuclear lymphocytes. The patient was transferred to the medical service for emergent care of meningitis. A subsequent culture revealed *Listeria* monocytogenes meningitis.

This case illustrates how important it is for a psychiatrist to rule out the presence of intercurrent medical illness, even in patients with known psychiatric illness.

Another example of the difference between inpatient and ambulatory practice involves patients with treatment-resistant depression. Because of managed care pressures and the need to relieve suffering, many patients admitted to the hospital have already failed to respond to several treatment regimens of antidepressants. When faced with these circumstances, clinicians need to consider whether some intercurrent medical disorder exists, whether a family or personal conflict has gone unrecognized, or whether ECT should be a treatment alternative. The long lag time before antidepressants begin to act makes these decisions difficult. Inpatient psychiatrists are then faced with a dilemma of determining whether or not a patient seems to be in the early stages of response to an antidepressant. If patients continue to be ruminative for over a week, show evidence of early morning awakening, or display other melancholic symptoms, ECT may be a preferred treatment.

A 70-year-old man with a history of recurrent depressive illness was admitted to the hospital; he had previously been treated for his depression, early morning awakening, and diurnal mood variation with an SSRI, and an SSRI in combination with a tricyclic antidepressant. Both medications had been used in adequate therapeutic dosages, and there were documented adequate tricyclic blood levels. There were no medical issues which prevented treatment with antidepressants, and the patient continued to be quite ruminative and in significant distress. Continued preoccupation with suicidality also raised concerns for his inpatient psychiatrist, who switched the patient's antidepressant to a more sedating agent in hopes of improving his sleep. However, the patient continued agitated, had frequent middle-of-the-night awakenings, and woke up ruminative and despairing. After a 5-day period of a new antidepressant, the psychiatrist determined that the patient's level of suicidality and other symptoms, as well as failure to show any evidence of response to his current regimen, warranted a course of ECT. The patient was treated with 8 unipolar ECT treatments and had an excellent response with complete remission of his depressive illness.

This case indicates that standards for changing one antidepressant for another or deciding on a course of ECT may differ in the inpatient setting. These decisions are made more complicated because new psychopharmacologic agents are rarely tested on inpatient populations with severe psychiatric illness. Therefore, hospitalized patients are treated with less available data than psychiatric outpatients. Additionally, concern over the medical complications of prolonged depressive illness—weight loss, aspiration, the risk of suicide, and/or continual anguish—must be considered as well in the decision to initiate ECT.

Managing Care under Limited Budgets and Capitation

Four major features are critical to caring successfully for patients under current cost constraints. These include: (1) high-quality initial evaluations; (2) access to real-time information, including information about the performance, the rules, and the activities of the provider network; (3) sophisticated case management that relies on information about the managed care organization and clinical information from the evaluation; and (4) effective linkages between the inpatient and outpatient staffs.

Initial psychiatric evaluations are like any other health care encounter. The skill of the clinician is critical in differentiating major psychiatric disorders from complaints related to problems in living or transient reactions to environmental stressors. Effective treatment requires careful diagnostic assessment and use of treatment modalities targeted toward resolution of specific problems.

A thorough initial evaluation, which lays out the difficulties and a plan at the outset, is an extremely effective way of forming an alliance with the patient. The clinician can educate the patient and family in a useful and collegial way, discussing such topics as long-term care (if required), expectations for outcome, the role of all elements of the health care system (including the patient and family), and the role of the case manager.

The clinical information derived from the initial evaluation needs to be complete and displayed in a manner that allows it to be discussed clearly and to be accessible over time as a case evolves. Development of a well-constructed form to collect data from the evaluations facilitates proper case management and provides meaningful information about trends in care so that management may be improved.

We have found that case management needs to operate according to the same principles as a high-quality evaluation. If the case managers are not highly skilled but are working from a script, they are likely to miss elements of diagnosis that a more skilled clinician might see.

The case management system needs to operate quickly when a complex patient needs care. Both the patient and the provider may need assistance in completing the evaluation and moving rapidly to a thoughtful plan. The case management systems should not be bound by a set number of visits for every situation, but should be flexible enough to allow more visits when the situation warrants. Case management should be able to mediate patient and provider expectations when provision of services has proven ineffective and decisions need to be made about better forms of treatment (Gabbard et al., 1991).

While much has changed in the management and care of psychiatric patients, including new trends in diagnosis, psychopharmacologic management, models of inpatient and ambulatory care, and management of patients under limited budgets, certain principles remain unchanged. First, the assumption of professional responsibility requires accurate, thorough, and multimodal diagnostic evaluation. Second, psychiatrists and other clinicians need to be aware that an initial diagnosis or treatment plan may need to be modified in the light of emerging conditions. Third, despite significant advances in the neurobiology of mental illness, neuroimaging, and diagnostic and psychopharmacologic methodologies, the general assessment of patients—including a psychodynamic formulation—is essential in understanding their psychiatric illness.

The future promises to bring increasing change to the systems which treat patients. While psychiatrists must be alert to the shifting economic aspects of medical practice, our primary concern must always be the well-being of the patient.

References

Adler, G., and Meyerson, P. G. 1973. *Confrontation in psychotherapy.* New York: Science House.

American Psychiatric Association (APA). 1997. Practice

guideline for the treatment of patients with schizophrenia. *Am. J. Psychiatry* 154(4 suppl.):1–63.

Anderson, W. H., and Stern, T. A. 1989. Psychiatric emergencies. In *Emergency medicine: scientific foundations and current practice* 3rd ed., ed. E. W. Wilkins. Baltimore: Williams & Wilkins.

Billig, N., Leibenluft, E. 1987. Special considerations in integrating elderly patients into a general hospital unit. *Hosp. Community Psychiatry* 38:277–281.

Curry, J. L. 1993. The care of psychiatric patients in the emergency department. *Journal of Emergency Nursing* 19:396–407.

Docherty, J. D., Marden, S. R., Van Kammen, D. P., Sires, S. L. 1977. Psychotherapy and pharmacotherapy: conceptual issues. *Am. J. Psychiatry* 134:529–533.

Dulcan, M. K., and Benson, R. S. 1997. AACAP official action: summary of the practice parameters for assessment and treatment of children, adolescents, and adults with ADHD. *J. Am. Acad. Child Adolesc. Psychiatry* 36(9):1311–7.

Eisenberg, L. 1986. Mindlessness and brainlessness in psychiatry. *Br. J. Psychiatry* 148:497–508.

Fogel, B., and Stoudemire, A. 1986. Organization and development of combined medical-psychiatric units. Pt. 2. *Psychosomatics.* 27:417–428.

Friedman, H. J. 1969. Some problems of inpatient management with borderline patients. *Am. J. Psychiatry* 126:299–304.

Gabbard, G. O. 1989. Splitting in hospital treatment. *Am. J. Psychiatry* 146:444–451.

Gabbard, G. O., Takahashi, T., Davidson, J., et al. 1991. A psychodynamic perspective on the clinical impact of insurance review. *Am. J. Psychiatry* 148:318–323.

Glick, I. D., Hargreaves, W. A., Raskin, M., Kutner, S. J. 1975. Short versus long hospitalization: a prospective controlled study. I. Results for schizophrenic patients. *Am. J. Psychiatry* 132:385–350.

Glick, I. D., Hargreaves, W. A., Drues, J., Showstack, J. A. 1976. Short versus long hospitalization: a controlled study. III. Inpatient results for non-schizophrenics. *Arch. Gen. Psychiatry* 33:78–83.

Gordon, C., and Beresin, E. 1983. Conflicting treatment models for the inpatient management of borderline patients. *Am. J. Psychiatry* 140:579–983.

Gunderson, J. G. 1974. Management of manic states: the problem of fire setting. *Psychiatry* 37:137–146.

Hall, R. C. W., and Kathol, R. G. 1992. Developing a level III/IV medical psychiatric unit: establishing a basis, design of the unit, and physician responsibility. *Psychosomatics* 33:368–375.

Hall, R. C. W., Popkin, M. K., Devaul, R. A., Faillace, L. A., Stickney, S. K. 1978. Physical illness presenting as psychiatric disease. *Arch. Gen. Psych.* 35:1315–20.

Hillard, J. R. 1994. The past and future of psychiatric emergency services in the U.S. hospital and community. *Psychiatry* 45:541–544.

Hyman, S. E. 1988. The role of molecular biology in psychiatry. *Psychosomatics* 29:328–332.

Hyman, S. E., and Tesar, G. E. 1994. *Manual of psychiatric emergencies.* Boston: Little, Brown.

Jayaram, G., Tien, A. Y., Sullivan, P., Gwon, H. 1996. Elements of a successful short-stay inpatient psychiatric service. *Psychiatr. Serv.* 47(4):407–412.

Jellinek, M. S., and Nurcombe, B. 1993. Two wrongs don't make a right: managed care, mental health, and the medical marketplace. *JAMA* 270(14):1737–39.

Jenike, M. A., Baer, L., Summergrad, P., et al. 1989. Obsessive-compulsive disorder: a double-blind, placebo controlled trial of clomipramine in 27 patients. *Am. J. Psychiatry* 146:1328–30.

Joffe, R., Sokolov, S., and Streiner, D. 1996. Antidepressant treatment of depression: a meta-analysis. *Can. J. Psychiatry* 41(10):613–616.

Kandel, E. R. 1983. From metapsychology to molecular biology: exploration into the nature of anxiety. *Am. J. Psychiatry* 140:1277–93.

Kathol, R. G., Harsch, H. H., Hall, R. C. W., Shakespeare, A., Cowart, T. 1992. Categorization of types of medical/psychiatry units based on level of acuity. *Psychosomatics* 33:376–386.

Kernberg, O. F. 1981. The therapeutic community: a re-evaluation. *NAPPH* 12:46–55.

Kessler, R. C., McGonagle, K. A., Zhao, S., Nelson, C. B., Hughes, M., Eshleman, S., Wittchen, U., Kendler, K. S. 1994. Lifetime and 12 month prevalence of DSM-III-R psychiatric disorders in the United States: results from the National Comorbidity survey. *Arch. Gen. Psych.* 51:8–19.

Kirshner, L. A. 1982. Length of stay of psychiatric patients: a critical review and discussion. *J. Nerv. Ment. Dis.* 170:27–33.

Klein, D. F., and Gorman, J. M. 1987. A model of panic and agoraphobic development. *Acta Psychiatr. Scand.* 76(suppl. 335):87–95.

Klerman, G. L. 1982. The psychiatric revolution of the past twenty-five years. In *Deviance and mental illness,* ed. Gove, W. R. Beverly Hills, Calif.: Sage. 177–198.

LeDoux, J. E. 1986. The neurobiology of emotion. In *Mind and brain,* ed. LeDoux, J. E., and Hirst, W. Cambridge: Cambridge University Press.

Leeman, C. P. 1983. The therapeutic milieu. In *Inpatient psychiatry: diagnosis and treatment,* ed. Sederer, L. I. Baltimore: Williams & Wilkins.

Lipowski, Z. J. 1989. Psychiatry: mindless or brainless, both or neither. *Can. J. Psychiatry* 34:249–254.

Maltsberger, J. T., and Buie, D. H. 1974.

Countertransference hate in the treatment of suicidal patients. *Arch. Gen. Psychiatry* 30:625–633.

Marshall, H. E. S. 1949. Incidence of physical disorders among psychiatric inpatients: a study of 175 cases. *Br. Med. J.* 1320:468–470.

Mattes, J. A. 1982. The optimal length of hospitalization for psychiatric patients: a review of the literature. *Hosp. Community Psychiatry* 33:824–828.

Mohl, P. C., Lomax, J., Tasman, A., Sledge, W., Chan, C., Summergrad, P., Notman, M. 1990. Psychotherapy training for the psychiatrist of the future. *Am. J. Psychiatry* 147:7–13.

Mountz, J. M., Modell, J. G., and Wilson, M. W. 1989. Positron emission tomographic evaluation of cerebral blood flow during state anxiety in simple phobia. *Arch. Gen. Psychiatry* 46:501–504.

Neuman, E. M., Reiman, M. E., Kebins, E., et al. 1986. The application of positron emission tomography to the study of panic disorder. *Am. J. Psychiatry* 143:469–477.

Perry, S., Cooper, A. M., and Michels, R. 1987. The psychodynamic foundation: its purpose, structure, and clinical application. *Am. J. Psychiatry* 144:543–550.

Persons, J. B., Thase, M. E., and Crits-Christoph, P. 1996. The role of psychotherapy in the treatment of depression: review of two practice guidelines. *Arch. Gen. Psychiatry* 53(4):283–290.

Regier, D. A., Goldberg, I. D., and Taube, C. A. 1978. The de facto U.S. mental health services system. *Arch. Gen. Psychiatry* 35:685–693.

Reiman, E., Raichle, M. E., Robins, E., et al. 1989a. Neuroanatomical correlates of a lactate induced anxiety attack. *Arch. Gen. Psychiatry* 46:493–500.

Reiman, E., Fusselman, M. J., Fox, P. T., Raichle, M. E. 1989b. Neuroanatomical correlates of anticipatory anxiety. *Science* 243:1071–73.

Rosenbaum, J. F. 1982. The drug treatment of anxiety. *N. Engl. J. Med.* 306:401–404.

Rush, A. J. 1996. The role of psychotherapy in the treatment of depression: review of two practice guidelines. *Arch. Gen. Psychiatry* 53(4):298–300.

Sederer, L. I. 1984. Inpatient psychiatry: what place the milieu? *Am. J. Psychiatry* 141:673–674.

Sederer, L. I., and St. Clair, R. L. 1989. Managed health care and the Massachusetts experience. *Am. J. Psychiatry* 146:1142–48.

Sederer, L. I., and Summergrad, P. 1993. Criteria for hospital admission. *Hosp. Community Psychiatry* 44:116–118.

Sheehan, D. V., Ballenger, J., and Jackson, G. 1980. Treatment of endogenous anxiety with phobic, hysterical, and hypochondriacal symptoms. *Arch. Gen. Psychiatry* 37:51–59.

Sifneos, P. E. 1966. Manipulative suicide. *Psychiatr. Q.* 2:1–14.

———— 1981. Psychosomatic aspects of attempted suicide: a clinical overview. *Psychother. Psychosom.* 36:735–785.

———— 1986. Psychosomatic aspects of manipulative suicide attempts. In *Proceedings of the 15th European Conference on Psychosomatic Research*, ed. Lacey, J. H., and Surgeon, D. A. London: John Libby & Co.

Stoudemire, A., and Fogel, B. S. 1986. Organization and development of combined medical-psychiatric units. Pt. 1. *Psychosomatics* 27:341–345.

Summergrad, P. 1991. Psychoanalysis and psychodynamic psychotherapy. In *Manual of clinical problems in psychiatry*, ed. Hyman, S. E., and Jenike, M. A. Boston: Little, Brown.

———— 1994. Medical psychiatry units and the roles of the inpatient psychiatric services in the general hospital. *Gen. Hosp. Psychiatry* 16:20–31.

Summergrad, P., Langman-Dorwart, N., and Kleinman, S. 1995. Failure of managed care or failure to manage care. *Harvard Review of Psychiatry* 2:341–346.

Summergrad, P., Herman, J., Weilburg, J., Jellinek, M. 1995. Wagons ho: forward on the managed care trail. *Gen. Hosp. Psychiatry* 17:251–259.

Thompson, J. W., Burns, B. J., and Taube, C. A. 1988. The severely mentally ill in general hospital psychiatric units. *Gen. Hosp. Psychiatry* 10:1–9.

Torgersen, S. 1983. Genetic factors in anxiety disorders. *Arch. Gen. Psychiatry* 40:1085–89.

Waldinger, R. J., and Frauch, A. F. 1989. Clinician's experience in combining medication and psychotherapy in the treatment of borderline patients. *Hosp. Community Psychiatry* 40:712–718.

Wellin, E., Slesinger, D. P., and Hollister, C. D. 1987. Psychiatric emergency services: evolution, adaptation, and proliferation. *Soc. Sci. Med.* 24:475–482.

Zarin, D. A., Pincus, H. A., West, J. C., and McIntyre, J. S. 1997. Practice-based research in psychiatry. *Am. J. Psychiatry* 154(9):1199–1208.

Recommended Reading

Hyman, S. E., and Jenike, M. A., eds. 1991. *Manual of clinical problems in psychiatry*. Boston: Little, Brown.

Stoudemire, A., and Fogel, B., eds. 1993. *Psychiatric care of the medical patient*. New York: Oxford University Press.

Stern, T., Herman, J., and Slavin, P., eds. 1997. *The MGH guide to psychiatry in primary care*. New York: McGraw-Hill.

PART FIVE

Special Populations

MICHAEL S. JELLINEK

DAVID B. HERZOG

The Child

Before the late nineteenth century, mandatory education, labor laws, and protective services for children (for abuse and neglect) were virtually nonexistent. Although children still suffer from self-serving decisions made by adults, there is an increasing recognition of their special medical, educational, and emotional needs. Psychiatric attention to children began in the early 1900s, when Drs. Henry Goddard and Lightner Witmer revised the evaluation and treatment of mental retardation. In 1909, 10 years after Illinois established courts specializing in juveniles, William Healy, supported by judges and philanthropic efforts, opened the Chicago Juvenile Psychopathic Clinic to treat delinquent children. State governments and foundations dramatically increased mental health services for children to include probation, special education classes, child guidance clinics, and foster homes. In 1912 the Federal Children's Bureau encouraged state programs in maternal and child health and welfare. In Boston the Judge Baker Guidance Center (1917) and the Thom Habit Clinic (1921) influenced child guidance centers nationally as they broadened their role to treat a wide range of emotional and behavioral disorders. At Johns Hopkins, Adolf Myer and Edward Park (1930) established the first child psychiatric clinic in a general hospital pediatric department; its head, Leo Kanner, later became the first professor of child psychiatry in the United States. Child psychiatry as a formal medical specialty emerged from the first mental health organization, the American Orthopsychiatry Association, through the establishment of the American Academy of Child and Adolescent Psychiatry in 1953 and a subspecialty board in 1958.

Child psychiatry, like pediatrics and other child-oriented disciplines, continues to face a number of economic, cultural, and technical challenges. What are reasonable goals and boundaries of responsibility for the medical care of children? How much does society want to invest in children's health care, safety, or schooling? How much should we allocate to population-wide prevention efforts, how much to early recognition of developmental and psychosocial difficulties, and how much to treatment of severe disorder? How do we balance parents' rights against the wish to protect children from the risk of ongoing abuse or neglect?

In practicing child psychiatry, do we base our judgments on behavioral observations as described by parents, a clinical psychiatric interview of the child, or teacher reports? Do we accept a child's verbal responses to questions, and do these responses mean the same at different ages, or should we interpret observations of play or unconscious themes based on the clinician's theoretical constructs? In light of a child's rapidly developing personality, how stable must a disorder be to warrant a diagnosis? Is a child's psychiatric diagnosis dependent on where the diagnosis is made (in an office, at school, at home)? Should we focus on symptoms or emphasize the child's functioning at home, in school, or with friends?

Although it is critical to prioritize according to reliable and valid diagnosis, the focus must also include treatment standards, efficacy, and cost-benefit analysis: Which treatment works, what is the cost, how does it benefit the child, and does it save future medical or social expenses?

Theoretical Perspectives

Child development is exceedingly complex and difficult to study. The processes of differentiation, maturation, and continuous integration take place over 20 years or more, and the capacity to adapt is lifelong. Biological, physical, environmental, psychological, interpersonal, and cognitive systems, each with distinct developmental structures and in various sequences, are constantly interacting. So much is intangible and evolving that until the recent advances in neurobiology and genetics, child psychiatry had to rely almost exclusively on theoretical inferences derived from the observations of dedicated and thoughtful clinicians.

The single most significant theoretical perspective continues to be psychodynamic, based on data derived from careful listening and clinical treatment. Anna Freud's writings, especially *Normality and Pathology in Childhood* (1965) and *The Ego and Mechanisms of Defense* (1973), continue to serve as the cornerstone of psychodynamic understanding of child development, psychiatric disorders, and treatment. The infant and child are seen as having a built-in set of instinctual needs, sexual and aggressive, that interact with an environment and inevitably evolve into a differentiated sense of ego (the "I"), a system of defenses, a personal/social conscience (superego, or "above the I"), and an active, influential unconscious life (id, or built-in "it"). Anna Freud's concept of developmental lines defines many of the child's basic psychological, interpersonal, and social tasks from birth to adult functioning. The prototypical developmental line is from "dependency" to "emotional self-reliance and adult relationships." The healthy child progresses through 7 steps:

Biological unity with the mother
An early, highly dependent stage of differentiation from the mother
The more autonomous functioning of early childhood (toilet training)
The "oedipal" period, which integrates relationships with both parents
The psychological and social separation of school entry
Increasing investment in school, sports, and activities beyond home
A several-year period of separation into adolescence and adulthood

A second developmental line is more social and traces the path from preoccupation with the self and internal stimuli (such as hunger) to a major emphasis on "others for companionship." Anna Freud defined a third developmental line starting again with the body, then progressing to toys and play, then to more purposeful activities building competency, and leading to the adult's investment in work. Anna Freud described the most common defenses that evolve to cope with unconscious wishes and feelings. For example, a child may use the defense of repression to block an unconscious wish from entering conscious life or a more mature defense such as displacement to suppress an unconscious wish and replace it with a less anxiety-producing conscious feeling.

Other major clinical theorists have emphasized different age ranges and specific aspects of the child's psychological development. Margaret Mahler, using both clinical material and observations in a research setting (Mahler,

Pine, and Bergman, 1975), focused on the infant's "separation and individuation" from the mother and defined a sequence of phases from birth to age 3:

Autistic: newborn experiences hunger and sleep
Symbiotic: mother's care creates memory islands of pleasure/good and painful/bad
Hatching: the alert 6-month-old looks through and beyond mother
Checking back: the 8-month-old scans and compares others with mother
Practicing: the 12- to 18-month-old walks freely, explores, experiences the world as pleasurable and frustrating
Rapprochement: the 2-year-old has mixed feelings—a growing awareness of being separate and a wish for constant closeness
Emotional object constancy: the toddler has a permanent, stable, positive inner image of mother
Individuality: the toddler develops a separate self-identity

Mahler related these normative observations, especially parental reactions to increasing autonomy and the child's ambivalence in rapprochement, to adult character psychopathology (e.g., turbulent interpersonal relationships and difficulties with intimacy).

D. W. Winnicott (1965, 1975), originally a pediatrician and then a psychoanalyst, emphasized that the essential clinical unit is the dyadic, inseparable, and survival-dependent relationship between mother and infant. The mother does not just "hold" the infant physically, but creates what the infant knows of the world: softness, warmth, comfort, time, satiation, wetness, cold, pain, smells, textures, and so on. From thousands of feelings, interactions, and caretaker responses, the infant learns that "something can be done about something." Being held eases fear, and food promptly provided rapidly relieves hunger. These are but 2 of many features of a relationship that make the infant feel loved and worthy of loving.

The infant has many moments of loving and feeling loved as well as feeling anger from hunger or other discomfort. Winnicott speculated that sometime toward the end of the first year, infants appreciate that the "hated" mother during times of distress (hunger) is the same mother loved for relieving distress. If so, then isn't it wrong to be so angry at someone so loved? According to Winnicott, this dawning sense of wrong is the earliest source of concern for others, an essential precursor to the older child's sense of guilt for angry feelings or destructive actions.

An infant devoid of "good enough" mothering, inadequately cared for, will feel that "nothing can be done about anything" and thus not worthy of being loved. As adults, such individuals will suffer from low self-esteem, be unable to treat themselves with care, cope in a passive manner with life events, and have difficulty establishing trust necessary for intimacy.

René Spitz (1983) and John Bowlby (1969) emphasized attachment and loss. In the early 1900s infants placed in foundling homes by unwed mothers were virtually all retarded or died from unknown or infectious causes after 1–2 years of apparently high-quality care. In sharp contrast, infants born to incarcerated mothers and raised in squalid prison nurseries were healthy and developmentally average or above. Spitz noted that the foundling homes provided sufficient food and warmth, but in a misguided effort to protect the infants from infection had deprived them of human contact. White sheets blocked out visual contact, nurses wore masks, and handling was kept to a minimum. The infants had developed what Spitz called anaclitic depression. In addition to food, the provision of human contact was, in fact, a life-and-death matter.

Bowlby (1969) extended studies on attachment to the hospital setting. In the 1940s he observed the behavior of infants and toddlers who had been hospitalized on pediatric wards. Hospital policies then in force permitted the mother only limited visiting hours, resulting in repeated day-long periods of separation. Bowlby defined 3 stages in the child's reaction to a mother's leaving:

Protest: minutes to hours of crying and agitated behavior
Despair: an extended period of quiet unhappiness and social withdrawal
Detachment: in children repeatedly hospitalized, rapid but superficial patterns of relating to adults

Bowlby's work indicated that infants as young as 6 months of age have specific attachment to a primary caretaker. (Frame-by-frame videotape analysis by T. B. Brazelton and his colleagues in 1973 and 1974 reinforced this finding, indicating defined and specific attachment behavior as early as the first month of life.) Bowlby's observations led to a dramatic revision of policies so that by the late 1960s, most hospitals permitted open visitation and began to encourage (and plan space for) mothers to "room in" with their children. Bowlby's work also led to related research on the stages of acute grief and served as a theoretical basis for clinical studies of death and dying.

Bowlby doubted that the separation anxiety experienced during loss of the mother was secondary to either sexual or aggressive instincts (as defined by psychoanalytic concepts), but instead was a primary, inborn psychological "instinct," paralleling the "fight-or-flight" response or even hunger. Given the life-and-death dependency between mother and newborn, he reasoned that an effective attachment system would carry significant survival value. A vigorous protest destined to be heard by a mother with her own built-in need to respond would have a special advantage in keeping the infant fed, cared for, and alive. Bowlby concluded that the infant's life depended on the attachment process which itself was safeguarded by protest behavior and separation anxiety. This biologic paradigm had roots originating in animal behavior which served as the basis for more differentiated human emotions and behavior.

Psychodynamic theorists placed strong emphasis on the quality of mothering and parenting. Parents meeting their own unconscious needs tend to recreate features of those conflicts in their marriage and in the mental life of their children. Poor parenting was seen as contributing to many disorders, including potentially severe developmental disorders such as autism. Alexander Thomas, Stella Chess, and Herbert Birch (1968) wondered whether some childhood disorders and difficulties in parenting result from the child's inborn temperament rather than solely from the psychological conflicts of the parents. Using pioneering research methodologies that included prospective design, reliable observations, and a large sample size, they followed over 100 children and their families for a period lasting years and defined key specific temperamental traits (rhythmicity, approach/withdrawal, adaptability, intensity, threshold, distractibility, persistence, and mood). These temperaments were observable in the first weeks of life, well before environment could have played a formative role. For example, some infants had a consistent rhythm in terms of physical habits and needs (such as naps and hunger); others were irregular. Infants also varied in adaptability to changes in daily routine or the environment (getting dressed to leave home for a walk) and in the intensity of their responses.

Thomas, Chess, and Birch noted that although most mothers could adapt to variation in their infant's temperament, some did not have such "goodness of fit." For example, although both infant and mother might be within normal limits of behavior independently, a baby's irregular and intense temperament might not fit well with the mother's need for regularity and a calmer, predictable daily routine. A few children were found at follow-up to be at greater risk for emotional problems because their temperamental traits were especially "difficult" and stressful for any mother. Correspondingly, infants with a calmer, more regular, and more adaptable profile were considered in general easy to care for and at lower risk for emotional disorders at follow-up during later childhood.

Profiles on the children repeated at intervals over years indicate some stability in temperamental traits in the pre-school age range, but not in childhood and adolescence. More recently, in direct observations initially using a research playroom and then again approximately 2 years later on the first day of school, Jerome Kagan and his colleagues (1986) found that one trait, behavioral inhibition—a shy reluctance to leave the mother's side for 20 minutes or so in unfamiliar situations—was a stable temperamental factor. Preliminary studies of young children whose parents have psychiatrically significant phobic disorders suggest a possible genetic basis for this short-term shyness.

Thomas, Chess, and Birch's work defined what the newborn brings to the relationship with the mother and, through emphasizing interaction, offered a welcome alternative to blaming parents for all aspects of their children's personality and emotional difficulties.

Psychologists have made many outstanding contributions to the understanding of child development, reliable assessment of academic abilities, research methodology, and behavioral treatments. The Swiss psychologist Jean Piaget (Flavell, 1963) derived his theories not from the treatment of emotional disorders, but from direct observation of children (especially his own) in a nonclinical setting. He wondered how children routinely develop a cognitive understanding of the world ("genetic epistemology"). How does a child at different ages develop concepts of object permanency, time, length, mass, causation, death, moral dilemmas, dreams (are they imagined, real)? Piaget held that every child has a built-in "need to function," an intellectual drive to make sense of the world by using the highest level of conceptualization available given the child's developmental level. Using thousands of observations and simple experimental conditions, Piaget defined specific stages, their invariable sequence, and the process of moving from one stage to the next. For each area of cognition, the child has a built-in schema that evolves through a process of accommodation and adaptation to the child's environment. While certain reflexes such as the patellar reflex remain fixed, others like the suck reflex differentiate to the shape of different nipples, cups, and eventually to eating a full diet. Where does a ball go when it rolls under a sofa? Is it gone? Does it still exist? Where would it exit given its entry point? The list of questions is endless when one considers a child's day-to-day

confrontation with the physical environment and the puzzlement of time and causation.

Piaget defined 4 major developmental stages:

Sensorimotor: body activity relates to mental image (0–2 years)
Preoperational: use of language/play as mental representation (2–7)
Concrete: concepts of weight, length, rules (7–11)
Formal operations: verbal reasoning, abstractions (11–15)

Piaget has heavily influenced elementary school curricula, the wording of interview questions used in research, and clinical issues such as assessing the child's ability to understand terms such as *adopted* or *other mother* (Nickman, 1985). Although his work is relevant to understanding how children learn, Piaget never intended it to accelerate children's educational process, remediate learning disorders, or suggest the need for special toys designed to hasten cognitive development. The child's understanding of the world evolves at a natural pace and is not meant to be "hurried" (Elkind, 1981) or overscheduled. Cognitive and affective theories of development are not automatically complementary. For example, infants develop emotionally relevant memories, such as those relating to their mother, sooner than more purely cognitive memory of object permanence.

Learning theory was born in the laboratory and uses objective measures and the experimental method to assess symptoms (Rutter and Hersov, 1994). Learning theory emphasizes the overt behavior of the child. Careful observation and methodologically rigorous frequency charting are core components of the behavioral assessments. The aim of treatment is to increase the frequency of adaptive behaviors and to decrease maladaptive ones. The behaviorist is committed to empirical evaluation of treatment, and treatment is specified in operational terms. In contrast to psychodynamic theory, learning theory does not focus on unconscious processes, traits, and personality structures but instead emphasizes the social, situational, and environmental factors that influence behavior. Learning theory includes 3 subtheories: classical (Pavlovian or respondent conditioning), operant conditioning, and social learning theory. In classical conditioning, a given environmental stimulus elicits an involuntary (often reflexive) response from an organism. Operant conditioning views behavior as contingent on positive and negative reinforcement and punishment. If an action provokes a positive response, it is likely to recur. For example, if a child cries and is then given candy to be quiet, he may begin to cry again the next time he wants candy.

According to social learning theory, children learn through observing and imitating both peers and adults in their social environment. Behavior modification uses natural sources of reinforcement, such as parental and peer approval, and models positive actions in an attempt to change behavior.

In recent years biological and epidemiologic research on child psychiatric disorders has blossomed. For example, the increased reliability and validity of the diagnostic criteria for adult depression, and the epidemiologic studies documenting the prevalence and morbidity of this disorder, led to a series of federally funded efforts to understand the nature of depressive disorders. This in turn led investigators to ask some of the same research questions about children, especially about the offspring of parents with well-defined depressive disorders. They developed methodologies of careful diagnosis, family history, and structured interviewing for children and conducted biologically oriented studies of genetics, neurotransmitter metabolites (as measured in urine and blood), and pharmacologic treatments.

The psychodynamic approach emphasizes the individual patient and unconscious factors, accepts a more interpretive approach to diagnosis, and criticizes biological work as potentially reductionistic or clinically irrelevant. The epidemiologic perspective emphasizes reliability and validity of diagnosis, structured evaluation, and a population base, and criticizes the psychodynamic approach as highly subjective.

In "Psychotherapy and the Single Synapse," Eric Kandel (1979) offered a perspective that integrates the biological and psychodynamic views. Kandel's study of the marine snail demonstrated that learning, habituation, and sensitization can readily take place on a simple neuronal level. He suggested that patients also may change on a neuronal level as the psychotherapeutic process encourages their learning through insight and feelings; thus he resolved the apparent antithesis between psychiatric and neurobiological perspectives.

Eisenberg (1995) presented a synthetic integration of the neurobiological advances since Kandel's work in a paper entitled "The Social Construction of the Human Brain." After noting the striking advances in molecular genetics and the emerging data based on magnetic resonance imaging (MRI) quantitative morphometry, Eisenberg reminds the reader that "precise neuroanatomic details are specified by activity-dependent competition between presynaptic axons for common postsynaptic target neurons." Thus certain core structures are built in, but their elaboration depends on environmental stimuli. Light, properly focused, leads to a chain of bio-

chemical, neurotransmitter, and neuronal events essential for vision. IQ may be genetically endowed, but motivation, achievement, and sense of success more likely stem from parenting, quality of schools, culture, opportunity, and social class. Is it far-fetched to think that certain inborn temperaments are related to specific neuronal patterns which can then be modified by experience, including the quality of the mother's "goodness of fit"? Although the mechanisms of nature/nurture are worthy of extensive study and hold therapeutic promise, arguing about a clear boundary is no longer relevant.

In terms of sweeping efforts to integrate theories of child (and adult) development, the contribution of Erik Erikson's "Eight Ages of Man" (1963) is unique. Erikson's "epigenetic" approach conceptualizes the genetic, biological, psychodynamic, interpersonal, cognitive, social, and cultural perspectives of human development as interwoven, much like a tapestry in which every thread connects and pulls every other. Individuals develop according to a "proper sequence of their enfolding" that lead to an ever-widening "social radius." The 8 major ages are:

Basic trust vs. mistrust (birth to about 2 years)
Autonomy vs. shame, doubt (2 to about 4)
Initiative vs. guilt (4 to about 7)
Industry vs. inferiority (7 to early adolescence)
Identity vs. role confusion (adolescence)
Intimacy vs. isolation (early, mature adulthood)
Generativity vs. stagnation (creative, productive adulthood)
Ego integrity vs. despair (later adulthood)

Each age includes a widening circle of personality development, family relationships, life tasks, and societal roles and obligations. Despite this breadth, each step also reflects a clinical perspective. Developmental failures throughout life are expressed in empathic clinical terms—mistrust, shame, guilt, inferiority, confusion, isolation, stagnation, and despair.

Diagnostic Classification Systems

Diagnostic systems reflect what is known about disorders and how that knowledge is conceptualized. Historically the classification of mental disorders was influenced by cultural values and priorities, so that alcoholism and senility were recognized long before child abuse. The first international effort to list presumed causes of death started in 1853 and was expanded in 1900 to include the causes of morbidity. The American Medical Association began a formal effort at diagnostic classification in 1928, and in 1952 the American Psychiatric Association published its first *Diagnostic and Statistical Manual of Mental Disorders* (DSM-I). The Group for the Advancement of Psychiatry (1966) proposed a diagnostic classification system (Rapoport and Ismond, 1984) based on a perspective of normal maturation, thoughtfully integrated many principles of child development, and attempted to be more descriptive. DSM-II, published in 1968, reflected a more descriptive approach but in some instances used interpretations of observed behavior, categories whose validity was questionable, and clinical diagnoses whose reliability was suspect. DSM-III, adopted in 1980, was a major effort to improve diagnostic validity and reliability to meet both clinical and research needs. Numerous expert subcommittees attempted to solve diagnostic issues using research data, criteria based on clinical care, and ultimately field trials involving thousands of patients. In addition to a descriptive rather than an interpretive or etiological approach, DSM-III instituted a "multiaxial" classification:

Axis I: clinical syndromes (example: attention deficit disorder with hyperactivity)

Axis II: personality and/or specific developmental disorders (example: developmental language disorder)

Axis III: physical disorders or conditions (example: asthma)

Axis IV: severity of psychosocial stressors (example: moderate parental discord)

Axis V: highest level of adaptive functioning in the past year (example: fair, difficulties in school, peer and family relationships adequate)

The 5 axes encourage the clinician to be more thorough and to complete a diagnosis that communicates a comprehensive perspective. In the example above, Axes I and II yield only a partial picture because the child's physical condition (Axis III) and psychosocial stressors (Axis IV) may be critical factors. Much of the practical importance of the diagnostic process is reflected in Axis V: how well the child is actually functioning in daily life.

DSM-III has been revised twice (DSM-III-R and DSM-IV) as part of a continuing effort to improve validity and reliability. Despite extensive field testing, DSM-IV remains controversial. Since the core definition of validity for psychiatric diagnosis depends on observation and some interpretation of behavior, there is still debate as to how much "clinical judgment" should influence diagnosis, especially with intrapsychic disorders (e.g., depression) that manifest little change in behavior. In addition, some clinicians complain that the basic descriptive approach of DSM-IV is oriented to research rather than to clinical practice, since mere lists of behavioral observa-

tions say little about childhood personality development, motivation, treatment approaches, or prognosis.

Although there have been marked advances in diagnostic classification, many questions remain unanswered. Using the more reliable descriptive approach does not ensure validity. Should clinicians base the diagnosis of childhood depression on the child's self-report, the parent's interview, or the teacher's observations? Should they depend on an empathic verbal interview, play sessions, or a reproducible structured interview that to some appears incongruent with clinical interviewing of children and parents? DSM-IV is a new, sophisticated starting point from which to address a series of complex questions concerning the criteria for child psychiatric diagnosis.

Diagnostic Interviewing

Interviewing a child and family is the core skill of child psychiatry (Simmons, 1986). The process of interviewing is essential to developing a therapeutic relationship (which starts in the first hour), and the content of the interview determines the diagnosis and comprehensive treatment plan. Knowing how to listen (or, with young children, to play), what question to ask, when to ask, and how to ask reflects the clinician's overall knowledge of child psychiatry, depth of experience, and personal self-awareness. When interviewing a child, the clinician attempts to build at least a temporary alliance with the child by listening, empathizing, and indicating an understanding of the issues. Virtually all interviewing includes an assessment of any danger, the child's daily functioning, family support/discord, risk and resiliency factors, and a formal diagnosis.

The potential number of questions is virtually infinite and can appear like a laundry list. On a microscopic level the skill of interviewing is an active process of choosing what questions to ask, and in what detail, sequence, and tone. If the child states he is "bored" in school, the clinician must decide when and how to pursue this issue. Is the boredom an excuse for disobedient behavior? Is the classroom work too easy for the child's abilities? Does the child have a learning disability that would impair his understanding of the material or its presentation? Is there a conflict with a particular teacher? Is the school behavior a consequence of family tensions or a pending divorce? Although much of this process is based on the clinician's objective knowledge, the quality of the interview depends on a sincere concern for the child, a capacity to engage the child on an emotional level, a balancing of empathy and professional judgment, an ability to bear anger and sadness, and an awareness of inevitable personal feelings when talking with a distressed child and making difficult clinical judgments.

The nature of the interview varies depending on the age of the child, the reason for referral, and the clinician's goal. A 4- or 5-year-old will have difficulty verbalizing a number of issues and will therefore require an interview with fewer words and greater use of play. The choice of toys, how they are used, and the themes of play may yield relevant information on the child's developmental level, psychological life, and the nature of distress. An interview at the bedside of a chronically ill adolescent would consist largely of discussion and would be more focused on the specific question raised by the referring pediatrician. With a child or family in crisis—for example, during a custody dispute in the midst of divorce—the goal may be supporting the child, negotiating agreement concerning visitation or school placement with angry parents, and, if a court is involved, advising on a settlement that could serve the child's "best interests."

Although the issues that bring children to psychiatrists are often quite serious, the clinician's tone should be not heavy-handed or stern but respectful, with more than a little room for humor and fun. Early in the interview, the psychiatrist should ask the child why he is being seen, what problems necessitated the evaluation, and give a brief explanation of goals. Older children and adolescents should understand what level of information will be kept confidential and how much control they will have over written and oral reports. Some experienced clinicians write reports that convey all necessary information in a readable manner and are designed to share with parents and the adolescent being evaluated.

If the same clinician is seeing parents and child, it is often best to begin the evaluation by talking first with older children and adolescents. For younger children, it is often more helpful to start by gathering history from parents.

One helpful structure in interviewing the child is to consider the age and developmental level, assess the major symptoms, and then review the major areas of daily functioning. For most children these include:

Family: What is the quality of family life, including relationships with siblings? How do people treat one another? with warmth or hostility? Are there reasonable rules? activities? fun? The child's perspective must be integrated with an extensive history from the parents that includes current behaviors, the child's developmental history, assessments of each parent's personality, and family history of psychiatric disorders.

Friends: Does the child have friends? how close? neighborhood and/or school? Do the friendships last the age-appropriate length of time? Who are they? how old? What do they do together? How do parents feel about the child's friends?

Play: What does the child enjoy doing? Are the activities age appropriate? fun? varied? shared with others in the family?

School: How is the child doing in school in terms of academics, relationship to teacher, friendships, rules, and homework? What is the parents' attitude toward school?

Mental status: General appearance, waiting room behavior with parents and separating for interview. How does the child relate to the clinician? How does the clinician feel about the child? What is the quality of the child's emotional life and thoughts (such as anxiety, worries), mood (depressed?), language, cognition (attention span, knowledge), and motor activity?

For many referred children, a considerable part of the information gathered will be negative; therefore, the clinician should also look for strengths and factors that may support the child's resiliency, e.g., a warm, supportive relationship with a parent or other adult, intellectual strengths, opportunities to enhance self-esteem, and so on.

Other key information includes the family's psychiatric history, as many childhood disorders, especially depression, substance use, and attention deficit hyperactivity disorder, have genetic antecedents. The clinician also needs to be aware of any risk factors such as poverty, divorce, or chronic illness in the child's past.

The clinical interview should be supplemented by appropriate information from other settings. For research purposes a structured interview that formally asks about a wide range of DSM-IV symptoms will often be more inclusive and reliable than clinician-directed interviews. Additional information from the child's teacher and psychological testing may confirm or modify a clinical judgment made in an office or based on observations from a single source. Often the most detailed and valid picture does not emerge until after several interviews; this result is not surprising given that the process is interpersonal and depends on a trusting relationship between 2 people.

General Treatment Options

Treatment should address specific goals. The goal may be reduction of targeted symptoms, return to baseline or improved daily functioning, enhanced self-esteem, or promotion of normal development. In individual psychotherapy the clinician may serve as a parent surrogate, teacher, and professional friend. The child feels understood, learns to master specific emotional conflicts, may see new options in reaching personal goals, and may have highly specific needs met. For latency age children and adolescents, groups can facilitate development of social skills and enhance self-esteem. Physical therapy, occupational therapy, and speech therapy have substantial roles in the identification and treatment of developmental disabilities.

Pediatric psychopharmacology research is a growing field. An increasingly broad range of medications is available to support the comprehensive treatment of attention deficit hyperactivity disorder, depression, obsessive-compulsive disorder, psychosis, and so on. Because childhood disorders often subsume a wide array of symptoms and behaviors, it is advisable to select target symptoms, since the choice of drug will often depend on those symptoms. Through reduction of symptoms, the antidepressants, antipsychotics, and antianxiety agents permit children to benefit from other therapies.

Family therapy has a definite role in the treatment of psychosomatic disorders and in other circumstances in which family disequilibrium contributes to the child's symptoms. Behavioral therapy has proved helpful for anxiety-based disorder, conduct disorders, attention deficit hyperactivity disorder, psychosomatic disorders, obsessive-compulsive disorder, and stress-related symptoms of chronic illness. Behavioral treatment is highly specific and can be especially helpful to control angry outbursts, rituals, or phobias.

Many childhood disorders require multiple modalities of treatment. For example, attention deficit disorder often requires psychopharmacologic management, psychotherapy, behavioral regimens, school consultations, and family work. A stimulant or antidepressant (Biederman, Gastfriend, and Jellinek, 1986) prolongs attention and reduces the motor hyperactivity. Psychotherapy allows the child to enhance self-esteem, understand more socially acceptable ways of dealing with frustrations, and be viewed by a respected adult as "not the bad kid." Behavior regimes help the child develop ways to anticipate and control behaviors. Psychological testing and school consultation set reasonable expectations for academic work and support self-esteem. The family therapist may modify the family's need to view this child as the scapegoat for a variety of family difficulties. The case manager, often the child's psychiatrist, must keep in regular contact with all clinicians involved in order to reassess the treatment and its goals. An occasional team meeting allows all the team members to feel valued: the "clinical family" can better "parent" the parents, who can then better parent their child.

Managed care has had a profound impact on outpatient and inpatient care. Up until the late 1980s, fee-for-service reimbursement encouraged long-term therapy and months-long inpatient lengths of stay. There was every philosophical and financial reason to set high expectations for treatment which then required time measured in developmental terms, months or years, with less emphasis on rapid return to functioning and a less realistic view of what kind of environment or services could be maintained over years. Among other potential contributions, managed care provides a range of services, often referred to as a continuum of care, that has the child in the least restricted, most local (and often least costly) setting. There is a clear focus on more limited treatment goals, less reliance on psychotherapy, and a greater readiness to use medication. These paths are "managed" by a caseworker who must approve any services for reimbursement. Only specific providers are "credentialed" and thus available in the particular company's panel of providers. Some reimbursement guidelines strictly control therapy visits and direct care to social workers and psychologists while deeming psychopharmacological visits as "medical" with relatively unlimited authorization (for brief visits). Overall cost savings have been dramatic, with a marked shift of care away from inpatient services, and clinicians have had to be creative both in working within the limits of the new system and in integrating local resources into the comprehensive treatment plan (Jellinek 1994).

The continuum of care for seriously disturbed children means that acute inpatient care will be rationed to those needing a secure setting for short periods of time (days rather than the weeks to months that was common not so long ago). The goal is rapid stabilization and preparation for transfer to a residential or partial hospital unit, then to day or outpatient treatment. Clearly these shifts in location and caregivers can be disjointed and stressful, especially to a severely disturbed child or adolescent. Thus there has been an increasing effort to have treatment teams follow the patient through each step of the process. Outcome data comparing past and current approaches to care or more subtle differences in technique or orientation are methodologically difficult and are not available.

Although the principles of managed care and the earliest implementation were promising, the introduction of profit and the separation or "carving out" of child psychiatrists from general pediatrics have crippled mental health services for children (Jellinek and Little, 1997). Marketplace dynamics result in a direct relationship between constraining services and increasing profits. It is also profitable to narrow the scope of services by shifting costs for care to schools, courts, and social service agencies already limited by recent tax cuts. Carving out mental health services from general medical care blocks pediatricians and child psychiatrists from working together, since many child psychiatrists are controlled or excluded from company panels. For-profit mental health HMO models have cut the total dollars spent on child psychiatric services, have failed to support research or training, and have done so without quality assurance.

Hospital treatment of childhood disorders offers multiple interventions simultaneously. Indications for inpatient treatment include:

Serious suicidal or homicidal ideation or behavior
Severe physical or sexual abuse
Psychosomatic disorders or somatopsychic disorders that have become life threatening
Severe socially unacceptable behavior associated with a psychiatric disorder that is unaffected by outpatient treatment or removal from home
Psychosis or severe developmental problem requiring continuous skilled observation not possible on an outpatient basis
Highly disturbed family situation that puts the child at substantial risk
Disabling symptoms, such as school phobia, that do not respond to outpatient treatment
Specific treatments, such as certain drug trials, that require close supervision

The aim of inpatient treatment is to return the child to life in his family, school, and community. The development of specialized units, such as family units (where the whole family stays), mother-child units, and daytime hospital units, has opened the way to work with children in their families.

Child Psychiatric Disorders

Attention Deficit Hyperactivity Disorder

Child psychiatric diagnoses and treatments, like disorders in other medical specialties, started with single case descriptions and continue to evolve through refinement of observations, theory, and research methodologies (Biederman and Jellinek, 1984; Rutter and Hersov, 1994). The history of attention deficit hyperactivity disorder (ADHD) and the complexity of its treatment are prototypical examples. What is now called ADD (attention deficit disorder) was first described by a physician, Hans Hoffman (1926), writing a diary about his school-age son. Hoffman was caring for his son while his wife was resting in the hospital after the birth of their second child. He noted the boy had trouble concentrating on homework, seemed impulsive in his behavior, had a short attention

span, and probably had what we would now call a learning disability, since he needed to copy repeatedly rather easy work in order to learn it. Although the symptoms were mostly cognitive, they occurred while the boy was separated from his mother and awaiting the arrival of his first sibling. This first clinical description lay dormant for many years and applied to children placed in residential care after suffering neurological sequelae following the 1917 worldwide flu epidemic. A number of postencephalitic and brain-damaged children displayed motoric hyperactivity, impulsivity, and a short attention span. Their disorder was sometimes called "organic drivenness."

In the 1940s and 1950s many more children were identified, mostly as outpatients, and diagnosed as having "minimal brain damage." When it became apparent that these children had no definable brain pathology, "minimal brain damage" became "minimal brain dysfunction," then "hyperkinesis," then "hyperactivity." In the late 1950s and 1960s pediatricians, child psychiatrists, and teachers broadened the use of this diagnosis to include 5% or more of all children. It is likely that this broad category included a small number with neurological damage, those who had a core attentional or motoric disorder, some reacting to anxiety, and others who were disobedient; probably the largest group, who appeared hyperactive when faced with unreasonable expectations in a school setting, would now be considered learning disabled. In the 1970s Michael Rutter, an outstanding British child psychiatric epidemiologist, began to wonder why there were so many hyperactive children in the United States and fewer than 1% in England. What accounted for this difference? Could all these children have the same disorder? Were the clinical criteria valid and reliable?

Using careful observation, and gathering data from multiple sources, Rutter and his colleagues (Sandberg, Rutter, and Taylor, 1978) discovered that each source of data—parents, teachers, child psychiatric interviewers, psychologists giving tests—had identified a different and only minimally overlapping group of children as hyperactive. Correlation between sources and settings was poor and raised serious questions that the diagnosis of hyperactivity (and, by implication, other less observable child psychiatric diagnoses) might not be valid or reproducible. The core disorder was redefined in the late 1970s, focusing on the cognitive issues of inattention and impulsivity rather than on harder-to-define and less specific motor manifestations. DSM-III attempted to mold many of the research findings into a descriptive approach to diagnosis with emphasis on each major feature of the condition confirmed by symptoms grounded in behavioral observations. DSM-IV uses many of the same criteria but deemphasizes clustering behavioral symptoms (impulsivity, motoric hyperactivity, inattention) in favor of a list of key symptoms. DSM-IV requires an onset before age 7; in fact some parents note ADD symptoms at age 2 and an ADD-like temperamental style in infancy.

Clinically, ADHD is more commonly diagnosed in boys than in girls and can be associated with learning disabilities in a substantial percentage of children. The ADHD child is criticized at home for "poor" behavior, inability to finish tasks, and not listening, and often feels like a failure in school. The symptoms and related impact on self-esteem are amenable to comprehensive treatment which includes medication, adjustments in school programs, helping parents set reasonable expectations, and ongoing follow-up. ADHD, with a current estimated prevalence of 3% (and with probably 1% or more being symptomatic in adulthood), is among the most studied disorders in child psychiatry. Findings relevant to frontal lobe functioning, family genetics, impact of multimodal treatment, new medications, and comorbidity are published monthly. An excellent, up-to-date clinical review has recently been officially adopted by the American Academy of Child and Adolescent Psychiatry (1997a).

ADHD as a diagnostic entity is the first child psychiatric disorder that has evolved from case description to clinical application to overuse to redefinition using higher standards of reliability and validity. Understanding the limitations of diagnosis and treatment permits accuracy, reproducibility in clinical and research efforts, targeting of interventions, and establishing reasonable long-term expectations for the child and family.

Conduct Disorders

Ten to 15% of children referred to psychiatric clinics are diagnosed as having a conduct disorder, which is often a difficult condition to treat successfully. DSM-IV describes conduct disorder as a persistent pattern (lasting 6 months or more) of non-aggressive behavior that causes property damage, deceitfulness or theft, serious violations of rules, or aggressive behavior toward others. There are 2 subtypes:

Childhood onset type: onset of at least 1 criterion characteristic of conduct disorder prior to age 10 years.
Adolescent onset type: absence of any criteria characteristic of conduct disorder prior to age 10 years.

The syndrome of conduct disorder has generated considerable controversy because of its lack of specificity and its overlap with attention deficit hyperactivity disorder and the learning disabilities. Common aggressive behaviors include fighting, temper tantrums, destructiveness, stealing, and running away. Fire setting is a rare but very dangerous symptom. Those with adolescent onset type, those behaving within a peer group, and those with fewer and milder symptoms tend to improve over time (Rapoport and Ismond, 1984).

Most children with conduct disorders are boys with academic and social difficulties. They often come from lower socioeconomic backgrounds, have experienced punitive child-rearing methods, and are temperamentally difficult, with high activity level and intensity of response. For example, their early history often includes domestic violence and real threats of abandonment. These children use aggressive behaviors as a means of testing the limits of safety. Other common antecedents are neonatal brain damage, specific learning disabilities, school failure, family history of substance use disorder or antisocial personality disorder, and marital discord. Given our culture's acceptance of firearms, 1 in 610 children will die by age 20 by gunshot (Children's Defense Fund, 1997).

Conduct disorder is linked with violence. Almost a third of severe crimes are committed by children under 18 years of age, although the perpetrators often represent a select group of repeat offenders. Delinquent males who grow up in an abusive family environment and who exhibit specific psychiatric, neurological, and/or cognitive vulnerabilities are more likely to commit violent crimes as adults (Lewis et al., 1989). A substantial segment of the growing and costly prison population can be traced to the lack of resources devoted to physical abuse, learning disorder, substance use, and conduct disorder earlier in these prisoners' childhoods.

Childhood conduct disorder is associated with adult psychopathology. Lee Robins (1978) reviewed follow-up studies of childhood behavior disorders and concluded that aggressive behavior in school-age children, particularly when accompanied by school failure, is predictive of later delinquency. Furthermore, she found that nearly half of seriously antisocial children are antisocial as adults. Antisocial behavior that is more moderate, isolated in the context of a troubled community, and with a prior history of better functioning has a more positive prognosis.

The treatment plan should be comprehensive and designed to suit the needs of the individual child's comorbid conditions; ADHD and depression especially need to be addressed. A professional highly invested in the child's long-term care is necessary to oversee and coordinate the multiple treatment modalities such as specialized education, behavior therapy, family therapy, and pharmacotherapy. Children with severe family pathology may require residential treatment. Recent practice and evaluation protocols have been issued by the American Academy of Child and Adolescent Psychiatry (1997a, b).

Pervasive Developmental Disorder

Pervasive developmental disorders (PDDs) refer to a continuum of developmental abnormalities that range from severe to mild. PDDs arise during infancy or the first few years of life and pervade language, social, intellectual, and emotional development. In DSM-III-R, the only PDD subcategory was autism; all other cases that did not meet specific criteria for autistic disorder were classified as "PDD Not Otherwise Specified." DSM-IV provides further differentiation of the PDDs and includes 3 new subclassifications: Rett's disorder, childhood disintegrative disorder, and Asperger's disorder.

The most severe subclass of PDD is infantile autism. Epidemiologic studies report that approximately 2 to 5 per 10,000 children have autism. Of these children, 75% are moderately retarded, with IQ scores in the 35–50 range (Gilman and Tuchman, 1995; Wong, 1993). Autism is about 4 times as prevalent in boys as in girls (Volkmar, Szatmari, and Sparrow, 1993; Wong, 1993). However, boys with autism may be less severely mentally retarded than autistic girls. In a study by Volkmar and colleagues (1993) examining 199 autistic individuals (mean age 13.3), males were 8.8 times more likely than females to have IQ scores in the normal (>70) range. The DSM-IV diagnostic criteria for autism are:

Limited capacity for social interaction
Impaired ability to communicate
Restricted repetitive and stereotyped behavior, interests, and activities
Delays in social interaction, language for social communication, and/or symbolic or imaginative play, with onset before age 3
Not due to Rett's disorder or to childhood disintegrative disorder

Seizures are also commonly associated with autism, and occur most often within the first year of life and in adolescence (Ballaban-Gil et al., 1991; Volkmar and Nelson, 1990). Volkmar and Nelson's (1990) study of 192 autistic individuals (mean age 14.1) showed that 21% developed seizures. They found a 29.3 per 1000 incidence rate in the under age 3 group and 20.4 per 1000 in the 11–14 age range.

Rett's disorder has been diagnosed only in females and is characterized by the development of multiple specific deficits, including diminished interest in persons or ob-

jects and the loss of previously acquired hand skills, following a period of normal functioning after birth. In most cases recovery is quite limited, and communication and behavioral difficulties persist throughout life.

Childhood disintegrative disorder has previously been termed Heller's syndrome, or dementia infantilis. In childhood disintegrative disorder, development is typically normal for at least the first 2 years of life, at which time there is a profound loss of previously acquired social skills and language and a development of stereotyped repetitive movements and mannerisms. Developmental regression usually stabilizes, after which time some limited improvement may occur.

DSM-IV, for the first time, provided distinct diagnostic criteria for Asperger's disorder, which historically had been considered a milder form of autism. Children with Asperger's disorder usually present with severe impairment in social interaction and with restricted, repetitive patterns of behavior, interests, and activities that typify autism. Unlike autistic disorder, Asperger's disorder is not associated with general retardation of language or clinically significant delays in cognitive development or in age-appropriate self-help skills, adaptive behaviors (other than those involving social interaction), and curiosity about the environment.

PDDs are extremely incapacitating, and the prognosis is poor. Approximately two-thirds of autistic children are still severely handicapped as adults. The prognosis is based on language and communication development and overall nonverbal intelligence (Gillberg, 1991). A child who has shown noteworthy improvement, demonstrates normal nonverbal intelligence (IQ >70), and communicates some useful language by age 5 will likely have good adjustment in adulthood (Gillberg, 1991).

PDDs require long-term multimodal treatment, including specialized educational programs, behavior therapy, pharmacotherapy, and family therapy.

Depression and Suicide

Depression can be described as a mood, a symptom, or a syndrome. As a syndrome, depression in childhood is characterized by a persistent mood disorder, dysfunctional behavior, and self-deprecatory ideation. These symptoms or behaviors should represent a significant change in the child's premorbid level of functioning and should not reflect a long-standing character trait, such as "low self-esteem" (Rapoport and Ismond, 1984). For children, the DSM-IV criteria for depression are the same as those for adults except that the mood can be irritable rather than depressed and there may be a failure to make expected weight gain rather than weight loss or weight gain. Other physiologic symptoms include abnormal sleep patterns, loss of energy, psychomotor abnormalities, and impaired concentration. Cognitive symptoms include feelings of guilt and worthlessness and suicidal ideation. Juvenile depression may be accompanied by difficulty in school, truancy, negativism, aggression, and antisocial behavior.

The child's experience and expression of depression may differ depending on his age. Children often appear depressed, with a sad or tearful face, report somatic concerns and phobias, and exhibit irritability, separation anxiety, and psychomotor changes. Adolescents, by contrast, more often lose interest in normally enjoyable activities, feel hopeless, experience hypersomnia and weight change, abuse drugs and alcohol, and utilize lethal methods to commit suicide (Ryan et al., 1987).

Although major depression is uncommon in preschoolers (< 3%), it does exist and increases in frequency with age (Fleming and Offord, 1990). For example, Velez and colleagues (1989) reported a 2.5% prevalence rate in 9- to 12-year-olds and a 3.7% rate in 13- to 18-year-olds. Others have reported rates from 9% in 12- to 14-year-olds (Garrison et al., 1992) to 10% in children 8–13 years old (Larrson and Melin, 1992), figures consistent with prevalence rates reported in adult populations (Nolen-Hoeksema, 1987).

In contrast to adults and adolescents, among whom females outnumber males, the gender distribution in children with depressive disorder is generally equal (Nolen-Hoeksema, 1987). There is evidence that a shift occurs around puberty, when the distribution changes to a higher prevalence of girls experiencing depressive symptoms (Kashani et al., 1987, 1989; Velez et al., 1989).

Beyond age, risk factors for depression in childhood include family history of depression, loss, stressful life events, family dysfunction, and low self-esteem (Fleming and Offord, 1990). Beardslee and colleagues (1988) observed that 30% of children whose parents had an affective disorder (versus only 2% of children of non-affectively disordered parents) suffered from major depressive disorder.

Various etiologies have been suggested for childhood depression, and it is probably best to conceive of it as multifactorial. The psychoanalytic view proposes that depression results from the loss of a highly valued person. Instead of directing anger at the person who has died, moved away, or otherwise become unavailable, the child turns the anger toward the most immediate and deserving target—himself (guilt). Sandler and Joffe (1965) suggested that depression is a psychological reaction to the loss of a previous state of self or expectation. In their terms, the child who is cognitively mature enough to distinguish adequately between himself and others may react to the birth of a sibling with depression. The learning theorists view depression as a function of inadequate or insufficient positive reinforcers. Thus the loss of mother as a source of primary reinforcement for the child may lead to depression. The cognitive view stresses a cognitive structure in which there is a negative attitude toward the self, the world, and the future. The learned helplessness model proposes that children who have a negative explanatory style and are then faced with negative life events may feel incapable of controlling their environment, thereby producing feelings of helplessness and depression (Seligman and Peterson, 1986). Genetic studies have demonstrated high rates of disturbance for children of depressed parents (Harrington et al., 1993), and neurochemical studies suggest that childhood depression is caused by a deficiency of norepinephrine or serotonin.

Both self-report questionnaires and structured interviews have been employed to diagnose depression in children. Self-report questionnaires have been used for screening and for quantitatively measuring severity. The Beck Depression Inventory, commonly used for adults, has been adapted for children and is called the Child Depression Inventory (CDI). Structured interviews have also been developed to create a more standardized information base. One of these is the K-SADS, adapted for children from the Schedule for Affective Disorders and Schizophrenia (SADS). Other instruments include the Interview Scale for Children (ISC), the Diagnostic Interview Schedule for Children-Revised (DISC-R), the Child Assessment Scale (CAS), and the newly developed Child and Adolescent Psychiatric Assessment (CAPA). A computerized version of the Diagnostic Interview for Children and Adolescents-Revised (DICA-R) is also available (Reich et al., 1995).

To date, no biological markers have been able to confirm a child's depression when the clinical diagnosis is in doubt. Since cortisol secretion is positively associated with age, children and adolescents rarely have elevated basal cortisol levels and less often suppress cortisol in response to the Dexamethasone Suppression Test (DST) (Puig-Antich, 1987; Puig-Antich et al., 1989). Both the sensitivity and specificity of responses on the DST have been inconsistent.

Another biologic marker often associated with depression is an altered electroencephalographic (EEG) sleep pattern. In general, depressed children do not consistently exhibit the abnormal EEG sleep pattern evident in depressed adults. These inconsistencies may be attributed less to differences between adult and childhood depression than to the changes in sleep patterns that occur with age (Puig-Antich, 1987).

It is difficult to evaluate the role of neurotransmitters in childhood depression because they, too, change with age. The catecholamine system does not fully develop until adulthood, and thus it cannot be used as an effective marker for childhood depression (Puig-Antich, 1987).

Pharmacotherapy, used in conjunction with individual and family psychotherapy and recreational programs, may hasten the reduction of symptoms in some depressed school-age children. However, the efficacy of antidepressants in depressed children is quite unclear (Ambrosini et al., 1993) and the superiority of tricyclic antidepressants (TCAs) over placebo has not yet been proven in several double-blind studies (Campbell and Cueva, 1995). Recent attention has focused on a new class of antidepressants, selective serotonin-reuptake inhibitors (SSRIs). Specifically, fluoxetine hydrochloride has been found to be relatively safe in children and to have fewer and more tolerable side effects than TCAs. Emslie and colleagues (1995) were the first to demonstrate the efficacy of fluoxetine over placebo in juvenile major depression.

Response to medication usually takes at least 4 weeks. Pharmacotherapy should be started at the lowest possible dose and reevaluated frequently during the initial phase of treatment. Children who do not respond to one antidepressant alone may benefit from the combined use of antidepressants from different classes. Finally, the need for continued drug treatment should be reassessed following a sufficient period of clinical stabilization (Spencer, Wilens, and Biederman, 1995).

There are few outcome studies on childhood depression. Fleming and associates (1993) compared the outcome of depression in a community-based sample of 652 adolescents who had major depressive disorder (MDD), conduct disorder (CD), MDD and CD, or neither disorder. At 4-year follow-up, these investigators found that 25% of the group who had a diagnosis of major depression continued to experience significant psychiatric and psychosocial morbidity. Juvenile depression though episodic is likely recurrent into adulthood.

Although accidents, especially those that are alcohol or motor vehicle related, are the leading cause of death among adolescents, suicide accounts for 12% of the mortality in this age group. Childhood seems to afford some protection from suicide. Some investigators have proposed that younger children do not possess the cognitive sophistication to comprehend what constitutes fatal behavior. While completed suicide is rare in childhood, Pfeffer and colleagues (1984) found that in a non-

psychiatric sample of 101 children aged 6–12, 8.9% had experienced suicidal ideation and 3% had made a suicidal threat or attempt. Campbell and associates (1993) found that greater family conflict, less family expressiveness, and less family organization were associated with an increased risk for suicidal behavior. Other risk factors include a diagnosis of depression, conduct disorder, ADHD, and drug and alcohol abuse (Shaffer et al., 1996). The presence of a stressful life event, such as concerns about homosexuality or achievement pressures, can trigger suicidal behavior in an already vulnerable adolescent (Sulik and Garfinkel, 1992). One group of investigators (Pfeffer, Normandin, and Kakuma, 1994) found that a history of suicide attempts was more common in first-degree relatives, most notably mothers, of hospitalized children who reported a suicide attempt than in children who were hospitalized for other psychiatric complaints and in a group of normal children. These findings support the use of family therapy with the suicidal child to assess the lethality of the family environment and to clarify the parents' behavior for the child.

The clinical assessment of a suicide attempt in adolescence requires developing a sense of trust with the patient, a detailed appreciation of the lethality of the intent, the patient's assessment of being rescued, and associated factors such as depression or substance use. The clinician needs to balance the short-term wish to protect or parent the adolescent with a respect for the teenager's developmental progression toward autonomy and responsibility for his or her own behavior and future.

From a public health perspective, suicide prevention is best accomplished by limiting access to lethal means (especially guns), making available treatment for depression and substance use, and fostering a sense of connectedness between the adolescent and his family and community.

Chronic Illness

All chronic illnesses present the child and family with psychological stresses (Schowalter, 1979). Chronic diseases can affect every aspect of a child's life. Severe asthma may limit participation in sports, cause school absence, require frequent medication, and, during attacks, threaten the child with death from suffocation. Cystic fibrosis, though better controlled in childhood, often requires up to 20 tablets a day to help digestion, 2 hours of pulmonary toilet, and occasional shocking looks into the future while in clinic waiting rooms observing adolescents in respiratory distress. School-age children with diabetes mellitus can have moderate to severe adjustment problems, commonly manifested in diet or insulin noncompliance.

Children overall cope well with chronic illness (Hobbs, Perrin, and Ireys, 1985), with most having only a moderate increase in behavioral symptomatology. However, children with seizure disorder have among the highest risk of psychiatric comorbidity.

Children's reactions to chronic illness vary. Some resistance to treatment is developmentally appropriate. The older child is beginning to strive for more independence and finds certain therapeutic interventions regressive. For example, the 10-year-old with cystic fibrosis who does not want his mother to pound on his back may be exhibiting age-appropriate behavior. Other common reactions are denial, passive-aggressive behavior, withdrawal, and depression. The clinical approach will of course depend on the child's reaction. Some denial is healthy and supports children's development in the face of congenital limitations, difficult medication regimens, surgery, or poor prognosis. When denial is more severe (for example, when it interferes with the medical care of the child or puts the child at risk for greater injury), it should be confronted gently and gradually. The timing and manner of confronting denial depend on the particular medical and psychiatric situation, the therapist's preferred style, and the family's needs and tolerance. The passive-aggressive reaction to the medical regimen, such as secret noncompliance, can be quite serious and is probably more common than expected. The psychiatrist should attempt to make the child's angry feelings more conscious and accessible so that the child can talk rather than act self-destructively. Like denial, anger may be positive if it does not interfere with medical care. Other avenues may be helpful in channeling the anger, such as sticking needles in puppets for a younger child or video games for an older child. Finally, withdrawal may represent a response to fear, to actual pain, to depressive thoughts, or to having all control removed by parents or medical personnel. The therapist must explore these various possibilities before deciding on an intervention.

Children with chronic physical disease warrant psychosocial screening, ideally at the time of diagnosis. Such assessment should examine the child's emotional development, including depression, self-esteem, and age-appropriate independence; relationships with family members; performance in school and other activities outside the home; and the child's response to the illness, including his understanding of it and willingness to participate in its treatment. It is also useful to find out about previous adaptation to stress because a history of successful coping strategies often predicts a good outcome.

The family's understanding both of the illness itself and of its impact on the family is another major consideration in the assessment and treatment of the child. Family perceptions may influence each member's ability to relate to the chronically ill child in a supportive manner. Providing effective education in order to minimize morbidity, maximize normal functioning, and ensure appropriate compliance is a basic goal in dealing with chronically ill children and their families (Brown, Fritz, and Herzog, 1997).

These children need guidance in learning how to talk about their health impairment. In addition, the psychiatrist can help the child's self-esteem through encouraging skills that have previously led to a sense of competence and by facilitating peer interaction.

Psychosomatic Disorders

Psychosomatic disorders are illnesses that affect both the psyche and the body. DSM-IV classifies the psychosomatic disorders as somatization disorder, conversion disorder, pain disorder, hypochondriasis, body dysmorphic disorder, psychological factors affecting medical illness, factitious disorder, and factitious disorder by proxy. Although diagnostic criteria are available for these disorders, they are often best understood through clinical descriptions. A hallmark of the psychosomatic disorders is the great pressure placed by the family on the doctor to define the disorder in biological terms and to do so without a total medical evaluation of the child, specifically without exploring the child's emotional or family life (Herzog and Harper, 1981). The families characteristically are unable to speak in psychological terms and deny the possibility of a relationship between the child's symptoms and the most painful and pressing issues in family life, such as threatened parental separation or extramarital affairs. These families pay expert attention to borderline test findings and constantly pressure the doctor to attend to these findings. Psychosomatic families rarely trust one physician and often see specialist after specialist.

Psychosomatic presentations vary according to the developmental stage. In the preschooler, failure to thrive, eczema, and encopresis are common. In the school-age child the symptoms are abdominal pain, spells, or seizurelike episodes, enuresis, encopresis, and asthma. In the preadolescent and adolescent, noncompliance and school phobia confound the presenting symptoms. As a way of either denying the illness or acting out, the teenage diabetic may not adhere to a rational diet or insulin regimen; the asthmatic may refuse his medications and may have substantial school absenteeism. Abdominal pain is a frequent complaint and may be primarily psychogenic or diagnosed sometimes years later as peptic ulcer, Crohn's disease, or ulcerative colitis. Teenage girls are increasingly reporting eating-disordered behaviors, at times associated with substantial weight loss, and the differential diagnosis should include anorexia nervosa and bulimia nervosa.

The psychiatrist must work with the primary physician, the patient, and the family. The primary physician may need assistance in defining a rational approach to treating both the family and the illness. It is not necessary to rule out every possible medical basis for these symptoms, and it is important that the psychosocial issues be addressed. Often the psychiatrist may intervene to protect the child from unnecessarily invasive tests. The therapist can also help the primary physician attempt the differential diagnosis of the source of anxiety that surrounds these cases. The concept of displacement can be applied as a way of understanding and managing his anxiety for the family. Displacement implies that the manifest anxiety about the vomiting or abdominal pain is magnified by unacknowledged anxiety about something else in the life of the child or family. The primary focus of the anxiety may be an emotionally traumatic issue such as impending divorce, and displacement occurs when the primary focus is too frightening to be acknowledged. The secondary focus for the anxiety, the child's symptoms, come to stand for the primary focus. During the diagnostic phase it is important to:

Be aware that it is not necessary to make the definitive diagnosis the first day, week, or month, despite pressures from the family.
Use caution in the investigation of equivocal organic findings, such as not hastily ordering an endoscopy in the face of minimal x-ray abnormalities.
Avoid reducing the symptoms to 1 disorder (the child may simultaneously have atypical asthma, family tension, and a depressive disorder).
Recognize that children often have shifting levels of functioning in different settings.

Therapeutic intervention should follow a medical-psychiatric team approach. Such an approach is often directly helpful and also serves as a graceful way out of a high-tension situation. Developing a working relationship with the child and family is critical. At times families will reject help if their defenses of denial and intellectualization are not adequately respected. Children with psychosomatic symptoms are at risk for medical abandonment, especially after psychiatric referral, and it is often useful to request another pediatric examination and to include both the pediatrician and the psychiatrist in treatment planning. Since the child's symptoms frequently serve to stabilize the family, the family may need therapy to avoid reinforcing the child's sick role and to allow the child to abandon that role. Family therapy helps parents regroup as a couple and puts the child's symptoms in perspective as they focus on their relationship. In addition, the healthy part of the child should be supported to help him relinquish the sick role. Developmentally appropriate activities and the use of physical or occupational therapy, or both, can increase the child's sense of mastery and self-esteem.

Child Psychiatric Consultation and Liaison to Pediatrics

The consultant's initial tasks are to clarify who requested the consultation, which usually comes from the primary care physician, and to define the issue being addressed (Rauch, Jellinek, and Herzog, 1997). The issue may involve a differential diagnosis, the development of a treatment protocol for the management of behavior problems, the appropriateness of certain illness behaviors, difficulties in the doctor-patient relationship, or assessment of parental stress. The psychiatrist may be asked to evaluate the "problem" family or "problem" patient, to determine how to manage a violent patient on a pediatric ward (Beresin, Jellinek, and Herzog, 1990), or to help convey tragic news to a family. The consultant should take the opportunity to discuss the request for the referral with the various staff members, although he should not see the patient until the primary physician agrees to write the order.

The child and family should be prepared for the consultation. It is essential that the referring physician discuss the reasons for the referral with both the child and parents so that the child does not feel that information is being withheld from him. The psychiatric consultant should interview the parents of the preschool and young school-age child (less than 8 years old) before interviewing the child.

The child may be active and verbal or shy and inhibited. The consultant should adapt his approach to the child's style of relating. The shy child may be engaged through drawings or games such as checkers or video arcade games. Information should be gathered about current and previous school attendance, school behavior, school performance, after-school activities, friends, mental health of family members, family problems, and interaction of family members in response to traumatic events. Consultations to a 6-year-old with a chronic disease such as leukemia will require several sessions before the child can trust that the psychiatric consultant will not be performing yet another invasive procedure. The leukemic child may also be extremely uncomfortable from the disease itself or its treatment. The first few sessions may be brief and consist of supportive comments, developmental assessment, observation of signs and discussion of symptoms, assessment of coping strategies, and suggestions for ways to deal with feelings and symptoms. The role of the psychiatric consultant for these children has many features of a "professional friend," and after a few sessions the consultant may only drop in for several minutes during rounds. In the inpatient setting, recreational therapy often plays a prominent part in helping children adjust.

On pediatric wards, patients, families, nurses, social workers, and physicians all experience tension. The inability to reverse a terminal illness, to provide a quality life for the severely brain-damaged infant, or to change an abusive parent frequently makes the caregiver feel helpless. The helplessness can arouse sadness, as a result of identification with the helpless infant or child; it can also engender intense anger at the child or family for making the caregiver feel inadequate or incompetent. The rage associated with feelings of helplessness in caring for the chronically or severely ill child is commonly projected onto other staff, spouses, or patients. Such feelings may affect both the quality of care provided and staff's interest in work (Herzog, Wyshak, and Stern, 1984). Liaison activities serve to (1) sensitize primary care staff to developmental and psychological needs of the child and family; (2) promote awareness of early signs of psychopathology; (3) broaden staff attitudes toward patient illness, clarify staff countertransference phenomena toward the patient or family, and support the pediatric medical and nursing staff; and (4) improve communication between staff members. The consultant can substantially influence the pediatric house staff team's ability to function through recognizing and managing discord (Jellinek, 1986). Weekly groups for nursing and house staff and multidisciplinary rounds provide regular opportunities for exchanging information, acknowledging feelings, and supporting one another.

The most challenging task of consultation liaison work is to bring child psychiatry and pediatrics closer together (Jellinek, 1982). Senior members of both disciplines have long advocated closer collaboration in both training and patient care. To this day, the training of a child psychiatrist does not require any pediatrics, and there is too little psychiatric input into pediatric training programs; many pediatric programs have limited or no child psychiatric consultation available. Given the growing emphasis on primary care, the very limited use of pediatric inpatient visits, and the 12–20% of children with psychosocial dys-

function, collaboration between pediatrics and the full range of mental health providers is essential.

Infant Psychiatry

Infant psychiatry has emerged as a specialty field (Rexford, Sander, and Shapiro, 1976). Because of advances in the technology of measurement in infancy, in infancy research, and in neonatal intensive care, requests are increasing for child psychiatrists to evaluate and consult on the problems of infancy. Studies of improved developmental outcome as a result of increased stability and sensitivity in the environment of infants have encouraged early intervention efforts. The present-day philosophy is one of intervention as early in life as possible to prevent developmental and emotional deviations from what is considered normal behavioral development.

The infant's environment is increasingly complex: teenage pregnancies are on the rise, working mothers and day care are the norm, divorce is common, adoption of children from foreign countries is possible, and foster care and adoption by single parents and by gay couples are becoming more acceptable. Since the average length of marriage is 6.8 years, many young children experience increasing stress earlier and earlier in their lives. James Herzog (1980), for example, in reviewing his psychotherapeutic work with 12 children between the ages of 15 and 30 months whose parents had recently separated, noted that loss of the father was associated with dreams of "father hunger" and nightmares. Emotional risk in infancy can now be identified through psychiatric assessment of the infant and its interaction with caregivers (American Academy of Child and Adolescent Psychiatry, 1997a, b).

In the early years of psychiatry, infancy was viewed through the retrospective reconstructions of patients; infants were passive and shaped by basic drives and parental handling. Over the past several decades, investigators into infancy have clearly demonstrated that infants play an active role in shaping environment. Their temperament, affects, and fit with caregivers are critical factors in development as described by Thomas, Chess, and Birch (1968), T. Berry Brazelton (Brazelton, Koslowski, and Main, 1974), and Daniel Stern (1977).

Psychiatric evaluation of the infant requires specific techniques and equipment as well as a detailed developmental and social history from the caregivers. In the newborn to 12-month-old, the assessment encompasses 3 areas: central nervous system reactivity (to the examiner and to standardized instruments), social interest and pre-attachment readiness, and temperament. To assess central nervous system organization, the clinician observes the infant's patterns of modulation during wakefulness and sleep and the infant's ability to soothe himself. Brazelton's Neonatal Assessment Scale (Brazelton, 1973) can be a useful guide in evaluating the newborn. The child psychiatrist can evaluate social interest and attachment readiness by comparing the intensity and quality of the infant's responses to the examiner and to the parent(s). Temperamental assessment is accomplished through parent interview, history taking, and observation, using Thomas, Chess, and Birch's (1968) 3 categories of infant temperament (easy, slow to warm up, and difficult).

In the 12- to 24-month-old, additional areas merit attention: affiliation and attachment behavior, and quality of spontaneous play. The psychiatrist should interview the child and caregiver in a free-play situation and carefully observe the child's degree of attachment to and separation-individuation from the parent. Mary Ainsworth's Stranger Situation Paradigm (1973) may be useful in this assessment. The child is observed as the parent or examiner leaves the room and again on the adult's return. Some 70% of American children are "securely attached" in this paradigm; 30% show "insecure attachment," protesting too little or too much at the time of separation.

Psychiatric diagnosis in infancy is still evolving. Some severe disorders, such as pervasive developmental disorder and mental retardation, are difficult to diagnose reliably in the first 2 years of life. Specific developmental disorders (motor delay, language delay, feeding difficulties) are much more common and more easily diagnosed, as are the psychosomatic disorders of infancy: failure to thrive, pica, rumination, eczema, and diarrhea.

Failure to thrive (FTT) is a relatively common syndrome manifested by failure to gain weight and to grow. Traditional studies attempted to distinguish between nonorganic and organic FTT. However, the disorder is better understood as multidimensional and includes the nonorganic risk factors of biological/genetic vulnerability in the infant, parental compromise, interactional difficulties, stress, poverty, and loss in the social environment (Rathbun and Peterson, 1987). These factors can be identified by the psychiatrist through a careful social history, record review, parent-infant observation during feeding and play, and developmental assessment. Because all FTT involves significant malnutrition, it necessarily leads to notable behavior change in the infant, which often generates further interactional deficits (Pollitt and Thompson, 1977). The diagnostic nomenclature for FTT has evolved since 1980, when DSM-III first offered a related diagnosis, Reactive Attachment Disorder of Infancy,

a diagnosis limited by its attempt to describe a unitary, nonorganic syndrome of growth failure, attachment disorder, and caregiving inadequacy. In 1987 DSM-III-R narrowed this diagnosis to one of failure to grow secondary to grossly inadequate caregiving; however, it was not until 1994 that DSM-IV finally separated growth failure from attachment disorder/caregiving failure, allowing multiple, and therefore more accurate, diagnoses in the multifaceted arena of failure to thrive. The 2 diagnoses now available are:

Feeding Disorder of Infancy or Early Childhood, a feeding disturbance with onset before 6 years of age and accompanied by significant failure to gain weight or loss of weight for 1 month or more.

Reactive Attachment Disorder of Infancy or Early Childhood, evidenced by inappropriate social relatedness and grossly pathological caregiving.

Depression also occurs in infancy. Some infants will manifest sad or expressionless faces, minimal social interaction, decreased activity, and sleep difficulties. Mothers of these infants often have significant physical or psychiatric illness or are in stressful environments that do not allow them to attend to their infant's emotional needs. An adequate psychiatric workup should include a medical evaluation because organic illness, such as cardiac or renal dysfunction, may be involved.

In the treatment of most infant disorders, the mother and infant are seen together. The mother-infant interview, as described by Selma Fraiberg (1980), involves not only the mother's description of her feelings but also the active demonstration of them to her infant. The psychiatrist addresses interactional concerns as they occur. The goals of therapy are to enhance the mother-infant attachment, stimulate the child's development, and educate parents to understand and facilitate their infant's development. With the parent, the psychiatrist addresses past and present feelings of pain, and the ways in which the infant contributes to those feelings. Fraiberg (1975) writes of "ghosts in the nursery," those difficulties with their own parents that individuals unconsciously bring to their own parenting. Parents can gain insight into such transgenerational issues and restructure their own interactions through intensive psychotherapy. Adjunctive programs that provide support for the infant, such as physical therapy, in-home early intervention, cognitive stimulation, and nutritional supplements, enhance both the child's physical and psychological development and the parent-infant relationship.

Contemporary Issues in Child Psychiatry

The pace and extent of social change exert a profound effect on family life and the well-being of children. The family unit is sustaining an accumulation of social, economic, and psychological blows that obscure, especially for research purposes, how any single social trend influences a later outcome. Increases in both the divorce rate and the number of households in which both parents work are placing younger children in day care for longer hours. Finding quality day care is difficult because of great demand and lack of financial support. In the midst of all this change, more children are living in poverty surrounded by violence and substance abuse. And this overwhelming list does not take into consideration the influence of television, the increasing number of adolescents having babies and abortions, and the dramatic decrease in the number of extended family members readily available to children.

Day care provides a window for understanding the impact of social forces on child development from psychodynamic, epidemiologic, sociocultural, and practical pediatric approaches. Over half of all mothers with children under school age work part or full time. Children are being placed in day care at younger ages and for more hours.

From a psychodynamic view the increasing use of day care places an increasing number of children at risk. Clinically oriented studies and extensive experience suggest that separations from the mother (or mother figure) cause children short-term and potentially long-term harm. Children, especially at earlier ages, cry and are anxious when taken to day care (Blehar, 1974) and are avoidant or need a transition time when they are picked up. Psychiatric clinics are treating more and more adults who sustained an early loss of a parent by death, disability, or emotional unavailability such as depression. Psychodynamic theories suggest that children experiencing frequent separations and the resulting inevitable inconsistency in care are more likely to feel rejected, develop lower self-esteem, and be less secure in later relationships.

An epidemiologic research approach challenges the broad clinical and psychodynamic conclusions as biased and unproved. Rutter (1971; Rutter and Hersov, 1985) reviewed the impact of day care and raised several precise questions:

What are the circumstances of using day care? economic necessity? legitimate career interests? Doesn't day care act as a relief for some women and thus make the mother more emotionally available?

What are the child's temperament, personality, and age? How many hours of day care does the child have per week? What is the child's life like at home—warm and supportive or tense and characterized by discord?

Is the caretaker warm? flexible in meeting children's needs? Does the caretaker set reasonable expectations? Is there enough adult attention and availability given the number and age of the children? How is the child introduced to day care—abruptly or with time to become familiar and comfortable?

How do any observable short-term effects, such as a brief protest at the time of separation, relate to long-term behavior or character development?

Intimacy and security are hard to measure, especially in individuals not requesting psychotherapy, and no methodologically reliable and valid study has been done using a normal population.

A third perspective is sociocultural and focuses on broad trends consistent over many years rather than on clinical experience or the specific impact of a single factor. A number of major trends may interact in a complex manner with multiple outcomes. Over a several-decade time frame the divorce rate has tripled (1 in 2 children will live with a single parent); use of day care is now the norm; 1 of every 5 children live in poverty; and the rate of violence, especially in urban centers, has risen dramatically (1 in 610 children die by gunshot). Furthermore, other factors such as the increasing incidence of adult and thus parental depression have changed as well. What will be the balance between rational use of medical resources and a too restrictive model that rewards underutilization? What will be the factors in allocating resources between older versus younger citizens (1 in 7 children have no health insurance)? How will we balance public health concerns with the cultural tradition valuing individual freedoms such as the use of cigarettes and alcohol (as well as a permissive attitude toward drunk driving)? All of these cultural trends and issues bear on the development and emotional well-being of children.

Divorce

The impact of divorce on children, families, and society is staggering (Jellinek and Slovik, 1981). Each year over 1 million children are involved in divorce (average 1 child per divorce), with the average length of first marriages being 11 years and second marriages being 7.4 (Children's Defense Fund, 1997). Although most children can cope with the divorce process and after a period of adaptation maintain their developmental progress, approximately 10–20% develop longer-term dysfunction in one or more areas.

Divorce is much more than a legal decree. It is a process that may reflect years of unhappiness and discord, many months of legal negotiations, and then a permanent change in the family's way of life. Often the family home is the major asset and is sold as part of the financial settlement. As a result children lose not only the consistency of both parents but also the home they grew up in, the neighborhood school, their friends, local after-school activities, and so on. Family disposable income drops, the mother's disproportionately, as legal fees and the cost of maintaining 2 households usually force both parents into a lower economic bracket.

The impact of divorce on parents is an additional critical issue. Both parents face multiple losses, including each other, their way of life, community relationships, and available income. Existing emotional disorders are likely to be exacerbated under the stresses of multiple losses, and approximately 20% of mothers may develop clinical depression.

The child's reactions to divorce are most influenced by developmental level and the quality of his relationship to the parent who has physical custody. Custody is awarded to the mother in approximately 70% of divorces, the father 10%, and jointly about 20% (Children's Defense Fund, 1997).

Infants and toddlers are highly reactive to the mother's ability to function. Wallerstein and Kelly (1981), in a study of 34 young children followed for several years after a divorce, reported that approximately half showed temporary reactions, including regression, increased irritability, and greater dependency. After a year most children were doing well except for 3 whose mothers were experiencing depression and both of whose parents were continuing to wrangle.

The young school-age child's vulnerability to divorce relates to his developmental level, which has gone beyond a one-to-one relationship with the mother and includes the concept of a family. From a cognitive perspective the 5- or 6-year-old does not understand complex motives, depends on an egocentric understanding of causation, and conceives of time in terms of hours or days rather than months or years. At this cognitive level the child is confused by the words and length of the divorce process. His increased verbal skills include a sense of conscience that is ready to accept blame for family events ("it's my fault . . . I'm bad"). The natural tendency toward self-blame is reinforced by the child's reaction to arguments overheard before the divorce in which his name was mentioned, especially to disagreements about his behavior or family events.

School-age children are cognitively more sophisticated and have an emerging ability not to feel directly responsible for the divorce. Instead children at this age feel frustrated by their helplessness and their inability to reunite the parents, and express a sense of loneliness when both parents are preoccupied by emotional, legal, and financial concerns. When overwhelmed, school-age children will show psychosomatic symptoms, depression, or dysfunction in school or in peer relationships.

The adolescent's developmental task is to separate from the family unit as part of the process of developing an adult identity. Given the multiple losses intrinsic in the divorce process, separation becomes difficult, and the natural evolution of individuation is markedly disrupted. At age 11 or 12, for example, the adolescent may react to the divorce by premature closure of school-age developmental tasks and adopt uncritically the absent parent's personality characteristics. Other young adolescents will act "pseudomature" by appearing aloof, overly controlled, and, frequently, overcontrolling. Pseudomature adolescents may select peer groups that are deviant from parental values or have an unusually wide age range that provides a more structured and superficially nurturant haven. Substance use may reflect a daily attempt to hide feelings of shame, suppress anxiety, dull depression, and test the limits of the new parenting system.

The long-term consequences of divorce on personality and sexuality are unknown. One can speculate that divorce at critical points in a child's psychosexual development could have a long-range impact. For example, does a divorce and a tenuous relationship with a father at age 6 or 12 have an effect years later on the child's identity? Are young children more adaptable while adolescents are more threatened as the divorce is closer to their own developmental experience? Studies of the long-term consequences and vulnerabilities that result from divorce are methodologically difficult to implement because the time period can be 20 or more years, and the number of intervening variables unrelated to the divorce process are difficult to control. The longer-term impact is harder to relate directly to any single influence but may include less security in heterosexual relationships, a need for counseling to overcome concerns about intimacy, and a lower quality of marriage (Wallerstein, Blakeslee, 1989).

After an initial period of shock and denial, most children begin to grieve for the loss of the family structure. Unlike death, this loss is not inevitable and is therefore more confusing. After the initial phase many children express anger and hostility. Except in cases of uncomplicated joint custody, most children are more ready to express anger at the parent of custody and are unable to conceptualize a rational apportionment of blame. Such children do not feel safe expressing anger at the visiting parent, lest they weaken what appears to be an already tenuous relationship. Children's concerns about visitation are frequently justified: studies indicate that 2 months after the divorce decree fewer than half of fathers see their children weekly, and after 3 years approximately half never see their children.

If the child, as part of coping, adopts the absent parent's role, there will be an increased level of tension between the custodial parent and the child. The mother may complain that her son is just like his father, and the result will be less support for the child's developmental needs.

Most children, after an initial period of grieving and mild to moderate symptomatic reaction, will return to their previous developmental trajectory within a year after the divorce decree. Peer relationships will improve, academic performance rise to appropriate levels, and family relationships stabilize in new patterns. In addition, the child will have adapted to either a new school or neighborhood, and family finances will be more predictable and not based on repeated negotiations or court decisions. Four factors increase the psychological risk during and after the divorce process: predisposing vulnerability, the quality of family life before the divorce, the extent of discord after the divorce, and the emotional stability of the custodial parent.

Predisposing vulnerabilities include genetic factors such as a family history of depression, a particular set of temperamental characteristics, or a history of previous losses. The divorce process may reawaken memories of a previously lost family member or loss of expectations, as in children having a chronic disease.

Divorce often serves only as a new marker of a hostile process active for years before the legal decree. It is difficult to know which impact on a child is greater—a divorce or living in an unhappy home. Preliminary epidemiologic work by Michael Rutter (Rutter and Hersov, 1985) indicated higher levels of delinquency in homes with high levels of tension and low levels of warmth. In a follow-up study of 65 families, he found that the rate of delinquency decreased along with the level of discord. Sometimes, however, divorce merely shifts continuing conflict from the home into the courts.

The last area of risk for the child is the parent's capacity to function. Parents may be temporarily dysfunctional, or the divorce may be symptomatic of more serious personality or psychiatric disorders. A child who requires extra support during the divorce process may be cared for by a parent who is temporarily overwhelmed or permanently unable to meet the child's physical and emotional needs.

Although the manner of telling the child about the divorce and discussing the specifics of visitation are important, parents' ability to maintain a clear perspective in terms of the child's needs is the overriding factor in easing emotional distress. When a child is used as a bargaining chip, the content of the issue is largely irrelevant. The clinical damage to the child results from the process itself—being used by one parent to harm the other—while the child's suffering goes largely unrecognized. Divorce can be a healing process if the child is not used and parental energies can be redirected away from fruitless arguments and toward meeting the individual needs of the parent and child. Unfortunately, because of continuing discord, decreasing involvement of the father, or remarriages that recreate destructive patterns and again end in divorce, the children who benefit from divorce are a minority.

Divorce is such a common and private process that pediatricians and even schools sometimes are not aware that the child is facing a crisis at home. The pediatrician may find out only when a bill is returned by the mother and a new address is given for the now separated or divorced father. Schools, because of daily contact with the child, may be told of the divorce by either the parent or the child, but it is still quite common for schools and teachers to be poorly informed about the major changes taking place at home. Many children face divorce alone, without an emotionally available adult to share feelings or answer questions. It is therefore important to ask explicitly about the quality of family life in the home, including the level of tension, hostility, and warmth. Child psychiatrists and psychologists can help the child through the divorce process by advocating for the child's needs, attempting to ease destructive tensions, and helping the child understand the process rather than feeling lonely and rejected.

Child Abuse and Neglect

The incidence of child abuse and neglect is alarmingly high: for physical abuse the rate is 3.4 per 1000 children, for physical neglect 1.7 per 1000, and for emotional neglect 1.0 per 1000. More than 2000 children in the United States die each year as a result of physical abuse (Rutter and Hersov, 1994).

The neglected child usually comes to medical attention before age 3 with numerous problems, including developmental delays, interactional difficulties, skin infections, and failure to thrive (starvation). The child at risk for neglect is often ill, has a difficult temperament, or is seen as damaged in some way. Parents who neglect their child are often depressed, expect the child to meet and gratify the parental needs for love and attention, and are disinhibited by alcohol or preoccupied by drug-seeking behavior.

The abused child may present with bruises, burns, fractures, lacerations, or abdominal or brain trauma. These children are often sad, cautious, and pseudomature. There is often a multigenerational disruption of positive mothering and a higher prevalence of a maladaptive but powerful identification of the abusing parent with his own abusing parent.

Sexual abuse refers to involvement, by an individual at least 5 years older than the child, in sexual activities that the child does not fully comprehend or to which the child is unable to give informed consent. Studies have found that approximately 38% of females will have some experience of sexual abuse before they are 18 (Russell, 1983). Female victims outnumber male victims by about 6 to 1, but the statistic may be inaccurate because of underreporting in boys who worry that being sexually abused makes them homosexual. Most of the victims are under age 6. Almost all the perpetrators are male and in nearly two-thirds of the cases are known to the victims.

The sexually abused child presents with physical symptoms resulting from trauma or infection or behaviors associated with post-traumatic stress syndrome. In 90% of these cases there is no physical evidence of sexual abuse at the time of presentation. The perpetrator typically has chronic low self-esteem and an intense need for omnipotence and control. Some have a compulsion for immature, undemanding, childlike sexual partners. Others become disinhibited through use of alcohol or drugs. Long-term consequences are frequent and include multiple personality, dissociative disorders, depression, sexual promiscuity, sexual inhibition, flashbacks, sexual abuse of their own children by abused males, and choice of abusive partners by abused females.

Initial treatment focuses on effecting change in the abusing parent(s), which may take the form of individual psychotherapy, group psychotherapy, or self-help programs such as Parents Anonymous. Family therapy can be particularly critical when the goal is to help the child remain with or return to the family. Parents who neglect or abuse their children are very difficult to treat but may respond to a supportive, nonjudgmental approach that provides them with the parenting they did not receive and helps increase their self-esteem. In long-term psychotherapy the child deals with themes of loss, guilt, betrayal, worthlessness, and rage.

The law requires the clinician to report all suspected abuse, and the child must be protected from intimidation or retaliation by the perpetrator, and possibly by other adults who have been complicit with the abuse. If the child is in the hospital, the physician, psychologist, or social worker can proceed with court action to keep the child in a protected setting.

Physical and sexual abuse raises complex legal issues. How does one decide when a child is a competent witness? How many times does a child need to go over sensitive material with different legal personnel? Does the child have to face the perpetrator in court? How much cross-examining of children should be permitted? In actuality many abused children are not considered competent witnesses, and in the absence of other witnesses or physical evidence many cases, especially those involving very young children, are not prosecuted. Some courts are now permitting, on an experimental basis, the use of videotapes of interviews between the psychiatrist and the abused child in order to provide data from the child, to decrease the number of different professionals questioning him, and to spare him the pain of facing the perpetrator, cross-examination, and the courtroom.

One of the major issues impacting abused and neglected children is adequate care and protection after the maltreatment has been discovered. Social service agencies and courts are overwhelmed, and there are inadequate treatment options for the children, perpetrators, spouses, and so on. If the child needs to be removed for foster placement or adoption, the process is slow and, given the current availability and funding of foster homes, often not protective (Jellinek, 1995). There are some innovative programs to prevent abuse by early identification and service provision including in-home teaching for high-risk pregnancies and birth as well as efforts to accelerate adoption if parents are unable to care safely for their children.

Poverty and Public Policy

The history of child mental health services in the United States reflects periods of rapid growth that were largely dependent on the funding of medical and education services for children. Private health insurance is oriented to inpatient care and procedures and provides either low or no benefits for "cognitive" outpatient pediatric or mental health services. The early rapid growth of child guidance units was supported by foundations and local governments to meet needs newly defined by innovative social policies (on delinquency) or to promote the care of poor, sometimes abused, children. These guidance clinics received additional momentum from research advances in child development and treatment and from the growth of child psychiatry as a recognized medical specialty. The second phase of major expansion was stimulated by the federal government in the 1960s and 1970s with a number of child advocacy programs, including funding for community mental health centers, Head Start for preschool children, Medicaid benefits for outpatient mental health services, mandates (but no funding) defining comprehensive care for physically and emotionally disabled children, and increased support of research through the National Institute of Mental Health. On a local level some state governments passed laws detailing a broad range of services for children with physical, educational, or emotional disorders, together with mandatory requirements for reporting and evaluating children suspected of being abused or neglected. In addition the federal government noted the shortage of child psychiatrists and encouraged new training programs through direct funding of fellowship stipends and faculty salaries. During the same period societal trends—the post–World War II baby boom and the concomitant rise in expectations, a sharp increase in the divorce rate, a growing emphasis on school achievement, and the newly discovered disorders such as learning disabilities—were among the many forces to work synergistically to increase the emphasis on mental health services for children. The net result of new needs, additional funding, and the training of more clinicians was a major increase in child mental health services through schools, hospitals, community clinics, and private practitioners.

In the 1980s, as part of a broad effort to decrease the cost of medical services and reduce state and federal taxes, there was dramatic reduction in emphasis on the availability and quality of child mental health services. As a result of these cuts at the federal level, funding for community clinics ended, Medicaid eligibility tightened, and outpatient mental health benefits were limited or rescinded; Head Start waiting lists grew so that only one-fifth of those eligible were enrolled (despite research findings documenting positive outcome and cost effectiveness); federal training grants for child psychiatry were funded at a very low level (by the will of Congress over the protest of the executive branch); and a greater number of children (1 out of 5) were living in poverty (U.S. Department of Commerce, 1996) despite a period of record-breaking economic growth.

Some states followed the federal government's example by not proceeding with innovative legislation or programs. Other states passed "tax caps" that forced local governments to choose between fire and police protection (in the face of a rising crime rate) and school budgets. The net result of such caps was inevitable: both routine and special educational services were frozen or cut.

Private and corporate funding of health care is following the same trend: efforts are focused on reducing rather than expanding insurance benefits. Government and corporate employers have capped or asked for "give-backs" in health coverage. Mental health services for adults and children were always limited to a specific number of inpatient days and few if any outpatient visits. In addition, recent growth of "managed care" through various prepaid groups has fostered price competition resulting in strenuous efforts to limit utilization of services. Not surprisingly there has been an increase in the management of mental health problems by primary care providers, in short-term therapy, and in "sector" therapy that sets rapidly achievable and less comprehensive treatment goals. Like a school system with a fixed budget, prepaid health and capitated plans help their bottom line by not finding problems and by stretching less treatment over a longer period (sessions biweekly or monthly).

The current status of educational, medical, and psychiatric benefits to children is bleak. More children are poor, many educational services face cost constraints, and medical and psychiatric benefits to children are often too limited (Jellinek and Nurcombe, 1993; Jellinek and Little, 1997).

It is to be hoped that the principles of managed care, cost-effectiveness, and the possibility that capitation may encourage the funding of prevention efforts will offer alternatives. Managed care allows for better tracking, often through computer-generated analysis of utilization. Pilot studies using psychosocial screening approaches (Jellinek, et al., 1995) are beginning to be used to balance the overwhelming financial incentive to do less or nothing. The political process on a state and federal level is pushing back on managed care corporations to define and provide reasonable service levels.

Ideally, children should have the availability and support of both parents and of society. But even though many parents, through natural affection and a knowledge of child development, are highly invested in their children's well-being, other factors such as divorce, career aspirations, and economic pressures may decrease their physical and emotional availability. Although society has more programs and protections for children than it did a generation ago, many are inadequately funded and contradictory. For example, federal law mandates that every child should have a full educational evaluation available on an as-needed basis; however, there are too few professionals to carry out this mandate, there is little funding for assessment, and local tax cuts are limiting educational services. More women than ever are employed outside the home; yet high-quality day care in the workplace receives a low priority. Similar contradictory patterns hold true for the medical and psychiatric care of children. Although immunizations are proven effective, and the cost of providing this resource is less than the cost of caring for ill children, not all children are immunized. Although recent advances in diagnosis and comprehensive treatment have made the psychiatric care of children more efficacious, the funding for such treatment is decreasing. We are concerned about accident prevention, suicide, and violence, yet drunk driving laws are lax, handguns are too easily accessible, and child psychiatric services for conduct disorder or substance abuse are limited. We know how to care for children in a humane and considerate manner; however, we often make short-range decisions that do not fulfill our responsibility to the future.

References

Advance report of final divorce statistics, 1989 and 1990. 1995. National Center for Health Statistics. 43 (9 suppl.):95–1120.

Ainsworth, M. D. S. 1973. The development of infant-mother attachment. In *Review of child development research*, ed. B. Caldwell and H. Ricciuti. Vol. 3. Chicago: University of Chicago Press.

Ambrosini P. J., M. D. Bianchi, H. Rabinovich, and J. Elia. 1993. Antidepressant treatments in children and adolescents I. Affective disorders. *J. Am. Acad. Child Adolesc. Psychiatry* 32:1–6.

American Academy of Child and Adolescent Psychiatry. 1997a. ACAP Official Action: practice parameters for the psychiatric assessment of infants and toddlers (0–36 months). 36(10):21S–36S.

American Academy of Child and Adolescent Psychiatry. 1997b.

ACAP Official Action: summary of the practice parameters for the assessment and treatment of children and adolescents with conduct disorder. 36(10):122S–139S.

American Psychiatric Association. 1980. *Diagnostic and statistical manual of mental disorders.* 3rd ed. Washington, D.C.: American Psychiatric Association.

——— 1987. *Diagnostic and statistical manual of mental disorders.* 3rd ed., rev. Washington, D.C.: American Psychiatric Association.

——— 1994. *Diagnostic and statistical manual of mental disorders.* 4th ed. Washington, D.C.: American Psychiatric Association.

Anders, T. F., and M. Niehaus. 1982. Promoting the alliance between pediatrics and child psychiatry. *Psychiatr. Clin. North Am.* 5:241–258.

Ballaban-Gil, K., I. Rapin, R. Tuchman, K. Freeman, and S. Shinnar. 1991. The risk of seizures in autistic individuals: occurrence of a secondary peak in adolescence. *Epilepsia* 32:84.

Bandura, A. 1969. *Principles of behavior modification.* New York: Holt, Reinhart and Winston.

Barkley, R. A. 1977. A review of stimulant drug research with hyperactive children. *J. Child Psychol. Psychiatry* 18:137–165.

Beardslee, W. R., M. Keller, P. W. Lavori, G. K. Klerman, D. J. Dorer, and H. Samuelson. 1988. Psychiatric disorder in adolescent offspring of parents with affective disorder in a non-referred sample. *J. Affect. Disord.* 15:313–322.

Beresin, E. V., M. S. Jellinek, and D. B. Herzog. 1990. The difficult parent. In *Psychosocial aspects of ambulatory pediatrics,* ed. M. Jellinek. Chicago: Mosby Year Book Medical Publishers.

Biederman, J., and M. S. Jellinek. 1984. Psychopharmacology in children. *N. Engl. J. Med.* 310:968–972.

Biederman, J., D. Gastfriend, and M. S. Jellinek. 1986. Desipramine in adolescents with attention deficit disorder. *J. Clin. Psychopharmacol.* 6:359–363.

Blehar, M. C. 1974. Anxious attachment and defensive reactions. *Child Devel.* 45:683–692.

Bowlby, J. 1969. *Attachment and loss.* New York: Basic Books.

Brazelton, T. B. 1973. *Neonatal behavioral assessment scale.* London: Heinemann.

Brazelton, T. B., B. Koslowski, and M. Main. 1974. The origins of reciprocity: the early mother-infant interaction. In *The effect of the infant on its caretaker,* ed. M. Lewis and L. A. Rosenblum. New York: Wiley.

Bronfenbrenner, U. 1974. The origins of alienations. *Sci. Am.* 53:61.

Brown L. K., G. K. Fritz, and D. B. Herzog. 1997. The somatoform disorders. In *Textbook of child and adolescent psychiatry,* ed. J. Wiener. 2nd ed. Washington, D.C.: American Psychiatric Press.

Campbell, M., and J. E. Cueva. 1995. Psychopharmacology in child and adolescent psychiatry: a review of the past seven years. Pt. II. *J. Acad. Child Adolesc. Psychiatry* 34:1262–72.

Campbell, N. B., L. Milling, A. Laughlin, and E. Bush. 1993. The psychosocial climate of families with suicidal preadolescent children. *Am. J. Orthopsychiatry* 63:142–145.

Centers for Disease Control. 1986. Suicide surveillance,

1970–1980. U. S. Department of Health and Human Services Public Health Service, Atlanta.

Children's Defense Fund. 1986. A Children's Defense Fund budget. Washington, D.C.

——— 1997. Twenty key facts about American children. Washington, D.C.

Eisenberg, L. 1980. Normal child development. In *Comprehensive textbook of psychiatry*, ed. H. Kaplan, A. Freedman, and B. Sadock. Vol. 3, 3rd ed. Baltimore: Williams & Wilkins.

——— 1995. The social construction of the human brain. *Am. J. Psychiatry* 152(11):1563–75.

Elkind, D. 1981. *The hurried child.* Reading, Mass.: Addison-Wesley.

Emslie, G., A. Rush, W. Weinberg, R. Kowatch, C. Hughes, and J. Rintelmann. 1995. Efficacy of fluoxetine in depressed children and adolescents. *Scientific proceedings of American Academy of Child and Adolescent Psychiatry,* vol. 11.

Erikson, E. 1963. *Childhood and society.* New York: Norton.

Flavell, J. H. 1963. *The developmental psychology of Jean Piaget.* New York: Van Nostrand.

Fleming, J. E., and D. R. Offord. 1990. Epidemiology of childhood depressive disorders: a critical review. *J. Am. Acad. Child. Adolesc. Psychiatry* 29:571–580.

Fleming, J. E., M. H. Boyle, and D. R. Offord. 1993. The outcome of adolescent depression in the Ontario child health study follow-up. *J. Am. Acad. Child Adolesc. Psychiatry* 32:28–33.

Fleming, J. E., D. R. Offord, and M. H. Boyle. 1989. Prevalence of childhood and adolescent depression in the community: Ontario child health study. *Br. J. Psychiatry* 155:647–654.

Fraiberg, S. 1975. Ghosts in the nursery. *J. Am. Acad. Child Psychiatry* 14:387–421.

——— ed. 1980. *Clinical studies in infant mental health.* New York: Basic Books.

Freud, A. 1965. *Normality and pathology in childhood: assessment in development.* New York: International Universities Press.

——— 1973. *The ego and mechanisms of defense.* New York: International Universities Press.

Fritz, G., S. Fritsch, and O. Hagino. 1997. Somatoform disorders in children and adolescents: a review of the past 10 years. *American Journal of Child and Adolescent Psychiatry* 36(10):1329–38.

Garrison, C. Z., C. L. Addy, K. L. Jackson, R. E. McKeown, and J. L. Waller. 1992. Major depressive disorder and dysthymia in young adolescents. *Am. J. Epidemiol.* 135:792–802.

Gillberg, C. 1991. Outcome in autism and autistic-like conditions. *J. Am. Acad. Child Adolesc. Psychiatry* 30:375–382.

Gilman, J. T., and R. F. Tuchman. 1995. Autism and associated behavioral disorders: pharmocotherapeutic intervention. *Ann. Pharmacother.* 29:47–56.

Group for the Advancement of Psychiatry. 1966. Psychopathological disorders of childhood: theoretical considerations and a proposed classification. Vol. 6, report no. 62. New York: Mental Health Materials Center.

Harrington, C., H. Fudge, M. L. Rutter, D. Bredenkamp, C. Groothues, and J. Pridham. 1993. Child and adult depression: a test of continuities with data from a family study. *Br. J. Psychiatry* 162:627–633.

Herzog, D. B., and G. Harper. 1981. Unexplained disability: diagnostic dilemmas and principles of management. *Clin. Pediatr.* 20:761–768.

Herzog, D. B., G. Wyshak, and T. A. Stern. 1984. Patient-generated dysphoria in houseofficers. *J. Med. Educ.* 69:869–874.

Herzog, J. M. 1980. Sleep disturbance and father hunger in 18 to 28 month old boys (the Erlkonig syndrome). *Psychoanal. Study Child* 35:219–233.

Hetherington, E. M. 1972. Effects of father absence on personality development in adolescent daughters. *Dev. Psychol.* 7:313–326.

Hobbs, N., J. Perrin, and H. T. Ireys. 1985. Chronically ill children and their families. San Francisco: Jossey-Bass.

Hoffman, H. 1926. Struwwelpeter. Frankfurt: Zerlog, Englerd and Schlosser.

Homer, C., and S. Ludwig. 1981. Categorization of etiology of failure to thrive. *Am. J. Dis. Child.* 135:848–851.

Jellinek, M. S., and L. Slovik. 1981. Divorce: impact on children. *N. Engl. J. Med.* 305:557–559.

Jellinek, M. S. 1982. The present status of child psychiatry in pediatrics. *N. Engl. J. Med.* 306:1227–33.

——— 1986. Recognition and management of discord within house staff teams. *JAMA* 256:754–755.

Jellinek, M. S., and Nurcombe, B. 1993. Two wrongs don't make a right: managed care, mental health, and the medical marketplace. *JAMA* 270(14):1737–39.

——— 1994a. The outpatient milieu. *J. Child Adolesc. Psychiatry* 33(2):277–279.

——— 1994b. Managed care: good or bad news for children. *J. Devel. Behavioral Peds.* 15(4):273–274.

Jellinek, M. S., M. Little, J. M. Murphy, and M. Pagano. 1995. The pediatric symptom checklist: support for a role in a managed care environment. *Arch. Pediatr. Adolesc. Med.* 149:740–746.

Jellinek, M. S., and M. Little. 1997. Supporting child psychiatric services using current managed care approaches: You can't get there from here. *Archives of Pediatrics* 152(4):32–326.

Kagan, J. S., J. Kagan, N. Snidmann, M. Gersten, K. Baak, and A. Rosenberg. 1986. Inhibited and uninhibited children: a follow-up study. *Child Devel.* 57:660–680.

Kandel, E. R. 1979. Psychotherapy and the single synapse: the impact of psychiatric thought on neurobiologic research. *N. Engl. J. Med.* 301:1028–37.

Kashani, J. H., W. R. Holocomb, and H. Orvaschel. 1986. Depression and depressive symptoms in preschool children from the general population. *Am. J. Psychiatry* 143:1138–43.

Kashani, J. H., N. C. Beck, E. W. Hoeper, C. Fallahi, C. M. Corcoran, J. A. McAllister, T. K. Rosenberg, and J. C. Reid. 1987. Psychiatric disorders in a community sample of adolescents. *Am. J. Psychiatry* 144:584–589.

Kashani, J. H., H. Orvaschel, T. K. Rosenberg, and J. C. Reid. 1989. Psychopathology in a community sample of children and adolescents: a developmental perspective. *J. Am. Acad. Child Adolesc. Psychiatry* 28:701–706.

Larrson, B., and L. Melin. 1992. Prevalence and short-term stability of depressive symptoms in schoolchildren. *Acta Psychiatr. Scand.* 85:17–22.

Lewis, D. O., R. Lovely, C. Yeager, and D. Della Femina. 1989. Toward a theory of the genesis of violence: a follow-up study of delinquents. *J. Am. Acad. Child Adolesc. Psychiatry.* 28:431–436.

Mahler, M., R. Pine, and A. Bergman. 1975. *The psychological birth of the human infant.* New York: Basic Books.

Najman, J. M., B. C. Behrens, M. Andersen, W. Bor, M. O'Callaghan, and S. Williams. 1997. Impact of family type and family quality on child behavior problems: a longitudinal study. *J. Am. Acad. Child Adolesc. Psychiatry* 36(10):1357–65.

Nickman, S. L. 1985. Losses in adoption: the need for dialogue. *Psychoanal. Study Child* 40:365–398.

Nolen-Hoeksema, S. 1987. Sex differences in unipolar depression: evidence and theory. *Psychol. Bull.* 101:259–282.

Pfeffer, C. R., L. Normandin, and T. Kakuma. 1994. Suicidal children grow up: suicidal behavior and psychiatric disorders among relatives. *J. Am. Acad. Adolesc. Child Psychiatry* 33:1087–97.

Pfeffer, C. R., S. Zuckerman, R. Plutchik, and M. S. Mizruchi. 1984. Suicidal behavior in normal school children: a comparison with child psychiatric inpatients. *J. Am. Acad. Child. Adolesc. Psychiatry* 23:416–423.

Pollitt, E., and C. Thompson. 1977. Protein-calorie malnutrition and behavior: a view from psychology. In *Nutrition and the brain,* ed. R. J. Wurtman and J. J. Wurtman. Vol. 2. New York: Raven Press.

Puig-Antich, J. 1987. Affective disorders in children and adolescents: diagnostic validity and psychobiology. In *Psychopharmocology: the third generation of progress,* ed. H. Y. Meltzer. New York: Raven Press.

Puig-Antich, J., R. Dahl, N. Ryan, H. Novacenko, D. Goetz, R. Goetz, J. Twomey, and T. Klepper. 1989. Cortisol secretion in prepubertal children with major depressive disorder. *Arch. Gen. Psychiatry* 46:801–809.

Rapoport, J. L., and D. R. Ismond. 1984. *DSM-III training guide for diagnosis of childhood disorders.* New York: Brunner/Mazel.

Rapoport, J. L., M. S. Buchsbaum, T. P. Zahn, H. Weingartner, C. Ludlow, and E. J. Mikkelson. 1978. Dextroamphetamine: cognitive and behavioral aspects in normal prepubertal boys. *Science* 199:560–563.

Rathbun, J., and K. Peterson. 1987. Nutrition in failure to thrive. In *The theory and practice of nutrition in pediatrics,* ed. R. Grand, J. Sutphen, and W. Dietz. Stoneham, Mass.: Butterworth's.

Rauch, P. K., M. S. Jellinek, and D. B. Herzog. 1997. Psychiatric consultation in pediatrics. In *Massachusetts General Hospital handbook of general hospital psychiatry,* 4th ed., ed. N. H. Cassem; section eds. M. Jellinek, J. Rosenbaum, and T. Stern. St. Louis: Mosby Year Book.

Reich, W., L. Cottler, K. McCallum, D. Corwin, and M. VanEerdewegh. 1995. Computerized interviews as a method of assessing psychopathology in children. *Compr. Psychiatry* 36:40–45.

Rexford, E. N., L. W. Sander, and T. Shapiro, eds. 1976. *Infant psychiatry.* New Haven: Yale University Press.

Robins, L. N. 1978. Sturdy childhood predictors of adult antisocial behaviour: replications from longitudinal studies. *Psychol. Med.* 8:611–622.

Russell, D. 1983. The incidence and prevalence of intrafamilial and extrafamilial sexual abuse of female children. *Child Abuse Negl.* 7:133–146.

Rutter, M. 1971. Parent-child separation: psychological effects on the children. *J. Child Psychol. Psychiatry* 12:233–260.

Rutter, M., and L. Hersov, eds. 1985. *Child psychiatry: modern approaches.* 2nd ed. London: Blackwell Scientific Publications.

——— 1994. *Child and adolescent psychiatry: modern approaches.* 3rd ed. London: Blackwell Scientific Publications.

Ryan, N. D., J. Puig-Antich, P. Ambrosini, H. Rabinovich, D. Robinson, B. Nelson, S. Iyengar, and J. Twomey. 1987. The clinical picture of major depression in children and adolescents. *Arch. Gen. Psychiatry* 44:854–860.

Sandberg, S. T., M. Rutter, and E. Taylor. 1978. Hyperkinetic disorders in psychiatric clinic attenders. *Dev. Med. Child. Neurol.* 20:279–299.

Sandler, J., and W. G. Joffe. 1965. Notes on childhood depression. *Int. J. Psychoanal.* 46:88–96.

Schowalter, J. E. 1979. The chronically ill child. In *Basic handbook of child psychiatry,* ed. J. D. Call, J. D. Noshpitz, R. L. Cohen, and I. N. Berlin. Vol. 1. New York: Basic Books.

Seligman, M. E. P., and C. Peterson. 1986. A learned helplessness perspective on childhood depression: theory and research. In *Depression in young people,* ed. M. Rotter, C. E. Izard, and P. B. Read. New York: Guilford Press.

Shaffer D., M. S. Gould, P. Fisher, P. Trautman, D. Moreau, M. Kleinman, and M. Flory. 1996. Psychiatric diagnosis in child and adolescent suicide. *Arch. Gen. Psychiatry* 53:339–348.

Simmons, J. 1986. *Psychiatric examination of children.* 4th ed. Philadelphia: Lea & Febiger.

Spencer T., T. Wilens, and J. Biederman. 1995. Psychotropic medication for children and adolescents. *Child Adolesc. Psychiatr. Clin. N. Am.* 4:97–121.

Spitz, R. A. 1983. *Dialogues from infancy: selected papers,* ed. R. Emde. New York: International Universities Press.

Spock, B., and M. Rothenberg. 1985. *Baby and child care.* 40th ed. New York: Pocketbooks.

Stern, D. 1977. *The first relationship.* Cambridge, Mass.: Harvard University Press.

Sulik, L. R., and B. D. Garfinkel. 1992. Adolescent suicidal behavior: understanding the breadth of the problem. *Child Adolesc. Psychiatr. Clin. N. Am.* 1:197–228.

Thomas, A., S. Chess, and H. G. Birch. 1968. *Temperament and behavior disorders in children.* London: University of London Press.

Trunnell, T. L. 1968. The absent father's children's emotional disturbances. *Arch. Gen. Psychiatry* 19:180–188.

U.S. Department of Commerce. 1996. *The national data book: statistical abstract of the United States.* 116th edition. Washington, D.C.: Government Printing Office.

Velez, C. N., J. Johnson, and P. Cohen. 1989. A longitudinal analysis of selected risk factors for childhood psychopathology. *J. Am. Acad. Child Adolesc. Psychiatry* 28:861–864.

Volkmar, F. R., and D. S. Nelson. 1990. Seizure disorders in autism. *J. Am. Acad. Child Adolesc. Psychiatry* 29:127–129.

Volkmar, F. R., P. Szatmari, and S. S. Sparrow. 1993. Sex differences in pervasive developmental disorders. *J. Autism Dev. Disord.* 23:579–591.

Wallerstein J. S., and S. Blakeslee. 1989. *Second chances.* New York: Ticknor and Fields.

Wallerstein, J. S., and J. B. Kelly. 1981. *Surviving the breakup: how children and parents cope with divorce.* New York: Basic Books.

Westman, J. C., D. W. Cline, W. J. Swift, and D. A. Kramer. 1970. Role of child psychiatry in divorce. *Arch. Gen. Psychiatry* 23:416–420.

Winnicott, D. W. 1965. *The maturational processes and the facilitating environment.* New York: International Universities Press.

——— 1975. *Through pediatrics to psychoanalysis.* New York: Basic Books.

Wong, V. 1993. Epilepsy in children with autistic spectrum disorder. *J. Child Neurol.* 8:316–322.

Recommended Reading

Green, M., ed. 1994. *Bright futures: guidelines for health supervision of infants, children, and adolescents.* Arlington, Va.: National Center for Education in Maternal and Child Health.

Lewis, M., ed. 1996. *Child and adolescent psychiatry: a comprehensive textbook.* Baltimore: Williams & Wilkins.

Winnicott, D. W. 1965. *The maturational processes and the facilitating environment.* New York: International Universities Press.

——— 1975. *Through pediatrics to psychoanalysis.* New York: Basic Books.

Wong, V. 1993. Epilepsy in children with autistic spectrum disorder. *J. Child Neurol.* 8: 316–322.

28

ARMAND M. NICHOLI, JR.

The Adolescent

Adolescence is the most confusing, challenging, frustrating, and fascinating phase of human development. This description holds true, unfortunately, not only for adolescents themselves and for their immediate families but also for clinicians attempting to understand their complexity and to diagnose and treat their disorders.

Adolescence plays a profoundly significant role in the life of the individual and in society as a whole. For the individual, the normal maturational processes occurring during adolescence involve the organization, synthesis, and crystallization of personality traits and qualities that ultimately constitute adult character structure. Furthermore, because of changing biological and sociological factors, adolescence now constitutes an increasingly large percentage of the average life cycle. If, as some authorities believe, adolescence begins with the onset of puberty and ends with the attainment of emotional and economic independence, then an individual may spend 10 to 15 years in this phase of development. For society as a whole, adolescents exert a strong influence in establishing the tone of our particular culture. Currently, adolescent dress, hairstyle, language, and music have a marked impact on the adult world.

If the adolescent influences the cultural tone of society, changes in society also significantly influence the adolescent's psychological development. During the sometimes smooth and sometimes turbulent passage from childhood to adulthood, the adolescent must accomplish a number of complex developmental tasks. These tasks include separation from parents and the establishment of a self separate from family (Larson, 1996; Katz, 1997; Flaherty, 1997); identity formation (Erikson, 1968; Rutler, 1980; Barber and Eccles, 1992); development of a capacity for intimacy (Erikson, 1968; Levy-Warren, 1996; Brown, 1997); formation of a stable and irreversible sexual identity (Erikson, 1968; Brooks-Gunn, 1997); the stabilization of character structure (Bryt, 1979); the development of a time perspective (Buhler, 1968); and the commitment to a set of life goals involving vocation and autonomy (Erikson, 1968; Medley, 1980; Katz, 1997). The primary task confronting every adolescent involves the integration of the many physical, emotional, and intellectual changes that occur during these years into a sufficiently clear and comfortable inner definition that facilitates the completion of the painful and lonely separation from parents. This process of separation "winds like a scarlet thread through the entire fabric of adolescence" (Blos, 1979) and results in a state similar to grief or mourning.

Recent changes in our society impede this process of separation, increase the ambivalence of children toward parents, and make completion of the grief work extremely difficult. Changes in child-rearing practices in the United States, for example, have shifted child care from parents to outside agencies. Cross-cultural studies indicate that American parents spend less time with their children than parents in any other nation in the world except England (Bronfenbrenner, 1970; Bronfenbrenner et al., 1996; Nicholi, 1980). Recent research demonstrates clearly that the emotional and physical inaccessibility of parents to their children in early life subjects those children not only to high risk for emotional and physical disorders in adolescence and adulthood but also to a considerably shortened life span (Schwartz et al., 1995; Hojat, 1996; Tucker et al., 1997; Russek and Schwartz, 1997).

The accelerating divorce rate in the United States results in over half the children under the age of 18 living in a home with one or both parents missing (Bureau of the Census, 1980, 1996). One of every 2 American children will live with a single parent, and 1 of 3 is born to an unmarried parent (Children's Defense Fund, 1997). The number of divorces in the United States in 1990 was 1.182 million, one of the highest numbers ever recorded (National Center for Health Statistics, 1996). An absent parent, studies show, is experienced by the child as rejection, and rejection inevitably breeds intense ambivalence, resentment, and anger. Sigmund Freud (1917) described how unresolved conflict owing to intense ambivalence toward a person makes difficult the separation from and loss of that person and may result in anger, depression, and suicide. This anger may be directed outward in the form of antisocial behavior and violent crime, or inward in the form of self-destructive behavior involving psychoactive drug use or suicide. A vast body of research, beginning with Dorothy Burlingham and Anna Freud's (1942) work in London, has demonstrated that the absence of a parent through death, divorce, or a time-demanding job contributes to the many forms of emotional disorder, especially the anger, rebelliousness, low self-esteem, depression, and antisocial behavior that characterize those adolescents who take drugs, become pregnant out of wedlock, or commit suicide (Wallerstein, 1980, 1991, 1997; Jellinek and Slovik, 1981; Goldney, 1982; Davis, 1983; Nicholi, 1983a, 1985b; Bronfenbrenner et al., 1996; Aseltine, 1996; Palosarri et al., 1996; Kessler, Davis, and Kendler, 1997). The explosive increase in this behavior among adolescents during the latter part of the twentieth century and the changes in society contributing to it will be discussed later in more detail.

This chapter considers (1) the definition of adolescence; (2) the current state of our knowledge about adolescence; (3) normal adolescence: early, middle, and late phases; (4) adolescent behavior patterns involving drugs, sexuality, and suicide; (5) the pathology of adolescence; and (6) basic principles of treatment of adolescents.

Definition

The 1988 edition of the American Psychiatric Association's *Psychiatric Glossary* defines adolescence as "a chronological period beginning with the physical and emotional processes leading to sexual and psychosocial maturity and ending at an ill-defined time when the individual achieves independence and social productivity. The period is associated with rapid physical, psychological and social changes" (p. 3). If the enormously complex experience we call adolescence can be defined at all, this definition is perhaps as satisfactory as any. It encompasses all those definitions that focus entirely on the biological aspects—"the period of life beginning with the appearance of secondary sex characteristics and terminating with the cessation of somatic growth," for example, from *Dorland's Medical Dictionary* (1994)—as well as those that focus solely on the psychological aspects, such as "the psychological state in personality and character development that follows the latency phase of childhood" (Josselyn, 1974, p. 382).

The modern concept of adolescence does not appear in the literature on child rearing until the late nineteenth century (Demos and Demos, 1969). Not until the early twentieth century did G. Stanley Hall (1904) first introduce the term and thereby formally recognize adolescence as a separate stage of human development. One year later, Freud published *Three Essays on the Theory of Sexuality* (1905). In this work he mentions "the transformations of puberty" and explains a number of features of the adolescent process. By introducing his then shocking notion that children have sexual feelings, he altered our understanding of adolescence. Before this work, authorities considered puberty and adolescence the beginning of an individual's sex life. From that time on, they considered adolescence not the beginning of sexuality but merely the bridge from a sexuality that begins at birth to that found in the adult. Some historians have more recently pointed to political and economic forces that help define adolescence for a particular era (Modell, 1990).

Current Knowledge

Although the duration and influence of adolescence appear to be increasing steadily, our knowledge of this stage of development remains sketchy and rudimentary. Making up perhaps 15–20% of the average life span, adolescence characteristically receives less than 1% of the space in most modern textbooks on psychiatry. The *Diagnostic and Statistical Manual of Mental Disorders,* fourth edition, of the American Psychiatric Association (DSM-IV) devotes no space exclusively to this topic.

In addition to being sketchy, our knowledge of adolescence remains confusing and controversial. There appear to be as many definitions of adolescence as authors writing about it. Even the boundaries of adolescence—that is, when it begins and when it ends—remain unclear. Some say adolescence begins with puberty, the onset of menarche in the girl and the equivalent changes in the boy (Anthony, 1974). Others say it begins as early as 2 or more years before the onset of puberty and includes all the physical and hormonal changes that immediately precede puberty (Josselyn, 1974). The upper boundary of adolescence remains even more vague. Clinicians and investigators define the end of adolescence in ambiguous and confusing ways, not in biological terms, as with its beginning, but in psychological and social terms. Adolescence ends when the individual "consolidates his identity as an adult," "achieves independence," "adopts an adult social role," "attains autonomy," "finds a nonincestuous love object," "marries and assumes a full-time work responsibility," "achieves an adult-adult relationship with the family," and so forth (Arnett, 1994). If we look carefully at these criteria, we see that adolescence can end at 18 years of age or continue throughout life.

Our picture of the exact nature of adolescence, of what is normal and what is abnormal, is also unclear. Some clinicians and investigators view the whole of adolescence as a period of acute and sustained upheaval. They believe such turbulence is not just healthy but necessary and inevitable; conversely, they believe the absence of intense turmoil to be unhealthy. This view, first expounded by Hall (1904) more than a half-century ago, and embraced since then by most psychoanalytic observers, has been perhaps most forcefully stated by Anna Freud. Describing the adolescent, she mentions "his anxieties, the height of elation and depth of despair, the quickly rising enthusiasms, the utter hopelessness, the burning—or at other times sterile—intellectual and philosophical preoccupations, the yearning for freedom, the sense of loneliness, the feeling of oppression by the parents, the impotent rages or active hates directed against the adult world, the erotic crushes—whether homosexually or heterosexually directed—the suicidal fantasies, etc." (1958, p. 260). She then asserts that these "upheavals" reflect normal maturational processes, necessary for the integration of "adult sexuality into . . . the individual's personality" (p. 264). The constant upheavals of adolescence "are no more than the external indications that such internal adjustments are in progress" (p. 264). Furthermore, she asserts that the absence of outer evidence of inner unrest in the form of intense moodiness and rebelliousness "signifies a delay of normal development and is, as such, a sign to be taken seriously" (pp. 264–265). She suspects the untroubled, considerate, and cooperative adolescent of having built up excessive defenses against his drive activities, of having been crippled by this process, and, perhaps more than any other, of being in need of therapeutic help. This view of the intrinsic nature of adolescence, which implies that the "craziness" of adolescence is normal and its absence abnormal, has influenced our understanding of and therapeutic approach to this age group for decades.

Recent research has questioned the validity of this view. During the past several decades, large-scale longitudinal studies of adolescence have raised serious questions about the inevitability of intense upheaval in the adolescent (Weiner, 1970). In reviewing the research accumulated on adolescents during the preceding 20 years, Offer (1992) found the incidence of turmoil and severe crisis to be unusually low. He observed the overwhelming majority of these adolescents (80%) to be relatively free of the dramatic conflicts described in the psychoanalytic literature as part of the normal adolescent process. Offer's own research on large samples of adolescents in public high

schools found relationships with parents to be "stable, consistent, and empathic" (Offer, 1969, p. 223). These adolescents came, by and large, from traditional families and stable communities. Using the guidelines and resources of their parents to help them adapt to internal and external pressures, they tended to be less dependent on peers for guidance and approval. And although they manifested mild forms of rebelliousness, primarily between the ages of 12 and 14, these episodes could in no way be interpreted as serious disturbances. These and other large survey studies of normal adolescents have led clinicians and researchers to realize that the traditional view of adolescence as a highly disturbed state is at best a vast overstatement, at worst a gross distortion. Perhaps this traditional view reflects the danger of making wide generalizations from a relatively few case histories of disturbed individuals.

If our view of the normal process of adolescence has been unclear, so have our views of pathology and treatment. Modern dynamic psychiatry has yet to establish a useful theoretical formulation of adolescence and an effective therapeutic approach. Attempts to fit adolescence into classical psychoanalytic theory—to see it as a recapitulation of infancy (Jones, 1922) or a reactivation of the Oedipus complex (Spiegel, 1951)—have proved disappointing. Anna Freud (1958), after reviewing the many theoretical contributions to the literature of adolescence, states that our knowledge remains unsatisfactory and our analytical approach to treatment disappointing. Erik Erikson's concepts of identity crises, identity diffusion, and psychosocial moratorium (1968), however, have been an exception and have proved helpful clinically, especially in understanding and working with late adolescents.

Clinicians have found it difficult to agree on when an adolescent needs treatment. If one considers normal adolescence to be a period of continual upheaval, then one will have difficulty distinguishing transient episodes that merely reflect the normal processes of maturation from states of deep-seated and persistent psychopathology. "The adolescent manifestations come close to symptom formation of the neurotic, psychotic, or social disorder," writes Anna Freud, "and merge almost imperceptibly into . . . almost all the mental illnesses. Consequently, the differential diagnosis between the adolescent upsets and true pathology becomes a difficult task" (1958, p. 267). Some theorists have felt that the normal upheavals of adolescence were so similar to any number of severe illnesses that they could be diagnosed only in retrospect. If the disturbance resolved itself in time, one could consider it a normal manifestation of adolescence. This view has led some clinicians to a rather casual approach to the treatment of the disturbed adolescent and has often led to less than happy relationships between psychiatry and the adolescent's family.

Normal Adolescence

To understand pathology, one must have a clear concept of normality. Because of the long-standing difficulty in distinguishing the normal from the pathological manifestations of adolescence, this section focuses considerable attention on the various phases of normal adolescence. Emphasis is placed on internal and external stresses that may contribute to adolescent disorder and on aspects of behavior that may reflect adolescent psychopathology.

Early Adolescence

Because the emotional development of the early adolescent involves coming to terms with the virtual explosion of biological changes occurring in his body, these changes merit consideration in some detail. Striking changes of face, limbs, and trunk; the increase of gonadal hormones; and the appearance of primary and secondary sex characteristics evoke a degree of bewilderment in the child.

These physical changes begin to make their appearance as early as 2 years before the onset of puberty (the term is derived from the Latin *puber,* meaning "adult"). This period immediately before puberty is considered here as part of early adolescence, although many authorities refer to it as "preadolescence" or "pubescence."

In the girl, preparatory changes begin at 10 or 11 years of age, sometimes as early as 8 or 9. Estrogen levels increase, and specific feminine characteristics begin to appear. The breasts begin to develop, and the areolae and nipples increase in size and pigmentation. Breast development may be the first sign of impending puberty, and the breasts may reach full size before menarche. The pelvis widens, and layers of subcutaneous fat alter the contours of the body (Rosenbaum, 1993). First pubic and then axillary hair appears. In the boy, the initial physical changes appear about 1 year after the cells of the testes begin to secrete testosterone. The shoulders broaden, the genitals enlarge slightly, and the voice begins to deepen as the larynx increases in size (Wolstenholme and O'Connor, 1967). The boy usually remains leaner and more angular than the girl. Pubic, axillary, facial, and chest hair gradually appear in that order.

In both sexes a growth spurt occurs just prior to puberty. The limbs and neck grow more rapidly than the head and trunk and produce the long-legged, awkward look of a young colt so typical of this age. In addition, the pores of the skin increase in size, the sebaceous glands become more active, and acne makes its first unwelcome appearance. One side of the body may change more rapidly and more fully than the other (Stone and Church, 1968), adding to the child's bewilderment.

The beginning of the menstrual flow (menarche) and the occurrence of seminal emissions mark the actual onset of puberty in girls and boys, respectively. For reasons not yet fully ascertained, the onset of puberty has been occurring at an increasingly early average age. For the past hundred years, the average age of menarche, for example, has been dropping by about 4 months every 10 years (Tanner, 1962). The average age for the onset of menses was 16.5 years in 1860; it is currently 12.5 years. The onset of puberty in boys generally occurs about 2 years later than in girls and manifests the same trend toward earlier onset (Blizzard et al., 1970). This change has been attributed to better nutrition, although other factors may also play a role. The trend toward earlier onset of puberty has psychological significance because it thrusts the extensive emotional adjustments of this phase of development on a child considerably younger than the adolescent of a century ago (Alsaker, 1996; Sussman, 1996).

The emotional adjustments demanded of the early adolescent have led researchers and clinicians to consider puberty a crisis period within the life cycle. Even when a young child has been sufficiently informed beforehand concerning the changes taking place in his body, these changes may still produce wonder about what is happening and apprehension about the possible outcome. The adolescent's body changes so rapidly that he feels strange and awkward in it, as though it belonged to someone else. Relatives who have not seen him for a while may comment on how much he has grown, intensifying his feelings of awkwardness and self-consciousness. Studies of this age group show that the majority are preoccupied and markedly dissatisfied with their bodies (Vincent, 1992; Paxton, 1991). The early adolescent may spend long hours looking into a mirror and wondering what he will look like in the future. In addition to physical changes, the early adolescent begins to acquire new capacities for thinking and reasoning that, in a sense, contribute to his stress. A part of the cognitive revolution that Jean Piaget (1958) describes in young adolescents, whom he calls preadolescents, is the ability to think beyond the present and to worry about the future. In the years preceding this phase, the child's thinking is more concrete and focuses primarily on the present and on external reality. As he approaches puberty, he develops the capacity to think more abstractly, to be more reflective and self-critical, to think not only of the present but of the past, and to think systematically. He may become more introspective and begin a rich fantasy life. He may become acutely aware of the passage of time and of his own mortality. Questions of meaning and destiny may cause him to think seriously about philosophical and religious issues (Nicholi, 1974b).

All in all, the physical changes of early adolescence evoke mixed feelings: the excitement of growing up is tempered by apprehension and occasional yearnings for the relative security of childhood. The young adolescent may display unusually mature thought and behavior one moment and regress to the behavior of a young child the next. Sometimes he may deal with his fears and other uncomfortable feelings by becoming defensive, irritable, and secretive. At this age he may confide only in a close chum, who often replaces the larger group he played with earlier.

Harry Stack Sullivan considers this "chumship" characteristic of the years immediately preceding puberty and necessary for developing the capacity for interpersonal intimacy. Earlier, the child's relationships were essentially exploitative, based solely on fulfilling his own needs. During early adolescence the nature of his relationships changes from what Sullivan calls cooperation, competition, and compromise to collaboration in reciprocally meeting others' needs. A special sensitivity toward the needs of others develops and provides the basis for the capacity to form real love relationships later on. Sullivan believes the experience of seeing oneself through the eyes of others helps correct false notions about oneself and not only facilitates emotional growth but actually prevents emotional illness. This period of "chumship," Sullivan wrote in 1953, is incredibly important in saving many handicapped people from serious mental disorder that might otherwise be inevitable. And E. J. Anthony emphasizes that every therapist working with this age group should keep in mind Sullivan's concept of "chumship" as the "essential therapeutic ingredient" (1974, p. 379).

The "gang" at this period usually consists of groups of two interacting with other groups of two. Sometimes the group may consist of three, with one of the three acting as the leader and model for the other two. Sullivan also considers this type of interaction vitally important to development, because it promotes for the first time what he calls "consensual validation of personal worth." The child often shares anxieties or other problems with the group and receives support from them. Sullivan believes this intimate communication between chums helps correct self-deception and leftover egocentricisms, especially those of the child who may have been on the fringes of larger

childhood social groups (1953). This pairing phenomenon has, in addition to its remedial and growth aspects, potential for trauma. The close, intimate relationship with a chum carries with it the possibility of rejection, ostracism, and consequent loneliness. The breakup of these early relationships can be exceedingly painful. Anthony states that "it is in this era that loneliness reaches its full significance and goes on relatively unchanged for the rest of life" (1974, p. 380). The defenses marshaled against loneliness at this age determine in some measure how the individual will conduct his relationships throughout his life.

The physical changes of early adolescence may begin at any point in a wide range of times, and their onset appears to relate to specific personality characteristics in the adolescent that may extend to adult life. M. C. Jones (1965) has studied the impact of early and late maturing in both boys and girls over a number of years. Her evidence indicates that early onset of pubertal changes results in distinct advantages for boys but distinct disadvantages for girls. At the peak of growth, the early-maturing girls are taller than both the other girls and the boys, and this difference apparently adds to their self-consciousness. Adolescent boys who mature early are found to be physically stronger and more athletic, whereas late maturers are less masculine and more childish. The late maturers were treated by both peers and adults as immature. When the researchers studied these same boys at 17 years of age, they found the early maturers to be more competent, less dependent, more popular, more responsible, and better athletes. Both peers and adults considered them more attractive. The late-maturing boys showed more personal and social difficulties, prolonged dependency, more rebelliousness, and deep feelings of rejection by their peers throughout adolescence. In contrast, the early-maturing girls were found to be submissive, listless, and lacking in poise. Such girls had little influence on the group and seldom attained a high degree of popularity, prestige, or leadership. More recent research indicates that they are also at greater risk for developing psychiatric disorder (Hayward, 1997). Late-maturing girls are relatively more confident, outgoing, and assured than the early-maturing girls.

One other possible relationship of biological change to personality concerns the relationship of hormones to mood. Some investigators believe that hostility, irritability, depression, and other signs of emotional lability may be more than a reaction to radical changes in physical appearance (Hamburg, 1974; Paikoff, 1990; Leffert, 1996). A significant increase in the level of gonadal hormones may be directly related to altered moods during early adolescence. The relationship of mood to changes in the level of such hormones has been well researched during other phases of life, especially during pregnancy and menopause (Lunde and Hamburg, 1972).

In addition to the extensive biological changes occurring in the early adolescent, certain environmental and social changes add external stress, especially the change from elementary to junior high school. During perhaps the most psychologically inauspicious age, the early adolescent has imposed on him the burden of adjusting to the strange environment of a new school—new and older peers, new teachers, new and imposing buildings, and a more demanding curriculum. At a time in life when he most needs the support of a stable and familiar environment, he is thrust into an unfamiliar one. (Unfortunately, many children are sent away to boarding school at this age, an event that some look back on as one of the most traumatic experiences of their lives.) The need for stable boundaries when both inner and outer worlds appear to be changing and unstable motivates the early adolescent to test his environment frequently, to probe its limits—not so much to defy them as to find out where they are and consequently to find out where he is, to help define himself. Poorly defined boundaries often increase his anxiety. For this reason a parent or teacher who allows the early adolescent (even one who may be constantly pushing for fewer restrictions) the same freedom and permissiveness afforded an older adolescent will often produce considerable anxiety, if not outright hostility, in the younger child. This reaction accounts in part for the seventh and eighth grades' reputation as the most difficult to teach and as those with the highest teacher turnover, as in the following case:

> The headmaster of a private girls' school called in a psychiatrist to help solve an unusual behavior problem between a particular seventh-grade teacher and her class of 12- to 13-year-old girls. With this teacher, the girls would yell, throw erasers and chalk, spill ink over the teacher's desk, and write obscene and insulting remarks about her. As the semester wore on, the class became more and more out of control, subsiding only when the teacher fled the classroom in tears. With another teacher they liked and respected, this same class would sit absolutely quiet and absorbed in their work. The psychiatrist's discussions with the teacher having difficulty and with several students revealed that early in the semester the students began to test the limits set by their teachers. This particular teacher, however, had taught college students and had

also had some difficulty accepting and exercising authority; she told the girls that she considered their behavior childish and "ignored it, hoping it would go away." Her failure to set firm limits and her inability to effect external control of their impulses intensified the anxiety the girls were experiencing as a result of their phase of development. They projected the intolerance and contempt they felt toward their own insecurity onto the teacher, whom they perceived, like themselves, as weak and insecure. Such feelings would ordinarily be reserved for a vulnerable peer. The girls said of the unfortunate teacher, "She was too soft. We never knew when to stop," and of the other teacher, whom they admired, "She liked us and joked with us, but she always made it clear how far to go. You always knew where you stood."

In summary, early adolescence is a period of rapid physical change that marks the end of childhood and the beginning of adulthood. The young adolescent experiences an intensification of impulses, develops a strong attitude of defensiveness, establishes a new intimacy with one or two peers of the same sex, and manifests a new and extended capacity for critical and abstract thought.

Middle Adolescence

Middle adolescence comprises approximately the years from 15 to 18, the period the average individual spends in high school. With the exception of a few large-scale studies of normal high school students, investigators have given this phase relatively little attention. Psychologically, a relative inner tranquillity prevails during these years.

In midadolescence the individual must come to terms with his new body image and with his sexual identity. The recognition and acceptance of what the boy perceives as features of masculinity and the girl as features of femininity contribute to a mature identity. If an individual does not adequately fulfill cultural stereotypes because of slow physical development or genetic and family variations, he may suffer negative feelings about his body. Since few individuals fit the stereotype completely, some degree of dissatisfaction with the body occurs frequently. Studies of high school students show that a large percentage expressed dissatisfaction with one physical trait or another—their weight, height, voice, or complexion—although dissatisfaction occurred less frequently than in junior high school students, that is, in early adolescence (Frazier and Lisonbee, 1950; Vincent, 1992).

The first serious effort to separate from parents usually occurs in mid-adolescence. This attempt may evoke feelings of loss and mourning and contribute to brief episodes of moodiness and irritability. Parents may also react to threatened separation in diverse and subtle ways that make separation more difficult. Feelings of loneliness and isolation may give rise to overindulgence in food or long periods of idleness alternating with self-denial and intense work. The influence of parents begins to wane at this age, and peer influence takes on increased significance. Studies have shown that the transition from parental influence to peer-group influence is occurring at an increasingly early age in the United States (Bronfenbrenner, 1970; Bronfenbrenner et al., 1996). Thus parents no longer serve as models and guides to behavior to the same extent they did a generation ago. Because the peer group is often in conflict with parental values, an adolescent today finds it difficult to ascertain what behavior is expected of him and thus suffers a kind of culture shock within his own culture.

The adolescent will attempt to cope with the confusion, loneliness, and isolation he feels by establishing relationships with adults and peers outside the family for support, guidance, and identification he previously received from his parents. Intense attachments or "crushes" may be formed with teachers, coaches, or older students, and not infrequently, in fantasy, with celebrities. The adolescent's tenuous identity often makes him feel uncomfortable, however, when a relationship with a firmly established identity becomes too close. Thus close adult relationships may change rapidly, not only because they arouse anxiety in the adolescent but also because they reactivate yearnings and unresolved conflicts with parents. The need to establish independence and a clear inner definition may cause the adolescent to devalue his parents in an effort to make separation from them easier. Relationships with parents and other adults may therefore alternate between great emotional warmth and cooperation and open defiance and rebelliousness.

Relationships with peers of the same sex take on special significance during these years, providing support needed for establishing independence from the family. Acceptance by the peer group is enormously important, and the individual will take great pains to conform to the musical taste, language, dress, and other customs of adolescent culture. This culture changes rapidly, and what is acceptable one year may be looked on with disdain the next. Long hours on the telephone with close friends or at the computer may consume a large segment of the day and help fill the void caused by loneliness and isolation. Activities with peers in athletic and other organizations also help overcome a sense of not belonging. Considerable sexual energy may be sublimated in athletic activities,

with an unusual willingness to engage in demanding training schedules. From this particular age group, therefore, may come world-class athletes, especially in sports such as gymnastics and swimming.

In mid-adolescence, emotional energy previously invested in the parents now finds a source outside the family. Although the adolescent yearns for close relationships, he may find them difficult to tolerate. Considerable time and energy may be spent daydreaming of someone who has been observed at a distance and idolized. The adolescent may reach out tentatively toward members of the opposite sex. When a friendship with such a person develops and dating begins, disillusionment often sets in quickly and another distant person is idolized. This pattern protects the adolescent from commitments he is unprepared for emotionally. The telephone, so popular with this age group, allows a degree of intimacy without concomitant physical closeness, which the adolescent may find threatening. The breakup of a relationship with a member of the opposite sex, tenuous though it may have been, may nevertheless prove exceedingly painful and cause a major emotional crisis.

Sexual impulses, intensified during puberty, remain intense during this phase of adolescence. Permissiveness, the lack of moral guidelines, the sexually stimulating aspects of the mass media, and other dimensions of today's society make control of these impulses particularly difficult for the modern adolescent. Recent research shows that television exerts a profound influence on the increasing sexual permissiveness of our culture, especially on adolescents (Brown, 1990). Here again the adolescent finds himself in conflict—a part of him desiring sexual intimacy and another part fearing it, feeling emotionally unready for it, and sometimes seeing such expression as contrary to parental values. How the adolescent handles these conflicting internal and external demands determines in large measure his future character structure. His ability to attain impulse control will determine the extent of this control as an adult (Blos, 1968; Brooks-Gunn, 1997). Character has been defined as "the habitual mode of bringing into harmony the tasks presented by internal demands and by the external world" (Fenichel, 1945, p. 467). A few years after the sexual revolution of the 1960s began, clinicians observed that most adolescents are unprepared psychologically for coitus (Group for the Advancement of Psychiatry, 1968) and that the new sexual freedom has a destructive effect on adolescents' ability to sublimate sexual impulses and establish a mature character structure (Deutsch, 1967; Nicholi, 1974b). Sublimation and control of impulses have become particularly difficult in a society that no longer considers the sublimation of sexual and aggressive impulses to be one of its civilizing tasks. An increasing number of young people seek psychiatric help because of inability to control impulses, in marked contrast to the inhibition of impulses that characterized clinical problems among the young in the past.

As the mid-adolescent enters late adolescence, he confronts the difficult task of leaving home, of choosing a college or finding a job, and of finding among the billions of people on earth someone with whom to share his life. He must make the difficult shift from responsibility to an outside parent to responsibility for himself—a change that makes failure harder to tolerate. Finally, he must cope with subtle maneuvers by his parents to keep him dependent and thus to avoid the pain of loss.

Late Adolescence

Late adolescence is an indefinite span of time beginning at approximately 18 years of age and extending well into the twenties. How far it extends varies with each individual and depends on how long he takes to accomplish the psychological tasks required to permit him to feel comfortable assuming an adult role in society. Some individuals struggle with these adolescent tasks throughout their lives.

Late adolescence begins for a large majority of individuals upon graduation from high school. Whether they obtain a job or go to college, they enter a phase dedicated primarily to the task of defining who they are and establishing some notion of what they want to become.

Erikson has focused considerable attention on late adolescence and has contributed concepts that have proved especially helpful in understanding its complexities. He considers the period of prolonged adolescence—the time most individuals in our society spend in college or job training—as a "psychosocial moratorium," a period of delay in human development. During this time, "through free role experimentation [the individual] may find a niche in some section of his society, a niche which is firmly defined and yet seems to be uniquely made for him" (1968, p. 156). Erikson sees this delay as necessary for the sexually mature adolescent to catch up with himself psychologically and socially—that is, to develop a "psychosocial capacity for intimacy" and a "psychosocial readiness for parenthood" (p. 156). Until he has some understanding of who he is, some concept of how others see him, the adolescent will not be ready to make the types of commitment to career and to a mate demanded by the adult world. "When maturing in his physical capacity for procreation," Erikson writes, "the human youth is as yet unable either to love in that binding manner which only

two persons with reasonably formed identities can offer each other, or to care consistently enough to sustain parenthood. The two sexes, of course, differ greatly in these respects and so do individuals" (p. 242). The singular task that the late adolescent must therefore complete before entering adulthood is to establish a unique identity of his own. Erikson's concepts of "ego identity," "identity crisis," and "identity confusion" shed light on the adolescent's struggle toward self-definition and maturity.

Erikson first used the term *identity crisis* to describe the condition he observed in veterans of the Second World War who experienced the loss of a "sense of personal sameness and historical continuity" (1968, p. 17). He called this a loss of "ego identity" because it involved impairment of functions attributed to the ego. He then observed the same state of confusion in severely disturbed young people, noting that at this age the condition was acute and usually transient in nature. He concluded eventually that an identity crisis occurred as a part of all normal adolescent development. The severity of the crisis determined whether it warranted psychiatric attention.

The clinical picture of severe, acute identity diffusion includes an inability to make decisions, a sense of isolation, a feeling of inner emptiness, an inability to establish satisfying relationships, a distorted concept of time, a sense of urgency, and a marked inability to work or concentrate. Sometimes the identity confusion finds expression in what Erikson calls a "negative identity." Here the adolescent takes on a role presented to him as most undesirable or dangerous. Sometimes the negative identity may be a reaction to excessive demands of overambitious parents. A parent with deep-seated conflicts may unconsciously foster a negative identity by continuously reminding the adolescent to avoid behavior he would not otherwise even consider or by subtly rewarding such behavior with increased attention. A mother with an unconscious need to behave promiscuously may subtly encourage her daughter in this direction by excessive warnings against it. Erikson describes a mother with an alcoholic brother who responded selectively to those traits in her son that seemed to point toward the son's following in his uncle's footsteps.

Adolescent Behavior Patterns

The concept of identity provides a framework for understanding many aspects of both normal and pathological adolescent behavior. When future historians study American culture, they may be most perplexed by the explosive increase in the use of psychoactive drugs, in unwanted pregnancy, and in suicide among adolescents during the last quarter-century. They may find it perplexing and paradoxical that, during an era of unprecedented leisure time and prosperity, millions of adolescents used psychoactive drugs to alter their feelings and to escape their environment (Nicholi, 1983a; Kandel et al., 1986, 1997); that each year during an era of unprecedented openness and frank discussion of sexuality, hundreds of thousands of unmarried teenagers became pregnant and experienced an abortion (Black and DeBlassie, 1985; Bronfenbrenner et al., 1996); and that during an era of unprecedented scientific discovery and opportunity, thousands of adolescents both attempted suicide and succeeded in killing themselves (Davis, 1983; Deykin, 1986; King, 1997). And historians may be even more perplexed by society's reaction to this behavior. For they will certainly observe that although our society—as mentioned earlier—has had access to a vast body of research clearly demonstrating that the absence of a parent contributes to those traits and emotional disorders that characterize adolescents who use psychoactive drugs, who become pregnant out of wedlock, and who commit suicide, child-rearing practices continued to shift child care from parents to outside agencies, and the high divorce rate continued to ensure that over half the children under the age of 18 (approximately 13 million) and more than a quarter of children under age 6 live in homes with one or both parents missing (Bureau of the Census, 1996; National Academy of Sciences, 1976; Nicholi, 1985b; Bronfenbrenner et al., 1996).

Drugs. The current widespread nontherapeutic use of psychoactive drugs began among a small group of college students in the early 1960s and spread with explosive force into an epidemic of extraordinary scope (Nicholi, 1983a; Harrison, Haaga, and Richards, 1993; National Institute on Drug Abuse, 1996). The use of most all illegal drugs by adolescents increased significantly between 1992 and 1996, representing a reversal of downward trends observed for several years. Among the graduating high school class of 1996, 50.8% of students had used an illegal drug, compared to 40.7% in the class of 1992 (National Institute on Drug Abuse, 1996). The drugs currently popular among adolescents include the inhalants, phencyclidine, LSD, MDMA, "Ecstasy," cocaine, and marihuana. (For more information on these drugs, see Chapter 18.)

Inhalants comprise a diverse group of chemicals producing psychoactive vapors that act as powerful central nervous system depressants. They produce an intoxication similar to alcohol but of shorter duration. The immediate and transient effects, which last from 5 to 45 minutes after cessation of sniffing, range from excitation,

loss of inhibition, and a sense of euphoria to symptoms of acute organic brain damage—dizziness, amnesia, inability to concentrate, confusion, and ataxia. Although the toxic effects of most inhalants are considered transient and minimal, several deaths resulting from the intentional inhalation of aerosol sprays have been reported (Nicholi, 1983b). This "sudden-sniffing death" syndrome appears to be related to the tendency of fluorocarbons to potentiate the effect of epinephrine on the heart, resulting in heart failure and death. Methods of inhalation vary with different ages, with the most common being to inhale fumes in a plastic bag. This method has resulted in a number of deaths from suffocation.

A national survey on drug abuse reported that during 1996 the lifetime prevalence of inhalant use (the proportion of people who had ever used inhalants) was 16.6% among high school seniors and 21.2% among eighth graders (National Institute on Drug Abuse, 1996).

Phencyclidine, which came to public attention during the late 1970s, is of major concern to public health officials because of its association with violent behavior and bizarre deaths. Inhaled or "snorted" intranasally, smoked, or ingested, phencyclidine may act as a depressant, a stimulant, or a hallucinogen, depending on such variables as route of administration and dosage. Low doses may produce paranoia and perceptual distortion, high doses catalepsy and convulsions. Some psychiatric emergency units in urban hospitals reported during the 1970s that in up to 70% of their admissions the urine has been positive for phencyclidine. In 1979 over 300 deaths apparently resulted from toxicity caused by the drug. Unlike the decline in the use of LSD and other hallucinogens during the 1970s, the use of phencyclidine increased. During the 1980s and 1990s, however, the reverse took place: use of LSD increased and PCP declined (National Institute on Drug Abuse, 1996).

Cocaine is a naturally occurring central nervous system stimulant extracted from the leaves of the coca plant and is second only to marihuana in its popularity among adolescents. The rate of increase during the 1970s in all age groups was actually higher than the rate for marihuana. During the 1990s use of cocaine among young adolescents (eighth graders) almost doubled, from 2.3% in 1991 to 4.5% in 1996. The proportion of high school seniors who had used cocaine at some time in their lives rose from 6.1% in 1992 to 7.1% in 1996 (National Institute on Drug Abuse, 1996).

Until recently, cocaine was available as a powder in the form of the hydrochloride (HCl) salt, prepared from the alkaloid present in coca leaves. "Snorted" intranasally, the drug caused vasoconstriction of the nasal mucous membrane and thus limited its own absorption. The cocaine powder, sometimes called "snow," was often diluted with talcum powder. The powdered form of cocaine, or cocaine HCl, could not be smoked because heat caused it to decompose.

However, a new form of cocaine has appeared called "crack." Crack is almost pure cocaine, made by preparing an aqueous solution of cocaine HCl and adding ammonia (with or without baking soda) to alkalize the solution and precipitate alkaloidal cocaine. The name "crack" derives from the popping sound made by heating the crystals of alkaloidal cocaine. The crystals vaporize at high temperatures, making crack suitable for smoking ("freebasing") in a "base pipe." Alternately the "rock" can be crushed, mixed with tobacco, and smoked in a cigarette. Smoking crack delivers large quantities of cocaine to the vascular bed of the lung, producing an effect comparable to intravenous injection, and has contributed to the rapid rise in addiction and death. The emergence of crack on the market greatly increased the use of cocaine among adolescents by making the drug available at a decreased price (Nicholi, 1984; Jekel et al., 1986; Bachman, 1996; Kandel and Davies, 1996). Crack cocaine among high school seniors increased from 2.2% in 1992 to 3.3% in 1996 (National Institute on Drug Abuse, 1996).

Marihuana is the most widely used illicit drug among adolescents and is discussed in detail in Chapter 18. The adverse effects of marihuana on physical health and on intellectual and psychomotor functioning have been widely reported but continue to remain little known among users and even among many in the medical profession (Nicholi, 1983a). Recent surveys indicate that among young adolescents (eighth graders) marihuana use increased from 10.2% in 1991 to 34.1% in 1995. Among older adolescents (high school seniors) use increased from 23.9% in 1991 to 35.8% in 1996 (National Institute on Drug Abuse, 1996).

A strong statistical association exists between the use of marihuana and the use of more serious drugs (Fishburne, Abelson, and Eisin, 1980; National Institute on Drug Abuse, 1996). A person who smokes marihuana is more likely than a nonuser to become involved in other illicit drugs. Among adolescents, marihuana is usually the third stage in a predictable sequence of drug use, regardless of the age of initiation. In the first stage beer and wine are used; in the second stage tobacco, cigarettes, or hard liquor; in the third stage marihuana; and in the fourth stage more serious drugs (Kandel and Faust, 1975; Kandel and Davies, 1996; Kandel et al., 1997).

Adolescents who use illicit drugs differ markedly from nonusers. Large-scale studies with a high degree of reliability have shown that important differences exist in attitudes and values, in personality traits, in home and school environment, in relationships with parents, and in overall behavior. Drug users in the 1980s and 1990s are shown to embrace a constellation of attitudes and values that reflect an openness to deviant behavior: they attempt to place a lower value on academic achievement and a higher value on independence than do nonusers, have less academic motivation, and are more involved in antisocial and delinquent behavior. As a group they possess personality traits indicative of maladjustment, including rebelliousness, depressed mood, and low self-esteem (Kaplan, 1980; Johnston, 1981; Nicholi, 1985a; Kandel and Davies, 1996).

What motivates such a vast segment of our adolescent society to inhale, ingest, or inject into their bodies this wide assortment of mind-altering substances? When asked this question, those who reported using marihuana daily said that they did so primarily to alter how they felt—to help cope with feelings of stress, anger, depression, frustration, or boredom (Johnston, 1981; Kandel et al., 1997).

In an attempt to explore the psychological reasons why young people, many of whom placed a high premium on intellectual functioning, took drugs that are potentially dangerous to the mind, a study (Nicholi, 1974a) investigated a sample of college students who had ingested LSD. This study attempted to ascertain who had influenced students in the initial ingestion of the drug and to determine the emotional factors that motivated its continued use. Findings include the following. The initial experience with LSD results from the influence of a peer who reports pleasurable reactions to the use of the drug. The influence of a roommate or friend carries considerably more weight than newspaper articles about the dangers of the drug or rumors about other students who have had unhappy experiences. A strong relationship exists between the specific emotional conflicts of these students and the claims made for the drug by its proponents. In the minds of the students, promises about what the drug can do for them far outweigh the risk. A few of the needs the students feel the drug can meet are helping them feel love for others and overcome a sense of loneliness, making them productive and creative, making them more socially and sexually effective, and filling a moral and spiritual void. However, "the failure of the drug [LSD] to meet these expectations plus its inconsistency in producing the desired mood alteration has led to a gradual decline in its use" (p. 225). As mentioned above, however, LSD use has subsequently been on the increase. In 1995, lifetime use of LSD among high school seniors was 11.7%, surpassing the peak years of the mid-1970s (National Institute on Drug Abuse, 1996).

In essence, people take drugs to alter or to escape from a less than tolerable reality and to meet intense emotional needs. We need to explore the origins and dynamics of the specific psychological needs and character traits of the drug-using population in reference to changing child-rearing practices in the United States and to changes in the family constellation (Nicholi, 1983a; Bronfenbrenner et al., 1996).

Sexuality. Throughout adolescence the individual struggles with an acute sense of not belonging. No longer a child and not yet an adult, he often feels that he is an outsider and that no one needs or wants him. The late adolescent who leaves the familiar surroundings of home for the strange environment of a college or a job often feels adrift and struggles with a profound sense of loneliness and longing. This feeling in turn intensifies his need or "hunger" for a close relationship, especially with someone of the opposite sex. This need motivates him to reach out for such a relationship—tentatively at first but, depending on the individual, with increasing persistence. The self-centeredness and the pervasive sense of inadequacy of early and middle adolescence gradually lessen and make more tolerable the risk of possible rejection inherent in reaching out for this closeness. In establishing these early relationships, the adolescent tends to idealize and overestimate new friends, to experience sudden intense episodes of "falling in love," to become suddenly disenchanted, and to change to new involvements. Although these heterosexual relationships of middle and late adolescence may be whimsical, capricious, and short-lived, they may nevertheless involve deep emotional involvement, and their termination may cause some of the most painful feelings an individual encounters.

For many adolescents today, the sexual freedom of our culture exacerbates a conflict-ridden issue. Because of the early onset of puberty, the adolescent is biologically ready for coitus at a considerably earlier age than his counterpart of a century ago. Yet his psychological and social readiness is considerably delayed. Many factors account for this delay, not the least being that the long years of education required to prepare for most careers today prolong emotional and financial dependence on the family and make early marriage difficult. In addition, the adolescent has been reared in a permissive society. In this society the mass media, for purposes of exploitation, tend to keep

sexual impulses at a high pitch and to encourage their free expression. Studies show that television exerts a profound influence on an adolescent's concept of acceptable sexual behavior (Brown, 1990).

The adolescent, especially the older adolescent, has an intense need not only for sexual expression but also for guidelines on how best to conduct this aspect of his social life. As part of his struggle for identity, he seeks a moral framework for his life and desires to know not only what behavior is expected of him but also what behavior is in his best interest. When he turns to the adult world, he often finds more confusion than enlightenment. Even when he turns to the medical profession, he may receive conflicting messages. The problem of sexual ethics within the profession itself is an issue of increasing concern (see Chapters 1 and 35), and the professional literature on adolescence often proves more confusing than helpful. This confusing literature began to be published in response to the new sexual freedom of the 1960s. For example, the Group for the Advancement of Psychiatry's *Normal Adolescence* (1968) raises the question of whether premarital intercourse fosters healthy psychological development in the adolescent. The authors speak of traditional sexual standards that discourage intercourse outside of marriage as "a set of taboos and prohibitions which historically may have been appropriate but today seem inappropriate in the light of medical scientific advance" (p. 85). Modern medicine, the authors imply, has made invalid the concerns upon which these standards were probably based—"concerns about venereal disease, illegitimate pregnancy and its destructive impact on the family" (p. 85). Even the more unsophisticated adolescents, however, realize that these concerns not only remain extremely relevant today but also present a greater problem to our society than at any time in the past. This kind of information has made many adolescents feel disillusioned and misled by proponents of the new sexual permissiveness and confused as to where to turn for reliable guidelines on how to conduct their lives.

H. Deutsch observed during the sexual revolution of the 1960s that young people caught up in this new freedom "suffer from emotional deprivation and a kind of deadening, as a result of their so-called free and unlimited sexual excitement," and that "the spasmodic search for methods by which to increase the pleasure of the sexual experience indicates unmistakably that the sexual freedom of our adolescents does not provide the ecstatic element that is inherent—or should be—in one of the most gratifying of human experiences" (1967, p. 102). She goes on to say, "The inadequacy . . . of the sexual experience as such is expressed not only in their needs for drugs but also in the increasing interest they show in sexual perversions" (p. 102). Deutsch refers to the new sexual freedom as creating "a psychological disaster" (p. 102) and interfering with "the development of real tender feelings of love and enchantment" (p. 103). She also refers to the "social and personal catastrophe of illegitimate motherhood" among young girls (p. 106) and expresses the fear that this phenomenon will increase. Her fears are confirmed by statistics that show over a million teenage pregnancies per year, with over a quarter of a million terminating in abortion. That 50% of teenage marriages end in divorce within 5 years makes these findings no less disturbing. The rate for births of unmarried versus married teenagers increased steadily over the past few decades and far surpasses the rate in England, France, Sweden, or the Netherlands. Studies indicate that changes in the American family, especially an absent parent, contribute significantly to this increase (Levy and Grinker, 1983; Plotnick, 1992; Cherlin, Kierman, and Chase-Lansdale, 1995). Deutsch points out that teenage pregnancies are "compulsive" and that sexual instruction and modern contraceptives will do little to prevent them.

Many who have worked closely with adolescents have realized that the new sexual freedom has by no means led to greater pleasures, freedom, and openness, more meaningful relationships between the sexes, or exhilarating relief from stifling inhibitions. Clinical experience has shown that the new permissiveness has often led to empty relationships, feelings of self-contempt and worthlessness, an epidemic of venereal disease, and a rapid increase in unwanted pregnancies. Clinicians working with college students began commenting on these effects in the early 1970s. They noted that students caught up in this new sexual freedom found it unsatisfying and meaningless. A study of normal college students (those not under the care of a psychiatrist) found that, although their sexual behavior by and large appeared to be a desperate attempt to overcome a profound sense of loneliness, they described their sexual relationships as less than satisfactory and as providing little of the emotional closeness they desired (Nicholi, 1974b). They described pervasive feelings of guilt and haunting concerns that they were using others and being used as "sexual objects." These students' experiences underscore Freud's observation that, when sexual freedom is unrestricted, "love [becomes] worthless and life empty" (1912, p. 188). The disillusionment of late adolescents with this sphere of their lives as well as with drugs has contributed to the recent religious preoccupation among youth, especially the trend toward traditional religious faith. Although the basic Judeo-Christian mo-

rality conflicts strongly with their past behavior and current mores, they find the clear-cut boundaries it imposes less confusing than no boundaries at all and more helpful in relating to members of the opposite sex as "persons rather than sexual objects" (Nicholi, 1974b).

Still another characteristic of sexuality in the latter part of the twentieth century that forces adolescents to consider seriously the "traditional" sexual morality is the epidemic of new and deadly sexually transmitted diseases. Highly resistant forms of gonorrhea and herpes make miserable the lives of those afflicted and puzzle the physicians trying to cure them. The rampant spread of the acquired immune deficiency syndrome (AIDS) has preoccupied the nation and produced panic and confusion among the young. Although authorities described the first case in 1981 and emphasized that the vast majority of the cases occurred among sexually active homosexual and bisexual men, cases increased most rapidly during the 1990s among those reporting heterosexual contact with an HIV-infected partner (Neal et al., 1997). Studies show that in 1995 women accounted for 19% of AIDS cases in adults and that the greatest increases in AIDS incidence rates were in women 14 to 18 years old (Wortley et al., 1997).

Here again the message of the adult world to the adolescent has resulted in distortion and confusion. During the 1980s and 1990s the media and other institutions encouraged adolescents of all ages to protect themselves against AIDS, to use condoms and thereby to practice "safe sex." Although we have no idea of the full range of meaning that individual adolescents will infer from this information, many know that a high percentage of condoms currently used in the United States have a 50% rate of failure (Koop, 1987). Furthermore, the many programs evolved over the past several years to educate youth in the means of protection fail to influence large numbers. Recent surveys indicate that about one-half of sexually active adolescents and young adults aged 12 to 21 years do not use condoms, thereby increasing their risk of contracting sexually transmitted diseases (National Center for Health Statistics, 1996). Efforts to evaluate school HIV prevention programs have been sponsored by the government (Collins, 1996).

Suicide. Between 1960 and 1980 the suicide rate among adolescents in the United States increased 150% (Deykin, 1986). In some U.S. cities the increase has been even more dramatic. In one city, for example, in the 4 years between 1976 and 1980, completed suicides among 10- to 14-year-olds increased 80% and in 15- to 19-year-olds 100% (Shafii et al., 1985). Authorities now refer to the explosive increase in adolescent suicide during the 1970s, 1980s, and 1990s as a "national tragedy" (Davis, 1983; Deykin, 1986; Culp, 1995). Suicide ranks as the third leading cause of death among adolescents in the United States (after accidents and homicides). A recent study of high school and middle school students reported that 33 of every 100 had thought of suicide and 6 of every 100 had attempted suicide (Culp, 1995).

Although thousands of adolescents take their lives each year, researchers emphasize that, because of stigma and guilt experienced by the family, a large percentage of suicides go unreported. Families often tend to report death by suicide as death by accident. Researchers also estimate that for every adolescent who succeeds in committing suicide, 50 to 100 times as many attempt.

The rapid increase in the rate of suicide over a relatively short period appears to be limited to children and adolescents; the rate of suicide among older age groups has actually decreased or remained stable. The rate of increase has also remained relatively stable in adolescent women, the increase occurring primarily in white adolescent men. During the mid-1950s to the mid-1990s, suicides more than tripled among men aged 15 to 24 years (Center for Disease Control and Prevention, 1995).

What causes boys to commit suicide more than girls? Research again points to early childhood experiences and changes in the home. Most single-parent homes have absent fathers, and studies show that sons of absent fathers develop difficulty in controlling impulses. Male suicidal behavior usually involves an inability to control angry impulses (Trunnel, 1968; Tennant et al., 1981). Other studies show that both among nursery school children and among adolescents, sons suffer more adverse effects than daughters when both parents work (McCord, McCord, and Thurber, 1963; Propper, 1972; Gold and Andres, 1978). Although adolescent men outnumber women in completed suicides by about 4 or 5 to 1, adolescent women outnumber men by about the same margin in number of attempts (Frederick, 1985).

What causes this incredible number of children and adolescents to kill themselves? Though all human behavior is complex and multidetermined, an overview of recent research in the field points—with unmistakable clarity—to the changes in child-rearing practices and in the stability of the home as a significant factor in the rapidly rising rate of suicide. First, the increase in suicide closely parallels the increase in the divorce rate over the same period. Second, the dramatic increase in the suicide rate among prepubescent children indicates that many determinants of teenage suicide occur before adolescence. In addition, cohort analysis shows that each 5-year cohort

entering adolescence has a higher rate of suicide than the preceding 5-year cohort, further suggesting that early childhood experiences play an important role in the increase in suicide (Murphy and Wetzel, 1980; Deykin, 1986). These data have prompted researchers to scrutinize the recent changes in child-rearing practices in the United States and in the homes of young children (Wagner, 1997; King, 1997).

Divorce and out-of-wedlock pregnancies contribute to over half the children in the United States growing up in homes with one or both parents missing. Recent research demonstrates that among children and adolescents who commit suicide, a statistically significant number come from fragmented homes with missing parents. The fragmented home often consists of a missing father and a working mother with young children. Cantor (1972) found that 50% of adolescents who attempted suicide came from broken homes with the father absent; Tishler, McKenry, and Morgan (1981) found that in a sample of 108 adolescents who attempted suicide, 49% came from homes with one parent missing; other studies have found that the early loss or absence of a father played a significant role in adolescents who killed themselves (Petzel and Riddle, 1981; Peck, 1982); still other studies have found a statistically significant incidence of separation and divorce among parents of adolescents who attempt suicide as compared with control groups (Marks and Heller, 1977; Goldney, 1982; Adams, Bouchoms, and Steiner, 1982; Deykin, 1986; Botsis et al., 1995).

Since the 1960s a vast body of research has stressed the importance to the developing child of the physical presence and emotional accessibility of both parents. This research has demonstrated clearly that the absence of a parent through death, divorce, illness, or a time-demanding job contributes to many forms of emotional disorder, especially the anger, the low self-esteem, and the depression that accompany adolescent suicide. The landmark report on families by the National Academy of Sciences (1976) predicted present-day family life when it stated "in addition to needing food, shelter and basic health care, every child under six requires the constant care of an adult . . . For millions of America's children, such care becomes problematic because . . . both parents work." An overwhelming body of research indicates that any understanding of the epidemic of adolescent suicide must consider the role of physically and emotionally absent parents in the homes of American children and adolescents.

Cars and motorcycles. No discussion of adolescence would be complete without mention of the significant role the motor vehicle often plays in the modern adolescent lifestyle. Erikson notes that "the most widespread expression of the discontented search of youth as well as of its native exuberance is the craving for locomotion." He writes that "the motor engine, of course, is the very heart and symbol of our technology, and its mastery the aim and aspiration of much of modern youth. In connection with immature youth, however, it must be understood that [the] motor car . . . offers to those so inclined passive locomotion with an intoxicating delusion of being intensely active . . . While vastly inflating a sense of motor omnipotence, the need for active locomotion often remains unfulfilled" (1968, pp. 243–244).

For the adolescent seeking a clear inner definition, the car or the motorcycle may assume intense symbolic meaning with many levels of emotional appeal. The adolescent's preoccupation with a car's external appearance—the constant taking apart and rebuilding, painting, and modifying its appearance and sound—often reflects the bodily dissatisfaction so characteristic of this age group.

The motor vehicle may be used to satisfy inner needs and to work out inner conflicts. Through the motor vehicle, the adolescent may express anger, defiance, power, mobility, and independence from the adult world. The automobile often provides not only an image of great speed and power but also the appearance of a self-contained, enclosed world allowing for the expression of feelings he would otherwise be unable to express. The automobile also provides privacy for dating and intimacy.

The motor vehicle, like drugs and sexual behavior, may be a means of expressing severe inner conflict. This fact may explain in part why motor vehicle accidents are the leading cause of death in late adolescence. Arnett (1994) discusses the developmental issues involved in reckless automobile driving. Although a vast number of studies have focused on the emotional and psychological causes of automobile accidents in the general population, few have focused solely on the adolescent, even though adolescent deaths constitute a large percentage of motor vehicle fatalities. One study on the motorcycle illustrates how adolescent pathology expresses itself via a motor vehicle and contributes to injury and death (Nicholi, 1970).

The motorcycle is a particularly good vehicle for understanding this phenomenon; although the number of adolescents who drive motorcycles is only one-tenth the number who drive automobiles, the motorcycle accounts for twice as many injuries as automobiles. It is 16 times more dangerous than the automobile and causes 5 times as many deaths per mile (Cracchiolo, Blazina, and MacKinnon; 1968; Rutter, 1996).

Nicholi (1970) presents findings of an in-depth study of a group of patients manifesting unusual emotional investment in the motorcycle, all of whom were accident prone and had experienced one or more serious motorcycle accidents. The motorcycle intruded into their daily activities, their repetitive dreams, and their conscious and unconscious fantasies. Among these patients, the striking similarity of the symbolic meaning of the motorcycle, the tendency to use the vehicle as both an adaptive and a defensive means of dealing with emotional conflict, and the remarkable number of other shared characteristics led to the designation of the clinical disorder from which they suffered as "the motorcycle syndrome." The essential features of this syndrome are the following: (1) an unusual preoccupation with the motorcycle; (2) a history of accident proneness extending to early childhood; (3) persistent fear of bodily injury; (4) a distant conflict-ridden relationship with the father and a strong identification with the mother; (5) extreme passivity and an inability to compete; (6) a defective self-image; (7) poor impulse control; (8) fear of and counterphobic involvement with aggressive girls; and (9) impotence and intense homosexual concerns.

These patients experienced a serious ego defect stemming from a distant and difficult father-son relationship. A tenuous masculine identification led them to perceive the motorcycle as an essential part of their body image. The motorcycle served to strengthen a fragile ego. The conscious attraction to and fear of the motorcycle was found to parallel unconscious conflicts relating to an ambivalence toward expression of what the patient considered the masculine part of himself. The relationship of the vehicle to these unconscious conflicts compounded the adolescent's anxiety, increased his tension, lessened his control, and made him more susceptible to accidents. In these adolescents, the motorcycle served as an extension of what the patient considered his masculine self—the assertive, active, aggressive, competitive parts of his psychological make-up. Each of the patients showed a lifelong avoidance of and tenuous identification with a highly competent and critical father that left the adolescent inhibited and unable to exercise the assertive components of his emotional make-up effectively. When the adolescent felt weak, the motorcycle gave him strength; when passive, a "sense of doing something and getting somewhere" (p. 594); when effeminate, a feeling of virility; when impotent, a sense of potency and power; when withdrawn, a sense of assertion and thrusting forward. These positive feelings, however, were never free from the haunting awareness of danger.

The motorcycle was found to serve both a helpful and a harmful function—that is, it was used both adaptively and defensively. Helpful or adaptive functions involve attracting attention, giving a feeling of strength, and improving, if only transiently, the patient's inner definition. The cycle helped him express the more assertive, more active part of himself—the part that, having been inhibited and paralyzed, could not otherwise find expression.

The maladaptive use of the cycle involves replacing relatively unconstructive activity with constructive use of time. Charging through the streets on a motorcycle gives the adolescent a sense of moving ahead, of doing, and of exerting himself; but it is finally a false sense and a poor substitute for concentrated effort. Racing a motorcycle into the middle of the night relieves the anxiety of rejection or failure, but it effects little change in the conditions causing the anxiety. A fast, noisy, breathtaking ride tends to relieve apprehension over exams, but it helps little in preparing for them. The cycle simulates sexual feeling and even helps the adolescent approach a girl, but it contributes little to forming a meaningful relationship with her. The cycle helps to express anger, but the destructive tendencies of these adolescents make a machine that can travel 125 miles an hour a less than adaptive means of doing so.

In addition to these maladaptive aspects, the patients' conscious fears of the motorcycle—often based on a realistic awareness of its dangers—reactivated unconscious fears, intensified anxiety, and lessened their control of the vehicle. The psychological factors made the motorcycle especially dangerous to these young people and contributed to the high rate of serious accidents among them.

The Pathology of Adolescence

Confusion surrounding the pathology of adolescence has led to frequent diagnostic errors in the past and, overall, to a less than completely successful therapeutic experience with this age group. Many factors have contributed to this confusion. First, some forms of adolescent turmoil do indeed mimic severe pathology, though not as frequently as was once believed. This similarity has sometimes led the clinician to diagnose a serious disorder one day only to be confronted with a completely recovered patient the next, or to dismiss as transient turmoil what later proves to be a persistent, serious disorder. Second, adolescence does not fit the classical psychodynamic theoretical concepts, which have therefore contributed relatively little to our understanding of either its normal state or its pathology. After trying unsuccessfully to fit the data into a preexisting theoretical framework, investigators attempted to modify the theory to fit the data. Some of these efforts—Erikson's concepts, for instance—have

proved helpful. Third, treatment of the adolescent has often been programmed for failure before it begins. The adolescent, frequently referred for treatment against his will by the parent with whom he is most in conflict, tends to see the therapist as an ally of the parent and as part of the adult world he is rebelling against. Struggling for autonomy, he finds enforced treatment a threat and often reacts to the treatment situation and the therapist with resistance if not open hostility. Partly out of confusion and misconception and partly out of frustration, some theoreticians have tended to view psychiatric symptoms in adolescence as part of the normal maturational process, and some have even suggested that the adolescent not be treated at all.

Research—spurred in part by the widespread unrest and drug use of the 1960s—has gradually changed these concepts of pathology. Large-scale studies of both normal and emotionally disturbed adolescents have called into serious question the traditional concept that intense upheaval mimicking all degrees of psychopathology is universally experienced in adolescence. On the contrary, as mentioned earlier, studies reveal that the vast majority of adolescents experience relatively little turmoil, and few manifest psychiatric symptoms (Offer, 1992). Although some rebelliousness, especially in early adolescent boys, and episodes of moodiness and irritability occur frequently, these episodes are short-lived and in no way approach sufficient intensity to be considered pathological.

Recent studies have made untenable the conviction long embraced by psychiatrists "that the upholding of a steady equilibrium during the adolescent process is in itself abnormal" (Freud, 1958, p. 267) or that adolescence involves by definition structural upheavals that may resemble any of the serious adult disorders. These studies have also led clinicians to pay closer attention to psychiatric symptoms when they do occur in the adolescent. Psychiatrists no longer quickly dismiss symptoms as transient manifestations of the normal adolescent process without first assessing them carefully. J. F. Masterson's studies (1967) have shown that severe psychiatric disorder in adolescence usually does not disappear with time. If left untreated or incompletely treated, most of these disorders tend to persist and become psychiatric disorders of adulthood.

Epidemiology

Although clinicians have expressed the need for epidemiologic studies of adolescence (Henderson, Krupinski, and Stoller, 1971; Patton, 1996), no comprehensive study covering all of adolescence has yet been conducted. One epidemiologic investigation of college students found that 10% of the undergraduate population suffered emotional conflicts sufficiently severe to prompt them to consult a psychiatrist during their undergraduate experience. Among 551 students who left college for psychiatric reasons, this study reports the following diagnostic categories: 35.7% (196 students) with a diagnosis of neurotic disorder; 23.6% (130 students) with a diagnosis of transient situational disorder; 22.1% (122 students) with a diagnosis of character disorder; 7.1% (39 students) with psychotic disorders; and 11.6% (64 students) with miscellaneous other diagnoses. By far the most prevalent of disorders among these students were adjustment reactions of adolescence (23.6%) and depression (22.1%). A little over 5% of these students suffered from various forms of schizophrenia (Nicholi 1967). On the basis of this sample—one that may to some degree represent all phases of adolescence—the pathology afflicting the adolescent runs nearly the entire gamut experienced by adults. The exception, of course, is that vaguely defined conglomeration of symptoms referred to as "adjustment disorder of adolescence."

Adjustment Disorder of Adolescence

Because the diagnostic category of adolescent adjustment disorder occurs most frequently and is the most difficult to diagnose with certainty, I will focus primarily on describing its features and discussing its differentiation from the other common disorders of this age group. For a further discussion of pathology, see other chapters in this book on the clinical syndromes.

The term *adjustment disorder* is listed in DSM-IV (1994) as the development of clinically significant emotional or behavioral symptoms in response to an identifiable psychosocial stressor that occurs within 3 months of the onset of the stressor. The reaction may cause impairment in academic or occupational functioning or in relationships with others. The symptoms must persist for at least 1 week but not for more than 6 months after the stressful condition has ceased. If the stressor is chronic, however, the symptoms may persist for longer than 6 months. The disorder may be associated with depression, with anxiety, or with a mixture of both. It may also be associated with disturbances of conduct such as truancy, vandalism, or reckless driving.

Clinical features. The outstanding clinical feature of this disturbance is a gradual or acute change in behavior indicating that the adolescent is having difficulty coping with internal or external stress. Its manifestations therefore vary with each phase of adolescence and with the stresses peculiar to that phase. In early adolescence, for example, the inability to cope may manifest itself in a marked increase in the open expression of aggression and defiance. Anger may lie close to the surface, and the slightest frustration or irritation may provoke an angry outburst or temper tantrum characteristic of a younger child. The intensity of such outbursts appears inappropriate to the precipitating circumstances. Defiance may be directed against all authority—parents, older siblings, teachers, coaches, or police—or it may be expressed in delinquent behavior within groups, where the risk of an untoward reaction from parents or other authority is lessened. The stresses characteristic of this early phase (discussed earlier in detail) include the biological changes of puberty, increased peer pressure to be popular socially and to compete athletically, and increased academic demands and family responsibilities that necessitate giving up time previously spent in play.

In addition to engaging in aggressive, acting-out behavior, the early adolescent may react to stress by becoming excessively passive and withdrawing from his usual interests and activity. He may manifest clinical signs and symptoms of adult depression. The breakup of an early adolescent "chumship" or the failure to make an athletic team or to attain academic goals can result in withdrawal, loss of self-esteem, moodiness, chronic fatigue, and feelings of anxiety and depression. Hyperactive behavior with great bursts of energy may alternate with periods of passivity and withdrawal. Suicide gestures, as a cry for help, are not uncommon reactions to stress during this phase.

In middle adolescence, regressive behavior, severe anxiety, or episodes of depression result from demands made to establish heterosexual relationships, to become independent of parents, or to make decisions about what college to attend. The breakup of a romantic relationship may precipitate a crisis of apathy and withdrawal; filling out applications for college or for a job and making plans to leave home permanently may evoke acute anxiety and fears of growing old, of parents dying, of being abandoned, or of being unprepared to face the outside world. Feelings of depersonalization may occur and be expressed in terms of strange sensations within the body. During this phase, strong attachment to a friend of the same sex may evoke doubts about sexual identity. The fear of sexual inadequacy and the need to test masculinity or femininity may lead to sexual experience for which the individual is emotionally unprepared and which may therefore result in anxiety, guilt, despondency, and feelings of worthlessness and self-contempt; these feelings may interfere with the adolescent's functioning and require psychiatric help.

In late adolescence the stresses that precipitate adjustment reactions involve primarily those processes concerned with forming an identity pattern, finding an answer to the questions "Who am I?" and "What am I to become?" The late adolescent may experience considerable stress moving from a home where he has received recognition, comfort, and security to a college or university environment where no one seems to be aware of his existence. The solitude of study may intensify loneliness—perhaps the most painful and intolerable of all human feelings. A highly competitive academic environment may create an underlying atmosphere of apprehension about the possibility of failure and about work that appears never to be done.

Other factors may also cause stress in the late adolescent. The pressure to choose a career, to make a lifelong commitment to a vocation, may overwhelm the adolescent. He often lacks not only a clear idea of his interests and abilities but also firsthand knowledge of what specific career choices involve. The inability to sustain a close relationship with someone of the opposite sex may also precipitate a crisis. As the late adolescent completes college, the internal and external pressure to find a mate intensifies, and the termination of a relationship may precipitate feelings of failure and inadequacy.

Many late adolescents today also find the moral confusion of our particular culture stressful. They complain of the absence of a moral frame of reference within which to conduct their lives, and they experience confusion and turmoil in attempting to live without moral guidelines. Others complain of a "vague restlessness" and confusion about the meaning of their college experience specifically and their lives generally. They often become preoccupied with questions of purpose and destiny and acutely concerned with the passage of time, aging, and death. The twentieth or twenty-first birthday often precipitates a mild crisis, perhaps because the former signifies leaving one's teens and the security of childhood, while the latter signifies entering adulthood with a burden of responsibilities and "impossible decisions." Late adolescents speak despairingly of feeling old, of having accomplished little in their lives, and, as students, of living a parasitical existence (Nicholi, 1974b). Distance from family, loneliness, a sense of moral and spiritual void, and dissatisfaction with themselves and their relationships precipitate a crisis with anxiety, intense turmoil, despondency, and other symptoms. Because these symptoms usually disappear once the internal or external stress lessens, they constitute the clinical features of an adjustment reaction of adolescence.

Mental status. Examination of a patient experiencing an adjustment reaction of adolescence may reveal a variety of signs and symptoms but no single pathognomonic feature. With an early adolescent, whose parents may refer him for evaluation against his will, the therapist may encounter considerable hostility and uncooperativeness. The patient may appear solemn and answer questions in monosyllables or with a shrug of his shoulders. Older adolescents are usually more cooperative, especially if they have been referred by a peer, an older friend, or an advisor. The adolescent often appears restless, irritable, and apprehensive. He may have difficulty talking because of dryness of the mouth. The patient may look sad, withdrawn, and extremely tired; these signs may appear separately or along with those described earlier. He may have dark shadows under his eyes, may appear frightened and confused, and may complain of difficulty concentrating. He may describe an acute sense of not belonging and manifest an inability to keep track of time. In addition to the frequent findings of confusion, anxiety, and depression, the examiner may find signs and symptoms that mimic those of the adult emotional disorders.

Etiology. Adolescent adjustment disorders may be conceptualized within different frameworks. For example, all adolescent psychopathology may be considered to result from attempts on the part of the individual to establish an identity, a clear inner definition of himself. Adjustment reactions of adolescence may therefore all be considered manifestations of an identity crisis. Erikson's concepts of identity diffusion, negative identity, and psychosocial moratorium are helpful, especially in understanding adjustment reactions occurring in late adolescence. Other theoreticians, however, have tended to conceptualize the causes of adolescent psychopathology within the framework of ego defenses against strong dependent feelings toward the parents (Freud, 1958). The particular defenses used determine the specific form of psychopathology. For example, the adolescent may react to anxiety induced by his dependence with flight to parent substitutes outside the family. This defense by displacement of feelings may lead to relationships with adults similar in age to the parents but opposite in all other respects, with persons between the adolescent's and the parents' generations who represent ideals, or with "gangs" of contemporaries. These gang relationships may lead to acting-out behavior that brings the adolescent into conflict with school and other authorities.

In addition, the adolescent may defend against his feelings toward his parents by turning them into their opposites—love into hate, dependency into rebellion, admiration into derision. Denial and reaction formation (see Chapter 10) are the common defenses used here. The clinical picture shows a hostile adolescent in open and compulsive rebellion against his parents.

Still another common defense is the withdrawal of feelings from the parents and their investment in the self. This process may result in inflated ideas of the self, in fantasies of unlimited power, or in hypochondriacal sensations; alternatively, the adolescent may react by regressive changes in all parts of his personality. Defense by regression may result in a lapse in ego functioning, in difficulty distinguishing between the internal and external worlds, and in a severe state of confusion and turmoil. Defense against the intensification of impulses that the adolescent experiences may result in adolescent asceticism, a state in which the adolescent denies himself all pleasures, even food and sleep, and lives a spartan existence for brief periods of time. Eating disorders, withdrawal, and other symptoms may result.

Differential diagnosis. The identification of adjustment reactions of adolescence presents one of the most difficult of all diagnostic problems. Unfortunately, this diagnosis has often been used as a "wastepaper basket," including all adolescent problems not understood by the examiner. Because an adolescent adjustment reaction may simulate or occur simultaneously with other psychiatric disorders, the adolescent must be observed over a period of time and assessed carefully.

In making this diagnosis, the clinician must keep in mind that the symptoms—primarily anxiety, confusion, and despondency—are reactions to internal or external stress; once this stress is reduced or eliminated, the symptoms will usually disappear and the patient will return to normal. If the symptoms are severe and seriously interfere with the patient's functioning, they may, if untreated, persist and develop into an adult psychiatric disorder.

The differential diagnosis must include consideration of all the major psychiatric disorders whose symptoms will become clear when the adolescent is observed over a period of time. It may be particularly difficult to distinguish between severe adjustment reactions and schizophrenia. A history of psychological trauma in early childhood may indicate the more serious pathology. Nicholi and Watt (1977), for example, have demonstrated a statistically significant higher incidence of parental death in the childhoods of adolescent schizophrenics than in those of other adolescent psychiatric patients and of normal adolescent controls. Childhood bereavement, this study concluded, though not specific in its pathogenic influence, was a contributing etiological factor in schizophrenia.

When the adolescent suffers from schizophrenia, the symptoms of this disorder (see Chapter 13) will become evident over time. Grinker and Holzman (1973) found that one-third of hospitalized adolescents eventually given the diagnosis of schizophrenia presented no diagnostic difficulty. The other two-thirds presented a clinical picture of adolescent reaction; however, the reactions produced unusually severe chaos and turmoil, so severe that they were considered to be of psychotic proportions. Close observation of these patients revealed the underlying schizophrenic process.

Personality disorders must also be differentiated from adolescent adjustment reactions. A careful history will reveal lifelong patterns of behavior that interfere with a patient's functioning; the type of personality disorder will depend on the particular patterns present (see Chapter 15). In addition, the various psychoneurotic disorders must be considered in the differential diagnosis. As previously mentioned, an adolescent suffering from a specific neurotic disorder will generally manifest the symptoms of that disorder (see Chapter 12). The onset of these symptoms can be traced to early conflicts. If an adolescent crisis occurs in an individual with such an underlying disorder, the crisis may precipitate or exacerbate the illness.

Adolescent depression. In evaluating the adolescent, the examiner must be alert to the presence of depression and the accompanying risk of suicide. As already noted, in recent years the suicide rate among adolescents shows the greatest rise of any age group, and suicide is currently one of the leading causes of adolescent death (Jacobizner, 1965; Culp, 1995). Despite these statistics, depression among adolescents has been a neglected area of study, partly perhaps because in the past many clinicians seriously doubted the existence of real depression in adolescence and therefore any real danger of suicide. Recent studies of late adolescence, however, show depression to be one of the most common disorders afflicting this age group. Research has focused on both the psychobiology of adolescent depression (Dahl, 1996) and the psychosocial determinants, especially family relationships (Monck et al., 1994; Greenberger, 1996; Kassen et al., 1996).

Depression in adolescence may be a transient, situational disorder or it may be a long-standing, severe, crippling disorder with all the signs and symptoms of depression in the adult. Manic-depressive psychoses are believed to be extremely rare in early adolescence. Furthermore, the clinical picture of adult depression may not appear before the age of 14 years. Depression in an adolescent of any age, however, may express itself in ways that make diagnosis extremely difficult. A young adolescent may appear bored, listless, or restless; avoid being alone; and find it difficult to become absorbed in any activity. Sometimes depression expresses itself in alcohol or drug abuse, in sexual promiscuity, in antisocial acting out, in careless automobile and motorcycle driving, or in poor academic performance.

The way internal and external stress can combine forces to effect depression in an adolescent has been illustrated in the study of students who drop out of college for psychiatric reasons. As mentioned earlier, research has indicated that depression is by far the most frequent and most significant causal factor in the decision to leave college (Nicholi, 1967). The types of depression among these dropouts (and perhaps most of the depressions in this age group) appeared not to be related to object loss and therefore were not best understood within traditional concepts. These students' depression seemed to be related more closely to a discrepancy between the actual state of the self, on the one hand, and the ideal state of well-being, on the other. The awareness, gradual or abrupt, of this discrepancy resulted in the clinical picture frequently observed in the dropout: feelings of lassitude, inadequacy, and hopelessness; low self-esteem; and inability to study.

Many of the adolescents in this study were intellectually talented. Their concept of the ideal self was based on both fact and fantasy. The fantasy frequently centered on the need to be perfect—"When I saw that I couldn't get an A, I no longer felt like trying." The concept of the ideal self was based on previous academic success; the home and the secondary school environment once provided maximum positive feedback for that success. The fantasy, the success, and the narcissistic feedback helped defend against strong feelings of inadequacy and deep-seated doubt about intellectual competence. The college environment, in contrast, provided a minimum of positive feedback. An array of awesome professors and highly competitive classmates threatened the student; the college became no less threatening when it provided him with his first less than perfect grade. The self-image that once provided satisfaction and a feeling of well-being was replaced by an image creating profound inner turmoil. Stress became so intense that the adolescent, striving to maintain or regain a state of well-being, saw no alternative to leaving college.

Treatment. The mild adjustment reactions of adolescence usually respond well to short-term supportive measures and to steps directed toward alleviating or eliminating the precipitating stress. In the young adolescent, reassuring the patient, the parents, and teachers or other adults caught up in the patient's turmoil will not only contribute to resolving the turmoil but also help the adults to be more tolerant of the patient during the process of resolution. In more severe adjustment reactions, more intensive

therapy may be indicated. Treatment of depression and the other major psychiatric disorders in the adolescent follows the same basic principles as in the adult, with some modifications in psychotherapy.

Therapy with Adolescents: Principles and Techniques

The basic principles discussed in Chapters 1 and 20 apply to psychotherapy with the adolescent. They need, however, to be modified according to the age of the adolescent and the particular disorder being treated. Opinion about treatment differs widely; some therapists believe the adolescent should be treated with the most intense and carefully modified analysis, whereas others feel he should not be treated at all (Anthony, 1969). Several general rules hold, in spite of differences of opinion: (1) the younger the adolescent, the more the basic principles of therapy for adults must be modified and the more flexible must be the approach of the therapist; (2) regardless of the age of the adolescent, or of how analytically oriented the therapist, therapy ought to be carried out face-to-face; (3) therapy should be focused primarily on the patient's current functioning, his testing of reality, and his current relationships and on conscious and preconscious material; it should concentrate relatively little on unconscious material; (4) interpretation should be used sparingly, support given through suggestion, and change effected through clarification and confrontation; and (5) a process of integration and synthesis should predominate over one of dissection and analysis. A mutual sharing of feelings between therapist and patient may often prove helpful, as will focusing on issues of self-esteem and responsibility.

Certain technical problems arise in therapy with adolescents. The first and most difficult task confronting the therapist is to establish initial rapport and to help the patient recognize his need for help, if such a need exists. With the young adolescent, an introductory phase of therapy is usually necessary before a working relationship can be established. With any adolescent, especially the younger one, the establishment of this relationship may prove extremely difficult. The adolescent seldom sees his need for help and is usually brought to the doctor against his will; in addition, he is usually brought by his parents, those most involved in his anger, defiance, and turmoil. If the therapist is a friend of the parents, the therapeutic effort, if not doomed to failure, will at best meet with considerable resistance. The young adolescent often feels the therapist is part of an adult conspiracy and approaches the whole therapeutic situation with a suspiciousness that sometimes borders on paranoia. It helps, therefore, to deal with the patient as directly as possible and not through his parents. Treating the adolescent like a human being with rights and privileges of his own will help. If the parents call for an appointment, the doctor can ask to speak with the patient, work out a convenient time with him, and let him make transportation arrangements with his parents. It is also best to see the adolescent—even the very young adolescent—first alone and then to ask him for permission to speak with the parents. Because the adolescent has an intense fear of becoming dependent on the therapist, asking his permission to speak with his parents gives him some sense of control over what is happening. If he requests the therapist not to speak with his parents, the therapist will fare better if he honors this request for at least the first session or two. If the therapist believes interviews with the parents are necessary—and many therapists in the case of young adolescents think such an interview mandatory—the therapist can work through the issue with the adolescent over a period of time, helping him to see why such interviews might eventually be helpful to him.

An adolescent who is acting out can also present difficult technical problems. Some therapists have found it helpful to set limits firmly in a nonpunitive manner (Bergen, 1964). The adolescent will often perceive such limits as an expression of concern for him. The limits will usually lessen anxiety in the patient and perhaps in the therapist as well. Many adolescents have difficulty controlling their impulses and often find relief in control from outside.

Adolescents frequently have difficulty recognizing their need for help, regardless of how obvious this need may be to teachers, parents, or advisors. If asked why he has come to see the doctor, the adolescent may quote the referring source but quickly disagree. If the therapist then explores this area in detail with the patient, the adolescent may come to understand how his difficulties have interfered with living his life as he wishes and thus come to recognize his need for help. Sometimes this area will be too charged emotionally for him to discuss it with the therapist until an element of trust has been established. The therapist may have to backtrack in such a case to find some less emotionally charged area to explore—perhaps some interest the patient has in common with the therapist. If such a subject can be found, a silent patient may quite spontaneously begin talking with considerable enthusiasm, and the difficult task of beginning a relationship will have taken a significant step forward.

The older adolescent presents fewer technical difficulties, and the therapist can usually proceed as he would with an adult. He will usually find it helpful, however, to be more directive and, because of the fragile self-esteem of most adolescents, considerably more supportive during the initial contact than he would be with an adult patient. Because the older adolescent usually recognizes his need for help and comes on his own initiative, he is generally more strongly motivated than the younger adolescent. For these reasons, treatment has been more readily available to the older adolescent than to younger ones, and until recently he has been the subject of considerably more attention from investigators.

Group therapy has been found to be effective with some adolescents. Because of their fragile self-image, however, the involvement of some younger adolescents in a group of peers who obviously need help may confirm their fears about their own inadequacy, and they may refuse to cooperate. Group therapy has been found to be effective for adolescents whose problems manifest themselves primarily in current interpersonal difficulties, who show a pattern of withdrawal and isolation, or who become involved in gangs bound together by destructive behavior. For example, an adolescent may be involved in a gang only because of its delinquent behavior or its involvement with drugs.

In recent years, family therapy has begun to play an important part in the treatment of adolescent problems. Therapists have realized that adolescent turmoil and other symptoms may often be a direct reflection of disturbed family functioning. In examining the adolescent, some therapists now also assess the family, with the result that the family may be treated as a unit, or particular members of the family may be directed toward individual therapy. Problems considered especially amenable to family therapy include adolescent school phobias and certain borderline and schizophrenic disorders.

Adolescence, barely recognized by the profession at the beginning of the century, has generated sufficient interest during the past decade to have become a subspecialty of psychiatry. The growth of knowledge about this stage of life has been slow and marked by controversy and misconceptions. With recent research now beginning to focus more on this age group, we have begun to attain a new theoretical and clinical understanding of the adolescent that is not only rapidly changing our concepts of normality and pathology but also forging a more hopeful and more efficacious approach to treatment.

References

Adams, K. S., A. Bouchoms, and D. Steiner. 1982. Parental loss and family stability in attempted suicide. *Arch. Gen. Psychiatry* 39:1081–85.

Alsaker, F. 1996. Annotation: the impact of puberty. *J. Child Psychol. Psychiatry* 37:249–258.

American Psychiatric Association. 1988. *A psychiatric glossary.* 5th ed. Washington, D.C.

——— 1994. *Diagnostic and statistical manual of mental disorders.* 4th ed. Washington, D.C.

Anthony, E. J. 1969. The reaction of adults to adolescents and their behavior. In *Adolescence: psychosocial perspectives,* ed. G. Caplan and S. Lebovici. New York: Basic Books.

——— 1974. The juvenile and preadolescent periods of the human life cycle. In *American handbook of psychiatry,* ed. S. Arieti. Vol. 1. 2nd ed. New York: Basic Books.

Arnett, J. 1994. Adolescence terminable and interminable: when does adolescence end? *J. Youth and Adolescence* 23:517–537.

——— 1995. Reckless behavior in adolescence: a developmental perspective. *Developmental Review* 12:339–373.

Aseltine, R. 1996. Pathways linking parental divorce with adolescent depression. *J. Health Soc. Behav.* 37:133–148.

Bachman, J. 1996. Transitions in drug use during late adolescence and young adulthood. In *Transitions through adolescence: interpersonal domain and context,* ed. A. Graber, J. Brooks-Gunn, and C. Petersen. Hillsdale, N.J.: Lawrence Erlbaum.

Barber, B., and J. Eccles. 1992. Long-term influence of divorce and single parenting on adolescent family- and work-related values, behaviors, and aspirations. *Psychol. Bull.* 111:108–126.

Bergen, M. E. 1964. Some observations in maturational factors in young children and adolescents. *Psychoanal. Study Child* 19:275–286.

Black, C., and R. DeBlassie. 1985. Adolescent pregnancy: contributing factors, consequences, treatment, and plausible solutions. *Adolescence* 20:78:281–290.

Blizzard, R., A. Johanson, H. Guyda, A. Baghdassarian, S. Raiti, and C. Migeon. 1970. Recent developments in the study of gonadotrophin secretion in adolescence. In *Adolescent endocrinology,* ed. F. Heald and W. Hung. New York: Appleton-Century-Crofts.

Blos, P. 1968. Character formation in adolescence. *Psychoanal. Study Child* 23:245–263.

——— 1979. *The adolescent passage.* New York: International Universities Press.

Botsis, A., R. Plutchik, M. Kotler, and H. van Praag. 1995. Parental loss and family violence as correlates of suicide and violence risk. *Suicide Life Threat Behav.* 25:253–260.

Bronfenbrenner, U. 1970. *Two worlds of childhood.* New York: Simon and Schuster.

Bronfenbrenner, U., P. McCelland, E. Wethington, P. Moen, and S. Ceci. 1996. *The state of Americans.* New York: Free Press.

Brooks-Gunn, J. 1997. Sexuality and developmental transitions during adolescence. In *Health risks and developmental transitions during adolescence,* ed. J. Schulenberg, L. Maggs, and K. Herrelmann. New York: Cambridge University Press.

Brown, B. 1997. Transformations in peer relationships at adolescence: implications for health-related behavior. In *Health risks and developmental transitions during adolescence,* ed. J. Schulenberg, L. Maggs, and K. Herrelmann. New York: Cambridge University Press.

Brown, J. 1990. Television and adolescent sexuality. *J. Adolesc. Health Care* 11:62–70.

Bryt, A. 1979. Developmental tasks in adolescence. In *Adolescent psychiatry,* ed. S. C. Feinstein and P. L. Giovacchini. Chicago: University of Chicago Press.

Buhler, C. 1968. The course of human life as a psychological problem. *Human development* 11:184–200.

Bureau of the Census. 1980. *Social indicators: selected data on social conditions and trends in the United States.* Washington, D.C.: U.S. Department of Commerce.

——— 1996. *Statistical abstracts of the United States.* 116th ed. Washington, D.C.: U.S. Department of Commerce.

Burlingham, D. T., and A. Freud. 1942. *Young children in war-time: a year's work in a residential war nursery.* London: Allen & Unwin.

Cantor, P. 1972. The adolescent attempter. *Suicide Life Threat. Behav.* 2:252–261.

Center for Disease Control and Prevention. 1995. *HHS News.*

Cherlin, A., K. Kierman, and P. Chase-Lansdale. 1995. Parental divorce in childhood and demographic outcomes in young adulthood. *Demography* 32:299–318.

Children's Defense Fund. 1997. 20 key facts about American children. In *The State of America's Children Yearbook,* 1997. Washington, D.C.

Collins, J. 1996. Evaluating a national program of school-based HIV prevention. *Evaluation and Program Planning* 19:209–218.

Cracchiolo, A., M. E. Blazina, and D. S. MacKinnon. 1968. The high price of the economical motorbike. *JAMA* 204:175–176.

Culp, Anne M. 1995. Adolescent depressed mood, reports of suicide attempts, and asking for help. *Adolescence.* 30:827–837.

Dahl, R. E. 1996. The psychobiology of adolescent depression. In *Adolescence: opportunities and challenges,* ed. D. Cicchetti and S. Toth. Rochester symposium on developmental psychopathology. Vol. 7. Rochester, N.Y.: University of Rochester Press.

Davis, P. A. 1983. *Suicidal adolescents.* Springfield, Ill.: Thomas.

Demos, J., and V. Demos. 1969. Adolescence in historical perspective. *J. Marriage Fam.* 31:632–638.

Deutsch, H. 1967. *Selected problems of adolescence.* New York: International Universities Press.

Deykin, E. 1986. Adolescent suicidal and self-destructive behavior: an intervention study. In *Suicide on depression among adolescents and young adults,* ed. G. L. Klerman. Washington, D.C.: American Psychiatric Press.

Erikson, E. H. 1968. *Identity: youth and crisis.* New York: Norton.

Fenichel, O. 1945. *The psychoanalytic theory of the neurosis.* New York: Norton.

Fishburne, P. M., H. I. Abelson, and I. Eisin. 1980. *National survey on drug abuse: main findings, 1979.* Department of Health and Human Services publication no. (ADM) 80–976. Washington, D.C.

Flaherty, L. 1997. *Adolescent psychiatry.* Vol. 21. *Developmental and clinical studies.* Hillsdale, N.J.: Analytic Press.

Frazier, A., and L. K. Lisonbee. 1950. Adolescent concerns with physique. *School Rev.* 58:397–405.

Frederick, C. H. 1985. An introduction and overview to youth suicide. In *Youth Suicide,* ed. M. L. Peck, H. L. Faberow, and R. E. Litman. New York: Springer.

Freud, A. 1958. Adolescence. *Psychoanal. Study Child* 13:255–278.

Freud, S. 1905. Three essays on the theory of sexuality. In *Standard edition,* ed. J. Strachey. Vol. 7. London: Hogarth Press, 1953.

———— 1912. On the universal tendency to debasement in the sphere of love. In *Standard edition,* ed. J. Strachey. Vol. 11. London: Hogarth Press, 1961.

———— 1917. Mourning and melancholia. In *Standard edition,* ed. J. Strachey. Vol. 14. London: Hogarth Press, 1949.

Gold, D., and D. Andres. 1978. Relations between maternal employment and development of nursery school children. *Can. J. Behav. Sci.* 10:116–129.

Goldney, R. D. 1982. Locus of control in young women who have attempted suicide. *J. Nerv. Ment. Dis.* 170:198.

Greenberger, E. 1996. Perceived family relationships and depressed mood in early and late adolescence: a comparison of European and Asian Americans. *Developmental Psychology* 32:707–716.

Grinker, R. R., Sr., and P. S. Holzman. 1973. Schizophrenic pathology in young adults. *Arch. Gen. Psychiatry* 28:168–175.

Group for the Advancement of Psychiatry. 1968. *Normal adolescence.* New York: Scribner's.

Hall, G. S. 1904. *Adolescence: its psychology and its relations to physiology, anthropology, sociology, sex, crime, religion, and education.* New York: Appleton.

Harrison E., J. Haaga, and T. Richards. 1993. Self-reported drug use data: what do they reveal. *Am. J. Drug Alcohol Abuse* 19:423–441.

Hamburg, B. A. 1974. Coping in early adolescence. In

American handbook of psychiatry, ed. S. Arieti. Vol. 2. 2nd ed. New York: Basic Books.

Hayward, Chris. 1997. Psychiatric risk associated with early puberty in adolescent girls. *J. Am. Acad. Child and Adolescent Psychiatry* 36:255–262.

Henderson, A. S., J. Krupinski, and A. Stoller. 1971. Epidemiological aspects of adolescent psychiatry. In *Modern perspectives in adolescent psychiatry,* ed. J. C. Howells. New York: Brunner/Mazel.

Hojat, M. 1996. Perception of maternal availability in childhood and selected psychosocial characteristics in adulthood. *Genet. Soc. Gen. Psychol. Monogr.* 122:425–450.

Jacobizner, H. 1965. Attempted suicides in adolescence. *JAMA* 191:101–105.

Jekel, J. F., D. F. Allen, H. Podlewski, N. Clarke, S. Dean-Patterson, and P. Cartwright. 1986. Epidemic free-base cocaine abuse. *Lancet* 3:459–462.

Jellinek, M., and S. Slovik. 1981. Divorce: impact on children. *N. Engl. J. Med.* 305:557–559.

Johnston, L. D. 1981. Frequent marijuana use: correlates, possible effects, and reasons for using and quitting. Paper presented at Conference on Treating the Marijuana-dependent Person, May 1981, Bethesda, Md.

Jones, E. 1922. Some problems of adolescence. In *Papers on psychoanalysis.* 5th ed. London: Balliere, Tindall & Cox, 1948.

Jones, M. C. 1965. Psychological correlates of somatic development. *Child Dev.* 36:899–911.

Josselyn, I. M. 1974. Adolescence. In *American handbook of psychiatry,* ed. S. Arieti. Vol. 1. 2nd ed. New York: Basic Books.

Kandel, D., and M. Davies. 1996. High school students who use crack and other drugs. *Arch. Gen. Psychiatry* 53:71–80.

Kandel, D., and R. Faust. 1975. Sequence and stages in patterns of adolescent drug use. *Arch. Gen. Psychiatry* 32:923–932.

Kandel, D., M. Davies, D. Karus, and K. Yamaguchi. 1986. The consequences in young adulthood of adolescent drug involvement. *Arch. Gen. Psychiatry* 43:746–754.

Kandel, D., K. Chen, L. Warner, R. Kessler, and B. Grant. 1997. Prevalence and demographic correlates of symptoms of last year dependence on alcohol, nicotine, marijuana, and cocaine in the U.S population. *Drug Alcohol Depend.* 44:11–29.

Kaplan, H. B. 1980. *Deviant behavior in defense of self.* New York: Academic Press.

Kassen, S., P. Cohen, J. Brook, and C. Hartmark. 1996. A multiple-risk interaction model: effects of temperament and divorce on psychiatric disorders in children. *J. Abnorm. Child Psychol.* 24:121–150.

Katz, P. 1997. Adolescence, authority, and change. In *Ado-*

lescent psychiatry. Vol. 21. *Developmental and clinical studies,* ed. L. T. Flahery and H. Horowitz. Annals of the American Society for Adolescent Psychiatry.

Kessler, R., C. Davis, and K. Kendler. 1997. Childhood adversity and adult psychiatric disorder in the U.S. National Comorbidity Study. *Psychol. Med.* 27:1101–1119.

King, S. 1997. Suicidal behavior in adolescents. In *Review of suicidology,* ed. R. Maris, M. Silverman, and S. Canetto. New York: Guilford Press.

Koop, C. E. 1987. Surgeon General of the United States. Personal communication.

Larson, R. 1996. Changes in adolescents' daily interactions with their families from ages 10 to 18: disengagement and transformation. *Developmental Psychology* 32:744–754.

Leffert, N. 1996. Biology, challenge, and coping in adolescence: effects on physical and mental health. In *Child development and behavioral pediatrics: crosscurrents in contemporary psychology,* ed. M. Borstein and J. Genevro. Mahwah, N.J.: Lawrence Erlbaum, Associates Inc.

Levy, S. B., and W. N. Grinker. 1983. *Choices and life circumstances—an ethnographic study of project redirection teens.* New York: Manpower Demonstration Research Corp.

Levy-Warren, M. 1996. *The adolescent journey: development, identity formation, and psychotherapy.* Northvale, N.J.: Jason Aronson.

Lunde, D., and D. Hamburg. 1972. Techniques for assessing the effects of sex hormones on affect, arousal, and aggression in humans. In *Recent progress in hormone research,* ed. A. B. Astwood. Vol. 28. New York: Academic Press.

Marks, P. A., and D. L. Heller. 1977. Now I lay me down for keeps: a study of adolescent suicide attempts. *J. Clin. Psychol.* 33:340–400.

Masterson, J. F., Jr. 1967. *The psychiatric dilemma of adolescence.* Boston: Little, Brown.

McCord, J., W. McCord, and E. Thurber. 1963. The effects of maternal employment on lower class boys. *J. Abnorm. Soc. Psychol.* 67:167–182.

Medley, M. L. 1980. Life satisfaction across four stages of adult life. *Int. J. Aging Hum. Dev.* 11:193–209.

Modell, J. 1990. Historical perspectives. In *At the threshold: the developing adolescent,* eds. S. Feldman and G. Elliott. Cambridge, Mass.: Harvard University Press.

Monck, E., P. Graham, N. Richman, and R. Dobbs. 1994. Adolescent girls. I. Self-reported mood disturbance in a community population. *Br. J. Psychiatry* 165:760–769.

Murphy, G. E., and R. D. Wetzel. 1980. Suicide risk by birth cohort in the U. S. *Arch. Gen. Psychiatry* 37:519–523.

National Academy of Sciences. 1976. *Toward a national policy for children and families.* Washington, D.C.

National Center for Health Statistics. 1996. *Advance report of final divorce statistics.* Washington, D.C.

National Institute on Drug Abuse. 1980. *A drug retrospective: 1962 to 1980.* Rockville, Md.

——— 1996. *Monitoring the future study.* Rockville, Md.

Neal, J., P. Flemming, T. Green, and J. Ward. 1997. Trends in heterosexually acquired AIDS in the United States, 1988 through 1995. *J. Acquir. Immune Defic. Syndr. Hum. Retrovirol.* 14:465–474.

Nicholi, A. M., Jr. 1967. Harvard dropouts: some psychiatric findings. *Am. J. Psychiatry* 124:105–112.

——— 1970. The motorcycle syndrome. *Am. J. Psychiatry* 126:1588–95.

——— 1974a. Emotional determinants of LSD ingestion among college students. *J. Am. Coll. Health* 22:223–225.

——— 1974b. A new dimension of the youth culture. *Am. J. Psychiatry* 131:396–400.

——— 1980. *Children and the family.* Report of the Massachusetts Governor's Advisory Committee. Boston.

——— 1983a. The non-therapeutic use of psychoactive drugs: a modern epidemic. *N. Engl. J. Med.* 308:925–933.

——— 1983b. The inhalants: an overview. *Psychosomatics* 24:914–921.

——— 1984. Cocaine use among the college age group: biological and psychological effects—clinical and laboratory findings. *J. Am. Coll. Health* 32:258–261.

——— 1985a. Characteristics of college students who use drugs for nonmedical reasons. *J. Am. Coll. Health* 34:43–49.

——— 1985b. The impact of parental absence on childhood development: an overview of the literature. *J. Family and Culture* 1:19–28.

Nicholi, A. M., Jr., and N. F. Watt. 1976. The death of a parent in childhood: predisposition to schizophrenia. *Proceedings of the American Scientific Association.*

Offer, D. 1969. *The psychological world of the teenager: a study of normal adolescent boys.* New York: Basic Books.

——— 1992. Debunking the myths of adolescence: findings from recent research. *J. Am. Acad. Child and Adolescent Psychiatry* 31:1003–14.

Paikoff, R. L. 1990. Physiological processes: what role do they play during the transition to adolescence. In *From childhood to adolescence: a transitional period?* Advances in adolescent development: an annual book series. Vol. 2, ed. R. Montemayor, G. Adams, and T. Gullota. Newbury Park: Sage Publications.

Palosarri, U., H. Aro, and P. Laippala. 1996. Parental divorce and depression in young adulthood: adolescents' closeness to parents and self-esteem as mediating factor. *Acta Psychiatr. Scand.* 93:20–26.

Patton, G. 1996. An epidemiological case for a separate adolescent psychiatry? *Aust. NZ J. Psychiatry* 30:563–566.

Paxton, S. 1991. Body image satisfaction, dieting beliefs,

and weight loss behaviors in adolescent girls and boys. *J. Youth and Adolescence* 20:361–379.

Peck, M. L. 1982. When a teenager gets really depressed. *Changing Times* (June):27–28.

Petzel, S. V., and M. Riddle. 1981. Adolescent suicide: psychosocial and cognitive aspects. *Adoles. Psychiatry* 9:343–398.

Piaget, J. 1958. *The growth of logical thinking from childhood to adolescence.* New York: Basic Books.

Plotnick, R. 1992. The effect of attitudes on teenage pre-marital pregnancy and its resolution. *Am. Sociological Rev.* 57:800–811.

Propper, A. M. 1972. The relationship of maternal employ-ment to adolescent roles, activities, and parental relation-ships. *J. Marriage Fam.* 34:417–421.

Rosenbaum, M. 1993. The changing body image of the ad-olescent girl. In *Female Adolescent Development,* ed. M. Sugar. New York: Brunner/Mazel.

Russek, L., and G. Schwartz. 1997. Perceptions of parental caring predict health status in midlife: a 35-year follow-up of the Harvard Mastery of Stress Study. *Psychosom. Med.* 59:144–149.

Rutler, M. 1980. *Changing youth in a changing society.* Cam-bridge, Mass.: Harvard University Press.

Rutter, D. 1996. Age and experience in motorcycling safety. *Accident Analysis and Prevention* 28:15–21.

Schwartz, J., H. Friedman, J. Tucker, C. Tomlinson-Keasey, D. Wingard, and M. Criqui. 1995. Sociodemographic and psychosocial factors in childhood as predictors of adult mortality. *Am. J. Public Health* 85:1237–45.

Shafii, M., S. Carrigan, J. Whittinghill, and A. Derrick. 1985. Psychological autopsy of completed suicide in chil-dren and adolescents. *Am. J. Psychiatry* 142:1061–64.

Spiegel, L. A. 1951. A review of contributions to a psycho-analytic theory of adolescence. *Psychoanal. Study Child* 6:375–393.

Stone, L. J., and J. Church. 1968. *Childhood and adolescence.* New York: Random House.

Sullivan, H. S. 1953. *The collected works of Harry Stack Sullivan.* Vol. 1. New York: Norton.

Sussman, E. 1996. Experience and neuroendocrine parame-ters of development: aggressive behavior and competen-cies. In *Aggression and violence: genetic, neurobiological, and biosocial perspectives,* ed. D. Stoff, and R. Carins. Hillsdale, N.J.: Lawrence Erlbaum.

Tanner, J. M. 1962. *Growth at adolescence.* 2nd ed. Oxford: Blackwell.

Tennant, C., A. Smith, P. Bubbington, and J. Hurry. 1981. Parental loss in childhood: relationship to adult psychiat-ric impairment and contact with psychiatric services. *Arch. Gen. Psychiatry* 38:309–314.

Tishler, C. L., P. C. McKenry, and K. C. Morgan. 1981. Ado-lescent suicide attempts: some significant factors. *Suicide Life Threat. Behav.* 11:86–92.

Trunnell, T. L. 1968. The absent fathers' children's emo-tional disturbances. *Arch. Gen. Psychiatry* 19:180–188.

Tucker, J., H. Friedman, J. Schwartz, M. Criqui, C. Tomlinson-Keasey, D. Wingard, and L. Martin. 1997. Pa-rental divorce: effects on individual behavior and longev-ity. *J. Pers. Soc. Psychol.* 73:381–391.

Vincent, M. 1992. Body image and adolescent pathology. In *Int. Ann. Adolescent Psychiatry* 2:132–135.

Wagner, B. 1997. Family risk factors for child and adoles-cent suicidal behavior. *Psychol. Bull.* 121:246–298.

Wallerstein, J. 1980. The impact of divorce on children. *Psychiatr. Clin. North Am.* 3:455–468.

——— 1991. The long-term effects of divorce on children: a review. *J. Am. Acad. Adolesc. Psychiatry* 30:349–360.

——— 1997. Parental divorce and developmental progres-sion: an inquiry into their relationship. *Int. J. Psychoanal.* 78:135–154.

Walters, P., G. Goethals, and H. Pope. 1972. Drug use and life style among 500 college undergraduates. *Arch. Gen. Psychiatry* 26:92–96.

Weiner, I. B. 1970. *Psychological disturbance in adolescence.* New York: Wiley.

Wolstenholme, G. E. W., and M. O'Connor. 1967. *Endocri-nology of the testis.* Boston: Little, Brown.

Wortley, P. 1997. AIDS in women in the United States. *JAMA* 278:911–916.

Zinberg, N., and A. Weil. 1970. A comparison of marijuana users and nonusers. *Nature* 22:119–123.

Recommended Reading

Blos, P. 1979. *The adolescent: passage.* New York: Interna-tional Universities Press.

Bronfenbrenner, U., P. McCelland, E. Wethington, P. Moen, and S. Ceci. 1996. *The state of Americans.* New York: Free Press.

Feinstein, S., P. Giovacchini, J. Looney, A. Schwartzberg, and A. Sorosky, eds. 1980. *Adolescent psychiatry.* Chicago: University of Chicago Press.

Flaherty, L. 1997. *Adolescent psychiatry.* Vol. 21. *Develop-mental and clinical studies.* Hillsdale, N.J.: Analytic Press.

Freud, Anna. 1958. *Adolescence: the psychoanalytic study of the child.* New York: International Universities Press.

Hamburg, D. 1997. Toward a strategy for healthy adoles-cent development. *Am. J. Psychiatry* 154:7–12.

Schulenberg, J. 1997. *Health risks and developmental transi-tions during adolescence.* New York: Cambridge Univer-sity Press.

29

The Elderly Person

ANDREW SATLIN

BENJAMIN LIPTZIN

MICHAEL JENIKE

CARL SALZMAN

STEPHEN PINALS

Geriatric psychiatry is one of the fastest-growing and most exciting areas of clinical practice and research in psychiatry. The most powerful force behind the development of the field is the "demographic imperative." The older population has been growing rapidly in all countries of the world. In the United States the number of persons 65 years and older increased from 3 million in 1900 to over 33 million in 1994. By the year 2030 there will be over 70 million elderly persons in the United States. Equally striking is the fact that the elderly constitute an increasing proportion of the U.S. population, rising from 4% of the total in 1900 to 12.7% in 1994, with a projection of 20% by 2030. This change partly reflects decreases in mortality but results even more from today's lower birth rates. Among the elderly, the fastest-growing group is the "old old," defined as those over age 85 (3.5 million in 1994). Elderly minority populations also are increasing at higher rates than the elderly as a whole, and are projected to represent 25% of the elderly population in 2030, up from 13% in 1990.

Other demographic statistics affect the types of patients seen by the geriatric psychiatrist, and the life circumstances and problems that these patients face. The elderly are mostly women, and the ratio increases with age. For all persons 65 and older there are 1.5 women for every man, whereas for the group 85 and older the ratio is 2.6 to 1. Life expectancy also differs for older men and women. At age 65 the life expectancy for men is 15 years and for women 19 years. Blacks have a shorter life expectancy at birth than whites but a longer life expectancy at age 75. In terms of marital status, 77% of elderly men are married, compared to only 53% of elderly women. There are 5 times as many widows as widowers. This reflects the longer life expectancy of women and their tendency to marry older men. Although divorced older persons represented only 6% of all older persons in 1994, their numbers had increased 4 times as fast as the older population as a whole since 1990.

Many myths and misunderstandings exist concerning the elderly population. Common misconceptions are that a majority live in institutions, are demented, are poor, and are poorly educated. In fact, the elderly in the United States represent a very diverse population that overwhelmingly lives in the community, is cognitively intact, in good spirits, and non-poor. With respect to living arrangements, only 5% of the elderly reside in institutions, primarily nursing homes; 68% live with family members, and 30% live alone or with nonfamily companions. Marked gender differences exist, with 40% of older women and 16% of older men living alone. Although 30% of the elderly dwell in substandard housing, poverty has been greatly reduced: 12% of the elderly live below the official poverty level, but if food, housing, and medical benefits are included, this figure drops to 3.5%, a lower proportion than for other age groups. With each succeeding decade the educational level of the group 65 and over has risen. Between 1970 and 1994, the percentage of older persons who had completed high school rose from 28% to 62%. Of the present cohort of elderly, 13% are college graduates.

In terms of life experiences, anyone who was over age 65 in 1997 was born in 1932 or earlier. This group includes several different cohorts with respect to major historical and cultural changes. Many lived through World War I. Many immigrated themselves or were the children of immigrants at the start of the twentieth century. Many lived through the relative prosperity of the 1920s, and all lived through the economic collapse of the 1930s but were affected differently depending on their age and their economic circumstances. The elderly were all at least 10 years old during World War II, and many of the men were old enough to have fought in battle. In contrast to the turbulence of early life for many of today's elderly, the decades of their lives since 1945 must seem relatively calm. The elderly today benefit from a wide array of publicly funded programs to meet their needs, including social security,

Medicare, elderly housing, and transportation, nutrition, homemaker, and other services. Although some elderly persons still live at or below subsistence level, for most the "golden years" are much more comfortable than their parents' old age or what they anticipated when growing up. In 1982, 71% of those 65 years and older reported themselves as highly satisfied with their standard of living. This level, which is much higher than for any other age group, has probably increased in the last 15 years. In fact, consideration of scaling back the rapid growth in entitlement programs that are partly responsible for these gains in living standards is high on the political agenda.

Clearly the elderly are more likely to have health problems than younger persons. Older people accounted for 36% of all hospital stays and 48% of all days of care in hospitals in 1993. Over 80% of the elderly have at least one chronic illness. These medical conditions increase the risk of developing psychiatric illnesses, and may hinder diagnosis by altering or masking their presentation. However, just as the elderly are a diverse group from a demographic and socioeconomic perspective, they are heterogeneous from a biomedical standpoint. Nearly three-fourths of noninstitutionalized elderly rate their health as good or excellent. Physiologic capacity and vulnerability to disease are very different for the average 65-year-old and the average 85-year-old. In addition, interindividual differences are much greater among elderly persons at any given age compared to younger adults at any given age. The tremendous variability that accompanies physical and psychological aging has led to the concept of "frailty," which is associated with age but is not age-specific. The combination of losses in organ system reserve and function that characterizes frailty is found in some, but not all, elderly. By remaining aware of the heterogeneity of the elderly in terms of their origins, life experiences, current socioeconomic circumstances, and present physiologic and medical conditions, the geriatric psychiatrist is able to approach his patient with dignity, compassion, and therapeutic optimism.

Changes in Old Age

Nervous System

Changes in sensory perception and cognitive function characterize aging of the central nervous system and are particularly relevant to psychological adaptation and participation in psychological treatment. For example, visual changes include decreased accommodation, decreased acuity, decreased color sensitivity, and decreased depth perception (Rubert, Eisdorfer, and Loewenstein, 1996). The elderly have more cataracts, glaucoma, macular de-

generation, and diabetic retinopathy. Changes in hearing include a decline in high frequency speech perception and auditory discrimination; increased reaction time; and increased prevalence of nerve deafness, dizziness, and tinnitus. Hearing impairment may lead to heightened suspiciousness, if not frank paranoid thinking, and visual or hearing impairment may lead to a restriction in activity, social isolation, and loss of self-esteem. At the same time, these declines in function make it more difficult for the older person to make use of psychotherapy to address the effect of these changes.

A substantial literature exists on the cognitive changes of aging (Birren and Schaie, 1990; Rubert, Eisdorfer, and Loewenstein, 1996). Results of studies of intelligence in the elderly vary according to the methodology and instruments used to measure intellectual functions. Cross-sectional studies have shown that intellectual performance peaks in the 30s, plateaus through the 50s or early 60s, and then begins a slow but increasingly rapid decline in the late 70s. However, longitudinal studies of the same persons over time have shown no change or minimal decline. This finding suggests that the differences in intelligence seen in earlier cross-sectional studies may reflect cohort differences in amount and recency of education, occupation, and familiarity with tests. The current consensus is that many intellectual functions, including attention span, everyday communication skills, lexical, phonological, and syntactic knowledge, discourse comprehension, and simple visual perception, show little or no decline in individuals over 60. By contrast, selective attention, naming, verbal fluency, complex visuoconstructive skills, logical analysis, cognitive flexibility, and the ability to shift cognitive set may decrease with age. Another major factor affecting the apparent decline in these functions with age is the increasing rate of physical illness that accompanies aging. Among persons of the same age group, healthier subjects consistently perform better.

Memory decline is the most frequent cognitive complaint of older people. The study of memory function has made increasingly sophisticated use of tasks to measure specific aspects of memory. Tests of primary memory such as digit span appear to be performed equally well in older and younger adults. Older subjects have more difficulty than younger ones on secondary or short-term memory tasks when asked to divide their attention or to reorganize the material presented. Memory for remote events is also diminished in the elderly, but recall and recognition of past events remains quite high. Mild forgetfulness, especially for names, is a normal phenomenon and should not alarm the patient or the clinician. Moderate or severe memory difficulties are not normal and suggest dementia.

Although decrements in performance occur with increasing age on many experimental learning and memory tasks, the actual deterioration among healthy older persons is not nearly as significant or extensive as once thought. One reason is that most studies of changes in learning and memory are done under artificial laboratory conditions, where some of the change may be due to speed of presentation or to motivational factors. Older subjects may develop greater anxiety in fast-paced tests and withdraw from the testing situation or provide fewer responses. More recent research has attempted to identify factors that facilitate learning in the elderly. These aids include slowing the rate of presentation and the expected speed of response or developing strategies for learning. A better understanding of how learning can occur even at advanced ages may improve the ability of older persons to adapt to new work or living situations.

Basic Body Functions

Many organ systems show functional decline with age, although it is sometimes difficult to separate the effects of aging per se from those due to age-associated diseases (e.g., cataracts, osteoporosis), environmental influences (e.g., air pollution or exposure to sun), or lifestyle choices (e.g., exercise and smoking) (Leventhal, 1996; Taffet, 1996). Regardless of cause, a decline in basic body functions such as mobility, strength, sleep, and sexual function affects self-perception and contributes to the psychological sense of aging. Important physical changes include decreased skeletal muscle strength and connective tissue flexibility that may lead to decreased mobility, falls, and functional decline (Fiatarone et al., 1994). Changes in skin, hair, and subcutaneous tissues result in the altered appearance that we associate with being "old." Blunted senses of smell and of taste may affect appetite. In turn, diminished pleasure in eating reduces the quality of life, and may result in poor nutritional intake that can contribute to physical frailty.

Important biological changes in sleep accompany aging (Miles and Dement, 1980). Older people spend more time in bed but show decreased continuity of sleep with increased brief arousals and decreased slow-wave sleep. There is a tendency for the major sleep period to occur earlier in the night and for REM sleep to occur earlier in the night. More fragmented nighttime sleep is associated with increased napping during the day. A healthy older person typically lies awake for one-fifth the night. Perhaps because of these frequent awakenings, by age 75 one-third to one-half of healthy people complain of insomnia. Primary sleep disorders such as sleep-disordered breathing and periodic leg movements of sleep occur more fre-

quently in the elderly, and common medical conditions such as congestive heart failure, chronic obstructive pulmonary disease, and arthritic pain may interfere with sleep. Since sleep disturbances are common in affective illness and in dementia, the clinician must rule out the presence of such disorders before attributing sleep complaints to aging alone.

Although age-related physiological changes may affect sexual functioning (Masters and Johnson, 1970), sexual interest, fantasy, arousal, and activity may continue into old age for both sexes (Renshaw, 1996). For older men a slower sexual response and decreased erection, seminal fluid volume, and excitatory pressure usually occur. Impotence may be caused by physical illness or medication. Older women usually experience a delay and decrease in vaginal secretions. The orgasmic phase may be shorter, and there may be painful spastic contractions of the uterus. Some of these problems may be helped by exogenous estrogens. Sexual activity declines with physical illness or if a partner is not available. Cultural taboos or upbringing may limit the frequency of masturbation as a sexual outlet, although this may be less true in the cohort raised with explicit sexuality in the media.

Drug Metabolism

The psychiatrist who prescribes medications to the older patient must be familiar with many factors that may affect the drug's effectiveness. First, most elderly patients will already be taking other medicines. Some patients may not fill yet another prescription because the rationale for the new medicine has not been adequately presented. Or they may hesitate to do so because of an unallayed fear that they will be taking too many pills, or because they cannot easily afford to pay for one more. Concern about adverse drug interactions may be realistic, especially if the patient is taking over-the-counter medications and the psychiatrist is not aware of their use. Memory loss may prevent patients from taking the medication correctly, and family or other caregivers may not be available to remind them. Thus, several factors may contribute to an elderly person not taking a prescribed medication. Poor "compliance" is an inadequate summary of these factors, or one that the elderly person may reasonably view as pejorative.

Physiological changes with aging affect the pharmacokinetics and pharmacodynamics of drug metabolism. Pharmacokinetic changes may occur in the absorption, plasma protein binding, distribution, biotransformation, and elimination of the drug from the body. Absorption from the gastrointestinal tract appears to change little with age. A decrease in the hepatic synthesis of albumin leads to reduced protein binding of medications and increases in the availability of free drug for entry into the brain or for access to metabolism in the liver. This change may be especially relevant for psychotropics that are highly protein bound, such as the selective serotonin-reuptake inhibitors (SSRIs) and valproic acid. The volume of distribution of lipid-soluble drugs increases with aging as the proportion of the body composed of fatty tissue increases with the loss of lean muscle mass and total body water. Since most psychotropic drugs are highly lipid-soluble, the amount of these drugs that accumulate in the body tends to increase with age for any given dose and body weight. Greater accumulation of a drug in fatty tissue results in longer half-life, a greater time to reach steady-state concentration, and longer pharmacologic activity. These factors are independent of the rate of clearance of the drug. However, in the elderly, clearance also is decreased because of reduced hepatic biotransformation (Von Moltke, Greenblatt, and Shader, 1993). Reduced clearance further increases half-life. In combination, these changes are the basis for the aphorism "start low, go slow" in prescribing and increasing doses for elderly patients.

Decreased hepatic metabolism does not affect all psychotropic drugs equally. In general, those drugs that require hepatic oxidation as the preliminary step in excretion will have longer half-lives in elderly patients because of declines in the activity of the microsomal enzymes responsible for that oxidation (Schmucker, 1984). However, drugs that proceed directly to glucuronide conjugation, making them water-soluble for excretion by the kidney without prior oxidation, will not necessarily have longer half-lives because this process does not seem to be affected by age. Thus, whenever possible, it is preferable to use drugs that do not require hepatic oxidation (e.g., short half-life benzodiazepines such as lorazepam) instead of those that do (e.g., long half-life benzodiazepines such as diazepam) in elderly patients.

Reduced clearance of drugs by the kidney affects 2 classes of medications. The first are those medications that are water-soluble in their administered state, such as lithium. Thus, in order to avoid cardiac and central nervous system toxicity, lower lithium doses must be used in elderly patients. The second class of medication affected by reduced renal clearance includes drugs such as the tricyclic antidepressants, which continue to have cardiotoxic effects even after they have been oxidized by the liver to water-soluble metabolites. With reduced renal clearance of these metabolites, patients may develop cardiac conduction delays even with low therapeutic concentrations of the active parent drug. The only reliable method for detecting these toxic effects is with an electrocar-diogram, which should therefore be checked regularly (e.g., after each dose increase) in elderly patients taking tricyclic antidepressants.

The aging process affects the central nervous system (CNS) in ways that can influence the response to medication (Taffet, 1996). The weight of the brain decreases significantly, and blood flow to the brain decreases 20%. Changes in synthesis, turnover, receptor binding, and synaptic neurotransmission occur in many parts of the brain. Although the exact clinical consequences of these age-related alterations are not known, evidence to date suggests that decreases in CNS norepinephrine, serotonin, dopamine, GABA (gamma-aminobutyric acid), and acetylcholine result in increased receptor-site sensitivity in areas of the brain associated with mood, cognition, and coordinated motor behavior. In addition to the possible pharmacodynamic effects of these changes in neurotransmitter synaptic function, researchers speculate that they may be associated with increased anxiety and depression as a response to stress, loss, or illness, as well as with a progressive decline in memory function.

Pharmacodynamic changes in neurotransmitter function also may result in increased peripheral side effects of psychotropic medications. Reduced noradrenergic function with aging may render the older patient more susceptible to orthostatic blood pressure effects from tricyclic antidepressants and antipsychotics. Reduced cholinergic function in the bowel and urinary tract may account for severe constipation (in some cases leading to impaction) or urinary retention, both of which are more common in older than in younger patients who take medications with anticholinergic properties.

Disease states may have additional effects on the action of psychotropic medications. Illness may affect the metabolism of medication, for example, by reducing blood flow to the kidneys and liver. Cardiac ischemia may result in a greater risk of ventricular irritability and sudden death when patients are given tricyclic antidepressants (Glassman, Roose, and Bigger, 1993). Other unknown or unpredictable effects also may occur. Unfortunately, most studies of new drugs are done in healthy adults, and little clinical experience in very old, frail, or medically ill patients is available at the time of the approval and marketing of new agents. Thus, caution always must be exercised in these populations, especially when combining new medications with older agents or with one another.

Psychosocial Changes

Alterations other than somatic changes impinge on the aging person. Of these, perhaps loss has the most significant impact. Not only do the elderly experience physical bodily losses, but they also sustain important emotional losses of significant people and love objects—spouse, children, friends, relatives, associates, and colleagues.

Changes owing to retirement also characterize this phase of the life cycle. The response to retirement depends on many factors including these: Was the retirement voluntary or involuntary? Was it health related? Are adequate financial resources available? Had the person anticipated and planned for retirement? How did the person feel about his or her job? Despite a deeply ingrained work ethic and the self-esteem that comes from working, more people now feel that leisure time is important and have the financial resources to enjoy their retirement. New or postponed hobbies and interests can be developed.

Developmental Issues

Psychiatrists have written about the psychodynamics of aging largely on the basis of psychotherapy with individual patients (Berezin, 1972; Colarusso and Nemiroff, 1987). As noted above, older adults suffer many losses in their life. The significance of each event or life change, whether somatic, interpersonal, or psychosocial, must be understood in the context of an individual's personality structure and life experience. The range of responses to age-specific conditions may vary from mature coping to complete psychological breakdown.

In his well-known work on life stages, Erikson describes the psychosocial crises or conflicts experienced by individuals at different ages (Erikson, 1959). The psychosocial conflict of late life is described as integrity versus despair. According to Erikson, integrity is

the acceptance of one's own and only life cycle and of the people who have become significant to it as something that had to be and that, by necessity, permitted of no substitutions. It thus means a new different love of one's parents, free of the wish that they should have been different, and an acceptance of the fact that one's life is one's own responsibility . . . Although aware of the relativity of all the various life styles which have given meaning to human striving, the possessor of integrity is ready to defend the dignity of his own life style against all physical and economic threats. For he knows that an individual life is the accidental coincidence of but one life cycle with but one segment of history . . . I can add, clinically, that the lack or loss of this accrued ego integration is signified by despair and an often unconscious fear of death: the one and only life cycle is not accepted as the ultimate of life. Despair expresses the feeling that the time is short, too short for the attempt to start another life and to try out alternate roads to integrity. Such a despair is often hidden behind a show of disgust, a misanthropy, or a chronic contemptuous displeasure with particular institutions and particular people—a disgust and a displeasure which (where not allied with constructive ideas and a life of cooperation) only signify the individual's contempt of himself. (p. 98)

Neugarten has studied adult development in large numbers of individuals (Neugarten, 1970). She noted that there is enormous diversity in lifestyles among the middle-aged and old. The timing of life events is becoming less regular, age is losing its customary social meanings, and the trends are toward a fluid life cycle and an age-irrelevant society. One can now see a 35-year-old grandmother, a 50-year-old retiree, a 65-year-old father of a preschooler, and a 70-year-old college student. Psychological change is continuous throughout the life cycle. Neugarten also demonstrated that most individuals cope well with major life changes (e.g., retirement or widowhood) when they occur "on time" in one's life cycle. She suggests that a changing time perspective starts in middle age. Time becomes restructured in terms of time left to live instead of time since birth. She describes the issues that arise in old age as

adapting to losses of work, friends, and spouse; the yielding of a position of authority and the questioning of one's former competences; the reconciliations with significant others and with one's achievements and failures; the resolution of grief over the death of others and of the approaching death of self; the maintenance of a sense of integrity in terms of what one has been, rather than what one is; and the concern over legacy and how to leave traces of oneself. In old age there are also the triumphs of survivorship; the recognition that one has savored a wide range of experiences and therefore knows about life in ways no younger person can know; the knowledge that in having lived through physical and psychological pain, one recovers and can deal also with the contingencies that lie ahead; and a sense that one is now the possessor and conservator of the eternal truths. The preoccupation with time left to live loses some of its poignancy. Dependency and deterioration, not death itself, is the specter of old age. In the innermost parts of the mind the acceptance of one's own death may be . . . impossible to contemplate, yet the old person seems relatively free to talk about death and to express concern not over the fact that death will come, but about the manner in which it will come. And there is, for many if not most, a sense of peace as much as protest. (Neugarten, 1979)

Vaillant has conducted empirical longitudinal research on white men who were originally interviewed during their sophomore year in college (Vaillant, 1977). Based on extensive interviews, Vaillant described a hierarchy of psychological defense mechanisms that are established very early and usually persist throughout life (see also Chapter 10). Psychotic defense mechanisms include denial of external reality, distortion, and delusional projection. Neurotic mechanisms include intellectualization (isolation, obsessive behavior, undoing, rationalization), repression, reaction formation, displacement (conversion, phobias), or dissociation (neurotic denial). Immature mechanisms include fantasy (schizoid withdrawal, denial through fantasy), projection, hypochondriasis, passive-aggressive behavior, and acting out. Mature mechanisms are sublimation, altruism, suppression, anticipation, and humor. Vaillant's research demonstrated that over time, these men tended to use more "mature" and fewer "immature" defenses. In later interviews with the same group of men, Vaillant demonstrated that successful aging at age 65 was associated with the use of more "mature" defenses before age 50 (Vaillant, 1990).

Colarusso and Nemiroff (1987) described the tasks that need to be dealt with in middle and late adult life. These include: the aging process in the body; increased awareness of time limitation and one's own death; illnesses or death of parents, friends, relatives; changes in sexual drive and activity; markedly altered relationships with parents, young adult children, and a maturing spouse; the assessment of career accomplishment and the recognition that not all personal goals will be reached; and planning for retirement. They suggest that these issues often come up in psychotherapy with older patients.

The findings of Erikson, Neugarten, Vaillant, and Colarusso and Nemiroff are remarkably consistent in suggesting that late life is a time of both loss and growth. Successful adaptation to early life challenges, and the use of more healthy defense mechanisms, predict successful adaptation to the crises of later life. The integrity that results may be diminished by severe and unanticipated loss, but can be enhanced by psychotherapy. The geriatric psychiatrist therefore must recognize that the older person shares common issues and concerns with others of his age, but also must be approached as an individual. Older patients may be as responsive to psychotherapeutic intervention as younger patients, and should not be assumed to be incapable of growth and change.

Death and Dying

It is said that one is old when time ahead is measurable, that is, when one's death draws near. A common assumption is that as a person ages he becomes more preoccupied with ideas of his own death and that old people are fearful and anxious about this matter. But in fact it is rare for old people to be afraid of approaching death. Imputations to the contrary usually arise from the projections of younger people. Old people are aware of approaching death, but they do not commonly have pathological reactions to it. Usually the concern is not about dying but about how death may come—whether it will be sudden or lingering, with or without pain, or whether one will be a burden to others. (See also Chapter 33.)

The facts of dying and loss may cause greater suffering in the people involved with the patient, such as spouse, children, siblings, relatives, friends, and colleagues. They are required to cope with poignant situations over which they have no control. Once a diagnosis of terminal illness is made, the final steps toward death and loss are usually progressive and irreversible. The awareness of irreversibility produces a feeling of helplessness, which can be the worst disease of all. Especially difficult for friends and relatives is the fact that full mourning cannot occur until the loss itself becomes final, and without mourning a final resolution of grief is impossible.

The concept of partial grief describes the state in which unresolved grief is precipitated by a partial rather than a total loss (Berezin, 1970). Partial grief need not have a direct connection to death itself but may be observed in situations that suggest the beginning of "the end of the road" or in retirement or birthdays in advanced years. Partial grief can also occur at fiftieth wedding or other significant anniversaries, when family members are reminded, consciously or unconsciously, that a person's previous identity has changed and time ahead is more finite.

The unresolved grief unfortunately may lead to regressive positions, aggressive and hostile outbursts, projection, and depression. Sometimes family members may make impossible demands for life-saving measures (or the opposite), or previously friendly siblings may become more quarrelsome and fight among themselves. Such manifestations are consistent with the family's sense of helplessness and their inability to cope with what may in fact be a hopeless situation in a sick or dying relative or friend. When such irrational behavior occurs in these states of partial grief, a family conference may be useful. With the psychiatrist (or other treating person) acting as a neutral, understanding, objective, and knowledgeable resource, the family confronts the reality of the situation and discusses the prognosis openly. Their reactions, especially their feelings of helplessness, are reviewed, and the need for family unity is stressed. The appeal is both to the realities of the aged person's situation and to the awareness of the uncomfortable struggles among those who grieve.

Psychiatric Assessment of the Older Patient

The general principles of careful psychiatric assessment apply to older patients as well as to younger ones. Any evaluation should include a thorough history of the presenting complaint, previous psychiatric illness, medical history, medication use, family history, social history, habits and use of alcohol, and a mental status examination including appearance, affect, behavior, mood, thought, and cognition. An essential element is the assessment of functional capacity, which aids in diagnosis as well as in treatment planning. Often, the referral of a geriatric patient will be initiated by family members, other caregivers, or social service agencies. These referrers, together with the patient's primary care medical provider, all must be involved in the assessment process. However, the development of the strong therapeutic alliance with both the patient and family that is essential to treatment begins with the method and style of the evaluation. Clinical staff must strike a balance between gathering information from outside sources and respecting the patient's confidentiality. Usually the extent to which cognitive impairment may interfere with obtaining an adequate history from the patient will only become apparent during the course of the initial interview. Thus, the patient should be interviewed privately first, and then family or other caregivers should be invited to join, with the patient's permission. In this way patients will be able to divulge confidential information, which can later be verified by family members. Family will be able to provide information about function that may corroborate apparent cognitive deficits. The interview with the family also will yield insight into the psychosocial dynamics and available caregiving and financial resources of the patient-family unit, which can be used to tailor recommendations for treatment, ancillary services, and the possible need for assisted living or nursing home care.

The initial interview should begin with asking the patient for his understanding of the reason for the evaluation. Lack of understanding, either from cognitive impairment or poor reality testing, points the clinician toward a focus on the mental status examination and more quickly involving the family in the assessment. The clinician should be alert to possible sensory impairments, such as loss of hearing or vision, that may require adjustments in the style of the interview. Observation of the patient will complement the initial description of the presenting illness in helping to determine the contributions of physical illness or disability to psychiatric decom-

pensation or psychological distress. Particular attention must be paid to recent environmental changes including separations, deaths, and changes in residence or supports. A list of all currently used medications, including over-the-counter medications, as well as the quantities of alcohol and caffeine regularly consumed, must be obtained.

Perhaps the most significant area in which the assessment of older patients differs from that of younger ones is in the evaluation of cognitive deficits. Cognitive impairment may be inferred from a patient's distractibility, apparent inattention to appearance, deferring to family members for answers to personal questions, or from lack of spontaneous, fluent, and logically directed speech. When impaired cognitive function is suspected, more detailed assessment is required. It is often assumed that any cognitive problem in an older person is due to dementia, and Alzheimer's disease is now often diagnosed in the absence of a careful and comprehensive workup. Numerous studies and extensive clinical experience suggest that a substantial proportion of such patients have treatable or reversible problems, such as drug side effects, infections, metabolic imbalances, endocrine disturbances, congestive heart failure, or other physical illnesses. Although treatment of these conditions may not completely reverse the observed cognitive deficit, the patient's functioning and overall well-being certainly may improve (Larson et al., 1984).

The geriatric psychiatrist should be familiar with a brief, standardized cognitive examination for regular use as a screening tool. The use of such an instrument ensures that all important areas of cognitive function are tested, and serves as a baseline against which later function may be compared. One such test is the Mini-Mental State Examination (Folstein, Folstein, and McHugh, 1975), which samples orientation, attention, concentration, memory, language, comprehension, and constructional ability, and can be completed in 10 minutes. Although scores under 24 (of a possible total of 30) are often considered indicative of dementia, other factors such as state of arousal, presence of depression, or level of education may influence performance. The Mini-Mental State Examination should therefore be used only for clinical screening, as part of a broader assessment of mental status and history. If deficits are questionable, or if cognitive dysfunction is still suspected despite high scores, more detailed neuropsychological testing is warranted.

Special Features of Psychiatric Disorders in the Elderly

The typical features of psychiatric disorders are described elsewhere in this book. The geriatric patient with a psychiatric disorder, however, often presents atypically, and it is these special features that are discussed here. Each section reviews the epidemiology, presentation, diagnosis, and treatment of the major psychiatric disorders affecting the geriatric population.

Depression

Depression is the most common psychiatric illness among the elderly. Recent controversy about the relative rates of depression in the young and the old should not obscure the fact that depression is a major cause of the increased morbidity, functional decline, and mortality that accompany aging. Much has been made of the fact that the Epidemiological Catchment Area (ECA) study found that the one-year and lifetime incidence of major and bipolar depression is lower in persons over the age of 65 than in those younger than 65 (Blazer, 1994; Myers et al., 1984; Weissman et al., 1991). However, a number of factors may account for this apparently surprising finding. First, the ECA study only surveyed individuals living in the community, and therefore did not sample persons living in nursing homes and other institutions, where rates of depression are much higher. Second, the elderly have a tendency to underreport depressive symptoms (Lyness et al., 1995). Third, lifetime estimates may be artifactually low for the elderly because of forgotten early episodes of depression, low rates of diagnosis or labeling of early life depression, and earlier death of people with affective illness. Fourth, depression in older persons may not be diagnosed because of attribution of neurovegetative affective symptoms to medical illness or dementia. Finally, atypical or "subsyndromal" presentations may lead to missed diagnoses; many depressed older people may not meet criteria for major depression because they lack a sufficient number of neurovegetative symptoms, but nevertheless may have clinically significant syndromes. If all of these factors could be addressed, the rates of depression in the elderly would certainly be very high. In fact, surveys that account for any of these factors consistently find higher rates. For example, among nursing home residents the prevalence of major depression has been estimated as 6–25%, and another 30% may have significant depressive symptoms (Parmelee, Katz, and Lawton, 1989). If depressive syndromes not meeting criteria for major depression are included, 8–15% of elderly in the community are found to have clinical depression (Blazer, 1994). Among hospitalized patients with medical illness, 11% have major depression and another 25% have clinical depression.

The factors that artificially lower the apparent rates of depression in the elderly also have important implications for clinical practice. For example, physicians who work in nursing homes should regularly screen their patients for depression. Any patients with new or worsening medical illness or who decline in daily functioning should be carefully evaluated for the presence of depression. When asking older patients about depressive symptoms, clinicians should be alert to the possibility of symptom denial, and should consider obtaining information from collateral sources. Finally, clinicians should rely on the degree of symptomatic distress and its effect on function, rather than on whether rigid diagnostic criteria are met, when deciding whether and how to treat their older patients with depressive symptoms.

Identification of depression in older persons may be difficult because many may not have classic constellations of neurovegetative symptoms and signs. For example, depressed older patients may have more somatic complaints and fewer expressions of guilt than younger patients (Small et al., 1986), and may exhibit more psychomotor agitation or retardation (Brodaty, Peters, and Boyce, 1991). Depression that first appears in late life more often may include delusions, especially of somatic illness or poverty, although this finding has not been consistent across studies. In the nursing home, depressive syndromes often are characterized by negativity, irritability, hostility, anxiety, complaints of pain, and requests for pain medication (Burrows et al., 1995; Parmelee, Katz, and Lawton, 1993). Patients may deny that they feel depressed, and focus on other complaints about the environment or their health. As a result, depression may be misdiagnosed or unrecognized. Because of the high rate of depression in nursing homes and the atypical presentation of many of these patients, screening should be routine and should emphasize global changes in affect and functioning. These changes are more likely to be recognized by nurses who interact with the patient on a daily basis than by physicians who see patients in the home briefly and irregularly. Clinical experience and research findings so far suggest that an efficient approach might include a combination of 2 screens: simply asking the patient's primary nurse whether the patient exhibits depressive symptoms such as looking sad and withdrawal from activities nearly every day; and asking patients to fill out (with the assistance of a nurse, nurse's aide, or other staff) a simple self-rating scale such as the short form of the Geriatric Depression Scale (Yesavage et al., 1983). This scale consists of 15 questions with yes-no answers; responses consistent with depression on 6 or more should prompt a more thorough evaluation.

Targeted screening is aided by focusing on populations with known risk factors for depression. In the elderly, these risk factors include female sex, unmarried status, recent stressful life events such as major losses or moves, including admission to a nursing home, lack of a supportive social network, and the presence of medical illness (George, 1994; Zisook, Schucter, and Sledge, 1994). Medical illnesses most commonly associated with depression are coronary artery disease and congestive heart failure; renal failure; endocrine abnormalities such as adrenal and thyroid disorders and diabetes mellitus; spinal cord injuries; anemia; autoimmune disorders; chronic pain; and malnutrition. Depression may occur in 25–50% of patients with cortical strokes and neurodegenerative disorders such as Alzheimer's disease, multi-infarct dementia, and Parkinson's disease. Many medications commonly used by elderly patients also are associated with depression, including antihypertensives (notably the beta-blockers), anti-parkinsonians, cimetidine, sedative-hypnotics, anticonvulsants, and steroids. Alcohol use is frequently underappreciated in older persons; many start to use alcohol in an attempt to improve sleep, and may induce or worsen depression instead. Sleep disorder itself is a risk factor for depression. Character disorders, or life-long maladaptive coping strategies, also may contribute to the risk of depression. There is some evidence that long-standing depressive personality traits may increase vulnerability to major depression in late life (Hirschfield et al., 1989).

Depression in older persons has serious morbidity. Depressed elderly patients take longer to recover from physical illness, have prolonged hospital stays, and have increased mortality, especially from cardiovascular causes. Later onset of depression also is associated with a greater risk of recurrence. Outcome studies find that, on average, elderly patients are as well at 1-year follow-up as younger patients, given adequate treatment (Baldwin and Jolley, 1986; Burvill, Stampfler, and Hall, 1986; Meats, Timol, and Jolley, 1991). However, those patients who have active physical illness or who develop a new physical illness during the year of follow-up, and those who suffer more adverse life events and have less extensive social supports, generally have poorer outcomes. Other factors that may predict failure to recover or increased relapse include more severe depression at onset, the presence of psychosis, and comorbid alcohol abuse.

The most serious result of depression is suicide. Rates of suicide are highest in the elderly, who constitute 12% of the population in the United States but account for 20% of all suicides. Rates in women tend to peak around age 50, but rates for men continue to increase into old age. Other risk factors for suicide in the elderly are low income, social isolation, alcohol abuse, delusions, and concurrent physical illness. Older persons who attempt suicide use more lethal means, such as firearms, and are much more likely than younger persons to be successful. They also appear to be less likely to communicate their intention to attempt suicide. However, a 1990 study of suicides in Cook County revealed that 20% had seen their primary care physician within 24 hours and 70% had seen their primary care physician within the month prior to suicide (Clark, 1991). These findings suggest that careful screening of at-risk elderly populations may offer the hope of identification and thus prevention.

Treatment of depression in older persons should combine psychotherapy, support and environmental manipulation, and pharmacotherapy. Despite the belief still held by many that the elderly are rigid and inflexible, and consequently cannot benefit from psychotherapy, there is evidence that personality traits remain relatively constant throughout life, and that rigidity of character is a function not of age but of personality structure. This finding is consistent with empiric studies documenting that elderly persons respond well to psychotherapy (Gallagher and Thompson, 1983; Lazarus, Sadavoy, and Langlsey, 1991). Brief insight-oriented approaches and cognitive behavior therapy are both beneficial in reducing depressive symptoms in older patients, although the benefits from cognitive behavior therapy may be better maintained at 1-year follow-up (Teri et al., 1994; Thompson and Gallagher, 1985). Psychodynamic therapy with older patients often takes the form of life review or reminiscence therapy, first described by Butler (1963). Such an approach may reduce depression and anxiety in some older patients, while increasing self-esteem and life satisfaction.

Special transference-countertransference issues may arise in psychotherapy with the elderly. Usually the therapist is younger than the elderly patient and may feel uneasy treating someone old enough to be his parent or grandparent. This countertransference issue can block good therapy because the psychiatrist's uneasiness is transmitted to the patient, who reacts in turn. With increased experience, therapists come to appreciate that transference may not represent reality and that the elderly patient is not guided by calendar age. In fact, much evidence supports the opposite: rather than viewing the young psychiatrist as a child figure, the elderly patient may see him as a peer or even as a parental figure (Berezin and Fern, 1967).

Supportive therapy for older persons may require that family members be involved, just as they often must be in the evaluation process. Ongoing family therapy provides psychoeducation that can enhance the understanding and cooperation of family members who are primary caregivers, thereby improving the patient's compliance with treatment and resulting in better outcomes. Helping patients and families deal with practical problems in caregiving, often by providing referral to community agencies, may complement the exploration of intrapsychic and interpersonal issues that constitute more traditional therapy. Other adaptations of traditional psychotherapeutic techniques often are required in treating the elderly depressed person. Impediments to the patient's involvement in psychotherapy may include impaired mobility that restricts access to the therapist's office, decreased hearing that interferes with the patient's ability to engage in therapy, and fatigue that may occur during the day as a result of inefficient sleep at night. Adaptations to deal with these problems include flexible scheduling of appointments, use of home or nursing home visits, appointments by telephone, and use of an external hearing aid in the office (Fogel, 1996).

Psychopharmacologic treatment of depression in the elderly is based on similar principles used to treat depression in younger patients. Selection of an appropriate agent is based on previous treatment response and an educated guess about which side effects may be most severe or difficult to tolerate for any given patient. The rate and increment of drug dose titration should be based on the pharmacokinetics of the drug. An adequate duration of treatment is required for therapeutic response, and patients may need support and encouragement to tolerate their symptoms until response is achieved. If an adequate trial does not result in improvement, the medication should be tapered and discontinued, and the patient should then be started on another agent, usually from a different class of drug. If partial response occurs at the maximally tolerated dose, augmentation strategies (i.e., combination of the antidepressant medication with other medications that may enhance its effect) may be considered. Once the patient has improved, maintenance therapy is required to prevent relapse.

In actual clinical practice, these principles must be tailored to the individual characteristics of any given patient. On average, older patients have some common characteristics that allow us to generalize about applying these principles to their treatment. For example, as described in the section above on drug metabolism, most elderly will be more intolerant of anticholinergic and cardiovascular side effects, and should not be given tertiary amine tricyclic antidepressants such as amitriptyline and imipramine. Therapeutic response may be slower in many older patients, and therefore adequate drug trials may need to extend for as long as 9–12 weeks (Georgotas et al., 1988), and the clinician must be more resistant to

pressure from the patient and family to abandon a medication before it has been given enough time to work. Finally, there is anecdotal evidence that elderly patients may be more prone to relapse, and the clinician often is wise to consider chronic maintenance antidepressant therapy more readily than in a younger patient. Chronic maintenance therapy may be more acceptable to older patients, whose other medical conditions requiring ongoing medication, such as hypertension and diabetes, may make them more comfortable viewing their depression in a similar way. Since relapse is associated with medical illness and lack of social support, ongoing monitoring of medication by the psychiatrist provides additional protection against relapse by allowing for frequent identification of these risk factors.

The literature on the effectiveness and tolerability of specific antidepressants in the elderly is small and of limited utility. Most published clinical trials of antidepressants in the elderly include many subjects who are between 55 and 65 years of age, free of significant comorbid medical illness, and not taking concomitant medications. Thus, these studies cannot be generalized to the very old, frail, medically compromised patient who is typical of geriatric practice. In addition, most clinical trials include only patients who meet criteria for major depression. As discussed above, many elderly patients with atypical presentations may not meet these criteria and yet may have clinically important depressive syndromes. Data about the responsiveness of these syndromes to pharmacologic treatment, and the most useful medications to treat them, are so far lacking.

The most extensively studied antidepressant medications in the elderly are the tricyclic antidepressants (TCAs), especially the secondary amines such as nortriptyline. Nortriptyline has been found to be an effective antidepressant even in frail, institutionalized elderly with an average age of 85 (Katz et al., 1990). However, 30% of patients in this study had significant side effects that limited the use of the medication. Although the secondary amine TCAs such as nortriptyline and desipramine cause less severe side effects than the tertiary amines such as amitriptyline, imipramine, trimipramine, and doxepin, they still may produce clinically significant sedation, anticholinergic effects, and cardiac effects. Elderly patients have reduced central and peripheral cholinergic function and are at increased risk for bowel impaction, urinary retention, blurred vision, tachycardia, and cognitive effects such as disorientation, memory loss, and even delirium with agitation and visual hallucinations. Adrenergic effects of the TCAs include orthostatic hypotension. The most dangerous potential toxicity of the TCAs is their effects on the heart. Like the Class 1A antiarrhythmics that they chemically resemble, they delay cardiac conduction, which may lead to higher degrees of block in patients with preexisting conduction abnormalities. In addition, evidence from the Cardiac Arrhythmia Suppression Trial (CAST) indicates that patients with cardiac ischemia are at increased risk for ventricular irritability and sudden death when given Class 1A antiarrhythmics (Glassman, Roose, and Bigger, 1993). By analogy, TCAs may confer a similar risk. Thus, these agents must be used cautiously, with electrocardiogram (EKG) monitoring, in patients with conduction abnormalities, and should be avoided in most patients with ischemic heart disease or recent myocardial infarction.

A number of new antidepressants have been studied and approved for use in the last 15 years or so. These have the chief advantage of reduced side effects compared to the TCAs, with generally comparable efficacy. The most commonly used of these medications are the selective serotonin-reuptake inhibitors (SSRIs), of which fluoxetine, sertraline, paroxetine, and fluvoxamine are available in the U.S. They have relatively weak effects at postsynaptic cholinergic, adrenergic, dopaminergic, and histaminergic receptors, which accounts for their low incidence of the side effects mediated by blockade at these receptors (Cusack, Nelson, and Richelson, 1994). Compared to the TCAs, however, they are more likely to cause serotonergic side effects such as loss of appetite, nausea, diarrhea, increased sweating and salivation, sexual dysfunction, anxiety, restlessness, and insomnia. Although these side effects are generally better tolerated or less severe than the typical side effects of the TCAs, some elderly patients who already have anorexia, or who have an agitated depression with poor sleep, may find that the side effects of the SSRIs make them feel worse. The SSRIs also have a number of potential drug interactions owing to their inhibition of various cytochrome P450 isoenzymes, leading to elevated and even toxic levels of some concomitantly used medications (Nemeroff, DeVane, and Pollack, 1996). Clinical trials in the elderly are compromised by the inclusion of many young-old subjects and by comparisons with high-side-effect–producing tertiary amine TCAs, often without a placebo group. Nonetheless, these studies document that the SSRIs are superior to placebo and comparable to TCAs in elderly patients (Dunner et al., 1992). However, there is some evidence that the SSRIs may be less effective than the TCAs in elderly patients with more severe, melancholic depression (Roose et al., 1994).

A newer class of drugs has effects on both the noradrenergic and serotonergic neurotransmitter systems, and thus may combine some of the therapeutic effects of the TCAs and the SSRIs, without significant effects at postsynaptic cholinergic or histaminergic receptors. The first drug in this class was venlafaxine, which inhibits the reuptake of both norepinephrine and serotonin. It may cause similar side effects as the SSRIs, including nausea, dizziness, anxiety, and insomnia. At high doses, hypertension may occur. Venlafaxine is reported to be safe in the elderly, but large trials documenting efficacy have not included many elderly patients. Nefazodone also inhibits the reuptake of both serotonin and norepinephrine, but more weakly than venlafaxine. Its primary effect may be antagonism at the postsynaptic serotonin-2 receptor, which may account for its antianxiety effect. This characteristic, together with nefazodone's beneficial effects on sleep, may make it a particularly useful drug for the agitated, restless, and sleepless older person with depression, but clinical trials in this population have not yet been done. Trazodone, an older drug chemically similar to nefazodone, also has beneficial sedative effects. However, it can cause significant orthostatic hypotension.

Bupropion is an atypical antidepressant that appears to modulate noradrenergic function at usual therapeutic doses. Unlike the other new agents, it has the advantage of having been studied in older depressed patients with preexisting cardiac disease. In patients with arrhythmias, conduction abnormalities, and ventricular dysfunction, doses of bupropion in the upper therapeutic range were effective and had minimal effects on blood pressure and no significant effects on cardiac rate, rhythm, or ventricular function (Roose et al., 1991). Bupropion has a short half-life, but the recent availability of a slow-release formulation allows for dosing twice a day.

Several older approaches to the pharmacologic treatment of depression have lost favor for use in the elderly with the advent of these newer agents. The monoamine oxidase inhibitors (MAOIs) can cause severe orthostatic hypotension. Acute and dramatic rises in blood pressure (hypertensive crisis) can occur when patients on MAOIs eat foods rich in tyramine, such as aged cheese, or when drugs with direct or indirect sympathomimetic action are taken. These substances often are found in over-the-counter cold preparations. Yet MAOIs are effective in elderly patients and may be better than TCAs for maintenance therapy (Georgotas, McCue, and Cooper, 1989). They also cause minimal anticholinergic side effects and for this reason may be better tolerated than the TCAs by some elderly patients. Psychostimulants can cause tachycardia, hypertension, and cardiac arrhythmias, as well as insomnia, restlessness, confusion, and even psychosis. However, they appear to help patients who are anergic, apathetic, and demoralized by medical illness, and their use may therefore aid medical recovery (Roccaforte and Burke, 1990). In this population, the rapid response to treatment that often is seen (24–48 hours) is a great benefit. Stimulants also are reported effective for patients in extreme old age (Gurian and Rosowsky, 1990). Antidepressant augmentation strategies, usually involving the addition of lithium or thyroid hormone, have become less commonly used as it has become simpler to switch to a new type of antidepressant. However, these approaches have the advantage of a relatively rapid effect once a partial response to the initial antidepressant has been achieved, and usually cause only minimal added side effects. Well-designed trials in older patients are lacking, but anecdotal evidence supports the use of lithium augmentation (Kushnir, 1986).

An older treatment that appears to be gaining in favor is electroconvulsive therapy (ECT). ECT often is the safest and most effective treatment for depression in elderly patients, especially when the patient is delusional or the depression is life-threatening and a rapid clinical response is necessary (e.g., the patient is suicidal, catatonic, or refusing food or water). One controlled study compared simulated ECT to real ECT in 35 patients who were 60 years of age or older, and found a significant difference in favor of real ECT on the Hamilton Rating Scale for Depression after 6 treatments (O'Leary et al., 1994). Geriatric patients with delusional depression may respond better to ECT than patients without psychosis (Wilkinson, Anderson, and Peters, 1993), and there is some evidence that older patients may respond better than younger patients (Black, Winokur, and Nasrallah, 1993). ECT may be used in medically ill patients, and even in patients with dementia. Hypertension and arrhythmias are the most common cardiovascular complications. Cognitive side effects include transient confusion immediately after the treatment, which persists for up to a few weeks in a minority of patients. Anterograde amnesia usually persists for the period of time when the ECT course is being given, but does not generally extend beyond this, and retrograde amnesia usually recovers gradually. The use of anticholinergic premedication, short-acting barbiturates for anesthesia, oxygenation during the treatment, muscle relaxants, low energy stimulus waveforms, and unilateral electrode placement all have resulted in decreases in the morbidity and mortality associated with ECT, without any loss of efficacy.

Clinical experience, together with the findings from the literature summarized above, suggest the following approach to the treatment of the depressed older patient. The first step, of course, is treatment of any underlying medical illness or substance abuse problem that may be causing or exacerbating the depression, or discontinuation of medications that may be contributing to it. If the depressive symptoms persist, a combination of psychotherapy and somatic therapy should be initiated. For patients who are in the young-old age group and medically healthy, any antidepressant will be safe and have an equal chance of being effective. Often, as with younger patients, the medication of first choice will be one of the SSRIs, because of their relatively low side effect profile and ease of dosing. Doses should start at one-third to one-half the usual adult starting dose, and be increased in increments equal to the starting dose every week for sertraline or paroxetine, and after a month for fluoxetine. However, if the patient has been depressed previously and responded well to a TCA or MAOI, it is entirely reasonable to try the same medication again. The preferred TCAs are nortriptyline, starting at 10 mg a day and increasing by 10 mg every 3–5 days, or desipramine, starting at 25 mg with similarly spaced 25 mg dose increases. These medications should be titrated to plasma levels of 50–150 ng/ml and at least 125 ng/ml, respectively, while monitoring blood pressure, EKGs, and clinical response (Alexopoulos, 1992).

For older patients with mild to moderate depression who have cardiovascular illness, especially ischemic heart disease, the TCAs should probably be avoided. Instead, an SSRI should be tried. If the SSRI is unsuccessful or causes intolerable side effects, a switch to venlafaxine, nefazodone, or bupropion is warranted. Nefazodone might be selected if the patient is agitated or unable to sleep, and bupropion may be preferred if there is underlying heart disease. If the depression persists or worsens, or if the initial presentation is of a severe depression with melancholic features, a TCA might again be considered next, but close cardiac monitoring will be required. In treating geriatric patients, it should be remembered that longer treatment trials may be needed; one study found that nearly half of patients who had not responded at 7 weeks improved during an additional 2-week period, and another third of the remaining nonresponsive group improved after 3 more weeks (Georgotas and McCue, 1989). Finally, for treatment-resistant depression, delusional depression, or for life-threatening situations, ECT should be the treatment of choice. A course of 6–12 unilateral treatments, followed by maintenance medication or ECT, is likely to result in sustained clinical improvement. Maintenance should last for at least 6 months, and patients who have had 2 recurrences over 2 years of follow-up probably should remain on medication indefinitely.

Mania

Mania in the elderly may be due to new onset bipolar disorder, recurrence of earlier onset bipolar disorder, or may be secondary to other conditions. When bipolar disorder first appears in late life, the mania usually follows several episodes of depression with a latency of 10–15 years. Many of these cases have evidence for some form of neurologic dysfunction (Shulman et al., 1992). Consistent with this association, many elderly bipolar patients will demonstrate some degree of cognitive dysfunction, and mortality is higher in elderly manics than in elderly depressives. Some new onset bipolar disorder first presents with mania; in these cases, neurologic or medical causes are common. Neurologic disorders most frequently associated with mania are cerebrovascular disease, epilepsy, neoplasm, trauma, and central nervous system infections such as human immunodeficiency virus (HIV) and neurosyphilis. Medical disorders that can cause mania include metabolic conditions such as vitamin B-12 deficiency, thyrotoxicosis, and Addison's disease. Medications also may cause mania; some of the more likely to do so are corticosteroids, dopaminergic drugs, sympathomimetics, psychostimulants, anticholinergics, and some illicit drugs and alcohol. Mania due to medical illness or medications has been commonly referred to as "secondary mania" (Krauthammer and Klerman, 1978), but the DSM-IV (*Diagnostic and Statistical Manual of Mental Disorders,* fourth edition) diagnoses are "mood disorder due to a general medical condition" and "substance-induced mood disorder."

Compared with depression, the rates of mania and bipolar disorder in elderly persons are low. Approximately 4–18% of inpatients on geriatric psychiatry units have bipolar disorder (Glasser and Rabins, 1984; Yassa et al., 1988). In the community, rates are generally very low when DSM criteria for bipolar disorder are applied, with prevalences of 0.1% in those older than 65 (Weissman et al., 1991). However, rates are higher when mania is defined symptomatically. The phenomenology of late life mania is similar to that of younger patients. No consistent differences are found in the degree of euphoria, grandiosity, or expansiveness, or in the frequency of psychosis or mania mixed with depression, when older manics are compared with younger patients. When the mania has an organic cause, however, it may have some characteristic clinical features. These include impairments of attention, concentration, or memory sufficient to meet criteria for either a delirium or dementia syndrome, a poor response to lithium, or the development of neurotoxicity at low therapeutic lithium levels. The natural history of organic or secondary mania also has some distinguishing features. These may include a chronic course, rapid cycling, and a negative family history. The presence of such features in a patient with a late-life onset of mania should always prompt a careful search for potentially treatable causes of this syndrome.

Mania in elderly patients should be treated with the same medications used in younger patients. As in depressed patients, the choice of drug will be based on previous response, anticipation of the tolerability of side effects, and concerns about interactions with other medical conditions and concomitant medications. The preferred treatment is with a drug that has both acute antimanic effects and long-term mood-stabilizing effects. Both lithium and the antiepileptic medications are effective. Lithium and valproic acid are approved for this indication in the United States, although neither medication has been studied in prospective, controlled trials in elderly patients. Most clinicians still use lithium as the primary first-line therapy because of greater experience with this drug. However, there is some evidence that the antiepileptic medications may be more effective in patients with secondary mania, mixed affective states, or rapid cycling (Pope et al., 1988; Yassa and Cvejic, 1994). In addition, these drugs are preferred in patients who have histories of nonresponse to lithium or intolerance of its side effects, and in patients who have medical conditions, such as underlying heart or kidney disease, that increase the risk of lithium-induced toxicity. Some patients may require adjunctive treatment with neuroleptic medications or ECT for acute control of severe manic symptoms or psychosis. These modalities also may be necessary for patients who do not respond to either lithium or any of the antiepileptics, or who develop toxicity at therapeutic doses of these medications.

Lithium is excreted by the kidney, and with age-related reductions in creatinine clearance the dose of lithium must be lowered. In addition, there is evidence that the elderly may respond to lower serum lithium levels, in the range of 0.4–0.7 mmol/l, and that levels in the usual adult therapeutic range of 0.8–1.2 may be associated with increased toxicity (Foster, 1992). For both of these reasons, starting doses may need to be as low as 150 mg/d. For patients with chronic renal failure, doses often will be even lower, and the use of liquid lithium citrate, measured by dropper, may be necessary. Lithium itself may cause changes in kidney function, with reduced concentrating ability seen at therapeutic doses, and possible decreased glomerular filtration rate at toxic doses. Patients also should be monitored for changes in sinoatrial node function and cardiac conduction, leading to bradycardia and dysrhythmias. Hypothyroidism and, more rarely, thyrotoxicosis are seen in a minority of patients treated with lithium. Neurologic side effects include cognitive impairment; movement disorders such as parkinsonian symptoms, eye movement abnormalities, and dyskinetic movements; and cerebellar dysfunction manifested as unsteady gait, slurred speech, and tremor. In elderly patients, such side effects may be the earliest sign of lithium toxicity, even when levels are in the low therapeutic range. Underlying neurologic disorders appear to increase the risk of lithium-induced neurotoxicity (Bell et al., 1993; Himmelhoch et al., 1980). Because of this risk, patients with dementia, Parkinson's disease, and perhaps other neurologic conditions probably should be treated with an antiepileptic instead of lithium. The most common drug interactions with lithium are elevated levels produced by concomitant administration of thiazide diuretics and nonsteroidal anti-inflammatory drugs. Since many of the latter are now available without prescription, elderly patients on lithium may present with toxicity that may be unexplained until the patient or family member is asked specifically about new use of these over-the-counter analgesics.

Use of the antiepileptic medications valproic acid and carbamazepine generally poses fewer problems in dosing, side effects, or drug interactions. However, monitoring for hepatoxicity, and for lowered white blood cell counts with carbamazepine, is necessary. Either of the antiepileptics may be used alone or combined with lithium in patients who have a partial response to monotherapy. Levels should be maintained in the usual antiepileptic range.

Anxiety

Formal investigations of the prevalence of anxiety disorders in elderly persons generally find rates to be lower than in younger persons. The Epidemiologic Catchment Area (ECA) study by the National Institute of Mental Health found 1-month prevalence rates for anxiety disorders as a group (including generalized anxiety disorder, panic disorder, phobia, obsessive-compulsive disorder, and post-traumatic stress disorder) to be 3.6% for elderly men and 6.8% for elderly women, compared to rates of 4.7% and 9.7% for the population as a whole (Regier, Narrow, and Rae, 1990). However, surveys using scales designed to identify clinically significant anxiety symptoms that do not necessarily meet criteria for any of these diagnoses find considerably higher rates. For example, an esti-

mated 10–15% of women over age 65 have sufficient anxiety to warrant medical attention, and up to 20% of all elderly have some anxiety symptoms (Himmelfarb and Murrell, 1984). Anxiety is more common in patients with depression, dementia, delirium, mania, and other psychotic illnesses. In the elderly, acute bereavement also may cause anxiety (Jacobs et al., 1990). Alcohol abuse and dependence may be associated with anxiety, although this association is not as robust in elderly patients as in younger ones (Flint, 1994).

Specific anxiety disorders in the elderly have received little attention. There is recent evidence that panic disorder may present for the first time in late life (Raj, Corvea, and Dagon, 1993). Late-onset panic disorder is similar to early-onset panic disorder in its clinical presentation and co-occurrence with depression, but is associated with less social phobia, and may be precipitated by medical disorders such as chronic obstructive pulmonary disease (COPD) and Parkinson's disease. It is unusual for obsessive-compulsive disorder (OCD) to start initially after age 50, but patients with long-standing OCD may first seek help in late life. A recent investigation of the longitudinal course of post-traumatic stress disorder (PTSD) in elderly survivors of the 1988 crash of Pan Am Flight 103 over Lockerbie, Scotland, found similar results to the few studies of younger populations of PTSD patients (Livingston, Livingstone, and Fell, 1994). One year after the explosion, 84% of the subjects met criteria for PTSD and 51% had coexisting major depression, but at 3-year follow-up the rates were only 16% for PTSD and 5% for major depression. Intrusive recollections and avoidance behaviors both recovered significantly. PTSD, but not depression, was associated with loss or injury to friends or family at the 1-year assessment, but at the 3-year assessment this association was no longer present.

Anxiety is frequently part of the symptom cluster of medical conditions that are common in elderly persons. Illnesses most commonly associated with anxiety are respiratory diseases such as COPD, asthma, and pneumonia; cardiovascular diseases such as angina, myocardial infarction, congestive heart failure, arrhythmias, and mitral valve prolapse; endocrine abnormalities such as hyperthyroidism, hypothyroidism, hypercortisolemia, and hypoglycemia; and anemia or other causes of relative hypoxia (Hocking and Koenig, 1995). Medications also may cause anxiety in elderly patients. Drugs most likely to be associated are the stimulants (including caffeine), corticosteroids, theophylline, thyroid replacement, digitalis, beta-adrenergic drugs, SSRIs, and anticholinergic medications. Neuroleptic-induced akathisia is often accompanied by anxiety. Withdrawal reactions, especially from sedative-hypnotics, alcohol, nicotine, and caffeine, also can cause anxiety. Identification of medical or medication-related causes for anxiety is the first step in resolving them, without the use of antianxiety drugs.

Many other factors, such as loss of friends and loved ones, failing health, financial decline, intellectual decline, feelings of helplessness and worthlessness, and loss of control over their environment, contribute to the risk of anxiety disorders in older persons. For many patients with these losses, however, anxiety is a natural response and should not be treated with medicine. When there is a clear precipitating event, discussion of the problem and suggestions for solution may be sufficient. Environmental manipulation, such as moving an anxious nursing home resident closer to the nursing station, may alleviate symptoms.

When medical causes have been ruled out or treated, and precipitating psychological events have resolved, residual anxiety symptoms should be treated with medication. For patients whose anxiety is associated with depression, antidepressant medications are the treatment of choice, although antianxiety agents may be useful adjuncts before the antidepressant has begun to work. Case reports now suggest that antidepressants, and in particular the SSRIs, are useful treatments for elderly patients with panic disorder, OCD, and PTSD (Calamari et al., 1994). For generalized anxiety disorder, and for patients with persistent anxiety associated with medical conditions, treatment will usually be with either a benzodiazepine or buspirone. The benzodiazepines can be divided into 2 classes, based on their metabolism. One class consists of drugs that are first oxidized by the liver, and are therefore affected by the reduction in the activity of hepatic microsomal enzymes that occurs with aging. As a result, the drugs in this category, which include diazepam, flurazepam, chlordiazepoxide, clorazepate, and prazepam, have long half-lives, long-acting active metabolites, and accumulate more readily to toxic levels in older persons. The other class of benzodiazepines consists of those drugs, including lorazepam and oxazepam, that do not require hepatic oxidation, but can be excreted in the urine after glucuronidation in the liver. Since this process does not appear to be as affected by the aging process, these medications have shorter half-lives, no active metabolites, and do not lead to accumulation with deleterious clinical effects. As a result, these benzodiazepines are preferred for use in elderly patients. As with most psychotropic drugs, initial and maintenance doses should be one-third to one-half of those used in younger adults.

Even the short half-life benzodiazepines, however, can cause serious adverse events in older persons. There is evidence for a strong dose-response relationship between the use of benzodiazepines and the risk of falls and hip fracture that does not depend on the type of benzodiazepine prescribed (Herings et al., 1995). Sedation, confusion, cerebellar ataxia, or a combination of these effects may contribute to the risk of falls. Benzodiazepines also are associated with cognitive impairment, and hospitalized elderly patients taking these medications are especially prone to delirium. Behavioral changes such as agitation and wandering can become prominent, and decline in memory function and symptoms resembling mild dementia also may occur. Because benzodiazepines depress respiration, especially during sleep, they may exacerbate sleep-related breathing disorders such as sleep apnea. Patients with underlying respiratory disorders such as COPD may be at increased risk for these adverse events. Since COPD is itself a cause of anxiety, and is common in the elderly population, these patients are at heightened risk for complications from benzodiazepine use.

An alternative to the benzodiazepines is buspirone, a nonbenzodiazepine anxiolytic with partial serotonergic agonist properties. In elderly patients with anxiety, buspirone has been found to produce long-term reductions in the Hamilton Anxiety Scale of over 60%, with minimal nausea, diarrhea, and headache (Bohm et al., 1990; Levine, Napoliello, and Domantay, 1988). Buspirone does not affect hepatic oxidative enzymes; does not cause significant sedation or effects on memory, balance, or coordination; does not depress respiration; and appears not to be addictive or to be associated with withdrawal reactions. Compared to the benzodiazepines, however, buspirone has a much longer onset of action (generally 2–4 weeks), and patients accustomed to the rapid anxiolytic effects of the benzodiazepines may tolerate this delay poorly. One approach to this problem is to combine both medications until the buspirone has been taken for enough time to achieve its therapeutic effect. Older patients usually require similar doses for therapeutic efficacy, as do younger patients (approximately 15–30 mg/d), consistent with the absence of an age effect on metabolism.

Choosing between a short half-life benzodiazepine and buspirone should be guided by the indication for treatment and by patient-related factors. Benzodiazepines, because of their greater side effects and the difficulty many patients have in stopping them after chronic use (possibly associated with addiction potential and withdrawal reactions), should be reserved for short-term use and to treat acute anxiety from psychosocial change or loss. Benzodiazepines also are preferred when medication is prescribed on an "as needed" basis, such as to treat the anticipatory anxiety expected with a planned medical procedure. When chronic use is likely to be necessary, buspirone is a better choice than the benzodiazepines. Thus, buspirone should be used in patients with generalized anxiety disorder or persistent anxiety due to chronic medical conditions that are not expected to resolve completely. Buspirone may be especially useful in patients with a history of falls, respiratory disease, dementia, and previous benzodiazepine or alcohol abuse.

Psychosis

Elderly patients with psychosis may have early- or late-onset schizophrenia, schizoaffective disorder, delusional disorder, unipolar or bipolar affective disorder, delirium, or dementia. As with other psychiatric syndromes in older persons, however, psychosis also may be due to medical conditions, prescription medications, or substances of abuse. Late-life schizophrenia includes recurrences of early-onset disease and schizophrenia first presenting with a late onset. Only 13% of patients with schizophrenia present in their 50s, with another 7% in their 60s and 3% after age 70 (Harris and Jeste, 1988). Late-onset schizophrenia is 6–20 times more frequent among women than men. It also has fewer negative symptoms but similar positive symptoms, course, and response to conventional neuroleptics (Jeste et al., 1996). Many late-onset schizophrenic patients have premorbid paranoid or schizoid traits and long histories of social isolation. However, they are more likely than early-onset patients to marry, hold a job, and raise children, probably because the delayed onset allows for extended presymptomatic opportunities to initiate and maintain relationships and to develop more mature ego defenses (Jeste et al., 1988).

Delusional disorder is characterized by nonbizarre delusions lasting at least a month in the absence of prominent hallucinations, thought disorder, affective symptoms, or a deteriorating course. It most often begins in mid-adulthood in men, but in late adulthood in women (Jeste, Manley, and Harris, 1991). Sensory deficits from auditory and visual impairments are common risk factors (Prager and Jeste, 1993). Psychotic features in delirious patients typically include visual hallucinations and disorganization of thought. Psychosis may occur in about 25% of patients with dementia, and may be more common in patients with cerebrovascular disease than in those with Alzheimer's disease. The delusions tend to be simple and concrete, involving the suspicion that others are stealing from the patient or spying on him, and do not have the elaborate systematization common in manic or schizo-

phrenic patients. Increased suspiciousness may be a defensive response to changes the individual perceives as unacceptable. For example, a patient may accuse others of stealing her purse to avoid acknowledging that she misplaced it and cannot remember where she put it. A patient with uncorrected hearing impairment may be more likely to believe that others are talking about him. Psychosis due to medical or neurologic causes may be phenomenologically indistinguishable from the psychosis of schizophrenia, but the presence of associated features suggestive of the underlying etiology is diagnostic. Disorders in which psychosis is common include epilepsy, stroke, central nervous system tumors, demyelinating diseases, metabolic abnormalities, endocrinopathies, vitamin deficiencies, and toxicity from medications.

After treatment of any underlying medical or neurologic conditions, treatment of non–mood-related psychotic disorders of any etiology in elderly patients should start with neuroleptic medication. In one chart review study of late-onset patients with schizophrenia who were treated with neuroleptics, almost half had complete remissions (defined as the absence of delusions, thought disorder, hallucinations, and catatonic behavior), and an additional quarter had a partial response (Pearlson et al., 1989). Neuroleptic drugs, regardless of chemical structure and class, are therapeutically equivalent and differ only in milligram potency and side effect profile. Selection of any one neuroleptic in preference to another, therefore, is based primarily on the different range, frequency, and intensity of side effects of each drug or each drug class, as well as on the patient's history of prior drug response or lack of response. Sedation, a side effect of some low-potency neuroleptic drugs such as chlorpromazine and thioridazine, may be employed to improve nighttime sleep temporarily. However, because of the prolonged elimination half-life of most psychotropic medications in older persons, sedating effects that are desired in the evening may carry over to the next morning and even to the afternoon, producing daytime sedation, hangover, confusion, and impaired thinking. Sedating neuroleptic drugs also tend to produce orthostatic hypotension, which may be potentially serious in the ambulatory elderly patient. For these reasons the nonsedating neuroleptics, including the high-potency drugs such as haloperidol and fluphenazine, tend to be preferred for the treatment of severe psychosis in older patients. These neuroleptics, however, are associated with a high incidence and severity of extrapyramidal symptoms, including parkinsonian tremor, akathisia (restlessness), and akinesia (decreased movement and affective response).

With conventional neuroleptics, the usual approach to

this therapeutic dilemma has been to start with an intermediate potency agent, such as perphenazine, which also is intermediate in its side effect profile. In addition, the lowest effective dose of medication should be used. However, some patients will develop significant side effects even at subtherapeutic doses of perphenazine. An alternative approach is to use one of the newer atypical neuroleptic medications, such as clozapine, risperidone, or olanzapine. In younger patients, these drugs cause fewer extrapyramidal side effects than the conventional neuroleptics, do not appear to produce tardive dyskinesia, and may be more effective for negative symptoms of schizophrenia. Few data are available on the use of clozapine in older patients, but 3 small open trials found moderate to good efficacy in elderly patients with chronic psychosis (Chengappa, Baker, and Kreinbrook, 1995; Pitner et al., 1995; Salzman et al., 1995). Clozapine can cause marked sedation and orthostatic hypotension, and elderly patients are at increased risk for falls and injury. For this reason, the starting dose of clozapine in older patients should be no greater than 6.25–12.5 mg/d. Open trials also have found risperidone to benefit older patients with schizophrenia (Berman et al., 1996; Madhusoodanan et al., 1995). Preliminary data support a positive effect on cognition in these patients. Risperidone lacks significant side effects at very low doses, but older patients may develop extrapyramidal side effects, sedation, and orthostatic hypotension at much lower doses than will younger patients. Clinical experience suggests that risperidone be started at 0.25 mg/d in older patients, and that the maximum daily dose should not exceed 2–3 mg. So far, published data on the use of olanzapine in older patients are not available, although its use has not been associated with greater side effects in the older patients included in large clinical trials.

Older age is associated with an increased risk for developing tardive dyskinesia, a complication of neuroleptic use characterized by involuntary, choreoathetoid movements of the face, mouth, and extremities. Age correlates with increased prevalence of this disorder, increased severity of symptoms, and lower rates of spontaneous remission after discontinuation of the neuroleptic agent (Smith and Baldessarini, 1980). In one study, the incidence of tardive dyskinesia in patients over the age of 45 was 26% of neuroleptic-treated patients after 1 year, 52% after 2 years, and 60% after 3 years (Jeste et al., 1995). Prior neuroleptic use at baseline, cumulative amount of high-potency neuroleptics, history of alcohol abuse or dependence, and the presence of subtle movement disorders such as tremor at baseline all increased the dyskinesia risk. If the newer atypical antipsychotics prove not to cause

tardive dyskinesia, or even to improve it when patients are switched from another neuroleptic, their use in older patients will receive added support.

Insomnia

Older persons commonly report difficulty in initiating and maintaining sleep. They are inclined to spend more hours in bed and to experience fragmented, interrupted, and often unrefreshing sleep. In part, these subjective complaints may represent developmental changes associated with aging of the brain mechanisms that regulate sleep's timing and duration. Objective evidence from polysomnographic sleep studies is consistent with these subjective complaints. Nocturnal awakenings and stage 1 sleep (lighter sleep) increase with age, while sleep efficiency and slow-wave sleep (stage 3 and 4, or delta sleep), which are associated with the refreshing function of sleep, decrease markedly with age. Contrary to popular myth, the changes that occur with age represent not a decrease in the need for sleep, but rather an inability to consolidate an adequate amount of sleep during the night. Since the basic problem in an insomniac older person is an insufficient amount of restful sleep during the 24-hour day, a nap in the afternoon can be an effective remedy. In order to prevent the nap from worsening sleep at night, it probably should be at a regular time and of a defined duration not exceeding 1 hour. Good sleep hygiene also requires that older persons have regular bed and rise times, and not remain in bed at night when they cannot sleep.

Primary sleep disorders such as sleep-disordered breathing (sleep apnea) and periodic leg movements of sleep (nocturnal myoclonus) are more common as people age. Both of these conditions cause increased arousals at night and impaired concentration and functioning during the day. Many elderly persons with subjective complaints of drowsiness during the day may be suffering from one of these disorders even in the absence of other symptoms. Studies of community-dwelling elderly without sleep complaints find rates of sleep apnea approaching 20% of those in their 80s, and nocturnal myoclonus may be present in more than 90% of persons in this age group (Hoch et al., 1990).

Insomnia, like anxiety and depression in the elderly, may be due to a variety of medical and psychological conditions. Congestive heart failure with nocturnal dyspnea and chronic obstructive pulmonary disease may make it difficult for the elderly person to lie comfortably flat in bed. Pain from arthritis, cancer, or bruxism, and nocturia from heart disease or urinary tract disease, may interrupt sleep. Mood and anxiety disorders, pathological bereavement, dementia, delirium, and substance abuse or withdrawal are common psychiatric disorders associated with insomnia. Hospitalization may lighten sleep: traction, chest tubes, plaster casts, intravenous tubes, and other devices requiring a fixed position in bed interfere with sleep and may aggravate preexisting insomnia. Older persons also commonly use medications that interfere with sleep. These include drugs with stimulant properties, such as the SSRIs and over-the-counter decongestants. The beta-blockers may sometimes induce vivid dreaming that can cause awakening at night. Sometimes, older persons will start to use alcohol in an attempt to improve sleep, which instead may worsen their insomnia by decreasing the amount of slow-wave sleep. Impaired hepatic metabolism can result in prolonged effects of stimulants. For this reason, some elderly find that a cup of coffee or tea at lunch may impair their nighttime sleep as much as a cup at bedtime.

As in younger patients, benzodiazepines are effective and rapid sleep-inducers in the elderly. However, they may change sleep architecture by decreasing the percentage of time spent in deep or slow-wave sleep. Since older persons already experience physiologic decreases in slow-wave sleep, this change may be more important in this age group, but clinical evidence supporting this hypothesis is not available. Long half-life benzodiazepines such as flurazepam tend to accumulate with age because of reduced oxidative metabolism in the liver. As described above for the use of benzodiazepines in anxiety disorders, short half-life drugs without active metabolites, such as temazepam, are therefore preferable. Although these agents may lose effectiveness after daily use for a month, elderly patients who are prone to experience withdrawal symptoms may find it difficult to discontinue their use (Salzman, 1990). With the development of tolerance, rebound insomnia may occur on the first night or even the first few nights after drug discontinuation. Some clinicians suggest that discontinuation may be easier if the hypnotic is used initially only 2 or 3 times a week rather than every night. Other adverse effects made more likely by the pharmacodynamic changes associated with aging include depressed mood, daytime sedation, impaired balance and coordination, and cognitive impairment. The benzodiazepines also can depress the central respiratory drive, especially in patients with underlying asthma or chronic obstructive pulmonary disease. As with most psychotropic drugs used for elderly persons, doses of one-quarter to one-half the usual younger adult dose should be used (e.g. 7.5 mg of temazepam; 0.125 of triazolam).

Some of the disadvantages of the benzodiazepines may be avoided by using a nonbenzodiazepine imidazopyridine hypnotic. Zolpidem is the first such drug to be available in the United States. It is believed to be relatively selective for the benzodiazepine type 1 receptor, which may account for its relative lack of muscle relaxant, anticonvulsant, and anxiolytic effects at doses adequate to achieve sedation. The metabolism of zolpidem in elderly persons is not substantially different from that in younger patients. Healthy geriatric patients without sleep complaints who take between 5 and 20 mg of zolpidem have decreases in sleep latency, increases in sleep efficiency, and subjective improvement in sleep quality without significant side effects (Scharf et al., 1991). In a double-blind, placebo-controlled trial of 119 elderly psychiatric inpatients complaining of insomnia, zolpidem at 10 mg/d improved total duration of sleep without significant daytime drowsiness or rebound upon withdrawal (Shaw, Curson, and Coquelin, 1992). There is some evidence that zolpidem may not decrease the amount of slow-wave sleep, but it is not yet known whether this property is clinically relevant.

Dementia

Dementia is a syndrome of acquired impairment of memory function associated with other cognitive deficits such as aphasia, apraxia, agnosia, and disturbances in executive function, including the ability to think abstractly and to plan, organize, and sequence behavior. For a diagnosis of dementia to be made, these changes must be severe enough to interfere with social or occupational functioning. Associated symptoms include disturbances of visuospatial skills, judgment, emotion, and personality. Most dementia is caused by illnesses that increase in frequency with advancing age, and thus dementia is predominantly a disease of late life. The most common cause of dementia, Alzheimer's disease (AD), is estimated to affect about 4 million Americans (Evans et al., 1989). The prevalence of AD rises dramatically with each decade of life after age 50, with rates of about 1% of those between ages 65 and 75, 10% of those over 75, and perhaps close to 50% of those over 85. Although a large number of medical and neurologic conditions may cause dementia, AD accounts for roughly 50–75%, depending on the age of the group studied, and vascular causes of dementia account for about another 25%, with some overlap between these two diagnoses.

AD is characterized by a gradually progressive decline in function, with the ultimate loss of all cognitive and voluntary motor activity after a course of 5–20 years. The initial presentation is usually with mild forgetfulness, repetitive speech, and the inability to learn new information, although some patients may have language dysfunction, visuospatial deficits, or personality change with or without depression as the earliest sign of disease. These changes may result in the patient getting lost, becoming agitated or irritable, and developing the belief that others are stealing from him, abandoning him, or being unfaithful to him. In any older patient who presents with any of these symptoms or some combination of them in the presence of cognitive dysfunction, a comprehensive workup to determine cause is essential. Cognitive testing must be sufficient to distinguish global change from abnormalities in specific cognitive domains that might indicate focal brain disease. Physical and neurologic examination is required to look for evidence of stroke, vascular disease, Parkinson's syndrome, or medical conditions that might lead to dementia. Laboratory tests, including brain imaging, can provide specific findings that might be associated with medical or neurologic causes of dementia. A diagnosis of AD is based on clinical diagnostic criteria established by a work group of the National Institute of Neurologic and Communicative Disorders and Stroke (NINCDS) and the Alzheimer's Disease and Related Disorders Association (ADRDA) (McKhann et al., 1984). Use of these criteria has improved antemortem diagnosis of probable AD to about 90% accuracy in specialized clinics. Definite AD can only be diagnosed by identifying the histopathologic hallmarks of the disease, senile plaques and neurofibrillary tangles, on brain tissue examination.

Vascular causes of dementia include cortical strokes and multi-infarct disease (MID) due to the presence of at least several lacunar infarcts in the basal structures of the brain. Hypertension and diabetes are risk factors for vascular dementia. This condition is distinguished from AD by its relatively abrupt onset and a stepwise deterioration, presumably associated with the occurrence of new small strokes that may not have other clinical manifestations. Often, however, the history as reported by family members is an unreliable guide to differentiating these two major causes of dementia. Focal neurological signs and symptoms suggestive of stroke and evidence for lacunes on brain imaging are more valid indicators of the presence of vascular dementia. Patients with dementia due to cerebrovascular causes may have more emotional lability, depression, apathy, and physical and cognitive slowing than patients with AD.

Dementia also occurs in about 30% of patients with Parkinson's disease (Huber et al., 1989) and in other subcortical brain diseases such as Huntington's disease and progressive supranuclear palsy. Although it often is difficult to distinguish the dementia due to these conditions from that due to AD on clinical grounds alone, the associated neurologic features will suggest the diagnosis. Patients with subcortical dementia also tend to have a relative preservation of insight and language early in the course of illness, but more depression, apathy, gait disturbances, dysarthria, and incoordination. Severe depressive disorders may present with dementia, more commonly in elderly patients than in younger patients. This dementia syndrome of depression is characterized by a relatively rapid onset (over days to weeks rather than the insidious onset typical of degenerative dementias), a fluctuating course, and a moderate to complete reversibility of the dementia with treatment of the depression. Since depression also is a common secondary feature of degenerative dementia, there is necessarily a great deal of overlap between these two conditions. Even among patients whose improvement with antidepressant therapy suggests that their cognitive dysfunction was part of the dementia syndrome of depression, many will subsequently present with a degenerative dementia (Alexopoulos et al., 1993). This finding suggests that depression may sometimes be the earliest symptom of incipient AD.

Treatment of dementia is best conceptualized as helping both the patient and family (or other caregivers) to manage a chronic disease. Education about the nature of the illness, its course, and the symptoms to be anticipated as it progresses should begin when the patient and family are told the results of the evaluation process and given the diagnosis. An assessment of caregiving resources allows for appropriate referrals to community agencies that can provide homemakers, personal care aides, visiting nurse services, respite care, day treatment programs, and various levels of institutional living when that becomes necessary. Patients and families also need information about legal and financial planning (e.g., durable power of attorney, health care proxy, and applications for Medicaid). Collaboration with the internist or family practitioner is essential to identify medical illnesses or medications that might be contributing to cognitive impairment or causing physical distress that may lead to agitated behavior. Optimizing general health status, and providing prosthetic devices such as hearing aids, may lessen the development of "excess disability" beyond that caused by the brain degenerative process alone. A discussion of the pros and cons of taking newly available medications to improve cognition in AD should be held as soon as that diagnosis is made, and patients and families should be informed about the availability of research studies of other new treatments. Behavioral and pharmacologic management of the secondary psychiatric symptoms of dementia, such as depression, psychosis, agitation, sleep disturbance, and other restless behaviors, is necessary when these symptoms are present.

The brains of patients with AD show selective loss of cholinergic neurons in the nucleus basalis of Meynert and reduced levels of the synthetic enzyme choline acetyltransferase and its product acetylcholine in the projection areas of these neurons in the hippocampus and other cortical areas. These changes correlate with the degree of memory loss, and their discovery has therefore led to the cholinergic hypothesis of memory dysfunction in AD. According to this hypothesis, therapies that restore cholinergic function may ameliorate some of the cognitive symptoms of AD, although they would not be expected to alter the degenerative process affecting neurons or slow the progression of the disease. Currently available treatments based on this hypothesis involve cholinesterase inhibitors that block the breakdown of acetylcholine in the synapse and presumably increase its availability for neurotransmission. The first of these agents, tacrine, has been reported to be effective in improving cognition as measured by standardized instruments in 3 published multicenter trials, 2 of which also demonstrated statistically significant improvement on a clinician's global impression of change (Davis et al., 1992; Farlow et al., 1992; Knapp et al., 1994). Tacrine now has been approved for use in patients with mild to moderate AD. However, clinical experience is consistent with the results of these clinical trials in suggesting that the improvement achieved with tacrine is usually small, at best returning the patient to the level of cognitive ability present 6–12 months earlier in the course of the disease. Tacrine also has a number of drawbacks in clinical practice, including a short half-life (requiring that it be taken 4 times a day); relative nonspecificity for brain acetylcholinesterase (resulting in limiting peripheral cholinergic side effects such as nausea and diarrhea in about a third of patients); and hepatoxicity (with elevations in liver enzymes greater than 3 times the upper limit of normal in about 25% of patients [Watkins et al., 1994]). For these reasons, a decision to use tacrine requires a detailed and careful discussion of the risks and benefits with the patient and family. Once treatment has begun, close supervision and biweekly blood tests are necessary.

Second-generation cholinesterase inhibitors have longer half-lives, no hepatoxicity, and more specificity, resulting in fewer and less severe peripheral side effects. Donepezil hydrochloride is the first medication of this group to be approved by the FDA for use in the United States. Its effects on cognition are similar in magnitude to those of tacrine. Another approach to correcting the cholinergic deficit in patients with AD is the administration of direct-acting cholinergic agonists. Several of these, generally somewhat specific for the M1 muscarinic receptor, are now being tested.

Treatment of the secondary psychiatric syndromes in dementia require a multimodal approach that combines behavioral techniques with pharmacotherapy. Environmental factors and life events may contribute to these symptoms. A change in routine, caregiver, or place of residence may precipitate behavioral disturbances. Patients with decreased cognitive abilities are less able to to adapt to these changes, and more likely to respond with fear, anger, and agitation. Identification of the immediate precipitant to such behaviors may suggest an environmental change that will lessen the behavior. When this is not possible, other strategies that may help include decreasing overall sensory stimulation, redirecting patients, restructuring or clarifying daily routines, and designating one trusted caregiver to interact with the patient. Environments that allow patients to pace, and activity programs that include regular exercise, may permit a safe release of motor restlessness. Social contacts should be frequent, brief (because of limited attention), and supportive. A calm, reassuring voice and an occasional gentle touch may reduce episodes of agitated behavior. Families and other caregivers should be educated not to argue with patients when they misperceive the environment, but instead to be accepting and attempt to direct the patient to a less threatening topic of conversation.

Major depression occurs in about a quarter of patients with AD, and can markedly exacerbate functional disability. Degenerative brain changes may be related to the onset of depression. For example, one study of depressed patients with AD found fewer noradrenergic neurons in the locus ceruleus (Zubenko et al., 1989). Unfortunately, there are few research data on the treatment of depression in dementia patients. One double-blind trial with a placebo comparison group used imipramine, and found equal improvement with both treatments (Reifler et al., 1989). The anticholinergic side effects of the tricyclics may worsen confusion and cognitive dysfunction in patients with AD, and therefore it is probably preferable to use the SSRIs or other newer agents. The only double-blind, placebo-controlled trial with positive results used citalopram, a very selective serotonergic agent not available in the United States (Nyth and Gottfries, 1990). In addition to improvement in depression, patients in this study had decreased irritability and restlessness. An open trial of sertraline in 10 patients with end-stage AD who had acute behavioral changes found improvement in 6, including 5 who resumed eating (Volicer, Rheaume, and Cyr, 1994). These results suggest that undetected depression may account for many of the acute changes in behavior or functioning seen in patients with severe dementia, and that empiric treatment with an antidepressant medication may have unexpected benefits.

Psychosis and behavioral disturbances in AD often become unmanageable by families at home, and are a common reason for admission to nursing homes and psychiatric hospitals. Antipsychotic medications are most often used for agitation in dementia, but their effectiveness is controversial. Most controlled studies of antipsychotics in agitated dementia patients have important methodological limitations, including diagnostic heterogeneity in the subjects, variable definitions of agitation, the use of unvalidated scales, and the lack of a placebo group. A meta-analysis of the published, well-designed trials concluded that antipsychotics were effective in reducing agitation in dementia, but the effects were modest, with improvement in only 18% of patients above the expected placebo response rate (Schneider, Pollack, and Lyness, 1990). Few studies have directly compared antipsychotics with other agents. Haloperidol, oxazepam, and diphenhydramine had roughly equivalent effects in one study, but the lack of a placebo group makes interpretation of the results difficult (Coccaro et al., 1990). Case reports document the efficacy of clozapine (Oberholzer et al., 1992) and risperidone (Allen et al., 1995; Jeanblanc and Davis, 1995) for agitation in dementia, but controlled studies have not yet been published. The risk of orthostatic hypotension, and the need for weekly blood monitoring, make clozapine difficult to use in demented elderly patients unless they are in the hospital. Risperidone is preferable, because it combines the safety of the high-potency neuroleptics with a relatively low risk of extrapyramidal symptoms. However, demented patients appear to be susceptible to parkinsonian side effects and blood pressure changes unless risperidone doses are kept very low (probably under 1–2 mg/d). Olanzapine, a typical antipsychotic structurally related to clozapine but without the risk of agranulocytosis, has only recently become available. Its moderate sedative effect and lack of significant anticholinergic or orthostatic blood pressure effects may make it a useful drug in this population.

Antiepileptic drugs are increasingly being studied in demented patients with agitation, analogous to their usage in elderly patients with bipolar disorder and psychosis. Carbamazepine reduced total BPRS scores by 25%, and factor scores for hostility-suspiciousness and activation by 44%, in an open study of 15 demented inpatients who had been unresponsive to antipsychotics (Lemke, 1995). Side effects were generally mild and well tolerated at mean daily doses of 323 mg, with mean serum levels of 4.1 mcg/mL, although 2 patients had to discontinue the medication because of leukopenia and allergic reactions. More than half of the patients from several case series improved with valproate (Lott, McElroy, and Keys, 1995; Sival et al., 1994). Minimal ataxia and sedation occurred

at doses averaging about 500 mg a day and levels slightly below 50 mcg/mL. Controlled trials will be needed to establish the place of these agents in the treatment of dementia symptoms. The need for blood monitoring for levels and liver and hematologic function with these drugs limits their ease of use in demented patients.

A variety of other agents have been tried in patients with dementia and agitation. Buspirone has lessened agitation in some open-label studies (Herrmann and Eryavec, 1993; Sakauye, Camp, and Ford, 1993). Doses of up to 60 mg are sometimes required for the treatment of demented patients, but side effects remain minimal even at these doses. In an open trial of trazodone in 22 patients with dementia and behavioral problems, 82% of the patients had moderate or marked improvement (Houlihan et al., 1994). The sedation commonly seen with trazodone may be helpful for some agitated dementia patients. However, orthostatic hypotension occurs frequently and may lead to falls. Benzodiazepines are sometimes useful in reducing the anxiety that may lead to agitation, and short-term use, especially in mildly demented patients, may be helpful. However, the risk of amnesia and confusion leading to greater agitation limits the usefulness of these drugs in later-stage dementia patients. Case reports suggest possible benefit from beta-blockers, lithium, selegiline, and ECT, but the indications for these remain unclear in the absence of well-designed trials. There is some evidence that estrogen may be useful to reduce aggressive physical behavior in demented men (Kyomen, Nobel, and Wei, 1991).

References

AARP. *A profile of older Americans.* Washington, D.C.: American Association of Retired Persons, 1995.

Alexopoulos, G. S. 1992. Treatment of depression. In *Clinical geriatric psychopharmacology,* ed. Salzman, C. 2nd ed. Baltimore: Williams and Wilkins. 137–174.

Alexopoulos, G. S., Meyers, B. S., Young, R. C., Mattis, S., Kakuma, T. 1993. The course of geriatric depression with "reversible dementia": a controlled study. *Am. J. Psychiatry* 150(11):1693–99.

Allen, R. L., Walker, Z., D'Ath, P. J., Katona, C. L. 1995. Risperidone for psychotic and behavioural symptoms in Lewy body dementia [letter; see comments]. *Lancet* 346(8968):185.

Baldwin, R. C., and Jolley, D. J. 1986. The prognosis of depression in old age. *Br. J. Psychiatry* 149:574–583.

Bell, A. J., Cole, A., Eccleston, D., Ferrier, I. N. 1993. Lithium neurotoxicity at normal therapeutic levels [see comments]. *Br. J. Psychiatry* 162:689–692.

Berezin, M. 1970. Partial grief in family members and others who care for the elderly patient. *J. Geriatr. Psychiatry* 4:53–64.

——— 1972. Psychodynamic considerations of aging and the aged: an overview. *Am. J. Psychiatry* 128:33–41.

Berezin M., and Fern, D. 1967. Persistence of early emotional problems in a seventy-year-old woman. *J. Geriatr. Psychiatry* 1:45–60.

Berman, I., Merson, A., Rachov-Pavlov, J., Allan, E., Davidson, M., Losonczy, M. F. 1996. Risperidone in elderly schizophrenic patients: an open-label trial. *Am. J. Geriatric Psychiatry* 4:173–179.

Birren, J. E., and Schaie, K. W., eds. 1990. *Handbook of the psychology of aging.* 3rd ed. San Diego: Academic Press.

Black, D. W., Winokur, G., and Nasrallah, A. 1993. A multivariate analysis of the experience of 423 depressed inpatients treated with electroconvulsive therapy. *Convulsive Therapy* 9:112–120.

Blazer, D. G. 1994. Epidemiology of late-life depression. In *Diagnosis and treatment of depression in late life: results of the NIH Consensus Development Conference,* ed. Schneider, L. S., Reynolds, C. F., Lebowitz, B. D., et al. Washington, D.C.: American Psychiatry Press. 9–19.

Bohm, C., Robinson, D. S., Gammans, R. E., et al. 1990. Buspirone therapy in anxious elderly patients: a controlled clinical trial. *J. Clin. Psychopharmacol.* 10(3 suppl.):47S–57S.

Brodaty, H., Peters, K., and Boyce, P. 1991. Age and depression. *J. Affective Dis.* 23:137–149.

Burrows, A. B., Satlin, A., Salzman, C., Nobel, K., Lipsitz, L. A. 1995. Depression in a long-term care facility: clinical features and discordance between nursing assessment and patient interviews. *J. Am. Geriatr. Soc.* 43(10):1118–22.

Burvill, P. W., Stampfler, H. G., and Hall, W. D. 1986. Does depressive illness in the elderly have a poor prognosis? *Aust. N.Z. J. Psychiatry* 20:422–427.

Butler, R. 1963. The life review: an interpretation of reminiscence in the aged. *Psychiatry* 26:65–76.

Calamari, J. E., Faber, S. D., Hitsman, B. L., Poppe, C. J. 1994. Treatment of obsessive compulsive disorder in the elderly: a review and case example. *J. Behav. Ther. Exp. Psychiatry* 25(2):95–104.

Chengappa, K. N. R., Baker, R. W., and Kreinbrook, S. B. 1995. Clozapine use in female geriatric patients with psychoses. *J. Geriatr. Psychiatry Neurol.* 8:12–15.

Clark, D. C. 1991. *Suicide among the elderly.* Chicago: Center for Suicide Research and Prevention, Department of Psychiatry, Rush–Presbyterian–St. Luke's Medical Center.

Coccaro, E. F., Kramer, E., Zemishlany, Z., et al. 1990. Pharmacologic treatment of noncognitive behavioral disturbances in elderly demented patients. *Am. J. Psychiatry* 147:1640–45.

Colarusso, C., and Nemiroff, R. 1987. Clinical implications of adult developmental theory. *Am. J. Psychiatry* 144:1262–70.

Cusack, B., Nelson, A., and Richelson, E. 1994. Binding of antidepressants to human brain receptors: focus on newer generation compounds. *Psychopharmacology* 114:559–565.

Davis, K. L., Thal, L. J., Gamzu, E. R., et al. 1992. A double-blind, placebo-controlled multicenter study of tacrine for Alzheimer's disease. The Tacrine Collaborative Study Group [see comments]. *N. Engl. J. Med.* 327(18):1253–59.

Dunner, D. L., Cohn, J. B., Walshe, T., et al. 1992. Two combined, multicenter double-blind studies of paroxetine and doxepin in geriatric patients with major depression. *J. Clin. Psychiatry* 53(suppl.):57–60.

Erikson, E. 1959. Growth and crises of the healthy personality. *Psychological Issues* 1:50–100.

Evans, D. A., Funkenstein, H., Albert, M. S., et al. 1989. Prevalence of Alzheimer's disease in a community population of older persons: higher than previously noted. *J. Am. Med. Assoc.* 262:2551–56.

Farlow, M., Gracon, S. I., Hershey, L. A., Lewis, K. W., Sadowsky, C. H., Dolan-Ureno, J. 1992. A controlled trial of tacrine in Alzheimer's disease. The Tacrine Study Group [see comments]. *JAMA* 268(18):2523–29.

Fiatarone, M. A., O'Neill, E. F., Ryan, N. D., et al. 1994. Exercise training and nutritional supplementation for physical frailty in very elderly people. *N. Engl. J. Med.* 330:1769–75.

Flint, A. J. 1994. Epidemiology and comorbidity of anxiety disorders in the elderly. *Am. J. Psychiatry* 151(5):640–649.

Fogel, B. 1996. *Old, sick, depressed . . . and badly in need of psychotherapy. Psychotherapy? Psychopharmacology? Which treatment for which depression in the older adult?* Boston: Boston Society for Gerontologic Psychiatry.

Folstein, M., Folstein, S., and McHugh, P. 1975. Mini-Mental State: a practical method for grading the cognitive state of patients for the clinician. *J. Psychiatr. Res.* 12:189–198.

Foster, J. R. 1992. Use of lithium in elderly psychiatric patients: a review of the literature. *Lithium* 3:77–93.

Gallagher, D., and Thompson, L. 1983. Effectiveness of psychotherapy for both endogenous and non-endogenous depression in older adult outpatients. *J. Gerontol.* 38:707–712.

George, L. K. 1994. Social factors and depression in late life. In *Diagnosis and treatment of depression in late life: results of the NIH Consensus Development Conference,* ed. Schneider, L. S., Reynolds, C. F., Lebowitz, B. D., et al. Washington, D.C.: American Psychiatric Press. 131–153.

Georgotas, A., and McCue, R. E. 1989. The additional benefit of extending an antidepressant trial past seven weeks in the depressed elderly. *Int. J. Geriatr. Psychiatry* 4:191–195.

Georgotas, A., McCue, R. E., and Cooper, T. B. 1989. A placebo-controlled comparison of nortriptyline and phenelzine in maintenance therapy of elderly depressed patients. *Arch. Gen. Psychiatry* 46:783–786.

Georgotas, A., McCue, R. E., Cooper, T. B., Nagachandran, N., Chang, I. 1988. How effective and safe is continuation therapy in elderly depressed patients? *Arch. Gen. Psychiatry* 45:929–932.

Glasser, M., and Rabins, P. 1984. Mania in the elderly. *Age and Aging* 13:210–213.

Glassman, A., Roose, S., and Bigger, J. 1993. The safety of tricyclic antidepressants in cardiac patients. *JAMA* 269:2673–75.

Gurian, B., and Rosowsky, E. 1990. Low-dose methylphenidate in the very old. *J. Geriatr. Psychiatry Neurol.* 3:152–154.

Harris, M. J., and Jeste, D. V. 1988. Late-onset schizophrenia: an overview. *Schizophr. Bull.* 14:39–55.

Herings, R. M., Stricker, B. H., de Boer, A., Bakker, A., and Sturmans, F. 1995. Benzodiazepines and the risk of falling leading to femur fractures: dosage more important than elimination half-life. *Arch. Intern. Med.* 155(16):1801–7.

Herrmann, N., and Eryavec, G. 1993. Buspirone in the management of agitation and aggression associated with dementia. *Am. J. Geriatric Psychiatry* 1:249–253.

Himmelfarb, S., and Murrell, S. A. 1984. The prevalence and correlates of anxiety symptoms in older adults. *Journal of Psychology* 116:159–167.

Himmelhoch, J. M., Neil, J. F., May, S. J., Fuchs, C. Z., Licata, S. M. 1980. Age, dementia, dyskinesias, and lithium response. *Am. J. Psychiatry* 1980; 137:941–945.

Hirschfield, R., Klerman, G., Lavori, P., Keller, M., Griffith, P., Coryell, W. 1989. Premorbid personality assessments of first onset of major depression. *Arch. Gen. Psychiatry* 46:345–350.

Hoch, C. C., Reynolds, C. F., Monk, T. H., et al. 1990. Comparison of sleep-disordered breathing among healthy elderly in the seventh, eighth, and ninth decades of life. *Sleep* 13:502–511.

Hocking, L. B., and Koenig, H. G. 1995. Anxiety in medically ill older patients: a review and update. *Int. J. Psychiatry Med.* 25(3):221–38.

Houlihan, D. J., Mulsant, B. H., Sweet, R. A., et al. 1994. A naturalistic study of trazodone in the treatment of behavioral complications of dementia. *Am. J. Geriatric Psychiatry* 2:78–85.

Huber, S. T., Friedenberg, D. L., Shuttleworth, E. C., et al. 1989. Neuropsychological impairments associated with the severity of Parkinson's disease. *J. Neuropsychiatry Clin. Neurosci.* 1:154–158.

Jacobs, S., Hansen, F., Kasl, S., Ostfeld, A., Berkman, L., Kim, K. 1990. Anxiety disorders during acute bereavement: risk and risk factors. *J. Clin. Psychiatry* 51:269–274.

Jeanblanc, W., and Davis, Y. B. 1995. Risperidone for treating dementia-associated aggression [letter]. *Am. J. Psychiatry* 152(8):1239.

Jeste, D. V., Manley, M., and Harris, M. J. 1991. Psychoses. In *Comprehensive review of geriatric psychiatry*, ed. Sadavoy, J., Lazarus, L. W., and Jarvik, L. F. Washington, D.C.: American Psychiatric Press. 353–368.

Jeste, D. V., Harris, M. J., Pearlson, G. D., et al. 1988. Late-onset schizophrenia: studying clinical validity. *Psychiatr. Clin. North Am.* 11:1–14.

Jeste, D. V., Caligiuri, M. P., Paulsen, J. S., et al. 1995. Risk of tardive dyskinesia in older patients: a prospective longitudinal study of 266 outpatients. *Arch. Gen. Psychiatry* 52:756–765.

Jeste, D. V., Eastham, J. H., Lacro, J. P., Gierz, M., Field, M. G., Harris, M. J. 1996. Management of late-life psychosis. *J. Clin. Psychiatry* 57(suppl. 3):39–45.

Katz, I. R., Simpson, G. M., Curlik, S. M., Parmelee, P. A., Muhly, C. 1990. Pharmacologic treatment of major depression for elderly patients in residential care settings. *J. Clin. Psychiatry* (51 suppl.):41–47; discussion 48.

Knapp, M. J., Knopman, D. S., Solomon, P. R., Pendlebury, W. W., Davis, C. S., Gracon, S. I. 1994. A 30-week randomized controlled trial of high-dose tacrine in patients with Alzheimer's disease. The Tacrine Study Group [see comments]. *JAMA* 271(13):985–991.

Krauthammer, C., and Klerman, G. L. 1978. Secondary mania: manic syndromes associated with antecedent physical illnesses or drugs. *Arch. Gen. Psychiatry* 35:1333–39.

Kushnir, S. L. 1986. Lithium-antidepressant combinations in the treatment of depressed, physically ill geriatric patients. *Am. J. Psychiatry* 143:378–379.

Kyomen, H. H., Nobel, K. W., and Wei, J. Y. 1991. The use of estrogen to decrease aggressive physical behavior in elderly men with dementia. *J. Am. Geriatr. Soc.* 39:1110–12.

Larson, E., Reifler, B., Featherstone, H., English, D. 1984. Dementia in elderly outpatients: a prospective study. *Ann. Intern. Med.* 100:417–423.

Lazarus, L., Sadavoy, J., and Langsley, P. 1991. Individual psychotherapy. In *Comprehensive Review of Geriatric Psychiatry,* ed. Sadavoy, J., Lazarus, L., and Jarvik, L. Washington, D.C.: American Psychiatric Association Press. 487–512.

Lemke, M. R. 1995. Effect of carbamazepine on agitation in Alzheimer's inpatients refractory to neuroleptics. *J. Clin. Psychiatry* 56(8):354–357.

Leventhal, E. A. 1996. Biology of aging. In *Comprehensive Review of Geriatric Psychiatry—II*, ed. Sadavoy, J., Lazarus, L. W., Jarvik, L. F., Grossberg, G. T. Washington, D.C.: American Psychiatric Press. 81–112.

Levine, S., Napoliello, M. J., and Domantay, A. G. 1988. An open study of buspirone in octogenarians with anxiety. *Human Psychopharmacology* 4:51–53.

Livingston, H. M., Livingston, M. G., and Fell, S. 1994. The Lockerbie disaster: a 3-year follow-up of elderly victims. *Int. J. Geriatr. Psychiatry* 9:989–994.

Lott, A. D., McElroy, S. L., and Keys, M. A. 1995. Valproate in the treatment of behavioral agitation in elderly patients with dementia. *J. Neuropsychiatry Clin. Neurosci.* 7(3):314–319.

Lyness, J., Cox, C., Curry, J., Conwell, Y., King, D., Caine, E. 1995. Older age and the underreporting of depressive symptoms. *J. Am. Geriatr. Soc.* 43:216–221.

Madhusoodanan, S., Brenner, R., Araujo, L., Abaza, A. 1995. Efficacy of risperidone treatment for psychoses associated with schizophrenia, schizoaffective disorder, bipolar disorder, or senile dementia in 11 geriatric patients: a case series. *J. Clin. Psychiatry* 56(11):514–518.

Masters, W. H., and Johnson, V. F. 1970. *Human sexual inadequacy.* Boston: Little, Brown.

McKhann, G., Drachman, D., Folstein, M., et al. 1984. Clinical diagnosis of Alzheimer's disease: report of the NINCDS-ADRDA work group under the auspices of Department of Health and Human Services Task Force on Alzheimer's disease. *Neurology* 34:939–944.

Meats, P., Timol, M., and Jolley, D. 1991. Prognosis of depression in the elderly. *Br. J. Psychiatry* 159:659–663.

Miles, L., and Dement, W. 1980. Sleep and aging. *Sleep* 3:119–220.

Myers, D. K., Weissman, M. M., Tischler, G. L., et al. 1984. Six-month prevalence of psychiatric disorders in three communities. *Arch. Gen. Psychiatry* 41:959–967.

Nemeroff, C. B., DeVane, C. L., and Pollack, B. G. 1996. Newer antidepressants and the cytochrome P450 system. *Am. J. Psychiatry* 153:311–331.

Neugarten, B. 1970. Adaptation and the life cycle. *J. Geriatr. Psychiatry* 17:71–87.

——— 1979. Time, age, and the life cycle. *Am. J. Psychiatry* 136:887–894.

Nyth, A. L., and Gottfries, C. G. 1990. The clinical efficacy of citalopram in treatment of emotional disturbances in dementia disorders: a Nordic multicentre study. *Br. J. Psychiatry* 157:894–901.

Oberholzer, A. F., Hendriksen, C., Monsch, A. U., et al. 1992. Safety and effectiveness of low-dose clozapine in psychogeriatric patients: a preliminary study. *Int. Psychogeriatr.* 4:187–195.

O'Leary, D., Gill, D., Gregory, S., Shawcross, C. 1994. The effectiveness of real versus simulated electroconvulsive

therapy in depressed elderly patients. *Int. J. Geriatr. Psychiatry* 9:567–571.

Parmelee, P., Katz, I., and Lawton, M. 1989. Depression among institutionalized aged: assessment and prevalence estimate. *J. Gerontol.* 44:M22–M29.

——— 1993. Anxiety and its association with depression among institutionalized elderly. *Am. J. Geriatric Psychiatry* 1:46–58.

Pearlson, G. D., Kreger, L., Rabins, P. V., et al. 1989. A chart review study of late-onset and early-onset schizophrenia. *Am. J. Psychiatry* 146:1568–74.

Pitner, J. K., Mintzer, J. E., Pennypacker, L. C., Jackson, C. W. 1995. Efficacy and adverse effects of clozapine in four elderly psychotic patients. *J. Clin. Psychiatry* 56(5):180–185.

Pope, H. G., Jr., McElroy, S. L., Satlin, A., Hudson, J. I., Keck, P. E., Jr., Kalish, R. 1988. Head injury, bipolar disorder, and response to valproate. *Compr. Psychiatry* 29(1):34–38.

Prager, S., and Jeste, D. 1993. Sensory impairment in late-life schizophrenia. *Schizophr. Bull.* 19:755–772.

Raj, B. A., Corvea, M. H., and Dagon, E. M. 1993. The clinical characteristics of panic disorder in the elderly: a retrospective study. *J. Clin. Psychiatry* 54:150–155.

Regier, D. A., Narrow, W. E., and Rae, D. S. 1990. The epidemiology of anxiety disorders: the Epidemiologic Catchment Area (ECA) experience. *J. Psychiatr. Res.* 24(suppl. 2):3–14.

Reifler, B. V., Teri, L., Raskind, M., et al. 1989. A double blind trial of a tricyclic antidepressant in Alzheimer's patients with and without depression. *Am. J. Psychiatry* 146:45–49.

Renshaw, D. C. 1996. Sexuality and aging. In *Comprehensive review of geriatric psychiatry—II,* ed. Sadavoy, J., Lazarus, L. W., Jarvik, L. F., and Grossberg, G. T. Washington, D.C.: American Psychiatric Press. 713–729.

Roccaforte, W. H., and Burke, W. J. 1990. Use of psychostimulants for the elderly. *Hosp. Community Psychiatry* 41:1330–33.

Roose, S. P., Dalack, G. W., Glassman, A. H., et al. 1991. Cardiovascular effects of bupropion in depressed patients with heart disease. *Am. J. Psychiatry* 148:512–516.

Roose, S. P., Glassman, A. H., Attia, E., Woodring, S. 1994. Comparative efficacy of selective serotonin reuptake inhibitors and tricyclics in the treatment of melancholia. *Am. J. Psychiatry* 151(12):1735–39.

Rubert, M. P., Eisdorfer, C., and Loewenstein, D. A. 1996. Normal aging: changes in sensory/perceptual and cognitive abilities. In *Comprehensive review of geriatric psychiatry—II,* ed. Sadavoy, J., Lazarus, L. W., Jarvik, L. F., Grossberg, G. T. Washington, D.C.: American Psychiatric Press. 113–134.

Sakauye, K. M., Camp, C. J., and Ford, P. A. 1993. Effects of buspirone on agitation associated with dementia. *Am. J. Geriatric Psychiatry* 1:82–84.

Salzman, C. 1990. Anxiety in the elderly: treatment strategies. *J. Clin. Psychiatry* 51(suppl.):18–21.

Salzman, C., Vaccaro, B., Lieff, J., Weiner, A. 1995. Clozapine in older patients with psychosis and behavioral disruption. *Am. J. Geriatric Psychiatry* 3:26–33.

Scharf, M. B., Mayleben, D. W., Kaffeman, M., Krall, R., Ochs, R. 1991. Dose response effects of zolpidem in normal geriatric subjects. *J. Clin. Psychiatry* 52:77–83.

Schmucker, D. L. 1984. Drug disposition in the elderly: a review of the critical factors. *J. Am. Geriatr. Soc.* 32:144–149.

Schneider, L., Pollack, V., and Lyness, S. 1990. A meta-analysis of controlled trials of neuroleptic treatment in dementia. *J. Am. Geriatr. Soc.* 38:553–563.

Shaw, S. H., Curson, H., and Coquelin, J. P. 1992. A double-blind, comparative study of zolpidem and placebo in the treatment of insomnia in elderly psychiatric in-patients. *J. International Medical Research* 20:150–161.

Shulman, K. I., Tohen, M., Satlin, A., Mallya, G., Kalunian, D. 1992. Mania compared with unipolar depression in old age. *Am. J. Psychiatry* 149(3):341–345.

Sival, R. C., Haffmans, P. M., van Gent, P. P., van Nieuwkerk, J. F. 1994. The effects of sodium valproate on disturbed behavior in dementia [letter]. *J. Am. Geriatr. Soc.* 42(8):906–907.

Small, G. W., Komanduri, R., Gitlin, M. W., et al. 1986. The influence of age on guilt expression in major depression. *Int. J. Geriatr. Psychiatry* 1:121–126.

Smith, J. M., and Baldessarini, R. J. 1980. Changes in prevalence, severity, and recovery in tardive dyskinesia with age. *Arch. Gen. Psychiatry* 37:1368–73.

Taffet, G. E. 1996. Age-related physiologic changes. In *Geriatrics review syllabus: a core curriculum in geriatric medicine,* ed. Reuben, D. B., Yoshikawa, T. T., and Besdine, R. W. 3rd ed. Dubuque, Iowa: Kendall/Hunt Publishing Co.

Teri, L., Curtis, J., Gallagher-Thompson, D., Thompson, L. 1994. Cognitive-behavioral therapy with depressed older adults. In *Diagnosis and treatment of depression in late life: results of the NIH Consensus Development Conference,* ed. Schneider, L. S., Reynolds, C. F., Lebowitz, B. D., et al. Washington, D.C.: American Psychiatric Press. 279–291.

Thompson, L., and Gallagher, D. 1985. Depression and its treatment in the elderly. *Aging* 348:14–18.

Vaillant, G. 1977. *Adaptation to life.* Boston: Little, Brown.
——— 1990. Natural history of male psychological health, XII. A 45-year study of predictors of successful aging at age 65. *Am. J. Psychiatry* 147:31–37.

Volicer, L., Rheaume, Y., and Cyr, D. 1994. Treatment of depression in advanced Alzheimer's disease using sertraline. *J. Geriatr. Psychiatry Neurol.* 7(4):227–229.

Von Moltke, L., Greenblatt, D., and Shader, R. 1993. Clinical pharmacokinetics of antidepressants in the elderly. *Clinical Pharmacokinetics* 24:141–160.

Watkins, P. B., Zimmerman, H. J., Knapp, M. J., Gracon, S. I., Lewis, K. W. 1994. Hepatotoxic effects of tacrine administration in patients with Alzheimer's disease [see comments]. *JAMA* 271(13):992–998.

Weissman, M. M., Bruce, M. L., Leak, P. J., et al. 1991. Affective disorders. In *Psychiatric disorders in America: the Epidemiologic Catchment Area study,* ed. Robins, L. N., and Regier, D. A. New York: Free Press. 53–80.

Wilkinson, A. M., Anderson, D. N., and Peters, S. 1993. Age and the effects of ECT. *Int. J. Geriatr. Psychiatry* 8:401–406.

Yassa, R., and Cvejic, J. 1994. Valproate in the treatment of posttraumatic bipolar disorder in a psychogeriatric patient. *J. Geriatr. Psychiatry Neurol.* 7(1):55–57.

Yassa, R., Nair, V., Nastase, C., Camille, Y., Belzile, L. 1988. Prevalence of bipolar disorder in a psychogeriatric population. *J. Aff. Disorders* 14:197–201.

Yesavage, J. A., Brink, T. L., Rose, T. L., et al. 1983. Development and validation of a geriatric depression screening scale: a preliminary report. *J. Psychiatr. Res.* 17:37–49.

Zisook, S., Schucter, S. R., and Sledge, P. 1994. Diagnostic and treatment considerations in depression associated with late-life bereavement. In *Diagnosis and treatment of depression in late life: results of the NIH Consensus Development Conference,* ed. Schneider, L. S., Reynolds, C. F., Lebowitz, B. D., et al. Washington, D.C.: American Psychiatric Press. 419–435.

Zubenko, G. S., Moossy, J., Martinez, A. J., et al. 1989. A brain regional analysis of morphologic and cholinergic abnormalities in Alzheimer's disease. *Arch. Neurol.* 46:634–638.

Recommended Reading

Erikson, E. H. 1997. *The life cycle completed.* New York: W. W. Norton.

Sadavoy, J., Lazarus, L. W., Jarvik, L. F., and Grossberg, G. T., eds. 1996. *Comprehensive review of geriatric psychiatry: II.* Washington, D.C.: American Psychiatric Press.

Salzman, C., ed. 1998. *Clinical geriatric psychopharmacology.* Baltimore: Williams & Wilkins.

JEAN A. FRAZIER

The Person with Mental Retardation

Mental retardation (MR) is a relatively common neuro-psychiatric disorder in children, adolescents, and adults. By definition, mental retardation is a condition associated with subaverage intelligence and with impairments in adaptive behavior. Epidemiologic studies indicate that approximately 2–3% of the school age population and 1% of the adult population have mental retardation (Cook and Leventhal, 1992; APA, 1994).

Mental retardation is a complex problem affecting millions of handicapped people. There are different severities of mental retardation, ranging from mild to profound, and a variety of etiologies. Advances in the field have been limited because studies are often confined to individuals with specific syndromic conditions which have MR as one manifestation, e.g., Down syndrome, Prader-Willi syndrome. Furthermore, most psychiatric studies assessing mood, thought, and behavioral disturbances exclude individuals with IQs below 70.

This chapter provides an overview of mental retardation. The disorder is defined, and its epidemiology, etiology, evaluation, prevention, and treatment are discussed.

Definition of Mental Retardation

In 1994 the American Psychiatric Association's *Diagnostic and Statistical Manual of Mental Disorders,* fourth edition (DSM-IV), defined 3 criteria necessary to diagnose mental retardation. An individual must have: (1) subaverage general intellectual functioning based on a standardized intelligence test (IQ), (2) concurrent deficits or impairments in adaptive behavior, and (3) the presence of both subaverage intellectual and adaptive functioning that must occur prior to the age of 18 years.

Subaverage intelligence is defined as a full scale intelligence quotient <70 (2 standard deviations below the mean). There are 4 specific diagnostic levels of retardation:

1. Mild: IQ from 50–55 to 70. These individuals develop social and communication skills. They frequently hold jobs and marry. Owing to their relatively normal functioning as adults, most of the patients disappear from medical care surveys.

2. Moderate: IQ from 35–40 to 50–55. This category includes individuals who can talk, but whose speech patterns are generally poor. They often have somewhat limited social awareness. They can be trained to take care of most personal needs such as dressing, feeding, and washing themselves. They can perform chores and often work in sheltered workshops. Moderate supervision is usually required.

3. Severe: IQ from 20–25 to 35–40. Early in life it is clear that the development in these individuals is abnormal. They generally have slow and poor motor development and limited or no speech. The severely retarded can attend to their activities of daily living under close supervision as well as perform certain tasks such as dumping garbage and drying dishes. They will often turn on the television or radio and rock rhythmically to the sounds.

4. Profound: IQ < or equal to 20–25. These persons show a high incidence of neurological deficits as well as poor cognitive and social capacities of a degree that makes them commonly unaware of who is caring for them. Speech is often absent. They require constant supervision. Most reside in special care settings. Measurable IQ scores are difficult to obtain.

A retarded individual's adaptive functioning must be equal to or below what would be expected for his or her IQ (APA, 1994). Although IQ is an important consideration in diagnosing the severity or subtype of mental retardation, differential classification according to subtype requires clinicians to consider adaptive functioning with great care. There are important and often subtle differences in adaptive functioning that can distinguish the mildly retarded individual from the moderately retarded individual, the moderately from the severely retarded individual, and the severely from the profoundly retarded individual.

Although in practice clinicians often use the full scale intelligence quotient (FSIQ) as the main criterion of developmental retardation, deficits in adaptive behavior are equally important for the diagnosis.

The DSM-IV places retardation on Axis II along with personality disorders (APA, 1994).

DSM IV multiaxial system
Axis I: clinical disorders including disorders first diagnosed in infancy, childhood, or adolescence
Axis II: Personality disorders and mental retardation
Axis III: General medical conditions
Axis IV: Psychosocial and environmental problems
Axis V: Global assessment of functioning

Intelligence

A fundamental aspect of mental retardation is lowered intelligence. Intelligence, however, is often difficult to define. According to Robinson and Robinson (1965), "intelligence refers to the whole class of cognitive behaviors which reflect an individual's capacity to solve problems with insight, to adapt himself to new situations, to think abstractly, and to profit from his experience . . . It is thus a forever emerging capacity which differs both in quality and in breadth with the individual's age and experience as well as with his constitution" (p. 15). The concept of intelligence must be treated in relation to other facets of personality.

Intelligence tests have limitations in that they focus specifically on cognitive mechanisms and abstract ability, as distinct from knowledge. Wechsler's test of intelligence, for example, emphasizes factual information and the ability to reason abstractly.

Epidemiology

Prevalence

Mental retardation is a relatively common neuropsychiatric disorder. Most epidemiologic studies estimate the prevalence as being 2–3% in the school age population (Cook and Leventhal, 1992). Approximately 80–85% of the MR population falls within the mild range, and 7–10% make up the moderate group. The severely and profoundly retarded groups combined make up 1–2% of the total MR population.

The prevalence rate of moderate to profound mental retardation in most studies is 3 to 5 per 1000 population (Kiely, 1987). The rate of moderate mental retardation is 2/1000, of severe mental retardation is 1.3/1000, and of profound mental retardation is 0.4/1000 (McLaren and Bryson, 1987). Lifelong prevalence of mental retardation varies with age, sex, and socioeconomic status (Kiely, 1987; McLaren and Bryson, 1987; Rutter et al., 1976). Prevalence increases from preschool to adolescence and decreases in early adulthood (Kiely, 1987; McLaren and Bryson, 1987).

Only 1% of the adult population is mentally retarded (Tarjan, 1966). Income levels for the mildly retarded approach those of normal individuals, signifying that many retarded persons learn to function well in the community. Charles (1953) has shown that many who have been considered mentally retarded during their school years succeed in leading independent lives in adulthood. Therefore, the diagnosis of mental retardation in childhood does not necessarily predict retardation in adult life.

Gender Ratio

The highest male-to-female ratio is seen among the mildly retarded (1.9:1) (Richardson, Koller, and Katz, 1986). In the severely to profoundly retarded range, the ratio is 1.5:1 (Rowitz, 1991). A male predominance exists, but the reasons for this are not entirely clear. Perhaps social and cultural prejudice leads to boys being labeled as MR more readily than girls. There also may be an overrepresentation of X-linked disorders, such as fragile X syndrome (Richardson, Koller, and Katz, 1986, McLaren and Bryson, 1987).

Socioeconomic Status

Mild mental retardation is overrepresented at the lower end of the socioeconomic continuum, implying social contributions to the retardation (Kiely, 1987; Bregman and Hodapp, 1991; Zigler, Balla, and Hodapp, 1984). Moderate to profound mental retardation is more equitably distributed across the socioeconomic strata.

Etiology

In approximately 25% of the mentally retarded population there is a known biologic origin. The etiology is less likely to be identified in those with mild mental retardation, and more likely to be known in those with moderate to profound MR. The etiology in the less severe forms of mental retardation may be related to environmental deprivation. The etiology for mental retardation is not known in only 25–40% of children with IQs less than 50 (McLaren and Bryson, 1987). Known etiologies can generally be divided into prenatal, perinatal, and postnatal factors. These factors are outlined in Table 30.1.

Prenatal Factors

During the period of fetal formation in pregnancy, a number of conditions may cause retardation. These prenatal factors are listed in Table 30.1. Best known among these is German measles, or rubella, a viral disease normally not of great consequence when it occurs in childhood. Occurrence in women during the first trimester of pregnancy, however, carries considerable likelihood that the unborn child will suffer central nervous system damage and consequent mental retardation.

Malnourished women tend to have smaller children than healthy women and to have premature children more often. Evidence indicates that insufficient amino acids for proper brain cell development, owing to protein-deficient diets during pregnancy, are a cause of mental retardation. In addition to dietary deficiencies, poor people are also likely to suffer from inadequate medical and obstetrical care, which increases the risk of mental retardation.

Noxious agents can also contribute to mental retardation. Some years ago the drug thalidomide, given to pregnant women, was found to result in the birth of deformed and retarded babies; the drug has since been withdrawn. Other agents produce similar effects, but most of these are now prohibited. X-rays of the mother's abdomen were given more commonly in the past to judge the size and position of the fetus, but this practice, too, has been found damaging to the developing tissues and has, for the most part, been discontinued. Sounding and amniocentesis are now used more commonly to evaluate fetal health.

Chromosomal abnormalities contribute to approximately 50% of prenatal etiologies in individuals with IQs less than 50 (Abuelo, 1991). Genetic disorders can involve either a single gene anomaly or complicated polygenic combinations of chromosomal abnormalities, with Down syndrome being the most common single factor (Bregman and Hodapp, 1991; Abramowicz and Richardson, 1975).

Genetic Disorders

The most common and well-known chromosomal abnormality that is associated with mental retardation is Down syndrome. This syndrome was first described a hundred years ago and is notable for the oriental shape of the eye, the palpebral fissures, and a fold at the inner corner of the eye. In addition, looseness of muscular tone, abundant skin around the neck, high cheekbones, and a protruding tongue are generally seen; hands tend to be

Table 30.1 Known etiologies of mental retardation

Prenatal Factors	Perinatal Factors	Postnatal Factors
Maternal infection (e.g., rubella, toxoplasmosis, cytomegalovirus, herpes simplex, hepatitis, human immunodeficiency virus, syphilis)	Asphyxia	Bacterial infections (e.g., hemophilus influenza, diplococcus pneumonia, viral encephalitis, meningitis)
In utero drug exposure (e.g., ETOH, heroin, cocaine)	Birth injury	Head trauma
Genetic disorders and chromosomal abnormalities (e.g., neurofibromatosis, Down syndrome)	Prematurity	Lead poisoning
Inborn errors of metabolism (disorders of lipid metabolism, mucopolysaccharide metabolism, oligosaccharide and glycoprotein metabolism, amino acid metabolism, e.g., phenylketonuria)		Metabolic abnormalities (low T4)
X-ray exposure		Gross brain disease (intracranial neoplasm)
Maternal mercury poisoning		Malnutrition
Maternal medication exposure (thalidomide)		
Maternal illness (malnutrition, emphysema, anemia)		

broad and thick and to have one thick line instead of the several creases that demarcate the normal palm, while the fingers are usually short and curve inward.

These physical characteristics are related to clearly demonstrated chromosomal abnormalities, although variations occur in the nature of these abnormalities and in the severity of the syndrome. At one time children with Down syndrome died before puberty; now, with better care, they are living into adulthood. Three basic etiological groups have been established: those with 3 of chromosome number 21 (trisomy); those in whom chromosome combinations of both normal and trisomic cells are found (mosaicism); and those in whom a translocation and fusion of 2 chromosomes, mostly numbers 15 and 21, is found. Overall these patients have extra chromosomal material, bearing 47 instead of the normal 46 human chromosomes, and the different combinations of this genetic material derange a variety of developing tissues. Some abnormal genetic material may be borne by parents free of the syndrome. In addition to hereditary factors, however, advanced maternal age increases the likelihood that a child will be born with Down syndrome. More recently an increased incidence of leukemia and Alzheimer changes have been reported in Down individuals.

The general characterization of these children as lovable and docile, calm and cheerful, is not altogether accurate. Although they will not be very troublesome if left alone with no demands placed upon them, when pressured to learn, to perform on a higher level, or to behave in more mature social ways, they can begin to show irritability and some of the negativism and reluctance seen in many children who are being taught.

The incidence of Down syndrome in the general population is approximately 1/1000 (Kinsbourne, 1985). Sex chromosome abnormalities often leading to subaverage intelligence include fragile X syndrome and multiple X (47XXX). Fragile X syndrome is the second most frequent chromosomal cause of mental retardation after Down syndrome (Goldson and Hagerman, 1992).

Perinatal Factors

Children injured by trauma to the brain during delivery or those who do not receive sufficient oxygen during this period may suffer internal bleeding. Death of brain tissue may result, leading to many defects in cerebral functioning and to mental retardation.

Children born prematurely may also suffer from mental retardation. An infant with a birth weight under 2300 gm tends to have less fully formed organs and to have gone through labor much more rapidly than larger newborns. A premature infant is particularly vulnerable to damage during labor and is also more likely to have central nervous system damage both because tissues are incompletely formed and because the infant may not be able to make the shift from being a dependent organism within the mother to being a self-sustaining, breathing system after birth. Almost one-quarter of children born with cerebral palsy have birth weights under 2500 gm. Neurological damage and retardation accompanied by electroencephalogram (EEG) abnormalities are more common in inverse ratio to birth weight. Modern advances in perinatal care have increased the survival of 1000 gm and even 500 gm fetuses, which have a 25% and 50% likelihood of mental retardation, respectively, entailing still another group of ethical problems. Thus modern technology and improvements in perinatal care combine with growing numbers of pregnant adolescents to increase the number of retarded children.

Postnatal Factors

Known biological postnatal factors are listed in Table 30.1.

The majority of children with mental retardation have mild MR with no evidence of organic brain syndrome. In fact, of the roughly 6 million retarded individuals in the United States, 80% are mildly retarded. This group comes predominantly from the lower socioeconomic strata of our society, and it is believed that many of its members are retarded owing to environmental deprivation. This underscores the fact that in all biological development an intrinsic factor exists that is stimulated to function by the environment. Development of each function of the body will vary according to the surrounding environment. For example, a child who is brought up in the dark or reared in isolation will be less "intelligent" when measured by the conventional social and academic standards. A child brought up in a minority group in the midst of severe poverty will often hear a grammatically different language, will be less well fed, and will get less medical care, less attention, and fewer opportunities to focus on intellectually stimulating objects and activities than middle-class children. It is the lack of proper nurturance, care, and environmental stimuli that causes much of the mental retardation in our society.

The purpose of presenting these categories is not to list all the physical causes of mental retardation but merely to indicate the principal ones and to mention the various ways in which intellectual function can be altered. All of the conditions presented can occur in mild or severe forms, so that the diagnosis of one syndrome does not necessarily determine the patient's level of intellectual functioning. A general correlation, however, does exist between more profound retardation and the presence of organic features; children who have suffered demonstrable brain damage, with definitive, visible loss of brain tissue, are more likely than others to have severe forms of mental retardation.

The Growth and Development of Retarded Children

A child born mildly retarded may show some signs of the condition at birth. If no physical abnormalities are apparent, as in the majority of cases, the parents will not notice anything remarkable. The typical course of development is one in which the parents find that the child is easy to manage. They may find him or her a bit quiet and undemonstrative, and often remark that "this has been the easiest baby." The child will tend to go through the normal stages of development slowly. The child is likely to play with his or her fingers, to follow objects, and to reach for people in a "lazy" manner. Children normally sit up at about the age of 6 months; the retarded child may not sit until 10 or 11 months. This developmental delay may not alarm the parents, because the child eats and sleeps in a smooth and rhythmic way. The child may manifest the same casualness in crawling and trying to walk; he or she may not seem to make the effort. Instead of being interested in standing and tottering about at 1 year, the child is still playfully sitting. Not walking is considered normal until about 17 months; the retarded child may begin to walk around this time or may not walk until age 2 years or later. Whereas speech comes to the normal child before the age of 2, the retarded child may not say anything significant until age 3 or 4. With the delay in these areas of development, most parents become worried and are likely to seek professional help (Work, 1983).

Traditional views have reinforced the notion that if a child is backward because of mental retardation, he or she will be uniformly backward in all developmental and intellectual functions. However, retarded children show different levels of functioning in different areas, although their developmental style is usually delayed and less energetic than that of normal children. Toilet training is slower, partly because the speech and communication pattern is absent and because the child may not get the sense of what is being taught as readily as the normal child; he or she may also enjoy mouthing and smearing more than other children.

According to Erik Erikson's (1950) developmental scheme, the first psychological phase is the oral phase, in which the mouth is the area for making contact with the world, for exploring and tasting, as well as for incorporating the food essential to life. The first mutual regulation between mother and child—the child's pattern of accepting things and the mother's or the culture's way of giving—occurs in this phase. During this stage, the child's basic sense of trust evolves. It is also in the oral phase that the child is most helpless and dependent on the caretaking abilities of the mother or other parenting individual. The retarded child has a prolonged period of dependency on caretakers.

Normally the child progresses in musculoskeletal development as he or she separates from others, gets up and starts moving around, and explores the world. The child learns to submit to certain rules of society, while becoming more competent in his or her adventures into the world. A fundamental need of the child is to achieve a sense of autonomy. The normal child may tussle and squabble over being trained on the toilet, but he or she proceeds with learning this and other things simultaneously. For the retarded child this evolution is slower, the tendency toward mouthing is greater, and dependency is more salient.

The poorly developed speech of the retarded child alters his or her conceptualization of the world. The delay in word usage by people of subaverage intellect is both the sign of their handicap and a cause of further handicapping. Earle (1961) observed that in the subnormal, weakness and simplicity in biological and psychic development tend to be inherent. This finding overlaps that of Webster (1963): retarded children studied in nursery schools tend to be more apathetic, to play with less initiative, to sit more quietly with a toy, and to be more self-involved or mildly autistic than others. They can be roused, but they require more stimulation to become involved than children of normal intelligence.

As the child develops, he or she begins to look around more, to play with other children, and to be treated by them according to his or her aggressiveness, physical skill, and temperament. A pecking order is established in the nursery, and it is clear that the retarded child is different. By this time parents have usually taken the child to a variety of specialists, including pediatricians, neurologists, psychologists, endocrinologists, or child psychiatrists either to obtain a diagnosis or to have the diagnosis of mental retardation changed to something they can tolerate more readily (Eaton and Menolascino, 1982).

For almost all parents the news that their child is retarded is a terrible blow. The reaction has been described by Olshansky (1962) as "chronic sorrow," the continuing sorrow of a parent who feels the lost hope for a perfect and "complete" child. Stages of shock, realization, and recognition are involved, and each will influence the way the child is handled as he or she grows up. Some parents overprotect and do not stimulate the child to use his or her fullest abilities. Others are too depressed to do much for the child. In still others, the sadness is interwoven with an impotent rage. Many parents are angry at the retarded child, although they try to cover this up, hating to admit feelings of anger toward one so helpless. Most try to do their best in spite of their personal sense of loss and sadness, but some become cool and distant and as a result withdraw from the child the sustained warmth and stimulation that he or she requires. Occasionally parents desperately peruse written material and medical journals and fly about both nationally and internationally seeking miracle cures. Others become engaged in mental retardation organizations and evade their own damaged offspring while helping in a social context outside the home. Some parents try to quash their own sadness and embark on brisk programs, pushing their child relentlessly toward speech training, toilet training, nursery school, exercises, and a host of other "stimulating" activities. In the process of pushing too hard, they overwhelm a vulnerable child and tend to make him or her withdraw further.

At no point does the child develop on his or her own; each developmental step occurs within a particular environmental matrix. We are progressively more aware of the influence of temperament, the endowed reactive style, on the interplay between parents and children. Some parents are particularly good with aggressive children and love the challenge; others feel comfortable only with "easy" children who have smooth rhythms. These factors set up resonances between parents and children that alter the style of development. The parents' tolerance for the slowness of a retarded child and their ability to identify with the child will aid in the effective use of the child's capacities during his or her more protracted developmental course.

During the oedipal phase, both male and female children become aware of their sexual organs and begin to explore them as part of their evolution of self-concept in relation to both parents. According to Erikson, issues of assertiveness and possessiveness are paramount during this phase. For all children this phase of development spans several years, and the patterns and ideas, the fantasies, the pokings, the teasing words, the explorations, and the fears are all part of a larger fabric. The retarded child will tend to move through the oedipal phase later than other children and to bear the altered self-esteem resulting from slowed maturation; the child's speech is still meager, often marked by an impediment, and his or her dependence on parents for care is still great. Studies in infant psychiatry indicate that the retarded suffer from problems of self-esteem as a result of negatively charged parent-child interactions (Demos, 1983).

The particular way in which the retarded child handles the oral and anal phases determines how he or she will handle later phases of development. Compared with normal children, the retarded child tends to be more fearful, more guilty, and more excited and bemused by the new and mysterious questions of sexual differences, the ways in which boys and girls differ, and where babies originate. By age 12 the child is also likely to have been made aware that the erotic aspects of life will be different for him or her. Parents often feel that they should protect their retarded children from sexuality. These feelings arise partly from sympathy and from the sense that their children will not likely marry or have normal sexual lives and partly from fear that the retarded, with their limited control and comprehension, will either be taken advantage of sexually or be sexually aggressive. Parental concerns about these matters begin early, with the result that the child who needs instruction and calm support is likely to get silence, abrupt instructions, and anxious lectures from parents who handle these matters more effectively with their other children. Consequently the child is more likely to inhibit questioning, and to keep his or her confused thoughts to himself or herself. This behavior is strikingly apparent in children growing up in schools for the retarded, where all the inhibiting pressures tend to be starker, no matter how well intentioned the staff.

The societal context in which all developmental changes occur shapes the retarded. Hurley (1968) points out that for the poor, constant awareness of their own abject status and the failure it implies leads to embarrassed withdrawal and isolation within society. This observation also applies to the retarded child, who responds to his or her own sociofamilial situation, the sister who is ashamed of him or her, the mother who feels burdened by him or her, the father who feels put off and annoyed by him or her. The retarded child comes to feel that people look at him or her differently, particularly if he or she has the "look," the haircut, or any of the organic signs that people associate with retardation. By the time the child gets to school, he or she is aware of a special educational status and will generally react by behaving in an inhibited manner. Whether this inhibition is part of a maturational process or whether the retarded are worn into submission by social circumstances remains open to question, as continuing pressure is brought to subdue most of their individuality and to make them less intrusive.

In spite of this attempt to outline a "normative" development in abnormal individuals, it is clear that, in

Kessler's words, "the term 'mentally retarded' embraces a range of patients, from the totally helpless child in the crib to the child whose handicap is apparent only in school. In addition to this variation in the degree and type of handicap, causes of the retardation vary and so do physical and personality characteristics associated with it . . . Mentally retarded children are as different from one another as are children of normal or superior intelligence" (1966, p. 166). Moreover, as Stevens and Heber (1964, p. 169) note,

the extreme paucity of experimental data bearing on the relationship between personality variables and behavior efficiency of the retarded person is indeed remarkable in view of the generally acknowledged importance of personality factors in problem-solving. Textbooks are replete with statements describing the retarded as passive, anxious, impulsive, rigid, suggestible, lacking in persistence, immature, and withdrawn, and as having a low frustration tolerance and an unrealistic self-concept and level of aspiration. Yet not one of these purported attributes can be either substantiated or refuted on the basis of available research data.

Evaluation

The evaluation and treatment of individuals with MR require the effort of a multidisciplinary team including primary care physicians, medical specialists, psychiatrists, psychologists, social workers, special education teachers, occupational therapists, and speech and language therapists.

Because individuals with MR often have limited verbal capacity to report any type of symptomatology, clinicians are dependent on laboratory measures, physical findings, information from caregivers, and their own powers of observation to detect problems.

The following are important components of a thorough evaluation of a mentally retarded individual:

1. History: The evaluation of an individual with suspected mental retardation should include a detailed history about pregnancy, delivery, postnatal health, and development, and details about past and current social and economic circumstance.

2. Physical: Physical examination is important to screen for stigmata of genetic syndromes and for underlying neurologic or metabolic/medical derangements. Physical handicaps are quite common in those with IQs <50.

3. Laboratory tests: Metabolic and chromosomal screening is indicated. Thyroid function test, electrolytes/Bun/Cre, glucose, FEP/lead level, serum zinc, magnesium,

CBC, urinalysis, urinary amino acids, and chromosomal studies should be pursued.

4. Neurologic and sensory: These individuals tend to have a higher rate of physical, neurologic, and sensory handicaps. For example, 10% of the moderately retarded and 50% of the profoundly retarded have seizure disorders (Rivinus et al., 1989). EEG, CT scan, and magnetic resonance imaging (MRI) studies should be done, as indicated, to rule out treatable progressive neurologic disorders. Blindness and deafness are common, particularly in those in the lower IQ range. Therefore, vision and hearing tests should be done.

5. Cognitive: Cognitive ability for school-aged children is usually assessed using a standardized instrument such as the Wechsler Intelligence Scale for Children III (WISC III) and the Stanford Binet, fourth edition. The Leiter International Performance Scale is used to assess the nonverbal child and the profoundly retarded (Frazier et al., 1997).

6. Adaptive behavior: Adaptive functioning is assessed using instruments such as the Vineland Adaptive Behavioral Scale (Sparrow, Balla, and Cicchetti, 1984) and the AAMD Adaptive Behavior Scale for Children and Adults (Nihira et al., 1975). An individual's education, motivation, personality, sociocultural background, associated handicaps, and level of cooperation all may bear on performance and need to be considered at the time of the assessment of adaptive functioning.

7. Speech and language: Speech and language problems are common in the mentally retarded and may be due to a variety of factors. Some factors are biological and attributable to the essential cognitive deficit while others may be social and may reflect important dynamic issues such as decreased parental verbal stimulation during a period of adjustment to the newborn handicapped child. Children with IQs <50 show marked deficits in information processing (Brooks, McCauley, and Merrill, 1988). Therefore, speech and language assessments are often indicated.

8. Emotional and behavioral: Although many individuals with mental retardation adapt well and function without too much difficulty, individuals with MR are at greater risk for behavioral disturbances and emotional difficulties. Those in the mild to moderate range are at increased risk for emotional distress that may arise from a sense of not being like everyone else and from peer and societal rejection that results in isolation. A careful mental status examination is important.

Psychiatric assessment. Retardation can coexist with other psychiatric conditions, and may predispose those who suffer from mental retardation to psychiatric disorders (Nuffield, 1983; Sovner and Hurley, 1983; Koller et al., 1983). Clinicians and researchers estimate that 30–60% of the MR population may have comorbid psychiatric conditions (Bregman, 1991). The lower the individual's IQ, the greater the tendency toward behavioral problems and psychopathology (Bregman, 1991).

The mentally retarded have a decreased capacity to process, problem solve, and self-manage, resulting in a greater susceptibility to behavioral disturbance and to mental illness. Physical, sensory, and cognitive handicaps can lead to impaired ability to understand and respond adaptively to the environment. The more severe the MR, the greater the impairment in expressing one's needs effectively, and the greater the tendency to misinterpret life events. Being different, societal nonacceptance, and other cultural-familial factors increase the risk of emotional disturbance in the mentally retarded person (Lewis and MacLean, 1982).

Psychopathology may be expressed somewhat differently from that commonly observed in the general population owing to both poorer communication skills and the tendency of individuals with MR to communicate depression, anxiety, agitation, and frustration in more primitive ways, such as self-injurious behavior, stereotyped rocking, aggression, and self-stimulation (Lewis and MacLean, 1982).

Additionally, there is a phenomenon called *diagnostic overshadowing* wherein clinicians wrongly attribute changes in mood and behavior to the individual's MR rather than to a comorbid psychiatric condition (e.g., depression, anxiety, bipolar disorder, attention deficit hyperactivity disorder, Tourette syndrome, psychotic disorder). Individuals with mental retardation develop psychiatric conditions like anyone else. For example, as many as 50% of noninstitutionalized individuals have been reported to meet criteria for an affective disorder (Bregman, 1991).

It is important for a mentally retarded child or adult with a marked change in behavior to have a full psychiatric evaluation. Common problems in MR patients that come to the attention of clinicians are self-injury and aggression. The basis of these behavioral changes must be discerned and treated. Etiologies of behavioral change include neurologic, medical, dynamic, and/or psychiatric. Underlying medical and neurological conditions need to be ruled out. It is also important to assess if there have been any life change events for the individual. If so, either individual psychotherapy (for those with IQ >50), behavioral therapy, or family therapy might be indicated.

Finally, behaviors may represent symptoms of a psychi-

atric disorder. The patient must be thoroughly evaluated for a psychiatric condition. Often such diagnoses require careful observation over a period of time, owing to the patient's limited ability to express problems verbally.

Family System

Numerous cognitive, physical, emotional, social, and behavioral challenges face mentally retarded individuals and their families during the course of development. The response of the family to the child, and the response of the child to the family, will shape the developmental pathway. Children with mental retardation by definition develop more slowly and reach a final level of development that is lower than that of their developmentally intact peers. Parents and siblings have the lifelong task of accepting their child's or sibling's developmental disability. Parents and siblings frequently experience varying periods of denial, anger, and sorrow once mental retardation is diagnosed in a child. Parental feelings tend to wax and wane with each developmental milestone that is or is not reached (Lewis and MacLean, 1982). This can lead to decreased emotional availability of the parents to the child, to each other, and to the rest of the family.

Families may require different levels of support at different phases of development which range from education to family assessment and therapy.

Prevention

Prior to pregnancy, we encourage genetic counseling for parents with known genetic disorders (e.g., neurofibromatosis), and for mothers of advanced age, given the increased incidence of Down syndrome with increased maternal years.

In the expectant mother, adequate intervention for any substance abuse problem, appropriate monitoring of prescribed medications and medical conditions, and adequate nutrition and prenatal care help to optimize the in utero environment. Once the child is born, active treatment of neonatal infections, metabolic abnormalities, and metal intoxication is indicated. Also, certain interventions can help ameliorate difficulties found in the mildly retarded individual, in particular, providing appropriate nutrition and infant cognitive stimulation.

Treatment Interventions

Clinicians must provide families with support especially during the initial adjustment period to the newborn child. Facilitating access to educational materials and information about services, providing emotional support, and at times providing family therapy can be very helpful. Families often need help with difficult decisions regarding school placement, and indications for out-of-home placement. The developmental challenges for children and adolescents with mental retardation can be anticipated and satisfactorily addressed if adequate planning has been undertaken and the proper family, social, and special education supports are available. Many families find benefit from contacting the local chapter of the Association for Retarded Citizens (ARC).

For the mentally retarded individual with a behavioral change, underlying medical and neurological disturbances need to be ruled out and then psychiatric evaluation should be undertaken. This may require careful observation over a period of time, owing to the patient's limited ability to express problems verbally. Once a diagnosis of a comorbid psychiatric condition is made, the question of selecting a treatment approach must be addressed. Operant behavioral interventions are often very helpful in treating the behavior problems common to the mentally retarded (Barrett, 1986). Intensive programs that involve differential reinforcement techniques may be particularly valuable (Cook and Leventhal, 1992). Behavior therapy has been used effectively for decreasing aggression, extinguishing a variety of maladaptive behaviors, and increasing prosocial behavior.

Cognitive behavioral therapy and psychotherapy can be particularly useful for children and adolescents in the mild range of mental retardation; these have also been helpful for adolescents and young adults diagnosed with moderate mental retardation (Barrett et al., 1992).

As a general rule psychopharmacologic intervention should not be used as a first approach to treatment. However, if target symptoms persist, clinicians should not hesitate to consider such approaches. Additionally, if a patient is already on medication(s), the medications must be reviewed and consideration should be given to the possibility that the target symptoms might be the result (or side effect) of the current medication regimen (Feinstein and Levoy, 1991). Many clinicians have reported that the mentally retarded child and adolescent populations require lower doses than usually prescribed and seem much more prone to untoward effects (Aman and Singh, 1988). Polypharmacy, drug interactions, and dose titration are likely to emerge as confounding variables in the treatment of individuals with MR (Rivinus et al., 1989). Tapering mentally retarded individuals off medication must be done gradually, as this population also seems particularly prone to withdrawal and rebound symptomatology.

When treating a disorder, a high enough dose over a long enough period of time should be administered for a valid assessment of treatment efficacy. Pharmacotherapy can lead to enhanced self-regulation. The goal of psychopharmacologic intervention is to decrease inappropriate behavior and relieve symptomatology. The overall aim is to improve quality of life of the mentally retarded individual.

In general, symptoms of a psychiatric syndrome, not an individual behavior, should be the targets of treatment with psychopharmacologic agents. For example, the individual behavior of self-injury may be a symptom of numerous psychiatric disorders (e.g., affective disorders, obsessive-compulsive disorder, psychotic disorders, Tourette syndrome, stereotypic movement disorder, etc.). Although neuroleptics are often used to treat self-injury, they are not always indicated and should be used judiciously given their side effect profile. One example of self-injury might be new onset head banging in a depressed patient. The head banging in this instance might represent suicidal behavior in a mentally retarded individual and would be more appropriately treated with an antidepressant than a neuroleptic. The etiology of the presenting behavior should be determined and viewed within the context of a composite of target symptoms of a psychiatric syndrome prior to psychopharmacological intervention.

Developmental Considerations for Treatment

Infancy

Secure attachment is often in jeopardy for an infant with mental retardation owing to parents' stress in adjusting to the birth of a child with developmental delays. Parents' internal struggle with the acceptance of their child can lead to decreased emotional availability to the child. Parents often require considerable support and education during these early days.

Preschool

Sometimes families need special support when they face the challenge of deciding whether the child can live at home or require placement.

School Age

Children with mild or moderate retardation sometimes remain undiagnosed until they face the academic and social challenges of school. At this stage teachers begin to note lagging school performance. Families and individuals require access to special testing and educational services. Peer rejection often occurs and can lead to decreases in motivation and withdrawal.

Adolescence

Peer acceptance and separation from family are two of the most important developmental tasks for adolescents. Most teenagers with mental retardation have experienced peer rejection and social isolation. These teens have cognitive deficits and may appear physically different owing to physical awkwardness, weight problems, and difficulties with complexion, making them easy targets of social derision (Shapiro and Friedman, 1987).

Teens with mild MR may eventually establish some independence from families, although teens with moderate MR range from being partly dependent to entirely dependent on caregivers. Total separation from families usually is not feasible. However, separation may be forced on families as parents may need to consider long-term planning for their developmentally disabled son or daughter.

Within the context of being partially dependent, the adolescent with moderate mental retardation needs help with establishing areas of personal and social independence. Teenagers with moderate mental retardation can and should be supported and educated to develop a preferred vocational skill as this can lead to the development of a feeling of personal usefulness and social constructiveness.

Sexuality is an important issue for all adolescents, including the adolescent with mental retardation. Teenagers with mental retardation clearly have typical levels of sexual desire and interest (Bernstein, 1970, 1979, 1985). What they often lack is sexual knowledge. It is critically important to provide sex education to adolescents with mental retardation, particularly the moderately retarded teenager. Many embarrassing and difficult social situations, as well as potentially dangerous and life-threatening circumstances, may be avoided if the adolescent with MR is well educated in the facts and responsibilities of sexual behavior and conduct.

Teens with MR are quite vulnerable sexually. They are likely to experience verbal ridicule and may experience physical and sexual abuse. Issues of safety are paramount and should be supported as a part of the special educational curriculum for all students with mental retardation.

To aid in sex education, it is important to help parents understand the feelings of their retarded children and to facilitate discussion of the problems of sterilization, abortion, child rearing, and sexual desires. Parents need to understand that for many mentally retarded individuals masturbation may be a safe sexual outlet. For some, marital experience may be feasible and desirable.

Adult

Many adults with MR remain dependent on families. Less retarded individuals can often live in community-based homes and work in workshops or in structured work settings. The more severely retarded often require ongoing dependent care.

Legal Issues in Treatment

The psychiatrist may become involved in problems of institutional care and administration, physical rehabilitation, special education or guardianship, and issues of legal competence. The psychiatrist can act as an advocate for the individual patient and for improved care for the retarded in general. Psychiatric consultation for the mentally retarded often requires knowledge of the systems affecting these individuals (Bernstein, 1988).

The field of mental retardation presents many challenges. There is a clear need for further research to acquire more information regarding neurophysiological and genetic factors of retardation. Social action is also required to deal with the sociogenetic causes of retardation (Hurley, 1968). Finally, physicians must work to minimize the prejudice toward these individuals which often leads to social ostracism and mistreatment, as well as to diminished access to adequate health care.

References

Abramowicz, H. K., and Richardson, S. A. 1975. Epidemiology of severe mental retardation in children: community studies. *Am. J. Ment. Defic.* 80(1):18–39.

Abuelo, D. K. 1991. Genetic disorder. In *Handbook of mental retardation,* ed. J. L. Matson and J. A. Mulick. 2nd ed. New York: Pergamon Press. 97–114.

Aman, M. G., and Singh, N. N. 1988. *Psychopharmacology of the developmental disabilities.* New York: Springer-Verlag.

American Psychiatric Association (APA). 1994. *Diagnostic*

and statistical manual of mental disorders. 4th ed. Washington, D.C.

Barrett, R. P. 1986. *Severe behavior disorders in the mentally retarded: nondrug approaches to treatment.* New York: Plenum Press.

Barrett, R. P., Walters, A. S., Mercurio, A. F., Klitzke, M. G., and Feinstein, C. 1992. Mental retardation and psychiatric disorders. In *Inpatient behavior therapy for children and adolescents,* ed. V. VanHasselt and D. J. Kolko. New York: Plenum Press. 113–149.

Bernstein, N. R. 1979. Intervention with the retarded. In *Basic handbook of child psychiatry,* ed. J. P. Noshpitz and S. Harrison. New York: Basic Books.

——— 1985. Sexuality in mentally retarded adolescents. *Medical Aspects of Human Sexuality* 19:50–61.

——— 1988. The mentally retarded person. Chap. 30 in *The new Harvard guide to psychiatry,* ed. A. Nicholi. Cambridge, Mass.: Belknap Press of Harvard University Press.

Bernstein, N. R., ed. 1970. *Diminished people: problems and care of the mentally retarded.* Boston: Little, Brown.

Bregman, J. D. 1991. Current developments in the understanding of mental retardation. Pt. II. Psychopathology. *J. Am. Acad. Child Adolesc. Psychiatry* 30(6):861–872.

Bregman, J. D., and Hodapp, R. M. 1991. Current developments in the understanding of mental retardation. Pt. I. Biological and phenomenological perspectives. *J. Am. Acad. Child Adolesc. Psychiatry* 30(5):707–719.

Brooks, P. H., McCauley, C. M., and Merrill, E. M. 1988. Cognition and mental retardation. In *Prevention and curative intervention in mental retardation,* ed. F. J. Menolascino and J. A. Stark. Baltimore: Paul H. Brookes Publishing Company. 295–318.

Charles, D. C. 1953. Ability and accomplishment of persons earlier judged mentally deficient. *Genet. Psychol. Monogr.* 47:3–71.

Cook, E. H., and Leventhal, B. L. 1992. Neuropsychiatric disorders of childhood and adolescence. In *Neuropsychiatry,* ed. S. C. Yudofsky and R. E. Hales. 2nd ed. Washington, D.C.: American Psychiatric Press. 641–644.

Demos, V. 1983. Perspective from infant research on affect and self-esteem. In *The development and sustenance of self-esteem in childhood,* ed. J. E. Mack and L. A. Steven. New York: International Universities Press.

Earle, C. J. C. 1961. *Subnormal personalities: their clinical investigation and assessment.* London: Bailliere, Tindall, and Cox.

Eaton, L., and Menolascino, F. 1982. Psychiatric disorders in the mentally retarded. *Am. J. Psychiatry* 139:1297–1303.

Erikson, E. H. 1950. *Childhood and society.* New York: Norton.

Feinstein, C., and Levoy, D. 1991. Pharmacotherapy of severe psychiatric disorders in mentally retarded individuals. In *Medical psychiatric practice,* ed. A. Stoudemire and B. S. Fogel. Washington, D.C.: American Psychiatric Press. 507–537.

Frazier, J., Barrett, R., Walter, A., and Feinstein, C. 1997. Moderate to profound mental retardation. In *Handbook of child and adolescent psychiatry,* ed. J. D. Noshpitz and N. E. Alessi. New York: Wiley and Sons. 397–408.

Goldson, E., and Hagerman, R. J. 1992. The fragile X syndrome. *Dev. Med. Child Neurol.* 34:826–832.

Hurley, R. L. 1968. *Poverty and mental retardation: a causal relationship.* New York: Vintage Books.

Kaplan, H. I., and Sadock, B. J. 1991. *Synopsis of psychiatry.* Baltimore: Williams & Wilkins.

Kaufman, D. M. 1990. *Clinical neurology for psychiatrists.* 3rd ed. Philadelphia: W. B. Saunders Company.

Kessler, J. 1966. *Psychopathology of childhood.* Englewood Cliffs, N. J.: Prentice-Hall.

Kiely, M. 1987. The prevalence of mental retardation. *Epidemiol. Rev.* 9:194–218.

Kinsbourne, M. 1985. Disorders of mental development. In *Textbook of child neurology,* ed. J. H. Menkes. 3rd ed. Philadelphia: Lea & Febiger. 768–774.

Koller, H., Richardson, S. A., Katz, M., and McLaren, J. 1983. Behavior disturbance since childhood among 5-year birth cohort of all mentally retarded young adults in a city. *Am. J. Ment. Defic.* 87:386–393.

Lewis, M. H., and MacLean, W. E., Jr. 1982. Issues in treating emotional disorders. In *Psychopathology in the mentally retarded,* ed. J. L. Matson and R. P. Barrett. New York: Grune & Stratton. 1–36.

McLaren, J., and Bryson, S. E. 1987. Review of recent epidemiological studies of mental retardation: prevalence, associated disorders, and etiology. *American Journal of Mental Retardation* 92(3):245–254.

Myers, B. A. 1987. Psychiatric problems in adolescents with developmental disabilities. *J. Am. Acad. Child Adolesc. Psychiatry* 26:74–79.

Nihira, K., Foster, R., Shellhaas, M., and Leland, H. 1975. *AAMD Adaptive Behavior Scale.* Washington, D.C.: American Association on Mental Deficiency.

Nuffield, E. 1983. Psychotherapy. In *Handbook of mental retardation,* ed. J. L. Mason and J. A. Mulick. New York: Pergamon Press.

Olshansky, S. 1962. Chronic sorrow: a response to having a mentally defective child. *Soc. Casework* 43:191–194.

Richardson, S. A., Koller, H., and Katz, M. 1986. A longitudinal study of numbers of males and females in mental retardation services by age, I. Q., and placement. *J. Ment. Defic. Res.* 30:291–300.

Rivinus, T. M., Grofer, L. M., Feinstein, C., and Barrett, R. P. 1989. Psychopharmacology in the mentally retarded individual: new approaches, new direction. *Journal of the Multihandicapped Person* 2(1):1–23.

Robinson, H. B., and N. M. Robinson. 1965. *The mentally retarded child: a psychological approach.* New York: McGraw-Hill.

Rowitz, L. 1991. Social and environmental factors and developmental handicaps in children. In *Handbook of mental retardation,* ed. J. L. Matson and J. A. Mulick. 2nd ed. New York: Pergamon Press. 158–165.

Rutter, M., Tizard, J., Yule, W., Graham, P., and Whitmore, K. 1976. Research report Isle of Wight Studies, 1964–1974. *Psychol. Med.* 6(2):313–332.

Shapiro, E. S., and Friedman, J. 1987. Mental retardation. In *Handbook of adolescent psychology,* ed. V. B. VanHasselt and M. Hersen. New York: Pergamon. 381–397.

Sovner, R., and Hurley, A. D. 1983. Do the mentally retarded suffer from affective illness? *Arch. Gen. Psychiatry* 40:61–67.

Sparrow, S., Balla, D. A., and Cicchetti, D. V. 1984. *Vineland Adaptive Behavior Scales.* Circle Pines, Minn.: American Guidance Service.

Stevens, H., and Heber, R. 1964. *Mental retardation: a review of research.* Chicago: University of Chicago Press.

Tarjan, G. 1966. Mental retardation: implications for the future. In *Prevention and treatment of mental retardation,* ed. I. Philips. New York: Basic Books.

Webster, T. 1963. Problems of emotional development in young retarded children. *Am. J. Psychiatry* 120:37–43.

Work, H. 1983. Consultation and mental retardation. In *Handbook of psychiatric consultation with children and youth,* ed. N. R. Bernstein and J. Sussex. New York: Spectrum.

Zigler, E., Balla, D., and Hodapp, R. 1984. On the definition and classification of mental retardation. *Am. J. Ment. Defic.* 89(3):215–230.

Recommended Reading

Aman, M. G. 1983. Psychoactive drugs in mental retardation. In *Treatment issues and innovations in mental retardation,* ed. J. Matson and F. Andrasik. New York: Plenum Publishing.

Barrett, R. P., Walters, A. S., Mercurio, A. F., Klitzke, M. G., and Feinstein, C. 1992. Mental retardation and psychiatric disorders. In *Inpatient behavior therapy for children and adolescents,* ed. V. VanHasselt and D. J. Kolko. New York: Plenum Press. 113–149.

Bregman, J. D. 1991. Current developments in the understanding of mental retardation. Pt. II. Psychopathology. *J. Am. Acad. Child Adolesc. Psychiatry* 30(6):861–872.

Bregman, J. D., and Hodapp, R. M. 1991. Current developments in the understanding of mental retardation. Pt. I.

Biological and phenomenological perspectives. *J. Am. Acad. Child Adolesc. Psychiatry* 30(5):707–719.

Frazier, J., Barrett, R., Walter, A., and Feinstein, C. 1997. Moderate to profound mental retardation. In *Handbook of child and adolescent psychiatry,* ed. J. D. Noshpitz and N. E. Alessi. New York: Wiley and Sons.

Rivinus, T. M., Grofer, L. M., Feinstein, C., and Barrett, R. P. 1989. Psychopharmacology in the mentally retarded individual: new approaches, new direction. *Journal of the Multihandicapped Person* 2(1):1–23.

GEORGE E. VAILLANT

The Alcohol-Dependent and Drug-Dependent Person

While there are many different drugs of abuse, there are no truly dangerous drugs; there are only people who use drugs dangerously. For this reason some clinicians have suggested that there are as many different addictions as there are people. Physicians, however, appreciate patterns of illness as well as individual idiosyncrasies, and generalizations become necessary. Thus, for heuristic purposes this chapter makes several generalizations about alcohol and drug dependence, although this oversimplifies complex individual patterns.

Definitions

Drug Dependence

Because the difference between self-detrimental drug use and socially disapproved drug use is often unclear, definitions are important. In 1969 the World Health Organization offered standard definitions of drug abuse, drug dependence, psychic dependence, physical dependence, and tolerance. The term *drug abuse* refers to excessive drug use, that is, a level inconsistent with acceptable medical practice. *Drug dependence* refers to a state, psychic or physical, of interaction between person and drug characterized by a compulsion to take the drug on either a continuous or a periodic basis in order to experience its psychic effects or to avoid the discomfort of its absence. *Physical dependence* is an altered physiological state brought on by frequent use of a drug and resulting in physiological symptoms on withdrawal. *Psychic dependence* is an often used but nonspecific term that refers to drug dependence without physiological evidence of dependence. *Tolerance* is an altered physiological state brought on by continuous use of a drug and resulting in the declining effect of a given dose.

No single formula fits all drugs. For example, drug dependence on tobacco results in modest tolerance, modest physical dependence, and marked psychic dependence. Heroin abuse produces far more tolerance than does alcohol abuse, but physical dependence on alcohol leads to signs of physical withdrawal more severe than those of withdrawal from heroin. Although using lysergic acid diethylamide (LSD) leads to marked tolerance, it does not produce physical dependence. Patterns of dependence of several commonly abused drugs are summarized in Table 31.1. The neurobiological basis for positive reinforcement by all abused substances appears ultimately to depend upon the dopaminergic pathways leading from the ventral tegmentum to the nucleus accumbens.

In order to encompass such differences and similarities, the American Psychiatric Association's *Diagnostic and Statistical Manual of Mental Disorders,* fourth edition (DSM-IV), offers a single multifactorial category, *substance dependence disorders,* designed to embrace all the major drugs of abuse, including caffeine. According to DSM-IV at least 3 of the following diagnostic criteria must be met within a 12-month period to identify a drug-dependent person:

1. Tolerance, as defined by either of the following:
   a. a need for markedly increased amounts of the substance to achieve intoxication or desired effect
   b. markedly diminished effect with continued use of the same amount of the substance.
2. Withdrawal, as manifested by either of the following:
   a. the characteristic withdrawal syndrome for the substance
   b. the same (or a closely related) substance is taken to relieve or avoid withdrawal symptoms.
3. The substance is often taken in larger amounts or over a longer period than was intended.
4. There is persistent desire or unsuccessful efforts to cut down or control substance use.
5. A great deal of time is spent in activities necessary to obtain the substance.
6. Important social, occupational, or recreational activities are given up or reduced because of substance use.
7. The substance use is continued despite knowledge of

Table 31.1 Effects of commonly abused drugs

Drug	Tolerance	Psychic Dependence	Physical Dependence
Alcohol	+	+ +	+ +
Amphetamines	+ +	+ +	0?
Barbiturates	+ +	+ +	+ +
Caffeine	+	+	+
Chlordiazepoxide	+ +	+ +	+ +
Cocaine	+	+ +	+
LSD	+ +	+	0
Marijuana	+	+	− +
Nicotine	+ +	+ +	+
Opiates	+ +	+ +	+ +

a. Symbols: 0, no effect; +, mild effect; + +, marked effect; − +, unclear or conflicting.

a persistent or recurrent physical or psychological problem that is likely to have been caused or exacerbated by the substance (e.g., current cocaine use despite recognition of cocaine-induced depression, or continued drinking despite recognition that an ulcer was made worse by alcohol consumption).

Among individuals who deny behavioral evidence of the disorder, a provisional diagnosis of dependence is warranted if there is evidence of a mental or physical disorder or condition that is usually a complication of prolonged substance use (for example, delirium tremens, cirrhosis, alcoholic neuropathy, or esophageal varices from alcohol use; needle marks or abscesses on the arms from intravenous opiate drug use).

Alcoholism

Alcoholism is the most ignored public health problem in America, but alcoholism is a treatable condition. Depending on the definition used, alcoholism affects between 5 and 10% of the adult population in the United States, including 20–40% of all adult patients admitted to general medical and surgical wards. In males aged 25–44, intoxication plays a major role in the 4 leading causes of death: accidents, homicide, suicide, and *alcoholic cirrhosis*. In the United States alcoholism results in greater health-related costs than all respiratory diseases and all cancers combined.

E. M. Jellinek (1960)—perhaps the greatest student of

alcoholism in the twentieth century—divided alcoholic drinking into the following categories: *alpha,* alcohol abuse for relief of psychic distress (such as depression); *beta,* physical damage from alcohol without dependence (as in hepatic cirrhosis); *delta,* inability to abstain, rather than loss of control (the 2-liter-a-day wine drinker, for example, rather than the "lost weekender"); *epsilon,* temporally spaced "bender" drinking; and *gamma,* alcohol abuse with tolerance, physical dependence, and loss of control. Over time, however, all 4 of Jellinek's other types may progress to *gamma*-type drinking. Thus, by offering a single category, alcohol dependence, DSM-IV encompasses all the chimerical forms in which alcoholism can present.

Intoxication or drunkenness should not be confused with alcoholism. Intoxication is often defined, especially in relation to driving offenses, as a blood alcohol concentration exceeding 100 mg per 100 ml of blood. Depending on gender, body weight, rate of drinking, and rate of gastrointestinal absorption, this blood level indicates recent ingestion of 3–6 ounces of gin or whisky, 3–6 cans of beer, or a 750 ml bottle of wine. (Since men metabolize a significant fraction of alcohol in the stomach prior to absorption, in contrast to women, men absorb only about two-thirds of the alcohol they drink.) Signs of intoxication include slurred speech, nystagmus, hyporeflexia, unsteady gait and other incoordinations, flushing, and a mental state fluctuating between somnolence and rowdiness. It is effectively treated with bed rest. Extreme excitement or violence may be controlled with 5 mg of haloperidol intramuscularly.

Sporadic, deliberate intoxication and voluntary heavy drinking (that is, *drunkenness*) must be distinguished from the illness or "disease" of alcohol dependence, wherein the individual may never become grossly intoxicated but cannot consistently exert control over alcohol ingestion. In oversimplified terms, the treatment for drunkenness is moderation; the treatment for alcoholism is abstinence.

Subjectively, alcohol use becomes an illness when the user either drinks when he wishes to refrain or continues to drink past the point at which he had earlier decided to stop. Objectively, alcohol use becomes "abuse" or an illness when alcohol ingestion impairs an individual's social relationships, health, job efficiency, or ability to avoid legal difficulties.

Polysubstance Use Disorders

Conventionally drug abusers are classified by the drug of abuse. But individuals who at one point in time abuse hallucinogens, barbiturates, or amphetamines may, over a lifetime, abuse a variety of drugs. For example, perhaps nine-tenths of the 1% of young Americans who have *used* heroin will also at some other time *abuse* sedatives, alcohol, marihuana, or cocaine.

Polydrug abusers constitute about 2% of the population and a much higher percentage of 2 very disparate groups: antisocial personalities and the medical profession. Although most alcohol abusers will not be re-labeled polydrug abusers, most polydrug abusers will at some point in their lives abuse alcohol. This can lead to confusion. Polydrug abusers tend to use those drugs that are available and in fashion and that exert the subjective effects they enjoy. For example, polydrug abusers often give a junior high school history of abusing inhalants and cigarettes because they were the first drugs available. Seeking some means of enhancing emotional response, some schizoid individuals say they prefer amphetamines and LSD. Some depressed individuals who fear loss of control and their own aggression choose opiates over alcohol and barbiturates. Other depressed, inhibited individuals seeking loss of control will choose barbiturates and alcohol for their disinhibiting effects. Cocaine is preferentially used by those seeking self-esteem or relief from depression. It is important to keep in mind, however, that polydrug abusers' patterns of drug abuse often change over time and may be greatly influenced by cost, availability, and social "status" of particular drugs.

In differentiating drugs of abuse, the terms *sedative* and *stimulant* are misnomers. A basic principle of psychopharmacology is that drug effect depends on the user's environment and activity pattern as much as on the pharmacology of the drug. For example, the "sedative" alcohol makes sitting still difficult if we are studying, stimulates us when we dance, and facilitates combat if we are provoked. In contrast, the "stimulant" amphetamine helps us to study, calms hyperactive children in a classroom, and at all but the highest doses may reduce the likelihood of physical combat.

Etiology of Alcohol Dependence and Polysubstance Use Disorders

Both alcoholism and polydrug abuse are as multidetermined and yet as actuarially predictable as whether an individual will develop heart disease or become an engineer. At least 8 broad etiological factors are known to affect alcoholism and polydrug abuse. Each of these factors interacts with the others and with the host. In treatment planning, the factors contributing to a given individual's alcohol or polydrug abuse must be taken into account.

First, availability is important. In Saigon during the Vietnam War, cheap, pure heroin was readily available, and abuse among U.S. troops dramatically increased. During World War II, owing to shipping restrictions, heroin abuse in New York City markedly declined. People who work near alcohol (such as diplomats and bartenders) have high rates of alcoholism. Altering the total alcohol consumption of a population has a direct effect on that group's rate of alcoholism.

But if drug abuse is profoundly affected by availability, effective social manipulation of supply to diminish abuse is complex. In Scandinavian countries, for example, altering contingencies affecting each drink (by increasing the price of alcohol) has reduced alcohol abuse. In the United States, putting emetics into airplane glue has made that form of inhalant use less attractive to teenagers. However, outright prohibition of alcohol consumption was ineffective during the 1920s and more recently has done little to contain alcoholism on American Indian reservations. High price and draconian prison terms have not deterred the importation of cocaine, and warning signs on packages have not significantly reduced cigarette sales. Only social experimentation can determine which legal or economic strategies will effectively alter drug availability or inhibit abuse in a specific cultural setting.

A second factor affecting drug abuse is whether the drug is slow or fast acting. The capacity of a drug to act quickly in altering consciousness increases its potential for abuse. Rapidly absorbed, high-proof spirits such as vodka and gin are more likely to lead to drug dependence than is the diluted alcohol in the more slowly absorbed beers and wines. Similarly, the use of fast-acting pentobarbital or intravenous heroin is more likely to result in dependence than the use of slower-acting phenobarbital or oral methadone. The available evidence suggests that the rapid-acting alprazolam (Xanax) has greater abuse potential than the slow-acting chlordiazepoxide (Librium) or more slowly absorbed oxazepam (Serax).

A third factor is the capacity of a drug to produce physical dependence. One of the factors maintaining alcohol and heroin abuse is the discomfort of the withdrawal symptoms. Once physical dependence is established, conditioning—both Pavlovian (classical) and Skinnerian (operant or instrumental)—plays a role in the maintenance of addiction. A wide variety of familiar stimuli will evoke conditioned withdrawal symptoms in a long-abstinent heroin addict, and some addicts report that they can get high just from a needle inserted in their arms (classical conditioning). Other individuals become habituated to the stereotyped but repeatedly reinforced "hustling" behavior that becomes the daily rhythm in the life of a heroin addict (operant conditioning). As with sport fishing, seeking becomes as fascinating as consumption.

A fourth factor affecting abuse is culture, especially peer culture. If the culture provides clear guidelines for nonabusive drug use, be it peyote, opium, or wine, abuse is less likely. Italian-Americans and Jews, for example, commonly allow children to drink but strongly prohibit drunkenness in adults; they enjoy low rates of alcoholism. In contrast, cultures that forbid children to use alcohol but accept drunkenness (such as the Irish and certain urban American cultures) have high rates of alcoholism. Culture also determines whether prohibition will be effective. For example, as long as only doctors said that "speed kills," intravenous amphetamine use by adolescents continued to increase. As soon as peers began to caution amphetamine users about intravenous use, abuse declined. Once doctors themselves began to stop smoking, other middle-class, middle-aged males, but not working-class women, followed suit. Culturally homogeneous Mormon universities can successfully forbid Coca-Cola and coffee, but prohibitions of far more dangerous heroin in culturally diverse urban high schools are ignored.

Heredity is a fifth factor known to affect alcoholism; however, it has not yet been clearly shown as a cause of other substance dependence disorders. The child of an alcoholic, adopted at birth into a nonalcoholic family, is at far greater risk of developing alcoholism than the child of nonalcoholic parents adopted into a nonalcoholic or even into an alcoholic family. Some Japanese or Chinese individuals but not ethnically related Native Americans exhibit more flushing and report more physical discomfort after ingesting moderate amounts of alcohol than do Caucasians. Such genetic intolerance to alcohol resulting from failure to metabolize acetaldehyde may help protect some individuals from becoming alcohol dependent.

In contrast to heredity, the sixth factor, deprived childhood environment, appears more important in polysubstance use disorders than in alcoholism. Alcoholics may justify their addiction by recalling childhood unhappiness. Early retrospective studies thus seemed to implicate poor nurture as a cause of alcoholism. Prospective studies that have followed teenagers into mid-life, however, have not found dramatic differences in the nurture received by those who eventually develop alcoholism. The increased incidence of broken homes among alcoholics can probably be explained as secondary to parental alcoholism. Yet childhood environment does play an important role in polydrug abuse. Heroin addicts have unhappier childhoods than do their socioeconomically matched nonaddicted peers. Juvenile delinquency can in part be explained by environmental deprivations, and, statisti-

cally, delinquents misuse all drugs earlier and more often than their socioeconomic peers. Cigarette, marihuana, and alcohol use and abuse all often precede adjudicated juvenile delinquency.

The seventh factor, personality, also plays a more important role in the genesis of polydrug abuse than in that of alcoholism. In the past, authorities have often maintained that people who developed alcoholism did so in part because they were premorbidly more passive, sociopathic, dependent, unaggressive, depressed, mother dominated, and latently homosexual than were controls. But prospective studies reveal that the prealcoholic person appears either quite similar to or somewhat more extroverted, aggressive, independent, and heterosexually oriented than his or her peers. Insofar as chronic alcohol intoxication produces dependency and irresponsibility directed toward the very individuals that the alcoholic most loves, alcohol abusers become lonely and depressed and often appear antisocial. These traits, however, are a *result* more often than a cause of alcohol abuse. Admittedly, the picture is complicated by the fact that most polydrug abusers, especially cocaine abusers, will at some point in their lives abuse alcohol.

In the United States the personality of the chronic polydrug abuser is not easily distinguished from that of the antisocial (male)/borderline (female) personality. For example, under the special circumstances of the war in Vietnam, as many as 40% of enlisted men in Vietnam abused heroin; after return to the United States, only about 5% of this relatively normal sample continued to use opiates. This fact sharply differentiates them from individuals who become dependent on heroin in the United States—a predominantly personality disordered sample in whom the majority repeatedly relapse. Significantly, the factors predicting persistent heroin dependence in Vietnam veterans did not include the amount of heroin used in Vietnam. The important factors predicting relapse to heroin were noncompletion of high school, a criminal record, or abuse of amphetamines and barbiturates (polydrug abuse) in Vietnam.

The available data also indicate that polydrug abusers who become abstinent have more severely impaired postmorbid personalities than do abstinent alcohol abusers. For example, Alcoholics Anonymous, run by abstinent alcoholics, is a remarkably stable, benign, and successful organization. In contrast, self-help organizations run by ex–drug addicts have tended to be short-lived and fragile, often dissolving or evolving into sadistic, autocratic communities.

The eighth factor, symptom relief, also differentiates alcoholism from polydrug abuse. Nicotine, alcohol, and barbiturates provide little real relief from psychological distress. Despite psychic dependence on cigarettes, heavy cigarette smokers often acknowledge that they enjoy few of their 30–40 daily cigarettes. The alcoholic is less insightful and may maintain that he drinks to combat loneliness, anxiety, and depression. Videotapes made before, during, and after alcoholic drinking demonstrate what many experienced clinicians and sober alcoholics have known for some time, namely, that from an objective viewpoint, chronic use of alcohol makes people more withdrawn, less self-confident, more depressed, and often even more anxious. In the treatment of chronic anxiety barbiturates are no more effective than placebos.

In contrast, amphetamines, cocaine, and opiates do provide symptom relief. Opiates effectively curb hunger, anger, and sexual desire; they soothe almost every aspect of suffering. Individuals on methadone maintenance are often able to lead more stable lives than when drug free. For brief periods amphetamines and cocaine are truly mood elevating.

These differences between the alcoholic and the polydrug abuser lead to an important, if tentative, conclusion. Because of poor childhood nurture, emotional distress, and sociopathic behavior, the polydrug abuser has always been lonely and seeks an effective anodyne. In contrast, the nondelinquent alcoholic becomes socially isolated as the result of abusing a drug that produces loneliness and sociopathy rather than relief from emotional pain. True, depression and alcoholism often occur together in the same families, but careful genetic studies do not support a genetic connection between the two illnesses. Rather, careful *environmental* studies suggest that children may grow up depressed if their parents (biological or adoptive) abuse alcohol. Thus, abuse of a single agent (e.g., tobacco or alcohol) may often be conceptualized as a "disease," and the primary purpose of treatment must be to facilitate abstinence and relapse prevention in the community rather than to relieve alleged underlying disorders such as depression and anxiety. Abuse of multiple substances, however, is usually a symptom of underlying psychosocial difficulties and personality disorder. Unless these difficulties are addressed, the removal of one drug of abuse often results in the substitution of another.

Treatment

Treating the Alcoholic

Diagnosis is the first step in treatment, but it is often the most difficult. In general medical and surgical settings perhaps three-quarters of alcohol abusers go undiag-

nosed. Several factors contribute to this lack of recognition: (1) different social groups regard alcohol abuse quite differently; (2) individual use patterns differ widely; (3) some alcoholics' denial is very convincing; (4) many physicians recognize only late-stage stereotypes of alcoholic drinkers; and (5) alcoholics are adept at concealing overt signs of intoxication.

In history taking the clinician must learn to conceive of alcoholism as a "disease" that causes depression, marital breakup, and unemployment, not as a symptom that results from such distressing events. In other words, to decide whether a person is alcohol dependent, it is important to ask, "Did your husband used to nag you about your use of alcohol before he left you?" rather than merely accepting the patient's explanation, "I did not drink really heavily until my husband ran off with our neighbor." Analogous to the futility of diagnosing obesity by asking people how much they eat, a diagnosis of alcoholism is rarely made by asking patients how much they drink.

No single symptom is sufficient, and the diagnosis of alcoholism can be reached only after the considered integration of evidence from all available sources. The interviewer must appreciate that individuals who drink alcoholically are very frightened and guilty; thus they may not divulge their symptoms freely. A series of questions has been devised that can identify the alcohol-dependent individual. These are reproduced in Table 31.2. The individual who answers affirmatively to more than 3 of the questions is very likely to be an alcoholic. The design of the questions minimizes guilt and circumvents the denial of many patients with alcoholism. Contrary to popular belief, a red nose, alcohol on the breath, "needing" one cocktail before dinner, and solitary drinking are not reliable indexes of alcoholism. In addition to Table 31.2 the 4 CAGE questions are a useful bedside screening test: Have you tried to *Cut* down?; Do you get *Annoyed* by people discussing your drinking?; Do you feel *Guilty* about your drinking?; Do you sometimes have an *Eye-opener* (morning drinking)? Although increased red blood cell mean corpuscular volume (MCV), serum gamma glutamyl transpeptidase (GGT), serum aspartate aminotransferase, and especially carbohydrate-deficient transferrin (O'Connor and Schottenfeld, 1998) are all associated statistically with alcohol abuse, their specificity and sensitivity are not as good as the CAGE questions.

Once the diagnosis of alcoholism has been made, it must be communicated to the patient. Alcoholism distorts the family equilibrium, and the resulting denial can reach extraordinary proportions. It is usually helpful to discuss the problem with the whole family together. Supporting the family in empathic objective confrontation of the alcoholic member is effective and ensures that all members receive the same message; but such confrontation requires an experienced leader. In discussing alcoholism, it is important to "keep it simple." Because of the associated guilt, alcoholism is an emotionally laden subject; also, most alcoholics suffer from a mild dementia ("wet brain") that after detoxification may not fully clear for 6 months. Thus, all instructions must be simple, unambiguous, and focused on alcohol as the primary problem—even when the term *disease* is an oversimplification. Until alcohol abuse is ceased, correcting any other problem in living is very difficult.

Whether or not to consider alcoholism a disease provokes controversy among clinicians. Nevertheless, it is important to explain to patients that their alcoholism, like a disease, has a life of its own and is not a moral or psychological problem. Repeated relapses that injure an alcoholic's loved ones generate enormous guilt and confusion. The ensuing shame aggravates denial. Thus, experience has shown that the concept of disease facilitates accep-

tance of illness and treatment. Patients do not use the disease model as an excuse to continue alcohol abuse, any more than diabetics use the disease model to excuse dietary lapses.

The analogy to diabetes is useful in another way, in that the battle for sobriety must be fought in the community rather than in the hospital. For in alcoholism, as in diabetes, hospitalization is most useful to interrupt episodes of decompensation and to provide education. The treatment of both glycosuria and alcohol dependence is not detoxification but the prevention of inadvertent relapse. Several weeks of inpatient treatment of alcoholics have rarely been shown to be more lastingly effective than detoxification and prolonged outpatient follow-up.

Alcoholism relapse prevention includes the following components: (1) offering the patient effective, nonchemical substitute behaviors to compete with alcohol dependence; (2) finding objective ways, in contrast to reliance on willpower, to remind the patient not to resume drinking (for example, self-help groups or prescribing disulfiram);

Table 31.2 Questions to identify the alcohol-dependent person

1. Do you occasionally drink heavily after a disappointment, a quarrel, or when the boss gives you a bad time?
2. When you are having trouble or feel under pressure, do you always drink more heavily than usual?
3. Have you noticed that you are able to handle more liquor than you did when you were first drinking?
4. Did you ever wake up the "morning after" and discover that you could not remember part of the evening before, even though your friends tell you that you did not "pass out"?
5. When drinking with other people, do you try to have a few extra drinks when others will not know it?
6. Are there certain occasions when you feel uncomfortable if alcohol is not available?
7. Have you recently noticed that when you begin drinking you are in more of a hurry to get the first drink than you used to be?
8. Do you sometimes feel a little guilty about your drinking?
9. Are you secretly irritated when your family or friends discuss your drinking?
10. Have you recently noticed an increase in the frequency of your memory "blackouts"?
11. Do you often find that you wish to continue drinking after your friends say they have had enough?
12. Do you usually have a reason for the occasions when you drink heavily?
13. When you are sober, do you often regret things you have done or said while drinking?
14. Have you tried switching brands or following different plans for controlling your drinking?
15. Have you often failed to keep the promises you have made to yourself about controlling or cutting down on your drinking?
16. Have you ever tried to control your drinking by making a change in jobs or moving to a new location?
17. Do you try to avoid family or close friends while you are drinking?
18. Are you having an increasing number of financial and work problems?
19. Do more people seem to be treating you unfairly without good reason?
20. Do you eat very little or irregularly when you are drinking?
21. Do you sometimes have the "shakes" in the morning and find that it helps to have a little drink?
22. Have you recently noticed that you cannot drink as much as you once did?
23. Do you sometimes stay drunk for several days at a time?
24. Do you sometimes feel very depressed and wonder whether life is worth living?
25. Sometimes after periods of drinking, do you see or hear things that aren't even there?
26. Do you get terribly frightened after you have been drinking heavily?

Source: National Council on Alcoholism.

(3) repairing the network of social support that has been destroyed by alcohol abuse; and (4) restoring self-esteem and hope.

As Table 31.3 suggests, Alcoholics Anonymous (AA) or its reasonable equivalent offers the simplest way of providing all 4 components. First, the continuous hope, the gentle peer support, and proof that abstinence is possible that is offered by AA provides a substitute gratification that takes the place of dependence on drinking and the barroom. Unlike clinic hours, AA meetings compete with barroom hours. Meetings are available daily, especially during evenings, weekends, and holidays. Second, AA single-mindedly underscores the special ways in which alcoholics delude themselves that it is now safe to drink. Thus, AA serves the same role as an external conscience or behavior modification to compete with the subliminal reinforcers that facilitate inadvertent relapse. Third, belonging to a group of caring but abstinent individuals who have found solutions to the typical problems that beset the newly sober alcoholic helps to alleviate loneliness, encourage better self-care, and provide a social network. Unlike the alcoholic's family, the new AA friends do not make the alcoholic feel guilty. Fourth, the opportunity to identify with helpers who were once equally or more disabled and then to help others stay sober provides hope and enhances self-worth. However initially annoying to some members, the spiritual component of AA reduces the alcoholic's inevitable shame and demoralization.

In Table 31.3 prolonged hospitalization provides the first 3 components of recovery but ignores the fourth. Psychotherapy and tranquilizing drugs provide the first component but ignore the second and fourth. Providing the anxious alcoholic with tranquilizers, for example, will give temporary relief of anxiety, but over the long term such prescription reinforces the belief that relief of distress is pharmacologic, not human; thus pharmacotherapy may serve to facilitate the chain of conditioned responses that leads to picking up a drink at the next point of crisis. Psychotherapy is limited both because alcoholics trying to stay sober often need help at odd hours and because their low self-esteem is worsened by feeling dependent on nonalcoholic individuals. In contrast, AA fosters sharing, not dependency. Disulfiram, 250mg q.d. (Antabuse), and similar compounds that produce illness if alcohol is ingested are reminders not to drink, but they take away a habit without providing an alternative behavior or dependency. The opioid receptor antagonist naltrexone, in a dose of 50 mg daily, has been shown to be a promising outpatient adjunct to preventing relapse in alcoholic individuals with alcohol dependence, but confirmation of long-term efficacy is needed.

In counseling alcohol abusers, some useful guidelines may be followed. The first is that once a clinician is sure that the patient's use of alcohol meets the criteria for alcohol dependence, he should not try to prescribe good advice about controlled drinking. An analogous situation is the futility of advising a 2-pack-a-day smoker to cut down to 5 daily cigarettes. Obviously the individual whose excessive drinking is truly voluntary or merely excessive for good health may be helped by advice about moderation and by education about the physical consequences of heavy drinking and consistent follow-up. Modification of

Table 31.3   Theoretical comparison of different treatment modalities in providing components for long-term alcohol abstinence

Treatment Components	Treatment Modalities[a]				
	AA	Hospitalization	Disulfiram	Psychotherapy	Tranquilizers
Substitute for alcohol dependence	+	+	−	+	+ +
Warning against relapse	+	+	+ +	0	−
Repair of social and medical damage	+	+ +	0	+	0
Restoration of self-esteem and hope	+ +	−	0	−	−

a. Symbols: 0, no effect; +, mild effect; + +, marked effect; −, negative effect.

heavy drinking can be enhanced by empathic, objective feedback of data, by working with ambivalence, by assessing barriers to change, by reinterpreting past negative experiences as alcohol related, by negotiating a follow-up plan, and always by providing hope.

In alcohol dependence, abstinence is the treatment of choice, but it can rarely be directly prescribed. Abstinence is a conclusion to which the patient must independently arrive through a process of negotiation. As a useful first step, the alcohol abuser may be instructed to conduct the following experiment: Drink daily if desired, but *never* more than 3 measured drinks (that is, 4 ounces of whisky, a half bottle of wine, or three 12-ounce cans of beer, or two-thirds of those amounts for women) in a 24-hour period. If the alcohol abuser cannot sustain such control for more than 3 months, it becomes objective evidence that the patient has lost voluntary control over alcohol use. Follow-up reevaluation is always an essential part of such a test.

In addition, clinicians cannot simply refer the alcohol-dependent person to Alcoholics Anonymous, any more than they could refer someone to a church or hobby club. Most people need to be introduced to AA, either by a treatment program or by another member. Few go to their first meeting by themselves. In addition, AA is a "program of attraction"; at first compulsory attendance is usually ineffective unless accompanied by other treatment. Many are initially put off by the religious overtones, or find going unpleasant, or initially choose an incompatible group. In recommending AA, therefore, clinicians should keep in mind that regular attendance at meetings may be as unpleasant and painful a prospect as going to an orthodontist; meetings should never be described as enjoyable—only potentially lifesaving. If a patient cannot accept AA, other forms of combined treatment—such as group therapy, a halfway house, disulfiram (0.25 gm per day), and vocational rehabilitation—can be devised to provide the 4 therapeutic components outlined in Table 31.3. Rational Recovery, a mirror opposite of AA, has been helpful to some.

The clinician must remember that the treatment of alcoholism requires patients to give up a substance that they truly, though ambivalently, have valued and enjoyed. For that reason abstinence should be prescribed "one day at a time." Proclamations that the individual may never again take a drink should be avoided. Threats of death or chronic illness are rarely effective and only add to guilt and denial. A more effective approach is to review with patients strategies and skills that in the past they have used to surmount difficult challenges. Any program of relapse prevention must be carried out for years, not weeks.

Last, clinicians are often unable to disguise their disappointment and resentment when their patients relapse—seemingly willfully. Clinicians should admit their own powerlessness over another person's drinking. To take an alcoholic's drinking personally, to see it as part of resistance or transference or as evidence of poor motivation, is to miss the point. Experienced workers in the field of alcoholism recognize that they are incapable of perceiving all the complexities of "motivation" and that relapse to or remission from alcoholism reflects a balancing of forces acting upon and within each individual, which vary from day to day. In alcoholism, as in much of medicine, we dress the wound; we do not heal it.

Alcoholism affects the entire family. In the past, because social workers and psychiatrists have viewed alcoholism as symptom and not disease, they have sometimes unwittingly implied that the spouse is the cause of the alcoholic's illness and needs treatment. Such an approach is not productive. The alcoholic's relatives will gain more strength and comfort if they understand that their relative cannot control his drinking and that no one understands why. Relatives can help and be helped in many ways. Both professional family counseling and self-help groups can be very effective. Clinicians who have several alcoholic patients may also find attendance at Al-Anon, a self-help group for family members of alcoholics, helpful. Al-Anon is a self-help organization in which the spouses and friends of alcoholics assist one another in understanding the "disease," learn how not to interfere with the recovery process, and, most important, discover how to take care of themselves. Alateen is a self-help organization in which adolescents in alcoholic families help one another to understand their painful home lives, build a network of support, and discover a wider set of coping strategies.

Because in the United States alcohol abuse is a contributory factor in roughly half of all suicides, it is important to assess the suicide potential of patients with alcoholism. Alcoholism, however, is a far more common cause of depression than depression is of alcoholism. Hence, treating a suicidal patient for his underlying alcoholism may be more effective than treating his overt depression. Some alcoholics with other mental illnesses will require antidepressants, lithium, or phenothiazines. However, there are virtually no circumstances when an alcoholic, once withdrawal is complete, should be prescribed sleeping pills or benzodiazepines.

Treating the Person in Alcohol Withdrawal

The withdrawal syndrome of someone physically dependent on alcohol is profoundly uncomfortable, may result in convulsions and delirium, can be life threatening, and often requires hospitalization. Withdrawal symptoms usually begin 6–24 hours after drinking ceases. Withdrawal seizures may occur in 5–15% of cases within the first 48 hours. On the one hand, patients may be in withdrawal and still have alcohol on their breath. On the other hand, alcoholic patients who are admitted for surgery, and therefore are given preoperative and postoperative medication, may have their withdrawal masked only to develop delirium tremens a week after admission.

On admission every alcoholic patient should be given 100 mg of intramuscular thiamine. Administration of high doses of benzodiazepines serves as a safe and effective means of treating the symptoms of alcohol withdrawal and preventing delirium tremens. As a guide for medication, measurable signs of withdrawal, rather than subjective complaints, should be followed. Sweating, tremor, fever, sensory distortions, tachycardia, impaired orientation, agitation, hyperventilation, nausea, and hypertension are objective findings that should be used to monitor the need for medication every 2 hours the patient is awake. Initially 15–30 mg of oxazepam (or the equivalent of another moderate- to long-acting benzodiazepine) should be given every 2–4 hours until the above objective symptoms are minimal to absent. On the second day, the first day's dose of benzodiazepine can usually be cut in half or by two-thirds and given only if objective signs return. Little medication is usually required after the third day. Inflexible regimens (such as 50 mg of chlordiazepoxide every 6 hours) can result in undermedication during the most dangerous stage of withdrawal and overmedication by the fourth day. If benzodiazepines are contraindicated, phenobarbital or Tegretol (200mg q.i.d. for 3–5 days) are effective alternatives.

Major complications associated with alcohol withdrawal are hallucinosis, mild dementia, seizures, and delirium tremens. Alcoholic hallucinosis may occur independently of delirium, and if so, like seizures, is most evident in the first 24–48 hours after the cessation of drinking. Hallucinations may be visual, auditory, and/or tactile, and usually occur in an otherwise clear sensorium. In rare cases auditory hallucinosis may persist for weeks or months after withdrawal and is often resistant to phenothiazines. Typically such chronic hallucinations are derogatory, accusatory, repetitive, and unusually concise. Although they occur in a clear, oriented sensorium, whether the condition is related to schizophrenia remains uncertain.

Should withdrawal seizures ("rum fits") occur, they may be treated symptomatically with parenteral diazepam. Routine administration of phenytoin (Dilantin) is not necessary or effective. If the patient was taking maintenance Dilantin before the onset of withdrawal, however, it should be continued.

For a few days to weeks after their last drink, patients who have been drinking heavily will exhibit a mild dementia. This condition can be distinguished from the memory defect of Korsakoff's psychosis by the fact that in mild dementia the memory and orientation defects are relieved by offering the patient clues. If the obtunded state following withdrawal does not progressively improve, or if it worsens, the possibility of a subdural hematoma should be vigorously investigated.

Clinically delirium tremens resembles most other acute deliria (see Chapter 16). The major difference is that delirium tremens is a hypermetabolic state; and the dangers of hyperpyrexia, dehydration, electrolyte imbalance, and mortality (up to 15%) are great. Delirium tremens usually occurs 50–100 hours after cessation of drinking and should always be treated in the acute medical service ward of a general hospital. It is commonly associated with another major illness, often pancreatitis, pneumonia, or recent surgery in the prior 2 days. It can be differentiated from severe withdrawal by the profound disorientation, markedly increased sweating, terror, and of course hallucinations and delusions. Adequate management includes close "flow sheet" monitoring of autonomic and metabolic function by the physician. Either haloperidol or parenteral benzodiazepines in adequately large doses should be used to control the hyperactivity and excitement of delirium tremens. Although oral benzodiazepines may prevent delirium tremens by allowing the patient to taper physical dependence slowly, they are generally ineffective in controlling delirium and psychosis, once present. Up to 10 mg of haloperidol or 50 mg of chlorpromazine intramuscularly every hour may be required to control the patient so that he is not dangerous to himself or others and so that other problems may be treated. Intravenous diazepam, though dangerous in inexperienced hands, is the most effective means of controlling the severe autonomic hyperreactivity of delirium tremens.

Once detoxification is complete, insomnia and anxiety may persist for weeks to months. In treating these symptoms, the physician should seek means that are not pharmacologic. Administration of minor tranquilizers and sleeping pills can rarely be justified.

In addition to conditions associated with withdrawal, other complications of alcoholism may occur. Infrequently, chronic alcoholics present with Wernicke-Korsakoff's syndrome (alcoholic amnestic disorder), presumably due to thiamine deficiency. Wernicke's encephalopathy can be of acute onset and potentially fatal. It is manifested by severe memory loss (often with confabulation), cerebellar dysfunction manifested by impaired gait, coma, and weakness of extraocular eye movements, especially of lateral gaze. It should be treated immediately in the emergency room with 50 mg of intramuscular thiamine and 50 mgm I.V. The coma and ocular findings may clear in minutes. Care should be given to administer the thiamine before intravenous glucose is administered; cellular metabolism of the glucose infusion will put increased demands on the already depleted brain thiamine and further impair neuronal function.

If the patient survives the Wernicke's encephalopathy, the residual state, Korsakoff's syndrome (alcoholic amnestic disorder), is characterized by marked disorientation and memory loss. The memory deficit is associated with confabulation and a characteristic lack of insight regarding the memory loss. The neuropathological changes of Wernicke-Korsakoff's psychosis are characterized by hemorrhages and neuronal loss in the mamillary bodies and in the gray matter adjacent to the third and fourth ventricles. Over a 6-month to 2-year period, full recovery may occur in roughly 25% of cases, and an additional 50% may improve significantly. Although prolonged vitamin supplementation is not needed, an adequate diet is essential. Thus Korsakoff's psychosis is one of the few psychiatric conditions that can actually improve on prolonged, involuntary hospitalization. The relatives of a patient who has been incapacitated by Korsakoff's psychosis should be advised that improvement may continue for at least a year.

The serious medical complications of chronic alcoholism are legion. The most common are acute and chronic liver damage, traumatic injury, gastritis, compromised immune system, cardiomyopathy (coronary artery disease), arrhythmias, pancreatitis, hypertension, various anemias, duodenal ulcer, esophageal varices, hepatic encephalopathy, polyneuritis, oropharyngeal cancers, cerebellar degeneration, and prolonged clotting time. For the management of these conditions, the reader is referred to medical texts.

Treating the Polydrug Abuser

Because polydrug abuse is symptomatic of underlying social or personality disorders and because various drugs may be involved, treatment is complex. Space does not permit a detailed discussion of the phenomenology and withdrawal from individual drugs, and the reader is referred to more specialized texts (see References). A few general guidelines are offered here.

Although chronic abuse of amphetamines, cocaine, and marihuana results in distress and sometimes psychosis, cessation of these drugs is not life threatening. Withdrawal of patients from these drugs usually requires only a drug-free environment, symptomatic relief, and psychological support.

Withdrawal from dependence on heroin or other opiates should be attempted on an inpatient basis in a strictly drug-free environment. Detoxification from heroin is rarely successful on an outpatient basis. On the first day of withdrawal, physiologically dependent heroin addicts rarely require more than 40 mg of methadone (a long-acting opiate) in divided oral doses. The dose of methadone may then be reduced by 5 mg a day in most cases. Methadone, buprenorphine, and clonidine are the drugs most commonly used to taper patients from opiates. In terms of discomfort and medical danger, opiate withdrawal has been compared to a week-long bout with influenza. The more immune the staff is to manipulation and game playing by addicts, the smoother the addict's own withdrawal will be.

Withdrawal from barbiturates and benzodiazepines may produce seizures and prolonged delirium and must be undertaken as carefully as withdrawal from alcohol. Therefore, individuals with a significant physical dependence on these drugs should be withdrawn in a general hospital with careful pharmacologic tapering. The severity of barbiturate dependence may be crudely assessed by giving a patient who has been without barbiturates for a few hours 200 mg of oral pentobarbital. If after an hour the individual is sleepy and manifests nystagmus, the likelihood of significant pharmacologic dependence is small. If in 1 hour the individual is fully alert and without nystagmus, physical dependence is present. A typical withdrawal regimen is 800 mg of pentobarbital in divided doses during the first 24 hours, with subsequent tapering by 50 mg a day. Signs of undermedication include a positive glabellar reflex, a pulse increase of more than 15 beats a minute after the patient moves from a supine to an erect position, hyperreflexia, twitching, sweating, agitation, and vomiting. In cases of combined alcohol and barbiturate (or other sedative) dependence, pentobarbital for the first 24 hours, followed by tapered doses of phenobarbital, appears to be a satisfactory regimen.

Physical dependence on diazepam (Valium), chlordiazepoxide (Librium), and especially alprazolam (Xanax) does occur. Because the first 2 compounds are long acting, withdrawal signs may not be seen for a week and may persist for 2 weeks or more. The support of a hospital treatment milieu and medication during withdrawal is usually necessary, and the patient's agitation and distress may be severe and prolonged.

Because polydrug abuse, like delinquent behavior, is symptomatic of underlying problems, especially familial dysfunction, these must be addressed. Youths steal cars or use heroin not just because their friends do or because it is fun, but because they lack psychosocial alternatives and because their parents are addicted, mentally ill, or absent. Unfortunately, at present society's approaches to both delinquency and polydrug abuse are inadequate; modern medicine is without adequate answers or effective treatment regimens.

Polydrug abuse can rarely be effectively treated with a single treatment modality, and drug use must be replaced with effective alternatives. For example, since narcotics are used in part for symptomatic relief, pure opiate antagonists are rarely effective. In contrast, methadone prevents the euphoric effect of "illegal" heroin, but it is also an active opiate that can both tranquilize the addict and "addict" him to a treatment program. Ideally, such a program will also include familial evaluation and involvement, vocational rehabilitation, group therapy, and medical care. Among heroin addicts, methadone has been more effective in reducing crime than in alleviating social disability.

Polydrug abuse, especially opiate abuse, dominates and provides a structure for the addicted individual's daily existence. Treatment, therefore, must provide an alternative structure for living. Neither prolonged imprisonment nor drug legalization is an effective alternative; neither prepares the individual for community living. Similarly, by themselves psychotherapy programs that involve at most only an hour or two of the addict's day are rarely effective.

Many opiate users have also given up narcotics through either short-term or long-term substitution of alcohol; but like the alcoholic, the polydrug abuser must ultimately substitute people for drugs. The families of origin of polydrug abusers, however, are often socially disorganized. Rather than returning to parents or former spouses, polydrug abusers are often helped by finding respectful employers, new loved ones, and more tolerant "families" such as the members of a halfway house.

Treating the addict *either* as a patient *or* as a criminal is usually futile. It is harmful, on the one hand, to excuse him from limits in time present or, on the other, to punish him too severely for past misdeeds. Making someone a patient *or* a criminal decreases self-esteem and makes less mature modes of adaptation more likely. Rather, programs for polydrug abuse should try to facilitate individual maturation. It is often helpful to ask the addict—with peer support—to condemn the drugs and self-deception that he once enjoyed, but such reaction formation is a potentially unstable solution. The army, therapeutic communities, sheltered workshops, Outward Bound, ideological movements, and employment enforced through parole all provide effective community structures that help polydrug abusers reorganize their lives. Ultimately, settings that allow the drug user to help peers altruistically, such as employment in drug rehabilitation programs and the Red Berets, are the most stabilizing and maturing.

In the treatment of polydrug abuse, coercion plays an unpredictable role. First, in masochistic personalities self-destructive behavior may actually relieve mental discomfort, and so punishment may accomplish little. Second, long prison sentences per se do little to promote subsequent community abstinence. However, prolonged parole that mandates regular employment and/or residential therapeutic communities are comparatively effective. Third, if coercion is to be successful, the penalties must be immediately enforced rather than existing only in the statute books. Thus if parole is enforced, it is far more effective than unenforced civil commitment laws. Fourth, for reasons not fully understood, coercion must be socially acceptable. Peer pressure is often more effective than controls imposed by prison wardens or head nurses. Today restaurants can forbid smoking; 40 years ago such prohibition would have led to their bankruptcy.

Finally, the fact that polydrug abusers are similar to delinquents limits the number of useful treatment alternatives. Often delinquents have received too little early supervision from both parents; such individuals cannot subsequently be ordered to do something they do not know how to do. We can, for example, pass laws against truancy but not against illiteracy. Thus, although residential self-help groups involve social coercion, they are effective not just because they require abstinence and provide limits but also because they offer training in alternatives to addiction. They give as well as take away.

Prognosis

A basic theme throughout this chapter has been that drugs and alcohol are ineffective substitutes for people. Any treatment that promotes supportive group membership in a drug-free environment is a far more effective means of treating drug addiction than are efforts to provide the drug-dependent individual with psychological insights or better drugs.

Because successful outcome depends on sustained community outcome, published treatment results are often misleading. Patients with the best prognosis (married, stable work history, no criminal history, first admission, stable social situation, no other psychiatric illness) tended to receive the most intensive inpatient treatments and made hospital care appear more effective than it is. Similarly, the shorter the follow-up, the better the outcome appears to be, but this is an illusion. In general, the treatment of cigarette smoking offers a useful analogy. Eventually more than half of all the afflicted nicotine addicts will recover; but the vast majority will relapse after a single treatment exposure, and in a majority of cases, long-term abstinence from cigarettes is achieved outside a formal treatment setting.

References

American Psychiatric Association. 1994. *Diagnostic and statistical manual of mental disorders.* 4th ed. Washington, D. C.

Bissel, L., and P. W. Haberman. 1984. *Alcoholism in the professions.* New York: Oxford University Press.

Bohn, M. J., T. F. Babor, and H. R. Kranzler. 1995. The Alcohol Use Disorders Identification Test (AUDIT): validation of a screening instrument for use in medical settings. *J. Stud. Alcohol* 56:423–432.

Brecher, E. M., and editors of *Consumer Reports.* 1972. *Licit and illicit drugs.* New York: Consumers Union.

Cahalan, D. 1970. *Problem drinkers: a national survey.* San Francisco: Jossey-Bass.

Clark, W. D. 1981. Alcoholism: blocks to diagnosis and treatment. *Am. J. Med.* 71:275–286.

Conigrave, K. M., J. B. Saunders, and J. B. Whitfield. 1955. Diagnostic tests for alcohol consumption. *Alcohol and Alcoholism* 30:13–26.

Edwards, G., and S. Guthrie. 1967. A controlled trial on inpatient and outpatient treatment of alcohol dependence. *Lancet* 1:555–559.

Goodwin, D. W. 1979. Alcoholism and heredity. *Arch. Gen. Psychiatry* 36:57–61.

Jellinek, E. M. 1960. *The disease concept of alcoholism.* New Haven: Hillhouse Press.

Lindstrom, L. 1992. *Managing alcoholism: matching clients to treatment.* New York: Oxford University Press.

McCrady, B. S., and W. R. Miller, eds. 1993. *Research on Alcoholics Anonymous: opportunities and alternatives.* New Brunswick, N.J.: Rutgers Center of Alcohol Studies.

Moore, M. H., and D. R. Gerstein, eds. 1981. *Alcohol and public policy: beyond the shadows of prohibition.* Washington, D.C.: National Academy Press.

O'Connor, P. G., and R. S. Schottenfeld. 1998. Patients with alcohol problems. *N. Engl. J. Med.* 338:592–601.

Robins, L. N. 1974. *The Vietnam drug user returns.* Special Action Office monograph series A, no. 2. Washington, D.C.: Government Printing Office.

Saitz, R., M. Mayo-Smith, et al. 1994. Individualized treatment for alcohol withdrawal. *JAMA* 272:519–523.

Schuckit, M. A., and T. L. Smith. 1996. An eight-year follow-up of 450 sons of alcoholics and controls. *Arch. Gen. Psychiatry* 53:202–210.

Stinson, F. S., and S. F. DeBakey. 1992. Alcohol related mortality in the United States, 1979–1992. *Br. J. Addict.* 87:777–783.

Tamerin, J. S., and J. H. Mendelson. 1969. The psychodynamics of chronic inebriation: observations of alcoholics during the process of drinking in an experimental group setting. *Am. J. Psychiatry* 125:886–899.

Vaillant, G. E. 1966. A twelve-year follow-up of New York narcotic addicts. IV. Some characteristics and determinants of abstinence. *Am. J. Psychiatry* 123:573–584.

Victor, M., R. D. Adams, and G. H. Collins. 1971. *The Wernicke-Korsakoff syndrome.* Philadelphia: Davis.

Walsh, D. C., R. W. Hingson, D. M. Merrigan, et al. 1991. A randomized trial of treatment options for alcohol-abusing workers. *N. Engl. J. Med.* 325:775–782.

World Health Organization. 1969. *Sixteenth report of the WHO expert committee on drug dependence.* Technical report series no. 407. Geneva.

Recommended Reading

Clark, W. D. 1981. Alcoholism: blocks to diagnosis and treatment. *Am. J. Med.* 71:275–286.

Edwards, G., E. J. Marshall, and C. C. H. Cook. 1997. *The treatment of drinking problems.* Cambridge: Cambridge University Press.

Jellinek, E. M. 1960. *The disease concept of alcoholism.* New Haven: Hillhouse Press.

Galanter, M., and H. Kleber. 1994. *Textbook of substance abuse treatment.* Washington, D.C.: APA Press.

Marlatt, G. A., and J. R. Gordon, eds. 1985. *Relapse prevention.* New York: Guilford Press.

Moore, M. H., and D. R. Gerstein, eds. 1981. *Alcohol and public policy: beyond the shadows of prohibition.* Washington, D.C.: National Academy Press.

O'Brien, C. P., and J. H. Jaffe. 1992. *Addictive states.* New York: Raven Press.

Vaillant, G. E. 1995. *The natural history of alcoholism revisited.* Cambridge, Mass.: Harvard University Press.

Wilsnack, S. C., and L. J. Beckman, eds. 1989. *Alcohol problems in women.* New York: Guilford Press.

32

DONALD C. GOFF

JON E. GUDEMAN

The Person with Chronic Mental Illness

Chronic, severe mental illness can take many forms, but is characterized by the persistence of disabling symptoms or impaired functioning. Most chronically ill patients suffering from major psychiatric disorders are unable to live independently and require considerable assistance from families and mental health care systems. The most basic aspects of living may be affected, such as providing for one's personal needs, maintaining interpersonal relationships, and pursuing work, schooling, or recreational activities. The illness may be of sudden onset, or may follow an insidious prodromal phase. The course, while persistent, can be continuously progressive or episodic in nature. The focus of this chapter is on schizophrenia, which is the classic chronic mental illness. Other diagnoses found among the chronically mentally ill include major affective disorders, paranoid disorders, and certain severe personality disorders, such as borderline personality. Substance abuse commonly results in chronic impairment but is discussed in Chapter 18. Similarly, antisocial personality lies outside the scope of this chapter but is reviewed in Chapter 15.

The difficulties encountered by individuals with chronic mental illness will be determined largely by the specific manifestations of their illness. To use schizophrenia as an example, symptoms tend to cluster into at least 3 groups: reality distortion (delusions and hallucinations), disorganization (formal thought disorder and inappropriate affect), and negative symptoms (apathy, social withdrawal, poverty of thought and speech, and flattening of affect) (Andreasen et al., 1995; Liddle, 1987). The majority of patients with schizophrenia display symptoms from all 3 categories and are classified as having "undifferentiated type." However, some patients may exhibit prominent symptoms from only 1 category, and the problems they struggle with will be determined by which cluster of symptoms predominates. In addition, the patient with schizophrenia whose illness follows a typical, unremitting course experiences a much different set of difficulties than the patient with an episodic affective disorder, who repeatedly faces unpredictable disruptions in his attempts to reestablish a more functional life.

Individuals with schizophrenia whose symptoms are restricted to complex delusional systems and hallucinations are subclassified as *paranoid type.* In the absence of overt disorganization and negative symptoms, the paranoid schizophrenic may go largely unnoticed by most observers. These patients often conceal their psychiatric symptoms and do not exhibit the bizarre appearance and speech which attract attention to other patients with schizophrenia. They may complete school successfully and hold jobs. However, difficulties arise when circumstances at work or within social relationships increasingly become complicated by delusional beliefs or by hallucinatory voices. The paranoid individual steadily incorporates more and more people into the delusional system until activities and relationships become impossible to sustain. The employed individual may become convinced that his boss is conspiring to harm him or may believe that he hears his boss taunting him when his back is turned. The young woman living at home may begin to believe that family members are poisoning her or have implanted a microchip and are monitoring her thoughts. Although the paranoid individual's life may become severely restricted by perceived dangers, mental health professionals often do not become involved until much later in the course of the illness, when the individual finally is apprehended for irrational behavior, or ceases to be able to care safely for himself.

The *disorganized patient* can exhibit profoundly disordered language and behavior which make independent living impossible. Thought disorders can range in severity from subtle peculiarities of logic to grossly incoherent speech. The idiosyncratic speech of some individuals with schizophrenia may give an exaggerated impression of cognitive impairment, whereas their capacity to understand specific issues and to make decisions may be adequate.

Impairment of judgment and of behavioral control can make the disorganized patient disturbing to others and possibly even dangerous. These patients may engage in inappropriate behaviors such as disrobing in public, stealing food, or smoking in restricted areas. Of even greater concern is the occasional violent or self-injurious behavior of agitated, disorganized patients. Unlike the individual with paranoid schizophrenia, the disorganized patient does not elude detection and usually remains under the close supervision of family or residential staff in structured settings.

Negative symptoms of schizophrenia include apathy, social isolation, poverty of thought and speech, flattening of affect, and neglect of hygiene. While these symptoms usually do not necessitate hospitalization, they can be quite disabling and may interfere with rehabilitative efforts in the community. Negative symptoms also tend to respond less fully than psychotic symptoms to conventional antipsychotic agents and may steadily worsen over time. Not only do negative symptoms profoundly impair an individual's ability to function in most realms and to participate actively in treatment, but also negative symptoms can alienate family and caregivers. Whereas hallucinations and delusions are readily recognized as symptoms of the illness, uninformed caregivers commonly view apathy, mutism, and poor hygiene as willful or as weakness of character. Parents become angry at their son with schizophrenia because of his repeated failures to clean his room, change out of his soiled clothing, or secure a job. Sustaining empathy and enthusiasm for the care of withdrawn, unemotive patients can be quite taxing for all involved, particularly if negative symptoms are not understood to be symptoms of the illness. A comprehensive plan must be developed to provide supervision for these avolitional patients who otherwise are unlikely to follow through with treatment.

Only recently has attention been paid to the role that *insight* plays in determining psychiatric outcome. Valid rating scales have been developed to measure patients' awareness of their illness; items include recognition of the impact of mental illness on one's life, the effect of medication, and awareness of aberrant behaviors or symptoms (Amador et al., 1994; Cuesta and Peralta, 1994). In a study of 412 psychiatric patients, Amador and colleagues (1994) found that over half of patients with schizophrenia were unaware of important aspects of their illness and 22% were almost completely unaware of the efficacy of medication. Patients with affective disorders exhibited less severe lack of awareness, although manic patients were quite similar to patients with schizophrenia in this respect. Schizophrenic patients in remission did not differ

from patients with active psychotic symptoms, implying that lack of awareness is a trait which tends not to respond to treatment. Lack of awareness is probably an additional component of schizophrenic illness, like psychotic or negative symptoms, and may be associated with neuropsychological deficits of the prefrontal cortex (Amador et al., 1994). As would be expected, severe lack of awareness of illness is associated with poor compliance with treatment and poor psychosocial functioning.

The History of Community Mental Health

The longest continuous history of community care for the chronically mentally ill began in Gheel, Belgium. According to legend, toward the end of the sixth century A.D., Dymphna, an Irish princess, and her priest confessor, Father Gerebran, fled to Gheel to escape her father, a petty king who sought incest and marriage with his beautiful daughter. The mad king discovered her flight and pursued her. The king and his soldiers assassinated the priest and with one blow beheaded Dymphna. An insane person watching this violent act was miraculously restored to sanity. Dymphna's martyrdom was considered a triumph of wisdom, and she was elevated to sainthood. Later a shrine and church were built in her honor. People with mental illness flocked to the church at Gheel to seek cures for their affliction. Unfortunately, after 9 days' penance at the church annex, not all mentally ill persons returned to sanity. Because the facilities were limited, families in Gheel considered it their religious duty to open their homes to care for the mentally ill. Thus the practice of family care for persons with mental illness began (Tuttle, 1891).

At Gheel, a psychiatric infirmary under church auspices developed, and in 1852 it became a state hospital and colony for the mentally ill. Patients are still committed to the town of Gheel. After evaluation at the hospital, they are placed in the homes of townspeople, but not more than 2 to a family. The families accept the mentally ill, ask them to work at simple tasks, and pay them a small wage. Today chronic mental patients have the resources of a social club and a small mental hospital. The colony at Gheel illustrates essential components of community care: adequate living arrangements, some economic support, daily work, social activity, and medical and hygienic supervision by the mental hospital services.

In America public responsibility for the mentally ill failed to develop until the latter part of the eighteenth century. Previously the mentally ill were kept in their homes. The Pennsylvania Hospital in Philadelphia, founded in 1752 for both the physically and and the mentally ill, was the first private hospital for the mentally ill person (Grob, 1973). In the early 1800s, the growth of cities, increased immigration, the large numbers of poor people, and a reform movement in Europe called "moral treatment" all paved the way for public mental hospitals in the United States.

In Worcester, Massachusetts, in 1833 the Boston Prison Discipline Society, an energetic reform group that sought an alternative to imprisonment for the mentally ill, helped to establish the first public mental hospital in America. Authorities at that time considered 120 beds the optimal size to provide good "moral treatment" for the mentally ill. They believed that the small hospital fostered a close personal relationship between the patient and the hospital superintendent and that this relationship, combined with good food, regular physical activity, and fresh country air, could alter the bad habits that produced mental illness. By 1848 the average daily census at the Worcester State Hospital was nearly 400, prompting the Massachusetts legislature to authorize the establishment of a second mental hospital at Taunton. During the latter part of the nineteenth century, public hospitals, as an alternative to prisons and almshouses, grew dramatically in number and size. The devotion and zeal of Dorothea Dix, a social reformer who spent 30 years lobbying for the establishment of mental hospitals, helped to build or expand 32 institutions.

Public institutions became overwhelmed by the psychological, social, physical, and economic burdens of caring for those with chronic mental illness. The striking increase in census in the public hospitals can be attributed to (1) commitment laws requiring institutionalization of dangerous mentally ill persons until they showed no evidence of illness (because the illness, in contrast to dangerousness, often lasted a long time, patients languished in the hospitals); (2) the failure to distinguish between patients who could benefit from treatment and those who were incurable; and (3) the increase in numbers of older persons with dementia as well as the public hospital's new responsibility for certain alcoholics and for patients with neurological disorders. In 1880 public concern about the numbers of chronically mentally ill resulted in the first "census for the insane," by which the federal government attempted to count the number of chronically psychotic individuals in the United States every 10 years. Data from these surveys, which were conducted up until 1963, have been used by contemporary researchers to study historical patterns in the distribution of psychotic illness in the United States (Torrey and Bowler, 1990).

In the United States the public mental hospital census grew to 144,000 in 1903 and then to its zenith of 559,000 in 1955. Estimates indicate that chronic patients occupied about 80% of the beds. Overcrowded and dilapidated facilities, inadequate staffing, and poorly managed programs led to abuse of some patients and made humane care difficult. These inadequate facilities provided only custodial care for dependent persons considered hopeless by both professionals and the community.

Deinstitutionalization

A number of developments in the 1950s led to the dramatic change in the treatment of the chronically mentally ill known as deinstitutionalization. The first of the antipsychotic drugs, chlorpromazine (Thorazine), became available in 1953. The new antipsychotic agents sufficiently suppressed delusions and hallucinations so that many patients with schizophrenia could be managed in the community. Later, the antidepressants and lithium helped patients with major affective disorders. At the same time, social psychologists and psychiatrists suggested that confinement in a hospital might itself produce dependency, apathy, isolation, irritability, and other symptoms of chronic mental illness (Goffman, 1962). Some even held that mental illness did not exist at all but was the product of hospitalization (Szasz, 1961).

New commitment laws and procedures designed to protect the civil rights of patients provided another impetus for deinstitutionalization. In general these laws restricted involuntary commitment to those who were dangerous to themselves or others and no longer included the protective or parental functions of the state commitment *(parens patriae)*. Instead, patients were encouraged to seek voluntary commitment to hospitals. New legal rulings which determined that patients had a right to treatment (*Wyatt v. Stickney,* 1971) imposed a significant financial burden on hospitals and thus encouraged them to discharge patients. Furthermore, the case of *Lake v. Cameron* (1966) ruled that patients had a right to the least restrictive environment, that is, to alternatives to public hospitalization.

The Joint Commission on Mental Illness and Health in its 1961 report *Action for Mental Health* also promoted deinstitutionalization by recommending that hospitals be limited to 1000 beds and that persons with serious illness be cared for in the community to the greatest extent possible. The president proposed and Congress funded the Community Mental Health Center Program in 1963 as an alternative at the local level to state hospitalization. In the mid-1960s new federal programs, especially Supplementary Security Income (SSI), Social Security Disability Insurance (SSDI), and Medicaid and Medicare health benefits, gave patients the financial resources to live outside the hospital. By 1988 combined spending on community care by state mental health agencies and the federal government totaled $3.5 billion (Hadley, Culhane, and Snyder, 1992).

Between 1955 and 1991 the state hospital resident population decreased by almost 80%, from approximately 560,000 to 100,000. The average length of stay became shorter, but the number of admissions to state hospitals increased, as did the number of readmissions. Some states, such as Vermont and Pennsylvannia, reduced the number of long-term state hospital beds by more than 90% (Hadley, Culhane, and Snyder, 1992). In the United Kingdom, funds released by closing psychiatric hospitals were reinvested in replacement services in the community; this was typically not the case in the United States (Leff, Trieman, and Gooch, 1996). One example of such a shifting of funds can be found in the Community Reinvestment Bill for New York State, enacted in 1993, which made $210 million available to community services as 5 psychiatric centers were closed. In most areas of the United States, the state hospital now serves mainly as a backup facility for chronic patients who have acute exacerbations; patients enter and leave the hospital as their symptoms worsen or improve (Bachrach, 1996; Goldman, Adams, and Taube, 1983).

Alternatives to Hospitalization

As is true of many social changes, deinstitutionalization of the chronically mentally ill took place in response to administrative fiat more than as a result of carefully performed experimentation. Critics have pointed to the lack of resources in the community and the tendency for many deinstitutionalized patients to receive no treatment or inadequate treatment (Weller, 1989). There are relatively few controlled studies comparing patients who remain in state hospitals with those who move into community programs. This is unfortunate, because deinstitutionalization has profoundly affected the care of the chronically mentally ill. Studies that are available generally show that outcomes for chronic mental patients in community programs are as good as, and occasionally better than, the outcomes for patients in traditional hospitalization programs. More firmly established is the finding that long hospitalizations generally are no more effective than shorter hospitalizations, although the definition of each category of hospital duration varies widely between studies, and the relevance of this finding to patients with schizophrenia is unclear (Hargreaves et al., 1977; Hirsch et al., 1979; Mattes et al., 1977).

Analysis of the outcomes of deinstitutionalization suggested 3 ways to reduce the need for hospitalization: (1) programs can provide an alternative "at the front door" of the hospital for patients who would otherwise be admitted to inpatient hospital services; (2) shorter length of hospital stay, or partial hospitalization rather than full-time care, can be offered once the patient is hospitalized; and (3) patients hospitalized for extended periods can be discharged and provided care in nonhospital settings.

As deinstitutionalization emphasized treating the chronically mentally ill in the community, recent trends in public psychiatry are shifting the emphasis from clinic-centered treatment of these patients to treatments directed out into the community (Santos et al., 1995). A pioneering model for an alternative to hospitalization "at the front door" was the Training in Community Living Program in Madison, Wisconsin, developed in 1975 (Stein and Test, 1980). Also known as the Program for Assertive Community Treatment (PACT), this model involves intensive support of the patient by a community-based team available 24 hours a day, 7 days a week. Program staff work long-term with patients, families, and agencies in the community to support the patients and to help them avoid hospitalization. A core professional team focuses on teaching patients to develop coping skills for community living. Randomized clinical trials of the first PACT project demonstrated benefits in clinical status, social functioning, medication compliance, employment, quality of life, and reduced hospitalization compared to conventional outpatient treatment (Marx, Test, and Stein, 1973; Stein and Test, 1980; Test and Stein, 1980; Weisbrod, Test, and Stein, 1980).

An early adaptation of the PACT model was the Threshold's Bridge Program, begun as a National Institute of Mental Health (NIMH) demonstration project in 1978 by a psychiatric rehabilitation agency in Chicago (Bond et al., 1988). The Bridge model, also referred to as "Assertive Outreach," differs by performing assertive community treatment within a larger care system. In contrast to the PACT model, in which all care is provided by the PACT team, the Bridge model integrates care delivered by affiliated service providers.

The Program for Assertive Community Treatment (Stein and Test, 1980) was a forerunner of the many innovative programs now generally referred to as "Assertive Community Treatment" or "Continuous Treatment Teams" (Santos et al., 1995). In these programs a multidisciplinary team closely follows a relatively small case load of chronic patients in the community, spending more than 75% of staff time out in the community. Medications are administered and monitored in the patient's home; shopping, cooking, and other living skills are taught in the patient's neighborhood; and family and other important sources of support are involved within the community. Clinicians advocate for the patient and share responsibilities with other members of the team. Some of the goals of this intensive community-based approach are to overcome the problems of missed clinic appointments, noncompliance with medication, and failure of traditional clinic-based treatment to improve the quality of an individual's life in the community. Families often report a sense of relief knowing that the ill family member is being closely monitored and that a clinical team is available to respond to emergencies at all times. A major advantage of this approach is that clinicians can monitor patients closely enough to identify early signs of noncompliance and relapse, thereby avoiding hospitalization or more serious morbidity.

Although quite costly, these intensive community treatment teams have substantially reduced hospitalization rates in several controlled trials and can be cost-effective when applied to patients with high rates of hospital utilization. In one study, the total psychiatric care of patients at a community mental health center randomly assigned to a community-based assertive case management program based on the Bridges model cost approximately $5500 less over a 6-month period than care for patients assigned to conventional aftercare services (Bond et al., 1988). Several reviews of outcome studies examining these models have been published (Burns and Santos, 1995; Olfson, 1990; Scott and Dixon, 1995), and important randomized trials are currently under way. McGrew and associates (1994) determined that fidelity to the original PACT model correlated with favorable outcome: results have tended to be less consistently positive than the original outcome trials reported by Stein and Test. However, Stein noted that converting clinicians to the PACT model can be like "swimming against a tidal wave" (Stein, 1992). Despite the difficulties of teaching traditionally trained clinicians to operate in this model, recent trials have indicated that PACT is superior to conventional approaches for several subgroups of patients, including the homeless, recent onset schizophrenia, and patients with substance abuse complicating major psychiatric illness (Burns and Santos, 1995; Drake, McHugo, and Noordsy, 1993; Teague, Drake, and Ackerson, 1995). Other studies have suggested that increasing investment in outpatient services without adopting the PACT model often fails to reduce overall hospitalization rates (Lawrence et al., 1991) or total expenditures per patient (Okin et al., 1995).

Day hospitalization also provides an effective alternative to traditional inpatient hospitalization for some chronically mentally ill patients (Herz, Endicott, and Spitzer, 1975; Lamb, 1967; Wilder, Levin, and Zwerling, 1966). Acutely ill patients can be admitted to a day hospital instead of the traditional inpatient unit (Hoge et al., 1992). Patients who are not stable enough to return home at night can be placed in an inn on the hospital's premises. Those who require 24-hour hospitalization because they are a danger to themselves or others receive care in a "crisis stabilization unit" and return to the day hospital as soon as they improve. While long-term day treatment has generally been replaced by social clubs and vocational rehabilitation programs, partial hospitalization is increasingly utilized as a short-term approach for stabilizing patients without requiring more costly hospitalization (Hoge et al., 1992).

In a landmark 1966 monograph, *Schizophrenia and Social Care,* a group of British psychiatrists reported the framework for a third approach to deinstitutionalization, which involves discharging patients from long-term hospitalization and providing care in nonhospital settings (Brown et al., 1966). In a quasi-experimental study the psychiatrists examined the discharge policies of 3 representative English psychiatric hospitals. Patients from the hospital with the most aggressive discharge policy did no worse than those in the other 2 hospitals, where patients stayed longer; no significant differences were observed in the course of illness, in disturbed behavior in the community, in employment, or in readmission, but the families of patients in the rapid discharge group reported more family problems. One follow-up study in Rhode Island of 53 patients with chronic mental illness discharged to the community after long hospitalizations determined that after about 7 years, 57% were living in community residences, 28% had moved to independent living, and 16% had returned to the hospital. Although these patients remained significantly symptomatic, and more than half had required rehospitalization at some time, they expressed almost unanimous preference for life in the community (Okin and Pearsall, 1993). Similar results were reported in the United Kingdom, where closure of 2 English psychiatric hospitals was closely studied in a 1-year follow-up (Leff, Trieman, and Gooch, 1996). As in the Rhode Island experience, more than 80% of patients preferred life in the community. Interestingly, while patients reported enriched social lives after discharge, contact with families decreased. Not all studies of deinstitutionalization have been as reassuring, however. A small follow-up study in Vermont of deinstitutionalized patients found an 87% rehospitalization rate within the first year despite concerted efforts to reintegrate and support patients in the community (Dewees, Pulice, and McCormick, 1996).

While it was originally assumed that, following deinstitutionalization, most patients would steadily advance along a continuum from highly structured, supervised residences to independent living, 2 studies have indicated that only a small proportion of chronically ill patients are able to progress to independent living (Geller and Fisher, 1993; Okin et al., 1995).

Another innovative program which has influenced the approach to caring for the chronically mentally ill in the community is the Clubhouse Model at Fountain House in New York City (Glasscote et al., 1971). Initiated by former state hospital patients, Fountain House provides housing, job training, socialization, and medical care. It leases inexpensive apartments where clients can live; if they improve sufficiently, they can take over the lease. The program offers job training at its midtown location and assigns clients to its own snack bar, cafeteria, thrift shop, and maintenance crews. After clients function well in the in-house job training program, they progress to supervised unskilled or skilled jobs at department stores, banks, or advertising agencies. Clients may go on to independent work after a period of supervision. The program staff maintains close collaboration with the New York State employment service and vocational rehabilitation services. Although many Fountain House members eventually require rehospitalization for psychiatric reasons, they stay in the community longer than those who do not participate in the program.

In a pioneering project at Boston University, the Center for Psychiatric Rehabilitation offers individuals with chronic mental illness a special education program on the college campus where they receive prevocational training in a "normalizing" environment (Unger et al., 1991). This project boasts impressive gains in employment following completion of this 4-semester program, although we emphasize that participants are carefully selected.

Scope of the Problem

The lifetime prevalence of schizophrenia is 0.85% and the incidence of schizophrenia about 0.4 per 1000 population per year. It has been estimated that in 1990 direct and indirect costs of schizophrenia in the United States totaled $33 billion, and treatment of schizophrenia accounted for almost 3% of all health care expenditures (Rupp and Keith, 1993). Most studies indicate that about 10% of patients with schizophrenia will become asymptomatic, 20% will remain severely disabled, and the remainder will experience a fluctuating course with varying levels of symptomatology and rates of relapse (Breier et al., 1991). As many as 1.3 million people reside in nursing homes,

and surveys indicate that over 100,000 have a primary psychiatric diagnosis such as schizophrenia. These figures indicate that to some extent the nursing home has replaced the state hospital for long-term placement of the chronically mentally ill. In addition, it has been estimated that between one-third and one-half of the homeless in the United States suffer from schizophrenia (Bachrach, 1992). The very high rate of chronic mental illness among the homeless is in part a consequence of almost a half-century of deinstitutionalization combined with inadequate resources for treatment and housing in the community.

Planning for the care of patients with chronic mental illness must take into account the scope of the problem and its unique nature. In the early years of deinstitutionalization, more than 50% of the patients in state hospitals returned to their families. Later, as the most seriously disabled patients were deinstitutionalized, the percentage of patients living at home dropped markedly. The prevalence of mental illness is highest in cities and in lower-class neighborhoods, largely owing to the "drift" of chronically ill patients toward urban environments and down the socioeconomic ladder. Deinstitutionalization has further contributed to this pattern, as aftercare for discharged patients has typically been concentrated in urban centers.

Systems of Care

The state hospital historically provided core services for the mentally ill. At a minimum, these services included control, containment, and domicile—so-called custodial care. Some mental hospitals also provided treatment and rehabilitation services. Today a range of community-based and hospital-based programs must provide all these services. The basic needs of the chronically ill include treatment, social rehabilitation, and domiciliary or housing services. To be effective, each need must be considered separately but linked programmatically with the others. Treatment entails diagnosis of illness and its symptom patterns; rehabilitative and domiciliary services require careful assessment of the patient's disability and level of functioning. Community systems work best when a centralized authority at the regional, county, or city level has overall responsibility for delivering care. Centralization makes it possible to link services, to develop new services, and to assign staff to meet patients' needs.

Because acute exacerbations and periods of remission characterize chronic mental illness, many patients require frequent hospitalization for short periods. Hospital-based services must therefore be integrated with community-based programs. One example, the Community Reentry Program, provides patients with chronic psychotic disorders training in fundamental skills while hospitalized in an effort to facilitate reentry into the community (Smith et al., 1996). Additional services required in a treatment system include emergency care (crisis intervention), outpatient and day treatment, social and vocational rehabilitation, and access to medical and dental care. Housing options must range from more intensely supervised settings, such as quarterway houses, group homes, and nursing homes, to less supervised settings, such as supervised apartments, foster care, independent apartments, and, when appropriate, home visiting in the patient's own home. To meet adequately the specific needs of the chronically mentally ill, such services must gain political support at the state and local level.

Continuity of care is another basic organizing principle for any system. Each patient needs to have an identified staff member (case manager, primary clinician, or clinical team) responsible for coordinating services involved in his care. Once a patient is hospitalized, the outpatient treatment team should remain directly involved in treatment planning and preparation for discharge. When decompensation occurs, programmatic and bureaucratic barriers should not hinder the patient from gaining easy access into more intensive treatment settings, such as a hospital. Central record keeping and tracking enhance this process and ensure that patients do not fall through the cracks. As much as possible, patients should have a choice of services, and complex funding arrangements or program barriers should not stand in the way. Persons who are legally incompetent to make judgments will need an appointed guardian or conservator who can make the necessary decisions. Financial arrangements should provide funding for the patient throughout the system.

The overall goal is to help patients achieve maximum independence, autonomy, and self-care while recognizing that illness and disability will often limit progress, that needs will be different at different stages of illness, and that some individuals will not progress despite the best efforts of the caregiving system. The long-term involvement of a case manager or treatment team will ensure that an individual patient's specific needs and vulnerabilities will be recognized and accommodated by the health care system.

Comprehensive Diagnosis and Psychiatric Treatment

The etiology and pathogenesis of the various conditions that constitute chronic mental illness are not known. The most useful assumption is that chronic mental illness derives in part from a biological predisposition, and that psychosocial factors contribute to its precipitation and influence its course and expression. This position is based on a biopsychosocial model that acknowledges no single therapeutic or rehabilitative form of treatment as the only correct one. Treatment of the person with chronic mental illness typically involves a combination of pharmacologic, psychotherapeutic, and psychosocial modalities.

Differential diagnosis of the specific disease entities that constitute chronic mental illness, such as schizophrenia, major affective disorders, or severe personality disorders, is discussed in other chapters. The psychiatrist must be familiar with all aspects of differential diagnosis, because many chronically mentally ill patients are limited in their ability to verbalize their signs, symptoms, behaviors, and emotional reactions. Many also lack insight into their illness, and their ability to provide a psychiatric history is compromised by their inability to recognize symptoms or evidence of impaired functioning. In addition to the careful assessment of the course of illness and specific psychotic, affective, and behavioral symptoms, it is very important to rule out organic pathology as well as comorbid substance abuse (Goff, Henderson, and Manschreck, 1997). The clinician must determine whether organic syndromes such as seizure disorders, endocrinopathies, or substance abuse are causing, exacerbating, or complicating the clinical picture, as chronically mentally ill individuals have a high incidence of physical illnesses and substance abuse (Bartels et al., 1993; Cuffel, 1992; Koranyi, 1979).

The clinician must rely on the clinical examination, history, mental status examination, psychological tests, and physical examination to arrive at a diagnosis and formulation and to develop a comprehensive treatment plan. History from other sources, including family and prior caregivers, is often essential when patients cannot provide an adequate history. The process works best if the physician assumes responsibility for the formulation and treatment plan but receives input from a multidisciplinary team. Treatment should be based on identification of the problems, the goals to be achieved, the interventions, and the anticipated outcome. Measures of outcome should be identified at the outset and actively monitored at specified intervals; a failure to achieve anticipated outcomes should result in a reassessment of the formulation and treatment plan by the multidisciplinary team. It is very important that the role of family and outside caregivers be incorporated into the treatment plan.

The following vignette illustrates this diagnostic process:

Mr. A. T. is a 28-year-old white single male who has been hospitalized continuously for the past 2 years. He was living in a supervised group home, but because of repeated stealing within the home and exposing himself to neighbors, he was hospitalized. Mr. T.'s illness dates back to his early school years, when he had trouble learning. He was initially diagnosed as having low normal intelligence and a learning disability (attention deficit disorder with hyperactivity) and was placed in special classes. His parents had difficulty acknowledging his special needs and to this day have unrealistically high expectations for him. Unfortunately they continue to blame schools, doctors, hospitals, and mental health professionals for his difficulties.

During Mr. T.'s adolescence he was repeatedly in trouble with the law for minor theft and prostitution. He was first hospitalized at age 20, when he experienced acute psychotic symptoms, including delusions and hallucinations. These were of a transient but recurrent nature. Since then his course has been stormy. When the patient lived at home, he struggled with his parents, who were frequently critical, demanding, angry, and intrusive. When he lived in group homes, his parents continued their involvement and made excessive demands on staff. At one point Mr. T. accused the staff of sexual abuse, which led to a series of legal court actions.

Mr. T.'s diagnosis on readmission 2 years ago was borderline mental retardation with an atypical psychosis and antisocial personality disorder. His initial treatment plan included low-dose phenothiazines, which were subsequently switched to an atypical antipsychotic agent owing to extrapyramidal symptoms, containment, low but consistent expectations geared toward activities of daily living, a reward system using spending money for good behavior, social service work with the family to help them set reasonable expectations, and supportive treatment by his primary clinician. This therapy was designed to address the patient's persistent feelings of vulnerability and deficit, help him to accept his limitations, permit him to grieve but not be overwhelmed with emotion, and set firm, consistent limits. The therapist was to take a practical approach and deal with problems of daily living. Because Mr. T. had shown little outward evidence of guilt, attention to appropriate behavior would be necessary.

With consistent, low expectations on the part of the staff, Mr. T. surprisingly left the hospital and obtained a job in a restaurant. For the past year he has worked as a busboy, his first work experience. His employer reports good performance. Mr. T. somewhat idealizes both employer and therapist. His earnings are deposited in an account, and he receives a daily allowance based on his behavior. The family, pleased with his progress and with the social service support, has been less intrusive. Mr. T. is requesting to live in a group home again.

A multidisciplinary treatment review was held with his psychiatrist, social worker, staff members from the inn at the hospital where he is living, the director of continuing care programs, managers of 2 group homes, and the apartment living director. Review of Mr. T.'s recent behavior reveals that he continues to be suspected of stealing at the inn and that he spends much time unsupervised. Group home leaders fear that he will be unmanageable if he returns to more independent living. A new plan is developed whereby he will have to participate in activities, assigned tasks, and chores. His hours will be supervised more closely. Simultaneously, alternatives to a group home will be explored, including a single room in the neighborhood. A very carefully supervised plan whereby Mr. T. could sleep outside the hospital and check in daily and nightly was formulated. His psychiatrist will tell him that he must take a number of steps before he can consider living outside, and will help him accept the anticipated disappointment.

Pharmacological Management

Antipsychotic medication is the cornerstone for treatment of schizophrenia, though insufficient as a sole treatment modality (Kane, 1996). Approximately 70% of patients will derive substantial benefit from treatment with conventional antipsychotic medication and can usually be managed outside the hospital. Preliminary evidence suggests that early initiation of antipsychotic medication may be associated with a better initial response and with improved outcome at 1-year follow-up (Loebel et al., 1992). While the conventional antipsychotic agents may substantially improve psychotic symptoms and prevent relapse, negative symptoms tend to be less responsive to these agents. In addition, parkinsonian side effects and akathisia can be quite troubling to patients and families. In one study, when asked to rate the relative advantages and disadvantages of antipsychotic medications, patients with schizophrenia reported that side effects outweighed therapeutic benefits, whereas families believed that therapeutic benefits outweighed side effects (Finn et al., 1990). Fortunately, the new "atypical" antipsychotic agents offer substantially improved side effect profiles and superior efficacy for negative symptoms. Clozapine is clearly more effective than conventional antipsychotic agents in certain treatment-resistant patients and has been found to be cost-effective despite the considerable cost of hematological monitoring (Kane et al., 1988; Meltzer et al., 1993). The financial advantage of clozapine results from reduced use of hospitalization in patients who respond. Clozapine may be particularly effective in preventing relapse compared to conventional antipsychotic agents (Essock et al., 1996). As with all psychotropic medications, effectiveness in preventing relapse is determined in part by the relative burden of side effects, since compliance rates can be quite low in the face of disturbing side effects. It is hoped that clozapine and the newer atypical agents will substantially improve the quality of life of patients with schizophrenia because of improved efficacy and improved compliance rates as a result of reduced levels of side effects (Goff, 1995).

Psychotherapy

Researchers generally agree that supportive psychotherapy alone is inadequate treatment for schizophrenia, but can be quite helpful when combined with medication. Although 3 of 4 controlled studies found no benefit for psychodynamic psychotherapy provided alone or in combination with medication, each study suffered from methodological limitations (Mueser and Bellack, 1995). Outcomes of "client centered therapy" and "major role therapy" have similarly been disappointing in controlled trials (Mueser and Bellack, 1995). One encouraging study by Tarrier and colleagues (1993) demonstrated a significant reduction of symptoms, which was maintained at 6-month follow-up, with a therapy emphasizing coping skills and problem solving.

Supportive psychotherapy plays an important role in the treatment of chronic patients, particularly if they are not involved in other modalities, such as Assertive Community Outreach Programs or Intensive Case Management. Emphasis is placed on establishing and maintaining an alliance, fostering compliance with medication, helping the patient cope with stressors, and attempting to assist with reality testing. Several specialized techniques are required to work effectively with schizophrenic patients, but these techniques can readily be learned by caregivers without professional degrees (Weiden and Havens, 1994). Forming an alliance can be quite difficult with a paranoid patient. Because delusional individuals are preoccupied with and distressed by their delusional beliefs, it usually is sufficient early on to engage them in a neutral, non-

threatening discussion about their current life and interests. Until a sufficient alliance is formed, the therapist should neither agree with the delusions nor attempt reality testing; impartial interest and concern alone are usually a welcome relief to a delusional patient. Fortunately, the therapist can often explore a patient's delusional system without becoming a part of it. As the therapist continues his empathic work and builds up the alliance, he helps the patient reality-test and solve problems in the here-and-now. The therapist learns about the patient's daily living, interactions with others, and basic activities. He lends support and at times gives advice. In this practical problem-solving approach, the therapist is an active participant in the patient's life. The assertive case management programs described earlier rely on frequent, brief educational and supportive interventions by clinicians in the patient's home environment rather than traditional scheduled psychotherapy sessions in the clinic.

The psychological understanding of patients with mental illness remains controversial. The late Dr. Elvin Semrad, professor of psychiatry at Harvard Medical School, taught that psychosis is a defense erected by the ego for protection from painful emotions. According to this model, the psychotic individual is limited to primitive defenses of projection, denial, distortion, and avoidance to cope with overwhelming drives, emotions, needs, and primitive fantasies. These defenses distort the patient's perception of reality. The therapist's role is to help the patient clarify this distorted reality, acknowledge his painful feelings, and gain insight into his illness. This therapeutic approach emphasizes support and insight and usually avoids any probing of the unconscious or attempts at resolving intrapsychic conflict. Many contemporary experts view psychotic symptoms as manifestations of the aberrant functioning of a compromised brain (see Chapter 13) and not as protection against emotional stress. Regardless of one's view, the clinician must always respect the psychotic patient's experience and his sometimes desperate attempts to find meaning.

Cognitive Behavioral Approaches

Traditional supportive psychotherapy has increasingly been supplemented or even supplanted by approaches utilizing cognitive behavioral principles. Best known and most established are programs emphasizing social skills and psychosocial education as developed by Liberman and colleagues (1995). Comprehensive treatment manuals have been developed, which include training videos and workbooks for patients. The program developed by Liberman and colleagues includes several modules which target different areas of social competency, such as medication management. After learning new skills and rehearsing within the group in role-playing exercises, patients are then expected to practice the skills during their daily interactions with caregivers, family, and friends. Social skills training is conducted in groups of 5–10 patients meeting 1–3 times per week, and each of the 6 modules takes about 10–20 weeks to complete. Most studies have indicated that social skills training successfully impacts patients' functioning and may reduce intensity of symptoms and frequency of hospitalization (Liberman, Spaulding, and Corrigan, 1995). However, evidence for reduced hospitalization has been inconsistent, and the efficacy of social skills training on symptomatology is debated (Mueser and Bellack, 1995; Penn and Mueser, 1996).

Recent work with cognitive approaches has been quite encouraging for the treatment of hallucinations and delusions. Following a model similar to that developed for the cognitive therapy of depression, patients are taught to reality-test their psychotic symptoms and practice strategies for coping with these aspects of their illness (Hole, Rush, and Beck, 1979). Several trials of cognitive behavioral therapy have demonstrated efficacy in treatment-resistant patients (Chadwick and Birchwood, 1994; Garety et al., 1994; Tarrier et al., 1993). These investigators have reported reductions in severity of hallucinations and delusions, in conviction about the reality of symptoms, and in levels of preoccupation with symptoms. In one study, reductions in psychotic symptoms were sustained at 6-month follow-up (Tarrier et al., 1993). Kingdon and Turkington (1994) have published a comprehensive treatment manual for the cognitive behavioral treatment of patients with schizophrenia.

Family Therapy

Families of patients with schizophrenia can be an invaluable source of information for establishing the diagnosis and identifying potential behavioral problems. Studies demonstrate clearly that educating families about the illness and helping them develop reasonable expectations for their member with schizophrenia significantly improves the course of the illness. Hogarty and colleagues (1991) found that while social skills training reduced hospitalization rates during the first year, only family therapy continued to reduce hospitalization rates during the second year of their study. Half of the relapses experienced by patients in these 2 psychosocial treatment modalities occurred after patients were placed in rehabilitation programs.

One study found that most families of patients with schizophrenia never receive a clear explanation of the illness or a clarification of prognosis (Atkinson, 1994). Whereas families of young adults who suffer more familiar and readily understood brain insults, such as closed head injury, experience a time-limited period of grief, families of patients with schizophrenia typically suffer from prolonged, unresolved grief reactions as they continually attempt to make sense of their loss (Atkinson, 1994). For these families, a clear, medically oriented discussion of the illness and referral to family self-help groups can bring enormous relief. This is particularly important in light of psychiatry's past blame of "schizophrenogenic mothers" as being responsible for the illness, a false view which persisted up until the 1970s (Neill, 1990).

In a series of classic studies, Brown and colleagues (Brown, Birley, and Wing, 1972) demonstrated that high levels of "expressed emotion" (EE) in families of patients with schizophrenia predict relapse. Expressed emotion, generally defined as criticism, hostility, or overinvolvement, has commonly been the focus of family therapy. Whereas high levels of expressed emotion have been conceptualized as an enduring trait characteristic of specific families, recent research suggests that qualities in the patient may determine the level of expressed emotion in the family to a large degree (Moore et al., 1992). Similarly, it has been shown that the distress experienced by the family and the burden of the patient's illness on the family correlate with ratings of expressed emotion (Jackson, Smith, and McGorry, 1990). This research suggests at least 2 important principles for working with families with a schizophrenic member. First, education about the illness is critically important to help families develop realistic expectations for the afflicted member and to reduce anger, fear, and criticism directed at misunderstood manifestations of the disease (Birchwood et al., 1992). Second, efforts should be taken to reduce the burden of the illness on the family by helping identify resources in the community and by providing a source of social support.

One very promising model for family therapy is the group model developed by McFarlane and colleagues (1995). In this approach, 6 families meet with 2 clinicians, first for psychoeducational programs and then as an ongoing treatment group. After families learn about the illness from clinicians, the group provides a setting for problem solving and support. Because many families become quite isolated owing to the stigmatizaton of mental illness, these psychoeducational groups can provide a valuable opportunity for families to share their difficulties and solutions with other families facing the same problems. In one controlled trial, patients from families participating in a group psychoeducation program relapsed at a significantly lower rate than patients whose families were in traditional single-family therapy (McFarlane et al., 1995).

Managed Care

Just as deinstitutionalization and the introduction of effective pharmacologic agents introduced a dramatic change in the treatment of chronically mentally ill patients between 1950 and 1970, we are now in a similar period of change largely resulting from the widespread implementation of managed care (Hoge et al., 1994). Community-based care for the chronically mentally ill became "unmanaged" after deinstitutionalization deemphasized state-sponsored control of services based at state psychiatric hospitals in favor of decentralized community care financed by federal welfare programs and provided by poorly integrated systems of providers. Managed care has focused on curbing escalating costs. The new pressures for "cost-effectiveness" have taken 2 forms (Clark, 1996). The first is a change in how treatment providers are paid, as prospective, capped payments to providers have resulted in decreased lengths of hospitalization. The second approach is to implement new and more effective treatment modalities based on research which measures cost-effectiveness. Examples of new treatments which bring about cost savings in most studies include assertive case management and clozapine. New psychosocial and pharmacological treatments increase the need to demonstrate cost-effectiveness. As managed care requires providers to implement more effective treatments in order to survive with lowered rates of reimbursement, serious risk exists that cost savings will be achieved by limiting access to treatment rather than by improving cost-effectiveness of treatment. In general, inadequate treatment of patients with serious mental illness results in increased rates of hospitalization and much higher costs to society. Managed care systems which are "capitated" so that resources spent on high quality care in the community are returned to the caregivers by reducing inpatient costs may, in theory, promote highly integrated and progressive treatment approaches. However, this process must be carefully monitored to ensure that the most vulnerable patients do not fall between the cracks, particularly when services are "privatized" (Dumont, 1992). For these reasons, managed care has also emphasized local mental health authorities to oversee care of the chronically mentally ill, allowing planners at the local level to make decisions about distrib-

uting resources to best accommodate the most underserved patients in each community.

Several examples of designs of state-funded managed care systems for patients with chronic mental illness have been described (Austin, Blum, and Murtaza, 1995; Quinlivan and McWhirter, 1996; Richman, Lucas, and Blum, 1995; Surles, Blanch, and Shepardson, 1992). In the case of San Diego County, San Diego Mental Health Services assumed the role of the local mental health authority in administering the Medi-Cal managed mental health system for 350,000 eligible clients (Quinlivan and McWhirter, 1996). Inpatient services were contracted with 14 private psychiatric hospitals, and a private contractor was hired to coordinate payments and approve transitional services. The design of the new system targets "high-cost clients," initially defined as those patients who were hospitalized 3 times or more during a 6-month period. The 113 patients who met this requirement accounted for 22% of all admissions and cost the system on average $27,189 annually. Among high-cost clients, 60% were diagnosed with schizophrenia or schizoaffective disorder, and 66% were dually diagnosed with substance abuse. Other problems which characterized this group of intensive users of inpatient services included medication noncompliance, violence, suicidality, self-mutilation, and, in 19% of patients, a diagnosis of borderline personality disorder. Specialized services addressing these problems within a system modeled after the PACT program are under development and will be evaluated for cost-effectiveness.

Violence in the Chronically Mentally Ill

Psychiatry has historically conveyed to the public that patients with psychiatric illness are at no greater risk for committing violence than the general public. This stance has probably represented an effort to fight stigmatization and has been important in reassuring communities questioning the placement of residences and services for the mentally ill within their neighborhoods. However, several studies have suggested that psychiatric patients are more likely to commit violent acts than the general population, and patients with paranoid schizophrenia may be particularly dangerous (Tardiff, 1992). Although psychotic patients appear to be at higher risk than the general population for committing violent acts, investigators have questioned the reliability of data on violence obtained from legal records or from self-reports (Swanson et al., 1990). More compelling are studies conducted in Europe and the United States of individuals who commit homicide. The prevalence of schizophrenia in samples of murderers has consistently been 5–20 times higher than in the general population (Taylor, 1995). Whereas primitive, assaultive behavior is probably more likely in disorganized patients as a result of impaired control of aggression, violent acts such as homicide, which involve some planning or complex behaviors, are much more likely in patients with persecutory or religious delusions when they are convinced that they have no alternative but to act violently—either to defend themselves or to obey God's command. Negative symptoms reduce the risk for violence, since such patients are far less likely to initiate activity. Command hallucinations appear to increase the risk of violence only when the individual interprets the voices within a delusional system in such a way that the voices cannot be disobeyed (Zisook et al., 1995). For example, a patient may believe that God's voice is giving orders to attack someone believed to be possessed by Satan. While the potential for violence from disorganized or delusional patients is cause for concern, fewer than 1% of patients with schizophrenia actually commit homicide, whereas 10% of patients commit suicide and as many as 50% attempt it. In addition to delusions and hallucinations, depression and substance abuse are also important risk factors for suicide.

Care of the chronically mentally ill is one of the most difficult and costly of all health-related problems in this country. During the second half of the twentieth century, the approach of long-term custodial care in state psychiatric hospitals gave way to community mental health models which improved the quality of life for many patients. However, fragmentation of care and diminishing resources have led mental health planners to redesign care systems either through changing funding mechanisms alone or by actively establishing local mental health authorities to administer managed care systems. Although the risk of reduced access to care is a serious potential consequence of the newer, more "cost-effective" systems, we hope that the many promising advances in the care of this population, including improved medications, assertive case management, and partial hospitalization programs, will increasingly be implemented.

References

Amador, X. F., Flaum, M., Andreasen, N. C., Strauss, D. H., Yale, S. A., Clark, S. C., Gorman, J. M. 1994. Awareness of illness in schizophrenia and schizoaffective and mood disorders. *Arch. Gen. Psychiatry* 51:826–836.

Andreasen, N. C., Arndt, S., Alliger, R., Miller, D., Flaum, M. 1995. Symptoms of schizophrenia: methods, meanings, and mechanisms. *Arch. Gen. Psychiatry* 52:341–351.

Atkinson, S. D. 1994. Grieving and loss in parents with a schizophrenic child. *Am. J. Psychiatry* 151:1137–39.

Austin, M. J., Blum, S. R., and Murtaza, N. 1995. Local-state government relations and the development of public sector managed mental health care systems. *Administration and policy in mental health* 22:203–215.

Bachrach, L. L. 1992. What we know about homelessness among mentally ill persons: an analytical review and commentary. In *Treating the homeless mentally ill,* ed. H. R. Lamb, L. L. Bachrach, and F. I. Kass. Washington, D.C.: American Psychiatric Press. 13–40.

———— 1996. The state of the state mental hospital in 1996. *Psychiatr. Serv.* 47:1071–77.

Bartels, S. J., Teague, G. B., Drake, R. E., Clark, R. E., Bush, P. W., Noordsy, D. L. 1993. Substance abuse in schizophrenia: service utilization and cost. *J. Nerv. Ment. Dis.* 181:227–232.

Birchwood, M., Smith, J., et al. 1992. Specific and nonspecific effects of educational intervention for families living with schizophrenia: a comparison of three models. *Br. J. Psychiatry* 160:806–814.

Bond, G. R., Miller, L. D., Krumwied, R. D., Ward, R. S. 1988. Assertive case management in three CMHCs: a controlled study. *Hosp. Community Psychiatry* 39:411–418.

Breier, A., Schreiber, J., Dyer, J., Pickar, D. 1991. National Institute of Mental Health longitudinal study of chronic schizophrenia: prognosis and predictors of outcome. *Arch. Gen. Psychiatry* 48:239–246.

Brown, G. W., Birley, J. L. T., and Wing, J. K. 1972. Influence of family life on the course of schizophrenic disorders: a replication. *Br. J. Psychiatry* 121:241–258.

Brown, G. W., Bone, M., Dalison, B., et al., 1966. *Schizophrenia and social care: a comparative follow-up to study of 339 schizophrenic patients.* London: Oxford University Press.

Burns, B. J., and Santos, A. B. 1995. Assertive community treatment: an update of randomized trials. *Psychiatr. Serv.* 46:669–675.

Chadwick, P., and Birchwood, M. 1994. The omnipotence of voices: a cognitive approach to auditory hallucinations. *Br. J. Psychiatry* 164:190–210.

Clark, R. E. 1996. Searching for cost-effective mental health care. *Harvard Rev. Psychiatry* 4:45–48.

Cuesta, M. J., and Peralta, V. 1994. Lack of insight in schizophrenia. *Schizophr. Bull.* 20:359–366.

Cuffel, B. J. 1992. Prevalence estimates of substance abuse in schizophrenia and their correlates. *J. Nerv. Ment. Dis.* 180:589–592.

Dewees, M., Pulice, R. T., and McCormick, L. L. 1996. Community integration of former state hospital patients: outcomes of a policy shift in Vermont. *Psychiatr. Serv.* 47:1088–92.

Drake, R. E., McHugo, G. J., and Noordsy, D. L. 1993. Treatment of alcoholism among schizophrenic outpatients: 4-year outcomes. *Am. J. Psychiatry* 150:328–329.

Dumont, M. P. 1992. Privatization of mental health services: the invisible hand at our throats. *Am. J. Orthopsychiatry* 62:328–329.

Essock, S., Hargreaves, W., et al. 1996. Clozapine eligibility among state hospital patients. *Schizophr. Bull.* 22:15–25.

Finn, S. E., Bailey, J. M., Schultz, R. T., Faber, R. 1990. Subjective utility ratings of neuroleptics in treating schizophrenia. *Psychol. Med.* 20:843–848.

Garety, P. A., Kuipers, L., Fowler, D., Chamberlain, F., Dunn, G. 1994. Cognitive behavioural therapy for drug-resistant psychosis. *Br. J. Med. Psychol.* 67:259–271.

Geller, J. L., and Fisher, W. H. 1993. The linear continuum of transitional residences: debunking the myth. *Am. J. Psychiatry* 150:1070–76.

Glasscote, R. M., Cummings, E., Rutman, I., et al. 1971. *Rehabilitating the mentally ill in the community.* Washington, D.C.: Joint Information Service of the American Psychiatric Association.

Goff, D. C. 1995. Have the serotonin-dopamine antagonists rendered traditional antipsychotic agents obsolete? *Harvard Rev. Psychiatry* 3:101–103.

Goff, D. C., Henderson, D. C., and Manschreck, T. 1997. Psychotic patients. In *The handbook of general hospital psychiatry,* ed. N. H. Cassem. 149–171.

Goffman, E. 1962. *Asylums: essays on the social situation of mental patients and other inmates.* New York: Doubleday.

Goldman, H. H., Adams, N. H., and Taube, C. A. 1983. Deinstitutionalization: the data demythologized. *Hosp. Community Psychiatry* 34:129–134.

Grob, G. N. 1973. *Mental institutions in America: social policy to 1875.* New York: Free Press.

Hadley, T. R., Culhane, D. P., and Snyder, F. J. 1992. Expenditure and revenue patterns of state mental health agencies, from 1981 to 1987. *Administration and Policy in Mental Health* 19:213–234.

Hargreaves, W. A., Glick, I. D., Drues, J., Showstack, J. A., Feigenbaum, E. 1977. Short versus long hospitalization; a prospective controlled study. VI. Two-year follow-up results for schizophrenics. *Arch. Gen. Psychiatry* 34:305–311.

Herz, M. I., Endicott, J., and Spitzer, R. I. 1975. Brief hospitalization of persons with families: initial results. *Am. J. Psychiatry* 132:413–418.

Hirsch, S. R., Platt, S., Knights, A., Weyman, A. 1979. Shortening hospital stay for psychiatric care: effect on patients and their families. *Br. Med. J.* 1:442–446.

Hogarty, G., Anderson, C., Reiss, D., Kornblith, S., Greenwald, D., Ulrich, R., Carter, M., Group, E. R. 1991. Family psychoeducation, social skills training, and maintenance chemotherapy in the aftercare treatment of schizophrenia. *Arch. Gen. Psychiatry* 48:340–347.

Hoge, M. A., Davidson, L., et al. 1992. The promise of partial hospitalization: a reassessment. *Hosp. Community Psychiatry* 43:345–353.

Hoge, M. A., Davidson, L., Griffith, E. E. H., Sledge, W. H., Howenstine, R. A. 1994. Defining managed care in public-sector psychiatry. *Hosp. Community Psychiatry* 45:1085–89.

Hole, R. W., Rush, A. J., and Beck, A. T. 1979. A cognitive investigation of schizophrenic delusions. *Psychiatry* 42:312–319.

Jackson, H. J., Smith, N., and McGorry, P. 1990. Relationship between expressed emotion and family burden in psychotic disorders: an exploratory study. *Acta Psychiatr. Scand.* 82:243–249.

Kane, J. 1996. Drug Therapy: Schizophrenia. *N. Engl. J. Med.* 334:34–41.

Kane, J., Honigfeld, G., Singer, J., Meltzer, H. 1988. Clozapine for the treatment-resistant schizophrenic: a double-blind comparison with chlorpromazine. *Arch. Gen. Psychiatry* 45:789–796.

Kingdon, D., and Turkington, D. 1994. *Cognitive-behavioural therapy of schizophrenia.* Hove, Sussex: Lawrence Erlbaum.

Koranyi, E. K. 1979. Morbidity and rates of undiagnosed physical illnesses in a psychiatric clinic. *Arch. Gen. Psychiatry* 36:414–419.

Lake v. Cameron. 1966. 124 U.S. App.D. C. 264, 364 F.2d 657 (D.C.Cir.).

Lamb, H. R. 1967. Chronic psychiatric patients in the day hospital. *Arch. Gen. Psychiatry* 17:615–621.

Lawrence, R. E., Copas, J. B., et al. 1991. Community care: does it reduce the need for psychiatric beds? A comparison of two different styles of service in three hospitals. *Br. J. Psychiatry* 159:334–340.

Leff, J., Trieman, N., and Gooch, C. 1996. Team for the assessment of psychiatric services (TAPS) project 22: prospective follow-up study of long-stay patients discharged from two psychiatric hospitals. *Am. J. Psychiatry* 153:1318–23.

Liberman, R. P., Spaulding, W. D., and Corrigan, P. W. 1995. Cognitive-behavioural therapies in psychiatric rehabilitation. In *Schizophrenia,* ed. S. R. Hirsch and D. R. Weinberger. Cambridge, Mass.: Blackwell Science. 605–625.

Liddle, P. F. 1987. The symptoms of chronic schizophrenia: a re-examination of the positive-negative dichotomy. *Brit. J. Psychiatry* 151:145–151.

Loebel, A. D., Lieberman, J. A., et al. 1992. Duration of psychosis and outcome in first-episode schizophrenia. *Am. J. Psychiatry* 149:1183–88.

Marx, A. J., Test, M. A., and Stein, L. I. 1973. Extrohospital management of severe mental illness. *Arch. Gen. Psychiatry* 29:505–511.

Mattes, J. A., Rosen, B., Klein, D. F., Milan, D. 1977. Comparison of the clinical effectiveness of 'short' versus 'long' stay psychiatric hospitalization. II. Results of a 3-year posthospital follow-up. *J. Nerv. Ment. Dis.* 165:395–402.

McFarlane, W. R., Lukens, E., et al. 1995. Multiple-family groups and psychoeducation in the treatment of schizophrenia. *Arch. Gen. Psychiatry* 52:679–687.

McGrew, J., Bond, G., Dietzen, L., et al. 1994. Measuring the fidelity of implementation of a mental health program model. *J. Consult. Clin. Psychol.* 62:670–678.

Meltzer, H., Cola, P., Way, L., Thompson, P., Banstani, B., Davies, M., Snitz, B. 1993. Cost effectiveness of clozapine in neuroleptic-resistant schizophrenia. *Am. J. Pyschiatry* 150:1630–38.

Moore, E., Ball, R. A., et al. 1992. Expressed emotion in staff working with the long-term adult mentally ill. *Br. J. Psychiatry* 161:802–808.

Mueser, K. T., and Bellack, A. S. 1995. Psychotherapy for schizophrenia. In *Schizophrenia,* ed. S. R. Hirsch and D. R. Weinberger. Cambridge, Mass.: Blackwell Science. 626–648.

Neill, J. 1990. Whatever became of the schizophrenic mother? *Am. J. Psychother.* 44:499–515.

Okin, R. L. 1995. Testing the limits of deinstitutionalization. *Psychiatr. Serv.* 46:569–574.

Okin, R. L., and Pearsall, D. 1993. Patients' perceptions of their quality of life 11 years after discharge from a state hospital. *Hosp. Community Psychiatry* 44:236–240.

Okin, R. L., Borus, J. F., et al. 1995. Long-term outcome of state hospital patients discharged into structured community residential settings. *Psychiatr. Serv.* 46:73–78.

Olfson, M. 1990. Assertive community treatment: an evaluation of the experimental evidence. *Hosp. Community Psychiatry* 41:634–641.

Penn, D. L., and Mueser, K. T. 1996. Research update on the psychosocial treament of schizophrenia. *Am. J. Psychiatry* 153:607–617.

Quinlivan, R., and McWhirter, D. P. 1996. Designing a comprehensive care program for high-cost clients in a managed care environment. *Psychiatr. Serv.* 47:813–815.

Richman, E. B., Lucas, N., and Blum, S. R. 1995. Toward managed behavioral health services in Philadelphia. *Administration and Policy in Mental Health* 22:345–356.

Rupp, A., and Keith, S. J. 1993. The costs of schizophrenia: assessing the burden. *Psychiatr. Clin. North Am.* 16:413–23.

Santos, A. B., Henggeler, S. W., Burns, B. J., Arana, G. W.,

Meisler, N. 1995. Research on field-based services: models for reform in the delivery of mental health care to populations with complex clinical problems. *Am. J. Psychiatry* 152:1111–23.

Scott, J. E., and Dixon, L. B. 1995. Assertive community treatment and case management for schizophrenia. *Schizophr. Bull.* 21:657–667.

Smith, T. E., Hull, J. W., MacKain, S. J., Wallace, C. J., Rattenni, L. A., Goodman, M., Anthony, D. T., Kentros, M. K. 1996. Training hospitalized patients with schizophrenia in community reintegration skills. *Psychiatr. Serv.* 47:1099–1103.

Stein, L. 1992. Innovating against the current. *New Directions for Mental Health Services* 56:5–22.

Stein, L. I., and Test, M. A. 1980. Alternative to mental hospital treatment. I. Conceptual model, treatment program, and clinical evaluation. *Arch. Gen. Psychiatry* 37:392–397.

Surles, R. C., Blanch, A. K., and Shepardson, J. 1992. Integrating mental health policy, financing, and program development: the New York State experience. *Administration and Policy in Mental Health* 19:269–277.

Swanson, J. W., Holzer, C. E. I., Ganju, V. K., Jono, R. T. 1990. Violence and psychiatric disorder in the community: evidence from the epidemiologic catchment area surveys. *Hosp. Community Psychiatry* 41:761–770.

Szasz, T. S. 1961. *The myth of mental illness: foundations of a theory of personal conduct.* New York: Dell.

Tardiff, K. 1992. The current state of psychiatry in the treatment of violent patients. *Arch. Gen. Psychiatry* 49:493–499.

Tarrier, N., Beckett, R., Harwood, S., Baker, A., Yusupoff, L., Ugarteburu, I. 1993. A trial of two cognitive behavioral methods of treating drug-resistant residual psychotic symptoms in schizophrenic patients. I. Outcome. *Br. J. Psychiatry* 162:524–532.

Taylor, P. J. 1995. Schizophrenia and the risk of violence. In *Schizophrenia,* ed. S. R. Hirsch and D. R. Weinberger. Cambridge, Mass: Blackwell Science. 163–183.

Teague, G. B., Drake, R. E., and Ackerson, T. H. 1995. Evaluating use of continuous treatment teams for persons with mental illness and substance abuse. *Psychiatr. Serv.* 46:689–695.

Test, M. A., and Stein, L. I. 1980. Alternative to mental hospital treatment. III. Social cost. *Arch. Gen. Psychiatry* 37:409–412.

Torrey, E. F., and Bowler, A. 1990. Geographical distribution of insanity in America: evidence for an urban factor. *Schizophr. Bull.* 16:591–604.

Tuttle, G. T. 1891. Two days at Gheel: twelfth annual report of the State Board of Lunacy and Charity of Massachusetts. Unpublished manuscript.

Unger, K. V. et al. 1991. A supported education program

for young adults with long-term mental illness. *Hosp. Community Psychiatry* 42:838–842.

Weiden, P., and Havens, L. 1994. Psychotherapeutic management techniques in the treatment of outpatients with schizophrenia. *Hosp. Community Psychiatry* 45:549–555.

Weisbrod, B. A., Test, M. A., and Stein, L. I. 1980. Alternative to mental hospital treatment. II. Economic benefit–cost analysis. *Arch. Gen. Psychiatry* 37:400–405.

Weller, M. P. I. 1989. Mental illness—who cares? *Nature* 339:249–252.

Wilder, J. F., Levin, G., and Zwerling, I. 1966. A two-year follow-up evaluation of acute psychotic patients treated in a day hospital. *Am. J. Psychiatry* 122:1095–1101.

Wyatt v. Stickney. 1971. 325 R. Supp. 781 (M. D. Ala.), enforced 344 F.Supp. 373 (M.D. Ala. 1972).

Zisook, S., Byrd, D., et al. 1995. Command hallucinations in outpatients with schizophrenia. *J. Clin. Psychiatry* 56:462–465.

Recommended Reading

Austin, M. J., Blum, S. R., and Murtaza, N. 1995. Local-state government relations and the development of public sector managed mental health care systems. *Administration and Policy in Mental Health* 22:203–215.

Carpenter, W. T., and Buchanan, R. W. 1994. Schizophrenia. *N. Engl. J. Med.* 330:681–690.

Hogarty, G., Anderson, C., Reiss, D., Kornblith, S., Greenwald, D., Ulrich, R., Carter, M., Group, E. R. 1991. Family psychoeducation, social skills training, and maintenance chemotherapy in the aftercare treatment of schizophrenia. *Arch. Gen. Psychiatry* 48:340–347.

McFarlane, W. R., Lukens, E., et al. 1995. Multiple-family groups and psychoeducation in the treatment of schizophrenia. *Arch. Gen. Psychiatry* 52:679–687.

Penn, D. L., and Mueser, K. T. 1996. Research update on the psychosocial treatment of schizophrenia. *Am. J. Psychiatry* 153:607–617.

Santos, A. B., Henggeler, S. W., Burns, B. J., Arana, G. W., Meisler, N. 1995. Research on field-based services: models for reform in the delivery of mental health care to populations with complex clinical problems. *Am. J. Psychiatry* 152:1111–23.

33

EDWIN H. CASSEM

The Person
Confronting
Death

Help the dying patient? Can one realistically hope to make a 35-year-old mother dying of cancer feel better? Feel better about what? At the bedside of the dying, the professional may feel overwhelmed by dread of the encounter or by the presumptuousness of the expectation to help. Yet because the dying have no less right to help than the living, their difficulties and needs require specific attention.

The science or study of death is called *thanatology*. Broadly conceived, it includes the study of dying as a psychophysiological process; the care of dying persons, including both adults and children; and the care of persons who seek death by suicide. The nondying directly affected by death—the bereaved and the care-giving personnel—are included, as are healthy persons whose lives are disrupted by irrational fears of death.

Psychiatric interest in the concrete problems of the dying is a recent phenomenon. Freud's agonizing 17-year struggle against oral cancer (Jones, 1957) is never reflected in his writings, even in those about death. S. Gifford (1969) has provided a historical review of psychoanalytic theories about death and also reports on the few individuals who became involved in empirical studies of the subject. In 1915 Freud, introducing his notion that the unconscious has no representation of death, explored unconscious convictions of immortality. In 1923, before he linked death and aggression in theory, Freud presented evidence that conscious fears of death represent underlying fears of helplessness, physical injury, or abandonment. Conversely, in depressive states conscious fears of punishment, castration, rejection, or desertion may represent underlying fears of death.

The first analyst to investigate the dying themselves was Felix Deutsch in 1933. Little further work was done in the field until Kurt Eissler's publication in 1955 signaled an era of empirical interest in dying patients. Beginning with the work of Herman Feifel (1959) and Dame Cicely Saunders (1959), significant contributions—from

Weisman and Hackett (1961; Hackett and Weisman, 1962), LeShan and LeShan (1961), Hinton (1967), Glaser and Strauss (1965), and several others—multiplied until 1969, when Elisabeth Kübler-Ross's now classic work evoked worldwide interest in the emotional concerns of the dying. The observations and recommendations that follow are based on the work of these investigators as well as my own (Cassem and Stewart, 1975).

The Psychophysiological Process of Dying

Dying is a process that keeps the body near the forefront of the mind. Having contracted a disease that may eventually cut him down (like heart disease) or devour him (like cancer), the patient interprets or even anticipates bodily changes as ominous. Symptoms are likely to produce fear when present, but fear is often experienced long before their arrival. The body, once regarded as a friend, may seem more like a dormant adversary, programmed for betrayal. Dying persons, even before disintegration begins, fear many things. Loss of autonomy, disfigurement, being a burden, becoming physically repulsive, letting the family down, facing the unknown, and many other concerns are commonly expressed. When all fears were compared for frequency in a sample of cancer patients (Saunders, 1959), the 3 that topped the list were abandonment by others, pain, and shortness of breath. These fears were expressed before the patients were symptomatic; they felt that as their illness progressed, family and hospital staff would gradually avoid them, their conditions would become increasingly painful, or the illness would encroach on breathing capacity and suffocate them.

Because physicians and families also worry about what will happen to the dying person, it is helpful to know which difficulties are in fact the most distressing when the patient is terminal. When Saunders (1959) documented the exact incidence of practical problems in terminal cancer at St. Joseph's Hospital in London, she found that the 3 most common complaints were nausea and vomiting, shortness of breath, and dysphagia. It was striking that pain did not appear high on the problem list; with proper medication, about 90% of her patients remained pain free. Largely because of her efforts, avoidance of dying patients decreased at St. Joseph's. Nausea and dyspnea are psychophysiological experiences in which the patient is usually miserable. Relief of these and other troublesome symptoms helps restore peace of mind.

Stages of Adaptation

In a work that stimulated worldwide interest in dying persons, Kübler-Ross (1969) presented a framework of 5 stages experienced by people after they receive news of their fatal illness: shock and denial, anger, bargaining, depression, and acceptance. Fear and anxiety are not represented. The concept of stages of adaptation is by no means new and is not restricted to dying. As a dynamic process, dying is a special case of loss, and the stages represent a dynamic model of emotional adaptation to any physical or emotional loss. A common misdirection in caring for dying patients is the attempt to help an individual through the stages one after the other. It is more accurate and therapeutically more practical to regard the stages as normal reactions to loss that may be present simultaneously, disappear and reappear, or occur in any order.

Questions far outnumber answers wherever the dying are cared for. Many controversies remain unresolved. The investigators mentioned earlier have outlined objectives in the care of the terminally ill that the physician can consider from the time treatment begins. Because the patient's bedside can be an uncomfortable place for the physician, several practical considerations for management are added in support of the goals.

Goals of Treatment

Deutsch (1933) observed in his clinical sample of dying patients that the decline in vital processes is accompanied by a parallel decline in the intensity of instinctual aggressive-erotic drives. Fear of dying is reduced as the pressures of inner instinctual demands diminish. The illness can be viewed by the patient as a hostile attack from an outside enemy or as a punishment for being bad (interpreted by Deutsch as inflicted from within by a harsh superego). Because the patient can worsen his predicament by reacting with increasing hostility toward outside objects or with self-punitive actions to offset experienced guilt, Deutsch's

therapeutic objective is a "settlement of differences." The ideal stage is reached when all guilt and aggression are balanced, permitting the patient a guilt-free "regression" to the love relationships of childhood and infancy. Deutsch judges this regression impossible without conflict under other circumstances because of the incestuous nature of the earlier relationships, but he infers that guilt is atoned for by the knowledge of imminent death. One could also infer that the patient's relationship to the therapist would fall under the same protective mantle.

For Eissler (1955) therapeutic success depends on the psychiatrist's ability to share the patient's primitive beliefs in immortality and indestructibility. In addition, sharing the dying patient's defenses and developing intense admiration for inner strength, beauty, intelligence, courage, and honesty are the main forces in the psychiatrist's supportive relationship with the patient.

Kübler-Ross (1969) speaks of the unfinished business of the dying—reconciliations, resolution of conflicts, and pursuit of specific remaining hopes. For Saunders (1969), the aim is to keep the person feeling like himself as long as possible. In her view dying is also a "coming together time," when family and staff are encouraged to help one another share the burden of the terminal illness. LeShan and LeShan (1961), choosing deliberately not to emphasize dying (the minor problem in their view), explore aggressively with patients what they wish to accomplish in living (the major problem).

Weisman and Hackett (1961) have coined the term "appropriate death," for which Weisman (1972) delineates the following conditions: the person should be relatively pain free; should operate on as effective a level as possible within the limits of his disability; should recognize and resolve residual conflicts; should satisfy those remaining wishes consistent with his present plight and ego ideal; and should be able to yield control to others in whom he has confidence.

Perhaps more important than any other principle in caring for the dying is that the treatment be unique and individualized. This goal can be accomplished only by getting to know the patient, responding to his needs and interests, proceeding at his pace, and allowing him to shape the manner in which those in attendance behave. There is no one "best" way to die.

Eric Cassell (1991) has observed that an individual life lived is a work of art. What sort of final time can best express the meaning of the person's life? How can the death be one the person can be proud of? How can the time left be for the bereaved a time they too can be proud of and begin a memorial with which they can live comfortably? Most frightening when death is announced on the horizon is the loss of the loved one, although other relationships may also be threatened. Help that rallies all to strengthen and improve their relationships addresses the most frightening aspect of death—loss that feels like abandonment. In the common effort to make the end of life meaningful, patient and loved ones can master death.

Recommended Qualities for Caregivers

Most of what is known about dying patients comes from them. In the realm of experiential reality, patients are the teachers; those who take care of them always have more to learn. Over the years, observations made by patients on various aspects of their management have helped in the recognition of the following 8 essential features in the care and management of the dying patient (Cassem and Stewart, 1975).

Competence. In an era when some discussions of the dying patient seem to suggest that "love" excuses most other faults in the therapeutic relationship, encouraging the misconception that competence in physicians and nurses is of secondary importance for dying patients would be unfortunate. Competence is reassuring, and when one's life or comfort depends on it, personality considerations become secondary. Being good at what one does brings emotional as well as scientific benefits to the patient. No matter how charming physicians, nurses, or intravenous technicians may be, for example, the approach of the person who is most skillful at venipuncture brings the greatest relief to an anxious patient.

Concern. Of all attributes in physicians and nurses, none is more highly valued by terminal patients than compassion. Although they may never convey it precisely by words, some physicians and nurses impart to the patient that they are genuinely touched by his predicament. A striking example came from a mother's description of her dying son's pediatrician: "You know, that doctor loves Michael." Compassion is a quality that cannot be feigned.

Although universally praised as a quality for a health professional, compassion extracts a cost usually overlooked in training. The price of compassion is conveyed by the two Latin roots, *con* and *passio,* to "suffer with" another person. One must be touched by the tragedy of the patient in a literal way, a process that occurs through experiential identification with the dying person. This process of empathy, when evoked by a person facing death or tragic disability, ordinarily produces uncomfortable, burdensome feelings, and internal resistance to it can arise defensively. Who can bear the thought of dying at 20? It

is therefore understandable that professionals do not encourage discussion of such a topic by the individual facing it.

In addition to guarding against the development of compassion, students are sometimes advised to avoid "involvement" with a patient. When a patient gets upset, hasty exits or evasions are thus more likely. Few things infuriate patients more, however, than contrived involvement; even an inability to answer direct questions may be excused when it stems from genuine discomfort on the physician's part. One woman, even though she wanted more information about how much longer she could expect to survive with stage IV Hodgkin's disease, preferred to ask her physician as few questions as possible: "Whenever I try to ask him about this, he looks very pained and becomes very hesitant. I don't want to rub it in. After all, he really likes me."

What are the emotional traumas a compassionate nurse or physician is required to sustain? They can be summarized by the "stages" the terminal patient goes through. Because the stages describe the emotional process in the terminal patient, it is only logical that they call forth similar reactions in a sympathetic observer. As physician and patient view the patient's predicament together, the physician, depending on his sensitivity, is likely to experience shock, denial, outrage, hope, and devastation. Involvement—"real" involvement—is not only unavoidable but also necessary in the therapeutic encounter. Patients recognize it instantly. As a hematologist percussed the right side of his 29-year-old patient's chest, his discovery of dullness and the recurrent pleural effusion it signaled brought the realization that a remission had come to an abrupt end. "Oh, shit," he muttered. Then, realizing what he had said, he added hastily, "Oh, excuse me, Bill." "That's all right," the young man replied. "It's nice to know you care."

Comfort. With the terminal patient, comfort has a technology all its own. "Comfort measures" should not indicate that less attention is paid to the patient's needs. In fact, comforting a terminally ill person requires meticulous devotion to a host of details.

Communication. Talking with the dying is a paradoxical skill. The wish to find the "right thing" to say is a well-meaning but misguided hope among persons who work or want to work with terminal patients. Practically every empirical study has emphasized the ability to listen over the ability to say something. Saunders summed it up best when she said, "The real question is not 'What do you tell your patients?' but rather 'What do you let your patients tell you?'" (1969, p. 59). Most people have a strong inner resistance to letting dying patients speak their minds. If a patient presumed to be 3 months from death says, "My plan was to buy a new [automobile] in 6 months, but I guess I won't have to worry about that now," a poor listener will say nothing or "Right. Don't worry about it." A better listener might say, "What do you mean?" or even "Are you saying you won't last till then?"

Communication is more than listening. Getting to know the patient as a person is essential. Learning about significant areas of the patient's life, such as family, work, or schooling, and chatting about common interests represent the most natural if not the only ways the patient has of coming to feel known. After a 79-year-old man of keen intellect and wit had been interviewed before a group of hospital staff, one of the staff said, "Before the interview tonight I just thought of him as another old man on the ward in pain." No esoteric skills are necessary to talk to a dying person. Like anybody else, he gets his sense of self-respect in the presence of others from a feeling that they value him for what he has done and for his personal qualities. Allowing the dying person to tell his or her own story helps build a balanced relationship. Effort spent getting to know patients almost always helps them psychologically.

The physician can help dissolve communication barriers for other staff members by showing them the uniqueness of each patient. Comments such as "This man has 34 grandchildren" or "This woman was an RAF fighter pilot" (both describing actual patients) convey information that can help the staff find something to talk about with the patient. Awkwardness subsides when patients seem like real people and not merely "a breast CA" or some other disease. This rescue from anonymity is essential to prevent a sense of isolation. Communication is more than verbal. A pat on the arm, a wave, a wink, or a grin communicates important reassurances, as do careful back rubs and physical examinations.

Patients occasionally complain about professional and lay visitors who appear more interested in the phenomenon of dying than in the patients as individuals. A woman in her early 50s, with breast cancer metastatic to bone, brain, lungs, and liver, entered the hospital for a course of chemotherapy. During her entire 6-week stay she was irascible, argumentative, and even abusive to the staff. She responded extremely well to treatment, experienced a substantial remission, and left the hospital. Apologizing for her behavior, she later told her oncologist: "I know that I was impossible. But every single nurse who came into my room wanted to talk to me about death. I came there to get help, not to die, and it drove me up a wall." A

wise caution is to take conversational cues from the patient whenever possible.

Children. Investigators have unanimously concluded that the visits of children are likely to bring as much consolation and relief to the terminally ill as any other intervention. A useful rule of thumb in determining whether a particular child should visit a dying patient is to ask the child whether he wants to visit. No better criterion has been found.

Family cohesion and integration. A burden shared is a burden made lighter. Family members must be assisted in supporting one another, although this process requires the effort of getting to know family as well as the patient. Conversely, when the patient is permitted to support his family, the feeling of being a burden is mitigated. The often difficult work of bringing the family together for support, reconciliation, and improved relations can prevent disruption when death of the patient initiates the work of bereavement. The opportunity to be present at death should be offered to family members, as well as the alternative of being informed about it while waiting for the news at home. Flexibility is the rule, with the wishes of the family and patient paramount. After death, family members should be offered the chance (but never pressured) to see the body before it is taken to the morgue. C. M. Parkes (1972) has documented the critical importance to grief work of seeing the body of the dead person.

Cheerfulness. Dying people have no more relish for sour and somber faces than anybody else. Anyone with a gentle and appropriate sense of humor can bring considerable relief to all parties involved. "What do they think this is?" said one patient of his visitors. "They file past here with flowers and long faces like they were coming to my wake." Patients with a good sense of humor do not enjoy unresponsive audiences either. It is their wit that softens many a difficult incident. Said one elderly man with a tremor, after an embarrassing loss of sphincter control, "This is enough to give anybody Parkinson's disease!" Wit is not an end in itself. As in all forms of conversation, the listener should take the cue from the patient. Forced or inappropriate mirth can increase a sick person's feelings of distance and isolation.

Consistency and perseverance. Progressive isolation is a realistic fear of the dying person. A physician or nurse who regularly visits the sickroom provides tangible proof of continued support and concern. Saunders (1969) emphasizes that the quality of time is far more important than the quantity. A brief visit is far better than no visit at all, and patients may not be able to tolerate prolonged visiting. Patients are quick to identify those who show interest at first but gradually disappear from the scene. Staying power requires hearing out complaints. Praising one of her nurses, one 69-year-old woman with advanced cancer said: "She takes all my guff, and I give her plenty. Most people just pass my room, but if she has even a couple of minutes, she'll stop and actually listen to what I have to say. Some days I couldn't get through without her."

Care and Management of the Dying Adult: Preliminary Considerations

Breaking Bad News

Because so many reactions to the news of diagnosis are possible, having some plan of action in mind ahead of time that will permit the greatest variation and freedom of response is helpful. The following approach is suggested. Begin by sitting down with the patient in a private place. Standing while conveying bad news is regarded by patients as unkind and an expression of wanting to leave as quickly as possible. Inform him that when all the tests are completed, the physician will sit down with him again. Spouse and family can be included in the discussion of findings and treatment. As that day approaches, the patient should again be warned. This warning permits those patients who wish no information, or minimal information, to say so.

If the findings are unpleasant—as in the case of a biopsy positive for malignancy—how can they best be conveyed? A good opening statement is one that is (1) rehearsed so that it can be delivered calmly; (2) brief—3 sentences or less; (3) designed to encourage further dialogue; and (4) reassuring of continued attention and care. A typical delivery might go as follows: "The tests confirmed that your tumor is malignant [the bad news]. I have therefore asked the surgeon [or radiotherapist or oncologist] to come by to speak with you, examine you, and make his recommendations for treatment [we will do something about it]. As things proceed, I will be by to talk with you about them and about how we should proceed [I will stand by you]." Silence and quiet observation for a few moments will yield valuable information about the patient, his emotional reactions, and how he deals with the facts from the start. While observing, the doctor can decide how best to continue the discussion, but sitting with the patient for a while is an essential part of this ini-

tial encounter with a grim reality that both patient and physician will continue to confront together, possibly for a very long time.

Telling the Truth

Without honesty human relationships are destined for shipwreck. If truthfulness and trust are so obviously interdependent, why does so much conspiracy exist to avoid truth with the dying? The paradoxical fact is that for the terminally ill, the need for both honesty and avoidance of the truth can be intense. Sir William Osler is reputed to have said, "A patient has no more right to all the facts in my head than he does to all the medications in my bag." Perhaps a routine blood smear has just revealed that its owner has acute myelogenous leukemia. If he is 25, married, and the father of 2 small children, should he be told the diagnosis? Is the answer obvious? What if he had sustained 2 prior psychotic breaks with less serious illnesses? What if his wife says he once said that he never wanted to know if he had a malignancy?

Most empirical studies in which patients were asked whether or not they should be told the truth about malignancy indicated an overwhelming desire for the truth. When 740 patients in a cancer detection clinic were asked (prior to diagnosis) whether they should be told their diagnosis, 99% said yes (Kelly and Friesen, 1950). Another group in this clinic was asked the same question after the diagnosis was established, and 89% replied affirmatively, as did 82% of another group who had been examined and found free of malignancy. Gilbertsen and Wangensteen (1962) asked the same question of 298 survivors of surgery for gastric, colon, and rectal cancers and found that 82% said they should be told the truth. The same authors approached 92 patients with advanced cancer, judged by their physicians to be preterminal, and 79% responded that they should be told their diagnosis.

How many do not want the truth or regard it as harmful? Effects of blunt truth telling have been empirically studied in both England and the United States. Aitken-Swan and Easson (1959) were told by 7% of 231 patients explicitly informed of their diagnoses that the frankness of the consultant was resented. Gilbertsen and Wangensteen (1962) observed that 4% of a sample of surgical patients became emotionally upset when they were told and appeared to remain so throughout the course of their illness. Gerlé, Lunden, and Sandblom (1960) studied 101 patients; members of one group were told, along with their families, the frank truth about their diagnoses, whereas with the other group an effort was made to maintain a conspiracy of silence between family and physician by excluding the patient from discussion of the diagnosis. Initially greater emotional upset appeared in the group in which patient and family were told together, but the authors observed in follow-up that the emotional difficulties in the families of patients "shielded" from the truth far outweighed those that occurred when patient and family were told the diagnosis simultaneously. In general, empirical studies do not support the myth that truth is not desired by the terminally ill or harms those to whom it is given. Honesty sustains the relationship with a dying person rather than retarding it. The following example is drawn from Hackett and Weisman (1962).

A housewife of 57 with metastatic breast cancer, now far advanced, was seen in consultation. She reported a persistent headache, which she attributed to nervous tension, and asked why she should be nervous. Turning the question back to her, the physician was told, "I am nervous because I have lost 60 pounds in a year, the priest comes to see me twice a week, which he never did before, and my mother-in-law is nicer to me even though I am meaner to her. Wouldn't this make you nervous?" The physician replied, "You mean you think you're dying." "That's right, I do," she answered. He paused and said quietly, "You are." She smiled and said, "Well, I've finally broken the sound barrier; someone's finally told me the truth."

Not all patients can be dealt with so directly. A nuclear physicist greeted his surgeon on the day following exploratory laparotomy with the words, "Lie to me, Steve." Individual variations in willingness to hear the initial diagnosis are extreme. And diagnosis is entirely different from prognosis. Many patients have said they were grateful to their physician for telling them they had a malignancy. Very few, however, react positively to being told they are dying. My own experience indicates that "Do I have cancer?" is a not uncommon question, whereas "Am I dying?" is a rare one. The latter question is more common among patients who are dying rapidly, such as those in cardiogenic shock.

Physicians today generally prefer to tell cancer patients their diagnoses. Donald Oken's study of 1961 documented that 90% of responding physicians preferred not to tell patients the diagnosis. When Novack and colleagues (1979) repeated this questionnaire 18 years later, 97% of responding physicians indicated a preference for telling the cancer patient the diagnosis, and 100% said that patients had a right to know.

Honest communication of the diagnosis (or of any truth) by no means precludes later avoidance or even denial of the truth. In 2 studies cited above in which patients

had been told their diagnoses outright (including the words *cancer* or *malignancy*), they were asked 3 weeks later what they had been told: 19% of one sample (Aitken-Swan and Easson, 1959) and 20% of the other (Gilbertsen and Wangensteen, 1962) denied that their condition was cancer or malignant. Likewise, Croog, Shapiro, and Levine (1971) interviewed 345 men 3 weeks after myocardial infarction and were told by 20% that they had not had a heart attack, though all had been explicitly told their diagnoses. For a person to function effectively, truth's piercing voice must occasionally be muted or even excluded from awareness. I once spoke on 4 successive days with a man who had a widely spread bone cancer. On the first day he said he did not know what he had and did not like to ask questions; on the second that he was "riddled with cancer"; on the third that he did not really know what ailed him; and on the fourth that even though nobody likes to die, that was now the lot that fell to him.

Truth telling is no panacea. Communicating a diagnosis honestly, though difficult, is easier than the labors that lie ahead. Telling the truth is merely a way to begin, but because it is an open and honest way, it provides a firm basis on which to build a relationship of trust.

A Comprehensive Approach to Palliation

The World Health Organization (1991) defines palliative (or hospice) care as "the active total care of patients whose disease is not responsive to curative treatments." The definition does not mention death, an acknowledgment of how this so upsets some patients that they will not accept hospice care even when it is desperately needed. This commonly presents an impasse to care. One may have to implore the patient to accept hospice care for the benefit of his family, and occasionally the physician and family may request hospice care despite the patient's opposition. The goals of palliative care can be simply expressed as aggressive minimization of the patient's burdens and maximization of quality of life. The latter generally constitutes an effort to maximize independence and the number of options available for the dying person, as well as an intense effort to make the most of the person's relationships. Although most understand "palliation" as aimed at physical comfort, this is gravely inadequate; palliation of psychiatric, psychosocial, and spiritual suffering requires formal consideration and effort.

Some persons, faced with death, come to regard suicide or euthanasia as the most appealing option. Why? The most frequent reasons why euthanasia is requested in the Netherlands are: loss of dignity, 57%; pain, 46% (but when pain is the only reason given, 5%); unworthy dying, 46%; being dependent on others, 33%; and being tired of life, 23% (Van der Maas et al., 1991). These reasons are all ultimately psychosocial. Psychosocial suffering, as we see from this study, is even worse than physical suffering, and requires in itself aggressive palliation. To cover all forms of psychosocial suffering, the multiaxial system of the *Diagnostic and Statistical Manual of Mental Disorders,* fourth edition (DSM-IV, 1994), is useful and is employed here for that purpose.

Axis I

Major depression. The more seriously ill a person becomes, the more likely he is to develop major depression (Cassem, 1990). Because few forms of human suffering match or exceed major depression, careful vigilance for its appearance is necessary, as is aggressive treatment when it appears. Suicidal ideation, rather than being accepted immediately as understandable, requires the same thoughtful examination demanded in any other circumstance. Avery Weisman (1992) formulated the wish to die as an existential signal that the person's conviction "that his potential for being someone who matters has been exhausted."

Ganzini (1994) documented that severely depressed patients make more restricted advance directives when depressed and change them after they reach remission. At Memorial Sloan-Kettering Cancer Center, Breitbart and others (1993) compared terminally ill cancer and AIDS patients with suicidal ideation to similar patients without suicidal ideation. The primary difference was the presence of depression in the patients with suicidal thoughts. When Chochinov and others (1993) in a Winnipeg palliative care unit studied patients who wished that death be hastened, 62% met diagnostic criteria for major depression.

Anxiety. Anxiety disorders may or may not intensify during a terminal illness, but clearly require psychiatric attention when they do. Impending death can generate severe anxiety in the patients facing it, in their families and their friends, and in those who take care of them. When panic, phobia, generalized anxiety, and other conditions have been sought and not found, the 4 commonest fears associated with death are: (1) helplessness or loss of control, (2) being bad (guilt and punishment), (3) physical injury or symbolic injury (castration), and (4) abandonment (Freud, 1923; Deutsch, 1933).

In clinical examination a severely anxious patient usually does not know what it is about death which is so frightening. Memories of someone who died of the same illness, or associations to the illness, may produce specific fears (e.g., that it will be painful or disfiguring). Truly disruptive anxiety states are usually related to the patient's developmental history—to a defective ability to trust or unresolved dependency conflicts (e.g., the fear of helplessness and loss of control). Conflicts over guilt and castration will be lifelong. The worst anxiety encountered may be that associated with defective maternal bonding, where abandonment appears to be the object of fear. Characteristic would be the dying daughter, now overwhelmed by anxiety she cannot pinpoint or understand, for whom separation from her mother had always been a major unresolved issue. Where the mother is available and willing, therapy for both simultaneously can be helpful, but since death's separation seems so irreversibly final, considerable discomfort may remain throughout the time left for treatment.

Increased anxiety may be associated with specific memories of and associations to the death of parents or others one identifies with (as for the woman with family members who died of breast cancer or the AIDS patient who tended a lover dying of it), where the patient pictures the same fate for herself, e.g., agonizing pain or a violent scenario with excessive use of technology. Such stories may not come to light without explicit questions.

Delirium and dementia. Cognitive difficulties are common. Concomitant confusion, wandering, sundowning, agitation, and belligerence add significant distress for everyone involved. Successful control of these difficulties (see Chapter 16) makes an invaluable contribution to the care of the dying.

Axis II

Individual traits are defining and are taken for granted. Some complicate relationships, and during the last phase of life they may pose serious obstacles—at least to some onlookers—to harmonious relations and quality of life. One skilled in handling traits such as dependency, passive aggressiveness, hostility, and a histrionic style can provide useful advice for caregivers and family that lighten the burdens of everyone. When the traits reach the realm of personality disorder, care may be halted until professional intervention comes to the rescue.

Dependency on others is hard for many to tolerate. It was third on the list of reasons given by those in the Netherlands who requested euthanasia (Van der Maas et al., 1991). One of the demands of maturity is to accept help from those we trust. Yet resolutions such as "If I have to be dressed and diapered by someone else, that is where I draw the line" are not uncommon when persons think about the end of life. It is perhaps inevitable that we fear being a burden to others, especially those we love. Nevertheless, it may be helpful to ask the patient who objects to the work imposed by the illness on family whether they feel that this is an unacceptable burden or an opportunity to give something back to the dying person. As such it may be one of life's more meaningful activities.

Among the most unfortunate of dying persons are those in the severely narcissistic or borderline range of personality, as well as some persons with a history of severe physical and sexual abuse. For such a person a fatal illness is but one more act of brutal victimization. Unfortunately, it may be difficult for such patients to believe that any physician, nurse, or caregiver will do anything to them but victimize them further. Help is therefore hard if not impossible to accept and trust. Only a professional with superior psychodynamic diagnostic and treatment skills may help such a person accept palliative care.

Axis III

Palliation of the effects of the medical illness is a complex challenge requiring extensive expertise. Freedom from pain is basic to every care plan, and should be achievable in 90% of cases. Unfortunately, palliation is often equated simply with pain control. Even though pain control in itself is so simple in concept that any medical student can master the principles in a few days, physicians are repeatedly indicted for undertreatment of pain, whether for outpatients with metastatic cancer (Cleeland et al., 1994), terminal AIDS patients (Kimball and McCormick, 1996), and patients dying in prominent academic center intensive care units (Desbiens et al. 1995). The same deficiencies are reported in house staff (Sloan et al., 1996) and nurses (Brunier et al., 1995), although nurses with more education know significantly more (Brunier et al., 1995). In his presidential address to the annual meeting of the Society of Critical Care Medicine, John Hoyt (1996) said that the ICU study "suggested that ICU physicians did not listen to families. They did not know when to stop treatment. They did not relieve pain and suffering." Fear of addiction and harsh regulatory threats continue to be cited as reasons for this perplexing failure (Hill, 1993; Reidenberg, 1996). Guidelines for cancer pain management are widely publicized and available (Jacox et al., 1994; Jadad and Browman, 1995).

Palliative care includes a vast number of problems more complicated than analgesia for nociceptive pain and

is the subject of several texts (Billings, 1985; Walsh, 1989; Woodruff, 1993; Doyle et al., 1993). Table 33.1 presents a list of the practical problems commonly found in the care of the terminally ill, listing the chapter titles from Billings (1985). If one claims to be committed to keeping the terminally ill person comfortable until death comes, one must be prepared, at the very least, to manage the difficulties listed in Table 33.1. The American Board of Internal Medicine (1996) has made available an educational resource document on palliative care for all physicians.

Axis IV

In DSM-IV Axis IV is used for "psychosocial stressors," and in this section the focus is the specific relationships that the dying person has with the psychosocial environment.

Table 33.1 Symptom control in terminal illness

Pain control

Nausea and vomiting

Hiccoughs

Anorexia and nutritional care

Constipation, diarrhea, GI problems
    Incontinence, obstruction, hepatic encephalopathy

Mouth problems, dysphagia

Dyspnea, cough, respiratory problems, "death rattle"

Urinary tract symptoms
    Incontinence, indwelling catheters, renal failure,
      obstruction

Skin problems
    Pruritis, pressure sores
    Fungating tumors, ulcerating wounds
      Odor, bleeding, drainage, fistulas

Fluid accumulation
    Edema, ascites, pleural/pericardial effusions

Dehydration

Neuropsychiatric symptoms, brain tumors

Weakness, fatigue
    Spinal cord compression, spasticity

Infections, fevers, sweats

Anemia and transfusions

Emergencies
    Superior vena cava syndrome, pathologic fractures

Source: Adapted from Billings, 1985.

Family. For family and close friends a fatal illness may be the only reality important enough to resolve long-standing conflicts. Comments to children such as "No mother wants to die with the thought that her children will never speak to one another again" may motivate individuals to rally to their mother and cooperate to ease her last months. Reconciliation may also result. Likewise saying to the family gathered around the patient, "And I hope many years from now none of you will think 'If only I had told Dad/Bill this or that.' You have time for that now." When conflicts are apparent, such direct comments can be made. Making peace should be high on the agenda. Specific plans for the family are important: wills, a correct family history, instructions about what sort of a funeral or memorial service to have, and so on.

The end of life is an opportunity to give a gift to the younger generation. When they are included in all the planning, the meetings, the discussions, the activities, the care, and final attendance at death, children learn that death need not be violent or terrifying, and that the answer to feeling threatened is contained in the loss itself, when all loved ones rally to put finishing touches on the relationships that are threatened. We face our losses best together.

Occupation and work. Work has been critical for the self-esteem of many persons. The relationships made in the course of one's occupation should be activated so that self-esteem can be maintained and the sense can be given of a life lived meaningfully. But the dying person is often too disabled to get around easily; hence mobilization of friends, especially friends who have been out of touch, needs deliberate attention. Many begin to feel less valuable when their work ceases or they retire. For them the end of life may intensify a sense of failure. Seeing old friends can remind a dying person who they are, what they accomplished, and that they are still remembered and respected regardless of their illness.

Role of religious faith and value systems. Investigation of the relationship between religious faith and attitudes toward death has been hampered by differences in methodology. Lester (1972b) and Feifel (1974) have reviewed much of the conflicting literature on the relationship between religious faith and fear of death. Other research has tried to clarify the way belief systems function within the individual. Allport (1958) contrasted an extrinsic religious orientation, in which religion is mainly a means to social status, security, or relief from guilt, with an intrinsic religious orientation, in which the values appear to be in-

ternalized and subscribed to as ends in themselves. Feagin (1964) provided a useful 21-item questionnaire for distinguishing these 2 types of believers. Experimental work (Magni, 1972) and clinical experience indicate that an extrinsic value system, without internalization, seems to offer no assistance in coping with a fatal illness. A religious commitment that is intrinsic, by contrast, appears to offer considerable stability and strength to those who possess it. Koenig et al. (1995) found that in elderly depressed patients religious coping was accompanied by significantly fewer cognitive symptoms of depression (e.g., feeling helpless or like a failure, boredom, social withdrawal, feeling downhearted and blue), while somatic symptoms showed no relation to religious coping.

Although psychiatric training has often made practitioners suspicious of, hostile to, or uncomfortable with anything associated with religion, people who have a strong internalized faith possess a resource that helps significantly to negotiate a fatal illness. Exploration of a person's religious or spiritual life is mandatory. Many patients are grateful for the chance to express their own thoughts about their faith. Faith is simply framed in psychological perspective as another personal relationship, this time between the person and God. The patient is asked about his relationship with God with the same questions used to assess the quality of relationships with a parent, friend, or any significant other: For you, what sort of a person is God? Do you picture God? Where? In what historical context was God introduced to you? Is God warm, secure, pleasant? Cold, scrutinizing, punitive? Does God regard you as a favorite? A black sheep? What sort of trust is there, you for God and vice versa? Does this sense of relationship give you confidence that God truly exists? What is the most powerful sense you have had of God's presence? Do you doubt? When you doubt, how is the sense of relationship affected? Do you communicate with God? Pray? Do you feel heard? Is communication a two-way process? Do you have any sense of God speaking to you? How? Do you get answers or ever feel certain of getting a message in return? Do you (ever) feel "in touch"? Cared about? Do prayers ever feel like "dead letters" sent to an unoccupied address? What then? In general, the person's ability to tolerate doubt is a good index of the maturity of his faith. If we *knew*, faith would be unnecessary. Doubt, as Gregory Baum said, is the shadow cast by faith.

Discussing the terminal illness provides an excellent chance to inquire about the patient's view of the age-old problem of evil. Given such a severe or life-threatening illness, just where does God stand in this? Sympathetic? If all good and loving, how could God permit it to happen to you? Do you feel supported? Punished? Justly punished? Betrayed? Are you still able to pray? How has all this affected your prayer or dialogue with God?

When conversation touches death, it is an opportunity to ask about the patient's belief in an afterlife. Is there anything after? Do you ever picture it? Does this comfort you somehow or in any way ease some aspects of this illness? In general, those persons who possess a sense of a benign personal presence of God, of being cared for and watched over, will continue to do so, and this belief will help to maintain tranquillity in their struggle with terminal illness. Firm religious convictions signal that a consultation with the chaplain should be discussed with the patient. The patient's own minister or rabbi, if available, usually can provide many valuable facts and insights about the patient and family and help uniquely to smooth the overall course before death.

Belief in an afterlife is another useful area for questioning and helps in assessing tolerance of doubt, an important quality of mature belief. In 1974 Kübler-Ross wrote: "Before I started working with dying patients, I did not believe in a life after death. I now do believe in a life after death without a shadow of a doubt" (p. 167). When M. G. Michaelson reviewed Kübler-Ross's book along with several others on death and dying, he quoted this passage and added: "Damned if I know what's going on here, but it does seem that everyone who's gone into the subject comes out believing in something crazy. Life after death, transformation, destiny, belief . . . These are the words of hard-nosed scientists fresh from their investigations" (1974, p. 6). Careful investigation of religious faith in the dying needs to be pursued.

Religious persons ordinarily have a community of believers who can be unusually thoughtful and generous in providing support. Again, they may not have been informed of the patient's plight and will need to be contacted. Does the person feel some need of reconciliation with God or with the community? Should the personal clergyperson be contacted?

For those without religious ties, strong convictions about life and values may be coded in a philosophy of life. What is important? What principles or guidelines have you tried to live by? Is there anything worth dying for? What are you proudest of? These issues are the material out of which a dying person may confirm a sense of a life lived well enough. If important persons have rallied to the patient, there may also be the sense of living on in their memories as an intact and valued person.

Recreational activities shared with others. Isolation can be painful and a source of suffering itself. The detailed personal information about a patient at the end of life should include the groups he or she joined to pursue interests or recreation. From bridge to bingo, sports as participant or fan, political activism, travel, the local "haunts" of the individual, activities generate clues to persons or groups who may be able to contribute meaning to the patient's last days. Having a serious illness is itself justification for forming new relationships, and self-help groups have been exceptionally helpful for all kinds of sufferers.

Society. A dying person may be burdened by shame for actions censured or disapproved of by others. A person who has committed a crime, hurt a loved one, abandoned a family, been disabled by a chronic disease, or for some other reason may feel disowned by society. The intense work with caregivers and friends to get through the end of life with courage and graciousness can establish in such a person a sense of being respected as a worthwhile, even admirable human being.

Psychoeducational group treatment. Cancer patients who participate in a psychoeducational treatment group gain significant advantages, including improvement in mood, reduction in anxiety, and learning more adaptive coping skills. The most dramatic benefit demonstrated so far is the significant prolongation of life demonstrated for both breast cancer (Spiegel et al., 1989) and melanoma (Fawzy et al., 1993) patients.

Axis V

In DSM-IV Axis V is an estimate of global function. Here "function" is used as synonymous with the goals of palliative care, namely, that quality of life be maximized, and to the extent that a person can function as he or she wishes, the work of others provides the critical assistance.

When things go well, care of the dying is a process of mutual growth. Just as the deterioration of another trapped by a fatal disease can be threatening (we feel both horrified at the prospect of the same happening to us and helpless to assist), the response of the dying person to the challenge may be not only edifying but also an invaluable lesson in coping.

Nonabandonment is one of the most important principles in this work. Despite frustration, seemingly unsolvable problems, and relentless deterioration, one must learn that presence itself is of value. Most patients who have lost the ability to communicate experience a period when they can still hear or perceive the presence of those in attendance. Although the patient may never be able to tell us how important that time is, an occasional incident will do so dramatically, as when a supposedly "unconscious" person suddenly smiles appropriately or even speaks. At those times one's knowledge of the person makes conversation with the family easy or, when the patient is alone for the regular visit, makes conversing possible, e.g., by reporting on something in the news known to be of interest, such as "The Red Sox are now only one game out of first place."

It is hoped that this mutual work at the end of life will have ratified the dying person's sense of self and has helped the family, friends, and caregivers achieve the sense that they have provided good care and safe passage.

Care of the Dying Child and His Parents

Fatally ill children pose poignant and difficult problems for their parents and caregivers. Easson (1970) and Spinetta (1974) have reviewed contributions to the understanding of these issues in a field that needs more empirical study. Any approach to helping a dying child and his family must be based on the understanding of the child's attitudes toward death.

The most common adult misconception is that children cannot comprehend the meaning of death. Even teenagers are often treated as though they did not understand mortality. Anthony (1940) and Nagy (1948) were the first to study empirically the development of the death concept in children. Table 33.2 summarizes the development of this comprehension in healthy children. Three phases characterize the gradual understanding of the death concept. Children 5 or younger regard death as reversible, comparable to a journey or sleep. Six months after the death of her father, a 3-year-old girl asked, "Mommy, will Daddy be home for Christmas?" Because of the inability of children in this age group to grasp the finality of death, I recommend that parents not compare death to sleep, natural as that is, because of the likelihood that a sick child with this association will be afraid to go to sleep at night. (This fear is a common feature of very sick adults troubled by specifically nocturnal insomnia. The fear is often unconscious, and its treatment is difficult.)

Between the ages of 5 or 6 and 9 or 10, the child personifies death as a ghost or bogeyman who comes to transport the dying person away. The causation is seen as external ("Who killed him?"). At this stage death becomes a definite fact of life, although it is common for the child to regard it as remote—as something that happens only to the very old.

Table 33.2 Concepts of death in healthy children

Concept	Age	Investigator
Reversible	3–5	Anthony, 1940; Nagy, 1948
Similar to sleep, journey, departure	3–5	Anthony, 1940; Nagy, 1948; and most others
Due to violence	3–5	Rochlin, 1965; Natterson and Knudson, 1960
Personified	6–10	Nagy, 1948
Externally caused	5–9	Anthony, 1940; Nagy, 1948; Natterson and Knudson, 1960; Safier, 1964
Fact of life	5–9	Most investigators
Inevitable	5–9	Most investigators
	3–5	Rochlin, 1965
Irreversible	9+	Nagy, 1948
	8	Portz, 1972
	7	Steiner, 1965
Universal	9+	Nagy, 1948
	8+	Anthony, 1940
	11	Steiner, 1965
	8½	Peck, 1966

The 2 most abstract elements in the concept of death, irreversibility and universality, are incorporated later. Comprehension of these elements is regarded as marking a complete grasp of the essential notions of the death concept. Acquisition of the concept of irreversibility marks the third and final phase in concept development and appeared after age 9 in Nagy's (1948) study. Steiner (1965) and Portz (1972) discovered its appearance at ages 7 and 8, respectively. Grasp of death's universality has been found as early as age 8.4 by Peck (1966), although other studies set it at 9 or later, and Steiner (1965) found its mean age of onset in her sample to be 11. The significance of these studies is great: the average child has a complete understanding of the essential notion of death between the ages of 8 and 11. Of course, a child's comprehension can be quite threatening to adults. Michele, aged 11 and dying of a brain tumor, said: "My parents won't tell me anything, but I know, I've got a tumor, people die of it . . . Of course I know that I won't get better. Children do sometimes die; I'm going to die, too" (Raimbault, 1972).

What fears accompany the growth of this comprehension of death in children? Table 33.3 presents a summary of fears specific to the phases of conceptual development outlined above. Children 5 or younger dread separation from parents. Minimizing the threat of death for them requires specific attention to maintaining contact with parents and reassuring the child about the return of a parent who must leave for short periods. One important application of this principle is the inclusion of children in all death rituals, such as wakes, funerals, *shivah,* and burial. Parents who fail to do so risk frightening the child far more by separating him from his family at a time when death has already caused one separation in the family. No child is too small to be included. As with visitation of the sick or dying, the child should be allowed to go unless he requests not to; he is usually a better judge of the situation than the parent.

Between the ages of 6 and 10, the child normally develops fears of bodily injury and mutilation, particularly as the victim of aggressive actions. The use of dolls in

Table 33.3 Specific fears associated with death in children and adolescents

Age	Fears
Up to 4 or 5 years	Separation
6–10 years	Aggression; mutilation; guilt; loneliness
10+ years	Own death; abandonment
Adolescence	Shame

describing surgical procedures to children in this age group is an effective method of neutralizing some of their fears. This is also the age in which parental discipline becomes formalized in the child's primitive conscience, where "good" acts deserve reward and "bad" ones punishment. The child, now very vulnerable to feelings of guilt, is likely to regard death or illness as a punishment for being "bad." Accordingly, children of this age should be reminded explicitly that illness does not befall them or their siblings because they were bad children. Similarly, all exhortations that imply guilt should be avoided, such as "If you are a good boy and take your medicine, nothing will happen to you." Finally, loneliness is listed here because it is, unfortunately, often experienced by fatally ill children. From around the age of 10 on, the concerns of children can be strikingly adult (as noted earlier in the case of Michele). They wonder what their own death will be like, particularly whether it will be painful and, even more, whether they will be left to face it alone when it comes.

Shame is listed as a special concern of the adolescent to emphasize how embarrassed and self-conscious the pubescent youngster can be with a new and rapidly changing body. To have this body threatened or disfigured by a fatal illness can result in feelings of intense shame, even revulsion, for the adolescent. All these age-specific concerns should be assumed to be present to some degree in ill children and great care given to their alleviation.

Like healthy children, fatally ill children understand the meaning of death and are usually aware of their own predicament. Eugenia Waechter (1972) studied 4 groups of 16 children, aged 6–10: those with a fatal illness, those with a chronic but nonfatal illness, those with an acute brief illness, and those with no illness (healthy group). The anxiety scale scores, as well as the derived-fear scores, from the Thematic Apperception Test of the fatally ill children were significantly higher than those of all other groups and demonstrated that the greatest anxiety was expressed by those children for whom death was the predicted outcome. The projective tests revealed significantly more specific concern about death among the fatally ill children. Moreover, every child in this diagnostic category (100%) used death imagery at least once in his responses to the protocol. Images of loneliness in this group also significantly exceeded those expressed by the other 3 groups. The main character in the stories of the fatally ill children died or was assigned a negative future significantly more often than in the other children's stories. Many parents had gone to great lengths to ensure that the diagnosis was never mentioned to the child and the illness never discussed with him. Waechter's study also demonstrated that the less opportunity the child had to discuss the illness at home, the higher his score on the general-anxiety scale. Avoiding talk about the illness appeared to indicate to the child that it was too terrible to discuss.

Even more difficult than discussing the illness with a dying child is the problem of remaining in his presence. What truth is there in the accusation that we avoid and isolate the dying child? What is the child's perception of this? To study these questions, Spinetta, Rigler, and Karon (1974) compared 25 children hospitalized for the first time with a diagnosis of leukemia and 25 hospitalized for a chronic, nonfatal illness; all children were aged 6–10. In an ingenious design, the experimenters used a 3-dimensional hospital room replica, scaled so that 1 inch equaled 1 foot. Using a child-patient doll matched for sex and race with the child, they presented sequentially father, mother, nurse, and doctor dolls with the instruction, "Here comes the nurse; put her where she usually stands." Distance from the child-patient doll was recorded in centimeters in each case. On the first admission, the 25 leukemic children placed the figures significantly farther away than did the control group of chronically ill children. The experiment was repeated with subsequent admissions. Although the distance of placement increased for both groups in the subsequent admission, the leukemic children increased the distance significantly more than did the chronically ill, lending strong support to the hypothesis that the child's sense of isolation grows stronger as he nears death. The implication of these empirical studies is clear. Effective care of the dying child must focus both on helping the child communicate his concerns and on helping the parents (and staff) deal with the personal fears that lead them to avoid or isolate the child.

Management of the dying child is an individualized matter, understood best by the parents. Days that can be lived normally will be the most enjoyable to the child, and for these days overindulgence may be just as damaging as neglect. Although professionals should not tell parents how to take care of their children, supplying them with a list of specific concerns, like the one in Table 33.3, is helpful. Discovering the child's specific fear is a basic objective. One 10-year-old girl with leukemia, who had done well emotionally up to the time her chemotherapy began to produce hair loss, went to bed in her room and did not come out. Promises of getting a wig proved of no help, but when she learned that the hair loss was an effect of medication, she promptly resumed her normal activities. She had associated loss of hair with death, and when her hair began to fall out, she thought she was dying. Children need encouragement to express and discuss specific fears

of this kind (Toch, 1964; Yudkin, 1967; Evans, 1968; Easson, 1970).

What does one tell a child about death or prognosis? Experienced pediatricians are too wise to answer this in any simple way, although most tend to shield the child from labels like "leukemia" or "cancer," and all are wisely careful to avoid predicting when the child will die. The discomfort over what to say to the child about illness and death, however, is often a primary obstacle for the parents and the medical caregivers. This uncertainty, coupled with the strong desire not to harm the child or make his predicament any worse, is a major obstacle to allowing the child to express specific fears. Children's questions are often blunt and alarming. "What is death like?" "Am I going to have a coffin?" "Are you and Daddy going to come to visit me when I'm in the grave?" are all questions that have been asked by children under 10. The most helpful technique in dealing with these confrontations is to ask for the child's own answer to the question. Thus, "What do you think it's like?" "What do you want done?" "What would you like us to do?" would be helpful initial responses to the 3 sample questions. Only in this manner can the adult learn more specifically what is on the child's mind. The boy who asked the first question said he thought that in death a bogeyman would come to take him away. Later he said he thought death would hurt. His mother was able to comfort him on both points. The 7-year-old girl who asked the second question said she wanted to choose the colors of the casket, while the 7-year-old girl who asked the third question said that she wanted visitors at the grave and promptly changed the subject to what kind of company she might have in heaven. Although it is painful and difficult to take children seriously, letting them say what is on their minds best guarantees understanding them and finding ways to comfort them. Imagined fears are almost always worse than reality, and astonishing equanimity has been seen in children who are confident that they will not be left alone, attacked, or regarded as bad.

Kübler-Ross has enlightened many about the symbolic language in a child's drawings. The same symbolism can be seen in dolls or other play objects. Sometimes children will talk about drawings, especially if the drawings, not the child, are made the focus of discussion by asking what the child in the drawing thinks, not what the artist thinks. One child who had undergone 6 major abdominal operations in 5 months introduced me to a grape named Joe. When I asked where his head was, she told me one pole of the grape was his navel, and in response to the repeated question said that the other pole represented his anus. When I asked what it was like for Joe to be contained between navel and anus, she replied with a smile, "Oh, it's not so bad, most of the time." She then declined to discuss Joe further. Some children will not discuss their drawings or play objects at all, and some are so eloquent that little need be added. Nonverbal communication can be more important at tense moments for the child. Children are reassured by being touched, hugged, or rocked (Kennell, Slyter, and Klaus, 1970), especially if the person doing it is relaxed and accepting. Various authors have pointed out the child's interest in toys, dolls, furry animals, and television; these absorbing objects do not lose their appeal when a child is sick.

Any support given to the parents will greatly benefit the child. While parents will find some understanding of the material presented above very helpful, they have their own needs. From the time they learn of the diagnosis, each may assume that the other will not be able to tolerate the tragedy of their child's illness and both will attempt to minimize any display of weakness and sometimes of any emotion at all. Often numb at first, parents may at times be filled with a sense of injustice or outrage. Repeatedly asking themselves whether they should have noted the illness earlier or acted on the symptoms sooner, and aware that they may have minimized the symptoms even to the extent of regarding them as trivial, emotional, or psychosomatic, the parents may have considerable feelings of guilt. Allowing them to state and explore these concerns is essential. Suicidal thoughts are probably the rule rather than the exception during the child's illness, particularly in the mind of the mother. These thoughts ("When Julie goes, I'm next") can be alarming but are far less threatening if expressed.

While helping parents to maintain as normal a life routine for the sick child's siblings as possible, it is necessary to remember that the well children in the family may become objects of unwitting resentment, another feeling whose emergence can cause considerable distress even in a parent who in no way acts it out. "Why couldn't it be Joe instead of Julie?" is a spontaneous feeling that may cause a parent to experience acute guilt and shame, sometimes for years. If allowed to verbalize such feelings, parents should be reminded that feelings are completely different from actions. Another source of parental discomfort is the need to seek further consultation about treatment for their fatally ill child. The death of another child on the same hospital floor, particularly if afflicted by the same illness, is likely to devastate the parents of a child who is enjoying a remission.

If parents request reading material to help deal with their healthy children, Jackson (1965) and Grollman (1967) are recommended; 3 useful texts have been designed to be read directly to children after a death has occurred: Grollman (1970), Harris (1965), and Stein (1974). In some cities, organizations exist in which parents of children who are dying or have died support one another; these include the Society for the Compassionate Friends (Stevens, 1973), Candlelighters, and One Day at a Time.

Who cares for the caregiver? Physicians, nurses, social workers, and chaplains who work with dying children have all been asked how they tolerate it. Two major difficulties must be overcome. First, how does one steer a course between incapacitating emotional overinvolvement and callous, detached withdrawal? John Schowalter (1970) observes that pediatric house officers who are parents themselves find the horror of a dying child more real than do those who are not parents, but they also tend to have more empathy and work better with the parents than their single peers. He finds a tendency in all house officers studied to avoid getting emotionally involved with dying children.

The second dilemma of health workers in this setting is how to obtain gratification from fighting a losing battle. Although they may actually deny for some time that it is a losing battle (and this denial can be useful), the ultimate reality remains. An interest in and respect for the child and his parents can be developed through encounters with them that provide gratification. This process, of course, implies emotional investment in the child and his parents. Parents of dying children frequently admit, though with embarrassment, that the desire to see a physician, nurse, or other member of the hospital personnel motivates their hospital visiting more than just seeing their own child. These encounters with parents as well as with the children provide the staff with specific feedback about their importance, effectiveness, and helpfulness in the situation. Flexibility is important. In a survey of pediatricians' attitudes toward the care of fatally ill children, J. M. Weiner (1970) notes that as pediatricians get older, they develop more flexible attitudes toward parental visiting hours and parental participation in actual child care. Another issue that parents need to discuss with physicians and staff is whether the child should die in the hospital or at home.

Mechanisms to ensure and promote growth in the ability of hospital personnel to take care of dying children and their parents should include formal training. As helpful as that may be, however, other mechanisms are necessary to optimize staff performance and morale in the treatment setting itself, whether inpatient or outpatient.

Schowalter (1970) advocates a multidisciplinary team meeting, including pediatric house officers, child psychiatry fellows, nurses, social workers, chaplains, medical and nursing students, and others who work in the setting. Such meetings are conducted by a staff child psychiatrist and senior pediatrician. In similar situations, nurses and house officers have stressed the need for a liaison person to deal with the parents and children directly, because both are likely to feel uncomfortable with the parents. Inviting a parent to a group meeting, either a multidisciplinary or a nursing group, can provide a model for allowing parents to discuss their concerns. Group members can also be invited to express their own feelings about children and parents and to arrive at specific management plans through sharing reactions and observations (Cassem and Hackett, 1975). Where parents' groups exist, the opportunity for staff members to visit maintains contact and provides a chance to see how parents cope with often incomprehensible tragedy.

Care and Management of the Suicidal Person

Death casts its shadow not only on the terminally ill but also on individuals determined or tempted to hasten its arrival. Care of the suicidal person represents a frequent health challenge. The tenth leading cause of death, suicide is known to claim from 22,000 to 25,000 lives annually, although the actual death toll (with many suicides disguised as accidents) may be about twice this number (Schneidman, 1975). For white males aged 15–19 it ranks second, and for physicians under 40 it ranks first, among causes of death. In the United States the recorded overall suicide rate is 10–12 per 100,000, placing this country midway in international suicide rates listed by the World Health Organization (1968). Japan, Austria, Denmark, Sweden, West Germany, and Hungary have rates higher than 20 per 100,000, while Italy, Spain, New Zealand, and Ireland have rates of 6 or less per 100,000. For every completed suicide about 8 attempts occur. Those who are widowed, divorced, or single kill themselves significantly more often than married people. In the United States, urban and rural dwellers are at equal risk, in contrast to Europe, where risk is greater in urban areas. The suicide rate among blacks, one-third that of whites 3 decades ago, is now more nearly equal, especially in urban areas. Protestants outrank Jews and Catholics among completed suicides. Half of American male suicides accomplish the act by firearms, a means used by one-fourth of women. More than one-third of female and about one-fifth of male victims use poisonous agents (including gas) to bring death.

Hanging or strangulation is chosen by about one-fifth of both men and women. The specific rise in the adolescent suicide rate is covered in Chapter 28.

Psychodynamics of the Suicidal Person

Self-destruction was seen by Freud (1917, 1920) as murder of an introjected love object toward whom the victim felt ambivalent. E. S. Schneidman (1975) reports that this classic and controversial theory stemmed from a statement by Wilhelm Stekel at a Vienna meeting in 1910 that no one killed himself unless he had either wanted to kill another person or wished another's death. Freud's initial conclusions stemmed from his work with depression, in which his discovery of hostility directed inward led to the prominence of aggression in his theory of the dynamics of melancholia. Not all depressed patients, however, engage in suicidal behavior, nor is the suicide attempter always depressed. Gregory Zilboorg (1938) points out that some suicidal patients have the unconscious conviction that they are immortal and will not die. In addition to hostility, he found an absence of the capacity to love others in suicidal patients (1937). S. Rado (1956) added the concept of expiation: suicide atones for past wrongs and becomes a way of recapturing the love of a lost or estranged object.

Karl Menninger's *Man Against Himself* (1938) extends the traditional psychoanalytic concept of self-directed aggression to include other self-destructive behaviors that stop short of suicide, classifying them as chronic (asceticism, martyrdom, neurotic invalidism, alcohol addiction, antisocial behavior, psychosis); focal (mutilation, multiple surgical procedures, malingering, accident proneness); and organic or psychological (masochism, sadism—with both self-punitive and erotic features). Despite the prominence of self-destructive behavior in everyday life, the relationships between such behavior and depression are not uncontroversial. In a series of careful empirical studies, for example, Aaron Beck (1967) was not able to confirm the presence of internalized aggression in depressed patients.

In addition to hostility, the withdrawal of social support—typified by sudden or intensified estrangement—places a person at much greater risk. Anniversaries of losses and holidays may reawaken all the original, keen feelings of abandonment, loneliness, fury, guilt, defectiveness, isolation, and hopelessness in the individual and increase his proneness to take his life. Beck (1963) stresses that suicidal behavior is most likely when a person perceives his predicament as untenable or hopeless.

What characterizes the state of mind of the person most likely to complete suicide? Buie and Maltsberger (1983) summarize by saying suicide results from 2 types of imperative impulses: murderous hate and an urgent need to escape suffering.

As psychoanalytic theories of narcissism and ego development expand, self-destruction has come to be viewed as an effort to restore the balance of wounded self-esteem. Avery Weisman (1971) points out that death itself may not be the wish of the completed suicide victim, but that the wish to die signals his conviction that "his potential for being someone who matters has been exhausted" (p. 230). Gregory Rochlin (1973), in a creative replacement of the "death instinct" theory, points out that suicide itself, like other forms of aggressive action, serves to restore bruised or shattered self-esteem. Self-inflicted death is, then, a preferred solution to and an honorable way out of the person's crisis of self-esteem, in which hopelessness and helplessness are not only the key subjective features for the individual but also the chief clues for the observer that suicide is about to occur.

Clinical Evaluation of Suicide Risk

In a thorough review of the literature of suicide prevention, Robert Litman (1966) concluded that, despite decades of interest and prolific writing on the topic, scientific study had barely begun. Six years later David Lester (1972a) could find no evidence that suicide prevention affected the suicide rate. Yet prevention depends on the accurate identification of the individual most likely to kill himself. Litman and associates (1974) suggest that the criticism of intervention programs may in part reflect a failure to differentiate between the acutely suicidal person, who is perhaps actually being rescued, and the chronically suicidal person, who, because of a somewhat lower profile, eludes detection and becomes the program's "failure."

Depression should always alert the clinician to his duty to assess suicide risk (Fawcett, 1972; Murphy, 1975b). A mental checklist should include age (men's suicide rates peak in the 80s; women's between 55 and 65); sex (men complete suicides about 3 times as often as women, while women attempt it 2 to 3 times as often as men); alcoholism; absence or recent disappearance of "fight," distress, or strong feeling (sudden calm in a previously suicidal person may stem from a definite resolve to die); refusal to accept help immediately; and prior experience as a psychiatric inpatient.

If the person has already made an attempt, its degree of lethality predicts the danger of a subsequent attempt. To assess this factor, the "risk-rescue" criteria of Weisman and Worden (1972) should be used. Information regarding the degree of risk (method used, degree of impairment of consciousness when rescued, extent of injury, time required in hospital to reverse the effects, intensity of treatment required) and the rescue circumstances (remoteness from help, type of rescuer, probability of discovery, accessibility to rescue, and delay between attempt and rescue) can be established in a careful history. Serious physical illness can increase suicide risk but does not diminish the importance of the foregoing points of assessment; it is the attitude toward the illness that requires explanation. Low tolerance for pain, excessive demands or complaints, and a perception of lack of attention and support from the hospital staff are danger signals in the assessment of suicide potential (Farberow, Schneidman, and Leonard, 1963).

Reich and Kelly (1976) analyzed 17 suicides in 70,404 consecutive general hospital admissions; the only ones without a psychiatric diagnosis were 2 cancer patients. The most significant warning of impending suicide was some sort of rupture in the patient's relationship with hospital staff, ranging from angry accusations and complaints to the perception (in the 2 cancer patients) that the staff was giving up on them.

Psychometric scales for assessment of suicide risk are available (Beck, Schuyler, and Herman, 1974; Zung, 1974). Beck, Kovacs, and Weisman (1975) provide a promising beacon to guide the physician in his search among so many variables. In a rigorous investigation of 384 suicide attempters, employing scales to measure hopelessness, suicide intention, and depression, this group demonstrates that hopelessness is the key variable linking depression to suicidal behavior. Therefore, encouraging physicians to focus on this particular clue may lead to new gains in suicide prevention.

Finally, one should always ask directly whether the person is considering suicide. Excellent evidence exists that a suicidal patient will admit his intentions to a physician if asked (Delong and Robins, 1961).

Contrary to popular belief, the physician is more likely than any other individual or agency to encounter the completed suicide victim shortly before his death. Analyzing all successful suicides in St. Louis County in 1968–69, George Murphy (1975a, b) discovered that 81% had been under the care of a physician within 6 months prior to suicide. By contrast, suicide prevention centers had contact with no more than 2–6% of the suicidal patients in their localities (Weiner, 1969; Barraclough and Shea, 1970; Sawyer, Sudak, and Hall, 1972). More soberingly, Murphy (1975a) documents that 91% of victims of suicide by overdose had been under the recent care of a physician (compared with 71% of controls), and in over half the cases, the physician had supplied by prescription the complete means for suicide.

Treating the Suicidal Person

Self-esteem or self-respect is the most basic psychic condition to be guarded if life is to continue. Therefore the restoration and maintenance of the individual's narcissistic equilibrium is the aim of the therapist confronted by a person tempted to destroy himself. Certain practical features of this relationship can be summarized from Schneidman (1975) and others.

1. The therapist should stand as an ally for the life of the individual and in a calm and gentle but firm and unequivocal way make clear that his role is direct and active, including intervention to prevent suicidal behavior when the person makes this known. This intervention may include sending the police to the patient's home, depriving him of the means of suicide (pills or weapons), or hospitalizing him by involuntary commitment. This approach is justified by those situations where suicidal communication is a cry for help (Farberow and Schneidman, 1965) and must be accompanied by equally forthright reminders to the patient of the therapist's drastic limitations—that he is only rarely able to control another's behavior; that responsibility for behavior belongs to its initiator; that unconscious hopes for someone else to stop the execution of a plan are very often disappointed; and that without the patient's actually cooperating (at least unconsciously), the therapist could not prevent or reverse a single suicide attempt.

2. This active relationship requires a delicate but deliberate violation of the usual confidences of the therapeutic relationship. Self-destructive plans are never to be held in confidence when their disclosure may prevent the death of the patient. It is not the plan that prompts action from the therapist (he can be content to hear in confidence innumerable variations) but the emergence of indications that execution of plans is likely.

3. Repeated monitoring of suicidal potential is an important feature of working with an actively suicidal patient. Suicidal intent, the extent of hopelessness, and events on the patient's "calendar," such as anniversaries of losses and most holiday seasons, require direct questioning for proper assessment.

4. Despite his status as an ally for life, the therapist must also have the capacity to hear out carefully and to tolerate the feelings of despair, desperation, anguish, rage, loneliness, emptiness, and meaninglessness articulated by the suicidal person. The patient needs to know that the therapist takes him seriously and understands. This understanding may require the therapist to explore the patient's darkest feelings of despair—a taxing empathic task.

5. Reduction of social isolation and withdrawal is essential. Active advice and encouragement may be required, as well as family, couple, or group treatment. Self-esteem develops through relationships with others, and internalization of a benign and supportive love object is an essential feature of ego development. A shortage of such love objects is often so prominent in the lives of suicidal patients that replacement of bad internalized objects may seem (and some say theoretically is) impossible. These persons are skilled at distorting interpersonal relationships and evoking rejection. For this reason the therapist's investment in and respect for them may mark the first and only relationship in which they can begin to eliminate distorting perceptions of all relationships.

6. Relationships, work, hobbies, and other individualistic activities enhance and maintain self-esteem. Community agencies may help the patient renew or initiate such activities.

7. Coexisting psychiatric disorders must be treated. Suicide does not respect diagnostic categories. Potential for completed suicide, while representing an escape from an intolerable, hopeless crisis of self-esteem, must be dealt with in a manner appropriate to the psychopathology of the individual. Thus with the suicidal schizophrenic, reality testing, increased medication, and even electroconvulsive therapy may be essential to prevent death. With the borderline patient or narcissistic personality, one is likely to spend even more time than usual interpreting negative transference or explaining the typical sequence of behaviors outlined by Gerald Adler (1973): highly idealized expectation, followed by inevitable disappointment and reactive rage, culminating in self-destructive behavior. Similar considerations for depression, anxiety, and other conditions must be made. If the patient has no psychiatric illness, as in the case of patients with cancer or dependence on chronic hemodialysis, attention to factors that can restore self-esteem and respect is also paramount.

8. Finally, the therapist himself must at times seek support or consultation when treating a patient with potential for completing suicide. Of all the difficulties encountered, the most troublesome is almost surely the countertransference hatred that suicidal patients often evoke in their caregivers (Maltzberger and Buie, 1974). When hostility is prominent in the patient, hypercritical, devaluating, scornful rage may be directed at the therapist

for long periods of time. Then the therapist's own reactions as well as the patient's feelings can make treatment seem like an ordeal.

Treating a suicidal person can be quite anxiety provoking for the therapist. The need to balance consideration for the patient's safety with the goal that he live his life independently in his own world reminds us how limited the therapist's powers are—that is, they are no stronger than the patient's desire to make use of help. The therapist who appreciates his ultimate inability to stop the person who really wants to kill himself is far more likely to be effective in restoring the person's sense of self-esteem and wholeness. Respect for independence, like investment in a patient's well-being, is itself therapeutic. Clarifying these limitations with the patient helps convey respect for his autonomy and reminds the therapist that a completed suicide can occur despite complete fulfillment of his responsibility. Both are thereby better enabled to see that the risks of their mutual encounter are worth taking.

Care of the Bereaved

William Heberden, listing the causes of death in London in 1657, assigned tenth rank to "griefe." Four centuries later, George Engel (1961) argued eloquently that grief should be classified as a disease because of its massive impact on normal function, the suffering it involves, and the predictable symptomatology associated with it. Parkes's *Bereavement* (1972) represents the most comprehensive contemporary summary of the empirical factors associated with the entire process. *Bereavement* refers to the process of accommodation to a specific loss, including anticipatory grief and mourning (Weisman, 1974); *grief* denotes the conscious impact of loss on an individual; *mourning* is the reactive process of coping with the loss.

How can one distinguish normal from abnormal grief? In his pioneer work with survivors of the Coconut Grove fire, Erich Lindemann (1944) describes pathognomonic features of normal grief: (1) somatic distress, marked by sighing respiration, exhaustion, and digestive symptoms of all kinds (C. S. Lewis wrote in 1961, after the death of his wife: "No one ever told me that grief felt so much like fear. I am not afraid, but the sensation is like being afraid. The same fluttering in the stomach, the same restlessness, the yawning. I keep on swallowing"; p. 7); (2) preoccupation with the image of the deceased, a slight sense of unreality, a feeling of increased emotional distance from others, and such an intense focus on the deceased person that the grief-stricken may believe themselves in danger of insanity; (3) preoccupation with feelings of guilt; (4) hostile reactions, irritability, and a disconcerting loss of warm

feelings toward other people; and (5) a disruption or disorganization of normal patterns of conduct.

In abnormal grief reactions, Lindemann found that the postponement of the experience or the absence of grief is usually associated with much more difficulty during bereavement. Parkes (1972) observes that hysterical or extreme reactions to loss (such as prolonged screaming and shouting, repeated fainting, and conversion paralysis) carry a prognostic significance as bad as the absence of grief. Cultural norms must of course be consulted to determine what is extreme in expressing grief. Lindemann (1944) lists 9 signs of abnormality, which he calls "distorted reactions": (1) overactivity without a sense of loss; (2) the acquisition of symptoms belonging to the last illness of the deceased, presenting as conversion (hysterical) or hypochondriacal complaints; (3) a recognized medical disease, such as ulcerative colitis, rheumatoid arthritis, or asthma (although Lindemann linked these diseases to the group of psychosomatic conditions recognized at the time, subsequent investigations have shown that after the death of a loved one, survivors are at a significantly increased risk of death and illness); (4) alteration in relationships to friends and relatives, with progressive social isolation; (5) furious hostility against specific persons, resembling a truly paranoid reaction; (6) such suppression of hostility that affect and conduct resemble a schizophrenic picture, with masklike appearance, formal, stilted, robotlike movements, and no emotional expressiveness; (7) lasting loss of patterns of social interactions, with absence of decisiveness and initiative; (8) behavior that is socially and economically destructive, such as giving away belongings, making foolish business deals, or performing other self-punitive actions with no realization of internal feelings of guilt; and (9) overt agitated depression. It is important to note that Lindemann was impressed by the rarity of these manifestations of abnormal grief among the families of the Coconut Grove victims.

Clayton, Desmarais, and Winokur (1968), in extensive investigations of bereaved persons, have firmly established in follow-up surveys how well most bereaved persons recover. At 3 months after the loss, the researchers found that 4 out of 5 patients were improved, and only 4% were worse. Rees and Lutkins (1967) have shown that widows and widowers have a significantly increased death rate for their age category in the first year following the death of their spouse. Holmes and Rahe (1967) have demonstrated that loss in many forms increases the risk of illness. Contrary to Rees and Lutkins's data, Clayton and associates failed to find an increase of morbidity among a sample of bereaved persons in the St. Louis area.

How long does bereavement take? A parent who recently joined a parents' group after the death of his child asked this question. Another parent replied, "My son died 30 years ago, so I don't know yet," eloquently expressing how feelings of loss and sadness can remain while behavior returns to normal. Treatment of the abnormal reactions is of primary importance.

Bereavement, according to DSM-IV (V62.82), focuses clinical attention on the reaction to the death of a loved one. In the case of the medical patient, of course, it is the self that is mourned after a narcissistic injury, e.g., a myocardial infarction. But DSM-IV unnecessarily restricts "bereavement" to loss of a loved one. After significant illness or injury one grieves for lost parts or aspects of oneself in the same way one grieves loss of a loved one.

The Process of Mourning

While many schemes are useful in conceptualizing mourning, that of John Bowlby (1961) is classic.

1. In the first phase, the survivor is preoccupied with the lost person. In accord with animal models of loss, this time is characterized by searching and protest. The behaviors may seem bizarre yet are entirely normal. One boy of 14 lost his best friend from nephritis. For 3 months thereafter he carried on prolonged conversations with his departed friend, with the conviction not only that his questions and discussion of future plans were heard but that his friend was present. Vivid hallucinatory experiences of the deceased person occur in about 50% of bereavement reactions. A mother who lost her 20-year-old daughter repeatedly found herself in the girl's room. She wore the girl's clothes and on occasion put on the girl's nightclothes and lay in her bed striving for some sort of meeting with her. The German artist Käthe Kollwitz described working on a monument for her younger son, who was killed in October 1914. Two years later she noted in her diary: "There's a drawing made, a mother letting her dead son slide into her arms. I could do a hundred similar drawings but still can't seem to come any closer to him. *I'm still searching for him,* as if it were in the very work itself that I had to find him" (Parkes, 1972, p. 39; emphasis added). Children of Israeli soldiers missing in action have been observed repeatedly to lose objects, complain loudly and tearfully about the losses, and, suddenly finding the object, carry it about on display, urging adults in the family to rejoice with them in the discovery; in one case the object was a picture of the missing father (reported by M. Rosenbaum at Psychiatric Grand Rounds, Massachusetts General Hospital, Boston, 1975). It is important for an observer to recall that even apparently bizarre behavior in

a bereaved person may represent the searching or protest phase of the mourning process.

2. The second phase described by Bowlby is one of disorganization, a preoccupation with the pain of the experience, characterized at times by turmoil or even despair. One father, 2 years after the loss of his 10-year-old son, told a group: "It hurts. I could tell you all about how you'd feel going through the whole thing, but I could never tell you about the emptiness that comes . . . afterward. That hurts more than anything—at times it aches." C. S. Lewis noted after the death of his wife, "Her absence is like the sky, spread over everything" (1961, p. 13). The pointlessness of life and the reasonableness of suicide are common in the minds of the bereaved in this period. Social interaction seems impossible, and yet solitude is intolerable. "I want others to be about me," Lewis observed. "I dread the moments when the house is empty. If only they would talk to one another and not to me" (p. 7).

3. Finally, a phase of reorganization occurs in which normal functioning and behavior are restored. Reversals during this time are the rule, and the reappearance of the earlier 2 phases should be expected. During the reorganization process, the bereaved person is caught off guard by memories and repeated realizations of the pain of loss. A widow, at the ringing of a phone, may be devastated by the sudden realization that her husband will never phone her again. Returning to scenes or sights shared with the deceased is a common occasion of grief and an opportunity to further the process of mourning. Death after a long illness, for example, may seem acceptable to a survivor because it terminates the pain and debilitation of the lost person. But return to a scene that recalls the lost person in a healthy state may precipitate new feelings and make the death entirely unacceptable. One widow used to carry the picture of her husband as he looked at his worst. When she felt sad, she would take the picture out and look at it "to remind myself that he couldn't be expected to go on."

Psychologically, death represents the rupture of the survivor's attachment to the lost person—a bond heavily laden with feelings, conveniently oversimplified as those of love and those of hate. For example, a wife dies. Because of her the husband felt loved, better, stronger, whole; her death comes as a personal blow, even to his own self-esteem ("narcissistic injury"). He now feels smaller, weaker, fragmented. He may feel cheated, angry, and desirous of lashing out. For all his hostile feelings toward her he now feels guilt, probably in proportion to his negative feelings ("I might have been angry, but I wouldn't have wished this for her in a million years"). In the classic view of Freud (1917), the libido invested in the lost object, through the process of mourning, was freed to allow the survivor to invest feeling in new love objects. Despite impressions given by some theorists, investment in the lost person is not forsaken. Rather, a progressive clarification of the attachment seems to occur, until both positive and negative feelings toward the dead person are restored to a realistic balance and the lost one is viewed with more perspective. In this clarification process, the survivor puts in perspective his own role and value in the relationship, thereby restoring his own damaged self-esteem.

Being Helpful to Those in Mourning

No less than the dying, mourners are outcasts of society. Their presence is painful to many who surround them, and efforts to silence, impede, or stop mourning are common. Most societies and subcultures have rituals for beginning the process of mourning, such as wakes or *shivah*, funerals, and burial services. These rituals have significant values (see Cassem, 1976): (1) They provide an occasion for the gathering of the social network of support that surrounds the family unit. (2) Those gathered activate important memories about the deceased, sometimes providing the bereaved with information and relationships not previously known. (3) Tributes paid to the dead person emphasize both his worth and the fact that he is worth the pain and stress of grieving. (4) Family units may be drawn closer together. (5) Rituals permit expression of sorrow, set some limits on grieving, and provide legitimate outlets for expressing positive feelings. (6) Rituals reemphasize the reality that the deceased person is dead and gone, often by providing a view of the body (failure to see the dead body generally retards grieving). (7) The funeral permits other people in the community to pay their respects and initiate their own grieving. (8) Death rituals for the community provide occasions to grieve for losses unrelated to the deceased, a chance to continue unfinished mourning. (9) P. C. Rosenblatt (1975) presents cross-cultural evidence from 78 societies that overt expressions of anger following a death are less common where ritualists deal with the body up to and during burial. (10) Because the bereaved generally remember nonverbal expressions of concern and affection more clearly than verbal expressions, rituals provide the formal occasion to bring others into the mourners' presence.

The task of the mourner is threefold: first, to experience and reflect upon his feelings toward the lost object during life and the feelings evoked by death; second, to review the history of the attachment; and third, to examine his own wounds, attend to their healing, and confront the task of continuing without the lost object. To help the bereaved, one need only facilitate the 3 parts of this process.

Allowing the bereaved to express feelings is essential. The most important part of this process is to avoid the maneuvers that nullify grieving. Clichés ("It's God's will"), self-evident but irrelevant reassurances ("After all, you've got three other children"), and outright exhortations to stop grieving ("Life must go on") should be carefully avoided. Some acquaintance with the nature of mourning is helpful, because many of the expressions of pain or seemingly aberrant behavior are necessary elements in the searching-disorganization-reorganization process. Tolerance of reversals from cheerful to grief-stricken feelings during the reorganization phase is essential.

Presence means more than words. Above all, the friend who can remain calm and quiet in the presence of a weeping or angry or bitter mourner is highly valued. Embarrassment only increases the discomfort of the grieving person. A touch can be worth a thousand words, as can moist eyes or a quiet tear. Friends who arrive at the home of the bereaved with food, or offer to take the children on an outing, or make some other tangible gesture do more than those who ask to be called if anything is needed.

Parkes and Weiss (1983) described 3 patterns of abnormal or blocked grieving in exhaustive interviews with 68 widows and widowers after their spouse's death. The syndromes of "unanticipated grief" (where loss is unexpected), "conflicted grief" (where the marital relationship was markedly ambivalent), and "chronic grief" (where dependency on the deceased was excessive) each interferes with 1 or more of the 3 tasks of recovery: intellectual acceptance of the loss, emotional acceptance of the loss, and the new development of an independent identity.

Sharing memories may help complete the memories of the deceased. The bereaved may be helped by looking through old photograph albums or collections of letters as they try to put the lost person into perspective. Persevering patience over the long haul is essential. Many acquaintances disappear after the funeral and burial rituals. Those who can continue to visit make a great difference. Letters or notes are valued by mourners. Anniversaries are key foci in the grieving trajectory. Special attention to the bereaved on that day is part of the most basic care of mourners.

Return to activity is usually an essential feature of the recovery process, both because it brings the mourner back into contact with concerned fellow workers and because the therapeutic effects of work on self-esteem help repair the narcissistic injury of the loss. Most bereaved persons benefit from returning to work within 3–6 weeks after the death of a loved one. Self-help groups continue to be among the most effective modalities for permitting expression of emotion, demonstrating that bereavement and its feelings are universal, and supplying the compassion and respect necessary for rebuilding self-esteem. The prototype for these groups is the widow-to-widow program (Silverman et al., 1974).

Reading can sometimes help bereaved persons. Often the most consoling books are stories of persons sustaining tragic losses, such as those by Anne Morrow Lindbergh (1973) or C. S. Lewis (1961). Edgar Jackson's *You and Your Grief* (1966), written for the bereaved family, provides helpful directives.

Distinguishing Depression from Mourning

In acute grief, major depression can be a difficult diagnosis to make, but when it is present it requires treatment perhaps even more than when it is present without acute grief. Clues helpful in determining the presence of major depression include: (1) guilt beyond that about actions taken around the time of the death of the loved one; (2) thoughts of death other than wanting to be with the lost person or feeling one would be better off dead; thus suicidal ideation should count in favor of major depression; (3) morbid preoccupation with worthlessness; (4) marked psychomotor retardation; (5) prolonged and marked functional impairment; (6) hallucinations other than seeing, hearing, or being touched by the deceased person.

Prigerson et al. (1995) have developed 2 very useful empirical constructs, *bereavement-depression* (depressive symptoms in the wake of a loss) and *complicated grief.* The first predicts the future medical burden of the person, while the latter predicts functional impairment at 18-month follow-up. The symptoms related to the bereavement-depression factor are hypochondriasis, apathy, insomnia, anxiety, suicidal ideation, guilt, loneliness, depressed mood, psychomotor retardation, hostility, and low self-esteem. The symptoms which are the principal components of the complicated grief factor are yearning for and preoccupation with thoughts of the deceased, crying, searching for the deceased, disbelief in the death, being stunned by the death, and inability to accept the death. Any patient with a Hamilton depression scale score ≥17 was treated with nortriptyline, at doses which averaged a low but therapeutic level of 68.1 ng/ml. Those treated showed significantly greater reduction in their bereavement-depression scores. This supports the clinical recommendation that any person who meets the criteria

for major depression should be treated. There is not and never has been any evidence that antidepressants retard the grieving process.

Sudden Death

Death with time to prepare is difficult enough, but sudden death inflicts a unique trauma on the survivors. Death on arrival at the hospital, stillbirth, sudden infant death, accidental or traumatic death, sudden cardiac arrest, death during or after surgery, murder, suicide—each carries its own set of horrors for the survivors, and in them the shock of death is dramatically intensified. Guilt is likely to be a much more serious problem because of the total absence of any preparation or opportunity to "do things right." Where violence and disfigurement are present, these feelings will be even further intensified.

General rules for dealing with the bereaved apply here, with certain specific emphases.

1. The chance to view the body, even when mutilated, should be offered to the family members. If severe mutilation is present, the family should be very carefully warned; they should be told that the body is disfigured and that they may not wish to view it but may do so if they desire. In addition, a chance to do something for the body can at times be very helpful to a survivor who has had no chance to do anything. Some funeral directors offer parents of children who have died suddenly the opportunity to wash and prepare the child's body for burial or to help in this procedure; most parents accept and benefit greatly from this opportunity. The need to view the body is greater when death is sudden.

2. Patience with the prolonged numbness or shock of the family is an essential feature of their care.

3. Physical needs can be attended to and may be the only avenue of communication. Leading the family to a quiet room, providing comfortable seats, bringing coffee, and other little acts of kindness performed in a compassionate and quiet way are helpful.

4. The numb survivor may also benefit from very gentle questions that help to review the last hours of the deceased. This review starts the searching process and leads to areas where guilt is present. What happened? Were there any prodromal symptoms? Any premonitions? Who saw him last? Families who do not wish to explore these crucial questions at the time should not be pushed.

Later issues are very similar to those mentioned above. The questions of guilt are usually more agonizing. The day may be relived thousands of times. In certain cases of sudden death, specific conflicts should be kept in mind. Parents stricken by a sudden infant death should receive all the available standard information on this syndrome, in which careful explanations emphasize that the causes are unknown and the usual self-accusations about what could have been done are groundless. Survivors of a murder victim often experience retaliatory murderous fury (sometimes unconsciously). Fear of not being able to control vindictive aggression can amount to panic in some individuals, with an inability to identify the feeling. Survivors of a person who has committed suicide are often the victims of an angry gesture and frequently must cope with their own hatred of the victim.

The main handicap for professionals is lack of an opportunity to develop a relationship with the survivors prior to the death of the victim. It is a time when close friends and relatives need to be mobilized.

Anticipatory Grief

Lindemann (1944) uses the term *anticipatory grief* to refer to a special case of separation in which death is assumed and later found to be untrue—a husband missing in action in World War II, for example. Having gone through the phases of grief, the mourner in this situation can be at a disadvantage if the lost person returns, for the grief work may have been done so well that she finds herself freed of her attachment to the love object and unready to receive him back. Since that time, the term has come to signify the reaction experienced in the face of an impending loss. Sudden death provides no opportunity for anticipatory grief. Parkes (1970), however, points out that most of the widows he studied knew in advance that they would lose a husband.

C. Knight Aldrich (1974) notes several differences between anticipatory and conventional grief. First, anticipatory grief is shared by both the patient or victim and the family, whereas conventional grief is experienced by the bereaved alone. Second, anticipatory grief has a distinct end point in the physical loss of death, whereas conventional grief may be prolonged for years. Third, the pattern of the 2 types may be different, with anticipatory grief often accelerating as death nears and conventional grief beginning at a high level of intensity and gradually decelerating. Fourth, hostile feelings toward the (about-to-be) lost person differ in the 2 states. If the lost person is still alive, as in anticipatory grief, the survivor's negative feelings tend to be experienced as more dangerous. Fifth, hope can accompany anticipatory grief in a way that it cannot once death has occurred.

Finally, the question arises in cases where death can be anticipated whether anticipatory grief can make conventional grief unnecessary or whether the work of mourn-

ing can be accomplished before death occurs. It is a fact that where anticipatory grief is possible, the intensity of the feelings of loss may actually decelerate as death draws nearer. In this case, death itself is viewed as increasingly acceptable. Aldrich notes, however, that the sample of Coconut Grove bereaved appeared to accomplish their mourning more quickly than did the sample of Parkes's widows (1970). No evidence can as yet satisfactorily answer the question whether unexpected loss requires longer grieving than anticipated loss.

Weisman (1974) reminds us of the importance of viewing grief and love as mirror images of each other. Each enhances the other. Rochlin (1965) has argued in detail that the powerful dynamic impetus produced by our losses is indispensable to emotional maturation. Mourning can lead to some of man's highest achievements as well as result in many pathological states when delayed or unresolved.

Difficulties of Those Who Care for the Dying

First in psychological importance among the caregiver's responsibility to the dying person is to understand. To do this, as Saunders (1996) says, is "above all to listen." What is the experience like? A suffering person often wants to communicate how awful a fatal illness is. Words are often irrelevant. "When no answers exist," says Saunders (1996), "one can offer silent attention."

The best way to recognize and acknowledge the person's worth is to get to know those features of his history and nature that make him unique, as mentioned earlier. The empathic effort takes its toll most often in the insights the patients give us about ourselves. Their needs and vulnerabilities bring us face to face with our own. The relentless approach of death for a patient with cancer or AIDS may leave him with feelings of terror, hopelessness, and despair—which tend to be contagious, intensifying our feelings of impotence.

At this point our own helplessness and despair may endanger the patient, causing us to avoid him, retreat, neglect him, or even, feeling he would be better off dead, convey to him how burdensome he is to us. This could be devastating to the helpless person who looks to his doctor or nurse for some sense of hope. Hence the greatest psychological challenge for caregivers is learning to live with these negative feelings and resist the urge to avoid the patients—actions which convey to the patient not that it is difficult for us but that he no longer matters. Fortunately, most patients, feeling that they are acceptable to their caregivers no matter how scared, disfigured, or miserable they are, find resources within and make what they can of each day. That sort of shared experience is an opportunity to grow for both persons.

Certain traits make these empathic difficulties hazardous for some caregivers. Dependent persons who expect patients to appreciate, thank, love, and nurture them are unconsciously prone to exhaust themselves regularly as they "can't do too much," a pattern which may be sustainable for a patient with the capacity to nurture the caregiver, but has a disastrous outcome when the patient is completely depleted or intractably hostile. The harder the caregiver strives, the less rewarding the work. Exhaustion and demoralization follow. Some caregivers want to please every physician they consult to and come to similar exhaustion because many of their patients cannot improve.

Criticism of physicians tends to be widespread and can generate unfortunate hostilities. Common accusations are that physicians are more afraid of death than other persons and that this fear prompted them to enter the medical field in the first place. Sophisticated critics refer to Feifel's (1965) study of physicians' attitudes toward death which showed that physicians spent significantly less time in conscious thought about death than did 2 control groups of professionals. Later researchers also found more unconscious fear of death in medical students than in 2 control samples. Dissatisfaction with physicians' communication patterns, their avoidance of patients, and their manner in the sickroom compound the alienation.

Although everyone is fascinated with death, physicians grapple with it more frequently than others and are sought out by those who wish to prevent or postpone it. Conflict or discomfort in the presence of death is intensified by the combination of 2 factors: frequent exposure and high responsibility. The findings of Feifel (1965) and others may also be accounted for by the increased exposure of medical students to death and to the widespread belief of the population that the physician is the last barrier against it. Disappointment that a terminally ill person cannot be saved may lead to resentment, and the physician may become the object of some or all of this resentment. Finally, those who accuse physicians of inability to communicate with the dying patient seem to forget that many have this difficulty, including members of the patient's family.

Hospice Care of the Terminally Ill

Dame Cicely Saunders traces the notion of hospice therapeutics back to *The Care of the Aged, the Dying and the Dead,* written by a family physician for Harvard Medical School students (Zimmerman, 1986). Using the work in pain control at St. Luke's Hospital in London, St. Joseph's Hospice continued development of the hospice concept. St. Christopher's opened in 1967 with Dr. Saunders as medical director, dedicated to enabling a patient, in her words, "to live to the limit of his or her potential in physical strength, mental and emotional capacity, and social relationships . . . It is the alternative to the negative and socially dangerous suggestion that a patient with an incurable disease likely to cause suffering should have the legal option of actively hastened death, i.e., euthanasia" (1969, p. xii).

Lynn (1996) provides a contemporary view of the hospice. Providing home nursing, support of the family, spiritual counseling, pain treatment, medication, medical care, and some inpatient care, hospice programs cared for approximately 340,000 dying persons in 1994, of whom 80% had cancer. The average patient enrolled about 1 month before death. Current hospice programs are not well adapted to meet the needs of patients dying from cardiovascular and pulmonary diseases, stroke, dementia, or chronic organ failure—largely because the timing of death is less predictable and their final phases less suited to hospice treatment (Lynn, 1996). Medicare requires that 80% of hospice care days be spent at home, which means that dying patients, to qualify, must have a home and a family capable of providing care. The more intensive the supportive services required for this, the less affordable it will be. Lynn advocates "a care delivery system . . . designed around the important priorities: relief of pain and other symptoms, maintenance of function and control, support of family and personal relationships, avoidance of impoverishment, trustworthiness and continuity, attentiveness to meaningful activities, and spiritual issues" (p. 202). Such a system would decrease priorities on medical treatment and increase them on "caring."

Ethical Decisions at the End of Life

Seven years after the automobile accident that left Nancy Cruzan in a persistent vegetative state, her feeding tube was removed. She died 12 days later. Her parents' request that the tube be removed initiated a journey that took them through the Missouri and federal courts, to the United States Supreme Court, and, ultimately, back to the original Missouri trial court, which once again authorized removal of the tube. Within an hour of the trial court's decision the hospital administrator, Donald C. Lamkins, tried unsuccessfully to move her elsewhere. When she died a few weeks later, 3 dozen armed guards patrolled the hospital premises to guarantee control at the scene, where unsuccessful legal attempts of several anti-euthanasia groups had failed to force reinsertion of the tube. Shortly before the sixth anniversary of Nancy Cruzan's death, another tragic note was sounded by the suicide of her father, Joseph.

The Supreme Court's decision in *Cruzan* reaffirmed most of the major lower court decisions that have helped patients, families, physicians, and hospitals resolve decisions about treatment for incurable illness (Annas et al., 1990), specifically: first, that competent patients have the right to refuse treatment; second, that forgoing nutrition and hydration is no different from forgoing other medical treatment such as artificial ventilation or pressor agents; third, that Missouri (and other states) could require "clear and convincing evidence" that the patient, while still competent, had rejected the idea of life-sustaining treatment under such circumstances, though states are also free to adopt less rigorous standards.

The *Cruzan* decision does not alter any of the standards, laws, or clinical practices that have evolved since the *Quinlan* case in 1976 (Annas, 1990). During this time, guidelines and principles have been established that enable patients, families, and physicians to reach medically sound, ethical treatment decisions in cases of irreversible illness. As a result, and despite widespread physician sentiment to the contrary, these treatment decisions are almost devoid of litigation danger. Nevertheless, physicians should work with their hospital attorneys to clarify the status of legislation and case law on these issues in their particular jurisdiction.

A Mini-course in Medical Ethics

A brief discussion of principles is not intended to supplant the need for concrete individualized judgments for every patient; clinical judgments are always practical. Principles provide anchor points from which clinical reasoning can proceed, specifically when limiting or stopping life-supporting treatment is proposed.

First principle. Traditional medical ethics express the primary obligation of the physician to the patient in both positive and negative terms. The negative goal, always referred to as "first," is not to harm the patient *(primum non nocere)*. The positive obligation is to restore health or relieve suffering, or both. Our contemporary dilemma, as Slater (1973) points out, arose because we now face many situations where these 2 aims come into conflict, i.e., the more aggressive the efforts to reverse an incurable illness, the more suffering is inflicted on the patient. If a 70-year-old man with large-cell cancer of the lung presents himself for treatment and is found to have metastatic spread of the disease to the other lung and to his liver, any treatment of the cancer is guaranteed to make him feel even worse while probably not even extending his survival. This first principle summed up the medical ethics of the 1950s and 1960s: Do what is best for the patient.

Second principle. The principle of autonomy has sometimes been stated: Let the will of the patient, not the health of the patient, be the supreme law. This principle guarantees any competent patient the right to refuse any treatment, even a lifesaving one. This has been the emphasis of medical ethics since the 1970s, and has focused on the patient's refusing life-prolonging treatment such as mechanical ventilation and, more recently, nutrition and hydration. Honoring such refusals presupposes that the patient is competent.

Forgoing vs. stopping. Patients and families need to know that treatments such as mechanical ventilation may actually clarify just how good the chances of recovery are, can be tried until the outcome is clear, and then stopped when it is apparent that health (or the extent of recovery acceptable to the patient) cannot be restored. Sometimes it is psychologically more difficult to stop such a treatment once it is started. But it is important to keep in mind that what justified its use in the first place was its relationship to recovery. The ventilator was used because the physician thought the patient might get better. Once it is clear that the patient will not recover, it is no longer necessary.

When the patient is not competent, there are several ways to resolve treatment decisions. The most help is provided when the patient has left a living will or advance directives, or appointed a durable power of attorney or a health care proxy, to help make decisions should he or she become incompetent.

Even when such clarity is not present, common sense should be followed, and the incompetent patient's next of kin should be asked to provide a substituted judgment about what the patient would have wanted.

When Should Treatment Be Limited?

Whenever the risks or burdens of a treatment appear to outweigh the benefits, use of that treatment should be questioned by both physician and patient. For example, the amputation of a poorly vascularized foot will ordinarily be postponed by patient and physician until life with the foot seems more burdensome than life without it.

Ordinarily, limitation of life-prolonging treatment is

reserved for 3 categories of patients. First, patients whose illness is judged irreversible and who are moribund need to be protected from needlessly burdensome treatments. This course is widely accepted for patients who will die with or without treatment, such as the patient with advanced metastatic cancer or the patient with end-stage cardiomyopathy where a transplant is not possible. Because of the right to refuse treatment, competent patients who are not moribund but have an irreversible illness have also been allowed to have life-sustaining treatments stopped. (Competent patients with a reversible illness have the right to refuse any treatment, including lifesaving treatments.)

Irreversible coma. When this diagnosis is established, the standard medical recommendation to the next of kin or surrogate would be to stop all life-sustaining treatment, including nutrition and hydration. Even where there is no family or next of kin for the patient with irreversible coma, standard medical practice would allow the patient to die, acknowledging the inevitability of death and the futility of any treatment to prevent it.

Persistent vegetative state. Typically the patient begins in coma, as after a cardiac arrest or severe head trauma, then enters a state of permanent unconsciousness with restoration of periods of wakefulness and physiologic sleep (Plum and Posner, 1980). The eyes may open spontaneously but do not track. The patient has a functioning brain stem with total loss of cortical function (American Academy of Neurology, 1989; Munsat, Stuart, and Cranford, 1989). The standard of medical practice remains less fully formed in this situation. The American Academy of Neurology (1989) has taken a position, adopted here, based on the pathophysiology of the condition, and recommends that all life-sustaining treatment, "because it is of no medical benefit to the patient," be withdrawn. The recommendation to withdraw treatments includes nutrition and hydration. The American Medical Association's Council on Scientific Affairs and Council on Ethical and Judicial Affairs provided a statement with diagnostic criteria and data supporting them which maintains the balance between patient preferences and the accuracy of the diagnosis, concluding that even if death is not imminent, "it is not unethical to discontinue all means of life-prolonging medical treatment" (American Medical Association Council on Scientific Affairs, 1990).

Judging when to limit treatment may seem impossible at times. An aortic valve replacement for an 80-year-old suddenly decompensated man in otherwise good health is usually imperative. If he has impaired renal and pulmonary function, both he and his physician will begin to wonder whether a decision to operate will only condemn him to a nightmare of suffering which will end in death. If he has widely disseminated large-cell cancer of the lung, valve replacement would be unethical and inhumane; the sudden cardiac decompensation would provide a merciful death. Abstract principles cannot solve clinical dilemmas. Rather, principles serve as points about which relevant clinical judgments and patient preferences become more sharply focused. Will benefit exceed suffering? Or does one condition (cancer, adult respiratory distress syndrome, AIDS) so overshadow another (gangrene, aortic insufficiency, pneumonia) that the benefits of a treatment (amputation, valve replacement, antibiotics) are negated?

Decisions to Maintain, Limit, or Stop Life-Prolonging Treatment

The guidelines for the framework below were developed through 24 years of experience by the Optimum Care Committee of the Massachusetts General Hospital (MGH) (Optimum care, 1976). From the President's Commission statement of 1983 (Deciding to forgo, 1983) through the Task Force on Ethics of the Society of Critical Care Medicine (Consensus report, 1990), a massive consensus has developed on the ethics of forgoing life-sustaining treatments in the severely ill.

Hospital admission. On admission to the hospital, both patient and family can be assured that any device or technology available to restore health will be used to its fullest potential. Yet, given the awareness that hospitals and intensive care units are often criticized for pursuing treatments that cause more harm than good, patients can be reassured that the hospital's and the physicians' policy is to protect patients from treatments that will not make them better but only make them suffer more.

Clinical judgment on irreversibility. At what point is the physician clinically sure that the patient is now going to die whether treatment continues or not? When is treatment only going to prolong dying? These are the questions that cause great concern to patients and families. These prognostic judgments are fallible clinical conclusions, but all turn to the physician to make them. At what point in recovery from coma is it clear that the chance of regaining significant cognitive function is virtually nonexistent? For the AIDS patient battling *Pneumocystis carinii* pneumonia (PCP), when does it bec resort to mechanical ventilation, once started, will become permanently essential for continued breathing? (This patient can be reassured that if he accepts the recommendation of a ventilator, he can indicate that it should be withdrawn once there is clinical certainty that he cannot live without it.)

The physician on whom this judgment falls bears a heavy responsibility. Reassurance is sometimes necessary, with the reminder that the questioner realizes that nothing can be foretold with 100% accuracy in clinical medicine. Unfortunately, where families are angry or litigation is feared, physicians with this responsibility may feel too vulnerable or intimidated to say what they think. The best clinical judgments of patient prognosis should be documented in the medical record. As they change, so should the documentation.

Consultation. Specialty consultation may be required to clarify further prognostic judgments. Sometimes patients or families ask for a second opinion. These consultants also need encouragement to be explicitly honest and state in the record that in their experience chances of recovery from an illness this severe are unprecedented, or virtually nil, or essentially nonexistent (e.g., "In my experience, neurologic damage of this extent is not compatible with recovery of cortical function").

Autonomy and the patient's preferences. Balancing the physician's judgment are the patient's view of acceptable risks, definition of quality of life, and attitudes toward pain. In the course of battling metastatic cancer with adjuvant chemotherapy, how many treatments will the patient accept, especially if the oncologist has begun to express reservations about the degree of response? One person might grasp at any chance of halting tumor spread no matter how debilitating the treatment. Another might, on hearing the oncologist's reservations, express relief at the chance to back off because of the unacceptability of the side effects of treatment. In this way patients and physicians together work out the risk-benefit calculus which will result in the final clinical decision about maintaining or forgoing treatment. Because patients' attitudes can change, ongoing dialogue is indispensable for clarifying understanding on both sides.

Autonomy applies to accepting or refusing appropriate medical treatment. Just as a patient cannot demand that a surgeon amputate an undiseased leg, he does not have the right to demand a treatment which his physician regards as inappropriate. Such a conflict can be painful. When an oncologist, discovering progressive cancer spread and severe treatment side effects, can no longer in conscience prescribe the treatment, and this decision is conveyed to the patient, many express acute dismay and protest, some insisting on continuing despite physician avowals that the chemotherapy can do nothing but harm at this time. Some physicians have resolved this conflict by lowering the dose to a nontoxic level, but find this choice unsatisfying because they feel it is dishonest. Usually the patient in this case feels that stopping anticancer treatment is stopping the fight against cancer, that it is "giving up," that without chemotherapy or radiation there "will be no hope." It is often beneficial to give this patient time (overnight) to consider the physician's advice, then to encourage him to describe exactly what it is that has kept him going satisfactorily to this point. Whatever it is, it has helped him even when chemotherapy seems to have been impotent against the tumor, causing only unwanted effects. In talking to those who say there will be no hope, my favorite question has been, "Hope for what?" Often such patients have then reviewed what has been told them from the beginning, e.g., that the malignancy cannot be cured, but that with aggressive palliation, the goal to maintain is the best possible existence for them.

Competent patients can make irrational choices (Brock and Wartman, 1990). On hearing that a patient refuses a simple and routine lifesaving procedure, physicians are obliged to explore further. The patient may be a Jehovah's Witness, legitimately refusing a blood transfusion. But it is also possible that the patient has completely misunderstood the situation, or has irrational fears of the treatment. More common is the occasional patient who will insist on cardiopulmonary resuscitation (CPR), i.e., will not agree to a do-not-resuscitate (DNR) order. Most of these patients do not understand the implications of the DNR order, thinking that after a cardiac arrest a simple procedure will restore them completely. Others may be overwhelmed and unable to process the conversation. Time, discussion with the patient and family together, psychiatric consultation, and recourse to an ethics committee can help resolve these dilemmas.

Incompetent patients. Conflict in discussions about forgoing treatment arises most often when the patient is incompetent. When patients have given no advance directives about life-sustaining treatment, surrogates may feel insecure, making decisions about life-prolonging treatments difficult. Conflicts tend to arise in such uncertainty, and can exist within the treatment team (e.g., nurses regard the treatments as inhumane, while doctors wish to pursue them), between the team and the primary physician, between specialties (e.g., anesthesia and surgery), between family members, and between family and the team. When decisions about life-prolonging treatment reach an impasse of intense conflict, most commonly the family is angry and distrustful of the caregiver team. If discussion cannot resolve the tension, the family can be asked to select a person they trust (e.g., family physician, clergyperson, or attorney) to confer with the team. This person may help clarify and resolve misunderstandings. The team may consult other specialists about alternate treatment options for the patient, or can consult an ethics committee (here the OCC).

Process for resolving conflicts over life-prolonging treatments. It is important that the treatment team agree on what its recommendation is and understand the source of the conflict. First, a meeting should be held with the entire family (especially if the conflict is primarily with the designated spokesperson while other family members have differing opinions), the team, essential consultants, ethics committee representatives (if invited), and the family's trusted person (if existent). Some partial agreement may occur, and another meeting may be scheduled, so long as there appears to be progress. Next, if there is no resolution, the family can be informed that the care of the patient can be transferred to another physician in the same hospital or to another hospital. If the family does not wish such a transfer or the patient cannot be transferred (e.g., if the other institution refuses to accept the patient, or if the patient is too sick), then the family can be informed that they can have recourse to the Probate Court for a determination. If the team remains clear about their treatment recommendation, there is no reason for them to consult the Probate Court at this point; if uncertain, they should have done so earlier.

Futile treatment. Conflicts that require the measures described above often center on treatments that either the family or the treatment team regard as futile, but agreement cannot be reached. In many cases when a patient is irreversibly ill and dying, resuscitation is simply not an option and is futile (Consensus report, 1990; Taffet and Teasdale, 1988; Murphy, 1988; Tomlinson and Brody, 1990). For example, for a patient whose glioblastoma has advanced to the point where he is semicomatose and will die with or without treatment, CPR is not a medical option, and application of it is contrary to the standards of medical practice, unethical, and inhumane. The family who asks that CPR and all lifesaving treatments be withheld or withdrawn from such a patient should be obeyed by the physician inclined to provide such treatment. Likewise, in such a case the physician does not have a duty to consult anyone before writing a DNR order. I recommend

that the physician take the opportunity to remind the family just how severe the illness is and that appropriate attention is being given to the needs of the patient. He can say, for example, "It is important for you to know that your father's condition has reached the point where he will die with treatment or without it. We will direct every effort to maintaining his comfort and dignity. Treatments like resuscitation or countershock would only brutalize him, and he has been protected from them by specific written order."

Defining futility is currently a major goal of medical ethics (Pellegrino, 1993). The negative right of refusal has become transformed by some into a positive right to demand of physicians any life-sustaining treatment. Others argue that doctors have a duty not to offer or provide treatments that are ineffective (Jecker and Schneiderman, 1993). Since most risk-benefit considerations of life-prolonging treatment involve value judgments, and the principle of autonomy requires that the patient's values come first, some argue that "objective" standards of futility are impossible to formulate and physicians should make no such judgments (Truog, Brett, and Frader, 1992). However, for patients in irreversible coma, and increasingly for those in a persistent vegetative state, life-prolonging treatments are generally seen to be futile. No physician is required to provide *harmful* treatments to a patient; the principle of beneficence obligates the physician not to do so. We would add that no physician is required to provide *useless* treatments either. CPR for the above-mentioned moribund glioblastoma patient is useless (and indeed harmful because it violates his dignity). If a moribund patient with breast cancer had metastasis-riddled ribs and disseminated intravascular coagulopathy, CPR would be harmful because it would probably kill her by causing fatal hemorrhage. Even if the patient were competent, a physician should not offer CPR if harm without resuscitation is the outcome judged clinically likely.

Informed consent is not necessary for either a useless or a harmful treatment. One could even argue that asking for consent (or enlightened refusal) could itself be harmful. The patient is likely to be confused as to why he has been presented with a treatment which the physician considers useless or harmful. So, too, one could argue that no substituted judgment is required when the treatment is either useless or harmful. One judge of the Massachusetts Superior District Court ruled that for a terminally ill patient who was going to die *with or without treatment within a short time*, life-prolonging treatments were futile.

Controversial questions about defining treatments as

futile will most likely be resolved as the Houston citywide consortium of hospitals has done, by setting up a panel of experts to judge the futility of a treatment after hearing all evidence presented by family, medical team, and others (Halevy and Brody, 1996).

Documentation. The medical record should be explicit and complete about the judgment of irreversibility and the prognosis, documenting that the patient, family, or both have been informed, as well as their reactions and wishes, the limitation of treatment and the reasons for it, and any discussion or dissent and how it was resolved. Orders given in the order book should also be explicit about which treatments should be stopped or not started. The latter is particularly necessary to guide house staff, nurses, and others who may be called upon in the absence of the primary physician to attend the patient in the event of acute worsening or cardiopulmonary arrest.

Agreement. Once agreement occurs, decisions can be made. If life-sustaining treatment is to be forgone, it is important to chart for the family the consequences of this omission. If no ventilator will be used should the PCP worsen in the AIDS patient, then a morphine intravenous infusion will be started as soon as there is sign of respiratory distress, and it will be increased enough to suppress breathlessness or any sense of suffocation. Of course, that may produce loss of consciousness, but if that is necessary, it is routinely done without hesitation. No further transfusions will be given to halt hemorrhage from a metastatic colon cancer lesion. But hemorrhage is one of the gentlest ways to die, and comfort can usually be assured without difficulty. Hydration can be cruel if maintained in the vegetative patient for whom feeding and all curative treatments have been stopped; hydration alone can prolong dying by 2 or 3 weeks. Hospice care avoids intravenous feeding in helping patients die at home; moisture for the mucous membranes is all that is needed for comfort. The point is to detoxify the concept of death, so often traumatic or violent in the minds of patients or families.

New therapeutic goals. Whenever a decision is made to limit treatment, the new goal must be clearly articulated, i.e., to relieve suffering and make the patient's life as dignified and becoming as possible. Foremost in this are the intensive nursing efforts which provide comprehensive, compassionate attention to breathing, secretions, pressure sores, turning, bathing, odors, and numerous other challenging problems for which they have such impressive remedies. All medical orders must be reexamined in light of the goal of providing comfort. Dressing

changes which are unnecessarily painful, venipuncture for laboratory tests, diagnostic procedures, antibiotics, and indwelling lines may be removed if not contributing. Pressor infusions may be stopped or maintained but not increased. Monitors may be removed unless their help in forecasting an arrhythmic death is required.

Death is now inevitable. The family's needs must also be examined and addressed. Even though time of death cannot be predicted very accurately, they must be asked if they wish to be present at that moment. Do they wish clergy to be notified? If they do not wish to be present, they may want to know that they will be informed quickly when the patient worsens or dies.

The Request for Assisted Suicide or Euthanasia

Sprung (1990), reviewing trends in critical care and reactions to them, concluded that active euthanasia programs would arise in the United States in the near future. Their popularity can be viewed as the public's condemnation of the way hospitals and physicians excessively treat the sick in their last days, making death a painful mockery, and/or of medicine's inadequate and ineffective treatment of suffering. It also represents a demand for more control over decisions about the end of life.

When a patient requests a prescription for enough medication to commit suicide or asks that his death be hastened, the physician must first seek to learn why. What is it that now makes death seem a better option than life? What was the last straw? What is it that must be avoided or escaped? Is the patient depressed? At what specific point does he believe that his potential for being someone who matters has been exhausted? These questions are critical when a nonterminal patient asks for pills to commit suicide. A terminal patient should not be excluded from the same sympathetic, gentle, but extensive search of his despair, his self-esteem, and his feelings of being valued by others. Are there financial considerations? Does he fear that he will become either a financial burden or a burden to care for, or both? Has any of this been discussed with his family? Where does his family stand in this regard? How would they understand his requests and be affected by them? How would they be affected by his suicide? If he considers his life devoid of value and meaning for himself, does it have meaning for certain others? Does this affect him? Has he made any effort to achieve consensus so that his death could be a meaningful, shared family experience?

Physicians, the public, and the Supreme Court are now debating the legalization of physician-assisted suicide in the United States. The numbers for and against appear roughly equal. All but 2 of 12 experts in a consensus report "believe that it is not immoral for a physician to assist in the rational suicide of a terminally ill person" (Wanzer et al., 1989). Mercy killing (euthanasia), however, is a crime in all 50 states and the District of Columbia. Even in the Netherlands, where physicians are allowed to practice euthanasia and do so commonly, it remains a criminal offense (De Wachter, 1989) . The reasons for my own opposition to the legalization are religious tenets and the conviction that the covenant between patient and physician will be seriously damaged if doctors are legally able to cause death. No matter one's side in the debate, every physician must be willing to identify and try to palliate the psychosocial and spiritual suffering that makes a sick person feel so bad that death seems the best option.

Fear of Legal Reprisal

When the physician makes a reasonable clinical judgment of irreversible illness and clarifies the wishes of the patient, or, if the patient is incompetent, the patient's proxy or surrogates who reasonably represent the patient's wishes concur that life-sustaining treatment is to be forgone or stopped, fear of litigation is neither reasonable nor a legitimate excuse not to proceed. The courts have made it quite clear over the last 15 years or so that these decisions are valid and should not be brought to court. It is irrational to demand guarantees that no litigation will follow. It is to be hoped, however, that physicians' energies will be invested in doing the best they can for the patient, in accord with the patient's wishes. Should litigation follow an action taken in accord with the above guidelines, they will be well prepared to defend their decisions in court.

References

Adler, G. 1973. Hospital treatment of borderline patients. *Am. J. Psychiatry* 130:32–35.

Aitken-Swan, J., and E. C. Easson. 1959. Reactions of cancer patients on being told their diagnosis. *Br. Med. J.* 1:779–783.

Aldrich, C. K. 1974. Some dynamics of anticipatory grief. In *Anticipatory grief,* ed. B. Schoenberg, A. C. Carr, A. H. Kutscher, D. Peretz, and I. Goldberg. New York: Columbia University Press.

Allport, G. 1958. *The nature of prejudice.* New York: Doubleday.

American Academy of Neurology. 1989. Position of the American Academy of Neurology on certain aspects of the care and management of the persistent vegetative state patient. Adopted by the Executive Board, American Academy of Neurology, April 21, 1988. *Neurology* 39:125–126.

American Board of Internal Medicine. 1996. *Caring for the dying: Identification and promotion of physician competency—personal narratives.* Philadelphia.

American Medical Association, Council on Scientific Affairs and Council on Ethical and Judicial Affairs. 1990. Persistent vegetative state and the decision to withdraw or withhold life support. *JAMA* 263:426–430.

Annas, G. J. 1990. Nancy Cruzan and the right to die. *N. Engl. J. Med.* 323:670–673.

Annas, G. J., B. Arnold, M. Aroskar, et al. 1990. Bioethicists' statement on the U.S. Supreme Court's *Cruzan* decision. *N. Engl. J. Med.* 323:686–688.

Anthony, S. 1940. *The child's discovery of death.* New York: Harcourt, Brace.

Barraclough, B. M., and M. Shea. 1970. Suicide and Samaritan clients. *Lancet* 2:868–870.

Beck, A. T. 1963. Thinking and depression. I. Idiosyncratic content and cognitive distortions. *Arch. Gen. Psychiatry* 9:324–335.

——— 1967. *Depression: clinical, experimental, and theoretical aspects.* New York: Harper & Row, Hoeber Med. Div.

Beck, A. T., M. Kovacs, and A. Weisman. 1975. Hopelessness and suicidal behavior. *JAMA* 234:1146–49.

Beck, A. T., D. Schuyler, and I. Herman. 1974. Development of suicidal intent scales. In *The prediction of suicide,* ed. A. T. Beck, H. L. P. Resnik, and D. J. Lettieri. Bowie, Md.: Charles Press.

Becker, E. 1973. *The denial of death.* New York: Free Press.

Billings, J. A. 1985. *Outpatient management of advanced cancer.* Philadelphia: Lippincott.

Bowlby, J. 1961. Processes of mourning. *Int. J. Psychoanal.* 42:317–340.

Breitbart, W. 1993. Suicide risk and pain in cancer and AIDS patients. In *Current and emerging issues in cancer pain: Research and practice,* ed. C. R. Chapman, K. M. Foley, et al. Bristol-Myers Squibb Symposium on Pain Research series. New York: Raven Press. 49–65.

Brock, D. W., and S. A. Wartman. 1990. When competent patients make irrational choices. *N. Engl. J. Med.* 322:1595–99.

Brunier, G., M. G. Carson, and D. E. Harrison. 1995. What do nurses know and believe about patients with pain? Results of a hospital survey. *J. Pain Symptom Manage.* 10:436–445.

Buie, D. H., and J. T. Maltsberger. 1983. *The practical formulation of suicide risk.* Cambridge, Mass.: Firefly Press.

Cassell, E. J. 1991. *The nature of suffering and the goals of medicine.* New York: Oxford University Press.

Cassem, E. H. 1990. Depression and anxiety secondary to

medical illness. *Psychiatric Clinics of North America* 13:597–612.

Cassem, N. H. 1976. The first three steps beyond the grave. In *Acute grief and the funeral,* ed. V. R. Pine, A. H. Kutscher, D. Peretz, R. C. Slater, R. DeBellis, R. J. Volk, and D. J. Cherico. Springfield, Ill.: Thomas.

Cassem, N. H., and T. P. Hackett. 1975. Stress on the nurse and therapist in the intensive care unit and the coronary care unit. *Heart Lung* 4:252–259.

Cassem, N. H., and R. S. Stewart. 1975. Management and care of the dying patient. *Int. J. Psychiatry Med.* 6:293–304.

Chochinov, H. M., K. G. Wilson, M. Enns, N. Mowchun, et al. 1995. Desire for death in the terminally ill. *Am. J. Psychiatry* 152:1185–1191.

Clayton, P. J., L. Desmarais, and G. Winokur. 1968. A study of normal bereavement. *Am. J. Psychiatry* 125:168–178.

Cleeland, C. S., R. Gonin, A. K. Hatfield, J. H. Edmonson, R. H. Blum, J. A. Stewart, and K. J. Pandya. 1994. Pain and its treatment in outpatients with metastatic. *N. Engl. J. Med.* 330:592–596.

Croog, S. H., D. S. Shapiro, and S. Levine. 1971. Denial among male heart patients. *Psychosom. Med.* 33:385–397.

Delong, W., and E. Robins. 1961. The communication of suicidal intent prior to psychiatric hospitalization: a study of 87 patients. *Am. J. Psychiatry* 117:695–705.

Desbiens, N. A., A. W. Wu, S. K. Broste, N. S. Wenger, A. F. Connors, Jr., J. Lynn, Y. Yasui, R. S. Phillips, and W. Fulkerson. 1996. Pain and satisfaction with pain control in seriously ill hospitalized adults: findings from the SUPPORT research investigations. For the SUPPORT investigators. Study to Understand Prognoses and Preferences for Outcomes and Risks of Treatment. *Crit. Care Med.* 24:1953–1961.

Deutsch, F. 1933. Euthanasia, a clinical study. *Psychoanal. Q.* 5:347–368.

De Wachter, M. A. M. 1989. Active euthanasia in the Netherlands. *JAMA* 262:3316–19.

Doyle, D., G. W. C. Hanks, and N. MacDonald, eds. 1993. *Oxford textbook of palliative medicine.* New York: Oxford University Press.

Easson, W. M. 1970. *The dying child.* Springfield, Ill.: Thomas.

Eissler, K. 1955. *The psychiatrist and the dying patient.* New York: International Universities Press.

Engel, G. L. 1961. Is grief a disease? *Psychosom. Med.* 23:18–22.

Evans, A. E. 1968. If a child must die. *N. Engl. J. Med.* 278:138–142.

Farberow, N. L., and E. S. Schneidman, eds. 1965. *The cry for help.* New York: McGraw-Hill.

Farberow, N. L., E. S. Schneidman, and C. V. Leonard.

1963. Suicide among general medical and surgical hospital patients with malignant neoplasms. *Med. Bull. Veterans Admin.* MB-9:1–11.

Fawcett, J. 1972. Suicidal depression and physical illness. *JAMA* 219:1303–06.

Fawzy, F. I., N. W. Fawzy, C. S. Hyun, R. Elashoff, D. Guthrie, J. L. Fahey, and D. L. Morton. 1993. Malignant melanoma. Effects of an early structured psychiatric intervention, coping, and affective state on recurrence and survival 6 years later. *Arch. Gen. Psychiatry* 50:681–689.

Feagin, J. R. 1964. Prejudice and religious types: a focused study of southern fundamentalists. *J. Sci. Study Religion* 4:3–13.

Feifel, H. 1965. The function of attitudes toward death. In *Death and dying: attitudes of patient and doctor. Group Adv. Psychiatry* symp. 11, 5:633–641.

———— 1974. Religious conviction and fear of death among the healthy and the terminally ill. *J. Sci. Study Religion* 31:353–360.

Feifel, H., ed. 1959. *The meaning of death.* New York: McGraw-Hill.

Fenichel, O. 1945. *The psychoanalytic theory of neuroses.* New York: Norton.

Freud, S. 1915. Thoughts for the times on war and death. In *Standard edition,* ed. J. Strachey. Vol. 14. London: Hogarth Press, 1957.

———— 1917. Mourning and melancholia. In *Standard edition,* ed. J. Strachey. Vol. 14. London: Hogarth Press, 1949.

———— 1920. Beyond the pleasure principle. In *Standard edition,* ed. J. Strachey. Vol. 18. London: Hogarth Press, 1955.

———— 1923. The ego and the id. In *Standard edition,* ed. J. Strachey. Vol. 19. London: Hogarth Press, 1961.

Ganzini, L., M. A. Lee, R. T. Heintz, J. D. Bloom, et al. 1994. The effect of depression treatment on elderly patients' preferences for life-sustaining medical therapy. *Am. J. Psychiatry* 151:1631–1636.

Gerlé, B., G. Lunden, and P. Sandblom. 1960. The patient with inoperable cancer from the psychiatric and social standpoints. *Cancer* 13:1206–17.

Gifford, S. 1969. Some psychoanalytic theories about death: a selective historical review. *Ann. N.Y. Acad. Sci.* 164:638–668.

Gilbertsen, V. A., and O. H. Wangensteen. 1962. Should the doctor tell the patient that the disease is cancer? In *The physician and the total care of the cancer patient.* New York: American Cancer Society.

Glaser, B. G., and A. L. Strauss. 1965. *Awareness of dying.* Chicago: Aldine.

Greenberg, D. B., H. S. Abrams, and E. H. Cassem. 1986. Psychologic and family complications of cancer. In *Can-*

cer manual. 7th ed. Boston: American Cancer Society, Mass. Div.

Grollman, E. A. 1970. *Talking about death.* Boston: Beacon Press.

Grollman, E. A., ed. 1967. *Explaining death to children.* Boston: Beacon Press.

Hackett, T. P., and A. D. Weisman. 1962. The treatment of the dying. *Curr. Psychiatr. Ther.* 2:121–126.

Halevy, A., and B. A. Brody. 1996. A multi-institution collaborative policy on medical futility. *JAMA* 276:571–574.

Harris, A. 1965. *Why did he die?* Minneapolis: Lerner.

Hill, C. S., Jr. 1993. The barriers to adequate pain management with opioid analgesics. *Sem. Oncol.* 20:1–5.

Hinton, J. 1967. *Dying.* Baltimore: Penguin Books.

Holmes, T. H., and R. H. Rahe. 1967. The social readjustment rating scale. *J. Psychosom. Res.* 11:213–218.

Hoyt, J. W. 1996. Critical care in 1996: Doing too much? Doing too little? Keeping the patient in focus during a time of smoke and fire. The presidential address from the 25th Educational and Scientific Symposium of the Society of Critical Care Medicine. *Crit. Care Med.* 24:890–892.

Jackson, E. N. 1965. *Telling a child about death.* New York: Channel Press.

——— 1966. *You and your grief.* New York: Channel Press.

Jacox, A., D. B. Carr, R. Payne, et al. 1994. Management of Cancer Pain: Clinical Practice Guideline No. 9. Rockville, Md.: U. S. Public Health Service, Agency for Health Care Policy and Research. AHCPR publication 94–0592.

Jadad, A. R., and G. P. Browman. 1995. The WHO analgesic ladder for cancer pain management. Stepping up the quality of its evaluation. *JAMA* 274:1870–1873.

Jecker, N. S., and L. J. Schneiderman. 1993. The duty not to treat. *Camb. Q. Health Care Ethics* 2:151–159.

Jones, E. 1957. *The life and work of Sigmund Freud.* Vol. 3. New York: Basic Books.

Kast, E. C. 1966. LSD and the dying patient. *Chicago Med. Sch. Q.* 26:80–87.

Kelly, W. D., and S. R. Friesen. 1950. Do cancer patients want to be told? *Surgery* 27:822–826.

Kennell, J. H., H. Slyter, and M. H. Klaus. 1970. The mourning response of parents to the death of a newborn infant. *N. Engl. J. Med.* 283:344–349.

Kimball, L. R., and W. C. McCormick. 1996. The pharmacologic management of pain and discomfort in persons with AIDS near the end of life: use of opioid analgesia in the hospice setting. *J. Pain Symptom Manage.* 11:88–94.

Koenig, H. G., H. J. Cohen, D. G. Blazer, et al. 1995. Religious coping and cognitive symptoms of depression in elderly medical patients. *Psychosomatics* 36:369–375.

Kübler-Ross, E. 1969. *On death and dying.* New York: Macmillan.

——— 1974. *Questions and answers on death and dying.* New York: Macmillan.

Kurland, A. A., S. Grof, W. N. Pahnke, and L. E. Goodman. 1973. Psychedelic drug-assisted psychotherapy in patients with terminal cancer. In *Psychopharmacologic agents for the terminally ill and bereaved,* ed. I. K. Goldberg, S. Malitz, and A. H. Kutscher. New York: Columbia University Press.

Kutscher, A. H., B. Schoenberg, and A. C. Carr. 1973. *The terminal patient: oral care.* New York: Columbia University Press.

Lack, S. A., and R. W. Buckingham. 1978. *First American hospice: three years of home care.* New Haven: Hospice, Inc.

LeShan, L., and E. LeShan. 1961. Psychotherapy and the patient with a limited life span. *Psychiatry* 24:318–323.

Lester, D. 1972a. The myth of suicide prevention. *Compr. Psychiatry* 13:555–560.

——— 1972b. Religious behaviors and attitudes toward death. In *Death and presence,* ed. A. Godin. Brussels: Lumen Vitae Press.

Lewis, C. S. 1961. *A grief observed.* Greenwich, Conn.: Seabury Press.

Lindbergh, A. M. 1973. *Hour of gold, hour of lead.* New York: Harcourt, Brace.

Lindemann, E. 1944. Symptomatology and management of acute grief. *Am. J. Psychiatry* 101:141–148.

Litman, R. E. 1966. The prevention of suicide. In *Current psychiatric therapies,* ed. J. H. Masserman. Vol. 6. New York: Grune & Stratton.

Litman, R. E., N. L. Farberow, C. I. Wold, and T. R. Brown. 1974. Prediction models of suicidal behaviors. In *The prediction of suicide,* ed. A. T. Beck, H. L. P. Resnik, and D. J. Lettieri. Bowie, Md.: Charles Press.

Lynn, J., J. M. Teno, R. S. Phillips, et al. 1997. Perceptions by family members of the dying experience of older and seriously ill patients. *Ann. Intern. Med.* 126:97–106.

Magni, K. G. 1972. The fear of death. In *Death and presence,* ed. A. Godin. Brussels: Lumen Vitae Press.

Maltzberger, J. T., and D. H. Buie. 1974. Countertransference hate in treatment of suicidal patients. *Arch. Gen. Psychiatry* 30:625–633.

Marks, R. M., and E. J. Sachar. 1973. Undertreatment of medical inpatients with narcotic analgesics. *Ann. Intern. Med.* 78:173–181.

Menninger, K. A. 1938. *Man against himself.* New York: Harcourt, Brace.

Meyer, J. E. 1975. *Death and neurosis.* New York: International Universities Press.

Michaelson, M. G. 1974. Death as a friendly onion. *New York Times Book Review,* July 21. 6–8.

Munsat, T. L., W. H. Stuart, and R. E. Cranford. 1989.

Guidelines on the vegetative state: commentary on the American Academy of Neurology statement. *Neurology* 39:123–124.

Murphy, D. J. 1988. Do-not-resuscitate orders. *JAMA* 260:2098–2101.

Murphy, G. E. 1975a. The physician's responsibility for suicide. I. An error of commission. *Ann. Intern. Med.* 82:301–304.

———. 1975b. The physician's responsibility for suicide. II. Errors of omission. *Ann. Intern. Med.* 82:305–309.

Nagy, M. H. 1948. The child's view of death. *J. Genet. Psychol.* 73:3–27.

Natterson, J. M., and A. G. Knudson. 1960. Observations concerning fear of death in fatally ill children and their mothers. *Psychosom. Med.* 22:456–465.

Novack, D. H., R. Plumer, R. L. Smith, et al. 1979. Changes in physicians' attitudes toward telling the cancer patient. *JAMA* 241:897–900.

Oken, D. 1961. What to tell cancer patients: a study of medical attitudes. *JAMA* 175:1120–28.

Optimum care for hopelessly ill patients: a report of the Critical Care Committee of the Massachusetts General Hospital. 1976. *N. Engl. J. Med.* 301:404–408.

Parkes, C. M. 1970. The first year of bereavement: a longitudinal study of the reaction of London widows to the death of their husbands. *Psychiatry* 33:444–467.

———. 1972. *Bereavement: studies of grief in adult life.* New York: International Universities Press.

Parkes, C. M., and R. S. Weiss. 1983. *Recovery from bereavement.* New York: Basic Books.

Peck, R. 1966. The development of the concept of death in selected male children. Ph.D. diss., New York University.

Pellegrino, E. D. 1993. Ethics. *JAMA* 270:202–203.

Plum, F., and J. B. Posner. 1980. *The diagnosis of stupor and coma.* 3rd ed. Philadelphia: F. A. Davis.

Portz, A. 1972. The child's sense of death. In *Death and presence,* ed. A. Godin. Brussels: Lumen Vitae Press.

President's Commission for the Study of Ethical Problems in Medicine and Behavioral Research. 1983. *Deciding to forgo life-sustaining treatment: a report on the ethical, medical, and legal issues in treatment decisions.* Washington, D.C.: U.S. Government Printing Office.

Prigerson, H. G., E. Frank, S. V. Kasl, et al. 1995. Complicated grief and bereavement-related depression as distinct disorders: preliminary empirical validation in elderly bereaved spouses. *Am. J. Psychiatry* 152:22–30.

Rado, S. 1956. *Psychoanalysis of behavior.* New York: Grune & Stratton.

Raimbault, G. 1972. Listening to sick children. In *Death and presence,* ed. A. Godin. Brussels: Lumen Vitae Press.

Rees, W. D., and S. G. Lutkins. 1967. Mortality of bereavement. *Br. Med. J.* 4:13–16.

Reich, P., and M. J. Kelly. 1976. Suicide attempts by hospitalized medical and surgical patients. *N. Engl. J. Med.* 294:298–301.

Reiss, D., S. Gonzalez, and N. Kramer. 1986. Family process, chronic illness, and death. *Arch. Gen. Psychiatry* 43:795–804.

Rochlin, G. 1965. *Griefs and discontents: the forces of change.* Boston: Little, Brown.

Rosenblatt, P. C. 1975. Uses of ethnography in understanding grief and mourning. In *Bereavement: its psychosocial aspects,* ed. B. Schoenberg, I. Gerber, A. Wiener, A. H. Kutscher, D. Peretz, and A. C. Carr. New York: Columbia University Press.

Safier, G. 1964. A study in relationships between the life and death concepts in children. *J. Genet. Psychol.* 105:283–294.

Saunders, C. 1959. Care of the dying: the problem of euthanasia, 1–6. *Nurs. Times* 55:960–961, 994–995, 1031–32, 1067–69, 1091–92, 1129–30.

———. 1969. The moment of truth: care of the dying person. In *Death and dying,* ed. L. Pearson. Cleveland: Case Western Reserve University Press.

Saunders, C., ed. 1978. *The management of terminal illness.* Chicago: Yearbook Medical Publishers.

Saunders, C. 1996. Foreword. In M. Kearney, *Mortally wounded.* Dublin: Marino Books, pp. 11–12.

Sawyer, J. B., H. S. Sudak, and S. R. Hall. 1972. A follow-up study of 53 suicides known to a suicide prevention center. *Life-Threatening Behav.* 2:227–238.

Schneidman, E. S. 1975. Suicide. In *Comprehensive textbook of psychiatry,* ed. A. M. Freedman, H. I. Kaplan, and B. J. Sadock. Vol. 2. 2nd ed. Baltimore: Williams & Wilkins.

Schowalter, J. E. 1970. Death and the pediatric house officer. *J. Pediatr.* 76:706–710.

Sheps, J. 1957. Management of fear in chronic disease. *J. Am. Geriatr. Soc.* 5:793–797.

Silverman, P., D. MacKenzie, M. Pettipas, and E. Wilson, eds. 1974. *Helping each other in widowhood.* New York: Health Sciences.

Slater, E. 1973. New horizons in medical ethics. *Br. Med. J.* 2:285–286.

Sloan, P. A., M. B. Donnelly, R. W. Schwartz, and D. A. Sloan. 1996. Cancer pain assessment and management by housestaff. *Pain* 67:475–481.

Spiegel, D., J. R. Bloom, H. C. Kraemer, and E. Gottheil. 1989. Effect of psychosocial treatment on survival of patients with metastatic breast cancer. *Lancet* 2:888–891.

Spinetta, J. J. 1974. The dying child's awareness of death: a review. *Psychol. Bull.* 81:256–260.

Spinetta, J. J., D. Rigler, and M. Karon. 1974. Personal space as a measure of a dying child's sense of isolation. *J. Consult. Clin. Psychol.* 42:751–756.

Sprung, C. L. 1990. Changing attitudes and practices in forgoing life-sustaining treatments. *JAMA* 263:2211–15.

Stein, S. B. 1974. *About dying: a book for parents and children.* New York: Walker.

Steiner, G. 1965. Children's concepts of life and death: a developmental study. Ph.D. diss., Columbia University.

Stevens, S. 1973. *Death comes home.* New York: Morehouse-Barlow.

Taffet, G. E., T. A. Teasdale, and R. J. Luchi. 1988. In-hospital cardiopulmonary resuscitation. *JAMA* 260:2069–72.

Task Force on Ethics of the Society of Critical Care Medicine. 1990. Consensus report on the ethics of forgoing life-sustaining treatments in the critically ill. *Crit. Care Med.* 18:1435–39.

Toch, R. 1964. Management of the child with a fatal disease. *Clin. Pediatr.* 3:418–427.

Tomlinson, T., and H. Brody. 1990. Futility and the ethics of resuscitation. *JAMA* 164:1276–80.

Truog, R. D., A. S. Brett, and J. Frader. 1992. The problem with futility. *N. Engl. J. Med.* 326:1560–64.

Van Der Maas, P. J., J. J. Van Delden, L. Pijnenborg, and C. W. Looman. 1991. Euthanasia and other medical decisions concerning the end of life. *Lancet* 338:669–674.

Waechter, E. 1972. Children's reaction to fatal illness. In *Death and presence,* ed. A. Godin. Brussels: Lumen Vitae Press.

Walsh, T. D., ed. 1989. *Symptom control.* Cambridge, Mass.: Blackwell Scientific Publications.

Wanzer, S. H., D. D. Federman, S. J. Adelstein, et al. 1989. The physician's responsibility toward hopelessly ill patients. *N. Engl. J. Med.* 320:844–849.

Weiner, I. W. 1969. The effectiveness of a suicide prevention program. *MH.* 53:357–363.

Weiner, J. M. 1970. Attitudes of pediatricians toward the care of fatally ill children. *J. Pediatr.* 76:700–705.

Weisman, A. D. 1971. Is suicide a disease? *Life-Threatening Behav.* 1:219–231.

——— 1972. *On dying and denying.* New York: Behavioral Publications.

——— 1974. Is mourning necessary? In *Anticipatory grief,* ed. B. Schoenberg, A. C. Carr, A. H. Kutscher, D. Peretz, and I. K. Goldberg. New York: Columbia University Press.

——— 1993. *The vulnerable self: Confronting the ultimate questions.* New York: Insight Books/Plenum Press.

Weisman, A. D., and T. P. Hackett. 1961. Predilection to death: death and dying as a psychiatric problem. *Psychosom. Med.* 23:232–256.

Weisman, A. D., and W. J. Worden. 1972. Risk-rescue rating in suicide assessment. *Arch. Gen. Psychiatry* 26:553–560.

Woodruff, Roger. 1993. *Palliative medicine: Symptomatic and supportive care for patients with advanced cancer and AIDS.* Melbourne: Asperula.

World Health Organization. 1968. *The prevention of suicide.* Geneva.

——— 1991. Palliative care: an urgent but neglected public health priority. *World Health Forum* 12:399.

Yudkin, S. 1967. Children and death. *Lancet* 1:37–41.

Zilboorg, G. 1937. Considerations on suicide, with particular reference to that of the young. *Am. J. Orthopsychiatry* 7:15–31.

——— 1938. The sense of immortality. *Psychoanal. Q.* 7:171–199.

Zimmerman, J. M. 1986. *Hospice: complete care for the terminally ill.* Baltimore: Urban & Schwartzenberg.

Zung, W. W. K. 1974. Index of potential suicide (IPS): a rating scale for suicide prevention. In *The prediction of suicide,* ed. A. T. Beck, H. L. P. Resnik, and D. J. Lettieri. Bowie, Md.: Charles Press.

Recommended Reading

Care for the dying: identification and promotion of physician competency. 1996. Educational resource document. American Board of Internal Medicine.

Doyle, D., G. W. C. Hanks, and N. MacDonald, eds. 1993. *Oxford textbook of palliative medicine.* Oxford: Oxford University Press.

Jacox A., D. B. Carr, R. Payne, et al. 1994. Management of cancer pain: clinical practice guideline no. 9. Rockville, Md.: U.S. Public Health Service, Agency for Health Care Policy and Research, publication 94–0592, March.

Parkes, C. M., and R. S. Weiss. 1983. *Recovery from bereavement.* New York: Basic Books.

Rochlin, G. 1965. *Griefs and discontents: the forces of change.* Boston: Little, Brown.

Weisman, A. D. 1972. *On dying and denying.* New York: Behavioral Publications.

Woodruff, R. 1993. *Palliative medicine.* Melbourne, Australia: Asperula.

PART SIX

Psychiatry and Society

34

CHESTER M. PIERCE

FELTON J. EARLS

ARTHUR KLEINMAN

Race and Culture in Psychiatry

Clinicians often fail to realize the significant role that race, culture, and ethnicity play in the etiology, diagnosis, and treatment of mental disease. Consequently, they may subject people of color, especially blacks, to inappropriate diagnostic and treatment standards. (To emphasize the salience of skin color in race relations and racism, the term "colored," or "people of color," is used to distinguish persons whose identity or ethnic origin is non-European.) Because of widespread racial and cultural tensions in the United States, patient care requires dedicated attention to these issues.

Standard nomenclature (*Diagnostic and Statistical Manual of Mental Disorders,* fourth edition, or DSM-IV) now provides a method to ensure comprehensive focus on ethnic and cultural considerations. DSM-IV fails, however, to recognize the importance of race and racism as ongoing components of daily existence. Because of predictions that within the lifetime of today's children the United States will no longer have a white majority, the twenty-first-century psychiatrist must be increasingly aware of a patient's race and culture.

This chapter presents a *method* to help clinicians become more aware of cultural issues and an *approach* to increase awareness of racial issues. Method refers to a system or outline for accumulating data as a routine part of case formulation. Approach refers to the preparation of the clinician's attitude and the proactive, anticipatory selection of factors which may have special pertinence in dealing with minority patients.

The "cultural methodology" and the "racial approach" are enhanced by using a "developmental context." Excellent patient care for people of color, therefore, rests on a triad. The triad consists of cultural assessment, racial sensitivity, and knowledge of how racial identity develops in both people of color and whites.

Because of space limitations, we do not review cultural influences on specific psychiatric disorders. (For relevant references, see Mezzich et al., 1996, and Kleinman, 1988.)

Key Words

"Race," culture, and ethnicity must be defined. *Race* is a biological definition of difference. The dictionary definition of race is, "any of the great divisions of mankind with certain inherited physical characteristics (e.g., color of skin and hair, shape of eyes and nose)." Also, "a number of people related by common descent" (Oxford Large Print Dictionary, 1992). But the term is hotly contested and difficult to define. Most biological anthropologists consider it an elusive concept. Although no gene pools in our heterogeneous society represent an isolated hereditary endowment, authorities agree that race in America nevertheless remains socially significant. "Race" often evokes stereotypes and stigmata that foster attitudes of racism. We define *racism* as the intentional or unintentional bias based upon skin color. *Culture* refers to the dominant set of symbolic codes (linguistic, moral, aesthetic) and material practices (dietary/behavioral) that characterize a group. Culture may refer to an entire society's codes and practices, as when reference is made to American or Japanese culture. *Ethnicity* refers to the particular reference group for individuals with a shared heritage: for example, Puerto Rican, African American, Irish American, or American Jewish groups. Some reference groups, e.g., those based on religion, may be voluntary. Other reference groups, e.g., those based on race, are usually involuntarily ascribed to the person. In multicultural America a person may identify with several groups simultaneously or with none. For example, a patient with one parent of Jewish Central European background and another parent who is American Indian may regard himself as white, American Indian, Jewish, all, or none of the above. Others, however, may also regard him as white, American Indian, Jewish, all, or none of these. Obviously, cultural issues become especially relevant when the patient is a recent immigrant who cannot speak English, requires an interpreter, and needs help in negotiating the new society. Although race, culture, and ethnicity may not always be clinically relevant, the clinician must nevertheless make an empirical assessment of these issues with every patient.

A Racial Approach

Background Issues in Racism

No compelling evidence exists to indicate that the racial identity of the psychiatrist, per se, confers advantage or disadvantage in the clinical care of minority patients. Colored or white therapists can give excellent or inept treatment to colored or white patients. The ability of the doctor to understand and appreciate broad, specific human needs and desires, such as envy or greed or how one justifies existence, is more significant than one's skin color. For the doctor-patient relationship to be successful, however, racist thoughts and actions in both doctor and patient must be acknowledged and controlled. Racism occurs whenever people's assumptions concerning the superiority or inferiority of skin color influences their ideas, feelings, and behavior. In the United States, the darker the individual, the more likely it is that he will be a target of discrimination and disdain. When large numbers of white and colored people accept this proposition as normative and act upon it, implacable tension results. When biases concerning skin color remain fixed—that is, unchanged even in the face of conflicting evidence—they may give rise to widespread delusional thinking. The psychiatrist may be called upon to help reduce the resulting psychological stress in the community. As the white majority becomes a minority during the next few decades, critical problems may arise.

The clinician's approach to people of color must embrace a knowledge of problems common to colored minority people (blacks, Asians, Latinos, Native Americans). The most comprehensive problem confronting all people of color concerns the degree of assimilation into the general culture that their group and each individual in the group desires. The therapist must accurately assess the degree of assimilation acquired by the patient, or that could be acquired by the patient, as well as the degree of traditionalism the patient wishes to retain; these may not be congruent or static. The great variety of ethnic, cultural, psychological, class, and socioeconomic attributes of individuals in each of the colored minorities makes assessment difficult.

Many practical problems result from this heterogeneity. Those germane to the psychiatrist include the difficulty the group has in naming or defining itself, the po-

tential for inter- and intraracial conflicts, and the wider reliance on "alternative" systems of medicine. Also the doctor must be more attuned to the sociopolitical history, migration experiences, and geographical influences on patients of color than in the case of white patients.

Perhaps chiefly, but not exclusively, these considerations loom large in the difficulty people of color experience in participating in available services. Memories of experiences that evoke feelings of being unwanted, trivialized, and demeaned will cause them to be suspicious, hesitant, and distrustful of the agents in a "white" facility. Frequently the reception the patient receives from a service institution reinforces this guardedness.

For these reasons, psychiatrists must convey respect and dignity in their approach to colored patients, especially to poor patients. Psychiatrists must also recognize that a person of color usually is more "culturally complicated" than a white patient. Colored people are likely to know and keep abreast of cultural traditions and changes in the general population to a greater extent than whites know or keep current about any colored population. The assumed notion among both whites and coloreds that whites take prerogatives because they know best what is needed for minorities has caused considerable tension in intergroup relations.

For people of color the principal cause of racial tension is that whites tend to control and command a colored person's space, time, energy, and motion. A complicated etiquette, backed by conscious and unconscious custom as well as by de facto law, fosters this tendency. An unwritten rule of our society is that a white person's time, space, energy, and motion take precedence over those of a minority person. To accomplish this whites incessantly use offensive mechanisms toward minorities which reduce their self-esteem, confidence, and security.

Often whites (both doctors and patients) deliver these offenses without intended hostility. The white person remains unaware of the insult and its consequences. Many of these subtle, stunning offenses, delivered as microaggressions, may appear minor and innocuous. The accumulation of these experiences by a colored person, however, is a crucial dynamic in influencing cross-racial interactions. When a young black in a white coat with a stethoscope enters a white patient's room, the patient may greet him cheerfully with, "Are you the barber?"

Frequently people of color contribute, often gratuitously, to their own catastrophe. By word and/or deed they comply, accept, and promote the notion that the white individual, agency, or institution is superior. When a black patient volunteers to her white doctor, "Black nurses don't know nothing," she is often without realizing it perpetuating her own and her group's suffering. More often the colored suffers casual degradation.

An Afro-American student was with a group of white classmates when their examination grades were returned. One of his peers excitedly asked each person present, "What did you get?" When he turned to the black peer he asked, "Did you pass?" Repetitive, routine, and multiple "put-downs" of this sort complicate even cordial, hetero-racial social situations. The recognition that one is perceived as peripheral to, different, and distant from the group contributes extra obstacles to adjustment and to the maintenance of self-esteem. The ongoing task for a minority member is to make a rapid assessment of these microaggressions and determine which ones require response and which ones are best ignored. When and how to respond to microaggressions can occupy much energy and thought. The doctor must become comfortable with discussion of what are appropriate responses in selected instances of such "innocuous" insults. Such an approach leads to insights which increase cooperation in cross-racial situations and positive self-evaluation by all participants. In the above instance merely supporting the student with the genuine acknowledgment "It must have been awful" prompted meaningful dialogue about feeling marginal and distinctive.

For colored or white doctors an approach, as opposed to a method, toward interacting with colored patients is based on acknowledging skin color differences, eliminating racist behavior, and customizing interactions depending on where the patient and doctor fall on a spectrum of psychosocial values. Support and relationship are paramount concerns in all clinical interaction. More support equals less stress. A strong relationship fosters mutual confidence, trust, and respect.

Skin Color Differences

In general, we recommend that the clinician explore skin color, especially skin color differences, early, comfortably and frankly with the patient. The doctor must elicit and listen for episodes of racial unfairness, especially less obvious offenses. Microaggressive insults and assaults are often unconscious or preconscious. Over time such racially inspired offenses are absorbed and result in an indisposable burden. They tend to cause the patient to feel paralyzed and defeated and to focus defensively and impotently on "what can't be done." That all members of the target group experience constant exposure to these insults helps to explain both the lack of social cohesiveness and the generalized hopelessness characterizing disenfranchised minorities. Patients need to become aware of

microaggressions, of their corrosive and energy-draining effect, and learn to anticipate and/or counter them. Virulent microaggressions when unattended produce lingering toxicity and contribute to a negative self-image and group identity. In this sense they constitute "psychotoxins" which can influence the social ecology of the entire community.

Eliminating Racist Behavior

The clinician may help colored patients increase their control of space, time, energy, and motion. As the doctor-patient relationship solidifies, the doctor, with gentleness and candor, may point out to patients when and how they contributed to their own degradation. Most colored people experience numerous examples of self-victimization, in which they are expected to display gratitude and good cheer. Knowing when, where, how, and how much to accept an affront constitutes an immense and never-ending dilemma for minority people. Support in helping the patient stand up for himself in an appropriate manner poses an important task for the clinician.

Treatment of disenfranchised minority persons, therefore, includes: assessing the cultural complexity of the patients, the degree of assimilation and traditionalism in their life and fantasies, how they respond to minor aggressions, and how the doctor can encourage the patients to stand up for themselves. This may prove difficult for several reasons. Although racial factors may dominate all aspects of the patient's existence, the patient will seldom present them as a chief complaint. Only the sensitivity, expertise and experience of the doctor can determine when and how ardently to pursue racial issues. To gain such expertise and experience requires openness, willingness, and encouragement by the doctor to discuss perceived and actual inequities. Not infrequently the doctor is in the position of needing instruction and enlightenment from the patient about particular social ills and their importance to the patient.

Throughout patient contact the doctor, therefore, must continually assess (1) how assimilated or acculturated the patient is and what degree of "orthodoxy" in therapy is required, and (2) the impact of the patient's and the doctor's skin color on their relationship. With these concerns in mind, the doctor catalogues psychosocial dimensions crucial in tailoring treatment to fit the specific needs of the patient. By following this approach, the clinician will avoid drawing conclusions merely from apparent racial phenotypes which differ significantly from the actual degree of assimilation, traditionalism, or identity with an ethnic or racial group.

Psychosocial Values

Transference and countertransference may complicate the interaction between the therapist and a patient of color. In addition, other seemingly minor issues may become important, e.g., rigidity about appointment times, questions about home visits, collaboration with an alternative healer, or allowing the patient to teach the therapist about ethnicity.

Two important cultural themes need to be explored openly with a minority patient. First, is the patient aware of how overt acceptance manifests itself in a cross-racial situation? Is the patient aware of the difference between being welcomed versus being tolerated? Second, is the patient aware of the interpersonal consequences resulting from the high probability that in cross-racial situations he or she will be made both peripheral to and fractionated across the main group? Grasping these 2 problem areas as they apply to specific situations may be exceedingly beneficial to the minority patient.

Finally, a therapist of any ethnic persuasion and a minority patient need to be able to explore how the patient thinks and feels (even when it conflicts with what the doctor thinks and feels) about a number of basic principles involving behavior in heteroracial settings. These include:

when to argue minority to minority in front of whites;
when to control laughter and smiling in intergroup contexts;
when to resort to selective silence in intergroup contexts;
when to curb publicity about self in intergroup contexts;
when to reveal plans in intergroup contexts.

To answer these questions patients may need to be encouraged to increase their knowledge of (1) their group's history and culture, and (2) methods to defuse negative racial propaganda that erodes their self-esteem. These questions are important because they force both doctor and patient to help clarify the advantages and disadvantages of their own skin color.

Customizing a treatment regimen away from standard or orthodox methods is more often required for people of color. To ensure such flexible possibilities, exploring questions like those listed above is a natural process. The patient learns that these are permissible, vital topics about prosaic, everyday happenings that the therapist recognizes as important and that usually are unattended to in any encounter with professionals of any sort. This paves the way for an enhanced doctor-patient relationship which leads to more honest, open, and meaningful exchange.

Living with never-ending major and minor acts of degradation inevitably produces feelings of diminished self-esteem and hopelessness. Because these pernicious hazards occur frequently, the clinician who treats colored patients should possess a sophisticated grasp of cultural and developmental determinants of racial identity.

Because of the variety of desires and perceived and actual degrees of assimilation in each patient, the approach to colored patients demands considerable individual customizing. Generally, the approach should first explore the patient's *feelings* before focusing on the patient's *behavior*. The approach should emphasize the patient's strengths before exploring weaknesses. Finally, the approach should focus more on motivations than on rationalizations over past or projected actions. Confidence in the approach is strengthened by one's knowledge of variables in the development of ethnic and racial identity.

Development of Identity

Ethnic identity refers to that part of one's self-concept that derives from membership in a social group or groups, together with the value and emotional significance attached to the membership (Tajfel, 1981). A specific language may or may not be part of that identity. Racial and ethnic identity achieved by experience in culturally bound events and settings, using a variety of coping skills learned through family and other mediating structures, strongly influences psychological development.

Several studies demonstrate the importance of ethnic identity to the self-concept of various white ethnic groups (Rosenthal and Hrynevich, 1985; Zak, 1973). Among minority groups in the United States, racial and ethnic identity increased in social significance during the civil rights movement of the 1960s (Laosa, 1984). Authorities differ in their opinions of how to incorporate racial and ethnic identity into concepts of development and how to measure it (Phinney, 1990; Rogler, Cortes, and Malgady, 1991; Vega et al., 1993).

In the United States whites have relatively little need for or interest in learning about subordinate cultures. Minority people, however, regardless of interest are obliged to learn a great deal about whites. Consequently, this may lead to vastly different perspectives, feelings, and expectations when whites interact with minorities.

Misinterpretation of research data often contributes to racial misunderstanding. For example, the original interpretation of the work of the Horowitzes and the Clarks during the 1930s and 1940s (see Cross, 1991, for an authoritative review) suggested a preference for white skin by blacks, as demonstrated in doll play experiments. More recent studies challenge the idea that these data reflect self-hatred among black children (Cross, 1991). Findings from these studies demonstrate considerable variability in the identity of black Americans and show that aspects of race and cross-race orientations often merge. These studies elucidate a more complex model of identification pointing to the development of possible bicultural and multicultural perspectives. The question whether such perspectives result in conflict and self-defeatism or enhanced social skill remains open. For instance, a person may be phenotypically colored and biologically half white. If he identifies his ethnicity as white but others identify him as black, he may experience "identity irresolution." The doctor's inaccurate "sensitivity" to racial concerns may also interfere with treatment.

A 19-year-old black male is encouraged by friends to seek psychiatric evaluation at a college health service because of recent onset dysphoria and suicidal ideation. A white psychiatrist, noting that the patient is biracial, focuses much of the initial session on how comfortable he feels about a recent escalation of racial tensions on campus. On further evaluation, the clinician infers that the presenting conflicts involve peer pressures regarding group affiliation and dating choices. He makes a provisional diagnosis of identity disorder and schedules a series of therapy sessions. The patient fails to appear for the first session, feeling that the psychiatrist did not fully understand his disappointment over poor academic performance and not living up to his family's high expectations for him. His symptoms eventually intensify and he leaves the college.

As our society becomes more racially heterogeneous, bicultural and multicultural perspectives become more significant as they involve a larger percentage of the population. Can racial or ethnic identity be conceptualized as a general phenomenon or must it be culture specific? Phinney (1992) identifies 4 components of general ethnic identity: (1) self-identification as a group member, (2) engagement in behaviors related to the group, (3) a sense of belonging to the group, and (4) attitudes toward one's group. All of these attributes are judged solely from the perspective of the individual, a limiting factor with this approach. Ethnic and race identity are also influenced by the degree to which one's own group and other groups accept or reject the individual's sense of belonging. Ethnic identity is as much a function of the social environment and interpersonal relationships as it is an intrinsic and internalized attribute of the individual.

Acculturation refers to the psychological adaptation of an individual to a host culture. While ethnic identity reflects the importance of cultural heritage to a minority individual's self-concept, acculturation also plays an important role. Because acculturation fails to discriminate between a variety of strategies employed by a person in becoming a member of a host society, the term must be used cautiously. For example, *assimilation* implies a rather complete transformation on the part of an individual in adopting the norms of a host society. By contrast, *accommodation* implies a weak or tentative acceptance of these norms. In addition, a person may appear to possess a high degree of acculturation, while at the same time feeling uncomfortable in the society. Acculturation as a process extends beyond developing skill in language use and acquiring the customs and habits of the dominant culture. The individual experiences a fundamental shift in belief and behavior as reflected in relationships with family and friends (in social activities).

The social psychology of groups suggests that conforming with the dominant culture proves more effective as a coping strategy than maintaining distance. Yet, as discussed earlier, this may also depict a form of defeatism. A strong sense of ethnic identity may serve as a protective factor, helping the individual manage the host culture more effectively (Recio Adrados, 1993). Higher degrees of acculturation have been related to poorer health outcomes, suggesting that adoption of the values and behavior of the dominant culture may place the individual at risk. For instance, in studies of adult Hispanics, those who reported higher degrees of acculturation also reported greater consumption of alcohol. The more acculturated also espouse more liberal attitudes than are found in their country of origin (Caetano, 1987), although length of residence in the United States appears to influence men more than women (Caetano and Media Mora, 1988). Higher degrees of acculturation have also been linked to increased risk for depression and suicide in Hispanic adolescents and young adults (Earls, Escobar, and Manson, 1990). However, ethnic groups tend to differ in the "distances" they maintain from the dominant culture. This makes difficult the comparison of acculturation of different ethnic groups.

To understand the development of ethnic identity in patients, the clinician must first define it and know the social context in which it becomes elaborated and differentiated. Psychoanalytic theories provide psychiatry with a set of constructs and a vocabulary that has been used for several decades by scholars exploring the origins and development of identity. Erikson (1968), in particular, made identity a focal point of his theory. Although he recognized that identity developed over the lifetime of an individual, his formulation emphasized adolescence as critical for consolidation of one's concept of the self in relation to the immediate social context. Present, past, and future representations of the self become integrated during adolescence and serve as a foundation for the psychological and social demands of adulthood. The failure to form "an inner solidarity with a group's ideals and identity" results in defects in character development. Any individual, therefore, of a dominated minority who attempts to develop ethnic integrity in a host society may suffer "identity confusion." Persistent intrusions by the dominant group's ideals and needs often conflict with the individual's efforts to admire and accept his own group.

Recent literature in developmental psychology emphasizes moving beyond the deficit or pathological models formulated in the older literature to more differentiated and health-promoting models (Cross, 1991; Harter, 1988; Spencer and Dornbusch, 1990). This perspective views identity formation as an active process in which children and adolescents, in response to the social context in which they are growing up, make active choices concerning the degree of their response to the demands of others. Racial minority groups view the attitudes and behavior of white Americans as obstacles to the achievement of healthy identity. These obstacles are, nevertheless, permeable and negotiable. The chief developmental task for people of color is to acquire confidence in their capacity to deal successfully with these obstacles.

Aktar and Samuel (1996) review the evolution of the concept of identity in clinical psychiatry. They describe different developmental periods from infancy to adolescence and maintain that identity originates in infancy and undergoes continuous elaboration during sensitive periods in childhood, adolescence, and adulthood. Body image, gender, temporality, and consistent attitudes and values combine with ethnicity to form a coherent structure to identity. These authors view the level of identity disturbance in a patient as a valuable indicator of psychopathology.

A solid, clearly defined and focused ethnic identity fosters mental health by helping the individual operate in an ongoing stressful environment with increased confidence and certainty. It may also give the individual greater freedom to use positive features in the host society.

The recent literature reflects the uncertainty concerning ethnicity in dominated individuals and their groups. Ethnic identity, particularly in reference to coloreds in the United States, is characterized by irresolution and variable resonance or penetration of ideals coming from outside their own group. The challenging task for the clinician is to estimate the degree of satisfaction and comfort minority patients experience with what they perceive to be their reference groups' ideals. At the same time, the clinician must also estimate how these perceptions match those of clinically relevant individuals and groups with whom the patient has interpersonal relations. Once he determines these complicated factors, the clinician must formulate them into practical treatment possibilities. Compounding this difficulty is the overarching responsibility of assessing what role, if any, ethnicity plays in the presenting psychiatric problem. Most of the time, despite the consuming conscious and unconscious importance it may have to a person's life, the clinician will elect to use the information only in history taking and assuring proper sensitivity and support to the patient's distress. However, the clinician can augment this sensitivity and support by making a cultural formulation.

A Cultural Methodology for Clinical Practice

For the practicing psychiatrist, DSM-IV contains a serviceable instrument to help the clinician take culture into account in diagnosing and treating patients and their families. The "Cultural Formulation" may be the single most useful practical contribution of cultural psychiatrists and anthropologists to patient care. Regrettably, it is buried in the DSM-IV's ninth appendix. Its proximity to the "Glossary of Culture-Bound Syndromes" may lend a sense of the exotic and tend to make "culture" appear less significant in daily, mundane clinical applications.

The Formulation provides a 4-step approach that supplements multiaxial diagnostic assessment. It provides a brief, systematic methodology to consider how an individual's ethnic and cultural context is relevant to patient care. The methodology requires the clinician to formulate a short narrative summary for each of 4 categories. No simple approach can describe the complexity of culture, class, and other social structural influences on the individual's psychopathology and treatment. Personal characteristics and those of families reflect culture differently. Yet the Formulation is a practical guide that deserves to be added to the core competencies of psychiatrists.

The Four-Stage "Cultural Formulation"

1. *Cultural identity* of the individual: the clinician should note the patient's ethnic and cultural group. For immigrants and refugees, the clinician should record the patient's and/or family's degree of engagement with both the host culture and the culture of origin. He should also note language abilities and preferences, dress, preferences

in music and reading, religious practices, dietary preferences, and health-relevant behavioral practices, where significant. The DSM-IV does not list economic matters, but because ethnicity and class frequently interact, clinicians need to be aware of limited financial resources and other socioeconomic constraints.

2. *Cultural explanations* of the individual's illness. The clinician should first describe the chief *idioms of distress.* These are the colloquial terms the patient expresses through symptoms and the need for social support. Examples of common idioms of distress are "nerves"; culturally emphasized somatic complaints and lay diagnoses such as neurasthenia, "attacks," or "weak blood"; and possessing spirits or religious construals of misfortune. Cultural explanations also convey the meaning and perceived severity and chronicity of symptoms in relation to group norms. Also frequently relevant are perceived causes and models of pathology that the person and the reference group use to make sense of illness and to formulate preferences for (and past experiences with) treatment—both professional and popular. Clinicians need to recognize that these explanatory models (Kleinman, 1988) often are fragmentary and changing, and may differ according to the particular situations and professionals with whom patients and families communicate. Disagreement among family members or with the practices of the reference group also can be significant.

Key questions to elicit patient and family explanatory models for an illness episode include:

What do you call this problem?
How do you think it affects your body? Yourself?
What is its cause?
What do you fear most about the illness? About the treatment?

3. Cultural factors related to the *psychosocial environment and levels of functioning.* Clinicians need to take into account culturally relevant interpretations of and experiences with social stressors and available social supports, as well as levels of functioning and disability. The role of kin networks, religious institutions, and welfare, disability, and other agencies can be important sources of support (emotional, instrumental, informational) as well as stress. Poverty and near-poverty along with trauma and losses can be critical elements, as can the chronic stress associated with racism.

4. Cultural elements in the *clinical relationship.* The DSM-IV format recommends that the clinician note and record "differences in culture and social status between the individual and the clinician and problems that those differences may cause in diagnosis and treatment (e.g.,

difficulty in communicating in the individual's first language, in eliciting symptoms or understanding their cultural significance, in negotiating an appropriate relationship or level of intimacy, in determining whether a behavior is normative or pathological)."

In addition, the culture of biomedicine and the institutional culture of the clinical environment may operate to create problems in diagnosis and caregiving. That is to say, the clinician in a cross-cultural encounter should be attuned to the way his value orientations, behavior rules, and cultural practices, including those of biomedicine and his institution, influence psychiatric care. Sometimes these values are greater and more problematic than those of the patient and family. For example, mind-body dualism, encoded into DSM-IV and used in the training of residents, frequently causes psychiatrists to treat the psychosomatic or somatopsychic integration of Chinese patients as "somatization." In fact, the psychiatrist may be the one who most somatizes episodes of depression or anxiety among Chinese. Chinese patients and families treat those conditions as both somatic *and* psychological. The clinician must keep in mind that most DSM-IV diagnostic categories are predicated on the model of a white middle-class male.

The *Cultural Formulation* should conclude with a discussion of how these cultural issues specifically affect diagnosis and treatment. The following vignette is illustrative:

Samuel Franklin (pseudonym) is a 36-year-old male postal employee with chronic low back pain. He is referred for psychiatric assessment to rule out major affective disorder as part of a disability evaluation. On examination he reports a history of weekend binge drinking of a decade's duration, but does not meet criteria for clinical depression. During the interview he is guarded and hostile.

Dr.: "What's your ethnicity, Mr. Franklin?"

Pt. (noticeably relaxing): "You're the first doctor to ask me that question, you know. I'm half American Indian—mixture of Coast Salish and other things—the other half split between Northern Irish, Protestant, and Jewish. My mother's parents were Polish Jews, mostly."

Dr.: "How do you identify yourself?"

Pt.: "It's interesting, really it is. I go by how I feel at times. I don't feel like I'm one thing only. I'm multiethnic. I felt most at home about it a few years back when I visited Poland. Then I could see how the Jewish side of me had the connection to race just like the American Indians' side here."

Dr.: "Do you think it relates at all to your health problem?"

Pt.: "When this problem started I was volunteering to fight a forest fire. We got caught behind the fire line, the fire was that fast. I thought we were goners. Finally, I saw a break in the burning trees, I yelled and pulled the other two guys with me. We got out, alive, hardly burned at all. Then this son-of-a-bitch says to me, 'You Injuns, you know what to do.' And then he made an ethnic joke, you know about how Indians are drunk and dirty. I could've killed the bastard. Thrown him back in the fire.

"Well that's how it began. That night I was so bloody angry, I drank and drank, and finally took my ax and started breakin' up wood. I guess I did something to my back. Ever since then I got me two problems—the back and these nightmares about the fire and about that bad guy. I'm angry just telling you about it all."

Mr. Franklin now opened up and acknowledged symptoms that made the criteria for depression. He responded to a course of short-term psychotherapy and antidepressant medication with improvement in his nightmares and flashbacks, his anger, and his chronic pain.

The Cultural Formulation of Mr. Franklin

1. Like an increasing number of Americans, Mr. Franklin preferred the self-description of "multiethnic" over identification with one group only. But he had great sensitivity (appropriate, it seems, given his personal experience) about the stigmatizing stereotypes connected in America with his American Indian heritage (and in Poland with his Jewish background). He was particularly concerned about racism, and his experience at the time of the forest fire confirmed his suspicions.

2. Mr. Franklin's explanatory model for his illness onset combined the traumatic forest fire experience with the negative experience of racism, which precipitated anger, alcohol abuse, and chronic pain. These aspects of the illness narrative gave the rationale for psychotherapy focused on this constellation of events and problems.

3. The traumatic experience of near-death in the forest fire combined with the experience of racism were central to his illness experience.

4. The clinical relationship was facilitated, as was the diagnosis, by attention to ethnicity and its relation to the illness onset.

This is a 36-year-old multiethnic American male whose American Indian and Jewish ethnicity made him sensi-

tive to racism, which he experienced in the context of a traumatic event that precipitated his pain, depression, and alcohol abuse. Culturally informed treatment ameliorated his symptoms and provided him with insight into their source as well as an occasion frankly to review his experiences with racism, his anger and sadness over it, and the role of that reaction to racism in the course of his illness experience.

This chapter assumes that the intellectual and clinical understanding of race is a legitimate necessity for any doctor practicing in the United States. For this to happen, adequate training about these issues and dedicated attention to them in all health delivery systems are mandatory. Such consideration is all the more important in times of increasing managed care and limited time for doctor-patient interaction.

Racism may be the most powerful and the most harmful of all cultural processes that influence the care of patients. We have, therefore, focused on *racism* and emphasized the significance of race, culture, and ethnicity for understanding normal and pathological development and for diagnosing and treating mental illness. In matters of ethnicity, race, and culture, most positive and negative features are nonverbal, kinetic, and attitudinal (e.g., a forbidding demeanor toward a colored patient by a white receptionist). This is particularly true about race. It might be argued that racism, the most negative feature in these matters, is a public health problem. It has dimensions touching virtually every life in this society and can leave lingering, serious damage. For this reason psychiatrists are urged to take a proactive, preventive stance against racism in all patient interactions. Because all medical practice takes place in a social matrix, the psychiatrist must, above all, be concerned with this dimension of the community.

By the end of the twentieth century authorities could predict that the white majority population in the United States was destined for minority status. The current nonwhite minorities are both neglected and inadequately served by psychiatry, a reflection of general conditions in our society that may in the next few decades lead to an unusually protracted, debilitating, and destabilizing struggle.

Psychiatrists must be more attentive to these demographic changes because they may become the advance retinue of grievous and implacable strife and contention. We suggest that in matters of research, service, teaching, and administration, psychiatrists (1) gather cultural data in a more deliberate, careful fashion following the formulation outlined above; (2) hone their sensitivity to racial problems and ethnicity; and (3) recognize the compounding complexity in human development resulting from widespread confusion and distortion regarding race, ethnicity, and culture. Finally, clinicians of all colors first and foremost must know as much as possible about their own race, ethnicity, culture, and development. Such rigorous, honest, and balanced self-appraisal will help them understand the hopes, fears, desires, needs, and wants of their minority patients.

References

Aktar, S., and Samuel, S. 1996. The concept of identity: developmental origins, phenomenology, clinical relevance, and measurement. *Harvard Rev. Psychiatry* 3:254–267.

American Psychiatric Association. 1994. *Diagnostic and statistical manual of mental disorders,* 4th ed. Washington, D.C., American Psychiatric Association.

Arce, C. H. 1981. A reconciliation of Chicano culture and identity. *Daedalus* 110:177–192.

Caetano, R. 1987. Acculturation and attitudes toward appropriate drinking among U.S. Hispanics. *Alcohol & Alcoholism* 22:427–433.

Caetano, R., and Media Mora, M. A. 1988. Acculturation and drinking among people of Mexican descent in Mexico and the United States. *Journal of Studies on Alcohol* 49:462–471.

Cross, W. E. 1991. *Shades of black: diversity in African-American identity.* Philadelphia: Temple University Press.

Earls, F., Escobar, J., and Manson, S. 1990. Suicide in minority groups: epidemiological and cultural perspectives. In *Suicide over the life course,* ed. Blumenthal, S. and Kupfer, D. J. Washington, D.C.: American Psychiatric Association Press. 571–598.

Erikson, E. 1968. *Identity, youth, and crisis.* New York: Norton Press.

Harter, S. 1988. Developmental and dynamic changes in the nature of the self-concept: implications for child psychotherapy. In *Cognitive development and child psychotherapy,* ed. Shirk, S. New York: Plenum. 119–160.

Kavanagh, K. H., and Kennedy, P. H. 1992. *Promoting cultural diversity: strategies for health care professionals.* Newbury Park, Calif.: Sage Publications.

Kleinman, A. 1988. *Rethinking psychiatry: from cultural category to personal experience.* New York: Free Press.

Laosa, L. 1984. Social policies toward children of diverse ethnic, racial, and language groups in the United States.

Mezzich, J., et al., eds. 1996. *Culture and psychiatric diagnosis.* Washington, D.C.: American Psychiatric Press.

Phinney, J. 1990. Ethnic identity in adolescence and adulthood: a review of research. *Psychol. Bull.* 108:499–514.

——— 1992. The multi group ethnic identity measure: a new scale for use with the diverse groups. *Journal of Adolescent Research* 7:156–176.

Recio Adrados, J. L. 1993. Acculturation: the broader view. Theoretical framework of the acculturation scales. In *Drug abuse among minority youth: advances in research and methodology,* ed. M. R. De La Rosa and J. L. Recio Adrados. Rockville, Md.: NIDA Research Monograph 130, USDHHS. 57–78.

Rogler, L. H., Cortes, D. E., and Malgady, R. G. 1991. Acculturation and mental health among Hispanics: convergence and new directions for research. *American Psychologist* 46:585–597.

Rosenthal, D., and Hrynevich, C. 1985. Ethnicity and ethnic identity: a comparative study of Greek-, Italian-, and Anglo-Australian adolescents. *International Journal of Psychology* 20:723–742.

Spencer, M. B., and Dornbusch, S. M. 1990. Challenges in studying minority youth. In *At the threshold: the developing adolescent,* ed. Feldman, S. S., and Elliott, G. Cambridge, Mass.: Harvard University Press. 123–146.

Tajfel, J. 1981. *Human groups and social categories.* New York: Cambridge University Press.

Vega, W. A., Zimmerman, R., Gil, A., Warhheit, G. J., and Apospori, E. 1993. Acculturation strain theory: its application in explaining drug use behavior among Cuban and other Hispanic youth. In *Drug abuse among minority youth: advances in research and methodology,* ed. M. R. De La Rosa & J. L. Recio Adrados. Rockville, Md.: NIDA Research Monograph 130, USDHHS.

Zak, I. 1973. Dimensions of Jewish-American identity. *Psychological Reports* 33:891–900.

Recommended Reading

Alarcon, R., ed. 1995. Cultural psychiatry. Special issue. *Psychiatric Clinics of North America* 18(3).

Helman, C. 1992. *Culture, health, and society.* 2nd ed. Boston: Wright.

Rogler, L. H. 1997. Making sense of historical changes in the Diagnostic and Statistical Manual of Mental Disorders: five propositions. *J. of Health and Social Behavior* 38 (March):9–20.

Willie, C., Rieker, P., Kramer, B., and Brown, B., eds. 1995. *Mental health, racism, and sexism.* Pittsburgh: University of Pittsburgh Press.

EDWARD M. HUNDERT

Ethical Issues
in the Practice
of Psychiatry

Psychiatric ethics has witnessed the biggest explosion of interest in both the scholarly literature and popular press since the last edition of this book, and so this new chapter has been added. Ethical principles and moral values permeate all aspects of psychiatric practice; the subject of psychiatric ethics is woven throughout much of the book, where ethical dimensions of specific topics—from psychosomatic disorders to sex therapy—are addressed. In order to capture psychiatric ethics as a discrete area of study, this chapter is divided into three sections.

The first section defines the scope of psychiatric ethics, with a look at what makes the *professional* relationship different from other relationships and what makes the *psychiatric* relationship unique even among doctor-patient relationships. The second section reviews major topics in psychiatric ethics such as informed consent, competency, involuntary treatment, confidentiality, professional boundaries, double agentry, conflicts of interest, and managed care. The third and final section deals with preventive ethics: the common sense way to solve ethical dilemmas by not getting into them in the first place.

The Scope of Psychiatric Ethics

The first question to ask about the subject of "psychiatric ethics" is whether it exists as a distinct field of inquiry. Because this subject is often viewed as a subset of the broader field of "medical ethics," one must first face the question of whether medical ethics is legitimately a field distinct from the even broader subject of "ethics" in general. After all, if Immanuel Kant left any legacy in the past 2 centuries, it is the notion that what counts as "ethics" must apply equally to anyone in a similar situation. We would quickly balk at a proposed separate field of "president's ethics" or "congressman's ethics," immediately insisting that the American Revolution was founded on the idea that the same rules should apply to all people regard-

less of their position. So what about medical ethics or psychiatric ethics?

Since academics and the media write as if a distinct field of medical ethics existed, we might consider a number of approaches to talking about it in a meaningful way. The least informative of these is to say that medical ethics is simply the application of the single field of ethics to people who happen to find themselves in the operating room with a scalpel in their hand or in a psychiatric hospital treating psychotic patients. This would shed little light on the obvious questions concerning the unique obligations of these individuals by virtue of their being physicians, and so would not get us very far. This is not merely a rhetorical point. As medical care becomes increasingly "managed" by nonphysician administrators, a significant question has emerged as to whether these nonphysicians should be bound by what has traditionally been called "medical ethics" or whether they are bound only by the ethical principles of the business world.

A more interesting approach comes from the idea that medicine as a profession is built upon a defining "ethic"—that of health promotion and disease prevention. In this approach, what makes medical ethics distinct from other areas of ethics is the particular value placed on alleviating the patient's suffering. When a suicidally depressed patient is hearing command hallucinations to kill himself, medical ethics might dictate involuntary commitment if the patient were refusing care and no less restrictive alternatives were feasible. In such a situation, medical ethics sometimes thus places more weight on relieving suffering and ensuring safety than on the patient's individual liberty and privacy, a pattern of value balancing that distinguishes it from legal ethics, for example. In legal ethics, values such as liberty, privacy, and justice tend to be given relatively more weight when they conflict with the characteristically medical values of promoting physical and mental safety and well-being. We can thus understand a "professional ethic" as a characteristic pattern of value balancing that defines the unique value system of the profession (Hundert, 1990).

Within medical ethics there is a parallel debate about the status of psychiatric ethics. The American Psychiatric Association has finessed this philosophical question by delineating its code of ethics as an "annotation" of the American Medical Association's principles of medical ethics (Table 35.1), adopting the same principles, but enhancing them with "annotations applicable to psychiatry" (American Psychiatric Association, 1995). Certainly these broad principles of medical ethics apply equally across all medical specialties: surgeons, internists, and psychiatrists share equally in the duty to "provide competent medical service with compassion and respect for human dignity," "deal honestly with patients and colleagues," "respect the rights of patients," and so forth.

Certain aspects of psychiatry, however, make it unique even among medical specialties. Because of their expertise, psychiatrists are given the awesome responsibility of assessing the state of other people's minds when a judg-ment is needed as to whether to deprive a person of his or her liberty for the sake of his or her mental health—a special status recognized in all 50 states and in most countries around the world. The very existence of psychiatric diagnoses has been defined as an ethical problem, since they relate so directly to subjective states and interpersonal behaviors in a way that the diagnoses of appendicitis and kidney stones do not. It is true that there is an ambiguous judgment call inherent in most medical conditions as to the precise border between normality and pathology (say, the defining limits of "borderline hypertension"), and these sometimes arbitrary judgments can carry important social consequences (whether an individual so defined can get life insurance or even employment, for example). But psychiatric diagnoses have historically carried a unique social stigma that may lead to complete exclusion or dehumanization, and in this connection psychiatry has also been pressed into the service of social control by courts and governments. Finally, psychiatrists more than any other physicians use themselves and their relationship with the patient as one of the most active in-

Table 35.1 Principles of medical ethics of the American Medical Association

Preamble
The medical profession has long subscribed to a body of ethical statements developed primarily for the benefit of the patient. As a member of this profession, a physician must recognize responsibility not only to patients but also to society, to other health professionals, and to self. The following Principles, adopted by the American Medical Association, are not laws but standards of conduct, which define the essentials of honorable behavior for the physician.

Section 1
A physician shall be dedicated to providing competent medical service with compassion and respect for human dignity.

Section 2
A physician shall deal honestly with patients and colleagues, and strive to expose those physicians deficient in character or competence, or who engage in fraud or deception.

Section 3
A physician shall respect the law and also recognize a responsibility to seek changes in those requirements which are contrary to the best interests of the patient.

Section 4
A physician shall respect the rights of patients, of colleagues, and of other health professionals, and shall safeguard patient confidences within the constraints of the law.

Section 5
A physician shall continue to study, apply, and advance scientific knowledge, make relevant information available to patients, colleagues, and the public, obtain consultation, and use the talents of other health professionals when indicated.

Section 6
A physician shall, in the provision of appropriate patient care, except in emergencies, be free to choose whom to serve, with whom to associate, and the environment in which to provide medical services.

Section 7
A physician shall recognize a responsibility to participate in activities contributing to an improved community.

Source: Code of Medical Ethics, American Medical Association, copyright 1996.

gredients in the treatment, and this raises unique and important questions about the boundaries of the professional relationship in psychiatry (see Chapter 1).

Theoretical Background

Before considering the practicalities of some of the major issues in psychiatric ethics, it is important to highlight briefly some historical and theoretical background. Ethics as a branch of philosophy has produced a glorious multitude of theories about what constitutes proper human conduct (MacIntyre, 1966). These theories are sometimes categorized as falling into one of two broad approaches to ethics: *teleological* and *deontological*. The term teleological comes from a Greek root which refers to a "goal" or "end" to be achieved. After defining this *telos* of human life, these theories call "ethical" those behaviors which lead toward the *telos* and "unethical" those which lead away from the *telos*. The most famous example of this approach is utilitarianism, the moral theory invented by Jeremy Bentham and developed by John Stuart Mill, which defines the *telos* as the greatest welfare for the greatest number of people (Mill, 1863). One can easily see how this utilitarian teleological approach has been so central to the field of medical ethics, since the promotion of human welfare forms the core of the profession.

In contrast to ethical theories which are teleological in their approach, there are also a number of important ethical theories which are *deontological*. This comes from a Greek root for "duty" and refers essentially to the duty to lead a "virtuous life." Deontological theories of ethics therefore define a concept of "the virtuous life," typically offering some list of virtues (honesty, courage, compassion, and so on) and vices (deceit, cowardice, selfishness, and so on). In these theories, the ethical life embraces the virtues and avoids the vices. In the medical context, a physician has certain duties to the patient which might be thought of in deontological terms (confidentiality, for example) in addition to the obvious teleological ethic of trying to improve the patient's welfare.

The values of these two historical approaches can collide in the ethical dilemmas faced by psychiatrists. In the example above, a psychiatrist may have to trade off the deontological duty to respect the autonomy of patients when this duty conflicts with the teleological value of safety and relief from suffering in the case of a psychotically depressed patient who hears command hallucinations to commit suicide: involuntary commitment may be the most appropriate medical response. In contrast, there may be cases when the deontological duty to preserve confidentiality must be upheld even when the psychia-

trist feels this would compromise the teleological value of disclosing confidential information—when, for example, such disclosure might be thought to benefit the patient clinically. The ethical dilemmas of psychiatry are properly called "dilemmas" because they entail such irreducible tradeoffs between important core values.

The Boundaries of Psychiatric Ethics

The field of ethics lacks distinct boundaries. Since a given case may raise questions that are simultaneously clinical, ethical, legal, financial, or technological in nature, these components often cannot be unambiguously distinguished. Indeed, the boundary of an ethical dilemma often blurs with questions of etiquette and local custom, and there are few ethical issues which are not grounded in cultural assumptions about proper behavior (from how doctors and patients address one another to the clothes they wear to the settings in which psychiatry is practiced). Even the AMA's first ethical principle, to provide "competent medical service," suggests a blurred boundary between those times when a physician may be practicing incompetently because of, say, impairment (psychiatric disability or drug addiction) and when that incompetence is more properly viewed as a breach of ethics, as when it stems from a drive to satisfy the psychiatrist's selfish desires at the expense of the needs of the patient. The "ethical principle" to provide "competent medical service" thus leaves ambiguous the issue of whether all incompetent care is *by definition* unethical, and this will always remain one of the blurred boundaries of the field of medical and psychiatric ethics.

Finally, there is obviously a sense in which specific ethical dilemmas in the practice of psychiatry are set within a larger field of the broader ethical questions of social policy. There is, for example, clearly an ethical dimension to the question of whether the allocation of resources for bypass surgery for octogenarian patients should be spent instead on depression screening programs to detect treatable psychopathology, which costs society vast resources in medical care, lost productivity, and social morbidity. While these larger questions can also be considered part of the field of psychiatric ethics, we will focus in the rest of this chapter on specific ethical issues in psychiatry which arise in everyday practice.

Major Topics in Psychiatric Ethics

The AMA's principles of medical ethics identify a number of broad headings which could be used to review the field of psychiatric ethics. Instead of surveying the field "principle by principle," this section reviews some of the major topics in psychiatric ethics, weaving those principles throughout the discussion. That is, the basic principles of respecting human dignity, truth telling, and treating patients with compassion are so central to medical and psychiatric ethics that they form a foundation underlying the discussion of any specific moral dilemma faced by psychiatrists. Although new technologies will continue to create new ethical dilemmas in medicine and psychiatry (the ethics of genetic testing is a good recent example), there exist certain long-standing issues which form the core of psychiatric ethics.

Informed Consent, Competency, and Involuntary Treatment

After the medical atrocities of the Nazis, the Declaration of Geneva established informed consent as one of the cornerstones of ethical medical care. The doctrine of informed consent is meant to allow patients to be partners in making treatment determinations that accord with their own needs and values. But as in most ethical domains, definitional gray areas immediately arise. In order to be meaningful, "informed consent" implies the *competent, voluntary* consent of a patient who understands all of the treatment alternatives, including the likely outcome of not pursuing any treatment. Terms such as "competent" and "voluntary" have clinical, ethical, and legal meanings which are not always congruent (Malcolm, 1988). Chapter 38, "Psychiatry and the Law," deals with issues such as legal competence and civil commitment. In the ethical domain, the issues surrounding competent, voluntary informed consent become highly charged in the setting of acutely depressed, anxious, paranoid, and psychotic patients. Such alterations of normal mental status may affect the patient's ability to understand the risks and benefits of a proposed treatment, or the patient's ability to make reasonable judgments about these risks and benefits.

Various legal mechanisms exist to try to deal with this problem, such as assigning a temporary legal guardian to make decisions for a patient whose judgment is grossly impaired by severe psychiatric illness. In practice, however, a psychiatrist must often use a considerable degree of judgment in determining just how much a patient understands of the treatment alternatives and risks and benefits involved. At one extreme, a psychiatrist may be faced with a competent patient in immediate danger of suicide who chooses to exercise his or her right to refuse treatment. At the other extreme, a psychiatrist may be faced with a severely psychotic patient who appears incapable of giving informed consent but who is quite willing to sign into the hospital.

While incapable of giving true informed consent, this latter patient is said to be giving "assent" to the treatment by entering the hospital and taking the medications provided. Situations like this raise the ethical dilemma of whether it shows more respect for the patient's dignity to insist on a guardianship or involuntary commitment in such cases (so as not to "take advantage" of the patient's lack of appreciation of his or her situation), or whether it shows more respect for the patient's dignity to accept the "assent" at face value (so as not to risk the therapeutic alliance by insisting on a guardianship or commitment with a willing patient). The intersection of the ethical, clinical, and legal aspects of such a case become apparent when the assenting incompetent patient, having been "voluntarily" admitted to the hospital, starts refusing to take the medication prescribed, and the doctors would then like to consider the guardianship option, even though they had previously regarded the patient as competent enough to make treatment decisions such as whether to sign into the hospital.

This example helps clarify the important point that "competent" is not a global attribute. When a question of competence arises, it is always important to ask the question: Competent to do *what*? Psychiatrists are considered competent to provide psychotherapy and medication for major depression, but not to perform an appendectomy for appendicitis. Similarly, in the American legal system, a person may be considered competent to get married or make out a will but still be considered incompetent to sign into a psychiatric hospital or refuse neuroleptic medication! In this system, *patients have both a right to refuse treatment and a right to treatment when they need it,* two legal rights that often play a central role in psychiatric ethics.

Confidentiality

Since the time of Hippocrates, physicians have upheld an ethical duty to maintain the confidentiality of their patients. The Hippocratic Oath states, "Whatsoever things I shall see or hear concerning the life of men in my attendance on the sick or even apart therefrom, which ought not to be raised abroad, I will keep silence thereon, counting such things to be as holy secrets" (Osler, 1922). *The Principles of Medical Ethics, with Annotations Especially Applicable to Psychiatry* states in Annotation 1 of Section 4 that "confidentiality is essential to psychiatric treatment. This is based in part on the special nature of psychiatric therapy as well as on the traditional ethical relationship between physician and patient" (American Psychiatric Association, 1995).

While confidentiality has long been considered one of the most vital ingredients to the trust between doctor and patient, this is all the more important in psychiatry, the specialty of medicine which has been most burdened by severe social stigma. Psychiatric records are often protected even more closely than other medical records, including protection of the very identification of a person as a patient. Even leaving a message on a patient's telephone answering machine to reschedule an appointment can be a breach of confidentiality when other family members are not aware of the treatment. Similarly, psychiatrists, more than other physicians, need to engage patients around questions such as whether the return address on a bill might unintentionally disclose their psychiatric treatment to a roommate.

Having emphasized the centrality of confidentiality to psychiatric ethics, it should not be surprising that most of the ethical dilemmas in this area concern instances when psychiatrists must disclose confidential information to others. For example, the insurance industry has for some time required patients to sign releases of information to validate the need for treatment in order to get that treatment covered by insurance. While this release of information has usually been kept confidential by the insurance company, this routine procedure has recently raised new challenges to the primacy of confidentiality in the era of electronic information systems and computerized records. Another common example comes from the split treatment model, in which one clinician provides psychotherapy and another prescribes medication. This model requires a very clear discussion with a patient about what information may be shared between the two practitioners.

Special ethical problems also arise around protection of confidentiality when treating minors, after a patient's death, and in child custody cases. Even in the academic literature, issues can arise when salient information must be changed to protect confidentiality in a case review, and such changes may compromise the ability to convey details relevant to an important clinical advance. The psychiatrist also has a duty to warn or protect other people who may be endangered by a patient, a potential conflict with the patient's confidentiality (see Chapter 38).

Maintaining Professional Boundaries

Boundaries have been defined as "the set of rules that establishes the professional relationship as separate from other relationships," such as social relationships (Frick, 1994). Boundary issues in psychiatry have received a great deal of publicity because of breaches of professional boundaries in the form of sexual relationships with patients. While there is now clear consensus that a sexual relationship with a patient is always unethical (see Chapter 1), many other boundary issues exist in the field of psychiatric ethics. The boundary conditions that define a professional relationship (in contrast to other relationships) include dimensions such as the appropriate time and place for the treatment; the doctor's billing the patient; appropriate physical contact, being limited to medically indicated examination and treatment; the absence of other business dealings or social contacts between doctor and patient; and perhaps most important the medical encounter's focus on the patient's problems, not the doctor's problems (Hundert and Appelbaum, 1995). Self-disclosure by psychiatrists about intimate details of their own lives is therefore considered a breach of professional boundaries (with the possible exception of substance abuse treatment, in which it has become common for treaters to talk about their own recovery from addiction). In the emotionally charged area of physical contact with patients beyond such legitimate medical interventions as checking blood pressure and examining patients for medication side effects, psychiatrists must be especially careful, for comforting pats of reassurance in particularly emotional sessions can blur into embraces more indicative of an intimate than a professional relationship (Simon, 1989).

It is important to note that it is the psychiatrist's, not the patient's, duty to maintain these professional boundaries (Gutheil, 1989). Psychiatrists must be vigilant about monitoring their own emotional lives as they make psychotherapeutic interventions. Boundaries must be maintained both to make the treatment effective and to guard against the exploitation of patients. It is only in the rare circumstance when a patient is becoming intrusive in the doctor's life, stalking the doctor or interfering with the doctor's home life, that the *patient's* breach of boundaries might become an indication for termination of a professional relationship. As one of the boundary conditions of the doctor-patient relationship, termination of that relationship carries with it a considerable ethical duty to ensure that patients are left in competent hands if they need continued care, or that patients understand why they no longer need care if they are not being referred to another treater. *Non-abandonment* is thus a central tenet of medical and psychiatric ethics.

The ethics of boundary issues can be understood in terms of the two general approaches to ethics discussed above. The teleological system reminds us that intentionally hurting patients instead of helping patients is unethical; the deontological system reminds us that breaching our duty and trust with patients is unethical. When psychiatrists find themselves slipping into a pattern of pushing the boundaries of standard therapeutic care, it is important that they seek assistance from a colleague and either get a consultation or consider terminating the treatment.

Double Agentry and Conflicts of Interest

The fundamental ethical principle that a physician always act in the patient's, and not in the doctor's own, interests (called the "fiduciary" relationship in the legal system) is central to psychiatric ethics. Double agentry occurs when a psychiatrist has a conflict of interest that interferes with this fiduciary responsibility to act in the best interests of the patient (Pope, 1991). In psychiatry, double agentry can occur when the doctor is conducting research using his or her own patients, when the doctor has a financial stake in the laboratory where blood tests are sent, when a doctor becomes an expert witness in a lawsuit involving a patient whom he or she has treated, or even when the doctor writes an academic article about a patient's case.

There are some highly specialized areas where an unavoidable dual relationship may entail conflicts with the psychiatrist's traditional duty to act only in the patient's best interests, such as in the practice of prison psychiatry (where assessments of patients' clinical progress may impact their parole) and in military psychiatry (where there is a need to get patients back into action). But psychiatrists who receive compensation from pharmaceutical companies or accept gifts or contracts from other industries put themselves into unnecessary dual relationships that may negatively influence the specific medications they prescribe or diagnostic studies they order.

While research ethics constitutes an important area of medical ethics generally, the questions about competence and informed consent discussed above in the treatment context make for unique ethical challenges in psychiatric research. In this research context, very complex determinations must be made both about the application of the informed consent doctrine and the ethical standard that clinical trials must have potential benefit to the patient and the minimum potential harm—determinations that will inevitably become confused if a single doctor fills the dual roles of treater and researcher.

Finally, as mentioned above, psychiatry has often been put in the position of having some agency of social control, protecting society from dangerous mentally ill patients (O'Brien-Steinfels and Levine, 1978). In light of the well-documented abuses of Soviet psychiatry in this context, every involuntary commitment case where a patient is assessed as "potentially dangerous" can be understood as a double agentry ethical dilemma, and psychiatrists must be particularly sensitive to power and authority issues before engaging in this practice. Psychiatry is notoriously inexact in the prediction of dangerousness. It is no small matter that this *uncertainty weighs asymmetrically* on the value scales in the ethical dilemma of involuntary commitment, and humility about our ability to predict a patient's future actions should always weigh on the side of pursuing less restrictive alternatives, even if the patient refuses needed treatment.

Managed Care

The advent of managed care has raised a number of important ethical concerns in medicine generally and in psychiatry in particular. While the fiduciary relationship discussed above is accepted as fundamental to medical and psychiatric ethics, certain types of managed care organizations establish a relationship between the physician and the health care organization that may be at odds with this traditional patient advocacy role. In some settings physicians are expected to be both allocators of resources and treaters; other systems even prohibit physicians by contract from disclosing the full range of treatment options necessary for fully informed consent. Physicians clearly engage in unethical psychiatric practice when more expensive but effective treatments are not disclosed to patients, or, indeed, when any financial incentives are not shared with all parties, thus keeping patients in the dark about important aspects of the clinical decision-making process.

This is not to say that managed care is by its nature unethical care. A well-designed health care organization may provide a framework for an even higher standard of ethical care (Massachusetts Medical Society, 1996). But this requires full disclosure to patients of all incentives, a realistic appeal mechanism if care is denied, and a focus on the primacy of patient welfare over any individual's financial interests. Ethical managed care requires that patients have real access to all of the benefits outlined in their insurance plan, and that benefits are presented to them in language they understand. Payments by or to physicians solely for the referral of patients, a type of fee splitting, is always unethical.

Specialized Topics in Psychiatric Ethics

In addition to the major topics discussed above, a number of specialized areas in psychiatry carry unique ethical considerations. The practice of child psychiatry (see Chapter 27), for example, has rather different boundary conditions from those outlined above. So does the practice of group therapy (Chapter 20). A well-developed and separate code of ethics exists for the practice of forensic psychiatry (Chapter 38) and for the practice of prison psychiatry and military psychiatry. In addition, unique ethical considerations exist in certain clinical subspecialties, including work in the consultation/liaison setting, psychoanalysis, the treatment of patients with mental retardation (Chapter 30), sex therapy (Chapter 23), and work with substance abuse patients (Chapter 18).

Other special clinical issues that often present ethical problems include the suicidal patient, the "VIP" patient, and such specialized treatment modalities as electroconvulsive therapy (Chapter 24) and psychosurgery. The relationship of psychiatrists to industry and the obligation to bill accurately for professional services rendered, by no means unique to psychiatry, must follow the ethical norms expected of all physicians.

Preventive Ethics

The best way to solve an ethical dilemma is to avoid being put in that situation in the first place. Some of the dilemmas described above are unavoidable, such as the dilemmas facing the military psychiatrist, or when a psychotically depressed patient presents with command hallucinations and a decision has to be made about involuntary hospitalization after the patient refuses treatment and no less restrictive alternative can be found. By contrast, many of the double agentry dilemmas faced by psychiatrists could have been prevented by avoiding the dual role that led to the problem. It just makes good ethical sense not to enroll your own patients in your own research protocols and not to engage in business ventures with patients.

Similarly, some psychiatrists find themselves in ethical dilemmas because they lack familiarity with the laws and statutes governing areas which impact clinical work. Psychiatrists can therefore practice their own "preventive ethics" through continuing education to maintain familiarity with these laws and statutes. For example, a thorough understanding of the laws regulating the reporting of suspected abuse, the duty to warn or protect, and the civil commitment statutes can often help psychiatrists avoid potential ethical pitfalls.

In the broader context, however, a basic question remains as to whether or not ethics can be "taught." Aristotle believed that, while ethics cannot be taught, it can be *learned!* To maintain accreditation, psychiatric residency training programs must include ethics training in the curriculum, and this often takes the form of case discussions and didactic seminars which review the ethical principles

and legal statutes psychiatrists need to know. However, Aristotle's belief grew out of his interest in character development over the first decades of life; the main literature on preventive ethics is probably better drawn from what is called "virtue theory" than from drilling residents in the 7 AMA principles of ethics.

In concrete terms, this means that psychiatrists need to remember some of the commonsense rules about maintaining their own health and well-being in order to be effective in the service of others. "Physician heal thyself" is not a bad motto for preventive ethics: preventive ethics for the psychiatrist who becomes addicted means not getting addicted in the first place. But the sine qua non of preventive ethics is adopting an attitude of constant humility so that when problems first arise, they are immediately identified and help is sought. The main enemy of ethical practice is not incompetence but arrogance.

References

American Psychiatric Association. 1995. *The principles of medical ethics, with annotations especially applicable to psychiatry.* Washington, D.C.: American Psychiatric Association.

Frick, D. E. 1994. Nonsexual boundary violations in psychiatric treatment. In *American Psychiatric Press review of psychiatry,* ed. Oldham, J. M., and Riba, M. B. Vol. 13. Washington, D.C.: American Psychiatric Press.

Gutheil, T. G. 1989. Borderline personality disorder, boundary violations, and patient-therapist sex: medicolegal pitfalls. *American Journal of Psychiatry* 146:597–602.

Hundert, E. M. 1990. Competing medical and legal ethical values: balancing problems of the forensic psychiatrist. In *Ethical practice in psychiatry and the law,* ed. Rosner, R., and Weinstock, R. New York: Plenum Press. 53–72.

Hundert, E. M., and Appelbaum, P. S. 1995. Boundaries in psychotherapy: model guidelines. *Psychiatry* 58:345–356.

MacIntyre, A. 1966. *A short history of ethics.* New York: Macmillan.

Malcolm, J. G. 1988. *Treatment choices and informed consent.* Springfield, Ill.: Charles C. Thomas.

Massachusetts Medical Society. 1996. *Ethical standards in managed care.* Waltham: Massachusetts Medical Society.

Mill, J. S. 1863. *Utilitarianism.* Reprinted in *Utilitarianism and other writings by J. S. Mill,* ed. Warnock, M. London: Collins, 1962.

O'Brien-Steinfels, M., and Levine, C., eds. 1978. *In the service of the state: the psychiatrist as double agent.* Hastings-on-Hudson, N.Y.: Hastings Center.

Osler, W. 1922. *The evolution of modern medicine.* New Haven: Yale University Press. 63–64.

Pope, K. S. 1991. Dual relationships in psychotherapy. *Ethics and Behavior* 1:21–34.

Simon, R. I. 1989. Sexual exploitation of patients: how it begins before it happens. *Psychiatric Annals* 19:104–112.

Recommended Reading

American Psychiatric Association. 1995. *Opinions of the Ethics Committee on the principles of medical ethics.* Washington, D.C.: American Psychiatric Association.

Appelbaum, P. S., Lidz, C. W., and Meisel, A. 1987. *Informed consent: legal theory and clinical practice.* New York: Oxford University Press.

Bloch, S., and Chodoff, P. 1991. *Psychiatric ethics,* 2nd ed. New York: Oxford University Press.

Epstein, R. S. 1994. *Keeping boundaries: maintaining safety and integrity in the psychotherapeutic process.* Washington, D.C.: American Psychiatric Press.

Gutheil, T. G., and Gabbard, G. O. 1993. The concept of boundaries in clinical practice: theoretical and risk-management dimensions. *American Journal of Psychiatry* 150:188–196.

Hundert, E. M. 1987. A model for ethical problem solving in medicine, with practical applications. *American Journal of Psychiatry* 144:839–846.

Reiser, S. J., Bursztajn, H. J., Appelbaum, P. S., and Gutheil, T. G. 1987. *Divided staffs, divided selves: a case approach to mental health ethics.* New York: Cambridge University Press.

Simon, R. I. 1991. *Clinical psychiatry and the law.* 2nd ed. Washington, D.C.: American Psychiatric Press.

Stone, A. A. 1984. *Law, psychiatry, and morality.* Washington, D.C.: American Psychiatric Press.

Szasz, T. S. 1988. *The theology of medicine: the political-philosophical foundations of medical ethics.* Syracuse, N.Y.: Syracuse University Press.

JANE M. MURPHY

MAURICIO TOHEN

MING T. TSUANG

Psychiatric Epidemiology

The years of publication of the *Harvard Guide to Psychiatry* have been a time of unprecedented activity for the field of psychiatric epidemiology. In the first edition, the chapter on psychiatric epidemiology (Beiser, 1978) reviewed the field up to the time of President Carter's Commission on Mental Health. The report of the Commission (President's Commission on Mental Health, 1978) emphasized the need for epidemiologic research, identified methodologic problems to overcome and gaps to fill, and laid the foundation for increased federal funding. In the same year, the *Archives of General Psychiatry* presented what has been described as a "classic issue for psychiatric epidemiology" in which a series of articles delineating emerging trends appeared (Weissman and Klerman, 1978; Robins, 1978).

In the second edition, the chapter on psychiatric epidemiology (Tsuang, Tohen, and Murphy, 1988) described the major products of the intervening decade. A centerpiece of that period was the publication of the third edition of *Diagnostic and Statistical Manual* (DSM-III) (American Psychiatric Association, 1980). This provided the conceptual basis through which the National Institute of Mental Health (NIMH) was able to develop the Diagnostic Interview Schedule (DIS) as a data-gathering procedure for large-scale epidemiologic studies (Robins et al., 1981). This schedule was then used in the Epidemiologic Catchment Area (ECA) Program (Regier et al., 1984; Robins and Regier, 1991). The ECA, conducted in 5 sites in the United States, was to date the largest of numerous studies concerned with providing epidemiologic data about psychiatric disorders.

The years leading up to this third edition have been a time of even greater activity. International collaborative efforts have come into the forefront. The World Health Organization (WHO) developed the Composite International Diagnostic Interview (CIDI), which is employed in numerous sites around the world (Robins et al., 1988). In modified form, the CIDI was used in the first nationwide investigation in the United States, the National Comorbidity Survey (NCS) (Kessler et al., 1994a, b; Kessler, 1995). In addition, genetic epidemiology of psychiatric disorders moved forward rapidly, and NIMH carried out a project to refine methods for a large-scale study of children and adolescents.

In order to present the field of psychiatric epidemiology, we divide this chapter into 4 parts. The first gives a general orientation to epidemiologic methods. The second describes a selection of cross-sectional studies of the prevalence of psychiatric disorders. The basic findings of these investigations are given, and the evolution of methods for case identification and diagnosis is also presented. The third part examines studies which go beyond cross-sectional prevalence and report findings about the incidence, clinical course, and mortality outcomes of psychiatric disorders. The fourth part describes research in the special areas of genetic epidemiology of psychiatric disorders, cross-national psychiatric epidemiology, and the epidemiology of psychiatric disorders among children and adolescents. In each part of the chapter, recent developments are described along with their historical background.

Methodologic Orientations

The purpose here is to provide a general overview of the field of epidemiology and the uses to which epidemiologic research can be directed. In addition, key concepts and their measurement will be discussed, and different strategies for designing epidemiologic research will be presented. This part ends with a review of issues concerning reliability and validity.

Definition and Uses of Epidemiology

Psychiatric epidemiology is the study of the distribution of mental illnesses in populations. The discipline takes its name from the word *epidemic,* meaning literally "on the people." The concepts of "exposures" and "outcomes" are fundamental to epidemiologic research (Tohen and Bromet, 1997). Often the subjects in an "exposed group" are those who have experienced a supposed causative factor which is hypothesized to have influence on a health "outcome," such as the emergence of an illness. Comparison of exposed and unexposed groups is therefore a crucial feature of epidemiologic analysis, whether in studies of large populations or in the growing field of clinical epidemiology.

One of epidemiology's classical studies involved an investigation of an outbreak of cholera in London during the middle of the nineteenth century. John Snow (1855) constructed a map of the Golden Square area of London at the site of the epidemic and, by plotting the distribution of cases, demonstrated that the outbreak centered on a well in Broad Street. He observed that a group of institutional inmates and the employees of a brewery, both of which had separate water supplies, remained free of cholera. This information suggested that contamination of drinking water might be related to the epidemic. By taking the handle off the Broad Street pump, Snow set in motion a series of events through which the epidemic was ultimately brought under control. At that point in time, the specific microorganism that causes cholera had not been identified, but the application of epidemiologic methods produced information about water contamination whereby effective prevention could be carried out.

Epidemiology today goes far beyond the study of sudden outbreaks of infectious diseases in populations (MacMahon and Trichopoulos, 1996). It can be thought of as having 3 overarching uses. One of these is to conduct research that may lead to etiologic knowledge and thereby to prevention. In view of contemporary evidence that most mental disorders are multifactorial in etiology, correlations between risk factors and rates of disorder are rarely enough. The strategy of epidemiology is usually a progressive one that grows incrementally toward gaining better and better clues regarding the complex factors involved in the origins and course of disorders.

A second important use is the contribution of epidemiology to understanding the clinical aspects of a disorder (Morris, 1957). In longitudinal studies of mental disorders identified in community populations, it is possible to investigate the natural history of a disorder in terms of course and outcome. Similarly in clinical epidemiologic studies treatment outcomes can be assessed. Information about course and outcome contributes to the evolution of psychiatric nosology by differentiating psychiatric conditions according to natural outcome or response to treatment.

The third main use of epidemiology relates to planning and evaluating health services and thus to the formation of policy. In this regard, epidemiology has become a central tool in the recent expansion of health services research. Epidemiology has not only the scientific purpose of contributing to knowledge about the origins, courses, and outcomes of psychiatric disorders but administrative purposes as well.

The language of epidemiology relies heavily on the word *disease*. Because the causes of most psychiatric conditions continue to be unknown, the language of psychiatry typically uses the word *disorder*. In this chapter, *disorder* will be used where in most epidemiologic texts *disease* would appear.

Prevalence and Incidence and Their Measurement

Several concepts and methods of epidemiology need to be presented as a basis for describing their application in psychiatric epidemiologic research. Enumeration plays a central role in epidemiology, and accurate demarcation between numerators and denominators is crucial to providing meaningful rates. Basic to epidemiologic inquiry are the concepts of *prevalence* and *incidence*.

Prevalence refers to the proportion of a population affected by a disorder at a given point in time (*point prevalence*) or over a period of time such as 6 months or a year (*period prevalence*). Prevalence disregards when the disorders had their onset and indiscriminately counts new cases, chronic cases, and recurrent cases so long as they are in evidence at the time of enumeration. Thus a prevalence rate counts all new and chronic cases in the numerator while the denominator refers to the total population at risk, including those with the disorder. A prevalence rate is a useful device for describing and comparing populations, especially when the purpose is to plan or evaluate services.

Recent psychiatric epidemiologic investigations have made extensive use of *lifetime prevalence*. The numerator for a lifetime prevalence rate consists of the number of persons who have ever had the disorder up to the time of investigation, including those who have recovered, while the denominator refers to the total population. The emergence of lifetime prevalence as an important product of epidemiologic research results from the need for population norms appropriate for family studies concerned with genetic contributions to a disorder. For example, lifetime rates among siblings and other first-degree relatives are uninterpretable unless compared with the norms for large general populations. Lifetime prevalence is not, however, free of interpretive difficulties owing to the fact that it is usually based on information gathered at one point in time from samples of the population with a broad age range. Lifetime prevalence among the elderly covers a much longer period of risk than that among younger people. Hence, problematic issues about retrospective recall are involved.

Incidence refers to the proportion of a population which becomes affected with a disorder for the "first ever" time during a specified period, and so can be thought of as dealing with "new cases" (Rothman, 1986). Incidence is especially useful in theoretical studies of causal factors. Because the point in time when a disorder first appears is the primary concern, it is sometimes possible to identify relevant events that are antecedent to the disorder and therefore possibly of etiologic significance.

An incidence study involves investigating persons who are known to be well at the beginning of an interval of observation and then following them over a period of time to see how many and when individuals become ill for the first time. It is necessary to take into account not only the number of persons observed but also the duration of observation for each person. The combination of persons in a population and the passage of time is known as "person-years" or "person-time."

Incidence is figured by dividing the number of new cases by the sum of the time periods of observations for all individuals in the population at risk. A hypothetical example of an incidence rate would be the number of suicides among 1000 manic patients who are observed for a 5-year period. While these patients may have attempted suicide earlier, completed suicide is clearly a "first ever" occurrence, and therefore it is appropriate to speak of the incidence of suicide. The numerator represents the number of patients who committed suicide and the denominator the 1000 manic patients times 5 years, or 5000 "person-years."

In psychiatric epidemiology, prevalence investigations far outnumber incidence studies. This is due to the fact that for an incidence investigation it is necessary to carry out a prevalence study as a first step followed by a longitudinal study in which all subjects are reassessed at a later time. Based on the results of the prevalence study, researchers can remove the persons who are or have been ill from the analysis in order to focus on those who had never been ill according to the first assessment. Those who had never been ill constitute the population at risk for a "first ever" occurrence of the disorder. The denominator consists of "person-years of observation" in reference to this population at risk, and the numerator consists of those who became ill during the interval of study.

When dealing with chronic or recurrent disorders, prevalence rates are higher than those for incidence. In fact, prevalence and incidence are formally related to each other through the duration of illness. Prevalence equals incidence times average duration. Thus prevalence is high relative to incidence owing to the accumulation of chronic and recurrent cases at any one point in time.

Design of Epidemiologic Studies

Although epidemiology is based on the concept of a population, studies often begin in hospitals or clinics. Especially in regard to rare disorders, it is more economical to identify cases where they are known to be concentrated. Depending on the purpose of the investigation, various strategies are used in which cases are compared to subjects selected as non-cases. The non-cases are frequently called "control subjects" or "normal controls" or more simply and accurately "a comparison group."

The main goal of epidemiologic research is to determine the level of association between exposures and outcomes. A commonly used measure of association is "relative risk," which is the ratio between the rate of a disorder among the exposed and unexposed groups. Figure 36.1 illustrates the concept of relative risk and its calculation.

Study populations in epidemiological research are selected according to disorder status or exposure status.

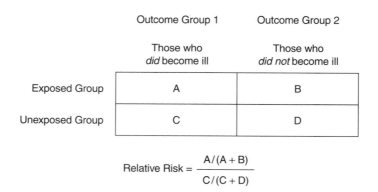

Figure 36.1 Calculation of relative risk.

A useful set of terms for referring to the designs of such investigations includes *experimental, quasi-experimental, cross-sectional, longitudinal cohort (prospective and retrospective),* and *case/control.*

A clinical trial is an example of an experimental design in which the study population is exposed to a specific treatment in order to measure an outcome. Essential elements for a valid clinical trial are: (1) randomization to ensure comparability of population, (2) use of a placebo to ensure comparability of effects, and (3) use of blinding to ensure comparability of information (Miettinen, 1985). The goal of randomization is to produce demographic and clinical comparability across study groups. The use of a placebo allows extraneous effects to be taken into account. To control for comparability of information, the investigator can use a single-blind design whereby patients are kept uninformed regarding the group to which they have been assigned (placebo, treatment X, or treatment Y). In a double-blind study, both the investigators and the patients remain uninformed about treatment assignment. In a triple-blind study, statistical analysts are kept similarly unaware of group assignment.

Many questions of interest in psychiatric epidemiology do not allow the use of experimental designs. Under some circumstances, however, quasi-experimental designs can be used in natural settings, as, for example, in disaster research. An outcome such as the development of post-traumatic stress disorder can be investigated where a portion of a population is exposed to a disaster such as an earthquake and another portion is not.

In contrast to experimental designs, *observational studies* are carried out in natural settings and can be divided into cross-sectional and longitudinal studies. Cross-sectional studies are carried out at one point in time and do not permit a clear-cut assessment of antecedent and consequent events, nor of the time interval between cause and effect. Cross-sectional studies are typically employed to obtain prevalence data. While useful for assessing service needs, they are of limited utility for causal inquiry.

Longitudinal research is characterized by a time interval over which subjects or patients are followed for further study. Often a longitudinal study is guided by a hypothesized cause, the effect of which is studied in terms of subsequent events. Such investigations are usually divided into *cohort* and *case/control* studies.

A cohort is a defined group of persons who are followed or traced over a period of time. In cohort studies, subjects are classified in terms of exposure or non-exposure status and are observed for a specified period of time to determine the presence or absence of an outcome. Cohort studies can be prospective or retrospective. A pro-

spective cohort study resembles an experimental design except that the exposure/nonexposure status is not based on random assignment. An example of such a study would be a cohort of patients with a first episode of mania where the exposure variable concerns the presence or absence of comorbid substance abuse and the outcome of interest would be relapse into another manic episode. Other comparison groups could include patients suffering from unipolar depression or schizophrenia.

One strength of a prospective cohort study is avoidance of selection bias. Since outcomes have not been determined at the beginning, there is no possibility that knowledge of outcome can bias assignment to exposed and unexposed status. Such studies also allow investigation of the temporal sequence between exposure status and disorder status, but they tend to be costly and sometimes are not feasible.

In a retrospective cohort study, subjects are assigned to exposure status after the outcome has occurred. Often archived medical records provide information about whether a given subject belongs in the exposed or nonexposed group. While retrospective cohort designs are low in cost and high in feasibility, their dependence on information collected in the past can be a disadvantage.

Longitudinal case/control studies utilize a design in which the *cases* are those who have a given disorder and *controls* are those who do not. Patients are then evaluated in terms of prior exposure or nonexposure. Such investigations are especially useful for studying rare conditions such as multiple personality disorder. Population-based investigations need to be extremely large in scale to provide a sufficient number of rare conditions for adequate investigation. A weakness of case/control studies, however, is the potential for recall bias. For example, in a study of teratogenic effects caused by a given substance, mothers who have given birth to congenitally malformed children may be more likely to recall exposure to the substance of interest than those mothers who delivered healthy babies.

Reliability and Validity

Whether an epidemiologic study involves a survey of a general population or a strategy in which cases and noncases are compared, issues about the *reliability* and *validity* of case identification and diagnosis are of paramount concern. Campbell and Fiske (1959, p. 83) describe these 2 concepts in a way which underscores their differences and similarities: "Reliability is the agreement between two efforts to measure the same trait through maximally similar methods. Validity is represented in the agreement between two attempts to measure the same trait by maximally different methods."

In shorthand, reliability refers to consistency of assessment and validity refers to accuracy and verifiability. Validity is a higher-order quality, but it cannot be achieved in the absence of reliability. It is possible, in other words, to be consistently wrong about something, but accurate assessment cannot be achieved if similar methods for testing it are in disagreement. Demonstrating validity is usually the more difficult task because it requires that the methods of assessment be genuinely independent.

Much research effort in psychiatric epidemiology has been devoted to questions about reliability and validity. Psychiatry is not alone in needing to demonstrate these qualities in its measurements, but the absence of biological markers for identifying most types of psychiatric conditions has had the effect of heightening awareness of these issues. In making diagnoses, psychiatrists mainly depend on what patients or their family members say in response to questions or on observations of behavior. Interviewing and observing are thus key methods of case identification. The strategies for showing validity in psychiatric assessments thus often involve comparison of different methods of interviewing and observing.

It is now well recognized that the reliability of psychiatric diagnoses has been improved by the advances in classification systems such as are available in DSM-IV (American Psychiatric Association, 1994) and in the tenth edition of the *International Classification of Diseases* (ICD) (World Health Organization, 1994).

The magnitude of the influence of these classification systems on the course of psychiatric epidemiology can hardly be overestimated. They have laid the foundation for improved case identification procedures so that much more comparability from study to study is beginning to be realized. This advance can best be conceptualized as having 2 levels, 1 general and 1 specific. At the general level is the fact that these systems indicate that a *syndrome* of symptoms is the basis for a diagnostic category and that a syndrome can be recognized through its *essential features* and *associated symptomatology* and by the fact that it has some persistence over time as *duration*. Gradually it is being recognized that it would be useful to include *disability* at this general level.

At the specific level is the fact that these classifications describe the substance of different diagnostic categories and spell out explicit criteria whereby they should be recognized. For example, DSM-IV identifies 9 features of the syndrome of major depression (depressed mood, loss of interest, weight loss or gain, insomnia or hypersomnia, psychomotor agitation or retardation, fatigue, feelings of

worthlessness, concentration difficulties, and recurrent thoughts of death). For a diagnosis of major depression, 5 of these symptoms must be present in a given 2-week period *(duration)* and at least 1 of these symptoms must be depressed mood or loss of interest (*essential features,* with the others being considered *associated symptoms*). Other criteria include that these symptoms do not meet the criteria for a "mixed episode," that they cause distress or impairment, that they are not due to the effects of medication or medical conditions, and are not better accounted for by bereavement. It can be seen in these criteria that *disability* is not absent, but neither is it a requirement, a point which is in line with questions about the role of disability in diagnosis.

With increasing evidence of reliability, validity is assuming the position of a primary target for research efforts. In the past, validation studies for psychiatric epidemiology were typically of 2 types. One type depended on comparison of the results of interviewing with a given protocol a series of patients and "presumed normals." Such a protocol usually involved interviewing methods which had some degree of "structure," by which is meant that the questions were formulated in advance and were asked in the same manner of all subjects. If the interview protocol clearly discriminated between the patients and the normal subjects, its validity was considered to be acceptable. The other type compared the results from such a protocol with an "unstructured" assessment carried out by a clinical psychiatrist on the same subjects. If the psychiatrist's assessments agreed with the protocol results, the validity of the protocol was considered adequate.

At the present time, validity studies typically use as the "gold standard" the results of having a psychiatrist or clinical psychologist interview a series of ill and well subjects using a "structured" interview schedule which calls for clinical judgments to be made at various points in the interview process. Such an approach was used, for example, in assessing the validity of the *Diagnostic Interview Schedule* (DIS) (Anthony et al., 1985; Helzer et al., 1985). The DIS is administered by "lay interviewers" who, although trained for the DIS, are not necessarily trained in a clinical discipline. Such "lay interviewers" are not allowed to make clinical judgments as they proceed through an interview. The difference between the "gold standard" and the procedure being validated is thus largely a matter of clinical judgment, since both the "lay" and "professional" interviewers make use of "structured" schedules.

Such strategies for validation are limited to information gathered at one point in time and utilize patient status or clinical interview as the criterion of validity. It has been emphasized by Robins and Guze (1970) that validation should draw on genetic evidence, laboratory investigations, and response to treatment, as well as interviewing procedures. Spitzer (1983) also pointed to the importance of expanding the components of validation studies. He proposed that 3 concepts should guide validation research: (1) that longitudinal data be incorporated, (2) that panels of psychiatric experts carry out the review, and (3) that all possible data be assembled. With an emphasis on Longitudinal, Expert, and All Data, he suggested that this approach be designated as using a "LEAD" standard.

Prevalence Studies

Cross-sectional studies of the prevalence of psychiatric disorders among adults in different places and at different historical periods are, by a wide margin, the most common type of psychiatric epidemiologic investigation. They involve estimates based on utilizing both treatment records (treated prevalence) and samples of general populations (sometimes called true prevalence studies). The purpose of this part of the chapter is to describe some of the well-known investigations and give a few findings from each. The studies are arranged chronologically so that the evolution of case identification methods can be shown and the historical periods of foment and change can be perceived. Common to all of the studies is the fact that they are oriented to the one point in time when data were gathered.

Before and during the Second World War

One of the earliest of the studies concerned with true prevalence was carried out in Massachusetts in the mid-nineteenth century. Cases were identified not only through hospital records but also through key informants, such as clergymen (Jarvis, 1971). Indicative of the language of psychiatric diagnosis at that time, the results indicated that there were 2632 "lunatics" and 1087 "idiots" in need of care.

Throughout the end of the century and into the next, most of the investigations drew solely on treatment records, although there were a few exceptions in Germany, Switzerland, and Scandinavia. Dohrenwend and Dohrenwend (1969) provide a review of these early studies.

In 1932 and 1934 a treated prevalence study was carried out in Chicago by Faris and Dunham (1939). This investigation found that the residential address given by patients on entering psychiatric hospitals was related to the diagnoses they received. Rates of schizophrenia were highest for those who lived in deteriorated, rooming house areas at the center of the city (36% of admissions), while such rates were lowest for those living on the peripheries (13% of admissions). This study provided early information about an inverse relationship between the prevalence of some types of psychiatric disorder and socioeconomic status, a relationship which continues to generate considerable research and theorizing.

During the Second World War, Bremer (1951) carried out an investigation of the total population of a community in northern Norway where he had been posted as a physician. His assessments were based on extensive firsthand knowledge of 1080 residents over the age of 10. His information indicated that, over his 5 years of observation ending in March 1944, 22% of this population suffered from some kind of recognizable psychiatric disorder, usually a chronic disorder. He noted that this percentage would increase to 23% if those who experienced "war neuroses" were added.

From the Second World War to DSM-III

World War II was a turning point in psychiatric epidemiology in the United States (Weissman and Klerman, 1978; Bromet, 1995). One formative influence was the emerging evidence that many recruits to the armed forces were being rejected for psychiatric reasons, and that a large number of soldiers were later discharged for psychiatric disability. After the war, the need for better information about the prevalence of psychiatric disorders irrespective of treatment was broadly appreciated not only in the United States but elsewhere as well.

One of the first postwar investigations was carried out between 1946 and 1948 in Taiwan and concerned a population of 19,931 persons (Lin, 1953). The method of case identification in this study relied heavily on leaders and other knowledgeable persons in different locales to identify persons who were believed to suffer from a psychiatric disorder. Subsequently psychiatrists interviewed those so identified. The total prevalence when all types of psychiatric disorders were grouped together (schizophrenia, manic-depressive psychoses, senile psychoses, other psychoses, mental deficiency, psychopathic personality, and psychoneuroses) was approximately 11 per 1000.

This prevalence rate is much lower than the 22 per 100 reported by Bremer. The difference probably reflects the difficulties posed for identifying less flamboyant symptomatology through key informants for a population of nearly 20,000 compared to firsthand knowledge by a physician of a population of approximately 1000.

Fifteen years later the same group of researchers carried

out a second cross-sectional study using the same methods relevant to a similarly sized Taiwanese population. They reported that prevalence had significantly increased to 17 per 1000 (Lin et al., 1969). The increase was largely due to disorders in the category which at that time was labeled "psychoneurotic." Nevertheless, these rates for Taiwan remained lower than those in most subsequent studies.

In 1947 the Lundby Study was started in rural Sweden (Essen-Möller, 1956). In this investigation, psychiatrists observed and interviewed all adults and children of a rural population that numbered 2550 residents. Using a biologically oriented approach to diagnosis, their enumeration included mental retardation, psychoses, personality deviations, neuroses, alcoholism, and so on. The estimates of prevalence ranged from 8.4% for the most obvious psychopathology to 28.2% when probable cases were included. Ten years later a repeated cross-sectional study was carried out (Hagnell, 1966). Lifetime prevalence at this time was summarized as consisting of 1.7% psychosis, 13.1% neurosis, and 1.2% mental deficiency.

In 1950 a treated prevalence study was initiated in New Haven, Connecticut. Making use of data about patients receiving treatment in both public and private facilities, Hollingshead and Redlich (1958) conducted an investigation focused on social class. A main finding was that patients from the lower socioeconomic levels were likely to be treated with pharmacotherapy or electroconvulsive therapy while most of the patients who received psychotherapy belonged to the upper social classes. Treated prevalence was highest for the lowest social class (1.7%), while the rates across the middle and upper classes varied only from 0.5% to 0.7%.

In North America at this time, considerable sociological experience had been gained in doing surveys with probability samples of populations using structured interviews. This approach meant that each sample member was asked the same questions, that the questions were worded in standard ways, and that the subject was requested to respond in predetermined categories. In addition, the war had provided experience in designing and utilizing methods for gathering psychiatric information from large populations. For example, a group of army researchers had constructed a symptom inventory to help screen recruits, the army's Neuropsychiatric Screening Adjunct (NSA) (Star, 1950). A similar civilian effort had produced the Cornell Selectee Index (Weider et al., 1944). While each of these inventories was administered as a paper and pen test, they were the forerunners of the type of systematic inquiry regarding psychiatric symptoms in-

tended for face-to-face interviews in which a schedule of questions would be asked by a trained interviewer in a "knock-on-door" survey.

In 1952 a study which utilized the survey method approach was started in Atlantic Canada in Stirling County, a rural area of 20,000 residents (Leighton, 1961; Leighton, Harding, et al., 1963). A sample of 1010 adults was visited by trained interviewers using a structured schedule which included a number of questions from the NSA and other schedules. In addition, the general physicians practicing in the county were interviewed about these same subjects. These materials were brought together so that they could be read and evaluated by psychiatrists. DSM (American Psychiatric Association, 1952) provided a catalogue of terms for describing disorders, but the evaluation process required the psychiatrists to rate their confidence in recognizing psychiatric syndromes through the pattern of essential features and associated symptoms, duration of illness, and functional impairment related to the disorder. When all diagnoses were enumerated together, current prevalence was estimated to be 20%.

Eighteen years later a repeated cross-sectional survey of a newly drawn sample was conducted (Murphy, 1980; Murphy et al., 1984). Focusing only on the common disorders of depression and anxiety, information about which came from interviews with subjects, the study reported that current prevalence remained remarkably stable: 12.5% in 1952 and 12.7% in 1970, when depression and anxiety were aggregated together. There were no significant changes in the 2 categories and no interactions of time, age, and gender.

The Midtown Manhattan Study was instigated in 1954 and concerned residents of a district in New York City (Srole et al., 1962; Langner and Michael, 1963). The interview schedule was similar to that used in the Stirling County Study, but the evaluation procedures were different. Drawing on Menninger's (1959) unitary concept of mental illness, in which disorders are conceived to vary more in degree than in kind, psychiatrists in the Midtown Study rated the assembled materials in terms of a continuum of symptoms, severity, and impairment rather than in diagnostic terms. Based on a sample of 1660 adults, the study indicated that the prevalence of cases with a level of symptom severity that could be thought typical of clinical disorders was 23.4%.

Inter-rater reliability was found to be satisfactory in the Midtown and Stirling studies, but comparability of case identification across the studies remained unknown. Each study also produced a short inventory of questions about symptomatology which was intended to be used for screening large populations. From the Stirling Study came the Health Opinion Survey (HOS) (Macmillan, 1957) and from the Midtown Study the Twenty-Two Item Scale Indicating Psychiatric Impairment (22IS) (Langner, 1962). In the years which followed, several studies were carried out which used one or another of these scales (Manis et al., 1964; Phillips, 1966; Dohrenwend, 1967; Dohrenwend and Dohrenwend, 1969; Husaini, Neff, and Stone, 1979; Schwab et al., 1979; Kessler and McRae, 1981). The number of symptoms reported were counted, and a cutting-point was used to identify cases.

A large number of such screening instruments now exist, such as the Center for Epidemiologic Studies Depression Scale (CES-D) (Radloff, 1977); the General Health Questionnaire (GHQ) (Goldberg, 1972); and the Hopkins Symptom Checklist (HSCL) (Derogatis et al., 1974). While this type of case identification is systematic, it differs markedly from having the materials evaluated by psychiatrists and from employing operational criteria for separate diagnoses. The cases are not diagnostically differentiated; durational features tend not to be clearly specified; and essential and associated symptoms are not distinguished. Most of the studies using the cutting-point method were presented as having measured "general mental health," "psychiatric impairment," or "psychological distress."

In the late 1950s some puzzling findings about case identification put diagnostic reliability in the forefront for more than a generation and led to a different type of instrument development. It was pointed out by Kramer (1961) that while the overall rate of mental hospitalization in the United States was similar to that in the United Kingdom, the diagnostic composition of the patients in U.S. hospitals was conspicuously different from that of patients in U.K. hospitals.

This discrepancy prompted the U.S.-U.K. Diagnostic Project, which was aimed at determining whether the difference was real or an artifact related to dissimilar diagnostic practices (Cooper et al., 1972). Though not an epidemiologic study in and of itself, the U.S.-U.K. study had a strong impact on the field by showing that the diagnostic criteria for schizophrenia were much broader in the United States than in Britain. In a New York hospital 61% of the patients were diagnosed as schizophrenic, while in a London hospital only 34% of the patients were so diagnosed. A major finding was that, when a structured interview was used with standardized diagnostic criteria, the differences became insignificant.

An interview schedule that played an important role in

the U.S.-U.K. study was the Present State Examination (PSE) (Wing, Cooper, and Sartorius, 1974). The PSE is a guide for structuring a clinical interview in order to assess the present mental state of patients who may be suffering from a neurosis or functional psychosis. It incorporates the diagnostic practices of psychiatrists in western Europe and many other parts of the world. Because this interview focuses on symptoms experienced in the previous month, it does not provide "lifetime diagnoses," and it does not cover substance abuse as well as some of the psychiatric categories which are usually included in current epidemiologic research.

The PSE needs to be administered by an experienced clinician, but the clinician's evaluation of the responses is recorded in such a fashion that analysis can be carried out by a diagnostic computer program named CATEGO. The computer program uses thresholds regarding the frequency and patterning of symptoms (Wing et al., 1978). Above the threshold used for case identification, the CATEGO program generates diagnoses compatible with the *International Classification of Diseases* (ICD) (World Health Organization, 1994). CATEGO does this by applying complex algorithms rather than by simply counting symptoms and using a cutting-point.

The PSE and CATEGO procedures have been used in several epidemiologic studies. For example, these procedures were used in a "two-stage" investigation in the Camberwell area of London (Bebbington et al., 1981). Typical of "two-stage" designs, a short set of PSE questions was used as a screening instrument, following which a subsample was interviewed by clinicians using the full PSE. Overall current prevalence was estimated to be 10.9%, which is a lower figure than that found in other studies which use diagnostic interviews. The smaller proportion of psychiatrically ill persons identified is partly due to the fact that the PSE does not cover alcohol abuse/ dependence and probably also due to the level of attrition associated with a two-stage design.

The PSE was also employed in a well-known study of depression among English women (Brown and Harris, 1978). In full or modified form, the PSE was also used in Australia (Henderson et al., 1979), Finland (Lehtinen et al., 1990), and Scotland (Dean, Surtees, and Sashidharan, 1983).

On this side of the Atlantic, efforts were also carried out to operationalize criteria for psychiatric diagnoses and produce interview schedules which implement the criteria. Among the first endeavors of this kind in the United States was the work of members of the Washington University Department of Psychiatry. Their criteria were published and are often referred to as the "Feighner criteria" in reference to the first author (Feighner et al., 1972). The Washington University group also produced the Renard Diagnostic Interview Schedule, which can be used to assess patients according to the Feighner criteria (Helzer et al., 1981).

Shortly thereafter, the Research Diagnostic Criteria (RDC) were developed as part of the Collaborative Study of the Psychobiology of Depression, sponsored by the National Institute of Mental Health (NIMH) (Katz et al., 1979). Although this study was a naturalistic investigation of patients, it influenced epidemiology by producing the means for more efficient and reliable diagnosis. The RDC criteria reflect collaborative efforts between members of psychiatric units at Columbia and Washington universities (Spitzer, Endicott, and Robins, 1978).

The Schedule for Affective Disorders and Schizophrenia (SADS) is an interview guide designed to provide information that can be analyzed according to the RDC (Endicott and Spitzer, 1978). It was a chief method of data collection in the Psychobiology of Depression Study. One version, known as the SADS-L, gathers information for lifetime diagnoses. Another version, SADS-C, was designed to measure change in psychopathology. The SADS was constructed with the intent that the interviewer would have clinical training and that the diagnostic decisions would be made by the clinician-interviewer after reviewing the RDC.

The SADS-L was used for an epidemiologic study in New Haven which demonstrated that an instrument designed for clinical investigations could be employed for case identification and diagnoses in an epidemiologic study of a general population (Weissman, Myers, and Harding, 1978). The SADS was also the main source of diagnostic information in a study of the Amish in Lancaster County, Pennsylvania, even though the initial screening in this close-knit group was carried out first by local informants (Egland and Hostetter, 1983).

DSM-III to the 1990s

The Second World War was described above as a major impetus for psychiatric epidemiologic studies of general populations. The next event which served as impetus, this time for improvement rather than initiation of studies, was the double circumstance of the Carter administration's President's Commission on Mental Health and the development of DSM-III, which was being circulated in prepublication drafts at approximately the same time. The commission outlined the mandate, and DSM-III provided a means for implementing improvement.

Following the commission's report, the Division of Biometry and Epidemiology of NIMH sponsored the development of the Diagnostic Interview Schedule (DIS) (Robins et al., 1981), which was used in the Epidemiologic Catchment Area (ECA) program. While the DIS contains questions pertinent to many diagnoses, the interviewers do not make clinical judgments and are not allowed to interpret the meaning of the responses. The diagnostic usefulness of the interview resides in the selection, sequence, and wording of the questions, as well as in the consistency with which it is administered from one individual to the next. Many instructions about how to proceed through the interview appear in the text of the schedule, including when and how to probe for further information or for clarification. These instructions are supplemented by a manual of specifications. Furthermore, interviewers receive an intensive period of training and practice before participating in a study.

The DIS gathers information for diagnoses that occur throughout the subject's life up to the time of interview and gives considerable attention to defining the age at onset of pertinent symptoms. By virtue of using predetermined response categories, the products of the interview are usually analyzed by means of a computer program. The DIS can be analyzed so as to produce diagnoses according to DSM-III, the RDC, and the Feighner criteria. This schedule has been updated periodically to match changes in diagnostic criteria and, at the present time, a version is available for implementing the criteria of DSM-IV.

The goal of the ECA program was to obtain prevalence and incidence data and to gather information about the use of health and mental health services (Regier et al., 1984; Shapiro et al., 1984; Eaton and Kessler, 1985; Robins and Regier, 1991). The sample was composed of approximately 20,000 community and institutional residents from 5 geographically defined mental health catchment areas. For each of these areas, researchers from a local university conducted the study: New Haven (Yale University), Baltimore (Johns Hopkins University), Raleigh-Durham (Duke University), St. Louis (Washington University), and Los Angeles (University of California at Los Angeles). Subjects were randomly selected at each site. The sampling was not, therefore, designed to provide national estimates but rather to gather information about these specific populations.

In Table 36.1, lifetime, 1-year, and 1-month prevalence rates are shown for the different diagnoses provided by administering the DIS to subjects at all sites (Regier et al., 1988; Robins, Locke, and Regier, 1991). The ECA estimated that 32% of adults in these catchment areas had suffered from some kind of psychiatric disorder at some point in their lives. The specific category with the highest lifetime prevalence (16.4%) is for substance abuse (mainly alcohol abuse and/or dependence), and the second highest (14.6%) is for anxiety disorders (mainly phobia).

The 1-year and 1-month rates are understandably lower, but they follow a somewhat different pattern. It is estimated that 15.4% had some kind of psychiatric disorder during the month when the interview was conducted. The specific category with the highest 1-month rate of 7.3% is, however, for anxiety disorders, the second highest at 5.1% is for affective disorders. Substance abuse is third in rank at 3.8%. The shift of substance abuse from having the highest lifetime rate to a much lower 1-month rate suggests that it is a less chronic disorder than the anxiety disorders.

When all of the ECA data were combined, several important and consistent findings were noted. One is that the overall and specific rates were very similar from site to site. Another was that both lifetime and current prevalence were higher among younger than older people. Another was that women had higher rates of major depression while men had higher rates of alcohol abuse.

Another interesting finding was the high prevalence of comorbidity, especially that involving substance abuse and non-substance psychiatric disorders. For example, individuals with an alcohol disorder had a high probability of having another DSM-III disorder, with anxiety being the most common combining disorder. Conversely, focusing on a non-substance disorder such as bipolar disorder, researchers found that those so diagnosed exhibited an exceptionally high level (61%) of comorbidity with substance abuse (Tohen, 1994; Tohen and Goodwin, 1995).

Of equal and major interest was evidence that a large volume of psychiatric disorders were untreated either by specialty or general health services. Only 19% of those with an active disorder in the recent year reported having been treated "for a mental problem" in either an inpatient or outpatient setting during that year. This evidence contributed substantially to the growth of the field of "mental health services research" and to the continuing evidence that general physicians play a prominent role in the delivery of services for psychiatric disorders (Regier, Goldberg, and Taube, 1978; Regier et al., 1993).

While the ECA investigations were in process during the 1980s, Dohrenwend and colleagues carried out a

Table 36.1 Prevalence rates per 100 by diagnosis from the ECA

Diagnoses	Lifetime	1-year	1-month
Any psychiatric disorder	32.2	19.0	15.4
Substance abuse disorders	16.4	—	3.8
Alcohol abuse/dependence	13.3	6.3	2.8
Drug abuse/dependence	5.9	2.5	1.3
Schizophrenic and schizophreniform disorders	1.5	1.0	0.7
Affective disorders	8.3	—	5.1
Manic episode	0.8	0.6	0.4
Major depressive episode	5.8	3.7	2.2
Dysthymia	3.3	3.3	3.3
Anxiety disorders	14.6	—	7.3
Panic	1.6	0.9	0.5
Phobia	12.5	8.8	6.2
Obsessive-compulsive	2.5	1.7	1.3
Somatization disorder	0.1	0.1	0.1
Antisocial personality disorder	2.5	1.2	0.5
Severe cognitive impairment	1.3	1.3	1.3

Sources: The rates for lifetime and 1-month assessment are taken from Regier et al., 1988 (*Archives of General Psychiatry* 45 [1988]: 977–986, copyright 1988 by the American Medical Association) and are standardized to the age, sex, and race distribution of the 1980 noninstitutionalized population of the United States aged 18 years and older and are based on interviews with 18,571 subjects. The 1-year rates are taken from Robins and Regier, 1991 (*Psychiatric Disorders in America* [1991], pp. 328–366, reprinted by permission of Simon and Schuster). Dysthymia and cognitive impairment have no recency information, and thus the rates are the same for all 3 time periods.

cross-sectional psychiatric epidemiologic study in Israel specifically to investigate the relationship between prevalence and socioeconomic status (SES) (Dohrenwend et al., 1992). In the first phase of a two-stage design, portions of the Psychiatric Epidemiologic Research Instrument (PERI) (Dohrenwend, Levav, and Shrout, 1986) were utilized. The PERI measures dimensions of psychopathology which may cross-cut the different diagnostic categories and was employed to screen a population of 4914 young adults, following which all those who scored positive (2741) were interviewed by means of the SADS. The findings suggested that schizophrenic subjects tended to drift down in the SES hierarchy, while the social circumstances and stress of living at the low end of the SES structure played a promotive and possibly causative role in depression among women and antisocial personality and substance abuse among men.

The 1990s

During the early 19902, while DSM-IV and ICD-10 were being prepared for publication, a new collaborative effort was undertaken by NIMH and WHO. The goal of this work was to lay the foundation for more systematic research throughout the world. A product of this collaboration is the Composite International Diagnostic Interview (CIDI), which joins together features of the PSE and the DIS (Robins et al., 1988). Like the DIS, the CIDI is intended to be used in large population surveys and administered by trained "lay" interviewers. Various of its features are being investigated such as the need to recall and date psychiatric symptoms from one's past history (Wittchen et al., 1989), cross-cultural and nosological issues (Cottler et al., 1991), and use of the probing system in different cultural settings (Rubio-Stipec et al., 1993).

Two new schedules designed mainly for clinical studies were also published. One is an outgrowth of the SADS and is named the Structured Clinical Interview for DSM (SCID) (Spitzer et al., 1992). It has become the most commonly used protocol for validation research in psychiatric epidemiology in North America. The other consists of the Schedules for Clinical Assessment in Neuropsychiatry (SCAN) (Wing et al., 1990), which represents improvements and updating in the PSE tradition.

By the 1990s, growing interest in comorbidity led to the initiation of the first psychiatric epidemiologic study to be based on a national sample of the United States (Kessler et al., 1994b), known as the *National Comorbidity Survey* (NCS). The goal was to study the comorbidity of substance abuse disorders and non-substance psychiatric

disorders among a sample of 8098 persons in the age range from 15 through 54.

A modified version of the CIDI, the University of Michigan Composite International Diagnostic Interview (UM-CIDI), was used. The modifications involved omission of diagnoses which had produced very low prevalence in the ECA (somatization) or were inappropriate to a younger sample (cognitive impairment) as well as the introduction of commitment and motivational probes and a few other adjustments designed to encourage subjects to report as accurately as possible their psychiatric histories.

Analysis of the CIDI information was geared to the specifications of DSM-III-R (1987). Such diagnoses are shown in Table 36.2. The NCS findings indicate that psychiatric disorders are more common than previous research suggested. For example, the NCS findings indicate that nearly 50% had suffered a psychiatric disorder at some time in their lives, and nearly 30% were active cases in the year when the survey was conducted. While these rates are higher than indicated in the ECA, there are a number of findings which are remarkably similar be-

Table 36.2 Prevalence rates per 100 by diagnosis from the NCS

Diagnoses	Lifetime	1-year
Any psychiatric disorder	48.0	29.5
Substance abuse disorders	26.6	11.3
Alcohol abuse	9.4	2.5
Alcohol dependence	14.1	7.2
Drug abuse	4.4	0.8
Drug dependence	7.5	2.8
Non-affective psychosis	0.7	0.5
Affective disorders	19.3	11.3
Manic episode	1.6	1.3
Major depressive episode	17.1	10.3
Dysthymia	6.4	2.5
Anxiety disorders	24.9	17.2
Panic disorder	3.5	2.3
Agoraphobia without panic	5.3	2.8
Social phobia	13.3	7.9
Simple phobia	11.3	8.8
Generalized anxiety disorder	5.1	3.1
Antisocial personality	3.5	—

Source: These rates are taken from Kessler et al., 1994 (*Archives of General Psychiatry* 51 [1994]: 8–19, copyright 1994 by the American Medical Association). The non-affective psychosis category includes schizophrenia, schizophreniform disorder, schizoaffective disorder, delusional disorder, and atypical psychosis.

tween the 2 investigations. In both studies the ordering of lifetime rates is similar, with substance abuse disorders being the most common, followed by anxiety disorders, followed by affective disorders.

Also similar to the ECA findings is the NCS evidence that only a minority of subjects with a disorder receive treatment for it. Within the previous year, for example, only 21% of those with a disorder had received treatment in any of the kinds of services queried, which included general, mental health specialty, and substance abuse facilities. The NCS also strengthened evidence that the burden of psychiatric disorder is especially high among young people, and that women outnumber men in major depression while men outnumber women in substance abuse (Kessler et al., 1993; Kessler et al., 1994a).

A major contribution of the NCS study is information about comorbidity among psychiatric disorders. For example, when focusing on lifetime diagnoses, researchers found that the 48% so reporting could be divided into the following proportions: 21% had only 1 disorder, 13% had 2, and 14% had 3 or more. Among those who reported having at least 1 disorder within the previous year, 59% had 3 or more. Defining "severe disorders" as those involving active mania, non-affective psychosis, or other types of disorders that either required hospitalization or created severe role impairment, researchers found that among those who had had at least 1 "severe disorder" within the previous year, 89% had 3 or more disorders.

Furthermore, it was learned that comorbidity was strongly related to use of health services. Again focusing on lifetime diagnoses, researchers found that 42% had at some time received professional help, but among those with 3 or more disorders, the proportion increased to 59%.

The UM-CIDI was also used in a provincewide survey of psychiatric disorders in Ontario, Canada (Offord et al., 1996). This investigation covered a probability sample of 9953 subjects in the age range from 15 to 64. The 1-year prevalence of 14 diagnoses grouped together was 18.6%, a figure that is lower than the NCS estimate of 29.5%. As in other recent findings, however, prevalence was highest among younger people, and the gender differences for substance abuse and depression were substantiated. Also replicated were findings that the majority of persons with a disorder do not receive care (Lin et al., 1996). A special interest in the Ontario survey was assessment of the disability associated with psychiatric disorder (Goering et al., 1996). It was found, for example, that those with comorbid disorders or with affective disorders have more disability than those with anxiety or substance disorders.

Themes in Prevalence Studies

To conclude this review of selected prevalence studies, a number of themes can be drawn together. A theme which has received much attention is the accuracy of the prevalence estimates. There continue to be notable differences across studies and across time when lifetime prevalence is used for comparison or when the focus is on a stringently delineated time frame such as "one-month."

More consistent information is available, at least for North America, Europe, and Scandinavia, about what can be called "current and/or recent prevalence," that is, prevalence estimates that are described simply as "current" and those that are presented as "one-year." A probable reason for such consistency is that rates which concern those disorders in evidence at the time of investigation or within a one-year frame are not seriously distorted by recall bias or by requiring extreme precision about time of onset or recovery.

When most types of psychiatric disorders are included in such estimates, current/recent prevalence varies only from approximately 20% to 30%. While there is greater clustering around 20% than around 30% (Dohrenwend et al., 1980), it is now appropriate to say that numerous studies of general populations suggest that *at least* 1 out of 5 adults suffers from a psychiatric disorder at any one time.

Another theme is the inverse relationship between prevalence and SES level. Beginning with the Faris and Dunham research in Chicago, most studies, whether of treated or true prevalence, have sought information on this topic, and numerous studies have reported that high prevalence (sometimes of all disorders aggregated together and sometimes specific disorders) is found in low SES level, especially among the poverty-stricken (Dohrenwend and Dohrenwend, 1969). ECA findings indicated, for example, not only that schizophrenia, alcohol abuse, and major depression were more common among the poor (Holzer et al., 1986), but also that over the subsequent year, individuals with incomes below the federal poverty level were at increased risk for a number of psychiatric disorders (Bruce, Takeuchi, and Leaf, 1991).

These findings have generated ongoing inquiry regarding the meaning of this association. Two hypotheses have been proposed. One, the "social causation" hypothesis, indicates that high prevalence is due to the causative force of a stressful environment. The "social drift" or "social selection" hypothesis indicates that high prevalence is due to the fact that the mentally ill drift downward owing to the disability associated with the psychiatric disorder.

Where schizophrenia is concerned, the weight of evidence suggests that selective rather than etiologic factors are probably relevant (Turner and Wagenfeld, 1967; Dohrenwend et al., 1992). Where other disorders are concerned, the evidence is much less clear-cut. Findings from a 16-year prospective Canadian study in Stirling County, for example, indicate that the relationship between depression and poverty remained remarkably stable over time and that both "drift" and "causation" are probably implicated (Murphy et al., 1991).

In addition to social class, there is continuing interest in prevalence correlations with ethnicity, educational level, rural versus urban residence, as well as other features of the social environment. It is appropriate to suggest, however, that the 2 other themes which have attracted the most sustained interest are those relevant to age and gender.

Numerous studies indicate that women predominate in rates of depression and the anxiety disorders while men predominate in rates of substance abuse and antisocial personality. Both biological and sociocultural explanations have been offered, but conclusive evidence has still not been achieved. If the gender differences were to change with time, however, greater weight would be given to the influence of social and cultural circumstances.

Regarding the influence of age, the growing evidence that young people are at particularly high risk for psychiatric disorders has profound public health implications. Evidence from numerous recent studies points to the fact that the onset of disorder occurs at a much younger chronological age and that prevalence is much higher among young people than was expected from earlier studies. Until these investigations, many studies showed that prevalence tended to increase with age. The new phenomenon of high lifetime prevalence among the young and low lifetime prevalence among the old is often called a "birth cohort effect."

It will be recalled that in describing designs of epidemiologic studies, we referred to a "cohort study" as one in which a defined group of persons is followed or traced over a period of time. The word *cohort* has similar meaning when modified as in "birth" cohort. A birth cohort consists of the component of a population born during a particular historical period. A "birth cohort effect" in epidemiology refers to health characteristics associated with period of birth which can be ascertained as the cohort moves through successive time and age periods. In order for an effect to be identified as related to time or generation of birth, it needs to differentiate the risks carried by one generation from those carried by another.

The information on lifetime prevalence in studies carried out after 1980 (the ECA and NCS) indicates that the risk for psychiatric disorders carried by persons born in the late 1950s and thereafter appears to be higher and therefore different from that for the cohorts born earlier. Questions remain as to whether this is a genuine finding or a methodologic artifact related, for example, to recall bias. If a genuine finding, it points to the influence of historical changes. Further, it has been suggested that the beginning of this phenomenon coincided in time with the emergence of the "drug culture," when young people began to exhibit increased involvement with substances of various kinds. It is possible that the "birth cohort effect" reflects that involvement with drugs is a risk factor for the development of other types of psychiatric disorders as well. Thus "comorbidity" and "birth cohort effects" may be intertwined phenomena.

Studies of Incidence, Clinical Course, and Mortality

In this part of the chapter, attention is directed toward studies which go beyond prevalence estimates and their correlations. These include studies of incidence and different types of outcomes such as chronicity and premature death. For the most part, such studies build on a baseline laid in a cross-sectional prevalence investigation.

Incidence of Psychiatric Disorders

Several decades ago Rema Lapouse urged psychiatric epidemiologists to turn from a focus on prevalence to one on incidence. Because incidence deals with the onset of disorder, she suggested that it gives better clues to etiology and therefore to the discovery of factors which may have potential for the control and prevention of mental disorders. The number of prospective incidence studies, however, remains small.

It can be perceived that lifetime prevalence is related to incidence because subjects are asked to review their whole life histories and to identify the "first ever" onset of relevant symptoms. Because lifetime prevalence is retrospective, however, it is customary to consider that incidence is better approached through follow-up studies. While prospective studies of this type have numerous strengths, retrospective dating is never completely avoided since subjects are still asked in the second assessment to date and describe the emergence of signs and symptoms.

The available incidence studies can be divided into those with a short interval of follow-up, usually a year, and those with a long follow-up, usually more than 10 years. Furthermore, the findings appear to vary systematically according to the duration of the interval. Surprisingly, a short interval seems to lead to higher incidence rates and a long interval to lower rates. This counterintuitive result means that accuracy of estimation is as much a theme for incidence as for prevalence.

More than any other study of psychiatric epidemiology, the 25-year Lundby Study in Sweden has concentrated on incidence and has produced evidence about most types of psychiatric disorders (Hagnell et al., 1982; Hagnell et al., 1990). For a comparative overview across studies, however, it is necessary to limit attention to depression.

The Lundby investigation involves 2 intervals over which incidence was calculated: one is the 10-year interval from 1947 to 1957, during which the average annual incidence of depression was 1.8 per 1000; and the other is the 15-year interval from 1957 to 1972, by which time incidence had risen to 4.5 per 1000. The Stirling County Study in Canada used a 16-year interval from 1952 to 1968 and reported for depression an average annual incidence of 2.3 per 1000 (Murphy et al., 1988). A study in Finland also followed a cohort over 16 years and reported the incidence of depression to be 2.0 per 1000 men and 2.7 per 1000 women (Lehtinen et al., 1996). The 15-year follow-up of the ECA sample in Baltimore reported the incidence of depression to be 3.0 per 1000 (Eaton et al., 1997). These findings not only are similar but also are congruent with evidence that incidence is low relative to prevalence when dealing with a chronic disorder such as depression.

Two studies which used a 1-year follow-up gave dissimilar results. One of these concerns the 5 sites of the ECA, where depression incidence was found to be 15.9 per 1000 per year (Eaton et al., 1989). The other 1-year study, which included only women, was carried out in Scotland and reported a very high rate, 78 per 1000 (Surtees, Sashidharan, and Dean, 1986).

Some investigators argue that a retrospective assessment over 1 year gives a more accurate picture than assessment over a longer duration. At the same time, others argue that interviews carried out over a relatively short interval may involve distortions. For example, subjects may "learn" what interests the interviewer and therefore try to provide such material.

A significant consideration is the implication of high rates of incidence. Rates as high as those given above from the 1-year studies indicate that nearly all persons in the general population will succumb to depression at some point in their lives. Because it seems unlikely that such is the case, a number of questions about incidence remain to be explored in further research.

Investigations of Clinical Course

A question of long-standing concern in clinical psychiatry has been prognosis, especially as it relates to schizophrenia and the affective disorders. Clinical observations have suggested that schizophrenic patients tend to experience a more consistently deteriorating course of illness than do patients with unipolar or bipolar depression. An adequate assessment of this question requires following a large number of patients over a considerable period of time.

Choosing a retrospective cohort design for a clinical outcome study, Tsuang and Winokur (1975) initiated the Iowa 500 Study, referring to the place of investigation and the number of subjects. They used the Feighner criteria for reviewing psychiatric hospital case records to select patients with diagnoses of schizophrenia, mania, and depressive disorder and chose surgical patients as a comparison group. In a 35-year follow-up, they used the Iowa Structured Psychiatric Interview (ISPI) for gathering information. The ISPI combines features of the PSE and Renard and was designed as an interview which can be administered by nonmedical personnel (Tsuang, Woolson, and Simpson, 1980). It covers information about psychiatric, social, and family history, as well as information about the frequency and duration of psychiatric symptoms.

Employing multiple features of clinical outcome such as stability of diagnosis (Tsuang et al., 1981), association with mortality (Tsuang and Woolson, 1977), and other aspects of long-term outcome (Tsuang and Dempsey, 1979), the researchers found that schizophrenic patients had a poorer prognosis than did affective disorder patients, and all psychiatric patients had poorer outcomes than surgical patients.

An important attribute of the Iowa 500 Study was the use of a comparison group. There are a sizable number of other clinical investigations of outcome that do not include comparison groups. Several of these concern unipolar depression and have provided evidence that persistence and recurrence in patient populations tend to be high (Keller, et al., 1984; Mann, Jenkins, and Belsey, 1981).

The perspective of general population studies on outcome is important, however, in light of evidence that many depressed persons do not receive treatment, and because cases in the community are not preselected for having the most serious disorders, as can be expected in clinical studies.

Several population studies indicate that high rates of chronicity and recurrence are typical of cases identified in natural settings (Amenson and Lewinsohn, 1981; Murphy et al., 1986; Surtees, Sashidharan, and Dean, 1986; Sargeant et al., 1990).

Findings from the 1-year follow-up of the ECA sample (Sargeant et al., 1990) indicated that 24% of those subjects who met criteria for major depression during the 6 months leading up to the interview carried out at Time 1 also met the same criteria at Time 2. Clinical characteristics such as comorbidity, the number of symptoms, and the length of prior episodes had greater impact on depression persistence than did sociodemographic characteristics such as age, gender, marital status, and education. An investigation of outcome over a 16-year period in the Stirling County Study indicated that 34% of those who were depressed at the beginning of the study were chronically or recurrently depressed over the ensuing years (Murphy, 1995). Thus, on the whole, population epidemiology tends to corroborate clinical studies in finding that unipolar depression often does not resolve into a full or stable recovery.

As a corollary to chronicity, increasing disability may be another facet of outcome. Based on the 1-year follow-up of the ECA subjects in North Carolina, those who suffered from major depression had nearly 5 times the amount of disability as those who were free of depressive symptomatology (Broadhead et al., 1990). Impairment was measured as days lost from work or "disability days" when the person spent all or part of the day in bed or was kept from usual activities because of depressive symptomatology. These findings complement the results of the Medical Outcomes Study, which indicated that depression was more disabling than any of the chronic medical conditions assessed with the exception of serious cardiovascular problems (Wells et al., 1989).

Psychiatric Mortality Studies

Focusing on the outcome of premature death, psychiatric studies have addressed not only the issue of suicide but also the question of whether psychiatric disorders carry a higher risk for other types of mortality as well. Mortality studies illustrate the use of epidemiologic methods in that death rates for a large population of reference are usually employed as a means for comparison. The Iowa 500 Study is one among a growing number of investigations which indicate that psychiatric patients have higher mortality than the general population and that such excess is not limited to suicide but includes other causes of death as well, especially accidental deaths (Tsuang and Woolson, 1977).

Population studies also provide evidence for an association between psychiatric disorders and mortality. For example, the Lundby Study reported that over a 25-year period there was an increased risk among men for suicide and accidental death associated with prior psychiatric disorder, mainly depression (Rorsman, Hagnell, and Lanke, 1982). A 9-year follow-up of subjects at the New Haven site of the ECA found that major depression, alcohol abuse, and schizophrenia were associated with mortality (Bruce et al., 1994). Although depression was associated with elevated risk for both men and women, the effect was stronger for men, as indicated in an age-adjusted relative risk of 4.2 compared with 1.6.

The Stirling County Study indicated that over a 16-year period, subjects who were depressed or anxious at baseline experienced 1.5 times the number of expected deaths, primarily owing to the fact that the standardized mortality ratio for depressed men was 2.1 (Murphy et al., 1987). Combining information on mortality with that about chronicity and recurrence, the findings further indicated that 83% of the depressed men either had died or had been chronically or recurrently depressed, according to the follow-up evidence, but only 42% of depressed women had a similarly poor outcome (Murphy, 1995). These figures about outcome contrast with those about treatment: 83% of the women had been in contact with medical services about depression but only 37% of the men. Such findings do not speak to the effectiveness of treatment, a topic which needs to be investigated using randomized procedures, but they do emphasize that psychiatric disorders identified in the general population appear to carry serious clinical consequences.

Special Topics in Psychiatric Epidemiology

In this final part of the chapter, 3 special topics are taken up for review. The first concerns the genetic epidemiology of psychiatric disorders. This is followed by a description of international work which has come to the forefront in recent years. Studies in this area tend to be called either cross-cultural or cross-national comparative investigations. The third topic is the newly emerging field of the epidemiology of psychiatric disorders among children and adolescents.

Genetic Epidemiology of Psychiatric Disorders

The field of genetic epidemiology investigates the distribution and determinants of psychiatric disorders in families. By doing so, the genetic epidemiologist seeks to locate disorder-predisposing genes and describe how they interact with the environment and lead to the onset of disorder. Such work often follows a logical progression from family studies, which show that a disorder is familial; through twin and adoption studies, which estimate the relative contributions of genes and environment; to molecular genetic studies, which locate genes and describe their disorder-generating mutations (Faraone and Tsuang, 1994). For many psychiatric disorders, genetic epidemiologic studies have implicated both genes and environment. Examples include schizophrenia, bipolar disorder, major depression, panic disorder, Tourette's syndrome, attention deficit hyperactivity disorder, antisocial personality disorder, Alzheimer's disease, obsessive-compulsive disorder, and autism.

The family study attempts to establish that a disorder runs in families by comparing relatives of patients having the disorder with relatives of subjects who do not have the disorder. Family studies can use a clinically referred sample or a population-based sampling frame such as is illustrated by a study of Irish families (Kendler et al. 1993).

The power of genetic epidemiologic designs is best illustrated by twin studies, which are based on the fact that monozygotic (MZ) twins are genetically identical but dizygotic (DZ) twins share, on the average, only one-half of their genes. Because of this biological fact, a higher concordance rate for a disorder among MZ compared with DZ twins provides strong evidence for the importance of genetic factors in the etiology of a disorder.

Taking schizophrenia as an example, Gottesman and Shields (1972) investigated a pooled sample of 550 MZ and 776 DZ twin pairs in a review of the literature. They reported concordance rates of 57.7% and 12.8% for MZ and DZ twins, respectively. Kendler (1983) summarized 9 twin studies from 8 countries involving 401 MZ twin pairs and 478 DZ twin pairs. Overall, 53% of the MZ twins were concordant for schizophrenia, whereas only 15% of the DZ twins were concordant. This significant difference between concordance rates for the 2 types of twin pairs strongly implicates genetic factors in the causation of schizophrenia. Although twin studies point to genetic factors, they also underscore the effects of non-genetic factors. Because the monozygotic twin concordance rate is less than 100%, environmental factors—whether biological or sociocultural—must play a critical role. Studies of twin pairs where 1 of the twins is adopted into a non-biological family are particularly useful for investigation of the gene-environment interaction.

Molecular genetic studies build upon family, twin, and adoption studies by finding the genes which underlie the predisposition to a disorder. The methodology for locating genes, known as linkage analysis, is now fairly routine. Linkage analysis has been successful for many medical diseases and has led to the discovery of 4 genes that predispose to Alzheimer's, as summarized by Tsuang and Faraone (1996). Thus far, however, linkage analysis has produced only suggestive findings for other psychiatric disorders.

Some studies suggest that genes for schizophrenia may lie on chromosomes 6, 8, and 22, with chromosome 3 having been considered but ruled out (Schizophrenia Collaborative Linkage Group [Chromosome 22], 1996; Schizophrenia Linkage Collaborative Group for Chromosomes 3, 6, and 8, 1996). Also, some studies have implicated a gene for bipolar disorder on chromosome 18 (Badner et al., 1995; Berrettini et al., 1997; Stine et al., 1995). Other work, however, cannot replicate these findings. Similar ambiguities exist for other psychiatric disorders. The conflicting results from linkage studies of psychiatric disorders indicate that, although developments in molecular and statistical genetics have made it straightforward to find and replicate linkage for simple single-gene disorders, it will be more challenging to find genes for etiologically complex disorders such as schizophrenia (Risch, 1990).

It is important to emphasize that defining the clinical and neurobiologic expression of genes causing psychiatric disorders (phenotype) remains one of the most crucial areas for genetic research in psychiatry, even though the identification of causative genes (genotype) is the ultimate goal (Tsuang, Faraone, and Lyons, 1993). Also, the elucidation of how environmental risk factors interact with genes to produce disorder remains a major challenge in the genetic epidemiology of psychiatric disorders.

Cross-national Comparative Studies

For a considerable period of time, investigators speculated that non-Western cultural groups may be free of psychiatric disorders, or may have very different expressions of disorders, or may have rates of disorder which differ markedly from those in the West. Early studies of hospital records and ethnographic observations tended to draw only abstract comparisons, as when reference was made to differences between "primitive groups" and "Western civilization" or between "the third world" and "the modern world."

Initial efforts to achieve concrete comparisons were directed toward the question of whether non-Western peoples observe and recognize phenomena which are comparable to clinical psychiatric disorders as conceptualized in Western medicine. Parallels for psychotic disorders were found to be strong, while words and concepts for other types of emotional and behavioral disturbances were more various (Edgerton, 1966; Murphy, 1972; Murphy, 1976).

As systematic research increased and large surveys were conducted using similar methods of data gathering, there has been a tendency to describe the work as "international" or "cross-national" rather than employing the earlier term, "cross-cultural." The International Pilot Study of Schizophrenia (IPSS) was the first of such large and coordinated investigations (World Health Organization, 1973). The intent of the IPSS was not to provide epidemiologic estimates but rather to investigate the question of whether a core profile of schizophrenia was found in different places around the world. In order to determine if international comparisons of psychopathology are feasible, the IPSS included 1202 first-admission hospital patients diagnosed as psychotic in 9 countries: Colombia, Czechoslovakia, Denmark, India, Nigeria, Taiwan, the Union of Soviet Socialist Republics, the United Kingdom, and the United States.

The criteria for patient selection were deliberately broad so that cultural differences in the definition of schizophrenia could be investigated. Most of the patients were diagnosed as schizophrenic, but affective psychoses were also represented. The psychiatrists making these diagnoses were themselves members of the same cultural groups as the patients, and they employed their typical standards for diagnosis. They interviewed each patient using the Present State Examination (PSE) and analyzed their findings by the CATEGO computer program according to the ICD system.

The results of the study indicated that patients diagnosed as schizophrenic in one country tended to have a symptom profile similar to that of patients so diagnosed in the other countries. Psychiatrists in the United States and the USSR were more often in disagreement with the CATEGO assessment than psychiatrists in the other countries owing to their broader definition of schizophrenia. In each country, however, there were patients whose original clinical diagnosis was schizophrenia and for whom the CATEGO analysis indicated that they shared a concordant type of schizophrenia.

A 2-year follow-up of the original sample indicated that patients in developing countries appeared to have a better outcome than patients in developed countries (World Health Organization, 1979). This finding led to hypotheses about whether schizophrenic outcome might be favorably influenced by such features of developing countries as agrarian economy, lack of upward social mo-

bility, presence of extended family structure, or absence of negative stereotypes.

While it was not the intent of the IPSS to conduct research on the prevalence of schizophrenia in the 9 countries, 2 population studies were carried out at about the same time focused on an empirical comparison between a Western group and a non-Western group. These investigations focused on prevalence estimates of the more common disorders involving depression and anxiety. One of these was carried out in West Africa among mainly rural Yoruba of Nigeria for comparison to the Stirling County Study (Leighton, Lambo, et al., 1963). The other was conducted in East Africa among the Baganda living in 2 villages in Uganda using the PSE so that comparisons could be made to the epidemiologic study in Camberwell, London (Orley, Litt, and Wing, 1979; Bebbington et al., 1981).

Combining depression and anxiety disorders, current prevalence was estimated at between 10% and 12% in Camberwell, Stirling County, and among the Yoruba. Among the Baganda, however, prevalence was 22%. This study was carried out prior to the strife in Uganda, and the appreciably higher prevalence is not well understood. Nevertheless, these investigations suggested that *nonpsychotic* disorders were as common or more common in these largely illiterate areas than in the Western areas which served for comparison.

After the DIS was constructed for the ECA study, it was used in a number of studies in other countries, Taiwan being one. It should be noted that the DIS study in Taiwan is the third cross-sectional study of that area mentioned in this chapter. The second study, it will be recalled, reported an increase in psychoneurotic disorders, but nevertheless the rates were much lower than in other studies of that time. Because the diagnostic information in the second study remained clinically based, it is difficult to know if this increase represented change in the definition of the disorders grouped as "psychoneurotic" or actual change in the frequency of disorder.

Problems of variable definitions were largely overcome when a new study in Taiwan used a Mandarin Chinese translation of the DIS (CM-DIS) (Hwu et al., 1984). The CM-DIS study involved a large sample of over 11,000 subjects selected to represent metropolitan Taipei, small Taiwan towns, and rural Taiwan villages. These data were combined with information from the ECA for a systematic and contemporary comparison between Taiwan and the United States (Compton et al., 1991). Using lifetime prevalence, investigators reported that Taiwan had a significantly lower overall rate (22%) compared to the U.S. rate (36%). The lifetime prevalence of each of the major psychiatric categories was lower in Taiwan than in the United States. The only serious exception to this generalization was that the rate for generalized anxiety disorder (GAD) in Taiwan closely approximated that for the United States.

Bearing in mind that GAD is referenced mainly through somatic symptoms of motor tension and autonomic hyperactivity, it is of interest that this diagnosis should be the one where prevalence was approximately as high as in the United States. Studies of neurasthenia among mainland Chinese and Taiwanese subjects by Kleinman (1977, 1982) suggested that in these countries patients tend to focus more on the somatic equivalents of depression and anxiety than on the features of disturbed psychological mood. Thus, the relatively high prevalence of GAD in Taiwan may be an expression of the tendency to use somatic symptoms as an overlying expression of psychiatric disturbance.

As the use of the DIS continued to spread, a group of researchers drew on information from 10 regions around the world for lifetime estimates of alcohol abuse and dependence (Helzer and Canino, 1992). Unlike the rates across the 5 sites of the ECA study, these rates varied considerably, with the highest being 23% among native Mexican Americans in the United States and the lowest being 0.45% in Shanghai. The remaining rates were as follows: Korea 22%; Christchurch, New Zealand 19%; Edmonton, Canada 18%; ECA-U.S. 14%; U.S. immigrant Mexican Americans 13%; Munich, Germany 13%; Puerto Rico 13%; and 3 sites in Taiwan ranging from 5% to 9%. While the amount of variation cannot be dismissed, most of the rates are in the high teens.

Investigators have also used the DIS to form a Cross-National Collaborative Group that represents investigations in Canada (Bland, Newman, and Orn, 1988), Puerto Rico (Canino et al., 1987), Germany (Wittchen et al., 1992), Italy (Faravelli et al., 1990), France (Lépine et al., 1989), Lebanon (Karam et al., 1991), New Zealand (Wells et al., 1989), and Taiwan (Hwu, Yeh, and Chang, 1989). Headed by Weissman, this group showed that 2 findings from the ECA have wide generalizability. One is that women are more prone to depression than are men in all the sites covered except Puerto Rico (Klerman and Weissman, 1989; Weissman et al., 1993). The other is that the "birth cohort" effect is clearly shown in each site (Cross-National Collaborative Group, 1992). Thus, it appears that young people in many parts of the world are at greater risk than previously expected and that the public health implications are worldwide in scale.

Recent work in cross-national comparison has been facilitated by using the same interview schedule for collecting data and the same computer algorithms for analyzing data sets. Furthermore, cross-national collaborations are making use of the Internet. Under the leadership of Kessler, for example, the Internet facilities associated with the Inter-university Consortium for Political and Social Research (ICPSR) of the Survey Research Center at the University of Michigan are being used. The CIDI findings of the *National Comorbidity Survey* can be accessed, and consultation and coordination in the analysis of CIDI databases developed from surveys in numerous countries can now be provided. With various trials of reliability and cultural appropriateness nearing completion, it can be expected that considerably more information comparing prevalence of a wide range of psychiatric disorders from different sites will be forthcoming.

Another international study of note is the World Health Organization Collaborative Study on Determinants of Outcome of Severe Mental Disorders (Sartorius et al., 1986). This study built on the work of the IPSS but extends the goal to provide more adequate information for estimating prevalence, incidence, and outcome of schizophrenia and other severe disorders. This work takes its orientation from the fact that population-based studies employing face-to-face interviews are not necessarily the best approach to gathering information about the more serious disorders which are less common and also more likely to be known to treatment facilities. This new WHO study pays particular attention to the incidence and outcome of schizophrenia in a network of treatment centers around the world.

It is appropriate to end this section on cross-national comparisons by reference to the *Global Burden of Disease* (Murray and Lopez, 1996), which details research directed at assessing the health of populations not only through death rates but also through the level of disability imposed upon the population. This type of analysis stands behind the projection that by the year 2020, depression will head the list of conditions creating a burden of functional impairment and lost quality of life.

Epidemiology of Psychiatric Disorders among Children and Adolescents

Childhood experiences and the treatment of children with psychiatric disorders have a long history in psychiatry, but epidemiologic investigations focused on pre-adult age groups are of rather recent origin. At the present time, studies of children and adolescents stand high in the agendas of both academic and national institutions. Evidence from studies of adults that the onset of most psychiatric disorders occurs early in life has contributed to making studies of children a top priority, as has evidence that a "birth cohort" effect may represent a historic change which puts children and adolescents at heavy risk.

Large-scale, population-based studies of children present challenging problems for accurate diagnosis. Because such studies focus on a phase of rapid physical and personality development, investigators find it difficult to determine which phenomena will turn into full-scale psychiatric disorders and which will disappear as development proceeds. In view of the focus on rapid changes occurring at this phase of life, researchers now refer to the pertinent studies as "developmental epidemiology." Most epidemiologic evidence about adults comes from asking subjects direct questions about feelings and behaviors on the assumption that adults are the best informants about themselves. With children, investigators draw on interviews with parents or teachers or both, as well as with children themselves, thereby opening up important issues about agreement between informants.

While epidemiologically focused studies of children date back to the mid-1930s (McFie, 1934), the modern era began with the work of Rutter and colleagues in England (Rutter, 1966; Rutter, Tizard, and Whitmore, 1970) and was carried forward by numerous researchers in both the United Kingdom and North America. A useful review by Angold (1988) focuses on depression. We describe 2 studies to illustrate this special topic, one in Canada and one in the United States.

The Canadian study, known as the Ontario Child Health Study, concerns a cross-sectional probability sample of 3294 children and adolescents aged 4 through 16 (Boyle et al., 1987; Offord et al., 1987). Methods for this study drew on the Child Behavior Checklist (CBCL) (Achenbach & Edelbrock, 1983). Four childhood disorders were assessed: conduct disorder, hyperactivity, emotional disorder (neurosis), and somatization. Conduct disorder and hyperactivity were based on DSM-III criteria for similarly named categories. Emotional disorder combined elements of DSM-III categories of overanxious disorder, major depressive disorder, and obsessive-compulsive disorder. Somatization involved 2 criteria: distressing recurrent somatic symptoms without evident physical cause and perception of oneself as "sickly." The overall 6-month prevalence of 1 or more disorders was 18.1%. Most of these children had not received psychiatric specialty care.

Further, the Canadian investigators found that the highest rate occurred among girls 12 to 16 and the lowest among girls 4 to 11 years of age. There was significant co-occurrence among the psychiatric disorders, and psychiatric disorders were associated with poor school performance, chronic health problems, substance use, and sui-

cidal behavior (Offord et al., 1989). A 4-year follow-up study was carried out among those who had been 4 to 12 years old in the original study (Offord et al., 1992). The results of the second study indicated that conduct disorder showed the most stability over time. Among those children who had been free of disorder at baseline, low family income predicted subsequent psychiatric disorder.

The U.S. investigation is known as the Great Smoky Mountains Study of Youth, referring to its location in the southern Appalachian mountain region of North Carolina (Costello et al., 1996a, b). A population of 4500 children aged 9, 11, and 13 years of age were screened using "externalizing" items and substance abuse questions from the CBCL. Those who scored in the upper 25% of the screening instrument and a 1-in-10 random sample of the others were selected for an original study which will serve as baseline for a 4-year follow-up. These U.S. researchers employed a number of data-gathering procedures such as the Child and Adolescent Psychiatric Assessment (CAPA) (Angold et al., 1995) with the goal of providing diagnoses based on DSM-III-R.

The 3-month prevalence of all DSM-III-R disorders combined was 20.3%, with the most common being anxiety disorders (5.7%), followed by enuresis (5.1%), tic disorders (4.2%), and conduct disorders (3.3%). Comorbidity among the psychiatric diagnoses was not uncommon. Boys had a higher overall rate than girls, owing mainly to the prevalence of behavioral disorders. The rates of separation anxiety, tics, and enuresis dropped significantly between 9 and 11 years of age. Poverty was the strongest demographic correlate of diagnosis in both urban and rural children.

The concept of "serious emotional disturbance" (SED) received considerable attention since it influences policies concerning the provision of services. "Serious emotional disturbance" is defined as a DSM-III-R diagnosis with impaired functioning in 1 or more areas. SED yields a considerably lower prevalence rate than when the focus is only on diagnosis (20% compared to estimates from 4% to 8%, depending on which of several measures of impairment were used). Despite this reduction in prevalence, only about 1 child in 4 or 5 with a "serious emotional disturbance" had recently received specialty care. Behavioral disorders, emotional disorders, and comorbidity increased the likelihood that criteria for seriousness would be met, but tics and enuresis did not. Children living in poverty were at significantly greater risk for such SED than those who came from more advantaged homes.

These 2 studies of children and adolescents produced a number of similar findings which are, in turn, similar to those in several studies of adults. At the same time, the studies of children make clear that a number of issues require further research, among them, for example, the issue of how to join diagnostic information with that about disability. Toward this end, NIMH has laid plans to initiate a new large-scale effort to be known as the Mental Health Service Use, Needs, Outcomes, and Costs in Child and Adolescent Populations (UNO-CAP). Prior to the launch of data gathering, a phase of methodologic refinement was carried out which was known as the NIMH Methods for Epidemiology of Child and Adolescent Mental Disorders (MECA) (Shaffer et al., 1996; Schwab-Stone et al., 1996). This study investigated the reliability and validity of the Diagnostic Interview Schedule for Children (DISC) version 2.3. Results suggest that, in general, the DISC shows moderate to good validity.

Another study under way in Chicago needs to be mentioned as we close this section on children and adolescents. Focusing on children growing up in "inner city" environments, this investigation explores circumstances that lead young people into delinquency and violence and, at the same time, attempts to measure the impact of victimization (Earls, 1991; Buka and Earls, 1993). Thus attention is paid not only to risk factors associated with becoming the perpetrator of criminal actions but also to the influence of witnessing and being a victim of crime.

Considerable consistency of findings in psychiatric epidemiologic research has emerged over the years since DSM-III. Such consistency has appeared in studies of adults as well as children and concerns evidence about the early onset of disorder, the "birth cohort" effect, gender differences for depression and alcohol abuse, the inverse relationship between prevalence and SES, the high degree of comorbidity, and the relatively low use of services.

While this includes an impressive array of common findings, questions persist about the validity of different diagnoses. Questions relevant to identifying "phenotypes" remain important for the growth of genetic epidemiology and its potential contributions to an understanding of etiologies. In and of themselves, validity questions will probably generate more efforts which follow subjects over long periods of time, using the "LEAD" standard. Furthermore, a question of paramount concern will be to determine the ways in which diagnosis and disability should be joined in measuring validity.

Recent years have seen relatively more epidemiologic attention paid to the young than to the old. Nevertheless, there is evidence of continuing effort to keep the latter phases of the life arc clearly in focus, not only through studies of Alzheimer's disease but also through investigations of the full range of psychiatric disorders.

It is also timely that the approaches of clinical epidemiology be more widely utilized. For example, there is increasing awareness that outcome studies benefit if the index cases are in a first episode of disorder and if there is adequate attention paid to comparison groups.

In addition, we anticipate that what we described here as the emergence of a broadly oriented psychiatric epidemiology will flourish, and will continue to concern itself with children as well as with adults, with nations throughout the world, and with historical trends over time.

As we look to the future and to the probability that depression will head the list of disorders that create a global burden, the roles of etiologic research and prevention take on increased importance. Psychiatric disorders have been particularly recalcitrant to being brought under the control of knowledge of their causes. We now fully recognize that the etiologic stream is a multifactorial one. Much work lies ahead to learn what mix of causes determines which types of cases.

Where prevention is concerned, already there is evidence that the technology of "preventive trials" is under investigation as a means of improving ability to implement preventive programs. Bearing in mind the experience of John Snow and the Broad Street pump, it is possible that effective preventive programs can be designed in advance of having complete knowledge about etiology.

References

Achenback, T. M., and C. S. Edelbrock. 1983. *Manual for the Child Behavior Checklist and Revised Child Behavior Profile.* Burlington: University of Vermont, Department of Psychiatry.

Amenson, C. S., and P. M. Lewinsohn. 1981. An investigation into the observed sex difference in prevalence of unipolar depression. *J. Abnorm. Psychol.* 90:1–13.

American Psychiatric Association. 1952. *Diagnostic and statistical manual of mental disorders.* Washington, D.C.: American Psychiatric Association.

——— 1980. *Diagnostic and statistical manual of mental disorders.* 3rd ed. Washington, D.C.: American Psychiatric Association.

——— 1987. *Diagnostic and statistical manual of mental disorders.* 3rd ed., rev. Washington, D.C.: American Psychiatric Association.

——— 1994. *Diagnostic and statistical manual of mental disorders.* 4th ed. Washington, D.C.: American Psychiatric Association.

Angold, A. 1988. Childhood and adolescent depression. I. Epidemiological and aetiological aspects. *Br. J. Psychiatry* 152:601–617.

Angold, A., M. Prendergast, A. Cox, R. Harrington, E. Simonoff, and M. Rutter. 1995. The Child and Adolescent Psychiatric Assessment (CAPA). *Psychol. Med.* 25:755–762.

Anthony, J. C., M. Folstein, A. J. Romanoski, M. R. Von Korff, G. R. Nestadt, R. Chahal, A. Merchant, C. H. Brown, S. Shapiro, M. Kramer, and E. M. Gruenberg. 1985. Comparison of the lay Diagnostic Interview Schedule and a standardized psychiatric diagnosis. *Arch. Gen. Psychiatry* 42:667–675.

Badner, J. A., E. S. Gershon, W. H. Berrettini, et al. 1995. Evidence of linkage disequilibrium between bipolar disorder and D18S53. *Psychiatr. Genet.* 5:S16.

Bebbington, P., J. Henry, C. Tennant, E. Sturt, and J. K. Wing. 1981. Epidemiology of mental disorders in Camberwell. *Psychol. Med.* 11:561–579.

Beiser, M. 1978. Psychiatric epidemiology. In *The Harvard guide to modern psychiatry,* ed. A. M. Nicholi. Cambridge, Mass.: Belknap Press of Harvard University Press. 609–626.

Berrettini, W. H., T. N. Ferraro, L. R. Goldin, S. D. Detera-Wadleigh, H. Choi, D. Muniec, J. J. Guroff, D. M. Kazuba, J. I. Nurnberger, W. T. Hsieh, M. R. Hoehe, and E. S. Gershon. 1997. A linkage study of bipolar illness. *Arch. Gen. Psychiatry* 54:27–35.

Bland, R., S. C. Newman, and H. Orn, eds. 1988. Epidemiology of psychiatric disorders in Edmonton. *Acta Psychiatr. Scand.* suppl. 338.

Boyle, M. H., D. R. Offord, H. G. Hofmann, G. P. Catlin, J. A. Byles, D. T. Cadman, J. W. Crawford, P. S. Links, N. I. Rae-Grant, and P. Szatmari. 1987. Ontario Child Health Study. I. Methodology. *Arch. Gen. Psychiatry* 44:826–831.

Bremer, J. 1951. A social psychiatric investigation of a small community in northern Norway. *Acta Psychiatr. Neurol. Scand.* suppl. 62.

Broadhead, W. E., D. G. Blazer, L. K. George, and C. K. Tse. 1990. Depression, disability days, and days lost from work in a prospective epidemiologic survey. *JAMA* 264:2524–28.

Bromet, E. J. 1995. Research training in psychiatric epidemiology and biostatistics. *Int. J. Methods Psychiatr. Res.* 5:93–101.

Brown, G. W., and T. Harris. 1978. *Social origins of depression: a study of psychiatric disorder in women.* New York: Free Press.

Bruce, M. L., D. T. Takeuchi, and P. J. Leaf. 1991. Poverty and psychiatric status: longitudinal evidence from the New Haven Epidemiologic Catchment Area Study. *Arch. Gen. Psychiatry* 48:470–474.

Bruce, M. L., P. J. Leaf, G. P. M. Rozal, L. Florio, and R. A. Hoff. 1994. Psychiatric status and 9-year mortality data in the New Haven Epidemiologic Catchment Area Study. *Am. J. Psychiatry* 151:716–721.

Buka, S., and F. Earls. 1993. Early determinants of delinquency and violence. *Health Aff.* 12:46–64.

Campbell, D. F., and D. W. Fiske. 1959. Convergent and discriminant validation by the multitrait-multimethod matrix. *Psychol. Bull.* 56:81–105.

Canino, G. J., H. R. Bird, P. E. Shrout, M. Rubio-Stipec, M. Bravo, R. Martinez, M. Sesman, and L. M. Guevara. 1987. The prevalence of specific psychiatric disorder in Puerto Rico. *Arch. Gen. Psychiatry* 44:727–735.

Compton, W. M., J. E. Helzer, H. G. Hwu, E. K. Yeh, L. McEvoy, J. E. Tipp, and E. L. Spitznagel. 1991. New methods in cross-cultural psychiatry: psychiatric illness in Taiwan and the United States. *Am. J. Psychiatry* 148:1697–1704.

Cooper, J. E., R. E. Kendell, B. J. Gurland, L. Sharpe, J. R. M. Copeland, and R. Simon. 1972. *Psychiatric diagnosis in New York and London.* London: Oxford University Press.

Costello, E. J., A. Angold, B. J. Burns, D. K. Stangl, D. L. Tweed, A. Erkanli, and C. M. Worthman. 1996a. The Great Smoky Mountains Study of Youth: goals, design, methods, and the prevalence of DSM-III-R disorders. *Arch. Gen. Psychiatry* 53:1129–36.

Costello, E. J., A. Angold, B. J. Burns, A. Erkanli, D. K. Stangl, and D. L. Tweed. 1996b. The Great Smoky Mountains Study of Youth: functional impairment and serious emotional disturbance. *Arch. Gen. Psychiatry* 53:1137–43.

Cottler, L., L. N. Robins, B. F. Grant, J. Blaine, L. H. Towle, H. U. Wittchen, N. Sartorius, and participants in the WHO\ADMAHA Field Trial. 1991. The CIDI-core substance abuse and dependence questions: cross-cultural and nosological issues. *Br. J. Psychiatry* 159:653–658.

Cross-National Collaborative Group. 1992. The changing rate of major depression: cross-national comparisons. *JAMA* 268:3098–3105.

Dean, C., P. G. Surtees, and S. P. Sashidharan. 1983. Comparison of research diagnostic systems in an Edinburgh community sample. *Br. J. Psychiatry* 142:247–256.

Derogatis, L. R., R. S. Lipman, K. Rickels, E. H. Uhlenhuth, and L. Covi. 1974. The Hopkins Symptom Checklist (HSCL): a self-report symptom inventory. *Behav. Sci.* 19:1–15.

Dohrenwend, B. P. 1967. Social status, stress, and psychological symptoms. *Am. J. Public Health* 57:625–632.

Dohrenwend, B. P., and B. S. Dohrenwend. 1969. *Social status and psychological disorder.* New York: John Wiley & Sons.

Dohrenwend, B. P., I. Levav, and P. E. Shrout. 1986. Screening scales from the Psychiatric Epidemiology Research Instrument (PERI). In *Community surveys of psychiatric disorders,* ed. M. M. Weissman, J. K. Myers, and C. E. Ross. New Brunswick, N.J.: Rutgers University Press. 349–375.

Dohrenwend, B. P., B. S. Dohrenwend, M. S. Gould, B. Link, R. Neugebauer, and R. Wunsch-Hitzig. 1980. *Men-*

tal illness in the United States: epidemiological estimates. New York: Praeger.

Dohrenwend, P. B., I. Levav, P. W. Shrout, S. Schwartz, G. Naveh, B. G. Link, A. E. Skodol, and A. Stueve. 1992. Socioeconomic status and psychiatric disorders: the causative-selection issue. *Science* 255:946–952.

Earls, F. 1991. A developmental approach to understanding and controlling violence. In *Theory and research in behavioral pediatrics*, ed. H. E. Fitzgerald, B. M. Lester, and M. W. Yogman. New York: Plenum Press.

Eaton, W. W., and L. G. Kessler, eds. 1985. *Epidemiologic field methods in psychiatry: the NIMH Epidemiologic Catchment Area Program*. New York: Academic Press.

Eaton, W. W., M. Kramer, J. C. Anthony, A. Dryman, S. Shapiro, and B. Z. Locke. 1989. The incidence of specific DIS/DSM-III mental disorders: data from the NIMH Epidemiologic Catchment Area Program. *Acta Psychiatr. Scand.* 79:163–178.

Eaton, W. W., J. C. Anthony, J. Gallo, G. Cai, A. Tien, A. Romanoski, C. Lyketsos, and L. Chen. 1997. The natural history of major depression: the Baltimore ECA follow-up. *Arch. Gen. Psychiatry* 54:993–999.

Edgerton, R. B. 1966. Conceptions of psychosis in four East African societies. *Am. Anthropol.* 68:408–425.

Egland, J. A., and A. M. Hostetter. 1983. Amish Study. I. Affective disorders among the Amish, 1976–1980. *Am. J. Psychiatry* 140:56–61.

Endicott, J., and R. L. Spitzer. 1978. A diagnostic interview: Schedule for Affective Disorders and Schizophrenia. *Arch. Gen. Psychiatry* 35:837–844.

Essen-Möller, E. 1956. Individual traits and morbidity in a Swedish rural population. *Acta Psychiatr. Scand.* suppl. 100.

Faraone, S. V., and M. T. Tsuang. 1994. Methods in psychiatric genetics. In *Textbook in psychiatric epidemiology*, ed. M. T. Tsuang, M. Tohen, and G. E. P. Zahner. New York: Wiley-Liss. 81–134.

Faravelli, C., B. G. Degl'Innocenti, L. Aiazzi, G. Incerpi, and S. Pallanti. 1990. Epidemiology of mood disorders: a community survey in Florence. *J. Affective Disord.* 20:135–141.

Faris, R. E. L., and H. W. Dunham. 1939. *Mental disorders in urban areas: an ecological study of schizophrenia and other psychoses*. Chicago: University of Chicago Press.

Feighner, J. P., E. Robins, S. B. Guze, R. A. Woodruff, G. Winokur, and R. Munoz. 1972. Diagnostic criteria for use in psychiatric research. *Arch. Gen. Psychiatry* 26:57–63.

Goering, P., E. Lin, D. Campbell, M. H. Boyle, and D. R. Offord. 1996. Psychiatric disability in Ontario. *Can. J. Psychiatry* 41:564–571.

Goldberg, D. P. 1972. *The detection of psychiatric illness by questionnaire: a technique for the identification and assessment of non-psychotic psychiatric illness*. London: Oxford University Press.

Gottesman, I. I., and J. Shields. 1972. *Schizophrenia and genetics: a twin study vantage point*. New York: Academic Press.

Hagnell, O. 1966. *A prospective study of the incidence of mental disorder*. Stockholm, Sweden: Svenska Bokförlaget Norstedts.

Hagnell, O., J. Lanke, B. Rorsman, and L. Öjesjö. 1982. Are we entering an age of melancholy? Depressive illnesses in a prospective epidemiological study over 25 years: the Lundby Study, Sweden. *Psychol. Med.* 12:279–289.

Hagnell, O., E. Essen-Möller, E. J. Lanke, J. Öjesjö, and B. Rorsman. 1990. *The incidence of mental illness over a quarter of a century: The Lundby Longitudinal Study of mental illnesses based on 42,000 observation years*. Stockholm: Almqvist & Wiksell.

Helzer, J. E., and G. J. Canino, eds. 1992. *Alcoholism in North America, Europe, and Asia*. New York: Oxford University Press.

Helzer, J. E., L. N. Robins, J. L. Croughan, and A. Welner. 1981. Renard Diagnostic Interview: its reliability and procedural validity with physicians and lay interviewers. *Arch. Gen. Psychiatry* 38:393–405.

Helzer, J. E., L. N. Robins, L. T. McEvoy, E. L. Spitznagel, R. K. Stoltzman, A. Farmer, and I. F. Brockington. 1985. A comparison of clinical and Diagnostic Interview Schedule diagnoses. *Arch. Gen. Psychiatry* 42:657–666.

Henderson, S., P. Duncan-Jones, D. G. Byrne, R. Scott, and S. Adcock. 1979. Psychiatric disorder in Canberra: a standardized study of prevalence. *Acta Psychiatr. Scand.* 60:355–374.

Hollingshead, A., and F. S. Redlich. 1958. *Social class and mental illness*. New York: John Wiley & Sons.

Holzer, C. E., B. M. Shea, J. W. Swanson, P. J. Leaf, J. K. Myers, L. George, M. M. Weissman, and P. Bednarski. 1986. The increased risk for specific psychiatric disorders among persons of low socioeconomic status. *Am. J. Soc. Psychiatry* 6:259–271.

Husaini, B. A., J. A. Neff, and R. H. Stone. 1979. Psychiatric impairment in rural communities. *J. Community Psychology* 7:137–146.

Hwu, H. G., E. K. Yeh, and L. Y. Chang. 1989. Prevalence of psychiatric disorders in Taiwan defined by the Chinese Diagnostic Interview Schedule. *Acta Psychiatr. Scand.* 79:136–147.

Hwu, H. G., E. K. Yeh, L. Y. Chang, C. T. Chen, C. C. Chen, and T. Y. Chen. 1984. The Chinese modification of the NIMH-Diagnostic Interview Schedule: reliability study on assessment of psychiatric symptoms. *Psychological Testing* 31:15–26 (Chinese).

Jarvis, E. 1971. *Insanity and idiocy in Massachusetts: report of the commission on lunacy, 1885.* Cambridge, Mass.: Harvard University Press.

Karam, E. G., M. Barakeh, A. N. Karam, and N. El-Khouri. 1991. The Arabic Diagnostic Interview Schedule. *Rev. Med. Libanasie* 3:28–30.

Katz, M. M., S. K. Secunda, R. M. A. Hirschfeld, and S. H. Koslow. 1979. NIMH Clinical Research Branch Collaborative Program on the Psychobiology of Depression. *Arch. Gen. Psychiatry* 36:765–771.

Keller, M. B., G. L. Klerman, P. W. Lavori, W. Coryell, J. Endicott, and J. Taylor. 1984. Long-term outcome in major depression. *JAMA* 252:788–792.

Kendler, K. S. 1983. Overview: a current perspective on twin studies of schizophrenia. *Am. J. Psychiatry* 140:1413–25.

Kendler, K. S., M. McGuire, A. M. Gruenberg, A. O'Hare, M. Spellman, and D. Walsh. 1993. The Roscommon family study. I. Methods, diagnosis of probands, and risk of schizophrenia in relatives. *Arch. Gen. Psychiatry* 50:527–540.

Kessler, R. C. 1995. Epidemiology of psychiatric comorbidity. In *Textbook in psychiatric epidemiology,* ed. M. T. Tsuang, M. Tohen, and G. E. P. Zahner. New York: Wiley-Liss. 179–197.

Kessler, R. C., and J. A. McRae. 1981. Trends in sex and psychological distress. *Am. Sociol. Rev.* 41:443–452.

Kessler, R. C., K. A. McGonagle, M. Swartz, D. G. Blazer, and C. B. Nelson. 1993. Sex and depression in the National Comorbidity Survey. I. Lifetime prevalence, chronicity and recurrence. *J. Affective Disord.* 199:85–96.

Kessler, R. C., K. A. McGonagle, C. B. Nelson, M. Hughes, M. Swartz, and D. G. Blazer. 1994a. Sex and depression in the National Comorbidity Survey. II. Cohort effects. *J. Affective Disord.* 30:15–26.

Kessler, R. C., K. A. McGonagle, S. Zhao, C. B. Nelson, M. Hughes, S. Eshleman, H. U. Wittchen, and K. S. Kendler. 1994b. Lifetime and 12-month prevalence of DSM-III-R psychiatric disorders in the United States: results from the National Comorbidity Survey. *Arch. Gen. Psychiatry* 51:8–19.

Kleinman, A. 1977. Depression, somatization, and the "new cross-cultural psychiatry." *Soc. Sci. Med.* 11:3–10.

——— 1982. Neurasthenia and depression: a study of somatization and culture in China. *Cult. Med. and Psychiatry* 6:117–189.

Klerman, G. L., and M. M. Weissman. 1989. Increasing rates of depression. *JAMA* 261:2229–35.

Kramer, M. 1961. Some problems for international research suggested by observations on differences in first admission rates to mental hospitals of England and Wales and of the United States. In *Proceedings of the Third World Congress of Psychiatry.* Vol. 3. Montreal: University of Toronto Press and McGill University Press. 153–160.

Langner, T. S. 1962. A twenty-two item screening score of psychiatric symptoms indicating impairment. *J. Health Human Behav.* 3:269–276.

Langner, T. S., and S. T. Michael. 1963. *Life stress and mental health: the Midtown Manhattan Study.* New York: Free Press.

Lehtinen, V., T. Lindholm, J. Veijol, and E. Väisänen. 1990. The prevalence of PSE-CATEGO disorders in a Finnish adult population cohort. *Soc. Psychiatry Psychiatr. Epidemiol.* 25:187–192.

Lehtinen V., J. Veijola, T. Lindholm, J. Moring, and P. P. E. Väisänen. 1996. Incidence of mental disorders in the Finnish UKKI Study. *Br. J. Psychiatry* 168:672–678.

Leighton, A. H. 1961. The Stirling County Study: some notes on concepts and methods. In *Comparative epidemiology of the mental disorders,* ed. P. H. Hoch and J. Zubin. New York: Grune and Stratton. 24–31.

Leighton, A. H., T. A. Lambo, C. C. Hughes, D. C. Leighton, J. M. Murphy, and D. B. Macklin. 1963. *Psychiatric disorder among the Yoruba: a report from the Cornell-Aro Mental Health Research Project in the western region of Nigeria.* Ithaca, N.Y.: Cornell University Press.

Leighton, D. C., J. S. Harding, D. B. Macklin, C. C. Hughes, and A. H. Leighton. 1963. Psychiatric findings of the Stirling County Study. *Am. J. Psychiatry* 119:1021–26.

Lépine, J. P., J. Lellouch, A. Lovell, et al. 1989. Anxiety and depressive disorders in a French population: methodology and preliminary results. *Psychiatry Psychobiol.* 4:267–274.

Lin, E., P. Goering, D. R. Offord, D. Campbell, and M. H. Boyle. 1996. The use of mental health services in Ontario: epidemiologic findings. *Can. J. Psychiatry* 41:572–577.

Lin, T. Y. 1953. A study of the incidence of mental disorder in Chinese and other cultures. *Psychiatry* 16:313.

Lin, T. Y., H. Rin, E. K. Yeh, C. C. Hsu, and H. M. Chu. 1969. Mental disorders in Taiwan fifteen years later: a preliminary report. In *Mental health research in Asia and the Pacific,* ed. W. Caudill and T. Y. Lin. Honolulu: East-West Center Press. 66–91.

MacMahon, B., and D. Trichopoulos. 1996. *Epidemiology: principles and methods.* Boston: Little, Brown.

Macmillan, A. M. 1957. The Health Opinion Survey: technique for estimating prevalence of psychoneurotic and related types of disorders in communities. *Psychol. Rep.* 3:325–339.

Manis, J. G., M. J. Brawer, C. L. Hunt, and L. C. Kercher. 1964. Estimating the prevalence of mental illness. *Am. Soc. Rev.* 29:84–89.

Mann, A. H., R. Jenkins, and E. Belsey. 1981. The twelve-month outcome of patients with neurotic illness in general practice. *Psychol. Med.* 11:535–550.

McFie, B. S. 1934. Behavior and personality difficulties in school children. *Br. J. Educ. Psychol.* 4:30–46.

Menninger, K. 1959. *A psychiatrist's world.* New York: Viking Press.

Miettinen, O. S. 1985. *Theoretical epidemiology.* New York: John Wiley & Sons.

Morris, J. N. 1957. *Uses of epidemiology.* Edinburgh: Livingstone.

Murphy, J. M. 1972. A cross-cultural comparison of psychiatric disorder: Eskimos of Alaska, Yorubas of Nigeria, and Nova Scotians of Canada. In *Transcultural research in mental health,* ed. W. P. Lebra. Honolulu: University Press of Hawaii. 213–226.

———— 1976. Psychiatric labeling in cross-cultural perspective. *Science* 191:1019–28.

———— 1980. Continuities in community-based psychiatric epidemiology. *Arch. Gen. Psychiatry* 37:1215–23.

———— 1995. What happens to depressed men? *Harv. Rev. Psychiatry* 3:47–49.

Murphy, J. M., A. M. Sobol, R. K. Neff, D. C. Olivier, and A. H. Leighton. 1984. Stability of prevalence: depression and anxiety disorders. *Arch. Gen. Psychiatry* 41:991–997.

Murphy, J. M., D. C. Olivier, A. M. Sobol, R. R. Monson, and A. H. Leighton. 1986. Diagnosis and outcome: depression and anxiety in a general population. *Psychol. Med.* 16:117–126.

Murphy, J. M., R. R. Monson, D. C. Olivier, A. M. Sobol, and A. H. Leighton. 1987. Affective disorders and mortality: a general population study. *Arch. Gen. Psychiatry* 44:473–480.

Murphy, J. M., D. C. Olivier, R. R. Monson, A. M. Sobol, and A. H. Leighton. 1988. Incidence of depression and anxiety: the Stirling County Study. *Am. J. Public Health* 78:534–540.

Murphy, J. M., D. C. Olivier, R. R. Monson, A. M. Sobol, E. B. Federman, and A. H. Leighton. 1991. Depression and anxiety in relation to social status. *Arch. Gen. Psychiatry* 48:223–229.

Murray, C. J. L., and A. D. Lopez. 1996. *The global burden of disease: a comprehensive assessment of mortality and disability from disease, injuries, and risk factors in 1990 and projected to 2020.* Boston: Harvard School of Public Health on Behalf of the World Health Organization and the World Bank.

Offord, D. R., M. H. Boyle, P. Szatmari, N. I. Rae-Grant, P. S. Links, D. T. Cadman, J. A. Byles, J. W. Crawford, H. M. Blum, C. Byrne, H. Thomas, and C. A. Woodward. 1987. Ontario Child Health Study. II. Six-month prevalence of disorder and rates of service utilization. *Arch. Gen. Psychiatry* 44:832–836.

Offord, D. R., M. H. Boyle, J. E. Fleming, H. M. Blum, and N. I. Rae-Grant. 1989. Ontario Child Health Study: summary of selected results. *Can. J. Psychiatry* 34:483–491.

Offord, D. R., M. H. Boyle, Y. A. Racine, J. E. Fleming, D. T. Cadman, H. M. Blum, C. Byrne, P. S. Links, E. L. Lipman, and H. L. MacMillan. 1992. Outcome, prognosis, and risk in a longitudinal follow-up study. *J. Am. Acad. Child Adolesc. Psychiatry* 31:916–923.

Offord, D. R., M. H. Boyle, D. Campbell, P. Goering, E. Lin, M. Wong, and Y. A. Racine. 1996. One-year prevalence of psychiatric disorder in Ontarians 15 to 64 years of age. *Can. J. Psychiatry* 41:559–563.

Orley, J., B. Litt, and J. K. Wing. 1979. Psychiatric disorders in two African villages. *Arch. Gen. Psychiatry* 36:513–520.

Phillips, D. L. 1966. The "true prevalence" of mental illness in a New England state. *Community Ment. Health J.* 2:35–40.

President's Commission on Mental Health. 1978. *Report to the President from the President's Commission on Mental Health.* Washington, D.C.: Government Printing Office.

Radloff, L. S. 1977. The CES-D Scale: a self-report depression scale for research in the general population. *Appli. Psychol. Measurem.* 1:385–401.

Regier, D. A., I. D. Goldberg, and C. A. Taube. 1978. The de facto U.S. mental health services system: a public health perspective. *Arch. Gen. Psychiatry* 35:685–693.

Regier, D. A., J. K. Myers, M. Kramer, L. N. Robins, D. G. Blazer, R. L. Hough, W. W. Eaton, and B. Z. Locke. 1984. The NIMH Epidemiologic Catchment Area (ECA) Program: historical context, major objectives and study population characteristics. *Arch. Gen. Psychiatry* 41:934–941.

Regier, D. A., J. H. Boyd, J. D. Burke, D. S. Rae, J. K. Myers, M. Kramer, L. N. Robins, L. K. George, M. Karno, and B. Z. Locke. 1988. One-month prevalence of mental disorders in the United States: based on five Epidemiologic Catchment Area Sites. *Arch. Gen. Psychiatry* 45:977–986.

Regier, D. A., W. E. Narrow, D. Rae, R. W. Manderscheid, B. Z. Locke, and F. K. Goodwin. 1993. The de facto U.S. mental and addictive disorders service system: Epidemiologic Catchment Area perspective one-year prevalence rates of disorders and services. *Arch. Gen. Psychiatry* 50:85–94.

Risch, N. 1990. Genetic linkage and complex diseases, with special reference to psychiatric disorders. *Genetic Epidemiology* 7:3–7.

Robins, E., and S. B. Guze. 1970. Establishment of diagnostic validity in psychiatric illness: its applications to schizophrenia. *Am. J. Psychiatry* 126:983–988.

Robins, L. N. 1978. Psychiatric epidemiology. *Arch. Gen. Psychiatry* 35:697–702.

Robins, L. N., and D. A. Regier, eds. 1991. *Psychiatric disorders in America: the Epidemiologic Catchment Area Study.* New York: Free Press.

Robins, L. N., B. Z. Locke, and D. A. Regier. 1991. An overview of psychiatric disorders in America. In *Psychiatric disorders in America: the Epidemiologic Catchment Area*

Study, ed. L. N. Robins and D. A. Regier. New York: Free Press. 328–366.

Robins, L. N., J. E. Helzer, J. L. Croughan, and K. S. Ratcliff. 1981. National Institute of Mental Health Diagnostic Interview Schedule: its history, characteristics, and validity. *Arch. Gen. Psychiatry* 38:381–389.

Robins, L. N., J. E. Helzer, M. M. Weissman, H. Orvaschel, E. Gruenberg, J. D. Burke, and D. A. Regier. 1984. Lifetime prevalence of specific psychiatric disorders in three sites. *Arch. Gen. Psychiatry* 41:949–958.

Robins, L. N., J. K. Wing, H. U. Wittchen, J. E. Helzer, T. F. Babor, J. Burke, A. Farmer, A. Jablenski, R. Pickens, D. A. Regier, N. Sartorius, and L. H. Towle. 1988. The Composite International Diagnostic Interview: an epidemiologic instrument suitable for use in conjunction with different diagnostic systems and in different cultures. *Arch. Gen. Psychiatry* 45:1069–77.

Rorsman, B., O. Hagnell, and J. Lanke. 1982. Violent death and mental disorders in the Lundby Study: accidents and suicides in a total population during a 25-year period. *Neuropsychobiol.* 8:233–240.

Rothman, K. J. 1986. *Modern epidemiology.* Boston: Little, Brown.

Rubio-Stipec, M., M. G. Canino, L. N. Robins, H. U. Wittchen, N. Sartorius, C. Torres de Miranda, and participants in the WHO\ADMHA Field Trials. 1993. The somatization schedule of the Composite International Diagnostic Interview: the use of the probe chart in 17 different countries. *Int. J. Methods Psychiatr. Res.* 3:129–136.

Rutter, M. 1966. *Children of sick parents: an environmental and psychiatric study.* London: Institute of Psychiatry Maudsley Monographs, Oxford University Press.

Rutter, M., J. Tizard, and K. Whitmore. 1970. *Education, health and behavior.* London: Longman.

Sargeant, J. K., M. L. Bruce, L. P. Florio, and M. M. Weissman. 1990. Factors associated with a 1-year outcome of major depression in the community. *Arch. Gen. Psychiatry* 47:519–526.

Sartorius, N., A. Jablenski, A. Korten, G. Ernberg, M. Anker, J. E. Cooper, and R. Day. 1986. Early manifestations and first-contact incidence of schizophrenia in different cultures. *Psychol. Med.* 16:909–928.

Schizophrenia Collaborative Linkage Group (Chromosome 22). 1996. A combined analysis of D22S278 marker alleles in affected sib-pairs: support for a susceptibility locus at chromosome 22q12. *Am. J. Med. Genet., Neuropsychiat. Genet.* 67:40–45.

Schizophrenia Linkage Collaborative Group for Chromosomes 3, 6, and 8. 1996. Additional support for schizophrenia linkage on chromosomes 6 and 8: a multicenter study. *Am. J. Med. Genet., Neuropsychiat. Genet.* 67:580–594.

Schwab, J. J., R. A. Bell, G. J. Warheit, and R. B. Schwab. 1979. *Social order and mental health.* New York: Brunner/Mazel.

Schwab-Stone, M. E., D. Shaffer, M. K. Dulcan, P. S. Jensen, P. Fisher, H. R. Bird, S. H. Goodman, B. B. Lahey, J. H. Lichtman, G. Canino, and M. Rubio-Stipec. 1996. Criterion validity of the NIMH Diagnostic Interview Schedule for Children, Version 2,3 (DISC-2.3). *J. Am. Acad. Child Adolesc. Psychiatry* 35:878–888.

Shaffer, D., P. W. Fisher, M. Dulcan, M. Davies, J. Placentini, M. Schwab-Stone, B. B. Lahey, K. Bourdon, P. Jensen, H. Bird, G. Canino, and D. Regier. 1996. The NIMH Diagnostic Interview Schedule for Children (DISC 2.3): description, acceptability, prevalences, and performance in the MECA Study. *J. Am. Acad. Child Adolesc. Psychiatry* 35:865.

Shapiro, S., E. A. Skinner, L. G. Kessler, M. Von Korff, P. S. German, G. L. Tischler, P. J. Leaf, L. Benham, L. Cottier, and D. A. Regier. 1984. Utilization of health and mental health services: three Epidemiologic Catchment Area sites. *Arch. Gen. Psychiatry* 41:971–978.

Snow, J. 1855. *On the mode of communication of cholera.* 2nd ed. London: Churchill.

Spitzer, R. L. 1983. Psychiatric diagnosis: are clinicians still necessary? In *Psychotherapy research: where are we and where should we go?*, ed. J. B. W. Williams and R. L. Spitzer. New York: Guilford Press. 273–292.

Spitzer, R. L., J. Endicott, and E. Robins. 1978. Research diagnostic criteria: rationale and reliability. *Arch. Gen. Psychiatry* 35:773–782.

Spitzer, R. L., J. B. W. Williams, M. Gibbon, and M. B. First. 1992. The Structured Clinical Interview for DSM-III-R (SCID). I. History, rationale, and description. *Arch. Gen. Psychiatry* 49:624–629.

Srole, L., T. S. Langner, S. T. Michael, M. K. Opler, and T. A. C. Rennie. 1962. *Mental health in the metropolis; the Midtown Manhattan Study.* New York: McGraw-Hill.

Star, S. A. 1950. The screening of psychoneurotics in the army: technical development of tests. In *The American soldier: measurement and prediction,* ed. S. A. Stouffer, L. Guttman, E. A. Suchman, P. F. Lazarsfeld, S. A. Star, and J. A. Clausen. Vol. 4. Princeton: Princeton University Press. 486–547.

Stine, O. C., J. Zu, R. Koskela, F. J. McMahon, M. Gschwend, C. Friddle, C. D. Clark, M. G. McInnis, S. G. Simpson, and T. S. Breschel. 1995. Evidence for linkage of bipolar disorder to chromosome 18 with a parent-of-origin effect. *Am. J. Hum. Genet.* 57:1384–94.

Surtees, P. G., S. P. Sashidharan, and C. Dean. 1986. Affective disorder amongst women in the general population: a longitudinal study. *Br. J. Psychiatry* 148:176–186.

Tohen, M. 1994. Bipolar disorder and comorbid substance

use. In *The decade of the brain*. Vol. 5. New York: National Alliance of the Mentally Ill. 1–2.

Tohen, M., and E. J. Bromet. 1997. Epidemiology. In *Psychiatry*, ed. A. Tasman, J. Kay, and J. Lieberman. Philadelphia: Saunders. 161–181.

Tohen, M., and F. K. Goodwin. 1995. Epidemiology of bipolar disorder. In *Textbook in psychiatric epidemiology*, ed. M. T. Tsuang, M. Tohen, and G. E. P. Zahner. New York: Wiley-Liss. 301–315.

Tsuang, M. T., and J. M. Dempsey. 1979. Long-term outcome of major psychoses. II. Schizoaffective disorder compared with schizophrenia, affective disorders, and a surgical control group. *Arch. Gen. Psychiatry* 36:1302–4.

Tsuang, M. T., and S. V. Faraone. 1996. Genetics of Alzheimer's disease. *J. Formosan Med. Assoc.* 10:733–740.

Tsuang, M. T., and G. Winokur. 1975. The Iowa 500: field work in a 35-year follow-up of depression, mania, and schizophrenia. *Can. Psychiatric Assoc. J.* 20:359–365.

Tsuang, M. T., and R. F. Woolson. 1977. Mortality in patients with schizophrenia, mania, depression, and surgical controls: a comparison with general population mortality. *Br. J. Psychiatry* 130:162–166.

Tsuang, M. T., S. V. Faraone, and M. J. Lyons. 1993. Identification of the phenotype in psychiatric genetics. *Eur. Arch. Psychiatr. Neurol. Sci.* 243:131–142.

Tsuang, M. T., M. Tohen, and J. M. Murphy. 1988. Psychiatric epidemiology. In *The new Harvard guide to psychiatry*, ed A. M. Nicholi. Cambridge: Belknap Press of Harvard University Press. 761–779.

Tsuang, M. T., R. F. Woolson, and J. C. Simpson. 1980. The Iowa Structured Psychiatric Interview: rationale, reliability, and validity. *Acta Psychiatr. Scand.* suppl. 283.

Tsuang, M. T., R. F. Woolson, G. Winokur, and R. R. Crowe. 1981. Stability of psychiatric diagnosis: schizophrenia and affective disorders followed up over a 30–40 year period. *Arch. Gen. Psychiatry* 38:535–539.

Turner, R. J., and M. O. Wagenfeld. 1967. Occupational mobility and schizophrenia: an assessment of the social causation and social selection hypotheses. *Am. Sociol. Rev.* 32:104–113.

Weider, A., B. Mittelmann, D. Wechsler, and H. G. Wolff. 1944. The Cornell Selectee Index: a method for quick testing of selectees for the armed forces. *JAMA* 124:224–228.

Weissman, M. M., and G. L. Klerman. 1978. Epidemiology of mental disorders: emerging trends in the United States. *Arch. Gen. Psychiatry* 35:705–712.

Weissman, M. M., J. K. Myers, and P. S. Harding. 1978. Psychiatric disorders in a U.S. urban community: 1975–1976. *Am. J. Psychiatry* 135:459–461.

Weissman, M. M., R. Bland, P. R. Joyce, S. Newman, J. E. Well, and H. U. Wittchen. 1993. Sex differences in rates of depression: cross-national perspectives. *J. Affective Disord.* 29:77–84.

Wells, J. E., J. A. Bushnell, A. R. Hornblow, P. R. Joyce, and M. A. Oakley-Browne. 1989. Christchurch Psychiatric Epidemiology Study. Pt. I. Methodology and lifetime prevalence for specific psychiatric disorders. *Aust. N.Z. J. Psychiatry* 23:315–326.

Wells, K. B., A. Stewart, and R. D. Hays. 1989. The functioning and well-being of depressed patients: results of the Medical Outcomes Study. *JAMA* 262:914–919.

Wing, J. K., J. E. Cooper, and S. N. Sartorius. 1974. *Measurement and classification of psychiatric symptoms: an instruction manual for the PSE and CATEGO program.* London: Cambridge University Press.

Wing, J. K., S. A. Mann, J. P. Leff, and J. M. Nixon. 1978. The concept of a "case" in psychiatric population surveys. *Psychol. Med.* 8:203–217.

Wing, J. K., T. Babor, T. Brugha, J. Burke, J. E. Cooper, R. Giel, A. Jablenski, D. Regier, and N. Sartorius. 1990. SCAN: Schedules for Clinical Assessment in Neuropsychiatry. *Arch. Gen. Psychiatry* 47:589–593.

Wittchen, H. U., J. D. Burke, G. Semler, H. Pfister, M. Von Cranach, and M. Zaudig. 1989. Recall and dating of psychiatric symptoms. *Arch. Gen. Psychiatry* 45:1069–77.

Wittchen, H. U., C. A. Esau, D. von Zerssen, J. D. Krieg, and M. Zaudig. 1992. Lifetime and six-month prevalence of mental disorders in the Munich Follow-up Study. *Eur. Arch. Psychiatry Clin. Neurosci.* 241:247–258.

World Health Organization. 1973. *International pilot study of schizophrenia.* Geneva: World Health Organization.

——— 1979. *Schizophrenia: an international follow-up study.* New York: John Wiley & Sons.

——— 1994. *International statistical classification of diseases and related health problems.* Rev. 10. Geneva: World Health Organization.

Recommended Reading

Anthony, J. C., W. E. Eaton, and A. S. Henderson, eds. 1995. Psychiatric epidemiology (special issue). *Epidemiol. Rev.* 17(1).

Compton, W. M., and S. B. Guze, eds. 1994. Psychiatric epidemiology (special issue). *Int. Rev. Psychiatry* 6(4).

MacMahon, B., and D. Trichopoulos. 1996. *Epidemiology: principles and methods.* Boston: Little, Brown.

Mezzich, J. E., M. R. Jorge, and I. M. Salloum, eds. 1994. *Psychiatric epidemiology: assessment concept and methods.* Baltimore: Johns Hopkins University Press.

Tsuang, M. T., M. Tohen, and G. E. P. Zahner, eds. 1995. *Textbook in psychiatric epidemiology.* New York: Wiley-Liss.

KEN DUCKWORTH

JONATHAN F. BORUS

Population-Based Psychiatry in the Public Sector and Managed Care

Psychiatry, like all of medicine, has traditionally focused the vast majority of its attention on the individual patient and on understanding the identification, etiology, and treatment of specific mental disorders. However, the nature of the funding for, and organization of, mental health care requires an understanding of the individual with a mental disorder as part of a larger geographic or economic population. Reductions in the amount of resources devoted to health care, the emergence of managed care, the changing role of government, the virtual disappearance of long-term state hospital care, the rise in consumer activism, and the rapid spread of homelessness are major societal forces that continue to impact the patient-psychiatrist dyad. Beyond the clinical encounter, these forces will, in part, determine both the identity of psychiatry and the nature and quality of clinical care. This chapter describes the organization of resources devoted to mental health care, the principles central to assuming responsibility for a population, and the ways in which psychiatrists directly and indirectly work with specific subsets of a population. Finally, we discuss problematic issues that the current organization of care presents.

Definitions

We begin by defining several key concepts that recur throughout this discussion. *Population-based psychiatry* is a care system with finite resources responsible for the mental health needs of a group of individuals defined by geography (e.g., catchment area), activity or occupation (e.g., university, corporation), or health care system (e.g., health maintenance organization). A psychiatrist choosing to work in such a system has responsibility both to individual patients and to the larger population in which these patients "reside."

Traditionally, *public psychiatry* is a government-funded care system of state hospitals and community mental health centers, serving patients who cannot access the pri-vate fee-for-service market and are therefore cared for in the *public sector*. The definition of the latter term is in flux, as many government agencies attempt to *privatize* (put out to private bid) public sector mental health services while retaining an important, but narrow, governmental oversight role. Public psychiatry has been increasingly focused on persons with severe and persistent mental illness, whether in hospital-based, community, or homeless settings such as shelters. *Community psychiatrists* work with populations, most often in the public sector, to organize service delivery systems to provide most efficiently care for patients with mental illness within their geographic or economic communities.

The term *managed care* refers to a variety of efforts to manage and monitor the cost and, at times, the quality of care provided to individuals within a population. This is usually done through contracting out responsibility for the care of the population to an organization for a set cost per period of time. In mental health, care has been most frequently managed as a "carve out" from the financing and management of general health care. Most managed care occurs on a capitation basis (*capitation* = "per head"), with a set amount paid to the managed care organization (MCO) for every member of the population. Critics describe managed care as being primarily "managed cost," because most efforts focus on limiting the costs, rather than improving the quality, of care. MCOs attempt to contain or reduce health care expenditures by using a variety of management strategies to alter provider and patient behavior. Typically for-profit businesses, MCOs assert the interests of the payor into the patient-doctor dyad, creating a more complex 3-way relationship. Pretreatment authorization, ongoing review of the need for services, and limiting access to specialists constitute 3 of the most familiar ways in which MCOs aim to reduce health care expenditures. MCOs often contract to manage the care of a privately or publicly insured population, usually working within a fixed budget.

The lack of consensus for a third-person term to describe people who have a mental disorder demonstrates the evolving nature of the mental health environment. *Patient* (from the Latin for "to suffer"), an acceptable and noble term in medical settings, is often perceived by people with mental illness as a passive or "one down" position vis-à-vis the physician. *Client* (from the Latin for "dependent") emphasizes the fiduciary aspect of clinical work, but reminds many of a legal setting. The term *consumer* ("to take wholly or completely"), used by many to better describe the "consumer activism" component inherent in receiving a service, is considered by others as a trivialization of human suffering, reducing it to a commercial transaction between providers and consumers. Employers, who ultimately purchase many services, often call users of service *customers.* Finally, some more radical groups who have had poor experiences with the mental health system describe themselves as *survivors* or *consumer-survivors.* This difficulty in agreeing on a third-person term demonstrates how the landscape of public sector psychiatry has continued to evolve, and how the psychiatrist working within a community must be respectful of the many conceptions Americans have about mental illness and its treaters. Although in this chapter we use the term *patient,* we encourage treaters to continue the dialogue with their patients about this issue.

History of Public and Community Mental Health Care

The history of care for people with mental disorders is a complex tapestry involving 3 broad areas of tension: (1) maintaining the afflicted as part of the community versus a containment/isolation mindset (Foucault, 1965); (2) the psychiatric field's focus on mental health (e.g., normal mental processes, the "worried well") versus mental illness (the most severely ill); (3) societal tolerance of maltreatment or neglect of people with mental illness versus scandal-induced reform movements (Morrissey and Goldman, 1984). While likely to shift over time as they have in the past, these tensions currently are leaning toward integration of individuals with mental illness into the community and a renewed professional interest in the seriously mentally ill population. Whether the present failings of the system (e.g., the large numbers of uninsured individuals and the growing population of homeless people with mental illness) can generate substantial reform remains to be seen.

Custodial care settings for people with mental illness, such as almshouses for the poor and Christian monasteries, appeared in Europe during the thirteenth to seventeenth centuries. The first public hospital for individuals with mental illness, Bethlehem Hospital, opened in England in the fourteenth century; the term *bedlam* derives from the nickname for this facility, where overcrowding, charging fees to witness the mad, and abusive treatment were common. Jails were also used to contain people with mental illness, mental retardation, or alcoholism.

Near the end of the eighteenth century, Philippe Pinel, a leading French alienist (psychiatrist), advocated the simple notion—later known as "moral treatment"—that shackles should not be employed and that humane treatment, fresh air, and involvement in working duties could restore a person from the stresses that caused mental illness. In the United States the first government-sponsored institutions specifically for individuals with mental illness were organized in the early nineteenth century for people with deviant behavior of whatever origin. Dorothea Dix, a prominent advocate, championed the building of state facilities to replace inhumane jails and almshouses; she persuaded several states to create institutions for the insane, many designed like villages, literally "asylums" from everyday life.

The latter half of that century witnessed a decline in the quality of these state institutions, as overcrowding made well-intentioned efforts to create "moral" and therapeutic asylums nearly impossible. As Godding wrote in 1890, "Day by day, year after year, I have seen the individualized treatment of special cases swamped by the rising tide of indiscriminate lunacy pouring through the wards, filling every crevice, rising higher and higher until gradually most distinctions and landmarks have been blotted out."

The dramatic rise in the state hospital population necessitated a move toward regimentation and efficiency, creating a custodial care environment (Grob, 1994). At the end of the nineteenth century, the industrial revolution placed an increased emphasis on productivity, and the "moral" paradigm was partially replaced with a more "scientific" model, often emphasizing useless somatic therapies. The heightened reliance on somatic treatment, coupled with the increased patient volume that encouraged custodial care, undermined the rest, recovery, and work ethic philosophy of the moralists.

The scientific model, however, produced 2 notable successes: the discovery by Wagner-Jauregg that the high fevers associated with malarial infection could cure tertiary neurosyphilis, with the result that numerous long-term cases of general paresis of the insane were discharged from institutions after this treatment; and the discovery by Freud and his followers that psychological approaches to human distress could help address conversion disorder and held promise for other conditions. Yet attitudes and treatment lagged far behind these therapeutic advances. In 1922, Briggs wrote of the many ill psychiatric patients who languished in jails: "It may be said that to be mentally ill was considered a crime, punishable by imprisonment, following court procedure" (p. xii).

Morrissey and Goldman (1984) observe that a recurrent pattern of periods of neglect in the treatment of individuals with mental illness leads to periods of reform. For example, the "mental hygiene" reform movement was galvanized by Clifford Beers's 1917 book, *A Mind That Found Itself.* This first-person account of recovery highlighted the overcrowded and poorly staffed conditions at mental hospitals and generated interest in prevention, application of psychodynamic constructs to patients, and outpatient evaluation. Outpatient mental health clinics began to open in the early 1900s, offering a different set of services than did the state institutions: evaluation rather than hospitalization, prevention efforts, and differentiation of acute from chronic cases. Increasing affiliation with medical schools also helped bring the field of psychiatry closer to the medical mainstream.

World War II provided a new impetus to psychiatrists working with a discrete population: the military. In 1943 the number of potential soldiers rejected through psychiatric screening and the number of psychiatric casualties and evacuees exceeded the pool of available new inductees into the armed forces. Consequently, authorities introduced 2 major changes in U.S. military policy concerning the psychiatric fitness and care of soldiers: they lowered significantly the screening threshold so that fewer inductees were excluded from service because of emotional problems, and they assigned psychiatrists to the combat zone to treat psychiatric casualties as soon as possible after the occurrence of their illness. Psychiatrists working near the line of combat reduced the number of psychiatric casualties by adhering to 3 now central tenets of community psychiatry: immediacy—patients should not wait for treatment; proximity—patients should be treated close to the place where they became ill; and expectancy—patients' social support networks should be utilized to expect and encourage them to improve and return to their prior roles.

The success of those principles, coupled with optimistic press accounts of narcotherapy, amnestic interview, and even lobotomy for mental illness, stimulated public interest in improving mental health care in the postwar era. In addition, the presence of large numbers of Veterans Administration patients, and a burgeoning awareness that mental disorders and psychiatric symptoms were common in the community, as demonstrated by the Stirling County (Leighton, 1959) and Midtown Manhattan (Srole et al., 1962) studies, fostered support for increased funding for mental health.

In 1946 the federal government enacted the National Mental Health Act, which allocated federal monies for research and training in mental health and set the foundation for the 1948 establishment of the National Institute of Mental Health (NIMH). During the 1950s, hospital-based care reached its zenith. In 1955, 550,000 patients lived in primarily custodial state mental hospitals. In 1948 Deutsch, in *The Shame of the States,* exposed the dehumanizing aspects of institutional life and compared it to the Nazi concentration camps. *The Snake Pit,* a film devoted to following one sympathetic female patient's journey through the back wards of an overcrowded state facility, raised public consciousness about the inhumane conditions of many mental institutions. These exposés of neglect again led to reforms. The 1955 Mental Health Study Act provided funding for a nationwide assessment of the treatment available to individuals with mental illness by the Joint Commission on Mental Illness and Health, whose report in 1961 emphasized the need to improve public hospitals by decreasing their size, increasing the resources available to them, and focusing new federal funding on improved treatment for patients with major mental illnesses.

Concurrently, researchers developed antipsychotic medications which promoted symptom reduction and highlighted the problems arising from long-term institutional care. In a classic study, patients with schizophrenia who were randomly assigned to treatment of home care and chlorpromazine rather than to the state hospital did better symptomatically, cognitively, and functionally than patients admitted to the hospital or provided with home care and placebo (Passamanick, Scarpitti, and Dinitz, 1967). Other studies demonstrated that long-term institutional care carried the side effects of inducing apathy, poor self-care skills, and asocial behavior (Goffman, 1961), unless specific "ego-stretching" activities and expectations were an intrinsic part of the inpatient milieu (Cumming and Cumming, 1962).

The political upheaval of the early 1960s provided an opportunity to reorganize the delivery of psychiatric care. The New Frontier, Peace Corps, and civil rights movement reflected the optimism and activism of the times. In 1963 President Kennedy delivered the first (and only) presidential message to Congress on mental illness and mental retardation. In line with the political mood of the times, Kennedy called for "a bold new approach" that "relies primarily upon the new knowledge and new drugs acquired and developed in recent years which make it possible for most of the mentally ill to be successfully and quickly treated in their own communities and returned to a useful place in society" (1963, p. 3). Contrary to the recommendations of the Joint Commission on Mental Illness and Health, Kennedy stated: "Central to a new mental health program is comprehensive community care. Merely pouring federal funds into a continuation of the outmoded type of institutional care which now prevails would make little difference. We need a new type of health facility, one which will return mental health care to the mainstream of American medicine, and at the same time upgrade mental health services" (p. 4). He recommended a temporary infusion of federal funds, until other methods of mental health financing through fees and adequate private insurance were developed, to establish a community-based mental health system. Shortly before his assassination, Kennedy signed legislation to provide monies to build this "new type of health facility," the community mental health center (CMHC).

The Community Mental Health Center Acts of 1963 and 1965 created funding for building and staffing CMHCs and established a set of community service principles that continue to have relevance for population-based care. Each CMHC was required to provide 5 essential services: inpatient care, partial hospitalization, outpatient services, emergency care, and consultation/education.

By the end of the 1960s, both federal and state governments began curtailing funds for health and social welfare programs. They often reduced staffing monies from federal, state, and local sources before the completion of a CMHC building, and the early plan to have 2000 CMHCs spanning the nation by 1980 was abandoned; ultimately, fewer than 800 were built. The unrealistic expectations of the CMHC movement also contributed to public ambivalence about psychiatry's role in the community; psychiatrists were criticized for overinvolvement in social issues at the expense of the treatment needs of people with mental illness.

By the mid-1970s, as the first wave of 8-year federal CMHC staffing grants began to expire, it was clear that the health insurance system would fail to provide a firm fiscal foundation for the care of patients with mental illness. In addition, the closing or downsizing of public mental hospitals under the policy of deinstitutionalization began to flood communities with large numbers of patients with chronic mental illness. In 1975 Congress passed legislation to revitalize and partially refund CMHCs, increasing the number of essential services a center had to provide in order to receive federal money, and explicitly mandating the provision of services to specific needy populations previously avoided by many

CMHCs. These services included specialized programs for children and the elderly, direct mental health screening services for the courts, follow-up care and transitional living facilities for deinstitutionalized patients leaving public hospitals, and specialized service programs for citizens with drug and alcohol abuse problems. The 1975 act provided a clear message that a publicly financed, community-based delivery system must give top priority to the care of those patients most disturbing to the community.

In 1977 President Carter established the President's Commission on Mental Health to assess the status of mental health care in the nation. Several of the commission's recommendations, incorporated into the Mental Health Systems Act of 1980, provided specific grant monies to improve services to underserved populations, including minorities, children, the elderly, and individuals with serious mental illness; to start new CMHCs; to link physical and mental health providers in order to improve the coordination of total health care; and to fund certain essential but non–revenue-producing community mental health services such as consultation, education, coordination of care, and community mental health center administration. In 1981, however, President Reagan's administration repealed this legislation before it could be implemented, ending almost 20 years of federal categorical funding for community mental health services. This federal pullback of funds, coupled with fiscal retrenchment by the states, decreased the resources available for the treatment of the seriously mentally ill in the community. Over the last 16 years, each state has developed its own response to this change in federal funding, and the emergence of managed care and privatization have considerably altered mental health systems.

Principles of Community Psychiatry

Although the 1960s vision of making community-based mental health services available to every American regardless of ability to pay was not realized, the following principles of care developed during the CMHC movement can be applied to efforts to treat a variety of patient populations.

Population Focus

CMHCs were charged with meeting the mental health needs of a geographically defined population, a "catchment area" of 75,000–200,000 people, regardless of ability to pay. Because of this mandate, all patients were theoretically the responsibility of one center from which they could not be turned away. Critics charged that CMHCs became overly concerned with treating the "worried well" who were interested in "emotional growth," underserved the severely ill, and in rural areas were often distant from much of the population. However, the principle of responsibility for a defined group of people is a central aspect of many treatment settings under managed care, capitation, and the public sector.

Prevention Orientation

In reaction to the custodial care of the earlier mental health delivery system in public hospitals, interventions in community mental health followed a public health model and were classified as any of 3 types of "prevention." *Primary prevention* strives to discover and eliminate the causes of mental illness. The formal aim of primary prevention is, therefore, to decrease the *incidence* of mental disorders (new cases of mental illness occurring in the population over a specified period of time). *Secondary prevention* is the early case finding and treatment of emotional disorders to minimize their duration and to prevent permanent disability. Its aim is to decrease the *prevalence* of mental disorders (total existent cases of mental disorder in the population at any one time). *Tertiary prevention* is rehabilitation to reduce and limit the rate and degree of residual defect and disability caused by mental illness. It aims to decrease the prevalence of disability due to mental disorder (the total number of disabled mentally ill in the population at any one time). In public psychiatry today there is little focus on primary and secondary prevention, with most resources prioritized to limiting disability in patients with persistent mental illness.

Community-Based Services

To maintain the patient's important ongoing relationships and support systems, a basic tenet is that treatment services should be provided in the geographic community where the patient lives. Unlike care in a geographically distant public hospital, treatment in the community strives to avoid isolating the patient and encourages him to retain ties to and roles in his family, workplace, and community. The growth of alternatives to long-stay inpatient care has been dramatic and includes intensive crisis intervention services, partial hospitalization, day treatment, community outreach, outpatient care, and "consumer"-run self-help services. Today, the option of long-term inpatient care is rarely available; both legal and funding mandates usually require sicker people to be in less restrictive settings than in the past, resulting in an in-

crease in the "revolving door" of multiple short-stay inpatient admissions. Within both the public and managed care sectors, there is widespread support for the provision of a continuum of care and increased focus on treating the patient in his home community.

Continuity of Care

Both the direct treatment of the patient and the coordination of all aspects of his care needs were the responsibility of the CMHC. Therefore, when a patient crossed boundaries between places or phases of care—for example, in moving from outpatient to inpatient status—information about the patient was to follow the patient. Similarly, discharge from an inpatient unit was to be coordinated with follow-up outpatient treatment in the community so that the patient did not get "lost" in the transition. Continuity also relates to the concept of a CMHC treatment network as a "closed system." The patient "belonged" to a single system of care for which all inpatient and outpatient clinicians had responsibility. This closed-system responsibility discouraged "dumping" of patients from outpatient to inpatient units or vice versa and encouraged system-wide coordination of the allocation and use of scarce resources. Today, as specific aspects of public care are being contracted out to different providers, critics have charged that care has become more discontinuous and that economically motivated "dumping" is widespread (Schlesinger et al., 1997). However, public and managed care providers are realizing that continuity of care can reduce unnecessary and costly services and affords better care for the patient.

Community Involvement

This principle was designed to encourage citizens to participate actively in the organization and delivery of mental health services in their community. Today, most CMHCs have a citizen advisory board who work with the mental health professionals to set the center's priorities. The professionals and the community board must agree on a division of power and must develop mutual respect; experience demonstrates that both are necessary for a successful public mental health delivery system. Citizens can help considerably in setting broad policies and treatment priorities for the CMHC, while mental health professionals define the therapeutic strategies and tactical treatment procedures most relevant to meet these priorities. Just as the citizen board clearly needs professional expertise to develop quality mental health care for the community, professionals need the citizens to help define what the center, with its limited resources and evolving mission, will and will not do. A strong alliance with the community is also essential, as it is the citizens who must lobby their political representatives to provide adequate public resources to the CMHC to enable it to carry out its programs.

Continuum of Services

Originally, as noted above, federal guidelines mandated that 5 essential services be provided to qualify for federal CMHC funding: inpatient care, outpatient care, partial hospitalization, 24-hour emergency services, and consultation/education to community agencies. Today the clinical trend in community-based public mental health systems no longer under federal monitoring is toward decreasing the frequency and length of expensive inpatient stays and increasing the use of intensive outpatient treatment, partial hospitalization, case management, "consumer"-directed clubhouses, and a continuum of residential services. Consultation and education services to community agencies, as non–revenue-generating activities, are now rarely included in contracts for discrete mental health services to populations.

The Emergence of Managed Care

Recent years have seen the growth of for-profit organizations competing for the health care dollar. With health care costs consuming an increasing portion of the nation's resources (currently estimated at 14% of the gross national product) (Lieberman and Rush, 1996), payors (employers, government, and individuals) have become increasingly concerned about the cost of care and its effects on the economy. This has led to a variety of efforts to "manage care," one intended side effect of which is to cap and, if possible, decrease the costs of a population's health care to payors. A basic premise of managed care is that if health care is carefully managed, many of the inefficiencies and excessive services that characterize a fee-for-service, charge-based reimbursement health care system can be eliminated, potentially improving the quality of care and decreasing its cost.

Mental health and substance abuse care delivery became an early focus of managed care because of the growth in the early 1980s of for-profit psychiatric and substance abuse hospitals exempt from the federal Diagnosis Related Groups (DRG) legislation. This legislation was intended to hold down the costs of inpatient medical care. The growth and profitability of these for-profit hospitals, paired with the fact that stigmatized persons with

mental illness are an unlikely group to protest effectively, made "behavioral health care" one of the initial targets of MCOs. Psychiatry's inability to delineate clear criteria to determine the amount and level of care required to treat specific illnesses also contributed to the field's vulnerability to such "management," as did the experience that many people seemed willing to trade extended mental health for other health care benefits when "menus" of coverage were offered by insurers, suggesting the public would be satisfied with short-term, symptom-oriented therapies for emotional problems. Manning et al. (1986) found that level of co-payment influences the amount of ambulatory care sought for psychiatric disorders; this convinced many in the payor community that mental health care would expand to the limits of coverage and, obversely, that demand would contract, with little effect on clinical outcome, when coverage lessened. Efforts to reduce spending on mental health continue despite the other major finding of the Manning study, that few individuals use mental health services (even when free), and the annual cost for this free care group is only $32 per person.

Since the end of the 1980s, for-profit behavioral MCOs have proliferated throughout the country, offering insurers and payors the opportunity to contain the costs of mental health and substance abuse care. For a specified amount, these MCOs contract to deliver "medically necessary" mental health and substance abuse care to a population of insured members of a health plan. Most MCOs develop networks of unaffiliated providers who agree both to see patients at discounted fee-for-service rates and have their care "managed" by the MCO. Patients needing mental health and substance abuse care, defined by themselves or by their primary care physicians, are usually required to receive prior authorization from the MCO for psychiatric evaluation; in many cases further care beyond initial evaluation is authorized only after review of either the evaluating clinician's written treatment plan or a phone discussion of that plan by the mental health provider with the MCO reviewer to determine the "medical necessity" for continued care. Each MCO has its own definition of what constitutes "medically necessary" mental health and substance abuse care, and the criteria for this determination are often not made available to network providers or patients. Private health care insurers, state mental health authorities, and welfare systems throughout the country have all utilized behavioral MCOs in order to provide care to populations of insured persons within fixed cost parameters.

Most behavioral MCOs provide care as a "carve out" from the provision and management of general health care, having a separate "pool" of money uninfluenced by general health care utilization or cost. Working with a fixed amount of money, behavioral MCOs that spend less on care than they have contracted for make a profit, while those that have costs exceeding their allocation lose money. Critics charge MCOs with inappropriately limiting access to, and the amount of, care in order to make a profit. Most monetary savings in behavioral health care have come from sharply decreasing the use of costly inpatient psychiatric and substance abuse services; consequently, inpatient lengths of stay, and the number of patients admitted to inpatient services in highly managed care markets, have fallen precipitously. Although many argue that needed inpatient care is increasingly difficult to access for a severely ill patient under managed care, others point to the lack of data demonstrating that lengthy hospitalizations provide better clinical outcomes although they clearly increase costs of care. While MCOs have found it most lucrative to "manage the inpatient benefit," many have had mixed results in managing outpatient care, especially in states which have a mandated outpatient mental health/substance abuse insurance benefit.

The better behavioral MCOs have recreated the continuum of care services in the private sector which community mental health systems, also serving a defined population with finite resources, created in the public sector some 20–30 years ago. Both provide clinically effective care in the least expensive manner. To achieve this goal, MCOs have had to set up closely linked, multilevel care systems which facilitate patients' moving rapidly to less intensive, less expensive care levels as soon as such movement becomes clinically appropriate. As in community mental health, offering care continuity, coordination, and efficiency, and helping patients traverse the interfaces between levels and settings of care are important components of an effective managed care system.

Today, however, most "carve out" behavioral health care networks are providers that are not tightly affiliated, and case management is performed by MCO reviewers via telephone and fax. Many providers feel that clinical review and resource allocation by reviewers who have not seen the patient (and often have less clinical experience than the treating clinician) short-changes patients and denigrates the expertise and judgment of the clinicians providing the care. Both providers and patients frequently complain about the intrusiveness of the MCO into the patient-provider relationship by requiring disclosure of the patient's symptoms and dysfunction to an anonymous reviewer in order to access care. Recent legislation in some states limits information MCOs can request (from patient or provider) to access mandated minimum mental health and substance abuse care benefits (Commonwealth of Massachusetts, 1996).

Behavioral MCOs have helped set standards for treatment planning and monitoring, record keeping, and clinical responsiveness, and have put a new focus on the relationship of the patient's symptoms to his functioning. Operating with the responsibility of serving a population with defined resources, MCOs, like CMHCs, have set priorities for their resources. They link the criteria for continued care to dysfunction due to treatable mental disorders rather than to diagnosis per se or desire for emotional "growth."

One disadvantage of the behavioral health care "carve out" strategy is that the financial bottom line of the behavioral MCO is not tied to that of general health care providers and insurers; therefore, the MCO has little incentive to coordinate mental health with physical health care or to prevent overflow of psychiatric and substance abuse problems onto primary care and other medical settings because the costs for such services do not affect the behavioral MCO's profits or losses. Several areas of the country, however, are moving toward a capitated method of payment for health care. The federal government is encouraging so-called "Medicare risk" agreements, in which insurers and providers agree to provide total health care to the elderly at a capitated rate (95% of the average annual per capita Medicare cost in the local area). Many insurers are beginning to contract with provider organizations for capitated care to non-elderly populations as well.

As capitation of general health care increases, some insurer-provider consortia are offering integrated physical health and mental health care under a single capitation. This provides incentives to both physical health and mental health care providers to facilitate coordinated care, and to provide sufficient mental health care to realize the "offset effect" on total health costs of appropriate treatment of psychiatric and substance abuse disorders (Borus et al., 1985). In such integrated systems primary care physicians have the major responsibility for managing health, mental health, and specialty care; this encourages psychiatrists and other mental health professionals (1) to work closely with primary physicians to assist them in treating those psychiatric and substance abuse disorders they can serve within their busy practices, (2) to provide consultation to assist the generalist in psychopharmacologic agents, and (3) to work collaboratively in referring patients for mental health care. This integrated approach may improve the quality and coordination of health and mental health care and contain total costs.

MCOs have generated considerable controversy. Legislative efforts to regulate them have become more common; e.g., 19 states have passed "gag" rules which prevent MCOs from restricting the clinical care options a physician can review with a patient. Other legislation has eliminated obstetric "drive through" deliveries, allowed patients to switch physicians within an MCO, and improved "due process" protections for people appealing negative determinations for care from their MCO. Other issues specific to behavioral MCOs concern record access and confidentiality, availability of expensive interventions (such as the new generation of antipsychotics or residential services), and medicolegal liability for decisions to deny or restrict care.

Advocacy and Self-Help: A New Landscape

One of the most interesting and welcome changes in population-based psychiatry is the recent growth of advocacy and self-help groups. Long-established advocacy groups, such as the American Cancer Society and the American Heart Association, have promoted research and improved services for people with specific physical disabilities or diseases. Advocacy groups for individuals with serious mental illness, however, have lagged behind; the social stigma of mental illness, coupled with past adversarial relationships between professional groups and patients and families, hindered their widespread growth. Self-help groups, from Alcoholics Anonymous to Recovery, Inc., to "clubhouse model" programs for people with serious mental illness, now form an important part of the modern world of psychiatry. Both advocacy and self-help groups seek to improve the political, social, and treatment conditions of people with mental illness. Each offers the public and the interested professional essential and compelling perspectives on the experience of family members, frustrations with the political aspects of the public sector, and the strengths and capabilities of people with mental illness.

Today, the most effective advocacy group is the National Alliance for the Mentally Ill (NAMI) and its statewide Alliance for the Mentally Ill (AMI) affiliates. Formed in 1979 by mothers of children with mental illness, NAMI now has over 150,000 members and advocates for increased funding for brain research, improved treatment services, and support for patients and their families. Families of patients with severe mental illnesses, formerly viewed by some practitioners as "schizophrenogenic," are now properly viewed as professional allies and key advocates for their relatives and for the shared goals of increased funding and improved treatment. NAMI has initiated a campaign to end discrimination against people with mental illness, and was instrumental in the adoption of the first insurance parity law, which requires that mental health coverage offered by insurance companies must have yearly and lifetime payment limits equal to those for physical health. Authorities predict that complete insurance parity for serious mental illness will result in a decrease in total health care costs by 10% for this population (National Advisory Mental Health Council, 1993). NAMI was also instrumental in having mental illness included in the Americans with Disabilities Act, and in the enactment of Public Law 99–660. This law requires all 50 states to include family and consumer participation in the development of community-based care for people with serious mental illnesses.

Self-help groups are composed of individuals who offer support, education, and problem solving to others with similar concerns (e.g., sexual preference), diagnoses (e.g., Alcoholics Anonymous, Recovery, Inc., HIV groups), or developmental issues (e.g., Parents Anonymous). About 10 million adults in the United States belong to self-help groups which offer an important adjunctive or even primary intervention for their psychological/behavioral concerns. Professionals interested in working with community or populationwide issues must be aware of the potential value of these groups to their patients. Emerick's study (1990) of over 100 self-help groups found that more than 70% reported little or no interaction with professionals; although these groups generally have little interest in a professional leader, their work tends to complement professional treatment interventions. Self-help groups emphasize the strengths of their members as each participant is both a giver and receiver of support, validation, and advice.

Related to self-help, and also to rehabilitation, is the "clubhouse model," initiated in 1948 at Fountain House in New York. In this model, former public hospital patients create an environment that emphasizes voluntarity, strengths, support, and return of patients to full roles in society (Beard, 1983). Replicated all over the country, clubhouses have "members," not patients, who decide on the degree of their involvement with the larger community and how best to organize the group's activities. For example, many clubhouses have an outreach component where members contact one another in the event of birthdays, prolonged absences, or hospitalizations. Others provide a temporary employment unit where members share jobs at selected businesses. Staff members also fill in at the job for a member who is too ill to participate, illustrating the role flexibility in clubhouse settings. The future of mental health in community or population-based settings will involve increasing interface with advocacy, self-help, and clubhouse style programs.

Providing Direct and Indirect Services to Populations

When working with a population-based system such as a public sector catchment, an HMO, or the insured persons in an MCO contract, clinical functions can be divided into services performed directly and those which indirectly promote the mental health of the group. In the direct service section, we focus on difficult or unique populations and attempt to address their particular concerns: outreach to the homeless population, community-based interventions for individuals with serious mental illness and for substance abusing adolescents, crisis intervention, and disaster relief. In the indirect service section, we review ways psychiatrists indirectly impact a population's mental health concerns, including consultation to primary care physicians and other caregivers, prevention, and the role of educating the larger community.

Direct Services for Specific Populations

Outreach to the homeless. Many people with severe mental disorder, including the homeless, avoid treatment at public sector clinics and fail to qualify for insurance-based private care. They avoid treatment because of paranoia, fears of involvement with the "system," poor insight, or unsuccessful (and often involuntary) treatment in mental health settings. This population is at increased risk of morbidity and mortality because of exposure to the elements, violence, and high rates of substance abuse; they are also disproportionate users of emergency room services. Many leaders in community mental health believe that outreach programs provide the only clinically sound and ethical approach to this challenging population.

Morse et al. (1996) define mental health outreach as "workers contacting homeless mentally ill individuals in non-traditional settings for the purpose of improving their mental or physical health, social functioning, or utilization of human services and resources." They describe the functions of outreach as establishing credible contact, identifying and engaging people with mental illness, conducting assessments, developing treatment planning, and providing ongoing services. Continuous and respectful contact as well as helping the patient make linkages to services and/or housing are essential components of effective outreach.

Professionals must also be cognizant of the potential need for role flexibility when working in nontraditional outreach settings. Susser's description of his work in a homeless transitional hotel, where residents and staff perceived referral to the psychiatrist as a humiliation, illustrates the point (Susser, Goldfinger, and White, 1990). To overcome this "stigma," Susser began running a well-attended and nonthreatening activity, the weekly bingo game; this role change allowed him to be accepted as an integral member of the community, as a "guest," and to be regarded with acceptance rather than fear. After he became an accepted part of the community, referrals for psychiatric care were made more easily.

Assertive community treatment. The clearest, most dramatic trend in community mental health over the past several decades has been the shift toward caring for people with severe and chronic mental illnesses in the communities in which they live. Innovative programs determine how best to service disabled patients living in group homes, independent apartments, their parents' homes, shelters, and so on. In the late 1970s, Stein and Test (1980) developed Training in Community Living (TCL), a groundbreaking treatment program departure from traditional hospital-based care. In TCL, most interventions occurred where the patient resided: pragmatic skills were taught in vivo (e.g., cooking, budgeting, negotiating the transportation system), and patient and family strengths were emphasized. Clinicians were charged with an "assertive" duty to ensure that patients did not get lost to follow-up. Stein and Test found that TCL "greatly reduced the need to hospitalize patients and enhanced the community tenure and adjustment of the [TCL] patients" (p. 392) when compared to treatment as usual. They also reported that 14 months after TCL was discontinued, hospital use rose "sharply," leading to the conclusion that severely ill patients living in the community require ongoing comprehensive support.

Assertive Community Treatment (ACT), also known as Community Treatment Teams (CTT), is a direct descendant of TCL and incorporates many of its ideals and strategies. Santos et al. (1995) document ACT's clinical effectiveness in which a team of clinicians provides flexible, patient-centered care to persons with severe mental illness in their residence, be it a home or shelter. By working with patients in their residences, they tailor the skills for daily living to a patient's actual living situation. ACT teams also emphasize medication compliance, maximal utilization of the support of family, friends, and neighbors, and close monitoring of the patient's medication intake and mental status. Not wedded to fixed appointment times in a clinic setting, the team can intervene to avert a crisis by providing additional supports, visits, or medication adjustments. Because this flexibility promotes a strong therapeutic alliance, the number of hospital admissions and length of stay of ACT patients have been reduced in comparison with similar patient populations. ACT programs are currently deployed statewide in Wisconsin, Michigan, Rhode Island, and Delaware, with several other states developing similar programs.

In their review of ACT, Santos et al. (1995) note that these programs do not easily lend themselves to traditional third-party billing. For this reason, leadership on the state level is required to create a reimbursement system that encourages such non-hospital, non–clinic-based treatment; i.e., the state director of mental health needs to arrange funding relationships with Medicare, Medicaid, and other major payors to support ACT activities such as home delivery of medications to avert a crisis. This kind of transition from a more traditional facility-based system takes time and commitment on the part of state administrative leaders who organize and pay for care systems.

Unfortunately, some innovative programs that provide alternatives to hospital/clinic-based care have lost support despite their demonstrated effectiveness. Reding and Raphelson (1995) describe how the addition of a psychiatrist to a mobile crisis team to provide 24-hour availability to perform assessments, on-site support, and medication prescription for patients in times of crisis led to a reduction in public and private hospitalizations for patients in the catchment area. After 6 months, however, the program was terminated, with a consequent increase in the hospitalization rate. Reasons for the defunding involved difficulties in integrating this nontraditional intervention with the existing CMHC service delivery system. One leading community psychiatrist blamed this program's demise on having been "killed by bureaucratic rigidity" (Diamond, 1995). Increased attention to outcome research is likely to promote and ultimately lead to funding of programs that are cost-effective, regardless of the institutional or conceptual hurdles they create.

Multisystemic therapy. Adolescents who abuse substances, and those with histories of delinquency, constitute a high-risk population that often fares poorly in traditional office-based settings and has high dropout rates. Barriers to treatment such as difficulties in accessing therapists, waiting lists, lack of evening and weekend treatment hours, and difficulties with transportation to an office for treatment reduce participation by all adolescents. In contrast, "home visits, less waiting time, more frequent client contacts, the provision of concrete services, and high levels of therapist commitment to and respect for the client" reduce the number of dropouts from substance abuse intervention (Henggeler et al., 1996, p. 427). Multisystemic therapy, a time-limited, home-based, and intensive intervention, aims to utilize those strategies for eliminating dropout from treatment by adolescent substance abusers and delinquents. This is an important strategy on both clinical and cost-effectiveness grounds since currently the majority of dollars spent on adolescent mental health care is devoted to residential services.

In multisystemic therapy, a master's level clinician has a relatively small caseload of adolescent patients to whom he is available 24 hours a day, 7 days a week. The therapist (and his supporting team) take active responsibility for engaging the patient and his or her family; different and flexible approaches are tried until participation is maximized. Intervention plans are individualized, but typically involve intensive work with parents, school, peers, and the adolescent, at the times and places that best promote participation and eliminate dropout, e.g., in-home meetings on weekends at dinnertime when an intervention may have high potential for impact. With this commitment to making the service system "user friendly," Henggeler et al. (1996) found a dramatic increase in the number of families who completed a full course of treatment in multisystemic therapy (98%, n=57) compared to families who received "treatment as usual" (78%, n=47, received *no* substance abuse or mental health services).

Like ACT, multisystemic therapy seeks to identify and support resources within the patient and his environment to maintain as much autonomous functioning as possible; unlike ACT, multisystemic therapy is a short-term, intensive treatment. Although this approach requires extensive support and supervision, as cost accounting assumes a greater role in the future of mental health services, continued development and assessment of such outpatient support programs are likely to continue.

Pluralistic brief therapies/crisis intervention. Another strategy for providing more economical direct services is cutting the costs in worker hours per patient by using group, family, and crisis intervention techniques. A community or mobile setting provides greater accessibility to patients, their families, and other important patient supporters and caregivers (clergy, employers, local physicians). A therapist may therefore work with an entire family unit or other group in a single therapeutic intervention. Too often, however, in an attempt to be economical, clinic-based providers offer only group or family therapies even when inappropriate to the needs of a particular patient or cultural group.

A cost-effective therapy used frequently in community mental health settings is crisis intervention. A crisis is a time of substantial stress and change in a person's life that requires both internal and external coping efforts for successful adaptation. Crisis intervention is a brief therapeutic input to facilitate healthy coping and prevent the deterioration of behavior into a defined mental disorder.

The population-focused psychiatrist must distinguish among 4 overlapping uses of the crisis concept in deciding how to help people: (1) an *identity crisis,* as described by Erik Erikson (1950), is a stressful turning point in normal development (for example, adolescence or midlife) during which one's internal priorities and external goals must be reevaluated and realigned; (2) a *situational crisis,* as described by Erich Lindemann (1944), refers to the stress experienced by a number of persons in a population when exposed to a precipitous change in social context caused by a disaster or a major social or economic change; (3) a *transitional life crisis,* a concept stemming from the work of Adolph Meyer (1952), refers to the stress inherent in predictable transitions from one psychosocial or physiological stage of life to another (e.g., stress experienced by kindergartners leaving the protectiveness of home, young adults going away to college, or parents of newborns); and (4) an *idiosyncratic emotional crisis,* which is an unpredicted state of emotional turmoil caused by an individual loss, such as the death of a parent or the loss of a job. We have described elsewhere in this chapter how assertive community work can intervene into a crisis with a seriously ill patient to avert hospitalization, and how interventions after disaster can avert long-lasting symptomatology following situational crises.

Crisis theory posits that in such stressful situations previous coping methods no longer work, and people feel overwhelmed, helpless, extremely anxious, and eager for help (Caplan, 1964). Crisis intervention as a therapeutic technique involves a brief, intense therapeutic input focused on the recent crisis only, sectoring out much of the rest of the person's life history. The therapist helps the person avoid using old, regressive, and inappropriate coping methods by suggesting appropriate new methods aimed at solving the current problem. The goals of crisis intervention are to foster mastery, to avoid prolonged dependence on therapy, and to enlarge the person's coping repertoire for dealing with both the current crisis and future situations.

Disaster relief. Mental health professionals increasingly provide support to those who suffer natural or manmade disasters (Ursano, Fullerton, and Norwood, 1995). The high incidence of post-traumatic stress disorder (PTSD) in people directly exposed to traumatic events has led local psychiatric societies to plan intervention and consultation strategies for disaster victims. For instance, psychiatrists from the Oklahoma Psychiatric Association's Disaster Committee quickly provided valuable on-site assistance to the victims of the April 1995 bombing of the Murrah Federal Building in Oklahoma City (Karel, 1995).

The fourth edition of the *Diagnostic and Statistical Manual of Mental Disorders* (DSM-IV) provides a new disaster-related diagnosis, Acute Stress Disorder (ASD). This diagnosis differs from PTSD primarily in the time course; the diagnosis of ASD requires symptoms (hyperarousal, avoidance, reexperiencing, dissociation, impairment or distress) within 4 weeks of the acute stress (these symptoms usually resolve within 4 weeks), an acknowledgment of the commonality of traumatic symptoms in communities exposed to disasters. Proximity to the disaster is the best predictor of psychiatric symptoms; for instance, in the case of the Mount St. Helen's volcanic eruption, Shore, Tatum, and Vollmer (1986) documented higher incidences of PTSD-generalized anxiety disorder and depression in victims who lived closer to the volcano, a finding consistent with the Vietnam era experience that PTSD occurred more frequently in wounded veterans. Other researchers (Palinkas et al., 1993) found a significant increase in psychiatric symptoms in 13 Alaskan communities 1 year after the *Exxon Valdez* oil spill, demonstrating that even a disaster not directly threatening to a population's physical safety can cause great psychological distress. For this reason, disaster support should be provided in close proximity to the stressful event.

Psychiatric interventions in time of disaster involve both direct and indirect services. Primary care settings proximate to the disaster can be an important place to identify and treat people at risk of PTSD. Support must also be provided for the rescue personnel, themselves at high risk of traumatization as they attempt to find survivors and remove the dead. Direct debriefing meetings with traumatized victims and families should be provided, but at appropriate times when people can adequately process the experience (Shalev, 1994). Assisting community leaders in normalizing the community's response, controlling rumors, and acting as liaison and advocate with state and federal health care units are indirect services psychiatrists can provide to help optimize community response to disaster (Ursano, Fullerton, and Norwood, 1995).

Indirect Services for Specific Populations

Mental health consultation. Mental health consultation, a clinical skill defined and developed by Gerald Caplan (1970) to stretch limited resources, provides indirect consultative services to a wide variety of health, welfare, religious, and legal system caregivers in the community. Working with community caregivers is especially important in light of studies demonstrating that people suffering emotional difficulties seek care first from clergy, primary physicians, and teachers rather than from psychiatrists and other mental health workers. The rationale for community mental health consultation to other community caregivers is illustrated by the following scenario. A schoolteacher in the primary grades is the societally sanctioned caregiver 6 hours a day for 30–40 children. In this role the teacher has an ongoing view of the children's development and directly observes their behavior and their emotional conflicts. Similarly, a primary physician, another sanctioned caregiver, sees 30–50 patients a day, longitudinally observes their behavior, follows their development, and elicits their problems. In an hour a week a consulting psychiatrist can help these professionals better understand both normal and aberrant behaviors in the classroom or the doctor's office. The consultant can suggest interventions for handling emotional problems relevant to the particular setting; for example, he can help the teacher deal effectively with behavioral problems in the classroom without labeling or expelling the child and help refer the child for specialized mental health treatment if necessary.

Mental health consultation is a complex skill that, to do well, requires time, training, and supervision. The consulting psychiatrist must be aware that by definition he is outside the line of decision-making authority, and therefore his recommendations may be accepted or discarded. A consultant's only power is gained by demonstrating that his expertise is helpful in finding realistic solutions to the behavioral problems faced by his consultee.

Caplan (1970) defines 4 types of mental health consultation. In *client-centered case consultation* the psychiatrist examines the primary caregiver's client and provides an evaluation and treatment recommendations. This familiar mode of consultation is best exemplified by a psychiatric consultation to a general physician about a hospitalized patient. *Consultee-centered case consultation* differs from the first mode in that the psychiatrist never meets directly with the caregiver's client. Instead, the caregiver describes the case to the consultant, and the latter helps him learn new ways to handle it. The psychiatrist determines why the professionally competent caregiver is having difficulties with this case (lack of knowledge, skills, confidence, or objectivity); he then addresses this problem through the case to prepare the caregiver to deal more effectively with such cases at present and in the future. *Program-centered administrative consultation* is analogous to the first mode in that the psychiatrist is called in to analyze a specific programmatic problem and make recommendations to management staff about how best to remedy it. *Consultee-centered administrative consultation* is analogous to the second mode in that the psychiatrist is asked to clarify organizational difficulties in administrative roles and tasks.

Both client and consultee-centered psychiatric case consultation is increasingly directed to primary care physicians (PCPs), the "gatekeepers" from whom patients often must get approval to access specialists in managed care settings. Such consultation helps make the psychiatrist's expertise available to the large number of people treated by PCPs, and focuses the psychiatrist's direct-service efforts on resistant and complex cases the PCP cannot handle. Evidence suggests that mental health and substance abuse issues consume a large part of PCP practice time, and that the psychological and behavioral responses to many illnesses (e.g., diabetes, heart disease, cancer) which increase the morbidity of these conditions are not being sufficiently addressed. The Epidemiologic Catchment Area study confirms that more patients with a mental health or substance abuse disorder seek treatment from a general health professional than from a mental health professional (Regier et al., 1993): in the prior 6-month period 56.7% of people with a mental disorder had an outpatient general medical visit, while only 12.4% had a visit to any mental health professional (Shapiro et al., 1984).

These data support the notion that population-focused psychiatrists should set a high priority on coordinating their care with that of PCPs in solo, group, or organized practices in the community. Providing mental health services in the same community settings as primary health care has many advantages (Borus, Burns, et al., 1979). People find it easier to seek mental health services in the general health care setting, where they can see a mental health provider without being labeled a "mental patient." They are more likely to accept referral for specialty mental health care when they are handed over from their trusted general physician to his colleague within the same service setting. The coordination of a patient's mental and physical health care is also more likely to occur when caregivers can meet on a regular basis to avoid fragmented treatment plans, conflicting medication regimens, and the like. Utilization of mental health services within primary health care settings is 2–5 times greater than that provided in freestanding CMHCs, a fact which supports the notion that the primary health care setting is a more acceptable and accessible site for patients to seek such care. PCPs, who often under- or misdiagnose mental disorders in their patients (Borus et al., 1987), benefit from the consultative and collaborative availability of on-site psychiatrists. Finally, "offset studies" suggest that improving access to specialty mental health care decreases the high utilization of general health services by patients with mental disorders (Borus et al., 1985). Greenberg and Paulsen (1996) have described how residency training programs can teach psychiatrists to work effectively in the primary care setting.

Multidisciplinary team approach/case management. Many public mental health agencies and HMOs have adopted a multidisciplinary team approach with caregivers from different mental health professional disciplines and paraprofessionals forming the treatment team. Such a team is economical and effective if less expensive caregivers can actually provide many of the direct services required by patients. Careful cost accounting, however, reveals that, despite salary equivalency, 4 mental health workers cannot fully substitute for 1 psychiatrist because the community service agency must also incur the costs of expert, "expensive" professionals to provide the mental health workers with training, supervision, consultation, and support. In many agencies the psychiatrist's role includes providing these essential indirect services to other clinicians who then provide most of the direct patient care. Although there is some overlapping of roles among the mental health professions, a functional team will pool its members' differing areas of expertise (psychiatrists' knowledge of medical, psychophysiological, and psychopharmacologic aspects of illness; social workers' knowledge of the welfare system and family dynamics; etc.) to avoid duplication of effort, denigration of expertise, and the development of false egalitarianism (Borus, 1978).

Community-based agencies may also use paraprofessional mental health workers from a wide variety of backgrounds (ranging from homemakers to humanities doctoral candidates) to help professionals provide mental health services. Some centers employ paraprofessional therapists and case managers who live in the community and can demonstrate warmth, empathy, and regard for

local patients. A study in an Italian-American neighborhood of Boston found that, despite these admirable personal qualities, such caregivers require clinical training and supervision to develop necessary therapeutic expertise to add to their knowledge of the culture, customs, and stresses of their community (Borus, Anastasi, et al., 1979).

As the locus of care for people with severe mental illness has shifted from the hospital, where all services occurred on one site, to the community, where many places and agencies are involved, the need for case management has expanded considerably. A case manager's role is in part supportive but primarily involves the coordination of the numerous agencies and clinical services involved in the care of seriously ill patients. For example, one of our patients, a 32-year-old man with schizophrenia who receives his clinical care at a state-funded CMHC day treatment program, receives federal support through Social Security Disability Insurance, and lives in a room in a vendor-operated group home. His expensive medication (clozapine) is paid for by the closely monitored state pharmacy budget when the pharmaceutical company's "low income" program is exceeded; if he were eligible for Medicaid, this government insurance for low income people would pay for all his medications. He attends a clubhouse model program operated by another private vendor, has his blood drawn at the CMHC and monitored by a separate vendor, and, if he were hospitalized (the inpatient setting determined in part by the type[s] of insurance he has), he would require a coordinated transition back to his group home and day treatment programs. Not surprisingly, many people with serious mental illness have difficulty navigating such a complex and ever-changing system without a case manager; yet, in some settings, case managers carry enormous caseloads which make individualized, responsible care coordination nearly impossible.

In many service systems, a relatively small number of patients use a high percentage of expensive inpatient services. In a San Diego study (Quinlivan et al., 1995), high users of services were randomly assigned to either traditional case management, involving coordination of caregiving agencies, or intensive case management, involving more frequent contacts, assertive outreach, and proactive intervention (e.g., ensuring that a patient who loses his medication gets a refill instead of just hoping that he does). The researchers found that the more intensely case managed patients incurred lower annual per capita costs ($9471) than either the group receiving traditional case management ($13,043) or the control group ($21,047). The intensive case management team also utilized consumer "community living aides," people with a major mental illness who had been previously hospitalized, as members of the case management team; these aides were successful in establishing rapport with high service users resistant to help offered by professionals. The model of employing "consumer/case managers" or "consumer/living aides" as adjuncts to outpatient teams has gained momentum nationwide as experience has proved its worth (Solomon and Draine, 1996).

Community education. Educating the community about mental disorders and their treatment is an indirect service that can improve identification of cases at an early stage of illness, increase community acceptance of people with chronic mental illnesses, and inform citizens about the availability and effectiveness of treatment. Education seeks to decrease the stigma of seeking care for a mental disorder, thus promoting early intervention, which is likely to be less costly and require fewer resources than treatment delayed.

Accurate information about psychiatric conditions continues to be misunderstood, ignored, or inaccessible to the public. For example, many believe that schizophrenia is synonymous with multiple personality disorder; this belief is so pervasive that 2 1993 dictionary definitions of schizophrenia include it as an adjective for having contradictory opinions or purposes (e.g., the public is "schizophrenic" in wanting to have more government services and to pay fewer taxes) (*Merriam Webster's Collegiate Dictionary* and *Collins Cobuild English Language Dictionary*). So prevalent are the misperceptions about schizophrenia, even among professionals in the field of psychiatry, that Harding and Zahniser (1994) wrote a classic paper challenging the 7 most common myths about schizophrenia "which impinge upon the perception and thus the treatment of patients." Depression entails similar misconceptions: a 1996 survey commissioned by the National Mental Health Association revealed that 54% of Americans believed that depression was a weakness, not an illness; and fewer than one-third of respondents were aware that anxiety, agitation, sleeping, and eating habits were associated with clinical depression (*Neuroscience News,* 1996).

These misconceptions result primarily from erroneous media portrayals of individuals with mental illness: evil psychotic killers, fools to be ridiculed, or failures. In the average American home, the television is on more than 7 hours a day; most people report that their main source of knowledge about mental illness comes from TV. A 10-year study of over 19,000 speaking parts on television

shows divided the characters portrayed into "heroes" and "villains." Characters with mental illness were portrayed as "villains" nearly 10 times as often as people who were physically disabled (Gerbner, 1993).

Because of the prevalence of these negative portrayals of mental illness in the media, 85% of Americans who need mental health services report that they failed to seek help because of the social stigma of mental illness (Clements, 1993). *Stigma,* a term used to describe the social process "marking" members of a group with undesirable attributes, originated in the ancient Greek era, when slaves were literally "marked" to denote their low status. While today's meaning is more metaphorical, the impact remains the same. Mental illness raises the specter of the unknown and incites anxiety and fear; people fear what they do not understand. It is to be hoped that the combined efforts of neuroscience, research, and public education will reduce these misperceptions.

Psychiatrists must support and participate in educational activities in community organizations, and utilize the media to convey accurate information about mental illnesses and treatment. National Depression Screening Day, the first and most successful example of a voluntary screening and education program for a psychiatric disorder applied to a large population, presents opportunities for psychiatrists to participate in community education. Depression is a common and treatable disorder which often responds to early intervention but can escape the awareness of the person who has it. In a review of the 1992 National Depression Screening Day data, Magruder et al. (1995) note that 76.6% of the 5387 adults screened had at least minimal depressive symptoms and 22.6% had severe symptoms; they found that few of the symptomatic volunteers were in any treatment. Another national educational project, Mental Illness Awareness Week (the first week of October), is an annual opportunity for psychiatrists and other mental health professionals to help demystify psychiatric issues via educational programs in schools, churches, and community organizations.

In addition to the work of psychiatrists, advocacy organizations, and self-help groups, grassroots efforts to combat the stigma surrounding mental illness are emerging. One of the most successful is the National Stigma Clearinghouse, which collects egregious examples of stereotypical and hostile portrayals of mental illness from popular advertisements, films, TV shows, and cartoons. Numerous retractions and apologies have resulted from the work of this socially conscious group, which was awarded the American Psychiatric Association's Assembly Speaker's Award in 1995. A recent proliferation of written and filmed first-person accounts of coping with psychiatric disorders has also helped to demystify these conditions and the people who experience them (Styron, 1990; Jamison, 1995). When speaking to a community, the psychiatrist should be familiar with these popular works and with lay audience-friendly professional texts and pamphlets that provide accurate and understandable information concerning mental illness and treatment.

Preventive intervention. Another attempt to stretch resources through indirect services has been preventive interventions that decrease the onset, severity, duration, and disability of mental illness. Primary prevention to decrease the incidence of new cases of mental disorders is an appealing but controversial area because it involves intervening before the onset of disorder, and it is always difficult to prove that what did not happen was prevented and would have happened without the intervention. Gaining the clear sanction of citizens for primary prevention programs is therefore essential. One important form of primary prevention is timely crisis intervention, as described above, for people who show symptoms of emotional disturbance before the precipitation of discrete illness. Helping the population to avoid known physical toxins that can lead to mental disorder (for example, through screening programs for lead and phenylketonuria, or PKU) is another primary preventive intervention. A third involves intervening with targeted populations at increased risk of developing a mental disorder (for example, pregnant teenagers or recent widows) (Borus and Anastasi, 1979).

Secondary prevention to decrease the prevalence of illness by reducing its length and avoiding disability focuses on efforts that facilitate early case finding and effective treatment. These efforts include close coordination between mental health providers and clergy, primary physicians, and teachers; providing an accessible and acceptable service system so that people will seek and receive care without delay; providing outreach services, including community education, to make contact with citizens hesitant to seek care; and screening procedures in settings where citizens at risk congregate (for example, preschool screening, premarital counseling, and outreach programs at senior citizen centers).

Tertiary preventive interventions—rehabilitative services to minimize the residual defect and disability caused by mental disorder—include a variety of services aimed at effectively caring for patients with chronic mental disorders. Such care has become a primary focus of public psychiatry in the last decade and is described above and in Chapter 32.

Current Issues

Disenfranchisement

Although the organization of public and private services appears to include all Americans, substantial gaps exist for disenfranchised subsets of the population. Estimates are that 40 million Americans have no health insurance (*Statistical Abstract,* 1995), and of that population, many have no identified system for mental health care except limited access to "free care." The private sector generally has assumed no responsibility for uninsured people. As public sector systems have increasingly focused their attention and scarce resources on the most severely and persistently ill population, individuals not "sick enough" are unable to gain access to public care. In this disenfranchised group are the working poor, temporary workers, and illegal immigrants functioning well enough to maintain a living but with no health insurance and not sufficiently ill to qualify for public sector care.

For example, Ms. M., an uninsured 36-year-old piecework seamstress and single mother of 2 small children, presented to a private hospital emergency room with symptoms of anxiety, depression, and drug cravings. She was neither acutely suicidal nor using drugs. She was not "poor" enough to qualify for free care at the hospital; neither was she chronic enough (symptoms had been limited to several weeks), impaired enough (she continued to work to avoid becoming homeless), nor did she have a severe enough diagnosis to qualify for the public sector system. Ironically, if she were to go untreated and become suicidal or homeless, she could qualify for the public sector; if she had to quit work and thus become poor enough, she could get free care at the private hospital. Another example is Mr. R., a 22-year-old college student having dissociative episodes in the context of recovering traumatic memories. While functioning at a reduced but still passing level in school, he has exceeded the school health system's ability to provide him with service. Too ill for the school health facilities, he may not be ill enough for the public sector CMHC in his area. If fortunate, people like Ms. M. and Mr. R. may benefit from a compassionate clinician or administrator who makes exceptions and absorbs the financial losses to provide them with care.

Unfortunately, not all disenfranchised people find such help, and most are, by definition, without a service system. Persons who speak different languages or come from other cultures are particularly at risk to go unserved. Sadly, because the aggregate system does not adhere to the first principle of community/population psychiatry discussed above (responsibility to a population), subsets of the population are left without treatment. This is an ethical challenge to the field of psychiatry and promises to be an area of increased political and social concern in the coming years.

Homelessness and Deinstitutionalization

The number of homeless Americans has soared in the last few decades. Point-in-time estimates of homeless individuals have been as low as 600,000 (Burt and Cohen, 1989). Yet recent research reveals that about 7 million Americans experienced being homeless at least once in the latter half of the 1980s (Link et al., 1995; Culhane et al., 1994). The proportion of homeless persons suffering from a major mental illness ranges from estimates of between one-fourth and one-third (Dennis, 1990) to one-fourth and one-half (Arce and Vergare, 1984) of the total; the percentage is higher for point-in-time estimates. Deinstitutionalization and socioeconomic changes contribute to these social problems.

In the late 1950s, states began closing and "downsizing" facilities for individuals with long-standing and serious mental illness. The forces that led to the transition of several hundred thousand people with mental illnesses to the "community" involved several factors: (1) the attempt to transfer the high cost of care of these individuals from the state to the federal government through the use of outpatient federal benefits (state-run, long-term inpatient psychiatry beds are not reimbursable by the federal government); (2) the advent of improved pharmacotherapy (first the antipsychotics, and later lithium and antidepressants) for persons with serious mental illness; (3) the public concern generated by exposés dramatizing the life of institutionalized patients; and (4) increased interest in the civil liberties of disenfranchised psychiatric populations, and case law which set a "least restrictive alternative" (*Lake v. Cameron*) standard for psychiatric care.

This transition created many problems. Deinstitutionalization attempted to reintegrate individuals with serious mental illness into the community, foster independent functioning, and increase family contact. Often, however, patients, families, and communities were unprepared for this sweeping system change which failed to provide follow-up care for many of the deinstitutionalized. Segal and Aviram (1978) found that fewer than one-third of former long-term state hospital patients received any kind of mental health follow-up care when discharged. Consequently, the number of specialized residential units required for this population never approached the demand. Many deinstitutionalized patients became "tran-

sinstitutionalized" to nursing homes, shelters, single-resident occupancy (SRO) units, and correctional institutions, moving from one custodial setting to another, while others ended up on the streets. Unlike the patients in the TCL program discussed above, few were taught how to remedy the atrophy of life skills that often accompanied long-term institutional life.

During this time, broad socioeconomic changes significantly reduced the number of low-cost housing units, with a resulting increase in rents. During the 1970s, over 1 million SRO housing units were lost. Vacancy rates in SROs dropped to less than 1% in New York City (Mapes, 1985). As the rent-to-income ratio increased for the poorest members of society (Carliner, 1987), federal subsidized housing monies were reduced by 60% from 1981 to 1985 (Mapes, 1985). Availability of low-cost housing decreased just as the economy saw a decreased demand for manufacturing and manual labor; low-wage service industry jobs replaced only some of these losses. Additionally, by the 1980s, New York hotel managers refused to reaccept old tenants who had been hospitalized and would not accept new tenants with psychiatric histories; in effect, contact with the mental health system actually contributed to homelessness (Cohen and Thompson, 1992).

These socioeconomic forces also led to a rise in the number of families who lost their homes and turned to shelters. In a 29-city survey, the U.S. Conference of Mayors (1987) reported that families, predominantly headed by women, constituted 34% of the overall homeless population. Bassuk (1990) argues that we are witnessing the "feminization of homelessness," typically involving female heads of households with young children under 5. Many of these families previously lived in overcrowded housing with relatives or friends. Those fortunate enough to gain access to state-sponsored housing are often placed in low-rent hotels, distant from their pediatrician, supermarket, and natural support system.

In 1987 the Stewart McKinney Homeless Assistance Act created numerous programs to protect and improve the lives and safety of the homeless. These included mental health care programs, education and job training, emergency food and shelter services, income assistance, transitional and long-term housing, substance abuse programs, and funding for a variety of housing programs. In its unique housing study, the Boston McKinney Demonstration Project challenges the mindset that previously homeless people with serious mental illness require custodial care and containment (Goldfinger et al., 1994). By designing a program where residents gradually assume responsibility for running their homes, the Boston Project has demonstrated the feasibility of lengthy housing tenure for previously homeless people. Termed "Evolving Consumer Households" (ECHs), the project starts with full-time staff who gradually transfer responsibility for managing the house to the residents. By "empowering" the residents with modeling, coaching, and training in specific skills (such as conflict resolution), staff gradually "fade out" of running the home. Residents of such homes report an increase in their overall quality of life, sense of control, and personal safety. Of note, those residents with serious substance abuse issues were most likely to be asked to leave the ECHs.

Training

The current trends in the financing and organization of care raise issues about how psychiatric residency training will be funded and how it should evolve. In a time when efficiency and cost-effectiveness are viewed as essential to medical care, psychiatric training, which is neither, faces a crisis (Borus, 1994). Funding streams for residency training are under pressure from all sides. MCOs evidence no incentive or mandate to invest in the creation of future practitioners and often refuse to pay for services delivered by trainees. At the same time, the federal government has reduced graduate medical education funding to the hospitals which train residents. Recent Medicare guidelines severely restrict the ability of residents to bill for clinical services unless an attending psychiatrist is present for the entire encounter. As a result, academic centers are being forced to assign residents away from Medicare-funded and MCO patients, raising questions about what population trainees will have access to as they learn their craft.

Public sector systems, which continue to shoulder most of the burden of care for patients with serious mental illness, may surprisingly offer some hope for funding future training. States have an interest in attracting high-level caregivers for the neediest members of society. Evidence exists that residents who train in academically related public sector settings are more likely to pursue careers in the public sector (Salzman, 1976). However, in the absence of substantial advocacy for continuation of public sector funds for training, such settings also are at great risk of being cut.

In a 1994 survey of 76 academic psychiatry residency programs (Douglas et al., 1994), 52 chairpersons reported that their departments had a significant relationship with a CMHC as a teaching site. Most respondents reported that the CMHC training experiences were "good" or "excellent," and believed that patient populations in public sector settings are important for residency training. As

psychiatry devotes more of its attention to people with serious illness, increased academic collaboration with CMHC and other public sector facilities will be welcome. Finally, the ascendance of the PCP as the pivotal member of new systems of care, the relative shortage of generalist medical practitioners, and the awareness that individuals with serious mental illness receive poor general health care have led to recent calls to redefine psychiatric training to include competence in primary care medicine (Shore, 1996).

Outcomes Research

Today's focus on cost containment and accountability to payors has led to widespread interest in understanding which interventions produce what clinical results and at what cost. Termed "outcomes research," the answers to these questions require rigorous study design, specificity of interventions, and valid assessment tools.

Even with increased research sophistication, a population-based focus is needed to place outcomes research in a larger context. For example, an expensive medication may promote symptom reduction and even reduce service utilization, but will be underutilized if the pharmacy budget at a CMHC bears no connection to the larger service budget (e.g., the pharmacy manager will attempt to reduce access to expensive medications, regardless of clinical or service utilization outcomes). In a study of 96 patients with treatment-resistant schizophrenia, Clozaril, an expensive and atypical antipsychotic agent, was found by Meltzer et al. (1993) to decrease total service costs by $8702 per patient; this reduction occurred almost exclusively from decreased inpatient usage. Only a coordinated service system responsible for an entire population is likely to invest in an expensive treatment in order to reap greater savings later in a different component of the system. Psychiatrists who attend to a population, such as a public sector catchment area or population of managed care enrollees, will increasingly be asked to be stewards of the finite treatment resources allotted for that group. By proactively leading the exploration of "what works and what it costs," psychiatrists can continue to contribute to improving the mental health of the populations they serve.

References

Arce, A. A., and M. J. Vergare. 1984. Identifying and characterizing the mentally ill among the homeless. In *The homeless mentally ill*, ed. H. R. Lamb. Washington, D.C.: American Psychiatric Association.

Bassuk, E. L. 1990. Who are the homeless families? Characteristics of sheltered mothers and children. *Community Ment. Health J.* 26:425–434.

Beard, J., T. V. Propst, and T. Malamud. 1983. The Fountain House model of psychiatric rehabilitation. *Psychosoc. Rehab. J.* 161:3–4.

Beers, C. W. 1917. *A mind that found itself.* New York: Plimpton Press.

Borus, J. F. 1978. Issues critical to the survival of community mental health. *Am. J. Psychiatry* 135:1029–34.

———— 1994. Economics and psychiatric education: the irresistible force meets the moveable object. *Harvard Rev. Psychiatry* 2:15–21.

Borus, J. F., and M. A. Anastasi. 1979. Mental health prevention groups in primary care settings. *Int. J. Ment. Health* 8:58–73.

Borus, J. F., M. A. Anastasi, R. Casoni, R. Dello-Russo, L. DiMascio, L. Fusco, J. Rubinstein, and M. Snyder. 1979. Psychotherapy in the goldfish bowl: the role of the indigenous therapist. *Arch. Gen. Psychiatry* 36:187–190.

Borus, J. F., B. J. Burns, A. M. Jacobson, L. B. Macht, R. G. Morrill, and E. M. Eilwon. 1979. *Coordinated mental health care in neighborhood health centers: Institute of Medicine series on mental health services in general health care.* Vol. 2. Washington, D.C.: National Academy of Sciences.

Borus, J. F., M. C. Olendzki, I. Kessler, B. J. Burns, U. C. Brandt, C. A. Broverman, and P. R. Henderson. 1985. The "offset effect" of mental health treatment on ambulatory medical care utilization and charges: month-by-month and grouped month analyses of a five-year study. *Arch. Gen. Psychiatry* 42:573–580.

Borus, J. F., M. J. Howes, N. P. Devins, R. Rosenberg, and W. W. Livingston. 1987. Primary health providers' recognition and diagnosis of mental disorders in their patients. *Gen. Hosp. Psychiatry* 10:317–321.

Briggs, L. V., and collaborators. 1922. *History of the psychopathic hospital, Boston, Massachusetts.* Boston: Wright & Potter Printing Co.

Burt, M. R., and B. E. Cohen. 1989. *America's homeless: numbers, characteristics, and programs that serve them.* Washington, D.C.: Urban Institute Press.

Caplan, G. 1964. *Principles of preventive psychiatry.* New York: Basic Books.

———— 1970. *The theory and practice of mental health consultation.* New York: Basic Books.

Carliner, M. S. 1987. Homelessness: a housing problem? In *The homeless in contemporary society,* ed. R. D. Bingham, R. E. Green, and S. B. White. Newbury Park, Calif.: Sage.

Clements, M. 1993. What we say about mental illness. *Parade* 31:4–6.

Cohen, C. I., and K. S. Thompson. 1992. Homeless mentally ill or mentally ill homeless? *Am. J. Psychiatry* 149:816–823.

Commonwealth of Massachusetts. Acts of 1996. Chapter 8.

Culhane, D. P., E. F. Dejowski, J. Ibanex, E. Needham, and I. Macchia. 1994. Public shelter admission rates in Philadelphia and New York City: the implications of turnover for shelter population counts. *Housing Policy Debate* 5:107–176.

Cumming, J., and E. Cumming. 1962. *Ego and milieu.* New York: Atherton Press.

Dennis, D. 1990. Exploring myths about "street people." *Access* 2:1–3.

Deutsch, A. 1948. *The shame of the states.* New York: Harcourt Brace.

Diamond, R. 1995. Some thoughts on "around-the-clock mobile psychiatric crisis intervention." *Community Ment. Health J.* 31:188–90.

Douglas, E. J., L. R. Faulkner, J. A. Talbott, C. B. Robinowitz, and J. S. Eaton. 1984. Administrative relationships between community mental health centers and academic psychiatry departments: a 12-year update. *Am. J. Psychiatry* 151:722–727.

Emerick, R. R. 1990. Self-help groups for former patients: relations with mental health professionals. *Hosp. Community Psychiatry* 41:401–407.

Erickson, E. H. 1950. *Childhood and society.* New York: Norton.

Foucault, M. 1965. *Madness and civilization: a history of insanity in the age of reason.* New York: Pantheon Books.

Gerbner, G. 1993. *Women and minorities in television: a study in casting and fate. A report to the Screen Actors Guild and the American Federation of Radio and Television Artists.*

Godding, W. W. 1890–91. Aspects and outlook of insanity in America. *Am. J. Insan.* 67:1–16.

Goffman, E. 1961. *Asylums: essays on the social situation of mental patients and other inmates.* Chicago: Aldine.

Goldfinger, S. M., B. Dickey, S. Hellman, M. O'Bryan, W. Penk, R. K. Schutt, L. J. Seidman, N. Ware, et al. 1994. The Boston project: promoting housing stability and consumer empowerment. In *Making a difference: interim status report of the McKinney Demonstration Program for Homeless Adults with Serious Mental Illness.* Washington, D.C.: Center for Mental Health Services, U. S. Department of Health and Human Services.

Greenberg, N. E., and R. H. Paulsen. 1996. Moving into the neighborhood: preparing residents to participate in a primary care environment. *Harvard Rev. Psychiatry* 4:107–109.

Grob, G. N. 1994. The mad among us: a history of the care of America's mentally ill. New York: Free Press.

Harding, C. M., and J. H. Zahniser. 1994. Empirical correction of seven myths about schizophrenia with implications for treatment. *Acta Psychiatr. Scand.* 90(suppl. 384):140–146.

Henggeler, S. W., S. G. Pickrel, M. J. Brondino, and J. L. Crouch. 1996. Eliminating (almost) treatment dropout of substance abusing or dependent delinquents through home-based multisystemic therapy. *Am. J. Psychiatry* 153:427–428.

Jamison, K. R. 1995. *An unquiet mind: a memoir of moods and madness.* New York: Knopf.

Karel, R. 1995. Psychiatrists plunge in after Oklahoma bombing. *Psychiatric News* 20:4, 28–29.

Kennedy, J. F. 1963. Message from the president of the United States relative to mental illness and mental retardation. Document 58, 86th Cong.

Lake v. Cameron, 124 U.S. App. D.C. 264, 364 F2d 657 (1966).

Leighton, A. 1959. *My name is legion.* New York: Basic Books.

Lieberman, J. A., and A. J. Rush. 1996. Redefining the role of psychiatry in medicine. *Am. J. Psychiatry* 153:1388–97.

Lindemann, E. 1944. Symptomatology and management of acute grief. *Am. J. Psychiatry* 101:141–148.

Link, B., J. Phelan, M. Bresnahan, A. Stueve, R. Moore, and E. Susser. 1995. Lifetime and five-year prevalence of homelessness in the United States: new evidence on an old debate. *Am. J. Orthopsychiatry* 65:347–354.

Magruder, K. M., G. S. Norquist, M. B. Feil, B. Kopans, and D. Jacobs. 1995. Who comes to a voluntary depression screening program? *Am. J. Psychiatry* 152:1615–22.

Manning, W. G., K. B. Wells, N. Duan, J. P. Newhouse, and J. E. Ware. 1986. *JAMA* 256:1930–34.

Mapes, L. V. 1985. Faulty food and shelter programs draw a charge that nobody's home to homeless. *National J.* 9:474–476.

Meltzer, H. Y., P. Cola, L. Way, P. A. Thompson, B. Bastani, M. A. Davies, and B. Snitz. 1993. Cost effectiveness of clozapine in neuroleptic-resistant schizophrenia. *Am. J. Psychiatry* 150:1630–38.

Meyer, A. 1952. *The collected papers of Adolph Meyer,* ed. E. E. Winters. Baltimore: Johns Hopkins University Press.

Morrissey, J. P., and H. H. Goldman. 1984. Cycles of reform in the care of the chronically mentally ill. *Hosp. Commity Psychiatry* 35:785–793.

Morse, G. A., R. J. Calsyn, J. Miller, P. Rosenberg, L. West, and J. Gilliland. 1996. Outreach to homeless mentally ill people: conceptual and clinical considerations. *Community Ment. Health J.* 32:261–274.

National Advisory Mental Health Council. 1993. Health care reform for Americans with severe mental illness. *Am. J. Psychiatry* 150:1447–65.

Palinkas, L. A., J. S. Petterson, J. Russell, and M. A. Downs. 1993. Community patterns of psychiatric disorders after the Exxon Valdez oil spill. *Am. J. Psychiatry* 150:1517–23.

Passamanick, B., F. R. Scarpitti, and S. Dinitz. 1967. *Schizo-phrenics in the community.* New York: Appleton-Century-Crofts.

Quinlivan, R., R. Hough, A. Crowell, C. Beach, R. Hofstetter, and K. Kenworthy. 1995. Service utilization and costs of care for severely mentally ill clients in an intensive case management program. *Psych. Services* 46:365–371.

Reding, G., and M. Raphelson. 1995. Around-the-clock mobile psychiatric crisis intervention: another effective alternative to psychiatric hospitalization. *Community Ment. Health J.* 31:179–187.

Regier, D. A., W. E. Narrow, D. S. Rae, R. W. Manderscheid, B. Z. Locke, and F. K. Goodwin. 1993. The de facto U.S. mental and addictive disorders system. *Arch. Gen. Psychiatry* 50:85–94.

Salzman, C. 1976. Alumni of the Massachusetts Mental Health Center residency training. *Arch. Gen. Psychiatry* 33:421–423.

Santos, A. B., S. W. Henggeler, B. J. Burns, G. W. Arana, and N. Meisler. 1995. Research on field-based services: models for reform in the delivery of mental health care to populations with complex clinical problems. *Am. J. Psychiatry* 152:8.

Schlesinger, M., R. Dorwart, C. Hoover, and S. Epstein. 1997. The determinants of dumping: a national study of economically motivated transfers involving mental health care. *Health Serv. Res.* 32:561–590.

Segal, S., and U. Aviram. 1978. *The mentally ill in community-based sheltered care: a study of community care and social integration.* New York: John Wiley & Sons.

Shalev, A. Y. 1994. Debriefing following traumatic exposure. In *Individual and community responses to trauma and disaster,* ed. R. J. Ursano, B. G. McCaughey, and C. S. Fullerton. London: Cambridge University Press.

Shapiro, S., E. A. Skinner, M. Vonkorff, P. S. German, G. S. Tishler, P. J. Leaf, L. Behma, L. Cottler, L. G. Kessler, and D. A. Regier. 1984. Utilization of health and mental health services: three epidemiologic catchment area sites. *Arch. Gen. Psychiatry* 41:971–982.

Shore, J. H. 1996. Psychiatry at a crossroad: our role in primary care. *Am. J. Psych.* 153:1398–1403.

Shore, J. H., E. L. Tatum, and W. M. Vollmer. 1986. Psychiatric reactions to disaster: the Mount St. Helen's experience. *Am. J. Psychiatry* 143:590–595.

Solomon, P., and J. Draine. 1996. Perspectives concerning consumers as case managers. *Community Ment. Health J.* 32:41–46.

Srole, L., T. S. Langner, S. T. Michael, M. K. Opler, T. A. C. Rennie, et al. 1962. *Mental health in the metropolis: the Midtown Manhattan Study.* Series in social psychiatry, ed. T. A. C. Rennie. Vol. 1. New York: McGraw-Hill.

Statistical Abstract of the United States. 1995. Washington, D.C.: Department of Commerce.

Stein, L. I., and M. A. Test. 1980. Alternative to mental hospital treatment. *Arch. Gen. Psychiatry* 37:392–397.

Styron, W. 1990. *Darkness visible: a memoir of madness.* New York: Random House.

Survey finds huge gap in what Americans know about depression symptoms, treatment. 1996. *Neuroscience News* 1:3.

Susser, E., S. M. Goldfinger, and A. White. 1990. Some clinical approaches to the homeless mentally ill. *Community Ment. Health J.* 26:463–480.

Ursano, R. J., C. S. Fullerton, and A. E. Norwood. 1995. Psychiatric dimensions of disaster: patient care, community consultation, and preventive medicine. *Harvard Rev. Psychiatry* 3:196–209.

U.S. Conference of Mayors. 1987. A status report on homeless families in American cities: a 29-city survey. Washington, D.C.

Recommended Reading

American Psychiatric Association Office of Economic Affairs and Practice Management. 1992. *The psychiatrist's managed care primer.* Washington, D.C.: American Psychiatric Press.

Barsky, A. J., and J. F. Borus. 1995. Somatization and medicalization in the era of managed care. *JAMA* 274:1931–34.

Jamison, K. R. 1995. *An unquiet mind.* New York: Knopf.

Minkoff, K., and D. Pollack, eds. 1997. *Managed mental health care in the public sector: a survival manual.* Amsterdam: Harwood Academic Publishers.

Secunda, V. 1997. When madness comes home: help and hope for the children, siblings, and partners of the mentally ill. New York: Hyperion Press.

ALAN A. STONE

Psychiatry and the Law

The traditional subject matter of law and psychiatry centered on the insanity defense and competency for various legal purposes. These basic topics continue to pose questions of practical and theoretical importance. The insanity defense is the most visible instance in which society confronts the question of when its citizens are to be excused from legal and perhaps moral responsibility for crimes. Competency determinations require that we examine the boundaries of rationality, reason, and the capacity of an individual to make autonomous choices and to act as an equal citizen. The legal question of competency is now of more practical significance than ever before. The Supreme Court has ruled that "competent" patients have a constitutional right to refuse life-prolonging treatments (*Cruzan v. Director, Missouri Dept. of Health,* 1990), and has left it to the states to decide whether competent patients have a right to physician assisted suicide (*Washington v. Glucksberg,* 1997). Determinations of competency to make such medical decisions may well become the most important matter at the intersection of law and psychiatry in the twenty-first century.

In practice, psychiatrists who are called upon to provide expert testimony about responsibility and competency have traditionally relied on a practical rule of thumb. When, in their clinical opinion, the person is psychotic, they are generally prepared to answer that the person lacks responsibility and is incompetent. Unfortunately, the reconceptualization of psychiatric diagnoses in the fourth edition of the *Diagnostic and Statistical Manual of Mental Disorders* (DSM-IV) has somewhat blurred the distinction between psychosis and other disorders. Despite this problem, the rule of thumb about psychosis remains an important criterion because psychiatry has *no coherent and generally accepted theory* about responsibility or competency. Neither does law or philosophy, as even a brief survey of the literature will demonstrate. The lack of such generally accepted theories demonstrates the inability of Western thought to reconcile its scientific and "de-terministic" conceptions of human nature with its moral conceptions of the human condition. Nowhere is this failure more obvious than in the controversies found in this traditional subject matter of law and psychiatry.

A new era in law and psychiatry began with the constitutional challenges of civil commitment in the 1960s (Stone, 1975). Psychiatric diagnoses and other clinical testimony about the need for treatment were criticized as too subjective, potentially biased, and therefore inadequate as a constitutional justification for the loss of liberty entailed by involuntary hospitalization. The courts began to insist on objective behavioral criteria emphasizing physical danger to self or others along with procedural safeguards for the "alleged" patient. These changes made civil commitment hearings more like criminal trials. A mental health bar emerged to defend the "rights" of the mentally ill. Constitutional challenges were raised against every other exercise of psychiatric discretion in the confinement, treatment, and management of involuntary patients. Courts accepted and attempted to apply the constitutional notion of "the least restrictive alternative." Any psychiatric intervention imposed on a patient had to pass the legal test of whether, in the given situation, it was the intervention that least restricted the patient's liberty. In this new era of patients' rights and psychiatrists' constraints, the vast complexity of constitutional law came to be a second area of law and psychiatry (Grinspoon, 1982).

The impact of these new constitutional rights was felt primarily in public sector psychiatry, but the rest of psychiatry was not unaffected. When the least restrictive alternative began to apply to involuntary confinement and treatment, the clinician in the private sector had to find new methods for dealing with many clinical problems previously solved by involuntary hospitalization and treatment. Legal reforms also significantly influenced the basic theory of clinical practice. The concept of a therapeutic contract, the values of patient autonomy, and the notion of less therapeutic paternalism were assimilated by the mental health professions as constructive clinical reforms. Law and psychiatry had become a subject of direct concern to all psychiatrists.

Legal reformers gave a constitutional emphasis to the litigation directed at the institutional practices of psychiatry because they sought to establish broad and enduring national precedents. But some of the cases that were litigated on constitutional grounds could equally well have been pressed as individual malpractice cases. Involuntary drug treatment, for example, can be the basis of a malpractice claim of battery (an illegal physical contact) or negligent failure to provide informed consent, as well as a violation of a constitutional right to privacy or self-determination. Some litigation pressed both constitutional and malpractice claims (*Rogers v. Okin,* 1979). As the wave of constitutional litigation began to recede, the smaller wave of malpractice claims grew and became more visible. Malpractice law emerged as a third important area of law and psychiatry.

These new developments—the relevance of constitutional law and malpractice—were only two aspects of a complicated new scenario. Equally important was the subsequent wave of legislative reforms. New fiscal incentives to deinstitutionalize and downsize state programs were generated by federal entitlement legislation, such as Medicare, Medicaid, and various disability programs for which patients in state and county mental hospitals were ineligible (Stone, 1985). The pressure to shift the burden of financial responsibility for patients from the states to federal programs was met with red tape and outright bias against the mentally ill.

Legal advocates for the mentally ill now had to contend with federal officials. Disability entitlements were eventually made available to patients with mental disorders and then extended to patients with substance abuse disorders. Entitlement programs multiplied and brought with them a legal maze of federal and state regulations. The mental health system, the welfare system, and even the educational system had become interlocking bureaucracies with overlapping responsibilities. These complex entitlement programs, accompanying regulations, and the attendant problems of gaining access to services and benefits in the community became a fourth area of law and psychiatry. Providers and patients had to find their way through a legislative and bureaucratic maze that required a new kind of legal expertise.

But the ultimate transformation of American psychiatry and its standards of practice came from federal legislation that when passed seemed to have little to do with health care or psychiatry. The Employment Retirement Income Security Act (ERISA) permitted private sector

regulation that emphasized cost-effectiveness achieved through managed care. Private regulation regimenting the practice of psychiatry is now a dominant concern of the profession. Power and authority have shifted from the physician's office to the health plan. Health plans regularly impose limitations on hospitalization, length of stay, number of office visits, and even which drugs shall be utilized. The legal and ethical aspects of managed care are a fifth area of law and psychiatry (Stone, 1995).

Law and psychiatry as it applies to children is now recognized as a separate subspecialty. It can be described as the sixth area of law and psychiatry. Not only do the 5 other areas apply in special ways to children, but also certain issues are unique to children, such as the special laws of the juvenile courts, adoption, custody disputes, child abuse, the claims of biological parents, and the probity of the child's testimony in court (Schetky and Benedek, 1992).

Given space limits, this chapter cannot adequately deal with all 6 areas of law and psychiatry. The field of entitlement programs and regulation now supplemented by the Americans with Disabilities Act reaches in too many directions for any concise summary. The same must be said of law and psychiatry as applied to children and their families. The reader, however, should be aware that the practitioner without specialized knowledge of these matters will be limited in his capacity to serve the aged, the indigent, the disabled, as well as children and their families.

Even in the 4 other sectors I have had to make difficult choices to avoid the bare cataloguing that would result from an attempt to include everything significant. The objective here is to present some of the critical issues and to orient the reader to the basic legal concepts. Equally important in this agenda is to demonstrate how issues in law and psychiatry are relevant not just to forensic psychiatrists but also to the basic enterprise of psychiatry: its theories, its practices, its standards, and perhaps most important its ethics.

As the law constrained and redefined the doctor-patient relationship, there was no generally accepted theory and no core of ethical principles to which the profession could turn for direction. There is now a plethora of medical ethicists and bioethicists but little consensus on controversial issues such as the ethics of physician assisted suicide or the ethical responsibilities of physicians under the economic constraints of managed care. The official "principles of ethics" promulgated by the American Medical Association and adapted by the American Psychiatric Association (1995) provide only limited guidance. These official ethics have long since abandoned the traditional and perhaps most important guiding ethical maxim of the medical profession: *primum non nocere* ("first of all do no harm").

The Building Blocks of Law

In order to appreciate the complexity of the relationship between law and psychiatry, it is useful to understand the 6 basic building blocks of law itself: (1) statutes, (2) the Constitution, (3) common law, (4) criminal versus civil law, (5) the adversary system, and (6) case law (Berman, 1971). The best approach is to examine these features as they arise in a case. I have chosen *State ex rel. Hawks v. Lazaro* (1974), which has the advantage of being typical of the judicial reform of civil commitment standards and procedures in the 1970s—reform premised on the growing legal concern for "patients' rights."

Statutes

Ronald Lee Hawks was committed to the Huntington State Hospital in West Virginia for an indeterminate period. He had been diagnosed by psychiatrists as both mentally ill and mentally retarded. Hawks was committed under a state statute that dictated civil commitment standards and procedures. Such statutes enacted by legislatures form one major ingredient of law. Every psychiatrist should be familiar with at least the statutory standards for civil commitment in his state and the procedures with which he must comply. *Hawks* and other cases in this kind of litigation challenged the existing statutory standards for civil commitment that embodied the so-called medical model—that is, the individual must be mentally ill and in need of treatment. State statutes now generally require that the person be not only mentally ill but also (1) dangerous to others, (2) dangerous to self, or (3) gravely disabled so as to be unable to meet basic needs. These standards are defined differently among state statutes. The American Psychiatric Association and the National Alliance for the Mentally Ill have endorsed a fourth standard to allow for the confinement of patients with serious mental illness who are "deteriorating" and have become incompetent to make medical decisions.

The Constitution

Hawks, through his lawyer, appealed to the Supreme Court of West Virginia, claiming that the procedures set forth in the statute had not been faithfully carried out and, furthermore, that those procedures were unconstitutional. The federal Constitution is, of course, a major component of law with which all state and federal statutes must comply. (A further complication is that each state also has its own constitution.) Hawks, in this case, claimed that he had been deprived of liberty without *due process of law* as contemplated in the Constitution. Essentially, due process of law demands that legal procedures be fair, and fairness demands a variety of constitutional protections for the person whose basic right to liberty is at stake.

Legal reformers have also argued that psychiatric hospitalization is stigmatizing and that citizens have a separate constitutional right to be protected against stigmatization by the state. Therefore, even a prisoner who has already lost his liberty is entitled to due process before transfer to a mental hospital that will result in stigmatization (*Vitek v. Jones*, 1980).

Common Law

The court, in deciding whether Hawks had obtained due process under these statutes, confronted the ancient doctrine of *parens patriae* ("father of his country"). It allowed the kings of England to stand in as parent to members of the nobility found to be "idiots or lunatics."

This English doctrine, transformed over centuries of judicial interpretation, has been accepted together with many others into what is called the *American common law*. The common law is a composite of ancient traditional doctrines and judicial opinions reformulated and accepted as part of the fabric of U.S. jurisprudence. The doctrine of *parens patriae* has come to stand for the broad proposition that the state can act in what it takes to be the best interest of a citizen who is mentally incapacitated or a minor. This doctrine is the basic legal justification for "paternalism" in mental health laws.

Under the *parens patriae* rationale, a legal distinction arose holding that when the state acted presumably to help under *parens patriae*, the state need not follow the same standards of procedural fairness applicable in a criminal trial, where the state acts to punish. Therefore, constitutional protections such as the right to remain silent and the right to confront one's accuser did not apply when the state acted to help the person, as in a civil commitment.

Criminal versus Civil Law

The involuntary hospitalization of Ronald Lee Hawks was carried out under a set of what are called *civil statutes* rather than *criminal statutes*. The legal procedures that the state must follow in civil cases are less exacting than in criminal cases. Reform in mental health laws in the 1970s rejected or radically narrowed the moral legitimacy and legal acceptance of the paternalistic doctrine of *parens patriae,* which justified the distinction between civil and criminal procedures (*Lessard v. Schmidt,* 1972). Reformers suggested that loss of liberty was at stake in these civil statutes, and therefore they attempted to provide the "alleged" patient with the same procedural safeguards as granted an "alleged" criminal. The most important of these safeguards is the right to legal counsel.

Adversary System

The hallmark of the Anglo-American system of justice is its adversary nature. This tradition is repugnant to many psychiatrists, particularly because it almost inevitably results in the expert witnesses for each side giving directly contradictory testimony. The psychiatrist unfamiliar with law often assumes that a neutral panel of psychiatric experts appointed by a judge would produce a more "scientific" and thus better result. But the adversary approach is the very foundation of our legal system. It affords every person brought before the court a legal champion who represents his client zealously within the bounds of the law. This right to legal counsel is guaranteed by the Constitution. The defense attorney and the prosecutor both present their most powerful case. In the process, they enlist helpful "experts" and confront each other's expert witnesses in a manner little resembling a scientific search for truth.

Before psychiatrists condemn the adversary system, they should consider its unique advantage: it is the key to invoking all the other rights that allow the individual to defend himself against the power of the state before any lawful tribunal. One might contrast the Anglo-American adversarial procedure with the Continental inquisitorial system, in which the judge more actively participates in the investigation and may appoint a "neutral" panel of experts. This tradition was followed in the former Soviet Union and produced much criticism of alleged political misuse of psychiatry. The clash of expert witnesses may not be the best way to formulate scientific truth, but it may be the best way to achieve justice.

Case Law

The Supreme Court of West Virginia made several rulings in the *Hawks* decision; these rulings subsequently formed the case law (law made by judges) in West Virginia. Based on the *Hawks* case precedent, every alleged patient in West Virginia must (1) be present at his commitment hearing, (2) be allowed to confront and cross-examine witnesses (including relatives and psychiatrists), and (3) have legal counsel. These procedures impose great expense on the state in terms of lawyers', judges', and psychi-

atrists' time, if civil commitment is to continue at any appreciable rate. If psychiatrists are in court testifying, they cannot be treating patients. Such procedural hurdles dramatically change the psychiatrist's discretionary authority and incentives to invoke involuntary confinement. Similar legal reforms in other states have contributed to the nationwide decline in involuntary confinement.

This cursory description of the 6 building blocks of law gives some sense of the law's complexity. Although the interfaces between law and psychiatry have always been more complicated than was appreciated, a new level of complexity has been imposed by the constitutional decisions intended to protect patients' rights. The psychiatrist should therefore accept with caution any simple assertions about psychiatry and law. Much of what follows here can only point the way. (Further specifics may be found in Stone, 1985; Appelbaum and Gutheil, 1992; Brakel, Parry, and Weiner, 1985.)

The Insanity Defense

Psychiatrists should understand that the insanity defense is a by-product of the basic legal theory of criminal guilt. Criminal guilt generally requires both the commission of a prohibited act and some accompanying mental "element" that is blameworthy. For example, killing in self-defense is not a crime because no blameworthy mental element is involved. The insanity defense has developed as a special branch of this basic legal theory of guilt. The fundamental legal and moral question is: What abnormal mental states are sufficient to negate the blameworthy mental element of criminal guilt? The law has looked to psychiatry for help in answering this question, and attempts to provide answers have caused controversy. At the outset, one should note that some psychiatrists have assumed that they were being asked a scientific question. Scientific knowledge may indeed be involved in assessing a particular defendant's abnormal state of mind. But whether that abnormality is sufficient to negate the blameworthy mental element is to some extent a legal or moral judgment that goes beyond mere scientific knowledge.

The insanity defense, despite its notoriety, is of little practical consequence; it is rarely invoked and is even more rarely successful. It provokes public attention because the defendant in most cases has obviously done the deed and yet seeks to escape legal punishment. To those concerned about "law and order," the insanity defense—"the abuse excuse"—is therefore a symbol of the failure of the criminal justice system to exact retribution and to control crime.

Beyond the law and order controversy, the insanity defense continues to pose moral, philosophical, and theoretical problems. The arguments struggled over on the battlefields of the insanity defense involve the basic theory of mind and human action and reflect the contradiction between the law's enduring free will theory of the morality of action and psychiatry's seemingly deterministic theories of its causes.

Such considerations, though of profound interest to anyone concerned with the great theories of mind and behavior, cannot be adequately discussed here. The reader interested in a serious philosophical analysis should consult Moore's *Law and Psychiatry: Rethinking the Relationship* (1984). Moore attempts to find in philosophy a common language for law and psychiatry. His analysis of the problems is more enlightening than his proffered solutions.

The insanity defense involves a test of criminal responsibility, and the legal tests have varied over the centuries. A useful way to conceptualize the historical development of the tests of criminal responsibility is to think of a very narrow and limiting test that gradually expands over more than a century and then begins to narrow again. The analysis begins with an ancient English test—the "like-a-wild-beast" test. The analogy to the wild beast as a test of criminal responsibility has 3 important characteristics. A wild beast, as distinguished from a human being, was considered, first, to be incapable of reason; second, to lack any control over its behavior; and third, to be totally emotionally deranged—in a "frenzy" (a term frequently employed in early psychiatric literature).

All 3 characteristics together—lack of reason (cognitive capacity), lack of control (volitional capacity), and frenzy (acute and total emotional derangement)—make up the "analogical" wild beast test of criminal responsibility. The analogy provides a vivid picture of a very narrow category of mental abnormality sufficient to negate blameworthiness. The analogy is reflected in another phrase of the early law and psychiatry statutes: the "furiously insane." Subsequent legal tests arguably emphasized at least 1 of the 3 characteristics of the wild beast test as they sought to expand the scope of the defense. The principal tests follow.

The M'Naghten Test (Daniel M'Naghten's Case, 1843)

[E]very man is to be presumed to be sane, and . . . to establish a defense on the ground of insanity, it must be clearly proved that, at the time of the committing of the act, the party accused was labouring under such a defect of reason, from disease of the mind, as not to know the nature and quality of the act he was doing; or if he did know it, that he did not know he was doing what was wrong. (8 Eng. Rep. 722–723)

This test expands the scope of the wild beast test by emphasizing the cognitive defect and eliminating the requirements of frenzy and lack of volitional control. Thus a person acting under a delusional system but able to plan and premeditate might come under this rule. Such a person would not be "furiously insane" and might not seem obviously mad to a jury of his peers, who would need guidance from expert testimony. Although *M'Naghten* expanded the scope of the insanity defense, in time it was attacked as too limited. Critics argued that *M'Naghten* placed too great an emphasis on the cognitive faculty and ignored emotional derangement or loss of volitional control.

The Irresistible Impulse Test (Smith v. United States, 1929)

[T]he degree of insanity which will relieve the accused of the criminal consequences of a criminal act must be such as to create in his mind an uncontrollable impulse to commit the offense charged. (36 F.2d 548, 549)

This test emphasizes the lack of volition and, to a lesser extent, the frenzy of the wild beast test. It expands the insanity defense by adding a new category of abnormal mental states to the category covered by *M'Naghten*. From a psychiatric perspective a person without a thought disorder might be included in this new category. The irresistible impulse test is nowhere relied on as the only test; it is used to supplement the *M'Naghten* test in many jurisdictions.

The Durham Test (Durham v. United States, 1954)

An accused is not criminally responsible if his unlawful act was the product of mental disease or mental defect.

The *Durham* rule had no obvious relationship to the wild beast analogy, and it can perhaps best be described as a "medical model" of criminal responsibility. Any mental disease or defect is sufficient to negate blameworthiness under *Durham*. This ruling was the high-water mark of judicial deference to the determinist conceptions of psychiatry, and many members of the profession viewed it with enthusiasm as a progressive development. However, the *Durham* rule quickly faced criticism as a symbol of the criminal justice system's softness on crime. It was replaced in 1972 by the following test.

The ALI Test (American Law Institute, 1962)

A person is not responsible for criminal conduct if at the time of such conduct as a result of mental disease or defect he lacks substantial capacity either to appreciate the criminality of his conduct or to conform his conduct to the requirements of law.

Before the controversial decision to acquit John Hinckley under this ALI standard (for his assassination attempt on President Reagan), all the federal courts and half the state courts had adopted a version of the American Law Institute (ALI) standard for insanity acquittal. The ALI test required only a substantial lack of *either* cognitive or volitional capacity, and thus was broader than traditional tests. The test did not specify the severity or nature of mental diseases that would be sufficient, but it did use qualifying language suggesting that antisocial personality should be excluded.

After the Hinckley verdict, public outcry demanded change. Congress considered 3 major alternatives. The first was to abolish the insanity defense altogether. The second was to create an additional alternative verdict—guilty but mentally ill. This option, adopted by some state legislatures, would permit a jury to find the defendant mentally ill but still criminally responsible. These defendants supposedly get treatment, but even if "cured," they serve out an appropriate sentence imposed by the court.

Congress eventually acted on a third option and in 1984 adopted a new, narrowed version of the insanity defense to be applied in federal courts. "The defendant as a result of a severe mental disease or defect, was unable to appreciate the nature and quality or the wrongfulness of his acts" (18 U.S.C. §17). Congress thus removed both the volitional alternative of the ALI test and the language of "substantial capacity," presumably narrowing the scope of the defense. They added the word "severe" to make clear that not every mental disease would invoke the defense. The APA had recommended this version and proposed that "severe" be equated with psychosis. Except for the ambiguity of the word "appreciate," Congress has returned to a version of the *M'Naghten* test, and psychiatry has returned to the rule of thumb that something like psychosis is necessary if not sufficient for insanity.

Reaction to the *Hinckley* verdict also influenced the legal standards under which insanity acquittees (those found not guilty by reason of insanity) should be confined and released from confinement. Throughout Anglo-American legal history, an insanity acquittee's most likely fate was to spend the rest of his life in an institution for the criminally insane. Legal reform in the 1970s created the possibility of an early release. A person found not guilty by reason of insanity could potentially go free immediately or after a few weeks of observation unless the state could prove that he still met the new strict standard for civil commitment.

The Supreme Court after *Hinckley,* in a clear reversal of its earlier position, held that insanity acquittees can be indefinitely confined regardless of the crime for which they were originally charged (*Jones v. United States,* 1983). The Court also accepted a lower standard of proof for confinement, a standard they had rejected as inadequate protection for ordinary civil commitment. Congress, in the Insanity Defense Reform Act of 1984, went even further and required insanity acquittees petitioning for release to assume "the burden of proof by clear and convincing evidence that [their] release [will] not create a substantial risk of bodily injury to another person or serious damage of property (18 U.S.C. §17)." Given the difficulties of predicting future dangerousness, the law prior to the *Hinckley* verdict favored the release of the insanity acquittee. The government then had the burden of proving that the individual would be dangerous if released—despite the known empirical difficulty of making such predictions. Congress simply turned the tables, placing the burden on the defendant, who is no more capable of proving that he is not dangerous than the government was capable of proving the opposite.

Legislatures in many states followed the lead of Congress and narrowed the insanity defense and took measures to ensure that insanity acquittees who have committed violent acts are confined. Further, at this writing 3 states have abolished the defense entirely. Civil libertarians have challenged these conservative reforms. The Montana State Supreme Court, rejecting such a challenge, has held that abolition of the insanity defense is constitutional (*State v. Kovell,* 1984). The supreme courts of Idaho and Utah have reached similar decisions.

In addition to tests of criminal responsibility, many states allow psychiatrists to testify as to whether the defendant had a mental disorder that might negate the requisite premeditation or malice for the specific crime charged. Thus, for example, a charge of first degree murder might be reduced to manslaughter on the basis of psychiatric testimony. The Supreme Court has ruled that all defendants in capital punishment cases have a constitutional right to the assistance of a forensics expert, even at the expense of the state (*Ake v. Oklahoma,* 1984).

Whether persons charged with crimes are criminally responsible or not, clearly many are mentally ill. Although civil libertarian critics of psychiatry emphasize the stigmatizing aspect of diagnostic labels, defense lawyers in the criminal courts look to psychiatry and diagnostic labels as a resource. Given the crowded dockets of the criminal courts and the scarcity of prison cells, prosecutors and judges are often amenable to any credible diversion from the criminal justice system. Even when diversion from the system is not possible, psychiatric evaluations may play a role in plea bargaining and in sentencing (Rosner, 1994). Thus the prudent criminal lawyer is a specialist in access to the mental health system and its resources. A diagnosis and a proposed treatment plan may be enough to avoid a prison sentence.

Although many ethical problems arise in this context, perhaps the most important one can go unnoticed. That problem involves race and class. If minority and lower-class criminal defendants do not get fair access to these preferred mental health alternatives to the prison system, then psychiatry is implicated in discrimination. These realities are of greater practical significance than the much-discussed insanity defense, and they are of greater importance to social justice.

Victim Impact Statements

Many jurisdictions allow victims of crimes and members of their families to make statements to the court at the time of sentencing the criminal defendant. Some psychiatrists believe that these so-called victim impact statements serve a healing function. Often, impact statements include psychiatric reports stating that the victim or family member now suffers from post-traumatic stress disorder. Other psychiatrists have misgivings about the possibility that victim impact statements relying on psychiatric expertise might persuade courts to impose the death penalty in capital punishment cases.

The Test of Competency to Stand Trial

While the test of competency to stand trial may vary among jurisdictions, essentially it involves the capacity to understand the proceedings and to consult with one's lawyer. The Supreme Court has formulated the test to be "whether the defendant has sufficient present ability to consult with counsel with a reasonable degree of rational understanding and whether he has a rational as well as factual understanding of the proceedings against him" (*Dusky v. United States,* 1960, 362 U.S. 405). This narrow test, like other modern tests of legal competency, is defined by the specific legal issues involved rather than by some general standard of competency.

Competency to stand trial has been the most frequent and consequential mental health inquiry pursued in the criminal law system. Once the question has been raised, the defendant must be found competent or be restored to competency in order to be tried—even if he pleads insanity. Traditionally, the law used incompetency far more often than insanity to dispose of obviously psychotic offenders. A defendant who could not be restored to competency was in the past indefinitely committed to an institution for the criminally insane, typically without any prospect of efficacious treatment and without even having had his day in court as to his guilt or innocence. The first cases on the right to treatment arose in this context (*Commonwealth v. Page,* 1959).

The Supreme Court (*Pate v. Robinson,* 1966) has held that the defense attorney, the prosecutor, and the judge have a legal duty to raise the issue of competency whenever they believe that the defendant may have a mental illness that might interfere with his capacity to stand trial. This supposedly benevolent duty has at times led to abuses. The law has no clear standard of mental incapacity to indicate when an inquiry into the competency of the defendant can be required. A court can sometimes preclude the possibility of bail by requiring a competency examination and committing the defendant to a mental health facility. Such an examination ordered immediately after arrest may provide the prosecution evidence as to the defendant's mental condition close to the time of the crime, which could be important if the defendant should later plead insanity. For these and other reasons, courts and prosecutors have had incentives to misuse competency evaluations.

The Supreme Court, recognizing the injustice in indefinitely confining incompetent defendants, held in *Jackson v. Indiana* (1972) that the confinement of alleged incompetents must be limited to a reasonable time, given the purpose of the confinement. If defendants cannot be restored to competency after such reasonable period of therapy, they must be treated like any other allegedly mentally ill person and be either civilly committed or released. Since *Jackson,* most abuses have been rectified. Most defendants are now rapidly restored to competency, and some facilities have programmed learning devices to provide the defendant a factual understanding of the lawyer's role and the proceedings.

Many defendants can be restored to competency by antipsychotic drugs, but this raises difficulties. Does a defendant have a right to refuse antipsychotic medication despite the state's interest in restoring him to competency and providing him a speedy trial? Model legislation proposed by the American Bar Association (1984) would provide a right to refuse treatment. In 1992 the Supreme Court determined that the state of Nevada had violated a defendant's constitutional right to refuse treatment by forcibly administering antipsychotic drugs (*Riggins v. Ne-*

vada). The Court implied that forced medication might be constitutionally acceptable if it were *necessary* to keep a defendant competent. However, in *Riggins* there were significant indications that the defendant would have been competent *without* the medication, and therefore forced treatment was not justifiable.

The *Riggins* Court, while it did not rule on the issue, also expressed strong concern about the effect antipsychotic medication may have on a defendant's demeanor at trial. Defense attorneys have argued that juries may interpret an impassive, indifferent demeanor that may be the result of medication as indicating lack of remorse. Further, the defendant's "medicated behavior" may be particularly problematic in an insanity defense. State courts have come to contradictory conclusions about these matters. Some have ruled that the problem of drugged demeanor can be mitigated by expert testimony explaining the impact of the medications. Videotape evidence of the defendant's mental state without medication has been considered.

Under current law in most states, the alleged incompetent defendant need not be confined at all, and if confined, not necessarily in a maximum-security facility. These laws, like the law of civil commitment, make confinement determinations turn on the question of dangerousness.

Other Issues in the Criminal Courts

The Fifth Amendment

The Fifth Amendment protects a criminal defendant from being forced, coerced, or misled into incriminating himself. Any pretrial psychiatric examination or intervention at the behest of the police or prosecution may violate the defendant's constitutional right if information obtained by the psychiatrist is used to make the state's case. In the course of a competency examination, the defendant may in some way incriminate himself or even confess to the psychiatrist. If that evidence is used to establish the defendant's guilt, then his constitutional right has been abrogated.

The police are required to give the well-known *Miranda* warning, "Anything you say may be used against you," to persons they arrest, and the same legal requirement can be imposed on psychiatrists. But a *Miranda* warning given by a psychiatrist may not be adequate protection. The arrestee may not recognize the legal consequences of talking to a psychiatrist, and the psychiatrist's interviewing skills may induce damaging revelations. Alternatively, the psychiatrist's *Miranda* warning might convince the defendant to remain silent, making the neces-

sary evaluations impossible. Defense lawyers have argued that they should be present at any psychiatric evaluation so that they can advise their client when to "take the Fifth" and remain silent as they do in other interrogations.

Courts have been sensitive to the importance of Fifth Amendment rights. At the same time courts recognize that if the defendant can cooperate with his own psychiatric experts but can "take the Fifth" with the state's psychiatric experts, then the prosecution may be unfairly disadvantaged. Different jurisdictions have reached various compromises. Usually, when the defendant seeks to introduce psychiatric testimony, as in an insanity defense, he must be available for evaluation by psychiatric experts for the prosecution. In a criminal trial the psychiatrist cannot testify about directly incriminating evidence revealed to him in the course of a court-ordered examination. Beyond these two basic premises the issues are complicated, as we shall see when we consider psychiatric testimony in the capital punishment context. The APA has taken the position that Fifth Amendment rights are appropriate in all examinations in the context of the criminal justice system and in special commitment procedures, such as those for sexual offenders, even though designated civil commitment. At the same time the APA has urged that the Fifth Amendment not apply to ordinary civil commitment. Should an ordinary civil commitment examination reveal self-incriminating evidence about a crime, that evidence would not be admissible in any other context (Stromberg and Stone, 1983).

The Supreme Court, disagreeing with the APA, has held that the Fifth Amendment does not apply in special commitments of sexual offenders because the commitments are civil and the state's goal is treatment (*Allen v. Illinois*, 1986). Nonetheless, the psychiatrist, whenever examining a patient in the context of a criminal or special civil commitment proceeding, should inform the defendant of the purpose of the examination. Indeed, ethics mandate that whenever one performs a psychiatric evaluation for a purpose other than treatment, one must inform the patient of that purpose. It is particularly important that the psychiatrist not allow his professional skills or role to be used for some prosecutorial purpose when the person arrested is not yet represented by an attorney. The ethical goal is to avoid exploiting the psychiatrist's role as therapist for any purpose other than therapy.

Predictive Testimony

Can psychiatrists reliably predict future dangerousness? Recent legal reforms have increased the importance of such predictions. Predictions of future dangerousness are central not only in civil commitment hearings but also in the criminal law. Future dangerousness is a criterion for capital punishment, for pretrial confinement of the mentally ill offender, and for everyday judicial decisions about probation and sentencing. Negligent failure to predict violence and warn potential victims or otherwise protect them has become a growing cause for malpractice suits against mental health facilities and professionals. Based on clinical considerations, it is useful to distinguish 3 time frames for prediction. The first is current assessment. Do the patient's mental status, past history, and present situation indicate that violence is imminent? In this time frame the crucial situational factors external to the patient are presumably known and do not have to be predicted. But even then, doubt may exist because of the patient's ability to conceal his dangerous intentions or because of the lack of a reliable history. The second time frame, short-term prediction, refers to a period of days or a few weeks, when external situational factors may change. The third time frame, long-term prediction, refers to months or years, when external situational factors are bound to change.

The existing empirical research, though recently more encouraging, does not demonstrate that "clinical" predictions of dangerousness are scientifically reliable (Monahan, 1994). The American Bar Association (1984) had proposed in its Criminal Justice Mental Health Standards that psychiatrists, psychologists, and other experts be prohibited from offering clinical testimony about future dangerousness in any criminal hearing. Courts have been reluctant to follow these proposals, and a majority of the Supreme Court has opposed the exclusion of clinical predictions as a basis for imposing capital punishment. The view of the justices is, first, that courts routinely make such predictions, and the idea that experts cannot and should not do so seems absurd. Second, the justices look to the adversarial cross-examination process, rather than to an exclusionary rule, to expose the supposed fallacies of prediction (*Barefoot v. Estelle*, 1983). Because capital punishment seems to present the strongest legal argument for excluding testimony that has no demonstrable empirical reliability, one can assume that the Supreme Court would not exclude such predictive testimony in any of the other legal contexts in which it is now employed.

Capital Punishment

Psychiatry is now deeply involved in legal and ethical complexities connected with the death penalty. Despite years of organized litigation by lawyers who oppose capital punishment, the Supreme Court has refused to abolish it on constitutional grounds. Yet the Court has struck down certain state statutes on the grounds that they imposed the death penalty in a racially biased manner. The Court eventually suggested the outlines of a permissible death penalty statute (*Furman v. Georgia,* 1972), and most states subsequently passed statutes that followed the Court's outlines. The statutes provide that after the defendant has been found guilty of a capital offense, a separate hearing on the death penalty must be held. The judge or jury at that hearing considers such racially neutral questions as whether the guilty defendant would pose a continuing threat to society. Thus the law, in its search for objectivity, has made prediction of future dangerousness a crucial consideration. The death penalty decision makers may also consider extenuating circumstances and whether the defendant shows remorse.

Attorneys looked to psychiatrists to provide expert testimony on these questions, and this has raised legal and ethical challenges. In amicus briefs to the Supreme Court, the APA contended that long-term clinical predictions of future dangerousness were more often wrong than right. Therefore, such testimony for the prosecution was unscientific and perhaps unethical.

These and other legal and ethical questions were presented to the Supreme Court in *Estelle v. Smith* (1981). A Texas judge had ordered a competency to stand trial evaluation of a man who was eventually found guilty and sentenced to death. The psychiatrist who performed the competency examination was called by the prosecutor at the sentencing phase of the trial, and on the basis of information obtained during the competency examination, the psychiatrist testified that the man was dangerous. The Supreme Court found that this violated the defendant's Fifth Amendment right against self-incrimination and his Sixth Amendment right to effective counsel. Neither the defendant nor his lawyer had been informed that the competency evaluation would be the basis for psychiatric testimony at the sentencing phase.

The Supreme Court's decision apparently disadvantaged the prosecution in subsequent cases. They could no longer obtain a psychiatric evaluation of a defendant without informing both him and his lawyer that damaging information could be used in the capital sentencing phase, and with such a warning the defendant would be unlikely to cooperate. But prosecutors, like defense attorneys, can be ingenious litigators. At a subsequent trial two psychiatrists were called to testify at the sentencing stage. Neither had personally examined the defendant, so there could be no violation of constitutional rights and no exploitation of their therapeutic role or skills during an evaluation. The prosecutor asked the psychiatrists for their expert opinions solely on the basis of hypothetical questions derived from what was known about the defendant. Both psychiatrists testified that the defendant had an untreatable antisocial personality disorder, and they predicted further acts of criminal violence. The death penalty was imposed. The case was appealed to the Supreme Court (*Barefoot v. Estelle,* 1983).

The APA once again informed the Court of the empirical evidence against clinical predictions of dangerousness and raised scientific and ethical questions about expert testimony based on hypothetical questions where the psychiatrist has not personally examined the patient to rule out alternative diagnoses. Justice White wrote the majority opinion upholding the death penalty verdict and gave vent to his feelings about psychiatry's disclaimer of any special ability to predict future violence: "We are being asked 'to disinvent the wheel.'" He emphasized the established role of clinical predictions of dangerousness in civil commitment and argued that if the APA's views were correct, there should be no shortage of expert opinion to contradict the prosecution's experts. As to experts answering hypothetical questions, he concluded that it was an accepted legal practice under the rules of evidence. Justice Blackmun, in dissent, essentially adopted the APA position, but Justice White dismissed the dissent as demonstrating insufficient confidence in the adversary system's capacity to resolve conflicts in expert testimony.

Competency to Be Executed

State law has always contained vague statutory language about competency to be executed, but it had rarely been invoked. In some states the issue was left to the governor under his clemency power. The Supreme Court considered this question in *Ford v. Wainwright* (1986). The Court held that executing the insane is cruel and unusual punishment and made determination of competency to be executed a constitutional requirement in all states. More important, the Court also required a hearing, allowing the prisoner to cross-examine the state's psychiatrists, to call his own expert witnesses, and to have a neutral fact finder—a judge rather than a governor. However, the Court left it to the states to articulate a clear standard for incompetency to be executed.

Competency of mentally retarded defendants to be executed has been particularly problematic. In 1989 the Supreme Court determined that a retarded adult with the mental capacity of an 8-year-old was competent to be executed (*Perry v. Lynaugh,* 1989).

These situations present difficult ethical questions for psychiatry. Should a person found incompetent to be exe-

cuted be treated by psychiatrists and restored to competency so that he can be executed? Is it ethical for a doctor to be involved in the process leading to capital punishment at all? Can psychiatrists rely on professional ethics to guide them through the new dilemmas posed by capital punishment? The principles of medical ethics and the ancient ethical maxims of the profession are based on the actual doctor-patient relationship. They do not directly address the role of the doctor in court or in other dealings with law and legal regulation. Forensic psychiatrists have attempted to formulate their own principles of ethics, as they deal with legal issues in non-clinical contexts (Rosner, 1990).

The Ultimate Legal Question

The basic legal justification for permitting experts to offer their opinions at a trial is that the judge and jury do not have the requisite technical knowledge to understand or interpret certain kinds of facts. But psychiatrists have often been asked not only to interpret facts but also to reach a legal conclusion. Thus psychiatrists have traditionally been asked, "Did the defendant know right from wrong?" or "Is the defendant competent to stand trial?" Answers to these questions are answers to ultimate legal questions. Some forensic psychiatrists believe that it is improper to answer such questions because they go beyond the boundaries of psychiatric expertise. Until the courts resolve the issue, however, psychiatrists who decline to express opinions about ultimate legal questions may disadvantage their side in the adversarial contest. Unfortunately, some forensic psychiatrists testify as though they were legal experts who have authoritative answers to ultimate legal questions.

Hypnosis and Recovered Memory

The legal effects of hypnosis have been the subject of considerable controversy. The courts are concerned that a witness whose memory has been restored or amplified under hypnosis may produce testimony tainted by the hypnotist's suggestion. California has barred testimony by any witness who has been hypnotized (*People v. Shirley,* 1982). Other jurisdictions have established less restrictive rules, such as requirements that the hypnotist be a qualified professional and that the hypnotic sessions be carefully documented to determine whether suggestion has occurred. The question remains, however, whether a memory recovered under hypnosis is like another memory or whether it has a special certainty or a quality of fixed belief. The witness might therefore be more convincing and less susceptible to cross-examination. Despite these concerns the Supreme Court has ruled that states cannot put an absolute ban on testimony by a *defendant* who has been previously hypnotized because of the traditional right to testify in one's own defense (*Rock v. Arkansas*, 1987).

In recent years courts have dealt with situations in which witnesses recover memory not through hypnosis but rather through psychotherapy or through some sudden spontaneous chain of associations. Recovered memory was used in a criminal prosecution in 1990, when a middle-aged California father was convicted of raping and murdering his daughter's childhood friend 20 years after the murder occurred. The daughter testified that she had repressed her eyewitness memories of the event for 20 years (*People v. George Thomas Franklin*, 1990).

Legal criticism of the probative value of recovered memory is mounting. Even the defendant in the landmark *Franklin* case has been released. One concern is the extent to which statutes of limitation (time limits on the viability of legal suits) should be set aside where witnesses or victims supposedly recover lost memories. Another concern is that there is no scientific basis for determining the validity of recovered memories. Psychiatric experts now disagree as to the accuracy of recovered memory, and some argue that many such "memories" result from the psychotherapist's suggestion (Ernsdorff and Loftus, 1993) (see the section on malpractice for more detail). Currently there is no legal consensus on the admissibility of recovered memory. Judges have decided the issue largely on a case-by-case basis.

Juvenile Courts

The juvenile courts were established in the United States at the turn of the century as the most explicit instance of *parens patriae*. Because the presumed goal of the system was to rehabilitate rather than to punish juveniles, the same concessions regarding due process safeguards were made as in the area of civil commitment. Unfortunately, owing to grossly inadequate institutional resources, the goal of rehabilitation has rarely been accomplished. The Supreme Court took note of this bleak failure in the famous *Gault* case (*In re Gault*, 1967). But rather than ordering the states to rectify the rehabilitative system's inadequacies, the Court imposed many of the procedural safeguards available in the adult criminal courts.

The American Bar Association (1977), in a massive reform effort, proposed new standards for the system. These standards acknowledge the failure of rehabilitation and give more emphasis to procedures similar to the adult system of criminal justice and to more "constructive" forms of punishment. This well-intended approach is unlikely to solve the central problem, namely, that despite legal intervention, juvenile offenders frequently go on to become adult offenders. Public opinion increasingly favors adult forms of punishment for juveniles who commit violent offenses.

Civil Commitment

Each state has its own standards and procedures for voluntary and involuntary entry into mental hospitals, and the psychiatrist must familiarize himself with the rules in his state. Since the era of patients' rights, exemplified by the *Hawks* case, discussed earlier, the alleged patient's constitutional rights are given greater legal protection. "Objective" legal standards must be met before involuntary confinement is permitted: typically, dangerous to others, dangerous to self, or so gravely disabled as to be unable to meet needs essential for survival. The length of confinement is specified, and periodic review is mandated when confinement continues.

Emergency commitment must be distinguished from other commitment proceedings. Most states permit any licensed psychiatrist (physician or psychologist) to initiate an emergency commitment (some states may require more than one). A few states (for example, California and Washington) have limited this authority to specially designated practitioners. The psychiatrist is usually required to have recently examined the patient and to certify that an emergency exists and that the patient is mentally ill and dangerous to others or to self. Virtually all patients entering the civil commitment system do so initially under these emergency provisions. Thus the mental health professional is the first to determine whether the patient meets the legal standard.

From the civil libertarian perspective this is a dubious delegation of the state's authority over personal liberty; an immediate judicial hearing would be preferable to determine whether "probable cause" for confinement exists or whether there is a less restrictive alternative (Brakel, Parry, and Weiner, 1985). Some courts have required such a hearing within 48 hours of emergency admission, but most states permit several days of confinement before any legal hearing. Where efficacious short-term treatment is available and permissible, the emergency may be dealt with or the patient may accept voluntary status before any court intervenes.

In *Zinermon v. Burch* (1990), the Supreme Court touched on the related issue of competency to commit oneself voluntarily to an institution. The Court determined that an obviously psychotic patient could sue a hospital for admitting him on a voluntary basis. The Court implied that institutions have some duty to ensure the competency of those committing themselves.

Once a court holds a hearing to determine whether civil commitment is appropriate, the court generally focuses on the "objective" standard of dangerousness. But this supposedly objective standard involves difficult and subjective predictions of future behavior (discussed earlier). The Supreme Court, acknowledging this difficulty, has required only the lesser evidentiary standard of "clear and convincing proof" for involuntary civil commitment, thus refusing to equate civil commitment with criminal confinement (*Addington v. Texas,* 1979). Most states, however, have imposed the "beyond a reasonable doubt" criminal standard, and some require proof of a past act or threat of violence in order to establish dangerousness. This past act requirement replaces subjective predictions of behavior with the same kind of objective inquiry as in criminal trials.

Civil libertarians oppose confinement based solely on serious and treatable mental illness, which constitutes loss of liberty based on one's status rather than one's actions. They also oppose confinement based solely on dangerousness (this is described as preventive detention). The Supreme Court has ruled that preventive detention is not a constitutional basis for committing an individual unless the dangerous patient is also shown to be mentally ill (*Foucha v. Louisiana,* 1992).

As we have seen, the procedures for civil commitment allow psychiatrists to initiate the emergency process. But the statutes increasingly define *emergency* in narrow terms of imminent physical danger and ignore other kinds of psychiatric emergencies. Additionally, states may limit the psychiatrist's ability to treat after an emergency admission (*Lessard v. Schmidt,* 1972). Civil libertarians argue that confinement is meant to deal with the danger, and that due process of law requires that any drug treatment should be delayed until a judicial hearing, at which time the patient, free of drugs, must be present and represented by counsel. Related arguments are discussed below in terms of the right to refuse treatment.

All states eventually require a full legal hearing for civil commitment, and the alleged patient has several constitutional protections, including the right to be present, the right to a lawyer, the right to have his own expert witnesses, and the right to a jury trial. The state's psychiatrist (or psychologist in many jurisdictions) will have to testify and be cross-examined in the patient's presence as to the diagnosis and the evidence of grave disability or of dangerousness to self or others. Other witnesses who testify,

such as family or friends, must also do so in the presence of the patient and are also subject to cross-examination. Many jurisdictions now provide the alleged patient with a lawyer, and some provide an independent psychiatric (psychological) expert. Very few courts have required that the examining psychiatrist for the state give the patient a *Miranda*-like warning that "anything the patient says may be used to commit him" (*Lessard v. Schmidt,* 1972).

Many states have also adopted least restrictive alternative requirements. Even if the patient meets the stringent standards of civil commitment, the law asks if there is some alternative to commitment less restrictive of the person's liberty (Brakel, Parry, and Weiner, 1985). For example, patients could be screened and treated at some less restrictive facility, such as a day care or night care program with crisis intervention services. Many jurisdictions have adopted mandatory outpatient drug treatment as a less restrictive alternative. In the modern era of managed care and privatization, mandatory outpatient treatment has become the norm in some states rather than the exception. It saves the cost of a bed, protects the liberty of the alleged patient, and satisfies the lawyers that they have accomplished something. However, whether it is good policy rather than expedient compromise remains debatable. One thing is clear: the least restrictive alternative emphasizes that involuntary confinement is to be the last resort.

The American Psychiatric Association has proposed a model civil commitment law that among other things would reinstate a version of the "medical model" (Stromberg and Stone, 1983). It would allow involuntary commitment of an individual who is suffering substantial mental or physical deterioration as a result of a severe mental disorder. The model law attempts to avoid the legal objections to the medical model by requiring that the individual's psychotic condition be *treatable,* that the individual be *incompetent to make medical decisions,* that there be a reasonable prospect *that treatment is available,* and that there be objective evidence of *psychotic deterioration.* The intent of the model law is to facilitate efficacious treatment of obviously psychotic patients. The APA model law deals with the patient's right to treatment and right to refuse treatment at the time of commitment.

In varying degrees, most states have turned toward involuntary *outpatient* commitment as a means of preventing relapse and enforcing compliance with treatment programs. Typically, lack of compliance requires depot injections of antipsychotic medication. Clinicians at treatment programs are authorized to call on law officers to bring noncompliant patients in, and can sometimes reinstitute proceedings for inpatient commitment. Although some studies indicate that when outpatient commitment is used, compliance with treatment has risen and rates of rehospitalization have fallen, others argue that the effectiveness of involuntary outpatient commitment may be limited, and perhaps unnecessary, when "high-quality" community treatment programs are "aggressively" provided (Swartz et al., 1995). There is no evidence that mandatory outpatient treatment can be effectuated in large urban areas with homeless mentally ill persons who are routinely discharged from hospitals to the streets.

Sexual Predator Statutes

A variety of non-criminal statutes and procedures for the indefinite confinement of sexually dangerous persons thought to be both criminal and mentally ill were adopted by the states in the mid-twentieth century. Those laws fell into disfavor after civil libertarians questioned their constitutionality, and psychiatrists questioned whether meaningful treatment was available. Relabeled as violent sexual predator confinement statutes, these laws have recently been "rediscovered" by some state legislatures as a method of dealing with sexual offenders. These laws reflect society's increased intolerance of child molesters.

The Supreme Court has held that these "special commitment" statutes are constitutional (*Kansas v. Hendricks,* 1997). In *Hendricks,* a Kansas statute permitted further confinement by civil commitment of a person who had served out a criminal sentence in prison but both was sexually dangerous and suffered from a mental abnormality. "Mental abnormality," however, was defined broadly by the legislature, such that the statute applied to sexually dangerous persons who were neither mentally ill nor treatable by psychiatric criteria. In light of *Hendricks,* many states are expected to enact similar legislation aimed at the indefinite confinement of recidivist pedophiles.

Because of the many legal and psychiatric difficulties and the failure to provide efficacious treatment, the American Bar Association (1984) had called for the abolition of all "special commitment" statutes, like the Kansas statute, in favor of standard criminal procedures and sentences. Ironically, the best argument against such abolition at the time was the danger of prison life for the sexual predator, since pedophiles are often targets for physical and sexual abuse in prison.

Another constitutional and medical controversy has arisen about the imposition of chemical castration on sexually violent criminals. In 1996 California passed a statute requiring weekly injections of the synthetic hormone Depo-Provera for repeat child molesters. Several other states are currently considering similar legislation. The California statute has encountered fierce criticism on the grounds that it constitutes cruel and unusual punishment. The statute applies to repeat child molesters convicted after January 1, 1997, and it is likely that the law will suffer constitutional attack the first time enforcement is attempted.

The Right to Treatment

The obvious purpose of involuntary confinement of citizens who are not convicted criminals is treatment. Unfortunately, many institutions inadequately provided it. The sometimes squalid and even tragic conditions in these institutions were generally ignored by the courts until the right to treatment was first articulated by the federal courts.

The first important case recognizing civil commitment followed by neglect as a matter of constitutional significance was *Wyatt v. Stickney* (1972). There the district court ruled that "to deprive any citizen of his or her liberty upon the altruistic theory that the confinement is for humane and therapeutic reasons and then fail to provide adequate treatment violates the very fundamentals of due process" (325 F. Supp. 781). Beyond that simple statement, however, the court neglected to spell out a constitutional theory.

The Supreme Court has never specifically endorsed a constitutional right to treatment (as opposed to a right to habilitation; see below), just as it has not endorsed a right to food, shelter, education, clothing, or health care. Federal courts are now increasingly likely to leave the burden of creating costly entitlements to the legislative process.

An activist constitutional theory of the right to treatment had been formulated by a federal court in *Donaldson v. O'Connor* (1974). The court articulated what is known as the "quid pro quo theory" of the constitutional right to treatment. This theory holds that deprivation of liberty by civil procedures (providing lesser safeguards than criminal procedures) is the "quo" that must be balanced by the "quid" of adequate treatment.

The Supreme Court never accepted the quid pro quo theory. In *O'Connor v. Donaldson* (1975), the Supreme Court dodged the right to treatment issue and dealt with the narrow issue of release, holding that "a State cannot constitutionally confine without more a non-dangerous individual who is capable of surviving safely in freedom by himself or with the help of willing and responsible family members and friends" (422 U.S. 563, 576). Some have interpreted the landmark decision as holding that dangerousness is the only constitutional basis for commitment, but that conclusion is not supported by a careful reading of the entire decision. The Court's language, "without more," could mean the presence of a serious mental disorder and the provision of efficacious treatment. This case did much to end the practice of involuntary custodial confinement in state mental hospitals.

In the 1980s the legally significant right-to-treatment cases involved the mentally retarded. In 1982 the Supreme Court ruled that institutionalized mentally retarded patients have a "right to habilitation" (*Romeo v. Youngberg,* 1982), specifically, the right to a safe institutional environment and to training necessary to ensure their safety and freedom of movement. Unfortunately, the Court made this right extremely narrow. The right explicitly did not include training necessary to prevent deterioration of their preexisting cognitive and psychosocial skills. Furthermore, this was not a "per se" right to treatment but rather a right not to be unnecessarily physically restrained and endangered. The Court indicated that the professionals responsible were not to be personally liable when restraint was necessary because of a lack of resources, and specifically gave room for professional discretion. The "reality" of habilitation has, however, come in generous measure from state and federal legislatures who have provided for "special needs" children, a generosity that has not been shown to adults with chronic mental disorders.

Some of the lower court decisions finding a right to treatment remain in place. Some states have found a constitutional right to treatment in the least restrictive setting—generally, community placement for discharged patients. Other states prefer to negotiate "consent decrees," whereby lawyers for plaintiffs and defendants join state authorities to create mutually acceptable plans, some of which replace large state institutions with community-based care. The consent decree plan is given the federal court's imprimatur, and its implementation can be enforced by the judge's power to hold state officials in contempt of court. Some of these lower court decisions have resulted in dramatic improvements; others have arguably led to premature deinstitutionalization without adequate planning or appropriate aftercare. Until mental health facilities provide humane treatment, the moral legitimacy of confinement remains dubious. Some state courts have found a limited right to treatment under state law (*Arnold v. Sarn,* 1985), but most state legislatures are unwilling to supply the necessary funds. The right-to-treatment concept ironically contributed to the dismantling of public mental health facilities and to the increase in the numbers of homeless mentally ill.

The Right to Refuse Treatment

Along with the growing concern about adequate treatment came a parallel concern about imposing treatment on unwilling subjects. The courts have confronted two kinds of cases over the same period of time: the right of committed psychiatric patients to refuse antipsychotic medication, and the right of terminal medical patients to refuse life-prolonging treatments. Psychiatrists are directly involved in the former cases and often indirectly involved in the latter cases when they are called on to make a determination of competency to refuse life-prolonging treatment.

Two legal theories protect all patients against involuntary treatment. The first comes from the common law, which has two strands. First, a doctor who treats a patient without consent except under special circumstances (typically in an emergency) is guilty of battery (an illegal touching) and can be sued for damages. Second, a doctor who treats a patient without *informed* consent except under special circumstances is guilty of negligence and is also liable (Rozovsky, 1990). The courts have also articulated a constitutional right of privacy or self-determination as a basis for the right of hospitalized mental patients to refuse treatment (*Rogers v. Commissioners of Mental Health,* 1983). Such a right is not absolute and must be balanced against the state's interests. Thus the state's interest in controlling imminent violence might outweigh the patient's right to refuse antipsychotic treatment. Courts have given less weight to other state interests, such as providing efficacious treatment.

A violation of the common law right may lead to a malpractice claim. The constitutional right, if violated under "color of law," may create a federal case for monetary damages. Thus, two legal protections exist against involuntary treatment, backed up by potential monetary claims against the offending doctor. These legal theories assume that the patient refusing medication is competent to make treatment decisions, but often the real clinical and legal question is whether the patient is competent to give or withhold informed consent. (Informed consent is discussed below in the section on malpractice.)

The Right to Refuse Antipsychotic Drugs

The law on the right to refuse antipsychotic drugs varies among jurisdictions (Appelbaum, 1988). First, what constitutes an emergency in which antipsychotic drugs can be given without consent? In some jurisdictions an "emergency" occurs only when there is imminent risk of physical injury or of immediate and irreversible deterioration of the patient's condition. Emergency treatment is limited to the emergency and cannot continue once the emergency has passed (*Rogers v. Commissioners of Mental Health*, 1983). Other jurisdictions permit somewhat greater leeway in defining an emergency. This is a legal issue in transition, and the psychiatrist must have up-to-date legal guidance.

Second, what legal procedure should be followed when an involuntarily committed patient refuses drug treatment? Rules among different jurisdictions vary along a spectrum. At a maximum, some courts require a legal hearing to determine incompetency. If the patient is found incompetent, the judge makes a substituted judgment using criteria designed to implement the particular patient's own decision were he competent. Concern about tardive dyskenesia weighed heavily in these extreme judicial determinations, and the courts may be open to reconsidering those precedents in light of the new classes of antipsychotic medication.

At a minimum, the patient who has been found incompetent by a doctor but not a court has a right to appeal to some other decision makers (a judge or another doctor, for example) about the proposed treatment and about his competency. Some courts, for example, have ruled that the mental health regulations must provide for a procedure by which a patient refusing treatment can have doctors not involved in his care review his proposed treatment and his competence to refuse (*Rennie v. Klein*, 1979). In *Washington v. Harper* (1990), the Supreme Court allowed a state procedure authorizing a hospital committee to make the determination. It is still possible for such hospital determinations to be appealed to a court of law.

These decisions do not exhaust the different legal answers (for example, some courts appoint a guardian to make proxy decisions), but they should provide a sense of the range and complexity of the legal solutions.

The constitutional issues involved in the right to refuse antipsychotic drug treatment are similar to those involved in the right to die. But the courts' distrust of psychiatry is demonstrated by the fact that in some jurisdictions the patient's constitutional right to refuse antipsychotic medication is more zealously guarded by courts than the patient's right to refuse lifesaving treatment. In Massachusetts a physician can determine that a patient is incompetent and then decide, in consultation with the family or guardian, whether to withhold lifesaving treatment. Only if the physician is unsure of what is ethically and medically appropriate must a court be consulted. Often a psychiatrist will be called on to provide the definitive opinion about the medical or surgical patient's compe-

tency. But a psychiatrist cannot decide that a committed psychiatric patient is incompetent. He must consult a court, and the court decides competency and treatment questions. Courts in practice, however, typically defer to the recommendations of the psychiatrist once the court decides a patient is incompetent.

Many states have special statutory or regulatory constraints on electroconvulsive therapy and psychosurgery. Aversive therapy has also been subject to litigation and regulation. State legislation on drugs that can be abused may limit the amount that can be prescribed and may require reporting or other special procedures. Psychiatrists in some states are not permitted to prescribe psychoactive drugs for themselves or members of their family household.

Right to Die and Physician Assisted Suicide

Beginning with *Roe v. Wade* (1973), the Supreme Court's abortion decision, there has been a new constitutional emphasis on a patient's rights to autonomy and self-determination. Difficulties arise when the patient is incompetent and unable to exercise these rights. Courts have addressed 3 broad categories of problematic cases: where patients involved (1) are permanently unconscious, (2) suffer from dementia or severe mental retardation, or (3) are competent but want to refuse life-prolonging medical treatment.

Initially, many cases involving the right to refuse life-prolonging treatment relied on the fundamental right to privacy recognized in *Roe v. Wade*. In the mid-1970s the Supreme Court of New Jersey decided that a patient in a permanent vegetative state had the same kind of privacy right to terminate mechanical respiration. The court delegated the decision to the family in consultation with the patient's attending physician and the hospital ethics committee (*In the matter of Karen Quinlan*, 1976).

While other state courts soon followed New Jersey's precedent, Massachusetts established a much more cumbersome procedure that required judges, rather than families, to make the decisions about terminating or refusing treatment (*Superintendent of Belchertown v. Saikewicz*, 1977). This approach, heralded by civil libertarians, soon proved unworkable, and Massachusetts now uses the court procedure only in novel situations or when the family is in conflict. The New Jersey Supreme Court next took a more dramatic step by ruling that senile patients in a nursing home could, under appropriate circumstances, have treatment withdrawn even when their life expectancy was 1 year (*In the matter of Claire Conroy*, 1985). The *Conroy* court also rejected the distinctions between refusals of extraordinary care (e.g., respirators) and ordinary medical treatment and between medical treatment and food and water. As the right to refuse treatment gained momentum, many other courts also rejected these distinctions.

In 1990 the Supreme Court addressed the issue of whether a patient in a permanently vegetative state has a constitutional right to refuse medical treatment. The Court assumed that competent persons had a right to refuse "lifesaving hydration and nutrition" (*Cruzan v. Director, Missouri Department of Health*, 110 S. Ct. 2841, 2852). However, the Court framed the right not as a fundamental right of privacy or self-determination as in *Roe v. Wade*, but as a "liberty interest" which could be outweighed by "relevant state interests" (110 S. Ct. at 2851). Then, turning to the issue of whether an *incompetent* patient could refuse medical care, the Court upheld a state statute that prohibited the withdrawal of treatment in these circumstances unless there was "clear and convincing" evidence that the patient would have wanted the withdrawal.

When courts have addressed the issue of what an incompetent patient would choose, the dominant legal trend has emphasized that the basis for "substituted judgment" should not be objective—what a reasonable person would do—but subjective—what that particular incompetent patient would decide were he or she competent (*Superintendent of Belchertown v. Saikewicz*, 1977).

Most legislatures now provide for advanced directives which allow patients to make these decisions before they become incompetent. There are also procedures to appoint a proxy medical decision maker to choose for the patient and to avoid family disagreement. After the *Cruzan* decision, Congress passed legislation requiring that patients be informed about their legal rights by hospitals.

Whereas the right to refuse life-prolonging treatment is now generally accepted, controversies arise when notions of patient autonomy are extended to an affirmative right to physician assisted suicide. Legal and ethical sanctions have rarely if ever been imposed in circumstances where the physician acts to provide palliative measures that hasten death when the patient is suffering, his condition is hopeless, and death is imminent. These practices are justified under the principle of double effect, which allows physicians to ease pain even when it may hasten death.

Unfortunately, recent surveys demonstrate that a substantial proportion of gravely ill patients in hospitals received inadequate pain relief and were subjected to invasive medical technology that prolonged the process of dying. Many people no longer wish to rely on their physician's compassion. They wish to control their own fate by way of physician assisted suicide. Most controversially, some wish to exercise this right before they are terminal.

Physician assisted suicide is legally distinguishable from voluntary euthanasia by the patient's intervening act. Instead of murder, the physician may be charged with the lesser crime of assisting in suicide. After a period of contention on the issue, the Supreme Court upheld statutory prohibitions on physician assisted suicide against constitutional attack (*Washington v. Glucksberg*, 1997), and the issue will be resolved on a state-by-state basis.

Oregon voters have approved legislation allowing physician assisted suicide, and at this writing more than a dozen other states are considering similar legislation. Most proposals would permit physician assisted suicide only when the patient is terminal, defined as having less than 6 months to live. Other more radical proposals would permit physician assisted suicide for patients who are suffering from incurable but not terminal afflictions. The proposed statutes would require competency screenings performed by a psychiatrist before allowing patients to terminate their lives.

Many practical and ethical problems await a psychiatrist who undertakes this screening. First, many psychiatrists feel it is difficult, even perhaps clinically impossible, to distinguish clearly between symptoms of depression and similar feelings of hopelessness stemming from a life-threatening illness. Second, although the recent literature on assisted suicide urges psychiatrists to accept the possibility that suicidality is not necessarily a symptom of mental disorder, the distinctions between the different kinds of suicidality are less than clear. Third, recent empirical evidence indicates that even patients with a confirmed diagnosis of severe depression may pass most legal tests of competency to make medical decisions. Thus, a diagnosis of depression may not be determinative even when it can be made.

Testamentary Capacity

The current trend in law, illustrated by the reforms in civil commitment, is to articulate different kinds of legal competency in different legal contexts and to assert that incompetency in terms of one legal function does not necessarily mean incompetency in terms of all. A person found "mentally ill" or "insane" or "psychotic" is not incompetent for all legal purposes. Reformers argue that each aspect of competency should be determined on the narrow legal standards applicable to the specific legal function. Thus, competency to vote, to contract, to marry, and to make a will would be separately delineated.

As noted earlier, legal questions can be fully understood only in the context of the doctrines, common law, and statutes specific to a given area of law. I have already dealt with competency to stand trial, competency to be executed, and competency to refuse medical treatment. Here I shall discuss competency to make a will—testamentary capacity. The current, almost universally accepted standard has been in use more than a century, and, not surprisingly, it emphasizes cognitive capacity.

The courts require that the testator:

1. Know, without prompting, the nature and extent of the property of which he is about to dispose.
2. Know the nature of the act he is about to perform.
3. Know the name and identity of any person who is to be the object of his bounty.
4. Know his relations toward them.
5. Have sufficient mind and memory to understand all of these facts.
6. Appreciate the relation of these facts to one another.
7. Recall the decision which he has formed.

Often the psychiatrist, when testifying as to testamentary capacity, will be asked a series of hypothetical questions incorporating the foregoing requirements—for example, "Assuming that Mr. Jones had episodes of confusion and recent memory loss, would it be possible for him to know . . . ?"

Wills are challenged only after the testator's death, which is often long after the will was drafted. Because wills are usually drawn up by lawyers (and not by the testator), the language contained in them will give little indication of the testator's cognitive capacity. Thus, unless detailed psychiatric evaluations contemporaneous with the creation of the will are available, the psychiatrist is forced to deal with inferences based on secondary sources. In this context, the reliability and validity of psychiatric testimony can surely be questioned.

Psychiatric Malpractice

"Malpractice is a special remedial category designed to regulate professional misfeasance. Its attributes are the measurement of lack of skill and care by a physician in a doctor-patient relationship against a professionally proved standard of community practice. It involves damages caused the patient by the act of a psychiatrist" (Dawidoff, 1973, p. 15). In virtually all cases of psychiatric malpractice, the plaintiff who brings the suit must retain expert witnesses to establish the professional standard of care and the defendant doctor's failure to meet that standard.

Throughout most of the twentieth century, psychiatric malpractice was a minimal problem compared with malpractice among other medical practitioners. Recently, however, claims of psychiatric malpractice have increased significantly, and rates for psychiatric malpractice insurance have begun to escalate.

Informed Consent and Medication

Informed consent to treatment involves at least 3 conditions. First, the consent must be *voluntarily given:* no coercion, explicit or implicit, may be involved. Second, it must be *knowing:* the patient must be informed of the relevant risks and benefits, the possible side effects, and available alternative treatments. Third, the patient must have the *legal capacity* to give consent; for example, he must legally be an adult (Rozovsky, 1990). When the patient does not have the capacity to give consent voluntarily and knowingly, the traditional practice had been to obtain the consent from the closest relative. These traditional practices have been rejected in some jurisdictions, and more complicated procedures must be followed. Most health organizations are aware of the more specific legal requirements in this area, and forms are usually available for obtaining written informed consent and for procedures to be followed when the patient is incompetent to give consent.

Doctors can treat patients without fully informing the patient of the risks in emergencies and when the doctor in good faith believes that the patient's condition would be endangered by full disclosure of the risks involved in a treatment that is clearly necessary. If the "emergency" or "therapeutic exception" does not apply and a patient is not informed of a risk of treatment, and that risk eventuates, the patient may bring a malpractice suit for negligence.

The crucial question arises of how much information the physician must provide. Courts have two different answers to this question, and neither is completely satisfactory. The traditional standard is that the doctor tells the patient what other doctors tell their patients in similar circumstances. This standard assumes that, just as there is a professional standard for treating pneumonia, there is a professional standard for disclosing risks, benefits, and alternatives to a proposed treatment.

The other modern "consumer-oriented" approach to informed consent in law requires the doctor to provide the patient what a reasonable patient would need to know in order to make an informed decision (*Canterbury v. Spence,* 1972). It is difficult to specify, however, what a reasonable patient would need to know. A malpractice case will arise only when a risk of treatment eventuates, and the patient may claim by that very fact that a reasonable patient should have been told of that risk. Thus, to the risk-averse physician, this standard suggests disclosure of every conceivable risk. Courts have held that very rare risks need not be disclosed under the "consumer standard," but a gray area still exists. Where patients are exposed to experimental or novel treatments, courts expect even more elaborate efforts to ensure that consent is voluntary and informed (Rozovsky, 1990).

Informed consent standards typically require that patients be informed about possible alternative treatments for their illness. This provision became controversial in psychiatry when it was interpreted to require psychotherapists to inform patients about alternative biobehavioral treatments (Klerman, 1988).

The unwanted side effects of drugs and other forms of treatment pose the same problems for psychiatrists as they do for the rest of medicine. Claims of negligence could be based on failure to obtain informed consent (Simon, 1992), failure to monitor the patient properly, failure to adjust drug dosage in light of the risks, prolonged use of drugs for conditions in which the risks do not justify the benefits (as with nonpsychotic patients), and administering drugs for convenience or expedience rather than for efficacious treatment of the particular patient (*Clites v. Iowa,* 1981).

Obtaining informed consent from disturbed patients is particularly problematic (Appelbaum and Gutheil, 1992). The patient's knowing and voluntary consent should be a continuing part of the treatment process. Informed consent should be viewed as an essential part of the therapeutic alliance, as well as necessary to minimize legal liability. The doctor must know how to monitor the patient for early signs of tardive dyskinesia and other unwanted side effects and should keep records of that effort and of the patient's cooperation. Except in emergencies, antipsychotic drug treatment should not be imposed until the appropriate legal procedures have been implemented. Any psychiatrist or physician who writes prescriptions for antipsychotic medication without personally examining and monitoring the patient invites legal liability.

A difficult question for psychiatrists prescribing antipsychotic drugs is when to withhold from the patient the risks under the therapeutic exception to informed consent. Some knowledgeable psychiatrists believe that, because tardive dyskinesia is not a short-term risk, informa-

tion about that side effect can be withheld from psychotic patients until a therapeutic effect has been achieved and the patient can deal with the information more rationally. This approach may be clinically reasonable but legally problematic. It seems appropriate to decide this question on a case-by-case basis after documenting in the medical record why the information was not given to this particular patient. Caution suggests that one should discuss the side effects with the next of kin and document that discussion.

Informed Consent and Recovered Memory

Psychotherapists are now facing liability for failing to secure informed consent for recovering repressed memories in patients. In 1995 a Minnesota jury awarded $2.4 million to a woman who "recovered" graphic memories of sexual abuse during her childhood, which she subsequently alleged were falsely implanted by the therapist's hypnosis, amytal interviews, and suggested readings. The jury found that the doctor negligently harmed the patient. In particular, the jury found that the doctor failed to get informed consent for what expert testimony characterized as risky experimental procedures when safer methods to treat general anxiety were available. Further, at least one psychotherapist has been successfully sued not by her patient but by the alleged sexual abuser supposedly identified in recovered memories. In light of these developments, practitioners should adhere to the highest standards of informed consent, seek consultation, and recognize that "narrative truth" worked out in psychotherapy is not always probative evidence in a court of law.

Other Malpractice Issues

Of particular interest to psychiatrists has been the development over the last few decades of a duty to protect society from the dangers posed by their patients. While malpractice suits involving the negligent release or escape of dangerous patients who harmed third parties have long been permitted, only recently has this been extended to an office-based or clinical practice.

The California Supreme Court, in the famous case of *Tarasoff v. Regents of the University of California* (1976), was the first to establish a duty to protect or warn third parties against the "predictable" violence of patients even when the therapist had no legal or physical control over the patient. To circumvent the legal tradition against imposing a duty in the absence of control, the court ruled that the psychotherapist-patient relationship was "special." According to the *Tarasoff* court, the psychotherapist must predict whether the patient is violent. In judging whether negligence has occurred, trial courts rely on expert witnesses who testify as to the prevailing professional standards in making such predictions. If the therapist makes (or should have made) such a prediction, he must warn the identifiable victims or take other unspecified measures to protect them.

The *Tarasoff* decision drew considerable attention in legal and psychiatric circles. Many other jurisdictions adopted similar holdings. The Virginia Supreme Court, however, ruled that the doctor-patient relationship is not "special" in the sense required by legal doctrine and refused to impose a *Tarasoff* duty (*Nasser v. Parker*, 1995). In addition, California and other states have enacted statutes limiting the scope of *Tarasoff*. Typically, these laws require evidence that the patient actually voiced a threat against a third party.

The increasing imposition of biobehavioral standards of care on psychotherapists merits brief description (Klerman, 1988). This parallels the increased focus the DSM-III, DSM-III-R, and DSM-IV have placed on symptom-oriented diagnosis (Axis I) and the literature on the efficacy of biobehavioral treatment. One controversial case illustrates this phenomenon. A patient diagnosed as having a severe narcissistic personality disorder with depression sued both a private hospital and his psychiatrist for treating him with psychoanalysis alone. Supported by distinguished psychiatric experts, 3 claims were made on his behalf: first, that he should have received drug treatment or electroconvulsive therapy for his severe depression; second, that informed consent included a duty to describe the alternative biobehavioral treatments; and third, that the hospital negligently failed to maintain staff competency in biological psychiatry. The case, which eventually settled, and other similar cases illustrate the risk of malpractice liability for failure to implement biobehavioral standards of care which have been further solidified by managed care protocols and practice manuals (Klerman, 1988). Information about alternative biobehavioral treatments should be made available to patients by psychotherapists as part of informed consent.

The major basis for claims against psychotherapists involves "undue familiarity" with their patients. During the late 1970s and 1980s a flood of such claims devastated the mental health profession, and large jury awards came close to bankrupting their malpractice insurance companies. Most policies now specifically exclude coverage of "undue familiarity," and the therapist may himself be liable for the damages. Undue familiarity in some states is now subject to criminal penalties and is commonly

grounds for a loss of licensure. Even after termination of therapy, sex with a former patient is unethical and may be grounds for civil and criminal liability.

Post-Traumatic Stress Disorder and Tort Litigation

Historically, courts have been reluctant to award damages for purely psychic injury without accompanying physical contact because of difficulties with proving causation and valuing psychic damages. However, the increasing legal recognition of post-traumatic stress disorder (PTSD) is breaking down the traditional barriers to recovery for nonphysical injury (Stone, 1993). Unlike the concept of neurosis, which emphasizes a complex etiology, PTSD posits a straightforward causal relationship that plaintiffs' lawyers welcome. The diagnosis takes matters that were once considered too subjective for legal resolution and seems to make them scientific and objective. As such, PTSD has become a lightning rod for a wide variety of civil claims of trauma-related psychopathology.

PTSD diagnoses have transformed the tort of "intentional infliction of emotional distress" into a significant compensable injury. Plaintiffs alleging PTSD in housing discrimination, sexual harassment, and similar suits now often obtain large jury awards, whereas before PTSD they might have received only a nominal amount, if anything. Lawyers are regularly using PTSD in routine personal injury cases, including cases of "negligent infliction of emotional distress" for automobile accident victims, bystanders who witness the accident, and similar plaintiffs.

PTSD has not borne its heavy forensic burden easily. The diagnosis poses for psychiatry some of the very problems it supposedly solves for legal purposes, including the illusory objectivity of the causative traumatic event and the expert's dependence on the victim's subjective and sometimes unverifiable reports of symptomatology for diagnosis. The disorder seems at first to provide a world of Manichaean moral certainty where evil people traumatize innocent victims, but of course it is not that simple. Even the victimizers claim to have been victims—that the abuser was abused (Stone, 1993).

Confidentiality

Confidentiality is a crucial consideration in psychiatry. But despite the efforts of the profession, confidentiality seems to be eroding. First, cost-control procedures by third-party payers demand increasingly detailed information, and utilization reviews, whether performed in-house or by external agencies, as well as computerized systems have increased access to sensitive patient information. Second, many jurisdictions have imposed mandatory reporting of child abuse; of impaired-physician patients, particularly physicians who are alcoholics or substance abusers; of patients obtaining certain prescriptions; and of potentially violent patients. Third, a variety of employment, licensing, insurance, and litigation contexts require patients to waive psychiatrist-patient confidentiality. Fourth, governmental investigators concerned about tax evasion as well as Medicare and Medicaid fraud have demanded access to patients' records to examine allegations of criminal conduct by mental health providers.

Present standards require psychiatrists to obtain written consent specifying the nature and extent of disclosure of confidential information, and substantiation that the consent was given voluntarily. Even with these precautions, many psychiatrists believe that there should be a duty to discourage patients from detailed revelations of sensitive material. However, patients (and, after the patient is deceased, their heirs in many states) have a right to obtain their medical records.

Issues of confidentiality have been much litigated. While a comprehensive discussion of all of these issues is beyond the scope of this chapter, I have selected one which illustrates the tensions between legal and psychiatric values.

Most states have created by statute a so-called psychiatrist-patient or psychotherapist-patient privilege provision. In essence it gives the patient the right, with certain exceptions, to prohibit the psychiatrist from testifying in court or supplying the patient's records. The privilege is the patient's; if he waives it, it cannot be asserted by the psychiatrist.

Psychiatrists may have their own professional and ethical reasons for not revealing the confidences of the therapeutic relation, but the courts have given these reasons only limited weight. This specific issue has been litigated in California (*Caesar v. Mountanos*, 1976). California law requires litigants in typical tort claims, such as automobile accidents, to waive all doctor-patient testimonial privilege. The law is intended to enable the court to consider the "best evidence" about the claimed injury. The "best evidence" rule serves the fundamental legal value of fairness.

Psychiatrists attacked this intrusion on the fundamental psychiatric value of confidentiality. They argued that such laws discouraged patients from obtaining needed psychiatric treatment and from making the kind of free, total disclosure necessary for psychotherapy. The California courts have heeded such arguments and have attempted to distinguish between psychiatric testimony about diagnostic material they will require and information that may be withheld, including broader psychodynamic material and detailed personal information. This distinction poses practical difficulties. The federal court of appeals having jurisdiction over California considered and rejected the subsequent claim that psychiatrist-patient communication was protected by the constitutional right of privacy (*Caesar v. Mountanos*, 1976). The APA dealt with these issues in "The Principles of Medical Ethics":

A physician may not reveal the confidences entrusted to him in the course of medical attendance, or the deficiencies he may observe in the character of patients unless he is required to do so by law or unless it becomes necessary in order to protect the welfare of the individual or of the community.

. . . When the psychiatrist is ordered by the court to reveal the confidences entrusted to him by patients he may comply or he may ethically hold the right to dissent within the framework of the law.

When the psychiatrist is in doubt, the right of the patient to confidentiality and, by extension, to unimpaired treatment, should be given priority. The psychiatrist should reserve the right to raise the question of adequate need for disclosure. In the event that the necessity for disclosure is demonstrated by the court, the psychiatrist may request the right to disclose only that information which is relevant to the legal question at hand. (1995)

The Supreme Court in *Jaffee v. Redmond* (1996) made the testimonial privilege part of the federal rules of evidence. The Court extended the privilege broadly to include licensed social workers as well. This ruling has no effect on proceedings in state courts, but may signal a legal trend toward protecting more patient-psychotherapist communications.

Disability Benefits and Protection

In 1984 Congress passed the Social Security Benefits Reform Act, which expanded the coverage of disability benefits for any individual whose mental or physical disability impedes "substantial gainful activity." Psychiatrists are called on to assess a patient's disability, functional impairment, and prognosis, for the purpose of assessing eligibility under the criteria promulgated by the Social Security Administration. These criteria are closely followed by the American Medical Association's *Guide to the Evaluation of Permanent Impairment* (1988). Psychiatrists also have a role in determining when an individual's eligibility ceases. Under current law, the government cannot withdraw support from a mentally disabled recipient unless it can demonstrate by substantial evidence that the disability does not exist or no longer impairs the ability to work.

A controversial policy question involves whether substance abuse disorder should be grounds for disability eligibility. In recent years such disorders have been compensable, although Congress required the payments to go to a representative, such as a clinic director or a legal guardian, rather than directly to the person disabled by substance abuse. Some psychiatrists and other experts, however, argued that subsidizing addicted patients was counterproductive, and in 1996 Congress acted to exclude substance abuse disorders. Affected patients must now reapply on the basis of other disabilities, and any money they receive will continue to go to a representative "payee."

Mental disabilities are also covered under private disability insurance and are increasingly the basis for claims. Large sums of money are involved, and insurers are more aggressively contesting these claims. Assessments of mental disability are also relevant to the issue of disability discrimination. The landmark Americans with Disabilities Act (ADA) of 1990 prevents public and private employers and programs from discriminating on the basis of disabilities that "substantially limit one or more major life activities." ADA also requires employers to make "reasonable accommodations to the physical or mental limitations of an otherwise qualified individual." Psychiatrists are increasingly being called on to determine when mental disorders qualify for the statute's protection. The question of adequate accommodation for a patient with a mental disability is not easy to resolve. The act is likely to keep lawyers and psychiatrists busy for years to come.

Managed Care and the Transformation of American Psychiatry

Managed care has transformed the legal and professional environment of the entire medical profession, including psychiatry. Only if we understand "private sector regulation" under both the Employment Retirement Income Security Act (ERISA) and the "market paradigm" of economic competition will we comprehend how that is possible (Stone, 1995).

ERISA: The Federal Statute That Changed American Health Care

The transformation of the health care industry was facilitated in the 1970s by the drafting and enactment of ERISA. Originally designed by the late U.S. Senator Jacob Javits of New York to protect employee pension funds, as the statute made its way through Congress it eventually included health care benefits as well. ERISA affects millions of insured Americans. According to U.S. Census Bureau statistics, 85% of Americans are covered by some form of health insurance plan, provided in most cases by their employer (Griner, 1991). While ERISA was meant to protect employees, in operation it actually protects the employer's control over health care benefits.

ERISA allows employers to establish, modify, or cancel employee medical benefits plans without governmental interference, so long as the plan's administration is consistent with ERISA's provisions. ERISA does not require that employers provide any specific health benefits, courts lack the power to mandate such requirements, and the state legislature cannot impose them.

Because of this ERISA protection, employers may limit coverage of mental disorders and may even discriminate between conditions, excluding from coverage diseases involving high-cost treatments such as Alzheimer's, schizophrenia, or even AIDS (Jameson and Wehr, 1993). More important, ERISA plans can regulate hospital and physician providers by establishing protocols for care that limit benefits.

Since ERISA was intended to impose uniform federal standards on employee benefits, it contained a provision preempting any state laws insofar as they relate to any employee benefit plan. This preemption provision and other provisions insulated the ERISA plan from malpractice claims and state legislation. ERISA provisions do allow for the recovery of benefits wrongfully denied to the patient but not compensation for any damages caused by the denial of treatment—the so-called "consequential damages" available in typical malpractice law. For example, if the plan limits the length of stay in a psychiatric hospital and the prematurely discharged patient commits suicide, his estate cannot sue the plan for negligence or the resultant damages available in a malpractice suit. They can sue only for the value of the denied benefits, e.g., 10 days of hospitalization. Doctors and hospitals can be sued, but the ERISA preemption clause generally protects the health plans and allows them to limit or ration care without liability for the consequences to patients. Some recent cases have bucked this trend (e.g., *Pappas v. Asbel*, 1996), and it remains to be seen if and how the law will develop in the future.

Despite these impediments to patient-plaintiffs, states were nonetheless still able to exercise some marginal control over ERISA plans under the so-called savings clause, which permitted the states to regulate health insurance companies under state insurance laws (ERISA, 1988). In *Metropolitan Life Ins. v. Massachusetts* (1985), the Supreme Court unanimously upheld a state statute requiring insurers to include minimum mental health benefits, but the decision also created a loophole from state regulations. The Court determined that plans that purchased insurance were subject to state insurance regulation under the savings clause, but plans that *self-insured* (described in the opinion as "uninsured") were exempt. Not surprisingly, most corporate ERISA plans used this escape hatch and became self-insured. Protected by ERISA, private sector managers of health care have regulated providers without risk of legal consequences and have been immune from state laws requiring parity in mental health benefits for more than 20 years.

The Role of Oligopsony Purchasing Power

Oligopsony and ERISA were twin blades of the scissors that cut the fabric of the American health care system. "Oligopsony" is a situation in which a few buyers control demand in a market with a large number of competing sellers. Oligopsony describes the market conditions that empower the current purchasers of health care. In the era of fee-for-service care, millions of individual patients subsidized by health insurance individually purchased health care from providers. But now the tables have turned and a small number of health plans purchase health care from hundreds of thousands of providers. These plans now have oligopsony purchasing power.

This health plan oligopsony purchasing power is most potent in regions of the country where there has been an oversupply of medical beds or professional services. Consider the case of the private psychiatric hospital, the institution that was among the first to feel the impact of managed care. All hospitals need to maintain a certain occupancy rate in order to survive financially. Below that rate (or "census"), the hospital, with its fixed costs and overhead, loses money. When managed care's utilization standards (i.e., private sector regulation) cut the median length of hospitalization for a psychiatric patient from 3 weeks to 1 week, the average hospital needed 3 times as many patients to maintain its previous census. During the 1980s, psychiatric hospital occupancy rates dropped from more than 70% to less than 50% as the result of managed care (Carpi, 1995). Desperate for more admissions, all of the psychiatric hospitals in a given geographical area competed for more referrals.

Any managed care health plan with a large number of potential referrals could approach such a financially troubled hospital and bargain for a discounted price since the plan wielded enormous oligopsony market power. The struggling hospital had a choice between an empty bed producing no income and a full bed producing a dis-

counted payment, e.g., 75% of the usual daily rate. In this fashion, powerful health plans were able to obtain reduced hospital rates and professional fees. During the era of fee-for-service some states had tried to regulate constantly escalating hospital rates by establishing price controls. This public regulation became superfluous as managed care drove down hospital rates and hospital use with their market power and utilization review. All health plans like HMOs further reduce their costs by limiting use of specialist services. For example, whenever possible the primary care physician, a less expensive social worker, or a psychiatric nurse will supply the necessary psychiatric service rather than a more expensive psychiatrist. This can be described as a "human economy of scale," a fundamental feature of managed care. Such "human economies of scale" inevitably mean that fewer psychiatrists will be needed to deal with the same number of patients. Fee-for-service health insurance plans cannot achieve similar economies and cannot compete in the new health care marketplace.

The 4 Stages of Managed Care

The market forces just described eventually pushed all of health care toward the HMO model or "capitated system." Managed care health plans consolidate the insurance and the provider function, as in an HMO. These large health plans now dominate American medicine. All of the other health care players—medical schools, hospitals, and physicians—must contract with the large plans or compete with them by organizing and controlling their own health plans. Independent psychiatrists and other specialists are struggling to find a place in some plan because they confront a shrinking demand for their services as managed care increases its enrollment and controls referrals. Despite the protean nature of health plans (HMOs, PPOs, POS plans, PAs, etc.), it is possible to describe the sequence of changes in managed care as occurring in 4 stages. Based on their impact on the psychiatric practitioner, these stages are: (1) fee-for-service care with external peer review; (2) horizontal networks to organize mental health providers and to contract selectively with managed care health plans; (3) vertically organized "carve-outs" of mental health care; (4) "carve-ins" reintegrating mental health care in one vertical health care plan.

Stage 1: external peer review. For psychiatry, the most important aspect of managed care in stage 1 was the increasingly intrusive role of "fourth-party" utilization review, i.e., the "outside scrutiny of physicians' medical decisions." In this "fourth-party" conception, the covered patient is the first party, the provider is the second party, and the insurer or self-insured ERISA plan is the third party. The "fourth party" is the utilization reviewer (UR), a company retained by the third-party payer to monitor the quality as well as the cost of mental health care at the hospital-patient and/or doctor-patient levels (Morreim, 1991).

An early, benign era of fourth-party utilization review that promised quality assurance as well as cost control inexorably gave way to URs which emphasized cost cutting. These fourth-party URs represented the start of a new type of business in medicine which would ultimately become managed care organizations (MCOs). URs made money not by providing care but by acting as middlemen who saved the money of third-party purchasers of health care by imposing limitations on physicians, i.e., by private regulation.

Over time, utilization review shifted from retrospective to concurrent to prospective authorization, each shift increasing the control of the utilization reviewer (Morreim, 1991). Eventually many URs were dictating the nature and duration of care—i.e., *how* to treat as well as *how much* to treat.

Working within self-insured ERISA plans, utilization reviewers were protected as previously described by federal law from malpractice liability for the consequences of their utilization decisions that changed the standards of care in psychiatry (Gordon, 1995). Some URs unprotected by ERISA remained in theory subject to malpractice liability. However, if some serious harm to a patient occurred as a result of a utilization decision, the legal case against the attending psychiatrist almost always seemed much stronger than the case against the UR. As a result, URs could regulate provider standards of care and reduce health plan costs without being overly concerned about the legal consequences.

Stage 2: horizontal networks to organize mental health providers and contract selectively with managed care plans. The second stage of managed care in psychiatry is characterized by discount pricing and selective contracting. Utilization review had helped to create an oversupply of both beds and service providers—an oversupply that paved the way for oligopsony purchasing power in the second stage. The emergence of a new form of health care organization, the Preferred Provider Organizations (PPOs), exemplified the use of oligopsony purchasing power.

The basic organizational strategy behind the PPO is to create a health plan "network" through *selective contracting,* which limits the panel of specialists and the choice of hospitals available to plan enrollees. Plan organizers ne-

gotiate with specialists and hospitals in order to obtain discounted fees for services in exchange for exclusive referrals to those hospitals or specialists, who become the plan's "preferred providers" (Loue, 1993). PPO enrollees who go to a physician or hospital outside the plan must pay a substantial additional co-payment.

The organization of Preferred Provider Organizations was one of many new horizontally integrated networking arrangements. Many new, loosely organized groups of mental health providers emerged, seeking to enter into selective contracts with PPOs. As demonstrated by the success of the PPOs, the advantages of oligopsony purchasing power were quickly and sometimes painfully obvious to third-party health insurers such as Blue Cross/Blue Shield. PPOs allowed more aggressive health insurers to offer lower premiums to ERISA plan corporate purchasers because the PPOs were paying discounted prices to providers. Although the pace of events varied in different regions of the country, these and other market pressures causing loss of market share and loss of low-risk patients were driving many Blue Cross/Blue Shield organizations into the red (for detailed treatment of topic, see Stone, 1995, "Paradigms, Pre-emptions, and Stages: Understanding the Transformation of American Psychiatry by Managed Care").

As external utilization review shortened the median length of stay, the style of psychiatric hospital practice had to adapt. To become preferred providers, hospitals found it necessary to alter their entire treatment approach. This contributed to the ongoing shift of hospital psychiatry toward rapid psychopharmacological interventions, short-term and symptom-focused psychotherapies, and behavioral treatments, as well as an increased biological emphasis in the biopsychosocial treatment model. This shift in treatment standards allowed general hospitals with excess beds to compete on an equal footing with psychiatric hospitals.

Stage 3: vertically organized carve-outs of mental health care. The developments that characterize stage 3 and lead to vertical integration of psychiatry can be seen in the following example. The managed care organization (MCO) of a major ERISA health plan sees the virtues in "bundling" mental health care rather than bargaining for and monitoring the separate services of the hospital, the psychiatrists, and other providers.

The bundle of services includes all of the mental health services needed by members of the plan. In the simplest case, an HMO that provides for all of its members' health care needs in exchange for an annual capitation payment (i.e. an amount per head, or per "covered life" [Shortell et al., 1994]), decides that its mental health services are unsatisfactory and not cost-effective. The HMO looks to contract out—i.e., to "carve out"—all mental health services. The mental health "carve-out" will provide all of the mental health care that the HMO members need, in exchange for a percentage of the HMO's annual capitation payment. Determining what percentage of these payments should go to mental health is a matter of fierce debate, and the needs of different populations vary. However, these carve-out arrangements are ultimately based as much on the market as they are on epidemiological considerations.

The "would be" mental health service carve-out that wants to compete at this level needs to be able to offer the HMO a vertically organized "one-stop shopping" partner who can provide for all of the mental health and substance abuse needs of enrollees. The mental health partner of the HMO then becomes responsible for providing all medically necessary mental health care, in exchange for a fixed percentage of the annual premiums. A horizontal network of psychiatrists and other mental health professionals providing only psychotherapy is not positioned to engineer a carve-out, and neither is a geographically isolated psychiatric hospital. Unless these providers are organized in such a way as to provide all necessary services, they will lose market power in stage 3.

Most important for the psychiatric profession, the carve-out, even when it is a teaching hospital or medical school department of psychiatry, now operates under the burden of the human economy of scale incentives. With its fixed budget, it has the incentive to replace psychiatrists with psychologists, psychologists with social workers, and social workers with nurse-practitioners whenever possible. Just like any other tight-fisted "insurer-provider," the carve-out will have little interest in paying psychiatrists to do long term psychotherapy. Cost-effective treatment and "medically necessary" treatment will be redefined relative to the fixed budget rather than in terms of traditional standards of care. As a result, the next generation of psychiatrists will learn a different role. The role played by the psychiatrist in a carve-out arrangement will emphasize *medical training*, primarily diagnosis and biological treatments. Anything else the psychiatrist provides can be obtained by the carve-out at a lower price from a non–medically trained professional. The economic pressures in the carve-out will intensify as carve-outs compete with one another.

Stage 4: reintegrating in one vertical health care plan. The basic feature of this stage is the predicted reintegration of mental health services into vertically organized total health care systems (i.e., the "carve-in"). Many medical school teaching hospitals prefer this arrangement as they try to compete with health plans for patients. They may offer their own health plan, become a regional branch of a national health plan, or work out a variety of other capitated packages to serve covered lives rather than identified patients.

If we look at how cost saving occurs under current arrangements, we can perhaps see the outlines of the future. At the core of most health plans that are gaining market share is the primary care physician functioning as gatekeeper. The primary care physician is surrounded by nurse-practitioners, physician extenders, and other less costly providers who increase the "productivity" of the primary care physician by providing most of the routine services and procedures. Likewise, many of the routine tasks of medical specialists are assumed by the lower-paid primary care physicians. In the framework of these gatekeeper plans, routine psychopharmacology will be taken care of by the primary care physician. The routine counseling and focused psychotherapies will be provided by nurse-practitioners and less costly professionals, rather than by more expensive psychiatrists, psychologists, or psychiatric social workers.

This version of the fourth stage carve-in requires even fewer psychiatrists than stage 3; furthermore, their expertise will be primarily neurobiological, and they will function as supervisory consultants who deal directly only with the most complicated cases. Once again this new and highly limited role will not necessarily be dictated by science or professional wisdom, but will be the result of the relentless market pressure that requires human economies of scale so as to maximize the cost savings of health plans.

Experts in health policy foresee many different possibilities along the way, but they seem to agree that market forces will lead to regional and national mergers of these new, vertically organized health care providers. Medical schools and teaching hospitals may not be able to control, or even influence, these vast organizations. The long-term result may be competing health care behemoths that are similar in many ways to the "big three" in the automobile industry.

Law and psychiatry is obviously in a state of flux and ferment. New law is being made every day. Courts have taken upon themselves not only the task of protecting the rights of the mentally disabled but also that of regulating the institutions in which the patients are treated. As this chapter was being written, the courts were dealing with physician assisted suicide, managed care was transforming the health care system, and freestanding psychiatric hospitals were on the verge of bankruptcy. The psychiatrist will find law and managed care intruding on everyday practice, and the future will bring more rather than less intrusion. The psychiatrist has no choice but to become familiar with the important junctures of law and psychiatry. A new generation of psychiatrists interested in policy issues will need to be schooled in law, economics, and financial transactions. If current trends continue, managed care and the courts will have more to say about the doctor-patient relationship than does the medical profession.

References

Addington v. Texas, 99 S. Ct. 1804 (1979).

Ake v. Oklahoma, 470 U.S. 68 (1984).

Allen v. Illinois, 106 S. Ct. 2988 (1986).

American Bar Association. 1977. *Standards relating to corrections administration.* Cambridge, Mass.: Ballinger.

——— 1984. Proposed criminal justice mental health standards. Paper presented at the 1984 annual meeting of the ABA.

American Law Institute. 1962. Proposed office draft of model penal code §401.

American Medical Association. 1988. *Guide to the evaluation of permanent impairment.* 3rd ed. Chicago: American Medical Association.

American Psychiatric Association. 1983. Statement on the insanity defense. *Am. J. Psychiatry* 140:681–688.

——— 1995. Opinions of the Ethics Committee on the principles of medical ethics with annotations especially applicable to psychiatry. Washington, DC: American Psychiatric Association.

Americans with Disabilities Act. 1990. 42 U.S.C. §12101.

Appelbaum, P. S. 1988. The right to refuse treatment with anti-psychotic medication: retrospect and prospect. *American Psychiatry* 145:4:413–19.

Appelbaum, P. S., and T. G. Gutheil. 1992. *Clinical handbook of psychiatry and the law.* Baltimore: Williams & Wilkins.

Arnold v. Sarn, no. C-432355, Ariz. Super. Ct. (1985).

Barefoot v. Estelle, 103 S. Ct. 3383 (1983).

Berman, H. 1971. *Talks on American law.* Rev. ed. New York: Vintage Books.

Brakel, S., J. Parry, and B. Weiner. 1985. *The mentally disabled and the law.* 3rd ed. Chicago: American Bar Foundation.

Caesar v. Mountanos, 542 F.2d 1064 (9th Cir. 1976).

Canterbury v. Spence, 464 F.2d 772 (D.C. Cir. 1972).

Carpi, J. 1995. Managed care pushes psychiatric care outside of hospital walls. *Clinical Psychiatric News* February:12.

Clites v. Iowa, 322 N.W. 2d 917 (Iowa Ct. App. 1981).

Commonwealth v. Page, 159 N.E. 2d 82 (Mass. 1959).

Cruzan v. Director, Missouri Department of Health, 110 S. Ct. 2841 (1990).

In the matter of Claire Conroy, 98 N.J. 321, 486 A.2d 1209 (1985).

Dawidoff, D. L. 1973. *The malpractice of psychiatrists.* Springfield, Ill.: Thomas.

Donaldson v. O'Connor, 493 F.2d 507 (5th Cir. 1974).

Durham v. United States, 214 F.2d 862 (D.C. Cir. 1954).

Dusky v. United States, 362 U.S. 405 (1960).

ERISA. 1982. §514(a). 29 U.S.C. §1144(a).

ERISA. 1988. §514(a)(2)(A). 29 U.S.C. §1144(b)(2)(A).

Ernsdorff, G. M., and E. F. Loftus. 1993. Let sleeping memories lie? Words of caution about tolling the statute of limitations in cases of repressed memory. *Journal of Criminal Law and Criminology* 84(1):129–174.

Estelle v. Smith, 451 U. S. 454 (1981).

Ford v. Wainwright, 106 S. Ct. 2595 (1986).

Foucha v. Louisiana, 112 S. Ct. 1780 (1992).

Furman v. Georgia, 408 U.S. 238 (1972).

In re Gault, 387 U.S. 1 (1967).

Gordon, M. S. 1995. Managed care, ERISA pre-emption, and health reform—the current outlook. *BNA's Health L. Rep.* 4:630–634.

Griner, D. D. 1991. Paying the piper: third party payor liability for medical treatment decisions. *Ga. L. Rev.* 25:861–922.

Grinspoon, L., ed. 1982. *Psychiatry 1982 annual review: law and psychiatry.* Washington, D.C.: American Psychiatric Press.

Insanity Defense Reform Act. 1984. 18 U.S.C. §17.

Jackson v. Indiana, 406 U.S. 715 (1972).

Jaffee v. Redmond, 116 S. Ct. 1923 (1996).

Jameson, E. J., and E. Wehr. 1993. Drafting national health care reform legislation to protect the health interests of children. *Stanford Law and Policy Review* 5:152–175.

Jones v. United States, 103 S. Ct. 3043 (1983).

Kansas v. Hendricks, 117 S. Ct. 2072 (1997).

Klerman, G. L. 1988. Depression and related disorders of mood (affective disorders). In *The New Harvard Guide to Psychiatry,* ed. A. M. Nicholi. Cambridge, Mass.: Belknap Press of Harvard University Press. 309–336.

Lessard v. Schmidt, 349 F. Supp. 1078 (E.D. Wis. 1972).

Loue, S. 1993. An epidemiological framework for the formulation of health insurance policy. *J. Legal Med.* 14:523.

Metropolitan Life Ins. v. Massachusetts, 471 U.S. 724 (1985).

Daniel M'Naghten's Case, 8 Eng. Rep. 718 (1843).

Monahan, J. 1994. *Violence and mental disorder: developments in risk assessment.* Chicago: University of Chicago Press.

Moore, M. 1984. *Law and psychiatry: rethinking the relationship.* Cambridge: Cambridge University Press.

Morreim, E. H. 1991. *Balancing act: the new medical ethics of medicine's new economics.* Boston: Kluwer Academic Publishers.

Nasser v. Parker, 249 Va. 172 (1995).

O'Connor v. Donaldson, 422 U.S. 563 (1975).

Pappas v. Asbel, 675 A.2d 711 (1996).

Pate v. Robinson, 383 U.S. 375 (1966).

People v. George Thomas Franklin, 1 Dist. A05226883. Div. 1 (Cal. 1990).

People v. Shirley, 181 Cal. Rptr. 243 (1982).

Perry v. Lynaugh, 492 U.S. 302 (1989).

In the matter of Karen Quinlan, 355 A.2d 647 (1976).

Rennie v. Klein, 462 F. Supp. 1131 (D.N.J. 1979).

Riggins v. Nevada, 112 S. Ct. 1810 (1992).

Rock v. Arkansas, 107 S. Ct. 2704 (1987).

Roe v. Wade, 93 S. Ct. 705 (1973).

Rogers v. Commissioners of Mental Health, 390 Mass. 489 (1983).

Rogers v. Okin, 478 F. Supp. 1342 (1979).

Romeo v. Youngberg, 102 S. Ct. 2452 (1982).

Rosner, R., ed. 1990. *Ethical practice in psychiatry and the law.* New York: Plenum Press.

——— 1994. *Principles and practice of forensic psychiatry.* New York: Chapman & Hall.

Rozovsky, F. A. 1990. *Consent to treatment: a practical guide.* Boston: Little, Brown.

Schetky, D. H., and E. P. Benedek, eds. 1992. *Clinical handbook of child psychiatry and the law.* Baltimore: Williams & Wilkins.

Shortell, S. S., et al. 1994. The new world of managed care: creating organized delivery systems. *Health Affairs* 13:46–60.

Simon, R. I. 1992. *Psychiatric malpractice: cases and comments.* Washington D.C.: American Psychiatric Press.

Smith v. United States, 36 F.2d 548 (D.C. Cir. 1929).

Social Security Disability Benefits Reform Act. 1984. 42 U.S.C. §423(f).

State ex. rel. Hawks v. Lazaro, 202 S. E. 2d 109 (1974).

State v. Kovell, 690 P.2d 992 (1984).

Stone, A. A. 1975. *Mental health and law: a system in transition.* Washington, D.C.: Government Printing Office.

——— 1985. Law's influence on medicine and medical ethics. *N. Engl. J. Med.* 312:309–312.

——— 1993. Post-traumatic stress disorder and the law: critical review of the new frontier. *Bulletin of the American Academy of Psychiatry and the Law* 21:23–36.

——— 1995. Paradigms, pre-emptions, and stages: understanding the transformation of American psychiatry by managed care. *International Journal of Law and Psychiatry* Fall:353.

Stromberg, C. D., and A. A. Stone. 1983. Statute: a model state law on civil commitment of the mentally ill. *Harvard Journal on Legislation* 20:275–396.

Superintendent of Belchertown State School v. Saikewicz, 373 Mass. 728 (1977).

Swartz, M. S., et al. 1995. New directions in research on involuntary outpatient commitment. *Psychiatric Services* 46:4:381–385.

Tarasoff v. Regents of the University of California, 551 P.2d 334, 131 Cal. Rptr. 14 (1976).

Vitek v. Jones, 445 U.S. 480 (1980).

Washington v. Glucksberg, 117 S. Ct. 2258 (1997).

Washington v. Harper, 110 S. Ct. 128 (1990).

Wyatt v. Stickney, 325 F. Supp. 781, 344 F. Supp. 373 (M.D. Ala. 1972).

Zinermon v. Burch, 110 S. Ct. 975 (1990).

Recommended Reading

Appelbaum, P. S., and T. G. Gutheil. 1992. *Clinical handbook of psychiatry and the law.* Baltimore: Williams & Wilkins.

Brakel, S., J. Parry, and B. Weiner. 1985. *The mentally disabled and the law.* 3rd ed. Chicago: American Bar Foundation.

Klein, J. I., J. MacBeth, and J. N. Onek. 1984. *Legal issues in the private practice of psychiatry.* Washington, D.C.: American Psychiatric Press.

Moore, M. 1984. *Law and psychiatry: rethinking the relationship.* Cambridge: Cambridge University Press.

Schetky, D. H., and E. P. Benedek, eds. 1992. *Clinical handbook of child psychiatry and the law.* Baltimore: Williams & Wilkins.

Stone, A. A. 1984. *Law, psychiatry, and morality.* Washington, D.C.: American Psychiatric Press.

——— 1986. Ethics in biological psychiatry. In *American handbook of psychiatry,* ed. P. A. Berger and H. K. Brodie. Vol. 8. 2nd ed. New York: Basic Books.

Index **841**

LAAM, 391
laboratory testing: dementia and, 330, 333; mental retardation and, 666
Lacan, J., 192–193
lactation: antidepressant drugs and, 483; antimanic agents and, 466–467; antipsychotic agents and, 457
lacunar state, 344
Lake v. Cameron, 686, 793
Lamkins, D. C., 721
language, 266; dementia and, 127; neural substrate of, 112; neuropsychological testing and, 337; paralinguistic aspects of communication and, 121–122. *See also* aphasia; speech
Lapouse, R., 764
Laudenslager, M. L., 368
law and legal issues: adversary system and, 801; capital punishment and, 806–807; case law and, 801; children and, 605, 799, 808; competency criteria, 798; competency to be executed, 807; competency to stand trial, 804–805; confidentiality and, 817; constitutional issues, 798–799, 800, 803, 805; criminal *vs.* civil law, 800–801; disability benefits and, 817–818; entitlement programs and, 799, 817–818; euthanasia and, 727; expert testimony and, 798, 805–807, 815; Fifth Amendment and, 805; hypnosis and, 807–808; insanity defense, 801–805; limitation of life-prolonging treatment, 727; malpractice and, 799, 811, 814–816; managed care and, 799; patient right to refuse treatment, 811–813, 814–185; plea bargaining, 803–804; practitioner familiarity with laws, 750; recovered memory and, 807–808, 815; sexual predator statutes, 810; *State ex rel. Hawks v. Lazaro,* 800–801; state statutes and, 800; testamentary capacity and, 813–814; treatment of mental retardation, 669; victim impact statements, 804. *See also* commitment law; confidentiality; informed consent; patient rights
LCH. *See* life change units
L-dopa, 454
learned helplessness, 291
learning disorders: DSM-IV codes, 74; neuropsychological testing and, 56; schizophrenia and, 266
learning theory, 526; child development and, 588–589; personality theory and, 193–194; sex therapy and, 526, 538. *See also* behavior therapy
"least restrictive alternative" standard, 793

Leff, J., 259
left hemisphere syndromes: aphasias and, 112–116; object aphasias and, 117
left-right comparisons, 57
legal issues. *See* law and legal issues
Leiter International Performance Scale, 666
LeShan, E., 700
LeShan, L., 700
Lester, D., 707, 714
Levenson, J. L., 381–382
Levin, D., 188
Levin, J. M., 92
Levine, S., 704
Levitan, S. J., 383
Lewine, R. J., 269
Lewis, C. S., 716, 717
Lewis, S. W., 264
Lewy bodies, 345
Liberman, R. P., 692
libido theory, 179, 181
Librium. *See* chlordiazepoxide
Lichtenstein, H., 188
Lidz, R., 242
Lidz, T., 242
Lief, H. I., 535–536
life change units (LCH), 366
life instinct (eros), 175–176
life-prolonging treatment, limitation of: conflict over, 725; decision guidelines, 723–726; fear of legal reprisal, 727; patient categories and, 722–723; patient rights and, 812–813. *See also* patient rights
lifetime prevalence, 753–754; incidence and, 764
lilliputian hallucinations, 35
limbic epilipsy, 104
limbic network, 103–112; autonomic function and, 107; emotional processing and, 138; emotion and, 121; limbic epilepsy and, 104–107; limbic system as term, 103; memory disturbances and, 107–112; motivation and, 104
limit setting, with adolescents, 616, 630
Lin, T. Y., 757–758
Lindemann, E., 376, 716, 720, 788
Lindsley, O., 497
Lipowski, Z. J., 377–378
listening: empathic, 426; impediments to, 15–17
lithium: adverse effects of, 464–467; agitation in dementia and, 655; antidepressant augmentation strategies and, 646; antidepressants and, 479; bipolar disorder and, 288; blood levels, 462–463; in

combination with other drugs, 464; ECT and, 477, 544, 548; elderly persons and, 638, 647–648; intoxication with, 464; mania and, 300, 647–648; OCD and, 231; renal tubular damage and, 465–466
lithium carbonate (Eskalith; Lithobid), 459; antidepressants and, 297; bipolar disorders and, 458–467; chemical structure of, 461; clinical use of, 461–464. *See also* lithium
lithium citrate (Cibalith), 459, 461. *See also* lithium
lithium salts: chemical structure of, 461; pharmacology of, 458–459, 460. *See also* lithium; lithium carbonate; lithium citrate
Lithobid. *See* lithium carbonate
Litman, R., 714
liver function, and treatment of mania, 300
LNNB. *See* Luria Nebraska Neuropsychological Battery
Loewenstein, R., 182
longitudinal studies, 755
long-term potentiation, 139
long-term treatment: antipsychotic agents and, 449–452; of anxiety, 488
loosening of association, 247
Lopez, A. D., 769
lorazepam (Ativan), 222, 450, 487; adverse effects of, 489; anxiety and, 484; dementia and, 350; dosages, 486; elderly persons and, 638, 649; molecular structure of, 485
loss, 701; divorce and, 603–604; elderly persons and, 638–639, 649; as stress, 372; as stressor, 367
loss of interest in usual activities, 247, 282
loxapine (Loxitane): chemical structure of, 447, 448; clinical use of, 450; dosage, 446; side effects of, 446
Loxitane. *See* loxapine
LSD. *See* lysergic acid diethylamide
Ludiomil. *See* maprotiline
Luisada, P., 249
Lundby Study, 758, 765, 766
Lunden, G., 703
lupus erythematosis, 382
Luria, A. R., 57, 58
Luria Nebraska Neuropsychological Battery (LNNB), 57–58, 337
Lutkins, S. G., 716
Luvox. *See* fluvoxamine
Lynn, J., 721
Lyons, M. J., 268

Neuropsychiatric Screening Adjunct (NSA), 758

neuropsychology, 53–60; abnormalities in schizophrenia and, 265–266; cognitive disorders and, 336–338; general aims of, 55–56; medications and, 59–60; pure word deafness and, 115; referral for evaluation, 336–338; relationship to other exams, 54–55; repeat evaluations, 59; research modalities, 90–93. *See also* neurobiology; neurology

neuroses. *See* anxiety disorders

neurosurgery, and OCD, 231–232

neurotransmitters: aging and, 638; childhood depression and, 597; complexity of, 136; dysfunction in schizophrenia and, 266–268; modulatory role of, 136; parallel and, 136; pathophysiology of depression and, 293–294; schizophrenia and, 150

Nicholi, A. M., Jr.: on adolescence, 611–634

nicotine, 675–676

nicotine-related disorders, 77

nightmares, 164

NIMH. *See* National Institute of Mental Health

NMS. *See* neuroleptic malignant syndrome

nocturnal myoclonus, 160, 651

nocturnal penile tumescence (NPT), 531

no diagnosis conditions, 82

Noguchi, H., 69

nomifensine, 474

non-abandonment, 748

nonbenzodiazepine imidazopyridine hypnotics, 652

"noncontrast" fMRI techniques, 91

non-fluent aphasia. *See* transcortical motor aphasia

"nonspecificity hypothesis," 365

noradrenergic pathways, 125

norepinephrine (NE): depression and, 293; monoamine system and, 136–137; schizophrenia and, 267; tricyclic antidepressants and, 294

norepinephrine-reuptake inhibitors (NRIs), 472

Norflex. *See* orphenadrine citrate

Normal Adolescence (Group for the Advancement of Psychiatry), 621

Norpramin. *See* desipramine

nortritplyine (Pamelor; Aventyl), 294; bereavement-depression and, 719; dosage for, 471; dose-response relationships and, 475; elderly persons and, 644, 646; molecular structure of, 469

nosology, 65, 72

Novack, D. H., 704

NPT. *See* nocturnal penile tumescence

NREM-REM cycle, 156–157

NRIs. *See* norepinephrine-reuptake inhibitors

NSA. *See* Neuropsychiatric Screening Adjunct

nucleus accumbens (NAc), 142

nursing homes: dementia and, 655; depression and, 642

nymphomania, 33

object libido, 175

object recognition deficit. *See* visual object agnosia

object relationships: Freud and, 173, 174, 178; Kernberg and, 183; Klein and, 180–181; May and, 192; object relations theory and, 185–187, 241–242; Rorschach studies and, 49; schizophrenia and, 241–242; TAT and, 50

observability, and behavior therapy, 499–500

observational studies, 755

obsession, definition of, 35, 229

obsessive-compulsive disorder (OCD), 164; antidepressants and, 476–477, 479; buspirone and, 488; characteristics of, 229–230; course of, 230; definition of obsession and, 35, 229; distinguished from obsessive-compulsive personality disorder, 230; ECT and, 547; elderly persons and, 648, 649; etiology of, 230; fMRI imaging and, 92; genetics and, 138; neural substrates of, 141; neurobiology of, 230; neurosurgery and, 231–232; with other Axis I disorder, 230; prevalence of, 230; prognosis with, 230; Tourette syndrome and, 128, 141; treatment of, 230–233, 503; undoing and, 210

obsessive-compulsive personality disorder, 323–324; course of, 323; definition of, 323; distinguished from OCD, 230; epidemiology of, 323; etiology of, 323; psychodynamics of, 323; treatment for, 323–324

obstetric complications (OCs): mental retardation and, 663; schizophrenia and, 261–262, 269. *See also* birth trauma

obstructive sleep apnea, 163

occupation: psychiatric history and, 28; psychosocial aspects of dying and, 707

OCD. *See* obsessive-compulsive disorder

O'Connor v. Donaldson, 810

OCs. *See* obstetric complications

oculomotor apraxia, 119

oedipal phase of development, 174–175; mental retardation and, 665; origins of, 218

Oedipus complex, 174–175, 178

Offer, D., 613

Oken, D., 704

olanzapine (Zyprexa), 150, 254, 449; agitation in dementia and, 655; chemical structure of, 447, 448; clinical use of, 452; dosage, 446; elderly persons and, 651; mania and, 300; side effects of, 254, 446, 453

olfactory hallucinations, 35

oligopsony, 819

olivo-ponto-cerebellar degeneration (OPCD), 128, 164

Olshansky, S., 664

Onstad, S., 261

Ontario, Canada, survey of psychiatric disorders, 763

Ontario Child Health Study, 770

OPCD. *See* olivo-ponto-cerebellar degeneration

operant conditioning, 510–514; addiction and, 674; aversive therapies and, 513–514; principles of, 510–511; within psychotherapies, 512–513; schizophrenic disorders and, 255

operational criteria, 70

operationalization, and DSM-IV, 66–67

opiates: adverse effects of, 391; categories of, 390; symptom relief and, 676; treatment for dependence on, 391; use of, 390; withdrawal from dependence on, 681. *See also* addictive disorders; substance abuse

opioid-related disorders, 77

optic ataxia, 119

oral-dental devices, and sleep disorders, 164

oral phase of development, 173–174, 664–665

Orap. *See* pimozide

organicity, concept of, 53–54

organic syndromes. *See* neurological disorders

organ neurosis, 362

organ transplantation: consultation-liaison psychiatry and, 380; psychiatric issues and, 381–382

orgasmic disorder: female, 533–534, 536; male, 534; treatment strategies for, 533–534

orgone theory, 181

orientation, psychiatric examination and, 32, 36

PERI. *See* Psychiatric Epidemiologic Research Instrument

periodic limb movement disorder (PLM), 160, 162

perioral tremor. *See* "rabbit" syndrome

Permax. *See* pergolide mesylate

perphenazine (Trilafon), 651; chemical structure of, 448; dosage, 446; side effects of, 446

perseveration, 34

persistent vegetative state, 721–722, 723, 813

personal history, 27–28

personality: adaptation to illness and, 378–379; alcoholism and, 675; categorical approach and, 73; coronary heart disease and, 370, 371; definition of, 67; development of psychiatric disorders and, 214–219; frontal lobe and, 122, 124; mood disorders and, 291–292; polydrug abuser and, 675; resistance to palliative care and, 705–706; temporolimbic epilepsy and, 105; theories of, 189–194. *See also* personality disorders; temperament; traits

personality assessment: objective tests, 51–53; projective tests, 47–51

personality development: developmental arrests, 214–218; mental retardation and, 664–666; regression and, 211–212; relationship of biological development to, 615–616; repression and, 208. *See also* personality theory

personality disorders, 308–325; in adolescence, 628; alternative systems for classification of, 311–314; antianxiety agents and, 490; antidepressants and, 490; as Axis II condition, 67; classification systems for, 310–314; comorbidity and, 309; defense mechanisms and, 199; demographics of, 309; development of, 309–310; dimensional models of, 312; DSM-IV and, 67, 81, 310–311, 314–325; integrative model for, 313–314; methodological advances and, 308; mood symptoms and, 289; prognoses for, 308; psychobiological model (Cloniger system), 313; resistance to palliative care and, 705; separate diagnostic axis (Axis II) for, 308; treatability of, 308; treatment modalities and, 310

personality measurement, 190–191

personality theory: classic psychoanalysis and, 171–178; clinically based theories, 171–189; ego psychology and, 182–184; existential theories, 192–193; factor analytic theories, 190–191; humanistic

theories, 190; learning theory and, 193–194; neo-Freudians and, 184–185; object relations theory, 185–187; phenomenological theories, 192–193; post-Freudian developments in, 178–182; psychological theories, 189–194; self psychology and, 187–189; systems-information theory, 191–192

Pertofrane. *See* desipramine

pervasive developmental disorders (PDDs), 74, 595

PET. *See* positron emission tomography

Petrie, W., 249

Pettinatti, H. M., 557

Pfeffer, C. R., 597

phallic phase of development, 174

phantom boarder syndrome, 341

pharmacotherapy: alcoholism and, 678; alcohol withdrawal and, 680; Alzheimer's disease and, 341–342; *vs.* behavior therapy, 499; borderline personality disorder and, 320–321; child psychiatric disorders and, 592; children and, 597; compliance and, 490; defense mechanisms and, 201; delirium and, 354; dementia and, 349–351, 654; dependent personality disorder and, 323; depression and, 597, 644–646; development of, 445; eating disorders and, 407; elderly persons and, 637–638, 644–646; generalized anxiety disorder and, 233–234; informed consent and, 814–815; limitations of, 445; mental retardation and, 668; OCD and, 230–231, 324; panic disorder and, 224–225; patient management and, 567–569; pediatric research and, 592; personality disorders and, 310, 320–321, 323; post-traumatic stress disorder and, 228–229; social phobia and, 227; specific phobias and, 235. *See also* antianxiety agents; antidepressant agents; antimanic agents; antipsychotic agents; drug interactions; medications; psychopharmacology

phencyclidine (PCP), 150, 268; adolescent use of, 619; adverse effects of, 396; substance use disorders and, 77, 395–396; treatment for overdose of, 396

phenelzine (Nardil), 222, 225, 227, 468, 470; dosages for, 471; molecular structure of, 469

phenobarbital, 486; adverse effects of, 489; alcohol withdrawal and, 680; molecular structure of, 485. *See also* barbiturates

phenomenological-existential theories of personality, 192–193

phenothiazines: chemical structure of,

448; clinical use of, 450, 451; introduction of, 446–447

phenotypes, definition of, 135

phentolamine (Regitine), 483

phenylbutylpiperidines, 447, 448

phenylpiperidines, 446

phobias, 35; avoidant personality disorder and, 322; behavior therapy and, 504–505, 519; counterphobia and, 211; displacement and, 209–210; distortion of psychic equilibrium and, 213; hypnosis and, 560; phobic personality, 322; specific phobias, 234–235; systematic desensitization and, 507; treatment of, 503. *See also* social phobia; specific phobias

physical dependence on a drug, 390

physician-assisted suicide, 726–727, 812–813

physicians: contact with suicidal patients and, 714–715; limitation of life-prolonging treatment and, 723–726; psychiatric consultation and, 789. *See also* medical conditions

physostigmine (Antilirium), 482

Piaget, J., 588, 614–615

Pick's disease, 335, 342

pimozide (Orap): chemical structure of, 447, 448; clinical use of, 450; dosage, 446; side effects of, 446

pindolol (Visken), 479

Pinel, P., 779

piperacetazine (Quide), 446

piperazine phenothiazines, 449

PLM. *See* periodic limb movement disorder

polysubstance use disorders: definition of, 673–674; etiology of, 674–676; prognosis and, 682–683; treatment of, 681–682. *See also* addictive disorders; drug use; substance use disorders

Popkin, M. K., 381

population-based psychiatry: advocacy groups and, 785–786; defined, 778; disenfranchisement and, 792–793; emergence of managed care and, 783–785; fate of innovative programs and, 787; history of public mental health care and, 685–686, 779–781; homelessness and, 793–794; principles of community psychiatry and, 781–783; self-help groups and, 785–786; terminology in, 778–779; utilization of mental health services and, 789–790. *See also* community mental health

positive emotional memory formation, 143

chosomatic process and, 364; as DSM category, 362; personality disorders and, 309; psychiatric consultation and, 383

somnambulism (sleepwalking), 158, 164

source of instincts, 173

Sparine. *See* promazine

Spark, R., 538

spatial orientation, 120; large-scale network organization of, 118–119; selective attention and, 126

Spearman, Carl, 191

specificity hypothesis, 181, 364

specific phobias: characteristics of, 234–235; course of, 235; prevalence of, 235; treatment of, 235

SPECT. *See* single photon emission computed tomography

spectrum concept, 251–252

spectrum disorders, 313, 314–316. *See also* cyclothymic disorder; paranoid personality disorder; schizotypal personality disorder

speech: mental retardation evaluation and, 666; poverty of, 247; psychiatric examination and, 32, 33–34

Spiegel, D., 383

Spinetta, J. J., 709, 711

Spitz, R., 587

Spitz, R. A., 292

Spitzer, R. L., 757

split treatment model, 748

Sprung, C. L., 726

SSE. *See* subacute spongiform encephalopathy

SSRIs. *See* selective serotonin-reuptake inhibitors

Stampfl, T. G., 507

standardized intelligence tests, 45–47; "premorbid IQ" and, 46; Verbal-Performance IQ discrepancies and, 46

State ex rel. Hawks v. Lazaro, 800–801

state function, 126

state-specific information, 124

static shift, 157

Steele-Olszewski-Richardson syndrome, 128

Stefano, G. B., 369–370

Stein, L., 688, 786

Stein, M., 368

Stekel, W., 713

Stelazine. *See* trifluoperazine

stereotypy, 33, 247

Stevens, H., 666

stigma, as term, 791

stimulants: ADHD and, 484; as antidepressants, 467–468, 474; depression

and, 484; drugs of abuse and, 674; elderly persons and, 646, 652; use with antidepressants, 477–478

stimulus fading, 517–518

stimulus flooding, 507

Stirling County Study, 758, 764, 765, 766, 768, 780

Stone, A., 21

STP, 394

Strachey, J., 197

Stranger Situation Paradigm, 601

Strauss, J., 258

stress: acute, 373; approaches to, 367–368; biological responses to, 367; concept of, 365–366, 375; defense mechanisms and, 196–201; depression in adolescence and, 629; heart disease and, 370–375; management of, 367–368; mood disorders and, 291; physiological responses to, 376–377; social support and, 366. *See also* acute stress disorder; post-traumatic stress disorder

stressful life events: depression and, 291; schizophrenia and, 258–259

stress reduction programs, 367–368

stroke: confusional states and, 127; dementia and, 343–346, 653; depression and, 381

structural brain abnormalities in schizophrenia, 264, 268–269

structural model, 187, 207–208

Structured Clinical Interview for DSM (SCID), 762

Studies on Hysteria (Breuer and Freud), 205

stuttering, 503

Styron, W., 281

subacute spongiform encephalopathy (SSE), 335, 347

subaverage intelligence, defined, 660

subdural hematoma, dementia and, 347

subjective units of distress (SUDs), 505

sublimation, concept of, 212

substance abuse: definition of, 390; ethical issues and, 750; as grounds for disability, 818; personality disorders and, 309; sedative tranquilizing agents and, 488–489; substance dependence disorders and, 390, 672–673; vulnerability to, 390. *See also* alcoholism; polysubstance use disorders; substance use disorders

substance dependence disorders, 390, 672–673

substance-induced disorders: mood disorder, 647; persisting dementia, 330; psychotic disorder, 248–249

substance-related disorders, 75–78

substance use disorders, 390–398; causes of use and, 390; physical dependence and, 390, 672–673; tolerance and, 390. *See also* polysubstance use disorders; substance abuse

Suddath, R. L., 149

sudden infant death syndrome, 719–720

"sudden-sniffing death" syndrome, 619

SUDs. *See* subjective units of distress

suicide and suicide risk: adolescent depression and, 622–623, 628; alcoholism and, 679; antianxiety agents and, 489; antidepressant treatment, 478; assessment of, 574–575; borderline personality and, 319; as cause of death, 713; in childhood, 597; clinical evaluation of, 714–715; countertransference and, 575; depression and, 283, 293, 294, 298–299, 714; discontinuation of lithium and, 463; elderly persons and, 643; ethical issues and, 750; hospitalization and, 574–575; in hospitalized medical and surgical patients, 380; manipulative suicide attempts, 575; patient management and, 574–575; prevention and, 597; psychodynamics of, 713–714; psychotic depression and, 286; "risk-rescue" criteria, 714; Rorschach index and, 48; schizophrenic mortality and, 258; TCAs and, 482; terminal illness and, 704–705; treatment and, 715–716; tricyclic antidepressants and, 294, 298–299. *See also* physician-assisted suicide

Sullivan, H. S., 184–185, 241, 615

sundown syndrome, 166

superego, 207; in Freudian theory, 177–178; primitive, 181; resistance and, 12

supportive psychotherapy, 429–431, 692; anxiety disorders and, 223; assessment of, 430–431; distinguished from psychoanalytic psychotherapy, 419; indications for, 429–431; mental retardation and, 667–668; for older persons, 643; outcomes with, 430; techniques in, 429–430

suppression *vs.* repression, 208

supranuclear ophthalmoplegia, 128

surgery, 553, 560. *See also* neurosurgery

Surmontil. *See* trimipramine

Susser, E., 786

Suzuki, L. A., 44

Sydenham, T., 68

Sydenham's chorea, 141

Symmetrel. *See* amantadine

symptom relief: alcoholism and, 675–676; polydrug abuse and, 675–676